*THE WESTMINSTER*
# DICTIONARY OF CHURCH HISTORY

# THE WESTMINSTER
# DICTIONARY
# OF
# CHURCH HISTORY

EDITOR

## JERALD C. BRAUER

*Naomi Shenstone Donnelly Professor and*
*Professor of History of Christianity*
*Formerly Dean of The Divinity School*
*The University of Chicago*

ASSOCIATE EDITORS

BRIAN GERRISH
*Professor of Historical Theology*
*The Divinity School*
*The University of Chicago*

ROBERT M. GRANT
*Professor of New Testament and*
*Early Christianity*
*The Divinity School*
*The University of Chicago*

RICHARD LUMAN
*Professor of Medieval History*
*Haverford College*

JULES LAURENCE MOREAU
*Professor of Ecclesiastical History*
*Seabury-Western Theological Seminary*

## THE WESTMINSTER PRESS

PHILADELPHIA

ISBN 0-664-21285-9

Library of Congress Catalog Card No. 69-11071


*Book Design by*
*Dorothy Alden Smith*

Published by The Westminster Press ®
Philadelphia, Pennsylvania

PRINTED IN THE UNITED STATES OF AMERICA

# PREFACE

THIS DICTIONARY does not intend to be definitive, nor do the entries pretend to be exhaustive. It has a modest but clear purpose: to give an immediate, accurate, introductory definition and explanation concerning the major men, events, facts, and movements in the history of Christianity. The Christian church in its institutional form is the dictionary's center of reference. However, church history is an essential part of our culture, and not only church members but many other persons as well are interested in it. This volume should therefore prove to be a handy, informative reference for anyone who is curious about the facts and explanations involving the Christian tradition in Western culture. It will be particularly useful for Christian laymen, ministers, theological students, and college students in religious classes.

The interplay between Christianity and Western civilization demands at least a certain number of key entries from such areas as the arts, politics, or philosophy. The history of the Christian churches cannot be understood apart from references to these topics. Such entries have been kept to a minimum, however; nor are there a great many entries on Christian doctrine or theology. Major doctrinal developments that have shaped the history of Christianity are included directly, but most theological subjects are handled indirectly through the biographies of outstanding Christian theologians or through crisis events in history.

Few Biblical materials are covered in this dictionary. Only such problems as different Bible versions or special archaeological discoveries are treated. For research on related matters, the reader can consult further the companion volumes: *The New Westminster Dictionary of the Bible,* the *Dictionary of Christian Ethics, The Westminster Dictionary of Christian Education,* and *A Dictionary of Christian Theology.*

An attempt has been made to eschew a particular bias or special interpretation in preparing the articles of this dictionary. The methodological studies of historians and philosophers make clear that there is no such thing as pure objectivity or simple facts. Nevertheless, a serious effort has been made to present all information as factually as possible and to avoid special pleading. The fact that most of the articles are short and by nature descriptive rendered the task less difficult. In a few cases, where interpretation could not be avoided, differing views on the subject are pointed out. No dictionary of this scope, written by so many hands, can fully approximate the ideal of objectivity.

Perspective reflecting a point of view is most evident in the weighting of materials in determining the general structure of the dictionary and the length of individual articles. A disproportionate amount of space had been allotted to the modern period of church history beginning with the eighteenth century, and to American developments. Several reasons can be given in defense of this unusual weighting. In terms of sheer quantity more has happened in the twentieth century than in any previous five centuries. One basic fact should not be overlooked—the tremendous and constantly escalating population explosion since the seventeenth century. In the history of the church, there are more people, more movements, more rapid changes, there is more action than at any other time. This in itself demands a fuller treatment for the modern period. It documents the increase in all facets of religious activity and involvement. The revolutionary impact of the modern age is as profound for the history of the church as was the Reformation or the founding days.

Finally, a defense can be made for the space given to the American scene. The dictionary was written primarily for an American audience. No other one-volume dictionary has as much material on the American churches and their history. Perhaps this division of materials will make it helpful to audiences in England or Europe. It is hoped that the dictionary will be widely used in congregations, in study groups, and by laity.

In keeping with the basic intention of supplying introductory factual information, most entries are no more than ten, thirty, or one hundred lines. There are only a few articles which were expanded to two hundred lines in order to deal with the major religious bodies of Christianity or to introduce the reader to a few key movements, such as the Reformation. Bibliographies are appended only to the one- and two-hundred-line articles, and the decision was made to limit references to four or five English titles. For those who wish to move to greater depth, the items in certain bibliographies contain titles in other languages. All Biblical quotations and references are taken from the Revised Standard Version.

The contributions came mainly from younger scholars, though many basic entries were written by established authorities. Careful use was made of the standard histories, encyclopedias, source collections, dictionaries, and the usual references. All entries were read by section editors and their staffs, and the general editor and his assistants also sought to verify and to spot-check all materials. In a volume containing so many facts, even the most careful editing will fail to uncover all errors, but much labor was expended to achieve the greatest accuracy possible.

The dictionary is a product of a continuous process of planning and work over a period of years. Initially the task was undertaken by the editor in company with Profs. Robert M. Grant, Jaroslav J. Pelikan, and James H. Nichols. That group sketched out the original format and balance of the dictionary. When the project was barely under way, the two latter gentlemen moved from The Divinity School and their work was picked up from the initial stages by Profs. Brian A. Gerrish and Richard Luman, and the work of Mr. Nichols by the general editor. Special thanks are extended to all these gentlemen for their conscientious assistance on the project.

As the volume now stands, Prof. Robert M. Grant, ably assisted by O. C. Edwards and John Helgeland, was responsible for the materials to A.D. 600. Profs. Richard Luman and Jules Moreau shared the editorial work of the medieval period, 600 to 1300, and they were assisted by William Carpe. Prof. Brian A. Gerrish carried out the editorial commitments for the period 1300 to 1700, with the competent assistance of Joseph Fitzer. The general editor was responsible also for the particular editorial work on the modern period and the American scene. He was ably assisted first by Ernest Sandeen and later by John Phillips. A special word of appreciation is extended to Mr. Phillips, whose great care and unflagging energy gave immeasurable help to the general editor in seeing the entire project through to a conclusion. All the editors have contributed articles. In the final stages, Kenneth East carried on the work of Mr. Phillips.

In a project of this magnitude, it is impossible to acknowledge properly all those who were involved in the effort. However, special mention must be made of several individuals. Trygve Skarsten directed a large group of advanced church history graduate students in The Divinity School of The University of Chicago in the immense labor of checking out all factual materials and references in the text. The articles, unsigned, went through the hands of a number of men in an effort to achieve a level of accuracy and uniformity. No effort was made to achieve uniformity of style, though a careful attempt was made to correct grammar. Thus the dictionary is the work of many men under the direction and guidance of the editors.

Without faithful and accurate secretaries and typists, a project such as this would have fallen into chaos. Two deserve particular mention for their outstanding service and help. Mrs. Tayna Davis and Miss Alma Obrikat provided the continuity and the care so important to the successful completion of the task. Above all, recognition must be given to the patience, forbearance, and constant help of the staff of The Westminster Press both in copy-editing and in proofreading. The plans for the dictionary had to be changed several times, for section editors moved away or other unforeseen circumstances occurred, but the Press graciously provided its support in seeing the entire project through to completion. The editors are grateful for this help and for the opportunity of continuous corrections as the manuscript has gone through the various phases of production.

JERALD C. BRAUER

# CONTRIBUTORS

ALDERFER, Owen H.

Professor of Church History
Ashland Theological Seminary
Ashland, Ohio

ANDREWS, Stephen T.

Instructor in Philosophy
Central Y.M.C.A. Community
College
Chicago, Illinois

ARNOLD, Harvey C.

Librarian
The Divinity School
The University of Chicago
Chicago, Illinois

BAMBURY, Ewart

Formerly Assistant Professor
Department of Religion
The Cleveland State University
Cleveland, Ohio

BANGS, Carl

Professor of Historical Theology
Saint Paul School of Theology
Kansas City, Missouri

BARRANGER, Milly

Assistant Professor of English
Tulane University of Louisiana
New Orleans, Louisiana

BATES, Robert L.

Graduate student
The University of Chicago
Chicago, Illinois

BEAVER, R. Pierce

Professor of Missions
The Divinity School
The University of Chicago
Chicago, Illinois

BERNARD, Paul P.

Professor of History
University of Illinois
Champaign, Illinois

BOOTY, John Everitt

Professor of Church History
Episcopal Theological School
Cambridge, Massachusetts

BRAUER, Jerald C.

Naomi Shenstone Donnelly
Professor and
Professor of History of
Christianity
The Divinity School
The University of Chicago
Chicago, Illinois

BREAKENRIDGE, Melvin L.

Graduate Student
The University of Chicago
Chicago, Illinois

BRIDSTON, Keith Richard

Professor of Systematic Theology
Pacific Lutheran Theological
Seminary
Berkeley, California

BROMILEY, Geoffrey W.

Professor of Church History
Fuller Theological Seminary
Pasadena, California

BRUINS, Elton J.

Assistant Professor of Religion
and Bible
Calvin College
Grand Rapids, Michigan

CAHILL, P. Joseph

Department of Religious Studies
University of Alberta
Edmonton, Alberta, Canada

CARPE, William D.

Assistant Professor of Medieval
Church History and Dean of
the Faculty
St. Meinrad School of Theology
St. Meinrad, Indiana

CARR, Anne

Instructor in Theology
Mundelein College
Chicago, Illinois

CHAPMAN, Julius Harley

Graduate Student
The University of Chicago
Chicago, Illinois

CHRISTIANSON, Gerald

Assistant Professor of Church
History
Lutheran Theological Seminary
Gettysburg, Pennsylvania

CLARKE, Robert J.

Assistant Professor of Art History
St. Louis University
St. Louis, Missouri

CLIFFORD, N. Keith

Assistant Professor of Church
History
University of British Columbia
Vancouver, British Columbia,
Canada

CLOUSE, Robert G.

Associate Professor of History
Indiana State University
Terre Haute, Indiana

CONHEADY, Eileen

Assistant Professor of History
Nazareth College of Rochester
Rochester, New York

COOPER, Robert M.

COVEY, Patricia

CROCKETT, W. R. K.

Professor of Systematic Theology
Anglican Theological College
Vancouver, British Columbia,
Canada

CRUM, Winston F.

Assistant Professor of Theology
and Lecturer in Biblical Languages and Ecclesiastical History
Seabury-Western Theological
Seminary
Evanston, Illinois

CULVER, Maurice E.

Professor
Epworth Theological College
Salisbury, Rhodesia

DANIEL, F. Harry
Graduate Student
Divinity School
Vanderbilt University
Nashville, Tennessee

DEAN, Eric
Professor of Philosophy and
 Religion
Wabash College
Crawfordsville, Indiana

DONAHEY, Mary
Graduate Student
Columbia University
New York, N. Y.

DOOLEY, Dolores
Graduate Student
University of Notre Dame
Notre Dame, Indiana

DRAKE, George A.
Associate Professor of History
 and Dean of the College
Colorado College
Colorado Springs, Colorado

DURNBAUGH, Donald F.
Professor of Church History
Bethany Theological Seminary
Oak Brook, Illinois

EAST, Kenneth A.
Graduate Student
The University of Chicago
Chicago, Illinois

EDWARDS, O. C.
Associate Professor of New
 Testament
Nashotah House
Nashotah, Wisconsin

ESSLINGER, Patricia
Assistant Professor of English
Texas Western University
El Paso, Texas

FIDDLER, Jeff
Graduate Student
The University of Chicago
Chicago, Illinois

FITZER, Joseph
Assistant Professor of Historical
 Theology
St. John's University
Jamaica, New York

FLOROVSKY, Georges
Professor Emeritus of Far Eastern
 Church History
Harvard University
Cambridge, Massachusetts

FOGDE, Myron J.
Associate Professor of Religion
Augustana College
Rock Island, Illinois

FORD, Austin

FORSE, James H.
Assistant Professor of History
Bowling Green State University
Bowling Green, Ohio

FREDERICKSEN, Linwood
Encyclopaedia Britannica
Chicago, Illinois

GERRISH, Brian A.
Professor of Historical Theology
The Divinity School
The University of Chicago
Chicago, Illinois

GODBEY, John C.
Assistant Professor of Church
 History
Meadville Theological School of
 Lombard College
Chicago, Illinois

GOEN, Clarence D.
Professor of Church History
Wesley Theological Seminary
The American University
Washington, D. C.

GORDH, George
Professor of Religion
Hollins College
Hollins College, Virginia

GOWAN, Richard D.
Graduate Student
The University of Chicago
Chicago, Illinois

GRANT, Robert M.
Professor of New Testament and
 Early Christianity
The Divinity School
The University of Chicago
Chicago, Illinois

GRITSCH, Eric W.
Professor of Church History
Lutheran Theological Seminary
Gettysburg, Pennsylvania

GROH, John E.
Assistant Professor of History
Concordia Teachers College
River Forest, Illinois

GUY, Fritz
Associate Professor of Theology
 and Philosophy
Loma Linda University
Loma Linda, California

HARBISON, Stanley L.
Instructor, Department of History
Eastern Michigan University
Ypsilanti, Michigan

HARDY, E. R.
Professor of Church History
Berkeley Divinity School
New Haven, Connecticut

HART, James F.
Graduate Student
The University of Chicago
Chicago, Illinois

HAWKINS, E. M.
Professor of Church History
The Graduate Seminary
Phillips University
Enid, Oklahoma

HELGELAND, John A.
Graduate Student in Church
 History
The University of Chicago
Chicago, Illinois

HERRING, Donald
Assistant Professor of English
The University of Chicago
Chicago, Illinois

HILLERBRAND, Hans J.
Professor of History and Modern
 European Christianity
Duke University
Durham, North Carolina

HOLDITCH, W. Kenneth
Assistant Professor of English
Louisiana State University
Baton Rouge, Louisiana

HOLMES, Urban T., III
Professor of Pastoral Theology
Nashotah House
Nashotah, Wisconsin

HYNES, William J.
Assistant Professor of Theology
St. Xavier College
Chicago, Illinois

IRWIN, Mary Ellen
Graduate Student
The University of Chicago
Chicago, Illinois

JORSTAD, Erling
Professor of History
St. Olaf College
Northfield, Minnesota

KARFF, Samuel E.
Rabbi, Chicago Sinai Congrega-
 tion
Chicago, Illinois

KAVANAGH, Aidan

Associate Professor of Theology
Director of Graduate Programs in
Theology and Liturgical Studies
University of Notre Dame
Notre Dame, Indiana

KESSLER, Herbert

Associate Professor of Art
The University of Chicago
Chicago, Illinois

KIRBY, James E.

Professor, Department of Religion
Oklahoma State University
Stillwater, Oklahoma

KOENIG, Duane

Professor of History
University of Miami
Coral Gables, Florida

KRODEL, Gottfried G.

Professor of History and Church
History
Valparaiso University
Valparaiso, Indiana

LANGER, Lawrence Nathan

Graduate Student
The University of Chicago
Chicago, Illinois

LANKFORD, John

Associate Professor of History
University of Missouri
Columbia, Missouri

LINDER, Robert D.

Associate Professor of History
Kansas State University
Manhattan, Kansas

LINKER, R. W.

Associate Professor of History
The Pennsylvania State University
University Park, Pennsylvania

LOCKHART, Arthur

LUMAN, Richard

Professor of Medieval History
Haverford College
Haverford, Pennsylvania

LYON, John

Associate Professor, General Pro-
gram of Liberal Studies
University of Notre Dame
Notre Dame, Indiana

MC CUE, James F.

Associate Professor of Theology
School of Religion
The University of Iowa
Iowa City, Iowa

MACLEAR, J. F.

Professor of History
University of Minnesota
Duluth, Minnesota

MAGAW, Malcolm O.

Associate Professor of English
Louisiana State University
Baton Rouge, Louisiana

MASSEY, James

Graduate Student
The University of Chicago
Chicago, Illinois

MERSCHEL, Carl

Assistant Professor, Science of
Society
Monteith College, Wayne State
University
Detroit, Michigan

MEYENDORFF, John

Professor of Patristics and
Church History
St. Vladimir's Orthodox
Theological Seminary
Crestwood, Tuckahoe, New York

MEYER, Charles R.

Professor of Systematic Theology
St. Mary-of-the-Lake Seminary
Mundelein, Illinois

MEYVAERT, Paul J.

Art History Librarian and
Lecturer
Duke University
Durham, North Carolina

MOREAU, Jules Laurence

Professor of Ecclesiastical History
Seabury-Western Theological
Seminary
Evanston, Illinois

MOYLAN, Prudence

Graduate Student
Indiana University
Bloomington, Indiana

MURRAY, Andrew E.

Professor and Chairman, Depart-
ment of Religion
Lincoln University
Lincoln University, Pennsylvania

NASH, Lee M.

Associate Professor of History
Northern Arizona University
Flagstaff, Arizona

NELSON, James D.

Associate Professor of Theology
United Theological Seminary
Dayton, Ohio

NICHOLS, Constance D.

Instructor in History
The University of Chicago
Chicago, Illinois

NORTH, James B.

Teaching Assistant, Department
of History
University of Illinois
Champaign, Illinois

O'BRIEN, John A.

Author in Residence and Special
Lecturer in Theology
University of Notre Dame
Notre Dame, Indiana

OSBORN, Ronald E.

Professor of Church History
Christian Theological Seminary
Indianapolis, Indiana

PEARSON, Samuel C., Jr.

Associate Professor of History
Southern Illinois University
Edwardsville, Illinois

PEDERSON, Phillip E.

Graduate Student
The University of Chicago
Chicago, Illinois

PENTON, James M.

Associate Professor of History
The University of Lethbridge
Lethbridge, Alberta, Canada

PFAFF, Richard W.

Associate Professor of History
University of North Carolina
Chapel Hill, North Carolina

PHILLIPS, John R.

Assistant Professor of Art History
and Humanities
Reed College
Portland, Oregon

PIERCE, Roderic H.

Associate Professor of the History
and Mission of the Church
Bexley Hall Divinity School
Kenyon College
Gambier, Ohio

PIPER, John F., Jr.

Assistant Professor, Department
of History
Lycoming College
Williamsport, Pennsylvania

RAITT, Jill

Assistant Professor of Religious
Studies
University of California
Riverside, California

ROGERS, Charles Allen

Assistant Professor of Church
  History
Evangelical Theological Seminary
Naperville, Illinois

RUFFIN, Joe David

SALLEY, Coleen Cole

Assistant Professor of Education
Louisiana State University
Baton Rouge, Louisiana

SANDEEN, Ernest R.

Associate Professor of History
Macalester College
St. Paul, Minnesota

SCHATTSCHNEIDER, David A.

Instructor in Church History
Moravian Theological Seminary
Bethlehem, Pennsylvania

SCHUELER, Donald G.

Associate Professor of English
Louisiana State University
Baton Rouge, Louisiana

SIMPSON, Robert L.

Professor of Philosophy and
  Religion
Phillips University
Enid, Oklahoma

SKARSTEN, Trygve R.

Assistant Professor of Church
  History
Divinity School
Yale University
New Haven, Connecticut

SMITH, Bernard S.

Associate Professor of History
Swarthmore College
Swarthmore, Pennsylvania

SMITH, Verlyn O.

Director of Campus Ministry
  Work for the Lutheran Church
  on the West Coast
Palo Alto, California

SMYLIE, James H.

Professor of Church History
Union Theological Seminary
Richmond, Virginia

SMYLIE, John

President
Queens College
Charlotte, North Carolina

SPIELMANN, Richard M.

Associate Professor of Church
  History and Liturgics
Bexley Hall Divinity School
Kenyon College
Gambier, Ohio

STAMMLER, Heinrich A.

Professor of Slavic Languages
  and Literature
University of Kansas
Lawrence, Kansas

STEECE, Arvel M.

Minister, Congregational Church
Bennington, Vermont

STEESZ, Willis R.

Associate Professor of Religion
Wright State University
Dayton, Ohio

STEIN, K. James

Professor of Church History
Evangelical Theological Seminary
Naperville, Illinois

STOREY, William G.

Associate Professor, Department
  of Theology
University of Notre Dame
Notre Dame, Indiana

STRAIN, Isaac

Deceased

SUTHERLAND, Randolph

Graduate Student
The University of Chicago
Chicago, Illinois

SWOMLEY, John M., Jr.

Professor of Christian Ethics
Saint Paul School of Theology
Kansas City, Missouri

TALLEY, Thomas J.

Associate Professor of Liturgics
  and Church Music
Nashotah House
Nashotah, Wisconsin

TODD, Wayne P.

TORBERT, Robert F.

Executive Director, Division of
  Cooperative Christianity
American Baptist Convention
Valley Forge, Pennsylvania

TUCKER, William E.

Dean, Brite Divinity School
Texas Christian University
Fort Worth, Texas

VAPORIS, Nomikos Michael

Assistant Professor of Eastern
  European History
Schools of Arts and Sciences
Hellenic College
Brookline, Massachusetts

VOLZ, Carl Andrew

Professor of Historical Theology
Concordia Seminary
St. Louis, Missouri

WAGGONER, Mary

Assistant Professor of English
Louisiana State University
Baton Rouge, Louisiana

WALLACE, Dewey D., Jr.

Associate Professor of Religion
George Washington University
Washington, D.C.

WATSON, Cresap

Professor of English and Chair-
  man of the Department
Louisiana State University
Baton Rouge, Louisiana

WECKMAN, George

Assistant Professor of Philosophy
Ohio University
Athens, Ohio

WERNER, Richard

Graduate Student
The University of Chicago
Chicago, Illinois

WHITBREAD, Leslie G.

Professor of English
Louisiana State University in
  New Orleans
New Orleans, Louisiana

WILTERDINK, Garret

Assistant Professor of Theology
Western Theological Seminary
Holland, Michigan

ZACEK, Judith Cohen

Formerly Assistant Professor
  of History
San Fernando Valley State
  College
Northridge, California

ZATKO, James J.

Professor of History
St. Mary's College
Notre Dame, Indiana

# THE WESTMINSTER
# DICTIONARY OF CHURCH HISTORY

# A

**Aachen, Synods of** (816, 817, 818–819). Three reforming synods of the Frankish Church, held under the direction of Louis the Pious. The first (816), attended probably by bishops and by laity, reformed the secular clergy by providing a rule (the Aachen Rule) establishing the common canonical life for nonmonastic clergy. A similar rule was provided for consecrated women, known as canonesses. Each metropolitan was to have an accurate copy of the rule and supervise its observance. The second synod (817) adopted the reform of monasteries proposed by Benedict of Aniane. All Frankish monasteries were placed under the direction of Benedict, then abbot of the imperial monastery of Inde. The third synod (818–819) considered matters relating to the administration and discipline of dioceses. Bishops were to be freely elected by the clergy and the laity. Serfs could be ordained only if previously freed by their masters. The education and the discipline of the parochial clergy were to be supervised by the bishops. Other canons provided for a minimum age for tonsure, clergy for proprietary churches, and the division of tithes. Several items relating to the monasteries were also discussed. Few of these reforms survived the disorders that arose from the civil wars between the sons of Louis the Pious.

**Aachen Cathedral.** A chapel built at Aachen by the emperor Charlemagne. This Palatine chapel served Charlemagne and his court and was dedicated to the Virgin Mary by Pope Leo III in 805. It has always enjoyed cathedral rank. The original structure was a high, vaulted octagon whose models were Byzantine and Roman. It incorporated marble columns and other antique elements brought from Ravenna and Rome. Although the mosaics have been restored and the church itself enlarged by a great Gothic nave, the Carolingian octagon survives almost entire.

**Abbasid Dynasty** (750–1258). Thirty-seven caliphs who ruled Islam from 750 to 1258. Marwin II, the last caliph of the Umayyad dynasty, was defeated in 750 and Abu-al-Abbas, who claimed descent from Mohammed's uncle Abbas, became the first ruler of the new line. The capital was moved from Syria to Baghdad, and a complex structure of government on all levels was established, centering around Islamic orthodoxy. The most famous of the Abbasids was Haroun-al-Rashid, though his reign marked the beginning of the decline of the dynasty, which was overthrown in 1258 by the Mongol invasion.

**Abbess.** The title of the head of a community of religious women who follow the Benedictine Rule. In the government of the community, an abbess holds the same authority as an abbot, although she may not administer sacraments. During the Middle Ages, abbesses exercised great power and were entitled to use the miter and the crosier. Many of the privileges of the abbess were revoked by the Council of Trent. The title is used also by superiors of the Franciscan Second Order.

**Abbey.** An autonomous monastic community (and its buildings) under the rule of an abbot. The traditional plan of the buildings includes an oratory (chapel), a chapter room (for assemblies of the community in which a chapter of the rule is read), a refectory, and dormitories all arranged around a cloister or an open inner court. In church jurisdiction, abbeys are independent of the local bishop.

**Abbot.** The title of the head of a monastery of the Benedictine tradition. The abbot (from *abba,* "father") is the father of the house, regulating the observance of the rule, governing the house and its outlying missions, and conferring minor orders and confirmation within the area of his jurisdiction. A Benedictine abbot is elected for life and receives a quasi-sacramental blessing from a bishop. The Benedictine Order is headed by an abbot primate, who resides in Rome.

**Abbot, George** (1562–1633). Archbishop of Canterbury. The son of a Guildford clothworker, he was educated at Balliol College,

Oxford (B.A., 1578), and became master of University College (1597). He was vice-chancellor of Oxford in the beginning years of James I (1600, 1603), and again in 1605. From the beginning he opposed the rising influence of William Laud, who was openly antagonistic to Calvinism and Puritanism, and he often showed affinities with the Puritan cause. In return for services to the king he was made bishop of Lichfield in 1609 and within a month was translated to London. In 1611, he became archbishop of Canterbury. Many of his contemporaries (e.g., Lord Clarendon and Anthony Wood) considered him ill-qualified for this elevation to office. Clarendon thought of him as being "totally ignorant of the true constitution of the Church of England." Wood thought that his ignorance of the priestly office was the reason for his showing more respect to "a cloak than a cassock." However, he seemed to be a man of inflexible honesty. He refused to allow the king's *Book of Sports,* which commended Sunday recreations, to be read in church at Croydon. He remonstrated with King James on the proposed Spanish marriage of the Prince of Wales, and was often a stubborn obstacle to the king's wishes. Abbot carried on a continuous conflict with the common lawyers, whose encroachments on the church's rights he believed to be a serious menace. Though he crowned Charles I, he was never in much favor with this monarch, and spent a great part of his later years in semiretirement at Croydon, further discredited by his accidental shooting of a gamekeeper in 1622. Abbot was a benefactor of Balliol College and a principal founder of Pembroke College, Oxford. His most enduring contribution is perhaps his translation of the Gospels for the Authorized (King James) Version of 1611.

**Abbott, Lyman** (1835–1922). Congregational clergyman, editor, and author. Abbott accepted modern Biblical scholarship, stressed the moral and spiritual values of Christianity, and was sympathetic to the current evolutionary hypothesis of Thomas Huxley, John Tyndall, and Herbert Spencer. In 1860, after a brief career in law, Abbott became pastor of the Congregational Church in Terre Haute, Ind., where he was given an unusual amount of pulpit freedom. Like Lincoln, he advocated a moderate reconstruction and in 1865 became corresponding secretary of the American Union Commission, formed to cooperate with the Federal Government in reconstruction. He also began to write for *Harper's Magazine,* and from 1870 to 1876 was editor of *The Illustrated Christian Weekly.* He then joined Henry Ward Beecher in editing the *Christian Union* (which became *The Outlook* in 1893), becoming editor in chief in 1881. Abbott succeeded Beecher in 1890 to the important pulpit of the Plymouth Congregational Church in Brooklyn, N.Y., but retired in 1899 to devote himself to editing and nationwide lecture tours on behalf of reform movements. He made *The Outlook* a powerful journal for "progressive and practical Christianity." Against denominational opposition, he supported Theodore Roosevelt and the Progressive Party, and advocated early United States entry into World War I. Abbott's books include *The Life and Literature of the Ancient Hebrews* (1901), *Theology of an Evolutionist* (1897), *The Other Room* (1903), and *The Spirit of Democracy* (1910).

**Abel, Charles W.** (1863–1930). Missionary to the Papuans. Abel lived part of his youth with the Maoris of New Zealand. He was educated at Chestnut College, England, and had some medical training at the London Hospital. In 1889 he was appointed by the London Missionary Society to new territory in New Guinea on the island of Kwato among the Papuans. Serving sacrificially and industriously, he introduced crafts and industries and the Christian faith, and realized the establishment of a strong indigenous Papuan church.

**Abelard, Peter** (1079–1142). Theologian. Born in Pallet, Brittany, he studied with the famous nominalist Roscellinus at Loches, then with William of Champeaux. He opened his own school at Melun, moving it later to Corbeil. In an encounter with William of Champeaux on the question of universals, Abelard made William look inconsistent. This caused Abelard's fame to spread, and the school at Mont Ste. Geneviève, where he became master, attracted many students. About this time Abelard studied under Anselm of Laon, but found that Anselm's method of glossing the texts of Scripture was old-fashioned. By delivering a lecture on Ezekiel, one of the most difficult books of the Bible for scholars, Abelard considered that he had vanquished Anselm. About 1115, Abelard was in Paris, living at the home of Fulbert, canon of Notre Dame, whose niece Héloïse he was teaching. Abelard and Héloïse had a son, Astrolabe, and were secretly married after his birth. Héloïse, realizing that marriage would hinder a philosopher's career, agreed to retire to the convent at Argenteuil. Abelard was castrated by the servants of the enraged Fulbert, and he withdrew to the monastery of St.-Denis. Here, shocked at the laxity in observance of the rule, Abelard received permission to open a school nearby, where he taught the arts and theology. In 1121, Lotulph and Alberic of Reims accused Abelard of heresy concerning the Trinity. Abelard was brought before the papal legate, canon of Praeneste, at Soissons. He was sentenced to remain in a monastery for a year, not for heresy but for teaching without a license. Abelard returned to St.-Denis, where he incurred the anger of the monks by proving from Bede that the patron of the monastery was not the bishop of Corinth associated with Paul. He had to flee the monastery, and took refuge with Theobald of Champagne. Dispensed from his vows at this time, he founded, not far from Troyes, an oratory dedicated to the Holy Trinity. So many students followed him that when invited to take charge of the monastery of St. Gildas at Ruits in Brittany, he accepted. Conditions at St. Gildas were unbearable, and Abelard returned to his oratory, which now became the refuge for Héloïse and some of her nuns who were driven from Argenteuil by the reforms of Abbot Suger. Together, Abelard and Héloïse founded the convent called the Paraclete, which was papally approved in 1131. In the 1130's he must have been engaged in teaching and in reworking his treatises. In 1139, William of St. Thierry, Cistercian at Signy, informed Bernard of Clairvaux that the writings of Abelard contained heretical statements on the Trinity and the Person of Christ. At Bernard's suggestion, Abelard was brought before the Council of Sens (1140), at which Louis VII and the bishops of the provinces of Sens and Reims were present. The condemnations were read. Abelard expected a debate, but seeing that there was to be none, he fled before he could be condemned. He hoped to appeal to Rome, but realizing on his way there that Bernard's letters had already arrived in Rome, Abelard retired to Cluny, where he died in 1142. Abelard was one of the most famous teachers of the 12th century. Among his pupils were Popes Celestine II and III, Otto of Freising, Fulkes of Dol, John of Salisbury, and some cardinals. He left an autobiography, *The Story of My Misfortunes.* This is one of the few autobiographies in the Middle Ages prior to the 13th century. In the *Dialectica,* Abelard developed a system of logic as far as it was possible without knowing the complete *Organon* of Aristotle. In the treatise *Know Thyself,* Abelard stressed the importance of the intention in determining the morality of an act. On the subject of theology he wrote *An Introduction to Christian Theology,* which attempts a systematic treatment of the doctrines of faith. He was the first to use the term "theology" to describe such a system.

Other works are the *Sic et non,* his exegesis on the letter to the Romans, and his letters to Héloïse. His love poems have been lost. Abelard has been hailed as the precursor of free thought, as the champion of reason over faith. A study of his writings shows that he was, rather, a man of faith who approached faith with new methods, and who sought greater understanding of his creed by the use of reason.

**Abercius** (Avircius Marcellus). Bishop of Hieropolis in Phrygia, c. 190. Vigorously opposed to Montanism, Abercius is also known from his tombstone, discovered in 1883. The inscription shows that Abercius traveled not only in the East (as far as Nisibis) but also to Rome; he shared in Eucharistic worship everywhere. The language of the inscription is intentionally cryptic, perhaps because of the danger of persecution.

**Aberdeen Episcopalians.** See SCOTTISH EPISCOPAL CHURCH.

**Aberhart, William** (1878–1943). Canadian Baptist layman and politician. Founder of the Prophetic Baptist movement and the Social Credit Party. He was born near Seaforth, Ontario, where he attended school. Thereafter he was at the Chatham Business College, the Hamilton Normal College, and Queen's University, where he obtained a B.A. in 1906. In 1902, he married Jessie Flatt, of Galt, Ontario. He was a schoolteacher from 1906 to 1914, and in 1915 became principal of Crescent Heights High School, Calgary, Alberta, where he remained until 1935. He founded the Calgary Prophetic Bible Institute in 1918 and organized the Social Credit Party in Alberta. In 1935, he became premier of Alberta and minister of education.

**Abgar.** Title given to many kings of Osroene (capital city, Edessa). The *Ecclesiastical History* of Eusebius of Caesarea contains apocryphal correspondence between Abgar V (A.D. 13–50) and Jesus, presumably placed in the royal archives after the conversion of Abgar IX (179–214) to Christianity. The Christian layman Julius Africanus met Bardesanes at the court of Abgar IX.

**Abolition Movement.** A movement in the United States before the Civil War, strongly opposing slavery and the slave trade. Although slavery had already been criticized on humanitarian and religious grounds, few voices were raised against the importation of Negro slaves into the American colonies. Accepted by Anglicans as an economic necessity for plantation colonies and by Puritans on the basis of divinely ordained human inequalities, it was first criticized by radical sectarians and such lonely figures as Samuel Sewall in Massachusetts. Before independence, Ralph Sandiford, John Woolman, and Anthony Benezet were vocal Quaker critics, joined by Benjamin Franklin and the Congregationalist Samuel Hopkins. In 1776, the Quakers sought to expel slaveholders from their ranks.

In time the abolition of slavery became tied to the doctrine of natural rights, democratic principles, enlightened humanitarianism, and evangelical religion. Benezet considered it particularly ironic that the Declaration of Independence proclaimed the rights of man without condemning Negro slavery. The writers of the U.S. Constitution did not debate over slavery, interpreting it as a state matter. David Rice, Kentucky Presbyterian leader, lost a fight for an abolition clause in that state's constitution, while in 1800 the Methodist bishop Francis Asbury noted that the religious bodies of America did nothing about slavery. The exponents of slavery used Scripture, religious tradition, and economic necessity to uphold it.

After the War of 1812, sectionalism became involved. The North saw slavery as incompatible with natural law, God's will, and the Declaration of Independence, whereas the South defended it as commensurate with Negro racial inferiority, the needs of Southern institutions, Scripture and history, and a romantic view of society. As positions hardened, the voice of abolition disappeared in the South and the Grimke sisters, James G. Birney, Levi Coffin, and Edward Coles exiled themselves. The founding in the North of the American Colonization Society (1816) represented a compromise, acknowledging the inferior race theory but also Northern guilt over slavery. It sought to return Negroes to Africa to develop their own culture. The Congregationalist Leonard Bacon was influential in the Society until drawn by S. S. Jocelyn to the idea of integrating Negroes into American society.

The first abolitionist newspaper was the *Philanthropist* (1817–1819), published in Ohio by the Southern Quaker Charles Osborn, later the editor of the *Manumission Intelligencer* in Tennessee. In 1820, the Quaker Elihu Embree established the *Emancipator* in Tennessee. Benjamin Lundy, also a Quaker, founded in 1821 the *Genius of Universal Emancipation* in Ohio and after moving to Baltimore made William Lloyd Garrison his assistant in 1828. Garrison's advocacy of immediatism and uncompromising emancipation led to the demise of the *Genius,* his imprison-

ment, and his move to Boston to publish the *Liberator* in 1831. Lundy's position was characteristic of these earlier abolitionists—not fanatical but unwilling to compromise. His seven points eventually were appropriated wholly or in part by most later abolition societies: abolition by the national government, no new slave states, prohibition of internal slave trade, the three-fifths compromise in the Constitution repealed, equal citizenship for free Negroes, aid to recolonizers, and black codes abolished in slave states. By 1830 the abolition movement became closely tied to the social reform programs of the "benevolent empire," a revival-oriented religious humanitarianism. Slavery was considered a sin of which all Christians were guilty. As it denied the worth of the individual and human equality, it was also conceived to be a menace to democracy. Marred by a "holier than thou" self-righteousness, it decried the cruelty and ruthlessness of slaveholders in many "authentic" tracts.

The abolition movement gained real impetus, not from Garrison and New England, but from the West and from New York philanthropists. George Gale, who had converted Charles G. Finney, founded Oneida Institute and Knox College, both centers of abolitionism. Theodore Dwight Weld was converted by Finney, studied at Lane Seminary in Cincinnati, and learned abolitionism at the feet of the Englishman Charles Stuart. His and other students' activities to aid Negroes in Cincinnati led to a break with the Lane authorities, including President Lyman Beecher. The students left Lane and with the help of Finney and the Tappan brothers of the "benevolent empire" formed a seminary at Oberlin College, which became the center of Western abolitionism. At the same time, Elizur Wright and Beriah Green made Western Reserve College another abolitionist stronghold. Meanwhile, Garrison formed the New England Anti-Slavery Society in 1832, which led to interest in a national society. This was attempted by the New York leaders of the "benevolent empire" but was frustrated through conflict over immediatism or gradualism. News of British emancipation in 1833 led to the quick formation of the American Anti-Slavery Society. Though Garrison was influential, its strength lay in the Western principle of avoiding hostility by stressing "immediate abolition, gradually accomplished." Quickly built up by the tracts, agents, local societies, and fund programs of the Weld-Finney group, it reached its peak in 1836 and then declined rapidly. It had been harmed by its association with Garrisonianism, a lack of centralization, disorganization, and a frustrating inability to draw leading abolitionists such as John Quincy Adams. A split between the Western group and the Garrisonians in 1840 was never healed and led to the formation of the American and Foreign Anti-Slavery Society. Both societies became largely ineffective. Many individual religious leaders were involved in abolitionism. William Ellery Channing, after a long silence, found that slavery contradicted justice and freedom. It is impossible to overestimate the effect of Harriet Beecher Stowe's *Uncle Tom's Cabin,* which was probably the most potent force in molding public opinion. Revivalistic lectures were second only to Uncle Tom. Weld presented slavery not as a political or economic issue, but a moral question. "If your hearts ache and bleed, we want you; you will help us; but if you merely adopt our principles as dry theories, let us alone." Weld's *Slavery as It Is* (1839) compiled "authentic" accounts of the sufferings of slaves.

There was also violence against abolitionists. It culminated in the murder of the Rev. Elijah Lovejoy, editor of an abolitionist paper in Alton, Ill., in 1837. This led to an identification of civil liberty and abolitionism, the participation of Horace Greeley, and the meteoric rise of Wendell Phillips as an abolition spokesman. Violence also marred the 1838 women's antislavery convention and brought Lucretia Mott, Maria Chapman, Angelina Grimke, and Abby Kelly to public attention.

Many clergy, while critical of slavery, repudiated abolition. They were epitomized in Leonard Bacon. Lyman Beecher deplored the violence and hatred it created and the disorganization of the entire antislavery movement. Francis Wayland insisted that slavery would peacefully disappear through the teachings of the love of justice and the fear of God. The Northern bishop John Henry Hopkins insisted that Negroes were better off and happier as slaves. Antislavery societies, their agents, and irregular lecturers were received only by the Baptists and the Methodists, while other denominations remained aloof. In 1836, Leonard Bacon promoted the "Connecticut gag law" preventing the use of pulpits by abolitionists. This practice spread to other states and led the Garrisonians to assail the churches as cages "of unclean birds," foes of God and man, and "bulwarks of American slavery." Parker Pillsbury, Stephen S. Foster, and George Stoors were imprisoned when their attempts to use pulpits led to riots. The Episcopal Church avoided the slavery controversy and in the South represented planter opinion. In 1818, the Presbyterians condemned slavery and recommended abolition, but this was smothered by rising Southern control headed by J. H. Thornwell, who linked abolitionism with atheism, socialism, communism, and Jacobinism. This conflict helped to foster Presbyterian schism in 1838. At first the Methodists rejected slavery, but growing Southern strength led to a gag rule in 1836 and a pastoral letter urging the clergy to avoid controversy. The Methodists divided in 1844 and the Baptists in 1841–1845. A few Southern clergy remained covert abolitionists, notably Robert J. Breckinridge, John G. Fee, and Moncure Conway. Most Southern clerical opinion was represented in Howell Cobb's defense in *A Scriptural Examination of Slavery* (1856). Quakers were the first to make extensive efforts to aid fugitive slaves, notably in Pennsylvania and Delaware. The Underground Railroad was centered in Ohio, Indiana, and Illinois, notably at Oberlin, Western Reserve, Illinois College, and Knox College. As open conflict drew near, Gerrit Smith, Franklin B. Sanborn, Thomas W. Higginson, and Theodore Parker went so far as to become involved in John Brown's adventure at Harpers Ferry. Because the Midwest, through revivalistic means, became antislavery, it won Lincoln the election in 1860.

BIBLIOGRAPHY: G. H. Barnes, *The Anti-Slavery Impulse: 1830–1844* (Gloucester, Mass., reprinted 1957); W. J. Cash, *The Mind of the South* (New York, 1941); A. F. Tyler, *Freedom's Ferment* (New York, 1962).

**Acacian Schism** (484–519). So called after the patriarch Acacius, who drafted the Henoticon of Zeno which was rejected at Rome. The Church in Italy, where German rulers governed in the name of the emperors, was thus for a generation out of communion with the imperial Byzantine Church. In 518, the Henoticon was repudiated at Constantinople and the Council of Chalcedon again accepted, and in the following year the schism was ended on the terms prescribed by Pope Hormisdas.

**Academies, Dissenting.** Educational institutions established by Dissenters. When the English universities were closed in 1662 to Dissenters, they developed an educational system of their own. At first these academies were small, seeking primarily to train theological students. Later, however, they responded to the needs of the upper middle class for a practical modern education. Although the universities continued to provide a classical education, the academies gave more attention to science, modern languages, and commercial subjects.

**Acadia, Expulsion of Roman Catholics from.** The driving out of the French Roman Catholic inhabitants by the English when the latter were in control of Acadia. Between 1598 and 1610 the French pioneered in the settlement of Acadia (Nova Scotia). The region became a bone of contention in the imperial struggles between France and England, the English gaining permanent control in 1713. Upon the renewal of hostilities with France prior to the Seven Years' War, the English, in 1755, removed over 6,000 Acadians, scattering them among the English colonies.

**Acarie, Mme.** (*née* Avrillot) (1566–1618). French mystic who introduced the Discalced Carmelites into France. She was the wife of Pierre Acarie, a councilor of the French Parlement. Their home served as the meeting place for some of the most noted Roman Catholics in the country, including Pierre de Bérulle and Francis of Sales. As a consequence of certain visions that she experienced, Mme. Acarie brought Teresa of Ávila's reformed (Discalced) Carmelites into France, and, when her husband died in 1613, she became a lay sister in that order, taking the name Marie of the Incarnation.

**Accommodation Plan** (1808). A plan accepted in 1808 to effect a uniform church government for congregations developing under the American Plan of Union by providing that a consociation of Congregational churches enter the Presbyterian synod in the same relation to it as that of a presbytery, its ministers to be members of the synod, and the delegates of its churches to have the same status as ruling elders. However, the consociation was to rule its internal affairs in the congregational manner.

**Acontius, James** (Jacopo Aconzio) (c. 1500–c. 1566). Anglo-European inventor and writer on religious subjects. He was born at Trent. All but his later years are obscure. He was in England by 1559. In 1565, he published his *The Stratagems of Satan,* advocating a distinction between fundamental and accessory dogma in Christianity, and an increase of toleration regarding the latter. Strongly influenced by humanism, he desired a rationalizing and moralizing of theology.

**Acosta, Joseph** (c. 1540–1600). One of the first Jesuits to work in South America. Acosta went to Peru in 1569 as a theology teacher, served for a time as provincial of his order in the territory, founded five colleges, and spent considerable time studying the land and its people. Acosta's merits as a naturalist rest on his *Historia natural y moral de las Indias.* Although it shows his interest in the physical and religious condition of the natives, the book nevertheless defends the Spanish colonial policy.

**Acta Sanctorum.** The name applied to two series of lives of the saints, arranged according to feast days, which assemble the known biographies and legends of each saint. The first series was conceived by the Jesuit Heribert Rosweyde, but was actually begun by John Bolland, S.J. (d. 1665). A small group of scholars, now known as the Bollandists, have continued the project, publishing the collected lives of the saints, as well as an auxiliary work *Analecta Bollandiana.* Work was suspended in 1773 when the Jesuits were suppressed. An attempt was made to establish the Jesuits at the Premonstratensian abbey at Tongerloo, Belgium, but this eventually failed. After the restoration of the order, work was begun again in 1837. Occasional suspensions of work have occurred because of European wars.

The second series was undertaken by the former Benedictine Congregation of St. Maur (Maurists). Primarily the work of Jean Mabillon and Luc d'Acherey, it was limited to saints of the Benedictine Order. The task was begun in 1668 and completed in 1701. Since the dissolution of the Maurists, no attempt has been made to reedit this work. It has been superseded by the more extensive compilations of the Bollandists. The auxiliary sciences of paleography, diplomatics, and archaeology were developed by these groups in order to prepare their works.

**Actio Catholica.** See CATHOLIC ACTION.

**Action Française, L'.** An intensely nationalistic French political movement begun in 1899 by Charles Maurras. Although an atheist himself, he believed that Roman Catholicism and a hereditary monarchy were essential to French civilization. The movement included many Catholics who viewed political democracy as a threat to the authority of the church. However, in 1926 the movement was condemned by Pius XI and its newspaper, *L'Action Française,* was put on the Index.

**Act of Uniformity** (1559). The third of a series of Parliamentary enactments prescribing the use of the Book of Common Prayer and attendance at Anglican services. It was a feature of the Elizabethan compromise which established the Anglican Church in England. This act required the use of a revised form of the Edwardian Book of Common Prayer of 1552. Clerical vestments, pictures, crucifixes, and church music were retained, while the earlier stand against the pope was modified. All clergy were required to adhere to the liturgy of this service book and all Englishmen were to attend church. (See UNIFORMITY, ACTS OF.)

**Acton, John Emerich** (1834–1902). Noted English historian. Acton was a member of Parliament and later Cambridge professor of modern history. As a Roman Catholic layman who was greatly concerned with the cause of religious liberty and free intellectual inquiry, he strongly opposed the Syllabus of Errors and in 1869 went to Rome to organize resistance at the first Vatican Council to the proposed definition of papal infallibility. He considered that he belonged more to the soul than to the body of the Catholic Church.

**Adalbert of Bohemia** (*known as* Voitěch) (c. 950–997). Bishop of Prague. The Slavs knew him by his baptismal name, Voitěch. He became bishop of Prague in 983 and was active in evangelizing the Magyars. Political difficulties led him to leave Bohemia and go to Italy, where he became a monk at Rome. After an unsuccessful attempt to return to Prague he went to Pomerania to evangelize pagan Prussians, by whom he was martyred in 997. His relics were transferred from Gnesen to Prague in 1039.

**Adalbert of Bremen** (c. 1000–1072). Archbishop of Hamburg-Bremen from 1045. He rose to prominence during the reign of Henry III. Adalbert helped Henry contend with the Saxon house of Billung, and Henry supported the diocese's mission to Scandinavia. Henry's pagan reaction and death (1056) complicated Adalbert's later life. The principal source for his life is the history by Adam of Bremen, Adalbert's younger associate.

**Adam of Bremen.** Author of the *History of the Archbishops of Hamburg-Bremen.* Little is known of his life, but he was probably born in upper Saxony and educated at Magdeburg. He came to Bremen in 1068. His *History,* which extends to the death of Adalbert (1072), is one of the best in the Middle Ages, and the principal source for the early history of the archbishopric and its northern mission.

**Adamson, Patrick** (1537–1592). Scottish church leader and foe of Presbyterianism. After studying philosophy and taking an M.A. at the University of St. Andrews, Adamson became minister at Ceres in 1563 shortly after the first triumph of the Reformation. In 1566 he left his charge and went to Paris as a tutor. On the occasion of the birth of James VI he wrote a Latin poem praising this son of Mary, Queen of Scots, as the legitimate ruler of Scotland, France, England, and Ireland. The French were offended, and Adamson spent six months in prison. At Bourges, upon his release he was again embroiled in French civil problems, and went then to Geneva. Here he met Beza and studied theology. About 1572, Adamson returned to Scotland as minister at Paisley. His outspoken opposition to Presbyterianism brought him into conflict with the General Assembly, which excommunicated him twice. His appointment by the regent to the archbishopric of St. Andrews heightened his conflict with the Assembly of the Kirk. Though he had great gifts as a writer and a speaker, he had little skill as an administrator. This weakness, joined with his increasing unpopularity with the Assembly, lost him the support of the Crown and eventually the revenue of his see. Adamson spent his final years under the cloud of heresy charges and supported by charity.

***Ad Apostolorum Principis.*** The encyclical (June 29, 1958) of Pius XII to the clergy and faithful in Communist China. It excommunicated all Chinese bishops who had consecrated progovernment prelates without Vatican approval and condemned the schismatic Patriotic Association of the Catholics of China, which was led by a Communist layman. The letter was circulated by underground means in China before publication at Rome on Sept. 8.

**Addai.** Legendary apostle of Edessa. He was said to have been sent by the apostle Thomas to the court of Abgar V of Osroene after the ascension. Eusebius of Caesarea got the legend from the Syriac Acts of Thaddaeus ( = Addai) (c. 280), but it grew independently later as shown by the *Pilgrimage of Silvia Aquitania* (c. 380) and the *Doctrine of Addai* (c. 400). The origin of the legend is to be sought in the 3d-century attempt to prove the apostolic foundation of the principal churches already in existence in the 2d century.

**Addams, Jane** (1860–1935). American humanitarian. Born and educated in Illinois, Jane Addams became interested in the problems of city slums while she was traveling in Europe. Having decided to try to develop a settlement house in Chicago, she studied Toynbee Hall, a settlement house in London, in 1888. In 1889, she returned to Chicago and with a friend, Ellen Gates Starr, secured the use of a house owned by Charles J. Hull and began the famous Hull House. She remained its director until her death. In the meantime she worked for other reforms—better sanitation, a tenement-house code, industrial education, and suppression of white slavery. Her work for world peace gave her a share of the Nobel Peace Prize in 1931. She held many national offices, received a multitude of honorary degrees, and died one of the most famous and beloved women in the land.

**Adelard of Bath** (early 12th century). English scholar and philosopher and an important figure in the history of science. Few details about his life remain except that he studied at Tours and Laon in France, and traveled extensively in Italy, Sicily, North Africa, and Asia Minor. He was especially interested in physics, astronomy, and mathematics, and was one of the first to make known to the West the scientific writings of the Greeks and the Arabs.

**Adiaphoristic Controversy.** A debate in 16th-century Lutheranism. *Adiaphora* is a Greek word meaning "things indifferent." In theology it refers to matters of religious life and worship (not of doctrine) which God neither commands nor prohibits. Luther, in a spirit of freedom, applied it to a wide range of "externals" which were to be left to church order to decide, but without binding the conscience. Controversy over this subject arose during the Leipzig Interim (1548–1552) imposed on the Lutheran churches by Emperor Charles V. Disappointed over the terms of the original Augsburg Interim, Melanchthon presented new terms that would permit the teaching of justification by faith to continue. To gain this, he had to concede the observance of many Romanist practices. He justified their inclusion by calling them "adiaphora." Matthias Flacius, objecting strongly to this interpretation, called Melanchthon a traitor for allowing the readmission of abuses. The Peace of Passau (1552) technically ended the Interim, but not until the Formula of Concord (1577) was the dispute settled among Lutherans. The Formula adopted the view that practices neither prescribed nor forbidden in Scripture should be matters of freedom, but are to be rejected whenever imposed as an obligation. A century later, Calvinists and Lutherans discussed whether or not secular amusements such as dancing should be considered "adiaphora," the former generally holding the stricter view, which the Lutheran Pietists adopted later.

**Adler, Felix** (1851–1933). Founder of the Society for Ethical Culture. German-born, Adler came to America as a boy and was educated at Columbia and in Germany (University of Heidelberg, Ph.D., 1873). He held professorships at Cornell and Columbia. His originating of the New York Society for Ethical Culture in 1876 set him upon a career of social service, lecturing, and writing. His most famous book was *Creed and Deed*.

**Admonitions to Parliament** (1572 and 1573). Two Puritan tracts presented to Parliament in 1572 and 1573. There was much unrest in England over the religious settlement which Elizabeth had effected. The Puritans looked to the Swiss models, desiring that the Reformed pattern be established in England. The *First Admonition*, written by John Field and Thomas Wilcox, condemned the Establishment for abuses in ecclesiastical usages and discipline. Positively, it advocated the Reformed pattern for the English Church. Appended to the tract were pro-Puritan letters by Beza and Gualther, Continental Reformers. Field and Wilcox were hurried to prison for their efforts, but the issues that they raised caused continuing controversy. The *Second Admonition* appeared the following year. It has been attributed to Thomas Cartwright, but that he wrote it is doubtful. The contents reveal a detailed exposition of the Presbyterian ideal of church government, with a request for relief from the subscription that Elizabeth required. Since the Puritans had achieved no success with Elizabeth in completing the Reformation, they hoped that Parliament might be the instrument to accomplish their purposes, but Elizabeth did not allow it. Though the *Admonitions* gave further intellectual support to the party, they accomplished little more.

**Adoptianism in Spain.** A doctrine originating in 8th-century Spain that Jesus became the Son of God by adoption at the time of his baptism or resurrection. The first indication of the Adoptianist controversy appears in the teaching of Elipandus of Toledo c. 780. At this time the Spanish Church was not in communication with the rest of Western thought, and seems to have been giving an Adoptianist interpretation to such authors as Augustine and Isidore of Seville. Elipandus regarded Christ's divine nature as the eternal Logos and his human nature as true humanity raised to the level of the divine. He was concerned to preserve the true humanity of Christ and accused his opponents of Docetism. The doctrines were further formulated by Felix of Urgel, who maintained that only the Adoptianist position preserved Christ's true humanity, without which man's salvation was impossible. If Christ was not the adopted human Son, then there was no possibility of other men being likewise adopted by the Father. Living in Arab domains, Elipandus was never brought to trial for his doctrines, but Felix was summoned before a Frankish council at Regensburg in 792, where he recanted. He returned to his diocese and began to teach Adoptianism again. The Council of Frankfurt in 794 again condemned his doctrine. His defense provoked a treatise against him by Alcuin. After recanting again, Felix retired to Lyons until his death. Adoptianism gradually disappeared in Spain after that.

**Adopting Act** (1729). A unitive action of the Presbyterian Synod in America in 1729 which provided that all ministers and licentiates subscribe to the Westminster Standards, but that if a person had scruples with regard to any article, he could at the time of admission state his views, and if the synod or presbytery judged this to affect only nonessentials, it would still admit him to the exercise of the ministry within its bounds.

**Adrian I** (d. 795). Pope from 772. He was born of a noble Roman family. After his election as pope, renewed harassment from the Lombards forced him to call upon Charlemagne and the Franks for military assistance. In 774, Charlemagne completely destroyed the Lombard kingdom and revived the Donation of Pepin, increasing the Papal States. Adrian, who presided over the Second Nicene Council, and the Franks disagreed sharply over the acceptance of the Nicene decrees of 787. The Franks misunderstood them as approving idol worship, and they were condemned by Charlemagne at Frankfurt in 794. Adrian did much to restore Rome and he established the temporal power of the pope.

**Adrian IV** (Nicholas Breakspear, c. 1100–1159). Pope from 1154. An English Augustinian, he became bishop of Albano in 1150 and papal legate to Scandinavia in 1152. The only Englishman ever to become pope, he was elected as Frederick I Barbarossa was entering Italy. He refused to deal with Arnold of Brescia, who was preaching against simony, the property rights of the church, and the efficacy of the sacraments under some circumstances, and put Rome under interdict. He exacted homage from Barbarossa in 1155 before crowning him, and had Arnold executed as a heretic. His claim that the Empire was a *beneficium* of the papacy started the long war between Barbarossa and the Lombard cities which lasted until their victory at Legnano.

**Adrian VI** (Adrian Florensz, 1459–1523). Pope from 1522. He was born at Utrecht, March 1, 1459, educated at Zwolle, with the Brethren of the Common Life, and at Louvain, where he studied philosophy, theology, and jurisprudence, being made Doctor of Divinity in 1491. He became a popular professor at Louvain and was tutor of future Emperor Charles V. Adrian was regarded as a saint when he was elected pope in 1522; his private life was simple and devout. As pontiff, he had four areas of concern: (1) reform of the Roman court and ecclesiastical administration, (2) reconciliation of the Christian princes, (3) arrest of the progress of Protestantism, (4) deliverance of Europe from the Turks. A climate of reform, however, did not yet exist in the Curia. Adrian's efforts to retrench expenses met with stiff opposition and ended in complete failure. His nuncio was received coldly when the pope proposed to assemble a general council in Germany. Vainly he tried to get the princes to execute the Decree of Worms and to proscribe religious novelties. Equally vainly he attempted to address Frederick III, Luther's protector. Finally, he failed in his call to the Christian princes to protect Rhodes, which fell to the Turks. Adrian was completely misunderstood by the Italian prelates, and was the last non-Italian pope.

**Adventism.** The doctrine held in common by various Christian groups that the Second Coming is to be expected immediately. The creed involves more than the belief in the Second Advent, however, and is bound up in a distrust of ameliorative social progress and in the belief that human ills are to be corrected by direct divine intervention and cosmic cataclysm.

Adventism in one form or another dates from earliest Christian times and is a leading tenet of so-called Fundamentalism, but as a denomination the Adventists date from 1831 when William Miller (1782–1849) first began to proclaim at Dresden, N.Y., that the Second Coming was imminent. On the basis of dates in the Old Testament and the prophetic words of Dan. 8:14, "Unto two thousand and three hundred days; then shall the sanctuary be cleansed," Miller set the date of the Second Coming on Oct. 22, 1843–1844. His group made many converts, held premillennium conferences, began a paper, *The Midnight Cry,* and when the year 1844 passed uneventfully, Miller suggested some later dates, always maintaining the imminence of the Second Coming. However, differences of opinion concerning the date and the character of the

Second Advent produced schisms, and a considerable shifting, splitting, and reconsolidation occurred in the original group. Disagreements over such matters as the inspiration of Mrs. Ellen G. White, the state of the dead, the observance of the seventh day as the Sabbath, and the Scriptural name of the church have created further branching of the Adventist bodies, and the Evangelical Adventists, the original Millerite group who retained a Catholic belief in an afterlife, disappeared from the scene about 1920.

The two largest bodies of Adventism are now the Second Advent Christians, or the Advent Christian Church, and the Seventh-day Adventists, both constituting themselves as separate groups after the 1844 failure. The former body believed that an error had been made in calculating the time of the Second Advent and thus set a second date of 1853 as that of the Second Coming, but when this too passed uneventfully they decided to remain separate and formed their own Advent Christian Association at Worcester, Mass., on Nov. 6, 1861. The Advent Christian Church holds doctrines similar to those of most Protestant churches, differing in their doctrines concerning the nature of man and the Second Advent, which they believe is indicated by Biblical prophecy. The Second Advent Christians also incorporated into their beliefs the doctrine that man is by nature mortal and that the dead lie unconscious in their graves until the resurrection.

The separate denomination of the Seventh-day Adventists also originated after the bitter disappointment of Oct. 22, 1844, but this group believed that the error had been made not in the year but in the nature of the event foretold. Under the leadership of Hiram Edson, this group decided that the prophecy of Daniel did not refer to a cleansing on earth but indicated an alteration in heaven, and that in the year 1844 there occurred a definite change in God's plans for mankind. After a close study of the Decalogue and in deference to Mrs. Rachel D. Preston, who had been a Seventh Day Baptist before joining Adventism, the group began to observe the Old Testament Sabbath from Friday sunset to Saturday sunset rather than Sunday as their day of rest and praise. The group was at first largely confined to the New England states, but in 1855 moved its headquarters to Battle Creek, Mich. In 1860, the group officially adopted the name "Seventh-day Adventist" and in May, 1863, became a formal denominational organization. It is the only body of Adventists to experience much growth, and now has well over 2,500 congregations, operates publishing houses, conducts high schools and colleges, a theological seminary, a medical school, hospitals, sanatariums, dispensaries, and clinics. The group is aggressively evangelistic and conducts missionary work in over 190 countries. Seventh-day Adventists condemn sensationalism and fanaticism and endorse a strict living code of total abstinence from liquor, tobacco, often tea and coffee, dancing, the theater, and related activities. The church believes that the Scriptures themselves provide an unerring rule of faith and practice, and insists upon adult baptism by total immersion as well as a tithe of 10 percent. The denomination holds that the exact time of the Second Coming cannot be discovered by a study of prophecy, but it retains the optimistic view that the return of Christ to earth will not be far away. Other Adventist denominations in the United States of much smaller membership than the Seventh-day Adventists are the various Church of God groups, usually distinct bodies identified by the additional name of their founder or church headquarters, such as the Primitive Advent Christian Church, and the Life and Advent Union, all of which adhere to the customary premillenarian doctrine.

BIBLIOGRAPHY: L. Froom, *The Prophetic Faith of Our Fathers,* 4 vols. (Washington, 1946–1954); A. A. Hoekema, *The Four Major Cults* (Grand Rapids, 1963); E. G. White, *The Story of Patriarchs and Prophets* (Mountain View, Calif., 1947); *Seventh-day Adventist Encyclopedia* (Washington, 1966).

**Advertisements, Book of** (1566). The regulations issued in 1566 by Archbishop Parker of Canterbury as an attempt to lay down minimum standards for clerical vesture, conduct of services, etc., to which the Puritan-minded clergy would conform. Queen Elizabeth prompted this action, but refused royal sanction for the provisions, thus weakening the authority of the *Advertisements.* Many of the clergy refused to conform to the book's stipulations.

**Advowson.** The right to nominate a cleric to an ecclesiastical benefice. Laymen who possess the right of advowson to a parish church may nominate a cleric for institution by the bishop. Bishops may possess the right themselves. The practice developed from the rights of feudal lords to appoint the clergy for churches on their own lands. Advowson has largely disappeared, except in the Church of England, where many lay patrons still hold this right.

**Aelfric** (c. 955–c. 1020). One of the outstanding figures of the 10th-century English

Benedictine monastic revival. A disciple of Ethelwold, he became the first abbot of Eynsham in Oxfordshire in 1005. He wrote the life of Ethelwold and other works in Latin, but is best known for his vernacular (Old English) compositions: homilies on the liturgical year, lives of saints, and doctrinal subjects; and translations from Holy Scripture and the works of Bede.

**Aelred of Rievaulx** (1109–1167). Abbot. After spending his early years in Scotland, Aelred entered the English Cistercian house of Rievaulx in 1133. He was elected abbot of Ravesby and, in 1147, abbot of Rievaulx. During his abbacy, the size of the monastery, as well as the entire order in England, increased greatly. He devoted himself to the visitation of English Cistercian houses and to writing. His most famous works are *Mirror of Charity* and *On Spiritual Friendship*.

**Aeterni Patris.** An encyclical issued on Aug. 4, 1879, by Pope Leo XIII, urging the study of "true" philosophy, especially that of Thomas Aquinas. Continued papal support, through various devices, strengthened the position of this philosophical system in the Catholic Church to the point where most of the opposition was forced to use Thomist terminology and redefine its position as just another interpretation of his thought. The effect has been to make Thomism the central subject of Roman Catholic philosophy.

**Aetius** (d. 366). Founder of the Anomoeans. His ordination to the diaconate at Antioch (350) challenged, he was inhibited. In dispute (356) with Basil of Ancyra, he was forced to flee to Alexandria, where he took on Eunomius as a pupil. Together they sought to clarify in a radical direction the ambiguities of Arius' system by means of syllogistic reasoning.

**Affair of the Placards.** See FRANCIS I.

**African Methodist Episcopal Church.** Oldest Negro denomination in the United States. It grew out of a protest of Negro members against racial discrimination in St. George's Methodist Church, Philadelphia, Pa. Under the leadership of Richard Allen, Bethel Church was begun in 1793. The first General Conference in 1816 chose Allen and Daniel Coker as bishops. Its doctrine and polity are similar to those of the Methodist Church. In 1951 it had over 1,000,000 members.

**African Methodist Episcopal Zion Church.** A church resulting from the withdrawal of Negroes from the John Street Methodist Church in New York City in protest against white control. In 1820, this group of Negroes (Zion Church) severed its ties with the Methodist Church and ordained its own elders. In polity and doctrine it is similar to the Methodist Church. In 1959 it reported some 770,000 members.

**Afrikaners.** A cultural group in the Union of South Africa which has descended predominantly from the early Dutch settlers. It maintains its identity through its language, Afrikaans, and its religion, Dutch Reformed. The group is currently noted for its conservative theological orientation and its extreme segregationist racial policies.

**Agape Work Camp.** Youth center in the mountains of northern Italy set up after World War II under the leadership of the Waldenses. It was completed in 1952 through the contributions and labor of youth from many countries and communions both Protestant and Roman Catholic. It is now used as an international conference center for Bible study, and for discussions on church renewal and various social issues.

**Agnosticism.** A view which holds that ultimate realities (the nature and existence of God, immortality, the origin of the universe) are both unknown and unknowable. The term "agnosticism" is usually attributed to Thomas H. Huxley, who is said to have coined the word in 1869 on the occasion of the formation of the Metaphysical Society. Huxley sought to indicate by agnosticism his rejection of all dogmatic isms whether atheistic or theistic. His scientific work led him to reject any statement as true unless it was supported by verifiable evidence. Huxley's agnosticism was more of a method than a creed. He was much influenced by William Hamilton's article "On the Philosophy of the Unconditioned" (1829), in which Hamilton extols the willingness to accept one's ignorance on ultimate matters as being evidence of man's supreme intellect and at the same time his most difficult assignment. Herbert Spencer maintained in his *First Principles* (1862) that neither science nor Christian dogma would be able to explain the ultimate nature of what lay beyond world processes and that in this realm of the unknowable, religion and science could join hands in reconciliation. By the mid-20th century, agnosticism had practically ceased to be used as a description of a person's creed or method and became a general term applied to all forms of skepticism.

**Agobard of Lyons** (c. 779–840). Theologian. Probably of Spanish stock, Agobard spent most of his career at Lyons, where he became archbishop (816). He took an active part in the polemics of his day. He was not an original thinker, but his twenty-nine surviving treatises show a sturdy common sense and a wide range of interests. He opposed popular superstition, the growing cult of pilgrimages, and trial by duel. He attacked the Jews, who enjoyed imperial protection, for alleged arrogance, and condemned the liturgical innovations of Amalarius of Metz.

**Agrapha.** A term derived from the Greek, meaning "unwritten [words]," which applies to such sayings attributed to Jesus as have been preserved outside the four canonical Gospels. The main sources of them include: (1) Other parts of the New Testament, the best examples of which are Acts 20:35; I Thess. 4:16 f.; and Rom. 14:14. (2) Ancient manuscripts of the New Testament in which are frequent interpolations, expansions, or intentional alterations of Gospel sayings, e.g., an addition to Luke 10:16 or the expansion of Matt. 20:28. (3) Quotations in the writings of early Christian authors, which provide the largest number of otherwise unknown sayings, e.g., Irenaeus, *Against Heresies* 5.33.3 f.; 2 Clem. 5.2–4; etc. Those occurring later in medieval authors and the Mohammedan agrapha are inauthentic almost without exception. (4) Discoveries of Greek papyri in the Egyptian desert, mostly at Oxyrhynchus, which have produced a half dozen sayings from the Gospel of Thomas, some expansions of canonical sayings (Pap. Oxy. 654), and two sayings closely related to John's Gospel (Pap. Egerton 2). (5) Miscellaneous sayings which appear in the Talmud (*Shab.* 116 a,b; *Abodah Zarah* 16b, 17a) and on a gate south of Delhi. Of all the several hundred agrapha, no more than twenty-one have good claim to authenticity.

**Agricola, Johann** (c. 1494–1566). German Lutheran Reformer. Attracted by Luther to Wittenberg in 1515, Agricola served as Luther's secretary at the Leipzig Debate (1519). In 1525 he became the head of the new Latin School in Eisleben. Here he began his famous collection of German proverbs. He chafed, however, under his removal from Wittenberg, which he blamed on Melanchthon. In 1527 he attacked the latter's stress on the law in the visitation plans for Saxony prepared by Luther and Melanchthon. Thus the Lutheran Church was rent by its first theological dispute, known as the Antinomian Controversy (literally, "antilaw controversy"). Luther succeeded in settling this dispute, but nine years later it broke out anew (1537–1540),

this time directed at Luther himself. Luther had not only come to stress the negative value of the law in preparing a sinner for the grace of God by making him aware of his sins, but over the years had increasingly emphasized the role of the law in disciplining Christians. Agricola denied even the law's negative value on the grounds that true repentance is effected by contemplating Christ's love in the gospel. In 1540, he was banished from Wittenberg and entered into the service of Joachim II of Brandenburg. For his role in formulating the Augsburg Interim (1548), he was considered by many as a traitor to Lutheranism. Plagued by his vanity and pride, he was nevertheless a gifted theologian who remained a convinced Lutheran all his life.

**Agricola, Mikael** (c. 1510–1557). First Lutheran bishop and leader of the Reformation in Finland. Sent by his reform-minded Roman Catholic bishop to study in Wittenberg, he introduced a conservative Lutheran reformation in the 1540's chiefly through his literary activity, which became the basis of the Finnish language. His writings included a manual for pastors (1545), the Finnish New Testament (1548), a catechism, and treatises on liturgy and the sacraments.

**Agricola, Rudolph** (Roelof Huysman) (c. 1444–1485). The "educator of Germany." Agricola was born near Groningen and educated there as well as at Erfurt, Cologne, and Louvain. A humanist in outlook, he spent much time in Italy. Thereafter he traveled extensively in the Netherlands and in northern Germany. His works include writings on education and philosophy, in opposition to Scholastic intellectualism, and a biography of Petrarch. He is thought to have been influential in the development of Erasmus.

**Agrippa von Nettesheim, Heinrich Cornelius** (1486–1535). German scholar. At various times a soldier, a magistrate, a physician, a lecturer on Hermes Trismegistus, and a theologian, Agrippa was a native of Cologne. He was educated there and at Paris. In 1529, Charles V made him his official historiographer. His *De occulta philosophia* (1510) is a mystical, Neoplatonic treatise; but his *De incertitudine et vanitate scientiarum et artium* is skeptical in character, teaching that truth is to be found only in Scripture.

**Aidan** (d. 651). Irish monk, bishop, and missionary. In 635, he went to Northumbria at the request of the Christian king Oswald to reestablish missions among the Angles after the pagans had been defeated. He established a monastery on the island of Lindisfarne, was consecrated its bishop, and the establishment soon became the center of English religious life. Aidan's missionary journeys to the mainland strengthened and extended the church in northern England.

**Aids to Reflection.** A book by Samuel Taylor Coleridge (1772–1834), published in 1825. In *Aids to Reflection,* Coleridge sees religion as something essentially ethical and intuitive. Religious certainty is to be found not in external proofs but in a religious consciousness arising out of a man's obedience to his own conscience. It is in such internally directed moral acts that man realizes the divine nature present in himself and thus can come into communion with God.

**Ailly, Pierre d'** (Petrus d' Alliaco) (1350–1420). French nominalist theologian. He was born at Compiègne and studied at the College of Navarre in Paris, where he obtained his doctorate in 1381. From 1389 to 1395 he was chancellor of the University of Paris. He was a conciliarist in his church polity, though among the rival popes at the time he supported the antipope Benedict XIII. He took little outward part in the Council of Pisa, but at the Council of Constance provided some assistance to his pupil John Gerson. His writings were considerable, but not of great originality.

**Ainslie, Peter** (1867–1934). American ecumenist. Ainslie was one of the most ardent proponents of Christian unity in America. As president of the International Convention of the Disciples of Christ in 1910 he proposed that they revive and intensify their original commitment to the cause of Christian unity and take steps toward the realization of that purpose. He became associated with several such endeavors himself, and was also editor of the *Christian Union Quarterly*.

**Aisle.** Properly, a lateral extension of a nave, opening into the nave by means of arches. A church may have one such aisle, but it is usual to have two. Aisles usually have separate roofs lower than that of the nave so that the upper side walls of the nave may have windows. In some cases an aisle may have a second-story opening into the nave, thus forming a gallery. Commonly, the word "aisle" means any walkway within a building.

**Aksakov, Konstantin** (1817–1860), and **Ivan** (1823–1886). Two ardent Russian Slavophile brothers. Konstantin attributed high Russian morality to the as yet non-Westernized and therefore unspoiled peasant. He sought to establish a Christian society while regarding the state as evil. Ivan was a Pan-Slavism publicist and tireless editor in its behalf, criticizing Western-style revolutions and the Russian government's conservatism.

**Alacoque, Margaret Mary** (1647–1690). A sister of the Visitandine Order who greatly promoted popular Roman Catholic devotion to the Sacred Heart. While at the order's convent at Paray-le-Monial, France, she claimed to have had frequent visions of Christ, in one of which he confided to her the mission to establish devotion to his Sacred Heart. She has been the subject of considerable controversy, but the devotion was eventually recognized and in 1920 she was canonized.

**Alain of Lille** (c. 1128–1202). Cistercian theologian and philosopher. Among his extant works are the treatise *On the Catholic Faith,* an apologetic against contemporary heresies; and *Rules for Sacred Theology* and *The Art of the Catholic Faith,* attempts at a deductive, systematic theology. Two poems are extant: *Anticlaudianus,* which describes the formation of the perfect man; and *Lament of Nature,* which allegorizes nature as the source of life, beauty, and order.

**Alaric.** From A.D. 395 king of the Visigoths. In 408 Alaric invaded Italy, threatened Rome, and in August, 410, captured the city and sacked it for three days. Though only a temporary occupation, this calamity shocked pagans and Christians alike; among the reactions to it was Augustine's great work, *The City of God.* Alaric died a few months later, and the Visigoths moved on to establish their kingdom in southern Gaul and Spain.

**Alban.** One of the few martyrs of Roman Britain. Alban was a citizen of Verulamium, near London, and according to tradition, much expanded in later legend, died during the persecution by Diocletian. His shrine, which existed as early as the 5th century, survived the Saxon invasions; around it grew up the medieval monastery (founded in the 8th century, refounded about 970) and the town of St. Albans.

**Albanian Orthodox Church.** A church of the Orthodox Christians established in 1922 in Albania. The southern part of what is now Albania has been associated with Orthodoxy since the 8th century, but the Albanian Orthodox Church emerged only in 1922 when the jurisdiction of the ecumenical patriarch was unilaterally repudiated. Archimandrite Theophan S. Noli (1882–1965) was consecrated metropolitan. He later came to the United States and headed up (1930) an independent Albanian Orthodox Church in America. Orthodox Christians in Albania, constituting perhaps 20 percent of the population, have been dominated by the patriarch of Moscow since 1949.

**Albert V** (d. 1579). Duke of Bavaria. Succeeding his father in 1550, Albert brought in Jesuits to reform the parishes of his duchy and employed the principle of the Peace of Augsburg (*Cuius regio, eius religio*) to expel Lutherans and Anabaptists. He informed the Council of Trent that he could not keep Bavaria faithful to Rome unless the chalice were given to the layman and marriage allowed for the clergy. Although his pleas fell on deaf ears, Albert's enthusiasm managed to keep Bavaria predominantly Roman Catholic.

**Albert of Brandenburg** (1490–1545). Margrave of Brandenburg, cardinal archbishop of Mainz and of Magdeburg, and bishop of Halberstadt. In return for his ecclesiastical benefices, held in pluralism, he was charged with the publication in Germany, especially in Brandenburg and Saxony, of the indulgence for St. Peter's Cathedral in Rome, it being agreed that he should retain half the proceeds to pay back the Fuggers for meeting the costs of his preferments. To promote the indulgence, he appointed the Dominican friar John Tetzel, whose preaching roused Luther to post his Ninety-five Theses in Wittenberg. Albert, a Renaissance man, was a liberal, seeing Erasmus as the restorer of theology, defending Reuchlin against the Dominicans, courting the friendship of humanists, in particular Ulrich von Hutten. He was friendly to the Protestant Reformation in its early stages. He received letters from Luther and allowed publication of Reformation tracts. Pope Leo X urged a change of attitude, but Albert wavered throughout the Peasants' War of 1525. Though he finally became a foe to Protestantism, he discouraged extreme measures, and was a moderating influence at the third Diet of Augsburg (1530). Helpless to stop the Reformation in his own diocese, he was driven from his home in Halle (1541). With his chapter and his creditors hard after him, he died almost in want.

**Albert of Prussia** (1490–1568). Last Grand Master of the Teutonic Order and first duke of Prussia. Won to the Protestant faith by Osiander and Luther's writings, he dissolved the order and on Luther's advice transferred Prussia (i.e., East or "old" Prussia) to Polish sovereignty as a duchy (1525). He promulgated the first evangelical Prussian church order and supported the evangelical forces in Denmark and Sweden. He also established schools and the University of Königsberg (1544).

**Albertus Magnus** (c. 1206–1280). Scholastic philosopher, theologian, and scientist. He entered the Dominican Order (1223) and after teaching in Germany was sent to Paris (1243), where he was made master in theology (1247). He organized the *studium generale* at Cologne (1248), his pupils including Thomas Aquinas. German provincial of his order (1254–1257), he returned to Cologne (1257–1260) and against the wishes of his general accepted the bishopric of Regensburg (1260), but resigned a year later. Ten years of itinerant duty for the papacy ended in his final return to Cologne.

He was a prolific writer on most subjects, his works including a commentary on the *Sentences* of Peter Lombard and five *Summae* on doctrinal subjects; commentaries on the writings of Pseudo-Dionysius; a commentary on *Nicomachean Ethics* and paraphrases of all the then known Aristotelian works; commentaries on the Major and Minor Prophets, Job, and the Four Gospels; two tractates on the Eucharist and an unfinished *Summa theologiae*. Recognized as *doctor universalis* even by Roger Bacon, he had mastered as no other medieval thinker had all the knowledge available at the time; but he was more than a mere epitomist—he showed excellent judgment. Not only did he do more than anyone to bring the new Aristotelianism to bear in medieval thought, but his tolerance and sympathy for Neoplatonism also made him the Western source to whom the later mystical traditions could trace their intellectual ancestry.

**Albigenses.** A heretical sect of the 11th to the 13th century, with doctrinal emphases resembling those of the Gnostic and Manichaean heresies of the early church. Medieval inquisitors identified this sect with the Catharist heresies appearing throughout Europe during this period, designating it by reference to the town of Albi, in the Languedoc region of southern France, where it arose. The "Catharist" identification was made on the basis of their separation of members into "believers," or the ordinary class of followers and workers, and "the perfect," or Cathari, assisted and served by the believers. "The perfect" were created by a rite called the Consolamentum, which involved a form of baptism and confirmation, confession and penitence, and the laying on of hands by other Cathari. One so set apart from the ordinary world pursued a life of maximum chastity, partook of only a minimum of food, and denied himself ordinary physical pleasures. Obviously not every believer was willing to undertake this drastic form of renunciation, and frequently the Consolamentum was postponed until a time near death. The endura, suicide by voluntary self-starvation, was the most highly recommended means of achieving liberation of the soul from its imprisonment in the body, the chief aim of life. Although the medieval churchman viewed such ceremonies with horror, there is little question that they combined practices of groups in or contiguous to the early church.

Their doctrinal reasoning was based upon an essential dualism asserting the coexistence of mutually opposed powers—good and evil —represented in spirit and matter respectively, and a theory of metempsychosis—the transmigration of souls upon death. Their ultimate goal was thus the freeing of all spirit from its imprisonment in the world of evil matter. Their avoidance of meat reflected the possibility that some fragment of spirit might become more earthbound by metabolism. The chastity expected of "the perfect" was not rigidly required; any form of incontinence was permitted to them, as long as it did not produce children and thus imprison more of the spirit in the world. The medieval inquisitors, of course, suspected the Albigenses and other Catharists of all forms of unnatural orgies, but such an attitude had been held toward every schismatic sect from the time of the early church.

It is probable that the resurgence of this dualistic heresy in so many areas of Europe was due to the characteristic occupations of the Cathars. Many of "the perfect" were weavers or physicians, for in spite of their contempt for the body, they seem to have practiced a form of faith healing similar to contemporary Christian Science. Both occupations involved travel and both offered ready access to the homes of noble families, where their doctrines could be easily promulgated.

Originally their doctrines may have traveled by such means from the heresy of the Bogomils in the Balkans, and brought there possibly from earlier Eastern dualism. In Europe itself, their practices also represented an ideal of freedom from the misery and repression of peasant life, but they likewise reflected the disenchantment of many of the upper classes with the lax state of both society and church in this period. When Cathar groups condemned the Roman Church and would not accept its sacraments or clergy, they then created their own clergy and their own sacraments, freed from the evil they saw in the church.

Innocent III preached a crusade against the known adherents of the Albigenses among the lower nobility of France, but the legalizing of the confiscation of the properties of the heretics indicates that plunder more than spiritual fervor motivated the crusaders.

By the 14th century, most Cathar groups had disappeared, lingering only in similar but diluted practices among some Waldenses. The major reason for their disappearance was less persecution than the greater success of the mendicant preaching orders—Dominicans and Franciscans.

**Albright, Jacob** (1759–1808). American preacher. A Lutheran layman of German extraction, born near Pottstown, Pa. Albright became a Methodist after his conversion experience in 1790, and then began preaching and organizing Methodist classes among his own people. As it became his intention to establish a German branch of Methodism, lack of Methodist approval meant only that he was ordained by his followers; and the Evangelical Church, emphasizing Arminian theology and Methodist polity, was organized in 1803.

**Alchemy.** A pseudoscience which probably began in the intellectual and spiritual ferment of the late Hellenistic period in Egypt. It is generally associated with attempts to change base elements such as lead or copper into silver or gold and the quest for the "philosopher's stone" by which such a feat might be accomplished. The roots of alchemy can be traced to the metaphysical speculations of gnosticism, Greek philosophy, and Egyptian science and technology. The literature associated with Hermes Trismegistus arising in the 2d century A.D. in Alexandria abounds with astrology, astral magic, numerology, and alchemy, which is its science par excellence. The Hermetic theme of the harmonious correspondence between man, the microcosm containing the Logos (or Word), and the universe, the macrocosm imbued with the Logos, was maintained in the Middle Ages. Such a view led alchemists to hold that out of man, the noblest creature of nature, should come the secret of gold, regarded as the most perfect metal of nature. The astral influence of the sun was a reason for the exposure of alchemical mixtures to the sun's rays in the hope that the color of the sun would be transmitted to baser materials and transform them into the precious yellow metal. With the translation of alchemical works preserved in Arabic and Syriac into Latin in the 11th and 12th centuries, practical alchemy, as noted above, produced both serious students and charlatans.

One of the most successful alchemists was Paracelsus, a precursor of modern pharmacology.

**Alcott, Amos Bronson** (1799–1888). American transcendentalist. Influenced by Plato, Coleridge, and Neoplatonism, Alcott believed in a radical transcendental idealism. Christianity, he believed, was the best religion, but could be improved. The world was created in fallen man, while man's soul was an emanation of God. The spirit was temporarily imprisoned in illusory matter and could be freed by intuitive self-knowledge and inspiration. Freedom of the spirit was to be achieved by moral education in the Socratic method to elicit innate rational ethical ideals. Alcott championed an advanced teaching theory, including harmonious development of physical, aesthetic, intellectual, and moral natures. Alcott achieved his best practical success as superintendent of schools in Concord, Mass. (1859), where he was able to put his views into effect. His most spectacular failure was his Fruitlands project (1844–1845). Alcott's most direct influence was on Emerson, Thoreau, Hawthorne, and Channing.

**Alcuin** (735–804). The greatest figure of the revival of learning in the Frankish empire. Alcuin was born at York and educated in the cathedral school, becoming head of it in 766. In 780, he was sent to Rome to obtain the pallium for the archbishop of York. While on this mission, he met Charlemagne at Parma and was persuaded to come to the court at Aachen to become master of the palace school. During his tenure as master (781–790) he was responsible for the education of the royal family, the children of the nobility and the clergy. He wrote numerous treatises on grammar and rhetoric, as well as liturgical and theological texts and Biblical commentaries. He was the inspiration for Charlemagne's directives for the establishment of schools throughout the empire. After a short visit to England, he returned and became involved in theological disputes. He is thought to be the author of the *Caroline Books,* an attack on the assumed Greek understanding of the veneration of images. He also wrote against the Spanish Adoptianists and succeeded in having them condemned at the Synod of Frankfurt in 794. He returned to England, but when civil disturbances forced him to leave, he went back to France and became abbot of St. Martin Abbey at Tours. There he established a famous school and scriptorium.

**Aldhelm** (c. 639–709). Abbot of Malmesbury and first bishop of Sherborne. Educated by Irish Christians in Wiltshire, he was an ascetic. Among the earliest Englishmen to pursue classical learning, he also wrote poetry in his native tongue. Association with Hadrian, Theodore's companion, made him a supporter of Roman versus Celtic customs. He converted many West Country Christians to Roman Easter, wrote in praise of virginity, and in a letter to Acircius illustrated rules of Latin prosody by verse riddles.

**Aleandro, Girolamo** (Hieronymus Aleander) (1480–1542). Italian cardinal and humanist. In his early life he was a scholar in classical languages and worked with Erasmus. In 1520, Pope Leo X sent Aleander as nuncio to Germany to present Luther with the bull *Exsurge Domine* and to lead the case against the Reformer at the Diet of Worms. He ordered Luther's books burned in several European cities.

**Alesius** (Ales), **Alexander** (1500–1565). Early Reformation figure in Scotland. At first, as canon of the collegiate church of St. Andrews, he opposed the Reformation, but he heard Patrick Hamilton argue reformatory views in 1528, and became convinced of the need for reform. He denounced clerical abuses, fled to Wittenberg, joined forces with Luther and Melanchthon, and signed the Augsburg Confession. Twice he lived in England, but each time his strong polemical views forced him back to the Continent. At the time of his death he was a professor of theology in Leipzig.

**Alexander II** (Anselmo da Baggio, d. 1073). Pope from 1061. A native of Milan, he was elected pope through the efforts of Hildebrand, then archdeacon of the Roman Church and later Pope Gregory VII, and under the new election law proclaimed in 1059 by a Lateran synod which declared that only the cardinal had a direct voice in papal elections. However, Alexander's election was contested by the Roman nobles and appealed to the German court. The court in turn nominated Bishop Peter Cadalus of Parma as Pope Honorius II. After three years, Alexander secured general recognition, the German regents repudiated the antipope, and the schism ceased to be important. Nevertheless, little was accomplished in Alexander II's pontificate because of his precarious situation. In 1066, the pope did become involved in the English succession when he supported William, duke of Normandy, against Harold I of England. Counseled by Hildebrand, Alexander condemned Harold as a usurper, excommunicated him and his followers, and blessed William's proposed invasion by sending him a consecrated banner and a ring containing a hair of St. Peter's head. As the former bishop of Lucca, Alexander had worked for the abolition of simony and the enforcement of clerical celibacy. In cooperation with Hildebrand and Peter Damian, Alexander laid the foundations of the reform movement. His deposition of the imperial bishop of Milan for simony was one factor that led to the investiture struggle between papacy and empire (see HOLY ROMAN EMPIRE).

**Alexander III** (Orlando [Roland] Bandinelli, d. 1181). Pope from 1159. He was a distinguished canon lawyer, diplomat, and scholar. He began his public career as professor of law at Bologna, and rose to become an influential adviser of Hadrian IV, whom he succeeded in 1159. His election, however, ran counter to the wishes of Emperor Frederick I Barbarossa and the Hohenstaufen candidate, Victor IV. A seventeen-year schism followed, but ended with complete victory for Alexander and his allies, the Lombard League, at the battle of Legnano (1176). In appreciation, the Lombard towns named the city of Alessandria after him. The most famous diplomatic problem he faced was the conflict between Henry II and Archbishop Thomas Becket. He probably thought Thomas too demanding, but upon the latter's murder, he imposed heavy penance on the king. He called and directed the Third Lateran Council (1179), which, among other measures, determined that papal elections thereafter would rest exclusively with the College of Cardinals. Fully as impressive as his administrative and diplomatic talents was his scholarly career. His commentary on Gratian's *Decretum* was one of the finer works of medieval canon law. He also wrote a theological treatise, the *Sentences of Roland,* in the style of Abelard, and strongly supported the 12th-century renaissance of learning.

**Alexander V** (Peter Philargès, 1339–1410). Pope from 1409. An advocate of conciliar reform during the Great Schism, Philargès played a leading role at the Council of Pisa (1409). Preaching the opening sermon, he presided over the Council's sessions. Pisa deposed the rival popes, Gregory XII and Benedict XIII, declaring the papal throne vacant, although this action was not recognized by the supporters of the two rivals. The Cardinals present elected Philargès pope in June, 1409. He died in May, 1410, with the Great Schism still unresolved.

**Alexander VI** (Rodrigo Borgia, 1431–1503). Pope from 1492. Born in Spain, Borgia was a nephew of Pope Callistus III, who made him a cardinal at the age of twenty-five. He quickly earned a reputation as one of the most corrupt clerics of his day. His reign as pope was marked by two great events: the Treaty of Tordesillas, dividing the New World between Spain and Portugal, and the execution of the fiery Florentine preacher Savonarola.

**Alexander VII** (Fabio Chigi, 1599–1667). Pope from 1655. He was born in Siena, where he later studied philosophy, jurisprudence, and theology. In 1628, he entered the papal service and in 1644 was made the envoy of Innocent X to the conference at Münster, where he defended papal concerns in the discussions leading to the Peace of Westphalia. In 1652, Innocent made him secretary of state, and in an eighty-day conclave in 1655 he was elected pope. His pontificate was marked by frequent clashes with Louis XIV of France. In 1662, the French ambassador at Rome occasioned one such disagreement, with the result that the pope temporarily lost Avignon and had to sign the Treaty of Pisa (1664). The French Jansenists were insisting that the Jansenist theses condemned in 1653 were not actually in Jansen's *Augustinus;* thus Alexander confirmed the condemnation, with particular reference to Jansen's book. He also sent a profession of faith to France to be signed by all the clergy and condemned an additional forty-five erroneous theses on grace (1666).

**Alexander VIII** (Pietro Ottoboni, 1610–1691). Pope from 1689. He was the son of the chancellor of the Republic of Venice. After serving for many years in the Roman Curia and becoming a cardinal and the bishop of Brescia, he was elected pope (1689). During his short reign, Alexander declared the Gallican Articles (of 1682) invalid, gave financial support to Venice in the war against the Turks, and was generous both to the poor and to his relatives. He revived the practice of sinecure offices, which his predecessor had suppressed.

**Alexander I** (1777–1825). Czar of Russia from 1801. Although espousing liberal ideals, Alexander was autocratic in temperament and able to accomplish few reforms during his reign. Despondent following the burning of Moscow in 1812, he came under the influence of Baroness von Kruedener, and from that time a mystical pietism permeated his policy. The Holy Alliance, a vague agreement that all sovereigns would act in a Christian fashion, was an offspring of his pietism.

**Alexander II** (1818–1881). Czar of Russia from 1855. Alexander was a moderate reformer who in 1861 abolished serfdom. This left the nobility dissatisfied, while the former serfs objected to the high cost and communal ownership of their small plots of land. Alexander also reformed the judicial system and allowed a considerable degree of local self-government in rural districts and large towns. In 1881 he was assassinated by a terrorist bomb.

**Alexander III** (1845–1894). Czar of Russia from 1881. He was the son of Alexander II but was unsympathetic to his father's ideals. His regime was known for its reactionary bent. Disenchanted with Western liberalism, he imposed the Russian language on all his subjects, destroyed various national traditions, and zealously promoted the Orthodox Church. Although much industrial progress was made during his reign, it is doubtful that this benefited more than a select few.

**Alexander, Archibald** (1772–1851). American Presbyterian theologian. A Presbyterian minister elected in 1812 as the first professor at Princeton Seminary, he then organized and taught all the courses, limiting himself in the following years to teaching didactic and polemic theology. He brought to the school not only scholarly attainments and an interest in rigid doctrinal orthodoxy but also a warmly pietistic religion, reflecting his own personal religious experience.

**Alexander Nevsky** (1219–1263). Prince of Novgorod. He led the Russians against the Swedes at the Neva River in 1236, for which victory he obtained the name Nevsky. During a German invasion in 1242, he routed the heavy German cavalry in a battle on the ice of Lake Peipus. He encouraged the Russians to follow a conciliatory policy toward the Tartars. He has been canonized by the Russian Church and is regarded as a national hero by the Soviet Government.

**Alexander of Alexandria** (d. 328). Bishop from c. 312. His short episcopate was marked by difficulties. The Melitian Schism might have been settled along the lines suggested at Nicaea but for the activities of Arius and his supporters, whom Alexander felt constrained to depose. He may have hesitated initially, but he did act to condemn the view of the Son as a being created in time, and he persevered up through Nicaea, with the increasing support of Athanasius, his deacon, who was to succeed him at his death in 328.

**Alexander of Hales** (c. 1180–1245). The first Franciscan professor of theology at Paris. Born at Hales, Gloucestershire, he studied in Paris, becoming master of theology in 1221, and was one of the first to lecture on Peter Lombard's *Sentences*. He joined the Franciscan Order in 1236, continuing to teach until his death. His thought, though primarily Augustinian, shows a thorough acquaintance with Aristotle and Avicenna. The *Summa* traditionally attributed to him is his only in part.

**Alexander of Lycopolis.** A platonist of the late 3d and early 4th centuries. He was a resident of Lycopolis in Thebaid. He is best known for a disputation he wrote which demonstrated how Manichaeism destroyed the basis of perception as well as knowledge, both being fundamental to Christianity and Platonism. Tradition names him a bishop of his native city, but nothing in his work is so exclusively Christian as to warrant the conclusion that he even became a Christian.

**Alexiad.** A lengthy account of the life and reign of Emperor Alexius I Comnenus, written by his daughter Anna Comnena. The fifteen books, encompassing the years 1069–1118, are a continuation of the "Historical Materials" collected by Anna's husband, Nicephorus Bryennius. Although the text is distorted by personal vanity, family pride, and strong bias, and the style is marred by pedantry and affectation, historians cite her account as a valuable source for Byzantine history. Her work vividly reflects the contempt and hostility of the Eastern Empire toward the Western Church and the Crusades. An English translation was made by E. A. S. Dawes, *The Alexiad* (London, 1928).

**Alexius I Comnenus** (1048–1118). Byzantine emperor. After a distinguished military career he forced Nicephorus Botaniates to abdicate in 1081, himself assuming power. His long reign led to the recovery of the empire from its previous state of decay. He defeated the Normans, recapturing Corfu and Dyrrachium, thwarted a Patzinak invasion of Thrace, and kept the Turks at bay. Extracting homage from the menacing first crusaders in return for supplies, he assured recovery of a substantial portion of Asia Minor for the empire. He forcefully opposed Paulicians and Bogomiles, but he seized church treasures to finance his war with the Normans and instituted grants of *charisticum,* a kind of benefice on monastic properties.

**Alfonso the Wise** (c. 1226–1284). Alfonso X, king of Castile and León from 1252. One of the most learned men of his times, he is famous as editor and coauthor of the *Alfonsine Tables* in the field of astronomy. He is also renowned for his historical works, the *Primera Crónica General* and the *General Estoria,* for the important legal works *Las Siete Partidas, El Sentenario,* and *El Fuero Real,* which were written under his auspices.

**Alford, Henry** (1810–1871). Dean of Canterbury and eminent English Biblical scholar. Alford's most important work was an edition of the Greek New Testament in which he made use of then current Continental scholarship. A versatile man and perhaps the most voluminous writer of his time, he was the first editor of the *Contemporary Review,* an accomplished poet, and a forceful preacher.

**Alfred the Great** (849–899). King of Wessex from 871. His victories against the Danes, especially at Ethandune (878), which led to the defeat and conversion of Guthrum, saved for Christianity a land ravaged by Danish attacks and almost bankrupt militarily and culturally. He could establish a strong monarchical rule and introduce effective reforms largely because there was no coherent system of feudalism as in Europe. He built up the navy with Flemish help, restructured the law, endeavoring especially to end the still prevalent vendetta, and encouraged foreign scholars to come to England, Erigena among them. He established monasteries to replace those destroyed by the Danes, e.g., Athelney and Shaftesbury where his daughter Elgiva became abbess. Skilled craftsmen were encouraged and good work in manuscript illustration was done in those monasteries. Half of his income was devoted to religious uses. He translated or encouraged translation into the vernacular of Boethius' *Consolation,* Gregory's *Dialogues* and *Pastoral Rule,* Orosius' *History,* and Bede's *Ecclesiastical History,* interpolating into some of them his own comments on geography or the nature of kingship. Like Charlemagne, he encouraged the collection of folk songs and promoted the writing of history, as is evidenced by the Anglo-Saxon Chronicle.

**Alice Movement.** An African cult that arose during the 1950's in an area of Northern Rhodesia where the Church of Scotland was strong. Its leader was Alice Lenshina Mulenga, who believed she had died and risen four times and had been called by Jesus to attack witchcraft. Thousands gave up their fetishes and were baptized. Polygamy and sorcery were also attacked.

**Allatius, Leo** (1586–1669). Greek-born Roman Catholic scholar and ecumenist. He was for many years custodian of the Vatican library, worked on several of its manuscripts, translated a number of Greek authors into Latin, and was much involved in the intellectual life of Europe. He earnestly sought to reconcile the Greek Church with Rome, and in his most important work, *De Ecclesiae Occidentalis atque Orientalis perpetua consensione,* tried to bring out the similarities and minimize the differences existing between the two churches.

**Allen, William** (1532–1594). One of the strongest defenders of Roman Catholicism in England during the reign of Elizabeth I. Forced to go into exile, he established a college at Douai to send missionaries to England (1568). Allen later helped Pope Gregory XIII to set up a similar school (the English College) in Rome. His political enterprises, however, did not meet with such success. He exhorted his Roman Catholic countrymen to side with Spain against England, only to see them participate instead in defeating the Armada (1588).

**Alline, Henry** (1748–1784). Itinerate Canadian preacher. He was called "the Whitefield of Nova Scotia." Uneducated, he was converted in 1775 and found himself "called to preach." Alline was typical of the radical revivalism of the Great Awakening and the source of "New Light" revivalism in Nova Scotia. He criticized uncooperative churches as "churches of Antichrist" and their ministers as "unconverted." He encouraged divisions and was ordained in 1799 by churches he had helped found. Alline had mystical and radical views on the genesis of souls and the relation of the spiritual and physical worlds. He published *Two Mites Cast Into the Offering of God for the Benefit of Mankind* (1804), an autobiography, his journal of the revival, hymns, and religious songs. Alline has been thought, falsely, to have founded a short-lived sect called the Allenites.

**Allouez, Claude** (1622–1689). Jesuit missionary. Born and educated in France, he came to Canada in 1658, did mission work on the St. Lawrence River, and in 1663 was appointed vicar-general for all of the northwest. In his vast travels he founded De Pere, Wis., and in 1675 succeeded Marquette in his work in Illinois. He has been called "the founder of Catholicity in the West."

**Almoner.** The title of an official who is in charge of the distribution of alms. Often the almoner was a cleric. An almoner was a member of the household of most bishops and high royal officials.

**Altenstein, Karl** (Freiherr vom Stein zum Altenstein) (1770–1840). Prussian statesman.

Born in Bavaria and educated at the universities of Erlangen and Göttingen as a student of law, he also found great delight in philosophy, especially the philosophy of religion, and became a Hegelian rationalist.

He gained reputation in financial matters and became Prussian minister of finance in 1808. However, he incurred the ire of Napoleon by laboring too effectively for the restoration and reconstruction of Prussia, and was pressured out of office. He resigned in 1810 from his position. In 1817 he was appointed first minister of the newly created department of public worship, education, and medicine in Prussia under King Frederick William III. In this capacity he served under serious difficulties yet with efficiency until 1840, the year of his death. One of his great achievements was the systematic improvement of primary and secondary education.

**Althusius, Johannes** (c. 1557–1638). German lawyer and political philosopher who taught at Herborn and Steinfurt. When he became an official of the city government of Emden, he sided with the city guilds in their struggle for political autonomy against the political absolutism of the nobles. In order to justify his action, he wrote a major work in 1603 entitled *Politics Methodically Arranged* (*Politica methodice digesta*), which introduced a new political theory. Influenced by the French Huguenot thinker Petrus Ramus (1515–1572), Althusius based his political theory upon an analysis of existing patterns of social and juridical behavior, which he tried to explain by way of Biblical examples and the tradition of classical antiquity that the humanists had rediscovered. Human experience, history, political contracts of various types, the question of active resistance to tyranny, and the Biblical idea of the covenant were among the topics of his philosophical reflections. He envisioned a society basically democratic in structure and built upon contractual agreements. Thus he can be regarded as a forerunner of Jean-Jacques Rousseau (1712–1778), while his dependence upon Calvinistic "federal (covenant) theology" links him with the Continental Reformation as well.

BIBLIOGRAPHY: Frederick Carney (ed. and tr.), *The Politics of Johannes Althusius* (Boston, 1964).

**Alumbrados** (Spanish for "enlightened"; Latin, *illuminati*). The name given to members of a rather heterogeneous group of mystics and pseudomystics who arose in Spain in the 16th century. In general they held that the human soul could become perfect enough in this life to receive a direct vision of the Holy Spirit. In such a state, sin would be impossible and good works and exterior forms of religion unnecessary. Many of the Alumbrados lived lives of holiness and moderation, but the claims of revelations and visions made by others caused the group to fall under the disfavor of the Inquisition.

**Amalarius of Metz** (d. c. 850). Liturgical scholar. A student of Alcuin, he was the author of several treatises on liturgy. His principal work, *De ecclesiasticis officiis*, attempted to explain the ritual of the Gallican and Roman rites by use of allegory. Many of these allegorical explanations were condemned by a synod at Quiercy in 838. He wrote treatises on the baptismal rite and the pontifical Mass. In 835 he was appointed administrator of Lyons during the exile of Archbishop Agobard.

**Amana Society.** German religious and communistic sect. One of the organized reactions to 18th-century orthodoxy in Germany was a blend of pietism and mysticism that took the name The Community of True Inspiration, which after nearly a century of quietude came to life again in 1817, and finding Germany inhospitable, emigrated to Buffalo, N.Y., in 1842. Another feature was the rigid communism practiced (1854–1932) at Amana, Iowa, where the community is still located.

**Amandus** (c. 584–c. 675). Merovingian bishop and abbot who evangelized Flanders and Carinthia. After spending several years as a hermit in the vicinity of Bourges, Amandus was consecrated a bishop without see in 628 and began his missionary activity. He was perhaps bishop of Maastricht for a short time. In his later years he founded two monasteries in Flanders and retired to one of them as abbot.

**Amann, Jakob** (c. 1644–c. 1730). Mennonite elder active in Bern, Switzerland. He spent the years from 1696 to 1708 in Alsace. In 1693, he formed a radical group which split the Swiss Mennonites and which advocated the exclusion of non-Mennonites from marriage and family ties, the washing of feet, the rejection of changes in fashion, and the growing of beards. Thus he was the spiritual father of the Amish, who still adhere to his teaching. (See ANABAPTISTS.)

**Amboise, Conspiracy of** (1559). Unsuccessful plot led by Louis de Condé, brother of Antoine de Bourbon, against the Guises. When in 1559 the fifteen-year-old Francis II succeeded to the throne of France, he entrusted the government to extremist adherents of the Roman Church, the duc de Guise and the duke's brother, Charles, cardinal of Lorraine. For both political and religious reasons, some of the Protestant nobility plotted an armed rebellion (which Calvin disapproved of). Word of the plot reached the king's ministers, and large numbers of the conspirators were executed, some of them being hanged from the battlements of the château of Amboise, where the court had retreated for safety. When the king died the same year, however, his ministers fell from power, and the Protestants had a period of respite until the outbreak of the Wars of Religion in 1562.

**Ambrose** (340–397). One of the traditional four doctors of the Western Church (with Jerome, Augustine, and Gregory the Great). He was born in 340 at Trier in the Rhineland, the residence of his father, Aurelius Ambrosius, praetorian prefect of the Gauls (i.e., governor-general of Britain, Spain, and Gaul). The family was both distinguished and devout. Ambrose was educated at Rome, probably after his father's death, and his sister Marcellina received the veil of a consecrated virgin from Pope Liberius. Ambrose was given a Christian training, but since he and his brother Satyrus were intended for a public career, they remained unbaptized, as often happened in such cases in the 4th century. Ambrose was still a catechumen, therefore, when he entered the imperial service as an advocate (c. 365). Some years later he was appointed governor of Emilia-Liguria, the province of northern Italy with its capital at Milan. The prefect Probus is said to have sent him with the words, "Go, not as a governor, but as a bishop." At Milan the bishop, Auxentius, was a survivor from the days of Arian dominance under Constantius. On his death, probably in the fall of 373, a stormy election was expected. When a childish voice was heard to say, "Ambrose bishop" (perhaps on seeing the governor at the episcopal throne), this was taken as providential, and Ambrose was elected by acclamation. In spite of his reluctance, the necessary arrangements were made, and in the space of a week he was baptized, ordained, and consecrated early in December (the date usually given, Dec. 7, 374, is probably wrong by about a year).

Milan in the late 4th century was the usual residence of Roman emperors in the West. Ambrose therefore found himself not only the pastor of a great metropolitan church, but adviser to the imperial family, and in matters of church and state often in a position of greater influence than the contemporary bishops of Rome. His episcopal career is closely connected with three emperors and two usurpers. In 375, Gratian succeeded his father, Valentinian I; Ambrose dedicated to him two important theological works, *On the Faith* and *On the Holy Spirit* (the latter partly based on the work of Basil of Caesarea on the same subject), which did much to establish the pattern and fix the terminology of Western Catholic theology. In 382, Gratian, as a zealous Christian, refused the title of Pontifex Maximus, and ordered the removal from the senate house at Rome of the altar of Victory, the symbol of traditional Roman paganism. Ambrose stiffened the emperor's rejection of the petition for its restoration brought by a delegation headed by the pagan leader Symmachus, prefect of the city (i.e., mayor of Rome).

In 383, Gratian was defeated by Magnus Maximus, a commander in Britain, and killed at Lyons. For several crucial years Maximus ruled the Gauls while Gratian's young brother, Valentinian II, reigned at Milan, largely directed by his Arian mother, Justina. Ambrose replied formally to a second pagan delegation from Rome, and on behalf of Valentinian and Justina he undertook a mission to Maximus at Trier, securing a temporary truce. Nevertheless, Justina demanded the concession to the Arians of one of the churches of Milan, first asking for a suburban basilica, and then, in Holy Week of 385, for one of the principal churches of the city. During this crisis, Ambrose kept his congregation assembled in protest in his cathedral, and to occupy them introduced the singing of the popular hymns that he had begun to compose. Justina was obliged to abandon her effort, as well as a second attempt to secure her aim by legislation in 386. To these years belong Ambrose's contacts with Augustine (converted in 386, baptized in 387). Maximus began to threaten Italy; on a second mission to Trier, Ambrose was annoyed (as bishop or as former official?) at being received in public consistory instead of private audience, and, like other church leaders, protested at the execution under Maximus' authority of the Spanish heretic Priscillian. The second embassy was unsuccessful; Maximus invaded Italy, and Valentinian and Justina fled to Thessalonica. There Theodosius, whom Gratian had made emperor of the East in 379, took up their cause, and Maximus was defeated and killed in 388.

Ambrose's close contact with Theodosius soon ripened into friendship. Nevertheless, he subjected the emperor to penance (though doubtless not to the full rigors of a public penitent) for the hasty order that caused a massacre at Thessalonica. In remorse, Theodosius enacted a law that thirty days should intervene before the execution of a capital sentence. Less admirable to the modern mind is Ambrose's successful protest against the emperor's decree that the church of Callinicum on the Euphrates should pay for the restoration of a synagogue destroyed by a Christian mob. In 391, Theodosius returned to the East and sent Valentinian to govern the Gauls. Here, Valentinian found himself dominated by the Frankish general Arbogast, and in fear of his life sent for Ambrose to come to his support and to baptize him. Before the bishop could arrive, Valentinian was killed (May 15, 392). In a memorial sermon Ambrose developed the doctrine of the baptism of desire for one whose intention of receiving the sacrament was involuntarily frustrated. Arbogast, pagan and barbarian, set up a lukewarm Christian, Eugenius, as emperor, and supported a pagan revival in Italy. During his control of Milan, Ambrose withdrew to Florence. Theodosius again marched west and defeated his enemies in 394; for a short time he and Gratian were once more together, until the death of Theodosius on Jan. 17, 395.

Ambrose was greatly admired as a preacher and teacher, though his style is that of a lawyer rather than an orator, unpretentious and sometimes crabbed. Many of his sermons expound the psalms, and a number were assembled to form the major part of his commentary on Luke. His ethical teaching is formally developed in the work in four books *On the Duties of the Clergy,* which follows the pattern of Cicero's work *On Duties,* adapting Stoic principles to Christian teaching, and providing Biblical examples. Many topics of personal and social ethics are treated in sermons on Old Testament characters. In dealing with the duties of the wealthy, Ambrose denies the absolute right of private property, and approaches a theoretical socialism, though scarcely expecting it to be put into practice in the conditions of his time. He supported the monastic movement, which was then beginning to enter the Western Church, and his treatises addressed to virgins and widows defend and direct the older forms of the ascetic life.

Ambrose's importance in the history of the church of Milan is reflected in the fact that its liturgical customs are still known as the Ambrosian rite, although the extent of his personal contribution is uncertain. His hymns were written in a simple balladlike meter, and in a rhythm closer to popular speech than to classical poetry (the "long meter" of English hymnody). The term *Ambrosianum* came to

be used for any hymn in this form, but seven or eight are indubitably by Ambrose, such as the morning hymn "O Splendor of God's Glory Bright." Ambrose is credited with introducing antiphonal singing of the psalms in the Latin Church, and may have devised the Ambrosian system of dividing the Psalter into groups of ten psalms for the morning office on weekdays (Saturday as well as Sunday was considered a festival at Milan). Ambrose's sympathy with the popular piety of the age is shown in the enthusiasm with which he welcomed the alleged discovery of the relics of the previously unknown martyrs, Gervasius and Protasius, and transferred them with great solemnity to the new church he had just dedicated. Two series of Ambrose's Easter-week sermons to the newly baptized are preserved: *On the Mysteries* and *On the Sacraments.* The latter was long ascribed to some lesser contemporary, but its genuineness now seems to be probable. It is of importance in liturgical history, since it quotes the central part of the Eucharistic Prayer, evidently giving an early form of the later Roman and Ambrosian canon, and contains the first formal exposition of the doctrine of consecration of the elements by the Words of Institution.

Besides presiding at several provincial councils at Milan, Ambrose took a prominent part in several more general meetings. The Council of Aquileia in 381 marked the end of Arianism in the Latin Church; those at Rome in 382 and Capua in 394 under Popes Damasus and Siricius dealt with the heresies of the time—Apollinarianism, Priscillianism, and the antiascetic teachings of Helvidius and Jovinian —and with less success attempted to intervene in Eastern disputes. In particular, Rome and Milan supported the minority party of Paulinus in the schism between two Orthodox bishops at Antioch, while Theodosius and the Eastern bishops recognized the majority group, in spite of its semi-Arian background, and were ultimately successful. At Aquileia, Ambrose was briefly taken in by the disreputable Maximus the Cynic, whose attempt to secure the see of Constantinople had been sternly repudiated at the Council of 381 in that city (later recognized as the Second Ecumenical Council), but he soon saw his mistake.

On the fortieth day after the death of Theodosius, Ambrose delivered as a memorial the last of his great sermons. His conspicuous days were over, but he continued to be active to the end. He addressed religious instruction and political advice to a Germanic convert on the northern frontier, Queen Fritigil of the Marcomanni (who started out to visit him, but arrived too late), and in the last of his letters, which have been an important source for his life, we see him arranging for a peaceful election to the episcopate in the distracted church of Vercelli. The new bishop of Vercelli, Honoratus, was at Milan in time to give Ambrose his last Communion on his deathbed, April 4, 397. His body was buried near the martyrs in the new church, now known as Sant' Ambrogio, where in a later building that succeeded his in the early Middle Ages it still lies. Soon after his death the Roman world and Christian empire which he had served loyally collapsed. However, we see in his career the beginning of the transition from early Christian bishop to medieval prelate, and he remains not only a great figure in the history of his age but a permanent influence in the forms and patterns of the Western Church.

BIBLIOGRAPHY: P. Schaff and H. Wace (eds.), *Nicene and Post-Nicene Fathers*, Series II, Vol. 10 (Grand Rapids, 1955); F. H. Dudden, *The Life and Times of St. Ambrose* (Oxford, 1935); A. Paredi, *Saint Ambrose: His Life and Times* (Notre Dame, Ind., 1964).

**Ambrosian Rite.** One of the few non-Roman rites surviving in the Latin Church. It is still in use at Milan. Although it bears the name of Ambrose, he was not its originator, nor did he leave any personal stamp on it. His writings are, however, an important source of information about the rite in the 4th century. Its origins have been disputed, but it is now understood to be basically Western, with some admixture of Oriental and other elements. (See LITURGIES.)

**Ambrosiaster.** Oldest Latin commentary on all the Pauline epistles. It originated in Rome in the time of Damasus, based on an Old Latin text, and of unknown authorship. Once attributed to Ambrose, the text was studied by Erasmus, who coined the name. It is a prime example of the pre-Augustinian interpretation of Paul, and its influence on the Pauline commentaries of Pelagius is evident.

**Ambulatory.** Properly speaking, the enclosed walk surrounding the apse in certain churches. Sometimes there are chapels that open onto the outer side of the ambulatory. By extension, the word has come to mean any covered walkway.

**American Anti-Slavery Society.** A society founded in Philadelphia in 1833, encouraged by Garrison's New England Anti-Slavery Society (1832) and British emancipation in 1833. While Garrison held the limelight and wrote the Society's declaration of principles, western reformers formed its backbone. This group, led by Theodore D. Weld and Charles G. Finney, included James G. Birney, William Goodell, Beriah Green, Elizur Wright, and Charles Stuart. Besides the Boston reformers under Garrison, important easterners were the Tappan brothers, Gerrit Smith, and William Jay. The Society's periodicals included *Human Rights, Anti-Slavery Record, Emancipator,* and *Slave's Friend.* Revival methods, initiated by Weld, effectively spread the Society's gospel. By its peak in 1836, there were 2,000 societies, 200,000 members, and 70 agents chosen and trained by Weld and John Greenleaf Whittier. Decline after 1836 was due in part to Garrison's radicalism, which included criticism of the churches for not condemning the slave system. The Society also suffered from its inability to draw prominent antislavery figures, particularly John Quincy Adams, or even a majority of those who opposed slavery. Steps toward a political party, opposed by Garrison, and his own zeal for unrelated reforms, led to a split at the 1840 convention. The moderates left to form the American and Foreign Anti-Slavery Society, and the Garrison-dominated Society declined rapidly.

**American Bible Society.** Interdenominational publisher and distributor of Bibles. The scarcity of Bibles in America, especially on the frontier, caused a number of Bible societies to be founded after 1808. A trip to the West and South by Samuel J. Mills revealed to him the need for a larger national organization, and his promotion of the idea led to a convention in May, 1816, out of which emerged the American Bible Society. Its purpose, as stated in its constitution, was "to encourage a wider circulation of the Holy Scriptures without note or comment." It immediately began its work with state and local societies serving as auxiliaries. In 1852, it built its headquarters, Bible House, in New York City. Today it publishes millions of Bibles and Bible portions throughout the world in over eleven hundred languages.

**American Board of Commissioners for Foreign Missions.** A missionary organization founded in 1810. A result of the Second Awakening in New England was the formation at Williams College of a band of men under the leadership of Samuel J. Mills who pledged themselves to devote their lives to missionary service. Upon graduation from Andover Theological Seminary in 1810 these men petitioned the Congregational General Association of Massachusetts to form an organization that would support them and future missionaries to the heathen. The suggestion was accepted, and soon several New England

Congregational Associations assisted in the formation of the American Board, which was soon enlarged to include Presbyterian and Reformed support. In 1812 a charter was secured from the Commonwealth of Massachusetts and the first contingent of missionaries left for Asia. The Board, which remained an agent of the churches for foreign missions receiving interdenominational support, also undertook work among the American Indians beginning in 1817, including the famous Whitman-Spaulding mission in the Northwest. The Christianization of the Hawaiian Islands was an early achievement and part of the work undertaken in the Pacific islands. Eventually the Board reverted to Congregational organization, and its missionaries were to be found in fields throughout the world.

**American College in Rome.** A college established in Rome for the education of North American clergymen. In response to the urging of several American bishops and with strong support from Archbishop Hughes of New York and Archbishop Kenrick of Baltimore, Pope Pius IX in 1859 established an American college in Rome similar to the other national colleges there. In 1884, it was raised to the rank of a Pontifical College. Since its beginning it has done much to promote uniformity between the Vatican and the Roman Catholic Church in the United States.

**American Colonization Society** (founded in 1816). A society dedicated to the purpose of freeing Negro slaves and transporting them to new homes in Liberia, which the Society had bought and organized as a free country. It had branches in several states and was supported by churches and some state legislatures. After the Civil War it served primarily as a trustee for the Liberian settlement.

**American Council of Christian Churches.** A body organized by Carl McIntire in 1941, its stated purpose "to enable evangelical Christians to accomplish tasks that can better be done in cooperation than separately, including joint witness to the glorious testimony to precious souls against denials or distortions of the historic Christian faith." Composed of fundamentalists, it is noted for its persistent attacks against the "soul-destroying modernism" and the so-called communistic tendencies of the Federal (and later, National) Council of Churches.

**American Home Missionary Society.** A society organized in 1826 when Congregationalists joined forces with the Presbyterian- and Reformed-supported United Domestic Missionary Society of New York. It quickly be-

came the most important single home missionary agency among Protestants in the United States before the Civil War undertaking an experiment in the cooperative conduct of missions. Being an interdenominational voluntary society, it was free of ecclesiastical control but nonetheless became the principal agency through which the Plan of Union functioned in the West. The area of work was confined primarily to New England and that part of the Western frontier where the New England element was most numerous, and hence facilitated the endeavors at transplanting New England religion and culture to the frontier. Its consistent policy was to organize and support churches, establish a settled rather than an itinerant ministry, give support only to ministers who refrained from secular employment, and encourage self-help by making grants in inverse proportion to the ability of a congregation to contribute to the support of its pastor. In 1837 at a time of heightened denominational consciousness the Old School Presbyterians withdrew their support, as did the New School Presbyterians in 1861, which led in 1893 to the new name of Congregational Home Missionary Society.

**Americanism.** A charge of heresy made toward the end of the 19th century against Catholics in the United States, accusing them of nationalistic tendencies. On Jan. 22, 1899, Pope Leo XIII addressed to James Cardinal Gibbons, archbishop of Baltimore, an encyclical letter commonly known as *Testem benevolentiae*. The letter was to be transmitted to all the members of the American Catholic hierarchy. It spoke specifically of "the opinions which some comprise under the head of Americanism." This supposed heresy might be looked upon as the American Catholic form of "Modernism." The issue was brought to the attention of the pope as the result of a furor in France between liberal and conservative Catholics over the proper stance to take toward the modern world. Abbé Felix Klein had written an introduction to the French translation of Walter Elliott's *Life of Isaac Thomas Hecker* (1898), the founder of the Paulist religious order and a convert to Roman Catholicism. In his introduction, Klein praised the more relaxed attitude of American Catholicism in civil and religious matters. From this the pope extracted certain tendencies which reputedly existed in American Catholic circles, tendencies that would relax the ancient rigor of the church and have it adapt itself to "modern" theories and methods. Cardinal Gibbons replied to the pope that the caricature of American Catholicism thus presented was entirely inaccurate.

**American Peace Society.** One of the organized expressions of the benevolence movement of the first half of the 19th century which was formed in 1828 on the basis of previous peace movements. It was designed to provide a forum for the development and promotion of ways of securing and ensuring world peace, although at first also involved in other issues, and became well known and was particularly active early in the 20th century.

**American Protective Association.** An organized reaction to the influx of Roman Catholic immigrants into the United States after the Civil War, formed at Clinton, Iowa, in 1887. By operating as a propaganda and political force promoting anti-Catholic legislation, it had some success in local elections but was rebuffed in its attempt to influence national politics, and after a decade lost what influence it had achieved.

**American Sunday School Union.** The most important extraecclesiastical body for the promotion of Sunday schools in 19th-century America. Governed entirely by laymen on an evangelical but nondenominational basis, it had a twofold purpose: to aid existing schools and "to plant a Sunday school wherever there is a population." Organized out of the Philadelphia Sunday and Adult School Union on May 25, 1824, the Union sought to strengthen Sunday schools by preparing and distributing improved uniform lesson materials and resources, and to improve the general quality of instruction by organizing county and state unions to train teachers in advanced methods of education. The "Union Question Books" and "Selected Lessons" were forerunners of the modern International Sunday School Lesson series. In addition to this aid, Union missionaries established over 67,000 new Sunday schools during the first fifty years of its existence.

**American Tract Society.** An American interdenominational publishing agency. Tract societies had been set up in Connecticut, New York, and Massachusetts, but the national organization bearing this name was founded in New York in May, 1825. It published leaflets, tracts, handbills, and, after 1828, volumes as well. By 1843 it was also issuing periodicals, the most famous being the *Christian Messenger*. It cooperated with temperance, missionary, and other societies by printing and circulating literature for them. Some of its materials were and are sold, but much has been given away, often by traveling colporteurs, to prisons, hospitals, incoming immigrants, mission churches, or distributed house to house. It has contributed greatly to the growth of Christianity in America.

**Ames, Edward Scribner** (1870–1958). American philosopher. Born at Eau Claire, Wis., he was educated at Drake University (B.A., 1889; M.A., 1891, LL.D., 1924), Yale University (B.D., 1892), and the University of Chicago (Ph.D., 1895). He was ordained a minister of the Disciples of Christ in 1890. From 1897 to 1900 he was professor of philosophy at Butler University. In 1900 he went to the University of Chicago, where he was professor of philosophy until 1935, when he became professor emeritus. Ames was a representative of the left wing of the liberal movement in theology associated with the University of Chicago. As an extreme modernist he embraced a naturalistic world view and a humanistic religion, which led him far from traditional Christianity. His works include *Psychology of Religious Experience* (1910) and *The New Orthodoxy* (1918).

**Ames, William** (1576–1633). Puritan theologian and casuist. Born at Ipswich in Suffolk of a Puritan merchant family, he was educated at Cambridge, where he distinguished himself and might have become master of his college had he not displayed Puritan traits. Leaving Cambridge, he went to Colchester and was sent from there to Leiden to dispute with defenders of the Church of England. About 1613, Ames began a controversy with Arminians at Rotterdam and also married the daughter of Dr. Burgess, whom he succeeded as chaplain to the English governor at Brielle, Holland. Dismissed from this position, he attended the Synod of Dort (1618–1619) as adviser to the Calvinists. Subsequently, he became a professor and then rector of the University of Franeker, which position he held until poor health forced him to move to Rotterdam, where he died in 1633. Ames left a second wife, a son, and a daughter, who emigrated to New England after his death. Ames has been known chiefly for his theological treatises, and in particular for his defense of Calvinism against Arminianism, for his presentation of Calvinist theology in his *Medulla theologiae* (1623; English tr., *The Marrow of Sacred Divinity*, 1642), and for his development of a reformed casuistry in his widely influential *De conscientia* (1632).

**Amiens Cathedral of Notre Dame.** Cathedral constructed in the French Gothic style. Regarded by many as the most magnificent in the French Gothic style, this cathedral was built at Amiens in 1220 on the site of four previous churches, three of which were destroyed by fire caused by lightning and one, the earliest, burned by the Vikings. The vertical lines of the building enhance the height of the structure, which extends nearly to the limits of the system of thrusts and counterthrusts employed in the Gothic style. The facade and interior are among the first in Gothic architecture.

**Amish** (*or* Amish Mennonite). Mennonite faction deriving from Jacob Amann, 17th-century Swiss dissenter. Amish groups arose in Germany, France, Russia, and Holland. Some Amish emigrated to America in groups with powerful social cohesion and determined separateness of dress and manner. There were three basic strains of Amish immigration: early 18th-century immigrants from Switzerland and the Palatinate to eastern Pennsylvania (1720); 19th-century Alsatian, Bavarian, and Hessian immigrants (Ohio, 1807 and 1812; Illinois, 1829; New York, 1845; Iowa, 1845); and Volhynian (Russian) immigrants in the last quarter of the 19th century (Kansas, 1873 ff.). Settlements also arose in Nebraska, South Dakota, Ontario, and elsewhere. Interstate immigration complicated the international movements. The greatest number of American Amish adhere to the Old Order Amish.

**Ammianus Marcellinus.** Roman soldier and historian. The preserved portion of his history (A.D. 353–378) is the best authority for the period covered. Ammianus was apparently a pagan, certainly an admirer of the emperor Julian (the Apostate) under whom he had served, but his general attitude was tolerant, and the occasional rather detached comments on religious affairs in his mainly political and military history are of considerable interest.

**Amphilochius** (c. 342–c. 395). Bishop. A Cappadocian by birth, student of Libanius at Antioch, and teacher at Constantinople, Amphilochius in 374 became bishop of Iconium, in the province of Lycaonia, which he organized and defended against the Messalians. He was an associate of the Cappadocian Fathers and a consistent champion of orthodoxy, thereby earning the imperial accolade in 381. His writings, few of which are extant, consisted chiefly of sermons and exegesis of Biblical passages.

**Amsdorf, Nikolaus von** (1483–1565). German Lutheran theologian and an intimate friend and loyal follower of Luther. Among the first students at the University of Wittenberg, he was ordained in 1524 and made superintendent at Magdeburg, where he actively promoted the Reformation, as he did later at Goslar and Einbeck. In 1541, Elector John Frederick appointed him bishop of Naumburg-Zeitz, but after the Protestant defeat at Mühlberg (1547) he fled to Weimar. He helped found a new university at Jena to counteract the mediating views of Melanchthon and the Wittenberg faculty and rigidly opposed all efforts to reconcile Lutherans with other Protestants or Roman Catholics. From Eisenach, where he was superintendent from 1552, he called Matthias Flacius to Jena and together they attacked the Leipzig Interim and the Adiaphorists, especially Melanchthon. Amsdorf was chiefly responsible for the break between Melanchthon and the more rigidly orthodox Lutherans at the colloquy held at Worms in 1557. In a controversy with Menius between 1554 and 1559 on the value of good works, Amsdorf finally adopted the extreme position that good works were detrimental to salvation. (See GEORG MAJOR.) When Flacius and his disciples were removed from Jena (1561), Amsdorf was allowed to remain because of his advanced age and great services in the early days of the Reformation.

**Amsterdam, Free University of.** A university established in 1880, free in the sense that it was founded by a group of individuals and not by any state or local governmental body. Rejecting the idea of a neutral education, the Free University of Amsterdam devoted itself fully to the Reformed principles as basic to all instruction and scholarly endeavor. These are defined as the principles of Holy Scripture. All instructors must subscribe to this point of view.

**Amsterdam Assembly** (1948). An assembly held from Aug. 22 to Sept. 4, 1948, to organize the World Council of Churches. One hundred fifty churches were invited, but only 135 denominations from 44 countries sent 351 official delegates. The Greek Church and the ecumenical patriarchate of Constantinople were the only representatives of the vast Orthodox tradition; a conference of Orthodox churches held in Moscow in July had charged that the goals of the World Council of Churches were political. The World Council of Churches was officially constituted on Aug. 23. There had been continual demands for its constitution since a synod of the ecumenical patriarchate in Constantinople had invited all churches to found a "league (*koinōnia*)" in 1920. Archbishop Nathan Söderblom of Sweden had urged the establishment of an "ecumenical council" at the same time, but many churchmen had felt that these demands were too radical. Only after the assemblies of Stockholm (1925) and Lausanne (1927) had it become evident that the two basic branches of the ecumenical movement—"Life and Work," "Faith and Order"—should be combined in a new constitution for the movement. Finally, the assembly of Utrecht had drafted the new constitution in 1938, which was voted upon and adopted in Amsterdam. Influenced by the events of World War II and its consequences, the Amsterdam assembly decided to study the theme "Man's Disorder and God's Design." A study commission, chaired by Henry P. Van Dusen, president of Union Theological Seminary, enlisted prominent scholars from various parts of the world to address the assembly—among them Karl Barth, Emil Brunner, Reinhold Niebuhr, John Foster Dulles, Josef Hromádka, Regin Prenter, and other famous men in the ecumenical movement.

The delegates and their alternates were divided into four sections and four committees to deal with subtopics. The sections, composed of delegates interested in the subject being studied, discussed: (1) "The Universal Church in God's Design," chaired by Bishop Ernest R. Lilje, of Hannover, Germany; (2) "The Church's Witness to God's Design," chaired by John A. Mackay, president of Princeton Theological Seminary; (3) "The Church and the Disorder of Society," chaired by Constantijn L. Patijn, minister of Economic Affairs of the Netherlands; and (4) "The Church and the International Order," chaired by Kenneth G. Grubb, executive chairman of the Commission of the Churches on International Affairs. The committees dealt with administrative matters: (1) "Constitution, Rules, and Regulations"; (2) "Policies"; (3) "Program and Administration"; and (4) "The Concerns of the Churches": (*a*) "The Life and Work of Women in the Churches," (*b*) "The Christian Approach to the Jews," (*c*) "The Training of Laymen in the Church," and (*d*) "Christian Reconstruction and Inter-Church Aid." The report of the first study section was especially significant, since it attempted to define the various meanings of the term "church," including both Protestant and Catholic traditions. Thus the church was defined in general as a gift of God founded by God's deeds of salvation in Christ. The assembly also adopted a statement regarding its own understanding of itself and that of the World Council of Churches, declaring: "The World Council of Churches is composed of churches which acknowledge Jesus Christ as God and Savior. They find their unity in him. They do not have to create their unity; it is the gift of God. But they know that it is their duty to make common cause in the search for the expression of that unity in work and life." A message was sent to all existing Christian churches calling for a commitment to the common cause of unity. The studies of the various sections are founded upon earlier work of the ecumenical movement, especially the Oxford assembly of 1937, which dealt with the theme "Church, Community, and State." They combined the two basic approaches of the ecumenical movement, "Life and Work" and "Faith and Order," in their attempt to deal with the problem of church unity and witness in the world. The results achieved at the Amsterdam assembly are contained in *Man's Disorder and God's Design* (The Amsterdam Assembly Series, 5 vols. in 2; New York, 1949).

BIBLIOGRAPHY: D. P. Gaines, *The World Council of Churches: A Study of Its Background and History* (Peterborough, N.H., 1966).

**Amsterdam Youth Conference** (1939). The first great cooperative effort to bring together a worldwide gathering of Christian youth. Sponsored by a number of lay youth organizations and the Provisional Committee of the World Council of Churches, it sought to introduce 1,700 young people to the meaning of the ecumenical church. Here, just before the outbreak of World War II, delegates from 71 nations searched for the significance in their time of the Conference motto, *Christus Victor*.

**Anabaptists.** A general designation for various 16th-century groups that desired a more radical reform of the church than the Protestants had undertaken. "Anabaptists" (i.e., "re-baptizers"), a term applied by their opponents, is misleading, first, because it was used to cover such diverse parties; second, because the Anabaptists rejected infant baptism and therefore, in administering baptism to believers, did not admit that they were "baptizing again." The typology of Anabaptism is a complex historical problem, but in general four major groups may be distinguished. Those who are sometimes called "main-line Anabaptists" (or, more tendentiously, "consistent evangelicals"), including the Swiss Brethren, the Mennonites, and the Hutterites, sought to establish voluntary communities of the regenerate according to a strict Biblical pattern. The spiritualists, such as Carlstadt, Müntzer, Schwenkfeld, and Sebastian Franck, appealed rather to the Spirit, who caused Scripture to be written. The rationalists, notably the Socinians, read the Scriptures in the light of reason and were led to deny the traditional beliefs concerning

Christ's deity and satisfaction of God's justice. The revolutionaries, such as the Münsterites, planned to bring in the Kingdom of God with the sword. Because of the extreme diversity of these religious bodies, it has become the tendency in much recent scholarship to restrict the appellation "Anabaptists" to the first group alone. (See RADICAL REFORMATION.)

**Anacletus** (from Greek, *anenklētos,* "blameless"). Pope from 76 to 88. He appears in the 2d-century lists as the second bishop of Rome, between Linus and Clement. Nothing more is reported of him, so the name merely represents the existence of Christian leaders at Rome in the generation after the apostles. The use of the shortened form "Cletus" led to a doubling of the name in later lists, which put Cletus before and Anacletus after Clement.

**Anagni.** A small town southeast of Rome in the hills away from the malarial swamps and the heat of summer, and therefore often used as a summer retreat by the popes. Its most significant moment was in September of 1303 when the enemies of Boniface VIII sought to seize (with a form of legality—the French) or kill (the Colonna faction) the old pope (Outrage of Anagni). He was held prisoner for three days and treated somewhat roughly. He died within a month after being freed, not from violence, but from shame and humiliation.

**Analogy of Religion.** A book published in 1736 by Joseph Butler (1692–1752), bishop of Durham. This work, an answer to the deists' criticisms of traditional theology, attempts to show that the rational difficulties raised concerning revelation can also be raised about the course of nature. Thus, if you accept God as the author of nature, as the deists did, there is no reason why you should not also accept him as the author of revelation.

**Anchorite.** One who withdraws from the world to live an ascetic and contemplative life. Although both the solitary hermit and the communal monk may be called anchorites, the term is usually applied to the former. In the early days of Christianity, the anchorites were free from hierarchical control and lived by no rule. Gradually they came under ecclesiastical control and were required to live according to a prescribed discipline.

**Ancren Riwle.** A treatise on the religious life written in Middle English for a small community of women. It is now generally dated in the middle 12th century, but its authorship is unknown. The rigorous life it prescribes is tempered by an understanding and gentle spirit. The last chapter contains rules for the administration of a monastery. It later came to be used by both male and female communities.

**Andover Seminary.** A school established as a reaction to Unitarianism at Harvard. It was founded in Andover, Mass., in 1808 to train Congregational pastors who would be well versed in strict Calvinist theology. Initially tied to the Westminster Standards and the Andover Creed, a restatement of Edwardean theology by Samuel Hopkins, the school became a training ground for revivalists. By the 1880's, however, it had come under the domination of contemporary liberal theological thought.

**Andreae, Jacob** (1528–1590). German Lutheran reformer and theologian, the only Lutheran pastor to remain at his post while the Spanish forces occupied Stuttgart in the Smalcald War (1547). Andreae corresponded with the ecumenical patriarch Jeremiah II. As the leader of the middle party between the Gnesio-Lutherans and the Philippists, he was eager to preserve Lutheranism by avoiding extremes. He coauthored the Formula of Concord (1577).

**Andreae, Johann Valentin** (1586–1654). Educator, reformer, theologian, and satirist. He believed that true religion was expressed in brotherhood and not in arid polemics. In 1619 he wrote *Christianopolis,* which was a description of the ideal Christian state. He believed that the purpose of education was best exemplified in Christian nurture rather than in indocrination, and he sought to make education of more practical value. Opposed to sectarianism, he pleaded for the reconciliation of all Christians.

**Andrewes, Lancelot** (1555–1626). Anglican prelate and theologian of the 16th and early 17th centuries. Born in All Hallows' parish, Barking, he was the son of Thomas Andrewes, a seafaring man, sometime master of Trinity House. Young Lancelot grew up in a devout Anglican household, the eldest son of thirteen children. His early education was received at Merchant Taylors' School, where he quickly showed himself to be a serious and studious pupil. After Merchant Taylors' he entered Pembroke College, Cambridge, in 1571, just at the time of the deprivation of Thomas Cartwright from the Lady Margaret professorship of divinity. All during young Andrewes' collegiate career the conflict between Anglican and Puritan grew in intensity. There are indications during this decade that he had some affinities with the Puritans, at least the more moderate variety. In common with the Puritans he was an early and earnest Sabbatarian. Cambridge at that time was the center of most of the Puritan thinking and activity, and gained increased encouragement in 1584 when Sir Walter Milmay founded Emmanuel College, which in time became the seminary for dissent. Andrewes became B.A. in 1575, and was appointed to a fellowship in Pembroke College. He was incorporated M.A. in 1578 and was made master of the college in 1589. Incongruous as it sounds, he was incorporated M.A. of the newly founded Jesus College at Oxford in 1581, though he never studied there or held residency. Further study and the presentation of a thesis led to his being made B.D. in 1585. On his becoming master of Pembroke he applied for the D.D., and though his application was challenged by some of the authorities, the degree was conferred nevertheless. Andrewes by this time was a zealous churchman and apologist for the Anglican cause. He rose rapidly in preferment, becoming dean of the Collegiate Church in Westminster in 1601, bishop of Chichester in 1605, bishop of Ely in 1609, and, upon the death of Archbishop Bancroft, a potential candidate for Canterbury, though the king preferred George Abbot. He was translated to the bishopric of Winchester in 1618, where he spent the remaining eight years of his life.

Bishop Andrewes was a diligent prelate and went about his episcopal duties with a quiet zeal. Many thought that he was too often quiet when he should have been outspoken for justice. He inaugurated many reforms in his dioceses, though not of the rigorous Puritan variety. When he was translated to Ely, which had in Elizabeth's time remained vacant for eighteen years, he set about instituting a program of rehabilitation in that then dilapidated diocese, both in the episcopal palace and in the parish churches. As a prelate he accepted without question the authority and headship of the king in ecclesiastical affairs. He had been one of the main supporters of King James I at the Hampton Court Conference of 1604. When the king decided on the appositeness of a new translation of the Bible, he gathered most of the distinguished Biblical scholars and linguists in England for this task. Lancelot Andrewes was appointed chairman of a "company" because of his great learning and intimate knowledge of ancient languages. The translation was the Authorized Version, known familiarly as the "King James," which appeared in 1611. Andrewes was now a confidant and courtier, and the king learned to rely on his wisdom in ecclesiastical matters. When the Gunpowder Plot was discovered in 1605, something like a panic struck England and awakened old memories of persecutions now a half century and more past. The king demanded an oath of allegiance from all recusants, and when the Roman Catholics challenged this, he appointed Andrewes to answer them. The pope chose his ablest polemicist, Cardinal Bellarmine, to confute the Anglicans, and verbal warfare was waged for several years until other issues attracted the attention of the Anglicans. Andrewes was at the height of his powers, and the aging cardinal was no match for his opponent's subtle wit. Andrewes argued against Rome for the antiquity and catholicity of the English Church, appealing often, as would the Caroline divines after him, to the Vincentian canon.

Distinguished as an able preacher, Andrewes was also a master of the spiritual life, his posthumously published *Private Devotions* (*Preces privatae*) becoming a classic of English spirituality. He was a scholar in Biblical languages, mastering, besides, most of the major European tongues, and was an astute theologian, though not a man of great originality. Possessing apostolic zeal and a saintly character, he was much given to meditation and quietism. His humanity shows through in his constant preferment of his brother, Roger, who was adjudged by all to be an incompetent and unworthy character. Andrewes wrought much in the reconstruction of the English Church after a period of bitter controversy and upheaval. He died on Sept. 26, 1626, and was buried in Southwark Cathedral. William Laud called him "a light of the Christian Church."

BIBLIOGRAPHY: Andrewes' works, edited by J. P. Wilson and J. Bliss in the *Library of Anglo-Catholic Theology* (11 vols., 1841–1854). The earliest life is by his pupil and secretary, H. Isaacson (1651). R. L. Ottley's *Lancelot Andrewes* (London, 1894) is an excellent treatment of the man, especially as a preacher and theologian. More recent treatments are by P. Welsby (1958) and M. Reidy, S.J. (1955).

**Andrew of Crete** (c. 660–740). Byzantine hymnologist and saint in the Eastern Orthodox Church. He was deacon of the Hagia Sophia in Constantinople, then archbishop of Gortyna in Crete. In 712, Andrew participated in the Monothelete Synod, but he recanted that heresy the following year. His writings include Scriptural commentaries, but he is most renowned for the invention of the canon, a new form of hymnology, to replace the traditional *kontakion*.

**Andrews, Charles Freer** (1871–1940). Missionary, teacher, and champion of the oppressed. An ambassador of interracial friendship throughout the world, but especially between India and his native Britain. He taught at St. Stephen's College, Delhi, where he sought to make the school a genuinely Indian institution. Objecting to proselyting and believing it infinitely more important to act out the Christian faith than to profess it, he sponsored the cause of oppressed Indians in South Africa and the Fiji Islands.

**Angela Merici** (1474–1540). Italian Roman Catholic, founder of the Ursulines. Angela entered the Third Order of St. Francis as a young girl with the intention of dedicating her life to penance for the sins of the world. Seeing the need to give a Christian education to girls, she set up a school in her own home. She was soon joined by other single women, and in 1535 the Ursuline Congregation was formally established at Brescia to continue their work. Angela was canonized in 1807.

**Angelico, Fra** (1387–1455). A painter of the Florentine school. He was born Guido di Pietro, but became Fra Angelico Giovanni da Fiesole when he entered the Dominican Order. He and his brother illuminated manuscripts and were influenced by Giotto. In 1435, Angelico was invited to decorate the Convent of San Marco in Florence by the patron Cosimo de' Medici. His work in Rome was sponsored by Eugenius IV and Nicholas V. His style is noble yet tender, his color brilliant and pure.

**Angelus.** A devotion in honor of the incarnation, recited three times a day, usually signaled by the ringing of a bell. The recitation consists of three Ave Marias, versicles, and a collect. The devotion may be found as early as the 13th century in Germany. Since the 17th century it has been in more general use.

**Anglican Communion, The.** The fellowship of autonomous churches and provinces that are in communion with the ancient see of Canterbury, some of which resulted from the severing of ties between members of the United Kingdom, some from the migration of Church of England people from the British Isles, and some from missionary activity of the Church of England or its daughter churches outside the British Isles. The Episcopal Church in Scotland, finally disestablished and permanently replaced as state church by Presby-

terianism in 1690, protected by an act of Queen Anne (1712) and officially recognized by George III (1788), is historically the first of the separate autonomous churches in the Anglican fellowship. The Protestant Episcopal Church in the U.S.A. was formally organized in 1789, but not until it had secured its first bishop, Samuel Seabury, from the Scots (1784) and its next three by English consecration through an act of 1786, making it possible for the archbishop of Canterbury to consecrate a bishop for service outside the British Isles. This church intended to continue to practice Christianity as it was understood in the Church of England except for establishment. Under the same act, Charles Inglis was consecrated bishop of Nova Scotia (1787), with jurisdiction over all of British North America, thus becoming the first colonial bishop, but the Church of England was reluctant to multiply colonial sees, creating only two more by 1823, Quebec (1793) and Calcutta (1814). The origin of the use of the term "Anglican Communion" is to be found in the 1850's in connection with the Jubilee of the Society for the Propagation of the Gospel and with the General Convention of the Protestant Episcopal Church in 1853. Although there was an assembly of some 108 bishops of Anglican churches for the Jubilee in 1852, the effective beginning of the Anglican Communion is to be dated from the first Lambeth Conference (1867), a meeting of Anglican bishops held decennially under the presidency of the archbishop of Canterbury. This Conference is not a legislative body, and the primacy of the archbishop is one of antiquity and honor only.

As presently constituted, the Anglican Communion consists of some eighteen autonomous churches, together with a number of overseas dioceses not yet included in provinces, the majority of which depend upon the archbishop of Canterbury for the appointment of bishops, and a control not unlike that of a metropolitan. The churches, with date of autonomy and composition, are: The Church of England (comprising two metropolitan sees, Canterbury and York), the Church of Ireland (1870; comprising two metropolitan provinces, Armagh and Dublin), the Episcopal Church in Scotland (1690; comprising seven dioceses over which an elected primus presides), the Church in Wales (1920; comprising six dioceses in Wales and Monmouthshire), the Protestant Episcopal Church in the U.S.A. (1789; 102 dioceses and missionary districts, several outside continental limits), the Church of India, Pakistan, Burma, and Ceylon (1930; metropolitan province of

Calcutta, with eighteen dioceses), Anglican Church of Canada (1893; four metropolitan provinces presided over by primate of all Canada), Church of the Province of South Africa (1847, declared independent 1863; metropolitan province of fourteen dioceses), Church of England in Australia and Tasmania (1872, independence 1962; four metropolitan and three separate dioceses under the Synod), Church of the Province of New Zealand (1857; seven dioceses and missionary dioceses of Melanesia and Polynesia), Church of the Province of the West Indies (1883; four dioceses), Holy Catholic Church of China (1912, limited relations with outside since 1955; fourteen dioceses), Japan Holy Catholic Church (1941; ten dioceses), Province of West Africa (1951), Province of Central Africa (1955), Province of East Africa (1960), Church of Uganda, Rwanda and Burundi (1961), Episcopal Church of Brazil (1965). The Jerusalem archbishopric comprising five dioceses in the Near East is now under close supervision of Canterbury, but has a plan for provincial autonomy. A half dozen more dioceses—two in South America, Bermuda, Gibraltar (supervision of English congregations in South Europe and North Africa), North and Central Europe (English congregations), and Madagascar and Mauritius—are included but under direct supervision of Canterbury. A council of Churches of Southeast Asia was formed in 1954 to include five dioceses still under Canterbury: Hong Kong (separated from the Church of China), Rangoon (still part of the Church of India, Pakistan, Burma, and Ceylon) as well as the Philippine Episcopal Church (in process of becoming a separate autonomous province), and Taiwan, both of which are related to the Protestant Episcopal Church in the U.S.A. and the newly constituted Philippine Independent Church; this council is not yet a separate province of the Anglican Communion but is rather a fellowship of common concern for mutual action.

While Lambeth Conference has no jurisdiction over churches in the Anglican Communion, its meetings have given rise to the Anglican Congress, a meeting of bishops, clergy, and lay people, originating in the Pan Anglican Congress of 1908 and subsequently meeting in 1954 (Minneapolis) and 1963 (Toronto). The Lambeth Conference of 1958 constituted a Consultative Body to meet in the interim between Conferences consisting of primates or presiding bishops of member churches. Since 1948, there has also been an Advisory Council on Missionary Strategy representing all the member churches meeting at intervals in connection with the Anglican Congress. This Council was strengthened by a report made to Lambeth Conference in 1958, and a continuing office was established, called the Executive Officer of the Anglican Communion, with headquarters in London, whose chief function is to provide liaison among the member churches and to devise and submit plans for interchurch cooperation in mission and union schemes. One important fruit of this office was the report *Mutual Responsibility and Interdependence in the Body of Christ* submitted to the Anglican Congress of 1963 and embodying the intention of member churches to be alert to the missionary challenge of being a worldwide church in the 20th century and the recognition of equality among all member churches in this enterprise. This document came out of deliberations of the combined meeting of the Consultative Body and the Advisory Council who agreed to meet biennially thenceforth, looking toward some official amalgamation of the two bodies by the next Lambeth Conference. In order to further the kind of cooperative activity represented by the 1963 report, it was recommended that year to appoint Regional Officers within provinces who should perform for the province work similar to that done by the Executive Officer for the communion as a whole. From almost haphazard and certainly unplanned beginnings, there has resulted among these churches a network of cooperation in mutual concern which has studiously avoided an authoritarian structure even to the point of limiting the authority of the see of Canterbury to a "primacy of honour," thus reflecting the peculiar structure of the Church of England but accommodating it to the nonestablishment of churches in those areas which have come under the missionary influence of that church.

Church union schemes in India and its environs, together with the recognition by member churches of this communion of other episcopally ordered churches whose traditions lie outside the sphere of influence of the Anglican Communion, has led in recent years to the establishment of the Wider Episcopal Fellowship. This is an association of churches and provinces which enjoy the historic episcopate and a measure of intercommunion with many, if not all, of the churches and provinces of the Anglican Communion. Upon the recommendation of the Lambeth Conference in 1958, the first meeting of this Fellowship was held in 1964 with half of the bishops from the Anglican Communion and the other half from other episcopal churches: the Church of South India, the Church of Nigeria, the Old Catholic Churches, the Spanish Reformed Episcopal Church, the Lusitanian Church of Portugal, the Philippine Independent Catholic Church, the Scandinavian Churches, and the Mar Thoma Syrian Church. As this Fellowship matures and closer relations are established among these churches and the Anglican Communion, a pattern for church union parallel to but distinct from the World Council of Churches and the Roman Catholic Secretariat for Unity emerges. In the meantime, a pattern of relations exists between the Anglican Churches and Rome as well as with the World Council of Churches, of which Anglican churches are members.

BIBLIOGRAPHY: R. S. Bosher, *The American Church and the Formation of the Anglican Communion* (Evanston, 1962); G. F. S. Gray, *The Anglican Communion* (London, 1958); S. C. Neill, *Anglicanism* (Baltimore, 1965); R. Rouse and S. C. Neill (eds.), *A History of the Ecumenical Movement: 1517–1948* (2d ed., rev., Philadelphia, 1967); *The Church of England Yearbook* (published annually).

**Anglicanism.** See ANGLICAN COMMUNION, THE.

**Anglicans in the United States.** The Church of England, one of the most powerful churches in America during the colonial period, was virtually destroyed during the American Revolution. Established in several colonies, it grew rapidly and played an important role in education and colonial politics, but it was weakened by lay domination, the lack of a native clergy, and its identification with royal intolerance. In 1782, William White, an acknowledged patriot, published *The Case of the Episcopal Churches in the United States Considered,* a plea for unity and reorganization. In 1783, the name Protestant Episcopal Church was adopted by a conference at Annapolis. A compromise was reached between lay and clerical parties at the Philadelphia Convention of 1789, where a constitution was adopted, the prayer book revised for American use, and self-government established. Samuel Seabury was consecrated bishop by nonjurors in Scotland (1784) and White and Provoost by Canterbury (1787). Low Church in emphasis under the leadership of White, the communion developed a strong High Church party under Bishop J. H. Hobart. With controversy threatening division, W. A. Muhlenberg, who called himself an Evangelical Catholic, brought reconciliation at the General Convention of 1835. The Epis-

copal Church was the only major denomination that remained undivided during the Civil War. It later pioneered programs of social amelioration, urban churches, and was a powerful element in the Social Gospel movement.

**Anglo-Catholic Movement.** The word "Anglo-Catholicism" was first used in 1838 to designate the High Church party in the Church of England. The Catholicity of the Church of England had been emphasized before, by some churchmen as early as the 17th century. This "older" High Church tendency can be associated with the names of Richard Hooker (d. 1600), Lancelot Andrewes (d. 1626), Archbishop Laud (d. 1645), and others. It was characterized by an emphasis on Catholicity in matters of authority, belief, and worship, but was bitterly opposed to Roman Catholicism. The older High Churchmen existed in Anglicanism as a small but significant minority.

*Oxford Movement.* In the first quarter of the 19th century the Church of England was in an enfeebled condition. Parish life was at a low ebb, ministerial zeal was lacking, and clerical education was greatly outdated. Secularity seemed to threaten the very existence of the establishment. The low state of the church was especially noted by a group of students and writers at Oxford University. They felt that the church was ready for and needed change and they seized the opportunity to publish their views. John Keble (1792–1866) was the founder of the movement, although about a dozen men had expressed views similar to his before 1833. However, it was Keble's assize sermon of July 14, 1833, which provided the spark and marked the beginning of the modern (or "younger") Anglo-Catholic movement. John Henry Newman, Richard Hurrell Froude, and later Edward Pusey were other famous members of the Oxford Group. Newman soon became the leader and began the publication of the *Tracts for the Times* (September, 1833) which stirred up a tempest in the Church of England. The argument of the early *Tracts* was intended to revive certain doctrines held by the great divines of the Church of England, but now held "obsolete with the majority of her members." Apostolic succession, the sacraments as the true source of divine grace, and both popery and Methodism as deviations from the true faith are positions taken in these writings. The superior nature of Anglicanism was made to rest on the apostolic succession of its bishops. *Tract 90,* written by Newman in 1841, represents a basic shift in the argument. Heretofore it was contended that Roman Catholics were not "true Catholics," but in *Tract 90* Newman interpreted the Thirty-nine Articles of the Church of England in a Roman Catholic fashion. On Oct. 9, 1845, Newman was received into the Roman Catholic Church, and Anglo-Catholicism has ever since experienced a steady number of conversions to Roman Catholicism.

*After 1845.* Edward Pusey took over leadership of the Anglo-Catholics (or Tractarians, or Puseyites, or simply the Oxford movement) after 1845, and Anglo-Catholicism slowly began to spread. The decades after 1845 were filled with controversy, of which the least edifying was the ritualistic argument that agitated many parishes. But the Anglican public had been greatly influenced and the Oxford movement had imparted a permanent "Catholic" dimension to the Church of England. The organization of Anglo-Catholicism began in 1860 and in 1920 yearly conferences were initiated. Most of the arguments and emphases of the Tractarians still characterize Anglo-Catholicism, for example, apostolic succession, sacramental grace, private confessions, an emphasis on asceticism, and so on. The Anglo-Catholic emphasis on ritual was not characteristic of the Tractarians. However, the ritualists united with Anglo-Catholicism and soon (by the 1870's) Anglo-Catholics were commonly spoken of as ritualists. Generally speaking, Anglo-Catholics have tried to establish as close an agreement as possible, in doctrine and practice, with the other churches of Catholic Christendom without sacrificing their Anglicanism. In any case, Anglo-Catholicism represents an instance in which a party changed the shape of a national church and a worldwide communion.

BIBLIOGRAPHY: Y. Brilioth, *The Anglican Revival Studies in the Oxford Movement* (London, 1925); J. H. Newman, *Apologia pro vita sua* (Garden City, 1956); S. L. Ollard, *A Short History of the Oxford Movement* (London, 1915); H. L. Stewart, *A Century of Anglo-Catholicism* (London, 1929); *Anglo-Catholic Congress Reports* (1920 ff.).

**Anglo-Prussian Bishopric of Jerusalem.** Joint bishopric set up in Jerusalem by Prussia and England. In 1840 an agreement was reached between Prussia and England to set up a joint bishopric in Jerusalem, the position to be filled alternately by English and Prussian nominees. However, the archbishop of Canterbury could veto German appointments and the ordination was always to be according to the Anglican rite. The project collapsed in 1886 when the Anglicans required that the bishop must also assent to the Thirty-nine Articles.

**Anglo-Saxon Christianity.** Origen and Tertullian both speak of Christianity in Britain, and there were British bishops at the Council of Arles in 314. Presumably, then, even as early as this there was some sort of ecclesiastical organization in Britain. Introduced perhaps by traders from the Continent or soldiers occupying the Roman garrisons, Christianity developed until Roman power declined and invading Saxons destroyed the Roman civilization and drove the older Celtic population to the Western reaches of the islands. Though they were Christians, they made no attempt to convert their conquerors. Not until the mission of Augustine (d. c. 604) to Britain in 579 was Christianity established more substantially. He was sent with forty monks to Kent by Pope Gregory I. After turning back once, he landed and was delighted to find that the queen, Bertha, was already a Christian. Her husband, Ethelbert, insisted on meeting Augustine in the open air to minimize the effect of any spells, but he was soon converted to Christianity and baptized.

Augustine was advised by Pope Gregory to set up two archbishoprics, one at London and one at York; each of them was to have twelve bishoprics under it. Unfortunately, Augustine antagonized the Celtic Christians by refusing to rise from his seat when they approached him and he had to work without their help. He was not a good organizer and failed to convert the north, the archbishopric of York not being established until 735.

The expulsion of Laurentius, Augustine's successor, from London led to the confirmation of Canterbury as the seat of the southern archbishopric. In spite of setbacks, most of England was Christianized in part within a hundred years of the original mission. Paulinus, who was sent to England by Gregory in 601, was through his acquaintance with the northern Christian queen Ethelburga mainly instrumental in this conversion. Ethelburga's husband, Edwin, was baptized in 627. Felix and Birinus carried the faith to East Anglia and the territory of the West Saxons. Christianity was of great importance in providing a single bond of unity for tribes and rulers of very different complexions, and it is largely true that England had one religion before it had a single political structure.

The different customs of the Celtic missions led finally to the Synod of Whitby (664), at which Roman customs were adopted in regard to the dating of Easter, the tonsure adopted by the clergy, and the form of baptism employed. The departure of Colman marked the end of the less organized Celtic Church and its replacement by the more highly structured Roman variety of Christianity. After the Synod of Hertford (673), the system of diocesan bishops resident in their own dioceses was adopted, and the wandering missionary bishop more characteristic of Celtic Christianity disappeared. For a time Offa tried to establish an archiepiscopal see in Mercia, at Lichfield, but this attempt failed to yield its anticipated fruits. In 669, Theodore of Tarsus, at age 64, was appointed archbishop of Canterbury and came to England with Benedict Biscop. Theodore was a scholar, having lectured in astronomy as well as in theology, in addition to which he was an indefatigable collector of books for the monasteries which he helped found at Wearmouth and Jarrow. A tradition of ecclesiastical and monastic scholarship was established in England within a generation. Theodore gave the church a sense of its unity through the Synod of Hertford, wrote a penitential, and among his practical accomplishments could number having divided large dioceses into smaller and more closely related fellowships, thus increasing the number of bishops, and ensuring a greater degree of supervision over diocesan life.

After Theodore, the story of Christianity in England is largely the story of the great monastic foundations and of sometimes even greater bishops such as the Venerable Bede, Chad, Dunstan, and others. With the conquest of the Danes, there was a setback until King Alfred, but English missionaries such as Boniface and scholars such as Alcuin at the court of Charlemagne powerfully influenced the development of European Christianity.

Most Anglo-Saxon institutions were abolished or replaced when the Normans invaded Britain in 1066, at this point only one Anglo-Saxon bishop, Wulfstan (c. 1009–1095), being retained.

BIBLIOGRAPHY: M. Deanesly, *The Pre-Conquest Church in England* (New York, 1961); and *Sidelights on the Anglo-Saxon Church* (London, 1962).

**Anglo-Saxon Chronicle, The.** A composite work giving a chronological history of England. About 891, during the reign of the English king Alfred (849–899), an attempt was made to write a national history based on early records. Copies were then sent to centers of learning and kept up to date as events occurred. These several manuscripts form the Chronicle. The events mentioned range from 60 B.C. to A.D. 1153. The Chronicle is important as one of the first major works in the English language and for its description of early English history.

**Anglo-Saxon Missions.** Primarily, Anglo-Saxon missionary activities on the Continent during the 8th century, and in a secondary sense the continuing influence of the Irish in Germany through the *Schottenkloster* of the later Middle Ages.

The Merovingian kingdom had already been introduced to Christianity with the baptism of Clovis, although the nature of the conversion was superficial. Under the veneer of Christian forms an active paganism lingered on. Columbanus (d. 615), an Irish monk, entered Gaul c. 590 and enjoyed some success in reforming the Gallican Church, establishing about forty monastic houses as mission centers. The most notable were at Luxeuil, St. Gall, and Bobbio. Although Columbanus rendered Christianity significant service in Gaul, his fiercely independent ways alienated him from both Frankish rulers and bishops. His autonomous Irish settlements tended to aggravate an already disorganized situation. Within a century of these labors the church in Gaul deteriorated. The late Merovingian period witnessed the decay of central authority, and the church tended to become territorial, controlled by disinterested lay princes. Ecclesiastical organization also broke down with the fragmentation of the kingdom, fostering a spirit of independence that was detrimental to the church's work. A threefold task awaited the missionaries from Britain: reconversion of Gaul, reorganization of the church, and the evangelization of the territories outside the old Roman Empire in the West.

The Anglo-Saxons brought with them the organizational experience of the Roman Church as it had been introduced to Kent by Augustine of Canterbury and subsequently to the entire Heptarchy by Wilfrid of York and Theodore of Canterbury. The impulse for mission activity came from the Irish who included in the monastic vocation the *peregrinatio pro Christi,* sacrificing life if necessary in the spread of the gospel. The missionaries came largely from monastic houses, so that their Continental activity bore the stamp of Irish zeal and Roman discipline radiating from monastic centers.

The first significant Anglo-Saxon missionary after Columbanus was Willibrord (d. 739), "Apostle of the Frisians," who came from Saxon Northumbria and spent some time with

Wilfrid at Ripon. In 678, Wilfrid had spent a year in the Netherlands, baptizing tribal chiefs and their followers. It is probable that his disciple Willibrord was influenced by the accounts of his missionary exploits. In 690, after spending twelve years in Irish monasteries, Willibrord embarked with eleven companions for the Low Countries inhabited by the Frisians. He visited Rome in 693 and received papal support for his activity, and in 695 he was consecrated archbishop of the Frisians by Pope Sergius. Pepin II supported him in his work and granted him Utrecht as his archiepiscopal residence. Although he spent nearly fifty years in Frisia, little is known of Willibrord's activities. He made an expedition to the Danes but met with little success. On his return journey to Frisia he was shipwrecked on Helgoland, "the holy island," and baptized two persons. His work was under continuous harassment by Radbod, prince of the Frisians, who saw in the success of the Christian gospel a veiled political threat to his position by Pepin the Frank. Radbod's successor made peace with Charles Martel and Willibrord. For the last three years of Willibrord's life he was assisted by Boniface. The earliest extant *Vita* we possess comes from Alcuin almost a century later. By the time of his death in 739, Willibrord and his colaborers had succeeded in bringing most of Belgium, Holland, and the German shores of the North Sea into the church.

By far the most significant Anglo-Saxon mission work was accomplished by Winfrid (Boniface), the younger contemporary of Willibrord. He was born in Wessex sometime before 680 and spent some time in the monasteries at Examchester and Nursling. In 716, he traveled to Utrecht and joined Willibrord. The following year he went to Rome and received authorization for mission work from Gregory II. In 722, he left Frisia for Hesse and Thuringia, where he realized some success in converting tribal chieftains to the faith. In the same year Gregory II consecrated him bishop and commissioned him to convert "the races in the parts of Germany and on the east side of the Rhine." The pope also wrote letters of commendation in behalf of Boniface to Charles Martel and to those bishops whose assistance would be helpful in his evangelistic work. This work embraced both the reform of the Gallican Church and the conversion of pagan Germany, in which he was supported by the papacy (Gregory II and Zacharias) and by the Frankish princes (Charles Martel and Pepin).

The method of Boniface consisted of preaching and founding monasteries. Following the tactics of his predecessors, he first attempted to convert the chieftains of an area, knowing that the tribes would follow their example. Perhaps his most famous exploit was cutting down the sacred Oak of Thor at Geismar, thus convincing the Hessians of the truth of Christianity. He was one of the first missionaries to employ women, notably Lioba, who founded a nunnery at Bischofsheim, and Walpurga, who became an abbess.

About 743, Boniface founded the monastery of Fulda as an outpost for the evangelization of Bavaria, an exempt house subject to the pope. Under its abbot, Sturm, this monastery grew to be the motherhouse for all of Germany and an influential center of Christianity. After the death of Charles Martel in 741, Boniface turned to the reform of the Gallican churches, which he accomplished through a series of councils, the first being the famous *Concilium Germanicum primum* of 742. He was fortified for this work by receiving the archbishop's pallium from Gregory III and the office of papal legate for Germany, taking Mainz as his archiepiscopal residence. It is a popular opinion that Pepin received regal coronation from Boniface when the Merovingians were displaced in 751. About 752, Boniface returned to Frisia, and in 754, while in the act of baptizing newly won converts, he died as a martyr at the hands of roving bandits. He was buried at Fulda, where his tomb remains to this day.

Boniface and his Anglo-Saxon followers brought organization, discipline, and reform to the Continent, and they assured future ecclesiastical stability through the foundation of numerous monasteries inhabited by local converts. They introduced a system of ecclesiastical provinces, insisting that all bishops be subject to the pope at Rome, and they attached the clergy to specific responsibilities. These missionaries also introduced that relationship between secular power and ecclesiastical institution which characterized the medieval period. The primary sources for Boniface's life and work are his correspondence and Willibald's *Life of St. Boniface*.

The Irish missionaries, following the example of Columbanus, continued to flock to the Continent. By the 12th century a number of Irish foundations were flourishing in Germany, intended primarily for Scotch and Irish monks. These houses became known therefore as *Schottenkloster*. Their motherhouse, or at least pioneering example, was Weih-St.-Peter at Ratisbon, founded c. 1072 by Marianus Scotus. This house became St. Jacob's (St. James's), which was to establish numerous daughter settlements in southern Germany.

BIBLIOGRAPHY: Alcuin, *The Life of Willibrord*, tr. by A. Grieve (London, 1923); Boniface, *Letters*, tr. by E. Emerton (New York, 1940); G. F. Browne, *Boniface of Crediton and His Companions* (London, 1910); C. H. Talbot (ed. and tr.), *The Anglo-Saxon Missionaries in Germany* (New York, 1954); Willibald, *The Life of St. Boniface*, tr. by G. W. Robinson (Cambridge, Mass., 1916).

**Anglo-Saxon Renaissance.** During the 10th century a revitalizing movement or scholarly renaissance, often called the Benedictine reform because of its monastic associations, spread from the Continent, in particular from the monastic centers of Cluny and Fleury-sur-Loire, into the religious houses of southern England. The movement was forwarded by three notable bishops, Dunstan, archbishop of Canterbury (d. 988), Ethelwold of Winchester (d. 984), and Oswald of Worcester and York (d. 992), and by the close sympathies of King Edgar (d. 975), aptly named "Father of the Monks." The Continental links were strong. Dunstan himself had spent two years at the reformed house of Blandinium in Ghent; Oswald studied the new monasticism at Fleury; and Ethelwold, prevented in his wish to go himself to Fleury, sent a representative to learn how the rule was administered there. When Oswald later founded a large monastery at Ramsey in Huntingdonshire, he invited a distinguished scholar, Abbo, to come from Fleury to teach his novices. When Ethelwold prepared a version of the Benedictine Rule, the *Regularis concordia,* with the aim of bringing uniformity to monastic usage, he was assisted by monks brought over from Ghent and Fleury. Among the aims of the reformers were the spread of the Benedictine way of life, the removal of corruption and laxity within the existing houses and the restoration of decayed ones, improvement in the standards of the parish clergy, the revivifying of the traditional monastic learning and its extension into the secular world. In matters of scholarship much was achieved. The considerable literary products of the Carolingian renaissance, the Latin writings of Alcuin, Hrabanus Maurus, Amalarius of Metz, and many others, in addition to the church fathers and classical authors, were made available to English students. Canonistic texts were particularly studied, and some of them translated into the vernacular. To the movement is due the proliferation of late Old English manuscripts and the voluminous homiletic writings of Aelfric, abbot of Eynsham (d. c. 1020), much of them aimed at improving standards of preaching outside the monasteries, and of

Wulfstan, bishop of Worcester and archbishop of York (d. 1023), who came to serve King Canute in the formulation of law codes. Much was done too in practical reforms. Secular clergy were largely turned out from the monasteries, and their places taken by professed monks pledged to the Benedictine vows of chastity, obedience, and poverty. The fenland abbeys of Ely, Peterborough, and Thorney, left desolate by the Viking invaders, were restored by Ethelwold. New houses were founded, Ramsey and Winchcombe by Oswald, Cerne Abbas in Dorset and Eynsham in Oxfordshire by wealthy lay patrons of Aelfric, Burton-on-Trent in the northeast Midlands by Wulfric Spott, a powerful Mercian landowner. On the secular side something like a religious revival was achieved, marked particularly by a new interest in education in much the same spirit as King Alfred's pioneering efforts of a century before. Much spiritual instruction was made available to the ordinary clergy. Wulfstan wrote a series of injunctions, the so-called Canons of Edgar, in addition to his homilies. Byrhtferth of Ramsey composed a treatise on computation expressly designed to win priests away from their dice games. Secular canons were provided with translations of the rules of Amalarius and Chrodegang in an effort to win them over to a communal life. Pastoral letters for circulation to diocesan clergy, pointing out what ecclesiastical canons required of them in their calling, were written by Aelfric for the use of Bishop Wulfsige of Sherborne and Archbishop Wulfstan himself.

The vitality of the movement persisted well into the 11th century. A sharp reaction against it took place, especially in Mercia, a short time after the death of King Edgar, but the nobility of the country in the main supported it, even though the Anglo-Danish landowners of the north showed little interest in the endowment of new monasteries. Neither the renewed attacks of the Vikings in the 980's nor the advent of a foreign king, Canute, soon after the turn of the century, gave much effectual opposition; Canute in fact proved a generous supporter of monasticism. One notable offshoot, though thinly documented, was the English mission to Scandinavia. The Normans when they reached England (1066) found an active and learned church.

BIBLIOGRAPHY: M. Deanesly, *The Pre-Conquest Church in England* (New York, 1961); and *Sidelights on the Anglo-Saxon Church* (London, 1962); E. S. Duckett, *St. Dunstan of Canterbury* (New York, 1955); J. Godfrey, *The Church in Anglo-Saxon England* (Cambridge, 1962); D. Knowles, *The Monastic Order in England* (Cambridge, 1940); T.

Symons, *The Monastic Agreement of the Monks and Nuns of the English Nation* (New York, 1953).

**Anicetus.** Bishop of Rome c. A.D. 154–165. During his time the prestige of the Roman Church was increased by the presence of numerous Christian teachers in the capital. Anicetus promoted the custom of observing Easter on the Sunday after the Passover, but remained in communion with the churches of Asia which retained the Jewish date, the 14th of Nisan, hence called Quartodeciman, and welcomed their leader Polycarp at Rome. The Quartodeciman practice was even tolerated in the congregations of Asiatic Christians at Rome.

**Annates.** The first year's income from an ecclesiastical benefice. Although annates could be collected from any benefice, the most common were those paid to the papal Curia by bishops and abbots in return for their appointments. The collection of annates led to many abuses, especially in the 14th and 15th centuries, and gave rise to much antipapal feeling throughout Europe.

**Anne, Queen** (1665–1714). Ruler of Great Britain, 1702–1714. The daughter of James, duke of York, and Anne Hyde. Raised a Protestant, she supported the revolution of 1688 and followed William III on the throne in 1702. Her religious policy was strongly Anglican, and "Queen Anne's Bounty" increased the livings of clergy from Crown revenues. She favored the Occasional Conformity and Schism Bills against dissent. On her deathbed she helped secure the peaceable succession of the Protestant Hanoverians.

**Annesley, Samuel** (c. 1620–1696). Puritan minister. In 1644, Annesley served as chaplain to the Earl of Warwick. Somewhat later he received the church at Cliffe in Kent, and in 1657 Cromwell appointed him lecturer at St. Paul's. In 1658, he was made vicar of St. Giles's, but when he refused to conform, following the Act of Uniformity in 1662, he lost this position. His daughter Susannah became the wife of Samuel Wesley and the mother of John and Charles, the founders of Methodism.

**Anno Domini** ("in the year of the Lord"). Commonly abbreviated A.D. and used to designate the years of the Christian era, counting from the date of Christ's birth as calculated by Dionysius Exiguus. It is now believed that he was in error by four to seven years. The Venerable Bede popularized the system of numbering from this date, and it became the accepted dating system in Anglo-Saxon England and the Frankish empire.

**Annoni, Hieronymus** (1697–1770). Swiss Pietist. Although early inclined toward radical Pietism and separatism, Annoni found his way to the official ministry of the church serving at Wallenburg and Muttenz near Basel, Switzerland. He published two volumes of popular pietistic hymns, but is best known for organizing the Fellowship of Good Friends in 1756 in Basel. Its members were to practice brotherly love, to gather news from mission fields, and to meet urgent practical needs in the community.

**Anomoeans** (from Greek *anomoion,* "dissimilar"). The Latinized name for the most radically Arian group of mid-4th-century Arianizers, derived from their use of the term to distinguish all other beings from God. Begun by Aetius, expounded by Eunomius, this view achieved dominance under Eudoxius of Constantinople (d. 370), persisting until the Second Council of Constantinople. (See HOMOEANS; ARIUS; ARIANS.)

**Anonymous of York.** Title usually given to the unknown author of an antipapal treatise, or tractate, written in the latter part of the 11th century. The work is one of the earliest to discuss the political theory of secular and ecclesiastical relations with a remarkable royalist bias. The writer, whether English or Continental, spent some time in England and applied his ideas particularly to the York-Canterbury dispute. The most recent editor (George H. Williams, "The Norman Anonymous of 1100 A.D.," *Harvard Theological Studies,* Vol. XVIII [1951]) would identify him with William Bona Anima, archbishop of Rouen (1079–1110).

**Anselm of Canterbury** (c. 1033–1109). Archbishop and Scholastic theologian. Born in Aosta, Italy, at the foot of the Great St. Bernard Pass, he was the son of Gundulph and Ermenberga, who were of noble birth. About 1056, Anselm went to Burgundy and then to Bec, attracted by the fame of the teacher Lanfranc. He entered the monastery at Bec (1060), succeeded Lanfranc as prior (1063), and Herluin as abbot (1078). While at Bec, Anselm composed *Meditations and Prayers,* a work of devotional piety, and judging from the number of extant manuscripts, popular among contemporaries. The treatise *Monologion* set forth three proofs for the existence of God. The first argument proceeded from the relative goodness of beings to a supreme good, God. The second proceeded from the fact that all objects had being in common and, therefore, there must be an ultimate cause of this being, which cause was called God. Thirdly, Anselm argued that the varying degrees of perfection in objects necessitated a supreme perfection called God. The *Proslogion*, originally to be called *Faith Seeking Understanding*, set forth the ontological proof for the existence of God. It is one of the most original pieces of theological writing in the whole of the Middle Ages. Although Anselm was influenced by Augustine, the finished treatises are distinctly original in that Anselm quoted no authorities, a departure from his predecessors and contemporaries. He depended upon logic to demonstrate the rationality of faith.

In 1093, Anselm was appointed by the dying William Rufus to the see of Canterbury, which had been vacant since Lanfranc's death (1089). Anselm protested that he was unsuited, but he acquiesced on the conditions that he would hold the see as it had been held by his predecessors, that William would listen to him as a spiritual father, and that Urban II would be recognized as pope. Invested with his see, Anselm asked permission to petition Urban for the pallium. This would imply recognition of Urban, a right William claimed for himself. At the Council of Rockingham (1095), Anselm received no support in this matter from his fellow bishops. William, however, sent for the pallium, but on the condition that Anselm be deposed. The papal legate brought the pallium and deposited it upon the altar at Canterbury, from which place Anselm received it. Upon the accusation that Canterbury had failed to send a proper contingent of forces to the war with the Welsh, Anselm went to Urban II, without permission from William (1097). While on the Continent in virtual exile, he wrote the *Cur Deus homo* and attended the Council of Bari (1098) and the Lateran Synod (1099). For the first time, an English prelate heard the decrees against lay investiture and homage. Anselm remained with Hugh of Lyons until he was recalled to England by the new king, Henry I (1100). Henry demanded that Anselm renew homage for, and be reinvested with, his see. Anselm refused and the struggle over lay investiture began in England. Four embassies went to Rome, Anselm undertaking the last in person. Although intransigent on investiture, Pope Paschal had shifted his position on homage from that expressed in his letter to Anselm (1102). In 1105, Paschal excommunicated the bishops invested by Henry, the Count of Meulan, and Anselm threatened to excommunicate the king. A meeting between Henry and Anselm was arranged at Laigle (1105) by Adela of Chartres. Negotiations lasted for two years and the final settlement was reached in London (1107). The London Settlement gave the right of investiture with ring and staff to the church, but allowed the bishop or abbot-elect to do homage for the temporalities before consecration. The last great struggle of Anselm's tenure occurred with Thomas of York, who attempted to secure the pallium before recognizing the primacy of Canterbury. Anselm died before that matter was settled. As archbishop, Anselm had lacked the ability to work with the secular authority as Lanfranc had done. He was intractable where the rights of his see were concerned and where the laws of the church were involved.

**Anselm of Laon** (c. 1050–1117). French theologian and teacher at the cathedral school at Laon. With his brother Radolf he conducted the first systematic exposition of theology, attracting pupils from all over Europe. He compiled a large part of the *Glossa interlinearis* of the Bible, and several of his *Sententiae* have been preserved. Abelard and many other great theologians studied under him. In turn, he became dean, chancellor, and archdeacon of Laon.

**Ansgar** (801–865). The "Apostle of Scandinavia." He was a Benedictine monk who began his mission to Denmark in 826. Louis the Pious commissioned him to Sweden, where, at Birka in 830, he built the first Christian church in the North. In 831, he became archbishop of Hamburg. He later established Danish congregations, but pagan reaction destroyed most of his work.

**Anthony, Susan B.** (1820–1906). American social reformer, organizer (1869) and president (1892–1900) of the American Woman Suffrage Association. Having parents who encouraged independent thinking, she early gave up teaching as too confining and began traveling, speaking, and writing, first for the cause of temperance and later for woman suffrage and the abolition of slavery. She never married. Vigorous and determined, she was arrested for voting in Rochester, N.Y., in 1872, but never paid the fine imposed.

**Antiburgher.** A member of the party of the Scottish Secession Church opposing the burgess oath. In 1747, the Scottish Secession Church split into two factions over the question whether church members should take the civil burgess oath, in which they must profess the "true religion" authorized by the laws of the state. The Antiburgher group held that the beliefs authorized were different from those of the Secession Church and consequently no member of that church could take the oath. The Burgher group did not object to the oath.

**Anti-Catholicism and Nativism.** Antagonism toward Catholicism was deep-rooted in America from the colonial period onward. Considered the symbol of persecution, it had been tolerated only in Maryland and Pennsylvania. Through immigration, Catholics grew to a million in number by 1840. Catholicism was contrasted unfavorably with the prevailing antisacerdotal and revivalistic evangelical Protestantism which was considered essential to democratic institutions and American destiny. Greater tolerance of Catholics in England, coupled with papal repudiation of liberal political movements and repressive secular policies, was seen as a Catholic victory and a threat to America. Roman Catholicism was portrayed as the leading adversary of the "American democratic faith," in spite of the attempts of Orestes Brownson and Isaac Hecker to reconcile the two. In 1830, the *Connecticut Observer* opened the floodgates of agitation by asserting that Catholicism was serving as the agent of European governments in a secret and subversive plot to overthrow the American form of government and the freedoms guaranteed by the Constitution. Lyman Beecher's *Plea for the West* (1835) spread these views widely. Herman Norton stated in his *Startling Facts for American Protestants* that Catholic emigration to the West was fostered by foreign powers. Samuel F. B. Morse, a most influential anti-Catholic, published *The Imminent Dangers to the Free Institutions of the United States Through Foreign Immigration* in 1835. Leading orators were W. C. Brownlee and John and Robert Breckinridge. Anti-Catholic societies included the Society for the Diffusion of Christian Knowledge (1835) and the Protestant Reformation Society (1836), which distributed vitriolic literature and sent out missionaries.

The result of this intensive agitation was discrimination, intolerance, fear, and hatred, which led to mob meetings, street preachers, rioting, and extralegal action. Churches and convents were burned, notably the Ursuline convent school in Charlestown near Boston in 1834. Protestant clergymen charged that the priesthood was corrupt and evil, the nuns immoral, and Catholicism itself base. Tales of horror in convents, though absurd and proved false, were highly incendiary. Most lurid was Maria Monk's *Awful Disclosures of the Hotel Dieu Nunnery of Montreal* (1838). The tales were believed because they fitted preconceived notions of Catholicism in spite of the critical efforts of Catholics and disinterested Protestants. Anti-Catholicism began to decline by 1856, but had already been absorbed as a weapon by nativism. Discrimina-

tion against the foreign-born was justified on the grounds that immigrants understood neither the privileges nor the responsibilities of American citizenship. They were suspected as economically competitive, socially inept, and participants in the Catholic plot. Burdened by poverty, illiteracy, and alien habits, they were considered the criminal scum of Europe, intentionally dumped on America by its enemies. Two important areas of conflict in New York and Philadelphia were control of education and church properties. These conflicts led to riots in Philadelphia and the rise in both cities of victorious anti-Catholic and nativist political parties. Violent action against immigrants was encouraged by Favazzi, Orr, and "the Fighting Parson" William G. Brownlow. Nativist secret societies were formed, such as The Order of the Star-Spangled Banner. The Know-Nothing or Native American political party arose out of the secret societies in the 1850's. It was strongest in the minority-conscious South and urban East. It possessed considerable power in 1854 and 1855, particularly in Pennsylvania, Massachusetts, Rhode Island, New Hampshire, Connecticut, Maryland, Kentucky, Texas, and California, but made a weak showing in the national elections of 1856. The party drew its membership and support largely from the old Whig Party and in its decline contributed to the rise of the Republican Party. Both anti-Catholicism and nativism were submerged in the rising slavery controversy. Both reappeared, however, with the flood of immigration from 1880 to 1920. In contrast with the growing fragmentation of American Protestantism, Catholicism was seen as a dangerous and alien power structure, with its unity, centralization, discipline, organization, control of education, and refusal to cooperate with non-Catholic bodies. The American Protective Association and the Ku Klux Klan were active in opposing immigration and Catholic growth. In spite of the proven adaptability to American institutions of such figures as Gibbons and Ireland, Catholicism remained suspect because of the papal Syllabus of Errors in 1864, the Vatican Council (1870), numerous encyclicals against liberalism, and the rejection of "Americanism" in 1899 and of "Modernism" in 1906–1907. The governorship of Al Smith in the 1920's in New York and the presidency of John F. Kennedy in the 1960's weakened anti-Catholicism by demonstrating that Catholic officeholders did not impose ecclesiastical policies on America.

BIBLIOGRAPHY: C. Beals, *Brass-Knuckle Crusade* (New York, 1960); R. A. Billington, *The Protestant Crusade: 1800–1860* (New

York, 1952); H. S. Commager, *The American Mind* (New Haven, 1950); J. T. Ellis, *American Catholicism* (Chicago, 1956); R. H. Gabriel, *The Course of American Democratic Thought* (New York, 1956); A. F. Tyler, *Freedom's Ferment* (New York, 1962).

**Anticlericalism.** Hostility to the influence of the clergy or hierarchy in public affairs. It became politically important during the Age of Reason when Voltaire, other *philosophes*, and Freemasons opposed what they thought to be the obscurantism, servility, and exactions of the clergy. Albeit Protestant cults were sometimes criticized, usually it was Catholicism that was censured for its supranationalism and alliances between throne and altar. Those attacking a dynasty attacked its supporters, the priests. Although the initial blow was against the Jesuit Society (1773), a general offensive came when the French Revolution (1789) placed church property "at the disposal of the nation," and soon subjected clerics to elections and oaths. Increasing revolutionary frenzy led to dechristianization and, at times, atheism. Napoleon restored order with the Concordat of 1801, but his Organic Articles (1802) and contumelies for Pius VI and VII contributed to anticlericalism in France and Italy. Joseph Bonaparte introduced Napoleonic religious reforms briefly to Spain. These became manifestos for 19th-century Spanish liberals. The Right was pious and the Left anticlerical as in France. After 1815 the writer Chateaubriand and the Romantic school renewed sentimental links with medieval Christendom and the Crusades. Yet there were assaults on churches and priests during and after the Revolution of 1830. Metternich found religion too useful a tool for keeping order in the Germanys and Hungary to neglect. Secret societies such as the Italian Carbonaria opposed cooperation between the state and the "parasitical" priests. The union of Italy was accomplished by liberals and nationalists who, if not flamboyantly anticlerical, aimed to reduce church claims. Bismarck united the German states under North German Protestant leadership against South German Catholic particularism. His Kulturkampf was an abortive campaign against the church during the 1870's and 1880's. Bismarck borrowed the techniques of anticlericalism popular elsewhere. The most bitter struggle was in France where, after 1870, war between partisans of monarchy and the Third Republic divided the land into two nations—reflected in the Boulanger and Dreyfus crises. Inflamed passions brought expulsion of religious orders, lay schools, civil marriage and divorce, and cancellation of the Concordat in 1905. The attempt of Leo XIII to detach Catholics from royalism, the Ralliement, succeeded slowly. The Second Spanish Republic of 1931 and the Civil War (1936–1939) saw atrocities against priests and nuns who were viewed as tools of the discarded monarchy. The Loyalists included many anticlericals in their camp; Franco had the support of the hierarchy. Conditions in Italy improved slowly after the royal occupation of Rome in 1870. The 1929 Lateran Pacts gave Mussolini's recognition to the Catholicity of the land. Marxian thought was always sharply anticlerical. The phrase "opiate of the people" is familiar. Antireligious activity took place in Béla Kun's Bolshevik Hungarian state (1919). Soviet Russia temporarily tried to use Catholic missionaries as a lever against orthodoxy. Atheistic manifestations became popular there and in other Iron Curtain countries following 1945. Fifty-three million Catholics formed a "Church of Silence," and their prelates—Stepanić (Yugoslavia), Mindszenty (Hungary), Beran (Czechoslovakia), and Wyszynski (Poland) were subject to arrest and repression. Nazi Germans were immediately concerned with anti-Semitism, reserving Catholics and Protestants for later severities. Their jailing of Pastor Martin Niemöller was a warning. Frequent anticlerical disorders took place in Latin American cities, especially in Mexico.

BIBLIOGRAPHY: A. Aulard, *Christianity and the French Revolution* (London, 1927); S. W. Baron, *Modern Nationalism and Religion* (New York, 1947); P. Guilday (ed.), *The Catholic Church in Contemporary Europe: 1919–1931* (New York, 1932); A. C. Jemolo, *Church and State in Italy: 1850–1950* (Oxford, 1960); J. S. Schapiro, *Anticlericalism: Conflict Between Church and State in France, Italy, and Spain* (Princeton, 1966); R. Soltau, *French Political Thought in the 19th Century* (New York, 1959).

**Anti-Masonic Movement.** An American political movement. Freemasonry was less suspect in early America than were some secret orders. A movement of opposition arose, however, in 1826, when one William Morgan, who was about to reveal certain Masonic secrets, suddenly disappeared. When a part of his exposé was published, it aroused the people. In New York, Masonic membership dropped from twenty thousand to three thousand. The anti-Masonic movement organized politically and in 1831 nominated candidates for president and vice-president of the United States. It founded journals to promote its views, the *Anti-Masonic Enquirer* (1828) and the *Al-*

*bany Evening Journal.* By 1840 it was absorbed into the Whig Party but was still a strong enough bloc in 1839 to defeat Henry Clay's nomination. Its greatest political success was the election of two state governors.

**Anti-Modernist Oath.** An oath imposed by Pius X in 1910 on all clergy and teachers in the Roman Catholic Church. This oath professed that miracles and prophecies were "most convincing" proofs of Christianity's divine origin. It rejected the idea of the evolution of dogma and any method of interpreting Scripture that did not place first the tradition of the church and the declarations of the pope. Many of those required to take the oath did so without any real conviction.

**Antinomian Controversy.** See AGRICOLA, JOHANN; HUTCHINSON, ANNE.

**Antinomianism.** The doctrine that by grace a Christian is freed from all forms of legalism or the need to observe any moral law. Theological systems asserting the abandonment of the Mosaic law are termed "antinomian." There have been several different justifications for such views: that Christ has raised the believer above the positive precepts of the law, and that he should therefore be obedient only to the immediate guidance of the Spirit, which makes him impeccable; or the teaching, derived from the contempt of the flesh, which argued that the material element should be destroyed by license; or that, since the law is the law of the Demiurge, it is a Christian duty to disobey it; or that, since sin is inevitable, it should not be resisted; or the view that the preaching of the law is opposed to that of the gospel and is unnecessary; or the view that God, in his eternal decree, willed sin, and it would therefore be impious to resist it—and so on. Antinomianism has appeared in Christian history from the beginning, and it has been a stock accusation made by Christian controversialists against their opponents, whether true or not (see, for example, JEROME).

Two important antinomian controversies should be noted: the controversy of Johann Agricola with Melanchthon in 1527 and with Luther during 1537 to 1540; and that in New England in the early 17th century, centering on Anne Hutchinson.

**Antioch, Council of** (341). Council of ninety-seven Eastern bishops assembled on the occasion of the dedication of the great church that Constantine had built for the city. Prominent Arians such as Eusebius of Constantinople were present, but the conservatives were in the majority. The second creed of the Council sought to exclude strict Arianism, using Scriptural terminology. However, the real targets were Athanasius and Marcellus, who were enjoying the protection of Pope Julius in Italy. A fourth creed was later drawn by certain attending bishops and became the basis for efforts to supplant the Nicene formula. The canon of the Council passed into church law.

**Antioch, Synods of** (264 and 268). Two synods of bishops subject to the metropolitan of Syria which were convened to correct the metropolitan and bishop of Antioch, Paul of Samosata. His Christology made Jesus an ordinary man in whom the divine impersonal Logos dwelt, thus denying any substantial union. Convoked by Helenus of Tarsus (264), the first synod, comprising several sessions and long enough for Firmilian to go home and return, failed to disclose the gravity of Paul's heresy because of his dialectical agility and its own irresoluteness following the death of Dionysius of Alexandria. It ended inconclusively with Paul's empty promises to correct his view. Protected by Zenobia, queen of Palmyra, under whom he was Procurator Ducenarius, he gathered support by persuasion and threat of recrimination until the bishops decided on further action, first by a letter to Paul expounding the orthodox faith and then by calling a second synod (268). Prior to and during this synod his chief adversary was Malchion, learned priest of Antioch. A synodal encyclical embodied the verdict: naming sixteen of the bishops, addressed to Dionysius of Rome, Maximus of Alexandria, and all the bishops of the *oikoumenē,* it outlines Paul's episcopate and teaching, and concludes with his deposition and the election of Domnus to succeed him.

**Antiphon.** A short liturgical verse or sentence, usually though not necessarily from Holy Scripture, said or chanted in its entirety both before and after the psalms in the proper of the Mass or the canticles in the offices of the Breviary. They vary with the liturgical season, giving particular point to the Mass or the office of the season. In the Western Church, there are presently in use more than a thousand of these antiphons.

**Antipope.** A person who claims to be pope while another who has been lawfully elected and enthroned holds the office. The antipope usually contends that the incumbent pope has been invalidly or unlawfully elected. Many disputes over the papal throne were not adequately settled during the lifetime of either claimant. There have been approximately twenty-five antipopes.

**Antirevolutionary Party.** A conservative political party founded in Holland in the 1870's by Neo-Calvinists and Roman Catholics under the leadership of Abraham Kuyper. They won state subsidies for their respective schools in 1887, which led to a confessionally fragmented educational system. The party, which controlled the government from 1901 to 1905, sought decentralization of the national government, social legislation, and an "ethical policy" that encouraged Christian missions and the economic welfare and education of indigenous populations in the Dutch colonies.

**Anti-Saloon League of America.** The climax of the movement within American denominations from temperance to total abstinence to a full-scale attack upon the saloon was organized in 1895. Manned by socially progressive Protestant churchmen and supported by liberal Roman Catholics, it became an instrument of sophisticated political action supporting candidates who voted "dry." Its ultimate aim was achieved in 1920 with national constitutional prohibition.

**Anti-Semitism.** A term that first appeared during the financial panic of 1873 which swept Germany in the wake of the Franco-Prussian war of 1870 and 1871. It is not to be understood as opposition to "Semitism," which designates language rather than race, but rather to "Judaism." The origins of anti-Semitism as a racist movement are associated with the Aryan-Semitic dichotomy employed by the French philosopher Joseph A. de Gobineau in his treatise *An Essay on the Inequality of the Human Races* (*Essai sur l'inégalité des races humaines*), published in 1853 and 1855, which had considerable influence upon the development of European anti-Semitism, particularly in Germany. But anti-Semitism already appears as a critique of Jewish religion in classical antiquity, beginning with the Greek epoch in the Near East (for example, in The Book of Esther, written between 300 and 50 B.C.); it reached its climax in the racist theory and practices of modern Nazism. The shift from religious to racial anti-Semitism becomes evident if its course through the three principal periods of Western history is surveyed:

1. *Classical antiquity.* Greeks and Romans opposed Jews mainly for religious reasons. The charge of "atheism" was frequently leveled against them because they refused to acknowledge either the national gods such as Zeus or Jupiter or the various emperors who considered themselves demigods to be worshiped in the imperial cult. However, Jewish colonies were generally tolerated by 30 B.C., when the Romans inherited the Greek lands in the Near East. Alexandria, for example, was populated by a significant number of Jews who were respected by both Greeks and Romans for their learning and commercial effectiveness. Roman emperors regarded Judaism as a sect to be tolerated; they respected Jewish religion even though they did not tolerate Jewish nationalism in their empire. Jews lived in safety in Rome while Jerusalem was being destroyed by Roman legions in A.D. 70.

2. *Middle Ages.* The advent of Christianity reintroduced religious anti-Semitism, and after the first Christian millennium major legislation was enacted against the Jews. The latent hostility of early church fathers (such as Justin in his *Dialogue with Trypho the Jew*) turned into a crusade against a people believed to have committed deicide by crucifying Jesus of Nazareth. By 1215, Jews were required to wear special dress; they were also suspected of witchcraft and ritual murders. Only the Moors in Spain tolerated them, so that a Jewish culture could survive. Christian anti-Semitism reached its height during the Crusades of the 12th and 13th centuries, when Jews were accused of allying themselves with the Arabs for the purpose of violating the Holy Sepulcher in Jerusalem. They were driven from England in 1290, and from France in 1394; for a time they were forced to wander through Europe, frequently hunted down by the Inquisition. The Renaissance, humanism, and the Protestant Reformation once again made toleration of minority groups possible. Jews were readmitted to English soil in 1657, after Holland had begun to tolerate them in 1593.

3. *Modern period.* In the period of the Enlightenment in the 17th and 18th centuries much of the religious anti-Semitism permeating Europe was abolished, and Jewish settlements were allowed to flourish in various parts of the Continent. By 1870, however, racial anti-Semitism had begun to appear in Prussian and Hapsburg territories. It was propagated by such tracts as August Rohling's *The Talmudic Jew* (*Der Talmudjude*) in 1871, by the poems of Carl Lueger in Vienna, and by the Christian Social Party, founded in 1878 by the court preacher Adolf Stoecker. The "anti-Semitic catechism" of Stoecker was popular with the Nazis, who in the 1930's instituted the systematic elimination of Jews resulting in the murder of six million Jews

in numerous concentration camps throughout the Third Reich.

BIBLIOGRAPHY: H. Arendt, *The Origins of Totalitarianism*, 2d ed. (New York, 1958); E. H. Flannery, *The Anguish of the Jews: Twenty-three Centuries of Anti-Semitism* (New York, 1965); C. Y. Glock and R. Stark, *Christian Belief and Anti-Semitism* (New York, 1966).

**Antitactae.** An antinomian libertine faction, mentioned only by Clement of Alexandria (*Miscellanies* 3, 34–39), who probably invented their name, deriving it from *antitassō* (from Greek, "range against") to describe their attitude toward prohibitive commandments. In refuting them, Clement uses the method of *reductio ad absurdum*, asking them why they do not "range themselves against" the positive commandments as well as the negative. The origin and issue of the group is unknown.

**Anti-Trinitarianism.** Movement variously denying the doctrine of the Trinity. At the time of the Reformation, anti-Trinitarianism grew to measurable proportions. Martin Cellarius (Borrhäus, b. 1499) was probably the first to publish his anti-Trinitarian principles (*On the Works of God*, 1527). Other early Anabaptists, including Hans Denck (b. c. 1495), David Joris (b. 1501; *The Wonderbook*), Johann Campanus (d. 1574; primitivist who studied under Luther), showed definite anti-Trinitarian tendencies. Some anti-Trinitarians (Simon Budny and Jakob Paläologus) in turn adopted Anabaptist Christology and social theory, including pacifism. Michael Servetus, a Spaniard who became a medical doctor, startled Protestants with his *De trinitatis erroribus* in 1531. Even though his *Dialogorum de trinitate libri duo* in 1532 retracted the earlier views somewhat, he hastened his Geneva execution by his severely anti-Trinitarian *Christianismi restitutio* which followed in 1553.

Anti-Trinitarianism gathered strength in the humanist environs of northern Italy. An anti-Trinitarian council was held in Venice in 1550, but the Inquisition suppressed the tiny group. Farther north in the Grisons of Switzerland, Francesco of Calabria, Tiziano, and Francis Stancaro (d. 1574; Hebraist) actively promoted the teaching. Geneva, the fortress of Reformed teaching, served as a temporary center for the new thought. Valentino Gentilis (d. 1566; *Antidota*), a humanist, engaged Calvin in personal disputation. Matteo Gribaldi (d. 1564), of Padua, a friend of Gentilis, visited Geneva briefly. Giampaolo Alciati, Gentilis, and Georg Biandrata (c. 1515–1588/ 1590) joined the Italian church in Geneva, a shelter for anti-Trinitarians. Biandrata and others subsequently moved to Poland and Transylvania.

Anti-Trinitarianism established its first substantial base in Poland. Although it made little progress among Polish Lutherans, the Reformed Church suffered great losses. Peter Gonesius (d. 1581) was summoned to preach at Wengrow by Jan Kiszka, an Arian noble. Gonesius established the first anti-Trinitarian congregation in Poland. Before long, Alciati and Gentilis found their way to the new haven. In 1565, the orthodox Reformed excluded the anti-Trinitarians from their congregations. The separated group formed a loose organization that year, but an internal struggle over the propriety of worshiping Christ summarily divided the group. Jakob Paläologus (d. 1585; in Poland after 1575) held the "nonadorantist" position, while Stanislaus Farnovius (d. 1615) opposed him. In short order the Arians and the Farnovians became opposition parties. Meanwhile, a Polish noble, Nicolaus Radziwill (d. 1565), came over to the anti-Trinitarian camp. Other nobles joined him, and by 1572 to 1573 it became a condition of the king's election that he preserve peace among the several religions, including anti-Trinitarianism. Raków was established in 1569; it became a city of refuge for harassed anti-Trinitarians. The arrival of Faustus Socinus (Sozzini, 1539–1604) in 1579 signaled a new age for the leaderless group. By 1588 he was the acknowledged leader. He organized the scattered adherents and created a dogmatic synthesis from the literary works bequeathed him by an uncle, Laelius Socinus (d. 1562). Raków assumed the character of a fortress, not a haven. A school was constructed in 1602, and a press established. Eventually the Polish Minor Church numbered about three hundred congregations. There were numerous public disputations with Reformed and Jesuit theologians, and "silent missionaries" traveled west to Continental universities, especially Altdorf. Socinus set out to revise the popular 1574 anti-Trinitarian catechism with Stoinski. The work was completed after his death by Schmalz, Moskorzowski, and Völkel, and appeared in 1605 as the Racovian Catechism. Roman Catholic counteraction gained impetus c. 1574. There was a general attack on Lublin in 1627, and Raków met destruction in 1638. Finally, in 1658, the diet ordered the expulsion of the Socinians. Many migrated to Transylvania, Silesia, the Rhine Palatinate, Holstein, Brandenburg, Prussia, and especially Holland, where Remonstrants and Mennonites came under Socinian influence.

Meanwhile, in Transylvania the party was flourishing. Biandrata was called as court physician to John Sigismund in Siebenbürgen in 1563. Sigismund issued an edict of toleration in 1568 which eventually led to full religious freedom for the anti-Trinitarians in 1571. Zápolya himself adhered to the party, and its influence spread to lower Hungary. Franz Davidis (d. 1579), first a Lutheran but openly anti-Trinitarian in 1566, assumed leadership in Transylvania. He was succeeded by Demetrius Hunyadi. From 1580 to 1635 there was a steady decline, but then anti-Trinitarianism flourished until Transylvania came under Austrian rule in 1690. In spite of the excellent guidance of Michael Szent Abrahami (bishop, 1737), Roman Catholic opposition prevailed. The besieged party corresponded with English Unitarians for the first time in 1821, and suffered greatly during World War I.

Germany proved nearly impenetrable to the new movement, even though Abraham Calovius, J. Hoornbeek, and others recognized its strength. The "young Hegelians," Feuerbach, and other German thinkers were acquainted with its spirit.

In England, Anabaptist activity and specifically the Church of the Strangers (1550) in London showed the influence of anti-Trinitarian thought. However, Socinianism entered the country primarily through Dutch intermediaries in the 17th century. An Anglican synod in 1640 adopted measures to check Socinianism, even though it was not organized, and the Long Parliament declared it a felony in 1648. John Biddle (1615–1662), frequently imprisoned, published *XII Arguments* (1647) and other anti-Trinitarian tracts. His *A Twofold Catechism* (1654) was carefully refuted by John Owen. He conducted meetings in London, but at his death the anti-Trinitarian movement faltered in spite of many publications financed by T. Firmin. Then two distinct anti-Trinitarian streams emerged. Within the Church of England a Trinitarian controversy developed especially over the Athanasian Creed. Publications were issued on both sides from 1687 to 1750 (William Whiston, Samuel Clarke, William Sherlock). In 1698, the Blasphemy Act was passed. Among other provisions it denied public office to anti-Trinitarians (repealed 1813). Meanwhile, among the Dissenters, anti-Trinitarianism grew to formidable proportions in the first half of the 18th century. At first the Dissenters haggled over "adorantist" and "nonadorantist" positions, but then became more radical. Exeter became a major center, and the movement made heavy gains among the Presbyterians.

Theophilus Lindsey (d. 1808), who had gathered signatures for the unsuccessful Feathers Tavern Petition to Parliament, opened the Essex Street Chapel in London in 1774 (attended occasionally by Benjamin Franklin). It was the first Unitarian chapel in England. Joseph Priestley (d. 1804) worked among Dissenters in Birmingham, London, and finally in America. The two English streams converged when Thomas Belsham (1750–1829) organized the Unitarian Society of London in 1791. James Martineau became the recognized leader upon organization of the British and Foreign Unitarian Association in 1825, but Unitarians were barred from the British and Foreign Bible Society in 1830.

American anti-Trinitarianism was in part a reaction to austere Calvinist theology and in part an English import. The doctrine of the Trinity was increasingly questioned among liberal Congregationalists in the East (1756–1776), but the Philadelphia Unitarian Society, organized c. 1796, was transferred full-blown from Britain. For the development of American anti-Trinitarianism, see UNITARIANISM.

**Antoine de Bourbon** (1518–1562). King of Navarre. As the duke of Vendôme, in 1548 he married Jeanne d'Albret, daughter of Margaret d'Angoulême, thus becoming in 1554 titular king of Navarre, which, however, the Spanish still held. A morally weak and vacillating man, he proclaimed himself Protestant in 1548, but eventually returned to Roman Catholicism. He was the father of Henry of Navarre, later Henry IV of France.

**Antonelli, Giacomo** (1806–1876). Cardinal secretary of state and chief political adviser to Pope Pius IX. Made a cardinal in 1847, Antonelli was appointed secretary of state the following year. With the support of a French army he was virtually the temporal ruler of Rome until 1870. He used his influence with the pope to favor a reactionary and ultramontane policy. He was a statesman rather than a prelate, but many considered him unscrupulous in his political maneuvers.

**Antoninus** (1389–1459). Archbishop of Florence from 1446, moral theologian, and economist. As a youth he joined the Dominicans, later directed several convents, and founded with Medici support the Convent of San Marco in Florence. He was a vigorous reformer, a widely sought counselor, and a compassionate leader during the Florentine earthquakes and distress. As a practical writer he published a compendium of moral theology, and a three-volume didactic history of the world. Of particular importance was his attempt to formulate an ethic of banking and commerce and to relax the traditional prohibition of lending at interest.

**Antoninus Pius.** Roman emperor (138–161). During his reign, in which few wars took place, Christians enjoyed almost complete freedom from persecution, though slanders against them resulted in the *Apology* of Justin and in four or five martyrdoms. The emperor's lack of enthusiasm for informers meant that it was dangerous to bring unfounded accusations against Christians. His reign has been regarded as the "golden age" of the Roman Empire.

**Antony of Egypt** (c. 250–356). Leader of the early hermits who, when the persecutions ended, went out to work and pray in the desert. After years in an isolated cell, the scene of his famous spiritual temptations, Antony became the guide of many other hermits, on whom he urged the importance of the saving grace of discretion. A life written by Athanasius is both a eulogistic biography of Antony and a pattern of the ascetic life.

**Antony of Padua** (1195–1231). Franciscan friar. Born in Lisbon, he entered the Augustinian order and received his education. Inspired by the activities of the Franciscans in Morocco, he obtained permission to enter that order. Ill-health curtailed his mission to Morocco, and he returned to Europe, where, chiefly in Italy, he became known as a great preacher. He spent his last days in Padua, where he is regarded as a patron saint.

**Anxious Bench.** A pew appointed at the front of the place of meeting where a person anxious about his religious life could come to be addressed particularly, made the subject of public prayers, and sometimes conversed with individually in the anticipation of his experiencing a definite religious conversion. It was one of the New Measures of revivalism in America developed by Charles G. Finney and widely used after 1835.

**Apelles.** A 2d-century disciple of Marcion. Eusebius hints that Apelles was a man of moral earnestness, impatient with doctrinal precision. He did seek to avoid the dualism of his master by teaching one God and a single "principle" and one derivative "power" who creates and serves as "god" of the Old Testament. In his *Syllogisms,* Apelles uses Aristotelian logic to show what he considered the ineptitude and falsity of the Old Testament revelation. His name is linked with that of a young woman, Philumene, whom he regarded as a prophetess.

**Aphraates** (*known as* "the Persian Sage"). A scholar of the East Syrian Church, a monk, and probably bishop in the territory of ancient Assyria, in his time a part of the Persian empire. His twenty-three *Homilies,* written in A.D. 336–345, are unique documents of a developed Syrian orthodoxy uninfluenced by Greek theology and controversies, with Jewish rather than Greek contacts. They also reflect the ascetic tendencies of the early East Syrian Church, in particular its refusal of marriage to adult converts after baptism.

**Aphthartodocetae** (Phantasiasts). Monophysite party holding Christ's body to be incorruptible (Greek, *aphthartos*) from the moment of incarnation. They were known as Julianists from Julian of Halicarnassus, who expounded this view. Upon the death of Timothy III (535), Monophysite patriarch of Alexandria, they chose Gaianus as their head, becoming thereafter Gaianites. This party later split again over whether the incorruptible body of Christ was created.

**Apocalypses.** Prophetic Jewish and Christian writings of 200 B.C. to A.D. 150 concerning an imminent messianic kingdom. The Revelation to John, the only apocalypse in the New Testament, did not acquire canonical status without controversy. Alongside it and using the same form, others were composed pseudonymously in the name of various apostles. Unlike apocryphal acts, only a limited number of these compositions are known and still fewer are extant: (1) Apocalypse of Peter. It was composed sometime between 125 and 150 and was highly regarded in antiquity. The complete text is extant in Ethiopic. It describes in colorful imagery the glory of heaven and the ugliness of hell, and depicts the blessedness of the faithful and the punishments meted out to sinners. Its store of imagery comes from the Orphic-Pythagorean cycle. (2) Apocalypse of Paul. Three apocalypses are condemned in *Decretum Gelasianum,* those of Paul, Stephen, and Thomas. Of several attributed to Paul, the best known is *Visio Pauli,* which recounts Paul's vision of heaven (II Cor. 12:2), his picture of hell (cf. Dante, *Inferno* 2.28), and a striking angelology. Written in Egypt, c. 250, it was revised sometime between 380 and 388 and republished (Sozomen, *Ecclesiastical History* 7.19). (3) Apocalypse of Thomas. Written probably in Greek c. 400 by a Gnostic, it tells of the message of the Lord to Thomas about the Last Days. (4) Apocalypse of Stephen. Fifth-century "invention" of relics. (5) Much later are Apocalypses of John and several Apocalypses of the Virgin.

**Apocryphal Acts.** Noncanonical stories parallel to the acts of the apostles related in the New Testament. The New Testament says little in detail about the lives, achievements, and deaths of even the best known of the apostles. In order to satisfy the natural curiosity of the faithful and to provide some spur to courageous piety, the early church composed numerous fanciful accounts of the acts of various apostles. Of these compositions, some with a definite heretical bias were written by sectarians in order to promote their own sects. Only a small selection of them are extant, and of these, few are even nearly complete. In form as well as in content, apocryphal acts resemble the Hellenistic romance, a popular form of secular literature in the early centuries of our era. The first five mentioned below formed a corpus for the Manichaeans, who substituted them for canonical acts; they were known to Photius (890), who criticizes them in his *Myriobiblion* and attributes all five to the presbyter Leucius, called an associate of John. He may have written the Acts of John, but the authorship of the others still remains an open question.

1. Acts of John. Earliest of those acts now available, composed sometime between 150 and 180 in Greek, in Asia Minor. A partial manuscript in Greek, supplemented in places by a Latin version, shows that it is a docetic document purporting to give a firsthand account of the ministry and missionary journeys of John in Asia Minor. It provides the oldest source for a Eucharist for the dead and gives a long Eucharistic prayer used at the celebration.

2. Acts of Paul. Written by an Asian presbyter before the time of Tertullian. It comprises three writings once thought to be independent: (*a*) Acts of Paul and Thecla, recounting the adventures of a Greek girl convert from Iconium, who assisted Paul; mostly legendary. (*b*) Correspondence of Paul with the Corinthians, comprising the answer to his second letter and a third letter from Paul dealing with two heretics by name. (*c*) *Passio Pauli*, a legendary account of Paul's work in Rome and of his execution there. The whole composition is now largely extant in Greek.

3. Acts of Peter. Composed c. 190 in Palestine or Syria, not in Rome. About two thirds of it has been recovered from various sources. The main part is in a Latin version which recounts Paul's leaving Rome for Spain, the activity of Simon Magus in Rome, and Peter's trip to Rome and eventual triumph. The martyrdom of Peter, comprising the last part of the document, is extant in Greek and contains the famous *"Domine, quo vadis?"* and the story of Peter's crucifixion head down. An earlier portion is somewhat docetic, while a long speech in the latter part shows Gnostic influence.

4. Acts of Andrew. A Gnostic writing from after 250 (c. 260?), less well preserved than the previous ones, recounting how the actions of Andrew led to his martyrdom in Patrae in Achaia. Like the Acts of Peter, it renounces marriage.

5. Acts of Thomas. Composed early in the third century, it is the only one of these five primary romances that we possess in its entirety. The consensus is that this work was written originally in Syriac by one of the Bardesanist sects in Edessa. Evincing both Gnostic and Manichaean influence, this document recounts in fourteen acts the legendary exploits of Thomas as he traveled to India to plant the gospel there. The ascetic ideal resembles that of the Acts of Andrew and the Acts of Peter. Most striking are the hymns it preserves, some of them originating probably before the actual composition of the acts.

6. Acts of Peter and Paul. Stemming probably from the third century, unrelated to either of the acts mentioned above, this writing may represent an attempt to replace them with a more orthodox tradition. It consists of the work and martyrdom of both apostles in Rome. Extant in Greek and Latin fragments.

7. Secondary Acts. Most important of these is the Acts of Philip, apparently a conscious imitation of the Acts of Thomas, at least in form. Much later there appear such works as the Acts of Andrew and Matthew, probable source of the Anglo-Saxon poem "Andreas" by Cynewulf (?), and the legendary Acts of Peter and Andrew and the Martyrdom of Matthew.

8. Minor Acts. Besides the Acts of John by Prochorus, based on the primary romance, there is the legendary Acts of Thaddaeus purporting to be a correspondence between Abgar, king of Edessa, and Jesus, asking him to come to Edessa (see ADDAI).

**Apocryphon of John** (before 180). A popular Gnostic composition, originally in Greek. It now exists in four manuscripts, each being a different translation into Coptic. The original underlies Irenaeus (*Against Heresies* 1.29). It purports to be what Jesus told John on the Mount of Olives about God and the emanation of lesser divine beings. In form, it is a kind of Gnostic midrash on Genesis, though on a higher intellectual and moral plane than later Gnostic writings.

**Apollinaris, Claudius.** Bishop of Hierapolis in Phrygia (c. 170–180). His writings, preserved only in fragments, show that he was a significant Christian leader who took a stand against the Quartodecimans and the Montanists, supporting and influencing decisions of the Roman Church. In his apology he insisted on the loyalty of Christians to the Roman Empire and told the story of the "thundering legion."

**Apollinarius of Laodicea** (c. 310–c. 390). First Christological heresiarch. He spent many years of his life as a pillar of orthodoxy. He was a friend of Athanasius and Basil the Great and a teacher of Jerome. The son of a schoolteacher of the same name, he lived in the Laodicea which was a Syrian seaport, not the Asia Minor city mentioned in Revelation. A priest in 346, he welcomed Athanasius, who was on the way home from exile, though his Arian bishop did not, and he was excommunicated for it. He and Athanasius began to correspond, having in common their great antipathy for Arianism. In 362, Apollinarius and his father helped foil Julian the Apostate. Julian tried to remove Christian influence from education by saying that it was unlawful for a man to teach what he did not believe; Christians were forbidden to teach pagan classics. Apollinarius and his father responded by writing a curriculum of textbooks in which Bible stories were exemplified in classical forms. The elder Apollinarius wrote a grammar, and he and his son composed heroic verse retelling Old Testament history. The rest of the Old Testament they rendered as Euripidean tragedies, Menandrine comedies, and Pindaric odes, while the Gospels and Epistles were presented in the form of Platonic dialogues. The only survivor of this body of literature is a hexameter Psalter. The vast majority of the works of Apollinarius are lost, which is unfortunate, since most of them were orthodox, and he was a man of distinguished intellect and style. Jerome said that he was the author of "innumerable volumes on the Holy Scriptures." His thirty books against Porphyry are generally accounted the greatest reply to that Neoplatonic critic of Christianity. He also wrote an apologetic work called *The Truth* which was directed against Julian. Most of what remains of his work is preserved either under the name of an orthodox author used as a pseudonym or in quotations by those who refuted him. G. L. Prestige has said, "Nowhere in patristic literature is there any document to compare with his *Detailed Confession of Faith* (*Hē kata meros pistis*) for terse expression, penetrating thought, understanding of the truth, and grasp of the reasons why the falsehoods are wrong" (*Fathers and Heretics* [England, 1940], p. 102).

It is common to describe Apollinarianism as the first of the Christological heresies. To do so, though, is misleading to the degree that it implies that Trinitarian controversies were unconcerned with Christology. The question behind these early Trinitarian controversies was the relation of Jesus of Nazareth to God the Father. The chief issue of the Arian controversy was the deity of Christ. That having been established, the next question to arise concerned his complete manhood. The swing of the pendulum can be observed often in the history of doctrine, as it can here; there is a sense in which Apollinarianism is only anti-Arianism gone overboard, for in it the assertion of the divinity of Christ was so strong as to deny his complete humanity.

Briefly put, the heresy of Apollinarius was the belief that the divine Logos took the place of the human soul in Jesus. It is probably a mistake to explain this error too much by recourse to its founder's facultative psychology; he appears in some places to utilize a trichotomy, but in others a dichotomy. The difficulty seems rather to have been the inability of Apollinarius to imagine perfect humanity and perfect divinity united in one person. He felt there would be a war of wills: there would be two Sons of God, one by nature and one by adoption. In order to avoid denying the divinity of Christ or postulating a divine-human half-breed, he settled on a doctrine that denied the full manhood of Christ. The process by which the Word became flesh has been graphically compared to electrolysis, in which the flesh was just a plating, as it were, for the Word. Apollinarius does not seem to have taught, as his opponents indicated, that the flesh was preexistent. His opponents, chiefly the Cappadocians, were quite right, however, in their grasp of the implications of his thought. That is, the gospel history in which our Lord did not appear omniscient would be denied by Apollinarius. An Apollinarian Christ could not save, since, as Gregory of Nazianzus said, he could not redeem the human soul he did not assume. Apollinarius did set the Christological problem, though, and his terms were those used throughout the whole debate. He was condemned in Rome in 374–380, Antioch in 378, Constantinople in 381, Rome in 382, and finally at Chalcedon. He led the schism of his followers himself, and they eventually joined the Monophysites.

**Apologists.** Name conventionally applied to a group of Christian writers, chiefly Greek, who from the 2d century onward defended their religion in treatises, often addressed to emperors, and tried to show that the current accusations of godlessness and immorality were unfounded. In the course of the defense they came to interpret the meaning of Christianity in relation to Greco-Roman culture, especially its philosophical aspects. The works of the various Apologists were little read after the times in which they wrote; their theology, while advanced in its own day, came to be regarded as primitive and the occasion for much of their writing vanished with the triumph of the church. Their value, then, is primarily historical; the treatises provide a bridge between: (1) the apostolic fathers and such theologians as Irenaeus, and the Alexandrians, and (2) traditional faith based on Scripture and its interpretation, and the philosophies of the Greco-Roman world. The attitudes of the Apologists varied in regard to the state: thus Melito and Claudius Apollinaris are "loyalists," while Tatian and Tertullian (both of whom left the church) were militantly opposed both to Greco-Roman culture and to the state. For pagan opposition to Christianity, see CELSUS, PORPHYRY, JULIAN; for the individual Apologists, see, besides those mentioned, ARISTIDES, ATHENAGORAS OF ATHENS, JUSTIN MARTYR, MINUCIUS FELIX, QUADRATUS, THEODORET, THEOPHILUS of Antioch.

**Apophthegmata Patrum.** A collection of sayings of the "desert fathers"—the early Egyptian monks (4th–5th centuries). The sayings are generally brief and pithy and are characterized by their practical attitude, loyalty to the "discipline," meekness, realistic understanding of the diabolical cunning of temptation, and anticipation of the life to come. They are arranged by author according to the Greek alphabet, though the original language and the date of the collection are disputed.

**Apostles, Epistle of the.** A writing of the middle of the 2d century from Asia Minor or Egypt. The epistolary form was soon dropped in favor of revelations made by Jesus to his apostles between the resurrection and the ascension. The New Testament, especially the Fourth Gospel, was the major source, but the author also used books marginal to the New Testament. The work is against the Gnostics and is a valuable source of information for early liturgical and sacramental usage. Originally in Greek, the document has survived only in translations.

**Apostolic Canons.** Extracts in the form of canons of the councils compiled by the author from the Apostolic Constitutions 8. 47. The eighty-five canons deal almost exclusively with the selection of clergy and their duties, echoing decisions of the Councils of Antioch (341) and Laodicea (c. 360). The Latin form of the canons provided the source for Western compilations of canon law as it pertained to conciliar decisions. Canon 85 contains a list of canonical books.

**Apostolic Chancery.** The office of the Roman Curia which is responsible for drafting and dispatching papal bulls and other official communications. It was instituted in the 11th century, being patterned after the civil chanceries of Imperial Rome. As an office of the Curia, it is responsible only to the pope. Until the 14th century, the head of the Chancery was known as the chancellor; at that time his title was changed to vice-chancellor. Except for two short intervals, the head of the Chancery has always been a cardinal. However, another official, the regent, was appointed, to whom a great deal of the responsibility has fallen. Originally the Chancery was concerned only with the preparation of certain official documents, but during the later Middle Ages, it came to play an important role in the fiscal policy of the Roman Curia by collecting the revenues associated with certain ecclesiastical offices. For this reason, the vice-chancellor's office was a profitable and influential one. However, in the modern period the Chancery has become much less important, particularly since its reorganization by Pope Pius X in 1908.

**Apostolic Church Order.** A typical church order of the early 4th century. It may have come from Syria but more likely from Egypt, where it was held in high honor. Like the Didache, it is a document of moral precepts, beginning with the "two ways"—to life or to death. The latter part consists of rules for selecting and ordering sacred ministers and regulations about church membership and the care of widows. The work purports to be by the apostles at the command of the Lord. (See HIPPOLYTUS.)

**Apostolic Constitutions.** The largest collection of legislative and liturgical regulations of the early church which claimed to be of apostolic origin. Comprising eight books, and compiled in Syria (c. 380) by Arian or Apollinarian Pseudo-Clement, it reworks and combines the *Didascalia Apostolorum,* the Didache, and the Apostolic Tradition. In addition, it contains a liturgy called Clementine, and the compilation of eighty-five canons known as Apostolic canons.

**Apostolic Fathers.** A title used following the 6th century to designate early Christian writers just after the New Testament, and since the 17th century for a group including

Clement of Rome, Ignatius, Barnabas, Hermas, Polycarp, and sometimes Papias. In the 19th century the Didache was added to this literature. It reflects a Christianity usually strongly influenced by Judaism but marked by striking diversity in thought as well as in style.

**Apostolici.** An ascetic sect that flourished in Asia Minor during the 3d and 4th centuries. Its members condemned marriage and private property and refused Communion to those who violated their rules; among their principal authorities were the apocryphal Acts of Andrew and Acts of Thomas. The significance of the sect lies chiefly in its name, which obviously implies the claim that they are the only true Christians. They also called themselves Apotactites ("renouncers").

**Apostolic Life.** The ideal life of poverty and celibacy (sometimes including also abstention from meat and wine) attributed to the earliest followers of Jesus, which several communities later strove to imitate as an ascetic discipline. Although monasticism in its various forms sought to reproduce this type of life, the more exaggerated expressions of the tendency usually led to heresy or schismatic sectarianism such as: (1) the Apotactites, a 4th-century Encratite sect of Cilicia, Pamphylia, and Phrygia, also known as the Apostolici, who required of their members abstention from private property, marriage, meat, and wine (Epiphanius, *Panarion* 61); (2) a 12th-century Manichaean type of sect centered in the lower Rhine and Brittany, opposed vehemently by Bernard of Clairvaux and persecuted by empire and church alike, which forbade infant baptism, marriage, oaths, meat, participation in Catholic services, and dealings with Catholic clergy; (3) the Apostolic Brothers, a distortion of the Franciscan ideal inspired by Joachim of Flora, which was founded by Gerhard Segarelli (c. 1260), proscribed by the church (1286, 1290), taken over after the founder was burned (1300) by Fra Dolcino, who was also burned (1307), and which disappeared in mid-14th century; (4) the Catholic Apostolic Church, a 19th-century English millenarian sect that sought the reinstatement of the charismatic characteristics of the early Christian church, including the speaking in tongues, prophetic revelations, and the twelvefold apostolate. They felt that the spirit of the early church must be recaptured before the Second Coming could occur. The New Apostolic Church is a German American branch of the Catholic Apostolic Church with almost identical beliefs.

**Apostolic See.** A term used interchangeably with "Holy See" and the "see of Rome."

A see is the official "seat" of a bishop, usually located in the cathedral of the diocese. The Apostolic or Holy See represents the diocese of the pope. An apostolic see is any see founded by an apostle and having the authority of its founder. References are made to the see of Antioch, founded by Peter, and to the see of Ephesus, established by Paul. In the see of Rome are centered the rites, the traditions, and the administration of the Roman Church.

**Apostolic Succession.** The concept of uninterrupted transmission of spiritual authority in the ministry through the episcopate from the apostles who were commissioned by Christ. Validity of holy orders is deemed to depend upon this unbroken succession. Clement of Rome in the 1st century emphasized the fact of the succession of the ministry from the apostles. Catholics hold that the Roman pontiffs come immediately after, occupy the position, and perform the functions of Peter and are therefore his successors. The Council of Trent (1545–1563) asserted that "bishops, who were by succession in the place of the Apostles, hold the principal degree in the ecclesiastical hierarchy being set by the Holy Spirit to rule the Church of God."

Anglicans claim continuity in apostolic succession through the episcopate with the undivided pre-Reformation church, although Pope Leo XIII in 1896 pronounced Anglican orders as "utterly null and void."

Apostolic succession is held to be maintained by the laying on of hands of at least three bishops at the consecration of a new bishop. Protestants in general deny the necessity of apostolic succession for ministerial authority. The Lambeth Quadrilateral has insisted that the historic episcopate is essential in any plan of church unity in which Anglicanism is involved.

**Apostolic Tradition.** A document describing the rites and practices of the church in the early 3d century. It was first known to the Western world in an Ethiopic version, but by 1906, Bohairic, Sahidic, Latin, and Arabic texts had been found. Egyptian Church Order, a name derived from the source of the versions discovered first, has been discarded in favor of the present name, Apostolic Tradition. Its authorship was unknown until the 1900's, when this church order was established as the work of Hippolytus. No Greek original is extant, but a reconstruction on the basis of a 6th-century Latin manuscript is now in general use (see HIPPOLYTUS).

**"Appeal to All Christian People."** A proposal for reunion with nonepiscopal denominations issued by the Lambeth Conference of

Anglican bishops in 1920. Although recognizing the "spiritual reality" of nonepiscopal ministries and desiring no repudiation of their form of ordination, the Conference suggested a mutual commissioning of ministers using both the Anglican rite and the rites of other communions. The discussions resulting from this proposal generally broke down over the meaning of episcopal ordination.

**Appellants** (English). In Elizabethan England, a group of Roman Catholic secular priests who in 1599, 1601, and 1602 "appealed" to Rome against their archpriest, George Blackwell. They hoped to achieve friendlier relations with the queen, Blackwell being under the domination of the much-hated Jesuits. After vicious recriminations, Clement VIII interposed, and suppressing the wrangling on both sides, severed the alliance between the archpriest and the Jesuits, and put appellant secular priests on Blackwell's governing council.

**Appellants** (French). French clergy who during the Jansenist controversy appealed against the bull *Unigenitus,* issued by Pope Clement XI in 1713. The bull condemned 101 propositions that he claimed were found in Quesnel's *Moral Reflexions on the New Testament.* Opposition arose among many French theologians and laymen who wished to defend the Jansenists. Under the leadership of the archbishop of Paris, Cardinal de Noailles, they sought to "appeal" to a future general church council. The group was excommunicated in 1718 and languished when the French king forced the submission of de Noailles.

**Apse.** The semicircular or polygonal extremity of a church or transept. Derived from the Greek word meaning "arc," the apse traditionally terminates the church on the eastern end, forming the part of the building in which the altar is placed and the clergy are seated. It is a normal feature of the true basilica. Some churches have three apses, a central one for the nave and one for each of the lateral aisles.

Small chapels radiating from the main apse, called apsidal chapels, are distinguished from those which open into the nave in that they are reserved for the clergy.

**Aquaviva, Claudius** (1543–1615). Superior of the Society of Jesus. The son of an Italian duke, he entered the Society at the age of twenty-five, and was elected its fifth superior (or general) in 1581. Regarded as its most outstanding administrator after Ignatius, he guided the Society during a difficult period of internal dissension and supervised the organiz-

ing of the Jesuit system of studies (the *Ratio studiorum,* 1593), which was employed in colleges throughout Roman Catholic Europe. Before his death the Society had grown from about five thousand to about thirteen thousand members.

**Aquinas, Thomas** (c. 1225–1274). Scholastic theologian. He was born near Aquinas, Italy, and offered by his parents as a Benedictine oblate in 1230. From that time until 1239 he studied with the Benedictines at Monte Cassino. Entering the recently founded University of Naples in 1240, he remained until 1244. While there he decided to seek admission to the Dominican Order, and it was as a Dominican that he spent his first years at the University of Paris, from 1245 to 1248. He studied under Albertus Magnus (Albert the Great), with whom he continued to work at Cologne from 1248 to 1252. In 1252, Aquinas returned to Paris, where he lectured on the Bible (1252–1254) and on the *Sentences* of Peter Lombard (1254–1256). In 1256 he became a Master of Theology. He stayed in Paris until 1259, returned there subsequently from 1269 until 1272, and in the intervals prior to his death in 1274 taught theology in several places in Italy.

Thomas Aquinas' most important writings may be grouped under the following headings: (1) Scriptural Commentaries: on several Old Testament books; on Matthew, John, and the letters of Paul. (2) Commentaries on the principal works of Aristotle. (3) Commentary on Peter Lombard's *Sentences.* (4) Systematic expositions of the whole of theology: *Compendium of Theology, Summa contra Gentiles, Summa theologiae.* (5) Studies of particular questions: *Quaestiones disputatae, Quaestiones quodlibetales.*

His thought does not lend itself to easy summary. He ranges over every topic which was then recognized as being of theological interest, and at every point his thought is highly technical and reflects a variety of influences.

Aquinas conceives of God as existence unlimited, *ipsum esse subsistens. Esse* (literally, "to be") is conceived of as the ultimate fullness of value and perfection, and the finite realities of our immediate experience are conceived of as limited imitations of and participation in *ipsum esse.* The reality of God is evident to man when he reflects upon the world that he knows. Aquinas articulates this evidence in "the five ways" or five arguments for the existence of God: the argument from motion to a first, unmoved mover; from the givenness of causes and effects to a first, uncaused cause; from contingent realities to a necessary reality; from the fact of varying degrees of certain perfections to a highest degree of those perfections; from purposeful action in even inanimate objects to an ordering creator. In addition to these arguments, there is the more elliptical argument in many places that the very finitude of things, which Aquinas articulates in terms of finite *esse,* reveals them as participating in the perfection of, and derived from the unlimited being of, God.

The God so discovered is, because infinite and altogether simple, beyond the power of human speech. All human speech implicitly affirms the finitude of its object; hence an unqualified (univocal) statement about God is not possible. Developing themes already worked out in some detail by Plotinus and by Dionysius the Pseudo-Areopagite, Aquinas maintains that all theological discourse must be affirmative (e.g., "God is good"), then negative ("But he is not one good among many, and good in the same way that these other things are good"), and finally, must go beyond the negation ("God is the source of good, and what these 'goods' are in a fragmented way God is simply and without restriction"). Thus we have no concepts or ideas that are clearly and straightforwardly applicable to God, though we can and do make true statements about God. This is the focus of Aquinas' doctrine of analogy.

Knowledge is correlative to the central concept of *esse.* It is conceived of as the possession of or presence of reality, one's own and whatever else there is. Hence both God and man are conceived of centrally as knowers, and the goal of man's creation is the fullness of the knowledge of God, the beatific vision. From this general orientation follows an understanding of revelation as primarily an embryonic communication to man of a knowledge of or about God as he is eternally and in himself, so to speak. Faith is primarily an acceptance in grace of this communication; theology is the speculative elaboration of this communication.

Revelation also includes what is known about the way in which God's purpose in man is to be fulfilled. Hence it includes the law and the gospel of grace. Aquinas' version of this topic is a blending of the Aristotelian ethics and the Pauline-Augustinian doctrine of grace. Virtues are habits tending toward good action; vices, habits tending toward evil; and good and evil are defined in terms of fulfillment or frustration of the basic tendencies of men and things. However, a habit tending toward action in harmony with the dynamisms of the things involved is genuinely or radically virtue only if it is rooted in what Aquinas calls the infused theological virtues of faith, hope, and love. Owing to original sin, man is incapable of fulfilling the basic law of love for God and men unless he is healed by grace. Only action rooted in and flowing from God's transforming grace is ultimately good. Thus man is not justified by the precepts of the law—the old law or the new—but by the work of the Holy Spirit within him. But the form that the working out of God's grace takes is the fulfillment of the commands of the law. To refuse to live according to the precepts of the law (the law of love for God and man, the Decalogue, and the natural law revealed to reason and conscience) is to repudiate God and constitutes sin (mortal sin).

The grace that makes the Christian life possible has been won by Christ, and it is principally via the sacraments that the work of Christ becomes effective in the lives of Christians. In Aquinas' thought, the sacraments are seven, all necessarily instituted by Christ. A sacrament celebrated by the church is, by Christ's promise, the effective presence of his grace to those participating in the celebration. The presence of Christ's grace in the sacrament is not conditional upon the faith of the individual participant, but the sacrament is efficacious with respect to this individual (infant baptism constituting something of an exception) only in and through the faith of this individual.

The doctrine of the church, or more specifically of church order, is underdeveloped in Aquinas, as it is generally in 13th-century Scholasticism. He considers the church infallible in its teaching and the pope the supreme teacher and authority, but these matters are discussed only cursorily.

The theology of Thomas Aquinas is commonly spoken of as "the medieval synthesis." In one sense this designation is quite apt, but in another it is profoundly misleading. On the one hand, Aquinas would seem to be far and away the greatest theological synthesist of the medieval period. Thought currents which in the 14th century tend to go their separate ways —Neoplatonism (in German mysticism), Augustinianism (Gregory of Rimini), and a systematic Aristotelianism (Latin Averroism)— interpenetrate at a basic level in Aquinas.

On the other hand, to suppose that Aquinas had the status of *the* theologian (in the way in which Aristotle was *the* philosopher and Averroës *the* commentator on *the* philosopher) is simply incorrect. Within Aquinas' own order this soon was the case, and his influence was not confined to the Dominicans; nonetheless, most post-Thomistic Scholastic theologians seem to have considered him as only one of their more important predecessors. Thus Duns Scotus, writing about three decades after Aquinas' *Summa theologiae,* clearly does not consider him to be *the* theologian with whom he must come to terms. For William of Occam, writing two decades later, Scotus is obviously a much more important figure than Thomas Aquinas. Thus Thomism constituted one, but only one, current in later medieval theology.

BIBLIOGRAPHY: T. Aquinas, *Summa theologiae,* Latin text and English translation, about 65 vols. projected (New York, 1964–    ); M. D. Chenu, *Toward Understanding Saint Thomas* (Chicago, 1964); F. Copleston, *Aquinas* (Harmondsworth, England, 1955); É. Gilson, *The Christian Philosophy of St. Thomas Aquinas* (New York, 1956); R. P. Scharlemann, *Thomas Aquinas and John Gerhard* (New Haven, 1964).

**Arch, Joseph** (1826–1919). A Primitive Methodist preacher. He organized the first Agricultural Trade Union in Warwickshire in 1872, and later became president of the National Union of Agricultural Labourers. He was supported by Gladstone in his drive to extend the franchise to agricultural workers. He aided some seven hundred thousand of them to emigrate to Canada between 1873 and 1882. In 1885, he was elected to Parliament as the first representative of the agricultural laborers.

**Archdeacon.** The chief administrative officer of a bishop. In the Middle Ages, the archdeacon frequently succeeded to the see. In early times, the archdeacon was simply chief of the deacons who assisted the bishop. However, by the 9th century he had acquired specified duties and was always a priest. The office remains in the Anglican Church, but has been replaced in the Roman Catholic Church by the offices of chancellor and vicar-general.

**Archimandrite.** The title of the head of a monastery or a group of monasteries in the Eastern Churches. In modern times the title has been extended to high administrative officials who are not necessarily monks. An archimandrite ranks just below a bishop. There is no direct equivalent to this title in the Western Church, although its honorific nature is similar to the title of monsignor.

**Architecture, Byzantine.** A style of architecture which dominated the eastern Mediterranean area from the 4th century when Constantine granted toleration to the Christian church until the 15th century when the By-zantine Empire fell to the Ottoman Turks. The term "Byzantine" is derived from Byzantium, the city whose name was changed to Constantinople when the capital of the Eastern Roman Empire was established on that site by Constantine in 330.

The ethos generated by the Constantinian patronage enabled the church to bring new design and function to the Roman basilica, or assembly hall. The design varied according to local liturgical requirements, social and economic conditions of the congregation, or patronage and building practices. As basilicas, the Christian churches were based upon an oblong plan with a longitudinal axis, had timbered roofs, either open or vaulted, and terminated in a tribunal that might be rectangular in form or an apse. The basilica was divided into a nave, aisles, and a high clerestory. The function was described as *basilica id est dominicum* ("an assembly which is of the Lord"). That function set the Christian assembly hall apart, to some degree, from other basilican structures. The large clerestory windows that illumined the interiors of the Christian basilicas were similar to those found in buildings of the 4th century which were dedicated to the emperor, the Sun of Justice. The mysticism of light connected with Christ as the Light of the World and as the King of Heaven found such imperial buildings structurally suitable for ecclesiastical purposes. The light provided by such architectural forms focused attention upon interior design in a manner that corresponded to the illumination of the interior life of the believer by Christ, the Sun of Justice. Thus much emphasis was placed upon mosaic decorations, elaborate furnishings, columnar designs, and gilded ceilings. Constantinian ecclesiastical edifices were not, strictly speaking, Byzantine. The architecture of this period was transitional, looking back to Late Antiquity and forward to Early Byzantine.

The Early Byzantine period was initiated during the reign of Justinian (527–565), an autocratic empire builder whose attempt to revive the Roman Empire through military reconquest, centralization of government, codification of law, and the enforcement of religious orthodoxy had an interesting side effect in architectural style. In the latter part of the 5th century the domed basilica was developed. It allowed more illumination for the interior, but it was still a basilica. Utilizing concepts of the Late Empire, the architects of Justinian created a bold new style based on a central plan with vaults and a central dome, a mark of what became known as the Byzantine style. The centrally planned building also lent itself

...turgical needs of Greek churches ...e numbers of clerics participated in ...ation of the Mass.

... foremost example of Byzantine architecture is Hagia Sophia, or Holy Wisdom. After the basilica in Constantinople had burned to the ground during the Nike Riot in 532, Justinian built Hagia Sophia over a period of five years at a cost equivalent to more than $150,000,000. When the church was consecrated, Justinian is reported to have said, "Solomon, I have vanquished you." Two non-professional architects, Anthemius of Tralles and Isidorus of Miletus, scholars trained in theoretical statics, kinetics, mathematics, and physics, designed a structure that has survived a series of earthquakes in spite of the fact that it went to the limits of safety coefficients. Structurally, Hagia Sophia is a large rectangle, 230 by 250 feet, composed of domes, half domes, arches, piers, and *conchae*. Traditionally-minded Early Byzantine architects concentrated on barrel and groin vaults and domes on pendentives in a cross-shaped compound.

After the iconoclastic period (726–867) the Middle Byzantine period was inaugurated under Basil I (867–886) and lasted until the Latin conquest of Constantinople in 1204. The use of mosaics, a practice noted in Early Byzantine churches, succumbed to that of fresco-painting. St. Mark's of Venice was created during this period. Dome mosaics of the characteristic five-domed churches generally emphasized the Pantocrater, Christ, as the Lord of all. The Late Byzantine period lasted from 1204 until the fall of Constantinople in 1453 and then continued in the regional styles where the Orthodox Church was found. After the Islamic conquests, many of the churches were converted into mosques.

BIBLIOGRAPHY: K. J. Conant, *A Brief Commentary on Early Medieval Church Architecture* (Baltimore, 1942); G. H. Hamilton, *The Art and Architecture of Russia* (Baltimore, 1954); R. Krautheimer, *Early Christian and Byzantine Architecture* (Baltimore, 1965); E. H. Swift, *Hagia Sophia* (New York, 1940).

**Architecture, Ecclesiastical.** No evidence exists for the development of a consistent church architecture prior to 313. Literary and archaeological materials indicate that Christian communities such as that of Dura Europas (Syria, c. 232) adopted local house forms to serve as the *domus ecclesiae* for worship and ritual. A diversity of functions, including large congregational halls and smaller memoria for holy sites and the graves of saints, as well as the new imperial status of the church after the conversion of Constan-

tine, created the demand for numero... monumental structures. Eschewing the temple form but working within the f... work of the late Roman development and cal building traditions, Christian architects the 4th century freely adapted two types public buildings associated with the empero cult—the basilica, which served as a meeting and indoor burial hall, and the central plan *hērōeion* for martyria and baptisteries.

Most significant was the fusion of these two forms in St. Peter's, Rome, where a T-shaped structure was built which consisted of a wooden-roofed basilica abutting an equally tall transverse hall containing an apse. The basilica served the congregational and funereal needs, while the transept enshrined the memoria of the apostle and sheltered the ceremony of the Mass. Western architecture during the following centuries focused on modest parish churches normally consisting of a long hall terminated by an apse. Justinian's churches (e.g., Hagia Sophia) typify the eastern dome plan that eventually evolved into the popular dome-on-cross church (Daphni). Governed by liturgical considerations, the nave was reserved for the clergy and the congregation was arranged on two levels around it. The dome, traditionally an image of the cosmos, ordered the structure, descending from the Absolute Power (dome), through the heavenly church (pendentives), to the terrestrial church. Inspired by Constantine and Justinian, Charlemagne introduced the T-shaped basilica (Fulda), the central plan palace chapel (Aachen), and even the triumphal arch (Lorsch) into Gaul. But changes were made. To the west facade of the basilica an impressive fortresslike structure of two towers and a raised imperial gallery was added (Corvey), and heavy arches, a Vitruvian module system, and a rectangular apse distinguish the Aachen chapel from its southern models. The gradual subdivision of monolithic early Christian spaces into a system of proportioned, interrelated bays, already begun at St. Michael's, Hildesheim (1010), represents a major step toward the medieval conception. Networks of churches along the pilgrimage roads and powerful monastic establishments maintained a certain uniformity among diverse local traditions of the 12th century. Following the injunctions of Bernard of Clairvaux, Cistercian churches were logical in construction and austere in design and detail. More elaborate were the churches dependent on Cluny or the massive basilica of St.-Sernin, Toulouse (1077), whose tunnel-vaulted nave and sheer walls pierced by round arches on simple piers and by small windows create a heavy, dark intethe aisles around the transept and apse numerous chapels accommodate pilgrims come to venerate the relics.

Gothic architecture stands as a near antithesis to Romanesque architecture. A new, geometrically ordered, diaphanous structure, which brought together such elements as the pointed arch, ribbed vault, exterior buttress, and double-towered facade, emerged from a series of constructional and visual experiments begun by Abbot Suger at St.-Denis (1137). Worked out in the Île-de-France (Sens, Laon), they culminated in the cathedrals of Chartres, Reims, and Amiens (1195–1220). Influenced by the Neoplatonic identification of God as the "superessential light" and by Scholastic principles of the homology of parts, Gothic architects opened the walls to stained-glass windows and established a unified relationship between facade, nave elevation, vault, arch, and pier. Particularly through the Cistercians, French Gothic was imported into other European countries and received local reinterpretations. By the mid-13th century, churches were reduced to delicate membranes of glass stretched between skeletons of tracery (Ste.-Chapelle, Paris). Gradually, decorative freedom and textural interplay transformed the earlier severe regularity into the restless, intricate, flamboyant style of the 15th century (Toul).

Classical antiquity, both Roman remains and the Hellenistic theories of Vitruvius, stimulated changes of form and of symbolic value in Renaissance architecture. In such a church as Sto. Spirito, Florence (1436), Brunelleschi not only used a formal vocabulary of Corinthian columns and classical moldings, but through a modular system, he organized the clearly disposed elements of the Latin cross basilica into simple, harmonious relationships. In his treatise, *De re aedificatoria,* Alberti argued that the church, a microcosm of the universe, should be based on the perfect forms of circle and square. For symbolic reasons, he and subsequent architects favored the domed, Greek cross plan (Todi) ornamented with classical borrowings. Inevitably, Bramante chose this plan for the rebuilding of St. Peter's (1506), using enormous, sculptural piers and a monumental dome to organize the spacious interior. Better suited to Neoplatonic ideas than to the liturgical and congregational needs of the church, central-plan buildings were repeatedly modified. Elliptical and irregular plans (Vignola, Bernini, Borromini) compromised the ideal of the central structure to focus on the altar and to separate congregation from clergy. The Latin cross plan with side chapels and a centralized, domed crossing

used by Vignola in Il Gésu, the Jesuit church of Rome (1567), became standard during the 17th century, and was introduced into France by Lemercier in the churches of Richelieu, Sorbonne, and Val-de-Grace. Sir Christopher Wren, influenced by French and Italian models, designed St. Paul's, London (1675), where again a dome dominates the crossing of an aisled basilica. The more fantastic, subjective forms of Borromini, Pozzo, and Guarini (ovals, interlocking curves, rich color play, and exotic details) penetrated Germany and Austria in the works of Fischer von Erlach (Karlskirche, Vienna, 1716) and Neumann (Vierzehnheiligen, 1743).

Early Protestant architecture was plain and restrained. It was not unusual for reformers to adapt Catholic churches by clearing them of sculpture and stained glass and by replacing the altar with a pulpit. In their own designs, Protestant architects introduced a variety of plans. At Willemstad, Holland (1586), an octagonal, brick church sheltered simple pews arranged in rows before the pulpit. Salomon de Brosse's Temple of Charenton (1623), built in Paris for the Huguenots, was based on Vitruvius' description of a Roman basilica. A simple rectangle with two tiers of galleries along four walls, its focus was on the pulpit and its effect was aural rather than visual. Demand that the congregation hear, see, and actively participate in the service affected the plans of the fifty-one city churches designed by Wren after the London fire of 1666.

Early immigrants to America carried with them the idea of the plain, well-lighted, nonliturgical Protestant church. Austere but handsomely crafted, the wooden, hip-roofed, rectangular "Old Ship Meeting-House," Hingham, Mass. (1680), is a witness to the Puritan spirit. Changes, first effected by the Episcopalians under English influence, but eventually generally accepted, transformed the meetinghouse into a more formal church during the 18th century. Christ Church, Boston (1723), and the more classical First Baptist Church of Providence, R.I. (1775), with pitched roofs, steeples, and entrances on the short ends, acquired longitudinal orientations.

The historical styles revived during the 19th century carried with them corresponding ecclesiastical significance. None was so closely identified with religious architecture, however, as Gothic, championed by the English convert to Catholicism, Pugin (1836), and later accepted, without a Roman Catholic bias, by Ruskin. By the end of the 19th century, expanded social and institutional responsibilities led most denominations to incorporate within the church complex a diversity of facilities.

The almost unlimited possibilities offered by constructional advances in the 20th century present opportunities for the development of meaningfully expressive structures. A few architects, resisting the temptation to rely upon historical clichés, have accommodated the new functional, liturgical, and psychological demands in their buildings. The striking shapes and peaceful interior of Le Corbusier's pilgrimage chapel, Ronchamp (1955), and the imposing power of Tange's Tokyo Cathedral (1965) are two examples of the new possibilities of ecclesiastic architecture.

BIBLIOGRAPHY: A. L. Drummond, *The Church Architecture of Protestantism* (Edinburgh, 1934); P. Hammond, *Liturgy and Architecture* (New York, 1961); R. Krautheimer, *Early Christian and Byzantine Architecture* (Baltimore, 1965); E. Panofsky, *Gothic Architecture and Scholasticism* (Latrobe, Pa., 1951); R. Wittkower, *Architectural Principles in an Age of Humanism* (London, 1965).

**Architecture, Gothic.** The architectural style developed during the middle of the 12th century when the groin vault, formed by two equal tunnel vaults intersecting to form a diagonal cross, was augmented by diagonal ribs. Ribs are arches that are formed on the surfaces of a vault. Though ribs, such as the cryptorib of Roman Antiquity, were used as reinforcements beneath the surface of the vaulting, the combining of the three-dimensional diagonal ribs with the groin vault marked the beginning of the Gothic style. The purpose of this combination was both aesthetic and functional. Aesthetically, the concept of diagonality lent itself well to the organic unity of the structure. Romanesque building techniques, from which Gothic architecture is derived, were directed toward the concept of the addition of units and antithetical forces. The Gothic style exhibited a wholeness of interacting divisions and synthetical forces. Functionally, the combination of diagonal ribs with the groin vault enabled the construction of churches that were vast in size in order to accommodate large numbers of people, including the pilgrims and crusaders. Another element peculiar to Gothic architecture in relation to size is the buttressing system.

The term "Gothic" is a misnomer. It was applied by Renaissance humanists to architectural styles that were nonclassical and therefore barbarian in origin. One theory was that the Gothic style originated in the German forests where the branches of trees were tied together to form a pointed arch simply because the Germans were not able to fell trees. Such fallacious reasoning was further enhanced by the Italian humanists, who claimed that the style was invented by the Goths who had sacked Rome in 410 and brought decadence to architecture. According to this view, most western European architecture for the next thousand years owed its origins to the Goths and the Germans. The real creators of the Gothic style, as it is still known, were the French, not the Goths or the Germans.

The Gothic period is divided into the Early Gothic of the late 11th and 12th centuries, the High Gothic of the late 12th and 13th centuries, and the Late Gothic of the 14th and 15th centuries. An early example of the use of diagonal ribs on a groined vault can be found in the choir of the Durham Cathedral in England, begun in 1093, only a short time after the Norman conquest of England. Another transitional church is that of St.-Etienne in Beauvais, begun in 1120. The bases and capitals of the shafts supporting the ribs are set diagonally and emphasize a vertical movement. These two, however, are examples of experimentation.

Recognized as the first church to be built in the Early Gothic style is St.-Denis, near Paris. The abbot of St.-Denis, Suger, wrote about the building c. 1144. The western entrance was too narrow for the traffic on feast days. The Carolingian entrance was torn down and a facade was reconstructed with three wide doorways and two towers, between which on the upper level was a chamber for storing valuable treasures. The chamber was illuminated by a large circular window. In the reconstruction of St.-Denis the pointed arch was introduced to the scheme of rib-vaulting. The sculpture of St.-Denis was also a part of the unified whole and therefore Gothic. Suger's interest in the mysticism of light led him to make much use of stained-glass windows for the chapels. The interiors of Early Gothic churches were the first to demonstrate the stylistic motifs of the pointed arch and diagonal rib-vaulting. Gradually the exteriors received stylistic attention. Pointed arches were exhibited in the windows and portals. Reduction of the weight and mass of the walls and the thrust of the vaulted bays led to the construction of the flying buttress (a quarter circle arch) to support the downward thrust. These external arches were first evidenced in Notre Dame in Paris.

The High Gothic style enhanced the interior of the buildings. The flying buttresses eliminated the necessity for galleries to uphold the thrust of walls and made possible the enlargement of windows. The stained-glass windows of the High Gothic churches are famous. The cathedrals at Chartres, Rouen, Paris, Amiens,

Reims, and Salisbury, as well as many more, are magnificent examples of the prodigious activities of the churchmen, architects, and craftsmen who produced these structures. Another facet of High Gothic style was the inclusion of gargoyles as integral parts of the structural system, and the wide use of other forms of sculpture. In the Late Gothic period nations other than France and England created their own versions of this type of architecture.

BIBLIOGRAPHY: K. Clark, *The Gothic Revival* (London, 1950); P. Frankl, *Gothic Architecture* (Baltimore, 1963); and *The Gothic: Literary Sources and Interpretations Through Eight Centuries* (Princeton, 1960); E. Panofsky, *Gothic Architecture and Scholasticism* (Latrobe, Pa., 1951).

**Architecture, Merovingian and Carolingian.** The Merovingian period in the West corresponded roughly to the Early Byzantine period in the East. Christianity became the norm for the Frankish settlers of the West after a king of the Merovingian dynasty, Clovis I, was baptized by Remigius in 496. The declining population of the Western centers of civilization militated against experimentation with new ideas in architecture. Most ecclesiastical edifices for the urban centers and villages were small in scale and constructed according to the traditional Roman basilican plan with wooden roofs. The small size of the urban centers, which were often episcopal sees, helped to maintain in the lands of the Franks a Roman tradition that the church should be of a size that could accommodate the community at the worship services. Monasteries, which were sanctuaries for the pursuit of prayer, farming, and the arts during a long period of population migration and wars, were able to undertake long-term programs to build monumental designs employing techniques that were utilized in the Carolingian Renaissance. Lantern towers with windows to illumine the altar space also served as fortification towers during this period of turbulence and were ancestors to the medieval spires. In addition, the towers were utilized as belfries, with the bells employed in the liturgy of the monasteries also calling the faithful to prayer at regular periods.

The Carolingian dynasty supplanted the Merovingians in 752 but maintained a continuity with the older dynasty. Pepin III the Short, son of Charles Martel, victor over the Moslems at Tours, was the first king of France anointed by the church. His son, Charlemagne, who held territories from the borders of Denmark to Rome, was anointed by Pope Leo III on Christmas Day, 800, and crowned as emperor of Rome. Though the imperial title was anachronistic, Charlemagne inaugurated a renaissance that was influential but short-lived. At his palace at Aix-la-Chapelle (Aachen), Charlemagne established a workshop for artists and writers. Just as he attempted to revive the Roman imperium politically, so also he aimed at a renewal of the classical ideals culturally. This contrived rediscovery of classical antiquity was felt in the architecture of the period.

The buildings constructed under the patronage of Charlemagne were revivals of Roman types, but with mixtures of Byzantine and Oriental themes as well as with Nordic and Celtic influences. The most famous building of Charlemagne's Renaissance is the Palatine Chapel at Aachen, designed by Odo of Metz and dedicated in honor of the Virgin Mary in 805. It was built according to Roman and Byzantine architectural styles, but because of restorations in 983 and 1881 it shows some Gothic and Renaissance influences. Although inspired by the church of S. Vitale in Ravenna, the chapel was more elaborate in design. Surrounding a central octagon was an annular vaulted aisle leading to a sanctuary. Twin basilican chapels, no longer in existence, were placed symmetrically on a cross axis on the north and south. The high arched central space was crowned by tunnel and groin vaults and by an octagonal cloister vault at the top. These techniques, plus the fact that building materials were obtained from Roman ruins, indicate the peculiar bent of the architectural style, even though thematically the chapel was constructed according to the design of S. Vitale.

The oratory at Germigny-des-Pres, built in 806 and inaccurately restored during the years 1867 to 1876, was constructed with some Byzantine and Oriental themes. A towered central square space was surrounded by eight vaulted compartments with tunnel vaults on the main and transverse axes. Horseshoe arches illustrate the Oriental inspiration. The tall lantern and belfry over the central space is of Germanic influence and may come from a later period.

The most characteristically Northern church design of the Carolingian Renaissance was the monastery church of Centula, or St.-Riquier, no longer in existence. Designed by the abbot Angilbert, St.-Riquier was basilican in scheme, with two axial towers about 180 feet high. The westwork, or entrance, with its boldly articulated facade, became a pattern that was followed in Western church architecture. Beyond the entrance was the narthex, or antechurch, containing a chapel with a high altar space dedicated to the Savior. The purpose of such a chapel was to emphasize the Savior in a period of superstition and cults of local saints.

The blending of Roman, Byzantine, Oriental, and Northern architectural themes in the Carolingian Renaissance led to the dynamic Romanesque designs.

BIBLIOGRAPHY: D. Bruggink and C. H. Droppers, *Christ and Architecture* (Grand Rapids, 1965); K. J. Conant, *Carolingian and Romanesque Architecture* (Baltimore, 1967).

**Architecture, Romanesque.** The Pre-Romanesque architecture of the Carolingian Renaissance (see ARCHITECTURE, MEROVINGIAN AND CAROLINGIAN) was experimental and devoid of a fully articulated style. With the accession of Otto I to the imperial throne in 936 the Romanesque period of architecture began and it continued until the middle of the 12th century when the Gothic period was initiated. Experiments in architecture during the Carolingian era and the destruction of buildings in western Europe by the Vikings and Magyars gave impetus to the Romanesque style. An answer had to be found to the combustible wooden roofs that were the rule.

The Early Romanesque period (950–1050) is distinguished from the Carolingian Romanesque by the widespread use of Roman types of vaulting for the roofs. Romanesque vaults were of masonry and replaced the inflammable roofs of the previous period. The heavy thrust of masonry roofs was supported by massive walls and arches. The round arch of Roman antiquity was a mark of the Romanesque style. As a distinctive style, Romanesque architecture began in the 9th century. Walls were constructed of a core of well-laid rough rubble, with the Byzantine oblong bricks or stones used for facing. S. Vincenzo, a columnar basilica in Milan, with its pilaster (a rectangular pier with a base, shaft, and column), arched corbel tables (a series of arches supported by a brick or stone cornice projecting from the side of a wall), rounded arches, and brick walls, is a 9th-century example of what was to come.

Under the Ottonians, with their considerable reliance on ecclesiastical authorities, a significant number of large cathedrals were built in Germany. The cathedrals at Mainz, Augsburg, and Strasbourg were constructed during this period. Stone sculpture and relief-work were occasionally employed both in the interior and on the exterior of many of the buildings. What the cathedral of Mainz was to the Ottonian rulers—a kaiserdom—the cathedral of Speyer was to their successors, the

Salian Franks. Begun under Conrad II about 1030, the cathedral of Speyer is one of the most imposing structures of both Romanesque and Gothic styles. The total length of Speyer is about 435 feet, with the nave being approximately 235 feet in length. The west wall is about 20 feet thick. When Speyer was reconstructed under Henry IV from 1082 to 1106, the timber roof was replaced by vaults in the nave. The supporting piers were increased from 8 to 10 feet across in order to sustain the nave vault, which measured about 107 feet high, higher than any other Romanesque nave vault. The vertical thrust of such buildings eventually aided in precipitating the Gothic style.

In France, after the "fury of the Northmen" subsided in the early 10th century, an intellectual and architectural revival ensued, especially in Burgundy and Aquitaine. When St. Martin at Tours was reconstructed, an ambulatory (an annular aisle surrounding the sanctuary on three sides) with radiating chapels was united with the sanctuary.

Monasteries as the cultural centers of the Romanesque period were influenced by the art and architectural trends of the era and in turn also influenced them. One of the most famous monasteries in terms of architecture was that at Cluny in southern Burgundy. Because it was comparatively free from external lay or ecclesiastical control and developed domination over other monasteries of the Benedictine Order under the abbot Odo in 931, the influence of Cluny became impressive. Cluniac interest in the liturgy engendered a preference for tunnel vaulting for acoustical effects. Cluniac churches were substantial in size and generally included ambulatories with radiating chapels, towered transepts, grouped piers with carvings on the capitals, and sometimes carvings on the portals.

The High or Mature Romanesque period (1050–1150) was international in scope. The interest in pilgrimages to sites of relic collections or burial places of venerated personages encouraged architectural activity in order that provisions might be made for the large numbers of the faithful. The churches of the "Pilgrimage Road," at Tours, Limoges, Congues, Toulouse, and Santiago de Compostela (recognized as the site of the tomb of James, the son of Zebedee), were imposing with their long aisles and galleries, wide transepts, rounded arches, impressive towers, and high tunnel vaulting. In nearly all the High Romanesque churches the walls were constructed of ashlar masonry and adorned with sculpture for decorative and didactic purposes. The style spread throughout western Europe.

BIBLIOGRAPHY: D. Bruggink and C. H. Droppers, *Christ and Architecture* (Grand Rapids, 1965); K. J. Conant, *Carolingian and Romanesque Architecture* (Baltimore, 1967).

**Archontici.** A Gnostic group from Palestine, according to Epiphanius, which flourished in Armenia in the 4th century. Its members made use of a typical Gnostic system of thought, along with Jewish-Christian apocryphal works such as the Ascension of Isaiah. The views of the Archontici seem to reflect much earlier kinds of gnosticism: Seth, the son of Adam and Eve, was taken to the heavens above, returning later to be present in Jesus.

**Archpriest.** The title of a priest who holds juridical or honorary preeminence over other priests. Archpriests were originally the senior priests of a city or rural area and exercised in that area an authority delegated by the bishop. The honorary title continues to exist, but the former duties of the archpriest have been assumed by rural deans.

**Arians.** So named for their support of the doctrinal position of Arius. The conflict engendered by Arius continued inside the church from c. 318 until 381; outside the church it continued with decreasing vitality until Arianism disappeared. Stages of the internal conflict are marked off by (1) First Council of Nicaea, (2) accession of Julian, (3) First Council of Constantinople.

1. From 318 to 325. Arius, an Alexandrian presbyter, was cited by a synod held at Alexandria (318) for teaching that the Logos was of a different nature (*ousia*) from the Father, was a creature and therefore not coeternal with the Father, but was the first and greatest of creatures, being created *ex nihilo;* thus his Trinity consisted of three hypostases of graduated rank. Excommunicated (319) by Alexander of Alexandria, Arius found asylum with Eusebius of Nicomedia; because of sympathies of Eastern bishops oriented toward Origenism, he was soon able to return to Alexandria. The demand of Constantine for settlement of doctrinal as well as constitutional problems in the church brought Arius' view before the Council of Nicaea (325), where it was anathematized. A symbol was adopted containing the term *homoousios* to describe the relation between the Logos and the Father; the Arian struggle henceforth turned on this term and variants introduced for it.

2. From 325 to 361. Just as there had been three parties at the Council, so in the period following it, there were also three: (*a*) the Arians led by Eusebius of Nicomedia; (*b*) the "orthodox" or "Nicenes" led by Alexander of Alexandria, Marcellus of Ancyra, and Hosius of Cordova; (*c*) a central party of somewhat indeterminate borders, known as semi-Arians and led by Eusebius of Caesarea, consisting mostly of the Origenists. Because of the excessive zeal expressed by the "orthodox" and the fears of the central party that theology would be sundered from philosophy, a thirty-five-year struggle ensued among the three parties for leadership of the church, with Athanasius, chief spokesman for the "orthodox," often the target of coalitions among segments of the two remaining parties. Constantine, under whose supervision the Council of Nicaea had met, began to lean toward the Arians and assisted in the reinstatement of banished Arian bishops and the restoration of Arian clerics. Arius died (336), however, before he could benefit therefrom. At the accession of Constantine's sons, a decidedly pro-Arian policy was pursued, resulting in replacement of "orthodox" bishops. After the synod at Rome (340) declared Athanasius and Marcellus to be orthodox, the West remained consistently non-Arian, but the Eastern Church declared itself to the contrary at Antioch (341). The upshot was the imperially summoned Council of Sardica in 342, which resulted in the East and West anathematizing each other, the West retaining the Nicene symbol and the East reasserting the stand it had taken at Antioch. In 344, the Eusebians (Arians) sought a *rapprochement* with the West, and at Antioch offered the Nicene West a new symbol called the *Macrostich,* containing the phrase, "The Logos is, in all respects, *similar (homoios)* to the Father"; *homoousios* seemed destined to extinction. After five years, when Constantius became sole emperor, the conflict flared again; at Arles (353) and again at Milan (355), the West agreed to drop *homoousios,* and those who, like Liberius, would not were banished. Athanasius drew condemnation again and was driven from his see (356). Instead of the intended unity, this synodal action divided the anti-Nicene group into three parties: (*a*) the radical Arians, called variously Anomoeans, Exoucontians, or Heterousiasts (because they averred that the Logos was of another, i.e., *heteros, ousia* than the Father); (*b*) the Homoiousians, so named because in the symbol adopted at Ancyra (358) *homoiousios* ("of similar *ousia*") replaced the *homoousios* of the Nicene symbol, a group including Basil of Ancyra, George of Cappadocia, Eustathius of Sebaste, and Eusebius of Emesa; (*c*) the Homoeans, who developed the view of the *Macrostich* as a compromise formula on politically expedient grounds, a view promoted

by Ursacius and Valens, representing imperial intentions of settling the controversy finally and peaceably. After contention between Homoiousians and Homoeans, Constantius at two separate synods, Ariminum (359) for the West and Seleucia (359) for the East, forced the adoption of the Homoean formula. Thus the central parties were united once more with both extremes left out; by such compromise the Arians had won a partial victory and the Homoeans remained in control until death of Constantius in 361.

3. From 361 to 381. The policy of complete religious freedom pursued by Julian the Apostate permitted the banished Anomoeans and the Nicenes to return to the fray on equal footing with the new central compromise party. During this period an alliance was concluded between the Homoiousians and the Nicenes, assisted by the reinterpretation of the old Nicene symbol by Athanasius at the Synod of Alexandria (362); the Nicene symbol was thus made acceptable to the Homoiousians. Further aid for this alliance was furnished through the speculative efforts to express Nicene theology in terms of Greek philosophical language carried out by the Cappadocians, Basil of Caesarea, Gregory of Nazianzus, and Gregory of Nyssa. Out of this alliance grew the "new orthodoxy" which, before it could become dominant, had to overcome sizable obstacles: (a) at Antioch the parties represented by "new orthodoxy" were in the minority and under the domination of Eudoxius, bishop there (358–360) and later at Constantinople, who was an extreme or Anomoean type of Arian; (b) growing out of the Athanasian declaration at Alexandria, many Eastern Christians refused the designation homoousios to the Holy Spirit, thus opening the struggle with the Pneumatomachi, or Macedonians, as they were called, since their leader was Macedonius; (c) many Western Christians feared that the "new orthodoxy" was more "new" than "orthodoxy" and with certain extreme Nicenes of the East opposed the mediating stance of Athanasius, giving rise to the Luciferian schism so called from Lucifer of Cagliari. The constant efforts of the Cappadocians drew the fringes of the new central group together so well that by 379 at Antioch the Eastern group could accept the formulary of bishop Damasus of Rome while condemning the Macedonians. The extreme Nicene party suffered great difficulty in trying to think out the Christology that would ensue from their strict homoousian position; the chief representative of this effort was Apollinarius, whose Christology protected homoousios but made impossible a real unity between divine and human in Christ. Successive condemnation of Apollinarius by Athanasius, the Cappadocians, and Damasus strengthened the position of the "new orthodoxy." The accession of Theodosius I as emperor of the East in 379 created the political climate for a victory for "new orthodoxy"; the anti-Arian policy of Theodosius eliminated extreme Arians from their churches. At the Council of Constantinople (381), the Nicene symbol was confirmed and a firm interpretation made to exclude Anomoeans, Eudoxians, Macedonians, Sabellians (see SABELLIUS), Marcellians (see MARCELLUS), the near-related Photinians, and chiefly, Apollinarians. The main result of the Council was to give a victory to the central Arianizing group while protecting against the extremes of either the Apollinarians or the Arians; "new orthodoxy" triumphed.

4. After 381. The West Goths, who had arrived in the Empire c. 382, remained Arian, since they had been converted through the Arian Ulfilas. Other invading tribes learned their Arianism from the West Goths. After a feeble attempt by Justina (386) to reinstate the Homoean symbol, the Arian conflict died away. The German tribes who were Arian were gradually absorbed into the orthodox imperial Catholic Church.

BIBLIOGRAPHY: P. Schaff and H. Wace (eds.), Nicene and Post-Nicene Fathers, Series II, Vol. 4 (Grand Rapids, 1957); R. W. Bush, St. Athanasius: His Life and Times (London, 1912); S. L. Greenslade, Schism in the Early Church (New York, 1953); H. M. Gwatkin, The Arian Controversy (New York, 1898); and Studies in Arianism (Cambridge, 1900).

**Ariminum and Seleucia, Synods of** (359). An ecumenical council in two sections, the Western at Ariminum in Italy, the Eastern at Seleucia in Asia Minor, summoned by the emperor Constantius. The emperor favored the moderate Arianism of the "Dated Creed," issued at his headquarters at Sirmium on May 22, 359, which declared the Son to be "like the Father" (homoios). But at Ariminum the majority supported the Nicene position, and at Seleucia the similar semi-Arian, or homoiousian. Under official pressure each Synod was persuaded to entrust its case to a delegation sent to meet Constantius at Constantinople. On Oct. 10 at the town of Nice in Thrace (perhaps chosen so the result could be called "Nicene") the Western majority delegates were brought to join the minority in a slightly revised form of the "Dated Creed," to which the remaining bishops at Ariminum hesitantly agreed. The Synod at Seleucia had adjourned, but on Dec. 31 its delegates accepted the same document, then proclaimed as the faith of the church. This is the moment described by Jerome in the phrase "The whole world groaned and was astonished to find itself Arian" (*Adversus Luciferianos* 19). A reaction soon set in, but as long as Arianism survived, the so-called Creed of Ariminum was its official confession of faith.

**Aristides of Athens** (2d century). Christian philosopher and Apologist. He addressed his work either to Hadrian (117–138) or to Antoninus Pius (138–161). Aristides' apology is probably the earliest that has come down to us. His work was known for a long time only through the statement of Eusebius that "Aristides also, a man of faith and devoted to our religion, has like Quadratus, left an Apology of the faith addressed to Hadrian. His writing, too, has been preserved by many" (*Ecclesiastical History* 4.3.2). In 1878, however, an Armenian manuscript of the 10th century which bore the title of Aristides' apology was published by the Mechitarists of San Lorenzo in Venice. Twenty-one years later a complete Syriac translation was found at St. Catherine's Monastery, Mt. Sinai, by Rendel Harris. On the basis of it, J. A. Robinson showed that the apology is paraphrased in the medieval romance *Barlaam and Joasaph*.

The form of the work is a contrast of Christianity with the non-Christian religions. On the basis of formulas resembling those of both Stoics and philosophical Jews, Aristides arrives at a description of God by the *via negativa* and then tries to see which religion measures up to the concept of God arrived at by this method. Not surprisingly, Christianity wins. He concludes with a brief description of Christian faith and practice. The naïveté of his apology was responsible for its neglect by later Christians. It is not likely that he wrote either the *Epistle to Diognetus* or the sermon *On the Thief's Cry and the Crucified's Response*.

**Aristo of Pella** (2d century). Author of a work now lost, called *Dialogue of Papiscus with Jason,* on the Jewish-Christian debate. As a native of Pella, Aristo probably belonged to the Jewish-Christian church that had withdrawn across the Jordan before the fall of Jerusalem in 70. Isolated fragments of his *Dialogue* seem to reflect a somewhat Judaistic theology. The anti-Christian writer Celsus condemned it, while Origen defended it.

**Aristotelianism in the Middle Ages.** Though Aristotle had some influence on Christian thought both before and after the Middle Ages, it was during that period especially that his influence in the West was prolonged and profound. During the patristic era Aristotle's voice was just one among the many in pagan philosophy. He was far less significant than Plato, the Stoics, or the Neoplatonists. In the postmedieval period, what influence Aristotle had was exercised largely, though not entirely, through medieval Scholastic intermediaries.

The *Corpus Aristotelicum* reached the Latin West piecemeal and by a number of routes. Aristotle's works on logic had all been translated into Latin by the early 6th century along with a number of commentaries on them. Only about half of these translations, "the old logic," survived until the renewal of interest in Aristotle in the 12th century.

In the mid-12th century, the rest of the Aristotelian logic, "the new logic," reached the West, principally in Arabic translations at the chief points of contact between Arabic and Latin culture, Sicily and Spain.

In addition to these works by Aristotle, a number of works by Arabic followers and interpreters of Aristotle were also available to Latin readers. Most important of these were Avicenna (980–1037) and Averroës (1126–1198). Throughout the 13th century the work of translation continued, and most of Aristotle's works were translated more than once, in some cases from a desire for a more accurate text, one less influenced by the peculiarities of Arabic Aristotelianism.

The introduction of Aristotle into the West was thus a rather gradual process, and though the pace accelerates rapidly in the early decades of the 13th century, there is no definite point at which Aristotle was introduced. Aristotle had to some degree defined the logic and influenced the vocabulary of medieval theology even before the 12th century. Again, it was Aristotle's logic that was principally involved in the 12th-century disputes over the place of "dialectic" in theology. However, it was in the 13th century and in the universities that the full-scale encounter between Aristotelianism and Christian thought took place.

In the universities an attempt was made to organize the principal areas of thought into coherent disciplines. Inasmuch as Aristotle presented a fairly coherent outline of everything from plants and animals to God, as well as an analysis of the way of investigating all subjects, it was inevitable that his system of thought would provide the 13th century with a unique challenge.

His writings on logic had already been accepted, but his other works met with considerable resistance in the early decades of the 13th century. At Paris, public and private lectures on Aristotle's writings on nature were prohibited in 1210 under threat of excommunication. By 1230, however, the *Metaphysics* and the works on nature had already been introduced into the curriculum there, and not many years later Aristotle's writings had come to constitute practically the entire philosophical curriculum not only at Paris but at most of the still young universities.

From this time on, there was a virtual identification of Aristotle and philosophy in the medieval universities, somewhat after the manner in which Euclid and geometry were identified down to more recent times. The philosophical faculties in these institutions by and large conceived of their task as the expounding of Aristotle, filling out if necessary the lacunae that he had left in his system. The faculties of theology in the main agreed in identifying Aristotle as *the* philosopher, with the result that their theologies were profoundly Aristotelianized or their criticisms of Aristotle were actually criticisms of philosophy and human reason in general. At least three distinct intellectual traditions can be discerned.

First, there was an attempt to develop an ideologically pure Aristotelianism. This work was done principally within the philosophical faculties and has been labeled, among other things, "Latin Averroism." The intention was not to see whether it was possible to read Aristotle in a Christian sense, but to discover and to explain what in fact Aristotle said and meant. The movement was suspected of heterodox intentions almost from the start and was condemned at Paris in 1270 and again in 1277, but it was never rooted out or even driven entirely underground. It continued, especially in the Italian universities, until it evolved into what is generally referred to as Renaissance Aristotelianism.

There is some question whether the movement was, at least in its early stages, quite as heterodox as it seemed. Some of the 13th- and 14th-century Averroists seem to have considered the heterodoxy of certain of their Aristotelian conclusions (eternity of the world, denial of the immortality of the individual soul and of God's knowledge of the world) a consequence of the fallibility of even this greatest of philosophers rather than as a philosophical refutation of the Christian faith.

Secondly, there was a synthesizing theological movement best represented by Thomas Aquinas (1225–1274). In addition to a large number of more strictly theological works, Aquinas lectured and wrote commentaries on most of Aristotle's major works, trying to show that an Aristotelianism true to its own basic insights (and thus perhaps different in some respects from the Aristotelianism of Aristotle)

would be in harmony with the Christian faith and could indeed be incorporated at many levels into a Christian world view. Though Aquinas' thought is not simply reducible to the thought of Aristotle, both the method and the content of Aristotelianism are visible on every page of Aquinas' work. So thoroughly did Aquinas integrate Aristotle's thought into his own that some of the condemnations directed against the Latin Averroists would seem to include Aquinas.

The third current was much more diffuse. It was a theological movement that, though obviously Aristotelian in many respects, grew increasingly critical of Aristotle and moved farther and farther away from the position developed by Aquinas. A logically more demanding conception of science and evidence was developed, to some degree by John Duns Scotus (c. 1270–1308), but especially by William of Occam (c. 1280–c. 1349). Much of this conception was derived from Aristotle's own works on logic, but its net effect was greatly to limit the cogency of the Aristotelian philosophy. Far fewer theological conclusions could be deduced from the necessities of things; more depended on the free will of God and, at another level, the teaching of the church. It is often asserted that Occam refused to use metaphysics in theology, but this is incorrect. Metaphysics, and a recognizably Aristotelian metaphysics, continues to function in theology, but it is a greatly reduced Aristotelianism.

These three currents were all quite well defined by the third decade of the 13th century. From that time on they dominated Latin intellectual life, or at least the universities, until the Reformation. For all their differences, they have in common a fundamental concern with the philosophy of Aristotle.

BIBLIOGRAPHY: É. Gilson, *History of Christian Philosophy in the Middle Ages* (New York, 1955); F. van Steenberghen, *Aristotle in the West: The Origins of Latin Aristotelianism* (Louvain, 1955); and *The Philosophical Movement in the Thirteenth Century* (Edinburgh, 1955).

**Aristotle** (384–322 B.C.). Disciple of Plato and founder of his own Peripatetic school. During the Hellenistic age his earlier, Platonizing works were read, while his more scientific treatises were lost. Not until the 1st century B.C. were they partially recovered and published. The conversion of Justin was influenced by genuine Aristotelian arguments, and the scientific treatises were used by Clement of Alexandria and Hippolytus. Most early Christian authors, however, regarded Aristotelianism as oversubtle and considered his science godless.

**Arius** (d. 336). Alexandrian presbyter, pupil of Lucian of Antioch. His writings include *Thalia* and occasional letters but no complete works are extant. Some of the existing fragments and quotations from *Thalia* are genuine. The heresy for which he was excommunicated was part of the Trinitarian struggle that began as early as the Monarchians but developed the Logos Christology that defeated the Monarchians. The ultimate solution of the Arian controversy by means of an Origenistic compromise indicates the base and direction of his doctrinal assertions. The controversy began when his former associates, the Melitians, cited him at a synod in Alexandria (318). At the time of his death (336) he was about to be reinstated, but imperial condemnation ratified at the Synod of Jerusalem (335) prevented immediate action.

**Arles, Synods of.** The city of Arles, situated on the banks of the Rhone River, was founded in pre-Christian times as a colony of Marseilles and has been the scene of at least fifteen councils. The earliest (314) was the first to be called by Constantine and an early abortive attempt to settle the Donatist controversy. The Council of 353 was an Arian attempt to replace the Nicene formulation and depose Athanasius. A council called in 813 was part of the Carolingian reform, and the Council of 1236 condemned the Albigenses. Another synod, in 1263, condemned the doctrines of Joachim of Flora.

**Armagh.** Primatial see of Ireland, founded by Patrick in 445. Many ecclesiastical foundations rose on the spot and the famous school there had some seven thousand students at one time. The Danes and Anglo-Normans burned the city at least seventeen times, and in the 11th century, power in Armagh was seized by a layman. The rivalry between it and Dublin, which goes back to Anglo-Norman times, has been resolved by calling the Anglican archbishop primate of *all* Ireland and the archbishop of Dublin primate of Ireland.

**Armenians.** Armenia was the first nation to embrace Christianity officially. Although its territories in northeastern Asia Minor were absorbed soon after by its neighbors, its people have maintained some unity of race, customs, language, and literature. The Armenian Church repudiated the Council of Chalcedon in 451 and since then has been thought to be Monophysite.

**Arminianism.** A movement that arose in 16th-century Dutch Reformed theology in opposition to the strict Calvinism of the day. It is named after Jacobus Arminius (b. Oudewater, 1560; d. Leiden, 1609), the son of a cutler who died while Jacobus was still an infant. Under foster parents, Arminius received his early education at Utrecht and Marburg. After his family was murdered by Spaniards in 1575, Arminius was sent to the University of Leiden, sponsored by some wealthy merchants from Amsterdam. An excellent student, he went to Geneva in 1582 and studied under Beza. After a short stay in Basel and a trip to Italy, he returned to Amsterdam in 1588 and was ordained in the Reformed Church. He became pastor at Amsterdam and soon was a popular preacher. While there he was asked to write a refutation of the views of Coornheert. As he made a thorough study of the issues involved, he came instead largely to agree with Coornheert and to question the strict Calvinistic doctrine that held sway in the Dutch Reformed Church. He began to preach that God's offer of grace was universal and that man possessed the freedom to respond in faith. In 1603, he was called to the position of professor of theology at the University of Leiden. There began the long and intense controversy with Gomar, a strict Calvinist and a colleague at the university. Gradually, Arminius began to set forth with growing clarity and conviction his opposition to the Calvinistic viewpoint on predestination and human freedom. He saw two great errors in the Calvinistic position: it made God the author of sin, and it did away with genuine human freedom. Under the leadership of Gomar, reaction against Arminius became intense. The church divided into two hostile camps and the whole populace became involved in the theological controversy. Gomar himself predicted that it might well result in civil war. In 1608, Arminius made a request to the States of Holland and West Friesland for the appointment of a national synod to consider the issues. In 1609 he appeared before the States General and gave a full explanation of his views. Before this conference was concluded, Arminius became ill and died at the age of forty-nine.

After Arminius' death, the leadership of the Arminians (also known as Remonstrants) fell to Simon Episcopius, who succeeded Arminius at the University of Leiden, and to Janus Uytenbogaert, who was the author of the *Remonstrance*. John van Olden Barneveldt, a leading Dutch statesman, and Hugo Grotius, the greatest scholar of the day, were also sympathetic to the Arminian cause. In 1610, the followers of Arminius sent a treatise, called the *Remonstrance,* to the States of Holland and West Friesland. In it they set forth their theological views and requested the appointment of a synod to settle these differences. Finally, the Synod of Dort was called in 1618. Overwhelmingly Calvinistic in composition, it condemned Arminianism and banned the Remonstrants. The Remonstrant Brotherhood continued its existence in exile and in secret for the next decade. When the ban was relaxed in 1626, the Remonstrant Brotherhood became a free church in the Netherlands and has remained so to this day.

Outside the Netherlands, Arminianism found its most fertile soil in England, where it became the general outlook of the Church of England. One stream of Arminianism in England led to Unitarianism and gradually lost its force. The other stream led to "evangelicalism" as seen in the General (or Arminian) Baptists and particularly in the Methodist movement. John Wesley grew up in an Arminian atmosphere. His parents were both outspokenly antagonistic to the Calvinistic doctrine of predestination. Through him, Methodism was stamped with a distinctly Arminian viewpoint. While some of the first American colonies were strongly Calvinistic in emphasis, the highly individualistic atmosphere of the frontier provided a rich soil for the Arminian emphasis of the Methodists and Baptists, accounting in part for their rapid growth in the land.

The Arminian controversy was another evidence of the age-old theological problem: the relation of divine sovereignty and human responsibility. The issues were essentially the same as those involved in the great Pelagian controversy of the 5th century. The Arminian position may be roughly compared to that of semi-Pelagianism, which came to be the prevailing position in Roman Catholic theology.

Although still highly Calvinistic in much of its theology, Arminianism claims that its distinctiveness lies in its Biblical, practical, and peaceful outlook.

BIBLIOGRAPHY: J. Arminius, *Works* (Auburn, 1853); C. Brandt, *The Life of James Arminius* (Nashville, 1857); R. L. Colie, *Light and Enlightenment* (Cambridge, 1957); G. L. Curtiss, *Arminianism in History* (Cincinnati, 1894); M. G. Hansen, *The Reformed Church in the Netherlands* (New York, 1884); G. O. McCulloh (ed.), *Man's Faith and Freedom* (New York, 1962).

**Arnauld.** A French family prominent in the Jansenist movement. The children of Antoine Arnauld (1560–1619), a lawyer, were the most important members of the Jansenist persuasion in France. Angélique

(1591–1661) joined a Cistercian abbey at Port-Royal, southwest of Paris. Under her leadership it became a Jansenist center, until it was closed in 1709. Five of her sisters also became nuns there. The sons of another sister, Catherine, were among the religious hermits who lived around Port-Royal. After a career as civil servant and author, Angélique's brother Robert Arnauld d'Andilly also retired to Port-Royal. Another brother, Antoine (1612–1694), was known as the Great Arnauld. His book *On Frequent Communion* (1643) was one of the most important manifestations of Jansenism in France. He wrote against Calvinism as well as against Jesuit Scholasticism. He was also a logician and mathematician. Pascal's *Provincial Letters* was written in Antoine's defense when he was attacked for his Jansenism. The whole family was influenced by Saint-Cyran. They were scholarly and ascetic, devoting all their considerable energies to the reform of their lives and their church.

**Arndt, Ernst Moritz** (1769–1860). German patriot and poet. Arndt achieved national fame when in 1806 he published *Spirit of the Times,* a book in which he called upon his countrymen to destroy French control and influence in Germany. In 1818, he was appointed professor of modern history at Bonn, but was later suspended for attacking the reactionary policies of the German princes. One of his fondest hopes was for a union of Catholics and Protestants in a German national church.

**Arndt, Johann** (1555–1621). German Lutheran pastor and devotional writer. Arndt accepted a call to Badeborn in Anhalt (1583) but was removed in 1590 because of his strict Lutheran views. He moved to Quedlinburg, Brunswick (1599), Eisleben (1609), and in 1611 became general superintendent for Lüneburg. It is on his devotional writings that his fame chiefly rests. As a boy he had eagerly devoured the works of Bernard, Tauler, and Thomas à Kempis. In his *True Christianity* (1606–1610), he asserted the inadequacy of an orthodoxy that neglected vital Christian experience, and he called for repentance and sanctification that would bring the soul into communion with God. Although he was a staunch Lutheran, his emphasis on sanctification and his borrowing from the medieval mystics brought him into disfavor with some of his colleagues. Nevertheless, he exerted a wide influence both inside and outside the Lutheran Church. *True Christianity* played a very important role in relation to German Pietism of the 17th century. Of prime importance is Arndt's influence in Scandinavia during the religious awakenings of the 18th and 19th centuries. Many of his writings have been translated into Asian and African languages as well as into most of the European languages.

**Arnobius** (d. c. 330). A teacher of rhetoric in Africa who perhaps numbered Lactantius among his pupils. He was later converted to Christianity, apparently by a dream in which proof from the miracles of the divinity of Christ was employed, and wrote an apology called *Adversus nationes*. Jerome tells us that the conversion of Arnobius, like that of Paul, was suspect, and that he was required by the local bishop to prove his faith. The proof he submitted was his hastily written apology (c. 303–310). In it he quotes no Christian writer, not even a Biblical author. His knowledge of the life of Christ is largely confined to miracle stories, but for him they are what is important. He believed that Christ took the form of a man, perfomed miracles to draw men to himself, and then promised them eternal life. In keeping with this rather Gnostic-sounding Christology is his belief that the flesh is the prison of the soul, and was not created by God, but by subordinate powers. Since Lactantius was not acquainted with this work or with the ideas of his old teacher, perhaps the "Christian Cicero" learned only rhetoric from him and that during Arnobius' pagan days.

The first two books of the *Adversus nationes* are a vindication of Christianity, which allows the work to be rated as an apology, but the other five books are a violent attack on pagan religion. They contain so much detailed information, however, that they are a valuable source book for historians of religion.

**Arnobius Junior** (5th century). A semi-Pelagian monk from Africa who about 450 attacked the doctrine of predestination which grew out of Augustine's doctrine of grace. Some believe Arnobius Junior to be the author of the work *Praedestinatus,* as it was called by its editor, the 17th-century Jesuit Sirmond. The purpose of this work seems to be to ridicule Augustine's doctrine by reducing it to absurdity. Arnobius Junior is also thought to be the author of several Biblical commentaries and a letter to a patrician lady.

**Arnold, Gottfried** (1666–1714). German Lutheran church historian, Pietist, and friend of Philip Jacob Spener. He is best known for his *Impartial History of Heresy and the Church* (1699–1700) wherein he sought to view heretics from their own writings rather than from what opponents said about them. He professed to see more truth in some of the old heresies than in more orthodox theologies.

He leaned increasingly toward mysticism but in later life became more orientated toward the church. In 1704 he assumed a pastorate, and in 1707 became a church inspector at Perleberg.

**Arnold, Matthew** (1822–1888). English poet and critic. The son of Dr. Thomas Arnold, he was born at Laleham, and educated at Winchester, Rugby, and Balliol College, Oxford. From 1847 to 1851 he was private secretary to Lord Lansdowne, who appointed him inspector of schools in 1851 (a position he held until 1886). From 1857 to 1867 he was professor of poetry at Oxford. His first two volumes of poetry (*The Strayed Reveller,* 1849; *Empedocles on Etna,* 1852) were published anonymously and afterward withdrawn by the author. Both volumes revealed his awareness of the contemporary "dialogue of the mind with itself," a dialogue destructive to faith and morality. Many poems were republished in *Poems* (1853). *Poems* (2d series) appeared in 1855; *New Poems* (1867) included "Thyrsis" and "Rugby Chapel." Although not directly involved in the Tractarian movement, Arnold recognized the weakness of religion as a moral and ethical force, which was indicated by this controversy as well as by later ones based on scientific criticism of Biblical texts. His major critical writings may be interpreted as an attempt to find a meaningful guide for conduct that would be both inspiriting and social. The critic's first duty is the "disinterested endeavor to learn and propagate the best that is known and thought in the world, and thus to establish a current of fresh and true ideas" (*Essays in Criticism,* 1865). Arnold objected to Bishop Colenso's criticism of the Pentateuch (1862–1879) because of its destructive rather than constructive nature. In *Culture and Anarchy* (1869), Arnold maintained that the critic's motivation had its origin in the love of perfection. Culture was a "study of perfection," and perfection was a "harmonious expansion of *all* powers and is not consistent with the over-development of any one power at the expense of the rest. Here culture goes beyond religion." Here and in *Essays in Criticism* (2d series, 1888), Arnold emphasized the role of poetry in the moral development of man: "In poetry, our race will find an ever surer and surer stay. Our religion has materialised itself in the fact, in the supposed fact; it has attached its emotion to the fact, and now the fact is failing it. But for poetry the idea is everything; the rest is a world of illusion, of divine illusion. Poetry attaches its emotion to the idea; the idea *is* the fact." Arnold's writings on specific religious topics are *St. Paul and Protestantism* (1870), *Literature and Dogma* (1873), *God and the Bible* (1875), and *Last Essays on Church and Religion* (1877).

**Arnoldi, Wilhelm** (1798–1864). Ultramontane German prelate and preacher. He irritated Prussia's king because of his rigid views on mixed marriage. By exhibiting Christ's holy tunic at his cathedral of Treves in 1844, he attracted a million pilgrims. The historian Heinrich von Sybel declared the relic false, assailed ultramontanism, and sparked a splinter German Catholic schism that numbered sixty thousand when merged, in 1859, with the Friends of Light.

**Arnold of Brescia** (c. 1100–1155). Italian political reformer and preacher. He was born in the last decade of the 11th century in Brescia. Little is known of his early life, although he may have studied in France as a young man. As an abbot in Brescia he participated in the revolt to replace episcopal autocracy by republican government. For this, he was denounced and deposed by Innocent II (1139). He fled to France, and was associated with Abelard when the latter was accused at Sens in 1140. Arnold stayed in Paris, teaching poor students. Dismissed by Louis VII, he took refuge with Cardinal Guido, legate to Bohemia. About 1146, Arnold was reconciled with Pope Eugenius III, who had been exiled in Viterbo by the Republicans at Rome. Arnold went to Rome, ostensibly to do penance and became associated with the Republic about 1148. For this he was excommunicated (1148) and was hanged as a heretic by order of Adrian IV (1155). Arnold was a persuasive preacher, inveighing against simony and worldliness in the clergy. He denied the right of property to the church, the efficacy of infant baptism, and the validity of sacraments administered by simoniacs. His belief in the *via apostolica* led him to participate in rebellions to sever the church from temporal duties. His austerity attracted many followers, especially women, and members of the sect founded by him were known as Arnoldists.

**Arnulf** (c. 580–c. 640). An official of the Austrasian court. He became one of the progenitors of the Carolingian family through the marriage of his eldest son to the daughter of Pepin of Landen. In 614, while still a layman, he was elected bishop of Metz, continuing to act as an adviser to the Merovingian kings. In 629, he was permitted to resign his see and retire as abbot of Remiremont.

**Ars, Curé of** (Jean-Baptiste Marie Vianney, 1786–1859). Parish priest. He was appointed to serve in Ars, France, in 1818, and in this remote village not far from Lyons he soon gained worldwide fame for his spiritual counsel. During the last years of his life he spent from sixteen to eighteen hours a day in the confessional. He was canonized in 1925 and later made the patron of parish priests.

**Art, Church.** See PAINTING AND SCULPTURE, ECCLESIASTICAL.

**Artemon** (Artemas) (3d century). A follower of Theodotus the Tanner from Byzantium and his namesake, called "the Money-Changer," in the Adoptianist form of the Monarchian heresy. He taught at Rome c. 235, and is credited with trying to give this heresy a more intellectual basis by the inclusion of the thought of Galen, Aristotle, and Euclid. His work was attacked by the *Little Labyrinth,* which survives only in a quotation in Eusebius. Lucian of Antioch associates Artemon with the Gnostic Ebion and Paul of Samosata.

**Arthurian Cycle of Romances.** Romances in prose and verse about King Arthur and his court, springing from obscure origins in Welsh history. Apparently the real Arthur was a 6th-century military chieftain. As the story of Arthur grew into a legend, he was elevated to kingship, and reports of his fabulous deeds spread throughout Europe. In the 12th century, Geoffrey of Monmouth made him the central figure of his spurious pseudohistory of Britain, which was developed by the Norman poet Wace and eventually appeared in the 13th-century English version, Layamon's *Brut.* In France less stress was laid on heroic deeds, and the court of Arthur came to serve as the general focus for an elaborate code of courtly love, as in the subtle 12th-century romances of Chrétien de Troyes. In the 13th century the legend crossed into Germany and was developed in Gottfried von Strassburg's *Tristan* and Wolfram von Eschenbach's *Parzival.* Perhaps the most brilliant romance is the 14th-century English *Sir Gawain and the Green Knight,* while the fullest account of Arthur is found in Sir Thomas Malory's 15th-century *Le Morte d'Arthur.* A recurring motif is the quest for the Holy Grail, the cup used at the Last Supper, which was brought to Britain by Joseph of Arimathea according to the popular tradition derived from the apocryphal Gospel of Nicodemus.

**Arundel, Thomas** (1353–1414). Archbishop of Canterbury. Made bishop of Ely at 21, he rose through family and personal political intrigue to occupy the sees of York and Canterbury. Impeached by the House of Commons for his opposition to Richard II and banished (1397), he was later reinstated (1399) and under Henry IV proved to be an able administrator. He carried on a bitter fight against the Lollards and supported their persecution through the passage of the act *De haeretico comburendo* (1401).

**Asbury, Francis** (1745–1816). American Methodist bishop. He was born and raised near Birmingham, England, in a home permeated by an atmosphere of evangelical piety, and at the age of thirteen he also experienced a religious awakening. When he was eighteen he became a local preacher, and three years later entered the itinerant ministry. In 1771, he was sent to America by Wesley, and a year later was appointed general assistant, a position that he held with the exception of a brief period until 1784. In 1775, he alone refused orders, which had been prompted by Wesley's Toryism, to return to England. His executive ability then proved invaluable in saving the Methodist movement in America when it became dependent on local leadership. He was an ardent advocate of discipline and itinerancy, both of which he strenuously practiced until his death, and which he imposed on his fellow Methodists. In 1784, he and Thomas Coke were appointed by Wesley as joint superintendents in America, a position he accepted only when so elected by the Methodist preachers at the constituting convention of the independent Methodist denomination in that year. He was then ordained a deacon, an elder, and consecrated a superintendent on successive days. Against Wesley's wishes, Asbury assumed the title of bishop, and, because Coke was often away, guided American Methodism until his death.

**Ashley Cooper, Anthony** (1801–1885). English evangelical social reformer. Succeeding his father as the Seventh Earl of Shaftesbury in 1851, Ashley Cooper's life, in and out of Parliament, was spent in the interests of philanthropy—as those interests were conceived from the viewpoint of an "Evangelical Tory." Initially interested in bettering the condition of the insane, after 1833 he became the Parliamentary champion of the movement to limit the hours of factory labor to ten. His general interest in bettering the condition of the industrial laborer involved him in agitation directed specifically at restricting or eliminating the labor of women and children in industry and mining. The Factory Act of 1833 —the first of its kind to provide for a force of inspectors to assure compliance with its regulations—was Shaftesbury's initial triumph. The Mines Act of 1842, which prohibited the

employment of women underground and restricted male labor there to those over ten years of age, also bore his influence, as did further acts to restrict the hours of labor, and a revolutionary act of 1851 which authorized corporations to erect municipal housing for the poor. He was long the president of the British and Foreign Bible Society, and was interested in the Y.M.C.A. and innumerable other charities.

**Aske, Robert** (d. 1537). Leader of the Pilgrimage of Grace, a popular uprising in northern England, especially in Yorkshire and Lincolnshire, to protest the suppression of the monasteries and other autocratic measures by Henry VIII's government. The first uprising in 1536 met with considerable success, and Aske was able to speak with the king's representatives on equal terms. The next year, however, the government won the upper hand, suppressed the movement brutally, and, despite an earlier safe-conduct, seized and executed Aske.

**Asmussen, Hans Christian** (1898–    ). German Lutheran Church leader. Together with Karl Barth, Asmussen led the opposition to Nazi control of the German Church. They held that the church could not conform to any state or party but only to Christ. To this end they helped organize the Confessing Church which in 1934 drew up a confession in opposition to the Nazis' "German Christian" program. Following World War II, Asmussen became head of the chancellery of the Evangelical Church in Germany.

**Associations, Law of.** A law passed by the French Government in 1901 aimed at restricting the activity of the Roman Catholic monastic orders in that country. Except for the five orders that had been previously authorized, the law required that all religious congregations whose members lived in common must be authorized by the state or their property divided. Most of the men's orders went into exile, and thousands of schools they had conducted were closed.

**Assumptionists.** A religious congregation also known as the Augustinians of the Assumption. The order was approved by Pius IX in 1864 and its purpose was to combat irreligion in Europe and the spread of schism in the East. It has produced a number of important scholars and promoted the study of the Eastern Church through its review, *Echos d'Orient*. It also maintains missions in Chile, Algeria, and Tunisia.

**Assumption of the Blessed Virgin Mary.** A dogma teaching that the Virgin was assumed bodily into heaven. Defined by Pius XII in 1950 in the bull *Munificentissimus Deus* as a dogma necessary for salvation, it was, most observers believe, the first exercise of papal infallibility since that doctrine was defined in 1870. The Assumption does not appear in the New Testament or in the early fathers. The first reference to it is late, in the 4th century. By the 6th century it had become a popular devotion in both East and West. There was never the opposition to this doctrine which there has been to that of the Immaculate Conception, and most of the medieval doctors support it. Therefore, although some Protestants thought the definition was untimely in view of ecumenical relations, the doctrine had in fact been generally taught and believed for many centuries.

**Asterius the Sophist** (d. after 341). One of the ex-students of Lucian of Antioch who became leaders of the Arian movement. Although his *Syntagmation* survives only in quotations by his opponents Athanasius and Marcellus of Ancyra, he appears to have been one of the more extreme Arians. He was the only one to call Christ a creature. A compromiser who had offered sacrifices during the persecutions and made concessions to the Catholics in the controversy, he remained a prolific pamphleteer in the Arian cause.

**Astrology and Numerology.** Astrology is the "science" that attempts to determine the course of future events by understanding the cosmic correspondence of the movements of the heavenly bodies with the earth. Originating in Mesopotamia in the third millennium B.C., it reached its height in the Roman era of the Hellenistic period and continued in influence in the Middle Ages in both the Christian and Islamic cultures.

In the Roman age, man regarded himself as caught up in forces that he could not understand, but that he could see at work. To these forces he gave such names as Fate, Chance, Fortune, or Providence. He believed that the movements of the sun, moon, and stars influenced the fortunes and fates of men. The deterministic theory incorporated in this belief was, in part, based upon the idea that from the earth, as the center of the universe, emanated forces which were reciprocated by the heavenly bodies. Scientific theories, such as the heliocentric theory of Aristarchus of Samos (lived c. 270 B.C.), gave ground to astrology, which did not accept as incomprehensible the vicissitudes of the Roman era. Also, the Stoic doctrine that the human soul contains the same divine substance, the Logos, which rules the universe, encouraged the as-

trological assumption that man and the universe are controlled by the same power.

The sun, moon, and stars were regarded as immortal divinities. Kronos, or Cronos, the mythological father of Jupiter and the son of Heaven and Earth, became confused with Chronos, or Time. Time was connected with the Creator and, in turn, became the sovereign of the destinies of men. The subdivisions of time (minutes, hours, seasons, years, centuries) gained a religious importance under the influence of astrology. Since time was so crucial in heaven's determinism of men's destinies, the seven planets then recognized (the moon, Mercury, Venus, the sun, Mars, Jupiter, and Saturn, or Kronos) were studied in relationship to time with great care. Each planet was thought to be the sovereign of a sphere, or heaven, encircling the earth, the highest being Saturn, or Time itself. To the influence of the seven planets was added that of the zodiac, considered to be of Greek origin. The zodiac was understood to be a belt of constellations, twelve in number, which contained forces that affected the heavens and, therefore, the destinies of men. In order that these destinies might be comprehended, professional astrologers arose to provide men with horoscopes (speculations in regard to the Horae, the keepers of the gates of the heavens) by which they might determine future fortune or fate. If the future, according to the horoscope, could be understood, then, since the planets were not all-powerful, the astrologers could advise their clients whether or not to act.

The impetus generated by the widely accepted views and practices of astrology during the Roman period when men felt unsure of their destinies carried the movement into the Christian era. There its practice can be traced through its condemnation by the early Christian councils. A large body of literature which was devoted to astrology, astral magic, and other occult sciences and philosophical discourses was developed during the period from the 2d to the 4th century A.D. under the name of Hermes Trismegistus. In these treatises can be found descriptions of the journey of the soul through the spheres of the planets and of the processes of spiritual regeneration by which the soul throws off the shackles of the material world and becomes filled with divine powers.

Astrology declined in the West during the period of the barbarian migrations. With the Carolingian Renaissance and its interest in antiquity and the rise of Islam and its preservation of ancient writings, astrology once more became a force to be reckoned with through the Middle Ages and the Renaissance period. Albertus Magnus in his *Speculum astronomiae* strongly criticized works ascribed to Hermes Trismegistus dealing with alchemy and astral magic, which he connected with a form of zodiac worship. Many of the writings ascribed to Hermes that were read in the Middle Ages were transmitted through Islamic literature.

Numerology is the application of astral mathematics to aid in the understanding of the supernatural, or spiritual, sphere. The superiority of numbers to natural things was first proposed by Pythagoras, a Greek philosopher of the 6th century B.C. The interrelationship of planetary numbers and those ascribed to men was an aid in comprehending the powers of the heavenly spheres.

BIBLIOGRAPHY: M. Eliade, *The Forge and the Crucible* (New York, 1962); L. Thorndyke, *A History of Magic and Experimental Science*, Vol. I (New York, 1929).

**Astruc, Jean** (1684–1766). Noted French physician. In 1753, he published a book anonymously in which he argued that Genesis was a compilation of earlier documents that had originally been constructed as a harmony, with the various sources arranged in columns and later put in consecutive form by some ignorant copyist. He did not question that Moses had brought the material together, since he felt that this was proved by New Testament passages attributing Genesis to Moses.

**Athanasius** (c. 296–373). Bishop of Alexandria and Greek theologian. 1. *Life.* Born in Alexandria, probably educated at the catechetical school there, he served Alexander as deacon and secretary at Nicaea (325), achieving fame at that Council as a vigorous disputant against the Arians (Socrates Scholasticus, *Ecclesiastical History* 1. 8). In 328, he succeeded Alexander as bishop and during the next forty-five years he was exiled from his see five times for his Nicene orthodoxy in the political struggle between the Empire and the church. Of these forty-five years, he was in possession of his see less than twenty-eight. (*a*) Refusing to restore Arius to the communion of the church, he was deposed by the Synod of Tyre (335) upon accusation by the Melitians, and then exiled by Constantine to Treves. When Constantine died (337), he returned to Alexandria. (*b*) Deposed again by a synod at Antioch (339), he fled (340) and was granted asylum in Rome by Julius I. The Council of Sardica (c. 343) sought his restoration, but Constantius would not grant it until the death of the intruded Arian bishop Gregory (345). (*c*) At the behest of Constantius, the Synod of Milan deposed him

again, and this time he sought refuge among the Egyptian monks of the desert. For five years of this time until his death (361) George of Cappadocia held the see of Alexandria. Athanasius was recalled upon the accession of Emperor Julian. (*d*) At the Synod of Alexandria (362), Athanasius encouraged reconciliation between the Homoeans and the orthodox Nicene group, but he was forced from his see because of the animosity of Julian and remained in exile until the death of the emperor (363). (*e*) A brief four-month exile (365) was terminated by popular demand, and he remained in Alexandria thereafter as its bishop until his death. During this period, he gave strength to the new Nicene party which was to achieve such a resounding victory at the Council of Constantinople in 381.

2. *Writings.* By 318, he had written two short treatises, *Contra gentes* and *De incarnatione*, which actually form two parts of a single work. The former resembles the 2d-century apologies, and it expounds the folly of pagan worship while pointing out the truth of monotheism. The latter explicates in classical formulation the doctrine of redemption as held by the ancient church. By his union with man, the Logos restored the image of God in which man had been created; by death and resurrection, the Logos overcame death which is the consequence of sin. As opposed to the Arian cosmological outlook, Athanasius represents the peculiar soteriological concern of the ancient orthodox fathers. His most significant polemical work, *Tres orationes contra Arianos*, written between 339 and 359, consists of one book defending against the Arians the Nicene doctrine of the divinity of both the Father and the Son; the second and third books are devoted to a discussion of the Biblical passages quoted and used by the Arians together with an orthodox interpretation of these texts. These *orationes* are amply summarized in the *Epistola de decretis Nicaenae synodi* (c. 351), where the Nicene term *homoousion* ("of the same substance") is expounded in an attempt to effect some reunion between the large semi-Arian party and the more conservative Nicene party. The success of this move is proved by the action taken at the Council of Alexandria (362). Among his other letters are also to be found four addressed to Bishop Sarapion of Thmuis in which the divinity of the Holy Spirit is stoutly defended against the Macedonians; there are also three others written at the request of various synods. His exegetical works are for the most part no longer extant except for citation in the various patristic catenae. As an

advocate of Antony of Egypt, whom he had known personally and with whose monks he had passed his third exile, Athanasius composed the semilegendary *Vita Sancti Antonii.* This work served two purposes: it defended Antony from his detractors, and it served to introduce asceticism into the Western Church and to further its spread. In accordance with custom, as bishop of Alexandria, Athanasius composed each year when possible an Easter or Festal Letter notifying the church of the date of Easter and the beginning of the Lenten fast, and including other pastoral matters. A full Syriac translation of thirteen of them (329–348) is extant. The thirty-ninth one (367) is most important, since it contains a list of the canonical books of the Bible, setting forth for the first time the twenty-seven books of the New Testament in the order in which they now appear. A large number of works have circulated under the name of Athanasius, the most famous of which is the so-called Athanasian Creed (*Quicunque vult*), a poetic and polemical rendering of what purports to be the Nicene faith. Attributed to Athanasius from about the 7th century on, it was shown to be spurious in the 17th century when it became apparent that this hymnodic creed had probably been composed in Latin subsequent to the time of Athanasius. Its probable point of origin is Milan, and it may well have come from the pen of Ambrose or someone in the Ambrosian school, thus stemming from the late 4th or early 5th century.

3. *Theological viewpoint.* Athanasius shaped the direction of the Christological and the Trinitarian doctrines through his vigorous and clear exposition of the Logos doctrine. While he carefully evaded the subordinationism of the Monarchians and the error of the Adoptianists, his Christology veered close to Sabellianism as is demonstrated by the proximity of his Trinitarian exposition to that of the later condemned Marcellus of Ancyra. This particular stance, especially with regard to *homoousios*, opened a wedge for the later Monophysites. By far his greatest theological contribution lies in the relation of theology to philosophy; he stemmed the rising tide of complete Hellenization of the Christian faith in an age that was just beginning to learn how to use its newfound tools of classical antiquity. He was much more successful in this enterprise than Origen, and the measure of his attainment is to be gauged by the *De incarnatione.* Despite the value of his theological contributions, however, they were in large part determined by his combination of theological stance and political viewpoint.

His theological adaptability was much greater than that of the radicals of either side of the Nicene settlement. The victory at Constantinople in 381, which he forged at the Synod of Alexandria in 362, demonstrated how much more the church of the conciliar period was concerned to counter each threat in the terms in which it was presented than it was to arrive at a complete systematization of Christian doctrine. The alteration in the thrust of his theological viewpoint between 318 and 362 was a characteristic of the conciliar period and makes of him a model disputant in the controversies of that period. If not the greatest of the conciliarists, Athanasius was the most typical among those who defended the Christian experience against its detractors whether from the side of complete Hellenization or of complete obscurantism.

4. *Significance.* As a bishop, he ensured the preeminence of the patriarchate of Alexandria over the Egyptian Church and won for it a position of prime importance in the imperial ecclesiastical structure. Against the claims of the rising Constantinople, he asserted a power second to none in the Imperial Church and exceeded only by the see of Rome in the opening years of the Middle Ages. Both his apologetic works and his polemical *Vita Sancti Antonii* created new literary forms for the Christian church and became the models for many later beloved works in Christian literature, e.g., Gregory's study of Benedict of Nursia. He anticipated the theological outlook of his later contemporaries, the Cappadocian Fathers, in most of its significant aspects.

**Athenagoras I** (Aristokles Spirou, 1886– ). Ecumenical patriarch of Constantinople and *primus inter pares* ("first among equals") of the Eastern Orthodox patriarchs since 1948. Ordained a bishop in 1922, he became the archbishop of the Greek Orthodox Church of North and South America in 1931. Athenagoras and Pope Paul VI met in Jerusalem on January 6, 1964, to establish a dialogue for the promotion of unity. It was the first encounter of a pope and a patriarch of Constantinople since the Council of Florence in 1439. Noted for his ecumenical spirit, Athenagoras again met with Pope Paul VI in Istanbul, July 25, 1967. Later in the year, after visiting the Orthodox patriarchates of Belgrade, Bucharest, and Sofia, he ended his mission with a return visit to Pope Paul in Rome.

**Athenagoras of Athens** (2d century). An Apologist who addressed his *Embassy* to the emperor Marcus Aurelius and Commodus, his son and coemperor, probably in the year

177. Christians were being accused of godlessness, cannibalism, and sexual immorality. Athenagoras devoted most of his treatise to an analysis of Christian Trinitarian monotheism —partly in contrast to pagan polytheism, partly in agreement with the best insights of poets and philosophers—and then briefly refuted the charge of immoral behavior. His work, neglected by almost all later Christians, was preserved in a 10th-century manuscript of apologetic writings and was first printed in 1557. It is especially valuable for the relatively high level of literary culture that it reflects. Athenagoras belongs to the "loyalist" Christian group; he thanks the emperor for the "deep peace" which (at the moment) the world is enjoying, and draws an analogy between Marcus and Commodus and Father and Son in the Trinity. Another writing usually ascribed to him (as in the oldest manuscript) is the *Oration on the Resurrection of Corpses*. In style and method of argument this treatise differs considerably from the *Embassy,* and some scholars have regarded it as directed against the views of Origen and written in the 3d or even the 4th century. Since ancient writers were proud of their ability to use different styles, the case is not settled.

**Athos, Mt.** A mountain at the tip of a peninsula that projects about thirty-five miles into the Aegean Sea from the coast of Macedonia. The peninsula belongs to twenty virtually independent monasteries of the Eastern Orthodox Church. It is famous for the medieval customs of the monks and for valuable collections of ancient manuscripts and Byzantine art.

**Atrium.** The entrance court of Roman houses. In Christian architecture it is a large court in front of the church, surrounded by colonnades. Usually there is a fountain in the center, where worshipers may wash themselves before entering the church. Penitents who were not admitted to the nave were allowed to gather there. The atrium was often used as a cemetery.

**Attila** (*known as* "the Scourge of God") (d. 453). From A.D. 433 chief of the Huns, the Mongol tribes who then dominated central Europe. After subjecting the Eastern Empire to tribute he invaded Gaul, but was defeated by Romans and Visigoths at the Catalaunian Fields (Battle of Châlons) in A.D. 451. In 452, when Attila invaded Italy, a delegation headed by Pope Leo I met the Huns, persuading Attila to withdraw beyond the Danube —perhaps mainly for military reasons, but the episode reflects the prestige of the church.

After Attila's death in 453 his empire rapidly dissolved.

**Auburn Affirmation** (1924). A document reflecting the fundamentalist-modernist controversy in American Presbyterianism. The *Affirmation* protested the action of the previous General Assembly in reaffirming the necessity of accepting certain "essential doctrines of the Word of God." It asserted that these formulations were theories and not the only interpretations allowed by Scripture and the Reformed confessions, and called for a spirit of toleration in the denomination.

**Auctorem Fidei** (1794). A bull issued by Pius VI condemning eighty-five articles of the Synod of Pistoia. This Synod, convened in Tuscany in 1786 under the leadership of Bishop Ricci, denied the right of the pope to intervene in civil affairs, held that ecclesiastical authority comes directly from the church at large, and condemned the use of Latin in the service. The proposals aroused considerable opposition, and following their condemnation in 1794, Ricci recanted.

**Audiani.** An anticlerical movement of the 4th century which broke away from the church over the worldliness of the clergy. It was founded by Audius, who himself was a layman. The members also favored the Antiochene method of dating the "Paschal Moon" condemned by Nicaea (325) and may have had an anthropomorphic view of God. After their schism they were banished to Scythia, where they evangelized the Goths. The movement survived into the 5th century.

**Aufklärung.** See ENLIGHTENMENT.

**Augsburg, Diets of** (1518–1555). Assemblies of the Estates of the (German) Holy Roman Empire held in Augsburg. In the period from 1518 to 1555, five assemblies were held. The first, in 1518, is notable for the interview of Martin Luther conducted by Cardinal Cajetan, papal legate at the Diet. The renowned general of the Dominicans failed to obtain a recantation of Luther's views expressed in the Ninety-five Theses. The second Diet, in 1525, was poorly attended, the Peasants' Revolt than demanding full attention. At the third, in 1530, the Lutheran princes and cities of the Empire presented the Augsburg Confession, drafted by Philip Melanchthon, to Emperor Charles V as their statement of faith. A papal Confutation was hastily written at the Diet to refute the Confession, which became the creedal standard in all Lutheran territories. The fourth Diet prepared the Augsburg Interim in 1548 to provide a compromise solution to the religious division of the Empire. Its Romanist bias defeated its intent. The final Diet (1555) promulgated the Peace of Augsburg, which ended open warfare temporarily and gave legal recognition to Lutheranism as a religion of the Empire. Other forms of Protestantism were still illegal. It also divided the Empire religiously according to the faith of the ruling prince, the principle later designated by the formula *Cuius regio, eius religio* ("Whoever rules, his religion").

**Augsburg, Peace of** (1555). The political settlement within the German Empire of the religious issues raised by the Protestant Reformation. It was concluded on Sept. 25, 1555, by the German electors and Ferdinand I, brother of Emperor Charles V. The strong position of Charles after the Smalcald War (1546–1547) was weakened by the return of Maurice of Saxony to Lutheranism and by the Peace of Passau (1552), which granted recognition to Lutheranism. The Diet of Augsburg laid down the conditions for peace between Roman Catholics and "the Estates belonging to the Augsburg Confession." All Roman Catholic spiritual jurisdiction in Protestant territory was suspended. Confiscated "spiritual" Estates not belonging to the emperor were to remain Protestant. Religious freedom was granted to the secular princes under the principle (later expressed in the formula, *Cuius regio, eius religio*) that the religion of each territory was to be determined by the ruling prince. But the conversion of a bishop or "spiritual" prince, to the Augsburg Confession meant the loss of his spiritual office and dignity and of the imperial fief. The lines were drawn between the two communions along strictly territorial lines. What gains the Protestant Reformation had made were thus secured, but further advance was checked. Moreover, individual religious liberty was not considered: other Protestants, who had not signed the Augsburg Confession, were not recognized.

**Augsburg Confession** (1530). The basic confessional statement of Lutheranism, written by Philip Melanchthon on behalf of the Protestant territories of northern Germany for presentation to Emperor Charles V at the Diet of Augsburg on June 25, 1530. Acceptance of this confession became the sign of the acceptance of Lutheranism in a particular territory.

In spite of papal excommunication (1520) and the imperial ban on his person and his books (1521), Martin Luther's reforming ideals spread rapidly through Europe. Not until 1529, however, was the emperor able to give attention to the growing rift between the papal and Evangelical parties. At the Diet of Speyer in the spring of that year, strict adherence to the 1521 Edict was required of the Evangelical princes and Estates. However, they were successful in lodging a formal protest (from which "protestant" is derived) demanding a hearing for their point of view. The emperor then called for a Diet of the Empire to meet at Augsburg in the spring of 1530 to hear the parties to the dispute.

Elector John of Saxony asked Luther, Melanchthon, Justus Jonas, and Johann Bugenhagen to draw up formal articles citing abuses in the church. These were presented to him at Torgau. Then there appeared 404 articles written by John Eck showing the Reformers to be guilty of ancient heresies. To counteract this assertion, Melanchthon prepared twenty-one articles, largely based on the Schwabach Articles approved by the Lutheran territories in 1529, to show that the Evangelical faith was the faith of the ancient church. With the addition of a preface by Saxon Chancellor Brück and the approval of Luther (although he commented that he could not "tread so lightly"), the full confession was read to the emperor in German on Saturday afternoon, June 25, by the Saxon vice-chancellor, Dr. Baier.

Melanchthon, wishing it to be an instrument for restoring the unity of the church, seemed willing to compromise some sections in favor of the papal position, but the princes would not allow it. The next year Melanchthon completed his *Apology for the Augsburg Confession* in reply to the Roman Catholic Confutation. Later, however, he felt it necessary to revise the confession itself. The most important of these revisions, the *variata* edition of 1540, marked a change in Melanchthon's view of the Lord's Supper, but his alterations were eventually judged unacceptable to most Lutherans (see CRYPTO-CALVINISM). The "Unaltered Augsburg Confession presented to the Emperor Charles V in 1530" has been the identifying confession of Lutheran churches to the present time.

The first twenty-one articles, the "doctrinal" articles for which Melanchthon drew on the Schwabach Articles of 1529, are designed to show the continuity between the Evangelical faith and that of historic Christendom. Doctrines concerning God, Jesus Christ, sin, the church, the ministry, the Lord's Supper, Baptism, free will, civil affairs, ecclesiastical order, and Christ's return were acceptable to the papal theologians of 1530 and continue today to demonstrate the common elements in the doctrines of the Roman Catholic and the Protestant Churches. However, other articles on justification, good works, the new obedience, confession, and repentance showed the effects of Luther's teaching on these subjects, as did the statements on the use of the sacraments and the proper honor due the saints.

The second section, seven articles dealing with abuses in the church which the Lutheran Reformers were working to remove, was fashioned from the articles presented by the Wittenberg theologians to their elector at Torgau in 1530. They call for both bread and wine to be given to laymen in Communion, for the removal of prohibitions regarding the marriage of priests, for cessation of the worst abuses in connection with the Mass (such as private Masses, endowed Masses, and the like), for a return to a type of confession that consoles consciences instead of burdening them, for dispensation from observance of human traditions regarding food and abstinence, for the easing of monastic vows and denial of their meritorious status, and for the limiting of the bishops' powers to spiritual matters. Throughout these latter articles, merit is denied to man's works and traditions, and the grace of God in Christ is stressed. Not until the Council of Trent (1545–1563) did Roman Catholicism make a definitive reply. Today the Augsburg Confession still symbolizes the faith of millions of Lutherans around the world. The edition of 1540 was widely accepted, even by the Reformed Church.

BIBLIOGRAPHY: F. Bente, "Historical Introductions," *Triglot Concordia* (St. Louis, 1921); M. Reu (ed.), *The Augsburg Confession* (Chicago, 1930); T. Tappert (ed.), *The Book of Concord* (Philadelphia, 1959).

**Augsburg Interim.** The provisional decree of the Diet of Augsburg (1548) imposing a religious settlement of Reformation disputes until a final determination in these matters could be made by a general council of the church. The victory of Emperor Charles V in the Smalcald War (1546–1547) enabled him to impose conditions favorable to Roman Catholicism on the Protestant Estates, but he could not ignore all the Evangelical demands without risk of further strife. He appointed Bishop Michael Helding, Bishop Julius von Pflug, and Evangelical theologian Johann Agricola to draft the agreement. The twenty-six articles they prepared were then revised by a team of Spanish monks and presented to the Protestant electors and to prominent Roman Catholics. Although favoring Roman Catholicism, the Interim did permit the cup to be given to the laity, the marriage of clergy, and a slight limitation of papal authority. The Roman Catholic princes would not be bound by it, but Charles enforced it vigorously against the Evangelicals in south-ern Germany. In Saxony the return of Elector Maurice to Lutheranism prevented its enforcement, and a modified form, the Leipzig Interim, was permitted there. It was accepted by Philip Melanchthon, but resisted by some. Both Interims were terminated with the Peace of Passau (1552).

**Augustine** (Aurelius Augustinus) (354–430). The most influential of the fathers of the Western Church. He was born at Tagaste, a small town in Roman Africa, Nov. 15, 354. His father, Patricius, was a leading local citizen, still pagan; his mother, Monnica, a devout Christian. Enrolled as a catechumen but not baptized, Augustine was related to the church but not a full member of it during the thirty years of growth and spiritual struggle later recalled and reflected on in his *Confessions.* Family and friends encouraged him to study for the career of rhetorician, which meant becoming a teacher of literature and philosophy as well as oratory, at Tagaste, at the larger town of Madaura, and finally in 372 at Carthage. Here all his problems found tentative solutions. A now lost work of Cicero's, *Hortensius,* converted him to the Platonic ideal of the beauty of the good, but for some years he embraced the Manichaean faith, whose dualism seemed both to explain theological and Biblical difficulties and to excuse moral lapses among those who were merely "hearers" as distinct from the "elect," the ascetics of the sect. Augustine took a mistress, who became the mother of his only child, Adeodatus ("gift of God," the Latin for "Theodore"). Augustine taught briefly at Tagaste, then at Carthage, and in 382 left for Rome, followed by his mother's prayers. Meanwhile he abandoned Manichaeanism for Platonism in its Neoplatonic form, theistic and mystical; but its remote deity did not give him the strength for moral discipline, which he came to admire in Christians. He was struck by the increasing trend of intellectuals toward Christianity, but it was the pagan leader Symmachus who recommended him in 384 for a professorship at Milan.

At Milan, the headquarters of Western emperors, Bishop Ambrose was a leading figure in both church and state. Augustine's own crisis approached. Monnica joined him, hoping that he would settle down respectably. He separated from his mistress (but briefly took another) and, inspired by Ambrose's preaching and example, began to see that the call to faith would mean for him a life of continence. On a summer day in 386 he heard a child's voice in an adjoining garden say, "Pick it up and read it"—and the summons came in the words of Rom. 13:13–14.

During the fall vacation, Augustine ended his academic career. With Monnica, Adeodatus, and a group of friends, he spent some time in a scholarly retreat at Cassiciacum, near Milan. At Easter, 387, he was baptized by Ambrose and started home. On the way Monnica died at Ostia, the port of Rome, now content at being the mother of a saint instead of a professor. On his return to Africa in 388, Augustine and his friends formed a semi-monastic community at Tagaste. Several of his associates were called to the episcopate, and Adeodatus died in 390. In 391, Augustine visited the city of Hippo on the coast, and popular demand secured his ordination as presbyter to assist Bishop Valerius, a Greek who found it hard to preach in Latin. Lest their brilliant preacher should be called elsewhere, the congregation in 395 secured Augustine's consecration as coadjutor to Valerius, whom he succeeded in 396. For the rest of his life he was not only pastor, preacher, and administrator at Hippo but a prominent figure in the councils of the African Church, partly because of his close friendship with Bishop Aurelius of Carthage.

Augustine's voluminous writings reflect his varied interests, partly successive, partly overlapping. He first came to terms with his own past. Largely at Cassiciacum he produced the philosophical dialogues that began to Christianize his Platonism: *On Order* (in creation), *Against the Academics* (the skeptics who controlled the Academy at Athens), *On Free Will,* and the *Soliloquies* addressed to God. Though his interests later changed, he renounced only minor parts of his early writings in the *Retractations* issued toward the end of his life. To the 390's belong the anti-Manichaean writings that attack the Manichaean idea of evil as a self-existent force, and its theological and ethical corollaries. Yet Augustine always retained a vivid sense of the conflict of good and evil in the world and in the soul, which can be considered a legacy of his Manichaean period.

Much of the first twenty years of Augustine's ministry was devoted to the conflict with Donatism, the African sect that claimed to be the true church of the martyrs, and had become the expression of North African nationalism. Numerous writings set forth Augustine's position, ranging from the popular *Psalm Against the Donatists* to the learned treatise *On Baptism.* He argued against the Donatists that the true church is the world-wide catholic communion, and is not composed only of saints. On the other hand, Augustine, unlike his opponents, recognized the formal validity of schismatic sacraments, so

that converts from Donatism did need to be rebaptized or reordained. Although Donatism was divided and beginning to decline, the efforts of Augustine and others had little effect in winning its adherents. To the Roman Government, Donatism was a political as well as a religious problem, since it had a revolutionary wing, and the Donatist hierarchy had supported separatist movements. After the failure of a grand conference presided over by imperial commissioners in 411, legal penalties were imposed on Donatists, which Augustine reluctantly supported. Donatism became unimportant, but its history is of permanent interest in connection with the theology of the church and the sacraments, and the problems of the relation of the church to nation and state.

Augustine's numerous sermons and letters contain much of his theological and ethical teaching, and reflect as well his pastoral labors. Many of his sermons relate to days in the church year and various pastoral occasions; others expound large parts of the New Testament, especially the great series of *Tractates on John.* These are fairly literal, while the *Thoughts on the Psalms,* largely made up of sermons preached at Hippo or Carthage, are highly allegorical. The hand of the old rhetorician appears not only in Augustine's style, adapted to the occasion, but in his systematic works on methods of Christian preaching and teaching. Though he was not strictly a monk, two of his letters, giving advice to a community of nuns at Hippo (*Letters* 210–211), were later used as the Rule of St. Augustine, and the common life he lived with his friends at Tagaste and later with his clergy at Hippo was the inspiration of the semimonastic Augustinian Canons. His letters include many on official business, many replies to inquirers on problems of faith and conduct, and a long exchange on Biblical questions with Jerome.

The last defenders of Roman paganism argued for their faith as not only a sound religion, but also as one under which Rome had grown great. This double issue was brought to a head by the Gothic sack of Rome in 410. Augustine began to comment on the crisis, and in the next fifteen years expanded his thoughts into *The City of God.* In ten books he defends Christianity and attacks paganism, popular or philosophical, and then in twelve more develops a philosophy of history based on the conflict of the two cities, that of God and that of the world. The powers of love and selfishness, of which church and empire are the visible expressions, have struggled since the fall of the angels, and will remain mixed together until finally separated in heaven and hell. In its effort to recognize the ambiguities of human existence, Augustine's great work has inspired many varieties of Christian thought on history and politics. To the same period belongs Augustine's one formal theological work, *On the Trinity,* though even here there was an immediate occasion for it in the revival of Arianism among Germanic soldiers and invaders.

Among the refugees from Rome who passed through Africa was the British monk Pelagius, with whom Augustine soon began his last great controversy. Pelagius and his followers appealed to man to use his own freedom to do the right, whereas Augustine had found this freedom only as a gift of divine love. In this conflict of two understandings of religion the opponents were forced to extreme positions, until in his last works Augustine comes close to the absolute predestinarianism which a series of admirers have found in him, from the Gallican Augustinians of the 5th century to Calvin in the 16th century and the Jansenists in the 17th century. Some consider this the crown of his teaching; others see in it the weariness of an old man. One should in any case remember that for Augustine the central act of redemption is always the victory of love in the "one mediator between God and men, the man Christ Jesus" (I Tim. 2:5, his favorite Christological text). Unity in love is his central theme—in God, in man, in state and church; and this he had found for himself when his restless spirit came to rest in God (*Confessions* 1.1). Against Pelagius, Augustine welcomed the support of the venerated Roman see, though he did not hesitate to challenge the apparent support of Pelagianism by Pope Zosimus in 417–418 when he probably drafted the firm letter *Optaremus* in which the African Church protested against Zosimus' inept interference in a judicial case, while not absolutely denying his rights in the matter.

Under the weak rule of Honorius (395–423), the Roman Empire in the West began to break up, though contemporaries could scarcely envisage its end. The Goths entered Spain, the Vandals passed farther south and ravaged the province still called Andalusia, and after Honorius' death Count Boniface, with whom Augustine had corresponded on the duties of a Christian soldier, rebelled in Africa against the central authority. The Vandals saw their opportunity—it may be, as alleged, that Boniface had foolishly invited them—and invaded the wealthy African provinces. Carthage and Hippo alone held out while Augustine lay on his deathbed in a town crowded with refugees—the penitential psalms written on the walls for him to read, and his last anti-Pelagian treatise incomplete (the "unfinished work," *Opus imperfectum,* against Julian of Eclanum). So he died, on Aug. 28, 430, an invitation to the Council of Ephesus arriving too late. With him the great days of the ancient African Church were over, though it did survive under Vandal persecution and Byzantine domination; but it left behind the influence of its greatest leader, secure in his place as an outstanding teacher of the Western Church. The Christian East knows him as a saint; but in theology it has not so much rejected his answers as failed to be interested in his questions.

**Augustine, Rule of St.** The name applied to three different documents: Augustine's Letter 211, addressed to a community of women in his diocese; the *Regula Secunda,* a brief description of monastic discipline; and the *Regula Tertia,* a longer adaptation of Letter 211 for use by a community of men. From the 6th century on, the two *Regulae* appear together in manuscripts and are called the Rule of St. Augustine. Only Letter 211 seems to be written by Augustine himself. The provenance and authorship of the *Regulae* are uncertain, but they seem to be nearly contemporary with Augustine. The rule was common through the 7th century when the common life of the clergy began to decline. It was known to Benedict of Aniane, who included it in his *Concordia Regularum.* With the revival of the common life among the canons regular in the 11th century, the rule became the standard of observance, although *Regula Secunda* was frequently omitted. The rule provides general regulations for a religious community, allowing considerable latitude for the development of differing customs of observance among the orders that use it. It is the basic discipline of the Augustinian canons and friars, the Premonstratensian canons, the Dominicans, the Servites, and several communities of women.

**Augustine of Canterbury** (d. c. 604). First archbishop of Canterbury, known as the "Apostle of the English." He was a monk at the monastery in Rome when Pope Gregory I chose him to head the mission to England for which the way had been opened by the Christian wife of King Ethelbert of Kent. In 597, Augustine arrived in Kent, and shortly after achieved the conversion of the king and many of his people. He was given a residence at Canterbury, consecrated to the episcopate at Arles, and returned to Canterbury as its first archbishop. Augustine was a typical Roman ecclesiastic of the period—conscientious and devoted, but lacking in diplomacy and imagination. He referred many problems to the pope, but did not follow Gregory's suggestions that local customs might be adopted in the church in England. Instead, Canterbury became a little Rome, with its cathedral, monastery, shrines, and schools, and a suffragan bishopric at Rochester. Augustine alienated the Welsh bishops, over whom he attempted to claim authority. In 604, he sent Mellitus as bishop to London, but Mellitus lost his see in a pagan reaction some years later. Augustine died in 604, or not long after, since his successor, Laurentius, was in office by 608. With all his limitations, Augustine had laid firm foundations for organized church life in England. From the fusion of the Roman tradition with the more enthusiastic if less disciplined Celtic mission was to come the Church of the English.

**Augustinian** (Austin) **Canons.** A general term describing those communities of canons regular which followed the Rule of St. Augustine. The revival of the common life in the West is contemporary with the reform movement centering about Gregory VII (Hildebrand). In France at St. Ruf in 1039, canons were established who lived a common life of absolute poverty. The same life was being promoted in northern Italy in the middle of the 11th century, primarily through the influence of Peter Damian. The Lateran Synod of 1059 discussed the matter of apostolic poverty among canons. Hildebrand urged the condemnation of those portions of the Aachen Rule which permitted canons to hold private property. The Synod, however, decided only to encourage poverty, not to require it. The Synod of 1063 recommended it also. The movement that had been developing in Italy and France was thus given formal approval by the church.

At this time there did not seem to be any observance of the Rule of St. Augustine. The common life of apostolic poverty was simply called the "Life of the Fathers" (*Vita Patrum*). It was justified by appeals to early councils and the writings of the fathers, especially Jerome and Augustine. Early references to canons living under the Rule of St. Augustine did not therefore imply that they followed the text now known by that title, but rather that they observed the ascetical and disciplinary ideas found in the writings of Augustine and other early authors. When the actual text of the Rule of St. Augustine was first used is uncertain, but it may have been by 1067 in the province of Reims. Its use

is well attested after the beginning of the 12th century. The *Regula Tertia* was the standard of observance, supplemented by the customs of several of the larger houses. The customary of St. Ruf was widely practiced. The directives of the *Regula Secunda* were regarded by some as more authentically Augustinian and were adopted as the basis of a more rigorous life. The first house to do so was Springiersbach, which developed austere customs of fasts, abstinence, silence, and dress. White replaced the traditional black dress. Influenced by this reform, St. Norbert of Xanten adopted many of these severe customs for his Premonstratensian canons. These conflicting ideals of the canonical life caused much disagreement among the canons themselves, as well as between the monks and canons, the more austere life of canons being indistinguishable from that of reformed monks. With greater emphasis upon the contemplative life, the performance of pastoral duties, long a part of the life of the canons, was seen to detract from their calling. However, the mixed life, with pastoral care in the world and a common life of contemplation, persisted for most canons. Secular canons felt threatened by these reforms, fearing that zeal for poverty among regular canons might undermine their rights to private incomes. Eventually the rights of both regulars and seculars were guaranteed by papal decrees.

Strictly speaking, there was no single order of Augustinian canons. Houses were organized into congregations, following the customs of the motherhouse. The largest congregations were those of Prémontré, the Lateran, St. Ruf, St. Quentin of Beauvais, Springiersbach, St. Victor of Paris, Windesheim, and the Gilbertines of England. A general chapter met annually at the motherhouse. The superior of a house was known by several different titles. In France the title of abbot was common, although such a monastic title was shunned by canons elsewhere. In Italy the title was prior; in Germany, provost.

The canons were noted for their piety and scholarship. In the 12th century, a school of mystical theology developed at St.-Victor in Paris. The congregation of Windesheim produced the great mystics of the 15th century, Thomas à Kempis and Gerhard Groote.

Communities of women were founded following the customs of various houses of canons. In some areas, double houses were common.

The dispersions and suppressions of the Reformation, the religious wars, and political revolutions have greatly reduced the number of houses of canons regular. Of the great medieval congregations, only the Premonstratensian and Lateran canons survive.

BIBLIOGRAPHY: J. C. Dickinson, *The Origins of the Austin Canons* (London, 1950).

**Augustinian Friars** (*or* Eremites of St. Augustine). A mendicant order founded in 1256 by a merger of several small Italian orders. The constitution resembled that of the Dominicans, although the friars followed the Rule of St. Augustine. The order spread throughout Europe and underwent several reforms. Martin Luther was a member of the German congregation of the order. Although it suffered great losses during the Reformation, the order continues to exist today.

**Augustinus Triumphus** (d. 1328). An Italian Augustinian who dedicated a famous polemical work, *Summa de potestate ecclesiastica,* to Pope John XXII c. 1322, containing the most extreme assertions as to the power and extensiveness of the papal monarchy. Pope and church are identified in the most extraordinary fashion. The pope is literally taken to be both pope and emperor with ordinary, direct, and plenipotentiary power over all bishops and princes.

**Aulén, Gustav E. H.** (1879–    ). Swedish churchman and theologian. In 1913 he was appointed professor of systematic theology at the University of Lund and in 1933 became bishop of Strängnäs. His chief theological concern is to find the essential Christian motifs behind a doctrine rather than to emphasize its particular form. He is most widely known for his Olaus Petri Lectures of 1930, which appeared in an abridged English version as *Christus Victor.*

**Aumbry** (*sometimes* "ambry"). A niche or closet in the wall of the sanctuary used in medieval times for storing sacred vessels, relics, or books. Sometimes, in the early Middle Ages, the reserved Sacrament was kept in it, but this practice has been abolished in the Roman Catholic Church. (See SACRAMENT HOUSE; TABERNACLE.)

**Au Milieu des Sollicitudes.** An encyclical issued by Pope Leo XIII in 1892. Written in French to avoid misinterpretation, it emphasizes the compatibility of Catholic doctrine with any form of government. Its intent was to urge French Catholics to accept the Third Republic, using their voting power to repeal the antireligious laws and prevent the separation of church and state. The majority failed to respond and continued to support efforts to reestablish the monarchy.

**Aurora.** See PETER RIGA.

**Ausonius.** Roman scholar and poet. He was born 310 in Bordeaux, where he became a teacher of grammar and rhetoric, and exchanged versified letters with his pupil and friend, Paulinus of Nola. A nominal Christian, he tutored Gratian, whom he served in civil office. His popular verses, though technically of superior quality, are pedestrian in content.

**Autocephalous.** A term used in the early church to describe bishops who were independent of any superior authority. Those bishops who did not come under the jurisdiction of a patriarch or metropolitan were the bishops of Cyprus, Armenia, and Iberia. Many of the newly converted Slav princes sought to establish independent churches. The Bulgarian khan Boris converted to Christianity in 864, and wanted to establish an autocephalous church. Although Byzantium reserved the right to consecrate the archbishop of Bulgaria, it held only nominal rule over the Slav Church. The conversion of the Kievan Grand Prince Vladimir in 987 or 988 seems to have left Russia for a time an autocephalous church. Consecrations of the Russian metropolitans did not begin until 1037. In 1448, Russia began to choose its own metropolitans, and in the late 16th century, the regent Boris Godunov created the Russian patriarchate.

Today "autocephalous" is used to describe those churches governed by their own synods and in communion with Constantinople. They are Russia, Constantinople, Antioch, Greece, Alexandria, Jerusalem, Cyprus, Bulgaria, Albania, Georgia, and the Serbian Church in Yugoslavia.

**Auxentius** (d. 373 or 374). Bishop of Milan. Cappadocian by birth, and Arian in theology, he was appointed bishop of Milan in 355 by Constantius. Hilary of Poitiers tried unsuccessfully to have him removed (364), but he remained bishop until his death when Ambrose succeeded him. Among works attributed to him is the *Epistola de fide, vita et obitu Wulfilae,* preserved in *Dissertatio contra Ambrosium,* which was composed in 383 by Maximinus, the Gothic and Arian opponent of Ambrose.

**L'Avenir** ("The Future"). A newspaper published in 1830–1831 by Lamennais and his associates Lacordaire and Montalembert. It sought to publicize the ideals of "Liberal Catholicism." Advocating democratic forms and liberties, these men believed that the church could more successfully control civil government through the Catholic masses than through a monarchy. The papacy was not yet ready for this tactic, and the paper was condemned by Gregory XVI in 1832.

**Averroës** (1126–1198). Arabian philosopher. One of the chief channels for the transmission of Aristotle's thought to Western scholars, and known by them as "the Commentator." Born at Cordova, he studied law, mathematics, theology, medicine, and philosophy, and became a judge and then physician to the caliph. He considered Aristotle the culmination of human intellect and devoted much of his life to making Aristotle's work intelligible to his contemporaries by means of three sets of commentaries. However, the impossibility of professing a belief in God as a mechanistic prime mover in the eternity of matter and in the unicity of the human intellect while avoiding charges of heresy from the Moslem orthodox led him to attempt a formal reconciliation of his beliefs with Islam. His formula provided that the same truth could be understood rationally in philosophy and allegorically in theology. Thus the Koran was seen to communicate by metaphor to the unlearned those truths which the learned could comprehend by analysis. This meant the subordination of the inspired text to the opinions of rationalizing philosophers, and in 1195, Averroës was exiled, the study of Greek philosophy was banned, and the books of logic and metaphysics were burned by order of the caliph. Having been stripped of all his honors, Averroës died in Morocco.

**Averroism.** In Christian philosophy a term applied less to the system of Averroës than to certain beliefs held by a group of teachers at the University of Paris, notably Siger of Brabant, Boethius of Dacia, and Bernier of Nivelles, who followed the interpretation of Aristotle advocated by Averroës. This included the beliefs that the eternity of the world can be philosophically demonstrated; that terrestrial events are determined by the heavenly bodies, thus denying Providence; that there can have been no first man; and that the rational soul, including the passive as well as the active intellect, is common to all men and survives death, thus denying individual immortality and individual moral responsibility. Attacked by Bonaventure and by Thomas Aquinas, who urged that Averroës had falsified Aristotle, the Averroists were forced to reply that they were only reporting Aristotle's words, or that if the irrefutable conclusions of reason in the natural order were incompatible with the revealed truths of the supernatural order, there must exist two kinds of truth. Etienne Tempier's condemnation in 1277 crushed Averroism in

Paris, but it survived in Padua until the 17th century in various forms. With John of Jandun stressing the divorce of theology from philosophy, and Marsilius of Padua that of the church from the state, the most durable contribution of Averroism to European intellectual life was the secularizing of natural science.

**Avicenna** (980–1037). Arab physician and creator of the first systematic Islamic philosophy. Born near Bokara, he was a child prodigy and by the age of sixteen had mastered Islamic theology and Greek science and was a practicing physician. He taught medicine and philosophy at Isaphan, was vizier to several sultans, and wrote over a hundred books. His *Canon of Medicine,* which gave universal currency to the belief that there was a close connection between the four humors in man and the four natural elements, was a standard textbook in Europe until c. 1500. His *Book of Healing,* a huge summary of Aristotle complemented by Neoplatonic metaphysics, exercised great influence on Scholastic philosophers. By fusing the mechanistic cosmos of Aristotle with the hierarchical, emanative universe of Proclus, he presented Greek science in a form acceptable to Christian tradition. He bridged the gap between the unity of God and the multiplicity of creation by showing God as absolute love creating via ten Intelligences, which gave motion to the ten celestial spheres, the last Intelligence giving form to matter in the sublunary sphere and acting as the active intellect in man, which communicates to the passive, individual intellect its knowledge of universals. Thus, physics, psychology, and theology were combined. His influence in Europe was felt most through three themes: matter as the principle of individuation; the relation between knowledge and illumination; and the relation between essence and existence.

**Avignon.** A town in southern France, the residence of the popes from 1309 to 1377. This so-called "Babylonian Captivity" of the papacy actually climaxed a long period of French influence on the Holy See. After the death of Boniface VIII, who had been humiliated by Philip IV of France, and the death of Benedict XI, who was more conciliatory in manner, the cardinals chose as pope Bertrand de Got (Clement V), who was intimidated by Philip and moved his residence to Avignon in 1309. Clement's successors John XXII, Benedict XII, Clement VI, Innocent VI, Urban V, and Gregory XI also lived at Avignon; Clement VI bought the town from Naples in 1348. The Avignon papacy did not enjoy a good reputation in the Christian world, partly because it was so dominated by the French king and partly because of its preoccupation with financial matters, particularly the taxation of ecclesiastical persons and property. Meanwhile, however, Rome was slipping into ruin and anarchy. At the urging of Petrarch, Bridget of Sweden, and Catherine of Siena, Gregory XI returned to Rome in 1377. Though he meant to go back to Avignon, he died in Rome the following year; the papal court thus found itself influenced by the Roman populace in its choice of a successor. The papacy remained at Rome, but the circumstances surrounding the election of Urban VI gave rise to the Great Western Schism.

**Avvakum** (c. 1620–1681). Russian archpriest, author, and leader of the conservative party in the Russian Church. He refused to conform when Patriarch Nikon revised the Russian service books according to the Greek forms and insisted on the use of three fingers instead of two in making the sign of the cross. Although condemned by the Council of Moscow in 1667 and eventually burned at the stake, he was revered by the masses. His autobiography has achieved a permanent place in Russian literature.

**Azariah, Vedanayakam Samuel** (1874–1945). Indian Christian leader. He was consecrated bishop of Dornakal in 1912, the first native Indian to become an Anglican bishop. He emphasized lay evangelism, self-support for native churches, and worked for a union of Protestant churches in India. Believing that Christianity must be presented in a way natural to the Indian people, he used Indian customs and tunes in worship and viewed the "mass movement" as the logical pattern of conversion in native villages.

# B

**Baader, Franz Xaver von** (1765–1841). Leading theologian of the early 19th-century German Catholic revival. Originally a mining engineer, he traveled to England in 1792, where he was introduced to the mysticism of the 17th-century Jakob Boehme. In 1820, he abandoned his successful mining career to devote himself to theology. His masterpiece, *Fermenta cognitionis* (1822–1825), combated the fundamental position of the German idealist philosophers and won him a chair of philosophy and theology at the newly organized university at Munich, Catholic rival to the Protestant university in Berlin. Proving to be an annoyance to the Crown, Baader was silenced in 1838 on the flimsy grounds that a layman should not lecture on theology. Although he left no systematic body of his ideas, he believed that authority and faith were found only in the Roman Catholic Church. Direct individual communication with the state resulted in anarchy. He felt that the true Catholic position had been preserved in the East, and his book *Eastern and Western Catholicism* (1841) was recently declared by one enthusiast to be "the greatest ecumenical writing of the 19th century." Although conservative in politics, Baader ascribed revolution to the poverty of the masses.

**Babylas** (d. c. 250). Martyr under Decius. While bishop of Antioch he is supposed to have refused Philip the Arabian entrance to the church and Holy Communion unless the emperor joined the ranks of the penitents. The story is doubtful, since it is unlikely that Philip was a Christian, although he and his wife did receive letters from Origen. The presence of the remains of Babylas in the sacred groves of Daphne on the Orontes were thought to interfere with the oracle and they were ordered removed by Julian the Apostate. Chrysostom was the eulogist of Babylas.

**Babylonian Captivity of the Church.** A phrase, derived from Petrarch, used to describe the papal residence at Avignon in the south of France (but not subject to the French Crown) from 1309 to 1377. There were seven Avignonese pontiffs, all French: Clement V (1305–1314); John XXII (1316–1334); Benedict XII (1334–1342); Clement VI (1342–1352); Blessed Urban V (1362–1370); and Gregory XI (1370–1378).

Clement V was forced to stay in France for several reasons, most important the delicate negotiations with Philip the Fair over the threatened posthumous trial of Boniface VIII for heresy, the suppression of the Templars, and the Council of Vienne. His successors remained in France because of constant disorder in Italy, their interest in attempting to end the Hundred Years' War between France and England, their conflict with the emperor Louis the Bavarian, and their natural preference, as Frenchmen, for the south of France. Their ties to and dependence upon the French court were important, but they were less puppets of Paris than has been supposed. The charges of great corruption (also dependent upon publicists such as Petrarch), although to some extent true, are exaggerated.

Increasing need for funds drove the popes to centralize ecclesiastical appointments in their own hands and to derive all possible income from the process of appointment. This led to the development of a highly sophisticated market in ecclesiastical futures (e.g., provisions and expectancies) which in turn attracted many office seekers to Avignon and led to or aggravated many abuses, such as influence-peddling, bribery, pluralism, and nonresidence (although not with the connivance of the popes). These tendencies are especially evident in the reigns of John XXII, one of the greatest of papal financiers, and of Clement VI. The money was needed for war in Italy, but also for great international projects (such as crusades) and for financing the great papal bureaucracy that had grown up in furtherance of the leadership of the papacy in the reform of the church and in the organization of ecclesiastical law and justice. Yet these developments led to conflict with temporal rulers (e.g., Statutes of Provisors and Praemunire in England), with extreme reformers within the church (e.g., the Spiritual Franciscans, William of Occam, Marsilius of Padua, and John Wycliffe), and with the Italian patriots (such as Petrarch and Catherine of Siena), who wished to see the papacy return to Rome. Blessed Urban V returned (1367–1370) but did not stay. Gregory XI, after much preparation, took the papacy back to Rome in 1377. His death there was followed by the Great Western Schism.

**Bach, Johann Sebastian** (1685–1750). German Lutheran composer, from a distinguished musical family. Born at Eisenach, Bach was orphaned at ten and blind at death. He was married twice and had twenty children. Serving as a choirboy in Lüneburg after 1700, he studied under Buxtehude in Lübeck in 1705. He became organist in Mühlhausen in 1707, but moved quickly to Weimar, where he was court organist from 1708 to 1717. During this period Bach composed short religious pieces, organ works, cantatas, and the famed *Toccata and Fugue in B Minor*. Then he became concertmaster at Köthen in Count Leopold's court until 1723. His compositions were primarily secular. Included were chamber music, sonatas, fugues, the *Brandenburg Concerti*, French and English suites, and *The Well-tempered Clavier* (I). From 1723 until his death Bach was cantor of the school of St. Thomas Church and university music director in Leipzig. During this time he composed deeply religious works, including the *St. John Passion* (1723), *St. Matthew Passion* (1729), *Mass in B Minor,* and longer church cantatas. Bach's body of work climaxed the art of baroque music and the Lutheran chorale. His

fugues offered insight into his style, which unified contrasting melodies in a deep harmony. His vocal works connected text and melody inextricably. He harmonized over 370 chorales, and wrote almost 300 cantatas, artfully combining subjectivity and the proclamation of objective wrath and grace. His most famous organ piece is the *Passacaglia in C Minor.* Known during his life as an organ virtuoso, Bach was brought to public attention c. 1800 by Johann Nikolaus Forkel's biography. Then Felix Mendelssohn reproduced his mighty *St. Matthew Passion* in an 1829 centennial performance. Bach societies became popular c. 1850, when his compositions came into their own. Although many of Bach's works are undoubtedly lost, he wrote no operas.

**Backus, Isaac** (1724–1806). Baptist leader. Converted during the Great Awakening while a youth in Connecticut, Backus began preaching tours in 1746 as a "New Light" Congregationalist. In 1748, he was ordained as pastor at Middleborough, Mass. Three years later he created controversy by becoming a Baptist, remained in Middleborough, and in time made it the strongest Baptist center in New England. He was one of the organizers of the Warren Association of Baptists and as its agent became one of the most important voices advocating separation of church and state, traveling thousands of miles, writing extensively, and officially representing the Baptists before the state on behalf of religious liberty. He is also remembered as a historian; his magnum opus was *A History of New England with Particular Reference to the . . . Baptists.*

**Bacon, Benjamin Wisner** (1860–1932). American clergyman and scholar. He was born at Litchfield, Conn., graduated from Yale University in 1881, and Yale Divinity School in 1884. He held Congregational pastorates from 1884 to 1896, then became instructor in New Testament Greek in Yale Divinity School. In 1897, he was named Buckingham professor of New Testament criticism and interpretation. His thirty-six-year career at Yale was spent in applying the method of "higher criticism" to the New Testament, in hopes that by this means he could arrive at a conclusive solution of the historical problems of the Gospels, his ultimate aim being the recovery of the historical Jesus and the beginnings of the Christian religion. He was the author of numerous works in this field, including *The Gospel of Mark* (1925) and *Studies in Matthew* (1930). He was resident director of the American School of Oriental Study at Jerusalem from 1905 to 1906.

**Bacon, Francis** (1561–1626). English statesman, lawyer, philosopher, and author. He was the youngest son of Sir Nicholas Bacon, lord keeper of the great seal under Elizabeth I. His mother was Anne Cook, a deeply pious Calvinist. After studying at Cambridge and Gray's Inn, Bacon served in Parliament as a member of Commons from 1584 to 1614. However, for various reasons, he never held an important post in government under Elizabeth. It was not until 1618, under James I, that he became lord high chancellor (the highest legal post in England). In 1621, he was impeached, found guilty of malfeasance in office, and forced to retire from public life. Because his character was a curious mixture of intellectual acuteness and moral obtuseness, Bacon has been difficult for historians to assess. His greatest literary works were his *History of the Reign of Henry VII* and his *Essays.* However, his chief claim to fame in the modern world rests on his work in the philosophy of science as expressed in his *Novum organum,* his *De augmentis scientiarum,* and his unfinished *New Atlantis.* Bacon was not himself a scientist but rather the prophet and propagandist of the scientific outlook. Although his system of scientific induction has been relatively insignificant, the general stimulus that he gave to scientific inquiry and the practical application of scientific knowledge to industry has been very important.

**Bacon, Roger** (c. 1214–1294). Philosopher and scientist. Born in Somerset, he studied at Oxford c. 1229 to 1235 and then taught at Paris c. 1240 to 1245, being the first to lecture on Aristotle there. He returned to Oxford c. 1247, abandoning theology for natural science, and possibly influenced by Grosseteste, spent ten years in the investigation of optics, alchemy, mathematics, geography, and medicine. About 1257 he joined the Franciscans. Hoping for official commendation, in 1267 he sent to Pope Clement IV, an old friend, his *Opus maius,* a compendium of knowledge and vast program of reform for all learning. In 1277, his *Speculum astronomiae* was condemned by his superiors, possibly because of its unorthodox views on astrology, and he was imprisoned until c. 1292. His last work, the *Compendium studii theologiae,* was unfinished at his death. A Neoplatonist with admiration for Avicenna, he was utterly out of sympathy with his Scholastic contemporaries and constantly denounced their work as abstract and divorced from experience, and above all negligent of Scripture. He advocated the study of Hebrew and Greek and a revision of the Vulgate for a proper understanding of the Bible, the source of all philosophy. This, with a knowledge of science, particularly mathematics, would lead to an understanding of God's handiwork and thus by Augustine's path to a knowledge of God.

**Bahaism.** The doctrine of a sect founded in Persia in the 19th century. Bahai originated in 1844, founded by Mizra Ali Muhammad (Bab), and succeeded by Mizra Husayn Ali (Bahaullah) and his son Abbas Effendi (Abdul-Baha). Bahai by the thousands suffered persecution and death at the hands of Moslems in the 19th century. Abdul-Baha was released from prison in 1908 and toured Egypt, Europe, and the United States. He broke ground for the first and major Bahai temple in the West at Wilmette, Ill., today the center of activities in the United States. Intended to combine the synagogue, cathedral, and mosque, the structure is based on the numeral 9, the symbol of perfection in Bahai, with 9 sides, 9 entrances, 9 arches, etc. The temple was dedicated in 1953 to the "unity of God, the unity of his prophets, the unity of mankind." The faith aims at three basic principles: the universal brotherhood of man, the unity of all religions, and world peace. It repudiates religious conflict, stating that God stresses unity and love. It maintains that one God spoke to Zoroaster, Mohammed, Buddha, Moses, and Jesus, and that the divine message was fulfilled in Bahaullah. Bahai emphasizes the "unfettered search after truth and the abandonment of all superstition and prejudice." It insists on compulsory education and equal rights and opportunities for both sexes in all walks of life. It advocates an international language, a universal league of nations, and an international parliament. Ecclesiastical organization is limited to teachers, local groups, and national assemblies.

**Bahrdt, Karl Friedrich** (1741–1792). German theologian. The *enfant terrible* of the *Aufklärung,* Bahrdt was trained at Leipzig and became professor of theology there (1766–1769). He held a number of ecclesiastical and academic posts from which he was dismissed for moral or doctrinal reasons. From orthodox beginnings he came to identify Christianity with natural religion. Attacked by such figures as Johann S. Semler, he was finally imprisoned under the Edict of 1788.

**Baillie, Robert** (1599–1662). Scottish church leader. Though not opposed to a moderate episcopacy for Scotland, Baillie protested firmly against the innovations proposed in the Kirk by the canons and liturgy of Charles I. In 1642, then a professor of divinity, he was appointed one of the Scottish commissioners to the Westminster Assembly. His *Letters and Journals* are historical sources of great importance.

**Baird, Robert** (1798–1863). American Presbyterian clergyman. Educated at Jefferson College and Princeton Seminary, he spent his life in extensive travel for the American Bible Society, the American Sunday School Union, and as agent of the French Association. In Europe he became a promoter of Protestantism and the American Union cause, writing many books, perhaps the most famous being *Religion in America,* a history of American churches.

**Baius** (de Bay), **Michel** (1513–1589). Flemish Roman Catholic theologian Baius was born at Meslin l'Évêque, became a priest, and eventually, from 1541 to 1551, a teacher of philosophy at Louvain. From 1551 to his death he taught theology, serving from 1575 as dean of St. Pierre's and vice-chancellor of the university. Desirous, perhaps, of combating Luther on his own ground, he elaborated a kind of anti-Scholastic Augustinianism, which, however, was less akin to the thought of Augustine than to a Stoic legalism. Thus, for Baius, Adam could keep the divine law without grace and could merit heaven; for fallen man, justification consisted in a restoration of Adam's state, justification being understood neither as divine acceptance nor as an infused grace of divine sonship, but simply as renewed ability to keep the law with meritorious works. Baius' doctrines were condemned in 1567 by Pius V, who, wishing to suggest a distinction between possibly orthodox and clearly heretical readings of Baius' works, allowed the absence of punctuation in the text of his bull to create ambiguity. Baius' views were condemned again by Gregory XIII in 1579. He received the correction humbly the second time it was given, although earlier he had demurred. Many have seen in Baius a forerunner of Jansenism.

**Bale, John** (1495–1563). Early proponent of Protestant views in England, bibliographer, playwright, acrimonious pamphleteer ("Bilious Bale"). Formerly a Carmelite, he was converted to Reformed principles, married, and fled to Germany in 1540 after the fall of his patron, Thomas Cromwell. He came back in 1547 on Edward VI's accession, and in 1552 was made bishop of Ossory; but the Marian reaction forced him to take refuge in Holland shortly thereafter. He returned to England in 1559.

**Ball, John** (d. 1381). English priest and a leader in Wat Tyler's revolt. Influenced by the teachings of Wycliffe, he became a fiery advocate of social equality. Despite excommunication and the proscription of his sermons, his popularity rose. In prison when the revolt began (1381), he was released by the rebels and was present at the murder of Archbishop Simon of Sudbury. After Tyler's death, Ball was captured, condemned for treason, and executed.

**Ballou, Hosea** (1771–1852). Universalist clergyman. Son of a Baptist minister, Ballou became interested in Universalist doctrine as a youth. In 1791, he was excommunicated and that year joined with John Murray at a Universalist Convention at Oxford, Mass. He began preaching and in 1794 was ordained. In 1797, while substituting for Murray at his church in Boston, controversy arose because Ballou departed from Murray in teaching anti-Trinitarianism (that Christ was not divine and man not depraved). After that his writing and preaching gradually made him the acknowledged theologian of the Universalists; his most important work was his *Treatise on the Atonement* in 1805. After 1818 he instructed ministerial students, since the Universalists had no seminary, and edited two journals. More than anyone, he shaped Universalism in America.

**Baltimore, Lord.** See CALVERT, CECIL.

**Bancroft, Richard** (1544–1610). Archbishop of Canterbury. Born at Farnworth, Lancashire, and educated in the local grammar school, he entered Christ's College, Cambridge, in 1564 and proceeded to his B.A. in 1567. He was tutor at Jesus College until 1574, received the M.A. in 1570 and the D.D. in 1585. Recognized early as an able administrator, he advanced rapidly in preferment, being rector of Tavisham, prebend of Ely, and archiepiscopal visitor of the diocese of Peterborough and Ely. He attracted the attention of Lord Burghley, and thus of Elizabeth. Bancroft believed in episcopacy, not as a matter of expediency, but of divine right (*jure divino*), and he entered the struggle against the Puritans and Congregationalists. Through his thorough investigative work he exposed the Puritan "plot" to Presbyterianize England and was instrumental in suppressing the Marprelate tracts in 1588–1589. He became bishop of London in 1597 and spent a great deal of his time prosecuting recusants and Puritans. He was a leading exponent of the king's party in the Hampton Court Conference in 1604 and the same year he was elevated to Canterbury. While in that office he carried through an earnest "reconstruction of the English Church," reforming abuses, especially among the clergy. Bancroft was at times a harsh prelate, though the years have softened the estimates of him. He was a genuine patron of learning and was himself something of a Renaissance man in his interests and ambitions.

**Banez, Dominic** (1528–1604). Spanish Dominican theologian. After making his Dominican profession in 1547, Banez' development of the thought of Thomas Aquinas caused many leading Spanish schools to consider him the brightest thinker of their country. Although important for his direction of Teresa of Ávila in her personal life and in the work of Carmelite reform (1515–1582), his leading role was in the controversy with the Jesuits concerning the relationship of divine grace to human freedom, a doctrine much discussed in the light of Protestant theology. By reason of his strong conservative adherence to Aquinas he was made the official examiner of *Concordia liberi arbitrii cum gratiae donis,* a book on this subject by Luis de Molina, S.J., which Banez allowed to be published only after notable revisions were made (1589). When the seriousness of the controversy had caused Rome (1594) to forbid all discussion pending its resolution by the pope, he successfully petitioned Pope Clement VIII in 1597 to allow the Dominicans to resume their teachings on the subject. He wrote criticizing Molina, chiefly for emphasizing man's freedom to the detriment of the omnipotence of God. His constant attempts to separate the thought of Thomas Aquinas from nominalist and Jesuit interpretations of it cause many to regard Banez as the founder of the modern Thomistic movement.

**Bangkok Conference.** Two meetings were held: (1) Eastern Asia Christian Conference, Dec. 3–11, 1949, called by the International Missionary Council and the World Council of Churches as a regional expression of ecumenism for study and action. Report: *The Christian Prospect in Eastern Asia,* New York, 1950. (2) Third Assembly of the East Asia Christian Conference, 1964, dealing with business and with the theme "The Christian Community Within the Human Community."

**Baptism.** The term employed to denote the rite of initiation into the Christian church. It is a direct transliteration of one or both of two Greek nouns coming from the same verb stem, one meaning the action of immersing or dipping, and the other the result of that action. Although the verb, with the meaning "to sink" or even "to drown," was common enough in pagan Greece, these two nouns are of strictly Jewish Christian Greek usage. Neither the practice of ritual cleansing, common in Juda-

ism, nor the particular use of water cleansing for proselytes ever acquired a sacral meaning, but remained a legalistic rite of purification. Christian baptism belongs to the class of rites of passage or initiation in religions, but any direct connection between them and the Christian rite is difficult if not impossible to establish.

The New Testament develops a wealth of synonyms for the noun as well as the verb, such as "washing" (Eph. 5:26; Titus 3:5), "sealing" (Eph. 1:13; 4:30; II Tim. 2:19; Revelation, *passim*), "anointing" (I John 2:20, 27), etc., to signify the various meanings attached to the rite. If Jesus was baptized by John, as the Synoptics have it, the Fourth Gospel modifies the event; this may testify to the early development of such sacral overtones to the rite as can be seen in Paul (Rom. 6:1–14). Baptism was a universal practice in apostolic Christianity, but the interpretation of it was not uniform. Five basic motifs in baptism receive individually more or less emphasis according to author or locale: (1) remission of sin; (2) sealing with the name of Jesus Christ; (3) conferral of the Spirit; (4) participation in the death and resurrection of Christ; and (5) rebirth or re-creation, a new beginning. It is questionable whether Paul is responsible for adding any of these motifs to the general Hellenistic Christian understanding of baptism, but it is quite clear that he intensified and probed more deeply into the theological significance of all of them. That a formal profession of faith was required before baptism is strongly suggested if not proved by the form and content of I Peter and Hebrews. In the deutero-Pauline literature such as Colossians and Ephesians, the process of theological expansion begun by Paul is carried much farther, perhaps because of the presence of proto-Gnostic tendencies and the consequently more articulate understanding of the nature of the church giving more emphasis to the three latter, more sacral, motifs mentioned above, without necessarily omitting the others (cf. Heb. 6:4–6; Col. 2:11–15). Baptism into the name of Christ (Acts 8:16; 19:5; cf. I Cor. 1:13,15) is expanded to include the Spirit (John 3:5 f.; cf. Acts 10:44–48) even in apostolic times, but the full Trinitarian formula (Matt. 28:19) did not emerge until the 2d century (Didache 7:1,3; Justin Martyr, *Apology* I. 61.3,11,13). Even in the first half of this century there was still no uniform theological assessment of baptism, although the rebirth motif, couched in the language of the mystery cults without any demonstrable effect upon doctrine, was progressively more evident. Just as in early Christological expressions, so in baptismal theology the early church employed numerous Biblical and eschatological images without settling exclusively on one or repudiating those not emphasized. Likewise, there was a movement parallel to Christology which discarded or left behind the eschatological, history-oriented baptismal terminology and moved toward the ontological categories.

During the first two centuries adult baptism was the norm, but the evidence for or against infant baptism in the apostolic and postapostolic eras is indirect and ambiguous. During the latter part of the 2d century a conflict arose over the increasing occurrence of infant baptism (Tertullian, *On Baptism* 18.5), and by the middle of the 3d century it had become normal practice (Cyprian, *Epistle* 64), theologically justified by ontological arguments (Origen, *Commentary on Rom. 5:9*), but not yet universally observed (Gregory of Nazianzus, *Orations* 40). Whether the growing predominance of infant baptism was its cause or a result of it (more likely both), there was a decided trend in the first four centuries to construe baptism as an *opus operatum* (a work effective in itself) whereby the baptized one not only entered a new life but was also changed in character. This development effectually eliminated the prebaptismal confession of sin and put increasing emphasis on what was done to and for the one baptized. One aspect of the trend is seen in the conflict over heretical and schismatic baptism in the mid-3d century.

Even before Nicaea (A.D. 325), the ceremonies attendant upon adult baptism were increasingly elaborated to include fasting and prayer before the rite, a vigil all the preceding night, renunciation of the devil at dawn, anointing the body against the devil, the actual immersion with first recitation of the baptismal confession, clothing with white garments, laying on of hands, signing with the cross in oil of chrism, acceptance by the bishop for the community, first participation in the Eucharist, and partaking of milk and honey. The shift to infant baptism caused an alteration in these ceremonies and the introduction of new ones. Hence exorcism played a large role, replacing the confession of sin, and regeneration was in the forefront of concern; likewise, a separation in the West was introduced between baptism and the laying on of hands with oil of chrism, forming a new sacrament, confirmation, reserved to the bishop. In the East the whole ceremony was performed by a presbyter using episcopally consecrated chrism.

The Eastern emphasis on baptism as incorporation into the divine Logos and the Western stress on forgiveness of sin and redemption from the devil were merged and conflated by Augustine, who saw Christ as the minister of baptism, active as "visible Word" in the external *sacramentum* and as "invisible grace" completing the "sacramental effect" in the one baptized. Thus the twofold action took place whereby redemption from sin and reconciliation with God was followed by the infusion of grace through the Spirit and incorporation into the church. This corresponded to the Pauline figure of dying to (original) sin and (the soul's) rising to (eternal) life, and it made possible the theological necessity of infant baptism. Scholastic baptismal theology as epitomized by Thomas Aquinas only spelled out in Aristotelian terms what Augustine had already expounded in Neoplatonic categories. For Aquinas, baptism delivers one from the guilt and punishment of original sin and makes him capable of virtue (*habitus virtutum*), and thus becomes an efficacious sign (*signum efficax*) imbuing him with indelible character. The Catholic baptismal doctrine reached its climax in the bull *Exultate Deo* (1439), which required for valid baptism water (matter), baptismal formula (form), and the intention of the minister.

In the Eastern Orthodox churches little theological reflection on baptism means that it is seen in pre-Augustinian terms, i.e., mystagogically. The medieval Catharistic sects added a "baptism of the Spirit" for the "elect," thus in a sense reflecting the Western division between baptism and confirmation, while the Waldenses rebaptized converts from Catholicism, emphasizing the necessity of "believers' baptism."

Luther's stress on "word" and "faith" moved away from the *opus operatum* concept of baptism, accentuating its covenantal character and the responsibility of each believer to reaffirm in regular response the effect of his baptism, while he avoided making the efficacy of the rite depend totally upon the believer by his emphasis upon the faithfulness of God's promise in the sacrament. The prevenience of divine activity undergirded his defense of infant baptism. Zwingli considered Catholic sacramental theology as magic, so he emphasized the *signific* side of the sacrament. Logically, he should have insisted on only adult baptism or at least only to older children instructed, but his conflict with the Anabaptists forced him to a defense of infant baptism. Calvin saw baptism as a *sign*, separating it from the conversion in faith that preceded it, and so infant baptism was less important for him than God's work on the child in a Christian context which was affirmed by baptism. The Heidelberg Catechism (qq. 69–72) spells this out, reiterating the "sign" concept of baptism, separating Calvinism from the reasserted *opus operatum* concept in the Baptismal Canon 10 of the Council of Trent. On their side, the Anabaptists carried to its fullest implications the Zwinglian idea, emphasizing the necessity of a profession of faith before baptism and thus radicalizing the *sola fide* concept of both Luther and Zwingli. Basing their stance on the New Testament, they contended that infant baptism was completely contrary to Scripture; at the same time, they countered a dogma that had grown more or less surreptitiously in Catholicism—that an unbaptized child was either damned or consigned to limbo—by their vehement denial of it.

With the emphasis on individualism concomitant with post-Enlightenment theology, greater attention has been paid to the preparation of the individual Christian for his proper role before he is baptized; yet the *pro forma* character of baptism has been more and more noticeable in this period. With the advent of dialectical theology and its recapturing of Biblical insights, baptism as well as confirmation has come in for greater consideration. The ecumenical movement brings together many different traditions from the Reformation and, in this context, the whole concept of church membership has been reexamined with the result that baptism has been a much discussed question in modern Protestant theology.

BIBLIOGRAPHY: K. Barth, *The Teaching of the Church Regarding Baptism* (London, 1948); O. Cullmann, *Baptism in the New Testament* (London, 1950); C. Davis, *The Making of a Christian* (London, 1964); A. Gilmore, *Christian Baptism* (London, 1959); "Baptism: Theology of," *New Catholic Encyclopedia,* Vol. II, pp. 62–68 (New York, 1967).

**Baptistery.** Originally a separate building either connected to or adjoining the church and used for baptisms. It was usually circular or polygonal in shape with a surrounding ambulatory and sometimes with radiating chapels. When affusion replaced immersion as the accepted mode of baptism, such structures became unnecessary. Then that part of the church in which baptism was administered was railed off from the rest of the church and called the baptistery.

**Baptist Missionary Society.** Founded in 1792 at Kettering, England, under the leadership of William Carey, "the father of foreign mission." The Society began its work mainly in India, but also sent missionaries to Jamaica, China, and Africa (the Cameroons, Congo). It branched out to form the American Baptist Foreign Mission Society in 1814. It is closely related to the British and Foreign Bible Society and to the modern ecumenical movement.

**Baptist Movements.** Among the diverse religious movements of the Hellenistic era, 200 B.C.–A.D. 200, are a number of small brotherhoods that can be grouped together because of the prominence of baptism or daily baths and washings. Several groups appeared and disappeared in the area of Palestine and Syria; all were derived from Judaism or Jewish Christianity. The members ceased to attend temple sacrifices and prayers; they adopted washings for purification or baptism as their central religious act. The most prominent were the Essenes. Philo reports that they lived east of the Jordan, were committed to poverty and celibacy, sustained themselves by agriculture, but neglected philosophy and science. They followed a strictly organized daily schedule. Philo estimates the existence of four thousand such "athletes of virtue." The Qumran community is generally regarded as a colony of Essenes. Other similar ascetics are mentioned by the ancients: Nazarenes and Nasoreans, Hemerobaptists, Baptists of the Morning, the hermit Banus. The disciples of John the Baptist (Johannites) persisted until the 3d century A.D. Some scholars regard the modern colony of Mandaeans in Iran and Iraq as one of these ancient baptist sects. More probably the Mandaeans arose in the 6th or 7th century A.D., but certainly inherited cultic practices from these early movements. In contrast to the ascetic practices of early baptists, the Mandaeans celebrate fertility, not celibacy.

**Baptists.** Members of a denomination of Christians that arose out of English Congregationalism in the 17th century. In 1965, more than three and a half centuries later, there were more than 27,000,000 Baptists in 122 countries. Approximately 24,000,000 were concentrated in the United States, about 90 percent of whom are included in four major conventions: the Southern Baptist Convention with nearly 11,000,000 members; the National Baptist Convention, U.S.A., Inc., with 5,000,000 members; the National Baptist Convention of America with nearly 3,000,000; and the American Baptist Convention with 1,600,000 members. The remainder are to be found in 23 smaller bodies.

*Early History.* There were two strands of the early Baptists, both having their roots in the English Reformation. The first emerged from the Separatist Puritans who had withdrawn from the Church of England, seeking renewal of the church in congregations of true believers separate from civil control. Their leader was John Smyth (c. 1554–1612), a clergyman who had left the state church about 1606 to become minister of a Separatist congregation at Gainsborough on Trent. To escape persecution, he and his people emigrated to Amsterdam in 1608. There, possibly under the influence of friendly Mennonites, Smyth rejected infant baptism as unscriptural and a stumbling block to a pure church. He disbanded his congregation, baptized himself by applying water to his head, and then baptized some forty of his followers. This was the first English church constituted on the principle of baptizing believers only.

When Smyth later became aware of a Mennonite church holding his view of baptism, he sought admission for his congregation. In this he was opposed by Thomas Helwys (c. 1550–c. 1616), who persuaded ten others to secede and return to London, where they established the first Baptist church in England. Because Smyth and Helwys held the moderate Calvinistic views of Jacobus Arminius regarding the atonement for all people, this church and those which sprang from its influence were called General Baptists.

The second strand of Baptist churches emerged out of a Puritan congregation established in 1616 by Henry Jacob (1563–1624) in Southwark, London. Unlike the Separatist Puritans, it acknowledged its association with the Church of England. In 1638, a group of six members withdrew to form the first Particular Baptist church under John Spilsbury. Its name derived from the more traditional Calvinistic view of its members that the atonement was for the elect only. Churches of this persuasion committed themselves by 1644 to immersion as the Biblical mode of baptism. Most of them were ecumenical in spirit, warning against schism and urging unity among all true believers. Some even practiced open membership, not requiring Christians from non-Baptist churches to be rebaptized.

During the period of Parliament's struggle against absolute monarchy and a state church (1640–1660), Baptists grew in numbers, the greatest gains being made by the Particular Baptists. After the Restoration of Charles II in 1660, they were subjected to disabilities until 1689 when the Act of Toleration provided partial relief.

For a time, in the decades that followed, the Baptists declined in numbers and influence. Then under the impetus of the Wesleyan Evangelical Revival, they came to new life. The Particular Baptists formed the English Baptist Missionary Society in 1792, with William Carey as their first missionary to India.

A New Connection General Baptist group was formed in 1770. A century later, this body united with the Particular Baptists to form the Baptist Union of Great Britain and Ireland (1891). Following World War I the Baptists, like other Free Churches, began to decline in influence and membership.

In the British Commonwealth, Baptists are to be found in Australia and New Zealand, where churches were begun in 1831 and 1854 respectively by missionaries of the English Baptist Missionary Society. They are also present in Canada, where the earliest churches were founded in the Maritime Provinces by New England emigrants in the latter half of the 18th century. Growth has been modest as churches have been established across the country. By 1944 most Baptists were united in the Baptist Federation of Canada; a minority remained aloof in independent fellowships of Evangelical (fundamentalist) Baptist churches.

*Development in the United States.* Baptist beginnings in the colonies constituted an extension of the reform movement that we have noted within English Puritanism. The first Baptist church was established at Providence, R.I., in 1639, by Roger Williams, a Puritan clergyman who had been expelled from the Massachusetts Bay Colony because of his protest against coercion in matters of personal religion. Other churches established in New England included a half dozen General Baptist churches in Rhode Island and a few Particular Baptist churches—at Newport, R.I. (1638?), Swansea, Mass. (1663), Boston (1665), and Kittery, Maine (1682).

The main center of Particular Baptist life was in the Middle Colonies. There the Philadelphia Baptist Association was organized in 1707. In later years, its membership included churches from Massachusetts to Virginia. Under the influence of the Great Awakening, the multiplication of churches prompted the Association to release groups of churches to establish in 1765 the Ketockton Association (Va.) and the Warren Association (R.I.) in 1767. Its leaders helped to organize the Charleston Association in South Carolina in 1751.

The associational plan of church life provided cohesiveness and guidance for struggling congregations in need of ministerial leadership, of mutual assistance in working out problems of polity and doctrine, and of cooperation in the struggle for religious freedom. The associations also served as evangelistic agencies, sending itinerant preachers into the South and West where new churches were established. They also founded numerous academies and colleges, the first college being Brown University at Providence (1765).

In 1814, the scattered associations were organized into a General Convention to support Adoniram and Ann Judson in Burma. This was the beginning of a worldwide mission overseas. In 1824, the American Baptist Publication Society was established to prepare Christian literature, distribute the Scriptures, and organize Sunday schools. In 1832, the American Baptist Home Mission Society was founded to plant new churches across the western expanse of the United States. In 1845, under the divisive influence of the slavery issue, the Southerners withdrew from the General Convention to organize the Southern Baptist Convention. Its work was to be accomplished through boards of home and foreign missions, education, and publication. The older body changed its name to the American Baptist Missionary Union, which today is called the American Baptist Foreign Mission Society.

At the close of the Civil War, Baptists of the North established several colleges in the South for the education of Negroes. During the postwar years, Negro Baptists began to establish their own churches. In 1880, the National Baptist Convention of America was organized. In 1916, it split over a dispute concerning the control of property and publications, the smaller of the two factions retaining the original name, while the larger body adopted the name of National Baptist Convention, U.S.A., Inc.

When the Southern Baptist Convention began to develop its own home mission and publication work toward the close of the 19th century, it protested the continued work of the older societies in the South. In a series of comity conferences, agreements were reached on a geographical allocation of work between Baptists of the North and the South. These agreements were continued when the various societies and state conventions in the North united in the Northern Baptist Convention in 1907 (after 1950 called the American Baptist Convention).

Theological controversy, adjustment to major social changes in American life, and a growing movement toward Christian unity marked the course of Baptists in the 20th century. These trends affected the Baptists in the North earlier and more intensely than Baptists in the South because they experienced greater acceleration of social and economic change. Two defections from the American Baptist Convention occurred in 1932 and 1947, resulting in the organization of the General Association of Regular Baptist Churches and the Conservative Baptist Association respectively.

Following World War II, the Southern Baptist Convention abandoned its regional limitations. Impelled by a need to follow its members to the growing urban centers of the North and West and motivated by a strong sense of mission to establish new churches, the Home Mission Board extended its influence into nearly all parts of the United States.

*Baptists in Other Parts of the World.* Through a vigorous missionary movement during the 19th century, British, European, and American Baptists were largely responsible for the development of younger churches in Asia, Africa, Latin America, and Europe. By 1965, the Baptist World Alliance, which had been organized in 1905 to give worldwide unity and cohesiveness to the Baptist witness, could report 1,132,265 Baptists in Europe and Britain, 418,700 in Africa, 911,600 in Asia, 489,000 in Latin America, and 105,200 in the Southwest Pacific.

*Distinguishing Features.* A number of features commonly recognized among Baptists give them their unity and self-consciousness: (1) an appeal to the Scriptures in matters of faith and practice; (2) a conviction that churches should be composed of convinced believers only; (3) insistence that Scripturally only believers should be baptized; (4) a belief that all Christians should share in the ministry and government of the church; (5) an understanding that the local congregation is equipped by Christ for the fulfillment of its mission; (6) belief in the separation of church and state to protect religious freedom.

BIBLIOGRAPHY: W. W. Barnes, *The Southern Baptist Convention: 1845–1953* (Nashville, 1954); H. Cook, *What Baptists Stand For* (London, 1961); W. S. Hudson (ed.), *Baptist Concepts of the Church* (Chicago, 1959); W. L. Lumpkin (ed.), *Baptist Confessions of Faith* (Chicago, 1959); E. A. Payne, *The Fellowship of Believers* (London, 1944); R. G. Torbet, *A History of the Baptists* (Valley Forge, 1963).

**Baptist World Alliance.** Organized in 1905 in London, England. It represents about 20,-000,000 Baptists and meets every five years. The organization consists of a president, nine vice-presidents, a general secretary, and several treasurers. The Alliance is only an advisory body discussing common Baptist problems, and is in close contact with the World Council of Churches and other ecumenical organizations.

**Barat, Madeleine Sophie** (1779–1865). Founder of a Roman Catholic religious order for women, the Society of the Sacred Heart (1800). The order was dedicated primarily to the education of young women, and consciously patterned itself on the regime of the Jesuits. Mlle. Barat became superior general of the order in 1806. Its constitution was approved by Leo XII in 1826, and its work expanded to America and Africa.

**Barclay, Robert** (1648–1690). Eminent Scottish Quaker. Barclay's father, David, had been a professional soldier, fighting under Gustavus Adolphus and with Middleton in the Scottish army. Under Cromwell, David Barclay forfeited his estates but sought and gained a seat in the Scottish Parliament in an effort to recover them. After the Restoration he was arrested, and during his imprisonment in Edinburgh he was converted to Quakerism by James Swinton. Robert Barclay, having finished his education in Paris, followed his father's example and in 1667 joined the Society of Friends. An excellent student, he soon found it his role to be the apologist for the Quakers in Scotland and beyond. He had considerable skill and success in public debate. It was not an easy time for Quakers, and Barclay was imprisoned several times. In 1675 he published fifteen *Theses theologiae* in which he argued that all true knowledge came from the divine revelation directly to the heart of the individual, and that the authority of reason and Scripture is second to that of the inward light. His greatest work, *An Apology for the True Christian Divinity* (1676), became the standard exposition of Quaker thought. He traveled widely and influenced prominent people, including the Princess Palatine and James II, who issued the patents for East Jersey to Penn and his colleagues.

**Bardesanes** (154–222). A Christian teacher of Edessa who was of suspect orthodoxy. The name "Bardesanes" is a transliteration of Syriac *Bar Daisan*. Many references to Bardesanes occur in the early literature, but their total impact is bewilderment. We hear that he was a good archer, the ablest writer in Syriac and father of Syrian hymnology, and an opponent of Marcion. The Neoplatonist Porphyry considered him to be a learned defender of Christianity who had a broad interest in other religions.

The principal question about him is his relation to Gnosticism. Eusebius says that he was a Valentinian for a while, but that he later returned to the orthodox fold, although "in fact he did not completely clean off the filth of his ancient heresy" (*Ecclesiastical History* 4.30.3). Hippolytus and Epiphanius believed that he remained a Gnostic, and Jerome

thought that he did return to orthodoxy for a while and then fell into a heresy of his own. It has been only in recent years that the Syrian evidence has forced a revision of the ascription to him of gnosticism. It is now seen that he was not an emanationist, nor was his Light/Darkness antithesis dualistic. He was not a Valentinian, and any Gnostic elements in his thought were more peripheral than central. He really seems to have more in common with Mani than Valentinus. His works include a selection on fate (for which we may have a number of different titles) and many hymns. He is not to be credited with the Odes of Solomon and probably not with the Hymn of the Pearl in the Acts of Thomas.

**Bar-Hebraeus** (Gregory Abu-l-Faraj, 1226–1286). Leader of the Jacobites in Syria. Son of a Jewish physician who became a Christian, he was popularly known by the name of Bar-Hebraeus, or "son of the Hebrew." A native of Turkish Armenia, he was consecrated bishop of Gubos in 1246 and became the primate (maphian) of the Jacobites in 1264. His *Chronicle* was intended as a history of southeastern Europe and western Asia from the creation to his own time. A scholar in a wide area of learning, Bar-Hebraeus also produced a commentary on Scripture, a study of Aristotle, and an autobiographical work.

**Barlaam and Joasaph.** An 11th-century romance intended to exalt monasticism. Falsely attributed to John of Damascus, it was written by Euthymius of Athos (d. 1028), describing the conversion of the cloistered Buddhist prince Joasaph by the Christian hermit Barlaam. The last of its three parts, presenting Christian truth in the form of ten parables, eventually became separated and in translated form circulated widely as *exempla* in homiletic and didactic works such as *Gesta Romanorum* and John Gower's *Confessio Amantis*.

**Barlow, William** (d. 1568). Bishop of St. David's (1536), Bath and Wells (1548), Chichester (1559). Formerly an Augustinian canon, Barlow proved as adaptable as was necessary under Henry VIII and Edward VI, but had to flee during Mary's reign. His principal importance is as the chief consecrator of Archbishop Parker in 1559; because no record of Barlow's own consecration as bishop survives, it has sometimes been proposed that the orders he transmitted to Parker were invalid.

**Barmen Declaration, The.** Statement of the first synod of the German Confessing Church, held in Barmen, May 29–31, 1934, which repudiated the program of the "German Christians." Precursors of the confession were Karl Barth's countertheses to the Rengsdorf Theses and his memorandum to the Pastors' Emergency League, both in 1933. The Barmen Synod met at the Gemarke Church in Barmen. Present were 139 delegates (86 theologians, of which 6 were professors, 53 laymen averaging c. 40 years) from 18 territorial churches, with Karl Koch presiding. The theological committee under Hans Asmussen steered the declaration through synodical floor action. It had drawn up the declaration May 15–16 under the dominating influence of Barth, although the document went through several drafts. Barth said little at Barmen, since the declaration spoke for him. It emphasized the discontinuity of throne and altar. The first combined confession of Lutheran, Reformed, and Union clergy since the Reformation, the statement contained in each thesis a Biblical passage, a positive confession, and a *damnatio*. Thesis One declared that the church's proclamation consisted only in Jesus Christ, not in the Nazi theory of blood and soil. The second asserted that all areas of life are under Christ's righteousness. The third confessed that the church is an assembly of brothers accepting Jesus as Lord, and the fourth that no one ecclesiastical ministry is superior to another. In the fifth is the statement that the state's role as a divine order does not extend to all the conditions of human life, and in the sixth that the church is not subservient to human purpose. Especially the first and fifth theses opposed the "German Christians." Reactions to the confession came first not from "German Christians" but from Lutherans, especially in Bavaria.

**Barmen Missionary Society.** See RHENISH MISSIONARY SOCIETY.

**Barnabas, Epistle of.** A 2d century work written in the epistolary literary convention and attributed by Clement of Alexandria and others of the early church to the apostle Barnabas. It is not an epistle nor can it be considered the work of Barnabas. It is a theological tractate with an anti-Jewish polemic quite inconsistent with the attitudes prevailing in the New Testament church. References in it to the destruction of the Temple mean that it must be later than A.D. 70, and the latest possible date is just after the Bar-Cochba rebellion. It was probably written around 130 and may be of Alexandrian provenience, since it was regarded as canonical there (it appears in Codex Sinaiticus just after the Revelation) and employs the alle-

gorical method of Biblical interpretation so esteemed there from the time of Philo on.

The work is divided into two main parts. The first seeks to prove that Jews cannot understand the Old Testament; Jewish Christians may say that the Covenant belongs to Jews and Christians alike, but it belongs only to Christians whose possession of the Spirit enables them to understand prefigurative language. Without the Spirit the Jews understand the institutions of the Old Covenant in a literal and almost idolatrous sense rather than in the allegorical sense that is correct. The second half of the book is a catechetical discourse on the "two ways" very similar to that in the Didache and undoubtedly based on the same source.

**Barnabites** (*or* Clerks Regular of St. Paul) A religious order founded in Milan in 1530 by Anton Maria Zaccaria, Barthelemy Ferrari, and Jacopo Morigia to renew the pastoral zeal of the clergy. The order soon spread to many European countries and was often given the task of trying to counteract Protestantism. The Barnabites are normally involved in preaching, teaching, hearing confessions, giving missions, and working in hospitals and prisons.

**Barnardo, Thomas John** (1845–1905). British physician, evangelist, philanthropist, and founder of the Dr. Barnardo's Homes for destitute children. He adopted Protestantism in 1862, studied medicine, preached, did settlement work, and established in London (1870) his first juvenile boys' home. Extending his activity to Canada, he had by the time of his death opened some 90 homes, rescued and trained 60,000 children, and otherwise aided over 150,000 persons.

**Barnes, Albert W.** (1798–1870). American Presbyterian clergyman. With degrees from Hamilton College and Princeton Seminary he served parishes in New Jersey and Philadelphia. Allegedly liberal views led to his trial for heresy, precipitating controversy contributing to the Presbyterian schism of 1837. He was author of many works, including an eleven-volume Bible commentary said to have sold over one million copies.

**Barnes, Robert** (c. 1495–1540). A chief English proponent of Lutheran ideas during Henry VIII's reign. Formerly an Augustinian friar, Barnes adopted "German" views at Cambridge in the 1520's. In the next decade his fortunes fluctuated with the usefulness of his beliefs to the king: sometimes in exile, sometimes a royal ambassador. Barnes was condemned by act of Parliament and burned as a heretic when Henry's position hardened in a more "Catholic" direction.

**Barnett, Samuel Augustus** (1844–1913). Church of England priest and social reformer. He was founder of the Charity Organization Society (1869), and cofounder of the Education Reform League (1884). His entire ministry combined Christian teaching with social reform activity. With the assistance of his wife, an associate of Octavia Hill, he wrote extensively on the relation of Christian faith to social responsibility. He aided in founding Toynbee Hall (1884), the first settlement house in the world. Barnett Hall, Oxford, is a memorial to him.

**Baro, Peter** (1534–1599). Anglo-Continental Protestant theologian. In 1574, having fled to England from his native France, he became a professor of divinity at Cambridge, where he attracted attention by his criticisms of the rigidly predestinarian positions of Calvin. The ensuing controversy with William Whitaker resulted in the Lambeth Articles of 1595, which condemned Baro's views. He was forced to leave Cambridge, but his Arminianism was influential on the subsequent generation of English divines.

**Baronius, Caesar** (1538–1607). Roman Catholic historian. He entered Philip Neri's Roman Oratory in 1557. Baronius managed to combine an amazing amount of historical research with his parish duties and such humble jobs as cooking and serving. In 1588, in reply to the Lutheran *Magdeburg Centuries,* he published the first volume of his major work, the twelve-volume *Annales ecclesiastici.* In 1593, he succeeded Philip Neri as head of the confraternity, and in 1596 he was made a cardinal. Soon afterward he became Vatican librarian and director of the new Vatican press.

**Barrow, Henry** (c. 1550–1593). Puritan Congregationalist reformer. He went to Cambridge as a profligate young man, but was converted when he wandered into a preaching service in London. He gave up law, and turned to the study of theology and the Bible. Both he and John Greenwood became indoctrinated with the thought of Robert Browne, and espoused Separatist views. In 1586, Greenwood was caught holding a conventicle in London, and was thrown into prison. When Barrow visited him, he was apprehended and detained. Greenwood, Barrow, and John Penry wrote a report of their trial before Archbishop Whitgift that stirred animosity against the Establishment. Arraigned on charges of intent to stir up rebellion, they affirmed that they had no such intent in any of their writings. However, an anti-Brownist bill was before Parliament, and Greenwood and Barrow, shortly to be followed by Penry, were hanged to persuade Parliament to pass the bill. Though Barrow was willing to separate from the Established Church in order to practice pure religion, he did not advocate complete separation of church and state. He felt that it was the task of the state to establish true worship, suppress false, and maintain morality, but that in matters indifferent or in the changing of the judicial law of Moses the prince had no rights. Barrow is usually considered one of the founders of the Congregational Church.

**Barsumas** (c. 420–c. 490). Nestorian bishop of Nisibis. A follower of Ibas of Edessa, he was condemned with his master at the Latrocinium but was not restored with him at Constantinople. Confusion is introduced into accounts of the "Robber Council" of Ephesus because this Barsumas was condemned by it for Nestorianism while another of the same name, the Monophysite archimandrite, dominated it with his monks. The Nestorian became metropolitan of Nisibis, was the only Christian welcomed by the Persian king, and made his see the center of the Nestorian missionary activity that eventually extended to China.

**Barth, Karl** (1886–1968). Swiss Reformed theologian, largely responsible for the revolution in 20th-century Protestant theology known as neo-orthodoxy (crisis theology). Born in Basel, the son of a professor of church history. He studied in Bern, Berlin, Tübingen, and Marburg, and was impressed by the liberal position of Wilhelm Herrmann. The period spent as a pastor in Safenwil (1911–1921) was crucial for a nearly complete reversal of this theological position. The subjective individualism of Herrmann was adequate neither to Barth's own social concerns nor to the moral perplexities of his people. At the same time, the shock of World War I destroyed for him the cultural optimism of 19th-century theology. Influenced by the Religious Socialist movement, the eschatology of the Blumhardts, and the thinking of Kierkegaard, the second edition of Barth's *Commentary on Romans* (1922) reflects a new approach, one which emphasizes the utter distinction between God and man, which places God completely beyond the reach of fallen man. The search for a natural knowledge of God is abandoned—man learns of God when he reveals himself to man as the Word: through Scripture or preaching by means of the Spirit. Man is more known than knowing. In the multivolume *Church Dogmatics* (1932 ff.), Barth has abandoned Kierkegaard's framework but maintains the basic dialectic or crisis in which God confronts man as judgment and mercy. Barth held academic positions in Germany after 1921 at Göttingen, Münster, and Bonn, until his expulsion in 1935 because of his opposition to the Nazis. He was professor of dogmatics at Basel until his death.

**Bartholomew of the Martyrs** (Bartholomew Fernandes, 1514–1590). Portuguese Dominican who taught philosophy and theology for many years in houses of his order. In 1559, he became archbishop of Braga and in 1561 attended the final sessions of the Council of Trent. He greatly influenced the Council's decrees on the reform of ecclesiastical life, especially in regard to the clergy. When he returned to Braga, he called a synod to carry out the new decrees and raise the moral and spiritual life of his priests. His familiar name, *de Martyribus*, was derived from the church in which he was baptized.

**Bartholomew's Day Massacre.** See HU-GUENOTS.

**Bartholomites.** A congregation of secular priests in Germany, founded in 1640 at Tittmoning by Bartholomew Holzhauser. Their aim was to renew the religious lives of both clergy and laity after the devastation of the Thirty Years' War. They lived a community life under a superior, but did not take vows. One of their chief works was seminary education. The Bartholomites were active in several European countries until forced to disband under Napoleon in 1803.

**Bartholomites, Armenian.** A refugee monastic group from Tarsus, which settled in Genoa (1307). A church was constructed for them, honoring Bartholomew, hence the name. Other Armenians settled throughout Italy. The Armenian Liturgy and Rule of St. Basil were replaced by the Roman rite and the Augustinian Rule (1356). After two hundred years, the congregation dwindled, and papal suppression, with the redistribution of incomes and property, was carried out in 1650.

**Bartolommeo, Fra** (1475–1517). Florentine painter, defender of Savonarola. He entered the Dominican Order after the reformer's death in 1498. His career as an artist was interrupted briefly, and his partner, Albertinelli, was left to finish his *Last Judgment*. Later he resumed painting at his prior's commission. He became a friend of Raphael, whom he greatly influenced. Illness marked his last years.

**Basedow, Johann Bernhard** (1723–1790). German educational reformer. Educated in theology at Leipzig and profoundly influenced by Locke, he attempted to apply the educational ideas of Rousseau to German education. His main contribution was in placing emphasis upon the development of body as well as mind, and upon positive rather than negative motivations for study. Though his reputation was diminished because of his identification with the Enlightenment, his influence on European education has proved broad and lasting.

**Basel.** The capital of the canton of Basel and the second largest city of Switzerland, located on the Rhine. It was mentioned in 374 as a Celtic settlement; in 1501 it joined the Swiss confederacy, and its university, the oldest in Switzerland, made it a center of humanism. A General "Reform" Council was held there (1431–1449) during the papal schism, which was frequently disrupted by the warring parties of papalists and conciliarists. In 1529 the city joined the Protestant Reformation under the leadership of John Oecolampadius. The university developed into a center of Reformed (Calvinist) theology after 1532. Famous humanists, philosophers, and theologians have taught there: Erasmus of Rotterdam, after 1521; Andreas Bodenstein, an early friend and later an enemy of Martin Luther; Friedrich Nietzsche, who proclaimed "the death of God"; and Jakob Burckhardt, famous historian. A spirit of toleration has permitted fruitful academic creativity at the university since the 16th century. In 1876 a "school for preachers" (*Predigerschule*), based on an ardent Biblicism, was founded in Basel to serve Mennonites and other free churches. In the 20th century such modern thinkers as Karl Barth and Karl Jaspers continued the tradition of creativity in the area of theology and philosophy. Today there are about 2,000 students and 190 professors at the university.

**Basel** (Basle), **Council of** (1431–1449). A council convoked by Martin V in response to the decree *Frequens* of the Council of Constance. Eugenius IV confirmed his predecessor's appointment of Cardinal Cesarini as president of the Council, which had for its purpose reform "in head and members," settlement of the Hussite question, and reunion of the Eastern and Western Churches. Very early, sharp conflicts arose between the Basel fathers and Eugenius IV on the question of superiority. Furthermore, in reforming the government of the church they reduced the papal income and the size of the Curia. An open break occurred over the question of union with the Greeks and the site of the projected council of unity. In 1437, Eugenius IV issued the bull *Doctoris gentium,* which moved the Council to Ferrara. A minority of the Basel members, including Cesarini and Nicholas of Cusa, joined Eugenius IV; the majority continued at Basel in opposition to the pope. In 1439, the Basel assembly declared it an article of the Catholic faith that a council was superior to the pope. Felix V was elected antipope. The neutrality of France and Germany prolonged the life of the Council, but eventually Eugenius IV gained full support, and the Council was disbanded in 1449.

**Basel Confession.** A moderate statement of Zwinglian doctrine. In 1531, Oecolampadius drafted a short formula, which was later reworked by Oswald Myconius in 1532 and issued by authority of the civil government of Basel in 1534. Its twelve articles were a short and moderate statement of doctrine, whose authority was confined to Basel and later to Mühlhausen. One of the earliest of the Reformed confessions, it is sometimes called the "First Basel Confession" to distinguish it from the more important First Helvetic Confession.

**Basel Missionary Society.** A pioneer mission society composed of Reformed and Lutheran elements and drawing support from Switzerland, Germany, and Holland. In 1815 a missionary training school was opened at Basel, with most of the early mission personnel serving in British mission societies. In 1822 it began mission work of its own which eventually came to include India, China, Borneo, Persia, Indonesia, Ghana, and the Cameroons. Basel missionaries also followed German emigrants to Brazil, Australia, Canada, and the United States. Between 1833 and 1881, 189 missionaries came from Basel to the United States and Canada. Several Basel-affiliated auxiliary mission societies in Germany eventually became independent, with their own overseas missions (e.g., Rhenish, Dresden-Leipzig, and North German societies). Basel influence was also felt in the formation of Lutheran mission societies in Denmark (1821) and Norway (1842). Basel missionaries were noted for their encouragement of economic advancement on the part of Christian converts, with Basel mission tiles and textiles becoming famous in southern India. In the 20th century the economic and political upheavals from two world wars and the new postwar status of missions have greatly affected the program of the Basel Missionary Society.

**Basilicas.** The name given to the first type of structure built for Christian worship. These churches were of two main shapes, rectangular and central. The latter were either octagonal or circular. All basilicas had a central section that had higher walls than the peripheral sections. The part of the walls that extended above the side aisles was called the clerestory, and it had windows. The nave opened into the aisles, separated from them only by the columns that held up the clerestory walls. At first the columns terminated in a horizontal architrave, but later there were arches. Normally there was a dome-vaulted, semicircular apse at the east end of the rectangular basilicas. Often there was an arcade on the street and an atrium separating the nave from outside noises. Usually there were outbuildings to the rear of the apse.

Not all basilicas were used for regular worship; many of them were martyria, built over "places of witness." These shrines could have been placed over the tomb of a martyr or the scene of a theophany, as was the Church of the Resurrection in Jerusalem. There was much variation in internal arrangement, depending on the purpose of the building and its geographical location. Although Christians owned buildings before the time of Constantine, no basilica churches before those which he built are known. There are various theories about the architectural antecedents of the churches, but the most likely explanation is that the architects combined the building types they knew to serve the new purpose.

**Basilides** (2d century). Influential Gnostic teacher who lived at Alexandria during the reign of Hadrian (117–138). He developed a strikingly original system of thought, according to which the nonexistent world was produced from the nonexistent by a nonexistent God. This "world" was a seed containing three divine "sonships," and the history of salvation is concerned with the third; when it is redeemed, the restoration of all will be accomplished, and cosmic ignorance and oblivion will come over everything that has been left below. The role of Jesus, "son of Mary," was that of mediating revelation—partly by his words, more importantly by his ascending and thus providing an example for all who belong to the third sonship. Such is, briefly, the system of Basilides as described by Hippolytus (c. 235). Chronologically, the account of his thought given by Irenaeus (c. 185) is earlier, but it disagrees with the account just given here and seems much more like other Gnostic systems; perhaps it is "Basilidian." The only famous disciple of Basilidea was his son Isidore, whose fragments reveal his interest in semiphilosophical ethics and in the history of philosophy. In the late 4th century the sect was still in existence, primarily in Egypt, north of Memphis, though from there some of its ideas had been taken to Spain by a certain Marcus. It probably died out soon afterward.

**Basil of Ancyra** (4th century). Physician elected bishop to replace the Sabellian Marcellus who was deposed at Constantinople in 336. Described as a man of great eloquence and learning, Basil belonged to the moderating party that tried to restore peace in the church over the Arian controversy. He presided at the Synod of Ancyra and signed the formulas of Sirmium and Seleucia. His homoiousian formula was defended by Athanasias and Hilary and represents the position arrived at by the Cappadocians. The Arians had him deposed in 360 and banished to Illyria, where he died.

**Basil of Caesarea** (c. 330–379). The first of the group commonly known as the Cappadocian Fathers. He came from a distinguished family in this frontier province, a land of great estates and ranches, and a few Greek cities. The chief of these, the former royal capital Mazaca, was renamed Caesarea after Cappadocia became a Roman province in A.D. 17. In the 4th century, Cappadocia was important as a source of horses for the imperial service, and was periodically traversed by emperors and armies on the way between Constantinople and Antioch. Basil's family, which had been Christian for several generations, also owned property in the more rugged province of Pontus to the north. His grandmother Macrina had received her religious instruction from Gregory Thaumaturgus, whose memory was kept alive in the family; his father, also named Basil, was a prominent lawyer at Caesarea. Basil was one of ten children; his older sister, Macrina, had an important influence on her brothers, three of whom became bishops—Basil of Caesarea, Gregory of Nyssa, and the much younger Peter of Sebaste in Roman Armenia.

Basil was still unbaptized, and presumably intended for a secular career, when he studied rhetoric at Caesarea and Constantinople, and later philosophy at Athens. There his friend Gregory of Nazianzus and Julian, later the Apostate, were among his fellow students and shared the rough student life of the time. On his return he taught briefly at Caesarea, but was urged by his sister to embrace not only the Christian profession, but also the ascetic life, which she later adorned as abbess of a large convent. After his baptism Basil visited the monastic communities of Egypt and Syria (c. 356–358), and then gathered several friends in an informal monastic settlement on the family estate at Annesi in Pontus. His actual monastic life was brief, but he always continued to be an ascetic, even to the damage of his health, and guided and organized the monasteries of Cappadocia and neighboring provinces on the moderate lines laid down in his Longer Rules. For Basil, the monastic model was the early Christian community as described in Acts. He definitely preferred the common to the solitary life on the ground that the gospel precepts of love and humility can be fulfilled only in community, but his monasteries also provided hermitages for those called to the solitary life. On the other hand, though the Rules mainly consider the monastery as a separate community, Basil employed his monks in the cluster of institutions outside Caesarea that came to be known as the New City (and became the site of the medieval and modern town). The 313 Shorter Rules are in the form of answers to questions on devotional and Biblical as well as monastic problems, and apparently come from meetings of superiors. Other briefer ascetic works are of doubtful authenticity, but Basil's practical teaching is further enshrined in the *Morals,* a collection of Biblical texts on Christian conduct for both monks and seculars. His Rules remain the classic document of Greek monasticism; early translated into Latin, they are an important source of the Rule of St. Benedict.

In 362 the pious but timid Eusebius became bishop of Caesarea, and called Basil to help him; he was ordained presbyter and began his active ministry about 364. Basil was soon famous as a preacher, and the recognized leader of what may be called the neo-Nicene party in Asia Minor, which aimed to unite the former semi-Arians who were now willing to accept the Nicene Creed with those who had always been loyal to it. Basil's prominence caused some coolness between him and his bishop, but this was ended before Eusebius' death in 370. Basil was his obvious successor; to those who doubted whether his health was equal to the position the older Gregory, bishop of Nazianzus, pointed out that they were not choosing an athlete but a bishop.

Basil's episcopate was largely spent in negotiations and struggles, the successful result of which he did not live to see. Though personally welcomed by Athanasius, he could not persuade the churches of Alexandria and Rome to recognize the former semi-Arian Melitius as bishop of Antioch instead of the rigid Paulinus, leader of the strict Nicene minority; and he had some difficulty in convincing Damasus of Rome of the heretical nature of the teachings of Apollinarius. He also met with difficulties from the pro-Arian policy of Valens, emperor of the East from 365 to 378. Valens supported the Arians at Constantinople, and expelled Melitius from Antioch and Athanasius' successor, Peter, from Alexandria. But Basil could not be touched at Caesarea, and emperor and bishop met and parted with respect, even when Basil refused to allow Valens to present his offering in the sanctuary, thus indicating that he considered him excommunicated. However, Basil suspected a personal attack when Valens divided the province of Cappadocia in 371, putting the cities of western Cappadocia in the new province of Cappadocia Secunda. The Canons of Nicaea assumed that the bishop of the civil metropolis would also head the church in the province, and Anthimus of Tyana, though no Arian, did not hesitate to claim his rights; the weakening of Basil's position as metropolitan bishop may not have been the emperor's main motive, but was certainly a welcome result of his action. Basil attempted to prevent it by installing bishops friendly to himself in some of the disputed cities, and was partially successful. His brother Gregory became bishop of Nyssa, but Gregory of Nazianzus never took possession of the church in the village of Sasima for which he was consecrated, and was left with a sense of grievance against his admired but dominating friend and leader.

The main monument of Basil's famous preaching is the *Hexaëmeron,* a series of sermons on the six days of creation. Other preserved sermons are on various psalms and gospel lessons and for special occasions. Basil's extensive correspondence is an important source for his public and personal life; it also includes several canonical epistles ruling on various points of church law and liturgy. His theological works are mainly occasional and controversial: *Against Eunomius* (c. 365) replies to the leader of extreme Arianism, and *On the Holy Spirit* (375) maintains the deity of the Spirit, especially against the Macedonians who accepted the deity of the Son but denied the same status to the Holy Ghost. An important brief work, the *Address to Young Men,* defends the study by Christians of classical literature in spite of its obvious pagan content. The Liturgy of St. Basil later assumes its present form, but its Eucharistic prayer seems to be at least in part the one which he used at Caesarea, and which was gradually adopted at Constantinople, backed by the prestige of his name.

The emperor Valens was killed at the battle of Adrianople in August, 378, and Basil's death on the following Jan. 1 slightly preceded the victory of the various causes he represented. With the accession of Theodosius, Nicene orthodoxy became the faith of the Eastern Empire, and in 381 the Council of Constantinople accepted the neo-Nicene theology, and recognized Melitius, just before his death at the Council, as bishop of Antioch. The theology that Basil had developed and taught was more systematically expounded after his death in the works of the two Gregories. The Eastern Orthodox Church properly venerates Basil as one of its great teachers; in its calendar, Jan. 1 is observed as St. Basil's Day, and is one of the occasions on which the Liturgy of St. Basil is still used.

BIBLIOGRAPHY: P. Schaff and H. Wace (eds.), *Nicene and Post-Nicene Fathers,* Series II, Vol. 8 (Grand Rapids, 1956); W. K. L. Clarke, *St. Basil the Great: A Study in Monasticism* (Cambridge, 1913); E. F. Morison, *St. Basil and His Rule* (New York, 1912); G. L. Prestige, *St. Basil the Great and Apollinaris of Laodicea* (London, 1956).

**Batak Church** (Indonesia). The result of mission work in Sumatra among the cannibalistic Batak people by the Rhenish Missionary Society. An outstanding example of Protestant missionary work under the pioneer leadership of Ludwig Nommensen (d. 1918), who came to Sumatra in 1862. Nommensen sought to work within the tribal structure of the Batak people and thereby to establish a "folk church." In 1877 a theological training school was founded. About 1899 a Batak missionary movement was begun which eventuated in the Zending Batak (Batak Missionary Society) in 1921. It now functions as a foreign missionary society of the church, with native Batak Christians going out as missionaries to neighboring islands in Indonesia and to India. In 1951 the church drew up its own confession of faith rather than adopt the Western (Lutheran) Book of Concord and on the basis of it was admitted into membership in the Lutheran World Federation. The Batak Church is growing rapidly, with over 1,100,000 members in 1967, nearly double its 1950 membership. It also conducts the outstanding Nommensen University in Sumatra.

**Bauer, Bruno** (1809–1882). German Biblical critic and writer. After Bauer had taught at Berlin and Bonn, his license to teach was revoked because of his 1841 work, *Kritik der Evangelischen Geschichte der Synoptiker*, which made of the Gospels a work of poetry. He was a leader in the "young Hegelian" school, an advocate of radical or absolute criticism, and an implacable enemy of the Jews (see his *Die Judenfrage*, 1843).

**Baumgarten, Otto** (1858–1934). Preacher and social reformer. Son of the historian Hermann Baumgarten, he served as pastor in Baden and Berlin, then as professor of pastoral theology in Jena (1890) and Kiel (1894). He worked hard for the reform of discipline and the application of Christianity to social and political life, acting as chairman of the Evangelical Social Congress. He was also a strong opponent of anti-Semitism, and wrote an autobiography in 1929.

**Baumgarten, Siegmund Jacob** (1706–1757). The most influential German dogmatician of the 18th century. Trained at Halle when it was a center of Pietism, he spent his mature life there as a professor of theology (1734 ff.). Strongly influenced by the English deists, Baumgarten attempted with much apparent success a systematic synthesis between orthodoxy and the rationalistic Wolffian philosophy. Highly reputed for his polished style of lecturing, he wrote in almost every realm of theology. A major portion of his literary work was published after his death by his now more famous pupil, Johann S. Semler.

**Baur, Ferdinand Christian** (1792–1860). German Protestant theological scholar. He was the founder of the Tübingen school of Biblical historians. During the years of his education at Tübingen he passed under the influence both of the old Tübingen school and of the new philosophy of Fichte and Schelling. In his early career while a seminary teacher he became preoccupied with the approach of Schleiermacher. Called to Tübingen in 1826, where he stayed for the rest of his life, Baur soon passed from the influence of Schleiermacher to that of Hegel, and from that point on his work was dominated to a greater or lesser degree by Hegel's philosophy of history. Baur brought about a revolution in the conception of the Scriptures and indeed in the treatment of all Christian history. Using Hegel's concept of history as a process in which conflicting forces are resolved in the emergence of a new synthetic reality, Baur set out to reach an understanding of the New Testament and early Christianity that was truly historical rather than merely literary or theological, i.e., to conceive of it as a living reality conditioned by historical forces and factors. In 1831, Baur, beginning with the apostle Paul and subsequently working his way through the entire New Testament, submitted the whole of early Christian literature to his theory that Christianity developed gradually from Judaism into a universal world religion, and that this took place when the thesis of Judaistic Petrinism was countered by universalizing Paulinism, finally giving rise to the synthesis of the ancient catholic church.

**Bautain, Louis Eugène Marie** (1796–1867). French theologian and philosopher. He won recognition as a professor of philosophy at Strasbourg (1819–1822). He was ordained in 1828 and became dean at the University of Strasbourg (1838), archbishop of Paris (1849), and professor of theology at the Sorbonne (1853–1863). His theory of fideism was that faith depended on feeling, not reason, and had superior truths inaccessible to reason. His ideas were condemned in 1838. After a temporary breach with the Roman Church he submitted, and in 1840 recanted in obedience to the church.

**Baxter, Richard** (1615–1691). English Presbyterian clergyman. He was largely self-educated and was ordained to the ministry of the Church of England in 1638. He began work as a teacher at Dudley and there came under the influence of nonconformists. At this time he could see rights and wrongs on both sides and retained such a view through most of his life. While at Bridgnorth, he indulged in nonconformist practices, refusing to make the sign of the cross, disdaining the use of the surplice, and expressing his conviction that the episcopacy of the Church of England bore little resemblance to that of the primitive church. In 1641 he became lecturer of the church at Kidderminster where he exercised considerable influence on the community. While he was there the Civil War began and Baxter sided with Parliament against the king, although approving of monarchy. For a time he fled, ministered to the Parliamentary forces, and in 1647 lived in retirement with friends. In ill-health and with divided loyalties, he nevertheless wrote much and in 1649 published his controversial *Aphorisms of Justification* and in 1650 his most famous work, *Saints' Everlasting Rest*. Toward the end of the interregnum he returned to Kidderminster and began to work on behalf of the Restoration. In 1660 he went to London, was appointed chaplain to Charles II, took a prominent part in the Savoy Conference, and proposed a Reformed Liturgy which won the admiration of Dr. Johnson. The rest of his life was lived under great handicaps, and much of the time he suffered persecution for his nonconformist convictions, but before his death he completed the *Reliquiae Baxterianae,* a powerful and moving account of his own life.

**Bayeux Tapestry.** A long narrow band of linen embroidered in colored wools which portrays events culminating in the struggle between the short-lived King Harold of England and Duke William of Normandy at the Battle of Hastings in 1066. Worked into the design is the name of William's half brother, Bishop Odo of Bayeux, who later died on the way to the First Crusade. The tapestry was embroidered within a few decades after the scenes detailed on it had occurred. Some 20 inches wide and over 230 feet long, it was brought to light in the late 1720's by the researches of the Maurist scholar Bernard de Montfaucon. Although it is called the Bayeux Tapestry, its place of composition is unknown. According to tradition it was displayed annually in the Cathedral of Bayeux as early as the 15th century.

**Bayle, Pierre** (1647–1706). French Protestant writer and critic. He was much admired by leaders of the Enlightenment, especially for his great *Dictionnaire historique et critique* (1st ed., 1695–1697). Bayle was in reality a skeptic on many issues both of religious tradition and of older scientific speculation. The articles in the *Dictionnaire* were respectful of orthodoxy and the proprieties, but the annotations were not. His views tended to divide morality and revealed religion, and often ridiculed or explained away those elements of religion (e.g., miracles) which seemed contrary to the new science.

**Bayly, Lewis** (d. 1631). Celebrated Puritan preacher and bishop of Bangor. He became chaplain to Henry, Prince of Wales, and after Henry's death, was chaplain to King James. As bishop in Wales, his Puritanism brought him into conflict with the people of his diocese. His fame rests on the devotional work, *Practice of Piety,* which went through numerous editions and translations. John Bunyan dated his first awakenings from the reading of this book.

**Bay Psalm Book.** The hymnal of the Massachusetts Bay Colony. The first book to be printed in English in the American colonies, it was authored by "the chief Divines" of Massachusetts Bay Colony and was provided with a preface by Richard Mather, and published in 1640 under the title *The Whole Booke of Psalms Faithfully Translated into*

*English Metre.* It was intended as a replacement for older versions and to be used in the worship services of the Puritans, where *a cappella* congregational psalm-singing was a distinctive feature.

**Bea, Augustin Cardinal** (1881–1968). German Roman Catholic cardinal. After studies in his native Germany, Bea joined the Jesuit Order in Holland, and was ordained in 1912. He became known for his work as a Scripture scholar and as rector of the Pontifical Biblical Institute (1930–1949). In 1959, Bea was made a cardinal by Pope John XXIII. As director of the Secretariat for Promoting Christian Unity established in 1960 in preparation for the Second Vatican Council, Cardinal Bea was a leader of the liberal faction.

**Beaton, David** (c. 1494–1546). Scottish anti-Reformation prelate and statesman. Educated in the universities of St. Andrews, Glasgow, and Paris, learned in canon and civil law, Beaton made rapid advancement as a churchman in Scotland. He was a trusted envoy of James V and in his missions to France gained the high regard of Francis I. In 1538, Pope Paul III appointed him a cardinal priest, and the next year he became primate of the Church of Scotland as archbishop of St. Andrews. When James V died, Beaton failed to obtain the regency, which went to the earl of Arran. He attempted to ally Scotland with England, but Beaton, who favored an alliance with France instead, was able to win Arran over to his views. Arran then dismissed the Protestant ministers by whom he had been surrounded. Since Beaton's ecclesiastical and civil power were threatened by the Scottish preachers who were denouncing Rome and urging reform, he relentlessly pursued, tried, and condemned many of them. Plots were laid against him, and George Wishart may have been involved in a famous conspiracy with Henry VIII to assassinate Beaton. In 1546, Beaton presided over the trial that condemned Wishart. After Wishart's execution Beaton was hated by many Scots and on May 29, 1546, he was murdered, the victim of his struggle to maintain hierarchal privileges at any cost in the face of popular demand for reform.

**Beaufort, Henry** (c. 1377–1447). Bishop of Lincoln (1398) and of Winchester (1404), cardinal in the Church of Rome. He was the son of John of Gaunt and Catherine Swynford, thus half brother of Henry IV. A shrewd church politician and financier, he attended the Council of Constance (1417) in addition to serving as papal legate to Germany, Hungary, and Bohemia, and three times occupying the chancellorship of England. As chancellor under Henry VI from 1424 he became the chief molder of foreign policy.

**Bebel, August** (1840–1913). German Catholic Socialist. He was an Opponent of Bismarck in the Imperial Reichstag. With Wilhelm Liebknecht (1869), he organized a Marxist workingmen's bloc. It fused at Gotha (1875) with the Lassalleans to form the Social Democratic Party—parliamentary before revolutionary action. Bebel rejected the Kulturkampf and militarism. Frequently in jail, he wrote *Women and Socialism* and *Christianity and Socialism*.

**Bec, Monastery of.** A Benedictine abbey in Normandy, consecrated in 1041. The abbey was expanded in 1060 and rebuilt in 1263 after being destroyed by fire. Among the notable monks of Bec were Lanfranc and Anselm, both later archbishops of Canterbury, and Pope Alexander II. The monastery was suppressed in 1790 and suffered extensive destruction. Monks returned to Bec in 1948 and restored the monastic life.

**Beck, Johann Tobias** (1804–1878). German theologian. Beck served pastorates in Waldtann and Bad Mergentheim, then went to Basel (1836) to oppose De Wette. In 1843 he assumed a chair in systematics at Tübingen, attracting many Finnish and Swiss students. From Bengel and Hahn he derived a strict Biblical realism and his *heilsgeschichtlich* methodology. Almost pietistic at times, he sought to retain a critical stance. Beck stressed the Kingdom of God in the world and the *imitatio Christi* as a practical penetration of culture. Against Hegel, he saw the flowering of the Spirit's power, not man's, in Biblical revelation. His works included *Die christliche Lehrwissenschaft nach den biblischen Urkunden* (1841).

**Beck, Vilhelm** (1829–1901). Danish Lutheran pastor and Inner Mission leader. Born at Ørsløv, Zealand, he studied theology at Copenhagen and was assistant to his father at Uby (1856–1865), where he sparked a spiritual awakening that was non-Grundtvigian in character. From 1866 to 1874 he served the parish at Ørum and from 1874 to 1901 was the pastor at Ørsløv, his childhood home. In 1861 he became active in the Danish Inner Mission movement (founded in 1853) and changed its emphasis from Grundtvigian to pietistic. Under Beck's leadership the Inner Mission movement developed into a religious party within the framework of the Lutheran State Church of Denmark. In 1872 the first mission house was dedicated by Beck. Thirty years later there were nearly four hundred such houses.

**Becket, Thomas** (c. 1118–1170). English archbishop and martyr. Becket was the son of Norman immigrants living in London and following his early education in England and Paris he returned home for practical business experience.

About 1141 he joined the staff of Archbishop Theobald of Canterbury and was sent to study law in Bologna and Auxerre. Upon his return he was ordained and became archdeacon of Canterbury in 1154. The next year King Henry II appointed him chancellor (secretary and adviser) and the two men became close personal friends. As chancellor, Becket carried out his duties with ability and zeal. Generally he followed a policy in line with the king's desires, even though this occasionally went against the interests of the church. Henry's trust in Becket was such that he often felt secure enough to travel abroad to look after his other lands. In his personal affairs Becket conducted himself more like a nobleman than a churchman.

In 1161, Archbishop Theobald died and Henry insisted that Becket take the office. Henry thus hoped to reduce the church's independence in his drive to consolidate his power. Under the reign of his predecessor, Stephen (1135–1154), the English Church had grown to enjoy a great degree of independence from royal control. Stephen had needed the church's support to attain the crown and he had paid for it by allowing church considerable freedom. In England the church's claims often seemed to border on encroachments upon the authority of lay courts. Occasional abuses occurred, since all clergymen accused of any crime were to be tried in ecclesiastical courts which could not pronounce any penalty involving the drawing of blood. The church seemed to be setting up a judicial system alongside of and detrimental to the lay courts and the king's authority. Henry hoped by having Becket as archbishop to bring the church's policy more in line with royal wishes. Becket reluctantly accepted election to the post, feeling that a clash with the king was nearly inevitable.

After becoming archbishop, Becket resigned the chancellorship as a conflicting interest and turned to live a life of personal piety. A serious quarrel soon arose between Henry and Becket over the question whether clergy in minor orders (clerks) accused of committing crimes should be tried in the lay or in the ecclesiastical courts. During a council held at Clarendon in 1164, Henry produced a set of laws (Constitutions of Clarendon), nicknamed the "grandfather's customs," which he claimed represented the traditional relationship between church and state. These laws limited the church's authority and gave the state more control over clergy accused of crimes. Becket, first accepting the laws, later changed his mind and refused to affix his seal to the propositions. This refusal angered Henry, who attempted, particularly through the Council of Northampton (1164), to undermine Becket's support by the bishops and ruin him financially. Becket finally fled to France and appealed his case to Pope Alexander III.

For the next six years Henry, Becket, and the pope intermittently carried on unsuccessful negotiations. Becket spent his time in a French Cistercian abbey until Henry threatened to expel all Cistercians from his domains. Becket then moved to a French Benedictine abbey which was under the direct protection of the French king.

In 1170 a brief reconciliation between Henry and Becket occurred, but was broken when a new quarrel erupted. The dispute arose when Henry's son was crowned his successor by the archbishop of York, thus usurping a traditional function of the archbishop of Canterbury. Although the king promised to make amends, Becket refused to protest papal orders suspending the archbishop of York and the bishops who had assisted at the ceremony.

Becket returned to England in November of 1170, still refusing to reinstate the bishops until they swore loyalty to the pope. Enraged by this action, Henry, then in Normandy, indicted members of his household, accusing them of accepting his hospitality but not avenging him when wronged. Four of his knights interpreted these words probably more literally than Henry intended and set out for England. They arrived in Canterbury and found Becket in his cathedral, where they murdered him (Dec. 29).

The assassination was a great shock to the church. Three years later Becket was canonized as a saint by Pope Alexander III and his tomb became the object of major pilgrimages. Henry, through an oath and submission to papal judgment, escaped direct guilt for the murder. Although he received no especially severe ecclesiastical punishment, he did public penance at Becket's tomb in 1174. As a result of Becket's murder, Henry's efforts to control the church were only partially successful.

BIBLIOGRAPHY: W. H. Hutton, *Thomas Becket, Archbishop of Canterbury* (Cambridge, 1926); M. D. Knowles, "Archbishop Thomas Becket: A Character Study" (Raleigh Lecture on History for 1949), in *Proceedings of the British Academy,* Vol. XXXV (1949), pp. 177–205.

**Becon, Thomas** (c. 1513–1567). English Reformer. Influenced by Latimer, Becon vigorously propagated Protestant doctrines in both preaching and writing (under the pseudonym Theodore Basille). He was forced to recant his opinions in 1540. In 1547 he became chaplain to the protector Somerset. In exile during Mary's reign, he returned to England in 1559. His views subsequently moved from the Lutheran toward the Zwinglian, and his writings enjoyed a marked popularity among English Protestants.

**Bede** (c. 672–735). English theologian and historian. By common consent he was referred to as "the Venerable Bede" within a few years of his death. Dedicated to the monastic life at seven, he became deacon at nineteen and priest at thirty. All his working life was spent as a monk at Jarrow. Educated by Benedict Biscop and Ceolfrith, he became the greatest historian of Christianity in England with his *Ecclesiastical History of the English Nation.* Bede puts his weight behind the attempt to abolish Celtic usages in favor of Roman ones, but he gives credit to the Celtic missionaries for their fervor. Where he uses the work of others he gives due acknowledgment and even asks copyists to preserve their names. He has a strong sense of literary form and loves the Bible for its beauty as well as for its usefulness. Biscop had introduced Roman music and liturgy into England. Bede gives full credit to English poets and musicians such as Caedmon and Cuthbert. He knew Greek and at the time he died he had just finished translating the last chapter of John. He may have known Hebrew. His forty-odd works are written in lucid Latin and his explanations tend to be rational rather than miraculous.

**Beecher, Henry Ward** (1813–1887). Congregational pastor. He was born at Litchfield, Conn., and educated at Amherst (1830–1834) and at Lane Theological Seminary (1834–1837) in Cincinnati while his father, Lyman Beecher, was president. In Cincinnati Henry wrote for a city daily and edited a Presbyterian weekly. Rejecting Old School Presbyterianism, he was ordained by New School Cincinnati Presbytery, and in two frontier pastorates (1837–1847) at Lawrenceburg and Indianapolis, Ind., revealed and developed traits that made his ministry at Brooklyn's suburban Plymouth Congregational Church (1847–1887) the most conspicuous in 19th-century America. His wife of fifty years, Eunice Bullard of West Sutton, Mass., and four children survived him.

A broad reader, Beecher succeeded through versatility, vitality, and wit rather than originality, mental depth, or disciplined work and thought. With the popularizer's synoptic gift, and the romantic's empathy and inclusive spirit, he excelled at oratory. He was an amateur art collector, gardener, and phrenologist.

Theologically, he made emotion and moral earnestness normative, not orthodoxy or rationalism. Influenced by frontier revivalism, he believed that God loves man in his sin for the sake of helping him out of it, not because of a covenant but "from the fullness of his great heart." His gospel of God's love displaced the righteous God and limited atonement of orthodox covenant theology. Beecher's Christ was "ever present," "always near . . . as a companion and friend, to uphold and sustain." The only necessary and essential thing was love of Christ as Savior, obedience to him as Lord, and sincere effort to advance his Kingdom. His *Life of Jesus the Christ* (1871) was never completed. He pleaded for openness to scientific facts and believed future creeds would "begin where the old ones ended: upon the nature of man, his condition on earth, his social duties and civil obligations."

Thus oriented, he influenced moral, social, and national issues more than theological and ecclesiastical ones. He early attacked personal vice on the frontier (*Seven Lectures to Young Men*, 1844). He condemned slavery but claimed constitutional protection for it in the South. He opposed the Compromise of 1850 and urged disregard of the Fugitive Slave Law and the use of rifles (Beecher's Bibles) to keep Kansas free. He campaigned for Fremont and Lincoln but condemned delay in emancipation after secession. His lecture tour of England (1863) helped dissipate anti-Union sentiment, and in 1865 he accompanied Old Glory's return to Fort Sumter. He angered radicals by urging the full and rapid reentry of the southern states into the Union, and by being content with gradual voting rights for Negroes and women while admitting the natural right of suffrage. In economics he opposed "protectionism" as "socialistic," and identified poverty with sin and prosperity with virtue.

Though several church councils asserted his innocence, after 1874 he labored under moral suspicion when a favorable but split jury failed to clear him completely of Theodore Tilton's charge of adultery. In later years he rejected doctrines of eternal punishment and verbal inspiration, became an early advocate of Darwinism (*Evolution and Religion*, 1885), and withdrew Plymouth Church from the Congregational Association in 1882. In 1884 he perplexed Republicans by stumping for Cleveland.

His style, analyzed in *Yale Lectures on Preaching* (1872–1874), combined verbal energy, almost comic humor, free self-revelation, and poetic figures with a revivalist's interest in results in an endless moral crusade. The spectacle of Beecher standing without pulpit or manuscript mentally and emotionally exposed on every public issue attracted the curious, but his contagiously earnest sermons and prayers kept them coming in numbers up to twenty-five hundred a week.

He created a national constituency with regular sermon reprints (*The Plymouth Pulpit*) and articles in the *New York Ledger*, the *Independent* (editor, 1861–1863) and the *Christian Union* (editor, 1870–1882).

Sincerity and carelessness of convention made Beecher a reformer and innovator, a popular symbol not only of new theology but of America. Yet commonsense avoidance of radicalism allowed him so to catch and reflect his countrymen's aspirations that in retrospect he appears more their mirror than their leader.

**Beecher, Lyman** (1775–1863). American Presbyterian minister and one of the leading revivalists of the Second Great Awakening. Born in New Haven and educated in Yale, Beecher, though he later moved far away from those precincts, remained throughout his life a Yankee and an exponent of the New England Theology. He went up to Yale College in 1793 and found it, as he said, "in a most ungodly state. . . . Most of the class before me were infidels, and called each other Voltaire, Rousseau, d'Alembert, etc., etc." (*Autobiography*, 27). Timothy Dwight, who was named president of Yale in 1795, put a stop to this and greatly influenced Beecher in the process. After graduation, Beecher studied for the ministry for nine months in Dwight's home. Beecher was continually on a crusade, but his life may be divided into three parts as he changed his field of labor. The first part of his ministry was spent attacking the forces of ungodliness (i.e., the Jeffersonian Democrats) which were attempting to achieve the disestablishment of the Connecticut Congregational churches. As a prelude to that contest, he served ten years in the Presbyterian Church of East Hampton, Long Island. It was not strange for a Congregationally trained minister to serve a Presbyterian parish, for under the 1801 Plan of Union these two denominations cooperated in missionary work in the West and were even then (1799) cooperating in their own states. It was under this Plan of Union that the remainder of Beecher's life was spent in the Presbyterian Church. His revival preaching often included attacks upon specific abuses, such as his first widely recognized sermon which attacked dueling, or a later famous series in 1825 which attacked intemperance. He moved to the parish of Litchfield, Conn., in 1810. Here, along with his old teacher, Timothy Dwight, and one of his closest friends and ministerial colleagues, Nathaniel W. Taylor, he launched his campaign to defeat the forces of disestablishment. The method perfected in this contest he utilized throughout his life: organizing the ministers to preach up a revival and write down the opposition. The campaign did not succeed in Connecticut. Beecher at first took it as a mortal blow, but later in recollection declared that "for several days I suffered what no tongue can tell *for the best thing that ever happened to the state of Connecticut*. It cut the churches loose from dependence on state support. It threw them wholly on their own resources and on God" (*Autobiography*, 252). The next step in Beecher's career was taken in accepting a call to Boston, the heartland of the Unitarian movement, to a new and very small congregation on Hanover Street. From 1826 to 1832 he carried on the same kind of crusade against the Unitarians as he had against disestablishment in Connecticut. He encouraged some drooping orthodox spirits, but did not have any great effect upon the direction of Unitarian thought. In 1831, he preached an unfortunate series of sermons against Roman Catholicism which was at least a contributing factor in the ensuing anti-Catholic riot that culminated in the burning of an Ursuline convent. In the third phase of his life, Beecher turned toward the West, becoming the president of the new Lane Seminary in Cincinnati in 1832. At this time he published probably his most important tract, *A Plea for the West,* in which he noted the danger from Catholic immigration and emphasized that the religious and political destiny of America would be decided in the West. His work at Lane was intended to affect this destiny, but his tenure as president was not uniformly successful. In 1834, over Beecher's objections, the Board of Trustees forced almost all the students to desert the seminary for Oberlin by forbidding them to discuss the abolition of slavery. More important was Beecher's own trial for heresy in 1835. It was actually more a preliminary skirmish in the civil war which was soon to break out in the Presbyterian Church and end in the schism of 1837. Beecher, as a representative of that

group of Calvinist churches which favored revivalism, was tried by the conservatives who opposed it. Beecher was cleared of the charges. He resigned the presidency of Lane in 1850 and spent most of the remaining years of his life in the home of his son Henry Ward Beecher. One of his daughters was Harriet Beecher Stowe, author of *Uncle Tom's Cabin*.

BIBLIOGRAPHY: L. Beecher, *Autobiography*, ed. by B. M. Cross (Cambridge, Mass., 1961); W. S. Hudson, *The Great Tradition of the American Churches* (New York, 1953).

**Beguines and Beghards.** Semimonastic associations of laywomen and laymen, respectively, existing in the 12th and 13th centuries in the Low Countries. The Beguine movement was a particularly representative example of high medieval lay "apostolic" ferment. Ultimately deriving from the Gregorian Reform but founded and nurtured in the Netherlands, it was a concrete realization of medieval aspirations to approximate the "apostolic life" as depicted in Acts 2:24–47; 4:32–37. It involved mostly pious women who embraced a common life of continence, poverty, and simplicity, of manual labor and the works of mercy, and of liturgical prayer, but without becoming nuns. Such women were largely from those socioeconomic classes not admissible to the typical Benedictine or Cistercian nunnery. Since the hundreds of beguinages that sprang up in the Netherlands and Germany had no single founder, rule, or congregation, the movement remained spontaneous and amorphous. It was essentially voluntary in nature: anyone of sufficient motivation could join and anyone was free to withdraw. Such semireligious or extraregular communities rarely transcended diocesan or even parochial boundaries. Although the informal character of the movement often worried the ecclesiastical authorities, its fervent attachment to dogmatic and sacramental essentials guaranteed it papal sanction. Houses of Beghards (male) were rather few in number. A small number of Beguine houses survived the Reformation and the French Revolution and continue to the present day in Belgium.

**Beissel, Johann Conrad** (1690–1768). German Pietist. Influenced in his native Germany by Pietism and inspirationalism, he came to America in 1720 and was baptized a Dunker. After being constantly repudiated for his advocacy of celibacy and Sabbatarianism, he withdrew from this denomination, and in 1728 organized the German Seventh Day Baptists, and in 1732 the Ephrata Community, in which semimonastic society he remained as leader until his death.

**Bekker, Balthasar** (1634–1698). Dutch Reformed minister and theologian. Bekker served as pastor to a congregation in Amsterdam from 1679 to 1692. The publication of his book *De Betoverde Wereld* (1691) led to his being accused of the Cartesian heresy, and as a result he was suspended from his pastorate. In this controversial work, Bekker, much in the manner of later rationalists, denounced belief in demonism, witchcraft, and other black arts.

**Belgic Confession** (1561). A Reformed confession growing out of 16th-century Spanish persecution of Protestants in the Low Countries. Written in 1559 by Guido de Brès (martyred 1567), with the help of Adrian Saravia, H. Modetus, and Godfrey van Wingen, it was printed in 1561 and presented to Philip II the following year in the vain hope of securing toleration for Protestants. With the Heidelberg Catechism and the Canons of Dort, it is a recognized symbol of the Reformed churches in Holland and Belgium, as well as of the Reformed Church in America and the Christian Reformed Church. Originally written in French, it was modeled on the Gallican Confession of 1559.

**Belinski, Vissarion Grigoryevich** (1811–1848). Russian literary critic and father of the radical intelligentsia in Russia. A disciple of both Schelling and Hegel, he attempted to understand the Russian cultural heritage and function with relation to a concept of universal history. Exhibiting a deep concern for the illiterate peasantry, he was instrumental in the inspiration and organization of efforts to relieve their situation. He was bitterly critical of the part played by the church.

**Bell, George Kennedy Allen** (1883–1958). Bishop of the Diocese of Chichester in the Church of England (1929–1958) and international leader in the ecumenical movement. He served as chaplain to the archbishop of Canterbury, Randall Davidson (1914–1924), and was his definitive biographer (2 vols., 1935). Widely known for his unusual ability and for his outspoken positions on various social issues, he was president of the World Council of Churches and editor of four volumes of *Documents on Christian Unity*.

**Bellamy, Joseph** (1719–1790). Connecticut Congregationalist pastor who was a Great Awakening evangelist and disciple of his mentor and friend, Jonathan Edwards. Nevertheless, he revised the latter's "consistent Calvinism" to provide a greater divine permissiveness regarding the Fall and a wider measure of human freedom in the salvation of the human race, about two thirds of which he felt might be elected to salvation.

**Bellarmine, Robert** (1542–1621). Jesuit prelate and controversialist. He was born at Montepulciano, Oct. 4, 1542, his mother the sister of the future pope Marcellus II. Bellarmine entered the Society of Jesus in 1560. Having studied philosophy at the new Roman College, he taught the humanities for three years at Florence and Mondovi, and in 1567 began his theology at Padua. In 1569 he was asked to finish his studies at Louvain to learn at first hand the heretical movements of the Low Countries. He lectured there until 1576, when he was recalled to fill the new chair of controversial theology at the Roman College. His studies resulted in *De controversiis* (3 vols., Ingolstadt, 1586–1593), his chief title to literary greatness, the earliest attempt to align traditional Roman Catholic doctrines systematically against the chief reformers of the times. The immensity of its impression may be gauged by the chairs founded in Germany and England to refute it. In 1590, however, while in France as theologian to the embassy of Cardinal Gaetano, he learned that Pope Sixtus V, having once given his approbation, was about to condemn Vol. I because it granted the papacy only indirect power over temporal matters. The sudden death of Sixtus prevented this, and Pope Gregory XIV gave the work his special approbation.

From 1591 to 1592 Bellarmine sat on the commission for the revision of the Vulgate text of the Bible prescribed by the Council of Trent. The impatience of Pope Sixtus with its slow progress had impelled him, though not a scholar, to take over the revision and print it along with the bull ordering its use. When the pope died before full promulgation, the commission recalled the texts and corrected the errors, reissuing it with a preface by Bellarmine that tried to smooth over the incident.

Bellarmine's reputation for scholarship, objectivity, and practical wisdom now led to a succession of appointments that were to give him a key role in important curial decisions until the year of his death. In 1592 he was made rector of the Roman College, in 1595 provincial of Naples, in 1597 theologian to Pope Clement VIII, as well as examiner of bishops and consultor of the Holy Office; in 1599 he became cardinal, "for the Church of God had not his equal in learning." But Bellarmine's curial work was interrupted when, as president of the congregation formed to judge the controversy between Jesuits and Dominicans over the relationship between divine grace and human liberty, he advised the pope against a final decision before there was more discussion in the schools. Clement at first agreed, then changed his mind; to save embarrassment he made Bellarmine archbishop of Capua in 1602.

In 1605, Clement died. He was succeeded by Leo XI, who reigned only twenty-six days, when Paul V was elected. Much against his wishes, Bellarmine was considered at both conclaves, but probably dislike for the Jesuits in some quarters prevented his election. He was again ordered to Rome, where his administrative positions made him the chief theological adviser to the Holy See. Before his death three major problems engaged his attention.

In 1606 the pope placed an interdict on the Republic of Venice, which had abrogated clerical exemption and withdrawn the church's right to hold property. Bellarmine and Cardinal Baronius defended the papacy in the ensuing pamphlet war against the antipapalism of Paolo Sarpi. The same year saw the English oath of allegiance whereby Roman Catholics in England were required, on pain of confiscation of possessions, to condemn as heretical the doctrine that popes could depose royalty. When Paul forbade the taking of the oath and King James defended it, Bellarmine's reply was based on the same theory of indirect temporal sovereignty as the *De controversiis*. In 1615 he informed Galileo of the condemnation of the heliocentric theory, although his own principles admitted the possibility that scientific discoveries could change the understanding of Scripture.

He attended one more papal conclave, electing Gregory XV in 1621, before bad health forced his retirement to the Jesuit novitiate in Rome, where he died September 17, 1621. He was canonized in 1930 and proclaimed a Doctor of the Church in 1931.

See J. Brodrick, *Robert Bellarmine* (Westminster, Md., 1961).

**Benedict** (c. 480–c. 543). Author of the Rule of St. Benedict and known as the "Patriarch of Western Monks." He was born at Nursia, near Spoleto, and was sent to Rome for his education. The immorality of Roman life shocked him enough to cause him to leave Rome and retire to the hills near the city, where he founded a hermitage at Subiaco (c. 500). After several years of learning the ascetic life from a friend, he was asked by nearby monks to become their abbot. They found his attempt to reform them too rigorous, and tried to poison him. He returned to

Subiaco to live again as a hermit. However, his fame as an ascetic attracted numerous disciples. From these disciples were formed twelve monasteries. Difficulties with a priest in the vicinity forced Benedict and his monks to leave Subiaco and establish a new monastery at Monte Cassino. There he is presumed to have written his famous rule which has become the classic text for Western monks. His sister, Scholastica, was a nun in the vicinity of Monte Cassino and frequently visited her brother for spiritual counsel. Both are buried at Monte Cassino. Benedict's life is known chiefly from the *Dialogues* of Gregory the Great. In 1965 at the rededication of Monte Cassino, Pope Paul VI proclaimed Benedict the patron saint of Europe.

**Benedict, Rule of St.** (*Regula Monachorum*). A rule for monks, written c. 530–540 by Benedict after the foundation of Monte Cassino.

*Text.* According to an account by Paul the Deacon, the autograph copy of the rule was brought to Rome by the monks of Monte Cassino when the abbey was destroyed in 580. In 720 when the abbey was restored, Pope Zacharias returned this copy to Abbot Petronax. When Charlemagne wished to have an authentic copy of the rule for the Frankish monasteries, he received a copy of the autograph that served as the archetype for several other copies. Today one cannot be certain that the exemplar of Charlemagne's manuscript was in fact the autograph of Benedict. However, the most reliable text of the rule is an early 9th-century copy of Charlemagne's text. This manuscript (MS. 914 of St. Gall, Switzerland), written in the vulgar Latin of Benedict's time, is thought to be the exemplar for most of the surviving manuscripts of the rule.

*Sources.* Benedict borrowed freely from earlier monastic writers. He was familiar with the *Vitae* of Antony and Pachomius and the collected sayings of the Egyptian fathers. He quotes from the Rules of Pachomius, Basil, Macarius, and Caesarius of Arles. Occasional references to Leo the Great, Augustine, and Jerome seem to indicate an acquaintance with their works. However, the existence of the Rule of the Master has raised questions about Benedict's use of sources. There are obvious parallels between Benedict and the Master, which is explained by Benedict's dependence upon the Master's text. Therefore, Benedict's firsthand acquaintance with his sources may be less than was once thought.

*Monastic Life.* The life conceived by Benedict is that of a large community of men who live together in one monastery under the direction of their abbot and relatively free from outside interference. The rule, consisting of a prologue and seventy-three chapters, regulates the life of this community in some detail. The mood of the rule is moderation and cooperation. Benedict writes in the Prologue: "We hope to ordain nothing that is harsh or burdensome." Any strictness of discipline was to be seen as necessary to the achievement of the goals of the monastic life. Excessive austerities, penances, or fasts were not permitted. The rule was designed for ordinary men, not for extraordinary spiritual athletes. The chapters of the rule may be summarized in the following outline: (1) definition of the kinds of monks and the declaration that this rule is for cenobites; (2–3) government of the monastery; (4–7) principles of the ascetic life; (8–20) order for the Divine Office; (21–22) deans and the dormitory; (23–30) penitential regulations; (31–34) administration of the monastery; (35–57) regulations for the daily life of the monks; (58–63) training of monks; (64–65) the appointment of the abbot and prior; (66–67) rules for enclosure; (68–72) rules for the community life; (73) Epilogue. The monks elect their own abbot, who is then the supreme authority in his house. He appoints the other officers of the community—the prior, the deans, the cellarer, and any others needed. Monks were not priests, but laymen living a special vocation. The abbot might select some of the brothers to be ordained by the bishop so that they could perform priestly functions for the community. All monks performed the *Opus Dei*, the Divine Office of prayers and psalms. While there was no vow of poverty, all property was held in common. The only vows required were: stability, which made the monk forever bound to his monastery; obedience to his abbot; and conversion of life, or the cultivation of the monastic ideals in his own life. Moderate clothing and an adequate diet were provided. The schedule of manual labor for each day was similar to that of the average Italian peasant of Benedict's day. Various sections of the rule have been modified to meet the needs of changing times and different locales. Commentaries have been written on the rule, the major ones being: Paul the Deacon (8th century), Augustin Calmet (1732), and Abbot Delatte (1913). There are several English translations of the rule, one of the better being by Abbot Justin McCann.

BIBLIOGRAPHY: C. Butler, *Benedictine Monachism* (London, 1919); D. Knowles, *Great Historical Enterprises* (London, 1963); H. B. Workman, *The Evolution of the Monastic Ideal* (London, 1927).

**Benedict XI** (Nicholas Boccasini, 1240–1304). Pope. Previously master general of the Dominicans, Boccasini was elected pope in 1303, following Boniface VIII. He was conciliatory with Philip the Fair and restored to the king and France the rights and privileges of which they had been deprived by Boniface. His leniency was not extended to William of Nogaret and Sciara Colonna, because of their role in the attack on Boniface at Anagni. His eight months' pontificate was brought to a sudden end by poisoning, which has been attributed to William of Nogaret.

**Benedict XII** (Jaques Fournier, d. 1342). Pope at Avignon. He came from an undistinguished family. Becoming a Cistercian monk, he gained a doctorate in theology at the University of Paris. Soon he became abbot of Fontfroide and then bishop of Pamiers in 1317. In 1334, on a surprising first ballot, the poor and obscure Cardinal Fournier was elected pope. As a cardinal and adviser to John XXII he had engaged in theological controversies aroused by the Fraticelli and by Pope John himself, who maintained that the beatific vision was postponed until the General Judgment. As pope, Fournier declared in a bull, *Benedictus Deus,* that the beatific vision was immediate for the souls of the just who had no faults to expiate. He wished to move the papacy back to Rome, but the factions among the Roman princes discouraged him. As Benedict XII he turned his zeal to reform. He revoked, except for cardinals, the practice of conferring benefices *in commendam* (whereby a cleric or layman had title to the revenues of a monastery, though he was in no way part of the community). He strove against the papal benefice system, against nepotism, against the profit obsession in clerics and monks; and he sought without success to disentangle the papacy from the control of the French king and to overcome the hostility of the emperor Louis IV of Bavaria.

**Benedict XIII** (Pedro de Luna, 1328–1423). Antipope. He was born in 1328, studied law at Montpellier, obtained a doctor's degree and later taught at the university. Attracted by his austere life and great learning, Gregory XI created him cardinal deacon in 1375. He participated in the election of Gregory's successor, Urban VI, in April of 1378 but in July joined the non-Italian cardinals at Anagni in protesting the election of Urban, giving his support to Clement VII, elected antipope on Sept. 20. He served Clement VII ably as a diplomat, winning support for the Avignon papacy and at the same time familiarizing himself with the endeavors of the University of Paris toward reunion.

He was elected to succeed Clement VII in September, 1394. On Oct. 3 he was ordained a priest, and on Oct. 11 he was consecrated bishop and enthroned as pope. At the time of his election he promised to end the schism, even by abdicating. Once enthroned, however, he remained independent of the efforts at reunion undertaken by the French court and the University of Paris. He entered into personal negotiations with three successive Roman popes, Boniface IX, Innocent VII, and Gregory XII, but no resolution of the schism was agreed upon.

Benedict withstood siege and imprisonment at Avignon. He was deposed by the Council of Pisa in 1408 and later by the Council of Constance in 1417. After the last of his adherents left him in 1417, he retired to the castle at Peñiscola in Spain, where he claimed to be the rightful pope until his death in 1423.

**Benedict XIV** (Prospero Lorenzo Lambertini, 1675–1758). Pope from 1740. After receiving his doctorate in theology and in civil and canon law in 1694, Lambertini held many curial posts under Clement XI and Innocent XIII. He was made bishop of Ancona in 1727, and cardinal the following year. In 1731 he became archbishop of Bologna. Upon the death of Clement XII in 1740 a division in the conclave between the forces of Austria and Spain, as well as other divisive factors, prevented the selection of a successor for six months. On the 255th scrutiny, Lambertini was chosen, taking the name Benedict XIV. Particularly interested in the arts and humanities, Benedict attempted to restore the glory that once had been Rome. He brought to life again the old *Accademia dei Lincei,* established four new academies in the city, and made changes in the Roman University. His interest in letters brought him into contact with the great men of the Age of Reason, such as Voltaire and Frederick the Great. His pontificate was vexed by struggles with the Jansenists and Gallicans, and Benedict involved the church in opposition to the rapid spread of Freemasonry. He published an encyclical against usury, established the canonical requirements for "mixed marriages," and was much devoted to missionary activities.

**Benedict XV** (Giacomo Giambattista Della Chiesa, 1854–1922). Pope from 1914. He received his Doctor of Laws degree from the University of Genoa in 1875, and was ordained three years later. He served with Archbishop Rampolla del Tindaro while the latter was nuncio to Spain, and once more when,

after 1887, Leo XIII made Rampolla a cardinal and papal secretary of state. In 1901, Leo made Della Chiesa his undersecretary of state. He was active in the struggle against "Modernism," and in 1907 became archbishop of Bologna. Upon the death of Pope Pius X in August, 1914, the conclave elected Della Chiesa his successor. He took the name Benedict XV. The seven years of his pontificate were blighted by World War I. His call for a peace free of the spirit of vengeance (Aug. 1, 1917) anticipated some of Wilson's proposals in the Fourteen Points. The legal training of his youth saw its fruition with the promulgation of the New Code of Canon Law in 1917, although the project had been begun under Pius X. During Benedict's pontificate the first steps were taken toward a relaxation of the tension between the papacy and the Italian state by the permission given Luigi Sturzo to form a "Catholic" political party, and by the *de facto* recognition of Italy.

**Benedict Biscop** (*also known as* Biscop Baducing) (c. 628–690). English ecclesiastic. Born to a noble Northumbrian family, he spent his early years in the court of King Oswy. In 653 he accompanied Wilfrid to Rome on the first of five visits. In 665 he became a monk at Lérins. He returned to England in 669 in the company of Theodore of Tarsus, who had been made archbishop of Canterbury. Benedict was appointed abbot of the Monastery of SS. Peter and Paul at Canterbury and later founded monasteries at Wearmouth in 674 and at Jarrow in 682. He was an advocate of Roman liturgy, church order, and architecture. Together with Archbishop Theodore and Wilfrid he promoted the reform of the Anglo-Saxon Church along the lines set forth by the Synod of Whitby. He was responsible for bringing the archcantor of St. Peter's to England to teach the English clergy Roman liturgical chant. He imported artisans from the Continent to construct churches and is said to have been the first to use stained glass in England. The development of Anglo-Saxon architecture owes more to Benedict's influence than to any other single figure. On his numerous trips to the Continent, he collected many manuscripts and relics for the monasteries of England. His biography was written by the Venerable Bede, who had been one of Benedict's students.

**Benedictine Order.** The name commonly applied to monastic foundations following the Rule of St. Benedict. The traditional black robes worn by the monks caused them to be called the Black Monks. Not a religious order in the strict sense of the word, the Benedictines are a federation of independent monasteries. A monk belongs not to the order but to a particular monastery.

*Origins.* Benedict founded a hermitage at Subiaco, where he lived for several years before a nearby monastery asked him to become their abbot. They found his regime too strict and attempted to poison him. Benedict then returned to his hermitage, where he soon attracted a band of disciples. From this group were formed twelve communities. Difficulties with a local cleric forced Benedict to leave Subiaco and establish a new community at Monte Cassino. Monte Cassino became the center for the new monastic movement built upon Benedict's Rule. During his lifetime, only one other monastery, Terracina, observed the rule. It is uncertain whether there was observance of the rule after Benedict's death. The monastery on Monte Cassino was destroyed by the Lombards in the late 6th century, and the monks fled to Rome, taking the rule with them. It was once firmly believed that Pope Gregory I established the Caelian monastery as a Benedictine house, that he himself was a Benedictine, and that Augustine of Canterbury, whom Gregory selected to head the mission to England, was also a Benedictine. All these assumptions have now been questioned. Gregory seems to have been more interested in the miracles of Benedict than in his rule, although he does comment on the rule's "discretion." There is insufficient evidence to assume that Gregory's monastery followed Benedict's Rule exclusively or primarily. The custom of Italian houses was to follow the precepts of the abbot and not a specific rule. The abbot might draw on various sources for his direction. Benedict's Rule may have been known to the Caelian monks, but it was not their exclusive rule. Therefore, it would seem that the English mission was not Benedictine.

*Expansion of the Order.* Even if one doubts the Benedictine character of Augustine's mission, it appears that the first Benedictine establishment outside of Italy was in England. Under Archbishop Theodore and his companion Abbot Adrian, the rule was established in the Saxon parts of England. The older Celtic monasteries tended to follow a more austere life as embodied in the Rule of St. Columbanus. Gradually the Benedictine life supplanted the Celtic, although traces of Celtic custom persisted. The English Benedictines were noted for their intellectual life, which produced such great scholars as the Venerable Bede. Outside England, the expansion of the order was less certain. A legend attributing the coming of the order to Gaul

to St. Maurus, a disciple of Benedict, is without foundation. In Gaul the monasteries tended to follow a variety of rules and customs. Monasteries founded by Celtic missionaries usually followed the Rule of Columbanus, while those founded from Lérins followed the Rule of St. Caesarius. As in Italy, several rules might be used by an abbot in the direction of his monks. Gradually the Benedictine Rule took its place among the other rules and eventually replaced them all. As in England, the older customs were incorporated into the Benedictine observance.

*Benedictine Missions.* From England, the Benedictine life spread to the Continent through the Anglo-Saxon monks who evangelized northern Europe: Wilfrid, Willibrord, and Willehad in the Netherlands, and Boniface and Willibald in Germany. These and hundreds of other monks established monasteries that served as centers to civilize and educate as well as to evangelize. From these monasteries other mission bands were sent deeper into Germanic and Slavic lands.

*Medieval Benedictines.* The turbulent years of the Merovingian kingdom had left their mark on the Frankish Church. The morality and educational level of the clergy had reached a low point. Church property had been confiscated and church offices granted in return for military or political favors. The Carolingian monarchs, beginning with Pepin III, sponsored a thorough reform of the church, the Benedictine missionaries being the chief agents of reform. The revival of learning under Charlemagne was to a great extent the work of such monks as Paul the Deacon and Alcuin. Under Louis the Pious an attempt was made at a synod at Aachen in 817 to bring all the Frankish monasteries into a common observance of the rule under the direction of the chief reformer, Benedict of Aniane. The reform succeeded for a time, but eventually failed as the supporting Frankish monarchy became weaker. However, many of these reform ideals were revived with the foundation of Cluny in 910. The Cluniac reform increased the time devoted to liturgical service and brought all affiliated houses under the direct control of the abbot of Cluny. In England a similar reform was carried out by Dunstan and Ethelwold through the *Regularis concordia* (970), based on the observances of Benedict of Aniane, Cluny, and Fleury. In reaction to the elaborate liturgical schedule and the wealth of these reformed houses and their concomitant laxity of observance, several orders of a more austere nature were formed (the Cistercians, Camaldolese, and Vallombrosans). Within the order there were reform movements such as that at Bec in Normandy. The Lateran Council of 1215 ordered the Benedictines to form provincial federations with chapters of abbots who would legislate for all houses in the province and provide for regular visitations. This program was augmented by Pope Benedict XII in 1336. Only in England was any successful attempt made to follow these directives. The English congregation survived until the Dissolution of the Monasteries (1536–1539). Elsewhere reform was not so successful. The Council of Constance called for additional reform of the religious life. In response several associations of monasteries were formed: the Bursfeld Union of 1420 in northern Germany, the Melk congregation of southern Germany, the St. Gall congregation of Switzerland, the St. Justina congregation of Italy, and the Valladolid congregation of Spain. Following the Reformation, the English congregation, the Scandinavian houses, and many German houses were suppressed.

*Modern Benedictines.* Two new congregations were formed after the Reformation: the St. Maur in France and the St. Vanne in Lorraine. Both congregations were noted for their scholarship, although the Maurists were far more famous, producing the great Dom Mabillon. The English congregation was revived in exile. By the end of the 18th century, the Benedictine houses had suffered extensively from the suppressions of Joseph II of Austria, the French Revolution, and Napoleon. Much monastic property was seized and secularized. Thousands of monks abandoned the monastic life. The French and German congregations were disbanded. In the early 19th century there was a revival of the Benedictine life. In 1830, Louis I of Bavaria restored several Benedictine houses. Dom Guéranger established the rule at Solesmes in 1833. From there the Benedictine life was reestablished in France. In Germany, the restoration came through the revival of Beuron in 1863. Colonies of Bavarian and Swiss monks established houses in the United States. The English congregation was restored to several abbeys in England.

The modern Benedictine congregation is a federation of independent monasteries headed by a president who is elected from among the abbots for a specified term. Each congregation determines the duties of its president and establishes the authority that the congregation has over individual houses. Some congregations are more highly organized than others. In 1893, Pope Leo XIII established an abbot primate for the entire Benedictine Order. He does not act as a superior general, but rather he represents the interests of the order in Rome, adjudicates disputes between congregations, and supervises the works of the entire order, such as the Benedictine college in Rome.

Among modern Benedictine scholars carrying on the scholarly traditions of the order are Abbot Marmion, Cuthbert Butler, Jean Leclercq, and David Knowles.

Benedictine nuns are said to have existed from the time of Benedict and his sister, the nun Scholastica. Benedictine convents have undergone reforms similar to those in the monasteries and are today organized into similar congregations.

In 1906 a community of Anglican Benedictines was formed. The order now is centered at Nashdom Abbey and has a priory in the United States.

**Benedict of Aniane** (c. 750–821). Benedictine reformer. The son of the count of Maguelone, he was sent to the court of Pepin III for his education. In 774 he entered a monastery near Dijon, where in 779 he was offered the office of abbot. He declined, desiring a more austere life. He founded a monastery on his family estate near Aniane. Visiting several monasteries nearby, he offered material aid and spiritual counsel, thereby beginning the system of grouping monasteries under one abbot. In 787 he began to follow the Rule of St. Benedict, supplementing it with Eastern customs. Several bishops requested him to build monasteries throughout the empire, all subject to his control. Louis the Pious, then king of Aquitaine, placed all the houses in Aquitaine under Benedict's direction. The Aachen Synod of 817 ordered the reform of all Frankish monasteries according to Benedict's program. Uniform customs were to be observed, all houses visited by imperial inspectors, and reports made to periodic synods. The hours of liturgical service were increased, while the hours of manual labor were decreased. He compiled all known monastic rules into a *Codex regularum.* Although his reforms did not survive the civil wars of Louis' sons, they were to a great extent revived by the reform of Cluny.

**Benefice.** The term used originally for a grant of land in return for some form of feudal service. In ecclesiastical law, "benefice" came to mean any church office for which there were specified duties in return for which the holder was to receive a specified income. Canon law forbade the holding of more than one benefice that involved the care of souls. The right to nominate the holder of a benefice is known as advowson.

**Benefit of Clergy.** The right of all tonsured clerics and nuns to be tried in an ecclesiastical rather than a secular court for charges of felony. For most of the Middle Ages, the ability to read was sufficient proof of clerical status to claim benefit of clergy. The right was abolished in England in 1827. It existed in America during the colonial period, but was abolished in federal courts in 1790.

**Benezet, Anthony** (1713–1784). Quaker philanthropist. A French Huguenot, Benezet fled to England, then to America in 1731, becoming a Quaker. After a short business career he taught school. At his own expense he published tracts to promote temperance, abolition, and Indian welfare. He joined John Woolman in the antislavery cause, succeeding him when he died. He founded the Negro school, Benezet House, in Philadelphia.

**Bengel, Johann Albrecht** (1687–1752). German Lutheran New Testament scholar. One of the Württemberg Pietists, he is widely recognized as the father of modern textual (lower) criticism of the Scriptures. It was he who first recognized families of manuscripts and attempted thus to classify and identify them. His *Gnomon Novi Testamenti* (1742), a verse-by-verse commentary, had wide and lasting influence. Bengel also showed great interest in Biblical eschatology and dated the coming of the millennium in the year 1837, an opinion that played a role in the Adventism of the 1830's and 1840's.

**Benjamin I** (1871–1946). Ecumenical patriarch (1935–1946). During his primacy, by his efforts the Bulgarian Church, considered schismatic, was declared autocephalous and in communion with Constantinople (1945), the Church of Albania was proclaimed autocephalous (1937), and the Uniate Carpatho-Russians were brought back into the fold of Orthodoxy (1946), thus gaining for him the reputation of peacemaker and conciliator among Eastern Orthodox Churches.

**Bentham, Jeremy** (1748–1832). Authority on jurisprudence and utilitarianism. Born into the family of a London attorney, Bentham was educated at Westminster and Oxford. In 1763 he began his legal studies at Lincoln's Inn and subsequently was admitted to the bar. Never a success in his profession, he gained prominence as a writer, his *Fragment on Government* (1776) providing an attack on Blackstone and inherited theories of jurisprudence and politics. As a result, Bentham came to the attention of Lord Shelburne, whom he influenced. While Shelburne's guest, Bentham was preparing his *Introduction to Principles of Morals and Legislation,* in which he defined "utility" and argued that the object of all laws was the total happiness of the community. Bentham's concerns were varied, including penal law; the "Panopticon," or inspection house, that he proposed for the supervision of industry; usury, which he defended; taxation; colonialism; poor law reform; and education. While living at Ford Abbey, sometime after 1814, he wrote suggesting that Paul had distorted primitive Christianity. In 1823 he aided in the founding of the *Westminster Review* and thereby promoted philosophical radicalism and the careers of James and John Stuart Mill. A staunch advocate of democratic government and of "the greatest happiness of the greatest number," Bentham spent his last years working on law reform and was engaged in writing his *Constitutional Code* at the time of his death.

**Bentley, Richard** (1662–1742). English classical scholar and literary critic. After his education at St. John's College, Cambridge, he was successively master of Spalding School, tutor to the son of Edward Stillingfleet, Boyle lecturer at Oxford, keeper of the royal library, and eventually master of Trinity College, Cambridge. In his Boyle lectures, *A Confutation of Atheism* (1692), he used the theories of Isaac Newton to prove the existence of an intelligent creator, and gained recognition as an able apologist for Christianity. In addition to his mastership he held the regius professorship of divinity from 1717. He defended the critical study of the Bible and denied that the existence of textual variants weakened its authority.

It was as a classical scholar that Bentley revealed his brilliant gifts. He combined wide learning with critical acuteness. He was able to do much to restore the ancient texts and point the way to new developments in scholarship. In his *Dissertation on the Epistles of Phalaris* (1699) he pointed the way to the historical and literary criticism of the 19th century. He authored an astonishing array of works. He was at his best dealing with texts rather than people. His Cambridge mastership was marked by continual tension and feuding, but he held his office until his death.

**Berdyaev, Nicolai Aleksandrovich** (1874–1948). Russian religious philosopher. He represented a position that may be called Christian existentialism. Strongly influenced by Marxian thinking in his youth and by Eastern Orthodoxy in his maturity, his life was marked by intermittent exile until he was finally expelled permanently by the Soviets in 1922. A major contributor to the religious and cultural revival in Russia following the humiliation of the Russo-Japanese War (1904–1905) Berdyaev became a convinced if not a conforming member of the Orthodox Church. After a short period of favor under the Soviet regime he was exiled, first going to Berlin, then shortly after to Paris, where he established his famous religious-philosophical academy in 1924. Under the influence of such various thinkers and literati as Jakob Boehme, Kant, Nietzsche, Dostoevsky, and Solovyov, Berdyaev made a strong affirmation of the primacy of a "transcendent world of spirit" over against the mere world of things or objects. Man, a participant in that spiritual world, may attain to a vision of truth, not by observation of things, but by a near-mystical creative act of intuition. The function of man is to bring about a reconciliation between this "truth" and the way "things" are. This theme is carried out also in his attempt to bring a synthesis between Westernism and Slavophilism, a question that has greatly troubled modern Russia, and in his ability to discern striking similarities between Marxist and czarist messianism.

**Berengar of Tours** (c. 1000–1088). Logician and theologian. By asserting the claim of logic to settle a doctrinal problem, he initiated the long debate between rationalism and fideism which was to characterize much of Scholastic philosophy. Berengar was born at Tours, studied under Fulbert at Chartres, became head of the monastic school of St. Martin at Tours and by 1040 was archdeacon of Angers. Having studied Aristotle, he was convinced that accidents could not exist without their subject, and in opposition to prevailing opinions on the Eucharist, which overemphasized the crude physical presence of Christ's body and blood, he denied a substantial change and asserted that the words of consecration added the beatified form of Christ's body to the bread. His argument proceeded from two current rules of grammatical analysis: that a pronoun stood for the substance of a thing apart from its accidents; and that a statement lost its validity if part of it was destroyed. Hence in the statement "This is my body," the pronoun "this" stood for the substance of the bread and could not cease to stand for it after consecration without the whole statement's loss of validity. Condemned by five separate councils and formally defeated by Lanfranc's doctrine of transubstantiation, he recanted before Gregory VII in 1079, living thereafter as a hermit under Gregory's protection until death.

**Berggrav, Eivind** (1884–1959). Norwegian Lutheran bishop and ecumenical leader. He was active in ecumenical affairs from 1917, a former president of the World Council of Churches, first chairman (1938) of the World Alliance for International Friendship Through the Churches. He founded the journal *Kirke og Kultur* which sought to maintain contacts between the church and its surrounding culture. After having served as a pastor and prison chaplain, he became bishop of Hålogaland in northern Norway (1929–1937) and later bishop of Oslo and primate of the Church of Norway (1937–1950). In the latter capacity, he gathered together the Christian forces assembled by Ole Hallesby and Ludwig Hope and led the church in its dramatic resistance to the Nazi regime during World War II. While in prison (1942–1945), he wrote *Man and State* (English tr., 1951), which presented Luther's doctrine of "obedience to the state" in a new light. During the 1950's he championed the church's autonomy in confessional matters.

**Bergson, Henri Louis** (1859–1941). French philosopher. Professor of philosophy at Clermont-Ferrand, and then at the Collège de France, Paris, Bergson created a philosophy of "creative evolution" which influenced most philosophical thought in his day and down to the present. He spoke of an *élan vital,* or force of life, which took possession of matter and drove it on to the various forms that it manifests. Life and matter, intuition and intellect, morality and religion, he pared off as primal forces engaged in a struggle out of which varying syntheses arose. The thrust of life was a force that acted counter to the laws of matter, he felt (here certain elements of the thought of Teilhard de Chardin are prefigured). His best-known works include *Essai sur les données immédiates de la conscience* (1889); *Matière et mémoire* (1896); *Durée et simultanéité* (1922); and *Les Deux Sources de la morale et de la religion* (1932). Bergson was a major influence on many of the Roman Catholic modernists such as Édouard Le Roy and Laberthonnière. Bergson himself slowly moved in the direction of Roman Catholicism, which he felt to be the fulfillment of Judaism. Yet, until his final illness, he was not baptized, preferring to maintain his ties with the Jewish people in their time of trial.

**Berlin Missionary Society.** The first missionary society in Germany. It was called into existence (1824) by Johann A. W. Neander under the impetus of Jänicke's Berlin mission school. East Prussian officials in church and government formed the core. Initially supporting other societies, the Berlin Society commissioned its first missionaries for South Africa in 1833, and expanded activities there until 1865. H. Wangemann, director from 1865 to 1894, organized novel home activities and extended the field to South China and the present Tanzania (1891). Genischen succeeded him, and the Society moved into Southern Rhodesia and northern China. Axenfeld, director from 1913 to 1921, was succeeded by Knaks, who encouraged Lutheran cooperation in East Africa. G. Brennecks assumed leadership in 1949 after the Society sided actively with the Confessing Church. The Society is predominately Lutheran.

**Bernadette of Lourdes** (Bernadette Soubirous, 1844–1879). French religious. The daughter of a poor miller of Lourdes in the French Pyrenees, Bernadette saw a series of visions of the Virgin Mary in the early months of 1858. At the sixteenth apparition (March 25) the Lady announced, in the local idiom, that she was the Immaculate Conception. Bernadette became a Sister of Charity at Nevers in 1866. She was canonized by Pope Pius XI in 1933.

**Bernanos, Georges** (1888–1948). French novelist. A student of the Jesuits at Paris, Bernanos made his first mark as a littérateur with the publication of his *Sous le Soleil Satan* in 1926. His work, translated as *The Diary of a Country Priest* (1936), and his letters, written from voluntary exile in Brazil and contained in the English volume *Plea for Liberty,* along with his *Dialogues des Carmelites,* have established his reputation in the world of letters.

**Bernardino of Siena** (1380–1444). Italian Franciscan. Born of the noble family of Albizeschi, he was orphaned at six and raised by pious aunts. After his training in civil and canon law, he entered a Marian confraternity, but later was professed as an Observantine Franciscan. In 1417 he preached in Milan and thereafter traveled through Italy, becoming an immensely popular street preacher. Elected bishop of Siena, he declined, but was made a vicar-general of his order. He was canonized in 1450. His extant sermons, *Prediche volgari,* are long, simple, direct, humorous, and witty.

**Bernard of Chartres** (d. c. 1130) French Platonist philosopher. A teacher at Chartres, Bernard was probably chancellor in the 1120's. His work is known only through the *Metalogicon* of John of Salisbury. Bernard taught through a grammatical analysis of selected texts, and assigned daily memorization and composition. He tried to harmonize Genesis and the *Timaeus,* maintaining that God created matter, but according to ideas existing eternally, not coequally, in His mind.

**Bernard of Clairvaux** (1090–1153). French ecclesiastic. He was born at Fontaines-les-Dijon of noble parents. With thirty companions, including three of his brothers and an uncle, he entered the monastery at Cîteaux (1112). Abbot Stephen Harding sent Bernard to found a house at Clairvaux (1115). The order spread rapidly; in Bernard's life sixty-eight houses were founded from Clairvaux alone. The popularity of the Cistercians brought them into conflict with the Cluniacs concerning the interpretation of the Benedictine Rule, which both orders followed, and the receiving of renegade monks. In answer to charges of lack of charity and justice toward Cluny, Bernard wrote the *Apology to William* (of St. Thierry) c. 1124. Although saying that both forms of observance were good, Bernard excoriated the abuses found among the Black Monks. In the second part of the treatise, he set forth the Cistercian ideal in observance and in architecture. Bernard first appeared as a power in the international sphere during the schism of 1130. Innocent II had been chosen by the younger members of the College of Cardinals in a hasty election after the death of Honorius II; Anacletus had been elected by older members. The Frangipani supported Innocent; the Pierleoni supported Anacletus. Louis VI asked Bernard to address the nobles and clergy gathered at Étampes (1130) to help the assembly decide which pope deserved the allegiance of France. Bernard espoused the cause of Innocent, basing his case on the election by the cardinal bishops, the priority in time, and the more virtuous character of Innocent. The French supported Innocent after this Council. Bernard persuaded the Milanese to back Innocent, and he received the submission of Peter of Pisa. The schism ended only with the death of Victor IV, successor to Anacletus (1138), so it is an exaggeration to credit Bernard with the healing of the schism. At this time Bernard was occupied with the rebuilding of Clairvaux (1136) on land given by Theobald of Champagne. He became involved in the episcopal election in Langres (1138) and the disputed election of William Fitzherbert in York (1140–1153). At the report of William of St. Thierry that Abelard's writings contained heresy, Bernard instigated proceedings by which Abelard was brought before the Council of Sens (1140). In this case, as well as in that of Gilbert de La Porrée at Reims (1148), Bernard showed that he did not trust philosophy as a means of understanding the doctrines of faith. The last international event in which Bernard played a part was the preaching of the Second Crusade. With the fall of Edessa (1145), the last stronghold of the Christians was lost in the Holy Land. Bernard was commissioned by Pope Eugenius III to preach a crusade in France, which he did at the Council of Vézelay (1146). He carried the preaching of the Crusade to Germany, although his commission to do so is less clear. Bernard extended the privileges of crusaders to those who defended the overland route against Wends, Slavs, and Moravians. The Crusade ended in failure with the defeat of the armies at Damascus (1148). Bernard died at Clairvaux, Aug. 20, 1153. He was canonized by Pope Alexander III (1174) and made a Doctor of the Church by Pius VIII (1830).

Among Bernard's extant writings more than five hundred letters remain, a vivid commentary on many facets of life in the years from 1120 to 1153. Sermons on the saints, and for the seasons of the church year number over one hundred. The sermons on the Song of Solomon, eighty-six in number, form a group in themselves. The language is so rich and ardent that it has been suggested, incorrectly, that this was a parent of the courtly love language. *Praises for a New Military Order* was a defense of the Knights Templars, an order of soldiers engaged in "malicide, not homicide." In *Grace and Free Will,* Bernard tried to determine how the will could merit salvation if good did not emanate from it, but could come only from God. The treatise addressed to Eugenius, *On Consideration,* was an exhortation to the former Cistercian to combine what he had learned as a monk with the duties of the papal office. The work *On the Degrees of Humility* was an elaboration of Benedict's teaching on humility. *Why and How God Is to Be Loved* set forth the reasons, origins, degrees, and ways of loving God. In all of his writing, Bernard showed a mastery of rhetoric and of Sacred Scripture unexcelled by his contemporaries.

**Bernard of Cluny** (*also known as* Bernard of Morval) (lived c. 1140). Monk at the great monastery of Cluny. Bernard is famous as the author of sermons as well as for the long poem *On the Contempt of the World,* which is some three thousand lines in length. In the poem he laments the vicissitudes of the earthly life as compared with the glory and eternity of the heavenly life. From it comes the well-known hymn "Jerusalem the Golden."

**Berryer, Pierre Antoine** (1790–1868). French Catholic lawyer and legitimist politi-

cian. An outstanding advocate and orator, Berryer helped his father defend Marshal Ney (unsuccessfully) and General Cambronne who was acquitted. He pleaded for press freedom in the cases of Lamennais and Chateaubriand, sustained liberty for labor organizations and religious congregations. Since he supported divine right kingship in various legislatures, his name was a byword for conservatism.

**Bersier, Eugène Arthur François** (1831–1889). French Reformed pastor. He served Free Church pastorates in Paris from 1855 to 1877. For a time he was an assistant of Pressensé. In 1877 he and his congregation joined the Reformed (Established) Church of France. A popular preacher, he wrote several books of sermons which were translated into English, German, Danish, Swedish, and Russian. He also wrote on Huguenot history and Reformed liturgy.

**Bérulle, Pierre de** (1575–1629). French cardinal. He was ordained a priest in 1599 and joined with Francis of Sales in trying to convert the Huguenots to Roman Catholicism. In 1611 he formed a French Congregation of the Oratory patterned after the one founded by Philip Neri in Rome. The Oratorians played a major role in reforming the French clergy. Bérulle was a much sought after spiritual adviser and took an active part in the French diplomacy of the time. He is best known today for his devotional writings, works (such as his *Grandeurs de Jésus*) which have merited him a prominent place in what is often called the French school of spirituality.

**Bessarion, John** (c. 1400–1472). Byzantine bishop, theologian, and Greek scholar. He began philosophical and rhetorical studies at Constantinople and became a monk (1423). Later he studied under the renowned scholar Gemistus Pletho. Having been elevated to the archbishopric of Nicaea (1437), Bessarion led the Greek delegation at the Council of Ferrara and Florence (1438), where he supported the Roman Church. A strong advocate of the union of the Greek and Latin Churches, he urged upon his colleagues the Western interpretation of the creeds. Many Greeks repudiated the union, but Bessarion remained in touch with Rome and made his home in Italy, where he often served as a papal emissary and in 1440 became a cardinal under Pope Eugenius. His home was a center for Greek refugees. With the fall of Constantinople to the Turks in 1453, he gathered together the remaining Greek manuscripts, giving the resulting sizable library to St. Mark's in Venice. Bessarion contributed significantly to the growth of the Italian Renaissance through his own writings and those of his pupils. He wrote an important defense of Platonism, attempting to show its compatibility with Aristotelian philosophy and Catholic doctrine. He also wrote a treatise on nature and art, several tracts on liturgical theology and Biblical exposition, and translated several Aristotelian works, as well as his own, into Latin. In 1463 he was given the title of (Latin) patriarch of Constantinople. His *Oration to Princes* (1470) was an abortive attempt to arouse the European rulers to a crusade against the Turks. He died at Ravenna.

**Bestiaries, Herbals, and Lapidaries.** Medieval books of science dealing, respectively, with animals, plants, and stones. On the whole, their scientific value was slight because of a tendency to allegorize and moralize the real or imagined characteristics of their subjects. They were quite popular and exercised an enormous influence on medieval art and literature. The later herbals were of some practical utility because they treated the medicinal properties of certain plants.

**Bethmann-Hollweg, Moritz von** (1795–1877). Prussian statesman and influential layman. He was instrumental in organizing the first German Kirchentag (1848), and his support of the Inner Mission made it possible for Johann Wichern, father of the movement, to speak at that gathering. Bethmann-Hollweg represented a moderate Lutheranism with strong emphasis on social responsibility for modern industrial society. In politics he argued for a constitutional monarchy on Christian grounds, rejecting both revolution and ultraconservatism.

**Beyschlag, Willibald** (1823–1900). German theologian. He studied at Bonn and Berlin (1840–1844) and thereafter rose to prominence, becoming in rapid succession vicar at Coblenz (1849), court preacher at Karlsruhe (1856), ordinary professor of theology at Halle (1860), and soon a prominent Protestant theologian of great renown.

Theologically he belonged to the Mediating school, whose leader and defender he remained until the end of his life. In 1886 he was an influential organizer of the Evangelical Alliance for the safeguarding of German Protestant interests. With Walters he founded *Deutsche Evangelische Blätter*, and became its editor. He was a voluminous writer, especially on New Testament theology subjects.

**Beza, Theodore** (1519–1605). Reformed pastor and professor, Calvin's successor at Geneva. He was born at Vézelay, Burgundy, on June 24, 1519, the son of Pierre and Marie

de Bèsze. At the age of nine he was placed at Orléans under the scholar Melchior Wolmar, with whom Calvin also studied briefly. When Marguerite d'Angoulême invited Wolmar in 1530 to become one of her group of scholars at Bourges, Beza accompanied him, there continuing his studies in Latin, Greek, and the Bible. Upon Wolmar's return to Germany in 1535, Beza took up the study of law at Orléans while simultaneously cultivating a literary talent. In August, 1539, he became a licentiate in law and began practice in Paris. Although his life was comfortable and his prospects brilliant, Beza was unhappy in the law and leaned toward literary pursuits. A collection of his light verse, *Juvenilia*, appeared in 1548, and was later to be a source of some embarrassment to him. He was not in orders, but since he held two benefices, his marriage to Claude Desnoz in 1544 was kept secret until he adopted the Reformed faith. A severe illness in 1548 led to his conversion and removal to Geneva.

At the request of Pierre Viret, Beza accepted a chair at the Academy in Lausanne, where he served as professor of Greek from 1549 to 1558. In 1550 he wrote a sacred tragedy, *Abraham's Sacrifice*, the first fusion of Greek tragedy with the medieval mystery. Four years later he defended the burning of Servetus in a treatise on the punishment of heretics. In his first conciliatory attempt in 1557 he sought to unite German and Swiss Protestants by reducing differences on the Lord's Supper to a minimum; but, although Calvin supported him, he succeeded only in alienating some of the Zwinglian Swiss.

In 1558, Beza returned to Geneva and became rector of the Academy when it opened in 1559. There he taught Greek and theology while being trained as Calvin's successor. Beza was invited in 1560 to Nérac to counsel the king and queen of Navarre on the Huguenot problem; from that time the French Protestants looked to him as a defender of their cause.

In 1561, Beza played his most important role as spokesman for the Protestants at the Colloquy of Poissy. Since Calvin would have been endangered by attending, Beza was requested by the Protestants to defend the rational and Scriptural foundations of Reformed belief. Before the eleven-year-old king, Charles IX, Beza defined the Lord's Supper as the sacrament of the body and blood—not in substance, but in the use and end for which it was ordained. In his criticism of transubstantiation Beza made no attempt at reconciliation, but stated that the body of Christ was as far from the elements as heaven was from earth. Nor was it a mere commemoration, for by faith men fed on the body of Christ. The Cardinal of Lorraine replied a week later with an air of superiority and condescension, and the conference ended in recriminations. Beza remained in France until 1563 as counselor during the Huguenot wars.

Upon the death of Calvin in 1564, Beza assumed leadership in Geneva. More conciliatory in spirit and gentler in his ways than Calvin, Beza softened the rigor of the great Reformer's administration. In theology, on the other hand, Beza's thought marked the development of Reformed teaching into a rigid Scholasticism. By his Biblical literalism, emphatic predestinarianism, doctrinaire presbyterianism, and doctrine of resistance to tyranny Beza perhaps did more than anyone else to shape the popular image of Calvinism. (See CALVIN, JOHN.) His literary output, though not great, contained some important works. His *Life of Calvin* was hastily composed and is unreliable for the early years. He produced an important New Testament translation in 1565, using the 6th-century Codex D (Codex Bezae), which he had rescued from a monastery in Lyons during the wars and presented to Cambridge University in 1581. His Latin versions and editions influenced the English versions of the Geneva Bible and the King James Version of 1611. Three volumes of *Theological Treatises* appeared in 1582, containing his controversial writings, among them the important *Confession of the Christian Faith*. With Clément Marot he prepared the Huguenot Psalter, and with Francesco Salluardo produced *The Harmony of Protestant Confessions,* showing the similarities of fifteen Protestant confessions. His conciliatory efforts should not, however, be taken as indicative of a belief in religious liberty, which he described as "a most diabolical dogma because it means that every one should be left to go to hell in his own way." In external affairs he remained active, working aggressively to establish Reformed strongholds in Lutheran areas. French refugees in Geneva kept his contacts with his native land alive, and he was sympathetic with the Presbyterian movement in England.

Impaired health forced him to resign his offices in 1600. He died on Oct. 13, 1605, after inquiring for the last time: "Is the city in full safety and quiet?"

BIBLIOGRAPHY: H. M. Baird, *Theodore Beza* (New York, 1899); P. F. Geisendorf, *Théodore de Bèze* (Geneva, 1949).

**Biard, Pierre** (c. 1567–1622). Jesuit missionary. He was born in Grenoble, France, and entered the Society of Jesus in 1583. He taught theology at Lyons and was named head of the Acadia mission which was organized in 1603 by the Huguenot De Monts. In 1611 he sailed to Acadia and helped to found the settlement at St. Sauver. He was taken prisoner by the English and forced to witness the destruction of Port-Royal, and on his return to France was accused of aiding the English in the destruction of the French settlements. His defense, *Relation de la Nouvelle France,* was published in 1616.

**Bible, Modern Translations of.** Translation, one of the oldest traditions in Christendom, has flourished enormously in modern times. Impetus for study and translation came as ancient manuscripts were discovered and made available in editions of the Greek New Testament by John Mills (1707), J. A. Bengel (1734), J. J. Wettstein (1752), J. J. Griesbach (1775 ff.), and others. Advances toward establishing a decisively ancient Greek New Testament text came with Karl Lachmann, who published Greek New Testaments from 1831 to 1850. In his footsteps came K. von Tischendorf and finally Westcott and Hort. Old Testament manuscript discoveries have remained static until quite recently.

A translation is judged by its source: Of what is it a translation? Some "translations" are, in fact, translations of translations. Others are revisions of translations, corrected against sources in the original language, but not fundamentally new. A few are fresh renderings of original language texts. Among these, quality and character of source text is of decisive importance. Fidelity to the original and stylistic legitimacy are the main goals of the translator's work, once a source is chosen.

English Bibles in the modern period are dominated by the King James Version (KJV), often called (from its title page) the Authorized Version (AV). James I, dissatisfied with existing translations, ordered the appointment of translators to produce a rendition "consonant . . . to the original Hebrew and Greek." They finished their work in 1611, complete with a lengthy preface stating clearly the methods, objectives, and qualifications of their labors. Because this preface is omitted from modern printings of KJV, the version has attained a sacrosanct authority its translators never intended.

The KJV translators did not start anew. Their basis was the Bishops' Bible (1568), itself a revision of the so-called Great Bible, instituted (perhaps) by Cromwell and printed by Coverdale in 1539. The translators say, "We never thought . . . to make a new translation, nor . . . of a bad one a good one; but to make a good one better."

All early English New Testaments go back indirectly to Tyndale's translation (1526) of Erasmus' Greek, and Erasmus worked hastily from a few late and faulty Greek manuscripts. But when the KJV translators wished to consult the Greek, they turned to a text essentially unimproved by comparison with that which Tyndale used almost ninety years earlier. No new data about the Old Testament Hebrew text was available, and the KJV translators did not value the Greek highly enough as a witness to early readings. Further, Hebrew scholarship was not then so far advanced as Greek. Still, there was improvement. Latin versions had been extensively used as a source for Old Testament renderings and had been especially influential in the Bishops' Bible. The Geneva Bible (1560) had been corrected at several points against the Hebrew but it was not popular in England, and James I especially disliked its commentary. The KJV at first had to compete with the Geneva Bible but eventually superceded it all over the British Isles.

Current forms of the KJV derive, not from the 1611 version, but from the revision of Blayney in 1769. Between eighty thousand and one hundred thousand alterations were made to bring the version into conformity with Samuel Johnson's dictionary of 1755.

After 1700, translations, especially of the New Testament, proliferated, spurred by the availability of better manuscripts and more comprehensive scholarship: Whitby (1703), NT; Wells (1718 f.), OT, NT; Mace (1729), NT; Whiston (1745), NT; Harwood (1768), NT; Wesley (1768), NT; Sharpe (1840 f.), NT, OT; Young (1862), OT, NT; Alford (1869), NT; Darby (1871 f.), OT, NT; Rotherham (1872 f.), OT, NT; Newberry (c. 1880 f.), OT, NT.

Whiston admired Codex Bezae, adding its interpolation, e.g., at Luke 6:5; Sharpe revised against Griesbach's Greek text; Alford had already edited an important Greek New Testament of his own; Rotherham used Tregelles' text in the New Testament for two editions, and Westcott and Hort for a third. In this period two English renderings of the Greek Old Testament (Septuagint) appeared— Thomson (1808) and Brenton (1844).

The KJV was revised in Britain in 1881 by a distinguished panel including Scrivener, Westcott, and Hort (cf. American Revised Version, 1901). They achieved an enormous advance over the KJV for accuracy, also using a better Greek text. In the Old Testament the revisers used the traditional medieval Hebrew,

making only conservative use of ancient versions. Still, the revisers, beyond 1611 by 270 years of Hebrew scholarship, produced a credible Old Testament revision.

*The Twentieth Century New Testament* (1898–1901) was the first "modern speech" English translation. Made from the Westcott and Hort Greek—the best then available— it reflected the social concern of its translators. Richard Francis Weymouth, editor of a Greek New Testament and later an independent translator, was a consultant. James Moffatt translated the New Testament from H. von Soden's Greek in 1913; his Old Testament translation appeared in 1924 (combined edition: 1928). In 1923, Edgar J. Goodspeed, a pioneering scholar of early Christian literature, translated the New Testament from Westcott and Hort under the title *The New Testament: An American Translation.* His work attracted great attention and was joined in 1927 by an Old Testament edited by Semitist J. M. Powis Smith and collaborators. In 1931 the two were published together (*The Bible: An American Translation*).

In 1946 another revision of KJV was published. The Revised Standard Version (RSV), like its predecessor of 1881, was the product of distinguished scholars working with up-to-date materials. It attained genuine popularity, arriving at English largely free of awkward and obscure locutions. In the New Testament the revisers used Nestle's *Novum Testamentum Graece* (ed. 17); in the Old, they had to use the medieval Hebrew text, but they paid less attention to the medieval vowel points, and more to ancient versions, especially the Greek (Septuagint).

After 1940 appeared many versions simplifying and modernizing the English or explaining it. These are not, in general, fresh renderings of ancient texts. We may mention *The Basic English Bible* (NT, 1940; OT, 1949), *The Plain English New Testament*, by Charles K. Williams (1952); Wuest's *Expanded New Testament* (1956–1959); *The Amplified New Testament* (1958), and the *New World Translation* (NT, 1950, OT, 1953 ff.). J. B. Phillips' *Letters to Young Churches* (1947), followed by renderings of the Gospels, Acts, and Revelation (1952, 1955, and 1957, respectively), is perhaps outside this category. Phillips' work paraphrases, often paying little attention to the nuances of the Greek. His version, nonetheless, was widely appreciated.

*The New English Bible* (NEB) New Testament appeared in 1961, the work of a joint British committee chaired by C. H. Dodd. Like the RSV committee, they began with a Nestle text. A few significant variants were translated in the margin. In 1964 the committee's composite Greek text was printed under the editorship of R. G. V. Tasker. The text of NEB represents no particular advance but the translation is fresh, vigorous, and usually exact. Critics have pointed to a few awkward or inaccurate renderings, and a sizable number of "Briticisms."

We have dealt so far with Protestant Bible translation. Since, in 1546, the Council of Trent canonized the Latin Vulgate for use by Roman Catholics, its text has dominated Catholic translations. The Vulgate is a 4th-century version partly attributable to Jerome. It renders New Testament text much earlier than that of the Erasmian editions. Until Karl Lachmann and others pushed the Greek New Testament back to the 4th century, the Vulgate provided, albeit in translation, the earliest ancient text available. The Vulgate Old Testament renders Hebrew older than the medieval texts, though not so different from them as that used by Greek translators.

Gregory Martin made, at Douai in northern France, toward the beginning of the 17th century, translations into English of the Vulgate. The New Testament was published in 1582, the Old in 1609 and 1610. (The New Testament, published when Martin was at Reims, is sometimes called the Reims New Testament.) Martin's version is heavy in literal translations and Latinisms. Revised into idiomatic English in 1749 by Richard Challoner, it is known as the Douay Version.

In 1941 an extensive revision was made of the 190-year-old Douay Version. The New Testament was revised with attention to new evidence for the Vulgate and for the Greek wherever it greatly differed from the Latin; and the Old Testament was newly rendered from Hebrew. This version is known as the Confraternity. In 1945 and 1949 respectively, P. A. Knox translated the New and Old Testaments from the Clementine Vulgate alone—i.e., the 1592 Vulgate authorized by Clement VIII. The Knox version is sanctioned by the Roman Church, but the official versions mentioned are superior to it in text.

Recently, Roman Catholic sanction has been extended to the RSV with no changes in the Old Testament (except the addition of the Apocrypha) and relatively minor changes in a few New Testament renderings.

Among non-English versions, Luther's Bible (1521 f.) is prominent. It unified Protestant Germany with a common standard overarching the dialects, paralleling Dante's influence on Italian literature, and it influenced most Germanic translations (see Werner Schwarz, *Principles and Problems of Biblical Translation,* Bibliography). On modern language versions, cf. further, O. M. Norlie, *The Bible in a Thousand Tongues* (1935) and B. M. Metzger, *The Interpreter's Dictionary of the Bible* (1962), Vol. IV, pp. 781 f.

BIBLIOGRAPHY: *The Translators to the Reader: Preface to the King James Version 1611,* ed. by E. J. Goodspeed (Chicago, 1935); F. F. Bruce, *The English Bible* (New York, 1961); F. C. Grant, *Translating the Bible* (Greenwich, Conn., 1961); I. M. Price, *The Ancestry of Our English Bible* (New York, 1956); E. Rumball-Petre, *America's First Bibles* (Portland, Maine, 1940); W. Schwarz, *Principles and Problems of Biblical Translation* (Cambridge, 1955).

**Bible Church Movement.** Organized activity springing from the fundamentalist controversy of the early 20th century. In 1929, J. Gresham Machen, a professor at Princeton Seminary, and a colleague withdrew to begin the conservative Westminster Theological Seminary. Later, offended by what they regarded as discriminatory treatment of fundamentalist candidates for missionary service by the Presbyterian Mission Board, Machen joined with J. Oliver Buswell and Carl McIntire to organize an independent mission board. For this action they were expelled from the denomination and in 1936 organized the Presbyterian Church in America. Six months later this body divided, and McIntire formed the Bible Presbyterian Church. It was racked by controversy in the mid-1950's. A crucial issue was the influence of agencies within the church which were not subject to synod control. At its general meeting in 1956 controls were voted over educational and missionary agencies and the church withdrawn from the American Council of Churches. In protest, McIntire organized a rival body but refused to separate. He was censured in 1957. The name of the original body was changed in 1961 to the Evangelical Presbyterian Church, which in turn merged in 1965 with the Reformed Presbyterian Church in North America.

**Bible Societies.** Agencies distributing unannotated Biblical texts. In *Britain* the interdenominational British and Foreign Bible Society was organized March 7, 1804, to provide Welsh Bibles and Bibles "for the whole world" (808 languages by 1955). An early secretary was Karl Steinkopf. The 1825 struggle over the inclusion of the Apocrypha was won by the anti-Apocryphal party. In *America* the Philadelphia Society (1808) was followed within a year by societies in Connecticut, Massachusetts, New York, and Maine. The groups merged into the American Bible Society (1816). It is currently supported by almost sixty denominations. In *Germany,* Bible societies were first organized to serve the poor at home. K. H. von Canstein's society in Halle (1710) distributed three million Bibles by 1799. The Württemberg Society (1812), organized under Steinkopf's influence, published the Nestle Greek New Testament in 1898 and the Kittel Hebrew Old Testament in 1921. The Bergic Society (1814) aided the Rheinish Mission Society. Among others, German societies included the Evangelical (1814), Saxon (1814–1919), and Altenburg (1852). The Verband der evangelischen Bibelgesellschaften in Deutschland was formed in 1948. A Roman Catholic society established in Regensburg by M. Wittmann (1805) was abolished by Pius VII (1817). Another was formed by Leander van Ess in Heiligenstadt (1815) with British aid, and others followed. Protestant societies, in addition to the above, arose in Scotland (1809, federated 1862), Ireland (1806), Australia (1817), New Zealand (1837), Canada (1807), Netherlands (1814), Norway (1816), Denmark (1814), Sweden (1815), Finland (1812), Russia (1813–1826, 1863–1917), and France (1819). The Gideon businessmen began work in 1898, and the Wycliffe translators (C. Townsend) in 1935. Recent foreign societies include China, Japan (1941), India (1944), and Pakistan (1956). The World Bible Society, established in 1946 in Britain, is a worldwide association. Bible societies have been influential in the ecumenical movement and in missions.

**Bibliander** (Buchmann), **Theodor** (c. 1504–1564). Swiss theologian. A native of Bischofszell in northeastern Switzerland, Bibliander was a linguistic genius, and in 1531 joined the faculty of the school of the Great Minster at Zurich. His translations included portions of the Bible, and even the Koran. He had an Erasmian position on predestination, which proved unsatisfactory to more rigid Calvinists, and led to his dismissal from the school (on salary) in 1560.

**Biblical Studies, Pontifical Commission of.** A group formally established by apostolic letter of Pope Leo XIII on Oct. 30, 1902. It had a number of purposes, especially: to defend the Roman Catholic faith in Biblical matters; to decide controversies on grave questions among Roman scholars; to give answers to any Roman Catholic who may consult it; to keep the Vatican library well equipped with Biblical tools and studies; and from time to time to publish studies on Biblical matters.

Known as the Pontifical Biblical Commission, it originally consisted of three cardinals and twelve consultors; later other cardinals and many more consultors were added. Some of its original actions included: support of Mosaic authorship of the Pentateuch (although admitting that Moses could have inspired others to write some of it); attribution of the authorship of the Fourth Gospel to the apostle John, with the Gospel itself to be accounted a historical document recording actual events and speeches of Christ; assertion that all Biblical books were written under inspiration of the Holy Spirit. Recently the Commission did much of the preparation for the Second Vatican Council's Constitution on Divine Revelation in which some recognition was given to modern Biblical discoveries in oral tradition and form criticism.

**Biblical Study in the Middle Ages.** Contrary to popular Protestant notions, the Bible occupied a central position in medieval studies. Its language and thought permeated everywhere; it became a set book for all levels of education; it served alike for devotion, allegory, and polemic; its text—first Greek, then Latin; finally Hebrew, Latin, and Greek— was regularly dissected, glossed, annotated, and corrected. The Latin Bible of the Middle Ages was largely the work of Jerome (d. 420). He learned Hebrew in Syria, studied under the Greek theologian Gregory of Nazianzus, and settling at Bethlehem in 386 with a devoted group of disciples, continued the task of translating the Bible (382–404). Reluctantly he added a hurried translation of Tobit and Judith, maintaining that the Apocrypha had no place in the Hebrew Bible. By the 7th century Jerome's version ultimately superseded the Old Latin versions, though in a somewhat corrupt form. With the addition of the Old Latin version of the Apocrypha, it became known as the *Vulgata* ("common," "ordinary") and was the version generally used by the Western Church throughout the Middle Ages. For the Hebrew Old Testament, a standard text, the product of Jewish Masoretic scholars in Babylon and Palestine, circulated from the 8th century onward. Not until the 12th century is there much evidence of Western scholars turning to either Greek or Hebrew. Private vernacular translations of single books of the Bible, particularly the Psalter and the Gospels, were frequently undertaken, alongside paraphrases and harmonies, but the great complete versions, such as the Catholic English Douay (1582 ff.), Luther's in German (1534), Tyndale's (1525 ff.), and the King James (1611), belong to Reformation times.

One predominant trend for medieval study of the Bible, its interpretation in terms of allegory and symbol, was already set in the 1st century by the writings of the Alexandrian Jew Philo (d. c. 45), eagerly followed by such Christian scholars as Clement (d. c. 215) and Origen (d. c. 254). The opposition to Alexandrian allegory by the so-called Antiochene school, notably Theodore of Mopsuestia (d. 428), had less influence, though some effect is seen in the studies of Hilary of Poitiers (d. 367) and Ambrose (d. 397). In patristic times, working on the basis of Jerome's materials, Augustine (d. 430) in his *On Christian Doctrine* pursues something of a middle course between literal and allegorical interpretation. The *Conferences* (or *Collations*) of John Cassian (d. 435) provided a Bible commentary on similar lines which proved particularly acceptable to the founders of Western monasticism such as Benedict (d. c. 543), who made Scriptural reading (*lectio divina*) a central part of his rule, and showed its influence also in the *Institutes* of Cassiodorus (d. c. 570), the *Moralia* of Gregory the Great (d. 604), and, with some sharpening of intellectual curiosity, in the popular exegetical writings of Isidore of Seville (d. 636) and the Venerable Bede (d. 735). The Carolingian Renaissance of the 9th century was marked by an organized revision of the Latin texts, evident in the group of scholars— Alcuin, Rabanus Maurus, Walafrid Strabo, and others—who occupied themselves with Scriptural commentary. The Cluniac reformers of the 10th century, though zealous for monastic scholarship in general, were more concerned with the Bible in its liturgical aspects. With the rise of the cathedral schools in the 11th and 12th centuries came a more concise and logical method of Bible interpretation: Fulbert of Chartres (d. 1028), his pupil Berengar of Tours, and Berengar's pupil Lanfranc (d. 1089), exemplify this approach. The school of Anselm of Laon (d. 1117) and its offshoot, the Abbey of St.-Victor in Paris, founded in 1113 with its three notable expositors—Hugh (d. 1141), Richard (d. 1173), and Andrew (d. 1175)—brought Biblical study to a formal science and exploited its value as a source of moral *exempla*. Peter Abelard (d. 1142) provides one instance of Bible students who made some attempt to fill out their studies by acquiring Hebrew and Greek. The Victorine tradition persists in such popular texts as the *Historia scholastica* of Peter Comestor (d. c. 1179) and the *Quaestiones* of Stephen Langton (d. 1228); even wider currency was achieved for the compilation known as the *Glossa ordinaria,* a running commentary on the Scriptures. The same source inspired the widening scope of Bible study at the university level, from 12th-century Paris to 13th-century Oxford. At Oxford especially the Bible lectures of the Franciscan and Dominican friars, notably Robert Grosseteste of Lincoln, showed an increasing awareness of Greek and Hebrew as aids to textual accuracy. The greatest of the teaching friars, Roger Bacon (d. c. 1294), was outspoken in his demand for a thorough revision of the Vulgate in the light of new developments. The next century, however, witnessed something of a return to the older symbolic and mystical methods of interpretation.

BIBLIOGRAPHY: H. Glunz, *The History of the Vulgate in England: From Alcuin to Roger Bacon* (Cambridge, 1933); H. W. Robinson (ed.), *The Bible in Its Ancient and English Versions* (Oxford, 1940); B. Smalley, *The Study of the Bible in the Middle Ages* (Oxford, 1952).

**Biddle, John** (1615–1662). English Unitarian. Upon graduating from Magdalen Hall, Oxford, Biddle was invited to be schoolmaster at Gloucester. While teaching there during the confusion of the Civil War, he began to expound anti-Trinitarian doctrine. Complaints were received from Presbyterians, and the magistrate called him in and required him to accept a confession of faith. The affair died down for a time, until someone stole a manuscript from him in which he had stated his religious opinions. He was immediately imprisoned, beginning a long pattern of alternating between jail and freedom. Called before Parliament to defend himself, he boldly published, while in their custody, "Twelve Questions or Arguments drawn out of Scripture, wherein the commonly received Opinion touching the Deity of the Holy Spirit is clearly and fully refuted" (1647). Biddle published other works soon after, and the Westminster divines requested Parliament to issue the death penalty against him. But personal friends intervened, procuring his release. Imprisoned and released once more, he organized a conventicle and conducted public worship. In December, 1654, he again was committed to prison, and after being in and out a few more times, he died in 1662 of the foul prison conditions. Though Biddle did not found the English Unitarianism, he is a forerunner of that movement.

**Biedermann, Alois Emanuel** (1819–1885). Professor of theology. Biedermann is usually identified as a follower of Hegel and a speculative theologian. His dogmatic writings concentrated on shaping intellectual concepts out of the raw material of religious experience. This was especially true in his construction of a speculative Christology. In so doing, Biedermann sought to meet the theological needs of the time as he saw them. He was professor of theology at Zurich from 1850 until his death.

**Biel, Gabriel** (c. 1420–1495). Late Scholastic theologian. Biel studied at Heidelberg, and later at Erfurt, learning there the Occamist *via moderna*. At Cologne he studied in the Thomist-dominated theologate. After some time in Mainz as cathedral preacher and vicar he joined the Brethren of the Common Life. From 1458 to 1477, he served as first provost of the Brethren's new house in Butzbach. By 1479 he was provost in Württemberg. In 1484 he joined the theology faculty at Tübingen, where he was instrumental in making the *via moderna* predominate over the *via antiqua*. In 1485 and 1489 he was elected rector of the university, after which he retired as provost to the Brethren's house at Einsiedel. His writings influenced two important Tübingen students: Johann Eck and John Staupitz. Biel stressed the power of the preached word to awaken faith and contrition, and the dominance of Scripture over its interpretation. On the other hand, his nominalist division of God's power into "absolute" and "ordinary" and the teaching based on this division concerning grace and merit opened the way to Luther's charge of Pelagianism in the Roman Church.

**Bielefeld.** A town in Westphalia near Bethel. Bethel is the location of the charitable institutions founded by the Lutheran pastor Friedrich von Bodelschwingh (1831–1910). These institutions consist of homes for epileptics, training centers for deaconesses and male nurses, and a college for theological students. The popular name of this institutional complex is Bethel bei Bielefeld.

**Bilderdijk, Willem** (c. 1756–1831). Dutch lawyer, lecturer, historian, philosopher, and poet. Bilderdijk practiced law at The Hague, was exiled in 1795, and returned to Holland from England in 1806. Sharply critical of liberalism, he urged authority in society, and interpreted his life and the world's history from a paternalistic perspective. Lecturing in Netherland history at Leiden (1817–1827), he influenced later leaders of the Awakening, including Da Costa and Capadose.

**Bilney, Thomas** (c. 1495–1531). The second Protestant martyr in England (Thomas Hilton, 1530). A Cambridge man like many other early English Protestants, Bilney led a society called the Christian Brotherhood, which, though orthodox in many of its views, opposed the cult of relics, pilgrimages, veneration of saints, etc. He recanted his opinions in 1527 and again in 1531, but relapsed in the latter year and was burned at Norwich.

**Bishop** (Greek, *episkopos;* Latin, *episcopus;* Old English, biscop). The term "bishop," now used to designate the head of a diocese or other geographical area of a church, can be traced to the New Testament (Acts 20:28; Phil. 1:1; I Tim. 3:2; Titus 1:7), but it is evident that there it designated a function rather than an office, and probably the function of presbyters (cf. Acts 20:17; I Peter 5:1). The very early association of "bishop," a quite common term in the secular community to indicate all sorts of oversight, with "deacon," a peculiarly Christian term (in both substantive and verbal form), suggests that its milieu may have been the Christian common meal which evolved in the Christian liturgy. The similar association with "pastor" or "shepherd" (Acts 20:28; I Peter 2:25; cf. 1QS 6.12,14,20; Damascus Fragment 13.9) may suggest another function of more ancient origin. There was likely still no sharp distinction of office between bishop and presbyter at the end of the 1st century (1 Clem. 44), although the basis for the distinction appears in Ignatius of Antioch. The 2d-century developments of the peculiar office of bishop are shrouded in darkness and mystery, but undoubtedly because the successive conflicts of the church with Montanism, Marcionism, and gnosticism necessitated the elimination of the charismatic ministries such as prophet and forced the regularization of an official ministry which was bound to a place and which would guarantee the church's teaching as apostolic. The 3d-century Syrian *Didascalia* and the more or less contemporary Apostolic Tradition of Hippolytus show a further crystallization of the office as order, the epitome of this development being reached in the compilation of the 4th-century Apostolic Constitutions. A new stage in the evolution of the office was reached with imperial recognition of the church, which fostered great expansion of the secular as well as the ecclesiastical authority of the bishops of the metropolitan sees (patriarchs and metropolitans) while promoting the organization of the Empire into episcopal jurisdictions. During the medieval era, the development of the papacy tended to overshadow collegiate episcopal authority which remained the norm in both the Eastern Orthodox and the non-Chalcedonian Churches.

In the Roman Catholic Church today, the appointment of a bishop lies in the discretion of the pope, and the bishop or his agent must report quinquennially to the pope on the state of his diocese. In many branches of the church, including the Roman, the practice has developed of appointing assistants to a bishop where circumstances have favored or required it. Thus an auxiliary bishop assists and a coadjutor bishop may also substitute for a diocesan; in all cases, in the Roman Church, such bishops are titular bishops, i.e., holding appointment to an ancestral see no longer existing (Codex Juris Canonici, Canon 329). In the Eastern Orthodox Church as well as in the non-Chalcedonian Churches, the method of selection varies from election by a synod of bishops to election by the secular clergy. At the time of the Reformation, few Protestant churches retained the episcopate. The Church of England maintained a succession of bishops in unbroken line in the changeover from papal jurisdiction to royal supremacy in the days of Henry VIII as well as in the transition from Mary Tudor to Elizabeth I. The election of a new bishop by dean and chapter of a diocesan cathedral follows nomination by the Crown. In the Protestant Episcopal Church in the U.S.A., bishops are elected by the clergy and the laity of a diocese in convention, but majority consent of the other bishops and dioceses is required before consecration. Some modification of these procedures obtains in the other provinces of the Anglican Communion. In the Reformed tradition, the office of bishop fell victim to the church reorganization undertaken by Calvin (cf. *Draft Eccl. Ord.,* LCC, Vol. XXII, pp. 58 ff.; *The Necessity of Reforming the Church,* ibid., 207 ff.; *Institutes* 4. 5. 11, etc.), although the function was preserved in the presbyterate. For Lutheranism, the episcopate was among the adiaphora; thus, while in Sweden there was maintained an episcopate recognized by the Church of England as within apostolic succession, the office in other Lutheran churches all but disappeared and where it has been revived it is a new entity. A similar phenomenon may be observed in the Methodist Church in the United States where episcopacy obtains but not as an order separate from the presbyterate. The Old Catholic Church and the Moravian Church have also maintained an episcopal succession.

The movement toward church union, begun in the late 19th century among Christian bodies that were the product of the Reformation, posed problems of ecclesiastical polity centering on the role and function of bishops. Much Anglican thought has considered the historic episcopate as of the *esse* of the church (cf. Lambeth Quadrilateral, 1888) and would enter into union schemes only upon general acceptance of this view; the more liberal view, that the episcopate is of the *bene esse* though not of the *esse* of the church is shared by many Anglicans and the majority of the churches stemming from the Reformation. A more recent view has seen the restoration of the episcopate as a goal of church union rather than a precondition for negotiation and has been called the *plene esse* view. This view has increasingly gained practical acceptance, if not articulate agreement, in the various union plans occupying Christian churches, especially since World War II. The event of Vatican II, particularly its Constitution on the Church, *Lumen gentium* (1964), pars. 18–27, has raised again the question of the role and function of bishops; although it maintained papal primacy, its decidedly collegial tone gave promise of a mollification of Rome's former intransigence, thus opening the door for a much wider discussion of the issue.

Traditionally, the bishop's ministry has been a sacramental one, including ordination, confirmation, and reserved blessings. His oversight (*episkopē*) has been highly organized, so that in most instances it amounts to governance. Church union schemes have forced a more theological evaluation of the ministry not only of bishops but of the entire church. Out of these discussions has emerged a new level of understanding of this particular office, leaving behind acrimonious debates over validity and regularity, *esse* and *bene esse,* and the legalistic interpretation of episcopacy.

BIBLIOGRAPHY: K. Carey (ed.), *The Historic Episcopate in the Fullness of the Church* (London, 1954); K. D. Mackenzie, *The Case for Episcopacy* (New York, 1929); A. J. Mason, *The Church of England and Episcopacy* (Cambridge, 1914); E. H. Peters (ed.), *De Ecclesia: The Constitution on the Church of Vatican Council II* (Glen Rock, N.J., 1965); K. Rahner and J. Ratzinger, *The Episcopate and Primacy* (New York, 1962); N. Sykes, *Old Priest and New Presbyter* (Cambridge, 1956).

**Bishops' Book** (or *The Institution of a Christen Man*). The second of the doctrinal statements pursuant to the English Reformation, issued in 1537 with Henry VIII's approval but not with royal authority. The general effect is rather more conservative than that of the Ten Articles (e.g., on the number of the sacraments), but the view taken of the universal church, as composed of independent national churches, provides an ideological basis for nonpapal polity. (See SIX ARTICLES and KING'S BOOK.)

**Bishops' Program of Social Reconstruction.** A platform of social reform written by John A. Ryan (1869–1945) but issued over the names of the bishops comprising the Administration of the National Catholic War Council in February, 1919. Considered radical at the time, the program advocated a legal minimum wage, social insurance for unemployment and illness, and labor's right to organize and bargain collectively and to a voice in aspects of industrial management.

**Bishops' Wars.** Two unsuccessful campaigns (1639, 1640) waged by Charles I of England to force the Scots to use Laud's Prayer Book imposed in 1637. By the terms of peace, Charles had to yield to the Scots free General Assemblies and Parliaments. The English Parliament, out of session after 1629, had to be convened, thus beginning the Long Parliament (1640–1653) which resulted in the downfall (1646) and eventual execution (1649) of the king.

**Bismarck, Otto von** (1815–1898). Prussian statesman. Bismarck studied at Göttingen and Berlin, then became a judicial administrator in Aachen. He represented Prussia at the Frankfurt federal diet in 1851, and observed that Austria did not respect Prussia as a partner. For him the Holy Alliance was dead, and Prussia should face the new situation. At diplomatic posts in St. Petersburg and Paris (1859–1862) he moved toward philosophical eclecticism and freedom from religious preconceptions.

During an 1862 constitutional crisis William I turned to Bismarck to implement programs of militarism and Junkerism in spite of a liberal majority in the diet. At first the liberals regarded the new chancellor as reactionary. They miscalculated his use of the new militant state as the primary instrument of a dynamic and aggressive policy. Bismarck ruthlessly crushed his opposition with a successful foreign policy of "blood and iron." He demonstrated his prowess during the Polish uprising in 1863 and in the Schleswig-Holstein affair in 1864. Naked power and self-interest were the watchwords of his *Realpolitik*. By 1866 Germany had become by and large subject to Prussia; even the liberals rallied around him in the defeat of Austria. Victory came again in the Franco-Prussian war of 1870, and the Second German Reich was declared in 1871. In the 1880's he pushed through social legislation with the aid of the Catholic Centre. Brusquely, William II dismissed him in 1890.

An unswerving monarchist, he was forced to bow to the monarchy. In retirement he showed himself to be the founder of a state but not an educator of the people.

Bismarck's religious life was indeterminate. His confirmation by Schleiermacher bore little fruit until he experienced a spiritual awakening at the deathbed of Maria von Blankenburg. He married a girl from a pietistic circle, but was never closely affiliated with the church even though he received the Lord's Supper from Büchsel, Gossner, and Knack in Berlin. His faith was highly individualistic.

Politically, Bismarck attempted to separate church and state. The famed Kulturkampf originated with a question over control of education. The Falk or May laws (1873–1875) were countered by the Catholic Centre, but Bismarck held firm. He supported the Old Catholics as "Germanic" in an attempt to subjugate the Roman Church, but finally he began to retreat in 1878. The last offensive act was removed in 1887 even though the Kulturkampf had actually ended in April, 1879.

**Bjørnson, Bjørnstjerne** (1832–1910). Norwegian poet and dramatist. After the death of W. A. Wexels (1866), Bjørnson became the leader of the Grundtvigian movement in Norway. In 1877 he broke with Christianity in a speech before the University Student Association entitled "To Abide in the Truth." In 1880 he wrote the novel *Støv* ("Dust") which attacked the Christian doctrine of the resurrection. His early works (1856–1872) dealt primarily with Norwegian sagas and country tales, but the plays *A Bankruptcy* and *The Editor* which were both produced in 1875 brought him into the field of social drama and realism. An outspoken critic of Christianity in the 1880's and 1890's, he became known as the "Robert Ingersoll of Norway." A contemporary of Henrik Ibsen, he never gained the international reputation of his fellow countryman.

**Black, John** (1818–1882). Scottish missionary. He was born at Dumfries, Scotland, and educated at the Delaware Academy, Delhi, N.Y., and Knox College, Toronto, where he obtained a D.D., Queen's. He was ordained in 1851 and was appointed to the Presbyterian Mission to the French at Montreal. Although unable to speak Gaelic, he was sent to the Scottish Red River Settlement, where he was the only Presbyterian minister until 1862. His ministry was deeply appreciated by the Selkirk settlers.

**Black Rubric, The.** A declaration inserted in the 1552 Book of Common Prayer explaining that the practice of kneeling to receive

Holy Communion is ordained to indicate reverence and humility, and not to suggest adoration of the consecrated elements. The rubric was introduced to placate Knox's followers. It was removed in 1559 and replaced in 1662, with altered wording. In the 19th century, when it became customary to print the rubrics in red, the declaration continued to appear in black because it was not strictly a rubric at all.

**Blackwell, George** (c. 1545–1613). Advocate of Jesuit policies in Elizabethan England. Blackwell was made archpriest in charge of the Roman Catholic clergy in England by Pope Clement VIII in 1598. It was hardly an enviable post, for a bitter rivalry between the Roman Catholic secular priests and the Jesuits threatened to disrupt the Roman mission to the English Church. Though Blackwell was not a Jesuit himself, his policies tended to favor the activities of the Jesuits, which were considered treasonable by the Crown, and this endangered the secular clergy's attempt to win the queen's confidence and negotiate a new settlement. A group of the seculars (Appellants) attacked the archpriest and appealed to Rome. Blackwell reacted with charges of schism. Some measure of peace was restored in 1602 when both sides were reproved by the Holy See. A few years later, however, Blackwell took the Oath of Allegiance to James I, and Pope Paul V removed him from office (1608).

**Blair, James** (1655/6–1743). First Anglican commissary in America. Reared in the Episcopal Church of Scotland and educated in Edinburgh, he went to Virginia in 1685 as commissary and there served congregations at Henrico, Jamestown, and Williamsburg. He was founder (1693) and first president of the College of William and Mary. For nearly fifty years he served influentially as a member of the colony's council.

**Blake, William** (1757–1827). English poet, engraver, and painter. Blake was the first of the English romantic poets, and his early work is full of the idealism and lyricism of that school. Faced with numerous disappointments in his career and personal life, however, Blake became more withdrawn as years passed. He turned to mysticism, and his work grew steadily more abstract. He became convinced that famous deceased persons (see SPIRITUALISM) and angels appeared before him and he drew their portraits and recorded their words. He insisted that Milton's spirit had entered into him, and Milton became a significant influence upon his work. Blake espoused a doctrine of love and liberty and interpreted the external world as merely a shadow of the world of the spirit. His later work is full of symbols, two of which are central: God (Urizen), the Jehovah of the Old Testament, representing law and strict morality; and Orc, the liberating spirit, exemplified for Blake by the revolutions in France and America. The prophetic books present a philosophy that is a strange blend of Christianity, Neoplatonism, and Swedenborgian mysticism. Among Blake's early works are the lyrical *Songs of Innocence* (1789), which are in marked contrast to the later sense of mystery and evil in the *Songs of Experience* (1794). Blake's final great allegorical poem *Jerusalem* (1818) and *Milton* (1804), also symbolic, were written within the last twenty-five years of his life.

**Blake-Pike Unity Proposal.** A proposal for a broad scale union of major American Protestant Churches made by Eugene Carson Blake, stated clerk of the United Presbyterian Church, in a sermon delivered at Grace Episcopal Cathedral in San Francisco in 1960 at the invitation of Bishop James A. Pike. The proposal was that the Methodist, the United Church of Christ, and other interested denominations join with the Protestant Episcopal and the United Presbyterian Churches in drafting a plan of union that would be "both catholic and reformed."

These four denominations were joined by the Disciples of Christ and the Evangelical United Brethren in an initial consultation in 1962. Another consultation two years later provided evidence that considerable progress had been made in adjusting points of tension, but it was also evident that many problems remained as serious obstacles to the realization of this ecumenical proposal.

**Blanc, Louis** (1811–1882). French socialist, politician, and historian. Blanc was a democratic socialist, opposed to the "class struggle" concepts of Marx, who hoped through state action to ensure the right to work and the establishment of a regime of cooperation to replace that of unlimited competition. He popularized the phrase, "From each according to his ability, to each according to his needs"—a deeply Christian sentiment.

**Bland, Salem Goldworth** (1859–1950). Clergyman, author, and one of the founders of the Social Gospel movement in Canada. He was born in Lachute, Quebec, and educated at Morrin College and McGill University (B.A., 1877; D.D., Queen's), and married Emma Levell in 1926. Ordained by the Methodist Church in 1884, he was professor of church history and New Testament literature at Wesley College, Winnipeg, Manitoba, from 1903 to 1917. From 1919 to 1927 he was minister at the Broadway Tabernacle and Western United Church, Toronto, and in 1925 he became a minister of the United Church of Canada. He was a staff writer on the Toronto *Daily Star* from 1927 to 1950.

**Blaurock, George** (Georg Cajacob) (c. 1495–1529). He was called "blue coat," or "strong George," and was the first to receive believer's baptism in the Anabaptist movement around Zurich (January, 1525). A former priest, he was the most zealous of a number of revivalist preachers during the movement's first months who proclaimed a faith issuing from repentance and resulting in a morally changed life. After an active career of bold preaching he was martyred in the Tyrol in 1529.

**Blavatsky, Helena** (1831–1891). Russian cultic leader. She was born in Russia, where she led an imaginative and erratic life. After visiting Tibet and India, she became interested in spiritualism while in the United States, and in 1875 with Henry Steel Olcott organized the Theosophical Society. She then continued her interest in the occult in Europe and India, claiming to reval the truths transmitted to her by certain "Trans-Himalayan Masters of Wisdom." She experienced both denunciation and veneration.

**Blemmydes, Nicephorus** (c. 1198–1272). Greek Orthodox theologian and teacher. Nicephorus was ordained a priest in Nicaea (c. 1223) and established a monastery in Ephesus which he was later to enter. He was a teacher of Theodore II Lascaris, emperor of the Eastern Roman Empire, upon whom he exerted considerable influence. His writings include a significant theological work in which he propounded the Roman Church's dogma of the procession of the Holy Ghost. His scholarship was sound, indicating a firsthand knowledge of the works of Plato and Aristotle.

**Bliss, William D. P.** (1856–1926). Episcopal clergyman and Christian Socialist. Son of Congregational missionaries in Turkey, Bliss became an Episcopalian in 1886 and was ordained in 1887. While a rector in Boston he was influenced by the English Socialism of Frederick D. Maurice and Charles Kingsley and in 1889 organized a Society of Christian Socialists, the first Christian Socialist society in the United States. After this, between pastorates he held a number of important socialist positions: national lecturer for the Christian Socialist Union (1894), president of the National Social Reform Union (1899), and with the American Institute of Social Service (1909–1914). He was an in-vestigator for the U.S. Bureau of Labor (1907–1909) and in charge of educational work among interned French and Belgian soldiers in Switzerland during World War I.

**Blondel, David** (1590–1655). French church historian. Educated at Sedan and the Genevan Academy, he served as country pastor at Roucy, but during his last decade he entered academic circles and in 1650 was appointed professor of history at Amsterdam. Among his writings were two treatises disproving the legend of Pope Joan, an attack on the Pseudo-Isidorian decretals, and a defense of Reformed polity.

**Blondel, Maurice** (1861–1949). French philosopher. While he was professor at the University of Aix, Blondel's *L'Action* (1893) formed the basis of the French school of the "philosophy of action," to which Père Laberthonnière and Édouard Le Roy later belonged. Though his philosophy was considered heterodox, and he was classed with the modernists, Blondel was never condemned. His apologetics were so valuable that Pius XII in 1945 even encouraged him.

**Bloy, Léon** (1846–1917). French-Spanish novelist and critic. Agnostic from his teens, Bloy tried art in Paris, became secretary to Barbey d'Aurevilly, and established himself as a writer in 1884. Joris Karl Huysmans, Baudelaire, and Fr. Tardif de Moidrey influenced him. His masterpiece, *La Femme pauvre* (1897), prefigured his return to faith. *Pilgrim of the Absolute*, journal selections edited by Maritain, whom he converted, appeared in 1947.

**Blumhardt, Christian Gottlieb** (1779–1838). Founder of the Basel Missionary Society (1804). He was the son of a pietistic shoemaker in Stuttgart. The Basel Missionary Society which he and two friends organized was one of the earliest German mission groups in the 19th century. Under his inspiration it took on a pietistic spirit with a relaxation of confessional differences. Blumhardt was chiefly responsible for the work of the Society in India and was an inspector for the Society from 1816 until his death.

**Blumhardt, Johann Christoph** (1805–1880). Evangelist and healer. A nephew of Christian Gottlieb Blumhardt, he taught at the Basel Mission Institute from 1830 to 1838. In 1838 he became pastor at Moettlingen. Here he gained fame as one who could cure by prayer and in 1852 he removed to Bad Boll, where sufferers from all over the world flocked to be cured by him. He worked there until his death, a man of kindly and pious nature whose motto was "Jesus is Conqueror."

**Bluntschli, Johann Kaspar** (1808–1881). Jurist and statesman. Educated at Berlin and Bonn, Bluntschli taught at Zurich in 1833, Munich in 1848, and Heidelberg in 1861. He was involved in the 1839 David Friedrich Strauss controversy, and in 1843 conservatively opposed Wilhelm Weitling and Bruno Bauer. With others he established the Protestant Alliance in 1863. A pacifist given to natural law, he helped found the Geneva Institute of International Law in 1873. He was president of the first Protestant Day and of the Baden church council.

**Bobbio.** A Celtic monastery in northern Italy founded in 614 by Columbanus with the assistance of the Lombard king Agilulf. Gerbert of Aurillac, later Pope Sylvester II, was elected abbot of Bobbio in 982. Since the 12th century it has been an episcopal see also. Bobbio was noted for its learning and its extensive library, which was dispersed in the 17th century to Rome, Milan, Turin, and Paris.

**Boccaccio, Giovanni** (1313–1375). Noted writer of the Renaissance. He is generally considered the first great Italian novelist and the founder of Italian prose. His most famous of many works was the *Decameron,* a collection of short stories that reflected the secular spirit of the age. The tales varied greatly in moral tone and subject matter. Most offensive to the church were those which satirized the clergy and ridiculed traditional Christian morality.

**Bodelschwingh, Friederich von** (1831–1910). Lutheran pastor and founder of the charitable institutions at Bethel bei Bielefeld. Of saintly character, Bodelschwingh not only sought to provide a refuge for the outcasts of society, but to minister to the displaced persons of modern industrialism. He was not a man of abstract theory, but an able administrator and organizer who spent himself in ministering to the needs of rapidly changing European society.

**Boegner, Marc** (1881–1967). Protestant professor and churchman. He was born in Épinal, France, and educated at the Lyceums of Orléans and St. Louis in Paris, the Faculty of Law, Paris (Lic. Law), and the Faculty of Theology, Paris (Th.D.) After ordination in 1905, he was appointed pastor of the Reformed Church at Aouste, Drôme, where he remained until made professor of theology at the Missionary School, Paris, in 1911. In 1918 he became pastor of the Reformed Church,

Passy, Paris, where he stayed until 1953. From 1920 to 1939 he was president of the French Protestant Churches Federation, from 1938 to 1950 president of the National Council of Reformed Churches of France, and from 1948 to 1954 copresident of the World Council of Churches.

**Boehme, Jakob** (1575–1624). German Lutheran theosophist and mystic. Born of a peasant family in Silesia, Boehme was placed at an early age as an apprentice shoemaker. He practiced cobbling at Görlitz for twenty-five years, married there, and had children. He read the mystics, such as Schwenkfeld and Paracelsus, and began to have visions himself, of which he wrote an account in 1612, entitled *Aurora, oder die Morgenröte in Aufgang.* It was circulated privately and Gregorius Richter, the Lutheran pastor in Görlitz, came across the piece. Denouncing Boehme, he persuaded the town council to demand a promise of silence from him and he continued to preach and agitate against Boehme for years. Boehme finally went to Dresden in 1624, where he was better received. He returned to Görlitz to die.

In spite of the obscurity of his writing, which used language adapted from the mystics, the astrologers, and others of that kind, Boehme has had a wide influence. He was read by the romantics, the German idealists, and Hegel, and some of his followers found their way among the Friends. Other important works of his are *Der Weg zu Christo* (1623), *Von den drei Prinzipien des Göttlichen Wesens,* and *Mysterium magnum.*

**Boers.** The name applied to South Africans of Dutch or Huguenot descent. The other large group of South African Europeans is of British ancestry. The Boers are served by three Dutch Reformed churches: the Nederduits Gereformeerde Kerk, the Gereformeerde Kerk van Suid-Afrika, and the Nederduits Hervormde Kerk. All have followed the government policy of apartheid, and a strict policy of "white supremacy" is characteristic of Boer history. The great trek from Cape Colony of about twelve thousand Afrikaners (1835–1843), which resulted in the founding of the South African Republic and Orange Free State, was partly inspired by the British policy of equality between the races. Anna Steenkamp records that this policy was "contrary to the laws of God and the natural distinctions of race and religion, so that it was intolerable for any decent Christian to bow down beneath such a yoke; wherefore we withdrew in order thus to preserve our doctrines in purity."

**Boethius** (c. 475–524). Statesman and philosopher, sometimes called the "last of the Romans." He was born about 475 and held high offices under Theodoric, king of the Ostrogoths and ruler of Italy. His translations and commentaries were important in transmitting ancient culture and philosophy (especially Aristotelian) to the Middle Ages. After the end of the Acacian Schism, however, prominent Romans, once more united with the imperial church at Constantinople, were suspect in the eyes of their Gothic (and Arian) ruler. Boethius was arrested on the charge of treasonable correspondence with the Byzantine court, and in 524 was put to death at Pavia. Having died under an Arian king, he is locally venerated as a martyr. In prison he composed his famous *Consolation of Philosophy.* The absence in it of specifically Christian ideas has cast doubt on the authenticity of the *Theological Tractates,* which carefully set forth the faith of the Council of Chalcedon, but there is nothing unchristian in its philosophical theism, and different circumstances may account for the different subject matter. Among Boethius' contributions are the classical definitions of "eternity" ("the perfect possession all at once of endless life," *Consolation 5, prosa* 6) and "person" ("the individual subsistence of a rational nature," *Contra Eutychen* 3).

**Bogatzky, Karl Heinrich von** (1690–1774). Lutheran pietistic devotional writer of Hungarian nobility. Bogatzky studied at Jena, and then took up theology under Franke from 1715 to 1718. Too sickly for parish work, he traveled widely as spiritual adviser in noble circles, and lived in the Halle orphanage after 1746. His writings include *Das Güldene Schatzkästlein der Kinder Gottes* (1718; widely published and translated), a seven-volume meditation on the New Testament and daily devotions. His "Awake, Thou Spirit" was among the first German mission hymns.

**Bogomiles.** A Balkan dualistic sect centered at Philippopolis. It thrived between the 10th and 15th centuries. The sect was founded in the mid-10th century by the priest Bogomile who was greatly influenced by the Massalians and Paulicians, sects that had penetrated the Balkans during the 9th century from Armenia.

Our basic information about the Bogomiles comes from anti-Bogomile writings such as Cosmas' *Sermon Against the Heretics,* and Euthymius Zigabenus' *Panoplia dogmatica.* The Bogomiles believed that God had two sons, the devil and Jesus Christ, who was the younger brother. The devil, in an attempt to imitate God, created the world. Hence, all material things are evil. Unlike other dualistic sects, the Bogomiles did not have two equal Gods (Good and Evil) vying against each other, but rather they believed in a rebellious son who continually struggled against the Father for mankind.

The Bogomiles rejected Jesus' incarnation and the holiness of his mother. They condemned the Trinitarian concept, the Eucharist and Baptism, the sanctity of apostolic succession, and spurned crosses, icons, marriage, and drinking wine. Their doctrines were mainly based on Paul's writings, and the Old Testament was scorned as the devil's work.

The Bogomiles were condemned at the Council of Turnovo in 1211 and disappeared under Ottoman rule.

**Bohemian Brethren.** Followers of John Hus. The death of Hus (c. 1415) attracted to his cause many Bohemians who had previously been neutral. The result was the formation of moderate as well as radical groups within the Hussite following. The moderates were the Utraquists, or Calixtines, the radicals were the Taborites, led by the blind general John Ziska (until his death in 1424). A long period of unrest followed, sparked by both a desire for ecclesiastical reform and an emerging Bohemian nationalism. In 1434 the Council of Basel was able to come to terms with the Bohemian rulers and the Utraquist churchmen. The Taborites rejected this agreement, but after their defeat by the Utraquists at the battle of Lipan in the same year they ceased to exert much influence. In 1437 the Bohemian nobleman George of Poděbrad became king of Bohemia and appointed John of Rokycana archbishop. John, a Utraquist, worked for church reform, and among his followers his nephew, Gregory, aided by Peter Chelčický, took a most active part, leading a group of zealous Christians in the establishment of a communal society at Kunwald, a village in northeastern Bohemia, in the winter of 1457–1458. They took to calling one another brother and sister, from which came the name Unitas Fratrum, or "Unity of Brothers."

Opposition, including the accusation of heresy by the king, compelled the Brethren to set up their own ministry, which they did at the Synod of Lhotka in 1467. Members who had been chosen by lot were ordained, and the overall supervision of the community was entrusted to a council presided over by a judge. Four elders had episcopal powers, and a committee of women supervised the activities of the other women of the community. A second persecution took place in 1468, and many of the Brethren were tortured and burned. Nevertheless, by the end of the 15th century there were over four hundred communities of the Brethren in Bohemia.

A dispute among the Brethren led to yet another persecution in the first decades of the 16th century. It was based, however, on a charge similar to an earlier one—that of reviving Taborite heresies. The meetings of the Brethren were prohibited, books ordered burned, and members imprisoned. At this point the Brethren contemplated joining one of the emerging Protestant groups. Thus they began corresponding with Luther and Zwingli. Luther refused any association with them because of their acceptance of seven sacraments, priestly celibacy, and rebaptism, and also because of their doctrine of the Eucharist. Upon further investigation, the Brethren rejected Zwingli's doctrine.

In 1528, John Augustana became leader of the Brethren, and modified their doctrines to make them acceptable to Luther. Luther, however, refused to adapt his views on good works to suit the Brethren, so that union was never achieved. When the Bohemian states were requested to join Charles V in the struggle against the Smalcaldic League, the Brethren refused. Instead, they organized attacks into Saxony against the emperor. The victory of Charles V forced them to submit to their king, Ferdinand I, who attempted, but without success, to bring them into the Roman Church. As late as 1609 they were nonetheless guaranteed freedom of conscience and of worship, and it was in part the royal violation of this freedom that led to the Defenestration of Prague and the Thirty Years' War. Early in the war the situation in Bohemia was resolved; by 1627 all forms of Utraquism were proscribed, and the Brethren were forced to go underground or to emigrate to Saxony or Silesia. The ideals of the Brethren, however, were revived by Zinzendorf in 1722. The Bohemians may be regarded as the spiritual ancestors of the Moravian Brethren.

BIBLIOGRAPHY: M. Spinka, *John Hus and the Czech Reform* (Chicago, 1941).

**Bollandists.** A group of Belgian Jesuits who edit and publish the *Acta Sanctorum,* an impressive collection of the lives and legends of the saints, with related documents, ordered according to feast days. The task was originally conceived by Heribert Rosweyde (d. 1629) and furthered by his successor, John Bolland (d. 1665), from whom the group took their name. The work of the early Bollandists has often been acclaimed as a landmark in the development of modern historical methods. A periodical on critical method is published and listings made of unpublished texts. In 1962 there were six Bollandists working in Brussels.

**Bologna, Concordat of** (1516). An agreement reached between Francis I of France and Pope Leo X whereby papal recognition was secured for many powers acquired by the Crown over the French Church after the Pragmatic Sanction of Bourges (1438). The pope, in turn, was assured of the withdrawal of the Sanction and the recognition of his position. Control of appointments in the French Church was shared, but the real power remained in the hands of the king.

**Bolsec, Jerome** (d. 1584). Antagonist of John Calvin. Bolsec was a Carmelite friar in Paris until objection to his Protestant preaching forced him to flee to Italy, where he began practicing as a physician. Later, in Geneva, he took issue with Calvin on the subject of predestination and was imprisoned. By December, 1551, he had been tried by the Little Council and banished from Geneva. In 1577, Bolsec published a defamatory *Life of Calvin.* (See CONSENSUS OF GENEVA.)

**Bolshevik Religious Policy.** "We have declared war once and for all on religion and on religious conceptions" (Engels), for "religion is the opium of the people" (Marx). "Marxism is materialism. As such, it is mercilessly hostile to all religion" (Lenin). These quotations from the Bolshevik troika serve as a guide to Communist religious policy. In more practical terms, this policy expressed itself in a crude, ruthless hostility and aggression in an attempt to destroy religion and religious belief. The initial period following the revolutions of 1917 witnessed the closing of all schools for religious training, the abolishment of religious marriage, the confiscation and in some areas the looting and desecration of church property, the prohibition of religious instruction, and the imprisonment and execution of thousands of clergy and many more faithful in an effort to create a "socialist society" free of all religion. When this policy failed, the Bolsheviks organized societies, such as the League of the Militant Godless, sponsored and seemingly favored rival church groups, and even tampered with the calendar to make worship difficult. More recently, they have used scientific achievement (sputniks) and material progress (tractors) as proof of the absence of God and the irrelevance of religion. On the other hand, they have used religion to further specific policies and to influence worldwide opinion. In the final analysis, however, a policy of hostility remains characteristic.

**Bompass, William Carpenter** (1834–1906). Missionary bishop of the Church of England in Canada. He was born in London, England. Though brought up as a Baptist, he was ordained by the Church of England in 1865. In the same year he was sent by the Church Missionary Society to the Mackenzie River district. In 1874 he was consecrated bishop of Athabaska and married Charlotte Selina Cox. When his diocese was subdivided in 1884, he became the first bishop of Mackenzie River, and in 1891 on further subdivision first bishop of Selkirk. He retired in 1905 but remained in the Yukon until his death.

**Bonald, Vicomte Louis Gabriel Ambroise de** (1754–1840). French restorationist. Along with Joseph de Maistre, Bonald represents the theocratic school of French conservatives. An opponent of Gallicanism in the church and liberalism in the state, Bonald rejected the rationalist doctrines of the 18th century and the revolutionary principles of thinkers such as Rousseau. For him, man was not born good, only to be corrupted by society, but a being tinged with evil for whom society and the traditional order were a remedy. A fideist and a traditionalist, Bonald published in 1796 his *Théorie du pouvoir politique et religieux dans la société civile* (3 vols.), in which he attacked the revolutionary principles of equality and the sovereignty of the people. In his view, kings were divinely given to rule over men, and the pope of Rome was the ultimate authority on earth. Like Edmund Burke, he stood aghast at the forces of dissolution loosed by the Age of Reason, forces that would inevitably lead to anarchy and atheism and culminate in the destruction of civilized life. Like René de Chateaubriand, he saw the beauty or utility of Christianity as a means of holding society together, and felt that the papacy had before it the prospect of a golden age of restored prestige and leadership.

**Bonaventure** (1221–1274). Mystical theologian and the last Christian thinker to produce a cohesive system in which all knowledge was subordinated to faith. Born near Viterbo, he joined the Franciscans c. 1238 and studied at Paris under Alexander of Hales. He began lecturing on the Bible c. 1248 and on the *Sentences* of Peter Lombard c. 1250, becoming professor in 1253. He was excluded from the university during the controversy between seculars and mendicants in 1255, and though readmitted, gave up teaching on being elected minister general of his order in 1257. In 1273 he was consecrated cardinal bishop of Albano. He died while attending the Council of Lyons. Following Francis, he saw the entire purpose of teaching as furthering the soul's progress to God and thus his aim in theology was Augustine's: to know God and the soul. All other knowledge, including philosophy, was pertinent only to the degree that it assisted this itinerary of the mind to God; sought for itself, it led only to error, for even knowledge of God gained by reason was erroneous without the light of faith. His metaphysics were based on the doctrines of exemplarism, emanation, and divine illumination, and he attacked Aristotle's divergence from them, whether advocated by the Averroists or by Thomas Aquinas. His last years were spent in reconciling the factions within his order and working for the reunion of the Greeks with Rome.

**Bonhoeffer, Dietrich** (1906–1945). German Lutheran pastor and theologian. For his part in an attempt to overthrow Adolf Hitler, he was hanged in the concentration camp at Flossenburg on April 9, 1945, after two years' imprisonment. He studied under Adolf von Harnack in Berlin and was influenced by Karl Barth. When anti-Jewish legislation was forced upon his church in 1933, he objected and in exile ministered temporarily to German congregations in London. Later, as head of a theological college in Germany, he made a lecture tour of the United States just before World War II and was offered political asylum. He refused, returned to Germany and became involved in the Resistance movement.

His published works include *Sanctorum Communio* (1930), *The Cost of Discipleship* (1948), *Ethics* (1955), and *Letters and Papers from Prison* (1953). In these he reinterprets Biblical concepts for a world that has come of age, in which neither the usual metaphysical nor psychological categories are adequate. He teaches a revolutionary understanding of Christian belief in which there is no separation of the religious realm from the secular realm. The Christian identifies with and suffers for the world as Christ did. Bonhoeffer's personal worldly commitment and execution tend to illustrate and emphasize his written ideas.

**Boniface I** (d. 422). Pope from 418 until his death. His predecessor, Zosimus, had been unpopular for supporting the Pelagians and for trying to establish a vicariate in Arles without regard for the rights of the Gallican metropolitans. After the emperor confirmed the election of Boniface instead of that of his rival, Eulalius, Boniface did much to reingratiate the papacy by his condemnation of Pelagianism and his recognition of the Gallican metropolitans.

**Boniface VIII** (Benedetto Caetani, 1294–1303). The climactic pope of the High Middle Ages. In his reign culminated most of the key aspects of two and a half centuries of the reform initiated by Popes Leo IX and Gregory VII. He inherited the full-blown concepts and the already long-standing legal practice of the papal monarchy, and as the most capable canonist of the Curia was determined to see the somewhat dubious triumphs of his latter-day papal predecessors transformed into total victories. Confident of his absolute claims, he lent a willing ear to such extreme proponents of papal absolutism as Giles of Rome (*De potestate ecclesiastica,* 1302) and James of Viterbo (*De regimine Christiano,* 1302). Their tendentious writings did nothing to abate his naturally overbearing attitudes.

Even before his election he had made many enemies, both political and curial. By replacing the saintly but inept Celestine V, who abdicated on his advice after only five months as pope, Boniface became the symbol of all that the evangelicals of the time found hateful, dangerous, and unspiritual in the life of the church. "Spiritual" Franciscans and all those who favored a radical reform of the Curia and the church combined to broadcast speculation that he had forced the saintly *papa angelicus* to abdicate. The fact that he subsequently kept the ex-pope under house arrest until he died and that he revoked all the special privileges granted to the Spirituals by Celestine confirmed them in their views that he was a kind of Antichrist. Their suspicions were also rooted in the awesome failures of papal diplomacy and warfare under preceding popes. The disastrous involvement of the Holy See with Charles of Anjou, the fateful Sicilian Vespers massacre (1282), and the attendant abuses of spiritual authority marked the pope, they felt, as a "man of blood" and a "slayer of Christians."

Both evangelicals and the lawyers supporting the rising national monarchies of France and England could only consider Boniface a menace to their aspirations. The combination was to prove fatal to his high-flown aspirations. Neither Boniface nor his advisers seemed able to grasp the changed mood of Christendom signaled by the Sicilian Vespers. This revolution had marked the end of the medieval hierocracy. Boniface's reign was to prove it.

The monarchical aspirations and the wars of France and England were to be his undoing. Philip IV (Philip the Fair) and Edward I were determined to use ecclesiastical property and revenues for national purposes. Partly to erode their bellicosity and partly to underline the supremacy of the papacy, Boniface was determined they should not do so without episcopal and papal consent. Once the issue was fairly joined, only naked power was to settle it.

Both kings were bitterly resentful of Boniface's blunt and arrogant claims and his interventions in their kingdoms, but only Philip IV was in a position to do him real harm. Two heavily disputed cases over taxation and clerical immunities in France occupied most of Boniface's reign and culminated in the "shame of Anagni," Sept. 7, 1303. Partisans of Philip IV and the alienated Colonna cardinals arrested the pope, maltreated him and tried to force his abdication. Vilified and discredited, the old man died a month later. The only practical upshot of his policies proved to be the "Babylonian Captivity."

His chief doctrinal legacy is one of the most famous dogmatic bulls of all time, *Unam sanctam,* Nov. 18, 1302. It is a succinct summary of a theological development that stressed the unitary nature of the *Respublica Christiana* and the direct and plenary authority of the pope in both spirituals and temporals. The fact that Giles of Rome helped compose it guaranteed that the bull would contain the quintessence of the extremist hierocratic claims. Its concluding dogmatic definition can hardly be interpreted otherwise than in the light of the whole document and its sources of inspiration. Like the tiara adorned with three crowns, *Unam sanctam* became the mark of the most advanced form of medieval papalism.

BIBLIOGRAPHY: T. S. R. Boase, *Boniface VIII* (London, 1933); W. Ullmann, *Medieval Papalism* (London, 1949).

**Boniface of Crediton** (Winfrid or Wynfrith, 680–754). Anglo-Saxon "Apostle of the Germans." Winfrid (he was to acquire the Latin name Boniface only later) was born at Crediton in Devonshire. At an early age he decided to become a monk and was entrusted to the care of the monastery at Examchester, where his life was most exemplary. He was a diligent student and soon had learned all that his masters had to teach; thereupon he moved on to the monastery of Nursling, where he continued his studies. He was such a successful student that he became a teacher himself. Upon reaching the canonical age, he was ordained to the priesthood.

However, the wanderlust that seems to have been a deep-seated characteristic of the Germanic peoples did not allow him to be satisfied with such a sedentary life. At length he asked permission of his abbot to lead a mission to the heathen Germans on the Continent. With reluctance his petition was granted and in the year 716 he set sail with twelve companions, landing on the coast of what is today the Netherlands. There he and his companions preached throughout the summer to the heathen Frisians, but with no success. Discouraged by their failure, they returned to their English monastery. Boniface remained there for more than a year. He then traveled to Rome, where Pope Gregory II commissioned him to make a report on the church in Thuringia. The church had not been completely obliterated in these areas by the migrations, and Boniface was to find out its condition. Crossing the Alps to Thuringia, he met with considerable success in converting the barbarians. When he had finished his work and had reported to the pope, he returned to Frisia, working for several years under one of his fellow countrymen, Willibrord (658–739), the "Apostle of the Frisians." Recalled to Rome in 722, Boniface was consecrated bishop of the Germans and took an oath of fidelity to the Roman see. This close relationship with Rome was to continue throughout his life and was to have momentous effects upon the Western Church in succeeding centuries. From Rome, he went first to Gaul in order to enlist the cooperation of the Carolingian house in the evangelization of the heathen. This alliance of the mission of the church with the political ambitions of the Carolingians was also to have great impact upon the church.

With the favor of the pope and the support of the Carolingian house, Boniface made his way to Hesse. His mission work among the Hessians seems to have been aided greatly by a dramatic event that took place soon after his arrival. During a heathen rite at the Oak of Thor, the sacred tree of the Hessians, Boniface boldly took an ax and felled the tree before the eyes of the worshipers. This demonstrated to them conclusively that the Christian God was more powerful than Thor. In accordance with the customary Christian practice, Boniface erected a chapel on the spot where the tree had stood. He was not alone in his work among the Hessians, for there was a steady flow of his fellow Englishmen who came to assist him. In order to evangelize the Germans, they founded monasteries in the countryside. The presence of devoted and often educated monks among the barbarians was very helpful in converting them. The most famous of Boniface's monastic foundations was Fulda, established in 743.

In 732, Boniface was made archbishop at large so that he could found episcopal sees and appoint bishops, thus consolidating the gains that had been made. The discipline of the church was greatly improved by a series of councils held under his leadership, beginning in 741. The authority of bishops over their priests was strengthened. Monasteries were reformed by placing them under the Rule of St. Benedict. About 747, Boniface was made archbishop of Mainz. Since this was the chief see of Germany, he could direct the church throughout the Carolingian domain. However, he could not forget his earlier failure at Frisia; in 752 he returned to his first mission field. He was martyred in Frisia in 754 along with a group of converts about to be baptized. He was buried at his beloved Fulda.

BIBLIOGRAPHY: Boniface, *Letters,* tr. by E. Emerton (New York, 1940); W. Levison, *England and the Continent in the Eighth Century* (Oxford, 1946); Willibald, *The Life of St. Boniface,* in C. H. Talbot (ed. and tr.), *The Anglo-Saxon Missionaries in Germany* (New York, 1954).

**Bonifatius Verein.** A German Roman Catholic home mission society. It was founded on Oct. 4, 1849, at the suggestion of Johann Joseph Ignaz von Doellinger, at that time an ardent champion of Rome and prominent church historian. Paderborn was chosen as the center of operation. Pius IX approved the society on April 21, 1852. The object of the society was to "promote the spiritual interests of Catholics living in Protestant parts of Germany, and the maintenance of schools." Such a society was deemed necessary because of considerable loss of Catholic membership to Protestant confessions in the 19th century. The society is financed by private donations and church offerings. Gradually it has expanded beyond the borders of Germany into the neighboring countries.

**Bonn Conference.** Second industrial conference conducted by Inner Mission at Bonn, June 14–15, 1870, with Erwin Nasse presiding. This marked the first effort of German industrialists to assess the grievances of labor. Included among one hundred participants were Fritz Kalle, evangelical clergymen, economists, Bonn theologians, and industrialists. Speakers were C. Stumm and Carl Sarasin. While the need for adequate housing was recognized, a paternalistic mood prevailed and no action was taken. *Concordia* (1871–1876), an industrialist journal, resulted from the conference.

**Bonosus** (d. c. 400). Bishop of Sardica in the second half of the 4th century who did not believe in the perpetual virginity of Mary. Our only known source for him is a letter to the Illyrian bishops from Pope Siricius, which was attributed to Ambrose. Bonosus was said to have explained that our Lord would not have committed his mother to the care of the beloved disciple if she had had other children. After the Synod of Capua in 391 Bonosus was condemned, but his sect continued to exist on into the 7th century, closely associated with the Photians.

**Book of Mormon.** A book of scripture in The Church of Jesus Christ of Latter-day Saints as well as the Reorganized Church. It is purported to be a record of the aboriginal inhabitants of the western hemisphere, including their Hebraic origin and subsequent destiny and apostasy during the years from 600 B.C. to A.D. 421. The account is said to have been compiled by the prophet Mormon and written upon gold plates which were hidden by his son, Moroni, in Hill Cumorah in New York State at the time of the demise of the faithful. That location was first revealed in 1823 to Joseph Smith, Jr., who later, after miraculously translating the record, had it published in 1830. It was upon the basis of the Bible, this book, and what were regarded as subsequent revelations that the church of Jesus Christ was considered by the followers of Smith to have been reconstituted.

**Booth, William** (1829–1912). English evangelist, founder and first general of the Salvation Army. He was born an Anglican, but became a Methodist at age fifteen. He went to London in 1849, where his fondness for outdoor preaching caused his withdrawal from the Wesleyans to join the Methodist New Connection. He was ordained in that body but found it too restrictive, so he withdrew from it also in 1861, becoming a traveling evangelist. Married in 1855 to Catherine Mumford, who was herself to become a preacher of note, Booth left London for a time after his break with the Methodists, to return in 1864. Then successively as the East London Revival Society, the East London Christian Mission, the Christian Mission, and finally in 1878 as the Salvation Army his main work evolved. Under military discipline modeled after that of the British Army, the tactics of this quasi-military organization are designed to reach the lowest strata of English society by (1) holding outdoor meetings and processions, usually accompanied by a musical band; (2) visiting bars, jails, and homes; (3) holding meetings in theaters, factories, and other unusual places; (4) enlisting each convert as an evangelist in his daily life. Though at first vio-

lently opposed, his book, *In Darkest England and the Way Out* (1890), did much to gain for the Army a very general sympathy, both public and private. In 1880 the movement spread to the United States and in 1881 to Australia. At Booth's death he was succeeded by his son, William Bramwell Booth.

**Bordeaux Pilgrim.** Author of the earliest known account of a pilgrimage from western Europe to the Holy Land. His *Itinerarium Burdigalense* tells of the trip in A.D. 333 and 334 during which he visited northern Italy, the Balkan peninsula, Constantinople, Asia Minor, and Syria. Although most of his account merely lists the stops he made, he does give a few notes on the Biblical sites he visited. He is, with Eusebius, one of our earliest sources for information about Constantinian basilicas such as the Holy Sepulcher and Anastasis, and the church on the Mount of Olives.

**Borgia, Caesar** (1475–1507). Renaissance prince. An illegitimate son of Pope Alexander VI, Caesar Borgia became a cardinal before the age of twenty. Resigning the cardinalate to become a secular prince, he became embroiled in a series of wars and intrigues involving the Italian states, the aim of which was to create a Borgia state in central Italy. He was killed in battle at the age of thirty-one. Caesar Borgia has been identified by some as the ideal civil ruler in Machiavelli's *The Prince.*

**Borgia, Francis** (1510–1572). Duke of Gandia and third general of the Society of Jesus. He was born in Valencia, a grandson of Pope Alexander VI (Rodrigo Borgia) as well as of Ferdinand of Aragon. A favorite at the court of Charles V, he was made master of horse to the empress, and later was given Eleanor de Castro in marriage. While accompanying the remains of the dead empress to Granada for burial, he was converted to a life of Christian perfection. Upon the death of his wife, he abdicated his dukedom in favor of his eldest son, and joined the Jesuits. In 1554, Ignatius appointed him commissary general of the order in Spain, Portugal, and the Indies. Between 1565 and 1566, he founded missions in Florida, New Spain, and Peru. He was elected general of the Jesuits in 1565, and his reforms earned him the title of "second founder." He established the Roman College in 1567 and died in Rome after a strenuous papal mission to Spain, Portugal, and France. He was canonized by Clement X in 1671.

**Borromeo, Charles** (1538–1584). Archbishop of Milan, cardinal, and papal secretary of state under Pius IV. He was born in Arona, Italy, the second son of Count Giberto Borromeo and Margarita de' Medici, whose younger brother became Pius IV. At twelve years of age, he was consecrated titular abbot of Sts. Gratinian and Felinus at Arona. In 1559, he finished his studies in civil and canon law at Pavia, whereupon his uncle, Pius IV, summoned him to Rome as secretary of state and made him a cardinal deacon. He became, in addition, administrator of the archdiocese of Milan. He helped to prepare the last session of the Council of Trent (1562–1564). Because of family pressure to marry, he was secretly ordained in 1563 and shortly consecrated bishop. He dedicated himself to the implementation of the reform decrees of Trent, and was himself an exemplary bishop, living austerely, frequently visiting his parishes, founding the Confraternity of Christian Doctrine for catechetical work, and most importantly, effecting the reform of his clergy and religious. He was canonized by Paul V in 1610.

**Bosco, John** (1815–1888). Italian religious leader. Born of peasant parents near Turin, John Bosco devoted himself to working with boys whose normal pattern of life had been adversely affected by the incipient industrial revolution. After ordination he worked in Turin. He founded the Congregation of Salesian Fathers, and cofounded the Daughters of Our Lady Help of Christians. The Salesians of St. John Bosco (Society of St. Francis of Sales) were dedicated to the care and education of orphan boys. The Society developed from a boys' refuge and night school which he organized. It was founded in 1841 under the patronage of Francis of Sales. By the time John Bosco died the Salesians had 750 houses and cared for 130,000 children. He was canonized by Pope Pius XI in 1934.

**Bosio, Antonio** (c. 1576–1629). Archaeologist. He was born on Malta but educated in Rome, where he did his great archaeological work in the catacombs. In 1593, fifteen years after the first accidental discovery of an ancient subterranean Christian cemetery in Rome, Bosio began the systematic exploration of the underground vaults. The posthumous publication of his detailed but not always accurate *Roma sotterranea* in 1632 aroused a lively and sustained interest in his findings.

**Bossuet, Jacques Bénigne** (1627–1704). French Catholic pulpit orator, controversialist, and bishop of Meaux during the age of Louis XIV. He was closely involved in the chief religious questions of the day: Protestant conversion, quietism, Jansenism, Gallicanism, and Bible criticism. Born at Dijon, he was from early life destined for holy orders. Taking his degree at Paris (1652) with distinction, he soon achieved renown for his closely reasoned sermons. His funeral orations were particularly noted, published, and glossed. Capable of prodigious feats of memory, he mastered the Bible, the church fathers (Augustine was his specialty), Tertullian, and John Chrysostom. Bossuet was greatly interested in the conversion of the Huguenots. Perhaps reflecting that civilization is more amenable to persuasion than to force, he tried to convince Protestants of the validity of Catholic claims. First in 1671 he outlined an *Exposition of the Doctrine of the Catholic Church*. Then seventeen years later he penned in two volumes the *History of the Variations of the Protestant Churches*. Bossuet thought Protestants erred in constantly changing their doctrines and that they could not properly be regarded Christians. In a pamphlet war on the topic, Bossuet's dialogue with the German scholar Leibnitz was most noted. He also found time to serve as tutor to the dauphin (using the occasion to outline from Biblical sources in his *Politique* the theory of the divine right of kings), to act as go-between for Louis XIV and Mme. de Maintenon, and to gain election to the French Academy. He exchanged literary blows over quietism with his friend Fénelon, archbishop of Cambrai. While the latter defended in *Maxims of the Saints* the Molinist ideas of Mme. Guyon, Bossuet authored *Reflections on Quietism*. Innocent XII settled the matter (1699) by censuring twenty-three of Fénelon's propositions. Some uncertainty exists on the questions of Jansenism. Bossuet denounced the five central statements of Jansen's *Augustinus,* yet thought Quesnel's *Moral Reflections of the New Testament* to be orthodox enough, though admitting their need for some corrections. While "soft" on Jansenism, he did not join that camp as did his nephew and namesake, the bishop of Troyes. The problem of the Gallican Church, pressed by Louis XIV, the Sun King, and based on ancient French claims for national religious autonomy, proved most difficult for Bossuet. He followed what some historians regard as an appeasing course. He authored the Four Articles of Gallican Liberties forced through the general assembly of the clergy (1682). The Articles rejected papal claims of suzerainty over kings, stated that the pope was limited by church councils and that the customs and privileges of the French Church and papal decisions on questions of faith were not always finite. It is said that Bossuet offered the Four Articles to stave off more radical ones from the throne of complaisant prelates. At the opening of the assembly he defended the unity of the church, but boggled at papal infallibility. The Jesuits as anticipated took a strong ultramontane stand against the Articles and their author. While compromise was ultimately achieved and schism avoided, Gallicanism was popular for long afterward. Bossuet was uneasy with the new critical scholarship of the Bible, and produced his *Defense of Tradition and of the Holy Fathers,* not finally available until 1862. Bossuet was not only a defender of faith who wrote *Reflections on the Gospels,* a sensible historian—his *Discourse on Universal History* (1681) is cited by historiographers for justifying the way in which Providence governs the earth, excusing God to man and especially to Frenchmen—but an exhorter of unbelievers. He labored even on his deathbed, leading the Duke of Saint-Simon to say, "He died fighting." Bossuet may be described as "a semiofficial exponent of much that was best in the religion of his time," but also as a scholar whose reputation declined subsequently as did the fortunes of the political ideas to which he was attached.

BIBLIOGRAPHY: P. Hazard, *European Thought in the Eighteenth Century* (Cleveland, 1965); E. E. Reynolds, *Bossuet* (Garden City, 1963); E. K. Sanders, *Jacques Bénigne Bossuet* (New York, 1921); W. J. S. Simpson, *A Study of Bossuet* (New York, 1937); N. Sykes, "Bossuet," in F. J. C. Hearnshaw (ed.), *The Social and Political Ideas of Some of the Great Thinkers of the Sixteenth and Seventeenth Centuries* (New York, 1967).

**Bound** (Bownde), **Nicholas** (d. 1613). Puritan divine in the Anglican Church. A graduate of Cambridge, he is best known for his work *True Doctrine of the Sabbath* (1595), which helped establish the Puritan position that Sunday is to be equated with the Jewish Sabbath as a day of rest. Recreation, sports, and feasting were all prohibited. The idenification of the Lord's Day with the Jewish Sabbath became a distinguishing mark of the Puritans in contrast to even the Continental Calvinists.

**Bourgeoys, Marguerite** (1620–1700). Founder of the Congregation of Notre Dame de Montreal. She was born at Troyes, Champagne, France. She came to Canada with Maisonneuve in 1653 and in 1658 opened her first school. To recruit companions for her sisterhood she returned several times to France. In 1675 she built a chapel dedicated to Notre Dame de Bon Secours. She resigned as superior of Notre Dame in 1693. She was declared venerable in 1878 and the official proclamation was made at Rome in 1910.

**Bourges Cathedral.** A structure ranking with Chartres and Notre Dame de Paris as one of the great monuments of Gothic architecture in France. Built between 1192 and 1275, it has no transept but has five aisles and five western portals, and is supported externally by great numbers of flying buttresses, many of them double. Its 13th-century glass rivals that of Chartres, but is marked by greater naturalism and dramatic sense (e.g., the "Sons of Jacob" window). The same realism is in the tympanum sculpture depicting naked figures rising with joyful countenance from the grave.

**Bourget, Ignace** (1799–1885). Bishop of Montreal. He was born at Pointe Levi, Lower Canada, and educated at the Quebec Seminary and at Nicolet College. In 1822 he was ordained by the Roman Catholic Church. He was appointed vicar-general of Montreal in 1836, and in the following year was appointed coadjutor bishop of Montreal. In 1840 he became bishop of Montreal, and two years later was a champion of ultramontane doctrines. He invited the Jesuits to return to Canada, and from 1858 to 1876 waged a bitter conflict with the Institut Canadien in Montreal. In 1876 he was appointed titular archbishop of Marianapolis.

**Bourignon, Antoinette** (1616–1680). Prominent quietist. She began life as a French Catholic, abjured convent life, and fled to Amsterdam. Severe, crippled, distrustful, she believed herself illuminated by God. She wanted to reestablish in its primitive purity the spirit of the gospel and to suppress external worship. Works such as the *Antichrist Discovered* brought followers in the Low Countries, Scotland, and France, and gave her quietist leadership.

**Bousset, Wilhelm** (1865–1920). German Biblical scholar. Educated at Erlangen, Leipzig, and Göttingen, Bousset taught at Göttingen, and after 1916 at Giessen. With W. Heitmüller he edited the *Theologische Rundshau* (1897–1917). As a scholar he was deeply interested in textual criticism, the history of tradition, and the early church, and studied especially the relation of late Judaism and early Christianity to contemporary Hellenistic religions. Bousset was a cofounder of the religiohistorical school; it relied heavily on his researches. His major works included *Die Religion des Judentums im neutestamentlichen Zeitalter* (1903) and *Kyrios Christos* (1913).

**Boutroux, Émile** (1845–1921). Respected Paris philosopher and educator. He taught a spiritual positivism ("man's spiritual life should dominate that part of his existence which is merely material and moral") which influenced Henri Bergson to call him *"cher maître."* A friend of William James, whose doctrines he interpreted to this country, he studied and criticized the history of ideas, science, and religion. He was an early Harvard exchange professor.

**Bowne, Borden Parker** (1847–1910). Methodist clergyman and philosopher. Founder of personalism, Bowne taught that personality was the reality behind all categories and laws. He emphasized the relativity of nature, the pragmatic test of truth, and that religion was the sanction of ethics and ethics the expression of religion. Professor at Boston University (1876–1910), he associated Methodism with modern theology. His writings included *Personalism* (1908) and *Immanence of God* (1905).

**Boxer Rebellion** (1900). An attempt on the part of traditionalist and nativist patriotic societies in China to eliminate foreign influence. It erupted with force in June of 1900. The dowager empress ordered all foreigners done away with, and several thousand Chinese Christians may have been killed as spreaders of the foreign contagion. Western nationals were besieged at the legations in Peking until relieved by an international force.

**Brabourne, Theophilus** (1590–c. 1661). English Puritan best known for his writing about the Sabbath. In his 1628 *Discourse on the Sabbath Day* he argued that Saturday is properly the Sabbath and should be so observed by Christians. For these opinions he was tried by the High Commission and imprisoned for eighteen months. Though he recanted, he continued to hold his belief. In spite of his radical views, he opposed Separatism and remained faithful to the Establishment into the Restoration.

**Bradford, William** (1590–1657). Colonial governor. Born in Yorkshire, England, he joined the Scrooby congregation of Separatists in 1606 and went with them to Amsterdam and thence to Leiden, Holland, where he worked as a weaver. In 1620 he sailed with the Pilgrims on the *Mayflower* and was elected governor of Plymouth upon the death of John Carver in 1621. He was reelected a dozen times, his last term ending in 1656. His administrations covered hard years for the colony, and his skill in befriending the Indians and in inspiring the colonists in large measure saved the colony. He represented Plymouth in the founding of the New England Confederacy and at the 1647 Synod at Cambridge.

His carefully written history *Of Plymouth Plantation* is a valuable source of information about the Plymouth Colony.

**Bradwardine, Thomas** (c. 1290–1349). Late medieval theologian and mathematician. A scholar before everything else, he was appointed in 1337 as chancellor of St. Paul's Cathedral and confessor to Edward III. In 1349 he was consecrated archbishop of Canterbury but died the same year. He earned the title of "Doctor Profundus" chiefly through his *De causa Dei adversus Pelagium* which attacked the Pelagian trends of his day. His argument is from Paul, Augustine, and traditional Scholastic metaphysics. The divine will is the efficient and sovereign cause of all being and act. Because God wills something, it is just, not the contrary. Therefore, if one wishes to understand justice, one must look to what God has said. The human will is absolute in the created order, subordinate only to the divine will. In order for God to be God he must have absolute power over the human will. It suffices for man to be free with respect to everything outside of God and to be a slave of God, though a willing slave, not a forced one. Thus Bradwardine argued that by faith alone, without preceding works, a man is just. Freedom essentially consists, not in complete independence, but in the reasonable capacity to judge rationally and choose voluntarily. To this latter we are not forced, and herein lies the possibility of sin.

**Brainerd, David** (1718–1747). Missionary to American Indians. Enthusiasm over revivals caused his expulsion from Yale, but he studied theology with a tutor and did mission work among Indians in western Massachusetts, Pennsylvania, and New Jersey. The publication of his diary inspired later Indian missions. His short, always frail life ended in the home of Jonathan Edwards, to whose daughter he was engaged to be married.

**Bray, Thomas** (1656–1730). Anglican priest. Educated at Oxford, he was appointed in 1696 as the commissary of Maryland. He lived in the colony for only one year but served it by recruiting pastors and collecting libraries, which led to the founding of the Society for Promoting Christian Knowledge (1699) and the Society for the Propagation of the Gospel (1701). He was largely responsible for Anglican establishment in Maryland.

**Brébeuf, Jean de** (1593–1649). Jesuit mystic and martyr. He was born at Condé-sur-Vire, in France. In 1617 he entered the Society of Jesus and in 1625 came to Canada with Samuel de Champlain, living from 1626 to 1629 among the Hurons. In 1633 he was made superior of the Huronian mission, where he remained until his death. He established his headquarters at Ihontatiria, which later became known as St. Joseph's Mission. On March 16, 1649, he was tortured and put to death by the Iroquois at St. Ignace near Georgian Bay.

**Breda, Declaration of.** A letter issued at the instigation of George Monck, Cromwell's lieutenant, by Charles II of England from Breda, Holland, just before the Restoration (April 4, 1660). To counteract antiroyalist sentiment the king offered general pardon to all insurgents, liberty of conscience in religious matters consonant with the peace of the kingdom, and a settlement of disputed land titles, all under conditions Parliament should dictate.

**Brent, Charles Henry** (1862–1929). Episcopal bishop. Canadian born and educated, he served parishes in the United States and as bishop in the Philippines, western New York, and over all American Episcopal churches in Europe. He distinguished himself in the cause against opium, as an Army chaplain in World War I, and as an ecumenical leader, organizing and presiding over the 1927 World Conference on Faith and Order.

**Brentano, Franz** (1838–1917). Philosopher. Nephew of the Catholic poet and novelist Clemens Brentano, Franz was ordained in 1864 and then taught at Würzburg. In 1873 he left the Roman Catholic Church over the question of infallibility. He then became professor of philosophy at Vienna. His works include *Psychologie vom empirischen Standpunkte* (1874) and *The Origin of Ethical Knowledge* (1889). Edmund Husserl was his pupil.

**Brenz, Johann** (1499–1570). Lutheran Reformer of Württemberg. He met Luther at the Heidelberg Disputation (1518) and became his staunch supporter. Called as pastor to Schwäbisch-Hall in 1522, he tactfully introduced the Reformation so that by 1536 his *Church Order* (1526) had been adopted throughout Württemberg. During the Peasants' War he criticized sharply both the princes and the peasants while pleading for clemency for the latter. In the *Swabian Syngram* (1525) he defended the doctrine of Christ's bodily presence in the Eucharist against Oecolampadius. Four years later he joined Luther at Marburg for the famous meeting with Zwingli. In 1536 he reorganized the University of Tübingen into a Lutheran institution. After twenty-six years of faithful service in Schwäbisch-Hall, the Augsburg Interim forced him to flee in 1548. In 1552 he journeyed to Trent in order

to defend his Württemberg Confession before the Council fathers. The next year he took an active role in reforming the Palatinate and accepted a call to the cathedral church in Stuttgart, where he remained until his death. Though taking an active part in the controversies of his day, he stood for a moderate, openhearted, pietistic type of Lutheranism that bore rich fruit in Württemberg and also influenced the Church of England.

**Brest-Litovsk, Union of** (concluded in 1596). An agreement between the Church of Rome and large numbers of Ruthenians in Poland and Lithuania. The union was due in large measure to Jesuit missionaries who worked among the people and persuaded many Ruthenian bishops to seek communion with Rome. In 1595, Sigismund III, king of Poland, granted the Ruthenian clergy the same rights as the Latin clergy, freed them of the excommunication of the Orthodox patriarch of Constantinople, and allowed them to keep their property and Byzantine liturgy. Pope Clement VIII approved these measures, and the union was solemnly proclaimed in Brest on Oct. 9, 1596.

**Brethren** (Dunkers). The Church of the Brethren was organized at Schwarzenau, Germany, in 1708 by Alexander Mack, who, influenced by contemporary Pietism, asserted that the Bible is the only guide to faith and life, and thus sought to develop a community to reproduce in faithful detail the exact conditions believed to have pertained in the primitive church. Exemplifying this was the importance and pattern of observance of the Lord's Supper, which was preceded by a love feast and the washing of feet, and was concluded with the "holy kiss" and "the right hand of fellowship." Among other Biblical practices that were observed were anointing the sick with oil, covering the heads of women during worship, wearing the plainest clothes, refraining from amusements, and refusing to take oaths, bear arms, or engage in lawsuits. Belief in adult baptism by trine forward immersion was also practiced, and from this came the popular name of Dunkers.

In America several religious bodies have arisen from this movement. The first appeared in Pennsylvania in 1719 and experienced considerable growth four years later as a result of a revival, at which time the first American congregation was organized. Then in 1729, Mack arrived to take over the leadership of what was termed the Conservative Dunkers, a name characteristic of the position that they have continued to espouse. The first defection from the main body was led by Johann Conrad

Beissel, who, in 1728, founded the German Seventh-Day Baptists, and later the semi-monastic Ephrata Community. A second division was the establishment of the Church of God (New Dunkers) in Indiana in 1848 by George Patton and Peter Eyman, which differed primarily in the insistence upon the Biblical name of Church of God. Other splinterings occurred during 1881 and 1882 when one group (Old German Baptist Brethren or Old Order Dunkers) claimed that the Conservative Brethren were departing from ancient Scriptural standards over such matters as personal attire and institutionalism, and another group (Brethren Church, Progressive Dunkers) advocated greater liberty in these areas. The major group occupied a middle position and remained in the original church, experiencing a doubling of membership in the first half of the 20th century.

**Brethren of the Common Life.** A later medieval religious fraternity. It was begun about 1374 when Gerhard Groote ceded the use of his house in Deventer to a group of poor women who wished to follow his exhortations to live an exemplary Christian life. In 1379, Groote wrote constitutions for them by which they lived in community, but were bound by no vows. They were to earn their livelihood but to have goods and money in common. With no change in their dress, they were to remain members of the local parish. Obedience, poverty, and charity were to characterize them. When Florentius Radewyns joined Groote, a community of men similar to that of the women developed. Death cut short further direction by Groote, who recommended that some of the men build an Augustinian monastery as a place of spiritual strength and renewal for those who remained working in the city. He had appointed Radewyns as their leader. Under him, the communities grew and moved their center to Zwolle. Daughter houses were founded in Flemish towns and grew with the type of school headed by John Cele, the "founder and originator of secondary schools," which became typical of the Biblically centered education of the Brethren of the Common Life. The Brethren ceased to function near the end of the 17th century, their educational activities having been taken over by other types of schools.

**Briçonnet, Guillaume** (1470–1534). French reforming bishop. Born in Paris of a noble family of Touraine. Briçonnet studied at the College of Navarre. After serving on a diplomatic mission for Francis I, he was made bishop of Meaux (1516). He vigorously undertook the reform of his diocese, inviting Lefèvre (Stapulensis Faber) and Farel to preach there, and encouraging the translation of the New Testament into French. More closely allied to humanism than to Protestantism, he was persuaded that the Protestants were going too far and (under royal pressure) actually condemned the works of Luther (1523). Attempts were made to impugn his loyalty to the Roman Church, but through the influence of the king were largely unsuccessful.

**Bridget of Sweden** (c. 1303–1373). Founder of the Brigittines. A member of an aristocratic Swedish family, Bridget felt called by God to bring back the papacy from Avignon to Rome. For this purpose, as well as to have the order she founded approved by the pope, she journeyed to Rome in 1349 and remained there until her death. She urged both Urban V and Gregory XI to return to Rome and to purify the church. The recipient of visions and revelations, Bridget exercised a great influence on popes and people in a turbulent era.

**Briggs, Charles Augustus** (1841–1913). American Presbyterian minister and professor at Union Theological Seminary, New York City. He was born in New York, educated at the University of Virginia, Union Seminary, and the University of Berlin. After a few years of pastoral experience, he was appointed professor of Hebrew and cognate languages at Union Seminary in 1874. Throughout his life, Briggs stood out as a champion of the new critical approach to the Bible, struggling to win a place in the Presbyterian Church for the study of the Bible according to the scientific standards of literary and historical criticism. Briggs himself was theologically conservative, his espousal of Biblical criticism being the only point at which he differed from his more conservative contemporaries, but his manner was frequently disputatious, brusque, and unguarded. In 1890 on the occasion of his being appointed to a new professorship of Biblical theology, Briggs delivered an inaugural lecture entitled "The Authority of Holy Scripture" which so alarmed his opponents that his election to the new chair was vetoed by the General Assembly of the Presbyterian Church and Briggs himself was convicted of heresy and suspended from the ministry. Briggs eventually joined the Protestant Episcopal ministry, and Union Seminary, unwilling to abide by the General Assembly's veto, cut itself off from any direct denominational control.

**Brightman, Edgar Sheffield** (1884–1953). American Methodist educator. He was born at Holbrook, Mass., educated at Brown University, Boston University, Nebraska Wesleyan University, and in Germany. He was ordained a Methodist minister in 1912. Primarily a philosopher of religion, he taught at various universities, and at Boston University from 1919 to 1953. He was associated with the liberal movement in theology, specifically the empirical modernists, using the empirical method to arrive at his concept of a personal but finite God.

**Brigittines.** Roman Catholic religious order founded by Bridget of Sweden and approved by Pope Urban VI in 1378. The order consisted of both monks and nuns, with each house being in effect two monasteries with a common church. The monks were present chiefly as spiritual advisers, however, and the supervision of each house was entrusted to an abbess. In the Middle Ages the order spread rapidly. At present it has fewer houses and only women members. Its rule is based on that of Augustine.

**Brilioth, Yngve T.** (1891–1959). Swedish Lutheran prelate. He taught church history at the universities of Uppsala (1919) and Åbo (Turku), Finland (1925). In 1929 he became professor of practical theology and provost of the Lund cathedral. His scholarly work was mainly in the field of medieval Swedish church history and the Evangelical and Tractarian movements of the 19th-century English church. In 1938 he became bishop of Växjö and from 1950 to 1958 he served as archbishop of Uppsala and primate of the Church of Sweden. A leader in the ecumenical movement (he was Nathan Söderblom's son-in-law), he was active in the formation of the World Council of Churches and was for a time chairman of its Faith and Order Commission and a member of its Central Committee.

**British and Foreign Bible Society.** Publisher of the Bible in almost every known language. Founded in 1804 upon the suggestion to the Religious Tract Society of an evangelist to Wales, its aim is "to encourage a wider circulation of the Holy Scriptures, without note or comment." Its founders came chiefly from the Clapham Sect. The Society is governed by a thirty-six-member committee of which six are non-British and half of the remainder Anglican. The decision of the Society to exclude the Apocrypha from its publications (1826) has profoundly affected the English canon.

**British Council of Churches.** "A fellowship of churches in the British Isles which accept our Lord Jesus Christ as God and Saviour." It has the same basis as the World Council of Churches, having been created in 1942 to further common action, cooperation in study, and the promotion of Christian unity. There are 112 members made up of official representatives from all the main British churches except the Roman Catholic.

**Brogne.** A monastery in Belgium near Namur, founded in 919 by Gerard (d. 959), a monk of St.-Denis. The reformed observance of Brogne attracted the attention of the Count of Flanders, who requested the monks to reform several monasteries in his domain. Approximately twenty houses were thus reformed from Brogne. With no formal affiliation to Brogne, the reform did not long survive in many of these houses after the death of Gerard.

**Brook Farm.** An American communistic community. Founded in 1841 by George Ripley, it was to be a community of intellectuals who would combine study with physical labor to support the enterprise. At its height in 1844 it included about seventy-five members. That year, however, it reorganized according to the social philosophy of Charles Fourier, lost its individuality, and began to decline. It was dissolved in October, 1847.

**Brooks, Phillips** (1835–1893). Episcopal bishop. After a brief period of teaching, Brooks entered the seminary at Alexandria, Va. He attracted considerable attention as a preacher in Philadelphia from 1859 to 1869 at the Church of the Advent and then as rector of Holy Trinity. In 1869, Brooks began a memorable ministry at Trinity Church, Boston. He gave the famous *Lectures on Preaching* at Yale Divinity School in 1877 and spent the rest of his career preaching in America and England, becoming in 1880 the first American to preach before Queen Victoria. In 1890 he preached noonday sermons for Wall Street businessmen at Trinity Church in New York City and in 1891 was consecrated bishop of New York. Brooks stressed personal religion and considered himself more a liberal preacher than a rational theologian. He felt no break with tradition and there is no record of a personal spiritual struggle. Influence by Coleridge, Tennyson, J. F. D. Maurice, F. W. Robertson, and Horace Bushnell, he was not so much a pioneer as an interpreter and popularizer of contemporary religious movements. Brooks did not enter into the conflict between science and religion, insisting that Christianity transcended such issues. Three religious convictions were central to his thought: the total immanence of God, man the child of God and capable of blessedness, and Christ the revelation of what God is and what man may be. Brooks wrote poetry and hymns (including "O Little Town of Bethlehem"), and his sermons were collected in numerous volumes.

**Brorson, Hans** (1694–1764). Danish Lutheran bishop of Ribe and Pietist hymn writer. In 1729 he began collecting Danish hymns and three years later published a volume of Christmas hymns including some of his own. He translated many hymns of German Pietism into Danish which were incorporated into Pontoppidan's hymnbook of 1740, thus influencing Norway as well. Together with T. H. Kingo and N. F. S. Grundtvig, Brorson rounds out the trio of famous Danish hymn writers. Two of his hymns, "Thy Little Ones, Dear Lord, Are We" and "Behold a Host," have become traditional within American Lutheranism.

**Brothers Hospitalers** (*or* Brothers of Charity). A religious institute founded by John Ciudad (John of God) in Granada, Spain, in the 16th century to build hospitals and take care of the sick. Founded as a lay society, it received the Augustinian Rule (1571) and was recognized as an order by Sixtus V (1586). While John provided the original impetus, it was his successor, Antonio Martino, who guided the Brothers as they increased in numbers and went out of Spain into France, Italy, and the New World. They took the three regular vows and the additional vow to serve the sick and dying.

**Brothers of Christian Instruction** (*or* La Mennais Brothers). An institute founded in 1817 at Ploërmel, France, by the abbés Jean Marie de la Mennais and Gabriel Deshayes. It was designed as a remedy for the regulation that Christian Brothers could not go on assignments singly. Its general motherhouse is now on the Isle of Jersey, England. Simple vows of poverty, chastity, and obedience are taken. The work is educational only. There were 2,220 members in 1966.

**Brothers of the Christian Schools.** A Roman Catholic teaching order of unordained male religious. The Christian Brothers were founded by Jean-Baptist de La Salle in Reims, France, in 1680. Their efforts have been expended largely on the education of boys from the lower and middle classes. Their educational regime was laid down in La Salle's *The Conduct of the Schools.* The order has spread throughout the world.

**Brown, William Adams** (1865–1943). American Presbyterian theologian and churchman. A student of Adolf von Harnack, Brown became Roosevelt Professor of Systematic Theology at Union Theological Seminary in New York City in 1898. He resigned in 1930 to become research professor of applied Christianity. He was a cofounder of Union Settlement (1895), a member of the Board of Home Missions (1910–1923), supported the New York Labor Temple, the Federal Council of Churches, the ecumenical movement, and foreign missions. He was concerned with reconciling intellectual freedom with loyalty to the standards of the church. A modernist, he accepted theological pluralism and insisted on the necessity of relating tradition to modern scientific modes of thought. Brown felt that the task of theology, once freed from metaphysics, was definition. His own theological emphasis was Christocentric. His major writings included *The Essence of Christianity* (1902) and *Christian Theology in Outline* (1906).

**Browne, George** (d. 1556). Advocate of the Protestant Reformation in Ireland. As provincial of the Augustinian friars (the religious order generally most sympathetic to the Reformation in England) he accepted the royal supremacy and supported Henry VIII's divorce. As archbishop of Dublin he tried from 1536 to promote acceptance of Reformation usages and legislation, but without conspicuous success. He resigned his see at Mary's accession, ostensibly because he had married.

**Browne, Robert** (c. 1550–c. 1633). English Puritan divine. Browne was educated at Corpus Christi College, Cambridge, and was influenced there by Thomas Cartwright. Subsequently he established several independent congregations, eventually emigrating to Middelburg, Holland, with one of them (1582). After only a short time there, he returned to England, where he was reconciled with the Church of England and episcopally ordained (1591). He died in prison, where he had been sent for assaulting a police officer. It is disputed whether Browne was mentally disturbed or simply quarrelsome. In any case, he was an astute theologian, influential upon the first British Congregationalists (or, as they were then called, "Brownists"). Browne emphasized that baptism alone did not make men members of the true church, and that it was hence necessary for devout Christians to form their own assemblies, ruled by officers of their own choosing. The basis of church membership was to be contractual (or covenantal), not residential. Browne's Separatist convictions were expressed in *A Treatise of Reformation without Tarying for Anie* (1582), in which he denied that the civil powers had spiritual jurisdiction over the church, whose sole Lord is Christ. In *A Booke which sheweth the life and manners of all True Christians* (also 1582), Browne argues that the sole Lordship of Christ is exercised through his members, all of whom participate in his offices as prophet, priest, and king. The priesthood of all believers thereby becomes, along with the idea of the covenant, constitutive of the church's essence, and the priesthood is interpreted in terms of fellowship or mutual concern.

**Browne, Sir Thomas** (1605–1682). Physician and author. Educated at Broadgates Hall (now Pembroke), Oxford, he left England, studying at Montpellier, Padua, and receiving his doctorate of medicine at Leiden about 1633. Settling at Norwich, his fame as a physician and author grew. *Religio medici* was first published in 1642. Revealing both skepticism and faith, it was the reflection of a cultivated physician upon faith. The book was widely read and translated into a number of languages. During the Civil War, Browne's loyalties lay with the Royalists, but he refrained from active participation. *Pseudodoxia epidemica,* more often called *Vulgar Errors,* was an attempt to eradicate commonly held superstitions and errors, according to the lengthy title; but the fact that Browne believed in astrology, alchemy, witches, and magic indicates that he himself was not yet completely free of superstition. By mid-century, learned men regularly consulted with him. Two other well-known works are *Hydriotaphia,* an antiquarian study of ancient burial customs, and the *Garden of Cyrus,* a history of horticulture. This was the last treatise he published (1658), though some things were printed posthumously. His style was Latinized English, ornate and sonorous, and though acclaimed in his day, does not have a continuing appeal.

**Brownson, Orestes** (1803–1876). American Roman Catholic apologist. Brownson had a varied career, being at different times a Presbyterian, a Universalist as well as a Unitarian minister, a religious radical, a social reformer, a Democratic publicist, and eventually a Roman Catholic convert. Sympathetic to the laboring classes and the common man, he sought social amelioration by moral suasion rather than political action. With his own church and journal in Boston in the 1830's, he condemned organized religion and preached "the church of the future," simultaneously attacking the social *status quo,* wealth, and the penal code. He was associated with William Ellery Channing, Thoreau, Aaron Bancroft, George Ripley, and John C. Calhoun, but broke with liberal politics and religion when he was converted to

Catholicism in 1844, becoming a leading Catholic apologist. Stages in his career are marked by *New Views of Christianity, Society and the Church* (1836), *Boston Quarterly Review* (1838), *The Mediatorial Life of Jesus* (1842), *Brownson's Quarterly Review* (1844), and *The Convert* (1857).

**Brunner,** (Heinrich) **Emil** (1889–1966). Swiss Reformed theologian and with Karl Barth cofounder of dialectic or neo-orthodox theology. Educated in Germany, Switzerland, and the United States, he held the post of professor of systematic and practical theology in Zurich from 1924 to 1955. From 1953 to 1955 he taught at the Christian University in Tokyo, Japan. During the first decade of his stay at Zurich he was closely associated with the thought and work of Barth, but in 1934 they parted company when Brunner rejected the Barthian exclusion of natural theology and his denial of man's possession of the image of God after the Fall. The initial attack upon Barth's position in *Nature and Grace* (1934) gave rise in that same year to Barth's *No!,* and the basic disagreement over the key issue remained keen through the years. As a result of this difference, many English and American theologians tended to find Brunner the more attractive. In the mid-thirties a new factor emerged alongside the emphasis upon the crisis of judgment and mercy which characterized any relationship between God and man. In his work *The Divine-Human Encounter* (1937), Brunner came under the influence of Martin Buber in making a distinction between knowing about something and knowing someone. He adopted Buber's concept of "I-Thou" as the key to a proper understanding of divine revelation. The most comprehensive statement of Brunner's mature thought is to be found in his three-volume *Dogmatics* (1946–1960). In the field of Christian ethics, Brunner is remembered for *The Divine Imperative* (1932), and in Christology *The Mediator* (1927) comes readily to mind.

**Bruno** (925–965). Archbishop of Cologne, eminent scholar, statesman, and ecclesiastic of the 10th century. He was the youngest son of Henry I (the Fowler) of Germany. At fifteen he became royal chancellor under his brother Otto the Great, and soon was one of his most trusted counselors. In 953 he was made archbishop of Cologne and duke of the turbulent duchy of Lorraine, which he sought to pacify and bind more closely to the Crown by overseeing appointment of loyal bishops while freeing their dioceses from the authority of local lay lords, thus accelerating the growth of prince-bishoprics within Germany. During

Otto's absence from Germany (962–965) when he was attempting to consolidate his hold on Italy, Bruno added to his duties those of regent of the German kingdom. He also represented German interests in France, and his intervention there, particularly in the disputes between his two nephews, the Carolingian king Lothair and the ambitious Hugh Capet, was so active that the period of his involvement has been referred to as the "regency of Bruno." Though primarily remembered as a politician, he also elevated the moral and intellectual caliber of the German clergy. As abbot of Lorsch and Corvey he undertook reform of those abbeys, and the monastery of St. Pantaleon which he founded in Cologne became a center for ecclesiastical reform. Through his reorganization of the chapel at the royal court, from which the majority of German bishops were to be drawn for the next two hundred years, he indirectly influenced the entire ecclesiastical reform movement throughout Germany.

**Bruno, Giordano** (1548–1600). Italian philosopher and polemicist. Bruno spent most of his life defending the new astronomy of Nicholas Copernicus as well as many of his own radical philosophical speculations. Bruno joined the Dominicans when he was fifteen but after a few years fled his monastery near Naples when the Inquisition began to investigate him on suspicion of heresy. In 1576 he began a peripatetic life which took him to France, England, Germany, and back to Italy. In 1591, he accepted an invitation from Giovanni Mocenigo to come to Venice and teach under his patronage. However, the next year Mocenigo turned Bruno over to the Inquisition. Initially imprisoned at Venice, he was later removed to Rome where he was incarcerated for a long period. Finally, in 1600, the Roman inquisitorial court under the presidency of Robert Cardinal Bellarmine declared Bruno guilty of heresy and ordered him burned at the stake. Bruno wrote a great deal, including his important *Heroic Inspirations* and *On the Infinite Universe and Its Worlds*. He was an ardent Copernican in a day when the works of the astronomer were still on the Index, even going farther than Copernicus by insisting that there were other worlds beyond the solar system. Bruno is seen in retrospect as a martyr for both philosophical liberty and the advancement of scientific thought.

**Bruno of Cologne** (c. 1030–1101). The founder of the Carthusian Order. He was educated at Cologne, where he was born, at Reims, and for a short time in 1050 at Paris. He became a canon at Cologne from where he was called in 1056 to be the *scholasticus* of Reims. In 1067, Manasses, a new archbishop who proved to be quite corrupt, was elected. Bruno led a reform group among the clergy and in an effort to pacify Bruno, the archbishop made him chancellor in 1075. Bruno continued his opposition and was deprived of all offices and expelled the following year. He returned to Cologne where he preached until Manasses was deposed in 1080. Bruno was nominated to succeed him, but the appointment was blocked by the king. With two friends, he then went to live under the direction of Robert of Molesme. Wishing a more austere life, he and six others left Robert and founded a house in the wilderness near Grenoble. This foundation was the beginning of the Carthusian Order. In 1090, his former pupil, Pope Urban II, called him to Rome to become a papal adviser. Bruno was offered the archbishopric of Reggio, which he refused. He was finally permitted to retire to the wilderness of Calabria near Squillace where he founded the monastery of La Torre and where he died.

**Bryan, William Jennings** (1860–1925). Politician and fundamentalist leader. Born and educated in Illinois, he practiced law in Jacksonville (1883–1887). From 1890 to 1894 he was in Congress and three times was the Democratic candidate for president of the United States (1896, 1900, and 1908). In 1912 he worked for Woodrow Wilson's nomination and served under him as Secretary of State (1913–1915). After 1894 he was in demand as a Chautauqua lecturer and in 1901 was the founder and editor of the *Commoner*. He was very active in his Presbyterian Church from 1900 onward, standing in favor of a literal interpretation of the Bible and in opposition to biological evolution. His fervent apology for Fundamentalism was climaxed by his part as prosecuting attorney at the famous Scopes trial in 1925. He died five days after his defeat there.

**Buber, Martin** (1878–1965). Jewish religious philosopher. Buber placed a strong emphasis upon the function of dialogue in community which afforded a valuable counterpoise to the stark individualism of existentialist thinking. Born in Vienna, grandson of a noted rabbinic scholar, he was reared in the bosom of a dual tradition of Enlightenment and Hasidism. Educated in Vienna and Berlin, he for a time was alienated from his religious heritage only to turn to active support of Zionism. From 1916 to 1924 he edited *Der Jude* in which he presented his Zionist views, which took cultural and religious rather than political form. From 1923 to 1933 he served as a professor of Jewish thought and ethics as well as history of religion at Frankfurt. With the coming of the Nazis to power he left Germany in 1938 to take a position at Hebrew University in Jerusalem where he retired in 1951 and died in 1965. Notable for his rehabilitation of Hasidic thought and for efforts to bring reconciliation between Jews and Arabs in the Near East, as well as for his exegetical works on the Hebrew Scriptures, his greatest influence upon Christian as well as Jew has been through his masterpiece, *I and Thou* (1923) in which he sets forth in classic form his concept of dialogue as the basis for community. He distinguishes between "I-It" as relation between subject and object and "I-Thou" (not thee) as a relation between subject and subject. This idea, which went on to see God as Eternal Thou, who may be known but not known about, has greatly contributed to the thinking of Protestant neo-orthodoxy.

**Bucer** (Butzer), **Martin** (1491–1551). German Protestant Reformer. Bucer was born on Nov. 11, 1491, at Schlettstadt in Alsace, son of a shoemaker, Nicholas Butzer. In his youth he became devoted to humanistic studies, which led him at the age of fifteen to choose a monastic life rather than that of a shoemaker. He became a Dominican in 1506, but hated the monastic life. In 1516 he was transferred to Heidelberg, and there found stimulating company among the humanists of the university. He studied Greek and took Erasmus for his personal model. He dined with Luther and heard him dispute in 1518 (see HEIDELBERG DISPUTATION) and became enamored of the doctrines of reform. After ordination at Mainz he traveled to Basel, where he met his lifelong friend Wolfgang Capito. Forced to flee from the disfavor of the Dominicans with the aid of Ulrich von Hutten he obtained refuge with Franz von Sickingen. Through the Roman Curia he obtained release from his vows in 1521 and became a secular priest. Life as court chaplain to the elector of the Palatine proved dull, and he obtained a pastorate at Landstuhl. He married Elizabeth Silbereisen, a former nun, in 1522, more for principle than for love, and had six children by her. His preaching at Wissembourg brought about his excommunication by the bishop of Speier in 1523 and forced his withdrawal to Strasbourg, where he joined his parents. There, under protection of the Council, he preached and lectured on the New Testament. By 1526 reform dominated the religious life of the city, and Bucer's part

in the Disputation at Bern two years later gave him a wide reputation. He took the Zwinglian side in the Eucharistic controversies of the 1520's, basing his position on the statement in John that "the flesh profiteth nothing"; but he held that the spirit is nourished by faith, that the Supper is more than a memorial. He always held the elements to be symbols, but expressed himself differently at various times. He was vague and evasive up to 1524, then leaned toward a Zwinglian position, speaking of symbols with a spiritual presence. By 1528 he was convinced that Luther actually agreed with Zwingli that there was no local presence, and felt that a colloquy might unite them. However, the Marburg Colloquy of 1529 produced no agreement on the Supper, and he was coldly rejected by Luther. It was Bucer's fate as a mediator always to feel the sides to be closer than they would admit, but his efforts continued. He helped draft the Tetrapolitan Confession for the Diet of Augsburg in 1530, which raised hopes for concord with the Lutherans, and he found a spirit of tolerance in Luther with whom he met at Coburg. At home he became head of the city clergy in 1531, and the Strasbourg Synod of 1533 gave him the victory in his long struggle with the Anabaptists. Bucer and Melanchthon met at Cassel in 1534 and agreed on the Cassel Formula, saying that Christ's body and the Eucharistic bread are sacramentally one, and that both are received. The Wittenberg Concord of 1536 brought Luther to agree on the nature of the real presence, but divided the radical Zwinglians from moderates such as Bucer. Bucer's remaining years were largely devoted (without success) to reconciling Roman Catholic and Protestant factions, notably at Worms and Regensburg in 1541, and he also assisted Hermann of Wied in the attempted reform of Cologne. He was sent to Augsburg to sign the Interim, an agreement between Roman Catholics and Protestants, in 1548, but opposed it (see AUGSBURG INTERIM). In consequent disfavor at Strasbourg, he accepted Cranmer's invitation to England, where he became regius professor of theology at Cambridge in 1549. He was well received, being shown favor by Edward VI and consulted on the revision of the Book of Common Prayer. His health failed in the English climate and he died on March 1, 1551. During the reaction under Mary his body was exhumed and burned, but Elizabeth ordered a ceremony of atonement in 1560. He was preceded in death by his first wife and three children in 1541, and had married Capito's widow the next year. A collected edition of his Latin and German works is currently in progress. His exegetical commentaries on the Gospels were published in a combined edition in 1530, followed later by works on The Psalms and Romans. They were hastily done and largely theological and homiletical.

BIBLIOGRAPHY: M. Bucer, *Instruction in Christian Love*, ed. by P. T. Fuhrmann (Richmond, 1952); H. Eells, *Martin Bucer* (New Haven, 1931); C. Hopf, *Martin Bucer and the English Reformation* (Oxford, 1946).

**Buchanan, George** (1506–1582). Scottish political theorist and historian. He was born near Edinburgh and educated at St. Andrews and Paris. His Protestant sympathies, evidenced in writings critical of monks, necessitated his leaving Scotland. He taught subsequently at Paris, Bordeaux, and Coimbra. Later returning to Scotland, he became tutor to Mary Stuart in 1562, and to the future James I in 1570. His principal works are a political treatise on constitutional monarchy (*De jure regni apud Scotos*, 1579) and his history of Scotland (*Rerum Scoticarum historia*, 1582). In his political theory Buchanan argued that the power of kings is derived from the people, to whom they remain responsible, so that popular resistance and even tyrannicide may be constitutionally justified.

**Buchman, Frank** (1878–1960). Lutheran minister. After a religious experience, Buchman organized the Oxford Group movement wherein he hoped other individuals could share the joys of such an experience in a fellowship setting. Then in response to the world tensions in 1938 he shifted his program to one of saving the world from destruction through Moral Re-Armament.

**Buddeus, Johann Franz** (1667–1729). German theologian. He was successively professor of moral philosophy at Halle (1693) and of theology at Jena (1705). Expert in classics, Orientalia, history, philosophy, and theology, he was acknowledged as the most widely talented German divine of his day. Representative of the transition period from orthodoxy to the Enlightenment and Pietism, he showed marked tendencies toward Pietism while he employed "natural religion" apologetically.

**Buell, Samuel** (1716–1798). A minister at Southampton, Long Island, who published a contemporary *Account of the Revival of Religion . . . in the Year 1800*. It documented some striking differences between earlier revivals and the Second Great Awakening in America which laid much less stress upon emotion and more emphasis on pre-

ceding prayerfulness, inward conviction, and moral reform. This was accomplished by pastoral counseling as well as at weekday and other special meetings.

**Bugenhagen, Johann** (*known as* "the Pomeranian") (1484–1558). German Lutheran Reformer, church organizer, and Luther's own pastor. Ordained priest in 1509, he joined Luther after reading his *Babylonian Captivity of the Church* (1520), came to Wittenberg in 1521 and lectured on the Old Testament. In 1522 he became the first of the Reformers to marry. The next year he assumed the pastorate of the church in Wittenberg where he stayed the rest of his life. Here he set a fine example of what an Evangelical pastor should be and came to share as Luther's spiritual counselor the joys and sorrows of his family. He assisted Luther in translating the Bible and published his own translation in Low German. In 1525 he became the first to write against Zwingli's views on the Lord's Supper. Endowed with rare organizing ability, he reordered the churches and schools of Hamburg, Brunswick, Lübeck, Pomerania, Hildersheim, Schleswig-Holstein, and Wolfenbüttel between 1526 and 1544. His church order also became the model constitution for many other Lutheran churches. In 1537 he went to Denmark, where he drew up a church ordinance for Denmark and Norway, served as university rector, consecrated seven bishops (thereby breaking apostolic succession), and crowned Christian III. In 1539 he returned to Wittenberg and was appointed superintendent general of Saxony.

**Bulgakov, Sergius N.** (1871–1944). Russian religious philosopher. As a young man Bulgakov studied law and political economy and taught briefly at the Universities of Kiev and Moscow. A member of the prerevolutionary intelligentsia, he renounced his Marxist views shortly after the turn of the century. Together with other former Marxists (including P. B. Struve, Nicolai Berdyaev, and S. L. Frank) he criticized many of the most cherished doctrines and traditions of the intelligentsia. Their most notable work was a volume of essays published in 1909 under the title *Vekhi* ("Signposts"), in which they called for a moral reeducation of the intelligentsia, for a legal order as the foundation of government, and for a merging of the state and the nation. Bulgakov's own essay reflected his growing attachment to Orthodoxy, for he condemned the intelligentsia's atheistic materialism and its blind borrowing of Western socialism without a Christian substratum of social morality and law. In 1918, Bulgakov was ordained a priest. After his expulsion by the Soviet Government in 1923 he lived in Prague and Paris, where he was professor of theology at the Russian Orthodox Theological Institute. Among his writings are *The Light That Never Wanes, The Tragedy of Philosophy,* and *The Philosophy of Language.*

**Bulgarian Controversy.** A 9th-century struggle between Rome and Constantinople for ecclesiastical jurisdiction of the Bulgarian Church. In 864 the Bulgarian khan Boris converted to Christianity. Hoping to use Christianity as a basis for uniting the ruling Bulgars and the Slav population, Boris sought a Bulgarian patriarchate which would enable him to control the church.

Pope Nicholas I offered to establish a Bulgarian archbishopric and sent a Latin mission composed of Formosus, bishop of Porto, and Paul, bishop of Populonia, to further Rome's interests at the khan's court. The pope was, however, unable to secure Byzantine approval for his activities in Bulgaria. The patriarch Photius convoked a church council in 867, anathematized the *filioque* doctrine of Rome, and excommunicated the pope. Photius' drastic action was an attempt to show Boris that Constantinople and not Rome was the "true" church.

The church schism was ended at the Synod of 869–870, which approved the deposition of Photius. But the Synod refused to give Rome ecclesiastical jurisdiction over Bulgaria. Furthermore, Boris, incensed at not receiving from Rome an archbishop of his own choice, turned to Byzantium for an archbishop and expelled the Latin mission. Boris allowed Byzantium nominal control over the Bulgarian Church, and in return, Byzantium permitted Bulgaria to use Slavonic in the services.

**Bulgarian Orthodox Church.** Bulgaria's conversion to Christianity is usually dated from the baptism of Khan Boris (864), although the Christian faith had many converts among the Bulgarians earlier due to the efforts of Greek missionaries from Byzantium. After some initial vacillation between Rome and Constantinople, Bulgaria chose Byzantium and the Greek Orthodox Church (870).

Shortly afterward, Bulgarian Christianity received new life with the arrival of the disciples of the Greek apostles to the Slavs, Cyril and Methodius, who had been expelled from Moravia. They brought with them the newly created Slavonic Christian literature which formed the basis for Russian, Serbian, and Romanian as well as Bulgarian Christianity.

Under Simeon, the Bulgarian Church secured its independence from Constantinople only to lose it when conquered by Basil II. Regained a century and a half later, it was lost again to the Ottoman Turks (1393). The latter placed the Bulgarian Church under the jurisdiction of the ecumenical patriarch who was made responsible for all Orthodox Christians. This was the situation until the middle of the 19th century when, due to the growing spirit of nationalism and supported by Turkey and Russia, the Bulgarian Church became autocephalous (1870). This action, however, was judged schismatical by the patriarchal Synod of 1872 because separation was based on nationalism. Relations were restored only in 1945.

Living in a Communist state, the Bulgarian Church, now a patriarchate, has nevertheless retained a semiofficial status, though restricted in its activities. In the United States, the Bulgarian Church is represented by the Bulgarian Eastern Orthodox Church.

**Bull.** The most important classification of documents from the papal chancery, formerly stamped with the official papal seal (*bulla*) in wax or lead. Letters of excommunication, convocations of councils, and letters of appointment of bishops and other high officials were thus sealed and known as bulls.

**Bullinger, Heinrich** (1504–1575). Swiss Reformer, successor to Zwingli. Born on July 18, 1504, at Bremgarten near Zurich, he was the fifth child of a clerical marriage between the parish priest, Heinrich Bullinger, and Anna Widerkehr. A good scholar, he was sent for advanced work to Emmerich-on-Rhine. He briefly considered becoming a Carthusian monk, undertook the study of Scholastic theology at the college of Bursa Montis in Cologne in 1519, and began patristic and New Testament studies independently. But through these studies, through his reading of Luther's early tracts and Melanchthon's *Loci communes,* and through his father's opposition to the indulgence-monger Bernardino Samson he grew interested in reform. By the time he received his B.A. in 1520 and M.A. in 1522 he had arrived at a nearly Lutheran position. He continued his studies at Bremgarten until invited to lecture on Melanchthon at the Cistercian monastery of Kappel, whose abbot favored reforms. In 1527, during a leave of absence in Zurich, he first heard Zwingli, and in 1528 accompanied him to the disputation at Bern. The same year he became pastor at Hausen, and in 1529 pastor at

Bremgarten. He married a former nun, Anna Adlischweiler, who bore him eleven children. During the next two years he served as pastor and began writing his New Testament commentaries. The defeat at Kappel forced him to seek refuge in Zurich, where he took over Zwingli's pulpit. He was to remain there for forty-four years, laboring to maintain the reforms already established, to clarify the new faith, and to tighten the bonds with other Protestant communities. Little needed to be added to Zwingli's practical and theological reforms, nor was Bullinger as aggressive for expansion as Zwingli had been. He was occupied chiefly in preaching, writing, correspondence, caring for refugees, and building a unified front for the Reformation. The First Helvetic Confession of 1536 was principally his work, and was accepted as authoritative by the German-Swiss churches. The Second Helvetic Confession began as a statement of his own position, but with changes was adopted in 1566 by all Swiss Reformed churches, and later in Scotland, Poland, and Hungary. Bullinger's friendly reception of the Marian exiles led to a continuing influence on the English reforms. In contrast to Zwingli, Bullinger's more moderate and conciliatory nature produced a steady and quiet development during his long leadership. His negotiation of the *Consensus Tigurinus* with Calvin and Farel in 1549 may be his most valuable work. Calvinistic in theology but partly Zwinglian in language, this agreement on the sacraments ended dogmatic disputes in Protestant Switzerland. Bullinger accepted the passage of leadership from Zurich to Geneva while preserving harmony. His exemplary private life was saddened by the deaths of his wife and three of his daughters by the plague in 1564 and 1565. Ill himself during the latter year, he remained in poor health until his death in 1575.

Bullinger's works comprise about 150 titles, some unpublished. His five books of *Decades,* fifty sermons on Christian doctrine, were widely known. The New Testament commentaries, treatises, and sermons on various doctrinal subjects, and controversial writings against Lutherans and Anabaptists make up the bulk of his work. He wrote a history of the Reformation up to 1534 that is a primary source for modern historians. More systematic than Zwingli, he built his arguments more solidly, but he was not an original and creative thinker, and his work lacks the vitality of the thought of Calvin and Zwingli. He described the sacraments as earthly signs which "represent the deep mysteries of the Gospel." In the Eucharist, Christ's body is in heaven, perceived with the eyes of the soul. We corporeally receive the signs, but spiritually partake of the things signified. The bread and wine are the body and blood mystically and sacramentally; by them we are reconciled with each other as well as with God. Bullinger supported infant baptism, saying that God imputes faith to the child; God in his mercy will save those dying unbaptized in infancy. His statements on the sacraments are generally more positive than those of Zwingli.

BIBLIOGRAPHY: Bullinger's *Second Helvetic Confession* may be found in A. C. Cochrane, *Reformed Confessions in the 16th Century* (Philadelphia, 1966).

**Bultmann, Rudolf** (1884–    ). German Protestant theologian and New Testament scholar. Bultmann is famous for his controversial demand that the New Testament be demythologized. Educated at Marburg, Tübingen, and Berlin, he has held academic appointment at Breslau, Giessen, and from 1921 until his retirement in 1951 at Marburg. He, with Martin Dibelius and Karl L. Schmidt, was a pioneer in the development of form critical methods for examining the Gospels in an attempt to go behind the text to the oral traditions of primitive preaching.

Under the influence of the existential philosophy of the early Martin Heidegger, Bultmann first in 1941 sounded an appeal for an existential understanding of the New Testament which he called "demythologization" (*Entmythologisierung*). This should not be seen as a simple elimination of elements in the Scriptural picture which are difficult for moderns to accept, but rather an attempt to interpret their significance in regard to their function in the primitive faith so that they may become formative for modern faith. Bultmann holds that elements of Jewish apocalyptic and Hellenistic gnosticism which once pointed toward the primitive faith of the believing community in the saving act of God in Christ now simply obscure that faith and its object, tending to make of faith a simple assent to the trappings of past faith rather than the direct act of man affirming his trust in God as revealed in the Christ event—for Bultmann the only key to "authentic existence."

**Bunsen, Baron Christian Karl Josias von** (1791–1860). Prussian scholar and diplomat. Interested in the ancient origins and institutions of the Germanic peoples, Bunsen also directed his energy to the mastery of languages, particularly those of the Near East. In 1816 he entered the diplomatic corps of Prussia, succeeding B. G. Niebuhr as ambassador to Rome (1823–1839). In 1828 he founded the Archaeological Institute at Rome. Upon the accession of Frederick William IV (1840), Bunsen found a kindred spirit in the Evangelical monarch. From 1841 to 1854 Bunsen was ambassador to the Court of St. James. One of his first projects was to try to effect some sort of union between German Protestants and the Anglican Church. This attempt issued in the controversial joint sponsorship (Prussia and England) of the Jerusalem bishopric. According to the plan launched in 1841, Prussia and England were to name alternately a bishop for Jerusalem who would then ordain German candidates for the ministry on the basis of their acceptance of the Augsburg Confession, and English candidates who could subscribe to the Thirty-nine Articles.

**Bunting, Jabez** (1779–1858). British Methodist leader. He was born and educated at Manchester and subsequently preached in the Midlands and London. A great organizer and statesman, he was four times president of the Conference, held many lesser posts in Methodism, and assisted in the founding of the Evangelical Alliance. "Pope Bunting" to his opponents, his autocratic methods, High Tory politics, and reluctance to accept change contributed to a succession of Methodist schisms.

**Bunyan, John** (1628–1688). English Puritan preacher. He was the writer of the popular religious allegory, *The Pilgrim's Progress*. The son of a tinsmith, he served briefly in the Parliamentary army and passed through harrowing religious crises before he found his vocation as itinerant preacher and leader of an Independent Bedford congregation. Jailed after the Restoration of 1660, he published the first part of *The Pilgrim's Progress* as an epic of Christian salvation in 1678. His other chief works were *Grace Abounding to the Chief of Sinners* (1666) and *The Holy War* (1682).

**Burchard of Worms** (c. 965–1025). Bishop and canonist. As bishop of Worms, he built the famous cathedral at Worms, published an edict of peace, and laid the foundations of the territorial power of the see. At the beginning of the 11th century he authored his *Decretum* in twenty books, probably the most important legislative collection before the work of Gratian. It reflected the laws of the Carolingian epoch and summarized the history of a time when the Frankish empire was the dominant influence in the church.

**Burghers.** A movement among 18th century Scottish Separatist Presbyterians who had been led out of the Established Church by Ebenezer Erskine (1680–1754). The crisis arose over an oath that the civil leaders were to take promising that they would support "the true religion presently professed within this realm." The Burghers felt that this oath was acceptable because it referred to evangelical Protestantism, but the Antiburghers objected to it because they thought it meant the Established Church of Scotland. Efforts to mediate this argument led to further divisions.

**Burial Hill Declaration.** The only Declaration of Faith approved by a body representative of American Congregationalism as a whole between 1648 and 1865 when it was made at the National Council in a session held at Plymouth, Mass. At a time of denominational consciousness and challenge the declaration was a restatement of the historic Congregational theology in terms of broad principle rather than of specific beliefs, but it was little known or used in local churches.

**Buridan's Ass.** A well-known problem perhaps posed by an opponent of John Buridan, a mid-14th century philosopher of the "terminist" or nominalist movement, which likened Buridan's doctrine of freedom of will in relation to the intellect to a hungry donkey placed between two loads of hay equal in quantity and quality and equally distant from the animal. The ass could not decide to which load he should turn, and so died of hunger.

**Burke, Edmund** (1753–1820). First Roman Catholic bishop of Nova Scotia. Born in Kildare, Ireland, he came to Canada in 1786, and was appointed first vicar apostolic of Nova Scotia in 1818. He thought that the hierarchy of Quebec was not sufficiently aware of the spiritual and cultural needs of the Irish Catholics and successfully appealed to Rome for independence. This Irish revolt had wide repercussions throughout the Roman Catholic community in Canada.

**Burnet, Gilbert** (1643–1715). English bishop. Born and educated in Scotland, Burnet entered the ministry there (1661), accepting the restoration of bishops, and becoming divinity professor at Glasgow (1669). He opposed the bishops' repression, seeking compromise with the Presbyterians. Having come to the notice of Charles II, he removed to England (1674), was made chaplain to the Rolls, but lost favor at court, joining the Whigs. He left England after the Rye House Plot (1683), which involved friends, and went again into exile on the Continent when James II became king (1685), but returned with William of Orange in the Glorious Revolution (1688). Rewarded with the see of Salisbury, he was dutiful as a bishop, advised William on Scottish affairs, and worked for toleration and the inclusion of Protestant Dissenters in the Church of England. Under Queen Anne, fearing Stuart restoration, he was an ardent Whig. A leader of the Latitudinarians, he was theologically liberal and nondogmatic against what he saw as Puritan "enthusiasm" and High Church "superstition." Among his works are treatises against Roman Catholicism, *An Exposition of the Thirty-nine Articles,* which was bitterly attacked by High Churchmen, a vindicatory *History of the Reformation,* and the partly autobiographical *A History of My Own Time,* a valuable source of background material.

**Burton, Ernest Dewitt** (1856–1925). Baptist minister. He taught New Testament Greek at Newton (Mass.) Theological Seminary for a decade before going to the University of Chicago, where he headed the department of New Testament and Early Christian Literature from 1892 to 1923, then becoming president of the university. He published extensively in his field of specialization, working with such men as William R. Harper and Edgar J. Goodspeed.

**Bury St. Edmunds.** A monastery northeast of London, founded c. 633 by the king of East Anglia. In 903 the body of King Edmund, killed in 870, was buried in the monastery. The abbey and the surrounding town were then named for the martyred king. A new abbey was built in 1020 and Benedictine monks established there. The abbot was secular lord of the town and was exempt from both episcopal control and feudal obligations. The abbey was famous as a religious shrine and a commercial center.

**Busch, Jan** (1399–1479). A leader and chronicler of the Brethren of the Common Life. Born in Zwolle, Holland, he entered the house at Windesheim and after ordination in 1424 he served as prior in various houses in Holland and Germany and as archdeacon over 120 parishes. Active in the monastic reform inspired by the Council of Basel, he was named by Nicholas of Cusa as an apostolic visitor to several German monasteries.

**Bushnell, Horace** (1802–1876). Congregational minister and theologian. During his youth on a New England farm, Bushnell planned to enter the ministry, but a four-year period of religious doubt following graduation from Yale (1827) found him teaching, serving as an editor in New York, and studying law at New Haven. Involved in a campus revival in 1831, he rededicated himself to the ministry and entered the Yale Divinity School. Here he was influenced by N. W. Taylor, com-

monsense philosophy and, above all, by Coleridge's *Aids to Reflection.* Ordained in 1833, he commenced a twenty-six-year-long pastorate in Hartford with a fastidious but loyal congregation. In 1847 he published *Christian Nurture,* a book evoking furious rebuttals from the Calvinists and revivalists whom he had accused of breeding an excessive individualism and of emphasizing conversion to the neglect of religious education. He denounced revivalism as a method in which God leaped forth like "a miraculous epidemic, a fire-ball shot from the moon," and he maintained that children should grow into Christian faith, it being impossible for a properly nurtured person to be anything but a Christian. Christian nurture, however, did not mean permissive "ostrich nurture," for parents as priests of Christ had the responsibility to create "the intensely religious character of the house"; the ideal youth would remember his father as "God's minister." Bushnell sought to replace radical conversion with a quiet faith inbred in persons who would feel "no struggle or hostility, but a new joy." Theologically, Bushnell's "nurture" rested upon a historical idea of revelation as progressive and continual; he argued that church dogmas had developed slowly and changed through the ages. In 1849, Bushnell had a vital religious experience that deepened his thought and, even amid numerous charges of heresy, reinforced his confidence. Despite his optimism about education, Bushnell did not neglect problems of evil and redemption. Unlike a New England contemporary, Ralph Waldo Emerson, he viewed the universe as "essentially tragic . . . [with] an overspreading curse at the beginning." Original sin was "a great and momentous truth," and evil malignly possessed men. In *Christian Nurture* he observed that men could overcome this evil by a quest for moral character and through the divine within them. Later he stressed the symbolic sacrifice of Christ, who neither was punished in man's place nor in any way bore man's guilt, but who had so identified himself with human suffering and misery as to reveal God's love for the world. Thus Bushnell broke with the moral government theory of atonement, a theory described by him as a "dry, stunted, half-conception . . . reducing Christ to a mere book-account compensation for suffering." Instead, the sinner must confront the immediate and personal misery of the cross which through "moral influence" compels the redeemed person to imitate divine virtue and to love God for his own sake. By being opposed to women's sufferage ("The Reform Against Nature," 1869), considering abolitionists rude persons whose conduct did not befit Christians, and interpreting the Civil War in terms of collective guilt, Bushnell seemed to be politically conservative. Although he declared that Jesus was not a liberal, Bushnell's influence on later liberalism and the Social Gospel is clear. Washington Gladden commented that without Bushnell's writings, no honest man could have remained in the ministry. Bushnell's emphasis upon human growth and upon doctrinal development, his concern for environment and family life, his condemnation of irresponsible individualism, and his insights into the demands and opportunities of the moral experience contributed to social Christianity.

Basic to Bushnell's use of orthodox symbols was an understanding of language, defined in *God in Christ* (1849). In 1847 he published *Christian Nurture* and a plea for education in the Western states called *Barbarism the First Danger*. His other major works included *Christ in Theology* (1851), *Nature and the Supernatural* (1859), *Vicarious Sacrifice* (1866), and *Forgiveness and Law* (1874). Some, however, find Bushnell's spirit best expressed in his published sermons.

BIBLIOGRAPHY: M. B. Cheney, *The Life and Letters of Horace Bushnell* (New York, 1880); B. M. Cross, *Horace Bushnell: Minister to a Changing America* (Chicago, 1958); T. Munger, *Horace Bushnell: Preacher and Theologian* (Boston, 1899); H. S. Smith (ed.), *Horace Bushnell* (New York, 1965).

**Buss, Franz Ritter von** (1803–1878). German Catholic theorist of social reform. He was professor of political science and international law (1836) and of canon law (1844) at Freiburg im Breisgau and intermittently active in German politics. Synthesizing liberal and conservative trends, on the basis of natural law and Christianity, he stressed personal responsibility in a corporate society thus making possible a resolution of traditional social antinomies such as authority vs. freedom.

**Butler, Joseph** (1692–1752). Anglican bishop. Though his father had intended him for the Presbyterian ministry, Butler opted for the Church of England, entered Oriel College, Oxford, and was ordained in 1718. In the course of his ecclesiastical career he was made dean of St. Paul's (1740), and, in 1747, was even offered the primacy, which he refused. In 1750 he accepted the bishopric of Durham.

Though works such as his *Fifteen Sermons* (1726) were popular in their time, Bishop Butler is best known to posterity for his classic work in apologetics, *The Analogy of Religion, Natural and Revealed, to the Constitution and Course of Nature* (1736). The method and argument of this volume deeply influenced men as different as James Mill and John Henry Newman, the latter stating in his *Apologia* that he had learned from Bishop Butler two great rules of life: that the world was a sacramental system, and that probability was the surest guide for man. Designed as a refutation of deism, *The Analogy of Religion* attempted to show the proportion between the various levels of being and the relationship between the natural and the moral universes. Though revelation alone brought certainty, very probable evidences for faith were given by reason, conscience, and nature.

**Buxton, Sir Thomas Fowell** (1786–1845). English Evangelical philanthropist and antislavery advocate. Educated at Trinity College, Dublin, he headed a family brewing firm before he turned to reform. He championed the London weavers, advocated prison reform, and sat in Parliament from 1818 to 1837. After 1822 he succeeded William Wilberforce as leader of the crusade to abolish slavery in the British Empire, successful in 1833.

**Byrd, William** (c. 1543–1623). English organist and composer. In 1575, with his former teacher, Thomas Tallis, he was granted by Queen Elizabeth a joint monopoly for the printing of music which lasted for twenty-one years. He also shared with Tallis the direction of music at the Chapel Royal. Although himself adhering to Roman Catholicism, Byrd wrote music for both the Latin rite (e.g., Masses for four and for five voices) and Anglican services. His music marks the high point of English polyphonic composition.

**Byzantine Architecture.** See ARCHITECTURE, BYZANTINE.

**Byzantine Empire.** The name applied to the Eastern Roman Empire after it became more Greek, Christian, and Oriental than classical, pagan, and Roman (a date much disputed by historians, but usually placed somewhere between Constantine I and Heraclius). The Empire lasted from the end of the Roman period until the fall of Constantinople to Mohammed the Conqueror, May 29, 1453. During this period (especially preceding 1071) it was the bulwark of Western civilization in Europe and of Christianity against Islam in the East. The Byzantines regarded themselves as Romans, and indeed had all the institutions of a great urban commercial civilization when Western Europe was largely rural and agrarian.

The great glory of the Empire was the city of Constantinople, founded on the site of the earlier Greek colony of Byzantium (hence the name) in 330 by Constantine the Great, as the "New Rome." Its situation is magnificent, not only for beauty but also strategically. It was from the first a Christian city, and was soon ornamented not only by great palaces and public places but also by churches, of which the most wonderful was Sancta Sophia, built by Justinian the Great between 532 and 537 and one of the great marvels of the world now as then. Theodosius II furnished the city with immensely strong walls which yielded to foreigners only twice in over one thousand years: in 1204 to the knights of the Fourth Crusade, and in 1453 to the cannon and the Janizaries of the Grand Turk.

The city was, and is, also the see of the ecumenical patriarch, the spiritual leader of Orthodox Christianity, and has been the site of several ecumenical councils.

# C

**Cadman, S. Parks** (1864–1936). Methodist and Congregational clergyman. Emigrating from England to the United States in 1890, he served the Metropolitan Methodist Temple in New York (1893–1901), making it an outstanding example of an institutional church. In 1901 he moved to Central Congregational Church, Brooklyn, where he began one of the earliest radio ministries. He was president of the Federal Council of Churches from 1924 to 1926.

**Caecilian** (d. c. 345). Bishop of Carthage over whose election the Donatist controversy was begun. Caecilian's predecessor having died on the way home from trial in Rome, the African bishops met to elect a successor without inviting the bishops of Numidia over whom the new bishop would exercise metropolitan authority. When the Numidian and Mauretanian bishops arrived and were met with a *fait accompli,* they elected their own antibishop. The ostensible issue was fidelity under persecution, but sectional and racial loyalties were involved.

**Caedmon** (d. c. 680). Earliest known author of Christian religious poetry in the Anglo-Saxon language. He was first a lay brother and then a monk at the famous monastery of Whitby in England. Bede records the miraculous way in which Caedmon acquired his ability to turn Scriptural passages into verse. Only one hymn known to be by Caedmon is extant.

**Caesarius of Arles** (d. 542). Bishop of the city of Arles from 502. He was a leader of the church in southern Gaul during the critical period of transition from Roman through Gothic to Frankish rule. He presided over a number of councils, the most significant for the church at large being the Second Council of Orange. His devoted pastoral ministry is reflected in his sermons, and his work as a monastic organizer in his rules for monks and nuns.

**Caesaropapism.** The doctrine and practice of the secular ruler's exercising authority in the church, even in its spiritual life and teaching. It is most commonly, though not exclusively, associated with Eastern Orthodox history.

Caesaropapism therefore stands at the opposite extreme from clerical theocracy which seeks to subordinate the government of the state to the rule of functionaries of religion. In English usage, the term "Erastianism," derived (somewhat incorrectly) from the writings of the 16th-century Swiss, Thomas Erastus, is more commonly employed to designate the civil magistrate's authority over the church. But Erastianism usually suggests more modest claims than Caesaropapism, and is associated with political control of church government and discipline. In Caesaropapism, by contrast, the ruler more boldly asserts a formal right to rule even in spiritual and dogmatic, as in ecclesiastical, causes. But any fast distinction is difficult to make, and the difference is largely one of usage and degree.

Caesaropapism appeared in Christian history immediately after the support of the state for the church had been secured. The emperor Constantine (d. 337), even while remaining unbaptized, assumed authority in the church, summoning and presiding over the Councils of Arles (314) and Nicaea (325), judging creedal formulas, and deciding theological issues of importance largely on the basis of political considerations. His successors continued these functions through the Christological controversies of the 4th, 5th, and 6th centuries. Constantius demanded the condemnation of Athanasius at Milan in 355 with the words, "Let my will be deemed a canon among you, as it is among the Syrian bishops." When theological issues swayed public sentiment as they did in the ancient eastern Mediterranean world, it was inevitable that the state should demand final decision, and that such decisions should be formed with a view to undergirding the political unity of the Empire.

Byzantine Caesaropapism is sometimes considered to have reached its zenith in the reign of Justinian (527–565). The great emperor had genuine theological interest and ability. Regarding the church as an arm of the state, he did not hesitate to define sound doctrine and condemn opponents on imperial authority. Another spectacular example of the same tradition came two centuries later in the reign of Leo III the Isaurian (717–740), who used military force to establish the imperial decision against icons, despite the opposition of church and people. Throughout Byzantine history, the patriarch of Constantinople was, with few exceptions, fully subordinate to the emperor. Curiously, this tradition continued in modified form after the Moslem conquest of Constantinople in 1453. Mohammed II appointed the new patriarch and invested him with the scepter of office. During the patriarchate of the famous reforming Cyril Lukar in the 17th century the sultan intervened repeatedly and finally had the patriarch put to death.

In western Europe princes sometimes made claims to high authority in the church. Charlemagne bestowed a Mosaic leadership on himself, and early Holy Roman emperors proclaimed an apostolic and sacramental kingship, responsible for the total health of the Christian community. Moreover, in practice later rulers sometimes assumed a dominion over the church in their realms which did not stop with externals. Philip II through his Inquisition was led to decisions concerning faith, while the French kings of the 17th and 18th centuries intervened significantly in the Jesuit-Jansenist disputes. Perhaps the best examples of a Western approach to Caesaropapism were the German Lutheran princes, whose extraordinary powers did not lack theoretical defenders among the theologians.

Modern Caesaropapism is most commonly associated with Russia, which acquired Orthodoxy from Constantinople in the 10th century. Like Byzantine emperors, Muscovite princes exercised control over their metropolitans, Vasily imprisoning the metropolitan Isidore who had favored the Florentine Union with the West in 1439. When Ivan III consciously absorbed all Byzantine traditions after the fall of Constantinople, this trend became stronger. Yet for a time in the 17th century the Czar's supremacy was challenged by the rise of the Moscow patriarchate. Established in 1589 in order to secure ecclesiastical independence from Constantinople, the patriarchate became particularly important during and after the civil wars and invasions of the "Time of Troubles" (1598–1613). The first Romanov, Michael, was the son of the patriotic patriarch Philaret. Patriarch Nikon forcefully advanced claims to ecclesiastical independence during the reign of Czar Alexius. The final deposition of Nikon in 1667 decisively reasserted the Cae-saropapist tradition, which Peter the Great made secure through his actions in 1700 and 1721. Refusing to permit a successor to be nominated or elected when Patriarch Adrian died, Peter at length established a Holy Governing Synod under a lay procurator. This body ruled the Russian church in the czar's interest until the 1917 Revolution.

Since World War I the Caesaropapist tradition has continued to find expression in Eastern Orthodoxy. Though the Russian Church was permitted to name a patriarch at the beginning of the Revolution, his resistance to communist policy and pressure led the Bolshevik Government to suspend the patriarchate again in 1925. It has since been revived, but the surrender of any independent witness is understood to be one of the conditions of survival for Orthodoxy in modern Russia. Similarly, Balkan Orthodoxy has been attentive to political direction, made easier by the establishment of independent patriarchates in Romania and Yugoslavia after World War I. The tradition has been reinforced by the determined policies of the new regimes set up after World War II.

BIBLIOGRAPHY: W. F. Adeney, *The Greek and Eastern Churches* (New York, 1908); J. S. Curtiss, *Church and State in Russia: 1900–1917* (New York, 1940); and *The Russian Church and the Soviet State* (Boston, 1953); B. J. Kidd, *The Churches of Eastern Christendom from A.D. 451 to the Present* (London, 1927); M. Spinka, *Christianity Confronts Communism* (New York, 1936); and *The Church and the Russian Revolution* (New York, 1927); J. W. C. Wand, *A History of the Early Church to A.D. 500* (London, 1963).

**Cahensly, Peter Paul** (1838–1923). Secretary of the St. Raphael Society, an organization to aid German immigrants. In 1891, Cahensly sent a petition to the pope, which was rejected, proposing that the national groups in America should have their own churches, parochial schools, priests, and bishops. The petition was based upon the claim that millions had been lost to the church through its failure to make provision for them in their own language.

**Cainites.** An antinomian Gnostic group mentioned by Irenaeus (c. 185). Rejecting the God of the Old Testament, whom they called "Womb," they praised his adversaries (Cain, the men of Sodom, Esau), calling them the children of Wisdom (cf. Luke 7:35). Violation of the Old Testament law was a positive duty for them, and Judas was their hero, for without his work the crucifixion would not have taken place. Cainite influence does not seem to have been significant.

**Caird, John** (1820–1898). Minister of the Church of Scotland (1845) and professor of divinity at Glasgow (1862). In 1873 he became principal of the University of Glasgow. Although he was less the philosopher and more the theologian than his younger brother Edward, both were neo-Hegelian. Deeply religious, he contributed much to the intellectual strength of Scottish Presbyterianism during the latter part of the 19th century.

**Cajetan** (Gaetano da Thiene) (1480–1547). Cofounder of the Theatines. As an Italian jurist, Cajetan participated in a number of diplomatic missions for Pope Julius II. In 1516 he was ordained and shortly after formed the Oratory of Divine Love to revitalize Christian life and awaken concern for the sick and the poor. In 1523 he helped found the Theatines and became head of the order seven years later. He established a Theatine settlement in Naples to impede the growth of Lutheranism. He was canonized in 1671.

**Cajetan** (Thomas de Vio) (1469–1534). Dominican theologian. Born of Italian nobility at Gaeta (hence Cajetan), he entered the Dominican Order against his parents' wishes when he was only sixteen. His early attack against the Averroist tendencies of the Italian philosophical Renaissance in his *De ente et essentia* (written while he was professor of metaphysics at the University of Padua) set the main goal for his career: to defend orthodox philosophy and theology intellectually. Becoming general of the order in 1508, he reemphasized theology as the chief means of attaining its ideals, and, before the Council of Pisa (1511), he denounced the disobedience of the cardinals and bishops by intellectual arguments in defense of the monarchical supremacy of the pope. In 1517, Pope Leo X created him cardinal, and in 1518 sent him as apostolic legate to Germany, where he met with Luther, but was not successful in bringing him back to the old faith. Cajetan's commentaries on the *Summa theologiae,* on which he labored from 1507 to 1522, were primarily in defense of Thomism against Duns Scotus and the Protestant Reformers. Despite his orthodoxy, the freedom of his Biblical interpretation (designed to meet the Lutheran arguments against authority and tradition) and the originality of his theological thinking brought anxiety to his more conservative contemporaries. He died at Rome in 1534.

**Calamy, Edmund** (1600–1666). One of the Puritan authors of *Smectymnuus,* a pamphlet arguing against the divine right of episcopacy, and a member of the Presbyterian party in the Westminster Assembly. After graduating from Pembroke Hall, Cambridge, he became lecturer at Bury St. Edmunds. A popular preacher, he held the ideal of constitutional freedom as against any arbitrary government, but opposed the execution of Charles I and supported the Restoration. After considering a bishopric, he became a nonconformist, the first to be jailed for disobeying the Act of Uniformity.

**Calendar Reforms.** A reform of the Julian calendar was authorized at Trent. In 1577, Gregory XIII appointed a commission to carry out the plans of the Calabrian astronomer, Aloysius Lilius. Christopher Clavius collaborated in the reform. The *Tabulae Prutenicae* of E. Reinhold, Lutheran professor at Wittenberg, provided the basis. On Feb. 24, 1582, in *Inter gravissimas,* Gregory ordered the suspension of the days between Oct. 4 and 15, 1582, so that the vernal equinox would be restored to March 21. Only century years divisible by 400 were to be leap years. To correct the spring full moon, the new moons were set back three days from Jan. 3 to Dec. 31. Henceforth the new moon was to be retarded one day on eight separate occasions in 2,500 years. New Year's Day was moved from March 25, Annunciation, to Jan. 1. The reform was quickly adopted in Roman Catholic countries. In Germany there were "old" and "new" calendars, and in 1700 the Protestants offered a third. It caused special bitterness in 1724, 1744, and 1788 because of a week's divergence between Gregorian and astronomical Easter dates. Frederick the Great suppressed the Protestant calendar (1775), and the Gregorian calendar went into effect. England adopted it (1752), as did the Soviet Union (1918). In 1924 the Eastern Orthodox Churches of Alexandria, Antioch, Greece, Cyprus, Romania, and Poland adopted the Gregorian calendar. Although most individuals in Roman Catholic churches of Eastern rites have not yet accepted the calendar, some churches adopted it before the 19th century. Current calendar reforms include the quest for a fixed Easter date, and the United Nations World Calendar which divides the year equally.

**Calixtines.** A party among the Hussites. After the betrayal of John Hus, a movement of rebellion and reform occurred in Bohemia, in which the Calixtines were the more conservative force (see UTRAQUISTS). As moderate Hussites, they sought remedies for religious grievances such as the withholding of the Eucharistic cup (Latin, *calix*) from the laity. This demand was granted at the Council of Basel.

**Calixtus, Georg** (1586–1656). Theologian at Helmstedt and principal figure in the "syncretistic controversy" which agitated the Lutheran Church throughout the early part of the 17th century. He came to believe that a compromise theology, based on the Creed and the fathers of the ancient undivided church—because they were ancient and universally received—would reunite the three great confessions (John III of Sweden had urged a similar program). He therefore thought the Augsburg Confession superfluous. Calovius and other Orthodox Lutherans denounced him as "crypto-Romanist" or "crypto-Calvinist" or as sacrificing the distinctive views of the Reformation in favor of irenicism. His ideas were later championed also in vain by Leibnitz.

**Calling, Effectual.** In classical Reformed theology, a phrase referring to the secret operation of the Holy Spirit whereby faith is produced in a man so that he is persuaded to accept the gospel according to God's gracious purposes. The subjects of this work, or the "called," are the elect. This is the first act in the process whereby those who have been elected receive the benefits of redemption.

**Callistus I** (d. 222). Pope from 217. The chief source of our information about him is his archenemy, the antipope Hippolytus, and may be more reliable for chronology than for imputing his motives. Callistus appears to have been a Christian slave of a Christian master and to have been sent to the salt mines in Sardinia. After his release and a rest period, he was ordained and was principal adviser to Zephyrinus, whom he succeeded. Hippolytus objected to his laxity toward Sabellius and his policy of absolving adulterers. He may be the "Praxeas" against whom Tertullian wrote, since the name could mean "busybody."

**Callistus II** (Guido of Burgundy, d. 1124). Pope from 1119. The son of a noble family, he became an important champion of the Gregorian reform and worked with vigor against lay investiture. He was present at the Third Lateran Council of 1112; later in that year he presided at a synod at Vienne which condemned investiture by laymen as heretical. Elected pope in 1119, he immediately took up the long-lived dispute over investiture with the German emperor. The struggle was brought to an end by his compromise settlement with Henry V in the Concordat of Worms in 1122.

**Callistus III** (Alfonso de Borgia, 1378–1458). Pope from 1455. Born at Valencia in Spain, Callistus was the first of the Borgia popes, elected in 1455, when he was seventy-seven years of age. His reign was dominated by two great concerns, the first of which was his crusade against the Turks, who continued to advance into eastern Europe after the fall of Constantinople (1453). Callistus attempted to unite Europe against them, but lacking tact, he met with little success. The Christians failed to take the initiative after the Turks were defeated at Belgrade in July, 1456. Callistus' other great concern was for his family and he showered offices and benefices upon his relatives. His nepotism exceeded that of the earlier popes. He made two of his nephews cardinals in 1457. One of them, Roderigo, later became the notorious Alexander VI. A third nephew he made a duke and prefect of Rome. From that time onward the Borgias played a leading role in Rome and the church. Callistus cared little for learning. He scattered the library gathered by previous popes, ignoring the enthusiasm of the Renaissance. He did reverse the decision of the trial of Joan of Arc. However, Callistus is primarily remembered for his nepotism, which continued to plague the papacy for over a century.

**Calovius, Abraham** (1612–1686). A German Lutheran theologian at Wittenberg. He was known for his exegetical endeavors in the interest of dogmatics, which when combined with his scholastic ability, produced a rigid, Bibliocentric orthodoxy as seen in his major systematic work, *Systema locorum theologicorum* (1650). He was also an incessant polemicist against what he considered the errors of syncretists, papists, the Reformed, Socinians, Arminians, and mystics.

**Calvert, Cecil,** Second Lord Baltimore (1604–1675). The son of George Calvert, the original possessor of the royal grant of land called Maryland, Cecil was responsible for the establishment of the first settlement in that territory (St. Mary's, 1634). One of the purposes of the founding of this proprietary colony was to provide English Catholics with a haven of refuge from religious persecution in England.

**Calvin, John** (1509–1564). The Reformer of Geneva, Calvin was born on July 10, 1509, at Noyon, about fifty miles north of Paris. His father, Gérard Cauvin, a lawyer for the local cathedral chapter, ensured his education by securing for him a church benefice in 1521 and another in 1527. In 1523, to escape the plague and to study theology and philosophy, Calvin went to Paris, where after five years at the nominalistic Collège de Montaigu he received the degree Master of Arts. On the advice of his father, then at odds with the cathedral chapter at Noyon, he decided not to enter the priesthood as planned but to study law at Orléans. During 1529 his studies were augmented by growing humanist interests, and the strain of excessive work adversely and permanently affected his health. The same year he transferred to Bourges, where he remained until the fatal illness of his father in 1531 brought him back to Noyon. He then went again to Paris and in 1532 published his first book, a commentary on Seneca's *De clementia,* by which he sought (not very successfully) to establish his reputation as an accomplished humanist. He returned to Orléans long enough to take a law degree, but spent most of his time in Paris until Oct. 31, 1533, when a sermon with a Lutheran sound by the new rector of the university, Calvin's friend Nicholas Cop, raised a furor that forced both to flee. Among the places Calvin visited during the following months was Noyon, where he resigned his benefices, and Orléans, where he stayed to finish his first theological work, *De psychopannychia* ("On the Sleep of the Soul," 1534). About the same time he also wrote, as a preface to a French New Testament by his cousin Olivétan, his initial Protestant credo, and he began work on the first edition of the *Institutes of the Christian Religion,* completed in 1535.

Thus Calvin's intellectual and religious development had taken him from nominalism through law and humanism to Protestantism. His "conversion" probably occurred in 1533, but he still thought of himself as—and was— a Christian humanist, not a reformer. In 1536 a detour on a journey from Paris to Strasbourg led him through Geneva; there Farel persuaded him to assist in the reform of the city. Holding at first only a minor position, Calvin soon became one of the city's three pastors, and in 1537 submitted articles for a new church organization. When he endeavored to have all citizens sign the Geneva Confession, however, a reaction developed which, with hostilities engendered by theological and political conflicts, led to the expulsion of Calvin and Farel from Geneva in 1538. Urged by Bucer, Calvin went to Strasbourg and spent there his most untroubled years, publishing a revised edition of the *Institutes* (1539) and the first of his Bible commentaries (on Romans, 1540). Also, in 1540 he married Idelette de Bure, the widow of a convert from Anabaptism.

Continuing unrest in Geneva led to an official entreaty for Calvin to return as a means of restoring peace. After ten months' hesitation he agreed, convinced that it was God's will, and arrived in September, 1541, to remain there until he died of tuberculosis on May 27, 1564. Almost the whole period involved political, ecclesiastical, and theological controversy. Calvin fought for the independent but cooperative functioning of the church and the magistracy, for the moral reform of the citizenry, and for the acceptance of his understanding of Biblical interpretation, the Trinity, sacraments, and predestination. In 1548 his opponents won a majority in the city councils and retained it for several years. Then the trial and execution of Servetus, widely endorsed as appropriate reaction to the blasphemy of denying the Trinity, strengthened Calvin's political position, and in 1555 his supporters regained control. Throughout the various conflicts Calvin maintained a prodigious literary output, climaxed by the final Latin edition of the *Institutes* in 1559. He also continued his pastoral activity, preaching regularly and conducting weddings and baptisms. In 1559 he established the Geneva Academy for the training of pastors.

Calvin's theology, clearly and completely expressed in the *Institutes* on the successive editions of which he worked for twenty-five years, was uniquely saturated with Biblical thought; it was a Biblical theology formulated not by identifying and elaborating key ideas but by ranging over the Old and New Testaments and affirming all their theological complexity. However, Calvin often read the Biblical text through the eyes of Augustine, whom he cited continually, especially in the doctrines of free will, grace, and predestination. He also knew medieval authors, although not as well. The effect of his early nominalist training is disputed, but there are at least some points of contact with Duns Scotus. He was also influenced by Erasmus and Budé. As a second-generation Protestant, he greatly admired Luther and read him diligently in Latin; although there is no direct acknowledgment in the *Institutes,* Calvin's doctrine of justification is certainly indebted to Luther. In his exposition of the law, baptism, and Christology, Calvin shows similarities to his friend Melanchthon. Where he differed from Lutheran thought, he inclined toward Bucer, especially in regard to the church, liturgy, and sacraments. Calvin owed little directly to Zwingli, whom he succeeded as the dominant force in the Reformed tradition; but some influence by way of Farel is likely.

Calvin's theology has no central principle from which a whole system develops. The *Institutes* is rather a comprehensive treatment of Biblical ideas in succession under the rubrics God the Creator and Ruler, redemption in Jesus Christ, the work of the Holy Spirit, and external helps to faith; but there is no rigorous consistency or even continuous argument developed by logical necessity. Calvin's primary concern was the divine object rather than the human subject of religion; yet his aim was always practical piety. The two interests were held together by the conviction that God is glorified by gratitude and obedience. Although justification is perhaps the most prominent doctrine, centrally placed and extensively explained in the *Institutes*, Calvin did not make it the whole of religion. He understood faith to be confidence in Christ as he "clothes himself" in the gospel. This faith makes self-renunciation possible. The law serves as a continuous useful guide in the Christian life; even one's secular vocation is a means of religious service. Yet Calvin insisted that the Christian never ceases to be a sinner; his "good works" are acceptable only by divine grace. Thus he saw a double justification: of the sinner, and of the justified sinner's works. The doctrine of predestination was an attempt to account, in the light of certain Pauline statements, for the diversity of human response to the gospel.

A pervasive idea in Calvin's thought was the distance between transcendent Creator and sinful creature, a distance overcome only by the revelation communicated in Scripture and certified by the inner witness of the Holy Spirit. Although every man has within him a sense of the divine and around him the signature of God in nature, he is so blinded by sin that he could respond only in terror or idolatry were it not for revelation, in which God condescends to use human language. Even so, man cannot know God as God is in himself, but only as God is toward man. Seeing the sacraments as the "visible word" of the divine good will, Calvin argued for infant baptism as a promise of grace yet to be seen in the life, and as a sign of initiation into the church. The Lord's Supper he understood as a means of grace in which the body and blood of Christ are really, but spiritually rather than locally, present. He emphasized the distinction between the divine and the human nature of Christ, yet he insisted that Christ saves us, by God's grace, through his obedience as the Righteous Man. Word and sacraments are understood as the means by which Christ communicates himself, with his benefits, to the believer. (See BEZA, THEODORE.)

BIBLIOGRAPHY: F. W. Battles and J. T. McNeill (trs. and eds.), *Calvin: Institutes of the Christian Religion*, 2 vols. (The Library of Christian Classics, Vols. XX–XXI, Philadelphia, 1960); J. K. S. Reid (ed.), *Calvin: Theological Treatises* (The Library of Christian Classics, Vol. XXII, Philadelphia, 1954); D. W. and T. F. Torrance (eds.), *Calvin's New Testament Commentaries* (Grand Rapids, 1960); E. A. Dowey, *The Knowledge of God in Calvin's Theology* (New York, 1952); J. T. McNeill, *The History and Character of Calvinism* (New York, 1954); W. Niesel, *The Theology of Calvin* (Philadelphia, 1956); B. B. Warfield, *Calvin and Calvinism* (New York, 1931); F. Wendel, *Calvin: The Origin and Development of His Religious Thought* (New York, 1963).

**Calvinism.** See CALVIN, JOHN.

**Calvinism in America.** This branch of Calvinism ought not to be identified solely with the thought and practice of John Calvin, nor with the Calvinist orthodoxy of the 17th century. Early American Calvinists were advocates of a broader Reformed tradition which included Zwingli (Zurich), Bucer (Strasbourg), Calvin (Geneva), Knox (Scotland), and the Puritanism of England and Holland. Major American denominations stand in this tradition—Presbyterian, Congregational, and Baptist—while several smaller churches, such as the Christian Reformed Church, evolved out of Scholastic orthodoxy, and later the German Reformed out of 18th-century Pietism. Distinguishing emphases include the sovereignty of God, human sin, Biblical authority, evangelical fervor, strict morality, representative government, and a positive position on the state and society. Much of American religion, and many political, social, economic, and intellectual trends have been decisively touched by Calvinism. In turn, Calvinism itself has been modified by American traits—optimism, individualism, and democracy.

Colonial Calvinism in New England and among the Middle Colonies Presbyterians exhibited a strong Puritan flavor. It was preoccupied by "experimental" and "experiential" religion which eventually erupted in the Great Awakening. Its greatest colonial theologian was Jonathan Edwards, who established a synthesis of Augustinian Calvinism, Enlightenment empiricism, and religious enthusiasm. Edwards' accomplishment temporarily delayed the move of some Calvinists toward the popular rationalist and naturalist religion of the Age of Reason, but the polarities between objective grace and personally executed repentance drove Calvinists into revivalist and rationalist camps. Meanwhile, the social and political implications of Calvinism encouraged the colonists to rebel against British tyranny and establish a representative form of constitutional government because of its equalitarianism (under God) and Reformation emphasis upon (Christian) liberty.

By the 19th century, the Calvinist denominations (Presbyterian, Congregational, and Baptist) had made highly successful adaptations to the dramatic challenge of separation of church and state and religious liberty in the new nation. Colonial theological polarities continued, with Nathaniel W. Taylor's New Divinity and Charles G. Finney's New Measures providing the revivalist wing with a new focus on human agency. The wing turned away from naturalist religion toward 17th-century Calvinist Scholasticism. The leading exponent of this position was Charles Hodge, who advocated a dogmatic confessional theology as the heart of the Calvinist tradition. A unique strain of Calvinism appeared in the Mercersburg movement of John W. Nevin and Philip Schaff. They attempted to counteract the effect of both Finney and Hodge by calling the Reformed tradition back to a pre-Puritan position, the Christocentric, churchly, sacramental, and Catholic stand of Calvin. At mid-century Horace Bushnell attempted a marriage between romanticism and Calvinism. He was deeply indebted to Schleiermacher, the German liberalizer of the Reformed tradition. Late 19th-century Calvinism became preoccupied with the challenges of the evolutionary hypothesis, historical criticism, the scientific revolution, and an urban industrialized society.

Calvinism once again became polarized into opposite positions, this time between Liberalism and Fundamentalism. The former, led by William N. Clarke and Walter Rauschenbusch, appropriated new evolutionary, social, and scientific thought for religious purposes, and emphasized an optimistic view of man, a developmental philosophy, and a religion centered on education and morality. In contrast, the Fundamentalism of J. Gresham Machen sought the "recovery" of traditional confessionalism, and the repudiation of new trends in Biblical criticism, scientific naturalism, and social action. Disillusionment with liberal Calvinism after World War I and the Great Depression encouraged an American response to the "crisis theology" of the Swiss theologian Karl Barth, particularly in the dialectical and paradoxical thought of Reinhold Niebuhr. Niebuhr reaffirmed the sovereignty of God, the sin of man, and the encounter between God and man in history.

In sum, Calvinism encouraged American independence with its evangelical activism, the Constitution with its equalitarianism, capitalism with its stress upon work and the equality of all professions under God, and most theology and revivalism took place under Calvinist auspices.

BIBLIOGRAPHY: S. A. Ahlstrom, "Theology in America," in J. W. Smith and A. L. Jamison (eds.), *The Shaping of American Religion* (Princeton, 1961); A. Heimert, *Religion and the American Mind* (Cambridge, Mass., 1966); L. A. Loetscher, *The Broadening Church* (Philadelphia, 1954); J. T. McNeill, *The History and Character of Calvinism* (New York, 1954); L. J. Trinterud, *The Forming of an American Tradition* (Philadelphia, 1949).

**Calvinistic Methodists.** George Whitefield (1714–1770) and John Wesley (1703–1791) argued concerning predestination and became temporarily estranged, Wesley supporting the Arminian position while Whitefield sided with the more orthodox Calvinists. This caused a controversy in the early Methodist movement and resulted in its dividing into the Wesleyan Methodists and the Calvinistic Methodists. Later, the break between Wesley and Whitefield was healed, but the divided groups still continued. As long as Whitefield lived he was the leader of the Calvinistic movement, although he left the work of organization to others. After his death, there was a division into three groups. One of these was known as the "Countess of Huntingdon's Connexion," another as the Tabernacle Connexion, and a third as the Welsh Calvinistic Methodists. The most interesting of these groups was the first, which sprang from the religious interest of Selina Hastings, the Countess of Huntingdon (1707–1791). An influential convert to Methodism, she had opened her London house to Whitefield for his preaching activities and later established a seminary and erected chapels. In 1779, she was forced out of the Church of England and started the association that bore her name, taking refuge under the Toleration Act.

**Camaldolese.** An eremite religious order of Benedictine origin founded c. 1012 by Romuald at Camaldoli (*Campus Maldoli*). Beset by tensions between strict eremites and cenobites, the order split into two independent communities in the 15th century, and the eremites subsequently split again. Since 1935, eremites and cenobites have been united under the headship of Camaldoli with two branches, the Montecorona (eremite) and Camaldoli (cenobite).

**Cambridge Platform and Synod (1648).** A synod of New England churches, meeting on Aug. 15, 1648, in Cambridge, Mass., adopted "The Platform of Church Discipline," written by Richard Mather, with a preface by John Cotton. It subscribed to the doctrinal statements produced by the Westminster Assembly (1643–1653) and defined the organization of the churches represented as Congregational.

**Camerarius, Joachim** (1500–1574). German humanist, classical scholar, and Lutheran theologian. A pupil, lifelong friend, and biographer of Melanchthon, he taught at Nuremberg, reorganized the universities at Tübingen (1535) and Leipzig (1541), and attended the Diets of Speyer (1529) and of Augsburg (1530, 1535, and 1555). He discussed church reunion with Francis I (1535) and Maximilian II (1568). His collection of letters is a valuable resource on the Reformation.

**Cameron, John** (c. 1579–1625). Scottish theologian. Born and educated in Glasgow, Cameron taught Greek in the university there for a year. Then he went to France, where he taught at Bordeaux and Sedan. The Protestant churches of southern France offered him four years of study at schools of his choice, a means of support that enabled him to attend universities in Paris, Geneva, and Heidelberg. In 1608 he joined the faculty of the University of Bordeaux. Ten years later Cameron became professor of divinity at Saumur, but in 1620 civil strife in France forced him to go to England. James I appointed him principal of the university at Glasgow in 1622. His willingness to accept episcopacy for the church in Scotland and his adherence to the doctrine of passive resistance made him unpopular. He resigned after a year and returned to France. He taught at Saumur and Montauban, where again his political views made him disliked. He was stabbed in Montauban and died of the wounds. A man of great learning, he was often dubbed "the walking library." His two most distinguished pupils were Louis Cappel and Moïse Amyraut (see SAUMUR ACADEMY). In his doctrine of grace he dissented from Calvin, approaching Arminius. Cameron's eight theological works formed the foundation of Amyraut's doctrine of universal grace.

**Cameron, Richard** (c. 1648–1680). Scottish Covenanter. In 1679 a fanatic band of Scottish Covenanters killed Archbishop James Sharp. Their rebellion was put down by Charles II's forces at Bothwell Bridge, but Richard Cameron maintained the fight by leading one party of Covenanters who disowned the king and were pledged to fight tyranny. In July, 1680, a small band of his forces were caught and Cameron was killed. His name was revered as a symbol of the fight against episcopacy, and the Cameronians eventually formed themselves into a Reformed Presbyterian body independent from the Church of Scotland.

**Camillo de Lellis** (1550–1614). The founder of a Roman Catholic brotherhood for the care of the sick. De Lellis was born in humble circumstances in Bucchianico, in Abruzzi. He was orphaned early and did not receive a good education. From 1569 to 1574 he served in the Venetian army against the Turks. Leaving military service a poor man, he accepted, in 1574, a caretaker's position in a Capuchin monastery in Manfredonia, and subsequently became a monk. Because of illness, he was sent to the hospital of St. James in Rome, and after regaining his health, joined in the work there, eventually becoming hospital master. In 1582 he founded his own religious society, later called the Camillians, and was its superior until 1607. At the urging of Philip Neri he had accepted ordination to the priesthood in 1584. He died in Rome in 1614, but the benefits of his work continued to be felt throughout Italy in the care of souls and of the sick. He was canonized in 1746.

**Camisard Wars** (1702–1705). A rebellion of French Calvinist peasants in Languedoc against the religious persecutions of Louis XIV. They were led by two men, Jean Cavalier and Roland. Atrocities were committed by both sides until the veteran soldier Marshal Villars by offers of amnesty induced Cavalier to surrender (1704). A few rebels held out until 1710.

**Campanella, Thomas** (1568–1639). Italian philosopher. Campanella was a Dominican friar who rejected the Aristotelian philosophy of his order and who was suspected of sedition by civil authorities. He spent the years from 1599 to 1626 in prison, and upon his release went to Paris, where he lived for the rest of his life. His most celebrated work, the *Civitas Solis* ("City of the Sun," 1623), presents a theocratic, utopian social order presided over by the pope; Campanella's ideas were drawn largely from Plato and Augustine. In several ways Campanella anticipated the direction of modern philosophy: for instance, in his notions that philosophy begins from universal doubt, by which self-consciousness is established as the basis of knowledge (see DESCARTES, RENÉ).

**Campanile.** Italian word for "bell tower." It has been generally adopted to specify any bell tower, but particularly those towers which are detached from the church.

**Campanus, Johann** (1500–c. 1575). Anabaptist noteworthy for his binitarian Christology and for his view of baptism as a lifelong covenant betrothal to God. His writings gave wide currency to the idea that the church had fallen from original purity just after the times of the apostles and that in his own times a restitution was being made. This was understood in apocalyptic terms by leaders of the Münster revolt, though Campanus' own thought was spiritualizing and nonsectarian.

**Campbell, Alexander** (1788–1866). A founder of the Christian Churches (Disciples of Christ). Born in Ireland, he withdrew from the Seceder Presbyterian Church, emigrated to the United States in 1809, and joined his father, Thomas Campbell, who had arrived in America two years earlier. They and several others formed the Christian Association of Washington (Pa.), a fellowship of Christians unrelated to any denomination. In 1811 the group constituted itself as a church and selected Alexander Campbell as its minister. Having adopted immersion as the only valid form of baptism, the Reformers, as they called themselves, united with the Regular Baptists in 1813, but the two groups separated in the 1820's. About 1832 the Reformers united with Barton W. Stone's Christians, and Alexander Campbell became the most forceful leader of the new movement. Campbell's debates with such prominent men as Robert Owen, Archbishop Purcell, and N. L. Rice attracted public attention. He founded Bethany College, W. Va., in 1840, and served as its president for over twenty years. An editor and publisher, he began the *Christian Baptist* in 1823 and changed the journal's name to *Millennial Harbinger* in 1830. Campbell rejected creeds as tests of Christian fellowship and advocated the restoration of primitive Christianity as the only sure means of uniting a divided church.

**Campbell, John McLeod** (1800–1872). Scottish clergyman and theologian, incumbent at Row, Dumbartonshire (1825). For preaching "assurance of faith" and "unlimited atonement," he was convicted of heresy by the General Assembly (1831). He was a pastor of an independent congregation in Glasgow (1833) until his health forced his retirement (1859). His theory of atonement won him recognition beyond Scotland and stressed the "spiritual essence of Christ's sufferings" while minimizing their penal character.

**Campbell, Reginald John** (1867–1956). Minister of the Congregationalist City Temple, London (1903–1915). Convinced of the contemporary church's irrelevance, he wrote his controversial *The New Theology* (1907), advancing the doctrines of divine immanence and man's fundamental religiousness as bases for revitalizing Christianity through moral action and social reform. His views were criticized by Bishop Charles Gore and the Congregationalist P. T. Forsyth.

**Campbell, Thomas** (1763–1854). Father of Alexander Campbell, and a founder of the Christian Churches (Disciples of Christ). A Seceder Presbyterian minister in Ireland, he emigrated to the United States in 1807. He, his son, and several others formed a separate fellowship which, about 1832, united with the Christians of Barton W. Stone. Author of the *Declaration and Address,* Campbell stressed Christian unity and the restoration of primitive Christianity.

**Campeggio, Lorenzo** (c. 1472–1539). Cardinal, Roman Catholic churchman, and diplomat. A doctor of canon and civil law at twenty-six, he married Francesca Vastevillani, by whom he had three sons. In 1509 his wife died, and he entered the clerical estate. He was appointed nuncio to the court of Maximilian, whom he persuaded to join the Holy League with Henry of England against France. He was rewarded with the see of Feltre and created count palatine of the Lateran Palace. His political career brought him into contact with the kings of Europe as well as into frequent attendance upon the emperor. His work earned him gifts and titles and involved him in negotiations concerning such diverse matters as a league against the Turks, Henry VIII's divorce, and the reform of the church. His fire-and-sword policy at the Diet of Nuremberg, as well as in Austria and Hungary, nearly cost him his life. Meanwhile, the imperial army sacked Rome, and while the pope took refuge in Sant'Angelo, Campeggio negotiated the departure of the troops. His last years were spent, first in England, attempting to straighten out Henry's marital problems, and then at the Diet of Augsburg, where his disagreement with Charles V about how to handle heretics caused him to resign as legate. His last work was to prepare a manual for the general council, soon to convene.

**Campion, Edmund** (1540–1581). Jesuit martyr. The varied career of this Oxford humanist led him from England, where he was suspected of "popery," to Ireland and then to Bohemia, where he entered a Jesuit novitiate. He was among the first of the Jesuits sent to England to minister to the remaining Roman Catholics and to attempt to win the country as a whole back to the Roman Church. Apprehended in 1580, he was racked three times and subsequently executed at Tyburn, praying for the queen. He was beatified in 1886.

**Camp Meeting.** The camp meeting was a result of the confrontation of religious revivalism and Methodist open-air preaching with the frontier in the trans-Allegheny west. Its rise may be traced to the beginning of the Second Great Awakening. The first organized camp meeting occurred in July, 1800, at the Gaspar River Presbyterian Church in Logan County, Ky., under the direction of James McGready. In the next five years the camp meeting movement spread throughout the settlements in the West among the Presbyterians, Methodists, and Baptists. In August, 1801, the best-known and largest encampment was held at Cane Ridge, Bourbon County, Ky., under the leadership of Barton W. Stone. The camp meeting as it was founded was an instrument by which these Protestant denominations jointly sought to bring a vital Christian faith into a rough and newly settled country.

The characteristic setting of a camp meeting was a clearing in the forest containing one or more preaching stands, before which were placed hewn logs for seats, those in front for the "mourners" and the rest divided between the men and the women. Around this were located in widening circles the fires for light and cooking, the tents or makeshift shelters for the campers, their wagons, and finally their grazing horses. The meetings usually began on Friday and lasted until Monday, though sometimes they extended for longer periods. Life at the camp was regulated by a schedule that called for early rising followed by family devotions and breakfast. Then there were prayer groups, after which came formal public preaching and the singing of camp songs. Following the noon meal another more informal preaching service was held, and also one at candlelighting after supper. This latter service in the setting of campfires often provided the occasion for the greatest emotionalism.

The preachers were urgent and emotional, clearly depicting the horrors of hell and the joys of heaven with the avowed purpose of bringing the independent, self-sufficient frontiersman to his knees as a "mourner" under conviction of sin, and then waiting upon him to experience a glorious and noisy release from this bondage. To this and the time in between the preaching services was often spent in prayer about the one under "conviction." At times religious excitement was so strong that preaching, exhorting, and singing by many continued day and night. Also, the preaching met with such pronounced physical manifestations as falling, jerking, rolling, running, dancing, and barking as well as visions and trances. A prominent part of the religious observance was the partaking of the Lord's Supper, usually on Sunday. To this only the members of congregations were invited, the Presbyterians and Methodists communing together, while the Baptists drew apart for their observance.

The camp meeting was not only a religious institution, but also a social gathering. People came out of the woods from as far away as a hundred miles. Here it was that lonely frontiersmen, separated from one another for long periods of time, living in fear of Indians and disease and overburdened with work could gather to spend several days in social intercourse. This brought many to the camp grounds who had no interest in religion, and though some were converted, others attempted to disturb and discredit the meetings.

About 1805, following the decline of the Awakening, dissension over the camp meeting became prominent. The Presbyterians were rent asunder by the revival question. Some became followers of Barton W. Stone and the Shakers and continued the revival methods for a time. Another group, the Cumberland Presbyterians, made extensive use of the camp meeting, but the denomination as a whole disowned the method, as did the Baptists, because of the unacceptable Arminian tendencies that predominated. Then, too, as denominational loyalty rose, union meetings became impossible, so that by the 1820's the movement became largely an annual tool of the Methodists for the spread of their denomination.

Also, the meetings became more subdued, refined, and regulated, lacking in the excesses that had been so prevalent in the first years. As the frontier continued to move westward and as more settled and cultured conditions came to prevail, the camp meeting became less effective, and often protracted meetings held within church buildings were introduced. Nevertheless, throughout the first four decades of the 19th century the camp meeting was an important socioreligious institution in backwoods America.

BIBLIOGRAPHY: C. A. Johnson, *The Frontier Camp Meeting* (Dallas, 1955); P. Cartwright, *Autobiography* (New York, 1956); W. W. Sweet, *Religion on the American Frontier* (4 vols.): *The Baptists; The Presbyte-*

*rians; The Congregationalists;* and *The Methodists* (New York, 1964).

**Camus, Albert** (1913–1960). French novelist, playwright, and essayist who received a Nobel Prize for Literature in 1957. He was raised in North Africa, the setting of two novels, but moved to France in 1939. During World War II he participated in the Resistance. Until his essay *The Rebel* (1951; English translation, 1953), he was recognized by Sartre as a fellow existentialist. He is noted for his penetrating atheistic analyses of the predicament of the contemporary conscience.

**Canada, Church Union in.** Early in the 19th century church union began with a series of interconfessional unions. As early as 1818 the Secession Churches of Nova Scotia had started to consider church union. This initial enthusiasm, however, was seriously dampened by the disruption in 1843 of the Established Church of Scotland. Consequently, it was not until the 1860's that any significant moves were made toward union. In 1860 the Secession Synod of Nova Scotia and the Free Church Synod were united to form the Presbyterian Church of the Lower Provinces of British North America, and in 1866 this Synod was joined by the Synod of the Free Church of New Brunswick. In 1861, the United Presbyterian Church in Canada (Secession) and the Synod of the Presbyterian Church of Canada (Free Church) united to form the Synod of the Canada Presbyterian Church. The Established Church of Scotland Synods initially remained aloof from these developments but eventually in 1874 all the Presbyterians in Canada were incorporated into the General Assembly of the Presbyterian Church in Canada. The Methodists went through a similar development. Tension between the American and the British Methodists led to a split in 1840. They were reunited in 1847 and this action paved the way toward the creation of an autonomous Methodist Church in Canada. Later, the Methodists in the Maritimes and the Canadas united in 1874 to form the Methodist Church in Canada. Following these interconfessional unions which created national denominational structures, the next step was the organic union of these national bodies with one another. After twenty years of negotiations, the organic union of the Methodists, Presbyterians, and Congregationalists was accomplished in 1925 and the United Church of Canada came into being. Since 1943 conversations between the Anglican Church of Canada and the United Church have been exploring a further organic union of these two churches. In 1965 their Joint Committee produced the Principles of Union and both churches have now accepted these principles as the basis upon which further discussions will proceed.

**Canada, United Church of.** A union formed in 1925 by the Methodist, Presbyterian, and Congregational Churches of Canada and Newfoundland. The movement toward union grew out of a common desire to avoid rivalry and waste in mission work on the rapidly expanding northern and western frontiers. In 1904 negotiations were set in motion toward a possible organic union and by 1908 a basis of union that covered doctrine, polity, administration, and law was drawn up for presentation to the various churches. From the votes of the church courts and congregations it appeared that sentiment was predominantly in favor of union, but a minority within the Presbyterian Church formed a vigorous opposition. In spite of efforts to overcome this opposition, it became clear by 1921 that it had hardened into an organized cause. On the other hand, over one thousand union congregations had been formed on the prairies in anticipation of the larger union. Not to have moved forward, therefore, would have forced these union congregations to form themselves into a separate denomination. Consequently, the decision was made to proceed with the union. In 1924 the Canadian Parliament passed the United Church of Canada Act, and similar bills were enacted in the various provincial legislatures. On June 10, 1925, the inaugural service of the United Church of Canada was held in Toronto. All the Methodists and all the Congregationalists entered, but only two thirds of the Presbyterians came into the union. The property settlement with the nonconcurring Presbyterians was supervised by a commission that was provided for in the United Church of Canada Act. This commission had exclusive power to determine all questions of property, and eventually it reached a unanimous decision on the settlement.

The government of the United Church of Canada is presbyterial in form and its courts are made up of an equal number of ministerial and lay representatives. At the congregational level the session has control of public worship and the administration of the sacraments. The presbytery exercises supervision over all ministers and pastoral charges within its boundary and is the primary court of discipline for ministers. The power to ordain and to receive ministers from other churches is vested in the eleven territorial conferences. The General Council, which meets biennially, is the lawmaking and policy-making court of the church, but it may not amend any provision of the Basis of Union without the consent of a majority of presbyteries.

The doctrinal basis agreed upon by the negotiating churches contained twenty articles couched in terms of conventional orthodoxy. The main desire in composing these articles was to restate the ancient faith and to do justice both to Calvinism and to Arminianism. The Congregationalists opposed making the twenty articles an absolute test of faith. Consequently, candidates for the ministry must simply declare their "essential agreement" with the statement of faith. A Book of Common Order based on the best traditions of the Reformed Church liturgy was compiled in 1932 and is used for the services of marriage, burial, ordination, and Holy Communion, among others. No set form of corporate worship, however, may be imposed on the congregations.

The first five years following the union were a period of adjustment. Seven boards were set up with secretarial staffs to administer religious and higher education, evangelism and social service, home and foreign missions, pensions and publications. A unified plan of finance was adopted, and annual offerings are apportioned year by year to the several administrative boards on the basis of need and the amount available. The United Church inherited the overseas missionary work of the three denominations as well as extensive obligations in home missions. It maintains eight theological colleges, three arts colleges, and ten secondary schools.

In the years from 1930 to 1940, the depression severely tried the financial resources of the United Church. Its income declined steadily, and the church accumulated a $1,700,000 deficit. The years from 1940 to 1945, however, marked a return of prosperity, and the church managed to liquidate its deficit. In the postwar years a campaign was launched to provide $5,000,000 to place the pension fund on a sound actuarial basis and in 1951 a campaign to raise $3,300,000 for church extension was successfully carried out. In the late '50s and early '60s the major concerns of the church have been with the problems of restructuring its life and work for more effective mission, the recruitment of men for the ministry, and the prospects of further organic union with the Anglican Church of Canada.

BIBLIOGRAPHY: G. W. Mason, *The Legislative Struggle for Church Union* (Toronto, 1956); G. C. Pidgeon, *The United Church of Canada* (Toronto, 1950); C. E. Silcox, *Church Union in Canada* (New York, 1933).

**Canadian Council of Churches.** The first step toward the formation of this Council was taken when the Canadian Committee of the World Council of Churches, the Christian Social Council of Canada, and the Joint Committee for the Evangelization of Canadian Life decided to share one office and one secretary among them. Rev. W. J. Gallagher was appointed to the joint secretaryship of these three agencies of ecumenical cooperation in July, 1942. The second step was taken when the Canadian churches rejected a proposal for the formation of a "North American Council of Churches" drawn up by the American Federal Council of Churches meeting at Cleveland in December, 1942. Following the rejection of this idea, a constitution was drawn up and presented to the various denominations, and the Canadian Council of Churches came into being in 1944 with Rev. W. J. Gallagher as its general secretary. The Council has no authority over its member churches, but it is representative of them and responsible to them. It provides an instrument for their cooperation and acts as the agency of the World Council of Churches in Canada. The work of the Council is administered by five departments: Evangelism, Christian Education, Social Relations, Ecumenical Affairs, and Overseas Missions. It is supported by grants from the member churches and contributions from other sources. Any communion in Canada that "accepts our Lord Jesus Christ as God and Saviour" is eligible for membership if it has autonomy and a Canada-wide organization.

**Canisius, Peter** (1521–1597). Dutch Jesuit. Born at Nijmegen, he was sent by his burgomaster father to Cologne to study arts, civil law, and theology. In 1543, after Peter Faber had guided him through the *Spiritual Exercises,* he entered the Society of Jesus. Canisius was ordained in 1546 after helping to found the first German Jesuit house at Cologne, where he taught and preached until 1547, when he participated in the Council of Trent. After his solemn profession in Rome in 1549, he was sent to Ingolstadt, where he became rector in 1550. Sent to Vienna in 1552, he three times refused its see, offered to him by Ferdinand I. The career of Canisius, whom Leo XIII called "the second Apostle of Germany after Boniface," included participation in the Diets of Augsburg and Worms, the foundation of numerous colleges, appointment as first provincial of Upper Germany, and service as papal theologian at Trent and secret nuncio to the German princes, to persuade them to enforce Trent's reform. He died at Fribourg, where he was court preacher to Ferdinand II. His major work was education through writing and preaching. His three catechisms were widely used; during his own lifetime they went into two hundred editions and twelve languages. Canisius was a major agent of the Counter-Reformation in southern Germany.

**Cano, Melchior** (1509–1560). Spanish Dominican theologian. Cano entered the Dominican Order in 1523. As a highly honored professor of theology at Salamanca he was sent by the Spanish emperor in 1551 to the Council of Trent, but disfavor with the Holy See, prompted by his support of the Spanish Court in certain disagreements, caused Pope Paul IV in 1557 to annul his election to the Spanish provincialate. Only at Paul's death was he able to obtain approbation of his election from the new pope, Pius IV. Always an object of controversy because of his vehemence and energy in Spanish political and ecclesiastical problems, he made enemies by his strictures on the Jesuits, which gained popularity at the time of the Jesuit suppression, and by his accusations of heresy against Bartholomew Carranza, a fellow Dominican and his theological rival for twenty-five years. Cano's major work, *De locis theologicis* (published in 1563), gained immediate publicity and is read today as a pioneering work in the development of scientific theology. To establish the foundations of theology, Cano attempted a treatise on theological method, consciously distinguishing the arguments from authority from those based on human reason alone.

**Canon.** 1. A term first applied to the clerics of the bishop's household, but later applied to any cleric who served a cathedral or collegiate church and did not follow a monastic rule. The word derives either from the rule (*kanōn*) which bound the clergy to a common life or to the list (also *kanōn*) of those who received their living from the bishop's treasury. Clerical communities were found in many cathedral churches, especially at Hippo under Augustine and at Vercelli under Bishop Eusebius. Councils of the late 6th and the 7th century legislated that these clerics should have a common refectory and dormitory. Colleges of canons were to be found in the numerous rural basilicas of Merovingian Gaul. The first formal rule for canons was written by Chrodegang of Metz for his own cathedral. This rule, adopting many customs of the Benedictine Rule, permitted the clerics to retain revenues from private property. In 816 the Synod of Aachen modified this rule and imposed it upon all nonmonastic clergy in the Frankish empire. While the extent to which the rule was followed is uncertain, it seems that by the beginning of the 12th century most chapters of canons had either divided their revenues into separate portions for each canon, thus ending the common life, or had adopted the Augustinian Rule which completely forbade private property. (See AUGUSTINIAN CANONS; PREMONSTRATENSIAN CANONS.)

2. The Greek word *kanōn* means both "rule" and "list," and in the second capacity came to be used by the church at a rather late date (Council of Trent, 1545–1563) to designate those Scriptural books which were regarded as inspired. The Protestant canon and the Roman Catholic New Testament canon are identical, but Protestants follow the Old Testament canon of the Hebrew Bible, while Roman Catholics endorse the Septuagint Old Testament canon, including the books of Tobit, Judith, Wisdom, Sirach, Baruch, and I and II Maccabees.

**Canoness.** A name first applied to a member of a community of religious women who lived according to the Aachen Rule. They differed from Benedictine nuns in that they were not bound to poverty, being permitted a certain amount of private property. During the reform of the canons regular, several orders of canonesses regular, parallel to the orders for men, were begun.

**Canonist.** The two centuries from the publication of Gratian's *Decretum* (c. 1142) to the death (1348) of Johannes Andreae, whose *Novella commentaria* (1338) became the critical apparatus for the period, are known as the classical period in the study of Western canon law. Those engaged in codification of and commentary on canon law in this period are known as canonists, but also because of their method, they are known as glossators. The period has three stages of canonistic activity: (1) the decretists, who wrote glosses and commentaries on the *Decretum*, of whom the most important was Huguccio of Pisa (d. 1210); (2) the early decretalists, who gathered and synthesized canonistic material (either unknown to Gratian or produced after him until the ten books which were issued by Gregory IX, 1234), chief of them Bernard of Pavia (d. 1213); (3) and later decretalists who made commentaries on other material than the *Decretum*, notably Peter of Spain (lived c. 1200), Richard de Mores (Richard the Englishman, d. 1242), and Bernard himself. Three schools of canonists are to be distinguished according to where they did their work and the manner in which it was done: (1) the school of Bologna, of significance from Gratian to Johannes; (2) the French school, or school of Paris, which flourished in the late 12th and early 13th centuries; (3) the Anglo-Norman school which was significantly active only in the late 12th century.

**Canon Law.** The body of ecclesiastical law for the government of a Christian church. The origins of canon law lie in the enactments of the early church councils. In addition to their definitions of doctrine, general or ecumenical councils drew up canons, or rules, dealing with organization and discipline. The Council of Nicaea, for example, summoned by Constantine in 325, issued twenty such miscellaneous statements prescribing for practical situations. As regulations for the earthly life of the church, canons did not possess the unalterable validity of doctrinal definitions, and they came to be constantly added to or modified, in the light of local and individual circumstances, by papal decretals and the pastoral letters of local bishops. Attempts were made from time to time to collect the relevant material, at first mostly in a chronological order which had its disadvantages for practical study and application. In the early Eastern Church, for instance, Theodore Balsamon, Zonaras, and others compiled and circulated such collections, with explanations and commentary, on what was essentially a private basis. The modern Eastern Orthodox commentary on canon law, the Greek *Pēdalion* ("Rudder"), compiled by the industrious Nichodemus of the Holy Mountain and published in 1800, may be called a standard statement, but remains in the private tradition insofar as it includes archaic material, difficult or impossible to apply to modern times, and stands in need of some revision and clarification, which perhaps only the systematic scrutiny of a church council could supply. Similarly in the Western Church, much of the earlier canonistic writing drew on local as well as ecumenical sources and incorporated matter that was dubious and unofficial. In England, for instance, canon law was frequently supplemented with local decrees issued from the provincial center of Canterbury. A decisive stage in regularization came about with the rise to importance of the medieval universities, which specialized in both secular and ecclesiastical law. As a scholarly and systematic reinterpretation and codification of the canons, the *Decretum* of Gratian (c. 1140), both a collection and a commentary, circulated widely and for a time achieved some degree of international

authority. During the 11th century, with the spirit of reform much in the air, the feeling for a thoroughgoing revision had arisen which, while basically dependent on the ancient prescriptions of the church, might provide more specific guidance on such later problems as the clerical obligation of celibacy, simony, and the controversies concerning lay investitures. In church libraries and monasteries were to be found a wide variety of canonistic texts, incorporating still much contradictory material, some still chronologically arranged, such as the collections of Dionysius Exiguus and Pseudo-Isidore, some more serviceably systematic, such as the popular *Decretum* of Burchard, bishop of Worms, compiled about 1012; the work of Abbo, abbot of Fleury-sur-Loire; and various Italian collections. In the age of the reforming pope Gregory VII (1073–1085), attempts at discarding unofficial material from the canons were made by Cardinal Atto in his *Capitulary* and by his colleague Cardinal Deusdedit. Before becoming pope, Gregory had commissioned Peter Damian to collect in a single manageable volume the canons relating to papal authority. Damian set aside the task, and Gregory as pope called for new canonical collections. The three main compilations which resulted—those of Atto, titular cardinal of St. Mark's; Anselm, bishop of Lucca; and Cardinal Deusdedit—achieved a modernized code which, while still firmly dependent on Roman tradition, was comparatively free of doubtful additions. The ultimate position, Roman canon law as a body of official church regulations on matters of faith and practice, ratified by the pope, was reached with the issue of the Codex Juris Canonici in 1917 under the aegis of Pope Benedict XV.

BIBLIOGRAPHY: Z. N. Brooke, *The English Church and the Papacy* (Cambridge, 1931); C. Duggan, *Twelfth Century Decretal Collections* (New York, 1963); R. Metz, *What Is Canon Law?* (New York, 1960); R. C. Mortimer, *Western Canon Law* (Berkeley, 1953); J. J. Ryan, *Saint Peter Damiani and His Canonical Sources* (Toronto, 1956).

**Canons, Anglican Book of.** The 151 canons passed in 1604 by the Convocation of Canterbury to clarify the confusions resulting from the partial abrogation of medieval canon law by English Reformation legislation. The canons, which are not systematically complete, deal with such matters as the ministry, ecclesiastical courts, and the administration of the sacraments. The majority are still technically binding in the Church of England, though some have fallen into disuse.

**Canons Regular.** A group of men, living a common life under a rule, bound by the traditional monastic vows and differing from secular canons by their insistence upon absolute poverty. The movement began in the 11th century and was closely related to the reform of Gregory VII. During the 12th century, most of the communities of canons regular adopted the Rule of St. Augustine, and were known as the Augustinian, or Austin, Canons.

**Canossa.** A fortified castle belonging to Countess Mathilda of Tuscany. Here in January of 1077, Pope Gregory VII, on his way to Germany, encountered Emperor Henry IV, who had come to Italy to have his excommunication lifted. Henry is said to have stood in the snow for three days as a penitent before Gregory absolved him from his excommunication. The incident is now seen as a major victory for Henry in the investiture controversy with Gregory.

**Canticle to the Sun.** A hymn of praise composed by Francis of Assisi, lauding God for the beauty and wonders of creation.

**Capadose, Abraham** (1795–1874). An important figure in the Dutch Réveil. From a Portuguese Jewish family, he, like Da Costa, allowed himself to be baptized in 1822 under the influence of their teacher, Willem Bilderdijk. He helped establish a Sunday school (1836), a mission to Jews (1846), the Dutch Inner Mission (1853), a mission to evangelize Spain (1869), and continually supported efforts to suppress slavery. In his last years he severed all contact with the organized church.

**Capetian Dynasty.** Upon the death of Louis V (987), the last Carolingian monarch in France, Hugh Capet, son of Hugh the Great of Neustria, was crowned king of the French at Noyon. Though initially faced with overmighty vassals, the dynasty had become, by the opening of the 13th century, the greatest political force in France. The senior line of the family ended with the death of Charles IV in 1328, when it was succeeded by a cadet line, the Valois.

**Capitalism.** Term designating a particular organization of economic activity, the use of which was hardly known among academic economists prior to the publication of the *Communist Manifesto* by Marx and Engels (1847). Although the term "capital" had been in use since the 16th century, the term "capitalism" was not even employed by Adam Smith (*Inquiry Into the Nature and Causes of the Wealth of Nations,* 1776). The term "capitalism" became more prevalent in the 19th century, but the concept was not demonstrated as fundamental until Werner Sombart's work on modern capitalism (1902). Since that time it has been used to designate a system in which (1) the nonpersonal means of production are privately owned, (2) production is undertaken by private initiative for private profit, (3) bank credit at appropriate rates of interest is extended to producers, and (4) prices of labor, materials, and product are permitted to seek their own level in a free and unregulated market (sometimes referred to as laissez-faireism). The term has gained further meaning as a contrast to the various socialist alternatives in which one or more of the previously mentioned features is modified or even intentionally reversed as, e.g., public ownership of productive means. Modern capitalist economies are largely the result of the industrial revolution, the managerial revolution, and the more recent cybernetic revolution; yet there is hardly a capitalist economy in which some measure of public control has not been introduced to modify the system and to correct inequities consequent upon its free operation. This modern tendency poses again the question raised so acutely by Marx, whether inherent proclivities in the process, if permitted to run their course, will not finally destroy it and produce socialism.

The appearance in 1904 of Max Weber's *The Protestant Ethic and the Spirit of Capitalism* reinforced from a religiosociological standpoint the critique of capitalism by Marx. In this essay, Weber advanced the theory that capitalism, including its laissez-faire dogma, its autonomy of economic activity subject to no law but its own, and its conception of business as a religious vocation or calling, was traceable not only in root but also in sanction to the ethics of Puritanism. This view adapted by R. H. Tawney's *Religion and the Rise of Capitalism* (1927) which, while noting the more ancient rootage of capitalism, contended that Puritanism supplied the context in which the spirit of capitalism achieved a high degree of respectability. Criticizing Weber and Tawney, H. M. Robertson showed in *Aspects of the Rise of Economic Individualism* (1933) that the development of Jesuit casuistry was of equal importance in undergirding the rise of modern capitalism. This debate over the fixing of responsibility between Protestant and Catholic tended to obscure the idea, hinted at already by Weber, that the autonomy of economic activity separated from the control of a religiously based ethic made the spirit of capitalism almost a demonic force.

The modern liberal voices within capitalist economies have responded variously to the tragic occurrence of the depression of 1929–1933. Out of this experience, the purely secular liberal has accepted the necessity of some external control on economic autonomy such as federal price controls. Curtailment of large fortunes by graduated income tax and the wider base of corporate ownership have tended toward the democratization if not the socialization of productive means. It was Reinhold Niebuhr, however, who penetratingly demonstrated that a theological issue about the nature of man lay at the root of the question and that this question has been debated but hardly resolved since the Reformation. A dialectical theologian, he offered a theological understanding of the secular order based on a concept of grace, and inveighed equally against the polarities of individualism and collectivism (*The Children of Light and the Children of Darkness,* 1944). Contemporary Christian social ethics reflects the concerns emphasized by dialectical theology when it puts stress upon responsibility both as a corporate characteristic and as an individual demand. Thus, while capitalism has been locked in a profound struggle within a world polarized between East (communism) and West (capitalism), both secular and religious critiques of the system have tended to effect modifications which have moved capitalism toward the center of the context defined by the poles of "pure" socialism and "pure" capitalism.

BIBLIOGRAPHY: V. A. Demant, *Religion and the Decline of Capitalism* (New York, 1952); A. Hyma, *Christianity, Capitalism and Communism* (Ann Arbor, 1937); R. Luxemburg, *The Accumulation of Capital* (New Haven, 1951); F. M. Stern, *Capitalism in America* (New York, 1951); F. Sternberg, *Capitalism and Socialism on Trial* (New York, 1951).

**Capito, Wolfgang** (1478–1541). Protestant Reformer. A Biblical humanist like Erasmus, Capito became preacher and professor of theology at Strasbourg in 1523. He was the early Protestant leader in that city, and his visit to Luther in 1536 helped to resolve difficulties between Lutherans and southern German Protestants. He was tolerant of other groups, persuading the city council of Strasbourg not to use force against the Anabaptists.

**Capitulations** (Turkey). Name given to the extraterritorial rights granted by the Turkish sultan, Suleiman, to France in 1535. They included the privilege of trading unmolested throughout the Ottoman Empire,

immunity from Turkish law and the right to be tried by French courts, and the special protection of Roman Catholics within the Empire. The latter was one of the irritants that led to the Crimean War in 1854 against Russia.

**Capreolus, John** (c. 1380–1444). Thomist philosopher. Capreolus was one of the outstanding agents of the revival of Thomism at the close of the Middle Ages. His highly praised exposition and defense of Thomas Aquinas, which had the form of a commentary on Peter Lombard's *Sentences,* earned him the name "Prince of the Thomists." He was the first interpreter of Aquinas whose intention it was to restate Thomist doctrine as it is found in Aquinas' writings. Capreolus worked mostly at Rodez until his death.

**Capuchins.** A branch of the Franciscan Order. In 1525, Matthew of Bascio, an Observant Franciscan friar, asked Pope Clement VII for permission to follow the Franciscan rule "to the letter." His request granted, four years later he and some like-minded companions had an approved rule. Their reform of existing mendicant life insisted on strict poverty and simplicity: they wore a coarse habit with the characteristic peaked hood, beards, and little or no footgear; and they practiced unadorned communal prayers. Preaching and care for the poor in the war- and plague-ridden Italy of the 1520's accentuated the pristine Franciscan character of their life and increased their popularity. A crisis occurred in 1541, however, when the vicar-general Ochino espoused Protestantism and fled to Geneva. Nevertheless, the order grew and was a strong force in the Counter-Reformation. Capuchins have been less scholars than preachers to the poor. As foreign missionaries since the 17th century they have been successful, especially in India. *Cappuccinorum* added to the usual abbreviation for the Franciscan Order may come from the pointed cowl, *cappuccio,* or from *scapuccini,* "hermits," as Italian children called Matthew and his companions.

**Carafa, Gian Pietro.** See PAUL IV.

**Cardijn, Joseph** (1882–1967). Belgian Roman Catholic leader. The son of a Belgian miner, Cardijn was trained at the seminary at Malines and ordained in 1906. He then studied in the social sciences at Louvain, observing always the disruption of life and faith brought about in the wake of industrialization. He was made curate in a working-class parish in Brussels, and in 1912 laid the foundation for what became the Jocist movement

(Jeunesse Ouvrière Chrétienne, or "Young Christian Workers"). His first group of lay people were dispersed by World War I, and he himself was imprisoned by the Germans. After the war he was put in charge of social work in Brussels and was able to elaborate the specific plan of formation and action for his lay groups which he had worked out while in prison. This approach to the apostolate he captured in the three verbs, "See—Judge—Act." One must accurately observe the situation, pass judgment on it in accordance with the canons of the gospel, and then act so as to make the situation more like the ideal. The basic unit of the movement was the cell, a militant discussion-action group. The movement spread throughout the world, its specialized approach to Catholic Action serving as an attempt to reverse the de-Christianizing tendencies of industrialism. Cardijn was made a cardinal by Pope Paul VI in 1965, two years before his death at Louvain.

**Cardinal.** The second highest ecclesiastical office in the Roman Catholic Church. Originally the term (Latin, *cardo,* "hinge") was applied to any priest permanently attached to an important church. By the end of the 5th century the cardinal priests of Rome were also assisting the pope in his duties. Soon the deacons who administered relief to the poor through the churches of Rome and assisted the pope came to be called cardinal deacons. From the 8th century onward the bishops of the dioceses surrounding Rome who assisted the pope were called cardinal bishops. Although the term continued to be used for clergy elsewhere, it was in Rome that the cardinals began to develop power. In 1150 they formed a College (corporation) with its own officers. The Roman cardinals soon came to form a permanent synod (Consistory) to assist the pope in church administration. After the 14th century when the cardinal bishops allowed cardinal priests and deacons the same rights that they enjoyed, the cardinals grew to be the most powerful body of clergy, and the term ceased to be used for clergy outside Rome.

Cardinals are created and deposed only by the pope and enjoy the rights of bishops. They are supposed to live in Rome unless they are bishops of foreign dioceses. They serve as papal counselors, envoys, and administrators of church affairs. Upon the death of a pope they meet in Conclave to elect a successor, governing the church in the interim. Until recently there were seventy cardinals, but Pope John XXIII created several in excess of this number. In 1966 there were 99 cardinals, and by 1967, some 120.

**Carey, William** (1761–1834). Baptist missionary. A cobbler in Northamptonshire, England, where he was born, Carey was converted in 1779, becoming a preacher and teacher (1783), and cobbling by night for a livelihood. Without schooling he learned the Biblical languages, Latin, Dutch, and French. Instrumental in founding the Baptist Missionary Society (1792), he went as its first missionary (1793) to India in a Danish ship. There he ran an indigo factory and a mission station in Bengal (to 1799) while translating the New Testament into Bengali. At Serampore (1801) he published a Bengali New Testament. Fort William College, Calcutta, founded in that year appointed him professor of Sanskrit, Bengali, and Marathi (until 1831), during which tenure he completed the translation of the Bible into Bengali (1809), and partial translations into twenty-four other dialects and tongues. A competent, though self-taught, philologist and grammarian, he published grammars and lexica in the Indo-European tongues of Bengali, Marathi, Punjabi, and Sanskrit, the Dravidian language of Telugu, and the Sino-Tibetan dialect of Bhotani spoken by the Bhutan invaders of Bengal. His continued political and social activity among Indian peoples helped toward the abolition of suttee (1829), the Hindu custom of cremating a widow on her husband's bier. From the Serampore printing press almost 250,000 Bibles and Testaments were published under his editorship.

**Carlstadt, Andreas** (Andreas Rudolf Bodenstein, c. 1480–1541). German Protestant Reformer. He began his career as a Thomist and a leading light of the University of Wittenberg. He was overshadowed by Luther, losing his nominal leadership after the Leipzig Disputation. Emerging differences from Luther led him to espouse liturgical and social changes in Wittenberg which Luther repudiated on his return from the Wartburg. From 1523 to 1525 he wrote a series of German tracts that became influential in the radical movement. Though he espoused the cause of the common man after taking a parish in Orlamunde in 1523, he opposed the violence of the Peasants' War as well as the apocalypticism of Thomas Müntzer. In opposition to Luther he (1) called for a "faith rich in love and a love rich in faith," charging Luther with being lax on moral reform; (2) vehemently denied the Real Presence, describing as idolatrous Luther's (and the Roman Catholic) view of the sacrament; (3) called for the believer's experience of the Spirit for faith to be genuine and challenged the usefulness of rites and ceremonies; and

(4) disavowed Luther's reliance on secular authority. His views spurred the iconoclasm of the Radical Reformation, but through his influence on Hans Denck and others he also supplied positive content to Anabaptism. The influence of Augustine and of the Rhineland mystics upon him is clear.

**Carlyle, Thomas** (1795–1881). Scottish essayist, historian, and philosopher. He is best known for his collected essays *On Heroes, Hero-Worship, and the Heroic in History,* and his studies of *The French Revolution* (1837) and the *History of Frederick the Great* (6 vols., 1858–1865). Carlyle is the classical exponent of the "great man" theory of history. Though his research is dated and inaccurate, his historical prose remains the most vivid in the English language. His autobiographical *Sartor Resartus* was a speculative discourse on creeds and human institutions as "clothes" and therefore temporary, with notable chapters on the "everlasting no" and "everlasting yea," describing a spiritual crisis such as was experienced by Carlyle himself. Although he gave up his earlier studies in the ministry, he retained a deep sympathy for the moral teachings of Christianity. His faith in the religious principle in the hearts of all good men, his opposition to all materialistic philosophy, and the idealism exemplified in his writings were widely influential.

**Carmelite Order** (*or* Order of Our Lady of Mount Carmel). A religious order founded on Mt. Carmel in Palestine c. 1154. Although the order once claimed to have descended from Elijah and the community of prophets who lived on Mt. Carmel, it was actually founded in Palestine c. 1154. The fall of the Crusader States forced most of the members to migrate to Europe. Under the sixth general, Simon Stock, the order was transformed into a mendicant order (1247) and the austerities of the rule adapted to the rigors of European climate. In 1452 an order of Carmelite nuns was founded. A third order for laymen was established, and after the 16th century they were encouraged to wear the scapular. Gradually discipline became lax and the order fell into decay. In 1562, Teresa of Ávila formed a new convent of Carmelite nuns which intended to follow the primitive discipline. Her return to the contemplative life attracted many followers, including John of the Cross, who extended the reform to the male houses of the order. This movement, known as the Discalced ("Barefoot") reform, succeeded in most of the houses of the order. The conflict between the two observances was resolved only by forming two independent divisions. The habit of the order consists of a brown robe and scapular with a white cape (from which they derive the common name of White Friars).

**Carmelites** (Discalced). A reformed order of the Carmelites begun c. 1562 in Spain by Teresa of Ávila and John of the Cross which emphasized asceticism and mystical piety. The name Discalced ("Barefoot") comes from their practice of not wearing shoes (though sandals are nearly always worn today). In 1593 the Discalced Carmelites obtained their own general thus marking the final break with the Calced (Observatine) Carmelites.

**Carnegie, Andrew** (1835–1919). American manufacturer and philanthropist. He was born in poverty in Scotland, then taken to Allegheny, Pa., where his family settled in 1848. Self-educated, he rose through profits from oil and railroads to become king of the steel industry. His view of wealth as a stewardship, stated in *Wealth,* became famous and prompted him before he died to give $350,000,000 for education, music, libraries, and the cause of peace.

**Caroline Books, The.** A treatise written at the court of Charlemagne c. 790, purporting to be written by Charlemagne himself, but more likely the work of Alcuin. It attacks the Second Council of Nicaea for its statements on images. A faulty translation of the Greek decrees had given the Franks the impression that the Council had condoned the adoration of images.

**Caroline Divines.** Anglican theologians in the 17th century who sought continuities with the older Catholicism rather than with the Reformed theology. They were the originators of the *via media* that became characteristic of later Anglicanism. The leading figure was Archbishop William Laud. Other prominent Caroline divines were George Herbert, Jeremy Taylor, John Bramhall, and John Cosin. They flourished from 1625 until c. 1700. They were especially dominant during the reign of King Charles I, whence the name "Caroline."

**Carolingian Architecture.** See ARCHITECTURE, MEROVINGIAN AND CAROLINGIAN.

**Carolingian Renaissance.** In the most general sense, the term "Carolingian Renaissance" refers to the reigns of the Frankish dynasty of Carolingians, who for several generations during the 8th and 9th centuries reversed the trend toward cultural stagnation and political anarchy that characterized western Europe in the period following the breakup of the Roman Empire.

Charles Martel (palace mayor, 714–741), who established himself as the most powerful hereditary official of the Franks, evolved a policy that included the reunification of the Frankish kingdom, the expansion of its territories, the reorganization and centralization of its secular and ecclesiastical administration, the encouragement of missionaries, and support of the papacy. His heirs furthered these policies. Pepin III, "the Short" (mayor, 741–751; king, 751–768), succeeded in casting off the last of the weak Merovingian rulers and had himself crowned king. This step was made possible through the influence of Pope Zacharias, who gave Pepin the sanction and support that he needed for the wholly illegal act. His ascendancy was further sanctified by the famous missionary Boniface, who anointed him king in 751. In return, Pepin gave Boniface full support in reforming the still badly disorganized and corrupt Frankish Church. In 754, Pope Stephen II, hard pressed by the increasingly menacing incursions of the Lombards, journeyed to Metz and there personally reanointed Pepin as Frankish king. Pepin, in return, promised Stephen a gift to the papacy of all lands taken from the Empire by the Lombards. After two years of military campaigns against the Lombards, Pepin made good his promise and in 756 presented Stephen with a deed to much of northern Italy (the Donation of Pepin). Pepin's achievements might not have survived the fratricidal strife of his two heirs, Charles and Carloman, if the latter had not died in 771, leaving Charles, Charlemagne, as sole ruler of the now greatly expanded Frankish empire. Charlemagne was the most brilliant and ambitious of the Carolingians. His long reign (768–814) is a chronicle of incredible energy and achievement. In a series of conquests he absorbed northern Italy into the Frankish empire, conquered and reconquered the pagan Saxons, won Bavaria, strengthened the eastern frontier against Slavs and Avars, and invaded Islamic Spain. This insatiable appetite for conquest was combined with rare administrative abilities, and in spite of the limitations of his treasury and frequent outbreaks of revolt, he managed to achieve a degree of centralized power unknown since antiquity. His lordship was both secular and religious. The papacy was greatly strengthened by its alliance with him. On an occasion that was to have great historical consequences, Pope Leo III, who was indebted to Charles for his rescue from hostile elements in the Curia, crowned him on Christmas Day, 800, while he was praying in St. Peter's. To the king's ostensible surprise, if we are to believe his biographer Einhard, Leo proclaimed him "Emperor of the Romans." The grandson of the palace mayor had become ruler of a new, still intangible, political and religious concept: the Holy Roman Empire.

The most immediate result of Charlemagne's reign was to establish western Europe as a distinct political and cultural unit, to provide it with an identity which it has never lost. In the relatively stable atmosphere of his reign, the church grew in influence and its missionaries converted much of heathen Europe. Under his sponsorship, the so-called palace school was instituted. To his court came the leading scholars of the day, notably the Northumbrian Alcuin and the Lombard Paul. The revival of learning which ensued, and which spread throughout Europe, was not notable for its originality, but for its spirit of rediscovery and assimilation. Innumerable works of the church fathers and Latin secular writers owe their continued existence to the efforts of Carolingian scribes and copyists. The corruption of classical and early Western Christian texts was remedied; the correlation of ancient sources was begun; monastic libraries began to grow and spread; and medieval Europe was for the first time provided with a common fund of ideas. Although the Carolingian Empire did not survive the death of Charlemagne, the scholarship and learning that he encouraged were destined to endure the shock of centuries of chaos, and become cornerstones of western European civilization.

BIBLIOGRAPHY: E. S. Duckett, *Alcuin, Friend of Charlemagne* (New York, 1951); and *Carolingian Portraits* (Ann Arbor, 1962); H. Fichtenau, *The Carolingian Empire* (Oxford, 1957); L. Wallach, *Alcuin and Charlemagne* (Ithaca, 1959); A. F. West, *Alcuin and the Rise of Christian Schools* (New York, 1892).

**Carolingian Schools.** Schools established by Charlemagne for the education of the clergy and the improvement of Biblical, liturgical, and theological texts. By a series of capitularies, especially that of 787 addressed to Abbot Baugulf of Fulda (*De litteris colendis*), Charlemagne ordered schools to be established in monasteries and in the residences of bishops. Students were taught to read Latin, to chant properly, and to compute the dates for holy days. Study of the liberal arts was promoted at certain monasteries which acquired excellent teachers and large libraries. First among these schools was the palace school of Aachen, where laymen as well as clerics were educated. Charlemagne's chief educational adviser was Alcuin of York. From Italy he acquired Paul the Deacon, Peter of Pisa, and Paulinus of Aquileia. Other important centers and their great masters were Tours (Alcuin), Orléans (Theodulf), Fulda (Rabanus Maurus), and Ferrières (Lupus Servatus). To meet the increased demand for texts, both classical and theological, numerous manuscripts were collected and copied. While Charlemagne's educational program did not long survive, the monasteries remained the centers for the preservation and dissemination of learning in the West. Much of classical literature has been transmitted to us through the scholars of these Carolingian schools.

**Carpocrates.** Libertarian Gnostic teacher of the 2d century. In his view the divine soul of Christ, present in Jesus (son of Joseph and Mary), enabled him to understand the Jewish law and terminate it; Gnostic Christians were therefore free from law in general. To his son Epiphanes (perhaps locally deified after his death at 17) was ascribed a treatise *On Justice* which explained that the commandments not to commit adultery or to steal were contrary to nature.

**Carpzov, Benedikt** (1595–1666). One of a family of German theologians and lawyers who in the 17th and 18th centuries were noted for their Lutheran orthodoxy. In 1638, Carpzov formulated the first system of German criminal law and in 1645 joined the law faculty at Leipzig. Four years later he summarized the legal development of Protestantism after the Reformation by drawing up the earliest complete system of Protestant church law.

**Carpzov, Johann Benedikt I** (1607–1657). German theologian, brother of Benedikt Carpzov. After studying at Wittenberg and Leipzig, he became pastor first at Meuselwitz and then at Leipzig, where he served St. Thomas Church and attained high church office. He was professor at Leipzig from 1641. His Latin textbook on systematic theology won him the title "father of symbolics," but he is better known for his homiletical work on arranging sermons.

**Carroll, Charles** (1737–1832). American Roman Catholic layman and Revolutionary leader. Educated by the Jesuits in Maryland, he continued his studies in Europe. Returning to America in 1765, he soon took up the colonists' side in the struggle over taxation and representation. He was a delegate from Maryland to the Continental Congress and a signer of the Declaration of Independence, writing his name in his usual way, Charles

Carroll of Carrollton. One of the wealthiest men in the colonies, he served his newborn country well.

**Carroll, John** (1735–1815). First Roman Catholic bishop in the United States, first archbishop of Baltimore, and a cousin of the Revolutionary leader Charles Carroll. Trained as a Jesuit in France, he took his final vows and was ordained in 1769. When the Society of Jesus was suppressed in 1773, he returned to seclusion in America. In 1776, he accompanied Benjamin Franklin and others on a futile mission to Canada to obtain the aid of the French Canadians. An ardent patriot, he wrote the notable *An Address to the Catholics of the United States* in 1784 and was an influential apologist for Roman Catholicism when it was under severe attack as an alien influence. He pointed out the considerable services of Catholics in the Revolution. After many pleas for more local authority, he was named prefect apostolic by Pius VI in 1784–1785. In 1790 he was consecrated bishop to forestall attempts to place American Catholicism under French control. In 1791 he presided over the first Roman Catholic Synod in the new nation. In 1795 he made plans for a cathedral, which was completed in 1821. In 1808, Baltimore was made an archdiocese and Carroll was named archbishop. From this post he came to dominate early American Catholicism. He paid considerable attention to education for Catholics, helping establish native seminaries and colleges, notably Georgetown in 1791. He was also instrumental in establishing a unified American church in opposition to French, English, Irish, and German demands for a church organized along nationalistic lines.

**Carthage, Councils of.** The first synods at Carthage were the seven held during the episcopate of Cyprian which legislated concerning the softening of penances, the authority of Rome, and the rebaptism of heretics. We still have the canons of the Councils of 348 and 390. A series of synods was held during the episcopate of Aurelius which included a condemnation of the Pelagianism of Celestius (c. 412) and the Council of 418 which forbade the appeal of clergy to Rome against their bishops. There were also councils under Boniface in 525 and 534.

**Carthusian Order.** An austere religious order founded by Bruno of Cologne, a competent teacher and administrator opposed to simony and believing ambition to be a form of dishonesty. In 1084 he established himself with a few companions in a mountain retreat near Grenoble. In 1104 there were still only thirteen monks there. They avoided meat, drank watered wine, and wore hair shirts, conversing rarely and giving themselves up to the discipline of internal prayer. Unlike other orders, the monks lived in separate cells with gardens attached and sought to combine the solitary life of the Egyptian desert ascetics with the disciplined order of later monastic foundations. Their physical needs were attended to by a community of lay brethren who lived farther down the mountain. Their abbot was the bishop of Grenoble, and the head of the order was an elected prior. They began very soon to collect a good library, from which simple origin grew La Grande-Chartreuse of later times.

The monks met in the chapel to sing the offices and especially the Night Offices for the Dead from 11:30 to 2:00 or 3:00 A.M. The chapel was simple, and rich vestments and ornaments were eschewed. In 1104 the abbot of Nogent said that only the chalice was of silver.

The most famous of the early accounts of the Carthusians is that of Peter the Venerable in about 1124. He stated that the fasting of the monks was almost continuous. They ate cheese and eggs only on Sundays and Thursdays, with cooked vegetables on Tuesdays and Thursdays and on other days only bread and water. They performed manual labor and gave much attention to the production of books. Their dress was the roughest of any worn by the religious orders. The boast of the Carthusians is that their order has never needed reformation: *"Nunquam reformata quia nunquam deformata."* This is true, although when Bruno was called to Rome by Urban II in 1091 to assist him with counsel, the strain was too much for the community and after defections it had to be reconstituted. A split in the order occurred between 1378 and 1400, known as the Great Schism, but it was healed by the resignation of both generals and the election of another to take their place.

The rigor of the life has meant that the order has never been widespread, most of its foundations being in France. In 1300 there were thirty-nine foundations, and a little over a hundred were established in the 14th century. At maximum there were only some two hundred houses.

There was no special rule at the beginning. In time, collections of the customs of the order were made, the *consuetudines,* and one of these was approved by Innocent II in 1133. Very few changes are to be found in the three original collections of customs.

The writings of Benedict, Jerome, and Cassian were prized among the early Carthusians

and they claimed to have some relics of Antony of Egypt. One month was passed as a postulant, simple vows were taken after one year, and final vows after four. It was also possible to be a professed lay brother, but ten years were required for final vows.

The general of the order was the prior of La Grande-Chartreuse. A general chapter was held each year consisting of all the priors plus any visitors appointed by the chapter itself. The latter visited each foundation every two years. In theory the prior was elected by the monks of each house, but in practice he was often appointed by the general. The general was assisted by the vicar, his deputy, a procurator who looked after the temporale and supervised the lay brothers and various other officers, such as the coadjutor who looked after guests. No woman was allowed within the buildings.

There was an attempt to extend the order to women, but in 1400 there were only nine houses for women. Widows were not permitted entry to a Carthusian nunnery.

Although encouraging members to sever every worldly tie and all personal ambition, the order produced some eminent administrators such as Hugh of Lincoln and Stephen of Die. The order encouraged a great labor of copying but discountenanced personal literary ambition, Carthusians at one time being forbidden to publish.

BIBLIOGRAPHY: C. Boutrais, *The History of the Great Chartreuse* (London, 1934); and *The Monastery of the Grande Chartreuse* (London, 1893).

**Cartwright, Peter** (1785–1872). American Methodist clergyman. Born in Virginia, he was raised in Logan County, Kentucky, in a section described as "Rogues' Harbor." At the age of sixteen he came under the conviction of sin, and experienced conversion at a camp meeting. Joining the Methodist denomination, he received an exhorter's license in 1802 and then soon became a circuit rider in Kentucky, Tennessee, Indiana, and Ohio. Known as the Kentucky Boy, he was characterized as an independent, tough frontiersman with a lively sense of humor and an unhesitating tongue, whether preaching the gospel or attacking sin and other denominations. In 1806 he was ordained a deacon and in 1808 an elder, in which year he also married. He continued as a circuit rider in Kentucky and Tennessee until 1824, when in his opposition to slavery he settled permanently in Illinois, serving for forty-five years as a presiding elder. He was a member of twelve General Conferences and two Illinois legislatures. In 1846 he was defeated by Abraham Lincoln for a seat in Congress. An ardent Methodist, he was thoroughly confident that through its organizational structure and practices the gospel could be spread across the land.

**Cartwright, Thomas** (1535–1603). Elizabethan Puritan Reformer. Cartwright was a brilliant student, and two Cambridge colleges, St. John's and Trinity, vied to secure his services. Appointed Lady Margaret professor in 1569, he began to criticize the structure of the English Church in his lectures and from the pulpit. He insisted that all ministers are essentially equal in rank; that bishops should exercise spiritual functions, not political; that deacons should care for the poor; and that church government should be in the hands of the local presbyteries, with each congregation choosing its own pastor. The authorities censured him, refused to grant him his D.D. degree, and deprived him of the professorship and fellowship. He left the country for Geneva, but was back in time to participate in the *Admonitions* controversy in 1572, engaging in a pamphlet duel with Whitgift. A warrant for his arrest was issued, and he again fled, settling at Middelburg, and then Antwerp, where he accepted the pastorate of the English church. In 1585, he returned to his homeland, eventually settling at Warwick, where he died an honored patriarch. Cartwright was a moderate Presbyterian, disavowing the Martin Marprelate tracts and the Separatists, but advocating a Presbyterian union of church and state. Undoubtedly, he was the most influential Puritan teacher of his time.

**Casaubon, Isaac** (1559–1614). Classical scholar and church historian. Born in Geneva of Huguenot parents, he received his education there, later becoming professor of Greek at the university (1581). In 1596 he accepted a teaching post in Montpellier, and in 1599, hoping for a similar position in Paris, moved to that city. Although his unyielding Protestantism frustrated these hopes, he was made a librarian by favor of Henry IV. When Henry was assassinated in 1610, Casaubon, after considering posts at Heidelberg and Leiden, chose, upon the invitation of Richard Bancroft, to go to England. Under the patronage of James I, he pursued his scholarly endeavors until his death in 1614.

Casaubon's primary scholarly competence was classical languages and literature. His editions of Suetonius and Polybius established for him an international reputation. In addition to the classics, his interests included theology and church history. He wrote several pamphlets defending Anglicanism in its controversy with a resurgent Roman Catholicism (1611). An extensive knowledge of the patristic period led him to begin his *Exercitationes,* an erudite corrective to the pro-Catholic historical work of Caesar Baronius. Casaubon was one of the earliest Anglo-Catholic scholars to emphasize the authority of the early church for contemporary Christianity.

**Case, Shirley Jackson** (1872–1947). American theologian. He was born in New Brunswick, Canada, educated at Acadia University, Yale University, and the University of Marburg, Germany. He was ordained a Baptist minister in 1900. As a scholar, his field was New Testament interpretation and early church history. He taught at the University of Chicago from 1933 to 1938, and was associated with the Chicago school of liberal theology, emphasizing the sociohistorical approach to Christianity.

**Casel, Odo** (1886–1948). Monk of Maria Laach in Germany, best remembered as the proponent of the *mysterium* theory, or the "theology of mysteries." Learned in patristics and in the theology of the Bible, he succeeded in giving a basis in doctrine to the liturgical movement in the Roman Catholic Church. In his view, Christ, the great sacrament or *mystērion,* continues his salvific action through the sacraments and liturgy.

**Cassander** (Cassant), **George** (1513–1566). Flemish-born irenic theologian. A teacher of the classics, he turned to Biblical and theological questions in an attempt to restore peace between Luther and Calvin and the Roman Church, only to be attacked by both sides. In his many writings Cassander tried to distinguish essential from nonessential doctrines and to emphasize the rights of individual judgment within the limits of a primitive consensus (Scripture, Apostles' Creed, and the fathers). In his role as mediator he argued that the papal primacy was of human origin. His works were put on the Index in 1617.

**Cassian, John** (c. 360–435). A Latin-speaking monk and theologian from Scythia (modern Romania). He lived for some time in Palestine, visited Egypt about 400, and later became abbot of St.-Victor's at Marseilles. His *Institutes* and *Conferences* (or *Collations*) brought to the West the experience of Eastern monasticism. They are used and praised by later monastic writers such as Benedict and remain important documents of moral theology and classics of Christian devotion and mysticism. Cassian was, however, attacked by the ultra-Augustinians of Gaul (especially by Prosper of Aquitaine in his *Contra Collatorem*) for what seemed excessive emphasis on free will in some of the *Conferences*. Nevertheless, he was respected at Rome and his final work, *On the Incarnation*, was written at the request of the archdeacon Leo, afterward pope, to inform the Western Church of the issues involved in the Nestorian controversy.

**Cassiodorus** (c. 475–c. 570). A Roman noble whose long life encompassed two careers. Under Theodoric and his successors he held high political office. His highly rhetorical official correspondence (*Variae*) is an important source for late Roman administration, and a work *On the Soul* reveals his intellectual interests. When the Gothic rule collapsed after 537, Cassiodorus withdrew from the subsequent wars to his ancestral estate near Scyllacium (Squillace) in Calabria, on which he founded two monasteries. These he made centers not only of devotion but of scholarship, on the lines of his *Institutes of Divine and Human Letters*. His own intellectual work is derivative, as in a commentary on the psalms, mainly from Augustine, and the *Tripartite History*, compiled from Greek ecclesiastical historians. He was, however, largely responsible for spreading the idea that manuscript-copying was a suitable form of labor for monks, and the preservation of secular as well as sacred literature a proper monastic activity. Though he seems to have had no contact with his contemporary, Benedict of Nursia, he made an important contribution to the future development of Benedictine monasticism and medieval culture.

**Castellio, Sebastian** (1515–1563). Humanist theologian. Originally from Savoy, he went to Strasbourg, where after meeting Calvin in 1540 he became Protestant. Shortly after Calvin's return to Geneva, Castellio was called to head the old Genevan college. He did his work well, but trouble started in 1543 when he sought admission to the pastorate, for among other differences of belief Castellio doubted the allegorical interpretation of the Song of Solomon, which he felt to be a description of royal amours. Calvin consequently convinced the Little Council that he should not be appointed. Castellio looked for other work, and after some hardship became professor of Greek in the University of Basel in 1553. Here he brought out a Latin Bible in which he strove for stylistic elegance but aroused opposition because of indifference to traditional teachings. Always ready to stand up for religious tolerance, Castellio presented his views against persecution after the death of Servetus in *De haereticis,* his most important work. This signaled his final break with Calvin and marked him as the leading 16th-century exponent of religious toleration. He argued that the Bible is not sufficiently clear on all points, and that a distinction should be made between things essential and things nonessential to salvation.

**Catacombs.** The name generally applied to the early underground burial places for Christians near Rome and later elsewhere. It was derived from the geographical location of the tombs under the church of San Sebastiano, which were described as *kata kumbas,* "by the hollow."

Until the time of Hadrian, cremation was the normal burial practice of the Romans; cinerary urns were placed in the niches of the vaults, called columbaria, which were built for the purpose. The Jews in Rome, however, practiced inhumation, and it may be from them that Christians adopted the idea. In deference to Roman custom, burials were not made inside the city walls. Volcanic sand, stone, and granular *tufa* compose the plain surrounding the city; only the *tufa* is soft enough to excavate yet firm enough to remain standing. The characteristic form of a catacomb is that of a network of interconnected corridors and chambers containing burial niches. The ground plan is often in the form of a gridiron, and there may be several levels. Graves may be simple loculi—recesses made in the walls to contain the wrapped corpses—which were closed in with brick or marble slabs. Normally the catacombs were for the poor, but as they developed into shrines the wealthy made elaborate tombs in them.

After the barbarian invasions the catacombs fell into oblivion and were not rediscovered until 1578. Modern study of them dates from the work of the de Rossi brothers in the last century. They counted over 500 miles of catacomb corridors and now we know of more than 35 catacombs at Rome, besides a number of others throughout the Empire. The Roman tombs are located along the roads that lead out of the city. Some of the older catacombs appear to have been pagan burial places before they were acquired by the Christians; the oldest tombs are those of Lucina, Callistus, Domitilla, and Priscilla. The crypts of Lucina are excavated beneath the impressive tomb of a prominent Roman of the 1st century. The first stage of the excavation included provision for only about fifty loculi. It consisted of a main passage with two branches. About a generation later additions were made, including the "Y" chamber, named for an unidentified saint, in which are some of the earliest known examples of Christian art. In later years it was expanded even more, and the remains of Pope Cornelius are there. In the same field is the catacomb known as the cemetery of Callistus, which derives its name from its administrator, who later became pope, and which contains the "Crypt of Popes." The tomb of Cecilia is also there. Six chambers known as Sacrament Chapels from their frescoes were probably used by Christians who came to them to eat meals in honor of the deceased. The Catacomb of Domitilla has excited speculation over whether it commemorates Domitilla, wife of Flavius Clemens, the Roman noblewoman who was exiled for her religion and who may have been a Christian. The catacomb seems later than her time and it was first used as a pagan burial place. The Catacomb of Priscilla is more extensive than the other three and consists of three definite parts, the Hypogeum of the Acilians, the Greek Chapel with its wealth of decoration, and another section which began in an abandoned sand quarry. Other catacombs which appear to be of Christian origin include the tombs of Praetextatus, Sebastian, and Peter and Marcellinus among their more notable examples.

The catacombs are the repositories of most early Christian art that has come down to us. Surprising to the neophyte is the number of pagan motifs that were taken over apparently without question by the Christians. Distinctively Christian designs included the fish anagram and, after the time of Constantine, the Chi Rho monogram. The woman with her arms lifted in prayer and the young shepherd with a lamb on his shoulder were familiar in Hellenistic art, but they had special significance for Christians. Many Old Testament stories that were considered typical of New Testament events were popular, and some New Testament stories appeared. The Christian art of the catacombs can be dated closely by reference to the style of pagan art. Most of the inscriptions are Greek.

During the 3d century, Christians sought refuge from persecution in the catacombs, and the Roman respect for graves often, though not invariably, protected them. Many martyrs were buried in them, which led to their beatification and the celebration of the Eucharist there on anniversaries. After Constantine the catacombs fell into disuse.

BIBLIOGRAPHY: G. M. Bevan, *Early Christians of Rome: Their Words and Pictures* (New York, 1927); W. I. Kip, *The Catacombs of Rome* (New York, 1854); O. Marucchi, *The Evidence of the Catacombs for*

the Doctrines and Organization of the Primitive Church (London, 1929); C. R. Morey, *Early Christian Art* (Princeton, 1942).

**Catechism** (from Greek *katēchein*, "to resound" or "to din in"). A manual for religious instruction. The catechesis, or oral instruction, of catechumens, i.e., those who were being trained in doctrine and discipline in the early church in connection with Christian baptism, occasioned the writing of manuals to aid in this religious instruction, or catecheses. Thus the catecheses denominated primarily a system of religious instruction but applied secondarily to the documents used in such instruction. Ancient texts relating to the catechumenate resemble in content and plan modern writings which have been called catechisms. Catechisms may be thetic in form or, more frequently, they are formulated in questions and answers.

The earliest systematic exposition of the theology of baptism is the small treatise by Tertullian, *On Baptism*. The *Mystagogical Lectures* of Cyril of Jerusalem is a collection of sermons on the three sacraments of Christian initiation as addressed to catechumens. In certain churches the custom was followed of imparting such instruction after, in others before, the reception of baptism.

The catecheses of Ambrose of Milan are found in *On the Mysteries* and *On the Sacraments,* the latter probably a set of notes taken by an auditor during the instruction. The *Catechetical Lectures* of Theodore of Mopsuestia cover the Credo, the Lord's Prayer, Baptism, and the Eucharist. Augustine's *De catechizandis rudibus* also presents comprehensive sacramental theology in what is essentially the form of a catechism. The *Ecclesiastical Hierarchy* of Pseudo-Dionysius the Areopagite, though also a catechetical treatise, differs from the preceding in that it develops a deeper theology for advanced believers rather than an elementary catechesis for the newly baptized.

Among the catechisms that have come down to us from the medieval church the following may be mentioned: the Weissenburg Catechism (789) and the *Disputatio puerorum per interrogationes et responsiones,* attributed to Alcuin. Catechetical aids also stemmed from the reforms of John Wycliffe (*Poor caitiff*), John Hus (the Hussite Catechism), the Moravians (Catechism of the Moravian Brethren), and the Waldenses (*Las interrogacions menors*).

The Reformation brought an emphasis on explicit faith on the part of every believer. A corollary was the development of new forms for the religious education of the young, centering about catechetical instruction. Martin Luther's Small Catechism appeared in 1529 as an epitome of the Large Catechism. It was designed for the education of the religiously illiterate laity. The catechisms were the outgrowth of thirteen years of pastoral work in the form of preaching, visitations, and writing. Luther preached catechetical sermons in the town church at Wittenberg and published booklets for laymen and children based on these sermons. The Small Catechism originated in posters that could be attached to the walls of the home, church, or school. In May of 1529 seven of these posters dealing with the Ten Commandments, the Apostles' Creed, the Lord's Prayer, the Benedicite, the Gratias, Baptism, and the Lord's Supper, together with a preface and Table of Duties, were published at Wittenberg in book form. A number of editions and revisions were published in the following months. Each article was presented in the context of the Christian gospel, and the gospel was related to the needs of everyday Christian living. The Small Catechism in much the same form remains the basis for religious instruction in Lutheran churches throughout the world. The Large Catechism was based on three series of catechetical sermons preached at Wittenberg in 1528. It was designed as an aid to the pastor, indicating how he might apply the catechism to the life situation of the parishioner. Lutheran church orders emphasized the thorough and regular catechizing of the congregation and accorded Luther's catechisms special significance. They were given confessional status by virtue of their incorporation into the Book of Concord (1580).

The Heidelberg Catechism (1563) stands as a classic and definitive statement of the Reformed faith. It reflects the influence of earlier catechisms and is the product of joint efforts. However, the major guiding spirits in its compilation were two Calvinist theologians, Caspar Olevianus and Zacharias Ursinus, who undertook the work upon the command of Elector Frederick III of the Palatinate. Although the elector planned it for use in the Palatinate as a means of conciliating Lutheran and Calvinist parties, it became the official catechism for the Reformed churches in Germany, Poland, Hungary, Transylvania, and the Netherlands. At the Synod of Dort (1619) it was revised and officially declared one of the symbolic books of the Reformed Church.

Of Calvin's two catechisms written in French, the first, his *Instruction and Confession of Faith for the Use of the Church of Geneva* (1537), was too compendious to be used extensively in the instruction of children. It was an abridgment of his famous *Institutes*. In 1542 he wrote a second catechism adapted more fully for use as an instructional manual. The English translation of this work, from a Latin text prepared by Calvin himself in 1545, became the official textbook for the Church of Scotland via the Book of Discipline of 1560.

The Westminster Assembly of Divines (1643–1649) adopted in addition to the Westminster Confession two catechisms: the Larger Catechism, for the use of ministers in explaining Christian doctrine from the pulpit, and the Shorter Catechism, for the instruction of children. As a result of the restoration of episcopacy in the Church of England in 1660 by Charles II and the consequent employment of the catechism included in the Book of Common Prayer, the influence of the Westminster catechisms was not extensive in England. But they were authorized by the General Assembly of the Church of Scotland in July, 1648, and by the Scottish Parliament in January, 1649. The Shorter Catechism is a summary of the Puritan interpretation of the Christian faith. What Luther's Small Catechism was for Lutheranism and the Heidelberg Catechism for the Reformed, the Shorter Catechism, the third great Protestant textbook, was for the formation of the Presbyterian faith.

A brief catechism for the Church of England was included in the first Book of Common Prayer in 1549. This contained a short explanation of the commandments and the Lord's Prayer. In 1604 a supplement consisting of questions on the sacraments was added. Convocation and Parliament approved this catechism, with some slight alterations, in 1661–1662. It is still part of the Book of Common Prayer and is the only authorized catechism for Episcopal churches throughout the world. These succeeded earlier Lutheran influences on catechetical developments in England, to be seen in Marshall's *Goodly Primer* of 1535 and in Thomas Cranmer's Catechism of 1548, a translation of Luther's Small Catechism and the Nuremberg *Sermons for Children* of 1533.

A summary of the tenets of Polish Unitarians appeared in the famous Racovian Catechism, published in 1605 at Raków. It was the work of Faustus Socinus and preachers associated with him at Raków, the headquarters of the Socinians. It sought to give a Scriptural version of a non-Trinitarian Christianity.

The Roman Catholic Church responded to the catechetical innovations of the Reformation churches by producing a number of catechisms. The Jesuits devoted themselves to this activity. Of particular significance is Peter Canisius' *Summa doctrinae Christianae* (1554). Later revisions of this catechism received wide use in the Roman Church for centuries. The Catechism of the Council of Trent, or Roman Catechism, published in 1566 upon the order of the Council of Trent, was not a catechism in the usual sense but a summary of doctrines defined at the Council for the use of priests. Cardinal Bellarmine's Catechism (1598), ordered by Pope Clement VIII, was proposed by Vatican I (1869–1870) as a model for a universal catechism. In the United States the Baltimore Catechism (1885) has exercised wide influence in the Roman Catholic Church. A catechetical renewal sponsored by the *Deutsche Katechetenverein* resulted in a new German Catechism approved for all German dioceses in 1954 in which new concepts of religious instruction are incorporated. Translations of it have been made into many languages, including English (A Catholic Catechism, 1957). In 1966 there appeared in the Netherlands a New Dutch Roman Catholic catechism, published by the Higher Catechetical Institute at Nijmegen. In narrative form, it differed radically from traditional Roman Catholic catechetical presentations, and its doctrinal orthodoxy was challenged by some Dutch traditionalist theologians. Subsequent investigation by a commission of cardinals, however, revealed no major doctrinal deviations, and the Dutch Catechism received the imprimatur (January, 1968). The impact of this new Dutch Catechism has been worldwide.

BIBLIOGRAPHY: W. A. Curtis, *A History of Creeds and Confessions of Faith* (Edinburgh, 1911); P. T. Fuhrmann, *An Introduction to the Great Creeds of the Church* (Philadelphia, 1960); B. A. Gerrish, *The Faith of Christendom* (Cleveland, 1963); *Fundamentals and Programs of a New Catechesis* (Pittsburgh, 1966).

**Catesby, Robert.** See GUNPOWDER PLOT.

**Cathari.** See ALBIGENSES.

**Cathedral.** The church where the bishop's throne (Latin, *cathedra*) is located and therefore the chief church of a diocese. The clerics of the bishop's household originally served the cathedral, but as the bishop tended to be present only on high ceremonial occasions, the cathedral clergy developed into an independent body known as the cathedral chapter.

**Cathedral Chapter.** A body of clerks called canons, who assist the bishop in the administration of the diocese. In the later Middle Ages there were two kinds of chapters—regular and secular. In a regular chapter the canons lived a common life in a cloister near the cathedral under the direction of a prior and the discipline of a rule, particularly the so-called Rule of St. Augustine. Their lives had many of the marks of the monastic community. Secular canons were not required to lead a common life and often lived in parishes which they served in the diocese. Canons were supported by shares of the cathedral endowment known as prebends. They elected their own officers, the chief of which was the dean. The chapter not only assisted the bishop in governing the diocese, but was in full charge when the bishop was absent from the diocese or when there was a vacancy in the bishopric. It was the chapter that elected the new bishop. In the later Middle Ages, the chapters often exerted their independence of the bishop, a fact that led to bitter conflicts. Such a dispute took place between Robert Grosseteste, bishop of Lincoln, and his chapter. It was finally settled only by intervention of the pope. Anglican and many Roman Catholic cathedrals continue to have chapters.

**Cathedral Schools.** In the Middle Ages these schools were of two classes: those for boys and those for clerical aspirants who had mastered the elementary subjects and wished to continue their education. The oldest of the elementary schools was probably York, which dates from the 7th century. Here there was a grammar school and a choir school run by lesser officials, while the bishop kept control over the theological education of the clergy. In time the officer charged with theological education was known as the chancellor and was one of the chief officers of the diocese, marked by his rank in processions. The syllabus of the schools adhered closely to the trivium and the quadrivium, the former comprising grammar, logic, and rhetoric, the latter astronomy, geometry, arithmetic, and music. These divisions date back to Martianus Capella in the 5th century and Boethius and Cassiodorus in the 6th. With the 12th-century revival of interest in humanistic studies, many cathedral schools especially in France (Laon, Reims, Chartres, Orléans, etc.) extended their studies beyond the traditional syllabus to include science and medicine. The cathedral schools with no entrance requirements waxed and waned with the reputation of their teachers, such as Gerbert at Reims and William of Champeaux at Paris. They provided a European network of humanistic culture and helped spread the ideal of a unified Christian culture. From them sprang the major universities, such as the one at Paris.

**Catherine II** (1729–1896). Empress of Russia from 1762. Born a German princess, Catherine married Czar Peter III in 1745. After the latter's murder she ruled alone. Initially, she instituted a number of reforms, but failed to solve Russia's most pressing problems, especially serfdom. Her reign witnessed the Pugachev uprising, two Turkish wars, and the partition of Poland. In the end, her liberal intentions became harsh reaction.

**Catherine de' Medici** (1519–1589). Queen of France (1547–1559). Orphaned at birth, Catherine de' Medici was raised by Cardinal Guilio de' Medici (later Clement VII), who in 1533 married her to the son of Francis I (later Henry II). The marriage was complicated not only by Henry's dullness but by his liaison with Diane de Poitiers as well. The deaths of Francis I in 1547 and Henry in 1559 were followed by the short reign of Francis II under the tight control of the Guises. In 1560, Catherine became queen regent, controlling the reigns of her sons Charles IX and Henry III. Attempting to moderate the explosive situation between the Roman Catholics and the Huguenots, she continually sought a policy of mutual toleration, for which she was castigated by both sides. In 1561 she issued an edict stopping all persecutions and calling a national church council at Poissy to study the early church and the problem of reform. Significant agreement was reached by both sides, but the results were nullified by papal interference. Some of these results were later contained in the Edict of January in 1562, which was often appealed to as a basis for settlement of the religious wars (1562–1598). On the other hand, chiefly for political reasons, Catherine is at least indirectly to blame for the Bartholomew's Day Massacre of 1572, when the Duke of Guise instigated the murder of Coligny, encouraging Paris to riot against the Huguenots.

**Catherine of Genoa** (Catherine Fieschi, 1447–1510). Medieval mystic. Catherine had been married to Giuliano Adorno, an easy-living nobleman, for ten years when her life was changed by a powerful experience of God. Her husband was also converted, eventually joining the Franciscan Order. Catherine began to work in a women's hospital. During the plague of 1493 she is reported to have performed numerous miracles of healing. Through her influence on some young admirers her ecstatic experiences of Divine Love were preserved and recorded in her *Vita, Dialogo,* and *Trattato del Purgatorio.* Baron von Hügel wrote an extended study of her visions and experiences.

**Catherine of Siena** (Catherine Benincasa, 1347–1380). Italian mystic. Born in Siena, the next to the youngest of numerous children, Catherine is credited by her confessor and biographer, Raymond of Capua, with mystical gifts from childhood. After taking the habit of a Dominican tertiary, she lived at home, first as a recluse and then as a woman actively influential in the church. At nineteen, she is said to have experienced the grace of "spiritual espousals" after which she increased her severe penances and her gentle, constant care of the poor and ill. In 1370, a "mystical death," which included visions of hell, purgatory, and heaven, contained for her a divine command to engage in a yet more active apostolate. She began to dictate letters to princes urging them to desist from civil wars. In 1376, as ambassador of Florence to the papal court at Avignon, she persuaded Pope Gregory XI to return to Rome. She wrote her *Dialogue,* a classic of Italian literature, in 1378. Urban II called her to Rome, where she spent her last days laboring for reform in the schism-torn church. Her writings, in the beautiful Tuscan dialect, include nearly 400 letters, 26 prayers, and the *Dialogue.*

**Catholic Action.** In the Roman Catholic Church a distinction has customarily been made between the "sending" or "apostolate" given by Christ to his chosen twelve apostles and that general mission given by baptism to all Christians and strengthened and brought to maturity in the sacrament of confirmation. The criterion by which one separates these missions today is supposedly the reception of a third sacrament, Holy Orders. Thus, in spreading the good news of the coming of Christ and in assisting others to procure the means of salvation, the hierarchy of the church is said to have the official role, while the laity possess only a secondary or subordinate role. However, with the increasing secularization of the modern world, the clergy have come, willy-nilly, to depend more than ever for the efficacy of their mission on the prior activity of the laity. Thus "Catholic Action" has entered the vocabulary of the church. Used first perhaps by Pope Pius X, the words received their classical definition from Pius XI, who, in a "Discourse to the Young Women's Section of Italian Catholic Action" in 1927, defined Catholic Action as "the participation of the laity in the apostolate of the Church's hierarchy." At the Second Congress for the Apostolate of the Laity (1957), Pius XII expanded the meaning.

**Catholic Apostolic Church.** A denomination that arose in England in the early part of the 19th century, in which Edward Irving and Henry Drummond were principal figures. The name was chosen to stress the unity of all Christians. Spiritual gifts and the Second Coming of Christ were emphasized. Governing the denomination were twelve apostles, and local churches had an "angel," priests, and deacons. Ordinations ceased with the death of the last apostle in 1901. Scarcely any churches now remain.

**Catholic Church.** See ROMAN CATHOLICISM.

**Catholic Foreign Mission Society of America** (Maryknoll). Until the year 1908 the United States had technically been a "missionary land" in the eyes of the Roman Catholic Church. As might be expected under such conditions, not much energy was devoted by the clergy of the United States to the work of "foreign" missions. However, three years after the termination of its mission status, the Catholic Church in the United States launched the Catholic Foreign Mission Society of America. Its origin is directly attributable to the plan of two men, Rev. James A. Walsh, of Boston, and Rev. Thomas F. Price, of North Carolina. In 1912 a major seminary was established at Ossining, N.Y., and named "Maryknoll." Speaking for the hierarchy, the American cardinals announced the opening of the seminary in that year, and emphasized the national scope of its work. The Society sent its first contingent of missioners to the Province of Kwangtung, China, in the fall of 1918. Two auxiliary groups, the Foreign Mission Brothers of St. Michael and the Foreign Mission Sisters of St. Dominic, were established to assist in the work of the Society. The Maryknollers are secular priests, and do not take the vows of the regular clergy. China, Manchuria, Korea, the Philippines, Japan, and Hawaii have been the scene of the Society's labor.

**Catholicism, Liberal.** The attempt of some Roman Catholics, especially in France, to relate the Revolution and the church. Liberal Catholicism was already afoot at the time of Gregory XV's election (1831), but its birth was in France, where Lamennais urged ultramontanism compounded with unbounded faith in the people. For him the causes of pope and people were one: truth and freedom against the pretensions of princes and aristocrats. Because he attacked a Gallican faith, Lamennais was suppressed until the reign of Louis Philippe in July, 1830. Then wider press coverage (see AVENIR, L') was permitted him and his friends Montalembert and Lacordaire. The victories of Belgian Catholics and of Daniel O'Connell in Ireland were inspiring. Freedom

of press, of association, of education, the extension of suffrage, the separation of church and state, and more elections were elements in liberal Catholicism. Lamennais' appeal to Rome came to nothing. *Mirari vos* (1832) implicitly condemned Lamennais' position. French liberals made some progress but also alienated many Catholics under Louis Veuillot. By 1860, ultramontanists and liberals were at odds over questions of liberty. Montalembert spoke at the Catholic Malines Congress (1863) and advocated religious tolerance and "a free Church in a free State." Doellinger conducted a similar congress in Munich. In the 1864 Syllabus of Errors with the encyclical *Quanta cura,* Pius IX condemned many elements in liberal Catholicism, and the movement, never organized, went underground to emerge more vigorously in Catholic Modernism.

**Catholic Reform.** See COUNTER-REFORMATION.

**Catholic Truth Society.** A group started by Herbert Vaughan and reorganized by James Britten and Msgr. Cologan in 1884. Its objectives are to spread devotional tracts among Catholics, to attract the uneducated poor to religion, to inform Protestants about Catholic practices, and to circulate good and cheap literature. Similar independent societies have been active throughout the English-speaking world.

**Cavour, Camillo Benso di** (1810–1861). The crafty prime minister of Sardinia-Piedmont who prepared the way for the unification of Italy as a constitutional monarchy under the rule of the House of Savoy. He was known as a Machiavellian politician. In 1860 he followed up the victories of Garibaldi in Sicily and Naples by incorporating all of Italy, with the exception of Venice and Rome, under the monarchy of King Victor Emmanuel.

**Caxton, William** (c. 1422–1491). First English printer. His translation, while at the court of Burgundy, of a French history of Troy led to an interest in the new art of printing, and the work was published at Bruges in 1474, the first book to be printed in English. In 1476, Caxton set up a press in London (Westminster) and issued numerous works, many of them devotional or liturgical. He also continued his work as a translator.

**Cecil, William** (Lord Burghley) (1520–1598). The principal political adviser and chief secretary of state to Elizabeth I of England (from 1558). Active in high office under both her predecessors, he became the most influential person in her reign. So keenly aware was he of the details of domestic and foreign intrigue that his vigorous policies, based on that knowledge, prevented papal subversion of the English break with Rome at a time when maintenance of it was in doubt.

**Celestine I** (d. 432). Pope from 422. He was known for his involvements in theological controversies. In 429 he sent Germanus of Auxerre to Britain to suppress Pelagianism. In 430 he formally condemned Nestorius. In 431 he supported the Augustinian party in Gaul against the semi-Pelagian tendencies of John Cassian. A synod at Carthage protested his interference in the case of an African priest who had been excommunicated by his superiors.

**Celestine III** (Giacinto Bobone, c. 1105–1198). Pope from 1191. A member of the Orsini family of Rome, he had been a cardinal for forty-seven years before his election as pope. He was a former student of Abelard, and defended his master at Sens (1140–1141). As a cardinal he advised a conciliatory policy toward secular monarchs. After his election, he crowned Emperor Henry VI, who shortly afterward invaded Sicily, uniting it to the Empire. He favored the Crusades and approved several military orders.

**Celestine V** (Pietro del Murrone, 1215–1296). Pope during 1294. A Benedictine monk, he became a celebrated ascetic in his retirement on Mt. Morrone. His numerous disciples formed the nucleus of the new Celestine Order. A divided Conclave elected him pope (1294), but after five bizarre months of incompetence, the aged man of solitude had alienated his supporters and was forced to abdicate. Arrested by his successor, Boniface VIII, he died in prison.

**Celibacy of the Clergy.** Although celibacy was not required of any Christians in the apostolic period, voluntary sexual continence was looked upon as a sign of extraordinary devotion to the Christian life. By the 2d century there were groups of virgins associated with many churches. It was in the 3d century that local synods first promulgated canons requiring celibacy of those in holy orders. The growth of the monastic movement with its required vow of chastity did much to spread the ideal. Thus it gradually came to be the custom throughout the Western Church to require a vow of celibacy from its clergy as they became subdeacons.

Throughout the Middle Ages there were continuing attempts to enforce the rule of celibacy among the clergy. This was particularly important so that church property would not be passed on from father to son, thus becoming the hereditary property of a family of priests. However, Roman Catholicism was never successful in achieving such celibacy of all its clergy until the modern era. Recently there has been increasing agitation within the Roman Catholic Church to relax the rule on clerical celibacy, but Pope Paul VI's encyclical *Sacerdotalis caelibatus* (June 24, 1967) reasserted celibacy in terms considered by many as intransigent.

The Eastern Orthodox Churches have always been less demanding of clerical celibacy than the Church in the West. Priests may not marry after they are ordained, but those who are married before they become priests may continue to live with their wives. Only bishops must be celibate.

**Cell** (from Latin *cella*, "small room"). Used of a monk's chamber which is to be simple but not necessarily uncomfortable. An outlying monastic house dependent on an abbey is also called a cell. A third use of the term "cell" is for the smallest unit of a social organization that implements the work of the whole.

**Cellarer.** According to the Rule of St. Benedict, the official appointed by the abbot to have charge over the supplies of the monastery. In a large monastery, the cellarer was permitted to have assistants. In actual practice, the cellarer was responsible for all the external business of the monastery and was allowed a certain freedom from the rule to carry out his duties.

**Celsus.** Middle Platonist philosopher. Celsus was the author, about 178, of *The True Account,* a bitter attack upon Christianity as irrational, antitraditional, and subversive. This work, based in part on Jewish sources and sometimes confusing gnosticism with "the great church," is known only through a refutation provided about seventy years later by Origen (*Contra Celsum*). Origen shared many ideas with his foe, but he insisted against him upon the importance of creation, incarnation, and resurrection.

**Celtic Christianity.** It flourished from the time of the withdrawal of the Roman armies from Britain in the middle of the 5th century until the time of the Synod of Whitby in 664 in England and the 9th century in Ireland when the Vikings attacked the churches there.

Although there were Christian bishops in England in the time of the Romans, and Germanus of Auxerre probably came to England to help stifle the heretical ideas of Pelagius, himself a British monk, the waves of Saxon invasions drove most British Christians into the west country.

Southern Ireland was probably Christianized before Patrick came, and his work was mostly in the north of the country. Because of the difficulty of communicating with the mainland of Europe after Patrick and the political disorganization there, Irish Christianity tended to go its own way and developed a number of peculiarities.

Chief of these was the monastic and ascetic character of Irish Christianity. Religion tended to be organized on a clan basis, and the diocesan organization had little importance. Large numbers of people lived in a monastic area, and the head of the church there was not the bishop but the abbot, though quite often the abbot was also a bishop.

Irish monks were very strict. They would recite the penitential psalms while immersed in icy rivers, or they would stand for hours with arms outstretched in the "cross vigil." This asceticism found its way into Europe with the great outburst of Irish missionary activity. Columbanus, for example, would not allow his monks any change of diet even when they were desperately ill. Irish missionaries went as far afield as Iceland and northern Italy. They were particularly active in Devon and Cornwall, and women, such as Eia, were active along with the men. St. Gall in Switzerland is an Irish monastery built on the site of the heritage of the Irish missionary Gall.

Ireland developed the system of penitential books which replaced in time the public confession and penance practiced in the early church. The most famous penitential books are those of Finan and Columbanus.

The offenses named are often bizarre, much space being given to penalties for eating food contaminated by animals. Long periods on bread and water are prescribed for sex offenses or spurning the church and its officers. The penalties are often impossibly severe, though tables of commutations were developed. However, murder and violence are not capital crimes. The use of penitentials spread with the arrival of the Irish missionaries in Europe. Irish monks cut their hair off in front of a line drawn over the top of the head from ear to ear. They had a date for Easter different from that of the Roman Church. Acting against a background of literary pagan bards, they developed good schools (Clonard, Clonmacnoise, Clonfert, etc.) and educated such

Roman Apologists as Aldhelm and Alcuin. The art of book illumination was far advanced, and the Book of Durrow (c. 700), the Book of Kells (8th century), and others are masterpieces in spite of their rather esoteric symbolic figures.

Although Ninian had worked in Scotland previously, the conversion of Scotland was almost wholly the work of Irish missionaries. Columba came to Iona about 565 and made it a vast missionary and educational center. Aidan, Eata, Finan, and others spread Christianity across the north as far as Lindisfarne. In the year of Columba's death, however, the Roman mission under Augustine began and the conflict between the two forms was settled at Whitby in 664 in favor of Rome. In 673 the Roman form of diocesan government was confirmed. Bishops were to stay in their dioceses and not wander everywhere like the Irish missionaries, who did not succeed in consolidating their gains. Enthusiasm was thereafter channeled into disciplined forms.

BIBLIOGRAPHY: Nora Chadwick, *The Age of Saints in the Early Celtic Church* (New York, 1961); and *Studies in the Early British Church* (Cambridge, 1958); Louis Gougard, *Christianity in Celtic Lands* (London, 1932); Kathleen Hughes, *The Church in Early Irish Society* (Ithaca, 1966); John T. McNeill, *The Celtic Penitentials* (Paris, 1923); W. D. Simpson, *The Celtic Church in Scotland* (Aberdeen, 1935).

**Celtic Missions.** During the 6th and 7th centuries the Irish Church was the most important source of Christian missionaries in western Europe. Although never a part of the Roman Empire, Ireland was probably first visited by Christians from the neighboring Roman province of Britain in the 4th century. The Roman withdrawal from Britain (c. 410) and its conquest by pagan Saxons left Ireland isolated from Christian areas and free to develop its own church life. Ireland remained politically independent until the Viking invasions of the 9th century, and the Irish Church maintained a separate organization and distinct customs until accommodation to Roman practices began late in the 7th century.

Among the unique practices of the Irish Church were the style of clerical tonsure, the date of celebrating Easter, and the presence of bishops without fixed dioceses. There was a strong emphasis on monastic life, and abbots were often the most powerful ecclesiastical figures. The monasteries were noted for their devotional life, scholarship, and art. Also present in the monasteries was a marked emphasis on ascetic discipline. One aspect of this discipline was the idea that voluntary exile from one's homeland was a mark of spiritual excellence. This concept, combined with the desire to spread the gospel, gave rise to the impressive work of the Irish missionaries.

These missionary monks were largely responsible for the spread of Christianity in much of modern Scotland and England, although their influence extended as far as France, Germany, Austria, Switzerland, and northern Italy. They worked in a variety of ways. Many of the monks established monasteries and served the surrounding population, some lived as hermits teaching those who visited them, and a few served as scholars and advisers at royal courts. Among many Irish missionaries, several deserve special mention.

About 562, Columba (c. 521–597), a native of Donegal, established a monastery on the island of Iona off the Scottish west coast. This institution soon became a center for training missionaries for England and Scotland. Columba himself made missionary journeys to the nearby mainland and there established other monasteries.

After spending twelve years in a monastery at Bangor, Columbanus (c. 550–615) set out for eastern France (c. 590) and established a monastery at Luxeuil, marked by strict rules for the monks. Columbanus carried on mission work and also attempted to revitalize the spiritual life of the Christian areas. This latter effort led to conflicts with the authorities, and Columbanus went first to Switzerland and then to northern Italy. Although his Irish Church customs sometimes led to conflicts with European churchmen, Columbanus' influence was extended through the nearly fifty monasteries which grew out of the work at Luxeuil and provided missionaries for western Europe. One of these workers was Ansgar (801–865), who went from the monastery at Corbey to do pioneer missionary work in Scandinavia. Gall (c. 550–c. 645), who had accompanied Columbanus from Ireland, remained as a hermit near Lake Zurich, where he did some mission work.

In 635 Aidan (d. 651) established a monastery on the island of Lindisfarne, off the northeast coast of England. The monks of Lindisfarne and two later bishops of Lindisfarne, Finan (d. 661) and Cuthbert (d. 687), did extensive missionary work in north and central England. Wilfrid (634–709), who was educated at Lindisfarne, was involved in the conversion of the last group of Anglo-Saxons, who lived on the Isle of Wight.

In the 8th century the tradition of the Irish missionaries was enthusiastically carried on by their most numerous converts, the English. The English monks, who had received the faith in monasteries founded by Irishmen, now carried it to Holland, Belgium, Germany, and Scandinavia (particularly Norway). Willibrord (658–739), who was educated in the monastery at Ripon while Wilfrid was abbot, did extensive missionary work in Holland and Belgium. Among Willibrord's helpers was the Englishman Boniface of Crediton (680–754), whose later work in Germany (where he occasionally had disputes with wandering Irish bishops) marked him as one of the most important medieval missionaries. Among Boniface's many assistants from England was Willehad (c. 730–789), who eventually became bishop of Bremen.

BIBLIOGRAPHY: L. Gougard, *Christianity in Celtic Lands* (London, 1932); K. S. Latourette, *A History of the Expansion of Christianity,* Vol. 2 (New York, 1938).

**Cenobite** (from Latin *coenobium,* "cloister," from Greek word for "common life"). Member of a religious community as contrasted to an anchorite; used technically of those who live in isolated cells within the confines of a community and assemble occasionally for common meals and worship. In this sense, cenobitic life is associated with the desert communities of Pachomius, Peter Damian, the Camaldolese, and the Carthusians. The general sense, which means those who live in a communally oriented religious order, is more common currently.

**Center Party.** A Roman Catholic political party in the German Empire (1871–1918) and the Weimar Republic (1918–1933), and the principal force opposing the policy of Bismarck in the Kulturkampf. After 1918 the Center held the balance of power and it provided eight of the fourteen chancellors of the Republic before the appointment of Hitler on Jan. 30, 1933. It vigorously opposed the Communists. The Nazi-Vatican Concordat did not prevent the victorious National Socialist government from suppressing the party as soon as it could.

**Cerinthus.** Jewish-Christian Gnostic of the early 2d century. According to legend he was opposed by the apostle John (especially in I John); later Christian critics of the Apocalypse, however, ascribed it to Cerinthus. He seems to have combined Jewish millenarian ideas with incipient Gnostic beliefs; in his view, Jesus was the son of Joseph and Mary and at his baptism the Christ descended upon him. The supreme Father, according to Cerinthus, was unknown, while the God of the Old Testament was an angel.

**Cesarini, Julian** (1398–1444). Italian ecclesiastical diplomat. Cesarini presided over the Council of Basel, but in 1437 he withdrew his support when he judged that the Council was furthering the Schism. He also played a prominent role in the Council of Ferrara-Florence. Subsequently he was appointed legate to Hungary, to promote a crusade against the Turks and to break the truce between them and the king. This proved disastrous for the Christian army, and resulted in Cesarini's own death.

**Chaadaev, Pyotr Yakovlevich** (1794–1856). Russian religious philosopher. He expounded his basic ideas in eight "philosophical letters" of which only the first could be published during his lifetime. His primary intuition was that history involves the realization of the Kingdom of God in this world. He longed for the unity of mankind through cooperation with a "higher consciousness," a cooperation in which Russia was to lead the way.

**Chad** (Ceadda) (d. 672). English prelate. He was a Northumbrian of a family important in Anglo-Saxon church life. A disciple of Aidan, he followed his brother Cedd as abbot of Lastingham in 664; the same year he became bishop of York to replace the long-absent Wilfrid. When the validity of his consecration was questioned by Theodore of Tarsus, he went back to Lastingham, but in 669 he was made bishop of Mercia, choosing Lichfield as his see city.

**Chakko, Sarah** (1905–1954). Indian Christian leader and devout member of the Syrian Orthodox Church of Malabar. A champion of Christian higher education in India, she taught at and became principal (1943) of Isabella Thoburn College in Lucknow. She earned international recognition as a leader of the Student Christian Movement. A delegate to the First Assembly of the World Council of Churches, she became one of six presidents of the Council in 1951.

**Chalcedon.** The modern Kadiköy, a town on the Asiatic shore of the Bosphorus across from Istanbul (ancient Byzantium, Constantinople), first settled by Greek colonists in the 7th century B.C. The later settlers of Byzantium with its much better harbor are said to have been told by the Delphic oracle to "settle opposite the city of the blind." Chalcedon, however, survived as a city in the Roman province of Bithynia, and was the seat of a bishop from at least the 3d century A.D. Its principal church in the 5th century was the magnificent basilica of St. Euphemia, a local martyr of the persecution of Diocletian. City and church are remembered in church history mainly as the seat of the Fourth Ecumenical Council in 451.

The crisis of the Monophysite controversy began in 448 when Eutyches was condemned by the local synod at Constantinople under Patriarch Flavian for refusing to confess the existence of two natures in Christ "after the union" as well as before. He appealed to the major sees of Christendom, above all to Alexandria and Rome. Leo of Rome in his own Tome on the doctrine of the incarnation supported Flavian, but Dioscorus of Alexandria supported Eutyches, and the emperor Theodosius II summoned a General Council to hear his appeal. The result was the Robber Council (Latrocinium) of Ephesus in 449, dominated by Dioscorus. It rehabilitated Eutyches and deposed Flavian (who died as the result of rough treatment at his arrest), as well as Domnus of Antioch, and two prominent Antiochene supporters of the two-nature doctrine, Theodoret of Cyrrhus and Ibas of Edessa. A reaction was already gathering force when Theodosius died in 450 and was succeeded by his sister Pulcheria, who with her husband Marcian was disposed to favor the other side. Leo would have preferred simple acceptance of his Tome or a council in Italy, but he agreed to send legates to a council that was summoned to meet at Nicaea on Sept. 1, 451.

The bishops were already assembling when Marcian, wishing to attend but at the same time to remain close to the capital on account of the danger of Hunnish invasion, transferred the Council to Chalcedon. Here it held sixteen sessions between Oct. 8 and Nov. 1. Over five hundred bishops took part —or six hundred, including proxies—more than at any other ancient council. A commission of civil dignitaries presided at most of the meetings, but the leading part was taken by the ranking bishops, especially the papal legates and Anatolius of Constantinople.

The proceedings of the Council fall into three parts. At the lengthy opening session the minutes of the Latrocinium, incorporating those of the Council of 448, were read amid disorderly protests. The Robber Council was repudiated and the condemnation of Eutyches thus reinstated. Dioscorus' position was changed from member of the Council to defendant before it. At the Third Session on Oct. 13 he was deposed on charges of personal misconduct. Theodoret was allowed to take part, though as one of the accusers of Dioscorus rather than as a member. Juvenal of Jerusalem and others who had been leaders at Ephesus were tentatively excluded.

The Council, thus constituted, proceeded to prepare its statement of faith. The papal legates insisted on acceptance of the Tome of Leo, which to many Eastern bishops seemed to repudiate the teaching of Cyril of Alexandria on the unity of the person of Christ. It was finally agreed to accept the teaching of both fathers and to add a new formula as well. The final form was drafted by a committee during the Fifth Session on Oct. 22, immediately adopted by the Council, and solemnly promulgated in the presence of the imperial couple—the "new Constantine" and "new Helen"—at the Sixth Session on Oct. 25. The Chalcedonian Decree begins by endorsing a series of classic theological statements: the Nicene Creed, both in its original text and in the expanded form connected in some way with the Council of Constantinople of 381; the Tome of Leo; and two of Cyril's less intransigent statements—the Second Letter to Nestorius, and the Letter to John of Antioch of 433. The latter includes the Antiochene Formula of Union which is the basis of Chalcedon's own profession of faith in Christ as "truly God and truly man . . . acknowledged in two natures without confusion, without change, without division, without separation."

After this climax the Council turned to personal and disciplinary matters. Theodoret and Ibas were restored, the former only after some hesitation consenting to the anathema on his old friend Nestorius demanded by the Eastern bishops. Domnus, whose conduct at Ephesus had been ambiguous, was not restored but was allotted a pension. Juvenal accepted the decisions of the Council, and was conceded an independent patriarchate in Palestine. Of the seventeen Egyptian bishops present, thirteen declared that they could not act without a partiarch; but four subscribed to the decisions of Chalcedon and agreed to install at Alexandria a bishop loyal to them. The Council adopted twenty-eight canons, mainly dealing with problems revealed by the recent disorders of the Eastern Church. They regulate the conduct of bishops and clergy, and provide for episcopal control of monasteries and for appeals from the metropolitan of a province to higher authorities— the exarch of the civil "diocese" (group of provinces) or the bishop of Constantinople. Canon 1 confirms the canons of previous Councils; the whole collection is the basis of later Eastern and, as far as relevant, Western

canon law. Canon 28 was adopted by the bishops in the Fifteenth Session, on the afternoon of Oct. 31, in the absence of the lay presidents and the papal legates. It gives Constantinople a patriarchate extending over the civil dioceses of Pontus, Asia, and Thrace, within which its bishop would ordain the metropolitans of each province and the individual bishops in territories occupied by barbarians; it adds that since Constantinople was New Rome and the imperial city, its bishop should have the same rights as the bishop of Old Rome and rank second only to him. At the final session on Nov. 1 the papal legates protested against Canon 28. Leo continued the protest, but nevertheless the canon was acted on in the East, and is the formal basis of the position of the "Archbishop of Constantinople, New Rome, and Oecumenical Patriarch" in the Eastern Orthodox Church. Under very different circumstances, Leo's successor Innocent III did finally recognize the position of Constantinople as the second see of the church at the Fourth Lateran Council in 1215.

In February, 452, Marcian gave the Council's decisions the force of law in the Empire, and in 453, Leo formally confirmed its decree on the faith. In theology the Chalcedonian formula marks the completion of classical Christology—all the more, perhaps, because it does not profess to answer all the questions involved, but lays down general lines, largely in a negative manner. The later Ecumenical Councils may be considered as giving greater precision to the decisions of Chalcedon—in particular the Fifth, which condemns the Nestorian tendencies of the Three Chapters, and the Sixth, which defines against the Monotheletes the existence of two wills in Christ. However, before the Fifth Council met, the faith of the Four Councils had become the civil standard of orthodoxy in the Code of Justinian, from which it passed into the tradition of Roman law and so, incidentally, into the standards of the Church of England. Neither in theology nor in politics, however, did Chalcedon secure complete acceptance in the Eastern Church, and the protest against its decisions is the beginning of the separate history of the Monophysites.

BIBLIOGRAPHY: J. S. Macarthur, *Chalcedon* (New York, 1931); R. V. Sellers, *The Council of Chalcedon* (London, 1953); B. Skard, *The Incarnation* (Minneapolis, 1960).

**Chalmers, Thomas** (1780–1847). Scottish Free Church leader. Educated at the Universities of St. Andrews and Edinburgh, he was ordained in 1803. At the Tron Church and

St. John's, Glasgow, he successfully reorganized the parochial system to serve a huge industrial parish through visitation, education, and assistance and rehabilitation for the poor. After 1823 he taught at St. Andrews and Edinburgh, advocated church extension, and opposed patronage. He was a leader of the Free Church party in the Great Disruption (1843) and presided over its subsequent organization.

**Chancellor.** In the Roman Catholic Church the ecclesiastical official who is responsible for the care and preservation of all the official documents of a diocese. He is always a priest. In ancient Rome, chancellors were officials of the law courts. As the administration of the church became more complex, ecclesiastical organization tended to be patterned on the Roman civil administration. Thus the chancellor became a necessary part of the administration of every diocese. Since both the doctrine and discipline of the church are largely based in tradition, the keeping up of records is very important. It is the chancellor who guarantees the maintenance of continuity in the diocese as bishop replaces bishop. In large dioceses the chancellor may be the head of a department called the diocesan chancery, which handles correspondence and maintains the archives. Depending upon the discretion of the bishop, the chancellor may act as the bishop's private secretary or have other functions in the government of the diocese. In the Anglican Church, each diocese also has a chancellor, although his functions are somewhat different from those in the Roman Catholic Church.

**Channing, William Ellery** (1780–1842). American Unitarian minister. Born in Newport, R.I., he graduated from Harvard in 1798 and was elected a rector of Harvard in 1801. In 1803 he became the pastor of the Federal Street Congregational Church in Boston. He defended the liberal Congregationalists in 1815 when Jedidiah Morse accused them of covertly agreeing with the theological views of Thomas Belsham. Channing preached his most famous sermon, "Unitarian Christianity," in 1819 at Baltimore for the ordination of Jared Sparks. This sermon gave the liberal Congregationalists a clear platform around which to unite, and Channing was soon recognized as their leader. When the American Unitarian Association was organized in 1825, however, he declined the offer of the presidency. He and Theodore Parker were the dominant influences in shaping American Unitarianism. His leadership continued until his death on Oct. 2, 1842.

The basic intellectual influences in his development were derived from Francis Hutcheson, Adam Ferguson, Richard Price, and (on certain points) Samuel Hopkins. The influence of Locke is seen in Channing's emphasis on the rational character of revealed religion.

Channing was deeply convinced of the unique, infallible authority of Jesus and of the validity of miracles as "Christian evidences"; he distrusted the transcendentalists' reliance upon immediate intuition. The concepts of the unipersonality and the moral perfection of God were crucial for his theology. It has been argued that Channing advocated a doctrine of the essential sameness of divine and human attributes.

In Christology, Channing was an Arian. He rejected the doctrine of the incarnation on Scriptural and rational grounds. Yet he held that Christ had both freedom of the will and that moral perfection toward which all men should aspire. Channing believed that Christ's life demonstrated that the achievement of moral perfection is possible for other men.

***Chansons de Geste.*** Medieval epic poems in Old French, dealing chiefly with the legends of Charlemagne. They were feudal in tone and celebrated battles and other heroic themes. The earlier poems of the 12th century were given over more to military events, while those of the 13th century were influenced by chivalry. Of the more than eighty *chansons de geste* that are extant, the most famous is the *Chanson de Roland* (late 11th century), which recounts the victory of the Christians over the Saracens and the death of Charlemagne's paladin Roland.

**Chant.** A monophonic song with a rather free rhythm that depends upon the text. It seems to have been adopted into the early Christian liturgy from the practice of the Jewish synagogues. Hebrew music was of a simple, though expressive, type and was well adapted to the singing of Scriptural texts. Originally there was considerable local variation in the chant. As a result of a program of liturgical revision in the 6th and 7th centuries, however, it became somewhat standardized. Pope Gregory the Great (d. 604) was in large part responsible for the systematization and revision of traditional liturgical music; the chant in the West has since been known as Gregorian chant.

Although all chants have much in common in that they are unaccompanied, nonharmonic, and flexible in rhythm, there are certain differences. There are three major types: syllabic, in which each syllable of the text has a separate note; melismatic, in which several notes correspond to each syllable; and neumatic, which is a mixture of syllabic and melismatic. Chants may be sung by one choir or antiphonally, that is, alternately by two choirs.

**Chantry.** The endowed chapel and priest established for the saying of Masses for the soul of the benefactor and his family. The chantry chapels were attached to churches, built close to cemeteries, or were special side altars in parish churches. The chantry priest might serve as a teacher, chaplain, or curate, but never as a parish rector. It is estimated that at the time of the suppression of chantries in England in 1547, there were 2,374 chantry endowments.

**Chaplains in U.S. Armed Forces.** With British precedents and chaplains in colonial militias, the Army chaplaincy was established in 1776 and the Navy in 1794. The first Army chaplain was John Hurt, and in the Navy, Benjamin Balch. The calling of chaplains was first unregulated. Many were unordained and uncommissioned. They also acted as secretaries, recreation directors, schoolmasters, and librarians. Worship was held at least weekly, and daily on ships. Most chaplains were Episcopalian, and the Book of Common Prayer was widely used. West Point received its first chaplain in 1818, whereas in the Navy, chaplains supervised the training of junior officers until the founding of Annapolis in 1845. The military chaplainship survived attempts to abolish it, but was limited in numbers, with no more than 24 in the Navy until 1914. After 1841 Navy chaplains had to be ordained (Army, 1862). The chaplaincy was securely established during the Civil War, with higher pay, officer status, uniforms, and formal regulations. Close cooperation with the major denominations and with the Federal Council of Churches followed. There were Roman Catholic chaplains after 1824 and Jewish chaplains after 1917. By 1860 each chaplain was permitted to conduct services according to his own denomination. The Navy Chief of Chaplains was established in 1917 and the Army Chief of Chaplains in 1920.

**Chapman, John Wilbur** (1859–1918). Presbyterian clergyman. He followed Reuben A. Torrey and preceded Billy Sunday as the most popular revivalist in the United States. A graduate of Lake Forest University and Lane Theological Seminary, he served as pastor of several churches, including the Bethany Presbyterian Church in Philadelphia and the Fourth Avenue Presbyterian Church in New York City, and was moderator of the Presbyterian General Assembly in 1917–1918.

**Chappot de Neuville, Hélène de** (*known as* Marie de la Passion) (1839–1904). French founder of a Catholic missionary order of religious women. Trained as a nun, she served in India before organizing (1877) the Institute of the Missionaries of Mary. In 1885 she affiliated her order with the Franciscans. At her death there were one hundred houses and three thousand women on four continents in her order.

**Chapter** (Monastic). The name for the assembled monks of a monastery, deriving from the custom of assembling to hear a chapter of the rule read each day. The chapter elects the abbot, carries on the business of the house, and has certain legislative rights. In some monastic orders the entire order is governed by a chapter of abbots and other representatives of the daughter monasteries.

**Chapter** (Religious Order). With the Constitutions of the Dominican Order, the chapter took on different characteristics from the monastic chapter. In the Cistercian Order, the priors of the houses met to conduct the business of the order. The canons of Prémontré adapted this idea, but the abbot of the motherhouse retained certain powers over the whole order. Visitors were appointed by the chapter to supervise houses in a specific geographical area. These ideas were adopted by Dominic for his order. Each religious house, the priory, had a chapter that elected its prior, who with an elected delegate met in the provincial chapter. The provincial chapter elected a provincial prior, who with an elected *diffinitor* was a member of the general chapter which elected the master general. Meeting on a three-year cycle, the general chapter consisted solely of the provincial *diffinitores* for two years and in the third solely of the provincial priors. Legislation for the order had to pass three consecutive meetings of the general chapter. An extraordinary meeting of *diffinitores* and priors (*capitulum generalissimum*) could in one meeting pass legislation. Between meetings of the chapters, the priors and the master general had complete power to act, although final authority always remained with the chapters. This plan was modified for use by other religious orders.

**Chardon, Louis** (c. 1596–1651). French Dominican. Born at Clermont-de-l'Oise, France, he was baptized John but was given the name Louis when he received the Dominican habit in Paris in 1610. Primarily a spiritual adviser, he was Master of Novices there until 1632. After a time spent preaching in Toulouse he returned to Paris in 1645, where, until his death of the plague in 1651, he devoted himself to pastoral duties and to writing. Best known of his seven books is *The Cross of Jesus,* which reflects the influence of Tauler as well as of Thomas Aquinas.

**Charity, Daughters** (Sisters) **of.** See VINCENT DE PAUL.

**Charlemagne** (Charles the Great) (742–814). King of the Franks and emperor of the West. Charles was the elder son of Pepin III, king of the Franks, and Bertrada, but nothing is known of his early life, except that he and his brother Carloman were anointed in 754 by Pope Stephen III, who had come to France to crown Pepin. In 768, Pepin divided the Frankish kingdom between Charles and Carloman. Shortly thereafter, Pepin died and the nobles elected each son to the kingship of that portion which he had received from Pepin. Relations between the brothers were strained. In 769, Carloman refused to aid Charles in his military campaign in Aquitaine. In 771, Carloman died and Charles became sole ruler of the Franks. Carloman's widow and sons fled to Lombardy and sought refuge with King Desiderius. Desiderius tried to enlist papal support for Carloman's family against Charles. The refusal of Pope Hadrian I brought an attack by the Lombards. The pope appealed to Charles for assistance. Charles attempted to pacify the Lombard king, since he was then engaged in his first campaign against the Saxons. When the Lombards continued their pressure upon the pope, Charles led an expedition into Italy in 773, the following year capturing Pavia, the Lombard capital, and forcing Desiderius to enter a monastery. Charles assumed the title of king of the Lombards. A revolution led by Desiderius' son was put down in 776. Charles then turned his attention again to the Saxon war, which had been carried on since the days of Charles Martel. Charles had first gone to battle with the Saxons in 772 and he fought intermittently with them until 804. The Saxons were eventually converted to Christianity and incorporated into the Frankish empire. In 778, Charles attempted to make inroads into Moslem Spain during some dissension among the Moslem forces. The expedition was a failure and the retreating army was ambushed by Basques and destroyed. Although only a minor defeat, this incident was the basis for a later romance named for a Frankish official, Hruotland (Roland), killed in the battle (see CHANSONS DE GESTE).

By 800, Charles had conquered the Avars, Pannonia, Brittany, northern Spain, and Bavaria. In the autumn of 800, he returned to Italy at the request of Pope Leo III, who the previous year had been attacked and beaten by some of the Roman nobility. Charles presided over a hearing at which charges against the pope were presented. Leo was exonerated and his enemies banished. Charles remained in Rome and on Christmas Day was crowned emperor by the pope in St. Peter's. Some contemporaries held that since Irene had usurped the throne of the Eastern Roman Empire, there was no legitimate emperor but Charles. However, Charles at times seemed reluctant to claim the title for fear of offending the Greeks. He was recognized as an emperor by Michael I in 812. He was on friendly relations with King Offa of Mercia and Haroun-al-Rashid, caliph of Baghdad, who once sent Charles a goodwill gift of an elephant.

Charles continued the ecclesiastical policies of his father. He remained the protector of the popes and their domains, the patron of reformers and missionaries, and the guardian of orthodoxy. The palace school at Aachen became the center for the Carolingian revival of learning. At this school were trained the civil and ecclesiastical officials upon whom the administration of the Empire depended. Under the direction of Charles, synods were held that reformed the morals and education of the clergy, standardized the liturgy, and combated heresy. The head of his palace school, Alcuin, was presumed to be the author of tracts attacking Adoptianism and the adoration of images. Charles established many monasteries and churches, the greatest being the court chapel at Aachen, which was modeled after S. Vitale in Ravenna.

Charlemagne was troubled in his later years by the jealousies and intrigues of his many children, wives, and concubines. His eldest son was implicated in an unsuccessful rebellion in 792. His daughters, whom he wished to keep close to him at Aachen, were of dubious virtue. His sons, whom he had trained to succeed him, died before him. He left the Empire to his sole surviving legitimate son, Louis, who became emperor after his father's death in 814. Charles's successors were unable to withstand the challenges of the nobility, the Normans, and their own families. Within a century, the Empire had disintegrated. Charles's success was due to a system of personal loyalties and overwhelming military strength. When his successors could no longer command the loyalty of the nobility and lost their military superiority, the Empire was dissolved.

BIBLIOGRAPHY: H. W. C. Davis, *Charlemagne* (New York, 1900); A. C. Grant (ed. and tr.), *Early Lives of Charlemagne* (London, 1926); T. Hodgkin, *Charles the Great* (New York, 1897); J. I. Mombert, *A History of Charles the Great* (London, 1888); C. E. Russell, *Charlemagne, First of the Moderns* (Boston, 1930).

**Charles I** (1600–1649). King from 1625 of Great Britain and Ireland, son of James I (Stuart, James VI of Scotland). After negotiations to marry the Spanish Infanta Maria had failed (1623), he married the French Henrietta Maria in 1625, promising on his accession to relax the recusancy laws. In order to repress a resurgent Puritanism he dissolved three successive Parliaments (1625–1629) while advancing High Churchmen to important posts in church and state, e.g., Laud, who furthered ecclesiastical uniformity even in indifferent matters, to Canterbury. Opposed to lay participation in ecclesiastical decisions, Charles permitted Laud to use the Star Chamber against the Puritans. In his relations with Scotland, the pressure toward uniformity in the imposed Prayer Book of 1637 and the oppressive English rule of the Scottish Church led to the National Covenant a year later which made Scotland Presbyterian. Presbyterian and anti-Royalist parliamentary forces united from 1640 to overthrow the king and the Church of England by 1646. Unable to coordinate resistance, the king surrendered to the Scots (1646), was seized by order of Oliver Cromwell and executed as a tyrant (Jan. 30, 1649). His exemplary behavior in death and the publication after his death of *Eikōn Basilikē* ("The Royal Image"), purporting to be the king's autobiography, aided recognition of him as a martyr for both church and royalism.

**Charles II** (1630–1685). King of Great Britain and Ireland, in exile from 1649, restored in 1660. The son of Charles I, proclaimed king in Scotland (1649), he accepted the National Covenant but was defeated in his attempt to overcome Oliver Cromwell (1651) and fled to the Continent. When conditions favored his restoration (1660), he issued the Declaration of Breda and returned as constitutional monarch. In 1662, by the Act of Uniformity, the Church of England was restored by a strongly Royalist and Anglican Parliament which, by a series of acts imprecisely called the Clarendon Code, proceeded to suppress nonconformity and dissent. Charles's attempts to remove the pressures from both nonconformist Puritans and recusant Roman Catholics (Declarations of Indulgence, 1662 and 1672) were rejected by Parliament. When Clarendon fell from favor (1667), the Cabal became the king's advisers, but the Test Act (1673) terminated their ascendancy and forced Roman Catholics such

as Clifford out of public office. The anti-Roman atmosphere favored Oates's accusations of a "popish plot," and Charles acquiesced in the execution of some thirty-five Roman Catholics (1678–1681). A parliamentary attempt to impeach Danby, one of the king's chief ministers, and exclude Charles's Roman Catholic brother James from the throne led to dissolution of Parliament for the rest of his reign (1681–1685). Charles's only children were the illegitimate ones produced by several extramarital alliances. In his last illness (Feb. 2–6, 1685) he became a Roman Catholic.

**Charles V** (1500–1558). Holy Roman Emperor (1519–1556), ruler of Hapsburg Spanish and Austrian territories. Religious unity was Charles's first concern at the Diet of Worms (1521) and at first he dealt more gently with Luther than his Roman Catholic advisers asked. He remained tolerant at the 1526 Diet of Speyer, letting the princes settle religious affairs in their own domains. An alliance against him headed by the pope forced him to an invasion of Italy in 1527 that ended in the sack of Rome, but he returned his territorial gains when promised a general council. After victory in France in 1529, he nullified the 1526 toleration at the 1529 Diet of Speyer. At the Diet of Augsburg in 1530 the German princes firmly confessed their new-found faith. Charles sensed danger in arousing them, as the Smalcald League, formed in 1531, confirmed. The Peace of Nuremberg (1532) restored the toleration of 1526. During the next nine years in Spain, Charles tried for a general council, which Pope Paul III finally promised him. When the Smalcald allies refused to take part, he defeated them in war (1547) and through the Augsburg and Leipzig Interims attempted a gradual Roman Catholic restoration. However, his troubles with Saxony, France, and with the pope discouraged him and he gave an amnesty to Lutherans at Passau in 1552, allowing his brother to conclude the Peace of Augsburg in 1555, which granted equality to Roman Catholic and Protestant princes. Charles abdicated in 1556 in favor of his brother Ferdinand, retiring to a Spanish monastery.

**Charles Martel** (c. 690–741). Illegitimate son of Pepin II of Herstal, mayor of the palace for Neustria and Austrasia. Upon his father's death in 714, he was imprisoned by his father's widow, who claimed the government for her own sons. During the ensuing anarchy, Charles escaped from prison and engaged the Neustrians in battle, defeating them in 717. He succeeded in overthrowing his half brothers and their mother, becoming mayor in

Austrasia. After 719, he was the effective ruler of the entire Frankish realm, although the Merovingian Clotaire IV was nominally king. He annexed Burgundy and formed an alliance with Aquitaine. In 732 he defeated the Saracens near Tours. Although he provided protection and aid to missionaries, his policies were not generally favorable to the church. He disposed of church lands and offices as was militarily or politically expedient. During his reign the papacy first turned to the Franks for aid against the Lombards. Although Charles refused to extend military assistance to Pope Gregory II, the papacy continued to look to the Franks for support. He never became king in name, although he ruled as one. He divided the kingdom, just as the king would have, between his two sons Carloman and Pepin, who did later take the royal title. Charles was buried at St.-Denis.

**Charles of Anjou** (1226–1285). Count of Anjou and Provence, king of Two Sicilies. The brother of King Louis IX of France, Charles longed to win a kingdom for himself. Answering the appeals of Pope Urban IV in 1266, Charles defeated and killed the Hohenstaufen Manfred of Sicily. Charles was then proclaimed king of Sicily. Two years later he defeated the last of the Hohenstaufen, Conradin, the grandson of Frederick II. With papal sanction, Charles beheaded the boy in the public square of Naples. Driven by ambition, Charles dreamed of conquering Byzantium. Throughout his reign he sought to form anti-Byzantine alliances and to gain papal approval for an expedition against Constantinople. To check Charles's schemes the Byzantine emperor Michael VIII Palaeologus formed an alliance with the king of Aragon (who had claims to Sicily through his wife) and subsidized malcontents within Sicily. Michael's most potent weapon, however, was his offer to unite the Greek Church with Rome, a ploy he used to gain the support of the papacy. At last Charles secured the election as pope of his own tool, Martin IV, who excommunicated Michael and proclaimed a crusade against Byzantium. As Charles was gathering his forces, however, a revolt, the Sicilian Vespers, broke out in 1282 in Sicily. Subsidized by Byzantine gold and aided by Peter III of Aragon, the Sicilians completely wrecked Angevin power in Sicily.

**Charron, Pierre** (1541–1603). Roman Catholic priest, humanist educator, and one of the best-known preachers and writers of his time. Trained primarily in law, Charron was put in charge in 1576 of all the schools in Bordeaux, where he worked in support of the reforms of the Council of Trent and preached at the court of Henry of Navarre. His first published work was in large part a proof of the purity of the Roman Church as the true representative of Christian religion, but he is better known for a work on natural wisdom (1601) in which he tried to find a basis in reason for agreement between Roman Catholics and Protestants. Wisdom, according to Charron, begins in the kind of self-knowledge that leads to a skepticism about man's ability to reach any firm natural knowledge; only in this way can man be open to the truth that is given by God in grace. Though this treatise was obviously intended to be a defense of orthodoxy, it was often associated with the more complete skepticism of Charron's friend Montaigne and was condemned for this reason by many later scholars.

**Charta Caritatis.** The instrument defining the elementary rules among the houses of the Cistercian Order. Stephen Harding, third abbot, formed this primitive redaction before 1119. The Rule of St. Benedict was to be observed in all houses as it was observed at Cîteaux. No house was to be established without the consent of the local ordinary. Charity was to be the sole bond among the houses and no relation was to be established through taxation. Two major innovations were the institution of the annual visitation of the daughter houses by the abbot of the parent house, and the convocation of the annual general chapter of abbots to consider community affairs. In the chapter, each abbot was equal, the abbot of Cîteaux being *primus inter pares*. The Charter also provided for the removal of unworthy abbots through the action of some abbots and the local ordinary. A second version of the Charter appeared sometime before 1152; it reflects the growth of the order. It included legislation giving more importance to the daughter houses of Cîteaux, provided exemption from the general chapter because of the inconveniences caused by travel from distant places, and established a committee system for considering abuses prior to the chapter. It eliminated the role of the bishops in deposing abbots and forbade papal exemptions. The Charter introduced the principle of filiation through the annual visitation, and federation through the general chapter.

**Charterhouse.** The name, derived from the French, *maison chartreuse*, commonly used in England for a house of Carthusian monks.

**Chartism.** An English working-class movement for political reform popular during the 1830's and 1840's. It focused on demands for adult male suffrage, secret ballot, equal districts, annual parliaments, removal of property qualifications, and salaries for members of Parliament. Agitation for parliamentary approval of a People's Charter reached a climax in 1848 and then quickly declined. Though opposed by most churchmen, the movement made some contribution to the Christian Socialist awakening.

**Chartres Cathedral.** Built in its present form almost entirely between 1194, when fire destroyed the old cathedral, and 1260. Only the St. Piat Chapel (14th century), the Vendôme Chapel (15th), the north spire (16th) and the clock pavilion were added later. Its 170 windows contain the finest stained glass in Europe, mostly 13th century and having almost 10,000 separate images. Its sculpture is nearly as remarkable as its glass. Dedicated to the Virgin Mary, the cathedral was the object of pilgrimages, but the holiness of the site precluded any burials there.

**Chartres, Cathedral School of.** In the period immediately preceding the rise of the universities, there were a number of schools attached to cathedrals in France. The most famous of these was at Chartres. Its chief teachers were Bernard of Chartres (d. c. 1130); Gilbert de La Porrée (1076–1154); and Thierry of Chartres, younger brother of Bernard. John of Salisbury probably studied at the school and was in any case bishop of Chartres for the last four years of his life (d. 1180).

The chief characteristic of the school was its Platonism and its belief in essences, plus a determination to enlist all knowledge in the service of Christianity and to express it in harmonious literary form. Thus astronomy, mathematics, and medicine were studied in some depth, and Thierry even used mathematical images to explain the Trinity and incarnation. William of Conches (1080–1154), a student of Bernard's, wrote commentaries on Priscian, Macrobius, Boethius, and aspects of Plato's *Timaeus*. While generally Platonist in approach, the teachers at Chartres did not ignore the philosophy of Aristotle, and Thierry tried to explain creation in terms of Aristotle's four causes. However, their overarching Platonism and their concept of God as the Form of all things did on occasion bring them close to pantheism. The school declined with the rise of such exciting teachers as Abelard in Paris, fifty miles away, and the development of the new university there.

**Chase, Philander** (1775–1852). Episcopal bishop. Originally a Congregationalist, he was educated at Dartmouth and ordained as an Episcopal priest in 1798. He served in New York State, New Orleans, and Connecticut. His most important work was that of first bishop of Ohio and later of Illinois, founding a new college in each state, Kenyon and Jubilee, respectively.

**Chateaubriand, Vicomte François René de** (1768–1848). French writer and political figure. After a youth in which he was exposed to the currents of French thought that were surging toward the Revolution, Chateaubriand, appalled by the excesses of that great movement, became a political "reactionary" and a literary romantic. He returned to the Roman Catholic faith of his childhood, a decision made as the result of the death of his mother in 1798. In 1791 he took a ship for the United States, where the omnipresence of nature in an untamed state deeply impressed him. He returned to France to fight in the army of Condé, and from 1793 to 1800 lived in exile in England. Upon his return to France in the latter year, he published the lengthy (five volumes) *Génie du christianisme* (1802), upon which much of his subsequent reputation was to rest. This work was a romantic apology for Christianity on aesthetic grounds, i.e., that it satisfied the deepest needs of man. *Génie* brought Chateaubriand to the attention of the emperor, and made him the best-known literary figure in France. He held several diplomatic posts under Napoleon and the restored Bourbons. The posthumously published *Mémoires d'outre-tombe* (twelve volumes) confirmed his literary position.

**Chaucer, Geoffrey** (1343–1400). Author of the *Canterbury Tales,* soldier, and diplomat. Chaucer reflects in himself and in his poetry the life and temper of the London of his day. He combined a love of the classics with a shrewd but kindly observation of nature and human nature. His tales criticize ecclesiastical abuses, but also commend sincere clerical dedication. His work was influenced by Boccaccio and Petrarch, who he may have met during a diplomatic mission to Italy.

**Chauncy, Charles** (c. 1589–1672). Colonial clergyman and second president of Harvard. Cambridge educated, he served parishes in England between 1626 and 1637, when he came to New England because of continued ridicule for his nonconformist beliefs. In America he again met opposition and after a twelve-year ministry was about to return to England when he was offered the presidency of Harvard. He held this office from 1654 to 1672.

**Chauncy, Charles** (1705–1787). American clergyman, great-grandson of the second President of Harvard. Ordained minister of First Church in Boston in 1727, Chauncy was its pastor for sixty years and the most influential Boston clergyman of his time. He became involved in three controversies: (1) Chauncy had no sympathy with the widespread revival known as the Great Awakening, and clashed with its chief apologist, Jonathan Edwards, over the subject of the role of emotions in religion. He defended "reasonable religion" in *Seasonable Thoughts on the State of Religion in New England* (1743). (2) Against Anglican claims of establishment in Massachusetts, Chauncy rejected episcopacy as the only divinely instituted form of polity, publishing the *Complete View of Episcopacy* (1771). (3) Critical of the trend of Edwardsian theology after the revival, Chauncy championed a liberal theology which he felt was more consistent with Puritan tradition. His views were published in *Salvation for All Men* (1782) and *Five Dissertations on the Fall and Its Consequences* (1785).

**Chautauqua Movement.** A post-Civil War movement designed to promote adult education for Christian leadership, named for its base of operations at Lake Chautauqua, N.Y. At first it provided a brief summer assembly for training Sunday school teachers. The program was soon extended and expanded to include lectures and courses on a variety of religious and cultural subjects. Finally it became a lyceum bureau promoting traveling lecturers.

**Chemnitz, Martin** (1522–1586). German theologian influenced by Melanchthon. He was ordained in 1554 as coadjutor to the superintendent at Brunswick and later himself became superintendent (1567–1584). A moderate in the adiaphoristic and Osiandristic controversies, he opposed crypto-Calvinism. An able author, his best-known works were on the Jesuits and the Council of Trent (*Examen concilii Tridentini*, 1565–1573). With Johann Andreae he also wrote the Formula of Concord and won its adoption (1577) to end controversies and theological deviation.

**Cheng Ching-Yi** (1881–1940). Prominent Manchu Protestant leader in China. The son of a pastor long connected with the London Missionary Society, he was extremely active in numerous Protestant organizations both in Europe and in China. He held important offices in the International Missionary Council, the National Christian Conference in Shanghai in 1922, and the National Christian Council. His most important contribution to Chinese Protestantism came in 1934 when he resigned the secretaryship of the latter organization to become the head of the Church of Christ in China.

**Chernyshevsky, Nicolai Gavrilovich** (1828–1889). Russian writer and politician. The son of a priest, he turned after the events of 1848 toward atheism, becoming a champion of the radical social reform known as Nihilism. He was influenced by Louis Blanc, Saint-Simon, Proudhon, Fourier, Robert Owen, and Feuerbach, and was praised by Lenin as "a guiding star leading toward Marxism." He held that all social ills were due to poverty, writing while imprisoned a classic of the Russian revolutionary movement, *What Is to Be Done?* (1863). He was exiled (1864) to Siberia for twenty-four years.

**Chevet.** The eastern extremity of a basilica, that portion which lies to the east of the nave. It thus includes the whole eastern end of the church.

**Chiang Kai-shek** (1887–    ). President of the Republic of China, Methodist layman. Born in Chikow, Chekiang, educated at Paoting Military Academy and Tokyo Military Staff College, he participated in the Revolution of 1911 and became closely attached to Sun Yat-sen. The year 1927 saw the marriage of Chiang Kai-shek to the daughter of a Methodist minister. His own baptism followed in 1930, influencing the growing significance of the Christian church in China. Commander of the Kuomintang army, he united the country in 1928. After weathering the Japanese war (1937–1945), he lost the mainland to the Communists in 1950 and transferred the government to Taiwan.

**Children's Crusade.** An expedition formed by the preaching of a twelve-year-old French shepherd boy, Stephen of Cloyes. At Vendôme possibly thirty thousand children, some of noble birth as well as great numbers of peasants, gathered to begin a march to the Holy Land. Many died on the difficult foot journey to Marseilles and others lost faith when the sea did not part for them as expected. Two merchants, Hugh the Iron and William the Pig, provided seven ships for them without charge. Two of the ships were wrecked, but the other ships reached Algiers, where the merchants had arranged to sell the children into slavery. Many were sent to slave markets in Egypt and Baghdad. It was said only one ever returned, a young priest who arrived in France in 1230. In the Rhineland a similar movement was begun by a youth named Nicholas of Cologne. His company, perhaps of twenty thousand, was slightly older and contained more girls and more disreputable elements. Less than a third reached Italy. When the sea did not part at Genoa or Pisa, many turned back, others stayed in Italy; a few found passage to Palestine. After reaching Rome, Nicholas' party was persuaded by the pope to return home. Few ever made their way to Germany. A second German party had no more success; a few embarked from Brindisi, but their fate is unknown.

BIBLIOGRAPHY: S. Runciman, *A History of the Crusades,* Vol. III (Cambridge, 1954); G. Z. Gray, *The Children's Crusade* (New York, 1898).

**Chillingworth, William** (1602–1644). Anglican divine. Educated at Oxford, Chillingworth delighted in disputes and entered a debate with the Jesuit John Fisher, who brought Chillingworth to doubt the truth of Protestantism. Attracted by the Roman Church's claim to infallibility, he was converted and went to Douai, where he was asked to write a polemical treatise on his change. Reviewing the arguments once more, he came to feel that the Roman Catholic claims to infallibility were after all unsound, so he retraced his steps back to Protestantism in 1634. As a result of a controversy with another Jesuit, Edward Knott, Chillingworth issued his most famous book, *The Religion of Protestants a Safe Way to Salvation* (1637), in which he inferred toleration and free inquiry from the principle that "the Bible only is the religion of Protestants." The points necessary to be believed are few and are clear from the Scripture—the existence of God, the atonement and the resurrection of Christ, the indwelling Holy Spirit, the universal church, and the revelation of God through Scripture. All else could be left to the individual Christian. Though errors would occur, such honest errors would not exclude men from God's grace. His thought was fundamental for later latitudinarian Anglicanism. During the Civil War he fought with Charles, was captured while ill, and died soon after.

**China, Church of Christ in** (Chung Hua Chi Tuh Chia Hui). Although the Church of Christ in China was organized in 1927, much prehistory led to this event. In 1901 the Presbyterian mission formed its Federal Council of the Presbyterian Church in China. It was from this that the various Presbyterian missions were led (1918) to merge into the Presbyterian Church in China. While the Presbyterian Church was prominent in the subsequent development, many elements were involved in the merger of 1927, the most comprehensive union achieved in the world to that date, exceeding in this respect the three other great Asiatic unions of the period (Japan, North India, and South India). The union that formed the Church of Christ in China embraced, in addition to Presbyterians, Congregationalists, Baptists, Methodists, and Lutherans. Later, other groups joined, including two churches affiliated with the China Inland Mission, and by 1950 some sixteen former missionary churches were in the Church of Christ in China.

Chiang Kai-shek's marriage in 1927 to the daughter of a Methodist minister was followed in 1930 by his own baptism, which was influential in the developing importance of the Christian church in China.

The doctrinal basis of the united Church of Christ in China recognized by its officers were three points: (1) faith in Jesus Christ as Redeemer and Lord, with an earnest commitment to spread his Kingdom; (2) acceptance of the Bible as God's Word and the supreme authority in faith and practice; (3) acknowledgment of the Apostles' Creed as the expression of evangelical faith. Church order resembled the Presbyterian, with equal lay representation in the ecclesiastical courts.

The history of the Church of Christ in China has been a steady "advance through storm"—or storms: the Japanese invasion, World War II, and the Communist take-over. The "advance" has not always been necessarily in numbers. In fact no satisfactory information is presently available on the life and statistics of the church.

A missionary spirit has characterized this church born of the missionary movement. For example, it began its successful work among three border tribes, the Chiang, Hsifan, and Lolos, in 1940, engaging as well in activities farther from home.

Not only has the Church of Christ in China suffered the tribulations and martyrdoms of the mid-century, but this has been done in such a way as to impress the Chinese nation. It is apparently still doing so under the Communist oppression according to visitors who are permitted to attend its services and converse with its leaders. Theological education continues, with one report claiming some eighty-five select students (see *The International Review of Missions,* "World Survey," Vol. LV [Jan., 1966]).

BIBLIOGRAPHY: A. J. Brown, *One Hundred Years* (New York, 1936); K. S. Latourette, *History of Christian Missions in China* (New York, 1929).

**China, National Christian Council of.** A council founded at the National Christian Conference, May, 1922, at Shanghai, called by the China Continuation Committee (founded 1913), of which it was the successor. Secretaries Ch'eng Ching-i and Edward C. Lobenstine provided continuity from the old agency to the new. The Council represented all major Protestant churches except the Southern Baptists, but soon the China Inland Mission and other conservative bodies withdrew, drawing off other fundamentalist and nondenominational elements. Nevertheless, it steadily gained stature as an effective ecumenical service agency and as a symbol of Christian unity. Its able staff and vigorous service departments were housed in its own building in the International Settlement in Shanghai. The largest part of the budget was always met by contributions from North America and Great Britain. During World War II it raised large sums to support "orphaned" European missions and was the relief agent of the International Missionary Council. The National Christian Council of China was an active member of the International Missionary Council, and Chinese leadership in international conferences and committees was outstanding from 1938 to 1950. When the Communist Government took over in 1950, it initiated "The Three-Self Movement" as the coordinating organ of the churches, and this displaced the National Christian Council of China, which was never formally disbanded but disappeared.

**China Inland Mission.** The London Missionary Society (founded 1794) in 1853 sent to China the physician James Hudson Taylor. Twelve years later Taylor established the China Inland Mission on the principles to which it still adheres.

Although nondenominational in character, it insists strongly on traditional, fundamental beliefs. Among these beliefs is a stress on the plenary inspiration of the Bible; also, the imminent visible return of Jesus Christ is central to its witness. The China Inland Mission hopes to hasten the return by speeding the preaching of the gospel in every part of the world (Matt. 24:14). Consequently, it places major importance on evangelistic witness and becomes somewhat reluctantly involved in the establishment of medical centers and schools. Another persistent principle of the movement is the "faith-mission" doctrine. Its missionaries must go out without assurance of financial support. At one time it had thirteen hundred missionaries on the field with no deficit in ninety years of faith-mission operation. There

is no doubt that some of its worldwide support comes from non-faith-mission denominations.

Its Far Eastern base was maintained in Shanghai until the Communist take-over of 1950 necessitated the move to Singapore. After this expulsion from China, the mission took up work in Japan, the Philippines, Vietnam, Malaysia, Thailand, and Taiwan, where it works especially among the Chinese.

**Chinese Rites Controversy.** A debate originating in the work of the Jesuit missionary Matteo Ricci (1552–1610). Under his leadership the Jesuits held that rites honoring Confucius and ancestors were essentially nonreligious and could be observed by Christians; that the adoption of European church practices and doctrines by converts could be gradual; and that the word "God" could be translated using Chinese philosophical terms. Accused of "compromising the faith" by rival mission orders, the Jesuits received from Rome in 1645 an injunction against these practices at the request of the Spanish Dominican Juan de Morales. Upon appeal the order was rescinded, but in 1704, Pope Clement XI approved another restrictive statement and sent his legate Charles de Tournon to China. Tournon offended Emperor K'ang Hsi, who favored missionaries following Ricci's ideas, and the legate threatened to excommunicate all who did. The issue was unsettled until 1715 when Clement issued the bull *Ex illa die,* which ruled against the Jesuits. The legate Jean Mezzabarba went to China but allowed eight exceptions to the bull with regard to the rites, and the situation remained ambiguous. In 1742, Pope Benedict XIV issued the bull *Ex quo singulari,* which confirmed *Ex illa die,* annulled the legate's exceptions, and demanded a loyalty oath from all missionaries in China, officially ending the debate.

**Chiniquy, Charles Paschal Telesphore** (1809–1899). A controversial convert to Protestantism from Roman Catholicism. Born at Kamouraska, Lower Canada, he was educated at the Quebec Seminary and ordained by the Roman Catholic Church in 1833. He led a French colony from Quebec to Illinois and became a minister of the Presbyterian Church in 1858. In 1877 he joined the Presbyterian mission to the French at Montreal. He married Euphémie Allard, of St. Anne, Kankakee County, Ill., in 1864. He was the author of many anti-Catholic tracts, several of which were translated into a number of languages and reached many editions.

**Choir.** That part of the church, usually in the east end, containing the chairs or stalls of the clergy. The choir was also used by the body of singers (*schola cantorum*) which became known itself as the choir. The term also refers to those members of religious communities whose primary responsibility is to attend all the liturgical offices of the community.

**Chorepiscopus.** The title of a bishop whose jurisdiction was limited to a rural district and who was theoretically subject to the local urban bishop. These bishops were common in the East and in the missionary areas of Germany in the 8th and 9th centuries. Their jurisdictional power was gradually assumed by the archdeacons, and by the 12th century they had disappeared. In the East, they continued until the 13th century.

**Chown, Samuel Dwight** (1853–1933). Canadian churchman. He was born in Kingston, Ontario, and educated at the Kingston grammar school and Victoria University (D.D., 1898) and ordained in 1879. He married Susie E. Hammond in 1879. He was field secretary, Brockville District, 1888–1889; financial secretary, Perth District, 1891–1892; chairman, Toronto West District, 1897–1899; and chairman, Toronto Central District, 1900–1902. From 1902 to 1910 he was secretary of the Temperance, Prohibition, and Moral Reform Committee of the Methodist Church, and from 1914 to 1925 was general superintendent of The Methodist Church, in which capacity he made a significant contribution to the formation of the United Church of Canada.

**Chrétien de Troyes** (12th century). One of the class of medieval French poets called trouvères. Little is known of his life except what can be drawn from his poetry. He was among the first writers of the chivalric romance, a form of literature drawing upon the traditions of knighthood and courtly love. The material of these romances came chiefly from Celtic sources, but use was also made of Roman and French legends. The most famous work of Chrétien de Troyes is *Perceval le Gallois,* which introduces the earliest known account of the legend of the Grail.

**Christian III** (1503–1559). King of Denmark and Norway from 1536. Christian was a convinced Lutheran who had witnessed Luther's stand at the Diet of Worms. In 1526 while duke of Schleswig, he set up a Lutheran seminary at Haderslev. Upon becoming king he immediately introduced the Lutheran Reformation by royal decree. In 1537 he invited Bugenhagen to reform the church, ordain seven Lutheran superintendents, and crown him and the queen.

**Christian and Missionary Alliance, The.** A perfectionist denomination that arose at the time of the Holiness movement in the 1880's, having its origin in the revivalistic work of A. B. Simpson among the unchurched masses of New York. Originally the group was no more than a mission society to propagate the main tenets of Simpson's theology, which espoused the customary fundamentalist positions, but which he articulated in the formula of the fourfold gospel: Christ the Savior, the Sanctifier, the Healer, and the Coming King. Preferring not to be known as a denomination, it was at first divided into two societies: the Christian Alliance for American missions, and the International Missionary Alliance for world missions. In 1897, however, the societies were merged into the present denominational organization. It is entirely independent of all other bodies, but is in fellowship with all who are sympathetic to its fundamentalist views. It regards other churches with a tolerance unusual among denominations of this kind. It has always been known for its fervent evangelical character, its work among neglected groups, and its promotion of foreign mission enterprises. Congregations are to be found throughout the United States and in numerous foreign mission fields, including New Guinea, Borneo, Japan, India, and various countries in Africa and South America. It has also been active in Cambodia and Vietnam since 1929. Its headquarters are located in Nyack, N.Y., where it maintains a Bible school for the training of its ministers and missionaries.

**Christian Commission, The United States.** An agency of the Y.M.C.A. established during the Civil War to provide northern soldiers with religious and humanitarian services. At the outbreak of the war many Y.M.C.A. branches lost virtually all their members to the Union armies, and concern for the well-being of these soldiers was natural for those who remained at home. Massachusetts volunteers passing through New York City had awakened a Y.M.C.A. leader, Vincent Coyler, to the soldiers' needs and the Association's potential role in meeting them. As a result, a special convention of delegates from fifteen Y.M.C.A. branches met in New York, Nov. 15, 1861, and agreed to establish the Christian Commission. What in effect happened was that many branches of the Y for the duration of the war transformed themselves into agencies for the raising of money, the collecting of books and other supplies, and the recruiting of volunteer field workers. The primary concern of the Commission was to provide the soldiers with Bibles, hymnals, and preachers, but a great deal else was also included, i.e., help in sending telegrams, arranging transportation, caring for the wounded, providing food and medicines. In the year of its greatest service (1864) the Commission collected $1,300,000 in cash plus an almost equal amount in contributed stores. By the end of the war, five thousand men and women had contributed an average of thirty-eight days of service with the troops.

**Christian Democratic Movement.** A movement originating from the post-1870 Christian trade unions and workers' movements. It sought to make the Christian conscience effective in the social and political realm, and was usually organized along confessional lines. The strongest Roman Catholic party was the Center Party in Germany organized against Bismarck during the Kulturkampf. Since World War I, Christian Democratic parties have been formed as conscious attempts to counter Communism.

**Christian Endeavor, Young People's Society of.** An international, interdenominational youth organization associated with Protestant evangelical churches. The first Christian Endeavor Society was organized on Feb. 2, 1881, in the Williston Congregational Church, Portland, Maine, by Francis E. Clark. The movement quickly spread, and in 1895 a World's Christian Endeavor Union was organized. There are now societies and unions in seventy-five nations and island groups with approximately three million members.

The movement, as a Christ-centered organization of Christian young people, has as its purpose: "To lead young people to commit themselves to Jesus Christ as Lord; to bring them into the life of the church; to sustain and train them for the service of Christ; and to release them through all channels of human activity in the service of God and man."

Each society is part of a local church that determines its theology, program, and activities. Societies are organized into local, county, district, state, and national unions. Conventions are held in different parts of the world quadrennially. In 1966, the convention was held in Belfast. The official publication is *The Christian Endeavor World,* issued monthly, and the society's motto is: "For Christ and the Church."

**Christian Freedom** (Luther's treatise). The third of Luther's "Reformation treatises," written in 1520. Unlike the two previous tracts

(*To the Christian Nobility* and *The Babylonian Captivity of the Church*), this one was written in a conciliatory yet unequivocal spirit. It was occasioned by Miltitz' request of Luther that he write a short summary of his faith and accompany it with an open letter to Leo X, assuring the pope that he had never meant to attack him personally. This Luther agreed to do in the Latin tract on *Christian Freedom* (or, from the German title, *On the Freedom of a Christian Man*). It was a confession of his own faith and of the freedom that faith in Christ gives to a justified sinner. The freedom of a Christian consists in his having been set free from reliance upon his works for salvation. Instead, he is saved from the guilt and power of sin through faith in Christ. Christian freedom, however, does not lead to license but to service. It imposes upon the man of faith the obligation to discipline himself and serve others "out of spontaneous love in obedience to God." Thus Luther says that "a Christian is a perfectly free lord of all, subject to none," and at the same time "a perfectly dutiful servant of all, subject to all." In this twofold manner Luther intimately connected Christian freedom with the privileges and duties of the priesthood of all believers.

**Christianity and Judaism in the Middle Ages.** Though the first Christians retained their Jewish observances and regarded their faith as fundamentally Judaic, differing only in their concept of Messianic fulfillment, the rift with traditional Judaism developed early and spread widely. By the 1st century the Pauline missions to the Gentiles and the view of Jesus as a sharer in the Godhead had alienated Jewish pride in their ancestral particularity and age-old monotheism. Political and cultural factors helped widen the rift. National hostility to the Roman yoke remained implacable, and uprising followed uprising. After the savage reprisals of Titus in the year 71 came the determined revolt of Bar-Cochba (132–135), then the persecutions under Hadrian, at times of genocidal intensity.

By the 4th century, Jerusalem had become a Christian capital and Judaism a political as well as a spiritual heresy. A powerful church in Palestine had long made life for the Jews intolerable, and the Jewish race was dispersed far and wide from its homeland. In 425, Theodosius II abolished the patriarchate of Palestine and effectively severed the head of world Jewry. For a while Babylon held the position of a spiritual second home, but by the 6th century this too was challenged by the rising rivalry of Zendicism. In their continued diaspora, Jews clung the more firmly to the one cohesive force left to them, the traditional lore of the Torah as restated in terms of the Talmud. When so much depended on the upkeep of traditional rites, Judaism remained separatist; in its contacts with Christians there could be little impulse to temporize or proselytize. Islam as it upsurged in the 7th century was not lacking in affinities and sympathies with the Jewish traditions on which it partly drew, and many Jews found a more tolerable condition of life under Islam than, for example, in the constant harassment of the Christian rulers of Byzantium or Visigothic Spain. But in Christian eyes the alliance was unholy and served to intensify past enmities. So grew the popular medieval attitude toward Jews as aliens, heretics, and intransigents. They were barely tolerated for their economic resources, but were regarded above all as Christ's betrayers who merited a righteous persecution. They were always suspect for dark dealings. Accusations of usury were commonplace. The scandals of alleged child victims of ritual murder (i.e., William of Norwich in 1144, Hugh of Lincoln in 1255, and the Italian Simon of Trento in 1475) were all too typical. Official attitudes of the Western Church, such as the regulations on Jewish life imposed by Innocent III at the Fourth Lateran Council (1215), often fostered popular and national feeling. With the Crusades, anti-Semitism became even more organized and fanatical. Jews were expelled from England in 1290, from France in 1394, from Spain in 1492. In Germany and France entire communities were slaughtered. Only Poland and to a lesser degree Italy served as havens of refuge.

Intellectually, however, the atmosphere of constant hostility was occasionally lightened, and Christian scholarship owed much to Jewish and Islamic thought. The writings of Philo (d. A.D. 40), who found some grounds for reconciling Jewish theology and Greek philosophy, were much studied by the church fathers. From the 8th century, Talmudic schools were established in several countries of western Europe, and many of their lines of inquiry penetrated into medieval Scholasticism. A 10th-century resurgence of Greek culture within the Moslem world affected Christian thought largely by way of Judaic philosophy, as reflected, for instance, in the *Sefer ha-Kuzari,* or "Book of Arguments," by Judah ha-levi, of Toledo (d. 1140); the *'Emunah Ramah* ("Exalted Faith") of Abraham ibn Daud, of Toledo (c. 1180); and the Rabbinical commentaries of Solomon ben Isaac, of Troyes (d. 1105), or Rashi, as he is often known, who offered practical advice on the problems of Jewish-Christian relations. Perhaps greatest of all was Maimonides, of Cairo (b. 1135), and his seminal *Guide for the Perplexed,* which in its use of Aristotelian reasoning influenced profoundly scholars such as Thomas Aquinas. The more speculative and symbolic Kabbalistic philosophies, such as the *Sefer Chassidim* ("Book of the Pious") attributed to the German Judah ha-Chasid (d. 1217), and the *Sefer ha-Zohar* ("Book of Splendor") assigned to Moses de Leon, of Granada (d. 1305), proved fruitful sources for the esoteric Christian mysticism that reached a special popularity in the 14th century. Jewish Biblical commentaries were extensively drawn upon by Christian Hebraists of the later Middle Ages and the Reformation. In particular, Rashi's commentary, constantly quoted as early as the *Commentaries* of the Christian Nicholas of Lyra (d. 1349), and the lucid textual studies of David Kimchi, of Narbonne (d. 1235), were among the main sources for both Luther's and the King James translations.

BIBLIOGRAPHY: L. Finkelstein, *The Jews: Their History, Culture, and Religion,* 2 vols. (New York, 1955); E. H. Flannery, *The Anguish of the Jews* (New York, 1965); I. Husik, *A History of Medieval Jewish Philosophy* (New York, 1916); J. Katz, *Tradition and Crisis* (New York, 1961); J. R. Marcus, *The Jew in the Medieval World* (Cincinnati, 1938); Moses Maimonides, *The Guide for the Perplexed* (New York, 1961); E. A. Synan, *The Popes and the Jews in the Middle Ages* (New York, 1965).

**Christian Nobility** (Luther's treatise). One of the three great reforming treatises written by Martin Luther in 1520. The full title is *To the Christian Nobility of the German Nation Concerning the Reform of the Christian Estate.* The urging of prominent laymen and the attacks by Alveld and Prierias, papal absolutists, may have led Luther to write the treatise, which was published on Aug. 18, two months after he started it. In the first section, Luther tears down the three walls protecting Rome and preventing reform: the supremacy of the spiritual over the temporal authorities, the pope's sole right to interpret Scripture, and his sole right to convoke a church council. Luther's answer to each of these three claims is the spiritual priesthood of all believers. The second section deals with abuses: the corruption of the papal court should be eliminated by constituting a German national church; the morally decadent monastic orders should be reduced and those who wished allowed to leave; church festivals and ceremonies should be simplified; priestly celibacy should not be required for ordination; education and the social and economic life of Germany must be improved. The impact on Germany was instantaneous. Luther had developed a total reform program incorporating many of the demands that others had made before him. He asked the princes of Germany to act, and he gave them theoretical justification for acting.

**Christian Reformed Church.** A denomination formed in 1857 by a group of dissatisfied members from the Dutch Reformed Church in Michigan. At first the church was called the True Holland Reformed Church, but in 1890 it united with a similar group from New Jersey and adopted the present name. The membership grew because of immigration from Holland.

Doctrinally, great stress is placed on a literal acceptance of such historic Calvinist creeds as the Heidelberg Catechism (1563), the Canons of the Synod of Dort (1618–1619), and the Belgic Confession (1561). Conservative positions are maintained on such issues as divorce, worldly amusements, and birth control. The church government is presbyterian in form as outlined by the basic creeds. Local congregations send both lay and clerical representatives to a district classis. These in turn send four delegates to an annual national synod. Christian service is emphasized not only in home and foreign missions but also by the maintenance of tuberculosis and psychopathic hospitals and homes for the aged. The church has a Christian school system with higher educational facilities at Calvin College and Seminary in Grand Rapids, Mich. In 1965 there were 610 churches in the denomination with 268,165 members.

**Christian Science.** An American sect founded by Mary Baker Eddy. Christian Scientists believe that only the "spiritual" entities of the world possess any truth or can be considered real, while matter is unreal and false. The motivating force in Christian Science is the belief that sin and evil are only forms of matter or, as they call it, "mortal mind," and can be conquered by discovering that they are not real or true. Thus God is good, life, truth, intelligence, while sin and evil are just the opposite. The Christian Scientist refuses to believe that sin and evil really exist, but acts as though they were only mistaken conceptions which may be banished by proper instruction.

Converts are won to the movement primarily by being healed, for the purely religious side of Christian Science is not so important as the fact that it claims to be able to heal disease. The therapeutic aspects of the movement are handled by practitioners, many of whom are women. Their treatment consists of bringing health through mental influence and suggestion. Each practitioner is trained briefly, approved, and registered by the authorities of the Mother Church in Boston. The teachings of Mrs. Eddy are not, however, organized in so orderly and logical a manner that her meaning is always clear. Her best-known work, *Science and Health,* has been the subject of many disputes among Christian Scientists, and a number of the followers of Mrs. Eddy do not accept the leadership of the Mother Church in Boston.

The Manual of the church prohibits the gathering and publishing of statistics of membership. Members of the church have come chiefly from urban populations and from the middle or upper-middle classes. Christian Science churches are uniformly substantial and relatively costly structures, for leaders in the movement feel that they ought to demonstrate their optimism and faith in God. Prosperity and success, just as much as health, are viewed as the fruits of Christian Science belief.

Practitioners give advice and treatments for business prosperity as well as for recovery from illness. Mrs. Eddy herself treated illness but gave up that aspect of the work in order to further her teachings through the printed page. Her famous work, *Science and Health,* first printed in 1875, is still published in great numbers and forms the principal material of Sunday worship for Christian Scientists. Among the many other periodicals issued by the Mother Church, none is as well known or as highly regarded as the daily newspaper, *The Christian Science Monitor.* All local congregations are linked to the Boston headquarters and receive publications from the denominational publishing concern. Membership in the Mother Church, the large Boston home church built expressly for Mrs. Eddy in 1895, is not limited to the Boston area, for every Christian Scientist leader is expected to become a member of this congregation as well as of his own local church. In this manner the directors of the Mother Church maintain close supervision over the practitioners and readers (the equivalent of pastors). Extremely self-conscious concerning public criticism of their movement, Christian Science leaders through their Committees on Publication bend every effort to see that no derogatory comments or books appear in public. The movement is intensely individualistic; no general social concern has been voiced by leaders, nor are there any charitable organizations that function through the church. In fact, no groups of any kind, even ladies' aids, are permitted.

BIBLIOGRAPHY: C. S. Braden, *Christian Science Today* (Dallas, 1958); R. Peel, *Christian Science* (New York, 1958).

**Christian Socialism.** A term employed in the 19th and 20th centuries to describe Christian attempts to meet the challenges of the industrialization and urbanization of modern society. Actually, it was a part of wider reform movements which found precursors in the communistic experience of the early church, the prophetic proclamation of the Kingdom of God, the radical sectarian experiments of the Middle Ages, and the utopian communitarian organizations of F. M. C. Fourier, Comte de Saint-Simon, Robert Owen, and J. H. Noyes. Immediate stimulation came from the sufferings of the dispossessed, the convulsions of 1848, and the emergence of the so-called "scientific socialism" of Karl Marx and Friedrich Engels. Some Christians began to oppose conceptions of immutable laws of individualism, competition, and profit-seeking, blessed by the laissez-faire economic theory of the 18th century and aggravated by the theories of evolution of the 19th century. They tried to combine some of the purposes of socialism with Christian Biblical, theological, and ethical convictions.

Roman Catholicism was generally suspicious of the democratic and socialistic spirit of the age and sought various means of practical charity to deal with social problems. Under the leadership of Bishop Wilhelm Emmanuel von Ketteler in Germany, Frédéric Le Play and Albert de Mun in France, Hilaire Belloc and G. K. Chesterton in England, and the powerful Austrian Christian Socialist Party, Roman Catholics began to advocate social legislation, "guild socialism" under ecclesiastical auspices with state financing, and the social survey method in the study of social problems. These tendencies were made more explicit in the encyclicals of Leo XIII (*Rerum novarum,* 1891 and Pius XI (*Quadragesimo anno,* 1931), which defended the natural right of the worker to organize and the duty of the government to regulate industry, and which supported in general the neofeudal "corporate states." In the United States, John A. Ryan, advocate of "essential economic socialism," stands out for his authorship of the Bishops' Program of Social Reconstruction (1919). This marked the end of the American hierarchy's defensive attitude

toward socialism and the beginning of a more aggressive involvement in social legislation and the development of labor schools and labor unions.

Protestant response was somewhat more varied. In England, Broad Churchmen first employed the term "Christian Socialism." After the failure of the Chartist uprisings in 1848, J. M. F. Ludlow, influenced by Louis Blanc's workshops, J. F. D. Maurice, and Charles Kingsley organized the Council for Promoting Working Men's Associations (1850) through which they encouraged producer and consumer cooperatives and profit-sharing in industry. They helped to pass the Industrial and Provident Partnerships Bill (1852) and also founded the Working Men's College in London to assist the education of laborers. Although this movement lasted only a short time, it made a wide impact even outside of England. The Anglo-Catholics, under the leadership of Stewart Headlam, united Puseyite and Maurician ideas in the Guild of St. Matthew (1877), while the Free Church encouraged closer relations with laborers and later, under John MacMurray in the Christian Left, showed more radical Marxist tendencies. The High Church Christian Social Union (1889) and the official Anglican Industrial Christian Fellowship (1919) attempted a more moderate solution to industrial problems. Archbishop William Temple organized Conferences on Politics, Economics, and Citizenship at Birmingham (1924) and Malvern (1941), while Christian layman Clement Attlee emerged as Labor Party leader and became Prime Minister after World War II. On the Continent, Protestants gave some leadership to various socialist movements. In France, T. Fallot and André Philip, economist and journalist, exercised tremendous influence in social reformation, while the Scandinavian countries, touched by the earlier cooperative movements in England, experimented with various types of control over industrial development. In Germany, Rudolf Todt and Adolf Stoecker, a Lutheran leader in the Evangelical Social Congress, favored a paternalistic state socialism in the throne and altar tradition, assisted by the political power of Otto von Bismarck. Friedrich Naumann, another German Protestant, moved toward the Left in support of "social democracy." In southern Germany and Switzerland, C. Blumhardt, Hermann Kutter, and Leonhard Ragaz started the movement known as "religious socialism," which came to include Karl Barth and Paul Tillich. Tillich participated in the League of Religious Socialists and the Kairos Circle. He immigrated to the United States in 1933 after protesting the neopaganism of Hitler's National Socialism.

Among Protestants in the United States, feudalistic and scientific forms of socialism did not play a large role. Many Protestants were active in the movement for social reform, earlier known as "applied Christianity" and then as the Social Gospel, e.g., Stephen Colwell, Washington Gladden, G. D. Herron, Henry George, Richard Ely, Francis G. Peabody, and Harry F. Ward. Episcopal priest W. D. P. Bliss organized the Society of Christian Socialists (1889), which was followed by a number of similar socialist organizations. Baptist Walter Rauschenbusch considered socialism as a power of the "coming age," although he made a distinction between a skeptical socialist and a Christian socialist who emphasized the Kingdom of God and the laws of Jesus, the sacredness of human personality, the solidarity of the human family, and the necessity of the strong standing with the weak. Some influences from this movement spread to South America, China, India, and Japan, e.g., with Toyohiko Kagawa. There was a utopian tendency among earlier Christian socialists to identify the democratized industrial order with the Kingdom of God. The Federal Council of Churches formulated the social creed of the churches in 1908, which was revised in 1932. Reinhold Niebuhr, with Tillich and Eduard Heimann, in the Fellowship of Socialist Christians (1932) reevaluated the Social Gospel with a more realistic theological perspective and the contributions of Karl Marx to social thought. These Protestant leaders, who wished to be known as Christians first, and then as Socialists, accepted some of Marx's economic insights, but rejected his determinism, messianism, and eschatology. They often supported former minister Norman Thomas, who was the Socialist Party candidate in six presidential campaigns.

As seen in the Life and Work Conferences of the ecumenical movement and the World Council of Churches (Stockholm, 1925; Oxford, 1937; Amsterdam, 1948; Evanston, 1954; New Delhi, 1961) and more recent Roman Catholic thought (John XXIII, *Mater et magistra*, 1961), Christians have contributed to the decline of laissez-faire capitalism and the de-Marxizing of socialism. They attempted to steer a course between earlier syndicalism, which did away with state power, and modern totalitarianism. They encouraged a responsible society with some form of guild socialism, social democracy, and the concept of the welfare state.

BIBLIOGRAPHY: T. Christensen, *The Origin and History of Christian Socialism* (Aarhus, Denmark, 1962); J. Dombrowski, *Early Days of Christian Socialism in America* (New York, 1936); E. Duff, *The Social Thought of the World Council of Churches* (New York, 1956); M. B. Reckitt, *Maurice to Temple: A Century of the Social Movement in the Church of England* (London, 1947); A. R. Vidler, *A Century of Social Catholicism, 1820–1920* (London, 1964).

**Christian Social Union.** An organization founded in 1889 by members of the Church of England, primarily under clerical direction and strongly Anglo-Catholic in tone. It sought to apply the moral truths of Christianity to pressing social and economic problems, and to establish the principle that the Christian faith has to do with the whole ordering of the life of a man in society. After World War I it merged with the Industrial Christian Fellowship.

**Christina** (1626–1689). Queen of Sweden from 1632 after the death of her father, Gustavus Adolphus. In 1644 she assumed full control and immediately sought to end the Thirty Years' War. At home she introduced educational reforms and supported learning by the patronage of foreign scholars and artists. In 1654 she abdicated her throne, converted to Roman Catholicism, and eventually died in Rome after having twice attempted to regain the Swedish crown.

**Christology.** The doctrine of the nature and work of Christ. When Jesus asked his disciples, "Who do men say that I am?" he received a variety of answers. Throughout the history of the church the question has continued to receive a variety of answers.

The nature of the gospel records is such that, taken out of the context of the history of the Christian community, the "Christ of faith" might seem to be an invention. Indeed, a frequently resurrected notion is that the simple "Fatherhood of God, brotherhood of man" teaching of an earthly Jewish rabbi was transmuted into a religion of a divine Savior. Among those for whom this notion has some appeal, the apostle Paul is usually accounted the culprit.

Whatever the problems of the canonical texts may be, however, it is clear that Christians from the very earliest times concerned themselves quite as much with the person as with the teachings of Jesus. To the extent that the gospel records emphasize the human characteristics of Jesus, it may well be that they self-consciously offset the earliest Christological heresy which would have made him divine to the exclusion of the human. This heresy, Docetism, is still rife among those sects which find it difficult to think of Jesus as having been limited to the extent of the scientific knowledge of his day.

The early doctrinal development of Christianity is typically thought of as the finishing of the doctrine of the Trinity. It is a fact, however, that the doctrine of the Trinity was principally hammered out over issues having to do with the nature and person of Jesus the Christ. From Peter's confession, "You are the Christ," the Christian community has had to attempt to say how the incarnation should be spoken of. The earliest debate, initiated by an affirmation of Arius that Christ was not coeternal with the Father, precipitated the Councils of Nicaea (325) and Constantinople (381). The product of these Councils, the so-called Nicene Creed, affirms that Christ is "of one substance with" the Father. Thus his complete divinity was affirmed.

The second round of debate, brought on by Eutyches and others, had to do with the person of the Incarnate One. Was there but a single divine-human nature? The Council of Chalcedon (451), in a fashion rather typical of orthodox theological statements, affirmed at some length the complete humanity and the complete divinity of the "Lord Jesus Christ." (It is perhaps worthy of note that heresies were often attempts to define *how* things are the case. The orthodox response was typically to affirm *that* they are so.)

In one form or another the whole debate has continued through the centuries. For example, Socinus in the late 16th century attempted to affirm the unity of the Godhead without denying the divinity of Christ. His followers frequently found it simpler to deny the latter. These are the origins of contemporary Unitarianism.

A peculiar form of Christological investigation arose from speculation concerning the Eucharist. The "real presence" of Christ in the sacrament had always been affirmed, and the Fourth Lateran Council (1215) had defined the real presence of Christ in the sacrament in the terminology of Aristotelian philosophy. This is properly known as the doctrine of "transubstantiation." As the philosophical categories came under attack from Occam and others, the "real presence" could no longer so conveniently be accounted for. How could the risen Christ, present at the right hand of the Father, be locally present under the species of bread and wine? The Reformers fell heir to the discussion, not least Luther, who was trained in the Occamist philosophical tradition.

While the Roman Catholic Church has continued to affirm the doctrine of transub-

stantiation, the problem remains unsolved, particularly in the metaphysically pluralist society of today. Attempts were made to meet the demands of reason by such categories as "the ubiquity of the risen Lord," but Calvin was satisfied to comment that the presence of Christ in the sacrament is a divine promise and that we need not be curious as to the means of its fulfillment.

Luther and Calvin represent two emphases within orthodox Christology. While certainly not failing to speak of Christ as Lord, Luther tended to speak of the comforts of Christ's presence to the believer. This experiential possibility is less the concern of Calvin, who tended to think always of the work of Christ in Trinitarian terminology. This difference of emphasis has been explained by reference to the personalities of the men, but it is, to a significant degree, perpetuated in the work of their followers.

For some time before the Reformation there had been pockets within the church in which a form of Christian devotion centered upon a sentimentalized picture of Jesus. This *Jesuanismus* became a peculiar mark of the Protestants stigmatized as Pietists. Such Pietists as P. J. Spener were not much given to a sentimental view of Jesus, but the sentimentalism was common in early Methodism and is typical of much sectarian Christianity today. This corrupt Christology is exemplified in such hymns as "In the Garden."

Beginning, perhaps, with the Enlightenment, Christological speculation underwent a significant change. Innumerable attempts were made to subject the texts of the New Testament to rigorous analysis sufficient to discover the "historical Jesus." In brief, it was to distinguish the "Jesus of history" from the "Christ of faith." Some of the investigators were attempting to write a new apologetic for the Christian faith; others were frankly destructive in intent. The former sought to show that the Jesus of history was credible, the latter that he could be explained away. Schweitzer's conclusion, generally accepted, was that all these attempts were necessarily unsuccessful.

Nevertheless, Adolf von Harnack and others attempted to show that changes had been introduced into Christian ideas as they came to be expressed in Hellenistic categories. This perpetuated an interest in the historical Jesus. Many attempted to demonstrate that the divinity of Christ consisted principally in the universality of his teaching or in the unsullied nature of his character. Thus, early in this century, Jesus was widely held to be a social reformer, a socialist innovator, and the like. It was in criticism of such views as theologically inadequate, while sympathizing with their social implications, that such individuals as Barth and Niebuhr brought to pass the theological revival known as neo-orthodoxy.

A reaction equally to the Modernism (see LIBERALISM) of Harnack and others and to neo-orthodoxy was an aggressive form of orthodoxy sometimes called Fundamentalism. Essentially, Fundamentalism does little to clarify the Christological problems as they are discussed today. Its tendency is to affirm the classical formulations under the misapprehension that they are simply Biblical.

Christology has been the preoccupation of recent theologians attempting to show how the Christian faith can be expressed in contemporary modes of speech. Subject to much criticism, Bultmann and his followers have attempted to show how one may reduce statements about God to statements about man, thus avoiding the problems of New Testament "mythology." Bultmann's attempt to demonstrate the relevance of Christ seen as the exemplification of authentic humanity has been found compatible with the interests of those theologians who prefer to substitute the categories of process philosophy or linguistic analysis for those of the more traditional substance philosophies.

Of some popularity among contemporary theologians who seek to be orthodox while yet speaking relevantly to the modern scene is a form of Christology known as Kenotic Christology. Emphasizing Christ's emptying himself of his Godhead (*kenōsis*), this view finds Christ's significance precisely in his completely identifying himself with man. More formally orthodox thinkers consider this view to be but half of what was affirmed at Chalcedon.

For some two centuries, of course, there have been those who disavowed all theological considerations and wished to see in Jesus a teacher of great stature, but a teacher to be compared with other historical figures. It is oddly true that some who consider themselves wholly orthodox, like these freethinkers, speak of little besides Jesus' ethical teachings.

Of most recent vintage is the attempt on the part of a few to show that the Dead Sea Scrolls cast significant light on Christian origins. It has been argued that the Teacher of Righteousness there spoken of constitutes the prototype for Jesus' ministry. Although the Christian theologian seems defensive in meeting the charge, it is unlikely that it can be shown that Jesus did, in fact, spend any time among the Essenes or that he patterned

his own life and teachings on those of the Teacher. This discussion has served to re-institute the quest of the historical Jesus.

BIBLIOGRAPHY: D. M. Baillie, *God Was in Christ* (New York, 1948); D. Bonhoeffer, *Christ the Center* (New York, 1966); E. Brunner, *The Mediator* (Philadelphia, 1947); H. R. Niebuhr, *Christ and Culture* (New York, 1956); S. M. Ogden, *Christ Without Myth* (New York, 1961); A. Schweitzer, *The Quest of the Historical Jesus* (New York, 1948); P. Tillich, *Systematic Theology* (Chicago, 1957).

**Chrodegang** (d. 766). An official of Charles Martel and Pepin III before his election in 742 as bishop of Metz. He headed a legation to Rome, bringing Pope Stephen III to Gaul to crown Pepin king of the Franks. Continuing the liturgical and disciplinary reforms of Boniface, he wrote a rule for the secular canons of his cathedral, which became the basis of the Aachen Rule of 817. He was the founder of the monastery of Gorze.

**Chronicles.** Compilations, unlike histories, in chronological order of as many historical details as are available to the writer. Early chronicles include those of Julius Africanus, Hippolytus, and Eusebius. Later ones take over previous chronicles and expand them to a new date, e.g., a chronicle by Hippolytus (to the year 234) extended to 334 by the Roman Chronographer of the year 354, but more important is the *Chronicle* of Eusebius of Caesarea from the birth of Abraham (2105 B.C.), which was translated and extended to the year 378 by Jerome, in which form it dominated medieval chronology. A much briefer chronicle is that of Sulpicius Severus (d. c. 420), outlining the period from creation to A.D. 400, written in Tacitean style. Also current in the Middle Ages was the work of Orosius. Prosper of Aquitaine excerpts Jerome and then continues to 455, and the *Chronicon* of Idacius does the same, adding the period from 428 to 468. That of Cassiodorus extends to 519. John of Biclaro continues during the period from 567 to 590 the *Chronicle* of Victor of Tunnuna, which reached to 566, while Marius of Avenches continues Prosper to 481. The last patristic chronicle is by Isidore of Seville to 615. Eastern chronicles include those of John Malalas (to 574); the Syriac Edessan *Chronicle* (133 B.C.–A.D. 540), continued by Pseudo-Dionysius to 754; *Chronicon Paschale* (to 629); and the *World Chronicle* of John of Nikiu (c. 700) in Coptic covering the 7th century.

**Chrysostom, John** (c. 347–407). Archbishop of Constantinople; theologian and preacher. Born in Antioch, he studied philosophy under Andragathius and law under the great pagan orator, Libanius, who also taught the emperor Julian as well as Basil and Gregory of Nazianzus. Chrysostom later studied theology under Diodorus of Tarsus. Disinterested in the law, briefly enthralled by the theater, he became attached while still in his youth to the bishop of Antioch, Melitius, and was baptized and confirmed at the age of twenty-three.

Chrysostom was attracted to the monastic life, but due to the pleadings of his mother, the widow Anthusa, he stayed with her, following a private rule. There he was a great influence on a number of people, including Theodore of Mopsuestia. Later he lived four years with a hermit, and then two years by himself, following the Pachomian Rule, but ill-health forced him to return to Antioch. Bishop Flavian ordained him deacon in 381 and priest in 386. It was during the period from 386 to 397 that he enjoyed his life's greatest productivity. He was appointed to preach in the cathedral, and for eleven years the people of Antioch enjoyed his great homiletical gifts.

Chrysostom's sermons were largely exegetical. Both at Antioch and later at Constantinople he preached a series each on Genesis, Psalms, Isaiah, Matthew, John, Acts, Romans, Corinthians, Galatians, Ephesians, Philippians, Colossians, Thessalonians, Timothy, Titus, Philemon, and Hebrews. He repudiated the allegorical method of interpretation, insisting that Scripture be understood literally. He held his hearers engrossed, and on occasions, such as that following the riots of 387, he swayed the whole city with his oratorical skill.

Chrysostom was not a systematic theologian. A reformer of society, a pastor, a preacher, he did not, however, show great theological originality. He was a moderate expositor of the Antiochene school of theology. His teaching often emphasizes the Eucharist, in part because his preaching was usually set within the liturgy.

In 397, Chrysostom, much against his will, was forcibly brought to Constantinople, and made bishop of the "New Rome." This was largely the work of Eutropius, then chief adviser to the incompetent emperor Arcadius. It was a mistake from the first. Chrysostom was not the man to deal with the intrigue of the imperial court or the machinations of his less scrupulous fellow bishops. He was honest, ascetic, and tactless. From the start he was opposed by Theophilus of Alexandria, and soon earned the wrath of the empress Eudoxia.

His feeble predecessor Nectarius had allowed ecclesiastical discipline to deteriorate to the point of collapse. Chrysostom's stringent efforts to correct this, as well as his refusal to entertain the court, alienated many. In 402, Theophilus came to Constantinople, ostensibly as a result of an imperial summons in regard to some monks residing in Constantinople whom he had expelled from Egypt. But Theophilus used his visit to gain the favor of the court and certain dissident bishops of Chrysostom's. As a result, Chrysostom was deposed at the Synod of Oak, a suburb of Chalcedon, and banished to Bithynia (403).

The sentence lasted only one day before public reaction forced the court to recall Chrysostom, but in less than two months he antagonized the empress again and was permanently exiled. The attempted intervention of Rome in this matter was of no avail. He was sent first to Cucusus in Lesser Armenia, where he gathered a circle of admirers from Antioch. This enraged his enemies, and he was ordered removed to Pityus, on the Black Sea. He never reached there, being intentionally made to suffer such severe deprivations enroute that he died in a chapel near Comana in Pontus. In 438 his remains were returned to Constantinople, and the son of Eudoxia, Theodosius II, did penance for the wrong of his parents.

We possess more writings from Chrysostom than from any other of the Greek fathers. Aside from the exegetical sermons, there are others on various topics. He also wrote treatises, including *On the Priesthood, On Monastic Life, On Virginity and Widowhood, Concerning the Education of Children, On Suffering,* and *Against Pagans and Jews.* A good number of his letters are extant. The Byzantine Liturgy named for him is, however, largely from the 8th and 9th centuries.

BIBLIOGRAPHY: P. Schaff (ed.), *Nicene and Post-Nicene Fathers,* Series I, Vols. 9–14 (Grand Rapids, 1956); J. Pelikan, *The Preaching of Chrysostom* (Philadelphia, 1966); W. R. W. Stephens, *Saint Chrysostom: His Life and Times* (London, 1872); B. Vandenberghe, *John the Golden Mouth* (Westminster, Md., 1958).

**Church.** The nature of the church has been a matter of significant debate particularly since the time of the Reformation. The terms of the debate, however, were anticipated in much earlier times. The earliest form of the debate had to do with the possibility of identifying the institution with the company of elect souls. In the later period there was considerable sentiment for the view that a proper understanding of the church excludes any institution superior to the local congregation.

The New Testament term "church," a translation of the word *ekklēsia,* occurs infrequently, and its precise significance is the subject of scholarly disagreement. Historically, the term signified an assembly, but New Testament writers seem sometimes to refer to a local congregation and sometimes to the whole body of believers. When the term is used in the latter sense, it is clear that the local congregation is not regarded as a part of the whole church as if the part were less than the whole. The local congregation is no less the church than the whole collection of congregations.

This conception is theologically profound, but perhaps difficult for everyday use, and as early as Clement of Alexandria we find a suggestion that the church is to be defined by the presence of the bishop. From this time on, the church is increasingly identified by the presence of the hierarchy, in particular the bishop. In the West by the time of the Middle Ages, one can speak of a "sacramental-sacerdotal system," i.e., the church is an institution conveying the sacraments as means of grace by the agency of men set apart for this function. The role of the congregation was essentially a passive one.

The traditions of the East, largely preserved in the Orthodox Churches of our day, did not tend to identify the church with the actions of the hierarchy. Maintaining a characteristic emphasis upon the church as "the body of Christ," the Eastern communions also preserved a corporate view of the church: the church is composed of all the faithful gathered to celebrate the sacred liturgy, as witnessed also by the faithful departed from this life. (Compare this view with that of the Free Church tradition.)

During the tense days of the Montanist and Pelagian heresies, there was an increasing tendency to emphasize theological tenets pointing in the direction of a well-formed doctrine of election. As a consequence it was necessary to affirm that the institutional church is not simply to be identified with the elect, those known only to God. The latter are the so-called "invisible church." This Augustinian emphasis upon election tended to undermine the authority of the institutional church, and helps to account for the problems which those sympathetic to Augustine's views have continued to experience. To cite only two examples, revived Augustinianism is seen later in Wycliffe in England and Luther in Saxony.

When the Roman Empire fell, the church was the only institution that was not purely local, and it thus assumed considerable influence in civil affairs. With the tendency toward the establishment of national governments at the end of the Middle Ages, the involvement of the church in civil affairs led to extended struggles with ambitious civil authorities. The struggles are symbolized in the investiture controversy, a long-continuing fight over control of church and state offices.

The creeds widely used through Christendom referred to the one, holy, catholic, and apostolic church. Increasingly, however, the authority of the church was being resisted. Whereas it was once possible to refer to the hierarchy as the repository of the church's divine status, the low moral state of the clergy in the late Middle Ages made this difficult to maintain. How, without being an intentional schismatic, might one resist an unworthy hierarchy? The Reformation answer was to define the church as the locus of evangelical preaching and valid sacraments. Thus, without asserting that the church had ever lapsed since the time of the apostles, it was possible to say that specific decisions of popes and councils were erroneous. All that the Reformers regarded as the debased accretions of the church could be attributed to the sinfulness of men, the essence of the church remaining unsullied. Neither Luther nor Calvin intended this view of the church to loosen discipline or to divest the church of all organization. Under Luther the organization of the church continued much as before, save that obedience to the pope was disavowed. Calvinist countries tended to adopt a form of representative government in the church as being most nearly that of the New Testament pattern. Less conservative spirits, however, were willing to go farther. Under a variety of names, there sprang up a number of loosely knit communions dedicated to the view that the local congregation is the essential unit of the church, and that no superior ecclesiastical authority is to be acknowledged.

Although none of the Protestant Reformers sought to deny the unity and catholicity of the church, it was obviously difficult to show that the church is united and worldwide in the absence of a united hierarchy. There was, consequently, a tendency to spiritualize the concepts. Sounder theological insight rested on the fact that the church was held to be a united worldwide communion before any institutional expression of its unity was present. There is the further fact, now better known in the West, that the Eastern Churches, commonly called Orthodox, enjoyed a sense of unity without the priesthood of any locality being subordinate to a single popelike metropolitan bishop.

From the time of the Reformation forward one has three distinct forms of ecclesiology (doctrine of the church): (1) *Episcopal.* The essence of the church lies with its ordained priesthood, primarily in bishops from whom power is delegated to priests (or vicars). Within this form of ecclesiology there is a type which finds the principle of unity in the bishop of Rome as pope, and that type, principally Orthodox and Anglican, which sees the unity of the church expressed in a synod of all the bishops. (2) *Congregational.* The essence of the church is here seen as the gathered community of believers, and this community is wholly competent to call and ordain its own minister. (3) *Synodical.* Here authority does not lie solely with the ordained clergy or solely with the local congregation. Regional bodies superior to congregations discharge the duties elsewhere carried out by bishops, such as ordaining men to the ministry and disciplining recalcitrant congregations. The peculiarly American institution, the denomination, is often an amalgam of these forms.

A marked feature of the theological revival of the 1930's was a "rediscovery of the church." The nature and the mission of the church have been central concerns since that time. Under the influence of Barth the church has been seriously studied in quarters not notably concerned for such "catholic" concerns in previous generations. As a consequence of this concern, groups not self-consciously grounded in historic traditions have recovered a sense of history and have thus been prepared for the new emphases found in Roman Catholicism.

Since the Edinburgh Conference of 1910 the church communities of the West in particular have moved increasingly in the direction of cooperative endeavors through such agencies as the World Council of Churches. Cooperation has been accompanied by a concern for a proper sense of church unity. Since the World Council of Churches is, by design, not a superchurch, the tendency toward unity has expressed itself in organic mergers of various denominations, sometimes from quite dissimilar origins, and also in "conversations" between Roman Catholic and other Christians.

Great impetus was given to all these sentiments with the election of John XXIII in 1958. By expressions of friendliness to all "separated brethren," the pope encouraged the furthering of ecumenical contacts, and these have been most significant among the separated brethren themselves. Initiated by a sermon preached by the stated clerk of The United Presbyterian Church in the U.S.A., Eugene Carson Blake, the Consultation on Church Union now involves more than the original eight groups in discussions seeking "a united church, truly catholic, truly evangelical, and truly reformed."

Many found great significance in the fact that the Roman Catholic Church, after generations of using the term "church" in the singular and with reference only to itself, has begun to use the term also to refer to other ecclesiastical communions. The Decree on Ecumenism of the Vatican Council II makes clear that the Reformation is not yet ended. Yet it may well be the case that the church of Christ is more unified today than since apostolic times.

After World War II, although churchgoing was largely on the decline, there was much popular interest in religious ideas. From some fragmentary writings of Dietrich Bonhoeffer, the idea of a secularized church gained currency. Many understood this as the end of the institutional church; others thought of it as the church really in mission to the world, as opposed to the church ministering only to its members.

BIBLIOGRAPHY: R. M. Brown, *The Significance of the Church* (Philadelphia, 1956); P. T. Forsyth, *Church and Sacraments* (London, 1917); A. G. Hebert, *Liturgy and Society* (London, 1935); H. Küng, *Structures of the Church* (New York, 1964); J. A. T. Robinson, *On Being the Church in the World* (London, 1960).

**Church and State in America.** See RELIGIOUS LIBERTY.

**Church Assembly** (England). The National Assembly of the Church of England created by Parliament in 1919 "to deliberate on all matters concerning the Church of England." However, it may not deal with matters of doctrine that are reserved to the Convocations of Canterbury and York. Its chief function is to prepare measures for presentation to Parliament. It has been influential in modernizing church structures, practices, and finance. It meets three times annually.

**Church Assembly** (Sweden). A national church synod (Kyrkomötet) established in 1863 to direct the affairs of the Lutheran state church. Membership is composed of approximately half each of laymen and of clergy. All enactments require the approval of Parliament and the king. Though it was intended to give the state church more freedom, it lessened the influence of the clergy in secular and cultural affairs especially after

1865 when Parliament was reorganized from a four-chamber house which included a clergy estate to a bicameral legislature.

**Church Congress.** An unofficial Anglican conference held annually in England from 1861 to 1913 and then sporadically through the 1920's. These were large assemblies which presented and discussed facets of the life and work of the Church of England. The addresses and records of discussion were published in report volumes. After World War II the Congress declined in popularity and significance, being displaced by the Church Assembly from 1919 onward.

**Churches' Commission on International Affairs.** See COMMISSION OF THE CHURCHES ON INTERNATIONAL AFFAIRS.

**Church History, Beginnings of.** The earliest example of church history that we possess is the two-volume work Luke-Acts, written at the end of the apostolic age in order to describe and defend the Christian mission from Jerusalem westward to Rome. Evidence for the writing of church history does not appear again until the decade between 160 and 170, when Hegesippus developed the theory that heresy arose only after the death of James of Jerusalem, and investigated the successions of bishops at Jerusalem and at Rome (possibly also at Corinth). A similar interest in succession is found in the letter of Dionysius of Corinth to the Athenians, and somewhat later in the writings of Irenaeus. The idea that heresy was later than orthodoxy—obviously anti-Gnostic—is also developed by Clement of Alexandria. For these early writers, church history was the history of tradition. Apart from the chronicles of Julius Africanus and Hippolytus, the first real church history was that written by Eusebius of Caesarea, an expansion of his earlier *Chronicle* and, like it, based on his researches in the church libraries of Caesarea and Jerusalem. Eusebius made little attempt to interpret his materials and for this reason his fragmentarily quoted sources are usually more valuable than his own comments. His work is intended to show the continuity of orthodox, episcopal tradition.

**Church Missionary Society.** An association founded in 1799 in an era noted for the establishment of missionary societies. This was the first and became the foremost among the religious societies for which the Evangelical wing of the Church of England was responsible. The Society was founded under the direction of John Venn, a leader of the famous evangelical group, the Clapham Sect, which then became very active in the work of the Society. The initial impetus for organization was the antislavery campaign that aroused interest in the spiritual condition of West African Negroes, among whom little missionary work had been undertaken. After a precarious beginning, the Society entered upon a vigorous campaign of pioneer work in the carrying of the gospel to the heathen. It became noted for its evangelical fervor and missionary goal, which was interpreted as preaching the gospel rather than extending the Anglican Church. It became the largest missionary society in the Church of England but was not limited exclusively to Anglicans. It retained friendly contacts with other Protestant missionary societies. Among the areas evangelized were West Africa, India, the American colonies, New Zealand, Western Asia, North Africa, and East Africa.

**Church Music.** The earliest church music that has come down to us in a reliable way is that of Ambrose, bishop of Milan (c. A.D. 340–397), and its abridgment and completion by Pope Gregory the Great (c. 540–604). To this monophonic, unaccompanied chant or plainsong which bears their names are sung not only the "psalms, hymns, and spiritual songs" of the early church but also the canonical hours and the entire Mass. Gregory established a *schola cantorum* at Rome which trained singers to go as missionaries throughout Christendom, hoping by a common music to create a united church.

In contrast to the many nameless monks who evolved the considerable body of plainsong, a composer who is still known to us is Perotinus Magnus (12th century). He wrote elaborate liturgical settings of the proper of the Mass for the Paris Cathedral of Notre Dame. His basic technique, that of adding one or more voice parts to a passage of plainsong called the *cantus firmus,* was to survive through all style changes to the present day. This French Gothic school continued throughout the Hundred Years' War with English-Burgundian composers predominating. With their style in demand, Flemish organists, composers, and singers took over many important positions abroad. German and Italian influences were brought back to form the pan-European style of the 16th century which later became known as the "golden age of polyphony."

The greatest of the 15th-century polyphonists and the earliest major composer whose works are still performed is Josquin des Prés (c. 1450–1521). He was able to fuse all the devices of his predecessors, notably tone-painting, the imitation of one voice by another, and the piling up of melodies and countermelodies to achieve new heights of expressiveness. His pupil, Adrian Willaert (d. 1562), became one of the many leading Flemish masters to settle in Italy. As master of the music at St. Mark's, Venice, he began that writing for instruments and double choirs which gave brilliance and color to festive music such as Europe had never seen. His pupil, Andrea Gabrieli (c. 1510–1586), and the latter's nephew, Giovanni Gabrieli (1557–1612), drew pupils from all the courts of Europe. Thus they transmitted their high Renaissance and early baroque style to the young Germans Heinrich Schütz (1585–1672) and Hans Leo Hassler (1564–1612), both of whom returned to lead Protestant Germany. Not less important was the Dutch Jan Sweelinck (1562–1621), who traveled to Italy to study the (originally) Flemish style with Willaert's pupil, Zarlino, and who returned to Amsterdam to write much important organ music in fugue as well as choral settings of the French metrical psalter.

Turning back to the elder Gabrieli's generation, we find yet another Netherlander coming to Italy, this time the young Orlandus de Lassus (1532–1594). From boy soprano to composer and conductor, he followed the usual steps of a distinguished career in Milan, Naples, and Rome until he was called to Munich, where he served the Bavarian court as conductor of the ducal *cappella* (the choir and orchestra) in both its sacred and secular functions. It is important to note that in this period of highest achievement, the music and the musicians for both were identical. Continuing in this manner until his death thirty-four years later, Lassus wrote an estimated total of fifteen hundred works (a complete edition has yet to be published).

Although surpassed in harmonic color by both Lassus and William Byrd (see below) and by the Spaniard Victoria (1548–1611) in emotional intensity, the preeminence of the Roman school was upheld for his own time by Giovanni Pierluigi da Palestrina (c. 1525–1594). With the exception of some madrigals, Palestrina's entire output was intended for the church. His life was the unremitting labor of writing an enormous body of work (thirty-three large volumes) and, thanks to his wife's inheritance, seeing a fair amount of it published.

Critics of the 19th century have written a good deal of imaginative nonsense about the musical reformers of the Council of Trent, and for a long time Palestrina was given credit for "saving" music from their hands.

Both the danger and the rescue now seem to have survived any proof. Perhaps because his genius lay in avoidance of any extreme, and because of his constant concern for euphony and normalcy in the polyphonic style which now reigned throughout Europe, an admiring posterity was led to link these universal elements together by the expression "Palestrina style." In this Platonic way can be summed up the best and most enduring of ritual music to the end of the 16th century.

Paralleling this long development on the Continent was the splendid flowering of composition and performance in England. Largely uniform with mainland practice until the Reformation, the Tudor musicians beginning with Christopher Tye (1500–1572) and Thomas Tallis (1505–1585) were the first to respond to Cranmer's reforms. At this time was born the English anthem (to take the place of the Latin motet) and the English service (to take the place of the canonical hours and the Mass). Many features of style in both anthems and service have persisted to the present, though each has undergone many changes. A few of these are: plain syllabic settings of important texts, use of organ accompaniment, sectional treatment, alternating solo and *tutti* passages, and, in the 17th century, growing use of orchestral interludes and accompaniments. This followed the Continental fashion and made the anthem indistinguishable from the cantata. The texts of the service received the same musical treatment as the anthem, even though some of the canticles retained from the Roman use are long and difficult to hold together in an elaborate musical treatment. The usual settings of the Morning Prayer are the Venite, Te Deum, Benedictus es; of the Evening Prayer, the Magnificat and the Nunc Dimittis; and in the Communion, the Kyrie, combined with the Decalogue, the Creed, and later with the Sanctus and the Gloria.

William Byrd (1542–1623), certainly the most brilliant Englishman of them all, wrote much for the new ritual while remaining faithful to the old. Throughout his long life his eminent position at court shielded him from the recurring shocks that traveled through the cathedral establishments. Many musicians lost their livelihood when the monasteries were dissolved; moreover, the training of the young was seriously disturbed. The effects of this were overshadowed for a time by the success of Tomkins, Weelkes, in service writing, and Orlando Gibbons (1583–1625), all of whom wrote definitive services in the old style. Gibbons wrote anthems, some of which explored all the new trends, and others which formed a last exemplar of the old Netherlands style.

But the forces of change were not spent. The Civil War in England dealt church music a blow from which it has really never recovered. After the Restoration of 1660, composers and performers alike found employment principally in court, ceremonial, and concert music. Chief among these was Henry Purcell (1659–1695). With his tragically premature death we must end the story of autochthonous English music.

Picking up once more the thread of our story with Sweelinck, we find his pupils becoming the leading organists of northern Germany. Samuel Scheidt (1587–1654) wrote settings of chorales for organ and Johann Hermann Schein (1586–1630) was also important in this regard. Germany now equaled Holland in building organs both rich in sound and number. Particularly, the pedal division was enlarged and the composers were quick to take advantage of the new possibilities. Praetorius and Schütz wrote enormous quantities of music which is sometimes thought of only as leading up to Bach, just as Purcell once figured as paving the way for Handel. What is more correct to say is that both Schütz and Purcell have a place of their own, and that it is not always necessary to view art from a developmental point of view. The sacred oratorio, with its dramatic choruses, orchestra colors, pastoral interludes, solo arias, and recitatives, most of which it shared with the secular oratorio and the opera, now came north to Germany.

Johann Sebastian Bach (1685–1750) built his prodigious work by writing definitively in every style and in every form used by his predecessors. Conservative Leipzig had changed little of its service since Luther, and he had changed even less. The Mass (Kyrie and Gloria) was still sung in Greek and Latin. The cantata based on the proper for the day was the main innovation. Bach wrote some two hundred of these. They, together with his organ music, the two *Passions* and the B Minor Mass, comprise the *summa musica* of the church. From the same Saxon-Thuringian roots that Bach came from arose his contemporary, George Frederick Handel (1685–1759). After a career of writing and producing Italian opera in London, Handel returned to his earlier training and wrote thirty-two secular and sacred oratorios. The latter have become the principal fare of English and American audiences ever since. Both Bach and Handel so thoroughly crowned the "age of the high baroque" that the next generation struck out in an entirely different direction. Many socioeconomic factors combined to make it clear that the lead in musical life had left the church for the concert hall. Composers who followed at the highest level have written little for church services. Large-scale settings of the Mass text continue to challenge major composers, and we rejoice to have nonliturgical but highly important works by Mozart, Beethoven, Verdi, Brahms, Stravinsky, and Hindemith.

BIBLIOGRAPHY: P. H. Lang, *Music in Western Civilization* (New York, 1941); E. A. Wienandt, *Choral Music of the Church* (New York, 1965); *Schwann L.P. Record Catalog* (Boston).

**Church of England.** See ANGLICAN COMMUNION, THE.

**Church of God** (several types). As a result of a revival among American members of the German Reformed Church, John Winebrenner founded several congregations which took the name Church of God in 1825. In these churches, which organized denominationally as the Churches of God in North America (General Eldership) in 1830, there were to be only regenerate members accepting the Bible as the only rule of faith and practice. However, most of the organizations bearing the name Church of God date from the post-Civil War era as the result of a series of revival movements emerging from the presumed religiously indifferent Protestant denominations, notably the Methodist churches. In the 1880's this took two directions: the formation of Holiness churches, and the appearance of the Latter Rain Movement eventuating in Pentecostal churches. The Holiness churches claim to be loyal to the true Wesleyan tradition by emphasizing a conversion experience and the baptism of the Holy Spirit resulting in entire sanctification, i.e., perfectionism, and rejecting all creeds and traditions but those articulated in the Bible, as for example, the Church of God (Anderson, Ind.), a secession from the earlier Church of God. The Pentecostal churches also emphasize a conversion experience including the baptism of the Holy Spirit resulting in entire sanctification, but insist that this is to be accompanied by the gifts of prophecy, speaking in tongues, and divine healing. Some also particularly accent the doctrines of Adventism and premillennialism as integral parts of Biblical understanding. Antidenominationalism was at times evident in these movements as many of the congregations took the simple Biblical term "Church of God" as their designation. Among the leaders of this movement were R. G. Spurling and A. J. Tomlinson.

When the movement gained momentum in the early 20th century under various leaders and with varying doctrinal emphases, the result was a bewildering array of Church of God organizations throughout America, some not larger than individual congregations and some referring to actual denominations.

**Church of Scotland Act** (1905). Legislation passed by Parliament rectifying the impossible situation created by the legal decision that awarded the properties of the Free Church to a small minority (see WEE FREES) which had refused to merge with the United Presbyterians in 1900. A rider clause gave the Established Church of Scotland power to change the subscription formula to the Confession of Faith required of its ministers.

**Church of South India.** A church formed in 1947 by the union of the South India United Church, the Methodist Church in South India (British background), and the Anglican dioceses in the region. It was the first merger to combine episcopal, presbyterian, and congregational elements of polity in a single church order. Thirty-one Indians and two missionaries met at Tranquebar in May, 1919, to discuss church union as the prime necessity for the evangelization of India. They issued a call to all the churches in South India, and the South India United Church immediately appointed a committee to confer with other churches. The Church of India, Burma, and Ceylon in 1920 appointed a similar committee. The Methodists entered the negotiations in 1925. After nine years of consultations the *Scheme of Union* was published in 1929. It went through seven revisions up to 1942, and some additions were made in a reprinting in 1944. The Anglicans were enabled to continue by the general, although cautious, approval of the Lambeth Conference in 1920 and 1930. Approval was voted by the Methodist Church in 1943, the Church of India in 1945, and the South India United Church in 1946. The North Tamil Council of the last remained outside, but joined in 1950. A community of Anglicans in the Nandyal area of Dornakal Diocese rejected union. The church was inaugurated at Madras on Sept. 27, 1947. At that time nine new bishops were consecrated by the three Anglican bishops.

It was agreed that all presbyters or ministers of the uniting churches would be accepted as equal, but that henceforth all ordinations would be done by bishops with presbyters assisting. It was expected that complete unification of the ministry would thus be effected in about thirty years. Anglican churches vary in their degrees of recognizing the clergy of the Church of South India, but other associated churches abroad grant full recognition. There are fourteen dioceses which have much autonomy within their own areas, and the churches have great liberty in following their former traditions and ways of worship. The Constitution lays much stress on the general ministry of the laity and the specific forms in which it can be performed. Laymen actually have greater numbers in the Synod than clergy, each diocese being represented by a minimum of two presbyters and four laymen and a maximum of six and eight respectively.

The pastoral, evangelistic, and teaching functions of the bishop are stressed even above liturgical, disciplinary, and administrative duties. The moderator is elected from among the diocesan bishops, is *primus inter pares* rather than a metropolitan, and he is the symbolic official representative of the church in its relations with other churches or organizations.

Statistics for the Church of South India in 1962 reported 8,523 churches; 336,405 communicant members; 1,141,144 total community including those baptized and under instruction; 878 ordained clergy; 2,185 men lay workers; 1,151 women lay workers; 172 associated lay foreign missionaries; and 89 ordained missionaries.

It was the conviction at the outset that the Church of South India must not rest content with being a united church, but should strive to be a uniting church, taking the lead in promoting a complete union of the Protestant and Orthodox Churches in South India. Conversations with the Lutherans and two Conventions of Baptists began in December, 1948. The Baptists suspended negotiations the next year. The Lutheran and Church of South India talks continued, and by 1966 had agreed in all matters of doctrine and had come to consideration of episcopacy.

The several portions of *The Book of Common Worship* were issued for use as they were completed and authorized, and the entire book was accepted by the Synod of January, 1962. The order for the Holy Eucharist, or Lord's Supper, bears evidence of the several traditions united in the church, but it transmits the essential elements from the early church, and it is influential in liturgical reforms abroad. There is nothing distinctly Indian about it, but the kiss of peace has been taken from the Syrian Orthodox Church.

BIBLIOGRAPHY: R. D. Paul, *The First Decade* (Madras, 1958); B. Sundkler, *Church of South India: The Movement Towards Union: 1900–1947* (London, 1954); *The Book of Common Worship* (London and Madras,

1963); *The Constitution of the Church of South India* (Madras, 1956).

**Church of the New Jerusalem** (Swedenborgian). A widely spread but numerically small religious body which follows the teachings of Emanuel Swedenborg (1688–1722). It insists that the Bible is concerned only with spiritual matters. It holds that whenever the Bible refers to historical, natural, or scientific matters it must be understood according to "the science of correspondence," which is the key to opening the spiritual meaning of the Scripture.

**Church Peace Union** (*now called* Council on Religion and International Affairs). An organization founded in 1914 through the efforts of Charles S. Macfarland and Andrew Carnegie's gift of $2,000,000. A pioneer in interfaith cooperation, it includes Protestants, Catholics, and Jews. It created and financed the World Alliance for International Friendship Through the Churches from 1914 to 1948, and then the interfaith World Alliance for International Friendship Through Religion. It publishes a periodical entitled *Worldview*.

**Church Socialist League.** An organization of members of the Church of England which was founded in 1906 to give explicit endorsement to the principles of socialism. It sought to represent Anglican involvement in social politics by affirming: "Christianity is the religion of which socialism is the practice." It was soon weakened by the lack of agreement among its members as to its theological position and program.

**Church Social Union** (*popularly,* Christian Social Union). An American offshoot of the British movement of the same name. Founded in 1891 for the scientific study and analysis of social problems, it sought to prod the General Convention of the Episcopal Church to recognize the claims of the Social Gospel. Its more than one hundred issues of *Publications* were very influential. When in 1910 the Episcopal Church set up a Commission on Social Service, the Church Social Union disbanded the next year.

**Church Unification in the United States.** There have always been attempts to manifest the larger unity of the church, as one, holy, catholic, and apostolic, in the United States. The most obvious single characteristic about religion from the earliest colonial period has been division and divisiveness. America inherited all the major religious divisions of Europe, e.g., between Jew and Christian, Eastern Orthodox and Roman Catholic (see

SCHISM, EASTERN), Roman Catholic and the innumerable Protestant bodies. These divisions were transplanted, perpetuated, and often aggravated in the United States by immigrants trying to keep some identity in a hostile environment through the preservation of language and liturgical customs. Moreover, liberty under American government (e.g., First Amendment, 1791) allowed for the expression of individual preferences in religious matters. Thus America has been home for literally hundreds of bodies calling themselves churches, existing because of differences in doctrine, worship, and polity, as well as for nationalistic, sectional, racial, social, and psychological reasons.

There has been a strong urge, however, to unify the church in America, to satisfy Biblical, theological, and practical demands for a manifestation of larger union among Christians. Transformations of various bodies, mutual interdependence, and new challenges have made earlier reasons for division no longer vital or viable.

In the colonial period of Protestant dominance, attempts were made to unify Lutheran (cf. Nicholas Ludwig von Zinzendorf and Henry M. Muhlenberg) and Reformed bodies (cf. Michael Schlatter). Cooperation, not unity, was achieved among the dissenters of English Protestantism, particularly during the Great Awakening and the agitation against the appointment of an Anglican bishop for the colonies. This cooperation continued as Christians faced the problems of the frontier. Stimulated by the Second Awakening (c. 1800) and within the political structure of the nation, they cooperated along denominational lines (e.g., Plan of Union, 1801, between Presbyterians and Congregationalists), and through many "voluntary" societies, organized across denominational lines by interested individuals for missionary (e.g., American Board of Commissioners for Foreign Missions, 1810), educational (e.g., American Bible Society, 1816), and reforming (e.g., American Temperance Society, 1826) purposes. While these societies fostered a common Christian spirit, they did not satisfy deeper desires for the reunion of the church.

Among more important suggestions during the 19th century for the unification of the church were: (1) Alexander Campbell's "restorationism" on the basis of the primitive New Testament church (cf. *Declaration and Address,* 1809); (2) S. S. Schmucker's *Appeal to the American Churches* (1838) for an "apostolic Protestant church"; (3) William A. Muhlenberg's "evangelical catholicism" and William Reed Huntington's "church idea" which led to the "Chicago-Lambeth Quadrilateral" as the basis for Episcopal church union; (4) and Philip Schaff, who gave hope that there would be a "reunion of Christendom" through his developmental view of history. Out of this ferment the Evangelical Alliance was organized in the United States (1867) by individual Protestants after a voluntary society pattern. Other organizations followed to encourage cooperation among denominations. The Federal Council of Churches (1908) was organized on a denominational basis to help coordinate Christian social concern. Its successor, the National Council of Churches (1950), incorporated into its structure many of the older voluntary agencies of the 19th century. In addition to helping member denominations fulfill the work of *diakonia,* it introduced discussion of faith and order matters considered excluded until 1959. Reacting to what was considered a liberal and activistic orientation of the Federal Council of Churches and the National Council of Churches, other Christians organized the National Association of Evangelicals (1942) more after the pattern of the older Evangelical Alliance.

There have been several important organic unions, involving denominations of the same family and several of different families. Among the most significant new bodies that have been formed are the following: The Methodist Church in the United States (1939), healing a sectional division that occurred before the Civil War; The United Presbyterian Church in the United States of America (1957), bringing together two branches of Presbyterianism; the American Lutheran Church (1960), uniting several bodies of divergent national origins; and the union of the Congregationalists with some Disciples of Christ (1931), and of the Reformed and Evangelical Churches (1934) which led to the formation of the United Church of Christ (1957). Interest in the unification of the church continued in the important Consultation on Church Union (1962) in an attempt to develop a body, catholic, reformed, and evangelical. In addition to major divisions of English Protestantism this discussion included Negro Methodism which had emerged for racial reasons at the beginning of the 19th century. While many particular denominational bodies still exist in the United States, most Christians are included among the ten larger denominational bodies.

Christians in the United States have been involved in international attempts to realize the unity of the church, for mission and as "partners in obedience," with other Christians (e.g., youth organizations, the International Missionary Council, 1921, and the World Council of Churches, 1948, which took the former into its structure in 1961). Moreover, in the United States, Eastern Orthodox have been involved in cooperative enterprises with Protestants. Recently in the spirit of John XXIII and Vatican Council II (1962; cf. the decree on Ecumenism), Eastern Orthodox, Roman Catholics, and Protestants have been engaged in dialogue about the unity of the church. Since World War II, with the persecution of the Jews and the establishment of Israel, Christians have joined in conversations with Jews about the relation of the church to Judaism.

BIBLIOGRAPHY: R. M. Brown and D. Scott (eds.), *The Challenge to Reunion* (New York, 1963); J. A. Hutchison, *We Are Not Divided* (New York, 1941); R. Lee, *The Social Sources of Church Unity* (New York, 1960); J. D. Murch, *Cooperation Without Compromise* (Grand Rapids, 1956); H. R. Niebuhr, *The Social Sources of Denominationalism* (New York, 1957); S. S. Schmucker, *Fraternal Appeal to the American Churches* (Philadelphia, 1965).

**Church World Service.** An organization formed in 1946 by joint action of the Foreign Missions Conference of North America, the Federal Council of Churches, and the American Committee of the World Council of Churches. It combined and integrated the work of the Church Committee for China Relief, the Committee on Foreign Relief Appeals (for Europe), and the Church Committee for Relief in Asia. When the National Council of the Churches of Christ in the U.S.A. was created in 1950, Church World Service became a department of it. A new organizational structure of the Council was adopted in 1964, and Church World Service was combined with the Division of Foreign Missions to constitute the Division of Overseas Ministries. Its purpose is stated to be "to carry on works of Christian mercy, relief, technical assistance, rehabilitation, and interchurch aid" on behalf of Protestant and Eastern Orthodox Churches. Eighteen churches were full members in it, and nine others were associated. The program in 1964 expended some $44,000,000. Since 1949 the appeal for funds has been largely concentrated in One Great Hour of Sharing on a Sunday in March when offerings are taken in local churches throughout the United States. There are varieties of continuing programs and emergency disaster services (twenty-three of the latter in 1964).

BIBLIOGRAPHY: H. E. Fey, *Cooperation in*

*Compassion: The Story of C. W. S.* (New York, 1966).

**Church Year.** The calendar that determines the focus of liturgical worship began with the early church's commemoration of the resurrection each Sunday. By the middle of the 2d century, Easter and Pentecost were observed, Christmas not until the late 4th century. Although reformers reduced the crowded calendar that developed through the Middle Ages, they did not eliminate it entirely. Most recently, especially in America, national holidays and special observances such as Mother's Day and World Communion Sunday have performed a function like that of the liturgical feasts, but with less direct association with Christ. The major cycle of observances depends on the date of Easter and thus varies from year to year, while commemoration of saints follows the dating of the common calendar.

The semester, or half year, of Christ begins with *Advent,* a season of semipenitential preparation for Christmas. Its color is violet and it starts on the Sunday nearest St. Andrew's Day, Nov. 30. *Christmas* and its twelve days include many lesser commemorations, such as those for Saints Stephen and John, leading up to the *Epiphany,* Jan. 6. It is followed by a number of Sundays until roughly seventy days before Easter. Its color may be white, like that for Christmas, or change to green after the Feast of Epiphany itself. Septuagesima, Sexagesima, and Quinquagesima are the Sundays of *Pre-Lent,* the color either green or violet. *Lent,* violet, a season of fasting and penitence in preparation for Easter, begins on Ash Wednesday. Passion Sunday, two weeks previous to Easter, and Palm Sunday, beginning Holy Week, mark earlier limits of the season of preparation. Maundy Thursday, named for the mandate from Christ to observe the Last Supper, then Good Friday, black, commemorate the events immediately surrounding the crucifixion. *Easter,* white, continues through a season of five Sundays (forty days) until the following Thursday, which is *Ascension Day.* A Sunday after Ascension and another week lead to *Pentecost,* red, in honor of the descent of the Spirit on the apostles. The following Sunday is dedicated to the *Trinity,* white, and begins the semester of the church, green, during which Sundays are numbered after Pentecost or Trinity, continuing until the next Advent. Among the prominent saints' days there is a minor cycle of feasts connected with Mary, including the Presentation or Purification, Feb. 2; the Annunciation, March 25; her Nativity,

Sept. 8; and Assumption, Aug. 15. Michaelmas, or St. Michael and All Angels, Sept. 29, and All Saints' Day, Nov. 1, are among the few exceptions to the consecration of feasts to one person or event. Feasts in honor of doctrines such as the Trinity include Corpus Christi, the Thursday after Trinity Sunday, but such observances are rare.

**Cid, El.** The titles Cid, from the Arabic *sayyid* ("lord"), and Campeador ("champion") were given to Rodrigo Díaz de Vivar (1043–1099), who is the epic hero of medieval Spain and the subject of *The Poem of the Cid.* Though the Cid was long regarded as the great warrior of the *Reconquista,* he was a typical medieval Spanish nobleman who fought equally well for both Christian and Moslem employers, though he was a faithful Christian and patron of the church.

**CIMADE** (Comité Inter-Mouvement auprès des Evacués). A movement founded in 1939 by French Protestant youth leaders. Teams worked in Vichy, France, internment camps to aid refugees, political prisoners, and Jews, and saved many by spiriting them into neutral countries at the cost of some lives. After 1945, CIMADE set up centers in the war-torn cities of France and Germany. Its chief aims are to aid all those in need without discrimination and to incorporate a Christian presence by ecumenical teams.

**Circuit Rider.** A Methodist preacher on horseback traversing the land on regularly appointed rounds. The circuit rider was a common sight in the early decades of the American republic. Itinerancy had been developed by Wesley for use in England, but was perfected in the frontier conditions of America, especially under the leadership of Francis Asbury. The circuits were large, often taking a month or more to travel, and the living conditions were usually very rugged. The characteristic circuit rider was often young and single as well as without formal education. If he were an experienced man, he had a younger companion, whom he instructed as best he could. He carried with him his Bible, the Methodist Discipline, and the hymnbook, and whenever possible devoted himself to study and meditation. However, most of his time was spent in traveling, preaching nearly every day where he could or had made an appointment, supervising the class meetings and Bible studies, promoting coordination and unity among the Methodist brethren, and serving as an agent for the Methodist Book Concern, which also helped supply his meager salary. His work was carefully supervised by his presiding elder and the

Annual Conference, and he was appointed to a new circuit by his bishop at least every other year.

**Cistercian Order.** An austere order begun when Robert of Molesme, dissatisfied with the laxness of his Benedictine foundation, left it and set up a group of monks who with himself strictly observed the rule. Finally in 1098 they went to Cîteaux ("Stagnant Pools," or "Cisterns"). Robert was the catalyst rather than the true founder of the movement, since he was presently recalled to his own monastery. Before going he released the monks at Cîteaux from their obedience and they continued with Alberic as their leader. Alberic, protected by Paschal II, and the White Monks, so called to distinguish them from those wearing the black habits of the Benedictines, began to settle down and even collect *conversi*, or lay brothers. The third abbot, Stephen Harding, drew up the foundation charter of the movement, the *Charta Caritatis* which defined the elementary rules of the Cistercian organization. It was during his rule in 1112 that Bernard entered the monastery with some thirty noble companions. The accession strengthened the movement so that in 1113 the first colony at La Ferté was established, in 1114 the second at Pontigny, and in 1115 the third at Clairvaux. These three, with Morimond, were granted power to examine the purity of Cîteaux itself.

Unlike Cluny, each Cistercian monastery was an independent unit. There was, however, an annual chapter attended by the abbots of all Cistercian foundations. This yearly chapter met regularly until 1411. At it an unsatisfactory abbot could be deposed. Each abbot had the duty of visiting the daughter houses of his own foundation. While there he took precedence over the local abbot. The four daughter houses of Cîteaux sent their abbots to examine and correct anything amiss there and took precedence over its abbot during their visitation. This ensured unity of custom and discipline throughout the order and avoided the overcentralization of Cluny and the relative independence of Benedictine foundations. The Cistercian houses were exempt from episcopal jurisdiction, a privilege confirmed by Innocent II in 1132. They proved to be popular and at the height of Cistercian influence there were over seven hundred of them in Europe.

The buildings were usually in a lonely and forbidding place, often at the bottom of a valley rather than on a hill like houses of other orders. The prescription for manual labor in Benedict's Rule was adhered to and the monks cleared forests, drained swamps, and in time became skilled breeders of cattle and producers of wool. Their buildings were plain, representing "the architecture of truth"; rich church plate and decoration were sedulously avoided. Bernard vigorously attacked Cluny for the "disgusting monkeys and spotted tigers" uselessly and expensively carved on the pillars there. Visits from wealthy laity were not encouraged; the Cistercians were against tithes and churches being given to them, and even avoided rhymed hymns. Because of their isolation, they did little to help educate Europe. Their efficient farming methods brought them in contact with the world of commerce eventually, and the existence of the *conversi* was always a threat to internal unity. The development of city and cathedral life, the coming of the mendicant orders, and the Black Death contributed to their decline in the latter half of the 14th century. In England they were suppressed by Henry VIII, along with the other monasteries (1536–1540), but the isolation of abbeys like Rievaulx saved some of them from desecration by local plunderers.

BIBLIOGRAPHY: L. Bouyer, *The Cistercian Heritage* (Westminster, Md., 1958); A. A. King, *Cîteaux and Her Elder Daughters* (London, 1954).

**Cîteaux** (Latin, *Cistercium*). A Burgundian monastery founded in 1098 by Robert of Molesme, which became the motherhouse of the Cistercian Order. The abbot of Cîteaux is head of the entire order.

**Civil Constitution of the Clergy.** The ecclesiastical settlement adopted by the National Assembly of France and accepted with reluctance by Louis XVI on July 12, 1790. It caused the clergy to be elected, made them salaried state officials, reorganized dioceses, and in other ways made the French Church, in all but dogma and respect for the office of the pope, independent of Rome. Opposition caused the Assembly to demand an oath of support from the clergy. The Constitution was condemned by Pius VI in April, 1791. The result was to divide the church into the "jurors" and "nonjurors." Napoleon's Concordat of 1801 healed the breach.

**Civil Law.** Roman law distinguished, on the one hand, from the canon law of the church, and on the other, from the common law of the Germanic peoples. Its basic collection in the medieval period was the Corpus Juris Civilis, a codification of Roman law made during the 6th century. The civil law continued as the legal basis of the Byzantine Empire until the fall of Constantinople to the Moslems in 1453. However, in the West, civil law fell into disuse in the face of the migrations of the barbarian peoples with their common law. Yet the civil law was not totally forgotten and did much to influence the canon law of the Middle Ages. In the 11th century there was a revival of the study of civil law in the West, particularly in northern Italy with its great school of civil law at Bologna. Civil lawyers came to take their places alongside the canon lawyers. Civil lawyers were particularly sought after by the nascent nation-states that arose in northern Europe during the last centuries of the Middle Ages.

**Civil Rights.** While the American churches have presumably benefited from separation of church and state and religious liberty, their historic participation in matters of race, suffrage, and poverty has been ambiguous. Although John Eliot, Samuel Hopkins, and John Woolman were early advocates of social justice for Indians and Negroes, the energies of the churches were devoted to the conversion of souls, not the emancipation of disinherited elements of society. With independence, civil rights in the United States gained momentum less from any Christian imperative than from Enlightenment conceptions of natural law, emphasizing equality, freedom, and natural human rights. The churches became deeply agitated by 1830 over the question of Negro slavery and emancipation, and seemingly persuasive arguments based on historical conditions, morality, and the Bible were made on both sides of the issues. The abolitionist movement, led by T. D. Weld and W. L. Garrison, together with southern attachment to a slave society as argued by R. L. Dabney and J. H. Thornwell, polarized differences within the churches. Schism among Methodists, Presbyterians, and Baptists was intensified by the Civil War and Reconstruction. Separate Negro religious bodies were formed and northern and southern Protestantism each took on distinguishing characteristics. After the Civil War the churches found themselves singularly unprepared to cope with the moral questions involved in the emergence of an industrialized urban society filled with civil strife between labor and capital. In response some turned to the Christian Socialism of G. D. Herron, others accepted the laissez-faire individualistic "gospel of wealth" of Andrew Carnegie and the revivalism of Dwight L. Moody, while still others found an answer in the Social Gospel, the liberal position of Washington Gladden, Josiah Strong, and Walter Rauschenbusch. The effect of World War I, the "religious depression" of the '20s, and the economic depression of the '30s shattered the optimism of these movements and led to the emergence of "Christian Realism" as propounded by Reinhold Niebuhr and John C. Bennett, based on the "crisis theology" of Karl Barth. This movement launched a sharp criticism of optimistic liberalism, laissez-faire capitalism, and nationalism as trends damaging to human rights. It was argued that the churches must take a responsible and active position in political, economic, and social affairs. The historic 1954 Supreme Court decision to end racial segregation in public schools led to renewed agitation for Negro civil rights. In the same year the all-Negro Central Jurisdiction of The Methodist Church was ordered to be diffused into the rest of the denomination. Negro clergy, notably the Baptist Martin Luther King, Jr., provided an ideal, a program, and leadership for the movement, beginning with the bus boycott in Montgomery, Ala., in 1955 and 1956. In 1957, King formed the Southern Christian Leadership Conference, which acted as a catalyst for civil rights action in the South. It led mass prayer demonstrations and operated clinics to educate Negroes in the techniques of nonviolent passive resistance. Sit-in demonstrations for public accommodations began in 1960 in Greensboro, N.C. Church leaders have also been prominent in other civil rights organizations, including the NAACP, CORE, SNCC, and COFO. In 1963 the National Council of Churches formed a Commission for Civil Rights and in 1964 sponsored the Mississippi Delta Project for community centers and educational programs in largely Negro areas. The year 1963 also marked the formation of the National Conference on Religion and Race, and the Negro revolt by mass demonstrations in Selma and Birmingham, Ala., with participation by national church leaders. In 1964, Martin Luther King, Jr., received the Nobel Peace Prize, twenty-four Negro churches were burned in Mississippi, prominent Catholic, Protestant, and Jewish leaders joined in a large-scale equal-rights demonstration in Washington, D.C., the Civil Rights Act was passed by Congress, and King noted that "there will be neither rest nor tranquillity in America until the Negro is granted his citizenship rights." There were churchmen and churches that were also active in movements directly opposed to the aspirations of the civil rights movement, notably in the KKK, the White Citizens Councils, the Black Muslims, and the tension between Black Power and White Backlash of 1965 and 1966. Church support of civil rights has increased in recent years, but the depth and effectiveness of participation remains ambiguous.

BIBLIOGRAPHY: K. Haselden, *Mandate for White Christians* (Richmond, 1966); M. L. King, Jr., *Strength to Love* (New York, 1963); J. La Farge, *The Catholic Viewpoint on Race Relations* (Garden City, 1956); B. Marshall, *Federalism and Civil Rights* (New York, 1964); P. Ramsey, *Christian Ethics and the Sit-In* (New York, 1961).

**Civiltà Cattolica, La.** An influential bi-monthly cultural review devoted to criticism and opinion (from a Catholic viewpoint) of modern civilization. Edited at Rome, Via di Porta Pinciana, by Italian Jesuits, the journal, long projected, was realized after the revolutions of 1848. Carlo Curci, with the blessing and financial aid of Pius IX, launched the organ, publishing first at Naples. Curci got suitable collaborators, and the initial issue, April 6, 1850, with a novel by Antonio Bresciani in the romantic genre, was an immediate success. Soon there were twelve thousand subscribers. The format has remained virtually unchanged since the beginning: articles, contemporary chronicle, press review, and bibliography (added 1856). The publication was transferred to Rome in October, 1850, where a good library and valuable archives are provided. The Jesuit circulation numbers some twenty thousand copies. As an unofficial weathervane to Vatican opinion, *La Civiltà Cattolica* forecast and gave authoritative discussion on such important theological events as the proclamation of the dogmas of the Immaculate Conception, papal infallibility, and the assumption of the Virgin Mary, and on the Syllabus of Errors, both Vatican Councils, Americanism, Modernism, the condemnation of the royalist paper *L'Action Française,* plus the Lateran Pacts. A cumulative index has been prepared to 1910.

**Claim of Right.** Part of the formal declaration adopted by the Estates of Scotland on April 11, 1689, the other part being an invitation to William and Mary to accept the crown of Scotland. The Claim, like its counterpart, the English Declaration of Right, asserted the right of the Estates to dethrone a ruler for violation of the laws of the kingdom and it enumerated fifteen counts on which James II had flaunted the constitution and thus "forfeited" the throne.

**Clairvaux.** The fourth daughter house of the Cistercian Order, founded by Bernard of Clairvaux in 1115. During Bernard's lifetime Clairvaux was the most important center of Cistercian life. The monastery was closed and its property secularized in 1790.

**Clapham Sect.** A group of politically influential and socially concerned Anglican evangelicals of the early 19th century. The name was applied by Sydney Smith because of the concentration of members of the circle in the parish of Clapham. Its chief members were John Venn (rector), Charles Grant, Zachary Macaulay, Hannah More, James Stephen, Granville Sharp, Lord Teignmouth, Henry Thornton, and William Wilberforce. The group concerned itself with, among other things, the abolition of slavery, the establishment of Sierre Leone for freed slaves, missionary efforts, the foundation of the British and Foreign Bible Society, poor relief, and Sunday schools.

**Clarendon, Constitutions of** (1164). A codification in sixteen clauses of Henry II's policy regulating the relations between ecclesiastical and lay jurisdiction, signed at Clarendon, Wiltshire, in 1164. They extended the power of royal justice at the expense of the church courts, and, most important, provided that a cleric, after conviction for a criminal offense in a church court, should then be punished by a royal court. This issue occasioned the quarrel between Henry and Thomas à Becket.

**Clarendon Code.** Persecuting acts against English Puritans after the Restoration, named after the earl of Clarendon, then lord chancellor. The Church of England was reorganized by High Church leadership, and Parliament acted against the Puritans, now feared as seditious. The Corporation Act (1661) required municipal officials to take the Sacrament by the Anglican rite, excluding Puritans from political power. The Act of Uniformity (1662) demanded full acceptance of the Book of Common Prayer by all clergy and the re-ordination of those not episcopally ordained, leading to the Great Ejection of Aug. 24, 1662 (about two thousand Puritan clergy were ejected, about seventeen hundred on that day, others before; of these, 170 were Congregationalists, the rest mostly "Presbyterians," i.e., conservative Puritans who still desired a state church but could not conform). The Conventicle Act (1664) forbade worship outside the Establishment. The Five Mile Act (1665) forbade nonconformist clergy from coming within five miles of former parishes. The result was the narrowing of the Church of England and the appearance of dissenting "denominations" outside of it—Presbyterian, Congregationalist, and Baptist—subject to persecution and civic and social discrimination.

**Clare of Assisi** (c. 1194–1253). Attracted by the example and preaching of her fellow citizen Francis, at eighteen this girl of noble birth became a disciple of "Lady Poverty" and with her sister Agnes composed the nucleus of the first convent of Poor Ladies, or Poor Clares. Francis himself drew up their "way of life," modeled on a literal imitation of the gospel. Clare exemplified the total poverty, charity, and joy characteristic of the early Franciscan movement.

**Clarke, James Freeman** (1810–1888). Unitarian clergyman. Raised by his stepfather, who was minister of King's Chapel, Boston, and educated at Harvard, he was ordained in 1833. He served a Unitarian congregation in Louisville, Ky., until 1840, when he moved to Boston and founded The Church of the Disciples, which he served, except for the years from 1850 to 1854, until his death. In Boston he became a famous community figure, serving in a number of important positions. From 1867 to 1871 he was a nonresident professor at the Harvard Divinity School. He carried on active crusades against slavery and in favor of temperance and woman suffrage. In 1845 he drafted a statement against slavery signed by 173 Unitarian clergy. Always tolerant, he befriended Theodore Parker, although he did not accept all of Parker's more liberal views.

**Clarke, William Newton** (1840–1912). Baptist clergyman and theologian. After serving a church in Keene, N.H., Clarke became the pastor of the First Baptist Church in Newton Center, Mass. In 1880 he moved to the Olivet Baptist Church in Montreal, a cosmopolitan position permitting him more freedom. In 1883 he taught New Testament and homiletics at the Baptist Theological School in Toronto. By 1887 he took a pastorate in Hamilton, N.Y., and taught theology at Colgate Theological Seminary. The year 1890 found him the J. J. Joslin professor of Christian theology. After 1863 he had been involved in independent study of the doctrine of the atonement. His major work, *An Outline of Christian Theology,* was published in 1898. An epoch-making work, it was the first broad survey of Christian theology accepting the modern world view. He substituted vital and dynamic concepts for the traditional mechanical and static views. He stressed experiential evidence and the historical approach to Scripture. Theology was to be subordinated to piety. In 1903 he gave the Dudleian Lectures at Harvard and two years later the Taylor Lectures at Yale. Significant publications included *Commentary on Mark* (1881), *Can I Believe in God the Father?* (1899), *What Shall We Think of Christianity?* (1899), *A Study of Christian Missions* (1900), *The Use of the Scriptures in Theology* (1905), *Sixty Years with the Bible* (1909), *The Christian Doctrine of God* (1909), and *The Ideal of Jesus* (1911).

**Clarkson, Thomas** (1760–1846). English antislavery agitator. The writing of a prize Latin essay on the subject at Cambridge (1785) led Clarkson to dedicate his life to the cause of destroying human slavery. In 1787, he with William Wilberforce and a number of leading Quakers formed a committee of twelve to that end. The victory of his agitation is seen in the regulation of slave trade (1788), its abolition in the British Empire (1807) and by the great powers at Vienna (1815), and the emancipation of slaves in the British Empire (1833), in all of which he played an active and influential part.

**Claudel, Paul Louis Charles Marie** (1868–1955). French playwright, lyric poet, and diplomat; a convert to Roman Catholicism. Claudel's religion informed his thought and his work. As a playwright he wrote of the Christian drama of man's struggle for salvation. Because of their religious significance, his symbolic plays stand out in an age of secular drama. *Break of Noon* (1906), *The Tidings Brought to Mary* (1912), and *The Satin Slipper* (1928–1929) are among his most notable plays. Published in 1949, Claudel's correspondence with André Gide is likewise infused with his intense orthodoxy. After an active and varied career, Claudel spent his last years studying the Bible and writing Biblical commentaries in which he rejected modern textual criticism in favor of symbolic interpretation.

**Claudius I** (10 B.C.–A.D. 54). Roman emperor from A.D. 41. Because he was reputed to have been governed by slaves and women, his own ability as an administrator has been obscured. His importance for the history of Christianity lies in his support of the old Roman religion, represented in his refusal of divine honors, his efforts to suppress druidism and astrology, and his expulsion of the Jews from Rome. Suetonius explains the last as due to riots instigated by "Chrestus," so the Jews that Claudius had in mind may have been Christians.

**Claudius, Matthias** (1740–1815). A northern German Pietist poet, journalist, and translator. Using the pen name "Asmus," he won attention for his popular editorials and poetry. A friend of Goethe and Princess Gallitzin, he fought against both the rationalist and classical modes of his day, desiring to preserve literature in a Christian, natural, and indeed "folk" atmosphere. He translated the works of Fénelon and Saint-Martin.

**Clement V** (Bertrand de Got, 1264–1314). The first of the Avignon popes (1305–1314). He was a member of a distinguished French family near Bordeaux. After studying law at Orléans and Bologna, he enjoyed a rapid advancement in the church, becoming bishop of Comminges in 1295 and archbishop of Bordeaux in 1299. Following eleven months' deliberation he was elected pope, June 5, 1305, and crowned at Lyons in the presence of the French king. Because of strife in Rome he resided in various cities of France until, in 1309, he settled at Avignon. His relationship with the French king, Philip IV, constitutes the most important aspect of his reign, though he is also recognized for his contribution of the *Liber Septimus* to the Corpus Juris Canonici promulgated in 1314.

Relations between Clement V and Philip IV focused chiefly on two demands of the French king, the removal of the condemnations issued against him by Boniface VIII and the dissolution of the Order of Knights Templars. Both of these demands were granted by Clement V, though not without a struggle.

The accusation against Clement of servility toward the French king is justified, although Clement's reasons for remaining in Avignon were better than those of his successors, and he was responsible for what little justice there was in the controversy over the Templars. The pope's poor health contributed to the general weakness of his character, which is manifested also in his nepotism.

**Clement VI** (Pierre Roger, 1291–1352). Pope at Avignon from 1342. Born at Maumont Castle, Limoges, he entered a Benedictine monastery at the age of ten. He became archbishop of Rouen in 1330, cardinal in 1338, and was elected pope in 1342. He was the second of the Avignon popes and was responsible for establishing a permanent papal residence there. In 1348 he purchased the sovereignty of Avignon from Joanna of Naples for 80,000 florins. His reign, like that of his predecessor, was characterized by French partisanship and nepotism.

After the outbreak of the plague in 1348, Clement VI gave evidence of both generosity in alleviating the distress of the poor and courage in defending the Jews, who were persecuted as the cause of the plague. He was more a prince than a pope, however, and his extravagant living led to an increase in taxes for ecclesiastical revenue, which was to prove a source of bitter resentment against the papacy.

During his reign he accepted the submission of William of Occam and the Franciscan Spiritualists and condemned the Flagellants as heretics. He extended the blessing of the church to newly discovered lands, establishing a bishopric for the Canary Islands in 1351.

**Clement VII** (Giulio de' Medici, 1478–1534). Pope from 1523. A nephew of Lorenzo the Magnificent, he was elevated to the cardinalate in 1513, at the same time that his cousin Giovanni de' Medici became Pope Leo X. Under Leo, Giulio became a leading framer of papal policy. A likely candidate for the papacy, Giulio was not elected after Leo's death in 1521, but only after the death of Pope Adrian VI in 1523. Attempting to practice Italian internecine politics by playing off the various sides against each other, Clement VII succeeded only in forming vacillating alliances and earning a reputation for indecision. This diplomatic wavering had disastrous results, as evidenced not only by the invasion of the Vatican by the Colonna cardinals in 1526 but also by Clement's relations with Henry VIII. Henry had commissioned Cardinal Wolsey to have the dispensation obtained from Julius II for Henry to marry Catherine of Aragon (1509) revoked so that with this marriage invalidated Henry could then marry Anne Boleyn. Clement was initially receptive to this proposal. Even after a first commission had decided against Henry, Clement appointed a secret commission consisting of Cardinals Wolsey and Campeggio. Although the commission was empowered to repeal Julius' dispensation, it was kept from doing so by the discovery of an additional brief by Julius which left no doubts on the issue.

**Clement VII** (Robert of Geneva, 1342–1394). Antipope. After some time spent as bishop of a smaller diocese, Robert of Geneva was named archbishop of Cambrai, and in 1371, cardinal. He served as the legate of Pope Gregory XI in Italy, where he brutally put down various feuds and civil disorders. When the French cardinals contested the election of Urban VI, they chose Robert as pope in 1378, thus beginning the Western Schism. Having returned to Avignon in 1379, Clement refused all offers of mediation, including those by the University of Paris and Catherine of Siena.

**Clement VIII** (Ippolito Aldobrandini, c. 1536–1605). Pope from 1592. Born at Fano of a Florentine family, he studied jurisprudence under his father. Having joined the papal service, he was made a cardinal and received the office of grand penitentiary in 1585. His success in gaining the release of the imprisoned Archduke Maximilian (an unsuccessful claimant to the Polish throne) earned him the goodwill of the Hapsburgs, and in the conclave of 1592 he was chosen pope through the influence of those cardinals who wished to free the papacy from the power of Philip II of Spain, a policy he himself was somewhat reluctant to pursue. In 1595, Clement received Henry IV of France into the Roman Church, thus hastening the end of the Wars of Religion (1562–1598) and gaining an ally in his struggle for the independence of the papacy in Italy. In 1598 he helped negotiate peace between Spain and France (the Treaty of Vervins), as well as between France and Savoy. He also aided the emperor in his war with the Turks in Hungary. Clement ruled the Papal States severely, saw to the revision of the Vulgate Bible and the Roman liturgical books, and took part in the controversy on grace (*De auxiliis*) between the Jesuits and the Dominicans (see EFFICACIOUS GRACE). A devout man, he was a long-time friend of Philip Neri.

**Clement IX** (Giulio Rospigliosi, 1600–1669). Pope from 1667. He was nuncio to Spain and secretary of state for Pope Alexander VII before becoming pope himself in 1667. Clement saw his role as one of pastor and conciliator. He heard confessions in St. Peter's and visited the sick. After the church in Portugal freed itself from Spain, Clement reorganized it and brought it unity and stability. He also mediated peace between France and Spain and established a temporary compromise with the French Jansenists (Clementine Peace). He did not, however, ignore his prophetic duties, but was quick to condemn the aggression of Louis XIV and his alliance with the Turks.

**Clement X** (Emilio Altieri, 1590–1676). Pope from 1670. He was involved in various papal diplomatic and legal duties before being made a cardinal by Clement IX shortly before the latter's death. The conclave that met to elect a new pope lasted for five months and finally chose Altieri as a compromise candidate. Clement X sought to preserve peace in Europe and supported Poland against the Turks. During the latter part of his reign he occasioned bitterness at Rome by turning much power over to an adopted nephew.

**Clement XI** (Giovanni Francesco Albani, 1649–1721). Pope from 1700. A native of Urbino, Italy, he attracted the attention of ex-Queen Christina of Sweden through his scholarship. He likewise won acclaim as bishop (Rieti, Sabina, and Orvieto) and secretary of papal briefs. Popular even with Protestants, he reigned during the difficult time of the War of Spanish Succession. He was caught between the rivalry of the Hapsburgs and Bourbons, and found his lands molested and his rights ignored, particularly at the Treaty of Utrecht (1713). Clement XI contributed to victories over Moslems by Prince Eugene in Hungary and by the Republic of Venice in Greece. He governed his territories well, avoided nepotism, built lavishly, aided the poor, and collected rare manuscripts. He refused to recognize the royal title assumed by Frederick I of Prussia, aided the exiled Stuarts of Britain, and raised Lisbon to the rank of patriarchate. He condemned Jansenism in the bull *Unigenitus* (1713), having forecast his position eight years before. The pope was interested in missions and pronounced on the Chinese rites controversy (1704, 1710, 1715) in favor of Dominicans and Franciscans and against Jesuits who favored accommodation to local customs. Similar conclusion was made of the Malabar rite difficulty in India (see SYRIAN ORTHODOX CHURCH OF MALABAR). Clement's twenty-one-year pontificate had lasted longer than any since the 12th century.

**Clement XII** (Lorenzo Corsini, 1652–1740). Pope from 1730. Elevated at the advanced age of 78, he succeeded Benedict XIII. A lawyer first of all, he held various curial offices before being selected pontiff. Albeit in failing health and losing his sight within two years, he displayed surprising energy for those expecting an interim pope. He jailed embezzlers, rationalized commercial laws, reintroduced the lottery to lower taxes, carried out public works including the embellishment of St. John Lateran Cathedral. Clement XII displayed interest in reunion with the Eastern Orthodox Church and established in Calabria a college for Greek priests. He likewise concerned himself with the Melchite and Maronite rites, extending patronage to them. Outside Rome, the Chiana marshes were drained, San Marino's independence restored, and Ancona favored. The pope issued the first decree (*In eminenti*) against Freemasons in 1738, and another the next year. He encouraged the Passionists and reunited some Egyptian Copts with Rome. Clement XII was unable to maintain papal claims over Parma and Piacenza, but forced the Bourbons of Naples to renew their annual tribute. Missions were established to Tibet and Tartary while free exercise of church jurisdiction was pressed in Bourbon-controlled Spain, France, and the Two Sicilies.

**Clement XIII** (Carlo Rezzonico, 1693–1769). Pope from 1758. A native of Venice, he was trained in early youth by Jesuits for papal service, achieved distinction, became a cardinal priest in 1737, and pope during the Seven Years' War. Although Clement XIII favored arts, artists, and antiquities, he placed on the Index the *Encyclopédie* of Diderot, Rousseau's *Émile*, and Febronius' (pseudonym) *De statu ecclesiae*. A powerful attack was launched by the Bourbon courts of Spain, France, Naples, and Parma against the Jesuit Society. *Philosophes* saw the Jesuits as leading supporters of a church that restricted freedom of conscience and thought. Princes saw them as opponents of national churches and episcopal patronage. Jesuit antagonism to Indian slavery in Latin America, monopolies in education, and competition in commerce and industry were issues. Portugal's Count Pombal accused the Jesuits of complicity in an attempt on King Joseph's life, jailed and deported them. France, at the behest of its *parlements* (superior courts) followed suit. Spain disembarked Jesuits abruptly on the shores of the Papal States. The Bourbon monarchs, united in a family compact to bring dissolution of the order, occupied the papal enclaves—Avignon (France), Pontecorvo, and Benevento (Naples)—or laid imposts (Spain). Clement XIII died leaving the thorny question to his successor.

**Clement XIV** (Giovanni Vincenzo Antonio [Lorenzo] Ganganelli, 1705–1774). Pope from 1769. A Franciscan, as pope he issued a decree dissolving the Jesuits in the 18th century. He was a member of the Curia and received the biretta from Clement XIII, his predecessor. A compromise candidate in the difficult three months' conclave of 1769 which was marked by the intrusion of two Hapsburg princes, Ganganelli was chosen after a score of cardinals had been rejected by the Bourbon courts and a siege of Rome threatened unless the new pope agreed to dissolve the Jesuits. Speculation still exists over whether Clement XIV gave any preelection pledges. In any case, under heaviest pressure, he permitted a tribunal with judicial form to examine the charges. The temper of politics was anti-clerical and the mood of society was secular. Finally the pope yielded to importunity, and a brief, *Dominus ac redemptor noster,* dated July 21, 1773, dissolved the Society of Jesus. Some Jesuits were protected for a time by Prussian and Russian monarchs, and even by the Grand Turk. Catholic historians view the ban as a moral defeat for the papacy, one that left notable gaps in education and foreign missions. The affair broke the health of the pontiff and he died fourteen months later. Rumors

of poisoning have been discounted. By the end of the reign the Bourbons had withdrawn from the enclaves, but Rome, badly administered, was full of complaints.

**Clementine Literature.** The ancient habit of publishing works under the name of great men to invoke their authority for the works, together with the high regard in which Clement of Rome was held, accounts for the rather large body of materials inaccurately attributed to him. Neglecting works that have also been assigned to others, we still have: (1) The Second Epistle of Clement, (2) two Epistles to Virgins, (3) the Clementine Homilies, (4) the Clementine Recognitions, and (5) excerpts from the latter two in various languages. Since these works have little in common except that the same authorship is ascribed to them, they will be inspected individually.

1. *The Second Epistle of Clement.* This work appears not to be an epistle at all, but a sermon written to be delivered orally to a congregation; it refers to what the speaker and his auditors will do when they return home and it speaks of passages of the Scriptures that have been read to the congregation in the course of the address. It is generally assigned to Corinth at about the time of the Shepherd of Hermas, that is, about 150. Jerome says, "There is a second letter circulating under Clement's name, but it is not acknowledged as such by the men of antiquity" (*Of Illustrious Men* 15). Its most interesting points are a doctrine of the church as preexistent and invisible before its earthly concretion, and an early presentation of the possibility of postbaptismal repentance.

2. Two *Epistles to Virgins.* The two letters are actually one work from the first half of the 3d century which treats of celibacy as a supernatural gift. The author, who may have been Palestinian, is practical enough to appreciate the difficulties of having male and female religious communities living under one roof. This work is valuable as one of our earliest accounts of Christian asceticism.

3. The twenty *Homilies,* together with the ten books of *Recognitions,* are a part of the apocryphal or fictional literature of the early church. These have more of a catechetical and apologetic purpose than some of the early Christian novels. The *Homilies* begin with Clement as a member of the imperial family who sets out to explore the various schools of philosophy in much the same way as Justin Martyr. Hearing of the birth in Bethlehem, he goes to the Holy Land, where he meets Peter, whom he accompanies on his apostolic jour-

neys. The encounter of Peter with Simon Magus gives an opportunity for polemic against that Gnostic sect.

4. The ten books of *Recognitions* continue the story of Clement and Peter and revolve around the separation and reunion of Clement's family. There is some question whether this is a work by the same author as that of the *Homilies*. The *Recognitions* are less Jewish and even have one explicitly Trinitarian passage (1. 69). Since we possess the work only in the Latin translation of Rufinus, we cannot be sure of the extent of his editing. Most scholars would agree that the two works are related, not by a dependence of one on the other but by a common dependence on the same source. Cullmann thinks that source was the Itinerary of Peter. There is a strong ascetic strain in the works which goes to the extent of making Peter a vegetarian and has him use water for the Eucharist—which was done by a number of more or less heretical sects of the late 1st and 2d centuries. The definite repudiation of virginity cannot be so certainly described as Jewish when Jewish sects often maintained the ideal and a number of Hellenistic Gnostic sects did not.

5. Excerpts from the *Homilies* and *Recognitions* exist in several collections and translations. We have two epitomes in Greek of the *Homilies* that expand the excerpts by the use of other sources. An Arabic version of the two works omits the discourses and tells only the story. The *Refutations* survive in a Syriac translation as well as in the Latin of Rufinus.

BIBLIOGRAPHY: R. M. Grant (ed.), *The Apostolic Fathers,* Vol. 1 (New York, 1964); A. Roberts and J. Donaldson (eds.), *The Ante-Nicene Fathers,* Vol. 8 (Grand Rapids, 1951–1952); E. J. Goodspeed and R. M. Grant, *A History of Early Christian Literature* (Chicago, 1966).

**Clement of Alexandria.** Greek theologian of the early Christian church. He was born about the middle of the 2d century A.D., probably in Athens, of pagan parents. Like many men of his time, he traveled about to receive instruction from various teachers. His journeys ended when he found Pantaenus, the head of a Christian school in Alexandria, about the year 180. He spent the following twenty years there, teaching in the Christian school, first under Pantaenus and then succeeding him as head of the school. This is the period of Clement's life during which he wrote most of his works. With the outbreak of persecution under Septimius Severus (c. 202), Clement fled from Alexandria. We next hear of him in two

letters written by Alexander, bishop of Jerusalem. The first, dated 211, speaks of Clement as the dispatcher of the letter, and the second, dated 215, speaks of "the holy Clement," one of "those blessed fathers who have gone on before us." The date of his death can thus be fixed as having occurred sometime between 211 and 215. The first letter refers to Clement as "the blessed presbyter," and so it appears that he was at some point ordained a presbyter.

Clement's chief extant writings are his great trilogy, the *Protrepticus* ("Exhortation to the Greeks"), the *Paedagogus* ("The Instructor"), and the *Stromateis* ("The Miscellanies"). The latter was originally in seven books, but later an eighth book was added, which consists of notes on logical questions and does not share the general character of the rest of the work. In the first chapter of the *Paedagogus,* Clement distinguishes three functions of the Divine Logos as *Protrepticus, Paedagogus,* and *Didascalus.* These three functions correspond to the three needs of mankind to be converted, to undergo a moral transformation, and to be taught the way of truth and salvation. The functions have traditionally been seen as reflected in the three works Clement wrote. The difficulty is that the works themselves do not carry this out in consistent fashion with respect to subject matter. This is particularly true of the *Stromateis,* which retraces ground covered in the earlier works and is generally unsystematic, not fulfilling perfectly the function of a *"Didascalus."* This has led to a number of theories concerning the date and composition of the *Stromateis,* all of which remain inconclusive for lack of external evidence. The controversy has not been without value, however, since it points up the fact that the three works cannot be read in facile fashion as simply carrying forward the indications given by Clement in the first chapter of the *Paedagogus.* Besides these three works, there survive to us a homily *Quis dives salvetur?* ("Whether a rich man can be saved?") written to show that Christ condemned not wealth in itself but only the wrong attitude toward wealth, and two collections of material, the *Excerpta ex Theodoto* and the *Prophetic Eclogues,* which, like the eighth book of the *Stromateis,* were probably intended as notes of a preparatory nature that Clement seems to have used already in the writing of the *Paedagogus* and the *Stromateis,* and which he intended to work up further into other finished writings. There are, lastly, some remaining fragments in catenae, and the like.

Clement's chief importance in the history

of the church lies in his successful attempt to bring Greek culture into a fruitful relationship with the truth of the faith at a time when his contemporaries, both theologians and ordinary lay Christians, were fearful of Greek philosophy and culture because it could and did sometimes lead to heresy. Thus Tertullian held that philosophy was the mother of all heresy, and Hippolytus that every heretic derived his ideas from some pagan philosopher. Clement saw, however, that if the church permanently shut itself off from the Greek intellectual tradition, it would have to give up its mission to the educated classes. Clement's own knowledge of Greek literature was so great that Jerome praised him as the most learned of all the fathers. Although he followed the practice of the time by taking many of his quotations from poetic anthologies and handbooks of philosophical opinions, he knew Homer, Euripides, Plato and the Stoics, and Philo at least at firsthand, if not the book of Heraclitus and perhaps part of Empedocles' works.

Clement has various opinions which he advances concerning the origin and role of Greek philosophy, but which he never wholly reconciles. He says that some attribute the fact that the Greeks expressed something of the true philosophy (Christianity) to chance, but chance is subject to Divine Providence, and hence Greek philosophy must have something of the nature of prophecy. The Greeks had also learned something of divine wisdom from reflection on the image of God within themselves which all men have, however, obscured. Clement also picked up the theory of the Jew Aristobulus, to which he devotes an inordinate amount of space, that the Greeks stole their wisdom from Moses, having plagiarized from the Old Testament. Thus he views Greek philosophy as really a dim reflection of the divine wisdom of the Jews. It is often obscure or only dimly aware of the truth, and frequently in error, but Clement treats it as a preparation for the gospel analogous to the divine revelation granted to the Jews in the Old Testament.

With regard to particular philosophers, Clement gives first place to Plato. In his portrayal of the Christian Gnostic many Stoic elements are present. He knows Aristotle, and he has several dozen quotations from the pre-Socratics, particularly Heraclitus, who assists him in correlating faith and reason. In many places dependence on Middle Platonism is clear, in which Stoic and peripatetic teaching is mixed with Platonic. Clement's "negative theology," i.e., his view that human concepts can never express the divine nature in its real essence but are useful only as pegs for the mind to hang on to, stems from the Middle Platonist Albinus. Epicurus is condemned for his ungodliness and his denial of Divine Providence. Generally speaking, philosophy is useful as far as it goes; it has a dim vision of the truth, but its knowledge of God is only a preliminary general sketch which can only be filled out by the wisdom that comes from Christ.

Clement also stands in a positive relation to the Gnostic teachers, particularly the heretical Christian Gnostics Basilides and Valentine, who had flourished as eminent teachers at an earlier date at Alexandria, but he rejects their excesses. He is willing, however, to describe the ideal Christian as a true Gnostic, and used the term freely in an orthodox sense. Origen did not follow him in this. Clement finds the term useful because his concept of the highest Christian life is expressed as the knowledge of God. Faith is the beginning step of the Christian life, but the knowledge of God is the perfection of faith. It is higher than faith because by it man participates in the life of God. The knowledge of God is perfected in love. Clement tends to pattern his Christian Gnostic after the Stoic wise man, and he teaches the value of *apatheia*, or the absence of passion. The true Gnostic will be ready to undergo martyrdom out of love because he will then sooner be assimilated to God.

Clement is a witness to the common tradition of the church, but churchly tradition does not play a large part in his writings as such. He took the apostolic tradition as his starting point in matters of faith, and besides the primitive Christian writings, he held the oral tradition to be part of the apostolic teaching. The Bible he used was in the main the Septuagint, and he interpreted the Scriptures allegorically, taking his cue from Philo and the Stoics. He knows of a creed in which the church's articles of faith are contained.

He has not arrived at the traditional doctrine of original sin as a solidarity of humanity in Adam's sin, but all men in fact use their free will wrongly and can be described as sick, blind, and gone astray. He denies the Gnostic teaching that sex or anything material is sinful in itself, on the ground that this impugns the doctrine of creation. He asserts that Christ is both God and man, but some of his practical statements about the humanity of Christ have a docetic ring. Clement speaks of baptism as imparting regeneration, enlightenment, divine sonship, immortality, and remission of sins. Baptism imprints the seal of the Spirit; the indwelling Spirit is a "shining impress" of the Christian's membership in Christ. The Eucharist is a participation in Christ's incorruptibility, and sanctification of soul and body. The elements are identified with Christ's body and blood. More often than not, however, in his writings, what seems to be a reference to the Eucharist becomes an allegory of the true Gnostic's knowledge; feeding on the flesh and blood of the Logos means apprehending the divine power and essence.

Clement's great merit is that he saved the church from intellectual alienation from culture. With a sure grasp of the fundamental Christian realities, his comprehensive mind brought all the human learning of his day into the service of the church. He may have lacked some perspective and he may have overdrawn certain positions, but he made Christianity a religion that could stand on its own intellectually and compete with the rival claims of the other philosophical and religious positions of his time, and he was himself an able teacher of his fellow Christians and a guide to the Christian life.

BIBLIOGRAPHY: C. Bigg, *The Christian Platonists of Alexandria* (Oxford, 1913); G. W. Butterworth, *Clement of Alexandria* (Cambridge, Mass., 1953); H. Chadwick, *Early Christian Thought and the Classical Tradition* (New York, 1966); E. Molland, *The Conception of the Gospel in the Alexandrian Theology* (Oslo, 1938); E. F. Osborn, *The Philosophy of Clement of Alexandria* (Cambridge, 1957); J. E. L. Oulton (ed.), *Alexandrian Christianity* (The Library of Christian Classics, Vol. II, Philadelphia, 1954).

**Clement of Rome.** Author of a letter addressed about A.D. 95 by the church of Rome to the church of Corinth in order to restore peace and proper order in a community upset by a rebellion against presbyteral authority. The letter, regarded as Scripture by several writers of the 2d and 3d centuries, provides examples from the Old Testament, from the lives of Peter and Paul (martyred because of "envy"), from the order of the universe, and from apostolic intentions to provide a succession of bishops (apparently equivalent to, if not precisely identified with, presbyters); these show that God intends order and punishes disorder. After the 4th century the letter was practically forgotten, since to Clement were now ascribed such documents as the Clementine *Homilies* and *Recognitions* (fictional presentations of Ebionite or semi-Ebionite doctrine) and the Apostolic Constitutions (a treatise on church order supposed to come from the apostles through Clement). By the 3d century his name had already attracted to

itself an anonymous sermon now known as 2 Clement (see HYGINUS) and two books of an anonymous treatise on virginity. Only in 1633 was the genuine letter, discovered in the Biblical Codex Alexandrinus, first published at Oxford by Patrick Young. In more recent times a more complete Greek text, not to mention versions in Latin, Syriac, and Coptic, has been found.

Practically nothing is known of Clement apart from this letter. Irenaeus regards him as bishop of Rome, but the letter says nothing of such an office, and in the time of Hermas "presbyters" governed the church there. Hermas mentions a certain Clement as in charge of correspondence with "those outside," and our letter may therefore have been written by the "foreign secretary" of a college of presbyter bishops at Rome. Clement has sometimes been related to the consul Flavius Clemens, executed in 95 (but not necessarily as a Christian); he may have been a freedman in the consul's service.

The letter is significant for three reasons: (1) It reflects a rather high level of Hellenistic and Jewish culture present in the Roman church by the end of the 1st century. Clement writes a good Greek and knows something of rhetoric. (2) It reflects a rather Roman concern for order and organization. Clement compares the church with the Roman army and insists upon succession as the principle of order (a question with which Romans were concerned in his time). He advocates prayer for the Roman state. It may even be that close commercial relations between Rome and Corinth encouraged the action of the Roman church. (3) It reflects the significant position of the Roman church, if not of the Roman bishop. Clement does not say that the Corinthians had sought Roman counsel, though it would appear that some leaders had gone to Rome. The Roman church sent not only the letter but also an embassy whose members were to take action and report to Rome. Since the letter was later read at Corinthian worship, it must have achieved its purpose. It may be that it also contributed to the movement toward monarchical episcopacy, both at Rome and at Corinth.

The earliest witness to the letter's title (Dionysius of Corinth) speaks of it as written "through Clement" by the Roman church. One person wrote it, but the authority it mentions was that of the church, not of an individual. The inspiration of the Holy Spirit of which it speaks was regarded as expressed in the words not of Clement as Clement or as bishop but of the Spirit-endowed community of which he was only the instrument.

The high value assigned to the letter in early times is shown by its use at Corinth and by references to it as Scripture by such writers as Irenaeus, Clement, and Origen. It comes at the end of the 5th-century Codex Alexandrinus but is not separated from Biblical books; a late Syriac manuscript also treats it as Biblical.

Clement is a witness to many Old Testament books (including Judith) and to some apocryphal writings now lost; he makes use of Hebrews (at a later date it was sometimes thought that he was the editor of the epistle) and of the Pauline epistles, especially I Corinthians. He quotes "words of the Lord Jesus" in a form which suggests either that he is combining several Gospels (especially Matthew and Luke) or that he uses oral traditions like those known to the Evangelists.

Evidence for his martyrdom is very late, and the supposed discovery of his relics in the Crimea during the 9th century reflects pious imagination, not historical fact.

BIBLIOGRAPHY: R. M. Grant (ed.), *The Apostolic Fathers,* Vols. 1–2 (New York, 1964–1965); E. J. Goodspeed and R. M. Grant, *A History of Early Christian Literature* (Chicago, 1966).

**Clerestory** (*also* clerestorey, clearstory). An outside wall of any room continued above the level of the surrounding roofs in order to allow for windows to light the room. An ancient building device (e.g., the temple at Karnak), it was adopted by the Romans (e.g., S. Maria degli Angeli, formerly the tepidarium of Diocletian's Baths) and so entered medieval church architecture. In Romanesque and Gothic churches, the clerestory with its many windows allows illumination for the nave which would otherwise be very dark.

**Clergy Reserves.** Lands set aside in Upper and Lower Canada under the Constitutional Act of 1791 "for the support and maintenance of a Protestant clergy." Though no definition of the term "Protestant clergy" was contained in the act, the Bishop John Strachan and successive colonial governors managed to retain a monopoly on the Reserves for the Church of England. In Upper Canada, where the majority of the population belonged to denominations other than the Church of England, this interpretation became a major grievance. The Presbyterians were the first to challenge this monopoly on the grounds that the Church of Scotland was also an established church and that they were therefore entitled to a share of the Clergy Reserves. This claim was eventually recognized and monopoly gave way to a compromise with state-church pluralism. This solution, however, was unacceptable to those who refused to recognize the principle of state support for religion and insisted that the Reserves were the collective inheritance of the inhabitants of the province. Such people raised the issue of voluntaryism versus any form of state-church establishment and demanded the secularization of the Clergy Reserves. In 1854 the MacNab-Morin Administration finally brought the struggle to a conclusion by passing the Clergy Reserves Act which secularized the Reserves. This act was not a clear victory for the supporters of the voluntary principle, however; it was instead a compromise, for both the Church of England and the Presbyterians retained the endowments that had been granted to them earlier.

**Clerical Abuses Bill** (1889). Anticlerical portion of the Italian penal code of that year dealing with clergy who in the exercise of their functions committed crimes. Under the title "Abuses of Ministers of Cults," specified as punishable were: arousing scorn or vilifying state laws, institutions, or acts of authority. The bill also provided for the punishment of any cleric performing acts of public worship contrary to the prescriptions of the government. Thus the secular power was to predominate over the ecclesiastical, and the clergy was to be reduced to the same level as the laity before the law. A muzzling of the Italian priests, the bill was updated by the 1930 penal code to shackle clergy in Catholic Action groups.

**Clericis Laicos.** Bull of Pope Boniface VIII issued in the spring of 1296 and directed particularly against the actions of Edward I of England and Philip IV of France in an attempt to put the property of the medieval church beyond the reach of the civil law. Under pain of excommunication and the interdict, it forbade the alienation of ecclesiastical revenue to the state without the prior permission of the papacy.

**Clericus of Leclerc, Jean.** See LE CLERC, JEAN.

**Clermont, Council of** (1095). A council called by Pope Urban II for ecclesiastical reform. The Council of Clermont occasioned the launching of the First Crusade. Envoys from the Byzantine emperor Alexius I Comnenus had approached Urban asking aid against the Turks. In one of the most effective speeches of history, Urban exhorted the assembled French knights to take up arms to wrest the Holy Land from the infidel Turks. At the end of his address hundreds shouted, "God wills it." The Crusades had begun.

**Clifford, John** (1836–1923). English Baptist minister and religious leader. Born into a poor family, he became a factory worker when eleven years old. He early studied the Bible on his own, entered the ministry in 1858, became pastor of Praed Street Church, Paddington. Under his leadership the congregation expanded and built Westbourne Park Chapel in 1877. Early in his ministry, Clifford graduated from the University of London with degrees in arts, sciences, and law. His belief that religion should permeate all of life led him into activities for which he was often criticized. He worked for social reforms; he championed Darwin, whom he considered a fellow seeker after truth; and he became a member of the Fabians. He led opposition to the 1902 Education Act which was subsequently defeated, as was its proponent, the Conservative Party, in 1906. When Charles H. Spurgeon withdrew from the Baptist Union on grounds that it was too liberal, Clifford supported the Union, arguing that liberty and lack of formal creed constituted the chief glory of the denomination. He opposed Protestant union movements, insisting that this would involve sacrificing too many basic beliefs. Clifford was first president of the Baptist World Alliance (1905–1911) and held many other important posts. He traveled extensively in the cause of Baptist unity. His ninety-nine pamphlets and books include *Is Life Worth Living?* (1880) and *God's Greater Britain* (1899), inspired by his world tour. In 1921, George V conferred upon him the Companionship of Honour.

**Cloister.** A covered passageway connecting the chapter house, refectory, or other parts of a monastery, church, or university, often running around an open court or quadrangle. A plain wall formed one side of this arcade, with the opposite side, which opened on the court, containing a series of windows between piers or columns which were covered with a vaulted ceiling. The cloisters served as places for quiet walks and contemplation or study and lectures. The word "cloister" also refers to a place of religious seclusion, such as a convent, or to the religious (or cloistered) life in general.

***Cloud of Unknowing, The*** (c. 1355). An anonymous treatise on mysticism, written in East Midland English. The writer appears to have been acquainted with the French mystical theologians of the Abbey of St.-Victor, yet assumes the ordinary sacramental and devotional life of medieval England. Reason seeks God, but only love can penetrate the "dark cloud" which prevents the contemplative from seeing God, so he must cling to God in loving faith. Another anonymous work, *The Book of Privy Counselling,* is thought to be a sequel to *The Cloud.*

**Clovis** (c. 466–511); **Clotilda** (474–545). King and queen of the Franks. Clotilda was the daughter of the Burgundian king Chilperic and had been reared as a Christian. She was able to convert her husband shortly after their marriage c. 492. His victory over the Alemanni was one of the things that convinced him that he should follow the God of his wife. He was baptized, together with three thousand of his subjects, by Remigius in 496. According to an ancient legend, Remigius anointed Clovis at his baptism with chrism from an ampulla brought him by a dove in answer to prayer. This same ampulla was supposedly used for the anointing of French kings at their coronation. At the same time Remigius is said to have given Clovis the power of curing the "king's evil" by his touch.

Clovis succeeded his father, Childeric I, as chief of the ferocious Salian Franks in 481. Five years later he defeated the Roman governor at Soissons and made that city the capital of his kingdom. Shortly after his conversion he fought the Visigoth king Alaric and ended the war by killing Alaric with his own hands. The emperor Anastasius then made him consul. The council Clovis called at Orléans was the occasion which established the peculiar privileges of the French kings against the pope. After spending his life in uniting the Franks, he redivided them in his will when he portioned them out to his sons. After his death in 511, Clotilda retired to the convent of St. Martin of Tours, where she gained a great reputation for holiness.

**Cluniac Buildings.** The great reform monastery of Cluny, founded in 910, the largest and most famous monastery in the West. The Romanesque basilica of St. Peter, completed in the 12th century was the largest church in Europe until the rebuilding of St. Peter's in Rome. Cluny was closed and largely destroyed during the French Revolution (1790), but recent excavations have made possible a reconstruction of the ground plan. Part of the basilica and a few of the other buildings survive as ruins.

**Cluny.** The founding of the abbey at Cluny in 910 is often cited as the turning point in the history of medieval Christianity. During the 9th and 10th centuries the prestige and influence of the church was declining. Princes of the church were often indistinguishable from secular warlords. Simony and clerical unchastity were commonplace. The German emperor and the feudal nobility controlled ecclesiastical appointments and often sold them to the highest bidder. Even the popes were little more than pawns of rival factions contending for the lordship of Rome. In such times, the charter of Cluny was remarkable for excluding many of the practices that had proved ruinous to other religious houses. Duke William of Aquitaine, the founder, specifically renounced his right of control and granted the monks the authority to elect their own abbots, specifying that they would be subject to no outside influence excepting that of the pope, and even he was not to have unlimited power to interfere. The monastery was fortunate in its succession of abbots. Berno (d. 927) was already experienced in the rule of abbeys, but his efficient administration would have come to nothing had not his successor, Odo (927–942), been the greatest religious force of his generation. Majolus (948–994), Odilo (994–1048), and Hugh (1049–1109) during their long reigns continued to enforce the strict Benedictine Rule and enjoyed enormous prestige and influence among the rough potentates of the time, who, whatever their own faults, admired asceticism and devotion in their spiritual leaders. Under the guidance of these abbots, Cluny became a model of the Benedictine observance. This spiritual preeminence led to the establishment, under Odilo, of a unique federation of Benedictine monasteries with Cluny at the head. Previously, the abbeys had been independent of each other, but now they became part of a great network of houses, possibly two thousand by 1100, which flourished throughout France, England, Spain, Germany, Poland, and Hungary. All were theoretically related to each other in a distinctly feudal system of graded relationships, with Cluny and its chapter at the apex. Priors of the daughter houses met annually at Cluny, and they themselves were subject to visitation by representatives of the motherhouse. The religious zeal and reforming spirit which accompanied this rapid growth was chiefly responsible for initiating a great age of monastic reform. It should be pointed out, however, that Cluny did not possess a monopoly on this reforming spirit. In England, the Rhineland, and elsewhere, there were independent, less widespread movements which coincided with that of Cluny.

The impact of the Cluniac federation extended far beyond the confines of the priories themselves. There is considerable justice in the remark that Cluny Christianized feudalism. In general, the monks administered their increasingly large holdings more efficiently and treated their serfs more humanely than did their secular counterparts among the feudal nobility. Their success encouraged emulation. Furthermore, their religious idealism was infectious, and the teachings of Christ began to modify the brutal practices of the day, and to color, among other concepts, the secular ideal of chivalry. It was during this period, and largely through Cluniac influence, that religion became an integral part of the codes and rituals of the knightly class, and the concept of the Christian knight as champion of the church and defender of the oppressed came into being. In some areas, the Benedictines were successful in enforcing the Peace of God and the Truce of God, Cluniac pronouncements which insisted that noncombatants be entitled to relief from the violence of war, that religious buildings be protected, and that hostilities must regularly be suspended on certain holy days and during entire half weeks throughout Advent and Lent. The alliance between the martial and the religious spirit became, in time, indissoluble, and when the moment arrived to preach the Crusades, Cluny had a large role to play. Indeed, the First Crusade has been described as a Cluniac enterprise, and it is significant that Pope Urban II, who proclaimed it at the Council of Clermont, had been a monk of Cluny.

The scope of Cluny's influence was also felt by the secular clergy. Clerical incontinence and marriage were so widespread that they had become symbolic of the corruption of the church. Both the example and the fulmination of the abbots of Cluny went a long way toward quelling these abuses. The abbots also worked to free the bishops from the patronage of the great feudal lords, and proclaimed that bishops should be elected by clerics and the people. The abuses of investiture were most noticeable in Germany, where the emperor even appointed the pope himself, but the teachings of Cluny influenced the efforts of Henry II and later, Henry III, to uproot simony and appoint churchmen on the basis of competence alone. Hugh of Cluny was the supreme example of the power and influence attained by the abbots of Cluny. A gifted mediator, he was the close confidant of a succession of popes, and the friend and adviser of numerous royal houses. His guidance helped Emperor Henry III in his attack on the simonists and his mediation almost managed to compose the differences between Emperor Henry IV and Pope Gregory VII (Hildebrand) in the fierce strife over investiture. Hugh, although only a lukewarm ally of Gregory (who was himself a former monk of Cluny), was present at the famous climax of the struggle, when Henry IV was forced to his knees at Canossa. Under Hugh, work was begun on a new abbey at Cluny which in later generations was to become one of the wonders of the medieval world, boasting the largest church in Western Christendom prior to the construction of St. Peter's in Rome.

The rule of Abbot Peter the Venerable (1122–c. 1156) saw the final golden age of the abbey. During this period it was second only to Rome as the chief center of the Christian world. Its very wealth became one of the causes of its decline as a seat of power during the latter part of the 12th century. By then, much of its early fervor and reforming spirit had passed to another less centrally organized Benedictine congregation, the Order of Cîteaux in Burgundy (Cistercian), which, under the leadership of Bernard, renewed the Benedictine Rule that had begun to weaken at Cluny.

Cluny continued to survive for centuries. Cardinals Richelieu and Mazarin were among its later titular prelates. They tried to restore its influence, but without success. At the suppression in 1790, the buildings themselves were virtually destroyed. A road now passes through what was once the nave of the monastery church.

BIBLIOGRAPHY: R. H. Bainton, *Early and Medieval Christianity* (Boston, 1962); C. Butler, *Benedictine Monachism* (New York, 1962); J. Evans, *Monastic Life at Cluny: 910–1157* (London, 1931); L. M. Smith, *Cluny in the Eleventh and Twelfth Centuries* (London, 1930); and *The Early History of the Monastery of Cluny* (New York, 1920).

**Cobbs, Nicholas H.** (1795–1861). Episcopalian bishop. The first bishop of Alabama in the Protestant Episcopal Church, Cobbs become known for extending the denomination by engaging in an aggressive missionary career. He also exemplified his nonpartisan moderate High Churchmanship by seeking to infuse his church with regard for its historic theology and traditions.

**Coblenz, Articles of.** In 1769 representatives of the archbishop electors of Mainz, Treves, and Cologne met at Coblenz and drew up thirty articles based on the ideas of Johann Nikolaus von Hontheim (Febronius). Although accepting the pope as titular head of the church, they held that ecclesiastical affairs should be kept largely under episcopal and civil control. The Articles were presented to Emperor Joseph II, but he took no action on them at the time.

**Cock, Hendrik De** (1801–1842). Dutch (1603–1669). Dutch theologian. He was a primary formulator, if not the founder, of federal or covenant theology. He received his early education in Germany, concentrating on Hebrew and rabbinic studies. In 1629 he came to Franeker, Holland, to complete his theological education. His Talmudic studies published there brought him to the attention and under the influence of Grotius. After teaching Biblical theology in Bremen for some years, he returned to the University of Franeker and the chair of Hebrew. In 1650 he moved to the University of Leiden, where he remained until his death. He never felt at home in the strict Calvinism of the Netherlands and withdrew almost completely from the life of the church. Philosophically he was a disciple of Descartes. He advocated and personally demonstrated a life of faithfulness to Biblical teachings rather than one devoted to the church and orthodoxy. He was a productive author. His emphasis was Biblical and practical, emanating from the central idea of the covenant. His views were influential in the later development of Pietism in Germany. He exerted a powerful influence on his time and on subsequent generations, not only by his theological views but by his peaceable character.

**Cochlaeus, Johannes** (Johann Dobenek) (1479–1552). Roman Catholic polemicist. He was a German priest and an ardent humanist, "Cochlaeus" being the name he used for his humanistic writing. One of the most zealous Roman Catholic theologians of his time, he wrote polemical works on free will, justification, the sacraments, the priesthood, etc., against Luther, Melanchthon, Zwingli, Henry VIII, and others. He united with Duke George of Saxony in opposing the Augsburg Confession (1530). His *Commentaria de actis et scriptis M. Lutheri,* first published in 1549, was the first biography of Luther and served for many years as a chief source for the Roman Catholic image of the Reformer.

**Cocceius, Johannes** (Johann Koch) Reformed pastor of Ulrum. He was the author of several tracts opposing the relaxation of the doctrine and discipline of the Reformed Church, e.g., hymns and indiscriminate baptisms. Deposed by the Synod of Groningen (1834), he led his congregation in secession to adhere rigidly to the principles of the Synod of Dort. Secessions of sympathetic congregations led by like-minded pastors eventuated in the organization of the Christian Reformed Church.

**Codex Juris Canonici.** Although there have been many collections of papal decrees and synodical legislation in the history of the

Roman Catholic Church, the current Code of Canon Law binding those in the Latin rite was issued by means of a papal bull, May 27, 1917. It takes the place of all previous collections. By a decree of Sept. 15, 1917, it has been provided that all subsequent legislation is to be inserted into this Code.

**Coelestius** (5th century). Disciple of Pelagius. While a lawyer in Rome, Coelestius was persuaded by Pelagius to join him in a life of asceticism and piety. Horrified by the depravity of society, they attempted to restore morals by insistence upon utter freedom of the will and personal responsibility. After the sack of Rome by the Goths (410) they made their way to Africa, where they met Augustine, who was soon to write the first of his anti-Pelagian works. The bold preaching of Coelestius provoked the first official condemnation of Pelagian doctrine. He was summoned before a synod of bishops at Carthage in 412 and excommunicated.

**Coenobite.** See CENOBITE.

**Coke, Thomas** (1747–1814). First American Methodist bishop, cofounder of the Methodist Episcopal Church. After graduation from Oxford (1768), Coke became a curate, a position he lost when he came under the influence of John Wesley. He joined Wesley, attended the Bristol Conference (1777), and was named first president of the Irish Conference (1782), an office he held many years. In 1784, Wesley appointed Coke first superintendent of the American Methodist Church and dispatched him to America with plans for the movement. Coke went on a thousand-mile preaching tour before attending the Baltimore Conference in which Francis Asbury, leader of Methodists in America, indicated that his followers desired a break with Wesley's group. The Methodist Episcopal Church was established with Coke and Asbury as bishops. Between 1784 and 1803, Coke crossed the Atlantic eighteen times, and despite constant disputes with Asbury, achieved much. He fostered the establishment of Cokesbury College in Maryland (1787), but the school was destroyed by fire eight years later. Because of his stand against slavery, Coke almost came to bodily harm on one occasion. In 1785, he and Asbury presented an antislavery petition to George Washington. In 1789, they issued on behalf of the Annual Conference a congratulatory address to the new President. Thus Methodism became the first denomination to endorse the new government. Coke's second major contribution to Methodism involved the establishment of foreign missions, to which he donated much of his large fortune. He died at sea on his way to establish a mission in Ceylon in 1814.

**Colenso, John William** (1814–1883). Anglican missionary bishop. Educated at St. John's, Cambridge, Colenso served several years as the vicar of a parish in Norfolk. In 1853 he became the first bishop of Natal.

To further his work, he studied the Zulu language and eventually published a Zulu dictionary and grammar. He also translated the New Testament and parts of the Old into Zulu, publishing commentaries in English as well. Faced with the difficulty of convincing his charges of the literal truth of the account of creation in Genesis, Colenso was finally forced to think through the problem of Biblical inspiration himself. The result was his publication of *The Pentateuch and Book of Joshua Critically Examined* (1862–1879), in which he concluded that much of the material in these books was not historical but poetic, the historical material having been introduced at a much later date than was customarily supposed. His conclusions drew the wrath of many upon him. Bishop Gray of Capetown attempted to depose him, but the Judicial Committee of the Privy Council upheld him. Troubles between white settlers and the natives plagued the last years of his life.

**Coleridge, Samuel Taylor** (1772–1834). English poet, critic, conversationalist, philosopher. He has sometimes been called the English Schleiermacher. His philosophical romanticism made a considerable impact on the 19th-century Church of England through the influence of his works (*Aids to Reflection, Confessions of an Inquiring Spirit*) on such men as Thomas Arnold and John F. D. Maurice. After some time at Jesus College, Cambridge, Coleridge spent part of a term of enlistment in the army, started to study for the Unitarian ministry, and met Robert Southey, whose sister-in-law he married. With Southey he developed a plan for an ideal pantisocratic community which was to be launched on the banks of the Susquehanna in Pennsylvania. The project never materialized, and in 1795, Coleridge met William and Dorothy Wordsworth, who were to have the greatest influence on his career. The following year Wordsworth and Coleridge produced a volume of *Lyrical Ballads*, containing Coleridge's *The Rime of the Ancient Mariner*. This same year he and the two Wordsworths left for Germany, where Coleridge fell under the influence of German thought, particularly that of Immanuel Kant. After a long spiritual pilgrimage, he returned to the Church of England and spent the last twenty years of his life as a practicing churchman.

**Colet, John** (c. 1467–1519). English scholar and clergyman. Colet was the leader of a small but influential group of Christian humanists at Oxford and London in the late 15th and early 16th centuries. He attended Oxford and later studied in France and Italy, where he became interested in Renaissance humanism. Returning to England in 1496, he lectured at Oxford for eight years before his appointment as dean of St. Paul's Cathedral in London in 1504, a position that he held for the remainder of his life. At St. Paul's, Colet refounded at his own expense the cathedral's grammar school, the first institution in England devoted expressly to Renaissance learning. Colet was not a great classical scholar. Rather, he stressed an evangelical Christian piety that led some to suspect him of Lollardy. He wrote little and exercised his influence almost entirely through lectures and sermons and through personal contacts with his numerous scholarly friends. In this manner he touched the lives of both Thomas More and Erasmus to a marked degree. His greatest contribution to the program of Christian humanism was his literary-historical method of Biblical exegesis. This method later gained international recognition in the hands of the great Biblical and literary scholar Erasmus.

**Coligny, Gaspard de** (1519–1572). Huguenot leader and French admiral. Coligny, a member of the noble Châtillon family, spent much of his early manhood in the service of the French court and the army, becoming a military leader of renown. Since he was a nephew of Connêtable Anne de Montmorency, his joining the ranks of the French Reformed Church shortly after the organization of the Paris congregation in 1555 brought prestige to the new group. He experimented with Huguenot colonies in the New World, but his expeditions in 1555 to Brazil and in 1562 to Florida both ended in disaster for the colonists.

When the Wars of Religion broke out, he was an acknowledged leader of the Reformed, and after the death of the Prince de Condé in 1569 his foremost position was unquestioned. After the Peace of Saint-Germain-en-Laye (1570), the new court policy was favorable to the Huguenots, and Coligny returned to court, where he was honored. His wholesome and noble character made a great impression upon the young king Charles IX. Fearful of his influence, Catherine de' Medici and the Guises plotted his assassination shortly

after the wedding of Henry of Navarre. The assassin on Aug. 22, 1572, only wounded him, but precipitated the wholesale massacre of the Huguenots two days later. Coligny was then slain, thrown from a window and decapitated.

**Collegiants.** Dutch religious group. In Holland about 1619 a small number of Remonstrants under the influence of Gysberg van der Codde established a congregation at Rhynsburg with neither pastors nor a confession. They baptized by immersion into the universal church, generally at their yearly meeting. They had a liberal theology, but their piety influenced both the English Baptists and Rhenish Pietists. The name "Collegiants" was given to them because they called their communities "colleges," thereby evading the penalties for Separatist churches.

**Collegiate Church.** A church served by a chapter of canons. Organized like a cathedral, the chapter is charged with divine service at the church and has no governing function and no bishop. The designation of churches to this dignity is either by papal mandate or by long-standing custom (Canon 391, Code of Canon Law). In the Church of England, several collegiate churches exist, e.g., Westminster Abbey. The origin of the notion is to be found in the reforms of Chrodegang of Metz.

**Collenbusch, Samuel** (1724–1803). German Protestant mystic and physician. He studied medicine at Duisburg and Strasbourg, at the latter place becoming interested in mysticism. In 1784 he moved to Barmen, where he was soon known for his deep and earnest piety. His theological works dealt with soteriology and eschatology. He rejected predestination and held to a thoroughgoing kenosis doctrine of Christ's self-humiliation. His influence was felt in the later Erlangen school of Thomasius and Hofmann.

**Collins, Anthony** (1676–1729). English deist. Educated at Eton, at King's College, Cambridge, and at the Temple, Collins became a justice of the peace in Essex. A freethinker, he was early influenced by his friend John Locke, whose principles he applied in the formulation of his own religious and philosophical beliefs. In a series of books he systematically presented his theory of the efficacy of human reason. The *Essay Concerning the Use of Reason* (1707) attacked the concept that certain matters of religion are above the comprehension of human rationality. In *Priestcraft in Perfection*, Collins asserted that the article guaranteeing the power of the church to establish rituals and settle religious disputes had been fraudulently inserted into the Thirty-nine Articles. His major work, *A Discourse of Freethinking* (1713), rejected the primacy and authority of ministers and argued that only through free inquiry could man arrive at truth. This significant defense of the deistic position elicited bitter responses from numerous influential Christian leaders, including Jonathan Swift. In 1715, Collins continued his iconoclastic attacks on Christianity with *Inquiry Concerning Human Liberty,* expounding the doctrine of determinism. His *Discourse of the Grounds and Reasons of the Christian Religion* (1724) disputed the validity of the Old Testament prophecies of Christ, the immortality of the soul, and, indirectly, the very foundations of the Christian faith. Though he was frequently disparaged on the grounds of faulty scholarship, Collins in his use of the principles of historical criticism became one of the most important apologists of deistic philosophy.

**Colluthus** (4th century). Priest of Alexandria who entered into schism during the episcopate of Alexander. He arrogated to himself the right and power of ordination, although he was only in presbyter's orders. The early laxity of Alexander toward Arius is said to have given Colluthus the courage to act, although he was not an Arian. He was deposed by the Council of Alexandria which Hosius of Cordova called. It is known that the Alexandrian bishops were elected by the presbyters until the time of Alexander, and some believe that our knowledge of Colluthus indicates that the Alexandrian priests also conferred orders.

**Collyridians.** A 4th-century sect of women who offered sacrifices of little cakes (*kollyridia*) to the Virgin Mary. The sect was Arabian, though its adherents seem not to have been native Arabs but immigrant Thracians and Scythians. Their extravagant devotion to the mother of Jesus may have been a vestige of the cult of Astarte or Ceres carried over into Christianity. Once a year the sect met to hold a solemn feast to Mary as a goddess and at that time they ate the sacrifice of the cakes.

**Colman** (d. 676). Bishop of Lindisfarne. A native of Ireland, Colman became a monk at Iona and later bishop of Lindisfarne (661). He led the Celtic party in Northumbria, and at the Synod of Whitby (664) defended Celtic usages (date of Easter, form of tonsure, etc.) against the Romanizing party, whose leader was Wilfrid. After King Oswy decided in favor of Roman usage at the Synod, Colman left Lindisfarne for Iona and later returned to Ireland, where he founded the monastery of Innisboffin (County Mayo).

**Colombini, Giovanni** (c. 1304–1367). Founder of the Gesuati. A wealthy merchant of Siena, he became committed to the ideal of poverty and cared for the poor and the sick. After a retreat of seven years with some companions, he began to preach the praise and peace of Jesus as his message to the then strife-torn land. His influence was profound, and he and his followers received papal approval in the year of his death.

**Colonna.** Noble Roman family of great antiquity and importance, descendants of the Counts of Tusculum. The first member of the family to be called Colonna (di Columna) was Pietro, who received a castle of that name in the Alban Hills in 1064. The family gained wealth and offices through the papacy; many were cardinals and senators. There were also, however, feuds with other Roman families, notably the Orsini and Caetani. A member of the latter, Pope Boniface VIII, tried to exterminate them, thus driving them into an alliance with Philip IV; it was Sciarra Colonna who led the attack on the pope, Sept. 7, 1303. Cola di Rienzi drove them briefly from Rome in 1347, but in the pontificate (1417–1431) of Oddone Colonna (Martin V) they received much power and land. His successor, Eugene IV, opposed them, and a century-long struggle with the popes ensued. Finally came peace, and many members of the family subsequently served with distinction, if not always propriety, in the papal court.

**Columba** (c. 521–597). Nobleman and abbot. He left Ireland in 563 to establish the monastery on Iona which became a center of missionary activity in Scotland and England. For two centuries it was the headquarters of the Celtic Scottish Church, presided over by its abbots. Stormy episodes are reported from Columba's early life, but he was later known for the gentleness suggested by his name (Colum, "dove"), and for his love of nature as well as of God and man.

**Columbanus** (c. 550–615). Irish monk and missionary. Leaving Ireland for the Continent about 590, he founded monasteries in France (Luxeuil) and Italy (Bobbio) which did much to revive religion and learning. The enthusiastic spirit of Celtic Christianity is reflected in his sermons, his rigid monastic rule, his learned and surprisingly sprightly poetry, and the prophetic vigor of his rebukes to kings and popes on matters of conduct and church discipline.

**Combes, Émile** (1835–1921). French prime minister from 1902 to 1905. He represented the rabid anticlericalism of the Third Republic, breaking off diplomatic relations with the Vatican in 1904. He pledged his government to work for the complete separation of church and state and rigidly enforced the Associations Act of 1901 by rejecting most authorizations and boasting that he had closed 13,904 schools run by religious orders. In 1903 many French nationals from these congregations began to go into exile.

**Comenius, John Amos** (Jan Komenský) (1592–1670). Bishop of the Moravian Brethren and one of the greatest educationalists of his day. He studied at Heidelberg, and became a teacher at Přerov and later at Fulneck. In 1621 he fled from the Spanish invasion to Poland, where he taught in the school at Lissa. In 1627 a Reformation Tribunal was established, and his was one of thirty thousand Protestant families driven out of the country. He went to Sweden in 1642 to reform the schools, but his ecumenical activities irritated the stricter Lutherans. In 1648 he returned to Poland, and was consecrated presiding bishop of the Moravians—the last of the Bohemian-Moravian clergy to hold the office. He was in Hungary from 1650 to 1654 establishing a school according to his ideas, but it did not become the model he expected, and the Netherlands sheltered his last years. His premise was that the religions must stop fighting and unite in doing God's will—which can be done only through universal education and the adoption of Christian love as the "one thing necessary" (*unum necessarium*). He believed in educating the whole person, and not in just memorizing facts. Development of Christian character was the ultimate educational aim. The educational philosophy he propounded and the reforms he introduced were of great influence in succeeding generations.

**Commendam, In** (Latin, "in trust"). The practice whereby a cleric or layman held the endowment of a benefice in trust and received its revenues during the vacancy of the benefice. It became customary for some bishops, abbots, and laymen to hold a benefice *in commendam* permanently. A vicar or provost would then be appointed to discharge the spiritual duties of the benefice. The practice has now disappeared, although honorary titles are held occasionally *in commendam*.

**Commissaries.** Church of England officials who serve as representatives and substitutes for the bishop except in his special duties of confirming and ordaining. This office came into existence in the 17th century when the need for clerical supervision and discipline in Anglican parishes in the British North American colonies led Bishop Compton to appoint James Blair of Virginia his first commissary. In an episcopally governed church, every parish must be under the supervision of a bishop. None, however, had been appointed for America; in 1632 all Anglican clergy who were there were put under the jurisdiction of the bishop of London. The first two commissaries fulfilled their tasks with a great deal of success. James Blair, who had been serving the parish in Henrico County, Virginia, was appointed in 1689 and performed his work with distinction until his death in 1743. Bishop Compton's second appointee, Thomas Bray, was not an American resident and remained in his assigned colony, Maryland, only a year, but was one of the most influential Anglican clerics in the pre-Revolutionary period.

**Commission of the Churches on International Affairs.** A commission created in 1946 as a joint agency of the World Council of Churches and the International Missionary Council for study and stimulating a relevant witness in the field of international relations. It maintains liaison with the United Nations and its specialized agencies. Its major work falls under six heads: international peace, human rights and religious liberty, advancement of dependent peoples, economic and social development, refugees and migration, and international institutions.

**Committee on Cooperation in Latin America.** An organization that came into being during the Congress on Christian Work held in Panama in 1916. It was designed to promote concord among Protestant denominations in Latin America. In the first decade of the 20th century, with the growth of Protestantism in Latin American countries, leaders felt the need for a united front to parallel that of the Roman Catholics.

**Commodian.** Christian Latin poet. There is some disagreement about the time and place of his activity, but the likelihood is that he was in Africa in the middle of the 3d century. His main claim to literary fame is not aesthetic but prosodiac; he based his rhythm on accent alone. His works reflect millenarian expectation and the heresy that God the Father suffered on the cross.

**Common Order, The Book of.** The prayer book also known as *The Forme of Prayers* which was authorized in 1562 by the General Assembly of the Church of Scotland. In

1564, when a full metrical Psalter had been added, it became the standard for all public worship in the Church of Scotland. Actually, the Scottish Common Order was just an edition of *The Forme of Prayers . . . used in the Englishe Congregation at Geneva*, which was printed in 1556. Although strongly influenced by Calvin's liturgy (itself based on the older Strasbourg models of Schwarz and Bucer), the Genevan *Forme* was not just an English translation of Calvin's services, probably because both Anglicans and Presbyterians, led by John Knox, helped compile it in Geneva. Knox brought the Genevan book to Scotland in 1559, and he championed its ensuing legal establishment. Although it went through more than seventy editions in the next sixty years, the book was replaced in 1645 by the Westminster Directory for Public Worship as the official standard for Scottish worship. In this century, the Church of Scotland, many English and American Presbyterian Churches, and the United Church of Canada have issued service books entitled The Book of Common Order. All in some way have been influenced by the original 16th-century book.

**Common Prayer, The Book of.** The liturgical book of the English-speaking churches of the Anglican Communion. All Anglican Prayer Books in current use stem from one or another of the first two English Prayer Books (1549 and 1552). These are, in turn, directly descended from the medieval Latin rites used in England for nearly a thousand years before the Reformation.

The Prayer Book was not the first distinctive liturgical prescription of the autonomous English Church after the rejection of papal supremacy. Experiments with the vernacular had resulted in the reading of a chapter of the English Bible at Matins and Vespers of Sundays and holy days from 1543, the English litany in 1544, and the Order for Communion (vernacular devotions for the people's Communion) in 1548. So the way was prepared for the first Prayer Book, which became the sole authorized service book of the English Church on Whitsunday, 1549. Cranmer (who, on the evidence of his earlier liturgical drafts, was almost certainly its chief compiler) retained many of the traditional elements, increased the Biblical content and tone, and incorporated some changes from Continental liturgical revisions, principally Cardinal Quiñones' revision of the breviary of 1535 and 1536, and Archbishop (of Cologne) Hermann's *Consultation* of 1543, largely the work of Bucer and Melanchthon.

He conflated the seven or eight daily offices into two—Matins, or Morning Prayer, and Evensong, or Evening Prayer. The basic elements were all traditional, but most of the non-Biblical accretions were omitted; the number of saints' days was drastically reduced, and the lectionary was arranged to provide for systematic reading through the Bible. Changes in the Eucharistic rite were more radical, especially in the canon, which was altered to deemphasize sacrificial and (especially) propitiatory elements, and to emphasize consecration by the invocation of the Holy Spirit (epiclesis), transubstantiation being implicitly denied. The forms that were provided for the occasional offices—baptism, confirmation, burial of the dead, etc.—were altered in ways similar to those for the Eucharist and daily offices, that is, in the direction of simplicity and the omission of ceremonies.

The second Prayer Book (1552) was a revision of the first in a much more Protestant direction. The most important changes were in the Eucharistic rite, where something of Cranmer's later Calvinistic (or "receptionist") opinions can be seen, especially in the words accompanying the giving of the elements. The prayers of the canon are rearranged, rendering the conservative interpretation such as Gardiner placed on the 1549 rite untenable. Some further traditional elements in the occasional offices (e.g., anointing at baptism) were omitted. A penitential introduction was added to the daily offices. The 1559 Prayer Book, which was made necessary by the reversion to the Latin rite under Queen Mary, is simply the 1552 book with three alterations designed to make it more acceptable to Roman Catholic-minded as well as Protestant-minded Anglicans. Minor revisions were made in 1604.

The next substantial version of the Prayer Book was that of 1662, after the restoration of the monarchy and the Established Church. Again the 1552 book provides the model, but with the Elizabethan changes retained and certain distinctively Anglican features strengthened. Further official revision of the English Prayer Book has been virtually confined to reform of the lectionary (1871, and subsequently); the 1662 book still contains the authorized liturgy of the Church of England.

Other versions of the Prayer Book can be divided into two groups: The first, consisting of those which have been widely accepted, includes the American, adopted first in 1789, and substantially revised in 1898 and 1928; the Irish (1927); the Scottish (1929); the

Canadian (1922 and 1961); and the South African (1929). Among the second group—those which have not received official acceptance or widespread usage—should be mentioned the Scottish (1637) book, officially imposed but stoutly resisted, which influenced the liturgies of the nonjurors and in turn the Scottish (1764) liturgy and the American rite; the various latitudinarian revisions, from 1689 to the proposed American book of 1785; and the English revisions of 1927 and 1928, approved by the Convocations and Church Assembly but defeated by Parliament.

BIBLIOGRAPHY: F. E. Brightman, *The English Rite,* 2 vols. (London, 1915); W. K. L. Clarke (ed.), *Liturgy and Worship* (London, 1932); F. Procter and W. H. Frere, *A New History of the BCP* (London, 1901 ff.); M. H. Shepherd, *The Oxford American Prayer Book Commentary* (New York, 1950); *The First and Second Prayer Books of King Edward the Sixth* (Everyman's Library).

**Communion.** See EUCHARIST.

**Comneni Dynasty** (1081–1185). The Byzantine dynasty, founded by Emperor Alexius I Comnenus, which restored Byzantine suzerainty over much of Asia Minor after approximately fifty years of domestic anarchy and eventual capitulation to the invading Moslem Seljuk Turks. The inspired leadership of Alexius and his son, John II Comnenus (reigned 1118–1143), strengthened Christianity in the East, but only temporarily. The dynasty gradually weakened, and by 1185 the interior of Asia Minor was again lost to the Seljuk Turks. Nevertheless, under the later Comneni there was something of a renaissance in art, letters, and scholarship.

**Compline** (from Latin *completorium,* from *complere,* "to complete"). The final office of the day, said by all regular clergy, all religious, and all priests of the Roman Catholic Church. Prime and Compline are of more recent origin than Lauds and Vespers. The contents of the office vary according to different breviaries and monastic usages. The Roman Breviary provides that after the short lesson (I Peter 5:8 f.) and the confession, three psalms (Ps. 4; 91; 134) be said, followed by a hymn, a lesson (Jer. 14:9), a responsory (varies with the season), the Nunc Dimittis, short prayers, and a blessing.

**Comprehension.** The ideal, widely advocated after the Restoration (1660), of an English Church that would "comprehend" (i.e., include) a large number of Dissenters. In 1660, Presbyterians and Anglicans met at Worcester House and agreed on a religious settlement to which Charles II also agreed. However, Parliament was in no mood for compromise, but imposed prewar Anglicanism and instituted the Clarendon Code, which severely restricted Dissenters. The next attempt occurred in 1667 when John Wilkins proposed two bills, one granting indulgence to Dissenters, and the other a comprehension bill. Dissenting ministers would simply declare that they approved of the doctrine, worship, and government of the Established Church. Certain objectionable parts of the liturgy would be considered optional, and their ordinations would be considered valid. Both bills were defeated. The king by this time was not favoring comprehension; he preferred toleration, for it would benefit Roman Catholics. Throughout the Restoration period various futile attempts were made to pass comprehension bills in Parliament. In 1688, the Dissenters and leaders of the Established Church finally agreed on a plan, but the advent of William of Orange destroyed the accord. In a compromise move, the Whigs and Tories agreed to pass a toleration act, but not a comprehension bill, leaving the Church of England unchanged.

**Comte, Auguste** (1798–1857). French philosopher, often referred to as the founder of positivism. A native of Montpellier, Comte studied and later taught mathematics. For a time he also served as Saint-Simon's secretary. In 1830 he published the first volume of his principal work, the *Cours de philosophie positive* (6 vols., 1830–1842). Comte's concern was to put an end to the intellectual and social chaos which he thought the French revolutionary period had brought; he undertook to set forth a philosophy in which all men could agree. This philosophy was to be the systematic presentation of the general laws of the sciences, including sociology. According to sociological principles, mankind passes through three stages: a theological stage, wherein everything is attributed to supernatural beings and of which the highest point is monotheism; a metaphysical stage, wherein everything is attributed to abstract forces; and the culminating scientific, or positive, stage, wherein the laws or relationships of phenomena are clearly known. In this final state of mankind, there will also be a positive social order, stressing orderliness and progress, and a positive religion, in which worship will be directed, not to God, but to humanity. To this end Comte wrote a *Catéchisme positiviste,* which included not only doctrine but directions for sacraments and feast days.

**Conciliarism.** A reform movement in the 14th and 15th centuries having as its central motif the superiority of an ecumenical council over the pope. The movement was rooted in the interpretation of certain Biblical passages (Matt. 16:18–20; Acts, ch. 15; Gal. 2:11) in the debates of 12th- and 13th-century canonists concerning the promise of the keys to both Peter and the apostles, and in the controversy over sections in Gratian's *Decretum* on the removal of a pope for heresy. Marsilius of Padua's *Defensor pacis* afforded an important impetus by teaching that doctrines of faith could be determined only by all the faithful. The opinion of Marsilius was supported by William of Occam's *Dialogus* and by the teaching of John Gerson and Pierre d'Ailly that the *plenitudo potestatis* of the church resided in the whole body as represented by a council. In an attempt to end the schism, the University of Paris in 1394 induced rival potentates and cardinals to relinquish their papal allegiances, and the Council of Pisa was called. Its failure ended in the Convocation of Constance, which elected Martin V, who, in turn, denied that a general council was superior to him, and who, like his successors, forbade an appeal to a general council over a pope. The principles of conciliarism were to some extent revived in Gallicanism.

**Conciliar Movement.** See CONCILIARISM.

**Conclave** (from Latin *cum clave*, "with a key"). The locked enclosure where the cardinals assemble to elect a new pope. The custom began in 1271 when after more than two years the politically deadlocked cardinals had failed to elect a pope. The cardinals were locked in a room until they reached a decision. The custom lapsed, but was revived by Celestine V in 1294 and modified by Clement VI in 1351. The practice continues today with some procedural modifications.

**Concord, Book of** (1580), and **Concord, Formula of** (1577). After the death of Luther, Lutheranism threatened to fragment as the result of bitter theological conflicts, many of them consequent upon the later views of Melanchthon. The need for a new confessional statement to settle these controversies was met in the Formula of Concord (1577), which rejected much of Melanchthon's theology but used his Aristotelian methodology and thus ushered in the era of orthodoxy. It provided definitive answers for Lutherans and drew firm doctrinal lines against Rome, the Calvinists, and others. The Formula did not, however, obtain confessional status everywhere (e.g., not in Denmark and Norway).

The Book of Concord (1580) is the collection of all those writings which were regarded as of confessional authority and includes: the three ecumenical creeds (Apostles', Nicene, Athanasian), the Augsburg Confession, Luther's Small and Large Catechisms, the Smalcald Articles, the Apology of the Augsburg Confession, and the Formula of Concord.

**Concordat, Cisalpine** (*properly* Italian) (Sept. 16, 1803). Napoleon, president of this republic centered at Milan, concluded with Cardinal Consalvi an accord favorable to Roman Catholicism, since there was neither conflict nor schism in northern Italy. Church lands were secularized, clergy salaried, and oaths of allegiance required. The unilateral Melzi Decrees four months later monitored the priests and took back most concessions.

**Concordat of Bologna.** See BOLOGNA, CONCORDAT OF.

**Concordat of 1801.** An agreement whereby Pius VII and Napoleon Bonaparte, First Consul, reestablished Roman Catholicism in France. It recognized the Catholic religion as that of the majority of Frenchmen. Dioceses were redistributed. On nomination by the state, the pope was to appoint bishops; in conjunction with the government, bishops were to appoint parish priests. The state was to pay the salaries of the clergy. The church was to have freedom of public worship subject to government regulations. The concordat marked the defeat of Gallicanism.

**Condé, Louis, Prince de** (1530–1569). He became the Huguenot leader, a role for which his brother, Antoine de Bourbon, was not suited. Because of his connection with the Conspiracy of Amboise in 1559, an ambitious plan aimed at eliminating Guise influence in the government, he was arrested and almost executed. A major Huguenot military commander, he was killed in the defeat of Jarnac.

**Condren, Charles de** (1588–1641). French spiritual writer and mystic. He was ordained in 1614 and joined the French Oratorians three years later. He was a close friend and follower of Pierre de Bérulle and when the latter died in 1629, de Condren succeeded him as head of the congregation and directed its final formation. Like Cardinal Bérulle, he was a popular confessor, and like him, too, he contributed to the French school of spirituality, the doctrines of the transcendence of God and the incarnation being central to his piety.

**Confessing Church.** Christians who resisted the advancement of the pro-Nazi "German

Christians" within the German Evangelical Church by creating a provisional counterpart during Hitler's regime. Late in 1932 the "German Christians" won overwhelmingly in Prussian church elections. Their April, 1933, convention in Berlin aroused their opponents to action. When Hitler's confidant, Ludwig Müller, was elected *Reichsbischof* of the German Evangelical Church in September, Martin Niemöller and others organized the Pastors' Emergency League to counteract the growing influence of the "German Christians." During Jan. 3 and 4, 1934, under the initiative of Karl Immer and others, 300 ministers and lay leaders from about 170 Reformed churches gathered for a free synod in Barmen to consider the situation. Karl Barth lectured. In February a Council of the Brethren, including Dietrich Bonhoeffer, decided to convene a gathering of all Christians who opposed the "German Christian" inroads and who adhered to reformational confessions. Thus the first synod of the "Confessing Church" met at Barmen, May 29–31, 1934. Present were 139 delegates from 18 territorial churches. Under the guidance of Hans Asmussen the Barmen Confession was adopted, and the "Confessional Church," as it was first called, became a reality. Subsequent conference-synods were held at Dahlem (October, 1934), Augsburg (January, 1935), and Bad Oeynhausen (February, 1936). The Council first numbered 12, then 22 at Dahlem, and finally 31 at Bad Oeynhausen, as the Confessing Church created a provisional administration to oppose the "German Christians." With Niemöller's arrest in 1937, its influenced waned, although recognition by outside churches at the Oxford Conference brought some relief. Members of the church variously interpreted the military oath, and the church, composed of Lutheran, Reformed, and union elements, was never free from internal discord. It lived through World War II, however, in spite of leadership losses, and some members participated actively in assassination plots against Hitler. Slowly the church was eclipsed by the more effective Lutheran Council created in 1934. The Confessing Church had laid the ground for the postwar Evangelical Church in Germany. Its October, 1945, Stuttgart declaration of guilt was characteristic of its direct approach to complex social and political questions.

**Confessional.** The enclosure that the confessor and penitent use during private confession in the Roman Catholic Church. Although auricular confession had been used in the Middle Ages, it was not until the modern period that the confessional in the sense that we know it came into use. Originally there was simply a partition with a small opening which served to separate the priest and the penitent. The confessional has evolved so that both parties are now completely enclosed to ensure privacy.

**Confessionalism.** The reaffirmation of historic creeds and confessions was a major phenomenon of 19th-century Protestantism both in Europe and in America. In Europe, confessionalism arose in part from the evangelical awakenings on the Continent and in Scandinavia (see, e.g., RÉVEIL; HAUGE, HANS NIELSEN; ROSENIUS, CARL OLOF), and from attempts to force Lutheran and Reformed communities into "union" churches (see, e.g., HARMS, KLAUS; LOEHE, JOHANN KONRAD WILHELM). Confessionalism in America was provoked by theological liberalism in the form of Unitarianism and Arminianism and by the increasing role of revivalism. Calvinists in Massachusetts sought to keep Andover Seminary's faculty orthodox by requiring affirmation of both the Westminster Shorter Catechism and the "Andover Creed." In Connecticut, orthodox Congregationalists established a seminary at East Windsor and in the Articles of Agreement excluded views approximating those of the New Haven theologians. Presbyterian conservatives rallied behind the theological system of Charles Hodge of Princeton, who sought to expound and defend the Westminster Confession and other Reformed confessions. They gained control of the Presbyterian General Assembly in 1837 and excluded New School synods viewed as too sympathetic to New Haven thought. Dutch immigrants at mid-century formed the Christian Reformed Church while German and Scandinavian immigrants established new Lutheran synods in the Midwest, expressing within these traditions a concern for a greater measure of doctrinal purity than was to be found in the General Synod.

**Confessions of Faith.** With reference to Matt. 10:32 and Rom. 10:10 this term is used to describe formal and authorized statements of Christian belief, usually of a rather more extended and explanatory character than creeds, and usually with reference to the religious manifestos of the Reformation period. A confession is thus the identifying mark of a certain Christian body. For Lutherans there is the Book of Concord; for the Reformed Church there are, among others, the two Helvetic Confessions, the Heidelberg Catechism, and the Westminster Confession. It is noteworthy that in the Baptist and Congregationalist traditions confessions are less authoritative than educational in character. Even where the normative character of confessions receives greater emphasis, however, these documents are understood as systematic expositions of the content of Scripture, not as strictly equal to Scripture. Thus the danger of rigid confessionalism may be avoided, the way being left open for a modification of confessions in the light of a deeper understanding and experience of the content of Scripture.

**Congé d'Élire** (French, "permission to elect"). A permit granted by a king to a cathedral chapter to elect a bishop. In England after 1214, a dean and chapter had to secure royal permission to proceed with the election, with royal confirmation of the election also required. Since the Reformation, the Crown grants permission and requires the chapter to elect the Crown's nominee.

**Congregatio de Auxiliis.** See MOLINA, LUIS DE.

**Congregationalism, British.** An ecclesiastical communion and an ecclesiology that grew out of 16th-century English nonconformity. "Congregationalism" is often used synonymously with "Separatism" and "Independency." Ecclesiastically, it designates churches that are governed by a polity of local autonomy, or those in which there is a great deal of congregational freedom of expression. Ecclesiologically, Congregationalism is the doctrine of a "gathered" church welded together by a covenant between God and his people. In theology the forerunners of Congregationalism were not greatly different from the Anglican Puritans, both of whom derived their thinking from John Calvin's Reformed tradition. The conforming Puritans responded to the Elizabethan Settlement by an attempt to "purify" the Church of England from within; the Congregationalists for the most part believed this to be impossible. They constituted a more radical wing of the Puritan movement and sought to "gather" churches and "separate" from the Establishment. In some respects they had affinities with the Anabaptists on the Continent and perhaps some continuity with the earlier followers of John Wycliffe known as Lollards. Whatever their rootage, after 1559 they sought to "finish" the Reformation on radical lines that soon brought them into conflict not only with the Anglicans but with their Puritan colleagues as well. They were everywhere embattled.

The exact beginnings of English Congregationalism lie in much obscurity even after more than a century's research by competent investigators. There are some fragments of evidence that in the decade of the 1550's during the Marian persecution small bodies of people were beginning to meet for worship, preaching, and exhortation, often in private homes, in fields and barns, and even on boats. Elizabeth's Act of Uniformity demanded complete obedience of her subjects in matters of church discipline and organization, though there was some latitude left for theological belief. The queen was still declared to be supreme head of the Church of and in England. There was to be no other polity or form of church life tolerated. The Presbyterian Puritans (called by their enemies "those precise men") sought to "purify" the life of the church by instituting preaching as basic to the service of God and modeling the polity of the church on Genevan-presbyterian lines. The Congregationalists were "separatists" seeking to gather out of the corrupt body the Lord's "poor people," a congregation of the faithful, who could give account of their faith and hope in Jesus Christ. The first glimpse that we have of their meetings as gathered churches is on June 19, 1567, when the sheriffs of the city of London paid an official visit to Plumber's Hall, where they had been notified that a nonconforming, dissenting "congregation" was in session. To their surprise they found about a hundred people holding a service. Representatives of the congregation along with their "ministers" were arrested, and after a night in the London jails, they were arraigned before the bishop of London (Edmund Grindal) and the lord mayor. In answer to the charges that they were meeting unlawfully, they urged their objections to the use of surplices and copes in church, which they styled "idolatrous gear." They further claimed that the queen had no right to make them withdraw this objection, and thus began the first self-conscious "dissent" against conformity that would lead in time to a schism in the English Church and portended the whole future of Congregationalism, both in its British and in its American form. Though it has been questioned whether they were genuine Separatists, it would seem from the remaining documents that they intended to be just that. Their basic Scriptural justification was the Pauline admonition to "come out from among them, and be ye separate." Not too long after this mention was made (by Bishop Grindal to the Swiss Reformer Heinrich Bullinger) that a secret congregation had been discovered in London ministered to by "Mr. Richard Fitz," who was something of the pioneer Dissenter. He declared against the "filthy canon law" and the whole entourage of archbishops, bishops, deans, and all forms of prelacy. Fitz and his congregation felt that all of this smacked of papal bondage and that long tutelage of tyranny from which they sought to be free in a true "Gospel freedom."

The next emergent in the development of Congregationalism was in the 1580's when a young Anglican cleric named Robert Browne (b. c. 1550) was preaching at the Church of St. Bene't in Cambridge. It seems that at this time he had already decided that a settled ministry in the Established Church was a form of "bondage." In early 1580 he was forbidden to preach. The letter of prohibition was delivered in person by Richard Bancroft, who would later play a significant role in the life of the Puritans and Dissenters. While in Cambridge, Browne met and was greatly influenced by a like-minded preacher named Robert Harrison, who was headmaster of the grammar school at Norwich. Browne went to Norwich. En route he paid a visit to a Puritan congregation at Bury St. Edmunds. In Norwich he too became a schoolmaster, and in time complaints were lodged with the archbishop that both he and Harrison were corrupting the minds of the children. It was while in East Anglia, the chief center of Puritan-congregational nonconformity outside of London, that Browne became convinced that the Reformation must be completed by separation from the church. Here was manifested that "arrogant spirit of reproving" which so many remarked about. Within a short time Browne was jailed, released, and jailed again. He was now convinced that England was not the place to carry forward this radical reformation that he envisaged. At the turn of the year 1582 he decided to go to Holland. Browne went to Middelburg, remaining for some eighteen months. At first he joined with a congregation of the followers of Thomas Cartwright, but he soon sought a congregation of his own, finding it difficult to serve even under Cartwright. While there he wrote his three famous tracts, which summarize the whole thrust of his radical reform: *A Treatise of Reformation without tarying for Anie; A Treatise upon the 23 of Matthew;* and *A Booke which sheweth the life and manners of all True Christians.* He soon became disaffected with his people there and returned, by way of Scotland, to England. The time between 1583 and 1585 is obscure, but he probably lived in Stamford some of this time. In 1585 he was charged before Archbishop Whitgift of being the author of an anonymous pamphlet written against Cartwright which was deemed seditious. Browne signed a recantation, and his

dissenting days seemed to be over. In time he was to be ordained priest (1591). After that he lived in relative obscurity at Achurch, Northamptonshire, until his death in 1633, though there are some evidences that he was intermittently involved in dissenting activities. Many consider him to be the first "Father of Congregationalism," but almost all Dissenters and Congregationalists have disavowed being "Brownists" from that day until the present. Erik Routley's judgment may not have been far from wrong when he said: "There, embodied in a single person, is sixteenth century English Dissent." Browne did set forth in almost classic form the early genius of gathered, covenanted Congregationalism. In a beautiful passage he calls the true church a "mutual using of friendship and callings . . . builded first by communion of the graces and offices in the Head of the church, which is Christ. . . . Secondly . . . by communion of the graces and offices in the body, which is the church of Christ. . . . Thirdly . . . by using the sacrament of the Lord's Supper, as a seal of this communion." This he asserted against Anglican authoritarianism and Puritan presbyterianism. After Browne's defection, other voices of nonconformity arose, and several suffered martyrdom for the cause, viz., Henry Barrow, John Penry, and John Greenwood in the spring of 1593. But churches were being gathered all during the decade of the 1590's, among them some that were to become famous in the 17th century—the meeting at Scrooby in particular, the congregation under the charge of Elder William Brewster which became the Pilgrim church of Pastor John Robinson, of Leiden. These groups came in time to settle in Holland, and from them were to develop the Baptists as well as the Independents. When Pastor Robinson's little band of Pilgrims set out for the new world in 1620, a nation was in the offing, and from the New England strand, Congregationalism was to become a major force in the future, not only of theology, but of politics as well.

During the period from 1600 to 1640 Congregational dissent was either in exile on the Continent or driven out of the homeland to America. Nonetheless, the Puritan cause gained strength in England and came to a climax in the conflict with Archbishop Laud and the outbreak of the Civil War in 1642. With the rise of Oliver Cromwell, who was an Independent, the free church forces gained ascendancy against the Presbyterians, who largely dominated the Parliament and the Westminster Assembly. During the time of the Commonwealth (established in 1649) the Independents were predominant in the ecclesiastical life of England, but they made no effort to organize the church. They allowed a great measure of freedom for most Christian peoples, though they prohibited papists and royalist Anglicans. All kinds of sectaries had free reign in this era—the Ranters, Familists, Muggletonians, Levelers and Diggers, Quakers, and Fifth Monarchy Men. With the death of Cromwell in 1658, and the failure of Richard Cromwell, the Restoration of King Charles II was inevitable. He returned to England on May 29, 1660, acclaimed by great multitudes of people, who were tired of the Puritan-Presbyterian-Independent prohibitions that had marked the life of the church during the preceding fifteen years or more. With the passage of the Act of Uniformity in 1662, English Dissenters and Nonconformists became at last distinct religious bodies, separate from the Establishment and subject to certain disabilities. From the time of the Act of Uniformity until the Glorious Revolution in 1688 the Dissenters in England suffered heavy penalties, though there were times of relaxation from the rigors of the law. After the accession of William and Mary, life for nonconformists became more tolerable, but they still suffered some disfranchisements from the common life. The 18th century was for Congregationalism generally undistinguished, though the names of Isaac Watts in hymnody and Philip Doddridge in preaching should not be forgotten. The 19th century witnessed something of a rejuvenescence among Congregationalists, as they more and more entered public life and politics. In Wales the Congregationalists were the major dissenting body, though in Scotland they remained a small and uninfluential minority. Local and county organizations developed. In 1831 the Congregational Union of England and Wales was established and became more and more pervasive in the life of the congregations. Congregationalists, both in England and America, have stood for a cultured and educated ministry and, as a correlate, and educated laity. They have entered wholeheartedly into ecumenical endeavors in the 20th century.

BIBLIOGRAPHY: Older histories of Congregationalism are still usable, though needing supplementation by more recent research, e.g., C. Burrage, *Early English Dissenters in the Light of Recent Research,* 2 vols. (documents and commentary, 1912); H. W. Clark, *History of English Nonconformity,* 2 vols. (rev. ed., New York, 1965); R. W. Dale, *History of English Congregationalism* (1907). The most recent and exhaustive treatment, especially from the period of 1662, is R. T. Jones, *Congregationalism in England, 1662–1962* (London, 1962).

**Congregationalists.** A Protestant body tracing its origin in the United States to the Puritan migration to New England in the 17th century. A small group of Separatists settled at Plymouth in 1620 and were joined by a much larger group of nonseparating Congregationalists who established themselves around Boston after 1629. Although disagreeing on the necessity of separation from the Church of England, Pilgrim and Puritan shared the basic ideas of English Puritanism. Their theology was Calvinism mediated through the works of Puritans such as William Perkins and William Ames. They elaborated a system of church life distinguished by its emphasis upon the covenant and by its insistence upon an evidence of election for church membership. A Synod at Cambridge in 1648 accepted the Westminster Confession of Faith as the doctrinal standard of Congregationalism and adopted a Platform of Church Discipline detailing the relationship of congregations to one another and of the church to the state. The polity of the Platform represented a middle position between Presbyterianism and Independency. Church councils were recognized as useful for discerning truth, but all judicial power was vested in the congregation. Magistrates were called upon to use the coercive power of the state in the service of the church. While church membership carried with it the franchise in Massachusetts and the life of the congregation was democratic, so great was the power of the clergy and aristocracy in the 17th century that the system has been termed a speaking aristocracy in the face of a silent democracy. The Halfway Covenant, adopted in 1662, reduced the stringent requirements for church membership, but the decline in religious vitality which precipitated this measure was not arrested until the Great Awakening of the 1730's. The Awakening intensified religious enthusiasm and increased church membership but led to controversy and schism. Revivalists often met with hostility in the established church, and many withdrew to form Separatist congregations. Meanwhile, the Awakening exacerbated theological controversies, led to the emergence of New England Theology, and hastened the drift of Boston area Congregationalists toward Unitarianism. During the Revolution, Congregationalists were generally enthusiastic for the colonial cause and independence from Anglicanism.

The early 19th century witnessed the disestablishment of Congregationalism in New England, the transition of most Boston area churches to Unitarianism, and the rapid migration of Congregationalists westward. Under the terms of the Plan of Union of 1801, Congregationalists at first cooperated with Presbyterians in the West through such agencies as the American Home Missionary Society and the American Education Society. However, Congregationalism was rapidly adopting a more liberal theology under the leadership of Nathaniel W. Taylor and Horace Bushnell, and as Congregationalism became less Calvinistic, conflict with Old School Presbyterianism ensued. Antislavery agitation intensified the conflict, for Congregationalists took a more hostile position toward slaveholding than did Presbyterians. Congregationalists from East and West met at Albany, N.Y., in 1852 and abrogated the Plan of Union. Thereafter Congregationalists vigorously encouraged their own polity in the West. A National Council was formed in 1871, and a creed expressing a liberal evangelical point of view was adopted at Kansas City in 1913. After merging with the Christian Church in 1931, Congregationalists merged with the Evangelical and Reformed Church to form the United Church of Christ in 1951. A small group of Congregationalists declined to participate in this merger and organized the National Association of Congregational Christian Churches in 1955.

BIBLIOGRAPHY: G. G. Atkins and F. L. Fagley, *History of American Congregationalism* (Boston, 1942); S. E. Mead, *Nathaniel William Taylor* (Chicago, 1942); P. Miller, *Orthodoxy in Massachusetts: 1630–1650* (Boston, 1959); and *The New England Mind: The Seventeenth Century*, 2 vols. (Boston, 1961); W. W. Sweet, *The Congregationalists*, Vol. 3 of *Religion on the American Frontier: 1783–1840* (New York, 1964).

**Congregational Union of England and Wales.** A liaison agent for the several County Unions, founded in 1831. Through effective service to the churches it eventually overcame the Independents' fear of associations and became the national voice of Congregationalism. It has, however, no authority over the churches. In 1962 there were 2,984 churches, 1,862 ministers, 212,017 communicants, 451,000 community. There is also a small separate Congregational Union of Scotland.

**Congregation of Picpus** (*known officially as* Congregation of the Sacred Hearts of Jesus and Mary and of Perpetual Adoration of the Most Holy Sacrament of the Altar). A religious congregation founded in 1805 in France with the motherhouse at Rue de Picpus, Paris. Primarily active in education and domestic and foreign missions, it has six Continental provinces and three overseas. A companion sisterhood is engaged in education. The Congregation publishes two journals devoted to Sacred Heart spirituality.

**Congregation of the Mission.** See LAZARISTS.

**Congruism.** A theory of grace promoted in the 16th and 17th centuries by the Jesuits, especially Suárez and Bellarmine, in an effort to solve the problem of relating free will and dependence on God's grace. According to Congruism, God gives his help under precisely those conditions in which he foreknows that the person will accept it and use it. (See EFFICACIOUS GRACE.)

**Conquistadors.** The Spanish soldiers who explored, conquered, and founded settlements for Spain in the Americas in the 16th century. Their leaders included such men as Hernando Cortes in Mexico and Francisco Pizarro in Peru, and they were usually accompanied by Dominican or Franciscan missionaries. The Spaniards were animated by two conflicting motives: they wished to convert the natives and treat them as fellow Christians, yet their lust for wealth tempted them to rob and exploit the Indians. The natives were slaughtered and enslaved, but defended by such men as Bartolomé de Las Casas. Ill-treated as the Indians may have been, they were to some extent benefited by Spanish culture, and not, as in North America, all but exterminated.

**Conrad of Gelnhausen** (c. 1320–1390). Conciliarist. He studied canon law at Bologna and theology at Paris, where he then taught. In his main work, the *Epistle of Concord* (1380), he argued that in view of the Schism, the church in council however assembled had the power to decide between rival popes. His thesis rejected by his king and his university, he left for the University of Heidelberg, where he became its first chancellor and the primary benefactor of the library.

**Conrad of Marburg** (c. 1180–1233). Papal inquisitor. A man of learning and rigorous asceticism, Conrad began his career in 1213 as a Crusade preacher. He was in charge of reforming convents in Thuringia and became a friend of the landgrave Louis IV. Later, Conrad was spiritual adviser for Ludwig's widow, Elizabeth of Hungary. After her death he was nominated the first papal inquisitor for Germany by Gregory IX, ruthlessly pursued his task until he was murdered in 1233, following his unfounded accusation of heresy against a nobleman.

**Consalvi, Ercole** (1757–1824). Cardinal, Vatican secretary of state, and a successful church diplomat and statesman. Gaining protection as a young cleric from the cardinal of York, he advanced in the Curia until the French occupation of Rome (1798). He visited Pius VI in exile and served as secretary of the Venice conclave (1800) that chose Pius VII. Raised to the cardinalate and named secretary of state, he administered the Papal States with considerable skill. In 1801 he matched talents with Talleyrand when negotiating the French Concordat. He was relieved in 1806 through French pressure, but was in France during the climax of Napoleon's reign. He was among a dozen "black" cardinals who refused to appear at the emperor's remarriage. Jailed for three years, he urged Pius VII to retract the Concordat of Fontainebleau (1813). He visited London, paving the way for ultimate Catholic emancipation, represented the pope with great ability at the Congress of Vienna, winning back all papal provinces except Avignon. Secretary of state (1814–1823), he reorganized the Papal States, maintained order against Carbonari menaces (1817), but saw the Austrians violate the Temporality (1821) en route to Naples. He drew up concordats with Bavaria and Sardinia (1817), Naples (1818), and Prussia (1821). He retired on the death of Pius VII in 1823.

**Consensus of Geneva** (1552). A Calvinist creed on predestination. After the disturbance caused by Bolsec, Calvin strengthened his position on predestination. He drafted this document, and by 1552 had the support of the Genevan ministers and city council. Although the controversy with Bolsec was the immediate occasion for the Consensus, Calvin's argument was directed chiefly against Albert Pighius, whose views on free will he had already criticized. A theological treatise rather than a creed in the normal sense, the Consensus acquired no authority outside of Geneva.

**Consensus Tigurinus** ("Consensus of Zurich"). In May of 1549, Calvin and Farel met with Bullinger at Zurich and agreed on this statement of faith, basically concerned with the Eucharist. Zwinglian and Calvinist concepts were combined to the satisfaction of both parties. Though Bern and Basel were displeased that a statement was drafted in their absence, they soon accepted the formula, as did all the Swiss Reformed Churches.

**Consistory.** Originally the chamber of the imperial palace where the emperor and his ministers administered justice; later ecclesiastical courts as well, and specifically the meetings of the pope with the College of Cardinals. These consistories have defined functions in the creation of new cardinals and the canonization of saints. In some Reformed churches, the governing body of a congregation is known as the Consistory.

**Consistory, Genevan.** A body composed of twelve elders and the ministers of the city which first met in December, 1541. It was soon the principal organ of church discipline, systematically supervising the morals and habits of the people. Its jurisdiction and harshness in petty misdemeanors has been attacked, but its decisions were no different from those on the statute books of many a late medieval city.

**Constance, Council of** (1414–1418). In 1409 the Council of Pisa left the church more divided than ever, for now there were three popes. The University of Paris, the cardinals, and the emperor Sigismund collaborated and urged the reluctant Pisan pope John XXIII to convoke a new council. On Nov. 5, 1414, the Council of Constance commenced. It was structured according to nations (Italian, French, English, German, and Spanish); each nation had a presidency and an equal vote, thus removing the imbalance of Italian votes. In 1415, John XXIII fled from the Council but the emperor held it together. There followed the famous Articles of Constance which declared that the Council, legitimately called in the Holy Spirit, represented the whole church and had its authority directly from God; all of its declarations which pertained to faith, the healing of the Schism, and reformation in head and members must be adhered to by every Christian (including the pope). Eventually the three popes were deposed or withdrew and the Schism ended. Martin V was elected and a decree passed (*Frequens*) which provided for a general council every ten years. The most notorious moment of the Council was the condemnation of John Hus which caused him to be burned at the stake in 1415. The Council concluded in 1418.

**Constans II** (*also known as* Flavius Heraclius Constans) (630–668). Emperor of the Eastern Roman Empire (641–668). During his reign he reorganized the provinces, but the Saracens made significant advances against the Empire. Sympathetic to the Monotheletes, he issued in 648 the Type or Typus, an edict banning religious discussion. It was designed to terminate the controversy between the Monotheletes and the Eastern Orthodox Church, which had increased after Heraclius had issued the Ecthesis in 638. Constans was assassinated by being drowned in his bath.

**Constantine and Family.** The Roman emperor Constantine the Great (c. 274–337) was the eldest son of Constantius Chlorus, a soldier who rose to the rank of caesar (vice-emperor), in charge of Britain and Gaul. Constantius was attached to the monotheistic cult of the Unconquered Sun, and enforced in his provinces only the first and mildest of Diocletian's edicts of persecution. In 305, Constantius became Emperor of the West, but his colleague Galerius controlled the choice of the new caesars. His son Constantine, fleeing from Galerius' court, reached York before Constantius' death in 306, and was proclaimed by the army as his father's successor.

In the confused struggles of the following years Constantine rose steadily. In 312 the defeat of Maxentius at the Milvian Bridge outside Rome made him ruler of the Roman West. On this campaign occurred the dream (or vision) of the cross in the sky which led him to put the sacred sign on his standards. In 313, Constantine and his colleague Licinius proclaimed toleration for the Christians, and Licinius defeated the persecutor Maximin Daia in the East. As Constantine increased his patronage of the church Licinius turned against it; he removed Christians from his service and encouraged paganism, but in 323, Constantine defeated him and became sole emperor.

Constantine cannot be considered either a saintly convert or a skeptical politician; he supported the Christian cult as the best means of securing the divine protection that he and his empire needed, and in turn expected the church to support him. Confronted with its divisions, he recognized the party that its Councils approved, and so confirmed the condemnation of Donatism in the West and Arianism in the East. He then temporized, largely for political reasons, gave practical toleration to the Donatists, and increasingly supported the imperialist bishops of the anti-Nicene party. In 326 his second wife, Fausta, and his oldest son, Crispus, were put to death for an alleged conspiracy. Pagan writers observed that he might well turn to a religion which offered forgiveness for every sin. However, his public policy was generally successful, and his reign was crowned by the refounding of Byzantium as Constantinople and the dedication of the imperial churches at Jerusalem. Shortly before his death on May 22, 337, he was at last baptized.

Constantine had planned to divide the Empire among the three sons of Fausta, with appanages for other relatives, but the army prevented this by a massacre of the latter except for two young nephews, Gallus and Julian. Constantine II and Constans ruled in the West, but they quarreled and the former was killed in 340. Constans, though a rough sol-dier, patronized the Catholic party in the church, while in the East his brother Constantius increasingly supported Arianism. Hence arose the impasse of 343 when a Council called to discuss the affairs of Athanasius broke into two sections at the frontier towns in modern Bulgaria, the Athanasians at Sardica (modern Sofia) and the Arians at Philippopolis (Plovdiv). In 350, Constans was killed in the rebellion of Magnentius; Constantius slowly moved west, and by the defeat of Magnentius in 353 became sole emperor. He was then able to develop fully his pro-Arian policy, which reached apparent success in 359 and 360 (see ARIMINUM AND SELEUCIA, SYNODS OF).

Meanwhile in 351, Gallus had been made caesar in the East; but proving inefficient and cruel, he was summoned to court and put to death on the way in 354. As Constantius returned to the East, Julian was sent to Gaul as caesar (for his personal career and religious policy, see JULIAN THE APOSTATE). He revealed unexpected military talents and saved the Rhine frontier for a generation. In 359, Constantius summoned Julian's best troops for the Persian War; suspecting Constantius' intentions, the soldiers proclaimed Julian emperor at Paris in February, 360. Conflict between the two cousins was prevented by the death of Constantius (shortly after his baptism) on Nov. 3, 361. After a long stay at Antioch, Julian advanced against the Persians in 363. He reached their capital, Ctesiphon on the Tigris, but finding himself too weak to attack it, retired northward and was killed in a skirmish on June 26. So ended the "second Flavian dynasty," which had produced at least four rulers of ability, two perhaps of genius, and by Constantine's success and Julian's failure inaugurated the Christian Roman Empire.

BIBLIOGRAPHY: A. Alfoeldi, *The Conversion of Constantine and Pagan Rome* (Oxford, 1948); G. P. Baker, *Constantine the Great and the Christian Revolution* (New York, 1930); N. H. Baynes, *Constantine the Great and the Christian Church* (London, 1930); J. C. Burckhardt, *The Age of Constantine the Great* (New York, 1949); J. B. Firth, *Constantine the Great* (New York, 1905); A. H. M. Jones, *Constantine and the Conversion of Europe* (New York, 1949).

**Constantine VII Porphyrogenitus** (905–959). Byzantine emperor and scholar. The son of Emperor Leo VI, he was excluded from all but nominal rule by his stepfather Romanus I Lecapenus until 945. A literary more than a political figure, he wrote or commissioned many reference works and anthologies.

His chief works were: "On the Administration of the Empire," a valuable source of geographical and ethnological information; "On the Themes," on the military organization of the empire; "On the Ceremonies at the Court of Constantinople," a description of church and court customs; and, under his direction, Simeon Metaphrastes' *Lives of the Saints* and the *Lexicon* of Suidas. As emperor he continued Romanus' policy of restoring land to peasants, and among the foreign legations he received one from the recently converted Russian princess Olga, thus inaugurating a new era in Byzantine-Russian relations.

**Constantinople, Councils of.** *First Council* (381). Although this Council is regarded as the Second Ecumenical Council, it is esteemed so more because of the importance of its decrees than for either the manner of its convocation or its composition. Our records for it are slight and their interpretation is not always certain. Some of the main facts, however, are indisputable. The purpose of the Council was to settle the Arian controversy which had plagued the church so long. When Constantius defeated Magnentius in 353 his interest in the peace of the church allowed the Arians to gain ascendancy. It was then that, as Jerome said, "the whole world groaned and was astonished to find itself Arian." When Theodosius I became emperor in 379, it was his desire to restore the Nicene party and he called this Council to effect his purpose.

For forty years before the accession of Theodosius to the purple the Arians at Constantinople had had such free sway that they began to argue with one another and to break into factions. The orthodox in the capital were without either a church or a bishop. When they heard that Theodosius was emperor, they began to prepare for the new order by calling Gregory of Nazianzus to be patriarch. He found the city in such a state of theological ferment that there were those who "if you ask the price of bread, tell you that the Father is greater and the Son subject to him, and if you want to order a bath, reply that the Son is made out of nothing." Gregory's justly famous *Theological Orations* were preached in the year before the Council and undoubtedly had much to do with the ease with which orthodoxy was established in Constantinople upon the arrival of Theodosius in the city in November, 380.

The Council was not called to be ecumenical and no Western bishops were present; the theory that Rome was represented by legates has been traced to a scribal error. There were 150 Orthodox bishops in attendance, including some from Egypt and Macedonia who did not stay through the end of the Council. Also present were 36 bishops of the Macedonian heresy who believed in the subordination of the Holy Spirit, but not in that of the Son. Theodosius had hope that they could be reconciled to the Nicene faith. Beginning in May and ending in July, the Council was called to restore the faith of Nicaea, settle the question of who was rightful bishop of Constantinople, and attend to several practical matters. Melitius of Antioch was the original president of the Council but died during its course. The question of who was to succeed him was complicated by the quarrels over who was the rightful bishop of Constantinople and what was the order of precedence among the great sees of the church. Timothy of Alexandria arrived late at the Council to challenge Gregory's right to the Constantinopolitan patriarchate on the grounds that the canons of Nicaea forbade the translation of bishops from one see to another and Gregory had been bishop of Nazianzus. Gregory left the Council and the city in disgust, thus simplifying the problem for those who stayed. Nectarius was elected patriarch and presided over the rest of the Council.

The major contribution of this Council is surrounded in mystery. The creed that is commonly called Nicene was read at Chalcedon in 451 as being the creed of the 150 fathers of Constantinople. Yet that is the earliest record we have of the creed. The question is: How is the baptismal creed of the East and the Eucharistic creed of the West related to the Council at which it is supposed to have originated? The answer seems to be that although Constantinople wished to reaffirm the teaching of Nicaea, it had no sense that it had to do so in the exact words of the Creed of Nicaea. The Niceno-Constantinopolitan symbol was taken as an equivalent expression of the Nicene faith which had some advantages over its predecessor.

The claim of the Council for ecumenical rank depends, of course, on its contribution of the most ecumenical creed of Christendom (the Apostles' Creed is not used in the East). It was not recognized by the East as ecumenical until Chalcedon. At that time Rome left Chalcedon, since it would not subscribe to the Constantinopolitan decree that Constantinople was the second see of Christendom in precedence of honor. Rome did not accept Constantinople as ecumenical until the Great Lateran Council.

*Second Council* (553). This Council is regarded as the Fifth Ecumenical Council. Like the earlier Council in the same city, it was called to put an end to a long-standing controversy—in this case, the Monophysite controversy. This controversy was the vestige of the continuing antipathy between the theological position representative of Antioch and that of Alexandria. The Monophysites came into separate existence after Chalcedon (451) but their belief that Christ had two natures before but only one after the incarnation was the teaching of Eutyches, who, in turn, only intended to reiterate the position of Cyril of Alexandria, who opposed Nestorianism in an orthodox manner. Nestorius considered himself the defender of the faith against the errors of Apollinarius and was the student of Theodore of Mopsuestia. In other words, the Monophysite controversy was merely a continuation of the running battle that had been going since the first distinctively Christological controversy.

The controversy had taken an unusual turn because the emperor Justinian was no mean theologian and he considered that being God's vice-gerent on earth gave him a theological responsibility. Justinian's ambition was the realization of the full potentialities of the Christian Roman Empire, and his ecclesiastical policy was part of his effort to achieve this ambition. Justinian's first attempt to heal the division was to call for a discussion of differences by leaders of the Orthodox and Monophysite factions. After that failed he tried persecution, which also failed, at least partly because of the secret intervention of the empress Theodora, who sympathized with the Monophysites. Procopius reports in his *Secret History (Anecdota)* that she had been born in a base estate, had been an actress and a prostitute before her marriage, and that she practiced sorcery as well, but he is too credulous to be very plausible. Theodora's sympathy for the Monophysites does appear to be historical. Since she exercised a great deal of power over Justinian, she may be responsible for his third effort to deal with the Monophysites, which was an effort to woo them back into the fold of the faithful. He wished for a statement of faith that would give the theology of Cyril in its essence without repudiating the Council of Chalcedon. Since the Monophysites were greatly annoyed by the fact that Chalcedon did not condemn the teachers of Nestorius (Nestorius, in fact, thought that Chalcedon had vindicated him), Justinian attempted to satisfy them on that score. About 543 he issued an edict on his own authority in which he condemned: (1) the person and writings of Theodore, (2) the anti-Cyrillian writings of Theodoret, and (3) the letter of Ibas to the Persian bishop Maris.

This was the first time an emperor had ever attempted to legislate dogma. The four Eastern patriarchs consented to it under pressure, but Vigilius of Rome objected. He followed a policy of vacillation dictated, according to Adolf von Harnack, by self-interest, becoming a Monophysite or Chalcedonian according to orders (*History of Dogma,* Vol. 4, p. 248).

The Council was called by Justinian to settle the affair of the "Three Chapters," as the writings he had condemned were called. Opening on May 5, 553, under Eutychius of Constantinople, the Council quickly proceeded to do what was expected of it. The 150 or so bishops, almost all Eastern, condemned Origen (though there is some debate about this), condemned the Three Chapters, and pronounced fourteen anathemas, instead of promulgating canons as previous Councils had done. The general result was that Chalcedon came to be given a Cyrillian interpretation. Some relief to the monotony of this rubber-stamp Council was furnished by Vigilius, who set up a sideshow. He issued a *Constitutum,* drawn up with the help of his deacon, who was to become Pope Pelagius I. He said that he would condemn the writings of the Three Chapters but not the writers. Since, however, Justinian would not let him go home until he accepted the decrees of the Council, he signed them after six months of hesitation and died on his way home to Rome. The Monophysite schism was not healed.

*Third Council* (680). This is the Sixth Ecumenical Council, third held at Constantinople. Instigated by Emperor Constantine IV Pogonatus, the Council was to settle the Monothelete controversy that had troubled the church for forty-odd years. The Monotheletes held that in Christ the divine will and the human will were one. The Catholic Church teaches that there are two distinct unseparable natures in Christ, and therefore two separate wills, the divine and the human. The author of this heresy was Sergius, the patriarch of Constantinople (610–638). It has been proposed that this doctrine was inspired by political rather than religious motivations in an attempt to bring the earlier advocates of Monophysitism (only *one* nature in Christ, the divine) back into the Orthodox Church. Monotheletism was denounced bitterly by church leaders such as Sophronius, Pope Severinus, and Martin I. Pope Agatho, in preparation for the Council, ordered synods to be held at Milan, Heathfield in England, and Rome, uniting the Western Church in its condemnation of Monotheletism. The eighteen sessions of the Council were largely debates conducted by the papal legates with Macarius, the patriarch of Antioch, who was a strong supporter of Monotheletism. Unable to substantiate his position from any of the decrees of previous Councils or from any writings of the church fathers, he, along with Sergius and other proponents of Monotheletism were anathematized by the Council. The Roman Catholic pope Honorius I (625–638) was also anathematized by the Council for having advocated the heresy of Monotheletism, thus furnishing a historical argument against papal infallibility. No canon laws were issued by the Council, since it concerned itself only with the question of Monotheletism. (See TRULLAN SYNOD.)

BIBLIOGRAPHY: A. Harnack, *History of Dogma*, Vol. 4 (New York, 1961); H. Jedin, *Ecumenical Councils of the Catholic Church* (Glen Rock, N.J., 1960); A. A. Luce, *Monophysitism Past and Present* (New York, 1920); W. A. Wigram, *The Separation of the Monophysites* (London, 1923).

**Contarini, Gasparo** (1483–1542). Cardinal. Born of one of Venice's most powerful families, Contarini first pursued the career of a patrician, serving on the Great Council and on various commissions of the Republic, and also as ambassador at the court of Emperor Charles V. When Pope Paul III in 1535 created him a lay cardinal, he used his diplomatic and political experience in leading church reform, both curial and diocesan. As a member of the newly created Commission for Reform, he presented to the pope in 1537 a document on reform (*Consilium de emendanda ecclesia*), largely his own work. He was partially responsible for the papal approbation of the Society of Jesus in 1540. As papal legate to the Colloquy of Regensburg (1541), his tendency to favor certain concessions to the Protestants led to a compromise doctrinal formula, which was, however, rejected by both Luther and Rome. His writings constantly tried to reconcile the views of Roman Catholics and Protestant Reformers; despite his strict orthodoxy, they brought him under suspicion. He died in Bologna.

**Convent.** The building where a religious community resides; also known as a cloister. The term can refer to the religious community itself. Although a convent may house either men or women, in popular usage the name is applied primarily to communities of women.

**Conventicle Act** (1664). A part of the Clarendon Code Restoration legislation which followed the English Civil War. Its purpose was to reestablish Anglican uniformity. It made illegal any religious gathering of five or more people, other than members of one household, which was not allowed by the Church of England. Offenses were punishable by fine, imprisonment, and, for a third offense, transportation to a colony.

**Conventual Mass.** The Mass said in a religious convent at which the entire community is present. It is usually a public High Mass rather than a private Low Mass as celebrated by the individual ordained members of the community. Such a Mass celebrated in a cathedral or collegiate church for the entire chapter, while properly called a capitular Mass, is popularly called a conventual Mass.

**Conventuals.** The name given to members of the Order of Friars Minor Conventual, one of the three independent branches of the First Order of Franciscans. They differ from the other Franciscan orders because of their liberal interpretation of the absolute poverty prescribed by the Rule of St. Francis. Unlike the friars of the older tradition (Observants) who rejected property altogether, the Conventuals (from Latin, "pertaining to convents") approved the acquisition and common holding of property. Although their policy was endorsed by Pope John XXII in 1322, the actual division of the First Order was not recognized until almost one hundred years later by the Council of Constance and was not formally sanctioned until 1517 when Pope Leo X allowed the Conventuals to elect their own master general (since 1587 called minister general). Their membership of approximately twenty-five thousand in 1517 declined significantly in the 16th and again in the 18th century for reasons associated with the general political and religious situations. The Conventuals in modern times profess the Rule of St. Francis in accordance with the so-called Urban Constitutions of 1625, which were officially decreed by Pope Urban VIII in 1628. Because of the color of their habit, they have been given the popular appellation "Black Franciscans."

**Conversi.** A term used of lay brothers in monasteries, sometimes synonymous with *barbatti* or *idiotae*. Introduced by the Vallombrosans and popularized by the Cistercians, the replacement of serfs by *conversi* reflected the determination of the orders to be free of manoral institutions. Although many dedicated laymen became *conversi* through religious conviction, others did so for economic reasons, freeing themselves from the bondage of the feudal system. Medieval monastic intrigues often were centered in the *conversi.* Their exact status is still a matter of controversy.

**Convocation.** An assembly of the clergy of the Church of England, belonging either to the province of Canterbury or to that of York, called together to consult on ecclesiastical affairs. Though there are traces of earlier large clerical assemblies, the Canterbury Convocation became established under Archbishop Theodore of Tarsus (668–690). York became a separate authority in 733.

Originally only prelates attended, but in 1225 under Archbishop Langton proctors of cathedral and monastic chapters were convoked, archdeacons in 1258, and in 1283, under Archbishop Packham, Convocation assumed its mature form, consisting of bishop, abbots, deans and archdeacon, two representatives of the clergy from each diocese and one from each provincial chapter. Originally a single assembly, from the 15th century on the Convocation split into two houses, the archbishops presiding over the bishops and abbots in the Upper House and a prolocutor over the other representatives in the Lower House. The new canons of 1921 ordered that the Lower House should be composed of the dean, or proctor, of every cathedral church and of the collegiate churches of Westminster and Windsor, the provost of Eton, if he is in priest's orders, the two archdeacons senior by date of appointment in each diocese, proctors for the clergy of each diocese, proportionally elected, provided that no diocese have fewer than three. Since 1936 the universities of Oxford and Cambridge have been represented in the Convocation of Canterbury.

Over the centuries the work of Convocation has been to legislate canons for the governance of the English Church. Among the most important were the canons of 1604 which have since then formed the basis of Anglican law.

The Reformation saw important changes in Convocation. After the Act for Submission of the Clergy (1534), Convocation could be summoned only by royal edict. The dissolution of the monasteries eliminated abbots from Convocation.

After the revolution of 1688 political disputes disrupted the Convocations until, in the Bangorian Controversy (1717), George I prorogued both Convocations to prevent the condemnation by the Lower House of a sermon and book by Bishop Hoadly. It required the combined influence of the Evangelical and Oxford movements, demanding clerical representation in the decisions of the Church of England, to renew the Convocations, that of Canterbury in 1852, of York in 1861.

The question of lay representation in the deliberations of Convocation was raised as early as 1857, but it was not until 1885 that the Convocation of Canterbury agreed to initiate a House of Laymen, representatives to be appointed by lay members of diocesan conferences and by the archbishop, to serve as a consultative body to Convocation. Such a House of Laymen came into existence in the Province of Canterbury in 1886 and in York in 1892. At the beginning of the 20th century the two Convocations began meeting together, and in 1904 a Representative Council composed of members of both Convocations and of both Houses of Laymen, sitting together, was initiated. The Council possessed no legal authority until Parliament passed the Enabling Act in 1919, conferring legislative power upon the Council, now renamed the National Assembly of the Church of England. Composed of the two upper houses of Convocation, a House of Clergy and a House of Laity selected every five years by the electors of the diocesan conferences, this body has its most important function in the preparation of legislation respecting the Church of England for enactment by Parliament. However, its influence is felt in almost every department of the Church of England. The Church Assembly encompasses the Convocations, but it does not altogether remove their separateness, pronouncements on theological matters being reserved to the Convocations alone. Convocations ordinarily meet about three times a year for two or three days. The Assembly meets in London, usually three times a year.

BIBLIOGRAPHY: E. W. Kemp, *Counsel and Consent* (London, 1961); A. F. Smethhurst, *Convocation of Canterbury: What It Is; What It Does; How It Works* (London, 1949); D. B. Weske, *Convocation of the Clergy* (New York, 1937).

**Conwell, Russell H.** (1843–1925). Clergyman and lecturer. Educated at Wilbraham Academy (Mass.) and Yale, Conwell became a Baptist pastor in 1879 after distinguished careers as a Civil War officer, a Minneapolis attorney, a foreign correspondent, and an editor. In 1884 he founded Temple University in Philadelphia. He lectured widely, giving his income to his university and to other philanthropic projects. His most famous lecture was "Acres of Diamonds."

**Cook, Joseph** (Flavius Josephus Cook) (1838–1901). Popular American lecturer. He was a native of Ticonderoga, N.Y., and a graduate of Harvard and of Andover Theological Seminary. Beginning in 1874, Cook for many years delivered the "Monday Lecture" in Boston's Tremont Temple. From this platform he assured the public that new insights in philosophy and science, including the theory of evolution, did not destroy the Christian faith. His addresses were published in eleven volumes.

**Coornheert, Dirck** (1522–1590). Dutch public servant and lay theologian. He was a strong advocate of Arminian views more than twenty years before Arminius himself. Profoundly influenced early in life by observing the execution of some heretics while he was on a visit to Spain, he came to feel strongly that the church had no right to shackle the conscience of anyone. A largely self-educated man, he worked at various times as an engraver, a secretary to the mayor of Haarlem, a secretary of the States of Holland, and a notary public. He was imprisoned in 1567 at The Hague with those who suffered for departing from the faith of Rome. So obnoxious were his views on religious liberty to the Spanish government that his name was excepted from the decree of amnesty in 1574. After settling in Haarlem in 1576, he began to make known his objections to the strict Calvinist teaching on predestination. He even declared that any church holding these views was no church at all. In 1583, because he had written against the Heidelberg Catechism, he came into conflict with the great Saravia, professor of theology at Leiden. A public debate with Saravia ended with both sides claiming victory. However, official displeasure with his views was indicated in the following year when he was forbidden to settle in the city of Delft. Maintaining his passionate concern for religious freedom, he wrote a pamphlet on liberty of conscience as he lay on his deathbed.

**COPEC.** The abbreviated name given to the Conference on Christian Politics, Economics, and Citizenship, held in Great Britain in 1924. Between the two World Wars the churches in Britain expended much energy in an effort to quicken the religious life of apathetic Protestants and also to reach the unchurched masses. One of the largest and most successful efforts of this kind was implemented through the joint cooperation of most of the churches of Britain at COPEC.

**Copernicus, Nicolas** (1473–1543). Renaissance astronomer, mathematician, and clergyman who revolutionized man's fundamental conceptions of the structure of the world by positing a heliocentric theory of the universe.

He was born in Thorn, on the Vistula River, his father apparently Polish and his mother German. His uncle, a bishop, financed his study of canon law, first at the University of Kraków and later at the Universities of Bologna, Padua, and Ferrara in Italy. While a university student he developed an intense interest in astronomy. Soon he began to doubt the almost universally accepted geocentric system of Ptolemy. Copernicus continued his scrutiny of Ptolemy after his return from Italy to his homeland in 1506. After 1512 he resided at Frauenburg in Prussia, where he served as a responsible member of the cathedral chapter until his death in 1543. His continued study of the heavens led him to reject the centuries-old Ptolemaic theory and to replace it with the concept that the sun was the center of the solar system. He spent thirty years on a book describing this discovery, his *De revolutionibus orbium coelestium,* published shortly before his death in 1543. Some of the Protestant Reformers rejected the Copernican theory, even though an unauthorized preface by Andreas Osiander emphasized that the *De revolutionibus* presented a hypothesis and nothing more. His book was put on the Index in 1616 at the time of Galileo's first encounter with the Church of Rome.

**Coppino Education Act** (July 15, 1877). An Italian law, named after a cabinet minister, instituting free elementary schooling. Parents were obliged to send their children aged six to nine to boys' and girls' schools. Three classes were introduced, one for each year. Communes were supposed to establish primary instruction where it did not exist. The scheme was not implemented until after the turn of the century. Teaching was secular.

**Coptic Church.** A Monophysite church in Egypt. The Christian church was late in winning significant influence in Egypt, although early church fathers had made many converts there. By the beginning of the 4th century, however, the Scriptures had been translated into several Egyptian vernaculars, so that the non-Greek-speaking majority of the population could be won to Christianity. Many early Egyptian Christians followed the Biblical precept of shunning material goods. They moved into the desert to lead lives of solitary meditation and prayer. Thus monasticism came to play a major role in the Coptic Church, and there is a tradition to the effect that a Copt founded the first monastery. By 400, Christians represented a large portion of the population of Egypt, and the patriarchs there exerted great power. After the Council of Chalcedon (451) declared the Monophysite position to be heretical, native Christians and the Greek Christians of Egypt united under one leadership to repudiate the decree and form the Coptic Church, which has remained an autonomous body ever since. Byzantine persecution of the Copts followed the separation, but this was alleviated somewhat by subsequent Arab invasions. In the 7th century, first the Persians and then the Arabs conquered Egypt, and under their persecution, many Copts abandoned Christianity to become Moslems. (See ISLAM.) Yet the Coptic Church has endured and retained to the present day its unique character, including distinct rituals and a distinct form of religious art.

**Corbey.** An abbey in Picardy, founded in 657 by Bathilde, widow of Clovis II. The first monks came from Luxeuil. During the 9th century, Corbey was an important intellectual center. Among the scholars were Adalhard and Paschasius Radbertus. The Saxon abbey of Corvey was established by monks from Corbey. The monastery was suppressed in 1790 and its famous library was moved to Paris.

**Cornelius à Lapide** (Cornelis Cornelissen van den Steen) (1567–1637). A Flemish member of the Society of Jesus and one of the most celebrated Biblical scholars of his day. He taught Scripture and Hebrew at Louvain for twenty years and from 1616 at Rome. He devoted his life to writing a series of commentaries on the entire Bible, except for Job and Psalms. He gives both the literal and the allegorical interpretations and makes use of the fathers and the scholars of the Middle Ages.

**Cornelius of Rome.** Pope (251–253). His election was the occasion of the Novatian schism. Although Novatian claimed to have withdrawn from the church because of the leniency of Cornelius toward apostates, he had himself been lenient earlier. The real cause of the schism seems to have been Novatian's disappointment over not having been elected pope. Cornelius wrote seven letters to Cyprian about Novatian, two of which survive, and they appear to be the earliest papal letters in Latin.

**Coronation Rites.** Consisting of the solemn investment of the sovereign with his power, the religious consecration of his authority, and the formal recognition of his sovereignty by the populace. With the conversion of Europe to Christianity, religion came to play a dominant role in coronation rites. The monarch swore a sacred oath, the ceremony itself became a religious one, and most important, the

king was anointed with holy oil. Anointing, which came from the Old Testament practice of anointing Hebrew kings, signifies God's consecration of the monarch. By giving divine sanction to his authority, the anointing makes the person of the king sacrosanct. After the monarch is anointed and invested with the symbols of his power—orb, scepter, and ceremonial sword—the high point of the ceremony occurs with the placing of the crown on the sovereign's head. This symbolizes the assumption of full royal authority. The king is then enthroned and receives the homage of his subjects. The role of the church is ever present in the ceremony. English kings after William the Conqueror have been crowned by the archbishop of Canterbury at Westminster Abbey; French kings were traditionally crowned by the archbishop of Reims in the cathedral of that city; and the Holy Roman Emperors were regularly crowned by the pope in St. Peter's, Rome.

**Corporation Act** (1661). The first act of the Clarendon Code passed by Charles II's Cavalier Parliament to disable nonconformists. It required each member of a municipal corporation to take an oath in which he abjured rebellion, declared the Solemn League and Covenant illegal, and stated that he had received Communion according to the Church of England during the year preceding his election. Frequently circumvented, the act was repealed in 1828.

**Corpus Christi, Feast of.** A feast in honor of Christ's presence in the Eucharist, celebrated on the Thursday after Trinity Sunday. It was first celebrated in Liège in 1246 as the result of the visions experienced by the nun Juliana. The hymns for the festival, "Lauda Sion" and "Pange Lingua," are attributed to Thomas Aquinas. The festival, marked by the carrying of the Blessed Sacrament in procession, has been observed throughout the West since the 14th century.

**Corpus Juris Canonici.** The standard collection of canon (church) law until it was superseded in the early 20th century. It was composed of six separate collections of the law: Gratian's *Decretum* of 1148; the *Decretals* of Gregory IX; the *Sext*, by Boniface VIII; the *Clementines* of Clement V; the *Extravagantes* by John XXII; and the *Extravagantes Communes* of various popes.

**Corpus Juris Civilis.** The basic collection of the Roman, or civil, law. It was essentially a codification and summary of ancient Roman law made during the reign of the emperor Justinian, consisting of four parts: the Institutes; the Digest; the Justinian Code; and the Novels, which were laws promulgated by the two emperors immediately succeeding Justinian.

**Cortes, Hernando** (1485–1547). Conquistador sent by Velásquez to Yucatán (Mexico) to explore the land and salvage what remained of two previous unsuccessful expeditions. He reached Tobasco in 1519 with eleven ships and some six hundred men. There he set up the colony of Veracruz with himself as head. Cortes then traveled into the interior, where he was taken for a god by Montezuma, emperor of the Aztecs. Though enemies in both Spain and Mexico tried to frustrate his efforts, Cortes managed to organize the land, study its many resources, and explore the Gulf of Mexico, lower California, and Honduras.

**Cosin, John** (1594–1672). Bishop of Durham and one of the leading Caroline divines. Born at Norwich, educated at Caius College, Cambridge, he became master of Peterhouse (1634). He rose rapidly in preferment and was elevated to Durham in 1660. Cosin was a distinguished liturgist and had great influence in the revision of the Prayer Book of 1662. His most famous published works are *The House of Prayer* and his polemical *History of Papal Transubstantiation,* written while he was in exile in Paris.

**Cosmas Melodus** (*also known as* Cosmas the Younger) (c. 685–c. 750). Author of Greek liturgical hymns. Together with his adoptive brother, John of Damascus, he entered the Sabas monastery near Jerusalem (c. 732). In 743, Cosmas became bishop of Maïuma near Gaza. He wrote *idiomela,* short songs with their own tunes, and at least fourteen canons after the example of Andrew of Crete, archbishop of Gortyna in Crete. A commentary on the poems of Gregory of Nazianzus is also attributed to him.

**Cotton, John** (1564–1652). Puritan. Born in Derby, England, and educated at Trinity College, Cambridge, he became successively lecturer, dean, and catechist at Emmanuel College. At Cambridge, Cotton encountered Puritanism and began to reconsider his preaching style and views of ceremonies. Chosen vicar of St. Botolph's at Boston, Lincolnshire, in 1612, he soon began instituting Puritan practices there. Summoned to appear before the Court of High Commission in 1632, he fled to London, resigned his charge, and sailed for New England. In Boston, Mass., he was designated teacher of First Church and rose to a position of prominence in the Bay Colony. He drew up for the General Court an abstract of laws patterned after the laws of Moses, but the code was rejected. He played a major role in the Cambridge Synod. In the antinomian controversy Cotton first supported Anne Hutchinson, but finding himself alone among the clergy, reversed his position. He was a nonseparating Congregationalist and objected to Roger Williams' contention that membership in the New England Church required renunciation of the Church of England. Cotton insisted that the coercive power of the state should extend over religious affairs. He wrote extensively in defense of the New England way in church and state.

**Council of 1551.** An ecclesiastical assembly called by Ivan IV (1533–1584) to reform the Russian Church. It was known as the Council of Stoglav (Hundred Chapters) after the one-hundred-part record of the Council's proceedings. The Council considered issues which were submitted by Ivan as thirty-seven questions. The intent of these queries was to correct faith, perfect discipline, and define ecclesiastical and civil jurisdictions. Clergy were charged with ignorance and illiteracy, indifference to social ills, and neglect of ecclesiastical duties. Variant liturgical uses and residual pagan practices were condemned. The church's judicial power in disputes between lay and ecclesiastical parties was curbed. To control its economic expansion, the church was required to obtain the czar's consent before accepting or purchasing land.

Some consider the Council a momentous move toward a national church, saying that the regulation of the church's business and the curtailing of its secular privileges helped to integrate its administration with the government of the state. Others are skeptical of the Council's practical results. It was unable to standardize ritual, eliminate local variances, inhibit economic expansion, or raise moral and intellectual achievement. Though admirable in exposing abuse and irregularity, the decisions of the Council seem barren of practical results.

Nevertheless, the Council had symbolic, if not practical, significance. After the fall of Constantinople (1453), the Muscovite state claimed the inheritance of Byzantium's mission, and efforts were made to endow the Russian Church with sufficient stature to eclipse both Constantinople and Rome. Though the church's moral and intellectual quality improved only slowly, by adopting canons at Stoglav at variance with Constantinople the Russian Church did show its absolute independence from patriarchal jurisdiction in ecclesiastical matters. Further, the recorded proceedings of the Council were important for their clear theoretical expression of the Byzantine ideal of the theocratic state adopted by the Muscovite empire. Church and state appeared inseparable as promoters of public morals and civil order. Though they retained separate controls, the czar, as son of the church, acted as the pivot between the two spheres, symbolically transforming secular power into an expression of divine will.

**Councils.** The first council in the history of the church is described in Acts, ch. 15. Attended by the apostles, it convened in Jerusalem to decide how far Gentile converts should be subject to the law of Moses. Such an assemblage of leaders was not repeated until 325 at Nicaea, but before then it had become customary in any particular province of the Roman Empire to hold a local or "metropolitan" council attended by the provincial bishops and presided over by the bishop whose diocese included the city selected. In the organization of the medieval church, distinction must be made between councils or synods of this sort, confined to the affairs of one diocese or nation, plenary councils called to deal primarily with national affairs but presided over by a papal legate, and the full ecumenical councils, of bishops and prelates, periodically summoned by the pope and making communal decisions on universal matters of doctrine which according to the Roman Church, are held to be infallible. The age of world church councils begins with the conversion of the emperor Constantine in 312 and the aim of his sons (337–361) to impose uniformity in the teachings and practices of what was after 337 the state religion.

Of the following general or ecumenical councils, only the first seven, the "seven pillars of the faith," are recognized as binding by the Eastern Orthodox Church: (1) The Council of Nicaea in 325 was summoned and presided over by Constantine, with an attendance of some three hundred bishops and churchmen. Its great achievement was the condemnation of the Arian heresy in favor of the views of Athanasius of Alexandria, which were later given formal expression in the Nicene Creed. (2) The Council of Constantinople in 381 had new heresies and disputed dogmas to face, in particular certain pagan Oriental influences. It attempted to settle rivalries of precedence between Rome and the old Eastern centers of Jerusalem, Alexandria, Ephesus, Antioch, and Constantinople, the "New Rome." The decision to give Constantinople second place to the bishop of Rome was to prove only a partial settlement

of the controversy. (3) At Ephesus in 431 the Nestorian heresy was set aside in favor of the views of Cyril of Alexandria. Feeling arose, however, that the claims of the bishop of Alexandria to primacy in the East were being too strongly pressed, and a further council at Ephesus in 449, in which these intentions became more specific, was not accepted as ecumenical by the church at large. (4) At the Council of Chalcedon in 451 the Monophysite heresy was condemned. Pope Leo I (the Great) gained recognition for the primacy of his bishopric, and a settled order of precedence was established for the five great sees of the church to which special honor was due: Rome, Constantinople, Alexandria, Antioch, Jerusalem. Some of the dogmatic decisions of Chalcedon were refined and reaffirmed at subsequent councils held at Constantinople. (5) Constantinople II in 553 and (6) Constantinople III in 680–681 had as their immediate concern the condemnation of Monotheletism, an offshoot of the Monophysite heresy. The last of the general councils acceptable to the Eastern Orthodox Church was (7) that held for the second time at Nicaea, in 787. The burning issue before Nicaea II was the iconoclast controversy, the struggle between the iconoclasts, or "icon destroyers," suspicious of the veneration of holy pictures or statues (icons) and its deeper implications, and the iconodules, who vigorously defended their place in the life of the church. The decision of Nicaea II to uphold the iconodulist position was later set aside by the Roman Church, which alone instigated and accepted later general councils. (8) The last council to be held on Eastern territory was Constantinople IV in 869. The dramatic council at Clermont in 1095, where Pope Urban II appealed for the First Crusade, was plenary rather than ecumenical in its purposes. The ecumenical series was resumed during the 12th century with the Lateran assemblages: (9) Lateran I in 1123, (10) Lateran II in 1139, (11) Lateran III in 1179, and (12) Lateran IV, the Great Lateran Council, in 1215. The first two dealt with topical problems such as the attitude of the church to usury. The latter two took steps to improve the morals of the clergy and the system of electing popes. Formal recognition was made at Lateran IV of the right of Constantinople to second place in the episcopal hierarchy. Among more internal decisions, the prohibited degrees of marriage were regularized, and a ban placed on the founding of new monastic orders. The latter was to be set aside by Pope Innocent III, who gave official approval to the organization of the Franciscans, Dominicans, and Carmelites. In the next century or so the deliberations of the councils mainly dealt with attempts to heal the breach between Rome and the East (see SCHISM, EASTERN). The negotiations at (13) Lyons I in 1245, (14) Lyons II in 1274, and (15) Vienne in 1311–1313 were largely inconclusive and served mainly to revive old dissensions. A series of councils held from 1409 on, collectively known as the conciliar movement, struggled with large problems of church doctrine, unity and morals, and with the complexities of the papal schism between the rival popes in Rome and Avignon. Negotiations of the first assemblage, at Pisa in 1409, at which a third pope, Alexander V, was elected, broke down. At (16) Constance in 1414–1418 the rival claimants to the papacy were successfully deposed and a new pope, Martin V, was recognized. John Hus of Bohemia was condemned to die at the stake for his reforming ideas and a decree (*Frequens*) was passed calling for regular, periodic councils. In another decree (*Sacrosancta*), it declared that an ecumenical council possessed the highest ecclesiastical jurisdiction in the church. Later historical circumstances caused this decree to become ineffectual. The long-drawn-out deliberations (17) at Basel, Ferrara, and Florence from 1431 to 1443 included a reassertion of papal supremacy, particularly by Eugenius IV. Further measures were taken against the Bohemian Brethren and renewed but ineffectual attempts were made to settle the Schism between East and West. The fall of Constantinople a few years later (1453) disposed of the chief incentive to any East-West *rapprochement*. The 16th century found the Roman Church struggling against the Protestant Reformation and becoming increasingly aware of its need to set its own house in order. These were the main issues before (18) the ineffectual pre-Reformation Council of Lateran V (1512–1517), and more especially (19) the Council of Trent, whose lengthy deliberations, interspersed with adjournments and delays, lasted from 1545 to 1563. Trent in particular was due to the insistence of the emperor Charles V that the challenge of Protestantism must be met by a united front. From the final sessions of this Council (1562–1563) emerged the settlement of a number of prevalent clerical abuses and a rigid and thoroughgoing statement of Roman Catholic dogma. Since the Reformation only two Ecumenical Councils have been summoned, the one (20) known as Vatican I, called by Pope Pius IX in 1869 and adjourned the following year, and (21) Vatican II called by Pope John XXIII in 1962. The main purpose of both was once again the restatement of dogmatic

issues and acceptable reforms in the light of modern conditions. In the modern organization of the Catholic Church the general arrangement and ordering of councils now comes under the control of the Sacred Congregation of the Council. Outside Rome, the World Council of Churches is an ecumenical agency for more than two hundred Protestant and Eastern Orthodox Churches, established at Amsterdam in 1948. Collective editions of the acts of councils have been compiled by J. Hardouin (1715), J. D. Mansi (1759–1798), C. H. Turner (1899–1939), and E. Schwartz (1914–1940).

BIBLIOGRAPHY: H. S. Bettenson, *Documents of the Christian Church* (New York, 1963); W. P. DuBose, *The Ecumenical Councils* (New York, 1914); K. J. von Hefele, *A History of the Councils of the Church*, 5 vols. (Edinburgh, 1871–1896); H. Jedin, *Ecumenical Councils of the Catholic Church* (Glen Rock, N.J., 1960); E. H. Landon, *A Manual of the Councils of the Holy Catholic Church*, 2 vols. (Edinburgh, 1909); E. I. Watkin, *The Church in Council* (New York, 1960).

**Counsels of Perfection** (Evangelical Counsels). In moral theology, precepts are those things which are obligatory for all individuals, such as the Ten Commandments as interpreted by the New Testament. Counsels are those things which while not obligatory are essential to those seeking a higher degree of perfection. The traditional counsels of perfection, binding on most monastics and religious, are poverty, chastity, and obedience.

**Counter-Reformation** (*or* Roman Catholic Reform). The movement, begun within the Roman Catholic Church in the 16th century, advocating renewal in all phases of its operation and return to the pristine vision of its mission and sanctity. It is contradistinguished from the Protestant Reformation which had its origins in religious leaders cut off from full membership in the Roman communion because of the alleged heterodoxy of their doctrine and methods. But it was precisely the Reformation that gave the chief impetus to the movement toward renewal within the church.

Interest in reform had been sparked from within the church well before the days of Luther. The 15th century saw attempts by such persons as Archbishop Antoninus of Florence, Lorenzo Giustiniani, Catherine of Siena, and the controversial Dominican Savonarola. Even the morally dissolute Pope Alexander VI, remorseful over the violent death of his son, Juan Borgia, became concerned and drew up a viable but unimplemented program of renewal. In France the provincial synod of Sens (1485) and the assembly of the clergy at Tours in 1493 pondered problems created by the laxity of Renaissance times. The *devotio moderna,* originating in the Lowlands stimulated within the church a new spirit of evangelical spirituality. An ecumenical council, Lateran IV, concluded just before Luther posted his famous Ninety-five Theses, focused its attention mightily but ineffectively upon the needs of the church to witness in a more authentic way to the message of the gospel.

It was undoubtedly in the defensive posture assumed against Luther and the other Protestant leaders, however, that Roman Catholicism received the great stimulus to action which gave birth to the Counter-Reformation movement.

Like the reform movement outside the Roman Church, internal renewal was pushed, not primarily by the authorities, but from below. The ignorance and ambivalence of the large majority of Roman Catholics in regard to traditional doctrine and practice, which facilitated the rapid spread of Lutheranism and Calvinism, challenged the hierarchy to respond and clarify. The work of reformulation and elucidation of the Roman Catholic position culminated in the Council of Trent, the apogee of the Counter-Reformation movement, in which what was to be Roman Catholic policy for the next several centuries was crystallized. Papal authority was reaffirmed and episcopal power strengthened. Exemptions from canon law, so numerous in the past, were suppressed. Presence of ecclesiastical authorities within their jurisdiction was required. The whole Roman Church was put into a state of militant vigilance. Prayer and the sacraments were highlighted as a means of sanctification. The rationale of human defectibility was explored in the decrees on original sin and justification. Superstitious practices were largely done away with. The work and the effectiveness of the Inquisition were enhanced. The needs were clearly recognized for the laity at large to have better education in the faith and for the clergy to have proper training.

One of the chief effects of the Counter-Reformation was the reorganization of the papal Curia. Pope Sixtus V prohibited once again the creation of lay cardinals and limited membership in the college to seventy. Decrees against nepotism were enforced. Sixtus also introduced fifteen Congregations to assist the papacy in the administrative work of the church and so discouraged prelates from becoming hangers-on and seekers of favor at the papal court. Through this businesslike parceling out of responsibility for various areas of the church's worldwide concern and the establishment of a clear-cut chain of command, efficiency of operation was ensured.

The Counter-Reformation found its chief exponents not only among leaders of the secular clergy such as the Cardinals Borromeo and Morone and Bishop Francis of Sales but also among the newly founded regulars, particularly the Jesuits, Theatines, and Oratorians. The Jesuits were especially outstanding in Counter-Reformation activities. They put into the field men such as Robert Bellarmine and Peter Canisius, while the Theatines and Oratorians matched them with their respective founders, Gian Pietro Carafa (Paul IV) and Philip Neri. Noteworthy also was Thomas of Villanova, the Spanish Augustinian. The Jesuit *ratio studiorum,* governing pedagogical philosophy and methodology, revolutionized the field of religious instruction and training both on the scientific and the popular levels. Seminary education was fostered by outstanding experimenters such as Vincent de Paul. Institutes for the clergy were set up by Olier, Bérulle, and Eudes. Colleges for the education of priests began mushrooming at Rome, especially during the pontificate of Gregory XIII.

Interest in historical research was spurred on by men such as Cardinal Baronius. Accounts of the lives of the saints, traditionally held up to Roman Catholics as examples for inspiration and emulation, were purged of spurious accretions by scholars such as Mabillon and Bolland. Literature and art, too, were profoundly influenced by Counter-Reformation ideas. The licentious freedom of the Renaissance era was abandoned. Above everything else it was restraint that characterized the writing of the post-Tridentine period. There was little sensuality, no sporting frolicsomeness, no overweening pride, no lusty outbursts of passion such as had prevailed before in both poetry and prose. Nature itself was downgraded. Reason triumphed over passion and feeling. Spontaneity gave way to preciosity. Religious devotion replaced humanistic loyalty. Erotic love gave way to charity, pride of achievement and heroism to zeal for the glory of God. In art, pious painting and works of sculpture appeared in place of the nudes that were so popular during Renaissance times. More ponderous themes obscured the *joie de vivre* of former days; suffering, martyrdom, death, judgment, heaven, and hell were the favorite topics of the Roman Catholic artists of Counter-Reformation times. Church architecture too was modified by the new religious attitudes, and ecclesiastical music, tainted by the introduction of popular melodies, was restored to its pristine grandeur by men such as Palestrina and Tomás Luis de Victoria.

One of the areas untouched by the Council of Trent was the question of the reform of the Roman Catholic princes who shared with the dissolute clergy of former times the responsibility of bringing disgrace upon the church. It is true that Pope Paul IV in 1559 made bold to depose all princes who held heretical doctrines or were in any way abettors of heresy. But it was Pius V in the bull *In coena Domini*, first published in 1568 and reissued every Maundy Thursday thereafter, who took the Roman Catholic princes to task for their irresponsible interference in ecclesiastical affairs and their unchristian way of life. Later on, a number of popes condemned the notion of state religions and protested against the unjust usurpation by civil authorities of church properties.

Notable also as part of Counter-Reformation activity was the liturgical renewal inaugurated by Pope Pius V. A new missal was published under his auspices. It added prayers to be recited at the foot of the altar at the beginning of Mass and appended the first part of the Gospel of John to the concluding prayers. The divine office—which consisted of antiphons, psalms, readings, and hymns and was chanted or recited by monks and priests every day—was greatly reduced in size, and a new official text, or breviary, was issued. In general, the penitential and sacrificial aspects of the liturgy were emphasized. Although the public nature of worship was stressed, personal piety gradually began to take precedence over communal prayer.

The Counter-Reformation gave rise to new kinds of spirituality in the Roman Catholic Church. The writings of Teresa of Ávila and John of the Cross opened the way to a new kind of mysticism, symbolically presented as a "spiritual marriage" and characterized by a sort of quietism. Italian writers, on the other hand, stressed the "spiritual combat" and highlighted the struggle of man against his passions. The need for spiritual direction was effectively pointed out in the writings of men such as Francis of Sales.

The Counter-Reformation was not a movement restricted to the 16th and 17th centuries. Its spirit pervaded the Roman Church down to the time of the Second Vatican Council. Its fruits included the static, monolithic, apologetic posture of the church that is now being dissipated in a new ecumenical era.

BIBLIOGRAPHY: H. Daniel-Rops, *The Catholic Reformation*, 2 vols. (Garden City, 1964); P. Janelle, *The Catholic Reformation* (Milwaukee, 1949).

**Countess of Huntingdon's Connexion.** A Calvinistic Methodist sect founded by Selina Hastings, Countess of Huntingdon (1707–1791). She became an outstanding protectress of Methodists within the Anglican fold. She knew the Wesley brothers and George Whitefield, who became her chaplain. The Connexion which she maintained emphasized the Calvinistic side of Methodism. After 1779 it was forced to take refuge under the Toleration Act as a dissenting sect. (See HUNTINGDON, COUNTESS OF.)

**Courtly Love.** In the 12th century the troubadours of southern France began to pay homage to their ladyloves. Like most medieval knights, they had married for practical reasons of political or economic advantage, so these ladies were not their wives but noblewomen prominent at the feudal courts. The troubadours glorified what we call romantic love, singing of moonlight and roses, incredibly beautiful heroines, and brave, handsome heroes who lived only to serve their ladies. Soon this concept of devotion to a ladylove became part of the chivalric ethic giving rise to the traditions of courtly love. Some troubadours, perhaps more cynical, carried this concept of romantic love to the point of condoning adultery. Ideally a knight was to serve his lady without reward or expectation of a physical relationship. True love was evidenced in the knight's absolute loyalty, self-denial, and labors and sufferings for his lady. Noblewomen such as Eleanor of Aquitaine helped to foster and propagandize courtly love. They held "courts of love" that were modeled on feudal courts and rendered judgments on the petitions of injured lovers. On the theme of courtly love the French troubadours and German minnesingers produced such masterpieces as the *Chanson de Roland, Parzival,* and the tales of King Arthur.

**Cousin, Victor** (1792–1867). French philosopher, publicist, and educator. His teaching of philosophy at the Sorbonne, which began in 1815, was twice interrupted by reactionary forces, first in 1821 and finally by Napoleon III. He was by intention an eclectic. His chief significance lies in his introduction of German idealism to the French philosophical scene and his efforts to bring it together with the Scottish sensualism which had until then dominated French thought.

**Covenant, National** (1638). In 1635, Charles I ratified the Book of Canons which aimed at asserting royal supremacy and establishing episcopacy in Scotland. Fearful of the new ritual and the king's designs, many nobles, ministers, and others met in Edinburgh to form and sign the National Covenant. Its foundation was the King's Confession of 1581. The Covenanters were not disloyal to the Crown. What they wanted was a binding covenant to guarantee the freedom of their Presbyterian Kirk.

**Covenanters.** The Scottish people have a long history of "bands" or "covenants." Concerted action in pursuit of a worthy goal was to be ordered and perpetuated by a written document to be signed. In the Reformation in Scotland the idea of the covenant was strong. The King's Confession as signed by James VI in 1581 became the foundation of the National Covenant signed by many Scots in 1638. The covenant was to bind every true Scot to a perpetual opposition against Romanism and episcopacy, to the Reformed tradition and presbyterial system, and to the monarchy. Devotion to the covenants became the ground of resistance to the anglicizing of the Church of Scotland as proposed by the Stuarts. Within the Kirk the party of Covenanters became distinct and powerful by 1640. Theirs was an especially difficult struggle, for in opposing prelacy they were opposing the will of the king to whom they were loyal. The Solemn League and Covenant of 1643 was the Scots hope for Presbyterian victory in England, but it was not rebellion against Charles I, for the Covenanters expected Charles I and his successors to keep the Covenant. However, Charles II and James II repudiated it and advanced their own plans for royal supremacy and episcopacy. The struggle of the Covenanters against the royal forces, civil and ecclesiastical, is a vivid story. The religious settlement of 1689 brought their cause a modest victory.

**Covenant Theology.** Often called "federal theology," from the Latin *foedus,* meaning a "covenant" or "alliance." It was the predominant type of theology underlying most of 17th-century Puritan and Congregational theology, especially in its American form. It maintains that the Biblical history tells of two covenants that God made with man: first, the covenant of works made with Adam; then, the covenant of grace in Jesus Christ. In the development of Reformed theology, especially in Calvin, the idea of the covenant of grace played a prominent role. The reformers in the Rhineland emphasized the concept of the two covenants—law and grace. The Puritans took this motif and made it an organizing principle of their doctrinal scheme. However, they gave it

their own emphases and nuances. The chief theoreticians of the covenant motif in the Continental Reformed theology, following the introduction of the Heidelberg Catechism (1563), were Maccovius, Alsted, Wolleb, and Wendelin. Francis Gomar, the Dutch champion against the Arminians, made much of the covenant idea, dividing the covenants into a *foedus naturale* and a *foedus supernaturale* (i.e., a natural and a supernatural covenant). The Arminians took up federal theology and gave it elaborate development, especially in Curcellaeus. However, the one man above all others with whom this idea is distinctly associated is Johannes Cocceius (or Koch), who produced his *Summa doctrinae de foedere et testimento Dei* in 1648. The English Puritans took up the covenantal idea in earnest in the early 17th century. Paramount among the Puritan covenant theologians was William Ames (1576–1633), whose *Marrow of Sacred Divinity* served as textbook for three generations.

**Coverdale, Miles** (1488–1568). Translator of the first complete English Bible. Coverdale's background includes two elements encountered among other early English Reformers: education at Cambridge and membership in the Augustinian Friars. He was arrested and tried for his opinions as early as 1526, and spent many of the subsequent years abroad. The first edition of his complete translation was published in 1535, probably at Zurich; it leaned heavily on Tyndale's New Testament and Pentateuch, and for the rest was based partly on the Vulgate and partly on Luther's German version. In 1537, Coverdale's Bible was twice reprinted in England, and the second English printing was issued by royal license. Parts of Coverdale's translation were used in the so-called Matthew's Bible (1537), which also had the king's license (see ROGERS, JOHN), and the Great Bible (1539), authorized by Thomas Cromwell for use in the churches, was largely his work. Distinguished for literary art rather than scholarship, it was not, apparently, based on the original Hebrew or Greek. Coverdale's translation influenced subsequent versions, including the Authorized Version of 1611 (King James), and his rendering of The Psalms is still used in the Book of Common Prayer. In 1551 he was made bishop of Exeter, but was deprived of his see two years later under Mary Tudor and fled to the Continent. On his return in 1559 he was given a London church, but forced to resign his living in 1566 because of his Puritan-minded opposition to Elizabeth's wish for liturgical conformity.

**Cowper, William** (1731–1800). English poet and hymn writer. The son of an Anglican clergyman, he was educated at Westminster and called to the bar in 1754. During his apprenticeship his life had been darkened by a forbidden romance with a cousin, but despite increasing melancholy, a playful side of his personality often appeared during the nine years of his legal practice. In 1763 incipient madness blighted his career and made of him an invalid for life. He was nominated to the clerkship of the journals of the House of Lords, but the dread of the customary examination of fitness caused him to attempt suicide. Dominated by a sense of divine reprobation, he suffered further attacks of illness. After two years in a private asylum he removed to Huntingdon in 1765, and in 1767 to Olney, where under the influence of his evangelical spiritual mentor, John Newton, he began to write hymns. In 1779 he cooperated with Newton in the publication of the *Olney Hymns.* At the suggestion of his friend Mrs. Mary Unwin, Cowper also began writing serious verse. His most famous poems are *The Task* (1785) and *The Diverting History of John Gilpin* (1783). He also made a translation of Homer (1791). His greatest hymns are "Hark, My Soul, It Is the Lord!" and "O for a Closer Walk with God."

**Craig, John** (c. 1512–1600). Scottish Reformer. After an education at St. Andrews, Craig became a Dominican. Suspected of heresy, he went to England and on to Italy, where Cardinal Pole secured his appointment as master of novices of a convent. He read Calvin's *Institutes,* adopted many Reformation tenets, and was condemned to be burned as a heretic. In the riots following the death of Pope Paul IV, Craig escaped to Vienna and eventually reached England under a safe-conduct guaranteed by Maximilian II. By 1560 he was back in Scotland. From the ministry at Holyrood he was called to be Knox's colleague in High Church, Edinburgh. He became a defender of church property rights against the claims of the Crown. After spending eight years in Montrose and Aberdeen, "illuminating the dark places," Craig became chaplain to young James VI in 1579. He assisted in the composition of The Second Book of Discipline and was the author of two influential catechisms (1581 and 1592). His most notable work was the composition of the King's Confession in 1581, which became the foundation of the National Covenant of 1638. In 1584 the so-called Black Acts were passed by Parliament restoring episcopacy. Craig denounced them but sought to mediate between

the king and the extreme Presbyterians. He was willing himself to accept the royal supremacy "in so far as the Word of God allows."

**Cranach, Lucas, the Elder** (1472–1553). German painter and engraver. Cranach executed many altarpieces and miniatures. One of his favorite themes was Christ blessing the children. A convert to Lutheranism, he painted portraits of leading Reformation figures. His style was realistic and he was a master of detail, but he lacked strength and the spirit of true greatness. He was appointed court painter for Elector Frederick of Saxony and served Wittenberg as councilor and burgomaster.

**Cranmer, Thomas** (1489–1556). Archbishop of Canterbury and English Reformer. Born at Aslacton, in Nottinghamshire, he was sent to Cambridge at the age of fourteen and, despite a relatively undistinguished academic career, remained there the next twenty-six years. In these years of preparation Cranmer laid the foundations of the Biblical, theological, and liturgical studies that were to be reflected in the course of the English Reformation. Cranmer became a fellow of Jesus College about 1515, and remained there (except for a year's suspension during his first marriage, terminated by the death of his wife in childbirth) until 1529. In that year he came to the notice of Henry VIII by his advocacy of the invalidity of the king's marriage to Catherine of Aragon. Cranmer insisted that the marriage was invalid on theological grounds, regardless of what the papal canonists might decide. Henry attached Cranmer to the household of Anne Boleyn's family, and sent him to the Continent on diplomatic errands in pursuit of the divorce.

Thereafter, Cranmer's rise was swift. In 1531 he became a royal chaplain, archdeacon of Taunton the next year, and archbishop of Canterbury, in succession to Warham, the year following (probably in part due to his connection with the Boleyns). In the previous year, while he was Henry's ambassador to the emperor Charles V, Cranmer had come under the influence of Lutheran theology and had married the niece of the German Reformer Osiander, so his position was potentially at variance with that of Henry, who favored neither Protestant theology nor clerical marriage. Sitting, with Henry's permission, as sole judge in the divorce case, he pronounced that the king's marriage with Catherine was invalid, and subsequently that Henry's secret marriage to Anne Boleyn, at which Cranmer did not officiate, was lawful.

Cranmer's loyalty to Henry made him invaluable in effecting the split with Rome and in striking the required balance in the shifting political and religious alignments of the time. Though the crucial pieces of Reformation legislation, such as the Act in Restraint of Appeals, were more the work of Thomas Cromwell (who was also chiefly responsible for the dissolution of the monasteries, in which Cranmer took little part), Cranmer assiduously accomplished the necessary background work: arguing the Act of Succession with Fisher and More, furthering publication of the English Bible, granting the required decrees of divorce and annulment for Henry's various marriages, tempting Continental Protestants with the idea of a united front joined by England, condemning heretics who persisted in beliefs on either side of the current government line, including beliefs Cranmer was coming to hold himself. In 1540, following the promulgation of the theologically reactionary Six Articles the year before, Cranmer nearly fell; his opinions, and particularly his marriage —an imperfectly kept secret—made his position precarious for the next several years. But Henry's anti-Protestant policy was relaxed toward the end of his life, and Cranmer's primacy was secure at the accession of Edward VI in 1547.

There was no longer further need to dissemble Reformed views. Still, Cranmer moved cautiously: the 1549 Book of Common Prayer, largely compiled by him, is of a more conservative tone than his opinions actually were at the time. The second Prayer Book (1552) reflects more closely the modifed Calvinism that came to characterize Cranmer's mature doctrine of the Eucharist (see RIDLEY, NICHOLAS), and the Forty-two Articles of 1553 are an unmistakably Reformed document. It should be added, however, that the interpretation of Cranmer's Eucharistic thought has been constantly debated.

Cranmer reluctantly submitted to the dying Edward's command to support Lady Jane Grey's claim to the crown. When this ill-judged coup failed, Cranmer was doubly in trouble with Mary—a traitor as well as a heretic. He was nearly executed on the former grounds in 1553; his obduracy in opposing the Roman Catholic doctrine of the Real Presence made inevitable his trial for heresy, a long-drawn-out process that lasted nearly two years, encompassing the deaths of Ridley and Latimer, extensive disputations, and protracted efforts to get Cranmer to recant. This he finally did, in a puzzling series of documents from which historians have variously deduced pusillanimity, duplicity, a genuine change of heart, or a pathetic last attempt to obey the wishes of his

sovereign. The truth seems to be that as Protestant he was bound to oppose the queen, but as Erastian to submit to her. In any case, on tne final day of his life Cranmer retracted his recantations.

BIBLIOGRAPHY: For a selection of Cranmer's writings, see G. E. Duffield (ed.), *The Work of Thomas Cranmer* (London, 1964). See also P. Brooks, *Thomas Cranmer's Doctrine of the Eucharist* (London, 1965); F. E. Hutchinson, *Cranmer and the English Reformation* (New York, 1951); J. Ridley, *Thomas Cranmer* (Oxford, 1962).

**Creeds.** Brief authoritative statements or formulas of religious belief. Creeds are usually thought of in terms of the lineage of currently familiar particular creeds, but their genesis is more informatively studied in the perspective of the creed-making activity of the church as a whole. The subject will be considered here under these headings: (1) the New Testament, (2) ante-Nicene literature, (3) the Old Roman Creed, (4) the Nicene and other synodal creeds, (5) The Apostles' Creed, and (6) the Athanasian Creed.

1. *The New Testament.* Not until the 15th century had anyone seriously questioned the legend that the apostles composed the creed attributed to them, each contributing an article. The questioning once begun, however, gathered momentum as it went, so that in the last part of the 19th and the early part of the 20th century, few would admit that before the middle of the 2d century anything more elaborate than a simple baptismal confession that "Jesus is Lord" or "Jesus is the Son of God" could be found in the way of a creed. Nevertheless, recent scholarship has come to recognize more and more that although there were no fixed creedal forms in the apostolic age, there was a corpus of distinctively Christian teaching. C. H. Dodd has shown that the kerygmatic outline of New Testament preaching had a creedal form. It is recognized that the corpus of belief was expressed in many activities of the primitive church in addition to preaching. While there were no creeds in the strict sense, the agreed body of belief came to be expressed in conventional summaries. These summaries appeared in preaching, baptism, catechetical instruction, the liturgy, exorcism, and the formal correspondence of church leaders with their flocks. The New Testament evidence comes from that correspondence and from the other activities reflected in it. Beyond the simple, one-clause Christologies mentioned above, there are more detailed confessions such as I Cor. 15:3 ff.; Rom. 1:3 f., 8:34; and II Tim. 2:8. "God,

who raised the Lord Jesus from the dead" is a recurring form of the third generation of the 1st century. Trinitarian faith was implicit in all these summaries, whether they were in three clauses or not. Thus the 2d-century conviction that the "rule of faith" was apostolic in origin was accurate if its content rather than its set form is referred to.

2. *Ante-Nicene Literature.* It has long been recognized that creeds arose in close relation to baptismal practices. Belief was considered the prime prerequisite for baptism. We do not find any evidence, however, for the use of declaratory creeds in the baptismal rite earlier than the 4th century; prior to that, when adult baptism was normal, the profession of belief at baptism took the form of response to threefold interrogation. The "tradition" and "redition" of declaratory creeds took place during the catechetical preparation for baptism. The word *symbolum* originally referred to the interrogation. Baptism, however, was not the only setting in which fixed forms of doctrinal statements began to develop. Antiheretical tests were incorporated into these statements, but the tendency is to overvalue their importance in the process. A survey of the literature of the period indicates that the apostolic fathers present much the same sort of witness which the New Testament produces—there are more quasi-creedal scraps than creeds. Justin Martyr indicates the rise of the baptismal interrogation, and Irenaeus and Tertullian speak much of the "rule of faith." The Apostolic Tradition of Hippolytus has what appears to be the first formal creed.

3. *The Old Roman Creed.* One of the earliest local creeds to take shape and be canonized was that of the Roman Church. It is the direct ancestor of all other local Western creeds, had great influence on Eastern ones, and is the direct ancestor of the Apostles' Creed. Our basic source for it is the *Commentarius in symbolum apostolorum* of Rufinus, which dates from about 404. This creed—known to scholars as R—appeared in Latin and Greek about the beginning of the 3d century. It has been demonstrated that R is a combination of a short Trinitarian confession and a primitive Christ-kerygma. The confession may be traced to the Matthean baptismal confession and the kerygma to the apostolic preaching. God is confessed in the first article as omnipotent, as *pantokratōr*— a term that originally referred more to his sovereignty than to his creative activity. The inclusion in the creed of the *gesta Christi* is probably more related to catechetical than polemical requirements. The string of miscellaneous credenda in the third article is a

list of the activities of the Spirit that tells of the redemptive community into which the baptizand is initiated. No Eastern creed was the source for later creeds in the manner in which R was determinative for the West. The main difference between the content of the creeds of the East and of the West is not so much that the East is more theological than the West but that the theological concerns are different. In the West the interest is in the primitive kerygma about the Savior, whereas in the East the concern is with the cosmic setting of redemption.

4. *The Nicene and Other Synodal Creeds.* The creed promulgated by the Council of Nicaea in 325 must be distinguished from the creed that is called Nicene. Nicaea put forth its creed as the first to be published by an ecumenical synod, so it was the first that could claim universal authority in a legal sense. The creed popularly called Nicene, however, is the creed that was read at the Council of Chalcedon in 451 as the creed of the Council of Constantinople in 381. For convenience we will refer to the two by their usual designations as N (Nicaea) and C (Niceno-Constantinopolitan). Eusebius has usually been read to mean that his baptismal creed from Caesarea had added to it the *homoousion* suggested by Constantine to create N. Since Eusebius had been placed under a theological ban by the Council of Antioch a few months before, it seems much more likely that his creed was approved only as demonstrating his orthodoxy. For other reasons, N appears to be based on a local baptismal creed of Syro-Palestinian ancestry. N differs from the more familiar C in that it has a shorter Christology, it gives "from the substance of the Father" as a paraphrase of *homoousios,* has a far simpler affirmation of belief in the Holy Spirit, and has anathemas against those who dissent from the faith it teaches. N is anti-Arian and is designed as a theological test. Since the Arians taught that "true God" applies to the Father only in the strict sense, the additions Nicaea made to the original baptismal creed were designed to exclude such teachings. Between Nicaea in 325 and Constantinople in 381 there were a large number of assemblies of bishops who met to pursue new developments in the Trinitarian controversy. During most of this period N was not invoked because it was regarded as having settled that stage of the debate and become irrelevant to later stages. With the defeat of Magnentius in 353, Constantius II was sole emperor and tried to establish tolerance in terms of a lowest common denominator creed. When its Arianizing tendencies were recognized, the broad central

body of bishops recognized the dangers of what has been called semi-Arianism and reacted in the direction of N. The one hundred and fifty fathers of Constantinople were glad to have an opportunity to reiterate the faith of Nicaea. In 451, C was read to the Council of Chalcedon as the creed of Constantinople of 381, but we have no record that a creed was made at that Council. The reason is probably that while Constantinople wished to reaffirm the teaching of Nicaea, it had no sense that it had to do so in the exact words of N; C was taken as an equivalent expression with some advantages over its predecessor. This creed became the baptismal creed of the East and the Eucharistic creed of the West. The Western insertion of "filioque" was part of the cause of the Great Schism.

5. *The Apostles' Creed.* This Western creed is known as the textus receptus, or T. It is simply an elaborate variant of R. The local Western baptismal creeds based on R made some amplifications which were incorporated into the Roman baptismal formula during the period of German and Gallic influence on Roman liturgy. The text has been known since the 8th century, but was not official in Rome until the 12th century.

6. *The Athanasian Creed.* A Western creed, this was not written by Athanasius, since it contains the language of debates after his time. It may, however, have been written by Ambrose. It seems to date between the Apollinarian and the Nestorian and Eutychian controversies. It treats of the Trinity and Christology and has anathemas pronounced against those who repudiate its teaching. It is recognized by Rome, by the Anglicans, and by the Lutherans, and to some extent by Orthodoxy.

BIBLIOGRAPHY: P. Schaff and H. Wace (eds.), *Nicene and Post-Nicene Fathers,* 2d Series, Vol. 14 (Grand Rapids, 1952–1956); O. Cullmann, *The Earliest Christian Confessions* (Chicago, 1949); B. A. Gerrish, *The Faith of Christendom* (Cleveland, 1963); J. N. D. Kelly, *Early Christian Creeds* (London, 1960); and *The Athanasian Creed* (New York, 1964); A. C. McGiffert, *The Apostles' Creed* (New York, 1902); P. Schaff, *The Creeds of Christendom,* 3 vols. (Grand Rapids, 1966).

**Cremer, August Hermann** (1834–1903). German Lutheran pastor and theologian. He was elected to the chair of systematic theology at Greifswald in 1870, where he also served as a parish pastor. Resisting theological liberalism, he took issue with Adolf von Harnack's *What Is Christianity?* Cremer rejected as well the Pietist view of justification and replaced it with a forensic Pauline doctrine. He is best known for his *Biblico-Theological Lexicon of New Testament Greek* (1878).

**Crespin, Jean** (c. 1520–1572). French Protestant writer and publisher. Born at Arras, France, he served for a time as a lawyer attached to the Parlement of Paris. He later returned to Arras, and being suspected of heresy, he removed to Strasbourg in 1545, and to Geneva in 1548. He started a press in 1550, and desired to publish Protestant works in French. In 1554 he completed his famous *Book of Martyrs,* which portrayed the heroic sufferings of the early Protestant martyrs.

**Cridge, Edward** (1817–1913). Canadian bishop. Born at Bratton-Heming, Devonshire, England, and educated at St. Peter's College, Cambridge (B.A., 1848), he was ordained by the Church of England in 1849. In 1854 he married Mary Winnella and was appointed chaplain of the Hudson's Bay Company on Vancouver Island and rector of the church at Victoria. Joining the Reformed Episcopal Church in 1874, he became rector of the Church of Our Lord at Victoria. He was elected bishop of the Reformed Episcopal Church in the following year. His diocese included all of Canada and the United States west of the Rocky Mountains.

**Criticism, Biblical Higher** (United States). A development that transformed American Protestantism in the late 19th and early 20th centuries, arousing interest and controversy which cut across denominational lines. Simultaneously condemned as an impious attack upon an inspired Scripture and praised as a valid historical and theological approach, higher criticism should be distinguished from lower, or textual, criticism, which is the attempt to determine from all available ancient manuscripts the original content and condition of a text. Higher criticism is the application to the Bible of the same kind of analysis that is applied to other writings, including questions of authorship, location and date of writing, intent of the writers, and the historicocultural environment. Higher criticism emerged out of the skeptical ethos of the Renaissance and Enlightenment, gaining widespread acceptance in the liberal theological movement initiated by the German Schleiermacher and developed by the researches and writings of Wellhausen, Semler, Strauss, and Baur. Pioneers of Biblical criticism on the American scene, such as Newman Smyth, Moses Stuart, and Edward Robinson, based their positions upon these European findings.

The battle over the historicocritical method reached its peak in the famous Briggs controversy. Charles A. Briggs, of Union Theological Seminary in New York City, while critical of the cold detachment of German scholarship, maintained in the 1870's that scholarly study of the Bible could not be fettered by the self-interest of traditional or dogmatic positions. In 1875 and 1880, higher criticism gained a wide audience through articles in the *Encyclopædia Britannica* written by the Scotsman W. Robertson Smith. In 1881, Briggs's fellow Presbyterians A. A. Hodge and B. B. Warfield argued vehemently against the new method and in favor of Biblical inerrancy on the grounds of direct divine inspiration. Briggs replied by rejecting confessional or dogmatic controls over critical studies and openly repudiated verbal inspiration. Henry Preserved Smith, of Lane Seminary, took Briggs's side, defended Wellhausen's documentary hypothesis, and soon became suspect for heresy. In 1891, Briggs brought the debate to a climax by specifically listing and condemning "superstitious Bibliolatry," "verbal inspiration," "divine authenticity," "inerrancy," "unnatural miracles," and "predictive prophecy" as positions destructive to scholarship and Biblical theology. The ensuing uproar led to his suspension from the Presbyterian Church (1891–1893), withdrawal of Union Seminary from Presbyterian jurisdiction in 1892, and the suspension of Smith in 1894. This controversy crystallized positions on Biblical criticism. The new method became a foundation stone for the Modernism of Shailer Mathews and William Adams Brown. It provided momentum for such movements as the Social Gospel through its emphases upon the Old Testament prophets as ethical leaders and of Jesus as primarily an exemplary reformer. Religious conservatives, notably fundamentalists, took the position that higher criticism undermined a necessary confidence in the Bible as the verbally and infallibly inspired Word of God. B. B. Warfield and J. Gresham Machen were early exponents of the conservative position, which was later carried on by Carl Henry and E. J. Carnell. Despite early widespread hostility to higher criticism in America and the derivative position of its American advocates, in recent years American critical scholarship has gained equality with its English and Continental counterparts, particularly through the efforts of W. F. Albright, H. R. Willoughby, G. E. Wright, F. W. Filson, F. C. Grant, R. M. Grant, and John Bright. Higher criticism was temporarily eclipsed with the decline of liberal theology and the Social Gospel, but has become a tool for neo-ortho-dox and Biblical theology in recent years. The latter position emphasizes an essential unity amid the diversity of ideas found in the Old and New Testaments, and argues that any attempt to impose dogmatic theological principles, liberal or conservative, upon the Bible is mistaken and misleading. Among American Catholics, Biblical criticism was initially cut off by papal encyclicals in 1893 and 1907, but it was revived by Pius XII's *Divino afflante spiritu* in 1939. In the same year the *Catholic Biblical Quarterly* was founded, and the studies of the Jesuit John L. McKenzie has established higher criticism in American Catholic circles.

BIBLIOGRAPHY: W. F. Albright, *History, Archaeology, and Christian Humanism* (New York, 1964); T. K. Cheyne, *Founders of Old Testament Criticism* (London, 1893); S. Terrien, "The Modern Period," *The Interpreter's Bible*, Vol. I (New York, 1952); H. R. Willoughby (ed.), *The Study of the Bible, Today and Tomorrow* (Chicago, 1947); G. E. Wright, *God Who Acts* (Chicago, 1952).

**Cromwell, Oliver** (1599–1658). Lord protector of England. Born at Huntingdon of gentry stock, he attended Sidney Sussex College, Cambridge, for a year, and sat in the 1628 and 1629 Parliaments, as well as in the Short and Long Parliaments of 1640. A consistent supporter of the Commons against the king, he raised a troop of light horse when arms were resorted to. The war was not progressing well, so Parliament created the New Model army, Cromwell being second in command. Fairfax, the commander, and Cromwell routed the Royalists at Naseby (1645). The following year, Charles capitulated; then the army and Parliament clashed. The latter decided to establish Presbyterianism without toleration, and the majority of the army were Independents. In the ensuing struggle, Cromwell supported his soldiers in a purge of Parliament and in the execution of Charles in 1649. The Rump Parliament abolished the monarchy and the House of Lords and declared England a commonwealth. Political deterioration caused the army to make Cromwell protector, and he virtually ruled the nation until his death. Cromwell was a devoted Puritan who desired religious toleration, a godly nation, and a representative government. Unable to achieve all three, and unwilling to give up either of the first two, Cromwell ruled personally. With his death, Puritanism as a political movement in England was dead.

**Cromwell, Thomas** (c. 1485–1540). Lord privy seal, lord chamberlain to Henry VIII, and earl of Essex. Trained in law, Thomas

Cromwell first rose to prominence as protégé and legal agent of Cardinal Wolsey. Facing oblivion because of association with Wolsey in 1529, he effectively transferred his services to the king (1531), first as privy councilor and in 1533 as intermediary between the king and the imperial ambassador, establishing amicable relations despite the king's divorce and remarriage. In 1535, he became vicar-general, with powers of visitation to enforce the Act of Supremacy. From 1536, as lord privy seal after Boleyn's downfall, he engineered suppression of the lesser and then also the greater monasteries, threatening charges of treason against reluctant priors and abbots. In 1539, as lord chamberlain, he arranged the marriage of the king to Anne of Cleves, for which he was made earl of Essex. New foreign alliances obviated the necessity of the marriage and it became the occasion for accusations against Cromwell by Norfolk. Awaiting in prison to learn whether he should die for heresy or treason, he sought the king's mercy by trying to prove that the marriage had not been consummated. The king turned a deaf ear and Cromwell was executed, having been abandoned by the sovereign whom he had served all too diligently.

**Crosby, Fanny** (1820–1915). American writer of popular hymns. Having lost her eyesight during infancy, she studied and taught at the New York Institution for the Blind, and in 1858 married one of her former pupils, Alexander Van Alstyne, a blind organist. At the age of forty-four she completed her first hymn. Of the thousands of hymns that she wrote, among the best known are "Safe in the Arms of Jesus," "Blessed Assurance, Jesus Is Mine!" and "Jesus, Keep Me Near the Cross."

**Crosby, Thomas** (1840–1914). Methodist missionary in British Columbia. Born in Pickering, Yorkshire, England, Crosby came to Canada with his parents in 1856. He was ordained by the Methodist Church in 1868 and spent the rest of his life working as a missionary among the Indians and isolated fishing and logging camps along the Pacific coast of British Columbia. His work firmly established a tradition of marine missions on the West Coast which has continued down to the present day.

**Crossing.** The place of intersection in a cruciform church where the transept crosses the nave. It is usually situated between the nave and the choir.

**Crotus Rubianus** (John Jäger) (c. 1480–1539). Theologian and humanist. He taught in Erfurt after 1498, and is considered a major contributor to the *Letters of Obscure Men.* Initially, Crotus strongly endorsed Luther. After 1521 or 1522, however, he turned against the Reformer, seeing him as a danger for the humanistic Reform program. He spent his last years in Halle as a canon of Archbishop Albrecht of Mainz.

**Crusader States.** The Latin or Frankish states existing in the Levant between the conquest of Jerusalem in 1099 and the fall of Acre in 1291. Although nominally in allegiance to the Latin kingdom of Jerusalem, the county of Edessa and the principality of Antioch in northern Syria were virtually independent. The Latins held most of Palestine, Lebanon, and Syria during the 12th century, but the inroads of Moslem attacks eventually reduced their territory to a strip along the seacoast. After Jerusalem was retaken by Saladin in 1187, Acre became the capital of the kingdom. The kingship, originally elective, tended to become hereditary, but was never strong in authority over the vassal lords. The High Court, composed of the chief vassals, established law, tried cases, and elected the king. In general, the political and social life of the outremer ("lands beyond the sea") was an importation of feudalism. Theoretically the pope was the overlord of the kingdom, and his influence was often sought in political quarrels. By 1187 the military orders were the chief landowners. The tenuous feudal connections, personal ambitions, and dynastic jealousies enfeebled the states, whose shadowy life was prolonged on Cyprus into the 15th century.

BIBLIOGRAPHY: J. L. LaMonte, *Feudal Monarchy in the Latin Kingdom of Jerusalem* (Cambridge, Mass., 1932); S. Runciman, *A History of the Crusades,* Vol. II (Cambridge, 1952).

**Crusades.** A series of military expeditions to recover the Holy Land from the Moslems. Although the crusading ideal persisted for many centuries, the period of major activity is usually delimited by the preaching of the First Crusade at Clermont in 1095 and the fall of Acre in 1291. Pilgrimage to Jerusalem had continued after the Moslem conquests of the 8th century, but with the rise of the Seljuk Turks in the 11th century access to the holy places became more difficult. At the request of the Byzantine emperor Alexius I for assistance in holding off the Turks, Pope Urban II, desirous also of turning the bellicose energies of Western barons against distant infidels rather than one another, urged the Frankish nobles present at the Council of Clermont in November, 1095, to take the cross and recover the Holy Sepulcher. Before the nobles could organize their expedition a motley crowd of some twenty thousand, following an itinerant monk, Peter the Hermit, and a poor knight, Walter the Penniless, set out across Germany. In Hungary their pillaging brought on reprisals from the populace, and Alexius had to send troops to control them as they crossed the Empire. Upon moving into Asia Minor they were almost completely wiped out by the Turks. Meanwhile, four expeditions of nobility had set out in 1096. Their leaders were Godfrey of Bouillon; Raymond of Toulouse and Bishop Adhemar of Le Puy, designated as leader by the pope; Bohemund of Taranto and his nephew Tancred; and Robert of Normandy, Robert of Flanders, and Stephen of Blois. Alexius had not wished armies of this size to be thrust upon him, and with apprehension but great tact he guided them through the Empire and into Asia Minor. Between sixty thousand and one hundred thousand men passed through Constantinople by the spring of 1097. In that year the armies marched across Anatolia, suffering from heat and Turkish attacks, and laid siege to Antioch, which fell in 1098. Bohemund set himself up there and refused to continue onward, while Baldwin of Boulogne made himself count of Edessa. Despite genuine religious motivation in many crusaders, others went in the hope of carving out estates for themselves or because of the promise of forgiveness of sins. After a short siege Jerusalem fell on July 14, 1099, with merciless slaughter of the inhabitants. Godfrey was named advocate of the Holy Sepulcher; his successors were known as kings of Jerusalem. His brother Baldwin of Edessa became king on Godfrey's death in 1100.

The Latin kingdom of Jerusalem was an importation of Western feudalism, a monarchy dependent for its strength upon the support of the High Court, composed of the chief barons. Not until 1130 did it gain suzerainty over Antioch, Tripoli, and Edessa. The rise of the Templars and Hospitalers as military orders gave the kingdom a professional fighting force to serve as the core of its armies.

When Edessa was taken by Zengi in 1144, the need for a new Crusade was seen. Louis VII of France and Conrad III of Germany set out with armies, but their forces were decimated in Anatolia in 1147. A misguided attack on Damascus, a Frankish ally, failed; by 1149 the Second Crusade was at an end. The next decades saw a struggle between the Franks and Nureddin for control of Egypt. His successor, Saladin, became the greatest Moslem leader of the period, unifying the Moslem world from Egypt to Syria. When the

Christians repeatedly broke truces with him, Saladin resolved to drive them from the land. After a crushing defeat at Hattin in 1187 the Franks could not prevent the recapture of Jerusalem later in the year. Reduced to a few coastal cities, the Franks once again appealed to the West for help. At the urging of Pope Innocent III, Philip Augustus of France, Frederick I Barbarossa of Germany, and Richard I of England began to move eastward. Frederick drowned en route, but Richard and Philip managed to raise the siege of Acre in 1191. Philip returned home after quarreling with Richard, but the latter checked Saladin's forces in a series of encounters which raised the fame of both to legendary heights. Although Richard left in 1192 without retaking Jerusalem, his conquest of Cyprus opened that island as a center of strength for the Franks in the next century. Eventually the crowns of Cyprus and Jerusalem became conjoined.

When Innocent III launched the Fourth Crusade he did not foresee that it would prove to be the most disgraceful episode of the era. Influenced by the Venetians, the Crusade turned against its fellow Christians of the Byzantine Empire and resulted in the barbaric sack of Constantinople in 1204 and the establishment of Baldwin of Flanders as the first Latin emperor there.

Another dark chapter in the story of the Crusades was the Children's Crusade of 1212, which resulted in thousands of children from France and Germany being sold into slavery while attempting to reach the Holy Land (see CHILDREN'S CRUSADE).

Beginning with the Fifth Crusade the goal of Western military expeditions was shifted to Egypt, seen as the center of Moslem power. In 1219, crusade armies took Damietta, but the delay of the German emperor Frederick II and the refusal of Cardinal Pelagius to treat with the infidels frustrated all attempts. Sultan al-Kamil's offer to surrender nearly all of the original kingdom of Jerusalem in return for Damietta was snubbed, nor did the intervention of Francis of Assisi produce results. Damietta was retaken in 1221 and the Crusade came to an end.

Frederick II finally arrived in the Holy Land in 1228, and, although under excommunication, made a treaty with al-Kamil giving the Christians possession of Jerusalem once again. Frederick remained in Palestine for fifteen years, having crowned himself king of Jerusalem against the wishes of the barons, with whom he quarreled while maintaining more friendly relations with the Moslems. When the truce ended, the Franks were defeated by the Mameluke Baybars and Jerusalem was lost for the last time in 1244. Again the call for a Crusade went out, this time accompanied by missions from Innocent IV to the Mongol khanates of the East, for the rising tide of Mongol conquests in central Asia was seen as a potential aid in the destruction of Islam. The great hero of the Seventh Crusade was Louis IX of France, a man of unquestionable devotion. After taking Damietta in 1249 he was captured and released only upon surrender of the city. At Acre he spent four years trying to strengthen the Franks, who were embroiled in dynastic quarrels and clinging only weakly to the coast. Forced to attend to affairs in France, Louis left in 1254. The demise of the Crusader States was delayed only by the power struggle between the Mongols and Baybars, now sultan of Egypt. Gaining the upper hand in 1260, Baybars next turned to pushing the Franks into the sea. In 1268 he took Antioch. Louis IX made a last futile attack on Tunis in 1270, but fell ill and died there with the words "Jerusalem, Jerusalem," on his lips.

The crusading spirit had now become debased to an urge to attack fellow Europeans; thus Gregory X could raise no response in 1274 for a new expedition to the East. Baybars died in 1277, but his successor Qalawūn continued the pressure on the Franks, with intermittent truces. He took Tripoli in 1289. His son al-Ashraf ignored a ten-year truce and led a huge army against Acre, which fell May 28, 1291. Acre had been the seat of government during the 13th century and its loss meant the end of Latin rule, although the kingdom nominally survived for another generation on Cyprus. Sporadic expeditions from many quarters during the next century were unavailing in stemming the Moslem tide. An expedition of nearly one hundred thousand men was wiped out by the Ottoman Turks at Nicopolis in Bulgaria in 1396, the last major effort of Western chivalry to stop the Turk.

The Crusades served as a stimulus in the shift of the center of civilization from the Near East to western Europe. While enhancing the reputation of the papacy, they also aided the rise of monarchies in Europe due to the absence of warring barons who had gone to the Holy Land. The capture of Constantinople in the Fourth Crusade brought a flood of Greek humanism into Italy (see FOURTH CRUSADE). Two centuries of intercourse with the East produced cultural and commercial contacts that were to have a lasting influence in the West. The blow to the Christian peoples of the East, however, was the darkest result of the Crusades, which had broken down the defenses of the Eastern Empire, allowing the Turks to overrun the Balkans. The barbarous behavior of the crusaders turned the Moslems against all Christians, and the churches that had survived six centuries of Moslem rule were wiped out.

BIBLIOGRAPHY: Ambroise, *The Crusade of Richard Lion-Heart* (New York, 1941); J. A. Brundage, *The Crusades* (Milwaukee, 1962); P. Dubois, *The Recovery of the Holy Land* (New York, 1956); M. R. B. Shaw (ed. and tr.) *Chronicles of the Crusades* (Baltimore, 1963); D. C. Munro, *The Kingdom of the Crusaders* (New York, 1935); S. Runciman, *A History of the Crusades,* 3 vols. (Cambridge, 1952–1954); K. Setton, *A History of the Crusades,* 2 vols. (Philadelphia, 1958–1962).

**Crypto-Calvinism.** The name given to the position of certain Lutheran theologians whose Eucharistic views resembled those of Calvin. Most prominent among them was Philip Melanchthon, who rewrote Article X of his Augsburg Confession (1540, ed.) in a manner later judged heretical by the strict Lutherans. At first, the so-called *variata* edition was used as the official Lutheran standard in conversations with the Roman Catholics, and it was widely used also by the Reformed. But the final decision of Lutheranism was against crypto-Calvinism, and the *Book of Concord* authorized the *invariata* edition of 1530.

**Cudworth, Ralph** (1617–1688). Cambridge Platonist and early Latitudinarian. A native of Somersetshire, he became a fellow of Emmanuel College, Cambridge, in 1639, master of Clare Hall in 1645, and regius professor of Hebrew in that same year. He was appointed master of Christ's College in 1654, and in 1678 was given a prebend's stall at Gloucester. Cudworth was in some ways the most prolific of the Platonists and did the most systematic writing among them. His unfinished *True Intellectual System of the Universe* (1678), an intricate and abstruse work, was an attempt to refute at once both dogmatic Calvinism and Hobbesian atheism. To Cudworth, Christianity was the only ultimately valid source of the most important realities: the divine ideas and the freedom of man. Cudworth thought of the world as being a "plastic medium" through which the transcendental God worked out his plans and purposes. Although he placed great emphasis upon the power of reason, he nonetheless argued for the necessity of divine revelation as the one real answer to atheism. He was primarily concerned with philosophical questions, but he also composed several theological treatises on the nature of the church and on the Lord's Supper.

**Cuius Regio, Eius Religio.** See AUGSBURG, PEACE OF.

**Cumberland Presbyterian Church.** An outgrowth of the Second Great Awakening on the Kentucky frontier. James McGready, a Presbyterian minister who arrived in Logan County, Ky., in 1796, was so persuasive and zealous as a preacher that the Cumberland revival followed in 1800. The Cumberland Presbytery, in order to meet the demand for more preachers which resulted from the revival ordained men to the ministry who did not have the educational qualifications considered necessary by the Presbyterian Church. Another aspect of the revival was the adoption of Arminian sentiments by several ministers who thus modified or rejected parts of Calvinistic Presbyterian doctrine. For these two reasons, the Kentucky Synod of the Presbyterian Church dissolved the Cumberland Presbytery. The revivalists in the presbytery, under the leadership of Finis Ewing and Samuel King, organized themselves into the Cumberland Presbyterian Church in 1810. The Cumberland Presbyterian Synod was constituted in 1813. The General Assembly was organized in 1829. In 1906, it merged with the Presbyterian Church in the United States of America. A large minority, however, continued as the Cumberland Presbyterian Church which now consists of 936 churches and 88,540 members (1967).

**Curate.** Anyone having the cure or care of souls, i.e., any minister is a curate; see the French *curé.* In English practice this term has been reserved for the assistant to a rector or chief pastor of a parish.

**Cur Deus Homo.** A treatise by Anselm of Canterbury, completed in 1098. Anselm tried to prove by logic the necessity of the incarnation. Denying the rights of the devil over man, Anselm argued that man owed a debt to God, since he had stolen from God's honor (a feudal term) by sin. The debt was greater than man could pay; only God could repay it. Since man ought to, and only God could, repay the debt, a God-man was necessary.

**Curia, Papal.** The governing body through which the pope administers the church. In the medieval church it was used in the same way that the *Curia Regis* assisted the feudal monarch in ruling his kingdom. At first the pontiff was assisted by Roman clergy and synods. In the late Middle Ages the popes used the cardinals, who became the court's most powerful members. By the 13th century the Curia was divided into three administrative departments: chancery; Camera, or apostolic chamber; and judicial tribunals. The Curia thereby handled secretarial, financial, and judicial matters. In 1967, Pope Paul VI revamped the Curia, providing for five-year appointments with worldwide representation to replace the small clique of elderly, ultraconservative Italian cardinals who have dominated the Curia and held lifetime tenure.

**Cuthbert** (c. 628–687). Celtic monk. He appears to have made an impact on his generation more by the immediate effect of his personality than by any great organizational or literary ability. Much of the information about him comes from the *Life* written by Bede which, unlike most of Bede's work, was hagiographic in form.

It is reported that the humbly born Cuthbert while still a shepherd saw Aidan's soul ascend radiantly into heaven. He entered Melrose Abbey, but later transferred to Ripon, where his adherence to Celtic practices led to his expulsion. He became prior of Melrose, but only after the ruling of the Synod of Whitby did he accept Roman practices. From 664, he was prior of Lindisfarne and Romanized that monastery. In 676, he became a hermit on Farne Island, closing his cell to every earthly sight. Recalled to active life as bishop of Lindisfarne in 685, he continued to live ascetically. He returned to the hermit cell just before his death, agreeing finally to be buried at Lindisfarne lest evil men claim sanctuary at his island retreat. There is no evidence that he left any writing. His body was moved from place to place during the Danish invasions, finding a resting place in Durham until the shrine was defaced in 1542.

**Cutler, Timothy** (1684–1765). Congregational and Episcopal clergyman. A graduate of Harvard and a highly regarded pastor of the Congregational Church in Stratford, Conn., he became president of Yale in 1719. When he renounced Congregationalism in 1722, the Yale trustees, appalled by the defection, excused him "from all further services." He then received Episcopal ordination from the bishop of Norwich and for the rest of his life served as rector of Christ Church (Old North) in Boston, Mass.

**Cyprian** (c. 200–258). Bishop of Carthage, Christian martyr. A Carthaginian trained in Roman law, Cyprian took the additional name of Caecilius in honor of the presbyter to whom he owed his conversion—hence his full name as a Christian was Thascius Caecilius Cyprianus. He was soon ordained presbyter, and in 249 became bishop of Carthage. His apologetic essay *To Donatus* reflects the appeal of Christianity to a practical mind in the collapsing Roman world.

During the persecution of Decius (250–251), Cyprian, who was in exile, continued to guide his church by letter. On his return he was confronted with the problem of the lapsi, those who had given way under the persecution, many of whom now desired readmission to the church. Cyprian insisted on penance but did not deny the hope of absolution, and thus avoided the extremes of either rigorism or laxity. Some of the confessors (i.e., those who had shown their willingness to die for the faith but had survived) claimed the right to share their merits with the lapsed, and jealous of Cyprian's rapid advancement, they joined some of the older clergy in a schismatic movement at Carthage. Cyprian was able to secure his authority, however, and gave his support to the new bishop of Rome, Cornelius, whose election was contested by the rigorist presbyter Novatian, the supporters of whom ultimately became the Novatianist Church. Cyprian's treatise *On the Unity of the Church* stresses the importance of unity with the episcopate, which inherits the commission given first to Peter and then extended to the other apostles. A crucial passage exists in two forms, one more Petrine than the other; but neither is papalist in the later sense, and the difference may merely be due to the fact that an edition was prepared for circulation at Rome as well as at Carthage.

During the following period of relative peace Cyprian was occupied in organizing the pastoral and charitable activities of his church, and advising on problems that arose after the persecution. His treatises and letters, largely on practical matters of conduct, became an important part of the literature of the Latin Church. *Epistle* 63 is in effect a brief treatise on the Eucharist, one of the earliest formal treatments of the subject. In 254, Cyprian found himself at variance with Cornelius' successor, Stephen of Rome. Stephen was willing to recognize the validity of heretical or schismatic baptism, while Cyprian maintained that only the true church could truly baptize. The problem may have been made more acute by the otherwise orthodox schism of Novatian. Previous heretical baptism had been mainly that of Gnostic sects who, even if they had used the Christian ceremony and the Trinitarian formula, scarcely intended to show Christian orthodoxy. Cyprian had no

hesitation in differing from the bishop of Rome on such a point. He rallied several well-attended councils of the bishops of Roman Africa to his side, and received much support from the East. Dionysius of Alexandria attempted in vain to reconcile the two parties. The Western Church, at least, was later to decide against Cyprian, though the problem of the precise line of church membership is a permanent one. The immediate dispute was still undecided when the death of Stephen in 257 was soon followed by the renewal of persecution under the emperor Valerian. There was now a definite attack on the leaders of the church, which Cyprian did not attempt to escape. He was first banished from Carthage, then recalled for trial in September, 258. On the morning of September 14 he made his formal confession of the faith before the proconsul Galerius and was beheaded. The simple eyewitness account that is preserved is one of the most authentic and moving of the Acts of the Martyrs.

Cyprian was one of the first great churchmen of the West, and in a sense the source of both episcopalian and papalist views of church order. Even more important is his straightforward expression of Christian devotion, marked by the combination of ethical responsibility and reliance on sacramental grace typical of so much later Western piety.

BIBLIOGRAPHY: A. Roberts and J. Donaldson (eds.), *The Ante-Nicene Fathers*, Vol. 4 (Grand Rapids, 1951); M. Bévenot, *St. Cyprian's De Unitate: Chapter IV in the Light of the Manuscripts* (London, 1938).

**Cyril** (c. 315–386). Bishop of Jerusalem from c. 349. He is best known for the *Catechetical Lectures* on the creed delivered to candidates for baptism, probably in 350. The most fully preserved specimen of this type of literature, they represent the moderate school which accepted the ideas of the Council of Nicaea but had not yet incorporated the key word *homoousios* into the baptismal creed. Cyril's episcopate was interrupted by two periods of exile—one from 357 to 361 due to personal charges brought by Acacius of Caesarea (who as bishop of the civil capital of Palestine tried to keep his jurisdiction over the rising see of Jerusalem), the other during the Arian predominance under the emperor Valens (367–378). Cyril's orthodoxy and canonical status were recognized by the Council of Constantinople in 381. He seems to have been largely responsible for organizing the observances of the church year into a series of historical anniversaries, as described in the *Pilgrimage of Etheria*, many of which spread from Jerusalem to the rest of the church. The series of *Catechetical Lectures* is completed by the brief *Mystagogical Lectures* on the doctrine and liturgy of Baptism and the Eucharist, delivered to the newly baptized during Easter Week. They represent the teaching and practice of Cyril's later years, though the actual composition may belong to his successor, Bishop John.

**Cyril** (c. 826–869) and **Methodius** (c. 815–885). Two brothers from Thessalonica who were the "Apostles of the Slavs." Both men were outstanding scholars and linguists, and had, in 860, participated in a missionary effort to convert the Khazars. Cyril, whose real name was Constantine until he became a monk in 868, held a chair of philosophy in Constantinople, while Methodius was an abbot of a Greek monastery.

In 862, the Byzantine patriarch Photius sent Cyril and Methodius to Moravia to help organize a Slav church. The *Life of Cyril* credits him with the creation of a Slav alphabet based on Greek uncials, the Cyrillic alphabet. However, some authorities believe this to be the work of one of Methodius' disciples, while Methodius himself is said to have devised the Glagolitic script, an alphabet derived from Greek cursive.

The German clergy opposed the Slav mission, and the brothers journeyed to Rome to justify their use of Slavonic in church services. The pope approved the use of Slavonic, ordained Cyril a monk (who died in Rome), and appointed Methodius archbishop of Pannonia.

In 870, Methodius was imprisoned for almost three years by the new ruler, Prince Sviatopolk, and in 880 he again journeyed to Rome to justify his work. Upon his death, the Slav mission was expelled, but his disciples later went to Bulgaria to help establish a Slav church.

**Cyril of Alexandria** (c. 370–444). Early Roman Catholic ecclesiastic and Doctor of the Church. An important though strangely ambiguous figure in church history, Cyril was the nephew of Bishop Theophilus of Alexandria. He grew up among the monks and theologians of Egypt, began his ministry under his uncle, and succeeded him as bishop in 412. His episcopate started with a series of conflicts with the civil authorities. He suppressed the Novatians at Alexandria and attempted to expel the Jews, and his quarrel with the prefect of Egypt, Orestes, led to riots in which there were victims on both sides, the most famous being the pagan philosopher Hypatia. Cyril was obliged to submit to the imperial authority, but remained the first citizen of Egypt.

In ecclesiastical affairs Cyril defended the primacy of Alexandria in the Eastern Church against the rising power of Constantinople and the rival theology of Antioch. In 428 his enmities were combined when the Antiochene Nestorius became bishop of Constantinople. In theology Nestorius as an Antiochene emphasized the humanity of Christ, and Cyril as an Alexandrian stressed the unity of Christ's divine person. Nestorius began his episcopate as a hammer of heretics, but was soon challenged by Cyril to correct his own teaching, symbolized by his refusal to call the Virgin Mary "Theotokos"—that is, one who, as mother of the one Christ, gave birth to God the Son. Cyril's anathemas and Nestorius' replies led to the summoning of a general council, called by the emperor Theodosius II to meet at Ephesus in June, 431. There were in fact two councils. Cyril arrived first, claiming a commission from Pope Celestine as well as his own authority, and held a council that deposed Nestorius, accepted Cyril's dogmatic letters as orthodox, and weakened the see of Antioch by recognizing the independence of the Church of Cyprus. John of Antioch came later, and with his Syrian bishops held a rival council that deposed Cyril. The emperor first compromised by banishing both leaders, but Cyril's influence, assisted by lavish gifts to court officials, soon secured the recognition of his council and the interment of Nestorius, later exiled to Upper Egypt. However, John of Antioch did not resume communion with Cyril until 433, after Cyril had accepted the orthodoxy of an Antiochene formula containing the crucial phrase "union of two natures." In this sense, further developed at Chalcedon in 451, the doctrine of the Council of Ephesus received general acceptance.

Cyril's sometimes ruthless politics should not obscure his contribution to theology, to which he owes his place in history as a saint and Doctor of the Church. His key idea may be said to be unity, whether in the external or the intellectual arena. His commentaries (preserved in whole or in part) on selected passages of the Pentateuch, on Isaiah and the Minor Prophets, and on the Gospels of John and Luke stress the unity of the Testaments. His dogmatic statements emphasize the unity of Christ in whom Godhead and manhood are joined "hypostatically" ("in one nature," as he would prefer to say) and not merely associated. This made the full humanity of Jesus something of a problem, so that "Jesus wept" was for him a difficult text, but led him to accept the paradox of the sufferings of the impassible God, who in Jesus "was impassibly making his own the sufferings of his own flesh." He therefore laid the foundation for important developments of both Monophysite and Chalcedonian theology. He is also the last of the ancient Christian Apologists in his reply to Julian the Apostate's *Against the Galilaeans,* now mainly of interest for its extensive quotations from his opponent.

Cyril died in peace, but it soon became clear how partial his victories were. The Council of Chalcedon made important modifications in his Christology, on lines that were accepted even by the heirs of his formulas, the moderate Monophysites of the school of Severus of Antioch; and the conflicts of the following period ended the splendor of the Church of Alexandria and its hegemony in the Eastern Church.

BIBLIOGRAPHY: W. J. Burghardt, *The Image of God in Man, According to Cyril of Alexandria* (Washington, 1957); A. Kerrigan, *St. Cyril of Alexandria: Interpreter of the Old Testament* (Rome, 1952).

# D

**Da Costa, Isaac** (1798–1860). Devout Dutch poet and historian. Da Costa was an aristocratic Sephardic Jew who was converted to the Reformed Church, becoming a leader of the spiritual awakening in Holland known as the *Réveil.* He sought to further Christian unity by discussion. Da Costa wrote a Jewish history, a Biblical commentary, and political and religious poetry. His *Israel and the Gentiles* brought him renown.

**Daillé** (Dallaeus), **Jean** (1594–1670). French Reformed scholar. From 1626 he was pastor at Charenton, where the Reformed Church of Paris was accustomed to meet. He is probably most famous for his attack on the use of the early church fathers, disparaging their authority, and maintaining that all authentic Christian doctrine must be traceable directly to the Scriptures.

**Damasus I** (c. 304–384). Bishop of Rome from 366. Damasus brought new importance to his office in spite of certain ambiguities in his position. A rival, Ursinus, disputed his election, claiming that, unlike Damasus, he had been loyal to the previous pope, Liberius, during his exile. Damasus' episcopate began with riots between the two parties, and it was troubled by lawsuits almost to the end. However, the civil authorities decided in his favor,

and in 378 the Western emperor Gratian confirmed his appellate jurisdiction over bishops. Damasus supported the Nicene party in the disputes of the Eastern Church and condemned the Apollinarians. In 379 the emperor Theodosius recognized Damasus and Peter of Alexandria as advocates of orthodox communion. But Western intervention in more personal disputes was neither welcome nor effective. Damasus encouraged pilgrimages to the tombs of the martyrs, for which he composed inscriptions in rather mediocre verse (see PHILOCALIAN CALENDAR). Under him the Roman Church finally became officially Latin-speaking. This made it more than ever the center of the Western Church, but tended to cut it off from the Eastern Church. The need for a standard version for worship may account for Damasus' greatest contribution, his commission to Jerome (who served as his secretary from 382 to 384) to revise the Latin Psalter and New Testament, a project that led to the Vulgate Bible.

**Daniel.** A widespread liturgical drama, or mystery play, derived from the Vulgate form of The Book of Daniel. The 12th-century Latin version by the students of the cathedral school of Beauvais fortunately survives with its music intact. The drama is noteworthy for the prefiguration of the Harrowing of Hell in Daniel's descent into the lion pit and the angel's prophecy of Christ's coming at its end. Pageant-like in form, it is strongly didactic in content.

**Danish Missionary Society.** A group organized in 1821 by the Lutheran pastor Bone Falck Ronne. Upon encountering some resistance from the state church, the Society limited itself to supplying missionaries and materials for missions already established in Greenland and Africa. By 1860 it had won state church support and in 1863 it undertook work in its own name in southern India. Its major work has been in India, though it has assisted missions elsewhere.

**Dante Alighieri** (1265–1321). Florentine poet, author of *The Divine Comedy.* Schooled in the Latin poets, Dante was also early attracted to the courtly love conventions of the Provençal troubadours. He found the supreme object of poetic exaltation in a young woman of Florence, Beatrice Portinari, whose perfections he celebrated in *The New Life.* This Platonic adoration did not prevent his marriage to Gemma Donati, by whom he had three or four children. He served in civic offices in Florence between 1295 and 1302, at which time he became a victim of political misfortune and was exiled on pain of death. The remainder of his life he passed in melancholy itinerancy as a guest of various noble Italian families, proving that "you shall find out how salt is the taste of another's bread, and how hard a path the going down and going up another's stair." During these years he became convinced that the solution to the turmoil of his time was the return of both papacy and empire to their respective, divinely ordained spheres of activity. His *Of Monarchy* stressed his belief in an empire centered on Rome, supreme in the secular sphere, and a papacy confined to its spiritual lordship. *The Divine Comedy,* written over a period of some ten years, dramatized these views in an extended allegory of man's journey to salvation.

**Darrow, Clarence** (1857–1938). Attorney. He was educated at Allegheny College and the University of Michigan. He practiced law in Chicago, where he became a member of counsel for Eugene V. Debs, leader indicted in 1894 for conspiracy in the Railroad Union case. A criminal law career began in 1924, when he defended Richard Loeb and Nathan Leopold. In 1925 he was chief counsel against William Jennings Bryan in the famous John T. Scopes trial in Tennessee. Darrow also defended the Negroes in the Scottsboro case.

**Darwinism.** An interpretation of life as an evolving process of change through natural selection, adaptation in struggle, and the survival of the fittest, described and formulated by Charles Darwin (1809–1882) in his works on biology, *On the Origin of Species by Means of Natural Selection* (1859) and *The Descent of Man* (1871). At first Darwin's facts and theories shocked many 19th-century Christians who interpreted them as threats to Biblical authority and traditional doctrines of creation, providence, and redemption.

Darwin's ideas were not completely new. Copernicus had expanded the concept of space in writing *On the Revolutions of the Heavenly Bodies* (1543); Lyell had expanded the concept of time in *Principles of Geology* (1830–1832); and with this scientific background critics raised serious questions about the authority of the Scriptures for adequate instruction concerning the natural order. Throughout these years many Christians continued to consider the Bible as such a text, and so-called providential empiricists who engaged in the scientific quest considered God as a necessary explanation of all the aspects of existence for which scientists had not discovered an explanation. Darwin's evolutionary theories and his evidence, anticipated by Lamarck in *Philosophie zoologique* (1809), seemed to provide

the explanation for creation and to question the Christian's understanding of the uniqueness of man's nature and destiny under God. Moreover, sociologists Herbert Spencer in England and William Graham Sumner in the United States employed the findings of biology to substantiate a "social Darwinism."

In the English-speaking world, the immediate response was almost outrage. Attachment to the older mechanistic views of Isaac Newton, William Paley's *Natural Theology* (1802), and the uncertainty of 19th-century scientists themselves about evolutionary processes did not help the discussion. Anglican bishop Samuel Wilberforce in the *Quarterly Review* (1860) and, after the Civil War in America, Princeton theologian Charles Hodge in *What Is Darwinism?* (1874) attacked the theories of Darwin as incompatible with the Word of God, contradictory to the revealed relations between God and his creation and creature, and a denial of teleology, the design of the Creator. Other Christians did not react so negatively. English Biblical scholar F. J. A. Hort and Scottish president of Princeton University, James McCosh, emphasized obvious aspects of development in life and "theistic evolution" as providing a fresh reason for adoring the power and wisdom of God. Still others began to interpret evolution positively in more systematic theological ideas. English professor Henry Drummond's "evangelical evolutionism" in *Ascent of Man* (1894) and American editor Lyman Abbott's "idealistic evolutionism" in *Theology of an Evolutionist* (1897) comforted and convinced many that evolution was "God's way of doing things" in a progressive redemption and sanctification of man from his brute inheritance. In the United States the debate over evolution sometimes led to bitter ecclesiastical and public conflict. Alexander Winchell, naturalist author of *Pre-Adamites* (1880), was removed from his position at Vanderbilt University; Crawford H. Toy resigned from the Southern Baptist Theological Seminary in 1879 because of disagreement over the plenary inspiration of Scripture; and James Woodrow was dismissed in 1886 from his chair at Columbia (S.C.) Theological Seminary after a heresy trial that involved a discussion of Paul's doctrine of the first and Second Adams, important for federal theology among American Calvinists. Sometime later, in 1925, William Jennings Bryan confronted Clarence Darrow in the famous Scopes trial in Tennessee over the "monkey bill" which outlawed the teaching of evolution in public schools. While the debate over Darwinism on the Continent was not always as direct as it was in England and

America, there was concern. Albrecht Ritschl, Adolf Schlatter, and Friedrich Loofs worried that Darwin's ideas simply reinforced the rationalism and materialism of the Enlightenment and undermined man's spiritual supremacy over nature.

Roman Catholic thinkers were generally hostile or reserved toward Darwinism, although St. George Jackson Mivart in *The Genesis of Species* (1871) and J. A. Zahm, *Evolution and Dogma* (1896), argued that a type of biological evolution did not contradict Catholic dogma. Pius XII reviewed the attitude of Catholics through his instructions in the encyclical *Humani generis* (1950). In any discussion of evolution, the Catholic must take for granted the spiritual soul of man, must leave the discussion to experts in theology and science, must not take for granted that evolution is a proved theory, and must be ready to submit to the judgment of the church on the issue.

It soon became evident that Darwin's idea of evolution had to be accepted, in some sense, and doing so stimulated a quest for origins in practically every intellectual discipline—in anthropology, psychology, and sociology. Social Darwinism, involving some competition by races, classes, and nations as well as by individuals, and as championed by Spencer and Sumner, soon fell into disrepute in the drive for social amelioration. Darwinism itself was influenced by various developments, particularly in the study of genes and mutations, although neo-Darwinians continued to insist that natural selection represented the truth about evolution. In order to deal with the problems of determinism, materialism, and mechanism implied in evolution, philosophers Hans Adolf Eduard Driesch developed "vitalism" an entelechy operating alongside the natural order; Henri Bergson described a life force in what he called "creative evolution," while in Lloyd Morgan's concept of "emergent evolution" new levels of life appear that cannot be explained in terms of previous levels. Out of these various views a "synthetic evolution" has emerged in the work of such scientists as George Gaylord Simpson.

Throughout the years, Christians began to listen, less threatened and with more humility and profit, to scientists who insisted that some form of evolution is basic to biology and to life. The discussion has continued, e.g., at the centennial celebration of Darwin's publication of the *Origin* at the University of Chicago (1959). There is a tendency among Christians to accept the Scriptures as a record of God's self-disclosure in history, a confession that the scientist cannot completely discount, and to interpret the Scriptures not in terms of a scientific account of origins but in terms of dependence and development in relation to God. Creative assistance in this approach has been given by Karl Heim in his *Christian Faith and Natural Science* (1953) and by Teilhard de Chardin, *The Phenomenon of Man* (1959).

BIBLIOGRAPHY: C. C. Gillispie, *Genesis and Geology* (New York, 1959); J. C. Greene, *Darwin and the Modern World View* (Baton Rouge, 1961); R. Hofstadter, *Social Darwinism in American Thought* (Boston, 1965); G. G. Simpson, *The Meaning of Evolution* (New Haven, 1949); S. Tax (ed.), *Evolution After Darwin,* 3 vols. (Chicago, 1960).

**Darwinism and American Churches.** Shortly after its appearance in 1859, Darwin's *On the Origin of Species by Means of Natural Selection* was consulted with a reverence usually reserved for Scripture. For almost a century Paley's argument from design had been the dominant proof of the existence of God. Darwinism seemed to demolish Paley's thesis and appeared to question the veracity of the creation narratives of the Bible, to undermine the traditional conceptions of sin and morality, and to disparage human dignity. When *The Descent of Man* appeared in 1871, the opponents of Darwinism pointed out that the application of Darwin's principles of natural selection to mankind could only lead to atheism. Charles Hodge championed this position in *What Is Darwinism?* (1874), the most popular anti-Darwin tract. Such figures as Dwight L. Moody, on the other hand, simply ignored the evolutionary hypothesis, and through their influence large numbers of Christians remained untouched by Darwinism. Anti-Darwinism itself was one of the roots of Fundamentalism, in which the literal inspiration and the inerrancy of Scripture were articles of faith, and where Darwinism was viewed as an unwarranted, immoral, and dangerous invasion of the realm of divine revelation by atheistic science. Darwinism won its chief victories among the churches that responded to the current liberal theology. As early as 1871, James McCosh of Princeton acknowledged the developmental hypothesis but remained dubious as to the application of natural selection to mankind because man's unique spiritual character was more plausibly explained by a special creation. John Fiske was a leading figure in the attempt to reconcile evolution and religion. Fiske asserted that evolution did not cancel faith, for it gave scientific support to man's spiritual knowledge. It illuminated progress but did not refute a first cause. In line with liberal theology, he said that it enhanced the glory of God by demolishing the arbitrary God of dogmatism and confirmed an enlightened view of a rational God. Evolution demonstrated the orderly connections and providential progress of God's universe. Fiske said that evolution proved that man was the ultimate object of the universe, the chief of God's creations. It affirmed that creation was not blind and chaotic, but carefully planned by God to come to a climax in the human soul. Evolution was to furnish a scientific foundation for morality congruent with Scripture: evil was destined to disappear into a greater good. By 1880 numerous liberal theologians supported Darwinism. They were encouraged by the theistic applications of evolution by such scientists as Darwin himself and Asa Gray, who insisted that natural selection did not refute the argument from design. Joseph Le Conte maintained that the argument from design had been enhanced by the evolutionary hypothesis. Washington Gladden, a disciple of Horace Bushnell, welcomed it as an ally to free Christianity from literalism and dogmatism, and to proclaim the reasonableness of Christianity. Henry Ward Beecher, won over by Darwin and the social evolution espoused by Spencer, was with Lyman Abbott and Phillips Brooks particularly effective in popularizing evolution for Christians. Beecher felt that man's religious spirit was not being threatened, and that theology would be corrected, enlarged, and liberated by evolution. Abbot proposed that the traditional view of sin be replaced by the notion that immoral acts were lapses into primitive action. Darwinism was a source for the Social Gospel movement, which emphasized a gradual and inevitable progress toward a better order in society. There were binding natural laws, it was argued, governing all human behavior. Bushnell's response to Darwinism was representative of the dilemma felt in some Protestant circles. He was convinced that evolution jeopardized religion because it implied a universe indifferent to man. Bushnell willingy surrendered Biblical literacy and inerrancy, and accepted the theory of inevitable progress, but repudiated the notion of "the eternity of Blunder." He acknowledged evolution only as far as it ascribed the necessity of progress to God. He tended to avoid conflict by repudiating "scientific theology" and emphasizing supernaturalism. Yet his concept of "Christian nurture" was welcomed for its emphasis upon a gradual growth in virtue and piety. To many liberals, evolutionary processes were a key to understanding history and the ways of God, but this weakened traditional emphases of radical divine interference in his-

tory, notably in the Fall and the cross. The acts of God were viewed as more fluid and nebulous. Sin became the failure to fulfill evolutionary designs, and intelligent adaptation was encouraged rather than contrition and confession. Evil was defined as maladjustment. Finally, Darwinism was instrumental in compelling religion to share its traditional claims to authority with science. It was a major step in the secularization of the modern mind.

BIBLIOGRAPHY: L. Abbott, *The Theology of an Evolutionist* (Boston, 1897); H. S. Commager, *The American Mind* (New Haven, 1950); B. M. Cross, *Horace Bushnell: Minister to a Changing America* (Chicago, 1958); J. Fiske, *Outlines of Cosmic Philosophy,* 2 vols. (8th ed., Boston, 1874); R. Hofstadter, *Social Darwinism in American Thought* (Boston, 1965); H. S. Smith (ed.), *Horace Bushnell* (New York, 1965).

**Davenport, Christopher** (*also known as* Francis Hunt, Francis Coventry, *and* Franciscus à Sancta Clara) (1598–1680). An English convert to the Roman Church who joined the Franciscan Order and taught philosophy and theology at St. Bonaventure's in Douai. Sent to England as chaplain to Queen Henrietta Maria, wife of Charles I, he became friends with many of the Anglican clergy and hoped to return the country to the Roman Catholic faith through some sort of corporate reunion. To this end, Davenport wrote a treatise in which he tried to show that the Thirty-nine Articles could be given a more traditional interpretation than was normally felt.

**Davenport, James** (1716–1757). Presbyterian revivalist. Graduated from Yale, he began his revival preaching under the influence of George Whitefield. Extravagances in method and preaching against "unconverted ministers" caused his expulsion from a number of communities, including his own congregation on Long Island. In 1744 he repented of his methods in *Confession and Retractions* and served as a parish pastor until his death.

**Davenport, John** (1597–1670). Puritan clergyman. Son of the mayor of Coventry, England, and educated at Oxford, Davenport was led by his nonconformism to move to Holland in 1633, but his opposition to infant baptism brought about difficulties in that country also. Along with a group of English Puritans, he sailed for New England and eventually settled at New Haven in what became Connecticut, where he became the first pastor.

**David of Wales** (d. c. 601). Patron saint of Wales and abbot bishop of Menevia

(Mynyw), the see that later took his name. He is the only Welsh saint who was canonized by a pope, and he appears in most Anglican calendars. His life was not written before 1090 when Bishop Rhygyfarch composed it to show that Wales was independent of the authority of Canterbury. Not a diocesan bishop in the modern sense, he was the abbot of a monastery who happened to be in bishop's orders. He led a holy life, spread the faith in Wales, and taught many Irish monastics.

**Davidson, Randall Thomas** (1848–1930). Anglican prelate. Davidson was a Scottish-born Presbyterian, educated at Oxford. He became archbishop of Canterbury (1903–1928), after having been bishop of Rochester (1891) and of Winchester (1895). His executive astuteness was demonstrated by his dealing with the Prayer Book revision (1904–1906, 1927–1928), the Kikuyu controversy (1913), the Enabling Act (1919), the disestablishment of the church in Wales (1920), and the Roman Catholic-Anglican conversations at Malines (1921–1925).

**Davies, Samuel** (1723–1761). Presbyterian educator and clergyman. Born in Delaware and educated at the Samuel Blair School in Pennsylvania, he was sent as an evangelist to Virginia, where as a Dissenter he founded strong Presbyterian congregations. He traveled in England on behalf of the College of New Jersey (Princeton) and later became its fourth president. He was known as the greatest preacher of his day.

**Day, John** (1552–1584). Printer in 1562 of the early complete edition, popularly known as Day's Psalter, of the metrical version of The Psalms by Thomas Sternhold (d. 1549) and John Hopkins (d. 1570). Called the Old Version after 1696, it was reissued by other printers and circulated for a century.

**Dead Sea Scrolls.** The name usually given to a great quantity of ancient Hebrew and Aramaic manuscripts and fragments found, beginning in 1947, in caves near the northwestern corner of the Dead Sea. Many of the manuscripts apparently constituted the library of a Jewish sectarian community established at Qumran between c. 135 B.C. and A.D. 68. The manuscripts may have been hidden in the caves for safekeeping when the destruction of the community was imminent. Although many of the manuscripts were stored in large earthen jars, none entirely without damage still exist and most survive only in tiny fragments.

All the books of the Old Testament except Esther are represented by at least a few fragments. The most complete manuscript is a scroll of Isaiah from beginning to end, which was probably made in the 2d century B.C. The Biblical fragments are significant for Old Testament studies because they are a thousand years older than any previous texts known, and they demonstrate the remarkable accuracy of transmission to the later tradition.

A number of other works, not previously known at all, reveal the nature of the sectarian community at Qumran. Among these are Old Testament commentaries, psalms of thanksgiving, an apocalyptic work usually designated as The War of the Sons of Light Against the Sons of Darkness, and a sectarian handbook, the Manual of Discipline. They provide new insights into some aspects of Jewish religious life at the time of Jesus Christ.

**Dean** (from Latin *decanus,* "head of ten"). Ecclesiastical title. It refers to: (1) senior cardinal bishop of the Sacred College of Cardinals; (2) senior of each of four classes of prelate in the Roman Curia, as established by Apostolic Constitution *Ad incrementum* (1934); (3) presiding priest of a cathedral or collegiate chapter; (4) head of a faculty; (5) priest who exercises a limited jurisdiction over a portion of a diocese, called rural dean (sometimes, archpriest).

**Decius** (d. 251). Roman emperor from 249. Philip the Arabian, who celebrated the thousandth anniversary of Rome only to find the Empire crumbling under him, decided that the one person who could save it was the wise senator G. Messius Quintus Trajanus Decius. The problem of the age was that the army had control of emperor-making. Ironically, the man whom Philip raised to protect him from the army was the man the army chose to replace him.

However reluctantly Decius began his rule, he sought to hold the Empire together. Since he saw the reason for the decline of Rome in the waning of the moral and spiritual virtues of the old Roman religion, he revived the office of censor and put into effect what became known as the Decian persecution, a title probably reflecting Christian self-consciousness. Whether by design or not, the procedure that was followed threatened the organization of the church severely. All inhabitants of the Empire were required to sacrifice to one of the Roman gods on a certain day in behalf of the emperor. The Christians were among those whose consciences forbade this act of citizenship. However, it was simple to procure *libelli pacis,* certificates falsely testifying that sacrifice had been offered, and even those who were tried for failure to sacrifice were offered every encouragement to comply.

The Christian community condemned the *libellatici*, who had purchased certificates, and more strongly the *sacrificati*, who had actually sacrificed, and when Decius was killed in battle against the Goths, he left a church greatly disorganized by the cowardice of many of its members under fire.

**Declaration, Royal** (*or* Declaration of the Sovereign). A coronation oath required of all sovereigns of England after William III and Mary (1689). Designed to ensure that no Roman Catholic should succeed to the throne, and based on a principle enunciated in the Declaration of Rights (1689), it was originally a simple acceptance of that principle. Later it was expanded into a detailed abjuration, but in 1910 it was simplified to its present form.

**Declaration of the Rights of Man and the Citizen.** Adopted on Aug. 26, 1789, by the French National Assembly as a preamble to the new French Constitution. The work of Lafayette, Mounier, Mirabeau, Rabaut-Saint-Étienne, among others, it contained an introduction about the "natural, inalienable and sacred rights of man" and seventeen articles, in all about five hundred words.

In the "presence and under the auspices of the Supreme Being" it acknowledged that "men are born and remain free and equal in rights." Thus it repudiated all legal and hereditary differences of rank or order except those based on "common utility." The state exists to preserve the natural rights of "liberty, property, security, and resistance to oppression." The Declaration then concerned itself with the nature of liberty, bounded by the rights of others, and the nature of law and authority. Rights belong not to "man" only but to man as "citizen" who possesses a share in sovereignty and in the formation of law. The Declaration has been called a "direction of intention," the death certificate of the old regime, the birth certificate of the new. There have been many controversies over (1) the sources of the Declaration, e.g., Calvinistic, American, or Rousseau's *Le Contrat Social;* (2) its basic impact, e.g., as individualist or collectivist; and (3) its influence upon other such declarations, e.g., the Declaration of the Rights of Man published by the United Nations in 1948. The French Declaration remains the chief single document of the 18th-century revolutions.

**Declarations of Indulgence.** Royal proclamations of post-Restoration England, three by Charles II and one by James II; because the last was republished with alterations there may be said to be five in all. (1) The first was issued on Oct. 25, 1660, announcing Charles II's intention of convening a conference to carry out the Declaration of Breda and of granting indulgence in some ceremonial practices until the conference (Savoy Conference, 1661) should have regularized these and other matters. (2) The second, Dec. 26, 1662, reiterated Charles's intention of fulfilling the undertaking of Breda and asking Parliament for greater freedom in suspending penal laws in matters ecclesiastical. Parliamentary action nullified the declaration (1663). (3) The third, March 15, 1672, granted indemnity to recusants and nonconformists, but it was viewed as a breach of the prerogatives of Parliament, which caused its withdrawal (1673). (4) The inclusive indulgence of James I, April 4, 1687, suspended penal laws for both Roman Catholic and nonconformist worship and lifted the Test Act restrictions for those in the king's service. (5) An altered form of the previous declaration, April 27, 1688, was required to be read in all churches. The five declarations, intended for relief of both Roman Catholics and nonconformists, paved the way for the Bill of Rights (1689), which ensured that relief would be legislative rather than by royal declaration.

**Decretals.** In the first and strict sense, the pope's answer to an appeal or his advice on a question of discipline. Such a response to a specific question addressed to him possesses binding force upon the recipient. The earliest decretal is the letter of Pope Siricius (384–399) to Himerius, bishop of Terragona in Spain. In a second sense, decretals refer to collections of papal responses to questions. Such collections are of later date than the false decretals (c. 850) and Gratian's *Decretum* (c. 1150). Between 1150 and 1234 five such collections were made, together known as the *Quinque compilationes antiquae.* The best known of these five was the last, made by Raymond of Peñafort under Pope Gregory IX, completed in 1234. Later authoritative collections were made by Boniface VIII (1298), *Sextus liber decretalium,* and Clement V (1317), *Liber septimus decretalium,* or known as simply *Clementinae.* The various collections were further codified by Jean Chappuis in 1500.

**Decretum Gelasianum.** The common title given to the Latin work *De libris recipiendis et non recipiendis,* which indicates an ancient attribution of authorship. The document deals with the relations of the Second and Third Persons of the Trinity, the canon of the Bible, Roman primacy, orthodox councils and fathers, and apocryphal writings of the Bible and the fathers. Its Biblical canon is the accepted one. The degree of Gelasius' responsibility for the decretal is in doubt. Dobschütz dates the work in the early 6th century.

**Defender of the Faith** (*Fidei Defensor*). A title conferred by bull of Leo X (Oct. 11, 1521) upon Henry VIII for his *Assertion of the Seven Sacraments,* an attack upon Luther's *A Prelude on the Babylonian Captivity of the Church* (1520). The title was sought by Henry as equivalent to titles assumed by the kings of France and Spain. It continued to be used after separation from Rome (1533), and by act of Parliament (1544) it became an official title borne by all English monarchs after that time.

**Defenestration of Prague** (1618). The incident that precipitated the Thirty Years' War. In 1609 the Hapsburg rulers of Bohemia had granted religious freedom to the Utraquist Church and the Bohemian Brethren. When, under an extremist Roman Catholic ruling council, this freedom began to be infringed upon, a group of noblemen broke into the room in Prague where the council was meeting (May 23, 1618) and hurled two of its most outspoken members from a window (Latin, *fenestra*) into a moat below. Religious as well as political turmoil in Bohemia provided a powerful impetus toward the Thirty Years' War. Very shortly, however, the hostilities turned to the disadvantage of Bohemian Protestantism when the forces of the emperor Ferdinand II won the battle of White Mountain (1620).

**De Haeretico Comburendo** ("On Burning Heretics"). An act of the English Parliament (1401) to put down Lollardy, the first English legislation to authorize the death penalty for heresy. If found guilty by an ecclesiastical court, the condemned man was to be released to the secular powers and burned "in a high place" to instill fear into the populace. The act was expanded by Henry V, rescinded by Henry VIII, restored by Philip and Mary, and at last repealed by Elizabeth I.

**Deism.** A theological attitude midway between traditionalism and radical skepticism (or atheism), generally signifying a belief in God, even though it is frequently used in contradistinction to theism. Historically, deism did not reflect the beliefs of a specific sect; as an attitude, it was almost exclusively confined to the intellectuals among the upper classes. These philosophers, instead of concentrating upon religion per se, sought to express their antagonism to the current conceptions of the Christian tradition. In mirroring the secular-ism of their day, they offered a philosophical and ethical substitute for revelation, based upon the power of human reason.

Chiefly in vogue during the 17th and 18th centuries, deism was foreshadowed by the humanists of the 16th century (Erasmus, for example) who had tried to create a purer theology through the use of reason and the exclusion of those "extraneous" traditions which had attached themselves to the simple Christianity of the Gospels. The later movement appeared first in England, just as the Anglican Church suffered the full weight of the Puritan assault. In 1624, Lord Herbert of Cherbury, the so-called "Father of English Deism," essayed to restore sectarian peace by preparing a confession of faith to which all rational men might subscribe. He and many like-minded thinkers were less concerned with spirituality than with ethics; they desired to discover a minimum creed that would put an end to the controversies which threatened to lead to armed conflict and civil war. The scientific rationalism of the late 17th century (the Newtonian revolution) reinforced the ideas of the early deists. The desire for social harmony seemed analogous to the harmonious proportions of the universe, revealed in Newton's famous *Principia mathematica.* Scientific discoveries also cast doubt upon the truth of traditional theology. Reason demanded a godly Prime Mover and a moral law with future punishments and rewards. This was "natural religion"; all else besides, as "revelation," was regarded as expendable. There followed a number of disputes between the deists, who wished to "purify" Christianity, and the orthodox, who sought to retain as much of revelation as possible. The deists attacked everything considered irrational; they assailed such buttresses of revelation as prophecies and miracles. They also criticized what they described as the inhumanity of historic Christianity. Traditional religion, devoid of right reason, had allegedly contributed little to the moral improvement of mankind. The orthodox replied by showing that natural religion possessed no more in the way of rationality than revelation: both were founded upon a set of assumptions that remained unproved; both were ultimately founded upon faith. In England, the deists hoped to reduce religion to an ethical code and to transform the Established Church into a quasi department of morality within the government. The movement lost momentum after the middle of the 18th century, owing to the rise of the Wesleyans and the Evangelicals, both of whom embraced a more enthusiastic religion than that afforded by the rational deists. They succeeded to such an extent, among the upper and lower classes alike, that they inspired the vital Christianity of the 19th century.

In France, deism served a political as well as an ethical purpose. Voltaire hoped, for example, that natural religion would shape a better citizenry; he also used rationalism to attack the corruption and anti-intellectualism of the entrenched Roman Catholic Church. The resistance of the Roman clergy in France was in marked contrast to the submissiveness of their counterparts within the Church of England. The French deists were held up to abuse as a danger to the fabric of society that had existed under the old regime.

In Germany, deism became fashionable among the upper classes after 1750; but there, as elsewhere in Europe, a spiritual reaction followed, generally referred to as the Romantic movement. Nevertheless, deism established an ideal of liberty and toleration that all right-thinking men might endorse. It promoted an improvement in public morals, and as a corollary of its rejection of revelation, it emphasized the value of scholarship as an aid to a purer religion. The monumental Biblical studies of the 19th century followed as a direct consequence. The deist's attempts to reconcile religion with science, as well as with many other intellectual currents, set a precedent for all subsequent reconstructions in religion.

BIBLIOGRAPHY: C. L. Becker, *The Heavenly City of the Eighteenth-Century Philosophers* (New Haven, 1959); G. R. Cragg, *The Church and the Age of Reason: 1648–1789* (Grand Rapids, 1962); P. Hazard, *The European Mind: 1680–1715* (Cleveland, 1964); A. C. McGiffert, *Protestant Thought Before Kant* (New York, 1962); R. R. Palmer, *Catholics and Unbelievers in Eighteenth-Century France* (Princeton, 1939).

**De La Taille, Maurice** (1872–1933). French Roman Catholic theologian. De La Taille entered the Jesuit Order in England, in 1890, and after further study at Lyons, taught theology at the Catholic Institute of Angers. From 1919 he taught at the Gregorian University in Rome. In his chief work, *Mysterium fidei* (1921), he emphasized the unity of the Mass with the acts of Christ at the Last Supper and on Calvary; the Mass is seen as simply the reoffering of Christ's sacrifice, not as a new sacrifice. De La Taille also worked out a general theory of the natural-supernatural relationship ("created actuation by Uncreated Act").

**Della Robbia.** Name of a talented Florentine family of artists and craftsmen that flour-ished during the Renaissance in Italy. Most famous and creative of them was Luca della Robbia (d. 1482), goldsmith and sculptor. His best-known surviving work, the *cantoria,* or choir loft, of singing angels and dancing boys sculptured in marble, is now in the Museo del Duomo in Florence. Luca also discovered a new technique for glazing terra-cotta. He was aided and later succeeded by his nephew, Andrea della Robbia (d. 1528), and his sons.

**Democracy, Catholic** (*or* Christian). A term approved by Leo XIII (1901) for Catholic groups aiming to comfort and uplift the lower classes. Growing out of church interest in labor expressed a decade before in *Rerum novarum,* it spurred Congress and Catholic Action groups in Germany, France, Spain, and Italy. Abuse was detected by the papacy when some Christian Democrats accommodated themselves to socialism and warred against ultramontane Catholics.

**De Motione Oecumenica** (Dec. 20, 1949). A Holy Office directive to bishops of the Roman Catholic Church dealing with ecumenism. It was a clarification after the World Council of Churches Assembly at Amsterdam (1948) had invited Catholic participation. Prelates were to watch over the ecumenical movement, to promote and direct it with prudence, to assist those seeking the truth, and to protect the faithful Catholics from dangers that could easily result from the movement.

**Denck, Hans** (c. 1500–1527). A "marginal Anabaptist" whose writings were esteemed in later Anabaptism. He began as a humanist and teacher, but in Nuremberg became an active discussant in radical lay groups reading Thomas Müntzer and Andreas Carlstadt. He thereafter preached a nonchiliastic "evangelical monism," seeking utter sincerity of expression of faith in believers' fellowships. For a time he defended rebaptism of believers. He died of the plague in Basel in 1527.

**Denmark, Conversion of.** The first missionary was Willibrord (700), followed by Ebo in 822. In 827, Ansgar began his work as the "Apostle of Scandinavia." After his death (865) the mission languished until Harold Bluetooth (960–985), who unified Denmark, and his son Sweyn Forkbeard (985–1014) championed Christianity. Under Canute the Great (1014–1035) the faith was established. In 1022 three bishops were consecrated for the Danish sees at Canterbury.

**Denominationalism.** The system and ideology founded on the division of the religious population into numerous ecclesiastical bodies, each stressing particular values or traditions and each competing with the other in the same community under substantial conditions of freedom. Thus denominationalism has usually been associated with religious pluralism, voluntaryism, mutual respect and recognition, and neutrality on the part of the state. Though these conditions were sometimes present in the 17th century, the word itself seems to have become current in the 18th-century Revival, as in John Wesley's wish, "But from real Christians, of whatever *denomination,* I earnestly desire not to be distinguished at all."

Sociologists of religion have made more technical use of the term, often employing it in revising or expanding the church-sect dichotomy developed by Max Weber and Ernst Troeltsch. Finding these classic types more appropriate to Continental Christianity than to the Anglo-American experience, sociologists have sometimes sought to establish the denomination as a discrete form, divorced (unlike the church) from privilege or domination in society, but also accommodated (unlike the sect) to its rivals and to the world. Under American conditions religious bodies beginning as churches, cults, or sects have ordinarily been unstable and have at length made their compromises, abandoned claims to universality or exclusiveness, and so evolved into denominations.

Historically, denominationalism has been a modern phenomenon. The collapse of Western Christian unity in the 16th century laid the basis for a plurality of competing ecclesiastical institutions. However, in most instances Reformation rulers were able to uphold a practical territorial uniformity until France, Holland, and England began to adjust to some religious diversity by the end of the century. The creative moment for the rise of denominationalism lay in the triumph and fragmentation of Puritanism in mid-17th-century England. Agreed upon the destruction of Laudianism, Puritans failed to agree on polity, worship, and theology, and finally formed competing congregations and connections. These assumed permanent form in the Restoration Settlement and (with the 1689 Toleration Act and the 18th-century Methodist secession) transformed Anglican uniformity into denominational pluralism.

The theory of denominationalism emerged from the same milieu. Building on the Reformers' cautions against hallowing particular churchly forms and on their acceptance of the several Protestant divisions as true churches, Puritan Independents argued for a necessary diversity *and* Christian unity. The denominational fellowship did not claim an exclusive identity with the true church but rather a true expression of the unity of faith. The believer followed Christ according to his light, but he did not condemn his brother of another way. In such diversity Christian communities might enlighten, correct, and enrich each other's vision. This view of the church resting in its various denominations underlay the Independent Cromwellian church experiment. Eclipsed at the Restoration, it soon came to dominate all nonconformity and ultimately to penetrate Anglicanism as well.

American religious history has displayed the richest development of denominationalism. From the beginning, numerous religious bodies, both British and Continental, found shelter in America. Toleration, a practical necessity, was widely practiced in the colonial era and triumphed in the new republic. Mobility of population and the collapse of Anglican and Congregational regional predominances established ecclesiastical equality and competition everywhere. This environment powerfully modified churchly tradition and eroded sectarian exclusiveness and isolation. All became denominations, especially as churches sensed the need for cooperation in common problems, such as that of reaching the unchurched. The denominational system came to fullest realization in 19th-century evangelical Protestantism with its competing national organizations, its sense of ecclesiastical mutuality, and its free voluntary societies for the pursuit of common Christian purposes. Thereafter, despite the usefulness of the system in accommodating indigenous churches and immigrant religions, conscious denominationalism weakened in the 20th-century decline of theology, the development of religious-cultural assimilation, the ascendancy of interdenominational agencies and projects, and the drive for structural unification of denominations.

BIBLIOGRAPHY: W. S. Hudson, *The Great Tradition of the American Churches* (New York, 1953); S. E. Mead, *The Lively Experiment* (New York, 1963); H. R. Niebuhr, *The Social Sources of Denominationalism* (New York, 1957); E. Troeltsch, *The Social Teaching of the Christian Churches,* 2 vols. (New York, 1960).

**Descartes, René** (1596–1650). French thinker and one of the fathers of modern philosophy. Born at La Haye, he received his education at the Jesuit College of La Flèche. He spent the years from 1612 to 1625 in military service and travel. After a short stay in Paris he moved to Holland in 1629 in search of solitude, remaining until 1649, when he went to Sweden. He died there the following year. Trained in Scholastic thought but dissatisfied with the controversies of the philosophical schools, he determined to reform philosophy by means of a consistent application of mathematical norms to its formation and findings, viz., to judge all ideas on the basis of their clearness and distinctness. First, by application of radical doubt to all existing ideas he reduced knowledge to the one irreducible intuition, the thinking self. From this intuition arose his basic affirmation: "I think, therefore I am" (*Cogito, ergo sum*). From this foundation he readmitted ideas that passed the test of clarity and distinctness and all ideas that could be deduced therefrom. The first distinct idea of which the thinking self is aware was, according to Descartes, God, whose existence may be deduced from the idea of him as all good, all wise, and all powerful. The presence of this rational and moral God was, for Descartes, the basis for the postulation of a rational and beneficial universe. Although he spent much time in observing nature and devising important mathematical and physical laws, the real basis for his thought was in this view of natural law founded upon the faithfulness of God rather than upon the observed regularity of nature. His rationalism was the sign of things to come in Western thought. A philosophical movement largely dependent on his thought, hence "Cartesian," developed in the late 17th and early 18th centuries on the Continent, especially at Utrecht and Leiden. Descartes's rational, mechanistic concept of the universe also influenced the development of English deism, particularly the thought of John Toland, who emphasized the rational element in natural religion.

**Desert.** A word descriptive of the austerity of life and habitation of certain ascetical communities such as the early Egyptian "desert fathers," of which Antony of Egypt (d. 356) was an example. The term "desert" was used by the followers of Nilus the Ascetic, who founded a monastery near Ancyra, and the followers of Romuald in Italy, as well as by the Carthusians later. The reformed (Discalced) Carmelites have also referred to their convents in this way, relating themselves to the first Christian hermits.

**Deventer.** Location of a community of lay Brethren of the Common Life established through the influence of Gerhard Groote. Unlike the monastic house at Windesheim, which received papal approval, Deventer struggled against the hostility of the Inquisition (1398), first because Deventer was a lay community without vows, and secondly because its devotion centered on the study of the Scriptures

in the vernacular. With certain minor exceptions, the work of the Brethren at Deventer was vindicated. They gave themselves to a spiritual life without withdrawal from the world and became especially noted for their labor as educators.

*Devotio Moderna.* A movement of religious renewal begun about the end of the 14th century. It emphasized a personal, interior spirituality in reaction against the supposed intellectualism of late Scholasticism. Its founders were Gerhard Groote and his Deventer circle, which included Florentius Radewyns, Zerbolt von Zutphen, and others. It was carried on by the Brethren of the Common Life and by the community of Windesheim. From the Netherlands, it spread to France, Italy, and Spain, where it influenced Ignatius of Loyola and Jiménez de Cisneros. Based on meditation on the life and passion of Christ, its classic expression is the *Imitation of Christ.* It was a powerful stimulus both to popular education, through the model Deventer school, and to the translation of the Bible into the vernacular.

**De Wette, Wilhelm** (1780–1849). Professor of theology at Heidelberg, Berlin, and Basel. De Wette was an influential teacher and prolific writer during his entire career. His theological position was originally rationalistic, and De Wette was removed from his post at Berlin in 1819, but influenced by his colleague Schleiermacher, he moved toward a more conservative position. He was appointed to a chair at Basel in 1822. His works include studies of the Old and New Testaments, systematic theology, church history, ethics, and even a novel. By holding that feeling was the basis of religion, De Wette tried to harmonize rationalism and belief in revelation.

**Diamper** (Udiamper), **Synod of.** A meeting that took place on June 20, 1599, in the village today called Udiamper, on the Malabar Coast of India. The purpose of the synod was to renounce certain Nestorian errors that had found their way into the Malabar tradition and to promise loyalty to Rome. The union was due in great part to the undaunted efforts of Alexis de Menezes, Latin archbishop of Goa, who brought in Jesuits to work among the natives, took over a see vacated by a Syrian (Nestorian) prelate, and himself visited parishes to talk with the people and give them the sacraments.

**Didache** (*or* "The Teaching of the Lord to the Gentiles Through the Twelve Apostles"). A manual of church discipline from a very early date which was first published in 1883.

In 1875, Philotheos Bryennios, metropolitan of Nicomedia, had discovered a manuscript of it written in 1056 by a notary named Leo. It was the property of the Greek patriarchate of Jerusalem (thus called Codex Hierosolymitanus) and had come from the hospice of the Holy Sepulcher Church in Constantinople. This codex also contains Barnabas, Clement, and Ignatius. Clement of Alexandria seemed to regard the work as Scripture, but he did not discriminate carefully between canonical and noncanonical books. The Didache became outmoded when its teaching was supplanted by the *Didascalia apostolorum* and the Apostolic Constitutions, and passed out of use except, to a limited extent, in Egypt.

The Didache begins with a catechetical description of the "two ways" of life and death, based in essence on Deut. 30:15. Many theories have been presented pointing to more immediate sources. There are obvious connections with Jewish apocalyptic literature, especially with the Manual of Discipline of the Qumran community. Some have suggested that the Didache was copied from the Epistle of Barnabas and others that they both depend on the Greek original of the *Doctrina apostolorum*. After a brief statement about baptism, the text sets forth two Eucharistic prayers closely related to Jewish meal blessings, but states that prophets do not have to follow these models. Then comes a discussion of the marks of true apostles and prophets and of the community's duties toward the latter, their "high priests." The ambivalence of the attitude of the Didache toward prophets has led some scholars to predicate a Montanist provenance for it, and others to contend that it was written against the Montanists. The ambiguities could be resolved by assuming that it is a Catholic reediting of a Montanist work, or that it comes from the 1st century. The ministry of itinerant apostles and of the more settled prophets needs to be coordinated with the (newer?) ministry of bishops and deacons. The document ends with a prediction of the imminent return of Christ. In the Coptic version there is also a prayer to be used with the baptismal chrism.

The date of the Didache, like that of other liturgical documents, is difficult to determine. If it has been archaized, it may well come from the latter years of the 2d century, though obviously before Clement. If it is a genuine reflection of the situation it purports to describe, the only *terminus post quem* is set by its reflection of the Gospel of Matthew, to which it refers as "the gospel." Like other similar documents, it may well be composite, expanded from an original nucleus. In general,

critics agree that it comes from Syria in the second half of the 1st century; the practices described in it are therefore even older.

If this is so, the Jewishness of the Didache reflects the church of Jerusalem or a church closely related to it, and the picture of the ministry resembles what Paul says of "apostles, prophets, and teachers" in I Corinthians, though in the Didache the main emphasis is on prophets. The ministry of these prophets is on the verge of being replaced by that of bishops and deacons, though wandering prophets are already being supplanted by those who remain in residence.

Baptism in the name of Father, Son, and Holy Spirit is already the normal practice, while the Lord's Prayer with the doxological ending is being recited thrice daily. Christians fast on Wednesdays and Fridays instead of on Mondays and Thursdays on which the Jews fast. The Eucharist described in the Didache contains no reference to the Words of Institution, and the blessing of the cup precedes the blessing of the bread (cf. I Cor. 10:16). One question is whether or not the Didachist describes everything to be found in the Eucharist of his time. If he does describe everything, some support is given to the view that not all Eucharists made use of the Last Supper as a pattern. The uncertainty of date, however, makes any argument about catechetical, liturgical, or hierarchical constitution that is based primarily on the Didache very much open to question.

BIBLIOGRAPHY: R. A. Kraft (ed.), *The Apostolic Fathers*, Vol. 3 (New York, 1965); E. J. Goodspeed and R. M. Grant, *A History of Early Christian Literature* (Chicago, 1966); J. A. Robinson, *Barnabas, Hermas and the Didache* (New York, 1920); F. E. Vokes, *The Riddle of the Didache* (New York, 1938).

**Didascalia Apostolorum.** "The Catholic Teaching of the Twelve Holy Apostles and Disciples of the Savior," otherwise called "Direction(s) of the Apostles" by Epiphanius (*Panarion* 45. 4. 5, *et passim*). It was written in the early 3d century for a Jewish-Christian church in northern Syria by its bishop. Except for minor fragments and quotations, the Greek original is lost, but a Syriac translation is extant, a partial Latin (less than half) version, and Coptic, Ethiopic, and Arabic versions. Similar to Pauline paraenesis, it directly addresses certain kinds of people, especially the bishop, so its form is not like that of church orders. Its viewpoint shows that certain problems were faced in the Syrian Church of the 3d century. Distinguishing between moral and ceremonial aspects of the law, it calls the latter *deuterōsis,* while its concern for penance reflects a laxist attitude toward postbaptismal sins. Further, it contains a long list of directions governing not only moral problems but liturgical and ecclesiastical questions as well, thus showing a strong hierarchical organization of the church. In point of time, the *Didascalia* stands midway between the Didache, which it employs as a source, and the Apostolic Constitutions, for the first six books of which it forms the basic outline.

**Diderot, Denis** (1713–1784). French writer and philosopher. Educated in Paris, Diderot several times intended to take up an ecclesiastical career, especially c. 1741. He was a close friend of Rousseau's (1743–1758). He served as chief editor of the grand *Encyclopédie* (1751–1772), with Jean Le Rond d'Alembert as associate in the early volumes. Diderot wrote many of the articles, including history of philosophy, mechanical arts, and social theory. Voltaire, Rousseau, Turgot, Holbach, and others were contributors. The encyclopedia proposed to further knowledge and strike a blow at reactionary forces in church and state. Firm trust in human progress and rationalism were underlying assumptions of the work. After the *Encyclopédie,* Diderot depended on Catherine the Great of Russia for income, visiting Russia in 1773. In an age of radical transition Diderot attempted to replace priestly teleology with a cosmic theory that conformed to the ideas of science. He stressed the versatility of material substance. His *Lettres sur les aveugles* (1749), emphasizing empiricism and atheism, was part of his slowly evolving philosophical materialism. He often argued on both sides of a moral question, reveling in the radical transitions of emphasis. His novels, plays, short stories, and correspondence were largely unpublished until the 19th century. Diderot worked to popularize deism, the mechanical universe, and socioreligious and moral reform in accord with enlightened ideals.

**"Dies Irae."** A hymn used as a part of the Requiem Mass and in the Mass for All Souls' Day. One of the most beautiful and moving hymns of the church, its first lines are: "Day of wrath, that Day, The world will be in ashes, As David and the Sibyls say." It dates from the 13th century, and has traditionally been ascribed to Thomas of Celano (d. 1255).

**Dietrich of Niem** (Nieheim) (1340–1418). German conciliarist. A native of Westphalia, Dietrich served as a curial official at Avignon. There, in addition to his other duties, he wrote a history of the Western Schism in 1409 and 1410. In 1410 he also brought out a theoretical work on church government that reflected the views of Occam and Marsilius of Padua. In 1414 he wrote a program of reform for the Council of Constance. He also made major contributions to the history of Germany.

**Digenes Akrites** (Basil Digenes Akritas; Basil, "born of two races," the "frontiersman"). The eponymous hero of a Byzantine epic poem which seems to be set in the 10th century. Digenes was the offspring of a Moslem father and a Greek Christian mother. His position is quite similar to that of the Cid in Spanish folklore. He died after a lifetime spent in keeping peace on the borders of Byzantium in Mesopotamia.

**Diggers.** The followers of Gerrard Winstanley (1609–1652), who believed that since the earth was God's creation, it was common property for all to use. Winstanley and his democratic, mystical group began digging up and planting the commons at George Hill, Surrey, in 1649, for which act they were arrested. This phenomenon broke out all across England, especially in Buckinghamshire, Middlesex, Berkshire, and Hertfordshire. They were considered "sectaries" by their contemporaries.

**Dilthey, Wilhelm** (1833–1911). German philosopher. He was professor at Berlin following Rudolph H. Lotze in 1882. His particular interest was in the examination and explanation of the human spirit and its expression in history and culture. He stood firmly against a mechanical or deterministic approach to these concerns, maintaining that the dynamic creativity of man defied such an approach. Strongly influenced in his hermeneutical theories and method by Schleiermacher, he has in turn influenced all modern discussions of the subject.

**Diocese.** An ecclesiastical administrative territory subject to the jurisdiction of a bishop. In Roman law the term was used to designate the area surrounding a city (*civitas*) and administered by it. The emperor Diocletian applied it to his twelve subdivisions of the Empire. In Christian usage, diocese was first applied in the East to the area subject to a patriarch (cf. Council of Constantinople, 381, Canon 2). In the West, the territory under a bishop's jurisdiction was first called *ecclesia,* but after the 4th century *parochia* and *diocese* were used interchangeably, the former falling into disuse by the 10th century. From the 4th century it was general practice for each *civitas* to have its bishop, so that civil and ecclesiastical boundaries were often coterminous (cf. Council of Chalcedon, 451, Canon 17). In early centuries the establishment of dioceses was regulated by synods or princes, but from the 11th century on in the West it was reserved to the pope (*Dictatus papae* of Gregory VII). The jurisdiction of missionary bishops was not limited to a diocese, e.g., Willibrord in the Netherlands, Boniface in Germany, Augustine in England, but they organized dioceses. Assisting the bishop in diocesan administration is a vicar-general, a chancellor, a chapter of canons, and especially in medieval times, the archdeacon. The bishop maintained an episcopal court of appeals which also served as a court of first instance for his own household.

**Diocletian** (245–313). Roman emperor (284–305). He was a Dalmatian of humble birth who rose in the ranks of the Eastern army. In 284 he was commander of the imperial guard, and upon the death of Numerianus was proclaimed emperor. In order to secure the boundaries of the Empire, it became necessary to evolve a new imperial system in which he shared the governance with others. Diocletian raised Maximian to the dignity of "Augustus," and Galerius and Constantius to that of "Caesar." Diocletian and Galerius, his caesar, ruled in the East; Maximian and Constantius, in the West. This arrangement was fundamental to a sweeping reorganization of the Empire into dioceses and provinces. The Empire became more efficient as a bureaucracy and lost much of the trappings remaining from the republic and the Augustan settlement. Diocletian made his capital Nicomedia; Maximian, Milan. The importance of Rome correspondingly declined, and the seeds of the separation of the Empire were sown. In 303 the Diocletian persecution of Christians began. Though centered in Nicomedia, the persecution, legally authorized, spread as far as Africa. Eusebius regards Galerius as responsible for the anti-Christian edicts. In 305, Diocletian (accompanied by Maximian) abdicated. He spent the last nine years of his life in retirement at Salona in Dalmatia.

**Diodorus of Tarsus** (d. c. 390). Ruler of an Antiochene monastery, and bishop of Tarsus from 378. Banished by the Arian emperor Valens in 372, but present at the Council of Constantinople in 381, he was the teacher of John Chrysostom and Theodore of Mopsuestia. Although evidence is fragmentary, he clearly stands at the threshold of the sober, nonallegorical, exegetical, and theological school of Antioch. It was this tradition which nourished the thought of Nestorius.

**Diognetus, Epistle to.** A composite apologetic work of unknown authorship originating in Asia Minor, no earlier than the 3d century in its present form. The first section (chs. 1–10) may be as early as Quadratus, while the remainder (chs. 10–12) is a homily probably arising in circles close to Hippolytus. The whole work, in the tradition of Ephesians and I Peter, is in good rhetorical style, though the naïveté of the earlier section regarding pagan religion reflects early 2d-century thought.

**Dionysius** (2d century). Bishop of Corinth (c. 170) and author of seven "catholic epistles" to churches in Greece, Bithynia, Crete, Pontus, and Rome, and another to a certain Chrysophora. Only Eusebius mentions them, but the fragments he quotes show that Dionysius was a militant anti-Marcionite, opposed to excessive asceticism, and an advocate of episcopal authority, especially as exercised in the Roman Church, whose charitable work he praised.

**Dionysius** (Denys), **the Carthusian** (Denys van Leenwen *or* Denys Ryckel, 1402–1471). Mystic and theologian. After studying at the University of Cologne, where he became a Master of Arts, he entered the Carthusian cloister at Bethlehem Mariae in 1424. Because of his literary zeal, which extended to all areas of philosophy and theology, and because of his God-filled life, the "Doctor Ecstaticus" gained a widespread reputation. He has been characterized as the "last Scholastic," and his mystical writings have had considerable influence.

**Dionysius Exiguus** (d. c. 544). A Roman monk of Scythian origin. He is supposed to have translated into Latin several works of Gregory of Nyssa and the *Life of St. Pachomius*. His collection of canon law, *Collectio Dionysiana*, remained in use for several centuries. He devised the present system for numbering years from the birth of Christ (see ANNO DOMINI).

**Dionysius the Areopagite.** Paul's Athenian convert (Acts 17:34), later assumed to have been the first bishop of Athens, and in legend a philosopher who had felt the earth tremble at the crucifixion; but the name is most commonly used in reference to a 5th-century Syrian mystic who issued his writings in the name of Dionysius, therefore called Pseudo-Dionysius the Areopagite. His use of the late Neoplatonist Proclus, and his references to church customs of his time, such as the use of the creed in the liturgy (introduced at Antioch about 475), indicate a date not earlier than 480. At a conference held at

Constantinople in 533 the Monophysite Severus of Antioch assumed, and his orthodox opponents denied, the authenticity of the Dionysian writings. For a thousand years thereafter they were given almost apostolic authority; their authenticity was not seriously disputed until the 15th century and was defended as late as the 19th century. The anonymous author seems to have intended to impress rather than to deceive, since he gives himself away by obvious anachronisms such as quotations from Ignatius of Antioch. The name of Dionysius and the rather histrionic impressiveness of his style, however, gave his writings an influence they might not otherwise have had.

Pseudo-Dionysius endeavors to combine with his Christian faith the Neoplatonic principle of the superessential, ineffable absolute, beyond personality and impersonality, but linked with the visible world by a hierarchy of being. His Christology seems to follow the Henoticon of Zeno, avoiding both Chalcedonian and Monophysite formulas. He discusses the manifestations of deity in the *Divine Names,* and its expression through the orders of angels in the *Celestial Hierarchy,* and through the orders and rites of the church in the *Ecclesiastical Hierarchy.* Finally, the brief *Mystical Theology* returns to his central theme, the mysticism of the divine darkness which is also the ineffable light. Gregory of Nyssa, one of Dionysius' sources, had given this idea a more profound as well as more Christian expression, but the Dionysian writings popularized it in ascetic and theological circles. The corpus is completed by ten brief *Epistles* on various points of the author's teaching. In Dionysius' Neoplatonic theology the Trinity is mainly a symbol of the ultimate unity of the one and the many, but his fascination with triads helped to popularize his ideas. He comments on nine orders of angels (made up by adding cherubim and seraphim to the lists found in the New Testament), and on three clerical orders (bishops, presbyters, and ministers, i.e., deacons), and three sacramental rites (Baptism, the Eucharist, and the blessing of chrism) as assisting the progress of the soul through purification and illumination to perfect union with God. Through his influence this latter scheme found a permanent place in Christian piety.

Pseudo-Dionysius was used and expounded by many writers greater than himself. Gregory the Great popularized the scheme of nine orders of angels, and among commentators were Maximus the Confessor in the 7th century, Thomas Aquinas in the 13th, and John Colet in the 16th. In France the Areopagite was identified in the Middle Ages with Dionysius of Paris (probably actually a 3d-century missionary). The interest in the Dionysian writings thus aroused led to an early Latin translation, which the 9th-century Irish scholar John Scotus Eriugena was commissioned to replace by a better one, thus being stimulated in his own Neoplatonic speculations. Finally, the Dionysian writings were valued by later medieval mystics, and early translated in whole or in part into English and other modern languages, and indeed are still read and appreciated for their own sake as classics of mysticism. The unknown Christian Neoplatonist of 5th-century Syria (obviously learned, probably a monk and cleric, but no more can be said of his personality, for efforts at identification have failed) has thus secured fame and success beyond what he could have hoped for.

BIBLIOGRAPHY: C. E. Rolt, *Dionysius the Areopagite on the Divine Names and the Mystical Theology* (London, 1920).

**Dioscorus of Alexandria** (d. 454). Archdeacon under Cyril and his successor as bishop in 444. He pushed to an extreme both the theological position and the political claims of the Alexandrian Church. His victory over Rome and Constantinople at the Robber Council of Ephesus in 449 was followed by his deposition at the Council of Chalcedon in 451. He was banished to Gangra in Asia Minor, where he died in 454, thus for Monophysites creating a vacancy at Alexandria.

*Directory of Church Government Anciently Contended For.* English translation (probably by Cartwright) of two short Latin works by Walter Travers. Not to be confused with his earlier and larger *Of Ecclesiastical Discipline,* the *Directory* was written about 1586 as a practical guide for those who wished to establish a Presbyterian framework of polity and discipline within Anglicanism. It was not published in English until 1644.

**Disciples of Christ.** Adherents of the movement originating with Alexander Campbell (1788–1866) and his colleagues. More narrowly, it denotes the largest of the three groups into which the fellowship has parted: (1) Churches of Christ (noninstrumental), (2) Christian Churches (independent or "New Testament"), and (3) Christian Churches (Disciples of Christ).

In 1807, Thomas Campbell fell afoul of the Seceder Presbytery of Chartiers, Pa., for latitudinarian practices. In his "Declaration and Address" he called for unity and for "complete conformity to the Apostolick Church."

His son Alexander accordingly insisted on believer's baptism, and this led to identification with the Baptists.

The dissolution of the Mahoning Baptist Association in 1827 marks the emergence of Disciples as a distinct religious community. In 1831 the Kentucky Disciples informally united with that part of the Christian Churches in the West led by Barton W. Stone.

Through his journal, *Millennial Harbinger,* debates, and preaching tours Alexander Campbell spread the "new Reformation," calling for the union of all Christians on the original faith and order of the apostolic church. This included immersion of believers, weekly Communion, congregational government, the eschewing of sectarian names in favor of designations drawn from Scripture, repudiation of creeds and of speculative theology, a local ministry of elders and deacons chosen from among the people, a general ministry of itinerant evangelists, a doctrine explicitly Biblical and limited to Biblical terminology.

In 1849 the first general convention formed the American Christian Missionary Society, a voluntary association of individuals. Similar societies were organized in the various states, as well as general boards for foreign missions, benevolence, ministerial relief, and other causes. These developments, obviously pragmatic and lacking Biblical authorization, polarized the movement between "progressives" and "conservatives." The latter resisted all "innovations," especially the introduction of musical instruments into public worship. The schism was acknowledged in the Federal Religious Census of 1906, which listed Churches of Christ separately from Disciples of Christ.

The Churches of Christ, adhering rigorously to Biblical authority, and renouncing any organization beyond the congregation, grew to an estimated 2,350,000 members by 1967, though suffering severe internal strains.

In 1917 the International (United States and Canada) Convention of Disciples of Christ was established as an annual meeting for reviewing the reports of agencies; in 1956 the name was changed to International Convention of Christian Churches (Disciples of Christ). Through the convention, Disciples participated in the Federal Council of Churches and in the subsequent National and World Councils of Churches. The United Christian Missionary Society (a coalescence of the agencies) entered into comity agreements abroad, and in the 1950's, Disciples missions were encouraged to assume the status of self-governing churches; several of these have entered into the new united churches, especially in southeast Asia.

Among mainstream Disciples, new tensions polarized around rival journals. In opposition to comity, open membership (acceptance of baptized Christians from other communions without immersion), and liberalism, the more conservative group formed the North American Christian Convention in 1927, launched numerous "independent" missions, and established Bible colleges "loyal to the plea." No formal schism has occurred, despite two parallel sets of institutions. The World Convention of Churches of Christ, meeting at five-year intervals, attracts both "independents" and "cooperatives" (but not members of the noninstrumental Churches of Christ), as well as persons from other countries, especially Great Britain, Australia, New Zealand, and South Africa. The total United States membership of Christian Churches was reported in 1967 as 1,918,000.

Cooperative Disciples have moved from their earlier congregational localism to a recognition of the churchly character of their general organizations. In 1966 the Convention amended its bylaws to change its assembly from a mass meeting to a body composed of voting representatives chosen by congregations. The Convention also received from its Commission on Restructure (for action in 1967) a Provisional Design for the Christian Church (Disciples of Christ).

The chief repository for materials pertaining to all phases of the movement is the Disciples of Christ Historical Society, Nashville, Tenn.

BIBLIOGRAPHY: W. B. Blakemore (ed.), *The Panel of Scholars Reports,* 3 vols. (St. Louis, 1963); W. E. Garrison and A. T. DeGroot, *The Disciples of Christ: A History* (St. Louis, 1948); J. D. Murch, *Christians Only: A History of the Restoration Movement* (Cincinnati, 1962); A. C. Watters, *History of British Churches of Christ* (Indianapolis, 1948).

**Discipline, Books of** (in the Church of Scotland). The Reformers in Scotland attacked what they judged to be papal errors and abuses, including the system of church rule by bishops. The first attempt to constitute the Kirk upon a Reformed base was the First Book of Discipline, presented to the Scottish Parliament in 1560 by John Knox and his colleagues. Under nine major heads it detailed "the policie and discipline of the Church" in conformity with the Word of God. It attempted nothing less than to apply to an entire nation the basic principles of the Ecclesiastical Ordinances of Geneva, but in addition to the ministers and elders recognized by the

Ordinances the Book of Discipline provided for lay "readers," where ministers were not available, and for "superintendents," who assumed some of the administrative functions of the bishops, but remained answerable to the General Assembly, the national synod of the church. Though Parliament did not ratify this document, many of its features became a part of Scottish church life.

When the struggle against episcopacy heightened, the General Assembly adopted in 1581 the Second Book of Discipline, which was essentially Andrew Melville's work. Here the fourfold ministry of presbyterianism is presented (pastors, teachers, elders, and deacons) and calling to the ministry is treated as the right of the people. The names "pastor," "bishop," and "minister" are said to refer to one and the same congregational functionary, whose duty is to preach the word and administer the sacraments.

**Dispensationalism.** A conservative movement which made inroads into practically all the American Protestant denominations after the Civil War by clinging tenaciously to the "essential" Biblical doctrines that were formally articulated at the Niagara Bible Conference of 1895. Combating the Social Gospel movement and theological liberalism, dispensationalism found its inspiration in the writings of the Englishman, J. N. Darby. The movement was greatly facilitated by the *Scofield Reference Bible,* which imposed a rigid schematization on the complex Biblical materials by relating each part of Scripture to a timetable of "dispensations" that were to culminate in the return of Christ to reign in glory. With this basis the movement was spearheaded by itinerant evangelists, popularized at "prophetic" Bible conferences, and supplied with leadership by the newly established "Bible schools."

**Dispensations.** Official relaxation of canon law in particular instances so that acts normally contrary to the law are allowed. The practice of granting dispensations is a recognition of the fact that the letter of the law is not applicable in all cases. It has been in use from an early time. During the Middle Ages it became subject to abuse, but was reformed somewhat by the Council of Trent. Of the various kinds of dispensations, some are reserved to the pope, whereas others may be granted by bishops or priests.

**Dissenting Deputies.** An official lobby representing nonconformist English Protestants. It was founded as early as 1732 to combat the civil disabilities inflicted upon the members of "the Three Denominations" (Baptist, Congregational, and Presbyterian) by the Corporation and Test Acts (1662). Two deputies were selected by each congregation within ten miles of London. Led by a committee of twenty-one London merchants and lawyers, the group motivated almost every judicial or legislative action relieving these disabilities down to the time of its dissolution in 1828 upon the repeal of the Test Act.

**Diuturnum Illud** (June 29, 1881). Encyclical of Leo XIII treating the origin of civil power. It rejected the rationalists' social contract theory, stating that all authority comes from God, though men have the right in some instances to select necessary forms of government. People ought to respect legitimacy. Christianity is a safeguard to public order, since naturalism leads to radical philosophies maintained by force and terror, such as Nihilism, Socialism, and Communism.

**Divine Comedy, The.** A 14th-century narrative poem by Dante Alighieri. Written in Italian during Dante's exile from Florence, it is at once a glorification of the ways of God and a sharp criticism of the ways of men who violate the divine plan. Dante's highly dramatic journey through Hell and Purgatory, guided by the poet Vergil, and through Paradise in the company of his idolized Beatrice, is an intricately detailed vision of the workings of God's justice and love. Dante populates the regions of the afterlife with figures of Biblical and classical familiarity, as well as with men of his own times, distributing them according to their adherence to or interference with God's plan, as Dante envisioned it. He saw the church and the Roman Empire as the two divinely ordained institutions by which men could live in peace on earth and attain their salvation. In assigning popes and politicians to Hell he was pleading for the restoration of both church and empire to their rightful spheres of activity and to their proper center, Rome. As allegory the *Comedy* shows how the soul, lost in a world of materialism, can by led by divine intervention to a recognition of the horrors of sin, a desire for the purgation of its own guilt, and an ascension to the beatific vision of the Godhead. See *The Divine Comedy,* tr. by Dorothy Sayers and Barbara Reynolds (Baltimore, 1962).

**Divine Right of Kings.** The theory that a monarch in the legitimate line has a God-given right to his kingship and authority and that to rebel against him is to rebel against God. If the ruler is evil, it is generally held that passive obedience of a subject is required. Monarchy by divine right has a long history extending well into pre-Christian times. Both Old and New Testaments contain this doctrine; traces of it are found in the ancient conception of king as simultaneously supreme lawgiver and supreme priest. Nevertheless, as a political theory the divine right of kings is of relatively recent origin. Emanating from the coronation and anointing of Christian emperors, divine right has been called a transitional theory of sovereignty between medieval empire and modern independent state. The Protestant Reformers held this view, though they were often ambiguous in its application; Luther argued that a subject may passively disobey his sovereign's command if it is clearly against God's word. Calvin qualified the theory by allowing that lesser magistrates could revolt against greater ones if God's word were being violated. The theory of divine right was highly developed during the English political controversies of the 17th century. Inherent in the English settlement of religion from Henry VIII to Elizabeth I, it came to the fore in the Stuart attempt to protect that settlement from Presbyterian attack. It became overt with Charles I, achieving its acme in the Canons of 1640. Checked by the course of events that culminated in the execution of Charles I, the theory went underground among High Churchmen, but it underlay the Restoration. The Revolution of 1688 forced abdication of James II, putting an end to the theory, which was confined in England henceforth to the Jacobites. Its end as a serious and widespread theory came with the French Revolution. Except for a few modern Jacobites, the Carlists of Spain and the French Royalists, the theory of divine right is now a completely dead issue.

**Divino Afflante Spiritu.** Encyclical letter of Pope Pius XII, "On the Most Opportune Way to Promote Biblical Studies," issued on Sept. 30, 1943. Urging exegetes to make themselves scholars in the languages of the ancient Near East, Pius stated that modern rules of grammar and classical philology were often not adequate for a true comprehension of the "spiritual significance" of passages in Holy Scripture.

**Doane, George Washington** (1799–1859). American Protestant Episcopal bishop. Doane was a strong advocate of the High Church party, demonstrating his friendship for the Oxford movement with the force of his personality. He was noted for his aggressive promotion of mission endeavors and church schools, although the latter were clouded in part by financial mismanagement. He was author of many hymns, among them "Softly Now the Light of Day" and "Fling Out the Banner!"

**Docetism.** Early Christian heresy that Christ's body only appeared to be real and that therefore he only seemed to suffer and die on the cross. The early Christian church moved in an atmosphere of distrust of the material, a view characteristic of the East generally, but also to be found in Greek thought, especially in Alexandria. Docetism (derived from the Greek verb *dokeō*, "to seem"), revolted by the thought of the union of the spiritual Christ with a human, material body, or offended by such teachings as the humiliation and crucifixion of Jesus, denied that the Christ was truly incarnated in a living human body and personality, arguing instead that the Christ only assumed a phantasm in human form like a mask or veil, and therefore only "appeared" to be human. Thus, either the sufferings and death were phantasmal only or they were in fact suffered by someone else (the man Jesus or Simon of Cyrene). This view is perhaps referred to in The First Letter of John, and is mentioned in the Alexandrian fathers. The heresy soon died out, but the basic impulse remained behind to trouble the church for many years.

**Doctors of the Church.** "Doctor" in Latin means "teacher." The Doctors of the Church are men chosen by either the pope or a council for their extraordinary contributions to the life of the church. Preeminent in the West are Ambrose, Augustine, Jerome, and Gregory the Great. The Eastern fathers were originally John Chrysostom, Basil the Great, and Gregory of Nazianzus. From time to time others have been given this title, so that there are now twenty-three Doctors of the Church, sixteen of which are from the West.

**Doddridge, Philip** (1702–1751). English nonconformist minister and hymn writer. The son of a London merchant of nonconformist background, he refused the offer of university training made after the death of his father by the Duke of Bedford, since this would have required him to compromise his nonconformist sympathies. He attended instead the liberal theological academy at Leicestershire. After holding several nonconformist pastorates he moved to Northampton, where he became the principal of the academy and the pastor of a large Independent congregation (1729). Besides his academic and pastoral work, he took part in early charitable efforts and worked out a plan to distribute Bibles in England and abroad. Although the author of a number of books, he is best known for his hymns, which can be found in almost every hymnbook. They include "Hark, the Glad Sound! the Saviour Comes," "My God, and Is Thy Table Spread?" "O God of Bethel, by Whose Hand," and "Ye Servants of the Lord." In 1751 he sailed for Lisbon, where he died soon after his arrival.

**Dodwell, Henry** (1641–1711). Irish scholar and theologian. Independent in thought, he became a significant figure in the nonjuror controversy. In 1691, he declined to submit to the oath of allegiance to William and Mary, forfeiting his professorship at Oxford, and became a pamphleteer. Major works concerned the oath, at first opposing the government (*Book of Schism, et al.*). Later, after his return to the Anglican Communion (1710), he urged others to follow his example.

**Doellinger, Johann Joseph Ignaz von** (1799–1890). German Roman Catholic church historian. Educated at Würzburg and the Bamberg seminary, Doellinger was ordained in 1822 to become the chaplain in Marktscheinfeldt and then in 1823 teacher at Aschaffenburg. He taught many subjects, but primarily church history, at Munich (1826) until his excommunication on April 18, 1871. He remained at Munich until his death. Doellinger served in the 1848 Frankfurt Parliament, agreeing to the permanent expulsion of the German Jesuits. In his earlier years he was ultramontane, well acquainted with Räss, Goerres, and Baader, and involved in the Cologne conflict over mixed marriages. Almost imperceptibly his views changed. He met the papal declaration on the Immaculate Conception (1854) with dampened enthusiasm. In the 1860's he drew closer to the "liberal Catholics," and showed concern over the centralizing policies of ultramontanism. Two lectures in 1861 attacked the temporal papal powers. Well known is his famous speech regarding Catholic theology at the 1863 Munich Congress. Several of his opinions were condemned in the 1864 Syllabus of Errors. He sharply criticized the Vatican definition of papal infallibility (1870) on historical grounds (*Letters of Janus* and *Letters of Quirinus*). After his 1871 excommunication he made overtures toward the Old Catholics. Although avoiding formal connection, he offered them frequent counsel. In 1873 he was appointed president of the Bavarian Royal Academy of Sciences. His writings included *Die Reformation, Die Papstfabeln des Mittelalters,* and *Christentum und Kirche.*

**Dom** (Latin, *dominus,* "master"). The title of address for a professed Benedictine monk and members of certain other orders. The term is common in Europe, but is rarely used in America.

**Dominic** (1170–1221). Founder of the Dominican Order. Born of a noble Castilian family, he studied for ten years at Palencia and then became canon, subprior, and prior of the cathedral chapter of Osma. In 1203 he met Innocent III in Rome and sought permission to go and convert the Tartars of the Volga. This was refused, and he was sent to convert the Cathari of southern France instead. He adopted a life of ascetic poverty to counter the rigorism by which the Cathari had attracted converts from the church. In 1206 he opened a hostel for women at Prouille to save them from Catharism. He continued to preach throughout the crusade against the Albigenses, but met with little success. By 1215 he had gathered a band of sixteen disciples and he attended the Fourth Lateran Council to obtain papal approval for a new monastic order. This was granted on condition that he adopt an existing rule, and the Friars Preachers therefore based themselves on the Augustinian Rule, which Dominic had followed at Osma, and certain of the constitutions of Prémontré. Since the order was devoted to study and preaching, the Divine Office was shortened and physical labor abolished. Mobility was ensured by having the members swear a vow to the order and not to any one house. Having traveled extensively to supervise the new provinces of his order, Dominic died at Bologna.

**Dominicans** (*or* Order of Friars Preachers). The order founded by Dominic as an outgrowth of his efforts during the first two decades of the 13th century to convert the Albigenses of Provence. With a few others, he labored long and hard to combat the deep-rooted heresy by means of preaching and argumentation. His success was limited, although he did manage to establish a convent of nuns at Prouille under the Augustinian Rule, and to draw a number of followers to his standard. He is said not to have taken any part in the bloodier aspects of the crusade proclaimed against the Albigenses by Innocent III in 1208. In 1215, Bishop Fulco of Toulouse took Dominic to Rome with him, where Dominic requested the pope's permission to found a new order devoted to the defense of the faith. The Lateran Council had recently ruled against the proliferation of orders, with the result that the pope several times refused to give his consent. However, permission was eventually granted Dominic to found an order under an already established rule. He and his associates chose the Augustinian Rule. The order was officially recognized by Honorius III in 1216. It was conceived as an "order of preachers," not a society of monks. Originally it was not a mendicant order, since it subscribed to the older conception of poverty which applied to the individual but not the community. Nor did it first have a "universal" character; it was several years before the brothers, armed with papal briefs, were allowed to preach or hear confessions in whatever diocese they wished. The first general chapter of the new order was held in 1220 at Bologna, at which sixty convents of preaching friars were represented. At this meeting, the brotherhood became a mendicant order by deciding to remove all property and fixed income and live by the voluntary alms of the people. However, despite the warnings of Dominic himself, the order never applied the vow of poverty with the severity that characterized the early Franciscans, with the result that the Preachers escaped some of the dissension that vexed the latter order.

A second chapter meeting was held at Bologna the following year (1221). At the meeting, a constitution was completed which differed markedly from that of older orders. It assigned to a master general, chosen for life, an unusual degree of authority, and required that the vow of obedience be made directly to him. Each province was to be governed by a prior provincial elected for four years by the provincial chapter, and each house was to be ruled by a prior chosen by its members.

The growth of the order was rapid, in part because its rule captured the imaginations of many pious people, but also because it was strongly supported by powerful kings and nobles as well as by a succession of popes. The Preaching Friars also made themselves useful as preferred inquisitors when Gregory IX began, in 1232, to replace the episcopal Inquisition with his own officials. This rapid advancement aroused hostility on the part of other orders, particularly the Cistercians and the Carthusians, and in the 14th century many cities in which the mendicants established houses greeted them with scant welcome. This was true in Paris where the university at first tried to bar the Dominicans, a contest that the order won in 1259.

During his lifetime Dominic had been concerned with the importance of learning as a weapon in the attack on heresy, and had sent six of his companions to the theological school at Toulouse. He had been particularly interested in establishing the order in centers of intellectual life, notably Paris, Rome, and Bologna. This concern with education was furthered by his successors, particularly the fourth in line, John of Wildeshausen (1241–1252), and the fifth, Humbert of Romans (1254–1263). Under them, the Dominican Order became the first to require study, at least of its priests, and regulated it in great detail. By the middle of the 13th century, each province had its own Dominican university, usually patterned on the University of Paris, with curricula that included the liberal arts as well as theology. Theological chairs were established at Bologna, Padua, Cologne, Prague, Salamanca, Oxford, and Vienna. The Preachers were the first religious order to take part in teaching at the University of Paris, and the only one possessing two schools. They were innovators in the teaching of language among the religious: Hebrew, Greek, and Arabic were courses of study at several of their provincial universities. One of the most obvious consequences of this educational bias was the impressive literary and scholastic output of the order. The most famous examples, of course, are the works of Thomas Aquinas and his teacher Albertus Magnus. The former's *Summa theologiae* (1265–1275) is still the single greatest masterpiece of theological thought, and his *De ortu et divisione philosophiae* is regarded as the most useful introduction to philosophy available during the Middle Ages. But the Dominican role in the 13th century was a many-sided involvement. Men such as Hugh of St. Cher undertook corrections of the Vulgate text, and numerous commentaries were written on the books of the Bible, among the most famous being those of Aquinas and Albertus Magnus. The Preachers, in keeping with their special role as opponents of heresy, produced the most powerful works in the field of apologetics. Aquinas was also active in this sphere, but there were many others, Meneta of Cremona, Raymond Marti, and Riccoldo di Monte Croce, to name a few. The Preachers were foremost in the composition of teaching manuals and biographies, the *Legenda sanctorum* ("Golden Legend") of Lacapo de Voragine being one of the most popular of medieval religious works, and the *Speculum sanctorale* of Bernard Guidonis one of the most scholarly. Bernard Guidonis was also one of the most astute of the Dominican historians, and his works are still notable for their unusually conscientious use of historical sources. Besides the great impetus they gave to medieval learning, the Preaching Friars also played an important role in the history of art. The order at first discouraged any manifestation of luxury or extravagance in the embellishment of its churches and monasteries, but this uncompromising attitude was generally relinquished during the second half of the 13th century. The most notable example of Tuscan Gothic (see ARCHITECTURE, GOTHIC), the Church of Santa Marie Novella in Florence, was the work of two Dominican friars, and throughout Italy, France, and Spain, Dominican edifices are among the most priceless examples of the architectural heritage of these countries. In painting, the names of two Dominican friars are well known: Fra Angelico and Fra Bartolommeo.

Theoretically, at least, the crucial part that the order played in the cultural and intellectual life of the Middle Ages and the early Renaissance was not an end in itself, but was meant to further their original function as preachers. Their work among heretics and heathens was for some time generally effective. They were largely responsible for the conversion of many thousands of Lombardian heretics; they had the special blessing of the church in preaching crusades against the Saracens; they sent successful missions to many parts of still heathen Europe, converting the Lithuanians in 1386; and they had even reached the court of Kubla Khan by 1272. The order is also indelibly associated with the most zealous and ruthless aspects of the Inquisition, although various master generals expressed concern at the consequences of this dubious ministry.

Worldliness made its inroads in the course of the order's history. Jealousy and controversy split the ranks of monks and secular clergy. Competition with each other, as well as intellectual disputes between Thomists and Scotists (see DUNS SCOTUS, JOHN), often led to debates that were, in their extreme theological subtlety, absurd. The immense wealth of the order played its part in the gradual lessening of its vitality. When the Counter-Reformation occurred, it was significant that the new order of the Society of Jesus took the lead in the fight against the Protestants. The feud between the Dominicans and the Jesuits continued for centuries, being waged both on the mission field and in the great theological controversy about grace (1588–1611).

In more recent times, the Dominican Order has once again assumed importance in its influence on theological learning, particularly under Pope Leo XIII, a great admirer of Thomas Aquinas. Four Dominicans have been popes: Innocent V (d. 1276), Benedict XI (d. 1304), Pius V (d. 1572), and Benedict XIII (d. 1730).

The Second Order, the Dominican Sisters, developed at Prouille and San Sisto during Dominic's lifetime. Their rule, orginally contemplative and ascetic, was intended to follow that of the brothers as much as possible. In time, the female houses undertook the education of girls, with a consequent mitigation in their contemplative rule. Generally, the history of the Second Order parallels that of the first in its successes and failures. At present, there are some 90 houses with 1,500 members.

The Third Order, composed of confraternities of people living in the world, was not welcomed by the early Preachers as a responsibility, but eventually, at the prompting of Honorius IV, a rule for tertiaries was drawn up in 1285, and known as the Penance of St. Dominic. The Third Order never became widespread, since the Preachers emphasized quality more than quantity. The Third Order still has a number of congregations, including several in the United States. Catherine of Siena was its most famous representative.

BIBLIOGRAPHY: A. T. Drane, *History of St. Dominic* (London, 1891); J. Herkless, *Francis and Dominic and the Mendicant Orders* (New York, 1901).

**Dominus ac Redemptor Noster** (1773). The name given to the papal brief that abolished the Society of Jesus. Under political pressure from the kings of France, Spain, Portugal, and the Two Sicilies, Clement XIV composed the brief between November, 1772, and June, 1773. It is said that the facts justifying the suppression were supplied by the Spanish ambassador, Joseph Menino. However, the brief does not condemn the doctrine, morals, or discipline of the Society; its stated purpose is to restore peace to the church by eliminating one of its most contentious factions.

**Donation of Constantine.** A document forged in the 8th century, probably in Rome, purporting to be a testament of Constantine granting to Pope Sylvester I (d. 335) the imperial rights over Italy and the "western regions." The document asserted the pope's supremacy over the West and his primacy over the other patriarchs. It was used in the late Middle Ages to support the claims of papal supremacy. It was demonstrated to be a forgery in the 15th century by Lorenzo Valla.

**Donation of Pepin.** A grant of supremacy made by King Pepin III to the papacy in 756. After defeating the Lombards, Pepin drew up a deed of donation for the former exarchate of Ravenna and the duchy of Rome. This document, together with the symbolic keys, was laid on the tomb of St. Peter. This donation was confirmed in 774 by Pepin's son, Charlemagne. It marked the formal beginning of the political authority of the papacy in Italy.

**Donatism.** An African schism with social and political as well as religious aspects. It formally began with a disputed election to the see of Carthage in 311 and 312, when peace had returned after the persecution of Diocletian. The local clergy chose the archdeacon Caecilian, without waiting for the arrival of more distant Numidian bishops who claimed a right to be present. The latter then attacked Caecilian's consecration on the ground that his consecrator, Felix of Aphthungi, had surrendered sacred books during the persecution, and as a traitor to the faith (traditor) could no longer administer its sacred rites. For their candidate, Majorinus, they claimed the donations that Constantine was about to bestow on the Church of Carthage. The emperor referred the question to a local Council at Rome in 313, and, on further appeal, to a general Council of the Western Church at Arles in 314. Both the specific charge and the theological basis were refuted, but with no effect on the party of Majorinus. The common name of the schism comes from its chief leader, Donatus, bishop of Casae Nigrae, in southern Numidia, who as Majorinus' successor at Carthage was later known to history as Donatus the Great (313–355). The movement appealed to the rigorist tendencies of North African Christianity, and absorbed into itself various forms of protest against Roman rule and influence—of native tribes against Latinized elements, of peasants against Roman landlords (at times taking violent action in the marauding bands of circumcelliones), of local chiefs and gentry against Roman rulers.

Constantine fell into a position of neutrality, and the Donatists soon became dominant in many areas. In 347 his son Constans, emperor in the West, sent the commissioners Paul and Macarius, who achieved an apparent unity by financial rewards and penalties and the repression of the circumcelliones. After Julian the Apostate suspended imperial intervention in church affairs (362) the Donatists returned to their previous position, or better. Many pagan civil officials were at least neutral, and several of the military commanders (counts of Africa) were supporters of the Donatist Church. Count Gildo, who worked closely with the Donatist bishop Optatus of Thamugadi (Timgad), revolted against the emperor Honorius in 397, and after his defeat in 397

the imperial government was prepared to take action against the Donatists.

During its years of apparent triumph, Donatism had weakened internally; several groups broke off from the main body, either toward a more rigorist or a less violent position. Meanwhile the anti-Donatist writings to which Augustine devoted much of his attention in the fifteen years after he became bishop of Hippo in 397 raised propaganda to the level of permanent contributions to theology. Building on the work of Optatus of Milevis, he challenged the Donatists, as a localized sect, with the authority of the church universal, and attacked their rigorist claims with the principle that it is Christ who works in the sacraments, even when they are administered by unworthy ministers. He could thus (contrary to the position of Cyprian) recognize the validity of the baptism and ordination of converts from Donatism, though he still held that these acts were spiritually ineffective until the schismatics were received into the Catholic Church, conceived as the fellowship of divine love.

A series of controversies and debates reached their climax in 411 in the inconclusive Conference of Carthage, attended by some four hundred bishops of each party. Thereafter Augustine came with some reluctance to the position that the civil arm might be appealed to where persuasion failed, to "compel people to come in" (Luke 14:23)—partly at least on the ground that the Donatist leaders themselves had attacked their opponents and held their followers in line by force or the threat of force. The following persecution was mainly limited to the confiscation of buildings and imposition of fines on the clergy and the wealthier Donatists. It was at least successful. Donatism had practically collapsed when the Vandals invaded Africa in 429, and does not figure in the history of the Vandal period, although there was a Donatist remnant in Byzantine Africa as late as the end of the 6th century. The permanent interest of Donatism is in the theological issues involved, and in the illustrations it affords from a distant age of the interlocking of religious divisions with political and social struggles, a point that was only obscurely grasped by contemporaries.

BIBLIOGRAPHY: G. Bonner, *St. Augustine of Hippo* (Philadelphia, 1963); W. H. C. Frend, *The Donatist Church* (Oxford, 1952); E. F. Humphrey, *Politics and Religion in the Days of Augustine* (New York, 1912); W. J. S. Simpson, *St. Augustine and African Church Divisions* (London, 1910); G. Willis,

*Saint Augustine and the Donatist Controversy* (London, 1950).

**Donne, John** (1572–1631). English poet and divine. Donne's career falls into two stages: the earlier as traveler, adventurer, unsuccessful courtier, and amatory poet; the later—after he had taken holy orders at the wish of James I in 1615—as churchman, writer of devotional prose and poetry, and the most celebrated preacher of his age. From 1621 he was dean of St. Paul's. His sermons are marked by great learning, complex rhetoric, and the restless intellectual energy that also characterizes his poetry.

**Dordrecht Confession** (*or* Confession of Dort) (1632). A statement adopted by Mennonites in the Netherlands in 1632 in the effort to provide common ground for disputing groups. Later Mennonites, never strongly creedal, often used it. Distinctive affirmations are the purity of the church (the ban, shunning expelled members, marriage only in the fellowship, believer's baptism), rejection of defense by force, refusal to swear oaths, and the ordinances of Baptism and the Lord's Supper, and foot washing.

**Dorotheus.** The most famous bearer of this name was the 6th-century writer on ascetical theory. Born at Antioch, he had a good education before entering the monastery of Seridos near Gaza. There he was in close contact with Barsanuphius and John the Prophet, who answered his many questions and formed his ascetical thought. After their death he founded his own monastery nearby about 540 and for twenty years gave the lectures to his monks which form his *Spiritual Instructions*.

**Dort, Synod of** (1618–1619). A national synod of the Netherlands Reformed Church called to deal with the Arminian controversy. It was held in Dordrecht (Dort) from Nov. 13, 1618, to May 25, 1619. The differences between the Arminians (Remonstrants) and the strict Calvinists on the doctrines of grace and freedom caught the attention of all Protestant Europe. Delegates came to the Synod from many countries in Europe. The Synod's composition was heavily weighted in favor of the Calvinists. Thirteen Remonstrant theologians were cited to appear before the Synod and were treated as defendants. Under the fiery leadership of John Bogerman, the elected president, the Synod found the Remonstrants guilty of heresy. About two hundred ministers were deposed and fifteen were placed under arrest and later expelled from the country. The Synod then proceeded to a positive statement of its Calvinistic views. These canons contain five heads of doctrine which flow from the principle of absolute divine sovereignty. They are: (1) Predestination is absolute and unconditional. (2) The atonement is effective only for the elect. (3) and (4) Through the Fall mankind inherits a depraved nature incapable of any saving good; his salvation comes solely from unconditioned and irresistible grace. (5) God's grace preserves all whom he calls so that they persevere in the faith to the end. After the departure of the foreign delegates, the Synod applied itself to many matters of church order. The Canons of the Synod of Dort were received with respect among European Reformed churches. They still hold symbolic authority for the Reformed Church in the Netherlands and for the Reformed Church in America and the Christian Reformed Church.

**Dorter.** The dormitory of a monastery. Usually it consists of a single large room in which each monk has his own bed. Since the Night Offices require easy access to the chapel, the dorter sometimes opens directly into the chapel. Nearby is the rere-dorter, the sanitary facilities.

**Dositheus, Confession of** (1672). A statement of faith drawn up by the Synod of Jerusalem in 1672 under the leadership of Patriarch Dositheus (1641–1707). It sought to eradicate the influence of Protestant theology which had entered the Eastern Orthodox Church through Cyril Lucar. In order to combat the theology of the Reformation, Dositheus tended to use the weapons of Roman Catholicism. Thus his Confession drew heavily upon Roman sources. Nevertheless, it has become one of the most important documents in the history of modern Orthodox theology. It sought to answer Lucar's Confession point by point, especially in the four areas where he and Lucar diverged: (1) the question of free will, grace, and predestination; (2) the number and nature of the sacraments; (3) the doctrine of the church; and (4) the veneration of icons. It adopted a synergistic view of salvation by stating that God "takes not away from [fallen] man the power to will —to will to obey or not to obey him." The sacraments are seven in number; they are effectual signs of grace not dependent upon the faith of the recipient; and in the Lord's Supper the elements are transubstantiated. The church is declared to be as infallible as Scripture and dependent upon the episcopal office and apostolic succession for its essence. In defending prayers for the dead, the Roman doctrine of purgatory is approximated.

**Dostoevsky, Fyodor** (1821–1881). Russian novelist and religious thinker. He was condemned to death for "revolutionary activities" (1849), a sentence commuted at the moment of execution to four years' hard labor in Siberia. His prison experience convinced him that his punishment was just (he loved suffering and wrote powerfully about it) and led him to adopt the ideas of the Slavophiles, which included the monarchy and the Russian Orthodox Church. He looked to the "virtue of the common people" for the salvation of society, and the realization of the true genius of Russian civilization. These ideas were apparent both in his later journalism and in his novels. He is often claimed as an ancestor of Christian existentialism, and his novels struggle profoundly with psychological and religious problems. His most famous works, *Crime and Punishment, The Brothers Karamazov* (from which the chapter "The Grand Inquisitor" is often abstracted), *Notes from Underground, The Possessed, The Idiot,* and others, are available in many popular editions.

**Douai, College of.** A school in Flanders, founded in 1568 by William Allen to educate English Roman Catholic clergymen. By 1600 it had sent nearly three hundred priests to England, almost one third of whom were executed. From 1578 to 1593 the College was located at Reims. It was at this institution that the old Roman Catholic, or Reims-Douay, translation of the Vulgate Bible was made. See ALLEN, WILLIAM.

**Double Monastery.** A religious community consisting of both men and women, living in separate houses but with a common discipline and superior. They were often found in the East and in the Celtic Church, where usually a nun presided over both houses. Double monasteries generally disappeared by the 16th century.

**Dowie, John Alexander** (1847–1907). Founder of the Christian Catholic Apostolic Church in Zion. While living in Scotland and Australia in 1878, Dowie began a career of revivalism and faith healing. In 1888 he came to San Francisco and thence to Chicago, where he organized his sect in 1896 and, about forty miles away, the town of Zion City, Ill., in 1901. After 1903 a series of failures resulted in the rebellion of his followers and his expulsion.

**Dreyfus Affair.** The trial and conviction in 1894 for treason of Captain Alfred Dreyfus, native of Alsace and member of a wealthy and influential Jewish family, which mushroomed into an ideological conflict that engulfed all of France. The *cause célèbre* exposed wounds as old as the earliest struggle between the Roman Catholic Church and Gallicanism, the French Revolution, and as fresh as the establishment of the Third Republic (1871). Even after it became evident that court-martial procedures had been irregular and the evidence fraudulent, it was very difficult for sympathizers of Dreyfus to obtain a retrial. The affair involved the honor of France, championed by conservatives and represented in the decision of the Ministers of War and of Justice, and the integrity of the Republic, aggravated on the one side by anti-Semitism and on the other by anticlericalism. Revisionists, or Dreyfusards, were led by intellectuals, e.g., Émile Zola (*J'Accuse*), and supported by Protestants, e.g., Georges Thiebaud and Ernest Renauld, who were able to cover their internal divisions in supporting this cause. Roman Catholics who desired revision were few; they were organized by Paul Viollet in the Catholic Committee for the Defense of Right. For the most part, bishops neither wrote nor spoke about the affair, while the lower clergy followed the lead of hard-hitting antirevisionist journalists, Paul de Cassagnac in *Autorité*, Edouard Drumont in *La Libre Parole*, and Père Bailly in *La Croix*, the paper of the Assumptionist Order. Generally, Catholics joined the nationalists and royalists, and these papers mixed a virulent anti-Semitism with a relentless opposition to Republican France. Charles Maurras, although an atheist, employed the situation to stir support for a clerical fascism under monarchy. The Jesuits were violently criticized by the revisionists, although their hostility to Dreyfusard opinions was less evident. Only in 1899 did Leo XIII deplore publicly the "international scandal" created by the partisan struggles. The *ralliement* of conservative forces did not succeed. Dreyfus, although again adjudged guilty at his second trial (1899), was immediately pardoned. The Dreyfus affair turned into the Dreyfus revolution. Anticlericals seized the opportunity to crush Roman Catholic orders by passing the Law of Associations (1901), which required a specific legislative act to authorize Roman Catholic monastic corporations, and the Law of Separation (1905), which ended the Napoleonic Concordat, denied the church legal privilege and public subsidy for the freedom of choosing bishops and holding assemblies without governmental control. Prophetically, Theodor Herzl, one of the fathers of Zionism, attended the first Dreyfus trial, and wrote during the anti-Semitic hysteria, *The Jewish State: An Attempt at a Modern Solution of the Jewish*

*Question* (1896). In 1906 the conviction against Alfred Dreyfus was quashed and he was restored to the army with pomp and ceremony.

**Droste zu Vischering, Clemens August von** (1773–1845). Roman Catholic archbishop of Cologne. He came under the influence of the Münster Roman Catholic Awakening gathered around Princess Adelheid Amalie de Gallitzin, and through her met Friedrich von Schlegel and L. von Stolberg. Taught by Johann Katerkamp, he was ordained in 1798. He became diocesan administrator in Münster (1815–1821) under French and Prussian rule. He organized the Company of Compassionate Sisters with motherhouse at Münster (1808). After 1815 he became critical of Prussian church policy. A conflict with Georg Hermes led him to resign his Münster office, but in 1827 he was made suffragan bishop of Münster. At the death of Archbishop Spiegel in 1835, the Prussian crown prince and Bunsen accomplished the appointment of Droste to the archbishopric of Cologne against the wish of the chapters and to the surprise of the Curia. At his elevation, a conflict arose that was an antecedent of the Kulturkampf. In 1834, Spiegel had agreed with the Prussian Government that the Roman ceremony was to be allowed in mixed marriages, but the children were not necessarily to be Roman. The suffragan bishop assented without the Curia's knowledge. When he became archbishop, Droste refused to honor the agreement. In addition, he took preventive measures against Bonn professors and priests who were following the Kantian interpretations of Hermes. He was imprisoned at Minden, Nov. 20, 1837, but released under full apology by the king in 1839. He was relieved by the coadjutor bishop, Johannes von Geissel, in 1841, and retired to Dorfield and Münster.

**Drummond, Henry** (1851–1897). Scottish theologian and evangelist. Educated at Edinburgh and Tübingen, he had a lifelong interest in work with student Christian movements. From 1873 to 1875 he assisted Dwight L. Moody and Ira D. Sankey in their English and Irish revival campaigns (again assisting Moody in 1882). From 1884 he served as professor of natural science in the theological faculty at Glasgow. In response to the impact of Darwinism he accepted the theory of evolution and attempted to demonstrate the natural basis for human dignity and divine presence.

**Dubourg** (du Bourg), **Antoine** (c. 1520–1559). French Protestant martyr. The son of a former chancellor, Dubourg became a member of the Parlement in 1557. By 1559 he had become sympathetic to the French Protestants. That same year, with Henry II present, he spoke in Parlement defending the Protestants. The angered king had him and several others arrested. Dubourg was executed—strangled and burned at the stake—in Paris, December, 1559.

**Duchesne, Louis Marie Olivier** (1843–1922). French Roman Catholic theologian. Ordained in 1867, Duchesne studied at the École des Hautes Études and at the newly created French School at Rome. In the course of his studies he acquired the historicocritical outlook that was to mark his works in archaeology and church history. In 1877 he returned to Paris to become a professor in the Institut Catholique, already a marked man because of his espousal of the historical approach. One of his first protégés at the Institut was the young Alfred Firmin Loisy, whom Duchesne encouraged in the pursuit of his Biblical criticism. Although Duchesne's career is intertwined with several currents of Modernism and he was looked upon as a modernist by many, he had apparently realized quite early in his professional life that Rome could not be cajoled into changing its traditional positions. His discretion served him well, although the first three volumes of his *L'Histoire ancienne de l'Église chrétienne* were put on the Index in 1912. In 1892, Duchesne became Director of Studies at the École des Hautes Études, and in 1895, Director of the French School at Rome. The Académie des Inscriptions et Belles-Lettres chose him as a member in 1888, and the French Academy in 1910.

**Duff, Alexander** (1806–1878). First missionary of the Church of Scotland to India. Duff made three tours there (1830–1834, 1840–1849, 1856–1864). On the first trip, he founded the English-language school (1830), which became in 1857 the University of Calcutta. After 1843, he joined the Free Church. He lost his mission property, but emerged as a leader in the Free Church. He occupied the first chair of evangelistic theology (missions) established by the Free Church at Edinburgh (1867).

**Dukhobors.** A Christian sect that originated in 18th-century Russia. The name, originally a derogatory nickname meaning "spirit wrestler" or "spirit fighter," has now been adopted by the group. They reject churches, Scriptures, elaborate ritual, and a specialized ministry. Holding that men are inherently good, they believe that all men may know the divine within them and have the capacity to follow its direction without interference from governments or any other form of human authority. They are pacifists, vegetarians, teetotalers, and nonsmokers, and their most rigid adherents deny the necessity of education. In the 19th century their refusal to bear arms caused several banishments from the Crimea and Georgia. With assistance from Tolstoy and the English Quakers, seven thousand Dukhobors in 1899 received land in Saskatchewan under the Homestead Act. Religious freedom was promised and their pacifism was recognized by Order-in-Council, but the Homestead Act required an oath of allegiance before title to the 160 acres permitted each man could be granted. Only a minority of the group were prepared to take this oath, and the land reverted to the government through failure to complete the claims. In 1908, Peter Verigin, the leader of the Sons of Freedom, the most radical Dukhobor group, instituted a purchase of land in the interior of British Columbia. Within five years nearly six thousand Dukhobors had moved to the area. Their refusal to send their children to school or to register births, marriages, or deaths has, however, led them into continual conflict with governmental authorities and has resulted in numerous Royal Commissions and other governmental investigations. Though many have been completely assimilated into Canadian society, the Sons of Freedom have reacted against assimilation and have protected against their loss of identity by such means as arson, nudism, and the dynamiting of railroads and power lines. This has led to conflict with law enforcement authorities and has resulted in many being sent to prison.

**Dunant, Henri.** See RED CROSS.

**Dunkers.** Any of the several German Baptist sects practicing trine immersion. One of the results of Pietism was the German Brethren movement that originated with Alexander Mack (1679–1735). Mack believed that the Pietist protest against the formalism and rationalism of the state churches could not effect reform, that it was necessary to withdraw from the state church and to organize separate congregations. Mack proceeded to do this in 1708 at Schwarzenau, Westphalia. Baptism was to be administered by triple immersion, hence the name Dunker, Tunker, Taeufer, or German Baptist Brethren. Because of political persecution, the Brethren (as they are officially called) emigrated to the United States (1719–1729). Here divisions occurred beginning in 1732 when Johann Beissel founded a separate community near Ephrata, Pa. There

are now four main Brethren groups. Beissel's original splinter party is listed with the Baptists as the German Seventh Day Baptists. The four are: the Church of the Brethren, the Old German Baptist Brethren, the Brethren Church, and the Church of God (New Dunkers). There is a variety of practices among these groups, but in none of them is doctrine stressed. Some characteristic practices are: baptism by triple immersion; the evening Eucharist preceded by foot washing and the love feast; the anointing of the sick with oil; total abstinence; nonparticipation in war, oaths, or civil litigation.

**Duns Scotus, John** (c. 1265–c. 1308). Medieval theologian and philosopher. Born at Duns, Scotland, he entered the Franciscan Order at an early age. In his short life, he achieved much that was to be significant in the future of Roman Catholicism. As a professor at Oxford and the University of Paris, he wrote a number of books, including commentaries on Scripture, Aristotle, and the *Sentences* of Peter Lombard. He was critical of previous Scholasticism, particularly Thomism. Aquinas and other 13th-century philosophers had relied on Aristotle to construct a systematized approach to religion, and Duns Scotus attacked the very foundation of Aristelico-Christian thought with his insistence on the practical. Faith, he argued, was a matter of will and not speculation and could not be established by any rational process. By restricting reason, he accomplished a separation between philosophy and religion that was to have far-reaching effects. From the deductive method he argued that since certain effects follow particular causes, there must be one cause from which all others spring, and that First Cause is God. All other knowledge of God must be taken on faith, including the resurrection and immortality. His disciples moved farther toward an ever intensified dichotomy between faith and reason, which led ultimately to the end of Scholasticism. Duns Scotus defended the Immaculate Conception against those Dominicans who attempted to disprove it, beginning a dispute settled fifty years later by a papal bull. When he died at Cologne, he had established himself as one of the greatest of the medieval Schoolmen. Because of the subtlety of his arguments, he came to be known as "Dr. Subtilis."

**Dunstan** (c. 909–988). Archbishop of Canterbury and leader of the monastic revival in England after the devastations of the Vikings. Born in Somerset, he studied at Glastonbury and was an attendant of King Athelstan (c. 925). He became a monk, chaplain to the bishop of Winchester and priest some time later, and then taught at Glastonbury. In 939 he became counselor to the new king, Edmund, who appointed him abbot at Glastonbury c. 943. Here he gathered disciples and organized a community based on the Benedictine Rule. After the accession of King Eadwig he was exiled in 956, for reasons now unknown, and took refuge first with Arnulf, Count of Flanders, and then at the monastery of St. Peter at Ghent, which had recently been reformed by Gerard of Brogne. In 957 he was recalled by King Edgar and made bishop of Worcester, then in 959 bishop of London and in 960 archbishop of Canterbury. With the close cooperation of Bishops Ethelwold and Oswald (d. 992), Dunstan was encouraged by Edgar to reestablish monasteries throughout England, and in 970 he promulgated the *Regularis concordia,* a uniform code of monastic observance, based on current Lotharingian usages, but unique in its provision for prayers for the king and queen. In 973 he crowned Edgar according to a new rite he had compiled, which stressed for the first time the priestly nature of the royal office and the king's obligations to his people.

**Dunster, Henry** (1609–1659). American educator. Born in Lancashire, England, and educated at Cambridge, Dunster emigrated to New England in 1640. Shortly after his arrival he was made the first president of Harvard College, a position that he maintained for some fourteen years. His opposition to infant baptism gradually ran him afoul of the ecclesiastical establishment and led to his resignation. He was a noted student of ancient languages.

**Duomo of Florence** (*or* Santa Maria del Fiore). The largest and most important of the numerous Florentine churches. "Duomo" (from Latin *domus,* "house") is a common Italian name for cathedral. Designed in 1294 by Arnolfo di Cambio, the cathedral at Florence is a blend of Italian Romanesque and Gothic architecture, illustrating how the Gothic style can be applied to various types of buildings. The dome, an octagonal cloister vault with only mechanical ribs, was constructed in the late Gothic period. Santa Maria del Fiore has been described as "stern and impressive" in that its minute details are recognized in relation to the monumental church.

**Dupanloup, Félix Antoine Philibert** (1802–1878). French Roman Catholic bishop. By the time he was appointed bishop of Orléans in 1849, he had already become well known throughout France. He had reputedly received

the adaptable Talleyrand back into the church, and had been a member of the commission appointed to draft the recommendations for that compromise educational measure which subsequently bore the name of the minister of public instruction, Falloux. Dupanloup's pulpit oratory was remarkable, his energy great. However, he is best remembered for his difficult role as leader of the French Liberal Catholics during a most trying period under the regimes of Napoleon III and Pius IX. Within France he was the bitter opponent of Louis Veuillot and the avid ultramontanes of the school centered around the newspaper *L'Univers.* In 1865 he composed a pamphlet interpreting the encyclical *Quanta cura* and its attached Syllabus of Errors, in which he opposed the "ideal" thesis to the "pragmatic" hypothesis. Though many felt that this simply explained away Pius' condemnations, Dupanloup was congratulated by the pope himself for his effort. His endeavors at the Vatican Council (1870) on behalf of the "Inopportunist" cause were doomed to failure, and he submitted to the decrees.

**Du Perron, Jacques Davy** (1556–1618). French cardinal. He was born at St.-Lô of Calvinist parents, and shortly after his birth the whole family fled to Switzerland. In the course of his education he was drawn to the study of the fathers, particularly Augustine, as well as Thomas Aquinas, with the result that he joined the Roman Church in 1577 or 1578. He was in the confidence of Henry III and Henry IV, and was instrumental in the latter's conversion from Protestantism. In 1591 he was made bishop of Évreux and continued to work for the conversion of Protestants. In a debate with Duplessis-Mornay at Fontainebleau on the Eucharistic doctrine of the fathers (1600), he was adjudged victor. In 1604 he was made a cardinal and went to Rome to serve with the Congregatio de Auxiliis (see MOLINA, LUIS DE) it is said to have been in large part his influence that kept the pope from condemning Molinism. Made archbishop of Sens in 1606, he defended the pope before the Parlement (1611) and urged the adoption of the disciplinary rules of the Council of Trent in France (1614–1615). He died in Paris. Included in his works (3 vols., 1620–1622) is a treatise intended to prove that James I of England could not truly maintain he was a "Catholic" by belonging to the English Church.

**Duplessis-Mornay, Philippe** (1549–1623). Huguenot statesman. His mother had leanings toward Protestantism, and he became a Protestant early in life. After escaping from the Bartholomew's Day Massacre, he fled to England for a year. On his return to France he wrote against the tyranny of the absolute monarchy, and aided the proceedings of the French Reformed Synods. Shortly he became attached to Henry of Navarre, becoming one of his chief counselors. In this position he was recognized as an influential adviser and outstanding Huguenot—popularly called the "Huguenot pope." He helped to reconcile Henry of Navarre and Henry III of France, and the former appointed him governor of Saumur in 1589. He was vehemently against the conversion of Henry IV to Roman Catholicism, but afterward continued to work for the protection of the Huguenots. Much of the favorability of the Edict of Nantes is attributed to him. He wrote a major work in 1598 on the Eucharist in the early church, but was charged by Jacques-Davy Duperron with hundreds of misquotations from the fathers, and was pronounced defeated in a public disputation—which, however, was not impartially conducted. His stand against Louis XIII's policy of *rapprochement* with Spain and the papacy lost him his prestige, and he was disgraced in 1621 when the governorship of Saumur was removed from him.

**Durand of St. Pourçain** (1275–1334). Medieval theologian. As a young man Durand joined the Dominicans and studied at Paris. After a short period at Avignon he successively held three bishoprics. In 1308 he wrote an anti-Thomistic commentary on Peter Lombard which aroused strong opposition among his fellow Dominicans. He corrected the work, but later, as a bishop, reissued it with his original opinions. Though his theory of knowledge is reminiscent of nominalism, he was primarily a disciple of Augustine.

**Dürer, Albrecht** (1471–1528). Influential, prolific, and internationally known German woodcut designer, painter, and engraver. He introduced into his works a deep understanding of the Italian Renaissance without destroying their essentially northern character. Best known are his engravings of *The Knight, Death, and the Devil* and *St. Jerome in His Study,* and his woodcut *Praying Hands.* Deeply religious, Dürer admired Luther but apparently never became a Protestant.

**Durham Cathedral.** Begun in 1093, it is the finest example of Norman architecture in England. Bede is buried in the Galilee Chapel, which projects from the west end and was constructed in 1175 at the end of the Norman era. The chapter house was built in 1140 and the upper west towers overlooking the river Wear in 1220. The sanctuary knocker on the north door was used by real or accused criminals seeking shelter in the church from their pursuers. Two janitors in tiny rooms over the door watched for those needing sanctuary. The custom continued until 1524.

**Durie** (Dury), **John** (1596–1680). Scottish advocate of church reunion. Durie studied at Sedan and Leiden, and in 1628 he received a pastoral appointment with the English Company of Merchants at Elbing, in Prussia. He was thus brought into contact with non-Presbyterian Protestants. The course of his life was filled with journeys and discussions aimed at the assembling of an evangelical council and the reunion of all Protestants, but without avail, partly because of the vagueness of the doctrinal basis by which union was to be accomplished. He participated in the composition of the Westminster Confession and Catechism, but at the Restoration he left England and lived at Kassel, which he made the center for further efforts at church union.

**Dwight, Timothy** (1752–1817). American educator and revivalist. He was born in Northampton, Mass., his mother one of the daughters of Jonathan Edwards. Dwight worked so hard at his studies both as student and tutor at Yale College that he ruined his health and permanently impaired his sight. One result of this breakdown was a series of horseback and walking tours through New England which formed the basis for his *Travels,* a mine of information about 18th-century New England. After service in the Revolutionary War as a chaplain, Dwight worked in Northampton and in Greenfield Hill, Conn., as a pastor and schoolteacher, his academies in both places rivaling Yale itself. In 1795 he was called to the presidency of Yale. Dwight's interests were always broad (two of his most important literary works were epic poems), and his encouragement of science and medicine were important for Yale's 19th-century growth. His most important contributions, however, were as a revivalist and polemical defender of the standing order in Connecticut. He found Yale at a spiritual low ebb, with students openly questioning the authority of the Bible and calling each other by the names of famous deists and infidels. The state was being infected politically by democratic sentiments and there was real danger that the established (Congregational) church would lose its state support (this did occur in 1819). Dwight attacked both manifestations as spiritual corruptions. Through sermons and discussions with students, through orations and lobbying, he attempted to turn back what he felt to be the forces of evil. His preaching to the students of Yale College was so successful that he has been credited with stimulating the Second Great Awakening in New England.

# E

**Eadmer** (d. c. 1130). English ecclesiastic and historian. A monk at Canterbury under Lanfranc and Anselm, he accompanied Anselm in his exiles. Eadmer's *History of Recent Happenings* and *Life of Anselm* are two of the most important sources for the history of the church in England after the Norman Conquest. He defended the Immaculate Conception of the Virgin Mary and wrote the *vitae* of the Anglo-Saxon saints Wilfrid, Odo of Canterbury, Dunstan, and Oswald of Worcester and York. His choice of subjects and treatment of them show his Anglo-Saxon origins.

**Eastern Orthodoxy.** The Eastern Orthodox Church's understanding of itself as the organic continuation of the original apostolic community, the early church, is based upon the assumption that the apostolic preaching implied the formation of local sacramental communities, each being the "body of Christ," with the head, or "bishop," fulfilling the ministry of Christ himself.

The local churches, however, do not live in isolation from one another. The identity of their faith and internal structure is being manifested in common action and common witness. In the early centuries, the councils were the normal instruments of this common life of the churches. After Constantine, ecumenical, or universal, councils began to be held to solve serious theological debates.

The Orthodox Church recognizes the first seven ecumenical councils as the authoritative witnesses to the uninterrupted Christian tradition: Nicaea (325), Constantinople I (381), Ephesus (431), Chalcedon (451), Constantinople II (553), Constantinople III (680), Nicaea II (787). The work of these Councils consisted in defining the doctrine of the Trinity; the two natures of Christ, united in his unique Person; the two wills, the divine and the human, in Jesus Christ; and, finally, the possibility of painting the image (or icon) of Christ-man and to venerate it, since it also represents God who assumed flesh. These doctrines are still considered by the Orthodox as the very basis of the Christian faith.

In the 9th century began the long final schism between the East and the West (see SCHISM, EASTERN). Thus in 862, Nicholas I, pope of Rome, refused to recognize the election of Photius as patriarch of Constantinople, and in 867, Photius excommunicated the pope who had given his support to the interpolation in the common Creed, approved by the Councils, of the Latin word *filioque* ("the Holy Spirit . . . , who proceedeth from the Father *and the Son*"). The problem was, however, solved on the basis of the original Creed in 879–880.

More incidents came later, among them the mutual anathemas uttered in 1054 and canceled in 1965 by Paul VI and Athenagoras I. The two halves of Christendom were developing apart from each other, and their differences were growing. Under the pressure of German emperors, the *filioque* clause was accepted in Rome, and the papacy meanwhile was developing as the supreme power over the entire West. In 1204, the Fourth Crusade, acting at least nominally in the pope's name, sacked the city of Constantinople.

Numerous attempts to close the gap between the two churches were unsuccessful, and in 1453, Constantinople, first recaptured by the Greeks from the Latin occupation, fell under Turkish rule. Since then it has been known as Istanbul and is now almost entirely a Moslem city, although it remains the seat of the ecumenical patriarch, a title of the bishop who enjoys a primacy of honor in the Orthodox world.

The conflict with the West did not prevent the Eastern Church from extending its missionary activity in vast areas of northern and eastern Europe. The Slavic nations of the Balkan peninsula, Bulgarians and Serbs, as well as the descendants of Roman settlers, known as Romanians, were converted to Christianity by Byzantine missionaries. In 864, Cyril and Methodius translated into Slavic both Scripture and the liturgical books. In 988, Russia followed the other Slavic nations into the Byzantine ecclesiastical fold. The principle of using the vernacular in the worship of the church provided Byzantine missionaries with a powerful tool ignored by their Western counterparts, who imposed Latin as the only language of prayer and culture. The Slavic nations thus developed their own Christian traditions, while continuing with Byzantium in unity of faith.

After the fall of Constantinople in 1453, Russia remained as the principal champion of Orthodoxy. The missionary movement, now sponsored mainly by the Russian Church, continued throughout Asia and reached Alaska and Japan.

In the 19th century, however, the Balkan States achieved their independence from the Turks, and the Orthodox Church today constitutes a commonwealth of churches, numbering some two hundred million baptized Christians united in faith and sacramental life, without any of them exercising any power over the others. These churches are very different in size and influence: the ancient patriarchates of Constantinople, Alexandria, Antioch, and Jerusalem are only vestiges of a glorious past (while preserving a certain traditional moral authority); the churches of Greece, Romania, Bulgaria, Serbia, and, above all, Russia are powerful national churches. In America, the original mission in Alaska has now grown, with the millions of immigrants from Eastern Europe, into a body of three million faithful, uniting around a Standing Conference of Bishops.

The weakening of the Orthodox Church in Eastern Europe under the impact of violently antireligious governments has been a factor contributing to the formation of a new Orthodox Church in America. Indeed, the Russian Revolution of 1917 to 1918 has put a final end to a secular alliance of the church with the state, which was the characteristic trait of Eastern Christianity, both Byzantine and Slavic.

The new communist government not only separated church and state but defined religion as the opiate of the people. Lenin deprived the church of legal identity and right of property. The law of 1929 made religious education of minors under eighteen a criminal offense. The constitution of 1936, which is still enforced, proclaims the freedom of "religious cult" and "antireligious propaganda," thus prohibiting any form of religious mission. However, the Communists underestimated the popular character of Orthodoxy in Eastern Europe. The Orthodox Church of Russia succeeded in rejuvenating itself in the midst of the revolutionary turmoil and even in 1918 reestablished the patriarchate of Moscow, which had been suppressed by Peter the Great in 1721 as a challenge to czarist autocracy. Although the church suffered greatly during the violent persecutions of the 1920's and 1930's Stalin again permitted its partial restoration in 1943, during the critical war years. In spite of a new and violent antireligious campaign started in 1959, Russian Orthodoxy can still gather millions of faithful in its churches and claim the adherence of intellectuals such as Pasternak and Senyavsky.

The communist regimes established in the Balkans are also obliged to be counted with the church's strength. Antireligious pressure never reached, in any of the "popular democracies," the same violence as in Russia, and the churches of Serbia, Romania, and Bulgaria have kept some of their former school systems and are allowed to publish a restricted amount of religious literature. Among the national churches, the Church of Greece is the only one preserving its alliance with the state, but the system is being challenged both by the secularistic tendencies of the state and by an increasing number of churchmen who consider this alliance antiquated.

In the recent decades, the Orthodox Church has played a growing role in the ecumenical movement. Although only a few of the local Orthodox churches were represented at Amsterdam in 1948 at the formation of the World Council of Churches, which was then violently condemned in Moscow, an opposite trend has developed since 1961, and practically all Orthodox churches take part in the Council's work. The contacts with Roman Catholicism have also received wide publicity in recent years.

BIBLIOGRAPHY: E. Benz, *The Eastern Orthodox Church: Its Thought and Life* (Chicago, 1963); V. Lossky, *The Mystical Theology of the Eastern Church* (London, 1957); J. Meyendorff, *The Orthodox Church* (New York, 1962); A. Schmemann, *The Historical Road of Eastern Orthodoxy* (Chicago, 1966); T. Ware, *The Orthodox Church* (Baltimore, 1964); N. Zernov, *Eastern Christendom* (London, 1961).

**Eberlin, Johann** (1470–1533). Popular writer of the Reformation. A former priest and Franciscan monk, Eberlin became an enthusiastic follower of Luther. He wrote fifteen popular tracts, reciting abuses in ecclesiastical, religious, and social life. His early radicalism, perhaps adding to the peasants' animosities, was later tempered by study under Luther and Melanchthon after 1522. He had a fine style and was an appealing preacher and writer.

**Ecclesiastical Vestments.** Although special clothing is not essential to liturgical worship, it adds to the extraordinary character of the event and inevitably develops because of the conservatism of formal worship. Special garments, particularly masks, have functioned in various religions to indicate the nonhuman forces or persons represented in liturgical representation. Finally, the importance of worship has led men to bestow the finest material and craftsmanship on its paraphernalia.

The Aaronic priesthood had symbolic and precious vestments. Christian use developed out of the secular formal clothing of the Roman world. The *cassock,* usually black, tied with a *cincture,* was everyday clothing until the 11th century. Strictly speaking, it is not a liturgical vestment as is the *alb,* a white garment that developed from the Roman tunic and carries the symbolism of the saved dressed in white in Revelation. The alb, like the cassock, covers shoulders to legs and is bound at the waist by a *girdle* of rope. The *surplice* (Italian, *cotta*) is a fuller and shorter form of the alb developed to fit over (*super*) the *pellicea* (a heavy cassock for use in cold churches). The *stole*, used with cassock and surplice for non-Eucharistic functions by Catholics and generally by other ministers, comes from the *pallium*, a scarf denoting office or honor in pagan Rome. It is of various colors to follow the church year. Full Eucharistic vestments in the Western Church begin with alb and *amice*, a white linen cloth that lies like a fallen hood at the back of the neck. A stole is worn over the alb, crossed and fastened in the girdle. A *maniple*, a formalized napkin, may be fastened to the left arm. The *chasuble* covers everything from the shoulders by one large piece of material of the proper color. The term comes from *casula*, "little house," and in Roman times was a large poncho used as an overcoat. These are the priest's garments. The deacon wears a *dalmatic* over the alb. Supposed to have come from Dalmatia, this is a tunic with short sleeves and of the proper color. The subdeacon wears a *tunicle*, like a dalmatic but with longer and narrower sleeves. Special gloves and shoes as marks of honor for priest or bishop were also adopted from Roman custom.

All the vestments mentioned thus far developed into normal usage from the 4th to the 8th centuries. They were made of good quality as befitted the public and festive nature of Christian worship after the persecutions, but they were still the ordinary dress of the day. No symbolism was necessarily involved, the one definite exception being the clothing of the newly baptized in white (hence White Sunday, or Whitsunday). Conservatism and the medieval love of symbolism perpetuated these vestments, added others, and found religious meaning in them and their decoration. Head coverings used liturgically include the skullcap, or *zucchetto*, and *biretta*, for priests, *miter* for bishops, and *tiara* for the pope. *Copes*, fine capes for use in non-Eucharistic functions and made in the liturgical colors, were adopted in the early Middle Ages. All the outer garments may be decorated with *apparels* or *orphreys*. The vestments of the Eastern Church are similar to those of the West but they have no dalmatic or tunicle. For example, the *sticharion* is comparable to the alb but is colored. There are unique vestments also: the *epigonation*, worn by bishops over the right thigh, and *epimanikia*, cuffs.

Protestant churches that have not used traditional Western vestments have often adopted the Geneva or academic gown, sometimes with "bands," a 17th-century innovation. Likewise, formal cutaways and other fancy dress have been adopted from secular use and ritualized, thus recapitulating early church history. In liturgical churches the altar, treated as a person, is vested also. The *fair linen* covers top and sides. A *frontal* of the color of the season originally covered all sides but now covers completely the front only. An *antependium* is a small frontal covering the center third. The *corporal* is a piece of linen on which the elements and their vessels are placed during Mass. A *pall* is stiff material placed over the chalice. *Purificators* are small napkins for wiping the chalice. All the vessels may be covered by a white or a colored *veil*. The corporal may be carried in a *burse*, a folder covered by colored cloth.

BIBLIOGRAPHY: G. Dix, *The Shape of the Liturgy* (London, 1945); H. Norris, *Church Vestments* (New York, 1950); A. C. Piepkorn, *The Survival of the Historic Vestments in the Lutheran Church* (St. Louis, 1958); C. E. Pocknee, *Liturgical Vesture: Its Origins and Development* (Westminster, Md., 1961); E. Roulin, *Vestments and Vesture* (St. Louis, 1931). Also, *Liturgical Arts Quarterly*.

**Eck** (Maier), **Johann** (1486–1543). German opponent of the Protestant Reformation. Born in Eck (now Egg), Swabia, he received his doctorate in theology at the age of twenty-four, joining the University of Inglostadt first as a theologian and later as prochancellor. Known only as a humanist and a defender of modest interest rates, Eck responded in 1518 to Luther's Ninety-five Theses with the tract *Obelisks,* to which Luther replied with his *Asterisk.* Debating with Carlstadt at Leipzig in 1519, Eck shifted his attack to Luther, who was also present. Largely through Eck's influence the debate moved from the question of indulgences to the problem of authority. Eck did not pursue Luther's statement that he would submit to Rome's authority if this were acknowledged as existing by human and not by divine right. Rather, Eck maneuvered the issue to the similarity of the positions of Luther and John Hus. Luther found himself admitting that certain controverted tenets held by Hus were Christian, which was to Eck an admission that the Council of Constance had erred. Eck showed himself an avid and adroit quoter of the Bible and the fathers, but Luther complained that the quotations were often out of context, invented, or inappropriate. Rewarded with the responsibility of publishing

*Exsurge, Domine* in 1520, Eck renewed the debate a year later with his treatise defending the papacy, *De primatu Petri* ("On the Primacy of Peter"). He continued his role as an apologist for the Roman Church until the end of his life, and he was present as adversary of the Protestant at both the Diet of Augsburg (1530) and the Colloquy of Regensburg (1541).

**Eckhart, Johannes** (*usually called* Meister, *or* Master, Eckhart) (c. 1260–c. 1327). German-born Scholastic, preacher, and mystic. His activity was divided among teaching, administration within the Dominican Friars, of which he was a member all of his active life, and pastoral oversight of associations of Dominican houses. Lecturer at Paris (1293–1294), master and teacher there (1302–1303, 1311–1313), and head of the *studium generale* at Cologne (1323–c. 1328), he wrote in Latin an extensive three-part theological *summa* consisting of (1) general propositions comprising over one thousand theses; (2) difficult questions raised in the *Summa theologiae* of Thomas Aquinas; (3) sermons and Biblical expositions; and also a commentary on the *Sentences* of Peter Lombard and several lesser works. Out of his pastoral-administrative years grew the German-language works, including a book on the religious life, one on divine consolation, and the famous sermon on Luke 19:12, *On the Noble Man,* as well as a host of other sermons. Accused of heresy in 1326 on the basis of twenty-eight propositions taken almost exclusively from his German (popular?) works, he was never excommunicated because of a general recantation of all heresy just before his death, although seventeen of the propositions were condemned in 1329. The amalgamation of Neoplatonism by way of Pseudo-Dionysius with his Aristotelian Scholasticism provided the foundations for a mysticism in which the Word is generated in the soul, which is itself a sort of divine spark; by this means, true contemplation yields unity with the Divine. Through his influence upon Tauler, Suso, and Ruysbroeck, and other followers, a mediated form of Eckhartian mysticism affected the Reformers, e.g., Martin Luther through the anonymous late 14th-century treatise *Theologia Germanica,* written by a priest of the Teutonic Order.

**Ecthesis.** Edict of Emperor Heraclius of the Eastern Roman Empire (638). It set forth the doctrine of Monothelism, belief in one divine will. Threatened by Arab invasion, Heraclius hoped by this measure to bring back Egypt and Syria, which had withdrawn and formed their own Monophysite Church after the Council of Chalcedon, into the Empire. Though Monothelism was generally accepted in the East after the Ecthesis, it was rejected in the West and declared heretical by three popes.

**Ecumenical Council.** A synod or assembly which, ideally, represents the whole Christian world and regulates matters involving doctrine, discipline, and cultic life. Most Christians recognize seven ecumenical councils: Nicaea I, II; Constantinople I, II, III; Ephesus; Chalcedon. Roman Catholics recognize fourteen others. A council's relation to the papacy has often been an issue in the West, e.g., the conciliar movement and the Reformation. Eastern Orthodox Churches by definition limit the number of ecumenical councils to seven.

**Ecumenical Missionary Conference** (New York, April 21 to May 1, 1900). This largest missionary conference ever held culminated the series of popular assemblies which began with New York and London in 1854. There were 2,500 members from 64 North American, 50 European, 35 British, and 13 other mission agencies, but 4,000 attended daily sessions, and total attendance exceeded 200,000. Here the term "ecumenical" was introduced into modern Protestant usage.

**Ecumenical Movement.** Designation given to the effort for both cooperation and unity among Christians. The word "ecumenical" is classical in origin, derived from a word meaning "the whole inhabited world." Its modern usage refers to that "which is concerned for the unity and renewal of the church."

*Before the 19th century.* Concern for the unity of the church and its renewal is not a matter of modern times only. Ever since the split between East and West, there have been persons sensitive to the oneness of the church as confessed in its creeds. The church council up to the 16th century was the instrument of unity; the Council of Ferrara-Florence (1438–1445) even managed to bring together the Western and Orthodox halves of the church for a time. The Reformers of the 16th century placed great hopes in an ecumenical council, but the Council of Trent only widened the gap between the old church and the new. Protestant efforts in the form of colloquies (especially Regensburg, 1541, and Poissy, 1561) were also unsuccessful, although they tended to dispel the Protestants' ignorance of one another and to promote toleration. The 17th and 18th centuries saw the appearance of certain ecumenically minded individuals; the Scot, John Durie (d. 1680), is the best example. Not until the 19th century was union actually achieved when an ecumenical individual wielding political power, Frederick William III of Prussia, forced a merger between Lutheran and Calvinistic churches in his lands (1817).

*Beginnings of the modern movement.* The 19th century was the age of great Christian geographical expansion carried out mainly by voluntary societies. On the mission field, the evils of competing denominations were especially evident and the first ecumenical gatherings occurred when missionaries met in the field for discussions and fellowship. The missions were often supported by interdenominational funds and soon the need for coordination led to worldwide meetings in New York and London (1854). Other meetings followed at irregular intervals, culminating in the World Missionary Conference at Edinburgh in 1910. Previously the meetings had been informal and composed of interested individuals. Edinburgh was a conference of delegates from the various churches (although it was not an official meeting) and it was thoroughly planned in advance by Joseph H. Oldham. A permanent Continuation Committee was established at Edinburgh to carry on the work, and this eventuated in the International Missionary Council (1921), the chairman of which was John R. Mott (1865–1955) who had presided at Edinburgh. That conference marked the beginning of the modern ecumenical movement. Another pioneering ecumenical thrust was the effect of certain youth organizations, such as the Y.M.C.A. (founded 1844) and the World Student Christian Federation. Almost all the leaders of the early ecumenical movement got their early training in interdenominational cooperation in these organizations. A third modern source of ecumenism was the concern for Christian service and common ethical action, especially felt because of World War I. The Evangelical Alliance (1846), although not particularly effective, expressed this concern, as did also the Federal Council of the Churches of Christ in America (1908). The most extraordinary figure in this effort was the Swedish archbishop Nathan Söderblom (1866–1931). Under his auspices and inspired by his leadership the first Universal Christian Conference on Life and Work was held in Stockholm in 1925. A continuation committee grew into the Universal Christian Council for Life and Work in 1930 (or simply "Life and Work"). A second world conference was called for Oxford in 1937. The fourth area of ecumenical concern was the field of Christian doctrine. Many were hesitant about raising problems of "Faith and Order," yet Christian unity demanded that division of belief also be considered. The

American Episcopal bishop Charles H. Brent (1862–1929) was the leader who had caught at Edinburgh the vision of a reunited church that would come about only through a discussion of doctrinal differences. After overcoming immense difficulties, Brent was able to chair the first meeting of the World Conference on Faith and Order (Lausanne, 1927). A continuation committee summoned the next meeting for Edinburgh in 1937.

*The World Council of Churches.* There were now three ecumenical bodies, the International Missionary Council, Life and Work, and Faith and Order. Plans were made to form a world council which would merge the last two groups, the first being associated with it. William Temple (1881–1944), archbishop of York at the time, was instrumental in plans for this future world organization. However, World War II intervened, and it was not until 1948 that the World Council of Churches was formed at Amsterdam, 147 churches from 47 countries participating. In 1961 the International Missionary Council was integrated with the Council, and probably the most significant group to join since its inception was the Orthodox Church of Russia.

The World Council is a limited organization. It does not contain the Roman Catholic Church or certain large Protestant bodies, such as the Southern Baptists in the United States. It does encompass most of the Eastern churches and almost all the churches stemming from the Reformation, as well as those of more recent development such as the Methodists and the Disciples of Christ. The World Council is not a church or a superchurch. It has no coercive power over its member churches and the authority of its studies on social and political matters exists only insofar as member churches wish to follow its conclusions. The World Council is not a hierarchical organization. Its objective is to work together with the churches in the interest of unity and renewal. As a forum for frank theological discussion, as a means for achieving cooperation, and as a resource for consultation, the World Council of Churches has proved its worth.

*Other forms of ecumenism.* The ecumenical movement has also expressed itself in other ways which, though not as extensive as the World Council of Churches, are very important. The first of these ways is the organic mergers within and across denominational lines which have taken place in many countries. The Presbyterian churches of Scotland finally achieved union in 1929, and in the United States conspicuous examples of union have been given by the Lutherans and Methodists. By crossing denominational lines, new configurations of church life have been created. Most noticeable of the interdenominational mergers are the United Church of Canada (Methodist, Congregational, Presbyterian) and the Church of South India (Methodist, Congregational, Presbyterian, Anglican). Secondly, worldwide denominational organizations have been formed, such as the Presbyterian Alliance (1875), the World Methodist Council (1881), and the Lutheran World Convention (1923). In the third place, other worldwide organizations also exist, some as protest movements against the World Council of Churches or its affiliates (for example, the National Association of Evangelicals in the United States), some as continuations of 19th-century voluntary organizations (The International Fellowship of Evangelical Students). Fourthly, the resurgence of the ecumenical vision of the Roman Catholic Church must be noted. The appointment of a special commission for ecumenical affairs in 1960, with Augustin Cardinal Bea as president, culminated in the Second Vatican Council. This marks, from the Roman Catholic side, an acknowledgment of the Protestant ecumenical movement and is of the greatest importance.

BIBLIOGRAPHY: R. P. Beaver, *Ecumenical Beginnings in Protestant World Missions* (New York, 1962); G. K. A. Bell, *Documents on Christian Unity*, 3 series (London, 1924, 1930, 1948); R. M. Brown, *The Ecumenical Revolution* (Garden City, 1967); W. R. Hogg, *Ecumenical Foundations* (New York, 1952); H. Küng, *The Council: Reform and Reunion* (Garden City, 1965); G. A. Lindbeck (ed.), *Dialogue on the Way* (Minneapolis, 1965); J. T. McNeill, *Unitive Protestantism* (Richmond, 1964); R. Rouse and S. C. Neill (eds.), *A History of the Ecumenical Movement: 1517–1948* (2d ed., rev., Philadelphia, 1967). Also, *The Ecumenical Review* (quarterly).

**Ecumenical Patriarch.** The Greek Orthodox patriarch of Constantinople (Istanbul) who is the holder of the primary place of honor among Orthodox bishops. Formally spoken of as "His All-Holiness," he is regarded as a symbol of unity but not as head of the whole Eastern Orthodox Church. Among Eastern prelates, he is first among equals; his post is not parallel to the Roman pope. Although according to legend the see was established by Andrew, it first achieved importance when Constantine dedicated Constantinople, on the site of the ancient town of Byzantium, as capital of his empire (330), emphasizing the principle that ecclesiastical organization should follow political organization. The Second Ecumenical Council (381) decreed that the bishop of Constantinople "shall have the privilege of rank next after the bishop of Rome; because Constantinople is new Rome." This meant that the title of patriarch, confirmed to bishops of Rome, Antioch, and Alexandria by the Council of Nicaea (325), accrued to Constantinople. In 451 the Council of Chalcedon gave the patriarch of Constantinople equal status with the bishop of Rome (though Rome might enjoy ceremonial precedence), jurisdiction over sees in Greece and Asia Minor, and the right to ordain subordinate prelates, to call provincial synods, and to be court of ultimate appeal for religious affairs in the East. It was the imperial rank of Constantinople that magnified its metropolitans. The ecumenical patriarch was never able to display the independence of secular authority that was exhibited by Roman pontiffs. Pope Leo I (440–461) refused to admit Eastern ecclesiastical parity to Rome, though *modus vivendi* had been achieved by the East.

Gregory the Great one and a half centuries later resisted the claims of the ascetic John the Faster to the title of "universal bishop." Definition of the term "ecumenical patriarch" was regularly in dispute between East and West, though it is doubtful that the bishops (then archbishops) of Constantinople ever sought supremacy over the entire Christian church. Meanwhile the Eastern Church was developing, as was the Byzantine Empire, customs of its own that would lead to permanent schism: use of Greek in the Mass, marriage of lower clergy, icons in preference to images. Groups that came to be called Uniats always admitted Roman hegemony. The Orthodox clergy did so less and less. From the point of view of the Byzantine rulers, the patriarchs were premier religious vassals to be made or unmade by imperial patronage.

Final separation from Rome came in the days of the patriarch Michael Cerularius (1054). When the Venetians in the Fourth Crusade captured Constantinople (1204), a Latin patriarch and dynasty were forced on the Empire and the schism was proclaimed healed. Actually, the Orthodox clergy resisted reunion. In less than a century the old order had been restored. When the Ottoman Turks captured Constantinople (1453), the patriarch became in effect hostage for his coreligionists in the expanding Moslem dominions. More often than not, simony was involved in his securing office. The authority of Constantinople declined in 1589 when Russian bishops in synod established the patriarchate of Moscow with the title of "universal lord" for their metropolitan. Phanariot Greeks officered the Orthodox churches in the Balkans until the 19th century when autonomous or autocephalous communions were set up by Serbia, Romania, and Bulgaria with their own order of service and patriarchs. Albania secured its autocephalous status in 1937. Establishment of the Turkish republic and the Greco-Turkish War of 1920 to 1922 with resultant population exchanges made difficult the position of the patriarch. Fortunately, with Turkey neutral until the close of World War II, exercise of the office was not impossible. A growing *rapprochement* with Latin Christianity was noted after this war, facilitated by the Second Vatican Council and culminating in the interview of the ecumenical patriarch and Pope Paul VI in the Holy Land (1964). Since then increased cooperation has been exhibited at every level. Patriarch Athenagoras I on Nov. 16, 1966, stated that reunion of Latin and Orthodox Christians would be achieved in the "foreseeable future."

BIBLIOGRAPHY: W. F. Adeney, *The Greek and Eastern Churches* (New York, 1908); A. Fortescue, *The Orthodox Eastern Church* (London, 1916); R. M. French, *The Eastern Orthodox Church* (London, 1951); B. J. Kidd, *The Churches of Eastern Christendom from A.D. 451 to the Present* (London, 1927); T. Ware, *The Orthodox Church* (Baltimore, 1964).

**Eddy, Mary Baker** (1821–1910). Founder of Christian Science. She was born into a Calvinist family in New Hampshire at a time when many were turning away from the old New England divinity. Although she was in somewhat delicate health, her childhood does not seem to have been abnormal. Because of illness, she did not obtain a good education, but she possessed ability as a writer, some of her poetry being published in women's magazines many years before she became known as a religious leader.

Her first marriage in 1843 to a family friend, G. W. Glover, ended tragically when he died within a few months of their wedding, leaving her pregnant and without resources. She returned home to have her child, but because of the recurrence of her illness he was raised in the homes of relatives. For many years Mary had no home of her own, no income, and poor health. When in 1853 she married a dentist named Patterson, she found herself worse off than before because of the improvident way in which he conducted his business and personal life, and she finally divorced him in 1873.

Her health had by this time become a constant preoccupation and source of anxiety. Medical terminology has changed so radically in the century since then that it is difficult to know what the exact nature of her illness was. She described it as a "spinal inflamation, and its train of sufferings, gastric and bilious." She spent some time experimenting with spiritualism, a common fascination of this period, but did not receive any relief from her malady until she met Phineas P. Quimby.

Quimby helped her a great deal, and his teachings are thought to have formed the core of what was later to become Christian Science, though Mrs. Eddy and officials of the Mother Church denied it in later years. He called himself a doctor, believing that by deriving strength from God he had the power to draw illness out of the body. Mary had a great deal of faith in Quimby, saw him often and copied some of his writings. When he died in 1866, she wrote an elegy for him that was published in the *Lynn* (Mass.) *Advertiser*.

A month after Quimby's death, in February, 1866, she fell on the ice and thought she was critically injured. Once again, her own reminiscences in later years do not coincide with verified witnesses, such as the doctor who attended her. Regardless of the seriousness of her injuries, however, she felt in later years that her career as a healer began on the third day after her fall when, trusting in God, she got out of bed and found herself well.

She began to practice healing herself with, apparently, some success, but soon gave that up in favor of writing. Still living with strangers for a few months at a time, facing what she considered betrayals by many early converts to her cause, she continued doggedly to write and revise her book which was eventually published in 1875 as *Science and Health*. She did not become a well-known figure overnight. The first editions of *Science and Health* lost money, and troubles followed her for many years. A. G. Eddy, whom she married in 1877, died five years later.

She was a genius in her own way, but she seems to have been jealous and somewhat vituperative, authoritarian, and liable to forget inconvenient things. Although her teachings developed during her lifetime, she did not vary from her fundamental conviction that Mind or God is the only reality, that sin, evil, sickness, and death are not real but only errors which can be overcome by the right beliefs—by Christian Science. Toward the last years of her remarkably active and long life, she withdrew from society and spent her time organizing the Christian Scientists into a religious society.

BIBLIOGRAPHY: C. S. Braden, *Christian Science Today* (Dallas, 1958); E. F. Dakin, *Mrs.*

*Eddy: The Biography of a Virginal Mind* (New York, 1930); S. Wilbur, *The Life of Mary Baker Eddy* (Boston, 1938).

**Eddy, Sherwood** (1871–1963). An American missionary and evangelist of a comprehensive Christian spirit. He combined evangelical piety with social passion in a concern for the wider relations of life. He was particularly known for his labors in the Orient, among American college students, in European seminars, and for his longtime connection with the Y.M.C.A. not only in America, but as national secretary in India (1896–1911) and secretary for Asia (1911 ff.). He became familiar to many through numerous books and magazine articles.

**Edelmann, Johann Christian** (1698–1767). German Neoplatonist. Initially a student of theology, Edelmann broke from the church and moved through Plotinus, the Stoics, Spinoza, and the physicotheology of B. H. Brockes. He wandered widely, but after 1749 stayed mainly in Berlin. Arguing heatedly with Christian Wolff, he maintained that the Logos was panentheistic (John 1:1, "In the beginning was reason"): reason is the power and wisdom of God come among men in Jesus; man must struggle free from flesh. Edelmann was one of the expositors in the eight-volume Berleburger Bible (1726–1742).

**Edict of Nantes** (1598). Treaty between Henry IV and the French Huguenots which granted religious liberty on condition of renouncement of foreign alliances. Signed April 13, 1598, the treaty ended the French Wars of Religion. The Reformed Church had suffered greatly in France, and Huguenots hailed the enthronement of Henry of Navarre (1589). When Henry became a nominal Catholic (1593), the situation worsened. Earnest negotiation preceded the Edict as Huguenot power increased. The Edict guaranteed that a man's faith was no reason for persecution. Private worship was allowed anywhere; public worship places were specifically designated, including some noble estates. The Huguenots were not to worship in Paris or within five leagues. They were given full civil rights, educational and hospital privileges. All offices of the state were made accessible, and mixed courts were established. With the king's permission, the Huguenots were allowed to enter political discussions. The state was to subsidize Reformed pastors and troops. Two hundred fortified towns were granted to the Huguenots as guarantees of these concessions. The Edict was ratified in the National Assembly with some difficulty. It was rather well enforced from 1629 to 1665, but gradually the concessions were withdrawn as Roman Catholic power in the government solidified. Louis XIV revoked the Edict on Oct. 18, 1685, and a mass exodus of Huguenots followed.

**Edict of Restitution** (1629). The culmination of the religious policy of the Holy Roman Emperor Ferdinand II in the Thirty Years' War. It marked the high tide of both his religious and his political fortunes in that conflict. The Edict demanded the return to Catholic authorities of all ecclesiastical lands that had passed into Protestant hands after the Peace of Augsburg (1555) and contrary to the "Ecclesiastical Reservation" of that document, which had exempted ecclesiastical lands from the force of its otherwise general principle *Cuius regio, eius religio,* if an ecclesiastical prince became Protestant, he was *not* allowed to change the religion of his lands. The opposition aroused by the Edict undoubtedly contributed to the deterioration of Ferdinand's position after 1629.

**Edict of 1788** (Prussia). A reactionary religious measure aimed to counteract the Enlightenment. *Das Edikt, die Religionsverfassung in den preussischen Staaten betreffend* (July 9, 1788), which was its official title, is also known as Wöllner's Religion Edict after its author Johann Christof Wöllner (1732–1800), a former pastor who had gained the confidence of Frederick William II through his role as head of the Rosicrucian lodge in Berlin. In 1788 he became privy councilor for state and justice and head of the spiritual department. Only six days later the Religion Edict was published. The object of this measure was to defend the liturgies and confessions of the three recognized churches in Germany against the "unbridled freedom" of the Enlightenment which had been so effectively promoted by Frederick the Great. The Edict forbade pastors to teach anything not strictly in conformity with the confessional books, set forth the necessity to protect the faith against the "enlighteners," and attempted to place education in the hands of the orthodox. Other measures were undertaken as well, including a censorship law, and in 1791 to what amounted to a "Protestant Inquisition." Although the Edict did not attempt to regulate private opinion, it tended to separate official proclamation of religion therefrom, requiring that it be orthodox even if the preacher's views were not. The failure of this reactionary measure was due largely to the resistance of the powerful theological faculty at Halle. In 1791 the king withdrew support from the Edict and the following year dismissed Wöllner.

**Edinburgh Conference** (1910). A world missionary conference. It was the first major delegated Protestant unity conference and a landmark in the ecumenical movement, a major event in the life of the church. "Edinburgh, 1910" was the focal point of a century's attempts at missionary cooperation. It set a determinative pattern for the future. At a critical juncture in world and church history the Conference released new creative sources to an emerging world Christian community supplying vision, leadership, and organization for a new era. It marked the metamorphosis from ecclesiastical colonialism to a global fellowship.

The Conference met at the University of Edinburgh's New Castle College. One hundred fifty-nine societies sent 1,200 delegates. It was a work conference to study, consult, and organize for unity in missionary endeavor. Studies included world evangelization, the "Native Church," the Christian message in relation to non-Christian religions, cooperation, and the promotion of unity. Many renowned church statesmen came out of this Conference, including John R. Mott and Joseph H. Oldham. The Conference realized a high degree of unity, an awareness of the urgency of the global task of the church, and a recognition that the church existed on "the mission field." It provided an international interdenominational Continuation Committee. A new desire for inclusive togetherness was born in the church.

**Edinburgh Conference** (1937). Second World Conference on Faith and Order. It was composed of the representatives of 123 churches sending 344 delegates. The Conference continued the work of the Lausanne Conference (1927). The program was set up by the Continuation Committee and its subjects were "Grace," "The Word of God," "The Communion of Saints," "The Ministry and the Sacraments," and "The Church's Unity in Life and Worship." The churches moved nearer agreement on the great themes that had been studied since Lausanne. The deepest consensus was reached on "The Grace of Our Lord Jesus Christ." The report on this section asserted that "there is in connexion with this subject no ground for maintaining division between Churches." However, on the crucial question of the ministry and the sacraments there was relatively little agreement. The principal obstacle in the way of achieving the aims of essential unity in faith and communion was found to be the opposition between the conception of the church as "authoritarian" and the conception of it as "personal."

The Conference drew up a memorable "Affirmation" of the church's union in allegiance to the Lord Jesus Christ. It also approved the proposal of a "World Council of Churches," which has since become a reality.

**Education Act of 1882** (France). The law of March 28, 1882, separating public education from the Catholic Church and associated with the name of Jules F. C. Ferry (1832–1893), minister of education. It made primary education free, compulsory, and secular. Subsequent laws of Oct. 30, 1886, and July 7, 1904, restricted teaching in both public and private schools to the laity and abolished all religious teaching in those schools. The 1904 law likewise placed secondary education under rigorous government controls, created an open breach with the papacy, and resulted in the 1905 Act of Separation.

**Education Act of 1902** (England). A constructive act measurably advancing education in England. It empowered local councils with new authority and subjected council and church-related voluntary schools to them. Maintenance of voluntary schools was put on the "rate charge." This aroused bitter antagonism from the nonconformist churches. Despite church discord, the act achieved integration of education with an increasing democratic community.

**Education Act of 1944** (England and Wales). A revolutionary education act centralizing authority, controlling standards, and strengthening the Christian foundations of education in England and Wales. The act unified the progressive levels of education and made secondary education compulsory. It gave full recognition to church-related voluntary educational work, modifying and elaborating it. It defined denominational privileges within the educational system.

**Edward VI** (1537–1553). King of England from 1547 during the progress of the Protestant Reformation in England. Though the boy king was undoubtedly influenced toward Protestantism by the protector Somerset and later by the duke of Northumberland, his own leanings were apparently in that direction and he was strongly interested in religious matters. Edward himself was, of course, without real political influence. His role as Supreme Head of the English Church, established by his father, Henry VIII, was delegated to the Privy Council and utilized to promulgate and enforce many ecclesiastical enactments, particularly of a liturgical nature. The most noteworthy of these were the first (1549) and second (1552) Books of Common Prayer, the latter much more "Protestant" than the former (see UNIFORMITY, ACTS OF; CRANMER, THOMAS). Some of this legislation aroused fierce opposition, especially in Devon and Cornwall. During Edward's reign some heretics (i.e., those erring on either side of the government's current ecclesiastical position) were burned, and some distinguished bishops were deprived of their sees, but there were no wholesale executions. Northumberland induced the young king, who was dying of tuberculosis, to name Lady Jane Grey as his successor, but the Crown was claimed by Edward's half sister, Mary, who reversed the religious policies of his reign.

**Edward the Confessor** (1003–1066). King of England from 1042. He lived at the court of his uncle, the duke of Normandy, where he was educated. Placed on the English throne through the influence of the powerful earl Godwin of Wessex, whose daughter he married, Edward excited opposition by his preferments of Norman prelates to English positions, especially Robert of Jumièges to Canterbury. Godwin objected and was banished in 1051, but restored in 1052, his supporter Stigand replacing Robert. A church had existed at Westminster since perhaps the early 7th century, but Edward encouraged the building of Westminster Abbey, which was consecrated shortly before his death in 1066.

**Edward the Martyr** (c. 963–978). King of England from 975. With the support of Archbishop Dunstan, he succeeded his father on the throne of England, despite the opposition of his stepmother Elfrida. The main ecclesiastical interest of the reign lies in the continued struggle of Dunstan to ensure unmarried and monastic clergy against the antimonastic faction led by Aelfhere, the earl of Mercia. Counseled by Dunstan, Edward defended the church and the monasteries. Although quick-tempered, he was personally popular and was murdered for political reasons, probably at the instigation of his stepmother, who was ambitious for her own son. Hurriedly buried at Wareham, he was removed two years later to Shaftesbury, with both Archbishop Dunstan and the earl of Mercia assisting at the elaborate ceremonies.

**Edwards, Jonathan** (1703–1758). American theologian, revivalist, philosopher, psychologist, and aesthetician. The contribution and controversy of Edwards can be summed up in the words "experimental religion." His public life and the life of his mind were cast in an orthodox New England Puritan mold. He was simultaneously experimental because he seized for his own use the new science and psychology of Newton and Locke. Caught up in the enthusiasm of the colonial awakenings while equally and deeply disturbed by contemporary tendencies to blur the harsh realities of God, Edwards concluded that his generation abounded with false conceptions of the nature of man. He devoted himself to an analysis of the means by which man acquires knowledge, what causes him to will good and evil, and what gives him intense emotions, whether with integrity or through "overheated imaginations." His thought and action rested on the Christian doctrines of original sin and irresistible grace, but he also believed, with the most sophisticated exponents of the new empirical science, that all knowledge was based upon sense experience. He came to believe in earnest that the revivals, whatever their excesses, were observable and therefore irrefutable manifestations of the reality of supernatural intervention in human affairs. He immediately came under attack by the new rationalist theologians for his defense of religious enthusiasm and for his advocacy of traditional Puritanism. Edwards was the most acute American analyst of the scientific, psychological, and philosophical achievements of the Age of Reason. He recognized and accepted the challenge given traditional Christianity by the physical discoveries of Newton, the epistemological observations of Locke, and the ever-growing popular acceptance of a "God more kind and man more worthy." He attempted to unite these divergent movements by his bold reliance upon a seemingly outdated Biblical revelation and Reformation theology. He admitted that many religious beliefs about man's "understanding" and "affections" had been inadequately explained. Yet he refused to exchange his strenuous Puritan theology for an Enlightenment moralism. Edwards nevertheless joined a select group of 18th-century intellectuals who recognized that the struggle for the contemporary mind would not result in a decisive victory for the physical scientist nor for those who were privy to the councils of heaven. The victor would have to produce a revolutionary concept of the workings of the human mind. Concerning the revivals, Edwards believed that the weeping and shouting were worthwhile human activities, considering the crises of the damned. The preaching of terror aroused the "affections," which are the "spring of men's actions." Edwards believed in both an unconditional God and an unconditional Nature, and the awakenings were the result of both. His energies were absorbed by his defense of revivalism and a lifelong battle with Arminianism. Convinced of man's helplessness, Edwards argued that men could be restored only through the divine gift of "a true sense of the divine excellence of things revealed in the Word of God and conviction of the truth and reality of these things." This "new sense" allowed man to participate directly in absolute truth, goodness, and beauty.

Educated at Yale, Edwards in 1727 became assistant to his grandfather Solomon Stoddard at the church in Northampton, Mass., and upon Stoddard's death, the regular minister. In 1731, Edwards gained widespread attention through his Boston sermon, "God Glorified in Man's Dependence." Deeply involved in the Great Awakening from 1735 to its conclusion, he defended it in four treatises: *A Faithful Narrative of the Surprising Work of God* (1737), *The Distinguishing Marks of a Work of the Spirit of God* (1741), *Some Thoughts Concerning the Present Revival of Religion in New England* (1742), and *A Treatise Concerning Religious Affections* (1746). Faced with dissension in his own church, Edwards was compelled to resign in 1750 and took a wilderness mission post in Stockbridge in 1751. There he wrote several major works, including *Treatise on the Freedom of the Will* (1754) and *The Great Christian Doctrine of Original Sin Defended* (1758). Edwards was named president of the College of New Jersey (Princeton) in 1757 but died from a smallpox innoculation after a few months. Posthumously published works include *The Nature of True Virtue* and *The End for which God Created the World* (1765). His intended synthesis, *A History of the Work of Redemption,* was never begun.

BIBLIOGRAPHY: A. O. Aldridge, *Jonathan Edwards* (New York, 1964); E. H. Davidson, *Jonathan Edwards* (Boston, 1965); D. J. Elwood, *The Philosophical Theology of Jonathan Edwards* (New York, 1960); P. Miller, *Jonathan Edwards* (New York, 1959); O. E. Winslow, *Jonathan Edwards* (New York, 1940).

**Edwards, Jonathan, Jr.,** "the Younger" (1745–1801). Son of the great philosopher and theologian and a rigorous Edwardsian. Ordained in 1769, he served churches in New Haven and Colebrook, Conn., and became president of Union College, Schenectady, N.Y., in 1799. Much of his theology was formulated in controversy, particularly with Charles Chauncy and his liberal successors. He sought to retain in modified form the doctrines of atonement, imputation, and depravity. Intolerant of opposition, his Edwardsianism was unmollified by a sympathetic piety. His rigorous legalism led opponents to label his theology as intemperate and immoral. He was the most skillful dialectician of Edwardsianism, but lacked his father's imagination and originality. His writings were largely polemical. He edited some of his father's works and published a defense of the elder Edwards' treatise on the freedom of the will. Many of his articles were published in *The New York Theological Magazine*. His most influential work was *On the Necessity of the Atonement and its Consistency with Free Grace in Forgiveness* (1785), which formed the basis for the Edwardsian theory of the atonement.

**Edwin** (c. 585–633). First Northumbrian king to become a Christian. He married Ethelburga, daughter of Ethelbert of Kent, Augustine's convert. Bede makes Bishop Paulinus, her chaplain, the chief instrument of the evangelization of Northumbria, but Celtic missionaries may have had more influence there than Bede's account would indicate. Edwin was baptized in York at Easter, 627, and slain at Heathfield in 633 in battle with the pagan kings of Wales and Mercia. He was venerated for many centuries as a martyr.

**Efficacious Grace** (post-Tridentine debates on). These debates in the Roman Catholic Church discussed the doctrine of predestination and were focused on the distinction between "sufficient grace," which merely *enables* the soul to perform a supernatural act, and "efficacious grace," which really *effects* the act. It was variously argued (1) that the efficacious grace given to the predestined is intrinsically different from the sufficient grace given indiscriminately to all; (2) that God predestines those whom he foresees will consent to the sufficient grace which is given to all; or (3) that to the predestined, God gives his grace under such circumstances as he foresees will guarantee their consent. Hence the efficaciousness of grace, wherever grace achieves its effect, was referred either to its special nature (the Dominican, or Thomistic, view) or to the activity of the human will (the Molinist view), or, finally, to the circumstances under which the grace is operative (the so-called congruist view). The second and third views, widely held among the Jesuits, both made use of the idea of God's foreknowledge, but in different ways. The first and third views agreed in making God's predestination independent of his foreknowledge of man's consent, whereas the second frankly subordinated predestination to foreknowledge of consent. It has been claimed that the congruist position, developed by Suárez and Bellarmine, was at least foreshadowed by Molina himself, and that what is commonly termed "Molinism" was more properly the view of

Lessius. The Thomistic position was ably defended by Banez. A commission to study the doctrine of the divine aid given to man (*Congregatio de Auxiliis*) was appointed by Pope Clement VIII (1597), and on the basis of its findings his successor, Paul V, allowed each party to teach its own view (1607). In 1613 the superior of the Jesuits, Aquaviva, required his order to teach the congruist rather than the Molinist doctrine. Subsequent commentators have pointed out that the Dominican and Jesuit positions are not strictly in opposition, the former being based primarily on metaphysical considerations, the latter being designed more with a view to usefulness in pastoral counseling.

**Egbert of York** (d. 766). Archbishop. A cousin of Ceolwulf, king of Northumbria, he was appointed to the see of York in 732, where he founded the well-known cathedral school. The Venerable Bede was his friend and adviser, and correspondence survives in which Boniface requests from Egbert the works of Bede. Alcuin was probably his pupil at York. Several works have come down to us under Egbert's name, including a penitential and a pontifical, but their authenticity is in doubt, at least in their present form.

**Egede, Hans** (1686–1758). Norwegian Lutheran pastor and pioneer missionary. After study at Copenhagen he became a pastor in the Lofoten Islands in Norway at the age of twenty-one. Reports about Greenland inspired him with a desire to preach to the Greenlanders. In 1710 he wrote "A Proposition for Greenland's Conversion and Enlightenment." The economic situation during the Great Northern War (1700–1721), however, delayed the implementation of his dream. In 1721, with 45 colonists and with the assistance of King Frederick IV, he established the colony of Godthaab (Good Hope) in Greenland. Finding no Norwegians on Greenland, he sought to evangelize the Eskimos there. On New Year's Day, 1725, he baptized the first converts. In 1731 three Moravian missionaries were sent to aid the mission but disagreements soon arose between them and the orthodox Egede. After fifteen years of labor Egede returned to Denmark because of poor health, his wife having already died in Greenland. In Denmark he was instrumental in founding a missionary college in Copenhagen and he became its superintendent. In 1740 he was named director of the Greenland Mission, retiring in 1747. His son, Paul, continued his father's work and translated the New Testament into the language of the Greenland Eskimos.

**Einhard** (c. 770–840). Frankish historian and one of the leading figures of the intellectual revival of the 9th century. He was educated at the monastery of Fulda and the palace school at Aachen. A close friend of Charlemagne's, he became influential at the imperial court, retaining favor through the reign of Louis the Pious. He was the author of a life of Charlemagne, which he modeled after the biographies of the Caesars by Suetonius.

**Einsiedeln** (from German for "hermits"). Benedictine abbey. On the site of the murder of the hermit Meinrad (d. 861) in Switzerland, Eberhard of Strasbourg in 934 incorporated the remaining hermits into a newly founded Benedictine abbey. After 965 the abbots of Einsiedeln were princes of the Empire. During the late Middle Ages the house declined, so that the last monk of that period fell on Zwingli's side in the war of 1531. Noted as a place of pilgrimage from 1314, it rose to its height in this respect in the 15th century. Reorganized in 1544, in 1602 it became the center of the Swiss Benedictine Congregation. From it three abbeys were founded in the United States in the mid-19th century.

**Ejection, Great.** See UNIFORMITY, ACTS OF.

**Eleanor of Aquitaine** (c. 1122–1204). Queen of France and later wife of Henry II of England. Heiress to the vast southern French duchy of Aquitaine, Eleanor married King Louis VII of France in 1137. A product of the more sophisticated southern culture, she scandalized her pious husband when she accompanied him on the Second Crusade (1147). She and her ladies-in-waiting dressed as Amazons, and there were rumors that at Antioch she engaged in a love affair with her uncle. Finally, her failure to bear Louis an heir coupled with his suspicions of her conduct led the French king in 1152 to divorce Eleanor on grounds of consanguinity. A few months later she married young Henry, duke of Normandy and count of Anjou, who in 1154 became Henry II of England. Thus Eleanor brought most of southwestern France into the hands of the English king, a fact that gave rise to the struggle between the French and English kings which ensued throughout most of the Middle Ages. Henry's infidelities brought about his estrangement from Eleanor, and during the latter years of his reign she often conspired with her sons against him. After Henry's death Eleanor had great influence in the affairs of state, particularly during the reign of Richard the Lion-Hearted. Eleanor has always been a romantic figure; it was at her court that great impetus was given to the courtly love traditions of the troubadours.

**Elections, Imperial.** With the creation of the Holy Roman Empire through the coronation of the German king Otto I as Roman emperor (962), it became tradition that election to the kingship of Germany by the German princes was *ipso facto* election as Holy Roman Emperor, the blessing and coronation by the pope being the formal assumption of the title. For a time, under the Saxon and Salian dynasties (918–1024 and 1024–1125 respectively) it appeared that election would give way to hereditary succession, but with the election of Lothair II in 1125 the elective principle became firmly established, and though after 1438 the choice was limited to members of the Hapsburg family, the election of the emperor continued as a matter of course until the end of the empire in 1806. In 1356 by the Golden Bull of Emperor Charles IV the electors of the emperor were limited to seven and the necessity of papal confirmation was denied. The seven electors were: the king of Bohemia, the duke of Saxony, the margrave of Brandenburg, the count palatine of the Rhine, and the archbishops of Cologne, Mainz, and Trier. Later an eighth elector, the duke of Bavaria, was named. The elective principle militated against the emergence of a strong imperial authority. It put enormous power in the hands of the great German nobles and contributed no little to the particularization of Germany until its unification in 1870.

**Eliot, John** (1604–1690). Missionary to the Indians in Massachusetts. A native of England and a graduate of Cambridge, he came to America in 1631 and served as teacher at the Roxbury Church from 1632 until his death. He organized settlements of "praying Indians," translated the Bible into the Indian language, and, with assistance from his sons, wrote *The Indian Grammar Begun*. He, Thomas Weld, and Richard Mather prepared the Bay Psalm Book.

**Eliot, Thomas Stearns** (1888–1965). American-born English poet, critic, Nobel Prize winner (1948). Educated at Harvard, Paris, and Oxford, Eliot expatriated to Britain before World War I, contributed to and edited several literary journals, and taught at Cambridge and Harvard. His transition from inherited Congregationalism to agnosticism is evident in the pessimism of *Poems* (1920) and *The Hollow Men* (1925). In 1927 he became a British citizen and an Anglican. *Ash Wednesday* (1930) and the drama *Murder in the Cathedral* (1935) demonstrate a renewed faith. Eliot's nontraditional poetry relied on suggestion and contrasting ideas; he sought new verse rhythms based on contemporary speech. He trusted the social function of poetry, and dealt with the fundamental questions of Christianity rather than its dogmas. His religious prose included *The Idea of a Christian Society*.

**Elipandus** (c. 718–802). Archbishop of Toledo. He became a leader in the Adoptianist controversy in Spain. Megitus of Seville had been teaching a Sabellian Christology to which Elipandus replied with an Adoptianist view. Because the controversy entered the Spanish March, Charlemagne called several synods to condemn the heresy. One of Elipandus' followers, Felix of Urgel, later renounced his doctrines. Elipandus retained his see until his death.

**Elizabeth I** (1533–1603). Queen of England from 1558, only child of Henry VIII by his second wife Anne Boleyn. The declaration of that marriage as invalid by Archbishop Cranmer in 536 made her illegitimate, a decision never legally reversed, although the Act of Succession (1544) gave her the right, with restrictions to succeed after Edward and Mary. Closely associated after Henry's death in 1547 with his last wife Catherine Parr, she was accused of complicity with Thomas Seymour, brother of Somerset and Catherine's husband, in an alleged plot (1548) to overthrow Edward. Having survived this ordeal, she found herself in new peril during her Roman Catholic half sister Mary's reign when she was imprisoned (1554) on suspicion of conspiracy in the rebellion fomented by Wyatt against the queen's marriage to Philip of Spain. Despite Spanish pressures to have Elizabeth executed, the case would not support such drastic measures.

When she succeeded Mary (Nov. 17, 1558), her dismissal of most of the Royal Council and her choice of a few men of moderate religious views, Cecil (later Lord Burghley) being her principal adviser, indicated the direction her reign would take. She would perhaps have preferred personally to return to the "popeless Catholicism" of the last years of her father's reign (1529–1547), but she realized that this was not acceptable to the increasing number of Protestants represented by Cecil; nor could she simply reinstate the 1552 settlement (see UNIFORMITY, ACTS OF; PRAYER BOOK REVISIONS), which would have alienated even moderate Catholics. Two Parliamentary acts—the Act of Supremacy, restoring approximately the religious situation of 1549 to 1551, and the Act of Uniformity, restoring in modified form the Prayer Book of 1552—and the Royal Injunctions, some fifty-three points for enforcement by visitors (based on the Edwardine Injunctions of 1547), all issued in 1559, became the statutory basis of the Elizabethan Settlement of religion. The selection of Matthew Parker as archbishop of Canterbury, a moderate deprived in Mary's reign, provided the ecclesiastical implementation of a comprehensive settlement. In 1562 he caused to be issued an augmented version of the *Books of Homilies* (first published in 1547), in 1563 he supervised issuance by Convocation of the Thirty-nine Articles, and in 1866 he issued his *Advertisements,* which pertained to the vestiarian controversy.

Although the official break with Rome occurred in 1561, it was not until 1570 that Pius V issued a bull excommunicating Elizabeth as a heretic and declaring her a usurper whose subjects need not obey her laws (*Regnans in excelsis*). However, the bull was a decade too late to be of value to the Roman Catholic rebels of the north. Effective Roman opposition came in the years following 1580 with the rising tide of Jesuit and seminary priests, the *Explanatio* of Gregory XIII confirming *Regnans in excelsis,* and the successive plots involving Mary Stuart. These activities led to harsher anti-Catholic laws and the execution of Mary Stuart after nineteen years of imprisonment on the occasion of the threatened Spanish invasion in 1587. Elizabeth's treatment of Roman Catholics during the rest of her reign was such as to minimize their political potential without insisting upon rigid application of all the statutory strictures upon them, except where religious fanaticism threatened either the realm, her person, or the religious settlement.

In her dealings with Puritans, Elizabeth faced a different problem. The settlement of 1559 was to them only a temporary stop on the road to Presbyterianism. Spurred on by Thomas Cartwright of Cambridge, the Puritan cause gained momentum and "prophesyings" were held regularly, especially after the two *Admonitions to Parliament* in 1572 and 1573 calling for the establishment of Presbyterianism. After Archbishop Grindal's refusal to issue orders suppressing the prophesyings and his suspension from office (1577) for that refusal, he was succeeded in 1583 by John Whitgift, a worthy opponent of Cartwright and the other Puritans. Following Elizabeth's policy of a comprehensive church protected against papal incursion as well as Puritan subversion, he issued a list of articles for compliance which were to be enforced by the Court of High Commission, and thus Puritanism was forced underground until the Millenary Petition in the first year of the reign of James I. The consistent refusal of Elizabeth in the first decade of her reign to enter into any of the several possible marriages proposed kept the succession question in the balance until her death.

BIBLIOGRAPHY: J. P. Hodges, *The Nature of the Lion* (London, 1962); C. S. Meyer, *Elizabeth I and the Religious Settlement of 1559* (St. Louis, 1960).

**Elizabeth of Hungary** (1207–1231). Daughter of Andrew II of Hungary and married at the age of 14 to Louis the IV, landgrave of Thuringia. After her husband's death in the Crusade in 1227, she was driven from her home by his brother. She settled in Marburg with her children, devoting herself to charity. Her spiritual director was Conrad of Marburg, who ordered physical and ascetic cruelties that led to her early death. She was one of the most popular saints of pre-Reformation Germany.

**Elkesaites.** A small group of Jewish Christians who flourished at the beginning of the 2d century A.D. Their name came from the Book of Elkesai, sacred writings said to have been revealed to Elkesai, who was perhaps their founder. They practiced asceticism and were interested in divination and astrology. They held a docetic view of Christ. Baths and washings were means of religious purification; they rebaptized for the forgiveness of sins. The Ebionites probably adopted baptist rites from them when they came to the Transjordan.

**Emancipation Acts, Catholic** (*also known as* Catholic Relief Acts). The freeing of Roman Catholics in England from civil disabilities by certain governmental acts. English Roman Catholics had suffered under civil disabilities ever since the 16th century, as also had nonconformists in general. Roman Catholicism in England followed Protestant nonconformity in enjoying the gradual removal of almost all civil disabilities. The most important Emancipation Act was passed in 1829 when the Irish situation was critical. Catholics were given the franchise and were permitted to hold most public offices. Acts had previously been passed in 1778 removing disabilities from Irish Catholics. Priests were freed from harassment by being no longer subject to persecution on the denunciation of a common informer; lifelong imprisonment for keeping a Catholic school was abolished; subjects were freed from taking an oath denying their religion in order to hold landed property. In 1791, Catholic worship and schools were tolerated in England, certain military and legal professions were opened, and the Oath of Supremacy was not required. In 1793, Irish Catholics won admission to the universities and the professions, and won the right to vote. The most sweeping emancipation act was passed in 1829 and remaining disabilities were removed by a law of 1926. Still retained is the law forbidding the king or queen to be Roman Catholic, nor can those holding the offices of Regent, Lord Chancellor, and Keeper of the Great Seal be Catholic.

**Emerson, Ralph Waldo** (1803–1882). American transcendentalist. After resigning from his Boston pastorate in 1832 because he felt that organized religion hampered his spiritual freedom, Emerson lectured widely on "the beauty, dignity, and infinite importance of the human soul." He wrote prolifically, including his *Essays, Representative Men,* and *The Conduct of Life.* His book *Nature* (1836) was the opening statement of transcendentalism. Influenced by Coleridge, Carlyle, Wordsworth, and through them by German idealism, he was also indebted to Neoplatonism and Oriental sacred writings, and was a disciple of American ideals. He stressed the new relations of man to the universe in a new land with new men and new thoughts. Oliver Wendell Holmes called his "The American Scholar" speech in 1837 "our intellectual declaration of independence." First know nature like a "transparent eyeball," Emerson said, for nature is the source of all power and wisdom. In a discourse before the Seminary at Harvard in 1838, he found the church dead and helpless. Such institutions were necessary, he acknowledged, along with religious sentiment, but Christianity was neglecting the soul, the only source of redemption. It preached a superannuated revelation when a new revelation more suitable to the times must be sought. The church only hindered the natural spiritual resources residing in man's moral constitution. Emerson broke with all organized religion, including liberal Unitarianism, and the feeling was mutual.

**Emmons, Nathaniel** (1745–1840). Congregationalist theologian and minister. Born in Connecticut, he graduated from Yale in 1767 and was licensed to preach two years later. Emmons combined a career as pastor with the training of students in theology ("consistent Calvinism," which he systematically expounded). He was a patriot for the American cause in the Revolutionary War and a vociferous Federalist afterward.

**Empire of Nicaea.** See NICAEA, EMPIRE OF.

**Emser, Hieronymus** (Jerome) (1477–1527). Roman Catholic theologian and opponent of Luther. At first Emser posed as a friend of Luther, but the break came at the Leipzig Debate (1519), where he identified the church with the papacy. He claimed to have been Luther's teacher at Erfurt in 1504. At the famous bonfire scene in 1520, Luther committed Emser's writings to the flames along with the papal bull of excommunication. In 1527, Emser published a rival German New Testament.

**Ems Points** (1786). A program, embodying most of the ideas of "Justinus Febronius," drawn up by representatives of the ecclesiastical electors (the archbishops of Mainz, Cologne, and Trier) and the representative of the archbishop of Salzburg. These men were all princes of the Empire as well as bishops, and sought to reduce papal interference in their affairs. They argued that nonspiritual (broadly interpreted) decisions of the Pope and his authority in that area should be binding in Germany only with the consent of the German bishops, that certain functions should be the monopoly of the bishops (e.g., appeals), not that of Rome. Had they been adopted by the Congress of Ems, the Ems Points would have created an independent "national Catholic" church in Germany.

**Enabling Act** (1919). A committee appointed in England by the archbishops led in 1916 to an address to the Crown asking a national assembly for the Church of England. Parliament in 1919 passed the Church of England Assembly, or Enabling, Act. The National Assembly is intended to initiate reforms and adapt church structure and ways to changing needs. Any matters except doctrine may be presented. If passed by Commons and Lords, the Assembly's recommendation becomes law on the assent of the Crown.

**Encratites.** A term meaning "abstainers," which was applied to several different groups of ascetics. The most famous sect of Encratites was that founded by Justin Martyr's disciple Tatian. It was a Gnostic group that condemned the use of meat in any form and wine-drinking to the extent of having a water Eucharist; it considered marriage to be adultery. Their curious Eucharist earned for them the sobriquet of *Aquarii.*

**Encyclopédie.** A reference work published in France (1751–1780) whose thirty-six volumes constitute one of the great achievements of the Enlightenment. Ostensibly a summary on the arts and sciences of the day, its main purpose was to propagate a rational and scientific point of view. The editor, Denis Diderot, and most of its contributors were supporters of an exclusively natural religion. Its influence on the intellectual classes of Europe was prodigious.

**Engels, Friedrich** (1820–1895). Cofounder of Marxism (dialectical materialism). Born in Barmen, Germany, the son of a wealthy manufacturer, Engels was brought up in strict pietistic circles and completed his formal education at seventeen when he graduated from the Elberfeld Gymnasium and was confirmed. At this point he began an apprenticeship in his father's business ventures. He was shocked by the disregard of his religious associates for the plight of the poor. While on military duty in Berlin in 1844 he made the fateful acquaintance of Karl Marx. It was chiefly through the popularization of the theories of Marx, who was to become a lifelong associate, that Engels is known to history. From 1849 to 1869 he worked, first as a clerk and finally as a director, in a textile mill founded by his father in Manchester, England. During this time, largely from an Irish emigrant girl who was his mistress, Engels developed a deep passion for the liberation of the industrial proletariat. He collaborated with Marx in the authorship of *The German Ideology, The Holy Family, Communist Manifesto,* and *Anti-Dühring.* He also edited Vols. II and III of *Das Kapital.* Strongly influenced by the "young Hegelians," especially Bruno Bauer and Ludwig Feuerbach, as well as by English economic theory (Adam Smith and David Ricardo), Engels always pointed to Marx as the real thinker and was willing to play a secondary role in promoting the theories and projects of his friend.

**England, Church of.** The historic national and legally established church in England (except Monmouth), particularly that church since the Protestant Reformation, and the parent body to the worldwide Episcopal, or Anglican, Communion. (See ANGLICAN COMMUNION, THE.)

A Christian community existed in the Roman province of Britain at least from the 3d century, and British bishops were present at the Council of Arles in 314. However, in the Anglo-Saxon invasions of the 5th century this ancient church, probably less vigorous than Continental churches, was overwhelmed in England together with other aspects of Romano-British culture. It survived, isolated, in the Celtic fringes of Cornwall, Wales, and southwestern Scotland, from whence it was to be carried to Ireland. The Saxons, adherents of Teutonic paganism, received Christi-anity in the 7th century from two sources. First, Gregory the Great sent a monastic mission, led by Augustine (d. c. 604), to Kent in 597. Kentish king and people were converted, and from this center the new faith entered other parts of England, not without setbacks. Second, Celtic Christianity penetrated Northumbria from Scotland. Differences between the two churches were resolved in favor of Roman Christianity at the Synod of Whitby (664), thus laying the foundations for one Church of England even before political unity was achieved.

The Saxon church was served by some notable men. It possessed a great scholar in Bede, a celebrated missionary, Boniface, and such able statesmen as Theodore of Tarsus and Dunstan. Yet it suffered greatly during the invasions in the 9th century by the Northmen and was slow to recover, despite the assistance of Alfred and his successors. On the eve of the Norman Conquest the church, while not without vitality, was inferior to the Continental church in learning, administration, and clerical life.

Extensive reforms took place under William the Conqueror's archbishop, Lanfranc. The building of churches, monastic reform, educational revival, and administrative improvements were all pressed, while separate ecclesiastical courts and Roman canon law were introduced into England. The 12th century witnessed serious church-state conflicts, notably the dispute between Henry I and Anselm over lay investiture and that between Henry II and Thomas Becket over jurisdiction of church courts. Both issued in compromises not unfavorable to the church. In wresting the Magna Carta from King John (1215), Archbishop Stephen Langton took the lead; the first article of the Charter guarantees that "the English Church shall be free." At the end of the century, when Parliament was forming under Edward I, the church received a consultative body of its own, "Convocation."

In the later Middle Ages the church was the target of mounting criticism. The Avignon period and the Great Schism eroded respect for the papacy. Papal appointments of foreigners to English livings brought countermeasures, the Statutes of Provisors (1351) and Praemunire (1353). Merchants and lawyers challenged church property and law. Reformers, such as John Wycliffe and the Lollards, demanded sweeping moral, ecclesiastical, and even doctrinal, reforms. Under the Tudors the Renaissance humanism of Erasmus, Colet, and More helped prepare the nation for the Reformation, as did the Lutheran writings smuggled in from Germany.

Henry VIII exploited this sentiment in his quarrel with Rome. Unable to obtain a marriage annulment, on which the hope of a legitimate male heir depended, Henry dismissed his chief minister, Cardinal Wolsey, and summoned the Reformation Parliament (1529). Parliament ended payments and appeals to Rome, and gave the king the supreme headship of the church. Thomas Cromwell, Henry's new favorite, dissolved the monasteries (1536–1539), seizing their property for the Crown. Yet Henry remained theologically conservative and opposed to Protestantism, despite the Reformation opinions of his archbishop, Thomas Cranmer, and the spread of Protestant doctrine in London, Cambridge, and the eastern counties. Even in Roman eyes, the church was schismatic rather than fundamentally "reformed."

Under Henry's immediate successors the pendulum swung wildly. During the brief reign of the boy king Edward VI the Protestant party triumphed. Roman Catholic bishops were jailed, chantries were dissolved, and most importantly, a reformed worship, accomplished under Cranmer's guidance in the first and second Books of Common Prayer (1549 and 1552), was imposed on the nation by the Acts of Uniformity. Protestant doctrine was officially embraced in the Forty-two Articles. The accession of Edward's sister, Mary (1553), meant a Roman Catholic restoration, carried through by Parliament but rendered odious to many Englishmen by persecution, of which Cranmer was one of the victims.

The modern Church of England is recognizable in the Elizabethan Settlement. Inclined to compromise, Elizabeth kept links with the past in a hierarchical church government and conservative liturgy, while doctrine, contained in the Thirty-nine Articles, was Protestant. Papal authority was denied, the queen made "supreme governor" of the church, and the episcopate, headed by Matthew Parker, filled with men agreeable to these changes. Accepted by most Englishmen, the Settlement drew fire from two parties. Roman Catholics remained hostile, more overtly so after Elizabeth's excommunication (1570). At the other extreme, Puritans, impressed by the Reformed Church abroad, worked for a full reformation in worship, discipline, and polity. Most of them agitated from within the church, but a few impatiently formed illegal conventicles. Here appeared the earliest English Dissenters. Yet by the end of Elizabeth's reign national sentiment had come to support her compromise, which was learnedly defended by such scholars as Richard Hooker and John Jewel.

The 17th century was marked by religious as well as constitutional upheaval. Stuart kings, supported by the church, quarreled with Parliament and courts and their Puritan allies. Religious contest was embittered by the favor shown to the High Church party, headed by William Laud, Charles I's archbishop, which stressed continuity with the pre-Reformation church and the authority of tradition and antiquity. In the Puritan revolution after 1640, Anglicanism was overthrown, but Puritanism, now divided into a number of competing groups—Presbyterian, Congregational, Baptist—was in a poor position to succeed. In the 1640's, Presbyterianism was officially established, and in the 1650's the protector Cromwell experimented with a national but unobtrusive Establishment which was comprehensively Puritan; yet the real situation in these years was that of free denominationalism.

Religious diversity was one of the principal problems of England throughout the remainder of the century. The Royalist Restoration in 1660 reestablished Anglicanism, excluding even moderate Presbyterians who desired "comprehension" through compromise. The Clarendon Code provided statutory basis for persecuting Dissenters, though dissent itself could not be liquidated. Truce between the two parties was achieved during the reign of the Roman Catholic James II, who was thought to threaten the security of both. After the expulsion of James in the Glorious Revolution of 1688, the Toleration Act (1689), protecting Trinitarian Protestants, provided a permanent settlement. However, six bishops and four hundred clergy were lost to the church. These nonjurors, predominantly High Churchmen, were unable conscientiously to support the deposition of James.

The 18th century was a more tranquil period in Anglican history. The church was securely established without serious rivals. Party spirit was dampened by the suspension of Convocation. An urbane rationalism settled over much Anglican theological writing. The growth of cities, the appearance of industrialism, and the decay of morals were problems with which the church was apparently unprepared to deal. Traditionally, but not with entire justice, this has been represented as the religious depression of English church history. Reaction came in the evangelical revival, led chiefly by George Whitefield and John Wesley. It resulted in a profound quickening of religious life in Britain, a growing evangelical party within the church, and the Methodist secession (ultimately) to the ranks of dissent.

Revival of another sort came in the 19th-century Oxford movement. Led by John Keble,

J. H. Newman, and E. B. Pusey, the movement was originally a protest against the government's undertaking much-needed reforms in the administration of the church. It stressed spiritual independence, exalted the apostolic succession, and recalled churchmen to the English Catholic traditions of the church. The movement aroused considerable hostility, especially after Newman was received into the Roman Church in 1845, but it revived under Pusey's leadership after temporary setback. In the later part of the century, the High Church party, though much troubled by ritualist controversy, became one of the dominant elements in the church.

Like other churches, the Anglican Church became increasingly preoccupied with problems of an industrial and liberal culture. The Anglican socialist movement, launched in 1848 by F. D. Maurice, Charles Kingsley, and John Ludlow, won increasing respect, notably among High Churchmen, and had some influence upon the unique quality of British socialism. Efforts to come to terms with modern scientific, philosophical, and historical studies began about mid-century, the chief milestones being *Essays and Reviews* (1860) and *Lux mundi* (1889). Church reunion also engaged the efforts of Anglicans. After 1832 a Broad Church tradition, inaugurated by Thomas Arnold, explored the possibility of widening the national church to include dissent, and in 1884 the Lambeth Conference appealed for unity on the basis of the Quadrilateral. Leo XIII's denial of Anglican orders (1896) and the running battle with nonconformity over education were disturbing factors, but some Anglicans provided leadership in the ecumenical movement.

Lastly, the church and state issue erupted after World War I. The church had been disestablished in Ireland (1869) and Wales (1914), but the great nonconformist campaign to achieve the same end in England had been unsuccessful. In 1919, Parliament provided for a church assembly of three houses to prepare measures for Parliament's consideration. A revision of the Prayer Book was rejected by Parliament in 1927 and again in 1928, despite substantial Anglican support for the measure. The situation produced much discussion of the rights of the church, threats of secession, conscientious disobedience, and continuing controversy.

BIBLIOGRAPHY: S. C. Carpenter, *The Church in England: 597–1688* (London, 1954); and *Church and People: 1789–1889* (London, 1933); R. B. Lloyd, *The Church of England: 1900–1965* (London, 1966); J. R. H. Moorman, *A History of the Church in England* (London, 1953); E. W. Watson, *The Church of England* (London, 1944).

**England, John** (1786–1842). Roman Catholic bishop. He was ordained in his native Ireland in 1808 and there fulfilled a distinguished ministry, including agitation for reform of prison ships going to Australia, which caused him to be called the founder of the Catholic Church in Australia, and agitation against allowing the English Government to have a part in the selection of Catholic bishops. This latter struggle created enemies for him, causing him to be made bishop of Charleston, i.e., the Carolinas and Georgia, a diocese of less than five thousand members. He developed his diocese, however, into a strong one, partly by identifying himself closely with America, which did much to minimize anti-Catholic feelings. In 1822 he founded the *United States Catholic Miscellany*, the first genuine Catholic paper in America.

**English Church Union.** An Anglo-Catholic society founded in 1859 as the Church of England Protection Society. Renamed English Church Union in 1860, it sought to defend and advance the High Church principles of the Oxford movement. It opposed the Erastian control of the church by the state, especially as exercised by the Privy Council. It also prosecuted Evangelicals as in the famous Gorham Case. In 1934 it merged with the Anglo-Catholic Congress to form the Church Union.

**English College** (Roman). See ALLEN, WILLIAM.

**Enlightenment.** The term refers to a specific epoch in the history of Western civilization (the 18th century) as well as to a particular mind-set. One might speak of the former as the age, of the latter as the spirit, of the Enlightenment. The term itself was already in use in the 18th century and expressed the self-confidence of the time which strove for a new understanding of man, society, and the universe. It was assumed that through a critical exercise of reason man could arrive at a reasonable and thereby natural understanding of himself, of law, of religion, and of philosophy. At the same time, extraneous authority was rejected and the uncritical perpetuation of past forms opposed. Since the use of reason had brought significant advances in the understanding of the natural world, optimism characterized the times which were persuaded that all of life could be structured reasonably. The notion of progress was thus an important characteristic of the period.

The sources of this new world view lay in the 17th century. The geographic discoveries brought Western man into contact with new peoples and cultures, thereby confronting him with the awareness that European culture was not the only one possible. More basic was the intellectual reorientation associated with the names of Descartes, Locke, and Newton which stressed critical inquiry and saw experience and reason as the "fountains of knowledge." This meant an epistemological basis for a new way of looking at the world.

The presence of Newton and Locke in England meant that Enlightenment ideas made their first appearance there, spreading to the Continent, especially France and Germany. In France they found their fullest expression; most of the great persons of the Enlightenment (e.g., Condorcet, Diderot, Montesquieu, Rousseau, Voltaire) were Frenchmen. In Germany the Enlightenment was a less widespread phenomenon, primarily a university movement, and not antireligious.

For church history, the Enlightenment is a distinct epoch, nestled between the age of orthodoxy on the one hand and the 19th century on the other. Since its ecclesiastical impact reached different countries at different times, however, a single chronology cannot be used to circumscribe the period. Thus in England by the middle of the 18th century the apex of the ecclesiastical Enlightenment had passed, at a time when Germany was only beginning to feel its impact.

Little happened with respect to the purely institutional history of the church during the time, except the disruption of the monolithic structure of ecclesiastical life in Europe that allowed the public exercise of one religion only in a given commonwealth. Several toleration edicts (United States, 1787; France, 1793; Austria, 1781) brought *relative* religious freedom.

At the same time, the relationship between the church and society underwent a significant change. The church had dominated the West for over a thousand years. The new situation of the Enlightenment was its challenge to the church, with respect both to its doctrines and to its social prerogatives. In France occurred the beginnings of an outright clash between the church and the state; for the first time since the 4th century the church faced persecution.

Most important were the theological developments. On the face of things, the Enlightenment was a theologically revolutionary period, perhaps the most significant one in church history, constituting a dividing line of major proportions. This was the case because the traditional consensus of an orthodox body of faith, to which all Christians subscribed, had

been disrupted. The break with the Christian tradition was thus radical, even though orthodox sentiment continued to prevail in many quarters and even dominated again in England in the second half of the 18th century. Although the Enlightenment did not replace orthodoxy, it brought a new alternative that was more than the sectarian dissent of a minority. This alternative was proposed from within the Christian community and the modification of the dogma was made by men who considered themselves Christian theologians. The common denominator of their various efforts was to adapt the true Christian faith to the new world view. Two major problems confronted the theologians: the problem of reason and revelation, and the issue of prophecy and miracles.

The former was precipitated by the postulate of the sufficiency of reason, for this meant that the necessary religious insights could be attained from reason and did not depend upon an extraneous source. John Locke (*The Reasonableness of Christianity as Delivered in the Scriptures,* 1695), John Toland (*Christianity not Mysterious,* 1696), and Matthew Tindal (*Christianity as Old as the Creation,* 1730) were among the important English writers who progressively modified the traditional notion of revelation, concluding with the assertion that revelation was only the confirmation of the religion of nature.

In Germany the theological development was similar. Its initial phase, in the beginning of the 18th century, was oriented by men who drew certain theological conclusions from the philosophical system of Christian Wolff (1679–1754), the "prince of the German Enlightenment." Here a distinction was made between the supranatural and the irrational aspects of a revelatory claim; the latter were rejected. A second phase, represented by J. S. Semler, found the content of revelation to comprise only the principles of natural religion, while not rejecting the concept of revelation as such. A final phase, exemplified by H. E. G. Paulus, did away with the concept of revelation as the communication of religious truth, and affirmed only natural religion. The issue of prophecy and miracles was posed by the new world view of causality. The Bible came under critical scrutiny. Historical exegesis examined the prophetic passages of the Old Testament (Grotius, Warburton, Collins, Whiston). A line of theologians (Annet, Collins, Chubb, Hume, Woolston) examined the Biblical record of miracles and concluded with the denial of any violation of the natural order. Thereby the understanding of God's relationship to the world underwent a drastic change. The immediacy of his presence and intervention in the affairs of men and the course of nature disappeared beneath the majestic regularity of his appointed laws.

A second stream of theological writings is associated with physicotheology and derives its name from Derham's important work with that title (1713). Here the effort was made to utilize competent scientific inquiry into natural phenomena in order to support religious assertions. The underlying assumption was that the perfection and order of creation allowed certain deductions about God. Derham's approach found imitators throughout Europe, each new wave of publications refining the particular aspect of the natural order (crystals, fish, reptiles, spiders, etc.) that was to supply support for theological affirmations: Crystal, Fish, Reptile, Spider, etc., "theologies" were not uncommon. The reinterpretation of the "true" faith meant the rejection of traditional theology but also a reflection on the historical development that had given rise to traditional theology. Coupled with the emerging historical temper of the time, such theologians as Walch, Woolston, or Semler concerned themselves extensively with Christian origins, the beginnings of dogma, the formation of the canon.

BIBLIOGRAPHY: C. L. Becker, *The Heavenly City of the Eighteenth-Century Philosophers* (New Haven, 1964); G. R. Cragg, *The Church and the Age of Reason: 1648–1789* (Baltimore, 1960); P. Hazard, *European Thought in the Eighteenth Century* (New Haven, 1954); and *The European Mind: 1680–1715* (Cleveland, 1964); S. G. Hefelbower, *The Relation of John Locke to English Deism* (Chicago, 1918); L. Stephen, *History of English Thought in the Eighteenth Century* (New York, 1927).

**Ennodius, Magnus Felix** (c. 473–521). Bishop of Pavia and a rhetorician. Born in Arles, France, of an important family, he studied in Milan. When he was sixteen, the aunt who had been his guardian died and in loneliness he married shortly afterward. He became a successful secular author who let success go to his head. During his most arrogant period he became seriously ill and was converted by Victor. After his recuperation his wife went to a convent and he to a monastery. He accompanied the bishop of Pavia on several trips and was called upon to defend officially the claim of Symmachus to the papacy at the fourth Roman synod. Becoming bishop of Pavia himself, he was sent by the pope to Constantinople twice to combat Monophysitism and to try to heal the growing rift be-

tween East and West. He was a passionate defender of classical pagan literature and also said that only God can judge a pope. His works include letters, discourses, and poems.

**Ephesus, Councils of** (431, 449). *First Council* (431). This Council was the third which is regarded as general and was called by the emperor Theodosius II to settle the Nestorian controversy. The manner in which the settlement was arrived at justifies the remark of F. J. Foakes-Jackson that "the Third General Council is proof that such assemblies, if infallible, are certainly not impeccable." The whole controversy appears to have been conceived in intellectual arrogance and provincial jealousy. Apparently neither party made the slightest effort to understand the other. In fact, each condemned the other for beliefs that the condemned denied, but which his accuser insisted were the implications of his position.

Nestorius, a monk of Antioch who was elevated to the patriarchate of Constantinople by Theodosius II in 428, shared the theological keenness and exegetical position of Antioch. His theology appears to contain nothing that was not at least implicit in the thought of Theodore of Mopsuestia. The difference was in personality and opportunity. From the moment of his consecration Nestorius set about the enforcement of his principles throughout his jurisdiction. Part of his anti-heretical activity was the attempt to suppress the description of the Virgin Mary as *Theotokos* (generally translated "Mother of God," but more accurately as "God-bearer"—that is, she bore One who was God, but she was not the source of his deity). The term had been used since Origen, but Nestorius objected to it as suggestive of Apollinarianism. Although he was guilty only of a pedestrian literalism, it sounded to many as though he were advocating Adoptianism. Cyril of Alexandria objected and the pope began to investigate. Instead of trying to grasp where he had been misunderstood, Nestorius wrote facetious letters to the pope. His teaching was condemned by a Roman synod in 430. Cyril, after launching a pamphlet attack, held a synod in Alexandria which likewise condemned Nestorius. The twelve anathemas against Nestorius branded him as an Adoptianist while Nestorius made countercharges that Cyril was an Apollinarian.

Theodosius called for a general council at Ephesus in the summer of 431 to deal with the dispute; all excommunications were to wait upon its decisions. Unfortunately, all the participants did not arrive on schedule. Nestorius came with only ten supporters to contend with Cyril's fifty. No one was content to use the time profitably. Memnon, the bishop of Ephesus, treated Nestorius' restraint as a *fait accompli* and closed the Ephesus churches to him. Cyril did not come to deliberate, but to impose a previously decided penalty. Nestorius did not consider himself on trial and made flippant replies to his interrogators. After a two weeks' wait Cyril received word from John, bishop of Antioch and friend of Nestorius, that he and his party were delayed and would not arrive for almost a week. He asked Cyril to wait to open the Council, but Cyril's patience was exhausted and he began immediately. His determination was not swayed by the protests of the imperial commissioner, since he felt that the Council was an affair of the church rather than the state. The deposition of Nestorius, who did not attend, was declared immediately. When John of Antioch arrived four days later, he opened a rival Council which, in turn, deposed Cyril and Memnon. Shortly afterward the Roman delegation came to reinforce Cyril, and there was a stalemate. A number of unsavory expedients were resorted to by both parties, and the impasse remained until a new commissioner appeared with orders to treat all the opponents as deposed and to imprison them. In September the emperor heard representatives of both sides, dissolved the Council, returned Nestorius to his monastery, appointing a successor for him in Constantinople, and allowed Cyril to return to Alexandria. During the following year negotiations between the two sides resulted in the complete victory of the Alexandrine party. Shortly afterward, the Nestorian schism began, although Nestorius himself died in the peace of the church, feeling that his position had been vindicated at Chalcedon.

*Robber Council of 449,* called the *Latrocinium* ("highway robbery"). Although there was an interval of almost twenty years between the two Councils of Ephesus, the latter can be viewed as a pendulum swing from the former. In reaction against Nestorianism the successors of Cyril of Alexandria pursued the course he set with as much vigor and less discretion. Their leader was Eutyches, the archimandrite of a monastery outside Constantinople. Described as imprudent and imperious, he opposed Adoptianism in a manner that sounded Apollinarian. At a session of the Standing Synod of Constantinople in 448, Eusebius of Dorylaeum told the other thirty-one bishops there that Eutyches confused the two natures of Christ to the scandal of the faithful. When Eutyches was given a chance to defend himself, he equivocated and temporized. When he was finally made to answer directly, he admitted that he believed that Christ was of two natures before but of only one after the incarnation. Eutyches refused to anathematize those who disagreed with the statement that after the incarnation Christ was of one essence (*homoousion*) after the flesh, since he did not believe this to be a teaching of the Bible or the fathers, although he himself could accept it. Eutyches probably did not intend to deny the manhood of Christ, but apparently he did not see that saying that Christ had lost his human nature at the incarnation could be so interpreted. Whether Eutyches was a Eutychian or not, the Synod decided that he did not really hold the orthodox faith and so deposed and excommunicated him.

Eutyches appealed to the emperor, Theodosius II, and to the pope, Leo I, to support him. The first appeal was the more successful. Theodosius made Flavian, the bishop of Constantinople, draw up a statement of his faith in answer to charges made by Eutyches. Leo, on the other hand, waited to hear Flavian's side before replying to the letter of Eutyches.

Theodosius called a council at Ephesus with the hope of exculpating Eutyches. It was presided over by Dioscorus, the patriarch of Alexandria and a good friend of Eutyches. Bethune-Baker says that Dioscorus had, in an exaggerated form, all the bad qualities attributed to Cyril, without Cyril's learning. Dioscorus had quite an army of Egyptian monks, soldiers, and servants and so overawed the 135 bishops that it has been said that he had them sign blank pages on which he would write what he pleased as decrees of the Council. Whether or not this was true, he certainly had his way with the Council. His monks under their archimandrite Barsumas (not the Nestorian Barsumas who was also present) accused Eusebius of dividing Christ. They also mobbed Flavian. Hearing of the plans for the Council, Leo wrote a letter to Flavian on June 13, 449, defining his position on the matter. This letter, the Tome of Leo, which was the basis of the definitions of Chalcedon in 451, was brought to Ephesus by Leo's delegates, but Dioscorus did not allow it to be read. Eutyches was received as a hero, declared orthodox and restored. His opponents were deposed and his teaching that there were no longer two natures in Christ after the incarnation was promulgated. So obvious was the intimidation that Leo referred to the assembly as no council at all but "highway robbery." Theodosius, however, was quite pleased with the results and exiled those who had been deposed. So violent was the reaction to this high-handedness that another council was demanded as soon as Theodosius was dead; this was to be the Council of Chalcedon.

BIBLIOGRAPHY: H. Jedin, *Ecumenical Councils of the Catholic Church* (Glen Rock, N.J., 1960); H. J. Margull, *The Councils of the Church* (Philadelphia, 1966); J. Stevenson (ed.), *Creeds, Councils, and Controversies* (New York, 1966).

**Ephraem Syrus** (c. 306–c. 373). A Syrian Biblical exegete and ecclesiastical writer. He lived at Nisibis until 363 when the Persians gained control of that area. In that year he withdrew to Edessa, living as an anchorite. Unreliable sources obscure his later life, but he became a link in the tradition of the Immaculate Conception of Mary, mother of Jesus. His theological writing is a source for the heresies of his day, among them Marcionism and Manichaeanism. He wrote in Syriac verse, which has been translated into Greek and Latin.

**Ephrata Community.** A semimonastic society formed under the leadership of the Palatine immigrant Johann Conrad Beissel near Lancaster, Pa., in 1732. Considering himself spiritually and rationally enlightened by his pietistic conversion in 1715, Beissel came to America in 1720 seeking to join the Society of the Woman in the Wilderness, founded by Johann Kelpius in 1694. Finding it disbanded, Beissel joined the Dunkers, who had immigrated as a group in 1719. In 1728 he formed the German Seventh Day Baptists and this evolved into the semimonastic Ephrata Community. It was founded on the principles of community of goods, celibacy, and the observance of the seventh day as the Sabbath. Other beliefs were drawn from the Dunkers, including trine immersion, refusal to go to court, foot washing, the Pax, the love feast, anointing with oil, refusal to accept interest on money, etc. There were many converts, including prominent German immigrants such as the scholar John Peter Miller, who when he succeeded Beissel as leader threatened the existence of the Reformed Church in Pennsylvania. The "brethren" and "sisters" lived in separate buildings, and both sexes wore clothes designed to conceal "that humiliating image revealed by sin." Weekly statements of individual spiritual condition were required. Worship consisted largely of singing hymns. By 1745 a gristmill, printing press, paper mill, and bookbindery were in operation. Hymnbooks, the *Blutige Schau-Platz,* and the *Chronicon Ephratense* were published. An excellent school drew students even from Philadelphia and Baltimore. After Beissel's death in 1768 the community began to decline and in 1814 the remaining members incorporated as the Seventh Day Baptists.

**Epictetus** (c. 55–c. 135). Stoic philosopher whose moral temper seems to resemble more nearly that of Christians. Born in Hierapolis, Phrygia, he lived at Rome, the slave of a freedman of Nero who abused him. He attended the lectures of the Stoic Musonius Rufus and was later freed. After expulsion from Rome by Domitian he settled in Epirus. His teaching was predicated on the principle that men must perceive their own moral weakness and inadequacy. His *Enchiridion* and *Discourses* were taken down and collected by his disciple Arrian, who is also the biographer of Alexander the Great. The influence of Christianity on him or vice versa is a moot question.

**Epicurus** (342–270 B.C.). Greek philosopher and founder of the school of ethics that bears his name. The Epicurean principle that man should seek pleasure is a counsel of prudence, not of indulgence, for the life of genuine pleasure is lived with prudence, honor, and justice, and a man's happiness attained by diminishing his desires. From the time of Justin, who considered Epicurus no true philosopher, Christian writers have regarded him as an atheist because, though believing in gods, he denied their relevance to life. Dionysius of Alexander used the Stoics against Epicurus, and Aristides and Theophilus of Antioch used Epicurus against the Stoics.

**Epiphanius** (c. 315–403). Bishop of Salamis. Born near Eleutheropolis (modern Beit Jibrin) in Judea, southwest of Jerusalem, he became a monk as a young man and c. 335 founded a monastery near his home. He was elected to the metropolitan see of Salamis by the bishops of Cyprus in 367, where he continued his keen interest in the ascetical life. During his episcopacy, Epiphanius was noted for ardent devotion to the Nicene faith and violent opposition to heresy. His best-known work, the *Panarion* ("breadbasket"), described every heresy from the beginning of the church. Epiphanius actively fought the Apollinarian and Melitian heresies, and in 392 joined Jerome in Rome in opposing Origenism. Later, in 394, he visited Jerome in Palestine, and became enmeshed in a controversy with John of Jerusalem. In 400, Epiphanius went to Constantinople at the instigation of Theophilus, bishop of Alexandria, ostensibly to see to the expulsion of some Origenistic monks. When he discovered he was being used against John Chrysostom, bishop of Constantinople, he started back to Salamis, but died on the way. Epiphanius also wrote the *Ancoratus*, a doctrinal work in which the Niceno-Constantinopolitan Creed may appear for the first time, as well as several other treatises. Both his works and his life reveal him to have been rigid and unimaginative, though zealous.

**Episcopal Church.** See ANGLICAN COMMUNION, THE.

**Episcopal Lists, Early.** The need of the church from the 2d century to find apostolic authority to distinguish between heresy and orthodoxy motivated certain Apologists to begin compiling succession lists, notably of the Roman see. Perhaps the earliest list was by Hegesippus (2d century) in his *Recollections,* to which Eusebius alludes (*Ecclesiastical History* 4. 22. 1–3). Some argue that a succession list by Epiphanius (*Panarion* 27.6) is based on Hegesippus. However, others insist that Hegesippus may never have compiled such a list and that even if he did, Epiphanius has not depended upon it. If this is true, the earliest list is by Irenaeus (*Against [All] Heresies* 3. 3. 3), which all existing lists up to 180 are dependent upon. From Irenaeus there are two lines of development: Eastern—as found in Julius Africanus (up to 221), Eusebius (early 4th century), and Epiphanius; and Western—as represented by the Pseudo-Tertullian (mid-3d century), the Liberian Catalogue (up to 366), and the first edition of the *Liber Pontificalis* (6th century). Some adjustments in the early names in several of the lists is evident. They all assume a monarchical episcopate from the apostles. The times assigned to the duration of office, as well as the particular dates, cannot be considered reliable until the mid-3d century.

**Episcopius, Simon** (1583–1643). Dutch Arminian theologian. He was one of the thirteen Remonstrants cited to appear before the Synod of Dort and was the principal exponent of Arminian views at the time. He received most of his education at the University of Leiden, studying under both Arminius and Gomar. His unusual ability brought an appointment as chaplain to Prince Maurice and preacher at The Hague. After Arminius' death, Episcopius was appointed professor of theology at Leiden. He took the Remonstrants' side in the conferences at The Hague (1611) and Delft (1613). At the Synod of Dort (1618) he gave an eloquent opening address defending the Remonstrant position and pleading for an open seeking for the truth. With the other Remonstrants he was banished from the country and lived for a time in Antwerp, Paris, and Rouen, until he was permitted to return to Rotterdam in 1626. In 1630, he consecrated a new Remonstrant church in Amsterdam and in 1634 became the head of a Remonstrant seminary in that city. He exercised great influence throughout the country from this position for the nine years until his death. In his writing, Episcopius maintained that theology is not speculative, but practical, and that any conception which cannot be applied to life is without value.

**Epworth League.** Name given to the official organization for young people in the leading Methodist denominations of America. The history of the League is complex, but it is generally agreed that it began about 1872 in pastor T. B. Neely's Methodist Episcopal Church in Philadelphia and spread among the churches of that city until a union was organized. In 1889 five diverse Methodist youth organizations were merged into a single society called the Epworth League, with an official organ, *The Epworth Herald.* The aim of the League is to win, to save, and to train young Methodists for Jesus Christ. The training is supervised under four departments: (1) promotion of evangelistic missionary work and training in the Bible; (2) Christian temperance, citizenship, and social reforms; (3) Christian philanthropy; (4) literary and social activities for young Methodists. The work of the League is maintained in weekly devotional meetings. The Epworth League has had a profound effect upon the Methodist churches in America through ministry and missionary recruits and devoted laymen.

**Erasmus, Desiderius Roterodamus** (c. 1469–1536). Christian humanist. Born out of wedlock, he was educated by the Brethren of the Common Life in Deventer and Bois-le-Duc. Apparently because of economic pressures, he became an Augustinian canon in Steyn, near Gouda (c. 1486), and was ordained in 1492. Under the patronage of the bishop of Cambrai, he began to study in Paris in 1495. By 1499 he visited England for the first time (accompanying his pupil, William Blount, Lord Mountjoy), where he was well received, especially by John Colet. Returning to the Continent, he drifted between Paris and Louvain, and finally revisited England in 1505, moving on to Italy in 1506. Returning to England in 1509, he stayed briefly with Thomas More, and was then appointed to the faculty at Cambridge. In 1516 he left England, and after some wandering finally made his home in Basel from 1521 to 1529. Fleeing the Reformation in 1529, he went to Freiburg im Breisgau, where he remained until 1535. Then he returned to Basel to supervise the printing of some of his work, and while there died in the home of his publisher and friend, John Froben.

Erasmus' life up to 1499, even the year of his birth, is obscure, since the major information available is from his retrospections, in which he tells of little but the misery of this early period. The young Erasmus was deeply impressed by the simple piety and the mystical tendencies of the *devotio moderna*. He was also a literary, aesthetically oriented humanist, who apparently from his earliest childhood had been thoroughly schooled in classical Latin, who was disgusted with Scholasticism, and who devoured the works of every classical author or church father that he could obtain. This interest in the literature of antiquity occupied Erasmus throughout his life. He also remained an aesthete, not only in his literary work (e.g., *Adagia*, 1500; *Colloquies; Style Exercises*) but in his habits of living as well.

Apparently through his encounter with Colet and the trip to Italy, Erasmus became the theologian of the "Christian humanity" reflected in his *Handbook of a Christian Soldier* (1501–1503, 1518), in the prefaces to his edition of the New Testament (*Methodus, paraclesis*, 1516; *Ratio seu methodus verae theologiae*, 1519), and in the *Paraphrases* to the New Testament (1517 ff.). As critical philologist with great potential, yet plagued by a lack of patient thoroughness, he published Valla's *Annotations to the New Testament* in 1505, and in 1516 he provided the first published edition of the Greek text of the New Testament (with grammatical, exegetical notes), which became the standard edition for generations to come. The publication of many of the works of the church fathers which he either prepared or supervised documents his continuous interest in patristic studies. From his roots in the *devotio moderna*, through his concentration on theological problems, and by the sheer experience of living, Erasmus the literary humanist matured to Erasmus the Biblical humanist and wise scholar who with sharp wit castigated man's sometimes foolish endeavors (*Praise of Folly*, 1511; *Colloquies*), and who had no use for the pagan humanism that developed in early 16th-century Italy (*Ciceronianus*, 1528).

Erasmus had reached the zenith of his scholarly and literary fame when the Reformation broke out. In the beginning paternally benevolent toward Luther, he became highly critical of the Reformer after the Leipzig Disputation (1519), and, being put on the defensive by pressures from all sides, publicly broke with Luther (*Diatribe on Free Will*, 1524; Luther's answer: *Bondage of the Will*, 1525; Erasmus' reply: *Hyperaspistes*, 1526–1527) and the Upper German Reformers (controversies on Hutten and on the Lord's Supper) in an attempt to maintain his independent position and to push his own reform program. In diplomatic moves (especially 1519–1521, 1524–1526, 1529–1531) and in many of his writings (e.g., *Inquiry Concerning Faith*, 1524; *On the Unity of the Church, Explanation of the Apostles' Creed*, 1533; *The Preacher*, 1535) he worked tirelessly to restore unity to a humanistically reformed Christendom, but could not accomplish this. His major theological concern was to revitalize a dynamic Scripture-oriented faith. His hermeneutical principles (influenced by the *devotio moderna*, Jerome, and Origen) centered on the Sermon on the Mount, and shaped his theology as a "Christian philosophy." In this theology the spiritual law of Christ is identical with the Law of nature, and this nature is basically good, though corrupted by carnal elements. The restoration of man's perfect nature is accomplished by grace alone, as embodied in Christ and his perfect law of love. Grace becomes effective only through faith (interpreted as meditation on and imitation of Christ, thus combining mystical and rational elements), by which man is reborn to his God-intended condition, the Christian humanity in which the image of God is restored in man. Erasmus interpreted the history of salvation as an educational process conducted by divine wisdom, in which man is led from flesh to spirit, from imperfection to perfection, from sinner to saint. Since according to Erasmus the systems of the Schoolmen contributed nothing to this perfection of man, he developed his thoughts in constantly biting, yet witty and therefore highly destructive, criticism of Scholasticism and Aristotelianism (and the Schoolmen were not slow in retaliating). On the other hand, he saw in Plato's spiritualism, in Cicero, and the Stoa true though incomplete parallels to the Christian philosophy. Consequently, this non-Aristotelian antiquity, together with Scripture, was to be made relevant to man if he were to reach Christian humanity, and Erasmus was wholeheartedly dedicated to this task.

The Christian philosophy of Erasmus was the organizing principle of his reform program. He demanded that the institutional church, in a gradual process of self-criticism (which he intended to bring swiftly about through his verbal lashings), abolish all abuses by returning to the standards of the early church, which were, so he argued, based exclusively on Scripture. Although he used the term *sola scriptura* before the Protestant Reformers did, he nevertheless did not challenge or clarify the function of ecclesiastical tradition itself. He further demanded that the church educate clergy and laity in the Christian philosophy and thus guide them to spiritual perfection. Erasmus saw in the church (the most complex, unclear, yet crucial concept in his theology and even in his life) a traditional sacred institution, extending through all ages, and charged with perpetuating the Christian philosophy. More specifically, he interpreted the church as a sacramental community of believing Christians, with its liturgical center in the Eucharist, that manifestation of the faith-communion between Christ and the individual and among the individuals themselves. In the state he saw the institution that was to guarantee the gradual permeation of society by the principles of the law of Christ. He strongly advocated toleration of and personal freedom for all who abided by this law. The main task of the state was to maintain justice and peace, to care for the socially underprivileged, and to educate everyone according to his ability (*Institutio principis Christiani,* 1516).

Erasmus' impact on the history of ideas needs to be studied more carefully than has been done in the past. Protestant and Roman Catholic reformations, left-wing Reformers, Enlightenment, ecumenicism, and the world-peace movement are indebted to him in one way or another. Already in his lifetime he had been claimed or condemned by many, yet he would associate only with those whom he found congenial. Seldom endorsing anyone, always suspicious and fearful, extremely sensitive to criticism, yet quick and merciless in uncovering what seemed to him weak and faulty, he was thus constantly involved in controversy. With age he became extremely pessimistic, cynical, and cantankerous, and above all lonely, although his fame as a scholar and writer has remained untarnished through the ages. Erasmus, who called himself a citizen of the world, can be properly judged only in the light of Hutten's famous statement that Erasmus is a man in a category all by himself.

BIBLIOGRAPHY: L. Bouyer, *Erasmus and the Humanist Experiment* (London, 1959); M. M. Phillips, *Erasmus and the Northern Renaissance* (London, 1949); Biographies by J. Huizinga (New York, 1924) and P. Smith (New York, 1924); F. v. d. Haeghen, *Bibliotheca Erasmiana* (Ghent, 1893); and *Bibliotheca Erasmiana,* 7 vols., incomplete (Ghent, 1897 ff.); J. C. Margolin, *Bibliographie Érasmienne* (Paris, 1963).

**Erastianism.** The subordination of ecclesiastical to secular power, named after Thomas Erastus (1524–1583), a Swiss Zwinglian and a physician. In 1558 he came to a professorship in the University of Heidelberg, and was soon a member of the elector's council, and the elector's personal physician. He was opposed to the Genevan type of constitution, and favored instead the system of Zurich, where discipline was a concern of the secular government. Under the elector's authority, the theologians Olevianus and Ursinus were setting up in the Palatinate a disciplinary system on Genevan principles. The occasion for controversy came over discussion of a doctoral thesis at Heidelberg on the subject of church discipline.

Erastus favored strong governmental control of doctrines and discipline. He felt that civil authorities alone had jurisdiction in all matters, either civil or religious, where there was only one religion in the state. Only they could levy punishments, and all censures, including excommunication, were subject to their approval. His main work was published only after his death, appearing in London in 1589. His doctrines were influential, particularly in England, where Richard Hooker defended the supremacy of the secular power.

**Erik IX.** King of Sweden (1150–1160). Though supported by the part-pagan Svea party, he sought to introduce Christianity into Finland through conquest and colonization (c. 1157). He brought along his bishop, Henry, from Uppsala to organize the Finnish Church. Erik seems to have favored a national church as opposed to the pro-Roman policy of the rival Sverker house. He was killed near Uppsala by the Danish prince, Magnus Henriksson. Legends surrounding Erik's translation to the Uppsala Cathedral in 1273 led to his status as patron saint of Sweden (never validated by Rome).

**Eriugena, John Scotus** (c. 810–c. 877). Neoplatonist philosopher and systematic theologian. Born and educated in Ireland, he was invited to Paris before 847 by Charles the Bald and in 851 was asked by Hincmar, archbishop of Reims, to write against Gottschalk. He produced *De divina praedestinatione,* which, based on the essential unity of God, asserted that since God could not know, and thus cause, evil, sin and its punishment did not come from him. Evil, being simply the absence of good, brought its own punishment—consciousness of the loss of good. This syllogistic rather than Scriptural argument led to his being suspected of heresy. At Charles's request he translated from Greek into Latin the works of Pseudo-Dionysius the Areopagite and his commentator, Maximus Confessor. He also translated Gregory of Nyssa's *De hominis opificio.* Certain that religion and philosophy were identical and that the philosopher should penetrate the metaphors of Scripture by rational analysis to discover truth, he undertook, in his *De divisione naturae,* a comprehensive explanation of God and the universe on Neoplatonist lines, the pantheistic flavor of which tended to predominate over Scriptural tradition and led to the work's condemnation by Pope Honorius III in 1225. His activities after Charles's death in 877 and the date and place of his death are unknown.

**Erlangen School.** Name applied to the confessional type of Lutheranism during the 19th century at the University of Erlangen. The best-known representatives of the school were J. C. K. von Hofmann and F. H. R. von Frank, who held that theology must be based upon proper exegetical study. The Erlangen school emerged as a positive and negative reaction to Pietism, the *Aufklärung,* F. D. E. Schleiermacher, G. W. F. Hegel, and F. W. J. von Schelling. Its major points are: (1) the totality of truth grows out of the totality of Scripture; (2) faith and the Bible are interpreted as an organic whole with its center in justification by grace alone; (3) through regeneration and conversion the Christian receives assurance in his belief, but this assurance must be founded on the knowledge of sin, the new life, the atonement of Christ and the church; (4) faithfulness to the Lutheran Confessions assures a dynamic moving forward in the direction indicated by the confessions and Christian experience. The influence of the Erlangen theologians has been far-reaching both in European and American Lutheranism. Among American Lutherans influenced were H. Offerman, C. M. Jacobs, M. Reu, A. Voigt, and Jacob Tanner.

**Ernesti, Johann August** (1707–1781). German Lutheran exegete and Latinist, the *"Germanorum Cicero."* Ernesti taught ancient literature and theology at Leipzig. He believed the Scriptures could not be understood theologically if not first understood grammatically. Criticism was a matter of philology or it was nothing. Associated with J. S. Semler, Ernesti is considered the founder of the grammatical and historical school of Bible studies.

**Erskine, Ebenezer** (1680–1754). Scottish Secessionist leader. Educated at Edinburgh and ordained in 1703, he opposed patronage and the action of the General Assembly in 1732 which sought to regulate the appointment of ministers when a vacant parish re- verted to the presbytery. He insisted on the right of the members of the congregation to choose their own pastor according to the teaching of the Books of Discipline. In 1733 he was censured by the General Assembly and that same year withdrew from the Church of Scotland and founded an Associate Presbytery which eventually became the Scottish Secession Church.

**Espen, Zeger Bernhard Van** (1646–1728). Professor of canon law at the University of Louvain. A leading figure in the development of Gallicanism, he advocated the supremacy of secular over papal authority in the temporal realm. His Jansenist theology and his support of the election of a Jansenist archbishop in Utrecht led to suspension from both priesthood and academic office. All his works were, in 1714, placed on the Index of the church.

**Established Churches in Colonial America.** Denominations that were state supported at some time during their American existence. Of the original thirteen colonies, eight had established churches, two partial establishments, and only three no established church at all. Most of these forms of state support were ended during the Revolutionary War, but establishment persisted in New England well into the 19th century, in Massachusetts until 1833. Thus the Congregational Church was established by law and supported by the state for over two hundred years. These established churches received at least three substantial advantages from their position. Most importantly, their ministers were paid and their church buildings erected, not by members alone, but by all residents of the colony or parish whether interested in the church or not. Secondly, the state supported the teachings of the church with legal enforcement when necessary. This meant that church and state cooperated in establishing and enforcing codes of conduct and morality (such as the hours during which taverns might be open), and also in very early colonial times in persecuting and repressing those inhabitants who tried to set up public worship in any but the approved way. Lastly, the church derived what might be called fringe benefits of social prestige from its connection with the government. Not every state-supported church in the colonies enjoyed all these privileges. Only during the early years of the 17th century were all Dissenters prohibited from worshiping in Massachusetts, for example. In the Carolinas and Georgia, establishment meant little more than that the royal governor worshiped at the Anglican church. Dissenters were in the majority in those colonies. The state-supported churches were divided between the New England colonies of Massachusetts, Connecticut, and New Hampshire, where the Congregational Church was established, and the southern colonies of Virginia, Maryland, the Carolinas, and Georgia, where the Anglican Church was established. New York and New Jersey had a form of Anglican establishment, but not a comprehensive or effective one. In Pennsylvania and Delaware, due to the Quaker William Penn, and in Rhode Island, due to Roger Williams, there was virtually complete religious liberty from the day of their founding. The established churches failed to perpetuate their positions for a variety of reasons. The vast space available on the American continent allowed those, like Roger Williams, who disagreed with the religious policies of the colonial officials to walk several miles into the wilderness and set up their own church and state. Even if no separate colony was founded, as occurred in the case of Rhode Island, dissidents on the fringes of all the colonies proved virtually impossible to control. The mother country also intervened frequently to prevent the establishment of a church or the too-severe enforcement of existing regulations. The Dutch West India Company insisted for the good of New Netherland's commerce that Peter Stuyvesant allow Jews, Lutherans, and Quakers to settle unhindered in that colony. Likewise, the English king forced Massachusetts Bay officials to tolerate Quakers in their commonwealth after 1661. By the time of the American Revolution, clearly no one church had been able to dominate the whole of the seaboard or to prevent Dissenters from settling within its boundaries. In addition, the two new factors of revivalism in the First Great Awakening and Deism had sprung to prominence in the 18th century, both having the effect of undermining religion enforced by law. The Great Awakening tended to unite many of the warring denominations in a new bond of fellowship and give them confidence that they could perpetuate themselves without the assistance of the state. Deism as voiced by men such as Benjamin Franklin and Thomas Jefferson argued strongly and persuasively that the only religion worthy of the name was that which won the adherence of its members freely and openly. These two movements tended to bring down the established churches, especially in the South. In Virginia, the Baptists from the Piedmont area collaborated with men such as Jefferson and Madison to obtain the passage of the Bill for Establishing Religious Freedom.

BIBLIOGRAPHY: E. B. Greene, *Religion and the State in America* (New York, 1941); W. S. Hudson, *The Great Tradition of the American Churches* (New York, 1953); W. H. Marnell, *The First Amendment: The History of Religious Freedom in America* (Garden City, 1964); S. E. Mead, *The Lively Experiment* (New York, 1963); A. P. Stokes and L. Pfeffer, *Church and State in the United States* (New York, 1950); W. W. Sweet, *Religion in Colonial America* (New York, 1947).

**Estienne** (*often Latinized as* Stephanus). A family of 16th-century French scholar-printers who worked first at Paris and, after 1551, at Geneva. The two most important Estiennes were Robert (1503–1559) and his oldest son, Henri (c. 1528–1598), both of whom illustrate the intimate relationship between humanism and the printing industry during the Renaissance in northern Europe. Robert was an erudite student of the classics and philology who early in his career was appointed royal printer by Francis I. While at Paris, Robert printed many of the works of the church fathers as well as a number of critical editions of the Bible. Also, he produced in 1543 a Latin lexicon in three volumes. In 1550, the theological faculty of the Sorbonne attacked him because of his Protestant leanings. He fled to Geneva in 1551, where he joined the Reformed Church and established a large publishing house. One of the first works he printed at Geneva was his Greek New Testament in which he introduced the division of verses arranged by himself which is still used today. After 1551, he published many books for the leaders of the Reformed Church. When Robert died in 1559, Henri took over his father's flourishing establishment. He continued to print religious books while at the same time publishing much classical material. In addition he personally edited fifty-eight Latin and seventy-four Greek authors. His greatest work was a five-volume Greek lexicon first published in 1572.

**Estius, William** (Wilhelm Hessels van Est) (1542–1613). Prominent Roman Catholic exegete, theologian, and educator. Born in the Netherlands, he taught first at Lausanne and then was called to the new university at Douai, where he was made professor of theology in 1582; in 1595 he was named chancellor of the university, a position he held until his death. In theology he was noted for his opposition to the Molinists and for his positive contributions to the doctrine of grace.

**Eternal Gospel.** The doctrine developed by Joachim of Flora (c. 1132–1202), who believed that human history would be divided into three ages or dispensations corresponding to the three Persons of the Trinity. The age of the Father was the dispensation of ancient Israel; the age of the Son was the Christian era, while the age of the Holy Spirit, based upon the "eternal gospel" of Rev. 14:6, was to begin in 1260.

**Ethelbert of Kent** (d. 616). First Christian English king. He became king of Kent in 560, and was married to the Frankish princess Bertha. She was a Christian and he allowed her to observe her religion. In 597, Augustine and his party arrived from Rome to begin missionary work in England. Probably through his wife's influence Ethelbert welcomed them and was soon baptized. He gave complete support during the rest of his life to the work of the mission.

**Etheria, Pilgrimage of.** An account by a Spanish abbess of her visit to the shrines of the Holy Land about 385 (in the last years of Cyril of Jerusalem or shortly thereafter). Though there are gaps in the unique manuscript, and the description is not always clear, the *Pilgrimage* is a valuable source of liturgical history. Of special interest is the report of services at Jerusalem, both the regular schedule and the special celebrations held between Epiphany and Whitsunday at the holy places.

**Ethical Culture, Society for.** The first such society was founded in New York City by Felix Adler in 1876. Since then societies have been formed in Chicago, Philadelphia, St. Louis, Brooklyn, Boston, Germany, England, Austria, and Switzerland. These societies have been organized into the International Ethical Movement. The movement seeks to promote personal and social morality apart from any and all religious doctrine.

**Eucharist** (from Greek *eucharistos,* "grateful"). The liturgical celebration of the Lord's Supper, otherwise called Holy Communion, the Divine Liturgy (Eastern Orthodox), or the Mass (Roman Catholic, also German Evangelical). The word itself comes from the Gospel narrative of the Last Supper (Mark 14:23; Matt. 26:27), where it denominates Jesus' "thanksgiving" over the cup. The derivation of "mass" is not agreed on, but it probably relates to the dismissal formula in the Roman liturgy, *"Ite, missa est."*

1. In the New Testament there are four accounts of the institution of the Lord's Supper by Jesus (Mark 14:22–25; Matt. 26:26–29; Luke 22:15–20; I Cor. 11:23–25) which may all come from a single source. Because these accounts all show signs of liturgical and theological modification, the question is still open as to whether Jesus actually observed a last meal with his disciples and if

so, under what circumstances and in what way. The Marcan account (earlier than Paul?) depicts that meal as a Passover, but the Johannine passion story, which omits the institution proper, disagrees with this (John 13:1 ff.). Although the earliest extant liturgies seem to depend upon the Last Supper for the origin of the regular repetition of the celebration, there is some evidence that another type of Eucharist oriented instead to resurrection appearances in table fellowship (cf., e.g., Luke 24:13–32) was assimilated to a Last Supper type, giving the impression of a uniform New Testament origin of later Eucharistic practice (see, e.g., Hans Lietzmann, Oscar Cullmann). Among other much debated questions are: At what point were the breaking of bread (before the meal) and the drinking of the cup (after the meal) lifted from the meal context (Is this the point at which the agape meal fell into disuse?)? When were the formulas that were said over the bread and the wine assimilated to each other (and the Dominical command to repeat it included?)? When was the whole put into a liturgical context? By mid-2d century (Justin Martyr, *Apology* 1.66) a rudimentary liturgical form had clearly emerged; the table-centered rite had been expanded by the addition of some readings from the then emerging New Testament. In the more developed rites, it would appear that this first part of the Eucharist had been patterned on the synagogue service consisting of prayers and readings from the Prophets and the Law interspersed with psalmody; as it developed, the Christian synaxis consisted of prayers, reading from the Epistles followed by a reading from the Gospel, with psalmody or other hymnody between. At the same time, the sermon assumed a central place in this part of the service; in the 3d century it still seemed to be the prerogative of the bishop. At that time, this portion of the service was concluded with the exclusion of the catechumens and those under penance for sin, from which practice derives the name for this part of the service, "Mass of the Catechumens." The origin of the divine office in the East is probably to be traced to this development in the Eucharistic liturgy. The growth of this part of the service is best seen in the modern Roman rite in which it begins with an introit psalm, Kyrie eleison, Gloria in excelsis (in season), collect and Epistle, gradual psalm or hymn, Gospel reading, and a sermon (if desired). Of these, the introit, collect, Epistle, gradual, and Gospel change with the day of the church year.

2. The center of the Eucharist proper is the thanksgiving prayer over the elements of bread and wine. The origin of this part of the Eu-

charist is to be found in the private Jewish table prayers of thanksgiving (*Tractate Berakoth* 6–8). This prayer, introduced by *Sursum corda* ("Up hearts!") and a preface relating to God's creative action and the Sanctus (Isa. 6:3b; since 4th century), includes an anamnesis of the redemptive activity of God in Jesus Christ, an institution narrative, and an invocation of the Spirit upon the elements (epiklesis). Ever since the 4th century, the Communion following this prayer is preceded by the Lord's Prayer, and as early as the euchologion of Serapion (4th century) a thanksgiving after Communion is usual. A blessing at the end is a quite late addition.

3. As the synaxis was expanded, so also was the Eucharist proper by the addition before the Eucharistic prayer of an offertory. Again, the developed Roman rite witnesses this expansion. The offertory begins this part of the Eucharist, and consists of the priest's preparation of the elements, which is the only surviving remnant of an offering of the elements by the congregation, an elaborate offertory anthem by the choir, the secret prayers of offering said by the priest, and the offertory prayer proper. The Canon (so called since the 8th century) follows, consisting of preface (anaphora), Sanctus and Benedictus, the prayer of thanksgiving (called *canon missae*) which since the 9th century has been said silently. The Roman Canon is actually a series of prayers strung together, including intercessions and memorials as well as Eucharistic elements. The Communion prayers follow, including the Lord's Prayer, the breaking of the bread and the mixing of a piece of it in the chalice (6th century), Pax Domini, Agnus Dei (7th century), the Communion of the priest, the Communion of the people (if there be any!), the ablutions, and the Communion proper hymn. The whole is completed by a post-Communion prayer and a dismissal.

4. Along with the rite itself, a theology developed in the West whereby the questions of the manner of the Lord's presence and of when consecration of the elements took place were solved. As part of the theology of sacraments, the real presence of the Lord was described in ever more objective terms until it became dogma (Fourth Lateran Council, 1215) that the substance of the bread was replaced by the substance of the Lord's body (transubstantiation); this is still the official dogma of the Roman Catholic Church. At the same time, it was set forth that the utterance of the words of institution effected this change. As Communions became less frequent (even annual!) a practice developed whereby the chalice was withheld from the laity, which

is still the norm in the Roman Church. With infrequency of Communions and increased devotion to the presence of the Lord in the bread, there developed also an ancillary service of blessing the congregation with the exposed Host (Benediction, 15th century), to the accompaniment of hymns such as "O salutaris hostia" and "Tantum ergo."

5. The reconception of the theology of the sacraments among the Reformers resulted in considerable change, not only in the form of Eucharistic liturgy but in an understanding as well of Eucharistic worship. The conservatism of Luther is reflected in the Lutheran Eucharistic liturgy, which is largely a translation and purging of the basic order of the Roman rite in order to emphasize the equality between Word and Sacrament. The Prayer Books of the various provinces of the Anglican Communion likewise evince their heavy debt to the Roman rite, although the English Prayer Book of 1662 still retains the Calvinist overtones consequent upon the more than century-long struggle with the Puritans. Zwingli's subjectivism and Calvin's mediating position both resulted in radical reconstruction of the ancient Eucharistic liturgy. The Free Churches elevated New Testament practice into a norm and patterned their Eucharistic celebrations more or less after the mandates of the New Testament.

6. The liturgical movement, more responsible historical study of Christian origins, and the renewed centrality of Biblical thought attendant upon the rise of dialectical theology have brought to the center of current thought about the Eucharist those elements of corporate worship which belong in the wider context of Christian discussion. Simultaneously, the sacrificial theology of the Roman Catholic Church has been mollified by similar trends while the non-Roman Churches have begun to see what was essential in this trend of thought. Hence, the abandonment of dogmatic positions with respect to matters that have developed historically bodes well for future dialogue within the nexus of divided Christianity.

BIBLIOGRAPHY: F. Amiot, *History of the Mass* (New York, 1959); Y. Brilioth, *Eucharistic Faith and Practice* (London, 1930); G. Dix, *The Shape of the Liturgy* (London, 1945); J. Jeremias, *Eucharistic Words of Jesus* (London, 1966); H. Lietzmann, *Mass and the Lord's Supper* (Leiden, 1953); H. Sasse, *This Is My Body* (Minneapolis, 1959); M. Thurian, *The Eucharistic Memorial* (Richmond, 1961).

**Eucharistic Congresses.** A modern international Roman Catholic development. The

Eucharistic Congresses aim to glorify the Sacrament by promoting public adoration and general communion. Martha Marie Tamisier, "The Beggar Woman of the Blessed Sacrament," set the pattern for the Eucharistic Congresses of which there have been 39: Lille (1881); Avignon (1882); Liège (1883); Freiburg (1885); Toulouse (1886); Paris (1888); Antwerp (1890); Jerusalem (1893); Reims (1894); Paray-le-Monial (1897); Brussels (1898); Lourdes (1899); Angers (1901); Namur (1902); Angoulême (1904); Rome (1905); Tournai (1906); Metz (1907); London (1908); Cologne (1909); Montreal (1910); Madrid (1911); Vienna (1912); Malta (1913); Lourdes (1914); Rome (1922); Amsterdam (1924); Chicago (1926); Sydney (1928); Carthage (1930); Dublin (1932); Buenos Aires (1934); Manila (1937); Budapest (1938); Barcelona (1952); Rio de Janeiro (1955). The theme at Munich (1960), "For the Life of the World," was summed up by John XXIII on radio and television to the usual final gathering of a million, after the new spirit between clergy and laity and among all Christians engaged in apostolic work had been signally explored (July 31 to Aug. 7). Paul VI appeared in person at Bombay (1964), and "The Eucharist and the New Man" was interpreted in the midst of an almost totally non-Christian environment. He also personally attended the Congress at Bogotá, Colombia (1968), the first visit of a pope to Latin America.

**Eucharistic Controversies.** The earliest significant Eucharistic controversy occurred in the 9th century between Paschasius Radbertus (d. c. 860) and Ratramnus (d. 868), both monks of Corbey. Radbertus wrote the first monograph on the Eucharist that we possess, *De corpore et sanguine Domini,* in which he supported the view that after the consecration the actual flesh of Christ which was born of Mary appeared on the altar, though the sensible forms of the elements remained. He is usually considered a forerunner of the doctrine of transubstantiation. Ratramnus opposed these views, maintaining that the body which was received together with the blood was spiritual rather than historical.

In the 11th century Berengar of Tours (d. 1088) stressed the concept of personal fellowship with Christ in the sacrament. The consecration added a spiritual dimension, but Christ's true body remained in heaven. His views were opposed by many, most notably Lanfranc of Canterbury. He was condemned at Rome and Vercelli in 1050, although Hildebrand, later Pope Gregory VII, defended

him at Tours in 1054. In 1059 and again in 1079, Berengar was compelled to recant. The doctrine of transubstantiation was formally declared dogma by the Fourth Lateran Council in 1215 (Canon 1).

**Eucken, Rudolf** (1846–1926). German professor of philosophy at Jena (1874–1920). He received a Nobel Prize for Literature in 1908. His many works on philosophy and religion all emphasize the necessity for a spiritual control of life. A famous author and lecturer in his day, Eucken is seldom heard of now. Part of the reason for the almost total eclipse of his popularity in recent times is his philosophical idealism, built upon the foundation of Kant and seeing man as a co-worker with the divine.

**Eudes, John** (1601–1680). Roman Catholic missioner. A native of Normandy, where he studied with the Jesuits, Eudes entered the Paris Oratory in 1623. Influenced by Pierre de Bérulle and Charles de Condren, he was ordained in 1625 and began outstanding missionary work in France. In 1643 he founded the Congregation of Jesus and Mary (Eudists) for the education of priests and missionaries. In 1666, Alexander VII approved his second foundation (founded in 1641), the Congregation of Our Lady of Charity of the Refuge for the care of penitent women.

**Eugenius III** (Bernardo Paganelli di Montemagno, d. 1153). Pope from 1145. A native of Pisa, he became a Cistercian abbot and a devoted disciple of Bernard of Clairvaux. He reestablished papal authority over the newly proclaimed Roman commune on his election, but left for France to preach the Second Crusade in 1147 and organize the Council of Reims in 1148, allowing the commune to revive under Arnold of Brescia. In 1153, he made a treaty with Emperor Frederick I Barbarossa, who guaranteed the rights of the church. His chief concern as pope was reform of clergy discipline.

**Eugenius IV** (Gabriele Condulmer, 1383–1447). Pope from 1431. Born in Venice, he entered the Augustinian Order when very young. In 1408, though still a priest, he was raised to the cardinalate by his uncle, Gregory XII. Elected to the papacy in 1431, he inherited a difficult situation.

The Council of Basel called by his predecessor, Martin V, convened at the outset of his reign. Acting on unfavorable reports, he dissolved the Council in December, 1431. Those who remained at Basel reasserted the Gallican conciliar theory of Constance, deposed Eugenius IV and elected Count Amadeus VIII, first duke of Savoy, as Felix V. The renewal of the Schism cost the Council much prestige and one by one the nations submitted to Eugenius IV. In 1438, Pope Eugenius transferred the Council to Florence, where a union between the Greek and Roman Churches was achieved, though it was to prove only temporary.

Driven from Rome by quarreling factions in 1434, Eugenius IV resided in Florence until 1443 when he returned to Rome. As a result of his experience in Florence he became a patron of literature and the arts. The Pragmatic Sanction of Bourges (1438) weakened papal ties with France, but the able Enea Silvio Piccolomini (later Pius II), as papal representative, established an alliance with the emperor. An ardent opponent of nepotism, Eugenius IV led a rigorous and devout personal life.

**Eunomius** (d. c. 395). Pupil of Aetius of Antioch and literary defender of neo-Arianism. He was appointed deacon of the see of Cyzicus in 360, and later elected bishop. Noted for his dialectical art and sophistical reasoning, his people soon tired of rhetoric and forced him to resign. After the death of Aetius he assumed leadership of the Anomoean party, i.e., those who taught that the Son was unlike the Father, in opposition to the Nicene declaration that the Son and the Father were one. He taught also that the Son created the Spirit. In his concern for doctrine he depreciated worship and the devotional life. His *Apology,* in which he defines God as the ungenerated and the Son as generated and thus not God, was refuted by Basil the Great. The *Second Apology,* a reply to Basil, is not extant. His works prompted many refutations by later writers and an imperial edict in 398 ordered that his writings be burned. In addition to the *Apology* a formal "Profession of Faith" to the emperor remains, but his other writings are lost. He was exiled by Theodosius I in 383 but he lived until 394.

**Eusebius** (c. 295–c. 359). Bishop of Emesa, a serious student of the Scriptures, and a disciple of Eusebius of Caesarea. The Arian Synod of Antioch (340) elected him to succeed Athanasius, but he refused and was later elected to the see of Emesa. He opposed pure Arianism, though he was himself semi-Arian. His writings are an important witness to the development of Trinitarian doctrine between 330 and 360.

**Eusebius** (d. c. 342). Bishop of Nicomedia. He was influential at the court of Constantinople in defense of Arius. He signed the Creed of Nicaea, though his own creed was rejected.

He became a member of the Eusebian party and was exiled to Gaul. On his return he had several orthodox bishops deposed. He was more of an ecclesiastical politician and diplomat than a theologian. He baptized Constantine in 337.

**Eusebius of Caesarea** (c. 263–c. 339). Theologian, scholar, and church historian. He was trained (and probably born) at Caesarea in Palestine, where the presbyter Pamphilus presided over the great library that Origen had established. During the persecution of Diocletian, Eusebius suffered imprisonment and exile but survived. Pamphilus died as a martyr, and in honor of his friend and spiritual father Eusebius took the surname Pamphili, "(son) of Pamphilus." Not long after his return to Caesarea its bishop died, and Eusebius succeeded him, about 313. To this relatively quiet decade belong the scholarly works that have made Eusebius famous—the first draft of the *Ecclesiastical History* (later revised and continued to 324), the *Chronicle* (preserved in Latin and Armenian versions), and the apologetic works *Praeparatio evangelica* and *Demonstratio evangelica;* the latter defend respectively the Bible against paganism, and Christianity against Judaism, but are chiefly of interest for their numerous citations from works now lost. Eusebius assisted Pamphilus in preparing an *Apology for Origen* which is lost, except for the first book which survives in the Latin translation of Rufinus; his *Martyrs of Palestine* is in abridged form attached to the *History,* and preserved in full in Syriac.

In theology, Eusebius was content with an undeveloped Origenism, for which the Son was a subordinate being. He sympathized with Arius, and seems to have been suspended from office at the Council of Antioch under Eustathius early in 325. He cleared himself at Nicaea by presenting the creed of his church, which may have made some contribution (though not as much as his account seems to suggest) to the formulation of the Nicene Creed. The Council also recognized the primacy of the see of Caesarea over Jerusalem. Eusebius accepted its creed with some hesitation, after it was commended to him by the emperor. After Nicaea he was not so much an Arian as an imperialist, opposing any action that might imperil the church's enjoyment of the imperial patronage now extended to it. He need not be accused of insincerity; it seemed to many that the succession of a pro-Christian ruler to a persecuting emperor meant that the kingdoms of the world were becoming the Kingdom of God and his Christ.

In the later years of Constantine, Eusebius

supported the reaction against the Nicene leaders. He attended the Council of Antioch, which deposed Eustathius in 330, but declined the suggestion that he might succeed him, and the Councils against Athanasius, which met at Caesarea in 334 and at Tyre in 335. His Biblical studies received a new impetus from the increase of pilgrimages to Palestine. Only fragments are preserved, however, of his commentary on the psalms and of his work on sacred geography (the *Onomasticon,* on Biblical place names), and the *Canones Evangeliorum,* in which he used a system of dividing the Gospels into sections to facilitate the study of their interrelation. In his last years he produced the *Theophany,* a shorter form of his apologetic works, and replied to the ultra-Nicene Marcellus of Ancyra.

As an orator Eusebius had long been in demand on special occasions. A great celebration occurred in 335 when Constantine combined his *tricennalia,* the thirtieth anniversary of his accession, with the dedication of his buildings at Jerusalem, in which Eusebius was prepared to see the fulfillment of the prophecy of the New Jerusalem. Eusebius delivered at Constantinople and Jerusalem his *Praise of Constantine,* a Christianized form of the customary imperial panegyric. Two years later the emperor died, and Eusebius began at once (or indeed even in advance) his eulogistic *Life of Constantine*—not strictly a biography, since it is professedly limited to the emperor's noble actions. But Eusebius himself died in a year or two, and the work remained to be finished by others. Eusebius is scarcely a heroic figure, though by his own standards a respectable one, perhaps best described as illustrating the reactions of an average man to the great events of his time. We remain indebted, however, to his conscientious scholarship, especially for the precious records of the early church, its leaders and writers, preserved in the *Ecclesiastical History.*

BIBLIOGRAPHY: P. Schaff and H. Wace (eds.), *Nicene and Post-Nicene Fathers,* Series II, Vol. I (Grand Rapids, 1952); K. M. Setton, *The Christian Attitude Towards the Emperor in the Fourth Century* (New York, 1941); J. Stevenson, *Studies in Eusebius* (Cambridge, 1929); D. S. Wallace-Hadrill, *Eusebius of Caesarea* (Westminster, Md., 1961).

**Eustathius** (c. 300–c. 377). Semi-Arian bishop of Sebaste in Pontus. As a youth he was a pupil of Arius. A strong supporter of monasticism, he advocated fasting, despised marriage, and depreciated worldly goods. He was a close friend of Basil the Great and

helped in the formulation of his rule. Later he participated in the Macedonian heresy. He was generally more interested in the ascetic life than in dogmatic questions.

**Eustathius** (d. c. 337). Bishop of Antioch, formerly bishop of Beroea, a confessor in the Diocletian persecution, one of the 318 fathers at the Council of Nicaea. He was the first to speak to the emperor when he entered the assembly. His strong anti-Arian theology, however, occasioned the displeasure of Constantine, resulting in his exile to Trajanapolis in Thrace after deposition by an Arian Synod. Except for *De engastrimytho adversus Origenem,* only fragments of his writings are extant in dogmatic florilegia. In this work against Origen he rejects Origen's interpretation of I Sam., ch. 28, and at the same time Origen's whole allegorical method. He is often regarded as the successor of Paul of Samosata and the predecessor of Nestorius in his theology, but modern studies have questioned this judgment. A conclusive answer concerning his Christology cannot be given. In later controversies his writings were used on both the Dyophysite and Monophysite side. In 787 the Second Council of Nicaea acclaimed him an unwavering defender of the true faith and an opponent of Arius. He is perhaps the most significant ecclesiastical writer in the third decade of the 4th century.

**Euthymius Zigabenus** (early 12th century). Celebrated theologian well known for his knowledge of grammar and rhetoric. A monk at the Peribleptos monastery, he wrote several commentaries on the New Testament, including treatises on the book of The Psalms and the letters of Paul. His best-known work, the *Panoplia dogmatica,* was written at the request of the emperor Alexius I Comnenus, who wanted a refutation of all existing heresies. The *Panoplia* contains to date the best information we have on the Bogomiles.

**Eutyches** (c. 378–c. 455). Archimandrite of a large monastery at Constantinople. He supported the Alexandrian party in both theology and church politics, and was influential at the court of Theodosius II during the supremacy of his godson, the chamberlain Chrysaphius (441–450). Charged with heresy at a local synod in 448, he refused to accept the existence of two natures in Christ "after the union," and only under protest would he agree that the humanity of Christ was of one substance with ours. He was deposed and banished; but his appeal led to the Robber Council of Ephesus in 449, which reversed the proceedings of 448. It was in turn reversed by the Council of Chalcedon, which thus reinstated the deposition of 448. Eutyches had by now dropped into the background, but was again banished from the capital in 452. He is last mentioned in 454 in a letter of Pope Leo I complaining of his continued activity. Already aged and infirm in 448, Eutyches probably died soon after. His historic importance is in the reactions he produced. The events of 448 to 451 mark the end of Alexandrian predominance in the Eastern Church. Later, Monophysites repudiated the extreme position ascribed to Eutyches, claiming that their doctrine of two perfect natures united into one followed a middle course between the opposing errors of Eutyches and Nestorius.

**Evagrius of Pontus** (346–399). One of the first learned monks. He left Constantinople about 382 for an Egyptian hermitage where he lived until 399, supporting himself by copying manuscripts. His writings, in the form of aphorisms, were influential in monastic circles, though Evagrius was later suspected of heresy on account of his interest in Origen. He is responsible for the psychological analysis of temptations which later became the list of "seven deadly sins."

**Evangelical Academies.** Conference centers or places of retreat that developed in Germany after World War II. Similar to Sigtuna Foundation in Sweden, Iona Community in Great Britain, Kerk en Wereld in the Netherlands, Kirkridge in the United States, the Evangelical Academies and institutes of Germany represent a fresh approach to lay involvement in a church often tradition-bound and clergy-dominated. Protestantism in Germany was badly disrupted after World War II, with the guilt of the past, the displacement of persons, the destruction of property, and new challenges of the postwar world. Pastors Eberhard Mueller and Helmut Thielicke, with the cooperation of the Württemberg Landeskirche, planned a two weeks' conference at Bad Boll near Stuttgart in 1945. The response was overwhelming and soon other academies were organized in Loccum, Arnoldshain, Hofgeismar, Tutzing, Harrenalb, Hamburg, Schleswig-Holstein. Still later others were begun at Muelheim, Iserlohn, Pfalz, Oldenburg, and Berlin. According to the constitution of their association, these Academies provide places of retreat in order to help modern man confront his everyday questions and "in the light of the gospel to bring these questions closer to clarification, and so to witness to the unity of life in the freedom of the gospel." Developing out of the Volkskirche, inclusive and unified parishes, organized regionally in Landeskir-

chen, the Academies gave freer opportunity for individuals (including Roman Catholics, Jews, and those estranged from the church), and for various groups (e.g., in labor unions, industry, education, politics, medicine) to meet for conferences. These conferences involved worship, Bible and theological study, and discussion of common experiences, problems, and possible programs of action. The Evangelical Academies served to build bridges between pastors and parishioners, between Christians and the world. To them has been attributed much of the renewal of the church in Germany.

**Evangelical Alliance.** A Protestant association of a voluntary character organized and active in the 19th century for the support and promotion of Christian unity and religious liberty. Founded in London in 1846, it aimed to find the "best methods of counteracting infidelity, Romanism and ritualism, and the desecration of the Lord's Day." At its founding conference, some nine hundred clergymen and laymen represented more than eight major denominational families from eight nations and numbered among them the most distinguished theologians, churchmen, and philanthropists of Protestantism. A nine-point doctrinal basis was agreed upon, including the following elements: authority of the Scriptures, individual interpretation thereof, the Trinity, the fall and depravity of man, the incarnation and atonement in Christ, justification by faith, work of the Holy Spirit, traditional eschatology, divine origin of the ministry and obligation of the "gospel" sacraments. This summary was not meant as a creed or an exhaustive definition of faith, nor did the Alliance aim to become either the basis for organic union in Protestantism or another denomination. Instead, it intended to be an expression of the spiritual unity that already was felt to exist among the churches. In this it was a forerunner of the modern ecumenical movement. Although the World's Evangelical Alliance still exists, its most lasting monument is the annual Week of Prayer which it promoted and which is still widely celebrated each January.

**Evangelical Alliance in the United States.** The American branch of a primarily British voluntary association of Christians formed to encourage the unity of Protestantism. The diversity of American religious life rather than its unity is usually stressed in surveys of American history, but unity, as a goal and culmination of the American experiment, is a strong theme in the 19th century. During the 1820's, clergy and a surprising number of laymen in many different denominations were active in the formation of the American Tract Society, the American Bible Society, and the American Sunday School Union. Missionary activity was also touched by this cooperative spirit. The American Home Missionary Society was supported by the Presbyterian, Congregationalist, and Reformed Churches. The American Board of Commissioners for Foreign Missions, which was responsible for sending overseas the first American foreign missionaries, was a similar ecumenical organization. Christians in various denominations also cooperated in an attack upon the notable evils of early 19th-century society, forming societies to combat intemperance, slavery, war, and dueling. Encouraged by the success of these cooperative ventures, some Christian leaders hoped to take one further step—the formation of a society uniting all Protestants. Samuel S. Schmucker, a Lutheran, in 1838 published a *Fraternal Appeal to the American Churches* to give visible expression to their deeply felt unity. Professional Schmucker proposed the formation of a group which, while respecting denominational differences, would allow all American Protestants to affirm a common creed and to practice intercommunion. Nothing came of this idea, but in 1846 seventy-five American clergymen traveled to London to participate in the founding of the Evangelical Alliance. The fact that approximately eight hundred American and European Christians were able to assemble in the same hall in a spirit of cooperation and brotherly love was a great joy and wonder to all participants. The American group came almost exclusively from the seaboard states (only four were from west of the Appalachians) and from the Calvinist denominations (forty-five of the delegates were Presbyterian, Congregational, or Reformed; sixteen were Methodist, six Baptist, and five Lutheran). There were not a great many other foreign delegates, the British nonconformists making up the bulk of the group. Each of these clergymen cooperated with the Alliance as individuals, their actions having no effect upon their denominations. This ignoring of the denominational differences was one of the greatest weaknesses of the movement. As individuals, however, they were able to agree to a very broad creedal basis. The organization was not to have any continuing secretariat, nor was there any long-range program established for the Alliance that a staff might have pursued. The delegates, having proclaimed their unity, seemed unable to conceive of any further steps. The session was virtually concluded with these steps taken when the question of the morality of slavery was injected into the discussion. British nonconformists had been active in the recently concluded campaign to free all the slaves within the British dominions. Now the British delegates wondered out loud why the Americans were not more forceful on the subject. A great controversy developed that wrecked the Evangelical Alliance as a worldwide organization. The best compromise that could be patched together was that each nation represented should form its own Evangelical Alliance. This was not accomplished in the United States until 1867. The Alliance functioned only to call conferences —in Pittsburgh in 1875; Detroit, 1877; St. Louis, 1879; District of Columbia, 1887; Boston, 1889; and Chicago at the Columbian Exposition in 1893. Probably the greatest of these meetings was held in New York in 1873, a conference to which all the European branches of the Alliance were invited to send representatives.

BIBLIOGRAPHY: R. Rouse and S. C. Neill (eds.), *A History of the Ecumenical Movement: 1517–1948* (2d ed., rev., Philadelphia, 1967); D. Schaff, *The Life of Philip Schaff* (New York, 1897); S. S. Schmucker, *Fraternal Appeal to the American Churches* (Philadelphia, 1965); A. R. Wentz, *Pioneer in Christian Unity: Samuel Simon Schmucker* (Philadelphia, 1967).

**Evangelical and Reformed Church.** A merger in 1934 of the Reformed Church in the United States and the Evangelical Synod of North America. Both churches had developed from German immigrant groups. In 1957, the Evangelical and Reformed Church merged with the General Council of the Congregational Christian Churches and the combined denomination is called the United Church of Christ.

**Evangelical Church in Germany.** A confederation of Protestant ecclesiastical bodies in Germany. The Evangelische Kirche in Deutschland (EKD) arose during the period following World War II on the foundation of 19th-century efforts at cooperation and union among the Protestant state churches of Germany. The term "evangelical" when applied to a church arose out of Luther's objections to the identification of the Reformation church by his name, and, although it never gained legal status, this term was used to identify the followers of Luther over against the Reformed and the Catholics down to the 19th century. During that century it came to be associated with efforts at union between the Lutheran and Reformed churches. Since that time it has been used as a general designation for Protestantism in distinction from Roman Catholicism in Germany, and the names Evangelical Lutheran and Evangelical Reformed have come into general use. The term has also tended to bear some significance touching upon Protestant union since that time.

The roots of the EKD go back to the Evangelical Alliance conference of 1846 at which twenty-six state churches were represented which led to the great Wittenberg Kirchentag of 1848 and to a more or less permanent structure to promote and facilitate the cooperation of the Protestant churches in Germany. These efforts gained much more significance when the "court churches" no longer were related to a royal court after World War I. The problems and opportunities of a partially disestablished church under the Weimar Republic led in 1922 to the establishment of the German Evangelical Church Confederation. To be sure, this was only a coordinating body with merely advisory powers, but it did have the aim of a more comprehensive unity. Unfortunately, when such "unity" was at last proposed, it was in the form of the German Evangelical Church (DEK) of 1933, designed as a tool for the mobilization of the Protestant churches in the Nazi program. Insofar as Hitler's German Christians were unable to dominate this body from the beginning, it was doomed both as a political tool and as an expression of Christian unity, and the stage was set for the rise of the Confessing Church in 1934 and the German Church struggle (1933–1945).

The Council of the EKD was established at a meeting held in Treysa in August, 1945, at the call of the fearless leader of the Confessing Church, Bishop Theophilus Wurm (1868–1953) of Württemberg. The new body gained a constitution in July, 1948, and its first synod took place in January, 1949. The confessional position of the EKD is the affirmation of unity on the basis of the Scriptures and the ancient creeds, and diversity on the ground of the Reformation confessions. It is not and does not pretend to be an organically unified church but, rather, a confederation of churches dedicated to the expressing of present unity and to the deepening of it by overcoming hindrances to union. Although it has been the subject of theological dialogue since 1947, full intercommunion has not been obtained in the EKD. Of the 27 member churches, 12 are United (union of Lutheran and Reformed), 13 are Lutheran, and 2 are Reformed.

The constitution of the EKD provides for three basic organs by means of which it is to function. The first of these, the Synod, is made up of 120 members, 100 appointed by the member churches and 20 by the EKD Council. This body meets annually and is the main legislative and moral voice of the EKD. The most significant statements it has issued were those on the church's responsibility for world peace, issued in 1950 and 1952. A second organ, and that which provides central leadership for the federation, is the Council, which is made up of 12 members selected by the Synod in conjunction with the Church Conference. Its members reflect the various confessional and territorial interests involved in the German Church. The Council has appellate authority with regard to Synod judicial decisions, and in general acts for the Synod when that body is not in session. Its main function, however, is to represent the EKD in ecumenical affairs and to supervise the operation of the administrative structure of the federation. A third constitutional body of the EKD is the Church Conference which functions at the discretion of the leaders of the member churches.

It should be noted that the EKD has taken responsibility for much of the work that was either carried on within the individual churches (students', men's, women's, and children's work) or fostered by voluntary nonecclesiastical bodies in the past (see INNER MISSION).

The clearly federative character of the EKD can certainly not be disputed, but the fact that it has weathered some extremely stormy Synods while gaining a deeper sense of unity and determination to stay together gives promise that the aim of organic unity for German Protestants may yet find expression through this "church."

BIBLIOGRAPHY: A. C. Cochrane, *The Church's Confession Under Hitler* (Philadelphia, 1962); S. W. Herman, *The Rebirth of the German Church* (New York, 1946); K. Hutten, *Iron Curtain Christians* (Minneapolis, 1967); F. H. Littell, *The German Phoenix* (Garden City, 1960).

**Evangelicalism.** A historical term and a movement within Christianity that has had a large variety of meanings. In actual historical perspective, evangelicalism began as a movement within Western Christianity in the 18th century, especially in Germany, as a reaction to the rigid orthodoxy of post-Reformation Lutheranism and Calvinism. It was generally called Pietism. At the same time it also originated in England as a reaction against the sterility and moribund character of both the Established and the nonconformist churches. The religious awakenings of Whitefield and Wesley, the rise of Methodism, and the organizing of an Evangelical party in the

Church of England were all parts of 18th-century evangelicalism.

Although European Pietists and English Evangelicals continued to give leadership, much of the fervor for Christian evangelicalism in the 19th century was found in America as a result of the religious awakenings going on there. In the last century, evangelicalism was spread throughout world Christianity by American, European, and English missionaries. Although the movement continued in most major Christian churches, by mid-20th century the term, at least, had been and continues to be applied to the fundamentalist churches and Pentecostal groups.

At its outset evangelicalism was based upon the Reformation doctrines of justification by faith alone, the priesthood of all believers, and the sinful depravity of man, which were proclaimed in the Biblical context of divine grace and forgiveness through the passion and death of Christ. The Bible has always been central and authoritative in the movement.

Strongly individualistic in character, evangelicalism has always emphasized personal commitment to God by the individual through a conscious conversion experience, often involving emotional characteristics. The fruit of conversion should be a personal moral and spiritual transformation which is revealed by disciplined living, strict morality, fervent personal prayer, and pious works of charitable philanthropy and service.

During the 19th century the movement achieved many accomplishments: foreign missions were established throughout the world, especially in Asia and Africa, and home missions were organized to reconvert the numerous baptized persons of all social classes who had lost interest in Christianity; the Sunday school was accepted and vigorously promoted; both the Bible, translated into many languages, and religious tracts were widely distributed, and various Bible and religious tract societies were organized; and schools and colleges were founded. In the matter of social and political action the movement was chiefly instrumental in winning legislation against Negro slavery, especially the slave trade; for prison reform; against work and recreation on Sunday; and for prohibition of gambling and alcoholic beverages wherever possible.

Within Christianity the chief criticism of evangelicalism has been its one-sided emphasis upon individualism which has often caused the movement to fail to support the fullness of the church and the Christian community. Another criticism has involved its emphasis on emotionalism, especially in the conversion experience, and in the present day its emphasis upon literal Biblical fundamentalism. The movement's social and political action has been criticized for its failure to take note of the social and economic structures of society that have caused so many of society's problems. Many proponents of the movement have believed that personal religion alone will overcome the worker's social and economic problems. It has also been criticized for its continued emphasis upon Sabbatarian laws and various social prohibitions. Its critics readily point to the fact that evangelicalism has always been a distinct minority movement within Christianity.

BIBLIOGRAPHY: G. R. Balleine, *A History of the Evangelical Party in the Church of England* (London, 1933); O. Chadwick, *The Victorian Church* (New York, 1966); L. Elliott-Binns, *The Evangelical Movement in the English Church* (London, 1928); and *The Early Evangelicals* (London, 1953); E. M. Howse, *Saints in Politics* (Toronto, 1952); R. A. Knox, *Enthusiasm* (New York, 1950).

**Evangelical Social Congress.** Founded by German churchmen in 1890 to show Christian concern for social and economic problems, especially those of laboring classes. Annual conferences were held to discuss Christian political and social action. Early leaders were Adolf Stoecker and Adolf von Harnack, but Stoecker left the group when younger radicals led by Friedrich Naumann dominated it. Harnack remained and later became chairman of the annual meeting.

**Evangelical United Brethren Church.** Church body constituted on Nov. 16, 1946, at Johnstown, Pa., by a merger of the United Brethren in Christ and the Evangelical Church. The United Brethren in Christ grew out of the work of Philip W. Otterbein (1726–1813), German Reformed pastor who with Martin Boehm (1725–1812) exerted vigorous evangelistic efforts among Germans in Pennsylvania. In 1800 an association of evangelists called itself the United Brethren. The first general conference of the body convened in 1815; subsequently the organization grew under the leadership of Christian Newcomer. The body was Arminian in doctrine and Methodist in polity. At the time of the 1946 merger, it was strongest in Pennsylvania, Ohio, and Indiana. The Evangelical Church was founded by Jacob Albright (1759–1808), a Lutheran turned Methodist who began preaching among Germans in Pennsylvania in the 1790's. The first council met in 1803 as sixteen followers acknowledged "Jacob Albright as a true Evangelical preacher in word and deed." Members of the group were variously called Albright People, Albright Brethren, and German Methodists even after the name Evangelical Association was officially adopted in 1816. The first General Conference met in 1807. Methodist polity was followed, including the circuit and itinerant ministry, and Arminian theology. After 1850 the Association extended its work to Württemberg, Bavaria, Switzerland, Alsace; missions were established in Japan, China, Africa, Central and South America, and Indonesia. By 1890 over half of the 130,000 members lived in Pennsylvania, Wisconsin, and Ohio. The United Evangelical Church broke away from its parent in 1891, but the schism was healed in 1922. The 1946 merger of the Evangelical Church and the United Brethren in Christ was long expected. The two bodies had much common ground in theology and polity, and their geographical boundaries overlapped. The present Evangelical United Brethren Church is divided into annual conferences. Its polity is Methodist; its highest authority is the General Conference. In 1968 the 750,000-member Evangelical United Brethren Church merged with the 9,600,000-member Methodist Church to form The United Methodist Church. The separate bodies have always had closely related organization and doctrine, and they have a long history of cooperative work behind them. It was mainly cultural barriers that remained to be overcome by the 1968 merger.

**Evans, James** (1801–1846). Missionary to the Indians in Canada. Born at Kingston-upon-Hull, England, he emigrated to Canada in 1823 and in 1828 became a teacher at the Rice Lake Indian School in Upper Canada. In 1833 he was ordained by the Methodist Church and in the following year became a missionary to the Ojibway Indians on the St. Clair River. He served among the Indians of Lake Superior (1838–1840) and was appointed general superintendent of the Northwest Indian Missions in 1840. At Norway House he invented the system of syllabic characters still in use among the Cree Indians.

**Evanston** (1954). Second Assembly of the World Council of Churches, held at Northwestern University, Evanston, Ill. The main theme was "Christ, the Hope of the World." The meeting was significant for its ability to accept and face tensions: theological tensions over whether Christ as "Hope" is to be understood only in eschatological terms or equally as the hope of the present world; international tensions in recognizing the division between East and West and sincerely lamenting the lack of delegates from China, Russia, and some East European countries; cultural ten-

sions in admitting the failure of Western Christianity to deal with Africa and Asia in their own cultural contexts; and ecclesiastical tensions in recognizing the real problems of intercommunion and of missionary strategy in Africa and Asia. It expounded a new evangelism which declared that man's social, economic, and political conditions directly affect his understanding and acceptance of the gospel of Christ. The Assembly's most prophetic document concerned a "Responsible Society" in which it condemned all racial segregation, set some standards for states and politicians about political rights and justice, and called for Christian concern for economic conditions, especially those of agricultural and factory workers.

**Evelyn, John** (1620–1706). English diarist. Born of the wealthy English gentry, he supported Charles I in the Civil War, advocated the return of Charles II, and held a number of minor offices in the Restoration government, though disapproving of the loose court manners. An intellectual, he was an early fellow and leader of the Royal Society. He adhered to episcopacy throughout the period of Puritan ascendancy. His diaries richly portray the conditions of his period.

**Ewer, Ferdinand C.** (1826–1883). A priest of the Protestant Episcopal Church noted for his zealous promotion of Anglo-Catholicism. He saw (non-Roman) catholicism as "a continent of certainty"; Protestantism as "an ocean of conjecture." In a series of sermons on "The Failure of Protestantism" (1868), he stated his hope for the ultimate reunion of Roman, Greek, and Episcopal Churches.

**Excommunication.** Censure depriving a church member of the rights of fellowship in the church community. Two degrees of ecclesiastical censure were used in the past: greater, involving exclusion from all sacraments (save Last Rites) and association with Christians, and lesser, liturgical limitation alone. Only the greater is used now in the Roman Church. Protestant churches also exercise jurisdiction over members, but infrequently and with the cooperation of clergy and congregation. For the Roman Church and many others, such censure does not mean that one's relationship to God is broken, although the need for discipline might indicate serious religious problems.

**Exemption.** The release of an ecclesiastical person or institution from the control of its normal superior (usually a bishop) to that of one higher, often the pope. The practice of exemptions arose when monasteries sought protection from episcopal oppression and appealed to synods or the pope. The first such privilege was given by Pope Honorius I in 628 to the monastry of Bobbio. From the 11th century, exemptions increased, sometimes including entire orders, e.g., Cluny, collegiate and cathedral chapters, parishes and individuals. Occasionally a bishop himself sought exemption from the authority of his metropolitan. From the 12th century, exemption of monasteries became the rule. The practice was a source of much friction between bishops and the exempt institution, resulting in considerable medieval litigation over conflicting claims of jurisdiction. The Council of Trent attempted to correct abuses of the practice by restoring ordinary and proper jurisdiction to the bishop (Session XXIV).

**Exile, Penitential.** In addition to the formal penalties imposed by the church as part of the sacrament of penance, the medieval sinner was often drawn to work out his true contrition, and gain fuller indulgence, by self-denials of a voluntary nature. Official prescription rarely went beyond pilgrimage, but the notion of temporary or permanent self-imposed exile of other kinds had great appeal. Missionary labor and withdrawal to the seclusion of the monastery or hermitage were often viewed in this light; the Crusades provided a secular equivalent. It was perhaps the special mark of the early Celtic Church to give literal expression to the voluntary penance of exile, based on the injunction of Matt. 19:29 to forsake both home and family for the love of Christ.

**Existentialism.** A tendency or attitude that seeks to emphasize the importance of individual human existence. In human personality, freedom and the will are more significant than the reason. Existentialism is a protest against rationalism, idealism, and scientism, or against views of the world and policies of action that regard individual human beings as helpless objects of historical forces or as determined by the regular operation of natural processes. Both in its 19th-century origins and its 20th-century flowering, existentialism was particularly a reaction against the system of Hegel.

Søren Kierkegaard (1813–1855) was the unwitting founder of modern existentialism. Under the influence of J. G. Hamann and Friedrich Schelling he rebelled against orthodox rational theology and the Hegelianism of the leaders of the established church of Denmark. In voluminous writings he reduced the individual human predicament to a simple dilemma of either Christ or the world. There are no logically compelling reasons why a man should decide for one rather than the other, but if a man should choose the world of pleasure or of cultivated humanism, he would be haunted by conscious or unconscious despair. If he should follow the path of duty, the individual would be led to accept general principles and collective aims that would be apt to obliterate the consciousness of individual responsibility. Religious seriousness is of first importance. All attempts to provide Christianity with a rational justification were fundamentally irreligious, indicating a lack of belief. From his own experience Kierkegaard emphasized the significance of the particular and the individual in such a way as to reevaluate profoundly the whole of human life.

In the 20th century, Kierkegaard was rediscovered and his writings were translated into German (1909 ff.), Italian (1910 ff.), French (1929 ff.), and English (1936 ff.). In the years after World War I, existentialism spread in Europe first of all without its original Christian orientation, in response to the moral and social upheavals of the time. Martin Heidegger (1889–    ) learned phenomenology from Edmund Husserl and applied its methods to human experience. Rooted in Kierkegaard's thought but without belief in God, he developed a pessimistic, almost morbid, view of man's condition which greatly influenced later existentialists. Karl Jaspers (1883–1969) worked out a more thorough philosophy of existence, although avoiding any attempt to systematize. He did not believe that any written or traditional revelation could help men in their actual dilemmas. French atheistic existentialism was led by Jean-Paul Sartre (1905–    ), whose *Being and Nothingness* (1943, English tr. 1956) was a major exposition of the position. The essays and novels of Albert Camus (1913–1960) also dealt with existential themes.

Existentialism has influenced 20th-century religious writers to a considerable degree. The French existentialist Gabriel Marcel (1887–    ) became a Roman Catholic in 1928 and introduced Kierkegaard to France. Through Socratic dialogue in his plays, he attempted to bring his audiences to grips with the actual options available to men. Nicolai Berdyaev (1874–1948), a loyal but nonconformist Russian Orthodox, spent the last twenty-four years of his life in Paris, where he published a number of Christian existentialist works. Martin Buber (1878–1965), well-known Jewish religious philosopher, in a short classic, *I and Thou,* used existentialist insights to enrich the meaning of dialogic relationships. Among Protestant theologians influenced by, and making use of existentialist philosophy are Rudolf Bultmann (1884–    ), Karl

Barth (1886–1968), Paul Tillich (1886–1965), and Reinhold Niebuhr (1892–1971). They believe in various ways that the essential aspects of the human predicament to which Christianity is addressed can be more adequately described through this philosophy than through any other.

BIBLIOGRAPHY: H. J. Blackham, *Six Existentialist Thinkers* (New York, 1952); R. Bretall (ed.), *A Kierkegaard Anthology* (New York, 1959); F. H. Heinemann, *Existentialism and the Modern Predicament* (New York, 1954); R. Jolivet, *Introduction to Kierkegaard* (New York, 1952); D. E. Roberts, *Existentialism and Religious Belief* (New York, 1957).

**Exoucontians** (from a Greek word meaning "out of nonbeing"). The followers of Aetius of Antioch and Eunomius of Cyzicus. They maintained an extreme Arian position, teaching that the Son is totally unlike the Father. The Son is begotten, created out of nonbeing, and therefore of a nature different from that of the Father. They are also called the Anomoeans ("unlike").

**Exsurge, Domine** ("Arise, O Lord"). Papal bull of Leo X issued June 15, 1520, condemning the teaching of Martin Luther and allowing him sixty days to recant on pain of excommunication. The bull condemns forty-one propositions from Luther's books; it orders the books burned, his supporters charged with heresy, and districts sheltering them interdicted. Eck, charged with publishing the bull in Germany, was received harshly, and Luther burned the bull publicly outside Wittenberg's Elster Gate on Dec. 10, 1520, thus provoking the bull of excommunication *Decet pontificem Romanum* (Jan. 3, 1521).

**Eznik** (5th century). Bishop of Bagrevand in Armenia. He is important in the history of Armenian Bible translations. His book *Against the Sects,* first published in 1762, opposes the pagans, the religion of the Persians, Greek philosophy, and the Marcionites. The discussion of the Marcionites is important for the history of heresy. He was a master of the Old Armenian style.

# F

**Faber, Frederick William** (1814–1863). Anglican convert to Roman Catholicism and hymn writer. Faber joined the Tractarian movement while a student at Oxford in the 1830's, was ordained an Anglican priest in 1839, and became a Roman Catholic in 1845 through the influence of Cardinal Newman and after a trip to Rome. He became a Roman priest in 1847 and in 1848 joined the Oratory of St. Philip Neri. He was made superior of the London branch of the Oratory, which was established in 1849, presiding over it until his death. He wrote many evangelical hymns, characterized by a love of Jesus and a strong sense of moral responsibility. Charles Wesley was the hymn writer whom Faber consciously emulated.

**Faber** (Heigerlin), **John** (1478–1541). Roman Catholic controversialist. The son of a German blacksmith, he changed his name to Faber (Latin, *faber,* "blacksmith"). He studied theology and law at Tübingen and at Fribourg, becoming a doctor of civil and canon law in 1509. As vicar of Lindau and the vicar-general for the bishop of Constance, he worked against the Protestant Reform and in 1521 presented the pope with his first work against Luther. In 1523 he debated against Zwingli in Zurich, and in 1526 and 1529 preached at the Diets of Speyer. A humanist and a friend of Erasmus, he advocated conciliar reform based on Scripture.

**Faber Stapulensis** (Jacobus Faber Stapulensis, *the Latin form of* Jacques Lefèvre d'Étaples) (c. 1450–c. 1536). French clergyman, philosopher, Biblical scholar, and humanist, in many ways the precursor of the Reformation in France. Born in Picardy, he was sent to Paris early in life to study for the priesthood. There he took his magisterial and doctoral degrees, after which he spent over a year traveling in Italy, where he became interested in Renaissance humanism. Returning to Paris in 1492, he became an active Christian humanist, attracting a large following because of his teaching ability and Christian piety. In 1521 he was censured by the faculty of the Sorbonne for criticizing the Roman Church and for alleged Lutheran tendencies. From this time on he led an unsettled life which took him to Meaux, then to Strasbourg, back to Paris, and finally to Béarn, where he remained until his death in 1536. Faber's greatest scholarly contributions were his *Psalterium quintuplex* of 1509, his commentaries on Paul's letters in 1512 and the Gospels in 1522, and his French translation of the New Testament from the Vulgate in 1523. In the preface to his commentary on the Pauline letters Faber propounded many of the principles of the Protestant Reformation five years before the appearance of Luther's Ninety-five Theses. However, Faber never formally left the Roman Catholic Church.

**Fabian** (d. 250). Bishop of Rome between 236 and 250. Though little is known of him, he is generally considered to have introduced the five lower orders of the clergy and to have divided Rome into seven areas, each the responsibility of a deacon. In *Epistle* 9, Cyprian speaks very highly of Fabian's administration of the Roman Church. He was martyred in the Decian persecution on Jan. 20, 250.

**Fabrique.** The church council characteristic of the Quebec parish that unites both the civil and religious aspects of the community into one corporation. This corporation is administered by a council composed of the parish priest, who is its president, and three churchwardens. Each year the parishioners elect a new warden who with the wardens from the two previous years join with the priest, forming the council for that year. This democratic system was in operation as early as 1645 in the parish of Notre Dame, Quebec.

**Faculty.** A grant of permission to perform an act or function that the recipient could not otherwise perform. A priest is granted a faculty to perform sacerdotal functions in a particular locality. A faculty may be granted permitting a person to be ordained who is below the canonical age. A bishop may grant a faculty to a priest to administer confirmation in the bishop's absence. Usually granted by the pope or a bishop, a faculty expires with the death of the granting authority.

**Faith and Order, World Conferences on.** Inspired by American Episcopal Bishop Charles Brent for discussion of approaches to church, creeds, sacraments, ministry, worship. The first conference was held at Lausanne (1927); the second, at Edinburgh (1937), decided to join with the Life and Work movement to form the World Council of Churches (1948). Subsequent conferences have been held at Lund (1952) and Montreal (1963), sponsored by the Faith and Order Commission of the World Council of Churches.

**Falk Laws** (May laws). So called because of Adalbert Falk (1827–1900), minister of public worship in Prussia, who was instrumental in getting them passed (1873–1875). The Falk (or May) laws were the legislative fruit of Bismarck's Kulturkampf, a violent quarrel between Prussia and Roman Catholicism. Religious education, clerical education, and clerical appointments were to be controlled by the state. Bitter resistance by the Roman Catholics was the result until peace was finally made with Pope Leo XIII. By 1887 most of the Falk laws had been nullified.

**Falloux Law** (March 15, 1850). French educational scheme, named for a liberal Catholic sponsor, which ended the secular monopoly of education. Private persons and religious orders could open schools of any level, the clergy teach without the usual degree, curés manage primary schools, and church-influenced councils monitor higher schools. One thousand new institutions soon appeared under the statute. Opponents labeled it "the greatest clerical victory of the 19th century."

**False Decretals.** See PSEUDO-ISIDORE.

**Familists.** The group founded by Henry Nicholas (Niclaes) in Emden in the 1540's which soon spread to England and later influenced the Quaker movement. The Family of Love cultivated a communal holiness in obedience to a "begodded" hierarchy of elders. The elders led a disciplined but Spirit-filled worship. The groups were often clandestine in the face of persecution. Charges of moral laxity are discounted by modern scholars.

**Family Compact.** A term applied to the governing class of Upper Canada prior to the Rebellion of 1837. There was in fact little family connection among those so designated, yet the expression persisted as an apt description of the alliance between the Established Church of England and the governing classes who desired, following the American Revolution, to suppress both radical political ideas and sectarian religion. "Family compact" is now used to describe the members of the Executive and Legislative Councils of Upper Canada.

**Farel, William** (1489–1565). French Reformer. He studied at the University of Paris, where he was strongly influenced by Lefèvre (Faber Stapulensis). Because of Farel's reformatory views, he fled France in 1523, going to Basel. There he preached Reformation doctrines, and was shortly banished from the city, partly through the influence of Erasmus. Later he went to Bernese territory, where he was active in the cause of reform, and helped make Bern a Protestant canton in 1528. Bern continued to be his base and patron. In 1530 he brought the Reformation to Neuchâtel, and at Orbe he won Viret to the Protestant camp.

In 1532 Farel began his work in Geneva. His provocative preaching brought mixed reactions, and for a while he was forced out of the town. By the end of the next year, however, he began to make progress, with Viret's help. In 1536 he threatened Calvin with God's condemnation if the young scholar refused the possibilities of Geneva, and persuaded him to stay. Thereafter Farel played a secondary role under the great Reformer, though he was fully implicated in the crisis of 1538 when they both had to leave Geneva. After Calvin's return to Geneva in 1541, Farel eventually went back to Neuchâtel. An ardent evangelist rather than a great scholar or gifted organizer, Farel was overshadowed by Calvin, whom he outlived by just over a year.

**Fascism and Christianity.** Attitudes of Fascists toward faith have ranged from ostentatious piety (L'Action Française), active support (Falangism), the use of faith as an instrument of social control (Fascism), to temporary accommodation (National Socialism). Fascists were normally secular in objectives and frequently shared the distaste of 19th-century liberals for religious dogma. In their view, clerical influences ultimately would be driven from public life. Mussolini, an agnostic, wrote in the *Enciclopedia Italiana*: "In the Fascist State religion may be considered as one of the most profound manifestations of the spirit." He made the Lateran Pacts recognizing Vatican City and accepting a Concordat with the pope (1929), yet two years later he attacked Catholic Action groups for meddling in politics. While General Francisco Franco allied himself with and sought aid from the conservative hierarchy in the Spanish Civil War, much later his constitution approved by plebiscite, Dec. 14, 1966, contained a proviso for toleration of non-Catholic public worship. The Holy See condemned the newspaper *L'Action Française,* voice of French monarcho-Fascism, in 1926. Although Hitler arranged a Concordat with Pius XI in 1933, he gradually became more repressive toward Catholics and Protestants: preoccupation with Jews perhaps spared Christians his closest attention. Some devout individuals saw Fascism as protection against Marxism; usually its collaboration with cults of Christianity was opportunistic rather than honorable. The entire question of the relationship between Fascism and Roman Catholicism in Italy, Spain, France, and Germany, and between Fascism and Protestantism in Germany is highly debatable. Some argue that there was a close relationship by mutual choice; others contend that the relationships were extremely complex and almost impossible to comprehend by a simple generalization.

**Fast Days.** Days on which Christians were to abstain from food and drink. As early as apostolic times Christians were accustomed to fast (Matt. 6:16; Mark 2:20; Acts 13:2; 14:23). The Jewish Christians probably followed the Jewish custom of fasting on Mondays and Thursdays. When the church reacted against its Jewish heritage, it apparently dropped these days and fasted on Wednesdays and Fridays, probably by the end of the first century (Didache 8:1). There are indications that even by the end of the 2d century these fast days were not universally enforced, and lasted only until 3 P.M. (Tertullian, *On Fasting* 1, 2, and 10). By the 5th century Saturday replaced Wednesday as a fast day in areas where the Sabbatarian controversy was most deeply felt. Lent grew in some places from two intensive fast days immediately before the Easter celebration in the 2d century to forty fast days in the 4th century. The Eastern Church also added Advent (from Nov. 15), Trinity Sunday until June 29, and the two weeks prior to Aug. 15, as fast days. The church at Rome early in the 3d century adopted the days of the chief agricultural operations in Italy as fast days, probably in opposition to pagan feasts. These, called the Ember Days, were the Wednesday, Friday, and Saturday following the First Sunday in Lent, Pentecost, and Sept. 14. A fourth season, following Dec. 13, was added later.

**Father Divine** (George Baker, c. 1880–1965). Negro cult leader. Born near Savannah, Ga., he founded the Peace Mission movement which spread during the 1930's. This racially integrated sect stresses fellowship banquets, separation of sexes, and communal living in "heavens" for its followers. Father Divine made few direct claims to divinity, but accepted divine titles from his followers. Members of the group take new names as "angels."

**Fatima, Apparition of.** A series of visions of the Virgin Mary alleged to have been seen in the Portuguese parish of Fatima. Between May 13 and Oct. 13, 1917, three children of the town of Aljustrel in the Portuguese parish of Fatima were said to have seen a number of visions of the Virgin Mary, in which she asked for repentance, the daily recitation of the rosary, and the consecration of Russia to her Immaculate Heart. On Oct. 13, some fifty thousand people saw a prodigious display of the sun which many claimed to be a miracle promised by Mary.

**Faustus of Melevis** (4th century). A leading figure in Manichaeism. He first taught in Rome and then in Carthage, where he met Augustine. Augustine was disappointed, however, and the encounter only hastened his movement toward the church. In 386, Faustus was charged with Manichaeism in Carthage and sent into exile. Though of humble birth, he was reputed to have attained great ability in rhetoric.

**Faustus of Riez** (d. c. 490). Abbot of Lérins in 433, later bishop of Riez in Provence, France, a leader of the French Church in the latter half of the 5th century. His *De gratia*, a refutation of Lucidus, is semi-Pelagian in theology. John Cassian calls him the most active champion of Pelagianism in its primitive form. Faustus was condemned at the Second Council of Orange in 529.

**Fawkes, Guy** (1570–1606). Folk villain of the Gunpowder Plot and subsequent celebrations of its anniversary. Following the banishment of Roman Catholic priests from England, a group of desperate Roman Catholics planned to blow up the Houses of Parliament and the king (James I) on Nov. 6, 1605 (the Gunpowder Plot). Fawkes, a Protestant who had been converted to Roman Catholicism and had served in the Spanish army, was the "technical consultant" who was to set the charge. He was apprehended on Nov. 5 with his bomb, and executed the following year. The result was widespread agitation, harsher anti-Roman Catholic legislation, and a more difficult time for the Stuarts, who were all inclined toward Roman Catholicism.

**Febronianism.** A form of German Gallicanism propounded by Johann Nikolaus von Hontheim, auxiliary bishop of Trier (1701–1790), in a work entitled *De statu ecclesiae* (1763), which was published under the pseudonym Justinus Febronius. He urged the pope to drop curialism and return to the spirit of primitive Christianity. He denied the monarchical constitution of the church and declared that papal primacy was limited in matters of doctrine by general councils and in matters of discipline by the national churches. In adopting this position he gave voice to the desire of the higher clergy to throw off their dependence upon the Curia. Rome prohibited the circulation of the book in 1764 and in 1778, Hontheim was asked to recant. He did so but his explanation of his recantation published in 1781 revealed no essential changes from his former views. In 1785 a Febronian program was set forth in the Ems Points. Joseph II (1780–1790) of the Hapsburgs was especially attracted to the ideas of Febronius.

**Fechner, Gustav Theodor** (1801–1887). German experimental psychologist. Educated at Leipzig, Fechner was professor of physics there from 1834 to 1839, when he resigned because of illness. Acquainted with R. H. Lotze, E. H. Weber, and C. H. Weisse, and influenced by Spinoza and Plotinus, Fechner advocated panpsychism under the pseudonym Dr. Mises. Even plants and stars shared an enveloping soul of which God was all-encompassing, he maintained. He contributed to early psychology through his further development of Weber's law, relating bodily and conscious movements, and strongly influenced Wilhelm Wundt. His writings include *Elemente der Psychophysik* and *Nanna oder Über das Seelenleben der Pflanzen.*

**Federal Council of the Churches of Christ in America.** Proposed to representatives of various Protestant denominations at the Interchurch Conference on Federation in 1905 and organized three years later. It was the culmination of the efforts of a relatively small group of men, led by Elias B. Sanford and William H. Roberts, who believed in church federation and who were convinced that Christian principles were relevant to the solution of social problems. Its constitution established these two concerns among its purposes: "To express the fellowship and catholic unity of the Christian Church"; and "To secure a larger combined influence for the churches of Christ in all matters affecting the moral and social condition of the people, so as to promote the application of the law of Christ in every relation of human life." The Council was the first large-scale explicitly interdenominational venture in American Protestantism. It was one of the first of those unitive efforts that make up the 20th-century ecumenical movement. It was racially inclusive from the outset, and comprised most denominations of size and influence. Several Eastern Orthodox bodies joined it in its later years.

The Federal Council merged into the National Council of Churches in 1950. Between its birth and its transformation in merger it led a full life, marked by the clear articulation of a social policy and a continuous attempt to give the policy concrete shape and form in terms of the social, economic, and political structures of American life. This social policy was never a fixed formula; rather, it was a flexible set of guidelines and directives, suggestive of possible courses of action. It was liberal in orientation and often prophetic in relation to the prevailing social standards. Its maintenance and extension for over four decades is one of the contributions of the Council to American religious life.

The social policy was formulated at the Council's first meeting in a report of the Committee on the Church and Modern Industry presented by Frank Mason North. The policy was the direct involvement of Christians and the churches in the social problems of the day. Section 9 of the report, later known as the Social Creed of the Churches, called upon the churches to work for "equal rights and complete justice for all men in all stations of life," "the abolition of child labor," "the abatement of poverty," and many other things. In 1912 the Creed was revised by extending its concerns to include protection of the family, conservation of health, and control of the liquor traffic. In 1932 the Creed was again revised, but this time it was thoroughly rewritten and renamed the "Social Ideals of the Churches." Among the new concerns included were those relating to social planning and farm problems. It condemned war and called for "the building of a cooperative world order."

The concrete applications of this social policy were numerous during the Council's history. Prior to World War I it focused on justice for industrial workers. During the war it worked for an adequate military chaplaincy, racial justice in the army, and a constructive peace. It supported Wilson's plan for a League of Nations. After the war it worked for industrial and international peace, racial justice, and many of the social programs that came to fruition in the New Deal. During World War II a Special Commission on a Just and Durable Peace under the chairmanship of John Foster Dulles proposed a forthright statement in favor of a peaceful international order. The Commission also advocated the formation of a United Nations.

The Federal Council was an experiment in unitive Protestantism of a practical rather than a doctrinal nature. It provided "a kind of laboratory or demonstration station for the Protestant churches, in which new ideas in many realms, especially social ethics, might be tried out." It suffered many vicissitudes in its history, but its continuation in the National Council testifies to the value of its structure and social policy.

BIBLIOGRAPHY: J. A. Hutchison, *We Are Not Divided* (New York, 1941); E. B. Sanford, *Origin and History of the Federal Council* (Hartford, 1916); *Federal Council Bulletin*.

**Felix of Urgel** (d. 818). Bishop of Urgel and a follower of Elipandus of Toledo in the Spanish Adoptianist controversy. He recanted at the Synod of Regensburg in 792 and later again before Pope Adrian I. He later began to teach Adoptianism again and was charged with heresy at Frankfurt (794) and Aachen (798). He renounced his errors in debate with Alcuin, but was regarded with suspicion until his death.

**Fellowship of Reconciliation.** An organization based upon social ideals, founded in England in 1914 and established in the United States in 1915. The Fellowship of Reconciliation has a following in many countries. United in their commitment to the ways of love and nonviolence, members of the Fellowship oppose war, seek to guarantee justice and civil liberty for all men, and strive to promote understanding between nations, classes, and races. The American Fellowship publishes a monthly journal, *Fellowship,* and maintains headquarters in Nyack, N.Y.

**Fénelon, François de Salignac de La Mothe-** (1651–1715). French mystic, archbishop of Cambrai. Trained at the Seminary of St. Sulpice, noted for preparing zealous and ascetic clergy, he was ordained to the priesthood in 1675. His career included educational appointments as superior of the Catholiques Nouvelles, a house for new converts from Protestantism, and tutor to Louis XIV's grandson. He spent two years on a mission to the Huguenots. In 1695 he became the archbishop of Cambrai. His chief contributions to his time were in education, spiritual counsel to earnest Christians related to the court of Louis XIV, eloquent sermons, loyalty to the pope and the church, and charitable works to the poor and suffering. His writings include the famous educational novel *Télémaque* (1699), and several pastorals defending the Roman Catholic Church in the Jansenist controversy. His distinct contribution is related to his writings on theocentric mysticism. Quietist tendencies characterized his thought, although in 1696 he signed the Thirty-four Articles of Issy which condemned quietism. As a follower and defender of Mme. Guyon, he became involved in a long and bitter controversy with J. B. Bossuet. In 1697 he published his *Maxims of the Saints,* a treatise on true and false mysticism. Assailed by Bossuet, this writing was condemned by the Holy See. Many of Fénelon's letters of spiritual counsel have been published.

**Feofan of Vysha** (1815–1894). Russian Orthodox bishop, eminent spiritual leader, letter writer, and translator of a five-volume version of the *Philokalia*. He was a major figure in Russia's 19th-century Orthodox Renaissance and was particularly active in the revival of patristic studies. Among the most distinguished *startsi* ("elders") of his day, he contributed significantly to the restoration of devotional and spiritual literature through his remarkable translation of the *Philokalia*. He also carried on a prodigious correspondence with those who sought his counsel in the life of the spirit. Published posthumously in seven volumes, his letters were extremely influential until 1917.

**Ferdinand of Spain** (1452–1516). Joint sovereign with Isabella of the united kingdoms of Castile and Aragon. Under their rule Spain became a major power. The kingdom of Navarre was annexed and the kingdom of Naples was recovered from the French. In 1492 the last Moorish stronghold in Spain, Granada, fell to the forces of Ferdinand and Isabella. During their joint reign the Inquisition was instituted by Sixtus IV, and the Jews and Moslems refusing to accept Christianity were expelled.

**Ferrar, Nicholas** (1592–1637). Founder of the quasi-religious community at Little Gidding in England. After promising starts in academic, government, and commercial careers, Ferrar was ordained deacon by William Laud in 1626 and went to live with his mother and other kinfolk at the Huntingdonshire manor house of Little Gidding. There an ordered life of devotional exercises and good works was practiced. The community was bitterly attacked by the Puritans, especially in a pamphlet, *The Arminian Nunnery* (1646).

**Ferrara-Florence, Council of** (1438–1445). Reckoned by Roman Catholics as the Seventeenth Ecumenical Council. The main documents for the history of this Council of unity are the Greek Acts, the so-called Latin Acts, and the memoirs of Silvester Sgyropoulos. They represent opposing sides but not in a disinterested manner. The background for understanding the Council is the conflict of Eugenius IV and the conciliarist fathers at the Council of Basel. Both parties urged the Oriental Church to join them in a synod of unity. The Eastern Church at this time was distressed by the threat of the Turk's mounting forces and sought Western aid. When Eugenius in 1437 transferred the Council to Ferrara, the Basel contingent hardened its opposition to the pope; but the papal move was strengthened when Eastern Church delegates opted for the papal council.

The assembly, which began its proceedings in January, 1438, reverberated the four-hundred-year-old clash that had occurred between Cerularius and Cardinal Humbert in 1054. After a four months' delay and at the urging of the Eastern Emperor, John VIII Palaeologus, the discussion of the Latin addition to the Creed (*filioque procedit*) was begun by Isidore, metropolitan of Kiev and all Russia, who presented the Eastern position that the Council of Ephesus had forbidden any addition to the Nicene Creed. The Latins understood this to mean a prohibition of changes in content, not in mere wording. No agreement was reached and because of the fear of the plague and lack of funds, the Council was transferred to Florence early in 1439. In the Sixth Session, Mark Eugenicus, metropolitan

of Ephesus, debated with John Montenero on the legitimacy of the addition, but no agreement was reached. From March until May the debate shifted from the wording of the Creed to the actual doctrine of the procession of the Holy Spirit. The Greek bishops reaffirmed the Scriptural statements that the Spirit proceeds from the Father. Some Greek fathers had used the phrase "proceeds from the Father through the Son." Later Greek theologians made the silence of the fathers into positive doctrine: the Spirit proceeds from the Father alone. The Greeks thought the Latins were saying that there were two causes of the procession of the Spirit. Montenero argued that the Father was principle of both Son and Spirit, but the Son, identical in nature to the Father, was also producer of the Spirit. Greek and Latin fathers were brought forth to support this view. In the private conferences of the Greek representatives the common witness of the variety of "saints" was admitted to be significant, for they all received of the same Spirit. The only alternative was to declare the texts corrupt, and this was realized by almost all to be a feeble response when no one could bring forth texts to support the claim of textual corruption. Eventually all the Greeks, with the exception of Eugenicus and three others, acknowledged the justification for the Latin belief.

There followed, for a month, impassioned debates on purgatory, the role of the epiklesis in the liturgy, and the primacy of the pope. On this last point the Eastern fathers objected to diminishing the dignity and autonomy of the patriarchates. Likewise, they stressed the importance of the patriarchs for the convocation of an ecumenical council. In July, 1439, after days of despair and hope, a Decree of Unity was issued (*Laetentur coeli*) which contained a formulation apparently agreeable to all the signing Greeks. Mark Eugenicus and a few others absented themselves from the elaborate ceremony. In September, Eugenius IV issued a bull, *Moyses vir*, condemning the truncated Council of Basel. Union with the Armenians, the Egyptian Copts, the Syrians, and certain Chaldeans followed.

When the Greeks returned home, the combination of the hesitancy and inactivity of the emperor John VIII toward the promulgation of the Decree of Unity, the ancient opposition of the people and uneducated clergy and monks, the polemics of the dissidents, especially of Mark Eugenicus, and the absence of strong personalities for the unionist cause created an abiding situation of discord. The situation continued until large numbers of Greeks were able to link the idea of union with Western aid against the imminent threat of Sultan Mohammed II. In 1453, however, the Turks laid siege to Constantinople and the union quest ended when Gennadius, a strong opponent to unity, was made the first patriarch invested by a Turkish sultan.

BIBLIOGRAPHY: J. Gill, *The Council of Florence* (Cambridge, 1959).

**Ferrar Society.** Anglican religious community founded in 1626 by Nicholas Ferrar (1592–1637). After abandoning a political career Ferrar established the society on his mother's estate (Little Gidding) near Huntingdon and was ordained deacon. The group was composed of about thirty of his relatives who lived under a strict rule of religious exercises and practiced bookbinding and charitable work. The community was dispersed after a Puritan raid in 1646.

**Ferry Laws.** Bitterly contested laws enacted in France in 1880 bearing the name of the anticlerical minister of education and future French premier, Jules F. C. Ferry. The laws eliminated clerical control of public education and made public primary education free and later compulsory. State secondary schools for girls were founded in every department. Only registered religious orders were allowed to run church schools, and the unauthorized Jesuit Order was expelled.

**Festivals.** Christians inherited from Judaism a weekly and an annual festival. Sunday ("the Lord's day," Rev. 1:10) replaced the Sabbath as a day of worship (not until the Middle Ages was the Sabbath law of rest as such applied to it), while the Passover was kept with a new meaning, celebrating redemption by the death and resurrection of Christ rather than the deliverance from Egypt. The paschal controversy of the 2d century revolved around the question whether Christians should celebrate the actual Passover day—the first full moon of spring—or the following Sunday, as the day of the resurrection. By the time of the Council of Nicaea in 325 the latter custom prevailed, and only details of the calculation remained to be determined. Pentecost, seven weeks after Easter, also continued to be observed, rather as marking the end of the festal season of the resurrection than as a separate feast. Along with the festivals, weekly fasts became customary, often on Wednesday and Friday, and a solemn fast of one or two days before Easter. From at least the time of the martyrdom of Polycarp (c. 156) Christians also took note of the "heavenly birthdays" of martyrs and remembered them year by year in the civil calendar. As a counterblast to pagan festivals, a feast of the Manifestation of Christ (Theophany, later Epiphany) was observed in Egypt by 200, at first it seems in Gnostic circles, and by 335 the calendar of the Roman Church marked Dec. 25 as the birthday of Christ. Late paganism celebrated the "birthday of the unconquered Sun" at the winter solstice, and Christians transferred the symbolism to the true Sun of Righteousness. The chronological argument that Christ was in fact born on Dec. 25 seems to have come later.

By the time of Constantine the essential principles of the Christian festal year had been developed—weekly and annual cycles revolving around Sunday and Easter, and anniversaries in honor of Christ and the heroes of the faith. During the 4th century the system gradually became more complex, with a certain shift from eschatology to history, from the foretaste of coming redemption to memorials of the past. At Jerusalem a series of historical commemorations were worked into the annual cycle, largely during the episcopate of Cyril (c. 348–386): Palm Sunday, Good Friday, Whitsunday as the feast of the Spirit, Ascension Day, and the Presentation in the Temple, forty days after Epiphany (later, forty days after Christmas, Feb. 2). Pilgrims brought the Jerusalem feasts to other churches, while Christmas was adopted in the East (except in Armenia) and Epiphany in the West given a special reference to the manifestation of Christ at his baptism and the adoration of the Magi. To their local martyrs each church added the famous martyrs of great centers; for instance, the Roman Philocalian Calendar of A.D. 354 includes Cyprian of Carthage, and the Roman feast of Peter and Paul on June 29, perhaps originally the anniversary of the transfer of relics to a safer place in 255, was widely adopted. The first to be commemorated who was not a martyr was Martin of Tours, whose cult began soon after his death in 399, thus establishing a new class of saints, those who confessed the faith nobly in time of peace. A sense of fitness led to adding feasts of apostles, which we hear of first in Syria about 375. The Virgin Mary, however, was long not commemorated separately, but remembered in feasts of Christ such as the Presentation and Annunciation (March 25); her nativity and heavenly birthday (Repose, or Assumption) was apparently first celebrated at Constantinople in the 6th century. Major churches celebrated their dedication anniversaries, which at Jerusalem became a feast of the Holy Cross. Meanwhile the pre-Easter fast became longer but less intense, until it coincided with the six weeks' period of preparation for baptism, hence the forty days of Quadragesima, or Lent. In the West by analogy the preparatory season of Advent was developed before Christmas.

On festivals as well as Sundays the Eucharist was celebrated, with special Scripture lessons for major occasions and a system of reading consecutively or by selection at other times. By 600 the Christian Year of festival and fast had reached the form that is still in use, subject to further additions within the framework.

BIBLIOGRAPHY: G. Dix, *The Shape of the Liturgy* (London, 1945); J. Dowden, *The Church Year and Kalendar* (Cambridge, 1910); A. A. McArthur, *The Evolution of the Church Year* (Greenwich, 1953).

**Fetter Lane Society.** A predominantly German Moravian group, begun informally in 1738 in London by James Hutton. The Fetter Lane Society soon attracted English members, including John Wesley, who introduced Peter Boehler, a Moravian minister, to Hutton. Asked by Hutton to preach to them, Boehler soon became an influential member of the Society, which was formally organized as the first Moravian congregation in England in 1742. Although Wesley broke with the Moravians and left the Society in 1740, Boehler had been instrumental in his conversion. The Fetter Lane Chapel, originally built in 1558 on the site of a sawmill on Fetter Lane where worshipers first met secretly, remained the Moravian headquarters in England until it was bombed in World War II.

**Feudalism.** A system of political organization from the 9th to the 15th centuries having as an essential ingredient the principle of direct reciprocity between individuals who were not equal to each other in power. This reciprocation was expressed by the contractual acts of homage and investiture. With the former, a tenant or vassal swore allegiance to an overlord, promising him a specified amount of military service and/or goods; with the latter, the overlord granted the vassal or tenant a part of his land to operate as the tenant's own, as well as a promise of protection. The overlord served in turn as the vassal of a still more powerful lord, and the tenant, depending on his importance and the size of his holdings, might be the overlord of individuals less powerful than himself, thus creating a hierarchy of interlocking dependencies. The conditional grant of land was the key to the system, and in this sense differentiated the feudal concept of ownership from that of ancient Roman law, in which ownership was exclusive.

The feudal system was essentially an improvisation, a means of establishing a minimum of order and stability in a society that lacked effective centralized government. Its evolution can conveniently be traced back to the breaking up of the Carolingian Empire in the 9th century, when, in an atmosphere of decaying central authority, western Europe was given over to civil war, barbarian invasions, and economic stagnation. In the ensuing anarchy, local strongmen, supported by groups of armed retainers, took control of relatively small areas in which they set themselves up as hereditary rulers. The only effective government became local government, and in terms of law, economy, and military might these principalities became virtually autonomous. However, the Carolingian system of lordship, in which bishops and counts owed their offices to the kings, was not utterly undone. Although the kings themselves, particularly in France and England, were at times reduced to being little more than local overlords, many links in the chain of power managed to survive or to be reestablished, so that in some areas huge domains were controlled by powerful nobles who exacted homage from lesser lords and continually added to their territories in wars with their neighbors. Within such principalities, notably in northern France, the process of feudalism was most firmly established: the great feudal courts managed to remain virtually independent of the kings while exacting ritual homage from a descending order of lesser nobility. There were enormous variations in the system: In some regions small landowners maintained their fiefs without any regard for overlords; in others, particularly in Germany, the monarchy managed to retain and even consolidate its power. Even in northern France, the holdings which an overlord conditionally granted to his barons and which they conditionally granted to tenants were soon regarded by vassal and overlord alike as a hereditary right rather than as a favor, providing always that the ritual of homage was renewed with each generation.

During the feudal centuries, the government of the church reflected that of Europe as a whole: in the Dark Ages, the bishops, like their secular counterparts, sought the protection of local magnates; the influence of Rome was at its lowest ebb. The clerical hierarchy assumed feudal characteristics and rituals, some of which the Roman Catholic Church retains to the present day. The church, through its bishoprics and monasteries, operated vast feudal estates in much the same way as secular landowners, though, in general, these holdings were more humanely administered. Christian ideals were also assimilated by the feudal aristocracy in the chivalric code. In practice, the feudal clergy were often in a state of vassalage to secular lords and kings, and simony was a commonplace. The concept of the universal church, however, like the idea of kingship, was never lost, and during many generations preceding the conflict between the German emperors and the popes, powerful representatives of the church sided with larger, more centralized political units against the localizing spirit of feudal autonomy. The feudal aristocracy themselves acknowledged at least in theory the concepts of kingdoms and kings, and these tenuous allegiances were destined to form the framework of modern nationhood.

BIBLIOGRAPHY: S. Baldwin, *The Organization of Medieval Christianity* (New York, 1929); R. Coulborn, *Feudalism in History* (Princeton, 1956); F. L. Ganshof, *Feudalism* (New York, 1961); H. Pirenne, *Economic and Social History of Medieval Europe* (New York, 1956); F. M. Stenton, *The First Century of English Feudalism* (Oxford, 1961); C. Stephenson, *Medieval Feudalism* (Ithaca, 1942).

**Feuerbach, Ludwig** (1804–1872). German philosopher and "antitheologian." The son of a noted jurist and groomed for the ministry from an early age, Feuerbach took up the study of theology at Heidelberg, where he fell under the influence of Karl Daub (at the time Hegelian) and in 1824 he transferred to Berlin to study with Hegel. The coincidence of his arrival and the most stringent exertions of Metternician repression played no small part in his bitter abandonment of both theology and church in the following year, this to the consternation of his father, who looked upon philosophy as a vocation "without bread or honor." Feuerbach completed his education at Erlangen in 1828 and was a lecturer there until 1832. The rest of his life was spent as a private scholar of modest means. This end to his academic career was related to his abandonment of Hegel and his attack upon Christianity. Rejecting the Absolute Spirit of Hegel, he saw man, a product of material nature, as the most real entity. Religion and Christianity are described in his classic *Essence of Christianity* (1841) as mankind's alienation of its own infinite essence and placement of it in an imaginary being: "The true essence of theology is anthropology." All the things that the individual man wishes and cannot obtain because of his finitude he projects upon this "god" who then delivers them back. Feuerbach was the thinker who furnished both Marx and Freud with a plausible explanation of religion, and his impact is to be observed on Nietzsche

and the radical theologians of the mid-20th century.

**Feuillants.** The reformed members of the Cistercian abbey at Les Feuillans, originally founded near Toulouse in 1145. By the 16th century the community had become lax in living the monastic ideal, and when Jean de la Barrière was abbot he took great pains (from c. 1570) to bring about a reform. The monks lived a life of silence and manual labor, ate very little, and what sleep they had was on the ground or on a wooden plank, with a stone for a pillow. As they grew in numbers, the Feuillants became independent of the Cistercians, and in time the rigors of their discipline were somewhat lessened. The reform was approved by Pope Gregory XIII (1581); his successor, Sixtus V, recognized the independence of the order in 1589. In France the Feuillants did not survive the aftermath of the Revolution (1789), and the daughter houses in Italy returned to the Cistercians. There was also a branch of the order, the "Feuillantines," for women.

**Fichte, Immanuel Hermann von** (1796–1879). German philosopher. He was professor of philosophy at Bonn (1836) and Tübingen (1842) until his retirement in 1863. In his philosophy he attempted to reconcile monism (Hegel) and individualism (Herbart) by means of theism (Leibnitz). An anti-Hegelian, he replaced Hegel's Absolute with Infinite Person. In the later part of his career he defended the possibility of harmonizing theism with the method of natural science. His philosophy is characterized by its historical and conciliatory approach to problems.

**Ficino, Marsilio** (1433–1499). Florentine clergyman, philosopher, and scholar who was the most widely known exponent of Platonism in Renaissance Italy. Ficino studied Latin, Greek, philosophy, and medicine at Florence. A child prodigy, he soon attracted the attention of Cosimo de' Medici. Conceiving of the idea of founding a native school of Platonic studies, Cosimo in 1462 gave the young Ficino a villa near Careggi, a library of Greek manuscripts, and a life endowment. Ficino devoted the remainder of his days to the task of reviving Platonism in Italy, both as a distinct philosophical doctrine and as an intellectual movement. He did this by studying, translating, publishing, and expounding the works of Plato and the Neoplatonists and by making his home a center of philosophical discussion frequented by the intelligentsia of Florence. Ficino's informal circle was later called the Platonic Academy of Florence, although there was no formal organization or systematic instruction. His two major works, the *De religione Christiana* (1477) and the *Platonic Theology* (1474), were attempts to fuse the Platonic tradition and Christianity into a single system. Ficino's pietistic Platonic mysticism inspired many of the leaders of northern Christian humanism such as John Colet, Faber Stapulensis, and Erasmus.

**Fideism.** A term applied to doctrines that deny the power of unaided human reason to reach certitude, affirming that faith is the primary form of human knowledge and that the criterion of certitude is authority with foundation in divine revelation. Papal encyclicals of 1832, 1834, and 1840 condemned fideism with the assertion that faith is posterior to revelation and that certitude of the existence of God and the validity of revelation depends upon human reason.

**Fifth Monarchy Men.** Millenarian party in mid-17th-century England. Opposing "human" government, they expected imminent rule of the "saints" on earth, along with the returning Christ, to last a thousand years—the "fifth monarchy." It was a radical version of the general millenarianism popular with many Puritans, especially in the 1640's, and an attempt to rally opposition to Cromwell. It led to agitation (1661) and abortive revolts.

**Filioque.** A Latin word meaning "and from the Son." It was added, in the West, to the Nicene Creed after the phrase: "the Holy Ghost, . . . who proceeds from the Father." The original Creed had been silent upon the procession of the Holy Spirit from the Son, perhaps because of the tendency in the East toward a certain subordination of the Son to the Father. The first known instance of its addition to the Creed was at the Third Council of Toledo (589). This was a council confirming the conversion of King Recaredo from Arianism. The *filioque* was doubtless added to make clear the distinction between the Arians and the Catholics on the issue of the Son. From that time, it spread to become an integral part of the Creed as used in the West. The Eastern Church, however, has never adopted the addition. Indeed, the *filioque* has been a source of much difficulty between the East and the West. The Eastern Church maintained that new dogma could not be added to the faith without a general council. There were, to be sure, other important issues involved in the schism between the East and the West, but the *filioque* played an important role in the separation of the churches. Protestant churches have followed the Western

custom in maintaining the double procession of the Holy Spirit.

**Fillmore, Charles** (1854–1948). Founder, together with his wife, Myrtle Page Fillmore (1845–1931), of Unity School of Christianity. He worked as a miner, a bank clerk, and eventually became a realty speculator in Kansas City, Mo. Influenced by Christian Science and New Thought, he founded the periodical *Modern Thought* in 1889, and in 1891 adopted the name Unity. In 1914 he formed the Unity School of Christianity and in 1927, Unity City. He considered himself a "representative-at-large for Jesus Christ," and his influence spread through the formation of Unity "centers," a prayer ministry called "Silent Unity," and the publication of pamphlets, magazines (e.g., *Unity*), and books, including *The Science of Being and Christian Healing* (1910) and *Prosperity* (4th ed., 1940). Developing physio-psychology, he emphasized rules of "mental discipline," human perfection, and success through "acquiescence" to "Divine Mind," and eternal life through bodily regeneration and reincarnation.

**Finan of Lindisfarne** (d. 661). Bishop and missionary. Finan, who followed Aidan in the see of Lindisfarne, the "Scottish" missionary station in Northumbria, was, like Aidan, consecrated and commissioned from Iona. He built a wooden church on Lindisfarne. He baptized both Paeda (son of Penda, the great pagan king of Mercia) and Sigbert of the East Saxons, organized the missionary staffs in those two kingdoms, commissioning Cedd and others. Finan vigorously championed the older Irish date for Easter against the newer Roman reckoning (Bede calls him a "hot-tempered man" and "obstinate"). He died in 661 after an episcopate of ten years.

**Finley, James B.** (1781–1856). Methodist clergyman. The son of a frontier minister, he was educated by his father in the classics and in medicine, which he practiced briefly. In August, 1801, he was "converted" at the Cane Ridge, Ky., camp meeting and began a traveling ministry. After acceptance into the Methodist clergy he rode the circuits and did mission work among the Indians for over thirty years. For twenty-one years he was superintendent of Methodist work in vast areas of the frontier. Eight times he was a delegate to the Methodist General Conference and was active in the 1844 session that dismissed Bishop James O. Andrew for owning slaves, leading to the North-South schism. He was author of the resolution that Andrew "desist from his office." His lengthy diary has been published in five volumes.

**Finney, Charles Grandison** (1792–1875). American Presbyterian revivalist and president of Oberlin College. Born in Warren, Conn., he spent his boyhood in Oneida County, N.Y., two years in a Connecticut academy, and some six years teaching school. Finney then apprenticed himself in a law office in Adams, N.Y., and by 1821 was launched on a legal career. He had been a leader in the Presbyterian Church in Adams, but his friends were not sure that he had been converted. In a characteristic action, Finney determined to set aside a day in which to settle the matter of his soul's salvation. He wandered into the woods to pray aloud and then, returning to his law office in the evening of Oct. 10, received, as he put it, "a mighty baptism of the Holy Ghost" which "like a wave of electricity going through and through me . . . seemed to come in waves of liquid love." Finney's reaction to this experience was immediate. He devoted himself to preaching, informing a client of his who came around the next morning, "I have a retainer from the Lord Jesus Christ to plead his cause and I cannot plead yours." Within a few years Finney was conducting revivals in New York State towns such as Evans Mills and Brownsville, and then, when he had become better known, in Rome, Utica, and Auburn. His success was due primarily to the vigor with which he called upon convicted sinners to help themselves. One of his most famous sermons was entitled "Sinners Bound to Change Their Own Hearts." This attitude differed radically from the Calvinism of the Congregationalists and Presbyterians who believed that, if one was to be converted, he must wait passively for the awakening of the Holy Spirit. This concept of free enterprise in religion had been born of the spirit of the times. Finney, who had refused to go east to Princeton Seminary, worked out his theology and revivalistic technique as he preached. His primary criterion of truth was, Will it produce conversions? His numerous opponents assailed his "New Measures" (praying for people in public by name, allowing women to pray in public, exciting the congregation into fainting fits and loud crying, appointing a pew in the front of the church as "the anxious bench" to which convicted sinners were drawn). Finney's methods, in fact, amounted to introducing the excitement of the camp meeting into the churches and, eventually, into the metropolises of the East. The big city has lured revivalists from the time of Finney to the present. A group of New England men, led by Lyman Beecher, attempted to restrain the ebullient Finney at a series of meetings in New Lebanon, N.Y., but he would not adopt their more cautious policies. In 1828 he moved to Philadelphia and, eventually, to New York City. These meetings were not like the later revivals of Dwight L. Moody and Billy Sunday, but similar to an evangelistic campaign held in a single church over a period of several months. Finney's efforts cannot be judged completely successful. His main accomplishment was to divide the New York and Philadelphia Presbyterians into revival and anti-revival factions, culminating in the creation of rival presbyteries within each of the cities. In 1830, Finney went west again to Rochester, N.Y., where he conducted the most successful revival of his career. Finney had lost much of his boisterous crudeness during the years in the East; there were no hysterical outbursts from his predominantly middle-class audiences. Contemporaries likened his appearance to a lawyer arguing before a jury. Although the number of converts cannot be ascertained accurately and Finney's own estimate of one hundred thousand is certainly quite exaggerated, the revival did make a deep impression upon the area. In 1831, Finney moved back to the East (to Boston), but his success was limited and the opposition vigorous. After eleven years of revivalistic campaigning, Finney seems to have become tired of the strain. He accepted a pastorate in New York City from 1832 to 1835 and then moved west again to become professor of theology and president of Oberlin College. The chief interest of this part of his career lies in his rather lukewarm advocacy of the abolition of slavery and the development of an interest in the doctrine of sanctification.

BIBLIOGRAPHY: C. G. Finney, *Lectures on Revivals of Religion* (New York, 1835); and *Memoirs* (New York, 1876); W. G. McLoughlin, *Modern Revivalism* (New York, 1959).

**Finnian of Clonard** (d. c. 550). Abbot. He first went to Tours and on his return spent some thirty years in Wales, settling the dispute between David of Wales and Gildas for primacy in Britain in favor of the former. On returning to Ireland he founded the school at Clonard, which had three thousand students at one point. He trained twelve disciples as apostles to Ireland. His *penitentiale* gives a good picture of disciplinary standards of contemporary Irish church life (see PENITENTIALS).

**Firmicus Maternus, Julius** (4th century). Author of the treatise *De errore profanarum religionum* (c. 347), addressed to the emperors Constantius and Constans, urging them to rid the Empire of heathenism. It is a valuable source for an understanding of pagan mysteries of late antiquity and an early witness of the demand for persecution of the heathen. He is perhaps responsible for the treatise *Matheseos Libri VIII* (c. 354) on astrology.

**Firmilian of Caesarea** (Cappadocia), (d. c. 269). One of the most esteemed bishops (c. 230) of the East. Only one of his letters remains. It was written to Cyprian concerning rebaptism. He agrees with Cyprian against Pope Stephen that those baptized by heretics should be rebaptized. A great admirer of Origen, he was president of the first Synod of Antioch (264) which condemned Paul of Samosata. He died shortly after the second Synod of Antioch.

**Fisher, John** (1469–1535). Bishop of Rochester, Roman Catholic martyr in the reign of Henry VIII. Fisher's career was largely academic; he studied at Cambridge and became its chancellor in 1504, encouraging the study of Greek and championing Erasmus. Much admired for his eloquence in preaching and his saintly character, Fisher was initially in favor with Henry VIII, and in 1527 he wrote against Protestant views on the Lord's Supper. When, however, as Catherine of Aragon's confessor, Fisher opposed the royal divorce, Henry turned against him. Fisher did what he could to mitigate the demands of Henry's reformatory legislation, while accepting certain parts of it, such as the Submission of the Clergy (1532). But Fisher, though undeniably loyal to the king, would not condone the extreme language of the preamble to the Act of Succession, and could not accept Henry's claim to be head of the English Church. He was imprisoned in the Tower in 1534, along with Sir Thomas More, and, having been named a cardinal by the pope, was beheaded the following year on a charge of treason. He was canonized in 1935.

**Fiske, John** (1842–1901). American philosopher, historian, and lecturer. He was a native of Connecticut and a graduate of Harvard. A disciple of Herbert Spencer and author of *Outlines of Cosmic Philosophy* and *Through Nature to God,* Fiske insisted that "evolution is God's way of doing things." His major historical interest was the American colonial experience. As historian and as philosopher, Fiske was a popularizer rather than a careful scholar.

**Fitz, Richard.** See CONGREGATIONALISM, BRITISH.

**Five Mile Act** (1665). One of the statutes of the Clarendon Code to secure the Anglican Church against Dissenters. The act prohibited any preacher "in Holy orders or pretended Holy orders" from teaching or coming within five miles of an incorporated town if he had not taken the oath of obedience. The act, which was designed to prevent any alteration of government in church or state, inflicted severe penalties on the Dissenters whose congregations were mostly located in the towns.

**Flacius, Matthias** (*usually known as* Flacius Illyricus) (1520–1575). Lutheran theologian born in Albona, Illyria. His conversion, like Luther's, was slow and painful. In 1541 he arrived in Wittenberg and became professor of Hebrew. He was much opposed to the Leipzig Interim (1548) and the concessions it granted to Roman Catholicism. He disagreed with Melanchthon on the question of adiaphora which he regarded as undermining the very structure of Lutheranism. In 1551 he went to Magdeburg, where he became, along with Amsdorf, the leader of the Gnesio-Lutherans. During this period the famous *Magdeburg Centuries* were begun. At the Conference of Worms (1557) which had been called to create harmony between Roman Catholicism and Lutheranism, Flacius accused Melanchthon of a number of errors. Canisius took note of the intransigence of the two Lutheran parties and began to lay plans for the Counter-Reformation. Flacius, who had become professor of New Testament at Jena not long before the Conference, was soon involved there in the synergistic controversy with Strigel. Four years later he was dismissed from Jena and spent the rest of his life traveling from place to place in search of a haven of rest, all the while continuing his work on the *Magdeburg Centuries* upon which his fame rests.

**Flagellants.** A radical sect of the 13th and succeeding centuries. The flagellants were so called for their practice of forming long processions of thousands of people and marching along while beating themselves. In the 13th century they appeared in Italy, partially in response to the great insecurity caused by war. In the following century they appeared in Germany after the Black Death (1348–1349). They were officially condemned by Clement VI in 1349, but survived far into the 15th century north of the Alps.

**Flatt, Johann Friedrich** (1759–1821). Representative of the older Tübingen school that sought to prove Biblical supranaturalism by use of reason while refuting rationalist criticism of the Bible. As professor of philosophy at Tübingen (1785) and of theology (1792), he lectured chiefly on exegesis and ethics. His works include a proof of the divinity of

Christ, a criticism of Kantian philosophy, an ethical treatise, and lectures on Paul.

**Flavian** (d. 449). Patriarch of Constantinople from 446, and an important figure in the events surrounding the Robber Council of Ephesus in 449. He presided over the provincial synod of Constantinople (448), in which Eutyches was condemned, only to find himself in a similar position at the Council of Ephesus the following summer under the presidency of Dioscorus of Alexandria. He died shortly after, not living to see himself restored.

**Fletcher** (de la Fléchère), **John William** (1729–1785). Associate of John Wesley and vicar of Madeley in Shropshire from 1760. Born in Nyon, Switzerland, and educated at Geneva for the ministry, he fled to Lisbon and enlisted in the army. About 1750 he settled in England and soon after joined the Methodist movement. He was ordained priest in 1757 and for the next few years preached for Wesley, becoming known as a supporter of the Methodist revival. In 1760 he accepted, against the advice of John Wesley, the living of Madeley, and until his death he labored there with singular devotion and zeal. From 1768 to 1771 he also exercised a general supervision over the Countess of Huntingdon's seminary at Trevecca, Wales, for the training of Methodist ministers, but resigned in 1771 on doctrinal grounds. In theology, Fletcher was an Arminian and his most important work, *Checks to Antinomianism* (1771), was directed against Calvinism and in support of John Wesley. Although he took no prominent part in organizing the Methodist movement, his simplicity and saintliness of spirit did much to establish Methodism in Shropshire.

**Fleury, Abbey of.** A monastery on the Loire, founded c. 640 by Leodebaldus. The abbey attained fame after the 7th century on the claim that the relics of Benedict and Scholastica had been translated there after the destruction of Monte Cassino by the Lombards. King Philip I of France is buried in the abbey church.

**Fliedner, Theodor** (1800–1864). Pastor at Kaiserswerth (1822–1849). The poverty of his small parish led him on fund-raising tours to Holland (1823) and England (1824). There he was impressed both by the suffering of the masses in the new industrial society and by the charitable institutions that ministered to them (especially the Dutch Mennonites). On his return to Germany, Fliedner first involved himself in the rehabilitation of criminals and prison reform, but he is chiefly remembered for his founding of the evangelical diaconate (1836), thus providing a place for women in Protestant charity. He founded deaconess homes and hospitals from Pittsburgh to Jerusalem. When he died, there were some 1,600 deaconesses and 32 motherhouses. Florence Nightingale studied at Kaiserswerth in 1851.

**Florence, Council of.** See FERRARA-FLORENCE, COUNCIL OF.

**Florilegia.** Works composed of collections of extracts, usually from patristic writings, Scripture, or commentaries on Scripture; a literary genre dating from antiquity and popular throughout the Middle Ages. The name is derived from the Latin *flores legere*, "to gather flowers," and is exactly equivalent to the Greek *anthologia*. The earliest collections were doctrinal in content and purpose, and some of them played an important part in the early Christological controversies. Florilegia sometimes preserve citations from works otherwise lost.

**Fogazzaro, Antonio** (1842–1911). Italian poet, novelist, and leading Catholic layman. He was greatly influenced by the Darwinian theory of evolution, and by the philosophical writings of Rosmini. A friend of Tyrrell, he was looked upon as a modernist, and his novel *Il Santo* (1905) was condemned by Rome. In *Ascensioni umane* (1898), he attempted to reconcile traditional Catholic positions with modern theories of evolution.

**Foliot, Gilbert** (d. 1188). English bishop. After a monastic career, he became bishop of Hereford (1148) and bishop of London (1163). In the struggle between Archbishop Thomas Becket of Canterbury and King Henry II, Foliot led the clergy who sided with the king against the archbishop. Becket excommunicated him twice (1169, 1170) and his second absolution (1172) was delayed by Becket's murder (although Foliot was not involved in the assassination). A trusted adviser to Henry, Foliot played a prominent part in ecclesiastical affairs until his death.

**Folk Schools.** A 19th-century Scandinavian experiment in progressive education for young adults. It was inspired by the Danish pastor and religious patriot, Nicolai F. S. Grundtvig, who strongly opposed the traditional Latin-school education and the Pietism and rationalism rife in the religion of his day. Grundtvig sought to awaken young adults to a proper attitude toward human life by seeking to educate the whole person, especially by helping the students to think for themselves. His system eschewed reading, and emphasized lectures, much informal discussion, and social gatherings and communal living. Although no specific courses in religion were offered, Christian virtues were basic to the educational atmosphere. He believed a thorough education in Scandinavian history, literature, and folklore would produce a Christian person. Grundtvig's ideas were put into practice by followers in Denmark beginning in the 1840's and in Sweden and Norway during the 1860's. The Folk High Schools, as they were called, were generally more popular in rural areas, and they did much to develop nationalism and progressivism among the middle and lower classes. Only a few folk schools remain today, but Scandinavian education still bears the marks of Grundtvig's ideas.

**Foreign Missions Conference of North America.** An organization formed in 1893 by which missionaries from North America sought to improve interdenominational cooperation. Beginning as an annual meeting of mission-society administrators and board members for the exchange of views, it eventually included a vast majority of the missionary societies in North America. A basis for continual consultation was made in 1907 with the establishment of a Committee of Reference and Counsel. Having powers of recommendation rather than legislation, it nonetheless became highly influential through its many committees for specific problems. It was especially noted for its work in educational institutions in foreign lands and in supervising orphaned missions. In 1921 it helped form the International Missionary Council, and in 1950 became a part of the National Council of the Churches of Christ in the U.S.A.

**Form Criticism** (form history, category criticism, tradition analysis). A method that investigates literary forms in order to place them in the history of literature and determine their religious setting. It presupposes that folk "memory" operated with small units which it derived from everyday life (funerals, weddings, victories, worship, etc.). In the 18th century, Robert Lowth isolated the forms and literary structure of Hebrew poetry. In the early 19th century, J. G. Herder, L. H. Jakob, Wilhelm Grimm, and others applied form criticism to classical and folk literature, while Alexander Geddes stressed the oral origin of separate literary units in the Bible but went unheard. The rise of the *Religionsgeschichtlicheschule* at the turn of the 20th century, emphasizing community over individual and worship over dogma, gave growth to form criticism. Hermann Gunkel (1862–1932) took up the term *Gattungsgeschichte* and applied form criticism to Old Testament literature in

writings extending from 1901 to 1932. He was indebted to Herder, Julius Wellhausen, Norden, and others. Prose and poetical forms were isolated. Especially Genesis and The Psalms were subjected to the criticism. Hugo Gressmann, A. Alt, and J. Hempel were additional leaders in Old Testament criticism. At the end of World War I the method was applied to the New Testament Gospels because literary criticism was blocked with the two-source synoptic theory. New Testament form criticism was a "child of disappointment." K. L. Schmidt (*The Frame of the Story of Jesus*), Martin Dibelius (*From Tradition to Gospel*), and Rudolf Bultmann (*The History of the Synoptic Tradition*) applied the method to the New Testament almost simultaneously in 1919. Paradigms, legends, apothegms, wonder tales, and other supposed forms were isolated. Ernst Lohmeyer (1890–1944) used the method in Biblical epistles to investigate creeds and hymns, and then liturgical forms were discovered in Revelation. Form criticism has resolved some of the doubts over the "historical Jesus" (Ernst Käsemann). Lately it has encouraged study of the Evangelist's or redactor's work. The method has found wider acceptance on the Continent and in America than in Britain, although it has been used extensively by many scholars.

**Formosus** (c. 816–896). Pope from 891. After a career as a papal emissary, he became a cardinal bishop in 864 and was elected pope in 891. Because he supported the claims of Emperor Arnulf in Italy, he was unpopular with Roman factions. After his death, his body was exhumed, tried for the violation of canon law in accepting election to a second bishopric (the papacy), and found guilty. After nullifying all his decrees, the court ordered his body thrown into the Tiber.

**Forster Act** (England, 1870). An educational measure, named for the Liberal member of Parliament, William Edward Forster (1818–1886). Designed to placate the contrary demands of those who sought a religious and those who wanted a secular education, the act empowered local school boards to demand a minimal education of those under thirteen years of age, and to provide the same. The "board schools" were to supplement those maintained by religious bodies.

**Forsyth, Peter Taylor** (1848–1921). British theologian and New Testament scholar. After holding five pastorates in British Congregational churches, Forsyth became principal of Hackney College, London, where he had studied with Albrecht Ritschl (1872). His early theology may be described as liberal; later he became more conservative and has been called "a Barthian before Barth." He was a prolific writer, who in thirty years produced twenty-five books and over three hundred articles, mostly on the New Testament, the person and work of Christ, prayer, missions, the church, and the sacraments. He wrote on other themes as well, but his center was always Christology. Within that center it was particularly the cross which provided the key to all of his work. He did not aim to found a new school of theology, but to revitalize the old orthodoxy, using Ritschl, Maurice, Calvin, and Luther for his guides. Nor did he write a technical, systematic theology, though certain dominant ideas can be discovered in his work. In his best-known book, *The Person and Place of Christ* (1909), these themes of Christology and the cross, and the holiness of God are to be found. In his other works, the church and sacraments and eschatology are dominant themes. In all these areas he anticipated many of the positions that would be commonplace twenty-five years after his death. During his own life he was out of step with the spirit of the times, but his work has demonstrated that he was a prophetic voice in early 20th-century theology.

**Forty-two Articles.** Doctrinal statement of the Edwardian Reformation, published in 1553. The articles, mostly drafted by Cranmer, are dependent on Continental Protestantism, firmly opposing both Rome and the Anabaptists. The clerical subscription that was to be required was never enforced because of Edward's death and the accession of Mary, a Roman Catholic. The articles were the direct precursor of the Thirty-nine Articles of 1563.

**Fosdick, Harry Emerson** (1878–1969). American Baptist minister. Ordained in 1903 as a Presbyterian, Fosdick became professor of practical theology at Union Theological Seminary, New York City, in 1915. His liberalism became widely known through his books, including *The Second Mile* (1908), *Christianity and Progress* (1922), and *The Modern Use of the Bible* (1924). In 1922 he preached the controversial sermon "Shall the Fundamentalists Win?" at the First Presbyterian Church in New York, which led the General Assembly to request his adherence to the Westminster Confession or resign. Fosdick resigned in 1925 and in 1930 became minister of Riverside Church, built for him by John D. Rockefeller, Jr. Fosdick was a major popularizer of "personal religion," Biblical criticism, and the psychology of religion. In 1935 he surprised many by stating that "the church must go beyond modernism," insisting that doctrine must always be open to revision. Later books included *A Guide to Understanding the Bible* (1938) and *The Living of These Days* (1956).

**Fountains Abbey.** A Cistercian abbey founded near Ripon, England, in 1132. Not completed until the 16th century, this magnificent church embodies examples of many architectural styles. Although the abbey is in ruins now, the great tower, which is in the perpendicular style, was built of limestone from nearby eastern hills by Abbot Huby in the late 15th century and is still standing.

**Fourier, François Marie Charles** (1772–1837). French social scientist and reformer. As seemingly utopian as a socialist could be, Fourier went from the reasonable premise that cooperation ought to replace competition to the view of the necessity of a complete reorganization of society into economic units called phalanxes. They were to be operated out of phalansteries which mixed private property and cooperative effort. The most famous phalanstery in the United States was Brook Farm.

**Four Orthodox Caliphs.** A title ordinarily given to the first four successors of Mohammed. They were: Abu Bekr (632–634); Omar I (634–644); Othman (644–656); and Ali (656–661). Associates and relatives of the Prophet, these four caliphs made Medina the first "capital" of the Islamic world. After Ali's death and the founding of the Umayyad caliphate, the Moslem community split into rival factions, Sunnite and Shiite.

**Fourth Crusade** (1202–1204). The expedition that was diverted from Palestine (or Egypt) and that sacked Constantinople, bringing it under Latin domination until 1261.

Four significant forces interacted in the Crusade: (1) Pope Innocent III, who called it, lamented its diversion into a conquest of Constantinople, but acquiesced in its settlements; (2) Philip of Swabia, who had married the daughter of the deposed Eastern emperor, Isaac Angelus; (3) the Venetians under the doge Dandolo, who sought monetary gain and redress of grievances against Constantinople; (4) the deposed and imprisoned Eastern emperor, who appealed for aid to Philip of Swabia, his son-in-law.

Because the crusaders were unable to pay Venice the required sum for transportation, they agreed to assist in the sack of Zara, a city along the Dalmatian coast that had recently rebelled against Venetian rule. After this initial diversion the crusaders were persuaded to travel to Constantinople, which was ultimately invested and pillaged because of its alleged failure to agree to the crusaders' demands. Baldwin of Flanders was enthroned as Latin emperor of Constantinople, and the Venetian Thomas Morosini was elected patriarch. The Crusade weakened Byzantium, which became prey to the forces of Islam, and it embittered relations between the East and the West (see SCHISM, EASTERN). The account of the Crusade by Geoffrey of Villehardouin is credited with being the earliest extant example of French prose. A second primary source is that of Robert de Clari.

**Fox, George** (1624–1691). Founder of the Society of Friends (Quakers). Fox represents an extension of the Puritan "spirit mystic" tradition, with its emphasis on the Holy Spirit working within. In 1643, he set out on a quest for faith, wandering about England for four years, finding no help from existing groups. In 1646, he experienced immediate communion with God, and came to believe that a man's life can be guided by the inner light, that is, by the Holy Spirit within. He felt that the religious controversies of his day dealt with peripheral matters; he labored to bring men into direct contact with God. His unconventional manners and dress were dictated by an ideal of simplicity and honesty. He traveled incessantly throughout England and abroad, preaching and organizing. He spent eight terms in jail, one for three years. Fox was a pacifist, opposed to oaths, scorned the idea of a professional class of ministers, rejected the material sacraments, and gave less credit to the letter of the Scriptures than to the Spirit who speaks through them. Macaulay's remark that Fox was "too much disordered for liberty, and not sufficiently disordered for Bedlam" is hardly objective. Fox was a religious giant, founding a society that has continuously leavened Christendom. The record of his spiritual progress is found in his famous *Journal*, published (1694) after his death.

**Foxe, John** (1516–1587). Author of *Actes and Monuments,* generally known as "Foxe's Book of Martyrs." Foxe, an ardent Protestant in exile during Mary's reign, gathered information about the persecution of antipapists after Wycliffe, and published a Latin account in 1554; this was expanded with grisly narratives of the Marian executions in the first English edition of 1563. The work achieved enormous popularity after the excommunication of Elizabeth in 1570.

**France, Union of Evangelical Churches of.** In the 19th century the French Reformed Church experienced a revival of a Pietist nature (see REVEIL) and a liberalism that attempted to accommodate the faith to the intellectual temper of the day. A result of the conflict which these contrasting views occasioned was the withdrawal of the more conservative elements in 1849 from the Reformed Synod, the renouncing of all endowments, and the establishment of the Union of Evangelical Churches supported by voluntary gifts.

**Frances of Rome** (Bussa di Leoni, 1384–1440). Founder of the Oblates of Mary. She was married at twelve to Lorenzo de' Ponziani, and while a wife and mother founded the Benedictine Oblate Congregation of Tor di Specchi, approved by Eugenius IV in 1433. A visionary, she is portrayed with her guardian angel whom she claimed to have seen frequently. After the banishment of her husband, the death of her sons, and the loss of her property, she retired to her convent. She was canonized by Paul V in 1608.

**Francis I** (1494–1547). King of France. He was born at Cognac, the son of Charles of Valois, count of Angoulême, and Louise of Savoy. Heir-presumptive upon the accession of Louis XII in 1498, he married Claude de France, Louis' daughter (1514), and upon Louis' death (1515) succeeded him to the throne, becoming the most powerful prince in Europe. He carried on the policy of Louis XII, engaging throughout his life in a series of self-defeating wars against the Hapsburgs in Italy and the Low Countries. He lost the election for the imperial crown to Charles V (1519), the Hapsburg claimant to the title of Holy Roman Emperor, and failed to obtain the support of Henry VIII of England (1520). After a long series of campaigns against the Empire he was defeated by Charles, forced to concede Burgundy, and finally Italy at the Peace of Cambri (1529), thereafter marrying Charles's sister Eleanor of Austria, his first wife having died in 1524.

In his religious policy Francis also showed instability, allying himself (1536–1538 and 1542–1544) with both the German Protestants and the Turks. He did much to strengthen royal absolutism in France, selling many offices to the bourgeoisie to finance his campaigns and (by the ordinance of Villers-Cotterets, 1539) making royal courts superior to all ecclesiastical courts. His Italian campaigns led him to invite many Italian humanists and artists to France, including Da Vinci and Cellini. In 1530 he founded the Collège de France, and at the request of Budé made sure that its lecturers in languages, medicine, and mathematics were independent of the Sorbonne. Up to 1534, encouraged by his sister, Margaret of Navarre, he was friendly to the reforming ideals of Briçonnet, but the Affair of the Placards in October, 1534 (when a group of reform advocates posted sharply critical notices against Catholics on the walls of Paris and other towns), inclined him to repress religious dissent. The hopes expressed in 1536 in the preface of Calvin's *Institutes* were in vain; under the guidance of Cardinal de Tournon edicts against the Reform appeared, books were proscribed, and dissenters put to death, among them, in 1546, Étienne Dolet. It can be said, however, that Francis' concern with religious matters was largely motivated by political factors, such as the need for unifying the country under royal authority.

**Franciscan Order.** Various foundations of religious, male and female, who profess the observance of the Rule of Francis of Assisi (1182–1226) in one of its forms. Francis is assigned the founding of these orders: the Friars Minor, the Poor Ladies or Poor Clares, and the Brothers and Sisters of Penance. The first of these was originally composed of the companions of Francis; their monastery was a collection of huts and a chapel donated by the Benedictines of Mt. Subasio in 1211. The actual existence of the Companions as an order dates from 1209, when Francis received the verbal approval of Innocent III for the simple rule he had composed. Francis later rewrote this rule and it was officially confirmed by Honorius III in 1223. It has been in effect among the Friars Minor ever since, but the order presently consists of three separate bodies: the Friars Minor itself, the Friars Minor Conventuals (1517), and the Friars Minor Capuchins (1519). The two latter groups, while generally adhering to the Friars Minor Rule, have their own constitutions and minister-generals.

The Franciscan Second Order of Poor Ladies was founded under Francis' guidance by Clare in 1221 at St. Damian's, near Assisi. Clare, a wealthy young heiress, had fallen under the spell of Francis' preaching, and beseeched him to allow her to follow the mode of life he espoused. He advised her to escape her father's house, and, when she had done so, he cut her hair, clothed her in the Minorite habit, and later provided her, and the women companions who joined her, with the retreat at St. Damian's. The chapel there, which he had rebuilt himself, was now donated to the incipient Franciscan Sisterhood. There is no evidence to support the idea that Francis ever drew up a rule for the Poor Ladies. Their rule was originally imposed by Cardinal Ugolino (later Gregory IX) in 1219, and later amended by Clare and approved by Innocent IV in 1253. All the monasteries of cloistered nuns professing this rule are included in this order, now generally known as "Poor Clares," although some have received dispensations that mitigate the original strictness of the rule.

According to tradition, the Brothers and Sisters of Penance was the last order to be founded by Francis. The motivation for its founding was his desire to afford a special order for those seculars who wished to follow his rule but were ineligible for admittance to the Friars Minor or Poor Ladies because of marriage or other such ties. It is uncertain whether Francis did or did not devise a rule for this Third Order. In any case, the rule approved by Nicholas IV in 1289 and modified by Leo XIII in 1883, was not the rule in its original form. The Third Order includes pious individuals of both sexes living either in community or in isolation as pilgrims and hermits. This order became known as the Third Order Secular to distinguish it from the Third Order Regular (see REGULAR CLERGY), a later development, whose founding is still the subject of debate. According to some, it was established in 1228 by Elizabeth of Hungary; according to others, in 1395 by Blessed Angelina of Marciano. Apart from the Third Order Regular, there are many widely different Franciscan tertiary congregations that have been founded since the 19th century.

The development of the three orders sketched above is the traditional account, but some recent students of the subject believe that the First and Second Orders actually evolved from the Third, the Brothers and Sisters of Penance, who composed the lay confraternity that Francis first envisioned. According to this view, the three orders resulted from a process of division, not addition.

As the foregoing indicates, the rule that Francis drew up for his companions has not survived in its earliest form. It was apparently a short and simple document on the gospel precepts that Francis most wished to exemplify: chastity, obedience, and poverty—with a particular emphasis on the last of these. The text of the different rules eventually adopted by the Franciscan orders can be found in *Serphicae legislationis textus originales* (Quaracchi, 1897).

BIBLIOGRAPHY: R. M. Huber, *A Documented History of the Franciscan Order* (Milwaukee, 1944); O. Kuhns, *St. Francis of Assisi* (New York, 1906); D. Muzzey, *The Spiritual Franciscans* (New York, 1908); V. D. Scudder, *The Franciscan Adventure* (London, 1931).

**Francis Joseph** (1830–1916). Emperor of Austria from 1848. He came to the throne amid the disorders of the revolution of 1848, which were put down in Hungary only with the help of Russian troops. His early years in power were marked by the ascendancy of conservative elements. This period was characterized by the rigorous suppression of all national movements in the polyglot Hapsburg monarchy and by a considerable expansion of the powers of the state. But after an initial success against the German aspirations of Prussia (Humiliation of Olmütz, 1850), his foreign policy met with serious reverses, notably the alienation of Russia after his failure to repay his debt to that country in the Crimean War and the disastrous Italian campaign against Napoleon III in 1859. This defeat led to a brief constitutional experiment, which was abandoned after the war against Prussia in 1866. In the following year he came to terms with his Hungarian subjects in the Compromise of 1867, which established the Dual Monarchy, making the Magyars virtually independent at the expense of his Slavic subjects. In 1879 he concluded an alliance with the German Empire, and thereafter his foreign policy was increasingly influenced by his much more powerful ally. In religious affairs he at first followed his strong Catholic convictions in concluding the Concordat of 1855, but in 1870 he all but put an end to the primacy of the Catholic Church in his dominions. In his later years he was unable to check the extremist elements at court and in the army which wished to challenge Russia in the Balkans. While not approving of the outbreak of war in 1914, he took no effective measures to prevent it. He died in 1916, two years before the dissolution of his empire.

**Francis of Assisi** (1182–1226). Founder of the Franciscan Order. The son of a wealthy cloth merchant, Pietro Bernadone, of Assisi in Umbria, he was christened Giovanni, but called Francis because his father had been on business in France at his birth. He lived the normal life of the fashionable youth of his city, taking part in the wars with Perugia, where he was held prisoner for a year. Soon after his release he joined an army to fight in Apulia under Walter of Brienne, but was forced to return by illness. His gradual conversion began soon after. He made a pilgrimage to Rome in 1205 and changed places with a beggar outside St. Peter's for a day. On another occasion he embraced a leper. In 1206 while praying in the derelict church of St. Damian in Assisi he felt he heard a voice from a painting of Christ tell him to repair it. He sold a load of his father's cloth and offered the price to the priest. On hearing of

this, his father disowned him. Under the protection of the local bishop he lived as a hermit near St. Damian for the next two years and rebuilt four churches with the proceeds of begging. In 1209 while assisting at Mass in a church at Portiuncula, some two miles from Assisi, he understood the words of Matt. 10:7–10 as a personal admonition to a life of apostolic poverty, and thereafter resolved to live as a beggar, preaching poverty, repentance, brotherly love, and peace. Having attracted a band of followers, he composed a short rule for them, consisting of a few precepts from the Gospels, and in 1210 went to Rome to gain Innocent III's approval and permission to continue his work. Innocent gave these on condition that Francis receive the diaconate and the other brothers minor orders. Thereafter the band called themselves the Friars Minor. They wandered all over Italy preaching and came together once a year at Pentecost for a chapter meeting at Portiuncula. In 1212 an heiress of Assisi, Clare, renounced all her possessions and was professed by Francis, founding at St. Damian a branch of the order for women, the Poor Clares. In 1214, Francis went through France and Spain to convert the Moslems of North Africa, but illness made him return. By 1216 the Friars Minor were established from Lombardy to Sicily and the simplicity of the rule began to be considered inadequate, particularly for those in the cities. In 1217, Francis met Cardinal Ugolino in Florence and found in him a protector against the many enemies the order was creating. In the following year he met Dominic, who suggested the two new orders be merged, an idea Francis politely refused. Ugolino attended the chapter meeting of 1219, the "Chapter of the Straw Mats," and prompted by some of the better educated brothers suggested that the rule be modified and amplified along the lines of the traditional monastic orders, with authority being delegated. Francis refused to depart from his original inspiration. Missions abroad were agreed on, and with eleven companions Francis set out for the Holy Land. Shocked by the lack of discipline among the crusaders, he tried to persuade them not to attack the Moslems. After they had done so and been defeated he crossed over to the Moslem camp to preach to the Sultan, who received him with hospitality. Returning to the crusaders, he was present at the bloody conquest of Damietta, but hurried off afterward to Syria for a brief visit to Bethlehem and further missionary work. The following summer a lay brother came to tell him that in his absence the two vicars he had left behind to govern the order had remodeled the rule, increasing the number of fasts and obtaining privileges from the pope. A rumor had been spread that Francis was dead. Hurrying back to Italy, Francis also found that brothers ignorant of the local language had been persecuted as heretics in France, Germany, and Hungary. This and Ugolino's advice persuaded him to accept official papal patronage and the transformation of the Minorites from a free community to a regular order governed by canon law. A new rule was drawn up and authorized by Honorius III in 1223, and Francis abdicated his leadership. In 1224 he retired to a hermitage on Mt. La Verna, and while in prayer allegedly received the stigmata. In spite of the pain, the severe stomach and liver ailments brought on by earlier austerities, and increasing blindness, he composed his Canticle to the Sun, his *Admonitions* to the brothers, and his *Testament,* the final statement of his ideal, before dying at Portiuncula. Less than two years later, his friend Ugolino, who had become Pope Gregory IX, canonized him.

BIBLIOGRAPHY: O. Englebert, *St. Francis of Assisi* (Chicago, 1966); R. C. Petry, *Francis of Assisi: Apostle of Poverty* (Durham, N.C., 1941); P. Sabatier, *Life of St. Francis of Assisi* (New York, 1917); L. Salvatorelli, *The Life of St. Francis of Assisi* (New York, 1928).

**Francis of Paula** (1416–1507). Founder of the Order of Minims. Born in Calabria, at thirteen he became a Franciscan Oblate, and a year later retired to a hermitage on his father's estate. In 1435 two friends joined him and in 1453 the order had grown enough to have a monastery and church. His rule was modeled after the Franciscan, but enjoined severe asceticism and humility; hence his followers were to be "minims" or "least." Persecuted by the king of Naples, he was summoned to the deathbed of Louis XI and remained in France at Plessis as an adviser to Charles VIII and Louis XII. He was canonized by Leo X in 1519.

**Francis of Sales** (1567–1622). French Roman Catholic bishop and devotional writer. Born of a noble Savoyard family at the castle of Sales, Francis studied under the Jesuits at Paris, and then proceeded to the University of Padua to study law. He was ordained in 1593, and in the following years did missionary work in Le Chablais, a region of Savoy under the spiritual influence of the Calvinists of Geneva. In his missionary work, and in his activities as bishop of Geneva after 1602, Francis emphasized the importance of the virtues of civility and charity in an age of religious extremism. Sought after as a preacher, he became acquainted with Pope Clement VIII and Henry IV of France. In 1610, with Jane Frances of Chantal, he founded the Order of the Visitation of Holy Mary. Insisting that sanctity was pertinent to and necessary in all human pursuits, Francis composed the works for which he is best remembered: *An Introduction to the Devout Life* and the *Treatise on the Love of God.* The example of his genial personality has long remained popular in the Roman Catholic Church, and several religious orders were founded upon his inspiration (e.g., the Salesian order founded by John Bosco in the 19th century). He was canonized in 1665, and declared a Doctor of the Church in 1877.

**Francis Xavier** (1506–1552). Jesuit missionary, called the "Apostle of the Indies." Francis was born at the castle of Xavier in Navarre, the youngest son of a high official, Juan de Yasu. In the French-Spanish struggle over Navarre, the Xaviers were ruined, and Francis left for the University of Paris to study law and theology. There he met Peter Favre and later Ignatius of Loyola, who became the spiritual master of the two younger students. With three others, they formed the Society of Jesus in 1534. In 1537, after ordination in Venice, Ignatius and Xavier traveled to Rome, where in 1539, at the request of John III of Portugal, Xavier was appointed papal legate to the East Indies. He arrived in Goa in 1542, beginning his ministry by preaching and serving the sick. After six months, he evangelized the pearl fishermen of southwest India, baptizing thousands, but his work was undermined by petty kings and the bad example of the Portuguese. In 1545, he left for the East, and in Malacca met Hachiro, who became the first Japanese convert. With him and two others, Francis voyaged to Japan, arriving there in 1549. By 1551, he had established a flourishing mission of two thousand Christians, but jealous bonzes, or Buddhist monks, drove him out. His zeal led him next toward China. He returned to India, was appointed provincial, settled difficulties at the Goa College, and set out in 1552 as "ambassador" to China. He was not allowed to enter, and, that same year, on the island of Sancian off the China coast, he died. This "greatest of the missionaries since the Apostles" was canonized in 1622.

**Franck, Sebastian** (1499–1542). Anabaptist. Originally a priest and then a Lutheran near Nuremberg, Franck pursued from 1529 an active free-lance writing career in several cities of southern Germany. He was a "programmatic Spiritualist," a pacifist and not chiliastic. His chief contention was that the church had fallen just after the times of the apostles and that the church fathers and every other spokesman for the organized church were "apostles of Antichrist." He welcomed the revolt against the traditional church but decried the setting up of the "four sects" (Roman Catholic, Lutheran, Zwinglian, Anabaptist). He was also against placing reliance in any "externals," such as ceremonies, doctrines, the words of the Scriptures, concern with tithes, and the power of the magistracy, all of which could be set in contradiction with one another as requirements. Rather, he said, the true church was a purely spiritual thing, being in truth what the external church was only in words. The faithful, scattered among the heathen and becoming faithful not by moral works but by the call of the Spirit, would be gathered together only at the end of the world. Franck displayed a certain world-weariness in some of his writings, but there was also a growing Germanicism in his geographical and historical works. He lived a harried life in Ulm and elsewhere until his death in Basel.

**Francke, August Hermann** (1663–1727). German Lutheran Pietist leader, educator, and social reformer. Early associated with the Pietists under P. J. Spener, he was in constant conflict with the Lutheran orthodox party. Driven out of Erfurt, he came to Glauchau, near Halle as pastor in 1691. Later, while a professor at the new university there, he founded influential charitable and educational institutions, sent missionaries to India, and aided in the establishment of a Bible society.

**Franco, Francisco** (1892–    ). Spanish generalissimo and lawgiver. He led nationalist forces to victory in the Civil War (1936–1939) with Axis help, restored the monarchy (1947), with himself as protector-regent for life. He admitted religious orders, brought back the Catholic calendar, lent state aid to the church, abolished divorce, and ratified episcopal nominations. Protestant and Jewish toleration remained permissive.

**Frankalomign.** A feudal land arrangement in which a church or other religious organization held land from a lord in perpetuity in return for prayers for the lord and his descendants.

**Frankfurt, Synods of.** As part of the constant supervision of his Frankish realm, Charlemagne rated his responsibility for the church very high. Since he had no true capital, traveling from one royal domain to another, he frequently assembled counts and bishops in synod wherever he happened to be. Records indicate that there were some sixteen such synods, at Frankfurt am Main during the Carolingian era, the most important by far being that of 794. Called for the purpose of reinforcing an earlier (792) synod's condemnation of the Adoptianist heresy which made its way across the border from Spain, it was attended by two specially invited papal legates and a number of non-Frankish bishops as well as by those from all over the Frankish kingdom. Two replies to the Spaniards, one by the Italian bishops and the other by the rest, were adopted as synodal letters condemning the heresy, and that condemnation was also alluded to in the first of the Synod's fifty-six canons. The second canon was a condemnation of the recently adopted decree of the Seventh Ecumenical Council (Second Nicene, 787) on icon worship. Unfortunately, the Synod attributed to the Council a doctrine diametrically opposed to that which had been, in fact, adopted. The remaining canons regulate the clergy, monks, and the rest of the faithful of the Frankish Church.

**Franklin, Benjamin** (1706–1790). American statesman, inventor, publisher, and patriot. Franklin also embodied popular American religious thought. During his youth in Boston, his articles in the anticlerical *New England Courant* teased New England's orthodoxy; after moving to Philadelphia in 1723 his views on religion, if not always skeptical, remained heterodox and deistic. Franklin adopted a pious work ethic from late Puritanism (e.g., Cotton Mather's *Essays to Do Good*) and developed it into Poor Richard's homespun moral idealism, a system of optimistic self-improvement that presaged later liberal thought. An excellent index to Franklin's spirit and faith is his *Autobiography*. He preferred sermons not of "the dogmatical kind" but those which "inculcated strongly to the practice of virtue, or what in the religious style are called good works." He advised men to seek moral perfection by self-imposed control of the will and by the observance of thirteen rules; the last rule was humility, attainable if one would "imitate Jesus and Socrates." Benjamin Franklin's essential creed is summed up in his statement that he "never doubted the existence of the Deity; that the most acceptable service of God was the doing good to man." Carl Van Doren's *Benjamin Franklin* (New York, 1938) is the standard biography.

**Frederick I Barbarossa** (c. 1123–1190). King of Germany from 1152 and Holy Roman Emperor from 1155. He was probably the greatest monarch of the Hohenstaufen. Regarding himself the heir of Constantine, Justinian, and Charlemagne, he determined to restore imperial authority over Germany, northern Italy, and the papacy, authority lost through the investiture conflict and the Guelph-Ghibelline civil wars in Germany. To this end he conducted a series of compaigns in northern Italy aimed at subjugating the Lombard communes. At first successful (in 1159 he forced the Italian communes to accept imperial podestas and in 1162 captured and razed Milan, the leader of the Lombard League), he was ultimately defeated by the communes in 1176 at Legnano. Although his authority in Italy was severely diminished, his ambitions in northern Italy and the marriage of his son Henry VI to the heiress of Sicily threatened the independence of the Papal States and earned for the Hohenstaufen the undying enmity of the papacy. Though successful in overcoming the rebellion of Henry the Lion of Saxony and in asserting feudal sovereignty over other German princes, he was ultimately unable to prevent Germany's disintegration into semiautonomous principalities. Leading the Third Crusade, he drowned in the river Saleph in Cilicia (1190). He became the symbol of Germany's era of glory, and legend later said that he did not die but was sleeping in a cave at Berchtesgaden to awaken in time of peril and lead Germany to greatness.

**Frederick II** (1194–1250). Holy Roman Emperor. Son of Henry VI of Germany and Constance of Sicily, he posed the most serious Hohenstaufen threat to the papacy. He succeeded (1198) to the Sicilian throne, and in 1220, on the promise of giving up that kingdom, he was crowned Holy Roman Emperor. As determined as his predecessors to establish authority over Italy, he sought to use Sicilian and German might to regain imperial control over northern Italy. A Sicilian Norman by temperament and upbringing, he apparently sacrificed his interests in Germany to concentrate on Italy. To secure German manpower and wealth for his campaigns against the Lombard communes he lavishly granted privileges to the German princes, severely weakening the feudal authority over Germany that had been gained by his grandfather Frederick I Barbarossa. His efforts to join Sicily and northern Italy squeezed the Papal States in a vise, and the popes feared for their independence. The result was that through most of his reign he was locked in a life-and-death struggle with the papacy, which sought to crush his power and destroy the union of Lombardy and Sicily. This conflict between emperor and pope resulted in strange paradoxes. Excommunicated in 1227 for failure to keep a crusading vow, in 1229 he led the Sixth Crusade and captured Jerusalem, but the pope reiterated his excommunication and laid Jerusalem itself under interdict. Later, as a result of Frederick's successes against the papacy and the Lombard towns, Pope Innocent IV preached a desparole crusade against him. Though himself successful in Italy, he brought down on his heirs the implacable hatred of the papacy, which after his death hounded his house to extinction.

**Frederick II the Great** (1712–1786). King of Prussia from 1740. The most successful and most imitated of the enlightened despots, he believed a monarch should not be absolute master, but first servant of the state. A skeptic, he admitted toleration, favored the *philosophes,* fostered learning, and policed the clergy. By reforming administration, aiding immigration, seizing Silesian (1740) and Polish (1772) territories, he enhanced Prussia's prestige.

**Frederick III the Wise** (1463–1525). Elector of Saxony, Luther's sovereign. He was the model of a pious medieval prince. Educated at an Augustinian monastery, he was a pilgrim to the Holy Land in 1493 and early began a collection of relics at Wittenberg that numbered 19,013 items by 1520. He became interested in the new learning and in church reform. Highly respected, his opinions were eagerly sought, and he was seriously considered as an imperial candidate in 1519. When Luther was cited to Rome in 1518, Frederick obtained a trial for him on German soil. From his innate sense of justice he refused to carry out the papal excommunication of 1520 and the imperial ban of 1521. In spite of his opponents, he would not suppress Luther, feeling that the Reformer's work might be God's will. He advocated no reforms but in 1523 ended the veneration of relics. Spalatin, his secretary, was most instrumental in acquainting him with Luther's theology. On his deathbed, Frederick sent for Luther, but Luther was in the Hartz mountains meeting with the peasants, whose revolt had embittered Frederick. He finally received Communion in both kinds from Spalatin, in this way openly avowing the Evangelical faith. Luther preached at his funeral, and Melanchthon gave a Latin oration praising him as the prince who had done more than any other to promote the gospel.

**Frederick William.** See GREAT ELECTOR.

**Frederick William I** (1688–1740). King of

Prussia from 1713. He promptly reentered the Great Northern War from which Prussia had withdrawn. In the Peace of Stockholm (1720) he recovered parts of Pomerania and the island of Rügen. In internal affairs he initiated rigorous economies which stood in sharp contrast to his father's extravagance. He devoted his energies to improving the financial condition of his kingdom. In 1723 he created, in the interest both of efficiency and of promoting a more centralized rule, a common ministry of finance, army, economic, and agricultural affairs. The civil service was expanded and the king himself oversaw the inculcation of a spirit of obedience, honesty, and punctuality in its ranks, qualities that were to become proverbial of Prussian officialdom. By far the greater portion of the revenues his reforms produced was spent on the army. He introduced conscription in 1733 and maintained a corps of recruiting agents abroad. At the end of his reign the Prussian army was in size second only to that of Austria among German forces and in quality unequaled. Huge sums were spent on assembling a royal guard made up of very tall men, the Potsdam giants. Yet in his later years his foreign policy was pacific. In 1728 he was among the first to adhere to the Pragmatic Sanction. His relations with his heir, the later Frederick the Great, were bad. Only after many vicissitudes did he reconcile himself to his succession. The king's religious policies were, on the whole, liberal. He granted asylum to seventeen thousand Salzburg Protestants, yet maintained good relations with the Roman Catholic Church.

**Frederick William II** (1744–1797). King of Prussia from 1786. He succeeded his uncle Frederick the Great, and won from Pius VI tardy papal recognition. A Lutheran, influenced by Rosicrucian favorites, he resisted rationalism, increased censorship, intervened in France and Poland, gaining from Polish partitions (1793 and 1795) the Catholic territories of Danzig, Thorn, and Warsaw. He left the army and treasury in disorder.

**Frederick William III** (1770–1840). King of Prussia from 1797. A nephew of Frederick the Great, he was not an effective ruler, but he desired and worked actively for a Protestant union in Prussia. In 1817, the union of the Reformed and Lutheran churches was accomplished as the United Evangelical Church. Frederick William proclaimed himself chief bishop, established a new liturgy, and worked throughout his reign to effect uniformity among Prussian Protestants. His efforts were to some degree rewarded, but there was considerable dissent against his decrees.

**Frederick William IV** (1795–1861). King of Prussia from 1840. He had little in common with most of his Hohenzollern forebears. As a young man he had received an excellent literary and philosophical education and he was never able to overcome his early dislike for the army and militarism in general. Yet his nature was decidedly conservative, albeit with a strong admixture of romanticism. As crown prince he came under the influence of a group that sought to combine the virtues of Christianity with those of the German past, and ultimately he emerged as a Pietist with strong reactionary leanings. He came to the throne in 1840 and although he furthered the arts and sciences and even relaxed the strict censorship, he refused to make any concessions to the increasing clamor for constitutional reform of the state. In March, 1848, he at first gave way to the revolutionaries in Berlin, but he put no obstacles in the way of his more energetic ministers who suppressed the liberals in November. In 1849 he refused the offer of a German imperial crown from the Frankfurt National Assembly, for he could not accept a crown from revolutionaries. Thereafter he attempted to create a union of German princes instead, but was forced to desist from this project by Austrian pressure at Olmütz in 1850. After this failure the internal governance of Prussia became wholly reactionary. In 1857 the king suffered a stroke, and his brother William governed in his name until his death, thereupon following him on the throne.

**Free Church Council.** A cooperative movement among English churches formed by a merger of the National Free Church Council of 1896 and the Federal Council of the Evangelical Free Churches of 1919. The council represents such groups as the Congregationalists, Methodists, Baptists, and Presbyterians. The views of the churches on matters effecting religion, education, moral standards, and ecumenism are set forth with more weight by the united group. The Council sponsors annual conferences, publications, youth work, advertising, and visual aids.

**Free Church of England.** A Protestant Episcopal church outside the Church of England which agrees with the Evangelical party within the church on matters of orders, doctrine, and worship. Founded in 1844 because of a dispute over the Tractarian movement within the church, it emphasized the attitude of the Protestant Reformation with a presbyterian form of ministry. In the late 19th century it was united with the Reformed Episcopal Church of America, but this association was not maintained.

**Free Church of Scotland.** A church produced by a schism in the Established Church of Scotland in 1843. The argument centered around the right of lay patrons appointing ministers to congregations. The Scots Church General Assembly declared that no pastor should be forced on a congregation contrary to the will of the people (1834). The government sided with the patrons and the dispute led to the secession from the Presbyterian Church of Scotland of 451 ministers out of 1,203 (1843). The group was ably led by Thomas Chalmers, who arranged for financing and the building of new churches. The theology of the Free Church remained the same as that of the state church except that in the licensing and ordination ceremonies the independence of the church was stressed. To educate its ministers, the New College at Edinburgh was built in 1847 and divinity halls were established at Glasgow and Aberdeen. The Free Church produced a number of fine scholars, among them W. Robertson Smith, A. B. Davidson, A. B. Bruce, Henry Drummond, and George Adam Smith. The progressive views of the group caused the secession of part of its membership in the Highlands to form the strictly orthodox Free Presbyterian Church of Scotland. The main body of Free Churches reunited with the Church of Scotland in 1929.

**Freedmen's Bureau.** An arm of the U.S. War Department (1865–1872). It was created to prevent the reestablishment of quasi-slavery of Negroes in the South. Its program included provision of food and medicine and the establishment of schools for Negroes, control of the Negro labor market, the administration of equal justice, and the control of confiscated land. Gen. O. S. Howard, a Presbyterian layman, was the commissioner, and the churches influenced the Bureau's creation and program. Negro education was largely through the missionary programs of northern churches and agencies, particularly the Congregationalists and the American Home Missionary Society. The education provided, however, fostered idealistic views of liberty and racial equality which under contemporary conditions increased racial hostility. This led to racial separatism, evidenced by Negro colleges and churches (Baptist and Methodist). The Bureau maintained absolute control over the ex-slaves for several years, and its unyielding and unsympathetic policies were a mixed blessing. The Negroes achieved a semblance of justice

and gained opportunities for education, but also a lasting animosity and separation between southern Negroes and whites. The cooperation between the Bureau and the churches was a rare example in a nation where education was considered exclusively a state affair.

**Freeman, James** (1759–1835). Pastor of the first Unitarian Church in America. A graduate of Harvard College (1777), Freeman became a lay reader at King's Chapel in Boston (1782). In 1785 he openly renounced the doctrine of the Trinity and revised the liturgy accordingly. Upon being refused Episcopal ordination, he was ordained by the senior warden of the church in 1787, thus removing the oldest Episcopal Church in New England from communion with the Church of England and creating the first Unitarian Church of America.

**Freemasonry.** Principles and practices that grew out of ancient guilds and relied heavily on deism and illuminism. Freemasons in London first merged four lodges into a Grand Lodge in 1717. The first German lodge was in Hamburg (1737). In France, where modern Freemasonry originated, and in Italy, relations between Freemasonry and the Roman Catholic Church were more hostile than in Germany, England, and the United States. The patriot Mazzini and other Italians were decidedly antipapal. Turin became an autonomous lodge in 1860. Freemasons called a countercouncil in 1870 and intentionally offended the papacy in the Giordano-Bruno celebration in Rome (1889). Among many papal pronouncements against Freemasonry, Leo XIII's *Humanum genus* (1884), inspired by Fava, is perhaps the most severe.

**Free Pews.** In America at one time the construction of church buildings was financed by selling pews in the completed building for the use of the owning families, and then maintaining the building through the annual rental of the pews. After the mid-19th century, when weekly offerings and other fund-raising techniques were employed, the policy of free pews open to any worshiper gained the ascendancy.

**Free Religious Association.** A loose federation of religious radicals formed in 1867 by a group primarily of Unitarian background after Unitarians in 1866 declared themselves liberal Christians, virtually excluding the Independents who could not accept this label. The leaders of the Free Religious Association were influenced by transcendentalism and the new science. They advocated complete freedom of thought without any restrictions, the scientific study of theology, and a religion of humanity. O. B. Frothingham served as their first president and was succeeded by Felix Adler. Providing a religious basis for scientific humanism, the Association gradually declined in significance as Unitarianism became more hospitable to radical thought and as the Ethical Culture Society drew away some of its constituency.

**Free Will Baptists.** A Baptist group that adheres to the Arminian doctrine of free will and practices adult immersion, baptism, and open Communion. Although some immigrants holding these views arrived from England and Wales early in the 18th century, the present denomination, known as The National Association of Free Will Baptists, traces its origin to the preaching of Paul Palmer in North Carolina in the 1720's and especially to the work of Benjamin Randall, a lay preacher, among Baptists in New England in the 1780's. Randall and seven followers formed an independent church at New Durham, N.H., in 1780, after formally separating from the Baptist association. Other churches were formed, and in 1783 they were organized in a Quarterly Meeting. The General Conference was organized in 1827.

**Frelinghuysen, Theodore J.** (c. 1691–c. 1748). Dutch Reformed revivalist. Born and educated in Friesland, he went shortly after his ordination to New Jersey. There he founded several Dutch Reformed congregations and precipitated an extensive revival, which has often been considered the beginning of the Great Awakening. He was an important influence in erecting an independent Dutch Reformed Church in America.

**French Confession.** See GALLICAN CONFESSION.

**Freudianism.** A term derived from the thought and work of Sigmund Freud (1856–1939), the originator and founder of psychoanalysis. Psychoanalysis has come to have an extensive and profound effect upon all the many facets of modern intellectual, social, and personal life, and Freudianism is one of the important results of the total impact of psychoanalysis upon thought and society. It is necessary, therefore, to recognize what Freudianism and psychoanalysis hold in common, and what are their points of difference so that the bearing of Freudianism upon church history can be clearly stated.

What is generally referred to as psychoanalysis began as a specific therapeutic technique for the treatment of psychological disorders, notably hysteria and obsessive-compulsive states. Today this technique remains as one of an increasing number of different forms of psychotherapy, although these newer forms incorporate many features basic to psychoanalysis. As Freud's therapeutic efforts developed, his thought moved beyond considerations of technique, so that psychoanalysis also became a school or system of psychology, taking its place alongside such other schools as behaviorism and Gestalt psychology. It became as well one of a growing number of theories of personality. Although a medical doctor himself, Freud considered his work more a psychology and less a specific type of psychiatric therapy.

Both the technique and the theory that appeared were revolutionary in relation to techniques and theories existing at the time. As Freud's work began to make itself known, it attracted followers who sought to learn the technique of psychoanalysis and to train others in its use. In this way psychoanalysis became institutionalized, creating its own leadership, centers of training, standards of practice, and professional journals. As a result, psychoanalytic ideas became increasingly available for appropriation by many people in different professions and academic disciplines, and especially by the public at large. Psychoanalytic ideas were applied to many diverse aspects of personal and social life. By the 1920's there were in the United States alone over two hundred popular books dealing with Freud. In this respect, psychoanalysis is not only a therapy and a system of psychology, but must also be considered as an ideology. The term "Freudianism" applies to this third aspect of psychoanalysis, and in this sense Freudianism may be thought of in much the same way as Marxism and Darwinism.

So understood, Freudianism consists of three basic tenets or assumptions, drawn from the body of writings of Freud and his early followers. First, it assumes the reality of an unconscious sphere or realm of mental life that exists alongside conscious awareness. Secondly, it asserts that conscious awareness is to a great extent, if not entirely, determined by unconscious strivings and wishes. And thirdly, it insists that such wishes take their origin in the early childhood of the individual and are sexual in nature.

Freudianism seeks to extend and apply in simplistic fashion these tenets to various problems of personal and social life, and especially to those of religion. The doctrines, rituals, and moral precepts held by the churches are found in Freudianism to be determined unconsciously by childhood sexual experiences. In this sense, religion is said to be a neurosis, a projection of unconscious infantile wishes. In such an elucidation of the origins of religious thought and practice, the claims of religion are denied.

Freud's writings on religion and his thought as a whole are far more complex than the tenets of Freudianism allow, yet much of his writing on religion, especially his earlier work, as well as the work of his early followers, was often reductive and discrediting in spirit. These studies usually attempted to analyze the unconscious, sexual roots of moral and spiritual life of religious figures. Consequently, the initial responses to psychoanalysis by churchmen were often equally ideological in spirit.

More careful and thoughtful attempts were first made by sensitive ministers who were concerned to use psychoanalytic insights to enhance their ability in the cure of souls. Following them, theologians have become interested in the study of psychoanalytic concepts, not only for apologetic purposes, but also in order to enhance and make more relevant theological understanding. Recently, biographical studies of religious personalities, using not only Freudian but neo-Freudian materials and concepts, have appeared. Most recent of all has been the use of Freudian ideas by the so-called "death of God" theologians.

As a result, Freudianism as an ideology is today a less powerful critique of religious life and thought. It remains, however, a very powerful ideological factor in current society, making its presence felt through the institutionalizing of psychotherapy, in the field of literature, and also in the advertising and entertainment industries. Here it appears as an ideology of psychotherapy, commending a detached, tentative, and "analytic" attitude toward any sense of unconditional obligation to one's neighbor, especially to those imperatives which have been embodied in the teachings of religious institutions. The final disposition of Freudianism, with regard to the history of the churches, has therefore not yet been determined.

BIBLIOGRAPHY: S. Freud, *Civilization and Its Discontents* (New York, 1962); and *The Future of an Illusion* (Garden City, 1957); and *New Introductory Lectures* (London, 1957); and "A Religious Experience," in his *Collected Papers*, Vol. 5 (New York, 1959); T. Altizer, *Mircea Eliade and the Dialectic of the Sacred* (Philadelphia, 1964); E. Erikson, *Young Man Luther* (New York, 1958); W. Oates, *The Christian Pastor* (Philadelphia, 1951); P. Rieff, *The Triumph of the Therapeutic* (New York, 1966); P. Tillich, *Systematic Theology*, Vol. 2 (Chicago, 1967).

**Freylinghausen, Johann Anastasius** (1670–1739). German Pietist theologian and hymnologist. Born in Gandersheim, he studied at Jena, Erfurt, and Halle. At Halle he assisted A. H. Francke and eventually became Francke's assistant and son-in-law. His fame comes from his hymns (forty-five are ascribed to him with certainty), which are characterized by Scriptural phrases and conceptions. Some of his hymns are found in both German and English hymnals.

**Friar.** The title of a member of a mendicant order, derived from *frater* (Latin, "brother"). The word "friar" is frequently used in connection with the color of the habit of the several mendicant orders in their popular names: Gray Friars (Franciscans), Black Friars (Dominicans), and White Friars (Carmelites).

**Friedrich Wilhelm I.** See FREDERICK WILLIAM I.

**Friedrich Wilhelm II.** See FREDERICK WILLIAM II.

**Friedrich Wilhelm III.** See FREDERICK WILLIAM III.

**Friedrich Wilhelm IV.** See FREDERICK WILLIAM IV.

**Friends of God.** Spiritual fellowships of the later Middle Ages. To many in the church, the 14th century seemed to be the century of God's judgment. It opened with the exile of the papacy to Avignon and ended with the Great Western Schism. Within this context several new movements sprang up in the church. The Friends of God was one such movement, taking its name from John 15:14–15: "You are my friends. . . . I have called you friends." It began in Basel sometime between 1339 and 1343. From there it spread down the Rhine Valley to Strasbourg, Cologne, and the towns of the Netherlands. It was a lay, democratic movement having no connections with the hierarchy of the church. The Friends of God were concerned with the Christian life as a life of holiness, piety, and love. Although essentially a middle-class movement, it included people from all classes of society. It was intimately connected with the rise of religious mysticism in Germany and the Low Countries. Its chief figure was Rulman Merswin, of Strasbourg, who wrote its most famous literary work, *The Book of the Nine Rocks*. Written in an apocalyptic vein, the book contrasts the corruption of the medieval church and the spiritual quest of a friend of God. Merswin's pupil Nicholas of Basel was tried for heresy, condemned, and burned as a heretic at Vienna in c. 1395.

As a response to corruption and abuse in the church, the movement was a forerunner of the Reformation of the 16th century.

**Fries, Jakob Friedrich** (1773–1843). German philosopher. Schooled with Schleiermacher, Fries attended Leipzig University and Jena, where he studied under Fichte. He lectured with Hegel at Jena (1805). At Heidelberg (1806) he was professor of philosophy and physics, and returned to Jena in 1816. His chief work was *Neue Kritik der Vernunft* (1807). He thought that Kant's transcendental philosophy was to be eliminated, and that observation of experience was the beginning of philosophy. He suggested further that there is a psychological exhibition of objective-synthetic relation. Religion finds its vital expression in social reforms. Politically liberal, Fries urged the formation of a united Germany.

**Fritzsche, Otto Fridolin** (1812–1896). German theologian. Educated at Halle, Fritzsche taught there, and then at Zurich (1837–1893). His interests were mainly New Testament exegesis and church history, but both fields benefited from his critical editions of Old Testament Apocryphal, church-historical, and Biblical texts. With W. Grimm, Fritzsche published a six-volume exegetical handbook on the Old Testament Apocrypha.

**Froben** (Frobenius), **John** (c. 1460–1527). German printer. Born at Hammelburg, Bavaria, and having studied at Basel, Froben established the first printing press in Basel in 1491, in time acquiring seven presses. His work was of high quality. From 1513 he was Erasmus' printer, bringing out his Greek New Testament in 1516, and later on his editions of the fathers. In all, Froben produced about two hundred fifty books, some of which were illustrated by Hans Holbein.

**Froissart, Jean** (c. 1338–c. 1410). French priest and chronicler of 14th-century life. His *Chronicles,* which continued the work of Jean le Bel, represents the best French writing of his time. A native of Valenciennes, he traveled through Europe collecting data for his vivid though often inaccurate chronicles. His love of the courtly life is reflected also in his romantic poetry. Chivalry is his theme, hence the careful detail of single combat and pageantry, with minor interest in such matters as the plague. Despite his undoubted defects as a historian, he succeeds in bringing alive the European scene in the first half of the Hundred Years' War.

**Frontier.** The region dividing the settled from the unsettled parts of the United States.

Frontier also pertains to a historical theory of the development of American institutions. The frontier was defined by the Bureau of Census as the boundary line between those areas of the United States with more and those with fewer than two persons per square mile. From about 1600 to 1850 the frontier was a nearly north-south line that moved gradually west. Migration into the South from the Gulf of Mexico tended to disrupt the regularity of this pattern as did the settlement of California, which was heavily populated long before many of the Rocky Mountain states. There are still today some areas of the United States that are virtually uninhabited, but these are not extensive or capable of fruitful settlement. The Bureau of Census officially declared the frontier closed in 1890.

In 1893, Frederick Jackson Turner first propounded the "frontier thesis." American history, at this time in its infancy, had previously been concerned almost exclusively with the colonial period (the slow growth of national consciousness and the eventual unification of the thirteen colonies). The focus had been on political events, primarily. Professor Turner's approach to American history signified a conscious and dramatic change of perspective. Turner felt that the Revolutionary War could no longer be looked upon as the culmination of American history; perhaps it was more the beginning. Turner was also strongly influenced by the trend toward economic explanations of history and viewed economic factors rather than political as the real driving forces behind long-term historical change. Lastly, Turner was concerned with the peculiarly American elements of American history and not with the manner in which British and European institutions had been altered during colonial days. All these concerns were united in Turner's analysis of the influence of the frontier. Up to about 1763 the frontier had been a European one, but, after the opening of the area beyond the Appalachians, American and not European families began to fill the open spaces; the new states were the offspring of older American communities. In their struggle with the new conditions, their old concepts dissolved and were remade. As Turner remarked in his brilliant lecture to the World's Congress of Historians at the Columbian Exposition of 1893: "American social development has been continually beginning over again on the frontier. This perennial rebirth, this fluidity of American life, this expansion westward with its new opportunities, its continuous touch with the simplicity of primitive society, furnish the forces dominating American character." Democracy, according to Turner, was the product of the American people's struggle with their environment.

This frontier thesis was influential in American historiography down to about 1930, when criticism became common and quite sharp. Oddly enough, it was just when "secular" historians of American life were abandoning or seriously modifying the frontier thesis that church historians first attempted to apply it to the development of American religious life. Peter Mode's *The Frontier Spirit in American Christianity* (New York, 1923) was the pioneer work, but William Warren Sweet (1881–1959), also teaching at the University of Chicago, made the greatest contribution in the attempt to understand America's religious life in this way. Sweet's analysis of the development of American religion, especially during the period from 1765 to 1840, has not been superseded, although historians in the 1960's have been expressing dissatisfaction with it. Sweet completely discarded Turner's interest in economic causation. In his hands, the frontier thesis, instead of accounting for the emergence of democracy, is used to account for the emergence of a peculiarly American form of religious life which has since come to be known as denominationalism. The frontier was also significant in determining the relative success of the various denominations. As Sweet remarked: "In the trans-Allegheny west new patterns emerged, and it was the success with which the several religious bodies functioned in the middle west that was to determine which of the American Churches were to be large and evenly distributed throughout the nation, and which of the Churches were to be typically American. The eastern Churches which failed to make a major impact upon the middle west tended to remain small and sectional." Professor Sweet never explained how literally he meant to interpret the concept of the frontier, but, if it is extended to virtually the whole of the United States during the early 19th century, as Prof. Sidney Mead has suggested, three aspects of its influence can be seen. Certainly, the frontier was a mission field. The people who marched across the mountains were potential if not actual pagans. In America there was after the Revolution no established church, no state support for religion. If Christianity was not to perish in the West and barbarism flourish, the denominations had to organize their membership into mission societies to reach these friends and neighbors who had left the home parishes. In this sense Professor Sweet was certainly correct: the Methodists and the Baptists grew to be the largest Protestant denominations in the United States because they were the best equipped to meet the conditions of the West. The Methodist circuit riders and the Baptist farmer preachers arrived in settlements almost as soon as the first campfires were lighted. Their informally trained, homespun leaders understood the mentality of the settlers because they were frontiersmen too. Second, the frontier provided space for experimentation. In America there was no theological orthodoxy, no establishment. People even in the East could think and preach as they pleased. In the West, free land and freedom from social constraints were added to this wider freedom. All these things proved an invitation to experimentation. The feeling that America was going to become the Kingdom of God was certainly born, in part at least, out of this feeling of unlimited freedom to cleanse what were considered the evils of the society the settlers had known and to create a new and perfect community for the future. This concept is basic to the religious teachings of the Mormons, the Disciples of Christ, and the dozens of Utopian communities such as Oneida, Ephrata, and New Harmony. Sometimes this idea of the wide open spaces is exaggerated; it would be wise to remember that the Mormons, for instance, were driven out of sparsely settled Missouri and Illinois into Utah because their neighbors would not tolerate their unorthodox behavior. Compared with Europe, however, the freedom provided by the open spaces of the West was great indeed. Third, the frontier acted as a solvent of society. Many people welcomed the freedom to experiment that they found on the frontier, and they discovered that it was impossible to perpetuate their old social and religious institutions. As Turner himself once wrote: "At the frontier the environment is at first too strong for the man. He must accept the conditions which it furnishes, or perish." How much we all depend upon the virtually unnoticed structures and habits of human society it is difficult for us to grasp; but the frontiersman learned by experience that life on the frontier was virtually life in a different culture. The wild extravagances of the camp meetings give eloquent witness to this new context of human behavior. The closest equivalent kind of conduct is found among primitive or peasant peoples who have known little or nothing of civilization. Little wonder that in these circumstances the structure of primitive Christianity as it is described in the book of Acts rather than the technical theology of Calvin or Arminius appealed to the religious sensibilities of the frontiersman. They did not choose to perpetuate the liturgies which they had inherited from Europe, but developed their own more extemporaneous forms. The frontier alone cannot be used as an explanation for the rise of denominationalism or the success of some of the evangelical churches, but its impact can never be ignored, nor ought its fascinating influence to be forgotten.

BIBLIOGRAPHY: P. Mode, *The Frontier in American Christianity* (New York, 1923); D. W. Noble, *Historians Against History* (Minneapolis, 1965); W. W. Sweet, *Religion in the Development of American Culture* (Gloucester, Mass., 1963); and *Religion on the American Frontier: 1783–1840,* 4 vols. (New York, 1964); F. J. Turner, *The Frontier in American History* (New York, 1963).

**Frothingham, Octavius Brooks** (1822–1895). Unitarian clergyman. He was born in Boston. After his graduation from Harvard College and Divinity School, Frothingham through the influence of Theodore Parker became a transcendentalist. In 1859 he formed the Third Unitarian Society of New York which reorganized in 1869 as the Independent Liberal Church. In 1867 he participated in the creation of the Free Religious Association and was its first president, retiring in 1879.

**Froude, Richard Hurrell** (1803–1836). An early Tractarian. Froude was educated at Eton and Oriel College, Oxford. While a tutor at Oriel he met John Henry Newman, and a close friendship followed. High Church and Romanizing in his ecclesiastical preference, Froude composed three of the *Tracts for the Times,* and contributed to the *Lyra apostolica.* Two years after his death from tuberculosis, his diary—or *Remains*—was published under the editorship of John Keble and Cardinal Newman. The *Remains* caused a tremendous furor because of Froude's outspoken criticism of the English Reformation.

**Fry, Elizabeth** (1780–1845). Prominent English Quaker, "minister," writer, and reformer. Born into an English family which had belonged to the Society of Friends for several generations, the Gurneys of Earlham, she became deeply interested in the improvement of prison conditions not only in England but on the Continent as well. At seventeen, after hearing William Savery, an American minister and abolitionist, she abandoned the social life of her liberal Quaker family, adopted plain garb, and began her work among the poor and sick of the neighborhood. In 1800, she married Joseph Fry, a London banker, to whom she bore eight children. Later she began an active ministry and work among prisoners. She accompanied her brother

Joseph John on a Continental tour to preach and spread prison reform. Her best-known work was among female prisoners at Newgate. She organized a relief association for them (1817), worked to supply clothing and other necessities, and established a school. She also aided prisoners being transported to New South Wales and the beggars and transients of London. She published *Female Prisoners* (1827), *Texts for Every Day in the Year* (1831), and other books.

**Fugger.** A German family that rose to power in banking and trade during the 15th and 16th centuries. The branch that descended from Jacob I established themselves at Augsburg in the spice and cotton trade and acted as financial agents for the Roman Curia. They reached the height of power under Jacob II (1459–1525), who created a monopoly on copper and silver mines, operated the papal mint, and financed various projects for the Hapsburg rulers as well as the Counter-Reformation.

**Fulbert of Chartres** (c. 952–1028). Bishop. He was a student of Gerbert at Reims. In 990 he opened the cathedral school at Chartres, where he taught fine arts, medicine, and theology, earning the cognomen of "the venerable Socrates." Made a bishop in 1007, he rebuilt the Chartres cathedral after the fire of 1020 and continued teaching. He opposed warrior bishops, defended the accused's right to a defense, and in his defense of philosophic essences and of the Platonism of Dionysius and Eriugena stands between the fathers and the Scholastics.

**Fulda.** A monastery in Hesse founded in 744 by Sturm, a pupil of Boniface, as a center for missions to the Saxons. The abbey received a charter of exemption in 751. During the 9th century, Fulda was a great intellectual center. Among its scholars were Rabanus Maurus and Walafrid Strabo. The famous library of Fulda was looted in 1631. Fulda is now an episcopal see, although the abbey itself was suppressed in 1802. Boniface is buried at Fulda.

**Fulford, Francis** (1803–1868). First Anglican metropolitan in Canada. He was born at Sidmouth, England, and educated at Exeter College, Oxford (B.A., 1827). He was ordained by the Church of England in 1826, and was rector of Trowbridge in Wiltshire from 1832 to 1842. From 1842 to 1845 he was rector of Croyden in Cambridgeshire, and from 1845 to 1880 minister of Curzon Chapel, Mayfair. He was consecrated first bishop of Montreal in 1850, and became first metropolitan of Canada in 1860. His province included the dioceses of Nova Scotia, Fredericton, and all the Canadian dioceses, though Newfoundland and Rupert's Land chose to remain under the jurisdiction of Canterbury.

**Fulgentius** (468–533). At one time a procurator, but later a monk through the influence of Augustine's treatise on the monastic vocation. Elected bishop of Ruspe, North Africa, in 507, he was soon banished by the attacking Vandals. He was a faithful defender of Augustine's teaching on grace and an opponent of semi-Pelagianism. He denied the Immaculate Conception of Mary. Ferrandus of Carthage wrote a life of Fulgentius.

**Fundamentalism.** A name given to the conservative elements within many denominations beginning about 1900. Because these groups never united in a single denomination of their own, because the name itself was avoided as offensive by many adherents of the cause, because time has altered the context of the controversy, historians have had great difficulty agreeing on a precise definition of Fundamentalism. The name itself has been traced back only to 1911, but, as a mood in the churches, Fundamentalism existed as early as the 1870's when Biblical criticism first became widely known in the United States. Fundamentalism is basically a movement of reaction against those who question the 19th-century definition of the inspiration of the Bible. In the process of its development, Christianity in America had cut itself off from most of the traditional forms of Christian authority (the enforcing power of the state, a developed theological tradition, belief in the church as a visible embodiment of God's will). American denominations, with the exception of a small segment of the Episcopalian Church and those foreign-language churches such as The Lutheran Church–Missouri Synod, had no other ground for their faith than an uncritical acceptance of the Bible as the Word of God. Biblical criticism seemed to attack this sacred tenet, and the forces that gathered to oppose Biblical criticism became known as fundamentalist.

Two strands of the movement have been identified, the Old School Calvinists and the Dispensationalists. The Old School Calvinists, especially at Princeton Seminary, developed the most respectable and consistent defense of the Bible as traditionally understood. The works of Charles Hodge, A. A. Hodge and B. B. Warfield, of Princeton Seminary, and to a lesser extent those of W. G. T. Shedd, of Union Seminary in New York, and Augustus H. Strong, of Rochester Seminary, were effective in giving theological respectability and precision to the common belief that the Bible was the verbally inspired and inerrant Word of God. The Presbyterian General Assembly in 1892 formally accepted the Princeton definition of the nature of Biblical inspiration and suspended several seminary professors, such as Charles A. Briggs, from its ministry for their refusal to accept this position. Later in 1910 the General Assembly formulated five points of Christian belief which they declared were necessary for every minister of the denomination to believe. They were (1) the inerrancy of the Bible, (2) the virgin birth of Christ, (3) Christ's atonement for sin, (4) his resurrection from the dead, and (5) his miracles. Dispensationalism, a theological movement that originated in Britain about 1830 with John N. Darby and the Plymouth Brethren sect which he founded, also opposed liberalism in the churches but on the basis of its own particular understanding of Christianity. Dispensationalism, in addition to a strong emphasis upon the inerrancy of the Bible, taught that God had appointed seven ages or dispensations of which the present age was the sixth. Every previous age had ended in disaster, with God bringing judgment upon most of the people while saving a few. Thus dispensationalists taught that the present denominations were corrupt and due to be destroyed at the coming of Christ while only the true Christians would be saved. This theology then gave some hope to people who no longer felt confident about the future of the organized church or the world. Dispensationalism was spread in a series of Bible and prophecy conferences that began in 1878, and have continued since then. Out of one such conference held in Niagara, N.Y., in 1895 came another five points of Christian belief very similar to the ones adopted by the Presbyterians in 1910 except that the dispensationalists included the premillennial return of Christ instead of a belief in Christ's miracles. Dispensationalism was further spread by the publication of the Scofield Reference Bible, which contained the full dispensationalist scheme in its notes, and by the founding of dozens of Bible institutes that trained dispensationally oriented pastors and laymen. From 1909 to 1915 both the Old School Calvinists and the dispensationalists cooperated in publishing a series of twelve small pamphlets called *The Fundamentals* which attempted to emphasize the need for retaining the old doctrines. After 1918 the controversy within the denominations was aggravated by the inclusion of a dispute over the truth of Darwin's theory of evolution. This particular dispute, although not carried on within the denominations as was the dispute over the fundamentals of Christian doctrine, involved many of the same people and was based upon the fundamentalists' belief that evolution conflicted with the Biblical description of creation. Several state legislatures were persuaded during these years to pass laws forbidding the teaching of evolution. The most famous event of the fundamentalist controversy occurred at the Scopes trial when a Tennessee high school teacher was tried in 1925 for breaking one of these laws.

The disputes and schisms that marked many of the denominational meetings during the decade after 1918 quieted after the Scopes trial, but Fundamentalism, although forgotten by the popular press, continued to exist within many congregations of the larger denominations and in some smaller churches that had been formed in protest against what was felt to be the apostasy of the larger groups.

BIBLIOGRAPHY: S. G. Cole, *A History of Fundamentalism* (New York, 1931); N. F. Furniss, *The Fundamentalist Controversy* (New Haven, 1954); C. N. Kraus, *Dispensationalism in America* (Richmond, 1958); L. W. Levine, *Defender of the Faith: William Jennings Bryan* (New York, 1965).

**Fürstenburg, Franz von** (1729–1810). German statesman and educator. He was vicar-general and curator of education in the prince-bishopric of Münster from 1770 to 1805. In that position he carried out a series of educational reforms, especially for the training of the clergy. He was particularly concerned because candidates for the priesthood were often taught by rationalistic professors. Fürstenburg's new University of Münster (1773), with the Jesuit Order providing faculty, was to solve this problem. His career was an early sign of the renewal of German Roman Catholicism in the 19th century.

# G

**Gabriel Severus** (1541–1616). Greek Orthodox theologian. Like many Greeks, Gabriel came to study in Italy. He became pastor of the Greek community of St. George in Venice. In 1577 he was named metropolitan of Philadelphia (then under Turkish domination), but he never ruled. He remained at St. George as pastor and polemicist. His most important writings were a defense of the theory that the Eucharistic bread is specially holy even before the consecration and a response to Bellarmine's charge that the Greek Church was schismatic and heretical.

**Gaius of Rome** (3d century). Presbyter during the time that Zephyrinus was bishop, and a militant opponent of the Montanists. Apparently in response to their claim of possessing John's tomb and authority, Gaius pointed to the monuments of Peter and Paul at Rome. He countered their interpretations of the Fourth Gospel and the Apocalypse by denying that John wrote either (the Apocalypse he ascribed to Cerinthus). He also rejected the letter to the Hebrews. His writings, now lost, were answered by Hippolytus.

**Galilee.** An outer porch at the entrance to English medieval cathedrals in which penitents awaited admission to the church. It was sometimes used as a storage area.

**Galilei, Galileo** (1564–1642). Italian physicist, astronomer, and mathematical philosopher, one of the most brilliant as well as controversial figures of his age. Galileo was also a student of medicine, a skilled draftsman, a painter of ability, and a splendid musician. After studying at the University of Pisa, he was appointed to a lectureship in mathematics there. Later he was forced from this position because he challenged the views of Aristotle and others in the fields of mechanics and dynamics. He fled to Florence and then in 1592 to Padua, where he was a university professor until 1610, when he accepted the chair of mathematics at the University of Pisa. Back at Pisa, he developed a primary interest in astronomy and his investigations led him to embrace the Copernican theory. However, in 1616, the Inquisition declared the heliocentric concept heretical and warned Galileo to forsake Copernicus. Galileo ignored the order and after years of study published his *Dialogue Concerning the Two Principal Systems of the Universe: the Ptolemaic and the Copernican* (1632). This work seemed to the church such a blatant and aggressive defense of the Copernican system that the following year Galileo was hauled before the Inquisition and forced to recant his unorthodox astronomical views. After his sentence of life imprisonment was suspended, he retired to Florence, ignored his recantation, and continued to write on astronomy until his death in 1642.

**Gall** (c. 550–c. 645). Celtic missionary. Born in Ireland, Gall became a monk at Bangor. He left Bangor for Gaul about 590 with Columbanus, and lived in the monastery that Columbanus founded at Luxeuil until the Irish monks were expelled from Burgundy in

610. Columbanus then crossed the Alps to found Bobbio in northern Italy, but Gall remained as a hermit in Switzerland, where he died. On the site of his hermitage, near the river Steinach, was built the famous monastery that bears his name.

**Galla Placida** (c. 390–450). Daughter of Theodosius I and Roman empress of the West. Captured by Alaric in 410, she married his successor, Ataulph, four years later. In 417, two years after his murder, she married Constantius. Upon his death her son Valentinian became emperor, though he was still a child. She ruled for him, waging a war against the Arians, schismatics, and heretics. After the Robber Synod in Ephesus (449), she supported Leo, bishop of Rome, in his battle for a two-nature Christology.

**Gallican Articles.** Four propositions drawn up by J. B. Bossuet, March 19, 1682, stating the rights of the French clergy. A dispute between Louis XIV and Innocent XI over revenues and the appointment of bishops precipitated the demands that (1) denied papal domination over things temporal, (2) declared the supremacy of ecumenical councils over the pope, (3) affirmed the validity of Gallican church laws and customs, and (4) declared the pope's judgment subject to church consent. Influential for a decade, the articles were suppressed by Alexander VIII in 1690 and by Louis XIV in 1693.

**Gallican** (*or* French) **Confession** (1559). Confession of the French Reformed Church. It was adopted as the definitive symbol of faith of the French Reformed Church at its first national synod held in Paris in 1559. The first draft was prepared by John Calvin and his Genevan colleagues on the basis of an earlier French confession of 1557. The first article of the Genevan draft was expanded into five by the Synod of Paris, and the confession was again revised and ratified at the seventh national synod held at La Rochelle in 1571 (hence it is also known as the Confession of La Rochelle). It remained the basis of faith for the French Reformed Church for its first one hundred years while it was permitted to hold national synods, and also through the subsequent two hundred years of persecution and state control. When the church was again permitted a national synod (Paris, 1872), there was much discussion and debate on the Gallican Confession. A liberal minority wished to have complete freedom from creedal subscription. The forty articles of the Gallican Confession are a faithful summary of Calvin's theology and are given a striking unity by

their strong Christological content. The additions made to the Genevan draft include a list of divine attributes, a statement on the canon of Scripture, and a assertion that God reveals himself in creation as well as in his Word.

**Gallicanism.** The collective name for the political and theological opinions peculiar to the Roman Catholic Church of France, which maintained that both the church and the state in France had ecclesiastical rights of their own, independent and exclusive of the jurisdiction of the pope. These theories were developed in opposition to ultramontanism. In regard to the church, it was held that infallible authority was committed to pope and bishops jointly; the pope decided the issue, but his judgments must be tacitly or expressly confirmed by the bishops before they had the force of law. In regard to the state, Gallicanism protested the theocratic pretensions of the medieval popes. The popes, especially Innocent III and Boniface VIII, claimed that they, as vicars of Christ, had the right to interfere actively in the temporal issues of princes and even to depose kings of whom they disapproved. Gallicanism answered that sovereigns held their power directly from God and therefore their secular concerns lay altogether outside the jurisdiction of the pope.

During the papal schism the French theologian John Gerson had presented a primitive form of Gallican doctrine that had been taught at the Sorbonne almost from the time of its foundation (1257). Early formal instruments of Gallicanism were the Pragmatic Sanction of Bourges (1438), by which Charles VII promulgated the decrees of the Councils of Constance and Basel for the reformation of the Christian church and the independence of the French Church, and the Concordat of Bologna, between Francis I and Pope Leo X in 1516, by which the French king's right to nomination to bishoprics and other high ecclesiastical offices was confirmed. During the troubles of the Reformation era, when the papal deposing power threatened to become a reality, the Gallican theories assumed a greater importance, and the constitutional decisions of the Council of Trent were not received in France.

Gallicanism was formulated as an established doctrine of the French Church by the theologians of the Sorbonne in 1663, and again, under the leadership of J. B. Bossuet, by the General Assembly of the Clergy in 1682, which published a declaration now known as the Four Gallican Articles. This document lays down (1) that the temporal sovereignty of the king is independent of the pope; (2) that a general council is above the pope; (3) that the ancient liberties and privileges of the church are sacred; (4) that the infallible teaching of the church belongs to pope and bishops together. This declaration, though it led to a violent quarrel with Rome and was officially withdrawn in 1693, remained the typical Gallican manifesto.

Gallican principles were preached throughout the 18th century by the opponents of the bull *Unigenitus* (Sept. 8, 1713). The Organic Articles added to Napoleon's Concordat with the papacy in 1801 included Gallican provisions, and Napoleon himself favored the Gallican party among his bishops. After the Restoration, however, the overthrow of Napoleon, the decline of the old regime, and the works of the Jesuits and such writers as J. M. de Maistre and H.-F. R. Lamennais reaffirmed a resurgent ultramontanism and undermined the Gallican position. Finally, in 1870, the Vatican Council I put an end to doctrinal Gallicanism by formulating the definitive statement that decisions of the popes in matters of faith and morals, when proclaimed ex cathedra, are infallible and irreformable of themselves and not by the authority of the church. With the repeal of Napoleon's Concordat in 1905 the importance of Gallicanism ceased, except as a historical movement.

BIBLIOGRAPHY: S. Z. Ehler and J. B. Morrall, *Church and State Through the Centuries* (London, 1954); W. H. Jervis, *The Gallican Church* (London, 1882); L. O'Brien, *Innocent XI and the Revocation of the Edict of Nantes* (Berkeley, 1930).

**Gallitzin, Princess Adelheid Amalie de** (1748-1806). Forerunner and instigator of the Catholic "romantic" revival in the Germanys. Although a German field marshal's daughter, baptized a Catholic, she accepted the principles of Illuminism. At the age of twenty she married Russian Prince Dimitri A. de Gallitzin, envoy of Catherine II to Paris, Turin, and The Hague. She had Franz Hemsterhuis, the eclectic and Platonistic philosopher, as guide during the early period of her cultural development. Animated by his concern and the educational innovations of Franz von Fürstenburg, she settled in the Westphalian town of Münster. Studying Scripture, meeting scholars, she came to know poets Matthias Claudius and Johann Wolfgang von Goethe. She returned, after serious illness in 1786, to Catholic orthodoxy and gathered a literary circle called the "Holy Family." These were important personages who were to contribute much to reinvigorating German Catholic life: L. von Stolberg, B. H. Overberg, and the three Von Droste zu Vischering brothers, of whom Clemens August was to become cardinal archbishop of Cologne. Her goal was to acquaint intellectuals with the glories and beauties of the church as she understood them. A missionary son, Demetrius Augustine (1770-1840), became the "Apostle of the Alleghenies."

**Gambetta, Léon Michel** (1838-1882). Leading anticlerical French politician of the 1870's. Descendant of a Genoese family, he earned popularity as a lawyer and orator. Unalterably opposed to monarchy, which he considered a prop of the church, he presided at the birth of the Third Republic (1870), exposed royalist plots, and served as premier in 1881 for sixty-six days. Gambetta's watchword was: "Clericalism, there is the enemy."

**Gandhi, Mohandas Karamchand** (1869-1948). Indian religious and political leader. Gandhi was born at Porbandar, Kathiawar. Upon completion of his law studies in London he was called to the bar at Inner Temple. After two years' practice in India, he went to South Africa in 1893, where he was shocked by the treatment of Indians, and founded the Natal Indian Congress in 1894. From 1906 to 1914, Gandhi developed his program of nonviolence, or *satyagraha,* as a political force for reform and justice. *Indian Home Rule,* published in 1909, set forth his political philosophy and program. When he returned to India in 1915, Tagore saluted him as "Mahatma," the title by which he is usually called. Gandhi supported Britain during World War I, but, disillusioned by the Rowlatt bills and the Amritsar massacre in 1919, he took the leadership of the independence movement, applying his techniques of nonviolence. He was the spiritual head of the Congress Party, while Nehru was its political leader. Gandhi was popularly considered the father of independence, achieved in 1947. All through these years he strove for the relief of the outcastes and for the restoration of an ideal village life self-sufficient and independent of industry and commerce. His headquarters for rural reconstruction was Sevagram Ashram at Warda. A great admirer of Jesus, Gandhi opposed conversion to Christianity. He was assassinated Jan. 30, 1948, at New Delhi.

BIBLIOGRAPHY: E. S. Jones, *Mahatma Gandhi* (New York, 1948); D. G. Tendulkar, *Mahatma: Life of Mohandas Karamchand Gandhi,* 8 vols. (New Delhi, 1963).

**Gannett, Ezra Stiles** (1801-1871). American Unitarian pastor and editor. He was the assistant and successor to William Ellery

Channing as pastor of the Federal Street Church in Boston. Exerting a strong influence as preacher, he helped organize the American Unitarian Association and the Benevolent Fraternity of Churches (a Unitarian missionary society in Boston). He vigorously opposed the transcendental movement and espoused "old-fashioned Unitarianism," holding to a firm belief in the miraculous mission and superhuman authority of Christ.

**Gansfort, Wessel** (c. 1420–1489). Dutch theologian. Born in Groningen, Wessel studied in the school conducted by the Brethren of the Common Life in Deventer, where he was introduced to the teachings of Thomas à Kempis. He continued his studies at Cologne (learning Greek and Hebrew), Heidelberg, Louvain, and Paris. At Paris he defended the nominalist position, a complete change from the realist outlook he had maintained at Cologne. In 1470 he visited Italy, where he came in contact with Renaissance humanism. In 1478 he returned to Groningen, spending his time in writing and discussion. He also paid frequent visits to a Cistercian abbey nearby which became a center for scholars. Here he met Hegius, Agricola, and Reuchlin. He gained the reputation of being an original and fearless theological preacher, although most of his time was spent within academic circles. He was drawn to mysticism, as his later writings show. He made several attacks on the theory of indulgences and the related doctrines of purgatory and personal satisfaction for sin. Known in his own time as the "Light of the World," he has been considered by some to be a forerunner of the Reformation through his great influence in the schools. Luther edited his works in 1521.

**Garbett, Cyril F.** (1875–1955). Anglican prelate. As a priest at Portsea (1899–1919) he became known for his work in the field of evangelism and his opposition to social evils. While bishop of Southwark (1919–1932) he sought to relate the ministry of the church to the largely slum area of south London which composed his diocese. From 1932 to 1942 he served as bishop of Winchester, where he became known for his walks through his rural diocese. As archbishop of York (1942–1955) he was drawn into national and ecumenical affairs.

**Gardiner, Stephen** (c. 1490–1555). Bishop of Winchester, diplomat, and statesman during the English Reformation. From positions of importance at Cambridge, where he espoused the humanist cause, Gardiner was drawn into government service, first as secretary to Wolsey and then on diplomatic missions, especially in connection with Henry VIII's divorce. In 1531, Gardiner was given the bishopric of Winchester, and for the next several years tried to follow a course of accommodation to Henry's antipapal legislation while restraining the more extreme Protestants. In the later years of Henry's reign Gardiner was a leader in the Catholic reaction, and because of this, spent most of Edward VI's reign in prison. Released and restored to his see under Mary, he was made Lord Chancellor and again struck a perilous balance, aiding in the reconciliation of England with the papacy but securing the retention of the dissolved monastic lands to their current lay owners. The accusation of vengefulness toward Protestants which since Foxe's time has often been leveled at Gardiner is now known to have been exaggerated; during the Marian heresy trials Gardiner was conspicuously merciful, particularly in his own diocese.

**Garrettson, Freeborn** (1752–1827). American Methodist preacher. Born in Maryland, reared as an Anglican, he came under the influence of Methodist preachers and after a profound religious experience was admitted to the Methodist ministry on trial and appointed to a circuit in 1776. After serving other circuits, he was ordained an elder in 1784. Subsequently, Garrettson continued to travel widely, though increasingly identified with the New York district of which he was made presiding elder in 1789. He retired in 1817 and died in 1827.

**Garrison, William Lloyd** (1805–1879). Abolitionist, reformer, and editor. Through Benjamin Lundy, a Quaker, Garrison turned to the slavery issue. As founder of the *Liberator*, first published on Jan. 1, 1831, Garrison became one of the earliest to demand "immediate and complete emancipation." He was a pacifist, an unbending moral idealist, and relied on the power of moral principles for the conversion of opponents. He devised no practical method of emancipation, repudiating political or military means. His uncompromising, inflammatory, opportunistic, and persistent character was his strength and his weakness. In 1833 he aided in the formation of the American Anti-Slavery Society. Lacking full cooperation from the churches, he accused the clergy of indifference toward slavery. He called the churches "cages of unclean birds, Augean stables of pollution." Disbanding his abolitionist activities after the Civil War, Garrison became deeply involved in protest against social and moral orthodoxy.

**Garth.** A small enclosed yard or court surrounded by the cloisters of a monastery.

**Gaul, History of the Church in Ancient and Merovingian.** The first Christian church in Roman Gaul was established at Lyons in the reign of the emperor Marcus Aurelius. Although this early church was initially weakened by many persecutions, its overall effect on Gaul was great because it satisfied a pressing need for an organized religious system. The Romans, in their conquest of Gaul, had destroyed the old Druid religion, but could offer no new religion to replace it. The Christian faith, however, which quickly gained many converts, was now to remedy this deficiency.

With the conversion of Constantine to Christianity in 313, the church in Gaul rested more firmly on its foundations. A council held at Arles in 314 and attended by bishops from all the Western Roman provinces successfully established many institutional canons. Thus organized, the church used its strength to launch attacks on those heretical groups, especially the Arians, which threatened it. The great churchmen of those times, such as Hilary of Poitiers (c. 351) and Martin of Tours (319–400), were instrumental in obtaining the victory of the orthodox cause.

Perhaps the greatest success was the conversion of the Arian Frankish peoples who invaded Gaul about 350. Gregory of Tours, in his *History of the Franks,* has set down a moving account of the conversion of Clovis, the leader of these Franks, in 496. Clovis, a brilliant military leader as well as a convert to orthodoxy, was able by the time of his death to extend his control over all of Gaul, and thus to consolidate this territory under orthodox auspices. It was also at this time that monasticism, which had been introduced into Gaul by the Egyptian ascetic John Cassian about 400, gained a firmer footing.

In the time of the Merovingians, as the house of Clovis and his descendants was called, the church came to be controlled chiefly by the bishops. The dioceses that had been established in the days of Roman Gaul corresponded roughly to the old Roman urban centers. From these urban bases, the bishops extended their control over the surrounding regions, which were under the jurisdiction of lesser clergymen. Until the 7th century when Pope Gregory the Great initiated measures to consolidate the church under papal authority, allegiance was to the bishop rather than to the pope.

Politically, the Merovingian period was one of constant strife. There was no sense of a "state" as we know it today. The Germanic conception of kingship was based primarily on property ownership. The domain, upon the death of a sovereign, was divided up among all his heirs, who usually thereupon fought each other for a larger share of the property. This civil strife, plus external attacks by neighboring barbarian tribes, prevented the establishment of any lasting order.

The church took upon itself the task of unification. Realizing that with the passing of the Roman Empire it alone could provide both a refuge and a bulwark for man in a chaotic world, the church began to concern itself with immediate social affairs. It became the sole provider of vast welfare assistance, ranging from care for the poor and widows to the establishment of hospitals. The strongest opponent of slavery, which was then still common in Gaul, the church thus successfully speeded the downfall of this institution. The power of the bishops came to rival even that of the king, and often rulers, faced with episcopal disapproval, changed their policies to make them more acceptable to their bishops.

This is not to say, however, that the Merovingian kings had no power vis-à-vis the church, for even amid the strife of the times the king was the supreme administrative authority. It was by virtue of this office that King Clotaire II proclaimed in an edict of 614 his right to appoint whom he pleased as bishops, thus legalizing a hitherto customary practice. In spite of this policy of secular election, most bishops were pious and able men who became both powerful and respected churchmen.

Uniform church doctrine in Gaul was secured by the frequent holding of church synods. Between the years 506 and 695 there were over fifty such councils, which were usually convened by royal proclamation.

Constant civil strife, however, was to undermine the strength of both the church and the crown. A series of especially weak and even mentally deficient kings came to the throne, throwing the kingdom into anarchy, while the practice of simony became prevalent and lowered the caliber of the clergy. The church was weakened to the point where Charles Martel, after gaining actual political control of the land, leaving the rightful king as only a figurehead, seized substantial amounts of church lands to finance his wars.

A new era was to dawn, however. With the ending of the Merovingian dynasty by the coronation of Charles Martel's son Pepin III in 751, a new church, formed under the guidance of Boniface, was to look to the authority of the papacy.

BIBLIOGRAPHY: Gregory of Tours, *History of the Franks,* 2 vols. (New York, 1965); F. R. Hoare (ed.), *The Western Fathers*

(Sulpicius Severus *et al.*) (New York, 1965); T. S. Holmes, *The Origin and Development of the Christian Church in Gaul* (London, 1911); K. S. Latourette, *A History of the Expansion of Christianity,* Vol. 1 (New York, 1938).

**Geddes, Jenny.** Scottish folklore heroine. Charles I authorized for use in the Scottish churches a new liturgy which appeared in 1636. The Scots resented its Anglican nature and its Roman innovations. Their anger grew when the Privy Council ordered the clergy to use it. On July 23, 1637, in St. Giles's, Edinburgh, the new liturgy was first used. Jenny Geddes started a riot by throwing her stool at the dean and accusing him of saying mass. Riots occurred all over Scotland and eventuated in the National Covenant.

**Geiler of Kaisersberg, Johann** (1445–1510). Celebrated German preacher. Geiler was born at Schaffhausen on the Rhine. After his studies at Freiburg he lectured there and at Basel. In 1478 he was made cathedral preacher at Strasbourg, a post he held until his death. His theology, which was influenced by that of Gerson, was Scholastic and orthodox. His preaching, often on extra-Biblical themes, was clever and earthy. Many works are attributed to him, but only *Der Seelen Paradies* ("Paradise of Souls") is certainly his.

**Gelasian Sacramentary.** A book containing the priest's prayers for Mass, named for Pope Gelasius I (492–496). The manuscript is from the 8th century in France. Although it is based on Rome's worship about 500, it is an adaptation for northern use. The reform of Gregory I may have been based on the Gelasian material, but in any event is later.

**Gelasius I** (d. 496). Pope from 492. Probably a native of Africa, he championed the primacy of Rome, declaring that though the emperor Anastasius I (494) ruled the world, priests had a greater responsibility for it, and they to Gelasius himself, whose responsibility was ultimate. He wrote against the Acacian Schism, and the Pelagians, and was author of *De duabus naturis in Christo.* The Gelasian Sacramentary and *Decretum Gelasianum* are falsely ascribed to him.

**Gelasius of Caesarea** (d. 395). Bishop of Caesarea c. 367. A nephew of Cyril of Jerusalem, Gelasius was expelled from his see because of his adamant Nicene theology during the reign of Valens (364–378), but was immediately restored when Theodosius became emperor in 379. His writings are lost, with the exception of a few surviving fragments.

Photius mentions that Gelasius wrote: (1) a continuation of Eusebius' *Ecclesiastical History,* and (2) a treatise against the Anomoeans, an Arian party which held that the Son was totally unlike the Father. In 381, Gelasius attended the Council of Constantinople.

**Gelasius of Cyzicus** (5th century). The son of a presbyter and the author of a church history (c. 475). Actually the history is little more than a compilation of material from Eusebius, Socrates Scholasticus, Theodoret, Rufinus, and Gelasius of Caesarea. It is divided into three books, which deal with the life of Constantine, the history of the Council of Nicaea, and the three edicts of Constantine. Highly imaginative, it is hardly trustworthy.

**Gellert, Christian Fürchtegott** (1715–1769). German poet and writer. A minister's son, Gellert studied theology at Leipzig (1734), but poor health kept him from a parish. He lectured at Leipzig (1751) in rhetoric and poetry, and wrote unsuccessful comedies, a novel, and artistic letters. Early fame came from *Fabeln und Erzählungen* (1746–1747). His hymns, at times rationalistic, stressed God as Creator and Father; "Jesus Lives" is an exception. Beethoven set some of his hymns to music. Gellert mollified strict rationalism and made it an ethic that drew on pietistic sensitivity.

**General Assembly.** The supreme ecclesiastical court in the presbyterian system of polity. The first Scottish Assembly met in 1560; a national synod of the French Reformed (a minority group) had already met the previous year in Paris. The General Assembly is a court of national extent, composed of ministers and elders, either a minister and an elder from each congregation (as in the Irish Presbyterian Church) or else representatives elected by the presbyteries (or regional courts). The Assembly, meeting annually, has total jurisdiction over the affairs of the national church. Its chairman, called the moderator, is elected from the body for the duration of the year.

**Geneva, Free Evangelical Church of.** A religious body evolving from the *Réveil* of 1813 to 1817. The preaching of Pastors L. Gaussen, César Malan, and others, drew from the Venerable Company of Pastors a Declaration that all ministers were required to sign in 1817 to retain standing. In reaction, free churches were founded in 1818 and 1824, and in 1831 an Evangelical Society within the state church. These elements formed the Free Evangelical Church in 1849. As of 1962, there were

25 churches, 56 ministers, and 94,000 adherents.

**Geneva Academy.** Forerunner of the modern University of Geneva. Founded by Calvin in June, 1559, with the support of the Little Council, it was mainly for the education of preachers and theologians, although a secondary school was included, where the young were trained in Christian fundamentals. The Academy became the center for the expansion of the Reformed Church, with students coming from all over Europe and taking back home the principles of the Calvinist program.

**Geneva Catechism.** The manual of instruction compiled by John Calvin in French (1542) and later translated by him into Latin (1545). Arranged in question-and-answer form, it is divided into five parts: on faith (the Creed), the law (the Ten Commandments), prayer (the Lord's Prayer), the Word of God, and the sacraments. An earlier work of Calvin, the *Instruction et confession de foi* (1537), which is a summary of the 1536 *Institutes* (not divided into questions), is sometimes called his "former catechism."

**Geneva Gown.** The long flowing black gown, loose fitting and with full sleeves, once a mark of scholars, which was adopted by the Reformed pastors as the appropriate dress for preaching and conducting worship after the former Eucharistic vestments had been discontinued. Its use emphasized the ministry of the Word as opposed to a sacrificing priesthood.

**Geneviève** (d. c. 500). Patron saint of Paris. The accounts of her life are largely legendary. She is said to have consecrated herself to the religious life at the age of seven, with the blessing of Germanus of Auxerre, and credited with saving Paris (451) during the siege of Attila's Huns by her prayers and encouragement of the inhabitants. Her influence with the father of Clovis was great, and she supported Parisian resistance to Clovis until he was converted to Christianity. Her relics were believed responsible for having ended an epidemic in 1129.

**Gennadius I** (d. 471). The twenty-first bishop of Constantinople, succeeding Anatolius. About 432, Gennadius led an attack on the Christological teaching of Cyril of Alexandria by writing *Against the Anathemas of Cyril* and *Two Books to Parthenius*. In 458 the emperor Leo designated him to fill the see at Constantinople. Timothy Aelurus, deposed from the see at Alexandria, schemed under pretense of orthodoxy to enlist Gennadius in an attempt to regain his office. Wisely, Gennadius consulted Leo, who banished Timothy and appointed Timothy Solofaciolus to that post in 460. Gennadius' nonpolemical writings include an encomium on the Tome of Leo I and an encyclical against simony.

**Gennadius of Marseilles** (d. 496). Theologian and presbyter. He continued Jerome's *Of Illustrious Men*. He discussed the ecclesiastical writers of East and West between 392 and 495. Most of his writings, largely against Nestorius, Eutyches, and Pelagius, are lost, but his *Epistula de fide mea* is extant. He was active in the semi-Pelagian school in southern France in the 5th century.

**Geoffrey of Monmouth** (c. 1100–1154). Chronicler and chief source for the Arthurian legends. Born in Monmouth and probably of Breton extraction, he was a secular Augustinian canon in Oxford from 1129 to 1150. Between 1136 and 1139 he wrote his *History of the Kings of Britain,* dedicating it to Robert of Gloucester, the natural son of Henry I, and sending a copy to his ecclesiastical lord, the bishop of Lincoln. He was appointed archdeacon of Llandaff in 1140. About 1148 he composed a *Life of Merlin* in Latin hexameters, and in 1152 was made bishop of St. Asaph in northern Wales. Probably because of unrest in the area he was unable to enter his diocese, apparently remaining in England until his death. The *History,* written in Latin, purports to be a translation from the Breton of a book brought to him from Brittany by his friend Walter, archdeacon of Oxford. It traces the history of the ninety-nine kings of the Britons from Brutus to the death of Cadwallader c. 689, and is in fact based on the works of Gildas, Nennius, and Bede, together with elements of Welsh legend and Geoffrey's own imagination. Four of its twelve books deal with King Arthur and are the first coherent presentation of Arthurian history and legend. The whole supplies a tradition for the Britons comparable to those of the Anglo-Saxons and Normans, and it had an enormous influence on later literature.

**George.** Christian martyr and saint especially revered by the English. Known through the legend of his combat with a dragon to liberate a princess, he became a popular saint in the 6th century, but it was not until the 12th century that he was called the dragon killer. Though there is still argument over his historic identity, he is generally regarded as having lived in the latter part of the 3d century.

**George, Henry** (1839–1897). American economist. When he was thirteen he left school, and at fifteen he went to sea. For a dozen years he moved from one printing or newspaper job to another, often experiencing bitter poverty. Finally he was made editor of the Oakland, Calif., *Transcript* and from this platform he began to voice the economic views that made him famous. Economic depression and poverty, he said, could be overcome by establishing what later came to be known as a "single tax" on land values, abolishing all other taxes. Land must be considered "common property" and taxed as rent. These views were set forth in the book *Progress and Poverty* (1879), which gained much public attention, made its author a national figure, and helped to create an atmosphere ripe for social reform. It had great influence upon the rise of the Social Gospel movement.

**George Hamartolos** (*also known as* George the Monk) (842–867). Byzantine historian. Of the life of Hamartolos (from the Greek word for "sinner") almost nothing is known. He is primarily significant because of his four-volume chronicle, entitled *Chronicon syntomon,* covering history from the Creation to the time of the emperor Theophilus. His study of history is based on the works of previous writers, but the contemporary material is of importance. Hamartolos was favorable to the worship of icons, and a large portion of his chronicle is devoted to this and other theological matters.

**George of Cappadocia** (4th century). A learned but avaricious Arian prelate who had been one of Julian the Apostate's Christian tutors. In 357 he was imposed on the Church of Alexandria during the third exile of Athanasius. He treated both Christian and pagan opponents harshly, and was killed by a mob when the news arrived of Julian's recognition as emperor in 361. Julian mildly condemned the action and asked his representatives to secure George's library.

**George Scholarius** (c. 1400–1468). Greek patriarch and member of the Council of Florence. While there he at first favored union with the West. Converted to antiunion views, he wrote several polemical works, some of which are important sources for the Council. He later entered a monastery and took the name Gennadius. After the fall of Constantinople he became the first patriarch under Turkish rule, but finally returned permanently to monastic life.

**Gerald of Wales** (*known also as* Giraldus Cambrensis *and* Giraldus de Barri) (c. 1146–c. 1220). One of the most engaging of medieval writers. Gerald was familiar with the courts of Plantagenet and Capet as well as the Curia at Rome. He was an unrelenting critic of monkish abuses, and his lifelong ambition of becoming bishop of St. David's in Wales was frustrated. He is best remembered for his *Journey Through Wales,* and for two works on Ireland.

**Gerber, Heinrich Nikolaus** (1702–1775). German Lutheran composer. While studying at Leipzig, Gerber was organ pupil of J. S. Bach. He became organist at Heringen (1728), and entered the court at Sonderhausen as organist and secretary (1731). In the course of his life he worked to improve the art of organ-building and to perfect the xylophone. His works, including chorale variations and music for piano and organ, are not highly regarded.

**Gerhard, Johann** (1582–1637). Chief representative of Lutheran orthodoxy during the century following the Reformation. When Gerhard was seriously ill at fifteen, Johann Arndt ministered to him and Arndt's influence persisted. After studying philosophy and medicine at Wittenberg, Gerhard went to Jena and Marburg, traveled widely in Germany (1605), then lectured at Jena. Duke Casimir of Coburg made him superintendent of Hedburg with required lectures in Coburg. Gerhard became general superintendent of Coburg in 1615, but in 1616 he took a lifelong theological professorship at Jena (rector and theological dean). He lectured in all theological disciplines, especially opposing Bellarmine and Georg Calixtus. He freely offered political advice and shared his wealth willingly. Among his works are *Loci communes theologici* (1610–1622), *Meditationes sacrae* (1606), *Confessio catholica* (1634–1637), and voluminous correspondence.

**Gerhardt, Paul** (1607–1676). Lutheran poet and hymn writer. After studying theology at Wittenberg (1628–1642), Gerhardt settled in Berlin (1643) and tutored until 1651. Then he assumed the superintendency at Mittenwalde, and finally a pastorate in Berlin (1657–1669), where he struggled with his elector over doctrine. In 1668 he moved to Lübben to serve as archdeacon until death. Gerhardt was trained in poetry by Buchner, the pupil of Opitz, but he adapted the methods. His hymns approached and sometimes superseded the mastery of Luther's, and he artfully wedded dogma and faith, relying heavily on the psalms. His passion hymns, including "O Sacred Head Now Wounded," were at times contemplative. He wrote 134 German and 14 Latin hymns still extant. The first were published and set to music by Johann Crüger in 1647.

**Gerhoh of Reichersberg** (1093–1169). German advocate of clerical and social reform. Born in Bavaria, he studied at Freising, Moosburg, and Hildesheim before being elected *scholasticus* of Augsburg in 1119. He soon became a canon of the cathedral, but resigned in 1124 to enter the Augustinian Order at Rottenbuch. In 1132 he became provost of the canons at Reichersberg. He carried out several reforms within the order, also advancing the reforms of Gregory VII. He was exiled from his monastery in 1159 for refusing to support the imperialist antipope.

**Gerlach, Leopold von** (1790–1861) and **Ernst Ludwig von** (1795–1877). Two brothers (a third, Karl, taught at Berlin and ministered among workers) who were Pietists and romantics influential at the court of Frederick William IV of Prussia. They were conservative and nationalistic in both politics and religion. Leopold became a general; Ludwig, a judge, and founder of the journal *Kreuzzeitung*. They were prominent in the successful attempt to overthrow the Revolution of 1848, but came to oppose Bismarck's policy as it developed after 1862.

**"German Christians."** Party organized by National Socialists (1932) in Germany to agitate for church union, nazification of teaching, and the purging of "non-Aryans." Predecessors of "German Christians" were the League for a German Church, organized in 1921 by J. K. Niedlich and Pastor Bublitz to free the church from Judaism; the Thuringian "German Christians," organized by Julius Leuthheuser and Siegfried Leffler; the Christian German movement, founded by Werner Wilm (1930); and other groups. Wilhelm Kube formed the Nazi party within the Prussian Church and campaigned to win the fall church elections in 1932. At the same time, a National Socialist Pastors' League was formed by Friedrich Wieneke and Joachim Hossenfelder, a Nazi after 1929. It issued its basis in February, 1932. Then Konopath and Hossenfelder worked to unite the German Christian League, "Christian Germans," and Thuringian "German Christians," adopting the last name under the recommendation of Gregor Strasser. The *Richtlinien* ("guiding principles") were published on June 6, 1932, and the movement became official under Hossenfelder's leadership. The party won one third of the seats in the fall Prussian Church election. When Hitler became chancellor in January, 1933, the "German Christians" were well organized; Hossenfelder was named Rust's adviser in church affairs. Hitler's Reichstag speech in March, followed by "A Mighty Fortress Is Our God,"

feigned church independence. The "German Christians" held their first convention in Berlin, April 3–5, 1933, with 211 Prussian pastors and some politicians (Goering, Frick) attending. Ludwig Mueller became leader of the group in East Prussia. Friedrich von Bodelschwingh was elected *Reichsbischof* in May, 1933, but resigned because of illegal "German Christian" moves. Mueller succeeded him at Wittenberg, Sept. 27, 1933, after "German Christians" won overwhelmingly in national church elections. In November, 1933, Reinhold Krause addressed a rally in the Berlin Sports Palace, and aroused high indignation by his call to "complete Luther's reformation." Finally, toward the end of 1933, the most radical "German Christians" (Hossenfelder, Krause) were dismissed in Hitler's attempt to pacify the situation, even though the evangelical youth were brought into the Hitler *Jugend* in December. Gradually the "German Christians" took over all territorial churches except Bavaria and Württemberg. Hans Kerrl was appointed Reichs minister of church affairs in July, 1935. The renaissance of the day evolved into an apologetic for the German nation. Although opposed by the Pastors' Emergency League and the Confessing Church, the "German Christians" remained in power until the end of the war.

**German Federation of Evangelical Churches.** An organization formed at Stuttgart in 1922 which included all the state churches and the Moravians, but excluded the free churches. It was a clearinghouse for the mutual concerns of these churches. Having gone out of existence under the National Socialist government, it was re-created in 1948 as the Cooperative Fellowship of Christian Churches in Germany, including the free churches and Old Catholics as well as the Evangelical Church.

**Germanus** (c. 496–576). Bishop of Paris from 555. Before becoming bishop he had been the abbot of St. Symphorian at Autun, his native city. He exerted a mediating influence between Frankish kings who were engaged in civil war at that time. It is likely that while a bishop he inspired the edict by Childebert against pagan rivalry on holy days, and perhaps the construction of the church of St. Vincent. This edifice was renamed St.-Germain-des-Prés in 754 when he was reburied in it. It was subsequently destroyed during the French Revolution.

**Germanus of Auxerre** (c. 378–448). French prelate. Like Ambrose, he was trained and active in Roman law and administration before being elected bishop of his native city by the clergy and the people of Auxerre (c. 418). He held office for thirty years and was active in the monastic movement and in the struggle against Pelagianism, in which cause he traveled to Britain in 429 and perhaps also in the period from 444 to 447. Patrick may have been his pupil. He died at Ravenna.

**Germanus of Constantinople** (c. 635–733). Eastern ecclesiastic. As bishop of Cyzicus (712), Germanus, under pressure from the emperor, professed Monothelism. After he became patriarch of Constantinople (715), he had the heresy condemned by a synod. In 730, Germanus was deposed because he was in favor of icons, and after his death he was anathematized along with John of Damascus by the iconoclastic Synod of 754. His dogmatic letters are important for the history of the beginning of the iconoclastic controversy.

**Gerson, John** (Jean le Charlier de Gerson) (1363–1429). French conciliarist. He was born on Dec. 14, 1363, in the hamlet Gerson-les-Barbey of Champagne, from which he was to take the name by which he is known to history. He studied at the College of Navarre at the University of Paris under Pierre d'Ailly. The early academic years were lived against the background of the Great Western Schism. The university would have preferred a general council as early as 1378 but supported the Avignon pope Clement VII. While progressing toward the doctorate in theology Gerson won a reputation for scholarship and gained the friendship of d'Ailly. In 1397, after being proctor of the French "nation" and almoner to the duke of Burgundy, he was made chancellor of the university. When, in the next year, a synod of bishops, clergy, and university representatives voted to withdraw obedience from Antipope Benedict XIII (an important step toward Gallicanism), Gerson disapproved. This he did in opposition to his patron, the duke of Burgundy. Gerson gradually gave wholehearted support to the coalition of rebellious cardinals that summoned the council of Pisa in 1409, for it was clear that neither Gregory XII nor Benedict XIII would abdicate for the sake of the church's unity.

At this time the French political situation complicated Gerson's life. His patron had died and John the Fearless, who had succeeded him, had in 1407 paid for the murder of his rival, the duke of Orleans. The deed was defended by John Petit, a university master, as an act of tyrannicide. Gerson not only hoped for eventual reconciliation, but was beholden to the new duke of Burgundy for his benefice. When the benefice was removed, it was not long before the university condemned the doctrines of Petit. From this time on, much of Gerson's energy was devoted to justifying the university's action. In 1415 he went to the Council of Constance as part of the university delegation. He was one of the major influences at the Council, even though his obsession with the Petit controversy worked directly against what he hoped the Council would achieve. Gerson was never to return to Paris, because John the Fearless had seized it and massacred many of his friends. After some time in Austria, Gerson resided for the last ten years of his life at Lyons, where his brother was prior of the Celestine Convent. He resumed there the goals of his youth—educating children and living the life of contemplation—until his death.

Gerson was involved in various theological controversies. Most significant were his ecclesiology and mystical theology. To overcome the schism he made use of whatever philosophical tools were available. His theoretical foundations were akin to Occamism when arguing "against the vain curiosity" of the Scotists who formalized and distinguished the essence of God beyond endurance. However, because the great theme of his ecclesiology was the church as the mystical body of Christ, he would seem not to have shared completely the nominalist denial of the ontological significance of universals. In his conciliarist treatises an important theme is the Aristotelian notion of *epieikeia*, an "equitable" interpretation of positive law according to the intention of the founder and lawmaker—Christ. Christ instituted the primacy of the church, and when the church itself is in danger a radical step must be taken and all else is subordinate: necessity demands that the letter of the law be overruled by the principle of "equity." The pope is the deputy of Christ, the spouse of the church; but should his presence and rule prove ineffectual or harmful to the church, then the church by divine law must gather together and provide an undisputed vicar at the general council. The council has the full power of the church and is its perfect expression. Scripture and history provide precedents.

Gerson's mystical writings fall into two periods. The later writings contain a doctrine not only of union but of identity between God and the soul in mystical prayer. Mystical theology has its origins in mystical rapture, as described by Pseudo-Denis (Dionysius). This view is a complete break with the pre-1425 writings which held the language of Ruysbroeck to be excessive and dangerous. The mystical union takes place in the virginal, inviolable realm of the soul.

BIBLIOGRAPHY: See J. L. Connolly, *John Gerson, Reformer and Mystic* (Louvain, 1928); J. B. Morrall, *Gerson and the Great Schism* (London, 1960).

**Gesenius, Frederick Heinrich Wilhelm** (1786–1842). German Orientalist, Semitic and Biblical scholar. Serving as professor at Halle after 1810, he was interested in the scientific study of the Semitic languages, especially Hebrew. He had the reputation of being the most popular teacher in his field in Germany. His Hebrew grammar and lexicon went through many editions and considerably influenced Old Testament studies.

**Gesuati.** Religious order founded in the 14th century. In 1367, Urban V, after having been assured that Giovanni Colombini and his followers were free of the errors of the Fraticelli, approved their religious order. They were popularly named Gesuati because of their constant refrain: "Praised be Jesus Christ." Their special devotion to Jerome gave them their longer title of Apostolic Clerics of St. Jerome. Their life was one of personal privation and service to the sick. The order passed out of existence in 1668.

**Gibbons, James Cardinal** (1834–1921). Roman Catholic symbol of "Americanism" and ranking prelate from 1886 to 1921. Gibbons was ordained in Baltimore in 1861, consecrated bishop of Adramyttium in 1868, of Richmond in 1877. The youngest member of the Vatican Council, he was impressed by the contrast between European and American handling of the church-state issue. His social and political views were similar to those of Leo XIII. At the Third Plenary Council of Baltimore in 1884 he issued a strong statement in support of American institutions. Gibbons was made the second American cardinal in 1886 and 1887, the appointment hailed because of his identification with the American system. In 1881 he had issued the first Catholic directive to celebrate Thanksgiving. He noted that Catholic progress in America was due in large part to American liberty. Knowledgeable of non-Catholic views, broadly tolerant, and a participant in public affairs, he was close to Cleveland, Roosevelt, and Taft. Gibbons supported social and economic reforms and was instrumental in restoring papal acceptance of the Knights of Labor, but he repudiated socialism. He sustained Ireland's experiment in cooperation with public school officials and opposed the Cahensly movement to appoint bishops on the basis of national groups. Gibbons marshaled Catholic influence against the popular election of senators, and against initiative, referendum, and recall. Of his numerous books, *The Faith of Our Fathers* (1877) was widely read.

**Gichtel, Johann Georg** (1638–1710). German mystic. Educated at Strasbourg, Gichtel inspected lowland missions with J. von Welz. Association with Friedrich Breckling of Zwolle turned him to mysticism and criticism of the Lutheran Church. Banished from Regensberg and Zwolle, he settled among followers in Amsterdam (with others in Berlin, Hamburg, Magdeburg, Altona, Nordhausen), organized the works of Boehme (1682), and took up Boehme's concept of God and cosmology. He stressed "spiritual marriage" and the Melchizedaic priesthood.

**Gilbert de La Porrée** (1076–1154). Theologian. Born at Poitiers, he studied under Bernard of Chartres and Anselm of Laon, then returned to Chartres, where he taught for twenty years. He was chancellor there from 1126 to 1137, lectured briefly at Paris in 1141 and was appointed bishop of Poitiers in 1142. His *De Trinitate*, a commentary on Boethius' theological tractates, aroused the hostility of Bernard of Clairvaux and he was accused of heresy. He was summoned to a council under Pope Eugenius III at Paris in 1147, but no conclusion was reached, and the investigation was adjourned to Reims in the following year. There the enmity felt by many of the cardinals toward Bernard helped secure Gilbert's acquittal. Primarily a logician, he attempted to reconcile the unity and Trinity of God by introducing formal distinctions between God, his divinity, and his attributes; by affirming a distinction between divinity and the Persons, asserting that only the Persons were eternal, he concluded that only the Person of the Son was incarnate, not the divine nature. Though it was not clear whether Gilbert's intention was solely to separate concepts or to make real distinctions, his opponents implied that he was teaching Adoptianism and tritheism. However, the indictment against him was destroyed and he continued in office until his death, his numerous disciples being known as a doctrinal family, the Porretani.

**Gilbert of Sempringham** (c. 1085–1189). Founder of the English Gilbertine Order. Appointed parish priest on his father's manor, he organized a community of nuns and later also lay brothers and sisters, and a group of chaplains living under the Augustinian Rule. This larger community became the double order of Gilbertines. The order was devoted to charitable works. There were over twenty houses of Gilbertines at the time of their suppression by Henry VIII.

**Gildas** (d. c. 570). A largely legendary figure considered to be Britain's earliest historical writer. His principal work, *The Fall of Britain,* was composed shortly before 548. Despite its name, the work deals only incidentally with history; it is primarily a denunciation of backsliders in Christian society, including its rulers. Research has shown that Gildas is often unreliable, but nevertheless informative for a period otherwise scantily known. His work was used as a source by Geoffrey of Monmouth and Bede.

**Giles of Rome** (Aegidius Romanus) (c. 1246–1316). The most influential of the extremist theologians who surrounded and buttressed the theories and practice of Pope Boniface VIII regarding the relations of the papacy with the monarchies of England and France. Although supposedly a disciple of Thomas Aquinas, his most important work, *De potestate ecclesiastica* (1302), was an unbridled argument for the direct power of the pope in both spirituals and temporals.

**Gillespie, Thomas** (1708–1774). Scottish Presbyterian clergyman. Born at Clearburn, Scotland, and educated at the University of Edinburgh, he received part of his training for the ministry under Philip Doddridge at Northampton. He was licensed for the ministry in 1740 and ordained in the following year. He was appointed minister to Carnock (1741–1752), but objecting to the law of patronage, he was deposed by the General Assembly. In 1761 he founded the Relief Church which continued until 1847 when it merged with the United Secession Church to form the United Presbyterian Church of Scotland.

**Gilson, Étienne Henry** (1884–    ). French medievalist, philosopher, professor until 1951 at the Sorbonne and Collège de France, member of the French Academy. A Thomist, he taught: "There is a spiritual order of realities whose absolute right is to judge even the state and eventually to free us of its oppression." He served at the United Nations. Gilson has written on Thomas Aquinas, Bernard, and Bonaventure. His *Forms and Substances in the Arts* appeared in 1966.

**Gioberti, Vincenzo** (1801–1852). Italian philosopher, priest, and politician, leader of the liberal Catholic neo-Guelph movement. Gioberti offered a scheme for Italian unity (1843) in the 700-page *Civil and Moral Primacy of the Italians.* He called for a confederation of constitutional Italian states chaired by a liberal pope. The papacy was the best instrument for regenerating Italian public life. The revolutions of 1848–1849 dashed his hopes.

**Gladden, Washington** (1836–1918). Congregational clergyman and Social Gospel pioneer. Licensed in 1859, Gladden felt himself freed from "the bondage of an immoral theology" by study of the "practical gospel" of Frederick W. Robertson and Horace Bushnell. Pastor in North Adams, Mass. (1866–1871), he wrote for the New York *Independent* and *Scribner's Monthly* and gained recognition through many books, including *Plain Thoughts on the Art of Living* (1868), which stressed the ethical questions of everyday life. In 1871 he joined the staff of the *Independent* and ministered to the North Congregational Church, Springfield, Mass. (1871–1882). He then became pastor to the First Congregational Church, Columbus, Ohio (1882–1918), and moderated the National Council of Congregational Churches (1904–1907). He helped popularize Biblical criticism and modern conciliatory theology in *Burning Questions* (1890) and *Present-Day Theology* (1913), and was known as a Social Gospel advocate by his *The Christian Way* (1877), *Applied Christianity* (1886), *Social Salvation* (1902), and *The Church and Modern Life* (1908). His own most cherished book was *Where Does the Sky Begin?* (1904). He advocated the right of labor to organize and encouraged cooperation of labor and capital, but repudiated socialism. He sought social amelioration by direct application of the ethic of love in individuals, as inculcated by the churches. "O Master, Let Me Walk with Thee" is perhaps the most famous hymn he wrote.

**Gladstone, William Ewart** (1809–1898). English statesman and four times prime minister of Great Britain. The son of an ardently evangelical mother, he was educated at Eton and Oxford. Some of his closest Oxford friends were among the Anglicans who left the Church of England for the Church of Rome under the impact of the Oxford movement and the Gorham case. Although he never became a Roman Catholic, he did, nevertheless, move to the High Church position and faithfully defended their Tractarian principles throughout his life. In his religious works, *The State in its Relations with the Church* (1838), *Church Principles considered in their Results* (1840), and *Studies Subsidiary to the Works of Bishop Butler* (1896), Gladstone upheld the visibility of the church, the certainty of the apostolic succession, the efficacy of the sacraments as well as the divine institution of the Church of England, and the doctrine of conditional immortality. In his public and private life he was an extraordinarily vigorous man who championed social and political reform, religious toleration, and humanitarianism.

**Glas, John** (1695–1773). Founder of a Scottish sect that spread to England and America. After ordination in 1719 to the ministry of the Church of Scotland, Glas became a popular preacher. By 1725 he had formed a society of persons from his parish for a monthly celebration of the Lord's Supper and for closer religious fellowship. However, his strong Biblicism moved him to oppose vehemently the state church, for which he found no warrant in the New Testament. He embodied his views in *The Testimony of the King of Martyrs,* published in 1727. His views and the book caused his suspension, then deposition from the ministry. At this point he formed his own church (popularly called the Glasites) in Dundee, and eventually congregations were established in Perth, Edinburgh, and other cities of Scotland. His son-in-law, Robert Sandeman, organized the sect's first congregation in England at London in 1760, and he established the first American congregation at Portsmouth, N.H. in 1764. The members of the sect were called Sandemanians outside of Scotland. Glas's views and his attempt to organize a church that followed New Testament texts literally had considerable later influence on Baptists in Scotland and the Campbellites and Disciples in America.

**Glasgow Missionary Society.** First Scottish agency for foreign missions, founded in 1796. The first two missionaries were sent to Sierra Leone in 1797. The next mission was Kaffraria in South Africa, where William Thompson and John Bennie arrived in 1821. After the secession of the Free Church from the Church of Scotland, the Glasgow Society in 1844 transferred its missionaries and the Kaffraria property to the Free Church's Executive Committee of Foreign Missions.

**Glastonbury Abbey.** Originally a Celtic house, it became Benedictine in 708 under the Saxon king Ina. Destroyed by the Danes, it was restored c. 944 by Dunstan. It continued to flourish under the Normans, becoming a center for pilgrimages to the presumed tomb of King Arthur. A 12th-century legend assigned the foundation of the abbey to Joseph of Arimathea. The monastery, once one of the largest in England, was suppressed in 1539.

**Glebe.** A term originally referring to any cultivated land, but later specifically to the land reserved for the maintenance of the parish clergy. The land could be cultivated by the clergy, rented, or leased, but could not otherwise be alienated. In modern times, canon law provides for certain circumstances under which glebe lands may be sold.

**Gnosticism.** Name given to a complex religious movement contemporaneous with the earliest period of Christian history and comprising a wide variety of systems. The origins of the Gnostic movement are difficult to determine because of the different elements, drawn from various sources, which were taken into the Gnostic systems. Scholars have attempted to trace the movement to Hellenistic philosophy, Oriental religion, late heterodox Judaism, and even to Christianity itself, because elements from all of these sources are present in the Gnostic systems. Gnosticism first appears in history as a Christian heresy, but a pre-Christian gnosis has been inferred from the existing documents. Although gnosticism represents a wide variety of religious phenomena, it is possible to group the various systems together under the name Gnostic because of certain tenets that they have in common, and because of the centrality of gnosis (Greek, "knowledge") in all the systems.

Until the last century our only knowledge of Gnostic teaching was derived from the accounts of the systems of Gnostic teachers given in the writings of the early Christian church fathers, who were obliged to oppose the Gnostics. In the 19th and 20th centuries, however, archaeological research has uncovered a number of writings of the Gnostics themselves, mostly in Coptic translation. The most important discovery was made in 1945 when a large jar was unearthed near Nag-Hammadi in upper Egypt which contained a 5th-century Coptic Gnostic library consisting of forty-six Gnostic treatises including gospels, epistles, apocalypses, secret traditions, dialogues, and theological treatises, among which are the now widely known Gospels of Thomas and Philip and the Gospel of Truth, the last perhaps written by the 2d-century Gnostic teacher Valentinus. Most of these Gnostic treatises are as yet unpublished.

The most significant feature that strikes anyone reading the Gnostic texts for the first time is the vast and bizarre mythology that characterizes the formulation of the Gnostic systems, but these strange systems all have at their center a doctrine of redemption, a doctrine that differs from the Christian doctrine of redemption in its view of man and the world. The world, according to the Gnostic view, is intrinsically evil, having been created by an inferior deity or Demiurge who fell from the supreme Deity. Man, as a part of the created world, is thus radically alienated from God, but there is in man a divine spark or spiritual element constituting his true inner self, which longs to free itself from its alienation and ascend to the ultimate God of light and goodness. Interposed between the supreme God and the world are a vast system of aeons, cosmic powers, angels, and semidivine beings who emanated by successive degrees from the supreme Father. This hierarchy of mediators and powers is variously pictured in the different Gnostic myths. Man, being in a state of alienation in this world, cannot deliver himself from his condition by his own efforts. He requires redemption. Redemption becomes in the Gnostic scheme a secret saving knowledge revealed only to the Gnostic. In Christianity, redemption centers around the two poles of grace and faith. In gnosticism, redemption centers around gnosis, or knowledge. The assumption is that if a man knows who he really is in his inner self, what his present condition is, and what his true destiny is, he is liberated by that very knowledge. It enables man to find himself, to see his place in the universe, and to know his true destiny. The function of the myth at the heart of a gnostic system is primarily to reveal to man who he really is. The Gnostic believer sees in the vast cosmological myth a picture of the universe wherein he can place himself; he can see how he became the way he is, and how he can get out of his alienated condition. Discovering that his true inner self is akin to the supreme Deity, he is liberated from the shackles of an alien self and an alien world. He now knows who he is, whereof he is, and why he is alienated, and is by that knowledge enabled to recover his true self and attain to his destiny. In some Gnostic systems a redeemer descends to earth from the supreme God to reveal this saving knowledge to man. In the Gnostic systems that made Christ the redeemer, Christ was seen as one of the aeons who descended upon the human Jesus in order to reveal to man the saving gnosis. He did not really become man or die upon the cross. It was this teaching about Christ, set against the background of the dualistic teaching of the intrinsically evil nature of the world and of man's full human nature, which made gnosticism the greatest single threat to the Christian church in the 2d century. In opposing it, the early Christian teachers saw clearly that the dualism which gnosticism found in the universe struck at the heart of the Christian teaching concerning the unity, love, and creative power of God, the essential goodness of the world and man as created by God, and redemption as entailing the redemption of the whole of man's nature—body, soul, and spirit.

Some of the principal Gnostic teachers are the following:

*Simon Magus.* The origins of his teaching are obscure. There is a Simon Magus, a sorcerer, mentioned in Acts 8:9–24. Other accounts of Simon Magus and his teaching are given by Justin Martyr, Irenaeus, and in the pseudo-Clementine *Homilies* and *Recognitions*. It is by no means certain that these are all the same Simon Magus. In the beginning, from the First God (who is held to be Simon himself) leaped forth the First Thought. She created the angels and powers, the world, and man, but was afterward held captive by the powers and passing through different human bodies finally became manifest in a prostitute. Her name was Helen. To free her, Simon, the First God, appeared as a man. He came also to offer salvation to men.

*Saturninus.* He taught at Antioch, probably during the reign of Hadrian (117–138). Irenaeus, our only source for his teaching, tells us that he sets forth one Father, unknown to all, who made a series of angels and supernatural powers. The world and man were created by a group of these angels. When man had been created, he wriggled on the ground like a worm because of the weakness of the angels in creating him, until the "power above" took pity on him and sent the "spark of life" into him. The God of the Jews was one of the angels who created man, and the unknown Father sent Christ the Savior, who appeared in the semblance of humanity, to destroy the God of the Jews and redeem such as were endowed with the divine spark. Because man's essential nature is the divine spark within him, Saturninus taught an extreme asceticism, rejecting marriage and the use of animal food.

*Marcion* (d. c. 160). Born at Sinope in Pontus, on the Black Sea, he came to Rome about A.D. 140, at first attaching himself to the Christian community there. During the next few years he worked out his own system, and breaking with the Catholic Church founded a church of his own. Interpreting the Old Testament according to the strictly literal sense, he saw an opposition between the God of the Old Testament, a God of wrath and law whom he looked upon as an inferior creator god, and the God of Love revealed in Jesus Christ. He thus rejected the Old Testament and retained only the letters of Paul and an edition of the Gospel of Luke, purged of all "Judaizing" tendencies. Marcion stands apart from the Gnostics in that his system does not have a mythological scheme characteristic of gnosticism, but he can be classed with the Gnostics, since his system shares some of the characteristic features of gnosticism. These include the distinction which he draws between the Supreme God and the inferior God of the Old Testament who created the world, his teaching that matter is evil and that Christ was not truly man, and an extreme asceticism.

*Valentinus.* The most important of the heretical "Christian" Gnostics, he taught at Alexandria and later at Rome in the middle decades of the 2d century. He is probably the author of the newly discovered Gospel of Truth. The Supreme God in the Valentinian system is the supreme Father, Bythos, the unbegotten monad and perfect aeon. From him proceeded by successive emanations a whole series of aeons which form the Pleroma, or fullness of the Godhead. The ultimate offspring of the Pleroma, which came into being by the fall of Sophia, one of the lowest of the aeons, was the Demiurge, the God of the Old Testament, who created the world and man. Some men were created only of the dust of the earth (earthly men); into others the Demiurge breathed a psychic substance (psychic men); and in some men was planted pneuma, or spirit (pneumatic men). To redeem man, the aeon Christ united himself to the man Jesus at his baptism to bring men the gnosis. Earthly men are incapable of salvation; psychic men attain salvation only through much effort; the pneumatics are the true Gnostics. (See ARCHONTICI, BASILIDES, CARPOCRATES, CERINTHUS, MARCION, and VALENTINUS.)

BIBLIOGRAPHY: F. C. Burkitt, *Church and Gnosis* (Cambridge, 1932); B. Gärtner, *The Theology of the Gospel According to Thomas* (New York, 1961); R. M. Grant, *Gnosticism: A Source Book of Heretical Writings* (New York, 1961); and *Gnosticism and Early Christianity* (New York, 1966); and *The Secret Sayings of Jesus* (Garden City, 1960); R. McL. Wilson, *Studies in the Gospel of Thomas* (London, 1960).

**Gobel, Jean Baptiste Joseph** (1727–1794). Alsatian French Revolutionary prelate and politician. Suffragan bishop of Basel, deputy to the States General (1789), he supported the Civil Constitution of the Clergy, consecrated juring bishops, and became metropolitan of Paris in 1791. Renouncing religion (1793), Gobel adhered to the Hébertist faction and participated in dechristianization demonstrations. Robespierre guillotined him along with Hébert, Cloots, and Chaumette on April 12, 1794. While in prison, Gobel was reconciled to Christianity and on the scaffold cried: "Long live Jesus Christ."

**Godfrey of Bouillon** (c. 1060–1100). Leader of the First Crusade and the first Frankish ruler in Jerusalem. He set forth with a large army in August, 1096, and joined forces with other armies at Constantinople. After the fall of Antioch he persuaded Raymond of Toulouse to move on to Jerusalem with him. When the city fell to them in July, 1099, Godfrey was named advocate of the Holy Sepulcher, refusing the title of king. He died there a year later.

**Goehre, Paul** (1864–1928). German pastor and Christian social reformer. While still a theological student Goehre became a laborer in a mill for three months. He wrote an account of his experiences which related poor working conditions to the economic, social, and moral problems of laborers. He studied rural poverty with Weber, wrote about Protestant social movements, becoming a friend of Naumann and general secretary of the Evangelical Social Congress.

**Goerres, Johann Josef von** (1776–1848). German apologist for Roman Catholicism. In early life Goerres was a political journalist supporting principles of the French Revolution and seeking the freedom of his native Rhineland. The Napoleonic era and the continued unrest in Europe disillusioned him and caused him to advocate a more conservative cause, maintaining that the Roman Catholic Church was the only power in Europe that could survive the times. In 1827, King Louis I of Bavaria made him a professor at the University in Munich and Goerres became a leader of the Catholic revival in Bavaria. He was chairman of a group of Catholic intellectuals at Munich which championed contemporary Roman Catholic causes, especially the church's liberty, the monarchy, and the spiritual life. In the 1830's he joined the archbishop of Cologne in strong opposition to the Prussian government's laws on mixed marriages. When the government finally arrested the archbishop, Goerres published his widely distributed *Athanasius* in which he sought to compare the archbishop with the 4th-century Alexandrian bishop and theologian. A devotee of the 19th-century romanticism, he wrote books on German and Indian myths and about medieval mysticism. In his later years he emphasized mysticism in opposition to the rationalism of his day.

**Goeze, Johann Melchior** (1717–1786). German Lutheran theologian and churchman.

Though a dedicated and learned pastor, Goeze is generally depicted as an obscurantist, and the term "bibliolatry" was coined to describe him. This essentially unfair picture of the Hamburg pastor results from his controversy with Lessing over the latter's publication of the work of the deist Reimarus. Goeze attacked Lessing directly and reaped the untempered invective of Lessing's *Anti-Goeze* writings.

**Gogarten, Friedrich** (1887–1967). German theologian. Educated at Berlin, Jena, and Heidelberg, Gogarten was a pastor in Stelzendorf, Thuringia (1917), and Dorndorf (1925). He taught at Breslau from 1930, then moved to Göttingen in 1935, where he remained until his retirement in 1955. In 1966 he traveled and lectured in America.

In early 1920, Gogarten attacked the primary assumption of liberalism, namely, that man's religious consciousness exists apart from the critical judgment of God. In 1922, with Eduard Thurneysen, G. Merz, and Karl Barth, he established the influential journal *Zwischen den Zeiten*. In 1926 he issued a blistering attack on historicism infused with idealism in *I Believe in the Triune God,* claiming that faith is history. He opposed the argument that a historical form contains timeless truth. Gogarten became a leader in the dialectical movement.

In his *Political Ethics* he set about to determine how his historical perspective affected human relations. He concluded that interpersonal relations were primary, and individuality secondary; ethics derives from the contingent relations of history. Properly understood, the state is the basis for the individual. During the years of National Socialism, he supported the "German Christians."

After World War II, Gogarten's interest shifted and he considered the relationship of secularization to Christianity. He relied heavily on Luther in attempting to distinguish the elements of secularization. Secularization properly includes the desacralization of the world and the proper distinction of faith and works. Man's selfish affirmation apart from faith is secularism. The world should be committed to reason; faith has nothing to fear. Only when secularization tends to become religious is it out of bounds. In time, Gogarten endorsed the demythologization of Bultmann. He emphasized that Jesus, God's revelation, must be approached through his humanity, his true Sonship. In addition to the titles cited, Gogarten's works also include *Von Glauben und Offenbarung, Die Kirche in der Welt,* and *Entmythologisierung und Kirche.*

**Gogol, Nikolai V.** (1809–1852). Russian (Ukrainian) author of short stories (*Mirgorod Tales, Arabesques*), plays (*The Inspector General*), and the unfinished novel *Dead Souls,* an indictment of serfdom. His early works were satirical with a blend of humor and melancholy. Later he experienced a religious crisis and psychological depression. After he renounced his former liberal views he was condemned by the intelligentsia. Ill and in despair, he burned the manuscript of Part Two of *Dead Souls* before his death.

**Golden Bull, The** (1356). The thirty-one-chapter constitution (twenty-three enacted on Jan. 23, eight on Christmas Day) issued by Holy Roman Emperor Charles IV, governing the selection of German kings by seven electors: archbishops of Mainz, Trier, Cologne; king of Bohemia, duke of Saxony, margrave of Brandenburg, count of the Palatinate. The document was thus named because of the seal (Latin, *bulla*) affixed in gold rather than the customary wax or lead. Although it theoretically continued in force until 1806, it was not effective after 1648.

**Golden Legend, The.** A story composed by James of Viraggio (Jacobus de Varagine) of the Dominican Order of Preachers in 1255. Designed primarily for preachers as an expansion of the standard lives of the saints, in the vernacular it became a staple devotional book and exercised noteworthy moral and artistic influence into early modern times. Such legends were intended as illustrations of the power of the risen Christ, not as history or biography in the modern sense.

**Golden Rose.** An ornamental rose fashioned of pure gold and studded with precious gems. It is blessed each year by the pope on the Fourth Sunday of Lent (rose-colored vestments). The origin of the custom is unknown, but Pope Leo IX in 1049 speaks of the custom as then being quite old. The blessed rose is sent as a sign of honor to a Catholic state, a religious community, a distinguished person, or a church.

**Goliards.** Wandering poets of the 12th and 13th centuries. They took their name from the mythical Bishop Golias, who was the head of an imaginary "monastic" order devoted to loose and jocular living. Most of them were students and young clerks, although some were men of position in the church. Their poetry was written in Latin and based upon classical and traditional Christian models, but it was infected with the vivacity of the vernacular. The Goliards were rebels against the traditional values and heaped poetic abuse and lampoons on monasticism and the church. Goliardic verse mirrors the rowdy life of the medieval university. A great feeling of freedom is evident in the ribaldry and satire of the poems, which, instead of extolling the Christian virtues, go to great lengths to praise the delights of wine, women, and song. But their verse shows genuine talent as well as freshness. Only a few of the Goliards have been identified. The most famous of them is known simply as the Archpoet; one of his poems, *The Confession of Golias,* ranks with the best of medieval poems.

**Golitsin, Alexander** (1773–1844). Russian prince, statesman, and philanthropist, closely associated with the "mystical" currents of the reign of Alexander I. In 1803 he was named chief procurator of the Holy Synod and in 1810 director of the Central Administration of Ecclesiastical Affairs of Foreign Creeds; thus he represented the state in its relations with all faiths. Although a self-confessed "Voltairian" in his youth, he became committed to an intensely pietistic "religion of the heart" in his adult years. In 1816 he was given the additional position of minister of public instruction; in 1817 his educational and religious posts were combined into a single ministry of ecclesiastical affairs and public instruction, which he held until 1824. In this capacity he sought to apply and enforce Christian principles (as interpreted by the government) as the basis for all education. From its founding in 1812 he served as president of the interdenominational Russian Bible Society, whose influence pervaded the Ministry in both its policies and personnel. His ecumenical approach to Christianity angered many Russian churchmen, who condemned his "religious indifference" and "derogation of Orthodoxy." Together with political opportunists, they succeeded in ousting him both as minister and as Bible Society president in 1824. He continued to serve in the State Council and in minor posts during the reign of Nicholas I.

**Gomar, Francis** (1563–1641). Dutch Calvinist. He joined the theological faculty at Leiden in 1594. Here he stressed the supralapsarian theory of predestination. At first siding with him, Arminius later dissented. This controversy spread throughout Holland, and in 1611, Gomar left the university. In later pastorates and professorships he continued to oppose Arminianism.

**Goodspeed, Edgar Johnson** (1871–1962). American New Testament scholar. Trained at Berlin and Oxford, and under W. R. Harper and C. R. Gregory, Goodspeed taught classi-cal languages, philology, and Bible. Professor at the University of Chicago (1905–1937), he was famous for his discovery of New Testament Greek as a vernacular, and for his translation of the Bible (1923, 1931), which stressed "the simple straight-forward English of everyday expression." His influence was also great on the Revised Standard Version of the Bible.

**Goodwill Industries.** An organization founded in 1907 by E. J. Helms, of Morgan Memorial Church (Boston), as a mission to the unemployed and handicapped to give them work in the reconditioning of cast-off materials. By 1910 it had become a national organization. In 1918 the Board of Home Missions of the Methodist Episcopal Church organized a Bureau of Goodwill Industries which in 1920 found its place in the discipline of the Methodist Episcopal Church. By 1934 this concept of Industrial Evangelism and Social Service had become both an interdenominational and international enterprise serving ninety-five major cities in the United States and ten other nations from Norway to Australia.

**Gordon, Adoniram Judson** (1836–1895). Pastor of the Clarendon Street Baptist Church in Boston from 1869 to his death. Under his leadership it became a center of revival and philanthropic work. He was a collaborator with Dwight L. Moody and a fervent advocate of missions and prohibition. The Boston Missionary Training School was founded by him and he supported the Industrial Temporary Home. Holding to the premillennial Second Coming of Christ, he opposed the Social Gospel movement.

**Gordon, Charles William** (1860–1937). He was born at Indian Lands, Glengarry Co., Canada West, and educated at the University of Toronto (A.B., 1883) and Knox College. He married Helen Skinner in 1899. After ordination by the Presbyterian Church in 1890 he served as a missionary in the Northwest Territories until 1893. The following year he became minister of St. Stephen's Church, Winnipeg, where he remained for the rest of his life. He was elected a fellow of the Royal Society of Canada in 1904, and moderator of the Presbyterian Church in Canada in 1921. He became a popular Canadian novelist writing under the nom de plume Ralph Connor.

**Gordon, George Angier** (1853–1929). Pastor of Old South Church, Boston, from 1884. Gordon helped introduce liberal theology into Congregationalism. Influenced by idealism and transcendentalism, he stressed man's free moral agency and the ethical character of religion. At the same time he was severely critical of sentimentalism. Representative works of his include *Immortality and the New Theodicy* (1897) and *Through Man to God* (1906).

**Gore, Charles** (1853–1932). Preeminent Anglican divine. Gore synthesized the tradition of Tractarian religion with historico-Biblical criticism and a keen social consciousness. Oxford-educated, a fellow of Trinity College (1875), he became first principal of Pusey House (1884). He edited *Lux Mundi* (1889), essays stressing incarnation as a clue to Christian faith, of which his own on Biblical inspiration and affirming kenosis was most startling to traditionalists. Monographs on the High Church doctrine of episcopacy, the incarnation, and the Eucharist followed. Gore founded the Community of the Resurrection (1893) and was its head until 1901. Elected bishop of Worcester (1902), he was instrumental in dividing the diocese and was first bishop of Birmingham (1905). He was translated to Oxford (1911) but resigned in 1919. *The Reconstruction of Belief,* a trilogy that he produced from 1921 to 1924, was a Trinitarian work outlining and arguing his "Liberal Catholicism," a reasonable and coherent faith resting on historical grounds. He lectured and was dean of theology at King's College, London (1924–1928), continuing to write and give voice to those peculiar tenets which marked him, namely his vigorous defense of the creeds against liberal criticism, his avid resistance to compromising episcopacy by union with Free Churches (e.g., South India), and his stalwart opposition to the Romanizing tendencies of Anglo-Catholics. At the same time he fervently advocated a High Church position in active dialogue with an enlightened world view.

**Gorham Case.** A minor issue over baptismal regeneration between a somewhat intransigent Tractarian bishop and a somewhat unorthodox Anglican Evangelical parson which became a national controversy between church and state and a cause of the defection of some significant Anglicans to the Roman Catholic Church. In 1848 the Tractarian bishop of Exeter, Henry Phillpotts, refused to institute a priest of his diocese, George C. Gorham, to a parish in Brampford Speke. After examining Gorham in December, 1847, and in March, 1848, Phillpotts claimed that Gorham held unorthodox views on baptismal regeneration. Apparently, Gorham believed that regeneration may or may not take place in baptism, which was in opposition to the English Prayer Book baptismal service. After losing an appeal to the Court of Arches, Gorham appealed to and was upheld by the Judicial Committee of the Privy Council on the ground that his teaching did not clearly violate Anglican formularies. The case further inflamed differences between Tractarians and Evangelicals in England, causing Tractarians led by John Keble, Edward Pusey, and others to question seriously the right of a civil court in a strictly ecclesiastical matter. It strongly influenced H. E. Manning, Robert Wilberforce, and others to become Roman Catholics.

**Gorze.** A monastery near Metz founded in 749 by Chrodegang, bishop of Metz. After a period of decline, the observance of the Benedictine Rule was restored in 933 through the abbot John of Vandieres (d. 976). With the aid of Bishops Adalbero of Metz and Gauzelinus of Toul, the monks of Gorze reformed many of the monasteries of Lorraine. The reform movement was eventually absorbed by Cluny and by a new movement led by Richard of Verdun.

**Gospel of Wealth.** The era following 1865 in the United States has been described as the "Gilded Age." It marked the emergence of an industrial nation, the reducing of the remaining physical frontier, and the continued exploitation of the natural resources—all of which was coated with an aura of progress and manifest destiny. The "gospel of wealth" was an attempt by some Protestant clergymen and businessmen to make peace between the reigning "rugged individualism," with its acquisitive urge, and the Christian concept of concern for one's fellowmen. It taught the sacredness of property; the unrestricted accumulation of wealth in a free, competitive society; and the law of stewardship, whereby those who were destined by God to achieve great material prosperity were to hold it as a trust from him for the people, and to use their wisdom in distributing it for the most good to the most people in a way better than they could do so for themselves, either individually or through the agency of the government. This gave a new impetus to the Puritan ideal of hard work and frugality, by giving the American business world divine sanction, and each man a divine responsibility to increase the wealth of the nation. A result of this was an increasing alignment of American Protestantism with the rising middle and upper classes of society.

**Gospels, Apocryphal.** Of all the New Testament documents, the Gospels were most frequently imitated by those who wished to supplement them or even to replace them. Not all of those known about are extant, nor are all of those which were written known about. The sources of information concerning the latter are patristic references and lists such as the *Decretum Gelasianum* and the *Stichometry* of Nicephorus. Some of them were written in or near orthodox circles, but apparently most of them arose in Gnostic or other heretical groups, thus accounting for their eventual disappearance. Recent discoveries at Nag-Hammadi (see GNOSTICISM) in Egypt have added to the number of those already extant a few more clearly Gnostic apocryphal gospels.

1. The Gospel According to the Hebrews. This gospel was current as early as the first quarter of the 2d century among the Nazarenes and the Ebionites. The origin of the name is difficult to trace, but clearly the gospel was first written in either Western Aramaic or Hebrew and later translated into Greek and Latin. In scope it was close enough to Matthew to have appeared to be the Semitic original of that Gospel, although this is unlikely, since it is shorter than Matthew and contains some things not in Matthew. It is unique among works of this kind in being close to the canonical Gospels.

2. The Gospel of the Ebionites. Epiphanius is our only source for this work, and it is not clear whether the gospel was a modification of one of the canonical Gospels (Matthew?) or an original composition. Epiphanius indicates that it presents a view altered in the direction of Ebionite practices—they were vegetarians. It is different from the Gospel According to the Hebrews and may be identical with the Gospel According to the Twelve cited by Origen and Jerome.

3. The Gospel According to the Egyptians. Our knowledge of this gospel comes from Clement of Alexandria, Hippolytus, and Epiphanius. The few fragments of it that still survive show that it was a product of gnosticism, since it is dualistic and enjoins a severe sexual asceticism. In one fragment, Jesus is quoted as saying that he came "to destroy the works of the female," which, interpreted, means "to destroy the lust of birth and decay."

Since the canonical Gospels say little about the infancy and childhood of Jesus or about the period just after his death, these periods are among the favorite topics of the writers of apocryphal gospels.

1. Infancy Gospels: (a) Protevangelium of James. This book was referred to by Origen as the Book of James and it extends from the conception of the Virgin Mary to the death of Zacharias, the father of the Baptist. It was originally written in Greek, and there is now extant no Latin version, although there must have been one, for one was condemned by the *Decretum Gelasianum*. The Protevangelium chiefly purports to establish the perpetual virginity of Mary and is the source of much lore about her, gathering together two groups of legends concerning her. It probably stems from the early 2d century. (b) The Gospel of Thomas. Not to be confused with the Coptic Gospel, this gospel gives an account of the boyhood of Jesus and consists of a series of miraculous acts performed by him. In its present form it is probably less docetic than its original, but it is also much shorter. (c) There are several other infancy gospels, but they are all either briefer or later, or both.

2. Passion Gospels: (a) The Gospel of Peter. A very brief fragment of a quite early (2d-century) work making use of all canonical Gospels, docetic in character and full of anti-Jewish polemic. (b) The Gospel of Nicodemus, or the Acts of Pilate. A composite work consisting of two parts, the first being a story of the passion and resurrection, the main intent of which is to furnish incontrovertible evidence for the resurrection. The second part is the story of the *descensus ad infernos,* the principal idea of which is the delivery of ancient worthies from Hades. The first part could have been written in the 2d century, and the second in the 4th; they were probably joined in the 5th.

3. Other Gospels: (a) The Gospel of Bartholomew is extant in three languages and combines a passion gospel, an infancy gospel, and a discourse; in its present form it is late. A further Bartholomew gospel is in Coptic and is a resurrection discourse, one of a large class of such works. (b) The Assumption of the Virgin deserves a place among this literature, although it exists in several recensions of which the Latin is attributed to Melito of Sardis. The rest are too numerous to mention.

BIBLIOGRAPHY: A. Roberts and J. Donaldson (eds.), *The Ante-Nicene Fathers,* Vol. 8 (Grand Rapids, 1951–1952); B. Gärtner, *The Theology of the Gospel According to Thomas* (New York, 1961); R. M. Grant, *The Secret Sayings of Jesus* (Garden City, 1960); K. Grobel, *The Gospel of Truth* (London, 1960); R. McL. Wilson, *Studies in the Gospel of Thomas* (London, 1960).

**Gossner Mission.** A foreign and home mission society begun during the 1830's by Johannes Gossner (1773–1858), a former Roman Catholic priest who became the Lutheran pastor of the Bethlehem Church in Berlin (1829). Here he established a missionary society which during his lifetime sent out over 140 missionaries, mostly to the Khols of East India. Today the strong indigenous Gossner Lutheran Church (a member of the Lutheran World Federation) stands as the fruit of the Gossner Mission. In Berlin the Gossner Mission conducted schools, asylums, a hospital, and engaged in a large benevolent activity. In the 20th century the Gossner Mission supported the Confessing Church during the Hitler era and worked for the Christian rehabilitation of Germany after 1945, seeking to relate Christianity to the conditions of contemporary Germany.

**Gothic Architecture.** See ARCHITECTURE, GOTHIC.

**Gothic Bible.** A translation of the Bible in the Gothic language made by Ulfilas, the Arian missionary bishop to the Goths. The Books of Kings were said to have been omitted, since he felt that the Goths needed no added incentive to warlike behavior. Today only fragments of the Gospels, the Pauline epistles, Ezra, and Nehemiah survive. One of the extant manuscripts, the Codex Argenteus of Uppsala, contains portions of the Gospels written in silver and gold on purple vellum.

**Gottschalk** (Godescalus) (c. 805–c. 868). German theologian and Benedictine monk. Son of a Saxon count, he was presented as a child oblate to the monastery of Fulda. He resisted the monastic life and was released from his obligations in 829. When Rabanus Maurus, abbot of Fulda, objected, Gottschalk was forced to resume the monastic life, but at the abbey of Orbais. He was ordained a priest c. 840. His doctrine of double predestination, i.e., that some are predestined to salvation and others to damnation and that Christ's death was beneficial only for the elect, brought him into conflict with his former abbot, Rabanus, who was then archbishop of Mainz. Gottschalk was condemned at a synod in Mainz in 848 and remanded to his metropolitan, Hincmar of Reims. At the first Synod of Quiercy, he was deposed from the priesthood for having been uncanonically ordained. Refusing to recant his doctrines, he was severely beaten and imprisoned in the abbey of Hautvillers, where he finally died in a state of mental derangement. The theological controversy continued after his imprisonment. His condemnation was affirmed at the second Synod of Quiercy (853). His supporters, Walafrid Strabo, Prudentius of Troyes, Ratramnus, and Lupus of Ferrières wrote in his defense. Their work and the growing dislike for Hinc-

mar of Reims resulted in a repudiation of the Synods of Quiercy by a synod held at Valence in 855.

**Gounelle, Élie** (1865–    ). French Reformed pastor and pioneer of the ecumenical movement. He was active after World War I in the Life and Work movement, German reconciliation, and the International Christian Social Institute. He favored the prophetic spirit over ecclesiasticism and aimed to lead the churches out of middle-class isolation. In the mid-1930's he warned: "What stands most in jeopardy is not bread but freedom; not the body but the spirit . . . social justice, love, and peace."

**Graham, Billy** (William Franklin Graham, 1918–    ). Famous revivalist of the religious "awakening" of the 1950's. Born of devout parents near Charlotte, N.C., Graham was encouraged from childhood to enter the ministry. His theological training was limited to a course of study at the fundamentalist Florida Bible Institute and a B.A. program at Wheaton College (Ill.), where his major was anthropology. After a few months as a pastor, he became a leader in the Youth for Christ movement, gaining experience in conducting mass meetings. With a group of other revivalists and musicians (his "team"), Graham in 1947 began to hold revival meetings in smaller cities across the United States. His name became famous in 1949 when at a Los Angeles crusade several Hollywood celebrities were converted. During the 1950's Graham conducted meetings in dozens of cities, his most publicized crusade being held in New York City in 1957. In many ways Graham duplicated the methods of Billy Sunday in his revival meetings (his use of an advance man, a large team of "associate evangelists," a soloist and song leader, for instance). His contributions to revivalism have been made in the arena of mass communications with a regular weekly radio program, *The Hour of Decision,* the production of motion pictures, and occasional television appearances.

**Grail, Legend of the.** A cycle of medieval romances dealing with the legendary, miraculous vessel variously identified with the chalice or other vessel used by Christ at the Last Supper. Although the origin of the legend is not known, it was undoubtedly non-Christian. The first work of literature to mention the Grail is the *Perceval le Gallois,* written about 1180 by Chrétien de Troyes. Chrétien associated the story of the Grail with Celtic legend. A short time later, Robert de Boron, in his *Joseph of Arimathea,* united the legend of the Grail with Christian legend. Robert tells how

Joseph, after the crucifixion, discovered the Grail, kept it with him during an imprisonment of forty years, and finally entrusted it to a friend, who carried it to England. The quest of the Grail later became an important motif in Arthurian romance, playing a significant part in Malory's *Morte d'Arthur*. Although there is no historical basis for the legend of the Grail, it was extremely popular in later medieval literature. It remained a tradition outside the church, however, for it never received ecclesiastical approbation.

**Grande-Chartreuse, La.** A monastery in Dauphiné, established in 1084 by Bruno of Cologne, founder of the Carthusian order. Until it was secularized in 1904, the monastery served as the motherhouse of the Carthusians. The present monastery, built in 1676, has been inhabited again by Carthusian monks since 1940.

**Grandmont, Order of.** A religious order founded by the followers of the hermit Stephen of Muret. After Stephen's death, a house was established at Grandmont in Normandy, from where the order spread into France, England, and Spain. An austere discipline with absolute poverty was observed. After a series of internal disputes, discipline became lax. A reform movement in 1643 failed. The order was finally suppressed during the French Revolution.

**Grant, George Monro** (1835–1902). Clergyman and educator. Born at Albion Mines, Nova Scotia, he was educated at Pictou Academy, the West River Seminary, and the University of Glasgow (D.D., Glasgow, 1877; LL.D., Dalhousie University, 1892). He married Jessie Lawson in 1872, having been ordained by the Church of Scotland in 1860, and from 1863 to 1877 was minister of St. Matthew's Church, Halifax. In 1877 he was appointed principal of Queen's University, Kingston. He was elected moderator of the Presbyterian Church in Canada in 1899 and president of the Royal Society of Canada in 1901. He became as outstanding in politics as he was in education.

**Gratian** (*Magister Gratianus*) (12th century). Father of the science of canon law. Gratian's writing and teaching initiated a new branch of learning, the study of church law as a discipline distinct from theology. Born in the late 11th century in central Italy, Gratian became a Camaldolese monk and lecturer at the monastery of Sts. Felix and Nabor in Bologna, center of the renewed study of Roman law. Gratian completed (c. 1140) his *Concordantia discordantium canonum*, better

known as his *Decretum*, a collection of nearly thirty-eight hundred texts on all fields of church discipline. It was a systematic arrangement of the laws and customs, the conciliar and papal decrees, of the church dating to 1139, so designed as to reconcile apparent contradictions. Gratian's work, therefore, did for canon law what Peter Lombard's *Four Books of Sentences* accomplished for theology. Although not accepted by the medieval church as a final authority, the *Decretum* became an indispensable text in teaching and in court practice. There were two chief reasons for its success: (1) Gratian introduced a logical order, the chief divisions of which he took from Roman law; (2) he included dogmatic exposition and discussion. Gregory IX, Boniface VIII, and Clement V added supplements to Gratian's work; these were published with Gratian's *Decretum* in 1582 as Corpus Juris Canonici, or the Code of Canon Law. Very little is known about Gratian's life. He is mentioned in 1143 as consultant to a papal judge, and there is evidence that he was dead before the Third Lateran Council in 1179.

**Gratry, Auguste Joseph Alphonse** (1805–1872). French liberal Catholic priest and philosopher who opposed papal infallibility. Gratry, a man of highest talents, was born at Lille, entered the church, and taught in seminaries at Strasbourg and Paris. He restored the French Oratory (1852) and became professor of moral theology at the Sorbonne (1863). He immediately won attention by contesting with Ernest Renan the historical character of Christ. In 1867 he was admitted to the French Academy, taking the chair that Voltaire had once used. Early in 1870 he wrote and published four letters to Msgr. Dechamps attacking infallibility, then being considered by the First Vatican Council. When Pius IX replied, polemics and pamphlets appeared on the subject. Gratry was condemned for living outside his religious community and obliged to leave the Oratorians. When infallibility was promulgated, he made public recantation. Gratry published half a dozen books on philosophy. He fought the Hegelian principle of identity or nonbeing. Induction or transcendence, he wrote, was necessary to attain the Infinite Being by means analogous to those required for infinitesimal calculus. He praised the French Revolution for giving the world a new meaning for the words "justice," "truth," and "liberty."

**Graves de Communi re.** The 1901 encyclical of Pope Leo XIII concerning Christian democracy. It attempted to clarify the meaning of popular Catholic Action by describing the position of the church on current social questions. Popular Catholic Action, according to this description, is organized action by Catholics, under Catholic leadership, for the well-being of the people. This action is not, under any circumstances, to be identified with a political movement. In modern times, however, the term "Christian democracy" has been subject to political exploitation, which has tended to distort the definition provided in the *Graves de communi re.*

**Great Awakening.** A revival of religious interest that spread across the American colonies from 1720 to the Revolutionary War. This revival was one of the great turning points in the religious history of the United States. By 1700 it had become clear that the pattern of religious life transplanted from Europe to the colonies was not functioning adequately. No one church had been able to obtain establishment throughout the colonies, nor even to maintain its own monopoly of religion within the colonies where it had been established. In addition, spiritual vigor within the congregations was lacking, and the great majority of the population in most colonies had no connection with the churches at all.

The years immediately preceding the revival marked the low ebb of the religious life of America. Historians usually point to New Jersey as the site of the revival's origin. There were really several independent sources that gradually coalesced, but it is convenient to note the congregations of the Dutch Reformed minister Theodore J. Frelinghuysen as one of the earliest manifestations of the revival. Frelinghuysen, beginning in 1720, preached earnestly and strenuously to his congregations in an effort to awaken them from what he viewed as dangerous torpor. Throughout the Great Awakening, ministers who favored the revival strove to bring members of their congregations to a crisis in which they dedicated themselves decisively to the Christian faith. The necessity for conversion was one of the unifying forces within the movement. The work of Frelinghuysen spread through much of the middle colonies, especially in the Calvinistic churches. Among the Presbyterians, the Tennent family was active in spreading the revival. Gilbert Tennent created a great controversy within his denomination by preaching a sermon entitled "The Danger of an Unconverted Ministry," in which he lashed out at ministers who did not support the revival, calling them blind leaders of the blind.

In the 1730's the revival spread into New England and the South, with many preachers of the middle colonies itinerating into neighboring areas with or without the invitation or permission of the ministers residing there, a step that served to increase ministerial animosities. The most prominent of these itinerants was the Anglican and Methodist clergyman George Whitefield, who came to America from England for the second of seven visits in 1739 and preached with astounding success to crowds of up to twenty thousand in almost all the colonies. Whitefield's ministry, appealing to such diverse personalities as Jonathan Edwards and Benjamin Franklin and spread across the whole eastern seaboard, more than any other one factor gave unity to the First Great Awakening. Before Whitefield's coming, the revival had broken out in New England, notably in 1734 in the congregation of Jonathan Edwards, who recorded its progress in his *Faithful Narrative of the Surprising Work of God.* Supported by many other Congregational and Presbyterian ministers in the Connecticut Valley and in Boston, the Awakening proceeded in spite of the active opposition of some ministers who, like Charles Chauncy of Boston, objected to the disorders and excitement. Although the New England clergy generally did not create or condone the disorders, several itinerant ministers, particularly James Davenport of Long Island, seem to have relished the pandemonium that broke out wherever they preached.

In the South the revival spirit was introduced by Presbyterians who were especially active in Hanover Co., Va., where Samuel Davies led the movement. Later in Virginia and the Carolinas the Baptists continued the movement with preachers such as Shubal Stearns, who had led a group of followers to Guilford Co., N.C., from New England. The Methodist phase of the revival also began in Virginia in the parishes of Devereux Jarratt, an Anglican priest who had been favorably influenced by Wesley. In the South the Awakening continued through the Revolutionary War in many parishes.

With the Great Awakening, the individualization of Christianity can be said to have begun. Preachers of this revival stressed that Christianity could not be understood as a body of knowledge to be discussed by a professional clergy or the church as an institution established to regulate community behavior. They insisted that Christianity was concerned primarily with the individual, that no man could count himself a Christian unless God touched him personally. Thus the principles of the old-line churches were alike all undermined and a new concept of evangelism and church order introduced into American religion. It is not surprising, then, that almost every denomination was rent by dissension and often schism while members of different denominations found in this experience unexpected areas of cooperation.

BIBLIOGRAPHY: E. S. Gaustad, *The Great Awakening in New England* (New York, 1957); W. M. Gewehr, *The Great Awakening in Virginia* (Durham, N.C., 1930); C. C. Goen, *Revivalism and Separatism in New England: 1740–1800* (New Haven, 1962); P. Miller, *Jonathan Edwards* (New York, 1959); W. W. Sweet, *Religion in Colonial America* (New York, 1947); L. J. Trinterud, *The Forming of an American Tradition* (Philadelphia, 1949).

**Great Ejection.** The removal of one fifth of the pastors from the Church of England after the passage of the fourth Act of Uniformity (1662). The Restoration Settlement had led to the Act of Uniformity, which reestablished Anglicanism and required ministers to assent to the Prayer Book of 1662 or be deprived of their churches. All ministers of the Anglican Church were to have episcopal ordination, give unqualified assent to a forthcoming revision of the liturgy, and swear that the League and Covenant was unlawful. Many of the clergy would not do this and they were consequently "ejected" from their parishes. Having been thus reduced to poverty, the dissenting clergy were further persecuted by the Conventicle Act (1664), the Five Mile Act (1665), and the Test Act (1673). By these measures, they were prevented from preaching before dissenting conventicles, attempting to alter church and civil government, or holding civil office.

**Great Elector** (Frederick William, 1620–1688). Elector of Brandenburg from 1640 and one of the founders of the Prussian State. To encourage emigration to his thinly populated lands, he pursued a policy of religious toleration that drew persecuted Lutherans, Calvinists, and Huguenots to Brandenburg-Prussia. The Huguenots were given substantial advantages in the Elector's Edict of Potsdam (1685), a retort to Louis XIV, who had revoked the Edict of Nantes.

**Grebel, Conrad** (c. 1498–1526). Anabaptist. Son of a leading Zurich family and humanistically educated, Grebel became a zealous follower of Zwingli in 1522. By 1523 he was a leader in a small group arguing in the name of the Scriptures against infant baptism and in favor of a believer's penitential baptism. A layman, he performed the first adult rebaptism in the home of Felix Manz at Zurich (January, 1525) and went on to preach and rebaptize widely until his death from the plague. (See BLAUROCK, GEORGE.)

**Gredja Protestan di Indonesia.** See PROTESTANT CHURCH OF THE EAST INDIES.

**Greenwood, John** (d. 1593). An English Separatist. A graduate of Cambridge, he was ordained an Anglican. In 1586 he was arrested for holding a private conventicle, and in his examination, he denied the Scriptural authority of the English Church and episcopacy. Released in 1592, he helped organize an Independent congregation (some date this as the beginning of Congregationalism) and was arrested again. The next year, along with Henry Barrow and John Penry, he was executed for sedition.

**Grégoire, Abbé Henri** (1750–1831). French Revolutionary cleric, humanitarian, and legislator. Sometimes forgetting piety for polemic, he aimed to reconcile Catholicism and political liberty. He was the first bishop to accept the Civil Constitution of the Clergy (1790), and moved to abolish the monarchy (1792) and reopen churches (1795). He abandoned his diocese (1801) and served in the Chamber after 1817. He quipped: "Kings are in the moral order what monsters are in the physical."

**Gregorian Calendar.** A revision of the Julian calendar promulgated by Gregory XIII in 1582; also called the New Style Calendar. It has gradually been accepted in most Christian countries and communities. Aloysius Lilius and Christopher Clavius were responsible for the computation. The calendar is in error one day in 3,323 years. It replaced the Julian calendar, which had been in effect since the Council of Nicaea, but which had accumulated an error of ten days.

**Gregorian Sacramentary.** A liturgical book containing the priest's prayers for Mass and other rites, named for Gregory the Great (pope, 590–604). This book was a modernization of the Christian liturgy, introduced by Charlemagne into his kingdom from Rome. Certain changes, probably by Gregory himself, concerned the Kyrie hymn, the placing of the Lord's Prayer after the Canon, and the polishing of texts and chants. The Roman rite is fully developed with Gregory's work.

**Gregory I of Rome** (*called by common consent "the Great"*) (c. 540–604). Pope from 590. Gregory strengthened the power of the papacy in the political vacuum left after the collapse of the Roman Empire, and in fact laid the foundations of the structure of the medieval papacy. Born about the year 540 of a prominent Roman family, he was given as good an education as the Rome of his day could provide. Although he knew no Greek and cared little for classical learning, he early showed marked administrative ability and was appointed by the emperor to head the civil administration of his native city of Rome. Though inheriting wealth through the death of his father, he turned his home into a monastery and gave the rest of his money to the poor. He was later appointed by the pope as one of the deacons of Rome, and subsequently he became the papal representative to the imperial court in Constantinople.

In 590, Gregory was elected pope, and accepted the office only after considerable reluctance. Immediately upon his accession he had to deal with a number of problems that would have appalled a weaker man. He had to attend to the feeding of Rome's poor and to the repair and maintenance of the churches. These labors were aggravated by an overflow of the Tiber that brought a plague upon the city. He managed not only to deal with these difficulties, but to put the church's large physical possessions on a successful financial basis. On top of all this the Lombards were attempting to expand their power in Italy, and Gregory raised armies to keep Rome secure from attack.

Gregory was also zealous for the welfare of the church beyond the Alps, and especially for the missionary expansion of Catholic Christianity. To this end he cultivated friendly relations with the Franks and with the Visigoths in Spain. He is perhaps best known for sending Augustine to establish the faith in England. He is noted for his insistence upon the supremacy of the Roman see, which caused strained relations between himself and the patriarch of Constantinople, to whose use of the title "Ecumenical Patriarch" he refused to give recognition. As a warm supporter of the monastic life, especially of the Rule of St. Benedict, he gave the monasteries increased liberty from the supervision of the bishops to govern their own internal affairs, and was zealous in reforming any moral or spiritual abuses that he found. His great interest in the liturgy caused him to reedit the Missal (the Gregorian Sacramentary) and to give the Roman Canon of the Mass the form that it still has to this day. He probably also revised the texts of the liturgical chant and produced a new edition of the Antiphonary. Whether or not he is the originator of the so-called "Gregorian" chant is a matter of dispute among scholars.

In addition to his administrative duties Gregory did considerable writing. A collection of 854 of his letters have been preserved, forming a valuable store of information about his character and the multitude of his official duties. His most famous work is his *Liber regulae pastoralis,* a manual for the pastoral conduct of bishops that had a wide influence as a guide to the medieval episcopate. His *Dialogues* contain accounts of the lives and miracles of Benedict and other early Latin saints. Their credulity set the pattern for hagiographical writing in the Middle Ages and fostered much of the mentality and practice of medieval piety. His other works comprise a commentary on The Book of Job and a collection of sermons, chiefly on the Gospels.

Gregory's doctrinal teaching is not important in its own right as a contribution to theology, but rather as a reflection of some of the doctrines that came into prominence in the Middle Ages. In the main, Gregory followed the teaching of Augustine of Hippo. He gave prominence to the doctrine of purgatory, popularized angelology, and fostered the veneration of the relics and images of the saints. As a man of great personal character and tremendous accomplishments he did much to give the papacy the prestige and position that it came to occupy in the medieval commonwealth.

BIBLIOGRAPHY: P. Schaff and H. Wace (eds.), *Nicene and Post-Nicene Fathers,* Series II, Vols. 12–13 (Grand Rapids, 1956); P. Batiffol, *Saint Gregory the Great* (London, 1929); F. H. Dudden, *Gregory the Great,* 2 vols. (London, 1905); H. H. Howorth, *Saint Gregory the Great* (New York, 1912); E. Spearing, *The Patrimony of the Roman Church in the Time of Gregory the Great* (Cambridge, 1918).

**Gregory VII** (Hildebrand, c. 1033–1085). Pope from 1073. He was born in Saona, Tuscany. It is generally thought that Gregory entered a monastery, since the anti-Gregorian polemicists referred to him as a false monk. The claim that he belonged to Cluny has been disregarded by modern scholars, since it rests on a misinterpretation of a passage in Bonizo of Sutri, and there are no references to the fact in Gregory's letters to Hugh of Cluny. Hildebrand accompanied Gregory VI into exile after the deposition at Sutri (1046). They went to Germany, probably Cologne, where Hildebrand came into contact with the ideas of church reform coming from Wazo of Liège, Humbert of Cologne, and the reformed monasteries in Lorraine. Leo IX appointed Hildebrand as deacon of St.-Paul-Without-the-Walls. He went as legate to France and heard evidence against Berengar of Tours (1053) and deposed six simoniacal bishops (1055). In

1057, Hildebrand accompanied Anselm of Lucca (later Alexander II) to Milan, where the Patarines and the imperialists had created a schism in the bishopric. Hildebrand proceeded to the court of the empress Agnes. Nicholas II made him archdeacon in Rome, and in this capacity he was in charge of the financial affairs of the papacy for the next thirteen years. He must have been skillful, for later polemicists were to refer to his financial ability. He negotiated the treaty of alliance with Richard of Apulia (1059).

Upon the death of Alexander II (1073), Hildebrand was chosen by the people of Rome as the successor, and the election was ratified by the cardinals. He was ordained priest and then consecrated pope in June, 1073. Henry IV wrote soon after, begging forgiveness for his offenses with regard to simony. Henry's letter is a proof that, at the time, Gregory's election was considered valid. At Brixen (1080) this validity was challenged on the grounds that the cardinals had not elected Gregory, and that Henry had not been informed so that he could give his assent, thus violating the election decree of 1059.

In 1075, Gregory issued the first decree prohibiting lay investiture; it was his response to the situation in Milan, where Henry had intruded his candidate Tedald into the see already held by Atto, the candidate of the Patrines and the pope. The decree was not well publicized, and Henry continued to appoint and invest bishops and abbots. Toward the end of 1075, Gregory threatened Henry with excommunication for violating the reform decrees. Henry replied by deposing Gregory at Worms (January, 1076). At the Lenten Synod (1076), Gregory excommunicated Henry and released his subjects from obedience to him. Whether Gregory intended an effective deposition or merely a temporary suspension of power is not clear. The *Dictatus papae,* found in Gregory's *Register* for that year, claimed among other papal rights the power to depose emperors. Gregory received Henry's submission at Canossa (1077) but never reinstated him in his royal office. That was to be decided at a diet of German nobles and bishops over which Gregory was to preside. The nobles met at Forscheim in the spring of 1077 and elected Rudolf of Swabia as king. The escort that was supposed to conduct Gregory to the meeting never came. Civil war broke out in Germany. After a second excommunication in 1080, and the election of the antipope, Clement III, Gregory suffered Henry's attacks on Rome for three years. His cardinals deserted him, and he was carried into exile by Robert of Sicily (1084).

Apart from his difficulties with Henry, Gregory tried to clarify the relation of the papacy to several monarchies. He chided Solomon, the king of Hungary (1074), for accepting Hungary as a fief of the German king when Hungary had been made a fief of Peter by Stephen of Hungary. To Demetrius, the king of the Russians, he wrote that he had conferred the kingdom of Russia, a fief of Peter's, upon the son of Demetrius (1075). Gregory requested Peter's pence and fealty from William of England; the tax was paid, but fealty was not rendered. Gregory extended the system of papal legates, and substituted the Roman rite for the Mozarabic rite in Spain. The dominant note in Gregory's pontificate was *justitia,* or righteousness, which meant, for him, obedience and humility in fulfilling God's ordering of the world. He considered himself the vicar of Peter, charged with maintaining the rights of Peter's see. He did not believe himself to be an innovator, although his pontificate proved to be a source of later innovations.

BIBLIOGRAPHY: A. J. MacDonald, *Hildebrand: A Life of Gregory VII* (London, 1932); A. H. Matthew, *The Life and Times of Hildebrand: Pope Gregory VII* (London, 1910); W. R. W. Stephens, *Hildebrand and His Times* (London, 1888); G. Tellenbach, *Church, State, and Christian Society at the Time of the Investiture Contest* (Oxford, 1940); J. Whitney, *Hildebrandine Essays* (Cambridge, 1932).

**Gregory IX** (Ugolino, Count of Segni, c. 1145–1241). Pope from 1227. Educated at the Universities of Paris and Bologna, and a nephew of Innocent III, he was appointed cardinal deacon in 1198 and cardinal bishop of Ostia in 1206. He served as papal legate in negotiations between the pope and imperial claimants Philip of Swabia and Otto of Brunswick. In 1220 when Emperor Frederick II took the crusaders' vow, Ugolini preached the Crusade in Lombardy and Tuscany. In 1227 (March 19) he was elected pope, though over eighty years old.

Gregory's pontificate was largely dominated by his struggle with Frederick II. In 1228 he excommunicated the emperor for failure to carry out the promised Crusade. In 1230 the treaty of San Germano reconciled pope and emperor, but in 1239, Gregory again excommunicated the emperor for his hostilities against the Lombard cities and the Papal States. The emperor subverted an anti-imperial council called by Gregory by capturing many of the prelates. Gregory died (Aug. 22, 1241) as the emperor was investing Rome.

Gregory issued statutes for the reform of

monastic houses and in 1233 he initiated the practice of papal inquisition by appointing the Dominicans official inquisitors of France. He was unsuccessful in his attempts to reunite the Greek and Latin Churches. In 1231 he modified the ban against Aristotle's works at Paris, and in 1234 he authorized the collection of papal decretals as codified by Raymond of Peñafort.

**Gregory X** (Teobaldo Visconti, c. 1210–1276). Pope from 1271. A native of Piacenza, he became archdeacon of Liège, accompanied Cardinal Ottoboni on his mission to England, and was elected to succeed Pope Clement IV while accompanying Edward of England on a pilgrimage to the Holy Land. In 1274, Gregory X summoned the Fourteenth General Council at Lyons for the purpose of considering the Eastern Schism, reform of church abuses, and the situation of the Holy Land. Every great state sent a representative to this Second Council of Lyons. The Byzantine emperor sent the heads of the Eastern Church to reaffirm its submission to the Roman see, thereby ending temporarily the Greek Schism (see REUNION ATTEMPTS). During the Council, Gregory X issued the constitution providing for a secret conclave of the cardinals within ten days after the pope's death in order to prevent delays in papal elections. Nationally, Gregory's accomplishments were prodigious in securing peace and harmony. He persuaded Venice, Genoa, and Bologna to end their wars; he reconciled Guelph and Ghibelline in Florence and Siena. In an effort to settle the affairs of the German empire, he secured in 1273 the election of Rudolf of Hapsburg as emperor and invited him to Rome to receive the imperial crown. Having presided at the Council in person, Gregory made his way from Lyons to Rome to crown Rudolf. He traveled as far as Arezzo, where he died.

**Gregory XI** (Pierre Roger de Beaufort, 1329–1378). The last of the Avignon popes. As a young man, he studied law at Perugia, becoming a skilled canonist. At eighteen he was made a cardinal by his uncle, Clement VI. He was elected pope at Avignon in December, 1370, while still in minor orders, ordained shortly after, and crowned on Jan. 5, 1371. He was principally concerned with pacifying the Papal States, which, under the leadership of Milan and Florence, were in revolt against his French officials. When his efforts met with no success, he excommunicated the people of Florence and sent Cardinal Robert of Geneva (later Antipope Clement VII) there at the head of an army. The Florentines appealed to Catherine of Siena to act as media-

tor, and she accepted the task, persuading the pope to return to Italy to restore order himself. Over the opposition of the French king and many of the cardinals, Gregory left Avignon in September, 1376, and entered Rome in January, 1377. Unable to quiet the rival factions in the city, he planned to return to Avignon, but was prevented from doing so by his death in 1378. The problem of electing his successor resulted in the Western Schism. It was Gregory XI who in 1377 condemned the doctrines of Wycliffe.

**Gregory XII** (Angelo Correr, 1325–1417). Pope from 1406 to 1415. A native of Venice, he was made Latin partiarch of Constantinople in 1390, and in 1405 a cardinal. He was elected to succeed Innocent VII, but was deposed by the Council of Pisa. Although he had agreed before his election that he would resign if the antipope Benedict XIII would do likewise, he did not trust Benedict to do so in 1409. He did resign, however, in 1415, at the Council of Constance, thus paving the way for the election of Martin V and the end of the Great Western Schism. Martin then named him cardinal bishop of Porto.

**Gregory XIII** (Ugo Boncompagni, 1502–1585). Pope from 1572. After studying law at the university of his native Bologna, he taught there from 1531 to 1539. Among his students were Alessandro Farnese (later Paul III), Reginald Pole, and Charles Borromeo. Paul III sent him to the Council of Trent in 1545, and from 1559 to 1563 he represented Pius IV there. Elected pope when he was over seventy, he established many seminaries and other institutions, much of the work being entrusted to the Jesuits. He supplied well-trained priests to Protestant countries and sent Jesuit missionaries to Japan; in 1582 he supervised the reform of the Julian calendar. Papal financial policies angered the nobility of the Papal States, however, and a period of turmoil followed. Gregory supported Henry III of France against the Huguenots as well as the revolt of the Irish against Elizabeth I of England. He condemned the teaching of Baius on grace and obtained the Flemish theologian's submission.

**Gregory XVI** (Bartolomeo Alberto—Mauro—Cappellari, 1765–1846). Pope from 1831. A reactionary after the pattern of Pius VII (1800–1823) and his successors, Gregory sought to return to the policies of the 18th-century pre-Revolutionary papacy. In a series of important encyclicals he condemned both political and theological liberalism. *Mirari vos* (1832) was directed against civil, political, and religious liberty; *Singulari nos* (1834) against Lamennais and his platform; *Dum* *acerbissimas* (1835) against the views of the deceased German scholar Georg Hermes. As a young man he had already written a strong treatise on papal infallibility, *Il trionfo della Santa Sede* (1799). As pope he contended that direct control of the Papal States was the only basis for independent government of the church. He did much to strengthen Roman Catholic missions.

**Gregory of Elvira** (d. after 392). Bishop of Illiberis in Baetica, southern Spain, and a vigorous opponent of Arianism. He was closely allied with Lucifer of Cagliari and took up the cause against Arianism after Lucifer's death. In recent years he has been shown to be the author of *De fide orthodoxa*, a *Homily on the Canticle of Canticles*, the *Tractatus Origenis*, and *De arca Noe*. He is noted for his christological interpretation by means of typology.

**Gregory of Nazianzus** (c. 330–389). Eastern Church ecclesiastic, theologian, and one of the Cappadocian Fathers. He was born near Nazianzus in Cappadocia, shortly after his father, also named Gregory, had become bishop of the city. The older Gregory was a leading citizen of Nazianzus and had belonged to the monotheistic Hypsistarian ("worshipers of God Most High") sect. Soon after his baptism, said to have been administered in 325 by bishops on their way to the Council of Nicaea, he was called to the episcopate and was thus one of the few conspicuous cases of a married bishop in the ancient church.

The younger Gregory was trained in rhetoric and philosophy at Caesarea and later at Athens, where among his fellow students were Julian, the future apostate emperor, and Basil of Caesarea. His eulogy on Basil gives a vivid picture of the undergraduate life of the time. On his return to Cappadocia, Gregory taught rhetoric for a while at Caesarea, and was at least a frequent visitor if not a resident at the monastic retreat that Basil had established on his family estate in the wilds of Pontus. In 361 he was ordained presbyter at Nazianzus in response to his father's need for assistance, and with fear and trembling preached his first sermon the following Easter. Soon he acquired a reputation as an able preacher.

This quiet ministry did not last, however. The emperor Valens in 371 transferred most of the cities of Cappadocia to the new province of Cappadocia Secunda. The bishop of Tyana, the new metropolis, claimed ecclesiastical independence from Basil, now bishop of Caesarea, who interpreted the whole action as an effort to weaken his position, and attempted to maintain it by installing friends as bishops in the disputed territory. Gregory allowed himself to be consecrated for the village of Sasima, but never took possession of his see, and retained a sense of grievance against Basil for pushing him into the situation. For a short time after his father's death in 374 he administered the church of Nazianzus, and then spent the next few years in retirement in a monastery at Seleucia in Isauria.

The death of the emperor Valens at the battle of Adrianople in 378 ended the imperial support of the Arians, and Basil's death on the following Jan. 1 left Gregory the ablest representative of the Nicene party in Asia Minor. He was soon called to reorganize the Nicene congregation at Constantinople, where the church had been dominated for a generation by Arians, themselves divided between the ultra-Arianism of Eunomius, the moderate Arianism of the official bishop, Demophilus, and the semi-Arianism of the Macedonians. Gregory began his work in a private house turned into the Church of the Resurrection (Anastasia) where, as he said, the orthodox faith was reborn. Here he delivered the *Theological Orations*, which expounded the Trinitarian doctrine of the Cappadocian Fathers, defending the deity of the Logos against Eunomius and that of the Spirit against the Macedonians, and displayed both rhetorical skill and remarkable familiarity with the Bible. Among Gregory's disciples at Constantinople were Jerome, who admired his Biblical learning, and the philosophical mystic Evagrius of Pontus, whom he ordained to the diaconate. A less happy associate was the adventurer Maximus the Cynic, who became the tool of Alexandrian hostility to Gregory and was clandestinely consecrated as a rival, according to Gregory, by Egyptian bishops who broke into the Anastasia at night.

At the end of 380 the emperor Theodosius arrived and handed over the great churches of Constantinople to Gregory, who now had a considerable following, although the Arians were still strong. The reorganization of the Eastern Church was begun by Theodosius' recognition of the Nicene faith, and completed by the Council that met at Constantinople in 381, later accepted as the Second Ecumenical Council. It recognized Melitius as bishop of Antioch and Gregory at Constantinople. When Melitius died during the sessions, Gregory took his place as president. The Council represented in both doctrine and politics a victory of the Cappadocians and the neo-Nicenes, some of whom had semi-Arian pasts, over Alexandria and the more rigid orthodox such as Melitius' rival Paulinus. Its canons condemn Arianism in various forms and the new Apollinarian heresy. The consecration of Maximus the Cynic was declared invalid, and the Church of Constantinople, as New Rome, was given a place of honor second only to that of Old Rome. The bishops of each diocese (or major division of the Empire) were told not to interfere in other dioceses. The Council's statement of faith has been lost, but from later references it is known to have propounded the doctrines of the Trinity and the incarnation as Gregory taught them. The expanded form of the Nicene Creed commonly used since the 5th century is ascribed to this Council by the Council of Chalcedon in 451; it may well have been Gregory's baptismal creed at Constantinople, and so used at the startling episode of the baptism of his successor.

Upon the arrival of Egyptian bishops, Gregory was subjected to renewed attacks, on the technical ground that he was formally bishop of Sasima and that therefore his transfer to Constantinople was contrary to the Canons of Nicaea. In disgust he resigned and left the city, where his place was hastily filled by the pious but still unbaptized civil servant Nectarius. In Cappadocia, Gregory again took over the administration of the church of Nazianzus, and when the long vacancy was at last filled in 384, he retired to a life of study and devotion on the family estate at Arianzus. There in 389 he died where he had been born. The date is fixed by Jerome's statement in 391 that Gregory had died "three years ago."

Gregory's somewhat romantic career has often attracted attention to his personality to the neglect of his importance as a theologian, though the Greek Church remembers him especially in that capacity as Gregory *Theologos.* It fell to Gregory to expound formally the ideas developed by Basil and later more speculatively presented by Gregory of Nyssa; the Cappadocian Fathers thus produced the orthodox Christian Platonism that has remained the main intellectual tradition of the Christian East. Gregory's preserved writings are sermons, letters, and poems. Several of the sermons, commonly called *Orations,* are of historical as well as homiletic and doctrinal interest, especially his eulogies on conspicuous figures such as Basil and Athanasius, and his discourses at crucial moments in his own career from his ordination to the *Last Farewell* to Constantinople. Among other items of more than personal importance, his letters contain his last contribution to dogma, the refutation of the Apollinarian doctrine of a partial humanity in Christ, on the ground that "what was not assumed was not redeemed," and incidentally defending the term *theotokos* for the Virgin Mary as mother of one who was true God and true man. The Apollinarians in the 380's were a party as well as a heresy, and had even set up a rival bishop at Nazianzus. Most of Gregory's verse was a monument of piety rather than of poetry, but some of the more personal poems have a gentle lyric charm, and the long autobiographical *Poem on His Life* is an important source for Gregory's career and the life of the time.

Gregory was a Christian gentleman and even something of an aristocrat. His will, drafted at Constantinople, shows that, ascetic though he was, he lived in some state with the deacons of his household. His convictions were firm, while his personality was gentle and even shy; hence the ambiguity of his relations with Basil, whose rather brusque leadership he accepted and yet somewhat resented, especially after the Sasima episode. There are elements of weakness in his character, but it is a weakness strengthened by faith.

BIBLIOGRAPHY: P. Schaff and H. Wace (eds.), *Nicene and Post-Nicene Fathers,* Series II, Vol. 7 (Grand Rapids, 1957); D. Brooke, *Pilgrims Were They All* (London, 1937); J. H. Newman, *Essays and Sketches,* Vol. 3 (New York, 1948).

**Gregory of Nyssa** (c. 330–c. 395). One of the three theologians of the late 4th century (the other two being Basil of Caesarea, who was the older brother of Gregory, and Gregory Nazianzus) who are called the Cappadocian Fathers. They appeared at a momentous period in the history of the church just after the Council of Nicaea (325) in the period of the last efforts of Arianism to assert itself against Catholic orthodoxy, and in the period before the final solution of the doctrine of the Person of Christ at the Council of Chalcedon (451). The Cappadocians championed the Nicene cause by asserting the full divinity of the Son. By their efforts the divinity of the Holy Spirit was as firmly asserted as the divinity of the Son, and they gave to the doctrine of the Trinity its final formulation for Eastern theology. They dealt with the Christological problem only in its earlier stage. Gregory of Nyssa is the most profound theologian of the three Cappadocian Fathers. In his own right as a theologian, apart from the particular contribution that he made to his time, he is a milestone in the history of Christian theology.

Gregory was born about the year 330 and was educated chiefly by his elder brother, Basil, whom he often called his teacher. After being a lector in the church he became a teacher of rhetoric. Later, under the influence of Gregory of Nazianzus, he turned his back on this secular occupation and returned to sacred studies and the life of prayer, entering the monastery in Pontus that Basil had founded. In the autumn of 371 he was raised to the see of Nyssa, a small town in his brother's metropolitan district of Caesarea. From the time of his election he became frequently embroiled, much against his will, in ecclesiastical politics and in struggles with the Arians. He was banished from his see in 376 on trumped-up charges by the Arian emperor Valens. After Valens' death in 378 he returned to his diocese. In 381 he appeared as one of the leading theologians at the Second Ecumenical Council at Constantinople, where he valiantly defended the Nicene orthodoxy against the Arians. He died about the year 395.

Gregory's literary production was considerable. He wrote a number of dogmatic and apologetic works that were largely controversial, since he had to define his position, notably in opposition to Eunomius, an extreme Arian who held that the Son was unlike the Father (Anomoeanism), to Apollinarius, who denied that Christ had a human soul, and against the Pneumatomachians, who denied the divinity of the Holy Spirit. His chief dogmatic work, the *Catechetical Oration,* is really a summary of Christian doctrine and deals with the doctrines of God, man, the Fall, the incarnation and redemption, the sacraments of Baptism and the Eucharist, and eschatology. His commentaries on Holy Scripture are not great in number but they are important, especially for his mystical theology. He also wrote a number of ascetical works. Thirty of his letters are extant, and many of his sermons, some of which are important for liturgical theology and practice.

No other father of the fourth century made so extensive a use of philosophy as Gregory did. Platonism is the chief philosophical system that molded his theology, but although he depends upon the teaching of Plato, Gregory's is a Platonism that has become transformed in the philosophical schools and by the Christian teachers before him through whom he received it. Plotinus and Philo are other influences, and there are some Stoic elements in his thought.

Gregory's theology is penetrated by a profound sense of the mystery of God. This expresses itself in his teaching that the essence of God is unknowable by man's intellect. This he asserted against the Arian attempts to reduce the divine nature wholly to human analogies. Reason, however, is capable of illuminating the mysteries of faith, and this point comes out clearly in Gregory's Trinitarian doctrine. It is based on that of Basil, which Gregory develops. Basil drew the distinction, based on a popularized Aristotelianism, between *ousia* and *hypostasis* to express the unity of the Godhead and the distinction of the three divine Persons. *Ousia* is commonly translated in English as "substance" and *hypostasis* as "person." God is *treis hypostaseis* ("three persons") in *mia ousia* ("one substance"). Gregory chiefly developed Basil's teaching in the direction of defending the unity of the Godhead against the charge of tritheism, while preserving the distinction of the Persons in so doing. The three divine Persons are three modes of being of the one Godhead. The Son derives from the Father by generation, and the Holy Spirit proceeds from the Father through the Son. Gregory developed the doctrine of the perichoresis (coinherence) of the divine Persons, whereby they have an inseparable will and activity. Gregory's doctrine of the Person of Christ is chiefly discussed in connection with the teaching of Apollinarius. Setting forth the figure of Christ as portrayed in the Gospels to exhibit his true human nature, Gregory defends the existence of a rational soul in Christ in order to safeguard the redemption, since if Christ's human nature did not possess a human soul, the whole of man's nature has not been redeemed. To express the union of the human nature with the divine nature Gregory uses the terms "mixture," "blending," "mingling." His doctrine of the unity of Person is not entirely coherent and awaited the later Christological developments.

Gregory's doctrine of man centers around the two notions of a pristine state in which man existed in Paradise before the Fall, and a doctrine of the image of God in man. Man was created in the image of God and endowed in his pristine state with all possible virtues and the faculties of reason and free will. Man by his free will fell when tempted by the devil. He thus became enslaved by his sensual nature. The incarnation is the assumption of human nature by God the Word in order to heal a diseased humanity. The incarnation is the principle of the redemption; the resurrection effects it. The death of Christ's human nature and its subsequent reunion with his Godhead in the resurrection is the touchstone of man's death to sin and his rising to share in a restored humanity. The incarnation is the beginning of a new human race. Christ's human nature becomes the fountainhead of a new humanity as Adam's was of the old sinful humanity. Gregory had a ransom theory of the atonement whereby Christ was supposed to have routed the devil by a ruse, but in the *Catechetical Oration* he was given a mystical interpretation of the shape of the cross which points to a profound understanding of its meaning. Gregory saw the four points of the cross as extending toward and encompassing the whole creation, and the figure of the Crucified as he who, being the center of all creation, in the act of his death restores all things to harmony and unity in himself. The new resurrection life is mediated to men through the sacraments. Baptism is a participation in Christ dead and risen again. The Eucharist is at once participation in Christ now by the impartation of his life to men and an earnest of the final resurrection of the body. In his eschatology Gregory taught the final universal restoration of the whole creation, including all men and all spiritual beings and the devil himself, to union with God.

Gregory's intellectual achievement reaches its climax and culminates in his mystical theology. He provided the ascetical and mystical theology for the vast current of spiritual life of his time which centered around his brother Basil's efforts to establish the monastic life in the Eastern Church. The possibility of mystical union with God lies in the affinity that man has with God through his possession of the divine image. Because man is fallen, he must go through the process of purgation from sin before he can enter upon the mystical ascent. In his *Life of Moses,* Gregory provides a type of the mystical ascent. Here the literal events of the exodus are applied to the stages of the journey of the soul toward God, from the leaving of Egypt (allegorically, sin) to the ascent of Mt. Sinai, and thus to the final intuition of God and the beatific vision.

BIBLIOGRAPHY: P. Schaff and H. Wace (eds.), *Nicene and Post-Nicene Fathers,* Series II, Vol. 5 (Grand Rapids, 1954); H. F. Cherniss, *The Platonism of Gregory of Nyssa* (Berkeley, 1930).

**Gregory of Rimini** (d. 1358). Augustinian theologian. After joining the Augustinian Order, Gregory taught in various Italian cities and at Paris. In 1357 he was made general of his order and undertook to reform it, but his efforts were cut short by his death in Vienna the following year. Some students of his work, including Capreolus, thought him a nominalist, but the extent of his nominalism is disputable. The principal influence on his thought, however, was clearly Augustine.

**Gregory of Tours** (c. 540–594). Bishop and historian. Educated for the church, he was elected bishop of Tours in 573 and became one of the most influential men in the civic and ecclesiastical affairs of the Frankish realm. He is chiefly important as the historian of the Franks. Since he had access to state and church documents, his *History of the Franks,* though uncritical, is invaluable for the early history of Gaul under the Franks. He also wrote a number of hagiographical works.

**Gregory Thaumaturgus** (c. 213–c. 275). One of the fathers of the Eastern Church. A convert and pupil of Origen's, he returned to his native province of Pontus as bishop of Neo-Caesarea, which he is said to have turned from a pagan into a Christian town. His brief *Statement of Faith* partially anticipates the Creed of Nicaea; his *Canonical Epistle* deals with problems raised by the Gothic invasion of 252–253. The surname Thaumaturgus ("wonder-worker") comes from stories of miraculous answers to his prayers. The sophisticated Greek Christian thus became something like a medieval missionary saint.

**Gregory the Illuminator** (c. 240–332). The Patrick of Armenia, its chief, though not its first, apostle. His career is shrouded in legend, but apparently under his influence King Tiridates and the Armenian nation formally accepted Christianity about 303. Gregory's son and successor, Aristaces, represented the Armenian Church at Nicaea. Early Armenian Christianity incorporated, among other national customs, a tendency to hereditary succession in the priesthood.

**Grenfell, Sir Wilfred Thomason** (1865–1940). English medical doctor and missionary. Grenfell was stationed in 1892 in Labrador as a surgeon by the Medical Service of the Royal National Mission to Fishermen. He fitted out the first hospital ship to serve fishermen in the North Sea, and cruised annually along Newfoundland and Labrador, stopping at the mission stations. He was instrumental in the establishment of hospitals, schools, orphanages, and co-op stores. In 1927 he was knighted and two years later was made rector of St. Andrew's University. He gained renown through many books, including *A Labrador Doctor* (1920) and *Forty Years for Labrador* (1932).

**Grey Sisters.** A French Canadian community founded by Mother Marie Margaret d'Youville in 1738. Five independent communities have developed since that time. There are four French-speaking congregations. First are the Grey Sisters of Montreal, who now have eighty-six houses in Canada and the United States; (2) the Grey Sisters of St. Hyacinthe, who have ten houses in Quebec, Manitoba, New England, and Haiti; (3) in

1845 were founded the Grey Sisters of the Cross, who administer thirty hospitals and orphanages and one hundred fifty educational institutions; (4) the same year saw the foundation of the Sisters of Charity of Quebec, with sixty-five houses in Quebec and the United States. The English-language congregation, the Grey Sisters of the Immaculate Conception, was founded in 1926 and administers hospitals and schools in Ontario, Saskatchewan, and British Columbia.

**Grindal, Edmund** (c. 1519–1583). Elizabethan archbishop of Canterbury. After an academic career at Cambridge, Grindal was just coming into national prominence when Mary's accession forced him into exile on the Continent. On his return in 1559 he was made bishop of London, being translated to the archbishopric of York in 1570 and that of Canterbury (as Matthew Parker's successor) in 1575. Grindal's sympathies were largely with the Puritans, and in his administration of the diocese of London he had been lax in his enforcement of discipline. But this policy did not befit Elizabeth's chief ecclesiastical adviser, and when, in 1577, Grindal tried to remonstrate with the queen over her severity in repressing Puritan "prophesyings" (meetings for the exposition of the Scriptures), he was suspended from the exercise of his jurisdictional functions. He was never fully active again, and, during his primacy, dissension and disaffection grew unchecked by any strong leadership. Both the Puritans and the queen expected more cooperation from Grindal than he could extend, given the pressures exerted on him by each side.

**Griswold, Alexander V.** (1766–1843). Episcopal bishop. Self-educated in law, Griswold left his practice to enter the ministry and served in Connecticut and Rhode Island. In 1811 he became bishop of the eastern diocese, which under his episcopacy quadrupled and was subdivided into five separate dioceses. In 1836 he became the third presiding bishop of the Episcopal Church in the United States, succeeding Bishop White.

**Grocyn, William** (c. 1446–1519). English clergyman and scholar instrumental in establishing Christian humanism at Oxford in the later 15th century. Grocyn studied in Italy from 1488 to 1490, where he learned Greek and became deeply interested in humanism. Although he wrote little of significance, he was an inspiring teacher who influenced a number of contemporaries, including John Colet, Thomas Linacre, and Thomas More.

**Groen van Prinsterer, Wilhelm** (1801–1876). Dutch Protestant statesman and historian. An aristocrat, educated at Leiden, Groen made Bilderdijk's acquaintance. He served as secretary to William I, although offered several professorships. At first liberal, his reading of De Maistre, Stahl, Lamennais, and especially Haller, and his association with the Brussels *Réveil* of Merle d'Aubigné, led him to Christian faith and political conservatism. Breaking decisively with liberalism, he formed a Christian-historical Antirevolutionary Party in active political life. In the lower house (1840, 1849–1857, and 1862–1865), he battled with the liberal Jan Thorbecke, contending for "school with the Bible," but the secularizing education law of 1857 disheartened him. His political goal was antirevolutionary, not contrarevolutionary; that is, he opposed all revolution in principle. In *Ongeloof en Revolutie* (1847), he saw revolution and unbelief as one. *Handboek der Geschiedenis van het Vaderland* (1852) discussed historically the mutual dangers of unbelief and revolution. In the state, God's sovereignty, not reason, must prevail. In the religious awakening (see RÉVEIL), Groen more than others was church-oriented, calling the Dutch Reformed Church back to its confessions and opposing the Groningen school and modernism. As director of the royal archives after 1833 he issued *Archives ou correspondance inédite de la maison d'Orange-Nassau* (1855–1862), an invaluable source for 16th- and 17th-century Dutch history. Of himself, Groen said, "Not a statesman—but a follower of the Gospel I am."

**Groote, Gerhard** (1340–1384). Organizer of the Brethren of the Common Life. Groote was educated at Aachen, Cologne, and Paris. His interests ranged from canon law and medicine to magic and astronomy. A successful citizen of Deventer and later of Cologne, living on the income of two prebends, Groote was at last converted by the persuasion of Henry of Calcar and returned to Deventer. For five years, he struggled for self-discipline, spending two years in a Carthusian monastery. John Ruysbroeck, Augustinian prior of Groenendael, directed Groote, who in 1379 was ordained deacon and began to preach to both clerics and laity. His reprimands of lax priests brought persecution, while his sermons to the people stirred them to conversion. He urged all to imitate Christ, to follow their consciences, and to preach by exemplary lives. The movement he thus began is known as *devotio moderna,* and out of it grew two fellowships: the Brothers and Sisters of the

Common Life and the Augustinian canons regular at Windesheim. John Cele's Deventer school developed new methods in popular education that included Bible instruction, while members of Groote's circle began translations of the Bible and of hymns into the vernacular. Although Groote was a reformer, he wished for reform within the Roman Church and he adhered to traditional theological doctrine.

**Gropper, John** (1503–1559). Roman Catholic priest and scholar, and an important figure in the early history of the relationships between Roman Catholics and Protestants in Germany. In 1528 he was made an assistant to Archbishop Hermann of Cologne. His combination of humanistic, legal, and theological training made him useful in the archbishop's attempt to reform the churches of his jurisdiction. He participated in the Diet of Augsburg and was the author of the first draft of the book that Charles V commissioned for the Regensburg Colloquy (1541). His position on justification was close to the Protestant understanding, but on the questions of the sacraments and the authority of the hierarchy he was not conciliatory. In later years he fought successfully against his archbishop's attempt to turn over his churches to the Protestants and after this affair wrote many works against Protestantism. On the other hand, he argued at Trent for a revival of the principle of synodical jurisdiction in an effort to democratize the government of the Roman Church.

**Grosseteste, Robert** (c. 1175–1253). English theologian and scholar. Little is known of Grosseteste's early life except that he studied at Oxford and perhaps also at Paris. Shortly after the turn of the 13th century he was a teacher at Oxford, where he achieved considerable fame. He also held several important ecclesiastical offices. At Oxford he became an avid patron of the new Franciscan Order, teaching in their school for some years and doing much to spread their influence. In 1235, he was elected bishop of Lincoln, at that time the most heavily populated diocese in England. As bishop he was tireless in visiting the religious establishments within his diocese, seeking to remedy abuses in the monasteries as well as among the secular clergy. Because of the zeal with which he sought to extend his jurisdiction he became involved in a lengthy dispute with his chapter. The controversy was finally settled only by a papal decree that confirmed Grosseteste's authority over the chapter. His reforming activities also included intervention in the affairs of Oxford University, which lay within the bounds of his diocese. In addition to being a reforming bishop, he was one of the most learned men of the Middle Ages. He knew Greek and some Hebrew and had a profound acquaintance with Aristotle as well as with the Christian fathers. He also did much to influence Roger Bacon through his work in experimental science.

**Grotius** (De Groot), **Hugo** (1583–1645). Dutch statesman, lawyer, and theologian. The son of an influential mayor, he was born at Delft and educated at Leiden and Orléans. He studied under Joseph Juste Scaliger, the French classicist and humanist. At the age of fifteen he accompanied John van Olden Barneveldt to Paris, and by 1599 he was well established as a lawyer. In 1607 he was named fiscal advocate for the Province of Holland. In 1613 he was appointed pensionary of Rotterdam and represented that city in the States of Holland and in the States General of the United Provinces. During this period he began to take a keen interest in theological questions, siding with Arminianism. His defense of Olden Barneveldt's ecclesiastical policy of moderation incurred the animosity of the Counter-Remonstrants, and in the political and religious revolution of 1618 Olden Barneveldt was executed and Grotius sentenced to imprisonment for life at the castle of Louvestein. Here he occupied himself with philological and theological studies. In March, 1621, he escaped by concealing himself in a book chest and lived for many years as a distinguished foreigner in Paris, protected by Louis XIII. Although Grotius was in sympathy with many Catholic doctrines, he did not take advantage of a Catholic conversion to enhance his position. In 1631 he returned to Holland, but after a brief period he left and lived in Germany and Sweden. From 1635 to his death he was the Swedish ambassador to Paris.

Grotius was a profound theologian, well versed in Christian literature. At Louvestein, as well as in Paris, he occupied himself with writing expositions of the Bible, which were published under the titles *Explicatio trium utilissimorum locorum Novi Testamenti* (1640), and *Commentatio ad loca Novi Testamenti quae de Antichristo agunt* (1640). These writings marked a new departure in the science of exegesis. He held that the Bible had nothing to do with dogmatism, and he dealt with the Bible as one would with literary writings, according to grammatical rules, explaining the words of Christ and his apostles by quoting passages from Greek and Latin authors. Discarding the then current belief of Biblical inspiration, Grotius adopted the method of philological criticism. At the same time, he stressed the necessity of ecclesiastical tradition for the right understanding of Scriptural traditions.

His principal religious work, *De veritate religionis Christianae* (1627), was designed as a practical manual to help sailors refute pagans and Mohammedans. In 1627 the Latin version was published, and the book has since been published again and again, and translated into many languages. Grotius attempted to uphold the evidences of natural theology and to establish the superiority of the Christian faith to all other religions.

Grotius' greatest religious desire was peace in the church and a Christianity without discord. He sought in many of his works, as well as by personal attempts, to heal the differences between the various Christian creeds, Protestant as well as Catholic. He was ecumenical in his sympathies, and with the Arminians he believed in the universality of divine grace. He regretted that the Reformation had divided the Christian world and brought so much quarreling among Christians. He wanted Protestantism to accept from Catholicism what was not repugnant to the gospel and to tolerate the Catholic organizations for unity.

His greatest work, *De iure belli ac pacis* (1625), severed law from theology. It gives a summary of the whole law of mankind and by itself has earned Grotius the title of "Father of International Law."

BIBLIOGRAPHY: C. Butler, *Life of Hugo Grotius* (London, 1826); W. S. M. Knight, *The Life and Works of Hugo Grotius* (London, 1925); H. Vreeland, *Hugo Grotius: The Father of the Modern Science of International Law* (New York, 1917); J. Ter Meulen, *Concise Bibliography of Hugo Grotius* (Leiden, 1925).

**Grottaferrata.** A monastery near Rome, founded in 1004 by Nilus the Younger. The monastery followed the Basilian customs of Greek monasteries and was a center for Greek learning throughout the Middle Ages. Later the monastery followed Western customs, but was reestablished in 1881 as a Greek rite house by Pope Leo XIII.

**Gruber, Eberhard Ludwig** (1665–1728). German pastor and leader of several separatist groups known as "The Inspired." In his book *Unterweisung von dem inneren Wort Gottes*, Gruber contended for the direct illumination of the heart by the Spirit. In 1719 he became head of a group of "inspired" communities in Swabia. Though evangelical in doctrine, these groups were influenced by 16th-century enthusiasm and mysticism.

**Grundtvig, Nikolai Frederik Severin** (1783–1872). Danish Lutheran pastor, educator, member of Parliament, hymn writer, and scholar in Nordic mythology. Graduating from the University of Copenhagen in 1803, Grundtvig broke with romanticism in 1811 and became an orthodox Bible Christian. In 1822 he was appointed pastor at the Church of Our Savior in Copenhagen. Three years later he made an "unparalleled discovery" whereby he sought to form an apologetic for orthodox Lutheranism on the basis of "the living Word" that had been confessed down through the ages by the church in the form of the Apostles' Creed. He despaired of defending the faith through use of the written Scriptures, feeling that they had been destroyed beyond repair by the rationalist attacks. He emphasized the role of the sacraments in the Christian life, through which one was initiated and sustained in the church. In 1826 he was placed under censorship for his attack on a work of H. N. Clausen, but the ban was lifted in 1837. During this period a Grundtvigian party arose within the Danish Church. From 1839 until his death he served as the pastor at Vartov, where he became known as an educator through his Danish folk school movement. He also worked for democratic reforms and religious liberty as a member of the Danish Parliament. The authorized Danish hymnbook of 1954 contains some 271 hymns (about one third of the total) by Grundtvig.

**Guardini, Romano** (1885–1968). Italian-born theologian. When Guardini was one year old his family moved from Italy to Germany where he spent most of his life. Ordained in 1910, he received his doctorate from Freiburg in 1915, and subsequently taught at Bonn, Berlin, Tübingen, and Munich. He became a figure of prime importance in Catholic intellectual circles both in Germany and wherever his works were translated. His concern was with liturgical renewal and modern humanism.

**Guéranger, Dom Prosper Louis Pascal** (1805–1875). Benedictine abbot. Ordained in 1827, Guéranger became the restorer of the Benedictine Order in France and the instigator of the liturgical revival in the Roman Catholic Church. He was abbot of the Monastery of St. Peter at Solesmes. Guéranger's works on *Les Institutions liturgiques* and *L'Année liturgique* became the "Bible" of an exclusive, aristocratic liturgical cult in the church.

**Guesthouse.** A separate room or building in a monastery in which guests are entertained. According to the Rule of St. Benedict, the standard monastic rule in the West, hospitality is to be extended to all who desire it. In order that they do not disturb the order of the community, however, they are isolated from the monks. A senior monk is assigned the duty of caring for the guest; the abbot acts as host and takes his meals with the guests.

**Guise, Charles** (1524–1574). Cardinal of Lorraine. The policies of Charles and his brother Francis were largely responsible for the persecution of French Protestants on the accession of Francis II (1559), for the revenge taken against the conspirators of Amboise (1560), and for the massacre of the Huguenots at Vassy, which signaled the outbreak of the Wars of Religion (1562). Charles also adopted an uncompromising Romanist position at the Colloquy of Poissy (1561). Nevertheless, he placed the interests of his family first, and when it suited him he courted the Lutheran princes; he was suspected of being in sympathy with the Augsburg Confession. At Trent in 1562 and 1563, possibly in the interests of Gallicanism, he demanded Communion under both species and prayers in the vernacular. When Pope Pius IV responded unfavorably, he accused Rome of being the seat of corruption and the main cause of the church's troubles. Yet he pressed for the enforcement of the Tridentine reforms in his homeland and invited Philip II of Spain to uphold the Roman cause in France. A less worthy man than his soldier-brother Francis, Charles earned a reputation for duplicity and intrigue.

**Guise, Francis, Duke of** (1519–1563). The warrior of the family, brother of Charles Guise. Henry II made him lieutenant general of France, and he won several contests with the Spanish before Henry signed the Peace of Cateau-Cambrésis (1559). Vehemently opposed to the Protestants and to the Bourbons, Guise became more powerful during the reign of Francis II (whose wife, Mary Stuart, was Guise's niece), but when Catherine de' Medici became regent for the young Charles IX, she showed tolerance toward the Protestants, and Guise organized a Triumvirate (1561) against her policies. This brought about the Huguenot war (see WARS OF RELIGION, FRENCH) and Guise was assassinated while laying siege to Orléans.

**Gunkel, Hermann** (1862–1932). German Old Testament scholar. Gunkel taught at Halle, Berlin (1894–1907), Geissen (to 1920), and again at Halle (to 1927). Indebted to Herder, Wellhausen, Norden, and others, he attempted to establish the original oral tradition of individual events (*Gattungsgeschichte*) prior to their literary embodiment. In writings from 1901 to 1932 his study of Old Testament forms influenced the literary-critical New Testament school as well. Gunkel was one of the founders of the religiohistorical school. Among his many works were *Genesis* and *Die Psalmen*.

**Gunpowder Plot.** A conspiracy, hatched in 1604 and undertaken by a group of English Roman Catholics under Robert Catesby, to blow up both houses of Parliament in session with James I on Nov. 5, 1605. The conspirators hired Guy Fawkes to set off gunpowder stored in the cellar of the Houses, and then planned to seize power. Lord Monteagle was alerted to the plot, which was thwarted. The principals were killed or executed and English animosity toward the papacy was heightened. Guy Fawkes Day (Nov. 5), observed by proclamation in the Book of Common Prayer until 1859, is still a folk festival.

**Gustav II** (*known as* Gustavus Adolphus) (1594–1632). King of Sweden (1611–1632). He was educated to be a strict Lutheran. After a short regency under Axel Oxenstierna he was declared of age and while still a teen-ager led his army to victory over Denmark (1613). In 1617 by the Peace of Stolbova he concluded a treaty with Russia. In 1621 he began a war against the Roman Catholic Vasas of Poland who claimed the Swedish throne. He made sure that Sweden was spared the ravages of war by fighting all his battles in Poland and the Baltic provinces. In 1629 he concluded a six-year truce with Poland. During these years he instituted many domestic reforms with the support of his ever-faithful chancellor, Oxenstierna. In 1630 his disciplined and religiously inspired army of Swedish veterans entered the Thirty Years' War against the Roman Catholic imperial forces. He rallied the demoralized Protestants and defeated Tilly at Breitenfeld (1631). Acclaimed the "Lion of the North" and the hero of Protestantism, he proceeded to drive deep into southern Germany, devastating Bavaria. The following year the Swedish army defeated Wallenstein at Lützen, but it proved to be a costly victory with the death of the king. Gustavus Adolphus' motivations have been variously interpreted, but it is certain that he saved German Protestantism and turned the Baltic into a "Swedish lake."

**Gustav Adolf Verein.** A German mission and aid society designed to defend and promote "diaspora" Protestantism. It was founded in 1832 by the Leipzig superintendent Christian Grossman and refounded in 1842 by the Darmstadt court preacher Karl Zimmermann, with headquarters in Leipzig. Pan-Protestant and international in its support and undertakings, the society has done work chiefly in regard to the construction and support of churches for minority Protestants.

**Gustav Vasa** (Gustavus Eriksson) (1496–1560). Founder of the Vasa dynasty, which ruled Sweden from 1523 to 1720. After the Stockholm bloodbath in 1520, he led a revolt against Christian II of Denmark and reigned as King Gustav I of Sweden from 1523 to 1560. In 1523 he invited the pope to reform the Church of Sweden. Four years later, partly for political and fiscal motives, he led the Protestant forces to triumph at the Diet of Vesterås, which authorized the public preaching of "the pure Word of God."

**Gutenberg, Johann** (c. 1400–c. 1468). German printer who is generally credited with the invention of printing from movable type at either Mainz or Strasbourg about 1450, although the technique had been developed independently several centuries earlier in the Orient. The best-known work of Gutenberg and his associates was his first printed book, a large 42-line folio Latin Bible, often called the Gutenberg, or Mazarin, Bible.

**Guthrie, James** (c. 1612–1661). Scottish minister and Covenanter. Educated at the University of St. Andrews, Guthrie became a regent there. He was at first Episcopalian and zealous for the full establishment of prelacy in the Church of Scotland. By 1639, mainly through the influence of Samuel Rutherford, Guthrie became a Presbyterian. As minister at Lauder and at Stirling he was active in national church affairs and was a member of the General Assembly. The civil and religious situation in Scotland was extremely confused just before and after the execution of Charles I. Guthrie became a leader of a party within the Kirk that saw Scotland's hope in the strict keeping of the Covenant and opposed the parliamentary resolution accepting into military service all but the obstinate foes of the Covenant. This party was called "Protesters" as opposed to "Resolutioners." Many of these strict Covenanters came to feel that their cause would be better furthered by Cromwell than by Charles, who had been crowned at Scone in 1651. Guthrie withdrew his allegiance to the king. After the Restoration, Charles II ordered his arrest and he was condemned for treason, the chief charges centering on his "Western Remonstrance" of 1650, his denial of the king's authority in ecclesiastical affairs, and his book, *The Causes of God's Wrath*. He was hanged June 1, 1661.

**Guyon, Mme.** (1648–1717). French mystic. A woman of personal charm and energy who was a leading propagandist of French quietism. Her mysticism attracted many. Her opponents considered her unbalanced and had her imprisoned. She was released, only to live under close episcopal supervision. She asserted that the essential activity of the Christian life was contemplation of God in which the soul would lose all concern for itself and instead yield "to the torrent of the forces of God."

# H

**Hadrian** (76–138). Roman emperor (117–138). Hadrian did not persecute Christians, though his visit to Athens may have occasioned the work of Quadratus. In 132 he began to rebuild Jerusalem as a Greek city. At this point Simeon bar Kosiba (called Bar-Cochba, "son of the star," from Num. 24:17) began a bloody revolt that lasted about three and one half years and ended with Roman victory. Much of Hadrian's reign was devoted to unifying the empire. He abandoned the policy of expansion.

**Haering, Theodor** (1848–1928). German theologian. Haering was a private tutor at Tübingen (1873) and a deacon in Calw (1876) and Stuttgart (1881). He succeeded Biedermann at Zurich (1886), and Ritschl at Göttingen (1889), then moved to Tübingen (1894–1920). Haering modified Ritschlianism, and gave a strong ethical significance to the life and work of Jesus. His works were primarily exegetical.

**Hagenau, Conference of** (June–July, 1540). A meeting called by Emperor Charles V to discuss Roman Catholic and Protestant differences. A papal legate was sent only as an adviser. The Roman Catholic princes refused any compromises. Charles wanted to arbitrate, but the Protestants insisted that only Scripture could judge doctrine. The conference was adjourned because the parties held irreconcilable views on the nature of the church, and another conference was called at Worms.

**Hagia Sophia.** See SANCTA SOPHIA.

**Hagiography.** The study and recording of the lives of the saints. The worship of the saints gave rise in both the East and the West to a considerable number of hagiographic documents that were religious in character and edifying in their moral purpose. Such were the lists of martyrs drawn up in the Middle Ages which became the nucleus of martyrologies and from which the literature of the saints' lives developed. Ancient Christian hagiography came into being when the ideal of sanctity represented by monks and bishops was added to that of the martyrs. Like the legends of the martyrs, the lives of the saints produced an immense and popular literature from the 6th to the 10th centuries.

Like the martyrologies, hagiographic literature came to be written under two distinct influences: the anonymous creator of oral tradition, and the man of letters developing a written tradition by recording and shaping the saintly legend in narratives, annals, and chronicles.

The 6th and 7th centuries were, par excellence, the centuries of hagiographers. The three saints' lives most influential in fixing the tradition of hagiography in the West were: Athanasius' *Life of St. Antony,* given to the West in the translation of the Antiochene author Evagrius; Sulpicius' *Life of St. Martin,* and Jerome's *Life of St. Paul of Thebes.* Basil the Great, Chrysostom, Ambrose, and other fathers contributed to this literature by their popular homilies on martyrs. In the East, Cyril of Scythopolis, among others, wrote several biographies of monks, such as his *Life of Euthymius* and *Life of Saba.* Some of the later historians among the church fathers wrote and collected several lives of the saints or included them in their church histories.

Among the most famous hagiographical collections of the Middle Ages are those of Gregory of Tours, under the title *Miraculorum libri VIII*; Gregory the Great's *Dialogi de vita et miraculis patrum Italicorum*; and the three books of Eulogius of Toledo, entitled *Memorialis sanctorum.* These collections use the historical order of the saints' lives or passions. Later hagiographic collections include the biographies of the saints according to the dates of the calendar. Other important hagiographical compilations dating from the Middle Ages are the *Sanctoral* of Bernard Guy, bishop of Lodève; the *Sanctilogium angliae* of John of Tynemouth; the *Sanctuarium* of B. Mombritius; and the compilations of Jean Gielemans under the titles *Sanctilegium, Hagiologium,* and *Brabantinerum.*

With the establishment of the Jesuit Bollandists in 1635 by John Bolland, hagiography arrived at a system of classification of documents in order to verify the degree of truth and historic value that the documents possessed. The hagiographer grouped documents of the saints' lives, for the most part, in the following descending order: (1) saints who have been canonically established by the church and have received the sanction of the centuries, for example, Lawrence, Cyprian, and Martin; (2) real personages to whom devotion was irregularly established, such as those mentioned in the writings of Gregory the Great and by the historian Theodoret; (3) imaginary personages to whom a real existence has ultimately been attributed. Supporting documents used to verify the above categories have been the official reports or archive records of the interrogatories of martyrs; the accounts given by trustworthy eyewitnesses or well-informed contemporaries; written documents; historical romances; imaginative romances; and lastly the forgeries.

BIBLIOGRAPHY: D. Attwater, *A Dictionary of Saints* (London, 1948); A. Butler, *The Lives of the Saints* (London, 1948); H. Delehaye, *The Legends of the Saints* (New York, 1907).

**Hahn, Johann Michael** (1758–1819). Württemberg Pietist and founder of the *Hahnsche Gemeinschaft* (Michelianer). A lay preacher, spiritual guide, and self-taught theologian, he won many followers despite state church disapproval. An author of exegetical works (15 vols., 1819) and some two thousand hymns, he emphasized sanctification within a framework of Boehmenist (see BOEHME, JAKOB) theosophy and Biblicism. His followers separated from the Lutheran Church, and number today perhaps ten thousand in three hundred communities in southwestern Germany.

**Haldane, Robert** (1764–1842), and **Haldane, James Alexander** (1768–1851). Scottish laymen active in the promotion of the Evangelical Awakening in the 19th century. They founded chapels, established Sunday schools, and were active in philanthropy. In 1816, Robert traveled to Geneva, Switzerland, and in 1817 to Montauban, France, precipitating the evangelical awakening known as the *Réveil* which later spread to Holland. Their influence also extended to Denmark and Sweden, and through Thomas and Alexander Campbell to the United States as well.

**Hale, Edward Everett** (1822–1909). Unitarian clergyman and writer. With a Harvard B.A., he entered schoolteaching, journalism, and then the ministry. His longest pastorate was in Boston, where he became influential as editor of several journals and author of many articles and books. He is best known for his short story *A Man Without a Country.* From 1903 until his death he served as chaplain of the United States Senate.

**Halfway Covenant.** A restricted form of membership permitted to those in the Congregational churches of New England who had been baptized as children but were "unconverted." Puritan Massachusetts limited church membership to visible saints, those who could personally testify to a working of grace in their lives. The covenant under which the church was constituted held that children of saints also were to be admitted to baptism. A personal conversion experience was, however, subsequently required before they could be admitted to the Lord's Supper. The religious fervor of the first generation of church organizers soon abated and few of the baptized children of saints could or would publicly testify to a conversion experience. When these children of saints came to maturity, a ministerial assembly of 1657 and a synod in 1662 agreed that such moral but unconverted members of the church might also present their children for baptism. These second-generation members had to affirm their loyalty to both the doctrine and discipline of the church, though neither they nor their children could participate in the Lord's Supper. This decision established the so-called Halfway Covenant, whereby the second- and third-generation New England Puritans maintained partial church membership.

**Hall, Joseph** (1574–1656). Bishop of Norwich, England. Educated at Emmanuel College, Cambridge, Hall prided himself on being the first English satirist, though his *Meditations* were his best work. He leaned somewhat toward Puritanism, but became the center of controversy over his advocacy of a moderate episcopacy in his *Episcopacy by Divine Right* (1640) and a pamphlet to the Long Parliament, *An Humble Remonstrance* (1640–1641). Five of his opponents applied with a pamphlet issued under a pseudonym (see SMECTYMNUUS).

**Halle.** See PIETISM.

**Haller, Berthold** (1492–1536). Protestant Reformer. A native of Aldingen in Württemberg and a fellow student with Melanchthon, Haller came to Bern, Switzerland, and allied himself with Zwingli in 1521. He was the leading contender for the Reformation in Bern, and suggested to Farel that he try the Reformation in the Vaud. Haller disliked controversy, but his last years were occupied with disputes against the Anabaptists.

**Haller, Karl Ludwig** (1768–1854). Swiss conservative Restoration theorist. In 1806, Haller went to Bern, where he was professor and publicist. In 1814, he became a member of the Municipal Great Council, from which he was ousted in 1820 because of his conversion to Roman Catholicism. He traveled to Paris, and settled in Solothurn. Challenging Rousseau's political theory of social contract, he urged a "patrimonial state" with an agrarian base. His self-help theory found wide acceptance with Frederick William IV, F. J. Stahl, the Gerlach brothers, and the Prussian aristocracy. The term "Restoration" derives from his six-volume *Restauration de Staatswissenschaften* (1816).

**Hamann, Johann Georg** (1730–1788). German literary figure and lay theologian, noted for his attack upon Enlightenment thinking and his influence upon the Romantic movement. After a mediocre public education, he studied at the University of Königsberg. Following service as a tutor for a leading merchant family in Riga, he was sent by them to England. In London he fell in with bad company and experienced deep moral and psychological suffering. This disillusioned him with his previous stance as a gentleman scholar. Thrown onto the resources of the Bible, he pursued intensive study of the Scriptures, which issued in a profound conversion. His studies were published as *Biblische Betrachtungen*. After returning to Germany, he earned a livelihood in several minor government administrative posts. A series of brief but brilliant pamphlets and newspaper articles soon brought him acclaim. He believed that wisdom must lead one to see what the Wise Men from the East saw in the star; hence he became known as the "Magus of the North" (Moser). His style, though sometimes obscure, was full of penetrating insights; it was freighted with allusions, making translation difficult. Hamann's thought profoundly affected the work of Herder, Goethe, and later Kierkegaard, as well as Lessing, Kant, and Hegel. Basic to his thought was the concept that as evil is within God's plan, it cannot be subdued by man's efforts. Also foundational was the emphasis upon God's condescension or accommodation to the world in his self-revelation in servant form. Over against the deistic tendencies of his contemporaries he stressed the event character of God's action in history.

**Hamilton, John** (c. 1511–1571). Roman Catholic martyr of the Scottish Reformation. As a power in Scottish politics he succeeded the murdered Beaton as archbishop of St. Andrews. His attempts to discipline and improve the church failed and he was unable to hinder Protestantism's triumph in 1560. He supported Mary, baptized the infant James

VI, and was hated for his Roman Catholic practices. Accused as a traitor, he was hanged in his pontifical garb in 1571.

**Hamilton, Patrick** (c. 1504–1528). First martyr of the Scottish Reformation. In Paris and Louvain, Hamilton had been influenced by the ideas of Luther and Erasmus. Back in Scotland he became associated with John Major but had to flee when Beaton charged him with heresy. He visited Luther and returned to Scotland with strong Protestant convictions. He was soon convicted of heresy and burned. In Scotland he represented the Lutheran stage of the Reformation.

**Hampton Court Conference.** A conference called by King James I at Hampton Court in January, 1604, between the English bishops and the Puritan leaders, to discuss matters concerning ecclesiastical reform. The Puritan leaders had presented the king with a Millenary Petition asking for certain reforms in liturgy and discipline. The Puritans were led by John Rainolds, while Archbishop Bancroft was chief spokesman for the bishops. The king conceded certain minor reforms in the Prayer Book and the promise of a new translation of the Scriptures, but nothing else.

**Handel, George Frederick** (1685–1759). Lutheran composer, impresario, and performer. Born in Halle in 1685 (the birth year also of Johann Sebastian Bach), Handel spent most of his life in England as a favorite composer of the new (1714) Hanoverian dynasty, dying in that country in 1759. He is perhaps best known for the oratorio *Messiah,* first played in Dublin in 1742, but he also wrote many operas, concerti, oratorios, suites, and other works, some sacred and some secular in character. Of the last group, perhaps his *Royal Fireworks Music* and *Water Music* are most often played. He was immensely popular in his lifetime (though he had feuds with other musicians and many vicissitudes of fortune), and his music, surely one of the noblest monuments of the baroque period, has had a lively revival in recent years.

**Hardenberg, Albert** (c. 1510–1574). Protestant Reformer. During his academic studies, Hardenberg met Laski at Mainz about 1538, after which he was accused of preaching Reformed doctrines. In 1547 he became cathedral preacher at Bremen, and initiated the Calvinist movement there. Because he did not uphold the Lutheran doctrine of the Lord's Supper, he was ousted from Bremen in 1561, and after an interlude became preacher at Emden in 1567.

**Hardenberg, Friedrich Leopold von.** See NOVALIS.

**Hardie, James Keir** (1856–1915). Scottish labor leader and journalist. After a childhood spent in the mines, Hardie turned his abilities toward the socialist organization of labor. Secretary of the Scottish Miners' Federation in 1886, by 1888 he had sparked the formation of the Scottish Labor Party. He became chairman of the Independent Labor Party in 1893, and first leader of the Labor Party in the House of Commons in 1906.

**Harless, Gottlieb Christoph Adolf von** (1806–1879). German Lutheran pastor and professor. As professor in Erlangen and Leipzig and later as president of the Church Consistory in Munich he promoted the Lutheran confessional revival of the early 19th century. While professor he founded the *Zeitschrift für Protestantismus und Kirche* and wrote his *Christian Ethics* (1842; English translation, 1868). He also wrote a new hymnal and order of service for the Church of Bavaria.

**Harms, Klaus** (1778–1855). German Lutheran pastor. As a young man he was influenced by Schleiermacher's *Speeches on Religion,* but later he turned to a strongly confessional Lutheranism. On the two hundredth anniversary of the nailing of Luther's Ninety-five Theses, Harms wrote ninety-five new theses in sharp criticism of rationalism and emphasizing forgiveness of sins and the sacraments. While many were advocating union between Lutheran and Reformed Christians, Harms called for a return to the pure Lutheranism of the Reformation era. Union, said Harms, was possible only for those who had fallen from faith. Of peasant origin, he always remained in close touch with the people as his major work, *Pastoral Theology,* demonstrates. Though he had a High Church view of the office of the ministry, he was popular as a preacher.

**Harnack, Adolf von** (1851–1930). German church historian. A student of Ritschl, he soon blazed his own trail in his monumental *History of Dogma* (1886–1889). Written when Harnack was only thirty-four, it was to become the classic work in this field. He argued that dogma was a product of the Greek spirit on the soil of the gospel; the simple spiritual and ethical religion of Jesus was obscured by the encrustations of church dogma. In 1889 he became a professor at Berlin, where he taught to the end of his life. In 1900, Harnack stated his views in more systematic and popular form in *The Essence of Christianity.* He located the essence in the teachings of Jesus rather than in a proclamation about Jesus. The recognized master of church history in the latter part of the 19th century, Harnack wrote countless volumes on all phases of ancient church history. Of these his *History of Ancient Christian Literature Until Eusebius* is still a standard reference work; *Texte und Untersuchungen,* which he edited, still publishes monographs, critical editions, textual studies, etc., on the church fathers. With Emil Schuerer he founded the *Theologische Literaturzeitung,* still considered one of the most important theological reviews in Germany. In later life he took on responsibilities ranging beyond his scholarly activities, becoming, for example, head of the Royal Prussian Library.

**Harnack, Theodosius** (1817–1889). Lutheran professor at Dorpat, a German-speaking university of the Baltic lands. Harnack was a strongly confessional Lutheran, his work *Luther's Theology* a forerunner of modern Luther studies. Though he was closely allied with the conservative Erlangen school of theology, his son Adolf von Harnack, the outstanding church historian, was to become famous for his liberalism.

**Haroun-al-Rashid** (766–809). Fifth caliph of the Abbasid dynasty, from 786. He was known in the West primarily through *The Arabian Nights.* His reign marks the turning point in this dynasty after which efficiency declined and disintegration set in. Under his rule, wars against the Byzantine Empire were carried on, literary output was at a high level, and the standard of living was superior, although it has frequently been romanticized. His alleged embassy to Charlemagne is not confirmed in any Arabic sources.

**Harper, William Rainey** (1856–1906). Hebraist and educator. In 1879, Harper accepted a position in Semitic languages at Baptist Union Theological Seminary in Morgan Park near Chicago. Here he began to develop his famous methods and texts for the study of Hebrew. In 1881 he accepted a position at Yale and from 1885 was prominent in Chautauqua. In 1892, Harper was called by John D. Rockefeller to become president of the new University of Chicago, with full academic freedom. By 1895 he had assembled a brilliant faculty and an outstanding library. Harper pioneered with university extensions, a university press, the four-quarter system, an integral summer school, faculty control of athletics, and emphasized graduate study and research. His writings include *The Priestly Element in the Old Testament* (1902), *Religion and the Higher Life* (1904), *The Prophetic Element in the Old Testament* (1905), *Amos and Hosea* (1905), *The Trend in Higher Education* (1905). Harper's theological position was informal and liberal.

**Harris, William Wadé** (c. 1853–1929). Native Methodist evangelist from Liberia, Africa. Harris began preaching in 1913 along the Ivory Coast and in Ghana on his own initiative and without any foreign support or sanction, calling for the destruction of all pagan symbols, belief in one God, observance of Sunday, and the cessation of adultery. Thousands heeded his message and were baptized, with his example inspiring other native Christians to go out and win their brethren.

**Harrison, Robert.** See CONGREGATIONALISM, BRITISH.

**Hartmann, Eduard von** (1842–1906). German philosopher. Inspired by the idealistic tradition of Schelling, Hegel, and Schopenhauer, Hartmann constructed a metaphysical system to synthesize elements of idealism and rationalism. He saw will and intellect in opposition to each other, but he resolved this conflict by rooting them in the unconscious. Besides his major work, *The Philosophy of the Unconscious* (1869), he also wrote a *History of Metaphysics, A Theory of Categories* where he seeks a common formal basis for philosophy and other disciplines, and many other historical works on ethics, aesthetics, and the philosophy of religion. A vigorous critic of the church, he regarded liberal Protestantism as the gravedigger of the church and considered Christianity a stage on the road to the religion of Absolute Spirit.

**Hase, Karl August** (1800–1890). German Lutheran church historian. He taught at Jena from 1830 to 1883. His *Kirchengeschichte* (1834) saw its twelfth edition in 1900. Visiting Rome often, he became an authority on Roman Catholicism. He stood for a scientific investigation of the gospel, and rejected external authorities for faith as well as 18th-century rationalism. He opposed many of the findings of F. C. Baur's Tübingen school, sharing Schleiermacher's concept of vital religion.

**Hauge, Hans Nielsen** (1771–1824). Norwegian lay preacher and leader of the first great Awakening in Norway. He came from a rural background and possessed a minimal education. In 1796 he sensed a call to become an itinerant preacher, which he was from 1796 until 1804, this in spite of the Conventicle Law (passed in 1741) that forbade lay preaching. He encouraged industry and thrift among his followers and helped them to establish factories and new business enterprises. In 1801, Hauge established himself as a successful businessman in Bergen and continued his itinerant preaching. After many arrests and much harassment, he was imprisoned in 1804 for derogatory remarks about the clergy and violation of the monopolistic trade laws. During his long imprisonment (he was finally brought to trial, sentenced, and released in 1814), Hauge remained loyal to the Church of Norway. In his last will and testament he implored his followers not to leave the state church. Thus the fruits of the pietistic Haugean revival remained within the Lutheran State Church of Norway and have had a marked influence upon that church to this very day.

**Havergal, Frances Ridley** (1836–1879). Gifted Anglican hymn writer. She dedicated all her powers to the task of bringing the unconverted to Christ. Among her correspondents was Fanny Crosby, blind American composer of popular hymns. After 1873, Frances Havergal sang nothing but sacred music. Her themes were faith, consecration, and service. Among her best-known hymns are "O Saviour, Precious Saviour"; "Thy Life Was Given for Me"; and "Take My Life, and Let It Be."

**Hawthorne, Nathaniel** (1804–1864). American novelist of Puritan descent. He was born in Salem, Mass., and graduated from Bowdoin College (1825). He did not find the Brook Farm transcendentalists congenial, nor was he much influenced by the Concord literati. In tales and novels he presented conflicts of egotism, nature, and sin, e.g., *The Scarlet Letter* and *The Marble Faun*. He sympathized with rebels against orthodoxy.

**Heads of Agreement.** A platform of points of agreement drawn up between the English Presbyterians and the Congregationalists in the 1690's. By this time many of the difficulties faced by nonconforming groups in England had been removed. They could have their own places of worship if they left the doors unlocked and notified the bishop of their activities, although they were not considered on equal terms with the Church of England. Two of the nonconforming bodies, the Presbyterians and the Congregationalists, sought to effect a merger by a common platform. Theological controversy, however, soon broke out between them and union became impossible. Though this effort at merger was unsuccessful, certain forms of "Presbygationalism" were to arise in the American colonies.

**Heber, Reginald** (1783–1826). Anglican bishop. Parish priest for a time, he became in 1815 the Bampton Lecturer at Oxford on "The Personality and Office of the Christian Comforter." He was appointed bishop of Calcutta in 1823, and worked for good relations between Christians and other religions in India. He is best known for his hymns, among which are "Holy, Holy, Holy! Lord God Almighty!" and "From Greenland's Icy Mountains."

**Hecker, Isaac Thomas** (1819–1888). Founder of the Paulists. Born in New York City of German immigrant parents, Hecker came early to an interest in transcendentalism. He was for a time part of the utopian experiments at Brook Farm and Fruitlands, and an intimate of the Thoreau household. Converted to Roman Catholicism in 1844 and ordained a priest in 1849, Hecker founded the Missionary Society of St. Paul the Apostle (Paulists) and the periodical *Catholic World* (1865).

**Hedge, Frederic Henry** (1805–1890). Unitarian minister, transcendentalist, and a translator of German literature. After graduating from Harvard in 1825 he studied at the Divinity School (1825–1829). He was ordained on May 20, 1829, and served Unitarian churches until 1872. He was editor of the *Christian Examiner* (1857–1861), professor of ecclesiastical history (1857–1876), and professor of German literature (1872–1884) at Harvard.

**Hefele, Karl Josef von** (1809–1893). Catholic church historian. Successor of J. A. Moehler at Tübingen (1840), he was also noted as an authority on the fathers and the late medieval church. His most famous work was his *History of the Ecclesiastical Councils*. Made bishop of Rottenburg in time (1869) to sit at the Vatican Council, he bitterly opposed the proposed dogma of papal infallibility and was the last of the German bishops to publish the decree.

**Hegel, Georg Wilhelm Friedrich** (1770–1831). German philosopher, proponent of absolute idealism. He was born at Stuttgart, the son of an obscure civil servant. It was determined that he should enter the field of theology, so he studied at Tübingen, receiving his Ph.D. in 1790 (certified in 1793). His examiners observed a particular deficiency in philosophy. The same year he became tutor for a Swiss family and moved to Bern, where he carried on a study of Christianity from which he emerged with a picture of Christ more Stoic than Hebraic. Under the guidance of I. H. Fichte he moved to a similar position in Frankfurt am Main in 1797, where his system (Hegelianism) first began to take its final form. In 1801 he took a university position at Jena, where he went as a disciple of Schelling. This relationship continued until the latter left Jena in 1803. As Napoleon entered Jena in October, 1806, Hegel was just completing his first great work, *The Phenomenology of Mind* (1807). When the university closed, Hegel took a temporary position as editor. In 1808 he moved to the rectorship of a school in Nuremberg (*The Science of Logic* appeared during the years 1812 to 1816), removing to Heidelberg in 1816 (*Die Enzyklopädie der philosophischen Wissenschaften im Grundrisse* was published in 1817). Finally, on the death of Fichte, he moved to Berlin in 1818, where he remained until his death from cholera in 1831. His work *The Philosophy of Right* was published in 1821; *Aesthetics, Philosophy of Religion, Philosophy of History,* and *History of Philosophy* were published posthumously. In his early career Hegel was not a successful lecturer and never mastered the art of easy delivery. During his "golden period" at Berlin (1823–1827), however, he enjoyed a position of the highest prestige and popularity.

**Hegelianism.** A speculative system of absolute idealism devised by G. W. F. Hegel and developed by his disciples. The almost universal impact of Hegel's philosophy on modern Western thinking is but a reflection of the scope and profundity of his undertaking and results. Kant had at the close of the 18th century deeply shaken the major premise of Western scientific and philosophical culture since Parmenides: the proposition that the universe is intelligible. In response to Kant's challenge, Hegel undertook an intellectual vindication of the rationality of reality. His first step was to reform and broaden the concept of reason. Then on the basis of his new logic he set out to comprehend all reality in its categories. The Hegelian premise that "the real is rational and the rational is real" was certainly no strange doctrine, but his intention of testing it by the construction of a consistent system comprehending all that exists, has existed, or will exist, was a bold stroke indeed.

The logic with which Hegel operated was one oriented to temporal and contingent existence rather than exclusively to timeless essence. In his "dialectic" the dogma of pure thought (thesis) is subjected to the negativity that characterizes actual existence (antithesis), and in the flux of history the two opposing elements give rise to a new reality in which the whole of each is incorporated (synthesis). In the application of this dialectic triad to the actual world a universal evolutionary scheme emerges. Reality appears as a continuous becoming in which all conflicting elements find their place and are ultimately transcended in the self-realization of the Absolute Idea. The entire flow of universal history is looked upon as the "biography" of the Absolute Idea or Absolute Spirit that stands at the beginning and at the end of history in a perfectly pure state. The events that have transpired in the meanwhile are the dialectic process by which thought has passed from potentiality to actuality. Absolute Idea stands before creation as purely contentless being in which *being* and *nothing* are identical, but are pitted against each other in the original dialectic from which the "synthesis" of *becoming*—of actual existence—arises. From that primordial "idea" comes nature, and ultimately existing mind or spirit arises from a combination of that "idea" and nature. Human history is seen then as the process by means of which *that* spirit comes to a consciousness of itself as *the* Spirit. The finality of Christianity for Hegel was in the very matter of the incarnation of God. In Christ, the God-man, is at last revealed the final issue of universal history in religious form—*spirit* and *Spirit* as identical. It remained only for this to come to realization on the ultimate plane of philosophy, and this seemed for Hegel to be very near. He was apparently convinced that the last in an infinite chain of dialectic triads was at hand. That the consummation did not come remained among other factors to give grist to the mills of the Hegelians who were to follow.

The schools of Hegelianism may be divided into "left," "center," and "right." The right wing, representing as it did supernaturalists and orthodox thinkers such as Gabler, Göschel, and Hinrichs, and the center, men attempting to develop Hegel's own line such as Rosenkranz (his biographer), Vatke, and Gans, are not of such lasting interest as the immensely creative left wing. On the left are found D. F. Strauss, Bruno Bauer, Ludwig Feuerbach, Karl Marx, and Søren Kierkegaard. Hegel also enjoyed great influence in England and America. The impact of Hegel upon the cultural tradition of the West in the 19th and 20th centuries has been felt in such widely divergent movements as Fascism and Communism. He has influenced economic, social, political, historical, and educational theory profoundly. His influence, it should also be noted, was formative as well for the first great school of modern church historians under F. C. Baur and the Tübingen school. Many present-day intellectual modes are little more than dim echoes of this giant's experiment in the radical secularization of Christianity.

Most of Hegel's important writings are

available in good English translations: *Hegel's Philosophy of Right* (New York, 1942); *Lectures on the History of Philosophy,* 3 vols. (New York, 1954); *Phenomenology of Mind* (New York, 1961); *Philosophy of History* (New York, 1956), *Philosophy of Religion,* 3 vols. (New York, 1962); *Science of Logic,* 2 vols. (New York, 1951).

BIBLIOGRAPHY: G. R. G. Mure, *An Introduction to Hegel* (New York, 1940); and *A Study of Hegel's Logic* (Oxford, 1950); W. T. Stace, *The Philosophy of Hegel* (New York, 1955).

**Hegesippus** (2d century). Antiheretical Christian author of the latter half of the 2d century. His *Recollections,* composed about an extended trip to Rome during the episcopate of Anicetus (c. 160) and visits to other Christian churches are extant only in fragmentary excerpts preserved by Eusebius. These extracts from a five-book work evince breadth of acquaintance with the 2d-century church. A Christian convert, he was born in Syria or Palestine and therefore discussed Jerusalem traditions at length.

**Hegira.** The departure of Mohammed from Mecca, his birthplace, to set up the first Moslem state at Medina. The word "hegira" means literally "emigration," but is often incorrectly translated as "flight." The year of the Hegira (A.D. 622), because it marked a new era for Islam, was subsequently established as the base year of the Moslem calendar. In Moslem writing, therefore, the abbreviation "A.H." (*anno hegirae,* "in the [specified] year of the Hegira") is applied to dates.

**Heidegger, Martin** (1889–    ). German existential philosopher. Born at Messkirch in the Black Forest of Roman Catholic peasant stock, Heidegger was schooled in the neo-Kantianism of Windelband and Rickert. He early developed a keen interest in the history of Western thought, which he has followed throughout his career. In 1915 he became a lecturer at Freiburg im Breisgau, where he came into contact with Edmund Husserl, from whom he adopted and adapted the latter's method of phenomenology. Largely on the basis of his reputation as a lecturer, Heidegger was invited in 1923 to a chair in philosophy at Marburg. During his stay there he produced and in 1927 published his basic philosophical work, *Being and Time.* This work, however, is merely a fragment, the first two of six proposed parts. In 1929 he was invited to succeed Husserl as professor of philosophy at Freiburg. Under the Nazi regime, he was elected rector of the University of Freiburg (1933), but resigned the post in 1934. In 1935, Hitler invited him to take a position in Berlin, but he declined, preferring to remain in his native region. In recent decades most of his time has been spent in the seclusion of an isolated ski hut atop a mountain in his beloved Black Forest, with only a few books, prominent among which are the works of the poet Hölderlin.

There is a major controversy among scholars over the basic continuity of Heidegger's thought. Some maintain that in the later works his preoccupation with "being" represents an essential break with a previous existentialism. There seems, however, no real justification for doubting the accuracy of his own statements that his interest in existence (man) was as an expression, or revelation, of being and not as the end of philosophy itself. Thus one might say that his existentialism is a philosophical method by which he hopes to approach the real end of philosophy—ontology (the nature of being).

Heidegger maintains that the entire Western philosophical tradition has been led astray from its proper object in that it has abstracted the things which are from the fact that they are, and has thus concentrated on the things, their manipulation, and their control, passing over with a bland assumption the more basic question of what it means *to be.* Heidegger wishes to reverse this objectifying trend, which has given rise to Western science, and in the examination of "that which is" to concentrate on the "is" rather than on the "that." In his quest for the "being" which is expressed in and through all "beings," he has adapted the phenomenology of Husserl. The central object of this approach as Heidegger uses it is to maintain a position of complete receptivity toward the phenomena which are under observation, withholding all classification or judgment, allowing them to express what they *are* in themselves, then only, on the basis of the received impression, obtaining or constructing an understanding. In the search for being, i.e., the *to be* of what is, Heidegger regarded man himself as the most accessible and expressive phenomenon. The fact that he never calls "man" by that name, but refers to him by what or where he is, that is, *Dasein* (being-there) or being-in-the-world, illustrates his intention of becoming mastered by rather than mastering that which he observes.

In *Being and Time,* which is only a fragment, Heidegger allows man, or *Dasein,* to teach him what being is. The fact that this fragment gives only a view of man "in-the-world," or existing man, has led many to regard Heidegger as an existentialist pure and simple, or as a humanist. Indeed, one would go far to find a more adequate account of the problems and possibilities of human existence than is to be seen in *Being and Time*. It is difficult to conceive of a better description of man's contingency and finitude than that found in this work. Man exists in this world projecting himself into the future, despite the threat that he no longer is what he was. He is in a state of anxiety (*Angst*), or dread, because of his freedom between real alternatives of being or not being. Oriented toward the future, which is the place where all his possibilities and projects lead his interest, man is faced with the impossibility of all his possibilities, the ultimate and inevitable nonbeing of death. Thus we see man as a being thrown into the world toward death. The expression of being here is in the face of nonbeing or nothingness. Its highest expression is found in man living hopefully in the daily presence of inevitable despair about death. It is this unaccountable positive character of *Dasein* through which being is most clearly revealed. Man is being-in-time despite what time means, i.e., death. As such, man is revelation.

Heidegger represents a disciplined application in philosophy of the insights of the earlier existential thinkers, especially Kierkegaard and Nietzsche. His structure, method, and aims are, however, his own. Although he calmly assumes that "God is dead," his approach has been particularly helpful to a number of theologians, notably Rudolf Bultmann and Heinrich Ott.

BIBLIOGRAPHY: M. Heidegger, *Existence and Being* (Chicago, 1949); J. J. Kockelmans, *Martin Heidegger: A First Introduction to His Philosophy* (Pittsburgh, 1965).

**Heidelberg Catechism, The** (published 1563). German Reformed catechism, named after the city of Heidelberg, then the capital of the Palatinate. The Palatinate had become a battleground of various Protestant views, particularly on the question of the "real presence" in the Lord's Supper. The conflict culminated in a fight at the altar by two opposing pastors. This was the immediate occasion for the writing of the Heidelberg Catechism. Frederick III, elector of the Palatinate, who favored the Reformed faith, directed the writing of a catechism to secure harmony among the churches. While the entire theological faculty at Heidelberg, the leading ministers, and Frederick himself were all probably involved in its preparation, the catechism appears to be primarily the work of two men: Zacharias Ursinus and Caspar Olevianus. Ursinus (1534–1583) was professor of theology at the University of Heidelberg and a man of profound learning and deep personal piety. Olevianus (1536–1585) taught theology, preached at the court, and was the elector's chief counselor in church affairs. The learning of Ursinus and the eloquence of Olevianus are reflected in the final product—a catechism of unusual power and beauty, an acknowledged masterpiece.

The Heidelberg Catechism has been translated into all European and many Asiatic languages. It is the most catholic and popular of all Reformed symbols. It sets forth the Calvinistic doctrine with wise moderation. The doctrine of election is included only incidentally (Question 54) and predestination, reprobation, and limited atonement are nowhere mentioned. The catechism is divided into three parts, following the letter to the Romans and the Christian attitudes of repentance, faith, and love. Part I deals with man's sin and guilt, Part II with man's redemption and freedom, and Part III with man's gratitude and obedience. It is still a widely recognized ecumenical standard of the Reformed Churches in Europe and the United States. It is included in the *Book of Confessions* of The United Presbyterian Church in the U.S.A. and is the authoritative guide for preaching in the Reformed Church in America and the Christian Reformed Church.

**Heidelberg Disputation** (1518). The academic disputation for which Martin Luther prepared twenty-eight theological and twelve philosophical theses to be discussed before the triennial chapter of the German Augustinian Eremites, the order to which he belonged. Luther presided and Leonhard Beier defended the theses with Luther's arguments. Following the furor created by the publication of the Ninety-five Theses, Pope Leo X asked the general of the order, Gabriel della Volta, or Venetus, to silence Luther. The order was passed on to John Staupitz, vicar of the German congregation and Luther's immediate superior. Luther agreed to write an explanation of the Theses and send it to the pope with an apology. Staupitz asked Luther to present his new insights, not on the controversial subjects, but on sin, free will, and grace, to the assembled order. Some of them later became active reformers. The theological articles emphasize that righteousness cannot be had through the law or through good works, that man must despair of his own powers and believe in Christ, and that theological understanding can come about only through faith and suffering (*theologia crucis*). The philosophical articles are mostly attacks on Aristotelian philosophy. The Disputation is important for understanding Luther's early theology and his use of Scripture in defense of his positions.

**Heiler, Friedrich** (1892–    ). German theologian and historian of religion. Originally Roman Catholic, Heiler lectured in Sweden in 1919 and soon joined the Lutheran Church. In 1922 he assumed the chair of comparative religion and religious philosophy at Marburg, which he held until expelled by the Nazis. His most important work, *Das Gebet*, is a thorough study of prayer. He has also published works on Roman Catholicism and Eastern Orthodoxy.

**Heim, Karl** (1874–1957). German Lutheran theologian. Pietistic in orientation, and evangelical in expression, Heim sought to relate Christian faith to the world views of the contemporary natural sciences. Influenced by the Jewish philosopher Martin Buber, he attempted within the categories of the "I-Thou" to discern how man apprehends supernatural truth. Many of his works have been translated into English.

**Heliand** ("The Savior"). An anonymous 9th-century paraphrase of the life of Christ in Old Saxon alliterative verse. Derived from the pseudo-Tatian harmony and other medieval commentaries on the Gospels, the story is told with the techniques and diction of Germanic heroic poetry. The Christ is presented as a heroic German warrior, and the twelve disciples as loyal thanes owing fealty to their prince.

**Héloïse** (d. 1164). The heroine of one of the most tragic love affairs of history. Héloïse was the niece of the canon of Notre Dame at Paris, who had employed Abelard to tutor her. Soon Abelard became her lover as well. After the birth of their son a secret marriage was arranged, but her uncle ended the matter with finality by having Abelard emasculated. Thereupon Héloïse became a nun and Abelard a monk, though her continuing love is shown by the letters she wrote to him afterward.

**Helvetic Confession, First** (1536). Earliest Reformed creed of national scope (see RE-FORMED CHURCH). Sometimes called the Second Basel Confession from its place of origin, it was composed in Latin by Heinrich Bullinger and others at a conference of delegates from several Swiss cantons and southern Germany. On the controverted doctrine of the Lord's Supper it taught, not a bare memorialization, but a real communion with the body and blood of Christ through the sacred signs.

**Helvetic Confession, Second** (adopted 1566). Swiss Reformed confession. The work of Heinrich Bullinger (1504–1575), pupil of Zwingli and after his death head of the Reformation in German Switzerland, it is the successor to and an expansion of the First Helvetic Confession. It was written by Bullinger in 1561 as his own abiding testimony, and appended to his will. It became public when Frederick III, elector of the Palatinate, under attack by Lutherans for becoming Reformed and for publishing the Heidelberg Catechism, asked Bullinger for a clear and full exposition of the Reformed faith. Bullinger sent him a copy of his confession, which greatly impressed the elector, and which he used in his defense before the Diet of Augsburg. Meanwhile, the Swiss churches felt the need for a new and fuller symbol of faith and called a conference to examine Bullinger's confession. Only a few changes were made, and with Bullinger's full consent. It was adopted and published in 1566 as the Confession of the Reformed Churches in Switzerland and the Palatinate. With the exception of the Heidelberg Catechism, it was the most widely adopted and most authoritative of Continental Reformed symbols. It assumes that the Reformed faith is in harmony with the true catholic faith of all ages. While uncompromising toward the errors of Rome, it is moderate in its dissent from Lutheranism, and tolerant toward minor differences. The preface to the confession, by Josias Simmler, Bullinger's son-in-law, takes pains to declare that the church is forced to vary the form of its confession, but always under the Word of God.

**Helvetic Confessions.** The Reformed Churches have been more prolific in the preparation of confessions than have been, for example, the Lutherans, and not all of them are universally acknowledged by Reformed Churches. There are two Helvetic Confessions. The First (1536), written largely by Heinrich Bullinger, was intended to represent all the Swiss Protestants. It naturally reflected Zwinglian views, but was conciliatory in spirit toward the Lutherans (1536 was also the year of the Wittenberg Concord between Bucer and the Lutherans). No permanent understanding between the two groups of Reformers grew out of it, however. The Second Confession, also by Bullinger (1566), celebrated the union of the Zwinglians and Calvinists of 1549 and looked toward the needs of such newly Reformed states as the Palatinate. Unlike the First, the Second Confession was widely approved and adopted among Reformed Churches outside Switzerland.

**Helvétius, Claude Adrien** (1715–1771). Philosopher of the French Enlightenment. He was closely associated with Voltaire, Diderot, and other *philosophes,* but he was more openly critical of religion and the church. His major work, *De l'Esprit* (1758), a study of man in society and as an individual, argued that every action of man is egocentric. As a purely sensuous creature, personal concern dictates every judgment. Translated into ethics, this anthropology considered ambition the motive for action and reduced religion to morality. Perhaps *De l'Esprit* was more scandalous in its expression than other writings of the time, but its ideas were already present among contemporary critics of religion. Its ancedotes, however, attracted widespread attention and led to its eventual condemnation by the church.

**Helvidius** (4th century). Roman churchman and disciple of the Arian bishop of Milan, Auxentius. His denial of the perpetual virginity of Mary brought violent attack from Jerome in *Adversus Helvidium, De perpetua virginitate Beatae Mariae.* He held that Jesus was conceived by the Holy Spirit, born of Mary (as a virgin), who afterward lived a normal married life with Joseph, giving birth to other sons. His followers were called Helvidians.

**Helwys, Thomas** (c. 1550–c. 1616). Early English Baptist divine. Helwys came from a good family in Nottinghamshire. He was educated at Gray's Inn. A Puritan for some time, he and his wife joined the Separatist congregation at Gainsborough, led by John Smyth. When the congregation removed to Amsterdam, Helwys went with them, evidently furnishing considerable money to make the move possible. He followed Smyth to the Baptist position, but refused to join the Waterland Mennonites and determined to return to England, with his supporters, to make the gospel known there. In 1612 the first Baptist church on English soil was organized in London. Helwys and his church accepted Smyth's Arminianism, and published a pamphlet expounding that position. However, he repudiated the Mennonite doctrine of free will and the succession of holy orders. In another tract, *A Short Declaration of the Mistery of Iniquity,* he contended for religious liberty. In an extant copy, which apparently was sent to the king, a penned inscription in the front states, "If the king have authority to make spiritual Lords and laws, then he is an immortal God." This is one of the earliest appeals for the right of free conscience. Helwys was soon in jail, and it is certain he was dead by 1616.

**Hemmingsen, Niels** (1513–1600). Danish theologian. He studied at Wittenberg and there became a disciple of Melanchthon. He wrote the first Danish pastoral theology in 1562. In 1571 he attacked the Lutheran doctrine of ubiquity and later persuaded the king to reject the Book of Concord for the churches of Denmark and Norway. As a crypto-Calvinist he influenced two generations of theological students in Denmark, Norway, and Iceland.

**Hengstenberg, Ernst Wilhelm** (1802–1869). German Lutheran professor and churchman. A Pietist in his youth, he later embraced conservative Lutheranism and became a leader in the Confessional party. As professor in Berlin and founder of the *Evangelische Lutherische Kirchenzeitung* he exercised this leadership for four decades. His theological conservatism was complemented by equally conservative political views.

**Henke, Heinrich Philipp Konrad** (1752–1809). German theologian and church historian. A native of Braunschweig, he studied at Helmstedt, serving as professor of philosophy and classics there, moving into theology in 1780. His chief work is the *Allgemeine Geschichte der christlichen Kirche* (6 vols., 1799–1808), which follows a consistent rationalist line. Its chief merit is its improvement in periodization. Henke was called to high church offices as abbot of the Michaelstein monastery (which had been transformed into an Evangelical seminary) and consistorial vice-president.

**Henoticon.** An act of union issued in 482 by Emperor Zeno. The Council of Chalcedon (451) formulated a unified Christology for Christendom, but religious controversy continued to pose serious problems for the Eastern Empire. Monophysitic sentiments were strong in Egypt, Syria, and Armenia. Under the influence of Acacius, patriarch of Constantinople, and Peter Mongus, patriarch of Alexandria, Emperor Zeno issued the Act of Union, or Henoticon, in 482. In the Henoticon, he ignored the Council of Chalcedon but asserted nothing contrary to its doctrines. He hoped that the Monophysites and their opponents would turn to the Councils of Nicaea (325) and Constantinople (381) for unified bases of belief. Zeno anathematized Nestorius and Eutyches, formally declared the truth and adequacy of the doctrines of Nicaea and Constantinople, and anathematized all who taught divergent doctrines "whether at Chalcedon or elsewhere." The inclusion of this clause was a tactical error, for it indicated the Monophysitic sympathies of its writers. Moderate Monophysites accepted the Henoticon, using it to denounce Chalcedon and the Tome of Leo I. Extreme Monophysites were not reconciled to the moderate policies of Acacius and Peter Mongus. Rome was offended by the document, which it considered a political intrusion into strictly ecclesiastical matters. It also rejected the implicit denial of the Tome of Leo. Pope Simplicius excommunicated both Acacius and Peter Mongus, and Emperor Zeno himself.

**Henry II** (973–1024). German king and Holy Roman Emperor. The son of Henry, duke of Bavaria, and Gisela of Burgundy, he was placed successively under the care of Abraham of Freising and Wolfgang of Ratisbon. He became duke of Bavaria upon the death of his father in 995, was chosen to succeed Otto III in 1002, and in 1004 was elected and crowned king of the Lombards. In 1014, he was crowned emperor by Pope Benedict VIII. Like his predecessors, Henry used the church to establish control within his territories and for submission of bordering peoples. He appointed bishops, either directly or by withholding approval of those elected. He revived the diocesan sees of Merseburg, Strasbourg, Magdeburg, and Hildesheim. In accord with the monastic reform movement emanating from Lorraine, he revitalized the monasteries of Gandersheim, Reichenau, Fulda, and Corvey. He secured the erection of the see of Bamberg in the territory of the Wends as a means of controlling those people. He used papal support to drive his rival Arduin of Milan from power in northern Italy. In 1022, he invited King Robert of France to join in a general assembly to reform the church. Henry was a just and pious ruler, and was venerated as a saint. He died in 1024, and was formally canonized by Pope Eugenius III (1146).

**Henry II** (1133–1189). King of England. Eldest son of the empress Matilda and Geoffrey Plantagenet of Anjou, he became king in 1154, being already by inheritance and his marriage to Eleanor of Aquitaine ruler of a large part of France. To restore the Crown's authority in England and to assure order during his absences in France he centralized the whole of English law and unified its administration by creating a permanent body of professional judges and a government machine run by a justiciar working through an exchequer. This assertion of the rights of royal justice was opposed by Thomas Becket, archbishop of Canterbury, who refused to permit lay jurisdiction over clerics, and would not assent to the Constitutions of Clarendon in 1164. The clash resulted in Becket's flight to France. To avoid a papal interdict Henry was publicly reconciled with him in 1170, but his rage on hearing that Becket had denounced

prelates who had assisted at the coronation of his son led four of his household knights to murder Becket. Henry was forced by the pope to do penance and to surrender his control over criminous clerks. The church courts regained many of the powers they had lost. From 1173 his sons, intriguing with Eleanor and Louis VII and Philip II of France, rebelled against him. He died after an unsuccessful campaign against them near Tours.

**Henry III** (c. 1017–1056). A Salian ruler in Germany (from 1039). The son of Conrad II and Gisela, he was designated king to succeed his father. He was married to Kunigunde of Denmark (d. 1038) and later to Agnes of Poitou. Victorious over the Bohemians, Hungarians, and Poles, he exercised some control over Lorraine, but his hegemony was tenuous in each of these areas, and his reign was troubled by a continuous series of revolts. In 1043, he declared a Day of Indulgence on two occasions, on which all his enemies were forgiven. In 1046, Henry entered Italy for the first time since 1039, called a synod at Sutri, and there deposed the three claimants to the papal throne. He named Suidger as Clement II. Clement crowned Henry emperor in the same year; the ancient title of *Patricius* was revived and bestowed upon him also. The reform popes—Damasus II, Leo IX, Victor II —were the choice of Henry. In naming the bishops for the sees of Ravenna, Pacenza, Strasbourg, Constance, Metz, and Trier, Henry sought the reform of the church as well as control of his Empire. He was a pious king, benefactor of many monasteries and churches. He left the Empire to his six-year-old son, Henry IV, under the regency of the empress Agnes.

**Henry IV** (1050–1106). King of Germany and Holy Roman Emperor. The son of Henry III and Agnes of Poitou, he was six years old when his father died. He assumed control of his kingdom (1065) after it had been weakened by the regency of his mother and the factions led by Archbishops Anno of Cologne and Adalbert of Bremen. Throughout his reign Henry was plagued by the combined opposition of the Saxons and the papacy, which he tried to offset by a coalition of higher clergy and the nobles of southern Germany and the Rhineland. For his violations of the decrees against lay investiture, Henry incurred excommunication by Gregory VII (1076) and thereby lost the support of the German episcopate. Although he did penance at Canossa (1077), the German nobles and bishops proceeded to elect Rudolf of Swabia as king at Forchheim (March, 1077). The ban was renewed in 1080 against Henry, who retaliated with the election of an antipope, Clement III, starting a schism that continued until 1100. Henry captured Rome in 1084, and crushed the Saxon rebellion finally in 1089. During the last years of his reign, he endured the rebellion of his son Conrad (1093), the renewal of the excommunication (1102), and the revolt led by his son Henry V (1104–1106). He died (1106) excommunicated, and was not allowed Christian burial in the Cathedral of Spires until five years later.

**Henry IV of France** (1553–1610). King of Navarre as Henry III and king of France. Through his father, Antoine de Bourbon, Henry was of the royal line, and through his mother he was heir to Navarre. He enjoyed a sturdy boyhood in southern France, where he learned his mother's Protestantism. Growing to maturity during the Wars of Religion, Henry came to know the valor of the field as well as the courtesies of the court. In 1572 he was selected to marry Margaret of Valois, the daughter of Catherine de' Medici. A few days after the wedding the Bartholomew's Day Massacre occurred, and Henry was held captive for three and a half years. When he escaped in 1576, he immediately became the recognized leader of the Huguenots, both militarily and politically. His fortunes thus wavered until 1589 when Henry III died without heirs and he was next in line. But four more years of warfare did not settle him on the throne—only his conversion to Roman Catholicism in 1593 did that. Much debate has ensued over Henry's real motives for his conversion, but it seems that his ultimate concern was not for personal advancement, but only for the salvation of divided France. He issued the tolerant Edict of Nantes, the most lenient up to that time for the Huguenots, and proposed a grand scheme to unite Europe against the Hapsburgs but was assassinated by a fanatic.

**Henry V** (1081–1125). German king and Holy Roman Emperor from 1106. The son of Henry IV, he allied himself with the papacy against his father, but upon his own accession to the throne he championed the imperial cause. In 1111 he forced Pope Paschal II to agree to the imperial right of investiture. His most significant act was the Concordat of Worms (1122), which settled the investiture controversy. He was the last of the Salian Franconian emperors.

**Henry VIII** (1491–1547). King of England and Ireland. The third child and second son of Henry VII, his brother Arthur having died in 1502, Henry succeeded his father in 1509.

Shortly afterward he was married to Catherine of Aragon, virgin widow of Arthur, to whom he had been affianced since 1503, the marriage having been postponed frequently. His aptness for learning as a youth, coupled with the Renaissance atmosphere in which he came to maturity, equipped him well to participate in the several contests that marked his reign. His learned Catholic sympathies showed in *Assertio septem sacramentorum* (1521) against Luther, earning him the epithet "Defender of the Faith." Remaining aloof from politics for some fifteen years, he began serious criticism of Cardinal Wolsey's successful, if expensive, foreign policy when the decline of France destroyed English influence in Europe (1525–1529). Catherine's failure to produce a male heir prompted negotiations for papal anullment of the marriage, but Wolsey's inability to procure it hastened his fall. Aware both of his own power, based on advancement of laymen to high office and popular approval, and of the powerlessness of the pope, Henry began systematic exclusion of papal jurisdiction from England. He thus facilitated both an English decision on the anullment and also a program of augmenting royal authority over the Church of England by a succession of legislative and royal acts as well as by organized expropriation of monastic and collegiate properties. With Henry as head of the church, the marriage was dissolved with the aid of Thomas Cranmer, who had been consecrated to Canterbury in 1533 by papal bulls secured through Henry's promise not to confirm the act against annates.

A marriage was concluded with Anne Boleyn, a member of a rising family. Dynastic considerations demanded a male heir, but Anne produced only Elizabeth. Her conduct, imprudent for a queen, allowed a jury to condemn her to execution for adultery (1536). Henry's next wife, Jane Seymour, produced Edward and died (1537). The Ten Articles (1536), the order for English Bibles in parish churches (Great Bible, 1538), and the negotiations for a marriage to Anne of Cleves, though the marriage lasted only a short six months (1540), showed Henry's tendencies toward Protestantism. The Act of Six Articles (1539), restoring rigid Catholicism, and his immediate marriage to Catherine Howard, a member of a Roman Catholic family, seemed to show the complete opposite. Catherine's indiscretions, though sustained as infidelity only by circumstantial evidence, brought about her execution in 1542. In the meantime Henry had incorporated Wales into union with England by a series of Welsh statutes (1534–1536), and after a successful campaign by

Skeffington (1535), he was made king of Ireland and head of the Irish Church. Intending to effect union with Scotland, he tried unsuccessfully to affiance Edward to Mary Stuart, but the French influence frustrated this effort and led to his ill-fated invasion of France (1544). In 1543, he married the twice-widowed Catherine Parr, a cultured woman who mothered all his children equally well and outlived him to marry again.

Henry's later years were marked by numerous efforts to reform the English Church without making it Protestant. His issuance of the King's Book (1543), a revision of the Bishops' Book of 1537 in a Catholic direction with fuller treatment of justification, his approval of the imposition of the use of the Salisbury (or Sarum) rite upon all the province of Canterbury (1543), his issuance of the English litany (1544), his further act suppressing chantries, colleges, and other religious foundations (1545), and the execution of Anne Askew for holding non-Catholic views on the Eucharist would all combine to justify the judgment that Henry was a thoroughgoing Catholic. The execution of Norfolk and Surrey, however, coupled with Cranmer's allegation that Henry intended to turn the Mass into a Communion service, would constitute evidence supportive of a contrary judgment. Taken together, the evidence goes far toward establishing Henry's preoccupation with the practical and political problems attendant upon maintaining the English realm against the changing constellations of Continental power, often at the cost of suppressing his private religious judgments. Despite his championing of the Catholic faith against compromise, however, it becomes increasingly evident that his intellect was distinctly secular.

BIBLIOGRAPHY: H. M. Smith, *Henry VIII and the Reformation* (London, 1948).

**Henry, Patrick** (1736–1799). American statesman. Born on the frontier, he began as a poor farmer in Virginia. Teaching himself law, he entered the bar in 1760 and came into fame by his defense against clergy suing for their salaries in 1763, a case that tended to increase dislike for Anglican clergy in Virginia. Active in politics, he was a champion of states' rights, slavery, the Bill of Rights, and colonial independence.

**Henry of Lausanne** (12th century). French heresiarch. Reputed to be an apostate monk, Henry appeared in 1134 before Innocent II at the Council of Pisa, where he was imprisoned and compelled to abjure his errors. Peter the Venerable wrote his *Epistola* (c. 1139) against the followers of Peter of Bruys and Henry of Lausanne, whom he accuses of preaching heresy in southern France. About 1145, Henry was rearrested, brought before the bishop of Toulouse, and probably imprisoned for life for his alleged attacks on the church.

**Heppe, Heinrich Ludwig** (1820–1879). German theologian. Devoting himself to Reformation studies, Heppe served as professor at Marburg and attracted attention by opposing the ideas of A. F. C. Vilmar and his disciples. His bibliography on German Reformation subjects runs to a score of titles. His views are summed up in a four-volume *History of German Protestantism* published in German (1853–1859). His popularity is attested by the appearance of his *Reformed Dogmatics* in 1950.

**Heraclitus "the Obscure" of Ephesus** (c. 536–470 B.C.). Pre-Socratic philosopher. He denied that there is an abiding substance, showing instead that change is so predominant that one cannot "step into the same river twice." He was noted for his obscure style, his religious interest, and his opposition to democracy. Justin Martyr thought the germinating seed of the Logos was active in Heraclitus, but Tatian spread tales about him. Both Tertullian and Hippolytus said that the God of the monarchians was like the monad of Heraclitus. Clement of Alexandria also quoted his sayings.

**Heraclius** (575–641). Emperor of the Eastern Roman Empire (610–641). As a result of a conspiracy between his father, the general Heraclius, and Crispus, son-in-law of Phocas, Heraclius succeeded to the throne when Phocas was forced to abdicate. Although Heraclius launched a brilliant campaign against the Persians, during his reign the Moslems made the first of their major advances against the Empire. In the last years of his life, Heraclius devoted himself to theology and ecclesiastical affairs. He issued the Ecthesis, an edict setting forth the doctrine of Monothelism, in 638.

**Herbert, Edward** (*known as* Lord Herbert of Cherbury) (1583–1648). Philosopher and diplomat. He was educated at Oxford and many of his early years were spent on the Continent soldiering and indulging his passion for dueling. In 1619 the earl of Buckingham made him ambassador to Paris, where he sought to keep peace with France and wrote his chief philosophical work, *De veritate* (1624). Always seeking recognition and reward, he was finally raised to the peerage in 1629, and in 1632, the year in which he began his history of the reign of Henry VIII, was made a member of the Council of War. During the Civil War he attempted to remain neutral, but under great pressure submitted to Parliament in 1645 and was granted a subsidy. Three years later he died and was buried at midnight in London at the Church of St. Giles-in-the-Field. He rejected all revelation, except for special revelation that might come to an individual. He believed all religion to consist of five innate ideas: that there is a God, that he ought to be worshiped, that virtue and piety are necessary to worship, that men ought to repent of their sins, and that there are rewards and punishments in a future life. Christianity he regarded as the best of all religions because it most nearly accorded with these ideas. He is considered a forerunner of English deism.

**Herbert, George** (1593–1633). English author and divine, brother of Lord Herbert of Cherbury. He seriously considered service with the state, being constantly at the court of James. Deciding on the religious life, he remained an ardent Royalist and Anglican. He is remembered for his poetry, which, like John Donne's, reflects the beauty, devotion, and rich spiritual experience of a segment of Anglicanism just prior to the Civil War. His best-known book of poems is *The Temple*.

**Herder, Johann Gottfried von** (1744–1803). German writer and philosopher. Educated at Königsberg under Kant and Hamann, and influenced by Spinoza, Herder was court preacher at Bückeburg (1771–1776), teacher at Rigle (1764–1769), and general superintendent at Weimar (1776–1803). He endeavored to rescue man's feelings and experience from 18th-century rationalism (Leibnitz, Locke, *et al.*). Humanity lay at the center of his thought; religion was humanity in its highest form; universal and macrocosmic history was his mode of measurement. Herder created a new understanding of revelation in harmonizing experiential reason and revelation. A powerful preacher with special Old Testament interests, he made no place for radical evil. He was the necessary precursor of Schleiermacher, De Wette, and the religio-historical school. His primary work was *Ideen zur Philosophie der Geschichte der Menschheit* (1784–1791).

**Heresy.** With its emergence as an institutional community, the Christian church was faced with the serious problems of determining what was the true or orthodox belief and opposing the many variant interpretations. The Greek terms *hairesis,* "heresy," literally, "a choosing," and *hairetikos,* "heretic," one who preferred a nonconformist belief, were commonly applied to dissenting elements, of whatever nature. Paul placed heresy among the works of the flesh (Gal. 5:20) and Peter lists it among the destroyers of faith (II Peter 2:1). Heresy, whether of the slighter, material kind (of the ignorant, without obstinacy) or the more serious formal kind (involving deliberate denial or doubt), was fought in many ways: by edicts of popes claiming the power to adjudicate in matters of faith, by councils summoned to deal with particular heresies, in the writings of church fathers concerned to defend orthodoxy, by the establishment of orders specially trained to investigate local and personal evidences of heresy, and by active militant assistance from interested secular leaders. Despite them, heresies continued to spring up, with the Roman Catholic Church viewing the theologies of the Protestant Reformation as representing perhaps their widest manifestation, and the Inquisition being used as the most rigorous of the antiheretical measures. Other measures used to combat heresy were preaching, moral suasion, excommunication, and interdict. Among the most troublesome heresies by which the early church was divided, **Arianism** stated that Christ, though of divine substance, was not the coequal of God. Condemned by the Council of Nicaea in 325, it persisted for many generations. **Gnosticism** was the belief that man might be liberated by his own knowledge (*gnōsis*) from the material to the spiritual world. **Pelagianism** taught that men were free of original sin and their moral destiny lay in their own control. As a lessening of the divine grace it was condemned by Augustine and others. **Nestorianism,** the belief that Christ had two harmonious but distinct natures, human and divine, was condemned at the Council of Ephesus in 431 on the grounds that it denied that the Virgin Mary was the mother of God (*theotokos*). **Monophysitism** held that Christ was of one composite nature, essentially denying his humanity. Its condemnation at the Council of Chalcedon in 451 so angered its Syrian and Egyptian supporters that they later gave little resistance to Islam. The Ebionites, Novatians, Manichaeans, and Donatists were among other early sects of heretical doctrine, and their later offshoots include the Albigenses (or Cathari), persecuted in France from the 13th century, and the Waldenses, who survived persecution and joined forces with Protestantism. The far-reaching reforms put forward by Wycliffe, Hus, Luther, Calvin, and Zwingli all inevitably came under the ban of the Roman Church, which forcibly reaffirmed its traditional doctrines, as well as internal proposals for reform, at the Council of Trent (1545–1563).

**Hergenröther, Joseph** (1824–1890). Roman Catholic cardinal scholar. Educated at Würzburg, Munich, and Rome, he taught theology, canon law, and church history in Germany after his ordination in 1848. An opponent of Doellinger, he helped prepare the schedule for the Vatican Council. He was made a cardinal in 1879, and later became first cardinal prefect of the Apostolic Archives when Pope Leo XIII determined to open the Vatican Archives to scholars.

**Hermann of Wied** (1477–1552). Archbishop of Cologne. The son of a noble family, Hermann obtained the archbishopric and electorate of Cologne in 1515. He was an able administrator, much in sympathy with the Lutheran reform. He attempted, while remaining within the Roman Church, to introduce Protestant practices, and even invited Bucer and Melanchthon to help him do so. He was forced to resign his see, however, by the opposition of his own clergy, Charles V, and Paul III. His writings were influential in the English reform.

**Hermannsburg Evangelical Lutheran Missionary Society.** A religious group founded in 1849 by Ludwig Harms in his congregation at Hermannsburg, Germany. Since missionaries were to be evangelists and colonizers, the Society opened a school to teach academic subjects and crafts, and graduates began work in South Africa in 1853. By 1857 the organization was administered through the state church. Its major work has been in South Africa, with a few missions elsewhere.

**Hermas** (2d century). Roman Christian apocalyptist and moralist, probably of Jewish origin. He wrote the *Shepherd,* which takes its name from an angel who appears to Hermas in the guise of a shepherd in the fifth Vision. Such an appearance was a commonplace of the Hellenistic mysteries. According to the romantic introduction to his work, Hermas was early sold into slavery; according to the Muratorian fragment (c. 190), he was a brother of Pius, bishop of Rome c. 150. Both could be true. His book alludes to his unhappy marriage and his anxiety about various postbaptismal sins which, according to his angelic informant, would be forgiven, once only, in the near future.

His three-part work is divided into five Visions, twelve Mandates or Commandments, and ten Similitudes or Parables. In the first four Visions a woman (old at first, but young at the last) appears to him who represents the church. In the fifth Vision the angelic shepherd appears. Both the Commandments and the Parables are also apocalyptic. The theme of the work is penitence. Hermas is worried about his own sins and those of his wife, who apparently was a veritable virago, and his children, who may have apostatized under persecution. Hermas is a witness to early Christian perfectionism in a form, primarily Jewish (though with some Hellenistic elements), which has been compared with the Dead Sea Scrolls. His work, included among the Apostolic Fathers, was often regarded as scripture in the early church. It survives in many papyrus fragments, in large part in Codex Sinaiticus (4th century), and almost entire in the 15th-century manuscript first published in 1856.

**Hermes, Georg** (1775–1831). German Roman Catholic theologian. He began teaching at Münster (1807), and in 1819 was called to Bonn, where he gained a wide following. Seeking to provide an apologetic on the basis of revelation and tradition resolved by reason, he appealed to many who were attracted to the Enlightenment yet who wished to remain Catholic. After his death Hermesianism was condemned by Gregory XVI in 1835 and a number of his works were placed on the Index.

**Hermetica.** Theosophical treatises generally presenting themselves as revelations of the god Hermes Trismegistus about the origin and nature of the world and the soul. Most come from the 2d and 3d centuries. Making some use of the Greek Old Testament, they reflect a development from religious-minded Middle Platonism in a direction incipiently Gnostic, though in the collection there are both monistic and dualistic treatises. Revelation is the source of all real knowledge. The treatises were known and used by Christian writers after the late 2d century, and some of them occur in the Gnostic library of Nag-Hammadi.

**Hermias.** Author of a short treatise deriding Greek philosophy and philosophers. Neither the date (possibly 5th century) nor the place of Hermias is known, and the work commonly found in school texts which is attributed to him consists of excerpts with a biting tone, which is his only contribution. It is thus inferior to the work of Tatian, with which it has sometimes been published.

**Hermit.** One who lives a secluded, solitary life. Christian hermits appeared in the third century in the Egyptian deserts. The most popular of these desert hermits was Antony of Egypt. Hermits followed no rule or uniform discipline, although more famous hermits occasionally attracted disciples who formed a loose community under the direction of the older man. Semi-eremitical orders appeared in the 10th and 11th centuries, especially in central Italy.

**Herrmann, Johann Wilhelm** (1846–1922). German theologian. Apologetically oriented in his thinking, he was deeply influenced by Immanuel Kant. Herrmann's thought led him into many problems at the forefront of theological discussion today, such as the significance of revelation and history. He has been influential on contemporary theology and on such contrasting figures as Karl Barth and Rudolf Bultmann. Of his translated works *The Communion of the Christian with God* (1886) is representative.

**Herrnhut.** In the Oberlausitz near Zittau in Saxon Germany lies Herrnhut, the place of origin of the Renewed Moravian Church (Unity of Brethren, Unitas Fratrum). In the early decades of the 18th century, the land on which Herrnhut was founded was part of the domain of Count Nicholas Ludwig von Zinzendorf. It was made available as a place of refuge for remnants of the persecuted Moravian Brethren. After 1727, Herrnhut ("the watch of the Lord") flourished as a communal settlement of the pietistic Moravians and as the headquarters for a far-flung missionary enterprise.

**Herron, George Davis** (1862–1925). Congregational clergyman. While a pastor in Minnesota and Iowa he became a famous exponent of the Social Gospel. As a professor at Iowa (later Grinnell) College he was the voice of "the Kingdom movement." His denunciations of existing institutions alienated many supporters, however, and he resigned his professorship in 1899. He was deposed from the ministry upon his unconventional second marriage in 1901, and his religious influence declined rapidly after his rejection of Christianity for Socialism. He was instrumental in organizing the Rand School of Social Sciences with Mrs. E. D. Rand in New York in 1906. He later also broke with the Socialist Party during World War I, becoming President Wilson's personal emissary during the ensuing negotiations for peace. Two volumes of his war papers were sealed and deposited in the Hoover Library of Stanford University.

**Herzen, Alexander Ivanovich** (1812–1870). Russian philosopher and socialist. Although in sympathy with the "Westernizing" inclinations of the 1830's, he viewed the peasant commune as a seedbed of socialism in Russia. Settling in western Europe in 1847, he never returned to Russia. He established the Russian Free Press in London and published the radical journals *The Bell* and *The Polar Star*. His memoirs are entitled *My Past and My Thoughts*. He was the chief spokesman for the radicals until the 1860's, when the younger generation of nihilists emerged.

**Hess, Johann Jakob** (1741–1828). Swiss pastor and theologian. A native of Zurich, he retired after his formal education and a brief career as a vicar to private life, enabled by an inheritance to carry on intensive Biblical and theological study. In 1777 he was called as pastor to the main Zurich church, where his preaching attracted large throngs. In 1795, against his will, he was made superintendent of the canton. His studies on the life of Christ were very popular, and achieved repeated publication and translation.

**Hesse, Hermann** (1877–1962). Novelist and editor. He was awarded the Nobel Prize (1946) for *Das Glasperlenspiel* (translation, *Magister Ludi*). From his early verse, *Romantische Lieder* (1898), he developed his own personal interpretation of psychoanalysis (*Demian,* 1919) and a synthesis of apparently disparate cultural motifs (*Siddhartha,* 1922; *Der Morgenlandfahrt,* 1932). A Swiss citizen after 1921, he accepted the Goethe Prize (1946), though disavowing "official Germany."

**Hesshus** (Heshusius), **Tilemann** (1527–1588). German Lutheran theologian, teacher, and pastor. He was an active polemicist against Calvinists and Philippists in the major controversies of his day. He was superintendent at Goslar and Heidelberg; pastor at Rostock, Heidelberg, Magdeburg, and Wesel; professor at Rostock, Jena, Helmstedt; and bishop of Samland. However, he was expelled from most of these posts because of the animosities he aroused. With Westphal he was Calvin's principal adversary on the doctrine of the Lord's Supper.

**Hesychius** (lived c. 300). Biblical textual critic. Jerome associates him with the recension of the text of the Septuagint (LXX), saying that he corrected it according to the Hebrew. He is probably not, however, to be identified with the "Alexandrian group" of witnesses for the LXX text. Eusebius identifies him with an Egyptian bishop, martyred in the Diocletian persecution, who was one of several signers of a letter to Meletius of Lycopolis.

**Hicks, Elias** (1748–1830). Quaker leader. He had little education and after 1771 he managed a farm on Long Island, where he was born. About this same time he began making "religious visits" to his neighbors and gradually gained widespread fame as a traveling preacher. About 1815 he began to differ from many of his fellow Quakers, whom he considered to have deserted traditional Quaker freedom and the doctrine of the Inner Light. He rejected their evangelicalism, their emphasis upon the Bible and upon original sin. In 1827 those who agreed with him left the Philadelphia Yearly Meeting and founded their own Yearly Meeting, splitting the Friends into two nearly equal parties. Hicks is also remembered as an early opponent of slavery, having taken part in the movement leading to its abolition in New York in 1827.

**Hierarchy.** The name for the ordering of the clergy of the Catholic Church. The orders of bishop, priest, and deacon were thought to be of divine institution, whereas the other orders were devised by the church. There exists also a hierarchy of jurisdiction within the Roman Catholic Church, from the pope, through the bishops, to such officials as legates, abbots, and vicars.

**High Commission, Court of.** The English "Commissioners Ecclesiastical," sitting as a quasi-legal ecclesiastical supreme court, from roughly 1560 to 1641. During the first half of Elizabeth's reign it was chiefly concerned with promoting visitations to repress heresy. Its subsequent development into a court of law was resisted by advocates of the common law, especially the jurist Lord Coke; the oath ex officio, which could compel subjects to incriminate themselves, was particularly hated.

**Hilary of Arles** (c. 400–449). Christian ecclesiastic. A monk of Lérins, he became bishop of Arles in 429. He was a noted preacher and disciplinarian, in theology semi-Pelagian, or at least opposed to strict Augustinianism. The position of Arles as chief city of Roman Gaul led Hilary into intervening in disputes outside his own province, and in consequence in 445, Pope Leo I suspended him from functions outside his own diocese. The informal primacy of Arles soon revived, however.

**Hilary of Poitiers** (c. 315–367). Christian prelate, one of the Doctors of the Church. He was known as the "Athanasius of the West" for his unrelenting struggle against Arianism. Elected bishop of Poitiers c. 350, he organized the Gallic bishops against the Arian views of the metropolitan of Gaul, Saturninus of Arles in 355, which provoked the emperor Constantius to banish him. His chief work,

*De fide adversus Arianos,* or *De trinitate,* was done during his exile in Asia Minor (356–359). He participated in the Synod of Seleucia in 359, and returned to Gaul in 360. He was present at the Synod of Paris (361), which saw the procurement of the excommunication of Saturnius and the return of Gaul to the Catholic faith. With Martin of Tours he established a monastery at Ligugé (c. 361). Under strong Eastern influence, Hilary must be counted as a great mediating and conciliating thinker in the development of Western theology. He pioneered in the doctrine of satisfaction and stressed the cooperation of man with God's grace in his redemption. Characteristic of his Trinitarian teaching is his insistence: "They are one, not by union of person, but by unity of substance." Yet the charge of Docetism has been leveled against him for his separation of the natures of our Lord in his earthly life; Hilary held that Jesus possessed unique, "heavenly" flesh.

**Hilda** (614–680). English abbess. Born in Northumbria of noble parents, Hilda was baptized by Archbishop Paulinus of York on Easter, 627. She did not enter the religious life until 649 when Aidan called her to become abbess of Hartlepool. She founded a double monastery at Whitby in 659, where among her subjects were John of Beverley, Caedmon, and Wilfrid of York. At the Synod of Whitby she supported Celtic customs. Her life is related in Bede's *Ecclesiastical History.*

**Hildebrand.** See GREGORY VII.

**Hilton, Walter** (d. 1396). An Augustinian canon of Thurgarton in Nottinghamshire, and author of *Scala Perfectionis* (*The Scale of Perfection*), a classic of English mysticism. The *Scale* attempts to present the whole of spiritual life: Part I, asceticism; Part II, more properly mystical. Like *The Cloud of Unknowing,* it insists on willing assent to grace. Hilton also warns against Richard Rolle's emotionalism: The goal is not to feel love, but "great rest and quietness of the body and of the soul" in God.

**Hincmar** (806–882). Archbishop of Reims. He was a pupil of Hilduin at St.-Denis. Loyal to Louis the Pious in the revolt of 830, Hincmar was appointed to the see of Reims (845) and received the pallium from Leo IV (846). The emperor Lothair challenged Hincmar's right to Reims by supporting the claims of Ebbo, deposed in 835 and 841. The Synod of Soissons (853) confirmed Hincmar in his office and declared the ordinations performed by Ebbo after 840 invalid. The decrees were confirmed by Benedict III (855) and Nicholas

I (863). Hincmar tried unsuccessfully to maintain his metropolitan rights against Nicholas I, who upheld the appointment of Wulfad to the see of Bourges, reinstated the deposed Rothade at Soissons, and confirmed the marriage of Judith of Burgundy with Baldwin of Flanders. Hincmar opposed the divorce of Lothair II from Teutberga, but Lothair died before the question had been settled. In the controversy over predestination, Hincmar opposed Gottschalk, Lupus of Ferrières, and Prudentius of Troyes. In 869 he crowned Charles the Bald king of Lorraine, but opposed his coronation as emperor (875). Among Hincmar's extant writings are about eighty letters, *The Annals of St.-Bertin Abbey,* a life of Remi, several exhortations to Charles on the ideal ruler, and the treatises *On Predestination and Free Will,* and *On the One and Not the Triple God.*

**Hinsley, Arthur** (1865–1943). Roman Catholic cardinal and primate in Great Britain. Ordained in 1891, Hinsley pursued a distinguished academic career in England and became rector of the English College in Rome. Becoming Visitor Apostolic to Africa in 1927, he was made archbishop of Westminster in 1935, and cardinal in 1937. He befriended workingmen, inaugurated the Sword of the Spirit movement for a moral international order, and opposed Nazi aggressions, and religious and racial persecutions.

**Hippolytus** (c. 160–236). A presbyter and teacher of the Roman Church, author of the *Philosophumena,* or *Refutation of All Heresies,* one of the last and longest of the anti-Gnostic treatises. Already under Bishop Victor (189–198), he seems to have hoped for the succession, in rivalry with the deacon Callistus, against whom Hippolytus supported a rigorist discipline, refusing absolution for mortal sins. He later attacked Callistus, a freedman who had been engaged in business, as a disreputable character, but the dispute seems basically one between the strict theologian and the more pastorally minded administrator. It is also an early example of the conflict of presbyters and deacons, who in the early church were lower in rank but as immediate assistants to the bishop often more influential. Under Zephyrinus (198–217), perhaps chosen as a compromise candidate, the policy of Callistus generally prevailed. Hippolytus' church order, the Apostolic Tradition, is in part his manifesto against it, perhaps in view of the next election. But Callistus was chosen bishop of Rome (217–222), and Hippolytus set himself up as a rival, the first antipope. A late chapter of the *Refuta-*

*tion* describes the "Callistans," who to most of the Christian world were the genuine Roman Church. When persecution broke out in 235, Hippolytus and Bishop Fabian were joined in exile and martyrdom; and thus, if not before, he was considered as reconciled to the church. His party does not seem to have survived him, though its principles were soon revived by Novatian.

Hippolytus' reputation was confused, and its revival in modern times has elements of romance. The Roman Church honored him as presbyter and martyr—by a natural confusion Damasus (c. 370) calls him a Novatianist. About 400, Prudentius describes the pilgrimages to Hippolytus' shrine, and gives a legend of his martydom based on the Hippolytus of Greek mythology. His works were described as those done by a bishop, but it could not be said of what see; some connected him with Portus at the mouth of the Tiber, where he may have lived, or he may be confused with a local martyr of the same name. His name was connected in different ways with several church orders derived from the Apostolic Tradition. After a thousand years of oblivion his memory was revived in 1551 by the discovery at Rome of a statue (headless unfortunately) erected by his admirers, with his Easter table and a list of his writings inscribed on the base. The *Refutation,* previously known in part, was published in full in 1851, and finally Schwartz in 1910 and Connolly conclusively in 1916 showed that the *Apostolic Tradition,* lost in Greek, can be reconstructed from ancient versions, especially Latin and Coptic.

Modern interest in Hippolytus is due largely to the fascinating description that the Apostolic Tradition gives of church life in the late 2d century. Except for a few matters involved in Hippolytus' controversies, such as the subordination of deacons, it does seem to be an honest recording of tradition. In spite of his great reputation in his own time as preacher and theologian, Hippolytus was on the whole a traditionalist rather than a creative thinker. In Christology he expounded but did not develop the Logos doctrine, tending somewhat to modalism. The *Philosophumena* (properly the title of the opening section of the *Refutation*) curiously anticipates Harnack's theory of the origin of gnosticism from Hellenic influence, but it is of value mainly for its accounts of Gnostic sects. Other preserved works include a brief commentary on Daniel, of interest for its effort to fix the year of the birth of Christ (in the authentic text not the day), and fragments of other commentaries and sermons. Hippolytus seems to have been the first Christian scholar to construct an Easter table independent of contemporary Judaism—perhaps a result of the Paschal controversy of the 190's in which Rome stood for the observance of Easter on Sunday instead of at the Jewish Passover. As a first effort it was remarkable, but it was based on the false premise that five lunar cycles (ninety-five years) were sufficient for a perpetual Easter table. Its errors became apparent by 240 and led to better attempts. This is perhaps typical of Hippolytus' general position in Christian life and thought—his contributions were valuable, but soon superseded.

**Hirsch, Emanuel** (1888–    ). German Lutheran theologian. Born in Brandenburg, he became a *Privatdocent* in Bonn in 1915, was called to Göttingen as professor of church history in 1921, and moved to a chair of systematic theology in 1935. A writer in philosophy and doctrine, he pursued studies in Luther and Kierkegaard. His major recent work is *Geschichte der neureren evangelischen Theologie* (5 vols., 1949–1954). After 1945, Hirsch fell into disfavor because of his approval of National Socialism.

**Historians of the Middle Ages.** The historians of the Middle Ages rarely show traces of the objective disciplines followed by the professional modern historian with his cautious sifting of evidence and striving for balanced judgment. Their historical writings are permeated with the religious spirit and its bias; their use of original sources is mostly quite uncritical; their record of fact all too often turns aside into the byways of folklore, hearsay, guesswork, and anecdote. Readability varies, yet the element of human interest is rarely lost. The antiquarian spirit that is basic to historical writing flourished within traditional institutions such as the church, and it showed itself in a wide variety of contexts: church histories, encyclopedic outlines, national records, letters, law codes, biography, hagiography, and personal reminiscences of contemporary events. These and other genres are abundantly represented all through the Middle Ages, at first exclusively in Latin and then later in the various vernaculars as well. Universal history stretches from the *Seven Books of History Against the Pagans* of the Spanish priest Orosius in the 5th century, the *Institutes of Divine and Human Letters* of Cassiodorus (d. 583), the *Etymologies* of Isidore of Seville (d. 636), through the *Antapodosis,* or survey of European history, by Liutprand, bishop of Cremona in the 10th century, to the romantic histories of the *Gesta Romanorum* in the 13th century, and

the ambitious *Polychronicon* of Ranulf Higden (d. 1364). National records, of varying reliability, run from Jordanes' account of the wars of the Goths in the 6th century, based on Cassiodorus; Isidore's history of the Goths and Vandals; the notable *History of the Franks* by Gregory of Tours (d. 594), continued by Fredegar in the next century; the *Fall of Britain* by the monk Gildas (lived c. 550) and its sequel the *History of the Britons* by the Welsh compiler Nennius, possibly of the 9th century; Paul the Deacon's entertaining *History of the Lombards* in the 8th century; the *History of the Archbishops of Hamburg-Bremen* by Adam of Bremen (d. c. 1076), of wider scope than its title would suggest; the histories of the kings of Britain by Geoffrey of Monmouth (d. 1154) and William of Malmesbury (d. c. 1143); and the *History of the Angles* by Matthew Paris (d. 1259), until we finally arrive at the far-reaching *Chronicles* of Jean Froissart (d. c. 1410). The Anglo-Saxon Chronicle, yearly records kept up continuously from Alfred's day to the 12th century, is the first of the many vernacular records. The church histories of Eusebius of Caesarea (d. c. 340), Bede (d. 735), and Ordericus Vitalis (d. c. 1142) exemplify a long tradition. In his judicious handling of sources Bede comes perhaps closest of all to the modern view of history. Asser, Alfred's contemporary, and for Charlemagne, Einhard (d. 840) and Notker of St. Gall (d. 912), provide anecdotal lives of sovereigns, while in the 12th century Fulcher of Chartres (d. c. 1127) and Guibert of Nogent (d. 1124) supply revealing pictures of the First Crusade, the first account enlivened by personal testimony.

**Historical Study in the Middle Ages.** The fathers of the church bequeathed to the scholars of the Middle Ages a view of history as the story of God's children on their way to salvation. In contrast to the classical view, it was universal and linear, moving in foreordained stages from the Creation to the incarnation, and thence to the Day of Judgment. Consequently, medieval historians, working from the basis of Scripture, and seeing the need to accommodate classical histories to the Christian scheme, were conscious from the beginning of problems of chronology and periodization. Moreover, viewing man less as an agent than as an instrument for God's purposes, they were more concerned to interpret events as clues to God's intentions than to seek social or political significance in them. Once the expectation of an imminent Second Coming had faded, and Eusebius had attached the hopes of Christendom to the success of the Roman state, the belief prevailed that submission to the vicissitudes of time was a Christian duty, since the world was clearly approaching its end, even though the precise day must remain hidden. Jerome interpreted Daniel's vision of the four beasts as representing the four ancient empires, with Rome as the last. Augustine divided all time into seven periods, corresponding to the seven days of Creation, with the period from the incarnation to Doomsday as the sixth and last before an eternity of rest. Orosius combined these schemes by identifying in his widely read history the sixth day with the duration of the Roman Empire. It followed, then, that the end of the Roman Empire, seen after Charlemagne's day as living on in the German state, would bring the end of time. The sense that the direction of history was predetermined, the tendency of medieval education to treat the written word as allegory, and the subordination of historiography to exegesis led to a concentration on the typical and recurrent to the detriment of the individual characterization or the revealing anecdote. The historian was charged with the duty of maintaining a record of events lest the memory of good examples, or bad ones, should perish. Hence the credulity concerning miracles and the attention paid to comets, floods, and other signs of divine displeasure. Hence also the widespread habit of incorporating whole paragraphs from Roman writers into descriptions of contemporary events. Though there were attempts at national histories, such as the account of the Goths by Cassiodorus and the history of the Franks by Gregory of Tours, the general shortage of books and absence of analytical training made the typical history, when it was not a simple annal, mainly a universal history, copied from the Bible, Eusebius, and Orosius, with an appendix of events in the writer's own area to bring it up to date. Bede's *Ecclesiastical History of the English Nation* was an outstanding exception, showing great care in the listing of sources, the separation of fact from hearsay, and genuine research. But in general the best history written was contemporary and local, usually of a monastery. In time many monasteries, particularly those near important cities, such as St.-Denis, or on main roads, such as St. Alban's, built up from personal observation and travelers' tales a continuous record of events over several centuries. With the rapid acceleration of change from the middle of the 11th century, many historians abandoned the traditional attitude toward novelty as the outcome of sin or a trial sent by God and attempted an exegesis of the changes of their times to discover what might be in store. The propaganda war of the investiture controversy stimulated a critical examination of the papacy's claims and an investigation of past records. The Crusades inspired several accounts in the vernacular. The revival of learning found expression in the carefully designed *Chronicle* of Otto of Freising, who saw the turbulence of his century as the logical outcome of all previous history and as clear evidence of the approach of Doomsday. Though the belief that the world was hastening to its end was to last well into the 17th century, the naturalism spread by the reception of Aristotle in the 13th century and the growth of the nation-state fostered the writing of national histories in which the universality and eschatology of earlier writing disappeared. From the 14th century onward, historians tended to be secular clerics rather than monks, often in close touch with national politics. In the *Chronicles* of Froissart, history became the secular and purely literary genre that was to be the norm of the Renaissance historians.

BIBLIOGRAPHY: J. T. Shotwell, *The History of History* (New York, 1939); J. W. Thompson, *A History of Historical Writing*, Vol. I (New York, 1942).

**Hoadly, Benjamin** (1676–1761). Latitudinarian English divine, successively bishop of Bangor (1716), Hereford (1721), Salisbury (1723), and Winchester (1734). His sermon against visible church authority (1717) provoked the Bangor controversy which issued in the proroguing of Convocation by Royal Writ. Mostly absent from his dioceses, he devoted himself to writing and speaking for such causes as the pure memorial character of the Eucharist, and against High Churchmen and nonjurors.

**Hobart, John H.** (1775–1830). Episcopal bishop. Educated at the College of New Jersey, he served several parishes, including Trinity, New York. In 1806 he founded the Protestant Episcopal Theological Society, which soon became General Seminary, where he taught after 1821. In 1816 he was made bishop of New York. He was High Church, a defender of orthodoxy against liberalism, and a devoted, energetic church leader.

**Hobbes, Thomas** (1588–1679). English philosopher. The precocious son of a country vicar, Hobbes was educated at Oxford, and in 1608 he became tutor to the young William Cavendish, later second earl of Devonshire, maintaining an association with the family through most of his life. With his pupil he traveled on the Continent and subsequently determined to devote his energies to the study of the classics and to writing. Acquainted with Bacon, Lord Herbert of Cherbury, and Ben Johnson, he began his career as a philosopher when about forty and at the same time began to study mathematics and the new physical sciences. In 1634 he visited Galileo in Italy and encountered the leading thinkers at Paris. He also became deeply concerned with political philosophy, composing his treatise *The Elements of Law* as he watched the quarrel develop between king and Parliament in England. In 1640 he fled to France, where he remained for eleven years, serving as tutor to the Prince of Wales, later Charles II. During his exile he wrote a political analysis called *De cive* as well as his greatest work, *Leviathan.* In 1651 he returned to England, having made his peace with the Council of State, completed his serious writing by 1658, and spent the rest of his life defending his writings. Holding a materialistic view of human nature, he argued that only the state, the Leviathan, the "mortal god," stands between man and nature. He thus subordinated the ecclesiastical to secular authority and accepted the creed of the national church only as an act of obedience to the law of the state.

**Hocking, William Ernest** (1873–1966). Philosopher and educator. He was professor of philosophy at Harvard and in 1932 editor of *Rethinking Missions,* which suggested, in reflecting a questioning of the mission enterprise as traditionally conceived, that educational and philanthropic work be commended, but that missionaries be freed from any responsibility for "conscious and direct evangelization." Instead, they were to foster intercultural penetration, which would bring about a synthesis of all religions.

**Hodge, Archibald Alexander** (1823–1886). American Presbyterian theologian. Named after Archibald Alexander, the first professor of theology at Princeton Seminary. A. A. Hodge continued the work of his father, Charles, who had been a student of Alexander's and later professor of theology at the Seminary. He became professor of theology at Western (Presbyterian) Seminary in Allegheny (now Pittsburgh), Pa., in 1864, and moved to Princeton in 1877 as continuator of the orthodox, Calvinist theology of the school.

**Hodge, Charles** (1797–1878). The professor at Princeton Seminary (1822–1878) who contributed more than any other single person to the shaping of American Presbyterianism. Initially an advocate of moderation, he remained so until the division of the denomination in 1837, after which he wholeheartedly supported the Old School, even opposing the reunion effected in 1869. Trained at Princeton and in Germany under F. A. G. Tholuck, E. W. Hengstenberg, and J. A. W. Neander, he developed a systematic theology that he believed was faithful to the Westminster Standards and other Reformed confessions, and he devoted his intellectual abilities to expounding and defending this in the classroom, in the periodical which became the *Princeton Review,* and in his three-volume *Systematic Theology,* which was published in the early 1870's and was the source of much of his later influence.

**Hoffmeister, Johannes** (c. 1509–1547). An Augustinian eremite and writer who labored strenuously to combat Lutheran influence on his order and to bring about reform within the Roman Catholic Church. Hoffmeister gained a reputation as a speaker and preached at the Diet of Worms in 1545. The tone of both his preaching and his writing, however, was decidedly polemical. He was made vicar-general of the Augustinian eremites in Germany (1546), but died within a year.

**Hofmann, Johann Christian Konrad von** (1810–1877). German theologian, active in the 19th-century Lutheran confessional revival, and a leader of the Erlangen school. In his *Interpreting the Bible* (1880) he maintained that true faith was a prerequisite for a correct understanding of Scripture. As a safeguard against subjectivism, there were the confessions of the Lutheran Church. In his *Prophecy and Fulfillment* (1841) he sought to relate dogmatics and Biblical theology more closely. Though he was a confessional Lutheran, his critique of the substitutionary view of the atonement laid him open to criticism from orthodox circles.

**Hofmann, Melchior** (c. 1496–1544). The most important inspirer of Netherlands Anabaptism after 1530. He was a lay student of Scripture and preached and wrote widely in Baltic lands in an earlier Lutheran phase. A passionate eschatology, a "heavenly flesh" Christology, a spiritualist view of Communion, and a strong claim to an experience of the Holy Spirit as a touchstone to Scripture distinguish him. He spent the last ten years of his life imprisoned in Strasbourg. (See MELCHIORITES.)

**Hohenstaufen Dynasty.** The Hohenstaufen emperors, coming from Swabia, ruled the Holy Roman Empire from 1138 to 1254. The dynasty ended with Conrad IV in 1268. The period witnessed feudal decentralization in Germany and the collapse of German power in Italy. The most notable Hohenstaufen rulers were Conrad III (1138–1152), Frederick I Barbarossa (1152–1190), Henry VI (1190–1197), and Frederick II (1215–1250). Throughout their intermittent struggles, supporters of the imperial party were known as Ghibellines, their opponents, the anti-imperial papal party, as Guelphs.

**Holbach, Paul H. D.** (1723–1789). French philosopher of German origin. One of the Encyclopedists, Holbach contributed in the area of natural science. A materialist in thought, he became famous for his attacks on Christianity and its philosophical connections. His most famous work, *Le Système de la nature* (1770), advances atheism founded on the purest and crudest materialism. Ethics is proposed as enlightened self-interest.

**Holcot, Robert** (d. 1349). Dominican theologian. Holcot studied and taught at Cambridge; later he taught at Oxford, where he entered into controversy with Thomas Bradwardine. Despite the Thomistic tradition of his order, Holcot was deeply influenced by the nominalism of Occam. It has been claimed that he distinguished so sharply between faith and reason as to maintain a doctrine of double truth, according to which a proposition could be theologically true, but philosophically false (or vice versa). Certainly, he held that natural (i.e., Aristotelian) logic could not deal with matters of faith, such as the Trinity, but this in fact led him to seek a higher logic, a "logic of faith," which would comprehend both philosophical and theological truth. It was a fundamental principle of his thinking that supernatural gifts are given to those who make fullest use of their natural endowments. Hence revelation is granted to the man who uses his reason to the utmost, and sanctifying grace to the man who first "does his best" (*facit quod in se est*). In neither case is God a debtor to man, but, rather, acts according to a covenant he has himself established, this being the sense of the distinction between the "absolute" and the "ordained" power of God. Both Holcot and his famous adversary, Bradwardine, died of the plague in 1349.

**Holiness Churches.** A term originally applied to those groups which revived and emphasized the Methodist doctrine of entire sanctification. Most of these groups accepted the doctrines of traditional Methodism, but laid particular emphasis upon the work of the Holy Spirit subsequent to baptism as a definite experience of divine grace. The largest of these bodies in the United States is the Church of the Nazarene. The term is also applied to Pentecostal churches, which grew out of the earlier Holiness movement and stressed a baptism of the Holy Spirit subsequent to regeneration, which was manifested in glossolalia (i.e., ecstatic speaking in unknown tongues). This latter movement arose in Kansas in 1901 and later became prominent in Los Angeles in 1906 through meetings led by W. J. Seymour, Frank Bartleman, and Joseph Smale. The Pentecostal movement has grown rapidly, making a special appeal to rootless and disinherited groups. It has grown from 23,000 members in 1906 to over 1,000,000 in 1948. The theology of the group is a conservative Biblicism that emphasizes experience as a test of orthodoxy. The largest United States bodies of this worldwide movement are the Assemblies of God, the Church of God, the Church of God in Christ, and the International Church of the Foursquare Gospel.

**Holl, Karl** (1866–1926). A German church historian. Trained at Tübingen, Holl became Harnack's junior colleague at Berlin in 1906. He was an important contributor in the realm of patristics (Epiphanius, John of Damascus) as well as the primitive church. Holl's greatest impact came through his introduction of students and scholars to Luther. This influence is almost ubiquitous in the formation of the so-called neo-orthodox theologians.

**Holland, Conversion of.** Attempts made in the early 7th century to convert the population of what is now Holland met with little success. The death of Radbod, the king of the Frisians, reduced resistance to Christianity and in 690 Willibrord and his companions began the effective conversion of Frisia. In 695 he was made archbishop with his see at Utrecht. Continuing pagan resistance can be seen in the murder of Boniface of Crediton in 754 at Dokkum.

**Holland, Henry Scott** (1847–1918). English preacher, theologian, and zealous advocate of social reform. Educated at Oxford and deeply affected there by the idealist T. H. Green, he continued as senior student at Christ Church (1870) until he became canon of St. Paul's Cathedral (1884), which post he occupied until his election as regius professor at Oxford (1910), where he spent the remainder of his life. The most original of the *Lux Mundi* group, Holland was more a preacher than a systematic theologian, but his writings show the touch of genius attributed to him by R. C. Moberly. No less than ten volumes of his sermons were published from 1882 until after his death. In his lectures at Oxford on Plato and the Fourth Gospel he evinced the type of thinking later to characterize his article "Faith" in *Lux Mundi* (1889). Concomitant with his intellectual apologetic was his avid social concern which was evidenced by his meetings in Oxford in the 1870's, his preaching in Hoxton and his care of the Maurice Hostel there, and the founding (1889) of the Christian Social Union of whose organ *Commonwealth* he was editor from 1895 to 1912. Here he related Christianity to socialism, attacking the economic ills of English society. Illness prevented him from writing substantial treatises supported by rigorous research but his powerful, succinct style and perceptiveness in occasional papers compensated somewhat for this deficiency.

**Hollatz, David** (1648–1713). The last of the 17th-century German Lutheran orthodox theologians. His major work, *Examen theologicum acromaticum* (1707), went through many editions, assuming the status of a dogmatic compendium. This work shows both preoccupation with the doctrine of the inspiration of the Holy Scriptures and excessive use of reason so characteristic of the later orthodox theologians.

**Holmes, John Haynes** (1879–1964). Pastor of New York City's Unitarian Church of the Messiah (1907–1949), which after 1919 became a community church open to all faiths, races, classes, and creeds. Sensitive to social injustices, Holmes helped create the National Association for the Advancement of Colored People and became a director of the American Civil Liberties Union. He remained a staunch pacifist during both World Wars.

**Holtzmann, Heinrich Julius** (1832–1910). New Testament scholar and professor at Heidelberg (1858) and Strasbourg (1874–1904). His critical work on the priority of Mark and the assumption of a sayings source common to Matthew and Luke laid the foundations of modern Synoptic studies. Although caught in the psychological interpretation of Jesus' life, Holtzmann showed signs of eschatological interpretation of the teachings. His *New Testament Theology* also displayed early hints of form-historical method.

**Holy Alliance.** An idealistic pact proposed by Czar Alexander I of Russia, under the influence of Franz von Baader and Barbara Juliana, Baroness von Kruedener, to European princes gathered at Vienna in 1815. The preamble of the document announced the princes' intention of making Christian love, justice, and peace the rationale of future political action. Alexander's proposal was almost messianic. The signers agreed that "the sole principle of force, whether between the said Governments or between their subjects, shall be that of doing each other reciprocal service." The alliance was signed by monarchs of Russia, Austria, and Prussia on Sept. 26, 1815. It was eventually accepted in principle by most fellow princes except those of England and Turkey. The pope refused to sign because he was unable, in the name of religion, to cooperate with Protestant and Orthodox sovereigns. The idea of the Holy Alliance was feeble and incoherent from the start. The alliance stimulated no intellectual movement and had little original literature of its own. Nevertheless, it became the instrument of reactionary policy in Austria and Russia, and tended to identify religion with reactionary politics. By 1822 the idealism of the war years had given way, especially in Britain, to realistic diplomacy. Canning's statement, "Every nation for itself, and God for us all," was the death knell for an alliance that was already impotent.

**Holy Apostles, Church of.** An architectural masterpiece of the 6th century, offering the most exact picture of Byzantium during the splendor of the Macedonian renaissance. Located in Constantinople, the edifice is remarkable for its five domes, for the richness of its marbles, metalwork, and magnificent mosaics, and for its sarcophagi of porphyry in which are buried ten generations of emperors. St. Mark's Church in Venice, an exact reproduction of the Church of Holy Apostles, was built in the 11th century.

**Holy Lance.** The lance used by the Roman soldier to pierce the side of Christ after his death. Supposedly authentic relics of this lance have existed in various places throughout the past. One formerly in Constantinople is now at the Vatican. Another which was in Ste.-Chapelle has been lost since the French Revolution. Another was uncovered at Antioch during the First Crusade. Still another was part of the regalia of the Holy Roman Emperors.

**Holy Office.** Because of fear of the spread of Protestantism in Italy, cardinals such as Caraffa thought it imperative that the papal Inquisition be centralized and made thoroughly efficient. Hence, in 1542, Paul III was persuaded to create a Congregation of the Curia as a final court in cases involving heresy. Formerly the Holy Office was charged with the censorship of books, and all matters affecting faith and morals.

**Holy Roman Empire.** Created in 962 when the king of Germany, Otto I the Great (936–972), was crowned Roman emperor by Pope John XII, the Holy Roman Empire represented medieval man's belief in the unity of

Christendom and his admiration for the past glories of Rome. Even with the dismemberment of the western half of the Roman Empire by the Germanic peoples and the deposition of the last emperor in the West in 476 the charisma of Rome remained. Almost every early Germanic king recognized the theoretical suzerainty of the emperor at Constantinople. In practice the West knew no political unity until the reign of the Frankish king Charlemagne (768–814). Charles succeeded in bringing much of western Europe, with the exception of Spain and southern Italy, under the authority of a single monarch. As the most powerful ruler in the West, Charlemagne became the protector of the papacy, and in return for his protection Charlemagne, on Christmas Day in 800, was crowned Roman emperor by Pope Leo III. In theory the Roman Empire had been restored in the West. Nevertheless, though his successors maintained the imperial title until 887, after Charlemagne's death his empire rapidly disintegrated. The title was claimed for a while by petty Italian princes, but for all intents and purposes imperial authority, even in Italy, was a phantom, and by the first decades of the 10th century no one bothered to claim the shadowy imperial honor.

In 962, however, the German king Otto I, like Charlemagne before him, crossed the Alps to come to the aid of a pope plagued by the factious Roman populace. Annexing Italy to his kingdom, Otto in February was crowned Roman emperor, thus reviving Charlemagne's title. In reality, however, Otto's empire was less universal and less Roman than that of Charles. West Frankland (France) was not included in the realm; the new empire was in actuality merely the union of Germany and northern Italy. Yet if not as majestic as the empire of Charles, Otto's empire nevertheless bore the name of Rome, and this Holy Roman Empire, as it came to be called, continued to live out an existence for the next nine hundred years.

During the 10th and early 11th centuries the Holy Roman Empire was undoubtedly the most powerful state in Europe. Under the Ottonian dynasty (918–1024) the emperors successfully mastered the powerful German dukes, used the German Church to create an instrument of royal authority, and in effect supervised the papacy itself. Otto the Great, for example, deposed two popes and nominated his own candidates, as well as elicited a promise that papal elections would be subject to imperial approval. Though the Ottonian line died out to be replaced by the Salian dynasty (1024–1125), the power structure built

up by Otto I remained in force during the reigns of the first two Salian emperors, Conrad II (1024–1039) and Henry III (1039–1056). Indeed, Conrad was able to annex the kingdom of Burgundy to his empire, and the reign of Henry III is often taken to mark the high point of imperial power and prestige.

Yet the very strength of the Empire (its alliance with and support by the church) proved also to be one of its most dangerous weaknesses. Royal officials were almost exclusively clerics; bishops and abbots, used as counterweights to secular lords, were granted privileges that made them great feudal lords in their own right. The system worked to the advantage of the monarchy as long as the emperor retained control over episcopal personnel. But the emperors, by freeing the church from local magnates and by lifting the papacy out of the morass of Roman politics, unwittingly created a powerful rival that would dispute imperial preeminence and ultimately eclipse it. The papacy, revitalized and dominated by a series of able and strong-willed pontiffs, sought to shake off imperial control and to assert its authority over the entire Western Church.

The conflict between pope and emperor that was to continue throughout the medieval period broke out in the reign of Henry IV (1056–1106). Pope Gregory VII, consumed with the desire to reform the church and to assert papal supremacy, believed that the subordination of the spiritual to the temporal authority was intolerable. Thus in 1176 he issued his famous bull *Dictatus papae*, which declared among other things that the pope has the right to judge and to depose secular monarchs, even the emperor. He then moved to strip Henry of his control over the German Church by promulgating a bull that forbade the investment of bishops by secular authorities. Henry was warned to cease investing bishops with the symbols of their spiritual authority—the ring and the staff—and when Henry repudiated Gregory's bull, the pope excommunicated the emperor and declared him deposed. Allied with rebellious German nobles, Gregory brought Henry to heel for a time. In 1077 the emperor, seeing his authority in Germany crumbling, appeared before the castle of Canossa, where Gregory was temporarily residing. For three days Henry stood before the castle gates in the garb of a humble penitent beseeching the pope's pardon and absolution. Gregory relented and lifted the sentences of excommunication and deposition. Later, Henry was able to defeat his rebellious nobles and even to drive Gregory from Rome. But the episode at Canossa was a tremendous humiliation of imperial authority. Henceforth political theorists would use the event to justify papal claims to supremacy.

A compromise with the papacy over lay investiture was reached by Henry V (1106–1125). By the terms of the Concordat of Worms (1122) it was agreed that episcopal elections would be free, but that an imperial representative would be present at each election. After election the bishop would swear fealty to the emperor for his lands and political authority; he was, however, to be invested with the symbols of his spiritual authority by fellow ecclesiastics. The Concordat did ensure that some imperial supervision of episcopal personnel would remain, but implicit was the fact that German ecclesiastics no longer owed primary allegiance to the emperor rather to the pope.

Until Henry V the imperial crown had been passed down more or less by hereditary succession to the descendants of Otto I. Henry V, however, died childless, and the German princes then seized the opportunity of asserting the elective principle, choosing Lothair II as emperor. The election was disputed by the closest relatives of Henry V, the Hohenstaufen, and thus was born the Guelph-Ghibelline struggle that would rend the empire for over one hundred years. The Guelph faction, which tended to support the elective principle and the papacy, though defeated more than once, was to remain a threat to the Ghibelline Hohenstaufen even after the family had secured the crown.

Under the Hohenstaufen it appeared for a time that imperial power might again be reasserted. The strongest member of the dynasty, Frederick I Barbarossa (1152–1190), managed to check the growing power of the German nobles and even secured for a short time a certain measure of control over northern Italy. Nevertheless, the Lombard communes, in alliance with the papacy, which was fearful for its newly won independence, ultimately smashed Frederick's army in 1176 at Legnano. Frederick was forced to recognize the autonomy of the towns of northern Italy. Yet the dream of subjugating Italy continued to dominate his house, and Hohenstaufen ambitions brought forth the implacable hatred of the papacy that henceforth sought to destroy the Hohenstaufen and to cripple imperial power. Frederick's son Henry VI (1190–1197) through marriage to the heiress of Sicily almost succeeded in uniting all of Italy under imperial authority. His premature death wrecked the promise of a resurgent empire, for his heir, the three-year-old Frederick II (1198–1250), was passed over in

Germany and was threatened in Sicily as well. Finally, however, after civil war in Germany (civil war fostered and prolonged by the papacy which sought to prevent the union of Sicily and the Empire and to further circumscribe imperial power) Frederick was chosen emperor. However, Frederick neglected Germany in a vain attempt to create an Italian kingdom, and at his death in 1250 the Empire had ceased to be a viable political entity. The elective principle had triumphed; with few exceptions no emperor attempted again to conquer Italy, and royal authority in Germany declined in the face of the ever-increasing power of the German princelings. The promulgation of the Golden Bull (1356) by the emperor Charles IV severed all ties with Italy. The papacy was excluded from any part in the selection of the emperor, and his election was placed in the hands of seven German princes (the archbishops of Trier, Mainz, and Cologne, and the king of Bohemia, the duke of Saxony, the margrave of Brandenburg, and the count palatine of the Rhine). All the princelings of Germany were henceforth guaranteed sovereign rights within their territories and imperial authority remained only as a titular vestige of German unity.

From 1273 until 1806 the imperial title was virtually monopolized by the Hapsburgs, who used the office to augment their Austrian possessions. During the reign of Charles V (1519–1556), who as king of Spain and Sicily as well as Holy Roman Emperor controlled much of western Europe, the Empire regained some prestige, but the Protestant Reformation shattered any chance that it might again become an effective force in European politics. By the terms of the treaties of Westphalia (1648), which ended the Thirty Years' War, the territorial independence of the German principalities was confirmed and strengthened. All imperial authority over the internal affairs of the German states was denied, and German princes were allowed to contract foreign alliances. The Holy Roman Empire was henceforth only a weak confederation of German principalities with a Hapsburg emperor as its titular head. Finally, in 1806, the Holy Roman Empire was dissolved by Napoleon. Although after 1250 the Empire had ceased to have any real political importance, it lingered on for another six hundred years as a testament to the aspirations and ideals of medieval man for a united Christian commonwealth in which the temporal and spiritual authority worked together for the benefit of Christendom.

BIBLIOGRAPHY: G. Barraclough, *The Medieval Empire* (London, 1950); and *Medieval*

*Germany*, 2 vols. (Oxford, 1938); J. Bryce, *The Holy Roman Empire* (London, 1950); H. A. L. Fisher, *The Medieval Empire*, 2 vols. (New York, 1898); G. Tellenbach, *Church, State, and Christian Society at the Time of the Investiture Contest* (Oxford, 1940); J. W. Thompson, *Feudal Germany* (Chicago, 1928); T. F. Tout, *The Empire and the Papacy* (London, 1914).

**Holy Spirit Fathers.** A religious order formed in 1848. This Roman Catholic religious order was created in 1848 by the fusion of the nearly defunct Congregation of the Holy Ghost (founded in 1709 by Claude François Poullart des Places) and the newly formed Congregation of the Immaculate Heart of Mary, which had been designed by the Jewish convert Francis Mary (Jakob) Libermann (1804–1852). Libermann became superior general and "second founder" of the Holy Spirit Fathers, popularly known as the "Black Fathers."

**Home Missions Council.** An organization founded in 1908 for interdenominational cooperation in home missions. Created amid a scene of fierce denominational competition in America, this was an organization of fellowship and conference consisting of churches or denominational missionary societies officially meeting to allocate mission fields through the principle of comity and to pioneer in other cooperative ventures. In 1950, the Home Missions Council was incorporated into the National Council of the Churches of Christ in the U.S.A.

**Homoeans.** Mediating party of Arianizers, supported by Constantius (sole emperor, 351–361), which tried to solve the *homoousion* controversy by omitting reference to *ousia*. At the Synod of Antioch (344), the Macrostich, a creed plus explications, was adopted, stating that Christ was "in all things like (*homoion*) the Father" (Athanasius, *De synodis* §26). Combining political dexterity with doctrinal ambiguity, the Homoeans were defeated at the First Council of Constantinople in 381.

**Honoratus** (c. 350–429). Archbishop of Arles. After his conversion to Christianity, Honoratus and his brother set out for a pilgrimage to the Holy Land. His brother's death forced him to turn back. He turned his zeal toward the founding of a monastery at Lérins (c. 410) which he continued to govern after his election as archbishop of Arles. He was succeeded by his student, Hilary of Arles.

**Honorius I** (d. 638). Pope from 625, elected successor to Boniface V. In England he con-

tinued the work of Pope Gregory I the Great. He conferred the pallium on the bishops of Canterbury and York, he commissioned Birinus to preach Christianity in Wessex, and he admonished the Irish for not following the church's teachings in the celebration of Easter. In the East with the aid of Emperor Heraclius (610–641), he ended the schism in Istria and Venetia by the deposition in 628 of the schismatic patriarch Fortunatus of Aquileia-Grado.

The support of Heraclius may have led the pope to misunderstand the formula of one will in Christ, the doctrine of Monotheletism, adopted by the emperor and advanced by Sergius, patriarch of Constantinople. Wishing to reconcile the Monophysite East with the orthodox West, the patriarch wrote Honorius, asking for a ruling on the doctrine. In agreement, Honorius replied that "there being only one principle of action, or one direction of the will in Christ, therefore there must be one will also," adding that the question of one or two wills was "a point which I leave to grammarians as a matter of very little importance." This was later called the Monothelete heresy. Forty-two years after his death, the Sixth Ecumenical Council, meeting at Constantinople in 680, repudiated monotheletism and condemned Honorius I as "a favorer of heretics." This action of the Council has been cited by historians to counter the claims of papal infallibility.

**Honorius III** (Cencio Savelli, d. 1227). Pope from 1216, successor to Innocent III. He continued the former's vigorous ecclesiastical and political policies. Alert to the problem of ecclesiastical reform, he gave approval to the new mendicant orders, Franciscans and Dominicans, while attempting to maintain Innocent's influence over the princes of Europe. His political activity was directed toward checking the power of Emperor Frederick II. His letters and survey of papal resources (*Liber censum Romanae ecclesiae*) are valuable sources for the secular activities of the 13th-century papacy.

**Honorius of Autun** (Augustodunensis) (early 12th century). A widely read and influential Scholastic theologian of the early 12th century. His theological works, based primarily upon Anselm and Eriugena, display the prevailing Platonism of early medieval theology. Although his name suggests that he came from Autun in Burgundy, he is thought to have come from Regensburg in Germany. Nothing more is known of his life.

**Hontheim, Johann Nikolaus von.** See FEBRONIANISM.

**Hooker, Richard** (c. 1553–1600). Anglican divine and apologist of the Elizabethan Settlement of religion. He was born of humble parents but through the patronage of John Jewel, bishop of Salisbury, was admitted to Corpus Christi, Oxford, in 1568. He was advanced to scholar in 1573, to fellow in 1577, and to deputy professor of Hebrew in 1579. In about 1581 he was ordained. His marriage to Joan Churchman in 1584 necessitated his resignation from Oxford. He became rector of Drayton Beauchamp, Buckinghamshire, and the following year master of the Temple in London. Here his theological acumen came to the fore as his morning sermons developed into a defense of the English Church against the Temples' famous Puritan afternoon lecturer, Walter Travers. This debate was on the highest level of personal regard, Travers having married Hooker's sister, but Hooker's deep respect for Calvin's doctrine of election was in this debate overshadowed by his sometimes acrimonious criticism of other facets of Calvin emphasized by the Puritans.

After Travers had been silenced in 1586 by an order from Whitgift, archbishop of Canterbury, Hooker set about developing seriously his defense of the Church of England's position on doctrine and polity, an effort that would issue in his *Treatise on the Laws of Ecclesiastical Polity*. Asking less arduous duty than the Temple, he was first made rector of Boscombe, Wiltshire (1591), and then rector of Bishopsbourne, near Canterbury (1592), where he spent his last days. From here he published the first four of the projected eight books of the *Treatise* in 1594, with a promise of the rest. In 1597, the fifth book, longer than the sum of the other four, was published. Much controversy has seethed over the authenticity of the last three books, published posthumously in a variety of editions. That these were quite possibly revised in a Puritan direction by his opponents is not altogether refuted by Spencer's preface to the 1604 edition of the first five which reports that the finished version of the last three was destroyed leaving only "dismembered pieces . . . of old draughts." The sixth book in its present form is the most highly contested, since the Table of Contents preceding the first volume promised that this book would handle the question of lay elders and presbyterian jurisdiction, although the now extant version only briefly discusses spiritual governance and moves rapidly to a lengthy exposition of penance. An Oxford manuscript commenting on the original confirms the doubt and implies that the original carried out the projected task. The present version may well have been derived from Hooker's notes made for another work. The seventh and eighth books are apparently compiled from Hooker's rather substantial previous drafts, but the quality of their style and outlook are decidedly below that of the first five.

Hooker's complaint against the Puritans, who contested episcopacy because it was unscriptural, developed into a complex theory of law in which natural law was the foundation and norm. The first two books of the *Treatise* argue, contrary to the Puritan notion that doctrines and institutions not expressly ordained in Scripture are in error, that natural law expressing God's supreme reason and accessible to man's reason and binding upon man's reason is the authority by which all human institutions, including the church, must be guided. The Scriptures must also be interpreted in the light of this authority, since instead of expounding the natural law, they supplement it by a supernatural law. His reference to the "common consent" understanding of government as applied to ecclesiastical polity forms the basis of the quite divergent *Treatise on Civil Government* by Locke. Book III denies that any unalterable form of church polity is found in Scripture, while in Book IV he justifies English polity against Reformed or Roman. At detailed length, Book V exonerates from all opposing charges the rites and ceremonies of the English Church; the seventh and eighth books respectively expound advantages of episcopacy over presbyterianism and the relations of church and state derived therefrom. The last is a defense of royal supremacy.

The continuing effect of Hooker's thought on Anglican theology, particularly upon High Churchmen, can be seen in the successive editions of his works: 1662, ed. by John Gauden; 1793, ed. by John Randolph; 1836, ed. by John Keble; 1888, ed. by R. W. Church and F. Paget (the last being the seventh and revised edition of the preceding and containing all literary remains).

**Hooker, Thomas** (1586–1647). Puritan churchman. A Cambridge graduate, Hooker was influenced by the Puritanism of John Rogers and William Ames. He first gained notoriety in 1626 as a "lecturer" at St. Mary's, Chelmsford, but conflict with Archbishop Laud led to his exile to Holland in 1630. He became pastor to an English nonconformist church at Delft. Hooker arrived in Boston, Mass., in 1633 with John Cotton and Samuel Stone. Later as minister at Newtown he participated in refuting Roger Williams' attacks on the "New England Way." Publicly critical of the limitation of sufferage to church members, Hooker moved his congregation to Connecticut in spite of the opposition of Cotton and the General Court. One of the founders of Hartford, Conn., he settled there in 1636, stressed the God-given power of the people to choose their magistrates, and maintained a stormy relationship with the Boston clergy. He nevertheless participated in the actions against Anne Hutchinson in 1637. During discussions for confederation of the New England colonies, Hooker came into conflict with John Winthrop over Erastianism and democracy. He insisted that the "foundation of all authority is laid in the free consent of the people." His views were embodied in the "Fundamental Orders" of Connecticut (1639). In 1643 he defended the "Congregational Way" against Presbyterianism, which led to his major work, *A Survey of the Summe of Church-Discipline* (1648).

**Hooper, John** (d. 1555). Bishop of Gloucester and Protestant martyr in the English Reformation. Hooper was educated at Oxford and entered a religious order (probably the Cistercian), but he early espoused Zwinglian views and was exiled on the Continent during the last years of Henry VIII's reign. At Zurich he made the personal acquaintance of Bullinger, Zwingli's successor, with whom he had already corresponded. In 1549 he became chaplain to the protector Somerset and the chief spokesman for the radical Protestant position in England. After being nominated for the bishopric of Gloucester, Hooper had to be imprisoned before he would accept consecration, because of his scruples about the oaths of the ordinal and the required vesture. In his diocesan administration at Gloucester, and later at Worcester into which it was subsumed, he tried to introduce a Zurich pattern of organization; he was also zealous in his opposition to ceremonies not authorized by the New Testament, such as kneeling for Communion. During Mary's reign he was imprisoned, deprived, tried for heresy, and, when he refused to recant, executed. He is sometimes called the "Father of Nonconformity," and his objection to "Aaronic vestments" anticipated the vestiarian controversy in the reign of Elizabeth.

**Hopedale Community.** A Christian socialist experiment, founded in 1841 at Milford, Mass., by Universalist Adin Ballou (1803–1890). A stockholding corporation whose members, in the spirit of Jesus, were bent on effecting the Kingdom of Heaven on earth, this community numbered nearly two hundred persons and gained moderate financial success by 1851. In 1856 it disbanded when private enterprise eclipsed its social idealism.

**Hopkins, John.** See STERNHOLD, THOMAS.

**Hopkins, John Henry** (1792–1868). Protestant Episcopal bishop. A native of Ireland, he came to America in 1800, and in 1832 was made first bishop of Vermont. He was noted for his versatile scholarship and initial support of the Oxford movement, but then later stated his thoughts in *The Law of Ritualism* (1866) by calling for a broad-mindedness. At the time of the Civil War he was loyal to the Union, but irenic in his attitude toward the South, which aided him as presiding elder in 1865 in healing the wounds in the church caused by the war.

**Hopkins, Mark** (1802–1887). Congregationalist clergyman and distinguished president of Williams College in Massachusetts (1836–1872). Hopkins was renowned for his lectures before scientific and literary societies, but his widest acclaim came in the classroom, where he employed the Socratic teaching method with excellent effect. He also served as president of the American Board of Commissioners for Foreign Missions (1857–1887).

**Hopkins, Samuel** (1721–1803). American Congregational minister and theologian. Graduating from Yale in 1741, he was given ministerial license in 1742 and appointed pastor in Great Barrington, Mass., in 1743. Hopkins was a close friend of Jonathan Edwards and spent much time with him after Edwards had moved in 1751 to the Stockbridge Indian mission a few miles north of Great Barrington. Hopkins, never a spirited or popular preacher, was dismissed from his pastorate in 1769. He moved to Newport, R.I., where he remained as pastor of the Congregational church until his death. This transfer from the backwoods to a busy seaport, although it did not affect his style of preaching, does seem to have made him more aware of social and ethical issues. Hopkins was one of the first New England leaders to denounce the slave trade as a moral evil. He was also an early advocate of foreign missions. His greatest contribution, however, was made as a theologian. His contributions to the New England Theology, often called Hopkinsianism, were associated particularly with the concept of "disinterested benevolence." The essence of sin, according to Hopkins, is selfishness, and the work of God's Spirit in the heart of man ought to produce instead concern for the good of all men or even, in his words, a willingness "to be damned for the glory of God."

**Hormisdas** (d. 523). Pope from 514. In ending the Acacian Schism in 519, he insisted that the Eastern bishops should sign the "Formula of Hormisdas," declaring that they accepted the true faith as always held by the Roman see. In the long run this was a significant step in the formulation of papal claims, but at the time it was at least one reason why the emperor Justinian was anxious to control the papacy when he recovered Italy from the Goths after 535.

**Hort, Fenton John Anthony** (1828–1892). English New Testament scholar. Educated at Rugby and Cambridge, Hort was a fellow at Cambridge from 1852 to 1857. In 1853 he began his famous work with B. F. Westcott on a new edition of the Greek New Testament which finally was published in 1881. In 1856 he was ordained as a priest in the Anglican Church and became the vicar of a parish near Cambridge until 1872 when he returned to Cambridge as a professor. In his early days at Cambridge, Hort became a lifelong friend and fellow worker with B. F. Westcott and J. B. Lightfoot. Of the three, Hort was known for his theological depth and his knowledge of patristic literature. His competence in other fields is also demonstrated by his being called six times to serve as an examiner in both moral and natural science. In his posthumous work, *The Way, the Truth, the Life* (1893), Hort revealed how an openness of mind could coexist with an unshaken grasp of central Biblical truths. Though it seemed at times that the Cambridge school became overabsorbed in the details of language, style, and the classification of New Testament manuscripts, the Cambridge trio always sought to keep before them the real end of theological study and to maintain that spiritual things were spiritually discerned. For Hort, the acquisition of truth in historical or linguistic matters was never an end but always a means, and he was especially anxious "not to drown literature and history in a textual flood."

**Hosius, Stanislaus** (1504–1579). Polish cardinal. Considered by Peter Canisius to be the most brilliant writer, most eminent theologian, and the best bishop of his time, Hosius was born in Kraków in 1504 and completed his studies in law and theology at Padua and Bologna. As bishop of Ermland (1551), he soon became the literary and practical leader of the Polish episcopate in its struggle against Protestantism. At the Synod of Piotrków (1551), he drew up a profession of faith, which he later expanded into his *Confessio Catholicae fidei Christiana*, a polemical work equating Roman Catholicism with Christianity, which saw thirty editions in his lifetime. He was created cardinal in 1561; in 1568, Pope Paul IV called him to Rome, where he became one of the most influential members of the Curia. As papal legate to Ferdinand I at Vienna, he arranged for the reopening of the last session of the Council of Trent. At the Council, he had much influence because of his powerful defense of papal authority, an influence he used to help bring the Council to a successful conclusion. He died near Rome in 1579.

**Hosius** (Ossius) **of Cordova** (c. 257–c. 358). Bishop and ecclesiastical adviser. Consecrated bishop c. 296, confessor in the Diocletian persecution (303), and participant in the Synod of Elvira, Hosius was Constantine's ecclesiastical counsel from 312 to 326. He was an influential orthodox protagonist against the Arians at the Synods of Alexandria, Antioch, Nicaea (presiding), and Sardica (author of some canons). Constantius ordered him to Sirmium (357), where, under threat and abuse, he subscribed an Arian formula but later retracted his signature. A Spanish synod condemned his behavior.

**Hospitalers.** The Knights of the Hospital of St. John, a military order of the era of the Crusades. Founded in 1048 to provide a hostel for poor pilgrims in Jerusalem, it received endowments from the Frankish state after the Latin kingdom of Jerusalem had been established in 1099. Originally Benedictine, the Hospitalers became an independent order, directly responsible to the pope. After 1118, when Raymond of Le Puy became master, the order took on military functions as well as those of hospitality to pilgrims, assisting the Templars in keeping the roads to Jerusalem open and furnishing the Frankish rulers with the most skilled fighting forces. As the power of the monarchy diminished, the Hospitalers, whose knights were identified by the white cross on their black tunics, became increasingly powerful, acquiring extensive lands in Palestine and Syria. Krak des Chevaliers, the best-preserved crusader castle, was their chief stronghold. After the fall of Acre in 1291 they sought refuge on Cyprus until 1308, when they conquered Rhodes. They controlled the island until defeated by Suleiman the Magnificent in 1522. Charles V allowed them to settle on Malta in 1530, where they remained until suppressed by Napoleon on his way to Egypt in 1798.

**Hospitals.** In the Christian world, institutions devoted to the care of the sick first appear during the reign of Constantine. These hospitals were attached to churches and also served as orphanages and almshouses. In the West, hospitals were usually found in monasteries and religious houses. Many hospitals were constructed along the customary routes of pilgrimages and Crusades.

**Hotman, François** (1524–1590). French jurist. Hotman enjoyed the friendship of Calvin, and for a time was on the law faculty of the Geneva Academy. Following the Bartholomew's Day Massacre, he became an ardent opponent of the French monarchy. In his *Franco-Gallia* (1573), he maintains that the Estates General could limit the king's power, and, if necessary, the people could depose the king and elect his successor.

**Houtin, Albert** (1867–1926). French priest and seminary professor. He was associated with Alfred Loisy in the movement within Roman Catholicism called Modernism. In 1902 he attacked the Biblical bases of the church and as a result lost his right to celebrate Mass. He soon left the reforming modernists, stating that "there is not and has never been such a thing as revealed religion." His books were placed on the Index, and in 1912 he gave up the priesthood, devoting his remaining years to historical and biographical writing.

**Hromádka, Josef** (1889–1969). Czech Reformed theologian. Born in Hodslavice, Moravia, and educated in Vienna, Basel, and Heidelberg, Hromádka began his teaching career in Prague in 1920. He served as professor of systematic theology at Jan Hus Faculty of Theology there from 1929 to 1939. Following this, he was guest professor at Princeton Theological Seminary until 1947, when he returned to Czechoslovakia, to Charles University, becoming dean of the Comenius Faculty of Theology in Prague in 1950. He was a member of the executive committee of the World Council of Churches, also serving with several other international religious groups. A special interest of his was the interpretation of the life of the church in Communist areas to those in non-Communist states.

**Hrotsvitha** (b. before 938–d. after 973). Benedictine nun, poet, and chronicler. A nun of the Saxon convent of Gandersheim, she was a product of the Ottonian renaissance in Germany. She wrote hagiographic poems and two historical poems, an encomium of Otto I the Great, and a description of the foundation of Gandersheim. She is chiefly remembered as an early medieval dramatist who produced Christian substitutes for the enjoyable but immoral pagan dramas, imitating Terence's style but using Biblical and martyrological subjects.

**Huber, Samuel** (c. 1547–1624). Swiss Protestant controversialist and champion of Lutheranism against the Swiss Calvinists. Huber was expelled from Switzerland in 1588 because of his emphasis on Christ's sacrificial death for the sin of all mankind, not for the elect only. Called to Wittenberg in 1592, he was banished in 1595 and spent the rest of his days wandering from place to place an "embittered martyr of universalism."

**Huber, Victor Aimé** (1800–1869). German social reformer. Baptized a Catholic but converted to Protestantism, Huber was called to Berlin (1843). He left in 1848 disaffected with monarchy but unreconciled to democracy. His unsuccessful ideas included an association of industrial workers as common property owners and the relocation of surplus workers to effect their redemption. Superficially similar to syndicalism, his conservatism was, however, rooted in his Christian faith.

**Hubmaier, Balthasar** (1481–1528). Anabaptist. From Friedberg near Augsburg, Hubmaier began his career as a favorite pupil of Johann Eck in Freiburg and ended it at the stake as an Anabaptist. He was a priest and an eloquent preacher at Regensburg before becoming a civic reformer at Waldshut in the manner of Zwingli. He debated at Zwingli's side in 1523 on the question of the Supper, but in 1525 and 1526, Zwingli put him to torture to get his (temporary) recantation of Anabaptism. From 1526 to 1528 he was the leading Reformer, as Anabaptist, in Nicolsburg in Liechtenstein, which was for a time an Anabaptist meeting and debating place. The writings of Luther and discussions with Erasmus and Zwingli and then with the Zurich radicals marked his development to an independent position. Among Anabaptists he was unique for defending the legitimacy of the sword, but his published arguments in favor of believer's baptism were widely repeated among them. He defended the importance of baptism, and in Waldshut instituted infant consecration. His theology of Baptism and the Supper made them expressions of covenant relationships with Christ and with fellow believers, and he defended the use of the ban for the sake of the purity of the church. He assumed a tripartite anthropology similar to that in Erasmus' *Enchiridion* and defended the freedom of the will.

**Hügel, Baron Friedrich von** (1852–1925). Roman Catholic Biblical critic and writer. Hügel's family moved to England in 1867, but, as with Lord Acton, his international connections and the scope of his mind gave a truly catholic cast to all he wrote. He was a close friend of the best-known modernists, his social prestige perhaps preserving him from condemnation. Though an arch-leader of the modernists, he kept his belief in Rome.

**Hugh** (c. 1135–1200). Bishop of Lincoln from 1186. He came from La Grande-Chartreuse via Witham in Somerset. The legend of the swan that guarded his sleep is evidence of his popularity. He cared for and ate with lepers, killed deer for the poor, and opposed the exactions of the king's foresters. First to refuse aid for the king's foreign wars, he objected to persecution of Jews in the city and began the present cathedral after the earthquake in 1185.

**Hughes, Hugh Price** (1847–1902). English Methodist. After pastorates in Dover, Brighton, London, and Oxford he became superintendent of West London Mission in 1887. A leader in Forward Movement, he waged campaigns against all varieties of social ills and individual vices, took active part in the controversy over Education Acts (1888–1902), and was a moving spirit in and first president (1896) of the National Free Church Council of England.

**Hughes, John** (1797–1864). Roman Catholic bishop. Coming to Pennsylvania in 1817 as a poor Irish immigrant, Hughes worked his way through school and was ordained in 1826. While a priest at St. Mary's in Philadelphia he became famous for his battle against trusteeism, which he helped to defeat after becoming bishop of New York in 1838. Less successful was his fight against public schools and in favor of tax support of parochial schools. In 1850 he became the first archbishop of New York and in 1854 took part in the Council in Rome proclaiming the immaculate conception. During the Civil War he went to Europe (1861) to represent the Union cause and when he returned was honored for his efforts. He considered the high point of his career to be the laying of the cornerstone for the Cathedral of St. Patrick in New York City.

**Hugh of Cluny** (*also known as* "the Great") (1024–1109). French Benedictine monk. Born in a family of minor Burgundian nobility, Hugh was trained as a monk from childhood and became abbot of Cluny at an early age. During his long abbacy (from 1049) the Cluniac Order reached its greatest extent and power. Hugh played an important role both in monastic affairs and in secular politics. In the investiture controversy he took

a moderate position and served as mediator between his godson, the emperor Henry IV, and Pope Gregory VII.

**Hugh of St.-Victor** (c. 1100–1141). The most distinguished scholar-teacher of the canons of the Abbey of St.-Victor, Paris, where he taught from about 1125 until his death. Called "a second Augustine," he conceived his task to be the reintegration of all learning as an introduction and guide to the study of the Bible. His *Didascalicon* was Augustine of Hippo's *De doctrina Christiana* brought up to date for 12th-century purposes. He underlined the need of all the liberal arts for the fundamental study of the literal sense of the Bible, and composed his own monumental *summa, De sacramentis Christianae fidei,* to provide the solid foundation stones of its allegorical interpretation. The old masters of the spiritual life, John Cassian and Gregory the Great, then provided him with materials for the tropological or moral consideration of the Scriptures.

Just as Hugh stressed the need for geography and history and a systematic exposition of salvation history for Bible study, so too he emphasized that all these preliminaries, and the special theological questions that demanded investigation, were only relative to the spiritual understanding and practical assimilation of Christian attitudes. The fuller development of his principles of exegesis and spiritual interpretation can be discovered in the writings of his chief disciples, Andrew and Richard of St.-Victor.

**Huguenots.** Name given to French Protestants, first applied about 1560. The word has been connected with the Swiss *Eidgenossen,* "confederates," and also with a jest made in allusion to the legendary nightwalking ghost of Hugh Capet, since the Huguenots often met at night.

Many early French Protestants immigrated to the more tolerant German states rather than endure persecution or martyrdom in France. John Calvin's early association with Strasbourg's Huguenot community was the source of his subsequent dominant influence on French Protestantism. The first Huguenot community within French territory (Meaux), founded in 1546, was modeled after Calvin's Strasbourg.

Though the first Paris Huguenot church was only organized in 1555, by 1559 a national synod was convened representing fifteen Huguenot churches. Inspired by the constitution of Calvin's Geneva, a surge of organizational energy emerged from this synod that resulted in an increase in the number of Huguenot congregations throughout France to 2,150 by 1561.

Huguenots were intermittently persecuted until finally the Massacre of Vassey in 1562 brought on the Wars of Religion. In August of 1572, during a temporary *rapprochement* between Protestants and Catholics, Margaret of Valois, sister of King Charles IX and daughter of Catherine de' Medici, was married in Paris to Henry of Navarre, a prominent Protestant leader. Catherine and members of the influential Guise family, jealous of Huguenot leader Admiral de Coligny's obvious influence over the king, took advantage of his presence in Paris for the wedding by arranging for his assassination. When the attempt was unsuccessful, Catherine and the Guises apparently convinced Charles of the threat of Protestant reprisal if their complicity was discovered. Charles was persuaded to order the elimination of the many Protestants still present in Paris. On the night of Aug. 23–24, the eve of the Feast of St. Bartholomew, the massacre began. It soon grew out of government control, and despite official attempts to end the violence, it continued for six weeks, spreading throughout the provinces. At least thirty thousand Huguenots were slain.

The religious civil war that followed ended only with the accession of Henry of Navarre as king of France. Though Henry IV converted to Catholicism in an attempt to consolidate his support, he published the Edict of Nantes (1598), which finally gave Huguenots civil and religious rights. Later Bourbons, however, did not abide by the provisions of the Edict and a new religious war broke out. It ended in 1628 when Richelieu took La Rochelle, the Huguenot fortified stronghold, and exterminated their last armies. After this, Huguenots' rights were constantly challenged. In the late 17th century a system of dragonnades was employed in the program of Huguenot persecution. Soldiers were quartered in Huguenot homes, with tacit permission to persecute their hosts. This system effected the forcible conversion of thousands of Protestants and led to the revocation of the Edict of Nantes by Louis XIV on the grounds that these reconversions had made the Edict unnecessary. The result was the immigration of over four hundred thousand French protestants to England, Germany, and the Americas. Though Huguenots experienced another period of religious and political toleration during the revolutionary period, it was followed by a conservative Catholic reaction that resulted in renewed persecution and immigration.

Huguenots laid great stress on education, and after Henry IV's death they led the literary fight against royal absolutism.

**Hulst, Maurice le Sage d'Hauteroche d'** (1841–1896). French priest and scholar. He examined and explained Biblical texts in the light of contemporary research. Chaplain in the War of 1870, he was active in opening the free Catholic University at Paris, becoming its rector in 1880. An outstanding preacher, D'Hulst became a member of the French Assembly and rallied to the Republic. He helped organize the International Catholic Scientific Congresses.

*Humani Generis.* Papal encyclical issued by Pius XII on Aug. 12, 1950, condemning certain modern tendencies in Roman Catholic theology. Establishing the moral necessity of revelation for truth about God, it argues that man's prejudice blinds him to the many evidences of the divine origin of the Christian revelation as well as to revelation itself. Though he is explicit in saying that evolution is an open question for Roman Catholic thinkers, he warns against those evolutionary views which consider the whole universe to be a process of evolution and thereby deny all absolutes. He further warns against existentialism; the use of Scripture to the extent of overlooking the valuable contribution of reason and the teaching office of the church; the distrust of the philosophy of the Schoolmen; and the denial that Adam was a historical person. In general the encyclical opposes those who attempt to appropriate the new without integrating it with the tradition received from the fathers. While recognizing the necessity among Roman thinkers of dealing with modern issues, Pius emphasizes the church's role in safeguarding the faith and interpreting the Holy Scriptures.

**Humanism.** An intellectual movement connected with the Renaissance. Originally a classical concept, the term "humanism" was revived by Renaissance scholars and popularized by modern historians. It comes from Cicero and was introduced into Renaissance usage by Leonardo Bruni in 1401 in his *De studiis et litteris.* Bruni used the classical term *studia humanitatis* to describe what Renaissance scholars offered as an alternative to the traditional curriculum of the Scholastics. Strictly speaking, humanism in the Renaissance meant a liberal arts education based on grammar, rhetoric, history, poetry, and ethics studied from classical texts. However, during the Renaissance the term broadened somewhat to include the study of both the form and the general content of classical literature. This differentiated it from 12th-century clerical humanism, which was concerned mainly with style, and from the Scholastic study of ancient Greek philosophy and science, which emphasized only intellectual content. Renaissance Italian humanism was primarily interested in the pagan classics. In northern Europe classical scholarship fused with evangelical piety to produce "Christian humanism," which differed in emphasis but not in kind from that in Italy. In modern times there has been a tendency to apply the word unhistorically to any philosophy that centers attention on man, and occasionally even to use it incorrectly as a synonym for "humanitarianism."

**Humanitarianism.** A term used to designate the various efforts to mitigate suffering in sentient life. Today it has become a component part of many diverse social attitudes ranging from animal humane societies to socialism. It seeks to demonstrate that humaneness and compassion are essential ingredients for moral life. In the Greco-Roman civilizations it emerged primarily as a philosophical abstraction, though occasional protests were made against slavery and the gladiatorial shows. During the Middle Ages the Christian church helped to keep alive and preserve a humanitarian consciousness in the midst of the cruelties of that age. Modern humanitarianism had its origin during the 18th century with the advent of the Enlightenment and the Evangelical revivals. Men such as William Wilberforce and members of the Clapham Sect were leaders in the abolition of slavery and the furtherance of social reform and unselfish philanthropy. Foreign missions had a strong humanitarian drive—witness the numerous hospitals and schools that were established and the native customs that were suppressed because they were deemed cruel and inhumane. Humanitarian impulses motivated the establishment of a host of voluntary social agencies such as the Red Cross (1863), which sought to alleviate human suffering resulting from industrialization, war, pestilence, and famine. In the United States the modern civil rights movement, the opposition to the war in Vietnam, and the attraction of the Peace Corps cannot be understood apart from humanitarianism.

*Humanum Genus.* Papal encyclical issued by Leo XIII on April 20, 1884, confirming previous papal condemnations of Freemasonry and secret societies. Catholics were forbidden to join the Masons, who (supposedly) taught supremacy of human reason, naturalism, un-certainty of both God and immortality, equality of men, civil marriage, and public schools. Catholics were to belong to church-approved groups. Actually anticlerical Latin, rather than milder American, lodges were suspect.

**Humbert of Silva-Candida** (d. 1061). Cardinal bishop. According to Lanfranc, Humbert was born in Lorraine; Berengar of Tours said he was born in Burgundy. He became a monk at Moyenmoutier, and when Leo IX, returning from the synod at Reims (1049), stopped at Mainz, he asked Humbert to join the papal service. Humbert was first appointed archbishop of Sicily, but this was not permanent. In 1051, he served as the papal legate to Benevento. In 1054, he, with Peter, bishop of Amalfi, and Frederick the Chancellor were sent as legates to the emperor Constantine IX to obtain an alliance against the Normans in southern Italy and to the patriarch Michael Cerularius to settle differences in rite and custom existing between the Roman and the Eastern Churches. Upon the refusal of Cerularius to recognize the jurisdiction of the Roman see, Humbert excommunicated the Greeks without further discussion. Humbert defended the Roman customs regarding fasting and unleavened bread in *Against the Calumnies of the Greeks.* He explained the necessity of clerical celibacy in *Against Nicetas.* His most extended work was *Against Simoniacs,* in which he differed from Peter Damian in declaring simoniacal orders invalid. He condemned the interference of the German emperor in Italy, lay interference in church elections and synods, and lay investiture. He described the relation of church to state as that of the soul to the body. His ideas were embodied in the reforms of Gregory VII.

**Humboldt, Baron Wilhelm von** (1767–1835). German educator, diplomat, and philologist. Educated in Göttingen, Humboldt traveled in France and Spain (1797–1801), and entered state service in 1801. In 1819 he was released because of his proposed constitution; he retired to private study of Indian philosophy and of philology. With Süvern he helped found the University of Berlin (1810). He accented Kantian philosophy, romanticism, and especially neohumanism (he worked for Jewish rights). His religious thought was humanistic and classical, not specifically Christian.

**Hume, David** (1711–1776). Scottish philosopher and historian. Born at Edinburgh, he was educated at the University of Edinburgh, but without taking a degree. From

1734 to 1737 he lived in France, where he elaborated his skeptical philosophical opinions and wrote *A Treatise of Human Nature* (3 vols., 1739–1740). In 1741 and 1742, Hume published his *Essays Moral and Political,* which attracted far greater attention than his *Treatise.* In 1748 he published his *Philosophical Essays Concerning Human Understanding,* which included his famous essay "Of Miracles." In this essay Hume argued that a miracle should be accepted only if the testimony for it is so strong that it would be miraculous for the testimony to be false rather than for the miracle to have happened, and that this condition is not satisfied in the case of any recorded miracle. In 1751 he wrote *An Essay Concerning the Principle of Morals,* followed by *Dialogues Concerning Natural Religion,* published posthumously in 1779. Hume wrote nothing of consequence thereafter on pure philosophy, but turned to history. His *Political Discourses* (1752) established his reputation, both in England and on the Continent. His celebrated *History of England During the Reigns of James I and Charles I* (6 vols.), written between 1754 and 1761, long remained the standard Tory interpretation of English history.

Hume's philosophical thought began from, and never questioned, John Locke's view that what we immediately perceive is always a sense impression. By reducing reason to a product of experience he destroyed its claim to sole validity, which had been put forward by the thinkers of the Enlightenment. Impressions exist only as objects of our mind; we have no direct experience of independent physical objects. Each impression is quite distinct from any other impression, so that experience reveals no necessary connection between them. The commonsense world, Hume concluded, is therefore not revealed to us by experience. At the same time, Hume argued that there can be no strict evidence of the existence of such a world, for reason is as powerless as experience. Although we can establish the relationship of ideas with certainty, the facts of reality cannot be established beyond the appearance of probability. Causality is not a concept of logic, but a result of habit and association. Nothing can be known except our own sense perceptions.

Hume's exploration of the ways of the human mind led him to skepticism. Reason really plays little part in life. He devoted a great deal of attention to moral philosophy and found that in regard to our actions reason "can never pretend to any other office than to serve and obey the passions." Reason can tell us nothing of values. Moral judgments rest on feelings of approval or disapproval, which relate to our pleasures and pains. At the same time, he did not regard the existence of God as demonstrable by reason. He did not claim to be an atheist and evidently thought it probable that there is some general principle of order in the universe based on intelligence. But this is only a guess and cannot be proved. We may choose to believe, but this is a sheer act of faith—"fideism." Both the deists and the rational Christians, according to Hume, were in error when they wrote about reason's supporting religion of any sort.

Hume's skepticism has had a profound influence on Western philosophical thought. It must be pointed out that Hume was far from drawing gloomy conclusions from his skepticism. He thought it a healthy sign that human beings are moral and believe in God because of instinct and the will to live. He was even skeptical of his own skepticism, calling his philosophical speculation "cold and strained and ridiculous."

BIBLIOGRAPHY: D. Hume, *Dialogues Concerning Natural Religion* (New York, 1948); J. Y. T. Greig, *David Hume* (London, 1931); J. Laird, *Hume's Philosophy of Human Nature* (London, 1932); E. C. Mossner, *The Life of David Hume* (Austin, 1954); J. A. Passmore, *Hume's Intentions* (Cambridge, 1952); N. K. Smith, *The Philosophy of David Hume* (London, 1941).

**Humiliati.** An order of penitents founded with the help of Bernard of Clairvaux in the 12th century. Papal approval for the order was secured at the beginning of the 13th century. The Humiliati practiced apostolic poverty and mortification of the body. They were an important force in combating the heresy of the Cathari. However, as time passed, their discipline became more relaxed and the disfavor of the papacy led to the suppression of the order in 1571.

**Hundeshagen, Karl Bernard** (1810–1872). German Reformed theologian and professor (Giessen, 1831; Bern, 1834; Heidelberg, 1847; Bonn, 1867). His book (1846) on the ill effects in post-Reformation Germany of the separation of intellect and ethics established his reputation even outside church circles. A later work on church polity (1864), written in the context of Baden Church Union, is still a classic in the contrast of Zwinglian-Calvinist and Lutheran polity.

**Hundred Chapters, Council of.** See COUNCIL OF 1551.

**Hungarian Reformed Church** (Magyarorszagi Reformatus Egyhaz). A communion brought into the Reformed family when the Synod of Debrecen in 1567 adopted the Heidelberg Catechism. The German minority was separately organized. The Counter-Reformation persecution was ended by the Edict of Toleration of 1781. The church was badly broken by the division of Austria-Hungary in 1918, large portions being in Romania, Yugoslavia, and Czechoslovakia. There are two million adherents.

**Hungary, Conversion of.** The Christian gospel was preached during the 4th century in the region which was to become Hungary, but the barbarian migrations made this effort of no lasting effect. In the 9th and 10th centuries Christian missionaries returned. It was a mission from the West that succeeded in converting the man who was to become Hungary's first king—Stephen (975–1038). Upon taking the throne in 997, Stephen began to Christianize the whole country. In the year 1001, he was recognized by the pope, and episcopal sees were founded throughout the country.

**Hunt, Robert** (c. 1568–1608). First American Episcopal clergyman. Cambridge educated, he served two parishes in England before going in 1606 as chaplain with the expedition that founded Jamestown, Va. He conducted the first English services of worship in the New World under a sail supported by logs. Though courageous and diligent, he was physically weak and died just thirteen months after arriving in America.

**Huntingdon, Countess of** (Selina Hastings, 1707–1791). English religious leader and founder of the Calvinistic Methodist known as the "Countess of Huntingdon's Connexion." Born at Stanton Harold, the daughter of Washington Shirley, she married Theophilus Hastings, ninth earl of Huntingdon. In 1739 she joined the Methodist movement, and after her husband's death in 1746, she devoted her life to social and religious work, hoping to introduce the aristocracy of England into Methodism. In 1747 she made George Whitefield one of her chaplains, and in the following years she placed Methodist chaplains in various parts of England. In 1768 she began Trevecca House (South Wales) as a Methodist seminary, but in 1779 the consistory court of London denied the Countess the right to employ her chaplains publicly and compelled her to register as a Dissenter under the Toleration Act. To perpetuate her work after her death, she organized her chapels into an association in 1790, and at her death bequeathed them, together with Trevecca House, to trustees.

**Huntington, Frederick Dan** (1819–1904). Unitarian clergyman and Episcopal bishop. Educated at Amherst and Harvard, Huntington joined the Harvard faculty in 1855 after a Boston pastorate. Following a great struggle, he resigned in 1860 and became an Episcopal priest in Boston. In 1869 he was made the first bishop of the diocese of Central New York and the same year founded St. John's School at Manlius, N.Y.

**Huron Mission.** A mission to the Huron Indians begun by the Recollet Father Joseph Le Caron. He arrived in 1615 and the following summer went back to France to get support for his mission. In 1623 he returned, but resources were lacking and the work was turned over to the Jesuits in 1625. In 1626, Brébeuf and Nouë arrived in Huronia, where the former remained until 1629 when the English captured Quebec and forced his return to France. When Canada was restored to the French, the mission was resumed. In 1634, Brébeuf and three companions reached Huronia, and others arrived in 1636. In 1638, Jerome Lalemant became the mission's superior and changed its strategy. Brébeuf, following the Recollets' tactics, had established separate mission houses with individual priests who identified themselves with the life of the village where they resided. Lalemant reversed these procedures, creating entirely new communities of converted Indians and erecting at St. Marie a permanent residence for the priests apart from the Huron villages. In July, 1648, the Iroquois destroyed the village of St. Joseph and slaughtered its inhabitants. A year later, they attacked St. Ignace and St. Louis, capturing Brébeuf and Gabriel Lalemant, who were brutally tortured to death. Following these attacks, the Hurons fled in terror. The mission moved its headquarters to St. Joseph's Island, but disease and starvation wiped out most of the Indians who were left. In June, 1650, the survivors moved back to Quebec and the Huron mission came to an end.

**Hus, John** (Jan Hus) (c. 1369–1415). Czech Reformer. Hus was born of peasant parents in Husinetz in southern Bohemia, where he attended school before studying theology at the University of Prague. An outstanding student, he was also known for his piety and moral character. He received the bachelor of arts degree in 1393 and the master's degree in 1396. During his student years he became acquainted with the writings of

Bohemian Reformers, such as Milíč (d. 1374) and Janov (d. 1394), as well as those of the English Reformer John Wycliffe. But it seems likely that before 1402 he knew Wycliffe only through his philosophical works on logic and metaphysics. In 1400 he was ordained a priest and in 1402 appointed rector of the university. He was also appointed preacher at the Bethlehem Chapel in Prague, which was founded for the purpose of maintaining the national religion in Bohemia and which provided sermons twice daily in the popular tongue. Hus used this opportunity to circulate his criticisms of the clergy, the episcopate, and the papacy.

Impressed now by the theological and reformatory writings of Wycliffe, brought back from Oxford by Jerome of Prague, Hus used them in his lectures at the university (as did other professors), until the proscription of certain Wycliffite propositions in 1403. He also translated the *Trialogus* of Wycliffe into the Czech language. Hus's career seemed to be advancing when Archbishop Zbynek (Sbinko) appointed him preacher to the Prague Synod (1405), where he was in a position to censure and exhort the members of the hierarchy.

Hus had continued to use Wycliffe's writings in his sermons. Hence when Innocent VII instructed the archbishop to take measures against the heretical teachings of Wycliffe in 1407, Hus was among those to receive a reprimand. However, the presence of two extraneous factors complicated the relationship between Hus and his superiors. First was the large popular following that Hus had acquired as a result of his sermons in the Bethlehem Chapel. Second was the rise of national sentiment and patriotism directed toward King Wenceslaus IV as a defender of the national church. The longer the king and the hierarchy delayed suppression of the heretics, the greater was their sense of national identity. In 1408, Gregory XII had to remind the archbishop that he was aware of the spread of the Wycliffite heresy. Then in June of that year the Synod ordered that all of Wycliffe's writings be handed over for correction. Hus complied and stated that he condemned whatever error the teachings contained.

Subsequent events set Hus first against the archbishop, then against the king. A split occurred at the University of Prague when Wenceslaus asked for approval of the neutrality plan, proposed by the Council of Pisa, to end the Schism by deposing both the rival popes. Hus consented, but Archbishop Zbynek, supported by the Germans, opposed the plan. Most of the German students and faculty left for other universities rather than renounce Gregory XII, the pope at Rome. Zbynek then obtained the assistance rather than renounce Gregory XII, the pope at Rome. Zbynek then obtained the assistance of the new ("Pisan") pope, Alexander V, in checking Wycliffite teachings. In 1409, through the mediation of the archbishop, Alexander ordered the cessation of all preaching except in specified churches. Hus was questioned and a report sent to Rome. In 1411, Hus and his followers were excommunicated by Alexander's successor, John XXIII. Hus then openly attacked the bulls of indulgence that Pope John promoted for monies to finance a crusade against Ladislas of Naples, and Hus's vehement criticisms began to alienate the king, who had previously been his supporter. In 1412, Hus left Prague and devoted himself to writing his *De ecclesia*. At the urging of the emperor Sigismund, and with a pass for safe-conduct, he went to Constance in 1414. There he was questioned, put into prison for eight months, questioned again, found guilty and burned as a heretic. Hus never recanted, and his death served to increase the devotion of his followers. The noted humanist, Poggio Bracciolini, has written a moving account of the proceedings.

Hus taught that Sacred Scripture was the sole final authority and denied the supreme authority of popes and even of general councils. He opposed traffic in indulgences and was charged (despite his disavowals) with denying transubstantiation. He encouraged a return to the simplicity of the early church and a continuation of the national liturgy, including the use of both species in the distribution of Communion. He strongly criticized abuses in the clergy, particularly in cases where the people were taken advantage of. Letters that he wrote during his imprisonment to friends in Bohemia became their guidelines in the following years.

In his major work, the *De ecclesia* ("On the Church," 1413), Hus borrowed freely from the writings of Wycliffe, but he used them with discrimination. Like Wycliffe, he identified the church as the whole number of the elect rather than as an outward, organized structure. In general he was less radical and less academic than Wycliffe, and he sought to dissociate himself from the Englishman's Donatist tendencies as well as from his polemic against transubstantiation.

BIBLIOGRAPHY: See further: M. Spinka (ed. and tr.), *John Hus at the Council of Constance* (New York, 1966); P. Roubiczek and J. Kalmer, *Warrior of God* (London, 1947); M. Spinka, *John Hus and the Czech Reform* (Chicago, 1941).

**Husserl, Edmund** (1859–1938). German Lutheran philosopher. He was born at Prossnitz and studied under Brentano at the University of Vienna (1884). He taught at the Universities of Halle (1887–1901), Göttingen (1901–1916), and Freiburg (1916–1928). In 1887 he joined the Lutheran Church, subsequently becoming a victim of the Nazi academic purge. He was the founder of the philosophy of phenomenology (the descriptive analysis of experience as presented) later used by Martin Heidegger, Jean-Paul Sartre, and Maurice Merleau-Ponty. His key work was *Investigations in Logic* (1900).

**Hut, Hans** (c. 1485–1527). Anabaptist. Hut was a colporteur who was caught up in radical religious discussion groups in central Germany from 1523 on, becoming critical of infant baptism. He was heavily influenced by Thomas Müntzer's eschatology and by the emotions of the Peasants' War. After being rebaptized by Hans Denck in 1526, he widely spread belief in penitential believer's baptism as an entry into the *eschaton* to occur three and a half years after Müntzer's fall at Frankenhausen.

**Hutchinson, Anne** (1591–1643). American religious liberal. She emigrated to Massachusetts Bay Colony in 1634, a devoted follower of her minister, John Cotton. An outspoken woman, she held informal meetings in her home to discuss sermons. Later venturing to expound her own views, she was charged with antinomianism, enthusiasm, and heresy by a synod that was called to bring her to trial. At first she was supported by Cotton, John Wheelwright, and Henry Vane, but her claims of special revelations alienated them and she was condemned in 1637 and banished by the General Court. Excommunicated, she emigrated to Rhode Island in 1638 and later to Pelham Bay, N.Y., where she was killed by Indians. Her teachings, coming at a time of religious conflict in England, were considered a threat to Massachusetts' solidarity. John Cotton, suspect as her pastor, was cleared by the clergy after he yielded on the issue of preparation for conversion. Covenant (or federal) theology, seeking a position between antinomianism and Arminianism, taught that salvation lay in fulfilling the conditions of God's covenant with man, including preparation for justification and a conscious effort toward sanctification. Anne Hutchinson condemned this as a covenant of works. Only Cotton and Wheelwright preached a covenant of grace in her eyes. Her excommunication and banishment were hastened by her claims of direct and immediate revelations and divine visions. She was tried on the grounds that the teachings of Scripture were so obvious that anyone opposing them must be perverse and saved from their own errors.

**Hutten, Ulrich von** (1488–1523). German nobleman, humanist, and patriotic poet. Having fled from a monastery in 1505, Hutten wandered through Germany and Italy, developing his poetic talent. Crowned poet laureate in 1518 by Emperor Maximilian I, he served briefly at the court of Albert of Mainz. His writings show a deep resentment of the papal church. He advocated a structural reorganization of the church in Germany, and a moral reform of its total religious life, seeing in both measures the necessary prerequisites for a nationalistic rebirth of the Empire. He saw in Luther a champion of his own dreams, and enthusiastically supported the Reformer's cause, popularizing it through German pamphlets. Attacked by Rome (which was seeking his extradition), deprived of any protection, abandoned by Erasmus (whom he had considered a friend and ally), and physically exhausted, Hutten, through Zwingli, found a final refuge on Ufenau Island in Lake Zurich. From there he charged Erasmus with treacherous cowardice, a charge that destroyed the unity of the upper German, humanistically oriented, intellectual world. He died a sick and lonely man.

**Hutter, Jacob** (d. 1536). Anabaptist leader. Hutter, an Anabaptist after 1529, united and organized disparate Anabaptist groups, aiming at communalism of production and consumption, so that a firm tradition was established which still today bears his name. Imbued with a powerful sense of divine vocation and sharing goods more consistently than other leaders, he drew his followers together in Moravia in the face of stiff Roman Catholic opposition until he himself was burned at the stake.

**Hutterites.** The followers and spiritual descendants of Jacob Hutter. This name continues to be given to those Anabaptists who developed the communitarian implications of one kind of radical Christianity, forming economically self-sufficient communities in which not only consumption but also production of necessities was in common. They were most numerous in the late 16th century and in the 17th century, declined under persecution and warfare, and were refounded in the 19th century in partial continuity with the older tradition. Among the earliest Anabaptists, brotherly love led to sharing of goods as there was need. Communitarian Anabaptism took shape under the leadership of Jacob Wiedemann among the faithful around Nicolsburg in 1527 and 1528 among those who counted themselves *stäbler,* or pacifists. When those Anabaptists who rejected the legitimacy of the magistracy were reluctantly asked to leave by Lord Liechtenstein, a communal church order was adopted in the new locale of Austerlitz in Moravia. There was instability of leadership in closely related groups until Jacob Hutter (d. 1536), possessed by a rocklike conviction of his divine vocation to be the leading elder, was able to unite most of them and in 1533 to organize them so that they ever after bore his name. After Hutter's martyrdom, Hans Amon was able to guide persecuted brethren in reestablishing communities and in sending out many missionaries. Peter Riedemann gave able leadership, together with Leonard Lanzenstiel. Another in a series of able theologian administrators was Peter Walpot, under whom the Hutterite churches reached their numerical and spiritual apogee, numbering at most an estimated thirty thousand. In 1592 an imperial decree banned them from Moravia, and many refugees began anew in Slovakia and Transylvania. During the Thirty Years' War, despite help from the Mennonites of Holland, their numbers decreased under harassment and looting, and during the 18th century many began practicing private property. In the late 18th century a Bruderhof was established in Russia, to be renewed after 1850 in Russia, and in the 1870's in the United States where also others in the Anabaptist tradition migrated from Russia. Many migrated from South Dakota to Canada in 1918, fleeing harshly administered military conscription laws. There are now about twenty thousand Hutterites in the United States and Canada and a few in South America. All are firmly communitarian.

The Hutterites cherish a distinctive literature produced mostly in the 16th century. This includes several chronicles which set their history in the context of all of church history; two confessions by Peter Riedemann, as well as epistles, tracts, and instructions for the common life by Walpot and others; and the *Ausbund,* a collection of lengthy hymns often expressing in an epic style their faith and hopes in times of sharp persecution, which is still in use among them and among the Amish. Hutterite thought turns on the conviction that the love which God looks for among his children cannot survive where there is concern for private possession. Arrogation to self of anything earthly would mean denial of God as the possessor of all

and of one's self. The genius of Hutter was able to transform the energies of people thus minded in a culturally productive direction. A high view of the church emerged. The church, through its elders elected for life, manages the common property and is able to act for God in conferring baptism on conscious believers and in administering discipline, including the ban. They were deeply concerned about the education of children, who were taught in common from the age of two to adolescence. Hutterite pedagogy for many generations has produced literate and convinced commune members able if necessary to die for their faith. It has also produced able craftsmen (*Haban* pottery had a wide reputation), and princes have valued their diligence and competence, sometimes harboring them contrary to imperial edict. Simplicity of dress and of speech has been cultivated to the present time, and all of life is understood to be under the guidance of the Spirit, always in subjection to the community separated from the world and guided by the Scriptures and by its traditions. Hutterites today maintain a minimum of contact with the rest of the world, and remain strongly conscious of their own traditions.

BIBLIOGRAPHY: P. Riedemann (Rideman), *Confessions of Faith,* tr. by K. E. Hasenberg (London, 1950); R. Friedmann, *Hutterite Studies* (Goshen, 1961); J. Horsch, *The Hutterian Brethren* (Goshen, 1931).

**Huxley, Aldous** (1894–1963). English novelist, essayist, and satirist. His early work was almost wholly negative (*Crome Yellow,* 1921). His second phase celebrated a positive source of value in balancing the claims of the body and of emotion over against those of the intellect (*Point Counter Point,* 1928). Noted for his interest in science and his warnings concerning the dangers inherent in the onward march of science (*Brave New World,* 1932), he became interested during his later life in mysticism and the Ramakrishna Mission in Hollywood, Calif., where he made his home in 1947.

**Huxley, Thomas Henry** (1825–1895). English scientist and popularizer of the theory of evolution. Known as "Darwin's bulldog," Huxley engaged in controversy with the English prime minister Gladstone regarding the Biblical account of the Creation. In his *Science and Christian Tradition* he saw himself called to break down the fence that the traditional Christian account had erected across the road leading to scientific knowledge.

**Huysmans, Joris Karl** (1848–1907). French Catholic novelist of Dutch descent. For thirty years a member of the French Ministry of Interior, Huysmans was noted primarily for his literary works. His early novels belong to the Goncourt-Zola school of realism. *En route!* (1895) reflected his conversion to Christianity as a result of a visit to a Trappist monastery. For a time he was an oblate in a Benedictine abbey. His later works reveal a strong interest in mysticism and religious art.

**Hyginus.** Pope from c. 136 to c. 140. Very little is known of the episcopate of Hyginus or of his relation to the Roman presbyters. In his time Gnostic teachers were active in the Roman church (Cerdo, Marcion, Valentinus). He may have written the anonymous homily II Clement, in which Jewish Christianity is combined with some proto-Gnostic expressions.

**Hypatia** (d. 415). Daughter of the mathematician Theon and leading philosopher of the Neoplatonic school at Alexandria. She commented on Plato and Aristotle, and wrote on mathematics and astronomy. The pursuit of logic and science enabled her school to find common academic ground with the famous Catechetical School at Alexandria. Her disciple, Synesius of Cyrene, became bishop of Ptolemais in 411. In March, 415, Hypatia was murdered by a fanatical mob of Christians.

**Hypsistarians.** Fourth-century Cappadocian sect that worshiped the "Most High God." The theology and the cultus of the sect were a strange mixture of Hellenistic and Jewish religious emphases. Observance of the Sabbath, dietary regulations, abhorrence of sacrifices and images, adoration of fire and light, and rejection of circumcision were primary cultic practices. Gregory of Nazianzus stated that his father was a member of the sect; Gregory of Nyssa also mentions the group.

# I

**Iamblichus** (c. 250–c. 330). Greek philosopher. Pupil of both Anatolius and Porphyry, he became the leading Neoplatonist of the Syrian School. His peculiar contributions consist in his modifications of Plotinus, especially in the system of mediation between noumenal and sensible worlds, and his introduction of a higher One above the Plotinian One. His chief extant works are predominantly exposi-

tions of Pythagoreanism showing the influence of Oriental systems and pagan mythology.

**Ibas** (d. 457). Bishop of Edessa from 435. His early life is obscure; he is first known as a presbyter in Edessa under the episcopacy of Rabbula. An admirer of the thought of Theodore of Mopsuestia, he translated the works of Theodore from Syriac. Because of his sympathy with Theodore, Ibas came into conflict with Rabbula and was condemned by the Council of Ephesus in 449. He wrote his theological views in a letter to Bishop Maris in Persia. It was this letter that the emperor Justinian condemned in an edict in 544.

**Iceland, Conversion of.** The first Christians were Irish hermits who fled upon the arrival of Vikings from Norway in 870. An attempt to introduce Christianity failed in 986. During 996 and 997, Olaf I Trygvesson sent Stevne Thorgilsson and Thangbrand to Iceland, but they failed also. In 1000, two native Icelandic Christians persuaded the *Althing* to adopt Christianity. This was the only instance of a people in western Europe accepting Christianity by ballot.

**Icon** (from Greek *eikōn*, "image"). A flat picture, executed in the formal Byzantine style, venerated in Eastern Orthodox Churches. Usually done in oil on wood, but often in ivory, stone (mosaic) or other material, the icon may represent the Christ, the Virgin Mary, or any other saint. Especially in Russia, a protective metal shield covers it, on which garments and nimbus are carved, leaving places for the painted hands and face beneath to show through.

**Iconoclastic Controversy** (iconoclast, from Greek word meaning "image breaker"; iconodule, "image worshiper"). The controversy over the worship of religious images (icons) in the Byzantine Empire during the 8th and 9th centuries. The iconoclastic movement comprises two phases: the first, beginning in 726 and ending officially with the Seventh Ecumenical Council (Nicaea, 787); the second, beginning in 813 and ending officially in 843 with Empress Theodora's "restoration of orthodoxy." In the late 6th century and during Byzantium's military crises of the 7th century, icon worship became a superstitious cult; icons were believed to possess miraculous powers. Especially strong opposition to icon worship arose in Asia Minor, probably as a result of Judaic, Islamic, and heretical Paulician influence in that region. In 726, Emperor Leo III, who had been born in Asia Minor, issued an edict against the use of images. Four years later he convened a council that promulgated another edict against images. Persecution of icon worshipers followed, and Leo's severe methods were continued by his son and successor, Constantine V (741–775). In 754, the Council of Hieria unanimously condemned image worship. With this formal sanction, Constantine V pursued iconoclastic policies with even greater severity until his death. Relations between Rome and the Byzantine Empire, already insecure, were severely strained by the imperial iconoclasm, which Rome strongly opposed. Constantine's son and successor, Leo IV (775–790), was an iconoclast, but his premature death resulted in the accession of his young son to the throne. Actual power passed to Leo's widow, the empress Irene, an icon worshiper. In 787 she and Tarasius, patriarch of Constantinople, convened the Seventh Ecumenical Council at Nicaea. Iconoclasm was anathematized and icon worship reestablished. The iconoclasts arose again after the accession of Emperor Leo V (813–820). Leo summoned a synod that reaffirmed iconoclasm (815). In 842, Emperor Theophilus died and, because of his son's minority, Empress Theodora became regent. Like Irene, she was an icon worshiper. In the following year she summoned a council that reestablished the use of icons as pictorial representations. Since 843 the Eastern Church has celebrated the first Sunday in Lent as the Festival of Orthodoxy.

No works of the iconoclasts are extant. Their theological treatises and the acts of the iconoclastic councils of 753 to 754 and 815 were destroyed by icon worshipers. Some of their beliefs are cited in the polemical works of their opponents. The iconoclasts supported their actions by pointing out the Second Commandment's prohibition against worship of graven images. They equated icon worship with pagan idolatry. Iconographic representations of Christ in particular were held to be heretical, since they separated Christ's human from his divine nature. Icon worshipers, on the other hand, emphasized the ornamental and mnemonic character of icons, which were simply a means for instructing the faithful. Against charges that the icons were made of material substance, they replied that these were an extension of the incarnation itself. Forceful supporters of icon worship included John of Damascus in the 8th century and Theodore of Studium in the 9th century.

Political motivations in the controversy appear to have been powerful. Some scholars argue that the iconoclasm of Leo III and his successors was an attempt to break the immense monastic power in Constantinople. Others argue that iconoclasm was a means by which the emperors tried to remove public education from the hands of the clergy.

BIBLIOGRAPHY: P. J. Alexander, *The Patriarch Nicephorus of Constantinople* (Oxford, 1958); E. J. Martin, *A History of the Iconoclastic Controversy* (London, 1930).

**Iconostasis.** The screen separating the sanctuary from the nave in Byzantine churches, which was originally a lattice of columns and a shelf. Since the late 14th century, it has become a solid wall covered with icons; hence its name. There are three doors in it: the central, royal door gives access to the altar and sanctuary area; the right one, to the diaconicon; and the left, to the prothesis.

**Ignatius** (c. 35–c. 107). Bishop of Antioch and martyr at Rome during the reign of Trajan. On his way to martyrdom Ignatius was able to visit several Christian centers in Asia Minor, and from Smyrna and Troas (cf. Acts 16:8) he wrote five letters to Asian churches, one to the Roman church, and one to Polycarp of Smyrna, who later made a collection of the letters for the church in Philippi. In them Ignatius pleads for the unity of the catholic, or universal, church (he is the first to use the term), which is based on the unity of God the Father with "our God Jesus Christ," on the unity of the hierarchical ministry of bishops, presbyters, and deacons, and on the unity of believers in the Eucharist, which he once calls the "drug of immortality, the antidote for dying." Because he insists upon a unity not only spiritual but also "fleshly," he is militantly opposed to heretical "infiltration," partly as expressed in Judaistic practices and ideas but especially as reflected in the notion that Jesus merely seemed to suffer. He is attacking either a kind of Jewish gnosticism or else two distinct types of heresy. In the 4th or 5th century his letters were used by Monophysites, and since others found them inadequately orthodox, they were filled with "orthodox" interpolations and supplemented by six more letters. The new version gradually replaced the authentic one, and it was not until 1644 that James Ussher, Anglican archbishop of Armagh, restored the originals by comparing the Greek text with a 13th-century Latin version; two years later the Dutch philologist Isaac Voss published the authentic text from the one surviving Greek manuscript. In the 19th century a Syriac abridgment was sometimes regarded as original, but the studies by Zahn and Lightfoot maintained the credit of the Ussher-Voss text, more recently confirmed by a 5th-century papyrus fragment.

Nothing is known of Ignatius' death at

Rome, though in the 4th century his relics were preserved at Antioch. In his letter to the Romans he asked the community (no mention being made of a Roman bishop) not to try to prevent his martyrdom. Polycarp implies that he was actually martyred, but the martyr acts that describe the event are no earlier than the 4th century.

Ignatius was obviously a witness to the existence of the monarchical episcopate in Asia Minor and Syria; he says that bishops have been appointed throughout the world. Their appointment comes from God and from Jesus Christ; Ignatius says nothing whatever about apostolic succession. His reference to himself as "bishop of Syria" may suggest that Antioch was already becoming a metropolitan see.

Modern critics have often suggested that Ignatius was obsessed by the notion of episcopacy and that in his time it was a novelty. Perhaps in the precise form found here it had not existed earlier, but the suggestion that Ignatius was neurotic is probably not verifiable. His style is a dramatic, vivid Asian or Syrian Greek, not necessarily due to neurosis. He exalts the office of the bishop (cf. I Tim. 3:1) but he does so in order to defend the unity of the church.

It has also been claimed that while attacking Gnostic ideas he falls under their spell and that his picture of Jesus is expressed in terms derived from a Gnostic myth of redemption. Isolated expressions may well be shared with Gnostic writings (all later than Ignatius himself), but what he says about Jesus is almost entirely derived either from the Synoptic Gospels or from the oral traditions used in them. Ignatius was probably acquainted with the Gospels of Matthew and John (possibly Luke also), and knew several of Paul's letters well. He usually refrains from giving exact quotations, but exactness is infrequent in early Christian writings and, in any event, should not be expected from a prospective martyr under Roman custody.

Ignatius' genuine letters were later known to Irenaeus, Origen, Eusebius, and other writers; Athanasius quotes him as a theological authority. Like Clement, he is one of the most important witnesses to the life of the church in the age just after the time of the apostles. The kind of Christianity he reflects is, like that of Irenaeus, essentially Pauline and Johannine.

BIBLIOGRAPHY: M. P. Brown, *The Authentic Writings of Ignatius* (Durham, N.C., 1963); R. M. Grant (ed.), *The Apostolic Fathers*, Vol. I (New York, 1964); A. Roberts and J. Donaldson (eds.), *The Ante-Nicene Fathers*, Vol. I (Grand Rapids, 1950); V. Corwin, *St. Ignatius and Christianity in Antioch* (New Haven, 1960); E. J. Goodspeed and R. M. Grant, *A History of Early Christian Literature* (Chicago, 1966); C. C. Richardson, *The Christianity of Ignatius of Antioch* (New York, 1935).

**Ignatius of Loyola** (1491–1556). Founder of the Jesuits. Born in the ancestral castle of the noble and wealthy Loyolas in the Basque province of Guipúzcoa in 1491, Ignatius was dominated in his early years by the ideals of martial valor and renown. In 1506 he became a page in the service of one relative, the treasurer of Castile, and in 1517 a knight in the service of another, the viceroy of Navarre. But the cannonball that fractured his left leg while he was defending Pamplona from the French in the spring of 1521 occasioned a radical reorientation of ideals.

Back at Loyola, he was in serious condition for a time, but when out of danger he underwent painful surgery to correct the mistakes of the first setting. During his long convalescence his time was divided between reading a life of Christ and lives of the saints, the only two books available, and dreaming of a great lady and martial valor. The connection between martial ideals and a life of holiness led in 1522 to a pilgrimage to Montserrat in northeastern Spain. After a general confession and the renouncing of the military life, he walked to Manresa, where he lived as an ascetic for eleven months. This was a decisive period of inward torture and light; its results were the sketch of his *Spiritual Exercises* and the decision to begin a life of combat for Christ by making a pilgrimage to Jerusalem. Leaving Barcelona in March, 1523, traveling by way of Rome, Vienna, and Cyprus, he reached Jerusalem in September, only to be refused permanent lodging by the Franciscan guardians of the shrines. After visiting the holy places, he left and returned to Barcelona in March of 1524.

It now became clear to Ignatius that he should lead an apostolic rather than a contemplative life. Convinced of the necessity of good training for leading souls, he began by studying Latin with schoolboys at Barcelona for two years. In 1526 he went to Alcalá for philosophy, but suspicion of his new followers and their distinctive garb, although they were exonerated, drove him to Salamanca at the end of 1527. There also he was apprehended; finally convinced that he should refrain from a public ministry until ordination, he left for Paris in February, 1528, where he was to study until 1535. Having received his theological license in 1534, he gathered his several new companions, including Francis Xavier and Peter Claver, at Montmartre (Aug. 15, 1534), where all vowed to live in poverty and chastity and to make a pilgrimage to the Holy Land within the next two years. Bad health prevented him from continuing study, so he left for Italy, where his companions met him at Venice in June, 1537, only to find that war between Venice and the Turkish empire made the pilgrimage impossible. There followed eighteen months of ministry, during which he and most of his companions were ordained, before the group decided to go to Rome to offer their services to the pope. In a small chapel on the way occurred his famous vision of God the Father asking Christ to accept Ignatius as his servant.

In 1539 the group decided to form a permanent union, adding the vow of obedience to the previous two. In 1540, Pope Paul III approved the plan; Ignatius was elected general in 1522. The most important work of his later years was the framing of the *Constitutions* of the new order. He worked on the first draft from 1547 to 1550, and revised the *Constitutions* on the recommendations of the others, finally completing them in 1552. The innovations in common rule required to make the Jesuits "ready to live in any part of the world where there is hope of God's greater glory and the good of souls" brought opposition both from within and from outside Roman Catholicism. Conservatives saw his exclusion of common penance and prayer as "Protestant"; the tremendous effect of the order against the Reformers in Europe brought their opposition.

Although as general he was frequently ill, and in 1551 he begged his associates to accept his resignation, they refused and he continued to direct the order until his death on July 31, 1556. He was canonized by Pope Gregory XV in 1622; in 1922, Pope Pius XI made him patron of all spiritual retreats.

BIBLIOGRAPHY: W. J. Young (tr.), *St. Ignatius' Own Story* (Chicago, 1956); J. Brodrick, *St. Ignatius Loyola: The Pilgrim Years* (London, 1956).

**Ihmels, Ludwig Heinrich** (1858–1933). German Lutheran pastor. Orthodox in his thinking, Ihmels was one of the representatives of the 19th-century Erlangen school of theology. He served pastorates from 1881 to 1894, became director of studies in Loccum (1894), and finally professor of systematic theology in Erlangen (1898). Of his writings, *Die christliche Wahrheitsgewissheit* is one of the most important.

**Illinois Band.** A group of seven young Yale theological students who in 1829 arrived in Illinois. They established Illinois College in Jacksonville the following year, and also planted Congregational churches in the surrounding territory. Among these men was Theron Baldwin (1801–1870), who helped create the Society for the Promotion of Collegiate and Theological Education in the West, of which organization he served as secretary for twenty-seven years.

**Illuminati.** See ALUMBRADOS.

**Ilminsky, Nikolay Ivanovich** (1822–1891). Russian Orientalist and religious educator. A graduate of the Theological Academy of Kazan, a prominent center of missions among the Tartar Moslems, he received a fellowship to study Turkic and Arabic languages and civilization at Damascus and Cairo. He then taught Oriental languages at the Institute for Missions among the Moslems at Kazan, where he was also a university professor for Turkic languages. In 1872 he was made director of the Kazan College for Teachers to the Oriental Minorities in Russia. He also became the founder of a Christian private school for Tartar children. Up to his time the efforts of the Russian Orthodox Church to missionize among the Moslems had remained haphazard and rather unsuccessful. Sometimes in opposition to the academic and ecclesiastical authorities, Ilminsky insisted that the propagation of the Christian faith among the religious and national minorities in Russia should proceed from thorough familiarity with their languages and cultures. He therefore advocated that the Scriptures, the liturgy, and other sacred writings be translated into the various vernacular idioms. He himself wrote a primer for the Christian Tartars as well as other textbooks and reference works. Furthermore, he translated the book of Genesis, The Wisdom of Solomon, the Gospel of Matthew, and the Orthodox Easter Liturgy into the Tartar language. In addition, he wrote numerous scholarly essays and articles about the folklore and literature of the Russian Moslems, questions of philology and linguistics, and archaeology. He was in later years supported in his work by Konstantine Pobedonostsev, the high procurator of the Holy Synod, with whom he exchanged a number of interesting letters shedding much light upon the missionary and general cultural policies of the Russian Orthodox Church in the second half of the 19th century.

**Il Risorgimento** ("The Revival"). Influential paper established in 1847 at Turin which advocated a united Italy and which lent its name to the entire nationalist movement under the leadership of Sardinia-Piedmont. The unification movement culminated with the establishment of the kingdom of Italy under the House of Savoy in February, 1861, and was finally completed when Venetia joined the kingdom by plebiscite in 1866 and the Vatican levies surrendered the city of Rome to overwhelming Italian forces in 1870.

**Imitation of Christ, The** (c. 1420). This book, the "Gospel of the *devotio moderna*" and finest product of the renewal in Flanders begun by Gerhard Groote, was second only to the Bible in popularity, going into more than three thousand editions and was translated into ninety-five languages. Although it is anonymous and its authorship has been disputed since 1500, scholars are now largely agreed that Thomas Hamerken, better known as Thomas à Kempis, is its author. He was a student of Florentius Radewyns at Deventer and became a monk of Mt. St. Agnes, an offshoot of the Windesheim Augustinian canons regular. The book is inspired by the teachings of Groote and stresses a simple interior following of the example of Christ. Written in Latin, it consists of four treatises, the first three concerning the progressive deepening of the inner life of union with God in Christ, and the fourth being devoted to the meaning and use of the Lord's Supper. It is cast in the form of maxims, prayers, and dialogues, and aims at the attainment of an effective spirituality free from intellectualism.

**Immaculate Conception.** Roman Catholic dogma defined on Dec. 8, 1854, by Pius IX in the apostolic letter *Ineffabilis Deus*. It teaches that Mary was freed from original sin by grace "in the first instant of conception." Augustine exempted the Virgin Mary from actual, but not original, sin. Duns Scotus defended the Immaculate Conception on Eadmer's principle, *"Potuit, decuit, fecit."* Franciscans instituted the Feast of the Conception of Mary (1263) and thereafter promoted the Immaculate Conception, but Dominican monks and Thomistic doctors strongly opposed them. The Council of Basel-Florence enunciated the doctrine; it was not promulgated by the pope. Sixtus IV declared (1483), after approving the Feast of the Immaculate Conception (1476), that either opinion could be held. In 1568, Pius V made the feast a holy day of obligation, while Trent stated only that the universality of original sin was not applicable to Mary, since Franciscans and Dominicans could not agree. Gregory imposed silence (1622) until the pope would decide. In the 17th century the papacy received requests, especially from France, to approve the

dogma. A novice's vision in the Rue du Bac (Paris), gave impetus to the evolving Marian devotion (see MARY, DEVOTION TO) and its dogmatic counterpart. On June 1, 1848, Pius IX appointed a committee, including Passaglia, to study the matter. In the encyclical *Ubi primum*, issued from Gaeta on Feb. 2, 1849, Pius stated that he had received many requests to speak on the matter and that he invited the prayers and opinions of the bishops. Pius' apostolic letter of 1854 defining the dogma was well received by ultramontanists, since the pope acted singly after consulting with the bishops.

**Immaculate Heart of Mary, Congregation of the** (*commonly known as* Scheut Missionaries). A missionary order founded at Scheutveld, Belgium, in 1862 by Theophil Verbist. Its main sphere of work was China. By the time of the final revision of its rule in 1923 it had over seven hundred members, nearly five hundred in missions. It produced such missionary pioneers as Konstanz of Decken, who crossed the Gobi desert in 1884, and Alphons Vermign, who compiled a Mongolian dictionary.

**Immigration.** Broadly speaking, colonial society was free from friction stemming from immigration. Only in Massachusetts Bay did the establishment maintain the purity of the faith by a rigid policy excluding all immigrants who did not adhere to Puritan theology and polity. This policy was relaxed by the end of the 17th century. In colonies such as Rhode Island and Pennsylvania, *de facto* religious toleration existed almost from the beginning. While there were sometimes civil restrictions on Roman Catholics and Jews, they were often observed in the breach.

Immigration became an issue for American Protestants in the 19th century as the result of the evangelical commitment to the idea of preserving and strengthening Christian civilization. In large part, this commitment developed as a response to shifting patterns of immigration which brought more and more Irish and German settlers whose religious and cultural values differed radically from those of evangelical Protestantism.

After 1830 a virulent strain of anti-Catholicism developed in America. This anti-Roman nativism found expression and leadership in both religion and politics. Lyman Beecher and Horace Bushnell, for example, detected a Catholic plot to take over the American Midwest. This stimulated attempts to provide home missions aimed at converting Catholics and strengthening Protestantism on the frontier. Other leaders feared the subversion of

American patterns in public education and the separation of church and state. The Know-Nothing party took these issues into politics in the 1850's.

Between 1865 and 1910 more than twenty-two million immigrants came to America. Although many were Protestants from central and northern Europe, an increasing number were Catholics and Jews from southern and eastern Europe. Most of the later immigrants settled in urban centers. Many individual Protestants and some church leaders met the situation with nativistic denunciations, but an increasing number saw the necessity for developing an adequate home missionary program to provide a ministry equipped to preach to the newcomers in their native language. Many denominations revised seminary programs to provide the necessary linguistic training. Still committed to a concept of Christian civilization, the churches embraced a program of Americanizing immigrants in which religion played a critical role.

The last stand of those committed to the idea of Christian civilization came in the 1920's. It was most clearly illustrated in the triumph of national prohibition and the activities of the Ku Klux Klan. Immigration restriction was also accomplished in this decade.

As a result of the acculturation of the various immigrant groups and the economic and political challenges of the 1930's and 1940's, ethnic and religious pluralism emerged as a new basis for American society. Ecumenical cooperation, a growing commitment to brotherhood, and the religious dialogue between all men of goodwill became increasingly important by the end of World War II.

BIBLIOGRAPHY: A. I. Abell, *The Urban Impact Upon American Protestantism* (Camden, Conn., 1943); R. A. Billington, *The Protestant Crusade: 1800–1860* (Chicago, 1964); R. D. Cross, *The Emergence of Liberal Catholicism in America* (Cambridge, Mass., 1958); M. L. Hansen, *The Atlantic Migration: 1607–1860* (New York, 1961); and *The Immigrant in American History* (New York, 1964); W. Herberg, *Protestant–Catholic–Jew: An Essay in American Religious Sociology* (Garden City, 1955); J. Higham, *Strangers in the Land: Patterns of American Nativism: 1860–1925* (New York, 1963).

**Immortale Dei.** Encyclical of Pope Leo XIII (Nov. 1, 1885). Concerned primarily with the constitution of the state, it aimed to refute the notion that the church is the enemy of the state and to compare Roman Catholic teaching with new theories of the state. Man

naturally forms a civilized society, says Leo, but an authority certified by God is necessary for the right government of society. Citizens are obligated to obey this authority, and rulers and people should honor the name of God and true religion. The state and the church govern their respective spheres, "one set over divine things, the other over human." If the governments of the two spheres conflict, the church cannot be subjected to civil authority. Such a Christian constitution, says Leo, causes peace to reign, assures good government, and makes possible the attainment of salvation and temporal well-being. Authority is not vested in the will of the people, and therefore they do not confer any right on those who exercise authority; rather, the authority of rulers comes from God. Finally, Leo brands as false the notion that liberty means that one can say and think anything one pleases. In conclusion he exhorts Roman Catholics to follow the guidance of the Roman see and the bishops of the church but also to become involved in the political and educational institutions of their respective states.

**Independency** (or Congregationalism). A term applying especially to the Congregationalists of Great Britain. It has never had any currency in the United States. It refers to their practice of local autonomy in congregational life. As a party the Independents were much in favor during the Commonwealth era. In the 18th century they were one of the three denominations (Congregationalists, Baptists, Presbyterians) that could send Dissenting Deputies to plead causes before Parliament.

**Index of Prohibited Books.** An authoritative list forbidding the reading or possession of books judged dangerous to faith and morals. Before the printing press and the Reformation it was possible to destroy books by public burning. As early as 1524 small lists of prohibited books were published in England and the Netherlands. The Paris faculty published a "catalog" in 1544. In 1559, Paul IV issued his own Index in Rome. The Council of Trent ordered an inquiry into "suspected and pernicious books" during Session 18 (Feb. 26, 1562). Session 25 constrained the pope to complete the work of the Council's committee. In *Benedictus Deus* (Jan. 26, 1564), Pius IV confirmed the Tridentine decisions concerning the Index, and issued Paul's Index revised, with a list of condemned authors and works appended. Rules concerning condemnation of publications, unauthorized Bible versions, and printery censorship were included. In March, 1571, Pius V established the Congregation of the Index. In 1590 and 1593 indexes were printed but never promulgated. Sixtus V (1585–1590) amended the Index to include objectionable passages. Benedict XIV issued a bull (July 8, 1753) that regulated in detail the procedures of congregational examiners. In 1917, Benedict XV transferred control of the Index to the Congregation of the Holy Office. Increasingly the indexing of books was the task of local bishops. After the first session of Vatican II the Index assumed less importance. At the second session, in 1966, the Index was officially abolished.

**India, Church of South.** A union church including four dioceses of the Church of India, Burma, and Ceylon (Anglican); the Methodist Church; and the South India United Church (Presbyterian, Congregational) created on Sept. 27, 1947, along the lines laid down by the Lambeth Quadrilateral of 1888 after more than twenty-eight years of negotiations. Despite reverses and difficulties, this union stands as the greatest monument of the modern ecumenical movement.

**India, National Christian Council of.** An organization formed at Ranchi (January, 1923) by the National Missionary Council (founded 1912) to be its successor. Provincial councils of churches and missions originally elected representatives to it, but the Council has come now to be composed entirely of churches with the missions excluded. Regional or provincial councils continue to function under it. The first two secretaries, K. T. Paul and William Paton, were men of unusual ability and ably guided it in its formative years. Through its membership in the International Missionary Council, the National Christian Council contributed notably to ecumenical fellowship, study, and action. Among its early achievements were famine relief, a youth movement, agricultural education and village improvement, literature, and the Christian Home and Family movement. It gained stature during World War II by its aid to interned German missionaries and to their institutions and churches. Audio-visual aids and mass communications were later concerns. Evangelism has always been central. The headquarters of the Council is at the Christian Council Lodge, Nagpur, B. S. The *National Christian Council Review* is published by the Council. The regional councils are Andhra, Assam, Bengal, Bihar, Bombay, Karnataka, Kerala, Madhya Pradesh, North West, Santal, Tamilnad, Utkal, and Uttar Pradesh. The Council occasionally publishes the *Christian Handbook of India*.

**India, United Church of Northern.** A union formed in 1924 in India by the joining of Presbyterian and Congregational churches associated with eleven missions and spanning the whole country from Gujarat to Assam. Statistics from 1962 are the latest ones available: India—424 churches, 208,770 communicants, 486,000 community; Pakistan—49 churches, 1,080 communicants, 2,764 community. There are 25 Church Councils in 7 linguistic area Synods under a General Assembly. The Moravian Church with its mission to Tibetans has also joined the United Church of Northern India. There is a confession of faith in twelve articles, but the church also recognizes the Westminster Confession, the Confession and Canons of the Synod of Dort, the Heidelberg Catechism, Luther's Catechism, and the Augsburg Confession "as systems of doctrine to be taught in our Churches and seminaries." This church initiated the large movement for church union in northern India, involving also Baptists, Anglicans, Brethren, Disciples, and Methodists, which got under way at the First Round Table Conference in 1929 and which is still being negotiated.

**Indians, American.** Although the Christian church sought to serve all Indians, its members often have shared white prejudices about red men and few have appreciated Indian cultures. Most missionaries, the main contact between church and Indian, have felt that their task was not only to convert heathens but also to transform aboriginal manners and economy. Following early relations with Roman Catholics, Indians encountered Protestants along the Virginia and New England coasts. Many colonial charters called for conversion of the natives, and to some Europeans this objective justified colonization. John Eliot and Thomas Mayhew, in part supported by English societies, gathered devout bands of "praying Indians," but these peaceful converts fared little better than their pagan brethren either against smallpox or against the whites in King Philip's War (1675–1676), a struggle that suppressed Massachusetts tribes and formally initiated two centuries of conflict between Indians and whites. In spite of the efforts of John Sergent at Stockbridge, the exemplary devotion of David Brainerd, and the support of Samuel Hopkins and Timothy Dwight, mission work was sporadic until 1820. The dilemmas of a Quaker government faced with frontier violence in Pennsylvania and the tragic story of Moravian missions in Ohio illustrate hardships shared by Christian magistrates and missionaries. Nevertheless, early white settlers insisted that they treated the Indians justly, paid them well for their forests, and then put the forests to a proper use:

cultivation. Others pointed to smallpox and Divine Providence to justify possession of Indian land. Unlike European romantics, Americans of the colonial, Revolutionary, and frontier periods did not always respect the native as a "noble savage"; preachers often described this "bond-servant of Satan" as the natural fruit of human depravity.

Cherokee removal during the 1830's created both moral indignation and confusion in the churches. Some leaders, such as the Baptist Isaac McCoy, favored relocation as the only means of saving Indians from white corruption; others, such as Jeremiah Evarts of the American Board, opposed the policy as immoral and unjust.

With Indian-white relations no longer complicated by foreign alliances, and aided by a federal "Civilization Fund," missionary effort was renewed after 1820. James Finley's Ohio Wyandot station, McCoy's work farther west, and Marcus Whitman's death near the Columbia River, drew public attention. Yet vicissitudes of removal, denominational arguments over the Indian vis-à-vis foreign missions, difficulties with nomadic Western tribes, and national preoccupation with abolition compromised the churches' effort to "Christianize and civilize" the so-called savage. The immediate post-Civil War period produced Helen Hunt Jackson's indictment *A Century of Dishonor* (1881) and President Grant's "peace policy" reform of the Indian Bureau (a policy that charged the churches with nomination and supervision of Indian agents). With the abolition of the treaty system (1871), the Indian ceased to be independent and became a ward of the Federal Government. Confronted with apparent linguistic and cultural extinction, the Indians of the 1890's responded to a new religion: the Ghost Dance. Messianic, pacifistic, and apocalyptic, Ghost Dance cults combined Christian and native elements. For three centuries Europeans had made little effort to understand native religions that they considered pagan, violent, and absurd; consequently, whites tended to condemn the Ghost Dance and its 20th-century successors, the peyote cult and the native North American Church. Mission and church opinion opposed the Indian Reorganization Act (1934), which attempted to treat Indians as Indians and to encourage indigenous culture. Most Americans incorrectly assumed that all Indians relished citizenship and wished to leave the reservation for a "normal" life. Even many missionaries had failed to determine the Indian's own viewpoint; by the late 1940's, however, this policy began to change, and, following a Quaker precedent, more emphasis was placed upon legislation for the rights of the Indians.

Until more is known about Christian attitudes and guilt feelings toward the Indians, and until mission studies are related to research in anthropology, this chapter in the church's history will remain unclear.

BIBLIOGRAPHY: H. Driver, *Indians of North America* (Chicago, 1961); H. Fey and D. McNickle, *Indians and Other Americans* (New York, 1958); E. Gray, *Wilderness Christians: The Moravian Mission to the Delaware Indians* (Ithaca, 1956); W. Hagan, *American Indians* (Chicago, 1961); J. Mooney, *The Ghost-Dance Religion and the Sioux Outbreak of 1890* (abridged, Chicago, 1965); R. Pearce, *The Savages of America* (Baltimore, 1965); R. Underhill, *Red Man's America* (Chicago, 1953); N. Burr, *Critical Bibliography*, Part II, pp. 425 ff.; W. LaBarre, Bibliography of peyote studies in *Anthropology Today* (Jan., 1960).

**Indulgences.** According to the Roman Catholic Church an indulgence, by drawing upon the merits of Christ and the saints, grants remission of temporal punishment due to sin. The practice is implicitly based on the assumptions that divine justice is of a retributive nature, that sin, though forgiven, still must be punished either on earth or in purgatory, that there exists a "treasury of merit" which is composed of the infinite merits of Christ, together with those of the Virgin Mary and the saints, and that the church by virtue of the communion of saints and apostolic succession has the right to administer to the faithful the benefits of this inexhaustible "treasury of merit" in consideration of prayers and other good works.

Modern practice in the Roman Catholic Church is to grant indulgences fairly liberally but only upon demonstrations of piety and good works. One may receive a plenary (complete) indulgence or a partial indulgence, that is, a partial remission of temporal punishment through reducing by a certain number of days or years the time one must spend in purgatory. But the church does not claim that the time granted in the indulgence exactly corresponds to time as reckoned in purgatory. However, it remains an article of faith among Roman Catholics that the church does have the authority to grant indulgences.

An indulgence is usually given to those who through confession and absolution have been restored to a state of grace and who then, as penance, say certain prayers, undertake good works, or visit a shrine. Often indulgences are attached to rosaries, medallions, and crucifixes, and to the observance of specified feast days. The faithful can also gain indulgences for the souls of the departed now in purgatory, but only through an act of intercession, for the church claims no authority over the souls of the deceased.

Although the doctrine of indulgences did not reach full development until the 12th century, as early as the 3d century the intercession of priests, confessors, and those expecting martyrdom at the hands of the Roman state was accepted by ecclesiastics as justification for shortening the canonical penalties of those undergoing penance. Later, penance itself came to be considered as substituting for punishment in purgatory, and with this development it was only logical that the belief arose that the intercessory prayers of the saints could shorten temporal punishment in purgatory. Thus, good works could substitute for penitential discipline and the merits of Christ and the saints could be called upon to supplement the good works themselves.

Nevertheless, there is no evidence of a widespread practice by the church of granting indulgences until the period of the Crusades. Indeed, one of the first examples of blanket indulgences occurs with the promise of Urban II when launching the First Crusade in 1095 that the crusaders would be granted remission of their sins. It then became the practice that a plenary indulgence (that is, one which completely washed away temporal penalties due to sin) was always given upon the penitent's taking the cross. The popes also granted other prelates the right to give partial indulgences for special occasions such as the dedication of churches, observances of certain feast days, and episcopal anniversaries.

The practice, however, lent itself to considerable abuse in the hands of unscrupulous ecclesiastics. Often to raise money a bishop, or even a pope, might grant commissions to "pardoners" who were to travel about, hear confessions and, upon receiving a monetary donation, grant an indulgence to the faithful. These pardoners seldom pointed out that an indulgence was a remission of temporal punishment. Rather, they tended to propagandize them as remissions of sin itself, with the result that the more gullible believed that they were buying licenses to sin. This scandalous playing upon the credulity and misconceptions of the uneducated is most remembered in the activities of Tetzel, the agent of Albert of Brandenburg, archbishop of Mainz. It was his preaching near Wittenberg that sparked Martin Luther's challenge of church doctrines which ultimately resulted in the Protestant Reformation. Even before Luther, however, such prel-

ates as Innocent III had attempted to end the excesses of the pardoners. It was not until 1567 when the practice of commissioning pardoners was proscribed by Pius V that the abuses of indulgences were finally ended. The current practice of granting apostolic indulgences, reserved to the pope alone, dates from a bull of Pope Sixtus V (1587).

BIBLIOGRAPHY: J. E. Campbell, *Indulgences* (Ottawa, 1953); H. C. Lea, *History of Auricular Confession and Indulgences in the Latin Church* (Philadelphia, 1896); A. H. M. Lepicier, *Indulgences: Their Origin and Nature* (London, 1906); P. F. Palmer (ed.), *Sacraments and Forgiveness* (Westminster, Md., 1960); N. Paulus, *Indulgences as a Social Factor in the Middle Ages* (New York, 1922).

**Ineffabilis Deus.** A bull issued on Dec. 8, 1854, after consultation with many bishops, by Pope Pius IX, who was deeply loyal to the devotion to the Virgin Mary. It defined as dogma the teaching that Mary was conceived immaculate, purified, it was said, "in view of" the merits of the Christ whom she would later bear. Most Doctors of the Church, including Bernard of Clairvaux and Thomas Aquinas, had opposed this devotion. The pope believed that his own authority and that of the current opinion of the church outweighed their dissent (a view reflected in his remark: *"Io sono la tradizione"*). Protestants have rejected the dogma on the grounds that it is not in Scripture and that it detracts from the uniqueness of the Christ. The character of the pronouncement, which depended for its authority on the pope, was an anticipation of the later decision (1870) of the First Vatican Council.

**Infallibility, Papal.** The Roman Catholic doctrine that when the pope speaks on faith and morals in his official capacity as head of the Roman Catholic Church, he is divinely safeguarded from error. This dogma was promulgated in 1870 by the First Vatican Council.

**Infidelity.** Sometimes identified with "unbelief," "free thought," or "skepticism." Its advocates usually have rejected a belief in revelation, especially Biblical, and questioned the obedience of believers to the sacerdotal authority of organized religion, arguing for the use of reason and critical inquiry as the only acceptable sources of truth. Although Christians have been accused of irrationalism since the early days of Celsus, Tertullian, and Julian, overt opposition to Christian supernaturalism gained momentum with the appearance of the Renaissance, the Age of

Reason, and the scientific revolution of the 19th and 20th centuries. Voltaire remains a representative infidel, crusading against the church, demanding that free men must *écrasez l'infâme* ("crush the infamous thing"). Other Enlightenment critics were Diderot, Locke, and Hume. Nineteenth-century opposition came from Jeremy Bentham's utilitarianism, Auguste Comte's positivism, Ludwig Feuerbach's psychological critique, Friedrich Nietzsche's "death of God," Karl Marx's economic materialism, Sir James Frazer's evolutionary naturalism, and, in the 20th century, Arthur Koestler's nihilism and Sigmund Freud's argument that religion is a psychological delusion.

Infidelity in America reached two peaks in the late 18th and late 19th centuries, with most critics striking at weaknesses in Christian Biblicism, ineffective morality, and antique social philosophy. The first American book directed against Christianity was Ethan Allen's *Reason the Only Oracle of Man; Or, A Compenduous System of Natural Religion* (1784). Allen sought to strip away obscurities in Christianity and uncover true reason as a guide to morality. Allen believed that the churches, through priestcraft and witchcraft, held men in ignorance for selfish purposes. Thomas Paine's *The Age of Reason* (1794–1795), however, remains the single most influential skeptical credo on the American scene. Paine called the colonial alliance of church and state an "adulterous connection," a tyranny from which men must be rescued. This first and widely influential age of American infidelity was based largely on British deism, rationalist and latitudinarian theology, moral libertarianism, German idealism, and popular native hostility to religious establishment. Such diverse figures as Jonathan Mayhew, Benjamin Franklin, and Thomas Jefferson were often accused of infidelity, but repudiated "that immorality." The Second Great Awakening (1797–1803) scattered the advocates of skepticism, although revivalists such as Timothy Dwight continued to use the threat of infidelity to encourage religious awakenings. Despite an apparent eclipse before the Civil War, the communitarian and socialist utopianism of Robert Owen was widely interpreted as an infidel attempt to build a free-thought society to counteract an ostensibly Christian society. Some contemporaries believed that Andrew Jackson represented political atheism, and his attacks upon property and aristocracy were considered elements of an infidel conspiracy. The revivalist Lyman Beecher formulated what came to be a definitive image of the infidel in American history. On the frontier he was a gambler, drunkard, immoralist, and blas-

phemer. Beecher advocated revivals and missions to the frontier in order to prevent its conquest by "unbelieving" infidels and Catholics. Skepticism gained a foothold in Kentucky, eventually leading to the American institution—the "village atheist." In the cities, Beecher believed that infidelity was the source of poverty, crime, and immorality. Infidelity meant that "there is no God, no resurrection, no future state, no free agency, no accountability, no virtue, no sin, no devil, no heaven, no hell, and death is an eternal sleep." Infidels, Beecher stated, denied the Bible, the Sabbath, marriage, and private property. Only Christianity could win a victory over this "loathsome disease and unutterable woe." In postwar industrial America, Robert Ingersoll (1833–1899) emerged as the national "infidel." Arguing that science and reason exposed the offensive and obscure nature of Christianity for all to see, Ingersoll believed that skepticism was not dying, but would soon triumph in an enlightened nation. He hit churches on their insecurity in an era of the evolutionary hypothesis, Biblical criticism, and technological success. Religion, he said, was the enemy of the people, leading to "softening of the brain and ossification of the heart." Ingersoll embarrassed such liberals as Henry Ward Beecher and Lyman Abbott, and was attacked by Thomas de Witt Talmadge and Cardinal Manning. Other late-19th- and early-20th-century "infidelities" include O. B. Frothingham's Free Religious Association, Humanist Societies, and Ethical Culture Societies. In the thirties, H. L. Mencken and Clarence Darrow condemned religion as a flight from reality.

BIBLIOGRAPHY: F. L. Baumer, *Religion and the Rise of Scepticism* (New York, 1960); M. E. Marty, *The Infidel* (Cleveland, 1961); R. R. Palmer, *Catholics and Unbelievers in Eighteenth-Century France* (Princeton, 1939); R. H. Popkin, *The History of Scepticism from Erasmus to Descartes* (New York, 1960).

**Infirmary.** In a monastery a room set aside for the care of sick monks. Since monasteries, particularly at an early period, were almost entirely self-sufficient communities, all the needs of the members had to be anticipated. In the Rule of St. Benedict, a chapter was devoted to the care of the sick. The rule required that there be an infirmary managed by an infirmarian. Those who were ill received special care, including better food than their brethren and frequent baths.

**Infralapsarianism.** A distinction arising in Dutch Calvinist theology in the 16th century relating to the order of the decrees of God in relation to the Fall. In opposition to supralapsarianism, this viewpoint maintained that the decrees of election and reprobation followed the decrees of creation and the Fall. It also placed the Fall among the "passive" decrees of God. Infralapsarianism is an attempt to soften the harshness of predestinarianism and to relieve God of the responsibility for the "lostness" of man.

**Inge, William Ralph** (1860–1954). Anglican churchman. Inge was a profound thinker who expressed himself in mystical and devotional literature. He was deeply influenced by Plotinus, about whom he wrote an important book. His published works ranged over many fields: ethics, mysticism, philosophy, the relation of religion and science, and Biblical theology. From 1911 to 1934 he was dean (known as the "Gloomy Dean") of St. Paul's, London.

**Ingersoll, Robert Green** (1833–1899). Lawyer, lecturer, "the great agnostic." Ingersoll complained of a harsh and Calvinistic childhood. A self-made man, he was attorney general of Illinois (1867–1869). In the midst of religious controversy over Darwinism, Ingersoll gained recognition as a leading orator, debater, and lecturer. He made "infidelity" attractive by his unimpeachable private and public life, his patriotism, and his participation in the Republican Party. In 1876 he nominated Blaine at the Republican National Convention and in 1879 moved his practice to Washington, where his most famous case was the successful defense of S. W. Dorsey, who was indicted in connection with the postal "star routes." Ingersoll conceived of himself as the successor of Paine and Allen, and was the only such figure to draw replies from leading churchmen, including Henry Ward Beecher, Cardinal Manning, and Dwight L. Moody. Typical lectures included *Some Mistakes of Moses* (1879), *Superstition* (1898), and *The Devil* (1899).

**Inglis, Charles** (1734–1816). First bishop of Nova Scotia. He was born in Glen and Kilcar, Donegal, Ireland, where he was educated. After teaching in a church school in Lancaster, Pa. (1757) he returned to England in 1758 for ordination and the same year was sent to Dover, Del. In 1765, he was appointed assistant to the rector of Trinity Church, N.Y. During the American Revolution his church was burned and his property confiscated. He went to Nova Scotia in 1783, returning to England the following year. In 1787 he was consecrated first bishop of Nova Scotia, and the next year he founded King's College at Windsor, Nova Scotia.

**Inner Mission.** A Lutheran home missionary movement (distinguished from "outer" or foreign missions) with the twofold interest of evangelism and social service. It drew together interests arising largely from the encounter of pietistic Lutheranism with the secular urban culture that emerged in 19th-century Germany. J. H. Wichern is recognized as the father of the movement because of his pioneer work at the Rauhes Haus near Hamburg and his impassioned appeal at the Kirchentag of 1848 which led in the following year to the establishment of the annual congresses and central administration for Inner Mission. In its early decades its interests were presentation of the gospel in preaching, literature, and acts of mercy, but in the years following 1875 the movement was agitated by the social questions raised by the problems of industrialization and the teachings of Marx. Yet the evangelical concern remained central. The enterprises of Inner Mission are extremely various, including operation of rescue missions, homes, hospitals, colonies, industrial and merchantile establishments, and finally theological seminaries. The movement has spread throughout the Lutheran world and has experienced an exchange of influences with movements of a similar type that found their origin in other communions.

**Innocent I** (d. 417). Pope from 401. He was a man who, because of his wide contacts in both East and West, greatly enhanced the position of the papacy through his insistence upon the role of Rome as arbiter in any major ecclesiastical disputes. He argued strongly for the Roman bishop's dominant position in sacramental functions. His belief in the primacy of Rome carried over into his promulgation of decisions in doctrinal questions, which had far-reaching consequences—particularly in regard to Pelagius, concerning whom the African Church had appealed to Innocent. Augustine asked his assistance in a controversy with Julian of Eclanum. In matters of polity and jurisdiction, Innocent opposed the deposition of John Chrysostom from Constantinople, demanding a synod of Eastern and Western bishops to inquire into the matter. When his demand was rejected, he and the Western Church broke communion with the Church at Constantinople, Alexandria, and Antioch. He supported Jerome against John, bishop of Jerusalem; and he brought East Illyricum under the ecclesiastical authority of the West with the aid of the bishop of Thessalonica. By his offices the emperor Honorius declared against the Donatists in 405, the decree becoming final at Carthage in 411. A letter (405) to Exuperius, bishop of Toulouse, indicates that he viewed the Apocrypha as Scripture.

Innocent III (Lotario dei Conti di Segni, 1160–1216). Pope from 1198. Born into a noble Roman family, he studied Scholastic theology under Peter of Corbeil at the University of Paris and civil and canon law under Uguccio of Ferrara at Bologna, the centers for these disciplines at the time. Returning to Rome, he quickly advanced in rank within the Curia through family connections, legal training, and acquired diplomatic ability. During an interval when he was without ecclesiastical office, he wrote the two famous treatises that epitomize the spirit of the man and his age, *De contemptu mundi* and *De sacro altaris mysterio,* expressing the emphases of the monk and the medieval churchman.

Upon the death of Celestine III in 1198, Lotario was unanimously elected pope, afterward being ordained a priest and consecrated bishop. As Innocent III, he based his ordination sermon upon Jer. 1:10 ("See, I have set you this day over nations and over kingdoms, to pluck up and to break down, to destroy and to overthrow, to build and to plant"), indicating then his lifelong zeal to bring all Europe together under one ruler and one Christian moral law.

His first efforts were directed toward the needed reform of the Roman Curia, then the only judicial body of final appeal in Europe. Although only thirty-seven years of age, he brilliantly succeeded in reorganizing the papal chancery courts and modernizing ambiguous canonical decrees. By ambitious attention to the detail of problems that came to Rome and businesslike oversight toward all judgments, he gave early indication of his determination. Accepting the premise that he was as "Vicar of Christ" appointed to convey the divine law to all mankind, he set out to make his authority uppermost in the feudal and ecclesiastical relationships that he reformed.

Confronted with Philip Augustus' intransigent refusal to fulfill his betrothal of marriage to Ingeborg of Denmark, Innocent used the interdict to force the capitulation of Philip and the French bishops who had supported the king. Upon the death of Emperor Henry VI in 1197, Innocent accepted the guardianship of the young Frederick II of Sicily, but extracted a promise from his preferred candidate for the emperor's throne, Otto IV, to respect the papacy's temporal power over the Italian states, summarized in the *Deliberatio* of 1201. When Otto violated this agreement, Innocent declared him deposed in favor of Philip of Swabia, justifying this action not as a temporal ruler but as a "spiritual judge" over all men. In the disputed election to the see of Canterbury, Innocent forced King John to

affirm the papal candidate, Stephen Langton, by the imposition of the interdict and the real possibility of a French invasion of England. Innocent at the same time gained the fealty of King John as a temporal lord. In a significant letter to John, Innocent expressed the principle that "the King of Kings . . . so established the kingship and the priesthood in the church, that the kingship should be priestly, and the priesthood royal . . . setting one over all, whom he appointed his vicar on earth." Determined to preach a Crusade, Innocent taxed the clergy, but the Fourth Crusade (1204) was diverted from the Holy Land by the Venetians, who had provided the ships, and proceeded instead to Constantinople, where it helped reestablish (1203) the dethroned emperor, thereby enabling Innocent to nominate a Latin patriarch. Even in nominating a Latin patriarch to Constantinople for the first time, Innocent stressed that "the Lord left to Peter governance not of the church only but of the whole world." Thus did Innocent make clear his claims.

It was in the centralization of the Inquisition at Rome, however, that Innocent exhibited his primarily spiritual aims, directing papal legates as well as the Dominican and Franciscan Orders to the extirpation of heretical "Catharist" Albigenses in southern France, after the repeated failures of the episcopal Inquisition in that area.

Innocent's leadership of the Fourth Lateran Council clearly represents the pinnacle of papal influence in the Middle Ages, and his famous analogy of "the two lights" (viz., the sun and the moon symbolize respectively the relative positions of the spiritual and the temporal powers in the world) was an ideal that the papacy was never again able to attain.

BIBLIOGRAPHY: C. R. Cheney and W. H. Semple (eds.), *Selected Letters of Pope Innocent III* (London, 1953); L. Elliott-Binns, *Innocent III* (London, 1931); C. H. C. Pirie-Gordon, *Innocent the Great* (London, 1907); C. E. Smith, *Innocent III* (Baton Rouge, 1951).

Innocent IV (Sinibaldo Fieschi, d. 1254). Noted canon lawyer at Bologna, elected pope in 1243, after a vacancy of the papal throne for over a year, due mainly to the machinations of Emperor Frederick II. Innocent immediately set out to combat Frederick and expel him from the Papal States. Refusing all peace overtures offered by Frederick, he determined to destroy the Hohenstaufen emperor. Forced to flee Italy for his safety, he journeyed north, stopping at Lyons, where, in June, 1245, he convoked an ecclesiastical council to deal with Frederick. Again, Innocent spurned the emperor's attempts to make peace. Reaffirming the earlier excommunication of Frederick and declaring the emperor deposed, he instructed the German princes to elect a new king. Ultimately, he even declared a Crusade against Frederick. After the emperor's death in 1250, Innocent was determined to crush the Hohenstaufen once and for all, vowing to "exterminate the viper breed," and during the last four years of his pontificate was embroiled in a constant struggle with Frederick's heirs, casting about among the princes of Europe for a papal champion who would take up arms against Frederick's illegitimate son, Manfred of Sicily. This unscrupulous use of papal spiritual authority, particularly of the Crusade as a political weapon, tarnished the moral prestige of the papacy. In his obsession to destroy the Hohenstaufen dynasty he neglected the internal affairs of the church, even closing his eyes to abuses whenever these could strengthen his political position.

**Innocent VIII** (Giovanni Battista Cibo, 1432–1492). Pope from 1484. A native of Genoa, he had spent some years as a bishop when, in 1473, he was made a cardinal through the influence of Giuliano della Rovere (later Julius II). When, in the conclave of 1484, Della Rovere saw that he himself could not be elected, he secured the election of Cibo by bribery. Innocent VIII, often in poor health, remained under the influence of Della Rovere and was not greatly interested in church reform. He opposed the Pragmatic Sanction of Bourges, condemned Pico della Mirandola, and unsuccessfully called for a crusade; but he ended by selling papal offices to pay for his own Italian wars.

**Innocent IX** (Giovanni Antonio Facchinetti, 1519–1591). Pope. He was born in Bologna, studied law and subsequently held various papal administrative offices, becoming a cardinal in 1583. He was elected pope as a compromise candidate, his pro-Spanish attitude being balanced against his advanced age. He died shortly after his election, however, so that his actual reign ran from Oct. 29 to Dec. 30, 1591.

**Innocent X** (Giovanni Battista Pamfili, 1574–1655). Pope from 1644. A Roman by birth, he held various curial offices and in 1627 became a cardinal. Over French objections he was chosen pope in 1644. He protested without avail against the terms of the Peace of Westphalia. In 1653 he condemned Jansenism. Although personally a pious man, he did allow his widowed sister-in-law, Olimpia Maidalchini, to gain much influence over him, a circumstance from which she derived considerable financial profit.

**Innocent XII** (Antonio Pignatelli, 1615–1700). Pope from 1691. Born in Naples, he became a member of the Roman Curia when only twenty years old. Later he was appointed archbishop of Naples. In 1691, after a lengthy conclave, he was elected as compromise pope between the contending Spanish-imperial and French parties. His reign was distinguished by a series of important acts and encyclicals and accompanied by diligence in reform of the church and a pastoral concern for men. Innocent made an effort to care for the poor; he built hospitals and schools, and worked for reform of the monastic orders. Of his decretals, *Romanum decet pontificem,* which opposed nepotism in any form, was one of the more important. In 1693, Innocent brought to a close the long strife over Gallicanism and won for the Curia a decided victory over the powerful Louis XIV. Symbolic of his victory was the concession by the French Crown of the pope's right to fill the bishoprics of the French Church. In 1699, Innocent's *Cum alias* condemned twenty-three propositions found in Fénelon's *Maxims of the Saints.* He also stood behind the judgment of his predecessor Alexander VII against Jansen (see JANSENISM). In contrast to his predecessors, his policies after the Gallican strife were favorable to France and cool to the Hapsburgs of Austria.

**Inquisition.** The ecclesiastical and judicial apparatus developed by the medieval church to deal with heresy. The establishment of this formal procedure was necessary for at least two reasons. Before the Inquisition there was no clearly defined policy for dealing with heretics and during the 12th, 13th, and 14th centuries there was a marked increase in the number of groups of doubtful orthodoxy.

Before the Inquisition, the church had held that excommunication was sufficient penalty for heresy, although occasionally secular rulers argued for confiscation of property or death. Lack of a clear policy made possible wide divergence in the treatment afforded heretics and sometimes left them to be executed by mob action or extra-legally condemned by secular rulers.

Heresy, in medieval thought, was considered a conscious denial of the Christian faith and a public and continuing persistence in erroneous ways. As such it threatened the social, ecclesiastical, and doctrinal order of Christendom. Church and state were two aspects of a single society and political and social unity were the results of ecclesiastical unity. To destroy heresy was thus to preserve the integrity of the faith and also the security of society. To the Christian monarch the heretic was a rebel; to the Christian church, the heretic was murdering his own soul.

Two of the major heretical groups were the Waldenses and the Albigenses (or Cathari). By the late 12th century the Albigenses had nearly gained control of Languedoc (southern France) despite their condemnation by several church councils. Pope Innocent III sent several missions to them in an attempt to win them back but when in 1208 the papal legate Peter of Castelnau was assassinated, Innocent finally organized a Crusade against them. The Catholic forces were led by the French nobleman Simon de Montfort. The Crusade soon lost all semblance of a "holy war" and became a struggle between various political factions that lasted until 1229.

The reign of Innocent III was also the time of a revival of interest in Roman law. This code emphasized that it was the duty of the state to protect orthodox religion and punish heretics. The state could use force, however, only when sanctioned by the church. Comparisons were soon made between heresy and treason, and Roman law clearly decreed the death penalty for the latter.

By early in the 13th century it was clear that the bishops who had been charged with the suppression of heresy by the Council of Verona (1184) had failed in this task, often through lack of training or hostility to Rome. The Albigensian Crusade disillusioned those who had sought to combat heresy in this manner. The revival of Roman law led to much legislation against heretics by both the Empire and the church, but as yet there was no widely effective way of enforcing the laws. Finally, in 1232 the Holy Roman Emperor Frederick II entrusted to political officials the routing out of heretics in the Empire. The next year, Pope Gregory IX, somewhat suspicious of Frederick's political plans, claimed this right for the church and appointed papal inquisitors. At this point the Inquisition formally came into existence.

Until well into the middle of the century the papal inquisitors were to be embroiled in struggles with local bishops over questions of jurisdiction; the prelates resented anyone working in their territory who was directly responsible to Rome and not to them. The bishops fought a losing battle, however, for the papal inquisitors were specially trained men drawn mostly from the Dominican and Franciscan Orders. With this training, and owing loyalty directly to the pope, they were lifted above local church politics; in addition, their monastic vows reduced the possibility of their being bribed. The inquisitors quickly gained great power; by 1259 they were formally exempted from all ecclesiastical control except the pope's and were given the right to interpret both civil and ecclesiastical law. Pope Alexander IV gave them the right to absolve one another from excommunication and irregular conduct. The Inquisition as such had no permanent headquarters, and the number of inquisitors was never very large.

Before the Inquisition began its operations in any area, a time of grace was proclaimed (usually about a month), during which the inquisitors toured the area urging heretics to make voluntary confessions. Those who confessed received pardons and light penances such as fasting or pilgrimages. Once the Inquisition began, suspects could be brought before it, provided that at least two witnesses accused them of heresy. At first, in order to protect them, the names of the witnesses were not revealed. Pope Boniface VIII, however, allowed the inquisitors to reveal the names if they felt there was no danger to the witnesses. During the trial the inquisitor acted as prosecutor and judge. Often a group of experts would view the proceedings, but they served the inquisitor only in an advisory capacity. All authority, including the determination of punishment, belonged to the inquisitor. The trial was actually the interrogation of the suspect by the inquisitor. The suspect had to prove himself innocent. He could summon witnesses in his favor, but he had no formal legal adviser and usually the witnesses against him were not present. The only appeal of an inquisitor's decision was to Rome and it was rarely made.

If the accused remained obstinate in the face of the evidence and the interrogation, he was subject to imprisonment and perhaps torture. These methods, particularly torture, were the inquisitor's last resorts. In 1252, Pope Innocent IV in his bull *Ad extirpanda* had allowed for the use of torture in inquisitorial proceedings. In adopting this practice of the secular courts the pope was careful to limit its use with various restrictions. Final discretion in the use of torture, however, rested with the individual inquisitor; some respected the limitations, some did not.

The formal pronouncement of the sentences took place at the act of faith (auto-da-fé), an impressive public ceremony. All the faithful of the region were expected to attend and "make an act of faith" (to pledge loyalty to the church and faith, to promise to pursue heretics and support the work of the Inquisition), being warned through the judgments passed against the heretics. The minor penances often consisted of fasting, pilgrimages, wearing of crosses on outer garments, and pious works. Major penances included excommunication, exile, confiscation of property, and imprisonment for terms up to life. Unrepentant heretics and those who had lapsed into a formerly abandoned heresy were sentenced to be burned to death at the stake. In 1254, Pope Innocent IV in the bull *Cum adversus haereticam* had approved the decrees of Frederick II that declared the stake as the punishment for such cases. The sentence was administered by abandoning the heretic to the "secular arm" (the state). Although it is difficult to determine the total number of cases considered by the Inquisition, perhaps the record of Bernard Gui, the inquisitor of Toulouse (France) from 1308 to 1323, is of interest. Of his 637 judgments, 67 were directed toward persons already dead and 40 resulted in death at the stake.

The Inquisition was successful in France, Spain, Italy, Germany, but relatively unsuccessful in England, Scandinavia, and eastern Europe. In 1312 the Council of Vienne issued laws correcting abuses in the use of torture, manipulation for political purposes, and excessive power claimed by inquisitors. Pope Paul III established in 1542 the Congregation of the Inquisition (Holy Office) as a final court of appeals for heresy trials. Following several reorganizations, it has become the Congregation for the Doctrine of the Faith, concerned with final judgments on issues of faith and morals.

The so-called Spanish Inquisition was a comparatively late development and differed from its predecessors in being closely bound to the state and having a tightly centralized organization under the Grand Inquisitor. Begun in 1479 by King Ferdinand V and Queen Isabella, it was originally directed against converted Jews (Marranos) and Moslems (Moriscos) suspected of secretly returning to their former faiths, and later used against Protestants. Its procedure was essentially the same as the Inquisition elsewhere. It was suppressed in 1820.

The Inquisition, always a source of controversy, bears little resemblance to modern court procedure. It was a penitential tribunal, not a penal court. The suspect was accused as a sinner, not as a criminal. The entire weight of the Inquisition was directed toward securing a voluntary confession of error for the sake of the soul. The heretic was always under the protection of the church and when he confessed, his penalties were prescribed under the rules that usually pertained to the confessional. When the suspect refused to confess, the inquisitor was forced to turn him over to the state for criminal punishment, since heresy was, in the state's eyes, a criminal offense. Confession was intended as the main concern, and when a heretic burned, a soul was lost, and the Inquisition had failed.

BIBLIOGRAPHY: G. G. Coulton, *Inquisition and Liberty* (London, 1938); H. C. Lea, *A History of the Inquisition of the Middle Ages,* 3 vols. (New York, 1888); and *The Inquisition in Spain,* 4 vols. (New York, 1908); A. L. Maycock, *The Inquisition from Its Establishment to the Great Schism* (New York, 1927); A. S. Turberville, *Medieval Heresy and the Inquisition* (London, 1920).

**Institute of Paris.** After seventy years of refusal, the French Parlement allowed private universities in 1875, whereupon a Catholic university of Paris was organized with faculties of law, letters, and science (1876). Denied the title of university and power to grant degrees (1880), it assumed the title of Catholic Institute of Paris. After suppression of Sorbonne's theology faculty (1886), the Institute established its own (1889). From 1893, upon the appointment of Alfred Loisy to this faculty, it came under censure through controversies later called Modernism, but after *Pascendi* (1907) the faculty was reorganized with Jesuits in principal chairs. The property was confiscated by the government in 1906 and was not repurchased until 1923. Upon the adoption in 1935 of the Apostolic Constitution *Deus scientiarum Dominus* (1931) and the *Ordinationes* implementing it, the Institute was declared a pontifical university by the Congregation of Seminaries and Universities. This action established three faculties of religious studies (theology, philosophy, and canon law) alongside the older profane faculties. Now the Institute could grant proper pontifical degrees in these and the other subjects of theological study. Governed by an episcopal commission under the archbishop of Paris, it comprises the six faculties and numerous associated schools and institutes.

**Institutes.** Popular name for John Calvin's great work, *Institutes of the Christian Religion.* The first edition was published in March, 1536, at Basel, when Calvin was twenty-six years old. It was a brief manual of six chapters intended as a guide for inquirers. In form it resembled Luther's Catechisms. However, the severe persecution of French Protestants at this time led Calvin to dedicate his work to King Francis I as an apology for the Reformed faith. Calvin's preface to the king stands among the greatest specimens of Christian literature of all time. Calvin expanded and rewrote the *Institutes* a number of times. The definitive edition, published in Latin in 1559, is about five times larger than the original. It contains eighty chapters in four books: Book I deals with the knowledge of God the Creator; Books II to IV, with the knowledge of God the Redeemer in Christ—that is, with the Person and work of the Mediator (Book II); the Holy Spirit and the application of salvation (Book III); and, finally, the means of grace (church, sacraments, and civil government, Book IV). While Calvin makes free use of reason and the church fathers, especially Augustine, he adheres faithfully to the Reformation principle of the sole authority of the Bible. The *Institutes* is the clearest and ablest systematic exposition of the ideas that inspired the Reformation. While Calvin's other writings, particularly his commentaries, have been valued highly through the years, it is his authorship of the *Institutes* that has earned him a place among the great theologians of all time.

**Institutional Church.** The name generally applied to a type of church that supplements its ordinary work by identifying itself in various ways with the secular interests of those whom it seeks to influence. This expansion of church work began in England as early as 1840, but was fully developed only in the latter years of the 19th century. In the United States the movement dates from about 1880, pioneered by William A. Muhlenberg as an experiment in charity for the underpriviledged, and it became a standard outlet for the expression of philanthropic concern in the post-Civil War era. St. George's Episcopal Church, New York; Berkeley Temple (Congregationalist), Boston; the Baptist Temple in Philadelphia; and the Metropolitan Temple (Methodist) of New York are outstanding examples of institutional programs in the 1880's and 1890's. They offered such services as industrial education courses, gymnasiums, reading rooms, day nurseries, employment bureaus, and social clubs, with great success. In 1894 a number of these institutional churches organized the Open or Institutional Church League on an interdenominational basis for the purpose of coordinating the various programs. Institutional churches multiplied toward the end of the century, encouraged by the activities of the League and by cooperative activities within denominations.

**Integralism.** Roman Catholic opposition to Modernism in the church in the early 1900's, especially in Germany. Integralism urged the rejection of secular advances of any kind. As a "religious totalitarianism," though unorganized, it emphasized the magisterial authority of the church. In literary circles it endorsed only literature that served Roman Catholic purposes (cf. the famous "literary strife," high point 1909, of Carl Muth, Richard von Kralik, and others). Politically, it advocated state-church unity approximating medieval *potestas directa*. It dismissed workingmen's unions before World War I ("integralists" in Berlin vs. "realists" in Cologne), since they were not church-dependent organizations. Benedict XV's *Ad beatissimi apostolorum* of 1914 rejected integralism. It refused to die, however, and arose again after World War II under violent opposition.

**Interchurch World Movement** (1918–1920). A development from the optimism and new world vision of the American churches at the end of World War I. Thirty denominations combined forces in a single campaign to finance the normal home, foreign, and educational work plus a tremendous advance program to be carried out both denominationally and in union projects. It was overambitious, and $336,777,527 was asked for 1920. The campaign failed disastrously, but experience in cooperation was gained.

**Interdenominational Conference on Social Service Unions.** An organization founded in 1911 under the leadership of Charles Gore, to bring together Anglicans and Free Churchmen to study and seek solutions to the many pressing social problems of the day. It directed a research seminar known as the "Collegium," led by William Temple and Lucy Gardner. These studies climaxed in the greatest conference of the Social Gospel movement in the English-speaking world, namely, the Conference on Politics, Economics, and Citizenship at Birmingham in 1924, which served as a forerunner to the first World Conference on Life and Work at Stockholm the next year.

**Interdict.** An ecclesiastical penalty that excludes the faithful from the sacraments but does not impose the more severe penalties of excommunication. Administration of sacraments is forbidden, except in cases of imminent death. The interdict, normally imposed by the pope, may be laid against individuals, groups of people, or whole geographical areas such as parishes, dioceses, or nations. Interdicts were used frequently by medieval popes.

**International Missionary Council.** An outgrowth of the Continuation Committee set up at the Edinburgh World Missionary Conference in 1910, constituted at a meeting in 1921 at Lake Mohonk, N.Y., upon plans made at the Crans, Switzerland, Conference. Members were national and regional missionary organizations. The stated functions of the International Council were: to promote missionary investigation and to share its results; to help coordinate missionary activity and promote united action; to foster freedom of conscience, missionary liberty, and international and interracial justice; to publish *The International Review of Missions* and study materials; and to call world missionary conferences as desired.

Such conferences have been held at Jerusalem (1928); Tambaram, near Madras (1938); Whitby, Ontario (1947); and Accra, Ghana (1957). From its inception the World Council of Churches and the International Missionary Council were "in association with" each other and cooperated in many undertakings. The final Assembly of the Council, Nov. 17–18, 1961, adopted the plan, and the act of integration with the World Council of Churches took place at the opening session of the latter's Third Assembly at New Delhi on Sunday, Nov. 19, 1961. The work now is done through the Commission of World Mission and Evangelism and the Division of World Mission and Evangelism.

**International Sunday School Association.** The modern Sunday school movement can be said to have begun in Gloucester, England, in 1780 by Robert Raikes and his pastor, Thomas Stock. The movement quickly gained supporters, and by 1785 the Society for the Support and Encouragement of Sunday Schools in England was formed. In America the First Day Society for the Establishment of Sunday Schools was founded in Philadelphia in 1790. Other local and state societies were founded to promote the Sunday school movement leading to the formation of a national society in 1823 called the American Sunday School Union.

As the work of the American Sunday School Union proliferated, national conventions were held from time to time to discuss the principles, methods, and curriculum of the Sunday school. In 1871, John H. Vincent proposed a series of "uniform lessons" wherein each Sunday school class in all the various denominations would be studying the same lesson each week. The plan was enthusiastically adopted at the next national convention held in Indianapolis in 1872. The "uniform" plan fostered an ecumenical spirit among the members of the various denominations and facilitated lesson preparation for teachers who assembled on Saturday afternoons to study the lesson that they were going to teach the next day. In 1908 the International Lesson Committee inaugurated a Uniform Graded Series of lessons for Sunday schools. (Some denominations did not use the "uniform" plan, notably, the Anglicans, Episcopalians, Lutherans, and the Church of Scotland.) John H. Vincent was also the driving force behind the establishment of teacher-training institutes such as the famous Chautauqua summer program founded in 1874. Moody Bible Institute of Chicago, founded in 1886, owes its origin to these teacher-training institutes. In 1875 the first "international" convention was held in Baltimore. Many of the subsequent triennial conventions were dominated by the spirit and person of Dwight L. Moody. In 1905 the eleventh International Sunday School Convention, meeting in Toronto and attended by almost two thousand delegates, decided to assume continuous authority and institutionalize itself rather than turn over responsibility to local, state, or denominational organizations. Thus the Convention became incorporated in 1906 and adopted the name International Sunday School Association.

**Investiture.** The juridical act by which one person transfers to another the rights over some specific thing. In the church, the term "investiture" came to be applied to the act by which a bishop was placed in charge of his bishopric; the term became current in the late 10th century, although the act itself was much earlier. The bishopric had, from the earliest centuries of the church, been an administrative division, and all revenues and lands associated with it were the property of the diocese. Through donation by pious people, lands and revenues accrued to the bishopric, making it a complex of many forms of real property and revenues as well as an office in the church for the care of souls. The Carolingians tried to bring this complex under their control, in order to have access to the revenues and produce of church lands. They extended their protection (*tuitio*) to bishoprics; the see with its complex of rights then came to be considered a part of the royal fisk. Charters extant from the reigns of Louis the Pious and his sons confer a bishopric on an elected bishop as a royal benefice. The king's dominion over the bishopric was not that of outright proprietorship; it was limited in that he could confer the see only on the person canonically elected. He could not alienate the see nor any part of it, and he could not use the church connected with it for any other than ecclesiastical purposes. Wala, abbot of Corbey (d. 836), Paschasius Radbertus (9th century), and Hincmar of Reims (d. 882) were each careful to remind king or emperor that he held limited rights over bishoprics. In the mid-9th century the first references are found to the investing of a bishop or abbot with the staff as the act by which the king placed the bishop in charge of his see. The staff had long been considered the symbol of episcopal authority as shown by the Council of Toledo (633) and by Isidore of Seville (d. 636) in his treatise *On Ecclesiastical Offices*. The staff of Caesarius of Arles (d. 543) was preserved in his church as a relic. In 865, Louis the German bestowed the bishopric of Bremen on the successor of Ansgar, commending it to the bishop "by the pontifical staff according to custom." This is one of the first notices of lay investiture extant. Similar accounts increased in the next two centuries. As royal power was diffused among lesser lords, they too assumed the right to invest. Humbert of Silva-Candida (d. 1061) was among the first to point out that the staff symbolized the conferring of the pastoral care, and therefore it should not be given by a layman.

Decrees prohibiting lay investiture were issued by Gregory VII (1075, 1078, 1080) and repeated by subsequent popes. The great controversy over investiture lasted from 1075 to 1122. As the controversy progressed, the component elements in a bishopric were recognized. Ivo of Chartres, in a letter to Hugh of Lyons (1097) defended the right of the king to add his assent to the election of a bishop by people and clergy in conferring the symbol that signified the transfer of worldly goods. Hugh of Fleury in the tract *On Royal Power* (c. 1102) agreed that the bishop should be invested with the temporalities of his see by a layman, but only after election and consecration. Hugh suggested a symbol other than the staff. With the London Settlement (1107) and the Concordat of Worms (1122) the investiture of a bishop was divided. The symbols of his pastoral office (staff and ring) were conferred by the consecrating bishops. The temporalities were conferred by secular authority through other symbols and in a ceremony separate from the consecration.

BIBLIOGRAPHY: See Bibliography of INVESTITURE CONTROVERSY.

**Investiture Controversy.** A struggle that occurred during the period from 1075 to 1122 over the right of lay investiture. Investiture was the juridical act by which a cleric became custodian of the complex of rights, spiritual and material, that were embodied in the bishopric, abbey, or parish. The right to invest was claimed by both secular and ecclesiastical rulers. Investiture by laymen had been prevalent since the reign of Louis the Pious, but it was not until the general reform movement in the church of the 11th century that lay investiture was condemned.

The first prohibitions against the practice were issued at the Lenten Synod of 1075. Gregory VII levied the sentence of excommunication on any cleric who received investiture from a layman. Henry IV of Germany, not knowing of the decrees, proceeded to invest Hozmann with the see of Spires, Henry with the see of Liège, and Robert with the monastery at Goslar. He inserted Tedald in the see of Milan after the candidate Atto had been elected by the people and approved by the pope. In November, 1075, Gregory threatened Henry with excommunication and the release of his subjects from obedience because of Henry's disregard of the decrees. Henry retaliated by calling a synod at Worms (January, 1076) at which the bishops present drew up a letter to "our brother Hildebrand," accusing him of violating the rights of bishops and of personal immorality. Henry addressed a letter to Gregory "not pope, but false monk," setting forth his claims to sacred kingship. At the Lenten Synod (1076), Gregory pronounced the ban of excommunication against Henry and released his subjects from obedience. Faced with the rebellion of the Saxons and also of bishops who had formerly been his supporters, Henry asked pardon of Gregory at Canossa, and through the intercession of Hugh of Cluny and Matilda of Tuscany, received absolution from the excommunication. The question of Henry's right to rule was deferred to a council of German nobles and bishops to be held at Augsburg at which Gregory was to preside. A preliminary council met at Forchheim, and having failed to send an escort for Gregory, proceeded to elect Rudolf of Swabia as king (1077). Civil war resulted in Germany.

The decrees against lay investiture were renewed at the Lenten Synods of 1078 and 1080, and the giver was bound by the prohibition, although he did not incur excommunication as did the receiver. In 1080, Gregory, stating that he had never reinstated Henry in his kingship, renewed the excommunication. Henry called the Synod of Brixen (1080), which deposed Gregory and elected Guibert of Ravenna as Pope Clement III. War between Henry and the papacy resulted. Henry attacked Rome (1081–1084); Gregory allied with Robert Guiscard. In 1084, Henry captured the city, all the cardinals deserting Gregory. Gregory was captured by Robert

Guiscard and died at Salerno in what was virtual exile (1085).

The struggle against lay investiture was continued by Urban II, who carried out the reform in Germany and France through papal legates. At the Council of Clermont (1095), Urban forbade not only lay investiture but also the rendering of homage to a layman by a cleric. Since homage was the act by which property came into the jurisdiction of secular rulers, this removed all church land and produce from lay control. These decrees were reissued at the Synod of Bari (1098) and the Lateran Synod (1099). At the latter, Anselm of Canterbury, exiled from England, first heard the decrees against lay investiture and homage. Upon his return to England (1100) at the request of Henry I, Anselm introduced the hitherto unheard of prohibitions into England. Investiture with ring and staff became the source of friction between Henry and Anselm for seven years. Paschal II, elected to succeed Urban, adhered to the policy of his predecessors, but went farther in advising Anselm in a letter (1102) that laymen could not invest even with the temporalities of a see. Although this specification did not occur in later directives from Paschal, Anselm remained firm in his opposition to any form of lay investiture.

After four legations to Rome, the last of which was undertaken by Anselm himself, and with no specific action of Paschal until 1105 when he excommunicated the bishops invested by Henry, a meeting between Anselm and Henry was arranged at Laigly (1105) by Adela of Chartres. Two years of negotiation issued in the London Settlement which provided that the higher clergy would do homage for the temporalities of their see or monastery and afterward be invested with ring and staff. The copy of the agreement has been lost, and it is from the Constitutions of Clarendon (1164) that the settlement has been reconstructed. In France the issue died out without specific settlement. Philip I was out of favor with the papacy for his marriage with Bertrada of Montfort, and having been reconciled with the church in 1104, he and his successors ceased to invest.

With Germany the struggle was more protracted, for here it was that the proprietary church was strongest and the issue of investiture had been so much a part of the bitter struggle between Henry IV and Gregory VII. In 1105, Paschal II gave his support to the rebellion of Henry V by receiving him into Communion, hoping thereby to settle the investiture controversy with Germany. Paschal invited the imperial party to a synod at Guastalla (1106) at which the legates from Henry asked for recognition of royal rights. Paschal replied by reiterating the decrees against investiture. At Benevento (1108) the giver as well as the receiver of investiture was to incur excommunication. Henry, desiring the imperial coronation, could not get it until some concordance had been reached on the question of investitures. Negotiations failed, with the result that Paschal finally offered to renounce all temporalities attached to the German sees if Henry would renounce investiture. The agreement was ratified at Sutri (1111), and Paschal agreed to crown Henry emperor. At the coronation ceremony (1111) in the Lateran when the terms of the agreement were announced, tumult broke out as the bishops and abbots realized the threat to themselves. The coronation could not proceed. Henry captured Paschal and after a two-month imprisonment, Paschal conceded to Henry the right of investiture and crowned him emperor. Henry returned to Germany, and left Paschal to face the opposition led by Guy of Vienne, Cuno of Praeneste, and the more moderate Ivo of Chartres. Paschal was forced to retract his concessions at the Lateran Synod (1112). In the same year a synod at Vienne declared that lay investiture was a heresy, and Paschal was pressured into confirming the decrees. He was also forced to agree with the excommunication of Henry announced by Cuno of Praeneste. Paschal died with the issue unresolved. His successor, Callistus II, reopened negotiations at Mouzon (1119), which failed because investiture but not homage was discussed. At the Synod of Reims (1119), Henry V was again excommunicated. The antipope Gregory VIII having been captured in 1121, Callistus had an undisputed claim to the papacy. Henry too had made peace with his nobles at Würzburg (1121). Both empire and papacy were in a position to negotiate peace, and the result was the Concordat of Worms (1122).

The investiture controversy had brought about a body of polemical literature on the relations of church and state, and an emphasis on canon law and administration in the church. The original reform of the church had been deflected to the issue of investiture. While investiture itself ceased to be an issue, the greater struggle of a self-contained, self-governed church, and the relation of that church to other forces remained unsettled.

BIBLIOGRAPHY: N. F. Cantor, *Church, Kingship, and Lay Investiture in England: 1089–1135* (Princeton, 1958); R. W. and A. J. Carlyle, *A History of Medieval Political Theory in the West*, Vols. 2–4 (Edinburgh, 1928–

1936); C. R. Cheney, *From Becket to Langton* (Manchester, 1956); A. Hyma, *Christianity and Politics* (Philadelphia, 1938).

**Iona Community.** A modern movement, founded by George MacLeod in 1938, of both clergy and laymen of the Scottish Church committed to seek through community life the way of obedience to Christ and the fulfillment of the church's mission in the world today. The island of Iona off the western coast of Scotland has been a holy place since earliest memory. Columba (d. 597) made it the principal seat of the Celtic Christian mission to Scotland and northern England. Neglected during the early modern period, Iona became the property of the Church of Scotland in 1899 through the generosity of its owner. In 1938 the partially restored buildings became the home of the Iona Community. Under the leadership of MacLeod, members dedicated themselves to mission work in industrial areas where working-class people have been alienated from the church. They have spent their summer retreats on the island, rebuilding the monastic structures by hand while preparing spiritually and intellectually for the missions of the winter months.

**Ireland, John** (1838–1918). American Roman Catholic prelate. Ordained in 1861, Ireland attended Vatican Council I and became bishop of St. Paul, Minn., in 1884. He encouraged westward migration from eastern slums and fought for Catholic acceptance of the labor movement, but condemned violence and picketing. An active and controversial participant in civic life, he fought for temperance and against political corruption. At the Third Plenary Council of Baltimore in 1884 he identified himself with American institutions, encouraging lay participation in church affairs. He strongly opposed "foreignism" and the Cahensly movement, which attempted to divide the church on national and racial grounds. Ireland became archbishop in 1888 when St. Paul was made an archdiocese. An address before the National Education Association in 1890 caused a lively debate when he stated, "I am a friend and advocate of the state school. In the circumstances of the present time I uphold the parish school," and urged a compromise by which the state would pay for secular education at regulated free parochial schools where religious teaching would be conducted by the denomination. He tried out his experiment with state support at Faribault and Stillwater in 1891, but in spite of support from the Propaganda, he was compelled to quit after strong Protestant and Jesuit opposition. Considered by non-Catholics as a bridge between America and Rome, Ireland stated at Gibbons' consecration, "The watchwords of the age are reason, education, liberty, and the amelioration of the masses."

**Irenaeus** (c. 130–c. 200). Bishop of Lyons in southern Gaul (c. 177–c. 200). He was born in Asia Minor at a date that is variously estimated to be anywhere from 97 to 147, although the scholarly consensus currently settles for sometime between 120 and 130. Since he and his friend Florinus were pupils of Polycarp, some of his early life must have been spent in Smyrna. He went to Gaul after studying in Rome. Many think that he could not have been at Lyons during the time of the persecution under Marcus Aurelius in 177 and escape martyrdom himself. Yet Eusebius says quite explicitly, "Irenaeus also, who was at that time already a presbyter of the diocese of Lyons, the same martyrs commended to the aforementioned bishop of Rome" when they wrote from prison in behalf of the Montanists (*Ecclesiastical History* 5. 4. 1). Irenaeus succeeded Pothinus, who had perished in the persecution, as bishop of Lyons and Vienne. He must have used Celtic in his preaching as well as in his everyday speech, since he apologized for his Greek on the grounds that he was "accustomed for the most part to use a barbarous dialect." The only event in his later life of which there is certainty is his defense of the Asian Quartodecimans on the grounds that Pope Anicetus had permitted Polycarp to follow his local usage even at Rome. Nothing is known about his death; the late legend that treats him as a martyr is confirmed by no early evidence. Since his last work seems to have come from c. 200, one can assume that he died later.

The poverty of biographical information, however, does not injure the reputation of Irenaeus as one of the foundation stones of Christian doctrine. In fact, Quasten calls him "the founder of Christian theology" (*Patrology,* Vol. 1, p. 294). A number of his minor works survive only in fragments, most of which appear in Eusebius. To his old school friend Florinus he wrote *On the Sole Sovereignty,* or *That God Is Not the Author of Evil,* in an effort to preserve him for orthodoxy. This failing, he wrote to him against his heresy in a treatise *On the Ogdoad.* His work *On Schism* written to Blastus is known by title only. There is a fragment of the letter he wrote to Pope Victor, asking him to suppress the writings of Florinus, and another fragment of the letter to him about the Quartodecimans controversy. Eusebius also knew his work *On Knowledge* and another work in which he quotes the letter to the Hebrews and The Wisdom of Solomon. C. M. Pfaff published what purported to be four newly discovered Irenaean fragments in 1713, but Adolf von Harnack showed that they were forgeries by Pfaff himself to support the Lutheran doctrine of the Eucharist.

The real fame of Irenaeus as a theologian, however, rests on his five books *On the Detection and Refutation of Knowledge Falsely So Called (Elenchos)*. Although many Greek fragments, some of considerable extent, are in existence, this work in its entirety is found only in a Latin translation. For that reason it is often called *Against [All] Heresies* from the Latin title *Adversus haereses*. The other major work of Irenaeus, which was known by name only until an Armenian translation was discovered and published in 1907, is the *Proof of the Apostolic Preaching*, or *Epideixis*. This latter work, however, adds nothing to the thought of *Against Heresies*, although it sometimes expresses it better.

The first two books of *Against Heresies* oppose Gnostics, especially the Valentinians, and the last three are an elaboration and defense of traditional theology. Until the recent manuscript discoveries at Nag-Hammadi, the work of Irenaeus together with that of Hippolytus constituted the chief source of information about the Gnostics after the *Syntagma* of Justin Martyr (on which Irenaeus drew) had been lost and Gnostic works had been suppressed. The discovery of the Apocryphon of John made it possible for Carl Schmidt to show in 1907 that Irenaeus had used its original form as the source for *Against Heresies* 1.29.

To the enlightenment soteriology of the Gnostics, Irenaeus opposed the salvation expected by the great church. His audience consisted of Christians who had enough sophistication to be impressed by the pseudointellectual trappings of Gnosticism, but not enough discrimination to see through them. The doctrine of Irenaeus is therefore no closely reasoned philosophical demonstration but an outgrowth of the religious life of the people.

Following the Platonic understanding of man as composed of *physis, psychē,* and *nous,* Irenaeus speaks of the body, soul, and spirit of man. Body and soul make up natural man. The perfection of man depends upon the reception of spirit, which is spoken of both as the spirit of man and the Spirit of God. This theory enables Irenaeus to distinguish between the "image" and the "likeness" of God in man (which were probably intended as a synonymous parallelism in Genesis). The image is the physical resemblance of the body of man to

God and the likeness is the spiritual similarity that is given to the man whose moral conduct is worthy of it. The gift of the spirit perfects man.

Through the fall of Adam, mankind became subject to sin and death and lost the likeness of God. He thus lost his incorruptibility (*aphtharsia*), which is his chief desire. In order to reclaim man from the power of the devil and to restore God's plan for man, God sent his Son to reinitiate the process begun and interrupted in Adam. This doctrine of recapitulation (*anakephalaiōsis*) is the most distinctive characteristic of the theology of Irenaeus. It has the effect of making the incarnation more efficacious in the soteriology of Irenaeus than the atonement. That is to say that what Christ did was not so much to suffer the penalty of man's sin as it was to renew the creation of man by his inner combination of godhead and mankind. All previous men were taken up into Christ and summarized in him to such an effect that Adam could be saved. It is in this connection that Irenaeus conveys his startling opinion that Jesus lived to be fifty years old; Jesus sanctified each age of man by his own experience of it. The Virgin Mary is taken to be a recapitulation of Eve, doing for her and humanity what she failed to do.

The relation of Jesus to God is that he is the Christ, the Logos, the Son of God, our Lord and Savior, the God-man. Drawing from Theophilus of Antioch, Irenaeus describes the Son and the Holy Spirit as the hands of God, although he does not imitate Theophilus in calling the Trinity *trias*. Yet, like most of the fathers, he thinks that "Let us make man in our own image and likeness" is addressed to the Son and Holy Spirit by the Father.

The benefits of the work of Christ are made available to men in the church through the sacraments. By Baptism the re-creation of the individual is effected. Our bodies are united to God and we receive the incorruptibility that we have so heartily desired. It would be improper to attach the terminology of later controversy to his understanding of the Eucharist, but there is no mistaking the fact that Irenaeus believes so strongly in the Real Presence as to make his doctrine of the resurrection of the individual grow out of it.

Christ as the head of the body includes the church within himself. Irenaeus considers the unity of the church to be so great that all orthodox churches will almost by nature (or grace) agree in the doctrine of the apostles that is passed down in the churches which they founded. Interpretation can only come from the bishops and priests of such churches. The foundation of the Roman community by two apostles gives it some sort of preeminence.

The Biblical interpretation of Irenaeus is important. His canon included the four Gospels, the Pauline corpus, Acts, the letters of John and the Revelation, First Peter, and even the Shepherd of Hermas. Against the fantastic speculation of the Gnostics he demanded that the Bible be understood in its obvious, natural sense. Sound interpretation would always agree with the "Rule of Faith," the Apostolic Tradition. He was the first Christian writer to make extensive use of Acts and the pastoral epistles.

Irenaeus is important not only in his own right but also as a link between the apostolic fathers and the Apologists (most of whom he used) and the later writers who had a more highly developed theology, such as Clement, Tertullian, and Hippolytus (who used his writings). Through all later periods the works of Irenaeus have been appealed to, since his theology points toward what became the main line of Christian thought.

BIBLIOGRAPHY: R. M. Grant (ed.), *The Apostolic Fathers,* Vol. I (New York, 1964); A. Roberts and J. Donaldson (eds.), *The Ante-Nicene Fathers,* Vol. I (Grand Rapids, 1950); E. J. Goodspeed and R. M. Grant, *A History of Early Christian Literature* (Chicago, 1966); F. R. M. Hitchcock, *Irenaeus of Lugdunum* (Cambridge, 1914).

**Irene** (c. 752–803). Empress of the Eastern Roman Empire. Irene married Leo IV in 769 and became regent to her son Constantine IV when Leo died (780). In 792 she abdicated to her son, but she was soon plotting to regain power. In 797, Irene arrested her son and her husband's five brothers, all of whom were subsequently blinded, and she served as sole ruler from 797 to 802 when she was dethroned and exiled to Lesbos. Irene restored the worship of icons (see ICONOCLASTIC CONTROVERSY) and summoned the Second Nicene Council in 787 to establish the veneration of religious images.

**Irish Articles.** The "articles of religion" compiled by Bishop Ussher and passed in 1615 by the Convocation of the Established (i.e., Anglican) Church of Ireland. One hundred and four in number and incorporating the Calvinistic Lambeth Articles, they were otherwise similar to the English Thirty-nine Articles. They were generally superseded by the Thirty-nine, which were adopted under pressure from Strafford in 1635. However, the influence of the earlier Articles can be seen in the Westminster Confession of 1646.

**Irving, Edward** (1792–1834). Famous preacher, controversial Church of Scotland minister, and close friend of Carlyle, Coleridge, and Lamb. He was born at Annan, Dumfries, studied at the University of Edinburgh, was several years a schoolmaster, and in 1822 became a highly popular preacher at the Caledonian chapel in London. In 1827 a new church had to be built to accommodate his swelling congregation. His popularity then waned because of the eschatological emphasis in his preaching. His published sermons on the incarnation of Christ and the Second Coming provoked violent controversy and opposition. His orthodoxy was challenged, and ecclesiastical courts charged him with holding "the sinfulness of Christ's humanity." Irving claimed that the charge was unjust and a misinterpretation of his words, but he was finally excommunicated in 1833 and deposed as a minister of the Church of Scotland. He then became a wandering preacher. Later he returned to London and assumed a minor office in the new Holy Catholic Apostolic Church that had been formed by some eight hundred members of his first congregation. He died in Glasgow and was buried there in the cathedral crypt.

**Isabella I** (1451–1504). Queen of Spain. With the marriage of Isabella of Castile and Ferdinand of Aragon, the kingdom of Spain was founded. Their reign inaugurated the golden age of Spain. Isabella ruled Castile directly, and the whole of Spain with Ferdinand. She was the patron of Columbus, financing his voyage of discovery which laid the basis for Spain's claim to America. Catherine, a daughter of Isabella, married Henry VIII of England.

**Isidore of Pelusium** (c. 360–435). A monk (or hermit) and presbyter of Pelusium in the northeastern corner of Egypt. His work as spiritual guide and Biblical interpreter is reflected in his letters, some two thousand of which are preserved. He supported the theology of Alexandria, but at times raised a prophetic protest against the worldly ambition he saw in its bishops Theophilus and Cyril.

**Isidore of Seville** (c. 560–636). Spanish prelate and scholar. He was brought up by his older brother, Bishop Leander of Seville, and their sister, the Abbess Florentina, and he succeeded Leander as bishop c. 600. He is best known for the textbooks he prepared for the cathedral schools of Spain, which preserved the essentials of ancient learning until the later medieval revivals. His *Etymologies* is a brief encyclopedia of general knowledge, and his *Sentences* and *On Ecclesiastical Of-*

*fices* are similar handbooks of theology and of church order and liturgy. To his brief *Chronicle* he added a *History of the Goths,* which is one of the first monuments of Spanish patriotism; the union of Arians and Catholics at the Council of Toledo in 589 made it possible for a Hispano-Roman to take pride in the achievements of his Visigothic rulers. Other works of Isidore are *On the Faith* (against Judaism) and a monastic rule marked by sanity and common sense; but he is not the compiler of the collection of canons later ascribed to him and interpolated with the false decretals, therefore called pseudo-Isidorian. Though not an ecclesiastical statesman like his brother, and a schoolmaster rather than a theologian, he is deservedly remembered as one of the Doctors of the Church. He ends the Hispano-Roman and begins the national period of Spanish church history.

**Islam.** One of the world's great religions, and, like Christianity and Judaism, part of the Semitic monotheistic tradition. The term "Islam" literally means "submission to God." A person who submits himself, thus an adherent of Islam, is called a Moslem (or Muslim).

The founder of this new religion was Mohammed, who began preaching in Arabia in the 7th century A.D. Convinced that both Judaism and Christianity had strayed from the initial divine message that had been made known to Abraham, the first Prophet, he believed that he and his people, the Arabs, as descendants of Abraham through his son Ishmael, had been accorded by God the task of leading mankind back to a pure monotheism.

The authoritative teachings of Islam stem from three separate sources: (1) The holy book, the Koran, which contains the precise revelations as uttered by Mohammed and written down by his disciples. It is the highest authority in all matters of law. (2) Sunna, or oral tradition of the Islamic community. The traditions stemming from Mohammed the man (as distinguished from his revelations from God) have been handed down in written form. These statements, Hadith, provide the Moslem legal system with an orderly set of precedents, which are applied in judicial cases. (3) Ijma, or unanimous consensus. This is the vehicle by way of which innovation in both religious and social matters can be legitimized. Upon these bases of authority Islamic law was established. Since Islam has no priesthood, the class of learned men, the ulama, assumed the role of professional interpreters of the law.

With respect to ritual, Islam requires five obligations of its adherents. These usually are called the "Five Pillars of the Faith" and include: (1) Profession of faith: All Moslems believe that there is only the one God, or Allah, that Mohammed was his greatest and last Prophet, and that there will come a Last Judgment. (2) Prayer: Islamic custom requires the performance of five ritual prayers daily. These may usually be performed wherever the Moslem is, but preferably in a mosque. (3) Almsgiving: The regular giving of alms, in the amount of one fortieth of a man's annual revenue, is required. (4) Fasting: Abstinence from food and drink from sunrise to sunset is required during the holy month of Ramadan. Those sick or on a journey may be exempted from fasting if they make up for the lost days by fasting at a later time. (5) Pilgrimage: Every Moslem must, if at all financially possible, make a pilgrimage to Mecca once in his lifetime. Some writers on Islam name as a sixth obligation that of waging holy war, jihad. Moslems were enjoined by the Koran to force the conversion of idol-worshiping pagans. Christians and Jews, however, because they are also believers in one God, were tolerated as protected subjects. Conversion of these peoples to Islam was not demanded and in return for a payment they were assured of their lives and property. This tolerance of Moslems toward Christians was often shown in the time of the Crusades, but Western sources usually fail to acknowledge this fact. (The crusaders actually learned much of the art of chivalry from their Saracen enemies.) Additional obligations for the Moslem include abstinence from pork and intoxicating beverages.

From the end of Mohammed's life and for many years after his death, the followers of Islam spread their faith to the surrounding peoples. By 644 the new empire included all of Arabia, Greater Syria (including Palestine), Cyprus, Persia, and Africa north of the Sahara. The rapid spread of Islam owes as much to the Western and Byzantine attitude toward the earliest Moslems as an insignificant, heretical Christian sect as to the Arabs' actual military prowess. By the 8th century the Moslems had come to control most of the Mediterranean islands and coastline, effectively hampering Western trade with the East and cutting off the Byzantine Empire from the West even more than before. The consequences of this for subsequent developments in both western Europe and the Byzantine Empire were immense. Arab power at this point in history was so great that, had it not been for such successes as Charles Martel's defeat of an Arab raiding party at Poitiers (Tours) in France in 732 and the Byzantine victory at Amisis in 863, all Europe might well have fallen to the Moslems.

On the internal scene the task facing the newly converted peoples was enormous. The first converts, the Arabs, had been basically a nomadic people ruled not by a central authority but divided into autonomous clan units. Mohammed's attempt to create of these people a single nation bound by a common religious code was many years in the making. After the remnants of the old Persian empire fell to the Moslems by 643, there arose the additional problem of assimilating the Persian peoples into the hitherto Arabian theocracy. While faced with these problems on the level of everyday life, Moslems were at the same time burdened with the task of standardizing the many points of religious doctrine.

The first leaders of the Islamic community after the death of the Prophet, who had made no arrangements for his succession, were those of his followers who had been among his earliest, most pious, and most trusted converts. The first successor, or caliph, was abu-Bakr, a well-to-do merchant who had been Mohammed's trusted lieutenant. He was succeeded in 634 by Omar, a most zealous and respected Moslem and a successful military leader. By the reign of the third caliph, Uthman, conflicts over succession erupted. Uthman himself was assassinated. With his death began a five-year civil war, the beginning of many such wars that were to divide the community into factions. One of these factions, which supported the claims of Ali, son-in-law of Mohammed, developed into a religious sect called the Shiites, who separated themselves from the "orthodox" believers, the Sunni. These two sects were to remain separate throughout the history of Islam, the Sunni always being in the majority. In addition to these two main sects, a third, the Sufis, ascetic mystics who on the whole remained true to the "orthodox" Sunni traditions, developed from the 8th century onward.

The civil skirmishes ended with the placement of the Umayyad Muawiyah on the caliphal throne. The Umayyad dynasty, which began with his reign, was characterized by extension of borders of the empire and the beginnings of purely Moslem culture. In 762 the Persian house of the Abbasids seized power. The period of Abbasid rule was one of great wealth and splendor, with an effective central administration and a budding cultural tradition bound by a common language, Arabic.

The period from 1000 to 1250 is considered the High Middle Ages of Islamic civilization. During this period, the now powerful empire extended its boundaries far beyond the Middle East, and Moslem society became truly international in its activities. Persian and Arabic flourished together as the languages of culture and politics.

As the Islamic empire outgrew its old boundaries, the centralized caliphate was weakened. With expansion came the establishment of local political units. By the Late Middle Ages of Islamic civilization (1250–1500) the empire, now fragmented politically, lost its former power, and by 1500 three separate empires had taken the place of Mohammed's community. These in turn were profoundly changed by modern nationalism.

**Islam in Medieval Spain.** From 711, when the Berber general Tariq defeated the last Visigothic king, Roderick, to 1492, when Granada fell to Ferdinand and Isabella, much of Spain was dominated by Islamic civilization under Moslem rulers.

Usually the Moors, as the Spanish Moslems were called, were quite tolerant, and large numbers of Jews and Mozarabs or Arabized Christians were permitted to live under their rule. But the Moors themselves (a mixed people of Arabic, North African, Slavic, and renegade Visigothic and Hispano-Roman origin) were responsible for the growth of the high civilization that developed in their part of Spain.

Under the Umayyad emirs and caliphs who resided at Cordova between 756 and 1010, Moorish Spain reached its cultural and political zenith. After the collapse of the Cordovan caliphate, however, central government disappeared and the center of Moslem civilization in the peninsula shifted to Seville. There it remained until that city fell to the Christian king Ferdinand III in 1212. Thereafter only the small and politically unimportant tributary kingdom of Granada existed as a last vestige of Islam in Spain until it too passed into Christian hands in 1492.

**Ivanov, Alexander** (1806–1858). Russian painter. A 19th-century Russian ideological and religious painter who attempted to combine the styles of Raphael and Michelangelo with those of his native Russia. He is especially known for his painting *The Appearance of Christ to the People,* which was completed after six hundred sketches and twenty-five years of labor. In his art, Ivanov strove for authenticity while at the same time he was haunted by the problem of depicting Christ on canvas.

**Ives, Levi Silliman** (1797–1867). A bishop of the Protestant Episcopal Church who became a controversial figure because of his expressions of affinity with the Oxford movement in his North Carolina diocese. He is best known for the resignation of his see in 1852 and his subsequent conversion to the Roman Catholic Church, being the most conspicuous of the American secessionists to Rome occasioned by the stir of the Oxford movement.

**Ivo of Chartres** (c. 1040–1116). Early canonist, student of Lanfranc at Bec, prior of canons regular of St.-Quentin at Beauvais, and bishop (1090) of Chartres. He was probably the greatest canonist before Gratian. In an era of forged documents and various collections, he gathered together three vital sets of canons: *Collectio tripartita, Decretum,* and *Panormia,* the last providing Abelard some of the material for *Sic et non.*

# J

**Jablonski, Daniel Ernst** (1660–1741). Moravian bishop. He was born at Nassenhuben, near Danzig, where his father was a minister of the Moravian Church. After studying at the gymnasium of Lissa and the Universities of Frankfurt and Oxford, he was appointed in 1683 as the Reformed preacher at Magdeburg. From 1686 to 1691 he was head of the Moravian college at Lissa, a position occupied earlier by his grandfather, John Amos Comenius. Appointed court preacher at Königsberg in 1691 by the elector of Brandenburg, and at Berlin in 1693, he became influential in court circles. In 1699 he was chosen senior of the Unitas Fratrum at the Synod of Lissa, and was consecrated bishop. He worked with Leibnitz to try to bring together the Lutherans and the Reformed Protestants. His consecration of Count Zinzendorf as bishop in 1737 acted as a transition between the Moravian Brethren and the younger Herrnhuters. He also exercised a wide influence on the development of the Prussian state.

**Jackson, Sheldon** (1834–1909). Presbyterian minister, missionary, and educator. Graduating from Union College, Schenectady, N.Y., in 1855 and Princeton Theological Seminary in April, 1858, he was ordained by the Albany, N.Y., Presbytery in May of the same year. He worked in Indian Territory, Minnesota, the Rocky Mountain area, and Alaska. In Alaska he introduced domesticated reindeer to aid the Eskimos and was appointed by the Federal Government as the first superintendent of public instruction. In this capacity he served as long as he lived.

**Jacobi, Friedrich Heinrich** (1743–1819). German philosopher and champion of the philosophy of faith and feeling. Born at Düsseldorf on Jan. 25, 1743, the second son of a wealthy sugar merchant, he was taught commerce, but preferred the literary and scientific circle of Lesage, the works of Charles Bonnet, Rousseau, and Voltaire. In 1764 he married and took over his father's business for a short time, but he retained his literary and philosophic interests, and with C. M. Wieland he founded the journal *Der Teutsche Mercur,* in which some of his earliest writings appeared. In 1785 his *Briefe über die Lehre Spinozas* (enlarged with important Appendixes, 1789), which expressed his objection to a dogmatic system of philosophy, was published. The Berlin clique of Moses Mendelssohn ridiculed the work for endeavoring to reintroduce belief into philosophy and denounced Jacobi as a Pietist. Thus his next important work, *David Hume über den Glauben* (1787), defended the term "belief." In 1794 he left Düsseldorf for Holstein, where he met Reinhold, to whom he wrote (Oct. 8, 1817): "I am a heathen in my reason and a Christian in my heart, and thus I swim between two bodies of water that will not combine to help by bearing me up, but while the one continuously holds me up the other lets me continuously sink." The accusation of atheism leveled at Fichte prompted his *Letter to Fichte* (1799), which outlined the relation of his philosophy to theology. In 1811, Jacobi's last philosophic work, *Von den göttlichen Dingen und ihrer Offenbarung,* appeared in Munich. He began his collected edition in 1812, but died in March, 1819, before its completion.

**Jacobites** (English). Scottish and English partisans of the Stuart claim to the English throne after the expulsion of the Catholic king, James II, in the Glorious Revolution of 1688. Within England, Jacobite support was drawn from three sources: Tories, who adhered to strict hereditary succession; nonjuring clergy of the Church of England; and Roman Catholics. The first two groups predicated allegiance on Stuart recognition of the Anglican Church, and the Stuarts lost much of their support by their continued adherence to Catholicism. Within Scotland, Jacobite support came both from Highland clans and from Scottish Anglicans. Besides the traditional loyalty to a Scottish line, many Highlanders were Catholic; Anglicans sought Stuart buttressing against the strong Presbyterian Church. Jacobites supported the rising of 1715 in favor of the Old Pretender and that of 1745 in favor of the Young Pretender. Both uprisings failed and left a stigma of treason upon the whole movement. There is still some romantic attachment to the Jacobite cause, but it is theoretical, for the only direct heir to the Stuarts is a Bavarian prince.

**Jacobites** (Syrian). Monophysite sect in Syria. After the Council of Chalcedon declared Monophysitism heretical (451), the Syrian patriarchate at Antioch withdrew from the Eastern Orthodox communion. Subsequently power was held alternately in the hands of the Orthodox and the Monophysite leaders until Justinian I imprisoned all suspected of the Monophysite heresy. The empress Theodora, wife of Justinian, was inclined toward the Monophysite position, however, and arranged secretly for the consecration of two monks who shared her feeling (543). One of them, Jacob Baradai, organized the Syrian Monophysites, and it is probably from him that they derived the name Jacobites, though many of them claimed direct descent from the apostle James and Christ's brother Jacob. Although the sect represented a small portion of the population, they gradually covered a wide geographical area as a result of the missionary ministers who traveled through Mesopotamia, Persia, and other Eastern countries. The 12th and 13th centuries saw a flourishing of literary activity among the Jacobites, including the work of their greatest scholar, Bar-Hebraeus (1226–1286). In the 14th century, the sect was persecuted by the Moslems and lost many of its adherents. Internal dissension resulted in a split among the Jacobites and there were rival patriarchs from 1292 to 1495; by the time the schism was mended, they were severely reduced in number. Many of the remaining members returned in the 16th century to the Roman Church.

**Jacob of Nisibis** (d. 338). Bishop of Nisibis. The teacher of Ephraem Syrus, Jacob was an ascetic, although not a "mountain" hermit. He participated at Nicaea as a leading protagonist against the Arians, enjoyed a favorable reputation, but left no writings. He probably did not establish the school at Nisibis, although his grave there was construed as a protective influence for the town.

**Jacob of Sarug** (c. 451–521). Syrian author and bishop of Batnae near Edessa after 518 or 519. Jacob translated the *Centuria* of Evagrius Ponticus, composed *Memre* (speeches), *Sogyatha* (dramatic poems), *Madrasche* (hymns), and biographies. One

metrical homily on Jesus' passion was thirty-three hundred verses in length. Orders of baptism and confirmation are incorrectly attributed to him. His letters indicate that he was probably a Monophysite; he firmly opposed the decisions of Chalcedon and zealously rallied his countrymen against the Persian persecution.

**Jacopone da Todi** (c. 1228–1306). Italian Franciscan poet. Born of a noble family, he studied law, began to practice, and took a wife. The death of his wife occasioned a change in his life; he became first a Franciscan tertiary and then a brother. He is famous for his poetry in the vernacular and for his well-known Latin hymn, "Stabat Mater Dolorosa."

**Jaenicke, Johannes** (1748–1827). Foreign mission director. Working as an assistant at the Bethlehem Bohemian Lutheran Church in Berlin from 1779 until 1792, when he became preacher, he was subsequently appointed director of mission in Germany by the London Missionary Society. He founded the first school for missionaries in Germany, which continued until 1849 and from which before his death some eighty missionaries went to already established foreign missions. He also founded a Bible society (1805) and a tract society (1811) which still endure in expanded forms.

**James I** (1566–1625). King of Scotland from 1567 and king of England from 1603. James succeeded his mother, Mary, Queen of Scots, on her abdication. After a stormy regency of sixteen years, he embarked in 1583 on his twin purposes of strengthening the Scottish crown and succeeding Elizabeth of England. Following an unsuccessful attempt to secure the support of Roman Catholic monarchs, he concluded an alliance with England (1586) while supporting Scottish Catholics against Presbyterians, but the audacity of the Roman Catholics forced him to curb them by granting a Presbyterian establishment (1592). In 1603 he obtained the succession to the English throne when Elizabeth died.

Arriving in England, he countered the Millenary Petition (1603) by resort to the doctrine of divine right which, he believed, was compatible only with an episcopal church. By the Hampton Court Conference the Puritans won little from him except that he sponsored the Authorized Version of the Bible (1611). James's inability to relieve the pressure on the Roman Catholics resulted in the Gunpowder Plot and the subsequent strengthening of recusancy laws. Moreover, although the Scots accepted episcopacy (1610) and the Articles of Perth (1618), James's manner of achieving this presaged ill for his son. Puritan mercantile interests wanted war with Spain, while he preferred peace and toleration. Thus he fought with his Parliaments, and because his lofty view of the monarchy prevented him from compromise, he was unsuccessful. His management of English affairs paved the way for the disasters that befell Charles I. James, called by Henry IV of France "the wisest fool in Christendom," was a learned man who left behind him a sizable body of undistinguished literature.

**James II** (1633–1701). King of England, Scotland, and Ireland (1685–1688), second son of Charles I. He was captured by Parliamentarians in the Civil War but escaped (1648) to Holland and served in the French and Spanish armies. At the Restoration he became lord high admiral, earning respect for his execution of that office. From 1668 he sought admission to the Roman Catholic Church, was apparently accepted in 1671, and resigned his admiralty upon the passage of the Test Act, which made membership in the Church of England mandatory for holding public office. Having become a widower, James married the Roman Catholic princess Mary of Modena (1673). Since Charles II was childless, a movement to exclude James from the throne was instituted but ultimately failed, and James received the crown in 1685.

After the abortive rebellion of the duke of Monmouth (1685), James began a repressive policy against all who had opposed him, having them tried under Judge George Jeffreys at what became known as the Bloody Assizes, and flouting the Test Act by appointing Roman Catholics to the army, state office, and Oxford. When Archbishop Sancroft of Canterbury refused to read James's Declaration of Indulgence, which exempted Catholics and Dissenters from penal statutes, and joined six bishops in petitioning against it, they were all imprisoned. Their eventual acquittal prompted James to reverse his policy, but it was too late. The English nobles offered the throne to his son-in-law, William of Orange, upon whose arrival in England, James fled to France (1688). After his plan to recover Ireland was defeated at Boyne (1690) James returned to France, where he became increasingly preoccupied by religious contemplation. He died in 1701.

**James, William** (1842–1910). American educator, philosopher, and champion of pragmatism. He found Spencerian naturalism and Hegelian idealism inadequate, and espoused "the philosophy of experience," in which ideas are to be judged by their results. Repudiating a priori reasoning, abstractions, and fixed principles, he advocated practicality, common sense, pluralism, and skepticism. James conceived truth not as an absolute but as a fact to be made and remade. His philosophy has been characterized as uniquely American, with its practical, democratic, individualistic, opportunistic, spontaneous, and optimistic character. James was particularly concerned with the contemporary discussions of the relationship of science, religion, and philosophy. He had no denominational ties, was uninterested in organized religion, and was not versed in theology. Yet he felt that some hopeful faith was necessary to mankind. In 1902 his Gifford Lectures, *The Varieties of Religious Experience,* were published, the most acute analysis of the psychology of religion since Jonathan Edwards (1703–1758). James concluded that religious experience was *sui generis,* with valid noetic claims. He revealed his mystical tendencies and his emphasis on the practical and experiential character of religion. His work was influential in the contemporary shift from dogmatics to person-orientated religion. His contributions won him a secure place in American philosophy with Edwards and Emerson.

**Jane Frances of Chantal.** See VISITANDINES.

**Jansenism.** A religious reform movement within the Roman Catholic Church, chiefly in France and the Low Countries during the 17th and 18th centuries. The movement takes its name from Cornelis Jansen (1585–1638), bishop of Ypres after 1636, who was for most of his life associated with the University of Louvain. Coming to Louvain in 1602, Jansen early exhibited strong Augustinian and anti-Jesuit opinions and formed a close friendship with a fellow student, Jean Duvergier de Hauranne, later abbot of St.-Cyran. Together they developed ideas of doctrinal and ecclesiastical reform that were further evolved during Jansen's sojourn in France. After 1616, Jansen taught Scriptures at Louvain and worked on his *Augustinus,* which was published posthumously in 1640. It did not at first attract unusual attention, although the papacy forbade its study in 1641.

In the *Augustinus,* Jansen claimed to restate the Augustinian interpretation of Catholicism in terms of the religious problems of his own time. In this he was following an earlier intellectual tradition at Louvain established by Michael Baius. Like Augustine, Jansen stressed the corruption and helplessness of man, his dependence on God, and the doctrine of grace. He argued the necessity for sincere repentance and condemned reliance on the ceremony or moralism that he ascribed to Jesuit teaching. Although Jansenist doctrine had Protestant parallels, Jansen repudiated the Protestant doctrine of justification by faith and taught the necessity of submission to the Roman Church. He remained a Catholic theologian and churchman, often in controversy with Dutch scholars.

France was to become the center of Jansenist controversy, and here the issue was to be partly religious and partly political and constitutional. In its later history, Jansenism was intimately associated with Gallicanism, which sought to diminish papal authority in the French Church. The doctrines were first introduced into France by Saint-Cyran (Jean Duvergier de Hauranne), who in 1636 became the spiritual director of the convent of Port-Royal near Paris. He contributed to a spiritual regeneration in the community, seeking perfect contrition in Communion and castigating the moral laxity of the Jesuits who allegedly gave easy absolution. In 1638, Saint-Cyran was imprisoned by the government, and his place was taken by Antoine Arnauld. Arnauld's book *On Frequent Communion* (1643) touched off violent controversy, publicized Jansenist teachings, and directed attention back to *Augustinus* as well. During the 1640's, Jansenism was winning a following among some bourgeoisie, lawyers, intellectuals, and a minority of bishops and theologians.

However, it had also incurred the hostility of the government. Richelieu and Mazarin both distrusted the breach of uniformity. Jansenists had been involved in the civil commotions of the Fronde. Louis XIV regarded Jansenism as both civil and religious rebellion against authority. Five propositions extracted from *Augustinus,* all relating to predestination, were condemned by the Sorbonne in 1649. Sent to Rome, they were condemned by Innocent X in 1653 as "false, temerarious, scandalous, derogatory to the Divine goodness." A legalistic controversy ensued. Jansenists accepted the condemnation but denied that the propositions were authentically Jansenist and argued, in response to a renewed papal assurance, that whereas the church might be infallible in matters of faith, it was not so in matters of fact. In 1656, Arnauld was officially deprived of his doctorate.

The Jansenist-Jesuit controversy and the popular interest that it aroused cannot be understood apart from the issues raised by the 17th-century science of casuistry. The development of moral theology and the prac-

tical problems in hearing confessions had led to the publication of manuals for the guidance of confessors. In this the Jesuits excelled, and some of their writers developed a system of probabilism whereby the penitent was given the benefit of the doubt in a course of action if any probability of moral justification could be demonstrated, even if the probability was less than that attached to another course of action. The system was defended as avoiding undue severity and freeing the priest from responsibility in difficult moral decisions for which he might be unprepared, but it was vigorously condemned by Jansenist and others as an affront to morality and truth. The chief literary monument to this phase of the controversy was the *Provincial Letters* of Blaise Pascal, a satiric attack on Jesuit teaching that circulated by thousands throughout France and created a sensation.

After 1679 repression of Jansenism became severe. Port-Royal was the center of Jansenist opposition, and in 1709 the nuns were deported and in 1710 the buildings razed and the graveyard destroyed. The final stages of the controversy centered around Pasquier Quesnel, the successor of Arnauld. In 1713, Clement XI, at the instigation of Louis XIV, condemned 101 propositions drawn from Quesnel's *Moral Reflections on the New Testament,* a devotional manual long in use. This bull, *Unigenitus,* divided the French Church, the "appellants" looking to a future general council. Louis died in 1715, but his policy was continued, and in 1730, *Unigenitus* was made a part of French law.

The quarrel dragged on throughout the 18th century. Later, Jansenism tended to move in three streams. Under repression Jansenism developed some marks of an enthusiastic cult, with miracles, hysteria, and prophecy. These were the so-called Convulsionaries. More important elements of Jansenism were combined with French Gallicanism in opposition to *Unigenitus* and papal authority. Jansenism in this form thrived until the Revolution, where it was represented prominently by Henri Grégoire. Some Jansenists migrated to Holland, where they were welcomed in the archdiocese of Utrecht, which had separated from Rome in 1702. The Jansenist Church in Holland continued and established relations with the Old Catholic movement when it arose in the 19th century.

BIBLIOGRAPHY: N. Abercrombie, *The Origins of Jansenism* (Oxford, 1936); M. Bishop, *Pascal: The Life of Genius* (New York, 1936); R. A. Knox, *Enthusiasm* (Oxford, 1951); L. Rea, *The Enthusiasts of Port Royal* (New York, 1912); H. F. Stewart, *The Holi-*

*ness of Pascal* (Cambridge, 1915); and *The Secret of Pascal* (Cambridge, 1941).

**Janus.** Pseudonym of Johann Joseph Ignaz von Doellinger (1799–1890), Munich ecclesiastical history professor. It was signed to several acute Augsburg newspaper articles (1869) opposing papal infallibility. These provided a rallying point for resistance to the dogma at the First Vatican Council. Under the label "Anti-Janus" the future Cardinal Hergenröther responded. The ultimate result was the Old Catholic schism. Doellinger never reconciled with the church.

**Japan, National Christian Council of.** An organization formed in 1923 as a result of the National Christian Conference of 1922. The Federation of Churches (founded 1911) immediately merged with it, and in 1925 the Federated Missions turned over the work of five committees. It is described as "the life-center for organic Protestant work on the national scale." Its first big task after organization was relief for the victims of the earthquake in the Tokyo area in 1923. Under pressure from nationalistic forces the National Christian Council in 1937 pledged support of the government, and under prodding from the government on Sept. 6, 1940, it committed the churches to complete autonomy from Western Church control and to union into a single body. When this single body, the Nippon Kirisuto Kyodan, was formed, there was no need for a council and the National Christian Council was in abeyance from 1941 to 1948. The reestablishment of separate denominations required its revival in 1948. The denominational members are the United Church of Christ (Nippon Kirisuto Kyodan), the Holy Catholic Church of Japan (Anglican), Evangelical Lutheran, Baptist Convention (Southern), Baptist Union, and the Korean Church, together comprising 60 percent of Japanese Protestants. It has Audio-Visual, Literature, and Education Commissions and a variety of committees for service. It publishes an English bulletin, *Japanese Christian Activity News,* and annually, the *Japan Christian Yearbook.*

**Japan, United Church of Christ in** (Nippon Kirisuto Kyodan). A nationwide church union founded in Japan in 1941. Japanese Christians sought unity in the early stages of mission work. The Presbyterian and Reformed Churches in 1877 merged in the United Church of Christ. A Commission on Church Union achieved little, and at the National Christian Conference in 1939, called expressly to deal with the subject, no action was taken.

That year, however, the government announced a law to control religious bodies to take effect in 1940, and official pressures were exerted on the churches to consolidate. On Sept. 6, 1940, the churches acted through the National Christian Council to form a single Protestant Church. The Nippon Kirisuto Kyodan held the founding General Assembly on June 24–25, 1941. Except for the Anglicans (in part) and Seventh-day Adventists, all the churches (34) merged. Flexibility in administration and freedom in doctrine allowed for continuation of the several traditions. After the end of the war the Lutheran, Anglican, and some Presbyterian Churches withdrew and reorganized, foreign personnel and funds exerting extreme pressure on exhausted Japanese. However, the united church still has within it one third of all Protestants. Communicant membership as quoted in 1968 was 11,636. The Church's Committee on Cooperation relates to the foreign mission boards, and the American boards (ten) have a Japan Interboard Committee for liaison.

**Jarratt, Devereux** (1733–1801). Episcopal clergyman. Rector in Bath, Va., from ordination in 1763 until death, he was unpopular with his colleagues for his Low Church beliefs and friendliness toward Methodists. Although he withdrew support of the Methodists when they separated from the Anglican Church, he has been called the true father of American Methodism for preparing the way for them in America.

**Jefferson, Thomas** (1743–1826). American statesman and president. After graduation from William and Mary in 1762 and admission to the bar in 1767, Jefferson served in a series of public offices, including the Virginia legislature and governorship, the Federal Congress, foreign ministry, and as secretary of state, vice-president, and president of the United States (1801–1809). He is especially remembered politically as author of the Declaration of Independence and for the Louisiana Purchase, and in relation to church history for his deistic views, which made him feared and hated by conservative Christians, especially in New England, and for his potent advocacy of separation of church and state. He considered his Bill for Establishing Religious Freedom (1779) in Virginia to be one of his three most significant accomplishments. Its influence charted a similar course in other states.

**Jehovah's Witnesses.** Known at first as Millennial Dawnists, Russellites, and International Bible Students until 1931, Jehovah's

Witnesses represent one of the most important Adventist and apocalytic sects that have emerged amid the pressures of the growing industrial and urbanized society of 19th-century America. Charles Taze Russell (1852–1916), a haberdasher, Congregationalist, and Y.M.C.A. worker, under the influence of Millennialists J. H. Paton and N. H. Barbour, began the movement in Pittsburgh in 1872. He organized the Zion's Watch Tower Society in 1884, edited *Zion's Watch Tower and Herald of Christ's Presence* in 1879, and published a series of books, *Studies in the Scriptures*. In 1917, Joseph Franklin Rutherford (1869–1942), Pastor Russell's attorney and better known as the "Judge," succeeded as the administrator and then the undisputed spokesman for the society, his prolific writings (cf. *The Harp of God*, 1921) gradually taking the place of those of the original leader. In 1942 with the passing of Rutherford, Nathan H. Knorr (1905–      ) assumed leadership. Witnesses base their urgent mandate on Isa. 43:10, "You are my witnesses." They trace their origin to Adam's son Abel, witness to a non-Trinitarian Jehovah God, and the rule of Jehovah in a theocracy. With their own *The New World Translation of the Holy Scriptures* (1955), inspired and inerrant, they support their own peculiar interpretations. Jesus Christ is not divine but, reminiscent of Arianism, as archangel and perfect man, he became God's agent for reconciliation. Relying upon the book of Revelation, they prepare for Armageddon, which will involve a great devastation followed by the thousand-year reign of Jesus Christ. The wicked will be destroyed. According to their figuring, one hundred forty-four thousand Witnesses will share as an anointed "little flock" in Christ's kingly, priestly, and judicial activities on a renewed earth after Armageddon. Witnesses include "other sheep" or "jonadabs" who will be spared the destruction of Armageddon if they work with the anointed. The vast majority of these will be gathered during the millennium. Baptism by immersion is required of all converts and may be administered by any male Witness. The Lord's Supper is celebrated only once a year as a "Memorial" on the Passover date of the Jews. These doctrines are explained in numerous books and pamphlets, e.g., *Let God Be True* (1946; revised in 1952) and *Jehovah's Witnesses in the Divine Purpose* (1959), which is the official history of the movement.

The organization of the Witnesses is authoritarian and hierarchical and exists as a missionary society. There are three legal corporations, reflecting the voluntary educational society pattern of the 19th century: Watch Tower Bible and Tract Society of Pennsylvania (1884), International Bible Students Association in England (1914), and the most important Watch Tower Bible and Tract Society of New York, Inc. (1939). A board of directors controls the movement, which is organized with "regional servants" and "zone servants." These servants supervise local "companies" or "congregations" whose "servants" meet with members in Kingdom Halls. Although each member is a minister, full-time propagandists are called "pioneers," while those who give part time are known as "publishers." These persons distribute literature door to door, e.g., *Watch Tower,* and *Awake!,* carry on Bible study with contacts in homes, and attempt to build up membership. Divorce is not approved. Witnesses are not allowed to use tobacco or liquor or to receive blood transfusions. The movement has spread throughout the world so that Witnesses claim to operate in approximately two hundred lands, and translate their materials into at least forty languages. Concerned for exact statistics, they have stated that they had in 1966, e.g., 24,158 companies with 1,109,806 ministers throughout the world, with 5,141 companies, and 330,358 ministers in the United States. They also keep exact accounts of the vast amount of literature published and distributed by their presses.

Because Jehovah's Witnesses claim exemption from military service, maintain the right to evangelize and proselytize, and acclaim Jehovah alone as sovereign, they have been persecuted in many countries. This is clearly demonstrated in the United States: (1) "Judge" Rutherford and other Witnesses were convicted of sedition and sentenced to twenty years in prison in 1918 (reversed in 1919) for encouraging Witnesses not to serve in the Armed Forces. Since then Witnesses who are not pacifists must show that they are occupied in full-time religious activity in order to qualify for 4-D exemption. During World War II many were imprisoned. (2) Because of the hostility that Witnesses showed to other religious groups and the irritating manner in which they presented their views, particularly under Rutherford, they began to run afoul of laws against peddling without a license, carrying on business on the Sabbath, disturbing the peace, and "group libel" statutes. Witnesses took their cases to court, relying primarily on the appeal to freedom of religion in their legal briefs. In Lovell v. Griffin (1938), Schneider v. Irvington (1939), and Cantwell v. Connecticut (1940), the Supreme Court provided some protection against local harassment. (3) Because Witnesses believe on Biblical grounds (Ex. 20:3–5) that flag-saluting constitutes an act of devotion, they suffered deeply during the 1940's. In West Virginia Board of Education v. Barnette (1943), the Supreme Court reversed Minersville School District v. Gobitis (1940) in support of the Witnesses' freedom of dissent.

There has been controversy over the significance of Jehovah's Witnesses. Some sociopsychologists consider Jehovah's Witnesses a negatively oriented sect that has appealed to the dispossessed—emotionally, economically, and politically. These people have become dissatisfied with dominant religious and civil value-systems. Witnesses have been incapable of participating in dialogue with such competing systems. This contention is usually supported with references to extreme literalness in interpreting the Scriptures, preoccupation with exactness in numbering Witnesses and Society publications, and emphasis upon apocalyptic themes, all exposing a quest for security and an escapist approach to life's problems. Other observers suggest that change to a more irenic strategy under leader Nathan H. Knorr and the appearance of Kingdom Halls in suburban communities indicate that Witnesses may be passing through a period of transition.

BIBLIOGRAPHY: D. R. Manwaring, *Render Unto Caesar* (Chicago, 1962); W. R. Martin, *The Kingdom of the Cults* (Grand Rapids, 1965); W. J. Schnell, *Thirty Years a Watchtower Slave* (Grand Rapids, 1956); H. H. Stroup, *The Jehovah's Witnesses* (New York, 1945); W. H. Whalen, *Armageddon Around the Corner* (New York, 1962).

**Jeremiah II** (1536–1595). Patriarch of Constantinople. Jeremiah was patriarch during the confessional crisis of the Western Church, and he rejected both the attempt of Rome to bring the Greek Orthodox under papal influence and also the repeated overtures of the Lutherans. In the first of his three "Answers" to the Lutheran theologians Jacob Andreae and Martin Crusius (1576), he severely criticized the Augsburg Confession, and further correspondence from the Lutherans proved fruitless. On a tour through Russia, undertaken to win financial support for the oppressed Byzantine Church, Jeremiah agreed to elevate the metropolitan see of Moscow to a patriarchate (1589). His action, performed in part to counter Roman Catholic influence in eastern Europe, was of momentous significance for the history of the Eastern Orthodox Church.

**Jerome** (Hieronymus) (c. 348–c. 420). One of the greatest scholars and most unre-strained controversialists of the ancient church. He was born at Stridon in Dalmatia about 348. He completed his classical education at Rome, and was there baptized, about 365. On a visit to Gaul he made his first acquaintance with monasticism, then for some years was associated with a group of ascetically minded clergy at Aquileia in Istria, near his home. In 372 he left for the East, settling among the hermits of the desert near Antioch. Here he developed his knowledge of monastic traditions and began the study of Hebrew. In an exuberant letter he consulted Pope Damasus as to which of the rival bishops of Antioch he should recognize. He was referred to the strictly orthodox Paulinus, by whom he was ordained to the priesthood, although he seems never to have exercised the office. In later years, however, he defended the status of his order against the claims of bishops and the practical importance of deacons, being one of the first writers to maintain formally the essential identity of the presbyteral and episcopal orders ("except for the chair and ordination"). From 379 to 381 he was at Constantinople during the episcopate of Gregory of Nazianzus, who further inspired his Biblical studies. There he produced his first important work, a Latin version of the *Chronicle* of Eusebius, carried down to 378.

Returning to Rome in 382, Jerome was for two important years secretary to Damasus, under whom the Roman Church had finally abandoned Greek for the Latin vernacular in its worship. This is the background of Jerome's commission to correct from the Greek the versions of the Gospels and The Psalms in use at Rome, which made him aware of the need for a fresh translation from the original texts. His version of the Septuagint Psalter (in a revised form, the Gallican Psalter) has remained in use in the Roman liturgy down to our own day. At this time many of the leading families of Rome were turning to Christianity, and were attracted by the new monastic movement. Jerome became spiritual guide of many of them, conspicuous among whom were the noble widow Paula and her daughters Blaesilla and Eustochium. To his Roman years belong his reply to Helvidius, who had challenged the merit of virginity and the tradition of the perpetual virginity of Mary, and his defense of the church against the followers of Lucifer of Cagliari, who considered their leader to have been the one pillar of orthodoxy. After the death of Damasus in 384, the aristocratic-monastic party was out of favor at Rome (the death of Blaesilla in 385 was alleged to have been due to unwise austerities) and in the same year Jerome and several of his friends left for the East. After visiting the monks of Egypt and the shrines of Palestine, he settled as head of a monastery at Bethlehem in 386, while Paula presided over a neighboring convent.

As pilgrims and travelers came and went, the monk of Bethlehem remained in touch with current movements in the church and the Empire. In the 390's, Jerome again defended the ascetic life against the attacks of Vigilantius and Jovinian, on the principle that while (as against Manichaeans) marriage is good, continence in the virgin or widowed state is better (cf. I Cor., ch. 7). He had begun his scholarly career as an admirer of Origen, to whom he always remained indebted, but he turned increasingly against Origen's more speculative ideas and unrestrained allegorism. Unhappily, Jerome's anti-Origenism came to be involved with personal quarrels, with Bishop John of Jerusalem and with Rufinus of Aquileia, a fellow countryman and rival translator, a quarrel that distressed Augustine, who retained his admiration for both scholars. In 401, Jerome supported Theophilus of Alexandria in his attack on the Origenism of the more sophisticated monks. He himself had translated the Rule of Pachomius for Latin-speaking monks at Alexandria from a Greek version that had been made for him from the Coptic.

Through all these years Jerome continued to issue his version of the Bible from Greek and Hebrew, accompanying the work with prefaces and following it up with commentaries. In loyalty to the Hebrew text he came to reject the dogmatic authority of the books preserved only in the Septuagint, the deuterocanonical or apocryphal, though continuing to use them for edification—a position revived by Renaissance writers, who were fascinated by Jerome as saint and scholar, and adopted by Lutherans and Anglicans. Except for the Psalter, his translation became the standard and popular version of the Latin Church, and so is still known as the Vulgate. It is a massive work of scholarship and a masterpiece of clear Latin style which still retains its importance, though Catholic as well as Protestant scholars now follow Jerome's example in working directly from the original tongues.

Unlike Augustine, who achieved a certain synthesis of classical and Biblical culture, Jerome never resolved the tension of the two elements in his education. He always remembered the warning that he heard in a dream during his stay in the desert, "You are not a Christian but a Ciceronian," but it never led him to renounce the methods of Latin rhetoric or to refuse to make use of his store of literary references. He taught the Latin classics to Roman boys at Bethlehem, but recommended a strictly Biblical education for Paula's granddaughter and namesake (who was, however, being brought up to be a nun). He followed classical patterns in his historical writings, in the dictionary of authors in his catalog of Christian writers (*Of Illustrious Men*), and in the eulogistic biographies in his semifictional lives of monks. Of these, Hilarion of Gaza was doubtless historical, Paul the first hermit perhaps a symbolic figure, Malchus the Syrian monk a fictional but typical character—to him belongs the story of the tame lion, representative perhaps of life in the desert, which legend has been transferred to Jerome himself. His extensive correspondence contains many answers to Biblical problems, and makes use of many of the forms of literary letter writing (the consolation, the eulogy, the letter of advice). Interspersed in his letters and controversial writings are vivid pictures of the life of the time, sometimes unfair to his opponents, which put him in the tradition of Roman satirists.

Loyal Roman as well as Christian, Jerome saw the barbarian invasions as signs of the end, and felt the sack of Rome, where he still had friends, as a deep personal blow. However, he retained his vigor in his old age, devoted the resources of his monastery to the physical and spiritual needs of the refugees who came as far as Palestine, and entered into the opening phases of the Pelagian controversy. By letter and treatise he attacked Pelagius, the British heretic ("all stuffed with Scottish porridge," he says in the prologue to his commentary on Jeremiah) who had succeeded in persuading the church authorities at Jerusalem of his general orthodoxy, which indeed was not in question. Jerome's position, however, was less extreme than that of Augustine's anti-Pelagian writings. Surrounded by admiring disciples, Jerome died in peace in 419 or 420, on Sept. 30, which became St. Jerome's Day, since in the charitable mind of the church his service to Christian scholarship and zeal for the ascetic life has been allowed to outweigh the ambiguities of his character. In art he is often shown as a cardinal, but this is a double anachronism, since the costume is of much later origin, and although Jerome was a member of the Roman Church by baptism, he was not one of its clergy. The figure of the hermit surrounded by books represents him more accurately.

BIBLIOGRAPHY: P. Schaff and H. Wace (eds.), *Nicene and Post-Nicene Fathers*, Series II, Vol. 6 (Grand Rapids, 1954); E. L. Cutts,

*Saint Jerome* (London, 1897); L. Hughes, *The Christian Church in the Epistles of St. Jerome* (New York, 1923); C. C. Mierow, *Saint Jerome: The Sage of Bethlehem* (Milwaukee, 1959); P. Monceaux, *St. Jerome: The Early Years* (London, 1933); F. X. Murphy, *A Monument to Saint Jerome* (New York, 1952).

**Jerome Emiliani.** See SOMASCHI.

**Jerome of Prague** (c. 1370–1416). Bohemian Reformer. He studied at Prague with Hus and at Oxford, where he absorbed Wycliffe's teachings. Returning to Prague in 1402, he vigorously propagated the English Reformer's theological doctrines. (Hitherto Wycliffe had been known in Bohemia as a logician and metaphysician.) Traveling to the European centers of learning, he aroused much opposition for his Wycliffism and his realism. An eloquent critic of a degenerate church, he was charged with heresy and forced to recant by the Council of Constance (1415). Later he took back his recantation and died courageously by fire.

**Jerusalem, Council or Synod of** (1672). A synod of Greek Orthodox churches which adopted a doctrinal statement in eighteen canons, sometimes known as the Confession of Dositheus from the name of the Council president. This document was aimed at refutation of the influential Calvinistic Confession of Faith of Cyril Lucar, ecumenical patriarch (d. 1638), which had been published in both Greek and Latin. The Council rejected predestination and justification by faith alone.

**Jerusalem Conference** (1928). Conference of the International Missionary Council which met in a German Protestant sanatorium on the Mount of Olives, March 24 to April 8, 1928. It was a working conference attended by fewer than 250 members representing 51 countries, with prominence given to younger churches of Asia, Africa, and Latin America. Secularism, industrialism, education, race relations, and world religions were considered. "Our message is Jesus Christ" summed up its outlook.

**"Jesu Dulcis Memoria"** (properly, "Dulcis Jesu memoria"). A late 12th-century hymn of English Cistercian origin. The original 42 rhyming quatrains (9 added, 15th century) contain the essence of the mellifluous spirituality of Bernard of Clairvaux and his school of divine love. They are an extended paraphrase of his words, "Jesus is honey in the mouth, melody in the ear, a shout of gladness in the heart." Since the 16th century it has been the proper breviary hymn for the office of the Feast of the Holy Name.

**Jesuits.** See JESUS, SOCIETY OF.

**Jesus, Society of** (Jesuits). A body of priests organized for apostolic work, following a religious rule and relying on alms for support, founded by Ignatius of Loyola. The story of the Jesuit beginnings parallels the life of Ignatius. When his desire to do battle for Christ did not find its outlet in Jerusalem (1523), he began to study in preparation for the apostolic life. On Aug. 15, 1534, at Montmartre in Paris he and his six companions vowed to live a life of poverty and chastity, and to make a pilgrimage to the Holy Land. When war made this impossible, the small band proceeded to Rome to offer their services to the pope. In 1539 they decided to form a permanent community, binding themselves by a further vow of obedience to a superior. Pope Paul III approved the preliminary plan, and on Sept. 27, 1540, finally approved the new order. In April, 1541, Ignatius was elected general, empowered to draw up its Constitutions.

In 1547, after experience had taught him what would work, Ignatius began to formulate the Constitutions. In 1551 he submitted the first draft, revised it in 1552 on the recommendations of the other members, made further revisions until 1556; in 1558 the first general congregation adopted his *Constitutions of the Order* as the fundamental law of the Society. The uniqueness of their emphasis lies in their reliance on the internal and external activities of the apostolate as the primary means to perfection. Of prime importance, therefore, is a complete mobility and adaptability that enables the Jesuit to work at any task where he is most needed. To accomplish this, Ignatius abandoned traditional religious forms such as communal chanting of the Divine Office, a common rule of penance and garb, and forbade accepting ecclesiastical dignities. The universality of the Jesuit apostolate is complemented by the spirit of personal loyalty to Christ inculcated by Ignatius' *Spiritual Exercises*. Although at first against tying the order to colleges, Ignatius gradually recognized the value of the educational ministry, and in his last years laid the groundwork for the system of education that was to give the order its greatest reputation.

The new order expanded rapidly. Ignatius, encouraging the missionary activity that is still a primary work, sent men to India, China, Japan, Abyssinia, and South America. At his death (1556), it numbered 1,000 men in about 100 houses, although its rigorous ministry for

Roman Catholic reform had already brought inner and outer opposition. Under Claudius Aquaviva, its fifth general (1581–1615), it reached a high point, its missionary activities spreading from China to Canada, and many of its European members leading their intellectual fields. Between 1730 and 1773 it became clear that the enemies of the Jesuits, the Italian and French Jansenists, the Gallican French politicians, many Enlightenment philosophers, and the ministers of state of Spain, France, and Portugal desired its total destruction. Perhaps because of anticlericalism, antipapalism, and in an attempt to stem the tide of the profound change that was to be the French Revolution, the three ministers pressured Pope Clement XIII by threatening to form independent national churches. Although Clement resisted, his successor Clement XIV could not. In 1773 the papal brief *Dominus ac Redemptor* ordered the suppression of the Jesuit Order. Only in Russia, where Empress Catherine II because of her need for educators forbade the promulgation of the bull, did the Jesuits remain intact. In 1783 they received the secret approbation of Pius VI; Pius VII in 1801 publicly approved their existence. In 1814, acceding to the growing demand that the Jesuit Order resume its work, Pius VII reestablished it throughout the church. The order's principal rebuilder and revivifier was John Roothaan (general, 1829–1853), who had received his training in Russia. Although suffering a series of expulsions and martyrdoms in both Europe and the mission fields in the 19th century, the order is expanding especially in English-speaking countries. Its high schools and colleges make it the largest teaching order in the United States.

BIBLIOGRAPHY: J. Brodrick, *The Origin of the Jesuits* (New York, 1941); and *The Progress of the Jesuits* (New York, 1947); T. Hughes, *The History of the Society of Jesus in North America* (New York, 1907–1910).

**Jeu, Books of.** A Gnostic work mentioned in Pistis Sophia, where it is assigned to Enoch. In 1905, Carl Schmidt identified the work with the two books of the *Mystery of the Great Logos,* which comprise the first half of Codex Brucianus, brought from Egypt by the traveler James Bruce and now in the Bodleian Library at Oxford. Purportedly revelations of "the treasures through which the soul must pass," they are such a hodgepodge of meaningless diagrams, numbers, and letters as to be virtually unreadable.

**Jewel, John** (1522–1571). Outstanding Anglican spokesman of the English Reformation. Jewel was an Oxford man who had been much influenced by Peter Martyr, and became one of the most respected and articulate proponents of moderate reform. Though he signed a series of anti-Protestant articles in 1554, after the accession of Mary, he remained under suspicion and in 1555 he fled to Frankfurt, opposing there the more radical party in the congregation of English refugees. At Strasbourg he met Peter Martyr and accompanied him to Zurich. After Elizabeth's accession he was made bishop of Salisbury, and administered his see with distinction. In 1562 he published in Latin his *Apology of the Church of England* (though his name did not appear on the title page). A vernacular translation appeared the same year; a second and superior version followed in 1564. Jewel's chief claim to fame, the *Apology,* is regarded as one of the classical statements of the Anglican position against the Church of Rome. Basing his appeal on the Scriptures, the early Councils, and the consent of the fathers, Jewel argues that in departing (or rather being cast out) from the Roman Church the English have not forsaken the church of antiquity. Jewel also wrote an attack on the Puritan Cartwright, which was published posthumously by Whitgift.

**Jewish Christians.** Originally all Christians were Jews and primitive Christianity could be properly described as a Jewish sect. Within the church of Jerusalem, however, there were disagreements between "Hellenists" and "Hebrews" (Acts 6:1), intensified after the mission to Gentiles got under way. At this point the circumcision of converts became a problem, as did table fellowship between Jews and Gentiles. The so-called Council of Jerusalem, in about A.D. 47, decided that circumcision was unnecessary for Gentiles but required the observance of the "apostolic decree" (Acts 15:29), based on the holiness code of Lev., chs. 17 to 19. Apparently some of the problems reflected in Paul's letters to the Thessalonians and the Corinthians are related to the enforcement of these requirements, which are reflected in the later Jewish Christian Clementine Homilies. In Galatians, Paul vigorously defended the freedom of Gentile Christians from the necessity of being circumcised, but in Romans he was concerned in part with maintaining the central role of Jews and Jewish Christians in the history of redemption.

The center of Jewish Christianity was, of course, Jerusalem, and there James the Lord's brother headed the church from about A.D. 44 until the year 62, when he was put to death. His close connection with temple worship and with the Jewish law is stressed by Hegesippus, whose account of Jerusalem Christianity, while largely legendary, correctly reflects its general position. Presumably The Letter of James comes from this environment.

At the time of the revolt of 66 to 70 the Christians of Jerusalem fled to the Gentile town of Pella, although some evidently returned. Eusebius has a list of fifteen Jewish bishops before the revolt of 132 to 135. In spite of such vicissitudes, Jewish influence remained strong: the Didache is essentially a Jewish-Christian document, while Clement of Rome reflects Hellenistic Judaism and Hermas is based on Jewish apocalyptic ideas. In Asia Minor, Christians continued to follow the Jewish calendar, and at Antioch (though Ignatius explicitly opposed Judaism) Theophilus was deeply influenced by Jewish ideas. His successor, Serapion, had to write against conversion to Judaism. For many Christians, in spite of the work of theologians the line between Judaism and Christianity remained obscure.

Something of a break took place, however, during the revolt of 132 to 135, when Bar-Cochba persecuted Christian Jews who did not recognize him as the Messiah. Though Christians continued to treat the Old Testament as Scripture, many Gnostic leaders rejected it and claimed that Yahweh was merely a Demiurge inferior to the supreme God. After this point, Jewish Christians came to be viewed by many as heretical. Irenaeus, for example, calls them "Ebionites" and says that they observe the law and live in Jewish fashion, regarding Jerusalem as "the house of God." In the 4th century, there were still such groups as the Nazarenes, but with the establishment of Christianity they gradually disappeared.

**Jews.** See JUDAISM.

**Joachim of Flora** (Fiore) (c. 1132–1202). Italian mystic. Converted to the spiritual life while on a pilgrimage to the Holy Land, he took the Cistercian habit and ultimately became abbot of Corazzo. He founded the Abbey of Fiore in Calabria, which became the center of an austere branch of Cistercians.

His three chief works, *Liber concordiae Novi ac Veteris Testamenti, Expositio in apocalypsim,* and *Psalterium decem cordarum,* derive their meaning from his interpretation of Rev. 14:6. In 1254 his works were published under the title *The Eternal Gospel.* Joachim interpreted history according to the tripartite division corresponding to the Trinity. The first age of the world, that of the Father, corresponded to the Old Testament and was an age of fear under the law; the second, that of the Son, was the age of the church under

grace, the New Testament, which was to last forty-two generations of about thirty years each; the third, the age of the Spirit, was to begin c. 1260 and would be an age of love in which all men would dwell together in peace. Although Joachim never pressed his third age to the point of anticlericalism, his ideas inspired the later Spiritual Franciscans and Fraticelli to stress the role of spiritual men in the new dispensation. His ideas lost much of their influence when the year 1260 passed without incident.

The Fourth Lateran Council (1215) condemned certain of his doctrines on the Trinity, and in 1265, Alexander IV condemned his central teachings.

**Joan, Pope.** The name of a legendary medieval female pope. According to the story, she had a successful career as a scholar while disguised as a man and about 1100 was elected to the papacy, reigning for two years, after which she died in childbirth during a procession in Rome. The first written version of the tale appeared in the 13th century, and although widely believed in the Middle Ages, the legend has no basis in historical fact.

**Joan of Arc** (c. 1412–1431). French national heroine. A peasant born in Domrémy-la-Pucelle, Joan was influenced from 1425 to 1428 by voices and visions encouraging her to save France, then involved in the Hundred Years' War. By 1429 she had been approved by an ecclesiastical commission at Poitiers, had defended Orléans from siege, and had seen Charles VII crowned at Reims. She was captured and sold to the English, who imprisoned her for a year. She was then tried in the ecclesiastical court of the bishop of Beauvais, found guilty, and burned as a heretic. Her sentence was later declared unjust by Pope Callistus III. She was canonized in 1920.

**Jocists** (Jeunesse Ouvrière Chrétienne). The popular designation for a group of young working adults created in Belgium between 1912 and 1925 by Msgr. (later Cardinal) Joseph Cardijn. The movement is known in the English-speaking world as the Young Christian Workers. Cardijn's "See—Judge—Act" methodology had proved quite successful in this specialized apostolate to the workers which is attempting to counter modern industrial materialism.

**John** (d. 441). Bishop of Antioch from 428. A friend of Nestorius, he arrived too late to aid him at Ephesus in 431; Cyril of Alexandria had already convened the Council and deposed Nestorius. John held a rival Council, but Cyril secured general recognition for his.

John then abandoned the personal cause of Nestorius, but in 433 insisted on Cyril's acceptance of the Formula of Union incorporating the Antiochene doctrine of the full humanity of Christ, later enforced at the Council of Chalcedon.

**John III** (1537–1592). King of Sweden from 1568, second son of Gustav Vasa. While duke of Finland, he married a Roman Catholic princess and thus opened the door for the Counter-Reformation. He was much attracted to Rome and authorized a bilingual Mass known as the "Red Book" (1576), but he was unable to obtain the concessions from the post-Tridentine popes that he felt were essential before Roman Catholic reform could succeed in Sweden.

**John VIII** (d. 882). Pope from 872. After his election, he was under constant attack from the nobility of Spoleto and Tuscany as well as from the Saracens. His support of Charles the Bald brought repeated controversy with Charles's Italian rivals. To gain Byzantine protection, he agreed to the restoration of Photius, but later withdrew his support. Charles the Fat, whom he crowned in 881, was unable to protect him and he was murdered in 882.

**John XII** (Octavius, d. 964). Pope from 955. Son of the secular ruler of Rome, Alberic the son of Marozia, he united his father's power to that of the papacy. He called on Otto I for protection, but after Otto's return to Germany, began to negotiate with Otto's enemies. Otto returned to Rome, deposed John for gross immoralities, and established a new pope, Leo VIII. John returned to Rome and deposed Leo, but died suddenly before Otto returned. He is the first pope to have assumed a new name upon election.

**John XXII** (Jacques d'Euse, 1249–1334). Avignon pope. A native of Cahors, he was educated by the Dominicans, studying theology and law at Paris. After teaching at Toulouse and Cahors, he was appointed chancellor of Cahors in 1309. He supported Boniface VIII and the bull *Unam sanctam*. After a two-year interregnum he was chosen pope in 1316 as a compromise candidate, being seventy years old at the time. John set about centralizing and otherwise improving the papal financial system, a project in which he was successful but which did not add to the reputation of the Avignon papacy. He attempted to insist on the supremacy of the papacy in temporal affairs, and as a result became involved in a bitter quarrel with Louis IV of Bavaria. Not waiting for papal approval, Louis

marched to Rome in 1328, where he was crowned Holy Roman Emperor by a Colonna. He then declared John deposed and called a council to elect a successor (who, however, had little support elsewhere). John now excommunicated Louis, just as earlier he had excommunicated Louis' theoretician Marsilius of Padua. In the quarrel between the Spiritual and Conventual Franciscans, John favored the latter. He incurred strong opposition from theologians for holding that the souls of the blessed do not receive the beatific vision until the Last Judgment.

**John XXIII** (Baldassare Cossa, 1370–1419). Antipope. Born of Neapolitan parents, he studied at Bologna, where he received a degree in law. He was one of nine cardinals who deserted Gregory XII in 1408 to convene the Council of Pisa. This Council made an attempt to end the Western Schism by deposing the current popes and electing a new one, Alexander V. When Alexander died in 1410, Baldassare was chosen to succeed him. He then supported Sigismund in the election for Holy Roman Emperor, on the assumption that Sigismund would in turn support his bid for the papacy. John agreed to call the Council of Constance (1414–1418) and participated in the judgment against John Hus. However, when he found he could not control the Council, he fled in disguise. The Council, angered by this act, deposed him and ordered his arrest. His friends Frederick of Austria and Charles the Bold of Burgundy were unable to help him, and he was put in the custody of Louis of the Palatinate for three years. He offered a full resignation from the papacy, and when finally released from prison, he put himself at the mercy of Martin V. He was made cardinal bishop of Tusculum, but died a few months later in Florence.

**John XXIII** (Angelo Giuseppe Roncalli, 1881–1963). Pope from 1958. He received his doctorate in theology and was ordained in Rome in 1904, after which he served as secretary to the bishop of Bergamo, a town northeast of Milan. In 1921 he took over the direction of the Congregation for the Propagation of the Faith in Italy, and then moved on to a career in the papal diplomatic corps. Pius XI appointed him to a minor position in the delegation to Bulgaria in 1925, and six years later he became apostolic delegate there. In 1934 he was appointed apostolic delegate to Turkey and Greece, in which post he served until made nuncio to France late in 1944. Pope Pius XII brought him back to Italy in order to make him a cardinal and patriarch of Venice in January, 1953. After the death of Pius XII, Roncalli was elected pope on Oct. 28, 1958, taking the name John XXIII. John's papacy was a most critical period for the church, his call for *aggiornamento* finally turning the face of the Roman Church toward the specific problems of the modern world. He is best remembered for his calling (and prodding) of the Second Vatican Council, and his call for unity, peace, and social justice in his encyclicals *Pacem in terris* and *Mater et magistra*.

**John Chrysostom.** See CHRYSOSTOM, JOHN.

**John Climacus** (579–649). A saint of the Byzantine Church. A Syrian abbot, John Climacus derived his name from his work entitled *The Ladder* [climax] *of Paradise*. Also known as John *scholasticus* and John the Sinaita, he dwelt for many years as a hermit at the foot of Mt. Sinai. For four years (600–604), he served as the abbot of the monastery on the famous mountain, where he died after resigning that position.

**John Frederick, the Magnanimous** (1503–1554). Elector of Saxony (1532–1547). A loyal Lutheran, he was tutored by Georg Spalatin, signed the Augsburg Confession, and was aggressive in spreading the Reformation. Not an astute politician, he rejected all imperial pleas for reconciliation, was defeated in the Smalcald War (1547) and imprisoned until 1552. He planned the University at Jena while in prison, and urged publication of Luther's works.

**John Gualbert** (c. 990–1073). Founder of an austere religious order at Vallombrosa. The son of a Florentine nobleman, he was moved to pardon his brother's murderer, whom he had captured on Good Friday. The experience so moved him that he entered a monastery. He later went to Camaldoli and then to Vallombrosa, where within the framework of the Benedictine Rule he established a semi-eremitical life for his monks. He was one of the early opponents of simony.

**John "Lackland"** (c. 1166–1216). King of England from 1199. The youngest son of Henry II and brother of Richard I, John succeeded to the throne upon the death of his brother. His reign saw the loss of many family ("Plantagenet") possessions on the Continent to the able French king, Philip Augustus. Faced with a revolutionary situation in England, John nominally announced his acquiescence to baronial demands by signing the Magna Carta, June 15, 1215.

**John Malalas** (6th century). Syrian chronographer born in Antioch; sometimes identified with John Scholasticus (d. 577), who was appointed patriarch in Constantinople (565). Malalas' *Chronographia* was the first of many Byzantine and Western annals. Primary sources were used uncritically in the extant text, which extends to 563. The first seventeen books center in Antioch and reflect Monophysitic views; part of the eighteenth book is concentrated in Constantinople and oriented toward orthodoxy. An earlier form of the chronicle is preserved in the church Slavonic version translated before the textual abbreviation.

**John Moschus** (c. 550–619). A monk, at various times in Egypt, Jerusalem, Antioch, and on Mt. Sinai. In 614, after the conquest of Jerusalem by the Persians, he went to Rome with his friend Sophronius, where he died. His chief work is *Pratum spirituale* (in Greek, *Leimōn*, "The Meadow"). It contains over three hundred edifying anecdotes about, and miracles of, contemporary ascetics. With Sophronius he wrote a biography of the Alexandrian patriarch John Eleemosynarius (d. 619).

**John of Ávila** (1500–1569). Spanish mystic. Born at Almodóvar del Campo, Spain, John studied at Salamanca and Alcalá. He wanted to go to the American missions, but was retained by the bishop of Seville. Called the "apostle of Andalusia," he helped organize the university of Granada and colleges in Andalusia, with the object of providing not only education but popular missions. He was spiritual adviser for John of God and Francis Borgia, and helped Teresa of Ávila in her work of reform. His writings include a mystical treatise entitled *Audi filia*, sermons, letters, and recommendations on ecclesiastical reform for the Council of Trent. He was beatified in 1894.

**John of Capistrano** (1386–1456). Franciscan preacher. Born in the Abruzzi, Italy, John studied law at Perugia. A dramatic conversion experience led him to join the Franciscans in 1415. Shortly afterward, in partnership with Bernardino of Siena, he began a lifelong mission of itinerant preaching. He undertook a number of missions for Eugene IV, and in 1451 was sent to preach to the Hussites in Bohemia. From 1454 he preached a Crusade against the Turks, which resulted in a Christian victory. Shortly afterward he died at Ilok, on the Danube.

**John of Damascus** (*also known as* John Damascene) (c. 675–c. 749). John was the last of the great Eastern fathers of the church. He was the son of a Christian official in the court of the caliph at Damascus, and succeeded his father in that post. However, he became dissatisfied with such a life and, at about the age of forty, became a monk in a Palestinian monastery. He took holy orders and became one of the greatest theologians of the church. In the iconoclastic controversy, which kept the Eastern Church in turmoil for more than a century, he was an avid defender of the use of icons. His chief contribution to the church, *The Fount of Wisdom,* consists of three parts which treat of philosophy, heresy, and the orthodox Christian faith. In the last part of this work he did much to systematize previous Eastern theology. His work was not particularly original, but it was encyclopedic. In a profound sense, the development of Christian thought in the Eastern Orthodox churches ended with him. John not only exercised great influence in the East but he had considerable impact in the West, particularly upon the medieval theologians Peter Lombard and Thomas Aquinas, who knew in a poor translation, *The Orthodox Faith,* the third portion of *The Fount of Wisdom.*

**John of God** (John Ciudad, 1495–1550). Founder of the Brothers Hospitalers. He spent most of his life as a soldier and a man without religion. When he was about forty years old, John decided to alter the course his life had taken and he began to walk through Granada selling pictures and books in order to raise money for the poor. He was greatly affected by the preaching of John of Ávila, but became so obsessed with grief over his previous life of dissipation that he was put in an asylum. John of Ávila helped him gain a more balanced perspective and turned him toward feeding and housing the sick and poor. John soon had many followers and the Brothers Hospitalers came into being.

**John of Jandun** (1275–1328). Foremost Latin Averroist of his day. He gave assistance to his Paris colleague Marsilius of Padua in his *Defensor pacis* and was specifically mentioned in the bull condemning it. Fleeing from Paris (1324), he sought refuge with Louis of Bavaria. His writings—commentaries on half a dozen of Aristotle's works, one on Averroës' *De substantia orbis,* and several scientific works—all exhibit the theory of double truth evolved by heterodox Aristotelians.

**John of Parma** (1209–1289). Franciscan minister general. After several years of teaching, John entered the Franciscan Order in 1233 and was elected minister general in 1247. He carried out a number of reforms

in the order, trying to restore the ideals of Francis. His sympathy with the thought of Joachim of Flora brought him under suspicion of heresy. He resigned his office in 1257, but was permitted by his successor, Bonaventure, to retire to any convent he chose. He was eventually cleared of any charges of heresy.

**John of Salisbury** (c. 1115–1180). Medieval philosopher, historian, and churchman. He studied at Paris under Abelard, Gilbert de La Porée, and Robert Pullus; at Chartres under William of Conches. After a few years at the papal court he returned to England to serve archbishops Theobald and Thomas Becket as secretary. From 1176 he was bishop of Chartres. He supported Becket against Henry II. Among his writings were *Policraticus,* the statesman's handbook, and *Metalogicon,* a philosophical treatise in defense of the study of logic. A polished Latinist and man of letters, he was a leading figure in the 12th-century Renaissance.

**John of the Cross** (Juan de Yepisy Álvarez, 1542–1591). Spanish mystic. The son of a noble father and a seamstress, John was early taken by his widowed and impoverished mother to Medina, where he was educated by Don Alonzo Álvarez de Toledo. In 1563, he became a Carmelite, taking the name John of St. Matthew. In 1567, when he had completed his studies at Salamanca, he met Teresa of Ávila, whom he agreed to assist in her newly approved order of Discalced Carmelites. In 1568, John became one of the first friars of the Carmelite reform, changing his name to John of the Cross. His activities involved him in the struggles of the reform which, in spite of his gentleness with recalcitrant nuns and monks, resulted in persecution and imprisonment. During nine months of great deprivation in a monastic prison, he wrote most of *The Spiritual Canticle.* After his escape, John took part in the Chapter of Almodóvar in order to defend the Discalced Carmelites. Powerful opponents, however, persuaded the pope to excommunicate him, an action of which John apparently never learned. Called to Baeza in 1579, he served as rector of the Carmelite college there and unified his four major works: *The Ascent of Mt. Carmel, The Dark Night of the Soul, The Spiritual Canticle,* and *The Living Flame of Love.* These lyrical treatises on the way of contemplation are remarkable for the great gentleness with which he expresses the stern demands of consuming divine love. Through the "nights" of the senses and the understanding, the soul is led, by divine grace, to depend wholly on God in faith and love. John died after a long illness, to which was added the grief of calumny from members of the reform itself. He was canonized in 1726.

**John of Wesel** (Johannes Ruchrath or Ruchrad, c. 1400–1481). Medieval reformer. A native of Oberwesel am Rhein, he studied at the University of Erfurt, receiving his doctorate in theology in 1456 as well as the position of rector. His reputation as an important theologian was maintained in later years, and Luther was among those who studied his works. Toward the end of 1460, John was a canon at Worms and in the next year a professor at Basel. In 1463 he returned to Worms to preach in the cathedral but was rebuked by Bishop Reinhard for his attacks on the church and the sacraments. Invited to the cathedral pastorate at Mainz, he was charged a second time with preaching Hussite doctrines. When he was tried by the Inquisition, his defense was vague and inconsistent (he was near eighty). Although he recanted, he was ordered to a life of repentance at an Augustinian monastery at Mainz, where he died two years later. Wesel followed nominalist teachings concerning penance and criticized the abuse of indulgences. He held that Sacred Scripture was the final authority in matters of faith, not the fathers or the general councils. He condemned the teaching concerning original sin, transubstantiation, Extreme Unction, long prayers, feasts, fasts, holy oil, consecrated water, and the ceremonies of the Mass.

**John Sigismund** (1572–1619). Elector of Brandenburg from 1608. For some time this elector flirted with Calvinism as either a substitute for or a complement to his Lutheranism. When the duchies of Jülich, Berg, Cleves, Mark, and Ravensburg fell vacant in 1609, he became an avowed Calvinist to win support for his claim to them. In the end he permitted Lutheranism to continue on his lands, favoring the idea of equality between the two.

**Johnson, Gisle** (1822–1894). Norwegian Lutheran theologian and churchman. A professor of theology and church history at Christiania Oslo from 1849 to 1894, Johnson combined existential faith with Erlangen confessionalism. He led the Second Great Awakening in Norway during the 1850's and 1860's, strongly opposing Grundtvigianism. He founded the Christiania Inner Mission in 1885 and its national counterpart (Lutherstiftelsen) in 1868, and was active in church reform attempts.

**Johnson, Samuel** (1696–1772). Anglican minister, first president of King's College (Columbia University). Graduating from Yale, where later he was a tutor, he entered the Church of England in 1722 and went to Stratford, Conn., as a missionary. He was president of King's College from 1754 to 1763. He was in favor of bishops in the colonies, wrote an English-Hebrew grammar, and spread the idealistic philosophy of Dean George Berkeley.

**John the Faster** (John IV of Constantinople) (d. 595). Patriarch of Constantinople from 582. John received his name from his austerity of life. He is venerated as a saint in the Eastern Orthodox Church. In the West he is chiefly known through the correspondence of Pope Gregory the Great, who took exception to John's assumption of the title "ecumenical." Apparently the term originally meant "imperial," but Gregory understood it as "universal." His protests did not prevent its continued use by the patriarchs of Constantinople.

**Joinville, Jean de** (1221–1319). French nobleman, historian, and seneschal of Champagne. He was an intimate friend and counselor of Louis IX, whom he accompanied to Egypt and Palestine in 1248 on the Sixth Crusade. The venture ended in disaster when both were imprisoned for five years, after which they returned to France. Although he declined to join the king on the Crusade of 1270, he remained loyal to him, as evidenced by his serving as one of the chief witnesses for Louis' canonization. He also wrote the now famous *Memoirs of St. Louis,* a charmingly graphic account of the hero's life as well as of the Crusade of 1248.

**Joliet, Louis** (1645–1700). French-Canadian *coureur de bois* and explorer. Though he studied under the Jesuits at Quebec, Joliet became a fur trader in the wilderness about the Great Lakes. Commissioned by the governor of New France, Joliet and the Jesuit father Jacques Marquette undertook in 1672 an exploration of the Mississippi River, which they followed to the mouth of the Arkansas, ascertaining by their latitude that it flowed into the Gulf of Mexico.

**Jonas, Justus** (1493–1555). German Lutheran Reformer. Appointed professor of canon law and theology at Wittenberg in 1521, he accompanied Luther to the Diet of Worms (1521) and the Marburg Colloquy (1529). He reformed Halle in 1541, translated many works by Luther and Melanchthon, furthered Luther's ideas on worship and liturgy, and opposed crypto-Calvinism. In 1546 he stood at Luther's deathbed and later preached the funeral sermon.

**Jones, Eli Stanley** (1884–      ). Methodist missionary. After his education at Asbury College, Wilmore, Ky., he became a missionary to the high castes of India in 1907. Elected a bishop of the Methodist Church in 1928, he resigned to continue missionary work. He has been active in the Christian ashram movement and the ecumenical movement. He is the author of many devotional books, and a proponent of the Greenwich Plan for federal union of religious denominations.

**Jones, Griffith** (1684–1761). Anglican priest of Llanddowror, Carmarthenshire, Wales. His sympathies for nonconformity fostered the development of Calvinistic Methodism in Wales, and earned the harassment of the Ecclesiastical Court. He was the inventor of Welsh circulating schools (1730), which sent the schoolmaster to town to teach Scripture in Welsh, to catechize, and otherwise to promote religion and learning. At his death, there were 218 such schools and the students who were taught by them enlarged Welsh Methodism.

**Joseph II** (1741–1790). Archduke of Austria, king of Bohemia and Hungary, Holy Roman Emperor. The eldest son of Francis Stephen and Maria Theresa, he was given a broader education than was customary with Hapsburg princes, and by his late teens he gave evidence of having a questing mind and a spirit critical of established values. Upon his father's death in 1765 he was elected emperor and appointed coregent with his mother. Later he clashed with her, for although she had found it necessary to acquiesce in a number of reforms in order to strengthen Austria against the challenge of Prussia, she was deeply suspicious of change. Restricted to the direction of military and foreign affairs, and lacking much talent for either, he presided over an abortive attempt to acquire Bavaria, which resulted in the indecisive Potato War against Prussia. At Maria Theresa's death in 1780 he was free to institute the reforms he thought necessary. Most importantly, he abolished serfdom, issued an edict of religious toleration (1781) that allowed members of major sects to worship freely, reduced radically the number of monastic establishments, overhauled the whole of the educational apparatus, introduced a diverse program of social services, restricted drastically the political influence of the landed aristocracy, and liberalized the censorship. Toward the end of his life he involved himself in a losing war against the Turks which, together with the police measures that accompanied his centralizing reforms, compromised his popularity to such an extent that on his deathbed he was constrained to repeal many of his innovations.

**Joseph Calasanctius** (1556–1648). Founder of the Piarists, an order formed in Italy to educate poor and homeless children. In 1597 Joseph opened the first free school in Europe. The group and its work had a number of enemies, but it was supported by the pope and given formal recognition as a religious order in 1621. Joseph was the first superior of the congregation but was ousted when dissension arose in the ranks. He was finally given back his earlier position and authority three years before his death.

**Josephinism.** Broadly, the whole tendency of liberal, centralizing reformism associated with the reign of Joseph II of Austria (Holy Roman Emperor, 1765–1790). More narrowly, it was the doctrine of Joseph's chancellor, Prince Kaunitz, that in all questions not directly related to dogma the church must be subservient to the state and that its clergymen were to lay claim to no privileges not accessible to the ordinary citizen. In Austria these views survived their creator by more than half a century and were not formally abandoned until the Concordat of 1855.

**Joseph of Volokolamsk** (c. 1439–1515). Russian monk and advocate of the social and political influence of the church. Joseph founded a monastery at Volokolamsk in 1479 and led it to a position of worldly power. He saw in a cordial alliance of church and state the best guarantee of religious uniformity in the newly independent dukedom of Moscow (see THIRD ROME), and he justified monastic property and wealth as the means to political influence. The position of the "Josephites" or "possessioners" was sharply contested by Nil Sorssky, who advocated an otherworldly piety and opposed both the persecution of Dissenters and the acquisition of wealth by the monasteries.

**Josephus, Flavius** (c. 37–c. 100). Jewish historian, born in Palestine. After serving the Jews as emissary to Rome (64), he fought in the Jewish War and was taken prisoner by Vespasian (67), for whom he acted as an interpreter. Pensioned by the Romans, he spent the remainder of his life in writing. His chief works were *The Jewish War* (77–78), *Antiquities of the Jews* (c. 94), an autobiography, and *Against Apion*. His books were sources widely used by Christian writers.

**Jovinian** (d. c. 405). An Italian ascetic who warned against the dangers of asceticism. Jovinian emphasized the unrestricted habitation of God in all baptized Christians. The rigid corollaries of this theme included: emphases on the equality of virgins, wives, and widows; one heavenly reward for all; impotence of the devil over the baptized; unimportance of fasts and foods. According to Ambrosius, he also denied the perpetuity of Mary's virginity. Jovinian found adherents in Rome, Milan, and Vercelli, but was excommunicated in Rome and Milan in 390 and 391. The Synod of Siricius issued an encyclical against him c. 390, Jerome wrote against him c. 393, and Augustine opposed his disavowal of virginity in 401. The emperor Honarius effected his island exile in March, 393.

**Jowett, Benjamin** (1817–1893). English scholar and theologian best known for his translation of Plato and as master of Balliol College, Oxford. Ordained an Anglican priest in 1845, he became noted for his independent mind, and his essays on the atonement and on the Scriptures in *Essays and Reviews* placed his orthodoxy under grave suspicion. Although his formal prosecution by church authorities came to nothing, he ceased to write on theological subjects and busied himself with his academic affairs.

**Judaism.** One of the oldest existing religions, and a strict form of monotheism, the religion of Jews and the parent religion of both Christianity and Islam. Exodus-Sinai, the primary revelatory experience of the Jew, gave birth to a people who believed that Yahweh, the nameless one (Ex. 3:14), had delivered them from Egyptian bondage that they might acknowledge his redemptive power and consecrate their lives to his service. Yahweh's relation (covenant) with Israel is at once a demand and a promise: "If you will obey my voice and keep my covenant, . . . you shall be . . . to me a kingdom of priests and a holy nation" (Ex. 19:5 f.).

The demand is embodied in Torah (teaching or revelation) of which the Ten Commandments (Ex. 20:1–17) is a classic paradigm. Torah is the fullness of affirmation and deed for which a son or daughter of the covenant may be held accountable.

Regulating every sphere of life, the Torah's injunctions include a celebration of Yahweh's creative and redemptive power (Sabbath, Passover), the regulation of diet (Ex. 22:30 f.), and the definition of one's obligation to an enemy (Ex. 23:4).

From its inception the covenant required ultimate loyalty to Yahweh (Ex. 20:3), who differed radically from the deities of Israel's contemporaries. Yahweh has no mythological counterparts, transcends the power of magic or fate, and is sovereign of nature and history.

Moses was the first of the apostolic prophets through whom Yahweh chose to make known his will. Later prophets refined the terms of the covenant. Amos (750 B.C.) sternly foresaw the destruction of the Northern Kingdom (722 B.C.) as a consequence of Israel's failure to obey Yahweh's primary demand for social justice (Amos 2:6–7a, 8). Hosea, a younger contemporary, affirmed Yahweh's *ḥesed* (steadfast love) and pleaded for the people's rejection of idolatrous cults (Hos. 4:9–14).

Biblical prophecy developed the universal dimensions of Israel's faith and prepared the Hebrew people for a mission to the nations. Amos explicitly affirmed that the God of Israel was active in the history of other peoples (Amos 9:7). To the Babylonian exiles, Jeremiah (597 B.C.) offered assurance that Nebuchadnezzar's victory revealed not Yahweh's impotence but his chastening purpose (Jer. 33:6–11). The prophet further advised the exiles that Yahweh could be worshiped outside the land of Israel (ch. 29:5–7). It remained only for Second Isaiah (539 B.C.) to interpret Cyrus' conquest of Babylonia and the return of the exiles to Palestine as Yahweh's redemptive act in order that a restored Israel might bear witness to his incomparable power among the nations (Isa. 42:5–8; 45:4–7).

Thus, the Babylonian exile transformed Israel from a people whose God was Yahweh to a prophet-people through whose word and witness all nations would acknowledge the one and only God.

Prophecy also reshaped Israel's understanding of the divine promise. What began as the confidence that Yahweh would secure his people in a land of milk and honey (Ex. 3:8) blossomed into a hope for messianic redemption (Isa. 2:2–4). Varied in nuance, the hope embodied these common elements: a restoration of Israel to the land of its fathers, a vindication of Israel's loyalty to the covenant, and the universal acknowledgment of Yahweh.

The vision (Isa. 9:6) of a divinely anointed Davidic monarch (messiah) projected a time when power would be united with love in the conduct of human affairs. In the late postexilic age, hope deferred engendered apocalyptic visions (Dan., chs. 7 to 12).

Our knowledge of early postexilic Judaism is ambiguous. It seems, however, that by the time Ezra (397 B.C.) assembled the Judean remnant for a covenant renewal ceremony (Neh., chs. 8 to 9) the Temple had been rebuilt, attempts to restore the Davidic monarchy foiled, and prophecy ended. When Ezra read from a Torah scroll, God's revelation was complete. It became the task of the priest-scribe to preserve the written text, interpret and transmit it from generation to generation.

By the 2d century B.C. the authority of the priest had been challenged by a new scholar class. Although stigmatized as dissenters (*perushim*, or Pharisees) by the established priestly descendants of Sadok (Sadducees), this group of sages won the confidence of the Judean masses.

Following the destruction of the Temple (A.D. 70), the Pharisees, now called rabbis, emerged as the undisputed leaders of the covenant community. Although they canonized the Hebrew Bible (A.D. 90), the Pharisees' contribution to Judaism is enshrined in that vast Talmudic compendium of law (halakah) and lore (haggadah) containing the teachings of some two thousand rabbinic sages from the 3d century B.C. to the 6th century A.D.

Under the aegis of Pharisaism the synagogue emerged triumphant, a learned laity supplanted the priesthood, and prayer and study were substituted for the sacrificial cult.

The Pharisees personalized the relation of the individual Jew to the God of the covenant. They transformed Rosh Hashanah from a Yahweh enthronement ceremony to a day when each man stands in judgment before the God of life. Under their tutelage postmortal reward and punishment became part of normative Judaism. In rabbinic literature new names for Yahweh appeared, betokening a new intimacy between God and man: *shekinah* (the divine presence), "Our father who art in heaven," and *makom* (the one who is always present).

To the rabbis must be credited that ingenious hermeneutic system by which the Biblical text yielded commandments relevant to the demands of the new age. Maintaining that there were two revelations at Sinai, written and oral, the Pharisees rooted their most far-reaching interpretations in the Sinaitic covenant. Armed with this concept of revelation, they virtually abolished the Biblical provision for capital punishment, defined the *lex talionis* as monetary compensation, and liberalized the observance of the Sabbath.

No less significant was the Pharisaic refinement of covenant theology. The myth-laden pages of the haggadah project a God-Israel relation grounded in a creative tension between contractual justice and unconditional love. The rabbinic understanding of repentance (*teshubah*) is indicative: God both demands acts of penitence and passionately pleads for the return of a people whom he loves and will not forsake. The conditional dimension of the covenant is a hallmark of man's dignity as copartner with God; the un-conditional dimension affirms man's reliance on divine love.

The rabbis prepared Judaism to endure Roman captivity and survive the destruction of the Temple. After the failure of the Bar-Cochba insurrection (A.D. 135) the messianic hope became decisively eschatological. Rabbi Johanan b. Zakkai (A.D. 90) and his disciples taught that to fulfill his mission the Jew needed only to observe the Torah and bear divine witness until the day of redemption.

With the birth and official recognition of Christianity by the Roman Empire, Jewish missionary efforts ceased entirely, and the covenant's validity itself was seriously challenged. The rabbinic response is obliquely embodied in Talmudic literature. Jesus' Messiahship, Sonship, and atoning death were unequivocally rejected. To the claim that a new elect had displaced Israel, Joshua b. Levi's answer is characteristic: "Not even a wall of iron can effect a separation between Israel and its father in heaven." Paul's claim that the law had been abrogated by God's revelation in Jesus Christ was equally denied. Commenting on Deut. 30:11–12, the rabbis conclude: "Do not say that there has arisen another Moses who brought another Torah from heaven."

The Jews' relation to Western Christendom alternated between periods of privileged toleration and harassment. That suffering which the church saw as a sign of Israel's divine rejection, the Jew attributed to God's chastening love and an unredeemed world.

During periods of relative freedom a segment of the Jewish community felt challenged by the philosophic currents of the dominant culture. Even as Philo (c. 25 B.C.–c. A.D. 45) had allegorically reconciled Biblical texts with the writings of Plato, Saadia ben Joseph (892–942) developed a synthesis between faith and reason in the idiom of the Arabic Mu'tazilite tradition. Centuries later, Maimonides (1135–1204) created an even more impressive synthesis between Aristotelianism and covenant theology.

Jewish apologetic literature has always reflected the culture and temperament of its authors, but even Maimonides, the rationalist, and Judah ha-Levi (c. 1085–c. 1140), the romantics' mystic, shared the conviction that the Torah, written and oral, was the revealed word of God, its commandments binding on God's chosen people, and its promise of redemption worthy of abiding trust.

This theological consensus enabled a dispersed people to maintain a remarkable continuity of observance and belief, spanning many centuries and a multitude of civilizations.

The relation of the Jew to persons outside the covenant was normatively defined in Talmudic literature. God's covenant with Noah bound all men to observe seven laws, including the prohibition of murder and idolatry. Maimonides reformulated the accepted Talmudic principle in his code: "Whoever professes to obey the seven Noachide laws and strives to keep them is classed with the devout among the Gentiles and has a share in the world to come."

Western Jewry's emancipation at the end of the 18th century threatened the consensus that had prevailed during the Middle Ages. The binding character and scope of the Torah tradition (revelation) was itself called into question, and the political establishment no longer underwrote the judgments of a rabbinic scholar class.

Modern Jewish sectarianism in its Orthodox, Conservative, and Reform manifestations arose as an attempt to negotiate the perils and reap the promises of emancipation. Its early spokesmen, Abraham Geiger (1810–1874), Zacharias Frankel (1801–1875), and Samson Raphael Hirsch (1808–1888), initiated a dialogue that may be reduced to the following as yet unresolved question: What does the God of the covenant require of the Jew at this time and in this place?

For the 20th-century Jew, that question has in part been preempted by the revelation at Auschwitz. Against the backdrop of Nazi genocide, the survivors of the holocaust must struggle anew for the power to trust and serve the God of the covenant.

Israel's rebirth (1948) enabled the Jew for the first time in two thousand years to constitute a self-determining culture-creating majority in a corner of the globe. Orthodox leaders of the 19th century had viewed the Zionist movement as a prideful usurpation of the Messiah's throne. Classical Reform had opposed it as a parochial betrayal of the Jew's universal mission. The verdict of history has virtually dispelled that controversy. Martin Buber (1878–1965), the Jewish existentialist, and David Ben-Gurion (1886–    ), the political secularist, shared the hope that in this land a community would emerge nourished by the vision of the Biblical prophets. Each believed that the second commonwealth was a sign of redemption.

In America the thoughtful Jew seeks to rediscover his distinctive witness even as he strives to share fully in the communal life of a free society. The secular city challenges Christian and Jew to affirm the positive role of each covenant community in the mystery of the divine economy and until the coming of the divine Kingdom.

Franz Rosenzweig (1886–1929) suggested that the Jew is God's primal and enduring witness, and the Christian, God's active missionary unto those who knew him not. Without denying the validity of God's covenant with other men, the Jew attests by faith and deed to man's copartnership with God in a world that has not yet been redeemed.

BIBLIOGRAPHY: J. L. Blau, *The Story of Jewish Philosophy* (New York, 1962); A. Cohen, *The Natural and the Supernatural Jew* (New York, 1962); J. Guttmann, *Philosophies of Judaism* (Philadelphia, 1965); M. Kadushin, *The Rabbinic Mind* (New York, 1952); Y. Kaufmann, *The Religion of Israel* (Chicago, 1960); H. Orlinsky, *Ancient Israel* (Ithaca, 1954); H. J. Schoeps, *The Jewish-Christian Argument* (New York, 1963).

**Judson, Adoniram** (1788–1850). Pioneer American foreign missionary. Judson was born in Malden, Mass., where his father was a Congregational minister. At Andover Seminary he met and joined a group of Williams College graduates who had become concerned about the need for preaching the gospel among the non-Christian peoples of the world. After helping to establish the first foreign mission board, the American Board of Commissioners for Foreign Missions (1810), and traveling to London for discussions with missionary leaders there, he embarked for India with his bride of two weeks, Feb. 19, 1812. Since the English missionaries in India were Baptists, Judson spent time on board ship studying the Bible in order to be able to meet arguments against infant baptism. The inquiry, however, undermined his own belief and he received believer's baptism on his arrival in India. The effect of his conversion was to spur American Baptist interest in foreign missions. Judson was not permitted by British authorities to remain in India and he settled, as an alternative, in Burma, where he remained, with the exception of one visit to America in 1845 and 1846, until his death. Although his life in Burma was very difficult and converts were not many, Judson accomplished much through literary endeavors, translating the entire Bible into Burmese, preparing other works in that language, and compiling a well-respected English-Burmese, Burmese-English dictionary. As a result of Judson's pioneer work, American Baptists have since regarded Burma as an area of special missionary responsibility.

**Juelicher, Adolf** (1857–1938). German New Testament scholar, and professor at

Marburg (1888–1923). Best known of his works are: two volumes on the parables of Jesus (1888–1899), his *Introduction to the New Testament* (1894; English translation, 1904), which went through seven editions, the last in conjunction with E. Fascher, and the reconstruction of the Old Latin text of the New Testament begun in his later years and subsequently continued by his students.

**Julian of Eclanum** (c. 386–454). Bishop of Eclanum from c. 416. His continued support of Pelagianism after its condemnation by a Carthaginian synod in 418 brought upon him the fury of Augustine. Julian insisted on the goodness of God and man's independence by virtue of his free will, citing the Greeks, especially the Gregories, in his support. His works, which exist only as fragments in Augustine's writings, indicate that he was an able dialectician and philosopher (Stoic).

**Julian of Halicarnassus** (d. after 518). Bishop deposed from his see in Halicarnassus in 518. He went to Alexandria, where he became leader of the Aphthartodocetae (who taught the incorruptibility of Christ's body) or the Phantasiasts (who taught that the body of Christ was an apparition). Julian in four works attacked Severus of Antioch, who was also in exile. Severus led the party which held that Christ's body was corrupt. This dispute led to a division in the Monophysite party which remained until the 7th century.

**Julian (Juliana) of Norwich** (c. 1342–c. 1413). English anchoress and mystic who lived outside the walls of St. Julian's Church, Norwich. Her book, *The Sixteen Revelations of Divine Love,* arose out of her mystical experiences or visions in 1373 during a prolonged illness in which Christ manifested to her his great love for all men. The *Revelations,* which was completed some twenty years later, has been called "the most perfect fruit of later medieval mysticism in England." The work bears the marks of Neoplatonic influences common among Christian mystics. She was perhaps acquainted with the anonymous mystical treatise *The Cloud of Unknowing,* written in East Midland English, or Walter Hilton's classic, *The Scale of Perfection.*

**Julian the Apostate** (331–363). Roman emperor from 361. A nephew of Constantine, he and his brother Gallus survived the massacre of other relatives in 337 (for his public career, see CONSTANTINE AND FAMILY). Trained by Arian tutors, he was increasingly attracted to Neoplatonic philosophy and pagan mysteries; he was never happier than during his brief stay at Athens in 354 and 355. When called to rule, however, he rose to his duties successfully. As emperor he could display his true sentiments, so he last attended Christian worship early in 361, and then proclaimed his return to Hellenism, developing an anti-Christian policy. At first he hoped that the Christian parties, left alone, would destroy each other. When this did not occur, he took further measures—restoring property to temples, forbidding Christians to teach the pagan classics, and attempting to organize a pagan hierarchy that would rival the Christians in good works. This artificial movement ended with his death in 363. By disposition Julian was a scholar and an ascetic; his writings include orations, some official and others expressing his religious views, satires (on previous emperors, and on the frivolous Christians of Antioch), and an interesting collection of letters. His *Against the Galileans,* the last considerable work of pagan apologetic, is largely preserved in quotations in the reply by Cyril of Alexandria.

**Julius I** (d. 352). Pope from 337. He is especially noted for his role in the development of the power of the Roman see and his support of Athanasius during the Arian controversy of that time. When Athanasius was forced out of Alexandria in 339, he met Julius while taking refuge in Rome. In the Council of Sardica (c. 343), called by Julius and the emperors Constans and Constantius, it was held that the Roman see was to become a court of appeal. Two letters written by Julius survive, one to the Eusebians and one to the Alexandrians.

**Julius II** (Giuliano della Rovere, 1443–1513). Pope from 1503. He began his ecclesiastical career by following his uncle, Francesco, into the Franciscan Order. He was made a cardinal when his uncle became Pope Sixtus IV in 1471. After the death of Sixtus (1484), Della Rovere managed by bribery to have Innocent VIII elected. Controlling the papacy until Innocent's death in 1492, he was forced to flee Rome when his enemy Rodrigo Borgia became Pope Alexander VI. Following Pope Pius III's brief reign, Della Rovere achieved his own election as Pope Julius II in 1503 by means of bribery and extensive promises. He agreed to call a council within two years and to make no decisions on war or on the location of a council without the concurrence of two thirds of the cardinals. In fact, this council, the Fifth Lateran Council, was not called until 1512. In 1506 the construction of St. Peter's was begun and a special indulgence was proclaimed to help pay for it. The main objective of Julius' reign was to reestablish the papal power by the restoration of the Papal States. By means of war, interdict, and excommunication Julius subdued Bologna and Venice. Creating the Holy League, he ended French power in Italy at Ravenna, in 1512. These activities earned Julius the name of Pontefice Terribile and made him the object of satirical writings, such as the dialogue *Julius Excluded* (i.e., shut out of heaven), which was attributed to Erasmus.

**Julius III** (Giovanni Maria Ciocchi del Monte, 1487–1555). Pope from 1550. A native of Rome, he studied law at Perugia and Siena. In 1542 he had been charged with preparatory work for the Council of Trent, and as its first president he presided at the opening on Dec. 13, 1545. At the Council he spoke for the pope in opposition to the emperor Charles V, particularly when the Council was moved to Bologna in March, 1547. Made a cardinal by Paul III in 1543, he succeeded him in 1550. In accordance with an agreement made prior to his election, he restored Parma to Ottavio Farnese, but when Farnese asked the French to aid him against Charles, Julius sided with the emperor, had Farnese driven out, and moved the Council to Trent again. He was forced to call a recess in April, 1552, however, because the French bishops would not take part in the meetings. When French military victories in northern Italy forced Julius to come to terms with France, he was disheartened and made few subsequent attempts at reform. He sent Cardinal Pole to England to represent him at the court of Queen Mary, and Cardinal Morone to speak for the interests of the Roman Church in the discussions preceding the Peace of Augsburg.

**Julius Africanus** (c. 160–c. 240). Christian writer. Probably born at Jerusalem, he migrated to Emmaus (Nicopolis), and eventually to Alexandria and to Rome. His wide associations gave him access to many courts, including Edessa. His chief work was a world history in five books, fragments of which are scattered through Eusebius' *Chronicle*. Other works include an encyclopedia of twenty-four books, extant in fragments, and two letters showing critical acumen.

**Jung, Carl Gustav** (1875–1961). Swiss psychiatrist and psychologist who broke with his teacher, Freud, over the concept of the unconscious, which he could not accept as merely subliminated sexuality. Jung postulated that there is a collective unconscious common to all men throughout history, which is expressed through basic forms or archetypes. These archetypes are present in certain Christian symbols and doctrines throughout Christian history. He developed a psychological theory that makes possible a Christian use of myth with a scientific psychological basis. Jung is one of the most important scholars who sought to interrelate psychological data and Christianity.

**Jung-Stilling, Johann Heinrich** (1740–1817). German Pietist, mystic, and devotional writer. He gave up a successful secular career for an annuity from Elector Karl Friedrich of Baden to write and promote a religious awakening in Heidelberg (1803–1806) and Carlsruhe (from 1806). In later years, he sublimated religious experience to supranaturalism under Kant's influence and finally moved to predominantly apocalyptic-eschatological motifs in his writing.

**Justification.** A doctrine dealing primarily with the conditions of man's salvation, his entrance into a right relationship with God. In distinction from the doctrine of redemption, the saving work of Christ, justification concerns man's appropriation of that work. Insofar as the term is drawn from the language of the law court, it points to the basis on which a man is declared to be just or acceptable by the judgment of God. Three motifs have historically regulated the formulation of this doctrine: (1) Morally, man is judged righteous on the basis of a virtuous life; (2) forensically, man is declared righteous by the gracious judgment of God; and (3) dynamically, man is made righteous through God's gracious creative activity within his life.

In the patristic period, formal statements about justification repeated the forensic language of Paul: Christ's death has made possible the imputation of righteousness and justification by faith apart from works. However, in the association of justification with the baptismal remission of sins rather than with a final gracious judgment, a moralist understanding of Christian life is implied. To be sure, the fathers asserted the universal subjection of Adam's descendants to sin and the necessity of divine grace as an infusion of the divine nature into humanity for a restored fellowship with God (the physical theory of atonement). Even so, in the broader discussion of salvation, Christ's role was also that of teacher (Clement of Alexandria) or lawgiver (Tertullian) who calls men to a repentance possible through the exercise of their free will. This universal patristic emphasis on free will and on man's consequent moral responsibility underlies the discussion of both penitential preparation for baptism and the subsequent life of obedience to the divine will as contributing to final salvation. This interpretation reflects a partially non-Pauline view: grace and free will cooperate in the process of salvation, with grace retaining the priority, since God creates the context within which man responds. This view also was operative in the development of the postbaptismal penitential discipline (Hermas, Tertullian).

The easy conjunction of grace and free will was severed for the Western Church in the 5th-century Pelagian controversy. Pelagianism, with its primary stress upon free will and moral responsibility, taught that salvation is the reward bestowed upon man for the exercise of his God-given capacity to will and to do the good works of God's law. Against such one-sided moral optimism, Augustine interpreted justification as the infusion of grace into the individual so as to make him righteous. This development of the dynamic motif includes as its elements: (1) the presupposition of man's total moral depravity and the corresponding necessity of grace for divine acceptance (thus climaxing the tendency of his 4th-century Latin predecessors); (2) an obvious shift from concern with the atoning work of the cross, apprehended through faith (the forensic view to which he gives passing attention only); and (3) the description of the effects of grace as the perfecting of man's love for God with the consequence that man's good works become acceptable to God—although, in effect, God rewards the merit of works he himself has ultimately performed. According to such a description, it is evident that man contributes nothing to his own salvation and that the figure of the Living Christ, in whom the divine love is revealed, is secondary for Augustine's own religious experience. Further, herein is implied both the foundation of medieval sacramental theory and Augustine's doctrine of election.

The formal statement of the doctrine of justification in the Middle Ages retained an Augustinian flavor. Man's problem was still defined in terms of sin—whether as an offense against God's honor (Anselm) or as a flaw in man's fallen nature (Thomas Aquinas); moreover, the grace by which man's restoration to God is achieved was conceived in substantive terms. Justification, accordingly, referred to the dynamic process by which grace is infused into man, its effects being the production of love for God. Such a process was firmly connected to the sacraments as the means for obtaining grace and therefore as essential factors in the process of man's being made righteous. However, to this Augustinian substructure medieval theology added a developed theory of merit according to which man's will and the good works of love, whether by preparing for the reception of grace or in cooperating with the Holy Spirit for the increase of justice, contribute to the obtaining of eternal life. Justification in reality, then, is based on the gift of love, which enables man to perform meritorious works. Thomas Aquinas denied that fallen man could, without the aid of grace, obtain the enduring gift of love itself. But, despite formal Augustinian expression, later Scholasticism (see NOMINALISM) gave greater emphasis to the merit attained through the exercise of man's will and its preparatory role. The Roman doctrine was finally formulated as dogma at the Council of Trent in terms calculated (1) to exclude the alleged Protestant heresy of a divine grace that excludes human cooperation; (2) to reconcile the Augustinian heritage with nominalism; and (3) to condemn the forensic interpretation while asserting officially the dynamic view in which grace and meritorious good works cooperate for man's salvation. The Roman Catholic doctrine thus leaves man no assurance of his justification.

The Reformation was characterized by a radical rejection of this entire medieval view. Indeed, justification by faith alone (*sola fide*) became the battle cry of the Reformation and in consequence the normative principle of Protestant theology. Here the forensic interpretation became predominant. Justification was made entirely dependent upon the judgment of God, as deserved condemnation was suspended by the forgiveness of sins and the imputation of the righteousness or merit of Christ to sinners. Accordingly, the Reformers stressed the understanding of grace as divine favor toward man rather than as some infused power. Their view suggests that God places sinners in right relationship to himself without any reference to good works, either moral or ceremonial; man's sinful condition precluded his ability to perform any such works as the basis of acceptance. Although Martin Luther could speak in terms of justification as a daily renewal in which the Holy Spirit makes us righteous (the dynamic view), John Calvin maintained a more completely forensic view in his struggle against the notion that Christ's essential or natural righteousness is imparted by some process of infusion and by his conclusion that our works are approved as the works of the Holy Spirit rather than identified as part of the process of regeneration. It is evident, then, that the Reformers conceived of faith as the subjective certainty or confidence with which one grasps, or rather is grasped by, a justifying God, instead of as a meritorious work.

The Reformation understanding of justification by grace through faith has continued to dominate Protestant thought, despite occasional exceptions (Pietism). Thus John Wesley regarded justification, the forgiveness of sins apprehended through faith, as the first element in salvation, with the process of perfection consequent to it. In liberal theology, also, justification has been treated in forensic terms as the declaration through Christ of divine love and forgiveness. However, in liberalism a perceptible change may be noted: justification also involves a subjective dynamic element—a change in the inner condition of man, whether the God-consciousness replaces the consciousness of sin in a position of predominance (Schleiermacher) or the attitude of mistrust toward God is replaced by one of trust (Ritschl). In such a view, then, it is man who is affected by Christ's death rather than the objective structures of God's justice. This liberal understanding has been challenged during the 20th century by neo-Reformation theology; here, a renewed emphasis upon the objective achievements of the death and resurrection of Christ lifts a forensic theme to dominance once again: justification is imputed in one's identification with Christ, in whom the divine righteousness was communicated to man (Karl Barth), new potentialities were opened to man by Christ's assumption of man's guilt (Dietrich Bonhoeffer), or a new self-understanding frees one from the bonds of inauthentic existence (Rudolf Bultmann).

BIBLIOGRAPHY: See G. C. Berkouwer, *Faith and Justification* (Grand Rapids, 1954); H. Küng, *Justification* (New York, 1964); G. W. Lampe (ed.), *The Doctrine of Justification by Faith* (London, 1954); H. R. Mackintosh, *The Christian Experience of Forgiveness* (New York, 1927); A. Ritschl, *The Christian Doctrine of Justification and Reconciliation* (Edinburgh, 1902).

**Justinian I** (483–565). Roman emperor from 527 and chief influence in ecclesiastical policy under his uncle Justin I (518–527). He left his mark in history as much by the results of his failures as by his achievements. His most splendid period came in the few years of peace with Persia (532–540); his architects planned the great church of Hagia Sophia, his lawyers drafted the classic code of Roman law, and his generals undertook the reconquest of North Africa from the Vandals (533–534) and Italy from the Goths (535–554). The long Gothic War left the exhausted peninsula a prey to the Lombards in 568. In the church, Justinian supported Chalcedonian orthodoxy, but the Monophysites continued strong, efforts at conciliation were ineffective (see THREE CHAPTERS, THE), and after Justinian's death the schism was soon complete. Among the expressions of Justinian's own theological interests was the condemnation of Origenistic speculations in a treatise issued as an edict in 543. He considered himself supreme governor of a Christian commonwealth in which emperor and priest would work together, under the practical direction of the former but in loyalty to the orthodox faith. From such principles developed the Byzantine ideal of "symphony" of church and state in one united body.

**Justinian Code.** See CORPUS JURIS CIVILIS.

**Justin Martyr** (c. 100–c. 165). Roman Apologist. Martyred between 163 and 165. Born in Hellenized Samaria, Justin received a conventional Greek education that did not include philosophical studies, which he entered upon in later years. After minimal contacts with other schools, he embraced Platonism because of its goal, the vision of God. A Christian teacher led him toward conversion by undermining Platonic teaching through the use of Aristotelian arguments and by pointing to the inspiration of the Old Testament prophets. Justin also admired the constancy of uneducated martyrs, and he became the most important Apologist of the 2d century, teaching first at Ephesus and later at Rome, where he headed a school and produced his now lost treatise against heresies (c. 145), his *First Apology* (c. 150), his *Dialogue* with the Hellenistic Jew Trypho (c. 160, based in part on a much earlier debate), and his *Second Apology* (c. 160; an appendix to the first). Eusebius knew other works, now lost; the genuine writings, largely supplanted by Byzantine forgeries, are preserved only in a manuscript of the year 1364 and were first published in 1551. In addition, the acts of his martyrdom have survived.

The importance of his works lies primarily in his Christian exegesis of the Old Testament and in his use of the Gospels as providing historical confirmation of the fulfillment of prophecy; in his willingness to describe Christian worship in order to show that it was not immoral; and in his effort to show that Christianity was not alien to the best of Greek philosophy ("Whatever has been well said belongs to us"), especially a kind of religious-minded, eclectic Platonism mixed with Stoicism which was characteristic of the 2d century. His philosophical approach was not unlike that of Philo and it was carried forward in the Christian school of Alexandria, especially by Clement.

In setting forth the meaning and nature of revelation, not confined to the Old Testament but also present among some Greek thinkers, he made use of the Stoic conception of the "seminal Logos" which, in part speaking through Greek martyr-teachers such as Socrates, Heraclitus, and the 1st-century Stoic Musonius Rufus, was incarnate only in Jesus (to whom in the *Dialogue* he applies the Philonic title, the "second God"). Justin does not quote the Prologue to John in support of this doctrine, but since he knew the book, he must have interpreted the Johannine Logos in this way. At least implicit in his combination of Logos doctrine and fulfillment of prophecy is a Christian theology of history, though he did not fully work it out.

In describing Christian worship, he discusses Baptism and the Eucharist, mentioning the Words of Institution and intimating that the elements were closely related to the body of Jesus. During Eucharistic worship, conducted by a "president," readings were provided from the writings of "prophets or apostles." He never mentions the Pauline letters, though he alludes to them; more important are the "reminiscences of the apostles," written either by apostles or by their disciples. He quotes from or alludes to all four Gospels, and in addition he makes use of oral tradition still circulating in his time.

Because of his fame among Christians as a philosopher (his pupil Tatian referred to him as "most marvelous"), later writings were sometimes ascribed to him by those who wanted them to acquire the prestige of antiquity. Thus the *Exposition of Orthodox Faith*, written in the 5th century by Theodoret, was regularly ascribed to Justin in the 6th century and later.

In fact he was not a philosopher. He made use of some philosophical terminology and ideas in order to commend Christianity to its opponents, but his starting point was the revelation provided by God through the inspired prophets of the Old Testament and confirmed by the incarnation. It is significant that his martyrdom took place in the reign of a philosopher-emperor (Marcus Aurelius) and under a prefect of Rome who was also concerned with philosophy. The martyr acts, however, are not concerned with philosophy but with acceptance or rejection of the Christian faith and its eschatology. Justin's judge advocated "piety"; Justin spoke of the Lord Jesus Christ and was beheaded.

His intention as a Christian teacher was to press philosophy into the service of faith; he thus stood at the beginning of the line of those who developed philosophical theologies. Even the later writers who criticized philosophy more severely than he did made use of his method and of his works (Tatian, Tertullian), for his theology was intended to be both Biblical and rational.

BIBLIOGRAPHY: R. M. Grant (ed.), *The Apostolic Fathers*, Vol. 1 (New York, 1964); A. Roberts and J. Donaldson (eds.), *The Ante-Nicene Fathers*, Vol. I (Grand Rapids, 1950); L. W. Barnard, *Justin Martyr: His Life and Thought* (Cambridge, 1967); H. Chadwick, *Early Christian Thought and the Classical Tradition* (New York, 1966); E. J. Goodspeed and R. M. Grant, *A History of Early Christian Literature* (Chicago, 1966).

**Juvenal of Jerusalem** (d. 458). Bishop of Jerusalem from c. 421. Cyril of Alexandria disapproved of Juvenal's desire to elevate the see of Jerusalem above metropolitan to patriarchal rank, yet needed Juvenal's support in the controversy with Nestorius. For political advantage, Juvenal switched his support in the interim between the Councils of Ephesus and Chalcedon, moving from the Monophysite to the Orthodox position. For a time the Monophysites under the monk Theodosius were able to hold the upper hand in Jerusalem, but in 453 the emperor reinstated Juvenal.

**Juvencus, Caius Vettius Aquilinus.** Early 4th-century Christian poet and Spanish presbyter. During the reign of Constantine he wrote the *Historica Evangelica*. A poem in hexameters and exceeding 3,000 lines was attributed to him by Jerome. It pictures events in the life of Christ, taking considerable material from Matthew, but also including substantial parts of John. The author shows a knowledge of the Latin poets Ovid and Vergil.

# K

**Kabbalah.** Jewish mysticism. Its major expression is the *Sefer ha-Zohar* ("Book of Splendor," late 13th century), which sums up the development of Hasidism and mysticism after, at the latest, the 12th century. Kabbalah flourished in Spain, and, after the expulsion of the Jews in 1492, developed even more richly in Safad in Galilee. Christians, of whom the first was Pico della Mirandola, followed by Reuchlin and Paracelsus, were fascinated by this teaching. It reflected Neoplatonic and even Gnostic speculations, and interpreted the letters of the Hebrew alphabet and the text of the Old Testament mystically to reveal secret teaching.

**Kaehler, Martin** (1835–1912). German systematic theologian. He taught at Halle from 1860 until 1864, spending the next few years at Bonn and returning to Halle in 1867. His most important writing, *The So-called Historical Jesus and the Historic Biblical Christ* (1892, 1896; rev., 1956; English translation, 1964), an antiliberal work, was rooted in his view of the Bible as "documents of Church-founding preaching." Along with Kaehler's other books, it was misunderstood by his contemporaries, but brought him posthumous fame in the post-Bultmannian era.

**Kagawa, Toyohiko** (1888–1960). Japanese religious leader and social reformer. Born in Kobe, Japan, of a wealthy family, he was educated in Buddhist monasteries and became Christian at fifteen, greatly influenced by the American missionaries C. A. Logan and H. W. Myers. Disinherited by his family, Kagawa studied at Meiji Christian College in Tokyo and the Presbyterian seminary at Kobe, where he became conscious of Christian responsibility amid social evil. In 1909 he entered the Shinkawa slums to work among the poor. From 1914 to 1916 he studied at Princeton Seminary, but returned to Japan in 1917 to help improve social conditions. He established churches, schools, missions, kindergartens, nurseries, and in 1921 founded the first Japanese Labor Union and first Peasant Union. In 1923 he organized relief work after the Yokohama earthquake; in 1928 he founded the National Anti-War League; in 1930 he established the Kingdom of God movement to promote Christian conversion and received 225,000 Japanese decision cards. He later became chairman of the Mission to Lepers, of Medical Co-operative, of Credit Co-operative, of Tree Crop Agricultural Research Institute; president of All Japan Farmers' Association; of *Christian News Weekly*. During the war he was arrested twice and was forbidden to preach. After the war he became a leader of the democratic movement in Japan and was appointed to the Japanese House of Peers in 1946. He is the author of 180 books on religion, social conditions, science, and poetry which reflect many spiritual writers and mystics of the West.

**Kaiserswerth.** Rhineland town now incorporated into Düsseldorf, where Theodor Fliedner, founder of the diaconate order in the Lutheran Church, established the first motherhouse in 1836. It is now the headquarters for the German branch of the order comprising some 28,000 sisters in 72 motherhouses. The order is associated with the Kaiserswerth General Conference, established in 1861 by Fliedner, comprising some 22 overseas houses organized for hospital services.

**Kandy, Pontifical Seminary of.** A school established at Kandy, Ceylon, in 1890, by Pope Leo XIII to standardize on a higher level the theological education of native secular priests recruited in the Far East. Staffed by professors of the Society of Jesus, it is one of three colleges entitled to the designation "pontifical" and is under the immediate direction of the Sacred College of the Propagation of the Faith, which is charged with missionary responsibility.

**Kant, Immanuel** (1724–1804). German philosopher. He was born and educated, taught and died, in the city of Königsberg; during his entire life he apparently did not set foot outside the province of East Prussia. The son of a poor harness maker, he entered the University of Königsberg in 1740 as a student of theology and completed his doctorate, becoming a lecturer at the university in 1755. Not until 1770 did he gain promotion to a full professorship in philosophy. During his early career he was almost completely under the influence of the Enlightenment (particularly the thought of Leibnitz and Christian Wolff); his was a thoroughgoing rationally governed system of knowledge based on an a priori metaphysical structure. Wolff had, with Scholastic orthodoxy, assumed the ability of reason to operate beyond the circle of human experience without ever examining its competence to do so. The positive contribution of Kant to philosophy came as a result of his examination and rejection of that competence. After a decade of nonproductivity following his inauguration address, Kant in 1781 published the first work of his "critical" period, the *Critique of Pure Reason*; then in succession followed his *Critique of Practical Reason* (1788) and the *Critique of Judgment* (1790), and in 1793 his *Religion Within the Limits of Reason Alone*. In these works this philosopher, who never departed from his basic rational assumption of the intelligibility and rationality of all that is and the unity of all truth, set forth the problems of knowledge with which philosophy has wrestled ever since. For this act alone Kant may properly be known as the father of modern epistemology (theory of knowledge).

As Kant struggled with the problem that lay behind the rationalistic system of his early years—the competence of reason to gain theoretical knowledge of that which lies beyond experience, i.e., to construct metaphysics—he came in contact with the thought of the Scot, David Hume, who, according to Kant, "awakened me from my dogmatic slumber." The influence of Hume here should not be overestimated, for he apparently substantiated more than originated Kant's thinking. Kant did not follow Hume into his radical phenomenology, not being willing to relegate reason to a purely analytic function.

The question that gives rise to the "critical" works is, How are the ideas within the human mind which we associate with reason and which are present there before the mind is stimulated by a particular sense experience (a priori) united (synthesized) with sense experience in the making of a theoretical judgment about that experience, as is done particularly in Newtonian physics? Kant was conscious of such a network of ideas through which all experience passes and by means of which it is ordered in the natural sciences. First of all, sense data come in terms of time and space and then are judged or "understood" in terms of twelve rational categories (twelve in all arranged under the heads: quantity, quality, relation, and modality). These are not found in sense experience but are joined with it in the act of cognition. For Kant, this meant two things: first, that man does not know the objects from which sense experiences arise (*Dinge an sich* or noumena), but knows them only as mingled with his ideas or reason as they appear to him in terms of time and space, etc. (phenomena). Secondly, since all theoretical knowledge is a synthesis of reason and sense stimulation, that kind of knowledge cannot be extended beyond the circle of sense experience, for reason is there required to work in a vacuum. On this basis, Kant proceeds to annihilate the Scholastic arguments for the existence of God (ontological, teleological, and cosmological). In short, he undercut the metaphysical basis for orthodox and rationalistic dogmatics.

In so doing, it was not Kant's intention to destroy, but to make way for something better —"to remove knowledge to make room for faith." To be sure, God, freedom, and immortality are not discovered by means of pure reason, but on the other hand may be seen as necessary postulates of the "practical reason," the moral consciousness. Kant held that within man is immediate consciousness of unconditioned "oughtness" (categorical imperative) which requires, first, that he be free to follow its command, second, that a validator for that moral sense exist (God), and, finally, that a realm exist in which that moral law will be vindicated (immortality). On this ground,

Kant proceeds to the construction of his "religion within the bounds of reason alone."

Finally, in his *Critique of Judgment,* Kant pulls his system together by postulating the drawing of all discordant elements in moral and theoretical reason into a harmonic whole that is expressed subjectively in the symbol of beauty, reflecting the true unity of all reason.

BIBLIOGRAPHY: I. Kant, *Lectures on Ethics* (New York, 1963); and *Religion Within the Limits of Reason Alone* (New York, 1960); G. Rabel (ed. and tr.), *Kant* (New York, 1963).

L. Beck, *Commentary on Kant's Critique of Practical Reason* (Chicago, 1960); H. J. Paton, *The Categorical Imperative* (New York, 1947).

**Karlovtsy Sobor.** Synod of the Russian Church Abroad held at Sremski Karlovtsy, Yugoslavia, in 1921. In opposition to the Bolsheviks and to those within the church who sought a *modus vivendi* with the Communist regime, the council elected a synod of bishops to appropriate the administrative powers of the church and called for a restoration of the monarchy.

**Kasatkin, Ivan** (1836–1912). Russian missionary bishop. He took monastic vows in 1859 and changed his name to Nikolay. In 1861 he was sent as chaplain to the Russian Embassy, first in Hakodate and then in Tokyo, where he began missionary work among the Japanese. He won the support of the Holy Synod for his missionary enterprise and was made bishop in 1880 and archbishop of Japan in 1906. From the very beginning he stressed the importance of training Japanese catechists and priests. Thanks to these farsighted policies, the Orthodox Church in Japan survived the subsequent crises of the 20th century, and has continued its progress to the present day.

**Kattenbusch, Ferdinand** (1851–1935). German historical and systematic theologian. Kattenbusch modified only slightly the views of Ritschl, whose pupil he was, becoming professor at Giessen in 1878, at Göttingen in 1904, and in 1906 at Halle. Kattenbusch's main work, *Das apostolische Symbol* (2 vols., 1894, 1900), was a historical study of the old Roman baptismal creed. Other works discussed the Reformation confessions, the theology of Luther, which he considered of paramount importance, and various systematic and historical problems.

**Kaunitz, Wenzel Anton von** (1711–1794). Chancellor of Austria (1753–1792), count of Rietberg (1764), a prime figure in the politics of late 18th-century Europe. Kaunitz was deeply influenced by the Encyclopedists. He was associated with Voltaire and Rousseau, and was a student of the rationalist politics of the Enlightenment. In the time of Maria Theresa he shaped the church-state relationship in Austria which came to be known under her son and successor as Josephinism.

**Keble, John** (1792–1866). Anglican priest and leading figure among Tractarians. Following a brilliant career at Corpus Christi, Oxford, he was named to Oriel as fellow (1811) and tutor (1817) after ordination (1816). Upon the death of his mother (1823), he resigned his fellowship and returned to the Cotswolds to live with his father, assisting him in his rural parish and with his brothers serving some small curacies near Coln. There he composed the poems published in *Christian Year* (1827). He was professor of poetry at Oxford from 1831 to 1841 and among his associates found others like himself conscious of the threat to the Church of England in liberal and reform movements. After his assize sermon in 1833, published under the title *National Apostasy*, he assumed a leading role in the Oxford movement and assisted John Henry Newman in writing *Tracts for the Times* of which some seven were his. He was vicar of Hursley, Hampshire, from 1836. His publications included an edition of the *Works* of Richard Hooker and he assisted Newman and Pusey in editing the *Remains* of R. H. Froude, the latter arousing a storm of protest because of its Romanizing tone (1838–1839). After Newman's submission to Rome (1845), Keble joined forces with Pusey to prevent further secessions. Of his remaining works, e.g., poetry (*Psalter*, 1839; *Lyra innocentium*, 1846) and biography (a life of the 18th-century bishop of Sodor and Man, Thomas Wilson), none reaches the importance of his controversial writing on the necessity of apostolic succession in the Church of England and the centrality of the Eucharist as a means of salvation stressing Real Presence. After his death a college was founded at Oxford (1870) in his memory and named for him.

**Keith, George** (1638–1716). A Scotsman who became a Quaker c. 1664. Keith was disowned by his coreligionists for his insistence on objective theological foundations after he came to America in 1685. However, a schismatic group followed him, and he went to England, where he was ordained an Anglican priest. In 1702 he became one of the first missionaries of the Society for the Propagation of the Gospel to labor in the American

colonies, working particularly among the Quakers.

**Keller, Adolf** (1872–    ). Swiss Reformed minister. Keller was a member of the group which prepared the New Testament text used in Moffatt's translation. He was pastor in Geneva (1899–1909) and Zurich (1909–1924), director of the European Central Bureau for Relief (1924–1945), and consultant to the World Council of Churches Department of Reconstruction and Inter-Church Aid from 1945. From 1925 to 1937 he was European representative to the Federal Council of Churches. Author of half a dozen books, he interpreted the theological and ecumenical life of the European churches to America in the twenties and thirties.

**Kells, Book of.** An illuminated manuscript of the text of the Gospels in Latin, with some local Irish records. The work received its name from the monastery of Kells in eastern Ireland, where it was written sometime during the 8th century. Now in the library of Trinity College, Dublin, this manuscript is one of the best surviving examples of early Christian art. The ornamental illumination of manuscripts flourished in Irish and Northumbrian monasteries during the 7th and 8th centuries.

**Kenry of Langenstein** (d. 1397). German ascetic theologian, scientist, and conciliar theorist. He denounced the use of comets as omens and was unsympathetic to popular prophecy and astrology. He wrote eighteen treatises on the Great Western Schism, the most important the *Epistola concilii pacis* of 1381. He argued, on the basis of the work of his friend Conrad von Gelnhausen, that a general council was the most convenient and the best way of solving the Schism and the one authorized by the fathers. He added the demand that reform was as important as unity and that regular reform councils would be necessary even in a united church. He had to leave Paris because of his position. He died in 1397 while teaching in the theological faculty of the University of Vienna.

**Kepler, Johann** (1571–1630). German astronomer and mathematician whose discovery of the working of the solar system was a major achievement of supreme importance to astronomy. Originally intending to become a Protestant pastor, Kepler attended the University of Tübingen, where he became deeply interested in astronomy instead. In 1594, he began his career as professor of astronomy at Gratz, after which he served for a time as the assistant of Tycho Brahe, the noted Danish astronomer. Brahe died in 1601. Kepler, building upon the work of his former master, enjoyed a distinguished and fruitful career of his own during which he discovered a nova since known as Kepler's star, wrote many books on astronomy in general, studied comets, produced a treatise on optics propounding the first correct theory of vision, exchanged ideas with Galileo, defended Copernicus, and formulated his now famous three laws of planetary motion. His laws were probably his greatest contribution to astronomy, since they removed many objections to a heliocentric solar system while at the same time demonstrating Kepler's talent for applying hypothesis to observation. The first two of these laws appeared in Kepler's *New Astronomy* in 1609, and the third ten years later in his *Epitome of Copernican Astronomy*. In his religious views, Kepler inclined toward pantheism, taking the solar system, particularly, as a manifestation of the divine.

**Keswick Convention.** A convention organized after the first preaching tour of Moody and Sankey by some Church of England Evangelicals for the "promoting of practical holiness" with prayer, Bible study, and preaching. It has met annually on the grounds of St. John's, Keswick, Cumberland, England, for a week in late July, attracting a large number of foreign visitors. Conservative in orientation, the convention publishes an annual report, *Keswick Week*.

**Ketteler, Baron Wilhelm Emmanuel von** (1811–1877). German Roman Catholic bishop and social reformer. After a brief career in the Prussian civil service, Ketteler studied theology at Munich and was ordained in 1844. He first came to the public eye as a delegate to the Frankfurt Parliament in 1848. In that same year, at Mainz, he gave a series of sermons which became the foundation for German Catholic social reform. Made bishop of Mainz in 1850, he increased his writing and action against the structure created by liberal capitalism. He felt that the Christian life could scarcely be lived under the "slave market" economy of modern industrial society, and in 1869, at a conference of German bishops, proposed certain features of the economic regime that would have to be changed. His great contribution was to awaken the social conscience of Catholics, but he was active in other areas. Though not taken with the views of liberal Catholics, he was an "inopportunist" at the Vatican Council. He sat as a deputy in the Reichstag until the coming of the Kulturkampf. His *The Catholics of the Empire* (1873) helped form a basis for the Catholic Center Party. He founded the

Sisters of Providence and the Brothers of St. Joseph. His great concern was for the "social deaconry" of the church.

**Khlysty** ("Flagellants"). Russian dissident sect originating at the end of the 17th century. It recognized both male and female spiritual leaders (Prophets and Prophetesses), those who had received the visitation of the Holy Spirit. The members believed in the perpetual reincarnation of Christ in the person of the Khlysty leader. The ritual aspect of their faith was strongly infused with elements of paganism and religious frenzy.

**Khomiakov, Aleksei S.** (1804–1860). Russian philosopher, poet, and lay theologian. The foremost advocate of Slavophilism, he championed the view that Russia's mission was the salvation of Western civilization. Russia alone could escape the decay that was enveloping the West as the result of its false philosophical foundations, for native Russian institutions avoided both the "unnatural tyranny" of Roman Catholicism and the "unprincipled revolt" of Protestantism. On the spiritual level, Russian moral superiority was evidenced by the concept of *sobornost* (conciliarity) pervading the Russian Orthodox Church, the fusion of the individual in the congregation of believers. Valid religious experience derived from the social and spiritual harmony of the individual and the community of the faithful. On the secular level, a counterpart of *sobornost* existed in the native Russian peasant commune, the *mir*. Unlike other Slavophiles, Khomiakov did not oppose all elements of Western culture. An amateur inventor and engineer, he welcomed material progress and praised Peter the Great for having prodded Russia out of its cultural stagnation, but at the same time he decried the materialism that had subjugated spiritual values, social harmony, and justice.

**Khrapovitsky, Anthony** (1863–1936). Metropolitan of Kiev, leader of the conservative faction of the Russian Church. At one time rector of the Moscow Theological Academy, he later became metropolitan of Kiev. After the Revolution he left Russia to become president of the Synod of the Russian Church Abroad, which met at Sremski Karlovtsy in Yugoslavia in 1921. This group saw the Revolution as God's punishment of the Russian people for their infidelity and urged the prompt restoration of the monarchy.

**Kierkegaard, Søren** (1813–1855). Danish author and philosopher known as the father of modern existentialism. He was born in

Copenhagen and spent most of his life there. The youngest son of a wealthy woolen draper, he was inheritor of his father's near-pathological melancholy and Christian piety dominated by that same spirit. During his stay at the university he rebelled against his pietistic upbringing by profligate living and Hegelian philosophy. His ultimate rejection of subethical living and the "system" of Hegel furnish major clues to his subsequent life and thinking. In 1838, Kierkegaard experienced a religious conversion and completed a theological education, passing his examination in 1840. His thesis was on Socratic irony, a factor which, added to his Christian sense of guilt, formed the style that was to characterize his literary efforts. During the year that followed he became engaged to Regina Olsen but in a rather unusual manner broke the engagement, apparently because he felt that his melancholy and some secret that underlay it must certainly destroy his mate. Very closely related to this event, his literary career took its genesis from it. In conjunction with short stays in Berlin (1841–1843) Kierkegaard began the feverish literary activity which was to continue through the next dozen years and in which he embodied his thought. Major among these works are *Either/Or, Fear and Trembling,* and *Repetition* (1843), *Philosophical Fragments* (1844), *Stages on Life's Way* (1845), *Concluding Unscientific Postscript* (1846), *The Sickness Unto Death* (1849), *Training in Christianity* (1850), and *Attack Upon Christendom* (1854–1855). The later years of his life were embittered by conflict: first, with the radical satirical weekly *The Corsair,* which in response to his attack of New Year's, 1846, made him the object of malicious ridicule for a number of months and subjected him to deep injury. His second conflict was with the church. In response to a eulogy delivered by Professor Martensen at the death of Bishop Mynster, Kierkegaard penned a newspaper article full of the most indignant protest (Dec. 18, 1854). This began a battle in which he embodied his "attack upon Christendom" first in journal articles and finally in a series of pamphlets entitled *The Instant.* Completely drained by this conflict, the forty-two-year-old philosopher collapsed in the street in October, 1855, and died a month later, refusing to the last to accept the ministrations of a "fallen" church.

Kierkegaard's attack upon the church must be seen as the culmination of his life and teachings. The rationalistic conception of Christianity that had dominated the Western Church since Aquinas had met an impasse in Kant's separation between theoretical reason and actual existence, rejecting knowledge of the latter. Hegel had attempted in his system to bring existence back into play by superimposing thought upon it in "history." Kierkegaard rejected on the one hand Kant's choice of reason over existence, and on the other Hegel's effort to reconcile the two. The melancholy Dane's choice of the existing subject over the intelligible object as the locus of reality marks what may ultimately be seen as the end of a line of thinking that dates back to the ancient Greeks. With reason relegated to the lowest plane of human operation, Kierkegaard saw life as lived on three planes. On the lowest, the "aesthetic" (feeling and thinking) plane, the individual is merely a spectator, even of his own life. This is the level at which Kierkegaard finds almost all his contemporaries living, encouraged both by their infatuation with Hegelian speculation and by "churchly" Christianity. The second plane is the "ethical," at which the person by means of decision takes responsibility for himself. This is the stage of authentic existence. Yet, broken by ethical failure, finite man is driven in despair to cast himself upon the one instance of infinity available in finitude—the God-man, Jesus Christ. This is the ultimate decision for Kierkegaard and is constantly in the process of renewal—an act of raw nerve born of despair. With such a view of Christian faith, the ease and complacence of his church with its debasement of the Holy God and its well-lubricated facilities for effecting faith was for Kierkegaard the ultimate offense. Thus he attacked first the Hegelian system that it was using and, finally, with the full wrath of his Attic wit, the church itself. Kierkegaard was ignored by his age, and it remained for the 20th century to appreciate his genius.

BIBLIOGRAPHY: R. Bretall (ed.), *A Kierkegaard Anthology* (Princeton, 1946); J. E. Hohlenberg, *Sören Kierkegaard* (New York, 1954); R. Jolivet, *Introduction to Kierkegaard* (New York, 1952); W. Lowrie, *Kierkegaard,* 2 vols. (New York, 1962); R. Thomte, *Kierkegaard's Philosophy of Religion* (Princeton, 1948).

**Kiev Academy.** A school founded in 1631 by Peter Mogila on the model of Western universities. It was the center of Orthodox culture and the disseminator of European learning. Former pupils played a role in the reforms of Nikon and Peter the Great. The Academy served as a pattern for schools in Russia and the Ukraine and survived as a theological school until after the Bolshevik Revolution.

**Kievo-Petcherskaya Monastery.** The famous Cave Monastery at Kiev. Hilarion, the first native Russian metropolitan, seeking a solitary dwelling in which to meditate, dug a cave near Kiev. Not far from the site of Hilarion's hermitage, the abbot Theodosius (d. 1074) established the Monastery of the Caves. The rule was patterned on that of the monastery which Theodore of Studium had built at Constantinople, and it set the pattern for future monasticism in Russia.

**Kikuyu Controversy.** A missionary conference of Anglicans, Presbyterians, and other Christians held at Kikuyu, British East Africa, in 1913, which under the guidance of the bishops of Uganda and Mombasa proposed intercommunion and federation of the churches. The bishop of Zanzibar, who opposed the plan bitterly, appealed to the archbishop of Canterbury. He ruled that nonconformists might receive Communion in the Anglican churches but Anglicans could not do so in nonconformist churches.

**Kilian** (d. 689). One of the Irish missionary bishops who worked at Würzburg in Franconia together with eleven companions. He converted Duke Gozbert, but made an enemy of the duke's wife, Geilana. Through her influence Kilian and two of his companions, Colman and Totman, were beheaded while the duke was absent. Kilian's reputation for ascetic sanctity caused many to seek burial near his tomb at Würzburg, where the three are still venerated.

**King, Henry Churchill** (1858–1934). American educator and theologian. Born in Hillsdale, Mich., King studied at Hillsdale College, Oberlin College, Oberlin Theological Seminary, Harvard University, and in Germany, where he came under the influence of Lotze's philosophy and Ritschl's theology. In 1884 he returned to Oberlin, where he served in various capacities until his retirement in 1927. In 1902 he was elected sixth president of Oberlin. King became nationally prominent as a theologian with the publication of *Reconstruction in Theology* (1901) and *Theology and the Social Consciousness* (1902). He was in demand as a lecturer and leader of religious and educational movements. A spokesman for "evangelical" liberalism in theology, he believed that historic Christianity could and must come to terms with the modern world without giving up essential orthodoxy.

**King's Book** (or *Necessary Doctrine and Erudition for any Christian Man*) (1543). The fourth doctrinal statement of the Henrician reformation, issued with royal authority. Basically a revision of the Bishop's Book, it denounced papal abuses as well as Luther's "solifidianism." "Catholic" doctrines such as transubstantiation are affirmed, but papal claims are rejected. The book was promulgated as "a true statement of the old catholic doctrine free from both the leaven of papacy and the poison of heresy."

**King's Confession** (or Second Scots Confession). A statement drawn up in 1581 among the Scottish Presbyterians to forestall a revival of Catholicism upon the recent coming of the French duke of Lennox to Scotland. In 1560 the Scottish Parliament had ratified a confession of faith that was largely the work of Knox. Its twenty-five articles incorporated the theological views of the Reformed Scottish churches. In 1581 a second confession was drafted by John Craig. It was signed by James VI and called the King's Confession. Incorporating the older confession, it further rejected alleged "popish errors" and all episcopal theories of church government. It provided the basis for the National Covenant of 1638.

**Kingsley, Charles** (1819–1875). English cleric, social reformer, and novelist. Born at Holne and educated at King's College, London, and Cambridge, Kingsley was ordained in 1842. From that moment until his death Kingsley led a varied life as playwright, novelist, chaplain to Queen Victoria (1859), professor of modern history (1860–1869), and canon of Westminster (1873). Under the influence of F. D. Maurice, he became a leader in the Christian Socialist movement. During this period he wrote his novels *Alton Locke* (1850) and *Yeast* (1851), in which he showed sympathy with the aims of the Chartists for political reform, though disapproving of their violent policies. His reforming spirit was tempered, however, by the fact that in his view a peer and a dean were the true leaders of the people, and he looked to the extension of the cooperative principle and to sanitary reform for the amelioration of the poor. He was, moreover, bitterly opposed to all forms of asceticism and therefore argued forcefully with the members of the Tractarian movement and J. H. Newman. In time he came to be an advocate of what was somewhat derisively called "muscular Christianity." His chief theological works were *Twenty-five Sermons* (1849), *Sermons on National Subjects* (1852 and 1854), *The Good News of God* (1859), and the posthumously published *All Saints' Day and Other Sermons* (1878).

**Kino, Eusebio Francisco** (c. 1645–1711). Italian Jesuit missionary to America and cartographer. He joined the Society of Jesus in 1663, and studied at Innsbruck and Ingolstadt in Germany, later taking up astronomy at Cádiz, Spain. In 1681 he landed at Veracruz, Mexico, and two years afterward charted lower California, which he thought at first was a "large island." In 1687 he went to the province of Sonora, Mexico, and established a series of missions, the most famous being San Xavier del Bac outside of Tucson, Ariz., which is still used as a mission church for Papago Indians. He died in Magdalena, Ariz.

**Kirchentag.** A general term in German applying to any assembly of churches or churchmen, now more specifically used of the Deutsche Evangelische Kirchentag (German Evangelical Church Assembly), a movement begun in 1949. Kirchentag is to be distinguished from two previous movements bearing the same name: (1) one from 1848 to 1872 begun under the leadership of P. Wackernagel; (2) one from 1919 to 1930, a series of rallies sponsored by the German Evangelical Church Federation. At the conclusion of the Evangelical Week of the German Student Union at Hannover in 1949, a new organization was founded, the German Evangelical Church Assembly independent of the German Evangelical Church, with the purposes of renewing personal faith and commitment to the church and of encouraging the laity to effectuate Christian responsibility in all secular activities. Held annually from 1949 to 1954, these assemblies combined study and discussion on the part of a central core of participants, lasting some five days, with a great final rally on Sunday. Meeting biennially since 1954, they alternate with the Catholic counterpart that assembles on intervening years. Each assembly has a central theme developed by some six commissions that are a part of the continuing organization located at Fulda. Stressing ecumenicity and lay action, the Kirchentag movement has not only revitalized German Christianity and strengthened ties between East and West German Christians, but has also inspired similar movements in Switzerland, France, Denmark, Scotland, Holland, and Indonesia.

**Kireyevski, Ivan** (1806–1856), and **Peter** (1808–1856). Russian philosophers and early advocates of Slavophilism. Ivan was initially an enthusiastic admirer of the West and an adherent of German philosophy, condemning the Russia of his own day and insisting that its only hope lay in emulating the West. A religious crisis in the late 1830's led him to revise his views. He remained critical of contemporary Russia but thereafter declared that its necessary social and spiritual transformation could be achieved only by a return to the principles and values of pre-Petrine Russia. Peter the Great had disrupted the organic evolution of Russian society by introducing alien (Western) principles and institutions which were leading Russia toward the same decadence that had enveloped the West. His adulation of "old Russia" was viewed by the reactionary regime of Nicholas I as a radical (rather than a conservative) critique, since it involved a rejection of the secular, autocratic, and bureaucratic assumptions of the Russian state.

Peter wrote little, but expressed his Slavophile views by seeking to revitalize popular customs and ancient native traditions. He is best known for his collections of old Russian folk songs which had never before been written down.

**Kirk, Edward Norris** (1802–1874). A popular antebellum Congregational evangelist. Unlike most revivalists of his day, Kirk responded to the panic of 1837 by emphasizing the importance of ferreting out the causes of poverty and applying a remedy. When he settled in a Congregational church in Boston in 1842, his work among some young men there became the setting for the organization of the first Young Men's Christian Association in the United States (1851), which served as an exemplification of his concerns.

**Kliefoth, Theodor Friedrich Dethlof** (1810–1895). Lutheran ecclesiastical reformer. He was associated from 1850 with the superior ecclesiastical court of Mecklenburg and was its president from 1886. A strict Lutheran, he fought against state domination of the church and absorption of his church into union schemes. The reforms he instituted in polity, liturgics, and theology aroused the opposition of liberals, Pietists, and those suspicious of hierarchicalism.

**Klopstock, Friedrich Gottlieb** (1724–1803). German religious poet. His *Der Messias*, the first epic in modern German, was based on a translation of John Milton's *Paradise Lost*, and consists of some twenty thousand lines in twenty cantos spanning the passion of Jesus and the forty days following the resurrection. Other poems include religious lyrics, panegyrics of earlier Germany, and a number of religious dramas in the bardic tradition.

**Knapp, Albert** (1798–1864). German writer, reviser of hymns and lieder, religious poet of renown. An orthodox Christian pastor, he avoided extremes of confessionalism as is evident in some eight volumes of spiritual poetry and an Evangelical hymnal (1837) in which he selected and revised over three thousand hymns. The "modernism" of his hymnody aroused the opposition of church officials, although the hymnal went through several editions.

**Knapp, Georg Christian** (1753–1825). German theologian. After studying at Halle and Göttingen, he became professor of New Testament and dogmatics at Halle (1777). He resisted the introduction of rationalism into Pietist Halle, and strongly championed supernaturalism. He also displayed a keen interest in missionary work. His main writings are expositions of orthodox belief according to the Biblical norm.

**Knights of Columbus.** Probably the best known of Roman Catholic fraternal organizations in the United States. The Knights of Columbus was organized in Connecticut in 1882 and spread rapidly to every state in the union and to much of the rest of the hemisphere. Their charitable work, their nation-wide proselytizing campaigns on behalf of the Catholic faith, and their insurance program have become well known.

**Know-Nothing Party.** A political party that emerged in the 1850's as an expression of periodic American anti-Catholicism. The Order of United Americans, popularly designated as the Know-Nothings, was not only openly anti-Catholic but advocated that only native-born Protestants should be eligible for public office. The party gained control of several state legislatures, but saw its influence rather quickly abate in favor of more pressing issues.

**Knox, John** (c. 1513–1572). Scottish Reformation leader. Little is known of the early life of Knox. Reared at Haddington, he attended the University of St. Andrews and studied under John Major. Returning to his home, he pursued the work of schoolmaster and notary. He was confronted with Reformation views by his association with George Wishart, who refused to let Knox become involved when Archbishop Beaton instigated his arrest and subsequent execution. Knox's first preaching was to the Scots who were taking refuge in the castle of St. Andrews after the retaliatory murder of Beaton.

Scotland had been well prepared for revolution. Touched by the intellectual ferment of the day and shamed by clerical excesses, the Scots were straining toward a purer and simpler faith. James V, suspicious of Henry VIII, had refused to lead Scotland in a separation

from Rome and had come to rely more upon Roman Catholic France. His death in 1542 left his infant daughter, Mary, as heir, under a regent holding some Reformation sympathies. However, the assassination of Beaton caused the regent to call in the French fleet, which subdued the Scots at St. Andrews (1547), at the same time making Knox a prisoner. He had been caught up in Scotland's political and ecclesiastical struggles.

Knox spent nineteen months as a prisoner in a French galley. English influence during the reign of Edward VI effected his release. With the Reformation tide so strong in England, Knox became a royal chaplain there and a preacher of some repute. On the accession of Mary Tudor he fled to the Continent. Eventually he became minister to the English congregation in Geneva, working in full accord with Calvin and endorsing most of his religious and political views. Enthusiastic for Calvinism, Knox returned to Scotland for ten months in 1555 and 1556. Since many of the nobility had accepted Protestant views, the preaching of Knox was tolerated, but when he wrote a letter to Mary of Lorraine, the queen-mother regent, urging her conversion, he was forced back to Geneva. At Knox's suggestion many of the nobles banded together for mutual support. This covenant of 1557 was the first of the bands that were so very important in Scottish Reformation history. These "lords of the congregation" invited Knox to return and complete the Reformation. In opposition to England's Elizabeth I, the policies of the regent had become even more Roman Catholic and French. In 1559, the year Knox came back to Scotland to stay, the regent summoned the Reformation preachers to stand trial at Stirling. Instead, they met at Perth, where their presence sparked a demonstration against religious houses. Scotland was divided between the party of Knox and that of the regent. The French, supporting the regent, and the English, seeking advantage through the Reformers, contended unsuccessfully and finally settled their differences by withdrawing from Scotland.

Left alone, the Estates of Scotland met in 1560 and overwhelmingly adopted the Scots Confession which Knox had helped to draft. The authority of the bishop of Rome was refused. The Reformed Kirk adopted the Book of Common Order (known as Knox's Liturgy) and the First Book of Discipline. Knox had led the Scottish Church into a reformation following the Calvinist tradition.

As preacher at St. Giles's, Knox boldly denounced Mary Stuart's private Mass at Holyrood as a revival of Romanism. Her Roman

Catholic loyalty and her designs on England were well known, including her marriage to the Roman Catholic Darnley, who stood next to her in line for the English throne. Knox opposed her, an opposition that encouraged the Scots to force her abdication in 1567. Until his death in 1572, Knox continued as a force within the unsettled political and ecclesiastical situation. The fervent preaching of Knox was irresistible to the Scottish chieftains with their traditions of semi-independence. His fearless and successful opposition to regent and queen marked him as a true patriot, but the man himself was the key to his great achievements —tireless, sincere, simple, practical, the real "dour Scot," not without humor and tenderness. His *History of the Reformation of Religioun within the Realme of Scotland* (1584) is an invaluable, but scarcely impartial, chronicle of the events in which he himself played a major role.

BIBLIOGRAPHY: G. MacGregor, *The Thundering Scot* (Philadelphia, 1957); G. R. Preedy, *The Life of John Knox* (London, 1940); E. Whitley, *Plain Mr. Knox* (Richmond, 1954).

**Knox, Ronald Arbuthnott** (1888–1957). English Roman Catholic prelate and writer. The son of a Low Church bishop, Knox took Holy Orders in the Church of England. In 1917 he became a Roman Catholic, driven there by the question of authority. Looked upon by many as the successor of Newman, he translated the Bible for the Catholic hierarchy of England. In addition to three volumes of commentary on the New Testament, his works include *Enthusiasm* and *Let Dons Delight*.

**Koch, Hal** (1904–1963). Danish Lutheran theologian. After study abroad, Koch returned to Copenhagen (1937) as professor in church history, a post he held the rest of his life. From 1940 to 1946 he led the Danish Youth Cooperation and in 1946 founded the Krogerup Folk High School, which he supervised until 1956. In the latter year he founded the Institute for Danish Church History. Influenced by Barth and Grundtvig, he wrote extensively in the field of patristics and Danish church history. From 1938 to 1952 he edited the *Dansk teologisk Tidsskrift* and together with Georg Christensen edited Grundtvig's works.

**Kölping, Adolf** (1813–1865). Father of the Gesellenverein, an association of German Catholic young workers societies dedicated to religious, moral, and professional education of journeymen craftsmen. Of humble birth,

apprenticed as a shoemaker, Kölping finally became a priest (1845) and established the international organization with headquarters at Cologne for which he edited a regular paper. Surviving World War II, the society still continues.

**Koran.** The holy book of the Moslem religion which comprises the verbal revelations of Mohammed as written down by his disciples. Divided into 114 chapters, called "surahs," the Koran is organized not chronologically but roughly according to the length of each surah, progressing from the shortest, the fatihah, to the longest. The subjects dealt with are vast, including both passionate prayer in rhymed meter and rhetorical injunctions. Many of the parables contained in the verses are similar to those found in the Old and New Testaments, which shows that Mohammed was familiar with Semitic religious tradition and considered his religious beliefs to be an extension of that tradition.

The dictates of Mohammed's revelations are not consistent throughout the Koran. This is due to the fact that even though the Prophet often received revelations which in content negated earlier ones, care was taken to record everything he uttered without omission or subtraction. The resulting inconsistencies have posed great problems for interpreters of Moslem law, for whom the Koran is the social and political code of the theocratic state as well as a code of personal ethics.

For purposes of analysis, interpreters of the Koran usually contrast the surahs of revelations that Mohammed received in Mecca with those he received later in Medina. Stylistically, the Meccan surahs are richer in poetic content and, on the whole, convey otherworldly ideas, particularly descriptions of such events as the Last Judgment. Those of Medina, received while Mohammed was in the process of establishing a theocratic state, are often more direct in style and deal with more immediate social topics.

**Kottwitz, Hans Ernst, Baron von** (1757–1843). Leading personage of the Berlin Awakening in the 19th century. In attempting to help the poor by giving them employment, Kottwitz lost much of his industrial substance, but his accomplishments have marked him as a forerunner of the Inner Mission. Influential in high places, he used his connections to secure appointments for theologians of the Awakening and has been credited with preventing that movement from becoming a sect.

**Koven, James de** (1831–1879). Episcopal priest. Koven was a leader of the "ritualistic group" in the post-Civil War period. Graduating from Columbia College (1851) and General Theological Seminary (1854), he was ordained by Bishop Kemper (1855) and taught ecclesiastical history at Nashotah House until he became warden of Racine College (1859). He successfully opposed Low Church efforts to dictate uniformity.

**Kraemer, Hendrik** (1888–1965). Dutch lay missionary and theologian. Serving the Dutch Bible Society in Indonesia from 1921 to 1935, he acted as general adviser of missions. He was a keen student of Islam and Indonesian culture and religion. Under the theological influence of Karl Barth, he prepared a preliminary report for the Tambaram Conference of the International Missionary Council in 1938. In 1937 he became professor of the history and phenomenology of religions in the theological faculty at the University of Leiden, but was interned by the Germans from 1939 to 1945. He was the first director of the Ecumenical Institute at Bossey (1947–1956). Well known as an apologist for Christian doctrine, he was also an ardent promoter of the active role of the laity in the church.

**Krafft, Johann Christian Gottlob Ludwig** (1784–1845). German Protestant theologian. From his professorship at Erlangen after 1818, he exerted great influence as a firm believer in Biblical supranaturalism, convinced that Scripture was wholly the work of the Spirit. Lecturing on almost all phases of theology out of his exegetical studies, he affected a wide circle of thinkers who were responsible for that combination of Scripture and religious experience known as the Awakening.

**Krauth, Charles Porterfield** (1823–1883). American Lutheran theologian. He was successor to his father, Charles Philip Krauth, in his role as the leader of conservative Lutheran forces in the successful struggle to retain the historic Lutheran faith in an American environment. He explicated his theological position in *The Conservative Reformation and Its Theology* (1871), and also devoted his attention to inaugurating a liturgical and sacramental renaissance among Lutherans in America.

**Kruedener, Barbara Juliana, Baroness von** (1764–1824). Russian-born mystic and chiliast who influenced history through the remarkable ascendancy she acquired over Czar Alexander I, whom she met in 1815. Her views were strongly millennial (indeed, she preached the millennium throughout Europe for many years after her conversion by a Moravian shoemaker), and she pictured the conflict between Russia and France as a struggle between the Antichrist (Napoleon I) and the czar, whom she believed to be the destined victor. She also urged upon the czar the project of the Holy Alliance, which was to be a grand alliance of conservative Christian powers in Europe against irreligion and revolution, and which, as a result of the czar's patronage, was adopted by the victorious powers after the defeat of Napoleon.

**Krummacher, Friedrich Adolf** (1767–1845), **Gottfried Daniel** (1774–1837), and **Friedrich Wilhelm** (1796–1868). Family of German Reformed clergymen, leaders in the Awakening on the lower Rhine. Born on July 13, 1767, into a Pietist home, Friedrich Adolf studied theology at Lingen and Halle, and became successively rector of the gymnasium at Mörs (1793), professor of theology at the University of Duisburg (1800), pastor of a rural congregation in the Ruhr, and after declining an invitation to the University of Bonn, one of the ministers in a Bremen congregation (1824–1843). He had great reverence for Scriptural Christianity, which is shown in his religious works, the best known of which are his religious poems for children, *Parabeln* (1809; English translation, 1824). His brother Gottfried studied at Duisburg, where Pietism was strong, and in his first parish at Bärl (1798) he met a Pietist layman who was the first to make him aware of the depth of the Christian experience. In 1801 he became pastor in Wülfrath, and in 1816 he was called to Elberfeld, where his preaching prompted a Pietist revival. He published several volumes of sermons that show his anguish and deep conviction of sin. Friedrich's son, Friedrich Wilhelm, studied at Halle and Jena, and became successively pastor at Frankfurt (1819), Ruhrort (1823), Gemarke in the Wuppertal (1825), and Elberfeld (1834). In 1847 he received an appointment to Trinity Church in Berlin, and in 1853 he became court chaplain at Potsdam. He was an influential promoter of the Evangelical Alliance.

**Kuenen, Abraham** (1828–1891). Dutch theologian and Biblical scholar. Professor in New Testament at Leiden from 1852, also in ethics from 1860, with the reorganization of the faculty he became professor of Old Testament from 1877. One of the leading proponents of the modern school in the debate between the orthodox and the liberals, he developed the Graf hypothesis regarding the P document in the Pentateuch and expounded the Prophets in an anticonservative direction He helped found *Theologische Tijdschrift,* to which he contributed heavily.

**Kukkonen** (Renqvist), **Henrik** (1789–1866). Finnish Lutheran pastor and revival preacher. Changing his name to Renqvist ("clean branch") after his conversion, he insisted that repentance and faith must be followed by a visible purity of life. He demanded total abstinence from alcohol and tobacco. His revival centered around the Karelia district, where the adherents were known as "praying people" because of their custom of kneeling in prayer during their meetings.

**Ku-Klux Klan.** At first a secret association of whites who opposed reconstruction and acted as vigilantes in the absence of civil law. Founded in Tennessee in 1865, the organization adopted a hooded garb and bizarre ritual that was effective in cowing opposition, especially among Negroes. Many members became outlaws and in 1871 and 1872 Congress enacted the Force Bill to break the Klan up. It nevertheless continued to exist with the objectives of protecting whites, limiting the Negro vote, gaining control of government, expelling carpetbaggers and scalawags, and nullifying federal statutes giving Negroes political power. The Grand Wizard was Gen. N. B. Forrest. The second Klan was formed by W. J. Simmons in 1915. A crusade for Protestant Christianity, white supremacy, and nativism, it used extralegal means to bypass "miscarriages of justice." Strongest in the Midwest and South, the Klan had 100,000 members by 1921. It was politically powerful in the 1920's, but faded rapidly after 1928 because of dissensions, power abuses, acts of violence, and corruption. Disbanded by 1944, the Klan was revived by Samuel Green in 1946 and encouraged racial and religious intolerance, opposed civil rights, and formed vigilante groups against radicalism. Violence was often employed. Largely ineffective because of adverse public opinion, the Klan also had its state charters revoked. It was put on the subversive list by the Department of Justice, and was actively prosecuted.

**Kulturkampf.** The anti-Catholic struggle in Germany between state and church during the 1870's. The decree of papal infallibility promulgated by the Vatican Council (1870) and increased Jesuit ecclesiastical power set off violent nationalistic reaction. The nationalistic, anticlerical Liberal Party in the new German empire maintained that political unity depended on unity of religion, language, and education. Bismarck, aware that Protestant Prussia had accomplished the unity of Germany, considered that his empire now stood over against the papacy. Anti-Catholic legislation expelled the Jesuits and brought education under state control. The famous Falk or May laws (1873) were enacted to destroy Catholic power in the country. In response to a condemnatory Vatican encyclical *Quod nunquam* (1875) the state withdrew all financial aid to the Roman Catholic Church.

The political character of the struggle was shown when Bismarck, impressed by the strength of the opposition, made a tactical change in policy to gain Roman Catholic support against the new threat of Social Democracy. He made peace with the new pope, Leo XIII, and entered into a concordat with the Vatican. By 1887 most of the repressive laws, with the exception of the expelling of the Jesuits, had been nullified. The Kulturkampf revived Catholic zeal and resulted in their new interest in national and cultural affairs.

**Kutter, Hermann** (1863–1931). Zurich pastor and leading figure in the development of a socially oriented Christianity. Taking his start from a Christian eschatological view and the socialist optimism for the future, he developed in the context of German idealism a "theocentric theology" in which God "is the only reality of life," explaining human misery as the result of falling away from God. He saw the extraecclesiastical struggle for human justice as indication of an active God.

**Kuyper, Abraham** (1837–1920). Dutch Reformed theologian, churchman, and statesman. A dominant figure in the Netherlands during the last decades of his life, he represented a consistent conservatism. Born in Maassluis and educated at Leiden, he committed himself while still a student to theological orthodoxy. Although the Dutch Reformed Church at the time of his involvement in it as a pastor (1863–1874) was experiencing a renewal of orthodoxy, he was not satisfied. It became his mission to reestablish the Dutch Church on the Confession and Constitution of Dort (1619) as a supralapsarian, neo-Calvinist church with built-in safeguards against any future "corruption." Protesting the control of theological professorships by the state, he founded the Free University of Amsterdam (1880) on strict confessional lines. Failing to obtain the kind of guarantees that he desired in the state church, he first attempted to lead the Reformed congregations of Amsterdam out of that body, and failing also in this (1886), he led a mass exodus of "believers," the so-called Doleantie ("sorrowers"), out of the establishment, forming the Low Dutch Reformed Church. In 1892 this group united with the Christian Reformed Church (1834 schism) to form the Reformed Church (Belgic Confession, Canons of Dort, and Heidelberg Catechism). Kuyper desired also a reconstruction of the whole country on a "Christian" basis. He inherited the leadership of the Anti-Revolutionary Party and became its parliamentary leader in the Lower House in 1874. In opposition to liberalism and socialism he formed an alliance with the Catholic State Party and the Reformed Christian Historical Party. He was successful in gaining equality of support for sectarian schools in 1920 and served from 1901 to 1905 as prime minister of the Netherlands.

**Kyodan.** See JAPAN, UNITED CHURCH OF CHRIST IN.

# L

**Labadie, Jean de** (1610–1674). Reformed Pietist leader. Born near Bordeaux, France, he studied in Jesuit schools and served as a priest in Bordeaux and Paris. In 1640 he became a professor of theology at Amiens. In 1650, influenced by Calvin's *Institutes,* he became a member of the Reformed Church and taught at their academy in Montauban. In the years that followed he served pastorates at Geneva, London, and Middelburg (Holland). During this time Labadie's former Jansenist piety blended with Reformed Pietism to form a strong experiential, otherworldly, mystical type of Christianity that emphasized the importance of separatism and conventicle meetings. The movement spread in Holland, and some groups began to practice community of property. By the early 18th century, however, Labadism had disappeared. Labadie's influence on Pietism has been much debated. His program is outlined in his influential tract *The Reform of the Church Through the Pastorate* (1667).

**Laberthonnière, Lucien** (1860–1932). French Roman Catholic liberal. Along with Maurice Blondel and Édouard Le Roy, he espoused the "philosophy of action," and was thus involved in the modernist movement. His *Essais de philosophie religieuse,* in which he developed his theory of "immanence," was put on the Index, as were the *Annales de philosophie chrétienne,* a review that he edited, and his *Le Réalisme chrétien et l'idéalisme grec.*

**Lacordaire, Jean Baptiste Henri Dominique** (1802–1861). French Roman Catholic liberal. After preparing for a legal career, Lacordaire, moved by a reading of Lamen-nais's *Essai sur l'indifférence en matière de religion,* studied for the priesthood. Upon his ordination he was offered a post on *L'Avenir,* the daily newspaper inspired by Lamennais. Lacordaire, along with Montalembert and Lamennais, contributed to this journal, proposing the separation of church and state along with freedom of religion and of the press. After the condemnation of this program by Pope Gregory XVI in the encyclical *Mirari vos* (1832), Lacordaire retired for a time. He joined the Dominican Order in Rome in 1840 and began the revival of that order in France. A series of lectures given at Notre Dame in Paris over a period of many years gained for him a reputation as a great pulpit orator. Heartened by the Revolution of 1848, he edited *L'Ere nouvelle,* and even sat in the Assembly for a time. His hopes for an alliance between Catholicism and republicanism finally shattered by the accession of Napoleon III and the identification of the church with his regime, Lacordaire ended his series of sermons in Paris and retired to direct a military academy at Sorèze until his death.

**Lactantius, Lucius Caecilius Firmianus** (c. 240–320). African rhetor and master of Ciceronian style. A disciple of Arnobius called to teach rhetoric at Diocletian's capital city, Nicomedia, Lactantius was forced to resign when persecution ensued because of his conversion to Christianity. He remained in Nicomedia until c. 317, then moved to Treves as tutor of Constantine's son. His principal work, in seven books, was *Divinae institutiones* (304–313), an apology and introduction to the chief articles of faith. The first two books expose the absurdity of pagan practices, the third, the contradictions of heathen philosophy. Christ, the true Wisdom of God, is the theme of the fourth book. The last three discuss the absence of earthly justice and the possibility of its rebirth within the family of God, the essence of true worship, eschatology, and immorality. Other works by Lactantius include *Epitome, De opificio Dei* (theistic discussion of human anatomy without specifically Christian orientation), *De ira Dei* (exposition of God's jealous nature), and *De mortibus persecutorum* (cruel deaths awaiting the church's persecutors). Some attribute to him *De ave Phoenice,* a rehearsal of the Phoenix legend. Lactantius displayed a negative attitude toward the world and tended toward theological dualism. He pictured Christ as "teacher of virtue and righteousness," and knew the Holy Spirit only as the Son. His chiliasm is evident in the *Divinae institutiones.*

**Ladislas I** (c. 1040–1095). King and saint of Hungary. Born in Poland of noble Hungarian parents, he was elected king of Hungary in 1077. During the controversy between the papacy and the emperors, Ladislas supported the popes against Henry IV. He fought against the Cumans and Petchenegs and extended Christianity into Transylvania and Croatia. He died before setting out on the First Crusade.

**Lady Chapel.** A chapel, dedicated to the Virgin Mary, within a cathedral or parish church. Common from the 13th century, Lady Chapels were at first constructed east of the high altar (e.g., Henry VII's chapel in Westminster Abbey). In more recent times, they have been built at the east end of one of the aisles, frequently becoming the repository for the reserved Sacrament when it was not on the high altar. The reredos sculpture in many of them are fine examples of devotion to the Virgin Mary.

**Laestadius, Lars Levi** (1800–1861). Swedish Lutheran revivalist. He studied botany and theology at Uppsala and became pastor of Sweden's northernmost parish, Karesuando (1825–1849), and from 1849 to 1861 at Pajala. In 1844, after years of spiritual struggle, he came to the assurance of faith through a conversation with a simple Lapp girl named Maria. Shortly thereafter a revival broke out in Swedish Lapland that spread during the 1850's into Norway and Finland. Strong emphasis was laid upon confession of sin, individual absolution, and agape (love feasts). Bible studies were not stressed because of the illiteracy of the Lapps. Moral regeneration was considered as evidence of a true conversion, with drunkenness the chief target of Laestadius' preaching. Though the movement developed some unusual practices such as ecstatic trances and lively dances, the awakening was kept within the Lutheran Church and has left a rich spiritual legacy, especially in Finland.

**Lagarde, Paul Anton de** (1827–1891). German Biblical scholar, philologist, and writer. His real name was Bötticher, the pseudonym "de Lagarde" having come from his mother's side of the family. Though he studied widely and did work on, among other things, an Arabic translation of the Gospels, he was best known for his writings concerning secular culture. Concerned with the role of the *Volk*, he wanted a new religion purged of Judaism and Romanism.

**Lagrange, Albert** (1855–1938). Brother Joseph Marie of the Dominican Order. A Frenchman, he organized in 1890 the École d'Études Bibliques in what is now Jordanian Jerusalem. Opposing the sometime Catholic view that to study the Bible is to damage it, he founded the *Revue Biblique* and turned out a substantial bibliography of exegesis. He paved the way for Dominican scholars to publish (1948–1956) the *Bible de Jérusalem* and the 1966 translation, *The Jerusalem Bible*.

**Lainez** (Laynez), **Diego** (1512–1565). Spanish Jesuit. Born in Castile, he studied at Alcalá and then with Salmerón went to Paris to join Ignatius of Loyola. After teaching in Rome, Lainez was one of three papal theologians sent to Trent, where he was the principal author of the decree on justification, returning to take a major part in Sessions XIV and XXII on the Eucharist. In 1551, he was elected provincial in Italy; in 1556, vicar-general; and in 1558, the second general of the Society of Jesus.

**Lalemant, Gabriel** (1610–1649). Jesuit martyr, the first superior of Jesuit missions in Canada. A nephew of Jerome and Charles Lalemant, he was born in Paris, becoming a Jesuit novice in 1630 and an instructor at Moulins from 1632 to 1635 and again from 1641 to 1644. He was also prefect of the college at Bourges and at La Flèche. In 1646 he went to Canada, where he joined Jean de Brébeuf in the Huron mission at St. Ignace. He was tortured to death with Brébeuf by the Iroquois on March 17, 1649.

**Lalemant, Jerome** (1593–1665). Superior of the Huron mission. Born in Paris, he entered the Jesuit novitiate in 1610 and was sent to Canada as a missionary to the Hurons (1638–1645). Thereafter, until 1656, he assumed the office of superior of the missions in New France. He returned briefly to France to become rector of the college at La Flèche (1658–1659), then returned to Canada with Laval and was again appointed superior of the Jesuit mission in Canada. He wrote the *Relations* on the Huron missions (1639–1643) and New France (1646–1648 and 1660–1664).

**Lambert, Francis** (1486–1530). French Reformer at Hesse. A Franciscan novice at fifteen, he read Luther's works (1520) and left the cloister. Later he studied at Wittenberg (1523–1524). He translated Reformation tracts into French and Italian. Philip of Hesse appointed him professor at Marburg (1527), one of the first teachers of theology at the new university. Suspected of Zwinglian views on the Lord's Supper, he nevertheless was favored as a teacher of practical Bible exegesis.

**Lambert of Hersfeld** (d. c. 1088). Medieval German historian. A Thuringian who entered the monastery at Hersfeld in 1058, he wrote several works of a historical nature, the most important being his *Annals.* He freely copied other annals for the period prior to 1040, but the period from 1040 to 1077 is an original, although biased, account of the controversy between Gregory VII and Henry IV.

**Lambeth Articles.** A set of nine propositions dealing chiefly with predestination and related questions, issued in 1595 with the support of Archbishop Whitgift of Canterbury. Their occasion was a dispute at Cambridge between the Orthodox Calvinist William Whitaker and Peter Baro, who questioned Calvin's doctrine of election. The Articles, which adhere uncompromisingly to double predestination, never had any official authority, and were disliked by Queen Elizabeth. (See IRISH ARTICLES.)

**Lambeth Conferences.** Assemblies of the bishops of the Anglican episcopate, held approximately every ten years under the presidency of the archbishop of Canterbury and named from their usual place of meeting, the archbishop's palace at Lambeth. The demand for these conferences came from the Synod of the Anglican Church in Canada (1865). The resolutions of the Conferences are significant expressions of the Anglican Church on theology and on problems of the day.

**Lambeth Quadrilateral.** The four articles accepted in 1888 by the Lambeth Conference of the Protestant Episcopal Church for any discussion of a reunited Christian church. The four articles are: (1) the Bible as the ultimate standard of faith; (2) the Apostles' Creed and the Nicene Creed as statements of the Christian faith; (3) the sacraments of Baptism and Holy Communion; (4) the historic episcopate.

**Lamennais, Hugo-Félicité Robert de** (1782–1854). Influential French political and social theorist; Roman Catholic writer. Influenced in childhood by Rousseau, Lamennais was converted to Catholicism by his brother priest and received his first Communion at twenty-two. His *Réflexions sur l'état de l'Église* (1808), urging religious revival, was highly clerical; it gave impetus to ultramontanism. Lamennais was ordained in 1816. In *Essai sur l'indifférence en matière de religion* (1817) he argued that knowledge depends on membership in community: there is no right of private judgment in the proposed Catholic restoration. Three later volumes became more radical and ultramontanist as Lamennais continued to link two unlikely partners, ultramontanism and liberal Catholicism. With Lacordaire and Montalambert, Lamennais established *L'Avenir* (1830–1831), a publication asserting that freedom is the essence of Christianity and that the church must be free from the state. He traveled to Rome (1832) to defend his ideas, but was reprimanded in Gregory XVI's *Mirari vos* (1832). Submitting outwardly, Lamennais answered in *Paroles d'un croyant* (1834) and attacked the church's political authority. The work swept Europe. When the pope condemned him by name in *Singulari nos* (June 25, 1834), Lamennais left the church but continued to write. He espoused the people's sovereignty, and moved gradually toward an indeterminate pantheism. He served in Parliament for a time, while his works turned increasingly to the sociopolitical sphere.

**Lamentabili Sane Exitu.** A list of sixty-five specific propositions supposedly drawn from the writings of Roman Catholic modernists, which were condemned and proscribed by the inquisitors of the Holy Office and by Pope Pius X, July 4, 1907. This decree singled out for condemnation propositions and tendencies in Biblical criticism and the history of dogma, in particular those which emphasized evolution.

**Lammers, Gustaf Adolf** (1802–1878). Norwegian Lutheran pastor and revival preacher. Ordained in 1827, Lammers was converted in 1848 by Johannes Gossner while on a trip to Berlin. He began a revival upon his return to his parish in Skien. He built the first "prayer house" in Norway in 1850 and founded the first local Inner Mission society in 1853. He left the state church in 1856 and founded the first Dissenter congregation in Norway, but he returned in 1860 to the state church, which he served until his death.

**Lampe, Friedrich Adolf** (1683–1729). German Reformed theologian. Product of the Rhineland, he pastored several parishes in that part of Germany, two in Bremen, and was professor (1720–1727) of dogmatics and church history at Utrecht (Holland). Instrumental in the spread of federal (covenant) theology to Germany, he looked upon it as a weapon to overcome the Enlightenment. Though legalistically Scriptural and dogmatically orthodox, he was himself an early product of the Enlightenment in theology.

**Landrecht** (Prussia). A legal code introduced in 1794, known officially as the *Allgemeines Landrecht für die preussischen Staaten.*

Its general temper was set by the rationalist Frederick the Great, though it appeared after his death. In church affairs it marked the end of the Edict of 1788 and its oppression of clerical consciences by assuring the right of freedom of conscience—even that of the clergy —thus minimizing the confessional character of the churches. It further placed all stress on the local congregations, connecting them through the administrative structure of the state.

**Lanfranc** (c. 1005–1089). Italian-born prelate and scholar in England. He was born in Pavia and studied with Berengar of Tours. Later, he opened his own school at Avranches. He was made prior of Bec c. 1045, where he started a school that became famous throughout western Europe. In 1063 he founded the monastery at Caen, from which he was called by William the Conqueror to become archbishop of Canterbury (1070). Lanfranc won recognition of the primacy of Canterbury over York at the royal Council at Winchester (1072). He revitalized diocesan organization in England. At the church Council of London (1072), Lanfranc ordered each bishop to hold two synods yearly and to appoint archdeacons. The latter foreshadowed the establishment of chapters in nonmonastic cathedrals. At the Council of Winchester (1076), Lanfranc ruled that major orders were not to be conferred on married men, but that those clerics already married might keep their wives. Ecclesiastical courts, an innovation in England, were established. Lanfranc also moved the sees of Lichfield, Selsey, and Sherborne to the cities of Chester, Chichester, and Salisbury. With regard to monastic reform, Lanfranc introduced the *Consuetudines* to the monks of Christ Church, Canterbury. Lanfranc worked with William in the appointment of suitable men to church office. Their reform of the Church in England was effective although independent of the Gregorian reform.

**Lang, Cosmo Gordon** (1864–1945). Anglican prelate. Born in Scotland and raised a Presbyterian, Lang was educated at the University of Glasgow, Balliol College, Oxford, and the Inner Temple, London. After being ordained by the Church of England in 1890, he was curate of Leeds Parish Church until 1893 when he was made fellow and dean of divinity at Magdalen College, Oxford. From 1896 to 1901 he was vicar of Portsea and suffragan bishop of Stepney from 1901 to 1908. In 1908 he was made archbishop of York, where he remained until his translation to Canterbury in 1928. He played an im-portant part in connection with the abdication of Edward VIII.

**Lange, Johann Peter** (1802–1884). German Protestant theology professor. He taught at Bonn after 1854. An opponent of rationalism and higher criticism, he contested with David Friedrich Strauss, whose researches on the "historical Christ" seemed to attack the traditional bases of faith. Lange has a lengthy bibliography, his most frequently quoted books being a *History of Materialism* and another of *Rationalism*. He was also known for his Biblical commentaries, which have been translated into English.

**Langton, Stephen** (c. 1155–1228). Archbishop of Canterbury, theologian, and chief mediator between King John (Lackland) and the barons negotiating for the Magna Carta. Born in England, he was teaching as a doctor in arts and theology in Paris by c. 1180. He introduced the present chapter divisions into the Vulgate and produced a series of glosses and commentaries on most of the Old Testament. Innocent III, whom he had known in Paris, made him cardinal priest of St. Chrysogonus in 1206 and consecrated him archbishop of Canterbury in 1207. Refused permission to land in England by King John, Langton lived with the Cistercians of Pontigny until 1213, when John, threatened by papal deposition and a French invasion, capitulated to Innocent and accepted him. Almost immediately Stephen had to intercede for the barons with John and thereafter he found himself on their side against John and Innocent, who condemned the Magna Carta and suspended him for not excommunicating the king's enemies soon after it was signed. He was reinstated in 1218 and crowned Henry III in 1220. In 1221 he secured the withdrawal of the papal legate Pandulf, who had been prominent in the administration, and persuaded Pope Honorius III to permit Henry III, age fifteen, to come legally of age and rule in 1222. He held a synod at Osney to promulgate the decrees of the Fourth Lateran Council and special canons for the English Church. He died at Slindon, Sussex.

**La Rochelle, Confession of.** See GALLICAN CONFESSION.

**Lartigue, Jean Jacques** (1777–1840). First Roman Catholic bishop of Montreal. He was born at Montreal and ordained in 1800. In 1806 he joined the Sulpician Order and was consecrated bishop of Telmesse, with oversight of the district of Montreal, in 1820. He was created bishop of Montreal in 1836 and in the following year denounced Papineau and his *patriotes* in the Rebellion.

**La Salle, Jean-Baptiste de** (1651–1719). French Roman Catholic reformer. After receiving the M.A. degree from the College des Bons Enfants (Reims) in 1669, La Salle went to the Sorbonne to study for the priesthood. Upon ordination in 1678 he worked in his hometown of Reims, directing several charity schools and a newly organized order of teaching sisters. He founded an institute of teaching masters which in 1684 took the name "Brothers of the Christian Schools." La Salle composed a rule for the order in 1695. The rule was revised in his last years and approved by Pope Benedict XIII in 1725. It emphasized the fact that teaching should be looked upon as the normal means of sanctification for a member of the order, and as the performance of a divine service. The teaching order founded by La Salle went through many difficulties before his death, being sued by the teaching masters of Paris, for example, for violating their ancient privileges. The order, limited to those who had not taken priestly orders (1690–1691), was given a precise teaching methodology by La Salle in 1695 in his *The Conduct of Schools.* By the time of his death the order had spread throughout France and, subsequently, throughout the world, in an attempt to provide free schools for the poor.

**Las Casas, Bartolomé de** (1474–1566). Spanish missionary. He was born in Seville of a family of French ancestry. His father had gone on Columbus' second voyage and brought back an Indian boy as a slave. After taking a law degree at Salamanca, Bartolomé became friendly with the governor of the Antilles, and in 1502 went to the island of Hispaniola as a legal adviser. He became interested in improving the conditions of the natives, who were oppressed with overwork and disease. Perhaps to gain greater freedom and influence, he became a priest, and in 1519 he obtained the support of the Spanish Crown to set up a church-controlled Indian settlement. When the Indians revolted and destroyed it, he blamed the ill will of his fellow Spaniards, shortly afterward joining the Dominicans and preaching that colonization was sinful. He traveled widely in the Spanish colonies, and by his fanaticism on behalf of the Indians, about whose language and culture he had taken no great pains to inform himself, succeeded in alienating nearly everyone but his supporters back at the Spanish court. He spent the last ten years of his life in retirement in Madrid. In 1552 his best-known work had appeared, a violent attack on colonialism, *Brief Relation of the Destruction of the Indies.* He has been called both the "Apostle of the Indies" and the initiator of Negro slavery in the Americas, neither of which appellations is correct. Negro slavery had already been in existence, although for a time he advocated it as a way of sparing the Indians.

**Laski** (a Lasco), **John** (1499–1560). Calvinist Reformer. A Polish nobleman, he studied at Wittenberg, and was at Bologna (1514–1517). He visited Erasmus in Basel in 1523, and spent the year with him in 1524. Though exposed to Protestant views, he was not at first wholly persuaded. Laski returned to Poland, where he became bishop of Vesprim in 1529 and archdeacon of Warsaw in 1538. However, that same year he declined another bishopric, and declared himself a Protestant. He had cordial relations with all the leading Reformers, but his sympathies were chiefly Calvinist. He came to Emden, where he was appointed pastor in 1542, and from here his teaching had an influence in the Netherlands. At Cranmer's invitation in 1548, Laski went to England, and returned to London again in 1550 to minister to the Church of the Strangers, a refugee church of mixed nationalities (really several churches in one). He stayed three years, and possibly had some influence on the Book of Common Prayer of 1552. Fleeing Mary's accession, Laski returned to the Continent, was refused shelter by the Danish Lutherans, and worked for a while with the English refugees at Frankfurt. In 1556 he went back to Poland, where he hoped to unite all Polish Protestants—Reformed, Lutheran, and the Brethren. He drafted several important statements of doctrine, but his unification effort was a failure. His Emden Catechism (1554), modeled on the Geneva Catechism, was in turn used by the authors of the Heidelberg Catechism.

**Lasuen, Fermin Francisco de** (1736–1803). Spanish Franciscan missionary. Born in the Basque province of Alava, Lasuen became a Franciscan in 1751. He went to Mexico in 1759, where he did missionary work, laboring also in the two Californias until his death. In 1785 he succeeded Junípero Serra as father president of the missions. An able administrator, Lasuen founded nine missions in Upper California, including Santa Barbara, San Fernando, and San Jose.

**Lateran Basilica** (Church of the Holy Savior, or St. John Lateran). The cathedral church of the Roman patriarch, the pope, who refers to it as "mother and head of all the churches of the City and of the world." Shortly after the peace of the church (313), Constantine gave his Lateran palace to the bishop of Rome as his official residence and constructed this first large basilican church next to it. It was to serve as a model for the classical basilicas that sprang up all over the Empire after 350.

**Lateran Councils.** A number of church councils which took place from the 7th to the 18th centuries at the Lateran Palace in Rome. Of the fourteen synods held or reputed to have been held there, five are numbered and included in the Roman Catholic list of ecumenical councils, and the remaining nine are of less importance.

NONECUMENICAL: (1) 313, called by Miltiades to deal with the Donatists; (2) 649, condemned Monotheletism; (3) 769, regulated papal elections and repudiated the iconoclastic Synod of Hieria (754); (4) 1059, restricted papal election to cardinals; (5) 1060, forbade ordination to simonists; (6) 1079, enacted Eucharistic doctrine; (7) 1102, condemned Henry IV and demanded the loyalty of metropolitans to Paschal II; (8–9) 1112 and 1116, repudiated the Treaty of Ponte Mammolo extracted from Paschal II.

ECUMENICAL: (1) *First Lateran* (1123), Ninth Ecumenical, formally ended the investiture controversy, confirming the Concordat of Worms. Among its canons, it set penalties for breaking the Truce of God, and regulated the dispensing of sacraments and the investing of clergy. (2) *Second Lateran* (1139), Tenth Ecumenical, settled the schism of Anacletus II; spelled out Gregorian reform by regulating the activities of nuns, denying Christian burial to usurers and knights killed in tournament, condemning clerical marriage and dictating avoidance of services of married clerks; condemned Arnold of Brescia and invoked the secular power to aid in the detection of heresy. (3) *Third Lateran* (1179), Eleventh Ecumenical, convoked by Alexander III, appears to have acted in a more orderly and legal way than its predecessors. The papal election procedure of 1059 was clarified, a two-thirds majority being sufficient to elect (as now!). A serious attempt was made to cure irregularities in benefices: no pluralities permitted and only one occupant even in benefices having multiple patrons; expectancies forbidden; vacancy of benefices limited to six months; installation fees and the willing of benefices abolished. The Council's regulations also set an ordination age, thirty years for bishops and twenty-four for priests; curtailed the size of bishops' retinues on visitation; forbade hawks and hounds; heavily condemned clerical concubinage; ordered priests not to meddle in civil law or medicine; restricted monks' activities to proper functions of their monasteries;

abolished monetary demands for such church services as burials; denied Christian slaves to Jews and Moslems and refused the word of a Jew in testimony against a Christian, although requiring proper treatment of Jews; took notice of the Cathari by enacting measures against the Albigenses. An indication of the Council's concern for the education of clergy was its requirement that every bishop have on his staff one man entrusted with teaching clergy and poor students. (4) *Fourth Lateran* (1215), Twelfth Ecumenical, was the most important in this series of Councils. All but two bishops in each province were ordered to be present, together with some eight hundred abbots and ambassadors of secular rulers. The confirmation of Frederick of Sicily as emperor was enacted and Innocent III's condemnation of Stephen Langton for his refusal to oppose the Magna Carta was ratified. Perhaps its most important act was to settle on transubstantiation as the interpretation of the Eucharist, the first time this term was used officially. In addition the Council required annual confession and Communion of all Christians. Further disciplinary regulations of clergy were enacted, including the suspension of all priests living with concubines and the regulation of the personal life of clergy. All sacraments were to be given free of charge and relics to be authenticated. To prevent intermarriage of Christians with Jews and Moslems, nonbelievers were to wear distinctive garb. The other decrees filled out and interpreted regulations of former Councils. (5) *Fifth Lateran* (1512–1517), Eighteenth Ecumenical, was papally dominated, largely Italian in its makeup, and promulgated its decrees as papal bulls. Composed of no more than eighty bishops and fifteen cardinals at any time, it reaffirmed *Unam sanctam* and soundly condemned conciliarism. It has been severely criticized even among more liberal Roman Catholics as a council reechoing in a rigid way the ills that conciliarism sought unsuccessfully to cure.

The Lateran Councils that are considered ecumenical began the marked development of the supremacy of the papacy in the West, and gave the Roman Church its understanding as *the* Catholic Church.

BIBLIOGRAPHY: K. J. von Hefele, *A History of the Councils of the Church,* 5 vols. (Edinburgh, 1871–1896); A. Henze, *The Pope and the World* (New York, 1965).

**Lateran Pacts** (Feb. 11, 1929). The accords between Italy and the papacy, consisting of three parts, resolving the fifty-nine-year-old Roman question. The Treaty of Conciliation gave the pope Vatican City (108.6 acres) in total sovereignty with full diplomatic privileges. A financial convention awarded the Holy See the sum of $91,875,000 for loss of the former Church States. The Concordat recognized Catholicism as the state religion, approved religious instruction in the public schools, and enforced canon law.

**Latimer, Hugh** (c. 1485–1555). Celebrated preacher, English Reformer, and bishop of Worcester. Latimer first attracted attention at Cambridge for an oration against the teachings of Melanchthon, but he was won over to the Protestant side by Bilney and others. His support of Henry VIII's divorce won him royal favor, and in 1535 he was made bishop of Worcester. During the Catholic reaction of the later years of Henry VIII, Latimer's fortunes were in eclipse. He opposed the Six Articles in 1539 and resigned his see. In 1546 he was imprisoned. On Edward VI's accession, however, he once again enjoyed prominence as court preacher, though he refused to resume his episcopate. Latimer was one of the first divines to be arrested in Mary's reign (having refused the opportunity of escape that was offered to him), and, with Ridley, was burned at Oxford in 1555, chiefly for his views on the Mass. His exhortation to Ridley ("We shall this day light such a candle . . . as . . . shall never be put out") has become famous.

A man of great probity and considerable learning, Latimer was no rabble-rouser. His preaching, seen to best advantage in his famous *Sermon on the Plough* in 1548, is marked by a directness and natural facility with the vernacular, though medieval characteristics are not lacking.

**Latin Empire.** A short-lived empire established at Constantinople by the crusaders under Baldwin of Flanders in 1204. The objective of the Fourth Crusade was Egypt as the new center of Moslem power, but the Venetians who gained control of that Crusade directed the force first against their Adriatic rival Zara and then against Constantinople. The city was captured in 1203, the emperor replaced by the son of a recently deposed emperor, but the arrangement proved futile. A second assault viciously sacking the city was mounted (1204), and the crusaders put Baldwin of Flanders on the Byzantine throne as the first emperor of the newly created Latin empire of Constantinople. Under its first two kings it fared moderately well, but increasingly this intruder kingdom was threatened by the rise of three new Byzantine states, Nicaea eventually defeating the Latin empire in 1261. Because of its transitoriness, the Latin empire permanently enfeebled the old Byzan-

tine Empire which on its return never again rose to the former heights, and in its weakened state became a victim of the rising forces from the East.

**Latin Kingdom of Jerusalem.** A weak feudal state created by the crusading Franks after their conquest of Jerusalem in 1099. The term also included the three other crusader states established in Syria (Tripoli, Antioch, and Edessa). Because of its feudal decentralization, the Latin kingdom never functioned with any sustained authority over the native Moslems. Indeed, the majority of the second Frankish generation forgot their religious fanaticism and adopted a policy of conciliation toward the Moslems. Although later crusaders restored Latin control briefly from time to time, the kingdom finally collapsed in 1291 when the Moslems overthrew Acre, the last stronghold of the Franks.

**Latin States of Greek East.** Offspring of the Fourth Crusade, the weak confederation of Latin states organized after the crusaders' destruction of Constantinople in 1204, and remaining intact for only half a century (1204–1261). Although the crusaders were motivated at the outset to guard the Holy Land against Moslem invasion and to bring religious reunion between Rome and Constantinople, the political machinations of Enrico Dandolo, doge of Venice, and a complexity of internal political disorders in the Greek empire itself combined to precipitate the Latins' destructive attack upon the capital of Eastern Christendom. Thereafter the stubborn Greeks, in spite of their own disunity, rebelled with ultimate success against the affronts of the Latins and their partition of the Byzantine Empire, and the existence of the Latin States was finally terminated when Michael VIII Palaeologus expelled the crusaders in 1261 and reestablished Greek control in Constantinople. The short duration of the Latin States, however, was the result also of extreme weakness within the confederation itself, decentralized as it was in its feudal structure.

**Latitudinarianism.** The name given, often in opprobrium, to an outlook among some 17th-century Anglican churchmen who were undogmatic in theology and lax in matters of liturgy and discipline. The term was applied to the Cambridge Platonists, who were called "latitude men." They were sympathetic to Arminian theology after the Synod of Dort. Archbishop John Tillotson was the leading representative of this attitude. The Latitudinarians were forerunners of the Broad Church movement of the 19th century.

**Laubach, Frank Charles** (1884–1970). American missionary and apostle of literacy. He was educated at Princeton, Union Theological Seminary, and Columbia (Ph.D., 1915), and was sent by the American Board of Commissioners for Foreign Missions to the Philippines, where he served as "missionary at large" in the field of literacy (1915–1954). Working with the Committee on World Literacy and Christian Literature, Laubach originated and carried out plans for teaching groups to read in their respective vernaculars in Asia, Africa, and Latin America. A practical Christian idealist, he was author of many devotional books and works to aid literacy.

**Laud, William** (1573–1645). Archbishop of Canterbury and High Churchman. Born at Reading, Laud was educated at St. John's, Oxford. He became an advocate of "the beauty of holiness," in the sense that the English Church should return to the forms of ritual and the hierarchical organization that existed before the Reformation. Regarding the doctrine of grace, he was an Arminian. At no time, however, did he recognize the authority of the papacy. Under Charles I he rose rapidly, becoming bishop of Bath and Wells, chancellor of Oxford (1629), and archbishop of Canterbury (1633). Misgauging the strength of Puritan sentiment, he aroused considerable hostility by his obstinate attempts at liturgical reform; opposition was particularly strong in Scotland, leading to the National Covenant in 1638. In 1640 he introduced an oath binding the church to government by "archbishops, deans, and archdeacons, &c" (the famous "et cetera oath"), which brought him into further discredit, and the same year he was impeached by the Long Parliament. The following year he was imprisoned, but he was not tried until 1644. The Commons forced the Lords to agree to his execution by beheading, which took place in 1645.

**Lauds.** The hour of prayer for daybreak in monastic usage. It is a counterpart to Vespers and contains psalms, a hymn, lessons, canticle, and prayers. It was combined with Matins by the Reformers to make the Morning Prayer service in Anglican and Lutheran use. Worship at the "hinges of the day" is widespread, e.g., in India, where Christians have in places adopted the native custom.

**Lausanne Conference** (1927). First World Conference on Faith and Order. The culmination of the movement led by Bishop Charles H. Brent after the Edinburgh Conference of 1910, it used the device of an ecumenical conference for the exploration of the areas of agreement and disagreement between churches as a means toward achieving unity. Brent induced the Protestant Episcopal Church in 1910 to take the lead in enlisting cooperation, which was forthcoming from other American churches, the Church of England and British Dissenters, the ecumenical patriarch, and others. World War I caused the indefinite postponement of the Conference. In 1920 a fruitful preparatory meeting was held at Geneva, and the Conference, which established the Faith and Order Movement as a going concern, was held in 1927. Rome refused involvement. This was the very first conference of churches as churches, represented by official delegates. It brought the Orthodox churches into the ecumenical movement. It was widely inclusive, from Orthodox to Friends. The most significant document was "The Church's Message to the World—the Gospel." A continuation committee was created, with Brent as chairman, but he died at Lausanne in 1929.

BIBLIOGRAPHY: H. N. Bate (ed.), *Lausanne 1927: First World Conference on Faith and Order* (New York, 1927).

**Laval-Montmorency, François Xavier de** (1623–1708). Canadian Roman Catholic bishop. Born and educated in France, where he served several years as priest, he came to Canada in 1659 as apostolic vicar with the partial powers of a bishop. In 1663 he founded Quebec Seminary (which became Laval University in 1852), and in 1674 became first bishop of the diocese of Quebec. He was a respected leader in both government and church.

**Lavater, Johann Kaspar** (1741–1801). Swiss pastor, casuist, mystic, and spiritual counselor. Lavater conceived of the Protestant ministry as a cure of souls. Incapable of identifying a deity apart from the Savior, he was indifferent to historical Christianity. A friend of Goethe, an enthusiast for physiognomy, he held pulpits in and around Zurich. William Blake admired his quotable *Aphorisms* (e.g., "The public seldom forgives twice").

**Lavigerie, Charles M. A.** (1825–1892). French Roman Catholic missionary leader. Professor of ecclesiastical history at the Sorbonne (1854–1856), he was made bishop of Nancy (1863) and archbishop of Algeria (1867). In 1868 he founded the missionary order popularly known as the White Fathers, and in 1869 the Missionary Sisters of Africa. He became metropolitan of Carthage and primate of Africa, was active in the antislavery movement, and a supporter of the *ralliement,* Pope Leo XIII's attempt to persuade French Catholics to drop their monarchist sympathies and "rally" in support of the Republic.

**Law, William** (1686–1761). English controversial and spiritual writer. He was born at Kings Cliffe, Northamptonshire, educated at Emmanuel College, Cambridge, and ordained and elected fellow of his college in 1711. On the accession of King George I (1714), Law refused the oath of allegiance, was deprived of his fellowship, and became a nonjuror. From 1727 to 1737 he was tutor to Edward Gibbon, father of the historian. In 1740 he retired to Kings Cliffe, where he spent the rest of his life in literary labors and works of charity. He was one of the most important English writers on practical divinity in the 18th century. His most famous work, *A Serious Call to a Devout and Holy Life* (1728), was an exhortation to all Christians to embrace the mystical Christian life. He held that all human activity, all virtues of everyday life (temperance, humility, and self-sacrifice), should be directed toward a complete glorification of God, the final goal of all religious belief. Law's religious thought had a profound impact upon his contemporaries, and his famous book was greatly admired and appreciated by numerous religious leaders, notably John Wesley and George Whitefield.

**Law of Associations.** A law promulgated by the French government in 1901 which stated that no religious congregation could be formed without authorization from the state. Congregations already recognized were allowed to continue if they presented annual lists of members, property, and financial status to the government. This law was a step in the final separation between church and state in France in 1905.

**Law of Guarantees.** Italian parliamentary law of May 13, 1871, which regulated Italian-papal relations until the 1929 Lateran Treaty. The law invested the pope with sovereignty, immunized him from arrest, guaranteed diplomatic autonomy, permitted personal guard and communications, and granted exclusive use of the Vatican, Lateran, and Castel Gandolfo. The state was no longer to nominate bishops or handle spiritual court cases, but Cavour's state/church separation was not fully implemented. Although the law appeared overly generous to anticlericals, the pope condemned it in *Ubi nos* (May 15, 1871) and rejected the first reparative payment.

**Law of Separation** (French). Legislative act (Dec. 9, 1905) officially abrogating the Napoleonic Concordat of 1801. The law applied to the Protestant and Jewish faiths as well as to Roman Catholicism. Church property was nominally acquired by the state, although it was specified that the use of all church buildings would be freely granted to religious associations customarily using them. The practice and support of religion was to be on a strictly voluntary basis on the part of the faithful.

**Lawrence** (d. 258). Deacon to Sixtus II. He survived him by four days and was martyred on Aug. 10, 258. He may well, as legend reports, have saved the treasures of the church from the persecutor by distributing them to the poor. The fire in which he is said to have been killed is perhaps symbolic of the fiery trial of martyrdom. Lawrence was one of the first martyrs to be annually commemorated at Rome, so that St. Lawrence's Day is one of the oldest in the Roman calendar of saints.

**Layman's Missionary Movement.** An interdenominational organization devoted to promoting foreign missions among laymen, founded in 1906. Its purpose is mission education; it holds conventions in major cities and promotes layman tours of mission fields. It also works through area and local committees, distributing literature and urging every congregation to have a missionary committee.

**Laymen's Foreign Missions Inquiry** (1930–1932). The unofficial project of thirty-five laymen associated with six denominations, who set up a commission chaired by William E. Hocking of Harvard and financed by a gift from John D. Rockefeller, Jr. Its object was to determine the right attitudes toward missions and to reconsider their functions. The report, *Re-Thinking Missions* (New York, 1932), called forth a storm of protest from the Boards, whereas Europeans have tended to think that it accurately portrays American attitudes.

**Laynez, Diego.** See LAINEZ, DIEGO.

**Lazarists** (*or* Congregation of the Mission). A congregation of secular priests (not a religious order) who take religious vows to work especially among people whose normal contact with the clergy is limited. Founded by Vincent de Paul in 1625, they were given the name Lazarists in most parts of Europe because of the priory of St. Lazare, in Paris, where Vincent stayed and did most of his religious work. In English-speaking countries they are called Vincentians. The Lazarists preach, give missions and retreats, and run schools and seminaries.

**League for Social Reconstruction.** Established in 1932 by a group of professors and business and professional men from Toronto and Montreal as a kind of "Canadian Fabian Society." The aim of the League was to be a nucleus for unattached critical spirits who could not accept the old parties and whose circumstances did not make it possible for them to join political labor or farm organizations. Its purpose was the promotion of research, the education of public opinion, and the development of political organizations seeking the establishment of a planned and socialized economy in Canada. It accomplished this purpose by publishing pamphlets, sponsoring discussion and study groups, and building up a body of information on matters such as public ownership, planning, and social services. The provisional executives of the League in 1932 consisted of Profs. F. H. Underhill, F. R. Scott, King Gordon, E. A. Havelock, and J. F. Parkinson, with J. S. Woodsworth as its honorary president. Although the League was dissolved at the beginning of World War II, it exercised a widespread influence on Canadian social and political thought. Its major contribution was the publication of *Social Planning for Canada* in 1935. The contributors to this volume were some of the most outstanding names in the Canadian university fields of government, law, history, and economics—Eugene Forsey, King Gordon, Leonard Marsh, J. F. Parkinson, F. R. Scott, Graham Spry, and F. H. Underhill. These authors were deeply influenced by the Social Gospel and freely admitted their debt to Fabianism, but they attempted to set out their analyses and proposals in specifically Canadian terms. The League also played an important part in the formation of the Canadian Commonwealth Federation, Canada's Socialist Party.

**League of the Militant Godless.** During the Bolshevik campaign against religion in Russia, the League of the Militant Godless was founded in 1925 to conduct antireligious propaganda. During the collectivization drive and the First Five Year Plan the members in the League increased to two million. It was headed by Emil Yaroslavski. By 1932 the League numbered five million members. However, with the growth of the German threat, pressure on religious believers was eased, and even the League decreased its activity. In 1937 the membership had dropped again to less than two million. After the German attack on Russia in 1942, the Orthodox Church threw its support to the government and to Stalin, and the League of the Militant Godless ceased publication.

**Le Clerc, Jean** (1657–1736). Protestant preacher and scholar. Born in Geneva of an academic family, he was credited at the age of twenty-two with a work on the Trinity. Virtually ousted from Switzerland because of his opinions, he refuged at Amsterdam, where he met John Locke, the English political scientist, and Philip van Limborch, a professor at the Remonstrant seminary. He wrote on the Hebrew language and Scriptural interpretation, rejecting Moses' authorship of the Pentateuch and Hebrew as the primitive tongue. His *Dissertation on the Statue of Salt* applied critical techniques to the story of Lot's wife. He anticipated modern geological and zoological ideas. He taught philosophy, belles-lettres, and Hebrew at the Remonstrant seminary and published (1693–1731) a series of Biblical commentaries having great merit. He showed the need for penetrating scientific study of original sources and documents. He also edited journals, provoking theological storms. When pressed by opponents, he sometimes stammered half recantations. The *Ars critica* and *Epistolae criticae et ecclesiasticae* demonstrated his methods. His broad bibliography (*Universal and Historical Library*, 25 vols.; *Selected Library*, 28 vols.; and *Ancient and Modern Library*, 29 vols.) represented a substantial contribution to early 18th-century Protestant theological writing.

**Lecomte du Noüy, Pierre** (1883–1947). French scientist who journeyed from agnosticism to Christian faith. His first scientific work was done during World War I in connection with the healing of wounds. Later he became famous for his research with protein solutions, blood serums, and immunization. In his *Human Destiny* (1947) and *The Road to Reason* (1948) he viewed the life of the spirit of man as the crowning achievement of the evolutionary process.

**Lectionary.** Any liturgical volume containing a schedule of Biblical passages to be read at designated times. Assimilating the Jewish custom of reading from the Pentateuch and the Prophets each Sabbath, early Christians added passages from the growing corpus of the New Testament also. Soon various systems evolved fixing lessons for special seasons. Originally, lessons were designated in Bible margins, but eventually manuscripts were copied with passages arranged in order. The Roman lectionary was retained in a revised form by many Protestant denominations, often substituting hortative lessons for more doctrinal passages. Continuous effort is being made within many denominations to renew traditional lectionary systems for meaningful use in the contemporary church.

**Lee, Jason** (1803–1845). Methodist missionary and pioneer in Oregon. In 1834 he founded an Indian mission on the Willamette, ten miles northwest of the present Salem, Oreg., and petitioned Washington, D.C., two years later for the establishment of a territorial government. In 1838 he journeyed to the East Coast to make a personal appeal for territorial status and to gather funds for the mission that had turned its attention to reaching the white settlers pouring into Oregon. Lee founded Willamette University and was a constant advocate of the Americanization of Oregon. He died while on a second trip to the East Coast. In 1906 his remains were reinterred in Salem, Oreg.

**Lee, Mother Ann** (1736–1784). Founder of the American Shakers. After persecution in England for Shaking Quaker activities, she came to Watervliet, N.Y., in 1774 with a group who became the first Shakers in the New World. Subject to ecstasy and visions, she was called "Ann, the Word" and believed to be the completion of the revelation through Jesus Christ. The group grew rapidly through her itinerant preaching.

**Legate, Papal.** A representative of the pope who holds authority delegated by him to fulfill a specific mission to a specific place. These representatives are known as legates *a latere* ("from the side of the pope"). Some dignitaries exercise delegated papal authority by reason of their office and are known as legates *nati* ("native" legates). Prior to the Reformation, the archbishop of Canterbury was *legatus natus* in England. Legates are today chosen from the College of Cardinals.

**Legion of Mary.** An association of Roman Catholic laity whose aims are the spiritual betterment of its members and participation in the apostolic work of the church. Founded in Dublin in 1921 by a layman, Frank Duff, the Legion is put at the disposal of the bishop and the parish clergy for the performance of any necessary work. It is peculiarly devoted to the Virgin Mary as the Mediatrix of All Graces.

**Leibnitz, Gottfried Wilhelm von** (1646–1716). German philosopher. Born at Leipzig, he was educated at Leipzig and Jena in jurisprudence, mathematics, and philosophy. A man of many interests, Leibnitz' attention was directed not only to logic, mathematics, and

science, but also to law, politics, and religion. After serving the elector of Mainz, he entered the service of the house of Brunswick as librarian at Hannover, a post he held for forty years. Unlike many philosophers, he did not present his system in any single work. A Protestant by upbringing, he engaged in correspondence with J. B. Bossuet on Christian reunion, and to this end he published *Systema theologicum* (1686). In his *Monadology* (written in 1714 and published in 1720), he tried to reconcile the mechanistic and teleological views of nature. Repudiating both the dualism of Descartes and the monism of Spinoza, he proposed a view of reality in which there is continuity but at the same time an infinite number of simple substances of force called "monads," each of which contains within itself the whole infinity of substance, each of which is a living mirror of all existence. The universe, for Leibnitz, therefore, is rational and harmonious because it is the creation of a benevolent God. He believed preestablished harmony a valid argument for the existence of God.

**Leighton, Robert** (1611–1684). Scottish mediating churchman in the struggle of presbyterianism and episcopacy. In 1661, Leighton was one of four bishops appointed by Charles II. A man of fine moral and intellectual qualifications, he tried unsuccessfully to persuade the Scots to accommodate to episcopacy. As archbishop of Glasgow he sought to dissuade Charles from harsh reprisals against the Covenanters. He failed and in despair resigned the archbishopric in 1674.

**Leipzig Debate.** Disputation between Johann Eck and the Wittenberg Reformers Andreas Carlstadt and Martin Luther. Held from June 27 to July 14, 1519, it marked the beginning of Luther's realization that an almost unbridgeable chasm existed between him and the hierarchy of the Roman Church. During the course of the debate, which centered on the question of authority, Eck forced Luther to admit that councils can and have erred, and that he found much truth in the works of the condemned heretic, John Hus.

**Leipzig Evangelical Lutheran Mission Society.** An organization founded at Dresden in 1836 upon an older association (1819), and moved to Leipzig in 1846. Karl Graul was the leading figure in formative years. Ultra-Lutheran, the mission long held aloof from mainstream missionary cooperation. When England bought Tranquebar from Denmark in 1845, the remnant of the Danish-Halle mission (1706) was entrusted to Leipzig and provided the base for its one big mission. In 1919 the indigenous Tamil Evangelical Lutheran Church was established.

**Leipzig Interim.** A temporary religious settlement adopted by Saxony in December, 1548. After the Lutheran theologians of Saxony had rejected the Augsburg Interim, and as the emperor pressed for compliance, Melanchthon drafted a substitute affirming justification by faith but permitting Extreme Unction, Mass, vestments, images, festivals, and fasts as nonessentials (adiaphora). The substitute Interim was accepted at Leipzig (December 21), but ended by the Peace of Passau (1552). Many Lutherans felt that it yielded too much. (See MAURICE OF SAXONY.)

**Lejeune, Paul** (1591–1664). Jesuit missionary to the Canadians. Born at Chalons-sur-Marne, France, of Huguenot parents, he was converted to Roman Catholicism and entered the Jesuit novitiate in 1613. He became superior of the Jesuit residence at Dieppe in 1630, and in 1632 he went to Quebec as superior of the Canadian mission, where he remained until 1639. Returning to France in 1649, he became *procureur* for foreign missions of the Society. His reports from Canada were published under the title *Relations* and stimulated great interest in the Jesuits' work among the Indians.

**Leloutre, Jean Louis** (1709–1772). French missionary to the Micmac Indians. He was born at Morlaix, France, educated at the seminary of St. Esprit, Paris, and ordained in 1737. In 1738, he became a missionary to the Micmac Indians. The English put a price on his head because he incited the Indians and Acadians against them. Captured by the English, he remained in prison on the island of Jersey from 1755 to 1763. Afterward he returned to France and participated in the settlement of the Acadians at Belle-Île-en-Mer.

**Leme da Silveira Cintra Sebastião** (1882–1942). Influential Brazilian prelate. Ordained at Rome (1904), he taught briefly in a São Paulo seminary, advanced to archbishop of Olinda-Recife, and then Rio de Janeiro (1930), becoming cardinal. The same year he went to the palace and persuaded President Washington Luiz to resign in the face of Getulio Vargas' successful revolution. Leme wrote about Joseph, Catholic Action, pastoral care, and the religious life.

**Leo I the Great** (d. 461). Pope from 440. The significance of Leo's pontificate lies in his assertion of the universal episcopate of the Roman bishop. In a squabble with Hilary of Arles over the appeal from Celidonius,

Leo appealed to the civil power for support, and obtained from Valentinian III a recognition of his jurisdiction over all the Western provinces. The decree recognized the primacy of the bishop of Rome based on the merits of Peter, the dignity of the city, and the decrees of Nicaea. In the renewal of the Christological debate by Eutyches, Leo extended the authority of Rome in the East. In supporting Flavian, Leo sent him a long letter, the Tome, which stated that in Jesus Christ there was neither manhood without Godhead nor Godhead without manhood, but two complete natures in one person, "without detracting from the proprieties of either nature and substance." Although Leo's Tome was denied a reading at the Robber Council of Ephesus (449) and at Chalcedon (451), it was accepted as a standard of Christological orthodoxy. When Attila invaded Italy (452) and threatened Rome, Leo met him and persuaded the Huns to withdraw beyond the Danube. When the Vandals took Rome (455), Leo's influence repressed arson and murder. His forceful nature gives validity to the title of the "first pope." Many of his sermons and letters survive.

**Leo III** (d. 816). Pope from 795. Succeeding Hadrian I, Leo made it his first act as pope to send to Charlemagne, as *patricius,* the standard of Rome together with the keys of the tomb of Peter. In 799, accusing Leo of various misdeeds, Hadrian's followers assaulted the pope in the streets of Rome. The object of his assailants was to deprive him of his eyes and tongue in order to disqualify him for the papal office. Escaping this fate, Leo fled for protection to Charlemagne. The king returned Leo to Rome under armed escort, ordering the pope and his accusers to appear before him in Rome the next year. In December, 800, the pope purged himself on solemn oath of the charges brought against him. On Christmas Day as Charlemagne knelt before Peter's altar in prayer, Leo placed the imperial crown on the king's head, raising him to emperor, thereby guaranteeing a closer protectorate by the Franks over the papacy. In so doing, Leo established the legal precedent, the source of later friction, that the pope alone could confer the imperial crown. In 809, approached by Charlemagne's theologians, Leo confirmed the dogmatic correctness of the *filioque* clause introduced into the Nicene Creed, although in the interests of peace with the Greeks, he requested that the creed not be chanted in the public liturgy.

**Leo III the Isaurian** (the Syrian) (c. 675–741). A vigorous, farsighted emperor of Byzantium who brought peace and stability to the Eastern Empire after twenty years of political turmoil and who defeated an almost overwhelming Arab attempt to capture Constantinople.

Influenced by a native antipathy against the widespread and popular use of icons and perhaps by certain Jewish and Moslem prejudices against all use of religious imagery, Leo used diplomacy, persuasion, and force in a long series of attempts to persuade the church to abandon the veneration of images. Resisted by Popes Gregory II and III, the patriarch Germanus of Constantinople, and John of Damascus, the greatest theologian of the century, Leo nevertheless persisted in his campaign and in 730 decreed the systematic destruction of all icons (iconoclasm) throughout his dominions.

His iconoclastic policies were sternly pursued by his even more violent son and heir, Constantine V (741–775), who summoned a packed council of bishops to back his views (754), savagely persecuted all its opponents, and finally forbade the cult of the saints entirely.

The restoration of icons by the Seventh Ecumenical Council (787) and by the Synod of Constantinople (843) was a victory both for Orthodoxy and for ecclesiastical freedom.

**Leo IV** (c. 750–780). Emperor of the Eastern Roman Empire from 775. Son of Constantine V, Leo was known as "the Khazar," a reference to his mother's nationality. In the military field, he initiated a strong policy against the Arabs and the Bulgars. Though Leo himself was opposed to the use of images in worship, his reign marks the end of the first iconoclastic era of the Empire, for his wife, the empress Irene, who as regent to their son succeeded Leo, was devoted to icon worship.

**Leo VI** (866–912). Emperor of the Eastern Roman Empire from 886. Referred to as Leo the Philosopher and Leo the Wise, he was a scholar and author of poetry and theological works. He issued the completion of Justinian I's digest of laws, entitled the *Basilica* (888). Leo's four marriages resulted in a long and complicated theological dispute within the church, ultimately concluded in his favor with the legitimatizing of his son, who succeeded to the throne as Constantine VII.

**Leo IX** (Bruno, 1002–1054). Pope from 1049. He was born in Egisheim, southeast Alsace. Through his father, Hugh, he was a cousin of Emperor Conrad II. In 1024, he entered the service of Conrad as a deacon; in 1026, he led imperial troops against the Lombards. He became bishop of Toul in 1027. Upon the death of Pope Damasus II (1048), Bruno was appointed successor by Henry III, the reigning emperor. Bruno agreed only if he were to be freely elected by the clergy and people of Rome. In penitential garb, he appeared in Rome, was acclaimed by the people and installed as pope. His biographer, Humbert of Silva-Candida, noted that his papal name Leo suited his courage in fighting simony and clerical marriage. Leo condemned both abuses at the Roman Synod, and in May, 1049, proceeded to Cologne and Reims, personally enforcing the decrees. Norman threats to southern Italy caused Leo to try mediation in 1053, but having failed, he led troops south and was defeated at Civitella (1053). Leo was kept in custody by the Normans until 1054 when he returned to Rome. The last years of his pontificate were troubled by Michael Cerularius, patriarch of Constantinople, who raised the old differences of ritual and jurisdiction between Eastern and Western Churches. Leo sent ambassadors, who excommunicated Michael, thus contributing to the Great Schism.

**Leo X** (Giovanni de' Medici, 1475–1521). Pope from 1513. The second son of Lorenzo the Magnificent, he was destined for a rapid rise in ecclesiastical circles. Made a cardinal at the age of thirteen, he became Pope Leo X at the age of thirty-eight. Leo X has the dubious distinction of being both the final Renaissance pope and the pope under whom the Protestant Reformation began. An avid patron of the arts and literature, Leo encouraged Raphael, Michelangelo, Machiavelli, and others, and established the University of Rome. His almost single-minded concentration on these matters caused political and religious affairs to be delegated to others. Under the skillful hand of his cousin Guilio (later Pope Clement VII), Leo sought to enlarge the Papal States. To obtain an alliance with Francis I, Leo arranged the Concordat of Bologna in 1516, negating the Pragmatic Sanction of Bourges, but continuing a large measure of royal control over the French Church. Leo's minimal attempts at reform during the Fifth Lateran Council and his condemnation of conciliarism in *Pastor aeternus* sharply dimmed prospects for reform. Leo reissued the indulgence for contributions toward the cost of rebuilding St. Peter's in 1517. Following Martin Luther's protest, Leo issued *Exsurge, Domine* in 1520, commanding Luther to recant within sixty days. The condemnation of Luther was then made final by the bull *Decet Romanum pontificem* of January, 1521.

**Leo XIII** (Gioacchino Pecci, 1810–1903). Pope from 1878. Ordained in 1837, he held several positions in the Curia, becoming bishop of Perugia in 1846, and cardinal in 1853. Upon the death of Pope Pius IX, Pecci was elected his successor (Feb. 20, 1878), taking the name of Leo XIII. Though he continued some of the more reactionary policies of Pius IX, Leo XIII is best known for his teaching encyclicals, in some of which a growing concern for the social problems of the age is visible. *Aeterni Patris* (1879) proposed a revived Thomism as the official philosophy of the Catholic Church. *Immortale Dei* (1885), though directed specifically at the political situation in France, marked the transition in papal politics from a position supporting "legitimate" monarchies to one of general indifference as to the form of government. *Rerum novarum* (1891) was concerned specifically with the social and economic problems of the age, advocating labor unions and state intervention while insisting nonetheless on respect for private property. *Providentissimus Deus* (1893) was a call for Catholic Biblical scholarship, and foreshadowed Leo's establishment of the Pontifical Biblical Commission in 1902. His policies seemed less rigorous than Pius IX's.

**Leonardo da Vinci** (1452–1519). Italian intellectual who in many ways was the embodiment of the Renaissance concept of a "universal man," that is, a versatile individual talented in a great number of different endeavors. Art historians consider Leonardo one of the greatest painters of all time, while most specialists in Renaissance studies heap praise upon him for achievements in other such diverse roles as sculptor, architect, engineer, musician, anatomist, mathematician, chemist, geologist, botanist, astronomer, geographer, inventor, and empirical scientist. In fact, his diversity of gifts and insatiable curiosity led him to occupy his mind with so many projects that few bore fruit. For all his multifarious activities, he regarded himself primarily as a painter. Of the many paintings he began, he completed only a few, including his masterpiece *The Last Supper,* his popular *Mona Lisa,* and his sensitive *Madonna of the Rocks.* Leonardo's wandering life paralleled his restless spirit. At various times he lived in Florence, Milan, Venice, Mantua, and Rome, finally dying in 1519 near Amboise in France, where he had gone in 1516 to accept the patronage of the French king. A man burdened with religious and emotional instability, he wrote many things in his later life which are full of lamentations and regrets.

**Leonine Sacramentary.** The oldest of the liturgical books that document the worship practice of the early Middle Ages. A sacramentary contains the celebrant's prayers at Mass and other rites. The manuscript for this book is 7th century but seems to show the liturgy of Rome of three centuries earlier. It is ill organized and offers many prayers for the same occasions. It gives a picture of worship before Gregory's reform.

**Leontiev, Konstantin N.** (1831–1891). Russian critic, writer, and philosopher. Shortly before his death he became a monk. Denouncing the culture of western Europe and those who sought to Westernize Russia, he condemned bourgeois democracy, liberal government, and industrial civilization. He predicted a brilliant future for Russia based upon militant Orthodoxy and unlimited autocracy, viewing these as Byzantine rather than Slavic traditions.

**Leontius of Byzantium** (*more properly* Leontius the Monk *or* Leontius Scholasticus) (c. 480–543). The chief theologian of the age of Justinian. His treatise in three books *Against the Nestorians and Eutychians* and other works defend the doctrines of Chalcedon but also bring into the Chalcedonian tradition the Monophysite emphasis on the unity of Christ. Deity and humanity are distinct yet united, like fire and wood in a flaming torch, and the humanity of Christ is neither impersonal nor a separate personality (hypostasis), but *enhypostatos,* made personal by its union with deity. This doctrine of enhypostasia is the basis of the definitions of the Fifth Ecumenical Council in 553 and of later developments of Orthodox thought. Little is known of Leontius' life. He may be identical with the Origenist monk Leontius of Byzantium (d. 543), who represented the monks of Palestine at Constantinople in the 530's and shared in several theological conferences there; but he cannot be the Leontius who was one of the Latin-speaking "Scythian monks" who advanced ideas similar to his from 518 to 520. A later writer developed his ideas in the treatise *On Sects,* describing the divisions of the Eastern Church as seen at Constantinople about 570.

**Leopold II** (1747–1792). Grand Duke of Tuscany and Holy Roman Emperor from 1790. His rule in Tuscany was prosperous and enlightened. As Holy Roman Emperor he effectuated a reconciliation between the papacy and Austria by repealing most of his brother Joseph II's anticlerical legislation, especially those measures dealing with Febronianism.

**Leopold Association** (Leopoldinen Stiftung). An organization established at Vienna in 1829 by the first German priest in the Northwest Territory, Frederick Rese (1791–1871), to support Catholic missions among German immigrants to the United States. It was named for the Austrian-born empress of Brazil. Members offered prayers and alms to send German priests to open churches and schools in America. Ultimately it fused with the Propagation of the Faith Congregation.

**Lepanto** (Návpaktos), **Battle of.** The sea engagement in which Christian naval forces in the mouth of the Gulf of Corinth defeated the Turks and dealt them a blow from which they never fully recovered (1571). In 1570 only Malta and Crete were left as Christian outposts in the eastern Mediterranean. Pope Pius V asked Genoa, Venice, and Spain for help. Responding for political and economic as well as religious reasons, they united under the Spanish commander Don Juan of Austria and, with over two hundred ships, met the fleet of Selim III off Lepanto on Oct. 7, 1571. The guns and strategy of the Christians won the day, and the Turkish warships were either sunk or driven ashore. Some twenty thousand Moslems supposedly lost their lives in the encounter.

**Lérins, Monastery of.** A monastery on an island off the coast of the French Riviera, founded c. 410 by Honoratus. The monastery served as a center for the training of missionaries and bishops, such as Patrick, Hilary of Arles, Vincent of Lérins, and Caesarius of Arles. The monastery was suppressed in 1788, but reopened as a Cistercian house in 1871.

**Le Roy, Édouard** (1870–1954). French mathematician and philosopher. He succeeded Bergson at the Collège de France in 1914. His teaching was looked upon as French Modernism in philosophical clothing. In *Dogme et critique* (1907) he proposed a nonintellectualist view of the meaning of dogma, a view influenced by Bergson's teaching on "intuition." The work was placed on the Index by the Holy Office in 1907.

**Le Sillon.** The name of a journal and a lay Catholic movement founded in France in the 1890's that was largely associated with Marc Sangnier. Its principles were liberal, revolutionary (i.e., it favored many of the tenets of the French Revolution), and republican. It was criticized for teaching that the basis of authority lay in the people, and in August, 1910, a letter of Pius X to the French hierarchy spelled its dissolution.

**Leslie, John** (1527–1596). Scottish Roman Catholic bishop, champion of the cause of Mary, Queen of Scots. Returning from study in France, Leslie became the defender of the Roman Catholic cause in Scotland. He was present at the disputation in 1561 with Knox and Willocks. He won the steadfast friendship of Mary and became her ambassador in Elizabeth's court but suffered banishment from England after Norfolk's arrest. He spent the rest of his life in France and Rome before retiring to a monastery near Brussels. In 1578, while at Rome, he published an important history of Scotland (in Latin).

**Lessing, Gotthold Ephraim** (1729–1781). German dramatist and critic, one of the principal figures of the *Aufklärung*. Born at Kamenz, the son of a prominent Lutheran pastor, he became a theological student at Leipzig in 1746, but soon devoted himself almost entirely to producing literary masterpieces. In his later years he was chiefly concerned with philological and theological problems. Under the influence of Spinoza, Leibnitz, and the deist Reimarus, Lessing developed a purely humanitarian religion founded on tolerance, benevolence, and generosity. His views were embodied in his famous blank verse play *Nathan der Weise* (1780). In his chief theological works, *Ernst und Falk* (1778–1780) and *Die Erziehung des Menschengeschlechts* (1780), he rejected Christianity as a historical religion because "accidental truths of history can never become the proof of necessary truths of reason." He expected a third stage in religious history, following Judaism and Christianity, in which a new and everlasting enlightened religious morality would be established, a period in which men would act rightly for right's sake.

**Lessius, Leonhard** (1554–1623). Belgian Jesuit theologian and moralist. He taught at Douai and Louvain and was involved in several of the theological arguments of his day. He believed in the idea of "subsequent inspiration," according to which a book written without the help of the Holy Spirit could still become Scripture if the Holy Spirit later made it clear that the book contained nothing false. Lessius also denied the Dominican doctrine of efficacious grace and taught the Molinist position on grace and free will. The faculties of Douai and Louvain condemned his theses and called him a semi-Pelagianist, but those of Ingolstadt, Mainz, and Trier supported his views. Pope Sixtus V forced silence on both sides.

**Letters of Obscure Men.** A satire written as a series of letters, published anonymously in 1515 and 1517, and addressed to Ortwin Gratius, who, though trained as a humanist, vociferously opposed Reuchlin. The authors, Crotus Rubianus, Ulrich von Hutten, and others, scathingly ripped the learning and the behavior of the Schoolmen, as well as general conditions in the papal church, which was thereby greatly discredited.

**Levelers.** Political group in mid-17th-century England, growing out of agitation in the Parliamentary army during the civil wars. Dissatisfied with Parliament's caution in remolding the nation, the Levelers advocated, in the army debates and the Agreement of the People (1647), the equal "natural" rights of all and therefore radical reforms, including freedom of religion and universal manhood suffrage. Fearing anarchy, especially after the 1649 army mutiny, Cromwell suppressed them, but leaders such as John Lilburne still pressed their demands. Lilburne (c. 1614–1657), influenced by Baptist Separatists, had taken part in the Puritan protest against Archbishop Laud, and was sentenced to whipping and prison in 1638; there he wrote tracts against the bishops. Released in 1640, he joined the Parliamentary army in 1642. His inveterate agitating led to imprisonment by Parliament (1645–1648) for unlicensed printing and contempt of the House of Lords. He then declared Parliament unrepresentative and maintained that all power was in the people. In 1649 he was tried and acquitted for attacking the army leaders. In his last years he joined the Quakers. Other Leveler leaders were William Walwyn, wealthy merchant and champion of religious liberty, and Richard Overton (d. 1663), Separatist printer and author of the controversial *Man's Mortallitie* (1644).

**Lewis, Clive Staples** (1898–1963). English writer, under the pseudonym Clive Hamilton. Born in Belfast, Ireland, and educated at Malvern College and University College, Oxford, he served as lecturer, University College (1924–1925), and fellow and tutor, Magdalen College (1925–1954). He was a fellow of the British Academy as well as a fellow of the Royal Society of Literature. A prolific author of popular religious and apologetic works (*Pilgrim's Regress, an Allegorical Apology for Christianity, Reason, and Romanticism,* 1935), he also wrote science fiction, children's stories, and scholarly works on medieval and Renaissance English literature.

**Lewis, John Travers** (1825–1901). Canadian bishop. Born at Garrycloyne Castle, Cork, Ireland, and educated at Trinity College, Dublin, he was ordained in 1849 and the following year came to Canada. In 1854 he became rector of St. Peter's Church, Brockville, Upper Canada, and was consecrated bishop of Ontario in 1862, becoming the first Anglican bishop to be consecrated in Canada. He was made metropolitan of Canada in 1893 and archbishop in 1894. He was the originator of the idea of the Lambeth Conferences, at which all the bishops of the Anglican Communion might be present.

**Liberal Arts.** The seven disciplines that constituted the basic course of education in the Middle Ages. The elementary disciplines were grammar, rhetoric, and dialectic (trivium). The technical disciplines were astronomy, geometry, arithmetic, and music (quadrivium). In a medieval university, the course in the liberal arts was prerequisite to study in the faculties of law, medicine, and theology.

**Liberalism.** As a general, though rather imprecise, characterization, this term implies that freedom is at the root of the type of thought so described. Originating deep in the history of Western thought, the notion of the freedom of the human will was championed by Pelagius (d. c. 419) against Augustine's insistence upon predestination and original sin. The victory of the Augustinian view over Pelagianism succeeded in submerging it throughout medieval Christian thought with only occasional brief appearances. As connoting freedom from external authority, the idea reappeared with humanism in the 15th century and achieved mature expression in such philosophers as Locke and Hume, Rousseau and the Encyclopedists, Lessing and Kant. As a political view, it achieved classic statement in the principles of the French Revolution.

Liberal theology is an attempt to incorporate into Christian systematic thinking the values that have been expressed in modern political and social movements while emphasizing the ethical over the doctrinal aspects of the Christian faith, thus stressing the freedom of man and his capacity for response to God's will and for shaping his own life in conformity thereto. The origin of liberal theology is to be traced to the early 19th century in Germany, where it comprised one of three directions of thought, the other two being mediating theology and confessional theology. Stemming from Schleiermacher, German liberalism passed through three phases. The first was dominated by the critical work of D. F. Strauss and the historical reconstructions of the Christian past by F. C. Baur depending upon Hegelian categories; the second was under the dominance of Albrecht Ritschl, whose separation of faith and knowledge, and dependence upon the former, amounted to a victory of Kant over Hegel; in the third stage the chief influence came from the "history of religions" school, whose liberal creed is so amply expressed by Adolf von Harnack in *What Is Christianity?* (1901). English liberal theology, coming out of deism and moralism, spawned Unitarianism on the one side and on the other, latitudinarianism, a school that began with S. T. Coleridge (d. 1834). The movement achieved a culmination with J. F. D. Maurice's universalism. A significant expression of this view was to be found in *Essays and Reviews* (1860), while it was carried on through Charles Gore and his *Lux mundi* school even to William Temple and *Doctrine in the Church of England* (1938). Another aspect of it was in the Modernism of R. J. Campbell. American liberalism in the 19th century came through the Unitarianism of W. E. Channing, the transcendentalism of R. W. Emerson, and the "later New Haven Theology" of Horace Bushnell. The movement developed in a characteristic way into the Social Gospel, espoused and advanced by Walter Rauschenbusch. As a more particularly theological movement, this direction of thought continued with Shailer Mathews and R. L. Calhoun, as well as with H. P. Van Dusen. The neo-orthodox eclipse of liberalism in Germany, accomplished by Karl Barth and Emil Brunner on one side and Rudolf Bultmann on the other, had its echoes in the American scene in the person of Reinhold Niebuhr and in his contemporaries. With a rather more strident tone, a renewed form of liberalism was to make its voice heard in "radical" or "death of God" theology, particularly in the work of William Hamilton, Thomas Altizer, and Paul van Buren, and to a lesser degree in Gibson Winter, Harvey Cox, and the situationists in Christian ethics. This typically American movement has had its echoes in Germany with the writing of Dorothee Sölle among others. As a revolt against neo-orthodoxy, this radical theology has stressed again the freedom of man but has been influenced by Dietrich Bonhoeffer in the direction of suppressing the transcendental dimension of earlier forms of liberalism.

BIBLIOGRAPHY: R. T. Calhoun, *God and the Common Life* (New York, 1935); K. Cauthen, *The Impact of American Religious Liberalism* (New York, 1962); L. H. DeWolf, *The Case for Theology in Liberal Perspective* (Philadelphia, 1959); D. E. Roberts and H. P. Van Dusen (eds.), *Liberal Theology: An Appraisal* (New York, 1942); C. R. Sanders, *Coleridge and the Broad Church Movement* (Durham, N.C., 1942).

**Liberalism in America.** The American expression of the theological movement associated with Friedrich Schleiermacher influenced northern urban Protestantism from the late 1860's, when the end of the Civil War left time to consider pending issues of the spirit, until the early 1930's, when increasing attacks from left and right produced a nemesis of creativity. Though owing its basic philosophic bent to the German school, American liberalism was indebted also to native forms of liberal thought, most importantly Unitarianism, and in its own social and religious setting developed a distinctive ethos and history.

In its beginnings the movement was primarily characterized by a spirit free from creedal commitments and hospitable to new truth, especially as attested by intuitive, perhaps mystical, religious experience. This spirit was exemplified by Horace Bushnell, "father of American liberalism," who absorbed his German romantic idealism mostly through Coleridge's *Aids to Reflection* (1825). Of open mind and heart, deeply conscious of the social and ethical dimensions of the gospel, dubious about emotional revivals, respectful of private mystical experience, unwilling to debate points of doctrine, Christocentric in emphasis, convinced that language was too imprecise outside a social context to be entrusted to form dependable creeds, Bushnell set directions for the liberal movement in *Nature and the Supernatural* (1858) and *Christian Nurture* (1860). His attitudes won wide acceptance, in part perhaps because they comported well with the strain of individualism in the American character.

In this expansive spirit, liberals set out to harmonize Christian faith with the facts and theories of modern scholarship. They found their methodology ready-made in the empirical, inductive scientific method whose increasingly wide application was producing the new scholarship. Liberals rejected the deductive rationalism common to the systematic theologies of Reformed Protestantism. If this spirit and method protected liberalism more perfectly from orthodoxy than from current culture, they built nonetheless an impressive record of accommodation from 1870 to 1900.

The uneasy truce of science and religion after Newton's synthesis was shattered by Charles Darwin's writings after 1859. In the lively American debate of the 1870's the concept of theistic evolution reconciled the theory with the liberal gospel. Evolution was not only God's way of doing things, but it supported rising liberal confidence in the possibilities in human nature for continued improvement, a confidence bulwarked also by generic American optimism. With the powerful blessing of pulpit idol Henry Ward Beecher by 1880, evolution was transformed from a threat into a triumphal key to knowledge of man, of religion, and of nature's God.

Belief in an inerrant Bible was destroyed among liberals not only by their concept of experience as authority, and by the implications of Darwin's theory for the traditional understanding of Genesis, but also by the application to the Bible of the principles of literary and historical analysis, called "higher criticism." This was scientific method in Bible study, and it brought into question the old conclusions as to authorship, accuracy, and chronology. The popularity of the higher criticism stimulated serious objective comparison of Christianity with other religions, whose sacred writings had long been subjected to such analysis. Interest in comparative religions was stimulated by James Freeman Clarke's *Ten Great Religions* (1871 and 1883), and liberals learned they could hold to a certain primacy of Christ while accepting other routes to the Kingdom.

Those who insisted that liberalism was a body of doctrine as well as a spirit and a method were obliged to deal with so many variations that they belied their contention. Yet most first-generation liberals could recognize their convictions in William Newton Clarke's *Outline of Christian Theology* (1898), the chief compendium of the new theology. Doctrine was minimized and was centered on Jesus as man at his best, an ethical influence rather than a risen Redeemer, the manifestation of the divine element in human nature, the crowning result of the evolution of Judaism, whose life and teachings provide a model for all and a standard by which the Bible, traditions, and creeds may be judged. The transcendence and judgment of God were replaced by divine immanence and love. Clarke did not promote social reform; 19th-century liberals were more apt to espouse "gospel of wealth" social conservatism than the nascent Social Gospel. The Social Gospel numbered conservatives as well as liberals among its founders, but by 1910 had become largely identified with liberalism. Both liberalism and the Social Gospel owed something to the pragmatic turn of the American mind.

The new theology provided the most exciting ideas of the age and captured the imagination of leading intellectuals in and out

of the church. Once accepted, the liberal faith became to many a new dogma, to be promoted with combative fervor against what was labeled "obscurantism." By 1900, liberalism had prevailed in the leading seminaries and had gained great influence in the central councils of most major denominations. Heresy trials were increasingly being won by liberals. After 1910 certain conservatives regrouped their forces for a final defense, and through the 1920's, lines were drawn and the fundamentalist-modernist battle raged. Modernists were the radical, humanistic liberals of the present century, some of them tending toward naturalism or Dewey's instrumentalism, rejecting the authority even of Christ, classic liberalism's last link with the historic faith.

By the 1930's, world affairs and the depression had revealed shadows in human nature and cast doubt on social progress. Serious American theologians arose, influenced by Barth's neo-orthodoxy, who successfully challenged the liberal neglect of historic doctrines and the damaging adjustments that conformed the faith to the contrary assumptions of modern secular thought.

BIBLIOGRAPHY: K. Cauthen, *The Impact of American Religious Liberalism* (New York, 1962); L. H. DeWolf, *The Case for Theology in Liberal Perspective* (Philadelphia, 1959); J. G. Machen, *Christianity and Liberalism* (New York, 1923); S. Mathews, *The Faith of Modernism* (New York, 1924); F. P. Weisenburger, *Ordeal of Faith: The Crisis of Church-Going America, 1865–1900* (New York, 1959); H. N. Wieman, *Religious Liberals Reply* (Boston, 1947).

**Liberian Catalogue.** A list of popes, modeled in its earlier part upon the one in the *Chronicle* of Hippolytus, compiled during the pontificate of Liberius (352–366). The compiler is known to us only as the "Chronographer of 354," the designation given to him by the scholar T. Mommsen. The Catalogue also includes the Roman holidays of the time, a list of consuls, an Easter table, a list of the Roman city prefects, a martyrology for Rome, and a chronicle of the ecclesiastical and the secular history of Rome.

**Liberius** (d. 366). Pope from 352. The first pope to become "the foremost Roman" (Harnack, *History of Dogma* V, 59), Liberius was so impressed with his authority that he tried to give directions to Athanasius and Constantius. He lived to be chastened, for Constantius sent him into exile for not condemning Athanasius and eventually compelled him to submit. It is not known what document he signed, but his doing so allowed him to return to Rome, where he found Felix ensconced in his see. After Felix retired in his favor, Liberius extended charity to the East and even toleration to the pagans.

**Liber Pontificalis.** A collection of papal biographies comprising several distinct editions, continuing to the 15th century. The letter at the beginning from Pope Damasus asking Jerome to write the history of the popes is regarded as false. Prior to the 8th century, the accounts are short and not contemporary. From the 8th century onward, they tend to be more detailed and are frequently written by contemporaries.

**Libertas** (June 20, 1888). Encyclical of Leo XIII on human liberty. The pope praised true and censured false ideas of liberty: limits exist to the freedom of worship, thought, speech, and press when liberals confuse liberty with license, placing error on a parity with truth. The result is a denial of divine authority and the suggestion that man is a law unto himself. "The eternal law of God is the sole standard and rule of human liberty."

**Lidgett, John Scott** (1854–1953). Methodist editor and writer. Born at Lewisham, England, and educated at Blackheath Proprietary School and University College, London, he was ordained by the Methodist Church in 1876. Together with Dr. Moulton, he founded the Bermondsey Settlement in 1891 and remained as its warden from 1891 to 1949. He was editor of the *Methodist Times* (1907–1918) and joint editor of the *Contemporary Review* (1911–1953). A member of the London School Board after 1897 and an alderman of the London County Council (1905–1928), he published many works on theological subjects, the best known of which was *The Spiritual Principle of the Atonement* (Fernley Lecture, 1897).

**Liebknecht, Wilhelm** (1826–1900). Founder of the German Socialist Party. A teacher in Switzerland when the 1848 revolution broke out, he led volunteers into Baden and set up a republic, but it failed. For thirteen years he lived in close association with Karl Marx in London. Expelled from Prussia in 1865, he settled in Leipzig. He was imprisoned for opposition to the war of 1870. The union of Socialists achieved at the Congress of Gotha in 1874 was his work. He was a member of the Reichstag (1874–1900).

**Lietzmann, Hans** (1875–1942). German church historian. Born in Düsseldorf and raised in Wittenberg, he early lost his father and was educated at great financial sacrifice by his mother. He was trained first in Jena but chiefly at Bonn, where his interest was mainly in classical philology and ancient history. In 1900 he became a lecturer in church history at Bonn, where he began publishing his *Kleine Texte für Vorlesungen und Übungen* and also engaged in and published his studies in the largely neglected Greek patristic catenae. In 1904 his study in Apollinarius of Laodicea revolutionized the interpretation of that church father. Called as professor extraordinarius of church history at Jena in 1905, he began publication there of the *Handbuch zum Neuen Testament* (1906 ff.), in which he authored the commentaries on Romans, Corinthians, and Galatians. In 1908 he became a full professor at Jena and while there produced a number of important monographs, among which his *Petrus und Paulus in Rom* (1915) stands out. Becoming editor of the *Zeitschrift für die neutestamentliche Wissenschaft* first in 1920, he carried forth that task until the close of his productive career. In 1924 he replaced Adolf von Harnack as professor of church history at Berlin. It was while there that he produced his famous treatment of the Mass and the Lord's Supper (1926) and the work for which he is best known to English readers, *A History of the Early Church* (4 vols., 1932–1944), on which he was still working when he died.

**Life and Work, Universal Christian Council for.** A council formed in 1930 by the reconstitution of the Continuation Committee set up by the Universal Christian Conference on Life and Work. The Council on Life and Work convened in the cathedral at Stockholm Aug. 19–30, 1925, gathering together over 500 delegates from 37 countries. The Universal Christian Council for Life and Work, without ignoring theological issues, seeks worldwide interdenominational cooperation on social issues without awaiting theological consensus. In its background are the World Alliance for Promoting International Friendship Through the Churches formed at an international conference at Constance at the outbreak of World War I (Aug. 2, 1914) and the Geneva Conference (Aug. 9–12, 1920), which first used the term "Life and Work."

The Council sponsored an international conference on "The Church and the State Today" in Paris in April, 1934, and convened the Second World Conference on Life and Work at Oxford on "Church, Community, and State" (July 12–26, 1937), consisting of 425 regular members representing 120 communions in 40 countries, plus associate delegates, visitors, and youth representatives. It appointed seven members and seven alternates to the Committee of Fourteen to implement merger with the Faith and Order movement. On May 13, 1938, at Utrecht it transferred its functions to the Provisional Committee of the World Council of Churches in Process of Formation.

**Lightfoot, Joseph Barber** (1828–1889). Anglican theologian. Born at Liverpool, he was educated at Trinity College, Cambridge. In 1857 he became a tutor at Trinity College and in 1861, Hulsean professor. He was Lady Margaret Professor of Divinity at Cambridge (1875–1879) and from 1870 to 1880 he worked as one of the revisers of the King James Version of the Bible. In 1879 he became the bishop of Durham. An outstanding New Testament scholar of the 19th century he produced a monumental five-volume edition of the apostolic fathers which is a standard work. He was a proponent of the historical-grammatical method.

**Liguori, Alphonsus** (1696–1787). Italian moral theologian. A potent influence on modern Roman Catholicism, he was a founder of the Redemptorists. His most significant works were his *Theologia moralis* and devotional treatises, especially those concerning the Virgin Mary (e.g., *The Glories of Mary*). The prestige of probabilism was due to him. Pius IX declared him a doctor of the Church in 1871.

**Lilburne, John.** See LEVELERS.

**Linacre, Thomas** (c. 1460–1524). English humanist and physician. Educated at Oxford and in Italy, where he learned Greek and studied medicine, he became Henry VIII's physician in 1509 and founded the Royal College of Physicians in 1518. As a friend of Erasmus, Colet, and More, and a tutor to Prince Arthur and Princess Mary, his influence on the English Renaissance was extensive.

**Lincoln, Abraham** (1809–1865). The 16th president of the United States (from 1861). While most American churchmen on both sides of the Civil War only displayed their provincial, short-range, and uncharitable views, Lincoln felt that North as well as South stood under divine judgment, and that America's religious destiny was at stake. Although influenced by conservative Baptist and Presbyterian traditions, Lincoln was independent and pragmatic in his personal encounter with the Bible. His inaugurals dwelt on moral and religious themes. He insisted on the essential spiritual unity of the nation and pointed out the tragedy of both sides reading the same Bible, praying to the same God, and invoking divine aid against each other when it was evident that neither side was to be answered ("The Almighty has his own purposes"). Replying to a clergyman, Lincoln said his hope was not that God was on the side of the North, but that the North was on God's side. Nevertheless, he acted under the premise that men must live according to God's will as they could estimate it in their finitude, admitting that certainty is impossible and self-righteousness self-defeating. Lincoln was unique in his ability to combine religious idealism with an effective concern for the practical realization of American institutions. He stressed freedom and national unity as "the last, best hope on earth" which Americans "shall nobly save or meanly lose." "American destiny under God" was an awesome challenge with unparalleled promise.

**Lindblom, Jacob Axelsson** (1746–1819). Swedish theologian and archbishop of Uppsala from 1805. His rationalistically revised catechism was authorized for general use in 1810 and had a wide influence for over forty years. During his primacy the Church of Sweden clergy became strongly influenced by Rationalism. He was the author of *Israel's Religion in Old Testament Times*.

**Lindisfarne.** An island off the extreme northeast coast of England and site of an important monastery founded in 635 by Aidan. This institution, which followed Celtic Church practices, soon became the center of English religious life, and many missionaries were trained there. Its influence began to wane after the Synod of Whitby ruled in 664 against the Celtic practices, though the monastery was not permanently abandoned until the time of the English Reformation.

**Lipsius, Richard Adelbert** (1830–1892). German Protestant theologian. He was a many-faceted person, a scholar and teacher (at Leipzig, Kiel, and Jena) of systematic theology who published critical editions of some sources for early Christian history. He became deeply involved in the issues of his own day as he worked for the Prussian Union of 1867 and helped found the Evangelical Alliance. His main concerns were the relation of philosophy to theology and of science to religion.

**Litany of the Saints.** An ancient form of prayer consisting of single intercessions with a short response. The traditional Western form began with invocations of the Trinity, Mary, and famous saints. This part was excised by the Reformers in making their litanies, but it is the sum of the litany under discussion which is used in the Roman Church. The naming of each saint by the officiant is followed by "Pray for us."

**Little Flowers of St. Francis of Assisi** (*Fioretti*). The collection of popular legends about Francis of Assisi and his early followers dating from about the beginning of the 14th century. Probably translated from a lost Latin original into the vernacular of Tuscany, the work is frequently praised as a glowing picture of religious life in the Middle Ages, successfully capturing the buoyant faith and childlike enthusiasm of Francis and his companions. It is still widely read.

**Little Labyrinth.** A name given to *Against the Heresy of Artemon*, an anti-Adoptianist work of the 3d century. The writer of a marginal note in Photius suggests that the author was Gaius, but since the description of this work as a "little" *Labyrinth* suggests comparison with a larger *Labyrinth*, and since that is another title for the *Philosophumena* of Hippolytus, many scholars believe the two works were by the same author. Our only quotations from the *Little Labyrinth* appear in Eusebius (*Ecclesiastical History* 5.28). There we are told that Christological orthodoxy was not a late innovation but had been maintained from the earliest times.

**Liturgical Books.** In the Old Testament, The Psalms are a hymnal and Leviticus a book of rubrics and rites. The Pentateuch, like much of the New Testament, was written to be read at liturgical assemblies. The discovery of the ritual purpose of many religious writings has helped to explain their arrangement and tone in contrast to books of instruction or meditation. After the canon was closed and as prayers and the structure of Mass and office became fixed, special books were developed for the convenience of priest, choir, and monk. The books that have been or are used for Mass are: *Missal*—all the parts used at Mass plus some blessings; *Kyriale*—the "ordinary" or unchanging parts with the various musical settings (plainsong); *Gradual*—chants and texts for the propers sung by the choir; *Homiliary*—sermons of the fathers; *Lectionary*—the pericopes of sections of Scripture appointed as Epistle and Gospel; *Liber usualis*—a compendium of chants and texts for the Mass and offices except Matins and Lauds. Books for the offices of Prayer: *Breviary*—all the offices, without music; *Antiphonary*—all the sung parts of the office; *Martyrology*—short lives of saints and martyrs, read at Prime. Other books are: *Ritual*—blessings and prayers not in missal or breviary

for priests; *Pontifical*—rites for a bishop; *Ceremonial*—ceremonies for bishop and others also. Books used by the Eastern Church include: *Typicon*—calendar and rubrics; *Euchologion*—priest's parts at Divine Liturgy; *Horologion*—common prayers and hymns for the office; *Menaion*—propers for saints in office; plus many books for the use of the choir. In Protestant worship three types of books have developed: *Hymnal; Service Book*—often bound with a hymnal, containing services of word, sacrament, and prayer for congregational use (e.g., The Book of Common Prayer); books of *Occasional Services* such as ordination and consecrations.

**Liturgical Movement.** Contemporary effort to enrich Christian worship and make it the center of life and piety, focusing especially on the Mass, Eucharist, or Lord's Supper.

In Roman Catholicism it emerged from Benedictine monasteries, first at Solesmes, France, with P. L. P. Guéranger (d. 1875); at Beuron, Germany, influenced by the theology of J. A. Moehler (d. 1838); and at Maredsous and Mont-César in Belgium. Gradually the movement became less monastic, medieval, romantic, and antiquarian, and more relevant to present needs. Its theology developed in the German abbey of Maria Laach with O. Casel's (d. 1948) "mystery theology," which stressed the whole liturgy as re-presentation of salvation events uniting man with God rather than the "making present" of Christ upon the altar. Scholarly liturgiology continued with P. Battifol, F. Cabrol, L. M. O. Duchesne, J. Jungmann, L. Bouyer, and others, but the movement as a program to change church life as a whole began with L. Beauduin in 1909 in Belgium, with the aim of centering parish life in the Mass properly understood. More congregational participation was favored (frequent Communion, vernacular Missals, dialogue Mass) and "extraliturgical" devotions discouraged (Rosary, Stations, Exposition, and Benediction of the Sacrament). Centers, institutes, and conferences popularized the cause. France, Belgium, and Germany were most favorable; in the United States, St. John's Abbey in Minnesota led. Papal sanction came: Pius X encouraged frequent Communion and reforms in church music; Pius XII gave cautious approval in *Mediator Dei* (1947), liberalized the rules for fasting before Communion, and had the Holy Week services revised and the Easter Vigil restored. Yet difficulties with local bishops were experienced. The Second Vatican Council went far in accepting the aims of the movement: use of the vernacular with the priest facing the people at Mass, congregational singing, emphasis on preaching, diocesan liturgical commissions, and, under certain circumstances, concelebration and Communion in both species were all authorized (1963). The movement was related to other currents of renewal: it spurred Biblical studies; liturgy as celebration of redemptive acts kindled theological emphases on revelation as event and salvation history; its corporate view of man bore on social concern; it inspired new art and music.

In Protestantism, the movement began as a return to earlier norms of worship (Reformation, patristic, or New Testament) in the Anglican Oxford movement; the Mercersburg movement among German Reformed in the United States; the books of C. Baird in American Presbyterianism; and in similar Lutheran movements in Germany (led by J. K. W. Loehe) and Sweden. Eventually many churches adopted service books to recapture their heritages: the American Lutheran *Common Service* (1888); the Presbyterian *Book of Common Worship* in the United States (1905) and *The Book of Common Order* in Scotland; the American Methodists' *Book of Worship* (1945); the English Congregationalists' *Book of Public Worship* (1948); and the Liturgies of Geneva (1946) and the Reformed Church of France (1955). Notable are the new liturgies of union churches, e.g., the United Church of Canada (1932) and the Church of South India. These have often been revised, stressing increasingly the centrality of Sacrament with Word, continuity with the whole church, and the need for relevance. In Anglicanism the weekly "parish Eucharist" became the norm, and the baroque excesses of Anglo-Catholics waned. Other aspects of the movement can be seen in the scholarship of Friedrich Heiler, Y. T. Brilioth, and Oscar Cullmann on the Continent and the Anglicans G. Dix and G. Hebert; in communities such as the French Protestant monastery of Taizé or Scotland's Iona; in societies such as the Order of St. Luke (American Methodist) or Brotherhood of St. Michael (German Lutheran); and in the growing preference for divided chancels, vested clergy, and use of the church year. Although this reflected theological concern for liturgy as response to the gift of redemption, often liturgy is also antiquarianism or desire for more "dignity."

BIBLIOGRAPHY: E. B. Koenker, *The Liturgical Renaissance in the Roman Catholic Church* (St. Louis, 1966); R. Paquier, *Dynamics of Worship* (Philadelphia, 1967); M. H. Shepherd (ed.), *The Liturgical Renewal*

*of the Church* (New York, 1960); M. J. Taylor, *The Protestant Liturgical Renewal* (Westminster, Md., 1963).

**Liturgical Revival in the United States.** A movement aimed at liturgical renewal, initiated by the Benedictines at the Abbey of Maria Laach in Germany, carried to the United States by monks of the order. St. John's Abbey, Collegeville, Minn., became the spiritual center of the Liturgical Apostolate. A periodical, *Orate Fratres,* renamed *Worship* in 1951, was sponsored by the abbey, beginning with Advent, 1925. This periodical has represented the objectives of the movement far beyond Roman Catholic circles, where the distinctive emphases of the revival first gained expression. The review's founder was Dom Virgil Michel, who combined interest in a renewed worship life with active social concerns. More recently Dom Godfrey Dieckmann has developed the broad program of renewal as editor of the periodical.

An earlier influence on the American scene may be traced to the foundation of the Pope Pius X School of Liturgical Music at Manhattanville College of the Sacred Heart in 1916. This was an outgrowth of Pope Pius X's *motu proprio* on sacred music issued in 1903. The *motu proprio* gave classic expression to the basic program that came to characterize the Apostolate; the faithful should acquire the true Christian spirit "from its first and indispensable source, namely, their own active participation in the sacred mysteries and in the solemn public prayer of the Church." A revived participation by the people should be realized, particularly in offering the sacrifice of the Mass, but the revival should extend to the other offices of the church as well (as distinct from participation in popular devotions). Pope Pius X presented the Gregorian chant as the liturgical chant par excellence of the Roman Catholic Church; he also sought to stimulate the faithful to more frequent Communion within the framework and celebration of the Mass.

The revival in the United States received an impetus in July, 1929, through the inauguration at St. John's Abbey of the first Liturgical Day. In 1928 the Liturgical Arts Society was chartered; the quarterly published by this society, *Liturgical Arts,* has contributed to the improvement of artistic standards in all media of liturgical arts, also among those not Roman Catholic. Dynamic exploration of new alternatives in church architecture and the plastic arts owes much to the stimulus of this periodical.

In 1940 the first Liturgical Week was held

in Chicago, permitting an exchange of views between Roman Catholic clergy, religious, and laity from all parts of the country. The conference has been held in various cities of the country since that time; in recent years the Liturgical Week has been scheduled each summer in a number of metropolitan centers. Local hierarchy have often been outspoken at these conferences in approving what they recognize as legitimate aims of the movement, but the history of the revival includes strong opposition on the part of local ordinaries to basic objectives of the renewal, e.g., the use of English instead of Latin in liturgical functions.

Two encyclicals issued by Pope Pius XII were significant for promoting and channeling the direction of the revival, also in the United States: *Mystici corporis Christi* in 1943, an interpretation of the church as Christ's mystical body, and *Mediator Dei* in 1947, an exposition of the Sacred Liturgy. Pius XII issued a new Latin Psalter in 1945 based upon a critical Hebrew text. In the 1950's the papacy authorized use of the vernacular in the occasional offices of the Roman ritual for various countries, including the United States. Thus such rites as Baptism and Unction as well as various blessings could be conducted in the language of the people. The revision of the Holy Week services and the restoration of the Easter Vigil in 1951 were important steps in correcting dislocations in the rite and in facilitating participation. The Second Vatican Council, in sessions from 1962 to 1965, demonstrated by its preoccupation with, and positive reaction to, problems emerging from the revival the remarkable vitality and potential of the renewal.

The worship revival has made significant contributions in the Anglican and Lutheran communions, as well as in the Presbyterian and Reformed Churches. Almost every Protestant body in the United States has participated in the reaction to an exclusive intellectualism and subjectivism in worship. The Protestant revival began in the 1920's, and has responded to particular cultural and theological traditions in each denomination. However, in all major Protestant bodies the revival may be seen as characterized by a renewed awareness of symbolism, an appreciation for the role of beauty in worship, by the use of vestments, a concern for better hymns and church music, and by an interest in the church year.

BIBLIOGRAPHY: L. D. Reed, *The Lutheran Liturgy* (Philadelphia, 1947); and *Worship: A Study of Corporate Worship* (Philadelphia, 1959); M. H. Shepherd (ed.), *The Liturgical Renewal of the Church* (New York, 1960); and *The Reform of Liturgical Worship* (New York, 1961); M. J. Taylor, *The Protestant Liturgical Renewal* (Westminster, Md., 1963).

**Liturgical Terminology.** Special terms and usages of terms developed for the direction and recording of liturgical worship in the church. *Rubrics* (from the Latin word for "red," since they are commonly printed in that color) are the directions for the traditional and orderly performance of worship, often printed with the texts or *ritual* or *liturgy,* i.e., the spoken or sung words.

The personnel: *Celebrant*—the president of the liturgy, in the earliest church the bishop only, now any priest or ordained minister. *Deacon*—the assistant to the president, who reads the Gospel and other prayers. *Subdeacon*—an assistant who reads the Epistle. *Acolyte,* or altar boy—the server of the celebrant and altar. *Crucifer*—the bearer of the cross in procession. *Thurifer*—the bearer of the thurible in which incense is burned.

Parts of the Western liturgy (usually the Latin word that begins the text): *Introit*—the opening processional chant after preparatory prayers or confession, consisting of a psalm verse with antiphons, and *Gloria Patri*—a sentence of praise to the Trinity added to psalms and canticles. *Kyrie*—Greek for "Lord" in "Lord, have mercy," said or sung in patterns of three or as a response to bids, or invitations to prayer. *Gloria in excelsis*—an ancient hymn of praise to the Trinity, beginning with the song of the angels to the shepherds in Bethlehem. *Collect*—a sentence prayer with address, petition, and closing formula mentioning Persons of the Trinity. *Epistle*—the lesson from New Testament letters or from the Old Testament. *Gradual*—portions of psalms with alleluia or special tract, the origin of the sequence hymns now suppressed. *Gospel*—the lesson from one of the four Gospels, accompanied by ceremonies. *Homily* or *Sermon*—exposition of texts of Scripture. *Creed*—one of three ecumenical creeds, usually the Nicene. *Offertory*—the reception of gifts, preparation for sacrament, prayers, and chants. *Preface*—versicles (president or leader says sentence, with sentence response by the congregation) including *Sursum corda* ("Lift up your hearts") introducing the *Sanctus* ("Holy," based on Isaiah's vision of heaven), followed by *Benedictus qui venit* ("Blessed is he who comes"). *Canon, Eucharistic Prayer*—a prayer of thanksgiving and consecration which includes or is replaced by the *verbum* or Words of Institution from the Biblical accounts of the upper room rite. *Pax*—a greeting of peace from president to congregation and sometimes also among the congregation. *Agnus Dei*—"Lamb of God," a meditative chant before the administration of the elements (bread and wine). *Benediction*—blessings of various degrees of solemnity following Communion or the whole liturgy. Texts for the Eucharistic Liturgy include the *ordinary,* used at every celebration, such as the Sanctus or the Gloria in Excelsis, which is omitted at penitential times, and the *propers,* such as the Introit, which change according to the particular observance in the church year. *Pericopes*—sections of Scripture appointed as proper lessons at Mass.

Special terms used of the offices of prayer: *Antiphon*—the phrase that preludes and follows a psalm or canticle indicating a theme for meditation sometimes based on the liturgical year. *Venite*—Psalm 95, traditionally the first psalm of Lauds or Morning Prayer. *Responsory*—meditation text following the church year in the form of versicles or choir chant, after lesson. *Canticle*—a psalm-like chant from the Bible other than the Psalter or a creation of the early church. *Intonation*—the indication of the tone by a cantor or soloist who begins the chant alone. *Psalm tone*—eight chant formulas that are used for the singing of psalms and canticles.

Locations: The altar end of a church is liturgically the East, the south being the Epistle side, and the Gospel side the north. The *choir* section, usually elevated, is the area between the nave, the place for the congregation, and the altar and its area, whether the singing choir is there or not. The *narthex* is the entrance hall into the nave. The *sacristy* is the side room for the preparation of the elements and the care of linens and hangings, also often serving as *vestry,* where liturgical vestments are put on and preparatory prayers recited.

**Liturgies.** The word "liturgy" comes from secular Greek, where it designated a public function or duty undertaken by or assigned to a prominent citizen, usually performed at his own expense, e.g., the production of a tragedy (Lysias, *Orations* 21.1 f.) or equipping of a warship (*ibid.,* 2). Eventually it was used for any public service, and in Roman times it could mean simply a beneficence (II Cor. 9:12). In the Hellenistic era, it acquired another technical meaning, that of a public service rendered to the Gods (Aristotle, *Politics* 7.9.7; Diodorus Siculus, *Historical Library* 1.21.7; cf. Tebtunis *Papyri,* No. 302). From this it got into the Septuagint (LXX) (Num. 8:25) to style priestly ministry and thence into rabbinical literature to denominate the synagogue service. The richest develop-

ment of the term came in postapostolic Christian literature where it was used almost exclusively of the order for the Eucharist. The term is used of worship forms beyond Judaism and Christianity only by analogy.

1. Uniform liturgies developed slowly and only out of regional uses. There are no demonstrable forms of liturgy immediately deducible from the New Testament, although attempts have been made to show that the passion narrative, the farewell addresses of the Fourth Gospel (especially John, ch. 17), and I Peter are based on liturgical form. Paul's discussion of the Corinthian assembly (I Cor. 11:17–34) may presuppose a fixed liturgy, but its outline is unrecoverable. The earliest recognizable liturgies stem from the East and are found in the Apostolic Church Orders, especially in Hippolytus' Apostolic Tradition (end of 2d century) and the Sacramentary of Serapion of Thmuis (4th century).

The most ancient complete liturgies are Syrian in origin. The oldest of these is the East Syrian Liturgy of Addai and Mari which has 3d-century roots and though originally without an institution of the Lord's Supper, acquired it through the influence of the Greek liturgies. At the end of the 4th century there appeared from northern Syria the Apostolic Constitutions containing the so-called Clementine Liturgy whose Eucharistic Prayer is a revised form of the one in Hippolytus. This region further produced the form that evolved into the Liturgy of St. John Chrysostom, the Eucharistic Prayer that underlies the Liturgy of St. Basil, and the liturgy that forms the basis of the *Catechetical Lectures* of Theodore of Mopsuestia. The Jerusalem Liturgy of St. James, first witnessed by the *Mystagogical Lectures* of Cyril of Jerusalem, belongs to the Syrian type and became the normative liturgy of the Syrian Jacobites.

The earliest Egyptian liturgy is the Alexandrian Liturgy of St. Mark, which was apparently the normative liturgy (cf. the Eucharistic Prayer of Serapion of Thmuis) in this region until it was replaced by the Liturgy of St. Basil, although it still enjoys popularity in Coptic and Ethiopic churches, where it is named for Cyril of Alexandria. The Liturgy of St. Basil and the Liturgy of St. Gregory were in use in Alexandria until its demise; both of these liturgies are also extant in Coptic.

The Byzantine Liturgy of St. Basil gradually took over all the Eastern Orthodox Churches that remained Chalcedonian. Originating in the environs of Antioch, it remained dominant in those churches until it was replaced in the 10th century by the Liturgy of

St. John Chrysostom, a Syrian liturgy that owes its origin to the Anaphora of the Twelve Apostles. This liturgy achieved wide use, since it was the one translated into Old Church Slavonic and used by all Slavic Orthodox.

2. In the West, there are two types of liturgies: the constrained, concise Roman-African type and the more poetic and mystical Gallican type deeply influenced by the East. Of the latter, there is the Spanish-Gothic or Mozarabic type, the Ambrosian use of Milan, the old Gallic Merovingian liturgy (cf. Pseudo-Germanus of Paris) and the Celtic liturgy of Ireland and the areas it influenced. These liturgies were all but obliterated by the determined liturgical imperialism of the see of Rome, one way in which that church achieved domination over the entire West. By 400, the Roman Church was using Latin exclusively, although its sacramentaries (Liturgical Books; Gelasian and Leonine Sacramentaries) showed the influence of the Gallican rites. In 600, Gregory I began a thoroughgoing reform to maximize liturgical uniformity in the Latin West. With the Ottonian Renaissance in mid-10th century, some Gallican flavor was restored (cf. Frankish *Ordines Romani* and the *Romano-German Pontifical* of Mainz). From the 11th to the 13th century under Gregory VII and Innocent III, a new movement to rid the Latin rite of all Eastern intrusions was given greater impetus by the Schism between East and West. This liturgy, used in Greek translation in parts of the East as the Liturgy of St. Peter, became a confessional standard of the West against the East. Developed in the Curia and promoted through the antiheretical struggles, this liturgy was carried across the Western world by the Franciscans. As a result of the decisions of the Council of Trent, a new missal was published (1570) which epitomized the Roman liturgical development, although it did not completely replace all local usages until the surge of Romanization accompanying the papacy of Pius IX in the late 19th century. This action left unaffected only the Eastern usages of a few Uniate churches, the Eastern Rite Catholics, the Ambrosian use of Milan, and the Mozarabic use at Toledo. No changes were undertaken in the Latin liturgy until the restoration of the ancient observance of Holy Week and the Easter Vigil (1955). Latin has been used exclusively in this liturgy since the 4th century; the permission for a vernacular liturgy granted by the Second Vatican Council (*Sacrosanctum concilium,* 1963) does not affect the structure of the liturgy or the uniformity of its use.

3. An important product of the Reformation was liturgical experiment. Luther meant less to revolutionize liturgy than to rid it of non-Scriptural medieval accretions and to eliminate the sacrificial tone of the Latin rite. Liturgical uniformity was confined to the regional churches, each of them adopting Church Orders, part of which was a liturgy. Although preaching was stressed, it was done in a liturgical setting which, after Thomas Müntzer (d. 1525), was in the vernacular. Zwingli's radical tendencies are nowhere more visible than in his liturgy for Zurich (1525) which is comparable to that of Oecolampadius for Basel (1525). Only what is specifically authorized by Scripture went into the liturgy, which was a preaching and prayer service, Communion being held only quarterly. Calvin's liturgical reform, influenced by his period at the Church of the Strangers in Strasbourg, was as radical as Zwingli's, although he did insist upon weekly Communion, which condition he was never successful in imposing on the Geneva community. Cranmer's liturgy of 1549, the Book of Common Prayer, was in large measure simply a vernacular rendition of the current Latin rite with some additions for devotions of the people. Although this liturgy was subsequently modified in 1552 (somewhat drastically), 1559, and 1662, it kept the Church of England closer liturgically to Rome than to the churches of the Continental Reformation. Among the Free Churches, liturgical innovation and modification were possible and occurred more frequently because of the greater community autonomy of these churches and their freedom from hierarchical and bureaucratic direction.

4. The historical and theological study of liturgy, as well as the vital concern for making liturgy more expressive of the church's faith, has brought about an awakening called the liturgical movement. From its beginnings among the Benedictines of Maria Laach, it has had widespread effect not only within the Roman Catholic Church but among Protestant and Reformed bodies as well. In a more cooperative atmosphere fostered by the various activities of the ecumenical movement, the results of historical inquiry have been concretized in the liturgical reforms of such groups as the Reformed cenobite community of Taizé in France, in the Michelbruderhof in Germany, and in the various liturgical reforms that are flowing from the deliberations of the Second Vatican Council. Another indication of this serious concern with liturgy is to be seen in the revised prayer books not only of the various provinces of the Anglican Communion but also among those churches in

the Wider Episcopal Fellowship. The second half of the 20th century should produce a new and exciting chapter in the history of liturgies.

BIBLIOGRAPHY: G. Dix, *The Shape of the Liturgy* (London, 1945); L. Duchesne, *Christian Worship* (New York, 1919); J. A. Jungmann, *Mass of the Roman Rite*, 2 vols. (New York, 1951–1955); and *Liturgical Worship* (New York, 1941); H. Lietzmann, *Mass and the Lord's Supper* (Leiden, 1953); B. Thompson, *Liturgies of the Western Church* (Cleveland, 1961).

**Liutprand of Cremona** (c. 922–c. 972). Italian prelate and historian. A noble Lombard, he was sent on a mission to Constantinople in 949 by King Berengar of Italy. After a public disgrace, he entered the service of Otto I, who made him bishop of Cremona in 961. He was sent to Constantinople to arrange a marriage for Otto II. His account of the mission *Relatio de Legatione Constantinopolitana* is a highly prejudiced view of Byzantine life. He wrote several historical works relating to Otto I.

**Living Church, The.** A schismatic movement arising in 1922 within Russian Orthodoxy, which favored cooperation with the Communists, believing that a *modus vivendi* with the Soviets could be found. In 1923, during the imprisonment of the patriarch Tikhon, a presbyterial form of church government was set up. In 1925 The Living Church claimed 12,593 parishes, 16,540 clergy, and 192 bishops. During the 1940's the leaders of The Living Church rejoined the patriarchal Russian Orthodox Church.

**Livingstone, David** (1813–1873). Scottish missionary and explorer in Africa. In 1840, under the auspices of the London Missionary Society, he established missionary stations in Bechuanaland. In addition to his missionary activities, he explored numerous rivers and lands and discovered Victoria Falls in 1855. In 1857 he published his *Missionary Travels and Researches in South Africa*, which aroused interest in his African adventures.

**Livonia, Conversion of.** Missions to Livonia began c. 1180 under the direction of the archbishop of Bremen. However, repeated pagan reactions hindered their success until the king of Sweden, Erik IX, lent his military support. A bishopric was established at Riga in 1201 which became a metropolis of Prussia in 1255. The Teutonic Knights were invited by a Polish prince in 1228 to assist in a war against the pagan Prussians. The order succeeded in defeating the Prussians, cutting the

Poles off from the sea, and introducing their own rule over Prussia. The eastward expansion of the Knights and of German colonization brought them into conflict with the Orthodox Russians and the pagan Lithuanians. A branch of the order, the Livonian Brothers of the Sword, engaged in a crusade against the pagans in order to bring them to the faith and under German control. The order succeeded in purchasing Estonia from Denmark in 1326, giving them a firmer hold on the Baltic. Their designs on Lithuania were thwarted in 1385 when the Lithuanian prince Jagello was converted to Catholicism, married the ruling princess of Poland, and himself became king of Poland. This conversion and union ended the crusading character of German expansion and led to the defeat of the Teutonic Knights by a Slavic army at Tannenberg in 1410.

**Locke, John** (1632–1704). English philosopher. Sometimes described as the intellectual leader of the 18th-century Enlightenment, Locke held theories of knowledge and political life that are still widely felt. Born at Wrington, Somersetshire, the son of an attorney who served as a captain in the Parliamentary army of the English Civil War, he was educated at Westminster School (B.A., 1656) and at Christ Church, Oxford (M.A., 1658). From 1661 to 1664 he lectured at Oxford on Greek, rhetoric, and philosophy, and in 1665, went as secretary of the English minister to the elector of Brandenburg. The next year he settled as a physician at Oxford, through his profession becoming a friend of Anthony Ashley Cooper (later first Earl of Shaftesbury), whose confidential adviser he became and under whose patronage he held various offices—fellow of the Royal Society (1668) and secretary of the Council of Trade (1673). When Shaftesbury went into exile (1682), Locke followed him and lived in the Netherlands until 1689. Returning to England after the accession of William and Mary, Locke spent the rest of his life publishing and writing his philosophical and religious ideas.

With the publication of his *An Essay Concerning Human Understanding* (1690), Locke became the leader of the English sensational school of English philosophy. His purpose was to investigate the origin, certainty, and extent of human knowledge. In this work he attacked the Platonist conception of innate ideas; the human mind, he argued, is a *tabula rasa,* and knowledge comes through experience and reflection. He was thus the originator of the empirical philosophy of the 18th century which greatly influenced the political and social theorists of western Europe. His *Two Treatises of Government* (1690), once thought to have been written to rationalize the Glorious Revolution of 1688, appears to have been written to justify Shaftesbury's opposition to the government of Charles II. Locke argued that government is a contract between the governor and the governed, and that if this contract is broken through arbitrary attacks on the life, liberty, and property rights of the people, revolution is justifiable. His political thought had a profound effect upon the American Declaration of Independence and the United States Constitution.

In religion, Locke was one of the foremost defenders of free inquiry and toleration. In his *Letters Concerning Toleration* (1689, 1690, and 1692), he proclaimed that "absolute liberty . . . is the thing we stand in need of." He did not stand firm on principle, however. He recommended the suppression of Roman Catholics, on the ground that they owed their first allegiance to a foreign authority, the pope; and of atheists, on the ground that their word on an oath could not be trusted. His religious ideal was a national church with a comprehensive creed that made ample allowance for individual opinion, in the belief that human understanding was too limited for one man to impose his beliefs on another. In his *Reasonableness of Christianity as delivered in the Scriptures* (1695), he maintained that the only secure basis of Christianity is its reasonableness. He had no belief in miracles, strongly distrusted mysticism and feeling in religious faith and people who had religious insights or visions. Locke had faith in reason and science, and, in fact, had no patience with anything more than the bare bones of Christianity. The essence of Christianity, he believed, was the acknowledgment of Christ as the Messiah who was sent into this world to spread the true knowledge of God. Everything else, according to Locke, was irrelevant.

BIBLIOGRAPHY: J. Locke, *The Reasonableness of Christianity* (Chicago, 1965); M. Cranston (ed.), *Locke on Politics, Religion and Education* (New York, 1965); S. P. Lamprecht, *The Moral and Political Philosophy of John Locke* (New York, 1918); H. MacLachen, *The Religious Opinions of Milton, Locke and Newton* (Manchester, 1941); N. K. Smith, *John Locke* (Manchester, 1933).

**Loehe, Johann Konrad Wilhelm** (1808–1872). German Lutheran theologian and preacher. Educated at Erlangen and Berlin, Loehe assumed a pastorate in Neuendettelsau, Bavaria, in 1837. He founded the Neuendettelsau Mission Society (1841) to train "emer-

gency pastors" for missions in the German diaspora, especially North America, Brazil, and Australia. His village teemed with missionary zeal. Loehe argued that "mission is nothing but the one church of God in its motion, the realization of a universal, catholic church." He established settlements in the Michigan Saginaw Valley (c. 1850) as Bavarian relief colonies and as Indian missions. In 1853 he agreed to transfer some colonists to Dubuque, Iowa, where the Iowa Synod was organized. Loehe sent Wyneken and numerous other pastors to America, some of whom organized the Lutheran Church—Missouri Synod. His "Church News from North America" was well read. At home, Loehe, along with Rudelbach, Scheibel, Petri, and Harms, fought for a strong Lutheran confessional basis in the Bavarian church struggle (1848–1852). In 1849 he formed a Lutheran Inner Mission to parallel Wichern's 1848 union mission. In 1854 he organized a diaconate in Neuendettelsau along with affiliated homes, hospitals, and educational institutions. In liturgics, Loehe's confessionalism led him to oppose Frederick William IV's removal of paraments. The Eucharist was central in his ecclesiology. His liturgical studies encouraged appreciation of historic collects, and he restored Vespers in his institution for deaconesses. His *Agende für christliche Gemeinden* (1844) was widely used in the Missouri Synod. It strongly influenced the liturgical studies of C. P. Krauth, S. S. Schmucker, H. E. Jacobs, and others who prepared the General Council's Church Book. Also important was his *Drei Bücher von der Kirche* (1845).

**Log College.** The name given in derision to the log cabin school begun by William Tennent in his own home at Neshaminy, Pa., about 1726 to educate young men for the ministry. In 1735 he bought 100 acres of land between Philadelphia and New York and in 1736 built his "Log College." The criticism of it and its graduates by European-trained Presbyterian clergy was one factor in the New Side–Old Side schism of 1741. This school became the pattern for many other "log colleges" and for the College of New Jersey, now known as Princeton University.

**Loisy, Alfred Firmin** (1857–1940). The best known of the French Catholic modernists. After ordination in 1879 he came under the influence of the church historian, Louis Duchesne, at the Institut Catholique. Biblical criticism particularly appealed to Loisy, and he attended the lectures of J. E. Renan at the Collège de France. In 1890 he was made professor of Sacred Scripture at the Institut

Catholique, where his adoption of the canons of historical criticism made him suspect among the orthodox. He was dismissed from the Institut in 1893, the same year that saw the publication of Leo XIII's encyclical on Biblical scholarship, *Providentissimus Deus,* to which, despite some difficulty, he submitted. In 1900 he became lecturer at the École des Hautes Études of the Sorbonne, and in 1902 published his *L'Évangile et l'Église,* which, designed as a criticism of Harnack's *Das Wesen des Christenthums* and a modern defense of Catholicism, drew down the wrath of the church upon him. In 1903, *L'Évangile* and four other works of his were placed on the Index. He was excommunicated on March 7, 1908, the year after Pius X's decree *Lamentabili* and encyclical *Pascendi* singled out the Modernism that he represented as "the synthesis of all heresies." His refusal to accept these decrees caused his excommunication.

**Lollardy.** Name given to the movement initiated by John Wycliffe. Oxford began to divide into parties (Lollards and Catholics) in 1379 when Wycliffe made more explicit his teachings on the Eucharist. By 1395 these Lollards had become an organized sect with specially ordained ministers and had considerable representation in Parliament. Members came from the middle and artisan classes as well as from the educated laity. They opposed the complex organization of the hierarchy and the holding of secular possessions by the church. They emphasized preaching and reading the Bible and discounted belief in transubstantiation. During the reign of Henry IV a small number were burned, and the statute *De haeretico comburendo* in 1401 ensured the use of royal troops in the destruction of the sect. Henry V decided against the Lollards in 1413, when he had John Oldcastle, a close friend, arrested for heresy. Oldcastle was condemned but escaped from prison and began to encourage a Lollard rebellion. The plan was betrayed, and the bands were scattered by royal forces. Oldcastle was finally captured in 1417 in Wales, where he was hanged. The subsequent history of Lollardy is not clear. Its adherents were forced into hiding because of strict persecution, but there is no concrete evidence that it was completely destroyed. The derivation of the term "Lollard" is unclear.

**Lombard, Peter** (c. 1100–c. 1160). Compiler of the most widely used textbook of theology in the Middle Ages and known as the "Master of the Sentences." Born near Novara, he studied at Bologna, Reims, and the Abbey of St.-Victor in Paris. He held the chair of theology at Notre Dame from c.

1135, writing commentaries on Paul's letters and The Psalms (c. 1140), and his *Four Books of Sentences* between 1150 and 1152. He was made bishop of Paris in 1159. The *Sentences,* the culmination of the systematizing work that had gone on for fifty years in theology, was a collection of the opinions of the fathers, set out in the dialectical method of Abelard, and arranged under four headings: God, Creatures, Incarnation and Redemption, and the Sacraments and Last Things. Nine tenths of the citations were from Augustine, though a few contemporaries (Abelard, Hugh of St.-Victor, and Gratian) were also quoted. Reverence for tradition, wide use of patristic, Biblical, and canonical sources for arguments, lack of any recognizably original doctrinal tendency, and power of synthesis ensured the success of the *Sentences.* Within twenty years it had become a subject for commentaries, and by the middle of the 13th century it was virtually the basis of university instruction. Lombard's fixing of the number of sacraments at seven and definition of them as symbols and means of grace were adopted by the church at the Council of Trent.

**London Missionary Society.** An organization founded in 1795 by Congregationalists, Anglicans, Presbyterians, and Wesleyans to promote Christian missionaries to the heathen. It had as one of its principles the freedom of each missionary to select the form of church government that he held to be right. In recent times the society has been maintained almost exclusively by the Congregationalists.

**Longinqua Oceani.** Encyclical of Jan. 6, 1895, in which Leo XIII discussed the Roman Church in the United States. The pope hailed the progress of American civilization and the American Roman Catholic Church, but rejected separation of church and state as a desirable arrangement. He praised the establishment of the Catholic University of America, the Apostolic Delegation, and signs of ecclesiastical growth. He spoke of the indissolubility of marriage and the need for frequent Communion. He approved labor unions, but not secret societies. He called for aid to Indians and Negroes.

**Loofs, Friedrich** (1858–1928). Lutheran church historian. Educated under C. E. Luthardt at Leipzig, Loofs also studied at Tübingen and Göttingen. He taught at Leipzig (1882) and Halle (1887), but remained active in church affairs as consistorial councilor in Saxony (1910). His chief interest was the history of dogma, especially Trinitarian dogma and reformational justification. Included in his writings were monographs on ancient church history, sermons, speeches, and numerous articles for the *Realenzyklopädie*. Loofs preferred Baur's definition of the history of dogma to Harnack's restrictive one, but distinguished the same from historical theology.

**Lords of the Congregation.** Scottish reforming nobles. Frequently in Scottish history, when the central government grew weak, groups of the nobles, or lords, bound themselves by a solemn, notarized covenant, or oath, to the achievement of some political end. When the preaching of John Knox moved the lords to swear, on Dec. 3, 1557, to "manteane, sett forward, and establish the most blessed word of God and His Congregatioun," they became known as the "Lords of the Congregation."

**Lord's Supper.** See EUCHARIST.

**Lotze, Rudolf Hermann** (1817–1881). German philosopher. Educated at Leipzig, Lotze taught philosophy there (1839), moved to Göttingen (1842), and was nominated for a Berlin post in 1881. As a teleological idealist who greatly modified Hegelianism, he attempted to give ultimacy to personal values while admitting the claims of natural science. Lotze opposed vitalistic theories vigorously and stressed the interdependence of ethics and metaphysics. He construed mechanism as the instrument of purpose, and was a pioneer in experimental psychology. Three of his major works were *Metaphysik, Logik,* and *Mikrokosmus.*

**Louis IX** (*known as* St. Louis) (1214–1270). King of France from 1226, among the greatest of all medieval kings. Deeply religious and of lofty principles, he led a life almost monastic in its simplicity, dressing modestly, shunning luxury and ostentation, personally giving alms to beggars, washing the feet of lepers, and constructing hospitals and churches. Best remembered for his passion for justice, he would sit under an oak tree in the forest of Vincennes, where anyone could approach him expecting a hearing and fair judgment. His reputation for impartiality spread throughout Europe, and at various times he settled disputes outside of France. Scrupulous in his observance of feudal law, he negotiated a territorial settlement with England unfavorable to himself because he believed the lands had been unjustly seized from the English by his predecessors. Eager to lead a crusade, in 1248 he launched the ill-fated Seventh Crusade against Damietta in Egypt. The expedition met with disaster, Louis himself being captured by the Mamelukes and held for ransom. Typically, he insisted on full ransom

payment even though its collection seriously drained his own royal revenues. In 1270 he led another Crusade, the Eighth, directed, for reasons not entirely clear, against Tunis in North Africa, where he died of a fever. He was so highly revered that, in 1297, less than thirty years after his death, he was canonized.

**Louis XIV** (1638–1715). One of the most famous kings in French history. His reign was superficially splendid but basically disastrous for France. His religious policy was essentially Gallican in nature, and he persecuted the Jansenists with the approval of Rome. In 1685, Louis issued the Revocation of the Edict of Nantes, which abolished religious toleration in France and forced the Huguenots either to convert to Roman Catholicism or to leave the land.

**Louis XVI** (1754–1793). King of France from 1774. His reign marked the beginning of the historic French Revolution. A devout Roman Catholic, he consistently upheld the independence and privileges of the French Church and the papacy against the encroachments of the Legislative Assembly, especially in his opposition to the Civil Constitution of the Clergy (1790). His support of the church undermined his power and was one of the contributing causes of his execution in 1793.

**Louis the Pious** (778–840). The son of Charlemagne and Frankish emperor from 813. Although Louis received military training and led armies while still young, his education and interests were more ecclesiastical than military or political. The early death of his older brothers left him heir to his father's empire. In 813, at the request of Charlemagne, Louis crowned himself emperor. After his father's death in 814 he became sole ruler and was crowned again in 816 at Reims by the pope. He made arrangements for the division of the empire among his three sons. The child of a second marriage upset this division, and his older sons deposed Louis in order to prevent further division. Louis was restored to his kingdom, but in 833 was again deposed and sent to a monastery. The following year he was once more restored. In 838, one of his sons died and the empire was reapportioned. His son Louis refused to accept this division and rebelled. After suppressing the rebellion, the emperor died. Under his patronage the Carolingian revival reached its greatest level of scholarship and creativity. He sponsored the reforms of Benedict of Aniane through synods held at Aachen during the early part of his reign. Throughout his rule he was at the mercy of his sons and the bishops. His personal piety was not sufficient for managing his family or his father's empire.

**Lourdes.** A town in southern France, in the Department of the Hautes-Pyrénées. In 1858 the young village girl Bernadette Soubirous saw a series of eighteen apparitions of the Virgin Mary on the banks of the River Gave near Lourdes. The vision was finally revealed to Bernadette as the Immaculate Conception. On Feb. 25, 1858, Bernadette's vision of Mary told her to go and drink from a spring underneath the rock of Massabielle, in a grotto where the apparitions had appeared. Though Bernadette could scarcely scrape up enough muddy water to moisten her lips, her efforts apparently loosened a spring which later that day made its way down to the Gave. The apparitions and the "miraculous" appearance of the stream made Lourdes a place of pilgrimage. From a town of some four thousand in Bernadette's time, the village grew tremendously. It has become the most popular shrine in the Christian world outside of the Holy Land itself. Several thousand seemingly miraculous cures have been recorded, drawing many hundreds of thousands of visitors to Lourdes every year, especially during the month of August.

**Louvain.** The foundation of the University of Louvain dates from 1425, though the theology faculty was not created until six years later. Suppressed by the French in 1797 after their annexation of the Netherlands, the university was reopened in an independent Belgium with the sanction of Gregory XVI in 1834. Later in the century, under the influence of Mercier, it became a center of neo-Thomistic philosophy.

**Lucar, Cyril** (1572–1638). Patriarch of Constantinople from 1620. A native of Crete, he studied at Venice and Padua, and taught theology at Vilna and Lvov. In 1596 he served as one of the representatives of the patriarch of Constantinople at the Council of Brest-Litovsk, where a majority of the Orthodox bishops went over to Rome. He was patriarch of Alexandria from 1602 to 1620. His experiences in Lithuania and Poland and the Jesuit activity in Turkey convinced him that the Orthodox needed to draw closer to the Protestants. In 1620 he was elected patriarch of Constantinople. The rest of his life is a story of stormy intrigue in which Rome, Geneva, France, Austria, Holland, and England all took part. Five times he was deposed and reinstated in his office. In 1638 he was strangled and thrown into the Bosporus by his enemies. Lucar was much interested in Protestant theology and published a Confession of Faith that appeared in Latin in 1629 in Geneva. It contained several Calvinistic articles later refuted by various Orthodox synods. Lucar's reign is the one outstanding example of Protestant-Orthodox contact during the Reformation era and also affords a vivid picture of the troubled state of Eastern Orthodoxy under the Ottoman Turks.

**Lucian of Antioch** (c. 240–312). Reputedly the founder of the Antiochene school of Biblical exegesis, which differed from the Alexandrian school in its insistence upon the literal meaning of the text before allegory. Born probably in Samosata, Lucian studied in Edessa but, forced by political pressures, left for Antioch in the 260's. That he was a pupil of Paul of Samosata is difficult to maintain. In 311 he was apprehended and taken to Nicomedia, where he suffered martyrdom in 312. His fame stems from his work as textual critic and theologian. The former is established by his recension of the Bible known as the Lucianic text. His editing of the Greek Old Testament produced a work that was standard in the East. His New Testament text is roughly that known as the Byzantine text and is thus represented in the Textus Receptus and in the King James Version; this text is characterized by smoothness in locution which has been achieved by elimination of barbarisms and by conflation of variant readings. Lucian's fame as a theologian is less easy to substantiate because only a few fragments of his works are extant; it is quite possible that the second of the four creeds proposed at the Second Council of Antioch (341) was ultimately composed by him. Christologically, he was a subordinationist, and taught Arius as a young man.

**Lucian of Samosata** (c. 115–c. 200). Rhetorician and satirist from Syria. He was acquainted with Christians, whom he favored as better than the charlatan Alexander of Abonoteichos but ridiculed as the dupes of another charlatan, Peregrinus Proteus. He tells how Peregrinus won the favor and support of Christians, but was finally expelled by them for violation of their (Jewish-Christian?) dietary regulations, perhaps c. 160.

**Lucifer of Cagliari** (d. c. 375). An uncompromising supporter of the Nicene position. He attended the Council of Alexandria in 362, held by Athanasius when exiles returned after the death of Constantius. He objected to its policy of welcoming the former semi-Arians, and perpetuated the schism at Antioch by consecrating Paulinus, leader of the strict Nicene faction there, to the episcopate. Lucifer died about 375, but his followers survived for some time as the rigorist sect of Luciferians.

**Ludlow, John Malcolm Forbes** (1821–1911). Originator of Christian Socialism in England. Although raised in France, he followed his father's wishes and remained an English subject, studying law and being admitted to the bar in England in 1843. A Christian Socialist from his youth, he was as dedicated to Christianity as he was to his political and social philosophy. He believed that true socialism must be based on moral righteousness, self-sacrifice, and common brotherhood, which he avowed were inseparable from religious faith. With Anglican theologian J. F. D. Maurice and preacher Charles Kingsley, he organized Christian Socialism in England in the early 1850's. Of the three, Ludlow was the most practical and the real leader. His contributions were as: supporter of the labor movement until the day of his death; founder and first editor of the penny journal *Christian Socialist* (1850); founder of workingmen's cooperatives and associations for which he helped to gain legal protection; founder and teacher in a workingmen's college in London; one of the organizers of the first cooperative congress (1869); the person responsible for persuading the Anglican Lambeth Conference (1888) to receive a report on socialism; one of the first to understand the essential relationship between Christianity and man's social and economic existence.

**Ludolph of Saxony** (c. 1300–1378). German spiritual writer. The prior of the Carthusian monastery of Coblenz, Ludolph resigned his office to live as a simple monk at Strasbourg for the last thirty years of his life. His *Life of Christ,* widely read in the late Middle Ages, condensed the commentaries on the spiritual life of numerous earlier writers. At the time of his death Ludolph was greatly revered for his holiness.

**Ludwig Missionsverein.** A German Catholic missionary society. Like the Austrian Leopold Association, this society was founded in response to an appeal made by Frederic Rese, then vicar-general of Cincinnati, during a tour in Europe (1828). Founded in Bavaria in 1828 and formally incorporated in 1838 under the protection of the king of Bavaria, the society collected money from the common folk to support missions in North America and Asia. Between 1844 and 1916 almost one million dollars was contributed, much of which came to the United States.

**Lugo, Juan de** (1583–1660). Spanish Jesuit, one of the most important figures in Roman Catholic theology in the first half of the 17th century. Born in Madrid, from 1611 to 1621 he taught theology in a number of Spanish seminaries and universities. Because of his reputation as a brilliant teacher, he was then called to an academic post in Rome. In 1643, in recognition of his scholarly achievements, he was made a cardinal, a rare exception to the practice of the Jesuits, and thereafter played important roles in the Holy Office and in his order. His theological work falls into two main categories: clear, systematic, and often original treatments of the principal Christian doctrines from a Thomistic standpoint; and compendious treatments of a great variety of specific questions, particularly those related to social ethics, the Eucharist, and the act of faith. He emphasized that an act of saving faith is possible for all men, non-Christians included. Alphonsus Liguori thought him the finest ethicist since Aquinas.

**Lull, Ramón** (*known as* Doctor Illuminatus, the enlightened doctor) (c. 1235–c. 1315). Mystic, missionary, and writer. A courtier of James of Aragon until the age of thirty, he then became a hermit and a tertiary of the Franciscan Order. His lifelong work thereafter centered on the conversion of the Moslems. He advocated the study of Arabic and Chaldean, founding the college of Miramar in 1276 for this purpose. He traveled extensively in North Africa (Tunis) and Asia, disputing with Moslems. He was stoned to death in Tunis.

Lull's literary activity (some three hundred works) attempted to show the errors of Averroism and the truth of Christianity. In his *Ars magna* he arranged theological propositions according to geometrical patterns so that his conclusions could be proved with mathematical precision. In general he tended to identify philosophy with theology, and he maintained that all the mysteries of the faith could be logically explained to the satisfaction of reason. His denial of the distinction between natural and supernatural truth was condemned by Gregory XI in 1376.

Lull's rationalism led him to a mysticism wherein he contemplated divine perfection, and he is considered a forerunner of Teresa of Ávila and John of the Cross. He was an enthusiastic proponent of the Immaculate Conception of Mary. His followers (the Lullists) for a time enjoyed considerable influence, especially in Spain. In recent years there has been a renewed interest in Lull's life and works.

**Lullus** (d. 786). Anglo-Saxon monk, bishop of Mainz. Educated at Malmesbury, he became the chief associate of Boniface in the mission to the Germans, and was designated as Boniface's successor at Mainz. After succeeding to the see in 754, he came into conflict with the monks of Fulda over their exemption from episcopal jurisdiction. He lost the dispute and founded a rival monastery at Hersfeld. Lullus received the pallium from Rome in 781.

**Lund Conference** (1952). Third World Faith and Order Conference. After an impasse had been reached in exploring agreements and differences, the Lund Conference sought a new approach to the question of unity in exploring the relation of Christ to the church, with the further intention of relating the doctrine of the Holy Spirit. A second gain was the discovery of the role of nontheological factors in inhibiting unity. See *Lund 1952, Third World Conference on Faith and Order,* ed. by O. W. Tompkins (London, 1953).

**Lupus of Ferrières** (c. 805–862). Abbot and theologian. He studied at Fulda under Rabanus Maurus and Gottschalk. Becoming abbot of Ferrières in 840, he made the abbey one of the great centers of learning in the Carolingian revival. He wrote *Liber de tribus quaestionibus* (c. 850) as a moderate defense of Gottschalk in the controversy over predestination. His letters and several other literary works survive.

**Luthardt, Christoph Ernst** (1823–1902). Lutheran scholar and churchman. Educated at Erlangen and Berlin as a student of J. C. K. von Hofmann, Luthardt taught at Marburg (1854–1856) and then at Leipzig. He became a leading figure in Leipzig Lutheranism with his editorship of *Allgemeine evangelisch-lutherische Kirchenzeitung* after 1868 and his presidency of the Leipzig Mission Society. He defended Lutheran rights when Prussian annexation in 1864 and 1866 threatened to impose the Union on certain areas. Among his many systematic and exegetical works was *Kompendium der Dogmatik.*

**Luther, Martin** (1483–1546). Leader of the Protestant Reformation in Germany. Born at Eisleben, Nov. 10, 1483, to Hans and Margarete Luther, Martin moved to Mansfeld in 1484, attended school there, afterward at Magdeburg with the Brethren of the Common Life, and at Eisenach. He entered the University of Erfurt in 1501. There he was exposed to the nominalist philosophy (William of Occam), which taught the inability of natural reason to establish articles of faith. Luther also sharpened his linguistic skills in

the classical tongues, but did not become a humanist then or later. He was made B.A. in 1502, and M.A. in 1505. In July, 1505, when knocked to the ground by lightning, he vowed to become a monk and entered Erfurt monastery of the Augustinian Eremites on July 17. His father objected, but he took the vows in September, 1506. Selected to study for the priesthood, he was made a deacon in February, 1507, and ordained priest on April 4. His father attended his first Mass on May 2, but rebuked him for disobedience to his parents.

Luther then began to study the theology of Peter Lombard and Gabriel Biel. In the autumn of 1508 he taught moral philosophy at Wittenberg and was recalled a year later to lecture at Erfurt. In November, 1510, he accompanied a fellow monk to Rome to request that their stricter houses not be compelled to admit the more lax houses of their order into their jurisdiction. As a pilgrim, Luther visited the major Roman shrines but was appalled by the spiritual laxity he observed, even among the clergy. At Wittenberg in the late summer of 1511, his vicar, John Staupitz, named him to study for the doctorate in theology in preparation for assuming Staupitz' professorship in Bible. In May, 1512, he was made subprior of the Wittenberg monastery and on Oct. 19 he became a doctor of theology, beginning his Genesis lectures on Oct. 25. Spiritual distress now plagued him. In the Bible he found an angry, judging God, but Staupitz directed him to the wounds of Christ, which help he always treasured. His lectures on The Psalms began in 1513. While preparing for them in 1513 or 1514, he discovered that the term "God's righteousness" could mean the righteousness by which God made man righteous. This insight enabled him to see the gospel as the message of God's work for man rather than as God's demand for man's striving. It determined the direction of all his subsequent preaching, teaching, and reforming activity. By 1515, in his lectures on Romans, his "theology of the cross" was becoming clear: the power and wisdom of God are displayed through human weakness and folly. He saw that works of love followed upon, rather than earned, justification. In Augustine, similar emphases convinced him that he was within the tradition of the church. Further, in 1516, John Tauler's sermons and an anonymous work *Theologia Germanica* (*A German Theology*), printed under Luther's supervision in Wittenberg in 1518, introduced him to mysticism. The mystic emphasis on Christ and the view that suffering was grace and sin was self-love pleased him, but much else he set aside. Luther's thinking won the support of the Wittenberg faculty by April, 1517, and of others of influence too.

His reforming activity began on Oct. 31, 1517, with his Ninety-five Theses against the abuses of indulgences. In April, 1518, Luther led a disputation on his theology for a meeting of his order at Heidelberg. He also wrote Pope Leo X respectfully, but in May the Dominican prior and inquisitor Prierias censured him from Rome. Cited there, he asked through Elector Frederick the Wise to be tried in Germany. Distortions of his tract on the ban led to an order for his arrest by Cardinal Cajetan, general of the Dominicans. The elector asked Cajetan to try him at Augsburg. There, in October, 1518, Luther refused to recant, arguing that the question of indulgences had no dogmatic status in the church, and thus was open to debate. Miltitz, without authority, unsuccessfully attempted a reconciliation between Luther and the pope and in June and July, 1519, Johann Eck of Ingolstadt drew Luther into his debate with Carlstadt at Leipzig, where Luther defended certain Hussite views and challenged papal primacy. In 1520, Luther produced four of his most important works. His *Treatise on Good Works* in March was a thorough discussion of ethics and faith. It praises faith as the greatest work. Without it, no work pleases God. From it flow truly good works, and faith itself flows from the wounds of Christ. In August, Luther's appeal *To the Christian Nobility of the German Nation concerning the Reform of the Christian Estate* denounced papal usurpation of spiritual authority and appealed to Christian princes to inaugurate specific reforms in the church. On Oct. 6, *A Prelude on the Babylonian Captivity of the Church* appeared, attacking the entire sacramental system of the Roman Church. A papal commission headed first by Cajetan and then by Eck published the papal bull, *Exsurge, Domine,* condemning Luther's views on June 15. It ordered his books burned and demanded that he recant. In November a few cities burned Luther's books, but these acts only served to confirm his denunciations. True, he wrote a conciliatory letter to Pope Leo, as suggested by Miltitz, along with the treatise on *Christian Freedom* (November), but he nonetheless condemned the bull in his *Against the Execrable Bull of Antichrist* and on Dec. 10, when books of canon law and Scholastic theology were burned outside the Elster Gate by the Wittenberg faculty, Luther threw a copy of the bull on the fire. Another bull excommunicating him was ready in January, 1521. When Frederick obtained a hearing for

Luther at the 1521 imperial Diet at Worms, he appeared before the emperor, electors, and princes, and refused to recant any of his writings without refutation by Scripture or reasonable proof. A commission, meeting privately with Luther, failed to draw a recantation from him. On the way to Wittenberg, near his father's ancestral home at Möhra, he was kidnapped on May 3 by Frederick's agents and taken to the Wartburg Castle. Here he was disguised as a knight, Junker George, and continued to write. In November, *On Monastic Vows* showed the meaning of religious vows and stated that monasticism should be free and priests should be allowed to marry. Most important at this time was his translation of the New Testament in German, using Erasmus' Greek text as a base (Luther's entire German Bible was not completed until 1534).

In December and January, Wittenberg was upset by disorders stemming from radical preaching by Carlstadt, the monk Zwilling, and the "prophets" from Zwickau, and Luther's attention was turned from the conflict with Rome to the need to combat other kinds of opponents. He returned and beginning on March 8 preached a series of sermons renouncing the use of force for religious aims. In 1524, peasant uprisings occurred in southern Germany and spread throughout the country the next year. His *Warning to Peace* went unheeded. By April, 1525, whole regions were terrorized. Luther preached in Thuringia without success. His tract *Against the Murdering and Plundering Bands of the Peasants* was a sharp, much criticized work. It was during the upheavals of the Peasants' War that Luther married Katherine von Bora, a former nun. Six children were born from their marriage.

An adversary of quite a different mettle was Desiderius Erasmus. Many humanists thought Erasmus and Luther should unite in reforming the church. Luther disapproved of Erasmus' theology, however, and Erasmus thought Luther too coarse and controversial. In 1524, Erasmus' *Diatribe on Free Will* stated his theological views, attacking Luther's dogmatic position on the impotence of man's will after the Fall. Luther responded with his *Bondage of the Will* in 1525, denying a role to the human will in salvation except as it acts under the moving of divine grace. Erasmus, offended, replied with *Hyperaspistes* in two installments (1526 and 1527), but Luther was content: he felt that his book was one of his best works.

After reformation was achieved at the university, Luther worked to implement reform throughout Saxony. Schools at Eisleben, Nuremberg, and Wittenberg established examples followed by all Saxony, providing better preparation for university work. Luther and Melanchthon prepared church visitation plans for Saxony in 1527. Luther's two catechisms of 1529 and his several church postils for pastors were used widely as correctives. Luther also encouraged congregational participation in the liturgy. His 1523 *Formula Missae* substituted a Lutheran Communion service for the Canon of the Mass. His 1525 German Mass was authorized by the elector for use in Saxony in 1526. Luther wrote hymns, arranged others, and promoted hymn-singing in worship.

A dispute over the presence of Christ in the Lord's Supper threatened to split the Reform movement. Luther's *Against the Heavenly Prophets* of January, 1525, answering Carlstadt's views, drew a reply from Zwingli in March. Bucer tried to mediate. After the 1529 Protest at Speyer, Philip of Hesse invited the contending parties to Marburg to attempt a reconciliation. But when the Diet of Augsburg met the following year, the Lutherans, the Swiss, and the southern Germans presented separate confessions of faith. Bucer and Melanchthon continued trying to unite the Swiss and German evangelicals. After a preliminary meeting in 1534, Luther invited Bucer and others to a conference in May, 1536. On May 23 at Wittenberg, concord was reached between the southern Germans and the Wittenbergers, and Communion was celebrated together. Melanchthon drafted the Wittenberg Concord, showing their agreement, but the Swiss and southern German Zwinglians were separated as a result.

Pope Paul III's call for a general church council at Mantua in 1537 induced Luther once more to show the sharp contrast between his theology and Rome's in his *Smalcald Articles,* and in 1539 the tract *On Councils and Churches* showed him still convinced that no organization, as such, could be identified with the true Christian church. Justification by faith remained his touchstone of authenticity. He never felt that he had founded a new church but that he had sought to restore the pure faith of the early church. His later years were hard. The bigamy of Philip of Hesse in 1539, which he and Melanchthon had condoned, was made public. His denunciation of the papacy grew more bitter, and he gave his approval to the persecution of the radical Reformers. He even wrote against the Jews. He died early on Feb. 18, 1546.

BIBLIOGRAPHY: J. Pelikan and H. T. Lehmann (eds.), *Luther's Works,* 56 vols. (Philadelphia and St. Louis, 1955 ff.); R. H. Bainton, *Here I Stand* (New York and Nashville, 1950); F. E. Cranz, *An Essay on the Development of Luther's Thought on Justice, Law, and Society* (Cambridge, Mass., 1959); B. A. Gerrish, *Grace and Reason* (Oxford, 1962); J. Pelikan, *Luther the Expositor* (St. Louis, 1959); R. Prenter, *Spiritus Creator* (Philadelphia, 1953); E. G. Schwiebert, *Luther and His Times* (St. Louis, 1950); G. Wingren, *Luther on Vocation* (Philadelphia, 1957).

**Lutheranism.** A term used to designate the worldwide communion of Christian believers who are the followers and spiritual descendants of the 16th-century Reformer, Martin Luther. Probably no other church of the Reformation has given such weight to its confessions as has Lutheranism. Its main doctrinal symbol (which was widely approved in the Reformed Church as well) is the Augsburg Confession first drawn up by Melanchthon in 1530. Luther's Small Catechism (1529) is also universally recognized by Lutheranism and is used as the basic manual of instruction in preparation for the rite of confirmation. In addition to these symbols, Lutherans adhere to the three ecumenical creeds (the Apostles', the Nicene, and the Athanasian). The above constitute the essential minimum in the confessional structure of Lutheranism. In an attempt to end the various theological controversies within Lutheranism during the 16th century, the Book of Concord was compiled in 1580. Though it is usually regarded as normative, it has not received universal acceptance within Lutheranism. The means of grace that God uses to call, enlighten, and sanctify the believer is the Word of God and the sacraments of Baptism and the Lord's Supper. Here lies the decisive, constitutive element in Lutheranism upon which the confessions themselves rest. The doctrine of justification by faith, although not a Lutheran monopoly, is heavily stressed and serves as a point of orientation for Lutheran theology. Good works are regarded as the natural consequence of genuine faith and result not in justification (which they presuppose) but in the fulfillment of joy and blessedness promised to those who live their lives in obedience to God and in love to their neighbor.

Unlike other churches that have made a certain form of ecclesiastical organization into a matter of divine right, Lutheranism, for all its creedal statements, includes polity among the adiaphora and uses the episcopal, presbyterian, and congregational forms of church government according to local preference. Another area of freedom within Lutheranism is the ordering of its worship. There is no uniform Lutheran liturgy, although Luther's *German Mass* (1526) has served as a basic model. His guiding principle was to preserve the traditional worship of the church purged of its Roman accretions and to give it to the people in their own language.

In accordance with his doctrine of the priesthood of all believers, Luther called upon the Christian nobility to reform the church in 1520. While it was not Luther's intention to substitute prince for pope, the temporary expedient whereby the prince served as *summus episcopus* (or "highest bishop") often became a permanent fixture. After Luther's death (1546) and the legal recognition of Lutheranism by the Peace of Augsburg (1555), a strict orthodoxy with its scholastically defined doctrines came to dominate Lutheranism and was in continuous theological conflict with Calvinism, Roman Catholicism, and the milder type of Lutheranism represented by Melanchthon and Georg Calixtus.

In 1675, Philip Spener published his *Pia desideria* and launched the movement called Pietism with its strong emphasis on personal piety and sanctification as opposed to "dead orthodoxy." Pietism proved to be a beneficial stimulus to the Lutheran churches of Germany and Scandinavia, and it never seceded from Lutheranism as did Methodism from the Church of England.

In the middle of the 18th century the rationalistic spirit of the Enlightenment made inroads into Lutheranism, but by the first half of the 19th century theological renewal and religious awakenings in Germany and Scandinavia brought about a revival of evangelical theology. With the publication of Klaus Harm's ninety-five theses against rationalistic theology in 1817 and the attempt to force the Prussian Union upon Lutheranism, a strong confessional movement arose in Germany. This new movement not only sought to combat "unionism" but also joined battle with the rising tide of Biblical criticism. In the 20th century the rise of neo-orthodoxy, the experience of religious persecution during World War II, and the influence of the Lutheran World Federation blended to revitalize the confessional principles within Lutheranism.

In the 18th century, Lutheranism began a worldwide expansion through emigration and foreign missions. In 1742, Henry M. Muhlenberg, "the patriarch of American Lutheranism," arrived in America to organize the infant Lutheran Church and give it stability. In the following century, Lutheran immigrants

began to arrive from Scandinavia, and the immigration from Germany increased to flood proportions. (Strong Lutheran churches were also founded by German immigrants in Argentina, Brazil, and Australia.) Much of Lutheranism's early growth in the United States was due to European immigration. With the cessation of immigration in 1930 and the discontinued use of foreign languages in its worship, American Lutheranism revealed its latent vitality as it grew in membership from four million people in 1930 to over nine million in 1965. Much of the history of American Lutheranism in the last century has been the story of church mergers which in 1966 found 96 percent of all Lutherans in the United States gathered within three synods. These three took a giant step toward merger in 1967 when they joined together in the cooperative agency known as the Lutheran Council in the U.S.A.

The other half of Lutheranism's worldwide expansion is the story of foreign missions that began when Bartholomeus Ziegenbalg went out to Tranquebar, India, as the first Protestant missionary in 1705. Though the spirit of rationalism dried up mission enthusiasm for a time, Lutheranism entered wholeheartedly into "the great century of missions" and produced some of the outstanding examples of mission work in Tanzania, New Guinea, and Indonesia.

As a result of two world wars in the 20th century, revolutionary changes have occurred in the heartland of Lutheranism. Following both wars, Lutheranism played a part in world relief and proved that *sola fide* need not discourage good works. (Indeed, this had been clearly demonstrated by the Inner Mission activity of German and Scandinavian Lutheranism during the previous century.) With the establishment of the Weimar Republic in Germany after World War I, the government of churches by territorial rulers disappeared completely. During the persecutions under Hitler many German Lutherans (sometimes in defiance of their church's own leadership) joined the Confessing Church in its opposition to National Socialism. In Norway, Bishop Berggrav led the Lutheran Church in a heroic struggle against Nazism, maintaining that when the driver has gone beserk it is the duty of the Christian to take over the reins for the sake of the others riding in the vehicle. With the division of postwar Germany, the birthplace of Lutheranism lay behind the Iron Curtain where 80 percent of the East Germans belonged to the Lutheran Church. Here, Lutheranism has been engaged in a struggle with atheistic Communism. In the years immediately following World War II some fourteen million refugees poured into West Germany. Large Lutheran minorities suddenly appeared in what had formerly been predominantly Roman Catholic regions. This movement of population has raised again the question of the right of confessionally bound territorial churches. In 1948 the overwhelming majority of the German territorial churches joined together to form the United Evangelical Lutheran Church of Germany. That same year it joined the federation of Protestant confessional churches known as the Evangelical Church in Germany. The spiritual isolation that Nazism endeavored to impose upon Lutheranism created a desire for Christian fellowship that knew no political or national boundaries. At Lund, Sweden, Lutherans gathered in 1947 and drew up a constitution for the Lutheran World Federation, which in 1963 included member churches from thirty-eight countries. In 1948 at Amsterdam, Lutheranism took an active role in the formation of the World Council of Churches, and most of the Lutheran bodies have since continued to take part in the ecumenical movement while remaining loyal to their confessional position.

BIBLIOGRAPHY: W. Elert, *The Structure of Lutheranism* (St. Louis, 1962); C. Lund-Quist, *Lutheran Churches of the World* (Minneapolis, 1957); A. R. Wentz, *A Basic History of Lutheranism in America* (Philadelphia, 1955); *Book of Concord*, ed. by T. Tappert (Philadelphia, 1959); *Encyclopedia of the Lutheran Church*, 3 vols., ed. by J. H. Bodensieck (Minneapolis, 1965).

**Luther's Catechism.** See SMALL CATECHISM, LUTHER'S.

**Luxeuil.** An abbey founded c. 590 by Columbanus. Under Abbot Walbert (d. 670) the Benedictine Rule was incorporated into the Celtic customs of the house. The influence of the monastery spread through the efforts of Queen Bathilde, who established several new houses with monks from Luxeuil. It was destroyed by the Saracens in 732 and reestablished by Charlemagne on strict Benedictine observance. The monastery was suppressed in 1790.

**Lyman, Eugene William** (1872–1948). American Congregational minister and educator. Born in Cummington, Mass., and reared in a Congregationalist home of "liberal orthodoxy," he studied at Amherst College and Yale Divinity School, and then in Germany for two years under Adolf von Harnack and others. In 1901 he was ordained a Congregationalist minister. He taught at the Oberlin School of Theology (1913–1918) and then at Union Theological Seminary in New York until 1940. Meanwhile, he had returned to Europe for more study under Bergson and Troeltsch. He was a representative of theological liberalism, of the type that was concerned to preserve Christian orthodoxy in the context of modern culture. Primarily a philosopher of religion rather than a systematic theologian, Lyman tried to incorporate a Christocentric religion into a defensible, modern philosophical outlook.

**Lyons, First Council of** (1245). The Thirteenth Ecumenical Council, as computed by the Roman Catholic Church. It is primarily remembered as an episode in the long struggle between the Hohenstaufen emperors and the papacy. Convoked by Innocent IV, who was fleeing from Frederick II, it reaffirmed the excommunication of Frederick, declared him deposed, and called for a crusade against him. Among religious matters dealt with were the institution of the octave of the nativity of the Virgin Mary and the decree that cardinals should wear the red hat.

**Lyons, Second Council of** (1274). The Fourteenth Ecumenical Council, according to Roman Catholic count. The Second Council of Lyons was most significant for its attempt to effect the union of the Greek and Roman Churches. Ecclesiastical union was sought by the Byzantines to ward off the threat of invasion posed by Charles of Anjou, who hoped to conquer Constantinople and restore the Latin empire with himself as emperor. The Greek emperor, Michael VIII Palaeologus, realized that ecclesiastical union with Rome would cause the pope to support him against Charles's ambitions. The Greek envoys at Lyons therefore declared the allegiance of the Greek Church to Rome, and vowed to accept certain Latin articles of faith. Chief among these articles was the addition of the *filioque* to the Greek creed—that is, the Greeks, like the Latins, declared that the Holy Spirit proceeds from both the Father and the Son. The Greek populace, however, rejected the union on the grounds that the four patriarchs of the East—of Constantinople, Antioch, Alexandria, and Jerusalem—were not represented. Thus, though Michael's envoys subscribed to the union in the name of the emperor and the Greek Church, the union never really took effect in the East. Indeed, Michael's attempts to force his subjects to accept union led to much civil disorder in Byzantium.

# M

**Mabillon, Jean** (1632–1707). A member of the Congregation of St. Maur, a scholarly Benedictine group of great influence in the development of church history. Mabillon is surely the finest of them, and one of the most eminent French historical scholars of any age. In his *De re diplomatica* (1681) he was the first to treat scientifically the problems of "diplomatics," i.e., that branch of history concerned with the evaluation, dating, authenticity, etc., of documents, thus making a major contribution not only to his own medieval studies but to the work of all historians. In addition, he was responsible for the collecting, editing, and publication of an enormous range of works of medieval writers, saints, and scholars, including the *Acta Sanctorum Ordinis S. Benedicti* and the beginnings of the *Annales.*

**Macarius Magnes** (4th or 5th century). Christian Apologist. In a work of five books (the *Apocriticus*) he challenged the objections to Christianity of a learned Neoplatonist. The chief value of the writing is in its preservation of sections of the original work under attack, which was probably by Porphyry. The Iconoclasts used Macarius' *Apocriticus* in support of their position (9th century). The text was lost, after being known and quoted by the patristic scholar and controversialist Francisco Torres in the 16th century. Rediscovered in 1867, the only manuscript of the work has now been lost again. The identification of this Apologist with Macarius, bishop of Magnesia, who was accuser of Heraclides of Ephesus at the Synod of the Oak (403), is probably a literary fiction.

**Macarius of Jerusalem** (d. c. 334). Champion of orthodoxy against Arianism. Macarius was condemned by Arius as early as c. 318, in a letter to Eusebius of Nicomedia. Macarius became bishop of Jerusalem c. 313. He attended the Council of Nicaea, and may have taken an active part in formulating its creed. Constantine commissioned him to build the Church of the Anastasis (Resurrection) in Jerusalem, to commemorate the discovery, by the empress Helena, of the supposed site of the crucifixion and the resurrection (c. 326). Later he shared with other Palestinian bishops in the construction of the Constantinian church at Mamre, after the visit made there by Eutropia, Constantine's mother-in-law.

**Macarius the Egyptian** (c. 300–380). A leader of Egyptian monasticism, wrongly regarded as the author of fifty spiritual homilies probably composed by the Messalian leader Symeon of Mesopotamia. The influence of the real Macarius was largely confined to Lower Egypt; that of Symeon was more widespread because of his spiritualizing light-mysticism and his criticism of contemporary monastic life. Further homilies were edited by G. L. Marriott in 1918 and a letter by W. Jaeger in 1954.

**Macaulay, Zachary** (1768–1838). Anglican cleric, social reformer, and father of the historian Thomas Babington Macaulay. He was a member of the Clapham Sect, a group of wealthy Anglican evangelicals who struggled for the abolition of the slave trade, the extension of missions in India and China, the foundation of the British and Foreign Bible Society, and the establishment of a model community in Sierra Leone. He was a founder of the University of London and editor (1802–1816) of the *Christian Observer,* the organ of the Clapham Sect.

**McCall Mission** (Mission Populaire Évangélique). An organization begun in 1871 by an English pastor, R. W. McCall, who sought to evangelize the lapsed and non-Christian workers of Paris. Meetings were held in shops, halls, etc., which would not remind workers of a church building. McCall wanted the gospel to confront the worker in a social rather than an ecclesiastical context. The Mission was successful at first, with 136 centers in France by 1892, but declined to 15 centers by the 1950's.

**McCloskey, John** (1810–1885). First American Roman Catholic cardinal. Educated at Mount St. Mary's College, Emmitsburg, Md., he was ordained in 1834. He studied further in Rome (1835–1837) and in 1843 was made titular bishop of Axiern, and in 1847 bishop of Albany. In 1864 he succeeded John Hughes as archbishop of New York and in 1875 was elevated to cardinal. He founded a seminary at Troy, N.Y., and completed St. Patrick's Cathedral in New York City.

**Macdonell, Alexander** (1762–1840). Canadian Roman Catholic prelate. He was born at Glen Urquhart, Scotland. Having been ordained by the Roman Catholic Church, he became the organizer and chaplain of the Glengarry Fencibles, a Roman Catholic Highland regiment that served in Ireland in 1798. In 1801 when the regiment was disbanded he obtained grants of land in Canada for men. He was chaplain to the Glengarry Light Infantry in the War of 1812, and in 1826 was consecrated bishop of Kingston. He was appointed a member of the Legislative Council of Upper Canada in 1831.

**Macedonian Dynasty** (867–1056). The Byzantine dynasty that marked the revival of Christianity in the Eastern branch of the Catholic Church after the disasters resulting from the collapse of the Roman Empire. Under this dynasty the Byzantine Empire expanded its borders, its economic power, and its prestige, and Constantinople became the wealthiest and most cultured city in Christendom. The last twenty-five years of the dynasty, however, saw a rapid decline, marked by domestic anarchy and the successful infiltration of the Moslem Seljuk Turks.

**Macedonius** (d. c. 362). After the death of Eusebius of Nicomedia, bishop of Constantinople (c. 341), Macedonius was acclaimed patriarch by the Eusebians. His election was not confirmed by the emperor Constantius, who regarded him with suspicion, but he was allowed to occupy the see. A strong supporter of the *homoiousion* party, Macedonius defended their position before the Council of Seleucia (359–360). The Arian Council of Constantinople (360) deposed him, along with Cyril of Jerusalem and Basil of Ancyra. His writings, if he left any, have been lost. For that reason, it is impossible to say whether he had any connection with the Macedonian heresy which has since the 5th century borne his name. There is no evidence to show that the discussion of the personality of the Spirit had become critical until about the time of Macedonius' deprivation and death. Athanasius' Synod of 362 required recognition of the consubstantiality of the Spirit, and the Pneumatomachoi ("spirit fighters"), a group that included many of the old semi-Arians, rejected this decision. But they did not become important until 373, when Eustathius of Sebaste, who had broken with Basil, became their leader. Pope Damasus condemned them the next year.

Socrates Scholasticus (*Ecclesiastical History* 2. 45) attributes to Eustathius the statement, which may summarize the opinion of this group, that he did "not choose to call the Spirit 'God' nor presume to call him a creature."

A law of Theodosius (Jan. 10, 381) deprived all heretics of their sees. This was followed by the Council of Constantinople (381). Here thirty-six "Macedonian" bishops were in attendance. They refused to accept the *homoousion* and withdrew. After 383 the heresy seems to have disappeared. Its adherents had often been under attack by the Cappadocians and by Didymus of Alexandria.

The historians Socrates and Sozomen are responsible for having identified the opinions of the Macedonians and the Pneumatamochoi. The identification was accepted by such later Latin writers as Jerome and Rufinus. It may be that the original Macedonians sought refuge in the larger Pneumatamochian party after the death of their founder.

**McGiffert, Arthur Cushman** (1861–1933). American church historian and educator. After teaching church history at Lane Theological Seminary from 1888 to 1893, he became professor of church history at Union Theological Seminary, New York. He served as its president from 1917 to 1926. In 1897 he published *A History of Christianity in the Apostolic Age*, which led to conservative criticism. The threat of a heresy trial led him to leave the Presbyterian Church to become a Congregationalist. Other major works were *Protestant Thought Before Kant* (1911) and *History of Christian Thought* (1931–1932).

**McGready, James** (c. 1758–1817). Presbyterian revivalist. A short pastorate in North Carolina preceded his going to Logan County, Ky., in 1796, where great revivals broke out immediately, climaxing in 1800 and resulting in conflict that led to the separation of the Cumberland Presbyterian Church from the older Presbyterian body in 1810. McGready left the new body two years later, however, and served the Presbyterian Church in Indiana.

**Machen, J. Gresham** (1881–1937). American Presbyterian minister, professor at Princeton Theological Seminary, and founder of Westminster Theological Seminary and the Presbyterian Church of America. Machen was born into a prominent Baltimore family and received his B.A. from Johns Hopkins in 1901. He enrolled at Princeton Theological Seminary in 1902 and, after three years there, wrote a prize essay on the virgin birth of Christ that enabled him to study in Germany for a year. At Marburg and Göttingen his orthodox faith was badly shaken, but he overcame his doubts on his return to the United States and began a long career as a professor of New Testament at Princeton. His best-known scholarly work was a fuller development of his prize essay, *The Virgin Birth of Christ* (1930). Machen was the last and most militant defender of the Princeton Theology in that seminary. He was an unremitting opponent of changes in the seminary and denomination which he thought sacrificed the essence of Presbyterianism and Christianity. Fighting a reorganization of the seminary until he was convinced that the cause was lost, he then resigned and organized Westminster Seminary in Philadelphia (1929). As a result of controversy over missions policy in the Presbyterian Church, Machen was censured by the General Assembly in 1936. He thereupon withdrew from the denomination and with his supporters founded a small rival denomination, the Presbyterian Church of America (later renamed the Orthodox Presbyterian Church). His own views of the issues involved were clearly presented in *Christianity and Liberalism* (1923). Deeply involved in the fundamentalist-modernist controversy, he did not consider himself a fundamentalist but rather a strict adherent of the Westminster Confession.

**Machiavelli, Niccolò** (1469–1527). Celebrated theorist of political science. He was born in Florence of a poor but distinguished family. From 1498 to 1512, when the Medici returned to Florence, he held various municipal posts. In the following year, he composed *The Prince*, which he dedicated to Lorenzo de' Medici to gain his favor. To some extent he succeeded, for Lorenzo's successor as ruler of Florence, Cardinal Giulio de' Medici (later Clement VII), gave him certain appointments. When the Medici were again driven from Florence (1527), Machiavelli had to go too. His literary style is often confused with the essential content of his writings, with the result that he is taken for a cynic. Actually, Machiavelli approved of the republican form of government, but saw only too clearly that the unsettled character of his time called for a prince who would subordinate all other considerations to those of policy. It is noteworthy that the foundation of Machiavelli's political doctrine is the concept of human nature as unchanging. *The Prince* may be said to have been inspired by the figure of Cesare Borgia, but it is scarcely a portrait of him. It is, rather, a sketch of the kind of government that the time seemed to demand.

**Machray, Robert** (1831–1904). Anglican archbishop of Rupert's Land and primate of Canada. He was born in Aberdeen, Scotland, and educated at King's College, Aberdeen (M.A., 1851), and Sidney Sussex College, Cambridge (B.A., 1855; M.A., 1858; D.D., 1865). Though brought up a Presbyterian, he was ordained by the Church of England in 1856. In 1862 he became vicar of Madingley, near Cambridge, and served there until 1865, when he was appointed bishop of Rupert's Land. The following year he arrived in Winnipeg. In 1875 he became metropolitan of Canada, and in 1893 archbishop of Rupert's Land and primate of all Canada. He revived

St. John's College, Winnipeg, and became the first chancellor of the University of Manitoba in 1877.

**MacIntosh, Douglas Clyde** (1877–1948). Baptist educator. Born in Breadalbane, Ontario, he studied at McMaster University, Toronto, and did graduate work in theology and philosophy at the University of Chicago. An ordained Baptist minister, he taught at Yale in various capacities from 1909 to 1942. MacIntosh is a representative of modernist liberal theology; in his commitment to the methods and standards of empirical science he rejected historic Christianity as the norm of theology.

**Maclaren, Alexander** (1826–1910). Baptist preacher. Born in Glasgow, he was educated there and at Stepney College in London. From 1846 to 1858 he was minister of Portland Chapel, Southampton; from 1858 to 1903 he was pastor of Union Chapel. He achieved a worldwide reputation for his sermons and writings, and was twice president of the Baptist Union. In 1905 he presided at the first Congress of the Baptist World Alliance.

**McPherson, Aimee Semple** (1890–1944). American evangelist. Converted by her first husband, Robert Semple, a Baptist missionary, she returned from China after his death. Her second marriage, to Harold McPherson, ended when she turned to full-time evangelism and healing. Settling in Los Angeles (1918) where she built the Angelus Temple, she preached to large congregations for twenty years. Founder of the Echo Park Evangelistic Association and the Lighthouse of International Foursquare Evangelism Bible College, she organized the International Church of the Foursquare Gospel in 1927. She entirely dominated the church during her lifetime and was succeeded by her son. Its teachings were set down in her Declaration of Faith, largely fundamentalistic in character. The sect is also Adventist, perfectionistic, and stresses literal acceptance of Scripture. Spirit baptism, glossolalia, prayer healing, a literal Second Coming, and rewards and punishment at the Last Judgment are also taught. She built a radio station, headed a Bible school, edited a magazine, wrote books and pamphlets, and was involved in extensive social service work. An attractive and charming woman, she was skilled in crowd psychology, bizarre ritual, and faith-healing ceremonies. She was a dynamic personality with prodigious energy. The sect was widely publicized and gained devoted followers in spite of the fact that her career was marred by scandal. She was often criticized for commercialism and untoward publicity.

**Madagascar, United Protestant Church of.** A confederation of Protestant churches in Madagascar, resulting from the concerted efforts of several missionary societies previously working independently. The effects were to strengthen and to coordinate the programs of Protestant denominations, to bring a higher percentage of indigenous leadership into the churches, and to increase substantially the active membership in the churches. Denominations did, however, preserve their nominal identities and their respective forms of ecclesiastical government.

**Madauran Martyrs.** Probably the first Christian martyrs in the Roman province of Africa, perhaps executed on July 4, A.D. 180. Their names (Namphamo, Miggin, Lucitas, and Samae) are recorded in a letter from Maximus of Madaura to Augustine and on several Numidian inscriptions, and reflect the spread of Christianity among the natives of North Africa. (See SCILLITAN MARTYRS.)

**Madras Conference** (1938). World Missionary Conference sponsored by the International Missionary Council at Tambaram near Madras in December, 1938. It was the major event in the development of modern world mission and church unity, chiefly because the younger churches were equal in representation to the older churches. The key subjects covered were the problems of an indigenous minority, theological education, and the economic basis of younger missionary churches.

**Magdeburg Centuries.** The first comprehensive history of the church. Published by Matthias Flacius and his colleagues between 1559 and 1574, each of its thirteen volumes covered one century. Calvin, among others, criticized this arbitrary arrangement of the material. The authors viewed all history as a struggle between God and Satan in which the pope was the Antichrist and the Roman Church his empire. Openly biased, it proved to be a stimulus to free historical inquiry and evoked a reply from the Roman Catholic historian Caesar Baronius.

**Maimonides** (Moses ben Maimon) (1135–1204). Philosopher and master of rabbinic literature. Born in Cordova, Spain, Maimonides and his family were forced to flee upon the seizure of the caliphate by a fanatical Moslem sect. Eventually settling in Cairo, Maimonides became the leader of the Jewish community there. Though a most notable student and practitioner of medicine, Maimonides is best remembered for his theological and philosophical work in attempting to reconcile the Jewish faith with the practice of consistent rational thought as presented by the Greek philosophers in the works of Arab commentators. In this work of synthesis he was to do for the Jewish community what Avicenna had done for Islam and what Thomas Aquinas would do for medieval Christianity. Though Aristotle was his sure guide in matters appertaining to reason, Maimonides held to the Jewish belief regarding matters of revelation, such as the creation of the world. In the best Semitic tradition, he insisted upon the transcendence of God, and, consequently, upon the impossibility of applying to him anything more than "negative" predicates. When necessary, he resorted to allegorical interpretations of Scripture. His work, chiefly that major composition written in Arabic and translated into English as the *Guide for the Perplexed,* gained for him the sobriquet of "the second Moses."

**Maistre, Joseph Marie de** (1753–1821). Roman Catholic apologist and social theorist of Napoleonic and Restoration eras. Driven from his native Savoy in 1792 by the Revolution, De Maistre took service with Sardinia, acting as envoy to Russia (1802–1817), where much of his writing was done. *Du pape* (published in 1819), his best-known work, rejected social contract ideas, stressed the priority of society to the individual, emphasized religious sanction in government, celebrated absolutism as the unique source of order, and located ultimate authority in the sovereign papacy, representative of God and implicitly infallible. De Maistre's logical approach made his works useful to the clerical and conservative revival in early 19th-century Catholicism.

**Major, Georg** (1502–1574). German Lutheran churchman. Educated at Wittenberg, he was ordained and became Wittenberg court preacher in 1537 and was appointed to the faculty in 1544. As superintendent at Eisleben (1552–1553) he was opposed by the clergy for teaching that good works are necessary for salvation, though not for justification. This controversy (Majoristic) drove him back to Wittenberg, where he was an active Philippist and dean of the faculty (1558–1574). The Formula of Concord accepted the truth in his view while deploring the wording.

**Major, John** (1470–1550). Scottish theologian and historian. The Scottish Reformation inextricably involved church and state. Its theology was Calvin's but its political views were greatly influenced by John Major, who was not an active participant in the work of reform. Reared in East Lothian, Major was educated in Cambridge and Paris, where he received the master's and doctor's degrees and began to teach the arts and Scholastic philosophy. In 1503 he published his first work, which was on logic. His greatest work was a commentary on the *Sentences* of Peter Lombard. When he became professor of divinity and philosophy in the University of Glasgow, he began to share his views with Reformation leaders. In 1522 he moved to St. Andrews, where John Knox and George Buchanan were students. During this period he completed a history of Great Britain, the first to be written in a critical spirit. By 1525 he was back in Paris, still supporting the Roman Church and opposing Lutheran views. Six years later he returned to St. Salvator's College but held aloof from the Reformation struggle. In political theory he taught that the sole source of civil power resided in the people and the popular will. As a churchman he was Gallican and conciliarist and approved the reform of ecclesiastical abuses. As a theologian he was a conservative Scholastic, generally sympathetic to the spirit of later medieval nominalism.

**Major Orders.** The name given to the three higher orders of the ministry in the Roman Catholic Church. They are the subdiaconate, the diaconate, and the priesthood. The episcopate was once considered a major order, but since the Council of Trent, Catholic doctrine has regarded it as a superior form of the priesthood. Those ordained to a major order in the Latin rite are bound to the daily recitation of the breviary and to celibacy (Canons 949–950, Code of Canon Law).

**Makarii** (16th century). Russian churchman, metropolitan of Moscow, closely associated with Czar Ivan IV. A disciple of Joseph of Volokolamsk, Makarii championed the concept of a national church that would support the autocracy and be subordinated to the state in return for recognition of the church's privileges, including retention of its lands. He supervised the preparation of a collection of church books and lives of the saints (*Chetia-Mineia*).

**Makarios III** (1913–    ). Greek Orthodox prelate and politician. Makarios received his education in Greece and America and was ordained a priest in 1946 and a bishop in 1948. In 1950 he became archbishop of Cyprus and advocated the freeing of Cyprus from British control and its union with Greece. These views led to negotiations with the British, a period in exile (1956), and eventual return to the newly independent island, where he became president in 1960.

**Makemie, Francis** (c. 1658–1708). Presbyterian clergyman. Glasgow-educated, he was sent by his Presbytery of Laggan, Ireland, to America c. 1683, and organized some of the first Presbyterian churches in the New World. He published a catechism on the Westminster Confession and was one of the founders of the first American Presbytery (1706) and its first moderator. He has been called the chief founder of the Presbyterian Church in America.

**Malan, César Henri Abraham** (1787–1864). Swiss Calvinist theologian and gifted preacher. Influenced by Quakers, he encountered difficulties in Geneva with the authorities over his emphasis on the primitive elements of Christianity. Interested in predestination, he joined the Scottish Church, and became concerned with missionary activities and debate. He wrote on the divinity of God and opposed Roman Catholic spiritual claims.

**Maldonatus, Johannes** (Juan Maldonado) (1533–1583). Spanish Jesuit theologian and Scripture scholar. He taught at the Collège de Clermont in Paris and did much to revive theology which was languishing under barren philosophical disputes. In his own theology Maldonatus avoided philosophy and put the stress on Scripture, the fathers, tradition, and the teaching of the theologians. His lectures were attended by Roman Catholics and Huguenots alike, and by people from all walks of life. However, he incurred the displeasure of the Sorbonne theologians, who suspected him of heresy.

**Malthus, Thomas Robert** (1766–1834). English cleric and economist. He was best known for his warning that unless population growth was controlled, it would increase more quickly than the world's food supply. Educated privately and in Cambridge, he was ordained in 1788. In 1796 he took a curacy at Albury, Surrey, and in 1798 published *An Essay on the Principle of Population as It Affects the Future Improvement of Society*, a work that brought him immediate fame. He argued that population growth was not always a desirable trend, since population tended to increase geometrically while the food supply increased only arithmetically. It was, according to Malthus, this race between population and food supply which helped keep down the standard of living and gave rise to famine, pestilence, and war. Because he believed that his "principle of population" was a natural law, he was opposed to any public or private aid that encouraged the poor to marry on an income that could not support a family. At the same time, he was opposed to birth control as a moral evil. He believed that only "moral restraint" (late marriages) could adequately deal with the problem of misery and vice created by overpopulation. Malthus, like other members of the "pessimist" school of economists, had a profound influence on contemporary European society.

**Malvern Conference.** A conference of 240 Anglican clergy and laity convened at Malvern, England, January, 1941, to discuss the relation of Christian faith to the contemporary world. Theologically oriented, it sought "maxims for conduct which mediate between the fundamental principles and the tangle of particular problems." Chairman Archbishop Temple said the chief result was the discussion raised by the conference within and without the church.

**Mamelukes.** The strong men behind the Ayyubid kings at Cairo, who were originally brought to Egypt as slaves. Gaining political control in 1250, the Mamelukes ruled as sultans until the Ottoman conquest in 1517. The Mameluke period is distinguished by commerce, far-reaching political influence in the Middle East, and significant literary and artistic (particularly architectural) development. This dynasty was the first to halt successfully the Mongols in their massive westward invasions in the 13th century.

**Mance, Jeanne** (1606–1673). French philanthropist. Born at Rogentle Roi, France, she went to Canada with Maisonneuve in 1641. There she founded the Hôtel-Dieu at Montreal in 1644, establishing a nursing tradition that is still an inspiration to her profession in French Canada.

**Mandaeans.** A Gnostic sect originating east of the Jordan out of Syrian Christianity. Today it comprises some five thousand members in Mesopotamia. Their name comes from Manda da Hayyê, the redeemer who once on earth defeated darkness and who will free men's souls for ascension. Mandaean writings stem almost entirely from the Islamic period. Despite the prominence of John the Baptist in their mythology, it cannot be maintained seriously that the sect is pre-Christian and goes back to the Baptist.

**Mani, Manichaeism.** Mani was the founder of a religion that he intended to become world-embracing. His father was a member of a semi-Christian baptist sect in south Babylonia. At the age of twenty-four Mani began his work in India, and here he was doubtless influenced by Buddhist ideas that have left numerous traces in his system. In 241 he returned to his native region and for more than thirty years worked as a missionary in the Sassanid empire. His disciples were sent out into the world. At the instigation of the Parsees, Bahram I had him crucified (c. 277).

Mani's system was an elaborate combination of Gnostic, Christian, Buddhist, and Zoroastrian elements. He believed that it would capture the allegiance of the whole world. In fact, he met with considerable response, and had numerous followers in places as diverse as China and North Africa. His work went on for a thousand years after his death, and was a major rival of Christianity. It cannot be shown that the Cathari, Christian heretics of the Middle Ages, had any organic connection with the original Manichaeism, but many of the doctrines of the two groups are identical. Mani couched his teachings in forms most likely to appeal to his hearers. Thus in Hellenistic places he employed the terms of Greek philosophy; among the Christians he used a New Testament phraseology. By such means he was able to convert men such as Augustine of Hippo. He taught that Jesus, Buddha, and Zoroaster were his own forerunners. He was the Paraclete that Jesus had promised, and he sometimes described himself as "an apostle" of Jesus—meaning "one who came after to complete." He taught that evil exists eternally along with absolute good. Light and darkness, God and matter, are forever in conflict. The world came into being as the result of the struggle of Darkness to reach the Light. Consequently, a universe came into being in which Light is held in chains of Darkness. Man reflects this dualistic pattern. God sent his envoy to earth to teach man how to liberate the light within himself. This was to be done through the practice of asceticism. If man could get loose from all material substance, he would be free. Hence, no animals were to be hurt or killed, no plants pulled up. Man was not to settle down in any fixed place, and was to refrain especially from procreation, for otherwise he would only bind more souls to the chains of matter.

Not all the disciples of Mani attained the standard of perfection. There was a graded hierarchy of auditors—the elect, priests, bishops, and apostles. The cult was simple, and worship consisted only in the recitation of certain prayers, the observance of prescribed fasts, and the confession of sins.

These redemptive procedures were clothed in an elaborate mythology. The two eternals are God, or the Father of Greatness (Light), and Evil, or the Ruler of Darkness. The material cosmos is a mixture of these two elements, but it has looked beyond itself, seen the glories of Light, and determined to be free. To aid these imprisoned elements of Light, God sent his Personified Powers (particularly Primordial Man) with the five Light elements of fire, air, wind, light, and water. But in the struggle, Primordial Man deserted the Light, which was then swallowed by the Darkness, and became intermingled with it, and the Light elements forgot their origin. Primordial Man also forgot himself, but was rescued by the Living Spirit sent from above. Then the process of redeeming the self-forgetful elements of Light was begun, and a part of the process was the creation of the world. It was fashioned from the skin, flesh, and bones of the elements of Darkness. The sun and moon were made of uncontaminated Light, and in them other elements of Light could be transported to their native home once they were freed of the Dark. (That is why the moon waxes every month: it is being filled up with passengers for the return journey.) At this point the Third Envoy descended with the work of redemption. The Elements of Light engaged in sexual intercourse with the Elements of Darkness, and thereby many Light elements were set free. Darkness, becoming anxious for its future, then created Adam and Eve, who took the germs of Light in them and bound them ever afresh, through procreation, to their material chains.

Jesus then came and taught Adam to recognize the Light in his soul. Jesus brought the divine nous to man, and created the elements of virtue and understanding in man's heart. With these weapons the soul would at last become free. Thus man began his struggle, but in the course of it he forgot himself. God continually sends messengers to earth to advise and redirect him in the right. These messengers are the founders of religions. The place and role of Jesus is confused. Sometimes he is the Third Envoy; sometimes a companion of the Third Envoy. Sometimes he is Primordial Man, or his son. He also appears as one of the messengers, and is the last in the succession of the founders of religions. The crucifixion is not regarded as a historic event. It represents the soul bound to matter. All things are now in the final stages of battle, and there awaits only the great day of the victory.

BIBLIOGRAPHY: P. Schaff (ed.), *Nicene and Post-Nicene Fathers,* Series I, Vol. 4 (Grand Rapids, 1956); F. C. Burkitt, *The Religion of the Manichees* (Cambridge, 1925); A. V. W. Jackson, *Researches in Manichaeism* (New York, 1932); S. Runciman, *The Medieval Manichee* (Cambridge, 1955).

**Manning, Henry Edward** (1808–1892). English cardinal. Educated at Harrow and Balliol College, Oxford, Manning spent some time at the colonial office. He ultimately chose a clerical career, however, and was ordained in 1832. In 1841 he became archdeacon of Chichester.

Manning's High Church tendencies were accentuated by the Tractarian movement, and in particular by the writings of John Henry Newman and William George Ward. The Gorham case of 1850 initiated a period of doubt for him, from which he emerged after having made a decision to join the Roman Catholic Church. He was received into that communion in April, 1851, and ordained two months later.

Though Manning rose rapidly within the fold of English Catholics, his mannerisms and his espousal of an extreme form of ultramontanism gained him the enmity of the more Cisalpine "Old" Catholics. Upon Cardinal Wiseman's death in 1865, Manning was made archbishop of Westminster.

In the Vatican Council of 1869–1870, Manning was a noted champion of the cause of papal infallibility. He was made a cardinal by Pius IX in 1875. In the last years of his life he became directly involved in problems of social welfare in England.

**Manz** (Mantz), **Felix.** See GREBEL, CONRAD.

**Manzikert, Battle of** (1071). A crucial encounter in which the Byzantine army was soundly defeated by the invading Moslem Turks, who thereupon became permanently established in Asia Minor. The immediate result was the Turks' intimidation of Christian pilgrims traveling through Syria to the Holy Land, an intimidation marked by thievery and the leveling of outrageously high visitors taxes. More abstractly, the result was the undermining by the Moslem Turks of Christian authority in the Byzantine Empire. It was this intolerable situation which ultimately precipitated the First Crusade (1096) and indirectly the Crusades that followed it. The military purpose of the Crusades, in short, was to serve as a corrective to the chaotic conditions that emerged from the defeat of the Byzantine army at Manzikert.

**Map** (Mapes), **Walter** (c. 1140–c. 1210). Ecclesiastic and author. Of Welsh background like his friend Giraldus Cambrensis, Walter Map served King Henry II of England as an itinerant justice and in other capacities. Although tales of the Arthurian cycle and certain scurrilous medieval stories are attributed to him, he is best known for his composition of a volume of remembrances of episodes at the court, the *De nugis curialium.*

**Marburg, Colloquy of** (1529). A conference summoned by Philip of Hesse to achieve unity between the Saxon and the Swiss Reformers. The Swiss were represented by Zwingli and Oecolampadius and supported by Martin Bucer of Strasbourg. The Saxons were led by Luther and Melanchthon. After agreement had been reached on fourteen articles, unity was not achieved because of inability to reconcile divergent views on the bodily presence of Christ in the Eucharist.

**Marcel, Gabriel** (1887– ). French Roman Catholic existentialist. After his conversion to Roman Catholicism in 1929, Marcel became the prime expositor of what has come to be called "Christian existentialism," a philosophical movement that attempts to tread between the extremes of Scholastic abstraction and the hopelessness of atheistic existentialism. Marcel has adumbrated his philosophical position in plays as well as in his more rigorous works.

**Marcellus** (d. c. 374). Bishop of Ancyra and the chief representative of the extreme wing of the Nicene party. He lost his see after the publication of his work attacking the Arian Asterius. At the death of Constantine he was restored (337), but was deposed again in 339. He held that the Scriptures were the only source of theological opinion. From the New Testament he deduced a doctrine of God comparable to Sabellianism, though it was also reminiscent of the teaching of Irenaeus and Tertullian. He taught that the Logos was not a hypostasis, but only an extension or expression of the Divine Monad. Consequently, he refused to use the word "generation" of the Son. The Son and the Spirit became independent entities for the purposes of creation and redemption, after which they were to become one with the Father once more. He maintained, but without being able to describe, a difference between Incarnate Logos and the Spirit. At councils in the West (Rome, 340, and Sardica, 343) his orthodoxy was accepted, but in the East he was detested by the Eusebians, and was a source of embarrassment to the supporters of the *homoousion.* Origen had taught the East to take the implications of doctrinal speculation with seriousness. In the West a more matter-of-fact and practical approach to these subjects still prevailed in the 4th century, and Marcellus' friendly treatment at the hands of the West may be explained by the fact that he stood in the tradition of an earlier, economic Trinitarian orthodoxy.

It was as a denial of Marcellus' belief in the reabsorption of the Son that the words "whose Kingdom shall have no end" were placed in the Nicene Creed. Marcellus' own creed, sent in his letter to Pope Julian, is thought to be the best witness of the form of the Old Roman Creed.

**Marcian** (*also* Marcianus) (392–457). Emperor of the Eastern Roman Empire from 450. Of a peasant background, Marcian became the consort of Pulcheria when her brother Theodosius II died. During their reign, the Council of Chalcedon was called (451) and the Monophysites were declared heretics. Subsequently, Palestine and Egypt, adherents of Monophysitism, withdrew from the Empire and Marcian's military attempts to regain them were by and large ineffectual. Marcian's refusal to pay tribute to Attila was to result in later encroachment on the Empire by the barbarians.

**Marcion.** A mid-2d century defector from the orthodox strain of Christianity who founded a rival movement that survived until the 4th century and was one of the most dangerous threats to the Christian church. The dates of both his birth and his death are uncertain, but the period of his activity would seem to confine his life to the first two thirds of the 2d century. Sinope in Pontus, Asia Minor, is his early sphere of action, where tradition says he was a shipowner. In Pontus he began to develop some of the peculiarities that were to mark his particular heresy: the overaccentuation of the Pauline viewpoint and a Christology of the modalist variety. These features of his system brought him into sharp conflict with the orthodox bishop of Sinope (said by some to be his own father), and the result of this altercation was excommunication. Leaving Sinope, he went to Rome (c. 137), where he enjoyed the hospitality of the Roman Christian community at first, then later was excommunicated by this church also (144). The chief characteristics of his teaching that led to his excommunication were a deep-seated opposition to all that Judaism stood for and his consequent rejection of the Old Testament. It was on this ground that he founded his own church and provided it with a scripture and a systematic theology.

Should Marcion be called a Gnostic? The answer to this question will depend upon the definition given for gnosticism. According to both Irenaeus and Hippolytus, he was indebted to Cerdo, the Syrian Gnostic who was in Rome (c. 140) and to whom the opposition between the wrathful God of the Old Testament and the "good" Father of Jesus Christ is to be attributed. This salient feature of Marcion's system may be due to Cerdo's influence, but it also seems to have had a prehistory in the rabbinic distinction between the names Yahweh and Elohim, the first characterizing the goodness of God and the latter the righteousness of God. The same idea appears to underlie a passage in the Apocryphon of John (62.10 f.). Marcion differs from the Gnostics, however, in that his scripture is taken entirely from those documents which the orthodox church ultimately canonized, although *Antitheses,* the systematic work he wrote, sets forth the oppositions between the Old Testament and the New Testament. In the Old Testament he finds revealed a creator God whose wrathful justice indicates that he must have been less than perfect. Just as this creator God was imperfect, so he could produce only an imperfect creation out of matter. As a result of this imperfection the whole creation and those who dwell in it are under sentence of condemnation to complete annihilation. The true God then reveals himself, and he is at once perfect, completely good, and utterly unknown to the creator God as well as to his creation. In the fifteenth year of Tiberius Caesar, this good God made an appearance in the person of Jesus and taught men to acknowledge his superiority and in this way to overcome the sway of legal justice by means of redeeming love. Because he did not know the Redeemer, the creator God allowed him to be crucified, thus permitting him to carry out his work of redemption in the underworld from which he brought with him those he had redeemed from death. Although these souls are exempted from death, the destiny of all who reject the Redeemer, as well as that of the whole creation, is ultimate destruction. The revelation of this good God, Marcion finds in the "Pauline" Lucan "Gospel," which has to be edited, however, since it has been adulterated at an early date by followers of the creator God. Marcion takes his stand on the Third Gospel, purged of its anti-Paulinism, and upon the "Apostle," consisting of ten Pauline epistles (the fourteen minus Hebrews and the pastorals). The basis for authenticity is a formula making justice, legalism, and Judaism the marks of adulteration. In practice, the Marcionists, as they called themselves, differed in slight but decisive ways from the orthodox; their abhorrence of matter produced excessive ascetic demands and even celibacy for all baptized.

A later follower of Marcion, Apelles, expanded the teaching more in line with general Gnostic patterns. Persecuted along with the Christians, the Marcionites produced many martyrs, and with the 4th-century dominance of the orthodox their organization disappeared and those not killed joined Manichaeism.

BIBLIOGRAPHY: A. Roberts and J. Donaldson (eds.), *The Ante-Nicene Fathers,* Vol. 3 (Grand Rapids, 1951); E. C. Blackman, *Marcion and His Influence* (London, 1948); F. C. Burkitt, *The Gospel History and Its Transmission* (Edinburgh, 1907); J. Knox, *Marcion and the New Testament* (Chicago, 1942).

**Marcus Aurelius** (121–180). Roman emperor from 161. Trained in rhetoric but converted to Stoic philosophy, he spent most of his reign in warfare. After a rebellion in 175 he vigorously persecuted the Christians, whose martyrs he regarded as "obstinate." The apologies of Apollinaris, bishop of Hierapolis, Melito, and Athenagoras were addressed to him. In 177 many Christians in Gaul were put to death.

**Margaret of Scotland** (c. 1045–1093). Granddaughter of King Edmund Ironside of England, queen of Malcolm III of Scotland. She was born in Hungary, later coming to England. After the Norman invasion she fled to Scotland, where she married King Malcolm III. She was a benefactress of the Scottish Church and was credited with the reform of Scottish rites and customs. With her husband she also founded several monasteries. She died four days after her husband was killed in battle.

**Marheineke, Philipp Konrad** (1780–1846). German Protestant theologian. Born at Hildesheim, he studied at Göttingen, took a position at Erlangen in 1805, at Heidelberg in 1807, and at Berlin in 1811. In 1820 he became a colleague of Schleiermacher's at Trinity Church, and, like him, served there as pastor as well as professor until his death. The first edition of his *Die Grundlehren der christlichen Dogmatik als Wissenschaft* (1819) reflects the early influence of Schelling, but by the publication of the second edition in 1827 the influence of his philosophical colleague Hegel had made itself not only apparent but overpowering. Representing a position similar to that of Karl Daub of Heidelberg, he attempted to work out the theological implications of orthodox Hegelianism. It was his desire to explain and defend the orthodox doctrines of Christianity without distortion in terms of Hegel's philosophy. The result was more Hegelian than Christian. His classic work was his *Christliche Symbolik* (3 vols., 1810–1813). The chief content of his teaching in which he attempted to work out a speculative system of Christian thought and an apologetic on the Hegelian framework was included in his *Die Bedeutung der Hegelschen Philosophie in der christlichen Theologie* (1842) and in lecture notes published soon after his death by his pupils. A representative of right-wing Hegelianism, Marheineke looked with horror upon the work of the "young Hegelians," particularly that of D. F. Strauss.

**Maria Laach.** Modern liturgical and religious center near Andernach, Germany, established in 1093 by Henry II of Lorraine and later placed under monks from St. Maximin and Cluniac Benedictines from Affligem in Belgium. The cloister and its territorial possessions reverted to France and then to Prussia (1815). The Jesuits controlled the center from 1862 to 1873. Beuron Benedictines assumed ownership in 1892. The current fame of Maria Laach originated with the periodical *Stimmen aus Maria-Laach* in 1871, but the importance of the abbey as a liturgical-monastic center greatly increased after 1914.

**Mariana, Juan** (1536–1624). Controversial Spanish Jesuit. He taught at Rome and at Paris, and from 1574 lived in Toledo. His most famous work, *De rege et regis institutione* (1599), painted a vivid picture of the ideal king, but justified putting a tyrant to death. When Henry IV of France was assassinated (1610), a violent protest broke out against the book. It was burned publicly and Aquaviva, the general of the Jesuit Order, forbade his priests to preach the lawfulness of tyrannicide. Mariana also wrote a treatise, *De monetae mutatione* (1609), in which he opposed debasement of coinage. He was arrested and charged with treason, because his views allegedly tended to upset the economy, and he was confined to a Franciscan convent until shortly before his death. Apart from his controversial works on tyrannicide and economics, Mariana is noted chiefly for his important history of Spain (*Historiae de rebus Hispaniae,* 1592).

**Maria Theresa** (1717–1780). Austrian archduchess and wife of Francis Stephen of Lorraine, the Holy Roman Emperor. Maria Theresa succeeded Charles VI of Hapsburg in 1740. Her rights of succession were challenged in the War of Austrian Succession, which ended in 1748. She led Austria into war with Prussia (1756–1763). She was a religious woman, but early antipapal instruction at the hands of Gottfried Spannagl influenced her deeply, and she persisted in recalcitration against the papacy.

**Marie de l'Incarnation** (1599–1672). First superior of the Ursulines in Quebec, missionary to the Indians. A native of Tours, France, she was married to Claude Martin in 1616, but was widowed in 1619. After devoting herself for the next twelve years to her son's education, she entered the Ursuline convent at Tours in 1631. Coming to Canada in 1639, she founded an Ursuline convent at Quebec, and became its first mother superior. She was beatified in 1911.

**Mariology.** A Roman Catholic doctrine dealing with Mary's role in redemption. Most Marian thought has been based on her title "Mother of God" (Greek, *theotokos,* or "god bearer"). The ancient church developed this formula to guarantee the unity of man and God in Christ. Thus Mariology is an extension of Christology; Mary is not divine in the definitions of Catholic theology. However, the term "Mother of God" has meanings that its theological definition does not permit. The ancient Near East knew goddess figures with sons who died and rose. The power of nature, earth, and fertility were seen in the goddess. Such pagan ideas have never been recognized in Mariology, but her piety has sometimes looked like the old forms. It is noteworthy that Jung welcomed Marian dogmas as the incorporation of traditional female religious values into Christianity. Devotion to Mary is nevertheless carefully defined as "hyperdulia," not "dulia" for ordinary saints or "latria" for God alone. Ecumenically, the problem has been sharpened by the dogmas of the Immaculate Conception (1854) and the Assumption (1950). Some recent Catholic thought emphasizes Mary's obedience and receptivity to God's action, making her a symbol of the church. Luther's approach was similar in his *Magnificat.*

**Marist Brothers** (*or* Little Brothers of Mary). A teaching order founded in France in 1817 by Joseph Benedict Marcellin Champagnat. The Marist Order was one of the numerous religious orders devoted to teaching which sprang up in France during the generation after the Revolution in an attempt to recapture for the church the youth of that land. Subsequently their labor has been extended to Africa, Oceania, Australasia, and North and South America.

**Maritain, Jacques** (1882–    ). French Roman Catholic Thomist. Educated at Paris and Heidelberg, Maritain came under the influence of the philosophy of Henri Bergson, which he later opposed. Through the inspiration and example of Léon Bloy, Maritain and his wife, Raissa, became Roman Catholics in 1906. He was made professor of modern philosophy at the Institut Catholique de Paris in 1914. In 1923 he helped found the Thomist Society in an attempt to further the Scholastic approach of Thomas Aquinas, of whose philosophy Maritain has become the leading contemporary exponent. In the 1930's he taught at the Institute of Medieval Studies at the University of Toronto. He was made a representative of France to the United States in 1939, teaching at Princeton and Columbia Universities during the war. From 1945 to 1948 he was a French representative to the Holy See, returning to Princeton after this. His name is synonymous with the neo-Scholastic revival both in this country and in Europe. He is an advocate of Christian personalism and humanism. His works include the standard text of neo-Thomism, *An Introduction to Philosophy;* other philosophical works such as *A Preface to Metaphysics* and *The Degrees of Knowledge;* and such diverse volumes as *Man and the State, Art and Scholasticism,* and *True Humanism.*

**Marius Mercator** (5th century). Orthodox polemicist. A follower of Augustine, he wrote a treatise against Pelagius (c. 418). His most important work was done during the Nestorian controversy. These writings, collected a century after his death, are a primary source of Nestorian teaching. Little is known of Marius' life except that he probably came from North Africa and that he lived and worked in Constantinople.

**Mark the Hermit** (4th century). Author of ascetical works. He is said to have been a pupil of John Chrysostom. For a time he was probably an abbot in Ancyra, and later he became a hermit. His many writings on moral and theological subjects became popular. He taught that grace is given in baptism, and afterward in accordance with a man's obedience. As man is God's slave, he deserves nothing and owes everything. Therefore, all is of grace. The work *On Temperance,* sometimes assigned to him, contains precise language about the two natures of Christ, and so must be the work of some later author.

**Marmoutier.** An abbey near Tours, founded by Martin (c. 375). It was an important center for intellectual life in the Carolingian period. It was destroyed by Normans in 853, rebuilt for canons, and in 986 reformed by monks from Cluny. Directly subject to the Holy See through most of the Middle Ages, it was made part of the Maurist Congregation in 1637. The abbey was suppressed and its buildings destroyed in 1792.

**Marnix, Philipp van** (1540–1598). Dutch statesman and theologian. After studying at a number of universities, Marnix was about to take orders when he was won over to Protestantism. He returned to the Netherlands to help in the Reformation, but was driven to Germany, where he wrote a satirical book entitled (in English) *The Beehive of the Holy Roman Church.* He was later a friend of William of Orange, and also an important statesman and a translator of the Scriptures.

**Maronites.** Eastern rite Christians who are chiefly distributed in Lebanon, Syria, Palestine, and Egypt. Many immigrants also went to the United States. The church is governed by a patriarch of Antioch who is elected by the bishop of the Maronite church; the bishops are nominated by the patriarch. Their diocesan clergy are married, and there are religious who follow the Rule of St. Antony.

The Maronites believe that they have constantly retained perfect Orthodoxy, but this is hotly disputed by the other Christians of the area. The most damaging evidence against the Maronite position comes from William of Tyre who reported that they adhered to the Church of Rome in 1182.

Certainly from the 16th century their history and adhesion to Rome are clear. This dates from 1516 in the Eleventh Session of the Fifth Lateran Council. Gregory XIII established a Maronite college in Rome, to which the Maronite bishops could send six priests.

In 1616 a general council of Maronites at Kannobin legislated against abuses and introduced mild liturgical reforms. Maronite liturgical usages are strongly influenced by Roman usages: unleavened bread, Communion under one species (since 1736 when Communion under both species was forbidden).

Another council, under Patriarch Joseph IV (1733–1742), undertook to reform other abuses, e.g., marriage dispensations sold only for money, the remarriage of priests, the use of Arabic in the liturgy by the Maronites of Aleppo. The council introduced the *filioque* into the Creed and stipulated that altar bread was to be circular like that used in Rome. Today the Maronites are governed by one patriarch, two archbishops, ten diocesan bishops, and one apostolic administrator. In areas where there is no regular jurisdiction of their own rite, the Maronites are under the jurisdiction of the Latin bishops.

There are about 800,000 Maronites in the world.

**Marot, Clément** (c. 1497–1544). French court poet and hymn writer. He became acquainted with Protestantism early, and accepted it lukewarmly, but later reverted to Roman Catholicism. His French psalms were adopted by French Protestants and entered into the making of the Genevan Psalter. Calvin published twelve of them in 1539 while in Strasbourg. Following a flight for refuge to Geneva in 1542, Marot there finished his collection of forty-nine French psalms, which was later supplemented by Beza.

**Marozia** (d. before 945). The daughter of Theophylactus, prominent Roman senator, and Theodora the Elder, with whom she and her sister exercised control over the papacy and the civil government of Rome (see PORNOCRACY). In 931, Marozia assumed the titles *Senatrix* and *Patricia*. Her son, whose father was thought to be Pope Sergius III, was made Pope John XI but was deposed and died in prison (936). An older son, Alberic, drove Marozia and her third husband, Hugo of Italy, from the city in 932 and seized power himself. Nothing is known of her after this.

**Marpeck, Pilgram** (c. 1495–1556). Anabaptist. A successful civil engineer in the Tyrol, Strasbourg, and Augsburg, Marpeck was a chief protagonist of nonspiritualist, nonapocalyptic, noncommunalistic Anabaptism throughout southern Germany. Through theological writing and controversy and irenical church-building he ensured the success of the Anabaptist-Mennonite venture in the south. Succeeding generations did not often live up to his breadth of ecumenical sympathy and experience.

**Marprelate Tracts.** A series of seven anonymous Puritan tracts, issued in 1588 and 1589 under the pseudonym Martin Marprelate, attacking episcopacy in particular and the Established Church in general. The tracts were marked by a cheerful scurrility infuriating to supporters of the Establishment, but many moderate Puritans were eventually alienated by the intemperateness of the attacks, which irritated the government instead of persuading it. The precise authorship of the tracts is still unknown. (See PENRY, JOHN, and UDALL, JOHN.)

**Marquette, Jacques** (1637–1675). French explorer and missionary. A great admirer of Francis Xavier, he became a Jesuit and went to Quebec in 1666 to do missionary work among the Indians. His field covered much of northern Michigan and Wisconsin and in the company of Louis Joliet he went down the Mississippi to the Arkansas River. He died on Lake Michigan. His journal is an important source for early American history.

**Marsden, Samuel** (1764–1838). Missionary to the convicts of New South Wales (1793). In 1807, he procured from King George III the fifty-eight Spanish sheep that constituted the nucleus which developed into the large flocks of modern Australia. In 1814, Marsden set up a mission station in New Zealand. Such was his influence among the native Maoris and the English settlers that he deserves credit as a pioneer in the civilization of the new colony.

**Marshman, Joshua** (1768–1837). English missionary and Orientalist. He was the founder of the Baptist mission in Serampore, India, in the early 1800's. Understanding the language and culture of India was basic to his missionary method and he helped translate the Bible into Eastern languages. He initiated Eastern-language newspapers and journals, and helped organize schools, especially one for the instruction of Asiatic youth in Eastern literature and European science.

**Marsilius** (Marsiglio) **of Padua** (c. 1275–c. 1342). Author of the revolutionary political treatise *Defensor pacis* (completed on John the Baptist's Day, June 24, 1324). He left Padua, where he had studied, and went to Paris, becoming rector of the university in 1313, then fled to the emperor Louis of Bavaria when his responsibility for the *Defensor* became known. He was made imperial vicar of Rome (1328) during Louis' campaign in Italy, and then faded from history except for the condemnations he received later.

The *Defensor pacis* ("Defender of Peace") was a combination of Marsilius' political experience in Italy, especially in the commune of Padua, and Aristotelian political philosophy. He was convinced that there was one preeminent cause of civil disorder in his day: the political power and policies of the papacy. People by themselves fell into strife; the object of the state, therefore, was the preservation of order. Order was possible only if all diversities were ultimately controlled by a single authority with a monopoly of coercive law. Law and rulers derived their authority from the whole community or the *valentior pars* ("more worthy part") thereof, but no *part* of the community could resist validly made law or validly appointed rulers. Therefore the church could not be an independent conflicting authority within the body politic, for this could only result in strife. The church was a part of society, directed by the law and the rulers. Ecumenical councils were infallible but were assembled by the legislator and represented the community, and their decrees were effective only if received by the legislator.

Marsilius shifted interest from the final to the efficient cause in politics, thus undermining all political arguments derived from theological analysis of final moral arguments, and anticipated the thinkers of the Renaissance. He can be interpreted as a liberal or a totalitarian democrat, but his view of the papacy was eminently clear to his contemporaries, by whom he was seen as an archheretic.

**Mar Thoma Church.** Third largest of six divisions of Syrian Christianity in southwestern India. Of ancient but unknown origin, this type of Christianity is almost completely confined to the Malabar region and those speaking Malayalam. Belonging to East Syrian Christianity until the 17th century, these churches were Latinized by the Portuguese and subjected to Rome. From 1653 to 1665 a schism separated Syro-Malabar Catholics (Roman) from Syrian Orthodox (Jacobite). In the 18th century a splinter of the latter became the Independent Syrian Church (Thozhiur). In the mid-19th century, under the influence of Anglican missionaries from the Church Missionary Society, a reform movement began in the Syrian Orthodox Church. A significant minority aggressively sought to reform the church, but instead were finally separated from the church, and in the 1880's formed the Mar Thoma Church.

The new organization claimed to be the true successor of the church founded by the apostle Thomas, and to have preserved the faith uncorrupted as was asserted to be no longer true in the Syrian Church. Although new church buildings were erected, much of the historic liturgy and practice of the Syrian Church was retained. The new body, however, was more evangelistic, as is evidenced by the founding in 1889 of the Mar Thoma Evangelistic Association which grew to permeate the entire church with missionary zeal. This found expression in the drawing of converts largely from the depressed classes, and in the church's stand against caste distinctions by incorporating fully into its life all members regardless of previous backgrounds. Successful missionary effort and building campaigns have resulted in a vital community independent of either Rome or Antioch. This evangelical church now has a metropolitan, four bishops, and 250,000 members.

**Martin I** (d. 655). Pope from 649. He summoned a council to meet at the Lateran in 649 which condemned Monotheletism. When he refused to subscribe to the Type, the edict of Constans II which forbade all religious discussion, he was ordered seized by the emperor and was exiled to Naxos in 654. A year later he was brought to Constantinople and then banished to Cherson, in the Crimea, where he soon died.

**Martin IV** (Simon de Brie, c. 1210–1285). Pope from 1281. A canon at Tours, chancellor of France in 1260 under Louis IX, Martin became a cardinal in 1261. As legate he held reforming synods in France and was responsible for negotiating with Charles of Anjou concerning the kingdom of Sicily. Through Charles's influence he was elected pope in 1281, using his office to further Angevin ambitions against the Eastern Empire. His unpopularity with the Romans caused an uprising that forced him to flee to Perugia, where he died in 1285.

**Martin V** (Oddone Colonna, 1368–1431). Pope from 1417. As a cardinal, he took part in the election of the popes Alexander V and John XXIII at the Council of Pisa. After a conclave of three days at Constance, he was unanimously elected pope on Nov. 11, 1417, thereby ending the Great Schism. On April 22, 1418, he dissolved the Council. When, in May, Polish ambassadors expressed discontent with a papal decision and appealed to a future council for amends, Martin V replied that no one was permitted to appeal beyond the Holy See or to excuse himself from the judgments of the pope in matters of faith. However, in accordance with the decree *Frequens* of Constance, after five years he called the Council of Pavia, although the plague caused him to transfer it to Siena. The French conciliarist discussions there were hostile to papal privileges, and Martin used the small attendance and disagreement of the cardinals as a pretext for dissolving the Council on Feb. 26, 1424, but he agreed to summon the Council of Basel within seven years. He appointed Cardinal Cesarini president of the Council, but died before it convened.

**Martin, Gregory** (d. 1582). Translator of the Douay-Reims Bible. He was a talented scholar and linguist at Oxford for many years before he left for religious reasons and became tutor to the family of Thomas Howard, duke of Norfolk. When the duke was accused of being a Romanist and imprisoned, Martin left England and went to William Allen's college at Douai, where he was ordained in 1573. Martin headed the group of scholars who produced the Douay-Reims English translation of the Latin Vulgate and did the greater share of the initial draft himself.

**Martineau, James** (1805–1900). Unitarian minister, essayist, educator, and philosopher. His sister was the famous Harriet Martineau.

Ordained in 1828, Martineau served a congregation in Dublin, and then returned to his alma mater, Manchester New College, as professor of philosophy. He subsequently became president of the college (1869). He was a member of the noted Metaphysical Society, and the author of numerous works.

**Martyn, Henry** (1781–1812). Anglican missionary. He served in India after 1805. At Dinapore, he established schools for the natives and learned their languages. There followed his translations of the New Testament and the Prayer Book into Hindustani, The Psalms into Persian, and the Gospels into Judeo-Persian. Martyn died in Persia, just as he was preparing a Persian rendition of the New Testament. He was long remembered for his heroic missionary efforts in India.

**Martyr Acts.** Histories or stories of events in the lives of the church's martyrs. Numerous accounts of martyrdoms in the period of persecution have come down to us. One type was that of the eyewitness report of the trial and death of a martyr. The descriptions of the death of Polycarp and of the sufferings of the Christians at Lyons belong to this group. Sometimes, as in the case of the martyrdom of Perpetua, who died in North Africa in A.D. 203, the first part, descriptive of the sufferings, was written by the martyr in the first person, and the narrative was then completed by other Christians. A second type of these acta was written in a documentary style, somewhat like the shorthand record of a court reporter. This method may have been adopted in order to lend an air of immediacy and reliability to the narrative. A third type was legendary, and might contain only a kernel of historical truth or none at all. The first collection of Martyr Acts was probably produced by Eusebius of Caesarea. His principal work has been lost, but his lesser work on the martyrs of Palestine survives. In Africa at least the Acts were read aloud in churches.

**Martyrs.** A word meaning "witnesses" which initially referred to those who had witnessed the historic events of Jesus' ministry (Acts 1:8). Later it designated those who by their sufferings had witnessed to their faith in him. It came, finally, to be used only of those who had died under persecution, thereby witnessing supremely. Those who had been faithful under persecution, but had survived, were called "confessors." It was a common belief in pre-Christian times that a prophet must seal his witness with his death. At the time of death supernatural powers would come to his aid and soften the force of his sufferings. It was with this belief that their sufferings would actually aid their cause, and that they would be spared in their final agonies, that Christians embraced martyrdom. Lucian, the pagan satirist, noted the willingness of Christians to die and ascribed it to their arrogance in believing themselves immortal. In the letters of Ignatius, and in his expressed anxiety to avoid escape from death in the arena, this attitude is exemplified. Martyrdom was held by the church to be equivalent to baptism. The martyrs soon became venerated as intercessors. Their bones and relics were used to sanctify places of worship, and the use of relics for devotional purposes was sometimes carried to surprising lengths. The cult of the martyrs may owe its formal origin to the custom begun in Smyrna in 156 of commemorating the death of Polycarp by an annual celebration at his tomb. This devotional practice had spread through the East and into Africa before the end of the 2d century. It does not seem to have prevailed at Rome before 202. A calendar of martyrs in use in the Roman Church in 354 includes no names earlier than this date. The custom arose much later of including all the Christian heroes in these calendars. Consequently, anniversaries of the apostolic and sub-apostolic age began to be kept at a later time than those of the 2d- and 3d-century martyrs, although one early Syrian martyrology includes Ignatius of Antioch.

The first of the martyrs was Stephen, one of the original seven deacons. He was stoned for heresy by the Jews of Jerusalem. James the apostle was executed by Herod Agrippa, who reigned from 41 to 44, and James of Jerusalem was stoned in 62. Following this incident, the Christian community withdrew to Pella, and so escaped the devastation following the Jewish rebellion of 66. This severing of ties with Jerusalem no doubt helped to bring Christianity's status as a Jewish sect to an end, and thus exposed it to the laws requiring conformity to the Roman state cult from which the Jews were exempt. Jews sometimes participated in the imperial persecutions of Christians which began about this time and continued sporadically into the 4th century. The first great attack on the church was made under Nero. In July, 64, a fire broke out in Rome and burned for six days, ravaging the city. Rumors that the fire had been set by authority were noised about, and the emperor accused the Christians of incendiarism. Because they were regarded as enemies of the human race, many of them were put to death in various horrible ways. The legal status of Christians was confused. In 112, Pliny the Younger wrote to Trajan asking for clarification of this matter. The emperor replied that no general provisions could be made. Christians were not to be sought out, but if charges were brought, they must be investigated. Jews had been hated because they held aloof, and Christians were hated for the same reason. Their withdrawal from society, and the secrecy in which their worship was conducted, fed the popular belief that Christians engaged in acts of atheism, incest, and cannibalism. At times of public distress the Christians became the easy targets of popular superstition. The state was not much concerned with the morality of Christian actions, but was alarmed by the unwillingness of the Christians to participate in the state cult, thus becoming a cause of national disintegration. Christian apologists were never able to persuade the officials to take any interest in the righteousness and simplicity of Christian life.

Only sparse records of the martyrdoms have come down to us. At the time that Revelation was written, probably under Domitian, Rome was said to be drunk with the blood of martyrs. Ignatius of Antioch probably suffered in a persecution under Trajan. In 177, Christians were hunted out and butchered in Lyons and Vienne, but persecutions were mostly of local significance until the time of Decius (249–251). The emperor was convinced that the troubles of the realm were caused by the neglect of the gods. The higher clergy were seized and the bishops of Rome, Antioch, and Jerusalem were early victims. Many, both clergy and laity, recanted. The intent of the persecution was not to punish the Christians, but to convert them to paganism. After a little more than a year it became obvious that this intention on a broad scale was only a fond hope, and the persecution was dropped. In the end, the church was much strengthened by the heroic examples of the Decian martyrs. Another general and bloody persecution began under Valerius in 257 and continued until 261. The term "martyrs" is often most closely connected with the persecution that began in 303 by order of Diocletian. It began with the clergy, and the next year was extended to the laity. It was brought to an end by various edicts promulgated during the struggles that brought Constantine to power in the West (313). After a few years, persecutions broke out again in the East, and were finally ended when Constantine became sole emperor (324). The age of the martyrs, as classically understood, then closed.

BIBLIOGRAPHY: W. H. C. Frend, *Martyrdom and Persecution in the Early Church* (Garden City, 1967); R. M. Grant, *The Sword and the Cross* (New York, 1955); H. B. Workman, *Persecution in the Early Church* (Cincinnati, 1906).

**Marx, Karl Heinrich** (1818–1883). German economist, foremost working-class theorist of the 19th century, and founder of "scientific" socialism. He was born at Trier of Jewish parents who embraced Christianity in 1824. Educated at Bonn and Berlin, he took his Ph.D. at Jena in 1842. From graduation to his death Marx devoted his energies to journalism and to a systematic analysis of history and contemporary society. He edited and contributed numerous essays to liberal and communist journals in Cologne, Paris, and London, and earned his livelihood as a journalist for the *New York Tribune*. In 1847, Marx and Friedrich Engels published the *Communist Manifesto*, a tract that brought its authors worldwide fame; in 1867 appeared the first of the three-volume work *Das Kapital*, Marx's crowning work.

In *Das Kapital*, a monumental analysis of the capitalist era of economic development, Marx undoubtedly established himself as the founder of the modern socialistic school, in that he was the first to make definite scientific statements concerning the principles of socialism. The roots of his theoretical system came from G. W. F. Hegel, who believed that all life is a process of social change. Everything, said Hegel, is related to something else and every movement automatically produces its opposite, and from the inevitable conflict between opposites emerges the final synthesis. Marx enthusiastically accepted Hegel's "dialectic" with only one exception. Whereas Hegel emphasized the primacy of "ideas" in social change, Marx gave emphasis to the primacy of material conditions. By materialism, Marx meant that the basic element in society is economics. It is not primarily by having ideas that men create the social world in which they live; instead, their form of society predisposes them to have certain ideas. He thus concluded that the history of "all previous society is the history of class struggles." At all periods mankind has been divided into exploiter and exploited, master and slave, patrician and plebian, and capitalist and proletariat. The substructure of economics determines the superstructure of ideology, politics, culture, and society. The structure of the modern world, for example, reflects the domination of the bourgeoisie capitalist world. The capitalists exploit the working classes, turning personal dignity into a negotiable commodity to be bought and sold. Eventually, however, the workers will develop class consciousness and violent revolution will produce a utopian classless society in which the catalyst of social change—class struggle—disappears. History, according to Marx, true history, will then begin.

Marx was an atheist, and his "dialectical materialism" was a powerful force in destroying the foundations, including religion, on which the world believed itself to be standing. State, church, law, and morality became merely "bourgeois." Marx believed that morals were "bourgeois morals," that law was "bourgeois law," that government was an instrument of class power, and that religion was a form of psychological warfare, a means of providing "opium" for the masses. Therefore, the workers must not let themselves be fooled; they must learn how to detect their class interest underlying the most exalted institutions and beliefs. Everything in Marx's system became a phase or manifestation of something else. Permanent things were made to look transient, and absolute things to look relative, as in the world's great religions.

Marx's influence in philosophy, history, and economics has been prodigious. In addition, he is regarded by more than one half of the world as one of the greatest men who ever lived. By his ideas he has transformed the world into the communist and noncommunist blocs.

BIBLIOGRAPHY: K. Marx and F. Engels, *On Religion* (New York, 1964); and *Basic Writings on Politics and Philosophy,* ed. by L. S. Feuer (Garden City, 1959); E. Fromm, *Marx's Concept of Man* (New York, 1961); E. Kamenka, *The Ethical Foundations of Marxism* (New York, 1962); G. Lichtheim, *Marxism: An Historical and Critical Study* (New York, 1961).

**Mary, Birth of.** A document generally known as the Protevangelium of James but published in 1958 from a papyrus of the 3d century, with the new title. The book begins with a story of the birth of Mary to Joachim and Anna, describes her upbringing in the Temple, and tells of her being entrusted at the age of twelve to Joseph. It concludes with legendary accounts of the birth of Jesus and the murder of Zacharias, the father of John the Baptist. This apocryphal writing is important because of its use by Origen and later church writers; a parody of it circulated among Gnostics.

**Mary, Devotion to.** Pious practices which gradually developed in relation to Mary. Foreshadowed in the Old Testament, Mary was revealed in the New (cf. Matt., ch. 1; Luke, chs. 1 and 2) as the personification of faithful Israel, the virgin daughter of Zion, the espoused of Yahweh, the Tabernacle of the

Most High, the living Ark of the Covenant. Early fathers saw in the overshadowing of Mary by the Spirit her embodiment of Yahweh's supreme act of loving-kindness, and in her virginal childbearing a summation of all God's initiatives toward his chosen. They stressed her actual motherhood of the Savior against the Gnostics, her perpetual virginity, her personal sinlessness, her role as the new Eve. She was the prototype of the church and of every faithful soul. Praying to Mary, however, was apparently unknown in the pre-Nicene church.

After the Christological Councils of Ephesus and Chalcedon, Mary emerged in both theology and devotion as truly *Theotokos, Dei Genetrix,* Mother of God, the touchstone of orthodoxy, the help of Christians. In the East, poets and preachers vied with one another in singing her praises, churches were raised to her in every city, her feast days appeared in the liturgy, her relics were "invented" and venerated with enthusiasm. Miraculous icons of the "God-bearing Virgin" became the focal point of popular piety. As Byzantine theologians restored "Christ our God" to the bosom of the Trinity, Mary became more and more the primary intercessor before this remote and awful Deity.

For the first thousand years it was the Byzantine East that surpassed all other churches liturgically and theologically in exalting the Theotokos. The far more sober Latin West was slower to permit the fervors of rhetorical piety to influence liturgy and doctrine. Aside from such local innovations as the English celebration of Mary's conception and presentation, the High Middle Ages kept only the five traditional Marian feasts: Jan. 1, the octave of Christmas; Feb. 2, the Presentation; March 25, the Annunciation; Aug. 15, the falling asleep and Assumption of Mary; and Sept. 8, her nativity. Moreover, the Mass and office of these feasts were preeminently Christological in tone and emphasis. Mary was fully the handmaid of the Lord.

Although the dubious Council of Basel (1439) tried to extend the feast of the Immaculate Conception to the entire Latin Church and Pope Sixtus IV introduced it into the diocese of Rome in 1476, some two centuries were to elapse before it was generally observed.

The great Scholastic doctors too, such as Bonaventure, Albert the Great, and Thomas Aquinas, like the Latin fathers before them, were restrained and careful in their formulation of Marian teaching. They concentrated chiefly on doctrinal essentials that enhanced and clarified Christ's salvific role and were hesitant to speculate about notions that were not plainly Biblical in origin.

Despite such liturgical and theological conservatism, popular preaching, writing, and devotion became ever more luxuriant and influential. The fervors of concrete piety came to play possibly a more important part in the development of lived doctrine than did sound theological thinking. The creation and diffusion of such popular practices of piety as the Little Office of Mary, the five Marian anthems, e.g., the classic "Ave Maria" and "Salve Regina," new Marian litanies, and the gradual development of the Rosary propelled Mary into the forefront of Catholic devotional life. The widespread effect of the many naïve and even fantastic Marian miracle stories and the near absence of an intelligible liturgy were all factors in the extravagant nature of medieval Marian piety. "Never too much of Mary," said her devotees. Men were encouraged to vow themselves to be her vassals and even her slaves, to wear her liveries and to outdo one another in exalting her without measure. Above all, Mary was presented as the infallible lightning rod of God's anger and as the one intercessor who could *command* Christ. Although this fervent Marian piety may well have safeguarded such Catholic doctrinal values as divinization by grace and the mutuality of life in the mystical body of Christ (the communion of saints), in the actual medieval situation of a divorce between liturgy and piety it was not without real danger to other Catholic values.

BIBLIOGRAPHY: H. Graef, *Mary: A History of Doctrine and Devotion* (New York, 1963); J. Herolt, *Miracles of the Blessed Virgin Mary* (London, 1928); M. Thurian, *Mary: Mother of All Christians* (New York, 1963).

**Mary, Hymns to the Blessed Virgin.** Liturgical songs or hymns related to the devotion to Mary and the feasts observed in her honor. Although the Syriac, Byzantine, and other Eastern liturgies at an early date sang the praises and implored the merciful help of the Virgin Mother with grace and profusion (the Coptic liturgy even has an entire anaphora addressed directly to Mary), the Latin liturgies of the West, slow to admit any but Biblical psalms and canticles, knew no Marian hymns until probably the 9th century. The "Ave Maris Stella," first used for vespers of the Annunciation, and the "Quem terra pontus," first used for the Assumption, became the fixed hymns of the Marian common of feasts and of the Little Office of the Blessed Virgin Mary. They both sing of the marvelous mystery of the Word made flesh in the womb of Mary, the new and second Eve, the luminous gate of heaven, and beg her to be the mother of Christians.

In the course of the 12th and 13th centuries, largely under Cistercian and Franciscan influence, four antiphons or anthems with attached versicles and collects came to be sung at the close of the daily office. Their theme is essentially the same as the earlier hymns, with somewhat greater stress on Mary's role as the interceding Queen of Mercy. The poignant and compassionate "Stabat Mater" is the only other permanent medieval contribution to the Roman liturgy.

**Mary, Queen of Scots** (1542–1587). Queen of Scotland and heir to the throne of England. By 1560 the Reformation had effected in Scotland a new system of church government and worship, but the national administration remained monarchical and the Scots were loyal to the ruler. At nineteen, Mary as the legitimate successor to the throne after the death of her mother, who had been regent for eighteen years, was invited to return to Scotland to rule. She had been in France since the age of six to be reared in the French court, subsequently marrying the dauphin, Francis II. By making a claim to the English throne, she and her husband alienated Elizabeth. Meanwhile, the Reformed Church of Scotland had been living under a French Roman Catholic regent who was intensely anti-English and who was ruling for a daughter already pledged to Roman Catholicism and to France.

In 1561 when Mary returned to her native Scotland to reign, it was as a young widow, more French than Scottish, already an enemy of England, and on probation with the Reformers. Almost immediately Mary's Roman Catholic loyalty created a crisis. She observed a private Mass, incurred popular anger, and was introduced to the thunder of Knox. Hoping to control Mary's claims (1563) to succession to Elizabeth, England proposed that she marry the earl of Leicester. Instead, in 1565, she suddenly married her cousin, Lord Darnley, a Roman Catholic, and next to Mary in the English succession. The Roman Catholic powers in Scotland united behind her in this act of defiance to both England and the Reformed Church. The scandal following the murder of Rizzio, whose preferment by Mary had provoked Darnley's jealousy, prevented the complete collapse of civil power held by the Reformers. Though Mary survived this crisis, she could not escape Scotland's horrified reaction to the subsequent murder of Darnley and her marriage to his presumed assassin, the ruthless earl of Bothwell. Civil strife followed. Mary's forces were met by a superior army of the lords and she surrendered at Carberry Hill (1567) when Bothwell was permitted to escape. However, she was forced to abdicate in favor of her son (born on June 19, 1566), who was to rule as James VI of Scotland, and later as James I of England. The earl of Moray became regent. Another attempt was made to restore Mary, but her forces were defeated at Langside (1568) and she fled to England, seeking the protection of her cousin Elizabeth.

Mary's career as queen of Scotland was short and turbulent, and many of her actions defy explanation. Born a Scot but reared in France out of touch with the Reformation, she believed that a queen was above censure and had the right to set the religious beliefs of her subjects. Her confidence in powerful Continental Roman Catholic allies who would support her was unfounded. Nor would her own Scots defend the folly and ambition of a Roman Catholic queen.

From 1568, when Mary reached England, until her execution in 1587, she was held a prisoner. Her position in England was delicate. There was the chance that Elizabeth would use her cousin's forced abdication as an occasion to subdue Scotland in punishment for rebellion against a legitimate monarch. Mary's Scottish foes were forced to try to discredit her before the English in order to prolong her exile. For two years charges and countercharges were made and Mary was placed under "house arrest" in charge of the earl of Shrewsbury. Her situation worsened when the Scots refused to grant her divorce from Bothwell so that she could marry the earl of Norfolk, her English champion. With her strong Roman Catholic allies, Mary was a constant threat to Elizabeth's security. Ultimately, Mary was charged with complicity in a plot to assassinate Elizabeth and with conspiring with Spain against England. Although Mary conducted her own defense with courage and ability, the Privy Council ordered her execution. She died in the same remarkable manner in which she had lived.

Mary was a woman of contrasts. There was much in her that was worthy of the highest praise, but also there were actions and judgments subject to the severest reproach. In a sense she was the victim in the death struggle of an old order.

BIBLIOGRAPHY: M. Bowen, *Mary Queen of Scots, Daughter of Debate* (London, 1934); G. Buchanan, *The Tyrannous Reign of Mary Stewart* (Edinburgh, 1958); S. Zweig, *Mary Queen of Scotland and the Isles* (New York, 1935).

**Mary Magdalene of Pazzi** (1566–1607). Italian Carmelite mystic who took as her motto: "To suffer, not to die." Believing in the spiritual value of suffering, she felt she could endure any torment for the love of God and the salvation of men. She was often physically sick and was afflicted with spiritual desolation for long periods of time. Yet she also experienced interludes of vitality and ecstasy, during which she counseled her fellow sisters, who wrote down her utterances and published them after her death (*Maxims of Divine Love*).

**Mary Tudor** (1516–1558). Queen of England from 1553. Daughter of Henry VIII and Catherine of Aragon, she endured great humiliation during Henry's quest for annulment of his marriage with Catherine and subsequently when she was excluded from the succession as an illegitimate child (1534). The return of her household in 1536 came only after her public acknowledgment of all that the Act of Succession asserted. By 1544, she had been restored to the line of succession after Edward, whom she succeeded only after failure of the abortive attempt of Dudley, duke of Northumberland, to put Lady Jane Grey on the throne. Though determined at her accession to restore the old religion, her early policy was conciliatory if stern. After Wyatt's rebellion, she set herself on the course that was to win her the epithet "Bloody Mary." Married to Philip of Spain in 1554, she pressed for the restoration of the old religion, thus threatening those who benefited from suppression of the monasteries, and invited Cardinal Pole to reconcile the kingdom to Rome. From this point onward she proceeded against heretics and executed among many others four bishops—Hooper, Latimer, Ridley, and Cranmer—while cruelly suppressing actual and alleged plots against her. Philip, never an ardent husband, left her permanently after his campaign against France had failed (1558), and she died shortly thereafter.

**Massachusetts Bay Company.** A group which was granted a royal charter on March 4, 1629, to found a colony on Massachusetts Bay, in spite of the fact that it was dominated by Nonseparating Congregationalist Puritans of East Anglia. The original commercial concept of the colony had been replaced by the Puritans with an intention of establishing a church and state based on Scripture. The first governor, Matthew Cradock, proposed on July 28 the transferral of the Company's government and charter to the colony. This was agreed upon by the new leadership—Thomas Dudley, John Winthrop, William Pynchon, Sir Richard Saltonstall, and Increase Nowell—and the transfer voted on Aug. 29. Cradock resigned and nonmigrating stockholders withdrew. Winthrop was elected governor on Oct. 20. The usual restriction that the government and charter remain in England was removed "with much difficulty." The Company and charter sailed March 29, 1630. This provided the structure on which the "holy experiment" was attempted. The Company was composed of stockholders or "freemen," who governed as the General Court, electing officers (governor and assistants), which later included deputies who represented settlements. It was further decreed on May 18, 1631, that none could vote or hold office except members of the churches of the colony. The Massachusetts charter was revoked by James II in 1684, but was partially restored in 1691 by William III, with the governor by royal appointment.

**Massachusetts Proposals.** The statements of a convention of pastors in 1705 calling for tighter church government by establishing associations with final authority in dealing with controversial issues and in passing on ministerial candidates. Although approved by a Boston Convention in 1706, the Proposals were implemented only in part in Massachusetts, but they became the basis for a similar action at Connecticut's Saybrook Synod in 1708.

*Mater et Magistra.* Encyclical letter of Pope John XXIII on Christianity and social progress, given on May 15, 1961. Emphasizing the concern of Christianity with the whole man, Pope John alluded to the allocutions of his predecessors which dealt with the questions of private property and the rights of labor. The keynote of the pope's letter was his insistence upon the obligations of economically advanced regions toward those less developed.

**Mather, Cotton** (1663–1728). American Puritan leader. The son of Increase Mather and the grandson of John Cotton, Cotton Mather was ordained in 1685 and succeeded his father as the leading cleric of Massachusetts Bay. He played an important role in the Salem witchcraft trials, having helped initiate them in his *Memorable Providences Relating to Witchcraft* (1689), but he later became critical of "spectral evidence" and executions. Arrogant, priggish, and intolerant as only a man with his sense of moral mission can be, Mather sought to restore the stature of the clergy against growing secularism, but was not a skillful ecclesiastical politician. He spent much time in theological introspection and evolved a simplified theology epitomized in *Essays to Do Good* (1710). His reputation was extended abroad by his writings and scientific papers, the Royal Society electing him as a member in 1713. During the smallpox epidemic of 1721 he successfully defended inoculation, making possible its use in Boston. The author of 450 books, Mather produced his greatest work in *Magnalia Christi Americana* (1702).

**Mather, Increase** (1639–1723). American Puritan leader. Ordained in 1657, Mather became pastor of Second Church in Boston in 1664. A master of the jeremiad, he dominated Massachusetts religious life, a leading figure in the acceptance of the Halfway Covenant and in the Reforming Synod of 1679–1680. He vigorously opposed royal attempts to proscribe the colonial charter in 1683 and sought the support of William III for a restored charter in 1688. Mather was influential in the attempt to unite English Dissent in 1691. Though a believer in witchcraft, he criticized the Salem trials and influenced their course in *Cases of Conscience Concerning Evil Spirits* (1692–1693). Defender of Puritan orthodoxy and Boston suzerainty, he came into conflict with growing liberalism, Anglicanism, and Solomon Stoddard. A fellow of the Royal Society, he demonstrated his lifelong interest in scientific progress in 1721 by supporting the unpopular cause of inoculation against smallpox. Mather was president of Harvard from 1686 to 1701.

**Matheson, George** (1842–1906). Blind Scottish divine who through readers and secretaries overcame his infirmity. A brilliant preacher, he wrote at least two dozen books and composed several hymns. His writings fall into three categories: philosophical theology and comparative religion; expositions of Scripture to aid preachers; and devotional works and hymns, among them "O Love That Wilt Not Let Me Go" and "Make Me a Captive, Lord." Of these, the last category has endured, although his best work is a life of Christ in two volumes (1899, 1900).

**Mathews, Shailer** (1863–1941). American Baptist educator. After schooling at Colby and Newton Theological Institute, he taught at Colby from 1887 to 1894, interrupted by a year of study at the University of Berlin (1890–1891). In 1894 he joined the faculty of the Divinity School of the University of Chicago, where he remained until his retirement to emeritus status in 1933; he was dean of the Divinity School from 1908 to 1933. His fame as a champion of theological liberalism and of the Social Gospel began with the publishing of *The Social Teaching of Jesus* (1897), followed by more than twenty other volumes.

Always active in the life of the church, he served as president of the Federal Council of Churches (1912–1916) and of the Northern Baptist Convention (1915), and held many other important Baptist and ecumenical positions.

**Matthew Paris** (c. 1200–1259). Monk at St. Alban's, best of English monastic historians and illustrator of his own manuscripts. His major work, the *Chronica majora,* combines the now lost records of his abbey by Roger of Wendover with material Matthew gained at firsthand and continues the story until 1259. This work shows antipathy to foreign provision and other invasions of English church life. It has been abridged as the *History of the Angles.* Matthew also compiled the lives of the abbots of St. Alban's.

**Matins.** A form of prayer for morning that developed out of the early Christian practice of vigils (watching with prayer through the night before Easter, any Sunday, or feast). As a monastic office, Matins has three nocturns, each with lessons and psalms, making it the longest of the hours of prayer. The Reformers combined aspects of it and Lauds to form Morning Prayer. It contains psalms, lessons, hymns, canticles, collects, and prayers.

**Mauriac, François** (1885–1970). French Catholic writer and Nobel laureate of 1952. Producing prose, poems, and polemics, he won fame with his fifth novel, *Le Baiser au Lépreux* (1922). Frequently he depicted rough characters redeemed through divine grace in his romances. He was elected to the French Academy (1933), engaged in political journalism, and aided the underground in World War II. A liberal rather than a reactionary, he supported the Fourth Republic. His works are available in English.

**Maurice, John Frederick Denison** (1805–1872). English cofounder of Christian Socialism. Under the influence of S. T. Coleridge's philosophical and theological thought, Maurice, who had gone to Trinity College, Cambridge, in 1823, left the Unitarian faith of his parents and was baptized in the Church of England in March, 1831. He was ordained Jan. 26, 1834, after a preparatory course at Exeter College, Oxford. His subsequent work may be viewed from a theological or from a social point of view. In either case he represented those who would be neither revolutionaries nor reactionaries. Closely associated with Maurice from both points of view was Charles Kingsley. Together they began to publish a series *Tracts for Priests and People* (1854). The great Tractarian movement was now

over, and consideration of abstract points of theology gave way to a concern for the relation of Christianity to the problems faced by a society in the throes of industrialization. In the same year (1854), Maurice founded the Working Men's College. He was professor of literature and history at King's College, London, after 1840. *The Kingdom of Christ* (1842), his *Epistle to the Hebrews* (1846), *Theological Essays* (1853), and *The Claims of the Bible and Science* (1863) set forth his theology.

**Maurice** (Moritz) **of Saxony** (1521–1553). Elector of Saxony. Maurice succeeded his father as duke of (Albertine) Saxony in 1541. Although he had signed the Smalcald Articles, he refused to join the League, preferring, at the Diet of Regensburg, to make a secret alliance with Charles V. With Charles's help he drove out his cousin John Frederick, the elector of (Ernestine) Saxony, and obtained the title and territories for himself at the Diet of Augsburg, in 1548. Though he rejected the Augsburg Interim, he accepted the less uncompromising Leipzig Interim. For both political and religious reasons, however, he turned against the emperor in 1552, and obtained by force the concessions of the Peace of Passau. Maurice died shortly afterward of injuries sustained in battle with the margrave of Brandenburg, who would not accept the Passau settlement.

**Maurras, Charles** (1868–1952). French Roman Catholic conservative. Along with Léon Daudet, Maurras was largely responsible for the L'Action Française movement. Large numbers of French Catholics were attracted to this rightist, antirepublican cause. Although seven of Maurras' works were placed on the Index in 1914, the decree announcing this fact was not promulgated until 1926. Pope Pius XI had *L'Action Française* (the journal of the movement) condemned in the same year.

**Maurus.** A 6th-century monk, the chief disciple of Benedict, to whom he had been entrusted as a boy. Maurus is credited with the miraculous rescue of Placid, another monk, from drowning. The *Dialogues* of Gregory the Great are the only nearly contemporary source for his life. A later forged legend relates that he was sent to Gaul by Benedict and there founded a monastery. The former French Benedictine Congregation, the Maurists, derive their name from him.

**Maximilian I Joseph** (1756–1825). Elector (1799) and king (1806) of Bavaria. He showed strong sympathies with revolutionary France and liberal French ideas during his electorate. With his minister, Count von Monteglas, he fostered agriculture and commerce, reformed taxes and the criminal code, and restricted the privileges of the churches, using their revenues for educational and other useful projects. With the Treaty of Pressburg (1805), he gained important territory and received the royal title. When Monteglas fell from authority in 1817, Maximilian also restored the powers of the clergy by signing a concordat with the papacy. Upon meeting strong parliamentary opposition in 1818, however, he made some concessions.

**Maximum Illud.** Apostolic letter of Pope Benedict XV on the spread of the faith throughout the world, issued on Nov. 30, 1919. Insisting that missionary activity in one form or another was incumbent upon all Christians, the pope reminded missionaries that they were emissaries of Christ and not of any particular nation or culture. He spoke of the training of the missionary and of the necessity of forming a native clergy.

**Maximus of Turin** (c. 380–c. 465). Bishop. The historian Gennadius of Messilia (c. 470) enumerates his works, most of which survive. He attended synods at Milan (451) and Rome (465). Influenced by Ambrose, he wrote 116 sermons, 118 homilies, and 6 tracts. These short but popular articles reveal the survival of paganism in northern Italy. In 1929, newly discovered homilies were published by U. Moricca.

BIBLIOGRAPHY: For the works of Maximus of Turin, see J. P. Migne, *Patrologiae cursus completus, series Latina,* Vol. 57 (162 vols., Paris, 1857–1866).

**Maximus the Confessor** (c. 580–662). The chief theologian of the 7th century. He was in early life a civil servant (secretary to the emperor Heraclius). About 613 he became a monk at Chrysopolis (Scutari) near Constantinople. During the wars of the following years he traveled westward, finally settling in a community of Byzantine exiles near Carthage, still the capital of Roman Africa. Here he was brought into controversy with the Monotheletes, defending the doctrine of two wills in Christ against the ex-patriarch Pyrrhus of Constantinople (643–644), and supporting Pope Martin I at the Lateran Council of 649. With the pope, he was arrested in 655 by order of the emperor Constans. He was first interned in Thrace, then in 661 tried for treason, sentenced to mutilation of the hand and tongue, which had opposed the emperor, and banished to the Caucasus, where he died in 662. Of more general interest than his dogmatic treatises are his devotional and mystical works, such as *The Ascetic Life, Four Centuries on Charity,* and the *Mystagogia,* a mystical interpretation of the liturgy. The two sides of his teaching are connected, since his Christian Platonism emphasizes the redemption of man by return to his true nature, which demands the recognition of a perfect human will in Christ, and in us the purification of the fallen human will by love.

**Maximus the Cynic.** An ecclesiastical adventurer who claimed to be a monk and philosopher. After being welcomed at Constantinople by Gregory of Nazianzus in 380, Maximus was irregularly consecrated by Egyptian bishops as a rival claimant for the see. In 381 the Council of Constantinople declared invalid "all that was done for him or by him," but he was recognized at Rome and Milan for a year or two longer.

**Mayer, Johann Friedrich** (1650–1712). German Lutheran orthodox theologian. He worked successively as pastor in Leipzig (1672), professor in Wittenberg (1684), pastor in Hamburg (1686), and professor in Kiel (1701). He passionately opposed Pietism as a threat to *sola fide.* Yet he also worked for catechetical and pastoral reform and for better hymns. Mayer's writings are mostly in the pastoral and New Testament field.

**Mayflower Compact.** An agreement, similar to the covenants of Separatist congregations, signed by the passengers of the *Mayflower,* Nov. 11, 1620, to serve as the basis for combining themselves together "into a civil body politic." They had rights to land in Virginia but were without a charter. When they disembarked far north of the colony, they were without rights, laws, or government. The Compact served as a form of government and actually constituted the first written American constitution. It was democratic in form and was in force until 1691.

**Mayhew, Jonathan** (1720–1766). Congregational clergyman. A descendant of the famous Martha's Vineyard family, he was educated at Harvard and served West Church, Boston, from 1747 until his death. Here he became an outspoken opponent of revivalism, the Society for the Propagation of the Gospel, and the proposal for an Anglican bishop. He strongly advocated the unity of the colonies and resistance against British intervention in the colonies' affairs.

**Mayne, Cuthbert** (1544–1577). English Roman Catholic martyr. He was brought up and ordained in the Church of England. At Oxford he made friends with Edmund Campion and Gregory Martin, who sought to convert him to Roman Catholicism (1570). When Mayne's relation to the two men was found out, he fled to the English College at Douai, where he was ordained and eventually sent back to England for missionary work in Cornwall (1576). He disguised himself as a steward to one of the local landowners, but was soon discovered and taken to Launceston, where he was tried, convicted, and executed, chiefly for alleged denial of the queen's supremacy. He was the first of Douai's "seminary priests" to be put to death.

**Maynooth College.** The Royal Catholic College of St. Patrick, at Maynooth, County Kildare. It is the chief school for educating diocesan clergy for the Roman Church in Ireland. It was established and given a grant by an act of Parliament in 1795 and erected on the site of the old College of St. Mary (1518–1538). It led the Catholic resistance to Protestant domination. The Irish Church Act of 1869 freed it of state control and left its direction to the prelates.

**Mazarin, Jules** (Giulio Mazarini) (1602–1661). French diplomat. Born in the kingdom of Naples and educated by the Jesuits in Rome, Mazarin took minor orders and became active in the diplomatic affairs of the papacy. After a term as nuncio to France, he became a French citizen (1639), was taken under the wing of Richelieu and made a cardinal in 1641. In the following year, Cardinal Richelieu died, after securing the appointment of Mazarin as his successor. Mazarin survived the death of Louis XIII (1643) and of Pope Urban VIII (1644), as well as the intrigues of the French nobility and others. He inherited Richelieu's policy in the Thirty Years' War (1618–1648), and saw to the successful prosecution of it at the peace negotiations in Westphalia. He worked closely with the queen regent, Anne of Austria. However, his meanness and hauteur, along with the suffering brought upon France through excessive taxation and war, and the natural resentment on the part of the feudal nobility at the centralizing policies of Richelieu and himself, aroused the revolt of the aristocracy, which coalesced into the political party known as the Fronde. Although twice forced into exile by the Frondeurs, Mazarin survived to hand on to the young Louis XIV a modern, centralized nation-state and a minister (Colbert) to manage it.

**Mediator Dei.** An encyclical letter of Pius XII, issued on Nov. 20, 1947, concerning the liturgy of the Roman Catholic Church, defining the purpose, scope, history, and character of the liturgy. The pope implied that in order to correct abuses and encourage sincere devotion some of the liturgical alterations suggested by scholars and the newer liturgical movements in Roman Catholicism might be made, but he gave no blanket approval to widespread changes. Many carefully regulated changes have since been allowed, and the action of the Second Vatican Council has greatly enlarged the area of reform.

**Medieval Ideas of Reform.** The view that the Christian church, insofar as it formed a human society, was subject to sin and error, and its clergy to corruption, and was, therefore, like every human society, in regular need of revision and reform, played little part in its first apostolic age or in its early struggles to achieve authority and dominance. As the Middle Ages progressed, this view was more and more strongly felt and asserted. The Eastern branch of the medieval church, less centralized and energetic in its administrative interests, was always less involved than the Western branch with movements for reform. The first great period of Western reforms more or less coincides with the final schism with the East in 1054 (see SCHISM, EASTERN), and was in some sense stimulated by the feeling that its independent authority was in need of reassertion.

The monastery of Cluny in southern France was founded in 910 and in the next half century became the center of a revitalization in monastic life that radiated into many other Benedictine houses of the West and spread its reforming zeal into the general life of the church. The great leader of Cluniac reform was the monk Hildebrand, who from his youth had seen at first hand current corruptions among the German clergy and within the papacy itself, in particular the widespread abuse of simony—the buying and selling of sacred things and sacred offices. As cardinal he drew up the first rules for the conclave in papal elections, expressly to do away with such abuses, and later as Pope Gregory VII (1073–1085) he initiated a far-reaching program of further reforms. Of his associates and followers three figures who were imbued with a like zeal stand out: Pope Paschal II (1099–1118) and the cardinals Humbert of Silva-Candida (d. 1061) and Peter Damian (d. 1072).

The impulses of the Cluniac movement as they merged into the wider aspirations of the Gregorian reformers had far-reaching effects on the whole life of the church, both spiritual and administrative. The new insistence on regularity of observances and clerical celibacy led to a general improvement in the standards of the clergy and a rejuvenation in the religious life of the laity which in the 12th and 13th centuries amounted to an almost revolutionary upsurge of piety. This devotion showed itself in the founding of the great mendicant orders of Francis of Assisi (d. 1226) and Dominic (d. 1221), and in the proclamation of the First Crusade by Pope Urban II at Clermont in 1095. Administratively, the reforming spirit was responsible for the reassertion of papal supremacy and the settlement of such vexed questions as lay investitures and secular supervision. Here the high peak was reached in the papacy of Innocent III (1198–1216), as much feudal as spiritual overlord in the Europe of his day, and in the decrees of the great Council of Lateran IV in 1215, which in its seventy canons made many decisions concerning clerical and lay discipline still in force today. Papal leadership waned during the period of the papal schism (1378–1417); some measure of unity was again achieved at the Council of Constance (1414–1418), but the three years taken there in deliberating further reforms of the church were indecisive. By then powerful external impulses to reform, affecting the very foundations of the traditional theology, had begun to make themselves felt. The serious threat of religious unrest brought on by the Protestant Reformers, Wycliffe in England, Hus in Bohemia, and later, Luther and Calvin, at length induced the Roman Church to strengthen its organization and authority and attempt to eliminate what serious abuses remained. Some measures, such as the Inquisition, were mainly repressive. More constructive was the work of new orders dedicated to reform, such as the Theatines (founded in 1524), the Capuchins (1525–1528), and the Society of Jesus (Jesuits) organized by Ignatius Loyola in 1534. The Middle Ages were spent and the Reformation well under way before the Council of Trent (1545–1563) promulgated its extensive clerical reforms or Pope Paul IV carried through his wide changes in the organization of the Curia (1555–1559), the central governing body of the Catholic Church.

BIBLIOGRAPHY: Z. N. Brooke, *The English Church and the Papacy* (Cambridge, 1931); S. Z. Ehler and J. B. Morrall, *Church and State Through the Centuries* (Westminster, Md., 1954); M. Spinka (ed.), *Advocates of Reform* (The Library of Christian Classics, Vol. XIV, Philadelphia, 1953).

**Medina, Bartholomeo** (1527–1580). Spanish Dominican moral theologian whose writings dealt chiefly with the thought of Thomas Aquinas. Medina has been considered responsible for probabilism, an ethical theory designed to resolve doubts occasioned by an apparent conflict of obligations or interests. According to this view, a course of action may be approved of if taught by reputable ethical theorists, even though a greater number of ethicists prefer its opposite. Though the theory was designed to favor the liberty of the individual conscience, it easily lent itself to abuse, and was satirized by Pascal in his *Provincial Letters*.

**Medley, John** (1804–1892). Metropolitan of Canada. Born at Chelsea, England, he was educated at Wadham College, Oxford (B.A., 1826; M.A., 1830). He was ordained by the Church of England in 1829, and in 1845 was consecrated first bishop of Fredericton, New Brunswick. This diocese he administered for nearly a half century, and he became metropolitan of Canada in 1879. Medley was a convinced High Churchman at a time when most of the laity favored a Low Church evangelicalism.

**Megapolensis, Johannes** (1603–1670). Dutch Reformed clergyman. Converted from Roman Catholicism at twenty-three, he served parishes in Holland before going to New Netherlands in 1642. There he conducted the first mission work among the Indians. After 1649 he had a congregation in New Amsterdam, where with Governor Stuyvesant he often advocated religious intolerance. He stayed there even after British occupation in 1664.

**Melanchthon, Philip** (1497–1560). German Lutheran lay theologian, the closest associate of Luther at the University of Wittenberg, where he was professor from 1518 until his death. He was born at Bretten in the Palatinate on Feb. 16, 1497, to the elector's armorer, George Schwartzert. His granduncle Johannes Reuchlin named him Melanchthon (the Greek form of Schwartzert, both names denoting "black earth"). Philip completed his B.A. at Heidelberg when fourteen and his M.A. at Tübingen a year later. From his teaching position there he was called by Elector Frederick the Wise as professor of Greek at Wittenberg. From the beginning he made significant contributions to scholarship. He accompanied Luther to the Leipzig debate in 1519, the same year he won his B.Th. In 1520 he married Katherine Krapp. They had four children.

The first systematic presentation of Lutheran doctrine was his *Loci communes* of 1521. In its many editions it served as the basic textbook of Lutheran theology for over a century. During the winter of 1521–1522, he could not decide how to settle the disturbances created by Carlstadt and the Zwickau "prophets."

He proved unable to lead firmly in Luther's absence. The Peasants' War of 1525 appalled him. Although he mediated for them in the Palatinate, he emerged with strong authoritarian views justifying the suppression of revolt. He was active in the visitation of Saxon churches and schools initiated by the elector after 1525. His *Instruction to the Visitors* (1528) brought the Reformation into parish churches and set forth the plan for free public school education in Germany. He directed the reorganization of the Universities of Cologne, Heidelberg, Leipzig, and Tübingen, and planned new universities at Königsberg and Marburg. For his work in improving German education, he was named the Preceptor of Germany.

The Marburg Colloquy was called in 1529 to settle religious differences between Lutherans and Zwinglians. It was to prepare for a political alliance between them against imperial pressure. The chief participants, Luther and Melanchthon, Zwingli and Oecolampadius, failed to agree on the Lord's Supper, so that the desired result was not attained. Melanchthon's views on the Lord's Supper changed in the next seven years. The Wittenberg Concord between the Lutherans and the southern Germans in 1536 reflected his mediating views concerning the presence of Christ in the Eucharist, but the Zwinglians shortly after repudiated the agreement.

His most significant contribution as a theologian, apart from the *Loci communes,* is the Augsburg Confession and its *Apology* of 1530 and 1531. The former is his masterful compilation of the doctrinal Articles of Schwabach (1529) and those of Torgau (1530) against abuses in the church, both of which he helped to compose. The *Apology* is a more extended explanation of certain articles in the Confession which papal theologians attacked. These documents soon ranked as the primary confessional statements of Lutheranism. Melanchthon revised the Augsburg Confession several times. The 1540 edition, the *variata,* caused a reaction against his changes in Article X on the Lord's Supper. The unadulterated 1530 edition became the accepted version. His third confessional treatise is the *Power and Primacy of the Pope* appended to Luther's Smalcald Articles of 1537.

Following the emperor's victory over evangelical forces at Mühlberg (1547) and the imposition of the Augsburg Interim, Melanchthon aided in preparing the substitute Leipzig Interim (1548), which at least affirmed justification by faith. Roman Catholic practices were conceded as unessentials (adiaphora), however, and this roused the antagonism of

Matthias Flacius. He attacked Melanchthon as a traitor to Lutheranism even after the Interim was terminated in 1552. He also led the opposition to Melanchthon's synergism, his belief that man's will could accept or reject God's offer of grace and the Holy Spirit after it was given. Flacius finally discredited himself, but Melanchthon's reputation was damaged. These controversies saddened his closing years. After a brief illness, he died on April 19, 1560, and was buried next to Luther.

BIBLIOGRAPHY: P. Melanchthon, *Selected Writings* (Minneapolis, 1962); C. L. Manschreck, *Melanchthon on Christian Doctrine: Loci Communes 1555* (New York, 1965); and *Melanchthon the Quiet Reformer* (New York, 1958); R. Stupperich, *Melanchthon* (Philadelphia, 1965).

**Melchiorites.** Followers of Melchior Hofmann, who inspired a number of mostly lay preachers and Scripture students in the 1530's. Some of them were leaders in the Münster uprising. Melchiorites were marked by fervent eschatology, a spiritualist-metaphorical Scriptural exegesis sometimes leading to exhibitionist behavior, and insistence on believer's baptism. Their Gnostic Christologies were associated with insistence on the purity of their gathered churches.

**Melchites.** A term from the Syriac root *melek,* "king," applied to the Syrian Orthodox followers of the Council of Chalcedon. They were called "royalists" or "imperialists" as supporters of the church backed by the Byzantine emperors. Since the 17th century the term has been used primarily for the section of the Syrian Orthodox Church that has accepted papal jurisdiction.

**Melitian Schisms.** In the 4th century there were two schisms known as "Melitian." The first was in Alexandria in the early part of the century, and resembled the Donatist schism in the West. The patriarch of Alexandria, Peter, was imprisoned during the Diocletian persecution, in 305. Although Peter continued to govern the church from prison, Melitius, the bishop of Lycopolis, seems to have taken it upon himself to ordain clergy throughout the patriarchate. He too was imprisoned and banished to the quarries at Pheno in Palestine. In 306, Peter sent out instructions for the readmission of the lapsed. Melitius was apparently deposed about the same time. After Galerius' edict of toleration in 311, the imprisoned Christians were released. Melitius, as a confessor, refused to subscribe to Peter's views on the readmission of lapsed Christians. A rigorist church was organized, in schism from the church under Peter. By 325 there were twenty-eight bishoprics in the Melitian church. Arius was at first a Melitian. He later came to terms with Peter, but disagreed with Peter's view that the Melitians' administration of baptism was invalid. The Council of Nicaea recognized the Melitians' orders, but stipulated that the Melitian clergy function under the jurisdiction of the Alexandrian patriarch. Melitius himself was allowed to retain the title of bishop, but was not allowed to function as such. Despite this healing of the schism, the Melitian church again became schismatic in 328 after Athanasius' election as patriarch. The Melitian bishops had joined in electing Athanasius, but, perhaps disappointed in his subsequent attitude, withdrew their support.

The second "Melitian" schism is named after a patriarch of Antioch. This Melitius was bishop of Beroea. In 360, upon joint application of the Arians and the orthodox, Melitius was translated to the see of Antioch. It would seem that both parties expected him to assist them. Melitius' course was made clear when he preached his inaugural sermon. Taking a text from Prov., ch. 8, he used the word *homoousios*. Within a short time the Arians secured his deposition and he was exiled to Armenia. Euzoïus, an associate of Arius, was consecrated bishop in his place. When Julian became emperor in 360, all the Christian bishops returned from exile. At this point there were at least four well-defined churches at Antioch—an Apollinarian, an Arian under Euzoïus, an orthodox Nicene under Melitius, and a second orthodox group led by the presbyter Paulinus. This last church was the remnant of the Eustathian schism. Eustathius, who had become patriarch of Antioch (c. 325) and had been at Nicaea, had shortly thereafter been deposed and exiled at the instigation of Eusebius of Nicomedia's party. Although Eustathius did not return with the exiled bishops in 337, the party bearing his name remained. At the Council of Alexandria in 362 it was decided that the Eustathian and Melitian churches should unite as one orthodox church under the guidance of Melitius. However, the Eustathian leader, Paulinus, was consecrated bishop, and the two churches continued side by side. Paulinus was strongly supported by Rome and, to some extent, by Alexandria; Melitius, by what can be called the neo-Nicene party. The situation was ameliorated by the agreement of the leaders of the church to consider Melitius and Paulinus coadjutors, with the survivor to succeed as patriarch upon the death of the other. In 381, Melitius presided over the Second Ecumenical Council at Constantinople. The Council confirmed Gregory of Nazianzus as patriarch of Constantinople, and at this point in the proceedings Melitius died. Instead of honoring the Antiochene agreement and allowing Paulinus to become sole bishop, the Council, unwilling to yield to Rome and Alexandria, elected Flavian patriarch of Antioch. Thus, while the Melitian Schism was healed in favor of Melitius' party under Flavian, a second orthodox church (the Eustathians) continued to exist in Antioch under Paulinus. However, within two years Paulinus died. The schismatic group elected Evagrius bishop, but soon he too died. Thereafter for a short time a small schismatic church survived, but without a bishop.

BIBLIOGRAPHY: H. I. Bell, *Jews and Christians in Egypt* (London, 1924).

**Melito** (d. c. 180). Bishop of Sardis in Asia Minor from c. 170. He was famous for his writings (Eusebius lists about sixteen of them), including an apology expressing Christian loyalty to Marcus Aurelius and a paschal sermon recently discovered in Greek and Coptic as well as in a Latin summary. Thoroughly trained in rhetoric, Melito reflects the growing Hellenization of the Asian Church. Because of his fame, several forgeries were ascribed to him in the 6th and 7th centuries.

**Melville, Andrew** (1545–1622). Champion of Scottish presbyterianism in its victory over episcopacy. Knox built a national church with a Reformed theology and a quasi-episcopal polity. Melville led the fight against the rule by bishops to establish the rule of the Kirk through presbyteries.

Melville was reared in Montrose, a good student, brilliant in languages. At the University of St. Andrews he was an outstanding scholar. At the age of nineteen he went to Paris to study language and philosophy. At Poitiers he became a regent of the college and studied law. When Coligny besieged the town, Melville moved on to Geneva, where he was warmly received by Theodore Beza. Melville came from a Protestant home, but it was his five years in Geneva that prepared him for his leadership in Scotland. Geneva was filled with Protestant refugees after the Bartholomew's Day Massacre (1572), so that he associated with many of the great leaders.

He returned to Scotland in 1574, called to Glasgow to assist in reviving learning in Scotland. His was an immediate success. He reorganized the curriculum, delivered the theological lectures himself. The university was soon crowded with students. To achieve a similar revival he was called to St. Andrews and became principal of St. Mary's, the theological school. His educational reforms were among the most liberal and enlightened in Europe. He also proved himself to be an able disciplinarian and administrator. Insubordination from faculty or students was not tolerated. He scorned the tyrant but had a deep-rooted conviction of the need for order.

The Scottish Kirk was suffering from an internal struggle over polity. Prior to 1572 the Kirk had been essentially presbyterian, though a system of bishops with a civil status remained. The appointment of the tulchan bishops placed church revenues in the hands of the state and increased the financial problem of the churches. The regent, Morton, undertook to restore full episcopacy, a logical way to restore state control over the Kirk and to please Elizabeth by this degree of conformity with Anglican polity. The restored episcopate was two years old when Melville came to Glasgow, and the Kirk was chafing under the bishops. He attended the General Assembly of the Kirk in Edinburgh in 1575, when Parliament was insisting upon a more satisfactory polity for the church. The Assembly appointed a committee to prepare the new constitution. This was embodied in the Second Book of Discipline which the Assembly accepted in 1581. Melville had been the leading spirit in its preparation. His opposition to episcopacy had become apparent back in 1575 when a resolution authored by Melville and presented by John Durie had attacked the episcopal system as being devoid of Scriptural warrant. Melville remained at the center of the fight over church polity. He was the moderator of the General Assembly which in 1582 prosecuted one of the tulchan bishops. When he refused to cooperate with civil authorities, he had to spend twenty months in England to avoid prosecution. He returned to St. Andrews, where he remained for another twenty years.

Melville regarded his fight as one against the encroachments of the civil powers upon the liberties of the Kirk. Although he was in constant conflict with the king, he was not opposed to royalty. In 1606, James I summoned him and seven other ministers to London with the aim of restoring peace to the Kirk. Melville argued that the church needed the free and open assembly. After witnessing the elaborate ritual of a service at Hampton Court he wrote a sarcastic epigram about it. In anger James put him in the Tower. When released four years later, Melville was refused permission to return to Scotland. He spent the last eleven years of his life teaching in the University of Sedan.

Melville fought for the presbyterian system in Scotland and has to be recognized as one of the champions of the liberties of the Kirk.

BIBLIOGRAPHY: T. McCrie, *Life of Andrew Melville* (Philadelphia, 1840); W. Morrison, *Andrew Melville* (Edinburgh, 1899).

**Mendelsohn, Moses** (1729–1786). German Jewish philosopher. The self-educated son of a poor scribe, Moses Mendelsohn, more than any other man, was responsible for leadership in bringing European Jews out of the ghetto and into modern life. Early influenced by John Locke, he was a close friend of G. E. Lessing, and himself a leader of the popular Enlightenment in Germany. Eventually moving in the most select circles of Berlin society, he remained to the end a practicing Orthodox Jew and spent the efforts of his later years defending the Jew's right to be Jewish in a "Christian" culture.

**Mendicant Orders.** General designation given to those new religious associations arising in the 13th century as a response to the poor brethren and depending upon alms for complete support. Eschewing even communal property, the orders were not bound by the vow of stability of place either, since their ministry was exercised outside the cloister. Canon 22 of the Second Council of Lyons (1274) established four such communities *de jure communi:* Friars Preachers, or Dominicans; Friars Minor, or Franciscans; Carmelites; and Austin Friars, or Friars Hermits of St. Augustine. In the narrow sense, these are the only mendicant (Latin, *mendicare,* "to beg") orders, but the Servites, or Servants of Mary, were added to this number by Martin V in 1424. In the wider sense of the term, there are lesser orders of various types included in this category. They are the Tertiary Franciscans, or Third Order Regular of St. Francis (1521); the Capuchin Friars Minor (1525), which are a reform of the Observants, who are in turn a reform of the Conventuals; the Hieronymites constituted in 1373 and exempted in 1595; the Minims (1474); and the Order of Penance also known as Scalzetti (1781). In addition, there are the Brothers Hospitalers of St. John of God founded in 1572, a singular order, as well as two ransoming orders: the Trinitarians, or Order of the Most Holy Trinity for the Redemption of Captives, founded in 1180 and reconstituted in 1221; and the Mercedarians, or the Order of Our Lady of Mercy, founded by Peter Nolasco, approved in 1230.

**Menken, Gottfried** (1768–1831). German Reformed pastor. From 1802 in Bremen, his preaching and writing fostered a theology centered in a Biblical piety opposed to both rationalism and orthodoxy. Subordinating God's justice and holiness to his love, Menken held that sanctification was possible in this life on the basis of faith in Christ, who took on man's fallen nature and thus delivered him from the onus of Adam's fall and subsequent sin.

**Mennonites.** The followers and spiritual descendants of Menno Simons. The name "Mennonites" is applied to those Anabaptists of the 16th century and their descendants who were pacifist, Biblicist, noncommunitarian, and not anti-Nicene. The name is derived from that of Menno Simons, who emerged as an organizing leader of a band of Melchior Hofmann's followers among the Anabaptists a decade after Anabaptism arose. The term *"Mennisten"* was first used of Menno's group in 1545 in East Frisia to distinguish them from the spiritualizing followers of David Joris and from the survivors of the fanatical Münsterites. These Melchiorites believed in an imminent Second Advent, the celestial flesh of Christ, the possibility and need for a re-created and morally pure church gathered on the basis of believer's baptism; they observed the Supper in celebration of a re-created corporate inner life, seeking to make all human relationships utterly sincere expressions of the love of Christ, banning anyone from the fellowship who fell short. Menno turned them away from visionary apocalypticism toward sobriety and practical sincerity. He encouraged a use of the ban that was not arbitrary, but subject to the love of Christ. Communities tending to these ideals were established under his direction from the Lowlands eastward to the Vistula delta by the time of his death in 1561. There was not in his time a formal unifying organization; leadership by traveling elders gave way to elders recognized only in particular congregations. During these years there were many martyrs under Spanish Catholic rule, some of them recorded in a book called in its final form in 1660 the *Martyrs' Mirror.* A theology of martyrdom, by which they understood themselves as the suffering remnant of the true church, was long part of the Mennonites' tradition. Reaction to early stringent use of the ban gave rise to the increasingly tolerant Waterlander group, the *Doopsgezinden,* more congregationalist in polity. Toleration came in 1577, but many had migrated to the Danzig, where they were valued for two centuries as fine farmers and craftsmen. Melchiorite Anabaptism, however, was antedated by Swiss Anabaptism spreading north from Zurich from 1525 on. These Anabaptists began as Zwinglians discontented with what was

seen as Zwingli's compromise with an imperfect world in continuing infant baptism. Small Bible-study groups becoming churches through believer's baptism and simple observances of the Supper spread through southern Germany, growing in strength in the repentance of sins and in mutual encouragement in discipleship of Christ. The aim was a restitution of the New Testament church. Though the Nicene Creed was not rejected, the Constantinian settlement was. Swiss Anabaptism was augmented by the influence of Hut and Denck from central and southern Germany. Marpeck and his circle gave theological foundations to developing congregations, disciplined in inner life and protesting against state hegemony over faith. Southern German and Swiss Anabaptists differed from the followers of Menno in Christology and in less severity in the ban, but gradually in the following century they adopted the name "Mennonite" because of its pacifist connotations. From 1683 onward Mennonites from the Palatinate and elsewhere migrated to Pennsylvania and westward in America. In the late 18th century, growing militarism in Prussia led Mennonites to settle new land in the Ukraine. A divisive influence there was German Baptist revivalism. In the 1870's, military conscription laws in Russia led large groups to migrate to the United States and Canada, with later migrations in the 1920's also to Paraguay and Mexico. At issue was not only their concern to maintain a Biblical pacifism but also their freedom from state interference in matters of faith. The Amish Mennonites began in the effort of Jakob Amann in Switzerland in the 1690's to maintain more stringent moral and doctrinal norms. Common to all groups is the teaching of nonresistance to evil, a teaching that is today widely being interpreted in more positive fashion: the Mennonite Central Committee, a service organization in which nearly all groups participate, carries on extensive relief operations in areas of greatest world need.

BIBLIOGRAPHY: R. Friedmann, *Mennonite Piety* (Goshen, 1949); C. H. Smith, *The Story of the Mennonites* (rev. ed., Newton, Kans., 1950); *The Mennonite Encyclopedia,* ed. by H. S. Bender (Scottdale, Pa., 1955–1959).

**Menno Simons** (c. 1496–1561). Anabaptist leader. The name of Menno came to be attached to a main surviving wing of the Anabaptist movement that began eleven years before he joined it in January, 1536. He drew together a largely Melchiorite Anabaptism in the Lowlands and gave it a pacifist basis in a way that commended itself to others, so that, though not all his views were accepted and there were others more creative than he, the name "Mennonite" still applies to the largest group of Anabaptists today.

Born in West Frisia, Menno became a priest in 1524 and served parishes near his birthplace for nearly twelve years. Later he confessed that he had growing doubts, from 1527 onward, about the traditional view of the sacraments, first of the Mass and then of infant baptism. He was impressed also by the moral seriousness of the Melchiorites, especially of one Sicke Snijder, beheaded for his faith in 1531. Menno studied the Scriptures, and from 1535 preached a gospel of serious repentance, the experience of which must precede and validate Baptism and the Supper. In 1537 he accepted reordination from Obbe Philips. His move out of the traditional church was prompted by pastoral concern for many simple folk swept up by the Münsterites, who were willing to die for views close to his own but were dying foolishly because of the errors of their leaders. For twenty-five years he traveled about the Lowlands, from Cologne to the Vistula, gathering sober congregations, preaching, writing (volubly rather than well), for most of the time with a price on his head. From 1554 he settled in the village of Wüstenfelde in Holstein and had a regular printer.

Menno's thought centers around the idea and experience of the "new creature." He took seriously the Pauline teaching of dying to the Old Adam and rising in newness of life in Christ, speaking often of a spiritual resurrection in consequence of which a believer enters a new kind of reality. Menno largely accepted Hofmann's view that Christ possessed a body of heavenly flesh, and was convinced that a seed of the same Word incarnate in Christ became incarnate in the sincere believer. The consequence he saw was that the believer now had an "obedient flesh" in place of the old Adamic disobedient flesh. Though sins of weakness might still occur, sins of a "mortal" nature should not be expected. He understood the "new creature" in an eschatological sense, as the first installment of God's inaugurated restoration of his fallen creation. He also understood the church as a corporate new creature, and had a vivid sense of the eschatological joy with which the gathered congregation celebrated the ordinance of the Supper of the Lord whose pure and unspotted body—the fulfillment of the types and foreshadowings of the Scriptures—the gathered believers were understood to be. Menno participated in controversies during most of his career. He rejected the pretensions of John of Leiden to be a "third David," saying that Christ was King of the church and of the world. He appealed to the clear and written Word of God in opposition to those who claimed direct revelations, though in his soteriology he was not a Biblical literalist. He opposed the followers of David Joris, who defended the dissembling of their views in the face of persecution, for he counted no faith genuine that drew a distinction between inner conviction and outer expression or that drew back from suffering in witness to Christ. He discussed with representatives of an emerging Reformed Church order the nature of the church. He defended believer's baptism, the necessity for the moral purity of all members and the use of the ban, the worthlessness of all ministers not similarly pure, and the separation of the church from the civil order. Menno was an ardent defender of religious liberty, not on prudential grounds alone (because of persecution), but because the new creature stands in the liberty of Christ free from all sorts of external coercion. Newness of life proceeds from within, not from rearrangements of externals. Still, faith was to issue in obedience, including obedience to the Scriptural ordinances of Baptism, Supper, and the ban. Menno also contended with Adam Pastor, in his group, for denying the Trinity, and with other Anabaptists who refused his moderate use of the ban.

BIBLIOGRAPHY: *The Complete Writings of Menno Simons*, tr. by L. Verduin, ed. by J. C. Wenger (Scottdale, Pa., 1956); J. Horsch, *Menno Simons* (Scottdale, Pa., 1916).

**Mercedarians** (or Order of Our Lady of Mercy). A mendicant order of men devoted to caring for the sick and rescuing Christian captives. It was founded in 1218 by Peter Nolasco (d. 1256) at Barcelona. The constitutions of the order were devised by Raymond of Peñafort, who sponsored their approval by Gregory IX. At first an order of Christian knights, it became a mendicant clerical order after 1318. Several Mercedarian houses were established in Latin America.

**Mercersburg Theology.** The "High Church movement of the Reformed tradition," and the monument of John W. Nevin (1803–1886) and Philip Schaff (1819–1893). Nevin, of Old School Presbyterian origins, began teaching theology at the German Reformed Seminary, Mercersburg, Pa., in 1840, while Schaff, trained at Tübingen, Halle, and Berlin, accepted a call to the seminary in 1844. Nevin's *The Anxious Bench* (1843) directly challenged the prevailing revivalistic theology of American Protestantism. Finney's New Measures were condemned as "transient excitement," while Nevin stressed the "growing faith" of parish life. Nevin sought to avoid surrender to contemporary theological erosion by bringing the Reformed churches back to a "pre-Puritan" understanding of the church and sacraments. In *The History and Genius of the Heidelberg Catechism* (1847), Nevin assessed the extent to which Puritanism, rationalism, and revivalism had weakened the real direction of the Reformation. Schaff's *Principle of Protestantism* (1845), which viewed history as an organism guided by an inner unity, complemented Nevin's position. Protestantism was a valid development of the early and medieval church, not a break from it. The central focus of the movement is evident in Nevin's *The Mystical Presence* (1846), in which he insisted that both theology and piety were based on the Eucharist. He criticized the degradation of the sacrament by Edwards, Hopkins, and Dwight into memorialism and subjectivism, and sought a return to Calvin's objective and Christ-centered sacramental theology. The *Mercersburg Review* became a forum for debate with Hodge, Brownson, Bushnell, and "evangelical" Lutherans. The movement was indebted to Schleiermacher, Neander, Dorner, the Oxford movement, Coleridge, and the Cambridge Platonists. It was largely ignored in its own day outside the German Reformed Church.

**Mercier, Désiré Joseph Cardinal** (1851–1926). Belgian cardinal and philosopher. Born at Braine-d'-Alleud, educated at Malines and Louvain, ordained priest in 1874 and cardinal in 1907, he became professor of philosophy at Louvain (1882). A disciple of Aquinas, he helped to found the Institut Supérieur de Philosophie (1894) at Louvain, which published the *Revue Néo-Scolastique,* a journal of neo-Thomism that exerted considerable influence on Catholic thought all over the world. In addition to numerous works on theology and philosophy, he used his power to eliminate class distinctions between the Catholic bourgeoisie and laborers and to bring about a closer understanding between all Christians. During World War I, he vigorously upheld the morale and spiritual unity of Belgians against the German invaders. Prompted by the "appeal to all Christian people" issued by the Lambeth Conference of 1920, he was the leading Roman Catholic advocate to seek contacts between the Roman Church and Anglicanism (1921–1925). These informal meetings were cut short by his death and failed to yield positive results.

**Merle d'Aubigné, Jean Henri** (1794–1872). Swiss historian of Protestantism. The son of a French family living near Geneva, Merle d'Aubigné was educated at the University of Geneva and ordained to the ministry there. The three hundredth anniversary of the Reformation suggested to him the project of writing a general history of the movement; to this end he studied at Berlin with J. A. W. Neander and Wilhelm De Wette. He returned to Geneva in 1832 to serve as church-history instructor and pastor for a separatist congregation. His principal writings are his *Histoire de la Réformation du XVIᵉ siècle* (5 vols., 1835–1853) and *Histoire de la Réformation en Europe au temps de Calvin* (8 vols., 1863–1878). Though a careful student of the sources, Merle d'Aubigné is occasionally excessively partisan in his judgments.

**Merovingian Architecture.** See ARCHITECTURE, MEROVINGIAN AND CAROLINGIAN.

**Merry del Val, Rafael** (1865–1930). Roman Catholic cardinal. Born in London, son of the secretary of the Spanish legation there, he was educated at Bayliss House, at Jesuit colleges in Namur and Brussels, at Ushaw College, Durham, at the Roman Pontificia Accademia dei Nobili Ecclesiastici, and the Gregorian University. He was ordained priest in the diocese of Westminster in 1888, and gained his doctorate in theology in 1890. Entering the papal service, in 1891 he became *cameriere segreto partecipante* at the Vatican. In 1896 he was secretary to the papal commission of inquiry on Anglican orders. In 1898 he became president of the Accademia in Rome and in 1900, titular archbishop of Nicaea. In 1903 he was made secretary of the College of Cardinals and subsequently was secretary of state under Pius X. In 1903 he became cardinal priest and dealt with anticlericalism and Modernism, the papacy declaring firm opposition to both. In 1914 the cardinal was appointed archpriest of St. Peter's and during the pontificates of Benedict XV and Pius XI was secretary of the Holy Office, exercising discipline over the entire Roman Church. A pastor at heart, the cardinal was active in works of charity and promoted the church's work among men and boys.

**Mersenne, Marin** (1588–1648). French Minim friar, author, theologian, philosopher, mathematician, and scientist. He devoted the latter part of his life to research in the mathematical sciences, and was a close friend of such notable contemporaries as Pierre Gassendi (d. 1655), Galileo (d. 1642), and René Descartes (d. 1650). Mersenne was instrumental in turning the young Descartes from a life of dissipation to the more serious paths of philosophy.

**Mesrob** (c. 345–440). Inventor of the Armenian alphabet and one of the original translators of the New Testament into that language. He was a zealous opponent of heresy, helping to induce the exile of the radical teachers Barbarianus and Theodius. He also encouraged the spread of the monastic life. His disciples discovered early manuscripts of the Scriptures. In 440 he succeeded Patriarch Sahak, but died within six months.

**Messalians.** A term derived from the Syriac word for "men of prayer" and applied to one of the ascetic movements that arose in the 4th century. Its members had given themselves so fully to the life of prayer that they tried to fulfill literally all the precepts of the Sermon on the Mount. They were mendicants who slept in the street. This movement, which originated in Mesopotamia, spread rapidly and attracted the opposition of Amphilocius of Iconium, Basil the Great, and Flavian of Antioch. Basil called the members "straitlaced, world-repudiating bag-carriers." Their piety was incorporated in the writings of Symeon of Mesopotamia and was preserved in the church in the supposed works of Macarius the Egyptian.

**Metaphysical Poets.** An expression used to designate certain 17th-century Anglican poets, including Donne, Cowley, Herbert, Vaughan, Traherne, and others. These poets shared a personal, sincere devotion, but they often made use of varied artificial devices—incongruity, forced imagery, abruptness, novelty—that did not always serve as an adequate vehicle for the thought. Yet their fresh approach brought vitality and originality to religious poetry.

**Methodism.** (1) A means of inculcating the religious life by systematic discipline, practiced in the 17th century by the Amyraldists and certain Roman Catholic apologists. (2) Since the 18th century the denomination of Protestant Christians founded by John Wesley (1703–1791). Born in an Anglican parsonage, educated at Oxford, ordained to the priesthood in 1728, Wesley gave himself to a strenuous regimen of private study and devotion, group discipline and corporate worship, and regular ministrations to the poor and imprisoned. Finding satisfaction neither in the High Church piety of Oxford's "Holy Club" nor in his missionary labors in Georgia (1736–1738), he finally gained a heartfelt assurance in the famous Aldersgate experience of 1738. Having already begun to speak to small groups of serious-minded church members, he now started preaching in ever-widening circles the sufficiency of God's grace for all men and the moral demands of the gospel upon its adherents. He thus emerged at a propitious juncture in the rising tide of evangelicalism being created in England and America by George Whitefield and other awakeners.

As a loyal son of the Established Church, Wesley had no intention of creating a schism or founding a new church. He considered his special vocation to be preaching to people unreached by the church—in the fields, if necessary, when church pulpits were closed to him—and providing for the nurture and discipline of those who responded. Following the example of the Moravians, who had befriended him during his struggle for personal faith, he gathered his hearers into bands, classes, and societies (the first at Bristol in 1739). These met regularly, examined each other's religious earnestness, and studied to deepen their Christian understanding. Wesley selected as leaders for these groups laymen who could assist in his work of carrying the gospel to the masses. In 1744 the lay preachers began to meet in annual conference, and in 1747 their appointed fields of labor were designated as circuits. In this form early Methodism spread throughout the British Isles, entering Ireland in 1747. The defection of the Calvinistic Methodists in the 1740's, even though it presaged various later schisms, scarcely diminished the rapid growth of the Wesleyan movement. Still within the Established Church, it was firmly under Wesley's direction and control.

Methodist ideas were brought to America by two lay preachers from Ireland, Philip Embury, who began to evangelize in New York City in 1766, and Robert Strawbridge, who settled about the same time in Frederick County, Md. Thomas Webb, a British officer converted in 1765, planted Methodism in New Jersey, Pennsylvania, and Delaware. In 1769 the English Conference sent Richard Boardman and Joseph Pilmoor, two laymen licensed to preach by John Wesley, and two years later Richard Wright arrived with Francis Asbury (1745–1816), who was to become the great apostle of American Methodism. America thus became the fiftieth circuit of the English conference. As the Revolution approached, Methodists in the colonies were suspected because of their connection with the Church of England and embarrassed by John Wesley's widely publicized Tory sympathies. By 1778 all the English preachers had returned except Asbury, who retired in frustrated neutrality to Delaware for the duration of the war. Notwithstanding these handicaps, at the close of the war American Methodists had some 15,000 members and 80 preachers.

The most serious disability, however, was the lack of ordained ministers. Members were supposed to receive the sacraments in the Anglican Church, but now that the colonies were independent of England and boasted few Anglican clergymen—and fewer who were sympathetic toward the Methodist movement—this was usually impossible. John Wesley, failing to persuade the bishop of London to ordain men for America, concluded that he himself must do so. Justifying such a step on the ground that in the early church presbyters and bishops belonged to the same order, on Sept. 1, 1784, he ordained Thomas Vasey and Richard Whatcoat and sent them to America with Dr. Thomas Coke, an Anglican priest whom he designated as "superintendent," with instructions to ordain Francis Asbury. Arriving in Baltimore, Coke convened the famous Christmas Conference (1784) which marks the organization of the Methodist Episcopal Church in America. Asbury, after election by the sixty preachers present, was ordained deacon, elder, and superintendent on successive days. (Later he and Coke were called "bishop," though the Methodist episcopacy remains essentially a superintendency.) The Conference adopted the Sunday Service and the Articles of Religion that Wesley had prepared on the basis of the Anglican standards, and added their own rules governing the life and work of the church, thus creating the Book of Discipline.

Numerical growth and geographical expansion are reflected in the fact that after 1792 the annual conferences became regional, while the General Conference began to meet quadrennially and in 1812 became delegated. The connectional system, an *ad hoc* arrangement by John Wesley in England, was well suited to the American situation, especially on the frontier. Annual conferences supervised the work of the traveling preachers, sending them on circuits that reached farther and farther into the expanding nation. Though at first few preachers had any formal training beyond their own reading of Bible, hymnbook, and Discipline, they were second to none in their evangelical zeal.

In spite of the fact that Wesley disavowed schism and remained himself within the Established Church, English Methodism moved ineluctably toward separation. In anticipation of his death Wesley had executed a Deed of Declaration (1784) that provided for the self-government of the Conference, and with the Plan of Pacification (1795), English Methodists became an independent church. Evangelism, education, and foreign missions marked encouraging growth throughout the 19th century. There were, in addition to the Calvinistic Methodists, several other splinter groups: Methodist New Connection (1797), Primitive Methodists (1810), Bible Christians (1814), Protestant Methodists (1828), Wesleyan Methodist Association (1835), and Reformed Methodists (1849). But these divisions began to be overcome as the Protestant Methodists, the Wesleyan Methodist Association, and the Reformed Methodists united in 1857 to become the United Free Churches, which in 1907 merged with the Methodist New Connection and the Bible Christians to become the United Methodist Church. This body joined in 1932 with the Primitive Methodists and the original Wesleyan Methodists to form The British Methodist Church. Membership declined moderately in the first half of the 20th century. Official conversations with the Church of England exploring the possibility of eventual reunion began in 1956.

American Methodists also proliferated in the 19th century and regrouped in the 20th. While becoming by 1830 the largest religious body in the United States, they witnessed the formation of the Republican Methodists (1792), the African Methodist Episcopal Church (1816), the African Methodist Episcopal Zion Church (1821), and the Methodist Protestant Church (1830). As the slavery controversy rose to crisis proportions a group of abolitionists organized the Wesleyan Methodist Connection in 1843, while the annual conferences in the slaveholding states withdrew the next year to form the Methodist Episcopal Church, South. The organizing of the Free Methodist Church in 1860 presaged a post-Civil War dispute over the doctrine of sanctification, which would cost Methodism several defections to the rising Holiness movement later in the century. A notable reunion occurred in 1939 when the Methodist Episcopal Church, the Methodist Episcopal Church, South, and the Methodist Protestant Church came together to form The Methodist Church, the largest Protestant denomination in the United States until 1963. By that time strong movements were under way to unite other denominations of Methodist and similar heritage. A merger of Methodists and Evangelical United Brethren took place in 1968, forming The United Methodist Church.

On the wider scene, Methodists have participated in both the world mission of Christianity and the ecumenical movement. Methodism in Canada, dating from 1799, achieved independent organization in 1828, overcame its divisions in 1884, and entered into the United Church of Canada in 1925. Methodist bodies elsewhere in the world, most of them originating as missions from England or the United States, are now indigenous and locally cooperative while maintaining fraternal ties through the World Methodist Council (organized 1881). The Methodist Church has involved itself from the start in the Federal (now National) Council of Churches, which appropriated the Methodist Social Creed at its organization in 1908, as well as the World Council of Churches and the Consultation on Church Union. Representing the theological mood of evangelical Arminianism, Methodism stands historically not so much for a unique doctrinal position as for an earnest approach to the Christian life—evangelical conversion, serious striving toward the goal of "Christian perfection," and active concern for social reform. It is thus able to pursue its distinctive vocation in close relations with other bodies affirming the central verities of the Christian faith.

BIBLIOGRAPHY: A. C. Outler (ed.), *John Wesley* (New York, 1964); E. S. Bucke (ed.), *The History of American Methodism,* 3 vols. (Nashville, 1964); I. L. Holt, *The World Methodist Movement* (Nashville, 1956); J. S. Simon, *John Wesley,* 5 vols. (London, 1921–1934); W. W. Sweet, *Methodism in American History* (New York, 1954).

**Methodist New Connection.** A nonconformist sect that separated from the Wesleyan Methodists, owing to differences in regard to church organization. In 1795, Alexander Kilham (1762–1798) demanded for the laity the free election of class leaders and stewards (the chief officers of the two smallest units of the Wesleyan hierarchy). He further advocated equal lay representation with ministers at Conferences (the annual assembly governing the whole Connection). For him, the ministers should have served only as the spokesmen of their congregations; they should have possessed no priestly authority. He further insisted upon a final separation from the Church of England. For his democratic views, expressed in a series of offensive pamphlets, Kilham suffered arraignment before the Conference of 1796 and expulsion from the church. He was joined by three other ministers, who, all together, helped set up the Methodist New Connection. By 1798, the sect had some 5,000 members. In its Conferences, ministers and laymen were of equal number: the laity were chosen by the Circuits (the third smallest unit in the Wesleyan hierarchy). Aside from organizational differences, the New Connection shared identical doctrines with the Wesleyans. In 1907, the Methodist New Connection merged with the United Methodist Free Churches and the Bible

Christians to form the United Methodist Church.

**Methodius of Olympus** (d. c. 311). Bishop in Lycia. One of the earliest opponents of Origen, Methodius is almost unknown to us except through his writings. Traditionally, his see is regarded as having been Olympus, a little town in Lycia. Jerome and others identify him with Tyre. F. Diekamp, however, has made a case for his having been bishop of Philippi in Macedonia. His death came during the persecution of Diocletian, probably at Chalcis in Euboea.

Methodius' opposition to Origen was an effort to conform the theology of Alexandria to the ordinary faith of the people. Far from despising everything that Origen stood for, "he lived on the feast of good things Origen had provided, even while attacking him" (Lietzmann, *A History of the Early Church,* Vol. III, p. 172).

His works, which remain to us largely in Slavonic translation, are greatly influenced by Plato and there is often a rather pedestrian Christian revision of the dialogues. His *Symposium,* or *On Virginity,* follows the form of its model closely, but has the table talk on a subject that is felt to be more fitting for Christian maidens than *erōs.* The Slavonic title for the work translated from Greek as *The Treatise on Free Will* is in English *On God, Matter, and Free Will,* which gives a truer picture of the contents. The most important work of Methodius is *On the Resurrection* in which he refutes Origen's belief in a completely spiritual resurrection and offers a theory of radical recreation in which the body at death is compared to metal that is melted down to be remolded. He also wrote the first treatise against Porphyry, some exegetical works in the allegorical tradition, and other books, most of which are lost.

**Metrophanes Critopoulos** (1589–1639). Patriarch of Alexandria. Born in Berea, Macedonia, he was a monk at Mt. Athos when Cyril Lucar, then patriarch of Alexandria, sent him to study theology in England (1616–1624). His travels took him also to Germany, Switzerland, and Italy before he returned to Egypt in 1631. In 1636 he became patriarch of Alexandria. It had been Cyril's design, in cooperation with Archbishop Abbot of Canterbury, to equip Metrophanes with a Protestant education and so to counter the influence of the Jesuits in the Eastern Orthodox Church. In 1638, however, Metrophanes joined in the condemnation of Cyril's "Calvinizing" theology. He is chiefly remembered for his *Confession of the Eastern Church,* written while he was in

Germany and published at Helmstedt in 1661. It is anti-Roman, recognizing only three "necessary" sacraments, but is strictly Orthodox rather than "Protestantizing." It was never officially sanctioned by the Eastern Church.

**Metternich, Klemens von** (1773–1859). Conservative Austrian statesman and prince. He gave his name to the era, between 1814 and 1848. Foreign minister from 1809, he helped overthrow Napoleon, dominated the Congress of Vienna, and promoted peace through European concert. Using Catholicism for social control, he fought Josephinism, liberalism, and nationalism, confirming instruction by the clergy and enforced censorship. Revolution drove him from power (1848).

**Metzger, Max Josef** (1887–1944). Roman Catholic peace worker executed by Hitler for "high treason and aiding the enemy." It was World War II that made the Baden-born Metzger a leader of the Austrian (Graz) freedom movement (Volksheils Zentrale) which was to bring him into opposition to National Socialism. He was also active in the struggle against alcoholism as a campaigner for abstinence not morally required by his church.

**Miall, Edward** (1809–1881). English Congregational pastor. Miall became the outspoken enemy of the Established Church as a result of the imprisonment of one of his members in 1840. He founded *The Nonconformist,* a weekly newspaper, in 1841 and organized the British Anti-State Church Association in 1844 (later known as the Society for the Liberation of Religion from State Control). He was elected to Parliament in 1852 as the implacable foe of the Establishment.

**Michael VIII Palaeologus** (c. 1225–1282). Byzantine emperor from 1259. He was placed at the head of the state through a military revolution, supplanting the child-ruler John IV. The capture of Constantinople by the West in 1204 had forced the Eastern Orthodox patriarch to withdraw to Nicaea. In 1261 the Latin empire itself collapsed, and the Greeks under Michael recaptured Constantinople, reestablished the Byzantine Empire, and restored the patriarchs. Michael proved a capable ruler against strong opponents, but soon after 1272 he was obliged to call for papal assistance against the designs of Charles of Anjou. In return, at the Council of Lyons in 1274, his representative acknowledged the papal supremacy (see REUNION ATTEMPTS).

**Michael Cerularius** (d. 1058). Patriarch of Constantinople (1043–1058). He was a central figure in events leading to the schism between the Eastern Orthodox and the Roman

Catholic Churches (see SCHISM, EASTERN). The Normans had forced Greeks in Byzantine Italy to conform to Latin usage; in retaliation, Cerularius closed Latin churches in Constantinople (1052). To legates from Pope Leo IX hopeful of settling dogmatic differences, Cerularius proved obdurate. Negotiations broke down on July 16, 1054, he and his fellow patriarchs were excommunicated, and the lasting gulf widened between East and West.

**Michaelis, Johann David** (1717–1791). German Lutheran Old Testament scholar. He was a teacher of Oriental languages at Göttingen during the whole of his productive career and one of the most celebrated scholars of his time. Having gained note as a student of Syriac, he participated freely in ecclesiastical and academic affairs in Germany. The representative of a type of rationalistic orthodoxy, Michaelis was the first scholar of repute to apply the historicocritical method in the study of the Hebrew Scriptures, thus becoming the father of modern Old Testament studies.

**Michelangelo** (Michelangelo Buonarroti) (1475–1564). Italian sculptor, painter, architect, and poet. With Leonardo da Vinci and Raphael, he was considered one of the three greatest artists of Renaissance Italy. Despite widespread contemporary acclaim for his painting, Michelangelo thought of himself as primarily a sculptor. This sculptural frame of mind carried over into his frescoes which have often been described as "painted sculpture." Michelangelo spent most of his life working in either Florence or Rome. Almost all of his career as a painter until he was past sixty was centered on one colossal project: the frescoes on the ceiling of the Sistine Chapel in Rome. Commissioned by Pope Julius II, he worked tirelessly for over three years depicting on the chapel ceiling the story of Genesis from the Creation to the Flood. The completed work covered about ten thousand square feet of surface and included 343 figures, some of them twelve feet high. Michelangelo's two best-known pieces of sculpture are his devotional *La Pietà* and his enormous marble *David.* Most of Michelangelo's work reflected his belief in the nobility and godlike beauty of man. However, in old age, amid the turmoil created in Italy by the Reformation, he seemed to abandon his faith in man's intrinsic greatness, and his works emphasized more and more the themes of God's judgment and mercy.

**Migne, Jacques-Paul** (1800–1875). Patristic publisher. Migne was a French Roman Catholic priest and theologian who because of a controversy with his bishop on the liberty of priests left his diocese and went to live in

Paris. There he established a printing press and produced low-priced editions of the church fathers and medieval Christian authors (217 volumes of the Latin fathers and 162 volumes of the Greek fathers). His work is especially valuable because, despite errors, it remains the one uniform collection of the fathers that even approaches completion.

**Mignot, Eudoxe** (1842–1918). French prelate. Cultured and influential as a French prelate (Albi) at the close of the 19th century, Mignot urged accommodation between his church and the Third Republic. He accepted separation of church and state (1905) and urged synthesis between Catholicism and Biblical criticism. A friend of Alfred Loisy, he protected the review *Le Sillon*, favorable to the Christian Democratic movement. When it was condemned for Modernism (1910), he abandoned it.

**Mikhailovskii, Nikolai K.** (1842–1904). Russian journalist, literary critic, and sociologist. He advocated "critical populism" based upon the Russian peasant commune, which he believed would serve as a model for democratic, socialist communities in which the harmonious development of the individual personality could be festered. His ideas were formulated in his *What Is Progress?*

**Milan, Edict of** (A.D. 313). The name given to a document found in divergent form in Lactantius (*De mortibus persecutorum*, 48.2–12) and Eusebius (*Ecclesiastical History* 10.5.4–14), whose origin is to be traced to a meeting at Milan between Constantine and Licinius (313). The result of the meeting was that toleration was granted to all religions alike in the Empire, that Christian churches were recognized and the property of churches and Christians restored.

**Militant Atheists.** See LEAGUE OF THE MILITANT GODLESS.

**Military Orders.** The military orders represent a synthesis of the twin medieval occupations, war and religion, combining the ideals of knightly chivalry with those of monasticism. Although more than a hundred such orders have been discovered, the three most famous are the Knights Templar, the Knights Hospitaler, and the Teutonic Knights, all originating in the Crusades. The Templars were founded in 1119 by Hugues de Payens to defend Jerusalem against recapture by the Moslems. In 1128, Bernard gave them a form of the Cistercian rules. By the 13th century they had become influential bankers of Europe because of their own accumulated wealth and the confidence placed in them by princes. Philip IV of France brought various charges against them, and the order was suppressed by Pope Clement V at Vienne in 1312. The guilt of the Templars is still a matter of controversy. The Hospitalers were founded to defend pilgrims to Palestine and to tend the sick. In 1309 they established themselves on the island of Rhodes which they defended against the Turks until 1522. In 1530 they received Malta from Charles V. The Order of Teutonic Knights, founded c. 1190, was organized to care for the sick and to fight the infidels. Its first Grand Master was Herman of Salza (d. 1239). Modern Prussia owes its foundation to the activities of the order.

**Mill, James** (1773–1836). Utilitarian philosopher and father of John Stuart Mill. In 1802 he left Scotland for a writing career in London, becoming in 1808 a disciple of Jeremy Bentham. They broke the monopoly of Oxford and Cambridge by helping to found the University of London. Mill became the acknowledged leader of utilitarianism. One of his last articles, published in 1835, was a plea to reform the church along utilitarian lines.

**Mill, John Stuart** (1806–1873). Utilitarian philosopher and economist; the eldest son of James Mill. Educated exclusively by his father, he learned the Greek alphabet by the age of three and was familiar with important Greek and English literature by his eighth year. Through his father's influence he became a clerk at India House in 1822. In 1828 he was promoted to assistant examiner, and in 1856 became chief of the examiner's office. According to his *Autobiography* (1873), most of Mill's early thinking was dominated by his father. His mature political philosophy took shape after 1830, stimulated by his first-hand observation of the effects of the July Revolution in France. His writing was shaped by an attempt to achieve, within the moral and social sciences, the clarity and certainty of the natural sciences. *Principles of Political Economy* (1848), *On Liberty* (1859), *Utilitarianism* (1863), *The Subjection of Women* (1869), and *Essays on Religion* (1874) are among his most famous works. In his writing, Mill applied the rigorous utilitarian method to pressing social, economic, and political problems. Many regard him as the most "humane" of the utilitarians. From 1865 until his defeat in 1868 he served as a member of Parliament for Westminster. Retiring to Avignon, he died on May 8, 1873.

**Millenary Petition.** A petition presented by the Puritan leaders to King James I en route to London from Scotland in April, 1603.

Though the petition was unsigned, it claimed to represent a thousand ministers (hence, "millenary") "praying to be relieved from their common burden of human rites and ceremonies." The petitioners asked to have abolished the cross in baptism, the wearing of the surplice, the ring in marriage, etc., but to avoid offense nothing was said against episcopacy. The petition led to the calling of the Hampton Court Conference.

**Millennialism.** The Christian belief in a thousand-year reign of Christ upon earth to occur at the end of this age and to be marked by peace, happiness, and freedom from want and disease. However, not all Christians have been millennialists. The belief in the millennium has been only one among several kinds of eschatological teaching found in the history of the church. Furthermore, not every millennialist eschatology has been apocalyptic, i.e., not every millennialist has believed that the world is presently and irretrievably controlled by the power of the devil and that God's purpose for this world can and will be accomplished only by the direct and decisive intervention of God in history. Though types of nonmessianic millennialism have existed, Christian millennialism has always been messianic, i.e., has always included as one of its principal features the Second Advent of Christ to complete and fulfill his mission. Christian millennialism can be most fairly defined, then, as the belief of some Christians in all ages and most Christians in some ages that Christ would appear on earth a second time at the end of history and that a thousand-year period of extraordinary bliss would be associated with that advent. There has been great disagreement, however, concerning whether this advent would precede or follow the millennium and whether this millennium would result from the gradual improvement of the human condition, the sudden decisive overthrow of a desperate and wicked world order, or whether both the millennium and Second Advent of Christ ought to be interpreted as metaphors and thus not expected in any literal way. In tracing the history of millennialism, one can see plainly how these variations in millennial definition have succeeded one another.

The millennium is referred to directly only once in the New Testament (Rev. 20:4–6), where the enjoyment of the thousand years of bliss seems restricted to special martyrs in the early church. One other New Testament passage (I Cor. 15: 24–28) mentions a messianic rule on earth in connection with the Second Advent, but this is the limit of canonical evidence. There are a number of apocalyptic descriptions of Christ's Second Advent (cf. Mark, ch. 13; I Thess. 4: 13–18; II Thess. 2: 1–12; and II Peter 3: 1–12), but none of these refers to a millennium. In the early church, however, a great many noncanonical apocalyptic writings were known and read. In the extratestamental literature of Judaism, I and II Enoch, II Esdras, and the Apocalypse of Elijah describe a period something like a millennium at the end of history, and, in works not now considered a part of the Christian canon, but very influential at the time (the Epistle of Barnabas, the Apocalypse of Peter, and the writings of Justin and Papias), this millennial chronology was taken over. For at least the first two hundred years of Christian history, apocalyptic millennialism dominated the church's outlook. This eschatology, often called chiliasm, was accepted and taught by, among others, Irenaeus, Tertullian, Montanus, and Lactantius. Gradually, however, chiliasm died out—by the time of Origen in the East and by the time of Augustine in the West. Chiliasm was one of the principal emphases in the teaching of the Montanists in Asia Minor (c. 160–220), and the condemnation of Montanism as a heresy had the effect of discrediting that kind of millennialism. The book of Revelation was discredited in this controversy, and this deprived chiliasm of its strongest Biblical support. Both Augustine and Origen gave an allegorical interpretation to millennial prophecies. The thousand-year reign of Christ, they taught, was actually occurring within the church; Christ dwelt within the hearts of all who had received the gift of faith. It seems clear that this transformation of expectations was related to the triumph of Christianity within the Roman Empire, the end of persecution, and the rising social status of Christians. Chiliasm or apocalyptic millennialism is usually found in those communities whose ordinary socioeconomic ambitions are blocked and who can conceive of the triumph of Christ only as a revolutionary act.

Millennialism during the Middle Ages in Europe conforms to this analysis. Augustine's interpretation of the millennium remained the orthodox view and served to bolster the authority of the pope and the hierarchy of the church. But revolutionary millennialism did not die out. Especially in the Rhineland and commonly after the 11th century, groups of chiliasts (who were usually treated as heretics) once more taught the lowly and oppressed to look for a radical and sudden deliverance from their trials. These groups sprang up in areas marked by rapid social change, industrial and commercial expansion, and the growth of population. The best-known exponents were Joachim of Flora, who had a great impact upon the Spiritual Franciscans, the sect of the Flagellants, and the Taborites of Bohemia; but there were hundreds of other little-known groups who have left some record of their teachings.

Millennial interest did not subside in the Reformation, but neither did Protestantism formulate a consistent view of millennialism. The same division that marked the church of the Middle Ages was carried over into Protestantism. The right-wing Reformers (e.g., Luther, Calvin, and the Anglican leaders) upheld an Augustinian position, but many enthusiastic prophets of apocalyptic millennialism (Thomas Müntzer, Melchior Hofmann, and leaders of the Münster experiment such as John of Leiden drew a large following. In the English Civil War (1640–1660) millennial teachings became popular, and some leaders of the army (the Fifth Monarchy Men) embraced a form of apocalyptic millennialism.

Nineteenth-century European and American history is marked by a decided revival in millennial movements and expectations. This can be explained, in part, by the profound changes brought to Western civilization by the industrial revolution, the French Revolution, and the Napoleonic wars. In many cases millennialism appeared disguised as a secular philosophy, as in the case of Marxism, for example, offering the same kind of revolutionary apocalyptic view of imminent salvation that had been the keynote of ancient and medieval chiliasm.

In America, however, hope rather than despair characterized the view of the future. Jonathan Edwards, the great preacher of Northampton, Mass., popularly associated with teaching about the torments of hell, wrote an optimistic *History of the Work of Redemption* which has been called the first postmillennial work in American history. Postmillennialism rejects the Augustinian view and looks for a literal millennial reign of Christ, but, in contrast to chiliasm (or premillennialism, its more common 19th-century name), does not anticipate a revolutionary upheaval or apocalypse. Rather, the millennium is expected as the product of the gradual evangelization of the world and the total triumph of the Christian message. So strong was American optimism in the 18th and 19th centuries that this postmillennialism became a part of the vocabulary of almost every religious group in the new nation. Alexander Campbell, father of the Disciples denomination, edited a periodical entitled the *Millennial Harbinger*. Joseph Berg, a Dutch Reformed pastor, predicted that "this world would be renovated by the power of holiness. . . . Oh! this is the reign of Jesus."

The Mormons even gave a definite location to the millennial kingdom, setting out to establish Zion in Utah. There was a minority report on the state of America, however, by some who felt that only the return of Christ would effect the millennium. The most famous of these was William Miller, who predicted the return of Jesus in 1844. The Seventh-day Adventists trace their history back to Miller. Another more recent advocate of apocalyptic millennialism, Charles T. Russell, also became convinced that the end of the world was coming—in 1914; his followers called themselves Jehovah's Witnesses. Fundamentalism has also been marked by apocalyptic millennialism. Primarily through Bible and Prophetic Conferences in the late 19th century, the expectation of the imminent (though not dated) coming of Christ was encouraged. The movement reached its peak from 1914 to 1918, when the coming of the war drove many to abandon their optimism.

BIBLIOGRAPHY: S. J. Case, *The Millennial Hope* (Chicago, 1918); N. R. C. Cohn, *The Pursuit of the Millennium* (New York, 1961); C. N. Kraus, *Dispensationalism in America* (Richmond, 1958); F. D. Nichol, *The Midnight Cry* (Washington, 1944); S. Thrupp (ed.), *Millennial Dreams in Action* (The Hague, 1962).

**Millennialism in the United States.** Belief in the millennium has occupied an especially prominent place in theology because of its mixture with the popular belief in America's destiny. The first Puritan settlers in America were imbued with a strong conviction that they were a chosen people. Americans did not abandon their enthusiastic optimism about America's future from the time of the colonial settlements through the Revolutionary War, the period of manifest destiny, and the Spanish-American War. It is interesting to note how rapidly the concept of America's destiny was reflected in American theology. By the time of Jonathan Edwards, American theologians were beginning to equate the Christian millennium with the American future. Undoubtedly, Edwards' experience in the First Great Awakening influenced his expectations of a golden age for the church on earth, and, as revivalism became increasingly effective as an evangelistic tool, the revivalistic ministers of every denomination were swept along on the tide. Their form of millennialism is called postmillennialism, for they looked for the coming of Christ at the end of a thousand-year period of Christian progress and growth. They were quite hopeful of the outcome of their endeavors to proclaim the gospel. A moderator of the General Assembly of the Presbyterian Church, Samuel H. Cox, while visiting Britain in 1846 remarked, "I really believe that God has got America within anchorage, and that upon that arena, He intends to display his prodigies for the millennium."

Not everyone in America, however, thought the frontier a utopia, and, in the midst of a serious economic depression following the panic of 1837, William Miller won thousands of converts by teaching that Christ would return to earth about 1843 or 1844. Miller is sometimes called a premillennialist, which is not strictly correct. Miller had little to say about the millennium at all, but simply proclaimed his belief that the return of Christ, which almost all Christians were expecting in some distant future time, was an immediate possibility. The chief result of Miller's movement was to discredit the idea of a premillennial return of Christ and to make postmillennialism, for the immediate future, the only respected doctrine of the last times.

In fact, for most Christian theologians, postmillennial hopes about the future of the church can be said to have remained very lively until the decade of disillusionment in the 1930's. The Civil War, although it gave some a rude shock, was viewed by most Northerners as only another form of progress: "Mine eyes have seen the glory of the coming of the Lord." During the late 19th-century period of industrialism, liberal theologians developed the doctrine of the Kingdom of God in perfect harmony with the millennium. Social Gospel leaders, such as Walter Rauschenbusch, entertained the same optimistic hopes about the outcome of their Christian service as had Edwards.

Beginning in 1878 at a conference held in New York City, there did develop a doctrine of the last times that was not built upon an optimistic view of the world. Leaning heavily upon conservative European theologians such as Henry Alford and Franz Delitzsch, these American clergymen, mostly conservative Calvinists, expressed doubt in the cult of progressivism and set out an opposing theory of premillennialism. The steady decline of the church could be halted only by the Advent of Christ, whose coming would initiate the millennium. There were many things about the American scene that disturbed these men, but probably the most important factor was the growth of Biblical criticism and liberal theology. It is not surprising to note, then, that Fundamentalism was largely premillennial. In fact, there seems to be a definite correlation between each age's view of the future and its understanding of the nature of the millennium.

BIBLIOGRAPHY: S. J. Case, *The Millennial Hope* (Chicago, 1918); N. R. C. Cohn, *The Pursuit of the Millennium* (New York, 1961); C. N. Kraus, *Dispensationalism in America* (Richmond, 1958); C. Larkin, *Dispensational Truth* (Philadelphia, 1920).

**Miller** (Müller), **John Peter** (1709–1796). Baptist sectarian leader. Educated at Heidelberg, Miller emigrated to North America in 1730. He soon came under the influence of the Baptist Johann Conrad Beissel (1690–1768) and joined Beissel's Ephrata Community upon its foundation. When Miller publicly renounced the Reformed Church, its existence in Pennsylvania was threatened, for Miller was considered a learned theologian, with friends in the most prominent ranks of American society, and his prestige was great. He succeeded Beissel as head of the Community in 1768.

**Miller, William** (1782–1849). American millennialist and revivalist. He was born in Massachusetts but spent his life in northern New York at a time when religious excitement was so prevalent that the area received the name "burned-over district." Miller was converted in a revival in 1816 and began to study the Bible, especially those books, such as Daniel and Revelation, which seemed to contain the secrets of the future. After fourteen years of study and calculation, Miller began to preach the imminent return of Christ. At first he did not set a date, but eventually he became more specific as to year and day. His message excited much interest, especially after he met and converted a Boston minister, Joshua V. Himes, who had a good deal of organizational ability and began to manage Miller's movement. At first Christ's return was expected between March, 1843, and March, 1844. Miller's followers, estimated to be about fifty thousand, were exceptionally excited by portents such as a comet, but their hopes were disappointed. A new date was set, however, on the basis of a new calculation, and the people once more waited for Christ to come —this time on Oct. 22, 1844. Although there seems to have been no mass hysteria, many did make definite preparations for the day. When the event did not occur, a large number of them became disillusioned, while others, feeling the return of Christ still imminent, banded together in the first Adventist churches.

**Mills, Benjamin Fay** (1857–1916). American minister, evangelist, and liberal social reformer. Mills resigned a Vermont pastorate in 1886 to become an itinerant evangelist for ten years. By 1893 he had become a liberal in his theology and an all-out advocate of the Social Gospel. He withdrew from the evangelical ministry in 1897 to become a Unitarian pastor in California. In 1903 he became an itinerant lecturer on liberal religion. Following his reconversion to the Christian faith in 1915, he began preaching as a Presbyterian evangelist.

**Mills, Samuel J.** (1783–1818). Congregational clergyman. Mission interest while a student at Williams made Mills a contributor to the founding of the American Board of Commissioners for Foreign Missions. After graduation from Andover he traveled widely on the frontier; seeing need, he founded the American Bible Society. He went to Africa for the American Colonization Society and secured the land later called Liberia.

**Milner, Joseph** (1744–1797), and **Isaac** (1750–1820). Two brothers who helped to promote the cause of evangelicalism within the Church of England. Although born of poor parents, Joseph managed to attend Cambridge University and later assisted in the education of his brother at Queen's College. He served the church at Hull, which, under his auspices, became a center of evangelicalism. There he wrote *The History of the Church of Christ* (1794–1797), a three-volume work devoted to the bright side of Christian endeavor rather than to a reprise of past polemics. Isaac Milner excelled as a student and ultimately held several offices at Cambridge. In holy orders, he manifested a professional competence in mathematics, practical mechanics, and chemistry. He was appointed professor of natural philosophy and president of Queen's College. A close friend of Wilberforce, he accompanied him on an expedition to the south of France (1784–1785). Isaac ruled his college despotically, but with good humor; all his efforts centered upon the advance of evangelicalism and efficiency. In 1791, he was appointed dean of Carlisle, and, although nonresident, he introduced improvements into the cathedral chapter. Very much involved in university affairs, he was elected vice-chancellor of Cambridge in 1792. After the death of Joseph Milner, Isaac edited, with additions, his brother's monumental *History*.

**Miltitz, Karl von** (c. 1490–1529). Papal nuncio. Born near Meissen of a noble German family, Miltitz served as agent for Frederick the Wise in the Curia and was sent by Leo X with the golden rose to win Frederick's favor. In January, 1519, he entered into unauthorized negotiations with Luther, who agreed to submit his views to a German bishop, to write a submissive letter to Leo X, and to keep silence if his opponents would. But Luther did not recant, and the negotiations proved fruitless.

**Milton, John** (1609–1674). English poet. Educated at Cambridge, he backed Parliament in the Civil War and in 1649 became Latin secretary to the Council of State; in peril at the Restoration, he was thereafter retired.

Milton's poetry represents the flowering of Christian humanism in the English Renaissance. Among his short poems are "On the Morning of Christ's Nativity" (1629), expressing his deep piety and personal consecration; "L'Allegro" and "Il Penseroso," aesthetic in tone; and many sonnets, often conveying his own feelings, as "On His Blindness." Major poems are *Paradise Lost* (1667), which, in order to "justify the ways of God to men," recounts in the form of a classical epic the fall of man, making human responsibility clear; *Paradise Regained* (1671), which tells of man's restoration by Christ's victory over temptation, and *Samson Agonistes* (1671).

Milton was an "advanced" Puritan, as his prose shows: his pamphlets attack episcopacy, justify the execution of Charles I, and *Areopagitica* praises a free press. A political thinker, he held the contract theory. *De doctrina Christiana* shows his theological affinity with many currents of radical Puritanism, rejecting Church Establishment and the orthodox Trinity (although teaching the Son's subordination, he nevertheless affirmed Christ's divinity and atonement).

**Mindszenty, Joseph Cardinal** (1892–    ). Hungarian Roman Catholic prelate. Ordained in 1915, Mindszenty was imprisoned by the Béla Kun regime in 1919. Made bishop of Veszprém in 1944, he was jailed by the Nazis in that year for his opposition. He became primate of Hungary in 1945, and cardinal in 1946. Accused of plotting, treason, spying, and black-marketeering by the Communist regime, he was condemned to forced labor by the Soviets in 1949. An agreement between the church and the government later in 1949 assured the church liberty to carry on its work, and Mindszenty was released. In 1955, however, he was once again placed under house arrest. Liberated during the briefly successful revolution of 1956, Mindszenty thereafter took refuge in the United States legation in Budapest. Despite repeated government overtures to leave the country, Mindszenty has refused. He regards his continued presence in Hungary as a living protest against the church's subjugation.

**Minims** (Minimi). Religious order founded by Francis of Paōla in 1435. The original rule of the members was based upon that of Francis of Assisi. Dedicated to the humility that their name suggests, their rule enjoins perpetual abstinence, penance, and abnegation. From Italy the order spread rapidly into France, where its founder was invited to come by the king. The order suffered greatly from the French Revolution, the number of its members being considerably diminished thereafter.

**Ministry.** Although it is relatively simple to describe the nature of the ministry in later centuries of church history, the earliest times are subject to differing interpretation depending on the tradition in which the interpreter stands. At the very least, the resources for the earliest times are slight and are not often interested in the kinds of questions that are subsequently influential.

In the New Testament itself, terminology is fluid. No clear distinctions appear between offices that are later quite distinct. For example, while Hippolytus and Irenaeus refer to the bishop as the successor to the apostle, it is difficult to determine in what sense he is to be considered the apostle's successor.

It would appear that the church in the 1st and 2d centuries possessed two classes of ministers: those whose functions and authorization were charismatic, and others whose role was more formal and more nearly defined. The first group cannot be exhaustively defined. They were "gifted" individuals of various kinds. The Didache mentions prophets, perhaps a class of itinerant preachers. The terms used to refer to them suggest that they were a class prone to be disorderly. Perhaps much of the ministry of the earliest days was of this highly personal nature. Toward the end of the 2d century, on the other hand, we see the role of the bishop rather clearly defined: he is teacher and celebrant of the Eucharist. A plethora of secondary offices seems to continue, but it is difficult to know much of them. Quite clearly, the ministry of the church is defined largely in relation to the sacraments, in particular the Eucharist.

Although early writers regard the Eucharist as the act of the whole Christian assembly, it is clear that the bishop is a necessary element: it is his office to offer the thanksgiving. As the number of Christians in a city increased, it was necessary to celebrate the Eucharist in several different places and for this purpose the bishop appointed representatives. It was soon the case that these vicars of the bishop were referred to as "presbyters" (in English, "priests"). The office of deacon, in New Testament times quite different, becomes a probationary period to the priesthood.

It has been typical of the West to assume that the powers of the priesthood are essentially those of the bishop as delegated to priests. Yet some functions which, in the West, are exclusively those of the bishop are done in the East—as they have always been—by the priest. Confirmation is an example of such a function. It would seem, therefore, that the powers of the ministry are not necessarily to be understood as deriving from the office of bishop. An alternative view, of increasing influence, is that the powers of the ministry are possessed jointly by the presbytery as symbolized in the office of one of their number, the bishop. The role of bishop understood in this fashion is approximately that of the chairman of a body: without the action of the chairman the body is incompetent to act, but the powers of the chairman are not his in his own personal right apart from the body. A similar notion was influential at Vatican II as the "principle of collegiality." As earlier indicated, the typical understanding of the bishop in the West is still tinged with monarchial characteristics.

There is the further question of primacy among the bishops themselves. In the East there was always a sense of parity. The metropolitan bishop of Constantinople (the "New Rome") was the "first among equals." In the West, on the other hand, there is a perceptible trend according the bishop of Rome a primacy by virtue of his office. The dogmatic teaching asserts that he has this role in Christendom because as bishop of Rome he is successor to Peter, yet the primacy of the bishop of Rome was never simply acknowledged by the Eastern churches, and was often resisted in the West.

The charismatic form of the ministry was manifested briefly among the Montanists of the 2d century before the whole movement was found to be heretical. The most exacerbated issue concerning the nature of the ministry in this early period was raised by the Donatists early in the 4th century. The Donatists questioned the validity of ordinations received from individuals who had, at least temporarily, failed to resist persecution. If the validity of sacraments depended upon the personal character of the celebrant, an unworthy bishop would allow a hiatus in the succession of the priesthood from the days of the apostles. The Donatists were condemned; however, the problem of the intention with which a sacrament is celebrated continues to haunt any consideration of validity.

The "high" doctrine of the ministry typical of the West holds that the priest's office is received as an indelible character at his ordination, that his ordination places him in the succession of the apostles, and that (excepting Baptism under extreme conditions) sacraments are invalid unless performed by a priest. From the time of the Reformation, however, there were some alternative views. The Reformers' principal criticism of the priesthood of their day was not doctrinal; they held that most of the ordained men of their day were insufficiently educated to perform properly their priestly functions. The Council of Trent did, it is true, order a thoroughgoing reform of priestly education. Certainly the Reformers advocated no "lower" view of ministry; their inclination was, however, to stress the dignity of the function rather than the personal privilege of the functionary.

Among Calvin's followers in particular, little stress was placed upon some traditional elements of the ministry. For Calvin, a settled ministry was more a matter of propriety than of theological niceties. To be in the succession of the apostles was, for Calvin, a consequence of doing what the apostles did. Tactile succession by the laying on of hands at ordination was no guarantee of apostolicity.

The greatest contribution of the Reformation in this connection was, perhaps, a broadened understanding of the nature of vocation. Whereas vocation has frequently been understood only in relation to churchly vocations, Luther and the other Reformers were prone to assert that all men are called to ministries only some of which are ministries within the congregation. In the present day, emphasis is being placed upon a theology of the laity, that is, a broadened understanding of Christian ministry.

Specifically with respect to offices within the church, however, the Reformers claimed to restore the ministry to its proper dignity by insisting that only such men be ordained as were manifestly capable of discharging their duties, with emphasis on their role as teacher and preacher to the congregation.

If the matter of apostolic succession was assumed in earlier years, it has—since the Reformation—become a problem among Anglicans and Protestants. There is the fact, for example, that Anglican orders are recognized as valid by Orthodox communions but have specifically been declared defective by a papal decree. On the other hand, a common Anglican view that apostolic succession is the essential mark of Christian ministry, and the insistence that Anglican orders possess this mark, has led to some Anglican resistance when union with various denominations has been broached.

The term "ministry" obviously denotes service. This service is both of the people of God and also (as the Reformers particularly stressed) of the Word of God. Yet the tendency was often in the direction of a monarchial clergy. Bishops were often spoken of as the princes of the church, by analogy to the Kingdom of God. The primacy of the pope in Christendom was, especially for Protestant controversialists, the logical extension of this monarchialism. As a reaction, Protestants placed specific emphasis upon the ministry as service. This note of Christian ministry was well comprehended by John XXIII when he stressed the age-old but little-used papal title "servant of the servants of God." This understanding of the papal office suggests possibilities of a *rapprochement* with Protestant groups which earlier polemics obscured.

The difficulties experienced by the institutional church in the 20th century have led many to the view that ideas concerning the nature of the church's ministry must be radically altered. Quite apart from the very specialized forms of ministry that have been developed—hospital chaplaincies, directors of religious broadcasting, etc.—many have felt that congregational worship as it has been practiced for centuries will gradually disappear, or that, to the extent to which it is retained, it need not be the prime function of a particular group of men. These ideas, together with an increasing entrance of women into the sacramental ministry of some communions, promise radical changes in years to come.

BIBLIOGRAPHY: *Calvin: Institutes of the Christian Religion,* ed. by J. T. McNeill (The Library of Christian Classics, Vols. XX–XXI, Philadelphia, 1960); H. G. Goodykoontz, *Ministry in the Reformed Tradition* (Richmond, 1963); A. G. Hebert, *Apostle and Bishop* (New York, 1963); J. T. McNeill, *A History of the Cure of Souls* (New York, 1965); H. R. Niebuhr and D. D. Williams (eds.), *The Ministry in Historical Perspective* (New York, 1956).

**Minocchi, Salvatore** (1869–1943). Italian Biblical scholar and priest. Ordained in 1892, Minocchi was suspended in 1907 for rationalist and modernist ideas, abandoning his habit the next year. He wrote on the origins of Christianity, subjected the Pentateuch to scrutiny, and gave especial attention to explication of the Song of Songs. Working from ancient texts, he produced in 1900 an annotated translation of the Gospels.

**Minor Orders.** The four lesser orders of the Christian ministry which include: ostiary (or porter), lector, exorcist, and acolyte. In the

Orthodox Church there exists also the order of cantors. Since the former functions of the minor orders have been assumed by laymen or those in major orders, the minor orders are regarded as preparatory steps to the priesthood and are conferred on seminarians. Celibacy is not required of one in minor orders, nor recitation of the breviary office (Code of Canon Law, Canon 949).

**Minucius Felix** (2d or 3d century). Author of a Latin apology entitled *Octavius,* part of which is paralleled in Tertullian's *Ad nationes* and, like it, makes extensive use of Cicero, *De natura deorum.* Anti-Christian arguments, largely philosophical, are developed at length by a pagan speaker, then refuted by a Christian; the protagonists finally agree to disagree. It is not certain whether the work belongs to the 2d century or to the 3d; few later Christians read it.

**Miracle Plays.** Medieval dramatizations of sacred history or episodes from the lives of miracle-working saints. Religious drama in the Middle Ages evolved from tropes, which were dramatic enactments of Scriptural stories inserted into the Mass. As these tropes developed, religious drama came to have an existence of its own apart from the Mass; finally the plays moved outside the church. Upon leaving the church, the plays became vernacular. Miracle plays were particularly popular in France and England, where there developed four major cycles, one of which contained forty-eight plays.

**Mirari Vos.** Encyclical of Aug. 15, 1832, whereby Pope Gregory XVI condemned freedom of the press and implied censure of Lamennais's journal *L'Avenir,* which only the previous year had been suspended and then recalled. The journal, containing articles by Jean Lacordaire, Montalembert, and Victor Hugo, was deemed dangerous to religion and was once more suppressed. When Lamennais replied to the censure with *Paroles d'un croyant,* the pope reiterated his condemnations in the encyclical *Singulari nos* (June 25, 1834).

**Mission Covenant, Swedish.** A Free Church movement in Sweden founded by Peter Waldenström (1838–1917) in 1878 growing out of the spiritual awakening of Carl O. Rosenius. Though it has no official connection with the Lutheran State Church of Sweden, its members continue to function as members of the state church. By 1910 it had about 100,000 adherents and had built over 1,200 chapels or "prayer houses." In the United States the Swedish Lutheran Mission Synod and the Ansgarii Synod united in 1885 to form the Swedish Evangelical Mission Covenant of America. In 1937 the group assumed the name "Evangelical Mission Covenant Church of America," and in 1957 "Evangelical Covenant Church of America." The Mission Covenant movement stressed a subjective moral theory of the atonement, the necessity of spiritual life, the essential unity of all true Christians, the sovereignty of the Word over all creedal statements, and the urgency of the mission imperative. Among other institutions, the United States group supports North Park College and Theological Seminary in Chicago and has 65,780 members in 533 churches (1966).

**Missions.** Mission (Latin, *missio,* "sending") is the proclamation of the gospel to all men near and far. Since it aims at the discipling of the nations (Matt. 28:19–20; Acts 1:8), the sending of missionaries has been paramount. Present mission theory sees the mission of the church as part of the *missio Dei,* the Triune God's self-sending for reconciling the world unto himself in Christ. As the Father sent the Son, so they send the church under the guidance and inspiration of the Holy Spirit. Mission is a means of God's action in history for the consummation of his purposes for men. The immediate and lasting impulse to mission comes from the personality and teaching of Jesus and the postresurrection certainty of the church that Christ is Lord and Savior. Missions are the practical means by which mission is carried out. This has always included the preaching of the gospel, the gathering of converts into churches, the fostering of church growth, and the effort to make the faith indigenous in any given culture. The Biblical model for mission is the sending of Paul and Barnabas by the church in Antioch (Acts 13:2–3) and Paul's subsequent evangelistic activities.

Paul was the preeminent initiator of the mission to the Gentiles of the Roman Empire, but the whole early church was spontaneously evangelistic. There were itinerating missionaries known as apostles, but most churches seem to have been planted by laymen traveling on business or pleasure. The Roman peace, administration, and excellent system of communications favored expansion. Other favorable factors were the wide use of Greek, the cultural pluralism of the time, and much spiritual hunger. Sometimes the growing identification of Christianity with Hellenistic culture was an aid, as in Pontus in the 3d century (Gregory the Wonder-Worker). Persecution failed to stem the growth. After Christianity became the state religion under Constantine and his successors, governmental patronage, legal proscription of paganism, and local pastoral nurture under bishops eliminated all paganism within the Empire, leaving the Jews as the only non-Christians by the beginning of the 6th century.

Meanwhile, the faith had spread beyond the imperial borders. Osroene, with its capital, Edessa, became the first Christian state. From there Syriac Christianity spread eastward. Armenia was the first large kingdom to become Christian, through the efforts of King Tiridates and the missionary Gregory the Illuminator in the 3d century. By the 2d century the St. Thomas Christians were already established in southwest India. Ulfilas (d. 383) was the apostle to the Visigoths, and through them other Germanic peoples were won. Patrick (c. 389–c. 461) is the main figure in the conversion of Ireland, where a distinctive Celtic form of the faith flourished. Southward the cross was carried into Ethiopia, Frumentius being the apostle. Note that all the persons named above were monks, and monastic orders would henceforth provide the missionaries until the rise of Protestant missions.

Irish ascetic missionaries went to pagan Scotland (Columba at Iona, 6th century) and thence southward to the Angles and Saxons. Led by Columbanus (d. 615), they went to France and the Rhineland on a mission of revival. At the same time the Nestorians of Persia evangelized peoples in central Asia and reached the capital of China in 635. However, Christianity in the 7th and 8th centuries lost its heartlands in Asia and North Africa to Islam through the Arab conquest. Even then advance was being made east of the Rhine. Pope Gregory the Great had sent a mission to Kent under Augustine in 596. Conflict with the Celts over order and customs was resolved in favor of Rome by royal intervention. The young English Church, combining Celtic mission zeal with devotion to the papacy, then undertook a great mission to its Germanic relatives. Boniface of Crediton (d. 754), with a papal commission as archbishop, led the movement, converting pagans, civilizing the region, and establishing church order. The Viking conquest destroyed the English sending mission; but when the northern kings became Christian they used English missionaries in the conversion of their peoples, whereas a mission from the Frankish domain led by Ansgar (801–865) was thwarted by political involvement.

Constantinople sent Cyril and Methodius to Moravia, and in a short time the Balkan peoples were won but sadly divided by Roman, Byzantine, and German competition. The Russian ruler, Vladimir, was converted about 987, and national adherence followed. The Mongol invasion devastated the central Asian Christian communities, but when peace reigned from Russia to the Pacific the Nestorian missionaries refounded the church in China, while the Franciscan John of Montecorvino also reached Khanbalik in 1294. Meanwhile, Spain and the Mediterranean islands were recaptured and the Crusades were launched against the Moslems. Their effect was to erect a permanent barrier between Moslems and Christians. However, a mission of loving persuasion was attempted by Francis of Assisi and Ramón Lull (martyred 1315 or 1316).

It was Spanish and Portuguese imperialism during the age of discovery that first carried Christianity all the way around the globe. When Pope Alexander VI in 1493 divided non-Christian lands between the two powers, they accepted missionary responsibility. All the Americas except Brazil fell to Spain, and moving westward across the Pacific the Philippines also were occupied. Christianity and Spanish civilization were imposed by force, but many missionaries gave valiant service and, led by Bartholome de las Casas, put up a courageous struggle for justice for the natives. Portuguese commercial colonies in the Orient drew the older orders but especially provided a field for the new Society of Jesus. The Jesuit apostle to the Indies was Francis Xavier (1506–1552), who went on from India to Malaya and Japan and died off the coast of China trying to enter there. The Jesuits had marked success in Japan and in China, where Matteo Ricci and his successors experimented with adaptation to Chinese culture. In order to break the bottleneck created by Portuguese control of missions (the padroado), Rome sent out vicars apostolic, bishops who were personal delegates of the pope and not diocesan bishops, and the Sacred Congregation for the Propagation of the Faith was founded in 1622 to supervise the missions. A French society, the Foreign Mission Society of Paris, then sent secular priests to Indochina with a policy of raising up a native secular priesthood. Spanish missionaries from the Philippines entered Japan and China and attacked the practices of the Jesuits. The disastrous rites controversy ended with the condemnation of the Jesuits. This eventually led to persecution of Christians by the Chinese government and was a factor in the proscription of Christianity in Japan in the 17th century. The decline of Spain and Portugal and the rise of the Protestant powers brought an end to this Roman Catholic expansion.

However, Roman Catholic missions quickly revived after the end of the Napoleonic wars and many new missionary orders were founded. All missions profited from European colonialism and the prestige of European civilization. After World War II the American churches provided the major share of funds but not of personnel. The great new feature of the 20th century has been the fostering of native clergy, bishops, and national hierarchies, stimulated by papal encyclicals. The decree *Ad gentes* of Vatican Council II has redefined the mission, removing non-Roman Christians as objects for missionary approach, limiting the mission to non-Christians, and even calling for cooperation with other churches in mission. Missionary bishops are also to be given a collegial role in the propaganda. By 1960 a membership of over 65,000,000 was reported in Asia, Africa, and Oceania.

Among the Orthodox churches only the Church of Russia has been missionary in modern times. It extended Christianity through Russian Asia to Alaska and Japan. Bishop Nicolai founded the church in Japan in 1863. It suffered tremendously during World War II. A Greek mission was begun in Kenya in the 1960's.

Protestants were slow to undertake mission work after the Reformation. The continuing missionary enterprise began with the evangelization of the New England Indians by the Mayhews and John Eliot in the 1640's and with the work of the chaplains of the Dutch East Indies Company at the same time. The next impulse came out of German Pietism and brought forth the Danish-Halle Mission in which August Hermann Francke (1663–1727) trained the men at Halle and the Danish king Frederick IV sent them to Tranquebar in southern India beginning with Bartholomeus Ziegenbalg (1705). Next, the Moravian Church, under Count Nicholas Ludwig von Zinzendorf, sent its first men to St. Thomas in 1731 as the vanguard of a host in many lands. These efforts, along with revival movements, notably the Wesleyan, stimulated the founding of the Baptist Missionary Society by William Carey in 1792, the London Missionary Society in 1795, and the Church Missionary Society in 1799. American societies began to organize in 1787, and a student movement at Williams College and Andover Seminary resulted in the creation of the first American instrument for overseas mission, the American Board of Commissioners for Foreign Missions in 1810. Samuel J. Mills was the moving spirit among the students. Further organization came rapidly. In Europe voluntary societies were formed, whereas the American pattern has been that of official denominational boards. By the 20th century there were few churches without foreign missions, and by 1910 there were about 420 direct sending agencies. In the 1960's there were more than that number in North America alone.

India attracted the greatest number of missionaries from the most denominations and countries, and China was next and had the greatest concentration of Americans until its closing in 1950. The only countries in which there were no organized Protestant churches in the 1960's were Sikkim, Bhutan, Tibet, and Saudi Arabia. By 1960 there were reported for all the young churches 21,806,552 communicant members and a total constituency of 64,874,508. North Americans took first place in the mission from the British by 1910. United States and Canadian boards in 1960 raised $170,000,000 and had 27,219 missionaries or 65 percent of the grand total.

The Protestant missionary movement was characterized by a keen sense of unity that expressed itself in common objectives, identical methods, territorial comity, conferences for consultation on the field and at the home base, federations of missions, union agencies for joint services, union institutions (such as schools, colleges, seminaries, hospitals, etc.), and even church unions on the fields. From the mid-19th century the objective of missions was agreed to be that stated by Rufus Anderson (1796–1880, American Board of Commissioners for Foreign Missions) and Henry Venn (Church Missionary Society) as the fostering of national churches that would be "self-governing, self-supporting, and self-propagating." As these churches came into being they also tended toward regional or national cooperation and unity. Out of all this cooperation came the major influences that brought into being the ecumenical movement. The great World Missionary Conference at Edinburgh in 1910 gave rise to the International Missionary Council, the Faith and Order Movement, and the Universal Christian Council for Life and Work, all of which later merged into the World Council of Churches. What began as a unilateral sending movement out of a geographical Western Christendom has become the world mission of Christian communities in almost every nation. The role of the Western boards and societies is now principally that of interchurch aid in lending personnel and granting funds to younger churches. The moment has arrived for a new missionary advance, and it appears that Protestants, Roman Catholics, and Orthodox will show unity and practice cooperation in it.

BIBLIOGRAPHY: K. S. Latourette, *History of the Expansion of Christianity*, 7 vols. (New York, 1937–1945); S. C. Neill, *A History of Christian Missions* (Grand Rapids, 1965).

*Bibliografia Missionaria* (Rome, 1933 ff.); *Bibliotheca Missionum* (Freiburg, 1916 ff.); *International Review of Missions* (New York, 1911 ff.).

**Missions in America** (Home Missions). An integral part of the earliest colonial ventures, home missions initially followed a European pattern as the Virginia colony was divided into Anglican parishes, and the towns in New England were organized with a Congregational church established in each. However, it proved to be impossible to develop fully or maintain such a pattern; there soon emerged indications of competition, as seen in the pre-Revolutionary work, particularly in New England, of the Anglican-founded Society for the Propagation of the Gospel. That many areas were not being reached at all was noted by the first American Presbytery, which stated in 1707 that all its clergy should supply "desolate places where a minister is wanting." Pastors throughout the colonies recognized the situation and undertook missionary tours to areas where there were no churches, or none of their denomination, and this pattern was expanded as a result of the Great Awakening.

Further acceleration occurred by 1800 with the opening of the Ohio-Mississippi river valley and was promoted by new denominational organizations reflecting a nationalistic spirit and by voluntary societies that gave structure to a new religious fervor and humanitarian interest. A fear of Roman Catholicism also became a factor.

The recently arrived Methodists articulated their mission program as one based on itinerancy. Soon the untiring, ubiquitous circuit rider, working under a carefully defined ecclesiastical structure, was proclaiming a religion that was based on a dynamic, emotional, and evangelistic appeal. America was covered by a network of circuits wherein local preachers developed the work, and, when augmented by camp meetings, often built the denomination out of the raw materials of the frontier. Also employing a method that enabled the denomination to move readily with the people were the Baptists with their more rigid theology and congregational polity. Their approach centered on the farmer-preacher who toiled on the soil six days a week and preached to his neighbors on the seventh. A similar program was carried forth by the native American Disciples of Christ.

Other mission policies were enunciated by Eastern denominations that demonstrated a strong paternal instinct. Concern about the migratory habits of the frontiersman and the attendant reversion to what was called "barbarism" found expression in 1798 in the organization of the first of many state and local voluntary mission societies. The programs undertaken were a continuation of the pattern of sending out clergymen on short missionary tours, with the determination that New England culture as well as religion be brought to bear.

Following the War of 1812 came the era of national societies to avoid the duplication and areas of neglect resulting under the separate societies. It was the policy of such bodies as the American Home Missionary Society to establish and support a settled rather than an itinerant ministry, and to grant aid to congregations in inverse proportion to what they could contribute to the support of a minister. It was deemed essential that only congregations with a promise of permanency be encouraged.

In the decades preceding the Civil War, denominational consciousness continued to gain, with each denomination wishing to promote missions through its own distinctive organizations and programs, and expending some effort among the Indians, though this had primarily been considered foreign missions. The use of the Sabbath school, the "protracted meeting," and publications as mission tools increased. The Episcopal Church reasserted itself by sending missionary bishops to initiate work and to develop fields for later dioceses, while other Protestants used mission superintendents to oversee the work on new fields. The work of the Roman Catholic and Protestant foreign-language churches continued to be largely confined to attempting to meet the needs of the immigrant and his children, with Catholicism especially receiving men and funds from European mission societies.

After the Civil War, enlarged programs of Negro missions led to the establishment of separate denominations. Denominational competition also continued to be severe in urban areas as well as in such often transient Western communities as mining camps, railroad towns, and among homesteaders. This was augmented by the formation of extension societies to aid in financial matters. Finally, in 1908 the Home Missions Council was organized to assist in comity arrangements to avoid duplication and to assign undeveloped areas to specific denominations.

The 20th century has seen the emphasis placed on continuing assistance to weak congregations, to developing urban missions in suburban areas and inner-city cores, and a new outreach of Roman Catholicism and Lutheranism.

BIBLIOGRAPHY: C. E. Drury, *Presbyterian Panorama* (Philadelphia, 1952); C. B. Goodykoontz, *Home Missions on the American Frontier* (Caldwell, Idaho, 1939); W. R. King, *History of the Home Missions Council* (New York, 1930); J. R. Scotford, *Spanning a Continent* (New York, 1939); W. W. Sweet, *Religion on the American Frontier: 1783–1840,* 4 vols. (New York, 1964).

*Mit Brennender Sorge.* Encyclical letter of Pope Pius XI addressed to the hierarchy of Germany, March 4, 1937. In this letter, Pius warned the German people against the cult of blood and race, and against attempts to revivify pre-Christian Teutonic myths and a pagan concept of heroism. He spoke out bitterly against the Hitler youth organizations, and complained of the many violations of the Concordat of 1933.

**Modernism, Catholic.** Although an amorphous movement, to say the least, Catholic Modernism might be looked upon as the logical successor to the liberal Catholic movements of the middle of the 19th century. It was an attempt at *aggiornamento* before its time. Philosophically, the movement was predicated on non-Thomistic grounds, emphasizing the role of the will and of action in the apprehension of "truth." Its roots might be looked upon as Kantian, and it was not unaffected by Bergsonian "intuition." The best-known modernists in England were Tyrrell, Von Hügel, and Petre; in France, Loisy, Blondel, Le Roy, and Laberthonnière; and in Italy, Fogazzaro. One of the touchstones in understanding the movement is the emphasis on "evolution," in the broadest sense of that word. In Biblical interpretation, church history, and the history of morals or dogma, modernists held that as the techniques applied to the secular sciences became more sophisticated and were applied to the sacred sciences, the church had to be prepared to allow for what might seem radical reinterpretations of positions it once held. Extremely dangerous and unpalatable to the "establishment," Modernism was condemned in the papal decree *Lamentabili* and the encyclical *Pascendi* in 1907.

**Moehler, Johann Adam** (1796–1838). Roman Catholic church historian. Educated at Ellwangen and Tübingen, Moehler taught at Tübingen and Munich. He stressed an organismic understanding of history and tradition, and viewed the church as a mystical body. His *Symbolik* (1832), controverted by F. C. Baur, awoke a new confessional consciousness among German Protestants as it contrasted the Roman Catholic teaching office with Protestant immediacy of Spirit. A forerunner of ultramontanism and Catholic Modernism, Moehler is studied in German and French ecumenical circles.

**Moeller, Johann Friedrich** (1789–1861). German Lutheran churchman. After a pastorate in Erfurt, Moeller served there as chairman of evangelical ministry and endeavored to reconcile a state church with Grabau-Lutheran separatists. As general superintendent in Magdeburg (1843) he was involved in conflict with *Lichtfreunde,* an aftergrowth of rationalism that demanded parish autonomy. Attacked by Wislicenus, Uhlich, and Sintenis, Moeller moved toward the confessionalist camp. He wrote in catechetics, and was a follower of J. Draeske.

**Moffat, James Clement** (1811–1890). Protestant church historian. Born in Scotland, Moffat emigrated to America in 1833 and acquired his formal education at Princeton and Yale. He taught at Lafayette College and Miami University in Ohio, where he was ordained a Presbyterian minister in 1851. He returned to Princeton (1852) as professor of Latin and Greek and in 1861 was appointed professor of church history at Princeton Theological Seminary. He published several books on aesthetics and church history and a lengthy autobiographical poem, *Alwyn: A Romance of Study* (1875).

**Moffat, Robert** (1795–1883). A Scottish Wesleyan who devoted himself to missionary work in South Africa. He sailed for Capetown in 1816 as an agent of the London Missionary Society. Destined for Namaqualand, he journeyed into the interior and lived for one year with the native chieftain, Afrikaaner. In 1819, Moffat brought Afrikaaner to Capetown as a Christian convert. This proved to the authorities the value of missionary enterprise. In 1825, after many skirmishes with the hostile tribes of Bechuanaland, Moffat established a station at Kuruman. Here he perfected himself in the native tongue; by 1830 he had translated into the Sechuana language the Gospel of Luke and a selection of other Scriptures. There followed strenuous efforts to get his work into print. By 1845, Moffat had completed his Sechuana versions of the New Testament and The Psalms as well as portions of the Old Testament and *The Pilgrim's Progress.* From 1839 to 1843, Moffat was in England; here he published his *Labours and Scenes in South Africa* (1842). After his return to Kuruman (1843) he was assisted in his work by David Livingstone, who married one of his daughters. He went back to England in 1870 to receive credit as the father and pioneer of mission work in South Africa. He was long remembered as a compassionate friend of the natives, a scholarly translator, a devoted teacher, and an inventive organizer.

**Moffatt, James** (1870–1944). Theologian and Bible translator. Born in Glasgow, Moffatt was ordained in the United Free Church in Scotland in 1896. He taught at Mansfield College, Oxford, and the United Free Church College, Glasgow, before emigrating to the United States in 1927. He became professor of church history at Union Theological Seminary, New York, a position he held until 1939. His books include *The Historical New Testament* (1901) and *Presbyterianism* (1928). His most famous work was his translation of the Bible: *The Moffatt New Testament* (1913) and *The Moffatt Old Testament* (1924).

**Mogila, Peter** (c. 1597–1647). Russian Orthodox theologian and metropolitan of Kiev. Born in Moldavia, he studied in western Europe (especially Paris) and after his return home became archimandrite of a monastery at Kiev (1627) and subsequently metropolitan of Kiev (1633). Mogila's most important work was his Orthodox Confession of the Catholic and Apostolic Eastern Church, written in 1638 and first published in 1645, which was officially sanctioned on several occasions (sometimes with revisions) by Orthodox synods and patriarchs. Resisting both Jesuit and Calvinist (Cyril Lucar) influences, the Confession presents the Orthodox faith under three headings: faith (on the Nicene Creed), hope (on the Lord's Prayer and the Beatitudes), and love (on the virtues, sins, and Ten Commandments). Mogila also wrote a Russian catechism (1645). He is credited with being "the father of Russian theology," importing Western theological scholarship, but preserving the integrity of the Orthodox faith.

**Mohammed** (c. 570–632). The last of the great line of Semitic prophets which began with Abraham and includes Moses and Jesus, according to Moslem revelation. Mohammed's mission, like the missions of the earlier prophets, was worldwide—to make known the word of God as revealed to him, and to correct or purify the corruptions of the divine message that were present in the life of his day. He believed that his people, the Arabs, were the inheritors of the Semitic religious tradition that had previously passed down through the Jews and the Christians.

Born in Mecca, a member of one of Arabia's strongest clans, Mohammed became a successful merchant. He received his first revelations at the age of forty, transmitting them orally to his immediate family and later to the pagan populace of Mecca, where his words were largely spurned. In 622, he was invited to go to Medina to mediate a long-waged civil war. There he gained an opportunity to establish his conception of an ideal state, which was founded on a fusion of the religious and secular ways of life. From this base of power, Mohammed spent his remaining years improving his governmental system and successfully converting the surrounding pagans. By the time of his death most of Arabia had adopted Islam.

**Molanus, Gerard Walter** (1633–1722). German Lutheran churchman. Educated at Helmstedt under Calixt, Molanus was professor of mathematics at Rinteln in 1659 and of theology in 1664. He assumed directorship of the Hannover consistory in 1674, and became abbot of the cloister at Loccum (only Protestant cloister in Germany under Benedictine rule) in 1677. Molanus worked actively with Leibnitz and Jablonski in unity negotiations with Roman Catholics such as Spinola and Bossuet, but without firm results. He urged the independence of ecclesiastical administration from sovereign control.

**Molina, Luis de** (1535–1600). Spanish Jesuit theologian. Born of Spanish nobility, Molina entered the Society of Jesus in 1553, was professor of philosophy at Coimbra from 1563 to 1567, and received the chair of theology at Evora in 1568. Thirty years of labor to vindicate, against Protestantism, the Tridentine doctrine that man retains his freedom to resist or accept grace produced his *Concordia liberi arbitrii cum gratiae donis* ("The Harmony of Free Will with the Gifts of Grace"), the obscurity of which was the catalyst for a bitter controversy with the Dominicans. The book was written as a commentary on the *Summa theologiae* of Thomas Aquinas, the first by a Jesuit, and followed the advice of Ignatius Loyola against allowing the Protestant sense of the power of God to obscure the reality of man's freedom of choice. God, said Molina, gives grace in the light of his knowledge of what a specific man will do in various hypothetical situations (*scientia media*). Molina thus thought to retain man's freedom of choice as an element in the reception of grace, the grace being conferred in terms of a divine foreknowledge of how man will react, not, however, *because* of man's action in the sense of its exerting a claim upon God. The *Concordia* met immediate trouble upon publication (1588), and was reissued the following year in a revised version, with an appended defense. However, the battle quickly spread over Spain, until Pope Clement VIII silenced both sides (1594) and ordered all the pertinent documents to be studied by a special congregation at Rome (1597). On the day that Molina died in Madrid (Oct. 12, 1600), the Congregatio de Auxiliis, after their second examination of the case, reported adversely on the *Concordia* to Clement; but its contents were exonerated by his successor, Paul V, in 1607.

**Molinos, Miguel de** (c. 1640–1697). Spanish mystic who popularized quietism by his *Spiritual Guide.* He taught that the soul experiences Christian perfection when it abandons all effort and desire and in thus assuming a position of complete passivity becomes lost in God. He was charged with attacking the teachings and practices of the church, and for asserting that acts of the body do not taint the soul. Finally he was arrested and imprisoned by the Inquisition in 1687.

**Molokans** ("milk drinkers"). A Russian sect that rejected sacraments and scorned ceremony and icons. Matwei Semjonowitch, a martyr, founded the group in the 16th century. Semjon Uklein was a reformer in the 1700's; their chief teacher was Dimitrij Tweritinow, who was strongly influenced by rationalism and "enlightened" Protestantism. The Russian Orthodox synod in 1714 condemned the sect, which interpreted miracles allegorically, conducted simple services, and followed only a human Jesus. Currently the group is recognized by the Soviet Government. Some Molokan groups are found in the Midwest in the United States.

**Monarchians.** Adherents of one of the various forms of the anti-Trinitarian theory in the 2d and 3d centuries that God is a single person as well as a single being. The first known attempt at an "orthodox" Christological statement against the Gnostics in an attempt to preserve monotheism in Christian belief comes from the 2d-century Theodotus, a tanner of Byzantium. A logical statement regarding the divinity of Jesus which would preserve the unity (monarchy) of God was necessary. Theodotus' statement gave rise to monarchianism, which spread rapidly from Asia Minor westward to Rome. Monarchians are divided generally into two schools, though variations existed within both: (1) Dynamic monarchians, including Theodotus, Artemon, and Paul of Samosata, who taught that in the man Jesus there came to reside the power (*dynamis*) of God whereby he is designated "Son of God," his divinity an ascription of status or quality rather than an essential nature. (2) Modalistic monarchians, including Noetus, Praxeas, Callistus (according to Hippolytus), Beryllus, and Sabellius, who, noting that the dynamists had destroyed the doctrine of the full divinity of Jesus, maintained that of the Godhead, "Father," "Son," and "Spirit" were but descriptions of the successive modes or manifestations of God's coming to man, thus proclaiming the full divinity of Jesus, but doing so at the expense of individuality within the eternal God. As an answer to the plain man's fear of polytheism, modalistic monarchianism had immense popularity. The modalistic monarchians were called Sabellians and also Patripassians, from the logical conclusion of their doctrine that the Father suffered as the Son.

**Monarchy by Divine Right.** See DIVINE RIGHT OF KINGS.

**Monastic Architecture.** Since the chief feature of monastic architecture is its utility, its evolution has followed the course of the development of the monastic ideal. The first monks took refuge in caves or ruins, but as the monastic life became more popular, it was necessary to build huts or cells. These cells were gradually grouped in an arrangement called the "laura." The rise of cenobitic monasticism necessitated the construction of sufficient buildings for the use of the community —these buildings were usually built within a surrounding wall. The Rule of St. Benedict, the standard rule in the West for centuries, requires at least the following buildings: chapel, refectory, dorter, guesthouse, scriptorium, and infirmary. By the 9th century it had become the custom for the monastic buildings to be arranged around a central cloister. This has remained the basic plan for Western monasteries, although modifications are made for the particular requirements of the various monastic orders.

**Monasticism.** A word derived from the Greek *monazein,* "the act of dwelling alone." Monasticism is strictly applicable to the eremitical life, though in common usage it refers also to communal religious vocation.

1. *Factors encouraging its growth.* Literal acceptance of the Scriptural injunctions not to love the world; preparation for the immediate return of Christ; interpretation of such New Testament passages as Luke 9:23; Matt. 19:12; Gal. 6:14; I Cor., ch. 7; the example of the rich young ruler (Matt. 19:18–22) and of Christ. Extra-Christian influences may be seen in Neoplatonism and its renunciation of the flesh; in the end of persecutions ("red" martyrdom) by the state dur-

ing the 4th century, thereby encouraging the "white" martyrdom of asceticism; in the laxity of morality within the church as a result of the 4th-century mass conversions, against which monasticism was a witness. Earliest monasticism was a lay movement and somewhat anticlerical, being a protest against the increasing bureaucracy in the church and clerical domination.

2. *Monasticism in the fathers.* Ignatius already refers to virgins dwelling at Smyrna about A.D. 110; Justin Martyr pointed to Christian men and women who lived celibate lives, and they came from all classes of society (*Apology* 15.6); Hermas, Minucius Felix, Tertullian, Cyprian, and, above all, Origen, encouraged asceticism. These early ascetics observed special fasts, prayers, and vigils while they remained living at home. Athanasius (d. 373) was a friend of the Egyptian monks and introduced monasticism to the West (c. 340) while visiting Rome. Augustine devised a communal life for priests attached to his episcopal residence, thus anticipating the future chapter organization. Ambrose, although himself never a monk, was an enthusiastic supporter of the religious life; with few exceptions the fathers of the first four centuries were all in some way associated positively with monasticism. Later theologians, notably Thomas Aquinas, spoke of observing precepts and counsels. The former included all obligations binding every Christian without exception, including the Ten Commandments. The counsels were optional, part of the law of liberty, a means toward the end of *caritas,* the more perfect way. They are usually classified as poverty, chastity, and obedience, constituting the threefold vow popularly associated with monasticism, though few rules explicated all three, since it was understood that the religious life required observance of the counsels.

3. *Egyptian monasticism.* Paul of Thebes is traditionally considered the first Christian hermit (d. c. 340), but Antony of Egypt (d. 356) is called the father of monasticism. His importance lies as much in Athanasius' Life of Antony and its influence as in the deeds of Antony. He followed a type of eremitical life with no organization or rule. In this primitive form hermits usually lived in huts or caves in the desert, coming together for weekly worship. The first to organize the hermits along communal lines was Pachomius (d. 346), who built nine monasteries in which the monks were divided according to the various tasks they performed. He also wrote a rule, which comes to us through Jerome, in which the rigorous and austere nature of

Egyptian monasticism is reflected. Shenoute (d. c. 450), abbot of the White Monastery and leader of 2,200 monks and 1,800 nuns, introduced the written profession of obedience from each monk. Egyptian monasticism was characterized by some eccentricities. It was predominantly a lay movement, attracting numerous followers who often intervened in the ecclesiastical controversies of the day. It was more interested in personal sanctity and austere practices than in intellectual activity. The most important single primary source is Palladius' *Lausiac History* (c. 420).

4. *Origins of Eastern monasticism.* Hilarion (d. 371), the founder of the anchoritic life in Palestine, was strongly supported in this by Epiphanius of Salamis (d. 403). Eustathius of Sebaste (d. 377) is credited with influencing Basil of Caesarea (d. 379) toward monasticism. Basil, considered the father of Eastern monasticism, stressed the values of the communal over the anchorite life, since the former made possible the exercise of charity, patience, humility, and service. His Longer and Shorter Rules (Migne, *Patrologia Latina,* Vol. 31) have remained normative in Eastern monasticism. Jerome (d. 420), although a Latin theologian, spent thirty-five years in Bethlehem as a monk, encouraging the monastic vocation through his literary productions.

5. *Early Western monasticism.* Martin of Tours (d. 397) was the father of Gallican monasticism. Although he wrote no rule, following Egyptian practices instead, he popularized the religious life through his establishments at Ligugé and Marmoutier. Many of his monks became bishops and missionaries. Honoratus (d. 429) founded a house at Lérins, patterned on the Egyptian model, which became an influential theological center. Cassian (d. 435), who founded the Abbey of St.-Victor at Marseilles, is especially noted for his *Institutions,* on the general obligations of the monastic life, and *Conferences,* an account of three conversations with Egyptian solitaries. His writings have exercised a considerable influence in monastic history. Caesarius of Arles (d. 542) was the most influential monastic lawgiver in Gaul. Two of his rules are extant, one for men and one for women. He attached great importance to preaching and to the vow of stability.

6. *Celtic monasticism.* In general the Celtic monks observed the more primitive austerities associated with the Egyptian hermits. Ninian (d. c. 432), missionary to Scotland, founded Whithorn (Candida Casa), from which northern Britain was converted. Patrick (d. 461) is famous as the patron saint of Ireland. He

established his center at Armagh, which became the administrative and educational center of the Irish Church. In preaching, he aimed at the conversion of the tribal chiefs. Finnian (d. 550) "the wise" of Clonard is especially noted for his books of penitentials. Columba founded a monastery at Iona in 563 which became the center of mission activities for England and Scotland. Columbanus (d. 615) was one of the first Irish monks to evangelize the Continent. His introduction of Celtic practices there came into sharp conflict with the established Roman usages in Gaul. He also introduced the Continental Church to his rigorous rule. Celtic monasticism was based upon tribal organization; it encouraged study, fostered mission work, and formed the basis of Celtic ecclesiastical administration.

7. *Benedict of Nursia* (d. c. 544). The Rule of St. Benedict ultimately became the basis of monastic life in the West. It emphasized three occupations of the monk: (*a*) the *Opus Dei,* that is, the worship of God; (*b*) the *lectio divina,* spiritual reading for the personal edification of the monk; (*c*) *opus manuum,* the manual labor required of a self-sufficient community. Benedict modified Egyptian monasticism by stressing communal life, by discouraging excessive and flamboyant asceticism, and by insisting on the vow of stability. The Benedictine way of life became the norm for most Western houses until the 11th century.

8. *Ninth- and 10th-century reforms.* Benedict of Aniane (d. 821) succeeded in gaining imperial approval for the use of Benedict's Rule in all the monasteries of the Empire through the *Capitulare monasticum* enacted at Aachen in 817. He also made a collection of all known monastic rules, the *Codex regularum.* He advocated a return to the simplicity of Benedict's usages, although he discouraged agricultural labor by the monks, forbade them to teach any except oblates of the house, and added considerably to the daily prayer life. His *Concordia regularum* contains his own additions to the rule.

Three important monastic reformers emerged in England during the 10th century—Dunstan of Glastonbury (d. 988), Ethelwold of Abingdon (d. 984), and Oswald of Westbury (d. 992). From a meeting of ecclesiastics held at Winchester about 970 there came a comprehensive code for English monasteries known as the *Regularis concordia Anglicae monachorum sanctimonialiumque.* The king was acknowledged as the protector of the monasteries, abbatial elections were subject to royal consent, and the chief work of the monks was considered the liturgy of the church. The influence of Cluny is apparent in the latter emphasis.

In 910, Berno of Baume (d. 927) founded an abbey at Cluny which became the center of a reform movement and the motherhouse for over one thousand five hundred priories at the height of its development. Cluny's primary significance lay in its being an exempt order, and as such it was in a position to advocate the independence of the church from secular control. It was the first order since that of Pachomius with the abbot of Cluny exercising direct jurisdiction over every other house, although some houses were incorporated into the system with more flexible ties to the motherhouse. Cluny represented a return to the ideals of Benedict of Aniane, stressing prayer and liturgy, dispensing with the idea of manual labor for the monks. The order declined in the late Middle Ages, although the motherhouse survived until 1790.

9. *"Back to the desert" movements.* When the renewed austerity fostered by Cluny began to give way to more lax observances, there arose new monastic organizations given over especially to ascetical practices reminiscent of the early Egyptian forms. This movement was also a reaction to the influx of wealth into the church and too close an identification of existing houses with the feudal order. The "rightists" fled into remote regions to practice greater austerities, while the "leftists" became mendicants and practiced new forms of religious life in the cities. Examples of the former movement are: the Camaldolese, founded by Romuald of Camaldoli in 1012; the Vallombrosians, founded by John Gualbert in 1036; the Carthusians, founded by Bruno in 1084.

The most significant of these movements was the Cistercian Order founded by Robert of Molesme at Cîteaux in 1098. Their ideal was a return to the literal interpretation of the Rule of St. Benedict, cutting away excessive luxuries and building houses in remote areas to enable undivided concentration on worship, spiritual reading, and work. They introduced a system of lay brothers to farm their lands, or granges, thus emancipating the monks from feudal entanglements. The real founder of the order was Stephen Harding, abbot from 1109 to 1133. The Cistercian organization called for annual visitations of each monastery by its motherhouse, with the abbey at Cîteaux being visited by its four principal daughter houses. The decentralization of the order was carried farther by the authority given to the annual General Chapter. Because of their policy of seeking out remote areas for cultivation, the order contributed significantly to the internal development of Europe. In England and the Low Countries they were especially noted for raising sheep and producing wool. Bernard of Clairvaux (d. 1153), the most illustrious Cistercian, was influential in spreading the order's ideals, so that by his death there were over 340 houses scattered throughout Europe.

**Mongols.** An Asiatic people who under the rules of Genghis Khan (d. 1227) and Ogadai (d. 1241) established an empire from China to the Dnieper River. Pope Innocent IV sent two Franciscan friars, John of Plano Carpini and Lawrence of Portugal, to the court of the Kha Khan Guyuk (d. 1248) to seek an end to the Mongol incursions into eastern Europe. The embassy was unsuccessful and Guyuk contemptuously rejected the pope's plea that he be baptized.

The Mongol law code, the *Yasa,* prescribed religious toleration. Nestorians are known to have lived at the khan's court, and Guyuk left the conduct of state affairs to a Christian. In Russia, the Golden Horde respected the church. The first missionary effort was undertaken in 1253 by William of Rubruck and Bartholomew of Cremona. Under Kublai Khan's rule, an archbishopric in 1275 was created in Khanbalik (Peking), and with the arrival of John of Monte Corvino, soon after Kublai's death, a Catholic center was established. In 1307, Rome was given permission to consecrate the archbishop of Peking. The archbishopric lasted until 1369.

**Monk.** A term, derived from *monos* (Greek for "alone"), for a man who lives in a religious community under a rule and who has taken the vows of poverty, chastity, and obedience. In the East, the term is more freely applied than in the West, where it is used almost exclusively for members of orders of the Benedictine tradition. Members of orders of canons regular, regular clerks, or mendicants are not properly called monks.

**Monod, Adolphe** (1802–1856). French Protestant pastor. Born in Copenhagen and educated at Paris and Geneva, in 1825 he founded a Protestant church in Naples and two years later moved to Lyons, where his sermons on the duties of communicants led to his expulsion (1831). In 1836 he became a theological professor at Montauban and in 1847 he accepted the call as preacher at the Paris Oratory, where he remained until his death. He has been called the foremost French Protestant preacher in the 19th century.

**Monod, Frédéric** (1794–1863). French evangelical. He was born in Monnaz, Switzer-land, and educated in Geneva, where he came under the influence of Robert Haldane. In 1820 he became an assistant to his father in Paris and in 1832 pastor of the Paris Oratory. Known for his uncompromising Calvinist orthodoxy, he urged the separation of church and state and in 1849 (against his brother Adolphe's counsel) established a "free" Union of the Evangelical Churches of France after the General Synod of the Reformed Church in France had refused to become a creedal church.

**Monophysites.** Supporters of the doctrine that in Christ deity and humanity are fused into one entity, *physis.* The Greek word suggests the terminal result of growing personality, while the Latin *natura,* used as its technical equivalent, suggests the point of departure; this linguistic difference may in part account for the strength of the Monophysite tendency in Eastern Christendom and the predominance of the two-nature doctrine in the West.

From the first formulations of the apostolic fathers, orthodox theology has held that Christ is truly human and truly divine, yet at the same time a single being. Third-century disputes and discussions, however, were mainly concerned with the relation of the divine Son to the Father. In the 4th century the repudiation of Arianism, with its ambiguous Christ who is neither quite human nor quite divine, turned attention to the details of the doctrine of the incarnation, of the Word made flesh. Athanasius finds it natural to speak in New Testament language of the Word taking a human body (*sōma*), though it does seem that *sōma* meant for him most of what would later be described as the human nature of Christ. His terminology made it possible for Apollinarians to claim to be following his teaching and the Alexandrian tradition in their doctrine of a Christ in whom the divine Word took the place of the human spirit. From an Apollinarian work falsely ascribed to Athanasius came the phrase that was to become the watchword of Monophysitism: "one nature (*physis*) of the Incarnate Word." The Christology of Cyril of Alexandria moves along this line, and in the early 5th century Alexandrian theology stresses the unity of Christ even at the cost of obscuring his full humanity, while the Antiochene theology emphasizes his manhood even at the risk of seeming to divide his person. In the condemnation of Nestorius, Cyril enforced the doctrine of the inseparable union; the Formula of Union for which the Antiochenes secured his approval in 433 balanced this with the phrase "union of two natures." In 448, Eutyches was condemned at Constantinople for the extreme Monophysite position which asserted that there were two natures before the union but thereafter only one, and that Christ is thus not consubstantial with us in his humanity. The rehabilitation of Eutyches at the Robber Council of Ephesus in 449 was by implication a Monophysite victory. Two years later at Chalcedon, Rome and Constantinople combined to define the doctrine of a perfect union which is still "in two natures." Henceforward supporters of the Council of Chalcedon considered the Monophysite doctrine heretical, while for Monophysites, Chalcedon was a heretical assemblage that lapsed into Nestorianism.

For a century after Chalcedon, Monophysitism was both a theological movement and a strong party in the Eastern Church. Its theologians took up a more moderate position than that of Eutyches, asserting that Christ is fully human, but his humanity united with deity in "one nature." Indeed, careful Monophysites such as Severus of Antioch seem to differ from their Chalcedonian opponents only in wording and emphasis, whereas for others such as Julian of Halicarnassus the divine humanity is at some crucial points different from ours. The movement also has important political ramifications; the non-Greek parts of the Byzantine Empire were strongly Monophysite, Rome and the West, Chalcedonian, and Constantinople for a time torn between the two. The theological questions are genuine, but the partisan divisions clearly reflect national and cultural factors as well.

The apparent universal acceptance of Chalcedon soon turned out to be fallacious. On the death of the emperor Marcian (457), Timothy Aelurus, a Monophysite rival to the Chalcedonian patriarch Proterius, was set up at Alexandria, and the Monophysite party gained strength at Antioch. After the accession of the emperor Zeno (474) a usurper known as Basiliscus appealed to Monophysite support, allowing Timothy Aelurus to condemn Chalcedon at a Third Council of Ephesus. On suppressing the revolt, Zeno attempted a compromise; the Henoticon, issued in 482, stated the common doctrine and condemned those who had taught otherwise "at Chalcedon or any other synod." This was generally accepted in the East, though it led to the Acacian Schism with Rome—and on the other side extreme Monophysites demanded a formal anathema on Chalcedon. The next emperor, Anastasius (491–518), supported the Monophysites, who by the end of his reign were in possession of all the Eastern patriarchates. The situation is reminiscent of the apparent victory of Arianism under Constantius.

Conditions changed with the accession of Justin I, which brought ecclesiastical affairs under the influence of his nephew and heir, Justinian I. Chalcedonian patriarchs were installed at Constantinople and Antioch, and the Acacian Schism was ended in 519. Egypt could not be touched at first, but after a disputed election in 535, Justinian brought the patriarch Theodosius to Constantinople and installed a Chalcedonian rival at Alexandria. The Byzantine Church thus became finally Chalcedonian, as Greek Orthodoxy has since remained. For reasons still obscure, the empress Theodora was able to welcome Monophysite exiles at Constantinople—perhaps the emperor wished to keep under his eye the chiefs of what he hoped would be a dying party. In 541, however, Theodosius consecrated an adventurous monk, Jacob Baradai, as nominal bishop of Edessa but in fact with a roving commission to reconstitute the Monophysite party and renew its episcopate. Justinian's scheme of offering an olive branch to the Monophysites by condemning the Three Chapters was a total failure. After his death in 565 the double successions of patriarchs at Alexandria and Antioch were permanently established, marking the completion of the schism between Greek Orthodox and Oriental Monophysites.

The Monophysites were at least passive when the Persians invaded Syria and Egypt after the accession of Heraclius in 610. In consequence he attempted another compromise after his final defeat of the Persians in 628, offering the Monothelete doctrine of one will in Christ as a basis of reunion. This was acceptable to none, however; in Egypt especially the attempt of the patriarch Cyrus, who was also prefect, to secure the submission of the Copts seemed to them merely a Chalcedonian persecution. When the Arabs invaded Syria after 632 and Egypt after 639, they were welcomed by the Monophysites, who soon settled down fairly contentedly under Moslem rule.

The Monophysites are represented today by the Coptic Church of Egypt (with the Ethiopian Church, until recently dependent upon it) and by the Syrian Jacobites, so called by others with reference to their organizer (Jacob Baradai). In the Middle Ages the Jacobite Church was vigorous and learned. In modern times it has been less active, but since the 17th century a large section of the Syrian Christians of India have been attached to it. Their older connections were with the Nestorians of Iraq, but under Portuguese rule they were obliged to accept papal authority, which many of them repudiated in 1653. The Armenian Church is also in effect Monophysite. Being outside the Roman Empire in the 5th century, it was not involved in the early politicoreligious controversies, but it has never accepted the Council of Chalcedon, and its theologians do in general expound the doctrine of one nature.

The historical interest of Monophysitism is largely in its relation to the separation of the Oriental Churches, which has endured to the present day. However, the theological issue remains a genuine one for any theology committed to maintaining the full deity and full humanity of the one Christ. Now as in ancient times it remains a question whether theologians of the Monophysite confession differ only in language or more profoundly from those who accept the Chalcedonian definition. Perhaps the main achievement of the Council is that it remained content to proclaim a paradox attempting to resolve it.

BIBLIOGRAPHY: R. V. Sellars, *The Council of Chalcedon* (London, 1953); W. A. Wigram, *The Separation of the Monophysites* (London, 1923).

**Monotheletes.** Adherents of the doctrine that the human and divine wills in Christ were fused into one will (*thelēsis*)—a proposition obvious to Monophysites and attractive to some Chalcedonians of the school of Leontius of Byzantium. The idea was evidently in the air in the late 6th century, since it is repudiated in a Palm Sunday sermon by Eulogius, Chalcedonian patriarch of Alexandria from 581 to 607.

The term is commonly used, however, for the broader movement launched by the emperor Heraclius, the last of the imperial efforts to secure the loyalty of the Oriental provinces by a religious compromise (see ZENO; THREE CHAPTERS). During the Persian invasion that began in 610 the separated Oriental Christians, Monophysite and Nestorian, accepted or even welcomed the invaders. Heraclius recovered the lost provinces in a series of brilliant campaigns from 622 to 628. It seems that Armenian theologians suggested that the divided churches might be reconciled if less stress were placed on the question of one or two natures in Christ and the idea of one "operation," one "theandric energy," were emphasized instead. Supported by the patriarch Sergius (610–638) of Constantinople, Heraclius secured on this basis what a later Byzantine historian called a "watery union" with the Syrian Jacobite, the

Armenian, and the Nestorian Churches. The doctrine received a hesitant approval from Pope Honorius (the relation of this episode to papal authority is a delicate question) but was vigorously opposed by the patriarch Sophronius of Jerusalem. One of the originators of the movement, Bishop Cyrus of Colchis, was made prefect as well as patriarch in Egypt, and proclaimed the new doctrine in the Plerophoria, or Tome of Union, in 633. He failed to conciliate the Copts, to whom he seemed merely a Chalcedonian persecutor, and indeed alienated them further from the Empire by his attempts to force submission. In 638, Heraclius moderated his position in the Ecthesis, which confines itself to the Monothelete doctrine properly so called, of one will. By this time, however, the Moslems had already conquered Syria and Palestine (where the patriarch Sophronius had to receive the caliph Omar at Jerusalem), and Egypt was lost to them by 642.

The movement that no longer had a political reason continued as the imperial policy. In 647, Heraclius' grandson Constans attempted a compromise in the Type, ordering silence on the question of one or two wills or operations. By this time Chalcedonians were convinced that the full humanity of Christ must include a human will. In 649, Pope Martin I condemned the Type at a Lateran Council. He was seized by the Byzantine authorities who still controlled Rome and banished to the Crimea, where he died in 655, virtually a martyr, as was Maximus the Confessor seven years later. Finally, in conjunction with Pope Agatho, Constans' son and successor, Constantine IV, decided to bring the weary dispute to an end. After preliminary meetings at Rome, in one of which the English bishop Wilfrid of York took part, the Third Council of Constantinople (Sixth Ecumenical) met in 679 and 680. Its solid but verbose decisions proclaimed the existence of a true human will in Christ, though one always in harmony with the divine, and condemned Monothelete leaders, living and dead, including Sergius, Cyrus, and Honorius.

Though in some aspects the Monothelete controversy seems mainly political, and in others highly technical, it is not without significance. It came closer than any other of the ancient Christological disputes to raising the question of the human personality of Jesus, in the modern psychological sense, and the decision of 680 was based on the important principle that union with the divine did not deprive Jesus of any element of true humanity, but perfected it.

Every ancient heresy seems to have left some lingering trace. Isolated by the Moslem invasions, the Lebanese Christians who gathered around the monastery of St. John Maro remained loyal to Monotheletism until the 12th century. Brought into contact with the Latin Church by the crusaders, in 1181 they accepted not only the orthodox faith but papal authority, and so the Maronites became the first of the Eastern Catholic or Uniate Churches.

BIBLIOGRAPHY: I. A. Dorner, *History of the Development of the Doctrine of the Person of Christ,* 5 vols. (Edinburgh, 1872–1882).

**Montaigne, Michel Eyquem de** (1533–1592). The most famous literary figure in France in the second half of the 16th century. Educated in law, Montaigne spent his early years in politics, both as a councilor in the Bordeaux Parlement and at the court of France. In 1571, however, he retired to his family's castle for a life of contemplation and writing. Here he began his famous *Essays,* the first collection of which appeared in 1580. Although he spent some time traveling and was for four years mayor of Bordeaux, the rest of his life was devoted to this work, which he continually revised and expanded until his death. The *Essays* are unsystematic yet brilliant personal reflections of a man imbued with, though critical of, the spirit of his time, covering almost every important phase of human life and conduct. Though they are by no means doctrinaire in form or content, they generally combine a stringent Stoicism in morals and a skepticism about natural and metaphysical knowledge with a satirical but tolerant sense of humor. Though Montaigne, a conservative in religion and politics, was a confessed Roman Catholic, his *Essays* became a textbook for the Libertine movement in France in the early 17th century. Because of this, the *Essays* were condemned by the Roman Church.

**Montalembert, Charles** (1810–1870). Best known to non Roman Catholics as the author of *The Monks of the West* (*Les Moines d'occident,* 1860–1877), a very influential if impressionistic history of monasticism. Montalembert was (as were many historians of 19th-century France) active in the political life of the state and in the movement for reform in the church. He was early associated with Lamennais on *L'Avenir,* but he accepted the rebuke of *Mirari vos.* He represented his people for many years in the Chambre, where he continued to favor liberal programs even against the Second Empire. Although opposed to and by the ultramontanes, and although he disapproved of the Syllabus of Errors (he was not, however, a Gallican), he ultimately accepted the First Vatican Council.

**Montanus, Montanism.** Apocalyptic prophet of Phrygia and the movement that arose from his ascetic teachings. About the middle of the 2d century (c. 157) Montanus appeared in Phrygia, Asia Minor, proclaiming that as a representative prophet of the Paraclete (i.e., the Holy Spirit) he was about to bring the Christian church into the final stage of its revelation, namely, the age of the Paraclete. There is a tradition that prior to his conversion to Christianity, Montanus was a priest of Cybele, but the silence of the 2d-century sources on this matter lead to the conclusion that this idea was born in the antiheretical polemic of a later age. One of the features of the movement was the prominence of prophetesses. Maximilla and Priscilla (called Prisca by Tertullian) are the best known, and from a generation later we hear of one Quintilla. Speaking as representatives of the new prophecy, Montanus and his followers proclaimed in ecstatic language the proximity of the end of the world and called all who would hear to a more rigorous ethical life than that practiced in the orthodox church. Among their ethical demands were proscriptions against a second marriage and against flight from persecution. Part of their rigorism was a radical demand for more thoroughgoing rules of fasting. Their expectation of the end of the world included the arrival of the heavenly Jerusalem and the establishment of the Millennial Kingdom. Unfortunately, out of the numerous writings that Montanus must have produced, nothing seems to have survived save about a score of prophetic oracles which can with difficulty be reconstructed from Eusebius and Epiphanius with a modicum of help from Tertullian. In essence, Montanism represented a restoration of the eschatological fervor of the 1st century rather than an advance into a new stage for the church. It proved extremely difficult for the church to protect itself against this outburst not only from the eschatological standpoint but also from the ethical standpoint, since the church was just learning to employ the forms of thought peculiar to the classical world. Montanism soon spread all over Asia Minor and even to North Africa, Rome, and Gaul. The literature produced against Montanism was extensive, though not all of it is still extant. The movement was vehemently opposed by Apollinaris of Hierapolis, by Miltiades the rhetor of Asia Minor, and by Melito of Sardis, as well as by the Patripassian Praxeas. Eusebius quotes at great length from an anti-Montanist treatise addressed by an unnamed presbyter or bishop to one Avircius Marcellus (see ABERCIUS). The author may well have been Polycrates of Ephesus. There is also some evidence that Soter wrote a letter against the movement, and it appears that Eleutherus did the same. Later, Apollonius wrote opposing Montanus and then the Roman Gaius wrote the *Dialogue with Proclus the Montanist* during the time of Zephyrinus (d. 217).

The end of the first stage of Montanism was reached at the close of the 2d century. At this time the founder was dead and the arrival of the end of the world seemed farther off. During the early 3d century Montanism shifted its emphasis away from its prophetic preaching of the end of the world and put its stress upon its rigorist ethics. It was during this period (c. 207) that Tertullian was attracted to the movement and became an ardent adherent. For several decades this newly directed movement continued to harass the church as an ethical corrective to what appeared to the outsider or the discontent as laxity on the part of the orthodox. How long Montanism survived is not easy to determine, but it was apparently close to extinction by the end of the 3d or the beginning of the 4th century, when references to it in the legislation of the 4th-century church became sparse.

BIBLIOGRAPHY: A. Roberts and J. Donaldson (eds.), *The Ante-Nicene Fathers,* Vols. 3–4 (Grand Rapids, 1951); J. de Soyres, *Montanism and the Primitive Church* (Cambridge, 1878); B. B. Warfield, *Studies in Tertullian and Augustine* (New York, 1930).

**Monte Cassino.** A monastery founded c. 529 halfway between Rome and Naples by Benedict, which became the center of Western monasticism. It was razed in 585 by the Lombards, forcing the monks to flee to Rome. Rebuilt in 720, it was destroyed again in 884 by the Saracens and in 1046 by the Normans. A new abbey was dedicated in 1071. Demolished during World War II, though many treasures were saved, the abbey has been rebuilt and remains the chief house of the Benedictine Order. Benedict and his sister Scholastica are buried there.

**Montes Pietatis.** Credit institutions to aid the poor, established in the 15th century by the Franciscans in the struggle against usury. In 1462 the first "bank of pity (or piety)" was founded at Perugia, Italy, resulting from the preaching of Michele Carcano, who inveighed against the exorbitant current rates of interest (up to 60 percent). From this beginning, *montes* were established throughout Italy, France, and Germany, although their existence was controverted until they were approved by a papal bull of 1515.

**Montesquieu, Charles Louis Joseph de Secondat, Baron de la Brède et de** (1689–1755). French philosophical historian. He was born at Bordeaux and educated by the Oratorians at Juilly and Bordeaux. In 1713 he married Jeanne Lartique, a Protestant heiress, and in the following year he became a councilor in the Parlement of Bordeaux. In 1721 he published anonymously his *Lettres persanes.* In the guise of letters written by and to two Persians of distinction, he satirized unmercifully the social, political, and ecclesiastical follies of his age. The *Lettres* criticized the Catholic Church, ridiculing the dogmas of transubstantiation and the Trinity, and accusing the church of many crimes. In 1748 he published his most important work, *L'Ésprit des lois.* This book, which deals with law, government, manners and customs, economics, and religion, was essentially a defense of the English principle of the division of powers as the safeguard of liberty. The spirit of moderation that characterized his views is apparent in his more positive attitude toward religion. He attacked clerical celibacy and doctrinal intolerance, but he viewed Christianity as a powerful moral force in society, making for order and happiness. The book, placed on the Index in 1752, had a profound effect on European and American history.

**Montgomery, James** (1771–1854). English poet and journalist. Educated at the Moravian center of Fulneck in England, he became editor of the *Sheffield Iris* and was engaged in the affairs of this newspaper until it passed into other hands in 1825. His chief interest was poetry and he was esteemed as a popular but not eminent poet. He wrote many hymns, including "Go to Dark Gethsemane," "Angels, from the Realms of Glory," and "O Spirit of the Living God."

**Mont-St.-Michel.** The "mount in peril of the sea," a small granitic outcropping separated from the shore of Normandy at high tide, which has drawn pilgrims ever since the 8th century. The Norman dukes introduced the Benedictine monks in the 10th century and assisted in the construction of a shrine, but the great Gothic monastery of the French king Philip Augustus, known as La Merveille, has come to dominate the mount.

**Moody, Dwight Lyman** (1837–1899). American revivalist and founder of Moody Church and Moody Bible Institute of Chicago.

Like many revivalists, Moody was born on a farm. His birthplace was in an area (Northfield, Mass.) which he later much admired for its beauty and near which he founded a preparatory school for girls (1879) and one for boys (1881). When he was a boy, however, he was anxious to leave the farm for the more exciting city. He became an employee in his uncle's shoe store in Boston in 1854 with the understanding that he keep good company and attend his uncle's church regularly. Moody's Sunday school teacher visited him at the store and persuaded him to repent of his sins and join the church. His conversion experience was completely matter-of-fact. By 1856, Moody had tired of Boston and set out for Chicago, where, working in another shoe store, he set himself the goal of earning $100,000. Even though he later abandoned the idea, he never lost the entrepreneurial spirit of those earlier days.

Revivalism became a large-scale corporate enterprise in Moody's hands. He did not become a revivalist immediately, however. He began a Sunday school of his own in a neglected part of Chicago's north side. Financing it in a way typical of his methods, he sold 40,000 twenty-five-cent shares of stock in his enterprise to raise the money for expenses. He soon had hundreds of children coming regularly. A church grew out of this movement which eventually became the Moody Memorial Church. Moody served as its first pastor, although he had had no theological training and was never ordained. He also became involved in the Chicago Y.M.C.A., and during the Civil War gave a great deal of his time to the United States Christian Commission. By 1860 he was forced to make a choice between his two interests—becoming a wealthy tycoon or a lay preacher. Again like a shrewd businessman, Moody calculated that he could live for seven years on his savings and trust God after that. His work with the Sunday school, church, Y.M.C.A., and guest speaking engagements kept him busy until the Chicago fire of 1871 brought all his enterprises to a halt.

While waiting for new buildings to rise, Moody decided to accept an invitation to preach in England. Although he had crossed the Atlantic several times previously, Moody was virtually unknown in Britain. When he arrived in Liverpool with his chorister, Ira Sankey, he discovered that his sponsor had died. However, he managed to get an invitation to the north of England, and, after several months, was invited to hold a revival campaign in Edinburgh. The meetings were a success. Moody's stay was prolonged for two years; he and Sankey preached and sang in Glasgow, Dundee, Belfast, Dublin, Manchester, Sheffield, Birmingham, Liverpool, and (for five months) London. As was true also of his American revivals, Moody's triumph in Britain was more than a personal one. During his life Moody became fast friends with an astonishing variety of people, and very few who ever met him failed to like him.

There was more to Moody's success than a winning personality, however. Conservative Christians in both Britain and the United States were beginning to draw together in fear of growing criticism of traditional Christianity —especially from Biblical criticism. Because his message was nontheological, nondenominational, conservative, and popular, these people could unite in their support of Moody and, for a little while at least, forget about the enemies of the church. During his life Moody made a sincere effort to keep all parties in the church working together in a program of evangelism, but the outbreak of the fundamentalist controversy after his death marked the defeat of his policy. When he returned to America in 1875, Moody was besieged by offers to conduct revivals, offers that he continued to fill for twenty-five years until he died while returning from his last revival in Kansas City. His activities were not limited to these meetings. Toward the end of his life he spent much time building up the three schools that he had founded—two in Northfield and the Bible Institute in Chicago. He also held conferences in Northfield during the summer to which he invited young people to hear a great variety of Christian leaders. It was at one of these meetings that the Student Volunteer Movement for Foreign Missions was born.

BIBLIOGRAPHY: W. H. Daniels, *Moody: His Words, Work, and Workers* (New York, 1877); W. G. McLoughlin, *Modern Revivalism* (New York, 1959); W. R. Moody, *The Life of Dwight L. Moody* (New York, 1930).

**Moors.** See ISLAM IN MEDIEVAL SPAIN.

**Morais, Sabato** (1823–1897). Rabbi. Born in Italy of Portuguese parents, he came to Philadelphia in 1851 to serve a congregation. In opposition to current liberal tendencies he founded Jewish Theological Seminary, New York, in 1886 as a bulwark of traditional Judaism. He was an ardent abolitionist and for his work received many honors that no American Jew had ever received before.

**Morality Plays.** Medieval religious dramas related to the miracle and mystery plays. They were so named because the characters were personifications of vices or virtues. Their purpose was the inculcation of moral truths. The most famous of these plays is *Everyman,* which dates from the 15th century and is of Dutch origin. In it, Death summons Everyman, who is abandoned by Knowledge, Kindred, Strength, etc., and sustained only by Good Deeds.

**Moral Re-Armament.** A movement begun by the American Lutheran pastor Frank N. D. Buchman (1878–1961) about 1921. Influenced by Schwenkfelders, Keswick piety, and the Y.M.C.A., Buchman considered the movement as a quest for renewal within denominations. It passed through several phases: (1) Buchmanism, organized chiefly for "soul surgery" among college students and workers in religious organizations; (2) A First Century Christian Fellowship, about 1930, involving prominent young adults; (3) Moral Re-Armament, in 1938, at which time Buchman turned his attention to preparing democracy for the struggle against dialectical materialism, particularly. Known also as the Oxford Group (c. 1930), members carry on "house parties" for the purpose of "sharing" sins and temptations, for "surrender" to God's "guidance," for "life-changing," which includes "restitution" to all whom members have wronged. Members' lives must be marked by the "Four Absolutes" of honesty, purity, unselfishness, and love. Attempts to begin "at the top" with the very important people, and the use of testimonials and advertising techniques, have tended to curb otherwise inclusive characteristics. Since World War II, attempts have been made to capture the older enthusiasm and to keep democratic ideology alive, particularly at international centers, e.g., Caux-sur-Montreux in Switzerland and Mackinac Island in the United States.

**Moravians.** A Protestant church that traces its beginning back to the Hussites of the 15th century. There is a sense in which the Moravians were the first Protestants. They also led the modern missionary movement and two centuries ago raised a lonely voice on behalf of church union.

After the death of John Hus those who followed his teachings organized the Unitas Fratrum. This has remained the official name of the church down to the present day, although the term "Moravian" came to be more widely used during the 18th century. The early leaders of the Unity received ordination from a Waldensian and thus claimed apostolic succession through that group. Their beliefs were simple, including a strong emphasis on Scripture, a modified emphasis on politics, and a preference for pacifism. The medieval church did not look kindly upon groups that divided from it and the Moravians therefore experienced severe persecution.

Brother Luke, who joined the group in 1482 and later became a bishop, entered into correspondence with Erasmus and Bucer, and they helped the mainstream of 16th-century Christianity to know more about the Moravians. Luther clarified his own evangelical position through a study of Moravian confessions. During the 16th century the Unitas Fratrum spread beyond Bohemia and Moravia into Poland, East Prussia, and Hungary. They also came under the influence of Calvin's theology. The intolerance of the Thirty Years' War (1618–1648) fell heavily upon the Moravians, and their organization was crushed in Bohemia and Moravia. Some of the congregations continued in other parts of Europe under the leadership of John Amos Comenius (1592–1670).

In 1722, however, a revival in the fortunes of the Moravians occurred. A group of refugees from Moravia found asylum on the estate of Count Nicholas Ludwig von Zinzendorf, naming their location Herrnhut. Besides the Unity, other German Pietist groups found refuge there, and the Moravians adopted many of their views. They established not only a spiritual community but also industries and trading enterprises. Centers similar to Herrnhut were founded in England and America. Within a decade Zinzendorf's estate became the vital center for the inauguration of the modern missionary movement. The Moravians sent evangelists to Greenland, North and South America, and Africa. This vigorous missionary activity has caused the Moravian Church to become in our day a global operation despite its small number.

The Moravian Church is found in the following countries: Great Britain, Czechoslovakia, Germany, Holland, Switzerland, Denmark, Sweden, Tanzania, South Africa, West Indies, Guyana, Surinam, Labrador, United States (Northern and Southern Provinces). A conferential form of government is used, with provincial synods preceding Unity synods. The ministry is by apostolic succession and consists of bishops, presbyters, and deacons. The church has a liturgical service rich in music and hymnology. In colonial America at a time when most Protestant groups paid little attention to music the Moravians made outstanding contributions.

The modern Moravian Church has shied away from confessions but the cardinal points of doctrine may be found in its catechism, Easter litany, and the published results of the

General Synod. The Scriptures are regarded as the only guide for faith and practice. The following evangelical doctrines are among those held by the church: the depravity of man, the love of God, the Trinity, justification by faith, good works as the fruit of salvation, the Second Coming of Christ, and the resurrection of the dead to eternal rewards. The churches still observe the love feast (services of worship at which a meal is eaten), but they have abandoned communal societies, pacifism, the use of the lot, and austere dress. The denomination has continued the ecumenical zeal of such men as Comenius and Zinzendorf, who tried to achieve a union between the different groups of Protestants. The church was one of the founders of both the National Council of Churches and the World Council of Churches. In North America there are 180 congregations of Moravians with more than 66,000 members. The world total is 625 churches and 361,000 members.

BIBLIOGRAPHY: W. H. Allen, *The Moravians: A World-wide Fellowship* (Bethlehem, Pa., 1940); A. L. Fries, *Customs and Practices of the Moravian Church* (Bethlehem, Pa., 1949); J. E. Hutton, *A History of Moravian Missions* (London, 1923); E. Langton, *History of the Moravian Church* (London, 1956); A. J. Lewis, *Zinzendorf: The Ecumenical Pioneer* (Philadelphia, 1962); J. R. Weinlick, *Count Zinzendorf* (Nashville, 1956).

**More, Hannah** (1745–1833). English political propagandist, religious writer, and practical philanthropist. Early in her life, she came to know many of the great men of her generation, living often with the David Garricks, and meeting Samuel Johnson, Edmund Burke, Horace Walpole, and others. The decade immediately prior to the outbreak of the French Revolution proved to be the critical one in the development of her character. Garrick's death in 1779 opened this period, which saw her interests turn toward the evangelical activities of the Clapham Sect and away from the theater and secular letters. She and her sisters started a chain of Sunday schools in the west of England in which the poor were taught to read. True to her "evangelical Toryism," however, such instruction was designed in part to make the poor content with their lot in life, and prevent them from becoming social revolutionaries. This was patently the case with a series of popular pamphlets she composed during the period of the French Revolution and which the British government saw fit to subsidize. *Village Politics* was designed for those who would not read Burke but might be influenced by Paine. Her religious writings, such as *Practical Piety, The Spirit of Prayer,* and *Moral Sketches,* were very popular.

**More, Henry** (1614–1687). Early latitudinarian and Cambridge Platonist. Henry More is perhaps the most studied and the best known of this school. Born at Grantham of a gentleman's family, he spent his life in comparative quietude and contemplation at Cambridge, scarcely touched by the troubled times of the Civil War and its aftermath. At Eton he was a serious boy and early showed his preoccupation with philosophical questions. He rejected Calvinism while his peers were playing games in the fields. In 1631, More, "a tall thin youth with olive complexion and rapt expression," entered Christ's College, Cambridge, where he found congenial companionship with Benjamin Whichcote, Joseph Mede, and John Smith. He took his B.A. in 1635 and became a fellow in 1639, being ordained priest in that same year, though he never preached, believing that he could do more with the pen. He immersed himself in Aristotle, Plato, and Scaliger and early showed promise of reflective genius. Courtly, though for the most part a recluse, he shunned preferments, turning down the deanship of his college, a provostship, and two bishoprics. With the exception of trips to Ragley, he lived almost entirely within the walls of his college.

As a theologian and a philosopher, More sought to counteract the rising influence of Thomas Hobbes and wrote an "antidote against atheism." He was consistently antimaterialist and the most "mystical" of the Cambridge Platonists, finding in the Platonic and Neoplatonic tradition the remedy for skepticism. However, his writings also reveal strange superstitions and oddities.

**More, Sir Thomas** (1478–1535). English scholar, lawyer, and statesman who contributed heavily to the humanist movement in England. In many ways More was the embodiment of the most desirable characteristics of both the Italian and the northern European Renaissance. Born in London, he was educated at Oxford and the Inns of Court. His contributions to humanism were made mostly before 1516, after which time royal service and religious controversy began to claim his attention. During this early period he associated with some of the greatest humanist scholars of that day, including John Colet and Erasmus. More exercised considerable influence on Erasmus, and the great Dutch scholar dedicated his famous *Praise of Folly (Encomium moriae)* to More. More's greatest literary work was his *Utopia*. Published in 1516, the book has been variously interpreted, often according to confessional loyalty or political ideology. One view is that he was writing as a Christian humanist, using *Utopia* to satirize 16th-century English society. After 1516 his political star rose rapidly and in 1529 he became lord chancellor. However, he lost royal favor when he declined to approve the annulment of Henry VIII's marriage to Catherine of Aragon. Then in 1534, during the crisis of the English Reformation, he refused to accept royal supremacy in matters of religion, was charged with and found guilty of high treason, and beheaded on July 6, 1535. More was canonized in 1935 by Pope Pius XI.

**Morin, Jean** (1591–1659). One of the most learned French Roman Catholic authors of the 17th century. He was born of Calvinist parents, but became a convert to Roman Catholicism and in 1618 entered the Oratory in Paris. From this center he engaged in many controversies and sought to bring Jews and Protestants to Roman Catholicism. He was noted for his studies of Scripture and Oriental languages, and wrote also on theological and historical subjects. Summoned to Rome by Urban VIII to prepare for union negotiations with the Greek Church (1639–1640), Morin advocated recognition of orthodox ordination.

**Mormonism.** The doctrine and practice of the American religious movement founded by Joseph Smith in 1830 which is known officially as The Church of Jesus Christ of Latter-day Saints. In 1962 there were five groups of Latter-day Saints in the United States. The Reorganized Church with its headquarters in Independence, Mo., reported a membership of 155,291. The main group of Mormons, centered around the headquarters in Salt Lake City, Utah, reported a membership of 1,486,-887. The other three Mormon splinter groups are quite small.

All Mormons trace their origins to Joseph Smith, who discovered and translated the Book of Mormon from golden plates and organized the church around this inspired book and his own revelations from God. The Book of Mormon, which Mormons place on a par with the Bible, is divided into fourteen books and covers a period from 600 B.C. to A.D. 400. It describes the way in which several groups of Israelites during the 6th century B.C. crossed the Atlantic; some of them became the ancestors of the American Indians. The book teaches that Christ appeared to these people after his resurrection and established the Christian church on this continent.

The inhabitants of America, after living for centuries as Christians, turned away from the gospel and, as a punishment, lost their knowledge of the faith. This history survived only because it was written on the golden plates and buried until the angel Moroni revealed them to Joseph Smith. Such explanations of the origin of the Indians were quite common in the United States about 1800, and did not constitute the most radical part of the book. Within the historical framework of the narrative there lay a theme of the struggle of good and evil handled in such a way that almost every issue of consequence in New York in the 1820's was discussed and decided. Some critics have argued that the Book of Mormon could not have been written anywhere but in New York and at no other time than the third decade of the 19th century. This is a serious charge if, as the Mormons claim, the book was not written by Joseph Smith but merely translated from the writing on the plates. Whatever the validity of the criticism, it is obvious that the book appealed to thousands of Americans because it did provide answers to the great religious dilemmas of the day. In this sense, Mormonism is one of the most typical American religious movements of the 19th century. Like many others, Mormons looked to an infallible book as their final religious authority. Smith and his followers stressed the role of human freedom in deciding man's fate, just as the Methodists and the Baptists did. The Mormons felt a great need to restore Christianity to its apostolic simplicity and to heal the divisions between denominations. In this regard the Mormons very much resembled the Disciples of Christ, from whom many early converts to Mormonism were drawn. Furthermore, the Mormons looked for a speedy culmination of world history and the coming of the millennium. No note was more characteristic of this era. Like most American denominations, the Mormons expected the Kingdom of God to be established in the United States. Lastly, in common with dozens of other groups, the Mormons believed in a community ideal, a type of utopian socialism, in which all individual drives were directed toward the goal sought by the community, not the individual.

The Mormon faith was spread around New York and Ohio by itinerant missionaries. Two former Disciples' ministers, Parley Pratt and Sidney Rigdon, were especially successful in winning converts in Ohio. In 1831 these men persuaded Smith to move to Kirtland, Ohio, where the church prospered and became better organized. W. W. Phelps, a newspaper editor, assisted Smith with polishing and correcting the Book of Mormon and some of his other writings. Pratt and Rigdon compiled a Book of Doctrine and Covenants which did a great deal to clarify Mormon beliefs. All resources were placed in the hands of Smith, who set about constructing an ideal community, but these schemes ended disastrously when leaders of the church set up an illegal bank to provide themselves with badly needed cash. In the panic of 1837, this shaky institution collapsed and many of the Mormons turned on Smith and his circle of assistants. These few fled to Missouri, where another Mormon settlement had been established, but found no rest there either. The church was driven from three successive counties because of the antagonism of the "gentiles," the Mormon name for non-Mormons. Some of this antagonism was merited: Mormons frequently boasted that they would soon possess the whole state. However, nothing in Mormon conduct and belief justified the ruthless attacks launched against them with the consent of the governor of Missouri.

In Nauvoo, Ill., the next site of the Mormon Zion, the story was repeated. A new city was laid out (Smith was adept at town planning) and converts gathered. By 1843, Nauvoo was the largest city in Illinois. But gentiles in the surrounding country refused to tolerate the existence of the community. Their grievances centered upon Mormon political activity and polygamy. Joseph Smith controlled all votes within the Mormon community just as he controlled the finances. His use of these votes as a bloc to gain favors for his church was deeply resented by many. Just when things were becoming critical in Mormon-gentile relations, rumors began to spread that polygamy had been introduced into Mormonism. An armed mob marched on Nauvoo, Smith was taken to jail in Carthage, Ill., and a few hours later, June 27, 1844, shot in his cell by a group of masked gunmen. This marked the greatest crisis in Mormon history—their divinely inspired leader was dead, their own lives in danger, and their future in any settled community seemingly an impossibility.

In these circumstances there was much uncertainty. Most of the divisions within the Mormon Church date from this time. Many people united around Brigham Young and set out on a march across the Great Plains to the Great Salt Basin. At this point in Mormon history, Mormon ingenuity in providing for their needs, courage in the face of hardship, discipline and faith in the midst of enormous obstacles are impressive. The first contingent of thousands that were to cross the mountains in the next few years reached Utah

in 1847; by the date of Brigham Young's death in 1877 over 140,000 Mormons had settled in the Utah territory. Many of these settlers came from Europe, especially England and Scandinavia. Mormon missionaries had been sent abroad as early as the 1830's. Converts were put on well-run ships, brought up the Mississippi to St. Louis, and then taken overland to Salt Lake. Toward the end of his life, Joseph Smith had a series of revelations, of which polygamous marriage was only one, which separated Mormons theologically from American Protestantism. Instead of becoming something of a composite of many of the evangelical frontier faiths, Mormonism was turned by Smith into a cult quite separate from Christianity and he formulated a set of temple ceremonies to celebrate these doctrines. Smith taught that there was more than one God and that man could himself become a god. He also taught that the relationships and acquisitions of this life would be retained in the next. It was at this point that he introduced polygamy. Not many of the Mormons themselves seem to have welcomed the doctrine. In Nauvoo there was much resentment over it. After the trek to Utah, polygamy reappeared as a Mormon tenet and caused the isolation of their Utah existence to be broken again by interference—this time from the Federal Government. Because Mormons lived as a community and not simply as members of a church, they had always tended to create a state within a state. In Utah they nearly became a separate nationality. With the coming of the railroad and the California gold rush, Americans generally began to notice them again. Brigham Young was made the governor of the Utah territory in 1851, but was replaced in 1857 and 2,500 soldiers were sent to maintain order. A "war" almost resulted, but Mormon leaders decided on a policy of compromise after sporadic fighting. This brought to an end a good deal of Mormon independence. In 1862 an antibigamy law was passed and another more stringent measure in 1882. In the meanwhile, the Supreme Court had ruled in 1879 that a claim to religious freedom was not sufficient grounds for the practice of polygamy. Mormon authorities held out for many years, but in 1890, with the accession of a new Mormon leader, the group gave up the practice.

BIBLIOGRAPHY: N. Anderson, *Desert Saints* (Chicago, 1966); N. F. Furniss, *The Mormon Conflict: 1850–1859* (New Haven, 1960); W. A. Linn, *The Story of the Mormons* (New York, 1963); W. Mulder, *Homeward to Zion* (Minneapolis, 1957); T. F. O'Dea, *The Mormons* (Chicago, 1957); R. B. West, *The King-*

*dom of the Saints* (New York, 1957); K. Young, *Isn't One Wife Enough?* (New York, 1954).

**Morone, Giovanni** (1509–1580). Papal diplomat. A native of Milan, Morone studied for the priesthood at Padua and was nominated bishop of Modena in 1529. He was appointed nuncio to Germany and attended the conferences at Hagenau (1540), Regensburg (1541), and Speyer (1542). In 1542 he was appointed cardinal legate to Trent, and in 1544, to Bologna. From 1553 to 1560 he was bishop of Novara. With Beccadelli, Lainez, and Nadal he attended the 1555 Diet of Augsburg. Though a loyal son of the Roman Church, Morone was sympathetic to the cause of reform. Overzealous Pope Paul IV imprisoned him for heresy (1557–1559), but after Paul's death he was released. In 1563 he was appointed president of the Council of Trent and guided it to a successful conclusion. He served on the commission for the improvement of the Vulgate text of the Bible, became bishop of Ostia in 1570, and was legate to the Diet of Regensburg in 1576. He died at Rome in 1580.

**Morrison, Robert** (1782–1834). English pioneer missionary to China. The son of James Morrison, he was born at Buller's Green, Morpeth, in Northumberland. He was taught reading and writing by an uncle and apprenticed to his father as a last and boot-tree maker. He joined the Presbyterian Church in 1798. He attended Hoxton Academy (Highbury College) and Missionary Academy at Gosport. In 1805 he went to London to study medicine and astronomy and to learn Chinese. He made transcripts of manuscripts in the language. Soon after his ordination on Jan. 8, 1807, he embarked for Canton.

Morrison was, for a period, the sole Protestant missionary in Canton, where he maintained himself as translator for the East India Company. In 1817 he accompanied Lord Amherst to Peking as interpreter, and in the same year was made D.D. by the University of Glasgow. In 1818 he established the Anglo-Chinese College at Malacca for training missionaries to the Far East.

In 1824 he returned to England with a large Chinese library, ultimately bequeathed to the University College, and interested himself in the Language Institution in Bartlett's Buildings, London. In 1826 he returned to Canton, where he died Aug. 1, 1834. He had two children by his first marriage, five by his second.

He wrote voluminously in English and Chinese. His *Dictionary of the Chinese Language* appeared in 1815–1823. He published a Chinese grammar and several treatises on language. His important work was a Chinese translation of the Bible published in twenty-one volumes in 1823. He also translated hymns and the prayer book and wrote numerous tracts and serial publications.

**Morse, Jedidiah** (1761–1826). Congregational clergyman and early American historian, best known for his geographical studies. As an orthodox Federalist foe of "the overbearing influence of Republicanism," Morse felt that the New England clergy formed "a kind of aristocratical balance" against Jeffersonian dangers. His vehement opposition to early Unitarianism led him to found the *Panoplist* (1805), a periodical he edited for five years, and to assist in establishing Andover Seminary. Morse also helped organize the American Bible Society, and in 1822 he submitted the important *Report to the Secretary of War . . . on Indian Affairs.* Samuel B. Morse, the inventor of the telegraph, was his son.

***Mortalium Animos.*** Encyclical issued on Jan. 6, 1928, by Pius XI on principles of religious unity among Christians. It warns against methods of restoring Christian unity advocated by non-Roman Christians and condemns the belief that all religions are good. It restates the Roman doctrine of the church as a perfect, visible society, under one head, infallible in its teaching and having divine promises of perpetual duration, and incompatible with attempts toward church reunion that would place Rome on a par with other denominations.

**Mortmain** ("dead hand"). A legal term referring to the inalienable possession of land held in perpetuity by an ecclesiastical or charitable corporation. Such lands cannot legally be sold, even if the religious corporation no longer uses them. Through laws of mortmain, the church in time acquired large quantities of property. Such perpetual ownership of land by any corporation is now strictly limited by statute or forbidden altogether.

**Moscow Conference** (July 8–18, 1948). A conference highlighting the five hundredth anniversary of the autocephalicity of the Russian Orthodox Church. It brought together the heads or representatives of ten autocephalous Orthodox Churches, plus the catholicos of all the Armenians (an honorary guest). The following problems were discussed at length and pronounced upon: sources of tension between the Vatican and the Orthodox Church, the validity of Anglican Orders, calendrical variations within Orthodoxy, and Orthodox involvement in the ecumenical movement.

**Moscow Council** (1666–1667). Russian Orthodox Church Council which sought to bring to an end the struggle that had raged between Czar Alexis (1645–1676) and Patriarch Nikon (1652–1666). This had begun as a liturgical reform but had grown into a struggle over state and church relationships. Advised by Patriarch Paisius Ligaridis, a Greek, the czar submitted the case to the review of the four Eastern patriarchs, who returned only a conditional condemnation. The czar then requested the four Eastern patriarchs to come to Moscow to sit in judgment on Patriarch Nikon. However, only the patriarchs of Antioch (Macarius) and of Alexandria (Paisius) arrived to attend the Council which met in November and December, 1666. The Council proceeded to excommunicate the Old Believers who had opposed Patriarch Nikon's reforms and then deposed the patriarch himself on Dec. 12, 1666. The much venerated Council of the Hundred Chapters (1551) was declared nonauthoritative because it was alleged to have been composed of ignorant men. Finally, the Moscow Council established three new bishoprics in Siberia at Tobolsk, Tomsk, and on the Lena River, and forbade the rebaptism of Latins joining the Orthodox Church. In the year 1667, Joseph, the archimandrite of the Troitskii-Sergeievskaja Laura, was elected to succeed Patriarch Nikon. Many of the faithful felt that the Council had "abolished the ancient faith of the fathers and established the impious heterodoxy of Rome." Schism within Russian Orthodoxy was the inevitable result of the decisions of the Moscow Council. On the eve of the Bolshevik Revolution (1918), about one sixth of the population was found within the fold of the Old Believers.

**Moses of Chorene** (5th century). Armenian scholar. Thought to have been a nephew of Mesrob, he was the author of the history of Armenia to the death of Mesrob in 440, the only native source for the pre-Christian period of the country. Moses wrote a revision of the geography of Pappus. Other works attributed to him are a homily on the transfiguration of Christ, a treatise on rhetoric, and a collection of hymns used in the Armenian liturgy.

**Mosheim, Johann Lorenz von** (1694–1755). German Lutheran church historian. He is generally recognized as the father of modern church history. Educated at Kiel, he taught at Helmstedt for most of his career, moving to Göttingen in 1747. His classic work is the *Institutiones historiae ecclesiasticae* (1726) in which, largely under the influence of both Pietism and the Enlightenment, Mosheim looked upon the church as essentially an association of voluntary character. For more than a century his work was to stand as basic in its field.

**Mott, John Raleigh** (1865–1955). American churchman and Nobel Prize winner. A graduate of Cornell University in 1888, Mott became chairman of the Executive Committee of the Student Volunteer Movement for Foreign Missions, a post he held until 1920. He was also secretary of the International Committee of the Y.M.C.A. until 1931. In 1895 with Karl Fries of Sweden he organized the World Student Christian Federation and acted as its general secretary and chairman until 1928. In 1910 he presided at the World Missionary Conference at Edinburgh and was chairman of its Continuation Committee to 1920, at which time he became chairman of its successor, the International Missionary Council, until 1942. Mott played a leading role in organizing Christian youth and forming student movements throughout the world, but particularly in the Far East. For his welfare work among troops and prisoners of war during World War II, he received the U.S. Distinguished Service Medal. With E. G. Balch, Mott was co-winner of the Nobel Peace Prize in 1946 for his participation in world church and missionary movements. In 1948 he was made an honorary president of the World Council of Churches. Mott wrote many books, including *Liberating the Lay Forces of Christianity* (1932), *Five Decades and a Forward View* (1939), and *The Larger Evangelism* (1944).

**Mountain, Jacob** (1749–1825). Founder of the Anglican Church in Canada. Born at Thwaite Hall, Norfolk, England, he was educated at Caius College, Cambridge (B.A., 1774; M.A., 1777; D.D., 1793), and elected a fellow there in 1779. In 1793 he was appointed first Protestant bishop of Quebec, with jurisdiction over the Anglican Church in both Upper and Lower Canada. He married Elizabeth Wale Kentish in 1783 and they had five sons and two daughters. Three of his sons became clergymen and his second son, George Jehoshaphat, became bishop of Quebec in 1850.

**Mt. Athos.** Holy mountain of the Eastern Orthodox Church, center of monasticism. Mt. Athos is in reality a range of mountains on a peninsula stretching thirty miles southeast from Greece into the Aegean. The peninsula is ten miles across at its widest point, and the highest peak has an altitude of 6,670 feet.

Athos had been populated since pre-Christian days, but it was not until the 9th century that the first authenticated hermit of the mount, Peter the Athonite, came there to dwell in solitude, remaining for fifty years. By the time of his death, the first monastery, Klementos, had been established. In the 900's, Athanasios, member of a wealthy family, came to Mt. Athos to live a peasant's life alone, but Nicephoros Phocas, emperor to be and friend of Athanasios, furnished money and support for the building of the Great Lavra (963), which initially housed eighty monks. By this time, numerous communities as well as solitary monks had been loosely organized under a leader (*prōtos*), and in 972, a permanent capital was established at Karyai. Athanasios constructed harbors and buildings, and changed the pattern of monastic life. The mountain had now become a powerful center of monasticism, and through the centuries the number of communities and monks increased. In 1783, the autonomous government of the peninsula was granted its own constitution, which was renewed in 1926. In the present century, there remain twenty monasteries on the mount.

**Mourning Church** (*properly*, Low German Mourning Church). A rigid ultra-Calvinist group formed after a schism of the Reformed Church of the Netherlands in 1886, reacting against a relaxation of views about predestination and "modernizing" tendencies. After a separate existence of only six years the church united with the Christian Reformed Church in 1892 to form the Gereformeerde Kerken, or Reformed Churches.

**Mozarabic Rite.** A distinctive non-Roman liturgy used throughout Spain until the 11th century, when it was suppressed by the reforming zeal of Gregory VII. It was revived in the 15th century by Cardinal Ximenes, but its celebration (which continues today) was limited to the cathedral and a few parish churches of Toledo. Numerous manuscripts, now being studied and edited, preserve the ancient Mozarabic rite. Scholars have not yet succeeded in deciphering their musical notation.

**Mueller, Adam Heinrich** (1779–1829). German Romantic political philosopher. Educated at Göttingen, Mueller organized a "Christian German" club whose members opposed French revolutionary advances in all fields. Under the influence of the Romantic literary movement, Mueller emphasized tradition and history over rational ideals in politics. In *Elemente der Staatskunst* (1809) he welded Romanticism and Christian thought into a political theory: man's relation to spiritual destiny was the ultimate basis of politics. Mueller decried capitalism, contending with Burke that man apart from the state is nonexistent. Converted to Roman Catholicism in Vienna (1805), he lectured in Dresden and Berlin, and served as a devoted monarchist in the Austrian government after 1811.

**Mueller, Ludwig** (1883–1946). German bishop. The leader of the "German Christians" Faith Movement, he was an ardent supporter of Nazi doctrines of race. Born at Gütersloh and educated at Münster, he was the religious adviser of Hitler. In 1933 he was elected bishop of Prussia and *Reichsbischof*. His attempt to inject Nazism into German Lutheranism provoked wide-scale opposition, especially from the Confessing Church, and in 1935 he resigned his offices.

**Muggletonians.** A radical extremity of the English Puritan movement in the 17th century. Followers of Lodowicke Muggleton and John Reeve, the Muggletonians were a strange mixture of rationalism and literalism. They had no preachers or regular services of worship, but they met to read the writings of their founders. They rejected prayer, thought faith was divine and reason demonic, and believed that God seldom entered the human sphere.

**Muhammad, Elijah** (1897–    ). Leader of the Black Muslims (founded in 1931), a Negro separatist group of about 50,000 to 250,000 members drawn chiefly from lower social and economic groups. Muhammad was born Elijah Poole in Sandersville, Ga., and succeeded W. D. Ford as the charismatic "prophet" of the group in Detroit in 1934. Black Muslims follow many orthodox Moslem beliefs, but also advocate separation from the white race and retaliation if attacked.

**Mühlenberg, Henry Melchior** (1711–1787). Lutheran clergyman. Born and educated in Germany, he came to Philadelphia in 1742 to strengthen New World Lutheranism. This he accomplished against much opposition by extensive travel and by founding in 1748 the first Lutheran synod in America, the Ministerium of Pennsylvania. He has often been called "the Patriarch of American Lutheranism."

**Muhlenberg, William Augustus** (1796–1877). Episcopal clergyman. After graduation from the University of Pennsylvania he studied with Episcopal bishop William White and was ordained to the priesthood in 1820. He served parishes in Lancaster, Pa., and Flushing, N.Y.

Mühlenberg became rector of the Church of the Holy Communion in New York in 1846. He was active in the Memorial movement seeking liturgical reform. From 1858 until his death he devoted most of his time to St. Luke's Hospital, an institution founded by his parish.

**Mukyokai** ("No-Church movement"). An indigenous Japanese Christian fellowship of great vitality initiated by a reaction against Western denominational forms introduced by the missions. Its founder was Kanzo Uchimura (1861–1930). The central activity is Bible study, guided by the Holy Spirit, and a weekly journal. Each local group has a permanent teacher-leader. No statistics are gathered by the Mukyokai, but observers estimate membership at 75,000 to 100,000.

**Munger, Theodore Thornton** (1830–1910). Congregational minister and theologian. The "New Haven seer," Munger was minister to the United Church, New Haven, Conn. (1885–1900). Influenced by Maurice, Robertson, and particularly Horace Bushnell, he was a leading exponent of liberal and progressive theology. Critical of orthodoxy for its legalism and irrelevance, Munger stressed a personal God, human ability, and organic evolution. He rejected theological systems for a catholic human concern, and preached "a living incarnation active in all the processes of human life." Munger emphasized the common interests and goals of Christianity and culture. He sought a balance of Protestant individualism and modern social consciousness. He was particularly conscious of the need for a relevant moral theology and a modern commonsense faith. His writings included *The Freedom of Faith* (1883), *The Appeal to Life* (1887), and *Horace Bushnell* (1899).

**Munich, Catholic Conference at** (1863). A gathering of Roman Catholic scholars which debated the free use of historical criticism. In delivering the presidential address, Ignaz von Doellinger insisted upon the incorporation of historical criticism along with Scholastic theology as a means of interpreting the message of Christ. The reply was a papal brief that affirmed the right of the church to trammel scholarship in deference to ecclesiastical authority.

**Munificentissimus Deus.** Apostolic constitution of Pope Pius XII, issued on Nov. 1, 1950, announcing the solemn definition as a matter of dogma of the bodily Assumption of Mary, the mother of Jesus, into heaven. The constitution briefly traces the history of the devotion to the Virgin Mary, noting particularly the grounds for belief in Mary's conception without sin and her bodily incorruption after "death."

**Münster Revolt.** A brief religious and political uprising in Westphalia, organized within an apocalyptic community of Anabaptists who seized a large church in Münster and usurped the powers of the town council. From early in 1534 to June, 1535, Münster was the scene of an extraordinary "kingdom." It began as a widening of the political base accompanying social and economic changes in the manner of many German cities of the time, developing first as a Lutheran religiosocial reform. However, a radical party headed by Bernt Rothmann, who held out for believer's baptism, gained the initiative. Many Melchiorites imbued with apocalyptic zeal, balked elsewhere, now began to believe that Münster would be the focal scene of the eschatological denouement. Thousands of them flocked there at the call of Jan Beukels and Jan Mathijs, Melchiorites who soon emerged as the real rulers. They expelled all who would not receive a rebaptismal rebirth into their "incarnate Word" apocalyptic covenant, and apostles were sent out to spread the faith. Life in the city was restructured as a communalistic theocracy, with Beukels claiming direct revelations. Polygamy was instituted and Beukels anointed king of the "new Zion" amid grandiose trappings. Finally, the city was betrayed by a disillusioned apostle and the theocracy overthrown. Sober pacifists such as Menno Simons gradually emerged as leaders of Anabaptism, but the movement as a whole was long held suspect by Reformation leaders.

**Müntzer, Thomas** (c. 1489–1525). Anabaptist. Müntzer has long been denounced as a cause of the Peasants' War and hailed by socialists as an early hero. A balanced view sees him as a priest and a scholar, interested in liturgical renewal and moral reform but iconoclastic and apocalyptic. He used his eloquence also to denounce the excessive work requirements which prevented the common people from being schooled in faith. In his dependence on Franciscan chiliasm, on Tauler and other mystics, on Luther's early attacks on the papal church, and on his own study of the Bible, of Augustine, and of the church councils, Müntzer concluded that the church had fallen from purity just after the apostles, and that it would be restored apocalyptically in his own times at God's initiative. After a reform attempt by public demonstration in Prague had failed, he adopted a pastoral approach in Alstedt as a parish priest. He sought through a vernacular Biblical liturgy and by extensive preaching and counseling to deepen believers' sensitivity to the inner Word so that the eternal Word would rise to temporal effectiveness in selfless believers and God would vindicate his elect at the imminent *eschaton*. When princely officials interfered, he reacted defensively; his hostility to them caught him up in the Peasants' War and proved his undoing. He was beheaded after the defeat at Frankenhausen.

**Muratori, Lodovico Antonio** (1672–1750). Italian historian and antiquary. Regarded as the "father of Italian history," he was educated as a doctor of laws, ordained priest in 1695, and assigned to the Ambrosian library at Milan. He came as librarian to the duke of Modena in 1700, where most of his life was spent in the preparation and publication and treatment of original documents. He is best known for a fragment (85 lines) of early Christian literature (probably late 2d century) which gives a list of authoritative Christian writings—the so-called "Muratorian Canon" which he discovered in 1740 and published.

**Muratorian Fragment.** A partial list detailing the books of the New Testament, found in an 8th-century manuscript discovered in Milan by Lodovico Antonio Muratori (1672–1750). He published it, among other texts, in 1740. Written in poor Latin, perhaps a translation from Greek, it may represent the late 2d-century canon of the New Testament for the Roman Church. Beginning in the middle of a sentence which seems to refer to Mark and possibly to Matthew, it designates Luke as the third of the Gospels. Its omissions (Hebrews, James, I Peter?, II Peter) as well as its inclusions (Wisdom, Apocalypse of Peter) are of importance for the history of the canon of the New Testament.

**Murray, Andrew** (1828–1917). South African missionary and educator. After study at Aberdeen and Utrecht he was ordained to the ministry of the Dutch Reformed Church in 1848. He returned to South Africa to minister to congregations in Bloemfontein, Worcester, Cape Town, and Wellington, to participate in the struggle for independence, to found numerous educational institutions, and to exert the influence of his evangelical spirit over men, combating rationalism and Erastianism. The Cape Synod six times elected him moderator. His most popular book was *Blijf in Jezus,* translated as *Abide in Christ* (1864).

**Murri, Romolo** (1870–1944). Italian priest and social critic. Embracing Christian Democracy, he founded the review *Cultura Sociale* and soon broke with the conservative Catholic Congress leadership to organize the National Democratic League (a forerunner of the People's Party). Censured (1907) by Pius X, he abjured the cloth, married, and supported the political Left. Don Murri wrote extensively on Modernism and Catholic Action, reconciled with the church just before death.

**Musonius Rufus** (1st century A.D.). Stoic moralist and an exile under Nero. Because of the nature of his teaching and his career, he was greatly admired by both Justin and Origen. According to Justin, the "spermatic Logos" was responsible for his teaching. Clement of Alexandria never mentions his name but incorporates much of his teaching in his own writings.

**Myconius, Friedrich** (c. 1491–1546). Lutheran Reformer and historian. Born at Lichtenfels in Franconia, Myconius joined the Franciscans in 1510 and was ordained a priest in 1516. His preaching in Weimar made him well known, but his sympathy with Luther's work resulted in his leaving the Franciscans in 1524. He then became pastor at Gotha and contributed to the reform of the Thuringian Church. He was present at the conferences of Marburg, Smalcald, and Hagenau, and traveled to England to attempt to gain Henry VIII for Lutheranism. With J. Heller he composed a useful history of the Reformation (*Historia Reformationis*).

**Myconius** (Geisshüssler), **Oswald** (1488–1552). Swiss Reformer. Myconius studied at Basel, where he was a friend of Erasmus—from whom he received the name Myconius—and became the cathedral schoolmaster at Zurich in 1516. In this position he persuaded the chapter to elect Zwingli as people's priest. In 1532 he succeeded Oecolampadius as chief pastor of The Reformed Church in Basel. He produced the First Basel Confession (1534), and also a life of Zwingli (1536).

**Mynster, Jacob Pier** (1775–1854). Danish bishop and theologian. He studied theology at Copenhagen and as pastor of the Church of Our Lady in Copenhagen won fame as a preacher. He also taught psychology in the theological seminary in Copenhagen. His ministry was characterized by a mild evangelicalism. In 1834 he became bishop of Zealand. He opposed the liberalizing efforts of N. F. S. Grundtvig in the Danish Lutheran Church.

**Mystery Plays.** Medieval religious plays particularly popular in the 15th century which concerned themselves with three major themes: the Old Testament, the New Testament, and non-Biblical lives of the saints. There were a large number of mystery plays, some requiring several days for a complete performance. Special dramatic associations were formed to stage them. Perhaps the most famous were the passion plays, of which the Oberammergau play is a descendant.

**Mystery Religions.** The Hellenistic age was one of the most religious periods in the history of humanity. During that time there was a steady development of monotheism and a growing enthusiasm for ethical idealism. At the same time there was a notable tendency in the direction of dualism and two implications of that dualism—a need for revelation and a need for redemption. Add to these conditions the contemporary taste for archaism and the development of the cult of the Roman emperor in the East and you have all the requirements for the importation of Eastern mystery cults into Rome and the rest of the Empire. A number of different cults from all parts of the Empire are included in this category, and it is hard to include all their phenomena in any general description. Also, their secret nature makes our direct information about them scarce. Yet they did have enough in common to justify being lumped into a common category. They generally involved belief in the fallen condition of man, and the possibility of overcoming the effects of that fall by a sacramental dying and rising with the divine man recognized by the cult as savior. Among the more prominent of the cults were those of Dionysus in Asia Minor through the 1st century; of Isis and Serapis out of Egypt; of Cybele, the Great Mother of the Mountain, with its frenzied initiatory rites and blood baths; and the more majestic and ethically demanding rites of Mithras, the Persian god of light, which during the 2d and 3d centuries met with great response throughout the Rhineland among both the military and native population. The tendency of scholars of half a century ago to posit the mystery religions as the major source for Christian sacramentalism is now generally discounted.

**Mysticism.** A phenomenon appearing in various religions and in many cultural contexts. Its very nature makes precise definition next to impossible. An indication of its nature may, however, be suggested by pointing out certain characteristic notes that appear in a variety of forms.

A mystic is generally described as a person who experiences direct awareness of or union with the Divine. The experience is ecstatic. In a way that is analogous to sensory experience, the mystic may be aware of Divine Reality. The awareness involves transcendence of ordinary consciousness, either by a cessation of the latter or by some sort of awareness that is different from it even though it is concomitant with it. In the mystical moment the person may be aware of the Divine while his consciousness is closed to self and world, or he may be aware of the Divine at the same time as he is aware of self and world, though his awareness is of a different quality or kind. For some mystics, awareness itself is transcended. In the mystical moment even the separation of self and Divine which is implied by the term "awareness" has been overcome. Union is complete.

Certain ideas are characteristically associated with mysticism. Where union is held to occur, the Divine is regarded as impersonal; where awareness is averred, the Divine may be regarded as impersonal or quasi-personal. Stress is placed on inwardness. It is with the inward self that the Divine is related, and mystics often speak of a part of the soul that is peculiarly the organ of relatedness between man and God. The mystical life is said to be one that is lived from within, though the mystic may be vigorously engaged in outward activity. Discipline is also almost universally associated with mysticism, sometimes becoming exceedingly elaborate. Discipline is needed to develop inwardness and to concentrate the powers toward the unity of selfhood requisite to the mystic experience. Symbols may be important to the mystic, as pointers to the Divine. Indeed, mysticism may give rise to complex systems of symbols. Interest in symbols may be divorced from concern about them for the sake of mystic experience; they become intellectual curios, counters in complicated games.

Mysticism has been especially congenial to Eastern religions. Thus, in Hinduism the center of the self (atman) may experience union with the impersonal Divine Reality (Brahman) in an ecstatic moment. The Tao may also be an object of mystical awareness. Zen Buddhism places emphasis on a kind of consciousness (satori), though here mysticism is somewhat unusual, since no supposed Reality is held to be encountered.

In the West, mysticism has generally been associated with Neoplatonism with its notion of a transrational union with the Divine. In the great historical faiths of the West, however, with their emphasis on revelation, mysticism has been somewhat problematical. And yet these faiths have had their mystical movements, though usually under some influence from Neoplatonism. Sufism has appeared in Islam, Kabbalism and Hasidism in Judaism, and a variety of movements have appeared within Christianity.

So problematic is the status of mysticism

within Christianity, however, that theologians have been sharply divided on the matter of its legitimacy within Christendom. Some theologians exclude mysticism completely from authentic Christianity. Their arguments generally focus on such assertions as these: Christianity is a radically historical faith in which man's relation to God cannot be viewed as immediate; it always regards God as moving toward man, proclaiming the futility of all human attempts to reach God; it does not know of any center of the soul that is innocent of evil, much less one that is divine. At the other extreme are thinkers who regard mysticism as the purest form of religion and regard the differences among faiths as insignificant. To them any characteristic of Christian faith that is at odds with mysticism is nonessential. Some thinkers hold that Christian faith brings mysticism itself to its highest and finest expression. Most thinkers, however, probably take a position about midway between the extremes: while mysticism is appropriate within Christianity, they hold, it must be balanced with proper regard for theological and institutional matters.

Certain concerns, images, and problems have been fairly recurrent in Christian mysticism. The Bible has generally been interpreted in allegorical and anagogical fashion. Repeated efforts have been made to set forth a meaningful relationship between the impersonal Divine of mystical union and the "personal" Trinitarian Deity of classical Christianity. Mysticism has often spoken of a Christ in the soul, and this Christ has been related in some way to Jesus the Christ. Mystical experience has frequently been described as the birth of Christ in the soul and related to the eternal birth of the Son and to the birth of Jesus of Nazareth. The crucifixion has been regarded as reenacted in the mystical experience; sometimes the stigmata have appeared. The risen Christ has been encountered as a spiritual presence; likewise, the Holy Spirit has sometimes been the mystic's divine Companion. The way to the mystic vision has been described innumerable times, sometimes with great elaborateness. The general pattern of purgation, illumination, and union has been almost universal. The sacraments, especially the Eucharist, have often been interpreted as having mystical experience as their intent and fulfillment. The church has also been an occasion of mystic awareness, symbolic of the fullness of fellowship between God and men, and of men with each other. The eternal life has usually been defined by the mystic as *visio Dei;* indeed, the mystical experience has often been interpreted as a temporary transport to the heavenly realm.

Among the major branches of Christendom some have been more hospitable to mysticism than others, but mystics have appeared within all of them. The Eastern Orthodox Churches, with their stress on the incarnation as the sharing of the Divine Life, their joy in the resurrection, and their concern for the transfiguration of humanity, have found mysticism congenial. Mystics have also found a home in the Roman Catholic Church. Its stress upon the atoning sacrifice has meant that often the mystic way has been understood as a way of the cross. The great figure of Augustine has exercised enormous influence, as has the Syrian monk who was identified as Dionysius the Areopagite. Periods of marked mystical activity took place in the High Middle Ages (Bernard, Bonaventure, the Victorines, some English mystics), at the close of the Middle Ages (Eckhart, Tauler, Ruysbroeck), and during the Counter-Reformation (John of the Cross, Teresa of Ávila). Throughout the centuries appeared many, especially women, whose mysticism was visionary in character (Catherine of Siena, Bridget of Sweden, Catherine of Genoa).

During the Reformation, churches committed to the Word found little or no place for mystical emphasis, and mysticism found its Protestant home among the sectarians. In the 16th century appeared the strange figure of Jakob Boehme, setting forth a mysticism emphasizing the will and drawing into itself an interest in nature mysticism that had been developing during the Renaissance. The 17th century saw the activity of many mystics, among them George Fox, founder of the Society of Friends (Quakers), whose entire ethos was determined by a mystical outlook. Pietism appeared within the churches determined by the Word, giving their religiousness a mystical cast, even though it did not challenge their theological presuppositions.

Liberal Protestantism was generally favorable toward mysticism. Schleiermacher reinterpreted the entire range of Christian doctrine in terms of God-consciousness. Some liberals saw God in nature; others defined the faith in terms of ethical mysticism. Some, haunted by the dissolution of faith, found in mystical experience an answer to doubt.

Mysticism, finally, is not simply a religious phenomenon. Wherever it has appeared, it has been reflected in philosophy, art, and literature—indeed, in the whole of culture.

BIBLIOGRAPHY: C. Butler, *Western Mysticism* (New York, 1923); W. R. Inge, *Chris-*

*tian Mysticism* (New York, 1956); R. M. Jones, *The Flowering of Mysticism* (New York, 1939); R. Otto, *Mysticism East and West* (New York, 1932); R. C. Petry (ed.), *Late Medieval Mysticism* (The Library of Christian Classics, Vol. XIII, Philadelphia, 1957); E. Underhill, *Mysticism* (New York, 1930).

# N

**Nag-Hammadi.** Village some sixty-five miles north of Luxor, Egypt, near which in 1945 and 1946 was found, quite accidentally, a cache of thirteen manuscripts, written in Coptic and dating from the late 4th or early 5th century. Possibly the library of a Gnostic sect, the documents extend the knowledge of the early environs of Christianity and rate in importance with the Dead Sea Scrolls.

**Nantes, Revocation of the Edict of.** See HUGUENOTS.

**Napoleon Bonaparte** (1769–1821). Corsican-born French general and emperor (1804–1814). Promoted quickly through merit in the army during the upheavals of the French Revolution, Napoleon overran the northern Italian states, inflicting the bitter peace of Tolentino (1797) on Pius VI. Cynical of religions, Napoleon posed as a friend of Islam while in Egypt (1798–1799). As first consul (1799), he felt that France was fundamentally Catholic, that reconciliation with the church would benefit the people and further his policy, and that men required the authority of revealed religion to be happy or resigned. He arranged the Concordat of 1801, recognizing Roman Catholicism, ending schism, and placing the clergy, his "sacred gendarmerie," on stipend. Secularized church lands remained with their possessors. The Organic Articles attached to the Concordat without papal consent created a virtual Gallican Church. Ministers and rabbis were similarly salaried. Pius VII assisted at Napoleon's coronation (1804) only to find himself deported from Rome (1809) and his remaining Papal States annexed by the emperor. The pope responded with excommunication. Wherever Napoleon extended his system, he abolished the Inquisition and mortmain and offered toleration to religious minorities. He stated in his testament to posterity that he died a Catholic.

**Narses** (Narsai) **the Leper** (c. 399–c. 502). Nestorian theologian. In 437 he directed the theological school at Edessa. Barsumas in 457 invited him to found a new school at Nisibis, which became the chief institution of Nestorian theology. Narses was temporarily exiled after a disagreement with Barsumas. After returning, he stayed in the school for the remaining years of his life. He is said to have left behind 360 hymns, many of which are today used in Eastern Syriac liturgy.

**Narthex.** The western end of a basilica, separated from the nave by a wall or partition. Originally there was an outer portion, consisting of a court, and an inner narthex, which was a vestibule adjoining the nave. Historically, it was used by those who were not allowed to enter the nave during the Mass. The narthex has evolved so that it is now the porch at the west end of the nave.

**National Association of Evangelicals.** An association growing out of the efforts of conservative American Protestants to provide an outlet for their views which, they felt, were not adequately represented by the Federal Council of Churches. An organizing conference in 1942 was followed by a constitutional convention in Chicago in 1943. The group adopted a statement of faith that was typical of conservative Protestantism, affirming, among other doctrines, a belief in the inspiration and infallibility of the Bible, and in the full deity of Jesus Christ, including his virgin birth. One aim of the organization is to represent conservatives in dealing with agencies of the national government on such matters as chaplaincies and religious broadcasting. The Association was active in opposing diplomatic ties with the Vatican and maintains commissions that deal with such activities as evangelism, higher education, Sunday schools, Christian day schools, missions, and social welfare. Some forty churches are affiliated, including the Assemblies of God, Church of God, and the Free Will Baptists. A number of local churches belong to the association while retaining their membership in nonaffiliated denominations. The group claims to represent some 2,000,000 members and a constituency of 10,000,000.

**National Catholic Welfare Conference.** An agency of the American Catholic hierarchy. Upon the entrance of the United States into World War I, the American Catholic hierarchy formed the National Catholic War Council in an attempt to mitigate the distressing conditions caused by this disruption of civilized life. Though the National Catholic War Council lasted only two years, the experience of working together seemed to be an exhilarating one for many members of the hierarchy. When nearly eighty bishops gathered for the formal celebration of the fiftieth anniversary of the raising of James Cardinal Gibbons to the episcopate (Feb. 20, 1919), Pope Benedict XV sent an address in which he urged the American episcopate not to abandon their efforts at concerted Catholic action upon the termination of the war. The experience of the National Catholic War Council had been largely with welfare activities, and the pope hoped that such activities would continue into the postwar period in an organized fashion. The American bishops thereupon determined to hold annual meetings to discuss problems of common concern, and also established an intermediary committee which, in the course of 1919, saw to the establishment of the National Catholic Welfare Council.

The Council had its opponents from the start. There were certain members of the American hierarchy who felt that a national council threatened the autonomy of the dioceses of the country and compromised the position of the bishops. Popes Benedict XV and Pius XI were so impressed with the arguments of this latter group that they temporarily removed their approval of the Council. The difficulty was partially a semantic one, however. In 1923 the name of the organization was changed to the National Catholic Welfare Conference, the voluntary nature of episcopal involvement was emphasized, the distinction between statements issued by such a body and the decrees of a church "council" was stressed, and the approval and encouragement of the papacy were once more given to the Conference.

The National Catholic Welfare Conference, as an agency of the American Catholic hierarchy, functioned through an administrative board which was to oversee and coordinate the efforts of eight permanent departments and numerous episcopal committees. The eight departments consisted of the Executive department and the departments of Education, Legal Affairs, the Press, Immigration, Lay Organizations, Social Action, and Youth. One of the best known of the episcopal committees was the Bishops' Welfare Emergency and Relief Committee, which administers the activities of the Catholic Relief Services. Other committees of importance were the Committee on the Propagation of the Faith; the American Board of Catholic Missions; the Committee on the Confraternity of Christian Doctrine; the Committee on the National Organization for Decent Literature; and the Committee on Military Service Legislation.

Since the year 1941 the American Catholic bishops have followed their annual meetings with the issuance of a joint statement concerned with some particularly relevant national problem. These meetings have ordinarily taken place at the Catholic University of America in Washington, D.C. They are held in November. The forum provided by these annual gatherings of the hierarchy has proved to be most important and useful. At their meeting in November, 1966, important changes were made in the structure of the "national secretariat" of the American episcopate. The National Catholic Welfare Conference, which had acted as the secretariat, became a thing of the past. It was replaced by the U.S. Catholic Conference, Inc., which was to carry on the work previously done by the Conference. At the same time, the American Catholic bishops formed the National Conference of Catholic Bishops, an unincorporated body, which would concern itself with more directly "spiritual" problems than the U.S. Catholic Conference.

BIBLIOGRAPHY: A. I. Abell, *American Catholicism and Social Action* (Notre Dame, Ind., 1964); M. T. Boylan, *Social Welfare in the Catholic Church* (New York, 1941); *National Catholic Welfare Conference*, ed. by R. M. Huber (Milwaukee, 1950).

**National Conference of Christians and Jews.** An association founded in 1928 under the leadership of E. R. Clinchy, a secretary of the Federal Council of Churches. This organization has enjoyed broad Protestant and Jewish support and some Roman Catholic participation in promoting the unity of the human race by combating prejudice, ill-feeling, and strained relationships. It maintains that God is the Father of all; that all are brothers; that all religions have the same common principles; that Christianity is really the outgrowth of Judaism; and that therefore any form of anti-Semitism is at the same time a blow against Christianity. The 1930's witnessed the establishment of many local organizations, and the Conference has become well known for its national programs and the advocacy of an annual Brotherhood Week.

**National Council of Churches.** Created in 1950 and given an imposing home in the Interchurch Center in New York City a decade later, the National Council of the Churches of Christ in the United States of America is the most important result of a half century of experiments in cooperative Christianity. Most of these experiments were initiated in the first two decades of this century to deal with certain phases of the church's mission, such as stewardship, home missions, and higher education. One of them, the Federal Council of

Churches, was organized to make explicit the unity of the church and to federate the churches in an effort to apply Christian norms to social problems. By the 1940's the spirit of the church as united and one had become a vision held more and more widely by American churchmen. Moreover, many of the cooperative agencies were overlapping one another in their work. After considerable effort, the following eight major interdenominational groups merged into the National Council: the Federal Council of Churches; the Foreign Missions Conference of North America; the Home Missions Council of North America; the Missionary Education Movement of the United States and Canada; the International Council of Religious Education; the National Protestant Council on Higher Education; the United Council of Church Women; and the United Stewardship Council. These groups were soon joined by five others: Church World Service; the Interseminary Committee; the Protestant Radio Committee; the Protestant Film Commission; and the Student Volunteers for Foreign Missions.

The National Council was formed "to manifest oneness in Jesus Christ as Divine Lord and Savior," and to combine the interests and functions of the churches. In its message "to the People of the Nation" it defined itself as an "instrument of the Holy Spirit" and announced itself as "our Churches in their highest common effort for mankind." It is responsible to its member denominations, twenty-nine in number at its founding. It was ecumenical from the outset, since four of these churches were Orthodox. The Council has been most fortunate in its leaders. It numbers Luther A. Weigle and Douglas Horton among those who guided the merger to life, and Samuel McCrea Cavert as its first general secretary. The Council functions through a general secretariat and four divisions—Christian Education, Christian Life and Work, Foreign Missions, and Home Missions. Departments within these divisions direct the specific cooperative activities of the churches.

The programs, projects, and pronouncements of the Council defy cataloging. A few must suffice to suggest the range of its work. It authorized the publication of the Revised Standard Version of the Bible and promoted its circulation and use. It has continued and extended the foreign and home missionary work of the churches and has introduced innovative ministries to migrants and to visitors to the national parks. It has supported the work of state and local councils of churches. Aware of the continuing growth of the communications industry, it has significantly increased the churches' radio and TV ministry. It has been extremely active in three areas of concern which it inherited from the Federal Council: economic life, race relations, and international affairs. In 1954 it adopted a statement, "Christian Principles and Assumptions for Economic Life," as a revision of the Social Creed of the Churches. In 1952 it adopted a statement on "The Churches and Segregation," and later called for peaceful compliance with the 1954 decision of the Supreme Court. Since then it has organized a special Commission on Religion and Race, sponsored the Mississippi Summer Project in 1964, and initiated the Mississippi Delta Ministry. It has been a vociferous supporter of the United Nations and in 1958 called for the admission of Communist China in order to make the UN a truly worldwide forum. The National Council has functioned with great effect as the organ and voice of a significant number of American Protestant and Orthodox Christians.

BIBLIOGRAPHY: S. M. Cavert, *On the Road to Christian Unity* (New York, 1961); R. Lee, *The Social Sources of Church Unity* (New York, 1960); R. W. Spike, *The Freedom Revolution and the Churches* (New York, 1965); *Christian Faith in Action* (New York, 1951); *Yearbook of American Churches* (New York).

**National Free Church Council of England.** An organization formed in 1896 when the nonconforming churches of England, including Congregationalists, Presbyterians, Baptists, and Methodists united in a federal body, with the Society of Friends expressing interest and sympathy. The Council ceased to exist in 1940 when it was merged with the Federal Council of the Evangelical Free Churches (1919) to form the Free Church Council.

**Nativism.** The effort of a majority to create national unity by restricting minority groups as sources of foreign influence. In America, nativists have opposed newer immigrant groups that differed from the Anglo-Saxon majority. Fears roused by political and economic crises have often resulted in repressive measures against ethnic and religious minorities. Before the Civil War, nativism was directed largely against the growing Roman Catholic immigration, which was viewed as a threat to Protestant predominance. Spurred by propaganda, and marked by violence, this movement reached its peak in the Know-Nothing political agitation in the 1850's. After the Civil War, the rise of industry that stimulated an increase of immigration from southeast Europe shifted nativism from a religious basis to a racial one. Established on false racial theories, such as Social Darwinism, American nativism culminated in the restriction of immigration after World War I. These restrictions were based on national quotas that favored earlier immigrant groups. Nativistic pressure has also been directed against American Negroes by groups such as the Ku-Klux Klan. During World War II, Americans of Japanese origin were subject to internment because of wartime fears based upon deepseated racial prejudices.

**Natural Law.** The concept of natural law is rooted in the Hellenic philosophic thought that is so fundamental and decisive for the development of Western culture. As enunciated by the 5th-century B.C. Greeks, it pertained to the eternal, immutable law that regulated the activities of nature whether animate or inanimate. Already present in Heraclitus, it was further clarified by Plato in *Laws* (4, 715 f.; cf. 10, 890); with Aristotle's distinction between natural law and humanly enacted law (*Nicomachean Ethics* 1134b 18–1136a 9; cf. *Rhetoric* 1373b 1–18) the focus of natural law is turned toward the ethical on the principle that what is moral is that which is in conformity to nature. For Aristotle, however, man is understood as a citizen of the polis and his destiny is worked out in the context of political life in that community. Stoicism, on the other hand, advanced the concept of the individual man as a citizen of the world subject to its innate law, the law of nature. In this form, natural law theory entered the Rome of the 2d century B.C. with the conquest of that civilization by the Hellenistic viewpoint. Natural law developed in Rome with more concern for matters juridical and legal (*jus naturale*) than for man's conduct generally. In the first few centuries of the Christian era, the fathers were able to designate the source of natural law, thus overcoming the Stoic vacillation between pantheistic immanence and personal divine foundation. This development achieved a climax in Thomas Aquinas, who distinguished *lex aeterna* and *lex naturalis* in both Aristotelian-Stoic and Roman ideas of natural law. For Aquinas, *lex aeterna* became *lex naturalis* in relation to the way in which man perceived the *lex naturalis,* thus he evolved the principle that these two could never be in conflict, since there was one source of both. Along with this tenet operated the principle of analogy whereby man could rationally perceive the *lex naturalis* which was a sort of mirror image of the supernatural *lex aeterna.* Both the Scotists and the nominalists offered critical revisions of the Thomist conception of natural

law and the principle of analogy, but these criticisms remained minority opinions until the Reformation. The Protestant critique of the dominant Scholastic conception of natural law stemmed from the radically different conception of the nature and capacities of man held by the Reformers. Although they still maintained the general idea of natural law, they interpreted severally in accordance with their respective theologies, the Anglican Richard Hooker being the closest to Aquinas. The emergence of a conception of natural law sundered from the nexus of Christian faith and possessing an independent authority was to bring about in the 18th century a completely secular theory of natural law. By the 19th century the term "natural law" was almost exclusively associated with the observably regular pattern followed by natural phenomena under given conditions, thus reflecting the dominance of natural science in that era's thought.

The reassertion of Reformation insights in the theology of neo-orthodoxy resulted in a sharp criticism not only of its traditional adversary (the Scholastic natural law theory of Roman Catholic moral theologians) but also of the ethical theory evolved by the proponents of a secular idea of natural law. The severest critique of Scholastic natural law theory comes from Karl Barth and Jacques Ellul, whose doctrine of the Fall eliminates the use of analogy. Less severe is the objection of Reinhold Niebuhr that natural law principles are subject to historical conditioning and thus are relative rather than universally and eternally valid. From a somewhat different standpoint, Paul Tillich argues that natural law is grounded ontologically as man's essential nature, a nature that is "distorted in his actual existence." Each of these estimates of natural law contributes to the conclusion that Protestant thought has so reconceived the notion of natural law as to remove it from the realm of abstract universal principles and place it in the realm of concrete human encounter.

BIBLIOGRAPHY: J. Dalby, *The Catholic Conception of the Law of Nature* (London, 1943); J. Ellul, *The Theological Foundation of Law* (Garden City, 1960); R. Niebuhr, *The Nature and Destiny of Man,* 2 vols. (New York, 1964); P. Tillich, *Love, Power and Justice* (New York, 1960); A. R. Vidler and W. A. Whitehouse, *Natural Law: A Christian Re-consideration* (London, 1946).

**Naumann, Friedrich** (1860–1919). German social reformer and Christian Socialist. Naumann was educated at Leipzig and Erlangen, was pastor in Langenberg and chaplain in Christian Social work in Frankfurt. He attempted to reach the proletariat by joining its fight for better wages. His goal was to create mutual understanding between church and labor. His failure to unite Christianity and socialism prompted him to devote himself to politics. In 1903 he helped found the National Socialist Party, and in 1918 he founded the German Democratic Party.

**Nave.** The great central part of a church, lying between the entrance and the choir. In some architectural styles, there is a central nave with smaller minor naves running parallel. The nave is the part of the church in which the laity take their place. The word is almost certainly derived from the Latin *navis,* meaning "ship."

**Nayler, James** (c. 1617–1660). Quaker leader. Nayler joined the Parliamentary army at the outbreak of the Civil War in 1642. While in the army, he became an Independent, then a preacher. In 1651, he returned home on the sick list, joined a Congregational church, but became a Quaker the following year during a visit by George Fox. Convinced of a call to the traveling ministry, he began preaching, and was soon arrested for false doctrine. After being released, he traveled in the north, then journeyed to London, where his preaching quickly became famous. Nayler was a handsome man, whose appearance reminded many of a popular picture of Christ. A number of women asked him to become head of the London mission. Fox and Nayler fell out over the situation, and shortly thereafter Nayler was arrested because of the undue honor bestowed on him by his numerous followers—who bowed to him, kissed his feet, cried out hosannas. Brought before Commons in 1656, he was declared guilty of "horrid blasphemy." His punishment was two separate pilloryings, each for two hours, whipping, having his tongue pierced with a hot iron, and his forehead branded with the letter *B.* Released three years later a chastened spirit, he was reconciled to Fox and made public confession of his offense. A year later he became ill and died.

**Nazarene, Church of the.** Representing the "right wing of the Holiness movement," the Church of the Nazarene is the result of the merger of three Holiness and Pentecostal churches in 1907 and 1908: The Association of Pentecostal Churches in America, the Church of the Nazarene, and the Holiness Church of Christ. It dissociated itself from radical Pentecostal groups practicing glossolalia. Like most Holiness churches, it arose from Methodism, and continues to adhere closely to the 18th-century Wesleyan doctrines of holiness and sanctification. Regeneration being considered the first work of grace by the Nazarenes, they teach that sanctification is the second work of grace, and all ministers must have experienced sanctification. Other central doctrines include plenary inspiration of Scripture, which contains all truth necessary to faith and practice, universal atonement, the Second Coming, resurrection of the dead, and the Final Judgment. Baptism and the Lord's Supper are understood to be the only two ordinances instituted by Christ. Faith healing is practiced, but medical aid is not excluded. Tobacco and alcoholic beverages are forbidden. The ecclesiastical structure of the church is similar to that of the Methodist, with district and general superintendents, but local pastors are elected by local congregations. A General Assembly is held quadrennially, and its General Board administers the missionary, evangelistic, publishing, and educational functions of the church. Mission activities are extensively pursued.

**Nazi-Vatican Concordat** (1933). Until 1929, Roman Catholics held the balance of power in Germany with their Center Party, but as their strength weakened with the growth of Hitler's regime, a long period began during which the church and the Third Reich sought to establish a working arrangement between them. After lengthy and complex negotiations involving numerous important political and religious figures (Pope Pius XI; Cardinal Eugenio Pacelli, then Vatican secretary of state, later to become Pope Pius XII; Monsignor Ludwig Kaar; Vice-Chancellor Franz von Papen; etc.), a concordat was compiled. The conditions were agreed upon by both parties in July, 1933, and documents of ratification were exchanged on Sept. 10. The Concordat guaranteed freedom of worship for German Catholics, freedom of communication between the Vatican and clergy in Germany, freedom for German religious orders, and continued diplomatic relationships between the two powers. At Hitler's insistence, an article was finally included to ensure exclusion of the clergy from politics. The immediate results of the pact were a dissolution of the Center Party and a tremendous increase in prestige for Hitler and the Reich. Although the Concordat provided temporary limited benefits and protection for Catholics, the widening gap between the two ideologies soon became apparent, and the harmonious coexistence desired by the Vatican was not forthcoming. From the beginning, the Nazis violated article after article, and by 1935 they were largely ignoring the compact and had begun their systematic persecution of Catholics in Germany.

**Neale, John Mason** (1818–1866). Church of England clergyman and author. The son of an evangelical clergyman in London, he was educated at Cambridge and after gaining his degree became chaplain and assistant tutor of Downing College. Deeply affected by the Tractarian movement, he was one of the founders of the Cambridge Camden Society (1839), afterward known as the Ecclesiological Society, meant to stimulate interest in church architecture and Catholic worship, contributing to the liturgical and ceremonial revival in the Church of England. Ordained in 1841, Neale began parochial work in Surrey, not being licensed by the bishop on account of his association with the Camdenians. Because of ill-health, he was forced, with his wife, Sarah, whom he married in 1842, to seek a better climate, until presented in 1846 with the wardenship of Sackville College. Here he remained, caring for the poor and aged householders in the college, rebuilding the college chapel, incurring the wrath of his bishop and others not inclined to medieval ornamentation, and founding at East Grinstead the nursing sisterhood of St. Margaret. As a writer, Neale is best known for his hymns, found in most hymnbook collections. But he was remarkable in his day for his mastery of twenty languages, his knowledge of Eastern Orthodoxy, and his scholarship in liturgical and ecclesiological matters.

**Neander, Johann August Wilhelm** (David Mendel) (1789–1850). German Lutheran theologian and church historian. Born in Göttingen of poor Jewish parents named Mendel, he took the name Neander at his baptism in 1806. Under the influence of F. D. E. Schleiermacher he studied speculative theology, but soon turned to ecclesiastical history and taught this subject at Heidelberg (1812) and Berlin (1813). His literary labors were prodigious. In addition to his *General History of the Christian Religion and Church* (English ed., 5 vols., 1882), he wrote excellent studies on Bernard of Clairvaux (1813), gnosticism (1818), Tertullian (1824), and a life of Christ (1837) refuting the position of D. F. Strauss. As a church historian he held that individuals are more important in re-creating the past than are institutions. He believed that the history of the church was the history of the process of the interpenetration of man's life with the divine life of Christ. His learning, piety, and sympathies attracted many students,

and he did much to bring a less formal spirit into Lutheran teaching.

**Near East Christian Council.** A council for missionary cooperation created in 1929 by a reorganization of the Council for Western Asia and Northern Africa (formed in April, 1924) at a conference sponsored by the International Missionary Council under the chairmanship of John R. Mott. It is the regional ecumenical cooperative agency for the Protestant churches and missions in the Near East. A major contemporary concern is Christian dialogue with Islam.

**Near East Relief** (1915–1930). The first huge international relief project undertaken by the American people in voluntary association. Christian missionary and philanthropic leaders organized the movement to aid Armenians in Turkey. Greek refugees from Asia Minor in the 1920's and natural disasters prolonged what was expected to be a temporary emergency. Orphanages and schools were as important as feeding and housing refugees. The number of orphans cared for reached 132,000, and $116,000,000 was expended.

**Neesima, Joseph Hardy** (1843–1890). Japanese Christian and founder of Doshisha University. Born in Tokyo, he came to America in 1865, where he was befriended by Alphaeus Hardy, who sent him to Andover Theological Seminary and Amherst College. He was ordained in 1874, and with the aid of American religious and charitable organizations he established Doshisha University in 1875 in Kyoto, Japan, for the exposition of Christian teachings in Japan.

**Neff, Felix** (1797–1829). Swiss social reformer and Protestant evangelical pastor. Born in Geneva and educated locally, Neff originally planned a military career, but after a religious revival (see Réveil) he devoted his life to religious preaching. He was ordained in M. Clayton's Chapel in the Poultry, London (1823), and spent the remaining few years of his brief life in the valleys of Quéras and Freissinière in the Alps preaching religious revival.

**Negro Churches.** In America, Negro churches developed from the conversion of Negroes to Christianity within the limits of slavery and racial discrimination. The earliest missions to Negroes were conducted by Anglicans and Quakers, but such efforts were limited by the rule that conversion should not alter the status of slaves. With the growth of slavery in the southern states, efforts were made by a number of churches to reach slaves on the plantations through preaching and oral instruction. Some slave churches were established which made use of slave preachers, but these were strictly controlled to prevent slave revolts. In some southern cities Negroes were admitted to white churches, but they were usually restricted to the galleries, and had no share in the operation of their church. Other slaves were won to Christianity by attending revivals and camp meetings. In general, the denominational affiliations of slaves corresponded to those of their masters.

The first Negro denominations emerged in northern cities as a protest against racial discrimination in white churches. Two of the oldest and largest Negro churches (African Methodist Episcopal and African Methodist Episcopal Zion) resulted from the withdrawal of Negroes from Methodist churches in Philadelphia and New York City. After the Civil War, with the end of slavery, these Negro churches had a rapid growth among the freedmen. Negro Baptist churches also grew after the war, often through the secession of Negroes from white Baptist congregations. A few white denominations won small Negro constituencies, but their greatest contribution was the support of an extensive educational program for Negroes in the South. Relatively few Negroes became Roman Catholics.

After World War I many Negroes migrated to northern cities, where they joined established Negro churches, though some turned to storefront churches for closer fellowship. In general, most American Negroes became Protestant Christians, usually Baptist or Methodist, in about the same proportion to the general population as white Americans, although with a slightly higher percentage of women members. Most Negro Christians belong to Negro churches or to local Negro churches within white denominations. Although a few Negro cults have developed, most Negro churches reflect the traditional orthodoxy of their white counterparts. In winning the American Negro, Protestantism won a larger group than in all the rest of its foreign mission work in the 19th century.

The Negro church has served as an agency of acculturation to bring Negroes into American culture. Since the ministry was one of the first vocations open to Negroes, the Negro minister has had a unique role of social and religious leadership for his people. The church has also provided a means of social control for shaping its members according to prevailing standards of Christian morality. Although now challenged by other institutions, the church has a significant function in expressing the solidarity of the Negro community. The leadership of Martin Luther King, Jr., a Negro Baptist pastor, in the civil rights struggle, is an example of the Negro church's participation in movements of social protest and reform.

Through its experience with racial discrimination the Negro church has provided an interpretation of Christianity that expresses the tragedy and the hope of the dispossessed. In the spirituals and sorrow songs that transmuted the sufferings of slaves, as well as in colorful sermons that express the frustrations of urban Negroes, the church has provided an outlet for the aspirations of its people. In recent years there has come a new emphasis on the social relevance of religion to the problems of this life, along with the traditional stress on the supernatural and the otherworldly. While white churches are making new efforts to integrate their Negro members into denominational life, and are becoming more aware of racial problems, the Negro churches are becoming more active in working with white Christians for racial and religious unity.

BIBLIOGRAPHY: E. F. Frazier, *The Negro Church in America* (Liverpool, 1964); L. L. Haynes, *The Negro Community Within American Protestantism: 1619–1844* (Boston, 1953); B. F. Mays, *The Negro's God as Reflected in His Literature* (Boston, 1938); D. M. Reimers, *White Protestantism and the Negro* (New York, 1965); C. G. Woodson, *The History of the Negro Church* (Washington, 1945).

**Negro Colleges.** Although a few Negroes were admitted to white colleges before the Civil War, the great expansion of Negro higher education took place after the war. The first institution for the higher education of Negroes was Ashmun Institute (1854). After 1865 some 200 colleges were founded by northern white and Negro churches in cooperation with the federal Freedmen's Bureau, and, of these, 56 survived into the 1950's. Among them were Fisk and Howard (Congregational), Wilberforce (African Methodist Episcopal), and Spelman (Baptist). Most of these included white teachers on their faculties. Because of racial prejudice in the South, few public colleges were founded for Negroes. Until the 1890's most Negro colleges followed the classical curriculum of white colleges, but for a time the work of Booker T. Washington brought pressures for industrial education. After World War I, efforts were made to improve the quality of Negro colleges by seeking accreditation. Recently, more Negroes have attended white colleges in the North, and in the South efforts have been made to improve public Negro colleges. Recent gains in racial integration have opened more white colleges to Negroes, but at present approximately 58 percent of all Negro college students still attend Negro colleges. Most of these are now state-supported institutions.

**Nemesius** (late 4th century). Bishop of Emesa in Syria. He was an unusual figure among ancient Christian writers. *On the Nature of Man,* the work which preserves his memory, expounds the Christian view of man from the point of the best ancient science and psychology. It indicates that Nemesius had in earlier life been deeply interested in medicine, though probably as an amateur student rather than as a professional. He is possibly identical with the philosophical official, at that time still pagan, with whom Gregory of Nazianzus discussed religion about 385.

**Neology.** A term applied by contemporaries to the "new theology" of the Enlightenment in Germany. It applies strictly to the movement away from dogmatic orthodoxy in German theology during the years 1750 to 1790 (particularly the 1760's and 1770's). Marked by the drawing of a sharp distinction between Scripture and dogma, it goes on to admit only Biblical doctrines, and then only those of a reasonable character. Outstanding among the representatives of this movement are J. S. Semler, A. F. W. Sack, J. J. Spalding, and J. F. W. Jerusalem.

**Neo-Orthodoxy.** A 20th-century theological movement also known as "neo-Reformation," "crisis," or "dialectic" theology. Arising in Europe directly following World War I, it represents a violent rejection of the synthesis between Christian theology and modern Western scientific culture represented by theological liberalism. During the 19th century the metaphysical stability that had characterized Western culture was exchanged for an empirical one. This in turn was particularly vulnerable in the face of the cataclysm of instability and irrationality that World War I represented for European man. It seemed clear to neo-orthodoxy that Christianity had married itself to Western culture just in time to officiate at its funeral. In the analysis of this movement's protest against liberalism the catastrophe of cultural disintegration should not be emphasized to the detriment of a proper understanding of the inherent objections that neo-orthodoxy had to liberalism on theological grounds. The progenitors of neo-orthodoxy were keenly aware of the anthropological reduction into which the liberal strain of theology had fallen at the hands of Ludwig Feuerbach and others. As a result of its immanentalism (God present in world

processes) and its foundation of theology on the human capacity to experience and know God, the conclusion had been drawn that God was really "man writ large."

The manifesto of neo-orthodoxy appeared in the second edition of Karl Barth's *Commentary on Romans* (1919). This work, which expounded the religious intention of Paul to the modern reader, stressed the central theme of the movement—the holiness and transcendence of that God who is revealed as merciful in Jesus Christ. This emphasis was at the same time a rejection of liberalism and a reaffirmation of themes that had already been coming to light through a historical rediscovery of the Protestant Reformers, particularly Luther, and had been expounded in the 19th century by Kierkegaard. Known as dialectic or crisis theology because of the crisis or judgment in which man is placed in the presence of such a God, and the tension that a relationship between God and man represents, it is called neo-Reformation theology because of the similarity of this theme to that of the Reformers and the positive use that the movement has made of the 16th-century Reformation figures.

Because of the cultural crisis and the theological dilemma into which main-line Protestant theology had fallen by the year 1920, this "new orthodoxy" enjoyed a phenomenally rapid success. Soon capturing many of the major theological centers, it moved on to Britain, and by the early 1930's the movement had gained a foothold in the American scene as well. Most of the theological figures of significance in mid-20th century are either of this movement or have been profoundly influenced by it. Among the preeminent names that deserve mention in connection with neo-orthodoxy in Switzerland and Germany are Karl Barth, Emil Brunner, Rudolf Bultmann, Friedrich Gogarten, Paul Tillich; in England, C. H. Dodd; and native to America, particularly the Niebuhr brothers, H. Richard and Reinhold.

Neo-orthodoxy may not be properly described as a school of thought, but better as a movement dominated by a mood. It was unified in its rejection of the identification between Christianity and Western scientific culture in liberalism, and also in its attempt to reestablish Christian faith on the basis of Christian revelation in Scripture. Its members also shared a modern view of the Bible that was their heritage from liberalism and wished to interpret the "strange world" that they discovered between its covers with the aid of modern historical and philological science. Thus "neo" is a proper part of the name by which they are known. They have also inherited a social concern from their liberal forebears, which they, however, tend to base upon the Lordship and judgment of God rather than upon any effort to build the Kingdom of God on earth.

The positive teachings of the movement may be characterized with regard to its emphasis upon the transcendence and holiness of God and the sinfulness and lostness of man, which leads to reference to God as "Other." Into this dialectical opposition of God and man comes the revelation of God's Word (Logos) in Christ who is both the judgment and the salvation of man. This pure act of God cannot ever be comprehended in man's wisdom or words but is borne witness to in the Bible and by the church, both of which are "words" referring to the Word. Through them and the proclamation that they make, God reveals himself again and again to men in this world as he confronts them in the judgment and mercy of the Word made flesh.

In its emphases and method of operation, neo-orthodoxy may be seen as a synthesis of the 16th and 19th centuries. At its best it can be a realistic effort of modern men to present a distinctly Christian theology; at its worst it can be a dodge to avoid a serious struggle with the modern crisis in knowledge—the cause/effect of the breakup of Western culture.

BIBLIOGRAPHY: K. Barth, *Epistle to the Romans* (London, 1933); and *Evangelical Theology* (New York, 1963); E. Brunner, *The Theology of Crisis* (New York, 1929); W. Hordern, *The Case for a New Reformation Theology* (Philadelphia, 1959); H. N. Wieman, *et al., Religious Liberals Reply* (Boston, 1947).

**Neoplatonism.** During the 3d century many of the elements of earlier Alexandrian Platonism were incorporated into a systematic philosophy by Plotinus (c. 205–270). This philosophy is called Neoplatonism, because although Plato's general conceptions about the two worlds, the soul of man as the intermediate realm, and his derivation of the world from God were retained, Plotinus incorporated many other elements in his synthesis. He deemphasized the mathematical aspects of earlier Platonism and stressed the notion of a chain of being, a hierarchical series of strata extending with diminishing perfection from the One all the way down to the lowliest level of matter.

The bond of the universe for Plotinus was a two-way motion of Eros. Each level of the chain aspires upward toward unity; each spiritual level extends its generous love downward toward matter. The love and striving of the soul are thus reciprocated by the Eros of the One. Plotinus also reemphasized the value of the phenomenal world with his concept of beauty. Earthly beauty leads the soul to seek eternal beauty, and is therefore an avenue for ascent to the world of the One.

Plotinus presented the Godhead as absolute and wholly indescribable unity, the Final Cause of the universe through pure creative activity. God creates the universe out of himself by emanation, the overflowing of the divine essence into creation. The stages of emanation are spirit (including ideas as archetypes in the divine mind, and other spiritual potencies), soul, and matter. The soul is alienated from divine light by its association with matter, but it can begin the return to God through love of the beautiful and true, and thence love of the idea. But only by divine grace is the soul lifted to the final stage of ascent, ecstatic communion with the One.

Plotinus' pupil Porphyry published his master's thought in six *Enneads,* and wrote considerable commentary on it. Porphyry added a number of demons to Plotinus' spiritual level of emanation, and directed the Neoplatonic system against the Christians in fifteen books of polemic. Jamblicus (d. 330) expanded this demonology into a systematic theology of polytheism, inserting various allegories and mythologies into the spiritual levels of emanation between man and God. Julian the Apostate was a follower of Jamblicus' school.

The last important Neoplatonic philosopher of this era was Proclus (410–485), who returned to the study of the original texts of Plato and Aristotle, and tried to summarize the whole of ancient philosophy in the form of a synthesis between Plato and Plotinus. Proclus described the development of the world from the Godhead by a system of triadic chains, each stage containing a continual permanence, going forth to the stage below, and returning to the stage above. He specified the stages of redemption for the sinful soul as political virtue, scientific knowledge, divine illumination, faith, and finally ecstatic union with the One.

These Neoplatonic philosophers elaborated their systems with the same basic intention as the early Christian theologians. They wanted to develop a philosophical system proving a given religious conviction to be the one sure way of salvation for a soul needing redemption. There was a primary difference between them, however. Christian theology was supported by a religious faith organizing itself into a church, whereas Neo-platonism was an erudite religion, supported by individual scholars or associations of scholars. Where Christian thinkers tried to define a specific orthodoxy to differentiate their religion in the flood of Greco-Roman and Oriental mystical philosophies, the Neoplatonists attempted to assimilate as many of the existing cults as possible.

After the beginnings made by Justin Martyr and Athenagoras, Christian theology began to come into its own in the 3d century with the Alexandrian school of catechists, including Clement and especially Origen (c. 185–c. 254). Origen was a contemporary of Plotinus, and attempted the same kind of synthesis and crystallization of Platonic themes, this time into a system that would be specifically Christian. For Origen, Scripture was the source and measure of religious knowledge, but he elaborated levels of interpretation in the same manner as Philo of Alexandria. God is described as absolute transcendence, pure Spirit which reveals its own essence with the Logos, the archetype of creation. The universe itself is a graded series of spirits similar to that of Neoplatonism, but in Origen the various strata have fallen away from divine purity by their own sin. The soul striving to rise from matter needs divine grace, which is perfectly revealed in Jesus Christ. Stages of redemption are not expressed in the same way as those of Neoplatonism but first as faith and religious understanding, then knowledge of the Logos, and finally complete absorption in God.

Origen was very influential for the thought of the Cappadocian Fathers of the 4th century, Gregory of Nazianzus and Gregory of Nyssa, as was Plotinus. The 4th century saw the beginning of the full incorporation of the Platonic tradition into Christian thought, as can be seen by the Christian Neoplatonist Chalcidius, who wrote an influential commentary on the *Timaeus,* and Victorinus, the translator of both Plotinus and Porphyry.

Augustine, bishop of Hippo (354–430), marks the most authoritative and complete combination of Neoplatonism and Christian thought. He was influenced especially by Plotinus and Porphyry, although *The City of God* contains a lengthy polemic against the latter's demonology. Augustine described Platonism as the philosophy nearest to Christianity, and said that it had missed only the mystery of the incarnation. In Book 7 of the *Confessions* and Books 8 and 10 of *The City of God* the Neoplatonic influence is most clearly exhibited.

According to the *Confessions,* it was Neo-platonic philosophy that allowed Augustine to realize the incorporeal nature of God and refute Manichaean dualism, which gave evil a positive, and therefore created, existence. He adopted the theory of the two worlds, but de-emphasized the Platonic-Plotinian concept of earthly beauty and represented the phenomenal world as a much more degraded realm. The concept of Eros was used to emphasize God's activity in man's soul, in harmony with Augustine's emphasis upon the corruption of the will and man's inability to reach goodness without God's grace. Platonic ideas, interpreted as archetypes in the divine mind, allowed Augustine to show that immutable truth has its foundation in God, and that man's knowledge comes by divine illumination. The Neoplatonic conception of germinal forms enabled him to reconcile the successive creation of Genesis with the simultaneous creation of Ecclesiastes.

In addition to the authoritative statement of Augustine, the influential *Consolation of Philosophy* of Boethius (c. 475–524) used Platonic philosophy and helped transmit it to the later Middle Ages, as did his commentary and translation of Porphyry. The *Consolation* describes the creation in a manner suggesting Genesis, but by means of the *Timaeus* myth and without any explicit mention of Christianity.

The last influential Neoplatonic and Christian synthesis of the early Middle Ages is the text attributed to the first Athenian convert of the apostle Paul, Dionysius the Areopagite. The text was actually written in the late 5th century and is based primarily upon Proclus. Dionysius attempted to reconcile the Neoplatonic One with the Christian Trinity, and the Neoplatonic concept of emanation with the Christian account of creation. He emphasized the impossibility of forming rational concepts about God and developed a negative theology that was revived in the speculative mysticism of Nicholas of Cusa (see RENAISSANCE PLATONISM). The writings of the Areopagite were discovered in the 8th century, and translated by John Scotus Eriugena in the 9th. They formed the basis of Eriugena's influential philosophy. After the 9th century, Augustine and Dionysius were combined in a Christian transformation of Platonism that was to be influential through the 14th century.

**Nero** (37–68). Roman emperor from 54 to 68. Nero's importance for church history is due chiefly to his effort, after a disastrous fire at Rome in July, 64, to use Christians as scapegoats, thus averting the widespread suspicion that he had planned the fire in order to "redevelop" the area involved. An unknown number of Christians were martyred. Two years later, Jewish sacrifices for the emperor were terminated at Jerusalem, and a war broke out which was won for Rome only by Nero's successor.

**Nerses** (d. c. 373). Sixth catholicos of Armenia. He was called "the Great" to distinguish him from a number of others of the same name. Born in Vagharshabad of royal blood, he was also a descendant of Gregory the Illuminator. After a Greek education and service in the court, he was begged by the king and the people to become bishop and then catholicos. As such he founded schools and charitable institutions. As ambassador he once restored peace between the king and Valentinian I, but did not succeed in doing so with Valens, who banished him to a desert island. Theodosius the Great restored him and asked him to participate in the Second Ecumenical Council. Returning to Armenia, he found that he had been supplanted and is even believed to have been poisoned by the king.

**Nestorianism.** Little is known of Nestorius' life (d. c. 451) apart from his involvement in the controversy that bears his name. He was born in Germanicia toward the end of the 4th century, and pursued his studies in Antioch, where he was probably the pupil of Theodore of Mopsuestia. He entered the monastery of Euprepios near Antioch, and gained a reputation for preaching. In 428, Theodosius II appointed him patriarch of Constantinople. The only work of Nestorius that is extant in full is his apology, the *Bazaar of Heracleides*. In 428, Nestorius and Anastasius, his chaplain, began preaching against the use of the word "Theotokos" in connection with the Virgin Mary. Nestorius claimed that Mary was not the bearer of God, but merely bearer of the human nature of Christ. The monks of Constantinople, many of whom had Egyptian affiliations, could not acquiesce in Nestorius' point of view, and refused to relinquish their use of Theotokos. Various denunciations and appeals raised the controversy to worldwide proportions. In 430 a synod in Rome condemned Nestorius and authorized Cyril of Alexandria to anathematize him. The emperor was forced to summon a general council meeting in Ephesus in 431. Cyril had the Council convened before the arrival of John of Antioch (d. 441), who supported Nestorius. Cyril's group deposed Nestorius, but the remnant of the Council under John of Antioch then deposed Cyril. Nestorius retreated to the monastery at Antioch. Various attempts were made to reunite the opposing factions, but in 435 the issue was decided when Theodosius II sent Nestorius into exile. The deposed patriarch finally arrived in Upper Egypt, where he remained until his death. Despite Nestorius' removal from the scene, the controversy continued. An opponent of Nestorianism named Eutyches asserted that Mary was Theotokos and, as such, the bearer of a Christ of one nature after the union. Despite the opposition of Flavian of Constantinople and Leo I of Rome, Eutyches, supported by Dioscorus of Alexandria, was upheld in the Latrocinium, or Robber Council, of Ephesus in 449. However, in 451, after Theodosius II's death, the Council of Chalcedon, reversing the Latrocinium, condemned Eutyches and the Monophysites, and provided a Christological definition that can be thought of as embracing the viewpoints of both Nestorius and Cyril. Though in some sense reestablished, Nestorius was never formally restored and probably died before receiving word of the partial justification of his position at Chalcedon.

The history of the Nestorian controversy can be explained in several ways. At least two factors that are not entirely theological must be considered. First, there was a strong rivalry between Antioch and Alexandria, two of the most important cities in the world. Second, there was a bitter rivalry between the Alexandrian and the Constantinopolitan sees. The primacy of the Alexandrian church was threatened by the establishment of the upstart see of Constantinople, or New Rome. Apart from these factors a real theological issue was involved. The traditions of Alexandria and Antioch maintained two very different approaches to Christian theology. Under the threat of Arianism, the Alexandrians emphasized the full divinity of Christ, and did so in terms of Greek philosophical categories. The Antiochenes were more concerned with the heresy of Apollinarius and strongly asserted Christ's full humanity. Though both aims were correct, when pursued to excess both could lead to error. The Alexandrians tended to omit supplying Christ with a full human nature, whereas the Antiochenes tended to assert two separate natures without supplying an adequate statement of union. The Christology of Cyril tended to drift toward Apollinarianism, whereas that of Nestorius tended to become what can be called "textbook Nestorianism," i.e., the separation of the human and divine natures of Christ. Nestorius' ideas, as presented in the *Bazaar of Heracleides,* can certainly be held to be in accord with the Chalcedonian definition of Christ's person as two natures, human and divine, united so as to be neither confounded nor separated. After the final condemnation of Nestorianism at Chalcedon, no Nestorian Christian was to be tolerated within the Empire.

For many centuries the Nestorian Church flourished in Persia and sent missionaries throughout eastern and southern Asia; penetrating into India, China, and Japan. In 1625, Roman Catholic missionaries rediscovered the Nestorian monument in northwest China which tells of the arrival of Nestorian missionaries c. 635. The monument itself dates from 781. From the 11th through the 14th century Moslem and Mongol invasions made serious inroads into the Nestorian Church and mission enterprise. Nevertheless, there still existed 27 metropolitan sees and some 200 bishoprics throughout Asia in 1400. Today only a remnant of Nestorian Christians (known as Assyrian Christians) are left in Persia as a result of Mongol and Moslem extermination and Roman Catholic absorption.

BIBLIOGRAPHY: J. F. Bethune-Baker, *Nestorius and His Teaching* (Cambridge, 1908); J. Joseph, *The Nestorians and Their Muslim Neighbors* (Princeton, 1961); F. Loofs, *Nestorius and His Place in the History of Christian Doctrine* (Cambridge, 1914); A. C. Monle, *Christians in China Before the Year 1550* (London, 1930); J. A. Montgomery, *The History of Yaballaba III, Nestorian Patriarch* (New York, 1927); J. Stewart, *Nestorian Missionary Enterprise* (Edinburgh, 1928); W. A. Wigram, *An Introduction to the History of the Assyrian Church: 100–640 A.D.* (London, 1910).

**Nestorian Uniates.** See UNIATE.

**Netherlands Bible Society.** An association founded in 1814 by the union of several earlier societies. It has carried on a work of great magnitude but concentrated on the translation, revision, printing, and distribution of the Scriptures for the Dutch colonies in the East Indies (now Indonesia) and West Indies.

**Netherlands Indies, Church of the.** The Dutch East India Company was responsible for the establishment of the Reformed Church in the area, supporting clergy who preached to both Europeans and natives. A church arose which, after the Company was dissolved (1798), had the support of the state and in the main centers of Dutch rule included a large proportion of the population. In 1935 the church was separated administratively from the state and became related to the International Missionary Council and then to the World Council of Churches.

**Netherlands Missionary Society** (Nederlandsch Zendeling-Genootschap). An association founded in 1797 by John T. Vanderkemp as an expression of a revival of Continental Pietism. It was influenced by the London Missionary Society and has been an independent society sending missionaries, mostly of the Dutch Reformed faith, throughout the world; it has been particularly active in the Dutch colonies. Some societies have opposed it as being too inclusive, hence too lax to reflect accurately the Reformed faith.

**Nettleton, Asahel** (1783–1844). American evangelist. Born at Killingworth, Conn., and educated at Yale, he was ordained as a Congregational evangelist in 1817, thereafter converting thousands. A strict Calvinist, he made a serious appeal to the consciences of his hearers. He rejected the more emotional New Measures of Charles G. Finney, and also opposed the New Haven Theology as weakening Calvinism. He was a founder of the Theological Institute of Connecticut.

**Neuendettelsau Mission Society.** A German Lutheran missionary society. Officially the Society for Inner and Foreign Missions of the Lutheran Church, the Society was founded by Wilhelm Loehe in 1841 to represent distinctly Lutheran interests in missions. Like the Inner Mission of Johann Wichern, it found expression in charitable as well as evangelistic activities. It had an influential role in Midwest American Lutheranism during the 19th century and since 1876 it has been active in Australia. From 1886 in New Guinea it has conducted an outstanding work among the natives as well as the colonists.

**Nevin, John Williamson** (1803–1886). Presbyterian and German Reformed theologian. Educated at Union College and at Princeton, Nevin substituted for Charles Hodge at Princeton for two years and then taught ten years at Western Theological Seminary. A study of German theology, especially Neander, influenced him toward a churchly and sacramental theology. After moving to the German Reformed Seminary at Mercersburg, Pa., in 1840, he developed this emphasis as leader (with Philip Schaff after 1844) of the so-called Mercersburg Theology. Upon the appearance of his *The Anxious Bench* (1843) much controversy arose, and he continued to write in defense of his views against charges of Romanism and Puseyism. He retired in 1853 but in 1861 began teaching at

Franklin and Marshall College, where he served as president from 1866 to 1876.

**New Connexion General Baptists.** General Baptists had been steadily declining in England during the period of toleration after 1689. As a result of the Wesleyan revival, Dan Taylor (1738–1816) formed a society in 1770 called the New Connexion which stirred a vigorous new life among the Baptists of the eastern Midlands. They were Arminian in theology and insisted upon the doctrine of "general" atonement. In 1891 the New Connexion body joined with the Particular Baptists in England to form the Baptist Union of Great Britain and Ireland.

**New Delhi, Assembly at.** The Third Assembly of the World Council of Churches, held in the capital of India, Nov. 18 to Dec. 6, 1961. From the viewpoint of the developing ecumenical movement the most important event was the integration of the International Missionary Council with the World Council of Churches to form its Division of World Mission and Evangelism. New churches admitted brought the membership to 198 in 70 countries. The wording of the Basis of the Council was altered to read: "The World Council of Churches is a fellowship of churches which confess the Lord Jesus Christ as God and Saviour according to the Scriptures." In addition to attending to the business of departments and committees, the Assembly carefully defined religious liberty, sent a special message on segregation and discrimination to the churches of South Africa, and sent another to those of East Germany, expressing sorrow over their absence.

The theme of the Assembly was "Jesus Christ, the Light of the World," and 600,000 copies of a course of Bible studies were distributed around the world for preparatory use. Three sections dealt with this theme in terms of "Witness," "Unity," and "Service." The "Message" calls for witness in unity through service both to need and to the furtherance of justice and community.

BIBLIOGRAPHY: See *The New Delhi Report,* ed. by W. A. Visser 't Hooft (New York, 1962).

**New England Theology.** A late 18th- and early 19th-century Calvinist movement which attempted to bridge the gap between the traditional theology of Puritanism and the newer emphases in America upon individualism and personal freedom. The movement was the product of at least two dozen theologians, stretched over more than a century, was

quite diverse in some of its manifestations, and because of the technical language and involved arguments frequently found, has not been an appealing subject even for historians of the church.

Chronologically, the New England Theology began with Jonathan Edwards about 1750, dominated the teaching of theology in the orthodox Congregational seminaries in the United States during the first half of the 19th century, but quite suddenly disappeared about 1880 when the influence of German historical and critical theology took its place. Although theologians of the movement taught at Hartford, Andover, Oberlin, and Chicago Theological Seminaries, the New England Theology was most clearly associated with Yale University and Divinity School. Jonathan Edwards was trained there, as were most of the other important figures, and Timothy Dwight and Nathaniel W. Taylor, two of the most important figures in the movement, were president of the university and first professor of the Divinity School respectively. Traditional Calvinism, as imported into New England by the Puritan fathers, emphasized the work of God—the manner in which God controlled the world, his hatred for sin, his compassion in sending Christ to win salvation for men—but man's role in this theology was negligible. In 18th-century western Europe and colonial America, man was not any longer considered so unimportant a creature—either by the philosophers or by ordinary people. In particular, the development of experimental science in Europe and the immigrant's wrestling with the frontier in America created among men generally a belief that man was not so bad a creature as he was made out to be in the Calvinist system. Jonathan Edwards, sensing this drift away from the old standards, set it as his task to reformulate Calvinism in terms of the new science—the physics of Isaac Newton and the psychology of John Locke. Edwards understood this new science as did few other men in the Western world. The effect of Edwards' lifework was to perpetuate Calvinism as a vital theological force for at least a century after his death. One definition for the New England Theology, then, is that it was the lengthened shadow of Jonathan Edwards. His reformulation of the problems of human life in terms of Calvinist thought gave many generations of subsequent theologians problems to mull over and avenues of thought to explore.

After Edwards, the leaders of the New England Theology were Joseph Bellamy (1719–1790), Jonathan Edwards, Jr. (1745–

1801), Samuel Hopkins (1721–1803), Timothy Dwight (1752–1817), Nathaniel W. Taylor (1786–1858), and Edwards A. Park (1808–1900). Their work as a whole might be described as a strategic retreat. They attempted to save as much of the Calvinistic system as they could by giving up small parts of it very gradually. They, of course, looked upon these surrenders as qualifications or interpretations. Although a general change in the climate of opinion seems to have been basically responsible, the immediate forces before which Calvinism was forced to retreat were the Universalist-Unitarian movement and revivalism. The former made a great fuss about the fact that Calvinism taught that man was punished for Adam's sin, which seemed very undemocratic even to Bostonians, while the latter protested that man did have a role to play in his salvation and did not need to remain passively waiting for God to save him. Both movements attacked the Calvinist concept of a limited atonement and taught that Christ had died for all men. As a result of these developments, New England theologians were particularly preoccupied with the doctrine of the atonement, the nature of original sin, and man's capacity for free action. In general, the tendency of all the leaders of the New England school was to limit the effects of original sin, to make man responsible only for his own misdeeds, and to allow greater and greater scope for man's freedom.

BIBLIOGRAPHY: F. H. Foster, *A Genetic History of the New England Theology* (Chicago, 1942); J. Haroutunian, *Piety Versus Moralism* (New York, 1932); S. E. Mead, *Nathaniel William Taylor* (Chicago, 1942); P. Miller, *Jonathan Edwards* (Cleveland, 1963).

**New Haven Theology.** A phase in the development of a more liberal interpretation of Calvinism associated with the work of Nathaniel W. Taylor (1786–1858), a professor in Yale Divinity School. Unitarian criticisms of Jonathan Edwards' Calvinism, as well as the rise of revivalism, led Taylor to give a more positive explanation of the freedom of the human will. Unlike earlier Calvinists who had grounded the freedom of the will solely on divine revelation, Taylor sought to show that Calvinistic teaching was also compatible with human reason. According to Taylor, since holiness depends upon free choice, God has given man a free will, for only in this way can man become truly holy. This gift of freedom involves the possibility of sin (although God did not directly will sin). In Taylor's thought, the certainty that man will sin does

not destroy human power to will the opposite, i.e., holiness. This doctrine means that God has voluntarily limited himself by giving man the power of choice beyond any divine control. In this view, sin is only voluntary sin, and infants are thus incapable of sin. The most famous follower of Taylor was Horace Bushnell, who stressed the role of Christian nurture in enabling the child to grow up as a Christian. Taylor's views were strongly opposed by strict Calvinists such as Charles Hodge.

**New Life Movement** (China). A trend promoted by Chiang Kai-shek to rally the Chinese people against Communism. It was begun March 11, 1934, and was intended to contribute to the growth of industrious, austere life according to ancient virtues, especially courtesy, service, honesty, and high-mindedness. The first of eight principles was: Regard yesterday as a time of death, today of life; rid ourselves of old abuses, and build up a new nation. Chen Li-fu was its ideologist, Madame Chiang its promoter.

**Newlights** (Canadian). A religious movement in Nova Scotia during the American Revolution characterized by great enthusiasm for things of the spirit. The movement was originated by Henry Alline, a young farmer from Falmouth, Nova Scotia. Anglican officialdom viewed with alarm this outbreak of religious enthusiasm and impugned the loyalty of the Newlights. Consequently, they turned to the Baptists and became absorbed into the Baptist Church.

**New Light Schism.** The Great Revival in the West (1797–1805), with its "fervor, noise, and disorder," led to conflict within the Presbyterian Church over the doctrinal and educational standards of the ministry. Revivalists sought to modify doctrines of human ability to enhance their appeals, and pointed to a lack of clergy because of "unnecessary" educational demands. In 1801 and 1802, Richard McNemar was charged with Arminianism in the Washington Presbytery. The issue came before the Synod of Kentucky in 1803. When he and John Thompson came up for trial, they questioned the Synod's jurisdiction and with Barton W. Stone, Robert Marshall, John Dunlavy, and David Purviance led the New Light schism. Suspended by the Synod, they formed the independent Springfield Presbytery, based on doctrine and polity derived from the Bible alone. In 1804 the Presbytery was dissolved, with its famous "Last Will and Testament," in which "sectarianism" was abandoned for the sake of Christian unity. They took the name "Christian." Stone became the dominant figure as McNemar and Dunlavy became

Shakers and Thompson and Marshall returned to the Presbyterians. The revivalistic "Christian" body grew, and in 1832 effected a union with the Disciples of Christ. A similar division over revivalism also took place in the Cumberland Presbytery, which separated in 1810 and adopted the name Cumberland Presbyterian Church in 1816.

**Newman, John Henry** (1801–1890). English Tractarian and Roman Catholic cardinal. Born in London, the eldest son of a banker, Newman matriculated at Trinity College, Oxford (1817), becoming a fellow of Oriel College in 1822. He was made vicar of the university church (St. Mary's) in 1828. In 1833 he and his associates in the Oxford movement began the *Tracts for the Times* (1833–1841). Newman, who wrote twenty-four of the *Tracts,* also had a great impact through his sermons at St. Mary's (1834–1842). His major concern was to demonstrate that the Church of England embodied the tradition of the church fathers, the *via media.* Beginning in 1839, Newman increasingly had doubts about Anglicanism which finally led him to Roman Catholicism in 1845. These doubts were manifest in his famous *Tract No. 90* (1841), which announced the compatibility of the Thirty-nine Articles with Roman Catholic doctrine. Reproved by the bishop of Oxford, he retired to Littlemore outside of Oxford. Resigning his Anglican benefices (1843), he was later ordained a priest in Rome (1847). A leader of English Catholicism as he had been of Anglicanism, he was made a cardinal by Leo XIII in 1879. Among his writings are *The Idea of a University* (1852), the autobiographical *Apologia pro vita sua* (1864), and *The Grammar of Assent* (1870).

**New Measures.** A term applied to the revival techniques of the American evangelist Charles G. Finney (1792–1875). These practices included extemporaneous preaching, harsh invectives against sinful practices, long prayers in which individuals were mentioned by name, protracted meetings, the encouraging of women to pray and exhort in public, an "anxious seat" for penitents, and the invasion of parishes against the wishes of local ministers.

**New School and Old School Presbyterians.** During and following the 1830's there arose an increasing sense of denominational loyalty in the United States. Within Presbyterianism this came to a climax in 1837 when at the General Assembly the denomination was rent in two. The Old School party of predominantly Scotch-Irish background exscinded the New School synods which had largely New

England roots, and repudiated interdenominational cooperation. After an attempt the next year to rectify this situation had failed, the New School Presbyterian denomination was formed. The cause of this division may be seen in the Old School's interest in strict Presbyterian confessionalism and polity, which was felt to have been circumscribed in congregations formed under the Plan of Union or served by ministers aided by the American Home Missionary Society. It was felt that these two sources of interdenominational cooperation had allowed a liberalized theology and a quasi-Congregational polity to become entrenched within Presbyterianism. The New School adherents, who were products of these cooperative ventures, remained faithful to them, but the Congregationalists withdrew from the Plan in 1852, and the American Home Missionary Society became a Congregational society in 1861. Also as a consequence of the animosity, and contributing to the division, were the bitter heresy trials of 1828 to 1837 and the antislavery agitation that was coming to the fore among New School adherents and Congregationalists. In 1869, with the causes of the division largely removed, the two groups were reunited.

**Newton, Sir Isaac** (1642–1727). English scientist. The son of a yeoman from Lincolnshire, he went to Cambridge to study theology, but switched to astronomy and metaphysics. The publication of his *Principia mathematica* ("The Mathematical Principles of Natural Philosophy") in 1687, in which he demonstrated that laws of motion and gravitation keep the celestial bodies in their proper places, consummated the revolution in science. His discoveries raised new questions for Christianity. If the universe operates according to demonstrable laws of motion and gravity, is the world a field of divine activity? If the universe works on such laws, then perhaps our own world operates the same way, and the providence of God for individual life is not real. Epistemologically, scientific truth began to be preferred by some to revelation. Although Newton himself remained deeply religious, others came to different conclusions. A few traced causes back to nature, eliminating God. Others, such as the deists, held to the necessity for the great "clockmaker," but denied divine intervention in the course of nature. Newton's work prepared the way for the Enlightenment, when man looked to scientific method and reason to discover all he needed to know. In his own personal religious beliefs Newton doubted the doctrine of the Trinity and inclined toward a variety of exotic speculations, the extent of which was learned only after his death.

**Newton, John** (1725–1807). English Evangelical minister and hymnist. After a long career at sea, Newton was converted, came under the influence of George Whitefield and John Wesley, and was ordained a priest at Olney (1764). Later he accepted the benefice of St. Mary Woolnoth, London, where he converted many important figures to the evangelical movement. He published his *Review of Ecclesiastical History* in 1770 and with his friend William Cowper the famous *Olney Hymns* (1779), including his own compositions "Amazing Grace," "Glorious Things of Thee Are Spoken," and "One There Is Above All Others."

**Nicaea, Council of** (325). The first of the ecumenical councils of the church. The emperor Constantine, having secured the throne, turned his attention toward establishing the peace and unity of the Christian church. Politically speaking, Constantine must have felt that Christianity could best serve as the spiritual force unifying the various nationalities of the Empire. Such a force was desperately needed, and the divisions within the church itself proportionately reduced its usefulness. These divisions, particularly in Alexandria, the granary of the Empire, were a real threat to economic and political stability. Constantine summoned the leaders of the church, who met at Nicaea in 325. According to tradition, there were 318 bishops present, and the Council was convened on May 20. Few of the Western bishops were present, though the bishop of Rome was represented by two presbyters. There appear to have been some preliminary meetings, but the Council really began when the emperor himself arrived. Constantine produced letters from various bishops chiefly concerned with the Arian controversy. Symbolically destroying the letters, Constantine implored the members of the Council to rid the church of disunity. The Arian controversy and the drafting of an authoritative statement of belief were certainly the major subjects of the Council's deliberations. A creed was submitted by Eusebius of Nicomedia, but promptly rejected as unorthodox. Eusebius of Caesarea then presented the baptismal creed he was accustomed to use. After much deliberation, and the insertion of the word *homoousios,* this creed was accepted as orthodox. For Eusebius, this was in all likelihood a great triumph, as it seems quite probable that he had been condemned as Arian at a preliminary synod in Antioch. However, it would seem doubtful that Eusebius of Caesarea's creed was the same as that promulgated by the Council of Nicaea. There is a general resemblance, but a closer approximation can be found in the creed of Cyril of Jerusalem. Although it is usually assumed that Alexander of Alexandria and Athanasius were the leaders of the orthodox group at Nicaea, the word *homoousios* was probably introduced by Hosius of Cordova, supported by the emperor himself. Beyond rejecting Arius' teaching, the Council made two other major decisions. The Quartodeciman controversy was settled in favor of celebrating Easter on the Sunday nearest the 14th day of Nisan (the Passover) rather than on the 14th day itself. The bishops of Alexandria and Rome were given the task of notifying Christendom of the proper Sunday year by year. Second, the Melitian Schism in Egypt was settled. Melitius, the bishop of Lycopolis, had objected to what he considered lax terms for the readmission of Christians lapsed during the Diocletian persecution, and had become bishop of a schismatic church. The conciliar decision allowed the Melitian clergy to function, provided it was under the jurisdiction of the patriarch of Alexandria, and Melitius was allowed to retain the title but not the power of bishop. After dealing with these three major sources of division within the church, the Council enacted various other canons, all of which had as their aim some kind of regularization and unification of the church. Although the acta of the Council do not exist, the creed with its anti-Arian anathemas, the synodal letter, and the canons do. There are twenty authentic canons extant. Their force, like the other decisions of the Council, depended upon general acceptance more than anything else. A number of the canons deal with clerical regulations. Careful physical and moral standards are set for the clergy. No one who has voluntarily castrated himself can be ordained priest (Canon 1). No one can become a priest immediately upon his reception from paganism (Canon 2). Deacons must keep to their subordinate position (Canon 18). No priest may have a woman living with him who is not a close relative or "beyond suspicion" (Canon 3). At least three bishops must consent to the consecration of a bishop (Canon 4), and no bishop, priest, or deacon may pass from city to city (Canons 15 and 16)—ecclesiastical boundaries must be observed. Canons 6 and 7 spell out the patriarchal status of the sees of Alexandria, Rome, Antioch, and Jerusalem. Canons 10 to 14 are a kind of penitential code concerned with the practical matter of readmitting lapsed Christians. Canon 17 provides excommunication as a penalty for usury, and

Canon 20 states that prayers must be said standing up on Lord's Days and on Pentecost. Its business accomplished, the Council adjourned, probably July 25, 325.

Unfortunately, none of the decisions of the Council could be exactly enforced, and their ecumenicity depends more upon their acceptance over half a century later than upon any immediate effect. Most serious for the unity of Christendom was the fact that Arianism, far from disappearing, became the official imperial version of Christianity. For this reason, it is worthwhile to trace the development of the Arian heresy, and to consider in some detail the theological question as treated at Nicaea. The heresiarch Arius, who had been a Melitian, was priest of a large and influential parish in Baucalis, a suburb of Alexandria. He was quite obviously an extremely intelligent and well-educated man, and also one familiar with the Platonizing theology of Origen. He seems to have taken this as a basis for his speculations. Origen had stated that the Logos was the agent of creation, that is, that through his Son God created the world. The implication of this assertion was that the very existence of the Son (or Word) and the world were bound up with one another. God was thought of as eternally generating the Word, and the Word as eternally generating the world. Arius combined this view of the Godhead and creation with a strong emphasis upon the monarchy of God. God, he asserted, is uncreate and cannot be involved in any direct way in the creation. The Son, begotten of God, is, therefore, not uncreate, but a creature (*ktisma*). To use the most famous Arian slogan: There was a time when the Son did not exist. Even though he is the agent of creation, and the firstborn of all creatures, the Son is nonetheless created. The Arian Christ appears, then, as a sort of demigod or as some superior angel. The bishops at the Council of Nicaea were under the necessity of finding some way of stating the orthodox belief regarding Christ in such a way as to refute the theology of Arius. From the earliest times the church had considered Jesus Christ both a man in the true sense of the word, and also divine. As opposed to Arianism, the church was forced to find a proper way of asserting the full divinity of Christ. The baptismal creeds of the orthodox bishops were only partially successful, because in every case they were patient of an Arian interpretation. No matter who introduced the word *homoousios*, it seems to have been the shibboleth that separated orthodox from Arian. Even though the Council accepted the word as definitive of its anathematization of Arius,

there were a number of objections to its use. At least partly because of these objections (and the consequent inability of the orthodox to rally around the standard), the Arian controversy continued in full force after the Council of Nicaea. The objections to *homoousios* were as follows: In the first place, there was no Scriptural basis for the word. Secondly, *homoousios* had been used by Paul of Samosata, who was condemned in 268. It seemed unsuitable to many to use a word with so shady a background. Finally, many theologians believed that *homoousios* was capable of a Sabellian interpretation. "Of one substance with the Father" might assert the full divinity of the Son, but might it not also assert that there is but one substance? In other words, the monarchian heresy seemed to be implied by *homoousios*. Athanasius' association with Marcellus of Ancyra, who was considered by the East an out-and-out Sabellian, did nothing to quiet this fear. It remained for the Cappadocians to hammer out the distinction between *ousia* and *hypostasis*, thus providing a vocabulary that clearly avoided both Sabellianism and Arianism. Despite these objections to the *homoousion*, and despite the fact that the Council of Nicaea marks the beginning rather than the end of the struggle against Arianism, the Council did set down a foundation. That foundation, built upon by Athanasius and the Cappadocians, is the basis not only of an anti-Arian polemic but also of the whole framework of Christian theology as traditionally expressed.

BIBLIOGRAPHY: P. Schaff and H. Wace (eds.), *Nicene and Post-Nicene Fathers*, Series II, Vol. 14 (Grand Rapids, 1952–1956); W. Bright, *The Age of the Fathers* (London, 1903); A. E. Burn, *The Council of Nicaea* (New York, 1925); G. Forell, *Understanding the Nicene Creed* (Philadelphia, 1965).

**Nicaea, Empire of** (1204–1261). The name given to the Byzantine Empire during the Latin occupation of Constantinople, an event that grew out of one of the campaigns of the Fourth Crusade. (See LATIN EMPIRE.) During the occupation the Byzantine Empire continued with headquarters at Nicaea, a city in Asia some one hundred miles southeast of Constantinople. Refusing to submit to Rome except when military power forced it, the Greek Church continued under its own patriarch. The Roman occupation ended ignominiously when the Byzantines, headquartered at Nicaea, retook Constantinople in 1261.

**Nicaea, Second Council of** (787). The Seventh General Council, the last recognized by the entire church. Emperor Leo III's decrees against image worship (726, 730) had precipitated a violent controversy in the Byzantine Empire. The Synod of Hieria (754) condemned image worship, and the Roman see, strongly opposed to iconoclasm, turned from Constantinople and sought allies among the Franks. When Emperor Leo IV died (780), his son was still a minor. Effective political power passed to the empress Irene, an image worshiper. She and her patriarch Tarasius summoned a council in 786, intending to restore image worship, and invited Pope Hadrian I to attend. The Council, held in Constantinople, was disrupted by soldiers favoring iconoclasm; in the following year, the Council was reconvened at Nicaea, site of the First Ecumenical Council, Tarasius presiding and legates from Rome present. Image worship was restored, and all heretics, including Pope Honorius, and notable iconoclasts were anathematized. Icons were held to be objects of veneration (Greek, *proskynēsis*) but not adoration (Greek, *latreia*). The Council also enacted disciplinary canons intended to raise the morality of the clergy (e.g., against simony; forbidding sexually mixed monasteries). In the East this Council provided the victorious image worshipers with firmer theological grounds for their view. In the West, due to a faulty translation that they had received, the Frankish bishops understood that icons had been accorded the same reverence as that given the Holy Trinity, and at the Synod of Frankfort (794), they rejected the decree. The Second Nicene Council, long unrecognized in the West, is now considered by Rome to be ecumenical.

BIBLIOGRAPHY: E. J. Martin, *A History of the Iconoclastic Controversy* (New York, 1930).

**Nicephorus** (*also known as* Nicephorus Patriarcha) (c. 758–829). Byzantine patriarch, theologian, and historian. The son of Theodorus, Nicephorus, like his father, was a champion of the worship of icons. He was influential in the Second Nicene Council (787) in which the use of icons was restored to the worship service. Subsequently, he withdrew to a monastery, but came out of retirement to head a poorhouse in Constantinople. At the death of the patriarch Tarasius in 806, the emperor Nicephorus appointed the layman Nicephorus to that high office. In 814, the emperor Leo V revived iconoclasm and deposed and imprisoned Nicephorus in 815 when the patriarch refused to obey the imperial edict. The emperor Michael III released all imprisoned as a result of the icon controversy

and offered to restore Nicephorus to the patriarchate if he would ban discussion of image worship. Nicephorus refused, went into exile, and he died. The writings of Nicephorus include a brief history of the period between 602 and 729 entitled the *Breviarium* and a chronology of history from the Creation to his own time. His theological work for the most part dwelt on the controversy over the use of icons.

**Nicetas of Remesiana** (d. after 414). Bishop of Remesiana in Dacia, north of the Danube (Bela Palanka in Yugoslavia) from c. 370. His importance for church history is seen chiefly in two respects: (1) The fact that he had contacts with the church in both the East and the West. His friendship with Paulinus of Nola (d. 431), whom he instructed in hymnology, is an indication of this. Paulinus, in verse, praised him as an ardent missionary. Nicetas reportedly used hymns in the winning of pagan barbarians in his diocese. Some scholars have ascribed the *Te Deum laudamus* to him. (2) In the character of his writings, e.g., *De explanatio symboli,* six books of instruction for catechumens. These books are essentially an exposition and a history of the development of the church's creeds. He refers to the church as "the congregation of all the saints," holding out to potential converts the idea that the Christian hope consists largely in "communion of the saints" (*communio sanctorum*), the earliest known usage of that term. Among his other works are *De ratione fidei,* written against Arianism, and *De Spiritus Sancti potentia* against the Pneumatomachians.

**Nicholas.** Historically bishop of Myra in Lycia during the 4th century, but more important as a focal point for hagiography. He was said to have been so rich and benevolent that he anonymously provided dowries for three poor girls. In later times his festival in December came to be associated with Christmas, and his name in Dutch, Sinterklaas, gave rise to the modern American Santa Claus.

**Nicholas I** (*sometimes called* Nicholas the Great) (d. 867). Pope from 858. A distinguished figure among 9th-century popes, he upheld the right of clerics to appeal to Rome against the decisions of a provincial synod in the cases of Wulfad of Bourges and Rothad of Soissons. In so doing, Nicholas caused the powerful Hincmar of Reims to retract his opposition to these men. Nicholas deposed John of Ravenna for failing to answer a triple summons to the Roman court to answer charges brought against him, and also deposed the bishops Gunther of Cologne and

Thietgaud of Trier for sanctioning the divorce of Lothair II, the king of Lorraine, from Theutberga. In the East, Nicholas faced schism when Bardas, acting for his nephew Michael III, deposed the patriarch Ignatius and intruded Photius (858). Photius opposed the Western use of *filioque* in the Nicene Creed and certain customs in ritual and fasting. Nicholas wrote to the Eastern bishops asking for support of Ignatius (862) and excommunicated Photius in the following year. Photius in turn excommunicated the Latins (867). Photius was deposed in the revolt, which caused the downfall of Michael (967). In Bulgaria, Nicholas secured the adherence of Boris to the Western Church, but after Nicholas' death, Boris accepted the Byzantine rite. The position of authority gained for the papacy by Nicholas was lost by successive popes until the 11th century.

**Nicholas II** (Gerard, d. 1061). He was born in Savoy and elected pope in 1058 through the influence of Hildebrand (Gregory VII). In the Synod of 1059, Nicholas announced the election reform decree that gave the cardinal bishops the right of electing the pope (see SACRED COLLEGE), with acclamation by the Romans and recognition by the emperor. He also formed an alliance with the Normans at Melfi in 1059. Both measures were attempts to free the papacy from domination by, and dependence upon, the Roman factions and the emperor.

**Nicholas V** (Tommaso Parentucelli, 1397–1455). Pope from 1447. The son of a physician, he was born in Sarzana in Liguria. He studied at Bologna, with the exception of a few years that he spent tutoring in Florence, where he came into contact with humanism. After finishing his studies he was made bishop of Bologna and papal negotiator to the Holy Roman Empire concerning the reforming decrees of the Council of Basel. His familiarity with patristic and Scholastic theology was particularly useful at the Council of Florence. He succeeded Eugenius IV to the papacy in 1447 and by the use of conciliation was able to achieve the abdication of the schismatic Felix V. He crowned Frederick III in 1452, the last time that a German emperor was crowned in Rome. He sent Nicholas of Cusa to Germany and Bohemia to reform abuses and Guillaume d'Estouteville to France for the same purpose. Nicholas was known for his patronage of humanism. One of his projects was to restore Rome, and to this end he commissioned a number of architects and designated 1450 as a jubilee year. He was particularly interested in reconciling the new learning with religion. He founded the Vatican library and employed hundreds of copyists and scholars.

**Nicholas, Henry** (Hendrik Niclaes) (c. 1502–c. 1580). Founder of the Familist movement. He was a merchant's son who from childhood claimed to have visions from God, and though he read the writings of Luther, he aimed at an immanent experience of God such as Luther never avowed. He also sought a church composed only of believers sharing an experiential holiness. He believed that he himself had become a *homo novus* ("new man") signing himself "H.N." to indicate his experienced sanctification. He and his followers believed that they had become the living tabernacle of God in readiness for the imminent *eschaton*. He understood the whole Trinity to dwell within them, though he emphasized the Spirit most. He encouraged his followers in a communality or family of love, though at the same time he was vigilant against antinomian behavior. Worship in the often clandestine groups was carefully organized, with explicit place made for the inspired utterances of anyone present. Members were to give sincere "service of love" to one another, and were especially to obey the more deeply Spirit-filled elders of the group. Baptism was received at the age of thirty. Nicholas was active in Emden and elsewhere, perhaps visiting England in 1552 or 1553. At any rate, the Familists were most numerous in England, some of them later becoming Quakers.

**Nicholas Mysticus** (d. 925). Patriarch of Constantinople (901–906, 912–925), pupil of Photius. Deposed for his adamant opposition to the fourth marriage of the widower Leo VI, he was replaced by the pliable Euthymius, but was recalled shortly before Leo's death and restored as patriarch. A split over the question of the legitimate patriarch, seen by some as a continuation of the animosity between Ignatians and Photians, was reconciled at Constantinople (920) when Nicholas was recognized as patriarch and communications with the papacy restored. Although removed from the council of regency for the minor Constantine VII by the boy's mother Zoë (919), Nicholas remained patriarch until his death.

**Nicholas of Cusa** (1401–1464). German churchman and philosopher. Born at Cues on the Moselle River, he was probably educated first by the Brethren of the Common Life at Deventer. He studied at Heidelberg, where he was influenced by the Neoplatonism of John Scotus Eriugena and Eckhart, and the Occamism of Marsilius von Inghen. At Padua he earned a doctorate in canon law and there gained the friendship of Cardinal Cesarini, his teacher. Nicholas also absorbed the Paduan masters of mathematics, astronomy, physics, and Averroism. It was at Cologne that he studied theology under Heymericus de Campo, the Albertist, and became acquainted with the writings of Ramón Lull. During this time (1426–1429) he was also immersed in the Italian Renaissance.

Nicholas' first important work, *De concordantia catholica* (written in 1433), reflects his enthusiasm for general councils as agents of harmony in the church. He wrote that the Council of Constance was inspired by God to restore order, and that after its decisions the primacy returned to the see of Rome. The Council was able to act on its own if the pope failed or refused to implement its decisions and meet the needs of the church. He distinguished a patriarchal general council from that which is a strictly universal general council. The latter represented the whole church and had its power immediately from God and was superior to the pope even though the pope, as successor to Peter, received important privileges from Christ. Nicholas went to the Council of Basel in 1432 and was a member of the Deputation of the Faith that refused Eugenius IV's bull and prepared a decree of suspension of the pope. When Nicholas' legal case for the claims of Ulric of Manderscheid was not judged favorably, and when Cesarini and others began to turn toward Eugenius IV, Nicholas too eventually changed his allegiance—after having been elected judge for the Commission of the Faith. He thereby revealed his unwillingness to be associated with the new proceedings against the pope. Moreover, he was disenchanted with the Council because of its failure to achieve union with the Greek Church. He became a zealous champion of the papal supremacy. Because of his important role in establishing German neutrality in the Basel-Rome dispute, he was called the "Hercules of the Eugenians," and for his services to the papacy, Eugenius' successor, Nicholas V, made him a cardinal. As bishop of Brixen he inaugurated reform and renewal until 1458 when he became a member of the Curia. He was involved as the pope's legate in the political and pastoral disorders that beset Italy until the time of his death in 1464.

The key to Nicholas' speculation is in his theory of knowledge. In *De docta ignorantia* ("On Learned Ignorance," finished in 1440), his immediate concern is with the possibility of our knowledge of God rather than with that knowledge itself. Man ceaselessly desires truth; when intellect takes possession of the object of its natural desire, it knows truth. All certain knowledge presupposes comparison, which in turn is nothing but measurement. If the contents of our knowledge are to be measured by and through each other, however, the first assumption must be homogeneity; i.e., they must be in some way commensurable. However, this cannot be realized when the object of knowledge is no longer something finite and conditioned but an infinite and absolute object. Between the infinite and finite there is no proportion or graduation. Learned ignorance is knowing that the absolute truth is beyond our understanding. God as the Absolute Maximum embraces in himself his opposites so that he is also the Absolute Minimum, the finite and the other. Our apprehension of the "coincidence of opposites" is not by imagination and reason but by a simple intuition. In Christ we have the Absolute Maximum in a state of limitation, i.e., God and Creature, and this by a limitation that could subsist only by the subsistence of the Absolute Maximum. Human nature as microcosmic "complicates" the whole cosmos in itself and therefore is the fitting nature to be elevated to the Maximum, for by this coincidence of opposites the Absolute Maximum is coincident with every level of being in the universe. This humanity, being maximal, "complicates" each person in God and is the source of being of each man so as to be more intimate than ever brother or friend could be. The church is the explication of the "complication" of the roots of humanity in Christ's divinity.

BIBLIOGRAPHY: See H. Bett, *Nicholas of Cusa* (London, 1932).

**Nicholas of Hereford** (d. c. 1420). Follower of Wycliffe. Nicholas became acquainted with the teachings of Wycliffe about 1375 as a student at Oxford; after receiving sacred orders and (in 1382) a doctorate in theology, he began to preach these doctrines. The same year he was excommunicated. He journeyed to Rome to plead his case, but to no avail. In 1391 he recanted, and from 1417 he lived as a Carthusian monk in Coventry. However, the first version of the Wycliffite Bible, for which he translated the greater part of the Old Testament, remained as a monument to his Lollard period.

**Nicholas of Lyra** (c. 1270–c. 1340). Medieval exegite. Born at Lyra in Normandy, Nicholas joined the Franciscans and studied at Florence and Paris. Later in Paris he lectured and served as provincial. He is chiefly known for his *Postillae perpetuae,* a Biblical commentary that emphasized the literal meaning of the text against the extravagances of figurative interpretation then current. His work, printed in 1472, achieved wide popularity.

**Nicodemus the Hagiorite** (1748–1809). A Greek monk of Mt. Athos. Nicodemus is best known for his many religious treatises on hagiography, asceticism, liturgics, and canon law. His *Ritual for the Twelve Months of the Year* (Venice, 1819) is still an important source for the study of the veneration of saints in the Greek Orthodox Church. Most significant of Nicodemus' writings is his *Rudder of the Intellectual Ship of the One Holy Catholic and Apostolic Orthodox Church* (Leipzig, 1800), a work in which the Athonite monk compiled and codified the entire corpus of Greek Orthodox canon law.

**Niebuhr, Barthold Georg** (1776–1831). Prussian statesman and historian. Educated at Kiel, Niebuhr took a position in the Prussian service in 1806, but quickly resigned. His reputation as a historian was established by lectures on Roman history at Berlin (1810–1812). As Prussian emissary to Rome (1816–1823), he achieved a concordat in 1821 regulating the church in Prussia. After 1823 he lived in Bonn. His gift of analogy and his superb method of source criticism contributed heavily to the growth of German historical scholarship. His works included *History of Rome* (3 vols., 1811–1832). Niebuhr was an early supporter of Prussia's claims to German leadership.

**Niebuhr, H. Richard** (1894–1962). American theologian, and professor of Christian ethics at Yale Divinity School. As a historical theologian and leader in postliberal Protestant thought, he dealt critically with the church's role in society by emphasizing the tension between Christian consecration and secular involvement, while maintaining the need for Christian involvement in the reconstruction of society as well as in worship.

**Niebuhr, Reinhold** (1892–1971). American theologian. A Christian realist, reared in the tradition of conservative theology and also attracted to the ethical implications of the Social Gospel, he became vitally interested in the social witness of Christianity while serving as pastor of a congregation of factory workers in Detroit, Mich. (1915–1928). While at Union Theological Seminary in New York City (1928–1960), however, he analyzed the whole structure of liberal culture, and found it much too unrealistic to solve the problems

of a technological and industrial society. Becoming the foremost leader of neo-orthodoxy in America, he enunciated in *Moral Man and Immoral Society* (1932) and in *The Nature and Destiny of Man* (2 vols., 1941, 1943) a theology which took sin very seriously, and which while emphasizing the grace of God in a man's salvation at the same time left him involved in the struggle for social reform.

**Niemoeller, Martin** (1892–    ). German churchman and founder of the Confessing Church. A naval officer in World War I, Niemoeller later took up theological studies and in 1931 became pastor in Dahlem, a suburb of Berlin. Founding the Pfarrernotbund (Pastors' Emergency League) in protest against the Nazi church policy, he was arrested and placed in a concentration camp in 1938. An instigator of the Stuttgart Declaration of 1945 in which the German Church admitted war guilt, he opposed remilitarization and in 1954 became a pacifist. In 1961 he became one of six presidents of the World Council of Churches.

**Nietzsche, Friedrich Wilhelm** (1844–1900). German philosopher and critic of Christianity. Born at Röcken, the son of a Lutheran pastor, he was educated at Bonn and Leipzig. In 1869 he became a professor of philosophy at the University of Basel, Switzerland. Because he was in poor health, he lived for a number of years in various places—in Venice, Switzerland, Genoa, Turin, and Nice. In 1888 he was declared hopelessly insane, remaining thereafter in the care of his devoted sister at Weimar.

Nietzsche was a prolific writer, and his works have had a profound influence in modern religious and philosophical thought. He himself was deeply influenced by Schopenhauer's atheism and deprecation of reason in favor of the will to live. From these foundations Nietzsche constructed a philosophy on the premise that all human behavior was a manifestation of the will to power. What men desired, he held, is power over self and creative mastery. All concepts of eternal life after death, he argued, are merely compensations for failures in this life to achieve power. But this power is not a collective element of the masses; it is the power of the great individual whom he calls *Übermensch* ("superman"). The superman is a magnificent man, such as Caesar Borgia or Napoleon, who develops his personality and employs his creativity without regard for laws, institutions, or other individuals. He is the man who ruthlessly pursues his success without any moral scruples.

Nietzsche was a vocal critic of Christianity and the Christian ethic. He criticized Christianity for its otherworldliness and found resentment at the heart of the Christian religion—resentment of this world, of the body, of sex, of the critical intelligence, of everything strong and healthy. He attacked Christianity because he believed it to be a slave morality. He felt that in order to make his concept of the superman possible in the future, the present values of Christianity (humility, selflessness, pity, love, principles of right and wrong) must be abolished because they were the tools of the weak who proclaimed these virtues to keep themselves in power and to debase the strong. He found the clue to Christian ethics in the "slaves' revolt in morals," supposing that the underprivileged, who were often the first converts to Christianity, transformed Christian ethics to their own inadequacies. In *The Antichrist* (1888) he called Christianity "the one great curse, the one enormous and innermost perversion, the one great instinct of revenge, for which no means is too venomous, too underhanded, too underground, and too petty—I call it the one immortal blemish of mankind."

Nietzsche was not a systematic philosopher in the ordinary sense and therefore produced no school of devoted disciples. He has, nevertheless, exerted a remarkable influence on many 20th-century thinkers, notably French and German existentialists.

BIBLIOGRAPHY: *The Portable Nietzsche,* ed. by W. Kaufmann (New York, 1954); K. Jaspers, *Nietzsche* (Tucson, 1965); W. Kaufmann, *Nietzsche: Philosopher, Psychologist, Antichrist* (Princeton, 1950); F. A. Lea, *The Tragic Philosopher* (London, 1957); G. A. Morgan, Jr., *What Nietzsche Means* (Cambridge, Mass., 1941).

**Nightingale, Florence** (1820–1910). English reformer of hospital nursing. Born in Florence, Italy, daughter of a wealthy country gentleman, she was raised in England and as a girl displayed great interest in caring for the sick. About 1844 she began hospital-visiting, and came under the influence of the Sisters of St. Vincent de Paul and their hospital work in Egypt. In 1850 and 1851 she spent some months at Fliedner's Institute of Protestant Deaconesses at Kaiserswerth near Düsseldorf in Germany. She was then convinced that nursing was no menial occupation but a possible calling for ladies. In 1853 she became administrative head of the Hospital for Invalid Gentlewomen in London. The next year she volunteered her services for the care of invalid servicemen in the Crimea. With her center at Scutari, she organized hospital facilities, enforced discipline, introduced sanitation reforms, and fought successfully to obtain necessary supplies. The troops knew her as "the Lady with the Lamp," because of her relentless labors by lamplight through the night hours. In 1856 she returned to England, where the Nightingale School of Nursing was founded in her honor at St. Thomas' Hospital. Now a semi-invalid herself, she was sought after for advice in setting up hospitals and schools of nursing, and in working for sanitation reforms. Her book, *Notes on Nursing* (1859), went through many editions. In 1907 she was the first woman to receive the British Order of Merit.

**Nikon, Nikita M.** (1605–1681). Patriarch of Moscow from 1652 to 1666, influential figure in Russian church history. Nikon became a popular preacher in Moscow, but at his children's death he and his wife entered monastic life. He retreated to the isle of Anzersky, and then to Kozhuzersky, where he became abbot in 1642. The czar appointed him archimandrite of the Moscow Novospassky monastery in 1646, and metropolitan of Novgorod in 1649. He was elected patriarch of Moscow on Aug. 1, 1652, after receiving an oath of obedience from his electors. Nikon instituted sweeping reforms as patriarch. In 1654 he summoned a synod of experts to examine the liturgical service books of Patriarch Jasaf. The council of 1656 sanctioned his textual revisions. He reformed the signing of the cross, and waged war on the so-called "new icons" in common use at the time. His reforms caused the secession of the Old Believers, the Raskolniki. By the summer of 1658 he was no longer in the czar's favor. He resigned his post and retired to the monastery of New Jerusalem which he had founded. After several halfhearted attempts, the Council of Moscow finally deposed him and sentenced him to banishment in 1666. Recalled by the czar Feodor II, Nikon died on the way to Moscow. His career and his theory that spiritual power superseded temporal might were factors in Peter the Great's decision to abolish the patriarchy.

**Nilus the Ascetic** (d. c. 430). Abbot or archimandrite of a monastery near Ancyra (Ankara). He is incorrectly known as "Nilus of Sinai" from a now discredited tradition. The state of his writings is confused and only fragments are extant. Much of what appears under his name is the work of Evagrius of Ponticus. In an authentic letter, he refers to himself as a disciple of John Chrysostom. He coined the term "spiritual philosophy" for the ascetic life.

**Nilus the Younger** (910–1004). A Calabrian Greek, he entered a monastery in 940 after the death of his mistress. Increasing Saracen raids forced him and his monks to go to Monte Cassino from which they finally moved to a monastery near Gaeta. He revived many practices of anchorites, incorporating them into the cenobitic life. He is regarded as the founder of the monastery at Grottaferrata, a site he selected shortly before his death.

**Ninety-five Theses.** The title commonly given to Martin Luther's *Disputation on the Power and Efficacy of Indulgences.* According to tradition, he posted them on the door of the castle church in Wittenberg at noon on Oct. 31, 1517 (the eve of All Saints' Day), now widely observed as the birth date of the Reformation. The Theses were intended to be the basis for theological discussion, as Luther specifically stated and as their publication in Latin shows. Their immediate purpose was to stop the sale of indulgences by the Dominican monk John Tetzel, who was actively promoting them in Ducal Saxony. This indulgence was to provide income for building St. Peter's Basilica in Rome and to help Archbishop Albert of Mainz repay his debt to the Fugger banking house for obtaining the three sees of Mainz, Magdeburg, and Halberstadt. As a loyal Catholic, Luther wrote his Theses desiring, not the abolition of indulgences, but the correction of abuses in the indulgence traffic which led people to neglect true repentance and to imagine that forgiveness could be bought. Repentance was a lifelong matter. Not evasion of penalties but true contrition shown by a Christian life should be sought. Luther further mantained that the pope's authority did not extend to purgatory. He sent a copy of the *Theses* to Albert asking him to stop the sale of this indulgence. Copies were translated into German, thereby making them public and creating an immediate impact throughout western Europe.

**Ninian** (c. 360–c. 432). Missionary to Scotland. An admirer of Martin of Tours, Ninian learned from him the form of monasticism practiced at Marmoutier. He returned to Britain about 397, and founded a monastery (Candida Casa) at Whithorn in Galloway. He and his monks used it as a base for their missionary work among the Celts and Picts and in Ireland. The encouragement of a Christian culture at Whithorn had enduring influence upon Celtic monasticism.

**Nitzsch, Karl Immanuel** (1787–1868). German Lutheran theologian and one of the most influential representatives of the mediating theology of the 19th century. He was born at Borna and educated at Wittenberg. In addition to teaching at Bonn (1822) and Berlin (1847), he was one of the most active promoters of the Evangelical Union of the Prussian Church (1817). In 1829 he published *System der christlichen Lehre,* which defined his religious views toward rationalism, supernaturalism, and Schleiermacher. As an opponent of contemporary, unbelieving rationalism he rejected a purely speculative interpretation of Christianity and emphasized the immediacy of religious feeling, which he believed was the foundation of all religious knowledge. Despite his disagreements with Schleiermacher's doctrines of God's relation to the world and his divine attributes, Nitzsch was one of the principal representatives of Schleiermacher's theology. He was an active preacher and writer during his Berlin period. His most important works are *Urkundenbuch der evangelischen Union* (1853) and *Praktische Theologie* (3 vols., 1847–1867).

**Noailles, Louis Antoine de** (1651–1729). French archbishop of Paris. Born at the Château of Teyssière in Auvergne, France, he studied theology at the Collège du Plessis in Paris at the same time as Fénelon. He received his doctorate from the Sorbonne in 1676 and was provided with the Abbey of Aubrac. In 1679 he became bishop of Cahors and in 1680 bishop of Châlons-sur-Marne. In 1695 he was promoted to the archbishopric of Paris. In 1700, Innocent XII, on Louis XIV's nomination, made him a cardinal. He became prior of Navarre in 1704 and head of the Sorbonne in 1710. During the quietistic controversy he acted as mediator between Bossuet and Fénelon. Although he denied being a Jansenist, he was always favorably disposed toward them and opposed their Jesuit adversaries. In 1695 he gave his approval to Père Quesnel's *Moral Reflections on the New Testament,* which was strongly Jansenist in sentiment. When De Noailles was elevated to the see of Paris, the Jansenists, confident of his protection, published De Barcos' defense of the Jansenist doctrine of grace, entitled *Exposition de la foy.* In 1696, De Noailles condemned the book but published a treatise on grace and predestination that closely resembled it. Neither the Jesuits nor the Jansenists were satisfied by this and De Noailles found himself drawn into the Jansenist controversy. At first he refused to accept the bull *Unigenitus* and encouraged open opposition to it in his diocese. Finally, however, he yielded in 1728 and to prove the sincerity of his submission he restored the Jesuits to the faculties that he had deprived them of thirteen years earlier. He died shortly afterward a broken man.

**Nobili, Roberto de'** (1577–1656). Jesuit missionary to India. Born in Tuscany, he entered the Society of Jesus in 1597. After a brilliant record as a student, he sailed to India in 1604, where he mastered Tamil, Telugu, and Sanskrit. In order to overcome the idea that Christianity was a religion for the lower castes, he adopted the dress and life of a Brahmin. He translated fundamental Christian works and wrote catechisms in the three Indian languages while fighting for his manner of life against detractors in India and Rome. His methods were at first condemned in Rome, but subsequently approved through the influence of Cardinal Bellarmine.

**Noetus** (d. c. end of 2d century). A presbyter of Smyrna. Although Noetus was expelled by the presbyters of Smyrna, his disciples Cleomenes and Epigonus appeared in Rome teaching his errors, i.e., that the Father suffered in the Son and that God is substantially one but nominally three. According to Hippolytus, who was the arch opponent of Callistus I (d. c. 223), both Zephyrinus and Callistus—successive bishops of Rome in the early part of the third century—fell into these errors taught by Noetus.

**Nogaret, William** (c. 1260–1313). A civilian (i.e., a student of Roman law) and theorist of royal power in the service of Philip the Fair, the king of France. His family may have had Albigensian connections. He is famed for his role in the king's conflict with Boniface VIII and in the suppression of the Templars. In 1303, he was commissioned by the king with securing Boniface's person for a proposed general council to try him for heresy. Nogaret attempted to seize the pope at Anagni but failed, and was excommunicated by Benedict XI for his action, although Philip was not. He was not absolved until 1311.

**Noli, Fan** (Theophan) **Stylian** (1882–1965). Albanian prelate. Born in Eastern Thrace, he received his higher education (A.B., Mus.B., Ph.D.) in the United States. Having produced the first Albanian translation of the Liturgy, and after fifteen years in the priesthood, he was consecrated metropolitan (1923) of the newly independent Albanian Orthodox Church. Political developments forced him before long to leave Albania. In 1930 he founded and headed the Albanian Orthodox Church in America. He later envisaged a single "American Orthodox Church."

**Nominalism.** A theory of knowledge that denies extramental reality to universals and ascribes it only to individuals. The problem concerns the relationship between thought and reality and is primarily one of logic, but inevitably has metaphysical implications. It was presented to medieval thinkers through Boethius' translation of Porphyry's introduction to Aristotle's *Categories*, where both Plato's and Aristotle's explanations of the relationship between the general and the particular were presented without reconciliation. Platonic realism was generally accepted until the end of the 11th century when Roscellinus of Compiègne defined universals as "mere sounds," names given to classes for linguistic convenience. This extreme view, attributing universality only to the physical sound of the word naming the class, came to be known as nominalism. The danger it represented to Christian orthodoxy was realized when Roscellinus applied his theory to the Trinity, defining the divine nature as a universal and granting reality only to the three Persons. At the beginning of the 12th century Abelard dealt more subtly with the problem, maintaining that since a sound was a thing and a thing could not be predicated of another thing, a universal could not be only a sound but must be defined as a word, a sound considered in relation to its meaning, and thus something that could be predicated of several things. Therefore, the universal, as a general class formed by abstraction from several things, did have existence to the extent that it referred to a quality immanent in the members of the class. Universals were, he concluded, neither things nor terms, but conceptions. This view, a compromise between the extremes but leaning more to nominalism, was generally accepted by philosophers throughout the 13th century, when the controversy tended in any case to be overshadowed by the debate over Aristotelianism. It was William of Occam, developing Peter of Spain's terminist logic, who produced the most thorough statement of nominalism at the beginning of the 14th century, one that was eventually to act as the main solvent of the whole medieval philosophical tradition. Occam argued that universals were terms signifying individuals and standing for them in propositions. Since only individuals could be proved to exist, universals could not. No common reality could exist in two members of a class, for God could annihilate one man without having an effect on any other. The universal was simply an act of understanding, and there was no reason to postulate an external reality corresponding to it. There was indeed no reason to postulate any factors other than the mind and the individual for any argument. This principle of economy, "Occam's razor," coupled with his insistence that logic dealt only with the meaning of propositions that could not be shown to have any relation to existence, led to a divorce between logic and natural theology. If it was not possible to argue from concept to extramentally existent fact, it was meaningless to assume the existence of causality or of any of the other relationships between individuals on which rational theology depended. No reasoning from effect to cause, from creation to Creator, could be proved valid. This removal of the data of revelation from the operations of reason demolished theology as a "science," leaving the Christian with only revelation and faith. Occam thus vindicated the absolute power and freedom of God which he, in common with many other Franciscans, believed had been subjected to limitations by the claims of Aristotelians such as Thomas Aquinas to know Him via reasoning. The nominalists, or Occamists, of the later 14th and 15th centuries by refusing to attribute to God any qualities other than omnipotence and mercy shattered Scholastic philosophy. Deprived of the unifying discipline of metaphysics, Christian thinkers were left either with fideism based on Scripture or with mysticism, and the scientifically minded were bound to pursue their investigations convinced of the purely subjective nature of their discoveries. From Occam's assertion that God's freedom meant that ethical commands were only expressions of his will, it followed that acts were good or bad only because God had defined them as such: there could be no merit therefore in conduct. Theologians tended in consequence to concentrate on soteriological questions until the Reformation.

BIBLIOGRAPHY: M. H. Carré, *Realists and Nominalists* (New York, 1946); F. Copleston, *A History of Philosophy,* Vol. 2 (London, 1950); É. Gilson, *History of Christian Philosophy in the Middle Ages* (New York, 1955); E. A. Moody, *The Logic of William of Ockham* (New York, 1935); H. A. Oberman, *The Harvest of Medieval Theology* (Cambridge, Mass., 1963).

**Non Abbiamo Bisogno.** Encyclical letter of Pope Pius XI concerning Catholic Action, issued June 29, 1931. Pius deplored the suppression of Catholic Action groups in Italy by the Fascist Party, insisting that Catholic Action ("the participation and the collaboration of the laity with the Apostolic Hierarchy") was above and beyond secular politics. He viewed the suppression as an attempt to turn youth from the church.

**Nonconformists.** Technically, this term refers to those Englishmen who for reasons of conscience were unable to conform to the doctrine, discipline, and worship of the Church of England as established by law at the time of the Restoration of the monarchy and were therefore unable to take the oath prescribed in the Act of Uniformity of 1662 under Charles II: "I, A.B., do here declare my unfeigned assent and consent to all and everything contained and prescribed in and by the book entitled 'The Book of Common Prayer, and Administration of the Sacraments, and other Rites and Ceremonies of the Church, according to the Church of England, together with the Psalter or Psalms of David, pointed as they are to be sung or said in churches: and the form or manner of making, ordaining, and consecrating of bishops, priests, and deacons.' " Such persons, identified principally with the Presbyterians, Congregationalists, Baptists, and Quakers, were recognized in legislation subsequently enacted by Parliament, most importantly by the Act of Toleration of 1689 whereby protection was granted to nonconformists who would take oaths of obedience and supremacy, although not all restrictions were removed and further restrictions were imposed in the Occasional Communion Act and the Schism Act. Until the 19th century, nonconformists were prevented from holding office, Oxford and Cambridge were closed to them, they were compelled to support the Established Church through the payment of church rates, and they could not be married in their own churches or be buried without Anglican rites. During the 19th century such disabilities were removed, and today the nonconforming churches, represented by the Free Church Federal Council, are an important and respected part of Christianity in England, alongside the Churches of England and Rome, some of the nonconforming churches now working toward union with one another and with other Christian bodies. In modern times they have championed religious freedom and the disestablishment of the Church of England.

The essence of nonconformity has been variously defined, H. W. Clark contending that "the Nonconformist spirit is . . . the spirit which exalts life above organization." The basic reason for nonconformity in England is to be located in the resistance of persons to the Church of England and to its claim to be the "true" church of the land. With this understanding in mind, many scholars see the beginnings at least of nonconformity with Wycliffe and locate a basic nonconformist position expressed in *An Admonition to the Par-*

liament (1572), composed by Thomas Wilcox and John Field. The *Admonition* argues that the Church of England is faulty with respect to the essential marks of the true church, and in particular attacks the Book of Common Prayer for its popishness and the government of the church by bishops as non-Scriptural. The nonconformists thus faulted the Established Church and declared themselves to be anti-Roman and Biblically centered. Furthermore, they believed that nonconformity was a duty for those committed to true religion as they understood it.

There were varieties of nonconformists, ranging from Presbyterians to Quakers, later encompassing Methodists, among others. There were those who believed the Church of England to be the servant of Antichrist. There were many, however, such as the Presbyterian Richard Baxter, who did not condemn the Church of England outright and accepted the label of "nonconformist" with sorrow and against their wills.

BIBLIOGRAPHY: H. W. Clark, *History of English Nonconformity,* 2 vols. (New York, 1965); H. Davies, *The English Free Churches* (New York, 1952); E. A. Payne, *The Free Church Tradition in the Life of England* (London, 1944); W. B. Selbie, *Nonconformity: Its Origin and Progress* (London, 1912); J. T. Wilkinson, *1662, and After: Three Centuries of English Nonconformity* (London, 1962).

**None.** The ninth hour of prayer (about three o'clock) in monastic use. Both Jewish and apostolic observance of private prayer at this time is seen in Acts 3:1; 10:30. The appointed hymn remembers Christ's death. This office of prayer contains psalms, hymn, short lesson, and collect on the same pattern as Terce and Sext.

**Non Expedit** (Feb. 27, 1868). Decree of Pius IX, reaffirmed, 1874 and 1877, forbidding Italian Catholic participation in the political life of the kingdom. "Neither electors nor elected" was the formula. The ban prevented Catholics from taking state oaths that would imply sanction for the occupation of the Papal States. It was moderated by Pius X in 1905. Its disappearance (1919) paved the way for the formation of the Catholic People's Party.

**Nonjurors.** Members of the Church of England who, after the Revolution of 1688, refused to take the Oath of Allegiance to William and Mary. The nonjurors were advocates of the divine right of kings theory, refusing to violate what they regarded as a sacred oath to James II. They remained loyal to James as the divinely appointed and lawful king of England who had been deposed forcibly and illegally by William III. There were eight bishops and four hundred priests who refused the new Oath of Allegiance. The nonjuring bishops were Archbishop Sancroft of Canterbury, and Bishops Ken of Bath and Wells, Turner of Ely, White of Peterborough, Lloyd of Norwich, Frampton of Gloucester, Lake of Chichester, and Thomas of Worcester. All but Lake and Thomas, who died before the sentence could be carried out, were deprived by Parliamentary Act in 1689. The movement was not suppressed by these deprivations. Many nonjuring clergy continued to function and to recognize the deprived bishops. In 1694, the exiled James II granted a *congé d'élire* for the consecration of new nonjuring bishops. However, the movement lost strength after James's death and began to be absorbed by the Church of England in the latter part of the 18th century.

**Nonnus of Panopolis** (born c. 400). Pagan poet. He was born in Panopolis in the Thebaid in Upper Egypt, and the author of a forty-eight-book epic in Greek, the *Dionysiaca,* on the legendary journey of the god Dionysus, to India. After 431, and perhaps conversion to Christianity, he wrote a *Paraphrase of St. John's Gospel* in hexameters; in this he often refers to Mary as *Theotokos.*

**Norbert of Xanten** (c. 1080–1134). Ecclesiastic and founder of Premonstratensian Canons. Son of a noble family, he was ordained a subdeacon and became a canon at Xanten. He had no intention of continuing the clerical life, but sought the pleasures of the imperial court where Henry V made him court almoner. In 1115 he was thrown from his horse during a thunderstorm and nearly killed. He then determined to withdraw from the world and so entered a monastery near Cologne where he was ordained to the priesthood. He returned to Xanten and tried to reform the canons. In 1118 they denounced him for making innovations in discipline and preaching without permission. He resigned his canonry and set out to meet Pope Gelasius II who was then in exile in Languedoc. The pope granted him permission to preach anywhere he chose. The succeeding pope did not renew this privilege, so Norbert settled at Laon where the bishop asked him to reform a house of canons. When these canons resisted his discipline, he was granted the abandoned monastery at Prémontré, where with thirteen disciples he founded the Premonstratensian Canons. The new order, which then included several other houses, received papal approval in 1126. In that year he was named archbishop of Magdeburg. His reforms proved to be unpopular and after several attempts on his life, he fled the city. He supported the claims of Innocent II and with Bernard of Clairvaux entered triumphantly into Rome with the pope in 1133. He continued to direct the activities of Prémontré until his death.

**Norman Invasions.** The Vikings of Scandinavia invaded much of western Europe from the 9th to the 11th century. The term "Norman" (a softened form of "Northman") designates those who came near the end of this long period. They settled in an area of northern France today called Normandy (on the English Channel) and later conquered southern Italy, Sicily, and England.

After a period of attacking and plundering, the Vikings received their initial French land in 911 through the treaty of Saint-Clair-sur-Epte between King Charles (the Simple) and the Norman chief Rollo. The Vikings began to adopt the manners, customs, and language of the land they had conquered and soon appeared more like Frenchmen than Scandinavian raiders. Rollo had been baptized and his followers gradually accepted the faith of the inhabitants who had first received Christianity in the 4th century.

Despite their accommodation to prevailing culture, the Normans did not lose their conquering spirit. They began their invasion of Moslem-held Sicily in 1061, and it was completed in 1091 by Count Roger I. Their control of Sicily and neighboring southern Italy lasted until near the end of the 12th century.

In 1066, in order to assert a claim to the English throne, the Norman duke William I (the Conqueror) successfully invaded England. The expedition ended with the death of the English king Harold in the Battle of Hastings, Oct. 14, 1066. The conquest brought England into the mainstream of European civilization.

**North, Frank Mason** (1850–1935). Methodist clergyman. After nineteen years as parish pastor he served in several high offices in his denomination and in ecumenical agencies and became prominent in promoting the Social Gospel. He was president of the Federal Council of Churches from 1916 to 1920, having been previously the founder and chairman of its Committee on Church and Modern Industry.

**North German Missionary Society** (*also called Bremen Society from the location of its headquarters*). An organization founded in 1836 by a federation of local missionary unions in northern Germany. It was a union, i.e., Lutheran and Reformed, but gradually most of the Lutherans withdrew leaving it predominantly Reformed. After early attempts among Telugus in India and in New Zealand, the Society concentrated on the Ewe people east of the Volta in what is now Ghana and Togo.

**Norton, Andrews** (1786–1853). Conservative Unitarian. Graduated from Harvard in 1804, he became professor of Biblical literature there from 1819 to 1830. After 1830 he devoted himself solely to literary activities. He opposed Emerson's transcendentalism but was reluctant to press for a heresy trial within the Unitarian community. He objected to the name "Unitarian" and sought to forestall the formation of the Unitarian Association. He also attacked with vigor D. F. Strauss's *Life of Jesus.*

**Norway, Conversion of.** Unsuccessful attempts were made by converted Viking kings Haakon the Good and Harold Bluetooth in the 10th century to convert Norway. Olaf I Tryggvesson succeeded in 995 by use of harsh methods. Norway's patron saint and king, Olaf II Haraldsson (1016–1028), overcame the pagan reaction that set in after 1000 and with his bishop Grimkel built churches, staffed them with missionary priests, and wrote Norway's first set of church laws.

**Notker Balbulus** (*called* "the stammerer") (c. 840–912). A monk at the famous monastery of St. Gall in what is today Switzerland. He became monastic librarian and eventually head of the monastery's school. It was he who collected sequences—Scriptural passages set to music for use in the Mass—and introduced them into Germany. He wrote historical works, among which were a life of Gall and probably also the collection of stories on the deeds of Charlemagne.

**Notre-Dame de Paris.** The cathedral church of Paris until the end of the 17th century. It stands on the site where a Christian altar replaced a temple dedicated to Jupiter. Begun in 1163 by an unknown architect, it was finished in 1235. The cathedral, 426 feet long, 164 feet wide, and with a height of 315 feet, can hold twenty thousand people standing. Its chief beauties are its rose windows and its unexampled wealth of fine floral sculptures.

**Novalis** (*pseudonymn of* Friedrich Leopold von Hardenberg) (1772–1801). Early romantic poet. Raised by a Herrnhut father, Novalis studied law at Jena (1790) and met Schiller. He became closely acquainted with Schlegel at Leipzig, and concluded his philosophical studies at Wittenberg. Fichte's *Grundlage der gesamten Wissenschaftslehre* especially interested him. By 1797 he was auditor of the Weissenfels salt works. He entered a mining academy at Friedberg in 1800, and later became local magistrate in Thuringia. The death of his young fiancée in 1797 greatly affected him. He spoke of "following her," though not in order to leave the world. A rich stream of literary works flowed effortlessly until he became ill. Included were *Hymnen an die Nacht, Heinrich von Ofterdinger, Geistlichen Liedern, Lehrlinge zu Sais,* and the essay *Die Christenheit oder Europa.* Novalis' religious thought, mystical in character, showed familiarity with Plato, Boehme (*"heitrer Frölichkeit"*), Hermsterhuis, Baader, Zinzendorf, and Spinoza. "Mediation" is stressed in his writings: the poet ("messiah of nature") deals theologically with all of nature in its potentiality and history; the ideal monarch mediates between God and men. Novalis sought to fuse temporal-eternal, life-death, with "magical idealism," the independence of spirit from intellect and use of the former. Until nature returns to its original unity, it must be "romanticized." Schleiermacher, Hofmannsthal, Benn, and many romantics felt his influence. His "Jesus" poems contributed to the century's quest for the "historical Jesus."

**Novatianism.** The denial during the 3d century of a rigorist group of schismatics of the church's right to restore lapsed Christians to membership. It became a heresy that persisted for two centuries. Originating in the church at Carthage during the episcopate of Cyprian, the movement, which led to the development of a rigorist attitude toward those who had denied the faith during the Decian persecution (January, 250, to June, 251), was set in motion, paradoxically enough, by one who advocated mild treatment of the lapsi. Felicissimus, a deacon in the Carthaginian church, along with five presbyters, formed a schismatic group that advocated leniency toward the lapsi. Cyprian, their bishop, was insisting upon a period of penance before restoration to Communion. Novatus, a presbyter, was one of the schismatic group which gathered around itself those who were "confessors" in the persecution. They offered restoration to the lapsed on ridiculously easy terms. According to Cyprian, Novatus considered that these "confessors" comprised the true church. Novatus, however, soon embraced the opposite attitude toward the lapsi, viz., that of rigorism, and fled to Rome. There he joined the schism of Novatian.

Novatian, a Roman presbyter, had opposed the mild views of Pope Cornelius toward the lapsi. This was against the important background of the lenient attitude of Callistus, a previous bishop of Rome, toward those who had committed adultery or fornication and had subsequently sought readmission to Communion. Novatian's hostility toward Cornelius brought those of like mind into his circle; it is thought that they elected him a counter-bishop of Rome. A catacomb inscription, however, discovered in Rome in 1932 which states, *"Novatiano beatissimo martyri Gaudentius diaconus,"* would cast some doubt, if it is the same Novatian, on this view. He required rebaptism of those who came to him from the church, holding that Catholic baptism was invalid. Those in orders were received as laymen. He consecrated bishops who held their churches until the 5th century, when they were deprived, though some persisted after that in the East. Apparently he offered apostates life-long penance, without restoration to Communion.

Novatian was a rhetorician, philosopher (Stoic), and the first theologian at Rome to write in Latin. His treatise *De trinitate* appeared c. 250 and indicated that he was a theologian of considerable ability. It reflects the strong influence of Tertullian. He repudiated Adoptianism and modalism as well-meaning but erroneous attempts to maintain the Biblical doctrine of the unity of God. He taught that the generation of the Son is pretemporal. The term *communio substantiae* was used by him to express the relationship of the Father to the Son. He taught, in regard to Christ, that only his bodily human nature constitutes his humanity. In this he fell short of the doctrine on that point of Irenaeus and Tertullian. His doctrine of the Spirit was rudimentary and remained undeveloped. In his *De baptismo* he taught that the Spirit is the active force in our experience of God, working our regeneration, and indicating to us the quality of the life to come. Of Novatian's later life and death nothing is known.

In the 4th century, Ambrose and his contemporary, Pacian, criticized the severity of the Novatianists. Pacian's letters to Symphronian, a Novatianist, are especially informative. He writes against the position that Symphronian had previously set forth, viz., that (1) penitence after baptism is not allowable; (2) mortal sins cannot be remitted by the church; (3) to receive sinners back into the church, deviating from the severe attitude of the New Testament (e.g., in Hebrews), would inflict such injury upon it that it could not recover. The followers of Novatian (and Novatus) allowed some alterations in their doctrine regarding the lapsed. It is probable, though, that they continued to require rebaptism. For minor sins, they perhaps admitted absolution, but withheld restoration for more serious ones, keeping the penitent under lifelong penance. The later Novatianists took the name Cathari, from Greek *katharos*, "the pure." The controversy over their rigorist position persisted into the 5th century. The writings that grew out of it form the foundation for systematic moral theology.

BIBLIOGRAPHY: A. Roberts and J. Donaldson (eds.), *The Ante-Nicene Fathers*, Vol. 5 (Grand Rapids, 1951).

**Novice.** A member of a religious community undergoing a probationary period before professing vows. While a novice, a person observes the rule and customs of the community, but also receives special instruction from the superior or a novice master. During the novitiate, which usually lasts one year, the novice may leave at any time or be dismissed by the superior without incurring any censure. The novitiate is sometimes preceded by a period of postulancy.

**Noyes, John Humphrey** (1811–1886). Founder of the Oneida Community. After attending Dartmouth and Andover, Noyes was dismissed from Yale for his perfectionist views. He traveled two years, trying to organize perfectionists, and in 1836 at Putney, Vt., set up a little Bible School that later developed into a communistic society. In 1846 the society began practicing "complex marriage" (every man married to every woman, sex relations and the number of children rigidly controlled). This aroused such opposition that Noyes and his people fled to Oneida, N.Y., where they called themselves the Oneida Community. Here they prospered greatly under Noyes' rule. The society declined, however, in the 1870's, and in 1879, because of opposition, abandoned its marriage practices. Noyes escaped to Canada, where he lived his last years.

**Nuncio, Papal.** Formerly, a fiscal officer of the papal court, later becoming a diplomatic representative of the Holy See to countries maintaining formal relations with the Vatican. The nuncio has the status of an ambassador, but ranks below a papal legate. In those countries which do not maintain diplomatic relations with the Vatican, there is a papal representative without diplomatic status, known as an apostolic delegate, whose charge is limited solely to ecclesiastical matters.

**Oates, Titus** (1649–1705). English conspirator. He was the son of an Anabaptist preacher, and himself a sometime Anglican cleric, who fabricated the "popish plot" (1678). This was a story of an alleged Jesuit scheme to murder Charles II and replace him with his Roman Catholic brother James. The story won some credence and occasioned trials and executions of presumed plotters. Oates, sued by James, was imprisoned and flogged (1685). Pardoned and given a pension under William III (1689), he became a Baptist, but was also expelled by them (1701).

**Oberlin, John Frederick** (1740–1826). German Lutheran pastor and pioneer in Christian social work. Oberlin was born in Strasbourg and became pastor of Waldbach in the Steinthal district of Alsace in 1767. He devoted the rest of his life to increasing the educational, cultural, and living standards of the people in his parish by building schools and establishing savings banks and agricultural societies. He was eminently successful, serving both Catholics and Protestants.

**Oberlin Theology.** A perfectionist theology dominated by the revivalist Charles G. Finney, who became professor of theology at Oberlin College, Ohio, in 1837 and was president from 1851 to 1866. Finney, with Asa Mahan, J. H. Fairchild, William Cochran, John Morgan, and Henry Cowles, formulated a perfectionism defined as the preference of Christ to self. This perfectionism was achieved by the restoration of the Holy Spirit to human nature. According to Finney, "the perfect control of this perfection over all the moral movements of the mind brings a man back to where Adam was previous to the Fall and constitutes perfect holiness." He maintained that obligation and ability were commensurate and that it was possible for men to obey the command of perfection. Influenced by the "New Divinity" of N. W. Taylor, this perfectionism was complemented by emphases upon the freedom of the will and moral ability, governmental and general atonement, man's active role in regeneration, a faculty psychology, the moral power of the truth upon the heart, and a rigorous social ethic. In part a product of religious "ultraism," the Oberlin position was criticized by the Presbyterians and Congregationalists as antinomianism.

The Oberlin Theology is best expressed in the *Oberlin Evangelist*, Mahan's *Scripture Doctrine of Christian Perfection* (1839), and

Finney's *Views of Sanctification* (1840) and *Systematic Theology* (1846).

**Oblate** (from Latin *oblatus,* "offered"). The name applied to children placed in a monastery at an early age to be reared and educated by the monks. The custom, quite common in the early Middle Ages, was gradually abandoned. Later, pious laymen frequently retired to monasteries, living as monks, although not professing vows. They were also known as oblates. Some modern religious orders use the title "Oblates," but this has no connection with medieval meanings.

**Oblates of Mary** (*or* Oblates Regular of St. Benedict). A Roman Catholic religious community for women, founded by Frances of Rome in 1425. Dedicated to the care of the poor, they adopted a modified Benedictine rule but did not live under strict vows. When Frances' husband died, she entered the community and was made superior. After her own death in 1440 the community continued to grow. At present it has houses both in Europe and in America.

**O'Bryan, William** (1778–1868). Founder of the Bible Christian Connexion. An offshoot of Cornish Methodism, it spread by emigration to Canada and Australia to be eventually absorbed by Methodism even in England by 1906. After O'Bryan was rejected for itinerancy by the Wesleyans because of undisciplined evangelistic ardor, he founded the society of Bible Christians in 1815. It grew rapidly, but his autocratic intransigence separated him permanently from the movement after 1829.

**Observants, Observantines** (*or* Friars Minor of the Regular Observance). A strict group within the Franciscan Order. They opted for exact observance of the Rule of St. Francis, as it had been approved by Pope Honorius III in 1223. They opposed the bulls of John XXII in 1317 and 1318, which permitted Franciscans to own property jointly. The chapter called by Leo X in 1517 allowed the Observants to become independent. Finally, in 1897, Leo XIII sponsored their reunion with other Franciscans.

**Occam, William of** (c. 1280–c. 1349). Theologian and logician. Born at Occam in Surrey, England, he joined the Franciscan Order and was ordained subdeacon in 1306. He studied at Oxford from c. 1309 to c. 1315, lectured on the Bible from 1315 to 1317, on Peter Lombard's *Sentences* from 1317 to 1319, and from 1319 to 1323 composed works on logic and a *Commentary on the Sentences.* Although he had fulfilled all the requirements for the degree of Master of Theology, he did not occupy a chair, since his opinions had incurred the censure of Lutterell, the Thomist chancellor of the university, who, having drawn up fifty-six articles of accusation, reported him to the papal Curia at Avignon. William was summoned to Avignon in 1324 and Pope John XXII appointed a commission to investigate his *Commentary on the Sentences.* The examination lasted three years, but was never completed and none of the offending doctrines was condemned. While waiting for the outcome, William became closely acquainted with Michael of Cesena, a Franciscan minister-general who was involved in a conflict with the pope over Franciscan poverty. Asked by him to examine the past papal writings on the controversy, William concluded that John XXII's constitutions contradicted the opinions of earlier popes. When, in 1328, John ordered the Franciscans to elect another minister-general, William, Michael, and two other friars left Avignon secretly, sailed down the Rhone to Aigues-Mortes, where a ship was waiting to take them to the emperor Louis of Bavaria at Pisa. The emperor, long a victim of papal intrigues, gladly gave them asylum in Munich, which soon became the center of intellectual opposition to the papacy. From here, in the company of Marsilius of Padua and John of Jandun, William poured forth a stream of books and pamphlets on the errors and heresies of John XXII, evangelical poverty, the relations between papacy and empire, and the rights of secular rulers to tax the clergy. When Michael of Cesena died in 1342, William took possession of the seal of the Franciscan Order. However, when Louis of Bavaria died in 1347, William sought a reconciliation with the papacy, sending the seal of the order back and swearing, in a formal submission, his future obedience to the pope and his abjuration of the opinions of Louis and of Michael of Cesena, though making no mention of the teachings for which he had been condemned while at Oxford. The Curia drew up a form of recantation for him to sign, but it is doubtful whether it reached him before he died, apparently of the Black Death, in 1349.

A rigorous analytical thinker, William effected a major revolution within Scholastic philosophy by developing formal logic to the point where it destroyed totally the rational theologies of his predecessors. Starting with the axiom that nothing may be assumed to exist for the purposes of argument unless an unanswerable reason (factual observation, logical insight, or divine revelation) can be given for its existence, he insisted that "nothing can be known in itself save by intuitional knowledge" and concluded that universals were only mental constructs, that being did not exist as a metaphysical entity, and that therefore metaphysical knowledge was impossible. Since God could not be known intuitionally, and no rational proofs could be offered for his existence, man had to be content with what faith and revelation told him. Man's knowledge of the soul was similarly dependent on revelation. It followed that rationalist, e.g., Thomist, arguments, transferring concepts of order, law, and predictability from the universe to the divine nature must be rejected as undemonstrable, and as limiting God's absolute freedom. Not only could God produce an "effect" in the human mind in the absence of its natural "cause" if he so willed, but he could also change his ethical norms, for goodness was by definition simply what he willed and evil what he forbade. Murder could become ethically good at God's command. Since God cannot be under obligation, his rewards and punishments need bear no relationship to men's conduct in the world. All this was not meant to encourage skepticism, though many of William's followers interpreted it so, but to assert God's omnipotence against the necessitarian implications of Christian Aristotelianism, and the primacy of faith over the spurious certainties of reason. Within a few years of his death he was regarded as the originator of "the new way," which under the name of nominalism, or terminism, was to affect theology and science radically for two hundred years.

BIBLIOGRAPHY: W. Ockham, *Philosophical Writings,* ed. by P. Boehner (New York, 1957); and *Studies and Selections,* ed. by S. C. Tornay (LaSalle, Ill., 1938); T. B. Birch (ed.), *The De Sacramento Altaris of William of Ockham* (Burlington, Iowa, 1930).

M. H. Carré, *Realists and Nominalists* (New York, 1946).

**Ochino, Bernardino** (1487–1564). Protestant Reformer. Born at Siena, he sought religion in the monastic orders, and rose to prominence among both the Franciscan Observants and the Capuchins, being vicar-general of the latter in 1538 and 1541. He preached moving sermons on repentance that attracted great crowds. Protestant tracts, which the pope allowed him to read in order to refute them, and contact with Peter Martyr converted him to Protestantism, and he became a Lutheran in 1541. Summoned to Rome, he feared for his life, and instead fled to Geneva. Here he preached in a church of Italian refugees, as he later did at Augsburg. In 1547 he was invited to England, where he wrote against the papacy and also against the Calvinist doctrine of predestination. When Mary came to the throne, he returned to Switzerland, becoming a pastor in Zurich. In 1563 he published a short work that was judged heretical, and he suffered another exile. He went to Poland, but died the next year in Moravia. Like Castellio, he argued for a difference between essentials and nonessentials, and was against the persecution of heretics. In his later years he leaned more toward liberal speculative mysticism and moved away from Reformed doctrine, but remained a friend of Calvin.

**O'Connell, Daniel** (1775–1847). Irish statesman. A devout Roman Catholic, he was educated at the English colleges at St.-Omer and Douai in France. Returning to England in 1793, he entered Lincoln's Inn, and was called to the bar in 1798, soon becoming one of the most respected lawyers in Ireland. He was a powerful orator, building his reputation by speeches against the union between Ireland and Great Britain. He founded the Catholic Association in 1823, combining the strength of Irish Roman Catholicism with the movement for repeal. The immediate objective of the Association was Catholic emancipation. Even though O'Connell tried always to work within the law, the Catholic Association was proscribed by Parliament in 1825. O'Connell, however, continued his agitation, and in 1828 was elected M.P. for Clare. He took his seat even though as a Catholic he was barred from the House of Commons. His political power was such that it forced passage of the long-contemplated Catholic Emancipation Act (1829). He continued to lead the agitation for repeal, establishing, in 1840, the Repeal Association. O'Connell was briefly imprisoned in 1844, after which, broken in health, he lost his hold on the repeal movement. He died on May 15, 1847, in Genoa while on a trip to Rome.

**Odes of Solomon.** Mystical hymns probably related to baptism and combining Jewish, Christian, and Gnostic imagery in the manner of Valentinus and Bardesanes. The Odes, written perhaps in the mid-2d century, are extant as a whole only in a Syriac version; there are also quotations in Lactantius and in Pistis Sophia. A 3d-century Christian collection of miscellaneous writings (one of the Bodmer Papyri) contains Ode 11 in Greek.

**Odilo of Cluny** (c. 962–1048). Fifth abbot of Cluny. Elected in 994, three years after he first entered the monastery, he was responsible for extending the reforming influence of Cluny to other houses, bringing them directly under the control of Cluny, thus creating the Cluniac congregation. He devoted himself to the expansion of the order, promoting the Truce of God throughout France and Italy. He is thought to have been responsible for introducing the observance of All Souls' Day.

**Odo of Cluny** (879–942). Abbot of Cluny from 927. Born in Tours of a noble Frankish family, he became a canon there and went to Paris to study. In 909, after being deeply influenced by the Benedictine Rule, he entered the monastery at Baume. When he became the second abbot of Cluny some twenty years later, he set to work to make it a center of revival and reform. He was the first abbot to extend the reforming influence of Cluny to other houses: Monte Cassino, Subiaco, and St. Paul's, Rome. He also wrote several moral and theological works.

**Oecolampadius, John** (1482–1531). Protestant Reformer. Born in the Palatinate, Oecolampadius studied at Bologna, Heidelberg, and Tübingen. In 1515 he was appointed cathedral preacher in Basel and seemed to be a Lutheran, but he shortly changed and entered a monastery. In 1522 he again changed his mind, and the same year became a pastor in Basel, and later a professor in the university. It was he who brought about the evangelical reforms in Basel. At a disputation in Baden in 1526 he met Eck, Luther's former opponent, and although he went down in defeat, he won a tactical victory. Bern and other Swiss cities were not impressed with Eck, and the Bern Disputation of early 1528 was a stunning victory for the evangelical forces. Though not involved in the Disputation, Oecolampadius was the major leader in the move of Bern toward a Reformed position. The next year he was an active participant at the Marburg Colloquy. He corresponded extensively with the advocates of reform, and was constantly active in the cause. Early in 1531 he planned a synod of Swiss cities to discuss doctrinal matters. Oecolampadius was never in good health, and the news of the defeat at Kappel and the death of Zwingli hastened his own, and he died seven weeks after Zwingli.

**Oecumenius.** Sixth-century author of the oldest commentary now extant in Greek on the book of Revelation. Tradition has called him *philosophos* and *rhētōr*. The scanty evidence of his life suggests that he was a contemporary and supporter of Severus of Antioch. His commentary on Revelation, lost for centuries, was rediscovered early in the 20th century; it uses a continuous historical approach. He is to be distinguished from the 10th-century bishop of Thessaly.

**Oetinger, Friedrich Christoph** (1702–1782). German Lutheran mystic. Dissatisfied with the philosophy that he learned at Tübingen, he followed the teachings of Bengel, the Kabbalah, Boehme, Swedenborg, and the French quietists. On his numerous journeys he cultivated the acquaintance of various Pietists and Separatists, among them the Moravians at Herrnhut. From 1738 he held several ecclesiastical appointments in Württemberg, finally in 1766 becoming prelate in Murrhardt. The unique mark of his teaching was his view of the redemption of all nature in Christ.

**Offa** (d. 796). King of the Mercians from 757. By 779 he was overlord of the whole of England south of the Humber and east of Wales. Under his rule a third archbishopric was established at Lichfield for a time (787–802), sanctioned by Pope Hadrian I. Offa enjoyed cordial relations with the papacy, as well as with Charlemagne, and was generous to the English monastic foundations. After his death Mercia declined, and the kings of Wessex assumed the leadership in the heptarchy.

**Olaf I Tryggvesson** (969–1000). King of Norway from 995. He was a pagan Viking converted by a hermit in the Scilly Islands. After defeating the apostate Haakon Jarl, he proceeded to force Christianity upon Norway. He built the first church at Moster, founded Nidaros, and dedicated a church to Clement, patron saint of sea travelers. He also established Christianity in Iceland, the islands of Orkney, Shetland, and Faroe, and Greenland. He died in 1000 at the Battle of Svolder.

**Olaf II Haraldsson** (995–1030). Patron saint and king of Norway (1016–1028). A Viking from his boyhood, he was converted from paganism and baptized in Normandy. He went to Norway in 1015 to claim his throne and began ruthlessly to complete the establishment of Christianity begun by Olaf I. At the Mosterting (1022) he and his English bishop Grimkel drew up Norway's first set of church laws. Rivals forced him to flee in 1028. He died in the Battle of Stiklestad (July 29, 1030). Declared a saint, he was canonized in 1164.

**Old Believers** (Raskolniki). Schismatics or separatists who rejected changes in church customs and liturgy. Patriarch Nikon in 1653 reformed Russian Church ritual, changing the number of prostrations during the reading of a prayer and the number of fingers used in making the sign of the cross. The reforms were confirmed at a council in 1666–1667. The Old Believers or Old Ritualists resisted this form of Westernization and were put down with much bloodshed from 1660 to 1680. Nevertheless, they remained a large minority (about

20 percent) up to the Revolution and certain groups are still found in the USSR today. There are two divisions: (1) Popovtsi (priests), a sect accepting priests who had fled the established church, which in 1849 secured its own episcopate. (2) Bezpopovtsi (priestless), who said that apostasy had destroyed the order of the church and therefore limited themselves to rites a layman can perform, using consecrated wine and chrism maintained by dilution.

**Old Catholics.** In the 18th century, "Old Catholics" were those who retained certain doctrines and customs of Roman Catholicism but rejected papal authority and the Tridentine decisions. Cornelius Steenhoven, consecrated by Dominicus Maria Varlet, became bishop at Utrecht (1723) during the Jansenist struggle over grace and Augustinianism. Subsequently, the Utrecht chapter continued to elect archbishops independently of Rome. However, the term "Old Catholics" properly refers to dioceses that banded together on Sept. 24, 1889, in the Declaration of Utrecht. Included were representatives from the Netherlands, Germany, Switzerland, and Austria. When papal infallibility was declared in 1870 at Vatican I, some dioceses chose schism over submission. Roman Catholic theologians, including Friedrich and Messmer in Munich, Hilgers, Knoodt, Langen, and Reusch in Bonn, Baltzer, Reinkens, and Weber in Breslau, Menzel and Michelis in Braunsberg, and Doellinger, led the retreat after some were excommunicated. Reinkens was consecrated by the bishop of Utrecht as Old Catholic bishop in Germany. Old Catholic congresses followed, meeting at Königswinter (1870), Nuremberg (1870), Solothurn (1871), and Vienna (1871). Some state support was given the Old Catholics, who numbered about 70,000 in Germany (1875, mostly Bavaria), 73,000 in Switzerland (1876) with E. Herzog as bishop, and 6,000 in Austria (1881). Today, Old Catholics are active in Holland, Germany, Switzerland, the United States, Canada, and Poland, but their status in Czechoslovakia is indeterminate. Their liturgy is in the vernacular. Celibacy was abolished first in Switzerland, then Germany (1878), the Polish U.S.A. church (1921), and Holland (1923). Some Old Catholics receive the cup in the Eucharist. Old Catholic churches in Italy, France, England (A. H. Mathew was consecrated in Utrecht, 1908, but broke away, 1910), South America, Australia, Yugoslavia (begun 1923), and the Philippines have disappeared.

**Oldham, Joseph H.** (1874–     ). Scottish missionary, theologian, and ecumenist. With John Mott, he organized the World Missionary Conference, Edinburgh (1910). He was secretary of its Continuation Committee (1910–1921) and was first secretary of the International Missionary Council (1921–1938). He served as chairman of the Research Commission of the Universal Christian Council for Life and Work (1934–1938); he headed the Christian Frontier Council (1942–1947). He also wrote nine books and edited *The International Review of Missions* (1912–1927) and the *Christian News Letter* (1939–1945).

**Olevianus, Kaspar** (1536–1587). Co-author (with Zacharias Ursinus) of the Heidelberg Catechism (1563). He was born in Trier and studied under Calvin in Geneva. In 1559 he returned to Trier, taught at the university, and preached the Reformed faith. Driven from Trier, he accepted the invitation of Frederick III, Count Palatine of the Rhine, to Heidelberg, where he worked, taught, and preached until the elector's death in 1576. He helped organize the Reformed Church in the Palatinate.

**Olga** (Helga) (d. 969). Widow of Igor, prince of Kiev, and regent for her minor son, Svyatoslav. She was from a Viking family of Pskov and was distressed by Slavic paganism. In 957 she was baptized in Constantinople and attempted to introduce Christianity into Russia. Her son remained a pagan and finally assumed power. It was not until the reign of her grandson, Vladimir, that the Russians were converted.

**Olier, Jean-Jacques** (1608–1657). Founder of the seminary and Society of Priests of St.-Sulpice. Born in Paris, he was educated by the Jesuits at Lyons. After further studies in Paris he left for Rome. While on a pilgrimage to Loreto, Olier recovered from a temporary blindness and thought of becoming a Carthusian. The death of his father recalled him to Paris, where he began catechizing the poor in his home and helping Vincent de Paul in mission work. Ordained in 1633, he was directed by Charles de Condren and worked effectively for the religious revival of France. In 1641 he was made pastor of the large parish of St.-Sulpice. There he trained seminarians to act as a reforming leaven at the Sorbonne and to assist in relief work for the poor and in the conversion of the worldly rich. His efforts against the Jansenists drew their attack, but bishops asked him to staff diocesan seminaries, since the seminary of St.-Sulpice had become the model for all of France.

**Olivétan, Pierre Robert** (c. 1506–1538). Bible scholar and Protestant Reformer. Christened Pierre Robert, he was purportedly nicknamed "Olivétan" because he burned the midnight oil in school. Already exposed to Lutheran opinions at Paris, he became a Protestant during his studies at Orléans and was obliged to flee to Strasbourg. Later he removed to Neuchâtel and in 1532 began a mission among the Waldenses, for whom he made a French translation of the Bible from the original Hebrew and Greek. Olivétan was a fellow townsman and cousin of Calvin, who wrote, as his first confession of evangelical faith, a preface for Olivétan's New Testament (published in 1535).

**Omar** (c. 581–644). Islam's second caliph from 634. One of Mohammed's first and most zealous converts, Omar became a powerful ruler, successfully capturing Jerusalem in 637 and extending Moslem control over Syria and Egypt. He initiated what became standard Moslem policy toward *dhimmis* (literally, "protected subjects"), who were followers of religions tolerated by Islam (Christians and Jews were included). By his administration they were assured of the security of their lives and property in exchange for a payment of tribute.

**Omayyads.** See UMAYYADS.

**Oneida Community.** The most famous of all American religious communistic communities, which developed as an expression of early 19th-century revivalism channeled into the advocacy of perfectionism. It was founded by John Humphrey Noyes as the Association of Perfectionists at Putney, Vt., in 1842. As a part of its system of individual and community perfectionism a communism of property was practiced as well as the doctrine of "complex marriage," about which so much public opposition arose that the community was relocated at Oneida, N.Y., in 1848. Here an economic base was established in the production of small-animal traps and in other ventures, particularly in the production of silver plate (Community Plate). "Complex marriages" were abandoned in 1879, and communal ownership was replaced by a joint-stock company two years later.

**Onesimus of Ephesus.** Bishop. The chief source of information about him is Ignatius' letter to the Ephesian church written on his way to Rome and martyrdom at the beginning of the 2d century. Though the name was a common one in the ancient world, it is possible that the bishop of Ephesus was the same Onesimus of whom Paul spoke in his letter to Philemon. Such an identification would strengthen the proposal that it was he who instigated the collection of Paul's letters.

**Ophites** (from Greek *ophis*, "serpent"). A group of (Barbelo-) Gnostics, including the Naassenes, Peratae, Sethians, and Cainites, who worshiped the serpent. The Coptic writings found at Nag-Hammadi in Upper Egypt supply most of what is known about them. They generally rejected the Old Testament or gave it a strongly allegorical interpretation. The serpent that Moses held up in the wilderness was interpreted as having power over evil, and as a mediator, with the Son and the Word, between the Father and unformed matter. Hippolytus accused the Peratae of tritheism. (The Son, Word, and serpent is one of several triads, e.g., Adam, Eve, serpent; and Cain, Abel, Seth.) He attributes to the Sethians the doctrine that the serpent is "the originating principle of generation." Seth is also seen as the progenitor of the true children of God. The Naassenes worshiped the serpent in place of the God of the Jews who had cursed it. The Gospel of Thomas may have originated in a Naassene circle. They apparently held that the primal man (*archanthrōpos*) in all men was released upon initiation into the Gnosis. Interpreted against the background of a morass of astrological (Chaldean), sexual, and mythical (e.g., Homeric) elements, Christ is seen as mediator between God and men, and as reconciler of opposing powers.

**Optatus** (4th century). Bishop of Milevis in Numidia. He wrote (c. 370) and revised (after 385) a work *Against the Schism of the Donatists,* which is an important source for the history of Donatism, and lays the foundation for some of the theological arguments on unity and schism later developed more fully by Augustine.

**Optina Pustyn'.** A celebrated former Russian monastery situated in the oblast of Kaluga. Dating back to the Middle Ages, it declined in the 18th century because of czarist hostility. Revival came when Platon, metropolitan of Moscow (1787–1811), invited to Optina Pustyn' some reforming monks who demonstrated that Orthodox religious life was not mere external manifestation of affected piety. A reputation was gained by certain elders, or *startsi*. They were humble, intense, ascetic monks who were esteemed for holiness and wisdom and who served as spiritual tutors for younger monks or laymen. As the fame of the monastery spread, a large number of pilgrims were received. By the purity of their moral lives the monks exercised much influence on all classes. The *startsi* were visited and venerated by the most eminent 19th-century

Russian writers: Ivan Kireyevski, founder of the Slavophile School, came to Optina Pustyn' as did Leontiev, Tolstoy, Gogol, Dostoevsky, and Soloviev, to seek advice and counsel at a time when rationalism was winning advantage among the intelligentsia. The spiritual renascence was impressive. The *starets* Amvrosy was a prototype of the monk Zossima in Dostoevsky's *The Brothers Karamazov*. The monks, ultimately numbering three hundred, also edited moral and hagiographic works before the Bolshevik Revolution brought an end to their activity.

**Opus Dei** (Societas Sacerdotalis Sanctae Crucis et Opus Dei). An association of Roman Catholic laity and clergy whose members try to add "the counsels of the gospel to the precepts common to all Christians." Founded in Madrid in 1928 by its present director, José María Escrivá de Balaguer, Opus Dei now has members in over fifty countries. It insists that it is neither a secret society nor politically oriented.

**Orange, Second Council of** (529). On the surface an informal meeting of Caesarius of Arles and twelve other bishops who assembled in 529 for the consecration of a church, and took the occasion to issue a series of statements on the doctrine of grace, taken from the works of Augustine, and a further pronouncement of their own. It appears, however, that Caesarius had drafted the document in agreement with theologians at Rome, and planned it to end, as it did, the Augustinian controversy that had convulsed the church in southern Gaul for a century. Caesarius sent the decisions for approval at Rome to his friend the archdeacon Boniface, who in the meanwhile had become Pope Boniface II and as such gave his endorsement to the Council. The general line taken by the Council of Orange, which thus became highly authoritative for the Western Church, was that grace alone can begin and carry through the work of salvation, but that the lost are responsible for their own damnation. This position, paradoxical at least formally, has been that of most Catholic and much Protestant theology. It stresses the importance of God's sovereign call while hinting that man is still free to say yes or no to it.

**Oratories.** Religious societies in the Church of Rome. The first oratory was begun by Philip Neri (1515–1595) in 1551 in Rome, where, as chaplain in the church of Saint Girolamo, he gathered young men in his room for spiritual discussion and devotional exercises. As the group became larger, he changed the attic over the church aisle into an oratory; the name was soon applied to the people meeting there. In 1564 he was given charge of San Giovanni, the church of the Florentines, where his disciples, including the historian Baronius, were ordained. They celebrated Mass and preached four sermons daily, interspersed with hymns and popular devotions. In 1575, convinced of the necessity of a church and a definite rule of their own, the group obtained and rebuilt Santa Maria in Vallicella. That year Pope Gregory XIII established there "a congregation of secular priests and clerics known as the Oratory." In 1577, Philip was formally elected provost of the congregation, although he did not take up residence until 1583.

The rules of the Congregation, drawn up seventeen years after Philip's death and approved by Pope Paul V in 1612, rely more on personal influence than organization, and stress the spontaneous practice of perfection instead of its enforcement by vows. Although each house was completely independent, all were to have in common three ideals, the careful performance of the liturgy, frequent participation in the sacraments, especially penance, and daily preaching. Each of the four daily sermons lasted about a half hour. The first explained the readings of the day, the second, a Scripture text; the third dealt with ecclesiastical history, the fourth with the lives of saints. The houses following this rule spread largely through Italy, Spain, and Portugal, and into South America, India, and Ceylon, until 1800. Under Napoleon I they were despoiled and partially suppressed, but recovered to survive a second suppression in 1869.

The French Congregation was founded at Paris in 1611 by Cardinal Bérulle to help effect the rehabilitation of ecclesiastical life. It adopted most of the original rules, but placed the government of all houses under a superior general to meet the problems of the French Church. Approved by Pope Paul III in 1613, its more than fifty houses helped to establish the seminaries prescribed by the Council of Trent, to train candidates for "the pursuit of sacerdotal perfection." Bérulle was succeeded in 1629 by Father Charles de Condren, who completed the organization and helped in founding the institute of St.-Sulpice. Before it was engulfed in the French Revolution, its membership included the preacher Le Jeune and the philosopher Malebranche. In 1852 it was restored by Father Gratry and the new superior general Father Pététot.

In 1845, Pope Pius IX advised Cardinal Newman that an oratory would be best suited for his future work. After a short novitiate at Santa Croce, Newman returned to England in 1847 and established an oratory at Mary-vale, Old Oscott. In 1848 he was joined by Father Faber and his Wilfridian community; the group finally found a permanent home in 1849 at Edgbaston, a suburb of Birmingham.

In 1849, Newman sent a group to found a house in London. On May 31, Cardinal Wise-man celebrated and preached the first Mass, and Cardinal Newman preached at vespers. The first public church in the diocese served by a religious community, it seemed to many a hazardous innovation, but its popularity, especially of Father Faber's preaching, proved its worth. In 1854 it moved to its present site in South Kensington.

BIBLIOGRAPHY: R. Addington, *The Idea of the Oratory* (London, 1966); L. Ponelle and L. Bordet, *St. Philip Neri and the Roman Society of His Times* (London, 1932).

**Oratory of Divine Love.** A group of devout Italian churchmen (not to be confused with the Oratorians founded by Philip Neri) formed in Rome about 1517. Its members, among whom were Cajetan da Thiene, Carafa (later Paul IV), and Sadoleto, sought to reform the morals of the church, but not radically to alter its doctrine and structure. Cardinal Contarini did not join the group, but concurred in its aims, which found ex-pression in the recommendations for reform made in 1538 to Paul III.

**Ordass, Lajos** (1901–    ). Former Lu-theran bishop of Budapest and Hungarian primate. He was jailed by the Communists (1948–1950) for alleged currency manipula-tions because he resisted school nationaliza-tion. Released in 1950 and temporarily re-stored during the Hungarian revolt (1956), he was ousted again after a 1957 anti-Com-munist address at the Lutheran World Federa-tion Assembly in Minneapolis.

**Ordinal.** In the Middle Ages a manual for priests on the recitation of the office. Now used of an order of prayers and ceremonies for conferring holy orders, i.e., ordination to any of the ministries of the church (see MAJOR ORDERS; MINOR ORDERS).

**Ordinal, The Anglican.** "The Form and Manner of Making, Ordaining and Conse-crating of Bishops, Priests, and Deacons," issued originally in March, 1550, and, with revisions, bound up with the subsequent edi-tions of the Book of Common Prayer, 1552, 1559, and 1662. Though the rite retained many traditional elements, a number of the elaborate ceremonies of the Latin pontifical were abolished, along with the minor orders, and a few new elements were inserted, largely

under the influence of Bucer. Three separate forms were provided, one for each order, all within the context of the Holy Communion.

Important aspects include the oath of su-premacy, the laying on of hands, the pro-nouncement by the bishop of an authoritative formula ("Receive the Holy Ghost [except for deacons]. . . . Take thou authority to . . ." [the distinctive functions of each order are then specified]), and the delivery of a New Testament or Bible (the first Ordinal also included a chalice and a paten for priests, and a pastoral staff for bishops).

The ordinal was attacked by many Prot-estants from Hooper on, and by Roman Cath-olics as being defective in, variously, form, matter, and intention. The latter defect was cited as the principal reason for Pope Leo XIII's declaration in 1897 of the invalidity of Anglican orders.

**Ordinary.** The legal term describing an ecclesiastic who exercises the powers of juris-diction permanently attached to his office, that is, the powers of governing, adjudicating, and administering sacraments. The pope holds im-mediate and full ordinary jurisdiction through-out the Roman Catholic Church. Other ordi-naries are bishops and their vicars-general, abbots, administrators, and vicars apostolic.

**Oregon School Case.** A 1925 decision of the United States Supreme Court invalidating a referendum-approved statute in Oregon that required all children between the ages of eight and sixteen to attend a public school. The decision upheld the constitutionality of attend-ance by children at parochial and private schools, but also clearly implied the right of a state reasonably to regulate all schools.

**Oresme, Nicole** (c. 1320–1382). Bishop of Lisieux from 1377 and one of the most im-portant philosophers and antinominalist theo-logians of the 14th century. His writings on political matters were very important in the formation of medieval theories of economics. Influenced by John Buridan and Albert of Saxony, he was a forerunner of modern as-tronomy. He in turn influenced the thought of Pierre d'Ailly.

**Organic Articles.** Seventy-seven articles in four "titled" sections promulgated by Napo-leon (April 8, 1802), together with the papal concordat. Each article had the state as its denominator. The government asserted con-trol over papal documents, some clerical train-ing, clerical dress, processions, stipends, par-ish boundaries. Reformed churches with a minimum of six thousand members were or-ganized under consistorial systems. Lutherans received a special church order. The Articles were rescinded by law on Dec. 9, 1905.

**Oriental Churches, Congregation for.** One of eleven Sacred Congregations of the Roman Curia, one of three presided over by the pope. Created by Pius XI (1938) to render judgments on or to refer to other problems pertaining to any Near Eastern Church in communion with Rome, Latin or not, or to other similar churches and their members outside the Near East. Oriental churches of languages or rites other than Latin claim ten million faithful.

**Origen** (Origenes Adamantius) (c. 185–c. 254). Greek father of the church and one of the most versatile and accomplished men in the early history of the church. A man first of all of deep and ascetic personal piety, he was a great teacher of both sacred and secular subjects at introductory and advanced levels, the first real textual critic of the Bible, the most influential of its early commentators, the first theologian ever to set forth a systematic presentation of the faith, and one of the great Apologists for that faith. Origen was one of the pioneer students of the spiritual life, and the theoretical basis of monasticism grew in part out of his teaching. His lifelong admiration for martyrdom was satisfied in a death that was brought on by injuries suffered under persecution. In spite of all this, he was opposed in his lifetime by his own bishop, Demetrius of Alexandria condemned by several synods, including the "home" synod of Constantinople in 543, and his name was listed among those condemned by the Ecumenical Council of Constantinople of 553, although perhaps a later addition.

Origen is almost uniquely well known to us because of the preservation of several sources of biographical information. The most important of these is the sixth book of Eusebius' *Ecclesiastical History*. Pamphilius wrote an *Apology* for Origen with Eusebius, but all that remains of it is Rufinus' Latin translation of the first book. The apostle of Cappodocia, Gregory Thaumaturgus, was a pupil of Origen's in Caesarea and delivered a panegyric on him that is still extant. Jerome included him among his *Of Illustrious Men,* and in a letter to Paula (*Epistle* 33) listed eight hundred of his works.

Origen was an Egyptian, probably born in Alexandria. Although his name means "son of Horus," he came from a Christian family. His father, Leonidas, saw that he received a religious as well as a secular education. Included in his daily regimen of study was the memorization of verses of Scripture. When he

interested himself at an early age in the spiritual meaning of the verses, his father's counsel was to limit himself to studies appropriate for his age. After his father was captured during the persecution under the emperor Septimus Severus (202), Origen longed to join him but was restrained by his mother, who hid his clothes. Unable to become a martyr as he so strongly desired, Origen sent word to his father, "Take care not to change thy mind on our account."

At his father's death, the responsibility for his mother and six younger brothers fell upon the seventeen-year-old shoulders of Origen. The assistance of a wealthy woman of Alexandria left him free to continue his studies. During his eighteenth year, through the bishop Demetrius, Origen became the head of the catechetical school at Alexandria. It was probably not an established institution dispensing advanced theological learning under such masters as Pantaenus and Clement, but a lay-conducted program to prepare pagans for baptism. At any rate, Origen took his duties seriously; in time he gave up his classes in pagan literature completely and even sold his library of classics. He earned four obols a day copying manuscripts. This was well below the wages of a common laborer, but commensurate with his asceticism. He devoted himself entirely to his work, studying the Bible until late at night. It is not surprising that such a teacher produced many eager for martyrdom, and Origen ministered to such pupils at great risk to his own safety. During this period (probably before c. 210) Origen, whose very name is associated with the allegorical interpretation of the Scriptures, took Matt. 19:12 in what Eusebius calls "too literal and extreme a sense" and made himself a eunuch for "the sake of the kingdom of heaven."

So many pupils came to him seeking instruction that he entrusted the preparation of the catechumens to Heraclas and began a private *didaskaleion,* on the order of that of Justin Martyr at Rome, where he taught advanced students. Here secular studies could be undertaken as preliminaries to Biblical study. Eusebius writes that "thousands of heretics and many of the most eminent philosophers" flocked to hear him.

During Origen's twenty-eight years as a catechist in Alexandria he traveled widely. His first trip was to Rome, where, Jerome writes, he met Hippolytus, who may have inspired him to write commentaries. His fame spread, and the current interest in everything religious led prominent pagans (such as the governor of his province and Mamaea, the mother of Emperor Alexander Severus and aunt of Emperor Heliogabalus) to ask him to come and tell them his opinions. He also began his immense literary output, producing his first commentaries and perhaps his systematic work, *Peri archōn*. A wealthy convert named Ambrose hired secretaries to take down Origen's lectures and copyists to publish them. Meanwhile, Origen learned Hebrew and studied philosophy under Ammonius Saccas, the teacher of Longinus and Plotinus.

During the massacre of the citizens of Alexandria under Caracalla in 215, Origen visited Palestine. He was asked to preach there by Alexander, bishop of Jerusalem, and Theoctistus, bishop of Caesarea. When word got back home to Demetrius that Origen, a layman, was preaching before bishops, he was recalled to Alexandria. However, some years later (230), Origen returned to Caesarea, where he was ordained priest. This infuriated Demetrius, who had him deposed by a synod of three Egyptian bishops. This deposition, however, was not recognized universally, least of all in Palestine, where Origen lived out his life and practiced his priesthood.

In Caesarea, Origen founded a school like the one in Alexandria and continued to teach and to write. He was called upon to settle disputes and participate in councils, and he engaged in correspondence with the great men of the day. He also began to preach almost daily in the church at Caesarea. Eventually scribes began to take his sermons down, and they are the homilies which have been preserved. During the Decian persecution (250) he was captured and imprisoned. Eusebius writes that "the sufferings he underwent because Christ had commanded it were many and intense. He was put in chains, his body was tortured, he was tormented with the iron collar and kept in the innermost dungeon of the prison. For several days he was set in stocks with his feet in the fourth hole and threatened with burning" (*Ecclesiastical History* 6.39). Though he survived his imprisonment by several years, there is no doubt that his death was hastened by the rigors of the persecution and that the only difference between his martyrdom and that of others is that his suffering and death were more widely separated.

Origen was one of the most prolific writers in the history of the church. Jerome tells us that the list of his works given by Pamphilus runs to 2,000 items. Epiphanius estimated the total to be 6,000. Jerome himself lists 800. The vast majority of these works are lost, although fragments continue to be discovered. They were, for the most part, Biblical studies. His *Hexapla* was an attempt to establish a critical text for the Old Testament by publishing the Hebrew text, a transliteration of it in Greek letters (the LXX), and other Greek translations in parallel columns. His exegetical works included scholia on difficult passages, popular homilies preached in church, and the commentaries in which he gave his scientific exegesis. One of the many controversies presently going on about Origen is whether the sage guide to the spiritual life of the homilies or the allegorically fanciful expositor of the commentaries represents the "real" Origen. The obvious answer is that each displays a facet of a richly diverse personality. The former general deprecation of his allegorical interpretation of the Scriptures is currently undergoing reassessment.

Origen's great apologetic work was his *Contra Celsum*. Celsus was not an Epicurean as has been thought, but a Middle Platonist, which means that he and Origen shared the same general philosophical outlook. His main objection to Christianity was its arrogance in claiming to be unique. Origen's answer was that Christianity gives what philosophy only promises and gives it to all, not to just a few who are intelligent enough to receive it.

The most important of Origen's works and the one responsible for his theological disfavor is *First Principles* (*Peri archōn*). It proposes to be a systematic statement of the faith. In the first book, he treats of supernatural beings and has a subordination of the Logos and Holy Spirit to the Father. He discusses creation, fall, and redemption in the second book, and in the third gives an outline of moral theology. In the fourth book he states his theory of Biblical interpretation. Although some parts of this great work appear to be inadequate to later generations, it was nevertheless the trailblazer. It cannot be justly evaluated on the basis of the later orthodoxy which followed it. Its author admitted that he was exploring; his fertile mind shot off ideas like a Roman candle. Probably no one in the history of the church has so objectified the trait, assigned to Origen by G. L. Prestige as characteristic, of presenting "the claims of religious intelligence" (*Fathers and Heretics* [Naperville, Ill., 1940], p. 43).

BIBLIOGRAPHY: Origen, *On First Principles*, ed. by G. W. Butterworth (New York, 1966); A. Roberts and J. Donaldson (eds.), *The Ante-Nicene Fathers*, Vol. 4 (Grand Rapids, 1951).

C. Bigg, *The Christian Platonists of Alexandria* (Oxford, 1913); H. Chadwick, *Early Christian Thought and the Classical Tradition* (New York, 1966); B. Drewery, *Origen and the Doctrine of Grace* (London, 1960); R. A.

Norris, Jr., *God and World in Early Christian Theology* (New York, 1967).

**Original Seceders.** The Old Light Antiburghers. Originating with the Scottish Secession of 1733, they split from that secession (1747), refusing to take the oath acknowledging the truth of the religion authorized by Scottish law, thus beginning the Antiburghers. When New Light arose (1806), they separated, forming the Old Light Antiburghers, continuing as such until all but a remnant united with the Free Church (1852).

**Ornaments Rubric.** A directive placed in the 1559 edition of the Book of Common Prayer. It provided that the liturgical ornaments and vestments of the Church of England be those of the second year of Edward VI's reign. Precisely what was the intention of this rubric, however, has been disputed since the 16th century. It was nevertheless approved again by Parliament in 1604 and 1662. Apparently, it gave temporary warrant for the use of the "white alb plain, with a vestment or cope" authorized by the first Edwardian Prayer Book (1549), but abolished by the second (1552). The promised "other order" seems never to have been issued, unless it is identified with Matthew Parker's *Advertisements* (1566), and the reaffirmation of the rubric in 1662 has never been revoked.

**Orosius** (b. c. 385). Spanish presbyter, associate of Augustine. Orosius' *Seven Books of History Against the Pagans* was completed in 418. Though the author of other works, he earned his reputation from this apologetic history designed to expound the thesis of *The City of God* (Book 3). His history extends from the Creation to his own day. It is based largely on second-rate sources and handbooks. In it the church's triumph is foreseen.

**Orphaned Missions Fund.** World War II progressively cut off all Continental European missionaries except Swedes from homeland support. Some missionaries were interned under bad conditions. The International Missionary Council set up the Orphaned Missions Fund in New York, and Lutheran World Action worked in close conjunction with it. The total for 1940–1949 was $8,305,633, of which $4,016,693 came from Lutheran churches in the United States.

**Orthodox Churches.** See EASTERN ORTHODOXY.

**Orthodox Theological Institute** (Paris) (*popularly known as* St. Sergius Theological Academy). An institute set up in 1925 under the jurisdiction of the ecumenical patriarch. It soon became an important point of contact between the Orthodox and the Western Christian communions. Though not able to speak officially for their church, the exiled Russian theologians forthrightly voiced the tradition of the Christian East in the various ecumenical conferences of the Life and Work, Faith and Order movements. Western Christians quickly recognized their significance and offered the Institute generous assistance. Through the Y.M.C.A. press, the Russian theologians were enabled to appear in print. A list of books and articles published by the Institute between 1925 and 1947 numbers some 90 pages. The first rector of the Institute was Sergius Bulgakov (d. 1944). Three former members of the Institute, Georges Florovsky, Alexander Schmemann, and John Meyendorff, are now teaching in the United States. The Institute is also noted for its choir, which has sought to revive the ancient classical chants of Russia. Today a majority of the students at the Institute are non-Russian. Since 1958 lectures are being given in French as well as Russian.

**Osiander, Andreas** (1498–1552). German Lutheran theologian. A native of Bavaria, he studied at Ingolstadt and served as a teacher and priest in Nuremberg, where he came out in favor of Luther in 1522. Along with Lazarus Spengler and Wenceslas Linck he helped to reform Nuremberg. Later he attended the colloquies at Marburg (1529), Hagenau (1540), Worms (1540), the Diet of Augsburg (1530), and signed the Smalcald Articles in 1537. During the difficult times that followed the Augsburg Interim (1548) he was forced to leave Nuremberg and in 1549 became the leading professor of the theological faculty at Königsberg. The following year he published *On Justification*, which embroiled the Lutheran Church in one of the most violent controversies after Luther's death. Though in basic agreement with Luther's theology as over against Roman Catholicism and Calvinism, he insisted that justification was not by the imputation of Christ's merits but by the infusion of Christ's righteousness to the believer. God "makes the sinner just" by letting Christ dwell in him instead of merely "declaring" the sinner to be justified. In 1577 the third article of the Formula of Concord rejected Osiander's views and upheld the forensic doctrine of justification.

**Oslo, Second World Conference of Christian Youth at** (July 22–31, 1947, in succession to Amsterdam, 1939). Twelve hundred persons from 181 churches and agencies in 71 countries attended. The objectives were to further cooperation, to train a new generation of leaders for the quest for unity and cooperation, to stimulate youth to study the fundamental issues of the time, and to show that their only solution lies in the Lordship of Jesus Christ.

**Oswald** (c. 605–642). English martyr, king of the Northumbrians from 634. Converted to Christianity by the monks of Iona during his exile in Scotland as a boy, he returned to Northumbria after the death of Edwin, his uncle, in 633 and established himself as king by a victory at Havenfelt. In response to his call for missionaries, Aidan was sent from Iona and installed as bishop in Lindisfarne. Oswald was killed in battle in 642 by the pagan king of Mercia, and honored thereafter as a hero and martyr both in England and on the Continent.

**Oswald** (d. 992). Anglo-Saxon churchman, archbishop of York, and bishop of Worcester. After learning the Rule of St. Benedict in a French monastery, he aided his relative, Oskytel, archbishop of York, in carrying out ecclesiastical reforms. His impressive holiness, diligence, and kindly liberality earned him an appointment as bishop of Worcester by Edgar, king of the English, in 961. Oswald worked in conjunction with Dunstan, archbishop of Canterbury, and Ethelwold, bishop of Winchester, in promoting learning, establishing new monasteries, and enforcing a Benedictine monastic discipline. Oswald was especially concerned with replacing with monks all married clergy who possessed religious houses. King Edgar's decree effecting this reform was labeled "Oswald's Law."

**Otterbein, Philip William** (1726–1813). A German Reformed pastor who came to America in 1752 and expressed his pietistic emphasis by preaching the necessity of an inner spiritual experience. After becoming acquainted with Francis Asbury, he began to appropriate Methodist techniques, which led to the formation of a German revivalist body that in 1800 became the United Brethren in Christ, a denomination exemplifying Arminian theology and Methodist polity.

**Otto I** (*called* Otto the Great) (912–973). Emperor of the Western Roman Empire from 962. He succeeded his father, Henry the Fowler, as king of Germany after election by the Franks and Saxons (936). He revived the coronation ceremony, being crowned at Aachen by Hildebert of Mainz. He incorporated the dukes of the stem duchies into the ceremony of the coronation banquet. Otto quelled revolts in Bavaria, Franconia, Lorraine, and Saxony by 939. He took Franconia as a royal duchy, appointed Hermann Billung to administer Saxony, gained the allegiance of Burgundy by protecting the young heir Conrad, and married Adelaide, widow of Lothaire, one of the claimants to the throne of Lombardy. Otto was crowned king of the Lombards (951). He defeated the Hungarians at Lechfeld (955), and was crowned emperor by Pope John XII (962), at the same time obtaining the establishment of the metropolitan see of Magdeburg. Otto used the bishops to keep his kingdom loyal, as did Adalbero of Metz, Bruno of Cologne, and Adalbero of Lorraine in the wars of the 950's. Others led troops, built castles, fortified towns, and served as ambassadors. He brought many abbeys under royal control and appointed advocates to oversee their administration. A revival of learning known as the Ottonian Renaissance took place during his reign.

**Otto III** (980–1002). Holy Roman Emperor from 983. He was the son of the emperor Otto II and Theophano, a Byzantine princess. During the period of his minority, the empire was ruled by his grandmother and mother. Upon reaching his majority, he attempted to reform both church and empire. He favored the ascetic practices of Nilus (d. c. 430) and Romuald (c. 950–1027) and appointed to the papacy first his cousin and then his former tutor, Gerbert (Sylvester II). He died in Rome at twenty-two years of age and was buried beside Charlemagne at Aachen.

**Otto, Rudolf** (1869–1937). German Protestant theologian. Otto taught at Göttingen, Breslau, and Marburg (1917–1937). His interest in comparative religion, Oriental thought, and natural science influenced his most famous work *Das Heilige* (1917; translated into English in 1923 as *The Idea of the Holy*). Reacting against the rational and ethical currents of the liberalism of his day, he examined those elements in religion which are called "feelings." Otto felt that these experiences are a valid way of knowing something of the transcendental presence. Theology has the task of trying to express in concepts the experience of feeling. Some of these attempts refer to the thrill of awe or reverence, the feeling of the uncanny, the sense of dependence and nothingness, or again the feeling of religious rapture and exaltation. As Otto describes this experience he uses the term "holiness," stating that it means more than morality, for it includes as well the idea of the "numinous." To a greater extent than any other religion, Christianity recognizes this element in combination with a rational approach. Yet even Christians, Otto taught, are plagued with the paradox of awe and rationality and only in the experience of worship do the two elements come into harmony. Paul Tillich and others have been greatly influenced by Otto's thought.

**Ottonian Renaissance.** The revival of learning under the imperial Ottos (I: 936–973; II: 973–983; III: 983–1002). Bruno (d. 965) wrote lives of the saints and Biblical commentaries; Liutprand of Cremona (d. c. 972) wrote a life of Otto and *Relatio de legatione Constantinopolitana*, which constitute a chief source of 10th-century history; Widukind (d. 973) of New Corbey wrote a history of Saxony; Hrotsvitha, a Benedictine nun, wrote numerous poems and plays; Gerbert (Sylvester II, d. 1003), philosopher, theologian, and scientist, was the most significant light of this brief renaissance. Bishop Ratherius of Verona (d. 974) wrote interesting accounts of the time.

**Otto of Freising** (c. 1111–1158). Austrian bishop and historian. He began his career as a Cistercian monk (c. 1132) and abbot (c. 1136). In 1138 he became bishop of Freising in Bavaria. In addition to his episcopal duties he participated in the Second Crusade (1147–1149) and wrote two important historical works: *The Two Cities, a Chronicle of Universal History to the Year 1146 A.D.* and a partial account of his nephew's reign, *The Deeds of Frederick Barbarossa*.

**Overall, John** (1560–1619). Bishop of Norwich. A graduate of Trinity College, Cambridge, and regius professor of divinity, Overall participated in the Hampton Court Conference in 1604, and the addition (on the sacraments) to the Anglican Catechism which grew out of that meeting was his work. He also assisted with the King James Version of the Bible of 1611. A moderate Calvinist, he remained a staunch advocate of Anglicanism while allowing some flexibility with the Puritans in his dioceses.

**Overbeck, Franz** (1837–1905). German Protestant theologian. Born at St. Petersburg, Overbeck was professor of church history at Jena (1864–1870) and professor of critical theology at Basel (1870–1897). A close friend and admirer of Nietzsche, he expounded a "secular church history" which rejected orthodox Christianity. His most important works are *Studien zur Geschichte der alten Kirche* (1875) and *Christentum und Kultur* (posthumous, 1919).

**Overberg, Bernhard Heinrich** (1754–1826). The theological head of a devout Roman Catholic group usually known as the Gallitzin circle. Educated by the Franciscans and at the seminary of Münster, he was ordained priest in 1780. Appointed private chaplain to Princess Adelheid Amalie de Gallitzin in 1789, he readily established himself within her literary and theological circle, which included both Catholic and Protestant scholars.

**Owen, John** (1616–1683). Puritan Independent clergyman and theologian. He was graduated from Queen's College, Oxford. In 1637, refusing to submit to Laud's statutes, he left the university, becoming chaplain to Lord Lovelace. He began his pamphleteering in 1643, espousing strict Calvinism and Presbyterianism. However, when he became vicar of Coggeshall soon after, he modeled the church on congregational lines. He accompanied Cromwell as chaplain in the Irish campaign and in Scotland, was appointed preacher to the council of state—often preaching before the Long Parliament—and then assumed the deanery of Christ's Church, Oxford, in 1651. Appointed vice-chancellor of Oxford the same year, he served until 1658 when he was relieved of his position, also being ejected from Christ's Church the following year. Though offered preferment during the Restoration, he rejected it, favoring religious toleration. He and Richard Baxter explored the possibility of uniting the Presbyterians and Independents, but nothing materialized. Owen opposed the comprehension movement, for he believed that no bill would be inclusive enough to allow the toleration needed for Independent worship. A prolific writer and controversialist, he was yet temperate in his polemics and profound in his learning. Owen ranks as the outstanding Independent of the Restoration period.

**Owen, Robert** (1771–1858). English social reformer. Son of a saddler and ironmonger in North Wales, he was educated until nine years of age, becoming manager of a cotton mill when nineteen. He gained control of the New Lanark factory (1799), where he organized a community for his workers, improving their welfare and providing stores and education for their benefit. Subsequently, he formed another firm (1814), with Jeremy Bentham and William Allen as partners. In 1813 he published his ideas for educational philanthropy in *A New View of Society*. Dispensing with the formal creeds of Christianity, Owen composed his own and taught that man's character is made for him through circumstances beyond his control and that he cannot be rightly blamed or praised for his actions. The importance of character formation in early years was emphasized and governed Owen's work on behalf of education and social improvement. His experiments at New Lanark gained international attention and in 1817 he made his first ventures into socialism. He attributed the ills of society to competition and advocated self-contained communities based upon cooperative principles. His ideas had great appeal, but he lost much support when he declared his hostility to all forms of revealed religion. Communities such as he advocated were established in Scotland and at New Harmony, Ind. Both failed. For the remainder of his life he promoted his socialist and secularist views and left behind as a fruit of his labors the cooperative movement. He died professing belief in spiritualism.

**Oxenstierna** (Oxenstjerna), **Count Axel** (1583–1654). Swedish Lutheran statesman. He served Gustavus Adolphus from 1612 until that king's death in 1632, remaining as chancellor and regent until Queen Christina came into her majority in 1644, and as chancellor until his death. He sustained the Protestant side during the whole of the Thirty Years' War. He is regarded by some as having had a religious motivation in pushing on with the war after the death of Gustavus Adolphus on the battlefield; others see in his treaty with Richelieu (1631 and 1633) and his war with Denmark (1643–1644) a shift from religious motivation to one of dynastic and territorial aggrandizement.

**Oxford Conference** (1937). This was the second conference of the Life and Work movement and was held at Oxford, July 12–26, 1937, under the general title of "Church, Community, and State." A study conference, it was meant to further efforts toward common ethical, social action in line with the work of the first conference of the Life and Work movement which met at Stockholm in 1925. There were 425 regular members present at the Conference representing 120 communions in forty countries. There were no official representatives from the Roman Catholic Church or from the Nazi-controlled German Evangelical Church. John R. Mott provided overall leadership, and the Conference Message was drafted by a committee chaired by William Temple, then archbishop of York. J. H. Oldham stated that "the essential theme of the Oxford Conference . . . was the life and death struggle between Christian faith and the pagan tendencies of our time." Reports of the Conference were published in eight volumes, The Church, Community, and State series. Besides its regular work, the Conference provided for the appointment of representatives to cooperate with representatives of the Faith and Order movement in forming the World Council of Churches. As a result the Life and Work movement transferred its responsibilities and functions to the Provisional Committee of the World Council of Churches in Process of Formation, established at Utrecht in 1938.

**Oxford Group.** See MORAL RE-ARMAMENT.

**Oxford Movement.** See ANGLO-CATHOLIC MOVEMENT.

**Ozanam, Antoine Frédéric** (1813–1853). French Roman Catholic scholar and a founder of the Society of St. Vincent de Paul. Born at Milan and educated at Lyons and Paris, he was appointed professor of foreign literature at the Sorbonne in 1841. In 1833, while still a student, he founded the Society of St. Vincent de Paul, an organization of Catholic laymen for religious and social service among the poor. His great aim was to write a historical reply to Edward Gibbon's *The History of the Decline and Fall of the Roman Empire* (3 vols., 1776–1781), and to vindicate the Roman Catholic Church by means of a history of Christian civilization. He did not entirely succeed; but his works have had a profound effect in reassessing the medieval world. His *Dante et la philosophie catholique au treizième siècle* (1839) is a brilliant exposition of Dante's Christian philosophy; his *Poètes franciscains en Italie au XIII$^e$ siècle* (1852) is of much importance for the history of medieval spirituality; his *La Civilisation chrétienne chez les Francs* (1845) excellently describes the success and influence of the Christian church in educating the Germanic tribes. Ozanam was a political liberal, a friend of Chateaubriand and Montalembert, and one of the leaders of the revival of Catholicism in France in the 19th century.

# P

**Pacca, Bartolomeo** (1756–1844). Italian cardinal, diplomat, and historian. Nuncio in 1785 to Cologne, he defended papal prerogatives against Febronian agitation and opposed Protestant toleration. As Prosecretary of state, in 1808, when Napoleon occupied Rome, he circulated Pius VII's bull excommunicating the emperor. Pacca, punished by exile in 1814, came home to govern the Church States briefly and urge revival of the Jesuit Society. He held various curial posts after 1815. His memoirs are important sources of historical material.

**Pacem in Terris.** Papal encyclical issued in 1963 by Pope John XXIII. It constituted a plea for peace on earth based on a concept of divine order and the freedom that was man's as a part of natural law. The document's significance lies in its distinctly modern tone; its recognition of contemporary problems; its urging of an easing of tension between Catholics and non-Christians and Communists; and its insistence on the individual's right to believe according to the dictates of his conscience. The encyclical represented a major part of the ecumenical program of Pope John.

**Pachomius** (Coptic, *Pakhom*) (c. 290–346). The first great organizer of the cenobitic (common life) form of monasticism. A native of Upper Egypt, Pachomius served briefly in the army of Licinius, then entered the ascetic life, first under the guidance of an old hermit, then as the leader of his own disciples. His monastery at Tabennisi combined strict discipline with recognition of individual differences, and emphasized productive work as well as prayer. It became the head of a group of monasteries, and associated convents, with an organization under a "common father" and a council of superiors, such as was not reached elsewhere until the 12th-century Cistercians. Pachomius was a friend of Athanasius, to whom his monks gave refuge during Athanasius' third exile (356–361), but since Pachomius spoke Coptic, and the center of the Pachomian, or Tabennesiot, Order was in Upper Egypt, Pachomian influence on the rest of the church was limited. However, there were Greek-speaking monks at Tabennisi, to one of whom we owe the first Life of Pachomius, and even Latin monks at the great Metanoia monastery near Alexandria, for whom Jerome produced a translation of their rule. This is a collection of scattered aphorisms and directions rather than a systematic document, but it served to transmit a knowledge of Pachomian ideals to later monastic founders.

**Pacian** (4th century). Bishop of Barcelona. His episcopate is difficult to date, but he must have written sometime after the Novatian schism and prior to 392. In his three letters to Sympronian, who was a follower of the Novatian school, and in his *Paraenesis ad poenitentiam,* Pacian, a supporter of the Cyprian school, argues on the basis of Scripture for a distinction between mortal sins (blasphemy, murder, and fornication), which can be remedied only by repentance and forgiveness, and other sins, which can be remedied by the compensation of good works.

**Pacifism in Christian Thought.** The idea that commitment to love requires reconciliation with enemies and a refusal to participate in armed warfare. This was apparently the position of Christians in the 1st and 2d centuries. The writings of that period imply that the Christian life is incompatible with bloodshed for any purpose, and there is no record of Christians entering military service until about A.D. 170.

Origen in the 3d century wrote that "Christians have been taught not to defend themselves against their enemies." He added, "No longer do we take the sword against any nations, nor do we learn war anymore since we have become the sons of peace through Jesus, who is our author, instead of following the traditional custom by which we were strangers to the covenant."

Tertullian wrote that "Christ in disarming Peter ungirt every soldier." Some historians specifically exclude eschatology or objections to idolatry as motivations for rejection of military service by the early Christians, since the expectation of the Lord's speedy return had waned and soldiers in the lower ranks were not expected to sacrifice for the emperor.

After A.D. 170 there was increasing evidence of Christians in the Roman armies. The functions of Roman soldiers were so diverse that some Christians who entered military service did so without the intention of taking human life. The Canons of Hippolytus in the early 3d century required that "a soldier of the civil authority must be taught not to kill men and to refuse to do so if he is commanded."

In a gradual transition about the time of Constantine, the majority of Christians came to believe that some wars were "just," although in subsequent years the monks, who were regarded as the more perfect Christians, generally abstained from war.

During the Middle Ages, about the 11th and 12th centuries, there were nonresistant sects who taught that no injury should be done to anyone. The Albigenses were virtually wiped out in two cruel crusades. The early Waldenses, who followed Peter Waldo, were also pacifist. They too were persecuted.

John Hus was a nonviolent leader, but his burning (July 6, 1415) was the signal for armed revolt in Bohemia against the Roman Church. His spiritual heirs were the Bohemian Brethren. They maintained an essentially pacifist position until the Protestant Reformation. Their history merges with that of the Moravians. The Moravians were pacifist in their missions in Ireland and in the English colonies to which they had sent personnel as early as 1732. They were granted relief by Parliament from bearing arms.

In the Renaissance period, pacifism was held by Erasmus (about 1500) and some of the humanists. After the Reformation, the

Mennonites, beginning in the 16th century, the Friends, or Quakers, in the 17th, and the Church of the Brethren, or Dunkers, in the 18th, came to be known as the historic peace churches because of their pacifist witness which continued into the 20th century.

The Mennonites, whose leader was Menno Simons, made a distinction between those in the kingdom of the world who because of sin needed the restraint of coercive power and the Kingdom of Christ, where love and the Word of God replaced the sword. Since they had entered the Kingdom of Christ, they did not serve as magistrates or soldiers.

The Mennonites were peaceful as distinct from other Anabaptists. Frederick of Prussia in 1710 granted them freedom from military service as did Russia until about 1874, when many of them joined earlier Mennonite settlements in America.

The Church of the Brethren, which originated in Schwarzenau, emigrated in 1719 to America. Their leader was Alexander Mack. For most of their history they were nonresistants and political nonparticipants.

There were other pacifist Christian groups such as the Schwenkfeldians, who left Germany for America in 1734, and the Dukhobors, whose leader, Peter Verigin, came under Tolstoy's influence while in Siberia. The Dukhobors emigrated to Canada in 1899. There was also a small group of pacifists in France, about the time of the Revolution, known as the Camisards. They were descendants of the original Huguenots. Upon learning of the Society of Friends and its leader, George Fox, they became Quakers.

Fox, while in the "house of correction" because of his religious activities, was told of the idea launched by some of Cromwell's soldiers that Fox should be made a captain in the forces. Fox recorded in his Journal: "I told them I knew whence all wars arose, even from the lusts, according to James's doctrine; and that I lived in the virtue of that life and power which took away the occasion of all wars."

The Friends have had the greatest impact on modern pacifism because they pioneered in political and social activity based on nonviolent principles. The peaceful colony of Pennsylvania was led by Quakers until the French and Indian War. Friends were also active in antislavery movements. The American Friends Service Committee was organized during World War I, and its British and Canadian counterparts have earned worldwide reputations for their relief and reconstruction activities. They also organized peace education and action programs that have influenced many Christians in other churches.

The Fellowship of Reconciliation, born in England during World War I from Quaker influence, spread to America and other continents to unite pacifist Christians from all churches. In the 1930's, pacifism became a significant emphasis in British and American Protestant churches. At the beginning of World War II some 3,000 American clergymen were enrolled in the Fellowship of Reconciliation along with about 12,000 laymen. The Protestant churches were successful in persuading British and American governments to grant legal recognition to conscientious objectors.

The writings of Tolstoy, Henry David Thoreau, and the New Testament influenced Gandhi to accept a nonviolent strategy in India. In similar fashion, the Fellowship of Reconciliation influenced Negro Christian leaders such as Martin Luther King, Jr., in the United States and Albert Luthuli in the Union of South Africa to accept a nonviolent struggle for racial equality following World War II.

Some groups in the 20th century, notably the Jehovah's Witnesses, have resisted military service without being pacifist either in a nonresistant or nonviolent resistant sense.

The Roman Catholic Church has had a few pacifists among its members throughout its history. In the 20th century most Roman Catholic pacifists have based their position on the idea that modern wars no longer can fit into the concept of a just war. A few have taken a position of nonviolence on Biblical or theological grounds. The Second Vatican Council responded to the pleas of Roman Catholic pacifists by asking that "laws make humane provisions for the case of those who, for reasons of conscience, refuse to bear arms, provided, however, that they agree to serve the human community in some other way."

After the Constantinian era, pacifists were a tiny minority in the Christian church, often misunderstood and persecuted by their fellow Christians. In the 20th century they have continued to be a minority, but their influence on social movements and on the position of the Protestant churches with respect to peace, civil liberties, and relief work has been adjudged significant by a number of social scientists and historians.

BIBLIOGRAPHY: R. H. Bainton, *Christian Attitudes Toward War and Peace* (Nashville, 1960); C. J. Cadoux, *The Early Christian Attitude to War* (London, 1940); and *The Early Church and the World* (Edinburgh, 1955); C. M. Case, *Non-violent Coercion* (New York, 1923); G. J. Heering, *The Fall of Christianity* (London, 1930).

**Padilla, Juan de** (c. 1500–c. 1544). Spanish missionary. About 1528 he came with the first Franciscans to enter Mexico. In 1532 he began missionary work, founding several missions in Mexico and as a member of the expedition of Coronado also in the present New Mexico. When Coronado abandoned his New Mexico settlement in 1542, Padilla remained with a small party and was later killed by the Indians he sought to convert.

**Padroado** (literally, "patronage"). The right to nominate bishops granted by medieval popes to Portuguese kings. The privilege caused difficulties in Goa (India), where Portuguese ecclesiastical jurisdiction was encroached upon by apostolic vicars named by the Sacred Congregation for the Propagation of the Faith. When Gregory XVI declared Goanese padroado abolished, a so-called "Goanese Schism" resulted. It was settled (1886) when the archbishop of Goa was designated patriarch of the East Indies.

**Paganuzzi, Giovanni Battista** (1814–1923). Venetian lawyer, active defender of the church, and an organizer of the Italian Catholic Congress movement. Prominent in Catholic Action groups, he admired Ludwig Windthorst, German centrist leader. Paganuzzi abstained from direct political participation because of papal bans, contested with Romolo Murri, and laid foundations for what became, at the end of World War I, Luigi Sturzo's Catholic People's Party.

**Paine, Thomas** (1737–1809). Political writer and deist. Born in England, he left school at the age of thirteen. He took up his father's trade in London, and worked for a time in the state excise office. In 1774 he came to America, and while he was editor of the *Pennsylvania Magazine* he published a pamphlet, *Common Sense,* which contributed greatly to the movement for independence in the colonies and made him famous as a patriot. He served with Washington's army in December, 1776, stirring the colonists to determined action by his *The Crisis.* In 1793 and 1794 while in Europe he wrote *The Age of Reason,* which, though it won him many friends in France, changed him from hero to rascal among most Americans of the time. Its outspoken deistic attack upon traditional Christianity was considered a threat and undoubtedly contributed much to the popularizing of deism in America.

**Painting and Sculpture, Ecclesiastical.** Christian attitudes toward the pictorialization of sacred themes and personages have varied greatly. The Mosaic law and antipaganism contributed to the suspicion of images, but it was fundamentally spiritual concerns that governed iconoclastic arguments. During the first Christian centuries, however, even the Jews had adopted classical traditions of mural painting (synagogue, Dura-Europas) and manuscript illustration, and by Constantinian times, Christianity had accepted the idea of religious images, although free-standing sculpture was generally avoided until later in the Middle Ages. A notable exception, the 4th-century statue of Christ in the National Museum, Rome, shows how far toward a pagan conception of the cult image early Christian artists were willing to go. It is not surprising that narrative became the principal artistic mode. Narration had fewer idolatrous connotations and reflected the fact that at the center of the Christian faith is the book of sacred history, the Bible. Consequently, manuscript illustration remained the principal art form of the Middle Ages and the source for other arts such as ivory carving, metalwork, sculpture, and even monumental decorations (e.g., narthex mosaics, San Marco, Venice). Books other than the Bible (apocrypha, menologies, histories) also were illustrated, and heterogeneous works (exegeses, encyclopedias, specula) were provided with illustrative cycles compiled from various sources. Great narrative programs, often an Old Testament opposed to a New Testament cycle, adorned the walls (Old St. Peter's) or doors of churches (Hildesheim). Modified cycles, such as the feast pictures found in Greek lectionaries and on the walls of Byzantine churches, were constructed to suit liturgical practices. Churches of the Middle Byzantine period were conceived as images of the cosmos and received mosaic decorations revealing the divine hierarchy in three zones: heaven (cupolas and apse), containing Christ Pantocrator, the Virgin, and other holy subjects; the Holy Land (squinches and pendentives), containing feast pictures; and the terrestrial world (walls and lower vaults), showing saints. Symbols, originating independently of narration, perhaps in minor or heraldic art, were drawn from nature (plants and animals), from other cults (Orpheus), and from literature (especially from the Old Testament viewed as typological precursor of the New Testament). Symbolic programs related to the early liturgy (e.g., to the prayers of Cyprian) were introduced by the time of the catacombs, and symbols often substituted for literal depictions of humans as in the transfiguration mosaic in S. Apollinare in Classe (Ravenna) where a cross and three lambs stand for Christ and the apostles. Symbols such as the attributes of saints or the flowers in the Portinari altarpiece of Hugo van der Goes enrich the narrative by alluding to other contexts. Although the special subjects of iconoclastic attacks, devotional art forms, which attempt to elicit a direct emotional response in the viewer, developed gradually, supported by Neoplatonic arguments that the image is a mediator involving sense stimuli from material objects that remind men of divine activity. Like the imperial lauraton from which it derives, the Christian icon focuses on the face of the saint, whose staring eyes establish contact with the worshiper (St. Peter, Sinai). Stone and wood sculpture, evolving from ivory carving and metalwork during the 10th and 11th centuries, at first concentrated on devotional subjects such as the crucified Christ (Gero Crucifix, Cologne Cathedral) but eventually encompassed the narrative and symbolic modes as well (Orvieto Cathedral). Elaborate programs of sculpture and stained glass, rivaling the theological complexity and completeness of Scholastic *summae,* were developed in Gothic churches (Chartres). During the 14th century, a type of personal, emotional sculpture evolved which dwelt on the physical details of Christ's passion, reflecting the personal mysticism of the period. Most significant was the gradual fusion of the narrative and devotional modes in altarpieces and panels which forced artists to blend narrative with devotional expression. Private devotional panels, mass-produced illustrated prayer books, and printed graphic art ensured a broader audience for religious imagery from the 15th century. Postmedieval art also continued the development of church painting but tempered the personal emotionalism of Gothic with classical restraint (Washington triptych by Perugino). Artists such as Bosch, on the other hand, presented in his northern style an antimundane, anticlerical attitude paralleling that of the *devotio moderna* and prophesying the Reformation. In its simple design, its depiction of the moment when Christ announces his new commandment, "that you love one another," and in the prominently placed paten, emptied of the traditional sacrificial lamb, Dürer's Last Supper woodcut of 1523 represents a Protestant point of view and reflects Luther's "chalice controversy." In general, however, Protestants remained hostile toward, or at least suspicious of, art. Secular genres of landscape, portraiture, and still life developed in Protestant countries, and Rembrandt's subjective interpretation of the Biblical narrative is a personal expression that remains more or less unique. The Council of Trent (1563) reasserted for Roman Catholicism the didactic ends of art, and Ignatius of Loyola restated the spiritual value of images. From this developed a lavish, triumphal baroque church decoration based on illusionism, dramatic lighting, and rich color effects, and focusing on the glorification of the church (Il Gesù, Rome, Vierzehnheiligen). Sculpture such as Bernini's *St. Theresa* displays a characteristic interest in mystical visions and an emphasis on physical experience. Less assertive church patronage; the refined taste, rationality, and emotional restraint of neoclassical art; and the naturalism of Courbet and the Impressionists, and the personal-psychological and formalistic concerns of 20th-century artists, have almost precluded Christianity as a major artistic inspiration during the past one hundred and fifty years. A general revival of mystical Christianity during the 19th century is reflected in the conscious spiritualism and moralistic themes in the work of the Nazarenes in Germany and of Blake and the Pre-Raphaelites in England. The personal piety of individual artists such as Rodin, Rouault, and Barlach also has resulted in a number of exceptional religious works. Common to most modern religious painting and sculpture is a revival of medieval forms, both to make use of allusion and because of the appeal of the simple planar style. Less bound to the Gothic tradition but strongly influenced by Gauguin's intensified colors and simplified forms are the paintings of a group of French artists called the Nabis (whose principal spokesmen were Serusier and Denis) which sought to restore serious Christian art at the beginning of this century. Despite the spate of church-commissioned art, especially since World War II, a full reconciliation has not yet taken place between the didactic, spiritual, and liturgical needs of Christianity and modern stylistic trends. Only a compromise solution is suggested in the *Mediator Dei* of Pope Pius XII (1947). Meaningful religious art such as the church decorations of the small chapel at Vence by Matisse remain expressions of personal faith rather than of a viable Christian development, and even such progressive church-sponsored projects as the rebuilding of Coventry Cathedral are bound to tradition.

BIBLIOGRAPHY: J. Beckwith, *Early Medieval Art* (New York, 1964); O. Demus, *Byzantine Mosaic Decoration* (London, 1948); A. Henze and T. Filthaut, *Contemporary Church Art* (New York, 1956); E. Panofsky, *Renaissance and Renascences in Western Art* (Stockholm, 1960); H. Swarzenski, *Monuments of Romanesque Art* (Chicago, 1954).

**Palestrina, Giovanni da** (c. 1526–1594). Italian composer of sacred and secular music.

According to tradition (though perhaps not correctly), he so impressed the fathers of the Council of Trent that they decided, contrary to their original intentions, not to exclude music from the services of the church. He wrote over one hundred Masses, two hundred fifty motets, and many madrigals, and was commissioned by Gregory XIII to edit and purify the plainsong chant customarily used in the Mass (a task he did not complete). The profound religious inspiration of his music may be owing to the influence upon him of Philip Neri.

His birth date is not definitely known, but his birthplace was Palestrina. He sang, conducted, composed, and played the organ in Palestrina and in Rome at Santa Maria Maggiore, the Julian Chapel, and S. Giovanni in Laterano, and at the Villa d'Este in Tivoli. He married and had children, a fact that caused him difficulty with the rigid Paul IV, who wanted no married men in the papal choirs; but he served his earliest patron (Julius III) and his later employers (Pope Gregory XIII through Pope Clement VIII) without conflict on that problem. He died while in papal service, as maistro di cappella in the Cappella Giulia at St. Peter's.

His influence on later ecclesiastical music was great, and he has, since his time, served as a model of contrapuntal technique. His most famous works include the *Missa Papae Marcelli, Missa Tu es Petrus, Missa Assumpta est Maria, Adoremus te, Christe,* and his motets on the Canticle of Canticles. His music is austere and liturgical, intended for devotion rather than display.

**Paley, William** (1743–1805). Archdeacon of Carlisle, England, and theologian. Educated at Cambridge, Paley excelled in mathematics, was ordained, and was elected fellow of his college, lecturing on "metaphysics, morals, and the Greek Testament." In 1776 he became rector of Musgrave, Westmorland, and in the next year married Jane Hewitt. He then remained in the parish ministry and in 1782 was made archdeacon of Carlisle. In 1785 his Cambridge lectures were published and adopted as a textbook at the university. Subsequently, Paley was active in the agitation against slavery, published an original book called *Horae Paulinae,* and in 1792 his *Reasons for Contentment.* It was his *View of the Evidences of Christianity* (1794), however, which gained him the greatest fame. His understanding of morality was clearly utilitarian and made a considerable impression on Jeremy Bentham. His theology was heavily influenced by the arguments of the opponents of

18th-century deism. He was not an original thinker, but his summary of arguments for the validity of Christianity provided an antidote to the corrosive influence of Hume, Gibbon, and Paine. His *Evidences* remained as a prescribed textbook at Cambridge until 1919.

**Palladius** (c. 364–c. 431). An outstanding historian of monasticism. He was a pupil of Evagrius of Pontus. His *Lausiac History* (c. 419) is of great importance for our knowledge of Egyptian monasticism. About 400 he became bishop of Helenopolis in Bithynia, and later bishop of Aspuna in Galatia (412–413). His championing of John Chrysostom, on whose behalf he journeyed to Rome in 405, is reflected in his *Dialogue on the Life of St. John Chrysostom.*

**Palladius, Peder** (1503–1560). Ordained by Bugenhagen as the first Danish Lutheran bishop of Zealand (1537–1560). Palladius was noted for his faithful parish visitation and the instructions that he left in his *Visitatsbog.* He also wrote an altar book, a manual for pastors, and an explanation to Luther's Small Catechism. As primate of the Danish Church he was adviser to the king and professor of theology at the university.

**Pallium.** A vestment worn about the shoulders of the pope in the Latin rite. It is a circular band of white lamb's wool with pendants in front and back and ornamented with six black crosses. The pallium is granted by the pope to archbishops as a sign of metropolitan authority, and to certain bishops as a sign of honor. The wool is blessed on St. Agnes's Day in Rome, and the finished pallium is placed on the tomb of Peter for one night. A similar garment is worn by Eastern Orthodox metropolitans, known as an omophorion.

**Pallotti, Vincent** (1795–1850). Italian Roman Catholic cleric. He established the Pious Society of Missions (Pallottines) at Rome (1835) for the preservation of faith among immigrants. Though a secular priest, he followed Capuchin discipline and exhibited humility, self-abnegation, and charity. Projects included offices of religion, preaching in various languages, refuges for the poor and the sick, prison visits, and book distribution. There are also Pallottine nuns.

**Palmer, Elihu** (1764–1806). An American popularizer of deism, who sought to continue the work of Thomas Paine by carrying it to the general public. In 1802 he published *Principles of Nature,* in which he defined religion as the practice of ethics and morality, the basis for which man can uncover in the divinely established laws of nature. Though he was an aggressive missionary, his teachings never became popular, and, in fact, served as a catalyst for the dissemination of traditional Christian thought.

**Palmer, Phoebe** (1807–1874). American evangelist and humanitarian. Born in New York City, she lived there almost all her life. In 1827 she married Walter Clark Palmer, a New York physician. Being Methodists, the couple became interested in the Wesleyan doctrine of perfectionism and after 1830 publicized that doctrine by traveling, holding meetings, and by writing. Mrs. Palmer edited a monthly magazine, *The Guide to Holiness,* and in 1851 published a book, *The Way to Holiness.* Several efforts for social betterment and reform occupied her attention as well. She participated in the founding of the Methodist Hedding Church mission to the New York slums and in 1850 founded the Five Points Mission. She was also an active leader in the movement for equal rights for women during the 1840's and following.

**Palut.** Bishop of Edessa (c. 200). According to the *Doctrine of Addai,* Palut was ordained deacon by Addai the apostle, but the same document states that he was made a priest by Serapion of Antioch. The latter account presumably marks the point at which the church of Edessa moved toward the common "orthodoxy" of the Greco-Roman churches, then winning the favor of Abgar IX.

**Pamphilus** (c. 240–309). Pupil of Pierius at Alexandria, later presbyter at Caesarea in Palestine and founder of the church library, using as a nucleus the collection of Origen. He and his colleague Eusebius, later bishop, published Origen's *Hexapla* and five books of an *Apology for Origen,* now lost. Imprisoned in 307, he was executed in 309. Eusebius took the surname Pamphili in his honor and wrote his biography, which no longer exists. The library perished in 687.

**"Pange Lingua Gloriosi Lauream Certaminis."** A processional hymn in trochaic tetrameter composed by Venantius Fortunatus (c. 530–c. 609) for the triumphal procession that welcomed the emperor Justin II's gift of a large relic of the true cross to Queen Radegunde's convent at Poitiers. Its theme is the victory over sin and death won by Christ's cross. In the Roman rite it is used during Passiontide, the veneration of the cross on Good Friday, and on Holy Cross Day (Sept. 14).

**Pantaenus** (d. c. 190). Earliest known teacher at the catechetical school in Alexandria. Clement of Alexandria, in his lost *Hypotyposeis,* wrote that Pantaenus was his teacher. Born in Sicily, converted from Stoicism, Pantaenus became a missionary preacher and went as far as India. No works are extant, but some scholars attribute to him the *Epistle to Diognetus.* It is probable that he taught Clement his method of interpreting Scripture.

**Papacy, Development of.** The pope, as head of the Roman Catholic Church, is the bishop of Rome and thus, in Catholic teaching, the direct successor to Peter, its first bishop, and to the Holy See, its ancient seat of government. Thus the pope claims that he is the supreme pastor of all Christians, the representative (vicar or vicegerent) of Christ on earth, and that his solemn official pronouncements on matters of faith and morals are infallible, safeguarded from error by God.

In its steady assertion of such claims, the papacy throughout the history of the church has had to contend with both the rival claims of the Eastern Church and attempts at secular supervision and control. The Petrine doctrine of papal supremacy was clearly stated by Pope Leo the Great (440–461) and defended in the writings of certain church fathers, in particular Augustine (d. 430) and Gregory the Great (d. 604), who himself became pope in 590 and whose firm leadership set the tradition of papal guidance in both dogma and church organization. To the same general period belong the spread of monasticism in the West, with the monk owing his most direct loyalty to the pope, and the beginnings of the emancipation of the church from secular and state influences. At the Council of Chalcedon (451), Pope Leo I gained formal recognition for the primacy of Rome within the whole Christian church, and since no emperor then resided in Rome, none could claim the superiority of imperial power. A reassertion of papal supremacy was supported by forged documents in the 9th century (Donation of Constantine; False Decretals), whereby the pope's worldly authority in Rome and dominion over all church affairs and appointments had been bolstered, and again after the so-called Cluniac reform of the 10th century, which strove to set right the abuses within the church. The Cluniac movement also had some beneficial effect upon the growing separation between Eastern and Western hierarchies, already evident in the 7th and 8th centuries in the iconoclastic controversy and reaching a first climax in the 9th century when the Eastern emperor Basil I (d. 886) and his powerful patriarch Photius of Constantinople attempted to break away entirely from the influence of Rome. The rift was healed temporarily, but the threat long remained as a challenge to papal primacy. A new threat was to come in the 11th century with the revival of the Holy Roman Empire under Otto the Great. Though the revival failed to check the emergent spirit of political nationalism among the peoples of Europe, which in effect gave to the papacy the superior role of unifier in a diversified world, it led to a period of serious rivalry and conflict between emperor and pope. The battle of wills between the emperor Henry IV and Pope Gregory VII ended with Henry's dramatic submission (1077) in a public act of penance at Canossa. Gregory's triumph, though short-lived, pointed the way for what was to come. The high peak of unchallenged papal supremacy was reached in the pontificate of Innocent III (1198–1216), the authority of which, the result of the patient work of an intellectual elite over many generations, reached into every corner of Latin Christendom and represented as much a feudal as a spiritual overlordship. Within a few years of the death of the emperor Henry III (1056), the election of a pope had been firmly vested in a college of cardinals, and the emperor retained only the formal power of confirming their decisions (see SACRED COLLEGE). With the 13th century came a marked decline in papal authority and prestige. The crusading spirit, so fervently evoked by Pope Urban II at Clermont in 1095, had largely spent itself, and with it the hope of seeing the Eastern Church back within the Catholic fold. Negotiations for reunification at the Councils of Lyons in 1245 and 1274 merely served to give new prominence to East–West dissensions. The political maneuvers of Pope Boniface VIII, and his ill-timed assertion of secular as well as spiritual supremacy in the *Unam sanctam* bull of 1302, produced a vigorous reaction. By a show of force, King Philip IV of France unseated Boniface and secured the election of a French pope, who chose to reside at Avignon rather than at Rome. With Boniface died the effective political power of the medieval papacy. There began the seventy-year "Babylonian Captivity" of the popes (1309–1377), the establishment of rival pontiffs in Rome and France during the period of the papal schism (1378–1418), and sharply divided loyalties among nations and religious communities. Nonetheless, despite vicissitudes and periods of stagnation, the papacy remained through the Middle Ages the central figurehead of European Christendom and unity, the true inheritor of the Roman Empire, preserving both the imperial language and in the organization of the church a firm outline of the imperial system of government, still the mentor of monarchs and the inspiration of missionary endeavors. By the close of the 14th century, however, a threat to papal supremacy, spiritual as well as secular, a threat more comprehensive than any before, was beginning to make itself felt. The conciliar movement, the series of church councils begun in 1409, settled the schism in favor of Rome and hoped to restore to the papacy something of its old prestige, but failed to come to grips with the more insistent demands for the reform of church abuses or with the growing rivalry between church aims and national aspirations. Only the vigorous intervention of Pope Eugenius IV prevented the papal authority from being transferred into the hands of a permanent council. National feeling by that time was such that in many countries it was difficult for the papacy to be considered as more than an Italian institution which for its own ends relieved them of taxes. Even without the advent of Luther some form of breach with papal authority was inevitable. The great church council at Trent (1545–1563) reaffirmed the traditional dogmas and the position of the pope as leader, and initiated many reforms in church organization; but the Protestant Reformation was by then too far advanced for a general reconciliation to be possible. The First Vatican Council (1869–1870) only deepened the rift between Rome and Protestantism.

The position of the pope as a temporal ruler deserves special consideration. Between the fall of the Western Empire and the rise of the Carolingian emperors the popes had been given a number of territories in central and southern Italy; the feudal terms of the papal rule had been established at the election of Charlemagne in 800. A number of additions to the Papal States were made during the 11th century. The temporal powers of the pope were abrogated in 1797 by the French (who had granted them in the first instance), then restored at the Congress of Vienna in 1815. Subsequently, the Papal States were seized by the kingdom of Italy (1860–1870), and the popes remained "prisoners of the Vatican" until the establishment of an autonomous Vatican state came about through the Lateran Pacts with Mussolini in 1929.

BIBLIOGRAPHY: M. Deanesly, *A History of the Medieval Church* (London, 1954); E. Giles, *Documents Illustrating Papal Authority* (London, 1952); B. J. Kidd, *The Roman Primacy to A.D. 461* (London, 1936); J. T. Shotwell and L. R. Loomis, *The See of Peter* (New York, 1965); W. Ullmann, *The Growth of Papal Government in the Middle Ages* (New York, 1956).

**Papal Appointments.** Papal provisions were synonymous in the Middle Ages with the process whereby ecclesiastical government in the papacy was centralized and consolidated. During the Middle Ages, papal appointments embraced various levels of administration: cardinalates, bishoprics, benefices, papal courts, and councils. From the time of the creation of the office of cardinal, the pope appointed the cardinal bishops, cardinal priests, and cardinal deacons. These collations were made from three sources: the noble families of Rome, the relations of the pope, and the great archbishops of Christendom. At no time in the Middle Ages was there any legal limitation of the pope's sole right, implicit in the theory of the plenitude of pontifical power, to create cardinals, thereby forming the College of Cardinals (see SACRED COLLEGE) and the papal Curia. The pope likewise appointed the legates, those members of the clergy, usually cardinals, whom the pope by right of his primacy of jurisdiction sent as his personal representatives to the sovereign or to the hierarchy and faithful of a country.

In the early Middle Ages, because of the church's need for state or regal protection there developed lay control of ecclesiastical offices in the sense that the office was treated like any other fief (see FEUDALISM) and its occupant like any other feudal lord, with rights and obligations dictated by custom. The most important right—the one that permitted lay control of bishoprics—was the right to influence the choice of bishops. Canon law specified that election of bishops be by priests and people. Thus law and custom sanctioned secular intervention, and since the papacy was itself in need of state or regal protection, no protest could be expected. During the 9th and 10th centuries, ecclesiastical offices were brought into the power of the lay aristocracy and known as lay investiture, the bestowal by laymen of the insignia of office on a clergyman. This practice symbolized secular domination, the extirpation of which became a major aim of the 10th-century reformers and the source of the bitter investiture controversy. Significantly, the investiture controversy involved a question of jurisdiction over the hierarchy: whether king or pope should appoint bishops and prescribe their qualifications and duties.

Pope Gregory VII (1073–1085) appeared at what seems to be the climax of a long evolution by which he sought the emancipation of the church from lay control signified by papal appointment. At the Lenten Synod of 1075, Gregory VII promulgated a decree prohibiting lay investiture (probably reiterating and narrowing Canon 6 of the Lateran Synod of 1059), thereby strengthening the appointive power of the Holy See. His successor, Pope Urban II (1088–1099), continued the struggle for papal preeminence and publicly forbade laymen to invest bishops with their office. Successive popes established various precedents for their own intervention in elections. With the clarification of the theory of the plenitude of power, there gradually developed the idea that all ecclesiastical benefices were at the disposal of the Holy See. The way was thus paved for direct papal provision for ecclesiastical benefices. Direct papal provision without solicitation was not, however, a feature of the period before 1250. Finally, by the end of the 13th century the power of the papacy to confirm the appointment of all archbishops, and many bishops and abbots, had been established. The papal assumption of the right to appoint to all benefices throughout Christendom was clear indication of the extent of centralization. Through a series of papal bulls beginning with Clement IV (1265–1268) in the 13th century, patrons were deprived of their right of nomination and chapters lost the right of election as more and more offices were filled by direct papal provision. The Holy See was also by the end of the 13th century appointing to lesser ecclesiastical benefices in an increasing number of instances for purposes of consolidation as well as for financial advantage. By the time of Pope Urban V (1362–1370) few ecclesiastical benefices remained that the popes did not claim, although their actual control was often limited by compromise with secular authorities.

Under the guidance of the Avignon popes (1309–1376) the process of centralization and consolidation of ecclesiastical government in the papacy reached its medieval peak. The appointment of the special court known as the Rota to handle judicial work is in evidence after 1336. The Rota handled cases arising from disputes concerning the holding of benefices whose collation was in the pope's hands. Another major administrative agency, the apostolic penitentiary, was appointed by Benedict XII in 1338.

BIBLIOGRAPHY: M. W. Baldwin, *The Medieval Church* (Ithaca, 1953); S. Baldwin, *The Organization of Medieval Christianity* (Gloucester, Mass., 1962); W. E. Lunt, *Papal Revenues in the Middle Ages,* 2 vols. (New York, 1965); G. Mollat, *The Popes at Avignon* (New York, 1965); T. P. Neill and R. H. Schmandt, *History of the Catholic Church* (Milwaukee, 1957); W. Ullmann, *The Growth of Papal Government in the Middle Ages* (New York, 1956).

**Papal Curia.** See CURIA, PAPAL.

**Papal Revenues.** Sources of income established for the Roman Church through traditional practices and the papal courts. Until the Vatican Archives were opened by Leo XIII in 1881, material for a history of the papacy had to be gleaned from various chroniclers whose accuracy was not always to be trusted or from equally questionable secondary sources. The availability of the records of the papal camera (chamber where treasury was kept) and the advent of the *camerarius* (treasurer) in the early part of the 12th century, his advance to a position of importance in the second quarter of the century, and the centralization of fiscal authority in his office from the middle of the century until the end of the Middle Ages gave primary evidence of the vast reorganization that took place. At the same time the development of large banking firms provided adequate means for transmission of funds from the payers to the camera; when the camera borrowed money against anticipated revenues, collection of those revenues was assured by the banks as well as by the agents of the camera.

The revenues accruing to the camera were of diverse classes and came from rents, taxes, levies for services of manifold variety and from gifts. One of the earliest and abiding sources of income was the rent (*pensio*) which came from the patrimonies and the lands that began to accrue to the bishop of Rome shortly after the Peace of the Church (313). When those early patrimonies, such as the richest of them in Sicily, were lost to the Saracen or to confiscation by the Byzantine emperor, they were replaced by the growing Papal States which were gradually transformed into a rich fountain of regalian rights as these lands were feudalized. The general term for such payment was "census," but it was enhanced by collection of numerous other fees such as tolls, herbage, and pannage. The term "census" was applied analogously to four other sources of income: (1) protected foundations (protected by the pope); (2) foundations exempted from episcopal jurisdiction and thus episcopal assessment, e.g., monasteries; (3) protected temporal rulers; (4) Peter's pence, related to the tribute paid by temporal rulers but used later as a means of illustrating the dependence of all sees on Rome. Beyond this there developed a set of levies taxing benefices and their provision: (1) services—tax upon all clergy confirmed in any benefice, origin unknown; (2) visitation tax paid by all prelates whose office required a periodic pilgrimage to Rome; (3) annates— a portion of year's income due from a see on

provision of an incumbent; (4) quindennia— periodic (every 15 years) levy on foundations not changing hands, e.g., hospitals; (5) interim fruits—the income of any see during its vacancy.

The Crusades provided another source of income, especially since Innocent III adapted the French and English custom of levying an income tax to support Crusades. With the increase of indulgences for those who contributed to a Crusade, the way was opened for direct payment. This custom was expanded so that purchased indulgences became the order of the day in Jubilee years. Legacies given for the prosecution of war against Saracen and Turk came to the camera; closely related to these were subsidies for special needs begun in 1093. Chancery taxes levied for every step involved in preparation of bulls were common, as were compositions asked for special grants of dispensation or absolution. Likewise productive were the fruits of jurisdiction, such as proceeds from the confiscation of a heretic's goods, fines of the papal courts, and the numerous fees collected for the use of the cameral auditor's seal, necessary to establish that a man's finances were in order and that he was not in arrears in his taxes.

Later sources of income included: (1) the papal share of the oblations laid on altars of papal churches in Rome; (2) procurations— the exaction of entertainment fees from prelates visited by papal legates or nuncios in performance of their official duties; (3) the sale of offices in the papal court (15th century); (4) gifts and legacies made directly to the Holy See by the wealthy and the poor among the faithful equally. It took money to run this establishment, and the camera collected it on a rigid scale of taxation.

BIBLIOGRAPHY: W. E. Lunt, *Papal Revenues in the Middle Ages*, 2 vols. (New York, 1965).

**Papal States** (*or* States of the Church). A political designation for the area of central Italy, of varying size at different times, under the temporal sovereignty of the pope until the unification of Italy in the 19th century. Except for Rome and the surrounding Patrimony of St. Peter which remained under papal authority until 1870, it was annexed to the Italian kingdom in 1860. At that time it comprised about 16,000 square miles and extended about 130 miles from north to south and from the Mediterranean to the Adriatic Sea.

The gradual formation of the Papal States dates from the decline of imperial power in the West and the migrations of Germanic peoples in the 5th and 6th centuries. The Western

Roman Empire collapsed in the 5th century, and though imperial power was reestablished in Italy from Constantinople under the emperor Justinian (527–565), Byzantine authority was unsteady and visibly on the wane at the end of the 6th century. In the same period the invasion and settlement of northern Italy by Germanic peoples, chiefly Ostrogoths, took place. These developments threw Italy into great political confusion during which the papacy had opportunity to assert political prestige and leadership. Already demonstrated in Leo I (440–461), papal leadership reached new heights in Gregory the Great (590–604), who sought to defend the city against both Ostrogothic and Byzantine political domination and secured a large revenue by the careful management of papal estates in central Italy and elsewhere. By the 7th century, political power in Italy was officially vested in the exarch of Ravenna, the representative of the emperor at Constantinople, but practical political authority in Rome tended to devolve upon the papacy.

This trend was greatly advanced by the relation between the papacy and the Franks in the 8th century. Pressed by the Lombard power in northern Italy, the papacy appealed to the Frankish state for aid. In 754, King Pepin invaded Italy and forced the Lombard ruler to surrender Ravenna and other conquests to the pope. This Donation of Pepin was an official acknowledgment of the pope's temporal rule over the most important state in Italy. The legal position of the Duchy of Rome, with which it was joined, was more confused, but Rome was under the *de facto* rule of the pope and after 772 the style of papal documents no longer recognized Byzantine political authority over Rome. Dating from this period also was the famous Donation of Constantine. This document, purporting to be a charter from the first Christian emperor to Pope Sylvester I, invested the pontiff with rule over "all provinces, places and districts of the city of Rome and Italy, and of the regions of the west." "We determine," it declared, "that the same be placed at his disposal, and do lawfully grant it as a permanent possession to the holy Roman Church." The Donation was actually a forgery, probably originating in the papal chancellery in the third quarter of the 8th century. Nonetheless, it was regarded as authentic for seven centuries until discredited during the Renaissance and the Reformation.

Government of the Papal States during the Middle Ages was often weak and ineffective. Lay officials, placed under clerical administrators, were restless. Popes were unable to control their feudal vassals. Provincial towns attempted to establish their independence. The great noble families of Rome, such as the Colonna and the Orsini, feuded among themselves and vied for mastery of the papacy. The Roman populace, remembering the city's ancient grandeur, entertained republican ideas and attempted to set up a Roman commune on more than one occasion. The long contest between the papacy and the Holy Roman Emperors added to the insecurity, which probably became greatest when Emperor Frederick II (1215–1250) threatened to establish a united kingdom of Italy by crushing the Papal States between his Sicilian kingdom and his northern possessions. Even at the height of medieval papal power, the pontiff was sometimes obeyed by foreign princes but insecure at home. In the later Middle Ages the popes abandoned Rome and took up residence in Avignon in southern France (1309–1377). This prolonged removal introduced confusion and near collapse into papal administration in Italy.

The attempt to reestablish papal authority in the Papal States began with Innocent VI (1352–1362), who sent Cardinal Albornoz as legate to Italy. Albornoz's military and diplomatic skill restored some order, and in 1352 he issued the *Egidian Constitutions,* which outlawed feuds and imposed papal advisers on town governments. These laws remained the foundation of papal government until the 19th century. They made possible the return of the papacy to Rome in 1377. During the Renaissance, papal authority became more substantial. Fifteenth-century popes had the conventional political ambitions of Renaissance princes and sought security at home and ascendancy in Italian politics. Alexander VI's captain, Caesar Borgia, undertook extensive campaigns to cement the pope's hold on his territory, and the militant Julius II (1503–1513) warred against nobles, Venice, and French invaders. Yet by the end of the 15th century, Italy was becoming a battleground of conflicting European dynastic interests, and Rome itself was subjected to Hapsburg occupation in the sack of 1527.

While much of the peninsula passed under the domination of great powers in the 16th century and after, the Papal States remained independent and recognized as part of the European state system. Economically, the region was poor and almost wholly agricultural. Towns were small, feudal survivals strong, disorders frequent, and government feeble. Awakening and crisis came with the French Revolution. French ideas of liberalism and nationalism penetrated Italy, and French military power expanded southward. Both threatened papal sovereignty. In 1791, France annexed the papal enclave of Avignon, and in 1797, Pius VI surrendered the northern part of the Papal States and a large indemnity to General Bonaparte. This was the beginning of the end of the temporal power. In the following year Roman republican agitation, encouraged by France, forced Pius from Rome to a death in exile. In 1809, Napoleon, after prolonged conflict, decreed the annexation of all papal territory, and Pius VII was carried off to France as a prisoner. Here he remained until, like other European monarchs, he was restored to his domains at the end of the Napoleonic era in 1814.

In the 19th century the temporal power of the papacy became a central Italian and even a European issue. The restored papacy followed reactionary policies in both domestic and international affairs. Inefficient and burdensome, papal government drew the protests of the great powers in 1831 and increasingly alienated its subjects. For maintenance of the *status quo* in Italy, the papacy relied heavily on Austria, which was also the mainstay of the general European reaction. Meanwhile, Italian liberalism and nationalism roused the population, created secret societies, and staged revolts. Thus liberalism and national unification stood opposed to Catholicism and the temporal power. The papal argument maintained that independent administration of the international church was impossible without temporal sovereignty.

The accession of the experimental Pius IX (1846–1878) gave brief promise of a peaceful solution, but the revolutions of 1848, which produced a short-lived republic in Rome, confirmed the papacy's antiliberal policy. Led by Sardinia-Piedmont, the Italians finally achieved national unity in war with Austria (1859–1860). In the process the papacy was forced to surrender about two thirds of its territory and three fourths of its subjects to the new Italian kingdom. It retained Rome and the surrounding area only with the help of a French garrison supplied by Napoleon III. In 1870 the Franco-Prussian War gave Italy the opportunity to seize Rome. After token resistance, the temporal power collapsed, and Rome became the capital of Italy.

Although the Papal States had now been liquidated, Pius IX refused to accept these changes. He denounced the Italian state and government, rejected conciliation, and kept the Roman question alive in Italian and international politics. The issue continued to poison Italian-papal relations until the Lateran Pacts (1929) established the independent Vatican City.

BIBLIOGRAPHY: M. Creighton, *History of the Papacy,* 6 vols. (New York, 1903–1904); L. Duchesne, *The Beginnings of the Temporal Sovereignty of the Popes* (London, 1908); F. Gregorovius, *History of the City of Rome in the Middle Ages,* 8 vols. (London, 1894–1902); S. W. Halperin, *Italy and the Vatican at War* (Chicago, 1939); F. K. Nielsen, *The History of the Papacy in the XIX Century* (London, 1906); L. von Pastor, *History of the Popes,* 40 vols. (St. Louis, 1951–1953).

**Papias** (c. 60–130). Bishop of Hierapolis in Phrygia in the early 2d century. His *Exegeses of the Dominical Oracles,* known only from fragments preserved chiefly by Irenaeus and Eusebius, reflects a combination of Jewish-Christian apocalypticism and Greco-Roman literary criticism. The first element is evident in a saying traced back through John to Jesus: it predicts that in the Kingdom of God a vine will produce ten thousand grapes (later Christians, opposed to this kind of eschatology, allowed Papias' work to perish). On literary matters Papias stated that he valued oral tradition more highly than written documents; he had tried to learn everything he could from itinerant disciples of Jesus. According to him, Matthew compiled the "oracles" in a Hebrew dialect, of which several Greek versions were made. He also stated that Mark, Peter's interpreter, recorded everything he could recall from Peter's teaching but produced a document that lacked adequate arrangement (whether literary or chronological). This information, partly derived from the "presbyter John," seems to involve the comparison of Mark's outline with that of some other Gospel.

A few 6th- and 7th-century writers state that Papias interpreted the Creation story in relation to Christ and the church. If this is so, Papias clearly reflected many of the concerns of Jewish Christianity in his time.

**Papyri.** Ancient manuscripts or scrolls written on papyrus. Many of them are important sources of early Christian literature. Because of the dry climate of the Egyptian desert, a large number of scrolls were preserved there. In Egypt have been found many fragments of Biblical writings as well as parts of 2d-century literature (apocryphal documents, the Didache, Hermas, the writings of Ignatius, Aristides, Irenaeus), a complete homily of Melito, and the works of later fathers.

**Paracelsus** (1493–1541). German-Swiss physician, surgeon, and alchemist. His real name was Theophrastus Bombastus von Hohenheim. Once thought to be only a brilliant and conceited quack, he is now viewed by historians as a curious mixture of the modern experimentalist and the medieval alchemist, and at the same time is credited with laying the foundations of the important iatrochemical school of medicine of the 17th century.

**Paradise Lost** (1667). The epic poem that is the chief foundation for the fame of its author, John Milton. It relates how Satan caused man to sin, though making clear man's responsibility, bringing on him the punishment of God—expulsion from Paradise. Not only is the poem unequaled of its kind in English literature, it is important as the poetic expression of the Puritan concept of sin and its consequences. Milton later wrote *Paradise Regained* (1671), showing the remedy for man in Christ's resistance of Satan.

**Pareus, David Waengler** (1548–1622). Heidelberg Protestant theologian, early advocate of toleration and conciliation among Lutherans, Calvinists, and Anglicans. Pareus taught John Amos Comenius and John Bythner, and his house "Pareanum" served as center for those desiring Protestant union. His masterpiece, *Irenicum* (1614–1615), was a most valuable literary piece of the period urging ecumenism. He wanted rulers to convoke a synod for merging the Evangelical confessions.

**Paris, Protestant Bible Society of.** A society organized in 1818 among the French Protestants after they were given official recognition. As an expression of new life after the disturbances in France had abated, the Protestants began to work for a more active propagation of their faith. Although a French Bible society was formed in London in 1792, it was not until 1818, through the agency of the British and Foreign Bible Society, that the Protestant Bible Society of Paris was founded. During the Apocrypha controversy, the British Society withdrew its support. In 1864 a minority group formed the Bible Society of France because of disagreement over a new French version.

**Paris, University of.** The greatest and most influential university of the Middle Ages, which gradually crystallized out of the cathedral school of Notre Dame. It cannot be assigned a definite foundation date. The cathedral chancellor was in charge of education and had the right of granting a teaching license. This power was resented by the teaching faculty, and the history of the university in early times is largely a story of the struggle to obtain freedom from the local ecclesiastical dignitaries by a series of charters and concessions from king and pope, the earliest being from Philip in 1200. Popes tended to support the faculty against the local bishop. Innocent III in 1215 allowed the masters to discontinue the oath of allegiance to the chancellor, and they had to be consulted about the qualifications required to obtain a teaching license. Because of town-and-gown disturbances, the masters seceded from Paris in 1229, an action frequently threatened later; this brought new privileges from the pope, Gregory IX (1231). His *Parens scientiarum* gave the masters what amounted to the power of autonomy. Although they taught all the subjects, theology became the most honored. Dominicans arrived in Paris in 1217, soon followed by Franciscans, who in the dispersion of 1229–1231 captured the chairs of theology. The university's prestige was such that it could rebuke Pope John XXII for lack of orthodoxy and provide the main leaders of the conciliarist movement, such as John Gerson and Pierre d'Ailly, but in the 15th century its importance began to decline sharply.

**Paris Evangelical Missionary Society.** A nondenominational society for Evangelical missions among non-Christian nations, organized in November, 1822, by French Protestants. In 1824 it established in Paris an institution for the training of future missionaries. Its first three missionaries were sent to Cape Town in 1829. From here the work expanded over considerable territory in South Africa. Additional fields were entered: China (1859), Senegambia (1862), Tahiti (1863). Gradually but steadily the mission expanded into most of the possessions of France's ever-expanding empire overseas. It is the largest Protestant sending agency in France. In 1962 it listed 80 ordained men, 50 laymen, and 196 laywomen from Europe working in eight different fields in Africa (Union of South Africa, Basutoland, Rhodesia, Nyasaland, Malagasy, Cameroon, Gabon, Togo) and French Polynesia (New Caledonia).

**Paris Foreign Missions Society.** Roman Catholic missionary organization. This society of secular priests and laymen was founded in Paris about 1660 by François Pallu, Lambert de la Motte, and others, its objects being to furnish secular priests to missionary bishops, to train native clergymen, and to help reduce the influence of the Spanish court on Roman missionary efforts at the time. The members of the Society were principally active in the Far East, founding the first seminary for the training of native clergy in Thailand in 1665. The Society has continued to be active up to the present time.

**Parish** (from Greek *paroikia,* "district"). An ecclesiastical division, originally the district under the jurisdiction of a bishop, now known as a diocese. Prior to the 4th century, there was in each area only one church, served by the bishop and his presbyters. Occasionally, outlying churches and preaching stations were served by presbyters sent by the bishop. With the rapid growth of the church after the 4th century, the number of these outlying churches increased and presbyters were assigned to be resident pastors. Gradually the term "parish" was applied to the geographical area served by these new churches. In the Middle Ages, a parish was frequently coterminous with a manor, the parish priest being appointed by the lord of the manor. In effect, this exempted most of the parish clergy from the control of the bishops. The Third Lateran Council gave the bishops the right of instituting the parish clergy in their diocese, although once instituted a priest under the control of the lord remained independent of episcopal control. A portion of land was set aside for the support of the priest, but this was often appropriated by the lord or a nonresident pastor, who then hired a poorly educated vicar to discharge the spiritual duties of the parish. Parishes once also served as civil subdivisions. A remnant of this is the use of the term "parish" for the county structure in Louisiana.

**Parker, Daniel** (1781–1861). Restorationist. Reared a Presbyterian, he adopted a view of universal salvation about 1814 and began itinerant preaching. Later, while pastor of the First Restorationist Church, Cincinnati, he wrote *Familiar Letters to a Brother* (1844). Believing his views to be a middle ground between Universalism and the other churches, he never became a Universalist, though he was friendly to them.

**Parker, Matthew** (1504–1575). First Elizabethan archbishop of Canterbury. Parker had been relatively uninvolved in the earlier progress of the English Reformation during the reigns of Henry VIII, Edward VI, and Mary (during the latter he was deprived of the deanery of Lincoln for being married), and he was not a widely known figure when Elizabeth picked him to be her archbishop. His efforts were principally directed at maintaining the Elizabethan Settlement of the Church of England, and he was perhaps the first consciously to cultivate a policy of *via media*. His attempts to enforce a minimum of uniformity in liturgical usages and matters of clerical vesture, as in his *Advertisements* of 1566, were fiercely opposed by the Puritan party, while despite a policy of leniency toward the bishops remaining from Mary's rule, he received no cooperation from those who

had been in ascendance under Mary, as witness the difficulties encountered in trying to secure a sufficient number of bishops for his consecration. A considerable scholar and patron of learning, Parker amassed a magnificent collection of medieval manuscripts, many of which are now at Corpus Christi, Cambridge, his old college.

**Parker, Theodore** (1810–1860). Unitarian clergyman and liberal theologian. Ordained in 1837, Parker championed the view that Christianity did not rest on revelation, miracles, or prophecy but upon its expression of universal truths. The significance of Jesus was his affirmation of essential religious tenets. Christianity was but one of many expressions of the religious impulse. This impulse was a primary human characteristic experienced through the religious faculties, conscience, and the "religious sentiment." The existence of God is not to be proved by reason, but to be intuited as a fundamental truth of self-conscious human nature. "The felt and perceiving presence of Absolute Being infused itself in me." Parker's views created a conflict within Unitarianism, and he was excluded from the Boston Association of Ministers in 1843 for his 1841 sermon, "The Transient and Permanent in Christianity." In 1845 he became minister of the new twenty-eighth Congregational Society of Boston. Critical of rationalistic Unitarianism, he advocated a transcendental Unitarianism in which man's instinctive intuition of the divine was identified with the religion of Jesus. With his lecture "A Discourse of Matters Pertaining to Religion" (1842), he became more widely known in England and Germany than in the United States. Parker found German Biblical criticism congenial and translated the work of Wilhelm De Wette in 1836. He later became an influential and vigorous abolitionist.

**Parkhurst, Charles Henry** (1842–1933). Presbyterian clergyman. Amherst-educated, he also studied in Germany. After a pastorate in Massachusetts, Parkhurst went to Madison Square Presbyterian Church, New York City. In 1892 his frequent political preaching was climaxed by a series of sermons on corruption in city government, leading to the Lexow Investigation of 1894, the defeat of Tammany Hall, and extensive governmental reform.

**Parochial Schools in the United States.** The origin of the system of parochial schools maintained by the Roman Catholic Church in the United States may be seen in the early Spanish Franciscan mission schools of the Southwest and Florida, in the English Jesuit schools of Maryland, and in the French schools of New Orleans and mission schools in the Mississippi Valley and Great Lakes region. The influx of Roman Catholic immigrants to the United States in the 19th century forced the hierarchy to address itself to the problem of maintaining the faith of these deracinated Irish and Germans. One of the means adopted for this purpose was the parish school, an institution that the affluence of the American Catholic community spread across the face of the land, particularly in the 20th century.

Threatened by what they saw as the "sectarian" control of the nominally "public" schools, the American Catholic hierarchy turned to the teaching orders of men and women established in Europe to staff the newly founded parish and private schools in the United States. The first Provincial Council of Baltimore (1829) as well as the First (1852), Second (1866), and Third (1884) Plenary Councils of the American hierarchy held at Baltimore studied the problems presented by the attendance of Catholic children at the public schools where, it was felt, a danger to their faith and morals was to be expected. As a result of the action of the American hierarchy at these Councils, a system of parochial schools was established. The Third Plenary Council of Baltimore provided that each parish was to maintain a school unless extraordinary difficulties prevailed. Clerics who did not provide such schools for their charges were to be reprimanded, and Roman Catholic parents were instructed to send their children to such schools unless they could provide for their religious education in a manner acceptable to the diocesan authorities. Though the expenses incurred by such a system have always borne heavily upon the families of a parish, American Catholics have by and large willingly supported an educational system that has come to be a source of amazement to Catholics in other countries. Despite being hampered by lack of funds and often inadequately prepared teachers, the system survived the 19th century and expanded phenomenally in the early 20th.

The philosophy underlying the parochial school system is perhaps best presented in the encyclical letter *Divini illius magistri* ("On the Christian Education of Youth") issued by Pope Pius XI in 1929. The position maintained therein is that education is a process which is essentially an extension of certain rights and obligations of the family and the church (as well as the state), and that any system which attempts to limit the legitimate rights of family and church to choose and determine the content and method of education must be resisted.

Thus, when the public schools appeared to pose serious dangers to the religious beliefs and morality of the Catholic population (as the Congregation of the Propagation of the Faith indicated in its letter of Nov. 24, 1875, to the bishops of the United States), there was an obligation incumbent upon the church to provide an alternate system.

The Catholic population of the United States has grown from nearly 30,000 at the time of the Revolution to over 46,000,000 today. The parochial school system has grown in a similar proportion. In 1966 there were 1,506 parochial and diocesan high schools, enrolling 687,961 students, while 10,550 parochial and institutional elementary schools gave instruction to 4,409,476 pupils. The total number of students under Catholic instruction (including those under released-time arrangements) in that year was 10,911,213. These schools and programs employed some 203,791 full-time teachers, over half of whom were religious sisters.

Several Protestant denominations also maintain day schools, though these are usually underwritten and supervised by associations of parents. The Missouri Synod Lutheran Church, however, maintains actual parochial schools, as do the Mennonites, the Society of Friends, the Christian Reformed, and the Seventh-day Adventists.

BIBLIOGRAPHY: J. Fichter, *Parochial School: A Sociological Study* (Notre Dame, Ind., 1958); A. M. Greeley and P. Rossi, *The Education of Catholic Americans* (Chicago, 1966); R. A. Neuwien (ed.), *Catholic Schools in Action* (Notre Dame, Ind., 1966); A. C. Stellhorn, *Schools of the Lutheran Church—Missouri Synod* (St. Louis, 1963).

**Particular Baptists.** A sect that originated between 1633 and 1638 among members expelled from Jacob's Church in Southwark, London. Their leader was John Spilsbury (1593–c. 1668). He held to the doctrine of "particular" election and predestination. The members were opposed to the Arminian leanings of the General Baptists. The first Baptist churches in America—Roger Williams' at Providence, R.I. (1639), and John Clarke's at Newport, R.I. (1641)—were both Particular Baptist congregations.

**Pascal, Blaise** (1623–1662). French theologian, mathematician, philosopher, and mystic. Born at Clermont, the son of a magistrate, he was educated privately by his father, Étienne, and his two sisters, Gilberte and Jacqueline. He was a precocious child and at Rouen he engaged in various mathematical experiments, including those on the barometer and calculating machine. Pascal had been educated to believe that matters of religion were beyond reason. During the 1640's, however, he was brought into contact with the absorbing problems of the spiritual life through acquaintance with Cornelis Jansen's *Discours sur la reformation de l'homme intérieur,* Antoine Arnauld's *On Frequent Communion,* and Saint-Cyran's *Lettres spirituelles.* The Jansenist piety had a profound effect upon Pascal and led to his "first conversion"; it had an even greater influence upon his sister Jacqueline, who, after her father died in 1651, entered the convent of Port-Royal.

For a brief period Pascal returned to world-making discoveries and writing on scientific subjects. But on Nov. 23, 1654, he had his "second conversion." He suddenly realized that "the Christian religion obliges us to live only for God, and to have no other aim than Him." During that night he definitively embraced God, "the God of Abraham, Isaac, and Jacob, not the God of the philosophers and scientists . . . the God of Jesus Christ." From that moment Pascal sought strength and protection for his new inner life in the solitude of Port-Royal. In spite of the advice of his physicians, he subjected himself to the strict discipline of fasting, vigils, and self-torture. Although he was never one of the Solitaires, he spent most of his remaining life at Port-Royal.

The condemnation of Arnauld by the Sorbonne in 1655 prompted Pascal's famous attack on the Jesuits in his *Provincial Letters.* There were eighteen letters in all; the first appeared in January, 1656, the last in March, 1657. They were an immediate success and made Pascal known in the world as one of the most eloquent prosaists and witty polemists of his time. He attacked both directly and indirectly the Jesuits' theories of prevenient and sufficient grace (Molinism), and moral theology (probabilism). He claimed that the Jesuits undermined morality, that they constituted the ethical ideal not according to what a man should do but according to what the average man was able to do, that they degraded religion to politics and morality to casuistry, and that they justified the means by the end and accepted the doctrine of mental reservation. The *Letters* were condemned at Rome and publicly burned by the hangman at Paris. A great many people applauded Pascal, however, and even to this day the *Letters* constitute one of the most devastating criticisms of Jesuit ethics and politics.

Pascal's early death prevented him from completing his *Apologie de la religion chrétienne,* designed for the conversion of unbelievers, but the notes he had written were collected and published posthumously, under the title *Pensées* (1670). It is one of the great books of mankind, full of the deepest insights of human existence. Pascal did not attempt to convince man by intellectual arguments alone; instead, he wished to persuade men's hearts. He does not exclude the use of reason from demonstrating the truth of faith, but he did not believe in rational proofs of God. "It is the heart that experiences God, and not reason. That is what faith is: God felt by the heart, not by reason." Pascal's religion was centered on the Person of Christ as Savior, and based on personal, mystical experience: "The heart has its reasons which reason does not know."

BIBLIOGRAPHY: E. Cailliet, *The Clue to Pascal* (London, 1944); H. F. Stewart, *The Holiness of Pascal* (Cambridge, 1915); and *The Secret of Pascal* (Cambridge, 1941); C. C. J. Webb, *Pascal's Philosophy of Religion* (Oxford, 1929).

***Pascendi Dominici Gregis.*** Encyclical letter of Pope Pius X, "On the Doctrines of the Modernists," issued on Sept. 8, 1907. Chief among the modernist tendencies the pope specified agnosticism, immanentism, and evolutionism. Modernism was "the synthesis of all heresies." Among the remedies prescribed by the pope were Scholastic philosophy, strict censorship, and diocesan "vigilance committees."

**Paschal II** (Raniero, d. 1118). Successor to Urban II as pope in 1099. He was born near Ravenna and as a boy entered Cluny. Gregory VII appointed him cardinal priest of San Clemente, c. 1080. As pope, he witnessed the establishment of the Latin kingdom of Jerusalem and the substitution of the Latin hierarchy for the Greek in Jerusalem. Overtures for a settlement made by Emperor Alexis I Comnenus (1112) met with failure, since Paschal demanded recognition of the primacy of the Roman see as the basis of negotiations. Paschal forced Philip I of France to renounce Bertrada of Montfort (1104). He was intransigent in his opposition to lay investiture, and renewed the decrees of his predecessors against it. In England the question of investitures was settled by the London agreement (1107) to which Paschal acceded, although he did not conceive it. In Germany, repeated attempts at negotiation with Henry IV and V ended in failure. Paschal renounced the *temporalia* of all churches and church offices in Germany at Sutri (1111). A combination of French and Italian bishops forced him to retract this concession at the Lenten Synod (1112). Paschal crowned Henry V emperor (1111) and conceded to him the right of investiture. The last years of Paschal's reign show a progressive loss of command. He was forced to agree to the excommunication of Henry announced by Cuno of Praeneste, and died with the matter of investitures unsettled in Germany.

**Paschal Baylon** (1540–1592). Spanish Franciscan. Born in the Spanish kingdom of Aragon, he took care of his father's sheep until he was twenty-four years old, when he joined a local group of Franciscans as a lay brother. Paschal's life was one of prayer and penance, and he daily tended to the sick and the poor and performed tasks no one else wanted to undertake. His piety was centered on the Eucharist, and for this reason Pope Leo XIII declared him "Saint of the Blessed Sacrament."

**Paschasius Radbertus** (c. 785–c. 860). A monk and later abbot of Corbey. He wrote several treatises, the most important being *De corpore et sanguine Domini*, the first theological treatise devoted solely to the Eucharist. His emphasis upon the presence of Christ's flesh has been viewed as anticipating the doctrine of transubstantiation. The work provoked attacks from Rabanus Maurus and Ratramnus, who objected to Paschasius' emphasis upon carnal reality.

**Pashkov, Vasili A.** (d. 1902). Protestant leader in Russia in the latter part of the 19th century. Converted to evangelical Protestantism by the Englishman Lord Radstock, Colonel Pashkov, a member of the Russian Imperial Life Guards, founded the Society for the Encouragement of Spiritual and Ethical Reading in 1876. His attempts to unite Ukrainian Stundists, Caucasian Baptists, and Russian Molokans into one church failed, though he did have success among the poorer Russian classes. His followers, the Pashkovites, were suppressed in 1884. He died in exile in Paris.

**Passau, Peace of** (1552). See AUGSBURG, PEACE OF; AUGSBURG INTERIM.

**Pastor, Ludwig von** (1854–1928). Austrian Roman Catholic historian. Born at Aachen, he was educated at Louvain, Bonn, Berlin, Vienna, and Prague. In 1887 he was appointed professor of history at Innsbruck. In 1901 he became director of the Austrian Historical Institute in Rome. In his most famous work, *The History of the Popes from the Close of the Middle Ages* (English ed., 40 vols., 1891–1953), he gave a balanced representation of the history of Catholicism in modern times.

**Pastor Aeternus** (1870). Dogma defining the infallibility of the pope. The fourth and final session of the Vatican Council, called under Pius IX on July 18, 1870, passed upon the doctrine of papal primacy 533 to 2. The pope, as Christ's vicar on earth, guided by the Holy Spirit, whose presence had been promised by Christ to the apostles, was declared to be infallible when he spoke ex cathedra in defining any doctrine of faith and morality universally applicable to Catholics.

**Pastors' Emergency League.** A group organized in 1933 to oppose the gains of "German Christians." Martin Niemoeller, with Friedrich Mueller, sent letters of invitation on Sept. 21, 1933. Immediately, 1,300 pastors signed up as the League was constituted in October. By Jan. 15, 1934, fully 7,000 pastors (one third of the Protestant clergy) had joined, but few church leaders (Dibelius, Weirich). At least 2,500 clerics later capitulated to "German Christian" pressure, but the League gave birth to the Barmen and Dahlem Synods and to the Confessing Church. Niemoeller's pledge obligated the signers to the Reformation confessions, protested forceful takeover of the church, and explicitly refused to accept the "Aryan paragraph." The League labored until December, 1944.

**Patarines.** The name given to a league of common people of Milan (artisans, merchants, and peasants—*"patari"*) organized during the brief pontificate of Stephen IX (1057–1058) to purge the Roman Church of corruption and to deprive it of many of its intolerable civil powers. Regarded by the church as heretics, the Patarines had as their two main preoccupations the desire to expel from their positions all unworthy and scandalous clergymen and to remove the ecclesiastical restraints imposed traditionally on the freedom of the peasant population and more recently on the artisan and merchant middle class. The organization of the Patarines is noteworthy primarily for being among the first of its kind. It gave rise to religious reform movements in vast numbers which sought to undermine what they regarded as the corrupt authority of the established ecclesiastical order throughout Europe during the social revolution effected by the decline of the feudal aristocracy and the rise of the lower and middle classes. These popular reform movements, many of them led by members of the clergy itself, were legion from the 12th through the 14th century, and their wide range of activities serves to objectify the dramatic changes that were taking place in the milieu of Christian-centered ideas and ideals among the clergy and the laity in the late Middle Ages.

**Paton, William** (1886–1943). Missionary and ecumenical statesman. Born at Brixton, England, of Scottish parents, he was educated at Whitgift School; Pembroke College, Oxford; and Westminster College, Cambridge. He was ordained in 1917 by the Presbyterian Church for Y.M.C.A. service in India. After some years as secretary of the National Christian Council of India, he became secretary of the International Missionary Council in 1927, serving also as a secretary of the World Council of Churches (Provisional) from 1938 until his death.

**Patriarch.** The term used after the 6th century to designate those bishops who exercised jurisdiction over metropolitans (archbishops). The bishops of Rome, Antioch, and Alexandria were so recognized at the Council of Nicaea. The Council of Chalcedon recognized Jerusalem and Constantinople also. The pope holds the title "Patriarch of the West"; however, the bishops of Venice and Lisbon have the title of patriarch without exercising patriarchal authority.

**Patrick** (c. 389–c. 461). Apostle of the Irish. Son of a Christian family in Roman Britain, he was kidnapped by Irish raiders, and after his escape prepared to return to the land of his home. Though not the only founder of the church in Ireland, he is properly remembered as the great apostle of the Irish. There is a legend that the Druid wizards had a prophecy that a monk would come who would challenge their religion. Patrick's brief *Confessions* and *Epistle* reflect the qualities that were to mark the Celtic Church—enthusiasm, asceticism, and mission.

**Patrick, Simon** (1626–1707). Bishop of Ely. The son of an English merchant, he was graduated from Queen's College, Cambridge. After receiving Presbyterian orders, he became convinced that episcopal ordination was necessary, and was accordingly privately ordained in 1654 by Joseph Hall, bishop of Norwich. He accepted the rectorate of St. Paul's, Convent Garden, in 1662, which he held for thirty years. He was made royal chaplain, given a prebend at Westminster, and accepted the deanery of Peterborough all prior to 1680. Opposed to James II's movement toward Roman Catholicism, he welcomed William and Mary, though respecting the nonjurors. In 1689, he was installed in the office of bishop of Chichester, then two years later transferred to Ely. Patrick was one of the five founders of the Society for Promoting Christian Knowledge, and a supporter of the Society for the Propagation of the Gospel. He was one of the prime movers in the revival of the Anglican Church in the later 17th century. His written works fall into three areas. In polemics he argued against Roman Catholics and nonconformists. His Biblical work was ten volumes of Old Testament paraphrases from Genesis to the Song of Solomon. His finest pastoral literature, *The Parable of the Pilgrim*, published in 1664, was an allegory along the same line as *The Pilgrim's Progress*, but independent of it.

**Patrimony of St. Peter.** A term loosely applied to the Papal States, but referring specifically to those lands which had come under the control of the pope through donations and inheritance. These large estates were acquired early, although ecclesiastical land tenure throughout the persecutions was difficult. By 600 the papacy owned large tracts of land in Italy, France, and Illyria. This was greatly increased by the Donation of Pepin which conveyed lands formerly under Byzantine control. Income from these lands was used extensively for charity as well as for financing the papal court.

**Patronage Act.** A law passed by the British Parliament in 1712 which gave to the patron of a parish the right to appoint a minister of his own choosing. This led to the Disruption of 1843 in the Church of Scotland. In 1874 the (Anti-) Patronage Act was passed, which gave to the congregations of the Church of Scotland the right to elect their own ministers. Eventual reunion with the Free Church did not take place until 1929.

**Paul II** (Pietro Barbo, 1417–1471). Pope from 1464. A native of Venice, he had originally intended to become a merchant, but his uncle, Pope Eugenius IV, directed him to the service of the church, and in 1440 made him a cardinal. He was chosen pope in 1464. He was not an enemy of humanism, but his concern for moral and doctrinal rectitude did gain him the enmity of writers such as Platina. In 1465 he established the first printing press in Rome. He deposed George of Poděbrad, king of Bohemia, and engaged in war with the Turks.

**Paul III** (Alessandro Farnese, 1468–1549). Pope from 1534. Born at Rome or Canino, he was educated at Rome, Florence, and Pisa. His youth was irregular, and as pope he gave preference to his relatives. He was, however, fully conscious of the reform responsibilities of his office, and began a renewal of the papal court, naming many distinguished men to the cardinalate, and endorsing new religious orders. In 1535 he called for a general council to convene at Mantua, but the Protestant sovereigns and the duke of Mantua successfully forestalled his plan. Again he called for a council, this time for Vicenza, in 1538, but opposition between Charles V and Francis I again defeated him. When the Treaty of Crépy (1544) brought peace between the two sovereigns, Paul returned to his task; after numerous delays the Council of Trent finally opened in December, 1545. Whether because of a plague in Trent or a new conflict between the pope and the emperor, the Council was transferred to Bologna, outside the emperor's domains. When Charles forbade the bishops to leave Trent, Paul suspended the Council in 1549, but not before it had accomplished a number of important reformations of clerical discipline, remedied some abuses, and made certain doctrinal definitions. Paul died in Rome the same year.

**Paul IV** (Gian Pietro Carafa, 1476–1559). Pope from 1555. He was born at Capriglio of a noble Neapolitan family. His uncle, Cardinal Oliviero, obtained his appointment to the Roman Curia. From 1505 to 1524 he was bishop of Chieti; in 1513 he was nuncio to England; from 1518 he was archbishop of Brindisi; and he also served as a chaplain to the Spanish court, which may have influenced his subsequent opposition to Spain. Carafa was a member of the commission that examined the teaching of Luther. From 1520 to 1527 he was also a member of the Oratory of Divine Love, and, giving up his benefices, became in 1524 a cofounder of the Theatines. Under Popes Clement VIII and Paul III he was an active advocate of reform, becoming a cardinal, archbishop of Naples, and a member of the reform commission in 1536. In 1542 he reorganized the Inquisition against Italian Protestants. Elected pope in 1555, he proved himself something of a zealot, preferring the Inquisition to the Council of Trent as a means of reform; and he even imprisoned Cardinals Morone and Pole as heretics. In 1559 he began the Index of Prohibited Books. Politically, Paul allied himself with France against the Hapsburgs. He disagreed with the Peace of Augsburg, and thought Ferdinand's accession invalid; thus the duke of Alva led the emperor's army into the Papal States, forcing the pope to break off his French alliance. Mistrustful of others, he gave his nephew Carlo great political power in the Papal States, and when, in 1559, he was obliged to dismiss him for gross malfeasance in office, his grief hastened his own death.

**Paul V** (Camillo Borghese, 1552–1621). Pope from 1605. He was born in Rome of a Sienese family. After serving as an ecclesiastical lawyer in Rome, he was made cardinal legate to Spain (1596), bishop of Jesi (1597), and general vicar of Rome and inquisitor (1603). Elected pope in 1605, he did much to further reform in the church, approving new religious orders, insisting that bishops reside in their dioceses, encouraging missionary efforts to new lands. In 1607 he closed the celebrated Congregatio de Auxiliis (see MOLINA, LUIS DE), observing only that neither the Dominicans nor the Jesuits might call each other heretics in regard to man's cooperation with grace. In 1614 he issued a reformed Roman ritual. In 1616 it was by his administrators that Galileo was condemned. He was a noteworthy patron of the arts, completing St. Peter's, and building the Palazzo and Villa Borghese. He loaded his relatives with favors, and perhaps by that expedient kept them under his control. Basically neutral in politics, he tried to defend papal authority against national states. He supported Ferdinand II with money, and from 1605 to 1607 placed Venice under interdict and excommunicated its senate. This was the last time that a pope moved against a state as such, the Venetian problem being eased through French and Spanish mediation.

**Paul, Kanakarayan Tiruselvam** (1876–1931). Indian Protestant leader. Born at Salem, South India, a third-generation Christian, he was a graduate of Madras Christian College (1894) and Madras Law College. He taught in mission schools, was secretary of the National Missionary Society (1906–1913), national secretary for rural work, Y.M.C.A. (1913–1916), national general secretary (1916–1930), and received the Order of the British Empire (1919). One of the two first secretaries of the National Christian Council of India, he also became president of the United Church of South India (1925), and was active internationally in Y.M.C.A. and the International Missionary Council. In 1930 he was a member of the first Round Table Conference, London.

**Paulicians.** A dualistic sect of the Byzantine Empire of obscure origins, probably founded at Kibossa in Armenia in the mid-7th century. It was persecuted continually until nearly exterminated in the 9th century. Some joined Islam and others fled to Bulgaria in the 10th century, uniting with the Bogomiles. By the 12th century the Paulicians were extinct. Their name may be derived from Paul, whom, like Marcion, they venerated to the exclusion of the Old Testament, or more likely, from Paul of Samosata, whose teaching resembles theirs.

**Paul of Constantinople** (d. after 350). Fourth-century bishop. Born in Thessalonica, Paul came to Constantinople in 330 and was consecrated bishop by 335. Although a perennial friend of Athanasius, he condemned the theologian at a trial in Constantinople, then reneged. Exiled to Pontus for political misbehavior fifteen months before Constantine's death, Paul came back under the protection of Constantine the Younger. When Constantius took the city in 338, Paul's fate was sealed; he was exiled and replaced by Eusebius of Nicomedia. Paul wooed the Western bishops in Trier and Rome, then returned at Eusebius' death in 339 or 340. The Paulinists incited a general insurrection against the bishop designate, Macedonius, but without success. Paul was removed to Singara (342) in chains. He returned again (344) under the protection of Constans only to be exiled to Thessalonica by the prefect Philip. In 346, Constans supported his final attempt, but in 350, Paul was imprisoned at Cucusus and disappeared. Paul was a courageous orthodox theologian who opposed the palace in days when such activity was highly unpopular. He left no writings.

**Paul of Samosata** (3d century). Bishop and metropolitan of Antioch. He became bishop about 260 after the exile of Demetrianus (c. 257) and the Palmyrean defeat of Valerian. Retaining the see until Aurelian's recapture of the city (272), Paul was deposed (269) by the Council of Antioch I for monarchianism, which he advanced by liturgical innovation, and for preoccupation with civil duty as *ducenarius* under Palmyrean administration. He is reputed to have been a precursor of Arianism.

**Paul the Deacon** (d. c. 800). A leading figure in the Carolingian revival. From a noble Lombard family, he became a monk at Monte Cassino, where he met Charlemagne and later traveled to the latter's court to settle family matters. He remained there teaching until 786, when he returned to Monte Cassino. He was the author of a history of the bishops of Metz, a history of the Lombards, and a commentary on the Rule of St. Benedict.

**Paul the Silentiary** (6th century). A court official and poet under Justinian I. His poem of over a thousand lines on the great church of Hagia Sophia, the glory of Byzantine architecture, was delivered before emperor and patriarch in 562, soon after the dedication of the present building, later mosque and now museum. With a shorter work on the magnificent pulpit, Paul's verses, though not distinguished as poetry, are an important source for architectural history.

**Paulus, Heinrich Eberhard Gottlob** (1761–1851). German rationalistic theologian. He taught at Jena, Würzburg, and finally Heidelberg (from 1811). Influenced by J. S. Semler and J. D. Michaelis, he was a rationalist, notable for opposition to Schelling. He championed Christianity for its spiritual worship and the loftiness of the personality of Jesus. In exegesis he raised the question of Messianic consciousness, but his uncritical handling provoked the reaction of D. F. Strauss.

**Peabody, Francis Greenwood** (1847–1936). Harvard professor and early leader in the Social Gospel movement. In 1881, when sociology was taught in few American institutions and while college economics was still firmly controlled by the school of *laissez faire,* Peabody inaugurated the teaching of social ethics, in which he maintained that labor should be governed by the principles of Christian ethics.

**Peace of God.** A declaration originating late in the 10th century of the immunity from military attack of particular holy places or specific holy personages. It was taken up as a divine command and made part of the ecclesiastical law. In time it became part of the penitential system and is to be differentiated from the secular Public Peace declared by the emperor and from the Truce of God.

**Pearson, John** (1613–1686). Bishop of Chester. He attended Eton and graduated from King's College, Cambridge, in 1639. The following year he became rector of Thorington in Suffolk, then joined Charles I's army as chaplain. With the collapse of the Royalist cause, he lived in London, devoting himself largely to study. In 1659, he published *An Exposition of the Creed,* his most important work, which became normative for Anglican theology. During this period, he wrote defending the English Church from both Roman Catholics and Puritans. After the Restoration, he was appointed to a number of posts, including royal chaplain, master of Jesus College, and Lady Margaret professor of theology at Cambridge, and then master of Trinity College in 1662, a position he held for eleven years. He was elected a fellow of the Royal Society, but did not take an active part. In 1672, he published *Vindiciae epistolarum S. Ignatii,* which was a scholarly demonstration that certain letters attributed to Ignatius were authentic, thereby verifying the early date for episcopacy. The following year he was appointed bishop of Chester, a position that he filled without much involvement in political life. A quiet man who avoided polemics, he was one of the ablest scholars and theologians of his day.

**Peasants' War** (1524–1525). An uprising of southern German, Swiss, and Austrian peasants against growing economic and civil injustice by noble and clergy landlords. Deprivation of feudal hunting, fishing, and wood-gathering rights, added feudal services, and widening class differences were the basic grievances. Secondary religious overtones were added by belief that the Reformation was primarily the casting off of ecclesiastical bondage. Thomas Müntzer and others aroused radical religious feelings. In June, 1524, a thousand peasants from the estate of Count Sigismund of Lupfen revolted at Stühlingen. The news led to other uprisings around the Lake of Constance, then in Swabia, Styria, Franconia, and the Tyrol. The criminal Rohrbach led a massacre at Weinsberg, an atrocity repudiated by other insurgents. On March 7, 1525, the Evangelical Brotherhood was formalized and at Memmingen the Twelve Articles were adopted as their platform. After some early successes, the movement began to disintegrate. General George Truchsess crushed it in Swabia. At Frankenhausen, Philip of Hesse defeated the forces under Müntzer, who was executed. Philip and Elector John of Saxony showed restraint toward the peasants. Elsewhere they were crushed, about 150,000 perishing by July 20, 1526, when the "bloody assizes" at Radstatt ended the conflict.

**Pecock, Reginald** (c. 1393–c. 1461). Bishop, scholar, and adversary of the Lollards. Welsh-born and Oxford-educated, successively bishop of St. Asaph (1444) and Chichester (1450), he used his "cleer witt" and mastery of English to controvert the Lollards. His criticisms of traditional views and ecclesiastical policy and his opposition to the Yorkists resulted in his heresy trial (1457). Despite recantation, he was deprived of his see and confined to a monastery, where he died. Pecock's fundamental point against the simple Biblicism of the Lollards was that the interpretation of the outward Scriptures, like all else, must be subject to "the doom [i.e., judgment] of reason written in man's soul and heart." He was one of the first ecclesiastical authors to write in English, and was also a pioneer in his rejection of the Donation of Constantine and of the apostolic authorship of the Apostles' Creed.

**Péguy, Charles** (1873–1914). French author. Of peasant origin, Péguy eventually went to the École Normale Supérieure. One of the most passionate, integral, and fascinating characters of his time, Péguy was a socialist, poet, publisher, journalist, patriot, Dreyfusard, and mystic. From 1900 to World War I he published the *Cahiers de la Quinzaine,* and in 1910 *Joan of Arc.* His spiritual struggle led him back to Roman Catholicism.

**Peitilia, Antti** (1878–1932). Finnish Lutheran theologian. He taught dogmatics and ethics at Helsinki (1919–1932), seeking to combine the confessionalism of Erlangen with the Biblicism of J. T. Beck and the Pietism of L. L. Laestadius. He insisted on the necessity of personal faith in order to study theology aright. To him the heart of the gospel was forgiveness, but he rejected forensic justification and opposed the views of Ritschl, Söderblom, and Barth.

**Pelagius, Pelagians.** The founder and followers of a heretical system of theology which made man virtually the author of his own salvation. Pelagius (d. c. 419) was a British (perhaps Irish) lay monk who, probably well on in years at the time, settled in Rome about 400. He was shocked by Roman morals and, in working for more strenuous ethical standards, won a reputation for his great learning and moral earnestness. In 410, perhaps because of the sack of Rome by Alaric and his Goths, Pelagius went to North Africa and evidently tried to see Augustine. He soon left for the East, where he found considerable support and where he apparently died between 418 and 420. His chief followers were Coelestius, a Roman lawyer who became a lay monk and accompanied him to Africa and later followed him to the East, and Julian, bishop of Eclanum (Southern Italy), a man of exceptional ability and an acute polemic.

The teachings of Pelagius and his followers were not innovations and were in accord with the views of the East in general and with those of many in the West. The great controversy that arose about him revolved around the issue of the freedom of man's will and about the nature and operation of God's grace. Pelagianism shows a rationalism and moralism of an individualistic (or atomistic) character and generally reflects the popular Stoic concept of human responsibility. The Pelagians denied the concept of an original sin inherited from Adam and held that obligation and responsibility in religion necessitate the power to fulfill them. Man does have the power of contrary choice (formal freedom) and has the inherent capacity to do what is right without any absolute necessity to sin. Men become sinners because they follow the bad example of Adam and other evil examples. Recent study of Pelagius' *Commentary on Paul to the Romans* shows his emphasis on justification by faith, baptism, and the work of Christ. His use of these concepts, however, supports his contention that man needs only a good example and that grace consists of God's revelations, given in many ways (as through the law, and especially in Jesus Christ), which assist and facilitate man's choices and actions.

The most common summary of the heresies of the Pelagians is the list drawn up by Paulinus of Milan in 411 or 412 against Coelestius: (1) Adam was created mortal and would have died whether he had sinned or not; (2) the sin of Adam injured himself alone, and not the whole human race; (3) newborn children are in the same state in which Adam was before his fall; (4) neither by the death and sin of Adam does the whole human race die, nor will it rise because of the resurrection of Christ; (5) the law as well as the gospel offers entrance to the Kingdom of Heaven; and (6) even before the coming of Christ, there were men wholly without sin.

The controversy concerning Pelagius and Pelagianism may be traced in various writings and ecclesiastical actions involving them: (1) Writings: (a) Augustine—*De peccatorum meritis, De spiritu et littera* (both 412), *De natura et gratia* (415), *De gestis Pelagii* (417), *Contra duas epistolas Pelagianorum* (420), and *Contra Julianum* (421); (b) Jerome—three *Dialogi adversus Pelagianos* (415); (c) Marius Mercator—*Commonitorium super nomine Coelestii* (429). (2) Ecclesiastical actions: 412—Coelestius was accused of heresy and excommunicated by a synod at Carthage to which he had applied for ordination as a presbyter (though he was later ordained to this office at Ephesus); 415—Synods of Jerusalem and Diospolis (Lydda) cleared Pelagius of the charge of heresy; 416—Councils of Carthage and Milevis condemned the teachings of Pelagius on the basis of his newly issued *De libero arbitrio;* 417—Pope Innocent I (401–417) endorsed the actions of the Councils of Carthage and Milevis and excommunicated Pelagius and Coelestius, but Pope Zosimus (417–418) reviewed the case and, on the basis of Pelagius' *Libellus fidei,* pronounced him innocent; 418—a Council at Carthage condemned Pelagius, and Zosimus in his *Epistola tractoria* confirmed the actions of Innocent I, after which Pelagius disappeared and most of his followers sought refuge in the East; 429—Nestorius intervened with

the pope on behalf of Julian and the Pelagians; 430—Emperor Theodosius II banished the Pelagians; 431—the Council of Ephesus condemned Pelagianism; 529—the Second Council of Orange condemned Pelagianism.

BIBLIOGRAPHY: P. Schaff (ed.), *Nicene and Post-Nicene Fathers,* Series I, Vol. 5 (Grand Rapids, 1956); J. Ferguson, *Pelagius* (Cambridge, 1956); J. Müller, *Christian Doctrine of Sin* (Edinburgh, 1868); B. B. Warfield, *Two Studies in the History of Doctrine* (New York, 1897).

**Penance in the Middle Ages.** The traditional sacrament of penance, as reaffirmed at the Council of Trent in 1547, was derived from Christ's words in John 20:22–23. The rite signified a reentry into God's grace whenever the sinner had lapsed from his state at baptism. Though a private or interior act of penitence might achieve this, it was to be confirmed in a formal rite whenever this was available, with a priest-confessor in the role of judge and adviser. Confession of sin as the first step was already traditional in the 1st century: the Didache speaks of "confession in church," presumably a public declaration (*exomologēsis*) of wrongdoing. By the close of the 2d century, public confession had come to be regarded as difficult and embarrassing. Irenaeus tells of those who so feared it that "they withdrew into the silence of despair"; Origen speaks of the sufficiency of private revealing of sins "to the priest of the Lord"; and in 459 the practice of public proclamation was condemned by Pope Leo the Great. Origen, too, explains the role of the confessing priest, assigned his power by formal commission of his bishop as both *iudex* and *medicus,* as one who both gave judgment and absolution and supplied a remedy. The confessional "seal" of complete and lasting secrecy was long assumed before its formal statement at the Fourth Lateran Council (1215). In earlier centuries the confession was often heard openly in church or in the priest's room, as is the case still in the Eastern Orthodox Church, and the modern confessional with its greater anonymity dates back, at least in its use for men as well as women, only to the 16th century. The traditional formula of contrition involved, as now, confession, the receiving of some penance such as prayers or good deeds by way of token satisfaction, and some words of spiritual advice. Then followed, as now, the formal act of contrition and absolution. In the writings of the church fathers, going back to Tertullian (c. 200) and Jerome (5th century), the traditional symbol is a shipwreck, from which the sinner may always be rescued with the help of two floating planks, the first the grace of baptism and the second that of penance. Traditional too was the division between mortal sins, those which kill God's friendship until it is brought back to life through penance, and venial sins, minor faults of temperament or uncharitable actions that strain the friendship until the tension is removed through penance. From the days of Gregory of Nyssa in the 4th century, the church made a clear distinction between true contrition and mere attrition based on the fear of punishment, adequate for the rite of penance but far less perfect.

In the early church, penance often took a public, arduous form. Cyprian of Carthage in the Decian persecution (250) prescribed a penance "not less than the crime," to be determined by the bishop, for those who under pressure had denied their faith and then later sought reconciliation. Here already are to be seen the persistent medieval notions that the ecclesiastical authority had the power to determine the penance or good deed which would expiate the sin, and that penitential exercises performed on earth would counterbalance the purgatorial punishment of cleansing after death. Cyprian instances the wearing of sackcloth and ashes, and fasting and lamenting, as well as good works and almsgiving, as appropriate penalties.

The more arduous penances of the early church, and the custom of prescribing so many days or years for their duration, were at first decided on a local basis. The first general or "plenary" indulgence was probably that proclaimed by Pope Urban II at Clermont in 1095 at the inauguration of the First Crusade. From this time on, pilgrimage became common as a means toward indulgence, particularly pilgrimage to the Holy Land or to Rome. In 1300, Pope Boniface VIII proclaimed the first "holy year," with the granting of special indulgence to those who made the journey to Rome. Self-imposed penance, in its most extreme form the permanent abandonment of home and family ties, frequently had its advocates among those whose religious zeal was not satisfied by the formal penalties. In the medieval church of the East a somewhat different attitude toward the sacrament of penance grew up, with confession heard in any convenient part of the church, with the priest-confessor seen more as witness than as judge, and with the imposition of penances an occasional rather than invariable part of the rite.

BIBLIOGRAPHY: J. T. McNeill and H. M. Gamer, *Medieval Handbooks of Penance* (New York, 1965); R. C. Mortimer, *The Origins of Private Penance in the Western Church* (Oxford, 1939); O. D. Watkins, *A History of Penance,* 2 vols. (London, 1920).

**Penitentials.** Manuals setting forth penances for particular offenses, meant to be used by priests in assigning penance. From the beginning, penance has been a part of the discipline that the church has exercised over its members. Penitential canons were issued from quite an early date by church councils. Thus within a period of time there grew up a considerable corpus of penitential tradition. However, it was only in the 6th century and then in the Celtic Church that such canons were gathered into the manuals of penance known as penitentials. These penitentials represented not Continental usages, but the Celtic penitential practices, which, by reason of isolation from the Continent as well as the peculiar nature of Celtic Christianity, tended to be more severe than those of the Roman Church. The Celtic penitentials spread to the Continent at least as early as the 7th century and did much to influence the penitential practice of the Western Church as a whole. The early church had required public confession, and penance was not repeatable; in the Celtic view penance was both private and repeatable. Thus the penitentials were influential in the development of auricular confession and of the medieval penitential system. Celtic practices themselves, however, were looked upon as too severe and were mitigated by Roman influence.

**Penitential System.** The earliest stages of what has grown into the penitential system are rather obscure. It seems, however, that quite early in the history of the church a need was felt for some way to deal with the embarrassing presence of even gross sins among some of those who had been baptized. Even in the New Testament (especially in Paul's letters) there are some indications of this problem and the approach of the church to it.

By the 3d century a regular system of penance (from the Latin *poena,* "punishment") had been developed. In the East it seems that there were four classes of penitents —the "mourners," who stood outside the church; the "hearers," who were allowed into the narthex; the "kneelers," who knelt in the nave during the worship service; and the "co-standers," who participated fully in the service with the exception of receiving Communion. The time spent in each stage was determined by the nature of the sin and it frequently took several years to be restored to full Communion. In the West the penitents formed a special "order" and were placed in the west end of the nave between the catechumens and the congregation, being further distinguished by having close-cropped hair and wearing a special robe. These penitents were excluded from Communion and required to undergo an arduous and long period of fasting, prayer, and almsgiving. This penance, which could be undertaken only once in a lifetime, was regarded as a "second baptism" to cleanse a penitent of sins committed after his original baptism, and the penitent undertook certain lifelong restrictions such as perpetual continence or ineligibility to marry or bear arms. As a result of this system, penance was usually delayed until death was imminent, although some undertook it as a kind of ascetic vocation.

The next stage in the growth of the penitential system was usually marked by the introduction of penitential books, which were codifications of the elaborate network of law and disciplinary penalties associated with various mortal sins, covering both conduct and inward thoughts and purposes. The origin of these books and the detailed system of penalties to be assigned various sins has been attributed to the Irish cloisters and to Theodore, the Saxon archbishop of Canterbury. As the penitential system spread, other modifications were introduced. The Germanic nations, for example, accepted the payment of money in place of personal punishment even in criminal cases, and among them arose the practice of paying fines in lieu of doing acts of penance (the beginning of the system of indulgences). During this period the confession of sins came to be more and more specific and secret. Absolution, which had originally been granted upon the completion of the penance, was also changed during this stage so that it came to be given at the time of confession. This period provided the transition to the "private penance" which was formally adopted by the Fourth Lateran Council (1215). This Council also made, at least, annual confession mandatory.

When penance came to be regarded as a sacrament, it contained three elements—contrition of the heart, oral confession, and satisfaction by the offender (*satisfactio operis*). In later moral theology, "contrition" was no longer regarded as essential and "attrition" (sorrow that is based upon fear) came to be regarded as sufficient to produce pardon. The element of confession was not always regarded as necessary for forgiveness and could be made to a layman if a priest was not available, but by the 13th century oral, private confession became required. Through repentance and confession the penalty of eternal

death which is incurred for mortal sins committed after baptism is commuted to temporal punishment. Then the priest, as a judge with the power of the keys, pronounces absolution and designates the satisfaction required. The efficacy of this satisfaction, which is both penal and medicinal, is through Christ, although the Middle Ages saw the development of the doctrine of a treasury of supererogatory merits —compiled by Christ and the saints—from which merit might be dispensed to cancel temporal penalties. During the Crusades plenary indulgences were inaugurated and later the benefit of indulgences was extended to include souls in purgatory.

Although repudiated by the Reformation, the penitential system as it had evolved was given formal endorsement by the Council of Trent, which defined the Roman Catholic doctrine of the sacrament of penance.

BIBLIOGRAPHY: R. S. T. Haslehurst, *Some Account of the Penitential Discipline of the Early Church* (London, 1921); J. T. McNeill and H. M. Gamer, *Medieval Handbooks of Penance* (New York, 1965); R. C. Mortimer, *The Origins of Private Penance in the Western Church* (Oxford, 1939); T. P. Oakley, *English Penitential Discipline and Anglo-Saxon Law in Their Joint Influence* (New York, 1923); O. D. Watkins, *A History of Penance,* 2 vols. (London, 1920).

**Penitentiary.** A cleric whose duty is the supervision of the sacrament of penance and the judgment of cases of conscience. In European cathedrals, there is a canon penitentiary. A cardinal penitentiary has jurisdiction in matters relating to penance which are reserved to the Holy See. The office existed early in the West, but did not appear in the East until the 11th century. The Council of Trent required each diocese to have a penitentiary.

**Penn, William** (1644–1718). Quaker and founder of Pennsylvania. The eldest son of Admiral Sir William Penn, who had served Cromwell and also aided in the Restoration of Charles II, he was apparently radicalized early, and was expelled for nonconformity from Christ Church, Oxford, March, 1662. At Cork in 1666 he heard Thomas Loe preach on the "faith that overcometh the world," and was converted to Quakerism. He was arrested several times for his preaching.

On his father's death (1670) he became one of England's wealthiest nonconformists. He was active in religious disputations and traveled widely, seeking relief for all radical Protestants. In 1676 he became involved in the Quaker settlement of West Jersey and from this developed the plan of a "Holy Experiment." In March, 1681, in discharge of a debt of nearly £16,000 which the Stuarts had owed his father, Penn received Pennsylvania. It is conjectured that Charles approved the gift in order to send into quasi-exile those Dissenters who supported the Whig faction. The history of Penn's province is caught up in the tension of Penn's desire for a holy community and his wish to break even on his expenses. Penn wrote almost one hundred books and pamphlets published during his lifetime. He was always devoted to the ideals of toleration and religious liberty.

**Pennefather, William** (1816–1873). Irish Anglican minister. He was noted as a mission preacher throughout England, being equally successful in evangelistic and pastoral work. He performed a conspicuous ministry in alleviating distress among the victims of the 1845 famine irrespective of their religious background. His home became a meeting place for men of all classes and creeds. His pastorates were marked by an inevitable need to build larger church and school facilities.

**Penry, John** (1559–1593). Welsh Puritan pamphlet writer. He was graduated from both Cambridge and Oxford. Widely thought to have been the author of the biting Marprelate tracts (1588–1889), he explicitly denies both authorship and approval of them in his diary. However, he was a severe critic of Anglicanism, and became an adherent of Separatist Robert Browne. Arrested at a time when Elizabeth was suppressing Separatism, Penry was convicted on slim evidence and hanged for treason.

**Pentecostal Churches.** Fundamentalist sects emphasizing Spirit baptism as an experience different from conversion and evidenced by speaking in tongues (Acts 2:1–13). These groups also teach salvation by conversion and revival, instantaneous sanctification, and divine healing; they claim to be a restoration of original Christianity. Early Pentecostal meetings were informal outbursts of ecstatic enthusiasm featuring healings, speaking in tongues, and motoric movements.

Pentecostalism began at the turn of the century as an outgrowth of the Holiness movement. In 1900 a Bible school called Bethel College was started at Topeka, Kans., by Charles F. Parham. Bethel was the seedbed of the movement, for here, using no textbook but the Bible, Parham drilled his students in "Spirit baptism" teaching. These pupils carried the message of the Spirit into Kansas and when the school closed, both teacher and students went throughout the South preaching Pentecostalism. Houston, Tex., became the next center of Spirit baptism when Parham and a local minister, W. F. Carothers, opened a school. One of their converts, W. J. Seymour, brought the teaching to Los Angeles in 1906, where he founded a Pentecostal meeting on Azusa Street. Besides the many visitors, including ministers, who were influenced by the Azusa Street revival, publications were put out from this headquarters which aided the rapid growth of the movement. As other churches were started in different parts of the United States the importance of Los Angeles decreased.

The Pentecostals did not desire to be a new denomination, but rather felt it to be their duty to call all Christians back to the primitive apostolic faith. Everywhere the work was to be under the guidance of the Holy Spirit, which in practice meant the control of visiting evangelists. As their teaching was opposed by other groups, however, especially the Holiness churches, they began to organize denominations. Among the more important Pentecostal church groups can be listed the Assemblies of God, the Church of God in Christ, the Church of God (Tomlinson), and the International Church of the Foursquare Gospel.

The Assemblies of God is the largest of these groups, with a total of 555,000 members. Founded in Hot Springs, Ark. (1914), it today maintains a denominational headquarters in Springfield, Mo. The group has been active in foreign missions and publication activities. In contrast to early Pentecostalism, the Assemblies give careful attention to the training of ministers. The church combines congregational and presbyterian forms of government and represents the most cultivated group in the Pentecostal movement.

The Church of God in Christ is the largest and most influential Negro Pentecostal body. The founder and leader of this church, Elder C. P. Jones, received the baptism of the Holy Ghost while visiting Los Angeles in 1906. The group, organized in the same way as the Assemblies of God, publishes a periodical called the *Whole Truth* and in 1964 had 413,000 members. Among the other Pentecostal groups using the title "Church of God," one of the more interesting is that for which A. J. Tomlinson was the general overseer. Starting as a Holiness church in 1886, this Church of God turned Pentecostal and suffered many divisions. Fragmentation is typical of the Pentecostal movement as a whole, and it is believed that after Tomlinson's death in 1908 the Church of God divided into more than two dozen organizations.

The International Church of the Foursquare Gospel, with its leader, Aimee Semple McPherson (d. 1944), is the best-known Pentecostal body. The church, organized in 1927, centers at the Angelus Temple located in Los Angeles. The colorful preaching of Mrs. McPherson started the movement which continues today with 741 churches and over 89,000 members.

The fact that one of the more important denominations started with the work of a woman illustrates the role of women in Pentecostal churches today. On the whole, the movement has evolved from a lower-class, spontaneous ecstatic revivalism to an institutionalism that attracts higher social groups. Its dynamic ideals continue, however, and recently some Episcopalians and Lutherans have been "speaking in tongues" as they receive the "baptism of the Spirit."

BIBLIOGRAPHY: N. Bloch-Hoell, *The Pentecostal Movement* (Oslo, 1964); E. T. Clark, *The Small Sects in America* (Nashville, 1949); J. T. Nichol, *Pentecostalism* (New York, 1966).

**People's Party** (Italian). A group opposed to Fascism, organized in 1919 by Sicilian priest Luigi Sturzo (1871–1959) after Benedict XV lifted bans on Italian Catholic political participation. Made up of Christian Democrats, it quickly won second place to Socialists in Parliament. Suppressed by Mussolini, it emerged after 1943 as Italy's governing party. Friendly to peasants, the Popolari asked freedom for religious orders and schools, decentralization, and proportional representation.

**Pepin III** (d. 768). King of the Franks. Before his death in 741, Charles Martel divided the Frankish kingdom, over which he was mayor of the palace, between his two sons—Pepin, who received the western half; and Carloman, who received the eastern half. Both brothers had been educated at St.-Denis and showed more interest in the church than their father had. In a series of synods held from 742 to 747, the reforms of Boniface were made obligatory for the Frankish Church. In 747, Carloman abdicated and entered a monastery. Pepin then became mayor of the palace over both halves of the kingdom. In 751 with the approval of Pope Zacharias, he deposed the figurehead Merovingian king Childeric III and became king himself. In 753, he sent a mission to Italy to rescue Pope Stephen II (III) from the Lombards. The pope returned to France and crowned Pepin and anointed his two sons, Charles and Carloman. Pepin became the protector of the papacy and on two occasions

led expeditions into Italy. He granted the pope authority over the former exarchate of Ravenna (see DONATION OF PEPIN). Pepin restored lands to churches and monasteries that had been seized by his father. After his death at St.-Denis, the kingdom was again divided, this time between Pepin's two sons.

**Perfectionism.** A doctrine that sinlessness has been or can be attained during the earthly life. The language of perfection in the New Testament (as in Matt. 5:48; John 17:23; I Cor. 2:6; Eph. 4:13; Col. 1:28 and 4:12; Heb. 6:1 and 10:14; and I John 4:18) along with the doctrine of the Kingdom of God as historical realization (as in Matt. 6:10 and Luke 17:21) or as imminent expectation (as in Matt., ch. 24; Luke, ch. 22; and Revelation) has stirred recurrent concerns for the perfection of the believer either individually or in social embodiments of the Kingdom of God. In the early church the Biblical roots were intertwined with influences from Hellenistic or Gnostic sources, as in Clement of Alexandria, whose doctrine of the "Christian Gnostic" is typical of much perfectionism. At a time when the church was threatened by crowds of people whose moral level was low and by the Gnostics with their claim of spiritual superiority, Clement urged Christian believers to go on to a true Christian perfection of love, which he designated by the problematical term "knowledge" (*gnōsis*). Origen developed this idea in the direction of an ascetic renunciation of the world tending toward monasticism.

Perfectionism emerged as a social movement in Egypt when earnest Christians, disturbed by the debauchery of Alexandria, fled to the isolation of the desert caves to the west of the Nile. There such men as Antony of Egypt (c. 250–356) pioneered the monastic ascetic pattern of perfectionism in which sanctification is sought in physical isolation from urban society. Under Antony and others, hermitic monasticism was replaced by cenobitic or communal monasticism, in which perfection was sought in a community under discipline. Monasticism has remained the dominant perfectionist ideal in the Eastern Orthodox and Roman Churches, the vows of poverty, chastity, and obedience being termed "counsels of perfection" (Thomas Aquinas).

In medieval theology, ascetic perfectionism was linked with a Platonic and Aristotelian idea of contemplation, accentuating a mystical cast to the notion of perfection. In this period particularly, the histories of perfectionism and of mysticism merge.

The Reformers tended to associate the notion of perfection with an ascetic works salvation and thus emphasized the sinfulness of the believer. Perfectionist concerns were expressed, however, by Anabaptists and Christian humanists in the tradition of Erasmus. An evangelical view of Christian perfection was adumbrated by the Dutch theologian Jacobus Arminius (d. 1609), who distinguished between perfection "according to rigor" and "according to clemency." He followed the Reformers in rejecting the first and the early fathers in affirming the second. A similar distinction was made by John Wesley, who differentiated between "Christian" and "absolute" perfection, the latter being an evangelical perfection of love, conditioned only on faith, available to the believer both as growth in love and as a "second blessing" of entire sanctification. The Wesleyan emphasis on Christian perfection became a central feature of Methodism, although the rigor of primitive Methodism has often been tempered by neglect or by preoccupation with the ideal of social holiness. A rigorist and individualist version of Wesley's position has been promoted in and out of Methodism by the Holiness movement since the mid-19th century. Charles G. Finney also promoted a revivalistic perfectionism.

Protestant social perfectionism has taken many forms, such as the violent Münsterite kingdom of 1525, the gentle society of Nicholas Ferrar at Little Gidding (17th century), and the American communitarian experiments of the Rappites and the Oneida Community (19th century).

Both personal and social perfectionist impulses contributed to the moral rigor and the optimism of the more recent Social Gospel movement. The postliberal theological reaction of Karl Barth and Reinhold Niebuhr, among others, revived the Augustinian and Reformation emphasis on sin in believers in opposition to both the older perfectionism and piety and the newer evolutionary perfectionism of society.

BIBLIOGRAPHY: R. N. Flew, *The Idea of Perfection in Christian Theology* (London, 1934); D. Steele, *Love Enthroned* (New York, 1875); J. Wesley, *Christian Perfection* (Chicago, 1921).

**Perkins, William** (1558–1602). The most influential Puritan writer at the turn of the century. He had the facility for translating complex theology into understandable doctrine and clear practice. A powerful teacher and preacher at Cambridge, Fuller said of him, "The Scholar could heare no learneder, the Townsmen plainer Sermons." His style of preaching and his psychology of conversion became normative for the Puritan ministry.

**Perrone, Giovanni** (1794–1876). Italian Jesuit. Entering the newly restored Society of Jesus in 1815, Perrone became professor of dogmatic theology at Rome. He was influential in the Marian movement, which secured the declaration of the Immaculate Conception of the Virgin Mary in 1854. His *Praelectiones theologicae* (9 vols., 1835–1842) was one of the most popular theological manuals of the century, widely used in seminaries.

**Perth, Five Articles of** (1618). Regulations which James I sought to force upon the Scottish Kirk in order to bring about increased conformity with the English Church. In 1618 the king presented the following demands to the General Assembly: kneeling at Communion, private Communion for the sick, baptism on the Sunday after birth, episcopal confirmation of the young, and the observance of holy days. The Assembly adopted the Articles, but the Scottish people abhorred them and boycotted the churches whose ministers supported them.

**Perthes, Klemens Theodor** (1809–1867). German jurist and historian at Bonn. His father, publisher and patriot Friedrich Christoph Perthes, married the daughter of poet Matthias Claudius. Thus young Klemens met a group of Protestant scholars who exerted great sway over German religious thinking. He wrote of his father in *Political Life in Germany Before the French Revolution* and exchanged valuable letters (1864–1867) with the Prussian war minister, Albrecht von Roon. These were printed in 1895.

*Per Venerabilem.* Decretal by Innocent III (1202) to Count William of Montpellier in which the principle was the prerogative of the pope to exercise temporal jurisdiction outside the Papal States. On the basis of Deut. 17:8–12, Innocent III claimed the right to act as supreme judge in all cases, whether civil or criminal, spiritual or secular. The principle was subsequently incorporated into the canon law of the church (Corpus Juris Canonici, II, cols. 714–716, ed. by E. Friedberg; Leipzig, 1881).

**Pestalozzi, Johann Heinrich** (1746–1827). Swiss educator. Inspired by Jean-Jacques Rousseau's *Émile*, Pestalozzi gave up his study of theology and law to become a reformer in education. In 1805 he founded at Yverdon his famous boarding school which attracted students, scholars, and notables from all professions and countries in Europe. His fundamental principle was "sense impression," and his method was carried on by disciples who established Pestalozzian schools in Europe and America.

**Petau (Petavius), Denys** (1583–1652). Important Roman Catholic scholar and Jesuit theologian. Trained in the humanist tradition, he prepared new scholarly editions of both theological and classical texts. As a controversialist, he wrote against the Jansenists and the Protestants, and also defended the Scholastic method. He was a careful historian of doctrine, and one of the first to develop clear methods for the use of this history in contemporary debate, e.g., in defense of the positions of the Council of Trent on Scripture and tradition. His careful work in positive theology, which he did not live to complete, synthesized this minute historical interest with Scholastic method and contained some important original treatments, e.g., in the doctrines of grace and the Trinity. In both cases he drew fruitfully upon the Greek fathers.

**Peter, Memorial of.** Gaius, a Roman presbyter, early in the 3d century mentions a "memorial of Peter" which may be the same columnar monument under St. Peter's Basilica, traces of which have been found in recent excavations. Such memorials apparently originated in the 3d century as "victory memorials" (*tropaia*) to commemorate some event such as the martyrdom of Peter and were probably not associated originally with any relics, burial sites, or cult of Peter. Three areas—the Vatican Hill, the Ostian Way, and the Appian Way—are particularly associated with Peter.

**Peter I** (*called* Peter the Great) (1672–1725). Czar under whom Russia became a great European power. His relations with the Russian Orthodox Church were strained. He dissolved monasteries, revised the liturgy, and abolished the patriarchate in favor of the Crown-controlled Holy Synod. His church reforms resulted in the large defection of Russians called Old Believers, who were systematically persecuted during his rule.

**Peter Chrysologus** (406–450). A saint and Doctor of the Church. Born in Imola, Italy, he became bishop of Ravenna in 433. Famous as an author and orator, Peter was a vigorous enemy of Monophysitism. His works were collected by Felix, bishop of Ravenna, edited by Agapitus Vicentius, and published in Bologna (1534). Most of them are brief and concise explications of passages of Scripture.

**Peter Claver** (1581–1654). Jesuit missionary to the Negroes. Entering the Society of Jesus in 1601, he was persuaded by the "holy doorkeeper" of Palma, Alphonsus Rodríguez, to volunteer for the Spanish missions to South America. He arrived in 1610 at Cartagena in modern Colombia, the chief slave market of the New World, and was ordained there in 1615. To fill the conquerors' needs for laborers to till the soil and mine gold, one thousand or more slaves per month were brought in from Guinea, the Congo, and Angola. Dedicating his life to them as "the slave of the Negroes forever," Claver assembled a group of interpreters and catechists, and boarded every entering slave ship, feeding and tending to the medical needs of the slaves, defending them against cruelty, and teaching them Christianity. Against strong opposition, even ecclesiastical suspicion of indiscreet zeal, Claver labored there for thirty-eight years, baptizing perhaps 300,000 slaves before he died. In 1888, Pope Leo XIII canonized him, and in 1896 made him patron of all Roman Catholic missions to the Negroes.

**Peter Comestor** (Manducator) (d. c. 1179). Biblical scholar. Chancellor of the Cathedral School of Paris, he was also author of the *Historia scholastica,* a popular compendium of Biblical history which used the Bible, the fathers, 12th-century commentaries, and even non-Christian authors to provide a continuous narrative of salvation history. Along with the glossed Bible, the *Sentences* of Peter Lombard, and the *Decretum* of Gratian, it became one of the standard books of the medieval theological curriculum.

**Peter Damian** (1007–1072). Italian ecclesiastic and reformer. Born in Ravenna, he was left in the care of an older brother following the death of his parents. His brother forced him to tend swine until another brother, an archpriest of Ravenna, took him into his own home. Adopting the name Damian from this brother, he went to school at Faenza and Parma and soon became an outstanding teacher. In 1035 he entered the monastery of Fonte Avellana, a house reformed by Romuald. In 1043 he was elected prior of this semieremitical community and devoted himself to the establishment of similar communities elsewhere. His reputation as a reformer and opponent of simony caused him to be made cardinal bishop of Ostia in 1057. In spite of his desire to return to the life of a monk, he served frequently as a papal legate, enforcing reform measures in Italy and Germany. Finally his repeated petitions to be relieved of his office were granted by Alexander II. He retired to Fonte Avellana, but was called occasionally to carry out a mission for the pope. On returning from such a mission to Ravenna, he was taken ill at Faenza and died there. He wrote *Liber gomorrhianus,* a treatise against clerical marriage, and *Liber gratissimus,* upholding the validity of sacraments administered by simoniacal clergy. He represents a moderate voice in the reform movements of the 11th century, disagreeing with extremists such as Cardinal Humbert.

**Peter Martyr** (Peter of Verona) (1205–1252). Dominican inquisitor in Lombardy. Born in Verona of parents who were members of the Cathari, he attended the University of Bologna, and entered the Dominican Order, receiving the habit from Dominic himself. He was appointed inquisitor for Milan in 1234 by Gregory IX. Shortly after Easter in 1252, while traveling from Como to Milan, he was attacked by two assassins from the Catharist sect, some of whom he had forced into exile. Having received a blow to the head, he fell to the ground and is said to have written on the ground with his own blood the words: *"Credo in Deum."* A second blow killed him.

**Peter Martyr** (Pietro Martire Vermigli) (1500–1562). Protestant Reformer. Son of an Italian noble who had been a follower of Savonarola, he joined the Augustinians in 1516, later becoming abbot of one of their houses in Spoleto in 1530, and prior at Naples in 1533. His brilliant mind turned to a serious study of the Bible, and his reading of Bucer and Zwingli won his sympathy toward the Reformers. This interest was apparent in his lectures, and he was forced to flee Italy in company with Ochino in 1542. He went to Basel, then Zurich, and then with Bucer's aid secured a position as professor in Strasbourg. Again with Ochino, he answered Cranmer's invitation to England in 1547, where he lectured at Cambridge, and took part in discussions of England's ecclesiastical future. Upon Mary's accession he was arrested but released after six months, whereupon he returned to Strasbourg and resumed his old university position. However, his Eucharistic views caused controversy, and in 1556 he removed to Zurich, taking the late Pellican's place as professor of Hebrew. He was there during the difficulty centered around Bibliander, whose views on predestination he successfully opposed. He also had a minor share in the shaping of the Second Helvetic Confession in the months before his death.

**Peter of Alcántara** (Pedro Garavito) (1499–1562). Spanish Franciscan. Born at Alcántara in Estremadura, he studied at Salamanca University, joining the Observantine

Franciscans in 1515. Later he founded the discalced, or Alcantarine, reform of that order. He was a mystic and reformer of great austerity who influenced Teresa of Ávila, whom he met in 1558 and assisted in the Carmelite reform. His best-known work is *A Treatise on Prayer and Meditation.*

**Peter of Alexandria** (d. 311). Bishop of Alexandria from 300. He died as a martyr under the persecution of Maximinus. Because of conflicting accounts, it is difficult to be certain about the nature of the conflict between Peter and Melitius, bishop of Lycopolis. During the Diocletian persecution (303–313), Peter was absent from Alexandria (probably because he had fled for safety). With the imprisonment of the Egyptian bishops—Phileas, Hesychius, Theodore, and Pachymius—four other Egyptian dioceses were empty. Melitius assumed power in these dioceses as well as in that of Alexandria by removing the episcopal visitors and appointing his own. The ensuing power struggle between Peter and Melitius (which may have centered on the issue of the lapsi) finally resulted in the victory of Peter in 305 or 306 and the schism of the Melitian party.

**Peter of Bruys** (d. c. 1140). A heretical priest who preached for twenty years throughout southern France, gathering a band of followers known as Petrobrusians. He preached against the Mass, baptism of infants, the veneration of the cross, and the sacerdotal office. He is supposed to have been burned at St.-Gilles in a fire which he himself had prepared to burn crucifixes. After his death, Henry of Lausanne became leader of the movement.

**Peter Riga** (c. 1140–1209). Canon regular of St.-Denis (Reims) and Latin verse writer. His most famous production was *Aurora,* the popular versified allegorical and moral commentary on the Bible, composed (1170–1200) in three successive editions: (1) a preface, Genesis through II Kings, plus Maccabees and about a third (some 1,000 lines) of the *Evangelium;* (2) all of the first edition plus Daniel, Tobit, Judith and Esther after II Kings, the rest of the *Evangelium,* and the *Recapitulationes,* 23 lipograms describing Old Testament persons as types of later events which were based on the encyclopedia *Etymologiae* of Isidore of Seville; and (3) the addition of Acts, Job, and the Song of Solomon in rhyming hexameters contrasted to the distichs of the rest of the work. Though not original but a compilation of popular exegesis, it provided source material for many late medieval scholars and writers, including

John Gower, Macé de la Charité, and Jehan Malkaraume.

**Petersen, Fredrik** (1839–1903). Norwegian Lutheran theologian. Born in Stavanger, he was educated at Christiania (Oslo) and Berlin. Ordained in 1873, he became professor of theology at Christiania in 1875. Petersen was interested in the contemporary problems of Christianity and its relationship to modern science. His essay *How Should the Church Meet Contemporary Unbelief?* adopted an open attitude toward scientific inquiry while at the same time seeking to uphold the traditional faith.

**Peter's Pence.** An ecclesiastical tax on each hearth, paid to the popes by England, Poland, and Scandinavia. The tax was certainly English in origin and may have been levied as early as King Offa in 787. Occasionally the national bishops retained a large portion of the tax for themselves. The withholding or just the threat of withholding the tax was used by the kings to obtain concessions from Rome. The tax was abolished at the Reformation.

**Peter the Fuller** (d. c. 489). Intruded Monophysite patriarch of Antioch (470). Twice exiled, he was restored (482) after assent to the Henoticon. His chief claim to remembrance is the addition to the Trisagion of the Monophysite expansion "[Thou] who wast crucified for us." Theodore Lector (6th century) in his *Ecclesiastical History* (2.48) credits Peter with introducing a recitation of the Nicene Creed at the Eucharist, the solemn blessing of chrism, and the veneration of Theotokos.

**Peter the Hermit** (d. c. 1115). French hermit and monk. Although it is uncertain whether he heard Urban II at Clermont, he soon became a popular preacher of the First Crusade, especially among the poor. He led a band of paupers across Europe to Asia Minor, where the Turks destroyed them. He escaped to Constantinople and joined the main army. He was caught trying to escape from the siege of Antioch, but had regained favor by the capture of Jerusalem. He returned to France, where he died.

**Peter the Venerable** (c. 1092–1156). Eighth abbot of Cluny who resisted the violent attempt of his discredited predecessor to recapture the abbey. Born of the noble Montboissier family, he became prior of Vezelay (1120) and at the age of thirty abbot of Cluny (1122) when Cluny had some two thousand dependent houses. The title "venerable" was conferred upon him by Bernard of Clairvaux, who in his famous letter nevertheless vigorously attacked the Cluniacs for their departures from the Benedictine Rule with their ornate church, fine foods, and relaxed discipline. Peter's response to this attack was in terms of the human needs of his monks; yet he did introduce some reforms in his later life, particularly in the standards of admission and in liturgical practice, although he was unable to effect a complete reformation. He sheltered Abelard after the latter's condemnation at the Council of Soissons and worked with Bernard at the Council of Pisa (1134). He had the Koran translated into Latin, and though writing against the Jews, sought toleration of them. As a Biblical commentator he tended to de-emphasize allegory, giving less attention to the views of the fathers than most of his contemporaries. He was involved in the beginnings of the struggle against the revival of Gnostic tendencies by Peter of Bruys and wrote against him.

**Petite Église.** A group arising among French and Belgian Catholics opposed to the Concordat of 1801. It represented a schism from the church which has persisted to the present time. Bishops who, along with parish priests, rejected the provisions of the Concordat carried on their dioceses in opposition to the new order. The resulting body persisted in spite of persecution, and functions today under lay leadership.

**Petrarch** (Francesco Petrarca) (1304–1374). Early Italian humanist and poet, regarded as the first modern man of letters and often hailed as the first representative humanist. He spent his youth first at Pisa and then in southern France near Avignon. In adulthood his restless spirit led him to travel widely in western and central Europe before finally settling in Italy during his last years. He devoted the greater part of the sonnets for which he is so famous to a beautiful lady named Laura whom he had met in 1327 in a church at Avignon. He worshiped her for a lifetime, but the fact that she was both married and virtuous prevented any consummation of his love. The poetry resulting from this frustrating affair was not only an influential force in Italian literature but also made the vernacular sonnet a work of art. However, the best energies of Petrarch's life were spent in searching for classical manuscripts and purging them of mistakes. His favorite was Cicero, many of whose works he was able to recover and edit. A sincerely religious man, Petrarch had taken minor orders as a young man but never became a priest. His religious feelings are laid bare in his *Secretum*, a confessional work written about 1342 as he wrestled with the problem of reconciling his medieval piety with his enjoyment of the things of the world.

**Petre, Maude Dominica Mary** (1863–1942). English Roman Catholic writer. Coming from one of the best known of the old Catholic families of England, Miss Petre was the close friend and subsequently the biographer and literary executor of the English Catholic modernist George Tyrrell. In addition to her *Life of George Tyrrell* (2 vols., 1912), she described the cause to which she was devoted in *Modernism* (1918), *My Way of Faith,* and a study of Baron von Hügel and Tyrrell.

**Petri, Laurentius** (Lars Petersson) (1499–1573). First Lutheran archbishop of the Church of Sweden (1531–1573). Petri valued succession of apostolic doctrine more highly than episcopal succession. He, along with his brother Olaus, exerted a wide influence on the spiritual life of Sweden. The great achievement of Laurentius Petri was the 1571 church order, which contained his mature thoughts on the Eucharist and the various church ordinances.

**Petri, Olaus** (Olaf Petersson) (1493–1552). Swedish Lutheran reformer. Like his brother Laurentius, he studied at Wittenberg. Returning to Sweden in 1518, he was ordained a deacon at Strengnäs two years later. Soon complaints came from the neighboring bishop of Linköping about the Lutheran preaching in Strengnäs. Petri's own bishop had been beheaded during the "Stockholm bloodbath" in 1520. Not long afterward, Gustav Vasa led Sweden in a successful revolt against Denmark and was acclaimed king at Strengnäs in 1523, summoning Petri, to whom his attention had been drawn, to Stockholm the following year. Two years later Petri's Swedish translation of the New Testament and his Swedish hymnbook appeared. In 1527 he was appointed the king's secretary and in 1531 his chancellor. In 1529 he brought out his *Manual* for pastors and in 1531 published his Swedish Mass, which his brother, Laurentius, was to revise over the next four decades in his capacity as archbishop. Olaus Petri was a fearless preacher and in 1539 came into disfavor with the king, who threatened him with execution. So great was Petri's popularity with the people, however, that this threat was never carried out. In 1543 he became the senior pastor of the cathedral in Stockholm. Petri, who had studied under Luther before the Leipzig Debate and the Diet of Worms took place, introduced a conservative reforma-

tion in Sweden that sank deep roots and gradually transformed the medieval church into a strong evangelical church.

**Pfaff, Christoph Matthäus** (1686–1760). German Protestant theologian. After studies at home and abroad, he became a professor, later chancellor, at Tübingen. He was an outstanding 18th-century theologian, combining orthodox, Pietist, and rationalist features with an irenic trend. In his work on church law he favored collegialism. A fine administrator and prolific writer, he was probably led by ambition to forge the Irenaeus fragments allegedly found in Turin.

**Pfefferkorn, Johann.** See REUCHLIN, JOHANNES.

**Pfleiderer, Otto** (1839–1908). German Protestant theologian. From 1875 he was professor of systematic theology in Berlin. As opposed to Ritschl, he adopted the Hegelian concept of development, applying it to the rise and history of Christianity. A great advocate of the philosophy of religion, he rejected the uniqueness of revelation in Christ, and resisted such categories as apostasy and heresy. He welcomed the Hellenization of the original gospel.

**Pflug, Julius von** (1499–1564). German Roman Catholic humanist and churchman willing to make concessions in order to have peace with the Protestants. He was elected bishop of Naumburg-Zeitz in 1541 but John Frederick, the elector of Saxony, was a Protestant and would not let him take possession of his post. When the elector was defeated six years later and Pflug was finally able to enter his diocese, he found it almost entirely Lutheran, most of the priests married, and the secular authorities prepared to force reinstatement of any clerics he might try to remove. In his desire for conciliation Pflug asked the Roman Church to accept married priests and Communion under both species. He assisted in forming both the Regensburg Book (1541) and the Interim of Augsburg (1548).

**Philadelphians.** A 17th-century English Sect. The Philadelphian Society was founded by Mrs. Jane Lead (1623–1704), her chief disciple, Dr. Francis Lee, and an Anglican rector, John Pordage. From childhood Mrs. Lead had experienced visions, but after reading Jakob Boehme these mystical encounters came almost nightly. Her published diary, *A Fountain of Gardens,* won followers who drew up a constitution and held well-attended meetings, but the Society broke up permanently in 1704.

**Philaret** (Theodore Nikitich Romanov, c. 1553–1633). Patriarch of Moscow from 1619. A distinguished diplomat and soldier, he became a candidate for the throne of the czar in 1598, but was forced to yield to Boris Godunov and to enter a monastery under the name Philaret. After the overthrow of the Godunovs, Philaret's son Michael eventually became the first Romanov czar (1613); thereby the so-called "Time of Troubles" was ended. Philaret as patriarch of Moscow was virtual coregent, concerning himself with the domestic problem of peasant migration as well as the continuing interference of foreign powers in Russian affairs. He left his mark on Russian education and the church by founding the Patriarchal Library, establishing diocesan seminaries, and encouraging the study of theology.

**Philaret** (Vasily Mikhailovich Drozdov, 1782–1867). Russian Orthodox prelate and metropolitan of Moscow from 1826. He was a loyal reforming influence in the Russian Orthodox Church, opposing infiltration of Roman Catholic theology. He advocated the use of the Bible in the vernacular, and wrote a Russian catechism that was published under imperial order in 1839. Noted for his preaching, he was also assumed to be the author of the imperial decree that freed the serfs in 1861.

**Philaster** (Filaster) **of Brescia** (d. c. 397). Bishop of Brescia. He is chiefly known for his writings opposing heretical groups. His zeal in this regard is shown by the fact that he included in his lists of heresies many positions that men such as Augustine regarded as merely erroneous opinions. Most of our information concerning his life comes from a panegyrical sermon preached on an anniversary of his death. His *Book of Heresies* (c. 385), written against Jewish and Christian heresies, was used by Augustine as well as many other theologians.

**Phileas** (d. 306). Bishop of Thmuis in Lower Egypt. He died as a martyr during the Diocletian persecution (303–313). While Phileas was in prison, Melitius, bishop of Lycopolis, assumed power in Phileas' diocese (as well as in the dioceses of other imprisoned bishops) by removing the episcopal visitors of Phileas and appointing his own.

**Philip II** (1527–1598). King of Spain. He was born May 15, 1527, at Valladolid, the son of Charles V and Isabella of Portugal, and educated in Spain, receiving directions by letter from his busy father. He grew into a serious, self-possessed man, rather distrustful of others. Though beloved in Spain, he never succeeded in evoking the enthusiasm of his subjects elsewhere. He had a good moral character and immense, almost excessive, capacities for work—a quality that led him to concentrate too much of the commonplace business of the kingdom in his own hands. In 1543 he was married to his cousin Mary of Portugal; after her death he married Mary Tudor, who bore him no children. He became king upon the abdication of his father in 1556, and married Elizabeth of Valois in 1559. By and large, Philip's whole reign was a vast crusade in the name of Spain and Roman Catholicism. He was mostly unsuccessful, provoking French, English, and Dutch national sentiment, and suffering the defeat of the Armada and the campaigns of William of Orange. In Spain the Inquisition became a tool of royal political power. Philip died in 1598 in the Escorial, the vast palace-monastery complex he had built near Madrid.

**Philip II** (*known as* Philip Augustus) (1165–1223). King of France from 1180. In 1193, he married a Danish princess, Ingeborg, but immediately asked to have the marriage annulled. A synod of the church in France carried out his wishes. Pope Celestine did not approve, but took no action. However, upon the succession of Innocent III, an interdict was laid upon France, which forced Philip to accept Ingeborg as his queen, though not as his wife. The episode is illustrative of the power of Innocent III.

**Philip IV** (*called* the Fair) (1268–1314). King of France from 1285. An energetic ruler, he successfully maintained his position over against that of the pope. He secured a compromise agreement with Pope Boniface VIII so that the church in France could be taxed. He also humiliated Boniface by capturing and abusing him at Agnani. His power over Boniface's successor, Clement V, is shown in that he lured the papal court to Avignon and secured the suppression of the Templars in order to confiscate their vast wealth.

**Philip Neri** (1515–1595). The founder of the Congregation of the Oratory. Philip left home at the age of eighteen to live with a relative near Monte Cassino. From 1533 he spent the rest of his life at Rome, where for the first sixteen years he tutored the sons of a Florentine for room and board. His services in hospitals culminated in the founding of the Confraternity of the Holy Trinity in 1548, to help poor pilgrims and convalescents discharged from hospitals. Ordained in 1551 on the persuasion of his spiritual adviser, he began to gather his young followers, won by personal magnetism and work in the confessional, into discussion groups, with conversation punctuated by prayers and hymns. Greater numbers forced them into an empty church attic; hence the name "Oratory" (from Latin *oratorium,* "place of prayer"), which came to be applied also to the men and to the religious and charitable activities they later devised. While he was rector of the church of San Giovanni (1564–1575), the first members of the new community, including Baronius, the historian, were ordained. In 1575, Pope Gregory XIII established the Oratorians as a congregation of secular priests and clerics; in 1577, Philip Neri was elected its provost. The influence of his cheerful and open personality made him one of the outstanding figures of the Roman Catholic Counter-Reformation. He was canonized in 1622.

**Philip of Hesse** (1504–1567). Landgrave from 1509 on the death of his father. He was declared of age in 1518. Philip led in crushing the Peasants' War in northern Germany. In 1524 he detained Melanchthon on the road to Wittenberg to discuss theology. On later receiving from Melanchthon his *Summary of Christian Doctrine* Philip was won to the Protestant faith and vigorously promoted it in his territory. He and Elector John of Saxony led in forming an alliance of northern German princes in 1526. At the 1529 Diet of Speyer he was one of the signers of the "protest." It was largely due to his interest in a Lutheran-Zwinglian alliance that the Marburg Colloquy was held in 1529. In 1530 he was one of the original signers of the Augsburg Confession and a leader in forming the Smalcald League. He entered into a bigamous marriage in 1540 (with the grudging approval of Luther and Melanchthon) which cost him his position of leadership and forced him to submit to Emperor Charles V. Philip warned the League of Charles's plan to attack them in 1546, but lack of preparation led to a quick imperial victory in 1547. The defeat at Mühlberg led to Philip's imprisonment until the Peace of Passau in 1552. During his remaining years he devoted himself to reforming and reorganizing the church of Hesse and to aiding Protestants wherever possible.

**Philip of Side** (5th century). Christian author. Born at Side (Eski Adalia) and a pupil of Rhodon at Alexandria, he established a branch school at Side in 405. He was an associate of Chrysostom, and was nominated to the see of Constantinople three times, once against Nestorius. He composed a polemic against Julian the Apostate and a Christian history (36 books). Only fragments of his work remain, along with some disputed works.

**Philippine Independent Catholic Church** (Aglipayan Church). In 1902, Father Gregorio Aglipay and Don Isabelo de los Reyes led a great religious independence movement and broke away from the Roman Catholic Church in the Philippines. The movement became the Philippine Independent Catholic Church, also known as the Aglipayan Church.

Though a part of general nationalism, it was rooted in deep religious convictions. It was strongly anti-Roman and the leadership repudiated papal authority, introduced the vernacular languages into the services, and permitted the clergy to marry.

Theologically the church has swayed officially from Marcionism to Universalism, to Unitarianism, to Anglicanism, though its membership has remained basically in the traditional Roman teachings of Christianity. On Nov. 24, 1906, it lost all property to the Roman Catholic Church by a decision of the Supreme Court.

On April 7, 1948, three of its bishops secured apostolic succession through Anglican ordination and in 1961 a concordat established intercommunion with the Episcopal Church in the United States of America.

Its ministerial candidates train at St. Andrew's Seminary of the Episcopal Church in the Philippines. At present it claims a constituency of 3,000,000 members. It is served by 38 bishops and a large core of priests.

**Philippines, National Council of Churches in the.** A Council organized in 1929 as a result of the ministry of John R. Mott. It was formed as a local unit of the International Missionary Council and conformed in organization and function to similar councils throughout the mission world. In 1939 it became the Philippine Federation of Evangelical Churches. Toward 1960 it was reconstituted into the National Council of Churches in the Philippines. It represents the United Church of Christ in the Philippines, The Methodist Church, the Episcopal Church, and the Philippine Independent Catholic Church.

**Philippines, United Church of Christ in the.** Formed in 1929, it was originally a union of Presbyterian, United Brethren, Congregational, and Philippine Independent Methodist Churches. Since World War II, the Evangelical United Brethren and the Disciples of Christ have merged with the United Church. Its first moderator was a Filipino. It has a membership of approximately 100,000, with a community of 250,000. Its more than 800 churches are divided into four jurisdictions—North Luzon, South Luzon, the Visayas, and Mindanao—and into 22 conferences. The administrative headquarters are located in Manila. Its main training center for the ministry is the Union Theological Seminary in Manila. It constitutes the largest single Protestant body in the Philippines, and has departments of education, public welfare, and a board of missions.

**Philippists.** Supporters of the views of Philip Melanchthon on free will (synergism), the value of good works, and the nature of Christ's presence in the Lord's Supper (see CRYPTO-CALVINISM). The name was first applied by Flacius' followers to the faculties of Wittenberg and Leipzig at time of the adiaphoristic controversy during the Leipzig Interim. Philipists saw themselves as moderating between the extremes of Zwinglianism and strict Lutheranism.

**Philip the Arabian** (d. 249). Roman emperor from 244. According to Eusebius, he was a devout Christian who confessed his sins in order to take part in the Paschal vigil (at Antioch, says Chrysostom). Eusebius mentions letters from Origen to him and to the empress Severa. Philip was at least no persecutor; anti-Christian activities at the end of his reign seem to have been instigated by his enemies. It is unlikely, however, that he was really a Christian.

**Philo** (c. 25 B.C.–c. A.D. 45). Hellenistic Jewish philosopher of Alexandria. A voluminous writer, Philo tried to correlate the Old Testament revelation with philosophy (largely Platonic) and Greek piety by means of the allegorical method, thus opening the way (especially with his Logos doctrine) to the Christian school of Alexandria, which preserved his works. He headed a Jewish delegation to the emperor Caligula in 40.

**Philocalian Calendar.** A Roman almanac for A.D. 354 which contains Christian as well as pagan and secular material. The anniversaries of bishops from 257 (*Depositio episcoporum*) and other days, mainly feasts of martyrs (*Depositio martyrum*) observed at Rome, also an Easter table and a list of bishops of Rome from Peter to Liberius, then in office. The existing manuscripts derive from an elaborate copy prepared by the calligrapher Furius Dionysius Philocalus (or Filocalus), who also worked for Damasus on inscriptions in the catacombs.

**Philokalia.** A collection of writings from ancient experts on the contemplative life, published in Greek in 1782 in Venice. It has become important in the Russian Orthodox Church: a condensation translated into Slavonic by Paissi Velichkovski found wide usage in monastic communities; and another version, the *Dobrotoliubiye* prepared by Teofan, bishop of Vysha, in the late 19th century, has remained influential even after the 1917 Revolution.

**Philostorgius** (c. 368–c. 439). Arian writer. His lost works include an encomium of Eunomius, a defense of Christianity against Porphyry, and a twelve-book church history extant chiefly in epitome by Photius. The last is a partisan history of Arianism beginning with the conflict (317) of Arius and Alexander and ending in 425. It is less history than an apology against orthodoxy and against paganism, which held the church responsible for the decline of empire.

**Philoxenus** (d. 523). Christian leader of the Eastern Church. He was a vigorous defender of Monophysites against Nestorianism and Chalcedonian orthodoxy. As metropolitan (485–519) of Mabug (Hierapolis), he was banished by Justinian on political grounds. His works include a partial Syriac version of the Bible (prime source for text history) and an extensive collection of theological discourses, letters, etc., which show how close his Christology was to that of Severus of Antioch.

**Photian Schism.** A serious controversy in the 9th century between Rome and Constantinople over the ecclesiastical jurisdiction of the Bulgarian Church, the *filioque* clause, and the accession of a layman to the see of Constantinople. The schism was the greatest threat to the unity of the Eastern and Western Churches until the rupture of 1054 (see SCHISM, EASTERN).

In 858, the emperor Michael, supported by his uncle, the ex-regent and caesar, Bardis, deposed the patriarch Ignatius, and appointed a learned layman, Photius, as patriarch. The second iconoclastic period, which had just ended in 843, still left the Byzantine Church divided between the extremists, led by Ignatius, who opposed any concessions to the iconoclasts, and the moderates, headed by Photius. The moderates sought to integrate both factions, and they had the support of the emperor. Ignatius refused to recognize a layman who was given in six days all the priestly offices necessary for the patriarchal throne. Pope Nicholas I sympathized with Ignatius, but the pope's legates, Radoald and Zachery, agreed to the decision of the Council of 861 in Constantinople which recognized Photius' accession. Upon learning of his legates' actions, Nicholas convoked his own council in 863 and maintained that the legates had exceeded their authority. The pope annulled the proceedings of 861, declared Ignatius patriarch, and condemned Photius.

The basic reason for the pope's actions was, however, his failure to secure ecclesiastical jurisdiction over Bulgaria. The pope had demanded, in return for the recognition of Photius, jurisdiction over Illyricum, the patrimonies of Calabria and Sicily, and the right to consecrate the bishop of Syracuse. Having failed to sway Byzantium, his only recourse was to excommunicate Photius.

Boris, the Bulgarian khan who had converted to Christianity in 864, was intent on erecting an autocephalous church. In pursuit of this goal, he began to negotiate with Rome for a patriarchate. Although Rome decided not to grant a patriarchate, it was willing to establish a Bulgarian archbishopric.

In an attempt to discredit Rome, Photius in 867 convoked a council in Constantinople and condemned the Latin mission in Bulgaria. He also anathematized the *filioque* doctrine, which he considered a heretical innovation of the Nicene creed.

In the same year, the new court favorite, Basil, assassinated the emperor Michael and with the support of the extremist party, seized the throne. Basil I forced Photius to resign and reinstated Ignatius. At the same time, Nicholas died, and the new pope, Hadrian II, who did not learn of the acts of 867 until Basil asked for a condemnation of Photius, called a council in June, 869, and excommunicated Photius.

A few months later, Basil convoked a church synod which he hoped would end the church factions and improve his relationship with Rome. Papal legates were sent to the Synod of 869–870 and they succeeded in reaffirming Photius' condemnation. However, Basil insisted that Rome was not superior to the other patriarchates and he gave Ignatius the power to absolve the supporters of Photius. Furthermore, the papacy's hopes in Bulgaria failed to materialize as the Synod gave Byzantium jurisdictional control over the Bulgarian Church.

Photius was able to secure a reconciliation with Ignatius and after the latter's death in 877 he was once again appointed patriarch. The Council of 879–880, attended and approved by Pope John VIII's legates, recognized the accession of Photius. Rome thus joined Byzantium in annulling the decisions of the Synod of 869. It was once thought that John, feeling himself fooled by Photius' unkept promises to relinquish control of the Bulgarian Church, excommunicated him, thus creating the "second Photian schism." Recent studies have shown, however, that the "second Photian schism" never occurred. Photius had indeed offered Bulgaria to Rome, but Boris would not permit Latin rule over the Bulgarian Church. John accepted his defeat and did not in fact excommunicate the patriarch. Photius remained in office until the accession of the emperor Leo VI in 886. He died five years later and was canonized by Constantinople in the 10th century.

BIBLIOGRAPHY: F. Dvornik, *The Photian Schism: History and Legend* (Cambridge, 1948); S. Runciman, *A History of the First Bulgarian Empire* (London, 1930).

**Photius** (c. 820–891). Patriarch of Constantinople (858–867 and 877–886). Born of a noble Greek family, Photius began his career as a professor of philosophy at the Imperial Academy in Constantinople, and in 855 he participated in an embassy to the Caliph al-Mutawakhil. As patriarch he became involved in a dispute with Rome that resulted in mutual excommunications (see PHOTIAN SCHISM).

Photius' best-known works are the *Myriobiblion,* an extract and criticism of 280 works, and the *Amphilochia,* a treatise on doctrinal problems.

**Piarists** (*or* Ordo Clericorum Regularium Pauperum Matris Dei Scholarum Piarum). A Roman Catholic order for the education of the young. It was founded in September, 1597, when a priest, Joseph Calasanza, opened the first free elementary school in the parish house of S. Dorotea in Trastevere (Rome). He and his associates received full papal approval in 1617, a fourth vow, of fidelity to youth work, being added to the usual three. From 1632 to 1669 the order was troubled by misunderstanding and intrigue, but it expanded rapidly thereafter, especially in the first half of the 18th century. After a split during the 19th century, it was reorganized under Pius X in 1904. The popular name "Piarists" was taken from the last word in the official Latin title of the order.

**Pico della Mirandola, Count Giovanni** (1463–1494). Italian Renaissance philosopher and scholar who believed that the key to all truth was a positive intellectual syncretism. A precocious child, he early in life mastered Latin, Greek, Hebrew, and Arabic. He studied at the Universities of Bologna, Ferrara, Padua, and Paris. He became convinced that many different philosophers had some share in common truth. He set out on the task of creating a kind of Hebraic-Christian-Platonic synthesis into which he wished also to blend certain elements of Arabic, Pythagorean, and Zoroastrian learning. In 1487, some of his ideas were declared heretical by the pope. After fleeing to France, Pico the next year returned to Florence where he became a friend of Marsilio Ficino and frequented the Platonic Academy. A religiously sensitive youth, he was deeply influenced near the end of his life by the pietistic preaching of Girolamo Savonarola. He was contemplating entrance into a monastery when he suddenly died at Florence in 1494 under mysterious circumstances. His most enduring contribution to Renaissance thought was his *Oration on the Dignity of Man*, written in 1486 but published posthumously. The *Oration*'s pronouncement that man is absolutely free and can make of himself what he will evoked condemnation from most contemporary orthodox theologians.

**Pidgeon, George Campbell** (1872–      ). First moderator of the United Church of Canada. Born at Grand Cascapedia, Quebec, and educated at Morrin College, McGill University (B.A., 1891), and Presbyterian College, Montreal (B.D., 1895; D.D., 1905), he was a minister at Montreal West Presbyterian Church (1894–1898), Streetsville, Ontario (1898–1903), and Victoria Church, West Toronto (1903–1909). From 1909 to 1915 he was professor of practical theology, Westminster Hall, Vancouver. In 1915 he became minister at Bloor Street Presbyterian Church, Toronto, and from 1925 to 1945 at Bloor Street United Church. He was an ardent supporter of church union in Canada, and in 1925 was made the first moderator of the United Church of Canada.

**Pierson, Arthur Tappan** (1837–1911). American evangelist. An effective and popular preacher of conservative theology associated with the Niagara Bible Conferences and several missionary promotions, he was also noted for his work in an institutional church program at Bethany Presbyterian Church in Philadelphia. Upon the basis of his theological study he became a Baptist in 1896, and later was identified with the personal holiness emphasis of the English Keswick Conferences.

**Pietism.** As a descriptive term, "Pietism" has had various meanings according to its various uses. It was first applied to a movement within German Lutheranism led by Philip Jacob Spener (1635–1705) and August Hermann Francke (1663–1727). Here it was largely a manifestation of reaction against orthodox formalism, against a Protestant Scholasticism influenced by the rationalism of the age, wherein the Christian life centered upon the passive acceptance of closely defined dogmas, the reception of the sacraments, and participation in the ordinances of the church. The vital personal relationship between God and man preached by Luther, productive of a vigorous spiritual life, seemed to be lost. In contrast, as Carl Mirbt has said, "Pietism emphasized the duty of striving after personal and individual religious independence and collaboration, and declared that religion is something altogether personal, that evangelical Christianity is present only when and in so far as it is manifested in Christian conduct." Considered as a reaction against orthodox formalism in which the individual spiritual experience is allowed to languish, Pietism may be located in that English Puritanism and Dutch precisianism which preceded the Lutheran movement of Spener and Francke, for in both of these movements personal conversion and practical holiness were stressed. But it is to be noted that Puritanism passed into its Pietist phase only after the Restoration Settlement in England in 1662, when it became quite apparent that a national program embodying the chief tenets of Puritanism was impossible and that the Christian could not depend upon the ecclesiastical structure for the cultivation of the spiritual life but had to turn inward and seek for such cultivation as an individual in concourse with like-minded individuals. Pietism was thus representative of the new status of Christianity in modern Europe, when it was no longer possible to Christianize civilization, maintain a uniform state church, or build a Christian culture. Attention turned toward the individual, toward internal appropriation of the Christian faith which was to be manifested in a largely individual expression of the Christian life. Pietism was an evidence of the adjustment of Christianity to the new situation and it found expression in many varying forms.

It is well known that Spener read the writings of the Puritans and was influenced by them as well as by the Dutch precisianists. In 1675 he published his *Pia desideria* in which he attacked the Lutheran state church system, recommended the reform of ministry and seminaries, and urged the formation of gatherings where laity might pray, study the Bible, and discuss Sunday sermons in order to deepen the individual spiritual life and to find release from the sinful world. Such meetings were called *collegia pietatis* (hence, "Pietism"). From this beginning, Pietism spread throughout Germany, in spite of virulent opposition, particularly from the Saxon clergy and the Saxon universities of Wittenberg and Leipzig. At the University of Halle, to which he went in 1698, Francke built up a center for the movement and added to German Pietism a zeal for missions that became one of the chief marks of Pietism and helped start the modern Protestant missionary outreach. With Francke's death, Pietism waned in Germany, but not without having fostered a more vital piety, improving education of the young and of ministerial candidates, opening a way for a more active participation of the laity in the life of the church, and inculcating a more serious study of the Bible.

There were many offshoots of the German Pietist movement, but the principal of these was the revival of Moravianism under Count Nicholas Ludwig von Zinzendorf (1700–1760), godson of Spener and student of Francke, who gathered a colony of followers about him at his estate. Here the dominant note was that of passion mysticism, expressed in sensuous and sentimental language. It was through the Moravians that John Wesley received Pietist influence, first on his journey to Georgia and later at the time of his "conversion" in London. English evangelicalism and Methodism are both considered Pietist in their reaction to the rationalism and deism rampant in 18th-century England.

BIBLIOGRAPHY: R. A. Knox, *Enthusiasm* (Oxford, 1951); E. Langton, *History of the Moravian Church* (London, 1956); J. T. McNeill, *Modern Christian Movements* (Philadelphia, 1954); P. J. Spener, *Pia desideria* (Philadelphia, 1964); F. E. Stoeffler, *The Rise of Evangelical Pietism* (Leiden, 1965); J. R. Weinlick, *Count Zinzendorf* (Nashville, 1956).

**Pighius, Albert** (c. 1490–1542). One of the leading theological spokesmen for the Roman Catholic position during the early years of the Reformation. Born in the Netherlands, he studied natural science as well as theology. In 1523 he was called to Rome by Adrian VI, who had been his teacher at Louvain. One of his first important tasks involved laying theological groundwork for dialogue with the Eastern Churches. On completion of this work, he devoted his efforts to the Protestant-Catholic controversy, participating in most of the major doctrinal discussions (including the Colloquy of Regensburg) and writing several works. Among them was a thorough defense of the papal system in which he argued that the pope could never become a heretic. He also wrote polemical treatises against Luther, Bucer, and Calvin. The positions that he developed in his works were highly influential at the Council of Trent, especially his concept of tradition; his teaching on justification and original sin, however, was rejected.

**Pilgrimage of Grace** (1536–1537). A popular religious insurrection, begun in Lincolnshire, that soon engulfed northern England. It was occasioned by Henry VIII's suppression of the monasteries (1536). Under Robert Aske some thirty to forty thousand commoners held off a royal army sent to quell the riot and won promises of royal conciliation. Renewed outbreaks of violence in 1537 and alleged evidence of foreign collusion led to the execution of Aske and an end of revolt.

**Pilgrimages.** Journeys to sacred places prompted by devotion or some other religious motive. By no means limited to Christians, pilgrimages have an important place in many religions. However, the pilgrimage has been present as part of the Christian life from the beginning. The places that pilgrims visited were predominantly those hallowed by Jesus Christ; by the 2d century, pilgrimages to the Holy Land were very popular. The graves of martyrs and of saints were also objects of pilgrimages. It was not long until the working of miracles became associated with certain of these places; thus an additional incentive for pilgrimage came about. The church encouraged pilgrimages and made them a part of the system of penance. Since travel was difficult in the ancient and medieval world, pilgrimages were undertaken with some sacrifice and hardship. The church counted pilgrimages as penance in proportion to the difficulty and the hallowed character of the shrine. The significance of the pilgrimage in Christianity is shown by the fact that the Crusades were undertaken in part in order to make the Holy Land free for pilgrims. Despite their popularity, however, pilgrimages have always had their critics, among them John Chrysostom, Jerome, and Erasmus.

**Pilgrims.** Originally, wanderers in a foreign land; later, devotees traveling to a shrine or holy place (see PILGRIMAGES). The English Separatists called themselves pilgrims while they were sojourning in Holland and when they sailed to the New World aboard the *Mayflower* in 1620. Also, the word "Pilgrims" as a proper noun continues to refer to the *Mayflower* passengers. The classic use of the term is in William Bradford's *History of Plymouth Plantation*.

**Pilgrim's Progress, The.** The most famous of all English allegories, written by John Bunyan. It takes the form of a dream in which Christian, learning that the city where he dwells will be burned, flees, having failed to persuade his family to go with him. Part I describes what he found on his journey—including the Slough of Despond, the Palace Beautiful, Vanity Fair, and finally, the Celestial City. Part II shows his wife, Christiana, making her pilgrimage with her children. This epic represents the culmination of the Puritan tradition which pictured life as a journey during which the soul must engage in constant warfare. Since Bunyan was a man of limited education, but had been thoroughly immersed in the Scripture, it is not surprising that his masterpiece is steeped in Biblical language. It has dramatic unity, charming simplicity, powerful characterizations, and demonstrates a native genius shaped by conviction and personal experience. Though the non-Puritan literary world was slow to realize its greatness, its popular success was immediate. First published in 1678, it went into ninety-two editions in the following century. In 1682, it was translated into French and Dutch, and since that time it has reached a total of 108 languages and dialects. It has probably been read by more people in English Christendom than any book other than the Bible.

**Pionius** (d. 250). Martyr during the Decian persecutions. He preserved the *Letter of the Smyrnaeans* (*The Martyrdom of Polycarp*) and is the alleged author of the partially preserved *Life of Polycarp* which is significant chiefly because it counters the testimony of Irenaeus (and, therefore, Tertullian and Eusebius) on the Asian residence of the apostle John and his relation to Polycarp. The *Acta Pionii*, mentioned by Eusebius, are reliable documents describing Pionius' arrest, trial, and martyrdom at Smyrna.

**Pirckheimer, Willibald** (1470–1530). Patrician and humanist. He studied Greek and law in Italy, and served Nuremberg, his hometown, from 1496 to 1523. For his strong endorsement of Luther, he was also named in the bull that threatened the Reformer with excommunication. Influenced by Erasmus, Pirckheimer turned against the Reformation after 1521 or 1522. He fought bitterly with Oecolampadius and the Nuremberg Reformers during his last years.

**Pisa, Council of** (1409). A council convoked to reconcile the divisions of the church. After 1378 the Western Church was split by the Great Schism. Both Rome and Avignon claimed to be the see of Peter and to be the residence of the pope. The clearest solution that offered itself was the conciliarist theory which had both a muted tradition and a contemporary representation of canonists and theologians, especially at the University of Paris. Yet the motif of the Council of Pisa was not predominantly the superiority of a council to a pope, but rather the urgent need for peace and unity in the church, in spite of the two opposing and vacillating popes. King Charles VI of France and the University of Paris gave their firm support to four cardinals of the Avignon allegiance who initiated an eventual union between the cardinals of Avignon and Rome. Together they issued a summons in 1408 to all princes and prelates to come to an ecumenical council at Pisa on March 25, 1409. There were sharp divisions among princes and clergy but the Council gained considerable support. The opposing popes, Gregory XII (Rome) and Benedict XIII (Avignon) were deposed and Alexander V was elected, but now there were three popes, and each had his own spiritual and temporal followers. Nevertheless, the groundwork was done for the more effective work of Constance.

**Pistis Sophia.** Four books that appear in the 4th-century parchment manuscript Codex Askewianus, now in the British Museum. All four books claim to contain postresurrection revelations by Jesus. The fourth, however, is a separate work and must belong to the first half of the 3d century, whereas the others belong to the second half. Only the first three of these Egyptian Gnostic books refer to Pistis Sophia, a spiritual being rescued from the demon Self-Will.

**Pistoia, Synod of** (1786). A synod convened by Bishop Ricci of Pistoia in support of the reforms of Leopold II of Tuscany. It exalted civil power, the national church, and the independence of bishops, against Rome. It also attempted practical reforms (reduction of Masses, use of the vernacular). Under pressure, Ricci was forced to resign in 1790, and recanted in 1795 after eighty-five articles were condemned by papal bull.

**Pitkin, Horace Tracy** (1869–1900). American Congregational missionary. Educated at Yale and Union Theological Seminary, he sailed in 1896, accompanied by his wife, for northern China where they were to be stationed at Paotingfu. On July 1, 1900, he was martyred during the Boxer rebellion. Before he died he asked that word be sent to his wife (who had just returned to America) of his desire that their little son take his place in China when he became twenty-five years of age.

**Pius I** (d. c. 154). Pope from c. 140. Almost nothing is known about Pius or his rule, although the *Liber pontificalis* gives Aquileia as his birthplace and the Muratorian fragment says he was the brother of Hermas, who wrote his *Shepherd* during this time. Marcion arrived at Rome during or before Pius' rule and became known as a disciple of Cerdo, who was teaching in Rome about 140. A generally rejected tradition lists Pius as a martyr.

**Pius II** (Enea Silvio de Piccolomini, 1405–1464). Pope from 1458. Born in Corsignano (later Pienza) near Siena, he came from the landed nobility who had lost position and power to the new bourgeois merchant class. He was attracted to Florence to study under Filelfo and was greatly influenced by humanism. He entered on an ecclesiastical and diplomatic career as secretary to Bishop Albergati on a mission to England and Scotland. He then went to Basel, where he served as secretary to the antipope Felix V. When offered a position under Emperor Frederick III, he accepted, later becoming poet laureate as well as cardinal. He also managed to reconcile himself with Eugenius IV. Elected to the papacy in 1458, he denounced his former conciliarist position and defended the supremacy of the pope in the bull *Execrabilis*. Disturbed by the fall of Constantinople, he preached a crusade against the Turks at the Congress of Mantua in 1459. On his way to save the East, he died at Ancona. He was the only pope to leave an autobiography, and his *Memoirs* are filled with ecclesiastical and secular intrigues, a zest for life, and a natural skepticism. He exalted the dignity of the papal office, asking Christians to "reject Enea and accept Pius."

**Pius VI** (Giovanni Angelo Braschi, 1717–1799). Pope from 1775. He rose in the ranks of the Roman Curia and achieved the cardinalate (1773). He was elected pontiff, reputedly with French support, after a four months' conclave. His lengthy reign brought him to grips with Febronianism and Josephinism in the Germanys, revolution in France, and invasion in the Italys. Regarded as a friend of the recently dissolved Jesuit Society, Pius was badgered by Hapsburg schemes in Austria and Tuscany for national churches and monastic secularizations. He reluctantly visited Joseph II at Vienna (1782) to seek redress. Instead of benefits, embarrassments such as the Synod of Pistoia and the Ems Points followed. The French Revolution burst in 1789, the papal enclave of Avignon revolted, the Civil Constitution of the Clergy brought schism, confiscations took place. Pius VI protested to no avail. A diplomatic incident, the Bassville assassination (1793), warned of more trouble with France. General Napoleon Bona-

parte invaded Italy, defeated papal troops, and forced indemnities in cash and art objects on the Papal States (1797). The next year saw Rome itself occupied by French troops. A republic was proclaimed, and the pope arrested. Transported, Pius VI died at Valence, France, leaving papal prestige at the lowest point since the 11th century.

**Pius VII** (Barnaba—Gregorio—Chiaramonti, 1740–1823). Pope from 1800. A bishop of Imola and a Benedictine, he was elected by the conclave at Venice in 1800. Obliged to contest mightily with Napoleon and modestly with Metternich, he suffered both humiliation and adversity. He negotiated the French and Cisalpine Concordats (1801, 1803), assisted at Napoleon's coronation, (1804), and found his States occupied (1808) after he had objected to Napoleon's appointment of bishops, Jerome Bonaparte's divorce, and the Continental System. Arrested in the Quirinal palace with his aide, Cardinal Pacca, he excommunicated Napoleon before being dragged to exile at Savona and Fontainebleau. He resisted the emperor's divorce and remarriage, signed and then disavowed the Concordat of Fontainebleau (1813). Returning to Rome (1814), he restored the Jesuit Society, created an apostolic vicarate in Lutheran Sweden, regained his Italian states, and supported Cardinal Consalvi in reforming the administration. A humanitarian, Pius VII asked for lenient treatment of Napoleon on St. Helena, and he dealt mildly with the Carbonari and other secret political sects. Metternich, however, was willing to violate church territory to put down rebellion at Naples (1821). With Consalvi's help, Pius VII lifted papal prestige out of the nadir in which he had inherited it.

**Pius IX** (Giovanni Maria Mastai-Ferretti, 1792–1878). Pope from 1846. After studying at the Collegium Romanum, he was made priest in 1818 and served in Rome and Chile. He was appointed archbishop of Spoleto in 1827, bishop of Imola in 1832, created cardinal in 1840, and elected pope in 1846. Upon his accession he began much-needed reforms in administration. Beginning as a political liberal, he aided national unity but later found difficulty with the revolutionary party. After a two-year exile he returned and opposed liberalism in church and state, claiming for the church all control of science, culture, and education. He eventually lost the Papal States and after the seizure of Rome by Victor Emmanuel in 1870 he was virtually deprived of temporal sovereignty by the Law of Guarantees of 1871.

However, his administration carried out a number of important achievements. Many new dioceses were established in the United States of America; the hierarchies of England and Holland were reestablished. He conserved the traditional beliefs of Catholicism with the issue of the Syllabus of Errors in 1864, condemning eighty contemporary philosophical and theological propositions. His declaration of the dogma of the Immaculate Conception in 1854 greatly stimulated Catholic devotion. The greatest event of his reign was the definition of papal infallibility by the Vatican Council of 1869–1870.

**Pius X** (Giuseppe Melchiorre Sarto, 1835–1914). Pope from 1903. He had risen from parish priest to cardinal patriarch of Venice by 1893. Of great moral rectitude, he was interested in doctrine, the priesthood, and the Congress movement. Coming after Leo XIII, he had as his motto "to restore all things in Christ." Pius X dealt with French and Italian anticlericalism, condemned Modernism (1907), reorganized the Curia, and ordered canon law. He was canonized in 1954.

**Pius XI** (Achille Ratti, 1857–1939). Pope from 1922. An Italian scholar and diplomat, he served as nuncio to Poland and archbishop of Milan. Elected pope to succeed Benedict XV, he urged world peace, patronized education and the sacred arts, and supported missions, hoping to create an indigenous clergy in Asian and African lands. The 1929 Lateran Pacts with Italy solved the Roman question. His *Quadragesimo anno* (1931) updated Leo XIII's labor encyclical *Rerum novarum.*

**Pius XII** (Eugenio Pacelli, 1876–1958). Pope from 1939. A Roman trained in diplomacy, he rose to be papal secretary of state and succeeded Pius XI. In global war he sought peace, relief for suffering, protection of the church and faithful, and adaptation to a world with fifty-three million Roman Catholics in Iron Curtain lands. He negotiated the favorable Portugal Concordat of 1940 with Premier Salazar. He created the first Chinese and Indian cardinals, issued the declaration of the Assumption to heaven of the Virgin Mary, and canonized Pius X.

**Planck, Gottleib Jakob** (1751–1833). German Lutheran church historian. Born at Nurtingen and educated at Tübingen, he was professor of church history at Göttingen (1774). His greatest work was on the Protestant Reformation and the rise of Lutheranism. He considered himself a "rational supernaturalist"; he accepted the divinity of Christ, the reasonableness of Christianity, and the comprehensibility of divine revelation.

**Plan of Union.** A plan of accommodation adopted between certain denominations in America early in the 19th century to help supply the pulpits of pioneer congregations without a minister of their own denomination. Following the close of the Revolutionary War in America, there began a considerable emigration into western New York and the old Northwest Territory. Many of these pioneers were of Presbyterian or Congregational background and lacked pastoral care. In view of this, and of the similarity between these denominations and of some previous cooperation between them, the Presbyterian General Assembly and the Congregational General Association of Connecticut adopted in 1801 a Plan of Union, which was in turn adopted by the other New England Congregational Associations. Accordingly, in the new settlements of the West there was to be a spirit of accommodation so that the members of these denominations in establishing a congregation could call a minister of either denomination. He and the members of the congregation were to retain their own individual denominational affiliation, and were to be disciplined nearly in accordance with their own denominational procedures. With some later modifications, this course was widely adopted, though often resulting in the establishment of Presbyterian congregations. The Old School Presbyterians denounced interdenominational cooperation in 1837 because they felt that it permitted a liberalized theology and quasi-Congregational polity to develop within Presbyterianism (see New School and Old School Presbyterians). Cooperation was continued among the New School Presbyterians and the Congregationalists until the latter abandoned the arrangement in 1852. In both cases a stricter denominational loyalty gained the ascendancy.

**Plantin, Christophe** (c. 1520–1589). Noted French printer and founder of the important Plantin publishing house in Antwerp in the mid-16th century. Plantin was the first and greatest industrial printer in Europe in his century. At the height of his career he operated 22 presses, and over a period of thirty-four years printed more than 1,500 different works. Plantin's Roman Catholic faith did not deter him from publishing for both sides during the Reformation.

**Platina** (Bartolommeo de' Sacchi) (1421–1481). Italian humanist and historian. He was a native of Piadena. A papal official under Pius II, he was arrested and imprisoned by Pius' successor, Paul II, on the charge of paganism. Restored to favor under Sixtus IV, he was made librarian of the Vatican, and while there, produced his widely read *Lives of the Popes* (1479). He also wrote on numerous theoretical and practical subjects.

**Plato** (c. 427–347 B.C.). Athenian philosopher, friend and pupil of Socrates, whose ethical teachings are preserved in his early dialogues. In 387 B.C., Plato founded the Academy, which was to remain a center of philosophical activity until A.D. 529.

Four interrelated aspects of Plato's philosophy were to be particularly influential for the development of Christian thought: the theory of ideas (in the *Phaedo, Philebus,* and the middle books of the *Republic*); the concept of Eros (in the *Phaedrus* and *Symposium*); the teachings on the immortality of the soul (in the *Phaedo* and *Timaeus*); and the cosmology (in the *Timaeus*).

According to the doctrine of ideas, the essence of reality is incorporeal and inaccessible to the senses. It is a higher and purer realm, of which the phenomenal world is merely a shadow, an inferior copy. True reality is unchangeable, immaterial form or idea, it is the realm of being and unity. To attain true knowledge the rational soul must direct itself beyond material sensuous becoming to contemplation of these transcendent ideas, all of which are encompassed in the idea of the good, the Godhead.

Philosophy is knowledge of these immutable ideas. Since the soul can conceive of them, it must be related in some way to the ideal realm. For Plato, the soul occupies an intermediate position between being and becoming. The impulse to philosophy arises when the soul recognizes the imperfect copies of ideas present in material reality, and with longing love (Eros) strives to transcend the corporeal and reach the purity of ideal forms. The soul does evil when it allows its bestial, sensuous inclinations to deform its higher nature and deflect its striving for ideal purity and truth. The soul is also able, by goodwill and right reason, to rise above its material nature to contemplation of the good, but only temporarily. Complete identification with the world of ideas and recompense for a moral life are achieved when the immortal rational soul has been freed from the bonds of sensuous existence by death.

According to Plato's cosmology, the Demiurge, or God, created the world from nothingness, using the idea of the good as pattern and cause. Plato's emphasis upon the good as both the essence of God and the cause and purpose of all creation was attractive to Christian thinkers. The mythical account of creation in the *Timaeus* was easily harmonized with Genesis, as was the teleological motif with Christian doctrine.

The influence of these four aspects of Plato's philosophy, in perpetually different combinations and interpretations, can be seen in the history of Christian thought from the Gnostics through the 17th-century Cambridge theologians. (See PLATONISM; NEOPLATONISM; RENAISSANCE PLATONISM.)

**Platon** (Peter Levshin, 1737–1812). Russian Orthodox churchman and theologian. Onetime tutor of Czar Paul I, he served as metropolitan of Moscow (1787–1811). His efforts to protect the church bore fruit when he persuaded Paul I to reopen monasteries suppressed under Catherine II. His catechisms, in which he reflects the influence of the Lutheran Quenstedt, were the chief theological textbooks of the Russian Church for several decades. Platon also produced a history of the Russian Church up to 1720 (1805).

**Platonism.** The protean phenomenon called Platonism is seldom or never concerned with the pure, original philosophy of Plato himself. Rather, it is the result of a continual process of accretion and partial synthesis with other intellectual traditions. After Plato's death in 347 B.C. the Academy increasingly emphasized the ethical aspects of his thought at the expense of the epistemological. By the 2d and 1st centuries B.C., Platonism in the West was to be found most frequently in an eclectic blend with Stoicism, as in the thought of Antiochus of Ascalon and Posidonius. It was in this mixed and fragmentary form that Platonism was infused into Latin literature, and notably through some discussion of it in Cicero, was partially transmitted to the Latin Middle Ages. In the East, Platonism was mixed with various Oriental religious cults. It was these diverse strains of Platonism that were tapped and utilized by early Christian thinkers.

By the time of the birth of Christ the vital center of Platonic studies was Alexandria. Ancient philosophy was turning away from the rationalism and self-sufficiency of the Wise Man, and toward the desire for a saving faith, with emphasis upon a higher otherworldly power to give man blessedness. There were two different strains of this mystical religious Platonism, the Neo-Pythagorean and the Judaic.

The Neo-Pythagorean philosophy was a mixture of monotheism, mathematics, and Oriental demonology associated with Apollonius of Tyana in the 1st and Numenius in the 2d century. They brought about various changes of emphasis in Platonic philosophy which were later important for Christian thought. Ideas were described as archetypes in the divine mind rather than the independent metaphysical entities they had been for Plato. The Neo-Pythagoreans claimed authority for their philosophy on the basis of divine revelation granted to Pythagoras.

The Judaic strain of Platonism was associated with Philo of Alexandria (1st century). Philo's mixture of Judaic religion and Platonic philosophy made Platonism seem the natural ally of Christianity. He taught that God was absolutely transcendent and could be described only by the negation of all earthly attributes. God touches the world through various potencies emanating from him; these Philo equated with Platonic ideas and the angels of the Old Testament. The Logos was described as the second God, the unity of ideas active upon matter in creation. Philo taught that the spirit of man could be released from its confinement in the body only with divine help, and would proceed through a graded series of stages to the highest blessedness—the full surrender of individuality in ecstatic absorption in divine Being. Philo was able to harmonize Judaic religion with Platonic philosophy by insisting that the revelations of God in the Old Testament must be interpreted allegorically to gain their true meaning. Thus Plato was portrayed as the greatest of saints and the ally of Moses.

In addition to these two primary strains of Platonic thought, there were a number of even more eclectic Platonists in the 1st and 2d centuries. Included among these are the group of pagan philosophers who wrote the corpus attributed to Hermes Trismegistus. This *Corpus Hermeticum* combined mystical theology with magic and astrology and was transmitted to the West primarily through the mediation of Arabic thinkers. Hermetic philosophy was to become very important in the Platonic syntheses of the Renaissance. (See RENAISSANCE PLATONISM.)

Gnosticism may also be included in the efflorescence of salvation religions with a Platonic flavor at this time. Gnosticism includes demonology and the teachings of Oriental salvation cults in addition to Neo-Pythagorean and Philonic teachings. Its emphasis upon separate principles of light and darkness governing the world is detectable in the Gospel of John. However, Christian thinkers were usually explicit in their denunciation of this dualism, as can be seen from the attacks by Irenaeus, Clement, Origen, and extending all the way up to Augustine's polemic against the Manichaeans.

By the 2d century the tremendous flood of salvation religions provoked the formation of a theology for Christianity, in order to define the faith and defend it from the proud scorn of pagan philosophers. Philo had shown Platonic categories to be in harmony with the Old Testament, so it was mainly to Platonism that early Christian thinkers turned to find the philosophical tools for their defense.

The 2d-century defenders of Christianity, Justin Martyr and Athenagoras, used a number of notions originating with the Alexandrian Platonists, including the belief that divine illumination had been granted to Pythagoras, Socrates, and Plato, or at least that these pagan thinkers had been acquainted with the Mosaic writings. They identified the Biblical account of the Creation with the Logos operating according to Neo-Pythagorean categories. But only with Jesus was the Logos perfectly and completely revealed and become man to redeem humanity fallen in sin. This pattern of defense of Christianity by means of Platonic philosophy received further impetus with the philosophical systematizations of Plotinus and Origen in the 3d century. (See NEOPLATONISM.)

**Plenitudo Potestatis.** A phrase expressing the papal claim to authority in temporal as well as spiritual matters. Influenced by the renewed study of Roman law after the 11th century, both canonist and civilian lawyers prepared cases delineating the "plenitude of power" possessed by their respective masters, the pope and the emperor. Seen earlier in such documents as the *Dictatus papae* (1075) during the pontificate of Gregory VII, the papal assertions of their prerogatives of power are best expressed in the thought of Innocent III (1198–1216).

**Pliny the Younger** (Gaius Plinius Caecilius Secundus) (62–113). A nephew of the naturalist Pliny the Elder and imperial Roman commissioner in the province of Bithynia and Pontus (111–112). Book X of his *Letters* is an important source for Roman administration, comprising his official correspondence with the emperor Trajan. In *Letter* 96 he reports on the trial of the Christians; Trajan's reply, *Letter* 97, indicates the basis of the spasmodic 2d-century persecutions.

**Plotinus** (c. 205–270). Greek philosopher, pupil of Ammonius Saccas in Alexandria, and reputed founder of Neoplatonism. Although concerned with the doctrine of the One, his chief preoccupation was with the question of how and by means of what intermediate emanations the One manifested itself, giving rise to the Many. His works, consisting of fifty-four tractates, were edited by his pupil Porphyry and arranged into six groups of nine each, from which comes the name *Enneads*.

**Pluetschau, Heinrich** (1678–1747). German Lutheran pastor and pioneer missionary in India. Born at Wesenberg, he was educated at Halle and was a teacher in the Francke institutions for several years. In 1705 he left for missionary service in India. In 1711 he returned to Germany and accepted a pastorate at Beidenfleth in Holstein, where he worked until his death.

**Plunkett, Oliver** (1629–1681). Roman Catholic archbishop and primate of Ireland. He was educated in Dublin and in 1645 left for Rome. He was ordained in 1654 and deputed by the Irish bishops as their representative in Rome, where he was a professor of theology at the College of Propaganda. In 1669 he was appointed to the Roman Catholic primatial see of Armagh. There he worked untiringly to improve education and administer the sacraments of the Roman Church in spite of penal laws. Renewed persecution in 1673 drove him into hiding. Arrested in 1679, he was taken to London for trial and executed in 1681, the last of the Tyburn martyrs.

**Plymouth Brethren.** A body of Christians founded in Ireland (1827–1828) by J. N. Darby (1800–1882), a former priest of the Church of England, and first established in England at Plymouth in 1830. Their teaching is a combination of Pietism and Calvinism and often contains millenarian emphases. They possess no organized ministry, are Puritans in morals and conservative in their Biblical interpretation, and they emphasize the autonomy of the local body.

**Pobedonostsev, Konstantine P.** (1827–1907). Ultraconservative Russian statesman, political theorist, and legal scholar. He served as tutor to Emperors Alexander III and Nicholas II and as high procurator of the Holy Synod from 1880 to 1905. Denouncing constitutions, free press, democracy, and religious liberty, he was an advocate of the Russification of the empire's multinational and multireligious population.

**Poetry, Medieval.** It was the good fortune of medieval poetry to be the heir of two rich poetic traditions, the classical and the Teutonic. Poetry in the last years of the classical period had not undergone as great a decline as had Latin prose. Thus medieval poetry had good classical models to follow; however, its own genius was expressed as it became thoroughly Christianized and was used in the service of the church. By about the 10th century, Latin poetry had become less dependent upon classical models and thus more open to poetic traditions of the North. Especially important was Anglo-Saxon poetry, which is represented in the great epic *Beowulf* and in the Scandinavian poetry of the Eddas. It was at this point that the two traditions came to influence each other profoundly. Vernacular poetry came into its own in the 11th century with the troubadours and the trouvères; it was continued by the minnesingers and Meistersingers. Latin verse tended to change from quantitative to accentual measures, but it continued to be important as is shown by such great religious poems as the "Stabat Mater" and the "Dies Irae." That Latin poetry was influenced by the secular spirit, however, is shown in goliardic verse. By the 14th century, poetry in the vernacular had gained the predominance that has continued to the present time.

**Poiret, Pierre** (1646–1719). French Protestant pastor and mystic. He edited the mystical works of Antoinette Bourignon and Mme. Guyon and found Cartesian philosophy relevant to his own mysticism. His most valuable work, *Bibliotheca mysticorum selecta* (1708), reveals a widespread acquaintance with medieval and modern mystics as well as with minor French mystics and Pietists. His writings won respect for mysticism and forced theologians to take account of it. His most famous disciple was Gerhard Tersteegen.

**Poissy, Colloquy of** (1561). A conference between the French Catholic bishops and the Reformed ministers to discuss their differences. The Reform had progressed in France by 1561 to the point where Catherine de' Medici felt that it was wise to call a meeting between them. Beza headed the Protestant delegation and met the Jesuit general Laynez. Little was settled, but the discussion did make way for the Edict of January, 1562, which allowed some recognition and freedom to the French Reformed.

**Poland, Conversion of.** The beginning of the conversion of the Poles dates from the baptism of Prince Mieszko I in 966 by the chaplain of his Catholic wife. Under his son, Boleslav I, the Polish Church was organized, free from German control, with a metropolitan see and national shrine established at Gnesen, at one time the repository of the relics of Adalbert. Under Boleslav III (d. 1138) the Pomeranians were converted (see LIVONIA, CONVERSION OF).

**Pole, Reginald** (1500–1558). English Roman Catholic prelate. The third son of Sir

Richard Pole and Margaret, niece of Edward IV, he was educated at Oxford. In 1521, he left to study in Padua with the help of Henry VIII. Foreseeing the difficulties of Henry's divorce, Pole asked to study in Paris, whereupon Henry desired him to bring the university to his side, offering Pole the see of either York or Winchester. When Pole continued to resist the divorce, Henry allowed him to return to Padua. On the martyrdom of John Fisher and Sir Thomas More, Pole wrote a treatise (*Pro ecclesiasticae unitatis defensione*) in which he vehemently attacked the king. Henry sent for Pole, who refused to come, obeying instead the summons of Paul III to Rome. For this, the Pole family in England was imprisoned and his mother executed. Assassins were sent after Pole in Viterbo, from where, as vicar, he ruled the Patrimony of St. Peter. In 1542, Pole was one of three legates presiding over the Council of Trent. On the death of Paul III in 1549, Pole had at one point nearly two thirds of the cardinals' votes, but the conclave ended with the election of Cardinal del Monte as Pope Julius III, who appointed Pole legate to England in 1553 when Edward VI died and was succeeded by the Roman Catholic Mary. In 1557, Pole was ordained priest and then consecrated archbishop to replace Cranmer in Canterbury. He died in 1558, still involved in the political embroilments of Rome, the Empire, and England.

**Polish Concordat.** An agreement between the government of restored Poland and the Vatican, signed on Feb. 1, 1925. This agreement stipulated that Poland was to possess five metropolitan sees (Gniezno-Poznań, Warsaw, Wilno, Kraków, Lwów). These metropolitan areas included sixteen suffragan sees. The Concordat provided for a metropolitan Uniate see at Lwów with two suffragan sees, and an Armenian rite Uniate metropolitan see at Lwów. In 1934 a Uniate Apostolic Administration was established. It further provided that the higher clergy were to be appointed by Rome, but the government had the right of confirmation through the president of the Republic. On the local level, bishops were to appoint priests in consultation with the government. The Concordat freed the clergy from military service, but in case of crimes they were subject to the civil courts. The free city of Danzig was not included in the Concordat agreements. A decree of the ministerial council in 1945 declared this Concordat null and void because the Vatican had allegedly supported Germany during World War II. Relations between the government and the church were determined at first by certain articles of the 1921 constitution; and in the 1952 constitution the separation of church and state was decreed. This decree (February, 1953), regulating the appointment of clergy, and the *modus vivendi* in 1956 provide the framework for church-state relations in communist Poland today.

**Polish National Catholic Church of America.** A group that separated from the Roman Catholic Church in 1904 in a dispute over issues including clerical power and Polish nationalism. Led by Francis Hodur, who was later consecrated bishop by Dutch Old Catholics, the church retained a Roman position on many matters but did allow for more lay activity, the use of Polish in services, and married clergy. Its headquarters are in Scranton, Pa., and membership is 282,411, with 144 ordained clergy and 162 places of worship.

**Politiques, Les.** A French political party during the Wars of Religion in France (1562–1598) which advocated religious toleration, especially after the Bartholomew's Day Massacre (1572). Opposed to religious fanaticism, these moderate Catholics thought first of the good of the nation. They made an alliance with the Huguenots, and subsequently many of them supported Henry IV.

**Polycarp** (c. 69–c. 155). Bishop of Smyrna and martyr during the reign of Marcus Aurelius. According to Irenaeus, Polycarp was a disciple of John, the disciple of Jesus, though in his extant letter to the Philippian church there is no definite reference to John or any of his writings. Polycarp certainly knew the letter of Clement of Rome and was personally acquainted with Ignatius, Marcion, Anicetus of Rome, and Irenaeus. He was therefore a personal witness to the tradition of the church's teaching during most of his long life (according to his martyr acts, he had "served Christ" for eighty-six years) and his one writing reflects a conservative theology close to that of the pastoral epistles (which, according to a modern theory, he may have written in Paul's name, though it is unlikely).

His letter, largely preserved only in a Latin translation, seems to speak of Ignatius as both dead and alive, and scholars have therefore suggested that it is not one but two letters, especially since there are no references to Marcion (a generation later) in it. Because of the way it has been transmitted, however, we cannot be sure that (1) the Latin correctly renders the lost Greek and (2) that the letter is free from interpolations. The martyr acts (sometime between 155 and 167) may also have been interpolated, especially by someone who was impressed by the resemblance of Polycarp's suffering to that of Jesus.

**Polycrates** (2d century). Bishop of Ephesus c. 190 and leader of the Asia Minor Church in its struggle to preserve autonomous rites (see QUARTODECIMANS) in the face of Roman insistence upon uniform Easter observance. Polycrates appealed to local apostolic and episcopal tradition, but apparently was excommunicated by Victor. Eusebius does not say how the conflict was resolved; perhaps the successor of Polycrates was less insistent upon autonomy.

**Pombal, Sebastião José de Carvalho e Mello** (1699–1782). Portuguese statesman and actual ruler of Portugal during the reign of Joseph I (1750–1777). A man of the Enlightenment, he increased royal power by attacking the independence of the Roman Catholic Church. In 1759 he expelled the Jesuits from all Portuguese territory, dissolved their organizations and expropriated their possessions. The attacks upon the Jesuits were followed in France, Spain, Austria, and Italy.

**Pomponazzi, Pietro** (1462–1525). Philosopher of the Italian Renaissance, sometimes called "the last Scholastic and the first man of the Enlightenment." Born at Mantua, he studied at Padua, then taught there, and later at Ferrara and Bologna. Pomponazzi was the leader of a new generation of Aristotelians trained in an intellectual atmosphere impregnated with humanistic ideals. He and his followers turned from the impersonality of Averroism, with its teaching that only the intellect of man was immortal, to a consideration of divinity and immortality in relation to the individual soul. Pomponazzi's thinking on the problem of relating Aristotle to the Renaissance crystallized in his *On the Immortality of the Soul* and an *Apologia,* published in 1516 and 1517 respectively. On philosophical grounds, he argued that the soul cannot function without the body, therefore cannot be immortal. However, in order to save himself from trouble with the church, he accepted immortality as an article of faith but refused to teach it as a philosophy. To the argument that immortality was necessary in order to ensure ethical conduct he answered with a largely Stoic philosophy emphasizing a purely naturalistic morality: virtue was its own reward and vice its own punishment. Thus Pomponazzi helped prepare the way for a purely secular ethic independent of Christian dogma.

**Pontificalia.** Garments and ornaments proper to a prelate celebrating Mass. They consist of buskins (silk leg coverings), sandals, gloves, dalmatic, tunicle, ring, and pectoral cross. A bishop adds the miter and pastoral staff. He may celebrate in pontificals at any time, but lesser prelates may do so only with permission.

**Pontoppidan, Erik** (1698–1764). Danish-Norwegian Lutheran bishop and theologian. He became a royal chaplain in 1735 and a theological professor at Copenhagen in 1738. In 1745 he went to Norway as bishop of Bergen. Ten years later he was appointed chancellor of the university in Copenhagen. As a Pietist, he exerted a profound influence in Denmark and especially in Norway through his *Explanation* of Luther's Catechism called *Truth Unto Godliness* (1737) and his pastoral textbook *Collegium pastorale practicum* (1757), both of which were widely used also by Norwegian Lutherans in America. In 1842 his *Explanation,* often called "the layman's dogmatics," was translated into English.

**Poor Clares** (*or* the Second Order of St. Francis). An order of strictly enclosed, contemplative nuns founded by Francis and Clare c. 1212. The first rule was written by Cardinal Ugolino (Pope Gregory IX) in 1219, being replaced by two subsequent rules, the last in 1253 based upon Francis' Rule. In 1263 an abridged rule was permitted by Urban IV, but the stricter observance was restored in 1410 by Colette.

**Pope.** See PAPACY, DEVELOPMENT OF.

**Popish Plot.** See OATES, TITUS.

**Popovtsi.** See OLD BELIEVERS.

**Pornocracy.** The period of influence in Rome of Theodora, wife of a Roman senator, and her daughters Marozia and Theodora. From the elder Theodora's influence in the election of Sergius III in 904, until Alberic, the son of Marozia, began to rule Italy in 932, the popes and secular rulers of Italy were the husbands, sons, or lovers of these three women. The term was first used in 1704 by the Protestant historian V. E. Loescher.

**Porphyry** (c. 232–c. 304). Neoplatonic philosopher and a bitter critic of Gnostic sects (whose books he regarded as forgeries) and of Christians. His fifteen books against the latter survive only in fragments, since they were proscribed under Christian emperors. However, they contained his view (as reported by Jerome) that Daniel was written under Antiochus Epiphanes and his criticisms of the Gospels and the apostles, as well as attacks on contemporary Christian leaders.

**Port-Royal.** A convent of the Cistercian nuns founded in 1204. It acquired fame as the center of the Jansenist controversy and after 1661, when the nuns refused to subscribe to the papal condemnation of Jansenism, its inhabitants were systematically persecuted. In 1679, the convent was forbidden to accept novices; in 1709, after the nuns refused to condemn Jansenism without "mental reservations," the convent was closed. Its buildings were subsequently destroyed and its site desecrated.

**Portugal Concordat** (May 7, 1940). An agreement by Premier Salazar and Pius XII guaranteeing the legal personality of the church in Portugal: free exercise of its power, liberty of communication with the Vatican. Clerics were exempted from bearing arms, permitted to maintain parochial schools and seminaries, and to seek government grants. Religion was to be taught in the public schools and church marriage recognized. A missions accord was signed also.

**Postulant** (from Latin *postulare*, "desire"). A candidate for a religious order who is in a period of trial prior to entering the novitiate, the formal training period (see NOVICE). The term of the postulant, varying in the different orders, is only a few months. The name "postulant" is also used in some Protestant churches for a candidate for ordination (e.g., the Protestant Episcopal Church).

**Potestas Directa.** A theory, emerging during the period from the 11th to the 13th century in the church vs. the empire struggle, whereby all power, secular or spiritual, was said to be granted directly to the pope as vicar of Christ, who in turn bestowed the secular power on emperors and kings. Having its origin in the reform sparked by the investiture controversy (the *Dictatus papae* of Gregory VII summarized his doctrine of the primacy of the papacy), taking shape under Hugo of St.-Victor, Bernard of Clairvaux, and Pope Gregory IX, and achieving its extreme expression in Augustinus Triumphus (d. 1328), this theory implied that emperors published laws only by papal authority and could be deposed for cause by popes. Marsilius of Padua in his *Defensor pacis* completely reversed the claim attributing *potestas directa* to the secular ruler. The theory of *potestas indirecta* advanced in slightly different forms by Robert Bellarmine and Francisco Suárez, defending the pope's spiritual supremacy but denying him interference in secular matters except to protect the church's rights, had its origins in Aristotelianism and was articulated by Thomas Aquinas. In modified form, the latter undergirds most Roman Catholic theory on church-state relations.

**Potter, Alonzo** (1800–1865). Bishop of the Protestant Episcopal Church. He was noted for the statesmanship of his episcopate in Pennsylvania (1845–1865). While broadminded and tolerant toward those of differing opinions, he welded the widely divided diocese into a whole. He also combined a successful professorial experience with administrative ability in developing and promoting educational ventures, youth societies, and a hospital.

**Potter, Horatio** (1802–1887), and **Henry Codman** (1835–1908). Episcopalian bishops. Horatio, who was the brother of Alonzo Potter, was bishop of New York (1854–1887) and led in reuniting his church after the Civil War. His rapidly growing diocese was taken over by his nephew, Alonzo's son Henry (1883–1908), who is remembered for founding the Advent Mission, an Episcopal form of revivalism, and for starting work on the St. John the Divine Cathedral in New York City.

*Praedestinatus.* An anonymous 5th-century treatise (possibly written at Rome while Sixtus III was pope, 432–440) evidently composed by a semi-Pelagian to caricature Augustinian predestination. It comprised three books: the first setting forth the doctrine of predestination (largely a paraphrased reproduction of Augustine's *De haeresibus*); the second taking the form of a defense of Augustine's doctrine; and the third refuting, and showing the error of, the second.

**Praemunire, Statutes of.** Legislation enacted in England during the 14th century (1363, 1365, 1393), the purpose of which was to curb papal authority in England. When Provisors (1351), a statute prohibiting papal disposition of English benefices, was passed, it necessitated Praemunire, whereby a person who took any cause of which cognizance belonged to the king's court out of the realm for judgment would be given two months to reply for his contempt. Originally applied to the writ served on the accused, the term came to apply to the offenses prosecuted under such writs as well as the penalties incurred, and finally to the statutes as a whole. In 1365, Provisors was confirmed and suits in papal courts to secure benefices were specifically brought under Praemunire. In 1390, Provisors was widely extended and three years later Praemunire similarly broadened so that even papal bulls could be promulgated in England only with royal permission. The statute has been invoked frequently, the most significant cases being Henry VIII's employment of it against Wolsey for using his legatine authority and subsequently against the entire body of English clergy to secure their submission to the royal supremacy. It was last invoked in the Marriage Act of 1772, which requires the sovereign's approval in royal marriages, except in certain instances, under penalty of this law.

**Pragmatic Sanction of Bourges** (1438). An edict of the French king Charles VII in 1438 which supported the reforms of the Council of Basel. By this action Charles gave support to the supremacy of councils over popes and strengthened the national church of France, particularly in the matter of filling vacant benefices without papal permission. Eugenius IV, who had suspended the Council, questioned the authority of a national council over internal church matters and demanded the support of the French bishops. The question was not settled until 1516, when the edict was finally annulled.

**Praxeas** (2d–3d century). An Asiatic Christian who appeared in Rome c. 190 and later went to Africa. He gained the support of the Roman bishops Victor, Zephyrinus, and Callistus in opposing Montanism, and is usually identified as the first prominent teacher of modalistic monarchianism, or Patripassianism. Although Tertullian, in his *Against Praxeas* (our only source for the teachings of Praxeas), says Praxeas "crucified the Father," there is some question about identifying him as a strict Patripassianist.

**Prayer Book Revisions.** First produced in 1549, the Book of Common Prayer was given a strong Calvinist flavor in a revision of 1552. Repealed by Mary in 1553, Elizabeth I reestablished it in 1559. This Book was a compromise between the 1549 and 1552 versions. Dropped once again during the Interregnum, it was reintroduced with changes in 1662. This Prayer Book is still in use today, though an act of 1872 allows flexibility.

**Preaching of Peter.** Two documents bear this name: one underlies the Pseudo-Clementine literature (see CLEMENTINE LITERATURE), the other is cited by Clement of Alexandria and mentioned by Origen. According to Clement, it contrasts the false ways in which pagans and Jews worship the one God with the true way in which Christians worship him. It is probably a 2d-century pseudonymous apology.

**Prebendary.** A clergyman receiving an income from a benefice in a cathedral or collegiate church. When the common life declined among canons, the endowment was divided into portions (prebends) for each canon, who received the income from this portion. In the Middle Ages, teachers, chantry priests, and even choir singers were granted prebends. Although modern chapters may not grant prebends, the canons are still known as prebendaries.

**Precarium.** A grant of land made free of rent but reclaimable at any time by the owner. In the Middle Ages the term referred to church-held land which could not be alienated but could be let for cultivation by someone else. Precaria were granted only for a specified term, but the church frequently found it difficult to recover these lands when the grant expired. The grant was also used as a legal cover for the seizure of church land.

**Precentor.** The canon responsible for the direction of the choral service in a cathedral chapter. He ranked next to the dean and frequently, because of other duties, delegated his musical tasks to a vicar known as a succentor. In some English cathedrals, the precentor is only a minor canon with no additional duties and no vote in the chapter.

**Preces Privatae.** A book of private Latin devotions issued, with the approval of Elizabeth I, in 1564. Its contents are drawn partly from the Book of Common Prayer, and partly from medieval devotional manuals, especially primers. Though nothing distinctively "papist" remained in the contents of the book, the modes of expression more closely approximated the traditional Latin office than Reformed devotional language. *Preces privatae* is also the title of a famous devotional manual by Lancelot Andrewes.

**Precisianist.** One who is adamant and scrupulous in observing external religious regulations and forms. The term was originally applied to and became synonymous with English Puritans of the 16th and 17th centuries, but it has a more general usage. (See PURITANISM; PIETISM.)

**Predestination.** A term suggesting that act of will exercised prior to actual human historical life by which God as sovereign Lord determined from eternity the particular recipients of salvation and, in the case of double predestination, the recipients of condemnation as well. Historically, the doctrinal function of this idea has been to assert the priority of grace in man's salvation without reference to human achievement. In certain expressions the apparent arbitrariness of such election has been modified by associating it with prescience (the foreknowledge of whose good works will merit the divine favor) or with the general election of all who believe in Christ. Elsewhere the doctrine has been extended to include the control of God over all the particular conditions of human life as well as over the natural order, human free will as a causal agency being considered illusory.

In patristic theology, the doctrine was rejected at the level of both theology and piety. The doctrinal negation reflects primarily a reaction against the Gnostic view of man—that some men on account of a spiritual nature lacking in others were the predetermined subjects of salvation. This equivalent of predestination, it was claimed, limited divine freedom in the gracious work of salvation to a certain natural class of men (so Irenaeus). More significantly, it denied free will as an agency of salvation through man's response to divine command and exhortation; for the fathers, free will, although always operative within a context created by grace, remained a key notion in explaining human sinfulness, man's moral responsibility, and the ethical urgency of the Christian faith. In terms of piety, the patristic understanding of prayer, its necessity and its efficacy, similarly presupposed a genuinely open human situation; as Origen argued, prayer does not truly effect a difference if all events have been predetermined by God. Consequently, the fathers developed a view of providence according to which God foreknew whose petitions would merit satisfaction and so prearranged the order of events as to satisfy them.

A thoroughgoing predestinarianism first came to expression in the theology of Augustine. His teaching presupposed both his doctrine of God as absolute will and his interpretation of salvation as totally dependent upon grace. In emphasizing God's absolute will, Augustine intended to assert divine control over all reality and divine authorship for all that is good, man being left responsible for the pursuit of evil. In complementary fashion, Augustine worked out his doctrine of salvation in terms of the divine will by which God has eternally elected certain men to salvation and assigned others to the just condemnation that universal sinfulness merits. At every step, salvation rests quite completely on the will and activity of God himself; not only forgiveness but also the prompting to faith (prevenient grace), the performance of good works (cooperating grace), perseverance in the Christian life, and the final blessedness of the vision of God and of harmony with the will of God are gifts of his grace. Further, God has predestined that the elect will participate in the chosen sacramental instruments of salvation and be incorporated into the church. It is evident that such a theology held no place for either reference to human merit or individual presumption of one's inclusion in the company of the elect. Further, Augustine denied the reality of free will except for man's freedom to sin as he wills; indeed, free will contrasts sharply with genuine freedom—that final state in which man is free from sin because he is unable to sin.

Shortly before Augustine's death (430), a controversy that was to continue for a century erupted over his doctrine of predestination. Its opponents, incorrectly designated semi-Pelagians, attacked the doctrine for its novelty, its tendency to undermine moral teaching, and its negation of the church's proclamation that God's grace and the merits of Christ's death are universally available. Nonetheless, they confirmed both man's depravity and the necessity of grace, though not as irresistible nor as more than cooperating with the faith springing from man's initiative and with man's free will in moral effort. The final settlement of the controversy at the Synod of Orange (529) reflected a more Augustinian position: unmerited grace was recognized as the prevenient cause of faith and good works; even so, irresistible grace was bypassed, predestination was limited to the elect, and predestination to evil was declared heretical. Throughout that struggle an evident impulse operated to maintain free will, moral responsibility, and the sacramental system (with baptism consistently assigned the function of restoring man's weakened will to its potential for doing the works necessary for salvation). This formulation remained unthreatened throughout the Middle Ages despite occasional challenge (as in the 9th-century controversy provoked by the Frankish monk Gottschalk in his reassertion of double predestination) and despite a developing emphasis upon human merit as cooperating in salvation. Thus, Scholastic theology managed the assertion of both God's absolute predestining will (usually on the grounds of foreknown merit) and man's freedom and moral responsibility, although later Scholastics (Duns Scotus, William of Occam) betrayed the formulas they professed by associating predestination with meritorious work. The debate over the Augustinian heritage was revived in the Roman Church by the 18th-century Jansenist controversy.

In reaction to the medieval piety of fear and uncertainty, the religious impulse of the Reformation led to the recovery of double predestinarianism. Three basic elements were operative in this development: (1) Experientially and exegetically, the Reformers reclaimed the Augustinian doctrines of the glory of God, universal sin, the bondage of the will, and the corresponding necessity of grace for salvation, grace conceived, however, as divine favor rather than as gift (Augustine). (2) Certain medieval qualifications of the doctrine were strongly attacked, as in the rejection of the teaching that sin comes by permission rather than by God's predetermination (Thomas Aquinas) or in denial even stronger than Augustine's of all talk about meritorious work. (3) The doctrine of election became a source of hope and comfort rather than of fear, since for the Reformers only God-instilled faith—confident trust in God and his unfailing purposes—made possible the apprehension of the doctrine's truth and man's grasp of his own acceptance as righteous (Luther), as elected in Christ (Zwingli), or as engrafted into Christ (Calvin). Accordingly, the Reformers stressed election to life, with reprobation a subordinate concern (note that Calvin provided a Trinitarian formula for election only). Further, they warned against the effort either to determine the particular subjects of election and condemnation or to question God's mysterious justice on the basis of human standards.

Predestinarianism did not prevail universally in Protestantism but rather became the cause of continuing controversy. Rejected by the Radical Reformation and elsewhere limited to the assertion of election to life (as in the Thirty-nine Articles), the doctrine met its most influential opposition in the semi-Pelagian arguments of Jacobus Arminius (d. 1609). Despite condemnation of the Arminian schism and reassertion of complete predestination by the Dutch Reformed Church (Synod of Dort, 1618–1619), Arminian teaching in England and America helped shape both 18th-century rationalism (deism) and movements concerned with Christianity as a power for moral transformation (Wesley, for example, regarded Calvin's doctrine as blasphemous). Subsequent support of predestination was reinforced by the emerging scientific outlook; Jonathan Edwards, in the most profound response to Arminianism, combined his Calvinist concerns with a Lockean analysis of the will and the Newtonian principles of universal causal connection. Similarly, Schleiermacher treated predestination as an expression of the divine government of nature and thus as an element in the regenerate man's consciousness of dependence, while Rudolf Otto rejected the argument from causation in favor of a totally religious creature-consciousness. In yet another formulation Karl Barth, making predestination central for his idea of God, views

election as that eternal action (not Calvin's absolute decree) by which God chose the way of gracious love for himself and fellowship with himself for sinful man.

BIBLIOGRAPHY: M. J. Farelly, *Predestination, Grace, and Free Will* (Westminster, Md., 1964); H. G. Hageman, *Predestination* (Philadelphia, 1963); P. Maury, *Predestination* (Richmond, 1960); J. H. Thornwell, *Election and Reprobation* (Philadelphia, 1960).

**Prelate.** A high-ranking ecclesiastic, but formerly any high official. Once reserved to ordinaries such as bishops and abbots, the term is now used for several ranks of papal officials, both active and honorary (monsignori). Within the Anglican Church the term applies only to bishops.

**Premonstratensian Canons.** An order of canons regular founded in 1120 by Norbert of Xanten. The order followed the Augustinian Rule, but with customary observances that created a more austere life than was usual under that rule. Norbert was deeply influenced by his friend Bernard of Clairvaux, and incorporated many Cistercian customs into the life of his order. He adopted the Cistercian white habit, for which the order was known as the White Canons. In 1126 the order received papal approval. The government of the order was similar to that of the Cistercians, although the abbot of Prémontré exercised greater power than did the abbot of Cîteaux. Although the order was to engage primarily in preaching and ministry, a movement at the end of the 12th century showed a marked tendency toward the monastic life, with an increased emphasis on manual labor and strict enclosure. Monasteries were built in more isolated locations, which incidentally made the order quite influential in the settlement and conversion of the eastern frontiers. They grew rapidly in France and the Rhineland, drawing from the sons of the nobility. The order suffered great losses in the French Revolution and was nearly extinct. A contemporary revival centers about the Abbey of Tongerloo in Belgium, with one abbey in the United States.

**Presbyterianism.** One of the three main systems of church polity. The word "presbyter" is derived from the Greek word meaning "elder"; hence, a Presbyterian church is one governed by elders. The ordination of elders in the early days of Christianity is attested in Acts 14:23; 20:17; and Titus 1:5. Presbyterians maintain that the terms "elder" and "bishop" in the New Testament are interchangeable and do not distinguish separate offices. Presbyterianism assumes the apostolic form of government to have been rule by teaching elders (ministers) and ruling elders, elected by vote of the congregation. It was during the Reformation that Presbyterianism developed its identity over against episcopalian and congregational theories of polity. Believing the system of papal monarchy to be unscriptural, advocates of reform searched the Old and New Testaments to discover apostolic practice and divine institution. John Calvin set forth the system of government that has been followed by those churches bearing the names of Presbyterian or Reformed. The Consistory that he set up in Geneva had some resemblance to a presbytery, although interference by the City Council prevented complete freedom in election of elders. From Geneva the Presbyterian system spread into France. By 1559 there were two thousand churches with Presbyterian polity in France, which were organized into a National Synod in that year. In the Netherlands the influence of Geneva-trained pastors led to adoption of a Presbyterian constitution at Antwerp in 1563, its polity patterned on that of the French churches. The distinguishing feature in the Low Countries was the Collegiate Church system, in which all churches in a city were ruled by a single session. Other churches of Presbyterian polity sprang up on the Continent, notably in eastern Europe, but it was in Scotland that it struck deepest roots. John Knox organized the first General Assembly there in 1560, which produced the Book of Discipline that was the guide for the dominance of Presbyterianism in Scotland. The Church of Scotland was the chief source for the spread of Presbyterianism to the New World. Scottish commissioners also played a prominent role in the Westminster Assembly in England (1643–1649), called during the Puritan revolution to settle the form of polity for the Church of England. Although Presbyterianism has played only a minor role in England since the Restoration in 1660, the Westminster Confession of Faith, the Catechisms, the Form of Government, and the Directory for Worship have remained universal standards for Presbyterianism. It reached America with Scotch-Irish, Dutch, English, and French Huguenot settlers. Francis Makemie organized the first American presbytery at Philadelphia in 1706; the first General Assembly met in 1789. Major divisions over issues of evangelism, theology, and slavery resulted in the establishment of several denominations bearing the name "Presbyterian." At present, the major bodies in American Presbyterianism are The United Presbyterian Church in the U.S.A., strongest in the North, and the Presbyterian Church in the United States, predominantly southern.

Presbyterianism is generally identified with Calvinistic doctrine, although some ultra-Calvinist bodies observe a congregational polity. Presbyterianism is a representative form of government, in which the congregation elects ruling elders who, with the pastors, form the session, charged with maintaining the spiritual government of the church. The presbytery consists of all ministers within a district and representative ruling elders for each congregation. It is the focus of authority, having jurisdiction over ministers and churches in its district. The removal or installation of a minister is by mutual agreement of congregation, presbytery, and individual. The synod is a body of representative ministers and elders from an area of at least three presbyteries and has authority over the presbyteries within the synod area. The highest judicatory is the General Assembly, which supervises all the churches and the work of the denomination as a whole, such as missions and education. Every presbytery in the denomination sends ministers and elders as commissioners to the General Assembly. On the local level, deacons are elected to supervise the temporal business of the church, under the authority of the session. The minister is a member of the presbytery in which he labors, not of the congregation.

BIBLIOGRAPHY: J. Moffatt, *The Presbyterian Churches* (Garden City, 1928).

**Pressensé, Edmond de** (1824–1891). French Protestant pastor, politician, and author. He resigned his Paris pastorate (1847–1871) after being elected to the National Assembly, and in 1883 he became a life member of the Senate. He opposed monarchist and clerical restoration and championed the free-church system. After 1888 he became the president of the Left Center Party. During this time he continued to preach throughout France and served for many years as president of the Union of Evangelical Churches of France.

**Prester (Presbyter) John.** A legendary medieval Asian Christian king. According to the story, which became popular in Europe during the Crusades, John was a priest and king who had conquered the Moslems and was to bring help to the Christians in the Holy Land. Although the different versions do not agree as to the exact location of John's kingdom, the story may contain a core of historical truth in reference to some unknown Nestorian prince.

**Prierias, Sylvester** (1456–1523). One of the first theological opponents of Luther. As a professor of theology in Bologna and Padua, and later as a Dominican prior and inquisitor, he published a number of comprehensive theological works that established his reputation as an erudite Thomist; as a result, in 1514 he was made professor of Thomistic philosophy in Rome. In 1515 he was named master of the sacred palace, a position that empowered him to act as an official inquisitor and judge in matters of faith concerning the whole church. He helped secure the condemnation of Reuchlin; and when Luther's Ninety-five Theses on indulgences were published, he responded with a treatise supporting a rigid position on the authority of the pope, arguing, in effect, that anyone who denied that the church, in the person of the pope, could do what the church had indeed done was a heretic. He prepared trial briefs against Luther, and wrote several other polemical treatises against him. Luther responded to these works with ridicule; it was not until they received the approval of Leo X in 1520 that Luther treated the position of Prierias as representative of the Roman Church.

**Priestley, Joseph** (1733–1804). Presbyterian clergyman and scientist. As a scientist, he is best known as the "discoverer of oxygen" and as the author of *Experiments and Observations on Different Kinds of Air* (3 vols., 1774, 1775, 1777). As a clergyman he is best known for his unorthodoxy, his embracing of Socinianism, his editorship of the contentious *Theological Repository,* and for his part in the founding of the Unitarian Society in 1791.

**Primate.** The bishop of the principal diocese in a country or area. In the Roman Catholic Church, a primate holds only honorary preeminence over other bishops. In the Anglican and Scandinavian Churches, primates exercise also a limited jurisdictional power over other bishops. Primates have never been designated for France, Germany, or the United States. The Benedictine Order is headed by an abbot primate, resident in Rome.

**Prime.** The office of monastic prayer at the first hour of the day (about six o'clock). Cassian says it was instituted in the 4th century in the East so that monks would not be tempted to sleep between Lauds and Terce. It is a "little" office like Terce, with thoughts concerning the work of the day ahead. Chrodegang of Metz (d. 766) added the chapter office at the end in which the rule is read. Remembrance of the saints by a reading of the martyrology is also appended to Prime.

**Princeton Theology.** A 19th-century American variant of Calvinism which was born with the founding of Princeton Seminary (New Jersey) in 1812. Inspired by its first professor, Archibald Alexander, and given its most complete formulation by Charles Hodge in his *Systematic Theology* (3 vols., 1872–1873), the Princeton Theology was defended and modified throughout the rest of the century by a large group of competent scholars among whom Archibald A. Hodge, Benjamin B. Warfield and J. Gresham Machen are the most noteworthy. Although the Princeton scholars themselves never admitted that they were teaching anything but orthodox Calvinism, the rationalist philosophical orientation of their argument, and the emphasis placed upon the doctrine of the substitutionary atonement and, especially, the inspiration of the Scriptures, have been sufficiently distinctive to separate the Princeton teaching from the rest of American Calvinism. Faced with a growing movement of Biblical criticism that seemed to be undermining faith in the authority of the Bible, the Princeton Seminary professors forged a doctrine of inspiration that defended the Scriptures as the verbally inerrant Word of God. Their views were for a few years after 1893 adopted as the standard for Presbyterian orthodoxy and in the 20th century have contributed to the Biblical literalism of Fundamentalism.

**Prior.** An official of a monastery second in authority after the abbot. In a large monastery there may be subpriors also. In the Cluniac Order, there was a conventual prior who ruled a house subject to the authority of the abbot of Cluny. Among the canons regular, the Cistercians, and the Dominicans, the head of a house is known as a prior.

**Prioress.** A nun whose rank corresponds to that of a prior. She is either the first deputy of an abbess, according to the Benedictine tradition, or the head of a house of nuns, according to the mendicant tradition.

**Priory.** The house or unit of a religious community governed by a prior. In those orders which follow the Augustinian Rule, the priory is usually the basic unit. In the Benedictine tradition, the priory is a dependency of the mother-abbey, the prior being appointed by the abbot. However, conventual priories have certain privileges of self-government.

**Priscillian** (d. 385). Bishop of Ávila (from c. 380), founder of a heretical Gnostic sect whose beliefs became known as Priscillianism. A Spanish layman, Priscillian was admired for his austerity and learning, and gathered about him a group of ascetic enthusiasts c. 370. The movement met with its first real opposition about the time Priscillian was made bishop of Ávila. He and his followers were forced into exile in southern France in 381. They were refused a hearing at Rome by Pope Damasus, but managing to have the decree of exile against them canceled by the secular authorities, they returned to Spain, where they continued to grow. Most of what is known about Priscillianism has been reconstructed from the criticisms of its adversaries. It had features that could be characterized as dualistic, astrological, ascetic, and antimaterialistic. Condemned by a synod of Bordeaux (384), Priscillian and several of his companions appealed to the emperor Maximus, but were condemned again, tortured, and beheaded at Trier in 385, the first to suffer death for heresy in the church's history. They were immediately honored as martyrs and after the fall of Maximus (388), Priscillianism again flourished. Although condemned at a Council at Toledo (400), the movement continued in existence until at least 563, when it was condemned by the Council of Braga.

**Probabilism.** A theory concerned with the moral situation in which there is no absolutely certain right or wrong practice. In such ambiguous situations, there will be several opinions as to what is in fact right and wrong, some of which will be more *probable* (i.e., logical or having authoritative support) than others. The probabilist teaches that the Christian may perform any such act with good conscience if there is any opinion supporting its probable virtue, even if other opinions urging another course of action appear to carry more weight. Confessors who favored this position were inclined to be lenient with penitents, and after 1656 there was much criticism of the position, especially from Pascal and the Jansenists, but also by two popes. It declined and was identified with the Jesuits. (See MEDINA, BARTHOLOMEO.)

**Proclus** (c. 410–485). One of the last, and greatest, representatives of the Athenian school of Neoplatonism. He significantly influenced Christian thought through those who drew upon his ideas. His literary activity was chiefly devoted to explanation of the writings of Plato with the addition of modifications of Neoplatonic principles introduced by himself. The Pseudo-Dionysian writings, which greatly affected medieval theology and mysticism, were largely based upon the thinking of Proclus. The *Liber de causis,* falsely ascribed to Aristotle, which contributed to the revival of Neoplatonism in medieval philoso-phy, was an extract from Proclus' *Elements of Theology.*

**Proclus** (d. 446). Patriarch of Constantinople from 434. He was a leader in (1) promoting the acceptance of the definitions of the Council of Ephesus (431); (2) strengthening the union of the Orientals and Cyril of Alexandria; (3) reconciling the Johannites; and (4) settling the quarrel about Theodore of Mopsuestia which threatened the Church of Armenia. A popular preacher, he delivered (c. 428) a famous sermon on the Theotokos in the presence of Nestorius. He is said to have introduced the Trisagion into the liturgy.

**Procopius of Caesarea.** Byzantine historian during the reign of Justinian (527–565). In his *De bellis,* Procopius describes the campaigns against the Persians, Vandals, and Goths; in his *De aedificiis* he describes the architectural achievements of Justinian, one of which was the Sancta Sophia. The *Secret History* (*Anecdota*) ascribed to Procopius is a series of anecdotes that picture Theodora as a morally depraved woman with insatiable desires and describes Justinian as a destroyer of Roman institutions and a murderer of thousands of innocent people. Because of the exaggerated and scandalous picture of Justinian and Theodora in the anecdotes in contrast to the more objective and sometimes laudatory tone of *De bellis* and *De aedificiis,* and also because of certain internal inconsistencies, the Procopian authorship as well as the historical reliability of *Anecdota* has been doubted by some scholars (L. von Ranke, J. B. Bury), while on the other hand, others (Edward Gibbon, F. Dahn) have accepted the Procopian authorship though retaining some reservations in regard to his credibility.

**Procopius of Gaza** (c. 475–c. 528). Head of the school of rhetoric at Gaza. Besides the fact that he was the teacher of Choricius, little is known about his life. Procopius was the first to write exegetical catenae, which he produced by collecting and arranging writings of early church fathers to form continuous commentaries on the Biblical text. The parts of his works that survive are included in the J. P. Migne series.

**Procurator of Russia, High.** An office instituted by Peter the Great after abolishing the Russian Orthodox patriarchate (1721) and substituting a synod in its place in imitation of German Protestantism. The holder of this office, often a military officer ignorant of ecclesiastical affairs, represented the government, which frequently interfered in purely religious matters. The most famous of procurators was Konstantine P. Pobedonostsev, who was influential in the reigns of the last two Russian czars.

**Prohibited Degrees of Relationship in Marriage.** The degrees of relationship by blood or marriage making it unlawful for two persons to marry. Relationships of blood, or consanguinity, are calculated by the number of generations, or degrees, back to the common ancestor. Thus, first cousins are two generations from the common grandparent and are related to the second degree. Relationships through marriage, or degrees of affinity, are calculated in the same way. Present canon law permits marriage to the third degree of blood relationship and to the second degree of affinity.

**Pro Juárez, Miguel Augustin** (1891–1927). Mexican Jesuit. Born in the Mexican province of Zacatecas, Miguel entered the Jesuit novitiate in 1911, but was sent abroad to study in order to escape the anarchy and persecution that characterized the Mexican Revolution. Ordained in 1925, he returned to Mexico and went about in disguise ministering to the poor. Accused as an accomplice in a plot to assassinate President Obrégon, he was seized and shot.

**Prokopovich, Feofan** (1681–1736). Russian theologian and ecclesiastic, closely associated with the reforms of Peter the Great. After a temporary conversion to the Uniate Church, he took holy orders in the Orthodox Church and taught at the Kiev Academy, which he later headed. In 1718 he was named bishop of Pskov and in 1724 archbishop of Novgorod. Well-educated and erudite, Prokopovich won renown as a preacher, theologian, and dramatist. Of greatest significance was his advocacy of autocracy and his collaboration with Peter the Great in religious affairs. Influenced by Protestant doctrines regarding church-state relations, he engaged in a protracted polemic with S. Iavorsky. In his writings (*Justice Is the Monarch's Will, A Sermon on Royal Authority and Honor*) Prokopovich denied the supremacy of the spiritual power and insisted that the sovereign, "by the grace of God," has both the right and the duty to regulate his subjects' activities and to provide for their welfare. His ideas were embodied in the Church Statute of 1721, by which Peter the Great abolished the patriarchate and replaced it with the Holy Synod, headed by a layman, the high procurator. The Russian Orthodox Church thus became a bureaucratic appendage of the absolute state, devoid of any ecclesiastical independence.

**Prone.** A vernacular office usually inserted into the order of the Mass on Sundays and holy days following the reading of the Gospel. It appeared in the time of Charlemagne when the common people no longer understood the Latin of the Mass. Although there was no prescribed order, it usually consisted of bidding prayers, the creed, a sermon, and the Lord's Prayer. Popular throughout the Middle Ages, Prone was the model for several Reformation liturgies.

**Propagation of the Faith, Congregation for the.** One of the twelve departments of the Roman Curia that serve the pope in the administration and government of the Roman Church, established by Pope Gregory XV (1622). Its particular function is the worldwide promotion and direction of Roman Catholic missions. To assist in this work, a College of Propaganda was established by Pope Urban VII to train native clergy destined for religious work in their native lands.

**Proprietary Churches and Monasteries.** Institutions belonging to private owners in contrast to the practice of the early Roman Church in which all ecclesiastical property was owned and administered by the bishop as part of his diocese. The proprietary church originated among the Germanic kingdoms and probably started when a lord built a church on his property for himself and his dependents. The altar and land constituted the principal. The owner had rights in civil law over the church: he could appoint the cleric, bestow the church as a benefice or give it as a dowry. He could not, however, put the church itself to any other than ecclesiastical use. Under Charlemagne and his successors the idea of the proprietary church was extended to include abbeys. Although laymen exercised some proprietary rights over bishoprics, they never held them by pure and simple proprietorship. Legislation from Pepin to Louis the Pious protected the proprietary system, but forbade the division of rights or the appointing of clerics without the bishop's consent. Clerics were enjoined to attend the diocesan synod. Protests against lay ownership were made as early as the Council of Valence (855), but the proprietary system did not disappear until the legislation prohibiting lay investiture became effective. Patronage has replaced proprietorship.

**Prosper of Aquitaine** (c. 390–c. 465). Lay theologian who defended Augustine against the semi-Pelagians but in the end defected from strict Augustinianism. In 428 he sent Augustine information about the opposition being expressed to his doctrines of predestination and grace in the Gallic monasteries by Vincent of Lérins and John Cassian. About the same time he composed *Carmen de ingratis,* a poem of more than a thousand verses in hexameters expanding his ideas on grace contained in a letter to Rufinus. After the death of Augustine (430), he tried to get Celestine I to issue condemnation of Augustine's opponents but received only a letter commendatory of Augustine. His controversial works of this period (431–434) include one against Cassian, one against Vincent, and two against "Gallic slanderers." The latter part of his life was spent as secretary to Leo I, and his literary activity was almost completely confined to compilations. The compilations include *Expositio psalmorum,* a florilegium of Augustine's comments on Psalms 100 to 150; a catena of extracts from Augustine's theology not systematically arranged; and a later collection of Augustine's theology based on the former. His ultimate position on predestination and grace is to be found in the anonymous *De vocatione omnium gentium,* extolling the universal saving will of God.

**Protestant Association.** A body of popular anti-Catholic societies formed in Scotland and the environs of London in 1779 by the rabble-rousing Lord George Gordon to force repeal of the Catholic Relief Act of 1778. Gordon marshalled a mob of about fifty thousand, principally members and adherents of the Association, to march on Parliament on June 2, 1780, and present a huge petition. Riots and pillaging lasted for days, and more than 450 persons were killed or wounded.

**Protestant Church of the East Indies** (*now called* Gredja Protestan di Indonesia). A union formed in 1817 by order of King Willem I, of churches founded in the 17th and 18th centuries by chaplains of the East Indies Company. It was the official state church in contrast to regional churches founded by mission societies. Administrative independence was granted in 1935, and the Republic cut off financial support at independence in 1950. Membership was reported in 1962 at about 200,000. Recently most of the churches have been transferred into regional churches, and the remaining membership is small.

**Protestantism.** Usually, the principles or religion of all Christian churches which are not Roman Catholic or Eastern Orthodox. The name derives from the formal protest made by the evangelical princes and cities of the German Holy Roman Empire on April 19, 1529, at the imperial Diet of Speyer. Earlier, at the first Diet of Speyer in 1526, the religious division caused by the rapidly spreading Reformation led to the decision that until a general council of the church could be held in a German city to settle the matter, each state should conduct its religious life so as to be able to answer to God and the emperor, thus leaving the decision to the rulers of each territory. In 1529, the papal party recovered its strength and, by a majority vote, rescinded the action taken unanimously in 1526. The Evangelical party protested, six princes and fourteen imperial cities, some Lutheran and some Zwinglian, signing the protest. The word "protestant" was thereafter applied to those separating themselves from papal authority while claiming full recognition as Christians. Evangelical groups seldom used the expression themselves. All preferred to be called Reformed, or Evangelical, Churches, nor did they surrender the traditional name "Catholics." Against Luther's own wishes, his followers came to be known as Lutherans. Anglicans often object to the negative connotations of the word "protestant" and many of them do not regard their communion as a part of Protestantism.

**Proudhon, Pierre Joseph** (1809–1865). French socialist and political writer. He has often been regarded as the father of anarchism. Born of a poor laboring family, he was essentially self-educated. In 1837 his philological treatise *Essai de grammaire générale* resulted in a pension from the academy of Besançon. In 1839 he wrote *L'Utilité de la célébration du dimanche,* and *Qu'est-ce que la propriété?* in the following year. Proudhon believed that property is theft, that it allowed certain men the power to exploit the results of labor without giving an equivalent. His solution was to substitute individual possession for private ownership, for private ownership is the origin of inequality. His aim was to realize a science of society resting upon principles of justice, liberty, and equality. In 1842 he was briefly imprisoned for his revolutionary opinions. Proudhon lived unmolested in Paris under the Second Empire. However, the publication of *De la justice dans la révolution et dans l'église* in 1858 aroused a storm of protest from the Roman Catholic Church and other institutions that he attacked, and he was forced to seek refuge in Brussels. Pardoned by the amnesty of 1859, he returned to France in 1860 and died at Passy in 1865.

***Providentissimus Deus.*** Encyclical letter of Pope Leo XIII on Holy Scripture, given on Nov. 18, 1893. Though encouraging the study of Holy Scripture in seminaries and schools, Leo, disturbed by currents of Biblical criticism and Catholic Modernism, insisted that it was forbidden to Catholics to restrict inspiration to certain parts of the Bible or to concede that the "sacred writer" had erred in interpretation or aptness of expression.

**Province.** An ecclesiastical division made up of a metropolitan see and several dioceses. Some religious orders, such as the mendicant orders and the regular clerics, are organized into provinces, headed by a provincial who is subject to the superior of the order. Such provinces are not necessarily geographical, but may be organized by national origin or the nature of work done.

**Provincial.** The head of a province of a religious order who is subject to the superior of the order. Provincials are usually elected by a provincial chapter for a specified term. The provincial visits all houses, appoints all priors, and supervises the administration of property within his province.

**Provisional Committee of the World Council of Churches.** A committee formed at Utrecht, May 9–12, 1938, with Archbishop William Temple as chairman. War delayed the inaugural assembly until 1948 and forced the Committee to exercise wide responsibilities: chaplaincy to war prisoners, Ecumenical Refugee Commission, Department of Reconstruction and Interchurch Aid, and Study Department. The full Committee could not meet until 1945. Meanwhile, ninety-three churches had joined.

**Provoost, Samuel** (c. 1742–1815). First Protestant Episcopal bishop of New York. He was appointed assistant minister of Trinity Church, New York City, after the Revolutionary War. His election to the office of bishop followed and his consecration was held in Lambeth Palace in 1787. He was chairman of the committee that drafted the constitution of the Episcopal Church and was responsible for changes in the Book of Common Prayer.

**Provost.** A title once applied to any official, but later used to refer to the prior of a monastery. In cathedral chapters modeled after monastic organization, the duties of the provost were gradually assumed by the dean. In some cathedral chapters the terms are synonymous. In religious orders, "provost" is used interchangeably with "prior." The heads of some English colleges are known as provosts.

**Prudentius, Aurelius Clemens** (348–c. 410). Latin poet and hymnographer who also had a successful career as a lawyer in Spain. His poems include *Apotheosis* (on incarnation), *Hamartigenia* (against Marcion), *Contra Symmachum* (against paganism), all apologetic; the *Cathemerinon* (hymns for daily use) and *Peri Stephanon* (hymns on Spanish and Italian martyrs) demonstrate the didactic and reflective character of his hymns, all of which are quite long and in classical meter.

**Prussia, United Evangelical Church of** (*also known as* Old Prussian Union). It was founded in 1817 as a union between the Lutheran and the Reformed Churches in the Hohenzollern domains. John Sigismund, elector of Brandenburg and ruler of Prussia, was converted to the Reformed religion in 1613, but his subjects retained their Lutheranism. A stable element in the ecclesiastical policy of the Hohenzollern rulers which followed was the promotion of a union of the two branches of Protestantism into a single church. In carrying out this policy, Frederick William, the Great Elector, and his son, Frederick I, the first king of Prussia (1701–1713), encountered strong and concerted opposition from the orthodox Lutheran party. However, as a result of the inclination of both Pietism and the Enlightenment to minimize confessional dispute and disagreement, the stage was set at the beginning of the 19th century for the realization of the Hohenzollern program. The immediate background of the declaration of union in Prussia was the national awakening in Germany which had accompanied the War of Liberation against Napoleon. This spirit brought a religious awakening of a pietistic sort which gave rise to increased interest in religious affairs.

Frederick William III (1797–1840) exhibited an intense interest in church matters and with the aid of his minister of religion, Karl Altenstein (1817–1840), he sought to carry forth a variety of reforms, but in general all ranged around the central program of uniting the royal church (Reformed) with the state church (Lutheran) in the entire realm. A first step had already been taken in 1816 with the institution of a new ecclesiastical constitution. The new system was to include organization of presbyteries as well as district and provincial synods, all to be crowned by the holding of a general synod. Although a few synods were held, the plan was opposed from the start by the old governmental church administration and finally lost the confidence of the monarch when it proved difficult to control in the liturgy controversy.

The union itself took place when on Sept. 27, 1817, Frederick William III acting in his role as *Summus episcopus* of the Prussian churches issued a declaration that in the forthcoming Reformation Jubilee the union of the

Reformed and Lutherans should be celebrated by the holding of a common Eucharistic service. Such a service had already been planned by the Berlin Ministerium under Schleiermacher's leadership. Thus on Oct. 30, the ministers celebrated together a Communion service and on the following day such services were held in the churches of Berlin. The United Evangelical Church received general acceptance in Prussian territories, particularly in the Rhineland and Westphalian lands that had just been added to the kingdom, but the marriage of the two confessions was to be far from peaceful.

The first problem that came to trouble the union was the introduction by the king of a liturgy which he had devised to conform to an old Lutheran usage. Apparently a conscious imitation of the Anglican system of liturgical conformity with theological diversity, the king's liturgy was introduced to try to facilitate the union. It was hoped that the liturgy, which was first published at Christmastide, 1821, would be freely adopted in all congregations. The publication was met by a storm of protest, however, so Altenstein took measures to enforce its adoption. Despite his efforts, in 1826 there were 1,802 ministers out of 5,708 who were still against it. Schleiermacher, although a supporter of union, served as a rallying point for opposition to the liturgy. He objected to it as unsuitable and rejected the right of the king to introduce it. The final outcome of the struggle was the publication of an appendix to the service book offering alternate forms. The general effect of the controversy was to destroy enthusiasm for the union.

A second problem arose as the result of a revival in Lutheran confessionalism. This found expression first in the ninety-five theses of Klaus Harms (1817), attacking the rationalistic theological premises on which a similar union had been concluded in Hesse-Nassau. This was followed by the rise of a party known as the Old Lutherans under the leadership of Prof. J. G. Scheibel in Breslau, Silesia. When he was suspended, he formed a separate Lutheran church which failed to receive either toleration or permission to emigrate. It was this group which, under Frederick William IV (1840–1861), gained recognition as the Evangelical Lutheran Church of Prussia, and outgrowths from it emigrated to the United States to become antecedents of The American Lutheran Church and The Lutheran Church—Missouri Synod.

It was not until the reign of William I (1861–1888) that the Prussian Union gained a synodical constitution that had effect (1876).

This church became by far the largest Protestant body in Germany, numbering some twenty million members at the beginning of World War I, and still eighteen millions at the beginning of World War II. The profound political and ethnic dislocations in the lands formerly included in Prussia after the latter conflict have made the restoration of the United Evangelical Church in anything like its former integrity impossible.

BIBLIOGRAPHY: A. L. Drummond, *German Protestantism Since Luther* (London, 1951); K. D. MacMillan, *Protestantism in Germany* (Princeton, 1917); J. H. Nichols, *History of Christianity: 1650–1950* (New York, 1956); W. O. Shanahan, *German Protestants Face the Social Question* (Notre Dame, 1954).

**Prynne, William** (1600–1669). Puritan pamphleteer. Prynne studied at Oxford, combining theology and law. The first of his many rounds with the government came when he published *Histriomastix* (1632), a tome condemning the theater. Though fined, imprisoned, and pilloried, Prynne was not cowed. From his cell, he continued to pour out vituperative tracts against sundry subjects and soon found himself before the Star Chamber a second time (1637). He used the trials as the platform for publicity, and after further stiff punishment was exiled to the Isle of Jersey. One of the first acts of the Long Parliament was to recall Prynne and cancel his sentences. He became a leading defender of the Parliamentary cause, attacked episcopacy, and vengefully assailed his persecutor Laud. A man who did not know the meaning of tolerance or compromise, he poured out a series of pamphlets against both Independency and an unrestricted Presbyterian establishment. He opposed the execution of Charles, and denounced Pride's Purge of Parliament. After more time in prison, he regained his seat in Parliament, with the aid of George Monck in 1660. He advocated the return of Charles II, and held posts in the Restoration government. His two hundred works are of no literary value, but they remain important as historical sources.

**Przywara, Erich** (1889–    ). German Jesuit theologian and philosopher. His written works discussed such varied topics as existentialism, speculative theology, patristics, and mythology, and such thinkers as Kant, Goethe, Nietzsche, Luther, Kierkegaard, Eduard von Hartmann, and Martin Heidegger. A neo-Scholastic, Przywara seems especially attracted to the 19th-century English theologian John Henry Newman, in whom he sees the clash between Scholasticism and the more liberal, psychological approaches to religious thought.

**Psellus, Michael Constantine** (c. 1018–c. 1078). Author, philosopher, and political leader. As head of the faculty of philosophy at the University of Constantinople, he exerted considerable power during the reigns of the emperors Constantine IX, Isaac I, and Constantine X. He served as prime minister under the regency of Eudocia Macrembolitissa and the reign of Michael VII Ducas, who had been his pupil. Interested in a wide variety of topics, Psellus revived the study of Plato and published *Synopsis in Aristotelis logicam* and *Chronographia,* works of considerable historical interest.

**Pseudo-Dionysius the Areopagite.** See DIONYSIUS THE AREOPAGITE.

**Pseudo-Isidore.** Common designation for a collection of canon laws sometimes called the "false decretals." The name Isidore Mercator appears in the Preface of the collection, and hence the title "Pseudo-Isidore." It is now believed that the decretals were drawn up between 847 and 856 in response to the decision to reform the church reached at the Diet of Épernay (846), and that they were compiled by a group of men working at Le Mans or Reims. The decretals are a collection of the authentic canons of the Greek, African, Gallo-Roman, and Iberian Councils, plus a series of apocryphal and forged decrees. Among the preexistent apocrypha used by the collectors are the Canons of the Apostles and the Donation of Constantine. Among the forgeries invented are the series of letters attributed to the bishops of Rome from Clement (89–97) to Gregory II (715–731). The collection is not a complete code, for such areas as monastic life and parish organization are not considered. The decretals were intended to free the bishop from lay control by defining his position in his diocese, in the province, and before the pope. It was not until the investiture controversy that the decretals were used to strengthen the papal position. The veracity of the decrees was questioned by Nicholas of Cusa and John of Torquemada (15th century), and proved to be forgeries by David Blondel (1628). For eight centuries, they had served as part of the law of the church.

**Pufendorf, Samuel von** (1632–1694). German jurist. Born at Chemnitz, the son of a Lutheran pastor, he was educated at Leipzig and Jena, and taught the law of nature and nations at Heidelberg and Lund (Sweden). Influenced by Thomas Hobbes and Hugo Grotius, he published his famous work on natural and international law (*De jure naturae et gentium*) in 1672. His first important point was that natural law does not extend beyond the limits of this life and that it confines itself to regulating external acts. He considered human nature as the basis of all law, and human reason as its supreme authority. In *De habitu religionis Christianae ad vitam civilem* (1687), he traced the limits between ecclesiastical and civil power, and defended the absolute sovereignty of the state and demanded that all monarchs provide for the happiness of their subjects. The work also propounded for the first time the "collegial" theory of church government, which makes fundamental distinctions between the supreme ecclesiastical power of the state and the church, especially in regard to religious toleration. The theory was put into practice to a certain extent in Prussia in the 18th century and greatly helped toward the growing principle of religious toleration.

**Pulcheria** (Aelia Pulcheria Augusta) (399–453). Empress of the Eastern Roman Empire. A daughter of the emperor Arcadius, she reigned jointly with her brother Theodosius II (414–450). When Theodosius died, Pulcheria married Marcian, who became her coruler. Together they summoned and controlled the Council of Chalcedon, which declared the Monophysites to be heretics. She became a saint of the Eastern Orthodox Church.

**Purcell, Henry** (1659–1695). Noted composer of the late 17th-century English school of music. His compositions blended French and Italian elements into a native English style, producing a school of sacred music that has strongly influenced the choral tradition of the Anglican Church to this day, though it was largely overshadowed by the English veneration of George Fredrick Handel.

**Purgatory.** The antechamber to heaven, or "intermediate state" for the saved, but not for the damned, who go straight to hell. In purgatory those who have not been completely cleansed of venial sin and whose temporal punishments have not been satisfied by penance in this life are purged and purified before entering the visible presence of God and the saints. The belief in some sort of cleansing after death appears very early and received the approval of Augustine and Gregory the Great. A belief in purgatory was important to the development of the indulgence, and was much abused in later medieval indulgence preaching, which provoked Luther's protest.

Belief in purgatory was reaffirmed at Trent, but denied by the major Reformers.

**Puritanism.** A movement for further reformation in the Church of England, to purge it of the last vestiges of Rome and bring it in line with the Continental Reformation and a rigid adherence to the Bible. It began in the reign of Elizabeth I (1558–1603) and continued as a distinct program to the end of the 17th century. At first largely a university movement (especially at Cambridge), the Puritans were successors of the aggressive Reformers of Edward VI's reign such as John Hooper, with whom they were linked through the exiles of Mary's reign who returned from the Continent in 1558 seeking more radical reform. They were frustrated by Elizabeth's policy of an unmistakably Protestant church that made as many compromises with the old medieval structure in liturgy, polity, and ceremonial as possible, a policy dictated by politics. The resulting "national" character of the church was considered undesirable by the Puritans who maintained a militant internationalism. During Elizabeth's reign conflict between Puritan and Anglican (those Protestants content with the Crown's policy) erupted. In the vestiarian controversy, some Puritans resisted wearing the surplice; in the controversy over the "prophesyings" the queen opposed attempts to set up structures independent of her authority; in the "petition" and *Admonitions* controversies, Puritans sought parliamentary reform of such abuses as pluralism, nonresidence, and "ignorant and scandalous" clergy. Similar conflicts occurred with James I (1603–1625), who rebuffed the Puritan demands presented in the Millenary Petition at the Hampton Court Conference (1604), and continually harried them, as in the order to read publicly the *Book of Sports* (1618), which violated their Sabbatarianism. With Charles I, the royal patronage was given to the emerging High Church party, led eventually by William Laud, which not only acquiesced in the Compromise church policy but valued it, seeing in episcopacy, ceremonial, etc., the glories of the English Church, proof of its "catholicity." Puritan "lectureships" were broken up, obnoxious ceremonial enforced (e.g., kneeling to receive Communion and holy tables railed in as altars), and defense of "divine right" monarchy made the road to preferment.

Stymied by Crown and bishops, some questioned a church government that seemed to support abuses. They sought a new structure giving power to the frequently Puritan parish clergy and the "godly" laity developing under their tutelage. Episcopacy as such was attacked in the 1572 *Admonition* and the notorious Marprelate Tracts (1588–1589). Thomas Cartwright's "Presbyterianism" substituted rule by parish clergy and lay elders for bishops. More radical, Robert Browne called for separation from the corrupt Establishment and the "gathering" of independent "congregational" churches. Some of his followers went to Holland, and some eventually to Plymouth, Mass. The main body of the Puritans, however, wedded to church establishment, and determined to reform the church from within, regarded Separatism with horror. The Independents or "nonseparating" Congregationalists, beginning with Henry Jacob and William Ames, called for the "pure church" of "congregationalism" without rejecting a national church, and meanwhile "gathered" their state parishes as congregational churches. With the Laudian repression of the 1630's, this became difficult and only emigration made congregationalism without Separatism possible —abroad, they could do as they pleased and still see themselves as the Church of England. In Holland such an experiment flourished for a few years; in New England, led by John Cotton, Thomas Hooker, and John Davenport, there was more permanence. (The tradition of Massachusetts Bay converted to congregationalism by the Plymouth Separatists is wrong.) Probably most Puritans never rejected episcopacy completely before the 1640's, being "Presbyterian" only in desiring checks on the bishops and more power for parish clergy. The concern of men such as John Dod or Richard Sibbes was not primarily polity and reform but preaching and cure of souls. They stressed the themes of the necessity for conversion, life as a pilgrimage, and the divine-human relationship as governed by "covenants." Related to this was a moral intensity, an insistence upon creating the "Holy Commonwealth" (a pure state and church where the Bible was obeyed and the "saints" ruled), and a heightened millennial expectation, especially among Independents. Behind and uniting it all was a piety, the Augustinian, Calvinist piety of man's dependence upon the unmerited grace of God. This piety was ensured by a theology firm in such Calvinist distinctives as limited atonement, irresistible regeneration by the Holy Spirit, and predestination. Thus Puritanism was at heart a particularly intense version of the central evangelical affirmation of the Reformed Churches that salvation is by grace through faith alone. In the Armenian controversy, Puritanism found its basic piety challenged in an attack upon the theology enshrining it. During Elizabeth's reign Puritan and Anglican scarcely differed theologically; after 1590 this changed, with Calvinism attacked in the universities by the High Church party, which centered its piety in ritual and sacrament. In response, Calvinism was hardened into supralapsarianism by William Perkins and others. While Calvinists James I and Archbishop Abbot ruled, this conflict remained submerged, though surfacing at the universities and in the reaction to Dutch Arminianism. During the reign of Charles I and Archbishop Laud, this theological divergence was seen by both parties as the root of their differences, as the York House Conference and the 1629 Parliamentary Debates indicate. With the Civil War the dispute waned, to be revived after the Restoration.

By mid-17th century, Puritans were in power in both England and New England. But the dynamism of the movement had created tensions undermining effective rule. Victory in the Civil War followed by the rule of Cromwell gave the Puritans their opportunity; yet the deliberations of the Westminster Assembly and of Parliament, and the appearance of such new sects as Seekers, Levelers, Fifth Monarchy Men, and Quakers made clear the lack of consensus. Seizing power from the "Presbyterians," Cromwell, advised by the Independent leaders John Owen, Philip Nye, and Thomas Goodwin, set up a loose establishment of independent parishes regulated by boards for admitting and ejecting clergy. At the Restoration (1660), Puritanism, with its ejection from the Establishment and suppression under the Clarendon Code, began to take denominational shape outside the Church of England, legally recognized by the 1689 Toleration Act. At the radical edge were the Quakers; the others were the Baptists, led to adult baptism by the emphasis on conversion; the Congregationalists, firmly Calvinist as led by John Owen; and the Presbyterians, some still hopeful of a broader state church, and, led by Richard Baxter, relaxing their Calvinism. In New England, established Congregationalism was challenged by the Separatism of Roger Williams and the antinomianism of Anne Hutchinson. The 1648 Cambridge Platform did not achieve stability, as it was followed by controversies over the Halfway Covenant and wider admission to the Lord's Supper, and by the breakdown of uniformity with the coming of Quakers and Anglicans. Efforts to shore up the old way in the Reforming Synod (1679), the Saybrook Platform (1708), and the work of Cotton Mather failed.

Puritanism was a strong cultural force. Milton and Bunyan evidence its literary creativity. Politically, emphasis on the covenant and the right of resistance as well as congregational training in self-government contributed to democracy. Its morality leavened English life, stressing duty, diligence, plain living, and a responsibility for social well-being which belies any charge of insensitivity to poverty. It created a Biblically and theologically literate public and an emphasis on personal religion, and left as its legacy in England not only the older Dissenters but also Anglican Evangelicalism. In the United States, it was transformed by Jonathan Edwards, Timothy Dwight, and others into that voluntaristic Calvinism and sense of responsibility for the nation's life that characterized the dominant Evangelicalism of the 19th century.

BIBLIOGRAPHY: G. R. Cragg, *Puritanism in the Period of the Great Persecution* (Cambridge, 1957); W. Haller, *Liberty and Reformation in the Puritan Revolution* (New York, 1955); and *The Rise of Puritanism* (New York, 1957); M. M. Knappen, *Tudor Puritanism* (Gloucester, Mass., 1963); P. Miller, *Errand Into the Wilderness* (New York, 1964); and *Orthodoxy in Massachusetts: 1630–1650* (Gloucester, Mass., 1965); and *The New England Mind: The Seventeenth Century,* 2 vols. (Boston, 1961); G. F. Nuttall, *Visible Saints* (Oxford, 1957); A. Simpson, *Puritanism in Old and New England* (Chicago, 1955).

**Purvey, John** (c. 1353–c. 1428). Translator of the Lollard Bible. Educated at Oxford, he became a close associate of John Wycliffe and for a time worked as his secretary at Lutterworth. He has an important place in the history of the English Bible as the principal reviser, with "divers fellows and helpers," of the somewhat crude first Lollard translation, which had been undertaken by Nicholas of Hereford under Wycliffe's inspiration. (It is unlikely that Wycliffe himself contributed directly to either of the two Lollard translations.) Purvey's version was probably completed c. 1395, possibly later, and it is commonly referred to simply as "the Lollard Bible." Imprisoned for his Wycliffite activities, Purvey recanted (c. 1401) and was given a benefice. He later resigned it, resumed his Lollard preaching, and was imprisoned again in 1421. Little is known of his last days. Several manuscripts of his Bible survived the attempted suppression and, though it was based on the Vulgate, it exercised some influence on later English versions.

**Pusey, Edward Bouverie** (1800–1882). Regius professor of Hebrew at Oxford and canon of Christ Church. Born of a well-to-do family, he was educated at Oxford, graduating B.A. in 1822. In 1823 he was elected to a fellowship at Oriel where he formed friendships with John Keble and John Henry Newman. Between 1825 and 1827 he studied on the Continent and prepared a defense of orthodoxy against German rationalism. In 1828 he was ordained and was appointed regius professor of Hebrew, a position he retained for the rest of his life. When young he was a liberal in politics, but the triumph of liberalism in 1832 he regarded as threatening the church that he labored to defend. When the Oxford movement began in 1833, Pusey became one of its leaders, the members of the movement sometimes being called Puseyites. He contributed tracts on Baptism and the Eucharist in which he established the fathers of the early church and Anglican divines of the 17th century as touchstones for doctrine. Besides writing tracts, Pusey was busy at this time with the Oxford Library of the Fathers, with influential preaching, and with defending tractarians against opponents. With Newman's defection to Rome, the leadership of the Oxford movement fell to Pusey. From 1845 on he was engaged in holding the movement together, doing battle with liberals, defending ritualism, founding religious sisterhoods, reviving the practice of private confession, exploring the possibility of reunion with Rome, with the Wesleyans, and with Eastern Orthodoxy, and defending himself from numerous attacks, many unwarranted.

**Pym, John** (1584–1643). A Puritan Parliamentary leader. He first entered the House of Commons in 1614, but did not take a prominent position until the Short Parliament in 1640. At the opening of that session, he delivered a two-hour oration enumerating the civil and religious grievances of the nation for the previous fifteen years. Quickly assuming the leadership of Commons, he refused to grant supplies to Charles until the grievances were met, so Charles dissolved Parliament. When the Long Parliament met in November, Pym recapitulated his earlier performance, and took steps to safeguard the rights of Parliament. To ensure Parliament's power, Strafford, Laud, and others of the king's ministers were impeached. Though Pym originally favored a modified episcopacy, he later supported the abolition of bishops. Mutual suspicion between the contending parties caused both to seek control of the armed forces. When Charles's attempt to arrest the five leaders of Commons (including Pym) failed, the lines of conflict were drawn. Pym led the Parlia-

ment to prepare for conflict, and persisted in the struggle even when the war was going badly in the first engagements. His last political achievement was the alliance with Scotland against Charles, for Pym's death came a few months later. However, the political leadership of Pym had brought about the temporary triumph of Puritanism in England.

# Q

**Quadragesimo Anno.** Encyclical letter issued on May 15, 1931, by Pius XI, ostensibly confirming the teaching of *Rerum novarum* on its fortieth anniversary. The statement was foreshadowed in a papal letter to Cardinal Liénart, bishop of Lille, in 1929. In the encyclical the pope affirmed his right to deal authoritatively with social and economic problems. He stated that the excellent teaching of Leo was suspected by some, even Catholics, and gave offense to others. He affirmed the right of individual and social ownership with avoidance of either extreme. The state was to define the duties entailed in social and individual ownership, and he declared further that "public authority . . . can determine more accurately upon consideration of the true requirements of the common good, what is permitted and what is not permitted to owners in the use of their property." The role of the state remained a limited, but regulative role. Pius complained that society was separated into state and mass; he urged development of groups and guilds within the state to bridge the gap. The lay workman was to be the apostle to estranged workmen. Social justice and social charity were the guiding principles of economic life, which was to be subjected to and governed by an effective principle. Concentration of financial power in a few hands was the direct consequence of an unbridled dictatorship deriving from an individualistic spirit in economic life. Although some have considered the social program of the letter as a pattern for the "corporative state," much like the Italian fascist state of the day, such an interpretation is an overstatement, even though certain clerical fascists welcomed the encyclical and modeled their states after it.

**Quadratus** (2d century). Bishop of Athens. He is perhaps to be identified with the Quadratus who wrote the earliest known apology, presented to the emperor Hadrian in 125. Known only from a brief quotation in Eusebius, the work contrasted the miracles of the

Savior Jesus, real because permanently effective, with the unreal miracles worked by others regarded as saviors. Quadratus, a prophet of Asia Minor, is probably a different person.

**Quadrivium.** The four technical or scientific disciplines of the seven liberal arts—music, arithmetic, geometry, and astronomy. The three elementary disciplines were known as the trivium.

**Quakers** (*or* Society of Friends). A religious denomination originating in the Puritan religious ferment of 17th-century England and now found in many countries, but chiefly in the British Isles and America.

The beginnings of Quakerism presently appear to be more complicated than was once thought. Modern thinking qualifies the uniqueness of the movement and the originality of its founder, George Fox, and stresses instead its continuity with radical Puritanism. One tendency in Puritan piety was toward mystical religion. Preachers and devotional literature exalted Christian experience, especially the drama of conversion, and demonstrated renewed interest in the doctrine of the Holy Spirit by which the most intimate relating of the soul to God might be achieved. Even before the Puritan revolution in the 1640's extreme versions of these ideas had produced Spiritist "heretics" and sects, while Anne Hutchinson and the Massachusetts upheaval represented the working of the same ideas. In England, revolution and war after 1640 allowed this theme to become more common and more radical, and from this environment Quakerism emerged.

George Fox (1624–1691) was born and raised in the Leicester village of Drayton-in-the-Clay by parents in humble circumstances. Though intended for the church at one time, Fox remained unlearned and became a shoemaker. Locally notorious for his religious unsettlement before he was twenty, he looked vainly to ministers for help. For a time he left his relations and wandered. At last came the illumination recorded in the *Journal*: "But as I had forsaken all the priests, so I left the separate preachers also, and those called the most experienced people; for I saw there was none among them all that could speak to my condition. And when all my hopes in them and in all men were gone . . . Oh then, I heard a voice which said, 'There is one, even Christ Jesus, that can speak to thy condition,' and when I heard it my heart did leap for joy."

Fox began his ministry no earlier than 1647 (if that early), probably among the religion-seeking, "shattered" Baptist community in Nottinghamshire, from whom he may have derived some emphases later regarded as characteristically Quaker. From these beginnings, Quakerism spread rapidly through the northern counties, the conversion of the Westmorland Seekers, "the people in white raiment," being especially notable for later growth. In the 1650's Quakerism was the most aggressive and dynamic English religious movement, recruiting largely from dissatisfied Baptists and Independents. Sometimes preached in churches, but often in houses, barns, or open air, "truth" was carried throughout England and Wales, and to Scotland, Ireland, and English colonies overseas.

Quakerism presented in more coherent, systematic form what had been fragmentary in earlier radical Puritan mysticism. Fox preached a New Age of the Spirit which was shed in the hearts of men, guiding them in spiritual faith and moral rectitude. Dwelling in the Spirit thrust on men a radical perspective on church and society from which characteristic Quaker doctrines emerged. The worship of the Friends was a silent waiting on the Spirit, who might become vocal in any humble worshiper, man or woman. Accordingly, the ministry was never an "office," though in later Quaker meetings the names of those who had been specially called were "recorded." Scripture, though precious as the testimony of the Spirit in ages past, was necessarily of less importance to those who had the Spirit as their Teacher. Similarly, sacraments might be discarded by those who had been baptized in the Spirit and fed on Christ spiritually. The same perspective prompted an uncompromising social ethic. Quakers rejected "hypocritical" polite speech —"you" in place of "thou"—and declined to remove their hats in respect. They repudiated oaths, force, and war. The term "Quaker" may have come from a physical manifestation of the intense spiritual excitement which often dominated these communities.

Because their views were considered so subversive to accepted ideas of church and state, Quakers were vigorously persecuted. Moreover, since they were drawn from the lower social scale, they were regarded as spokesmen for political and social radicalism. Even under the relatively tolerant Commonwealth, thousands were jailed, and after the Restoration in 1660 treatment became much more severe. Many Quakers were ruinously fined, flogged, transported to colonies abroad, or imprisoned. Legally, they were especially vulnerable, often charged with plotting against the regime, vagrancy, blasphemy, contempt of the king's officers, refusing to take the oaths of supremacy and allegiance, interrupting ministers, withholding tithes, as well as holding illegal conventicles. Throughout the persecution they refused to suspend worship or make their meetings secret. Some relief was found in Charles II's Indulgence (1672) and James II's favor, and security was finally won in the Toleration Act (1689). Yet even after this date, Quakers had to labor for the removal of many disabilities.

These years of persecution were also years of Quaker growth and organization. Fox himself visited every county in England and Wales; he made journeys to Scotland, Ireland, the Continent, and in 1671 and 1672 to the West Indies and the American colonies. In Scotland success was greatest near Aberdeen. From this community came Robert Barclay, whose *Apology for the True Christian Divinity* (1676) was the most important philosophical defense of Quakerism. In Ireland the Dublin Yearly Meeting was set up in 1670. Beginning in the 1660's a national organization was worked out, eventually with Monthly and Quarterly Meetings, and a London Yearly Meeting for all Britain. To intercede with government, the special Meeting for Sufferings was established in 1675. Some Friends regarded this structure as binding the free testimony of the Spirit, and for about twenty years a vigorous opposition, led by John Wilkinson and John Story, disrupted the society.

As this development suggests, at the end of the 17th century Quakerism was losing its dynamic vision of a gospel for all people and becoming the tenets of a particular sect. Prosperity, some legal security, middle-class respectability, and the decline of intense spirituality all left their mark. At the same time much emphasis was placed on Quaker solidarity, discipline, and peculiar dress and speech. "We are now coming into Jewism," complained Margaret Fell, Fox's widow, in 1700. In the 18th century, Quakers excelled in trade and philanthropy, but the period of growth was past.

America was the scene of Quakerism's greatest influence and numbers. "Publishers of Truth" invaded Boston in 1656, but were immediately expelled, the General Court passing severe laws against Quakers. Friends returned, despite punishment, even executions, but success in Massachusetts was slight. Rhode Island, by contrast, became predominantly Quaker. In 1674 control of and migration to West Jersey began. But the most important experiment was Pennsylvania (1682). William Penn, the proprietor, was determined that the province should be a refuge for Quakers and others oppressed in conscience and should be free of war, oaths, and persecution. The colony was a success from the start, and despite heavy non-Quaker immigration, eastern Quakers remained in political control until their voluntary withdrawal in 1755 because of conscientious inability to support the imperial struggle with France. Quaker settlements were also important in Delaware, Maryland, North Carolina, and later in Ohio and Indiana.

By the 19th century, Friends in both England and America were affected by the Evangelical Awakening. In England, Joseph Gurney was prominent in promoting evangelical views among Quakers. In America similar tensions produced the Hicksite separation (1827–1828), named for Elias Hicks of Long Island, who resisted the evangelical emphases of Orthodox Friends in the name of conservative Quakerism. In later years of the century, Hicksites remained a small fraction of the Quaker community.

Throughout its history, Quakerism has demonstrated a keen humanitarian witness for reform. English Friends were prominent in the antislavery movement, law and prison reform, and popular education. Similarly, American Quakers participated in the rich variety of 19th-century reforms, their testimony against slavery, led by Anthony Benezet and John Woolman, being especially notable.

BIBLIOGRAPHY: G. Fox, *Journal* (Cambridge, 1911); W. C. Braithwaite, *Beginnings of Quakerism* (Cambridge, 1955); and *The Second Period of Quakerism* (London, 1919); A. Brinton (ed.), *Then and Now* (Philadelphia, 1960); B. Forbush, *Elias Hicks* (New York, 1956); R. M. Jones, *The Quakers in the American Colonies* (London, 1911); R. H. King, *George Fox and the Light Within* (Philadelphia, 1940); E. Trueblood, *The People Called Quakers* (New York, 1966).

**Quanta Cura.** Encyclical letter of Pope Pius IX, issued on Dec. 8, 1864. This brief letter warned against the main evils of the day as seen by the pope, namely, naturalism, liberalism, socialism, communism, and secularism. It was to the text of this encyclical that the eighty condemned propositions of the Syllabus of Errors were attached. The Syllabus detailed the errors alluded to by the pope in *Quanta cura*.

**Quarles, Francis** (1592–1644). Anglican poet and apologist of royalism. He began by writing paraphrases of the Bible and later contributed six metrical psalms to a New England psalter. Wide acclaim came with his poems in *Emblems* (1635). Equally popular was a prose manual of piety, *Enchiridion* (1640). Though not greatly admired outside religious circles, his poems exhibited enough devotion and literary ability to cause them to be constantly reprinted for a century after his death.

**Quartodecimans.** Those who celebrated Easter on the day of the Passover, the 14th day of the month Nisan, rather than on the Sunday nearest it. They were largely from Asia Minor, where Jewish example was more in evidence. When Polycarp of Smyrna came to Rome in the middle of the 2d century, he was surprised to discover that this was not the universal custom. Anicetus of Rome could not be persuaded to adopt it, but he allowed Polycarp to follow it.

The question arose again in the time of the more rigorous Pope Victor, who tried to impose the Sunday observance of Easter on the churches of Asia Minor and was met by the stiff opposition of Polycrates, bishop of Ephesus. Polycrates claimed that the tradition of John the beloved disciple, Philip the evangelist (whom he called apostle), Melito of Sardis, and others was on the side of the Quartodecimans. Victor, who did much to hasten the centralization of the church around Rome, promptly excommunicated him. Many objected to his high-handedness in the matter, including Irenaeus, who wrote that "the disagreement in the fast confirms our agreement in the faith." For the time being, the churches of Asia Minor continued their practice. The Quartodecimans eventually left the church and survived as a body until the 5th century.

**Quenstedt, Johann Andreas** (1617–1688). German Lutheran theologian at Wittenberg in the period of high orthodoxy, expressing this theological position in its ultimate form. His major work, *Theologica didactica-polemica* (1685), although rigidly orthodox and exhibiting comprehensive erudition, is not, however, as passionately polemical as were many of the writings of Lutheran orthodox theologians.

**Quesnel, Pasquier** (1634–1719). French Oratorian priest. His most important scholarly writing, an edition of the works of Leo the Great (1675), was put on the Index (1676) because of the Gallican views espoused in his commentary. His *Moral Reflections on the New Testament* (1st ed., 1672; rev. ed., 1692) developed a Scriptural spirituality, but its Jansenism brought condemnation of 101 propositions in *Unigenitus* (1713). Refusing condemnation, he lived in Dutch exile awaiting future exoneration of his narrow view of the church.

**Quiercy, Synods of.** Two synods held at Quiercy near Laon in 849 and 853 under the presidency of Archbishop Hincmar of Reims. Both synods were concerned with the teaching of double predestination by the monk Gottschalk. At the first synod, he was suspended from priestly duties for alleged irregularities in his ordination and sentenced to a public flogging before being confined to a monastery. His doctrines were condemned by four chapters which affirmed single predestination and free will. The second synod, in the presence of Charles the Bald, reaffirmed the actions of the first.

**Quietism.** The doctrine which declares that man's perfection consists of complete passivity of mind and will and abandonment to God in pure faith. This state is reached by passive forms of prayer in which the soul is brought to rest in the presence of God, and God works in the life as he wills. Absorption in God rejects all discursive meditation and even adoration of the Divine Persons. Love of God becomes a habitual state that is wholly pure and disinterested. God is loved for God's own sake, not for merit or for one's own sake or one's salvation. Such a state of holy indifference is the unitive life. Even as prayer is passive, so also all outward acts of mortification, almsgiving, and confession are superfluous. The ethical implications are radical. Once this state is attained, sin is impossible, action unnecessary. A man may be tempted and do that which would be sin for another, but as his will has become annihilated such deeds cease to be sin in him. Those who follow quietism in its extreme form feel no need for external worship or the sacraments.

The chief exponents of quietism were Miguel de Molinos, condemned by the church in 1687, Pietro Petrucci, condemned in 1688, and Mme. Guyon, condemned by the Conference of Issy in 1695. François Fénelon was considered a semiquietist.

**Quiñones, Francisco de** (d. 1540). Spanish cardinal and liturgist. Born in León of a distinguished family, Quiñones joined the Franciscans and rose to high office in that order. He negotiated between Clement VII and Charles V after the sack of Rome by the imperial troops, and was rewarded with the cardinalate in 1528. The following year he became involved in the divorce proceedings of Henry VIII as a defender of the rights of Queen Catherine. In 1535 he published a reformed edition of the breviary, in which the format was simplified and the Scripture readings ordered more logically. Although Quiñones' work was not adopted by the Roman Church, it did exercise notable influence on the liturgical revisions of Thomas Cranmer.

# R

**Rabanus Maurus** (c. 776–856). Frankish scholar and theologian. A monk of Fulda, he studied for a time at Tours under Alcuin. Upon his return to Fulda, he was made head of the school, and under his direction it became the primary intellectual center of Germany. In 822 he was elected abbot, but was forced to resign in 842 because of conflicts with temporal authorities. He retired from the monastery and lived in seclusion until he was elected archbishop of Mainz in 847. Although he was not an original thinker, he did represent the great breadth of knowledge that was characteristic of the Carolingian Renaissance. His writings, intended for instructional purposes, are a compilation of earlier authors. His theological works quote heavily from the fathers, while his *De rerum naturis* is based on the works of Isidore of Seville. He wrote some verse, although the tradition of his authorship of "Veni, Creator Spiritus" is erroneous. He composed a manual for the education of monks and priests, *De institutione clericorum*. In 848 he held a synod at Mainz at which the predestinarian doctrines of Gottschalk, a former oblate of Fulda, were condemned. He also opposed the Eucharistic doctrines of Paschasius Radbertus. Among his students at Fulda were some of the intellectual leaders of the age: Walafrid Strabo, Lupus of Ferrières, and Otfrid of Weissenburg.

**Rabbula** (d. 435). Bishop of Edessa (from 412), the center of Syrian Christianity and the site of the oldest known Christian building. Rabbula was one of the leaders of the Syrian Church during a period of considerable theological conflict. He had evidently been a follower of Nestorius at one time but broke away and wrote a sermon (extant) opposing him. Rabbula was also the head of the theological school at Edessa, where the Persian clergy were educated, and he exerted a great influence through this school, which was finally broken up (489) as a result of the conflict over Nestorianism. Rabbula inaugurated the attack on the teachings of Theodore of Mopsuestia (d. 428) shortly after the meeting of the Council of Ephesus (431) which condemned Theodore's doctrine of the incarnation. Rabbula's works include Syriac versions of some of the writings (such as *De recta fide*) of Cyril of Alexandria. Another work generally attributed to Rabbula is the New Testament portion of the Peshitta, which was produced to replace the widely used *Diatessaron* of the heretic Tatian. Other writings of Rabbula include numerous epistles and hymns. The theological position of the Syrian Church became even more confused after the death of Rabbula when Ibas became bishop of Edessa (435–457).

**Racovian Catechism.** A statement of Socinian views. Raków in Poland became a center of Anabaptist Christianity in 1569. By 1574 a *Catechesis* was produced which expressed a pacifist, communitarian, anti-Nicene faith opposed to participation in civil government. The Racovians were deeply impressed by the Hutterites, but developed out of Polish rationalistic Calvinism and out of the free discussions in the Vistula area which was for a time a refuge for Dutch and Silesian Anabaptists and for others such as Osiander, whose views had made them unacceptable elsewhere. The views of two such men, Laelius Sozzini (Socinus) and his nephew, Faustus, were expressed in the Racovian Catechism of 1605 which became normative for the Polish Minor Church. The earlier Racovian *Catechesis* had already gone in a unitarian direction. The Holy Spirit was understood to be pervasive and powerful in achieving a redeemed and disciplined church through faith baptism and the Lord's Supper and in a regenerated life, but was not to be worshiped as God. Christians were enabled to imitate Christ in his role as Prophet, Priest, and King because Christ was the creator of the regenerate life, but Christ was not to be seen as the Logos in creation. Baptism was by immersion, and the Supper was frequently observed; resurrection was believed to be of the righteous only.

**Radbertus.** See Paschasius Radbertus.

**Rade, Paul Martin** (1857–1940). German Protestant theologian. Son of a Lutheran pastor, he was educated at Leipzig, served as pastor, especially at Frankfurt, then from 1900 taught systematic theology at Marburg. His main activity was as editor of *Christliche Welt*; he was also assistant editor of *Zeitschrift für Theologie und Kirche*. Influenced by Harnack, he tried to work out the social and political implications of Christianity. He played a prominent part in the Evangelical Social Congress, and after 1918 became one of the few ecclesiastical champions of the democratic regime. During the interwar years he worked hard in church movements for peace. In the church conflict under Hitler, however, he took neither side, since his own hope was always for a better liberalism. Rade was a prolific writer with a wide range of interests. In the historical field he wrote on such varied characters as Damasus of Rome, Luther, Ulrich von Hutten, Philip Jacob Spener, and Schleiermacher. He also wrote on various moral questions, on Christianity in an industrial age, and on problems of sex. By his influence, activities, and writings, Rade thus played a pivotal role in church life in Germany during a critical transitional period, though he stood outside the main theological development.

**Radewyns, Florentius** (1350–1400). Leader of the *devotio moderna*. After studying in Prague and becoming a priest (1377), he was won for the *devotio moderna* by Gerhard Groote. On Groote's death in 1384 he assumed leadership of the Brethren at Deventer, who were organized as a lay community in 1391. Though he did not himself become a monk, Radewyns was influential in the founding of the congregation of Windesheim. He wrote little, but made a profound impression by his qualities of leadership.

**Radical Reformation.** The phrase "Radical Reformation" refers to those movements in Christian life and thought in 16th-century Europe which did not seek a traditional *rapprochement* with a continuing civil and political establishment but rather a restitution of faith and practice in accord with the precedent of the primitive church. The word "Reformation" applies because some of these movements were occasioned by the work of the major Reformers and to some extent grew out of them, and because changes in morals and worship were sought. The word "Radical" applies because there was an appeal to the precedent of the early church in conscious disagreement with centuries of tradition: many who may be described by the phrase "Radical Reformation" saw themselves returning to the root (*radix*) of Christian faith. Historical influences especially to be noticed are the precedent of Luther in appealing to Scripture and to a personally received faith in contradistinction to the traditional church structure; the demand among the northern Biblically oriented humanists for a general reform in morals; the Sacramentarian movement of the Netherlands which found expression also in Zwingli's denial of the traditional doctrine of the Real Presence; a Biblicism arising from the humanist "return to the sources" and accentuated by the fascination with new vernacular translations of the Bible which had developed among those who were formerly illiterate; and apocalypticism coming in part from the Taborites but emphasized by the

Turkish threat, Biblical literalism, and the same economic, social, and political changes that produced the Peasants' War of 1525. There was often an iconoclastic revulsion against traditional images and practices which were regarded as ethically fruitless and distracting from a transcendent God. A popularized mysticism coming from the tradition of Tauler played a part, and to a lesser extent contemporary rationalism and naturalism received some hearing through Socinus and Servetus. Publications of the writings of early church fathers such as Tertullian influenced the thought of some earlier leaders.

It is noteworthy how little national or sectional loyalties were present in the thought of the Radical Reformation. Some individualism may be discerned, but on the whole theology and experience moved around a widely felt demand for finding a fresh basis for social experience; characteristic features of popular revivalism often occurred. The Radical Reformation, not a single movement but a congery of movements, developed distinct emphases of its own. Prominent among these emphases was the tendency to think of the sacraments as focuses of the relation of God and man. The Mass, Baptism, and ordination of clergy came to be regarded as valid only after moral or spiritual criteria had been met by the recipients. Marriage came to be thought of widely as a covenanted relationship. Extreme unction, confirmation, and penance dropped away, though practices analogous to the latter two occurred. Traditionally ordained clergy were often reordained after having the approval of a community of faith, though early it was also common for local "servants of the Word" to receive ordination from itinerant apostles, sometimes in conscious imitation of New Testament practice. The Lord's Supper and Baptism were often justified as ordinances to be kept in imitation of Christ's precedent and as signs of faith's presence rather than as initiatory means of grace, though spiritualizers such as Schwenkfeld preferred to see such "outer observances" as unnecessary and bad because divisive. The theme of "discipleship of Christ" was common as descriptive of the completion, or even the expression, of the faith that justifies before God, though this was sometimes balanced, as with Menno Simons, by the eschatological theme of the "new creature," or as with Hans Denck, by the indwelling Word which makes available divine sources of moral renewal. There was a frequent sense of reliance on the Holy Spirit, and though there were many instances of fanatic and erratic behavior, charges of antinomianism are on the whole misplaced because the Radical Reformers widely engaged in an earnest search for morality on a community basis after New Testament precedents. A few writers, less specifically concerned with renewal of man in relationship with fellowman, looked mainly for a renewal of inner attitudes. Spiritualizers such as Schwenkfeld (on a conventicular basis) and Sebastian Franck (on an individual basis) sought an enjoyment of feeding on the inner or heavenly Christ, or an unction of the Holy Spirit within man. Still fewer others, such as Servetus and Socinus, specifically sought also a renewal of human rational capacities. An important emphasis in much of the Radical Reformation and a point of difference from the Protestant Reformers was a strong missionary activity. The most important point, however, at which the Radical Reformation differed from evangelical Protestantism is in the estimate of the relation of justification to moral renewal. Again and again Luther and others were charged with teaching and living a morally fruitless and therefore unreal relationship with God. Faith, it was widely claimed, was a living, socially constructive thing as justifying faith. Because moral renewal, taking shape from a reception of the enlivening Spirit of God, proceeds as an inner restructuring of life, the fellowship of believers should not seek the support of the political order. In confidence that effective and relatively complete renewal was not only desirable but possible, proponents of the Radical Reformation tended to withdraw themselves from compromise with an imperfect world. Startling and short-lived exceptions such as the Münster kingdom should not obscure a genuine and widespread moral and spiritual revival among common people.

The Radical Reformation began first among leaders of the Wittenberg group; Luther's reversal of some of the changes made while he was in the Wartburg led Carlstadt and Müntzer and others to seek what they saw as a more thorough revival of worship and life in Orlamunde and Allstedt. Members of the circle around Zwingli saw his defense of infant baptism as a compromise of true faith, and they instituted believer's baptism and believer's Lord's Supper after January, 1525, which spread widely in Switzerland and in the towns of southern Germany. Also contributing to this spread were the writings of Hubmaier, who accepted the support of political authority, the writing and preaching of Hans Denck, who furthered a theological strain arising from medieval Augustinian mysticism, and the preaching of Hans Hut, who contributed a strong apocalypticism. Michael

Sattler, in the tradition of the Zurich radicals, was central in the writing of the Schleitheim Articles. Development of this southern German and Austrian Anabaptism was slowed by persecution after 1528, but increased rapidly in the 1530's under the leadership of Pilgram Marpeck in the southern German cities and of Jacob Hutter in Moravia and eastward in communalistic Anabaptism. The eschatological preachings of Melchior Hofmann in the Netherlands led to a widespread parallel development of radical faith leading on its apocalyptic side to the Münster debacle and on its pacifist side to the work of Menno Simons. Anabaptism spread eastward along the Baltic coast; the Mennonites have remained to this day a part of the religious scene in the Netherlands. A relationship existed between them and the se-baptists (self-baptizers) of England in the 1580's. Polish Anabaptism, deriving from Mennonite, Hutterite, and other sources after the 1560's, became Socinianism by 1605. Everywhere Anabaptism flourished primarily among the lower classes, and almost everywhere, especially in Belgium and Holland until 1577, in southern Germany and in Austria, there was harassment from civil and churchly authorities. There were thousands of martyrs in the Radical Reformation.

Several issues divided the movements. One was the question of when the early church was understood to have "fallen." Was it immediately after the New Testament apostles? or only under Constantine? Most rejected the Constantinian settlement, and a few, such as Socinus and Servetus, rejected the Nicene Creed on rational and Scriptural grounds. How far could one trust the Spirit apart from the written Word? Relatively few followed Campanus, Franck, and Schwenkfeld toward a quietistic spiritualism, and antinomian behavior was less the rule than the exception. Most insisted that faith had to be expressed outwardly to be genuine, though a few sought only changed inner attitudes. Almost all were convinced that the *eschaton* was near, but relatively few felt that this justified them in violent action against existing society. On the whole, the Radical Reformation can be said to have advanced ideas and practices whose time had not yet come, and its direct lineal descendants are today relatively few in number.

BIBLIOGRAPHY: G. H. Williams and A. Mergal (eds.), *Spiritual and Anabaptist Writers* (The Library of Christian Classics, Vol. XXV, Philadelphia, 1957); G. Hershberger (ed.), *The Recovery of the Anabaptist Vision* (Scottdale, Pa., 1957); F. H. Littell, *The*

*Anabaptist View of the Church* (Boston, 1958); G. H. Williams, *The Radical Reformation* (Philadelphia, 1962).

**Radowitz, Joseph Maria von** (1797–1853). Prussian military officer and statesman. Born of Hungarian stock and trained in French military schools, he first fought for (1813) and then against (1814) Napoleon, and entered the Prussian army in 1823. He served in the diplomatic corps and was leader of the extreme right in the Frankfurt Parliament (1848). He was for a time minister of foreign affairs (1850–1852). A Roman Catholic, he was a member of the closest circle of advisers to Frederick William IV and stood in close relation to the Protestant *Erweckung* ("awakening") movement in Germany.

**Ragaz, Leonhard** (1868–1948). German socialist. A cathedral pastor in Basel (1902), Ragaz with others published *Neue Wege* (1906–1945) and led a religiosocialist movement. He was named professor of theology at Zurich (1908), and then joined the Social Democratic Party. In 1921 he laid teaching aside to work full time in the industrial section of Zurich. After 1918 he was prominent in the pacifist movement. Influenced by Tolstoy, Carlyle, Hermann Kutter, and the Kingdom theology of the two Blumhardts, Ragaz perceived divine revelatory signs in socialism.

**Rahner, Karl** (1904–    ). Roman Catholic theologian. Born in Freiburg, Germany, Rahner became a member of the Society of Jesus in 1922 and was ordained in 1932. Professor of dogmatic theology at Innsbruck University, he is personal theologian to Julius Cardinal Döpfner of Munich and Franziskus Cardinal König of Vienna. Editor of the *Enchiridion symbolorum,* the standard compendium of documents expressing the teachings of Catholicism, Rahner was named by Pope John XXIII to the select group of official theologians to the Second Vatican Council. Rahner has proved one of the most profound and stimulating theologians of his time. His own insights are scattered among some seven hundred books, articles, and essays. Among his most recent publications are *Christian Commitment, Nature and Grace: Dilemmas in the Modern Church,* and *Christian in the Market Place.*

**Raikes, Robert** (1735–1811). English social reformer and founder of Sunday schools. Raikes was born at Gloucester, England, and educated at the Cathedral College School. In 1757 on the death of his father, he succeeded him as publisher of the *Gloucester Journal,* a newspaper that he employed for the propagation of the reform of prisons. His chief interest and fame, however, lay in the training of children. Stimulated by the neglected condition of the local children and taking a hint from a Dissenter, William King, who had established a Sunday school at Dursley, Raikes and his curate, Thomas Stock, began a school at Asbury, Berkshire. In 1780 he started a school in his own parish, St. Mary le Crypt, open on weekdays and Sunday for the teaching of Scripture, reading, and other elementary subjects. His movement, after some initial opposition from conservatives and Sabbatarians, spread rapidly. In 1785 a London society was organized for the establishment of Sunday schools in England. The methods of Raikes were followed by others, notably Hannah More in Somerset, and before his death Sunday schools had been cheaply and successfully established throughout the country.

**Rainolds** (Reynolds), **John** (1549–1607). Puritan divine. Rainolds served as president of Corpus Christi College at Oxford and as dean of Lincoln Cathedral. He was a staunch Calvinist. At the Hampton Court Conference of 1604 he headed the Puritan delegation. Among other things, he proposed a new translation of the Bible, and subsequently he worked on the prophetical books of the King James Version.

**Rainsford, William Stephen** (1850–1933). Episcopal clergyman. A native of Ireland and Cambridge-educated, he was ordained in England and served there and in Canada before coming to St. George's Church in New York City in 1883. At St. George's he developed a superb example of the "institutional church," partially through J. P. Morgan's support. A broadly diversified program made it the largest Episcopal church in America. Meanwhile, Rainsford was engaged in a number of civic affairs, giving his support to labor and various social reforms to aid the poor. A breakdown in 1904 caused him to resign his parish and to vacation in Africa, where after 1912, when he requested and received dismissal from the ministry, he led an expedition for the American Museum of Natural History. He is remembered as a leader in the Social Gospel movement.

**Ramabai, Pandita** (1858–1922). Hindu feminist and social reformer. A Brahmin Sanskrit prodigy, widowed early, she visited England and was converted to Christianity. She founded the Sharada Sadan, a home for destitute high-caste widows, at Poona (1889). Soon she was charged with proselytizing, when several of her Hindu girls became Christians. She is remembered gratefully for service to young widows, female rights, and education.

**Ramón Lull.** See LULL, RAMÓN.

**Rampolla, Count Mariano del Tindaro** (1843–1913). Roman Catholic cardinal and diplomat. Appointed as a diplomatic representative to Madrid in 1875, Rampolla returned to Rome in 1877 as Secretary of the Propaganda for Oriental Affairs. He became nuncio to Madrid in 1882. Leo XIII made him cardinal and papal secretary of state in 1887. Although he was one of the logical successors to Leo upon the latter's death in 1903, the veto of Austria prevented consideration of him.

**Ramus, Petrus** (1515–1572). French humanist. Educated at the College of Navarre, he personified the reaction against Scholasticism and when taking his master's degree in 1536 defended the thesis "Everything Aristotle taught is false." In 1544 he was forbidden by Francis I to preach, and was interdicted for undermining the foundations of philosophy and religion. The next year, however, he was appointed president of the College of Presles, and in 1551 a professor in the Collège de France. In 1561 he embraced Protestantism, with the result that he was forced to flee from Paris, and in 1568 even from France. He found refuge in Germany, but returned to his homeland in 1571, in time to be killed in the Bartholomew's Day Massacre the next year.

On his return to France he led a dispute favoring a congregational type of church polity rather than the established government by consistory, but after the Massacre the subject was forgotten. Against the system of Aristotle, Ramus projected his own, a combination of dialectic and logic which abolished the distinction between probable and demonstrable argument. A school of "Ramists" existed in France, Germany, and Holland, and quarreled with the "Anti-Ramists" over his ideas for a number of years.

**Ranters.** An English extremist group that flourished around the middle of the 17th century. The Ranters were often confused at the time with other nonconformist groups, but in their teachings they seem to have resembled most the medieval Brethren of the Free Spirit. They rejected the authority of the Scriptures and tended toward pantheism. Among others, Richard Baxter wrote against them.

**Raphael** (Raffaello Santi *or* Sanzio) (1483–1520). Italian artist, architect, designer, and sculptor. Raphael is considered one of the three greatest painters (the other two are Leonardo da Vinci and Michelangelo) of the High Renaissance. He did his most important work in Rome in the service of popes Julius II and Leo X. Raphael's numerous madonnas and his large frescoes on the walls of the Signatura of the Vatican represent a culmination of most of the technical achievements of the age.

**Rapp, George** (1757–1847). Founder of the Harmony Society. A peasant in Württemberg, Germany, Rapp, because of his pietistic beliefs, was led to reject the state church, for which he and his followers were persecuted. In 1803 they came to America and settled in Pennsylvania, later founding New Harmony, Ind. (1814), and Economy, Pa. (1824). In 1805 they organized themselves as the Harmony Society, which Rapp led as virtual dictator for the rest of his life.

**Rappites.** An American communistic sect of German origin also called the "Harmonists," officially the Harmony Society. For a number of years the layman George Rapp (1757–1847) preached in his home in Württemberg to an increasing group of Separatist families who practiced community property and celibacy. He brought them to America in 1803 to Butler Co., Pa., where they built the town of Harmony and in 1805 organized themselves as the Harmony Society. In 1814 they moved to Indiana to found New Harmony, then in 1824 sold out to Robert Owen and moved to a site on the Ohio River below Pittsburgh, founding Economy. The group had dwindled, and in 1905 dissolved.

**Raskolniki.** See OLD BELIEVERS.

**Rasputin, Grigori Efimovich** (c. 1871–1916). Russian religious and political figure. Son of a Siberian peasant and never in clerical orders, he gained acceptance in the highest circles of St. Petersburg society in 1905, and after presentation at court in 1907 won a powerful hold over the royal household by means of his apparent power over the health of the heir apparent. Though he led a flagrantly immoral life, he was honored as a *starets* ("saintly elder") and exercised immense power over church and state. Rasputin was finally assassinated because of his anti-military, pro-German views.

**Ratione Peccati.** A phrase meaning "by reason of sin" derived from the *Decretales* (2. 1. 13) of Pope Innocent III. When John Lackland, king of England, appealed to Innocent III against Philip Augustus, king of France, the pope justified in the decretal *Novit ille* (1204) his right to intervene in the war between France and England in order to reestablish peace. He argued that he did not want to diminish the jurisdiction or the power of the king of France, but that the pope had superior jurisdiction over temporal rulers in all matters involving sin.

**Ratisbon Colloquy.** See REGENSBURG COLLOQUY.

**Ratramnus** (d. c. 868). A monk of Corbey. He wrote treatises on the important theological issues of the middle 9th century. Against the doctrine of the physical presence in the Eucharist as taught by Paschasius Radbertus, he wrote *De corpore et sanguine Domini liber.* He defended double predestination in *De praedestinatione Dei.* He also wrote a text attacking the supposed errors of Greek theology.

**Rauhes Haus** ("rough house"). A home for poor and delinquent boys. The first such establishment was founded by J. H. Wichern at Hamburg, Germany, in 1833 and provided the seed from which the Inner Mission arose. The ideal was the residence of the boys in "families" of twelve with a "house father." The boys were bound only by love, and the entire community was arranged around a prayer house or chapel. From 1833 to 1858 this model was much copied. Wichern set up a training school for house fathers and in 1844 a periodical to promote the work.

**Raumer, Karl Georg von** (1783–1865). German minerologist and educator. Educated at Göttingen and Halle but influenced especially by Fichte and Pestalozzi, Raumer became a professor at Breslau (1811). Slowly he turned from minerology to education. He taught at a private school in Nuremberg (1823) and established an institution for delinquents. In 1827 he assumed a professorship at Erlangen, but retained an interest in pedagogy. His educational writings were influential also in America.

**Rauschenbusch, Walter** (1861–1918). American clergyman and leader in the social application of Christianity. He was pastor of the Second German Baptist Church, New York City (1886–1897), and a professor at Rochester Theological Seminary (1897–1918). Though he was an effective pastor and a highly praised teacher, it was as the most successful exponent of the Social Gospel that Rauschenbusch was called one of the three Americans (with Jonathan Edwards and Horace Bushnell) who most influenced Christian thought before neo-orthodoxy.

The son of Augustus Rauschenbusch, a German-born preacher who changed from the Lutheran to the Baptist Church, Walter had a conversion experience at seventeen and shortly thereafter decided to enter the ministry. He was educated in Germany and at Rochester Theological Seminary, where he graduated in 1886. His first full parish was in "Hell's Kitchen," New York City, where individualistic piety failed to solve new urban problems. He turned to Henry George and other social critics for answers to poverty's problems, combining modern ideas with the teachings of Jesus. Rauschenbusch was co-editor of a workers' paper, *For the Right* (1889–1891). In 1892 he cofounded the Brotherhood of the Kingdom with other Baptists who wished to emphasize the social aspects of the gospel.

Called to join his father in the Rochester Seminary's German school, he taught New Testament, civics, science, and English until he was made professor of church history on the regular faculty (1902). Active in civic and denominational affairs, and the author of many articles, he became internationally famous with the publication of his first book in 1907, *Christianity and the Social Crisis.* Despite partial deafness, he made hundreds of speeches and published many works in the next decade, including *For God and the People: Prayers of the Social Awakening, Christianizing the Social Order, Unto Me, Dare We Be Christians?, The Social Principles of Jesus,* and *A Theology for the Social Gospel.*

Rauschenbusch combined social analysis, theological liberalism, and Biblical piety in a style that suited the progressive era of the early 20th century and made his books widely read. Convinced that Jesus preached social salvation for social sin, he demanded renewed stress on the Kingdom of God as Christianity's goal. He interpreted it as an evolutionary development in which God and men worked together against the forces of evil for a reign of justice, democracy, and brotherhood on earth. Though scholars such as Schweitzer argued that Jesus' view of the Kingdom was more otherworldly, Rauschenbusch's emphasis on the importance of social ethics in the Bible was a greatly needed corrective to the selfish individualism of the gilded age of industrialism. The church was also needed, but subordinate to the Kingdom.

Sympathy with the poor inclined him to Christian Socialism, but he attacked dogmatic political socialism, insisting that "social redemption of the race through Christ" was crucial.

Rauschenbusch lived in an optimistic age, and his idea that family, church, education, and government were already largely "Christianized" (leaving mainly business) led to charges of naïveté. However, he did not accept the then common belief in inevitable progress, and World War I caused him to view the stubbornness of sin with much of the sobriety of later exponents of "realistic" neo-orthodoxy, whereas many Social Gospelers who outlived him continued with optimism unabated.

With books translated into many languages, he was perhaps the most influential Christian of his time, reaching the Y.M.C.A., the Federal Council of Churches, and progressive politics especially. Theodore Roosevelt, Lloyd George, and Woodrow Wilson were among those who sought his counsel. More recently, Reinhold Niebuhr and Martin Luther King, Jr., expressed indebtedness.

BIBLIOGRAPHY: B. Landis (ed.), *A Rauschenbusch Reader* (New York, 1957); V. Bodein, *The Social Gospel of Walter Rauschenbusch and Its Relation to Religious Education* (New Haven, 1944); R. T. Handy (ed.), *The Social Gospel in America: 1870–1920* (New York, 1966); D. Sharpe, *Walter Rauschenbusch* (New York, 1942).

**Ravenna Mosaics.** Mosaics executed at Ravenna after the imperial capital of the western division of the Roman Empire was moved there in the early part of the 5th century. They are among the best preserved 5th- and 6th-century Byzantine mosaics in existence. The Byzantine emphasis on the mysticism of light noted in the architecture of that style is enhanced in the mosaics by the brilliance of the reflected light obtained by a technique employing small cubes of glass, enamel, marble, and mother-of-pearl. The symphonic motif of the Byzantine liturgy finds its counterpart in the symphony of color in the mosaics. Light, color, and the rhythm of the configurations plus the aesthetical transformation of spatial dimensional qualities are characteristic of the Ravenna mosaics. Of the structures that contain the mosaics—the Mausoleum of Galla Placida, the Cathedral Baptistery, the Baptistery of the Arians, the Basilica of San Apollinare Nuovo, the Basilica of San Apollinare in Classe, the Archepiscopal Chapel, and the Church of San Vitale—the last holds those most renowned for their technical detail and subject matter. Besides the portrayals of Biblical scenes, the landscapes of which are reminiscent of the style of Rouault, the panel depicting the emperor Justinian and his retinue is an expression of the Byzantine style that has seldom been surpassed. The figures have a mystical quality that makes them appear to belong to a realm not conditioned by space and time.

**Raymond of Peñafort** (c. 1175–1275). Spanish monk and theologian. After studying and teaching at Barcelona, he went to Bologna to study law. In 1222 he entered the Dominican Order. As grand penitentiary to Gregory IX, he was commissioned to make a collection of all the papal decretals. In 1238 he was elected general of the order and instituted a reform. Thomas Aquinas wrote his *Summa contra Gentiles* at Raymond's suggestion. Raymond retired in 1240, devoting himself to the conversion of Jews and Saracens.

**Raymond of Sebonde** (Sabunde) (c. 1390–c. 1436). Spanish-born theologian, philosopher, and physician. His last years were spent teaching at the University of Toulouse, France. Raymond's thought was indicative of the decadent state of Scholasticism on the eve of the Renaissance; he held that it is possible to discover the contents of Christian revelation by reason alone. His greatest work, *Theologia naturalis,* was translated into French in the 16th century by Michel de Montaigne in whose *Essays* is included the well-known "Apologie de Raymond Sebond."

**Realism.** A theory of knowledge that ascribes extramental existence to universals. It is traceable to Plato's belief in the objective reality of ideas. In the early Middle Ages, influenced by Augustine's Neoplatonism and the need to extract every possible nuance from the words of Scripture, philosophers tended to subscribe to an exaggerated version of this view, and assuming that the logical and real orders were exactly parallel, they held that every word in the language must refer to an existing entity, and that because in such statements as "A is a man" and "B is a man" the word "man" is the same, there was a substantial identity in the real order between A and B. Thus the concept *Humanity* was seen to reflect a reality, the unitary substance of human nature, in which all men shared, or of which they were accidental modifications. Such reasoning could clarify the doctrine of original sin by showing how all men shared in Adam's fall. Fredigisius of Tours (d. 834) taught that the "nothingness" from which God created the earth must refer to some thing, to the chaos of primeval matter existing from eternity. Similarly, Remigius of Auxerre (d. c. 908) held that eloquence had existed before Cicero and that he had received a modality of it. The basic tendency of exaggerated realism is still discernible in the thought of Anselm (d. 1109). In his argument that the degrees of a hierarchical scale of essences imply God as a supreme unity at the summit, and that the consciousness of God within the soul implies his real existence outside it, Anselm transfers outside the mind the attributes of being as conceived inside it. This kind of realism was banished from further discussion by Abelard's attack on William of Champeaux. William had held that the universal essence of substance was unique and identical in all its subordinate members, that its whole reality was contained essentially in each of them. Thus the individual was only an accidental modification of the species and the species an accident of the genus. Abelard objected that if each man is the human species, then it is whole and entire in Socrates in Rome and Plato in Athens, and that consequently Socrates is present wherever the human essence is found and individuality is destroyed. William abandoned his view by teaching thereafter that reality was contained in each individual not "essentially" but "in a similar fashion," thereby coming very close to Abelard's own teaching. From that time on, though exaggerated realism continued to be taught as part of the general Platonism of the School of Chartres, Abelard's arguments and a greater knowledge of Aristotle's logic ensured that, in general, varieties of moderate realism would prevail. Gilbert de La Porrée adopted Boethius' distinction between substance and subsistence to distinguish between things and their classifications. Genera and species were defined as subsistences, since they had no accidents: they subsisted but did not exist as individual beings. He went on to say that the mind builds its idea of a species by abstracting these subsistences from substances: it then compares a group of like species and conceives the subsistence of a genus. At the top of this scale of abstraction stand the eternal ideas in the divine mind. In this way Gilbert amalgamated the Platonic and Aristotelian answers to the problem of universals. Thereafter the topic ceased to be of major importance to philosophers, taking its place as one of many elements in the more elaborate systems being built up. Using the refinements offered by Aristotelian psychology, Aquinas reechoed Abelard in saying that human nature existed only in individual men and that the universality of the concept *Humanity* was the result of abstraction and was thus a subjective contribution. Nevertheless, since the foundation of the concept was the objective essence of the thing, freed by the mind of its accidents, it did have an existence apart from the mind, though only in individuals, and in a way it was more real than the thing, since as immaterial being it was logically prior to anything physical. Aquinas thus denied exaggerated realism while retaining Augustine's belief in the prior existence of ideas in God's mind. A return to extreme realism can be seen in Duns Scotus, who, in order to safeguard the objectivity of all knowledge, ascribed extramental reality to the distinctions recognized by the mind. However, with the general triumph of Occam's philosophy in the 14th century and consequent loss of concern for metaphysics, realism of any kind ceased to find any influential proponent.

BIBLIOGRAPHY: R. I. Aaron, *The Theory of Universals* (Oxford, 1952); M. H. Carré, *Realists and Nominalists* (New York, 1946); F. Copleston, *A History of Philosophy*, Vol. 2 (London, 1950); É. Gilson, *The Spirit of Medieval Philosophy* (New York, 1936).

**Recared** (d. 601). King of the Visigoths in Spain from 586. He ended the conflict of Catholic Romans and Arian Goths by bringing his people into the Catholic Church at the Third Council of Toledo in 589, thus uniting Romans and Goths into the Spanish Church and nation. On this occasion the Nicene Creed was used with the anti-Arian addition of the *filioque* ("and from the Son," used of the procession of the Holy Spirit from the Father) which has become established in the West, and a point of distinction between Eastern and Western Churches.

**Reconquista** ("reconquest"). The period of the *Reconquista* of the Iberian Peninsula from the Moors covers the nearly eight centuries from 718 to 1492 and is generally regarded as the formative period of Spanish history. Tradition holds that in 718 a Visigothic prince, Pelayo, successfully defeated a Moslem army at Covadonga in Asturias and established a dynasty of Christian kings. Thereafter as Christian exiles joined their cobelievers behind the Cantabrian Mountains and as Pelayo's successors began to reconquer other areas of northwestern Spain, new Christian states came into being. By 950, León, Castile, Navarre, and Aragon had been established, while the province of Barcelona—later to become the independent principality of Catalonia—had been taken by the Franks under Charlemagne and made capital of Spanish March in 801. Often these states quarreled and fought with one another, but they remained constant in their desire to wrest lands and riches from the Moors.

As long as the Moors remained strong and united, the Christian advance was slow and often suffered major setbacks. After the death of the great prince Almanzor in 1010, Islamic Spain separated into some twenty-six petty monarchies which proved unable to check the Christians. In 1085, Toledo fell to Alfonso

VI of Castile and León. Christianity seemed about to triumph over Islam throughout the peninsula. In 1086, however, the Moors of Al-Andalus (Moslem Spain) received succor from North Africa. A large and fervent group of Berbers known as the Almoravids crossed into Spain and checked the Christian tide. Sixty years later the Almoravids were followed by the Almohads, even more primitive and zealous Moslems than their predecessors. Once again the Christians were put on the defensive. Yet in spite of these important incursions from North Africa, the Christian kingdoms gradually grew stronger, while the Moorish states of southern Spain fell into corruption and decay. Finally, in 1212 the Christians inflicted a decisive defeat on the Moors at the battle of Las Navas de Tolosa. Thereafter only the small and politically weak Moorish kingdom of Granada remained, and even it passed into Christian hands when Boabdil el Chico surrendered the city of Granada to Ferdinand and Isabella in 1492.

The ultimate and complete success of the *Reconquista* was due to many factors. In the first place it must be recognized that the Christians of northern Spain were generally less sophisticated and more warlike than their Moslem adversaries. Also, the Christians developed more stable states and governments than did the Moors, at least after the first decade of the 11th century. Then, too, Christian Spain developed a number of specific institutions, such as the military orders of the church, which were created with the especial purpose of making war on the Moslem "infidel" and of reconquering the peninsula.

Of interest is the fact that the idea for the creation of the military orders—Santiago, Calatrava, and Alcántara—was probably borrowed from the Moors, as was the idea of the crusade, or holy war, itself. The crusade was no more than a Christian jihad, and the *Reconquista* was in fact a series of crusades.

The cult of Santiago Matamores, or St. James the Moorslayer, also contributed much to the *Reconquista*. In 813, according to tradition, the bones of James the Greater were discovered at Compostela in northwestern Spain. Shortly thereafter the apostle was said to have aided King Ramiro of Galicia in winning a miraculous victory over the Moors at Clavijo. Thus James became the patron saint of Spain and his sepulcher became a favorite shrine for pilgrims from all over western Europe. Spanish religious fervor was heightened and foreign warriors came to Spain to fight the Moors.

The results of the *Reconquista* were manifold. Spain became a nation of warriors par excellence and the tradition of the crusade continued to exist in the Iberian Peninsula long after it had died out in other parts of Christendom. Thus the Spanish were perhaps the best suited psychologically of all Europeans to carry out the conquest of much of the Americas (the last great crusade) and to lead the Catholic Counter-Reformation against 16th-century Protestantism.

BIBLIOGRAPHY: H. J. Chaytor, *A History of Aragon and Catalonia* (London, 1933); H. C. Lea, *The Inquisition in Spain,* 4 vols. (New York, 1908).

**Recusants.** The legal designation for Roman Catholics who refused to conform to the reformed Church of England. An Elizabethan statute defines a recusant as one "convicted for not repairing to some Church, Chapel or usual place of Common Prayer to hear Divine Service there, but forebearing the same contrary to the tenor of the laws and statutes heretofore made and provided in that behalf." In actual practice, however, the designation came to be applied to Roman Catholics only, not to Protestant Dissenters. Recusancy laws were in effect from the reign of Elizabeth I to that of George III, but they were not consistently enforced.

**Red Cross.** An international organization, the main goal of which is to prevent and alleviate human suffering. It had its formal beginning in the vision of a young Swiss, Henri Dunant, who, appalled by the unnecessary suffering of the wounded at the Battle of Solferino (1859), and inspired by the work of Florence Nightingale in the Crimean War, organized groups to serve the unfortunate soldiers. In 1862, Dunant published *Un Souvenir de Solférino.* This book and his untiring energies aroused the sympathy of the sovereigns of Europe, and brought about a conference in 1863 which led to the Geneva Convention of 1864. The Geneva Convention for the Amelioration of the Condition of the Wounded and Sick Armies of the Field was adopted by twelve nations. It provided for the neutrality of army and civilian medical corps, the humane treatment of the wounded, and for an international emblem (a red cross on a white background) to distinguish personnel and supplies. The original Geneva Convention has been revised and expanded several times, extending protection to victims of warfare at sea (1907) and to prisoners of war (1929). By 1949 the Geneva Conventions of the Red Cross had been signed by fifty-two nations around the world.

**Redemptorists** (*or* Congregation of the Most Holy Redeemer). A Roman Catholic religious order for men established by Alphonsus Ligouri in 1732. The missionary effort of the order was designed mainly to restore or increase the nominal faith of the already Christian masses. The work of the society was taken north of the Alps at the beginning of the 19th century by the Austrian Clemens Maria Hofbauer.

**Reductions of Paraguay.** The controversial Christian Indian State organized and maintained by the Jesuits in the east and south of Paraguay from 1608 to 1767. The state was formed of Indians who had been "reduced" (from Latin *reducere,* "to lead") from their forests, and was known as the Reductions. The Jesuit work began as an effort to overcome the inability of the Spanish missionaries to convert the conquered and exploited natives. To make their labors more lasting, the Jesuit general Aquaviva ordered a concentration of effort and the founding of mission centers in the best localities. As the means to education and conversion, the natives were freed from the oppressive Spanish political structure by being gathered into separate units far remote from Spanish colonies. Against continual oppression by local governors and by the Portuguese, who were trying to gain territory, the Spanish kings sponsored the mission, which was finally ratified and confirmed by Philip V in 1743. The Jesuits established about one hundred small towns. Organized in a theocratic communism, they were economically independent centers of culture and religion, raising the living conditions and moral standards of well over a million natives. In 1750, Ferdinand VI of Spain was persuaded by the anti-Jesuit Pombal of Portugal to cede a large part of Paraguay in exchange for territory elsewhere. After native resistance was crushed in 1756, the missions were finally destroyed by the expulsion of the Jesuits in 1767.

**Refectory.** The dining hall of a monastic community. It is usually large, since meals are taken there in common. In most cases silence is enjoined during meals, but someone usually reads aloud from edifying books for the good of the entire community.

**Reform, Medieval Ideas of.** See MEDIEVAL IDEAS OF REFORM.

**Reformation, Protestant.** The religious movement of the 16th century which gave rise to Protestantism. Although political, economic, and social factors all have their place in a proper interpretation of the Protestant Reformation, the writings of the Reformers reveal the distinctly religious initiative in the movement.

It was not an abrupt revolution and its followers never espoused a radical rupture with the church's immediate past or its institutions as did adherents of the Radical Reformation. Luther's Ninety-five Theses against the sale of indulgences (1517) were not something novel, nor were they the work of an irresponsible renegade monk. Rather, they came from the filial concern of a loyal son of the church who in order to be obedient to the message of the gospel had to protest against the abuses and corruption of the Western Church as he saw it. Others had preceded him in calling the church to reform. Wycliffe and the Lollards in England, John Hus in Bohemia, the Brethren of the Common Life in the Low Countries, Savonarola in Florence, humanists such as Erasmus, conciliarists such as Cardinal Pierre d'Ailly, and the various monastic reform movements in the Middle Ages, all bear witness to the widespread attempts to undergird the eroding prestige of the medieval church (see COUNTER-REFORMATION).

In his search for a gracious God, Luther had by 1517 relegated as insufficient the way of self-help through the mediation of the church and good works, and had come to assurance of salvation by casting himself completely upon the mercy of God, whose righteousness is revealed in the gospel and makes us righteous through faith. This was not a new doctrine, he maintained, but the one to which the Holy Scriptures and the church fathers (especially Augustine) bore witness.

At the Heidelberg Disputation (1518), Luther defended his views before his own Augustinian order. During the Leipzig Debate (1519), Johann Eck branded Luther as the "Saxon Hus" because of his attack on the authority of the papacy and his admission that not all the tenets of Hus were heretical. In 1520, Luther set out the principles of the Reformation in three famous treatises. While Luther was writing these tracts, the pope threatened him with excommunication (see EXSURGE, DOMINE), but Luther upon receiving the papal bull consigned it to a bonfire. Luther's quarrel with the church now entered the realm of politics, and he was summoned before the Imperial Diet at Worms (1521) by the Roman Catholic emperor Charles V, but he refused to recant. On his return journey to Wittenberg, Luther was secretly abducted by his elector, Frederick the Wise, who feared for his safety and hid him at the Wartburg Castle. In 1522, Luther returned to Wittenberg to lay the groundwork for a conservative reformation. The next five years saw a continued expansion of the Reformation, a growing disunity becoming apparent with the emergence of the Radical Reformation and the failure of Luther and Zwingli to agree at Marburg (1529). At Augsburg in 1530 the Lutheran princes presented their confession of faith (which has since become the confessional standard of Lutheranism) to the Imperial Diet. In 1531 the Smalcald League was formed by the Protestant princes but the emperor hesitated to attack because of the threat of the Moslem Turks. Finally he did attack in 1546, gaining a momentary advantage through the Leipzig Interim of 1548, but in the end he recognized Lutheranism as a *fait accompli* and the principle of *Cuius regio, eius religio* in the Peace of Augsburg (1555).

By this time Lutheranism had also become firmly rooted in the Scandinavian countries. In Sweden, Olaus Petri was teaching the doctrines of Luther as early as 1518. By 1524 the king's secretary and chancellor were both committed Lutherans. In 1527 the Diet of Vesterås decided in favor of the Reformation, and a gradual ecclesiastical transformation took shape. It was not until 1593 at the Diet of Uppsala that Lutheranism as such was officially recognized. In Denmark at the Diet of Odense (1527), Frederick I declared faith to be a matter of the individual conscience and refused to curtail "the preaching of God's Word." In 1536 his son, Christian III, introduced the Lutheran Reformation to Denmark and Norway by royal decree and invited Bugenhagen to draw up a Church ordinance (see LUTHERANISM).

Contemporaneous with these events within Lutheranism, a parallel reform movement was going on in Switzerland under the leadership of Zwingli in Zurich and Calvin in Geneva. In 1519, Zwingli, with the surprising consent of his bishop, began to attack the indulgence traffic. An open break eventually occurred in 1522 over the question of Lenten regulations. By 1526, Zurich churches were cleared of statues and shrines, and a simple worship service was inaugurated. The Swiss Reformation continued to spread and was led by Oecolampadius in Basel, Haller in Bern, and by Farel and Viret in the French-speaking cantons. In 1529, Zwingli and Oecolampadius journeyed to Marburg and were joined by Bucer of Strasbourg for the fateful colloquy with Luther. Two years later the Swiss Reformation suffered a serious setback with the death of Zwingli on the field of battle and the passing of Oecolampadius. In 1536 new impetus was received with the arrival of John Calvin in Geneva. For the next twenty-eight years, with the exception of a brief interlude from 1538 to 1541 when he resided in Strasbourg, Calvin put his tremendous talents to

work in behalf of the Reformation. Geneva became the model church for the Reformed communion and a haven for Protestant refugees. Through his *Institutes of the Christian Religion,* which he continually revised (1536–1559), Calvin left a theological legacy that embodied the essence and genius of the Reformed Church.

It was not until the successful establishment in French Switzerland of the Reformation that it became a serious threat to Roman Catholic France itself. In spite of Francis I's policy of suppression, Protestantism continued to grow. In 1555 it began to organize itself and in 1559 a general synod was held in Paris (see GALLICAN CONFESSION). Though always a minority movement, the Reformation claimed some of France's most gifted citizens. In 1562 the slaying of a group of Protestants worshiping in a barn at Vassy signaled the outbreak of the tragic Wars of Religion in France.

By and large the Low Countries remained faithful to the Roman Church until the oppressive rule of the "foreigner," Philip II (1555–1598), brought about a merging of religious and political motives. In 1561 the Calvinist congregations drew up the Belgic Confession and for the next six years were baptized by fire under the cruel regency of the Roman Catholic duke of Alva.

In Scotland the Reformation triumphed in 1560 when Parliament adopted the Scots Confession, drawn up mainly by John Knox and patterned after Calvin's theology. Here the Reformation and Scottish nationalism were allied against the Roman Catholic queen, Mary Stuart (see MELVILLE, ANDREW).

The protestantizing process in England had medieval precedents, and opposition to the papacy was nothing new. The enactments of Parliament in the 1350's, the political views of William of Occam (d. 1349), the doctrines of Wycliffe and the Lollards, combined with the outlook of the 16th-century English humanists and the Cambridge Lutherans to form a fertile seedbed for the Reformation in England. The necessity of obtaining a male heir and the question of the validity of Henry VIII's marriage led to a merging of the religious and political impulses that ushered in the Reformation. In 1529, Parliament was called into session and authorized the Anglican break with Rome in 1534. Protestantism made noteworthy gains during the reign of Edward VI (1547–1553), which saw the appearance of Cranmer's Book of Common Prayer and the Forty-two Articles (see THIRTY-NINE ARTICLES). In 1553 a Roman Catholic reaction set in when Mary Tudor became queen. However, in 1558, Elizabeth ascended the throne. During her long reign (1558–1603) a religious settlement was reached that established the Church of England (see ANGLICAN COMMUNION, THE).

BIBLIOGRAPHY: R. Bainton, *The Reformation of the Sixteenth Century* (Boston, 1956); H. Grimm, *The Reformation Era* (New York, 1964); T. M. Lindsay, *A History of the Reformation*, 2 vols. (Edinburgh, 1964); P. Smith, *The Age of the Reformation*, 2 vols. (reissue, New York, 1962); *Cambridge Modern History*, Vol. II, *The Reformation* (Cambridge, 1960).

**Reformation, Radical.** See RADICAL REFORMATION.

**Reformed Church.** Those churches whose theology and polity stem from the Swiss Reformation. Originating in the work of Zwingli, Calvin, Bucer, Bullinger, Oecolampadius, and others, the movement spread from Switzerland and the Rhineland to France, the Netherlands, and eastern Europe, contributing directly to Presbyterianism in England and Scotland as well. When Zwingli broke with Roman Catholicism in 1522, he set up in Zurich and in other cities and cantons the procedure of debate followed by the vote of the congregation on whether they would follow the Roman or the Reformed religion. Civil authorities became the heads of the Reformed churches. In defense against Roman Catholic coercion the Christian Civic League was formed, but it was defeated in 1531 and a settlement allowing coexistence was reached. Controversy over the Lord's Supper caused a break with the Lutherans of Germany, and it became evident that a new branch of the Reformation was developing.

Under Calvin, Geneva became the center of the movement. After clashes with the civic authorities over control of the church which once caused him to leave the city, Calvin returned in 1541 and by 1555 had gained the advantage. From the Academy at Geneva went forth refugee pastors trained in the Reformed faith who would return to their homelands and establish churches modeled on those of Geneva. After Calvin's death in 1564, Beza assumed the leadership in Geneva and of the French Protestants, but Geneva declined in importance, and ceased to be a center of motive force. The Swiss cantons have retained churches of a presbyterian nature, which were organized into a federation in 1948.

In France, the early concern for reform expressed by humanists such as the Group of Meaux opened the way for the evangelization of the country from Geneva after 1555. The French Huguenots were usually more impetuous than Calvin himself, especially in revolt against the monarchy. They converted Calvin's local system of polity into a national one, based on consistories, provincial synods, and a national synod. The Huguenots organized as a political and military force against Francis II. Bloody wars ensued for three decades, and the Protestants found peace only with the accession of Henry IV. His Edict of Nantes in 1598 gave them the right to exist. Its revocation in 1685 caused two hundred fifty thousand Huguenots to flee France, and Protestant rights were regained only in 1789. During the 19th century a split occurred between the conservative National Union of Evangelical Reformed Churches and the liberal National Union of Reformed Churches in France; they were reunited in 1939 as the Reformed Church of France.

Strasbourg was an early center of Reformed activity (1521–1549); Bucer and Calvin were there, and it served as a channel of influence between Switzerland and the rest of Europe. Frederick III, the elector palatine, made Heidelberg University the center of Reformed thought in Germany; the Heidelberg Catechism of 1563 became a model for the Reformed churches. Frederick secured rights for the Reformed faith equal to those of the Lutherans at the Diet of Augsburg in 1555. Brandenburg became Reformed in 1613. The Thirty Years' War brought final recognition for Reformed churches, whose strength was swelled by sixty thousand Huguenot refugees after the revocation of the Edict of Nantes. Dutch Pietism drew the German and Dutch Reformed communions together during the 18th century. In 1817, Prussia began uniting the Lutheran and Reformed churches. They promoted an active missions program up to World War I. Between the wars a theological revival occurred, led by Karl Barth, but the largest areas of Reformed strength fell into the Soviet zone after 1945.

The Reformed faith came to the Netherlands down the Rhine. With the defeat of Spain, the Netherlands became free and the Reformed Church was established, being a blend of Rhineland traditions, Genevan Calvinism, and the influence of the French Huguenots. The Belgic Confession of 1561 became the standard creed, but each state within the Netherlands had its own church, presbyterian in government. A theological dispute between Gomar and Arminius resulted in the Synod of Dort in 1618, whose canons rejected both extreme positions and gave the classic statement of Calvinistic theology. Pietism swept the country in the 18th century. A result of the Enlightenment was a split that produced the Christian Reformed Church in 1834. The Low German Mourning Reformed Church was organized in 1886, then merged with the Christian Reformed in 1892 to create the Reformed Churches in the Netherlands. A small group who resisted the merger became the Christian Reformed Church (Restored). The original Netherlands Reformed Church had about one and a half million members in 1948. In South Africa and the East Indies, as well as in the Netherlands, the Reformed Church represents conservative interests in politics and labor, where the tendency is to follow confessional lines.

Small Reformed churches also exist in eastern Europe. Hus and the Bohemian Brethren were 16th-century forerunners of Reformed faith in Czechoslovakia. Not until 1781, however, was there toleration for adherents to Reformed symbols. The Evangelical Church of Czech Brethren revived after the creation of the Czech state; the present Reformed communion of some 90,000 members is the Evangelical Church of Bohemian Brethren. In Hungary, most of the Magyars are Reformed. The Augsburg and Helvetic Confessions were adopted in the 16th century, but the churches suffered persecutions from 1677 to 1781. The Hungarian Church became nationalistic after the shattering effects of World War I, but since World War II it has turned from upper-class nationalism to evangelism among workers. It had a membership of about one million in 1948. A sizable Reformed community exists also in Romania (380,000), and there are small Yugoslavian and Slovakian churches.

The Reformed Church in America is an importation of Dutch Calvinism. Its Collegiate Church in New York, founded in 1628, is the oldest in America with an uninterrupted ministry. The Great Awakening split the church over the issue of colonial autonomy; the colonial group founded Queen's College (Rutgers) under Theodore Frelinghuysen in 1766. The factions reunited in 1771, with ultimate authority remaining in the Netherlands. In 1819 the Reformed Protestant Dutch Church became independent; Dutch gradually ceased to be used, and in 1867 the present name was adopted. Migrations to Holland, Mich., and Pella, Iowa, during the 1850's increased the strength of the Reformed Church in America. In 1963 it counted some 229,000 members. Its government is a modified presbyterianism. The elders, deacons, and pastor form the consistory. It sends delegates to the classis, which in turn sends representatives to the synod, of which there are five in the United States. The national body is the General Synod.

The Christian Reformed Church had its origins in a doctrinal dispute of 1822. Those who withdrew from the Reformed Church at that time were joined later by the Dutch Christian Reformed Church and augmented by other seceders in 1881. By 1963 it had 262,000 members.

German immigrants from the Palatinate brought the Reformed religion with them to Pennsylvania in the 18th century, where it became a self-sustaining church by 1793. In the West, German Reformed bodies united in 1863. Attempts to merge with the Dutch Reformed in 1891 and with the Presbyterian Church U.S.A. later were not successful. But in 1934 the Reformed (German) Church in the United States joined with the Evangelical Synod of North America to form the Evangelical and Reformed Church, a body combining both Lutheran and Reformed traditions. At the time of this merger the Free Magyar Reformed Church in America removed itself from the jurisdiction of the Reformed Church in the United States. Formed in New York in 1904, it had come under the Reformed Church in 1922 and consisted of only a few thousand members. The Evangelical and Reformed Church had a membership of over 800,000 in 1961 when its merger with the Congregational Christian Churches to form the United Church of Christ was completed.

BIBLIOGRAPHY: E. Corwin, *A History of the Reformed Church* (New York, 1895); J. Dubbs, *History of the Reformed Church, German* (New York, 1895); J. Good, *History of the Reformed Church of Germany: 1620–1890* (Reading, Pa., 1894); H. Harbaugh, *The Fathers of the German Reformed Church in Europe and America* (Lancaster, Pa., 1857); R. Kingdon, *Geneva and the Coming of the Wars of Religion in France: 1555–1563* (Geneva, 1956); D. Kromminga, *The Christian Reformed Tradition: From the Reformation to the Present* (Grand Rapids, 1943); J. T. McNeill, *The History and Character of Calvinism* (New York, 1962).

**Reformed Churches of the Netherlands.** A body of churches comprising the majority of Dutch Protestants. Their Creeds are the Belgic Confession, the Canons of the Synod of Dort, the Heidelberg Catechism. The Nederlandse Herformde Kerk (Reformed Churches of the Netherlands) is the original Reformation church. In the 1960's it had a million communicants and a community of 3,300,000. Nineteenth-century schisms produced the Gereformeerde Kerken (Reformed Churches), now reporting 500,000 communicants, and the very small Christian Reformed Church.

**Reformed Episcopal Church.** A church organized in December, 1873, as a secession from the Protestant Episcopal Church in the United States of America, by George D. Cummins (with seven clergy and some twenty laymen), assistant bishop of Kentucky, who was bitterly assailed in the press and by the House of Bishops for participating, Oct. 12, in a united Communion service for the Evangelical Alliance. This body epitomized the growing opposition of the Evangelical party to Tractarian influences in the Episcopal Church. The *Declaration of Principles* (1873) grounds this body in Scripture, the Apostles' Creed, two dominical sacraments, and the Thirty-nine Articles. It holds to episcopacy but only as "ancient and desirable," leaning heavily for its liturgy on the Book of Common Prayer of 1785, and specifically condemns five "erroneous . . . doctrines" of which four are decidedly Catholic and Tractarian, and the fifth denies baptismal regeneration.

BIBLIOGRAPHY: See the monthly magazine *Episcopal Recorder* (Philadelphia, Pa.).

**Reformers.** See REFORMATION, PROTESTANT.

**Regalia** (Regalian Rights). The rights ordinarily belonging to the king, but exercised by all feudal lords to receive the revenues of vacant ecclesiastical benefices, just as they received the revenues from vacant feudal benefices. Vacancies in bishoprics and abbeys were frequently prolonged in order to obtain more money. This practice was a point of contention in the investiture controversy. The term "regalia" also refers to the symbols of royal office, such as crown and scepter.

**Regalism.** The doctrine or practice of the supremacy of a sovereign in ecclesiastical affairs. The term comes from the Latin *regale* used in the Middle Ages to designate the rights and powers of a sovereign. It was applied especially to a sovereign's claim to the use of incomes from a vacant diocese. The alleged right was widened to include the appointment to all benefices becoming vacant in a bishopric during this period that did not involve the cure of souls. Regalism sprang from the concept that a diocese, monastery, or church was the property of the patron or temporal lord. Thus it was closely allied to the concept of investiture. The earliest claim to this alleged right was made by Henry V (d. 1125). In 1166, Frederick Barbarossa espoused regalism in his claims upon the archdiocese of Cologne. During the pontificate of Innocent III the German monarchs surrendered their claims to regale but their action did not prove entirely effective. In France, regalism led to much turmoil and strife, with Gallicanism further complicating the picture. Not until the separation of church and state in France in 1905 was regalism definitely abrogated. The term may also be applied in a general way to the influence and control over the ecclesiastical affairs of a nation by a sovereign, i.e., the case of the Lutheran state churches in Scandinavia where the highest church authority is the king.

**Regensburg** (Ratisbon) **Colloquy** (1541). The last important attempt by Protestants and Roman Catholics to reach doctrinal accord before the Council of Trent. Instigated by Charles V in an effort to remove the religious conflicts within his empire, the preparations and proceedings were presided over by the new papal legate to Germany, Cardinal Contarini, one of the few members of the Roman Catholic hierarchy who still felt reconciliation to be possible. In preliminary discussions, the Protestants agreed on the text of the Regensburg Book as the basis for the Colloquy, and Contarini conceded the possibility of married clergy and lay reception of the Eucharistic cup in Germany. In the opening formal sessions of the Colloquy, a formula on original sin was accepted by both sides, and after heated discussion a statement concerning justification was agreed upon. When the questions of church authority and the Eucharist were taken up, however, both sides were adamant; Contarini had been instructed from Rome not to compromise on those issues. The discussions were quickly broken off, and within a month the agreements that had been reached were repudiated by both Rome and Luther.

**Regula Pastoralis** (Pastoral Rule). The rule composed by Pope Gregory I to guide bishops (himself included) in the exercise of their pastoral duties. It had great influence throughout the Middle Ages, although Gregory's precepts were not always followed. The work reflects the qualities of Gregory's character and personality, his psychological insight, his openness to diversity within the church, and the humility that prompted him to view the exercise of authority primarily as service.

**Regular Clergy.** The tonsured clerics who have professed vows in a religious or monastic order and therefore live according to a rule (*regula*). This category includes all monks, mendicants, canons regular, and clerics regular. Clerics who have professed no vows and are incardinated to a diocesan bishop are known as the secular clergy.

**Regularis Concordia.** A code formulated by Dunstan to regulate the revived monastic life in England. Based upon the reforms of Benedict of Aniane, with influences from Lorraine and Cluny, the code altered some customs to accommodate to English conditions and added prayers for the royal family to most of the choir office. Under the patronage of King Edgar, the code was approved by a synod at Winchester in 970.

**Reichsdeputationshauptschluss.** Meetings of empire representatives held between Imperial Diets until 1806. The most important was held on Feb. 2, 1803. Representatives from Mainz, Bohemia (Austria), Saxony, Brandenburg (Prussia), Palatinate-Bavaria, and Hesse-Cassel, under French and Russian pressure, decided that all ecclesiastical principalities except Mainz, the Johannine Order, and the German Order, were to be abolished. They also secularized the church's possessions, and limited the number of imperial cities to six. Instead of the extinct principalities of Cologne and Trier, four new secular, and Protestant, principalities were created: Salzburg, Württemberg, Bavaria, and Hesse-Cassel. This action put an end to the superiority of Catholic princes and dignitaries in the Imperial Diet.

**Reimarus, Hermann Samuel** (1694–1768). German rationalistic theologian. After brief terms at Wittenberg and as rector of Wismar, he became professor of Oriental languages at Hamburg Gymnasium. Philosopher and theologian of the Enlightenment, he advocated a religion of pure reason and edited a work based thereon. Remains of his critical study on the Old Testament and the New Testament posthumously published as *Fragments of an Unknown* engendered controversy and initiated the "quest of the historical Jesus."

**Reims Cathedral.** The purest exemplar of French Gothic architecture. The Cathedral of Notre-Dame at Reims was built (1211–c. 1311) on the site of Hincmar's cathedral, with a triportal west facade richly decorated by some 530 sculptures and a 40-foot rose window. The cathedral was badly damaged in World War I but restored by 1927. Among its treasures, in addition to skillfully carved interior walls, splendid tapestries, and exquisite 13th-century stained glass, it boasts the 12th-century chalice of Remigius and the remains of the Sacred Ampoule.

**Reinhardt, Franz Volkmar** (1753–1812). German Lutheran professor at Wittenberg (1777–1792) and pastor at Dresden. His weekly congregation numbered as many as three thousand or more. In 1800 he preached a famous Reformation sermon which, though it did not break the predominant rationalism, contributed to the rediscovery of Luther. Reinhardt refused the offer of a high administrative post in Berlin in 1809.

**Reinkens, Joseph Hubert** (1821–1896). First bishop of the Old Catholics. Born at Aachen and educated at Bonn and the theological seminary at Cologne, he was ordained priest in 1848. He was a bitter foe of the definition of papal infallibility at the Vatican Council (1870), and in 1871 he signed the Nuremberg Declaration, which denied the policies of the Council. The signatories of the Declaration formed the nucleus of the Old Catholic movement.

**Relief Church** (of Scotland). A church founded in 1761 by Thomas Gillespie (1708–1774) "for the relief of Christians oppressed in their Christian privileges." Having been deposed by General Assembly in 1752, and having gained an independent congregation at Dunfermline, he joined Thomas Benton (the Younger) to form a presbytery. This church was known for its liberal spirit and was united with the Secession Church in 1847, forming the United Presbyterian Church of Scotland.

**Religion in Higher Education.** The practice by certain officials or others of wearing distinctive robes or gowns in court, in church, or at university functions reflects symbolically the medieval idea of the whole of human society unified under a threefold authority. Derived from the kingly, priestly, prophetic roles of Christ, this authority is exercised by three earthly but divinely established institutions: the state, representing law; the church, representing revelation; the university, representing reason. This idea of the coordination of the spheres of society, religion, and culture is not simply a novel theological concept developed by the medieval mind. It is preceded, and partly conditioned, by the Hellenistic assumption underlying the whole of classical education in the West that human fulfillment is to be found in the fullest and most complete realization of man's personality. This is to be achieved primarily through *paideia,* that is, "training," or "education." Significantly, when Varro and Cicero translate *paideia* into Latin, they use the word *humanitas.* This linguistic transfiguration evidences, as H. I. Marrou in *A History of Education in Antiquity* points out, the fact that the primary unity of the Greek world was eventually centered in "sharing a single idea, a common attitude towards the purpose of existence and the various means of attaining it—in short, from a common civilization, or rather, culture." Furthermore, with the shaking of so many other beliefs and corporate values (e.g., the lack of political unity after the time of Alexander) there arose the growing conviction that there was "one true unshakable value to which the mind of man could cling," Marrou continues. "Hellenistic culture, thus erected into an absolute, eventually became for many the equivalent of a religion."

The fact that the earliest Christian documents were written in Greek underlines the inextricable involvement of Christianity with classical Hellenistic (which includes Roman) civilization and culture. Classical culture was symbolized and synthesized in the form of Hellenistic education. This tradition extended throughout the eastern half of the Mediterranean world and remained unchanged, essentially, throughout the Roman era; even the triumph of Christianity did not lead to the kind of educational revolution that might have been expected. Thus, though "Christian education" (a term first used by Clement of Rome about A.D. 96) was shaped by additional models such as the Jewish rabbinical schools and was at first primarily considered to be the task of the family in conformity with Paul's injunction that parents should train their children, the eventual adoption of Greek and Roman educational institutions and methods was another example of that "cultural osmosis" which formed the church in all of its organizational and intellectual life. There was recognition of the problems which this involved. Tertullian asks, "What is there in common between Athens and Jerusalem, the Academy and the Church?" But even less rigorous intellectual guardians of the faith, such as Augustine, felt the ideological conflict. Nevertheless, Christian teachers, such as Origen, became engaged in classical education and in 264, Christians made their debut in higher education when Anatolius, a future bishop of Laodicea, was elected by the citizens of Alexandria to be ordinary professor of Aristotelian philosophy. The fact that Luther was in his early academic career a lecturer in Aristotelianism exemplifies the long-lasting and pervasive character of this marriage of Hellenistic culture and Christian theology in higher education.

It would, therefore, be an oversimplification to identify the introduction of religion in higher education with the rise of the various kinds of specifically Christian schools—the monastic and the secular, the presbyterial and the patriarchal, for example. The fact is that the whole of Western higher education bears not only the marks of its specifically Christian origins but, though perhaps less obviously, the Hellenistic conviction that education is itself a religious expression and its cultural content is permeated and informed by religious awareness. So, the Western European universities evolved out of concern for providing particular kinds of religious education but also out of the realization, not always clearly articulated, that there was an intimate and inescapable connection between the life and thought of the church and the cultural matrix, Hellenistically derived and symbolically embodied in the classical educational forms.

This connection between the purpose of providing specifically theological training and of providing general cultural education runs through the history of higher education in the West. When, for instance, the Puritans in New England took it upon themselves to bring about a *translatio studii* from the ancient seats of higher learning of the Old World to the American wilderness, they assumed the continuity of what they were establishing with earlier institutions. "The founders of Harvard took for granted the essential continuity of Western learning—the direct link between the colonial American college and earlier institutions, such as the schools of the Hebrew prophets, the Academy of Athens, the Palace School of Charlemagne, the medieval universities, and the Reformation academies." It was not simply the aim of the New England settlers to set up a theological seminary when they founded Harvard but to make a replica of a Cambridge college, with the purpose of providing general cultural learning. Both aims, as it has been indicated, must in the broadest sense be considered "religious," for both were directed toward fostering a literate and cultured community which in their minds meant both a literate ministry *and* a literate congregation.

In this latter sense, that is, in seeking to provide for study in the liberal arts on the basis of the humanistic tradition, there has never been a total absence of "religion" in higher education. However, in the more formal sense of religious instruction, a separation if not divorce took place between religion and higher education in the 19th century. Between the closing of the Greek schools in Athens by the Christian emperor Justinian in 529 and the formation of the first universities such as Bologna, Paris, Padua, Naples, Oxford, Cambridge, Montpellier, Toulouse, and others in the 12th and 13th centuries, the only real institutions of higher learning were the cathedral and monastic schools for prospective priests and monks. Though these new educational corporations were less closely affiliated with the church as contrasted with the episcopal and monastic schools of the preceding eras, nevertheless the students were professing Christians, the enterprise was conducted within the context of the Christian community and commitment, and theology was everywhere acknowledged to be the "queen of the sciences." Gradually, however, the spirit of humanistic secularism penetrated higher education and though the universities remained under Christian and even ecclesiastical control until the time of the American and French revolutions, one by one the various fields of study and academic disciplines became independent and autonomous. Above all, the outlook of natural science became the dominant intellectual mode of the university community.

New legal and organizational restrictions emerged which separated religion from higher education in a more formal way. For example, in England the new provincial "red brick" universities were founded by those who believed that theology should be excluded from the subjects studied in the university. This was based both on ideological grounds (many members of the academic community were scientific rationalists or agnostic liberals) and on the practical grounds that the restrictive religious tests set by the persecuting acts of the Clarendon Code (1661–1665) at the ancient universities of Oxford and Cambridge were inappropriate, tyrannical, and sectarian, and therefore antithetical to the universal ideals of higher education.

In the American educational scene a somewhat similar pattern developed. In the older universities provision for religious studies generally remained, which was consistent with their ecclesiastical foundations. However, the first real "state university," which Thomas Jefferson founded at Charlottesville in Virginia, was deliberately nonsectarian; it was on these grounds that Jefferson opposed any professorship in theology, though he suggested denominational houses of worship adjacent to the university campus. These fears of sectarian wrangling were well-founded. Bitter battles were fought between various religious groups over higher education in Illinois, Indiana, and Michigan. As a result of this bitter history, the teaching of religion has generally been restricted to church-related institutions and, though the legal situation differs from state to state, there has been up to recent times a general disinclination to provide instruction in religion in public-supported colleges and universities.

The first significant break in this American pattern was the founding of a school of re-

ligion at Iowa in 1925. But even by the mid 1930's only 10 percent of America's public-supported colleges and universities offered courses in religion. In 1966 over 90 percent did so. One of the factors that may have accelerated this trend, or at least given college administrators encouragement in providing facilities for studying religion, was the majority opinion of Associate Justice Tom C. Clark for the U.S. Supreme Court in the *School District of Abington Township* v. *Schempp* case in 1963. In that decision, the Court ruled 8 to 1 against local laws requiring the reading of prayers and the Bible in the classroom. Though the decision struck a blow against "religious proselytizing" in classrooms, it did not strike down the academic study of religion. Justice Clark's opinion was: "It certainly may be said that the Bible is worthy of study for its literary and historic qualities. Nothing we have said here indicates that such study of the Bible or of religion, when presented objectively as part of a secular program of education, may not be effected consistent with the First Amendment."

The present ecumenical environment, with the increasing tolerance and understanding between the religious communities that it has helped to bring about, is also conducive to a new *rapprochement* between religion and secular higher education. The ecumenical spirit has created an ethos in which it seems possible for public educational institutions to approach the study of religion both objectively and sympathetically, but without sectarian bias or prejudice. This new relation between religion and higher education may provide a new model for the educational institutions of the new nations of the non-Western world in Asia and Africa. Generally, they have followed Western models in their educational institutions. The exclusion of the study of religion is a severe handicap to educational institutions training those whose cultural background is so profoundly religious and for whose emerging patterns of community life the relation of the ancient religious traditions is of critical importance in hindering or promoting the new technological and political orders. The spectacular emergence of a truly world culture, one of the most striking facts of this historical period, means that all educational institutions, Western and non-Western, must increasingly incorporate the study of religion into their curricula in order to do justice to all the dimensions of this profound global cultural revolution and to meet it in an educated and responsible way. The educational ideals of the ancient Greek *oikoumenē* synthesized with those of the Judeo-Christian tradition thus appear to be peculiarly appropriate to the new global *oikoumenē* now rising.

BIBLIOGRAPHY: J. Baillie, *The Mind of the Modern University* (London, 1946); K. R. Bridston and D. Culver (eds.), *The Making of Ministers* (Minneapolis, 1964); J. S. Brubacher and W. Rudy, *Higher Education in Transition* (New York, 1958); J. Leclercq, *The Love of Learning and the Desire for God* (New York, 1961); H. I. Marrou, *A History of Education in Antiquity* (New York, 1964).

**Religious Bodies Law** (1940). A law recognizing Christianity in Japan and establishing it as the third national religion, after Shintoism and Buddhism. For many years, Japanese Christians had been striving for two goals: freedom from foreign control and unity among the various denominations. There was a strong feeling that the numerous sects, having grown to large proportions, should no longer be controlled as missionary adjuncts of churches in other countries, and the actions of the militarily inclined government made unity seem feasible and even necessary to survival. In 1939, the Imperial Diet passed the law that recognized Christianity as a national religion and made registration of Christian sects mandatory. There were obvious advantages to the churches from such official sanction, but a certain amount of state control over Christian activity was also implicit in the action. The Religious Bodies Law became effective in April, 1940. The many religious groups concerned were allotted one year in which to register themselves under the law. Thereafter, the denominations found it expedient, as a result of an ever increasing Japanese nationalism and growing war threats, to place Japanese leaders in all important positions in the various hierarchies. The unity movement, already strong, received a new impetus from the Religious Bodies Law, and as a result, the United Church of Christ in Japan (Nippon Kirisuto Kyodan) came into existence in June, 1941.

**Religious Liberty.** A freedom variously interpreted in church history (as, e.g., the church's unrestricted liberty, toleration for Dissenters, equality for all faiths, separation of church and state), but now commonly defined as the right to believe, exercise, or propagate any religion (or conversely, to abstain from or to oppose religious belief).

Practically, religious liberty has become a major issue in modern times with the rise of religious diversity. The Middle Ages neither produced significant religious dissent nor recognized the problem of finding theoretical bases by which dissent might be accommodated. Medieval thought assumed the unity and authority of Christ's visible church to which all faithful Christians must yield obedience, and justified the exercise of ecclesiastical discipline and political penalties in those cases where obedience was withheld. The Reformation introduced a new situation, shattering the church's unity and judging ecclesiastical authority by that of Scripture. Classical Protestant thought made only a limited contribution to religious liberty. Despite early support for free religious decision, Luther turned ultimately to reliance on the Christian prince for the repression of heresy and false religion. Calvin also argued for the magistrate's duty in defending true religion and supporting church discipline. On political grounds, secular princes believed that religious freedom was inconsistent with social stability. Accordingly, post-Reformation Europe organized into various territorial uniformities, evident for Germany in the Augsburg Peace (1555) but generally adopted by Catholic and Protestant governments everywhere. The persecuted radicals of the Reformation contributed more to religious liberty. The Anabaptist ethic, opposing Christianity to violence, oaths, and compulsion, precluded enforced religious conformity. Anabaptists, Socinians, and spiritual reformers testified against repression as wicked and futile, but largely in vain.

Notable progress in the development of religious liberty was made in the 17th century in the Netherlands and in England. In Holland, divisions between Reformed liberals and rigorists, rationalist intellectual traditions, and predominant economic goals fostered a religious freedom that made Amsterdam the refuge of many persecuted faiths. In England, religious freedom was advanced by the Puritan movement and the denominational variety which its fragmentation supplied. Some Elizabethan sectaries argued against forced conformity, but such demands became politically important only after the Revolution and victory of the army. Theories differed: some desired indiscriminative state support for all Protestant bodies; others founded magistracy solely on natural conscience. In practice Cromwell's regime supported some faiths, tolerated others, and penalized blasphemy. Renewed Anglican persecution after 1660 was followed by toleration of Trinitarian Protestants in 1689. Later Dissenters and Catholics labored to win "political emancipation," successfully in 1828–1829.

The American colonies sought uniformity in the Anglican South and Congregational New England, but Puritan radicals in Rhode Island, Catholics in Maryland, and Quakers in Pennsylvania offered religious freedom. In the 18th century the variety of denominations, growth of dissenter strength, and philosophical and political rationalism weakened state churches and hastened disestablishment after the Revolution (not until 1833 in Massachusetts). The First Amendment of the United States Constitution required that "Congress shall make no law respecting an establishment of religion, or prohibiting the free exercise thereof," a guarantee extended to the states by later judicial interpretation of the Fourteenth Amendment.

In Europe the advent of the secular in place of the confessional state raised the problem in new form. Revolutionary and Napoleonic France exhibited religiously uncommitted governments granting or withholding freedom according to political expediency. Liberal 19th-century states leaned toward equal treatment of religions, sometimes culminating in separation of church and state (as in France in 1905); but several great anticlerical campaigns restricted freedom on the plea of securing the state against a hostile church. Violent persecutions were launched in the 20th century by totalitarian dictatorships in Russia and Nazi Germany, and repression spread over eastern Europe following World War II. The same period also marked changes in Roman Catholic attitudes toward religious freedom as the hostility of *Mirari vos* (1832) and the Syllabus (1864) was qualified under Leo XIII and finally discarded in the Vatican Council Declaration on Religious Freedom (1965).

BIBLIOGRAPHY: R. H. Bainton, *The Travail of Religious Liberty* (New York, 1958); G. Dodge, *The Political Theory of the Huguenots of the Dispersion* (New York, 1947); W. K. Jordan, *The Development of Religious Toleration in England,* 2 vols. (Cambridge, Mass., 1936–1940); T. Lyon, *The Theory of Religious Liberty in England: 1603–1639* (Cambridge, 1937); J. C. Murray, *Religious Liberty: An End and a Beginning* (New York, 1966); A. A. Seaton, *The Theory of Toleration Under the Later Stuarts* (Cambridge, 1911).

**Religious Orders.** An organized form of religious life, and hence juridical units within the total church. The diversity of the orders is a reflection of the culture and the exigencies of the times in which they arose. Religious orders exist in the Roman Catholic Church, the Eastern Orthodox Church, the Anglican Church, and to some degree in Protestant communities. But this discussion will be confined to the religious order as it exists within the Roman Catholic Church.

*Juridical Structure.* In the Roman Catholic Church a religious order is an institute in which vows are actually or juridically present. Approbation by the pope, operating through the Sacred Congregation of Religious, affirms that the rule of the order does not contravene faith or morals, and that its goal is evangelical perfection. Generally the orders are exempt from local episcopal jurisdiction. By the Middle Ages the rules and internal hierarchical structure of religious orders were clearly delineated. The two major categories of religious order—mendicant and preaching—which theoretically continue today, were developments of earlier monastic forms where the religious were permanently attached to one monastery, and differ in this respect from, among others, the Dominican and Jesuit orders.

In all orders there is a general superior, subject to the pope, who is aided by a chapter or congregation, which is elected from the local chapters, and which holds the legislative power within the order. Subject to the general superior is the provincial, and to him the local superior of individual religious houses, who has the power to govern his members and dispose of the possessions of his house in accordance with canon law and the rules of the particular order.

All religious orders require vows of personal poverty, celibacy, and absolute obedience to the order and to the superior, who stands in the place of Christ. All orders have some regulations, such as the manifestation of conscience, which give the superior access to information so that he may command for the total, as well as for the individual, good.

The type of dress in and out of the house is generally specified. Most communities gather for Divine Office and conventual Mass at particular times of the day, though the length of time spent depends upon the purpose of the order. Contemplative orders such as the Cistercians spend most of the day in prayer. Active orders spend less time in communal worship, more in study and activity. Since all orders are determined by the spirit of the times in which they were founded, as well as by the spirit of their founder, one must turn to history for a better understanding of religious orders.

*History.* Christian monasticism began in 305 when Antony of Egypt founded a monastery. Pachomius (290–346) established a monastery on the Nile and a rule for his cenobites in 320. Basil of Caesarea (330–379) wrote a more developed rule based on asceticism during the period of 358 to 364 which is still followed by Eastern monks.

Western monasticism began with the gathering of hermits around Hilary near Poitiers, and Martin near Tours, in the late 4th century. At the start of the 5th century Honoratus established a primitive monastery on one of the islands of Lérins. Cassian, under the influence of Eastern monasticism, founded two monasteries at Marseilles.

The barbarian invasions of the 5th and 6th centuries led to a consolidation of isolated hermits and the admission to monasteries of those who simply wanted to escape.

In 451, Chalcedon attempted to put the monasteries under the control of bishops. About the same time Irish monasticism, marked by its independence and severity, was established around the clan, with its political and religious head. Using a similar pattern, Columba (c. 521–597) founded a monastery in Ireland and on Iona, off the west coast of Scotland. Columbanus (550–615), leaving Ireland, went through England to Gaul, founding monasteries at Anegray and Luxeuil, from which he traveled to Bregenz and Switzerland and to Bobbio, where he founded an influential monastery.

Benedict (c. 480–c. 544) went to Subiaco about 500 and founded twelve monasteries each with twelve monks and an abbot. In 529 he moved to Monte Cassino, where he formally drew up the Benedictine Rule. It was intended to provide the layman with monastic conditions under which he might seek God and surrender self-interest through obedience. There were no obligatory extreme austerities. The abbot was the elected representative of Christ. There were six hours for manual labor daily, four for private study and reading, and four for the recitation of divine office, around which the day revolved. The self-supporting stability of the monastery helped the uprooted people of the age.

After the death of Benedict and the Lombard invasions, Gregory I, a former monk, became pope. Under him the Benedictines became the official order of Rome, though there was a beneficial interaction with Irish monasticism, and they were further protected from the bishops and feudal lords. In the 9th century the monasteries themselves became feudal powers. Reform came from Cluny, founded by William of Aquitaine in 910. Odo (abbot from 927 to 942), succeeding Berno of Baume (abbot from 910–927), was influential in persuading monasteries in southern France and Italy to follow Cluny in the reform of the feudal monastery. This reform, based on the original Benedictine Rule and stressing above all divine worship, lasted into the 11th and 12th centuries and strongly influenced the secular clergy.

Faced by the ignorance and immorality of secular priests, Robert (c. 1027–1111), abbot of Molesme and founder of Cîteaux, attempted reform by distinguishing two types of monk: one to remain in the abbey and the other to go out and preach. About 1110, William of Champeaux (c. 1070–1121) established a congregation following the Augustinian way of life, which since the 5th century had been applied to the secular clergy, and brought it into the intellectual mainstream by locating it in Paris.

The excesses of the Templars, a military order, and the Hospitalers, products of the continued experimentation of the 12th century, led to the establishment of mendicant orders as living examples of the poverty of Christ himself.

Francis of Assisi (1182–1226), moved by a vision in 1208 which urged him to leave everything, and inspired by his love of God and his world, began to collect disciples. This rule, drawn from the gospel, was approved about 1209 or 1210 and spread to women through Clare. The actual organization of the Franciscans was left to others.

After much preaching under the Augustinian Rule, Dominic (1170–1221) formed his own rule, mainly against the Albigensian heresy. After obtaining papal approval for a new monastic order in 1216, he traveled through Italy, France, and Spain, organizing his order. As his rule replaced manual labor with the intellectual labor of preaching, there could be no vow of stability. He advocated reason in the service of God. His intellectual emphasis and the love of God stressed by Francis were the two main influences on religious orders and theology in the 12th and succeeding centuries. To these, though, must be added the mystical influence of the Carmelites, especially through John of the Cross (1542–1591), Teresa of Ávila (1515–1582), and Teresa of Lisieux (1873–1897). The Carmelite order, though tracing its origins as far back as Elijah, was founded by Berthold in 1154. The work of the order was contemplation, missions, and theological investigation. The Carmelite sisters, founded in 1452, lead an even more strictly cloistered life.

*The Reformation.* During the Reformation there was a proliferation of groups, such as the Capuchins, attempting to reform existing religious orders, and for the secular clergy such groups as the Theatines. Out of the conflict of religions and principles sprang a new order, the Society of Jesus. During a long convalescence from a wound Ignatius of Loyola, a soldier (1491–1556), determined to become a soldier of Christ. To this end he traveled and studied widely, and at this time wrote *The Spiritual Exercises.* In 1534 with six companions he made vows of poverty, chastity, and pilgrimage to Jerusalem. In 1540, after Ignatius had experienced a vision in which God the Father asked Christ to accept Ignatius as his servant, Paul III approved the new society. From 1547 to 1550, Ignatius drew up the Jesuit constitutions. The Jesuits were to reform the church through education and preaching, acting as an instrument of the church (hence their special vow to the pope). To allow flexibility the recitation of the Divine Office was omitted, and Jesuits were to adopt the same standard of living as secular priests.

In the light of the documents of Vatican II, religious orders are changing. Further developments will clearly be instigated through the dialogical situation now existing between religious orders and contemporary culture.

BIBLIOGRAPHY: W. M. Abbott (ed.), *The Documents of Vatican II* (New York, 1966); P. F. Anson, *The Call of the Cloister* (London, 1955); J. Canu, *Religious Orders of Men* (New York, 1960); D. Knowles, *Religious Orders in England,* 3 vols. (Cambridge, 1965); J. Leclercq, *The Love of Learning and the Desire for God* (New York, 1961); W. Nigg, *Warriors of God* (New York, 1959).

**Religious Tract Society.** A British interdenominational society founded in 1799 for the production and distribution of religious literature. Its earliest publications were tracts in English, but it soon expanded into the publication of books and periodicals and in vernacular translations for use in non-Protestant Europe and in the mission field. In 1935 the Society united with the Religious Literature Society for India (1858) and the Religious Literature Society for China (1884) to form the United Society for Christian Literature, proprietors of the Lutterworth Press, London.

**Reliquary.** A receptacle for relics of sacred people or things. The earliest reliquaries were boxes or ampules, rings or simple bags or purses; often made of precious metals and frequently adorned lavishly, they were the precursors of the jeweled or otherwise decorated glass cases of the baroque period. Gabled shrines for the whole remains of a saint or martyr were popular in the Middle Ages, e.g., the Marienschrein at Aachen. The ostensory variety is still in vogue for large relics, but the jeweled casket is currently in the widest use.

**Remigius** (c. 438–c. 533). Bishop of Reims (c. 465–530). He lived through the transition of the last days of Roman Gaul to the beginning of the Frankish monarchy, beginning his long ministry as a Roman gentleman and ending it as a feudal prelate. His sermons (now lost) are praised for their classic elegance by Sidonius Apollinaris, but he is chiefly remembered as the officiant at the baptism of Clovis, the first Christian king of the Franks, probably on Christmas Day, 496.

**Remonstrance.** A treatise written by Dutch Arminians in 1610. Drawn up by Janus Uytenbogaert (1557–1644) and signed by forty-six ministers, it was sent to the States of Holland and Friesland as an apology for their Arminian (Remonstrant) views. The *Remonstrance* first rejects the prevailing Calvinism of the day, then presents five positive articles, as follows: (1) God's election and reprobation are based upon foreseen faith or unbelief. (2) Christ died for all men, though only believers enjoy the forgiveness offered in Christ. (3) Fallen man is unable to do good or achieve saving faith without the regenerating power of God in Christ through the Holy Spirit. (4) Grace is the beginning, continuation, and end of all good, but is not irresistible. (5) Although God's grace is sufficient to preserve the faithful through every trial, it has not been proved from Scripture that man may not fall from grace and be lost. The *Remonstrance* included a request for a general synod to settle the dispute. The Calvinists issued a Counter-Remonstrance and the dispute continued to divide Dutch Protestants until it was officially settled by the Synod of Dort in 1619, where the Remonstrant viewpoint was condemned.

**Remonstrants.** The name applied to the Dutch followers of Jacobus Arminius, from the *Remonstrance,* a statement of Arminian principles drawn up at Gouda in 1610. The Remonstrants repudiated the name "Arminians," but upheld the principle that the free investigation of the Bible should not be bound by subscription to symbolical books. On the invitation of John van Olden Barneveldt, the Dutch statesman and sympathizer with the Remonstrants, forty-six ministers convened at The Hague to record their views concerning all disputed doctrines. The *Remonstrance* was compiled by Janus Uytenbogaert, endorsed by all, and presented to Barneveldt. In five articles, the *Remonstrance* attacked the Calvinistic doctrines of predestination and the belief that the saints could not fall from grace; they also ascribed authority only to the Bible and maintained that secular authorities have the right to interfere in theological disputes to preserve peace in the church. Under the leadership of Francis Gomar and Prince Maurice of Nassau, a Counter-Remonstrant movement succeeded in having the Remonstrants condemned at the Synod of Dort (1618–1619). After a period of persecution, the Remonstrants were officially tolerated (1795). There are still several thousand followers of the Remonstrants in the Netherlands today.

**Renaissance.** A transitional movement in European history of the 14th, 15th, and 16th centuries, or the period itself. The Renaissance has been called "the most intractable problem child of historiography" (Wallace K. Ferguson). Used as a historical concept, the word "Renaissance" does not lend itself to easy or simple definition. Etymologically it is a French word meaning "rebirth" (Italian, *rinascimento*). The term has been used by modern historians to describe a number of different periods in European history. The Carolingian Renaissance refers to the outburst of intellectual activity that occurred during the reign of Charlemagne and his immediate successors in the late 8th and throughout the 9th century in western Europe. The Ottonian Renaissance designates the literary and artistic movement in medieval Germany that began under Otto the Great in the 10th century. The Renaissance of the Twelfth Century describes that era's revived interest in the classics and the rise of the universities centering for the most part in France. However, the word "Renaissance" is most widely used among historians to describe a period of European history between the end of the Middle Ages and the unmistakably modern world of the 17th and 18th centuries. As early as the 16th century, the Renaissance artist and biographer Giorgio Vasari spoke of a "rebirth" of art in his own day. In later centuries others wrote of the rebirth of art and letters in Italy during the 14th, 15th, and 16th centuries. However, it was not until 1855, when the noted French historian Jules Michelet published the seventh volume of his *History of France* (19 vols., 1833–1867), that the word "Renaissance" was used to denote a distinct epoch that sharply contrasted in spirit with the preceding age. As Michelet put it, with the Renaissance came "the discovery of the world and the discovery of man" as the old medieval world receded into historical oblivion. After Georg Voigt, Jakob Burckhardt, and John A. Symonds popularized the concept in the last half of the 19th century, the Renaissance has come to be accepted, in general, as a distinct and useful division of European history. Some present-day scholars

reject altogether the idea that there ever was a Renaissance; others maintain that it began as early as the 12th century, and still others extend it to the end of the 17th century. However, the majority of modern historians feel that the period from about the beginning of the 14th century to the end of the 16th constitutes the era of the Renaissance in Europe. It was during this period that there was a "rebirth" of many aspects of civilization, which resulted in an essential change in the character of European life. It was an age in which medieval and modern elements coexisted in a constant state of flux. However, feudal and ecclesiastical institutions, though still strong, no longer were predominant. It was an age of transition from medieval to modern civilization from which a recognizably new, radically different and much more secular world gradually emerged.

The Renaissance generally is understood to have begun in 14th-century Italy with the literary labors of men such as Francesco Petrarch (d. 1374) and Giovanni Boccaccio (d. 1375). The movement was centered first in Florence and later spread to Rome, Milan, and Venice. Initially, the Italian Renaissance focused upon humanism, a movement concerned with the revival of the study of the classics, then spread to painting, sculpture, architecture, and even religion. The Renaissance in Italy produced some of the most celebrated names of European history. Along with Petrarch and Boccaccio, Lorenzo Valla (d. 1457) was one of the most influential exponents of Renaissance humanism. Niccolò Machiavelli (d. 1527) made a lasting mark on history with his book *The Prince,* still the bible of those who believe that politics is amoral. Marsilio Ficino (d. 1499) and Giovanni Pico della Mirandola (d. 1494) pioneered in using Renaissance techniques to reconcile the pagan wisdom of antiquity with the Christian faith. Leonardo da Vinci (d. 1519), Michelangelo (d. 1564), and Raphael (d. 1520), along with many lesser lights, made the Italian Renaissance one of the most spectacular epochs in the history of art.

The Renaissance in Italy was not especially antireligious, but it was basically secular. Most of the men of the Renaissance were Christians but tended to compartmentalize their religion, sealing it off from the Renaissance emphasis on man in the present world rather than on his ultimate destiny in the next. The popes themselves were deeply affected by this secular outlook on life. The period when the papacy was located at Avignon and not Rome (1309–1377) and the great papal schism (1378–1417) which followed both took their moral toll. Beginning with Nicholas V in 1447, the popes for the next hundred years were usually chosen for their abilities in such matters as politics, diplomacy, and administration rather than for their spiritual piety. The immorality of the Renaissance popes, with the possible exception of Alexander VI (d. 1503), has probably been overemphasized. However, they were more interested in Renaissance activities than in the spiritual aspects of their office. Their secular concerns were reflected in the college of cardinals and the papal Curia which contained many humanists and numerous patrons of the Renaissance. The result was a general secularization of the Western Church at the highest levels.

As the Renaissance spread from Italy to northern Europe it became in general less secular, more conventionally Christian. The majority of northerners tried to relate their humanism and artistic accomplishments directly to the traditional faith. For example, transalpine humanists were more interested in classical Christian literature such as the New Testament and the writings of the fathers than they were in Cicero or Plato. They were also concerned with reforming the medieval church according to the principles of apostolic Christianity. Because of their desire to apply the "new learning" to the church, these northern Renaissance scholars are generally called "Christian humanists." Among their number were such men as John Colet (d. 1519) and Thomas More (d. 1535) in England, Faber Stapulensis (d. 1536) in France, Rudolph Agricola (d. 1485) and Johannes Reuchlin (d. 1522) in Germany, and the man hailed by his century as the "prince of humanists," Desiderius Erasmus (d. 1536). Also, as a rule, northern art more consistently reflected religious themes and values than did that of Renaissance Italy.

The question of the precise relationship of the Renaissance to the Protestant Reformation is still debated. In northern Europe, certain common political, economic, and religious factors were partly responsible for the rise of both movements. Furthermore, the Christian humanists and Protestant Reformers shared a common desire to rid the church of corruption, and both stressed the inwardness of true religion. After 1517, the Renaissance and Reformation continued to have such common goals as the renewal of the Christian church and an expanded program of lay education. Coming first in point of time, the Renaissance did much to prepare the religious and intellectual soil of northern Europe for the planting of the Reformation. At the same time, the Italian Renaissance could also blunt the spiritual sensitivities of the leaders of Western Christendom and prevent them from perceiving the desperate need for reform in order to curb religious unrest among the faithful. When Martin Luther (d. 1546) finally took drastic steps in 1517, many northern humanists sympathized with his aims, even though most did not follow him out of the Roman Church. However, many young humanists did leave to become leaders of Protestantism, among whom were Philip Melanchthon (d. 1560), Ulrich Zwingli (d. 1531), John Calvin (d. 1564), and Theodore Beza (d. 1605). Thus, in some ways the Protestant Reformation was the most radical expression of the desire of Christian humanists to reform the church and restore its pristine purity.

BIBLIOGRAPHY: J. C. Burckhardt, *The Civilization of the Renaissance in Italy* (New York, 1929); K. H. Dannenfeldt, *The Renaissance: Medieval or Modern?* (Boston, 1959); W. K. Ferguson, *Europe in Transition: 1300–1520* (Boston, 1962); and *The Renaissance in Historical Thought: Five Centuries of Interpretation* (Boston, 1948); M. P. Gilmore, *The World of Humanism: 1453–1517* (New York, 1952); D. Hay, *The Renaissance Debate* (New York, 1965); A. Hyma, *Renaissance to Reformation* (Grand Rapids, 1951).

**Renaissance of the 12th Century.** The cultural revitalization that characterizes 12th-century learning was felt exclusively in the fields of jurisprudence, science, philosophy, and the arts. In the area of jurisprudence, one aspect of the vastly enlarged influence of the reformed papacy was its growing function as an ecclesiastical court whose decisions affected the lives of kings and peasants as well as the clergy on matters ranging from marriage and legitimacy to usury and tithes. A renewed interest in, and need for, canon law led to a series of classifications of the earlier, often conflicting, prescriptions of popes and synods; the most notable of these was Gratian's *Decretum,* published c. 1141. To such classifications there soon accrued an ever increasing mass of legislation and decisions by the papal Curia concerning cases from all of Latin Christendom, which made of canon law a living, continually changing product (see CANONIST). In the search for guidance and precedent the civil law of Justinian became a crucial subject for study, and its precepts helped to make the canon law the most civilized law of its time. Secular lawyers too, in Italy and later in France, began to study the Justinian Code. The consequences of the revival of interest in Roman jurisprudence were incalculably great: the concept of law as legislative act based on reason rather than the Germanic concept of law as custom based on tribal authority was eventually to create the social framework of the modern world.

Jurisprudence was only one aspect of the growth of medieval learning. Renewed interest in the ancients extended to the study of the sciences and philosophy as well. In the former category particularly, much of the ancient learning was slavishly accepted and adhered to, including misguided concepts of astrology, alchemy, and medicine; and where inquiry existed, it was deductive and abstract. In the long view, however, this wealth of "new" old learning was to have a liberating effect on the European intellect. The 12th century was distinguished at least by the desire to learn about science, which was a first step, a necessary background to the critical explorations of a later age. The methods of philosophy were closely related to those of science in the medieval mind, but the consequences of its study were far more strikingly apparent in the 12th century. Prior to that time, only fragments of ancient philosophy had been available, but the succeeding years saw the full recovery of the works of Aristotle, as well as an important Platonic revival; it also witnessed the elaboration of the Scholastic method by Abelard, Gratian, and Peter Lombard, which furnished the necessary superstructure for the great theological synthesis of the 13th century. Also during this period there developed the vastly expanded use of dialectic as a means of argument to resolve questions of doctrine, and an equally expansive development of the traditional seven liberal arts, with philosophy emerging as a discipline distinct from liberal arts and theology. The setting for these intellectual developments was the cathedral schools, which in the 12th century rapidly replaced the monastic schools as centers of learning. Quite apart from the contributions of the individual Schoolmen and Scholastics who gave them life, they were destined to be, as institutions, the most enduring of medieval creations. They were assemblies of clerks who had the privileges of clergy, and their appearance, and the extent to which they flourished in Bologna, Paris, Chartres, and elsewhere perhaps the most obvious embodiment of the intellectual vitality of the period. That vitality also had its expression in the arts, and most particularly in architecture: the new Gothic cathedrals (see ARCHITECTURE, GOTHIC) which began to go up beside the venerable Romanesque (see ARCHITECTURE, ROMANESQUE) structures were inspired by faith, but they were made possible by the discovery or rediscovery of structural principles governing the use of ribbed vaults, pointed arches, and flying buttresses.

These developments are mere hints of the inquiring and experimental spirit of the 12th century. There were innumerable other manifestations: e.g., the refinement of social habits; the impact of Christian teaching on military feudalism, from which developed the ethos of chivalry; the great proliferation of translations from the ancients and from Jewish and Arabic sources; the sophistication of Latin poetry dealing with subjects both sacred and profane; the meteoric rise of secular literatures, represented by such types as the *chansons de geste,* the troubadour love poetry, and the chivalric romances dealing with the matters of France, Britain, and Rome. As Maurice de Wulf remarks, it was "an age which constructs in all departments and destroys in none." By any standard of definition, it warrants the name of "renaissance."

BIBLIOGRAPHY: A. J. Carlyle, *Progress in the Middle Ages* (Oxford, 1916); M. de Wulf, *Philosophy and Civilization in the Middle Ages* (Princeton, 1922); C. H. Haskins, *The Renaissance of the 12th Century* (Cambridge, Mass., 1927).

**Renaissance Platonism.** The first important Renaissance thinker influenced by Platonism was Nicholas of Cusa (1401–1464). A cardinal of the church, possessed of a tremendous Platonic and Neoplatonic library, Nicholas' speculative mysticism established the first real demarcation between the original Plato and the murky eclecticism of the Platonic tradition. He reestablished the absolute separation of the realm of being from the world of becoming, with no gradation and no emanation. He also reestablished the absolutely opposite character of the two worlds with his concept of God as the *coincidentia oppositorum,* where all the contradictions and categories of the phenomenal world are transcended.

The name most commonly associated with Renaissance Platonism is Marsilio Ficino (1433–1499), conscious "reviver" of Platonism, founder of the Platonic Academy in Florence, and Latin translator of the complete Plato and Plotinus, as well as other Platonic and Hermetic texts. His main work, the *Platonic Theology,* is a Platonic *summa* of all these varied sources around a Christian theme —the immortality of the soul. For Ficino, Plato, Zoroaster, Plotinus, and Hermes Trismegistus were all included in a primordial divine revelation and constitute the sources for a unified truth, a *pia philosophia* harmonious with Christianity.

Ficino accepted the Neoplatonic hierarchical

conception of the universe: the inner ascent of the soul to God through love and contemplation; the experience of earthly beauty, love, and contemplation; the experience of earthly beauty and love in God. Knowledge of God is the ultimate goal of human existence. It may be achieved in this life through contemplation, but only for the few. God's love grants it to many for eternity with his gift of immortality. Ficino described Christianity as the most perfect of religions, but thought that all religions were related to the true God in some way. He even approached a conception of natural religion with his contention that love of one God is innate in all men.

Giovanni Pico della Mirandola (1463–1494), Ficino's younger associate in the Florentine Academy, never claimed to "revive" Platonism. Rather, he wanted to harmonize Aristotle and Plato in a syncretic philosophy using a multitude of religious and philosophical sources. Pico's conception of the unity of truth was more comprehensive than Ficino's. He included Aristotle and all his followers, and the Jewish Kabbalah, which he considered a parallel authority to the Bible, and the prophecy and confirmation of the truth of Christianity. He adapted all these sources to Christianity by adding number and letter mysticism and allegories of Greek and Oriental myths to the four-level scheme of Scriptural interpretation used in the Middle Ages.

In his later years Pico was increasingly concerned with religion, and was influenced by Savonarola. His conception of the relation between reason and faith was more mystical than that of Ficino. Where Ficino believed in the ability of unaided human reason to know God, Pico interpreted philosophical knowledge as only a preparatory stage that must be completed by religion in order to reach truth.

From Florence the influence of Platonic philosophy spread to the rest of Europe. Pico's influence can be seen in the Christian Kabbalism of Johannes Reuchlin. Ficino's Platonism influenced Sir Thomas More, Erasmus, and Kepler, to mention only a few. John Colet's interpretation of justification as reciprocal love between man and God shows Ficino's influence. There is Platonism in the mixture of mysticism, humanist philology, and Biblical scholarship of Faber Stapulensis.

During the 16th century there emerges a prominent strain of vernacular Platonism, in varying degrees of dilution. The poetry of Margaret of Navarre exhibits a combination of Ficino's Platonic love with Christian mysticism. In most of the Platonic poetry of the 16th century, for example that of the Lyons school and the Pléiade, the Eros theme is combined with the notion of poetic furor (*Phaedrus, Ion*), and only very diluted Christian content remains. In Giordano Bruno's *Eroici furori,* near the end of the Renaissance, even these mild Christian overtones disappear and Eros emerges as titanic human power and creativity.

**Renan, Joseph Ernest** (1823–1892). French philosopher and historian. He was born at Tréguier in Brittany. Intending to enter the priesthood, he studied at St.-Nicolas-du-Chardonnet at Paris until he lost his faith (1845). For the rest of his life Renan devoted his attention to the history of religions, to the study of Oriental languages, and to scholarly writings, most notably *Histoire des origines du Christianisme* (1863), *Les Apôtres* (1866), and *St. Paul* (1869). His most famous work, *La Vie de Jésus* (1863), was written while on an archaeological mission to Phoenicia under the sponsorship of Emperor Napoleon III. In this book Renan denied the divinity of Jesus Christ, portraying him as nothing more than a genial Galilean preacher. The publication of the book, considered a scandal by most Roman Catholics in France, caused a sensation in Europe and led to the dismissal of Renan from his professorship of Hebrew at the Collège de France. In later years Renan turned to scientific rationalism, accepting the concept of God, but denying the existence of a Personal Being.

**Renouvier, Charles Bernard** (1815–1903). French philosopher. He opposed the Spencerian notion of a necessary progressive evolution assured in advance independent of individual wills. Instead, he stressed free will as the root of moral and intellectual life, holding that no certainty is ever possible without it. He stated that only phenomena have any real existence, and since knowledge deals entirely with phenomena, reality is solely that of experience.

*Rerum Ecclesiae.* Encyclical (Feb. 28, 1926) of Pius XI on foreign missions. It endeavored to establish the church as a "native" institution in mission lands. Catholics were urged to give alms and pray for missionary vocations, bishops to favor missionary societies. Since colonial Africans and Asians would shortly sue for independence, seminaries for the training of indigenous clergy should be opened, convents established, and invalid and child care improved.

*Rerum Novarum.* The papal encyclical issued on May 15, 1891, by Leo XIII on social justice. Translated into English as *On the Condition of Workers,* it sets forth Catholic teaching related to conditions created by the industrial revolution. Applying traditional doctrines to contemporary situations at the close of the 19th century, it has become a classic of church pronouncements on social problems. Opening with a description of the grievances of the working classes, it defends the church's right to become involved in the social question because of its moral aspect. It deals with the relation of man to work, profit, masters, servants. It upholds wage settlements by free agreement and advocates remedies for social problems by the combined action of the church, the state, the employer, and the employed. It asserts that wages should be based on "a dictate of natural justice more imperious and ancient than any bargain between man and man, that remuneration should be sufficient to maintain the wage-earner in reasonable and frugal comfort." It furthermore proclaims private property a natural right.

The encyclical was revolutionary and was considered by many as subversive of the established order. Among Catholics and non-Catholics alike it has had a wide influence and has become the basis of much discussion and literature.

**Rescissory Act.** A law regulating the polity of the Scottish Church. It was enacted (1661) during the time of the Restoration with a view to bringing the practice of the Scottish Church into harmony with that of England, that is, by replacing the presbyterian form of government with an episcopal one. It was drafted by Archibald Primrose; its form was that of a repeal of all legislation bearing on church polity from 1633 to 1661.

**Reservation, Mental.** See SANCHEZ, THOMAS.

**Reservation of the Sacrament.** The practice in the ancient church of taking away, or reserving, from the weekly Communion celebration the bread, or Host, in order to receive the Sacrament daily at home. Thus the Sacrament was reserved in one species on their persons or in a special box in their houses. Reservation for the purpose of devotion in church begins in the early Middle Ages in England and France, with the bread being suspended in a pyx, often shaped like a dove, over the altar. The common Italian practice by contrast was reservation for Communion in an ambry or locked wall cabinet. In 1215, at the time of the formulation of transubstantiation, the pope ruled that the Sacrament be kept in a special place in all churches. In the Low Countries and Germany the sacrament house, a monumental tower situated near the altar, became the common place of reservation toward the end of the Middle Ages. After the Reformation, the tabernacle, a locked cabinet placed on the altar, became the general practice of the Roman Church, codified in 1863. In the same period, adoration and, after the 17th century, benediction, of the Sacrament has been encouraged. The monstrance, an elaborate holder for the display of the Host, is used for these purposes. Ritual reservation at a side altar is also observed after Maundy Thursday celebration until the first Easter Mass. Processions, as at Corpus Christi, are another form of ritual reservation.

**Reserved Case** (*casus reservati*). A term used in the Roman Catholic Church for certain extraordinarily grave sins which, because of their extreme offensiveness, constitute cases that can be absolved only by specially authorized bishops. To these bishops, absolution of such sins has been exclusively reserved. The Scriptural justification for this procedure is found in the Gospel of John, ch.20:21–23. Such sins must be external, consummated, and clearly defined by the pope or the bishop who has been given exclusive legislation over them. A penitent who is unaware that his particular case has been reserved in his own diocese and who innocently and in good faith seeks absolution from a priest in another diocese where the sin is not reserved remains in most instances unquestioned and his so-called unauthentic absolution accepted as authentic. The cases that the popes have reserved to themselves are usually those for which excommunication is the penalty and for which only the Apostolic See can release the sinner. The cases reserved to the bishops are always sins of an extremely serious nature, such as homicide and certain kinds of unchastity. In extreme emergencies, penitents whose cases are reserved can be absolved by any priest, but this practice is consistent only in instances where the penitent is in danger of death.

**Restitution, Edict of.** The law issued in 1629 by Emperor Ferdinand II which declared that Protestants had to return all ecclesiastical property taken from the Roman Church after 1552. As a result of the edict the Roman Catholics regained two archbishoprics, twelve bishoprics, and several monasteries. However, for a variety of reasons (chiefly political), the edict was never fully enforced.

**Restoration, The.** Reestablishment of the English monarchy in 1660. The use of the term is also extended to denote the period in English history following the Commonwealth and ending with the fall of James II (1688). Disenchantment with Puritan austerity and the chaos that followed Cromwell's death (1658) brought the Stuart monarchy (Charles II) back to the throne and restored the House of Lords. The religious tolerance of the Commonwealth was ended with the reestablishment of Anglicanism, which terminated Puritanism as a political movement in England.

**Reuchlin, Johannes** (1455–1522). Lawyer, judge, humanist, and Hebrew linguist. Born in Pforzheim, he studied the liberal arts, classical languages, and law in Freiburg im Breisgau, Paris, Basel, Orléans, and Poitiers, and entered the personal, diplomatic, and judicial service of the duke of Württemberg in 1482. After 1496 he briefly served the elector of the Palatinate, and was then one of the three supreme judges of the Swabian League until 1512–1513. From 1513 he was a lawyer in Stuttgart. In his literary efforts Reuchlin (the first humanist to master Latin, Greek, *and* Hebrew) is perhaps overshadowed by others, although his comedies show him in clear command of the poetic rules of antiquity. As a Hebrew linguist, however, he opened a new epoch in the knowledge of this language among non-Jews. Through repeated study with Jewish teachers, he became a thoroughly trained Hebraist, and in 1506 published his *De rudimentis Hebraicis,* both a grammar and a dictionary, which was the tool of future generations.

In several official trips to Italy, Reuchlin became deeply involved with the thought of Pico della Mirandola. Influenced by Florentine Neoplatonism and apparently also by Nicholas of Cusa, he was led through his linguistic work to the study of Jewish literature, especially the Kabbalah. In his *De verbo mirifico* (published in 1494) and *De arte cabbalistica* (published in 1517), he reveals himself as a "matured Hebraist and the leading Christian expert on the Cabala" (L. W. Spitz). Through identifying the Pythagorean system with the Kabbalah and reading both in the light of Scripture, he created a theistically oriented universalism and a concept of world history in which Christianity, Hellenism, and Judaism were seen as being unified from the beginnings of time, even in the mind of God himself.

In 1510, Reuchlin issued a brief for Emperor Maximilian I concerning the confiscation and burning of Jewish literature. He opposed a certain Johann Pfefferkorn, a convert from Judaism to Christianity, who fiercely demanded that all Jewish literature be burned, and that stringent inquisitorial measures be taken against the Jews living in the Empire. Reuchlin, on the basis of his universalistic concept of the spiritual unity of Christian and Jew, and on the basis of the Roman law as well as the early canon law, demanded toleration for the Jew and his culture, and suggested that only those books be confiscated in which Christianity is actually blasphemed. He further affirmed that the laws against heretics could not be indiscriminately used against the Jews, since they had never been Christians in the first place, and consequently could not become heretics. Finally, he argued that the Christian should love the Jew as his neighbor and fellow citizen. With this program, in which, as a typical humanist, he confronted the present with the past, Reuchlin went contrary to the whole late medieval legal and philosophical notions concerning the treatment of the Jew. The ensuing struggle, in which Pfefferkorn was supported by the University of Cologne through its most vociferous spokesman, Ortwin Gratius, was so bitter that it darkened the last decade of Reuchlin's life, and also tends to obscure his importance as linguist and philosopher. He was charged with heresy in 1513; the first round of his trial ended with a judgment that could, under certain circumstances, be considered a victory for him. Under the impact of the *Letters of Obscure Men,* however, and the excitement stirred up by Luther (whose case Cologne cleverly yoked with that of Reuchlin), the Curia finally condemned Reuchlin in 1520. Due to some countermoves on his part, and above all due to the increasing pressures of Luther's case, Reuchlin suffered no consequences of this judgment. Overshadowed by Luther, lonely and bitter, he spent the last two years of his life teaching in Ingolstadt (1520–1521) and in Tübingen (1521–1522).

BIBLIOGRAPHY: *Johannes Reuchlins Briefwechsel,* ed. by L. Geiger (reprint, Hildesheim, 1962); J. L. Blau, *The Christian Interpretation of the Cabala in the Renaissance* (New York, 1944); W. Maurer, "Reuchlin und das Judentum," *Theologische Literaturzeitung,* 77 (1952), pp. 535 ff.; L. W. Spitz, *The Religious Renaissance of the German Humanists* (Cambridge, Mass., 1963); Biographies by F. Barham (1843) and L. Geiger (Leipzig, 1871).

**Reunion Attempts.** Although the Eastern Schism had been a reality since 1054, it was not until the late 12th century that deep animosity infused the ordinary Eastern Christian. By his confirmation of Thomas Morosini as Latin patriarch of Constantinople, Innocent III thought to have effected reunion between East and West, but it was by imposition of Western liturgical customs as well as by doctrine. The first serious attempt after the fall of the Latin empire to repair the breach and to achieve reunion was made by Michael VIII Paleologus, whose interests were as much political as ecclesiastical. In his negotiations with

Gregory X (pope 1271–1276), he made a personal confession of the Roman faith and attended the Council of Lyons (1274) with likeminded ecclesiastics whom he had appointed. The failure of this attempt, due to the inability of the Byzantine emperor Michael VIII to enforce a theological view upon the Eastern Church, was dramatized both in the immediate reversion of the East to its separateness after his death (1282) and his excommunication by the French successor of Gregory X, Martin IV (1281). A similar and equally unsuccessful attempt was made by John V Paleologus (1341–1391), who made profession of the Roman faith (1369) without any consequence in either East or West.

Realizing that personal conversion of the emperor and his negotiation with the pope was no way to bring about reunion between East and West, the usurper John VI Cantacuzene (emperor, 1347–1355) proposed that conversations between both sides in conciliar setting, together with the exchange of ideas particularly by translation of some of the most important Latin theologians into Greek, would be the only fruitful approach to union. After his abdication, John pursued the matter and convinced the papal legate Paul of its feasibility, but Urban V, the Avignon pope (1362–1370), refused the idea. This attempt, though an utter failure, was of singular importance because it provided the model upon which the Council of Florence (1438–1445) was structured.

The most serious attempt at reunion was made at this Council, although the recognition of the necessity of a council by the pope was dictated more by his fear that the Council of Basel (1431–1449), dominated by the conciliarists, might effect a reunion with the Greeks thus leaving the curialist-papal forces in a precarious position. Eugenius IV (pope, 1431–1447) finally dissolved the Basel Council (1438) and transferred it to Ferrara (1438–1439), Florence (1439–1442), and Rome (1442–1445). At this newly convened Council, the question of union was uppermost and a discussion of the doctrinal differences was carried on by outstanding voices on each side, although the major portion of the Greeks present were mediocre theologians. Cardinal Cesarini and Juan de Torquemada upheld the Latin side. The Greeks were not unanimous, for Bessarion, archbishop of Nicaea and later cardinal, sought to remove the chief obstacle, the *filioque,* by demonstrating the unanimity of the fathers on the double procession, while Mark of Ephesus remained adamant on its illegality. The Greeks, wearied of extended theological discussion and eager to return to the East with some assurance that the West would support them in their bitter struggle with the Turk, finally agreed to a decree of unity, *Laetentur coeli* (1439), which included not only the *filioque* but also the primacy of the pope, which the Greeks accepted in a far more ceremonial and honorary way than the legalistic and canonical conception that undergirded the papal structure in the West. The lone dissenter, Mark of Ephesus, was far more representative of Byzantine thought than Bessarion and the second-rate theologians who had signed *Laetentur coeli,* as was proved by the utter rejection of the decree by the Byzantine synods.

Although the Council of Florence made other reunion agreements with the Jacobites (1442), Mesopotamians (1444), Chaldeans and Maronites (1445), these agreements were equally short-lived. Thus, from the middle of the 15th century until the most recent beginnings of conversation in the wake of the Second Vatican Council, reunion has not even been a possibility.

BIBLIOGRAPHY: J. Gill, *The Council of Florence* (Cambridge, 1959); J. Meyendorff, *Orthodoxy and Catholicity* (New York, 1966); and *The Orthodox Church* (New York, 1962).

**Reuss, Édouard Guillaume Eugène** (1804–1891). German Biblical scholar. Born at Strasbourg, he was professor of the Bible at Göttingen, Halle, Jena, and Paris. He published numerous scholarly works on both the Old and the New Testament. His most important work was *History of the Sacred Scriptures of the New Testament* (English ed., Edinburgh, 1884).

*Réveil.* A revival or awakening movement in the 19th century centering in Switzerland, France, and Holland. The main center of the revival was in the canton of Geneva, where the state church had become Socinian by 1800. As early as 1810 some theological students under the influence of Moravians had formed a "Society of Friends" (not Quaker) which became the core of the revival that was to come. The visit of the Russian baroness and traveling evangelist, Mme. Kruedener, in 1813 added impetus to the awakening. More important was a series of visits from British Evangelicals, notably Robert Haldane and Henry Drummond. The former, during a stay of four months (1816–1817), gained a hearing among theological students and promoted the doctrines of Calvin. The latter, though less Calvinistic, was more impetuous. César Malan, a Genevan minister and teacher, became the center of the movement when he preached an "offensive" sermon on justification by faith at the cathedral (1817) and the Venerable Company found it necessary to impose a gag against any sermon dealing with Christology, human corruption or original sin, justification by faith, or predestination. The "friends" withdrew in August, 1817, forming the Free Evangelical Church of Geneva. Malan himself left the state church in 1823 and founded the Chapel of the Testimony. Despite persecution and schism, the Evangelical party gained increased influence in Geneva until it controlled the Venerable Company by the close of the century. Through the efforts of Robert Haldane at Montauban (1817–1819) and the Continental Society, the *Réveil* also spread in France and permeated the French Reformed Church through such men as Henri Pyt, Felix Neff, and Frédéric Monod. In Holland a parallel awakening arose under the leadership of Willem Bilderdijk, Isaac Da Costa, Groen van Prinsterer, and Hendrik deCock in the 1820's. Close contact and fellowship was maintained with such leaders of the Swiss *Réveil* as Malan, Merle d'Aubigné, François Gaussen, and Alexandre Vinet.

**Revivalism in America.** A mass evangelism movement whose function it is to produce religious conversions and, indirectly, to reform morals. Originating in the First Great Awakening, it has dominated religion in the United States more than has any other single influence. The movement has been identified with and shaped by a series of famous preachers—George Whitefield, Charles G. Finney, Dwight L. Moody, Billy Sunday, and Billy Graham—and its history may be summarized through their careers.

Whitefield's preaching was extemporaneous and so was the organization of his schedule. When he entered a city, he hoped to find some ministers favorably disposed toward him so that he might speak from their pulpits, but, failing in this, he was quite prepared to preach in the fields or in some secular building. He did not restrict himself to any church—a continuing feature of revivalism. He depended almost completely on word-of-mouth advertising, and had no follow-up in his work. Whitefield was little more than a famous preacher who refused to settle in one parish but itinerated throughout colonial America and Britain, preaching in such a way as to bring his auditors to a crisis in their religious lives.

Within the next generations, Whitefield's methods were carried into almost every village and hamlet of America by circuit-riding Methodists, Baptist farmer-preachers, and a host of other denominational ministers. Their message, as Methodist Peter Cartwright said, was always the same: "Behold the Lamb of God, which taketh away the sin of the world!" Their application of the text was also similar: Repent, cry out for mercy to God and be converted. The manner of conversion during these early years of the 19th century often differed, but it was frequently quite boisterous and violent, especially in the frontier camp meetings. Men and women fainted, cried out, fell into fits of barking or jerking, or simply moaned tearfully. Whatever our opinion of these conditions of conversion, there can be no doubt that the meetings were the means of filling the churches on the frontier and raising the Methodists and Baptists from the position of despised sects to the largest Protestant denominations in the United States. The Calvinists had some difficulty in accommodating revivalism into their theological framework. Their traditional emphasis had been upon the work that God did and upon the inability of man to save himself. Revivalism, however, tended to emphasize man's part in salvation with its calls to the sinner actively to repent and accept Christ. During the early years of the 19th century, the Calvinist churches of America passed through a period of realignment as ministers strove to make room in their old theological system for the New Measures of revivalism, or else, if they opposed revivalism, to stem its advances into their parish and church.

In New England, men such as Lyman Beecher and Nathaniel W. Taylor led the fight for revivalism, while Charles G. Finney was its champion in the West. Finney was accused of bringing the camp meeting into the Presbyterian and Congregational churches of New York. He allowed women to pray in mixed public meetings, called upon individual sinners by name to repent and be saved, and instituted the "anxious bench," a bench in the front of the church to which he invited all who were anxious about their salvation. Opposing the traditional Calvinism of the day, Finney claimed that the Bible would not urge men to do what they could not or should not do—to take an active part in their own conversion. His own theological position toward the end of his life more resembled Methodism than Calvinism. His campaign in Rochester, N.Y., in 1830 marked the beginning of a new era for revivalism in America. He obtained the cooperation of all the Presbyterians in the city and many of the other denominations as well and, for the first time in American history, dominated the religious life of a large city for more than six months. In this campaign, revivalism became an urban movement.

Dwight L. Moody led the next wave of revivalism beginning in 1875. Moody was a layman who had spent many years in business, and his revivals were marked by lay leadership and business methods. During the first years of his success, Moody held his meetings in large auditoriums, many times specially prepared for his preaching. By staying away from churches he was able to lay even more stress upon the nonsectarian character of the revival, to free his audience from some of the inhibitions felt in church, and, of course, to address far larger crowds. The expenses were many and necessitated a great deal more preparation and financial backing. Moody usually established a laymen's committee to finance the crusade and audit its accounts. Other innovations of Moody's included a large choir, trained ushers, an inquiry room instead of the anxious bench, and the use of a chorister and song leader—in his case, Ira D. Sankey.

By 1900 most of the common features of urban revivalism had been put into practice and perfected. The work of Billy Sunday was based upon a recognized pattern to which only a few refining touches were added. Sunday introduced the use of a team of revivalists, employed an advance man to good purpose, and was fond of having groups come to his tabernacles in delegations. Billy Graham in the 1950's added only electronic improvements —microphones for preaching, television and radio programs, movies—and syndicated newspaper columns.

It would be incorrect to give the impression that all that was necessary for success as a revivalist was the mastery of organizational techniques. Revivals of religion, as distinguished from revivalism, have not occurred the moment the preacher stepped into the pulpit. The five great revivalists just discussed owed their success in large measure to the coincident occurrence of great waves of religious interest during their lives. This wave of interest crested, broke, and ebbed during Sunday's lifetime, leaving him practically as little known in the 1930's as he had been in the 1900's. A few men have been hugely successful as revivalists, but literally thousands of others less well known have followed a call from God to leave the pastorate or their job and spend their life itinerating from town to town calling sinners down the sawdust trail to repentance. In fact, the revivalist has become as much a folk hero as the cowboy— perhaps as famous a revivalist as any flesh-and-blood figure is Sinclair Lewis' Elmer Gantry. In the late 19th and early 20th century virtually every evangelical congregation in America had its annual revival conducted by an itinerant evangelist. During the early years of revivalism, millions of converts were added to the churches by this kind of preaching. Church membership figures have risen in almost every decade from 10 percent of the population about the time of the Revolutionary War to 64 percent in 1967. A great deal of this success is due to revivalism, but, at the same time, the success itself has altered the nature of revivalism. From a method of reaching the unchurched, revivalism has become a means of Christian nurture. The annual midwinter revival of the average 19th-century congregation might have saved a few "sinners," but its largest group of converts were the young people of the church. The same thing is true of the large citywide campaigns of revivalists such as Graham. Critics of revivalism since the days of Horace Bushnell and John W. Nevin have been severe in their judgment of the manner in which revivalism changes the nature of Christian worship and theology. Especially, critics have pointed to the manner in which all the subtleties of thought and fine distinctions of meaning in traditional Christian belief have been washed away in the revivalist's drive to make things plain and simple. Revivalists have always insisted that theological discussion divided men and interfered with the winning of converts. Revivalism has not wanted to take seriously the wider social implications of the Christian gospel. Most revivalists have argued that the great social issues would be solved automatically if only sinners would be converted. Thus all social dilemmas, from slavery and higher criticism to alcoholism and juvenile delinquency, have been declared solvable only through the salvation of individual sinners. And yet the revivalist continues to preach and the converts continue to file down the aisles to stand before the platform. Revivalism has been declared dead many times, yet it has managed to persevere.

BIBLIOGRAPHY: E. S. Gaustad, *The Great Awakening in New England* (New York, 1957); C. C. Goen, *Revivalism and Separatism in New England: 1740–1800* (New Haven, 1962); W. G. McLoughlin, *Modern Revivalism* (New York, 1959); T. Smith, *Revivalism and Social Reform* (New York, 1957); W. W. Sweet, *Revivalism in America* (New York, 1944); B. A. Weisberger, *They Gathered at the River* (Boston, 1958).

**Reynolds, John.** See RAINOLDS, JOHN.

**Rhenanus, Beatus** (1485–1547). German humanist. While a student in Paris he came under the influence of Faber Stapulensis. For a time he worked with John Froben, and after

1526 lived in retirement, devoting himself to writing and editing. Among his works are a biography of Geiler of Kaisersberg, an edition of Tertullian, a history of Germany, and a nine-volume edition of the works of Erasmus, with a biography added (1540–1541). Like Erasmus, he first sympathized with the Protestant Reformers, but subsequently changed his mind.

**Rhenish Missionary Society.** An organization originating in 1828 through the unification of small missionary societies in the Rhineland. It was strongly supported by laymen from various denominations in establishing missions in South Africa (1829), Borneo (1834), China (1846), and especially among the Bataks in Indonesia (1861). After World War I its activity was limited to the training of missionaries. Its seminary in Barmen now trains pastors for service in Latin America.

**Ricci, Matteo** (1552–1610). One of the first Christian missionaries in China. He was born in the Papal States, entered the Society of Jesus in 1571, and studied at the Roman College, where he specialized in mathematics, cosmology, and astronomy. He left for India in 1578, teaching at Goa and Cochin until 1582, when he began to prepare for the China mission. With Father Michele de Ruggieri, he resided at Chao-K'ing, the administrative capital of Canton. The missionaries first began to break down the Chinese prejudice that all foreigners were barbarians by displaying clocks, mathematical and astronomical instruments, maps, and books. Fascinated mandarins often visited the learned Western priests, who made no secret of their identity. Ricci began explaining Christianity by showing how the ancient wisdom of China agreed with it. Hundreds of thousands of copies of his dialogue between a Chinese sage and a European priest were distributed and, together with the exemplary lives of the missioners, contributed to the spread of Christianity. As a "wise man," Ricci was summoned by Emperor Wan-li in 1601 to Peking, where he worked until his death in 1610. The work of adaptation and tolerance of ancient customs begun by Ricci was undermined and later destroyed by contrary edicts from Rome (1704) which aroused the hostility of the Chinese court.

**Ricci, Scipione de'** (1741–1809). Roman Catholic bishop of Pistoia-Prato, social reformer, and a representative of the Enlightenment in Italy. Born at Florence, he was educated by the Jesuits and ordained priest in 1766. He attempted to raise the levels of morality in his parish by founding a liberal theological seminary at Prato, but his re-forms were opposed and in 1790 when he was deposed of his see, he retired into private life.

**Rice, Luther** (1783–1836). Baptist minister and educator. As a Congregationalist, he requested permission of the American Board of Commissioners for Foreign Missions to join a party sailing for Calcutta, India, in August, 1812. During the voyage Rice studied baptism, and after his arrival he as well as Adoniram Judson, who had embarked earlier, both became Baptists in the fall of that year. Rice then returned to America to secure Baptist support for their missionary endeavors. For the next twenty years his efforts were devoted to arousing the interest of the Baptists in missionary and educational work. His activities were largely responsible for the Triennial Convention in 1814, then the symbol of Baptist unity. Recognizing the importance of an educated ministry, he was instrumental in founding several Baptist schools, including Columbian College in Washington, D.C., which later became George Washington University.

**Richard, Timothy** (1845–1919). Welsh Baptist missionary and educator in China from 1869. Active in Shantung, Shansi, Tientsin, and Peking, he became (1901) chancellor of the university founded in Shansi (the first of several such schools), religious adviser to the Chinese Government (1901), and secretary of the International Red Cross (1904). His literary work includes extensive translation into Chinese. Theologically, he saw all religions as contributing to the revelation of God. He was appreciative of Chinese culture.

**Richard of St.-Victor** (d. 1173). Theologian and mystic of the 12th century. Presumably born in Scotland, Richard entered the Abbey of St.-Victor (see VICTORINES) outside of Paris and there he became a pupil of the great mystic Hugh of St.-Victor (1096–1141), known as the Augustine of his time. Richard became one of the great teachers of the Abbey of St.-Victor and succeeded as prior of the Benedictine house in 1162. In the *Paradise,* Dante placed Richard among the greatest teachers of the church. Among the best known of his writings are his mystical treatises and his work on the Trinity entitled *De Trinitate.*

**Richard the Lion-Hearted** (1157–1199). King of England and a leader of the Third Crusade. With Philip Augustus of France he relieved the siege of Acre in 1191. During his sixteen months in Palestine he demonstrated great prowess in contesting for control of the seacoast with the Moslem leader Saladin. However, his arrogance also increased dissension among the crusaders. After a truce with Saladin he left the Holy Land in 1192, never to return.

**Richelieu, Cardinal** (Armand Jean du Plessis) (1585–1642). French prelate and statesman. He was born the third son of an ancient family of lesser nobility of Poitou at Paris. Although at first wanting to emulate his father, who had fought in the wars of religion under Henry III and Henry IV in 1606, while only twenty-one he was nominated bishop of Luçon by Henry IV. Obtaining the necessary dispensation, he was consecrated at Rome in August, 1607, and in 1608 entered his poor bishopric to spend six years diligently carrying out his duties and showing great zeal for the conversion of Protestants. In 1614 he was elected by the clergy of Poitou to attend the States General, where he won the notice of the queen mother, Marie de' Medici, and was chosen to present the address of the clergy embodying its resolutions and petitions. In 1615 he became almoner to Anne of Austria, the child queen of Louis XIII, and in 1616 he was appointed a secretary of state to the king. He owed his rapid rise to Concini, a favorite of Marie, and his power ended with Concini's murder on Aug. 24, 1617.

As chief adviser to Marie in her exile at Blois, he unsuccessfully tried to regain favor, and so returned to his see. Exiled to Avignon in 1618, he wrote *A Defense of the Main Principles of the Catholic Faith,* but Marie's escape from Blois in February, 1619, reopened the door to power. Recalled by the Crown to Marie's side, he participated in the treaty of Angoulême by which Marie was given her freedom and entrusted with much land. When the death of the king's favorite, Luynes, in December, 1621, made possible a reconciliation between the king and his mother, Marie used her power to push Richelieu into the post that would give him virtual control of France until his death. He was created cardinal by Pope Gregory XV on Sept. 5, 1622; in 1624, Louis XIII named him a member of his council; in August he became president of the council of ministers.

For the next sixteen years, his inflexible policy was to establish the absolute supremacy of the royal power at home against the Huguenots and the feudal nobility while seeking to crush the rival European power of the Hapsburgs. His attitude toward his fellow clergymen was to protect their possessions against state encroachments unless the Crown needed money badly enough.

Although the Edict of Nantes gave the Hu-guenots religious freedom, the successful siege of La Rochelle and the peace of Alais (June 28, 1629) ended their political influence. Richelieu's first attack on the nobility had been in 1626 in his edict for the destruction of all castles not needed for defense against invasion; it met with little opposition. The same year, however, saw the first of the conspiracies challenging his power, which he was so ruthlessly to crush. The attempt ended in 1629 when the king's brother, Gaston of Orleans, fled the country, his two companions dying for their efforts. Richelieu's severest test soon followed. While Louis XIII lay seriously ill at Lyons in September, 1630, the two queens, Marie and Anne, obtained his promise to dismiss Richelieu, though not until after peace with Spain. Word of the truce came in November, 1630, and Louis went to his mother's apartments at Luxembourg, but Richelieu secretly gained entrance to the meeting. Marie demanded an ultimatum. For a time the king's actions seemed against Richelieu. When Louis finally sent for him at Versailles, the court of Luxembourg was expecting the end. The king, however, assured Richelieu of his continued support; thus this day was called the "Day of Dupes."

To humble the Hapsburgs, Richelieu aided the Protestant princes of Germany against the emperor, in spite of the opposition of the disappointed French Catholic party, which had looked to him as a champion of orthodoxy. Threatened by a united Germany, he entered into agreement with the young Gustavus Adolphus of Sweden in 1631. The Treaty of Prague in May, 1635, by which the emperor was reconciled to most of the German princes, finally forced Richelieu to declare war; he marched against Spain both in Italy and in the Netherlands. By the time of his death the French successes had given him the power to lay down the lines for the Treaty of Westphalia (1648), whereby the European balance of power changed from the Hapsburgs to the Bourbons.

Patron of the arts, founder of the French Academy (1635), but above all a diplomatic genius, Richelieu died on Dec. 4, 1642, and was buried in the chapel he had built at the Sorbonne.

BIBLIOGRAPHY: H. Belloc, *Richelieu* (London, 1929); J. C. Burckhardt, *Richelieu: His Rise to Power* (London, 1940); C. V. Wedgwood, *Richelieu and the French Monarchy* (London, 1954).

**Richter, Julius** (1862–1940). German Lutheran professor at the University of Berlin (1913). He was active in missionary circles, served as president of the Society for Missionary Science, and wrote over thirty books on missionary activities.

**Riddell, John Henry** (1863–1952). Methodist clergyman and educator. He was born near Bolton, Canada West, and was educated at Victoria University (B.A., 1890; B.D., 1892). After ordination by the Methodist Church, Riddell became professor of classics at Wesley College, Winnipeg, in 1896. In 1903 he founded Alberta College in Edmonton, but returned to Winnipeg as president of Wesley College in 1917. He made a significant contribution to Methodist education in western Canada.

**Ridley, Nicholas** (c. 1500–1555). English Reformer. One of the younger of the leading figures of the Reformation, Ridley does not seem to have been converted to Protestant doctrines until the 1530's. His preferment was steady: chaplain to Cranmer (1537), master of Pembroke Hall, Cambridge (1540), chaplain to the king (1541), bishop of Rochester (1547), bishop of London (1550). He was deprived by Queen Mary in 1553, not only for his religious opinions but also for supporting Lady Jane Grey, her rival for the crown. After refusing to recant his views on the Eucharist, Ridley was burned at Oxford in 1555, with Latimer. Ridley was strongly interested in Eucharistic theology, having initially been influenced by the ideas of Ratramnus; during his episcopate many altars were taken down and replaced by Communion tables. He was also instrumental in securing recognition of the royal supremacy at Cambridge. Ridley's rejection of a doctrine of corporeal Eucharistic presence in favor of a purely spiritual, yet quite real, presence strongly influenced Cranmer.

**Riemenschneider, Tilman** (c. 1468–1531). German sculptor. He spent most of his life in Würzburg, where he was a leading producer of fine late Gothic sculpture in the north. Working in wood, stone, and bronze, and using religious themes, he was noted for his many altar pieces, sepulchral monuments, and statues of madonnas. He became a Protestant about 1522. Active in politics, he later favored the rebels in the Peasants' War (1524–1525).

**Rienzo, Cola di** (c. 1313–1354). Italian patriot and revolutionary leader. Of obscure origin, he tried in the mid-14th century to restore the Roman republic and recreate the "grandeur that was Rome." The papacy had moved to Avignon in 1309 at the behest of the French king. In 1343, Cola was chosen a member of a special delegation to Avignon

to ask the pope to come back to Rome. Unsuccessful, Cola returned to Rome to find the city in utter chaos thanks to the constant fighting of the Roman nobles among themselves and against the common people. He determined to take drastic action. In 1347, he led a bloodless coup which swept the nobility from power and established him as "Tribune of the People" over a shadow republic. He brought peace and a measure of prosperity to the city. However, he overstepped himself when he summoned an Italian national assembly, proclaimed the coming election of a national emperor, and commanded the rulers of the world to bring their titles and documents to Rome for his inspection and approval. The pope, alarmed at this turn of events, effectively undermined Cola's popular support by excommunicating him. In December, 1347, he fled to the mountains. Cola reappeared in Rome in 1354 and again cast his spell over the people. However, his second republic was also short-lived because of his tyranny. He was killed by an angry mob in October, 1354.

**Rigdon, Sidney** (1793–1876). An early Mormon leader. He was converted to Mormonism in 1830 and was closely allied with its founder, Joseph Smith, until 1844. The ideas of Alexander Campbell concerning faith, repentance, and baptism came into Mormon theology through Rigdon, who wrote *Lectures of Faith*. Rigdon was excommunicated from the faith when Brigham Young became the head of the Mormon Church after the death of Smith in 1844.

**Right of Sanctuary.** The idea of sanctuary is connected with the notion of the inviolability of sacred places. It was not Christian in origin, for some Greek and Roman temples were recognized as providing sanctuary for criminals. The practice was adopted by the Christian church at an early date and was given imperial sanction in the Theodosian and Justinian codes. It received papal approbation under Leo the Great. In some cases sanctuary was limited to the choir of the church, although in most instances it included the entire church building. In other cases, it applied to a certain geographical area surrounding the church. The right of sanctuary was always limited to certain crimes, the more serious ones being excluded from the privilege. There was also a limitation of the time during which a refugee could maintain sanctuary. The church sought to uphold the right of sanctuary by making violation punishable by excommunication. Violations seem to have been rather frequent, however. There were certain local variations in the practice, but it was in effect throughout Europe. In certain parts of Europe it survived well into the modern era.

**Rights of Man, Declaration.** See DECLARATION OF THE RIGHTS OF MAN AND THE CITIZEN.

**Riley, William Bell** (1861–1947). Fundamentalist leader. A Baptist pastor, he served in Indiana and Illinois and finally after 1897 at First Baptist Church, Minneapolis. There he founded Northwestern Bible School (1902), Seminary (1935), and College (1944), and was their president until his death. A vigorous polemicist, he was after 1925 the acknowledged leader of antievolutionary and profundamentalist forces in America.

**Ripalda, Juan** (1594–1648). A Spanish Jesuit and one of the most noted and versatile scholars of his day. He taught philosophy at Monforte, theology at Salamanca, and moral theology at Madrid. He wrote on many subjects, but his main interest was the problem of the natural and the supernatural. In this area he opposed many of the ideas supposedly taught a century earlier by Michel Baius. He nevertheless taught that it is possible for God to create a creature to whom grace is strictly due, though such was not the case with Adam.

**Ripley, George** (1802–1880). Unitarian clergyman, social reformer, and literary critic. He entered the Unitarian Church after his graduation from Harvard College in 1823. During his ministry at the Purchase Street Church in Boston (1826–1841), he was a founding member of the Transcendental Club. The club founded Brook Farm, of which Ripley was the president (1841–1846). He became literary critic of the New York *Tribune* in 1849 and was an editor of the *New American Cyclopaedia* along with Charles Dana.

**Risorgimento.** The name applied to the political and intellectual movement for the unification of Italy prior to 1860. Its aim was to free Italy of foreign control and to unite the various states into a confederation. There was some support for the papacy to head the confederation, but after the Revolution of 1848, Pope Pius IX was hostile to the movement. In 1847, Count Cavour, chief architect of Italian unity, founded the newspaper *Il Risorgimento* to preach unification.

**Ritchie, Arthur** (1849–1921). Episcopal clergyman. He served as rector of St. Ignatius Church in New York City from 1884 to 1914. A founder of the Clerical Union for Main-

tenance of Catholic Principles, he was also active in the High Church movement of the Episcopal Church. His extreme Anglo-Catholic position resulted in the introduction of incense, holy water, and the confessional box into his parish. He was also the editor of *The Catholic Champion*.

**Ritschl, Albrecht Benjamin** (1822–1889). German Protestant theologian and founder of the "theology of moral value." He was born at Berlin and educated at Bonn, Halle, Heidelberg, and Tübingen. His religious thought evolved through the mediating theology of Karl Nitzsch and J. Mueller to the Tübingen school. In his early career he was a disciple of F. C. Baur, but by 1857 he had completely abandoned the Tübingen doctrines of Baur. Ritschl's theology is best characterized as a theology of moral value. His intention was to explicate the ethical implications which he was convinced were inherent in Christianity, and to indicate the relevance of these for the life of the church in contemporary society. He stressed Christian ethics and the "Christian Community" because of his conviction that the rapidly developing industrial-urban society needed to be informed of the ethical and moral values of God's Kingdom. He rejected the techniques of both philosophy and mysticism from his theology and insisted on the irreducibility of religion to other forms of experience. He argued that religion is comprehensible only by faith, not by reason, and that this faith rests on moral values. He elaborated his main religious ideas in *Die christliche Lehre von der Rechtfertigung und Versöhnung* (3 vols., 1870–1874); English translation, *Christian Doctrine of Justification and Reconciliation* (Clifton, N.J., 1967).

**Ritualism.** Religious worship conducted according to established ritual practices. Rite is religious ceremony. Since public ceremonies must be organized and since religious traditions try to preserve their vessels for the sacred, ritual comes to mean the prescribed patterns in word and action for ceremonies. As such, it is inevitable; but ritualism implies a concern for the structure of rite with sometimes less than appropriate attention to its purpose.

**Ritualist Controversy.** The controversy resulting from the Oxford movement's emphasis on higher standards of worship in the Church of England. A Royal Commission, constituted in 1867 to investigate ritual aberrations, invoked the *status quo* of the previous three centuries as liturgical standards. Criticism aborted such criteria, and the ensuing confusion led to the coercive Public Worship Regulation Act of 1874. A few arrests were made under its provisions, but it became virtually obsolete after 1887.

**Robert College.** An American-supported English-language institution for men opened in 1863 in Istanbul. It was founded by Cyrus Hamlin upon his resignation from the American Board of Commissioners for Foreign Missions in opposition to its vernacular schools policy, and named for a major donor, Christopher R. Robert. After an initial struggle with the Turkish government the school flourished, and has educated many leaders of the new nations.

**Robert of Arbrissel** (d. 1117). A priest of Rennes and founder of an abbey at Fontevrault in 1100. Made up of both men and women who had been his disciples, the abbey was similar to the Anglo-Saxon double monasteries, with the entire community under the direction of an abbess. Gradually the abbey developed into a convent of nuns with a college of clerics who served them. Under Robert's guidance the abbey became an order that drew its members primarily from noble families.

**Robert of Molesme** (c. 1027–1111). French ecclesiastic leader in founding the Cistercian movement. Born of a noble family in Champagne, he entered the monastic life at the age of fifteen. After serving as prior of his house, he was elected abbot of another, but failing to reform this house, he returned to the first. He later headed a community of hermits at Molesme. The lack of discipline at Molesme led him and several monks to withdraw in 1098, founding the house at Cîteaux. Later the monks of Molesme asked him to return to be their abbot.

**Robertson, Frederick William** (1816–1853). Anglican preacher. A graduate of Oxford, Robertson was ordained in the Church of England in which he was identified with the Broad Church movement. He served briefly as minister of the English Church at Heidelberg, but gained renown as the preacher at Holy Trinity, Brighton. Never a profound theologian, he was a sincere man with a gift for understanding the people to whom he ministered, including the largely unchurched working class of Brighton.

**Robertson, James** (1839–1902). Canadian Presbyterian. Born in Dull, Perthshire, Scotland, he came to Canada with his parents in 1855. He was educated at the University of Toronto, Princeton, and Union Theological Seminary, New York, and was ordained by the Canadian Presbyterian Church in 1869. From that time he was stationed at Norwich, Ontario, until 1874, when he became minister of Knox Church, Winnipeg. In 1881 he was appointed superintendent of missions in western Canada and in 1895 was elected moderator of the Presbyterian Church in Canada, in which position he supervised the establishment of the Presbyterian Church in western Canada.

**Robespierre, Maximilien** (1758–1794). French revolutionist, Jacobin leader, and member of the ruling Committee of Public Safety. An ardent advocate of the Reign of Terror, he identified revelation with superstition and rejected Roman Catholicism. No atheist, however, he opposed dechristianization, accepted freedom of religious opinion and conversion by persuasion. Robespierre inaugurated public worship of the Supreme Being on June 8, 1794. Six weeks later he fell before the Thermidorian revolt and was guillotined.

**Robinson, John** (c. 1575–1625). Separatist clergyman. Although the facts of much of his life are obscure, it is quite certain that he was educated at Cambridge and was in a church at Norwich before he joined the Separatist congregation at Scrooby. He was with the second party from that group to go to Amsterdam (1608) and from there to Leiden (1609) in Holland, where he was pastor of the Leiden congregation. When the plan to go to the New World began to develop in 1617, he was an enthusiastic supporter of it. He preached to the party of departing Pilgrims just before they sailed and carried on a lively correspondence with "the church of God at Plymouth, New England." He may have intended to go to America later, but he died in Leiden. Two of his sons did make the trip. Some of his works were republished in 1851.

**Rodeheaver, Homer** (1880–1955). Music director in the evangelistic campaigns of Billy Sunday (1909–1931). His proficiency with the trombone and his ability as song leader were important to the revival services led by Sunday. The Rodeheaver-Hall-Mack Co., of which he was president, published the gospel songs he wrote for the campaigns. He was founder of the Summer School of Sacred Music at Winona Lake, Ind.

**Roehr, Johann Friedrich** (1777–1848). German Lutheran theologian. Born at Rossbach and educated at Leipzig, he was chief pastor at Weimar (1820–1848). His importance lies in his defense of rationalism. He held that the final end of religion was pure morality; the divinity of Christ was denied.

His views were not well received and in later years he greatly modified his radical doctrines.

**Rogers, John** (c. 1500–1555). English Protestant martyr. Rogers graduated from Pembroke Hall, Cambridge. While serving as priest to the English in Antwerp, he met William Tyndale, and was converted to Protestantism. When his mentor was imprisoned in 1535, Rogers gathered Tyndale's translations, used the work of Miles Coverdale to complete the Old Testament, and published the first complete Bible in English under the pseudonym Thomas Matthew (hence, "Matthew's Bible"). Returning to England in 1548, he was arrested at the beginning of Mary's reign, and became the first Marian martyr.

**Rolle de Hampole, Richard** (c. 1295–1349). English mystic. He was educated at Oxford at the expense of Thomas de Neville, and possibly also at Paris. Ordained a priest, he obtained permission to live as a hermit. He was his own master and thus was limited by his own experience, which, according to Walter Hilton, never reached authentic contemplation. Though influenced by Augustine and Peter Lombard, he seems to have had no knowledge of the German mystics then writing, and took the beginning of contemplation for its fullness. He attacked corruption in the church, but his writings are wholly orthodox, remaining well within common teaching. His ideas and principles are few and simple and found in two of his major works, *De incendio amoris* and *Melos amoris*. Grace is wholly gratuitous, and yet the grace of contemplation must be prepared for. It is a mystery of Christ's eliciting love; love demands love. He was devoted to the name and passion of Jesus, wrote severely of the danger of women and yet directed several of them with kindly delicacy. His genuine writings include several treatises in Latin, a dozen commentaries and translations of Scripture, eight letters and essays in English, and a number of English lyrics. Many more works were attributed to this master of Middle English prose.

**Roman Catholicism.** In the sense of this article, the Roman Catholic Church is the Western, Latin, or Roman section of the Christian church under the presidency of the bishop of Rome, usually called the pope. In the era of the undivided church the Roman patriarchate (Western Europe and North Africa) corresponded to the patriarchates of Antioch, Alexandria, and Constantinople, and already had a somewhat distinctive character of its own. By ancient right, confirmed in particular by the Councils of Nicaea and Chalcedon, the chief hierarchs or patriarchs of these great administrative components of the church universal enjoyed a kind of primacy over the bishops and churches of their region. Principally this involved presiding over the greater synods, supervising the election and consecration of bishops, and hearing appeals from the lower courts. Although patriarchal rights and customs evolved somewhat differently in each region, there was a marked tendency for each patriarchate to develop a common pattern of worship and liturgical music, a common canon law, and, generally, a kind of religiocultural distinctiveness of its own.

Besides his patriarchal role for the Latin Church, the bishop of Rome occupied a unique place among the bishops in general, a place that was acknowledged by the other hierarchs to correspond to that which Peter had held among the Twelve. His was a special headship and hegemony, a "presiding in love," a liturgical and moral leadership that during the course of the patristic age seemed about to express itself juridically and institutionally. To what degree this special role would have found concrete expression is difficult to say. The early popes were slow to grasp their ecumenical significance or to give it actual substance. By the time of the assertions and interventions of Leo the Great (440–461), the formative age was over. Despite the theological program of this lucid apologist, the success of his initiative at Chalcedon, and the striking confirmation of his *patriarchal* rights by the emperor Valentinian III, the *papal* primacy was to remain largely theoretical as far as the Catholic East was concerned. Imperial precedents after the time of Constantine effectively prevented the logical development of the Roman primacy. Crowned theologians such as Anastasius, Justinian, and Heraclius could respect, use, and pressure "the most holy and blessed patriarch of great and elder Rome," but what they could not abide was an effective papal primacy over the church of the Greek *oikoumenē* centered on Byzantium. Their bishop of New Rome (Constantinople) would be encouraged in his constant encroachments upon the territories and prerogatives of the ancient patriarchal sees of Antioch and Alexandria, but old Rome was to be excluded from the East both by positive imperial hostility and by the growing political, economic, and cultural separation of East and West.

As opposed to the Jacobite and Monophysite Churches resulting from the Christological crises of the 5th and 6th centuries, the Roman Church was at one with the other Orthodox or Chalcedonian Churches in professing the Trinitarian faith of the great councils. Arianism was not a lasting phenomenon in the West. Like the Orthodox (and the non-Chalcedonian) East, the Roman Church acknowledged the all-sufficient mediatorship of the Lord Jesus, the incarnate Son of God, and the extension and application of his salvatory work in history in and through the church which is his body, the vehicle of his operative presence in time for all believers. This Spirit-filled mystery organism initiates new members in every generation into the deifying passion, death, and resurrection of the Savior by means of the sacraments of Baptism, Confirmation, and the Eucharist which are, like the church itself, the activation in the present of the once-for-all reality of Christ's saving act.

Each local church is an organized body of believers with a diversity of spiritual gifts and ministries designed to serve for the edification of the entire community. Its soul is the Holy Spirit who manifests himself by a variety of charismata, some abiding and institutional, some passing and epiphenomenal. The institutional charism of greatest note is the office of bishop (overseer, superintendent) conceived of as a kind of presence of one of the original Twelve. As the preeminent witness to the good news he is, on the one hand, a sacramental presence of Christ to the believing community and therefore the chief celebrant of the mysteries and the chief preacher of the word, and, on the other hand, the embodiment of the local church as such, its link with the Church Catholic, its representative at synods and councils. Whatever the preeminence of the bishop, however, he was assisted in the ministry of Word and Sacrament and government by a college of priests who were, so to speak, his senate or council. Naturally as the local churches grew and required the establishment of parishes, it would be one of these elders of the community who would be delegated by the bishop as his vicar in that locale. Even so, however, serious efforts were made to keep the local church centered upon the one bishop and the one Eucharist. Although baptisms were finally permitted in the parishes, confirmation remained reserved to the bishop in person; at Rome itself the pope sent portions of his Eucharistic loaf by means of runners to the dependent churches whose Eucharist could not proceed without it; on solemn occasions when the clergy assembled as a body about the altar, concelebration was the rule; at ordinations the unity and cohesiveness of the one priesthood was stressed. A great variety of lesser ministries underlined the coordinated diversity of the one corporate body. Deacons and deaconesses, in particular, shared responsibility for the tasks of charity, instruction, and worship which constituted the life of the church.

The church could be best seen as the body of Christ and the people of God as it stood to worship each Lord's Day. This was the weekly plenary assembly of all its members in all their ranks to celebrate the mystery of Christ's risen presence in Word and Sacrament. This Eucharistic celebration, the Supper of the Lord, was the core of the church's existence and meaning. In it and through it the assembly of God was convoked by God's Word, renewing the covenant established in the blood of "Christ our Passover," and eating together a communion-sacrifice, a fellowship meal of the highest possible significance and effect.

The focus of the Liturgy of the Word was the Bible on its lectern and the bishop-preacher on his magisterial chair (cathedra), the written Word of God read by lectors and deacons, and the preached word of God proclaimed in the bishop's homily. Following the great intercessions, the focus then became the bread and the cup on the altar table (usually standing down in the midst of the congregation) and the bishop-celebrant's great canon of praise, thanksgiving, and memorializing which was a prelude to the general communion of all the faithful. Only the catechumens and the penitents were not present for the Eucharist proper. They had been dismissed after the Liturgy of the Word.

The primitive simplicity, directness, and intelligibility of the early Western liturgies were remarkable. As long as Latin remained a living language and preaching a live, weekly event, these liturgies retained a maximum of meaning, participation, and effectiveness.

By the 5th century nearly all the local churches of the West were gathered into provinces and the provinces into rather roughhewn "national" churches, each with its own primate. By seeking the pallium at the hands of the pope, such primates and the metropolitan bishops recognized the jurisdictional supremacy of Rome and were, in turn, established in their own. They and their synods constituted the classic pattern of church government for the rest of the Middle Ages. Free elections by clergy and people were also the classic method of designation to the higher clergy. Once such elections were ratified by the metropolitan and the bishop-elect was consecrated to his apostolic office by his fellow bishops, he exercised his role there for life. Bishops were not transferred from one diocese to another.

Although such was the classic pattern, various medieval factors made the logic of it frequently inoperative. In the first place, from the 6th to the 11th century the popes were normally out of contact with their bishops. Not only was effective intercommunion impossible at that period but during subsequent centuries, too, distance, the jealousy of kings, and episcopal independence, often made the papal primacy more theoretical than practical. Secondly, cultural decadence and the interference of princes, prelates, and popes all tended to undermine the synodal system in the name of efficiency or centralism. Ideas and suggestions tending toward a consensus could hardly filter upward in the absence of meaningful channels of communication and discussion. Thirdly, free elections were preyed upon by all and sundry. Royal and papal provisors, especially, rendered the electoral system more honored in the breach than in the observance. Royal, episcopal, and papal convenience also all conspired to divorce bishops from their original sees in a search for more golden opportunities.

In the nadir of European civilization that was the 7th century, the Roman Church almost foundered. Besides losing some seven hundred sees of North Africa and all those of Spain to Islam, the remainder of Western Christendom sank into chaos. Wave after wave of conquest and the barbarization of all aspects of existence led to such an enormous loss of literacy and communication as to make normal ecclesiastical life impossible. Preaching expired, the penitential and catechumenal systems collapsed, unworthy and incompetent candidates filled church posts, synods ceased to meet, most men lost vital contact with the Latin liturgy. Only in southern Italy and in the British Isles did a few monastic lighthouses do a little to alleviate the gloom of a dying religious world.

In the late 8th century these monasteries initiated a movement of reform and evangelization on the Continent which was destined to bring all the remaining Germans and Scandinavians into the fold of the Roman Church. The Carolingian monarchy was the chief ally and beneficiary of this new effort. Charlemagne, in particular, insisted upon having a common Roman liturgy for all his dominions, a common monastic rule for all his monasteries, and an orderly system of ecclesiastical provinces and synods. Like his Byzantine counterpart, he wanted the European-wide church to be an ideological and organizational cement for his empire. The monk reformers and founders of this new age may well have planned that the restored system was to culminate in the pope; the popes themselves, in allying with the Frankish kings, had no intention of exchanging a Byzantine master for a Frankish one. In actuality, however, Charlemagne was "the governor and protector of the Church of God"; Pope Leo III was merely a kind of chaplain in chief of the Carolingian king-emperor.

Whatever the weaknesses of realization, however, the papacy, basing itself largely on forged decretals and the convenient but spurious Donation of Constantine, was destined to get the ideological and even practical upper hand after the turbulence of the first feudal age. The incipient reform movements of the 10th century in England, Burgundy, and the Rhineland finally attained the degraded and captive papacy in the latter half of the 11th century. Initially an imperial reform, the Gregorian papacy soon broke free from imperial tutelage and began to lay the foundations of the papal monarchy which was to triumph politically and ecclesiastically for a short while in the 13th century. In the name of reform on a Continental scale, the popes proposed centralization and a kind of papal feudalism, both canonical and political, which would make it the master of primates and princes and the court of final appeal for Latin Christendom. By the 13th century the pope was the juridical head of the Roman Church. By working through legates, regional and international councils, the papal Inquisition, the newly chartered universities, and the international orders of friars, the pope was able in large measure to collect fees and taxes from all the dioceses of Europe, to intervene at his discretion in their internal affairs, to encourage constant appeals from the inferior courts to his own, and to maintain a system of thought control. Moreover, he could, in the name of external or internal menaces to the established order, generate crusades against his enemies and overthrow, for a time at least, even the most powerful monarchs. It was a century of dramatic successes ending in drastic failure. The Sicilian Vespers of 1282 were a kind of final judgment on a papacy unmindful of its high spiritual mission and fatally entangled in the sordid power politics of this world.

Moreover, for all its beneficent aims, its international organization, and its financial solvency, the papal monarchy seemed unable to remedy most of the serious and endemic problems that afflicted the medieval church. Even worse, the Avignon papacy appeared to be the tool of French foreign policy and its Curia a hotbed of luxury and venality. In a period rife with prayer and poverty movements, the suppression of what was generally thought of as evangelical reforms by a worldly papacy could only be deeply scandalous. Even the fanaticism and eccentricity of the sects could not obscure the fact that the official and established church, from the Roman Curia on down, appeared dead set against any changes that might have cured the great evils which beset it. Despite the facade of religious uniformity and cultural success, the mutterings of discontent and doubt were waxing while the spiritual prestige of the established church was waning.

Abortive reform movements were plentiful in the late medieval church. Some failed to be more than local phenomena; others were quickly discredited for real or alleged heresy. Conciliarism, the theologians' answer *par excellence,* was stillborn. Nationalism, frantic partisanship, and frenzied papal opposition murdered it before it was viable.

Even the "magnificent" Renaissance papacy, so admirable for its artistic and intellectual leadership, was spoiled and ineffectual on the level of the Spirit. In an age of religious crisis its brilliant but hollow pontiffs found that their elegant and cultivated paganism was drastically inadequate. The virile Luther was more than a match for the effete Leo X.

Strangely enough, for all its revolutionary character and the enormous losses it caused the Roman Church, the Protestant Reformation did not seem to teach it any profound lessons. Not even the Council of Trent and the reforming popes, for all their sincerity, went more than skin-deep in matters of reform. Trent settled mostly for dogmatic assertiveness and the reinforcement of the closed-system mentality. The Roman Church was under siege everywhere. It could retrench, tighten up its system, lop off a few of the worst medieval excrescences, but aside from that little could be expected. A real ecclesiastical *metanoia* was not destined to appear at this moment in history. What was perhaps the church's most crying need, a reform of worship, was the most neglected. The "new" Roman Breviary and Missal were simply codified examples of decadent medieval liturgy imposed by law on the whole Latin Church. As such they not only set the pattern for public worship for centuries to come in all Europe but also for the millions of new members of Latin Christendom beyond the seas.

There were pieties aplenty in the post-Tridentine church—and without them the interior life of the church would have vanished —but the Bible and the Liturgy remained sadly neglected. Even great orders such as the Jesuits, the Dominicans, and the Capuchins seemed unable to focus their valiant efforts on fundamentals; their specialties were promoting the Sacred Heart devotion, the Marian Rosary, or the Way of the Cross. Private devotions flourished while the Mass and the Office became more fossil-like with each passing generation.

As for structures the post-Tridentine church was a strange anomaly. Side by side with a heavy papal emphasis was a system of "national" Catholic churches in the hands of the Catholic kings. For them the pope was largely a convenience for granting dispensations and indulgences; by and large he could be ignored—or managed. Even the theoretical primacy of the pope was widely attacked and with relative impunity. More and more as the 18th century wore on, the pope passed his time maneuvering to maintain the independence of his estates in Italy while the bishops spent their time as courtiers at the courts of princes.

Only in the aftermath of 1789 did the Roman Church as it is presently known come into its own. The Catholic kings disappeared one by one; cultural Catholicism began a dramatic demise as its props were removed; all local churches were brought under the direct supervision of the Roman Curia; papalists promoted a new centralism and a stronger concept of juridical unity which culminated in the definitions of papal primacy and infallibility by the Vatican Council in 1870. The concomitant and resultant "cult" of the pope has had extraordinary repercussions in the life of this worldwide church. It will take the judgment of history to decide whether it has done more to Romanize or, ultimately, to catholicize the Roman Catholic Church. On the one hand, the influence of the Roman Curia, the Roman universities, and bureaucratic centralization in general have seemed to stifle church life, to promote an excessive uniformity and lack of liberty and to make genuine progress, adaptation, and reform extremely difficult, if not impossible. On the other hand, the centralized papacy has apparently rescued the church from a debilitating "Modernism" which would devour its dogmatic core and, at the same time, managed to steer the Church toward a reconciliation with the modern world and its legitimate social and economic aspirations. Without the modern authority of the papacy, the Second Vatican Council, both in its conception and in its implementation, would have been quite unthinkable.

Only a decade ago it would have been relatively easy to give an account of the Roman ecclesiastical system. Vatican II has changed all that. It would be difficult to exaggerate the revolution inherent in the debates and documents of this momentous Council. Although muffled at times by traditional curial language, the explosive charges contained in the Constitution on the Church, the Liturgy Constitution, the Church in the Modern World, and the Decree on Ecumenism are more than sufficient to change the course of Roman Catholic history irrevocably.

In place of the siege or ghetto mentality of the post-Reformation past, there appear to be emerging open and welcoming attitudes toward all that is of value both in the world at large and in the other Christian churches. Roman exclusiveness and intransigence is giving way in favor of the new friendliness and freshness characteristic of Pope John XXIII (1958–1963). He said he wanted to let a little fresh air into his church's ancient edifice, to update it and adapt it to the needs of the times, and so to prepare it for the task of Christian reunion. The Johannine Council has already initiated two striking practical reforms. In conjunction with its profound and moving doctrine on the church as "the universal sacrament of salvation" (*Lumen gentium*, No. 48), they appear to be of universal promise for the future.

The liturgical reforms begun by Vatican II are the first creative developments of Roman Catholic worship since the 6th century. Even in their first tentative stages they have encouraged a remarkable revival of the sense of corporate worship. Catholic piety is once more in firsthand contact with its wellsprings: Biblical preaching and a meaningful celebration of the Eucharist. It can be expected that the older Roman devotionalism, especially the eccentric Marian emphases, will now simply wither away in the face of a more authentic, liturgical piety.

The reform of church structures promises to be just as notable. The revived doctrine of collegiality has already found expression in the establishment of a representative Synod of Bishops to advise and assist the pope, in real decentralization in the hands of episcopal conferences, and in the solid prospect of diocesan senates and synods representing both clergy and laity.

An essential part of this renewal is the long-awaited reform of the Roman Curia announced by Paul VI in 1967. The worst features of the curial system are already fast disappearing: secret condemnations without appeal and the Index of Prohibited Books have been abolished; indulgences are fading away; time-consuming appeals and the judgment of particular cases will devolve back upon the diocesan authorities; the Roman seminaries and universities will attain a measure of academic freedom.

The *aggiornamento* proposed by Pope John is an ongoing process. If Vatican II was a true work of the Spirit, as Pope John believed, its results will be irreversible.

BIBLIOGRAPHY: W. M. Abbott (ed.), *The Documents of Vatican II* (New York, 1966); K. Adam, *The Spirit of Catholicism* (New York, 1935); H. de Lubac, *Catholicism* (New York, 1964); H. Küng, *Structures of the Church* (New York, 1964); E. Schillebeeckx, *Christ the Sacrament of the Encounter with God* (New York, 1963).

**Roman Church.** See ROMAN CATHOLICISM.

**Romanesque Architecture.** See ARCHITECTURE, ROMANESQUE.

**Romanian Orthodox Church.** The Romanians were originally Latin rite Christians who were conquered by the Bulgars in the 9th century and became subject to Byzantine bishops. During the 15th century the Turks dominated Romania. In 1711, Peter the Great liberated Romania, but withdrew, and thousands of persons were massacred as collaborators. The church was placed under the control of the bishop of Constantinople in 1767, the Romanians managing to maintain an active missionary center at Niamets and a printing press at Jassy. Russia again pushed south (1806–1812) and remained in control until 1856, but the Romanian Church declared itself independent of Constantinople in 1859, and was recognized as such in 1885. In the Austro-Hungarian Empire there was another autocephalous Romanian Church and the two were united in 1925, with the bishop of Bucharest becoming Patriarch. Church life has changed under the Communist state. The church is disestablished but officially recognized. The clergy, numbering about 10,000, are supported by the state and in Bucharest alone there are over 300 churches. A high level of theological study is carried on in two institutes and eight seminaries. In 1960 a more atheistic policy began with the arrest of 4,000 monks; publications were stopped and new novices were forbidden. There are about 12 million faithful.

**Roman Question.** The thorny issue of papal sovereignty in the 19th century. With the drive on for Italian unification in the 1850's, the papal claim to temporal sovereignty (which dated from the Donation of Pepin in 756) became a delicate and difficult question to resolve. Pope Pius IX insisted that the papacy must possess the Papal States in order to have an effective voice in the world. Cavour and the Italian nationalists looked to Rome as the natural capital for their new state without which Italy would remain a mere torso. At the same time it was not deemed expedient to make any rash moves that would adversely affect worldwide Catholic opinion and provide an excuse for Austrian or French intervention. In 1860, Cavour sought to work out a compromise arrangement but it was rejected. Ten years later his dream of unification was achieved when King Victor Emmanuel II sent Italian troops into Rome following the withdrawal of the French protective garrison that was needed in the war against Prussia. Thus the pope became "the prisoner of the Vatican." In 1871 a unilateral Law of Guarantees was passed and scrupulously observed by the Italian government, but it was not until the Lateran Pacts with Mussolini in 1929 that the Roman question was finally resolved.

**Romanus** (d. 556). Composer of hymns. Born in Syria, he came to Constantinople during the time of Patriarch Anastasius I (d. 518) and became famous for the many hymns he composed. He was sometimes referred to as *Melodius.* Of his one thousand or more hymns, approximately eighty (each containing at least twenty-four strophes and based on accent and not the usual Greek meter) are extant. His Christmas Day Hymn was used for about six centuries at the Christmas Eve banquet in the Imperial Palace.

**Rome, Churches of.** Of the nearly fifteen hundred churches, chapels, and oratories in contemporary Rome, more than half are 20th century. Of the many that are medieval or earlier, each has some claim to historical or ecclesiastical fame. Of special historical interest are the four major basilicas and the three patriarchal basilicas.

*Major Basilicas:* (1) St. Peter's. Largest in the world, the official church of the pope in his universal role, burial site for some 130 popes; dating from the 4th century, though frequently rebuilt and enlarged. (2) St. John Lateran. Cathedral of the diocese of Rome, built on the site where the papal residence stood from the 4th to the 14th century. (3) Santa Maria Maggiore. On the Esquiline Hill; 5th century and the smallest of this group of churches but the largest of some eighty dedicated to the Virgin in Rome. (4) St. Paul's outside the Walls. On the way to Ostia; built in the 4th century, but destroyed by fire (1823) and rebuilt on the original design.

*Patriarchal Basilicas:* (1) Sessorian Basilica, Church of the Holy Cross. Probably 4th century but rebuilt (1144), restored (1370), and

modernized (1744). (2) St. Laurence Outside the Walls. In the Cemetery of S. Ciriaco, site of Pius X's tomb; probably 5th century, though rebuilt (7th century) and totally altered (13th). (3) St. Sebastian Outside the Walls. Probably 6th century, although the present church is 17th century.

Of another score of significant *tituli,* the following merit attention: (1) SS. Cosmas and Damiano. At the edge of the Forum, first church erected from pagan temples (*Sacra Urbs,* 1st century; Romulus, 3d century); dating from the 5th century. (2) S. Francesca Romana. In the Forum; dedicated to her (17th century), the former S. Maria Nuova replacing (9th century) the older S. Maria Antiqua. (3) The Gesù. Principal Jesuit church (16th century), most ornate in Rome. (4) S. Maria *sopra* Minerva. Only Gothic church in Rome (c. 1280–1453). (5) Two circular churches, formerly secular buildings—S. Stefano Rotondo, a church since the 5th century; and S. Maria ad Martyres, dating from Emperor Hadrian (d. 138), a church since 609 when it was the scene of the institution of All Saints' Day.

BIBLIOGRAPHY: E. Male, *The Early Churches of Rome* (Chicago, 1960).

**Romuald** (c. 950–1027). Founder of the Camaldolese Order. He was a nobleman of Ravenna who became a monk after his father killed an enemy in a duel. Life in the monastery proved too lax, so he retired to the surrounding marshes to practice a severe personal asceticism. Later he wandered about Italy, gathering disciples and founding monasteries. Campus Maldoli, from which the new order took its name, became the chief center.

**Rood Screen.** A screen bearing a large crucifix, or rood, which is used to divide a church between the nave and the choir. Such a partition serves to separate the church into two distinct parts, one reserved for the laity, and one restricted to the clergy.

**Root and Branch Petition** (1641). A demand, authored by London Puritans, which called for the complete ("root and branch," cf. Mal. 4:1) destruction of episcopacy in the English Church. Though introduced in the Long Parliament on Dec. 11, little was done for some time, for although most agreed that episcopacy must go, they could not agree on what should replace it. Only after the Civil War had started were bishops, deans, and chapters abolished and lands confiscated.

**Roscellinus** (c. 1050–c. 1122). French theologian. Born at Compiègne, he studied at Soissons and Reims and then taught at Compiègne. In 1092 he was denounced by a monk of Bec for teaching tritheism. He retracted this at a council at Soissons under threat of excommunication and was acquitted. He then spent a short time in England, became a canon at Bayeux and taught at Loches in Brittany, where Abelard was one of his pupils. He was later in Besançon and Tours. Only one work of his, a letter to Abelard, survives, and his views must be inferred from the comments of Abelard and Anselm, who were hostile, and from John of Salisbury. Following Priscian's definition of a word as "thin air or the sound it makes," he defined universals as "mere sounds." He was thought thus to have originated the view that genera and species were similarly mere sounds, asserting that their meaning had no extramental existence, a belief later labeled as nominalism. Applying this reasoning in theology, he attacked Anselm's realism and maintained that the three Persons of the Trinity were like accidents to the substance of God and were three independent beings, saying that "if usage permitted," one could call them three Gods—on the ground that every existing being is an individual—even though they had one will and one power. He seems also to have denied the logical unity of the syllogism, dissolving it into separate propositions.

**Rosenberg, Alfred** (1893–1946). German writer and Nazi theorist. Born at Revel, Russia, he studied at Riga and Moscow. In 1919 he joined the Nazi Party, and after he was appointed Reich minister of eastern occupied territories in 1941 he ordered deportations and executions of millions of people. He was violently anti-Christian and in *Der Mythus des 20. Jahrhunderts* (1930) he presented the incompatibility of Nazism with Christianity. He was executed in 1946 by order of the international tribune at Nuremberg.

**Rosenius, Carl Olof** (1816–1868). Swedish lay leader who was strongly influenced by the writings of Erik Pontoppidan and Martin Luther. He worked as a city missionary in Stockholm and with George Scott, an English Methodist, founded the journal *Pietisten* in 1834. The Lutheran Inner Mission movement in Sweden (Evangeliska Fosterlandsstiftelsen) was founded by Rosenius in 1856 to further the cause of spiritual awakening within the Lutheran State Church of Sweden. Today it carries out an extensive missionary program with its own training schools and "prayer chapels."

**Rosenmueller, Ernst Friedrich Karl** (1768–1835). German Lutheran Biblical scholar.

From 1792 until his death he taught at Leipzig. He wrote numerous commentaries bearing on Scriptural exegesis, which drew extensively on rabbinic and patristic sources. His most important works are *Scholia in Vetus Testamentum* (16 parts, 1788–1817), *Handbuch der biblischen Altertumskunde* (4 vols., 1823–1831), and *Analecta Arabica* (1824).

**Rose of Lima** (1586–1617). The first canonized saint of the New World. She was born of Spanish parents in Lima, Peru. When she was twenty years old she became a member of the Third Order of St. Dominic and lived a solitary life in a makeshift hut in her parents' garden. Rose did sewing to help support her family, and at the same time she fasted, wore a spiked crown and an iron belt, and slept on a bed of glass, stones, and brambles. Her austerities, seclusion, and mystical experiences found little favor with her parents and friends, but her evident sanctity attracted people from all over the city to her garden. She was the first American-born saint and is considered the patroness of the New World.

**Rose Window.** A round decorated window found in churches. Its introduction into the West seems to have been a result of Eastern styles which were brought back to Europe following the Crusades. Round windows were used in Romanesque buildings, but rose windows with their fragile tracery were a mark of Gothic architecture. They were particularly popular in France for decorating the western end of the cathedral nave above the main entrance.

**Rosicrucians.** A mystic society, and at one time a secret society, thought to have originated in the writings of a 17th-century Lutheran pastor, J. V. Andreae. Andreae's work appears to have been an allegorical, if not simply satirical, production, but some individuals took it literally and formed groups to study it. Andreae tells of one Christian Rosenkreutz, who, after studies with the Arabs, founded in 1418 a society whose emblem was a rose with a cross in its center, symbolizing the death and resurrection of Christ. Its doctrines were similar to Neoplatonic cosmological speculation.

**Rosmini-Serbati, Antonio** (1797–1855). Italian religious philosopher. Ordained in 1821, Rosmini seven years later founded the Institute of Charity which did apostolic work in Italy and England. He undertook a serious study of philosophy, his works *The Origin of Ideas* (1830) and the *Trattato della coscienza Morale* (1839) initiating a protracted controversy over his philosophic orthodoxy.

Such charges were dismissed in 1854, but were renewed later.

**Rothe, Richard** (1799–1867). German Lutheran theologian. Born at Posen and educated at Heidelberg and Berlin, he taught at Wittenberg, Bonn, and Heidelberg. A disciple of F. D. E. Schleiermacher and J. A. W. Neander, he combined a pietistic spirit and rational criticism to achieve a "living Christianity." In his work, *Theologische Ethik* (3 vols., 1845–1848), he emphasized the inseparable relation between religion and morality.

**Rothmann, Bernt** (c. 1495–1535). Anabaptist. Rothmann was a teacher and preacher in his native town of Münster in Westphalia, whose pronounced leaning toward Lutheranism in 1532 soon took a sacramentarian and antipedobaptist turn. Under the influence of Melchior Hofmann and of the Melchiorites he hailed in his *Restitution* of 1534 a restored rule of the saints relying on Old Testament materials and justifying polygamy. He lost his life in the downfall of the Münster "kingdom" in 1535.

**Rousseau, Jean-Jacques** (1712–1778). French philosopher. He laid the groundwork for the reaction against rationalism that resulted in 19th-century romanticism. Born in a turbulent working-class section of Geneva, he ran away from home at the age of sixteen and always felt himself to be alienated from society in spite of later popularity. He obtained his livelihood from the generosity of friends and the patronage of important people.

Rousseau's own unhappy life probably shaped his views of civilization. He maintained that man in his natural state is fundamentally good, for nature gives him a warmth of feeling and love for his fellowman, a feeling that society and reason have corrupted. The progress in the arts and sciences, of which the men of the Enlightenment were so proud, actually debases man, and the aspect of society that most served to destroy the primitive goodness of humanity was the introduction of private property. Rousseau maintained that the good qualities in man stem from his emotions, whereas the evil qualities come from reason. Thus, in his writings such as the *New Héloïse, Émile,* and the *Autobiography* he stresses the heart rather than the head.

**Royce, Josiah** (1855–1916). Professor of philosophy at Harvard from 1882. Royce was close to Fichte and Lotze in his thought, but Americanized by James, Peirce, and Protestant individualism. He developed a monistic idealism that found romanticism, positivism,

and evolution inadequate. In *The Religious Aspect of Philosophy* (1885), he defined monism as the one mind of which all others are parts of the whole: the ultimate being of metaphysics, the object of worship, and the standard of value. Royce consciously sought to provide new philosophical foundations for American democracy, largely in response to the determinism of Darwinism, industrialism, and mass society. Royce was also noted for his contribution to logic in the "principle of noncontradiction," his ethical stance in the "philosophy of loyalty," and his attempt to reorient Christianity to the modern world in *The Problem of Christianity* (1913).

**Royden, Agnes Maude** (1876–1956). The first woman licensed to preach in Great Britain. She served three years (1917–1920) as assistant preacher at the Congregationalist City Temple, London. Her primary involvements were in social work and in crusades for the rights of women in ecclesiastical and political affairs. She was editor of *The Common Cause* (1912–1914), the literary organ of the National Union of Women's Suffrage Societies.

**Rufinus** (c. 345–410). Born near Aquileia in northern Italy, he studied at Rome, where he met Jerome. After returning to Aquileia, he migrated (371) to Egypt and became a monk in the desert. At Alexandria, under Didymus the Blind, he first became acquainted with the work of Origen. Traveling to Jerusalem, he was ordained by Bishop John and got into controversy with Jerome over Origen, supporting Bishop John against Jerome and Epiphanius. On his return to Rome (397) he translated Origen's *De principiis,* excising contested passages as heretical interpolations, adding a preface alleging that Jerome was a supporter of Origen. The controversy reopened violently, and Rufinus narrowly missed condemnation. His chief importance is as a translator of Greek writings for the Latin Church, where the knowledge of Greek was declining, although his translations show no systematic selection. In addition to *De principiis* he translated over a hundred of Origen's works, and fifty or so others, including some by Basil of Caesarea, and the church histories of Eusebius and Gelasius of Caesarea. His own works include three apologetic writings for Origen, one against Jerome's translation, a commentary on the Apostles' Creed (first Latin text of the Symbol), a list of the books of the Bible, and an allegory called *De benedictionibus patriarchum,* an exegesis of Jacob's blessing (Gen., ch. 48).

**Rule of the Master.** A rather long and cumbersome rule for monks, known to Benedict of Aniane, who gave it the title *Regula magistri*. Its original title seems to have been *Regula sanctorum patrum*. The numerous similarities to the Rule of St. Benedict were ascribed to the Master's use of Benedict's text. However, recent scholarship has suggested that the Master antedates Benedict and served as his source. This rule was probably written between 500 and 520 in southern Gaul.

**Rum, Sultanate of.** The Sultanate established by the Seljuk Turks after the tragic defeat of the Byzantine emperor Romanus IV Diogenes at the battle of Manzikert (August, 1071). It was sometimes called the Sultanate of Iconium after the Byzantine city in Asia Minor which became its capital. At times reaching from the Black Sea to the Mediterranean, the Sultanate met its end in the course of the 13th century under pressure from the Mongols.

**Ruotsalainen, Paavo** (1777–1852). Finnish Lutheran lay preacher and revival leader. He came from a humble peasant background and had little formal education yet became the dominant leader in Finnish Pietism and the outstanding layman in the history of the Church of Finland. He opposed nominal Christianity and criticized all forms of spiritual hypocrisy. Christianity was not a set of rules or dogmatic propositions but rather the experience of God's forgiveness through Christ Jesus.

**Rupert of Deutz** (c. 1075–1129). Exegete and theologian. Born near Liège, he was oblate and then monk there. A series of visions in early youth convinced him of his infallible ability to interpret Scripture. After being ordained in 1106, he gained fame as a teacher and became known as an uncompromising opponent of the simonists who had grown in influence during the confusion of the investiture controversy. In 1115 he wrote an attack on the Laon school's teaching concerning the origin of evil, and having been forced to flee from Liège to Siegburg, probably by local simonists, was ordered to return and defend himself against charges of heresy prompted by Anselm of Laon. In 1117 he went to see Anselm and William of Champeaux and debated with their pupils in Laon. In 1120 he was appointed abbot of the monastery of Deutz by the archbishop of Cologne and continued, though still active in Liège's church politics, in this office until his death. An extremely prolific writer, he based his Biblical commentaries on his certainty of divine inspiration, and rejected the then current introduction of logical method into theological teaching, while at the same time refusing canonical authority to the fathers. He elaborated Augustine's idea of history as the story of salvation, defended traditional Benedictinism against its new critics and revivified traditional exegesis with a highly fertile literary imagination.

**Russell, Charles Taze** (1852–1916). Founder of Jehovah's Witnesses. He was attracted to studies about the Second Coming of Christ very early in life. His first pamphlet, *The Object and Manner of Our Lord's Return*, had a wide circulation. He founded the magazine *Zion's Watch Tower and Herald of Christ's Presence* in 1879. His followers were organized into the Zion's Watch Tower Society, with headquarters in Brooklyn, N.Y. The group was later called Jehovah's Witnesses.

**Russia, Conversion of.** There were probably Viking Christians in Russia during the early part of the 10th century. They had dedicated a church in Kiev by 945. Olga, widow of Prince Igor, became a Christian in 954, but her son Svyatoslav remained a pagan. The first widespread conversions of the Russian people came under her grandson Vladimir, who was baptized c. 987. During the rule of his son Yaroslav, the Russian Church was closely patterned after the Byzantine Church in liturgy, church order, and canon law. A metropolitan see was established at Kiev in 1037. The civil strife and Asiatic invasions that followed the death of Yaroslav (1054) resulted in a decline of the importance of Kiev as both a political and a religious center. In 1299, the metropolitan Kirill left Kiev to reside in Vladimir. In 1328 under the protection of Ivan I the metropolitans moved to Moscow. During the early days of the Russian Church, the monasteries were built mostly around the cities, Kiev itself having seventeen. As the center of church life moved to the north, the monasteries tended to be founded in isolated rural areas. During the period of Lithuanian-Polish power in the Ukraine (1461–1589), there was again a metropolitan at Kiev, more influenced by Western thought than were the metropolitans of Moscow.

**Russia, Holy Synod of.** A synod or committee governing the Russian Orthodox Church from 1721 to 1917. Following the suggestion of Feofan Prokopovich, Peter I (1672–1725) informed his bishops on Jan. 25, 1721, that he intended to create a spiritual college to govern the church in Russia. At the first solemn session on Feb. 14, 1721, he officially gave the college the title of Holy Synod. This Holy Synod was approved by the four Eastern patriarchs. In 1722 a layman was appointed as high procurator of the Holy Synod. Under the empress Anna the Holy Synod suffered an eclipse, but under the empress Elizabeth (1741–1762) it was restored to its original authority. Under Paul I (1796–1801), because of the efforts of Ambrose, the bishop of Novgorod and St. Petersburg, the office of high procurator lost importance temporarily, and the archbishop as first member of the Holy Synod had direct access to the emperor. Under Alexander I (1801–1825) there was a ministry of cult, and even though this was dissolved and a separate administration was restored for church affairs, the high procurator of the Holy Synod actually functioned as the administrative head of the church in Russia. The transformation of the Holy Synod into a ministry of government proceeded rapidly under high procurator Nechaev (1833–1836), who, however, had to resign in the face of strong synodal opposition. The new high procurator, Protasov, named at the request of the bishops, completed the task. The chancery of the Holy Synod was made subject to him, and this completed the subjugation of the Holy Synod to governmental and ministerial control.

In 1917 the Holy Synod declared that it stood on the ground of accomplished facts. In a preconciliar meeting in 1917 the Holy Synod was no longer monarchical-minded.

Among the famous high procurators were D. A. Tolstoy and K. P. Pobedonostsev. The last high procurator was V. N. Lvov.

**Rutherford, Joseph F.** (1869–1942). Leader of Jehovah's Witnesses. Known as "Judge" Rutherford, he succeeded Charles T. Russell as teacher and leader of the Zion's Watch Tower Society in 1916. Rutherford had served as legal counsel for the society. Like Russell, he wrote widely. His followers used phonographs to play transcriptions of his talks on their house-to-house calls. He instituted the name "Jehovah's Witnesses" for the society in 1931.

**Rutherford, Samuel** (c. 1600–1661). Scottish theologian and Covenanter. After graduating from the University of Edinburgh, Rutherford became professor of humanities there in 1623. He left his post and proceeded to study theology. In 1627 he became a minister in Galloway and was very popular. His first clash with the policies of Charles I came in 1630 when he was charged with not observing the Five Articles of Perth. His first major theological work came out in 1636. Its severe Calvinism angered the bishop, who brought Rutherford before the High Commission Court and secured his deposition from

the pastoral office. During the next two years he wrote most of his famous *Letters*. In the year of the signing of the National Covenant (1638), the assembly at Glasgow restored his parish. The next year he became professor of divinity at St. Mary's College. He was an ardent Covenanter, taking a leading role in the covenanting assemblies. His *Plea for Presbytery* defended the presbyterian system against Independency. A year later (1644) he wrote *Lex rex* (i.e., "Law is King"), vindicating the covenant rights of the people against absolute monarchy. He was one of the Scottish commissioners sent to the Westminster Assembly, and he remained in London for nearly four years. After the death of Charles I, he became a protester and spent the rest of his life in controversy. At the time of the Restoration his *Lex rex* was burned and he escaped prosecution for treason by illness and death. This dynamic, hard-driving Scot has been called "the saint of the Covenant."

**Ruysbroeck, John** (1293–1381). Medieval mystic. Known as "the Ecstatic Doctor" and the "foremost of the Flemish mystics," John was raised by a pious uncle, canon of St. Gudule's, Brussels. Ordained in 1317, he lived an austere life with two like-minded canons for twenty-six years. In 1343, they retired to the hermitage of Groenendael, given to them by John III, duke of Brabant. So many were attracted to their simple life that in 1349 they organized, joining the canons regular. With his appointment as prior, John began his active career, rapidly gaining fame as a contemplative and director of souls. His influence on Gerhard Groote, and through him the Brethren of the Common Life, was personal, whereas John Tauler was affected by his writings. Ruysbroeck's best-known work is *The Spiritual Espousals*, a commentary on the text "Behold, the Bridegroom comes." Although he ascribed all that he wrote to the direct motion of the Holy Spirit, his works are not so much novel as bold and marked by experience. He emphasized a loving union with God, for which he was accused of pantheism, even though he distinguished a union of love from one of nature or essence. He stressed humility, charity, flight from the world, meditation on the life and passion of Christ, and abandonment to the divine will.

**Ryan, John A.** (1869–1945). Roman Catholic educator. Ordained in 1898, professor at St. Paul Seminary (1902–1915) and at the Catholic University of America (1915–1939), he gained fame as an advocate of labor, co-ops, racial equality, and the New Deal. From

1920 to 1945 he served as director of the Social Action Department of the National Catholic Welfare Conference, an important influence for social legislation.

**Ryerson, Adolphus Egerton** (1803–1882). Canadian Methodist clergyman. He was born in the township of Charlotteville, Norfolk County, Upper Canada, and educated at the district grammar school. He was ordained by the Methodist Church in 1824, and became editor of the *Christian Guardian* in 1829. He was a powerful spokesman against the exclusive claims of the Church of England to the Clergy Reserves. He was appointed first president of Victoria College, at Cobourg, Ontario, in 1841, and became chief superintendent of education for Upper Canada in 1844. The educational system of Ontario was largely his creation.

# S

**Sa, Emanuel** (c. 1530–1596). Portuguese Jesuit theologian and Scripture scholar. He was employed for a time as tutor to Francis Borgia, duke of Gandia, and in 1557 became one of the first professors at the new Roman College. Pope Pius V made Sa a member of the commission in charge of preparing an authentic and definitive edition of the Septuagint. In his Biblical commentaries Sa stressed the literal sense of the Scriptures over the allegorical. He also did work in moral and pastoral theology, and one of his books was temporarily placed on the Index because in it he allowed for confession and absolution by letter.

**Sabatier, Louis Auguste** (1839–1901). French Protestant theologian. After study at Montpellier, Basel, Tübingen, and Heidelberg, and four years of pastoral work, Sabatier became professor at the University of Strasbourg (1867–1873), from which he was dismissed by the German authorities. Later (1877) he was made professor of reformed dogmatics at the Protestant theological faculty of the Sorbonne in Paris, afterward becoming (1895) dean of the faculty.

Though Sabatier began with an orthodox position, his desire to reconcile faith with science led him away from his conservative beliefs. He came to view religion as the attempt by man to reconcile what he is with what he wishes to be. Man's spiritual quest proceeded through several stages: mythological, dogmatic, and psychological. The last stage alone satisfies the requirements of spirituality and criticism. The task of theology is to strip away extraneous elements from the central core of religious experience by revising creeds that become obsolete. With such beliefs, Sabatier was influential in preparing the way for the modernist movement and was respected by Roman Catholics as well as Protestants. Among his writings are *The Apostle Paul, Religion and Modern Culture,* and *Religions of Authority and Religions of the Spirit.*

**Sabatier, Paul** (1858–1928). French Calvinist scholar and minister. After studying at Besançon and Lille, he enrolled under the Protestant faculty of the University of Paris, where his brother, Auguste Sabatier, and Ernest Renan were among his teachers. After serving from 1885 to 1889 as vicar of the Protestant church in Strasbourg, he was expelled from Germany. Returning to France, he was a pastor from 1889 to 1894, resigning to devote himself to a life of scholarship. His historical interests caused him to travel to Assisi in Italy, where he studied the life of Francis and the Franciscan Order. Later, he became professor of Protestant theology at Strasbourg (1919) and continued teaching there until his death. His *Life of St. Francis of Assisi* (1893; English translation, 1894) was an immediate success and went into forty editions within his lifetime. The biography shows a sympathetic understanding of Francis, but Sabatier has been accused of molding him after the image of a 19th-century liberal. This interpretation emphasizes Sabatier's sympathy with liberal causes such as the modernist movement within the Roman Catholic Church, on which he delivered the Jowett Lectures in 1908.

**Sabbatarianism.** The practice of keeping the seventh day of the week as holy in conformity with the Third Commandment (Fourth by Reformed reckoning). Those following Sabbatarian principles observe the Lord's Day by the public and private exercise of religion, excluding work and all otherwise legal pastimes and recreations. The beginnings of Sabbatarianism are usually associated with the English Puritans of the last two decades of the 16th century, but it is probable that the English found the doctrinal basis for their practice in the teachings of Continental Reformed theologians such as John Tremellius and Hieronymus Zanchius. The agitation for the rigid observance of the Sabbath seemed to have been focused in Suffolk and found its most avid propagandist in the Suffolk Puritan divine Nicholas Bound, whose book, *True Doctrine of the Sabbath*

(1595), became the handbook of the Sabbatarians. The controversy was enlivened by James I's *Book of Sports* (1618), which urged the cessation of work on the Sabbath but encouraged lawful recreation. The book was burned by Parliament in 1643, and the strict observance of the Sabbath was enforced by law in England during the Interregnum. There was some relaxation of Sabbatarianism with the restoration of the monarchy but the Evangelical Revival of the 18th century gave fresh impetus to it. Sabbatarianism exercised a strong but gradually waning influence upon Christians in English-speaking lands, with evidences of its influence still to be seen in our day.

**Sabbatarianism** (in the United States). Sunday legislation was universal in colonial America and was continued by the states upon gaining independence. Strict observance of Sunday was particularly characteristic of New England Puritanism. The practice was generally based upon the regulations of 17th-century England, which prohibited public and private activities not specifically religious or charitable in nature. The Puritan Sabbath, however, gave way before the decline of theological dogmatism and the rise of more liberal views. Its decline was accelerated by industrialization, urbanization, immigration, acceptance of the "Continental Sunday," improved transportation, Sunday railroad schedules, Sunday newspapers, commercialized sports and recreation. Sabbatarianism, although founded on religious grounds, was also defended on secular humanitarian grounds, and supported as a bulwark of the moral fiber of the nation. The Constitution made no special reference to Sunday observances, and the matter was left to the states by the Bill of Rights. Among the major clashes over Sabbatarianism was the petition campaign of 1828 by the major denominations against the carrying of mail and the opening of the post offices on Sundays. However, this practice was successfully defended in Congress in 1829 and 1830. The Sabbatarians were more successful in the debate over the use of federal monies for the Chicago World's Fair (1892–1893) if it was to be opened on Sundays. They were also victorious in Sunday legislation for the District of Columbia in 1907 and 1908. Strict Sabbatarianism declined after the Civil War and though many states continue to carry the statutes today, enforcement is notoriously lax.

**Sabellius** (3d century). A Christian teacher at Rome (c. 215) and the most famous leader of the modalistic school (modalistic monarchianism). He was excommunicated by Callistus (bishop of Rome, 217–222). Traditions that came mainly from Greek writers of the 4th and 5th centuries say that Sabellius was a native of Libya and that after his excommunication he returned to the East, where he found a large following for his views, especially in Egypt and Libya. Sabellius evidently took the highly popular but rather naïve modalism of Noetus and Praxeas, who were also teaching in Rome during the early years of the 3d century, and developed it into a consistent system. He was opposed by Hippolytus, a champion of the Logos Christology, but seems at one time to have had the support of Zephyrinus (bishop of Rome, 199–217) and Callistus.

The precise teachings of Sabellius are also rather obscure. Only a few fragments of his writings remain and most of the evidence for his views comes from a century or more after his death. By this time his theology had undergone many modifications and become hopelessly confused with teachings such as those of Marcellus of Ancyra. In essence Sabellius held that God is a Monad who in the Father reveals himself as creator and lawgiver and through expansion, or "dilation," projects himself in the Son as redeemer and in the Spirit as sanctifier. Whether or not Sabellius used the term *prosōpon* to describe the various activities of the Godhead is a moot point, but although Sabellius and Sabellianism were condemned, it is certain that Sabellius did influence later orthodoxy in its rejection of any form of the subordination of the Son and the Spirit, and in preparing the way for the acceptance of the Augustinian Christology, including the West's adoption of the homoousian formula.

**Sack, August Friedrich Wilhelm** (1703–1786). German Protestant preacher. After studying at Frankfurt and Leiden, he became a tutor in a Huguenot family. He served as pastor in Magdeburg, then became court preacher in Berlin (1740), where he helped instruct the future Frederick William II. He corresponded with such men as J. S. Semler and F. G. Klopstock, and joined the Berlin Academy of Sciences. Theologically he was a neologian, but though against confessionalism, he supported the Establishment.

**Sack, Friedrich Samuel Gottfried** (1738–1817). German Protestant preacher. The son of A. F. W. Sack, he served as pastor at Magdeburg from 1769, then as court preacher in Berlin from 1777. He was a typical neologian, opposing both naturalism and pantheism (Schleiermacher). He worked for an enlightened church by seeking ecclesiastical and educational reform. In discounting confessionalism he helped to promote the Reformed-Lutheran union on rational and pragmatic grounds.

**Sacramentarians.** A somewhat misleading term for those who allegedly belittled the sacraments. During the medieval period, "sacramentarians" alluded to those who held that any of the sacraments was merely a sign involving no change either in the Sacrament (e.g., Eucharistic bread) or in the recipient (baptizand or ordinand). During the Reformation it came to mean those who opposed the real presence of Christ in the Eucharist. Luther referred to Carlstadt, Oecolampadius, and Zwingli as sacramentarians.

**Sacrament House.** Since the inception of the feast of Corpus Christi (1264), a special tower-like structure, developed from the ambry, used to house the reserved Sacrament. Developed in France, Belgium, and Germany, the sacrament houses were frequently ornamented with reliefs of passion scenes. After the 16th century they passed out of use, being replaced by the Tabernacle.

**Sacraments.** The Latin term *sacramentum* has no precise equivalent in Greek, but was used to translate the Greek word *mystērion.* In classical Latin, it was a sum of money laid in a sacred place by a litigant which went to the gods if he lost the case. Thus it came to mean any consecratory act. Tertullian introduced the word into the Christian vocabulary as a means of showing how God and man are intimately bound in an obligatory relationship in the salvific process that culminated in Baptism and the Eucharist. Because it had legal overtones, the word tended to put Western sacramental thought into a legalistic framework. There was no precise definition of sacrament, however, until Augustine took up the term and tied it closely with his doctrine of grace, thereby setting not only medieval Western Catholic sacramental thought on its peculiar course but Protestant (and Orthodox) thought as well. He distinguished between *signum* (the external action) and *res* (the divine inner operation of grace). In his thought, *signum* and *res* were inextricably coupled through Christ, the Word (*Verbum*), which guaranteed them. The efficacy of sacraments depends for him on belief in the Word that constitutes them. Moreover, he establishes their necessity for salvation: without sacraments there is no church, and there is no salvation outside the church. Augustine's alternate leaning toward the poles of spiritual

significance and realistic effectiveness opened two streams of thought, the latter of which was to dominate the Middle Ages, as is illustrated in the victory of the realism of Paschasius Radbertus over the spiritualism of Ratramnus and the condemnation of Berengar of Tours. That ever-present but somewhat suspect spiritualism is to be found in the mystics, in the Waldenses, and even in Franciscans such as Bonaventure and Duns Scotus, but it reaches its culmination in the Albigenses, who developed to their logical conclusion the ideas of the Euchites and the Paulicians.

Whether in opposition to these movements or by sheer force of development, the number of sacraments grew from the original two: Baptism and the Eucharist. By the 10th century, penance (confession and absolution) and marriage as well as two types of anointing (confirmation and unction of the sick or dying) were added to the list of sacraments. During this period also, ordination was lifted to this level. Though there was yet no official enumeration, there were attempts to extend the number even further, Hugh of St.-Victor creating some thirty in various ranks of importance. It was the Scholastic development that set forth the precise function of the sacraments in the systematic understanding of doctrine as well as in the exact number of them. The enumeration of precisely seven sacraments (Baptism, Confirmation, Penance, Eucharist, Ordination, Marriage, and Unction) was first set forth explicitly by Peter Lombard, but henceforth it became a Scholastic dogma. Thomas Aquinas, taking the Augustinian distinction between *signum* and *res*, introduced further distinctions within *signum:* matter (the element, e.g., water or oil) and form (the formulary act, e.g., the baptismal formula). He also intensified the Augustinian doctrine of intention (the minister intends to do what Christ and the church mean) while insisting, unlike the Franciscans, upon the inseparability of *signum* and *res* and thus upon the effectiveness of the sacrament as a means of grace through the very accomplishment of the act (*ex opere operato*) because the spiritual power resides in the sacraments and they both represent and mediate that power. Official Roman Catholic declaration on the sacraments was not made until Pope Eugenius IV (*Exultate Deo,* 1439), and was confirmed finally at the Seventh Session of the Council of Trent. The *de fide* statement about the sacraments includes: (1) the number of seven; (2) dominical institution; (3) distinction of matter, form, and ministering of each; (4) that sacraments mediate grace; (5) the different graces bestowed by the several sacraments:

(6) their necessity for salvation; (7) their *ex opere operato* effect (provided the recipient does not interpose an insuperable barrier; (8) the bestowal of "indelible character" by Baptism, Confirmation and Ordination.

The Eastern Orthodox Church has been less precise and legalistic than the West, although in its negotiations with the West since 1274 it has developed a systematic treatment very close to the Roman statement without the Scholastic terminology. Even these categories were adopted in the *Confessio Orthodoxa* (1642) directed against the Calvinizing tendencies of Cyril Lucar, but this statement has never become dogma.

Although they differed in their several conceptions of the sacraments, as in so many other respects, the Reformers almost uniformly opposed the *ex opere operato* idea of the sacraments, restoring the balance between Word and Sacrament by the elevation of preaching to at least an equal status with sacramental action (note Calvin's overbalance in this respect in putting preaching in the dominant place) and eliminating from sacramental standing all but the two Gospel sacraments: Baptism and the Eucharist. Of all the Reformation Churches, the Lutherans and the Church of England remained closest to medieval Catholic sacramental theology, although neither of these traditions spelled out in great detail systematically either the manner in which sacraments effected grace or the relation between Word and Sacrament (cf. Augsburg Confession, 9–13; Articles of Religion, 25–31). In Anglicanism, the concern over episcopacy in the 16th century gives evidence of a sacramental understanding of ordination which has continued, while the renascence of Catholic thought and practice in the 19th century Oxford movement witnessed to an abiding intention to remain within the sacramental tradition that goes back to the Middle Ages.

Characteristically, Zwingli emphasized the signific quality of the two Gospel sacraments (though he eschewed the term as unbiblical), placing emphasis upon the memorial aspect of both ordinances and upon the faith of the individual Christian and the community. Calvin's conception mediated between the objectivism of the Lutherans and the subjectivism of Zwingli. Against the latter, he gave large place to the action of God in the sacraments, thus emphasizing their effective character; but at the same time, against the former, he confined this effect to reinforcement and confirmation of what had already been done by God. Thus, his emphasis upon the sovereignty of God both highly qualified the *ex opere operato* notion and guarded against the mere memorialism of Zwingli as he understood him (cf. *Institutes* 4.14.1–17; Heidelberg Catechism, 65–67; Geneva Catechism, *in loc.*). Among the Free Churches, sacramental theology tended to be understood in a decidedly subjective and individualistic way, although this direction of thought rooted in the 16th-century Radical Reformers was in part influenced by Pietism and in part by the philosophical trends of the Enlightenment. The drift toward individualism continued through Schleiermacher and into the liberalism of the 19th century, while orthodox Protestants and Reformed scholasticized the Reformation views.

With the advent of neo-orthodoxy in the Reformed tradition and its counterparts in Protestantism, a reassessment of the role of sacraments began to take place, although in the center of this movement the problem of the relation of Word to Sacrament has been raised in a new framework; the new emphasis upon kerygma came as a result of the insights into the life and practice of the early church afforded by modern historical study of the New Testament and contiguous materials. As in other theological questions, the contemporary, more free interchange among various church traditions, stemming from the Reformation, and between them and Roman Catholics, has opened up a much wider front along which the whole understanding of sacraments may be discussed and evaluated. The deepening effect of the liturgical movement upon an ever-increasing number of church bodies brings to the fore the older questions about sacraments, but they are discussed with greater historical responsibility by Protestants and with rather less dogmatism by Roman Catholics.

BIBLIOGRAPHY: D. M. Baillie, *The Theology of the Sacraments* (London, 1957); L. Bouyer, *The Word, Church and Sacraments in Protestantism and Catholicism* (London, 1961); G. W. Bromiley, *Sacramental Teaching and Practice in the Reformation Churches* (Grand Rapids, 1957); B. Leeming, *Principles of Sacramental Theology* (Westminster, Md., 1960); W. N. Pittenger, *Sacraments, Signs and Symbols* (Chicago, 1949); K. Rahner, *The Church and the Sacraments* (New York, 1963).

**Sacred College.** Although the cardinalitial dignity goes back to at least the 6th century in the case of cardinal priests and deacons and to at least the 8th century for cardinal bishops, these three orders of cardinals were not constituted as a collegium until the 12th century. The idea of a sacred college seemed latent in the reforms of papal election instituted by Nicholas II (1059) and Alexander III (1179), and the selection of bishops of foreign dioceses to be, in addition to their episcopal function, cardinal priests and deacons emphasizes the Roman nature of the Western Catholic Church from the 11th century. The number of cardinals in the 6th century was fourteen: chief priests of the seven ancient churches and the chief deacons of the seven diaconal regions of Rome. In the 8th century, the bishops of seven suburbicarian dioceses were associated with the Lateran basilica as suffragans to the pope. When the college was constituted, its number was set at six cardinal bishops, twenty-five (later twenty-eight) cardinal priests of titular churches and twelve (later eighteen) cardinal deacons, so that during the Middle Ages, the highest number possible was fifty-two (under Pius IV, it rose to seventy-six), although the reform Councils of Constance and Basel agitated to reduce the number to twenty-four and established the high standards for selection and admission that still obtain. The reform of the Curia begun after the Council of Trent by Pius V and carried to its conclusion by Sixtus V froze the membership of the college at seventy (six bishops, fifty priests, fourteen deacons), and that number has been constant up through the promulgation of the new Code of Canon Law by Benedict XV in 1917 (Canons 230–241). Canon 231, which sets this number, was revised, at least in practice if not in letter, by John XXIII, who in four consistories raised the number to eighty-seven, and by Paul VI whose 1967 consistory further increased the college to one hundred twenty members.

The functions of the sacred college as defined by canon law are to "constitute the senate of the Roman Pontiff and assist him in the government of the Church" (Canon 230) and to provide for as smooth a transition from the rule of one pope to another as can be accomplished under the governing papal directives (Canon 241). The authority of the college as a governing body, even if only as assisting, has been in serious doubt ever since the creation by Sixtus V (1588) of fifteen cardinalitial congregations which carry on all the official functions of the Curia. The ambiguity of the governmental role of the college was made even more apparent by the decision of the Second Vatican Council to provide the pope with an elective council or synod of bishops to assist him in making policy for the church, but the creation in 1967 of enough cardinals to increase the college to 120 members and the hint that it would be even larger by Paul VI appeared to offset the legislative downgrading of the college as a governing body. The main reason for the ambiguity both of the role of the college and of the projected episcopal senate lies in the inability or unwillingness of the Second Vatican Council to face up to and try to resolve the problem of collegiality or the relation of the pope's infallible position and the renewed understanding of the function of bishops made possible by ecumenical discussions and historical study.

The tendency to maintain a predominant number of Italian cardinals, although they are not a majority, assures that the church keeps the look of internationalism while it also answers the practical need for officers to carry on an administration still largely Roman. It is noteworthy that practically all the non-Italian cardinals retain their residence in their respective sees. One important change instituted by John XXIII just prior to the Second Vatican Council was the requirement that all members of the sacred college, regardless of their rank in the college, be consecrated bishop, although the curial cardinals have only titular sees.

BIBLIOGRAPHY: S. Woywood and C. Smith, *A Practical Commentary on the Code of Canon Law* (New York, 1952).

**Sacred Heart, Society of the.** Congregation of sisters founded at Paris (1800) by Madeleine Sophie Barat (1779–1865) for the education of girls. Emphasizing detachment from the world and devotion to the Sacred Heart, the rule prospered. By 1865 the order had expanded to eighty-six houses. Pius XI canonized Barat in 1925.

**Sacred Heart of Jesus, Devotion to the.** A form of piety that honors the human heart of Jesus as a symbol of his love. Its origins may be traced back as far as the 12th century. Gertrude (d. c. 1300) and later Margaret Mary Alacoque (d. 1690), a Visitandine nun of Paray-le-Monial in France, gave particular impetus to this devotion. It was emphasized by the Roman Catholic opponents of Jansenism. Pius XII's encyclical *Haurietus aquas in gaudio* presents the theological basis of this devotion.

**Sadoleto, Jacopo** (1477–1547). Roman Catholic scholar and ecclesiastical statesman, one of the leading figures in the hierarchy in the first half of the 16th century. Educated as a humanist and Latinist, he was brought into the Curia in 1513 by Leo X as domestic secretary, a position he also held under Clement VII. Taking up residence as bishop of Carpentras in 1527, he pursued his scholarly career in his spare time, producing both secular works and Biblical commentaries. The latter, however, were criticized by both Protestants and Roman Catholics because of their unsophisticated semi-Pelagianism.

Called back to the Curia and made cardinal in 1536 because of Paul III's plans for reform of the church, he was one of the most outspoken members of the committee that drafted the document on reform which was published in 1538. He was as critical of the contemporary state of the Roman Church as were many Protestant writers. In the same period he made several conciliatory approaches to Protestants, including his letter to Geneva, which elicited Calvin's famous *Reply*. He was censured by his colleagues for these attempts and spent his last years working on the preparations for the Council of Trent.

**Sailer, Johann Michael von** (1751–1832). Roman Catholic liberal leader of the evangelical movement among Bavarian Roman Catholics. Trained as a Jesuit, he won academic recognition at Ingolstadt and Munich, but missed high ecclesiastical preferment because of his liberal views. Though anxious to update faith, he defended papal supremacy and rights. He helped the church recover from earlier disorders and even earned praise from Basel-based Protestant evangelicals.

**St. Alban's Abbey.** The most famous monastery in England, commemorating Britain's protomartyr and built on the reputed site of his martyrdom. A church existed on the site of St. Alban's in the time of Bede; the monastery was founded by King Offa (c. 794) and rebuilt, beginning in 1077 by Paul of Caen. Adrian IV (Nicholas Breakspear) gave it precedence over all other English monasteries. It had a series of outstanding abbots and a school of historians of whom Matthew Paris is the best known.

**Saint-Cyran, Abbé de** (Jean Duvergier de Hauranne, 1581–1643). French Jansenist leader. Son of a wealthy family of southern France, he studied theology at Louvain, later becoming a close friend of another Louvain student, Cornelius Jansen. In 1620 he received the benefice of St.-Cyran, from which he took his name. In Paris he became the chief apostle of Jansenism, although Saint-Cyran's form of Jansenism was of a considerably less theoretical turn than that of Jansen himself. His life and writings were motivated by a desire for the reform of Roman Catholicism through the revival of the teachings of Augustine. He opposed Scholasticism and Jesuit moral theology,

but hoped to defeat Protestantism by returning the church to its true spiritual bases. He was especially critical of the abuses that gave some justification for Protestant polemics. The Jansenist emphasis on the helplessness of man regarding salvation made them seem in this respect close to Protestantism, one circumstance among many that occasioned persecution. Saint-Cyran's writings are disorganized in thought but indicate great spiritual depth; it was more in his person than in his writings that he was influential. He was the spiritual guide of the Arnauld family and of the convent of Port-Royal; through them he influenced Pascal. His greatness lay in leading individuals to a deeper religious experience than they had previously known. Richelieu thought him dangerous enough to imprison him from 1638 to 1643. The Jansenists thus thought of him as a martyr for their cause.

**St.-Denis.** A Benedictine abbey founded c. 625, dedicated to Dionysius, the presumed Areopagite. For questioning the authenticity of the patron, Peter Abelard was expelled from the abbey. It enjoyed the prestige of being the royal abbey of France, many kings having been buried there. The abbey was sacked during the French Revolution, but was restored as a national shrine by Napoleon III.

**Sainte-Chapelle** (Paris). Chapel built (1247–1250) for Louis IX to house the crown of thorns and other passion relics ransomed from the Venetians. It served as a royal chapel for French kings until 1791. An exquisite example of Rayonnant Gothic, its walls are almost entirely glazed. Though restored in the 19th century, Sainte-Chapelle still preserves much of its original glass. From this period comes also the restored baldachino, a superior specimen.

**St. Joseph's Society for Foreign Missions** (*or* Mill Hill Missionaries). The order was established at Mill Hill, England, in 1866, by Fr. (later Cardinal) Herbert Vaughan. The priests, brothers, and sisters of this congregation today number over 1,700 persons, who maintain mission stations in Africa, India, Pakistan, Borneo, the Philippines, New Zealand, Sarawak, and elsewhere throughout the world.

**Saint-Martin, Louis Claude de** (1743–1803). French mystic, teacher, and revolutionary. Freemasonry led him to a mysticism that was a mixture of Gnostic, kabbalistic, and Neoplatonic ideas. He was chosen a tutor to the Dauphin (1791), and taught in lay schools before his death. His interests led him to write on the philosophic and religious implications of the Revolution. Concerned with anthropology and primitive Christianity, he also wrote extensively upon these subjects.

### St. Peter's Basilica, Rome.

The basilica (the second on the site) was built around the shrine erected c. 160 on the Vatican Hill, commemorating either the site of the martyrdom or the burial of St. Peter, Prince of the Apostles, who was believed to have died in the Neronian persecution, about 67. The first church ("Old St. Peter's"), a five-aisled basilica, was erected by Constantine I in the second quarter of the 4th century. He excavated part of the Vatican hillside and filled part of the valley, and acting as Pontifex Maximus, suppressed a largely pagan cemetery—a vast enterprise demonstrating the solidity of the belief in Constantine's time in the tradition connecting Peter with this place. (Evidence of the early existence of the tradition and harmonious with its truth although not establishing it beyond dispute, has been gathered by excavations undertaken since 1940.) Constantine's church, remodeled by Gregory the Great, looted by the Saracens in 846, repaired again and again, stood until the 15th century, when the decision was made by Nicholas V to pull it down and replace it with a more splendid church in the new style. This second building, the largest church in the world (length, 694 feet, including portico; dome, 435 feet high; transept, 451 feet) and one of the greatest of Renaissance buildings (even though artistically flawed by the elongation of the nave against the advice of Michelangelo), was begun in 1506 and completed in 1614. The wonderful colonnades of the Piazza, designed by Bernini, were completed in 1667. The indulgence of 1515 which provoked Luther's theses was intended to defray in part the cost of this vast structure. The architects included Bramante, Raphael, Michelangelo, and Maderna (who added the facade). The basilica abounds in tombs of popes and kings and in works of art, of which the most famous perhaps are the *Pietà* of Michelangelo, the bronze statue of Peter (by Arnolfo di Cambio?), and the baldachino of the high altar and the Altar of the Chair, both by Bernini.

The basilica is not the cathedral church of the diocese of Rome—that is S. Giovanni in Laterano (the Lateran Basilica). However, owing to the residence of the popes in the Vatican palace (the first conclave held there was that of April 8, 1378) and the significance of the shrine of Peter, St. Peter's Basilica has come to stand as symbol for the pope's position as head of the universal church, successor of Peter, and patriarch of the West.

### Saints, Lives of.

Christianity has had an interest in biography from its very beginning. Whatever similarity the Gospels may have to any of the Greek biographical conventions, they nevertheless appear as a unique literary form. Their interest is not in merely recounting the life of Jesus or even in holding him up as a model for imitation. Instead, they present an offer of salvation. From that time on, Christianity has recounted the story of its heroes. The book of Acts is largely devoted to telling of the ministry of the two greatest apostles. By the end of the 2d century, apocryphal acts of the apostles began to be circulated. It appears that the purpose of these writings was not so much to supplement biographical information about the apostles as it was to present edifying entertainment to compete with the pagan romances that were popular at the time. Nevertheless, most of these apocryphal or fictional works betray heretical backgrounds and were undoubtedly used as propaganda. The Clementine *Homilies* and *Recognitions* belong to this genre. The next type of biography to appear in the church was the acts of martyrs. The first of these was the letter written (perhaps in 156) by the church at Smyrna to that at Philomelium to relate the events of the death of Polycarp. Probably the first saint who was not a martyr to have his life story written for the edification of the faithful was the hermit Antony of Egypt, whose biographer was no less a figure than Athanasius. This work had profound influence on the monastic movement. Eusebius not only included biographical sketches of holy men in his *Ecclesiastical History* but also wrote a life of Constantine, who enjoys Eastern canonization. Jerome's work *Of Illustrious Men* contains lives of saints and pagans.

Among the many records of the life stories of the saints, those which deserve the name of hagiography differ from all others chiefly in their purpose, which is to edify. Hagiographic saints' lives have been divided into six groups: (1) Official court proceedings. Though few in number, they are our most authentic witnesses to martyrdoms. Christians succeeded in copying the records of court reporters. In this category fall the Acts of Justin and His Companions, which records the trial of the Greek Apologist at Rome c. 165; the Acts of the Martyrs of Scilli in Africa, which is the oldest document of African church history, dating from 180; and the Proconsular Acts of Cyprian, the bishop of Carthage who was executed in 258. (2) Eyewitness reports called *passiones* or *martyria*. They include the Martyrdom of Polycarp; the Letter of the Churches of Vienne and Lyons to the Churches of Asia and Phrygia, which tells of the martyrs of Lyons in 177 or 178 and is preserved by Eusebius; the Passion of Perpetua and Felicitas, which is composed of the diary of Perpetua, some chapters by one of her companions, and the editorial setting by no less a person than Tertullian; the Acts of Carpus, Papylus, and Agathonice, from the time of Marcus Aurelius; and the Acts of Apollonius, the philosopher who was beheaded during the reign of Commodus. This category can be divided into: (*a*) documents in the first person singular, (*b*) documents in which the contemporary author quotes the testimony of others exclusively, and (*c*) documents in which the testimony of the author is combined with that of others. (3) Acts whose principal source is a written document of one of the preceding categories which has been set in literary form by an editor. Some of the lives in the menology of Metaphrastes fall under this classification. (4) Acts that combine real and imagined events into a historical romance. In these acts the name of the saint or the location of his shrine may be the only historical element. The stories are not necessarily fantasy, but they are unreliable. Often it appears that the stories of one saint have been transferred to another by a simple change of the names of places and persons. In this category belong the whole series of cycles in the Roman *Legendarium*. (5) Imaginative romances in which the saint himself is a product of the writer's imagination. Among such are Nicephorus and *Barlaam and Joasaph*. (6) Forgeries that have been written with the purpose of deceiving the reader.

There have been many efforts to collect the lives of saints and to arrange them according to some theory. The greatest work in the field has been done by the group of Jesuit scholars called the Bollandists, who have placed the lives in the order of the calendar in their *Acta Sanctorum*.

BIBLIOGRAPHY: D. Attwater, *A Dictionary of Saints* (London, 1948); A. Butler, *The Lives of the Saints* (London, 1948); H. Delehaye, *The Legends of the Saints* (New York, 1907).

**Saint-Simon, Count de** (Claude Henri de Rouvroy) (1760–1825). French socialist. A member of a noble family, educated by Jean Le Rond d'Alembert, he fought on the side of the colonists in the American Revolution. An enthusiastic supporter of the French Revolution, he abandoned his titles and changed his name. For the rest of his life he devoted himself to scientific inquiries and social writings. In his books, *L'Organisateur* (1820), *Du*

*système industriel* (1821), and *Le Nouveau Christianisme* (1825), he became the apostle of positive science, industrialism, socialism, and a humanitarian lay religion. In his ideal society, industry was to rule all. He believed that only the industrial classes work for the moral and physical welfare of mankind and that therefore they should be the privileged class. He advocated a social hierarchy in which each man shall be placed according to his capacity and rewarded according to his works. In religion he believed that the one divine principle in Christianity is that men must behave as brothers toward each other. True Christianity, he believed, consists in the amelioration of the conditions of the poor. The teachings of Saint-Simon were propagated by his followers, Olinde Rodrigues, Armand Bazard, and Barthélemy Prosper Enfantin.

**SS. Peter and Paul.** Monastic church in Canterbury founded by Augustine and the Kentish Crown in 598. It was dissolved as a monastery in 1538 by Henry VIII. The tombs of the first ten archbishops were there, and Cuthbert's breaking with this tradition led to disputes between the monks and the cathedral chapter. The abbey church claimed exemption from the jurisdiction of the archbishop, and since 1051 its abbot has been granted precedence over all but Monte Cassino. From 1061, he has been granted episcopal insignia.

**Saladin** (1138–1193). Sultan of Egypt who united the Moslem forces against the Latin kingdom of Jerusalem. After crushing the Christian armies at Hattin, Saladin proceeded to retake Jerusalem in 1187. The resurgence of the crusaders under Richard the Lion-Hearted resulted in a stalemate, but the Christians never again controlled more than the seacoast. Saladin's death came only a few months after the truce with his great nemesis, Richard, in 1192.

**Salazar, Antonio de Oliveira** (1889–       ). Portuguese premier after 1932. Sometime economics professor and parliamentary deputy, he was named finance minister in 1928. He set out to create a "new state," authoritarian, run by technicians on nationalist and Christian principles. By statute (1933) he was "responsible before himself and God." The Concordat of 1940 gave the Catholic Church a privileged position. Goa, Diu, and Damão were lost to India in 1961.

**Salmanticenses.** A group of reformed (Discalced) Carmelites in Spain in the 17th and early 18th centuries who taught at the theological college at Salamanca. They were fervent disciples of Thomas Aquinas and in order to provide for unity and consistency in their teaching they would take a vote whenever there was a difference of interpretation among them. Their chief written work, on which the group labored for seventy years (1631–1701), was the twelve-volume *Cursus theologicus Summan d. Thomae complectens,* a massive commentary on the *Summa theologiae* of Aquinas.

**Salmasius, Claudius** (Claude de Saumaise) (1588–1653). French classical scholar. He studied at Paris, where he was won over to Calvinism. He published a number of classical works, and later succeeded to Joseph Scaliger's chair at Leiden in 1632. Among his numerous works were two books setting forth a defense of usury on Christian principles and his vindication of the Stuart monarchy (*Defensio regia pro Carolo I*), which elicited Milton's reply, *Pro populo anglicano defensio.*

**Salter's Hall Conference** (1719). London synod of English Dissenters which debated theological freedom after hearing of the "Arianism" of some Exeter ministers. This "Arianism" taught that the divine Christ was subordinate to God the Father. The synod decided against doctrinal tests other than Scripture. The result was a division between Presbyterians and the more orthodox Congregationalists, and the drift of many Presbyterians into Unitarianism.

**Salvation Army.** The international evangelistic and social agency organized by William Booth in London in 1865. As a local preacher in the Wesleyan Methodist Church working in London, Booth was touched by the plight of the poor and he chafed at the reluctance of his denomination to preach to them. His zeal led him first into the reform movement of the Wesleyans and later into the New Connection Methodists, where he was ordained. In 1861 he withdrew from the New Connection to become a traveling evangelist. His work brought him back to London in 1865. That same year he organized the group that became the Christian Mission, and later the Salvation Army, to work in the slums of the Mile End Waste. Though the work was difficult, Booth gradually developed a style of evangelism that was appealing. He preached informal and colloquial sermons and learned that it was necessary to minister to the physical and social needs of men as well as to preach to convert their souls. Some innovations to assist evangelism, such as the use of brass bands and religious songs set to popular tunes, came naturally and were not contemplated in advance. Certainly no one at the time could have estimated their value to the movement. With these changes the "Hal-lelujah Army" was soon rapidly spreading across England.

Prior to 1877, Booth had no plans to organize his work into an army, and its military character was something of an accident. Between 1878 and 1880 the movement was reorganized into its present form. In 1878 the first edition of *Orders and Regulations for the Salvation Army* was printed. The Army's publication, the *War Cry,* was begun the following year. Mrs. Booth designed the first flag, and in the early 1880's the uniform was regularized. The basic unit of the Army is the corps, which is commanded by an officer. There may be more than one corps in a given location. These are in turn organized into divisions and territories. The central organization is headed by a "general." Officers, the Salvation Army's equivalent of ministers, are recruited mainly from the corps. A "cadet" is eligible to apply for officer's training after he has been a member six months. At present the normal training period for an officer is two years in residence in one of the Army's training colleges. New "recruits" are required to sign the "Articles of War," or creed of the Army.

Although the Salvation Army met severe opposition in its early years, it came to be a popular movement, with the Prince of Wales as patron.

In 1880 the Army invaded the United States. Australia and France were entered the following year, and India, Sweden, Switzerland, and Canada the next. Moreover, the social aspects of the work were continually being increased, until at present the Salvation Army operates hospitals, maternity homes, camps and farms, shelters, food depots, employment offices, social and treatment centers, canteens, and old folks' homes. At various times in its history it has launched crusades on behalf of prostitutes, criminals, the insane, and alcoholics. One of these of twenty-five years' duration produced the closing of the infamous prison, Devil's Island. Wherever there has been human need or suffering, the Army has been present.

In 1912, William Booth "laid down his sword" in death and was succeeded as general by his son Bramwell, who for years had been chief of staff. He served until 1929, and since that time the position has been elective. Leadership in America was for a long period provided by Booth's daughter, Evangeline.

BIBLIOGRAPHY: E. Bishop, *Blood and Fire! The Story of General William Booth and the Salvation Army* (Chicago, 1965); S. Chesham, *Born to Battle: The Salvation Army in America* (Chicago, 1965); St. J. Ervine, *God's Soldier,* 2 vols. (London, 1934); H. A. Wisbey,

Jr., *Soldiers Without Swords: A History of the Salvation Army in the United States* (New York, 1955).

**Salvian** (c. 400–c. 480). Presbyter and writer of Marseilles. Called "teacher of bishops," he wrote more than a score of volumes, including homilies and letters. He was born early in the 5th century in the Rhineland. His eight books *On the Government of God* rest upon Lactantius, recall Augustine's *City of God,* and make a two-pronged attack on the complacency of church and empire in the form of a review of world history to the time of writing (439–450). The style is rhetorical but clear.

**Salzburgers.** Protestants who were banished from the Roman Catholic archbishopric of Salzburg, Austria, in the 18th century. During the early part of the 16th century, Archbishop Mattheus Lang appeared to be sympathetic to the work of the Reformers Paul Speratus and Stephen Agricola. Although Lang had turned against the Reformation by 1520, adherents to Lutheranism multiplied. In 1588, Catholic authorities, with the knowledge of the pope, decided that Protestants would have to recant or be banished from the country. Many Protestants conformed outwardly but secretly and with much success continued to worship and to give Lutheran instruction to their children even though persecution was renewed in 1614. Archbishop Leopold Anton succeeded in getting approximately twenty thousand Evangelicals to identify themselves publicly in 1730. Alarmed, Protestants formed the Salzbund, or "covenant of salt," and vowed they would remain faithful to their religious convictions even if they were forced to live on a diet of salt and bread. In 1731, they were commanded to leave Salzburg in three months, thus facing financial ruin and the loss of their offspring not of age. Protestant Europe was shocked and promised protection. Frederick William I of Prussia welcomed and profited from some of the exiles who made a triumphal march to populate the Lithuanian plains.

Samuel Urlsperger, an Augsburg pastor, assisted by the Society for Promoting Christian Knowledge, interceded with the English government, which authorized a collection for the Salzburgers. Under a special commissioner, Baron Philip George von Reck, it then provided them free passage to Georgia, free care for a year, free use of certain lands for ten years, with rights of citizenship and freedom of worship. Several groups emigrated to Georgia between 1733 and 1741. On the Savannah River, the Salzburger community of Ebenezer thrived religiously and economically under the leadership of Halle-trained pastors, John Martin Boltzius and Israel Christian Gronau. Isolated geographically, the Salzburgers were nevertheless closely associated with the Moravians, and they helped to support the work of Henry M. Mühlenberg in the building of churches in Pennsylvania. Although there are descendants, they have been absorbed into larger Lutheran bodies.

**Sanchez, Thomas** (1550–1610). Spanish Jesuit moral theologian. Sharply criticized because of the indiscreet details of his treatise on marriage (*Disputationes de sancti matrimonii,* 1602), he was also accused of laxity with regard to "mental reservation" (speaking all or part of the truth in such a manner as to permit the hearer to derive a false understanding from what is said) in his treatise on the Ten Commandments (*Opus morale in praecepta decalogi,* 1613). The Venetian editions of Vol. 3 of the *Disputationes* were put on the Index in 1627, not, ultimately, because of their moral doctrine, but because certain passages displeasing to the Venetian authorities had been suppressed.

**Sancroft, William** (1617–1693). Archbishop of Canterbury. As a Royalist, he opposed Calvinism and the Commonwealth. Later he collaborated with Christopher Wren in building St. Paul's Cathedral while he was dean. An able and energetic archbishop (consecrated in 1678), he opposed the Roman Catholic politics of James II, even encouraging intervention by William III to effect peace. He refused to break his oath of allegiance to James, however, and led the nonjurors, after which he was deprived of his office.

**Sancta Sophia** (Hagia Sophia). The patriarchal cathedral of the Byzantine or ecumenical patriarch. It was erected by the emperor Justinian the Great in 537 as an architectural synthesis of the square, basilican, and cruciform styles. Earthquakes destroyed the great central dome in 558 and again in the 10th century, but the third dome has lasted for nearly a thousand years. As the mother church of Eastern Orthodoxy, it has with its liturgy, iconography, and basic structure dominated the ecclesiastical life of both Greek and Slavic lands.

**Sanctuary, Right of.** See RIGHT OF SANCTUARY.

**Sandeman, Robert** (1718–1771). Leader of a sect known as Sandemanians, Glasites, or Glassites. He was born at Perth and served as a linen weaver's apprentice before studying briefly at the University of Edinburgh. He considered both the church and medicine as future professions, but finally joined the religious movement of John Glas. In 1737 he married Glas's daughter and joined a brother in a linen-manufacturing partnership. He left business in 1744 when he became an elder in the Glasite church. After serving as minister in Perth, Dundee, Edinburgh, and London, he sailed to Boston in 1764. He founded several churches in America, the first at Portsmouth in 1765. However, he alienated many by advocating loyalty to Britain, and he was tried by Connecticut authorities in 1770. He died at Danbury, where his burial precipitated a political demonstration. Some feel that he gave the Glasite sect a distinctive doctrine concerning the nature of faith, but others think that he merely helped to give the movement vogue through his advocacy. He published a number of religious essays, tracts, letters, and poems.

**Sanford, Elias Benjamin** (1843–1932). American Congregational pastor and ecumenical leader. In 1895 he became secretary of the newly organized Open and Industrial Church League designed to promote interchurch cooperation and social service. Under his direction a conference was held in Carnegie Hall, N.Y., in 1905 which formulated a constitution for the Federal Council of the Churches of Christ in America, which became operative in 1908.

**Sangnier, Marc** (1873–1950). Leader of the liberal French Roman Catholic democratic movement known as Le Sillon which was condemned by Pope Pius X in 1910 because it placed authority in the hands of the people and tended to level the various social classes. Never personally condemned, Sangnier is considered the founder of French Christian Democracy, and after World War II its symbol.

**Sankey, Ira D.** (1840–1908). Evangelist and hymn writer. He was a choir director in the Methodist Church in Newcastle, Pa., when he attracted the attention of Dwight L. Moody in 1870. Sankey joined Moody as his song leader and served in the revival meetings in England and the United States. The simple gospel singing of Sankey was a contributing factor to Moody's success. Sankey's tuneful gospel songs such as "The Ninety and Nine" were published and achieved wide sale.

**Saracen** (possibly from an Arabic stem, *sh-r-q,* meaning "east"). A name used to designate the Syro-Arabian nomads who harassed the eastern borders of the Roman Empire. From the 8th century but more frequently from the 13th on, the word "Saracen"

was transliterated and adopted by the Latin writers to characterize all Moslems regardless of their national origin. The term fell out of the literary vocabulary after the fall of Constantinople but remained in the popular vocabulary of many European tongues.

**Saravia, Hadrian à** (1531–1613). Flemish theologian. A native of Artois, Saravia became a pastor at Antwerp and was among the framers of the Belgic Confession. Unrest in the Netherlands caused him to accept a pastorate on the Isle of Guernsey, and later the headship of a school in Southhampton. Upon his return to the Netherlands he received a theological professorship at Leiden. In 1585 he returned to England, where in 1590 he wrote a treatise favoring episcopacy, which involved him in controversy with Theodore Beza. Saravia also took part in the translation of the King James Bible.

**Sardica, Council of** (c. 343). A council convoked by Pope Julius I and the emperors Constans and Constantius to meet at Sardica (modern Sofia). It was fraught with difficulties from the very beginning when disagreement arose over the seating of Athanasius, Marcellus, and other bishops who had been deposed by the Eastern Church but were recognized by the Western bishops as members of the Council. Most of the Eastern bishops left Sardica and retired to Philippopolis in Thrace, where they reiterated the charges against Athanasius and his followers, raised the old objection to Western bishops ruling on internal matters that had been decided by Eastern synods, and reaffirmed and expanded the fourth formula of Antioch. The Western bishops, with Hosius of Cordova and Protogenes of Sardica serving as chairmen, cleared Athanasius and the other deposed bishops from the East of all charges, defined "Arianism" as a pejorative by accepting Athanasius' charge that the Eusebians were Arians, and adopted thirteen canons regarding the inner life of the church. The Council is usually said to have confirmed the Nicene Creed, and at one time the canons of the Council of Sardica were regarded as being canons of the Council of Nicaea although the Nicene Council, its creed, and the word *homoousion* are never mentioned in the "creed of Sardica," which consists of an encyclical letter describing the actions of the Council and a theological manifesto describing the views of the Council.

This Council is largely significant because it transferred what had previously been a political and church polity contest into the realm of theology. This was the first time in church history that the East and the West separated by formal decision, and it marked the beginning of a process that culminated in the final separation in 1054.

**Sarpi, Paolo** (1552–1623). Italian Servite and historian. Sarpi entered the Servite Order in 1565, later becoming procurator general of the order (1585–1588). The subsequent antipapalism of "the terrible friar" was successfully used to thwart Pope Paul V's interdict on the Venetian Republic (1606). When peace was restored, his literary energy produced the famous *Istoria del Concilio Tridentino* (1619), full of sharp criticism of what he viewed as the triumph of papalism at the Council of Trent.

**Sartre, Jean-Paul** (1905–    ). French philosopher, playwright, and novelist, who in 1964 declined a Nobel Prize for Literature. Among more than twenty published works of various kinds, his *Being and Nothingness* (1943; English translation, 1956) stands out as most significant. It is a philosophical discourse devoted to the development of an atheistic, existentialist theory of Being. He emphasizes the burden of individual human freedom. *The Words* (1964) is a brief autobiography of his childhood.

**Satire, Religious.** Flourishing in the verse of the 12th and 13th centuries, religious satire usually attacked not the church itself or its teachings but the particular abuses found in the institutions of the church and the increasingly worldly religious orders. The most vulnerable targets were the monks and friars who, instead of adhering to their vows, indulged in rich drink, food, and dress. The main purpose of the satirists, themselves churchmen, was the correction of abuses and a return to the ideals of the simple faith exemplified in the poor parish priests.

Wandering clerics embodied their satire in extremely impudent and disrespectful parodies of the Bible, daily offices, and the Liturgy itself. A more effective satire is found in Nigel Wireker's *Mirror of Fools,* where the worldliness and the pursuit of knowledge of erring monks is inoffensively represented in the wanderings of a stupid donkey, Burnel. In *The Canterbury Tales,* Chaucer gently satirized the social pretensions of the Prioress, but directed a more serious criticism toward the moral laxness and avarice of the Pardoner and the Friar in the execution of their offices. Bitter satire and invective is also to be found in Bernard of Cluny, *Contempt of the World*; William Langland, *The Vision Concerning Piers Plowman*; and the Wycliffite polemic *Piers the Plowman's Creed*.

**Saumur Academy.** Protestant theological school in Saumur, France, from 1604 to 1685. It was founded by Philippe Duplessis-Mornay, French Protestant statesman, soldier, and theologian, who was governor of Saumur. One of its first professors was the Scot John Cameron. Cameron's emphasis upon free and independent theological research became a primary characteristic of the Academy. Three disciples of Cameron—Moïse Amyraut, Louis Cappel, and Josué de la Place—developed the Academy to a position of renown. Amyraut advanced the concept of "hypothetical universalism." He maintained that God wills the salvation of all men, on the condition that they believe. Since all men reject this condition through depravity, however, God wills in particular the salvation of the elect. This viewpoint stirred up considerable controversy among Calvinists in Holland and Switzerland. Cappel was a Biblical researcher who established the first fertile school of criticism in modern theology. De la Place emphasized the responsibility and accountability of each individual and therefore opposed the idea of the imputation of Adam's actual sin to his descendants. Until it was suppressed by royal edict in 1685, the Academy was the most influential and important Protestant theological school in France, attracting students from other countries, especially Switzerland.

**Sava** (c. 1175–c. 1235). First bishop of Serbia. He was the younger son of the Serbian king. Retiring to Mt. Athos in 1191, he was later joined by his father, who had abdicated. Together they founded the monastery of Khilandari, which became the center of Serbian culture. After returning to Serbia, he founded monasteries and established an autonomous church with himself as archbishop. He was influential in the unification of Serbia under his brother Stephen II.

**Savonarola, Girolamo** (1452–1498). Reformer. He was born at Ferrara and died at Florence. Receiving a humanistic education, he started to study medicine, but in 1475 changed his mind and became a Dominican novice at Bologna. After completing his studies for the priesthood at Ferrara, he was sent in 1482 to preach in Florence. His pious sermons made little impression on the people of this Renaissance center so thoroughly imbued with the worldliness of the Medicis. After preaching in several other Italian cities, Savonarola returned to Florence in 1489 and there became prior of the Dominican convent of San Marco in 1491. The austerity of his life and the apocalyptic nature of his sermons began to have an effect upon the city. Despite the severity of Savonarola's regime, the choir stalls of San Marco were daily swelling with new postulants. Soon the Dominican church began to be jammed with townsfolk anxious to hear the prior's pronouncements against the Medicis and other loose-living princes and ecclesiastics of the period.

Savonarola's popularity reached a peak when he urged Charles VIII, king of France, to avenge the wrong suffered by the church because of the dissolute life of Pope Alexander VI. In 1494 a revolution forced the Medici family out of Florence. Under the tutelage of Charles VIII a new government was formed in the city-state. Savonarola occupied an influential position. Soon what had formerly been the gay capital of the Renaissance became virtually a monastery. Playing cards, dice tables, wigs and ornaments, cosmetics, lewd pictures, and the obscene writings of the pagans were collected and burned. Religious observance was ensured by a vigilante committee. Savonarola found himself the spokesman for God in what could best be described as a theocracy.

Having conquered Florence, the Reformer then turned his full attention to what he called the "harlot Church" at Rome. A series of papal briefs vainly attempted to silence him. Summoned at length to appear in Rome to explain his attacks upon the papacy, Savonarola excused himself on grounds of poor health. Pope Alexander's last resort, an attempt to bribe his formidable adversary with a promise of a cardinalate, served only to fan the flames of the friar's wrath. Excommunicated in May, 1497, the indomitable Reformer declared that only God himself could cut him off from fellowship with the faithful, and he continued to preach and say Mass. A threat of interdict upon the city alarmed the *Signoria,* or ruling body. For a while Savonarola respected their request that he refrain from preaching, but eventually he resumed his philippics with renewed vigor.

The Franciscan community in Florence became envious of the successes of the Dominican Reformer and angered by the friar's dramatic use of the Eucharist in his sermons. They demanded that he give a sign of his authority from God to do what he was doing. One of their members, a certain Francesco da Puglia, offered to undergo an ordeal by fire in order to prove that Savonarola was a fraud. The Dominicans, however, decided that their leader should not undergo such a test, and opted to send one of his lieutenants, Domenico da Pescia, as his champion.

On the morning of April 7, 1498, two piles of fagots some forty yards long were kindled in the Piazza della Signoria. There was just enough space between them for a man to get through. Soon the whole area was a raging inferno. The agreement stipulated that both Domenico and Francesco were to walk through the flames. If both men were killed, or if Domenico alone was killed, Savonarola's claim to a prophetic role would be proved false. Francesco believed he would die; but so too, he thought, would Domenico, and the power of the Dominicans would then be broken. When the time arrived, Domenico refused to enter the flames unless he could carry the Blessed Sacrament or at least a crucifix. But the Franciscans would not permit this. A prolonged argument delayed the event, and eventually a violent thunderstorm dispersed the crowd. For having failed to undergo the ordeal, the Dominicans lost face. The whole city turned against Savonarola. The *Signoria* received the legates of Pope Alexander VI. Savonarola and his champion were tried for heresy. After torture had been applied, they were both found guilty and condemned to death. They were hanged, their bodies burned, and the ashes scattered over the River Arno.

BIBLIOGRAPHY: R. Ridolfi, *The Life of Girolamo Savonarola* (New York, 1959).

**Savoy Conference.** A conference called into being by warrant of Charles II, issued on March 25, 1661, to seek for agreement between conformists and nonconformists with respect to the Book of Common Prayer. The conference, which met at the Savoy in London from April 15 to July 24, 1661, was composed of twelve bishops, led by Sheldon, bishop of London, and twelve Presbyterians, led by Richard Baxter, with nine assessors on each side. The Presbyterians were made to present their objections to the Book of Common Prayer, which they did in a list of *Exceptions.* Baxter drafted an alternative service book, and in a *Petition for Peace* suggested that clergymen not episcopally ordained should not be required to be reordained. The conference did not succeed in bringing about agreement between the parties. Baxter's proposals were rejected and all but seventeen of the *Exceptions* were refused, fifteen of those adopted being embodied in the Book of Common Prayer authorized by the Act of Uniformity in 1662. The Presbyterians were unable to accept the 1662 book, about two thousand of them being ejected from their churches.

**Saxon Confession** (1551). Protestant restatement of the Augsburg Confession by Philip Melanchthon, requested by Emperor Charles V for the Council of Trent. The

Saxon Confession emphasized more sharply than Augsburg the grounds of Protestant opposition to Rome. With reunion unlikely, the tone was not conciliatory. The Confession, signed only by theologians, was submitted, with Johann Brenz's Württemberg Confession, to a private congregation of the Council but achieved nothing.

**Saxon Visitation Articles** (1528). Articles drawn up by Melanchthon to serve as a guide for visitation commissions, pastors, and teachers. They contained the first Lutheran confession of faith and the first general school plan. The Visitation Articles became the model plan for establishing Lutheranism throughout Germany and were a monumental step in the progress of German education. By 1555 more than 135 plans had appeared based on the 1528 Visitation Articles.

**Saxon Visitation Articles** (1592). Four articles to be subscribed to by pastors, teachers, and certain civil officials in Electoral Saxony in order to root out crypto-Calvinism. They were written in 1592, their principal author being Aegidius Hennius, though they were modeled after the outline of a discussion between Beza and Johann Andreae. They emphasize conservative Lutheran views on the Eucharist, the person of Christ, Baptism, and predestination.

**Saybrook Platform.** A Connecticut Congregational document. Similar in content to the Massachusetts Proposals, it met a fate unlike theirs in that the colony's government adopted it (1708). Its effect was to make Connecticut church polity less congregational and more presbyterian, causing these churches gradually to look away from Massachusetts Congregationalism and toward Middle Colony Presbyterianism.

**Scaliger, Joseph Justus** (1540–1609). French scholar. Learned in many fields, he was master of the ancient classics. He became a Protestant in 1562 and occupied several important academic posts, finally accepting a research professorship at Leiden (1593). Scaliger's labors with classical authors marked an important advance in the disciplines of textual criticism, and in his *De emendatione temporum* ("On the Correction of Chronology," 1583) he set the study of ancient chronology on a scientific basis.

**Schaff, Philip** (1819–1893). Reformed Church historian. Swiss-born, he was educated at Tübingen, Halle, and at Berlin, where he taught before coming to Mercersburg, Pa., in 1844. There he and John Nevin developed the so-called Mercersburg Theology with its

churchly and sacramental emphases. In 1863 he moved to New York, where he was secretary of a Sabbath committee and after 1870 professor at Union Seminary. He wrote or edited over eighty or more publications, including an edition of Lange's commentary (1865–1880), an encyclopedia now known as *The Schaff-Herzog Encyclopedia of Religious Knowledge* (1882–1891); *The Creeds of Christendom* (1877); and a seven-volume *History of the Christian Church* (1882–1892). He is remembered chiefly as a gifted church historian but also as a leader in bringing German thought to America and as an advocate of church unity.

**Scheler, Max** (1874–1928). German phenomenologist. A student of Rudolf Eucken, Scheler taught at Cologne (1919) and Frankfurt (1928). He investigated man's spiritual experiences with Husserl's phenomenology. Among sensible, vital, spiritual, and religious values, religious values are *sui generis*. Man's eternity (*Von Ewigen im Menschen*) is his permanent potential for religion culminating in love. Scheler later advocated an evolutionary pantheism in which blind force and spirituality, God's attributes, appear in history and in man. His anthropological stress on "person" was taken up by existentialists.

**Schell, Hermann** (1850–1906). German Roman Catholic theologian. He was the most significant leader of the modernist movement in the German branch of the church. While professor of apologetics at Würzburg he wrote his two chief works, *Catholic Dogma* (3 vols.) and *God and Spirit*. Because of his anthropological and eschatological speculations, both of these works were placed on the Index in 1898.

**Schelling, Friedrich Wilhelm Joseph von** (1775–1854). German philosopher. After studying theology and philosophy at Tübingen and science at Leipzig, he served as professor at Jena, where he came under the influence of the Romantic movement and sympathized with the revolutionary sentiments of his students. Later he taught at Würzburg, Erlangen, and Berlin (1851). His thought is heavily influenced by Fichte, Kant, Spinoza, and Boehme.

Although never elaborating a consistent system of thought, he is very important in the evolution from the older idealists to Hegel. In Schelling's earlier view, reality was identical with the dialectical process of thought. Thus, by tracing the movements of nature and history one can understand the universal mind or absolute reality. Later, he became dissatisfied with this logical pantheism and changed his outlook. The universe, he taught, cannot be assumed to be a rational system. Rather, men try to fasten a logical system on an originally chaotic world. As he turned away from rationalism, Schelling placed more stress on the ideas of religion as a way to find ultimate reality. This later emphasis influenced Bergson, Kierkegaard, and the existentialists.

**Schenkel, Daniel** (1813–1885). German theologian. After study at Göttingen he returned to Basel in 1838, lecturing and editing the *Baseler Zeitung.* Much influenced by Wilhelm De Wette, whose student he had been, Schenkel succeeded him in 1850 as professor at Basel. The following year he was called to Heidelberg, where he took an active role in church-political affairs, remaining there until his death. He promoted "mediating theology" pugnaciously but capriciously, forcing R. Dulon out of the Heidelberg faculty and befriending Richard Rothe and Bunsen. In Baden he opened a liberal era in church government, and cofounded the Protestant Union of 1863.

**Schiller, Johann Christoph Friedrich von** (1759–1805). German poet, dramatist, and philosopher. Born into a deeply religious family, Schiller developed early an enthusiasm for the ministry. This ambition was thwarted when Duke Charles II demanded that the youth enter the military academy he had set up (1770), first to study law, and later, when the academy removed to Stuttgart, as a medical student. In 1780, Schiller was appointed surgeon to the army in Stuttgart, but he began to write, despite the duke's protests, and was jailed for two weeks for attending performances of his drama *Die Räuber.* Finally he fled the city, lived for a time under assumed names, and devoted himself exclusively to writing. With *Don Carlos,* he abandoned prose and the "storm and stress" of his earlier work for iambic pentameter and the drama of ideas. In 1791, Schiller began a study of Kant, attracted by the philosopher's theories of aesthetics. Between 1793 and 1796, Schiller published four philosophical studies (e.g., *Anmut und Würde*) in which he extended Kant's attitude into a belief that beauty is intrinsic and is associated with the good and true. Through the contemplation of beauty, he believed, man could rise to a state of peace. Later poems and plays conveyed this idea and exhibited his ability to give concrete expression to abstract ideas and ideals. Although aligned to the Age of Reason in equating virtue with the highest good, Schiller became the most significant literary representative of the religious aspect of romanticism's revolt against rationalism.

**Schism, Eastern.** The separation between the Eastern Church, with its headquarters at Constantinople, and the Western Church (Rome) cannot be assigned a precise date because it was not a single event but rather the result of an increasing estrangement that culminated in 1204 with the vengeful destruction of the Byzantine Empire by the crusaders (Latin empire) and the confirmation by Innocent III of the Venetian Thomas Morosini as first Latin patriarch of Constantinople. The origin and causes of the separation between East and West are equally difficult to determine with accuracy. Language differences and correspondingly different cultural outlooks are contributory, but the difference in political understanding between East and West is of almost incalculable significance; this was expressed in the rivalry for primacy between Rome as the ancient midpoint of the Empire and therefore of the church, and Constantinople, the parvenu capital of the Empire and second-ranking primatial see after the First Council of Constantinople (381).

During the basically doctrinal Acacian Schism (484–518), Rome argued its claim for the first time on grounds of its Petrine establishment and introduced the notion of the supremacy of the ecclesiastical over the secular power. This idea was in stark opposition to the Byzantine conception of relations between emperor and bishop, and it was a factor in the Roman opposition to Justinian's ecclesiastical policy and Hormisdas' refusal to attend the Second Council of Constantinople (553), the opposition being aggravated by the assumption by John IV of Constantinople of the title "Ecumenical Patriarch." The dissidence was furthered by the canons of the Trullan Synod (692) condemning Roman usages (resisted by Sergius I), the disagreements during the iconoclastic controversy, and the decidedly anti-Byzantine act of Leo III in crowning Charlemagne, but it reached a new level in the claim of ecclesiastical supremacy, even over emperors, implied in Nicholas I's presumption in judging the Photian Schism.

When the *filioque* was introduced into the Creed by the 11th-century German popes and the Creed containing it included in a letter written to Constantinople by Sergius IV announcing his assumption of office at Rome, Constantinople replied by dropping the name of the pope from the diptychs, a sign that his orthodoxy was in serious question. This act is frequently marked as the beginning of the final schism.

The reform movement begun at Cluny and championed by the popes favorable to the Ottonian emperors was expressed in a set of decrees issued by the Synod of Siponto (1050) assembled by Leo IX. Among those decrees, though not of prime importance, were some calling for the eradication of Greek customs that had crept into the usage of certain Latin dioceses. The patriarch Michael Cerularius, sensing the threat to the Greek rite churches of southern Italy, reciprocated by ordering all Latin churches and orders in Constantinople to adopt the Greek rite. The subsequent loss of southern Italy to the Normans through an alliance with the papacy that miscarried prompted an embassy from the pope to Constantinople. The embassy was headed by Humbert of Silva-Candida, an avid anti-Greek and ardent advocate of the reform. His intransigence on all the points of difference between Rome and Constantinople only hardened the opposition and resulted in his laying on the altar of Hagia Sophia an excommunication bull. Although this effected practical schism, neither pope nor patriarch considered it final as subsequent relations demonstrate (see REUNION ATTEMPTS), but the emperor's insistence upon supremacy in ecclesiastical matters was not to be argued by the 12th-century papacy. The Crusades complicated the situation when Antioch was seized by Bohemund (1098), who intruded a Latin patriarch. The end was in sight when citizens of Constantinople rose up in bloody attack upon the Latin crusaders (1182) and gave rise to the crusaders' conviction that nothing short of capture and reduction of Constantinople would assure the aim of the crusaders to free the Holy Land. The conquest and subsequent acts of 1204 did not achieve that end, but it made the Eastern Schism an enduring reality.

BIBLIOGRAPHY: F. Dvornik, *Byzantium and the Roman Primacy* (New York, 1966); and *The Photian Schism: History and Legend* (Cambridge, 1948); D. Geanakoplos, *Byzantine East and Latin West* (New York, 1966); J. Gill, *The Council of Florence* (Cambridge, 1959); S. Runciman, *The Eastern Schism* (Oxford, 1955); P. Sherrard, *The Greek East and the Latin West* (New York, 1959).

**Schism, Great Western** (Sept. 20, 1378, to Nov. 11, 1417). A breach in the Western Church during which there were two, sometimes three, rival popes.

Gregory XI died shortly after returning the papacy to Rome from Avignon (see BABYLONIAN CAPTIVITY OF THE CHURCH). The subsequent conclave and its consequences were disastrous, for Gregory's cardinals presented the church with two popes, each of whom it asserted was true, and a constitutional crisis that brought forth profound discussion of the meaning of unity, the place of the papacy in the church, and proposals for the reform and reordering of the church with significant implications for ecclesiology and political theory.

The sacred college in 1378 was internally divided: a large French majority could not agree on a French candidate. The Romans quarreled with papal authority in Rome, but were determined to have a "Roman or at least an Italian" who would keep the papacy in Rome. Violence and schism were threatened. Armed crowds milled in the streets and burst into the papal palace. On April 8, the college elected (twice!) Bartolomeo Prignano (Urban VI). He had always been a good servant to the lordly French cardinals, and apparently they expected that he would continue to be so. He wanted reform, but power seems to have unbalanced him, and soon his offended cardinals deserted him. They announced that they had been terrorized by the mob in April, that Urban's election was invalid, and, on Sept. 20, they held a second election in Fondi. They chose Robert of Geneva (Clement VII), a cousin of the French king. Although Urban VI had been universally accepted, the second election was not. France now received Clement VII. Europe divided (largely along lines of political interest) into two obediences. The Schism continued for nearly forty years. Clement VII was followed (at Avignon) by Pedro de Luna (Benedict XIII, 1394–1423). Urban VI was followed (in Rome) by Boniface IX (1389–1404), Innocent VII (1404–1406), and Gregory XII (1406–1415). Although it is conventional now to regard the Roman line as legitimate, it was uncertain during the Schism, and no competent authority (pope or council) has ever decided infallibly.

Clement VII proposed to solve the Schism by force (*via actionis*), but his campaigns in Italy failed. Governments and lawyers tried to decide who had in fact been elected (*via facti*): there were five investigative commissions in all. Withdrawal of obedience in France failed to coerce Benedict XIII, a brilliant and adroit lawyer and a stubborn old man. The way of negotiation or mutual resignation failed when Gregory XII, influenced by his relatives, avoided meeting Benedict in 1408.

Professors at the University of Paris (Conrad von Gelnhausen, Henry of Langenstein) suggested in the years from 1379 to 1381 that a general council be called to reunite the church, reform it in head and members, and soothe sorely troubled consciences. The obstacle that frustrated this call for the *via regalis concilii* was the canon law, which placed the papacy beyond any judgment other than God's, and which reserved the convocation of general councils to the pope. Those favoring a council argued that the real locus of authority in the church was the whole community of the faithful (*congregatio fidelium*) represented in a general council, that the authority of the pope was ministerial, delegated from the community, and that, in any case, the application of the law was to be governed by the intention of the legislator and the situation rather than the letter (*epieikeia* = equity). Langenstein also argued that regular reform councils must be called. This view (conciliarism) was formerly thought to be an adaptation of the constitutional practice of temporal kingdoms, an *ad hoc* but illegal reaction to the crisis of the Schism, or a development of heretical propositions derived from Marsilius of Padua or William of Occam. Recent research, by Brian Tierney and others, has shown that in fact the conciliarists drew upon the long tradition of canon law and Aristotelian theological-political theory at least as old as Thomas Aquinas.

Disappointment at the selfish maneuvering of Benedict and Gregory finally persuaded their two colleges of cardinals to leave them, unite, and summon a general council at Pisa (1409). The Council was a legal process deposing the two popes for stubborn schism, followed by an election of a third pope (Alexander V), who died shortly and was succeeded by Baldassare Cossa (John XXIII).

The spectacle of three competing popes, the mockery of unity and faith, the exactions of three hungry Curias, increased the demand for reform. The emperor-elect, Sigismund, forced John to call a general council at Constance (1414–1418). John hoped to pack the Council of Constance. The Council resisted, John fled, and the Council deposed him and declared itself legitimate, representing the church, with power immediately from Christ and superior to all (including the pope) in matters of faith, reform, and the Schism (*Haec sancta*, April, 1415). Negotiations secured the approval and resignation of Gregory XII and the abandonment of Benedict XIII by all his supporters. The Council then proceeded to the election of a universally recognized pope, Oddone Colonna (Martin V, 1417–1431), thus extinguishing the Schism but not the problems it had raised. It attempted to ensure reform by insisting on the convocation of regular reform councils, but itself did little (*Frequens*, October, 1417). The status and meaning of the great decrees of Constance are still debated among Roman Catholics.

BIBLIOGRAPHY: E. F. Jacob, *Essays in the Conciliar Epoch* (Manchester, 1943); L. Salembier, *The Great Schism of the West* (New York, 1907); B. Tierney, *Foundations of Conciliar Theory* (Cambridge, 1955).

**Schism Act.** An act of the English Parliament in 1714 forbidding Protestant Dissenters to operate schools, passed during the Tory and High Church reaction at the end of Queen Anne's reign. It was intended to keep Dissenters out of the professions, and eventually extirpate them, by giving an educational monopoly to the Church of England. With Anne's death that same year and the coming of the Whigs to power, it was not enforced, and was repealed in 1719.

**Schlatter, Adolf** (1852–1939). German Protestant theologian and professor at Greifswald, Berlin, and Tübingen. His chief importance lies in his belief that the only foundation of systematic theology rests in Biblical exegesis. His ideas anticipated, to a large extent, the dialectical theology of Karl Barth. His most important works are *Die Theologie des Neuen Testaments und die Dogmatik* (1909) and *Das christliche Dogma* (1911).

**Schlatter, Michael** (1716–1790). German Reformed clergyman. Swiss-born and educated in Holland and Germany, he came to Pennsylvania in 1746 and there organized the first German Reformed synod in 1747. He founded dozens of congregations, several schools, and made European tours to raise men and money for the colonial churches. After 1757 he was a British army chaplain but became a patriot in the Revolution.

**Schlegel, Friedrich von** (1772–1829). German Roman Catholic poet, critic, and apologist. Born at Hannover, he studied law at Göttingen and Leipzig, and together with his wife, Dorothea (a daughter of Moses Mendelssohn), he joined the Roman Catholic Church in 1808. In his numerous writings, notably *Gedichte* (1809) and *Philosophie der Geschichte* (2 vols., 1829), Schlegel was adamantly opposed to the development of political and religious freedom in Germany, was a vigorous defender of the medieval imperial ideal against the rise of the German national state, and was an eloquent preacher for a restoration of national life in Austria and Germany upon a Roman Catholic basis. When failure of a restoration became evident, Schlegel turned to literature and philosophy for a renewed Catholicism. In later years he became a keenly critical opponent of the pantheism of G. W. F. Hegel and developed his philosophical thoughts around Aristotle and Plato.

**Schleiermacher, Friedrich Daniel Ernst** (1768–1834). German philosopher and one of the most influential theologians of 19th-century Protestantism. He was born in Breslau, the son of a Prussian army chaplain of the Reformed Confession. He was educated at schools belonging to the Moravian Brethren and was to have become a Moravian pastor, but, beginning to doubt Christianity, he entered the University of Halle (1787), where he became a student of Kantian philosophy. In 1794 he was ordained and two years later he was appointed chaplain to the Charité Hospital in Berlin, where he came under the influence of Spinoza, Plato, F. von Schlegel and J. G. Fichte. He established his fame with *Reden über die Religion* (1799). In this work he attempted to reconvert the educated classes to religion, which, he maintained, was absolutely independent of knowledge and morality. Arguing that religion was based on intuition and feeling and independent of all dogma, Schleiermacher saw the religious experience in a sensation of union with the infinite. In 1800 his *Monologen* appeared containing the first statement on his ethical system. From 1802 to 1804 he was pastor at Stolp; from 1804 to 1809 he was professor of theology at Halle; and from 1809 until his death he was professor and dean of the faculty at the newly founded University of Berlin. He played a prominent role in the national movement against Napoleon and did much to promote the union of the Lutheran and Reformed churches in the Church of Prussia (1817). The remainder of his life was devoted to teaching and writing. Some of his important works are *Kurze Darstellung des theologischen Studiums* (1811), *Der christliche Glaube nach den Grundsätzen der evangelischen Kirche* (2 vols., 1821–1822), and *Theologische Studien und Kritiken* (1829).

At Berlin, Schleiermacher was overshadowed by Hegel as a philosopher, but in religious thought his influence was prodigious. He placed emphasis upon feeling as the basis of religion and thus strongly reacted against both the German rationalist tradition and the formalist orthodox tradition. He believed that self-consciousness was the source of all religion, because man in his self-consciousness knows that he does not exist from himself and,

therefore, feels himself absolutely dependent upon religion. All religious language, doctrines, and dogmas, therefore, are merely expressions of religious self-consciousness. Natural religion, or the religion of reason, is merely a pure abstraction; but religion is positive because religious feeling is experienced only in conjunction with sense consciousness and consequently every religious expression has its own particular character. Here Schleiermacher is defining religion as the feeling of absolute dependence, which finds its purest form in monotheism. The variety of expressions which this feeling creates in different civilizations and peoples is the reason for the great diversity of religious beliefs, of which Christianity is the highest, but not necessarily the truest.

What was especially striking in Schleiermacher was his versatility. He was at one time, and quite often at the same time, a brilliant theologian and philosopher and a great preacher and patriot. His influence on Protestant thought in the 19th century was enormous. Generations of theologians, including Albrecht Ritschl, Adolf von Harnack, and Ernst Troeltsch, developed and modified his ideas. In the 20th century his influence has diminished, primarily because of the reaction of Karl Barth and Emil Brunner to Schleiermacher's emphasis on feeling in religion.

BIBLIOGRAPHY: F. D. E. Schleiermacher, *Christmas Eve* (Richmond, 1967); *Speeches on Religion* (New York, 1958); and *The Christian Faith*, 2 vols. (New York, 1963); J. Dawson, *Friedrich Schleiermacher: The Evolution of a Nationalist* (Austin, 1966); R. R. Niebuhr, *Schleiermacher on Christ and Religion* (New York, 1964); W. B. Selbie, *Schleiermacher: A Critical and Historical Study* (New York, 1913).

**Schleitheim Articles.** An early attempt (February, 1527) to define a faith including believer's baptism but excluding eschatological fancies and antinomianism. The participating Anabaptists aimed at a pure and covenanted baptismal fellowship critical of reliance on ceremonies. Settled pastors, the ban, Baptism, Communion, nonswearing of oaths, the validity of civil authority, and "separation from the world" were professed.

**Schmidt, Johann Lorenz** (1702–1749). German rationalist. Schmidt studied theology (Buddeus), mathematics, and philosophy (he was influenced by Christian von Wolff). After 1725 he tutored in Wertheim and began an extended Bible translation which was to serve as the basis of a new theology. His Pentateuch appeared anonymously in 1735; the translation was greatly distorted. Schmidt's work was confiscated and he was imprisoned in 1737, but released. He moved to Hamburg and Altona while translating Spinoza's *Ethik* (1744), then became court mathematician at Wolfenbüttel under the pseudonym Schröd(t)er. G. E. Lessing attributed some of the *Fragments* to Schmidt.

**Schmidt, Wilhelm** (1868–1954). German Roman Catholic priest, professor of anthropology in Vienna and Fribourg. He joined the "culture circle" school of ethnology in opposition to "evolutionism." His major work, *Der Ursprung der Gottesidee* (12 vols.), argues that primitive people first believed in one supreme being and degenerated into polytheism. In 1906 he founded the Anthropos Institute and its journal.

**Schmolck, Benjamin** (1672–1737). Lutheran hymn writer. He was born in Silesia. Following theological studies at Leipzig, he became an assistant to his pastor-father. In 1702 he was called to Schweidnitz as pastor, where he remained. Schmolck wrote some twelve hundred hymns (published in 2 vols. in Tübingen, 1740–1744), several of which have become standard. A basic theme of his poetry was "the closer to the cross, the closer to heaven." The hymns are noted for their catechetical quality and moderately baroque style.

**Schmucker, Samuel Simon** (1799–1873). American Lutheran clergyman. When graduating from Princeton Seminary in 1820 he expressed three wishes: for a Lutheran seminary, a Lutheran college, and a dogmatics in English. All three were fulfilled. In 1826 he helped found and became president of the Lutheran seminary at Gettysburg, Pa., and in 1827 began what later became Gettysburg College. Also, in 1826 he translated a German dogmatics and in 1834 wrote his own *Elements of Popular Theology* and saw it become the text for much of Lutheran America. Controversy arose when a wave of German immigrants challenged his less confessional Lutheranism, and was climaxed in the appearance of his *Definite Synodical Platform* (1855), a proposal for a genuinely "American" Lutheranism and a revision of the Augsburg Confession. This document was so stiffly rebuffed that Schmucker never regained his theological leadership, although he did not retire from the seminary until 1864. Schmucker wrote over forty works, many of them devoted to this confessional controversy but others to his ecumenical interests. His *Fraternal Appeal to the American Churches* called for a federation of churches quite like the later Federal and National Councils. He also

helped organize the Evangelical Alliance in 1846.

**Scholastica** (c. 480–c. 543). Sister of Benedict. She lived in a convent at Plombariola, a short distance from Monte Cassino. She and Benedict were accustomed to meet once a year to discuss spiritual matters. All that is known of her life is from the *Dialogues* of Gregory the Great. She is buried with Benedict in a tomb at Monte Cassino.

**Scholasticism.** The normal designation for the Christian philosophy of the Middle Ages and early Renaissance, characterized by its systematic use of Aristotelian categories. More simply, Scholasticism is described as the systematic application of reason to revelation. A deteriorated Scholasticism is evident in nominalism and voluntarism, hence the pejorative use of the term. Etymologically the term comes from the Greek verb meaning to enjoy one's leisure by the pursuit of learning. The Greek noun for "leisure" was applied to the place where lectures were given, the school. As a method of study, Scholasticism is associated with organized textbook theology and the thesis method. Since Scholasticism is an analogous term, each of the above meanings is valid.

Scholasticism arose in a definite theological context. All theology is first of all historical theology, that is, individual questions arise and particular answers are given. Scholasticism is simply an organized and systematic historical theology. The early church councils were concrete instances of the theological question asked and answered. Scholasticism systematized these historically disparate questions and answers. Scholastics of the 12th and 13th centuries organized the theological thought of the preceding centuries. The apex of Scholastic endeavor was reached by Thomas Aquinas (c. 1225–1274). It was he who brought historical theology from the prescientific to the scientific, from the nonreflex to the reflex, from the unsystematic and unthematic to the systematic and thematic. The materials for a theological system were at hand when he appeared; after him follows the sterile period of nominalism and formalism typified by William of Occam (1300–1349). Scholastic methodology was revived somewhat from 1500 to 1700 by the work of Cano, Petavius, Banez, Molina, and Suárez. Overshadowed in Germany by the Enlightenment and in France by Cartesianism but still regnant in Spain through Dominican influence, Scholasticism experienced a renascence in the 19th century first in Italy, where by the middle of the century a new edition of the works of Thomas Aquinas was undertaken. Against rationalism and similar tendencies, this kind of theology was favored by Pius IX in several official dicta, but it remained the work of Leo XIII to rehabilitate it by his encyclical *Aeterni patris* (1879), which was incorporated into the requisite instruction of ordinands by Pius X. Since Pius XI, this exclusivity of Scholasticism has been progressively modified.

Scholasticism appeared in the cultural unity imposed by Christendom. The remote foundations of Scholasticism were laid in 529, when pagan philosophy as an institutionalized process disappeared after Justinian closed the Platonist Academy at Athens, the same year in which the first Benedictine abbey was founded at Monte Cassino. Under Gregory I (590–604) the church offered protection, leadership, and unity. This relatively stable order was refined by Charlemagne (768–814). Monasteries such as those emanating from Cluny (more than 200 by the 11th century), the reformed abbeys of the Cistercians (more than 340 by the middle of the 12th century), the emergence of the Franciscans, the growth of urban university centers such as Oxford, Paris, Bologna, and Salerno—all were part of the cultural ethos in which Scholasticism appeared. A Scholastic was a teacher in an urban university or a master around whom students gathered.

John Scotus Eriugena (810–877) organized a system of education based on Greek thought. Because of his emphasis on the use of reason in studying revealed data, he is commonly called the first Scholastic. The original Scholastic was Anselm (1033–1109), who repeated Augustine's dictum: "I believe that I might understand." Articles of faith were the data from which human reason began. After the work of Roscellinus (c. 1050–c. 1122), William of Champeaux (c. 1070–1121), and Abelard (1079–1142) followed a developed Scholasticism in the *Four Books of Sentences* of Peter Lombard (c. 1100–1160). Lombard developed the technical question and solved it by dialectics; in treating of God, creation, the incarnation, redemption, and the sacraments, he introduced the characteristic of all Scholasticism: the systematic approach in the solution of individual and seriated theological questions.

In the 13th century, Scholasticism came into contact with the Islamic thought of Averroës (1126–1198) and Avicenna (980–1037) as well as with the Jewish thinkers, Avicebrón (c. 1021–c. 1058) and Maimonides (1135–1204). These men too, with the help of Aristotle, were reasoning systematically about God's revelation. William of Moerbeke (1215–

1286) made Aristotle available to the Latin West. In fact, Aristotle was prescribed reading at the University of Paris. The university method of learning was primarily reading and the disputation. Thomas Aquinas was to point out the importance of the magisterial type of disputation where one asks the question, "What is the meaning of your affirmation?" To use the authoritative disputation to answer this question would send the student away, in Aquinas' words, *vacuus*, "without understanding." Although for Bonaventure (1221–1274) truth is primarily revealed truth, Aquinas distinguishes nature and grace, and thus he gives a completely independent domain to reason. For Aquinas, the object of the intellect is being. His philosophical basis is the analogy of being which enables man to know the transcendent God and the analogy of faith which means that the truths of faith may be assembled into a coherent whole. Aquinas began with the causes of knowledge and proceeded to the causes of being. His disputations are arranged according to the causes of knowledge, the *Summa* according to the causes of being. This analytical method of the disputation and synthetic method of the *Summa* are the essential characteristics of Scholasticism during its best period.

Though Scholastic procedure was more or less followed after Aquinas, later Scholasticism is generally associated with a method of systematically applying reason to revealed data. The controversialists of the Counter-Reformation were Scholastic in approach. More recently, Scholasticism came to be identified with the thesis method of learning and teaching philosophy and theology. It was to this method that Vatican II seemed to be referring when it modified certain schemata and terms because they were "too Scholastic."

Immediately following the Reformation, both Lutheranism and the Reformed Church experienced a period of Scholasticism when Protestant Orthodoxy was measured against Luther's teaching and Reformed Orthodoxy against Calvin's *Institutes,* both quite literally interpreted. The contest over doctrinal differences between Luther and Melanchthon, in which the former was represented by the Gnesio (Genuine)-Lutherans and the latter by the Philippists or Melanchthonians or crypto-Calvinists, was brought to a close by the Formula of Concord (1577), but the Formula was almost immediately developed into a system of doctrine resembling Scholasticism. This formalized system held sway in Lutheranism until the late 17th century when Spener's *Pia desideria* (1675) posed the challenge of Pietism to orthodoxy. Unlike Lutheranism, the

Reformed group was torn by continuous doctrinal struggle from the Consensus Tigurinus (1549) until the Formula consensus Helvetica (1675), during which time the major conflicts centered on predestination as witnessed by the Arminian or Remonstrant Church's advocacy of free will and the disciplinary authority of the church. Against all such opposition the theology of the Geneva Academy filtered through the Synod of Dort (1618–1619) and the Leiden *Synopsis purioris theologiae* (1624) ruled as Scholastic Reformed orthodoxy.

The essence of Scholasticism, then, is the placing of a genuine question, the sympathetic presentation of all contrary opinions, the articulated answer to the question, and the response to contrary opinions. The questions, objections, and answers are then systematized thematically into a coherent and total system open to future questions. Scholasticism is a method of procedure and a system emerging from the analytic and synthetic process. Because of the knowledge explosion and the fact that no one world view has a monopoly on truth, Scholasticism as method continues, but Scholasticism as total system comparable to the *Summa* of Thomas Aquinas has not been reproduced in modern times.

BIBLIOGRAPHY: D. J. B. Hawkins, *A Sketch of Medieval Philosophy* (New York, 1947); G. Leff, *Medieval Thought: St. Augustine to Ockham* (Baltimore, 1962); M. deWulf, *An Introduction to Scholastic Philosophy* (New York, 1956); F. van Steenberghen, *Aristotle in the West: The Origins of Latin Aristotelianism* (Louvain, 1955); and *The Philosophical Movement in the Thirteenth Century* (Edinburgh, 1955); P. Vignaux, *Philosophy in the Middle Ages* (London, 1959).

**Scholte, Hendrik Peter** (1805–1868). Dutch Reformed theologian. Born in the Netherlands and educated at Leiden, Scholte while pastor at Doeveren vigorously protested the secularism of the state church. He seceded from the church (1834) at the head of a dissenting movement, and edited a periodical. In 1847 he emigrated to America with a group of eight hundred and founded a colony in Pella, Iowa. He was influential in drawing Central University to the area, and took an active interest in community affairs. The colony merged with the Reformed Church in America in 1856.

**Schopenhauer, Arthur** (1788–1860). German philosopher. He was born at Danzig and studied at the Universities of Göttingen, Berlin, and Jena. By 1819 his principal work, *The World as Will and Idea,* had appeared, but it was not immediately accepted at centers of higher learning because of its opposition to the Hegelianism prevailing at the time. Fortunately, his family was of the wealthy merchant class, so he was not in need of a position and was therefore free to travel and write essays which he submitted for various prizes. It was not until 1851 that he attracted much attention, and he lived to see lectures given on his ideas at the Universities of Jena, Bonn, and Breslau. He secured an international group of devoted admirers. However, Schopenhauer remained a brooding, cynical, pessimistic man with a bad temper and many phobias. Philosophically, he was influenced by Kant, Plato, and Hindu mysticism. He felt that reality is characterized by a blind principle which actualizes itself in the infinite variety of living forms in the world. This principle or force may be called the "will to live" and explains the conflict that men experience in life. Schopenhauer's teaching aided the growth of romanticism and prepared the way intellectually for the nihilism of late 19th-century philosophers such as Nietzsche.

**Schrempf, Christoph** (1860–1944). German humanitarian. He taught philosophy at the Institute for Technology in Stuttgart, Germany. He was originally a pastor in Leuzendorf, but was dismissed by the Evangelical Church of Württemberg because he could no longer believe in the Apostles' Creed. He conducted a long literary feud with the church and preached humanitarian ideals which are now collected in the thirteen volumes of *Gesammelte Werke.*

**Schubart, Christian Friedrich Daniel** (1739–1791). German poet and musician. After studying theology at Erlangen, Schubart became active in music. Gradually he revolted in poetry against official methods of repression, governmental corruption, the caprices of princes, and became a leading representative of *Sturm und Drang.* He was imprisoned for ten years (1777–1787) by Prince Karl Eugen of Württemberg. When he died he was a music director in Stuttgart. Few of his fragmentary poems were titled.

**Schubert, Gotthilf Heinrich von** (1780–1860). German representative of a romantic philosophy of nature influenced by Schelling, Novalis, and Herder. He was a theologian, biologist, and physicist teaching at Erlangen, Dresden, and Munich. Drawn to the Protestant religious awakening centered in Nuremberg, he combined a simple Biblical faith with his work as a natural scientist through principles of German idealist philosophy.

**Schütz, Heinrich** (1585–1672). German musician. He was the most influential and prolific Protestant composer of his era, and a forerunner of J. S. Bach and George Handel. Studying in Italy under Giovanni Gabrieli as a youth, he returned to introduce new concepts into the music of his native land. He wrote the first German opera and gave Germany its earliest "passion music" and oratorios based on double choirs and various contrasting combinations of voices and instruments.

**Schwabach Articles** (1529). Seventeen doctrinal articles drafted by Wittenberg theologians, chiefly Melanchthon, on the order of Elector John of Saxony, to serve in negotiations with the Upper German cities. The desired doctrinal unity and a possible political alliance were not achieved, but Melanchthon used the Articles extensively in formulating the doctrinal section of the Augsburg Confession of 1530. They also bear a family likeness to the articles Luther prepared for the Marburg Colloquy (1529).

**Schwarz, Karl** (1812–1885). German theologian. Trained at Halle, Berlin, and Greifswald, Schwarz lectured at Halle (1842), was released, and then reinstated in 1849. He became court preacher at Gotha (1856), and general superintendent and member of the state ministry (1877). At the Frankfurt Parliament, and later, he urged freedom for the church in teaching, polity, and worship. Cofounder of the Protestant Union, he wanted to extend it to doctrinal matters. His "rational" theology, derived from Hegel and Schleiermacher, viewed Christianity historically and drew on experiences of heart rather than revelation.

**Schweitzer, Albert** (1875–1965). Protestant, Biblical scholar, theologian, philosopher, organist, and medical missionary. Born in Kaysersberg, Upper Alsace, he was educated at the University of Strasbourg, where he received his Ph.D. (1899), Lic. Theol. (1900), and M.D. (1912). He studied at Paris and Berlin under Adolf von Harnack. While serving as curate at the church of St. Nicolaus, he was *Privatdocent* in theology at Strasbourg (1902). An accomplished organist, he assisted in completing a definitive edition of the works of Bach, and published his epoch-making *Jean-Sebastian Bach, le Musicien-Poète* (1905; translation, *J. S. Bach,* 1911), in which he demonstrated the relation between Bach's music and his text. He was the author of *Kant* (1899); *The Problem of the Last Supper* (1901); and *The Secret of the Messiahship and the Suffering: A Sketch of the Life of Jesus* (1901) before he wrote *Von Reimarus zu Wrede* (1906; translation, *The Quest of the Historical Jesus,* 1910), which established his reputation as a Biblical scholar. In *The Quest,* a history of the modern research into the life of Jesus, he stressed futuristic eschatology and Jesus' resolution to suffer for others to bring about the coming of the Kingdom of God. Other Biblical writings included *Paul and His Interpreters* (1911) and *The Psychiatric Study of Jesus* (1913). He caught the admiration of the world when he left pastorate and professorship to serve at a station of the Paris Missionary Society, Lambaréné, Gabon, French Equatorial Africa. He went to Africa "in obedience to Jesus," although theological difficulties with the mission society made him serve as a surgeon. He represented missionary paternalism at its best prior to the development of African nationalism. Expansion of his medical work was supported in part through his publications: *On the Edge of the Primeval Forest* (1922); *Christianity and the Religions of the World* (1923); *The Decay and Restoration of Civilization* (1923); *Civilization and Ethics* (1923); *Out of My Life and Thought* (1933); *Indian Thought and Its Development* (1936); *Goethe: Four Studies* (1949); *Animal World: Jungle Insights Into Reverence for Life* (1950). In 1952, he received the Nobel Peace Prize. He practiced his key concept, "reverence for life," showed increasing interest in *Kulturphilosophie,* and was outspoken in *Peace or Atomic War?* (1957) against the development of nuclear weapons. Except for internment as a German citizen at Provence prison during World War I and occasional lecture tours to Europe and America (1949), he spent his remaining years in Africa.

**Schweizer, Alexander** (1808–1888). Swiss Reformed theologian. From 1835 he taught at the University of Zurich and after 1844 was also pastor of the Great Minster Church. Known as the most faithful disciple of Schleiermacher, Schweizer was involved in the controversy that surrounded the calling of D. F. Strauss to Zurich, and apparently for a time he hoped Strauss would return to theology. In his major works, Schweizer renewed the exercise of Calvinistic dogmatics which had for a century been neglected.

**Schwenkfeld, Kaspar** (1489–1561). Anabaptist. Schwenkfeld was a Silesian aristocrat, diplomat, and lay theologian who was an early Lutheran, helping to institute Lutheran reform in Silesia in 1522. After 1526 he defended Spiritualist views. Independently wealthy, he lived from 1529 in exile, traveling, writing, and discussing voluminously. He understood Christian faith from the viewpoint of a Eucharistic Christology. He saw faith as a perpetual feeding on the celestial flesh of

Christ which God had foreordained to be established in Jesus for the redemption of sinful man. This spiritual food changed the believer into a partaker of the divine nature so that he was sanctified, though not to perfection in this life. Participation in sacraments was unnecessary, and to be avoided where there was no unity among believers. Indeed, Christ was not a man like other men. Schwenkfeld advocated a withdrawal from parish church participation, though he built up study and prayer conventicles made up of the regenerate by faith. He urged the study of the Scriptures (defending the parity of the Testaments) and the preaching ministry, and though he attacked infant baptism, he never espoused rebaptism. He was a pious, courteous, confident, articulate —to some a tiringly insistent—spokesman for his views. Schwenkfeldians have never been numerous, though some remain today.

**Scillitan Martyrs.** Among the earliest Christian martyrs of North Africa (see MADAURAN MARTYRS). They were known from the authentic acts of their trial before Vigellius Saturninus, proconsul of Africa, on July 17, A.D. 180. The proconsul urged them to return to "Roman customs," while one of them stated that he did not acknowledge "the empire of this age." All twelve of them gave thanks to God and were executed.

**Scofield, Cyrus I.** (1843–1921). Congregational clergyman. A Civil War veteran, he was admitted to the Kansas Bar in 1869 and made U.S. attorney for Kansas in 1873. He was converted to Christianity in 1879 and ordained in 1882. Fame as a Bible expositor created wide demand for him as a lecturer. He is especially remembered for his *Scofield Reference Bible* (1910) and Scofield Correspondence Bible School.

**Scopes Trial.** The trial in which John T. Scopes, high school science teacher in Dayton, Tenn., was charged, tried, and convicted of violating the state law prohibiting the teaching of evolution in the public schools. The trial ran from July 10 to July 21, 1925, and Scopes was sentenced to pay a fine of $100. William Jennings Bryan, a leader of fundamentalist opposition to evolution, was the prosecutor, and Clarence Darrow, considered a skeptic, was counsel for the defense. The fundamentalists insisted that the very moral and religious fabric of the nation was being threatened by religious Modernism and scientific contradictions of Biblical literalism. They sought to reemphasize traditional doctrines and agitate for state laws to prevent public dissemination of liberalism. The debate centered on the doctrine of evolution, accepted by Modernism and secular opinion, but seen as the seed of materialism by the fundamentalists, for it denied a literal interpretation of the Biblical account of the Creation. On religious grounds, the trial tested the relative strength of Fundamentalism. Largely because of its inflexible stand and refusal to accept scientific evidence, Fundamentalism never regained the strength and stature it held before the trial. On secular grounds, the trial tested the right to teach scientific views that questioned prevailing mores, and how far a state could go in determining the nature of religious instruction in public schools.

**Scotland, Church of.** The historic, national, and legally established Scottish Church; more particularly, that church since the Reformation. Much of Scottish church history prior to the Reformation is obscure and confused. Until the end of the Middle Ages, Scottish society was politically and culturally backward. Tribal Highland life, Lowland feudalism, and weak central government were accompanied by a rather disorganized and ineffectual church. Unlike England, Scotland first received Christianity entirely in its Celtic form. Apart from possible penetration from ancient Roman Britain missionaries and from Candida Casa, the monastery founded at Whithorn, Galloway, by Ninian at the end of the 4th century, the conversion of Scotland traditionally began with the coming of Columba from Ireland in 563. Columba's monastery on the island of Iona contributed much toward spreading the new faith in western and northern Scotland, and from there Aidan carried Celtic Christianity to Northumbria in 635. After the English Synod of Whitby (664), the Celtic Church, with its different customs and calendar and its primarily monastic organization, retreated gradually before the Roman Church, and in the 8th century Roman authority was recognized.

During the Middle Ages, Scotland moved only slowly toward conformity with other European churches. Diocesan authority was introduced, the primacy vested in St. Andrews, parishes defined, tithes imposed, and abbeys founded. Against England the church resisted the ecclesiastical authority of York and Canterbury and the military invasions of the Edwards. In the 15th century, universities were established at St. Andrews, Glasgow, and Aberdeen. Yet on the eve of the Protestant Reformation, the church in some sections was in a precarious or ruinous state, and the need for episcopal supervision and adequate parish ministry was acute.

As in other countries, the Reformation in

Scotland derived from various causes, social and political as well as religious. The quickened economic life of the Lowlands, the ambitions of the barons, the emergence of nationalism, and the rivalry of pro-French and pro-English factions all played a part. Protestantism, from both Continental and English sources, was represented in the universities and confirmed by the martyrdoms of Patrick Hamilton (1528) and George Wishart (1546), whose mantle of leadership passed to John Knox (d. 1572). Before his return to Scotland in 1559, Knox had lived in England, Frankfurt, and Geneva, and was an ardent champion of the Reformed faith. With English help the Protestant Lords of the Congregation called the Reformation Parliament of 1560 which voided the heresy acts, the Mass, and the authority of the papacy, and established a new confession (the Scots Confession) and a new discipline. The First Book of Discipline (presented to Parliament in January, 1560) provided for superintendents, general assembly, presbyteries, lay participation, worship, poor relief, and a national educational system (the last not implemented). These arrangements were somewhat provisional, and in the following years the Crown and nobility strove to limit reform. Neither episcopacy nor lay patronage, both later issues of importance, was destroyed. On the other hand, the church, led by Andrew Melville (1545–1622), moved close to the classical Presbyterian order, attacking superintendency and vindicating the liberties of the Kirk. This was evident in the Second Book of Discipline, ratified by the General Assembly in 1581.

The 17th century was filled with controversy over the government and the independence of the church. During the first part of the century the Crown was largely successful in extending its authority. Bishops were maintained, the Assembly was dominated, opposition was silenced. After 1618, liturgical experiments to draw Scotland into uniformity with the English Church, more determined after the accession of Charles I, introduced a further issue. Archbishop Laud's service book of 1637 was the signal for national revolt. In Scotland, bishops were deposed, polity and worship reformed, and a national covenant bound men to defend the Kirk. The Solemn League and Covenant (1643), made possible by the English Revolution in 1640, promised the extension of the Scottish order to England. Though the Westminster Assembly prepared a common confession, liturgy, and polity, accepted in Scotland, opposition prevented an enduring triumph of Presbyterianism in England.

In the second half of the century some of the same issues and conflicts were repeated. Political and religious dissension at home and war with England helped pave the way for the Stuart Restoration and its religious policies in 1660. A Rescissory Act (1661) swept away the ecclesiastical legislation of the previous two decades, and episcopacy and patronage were restored. Resistance resulted in Covenanter conventicles, persecution, and reprisals. The Roman Catholic sympathies of James VII (James II of England) furthered distrust. Final settlement came in the Glorious Revolution of 1688, which was more extreme in its political and religious reaction than its English counterpart. In some places mobs turned clergy of the episcopal party out of their livings. By law the Westminster Confession was restored and episcopacy repealed. Dissenters from the new settlement formed the Scottish Episcopal Church.

By contrast to the 17th century, the 18th century was disturbed by few crises. The Presbyterian Establishment, a satisfied part of the Scottish Constitution, upheld the *status quo*. The union with England in 1707 contained guarantees for the Scottish Church, and Presbyterians performed loyal service in the Jacobite risings of 1715 and 1745. The dominant party in the church, the Moderates, long under the leadership of the historian William Robertson (1721–1793), stood for political accommodation and intellectual respectability; but though they contributed brilliantly to Scottish letters, they often lost touch with parish life. The patronage issue created the most difficulties, as the Moderate Assembly adopted the policy of compelling the presbytery to accept presentations regardless of the wishes of the congregation. As dissatisfied ministers and people left the church, small dissenting bodies formed, which, however, were not separated from the church by doctrinal issues. Toward the end of the century Moderate dominance was undermined by the growth of the evangelical movement. Wesley visited Scotland, but more important work was done by the Haldanes and Scottish preachers. Preaching, education in the Highlands, and foreign missions were promoted. Great efforts were made to establish new churches in the Highlands and the large industrial cities.

The greatest leader of the 19th-century Evangelicals was Thomas Chalmers (1780–1847). Chalmers defended the Established Church as providing the most effective parish ministry to the nation and headed a successful effort at church extension. But controversy over patronage led Chalmers to take the leading role in the Disruption of 1843. The Ten

Years' Conflict that preceded the Disruption centered chiefly about the Veto Act, passed by the Evangelical-dominated Assembly in 1834. The act prohibited the intrusion of a minister on a congregation against its will, but in 1838 a disappointed presentee successfully appealed to the Court of Session to overrule the act. Other cases followed, and Evangelicals believed that the freedom and discipline of the church were at stake. An appeal to Parliament having failed, Disruption occurred at the Assembly session in 1843, when over 450 ministers formed the Free Church of Scotland. The secession took about one third of the members of the national church, all the foreign missionaries save one, and about 400 teachers. Chalmers, whose Sustentation Fund helped carry the financial burden, was the first moderator of the Free Church.

Despite schisms, Scottish people were not seriously divided on religious issues, and the next century was to be one of reunions. In 1874, Parliament passed the Patronage Act, which acknowledged the necessity of the congregation's call, thus removing an ancient cause of secessions. Also in the 1870's, negotiations prepared a union of the Free Church with the United Presbyterian Church, itself a fusion of United Secession and Relief Churches, representing 18th-century protests against the patronage system. Discussions broke down because of disagreement on the "voluntary" principle, but union was finally achieved a generation later in 1900. The passage of the Church of Scotland Act (1921), recognizing the church's freedom, removed the last obstacle to the reunion of the United Free Church and the Church of Scotland, which was consummated in 1929. (See PRESBYTERIANISM.)

BIBLIOGRAPHY: G. Donaldson, *The Scottish Reformation* (Cambridge, 1960); J. A. Duke, *History of the Church of Scotland to the Reformation* (London, 1937); J. R. Fleming, *A History of the Church in Scotland: 1834–1874* (Edinburgh, 1927); Continuation, *1875–1929* (Edinburgh, 1933); and *The Story of Church Union in Scotland* (London, 1929); W. D. Simpson, *The Celtic Church in Scotland* (Aberdeen, 1935); H. Watt, *Thomas Chalmers and the Disruption* (Edinburgh, 1943).

**Scotland, United Free Church of.** An organization founded in 1900 by the merger of the Free Church of Scotland and the United Presbyterian Church. In 1929, when it rejoined the Established Church, some of its members withdrew and continued to function under the original name. In 1954 it had 121 congregations with approximately 25,000 members.

**Scots Confession.** A confession of faith ratified by the Scottish Parliament on Aug. 7, 1560. It marked the triumph of the Reformation in Scotland. A committee (of which John Knox was the leading spirit) had drafted this statement of Protestant principles, which was thought to be totally grounded on the Word of God. About ten thousand words in length, the Scots Confession contained twenty-five articles. The first twelve dealt with standard theological themes—God, creation, original sin, etc. The theology was Calvinistic and in harmony with Continental Reformed confessions. The final thirteen articles were intensely anti-Roman. It is affirmed that the true Kirk is distinguished by the true preaching of the word, the right administration of the sacraments (Baptism and Communion), and the upright maintenance of discipline. Transubstantiation is denied, as is the view that the elements are no more than "naked and bare signs." Only lawful preaching ministers can administer the sacraments. The civil magistrate has great authority which must be used in religion to uphold the true and suppress the false. The Confession does not deal with church order but affirms that ceremonies are temporal and ought to be changed when change fosters a fuller appreciation of truth. The Scots Confession was superseded by the Westminster Confession in 1647. See also the KING'S CONFESSION.

**Scott, George Gilbert** (1811–1878). Ecclesiastical architect. He was the grandson of the theologian and Biblical commentator Thomas Scott. Originally an opponent of the Gothic revival in England, he was won over in Cambridge and became its leading representative. His main works include the Martyrs' Memorial, Oxford, St. Nicholas at Hamburg, the Albert Memorial, and also cathedral restorations such as Ely and Salisbury. Preference for his own designs over originals, however, provoked resistance from the Society for the Protection of Ancient Buildings.

**Scottish Disruption** (1843). An outgrowth of the controversies within the Church of Scotland on the subject of lay patronage. After 1832, many Presbyterians demanded the repeal of a statute of 1712, which had restored to certain laymen the power to appoint ministers; these dissidents insisted upon a return to the "call," wherein each congregation would enjoy the option of approving or rejecting its pastors. In 1834, after a series of quarrels, the General Assembly of the church embodied the "call" in the Veto Act. Henceforth, the majority of heads of families in any church might veto the appointment of any presentee on reasonable grounds. There followed ten years of renewed conflict. In 1838, the Scottish Court of Session disallowed the Veto Act, thereby denying the Assembly's authority to legislate for the church. In 1842, the so-called Claim of Right, published by the extreme nonintrusion party, flatly discountenanced lay patronage and contended for the church's complete independence of civil control. In 1843, after the government's failure to mediate successfully between the Assembly and the Court of Session, the tangled dispute engendered the Great Secession or Disruption. Out of 1,203 ministers, 474 abandoned the church, arguing their inability to participate in anything but a free Assembly. Under the leadership of Dr. Thomas Chalmers, they convened the first meeting of the Free Church of Scotland. Not until 1928 was the schism finally healed.

**Scottish Episcopal Church.** Bishops were introduced to Scotland by James VI (James I of England) in 1610. In 1618 the General Assembly meeting at Perth, under pressure from James, ratified five unpopular articles authorizing such Anglican practices as observance of holy days and kneeling at Communion. In 1619 a Scottish Prayer Book was published by the archbishop of St. Andrews. It was not widely accepted and when Charles I tried, in 1637, to enforce its use he was met with open rebellion. The General Assembly and Scottish people subscribed to a National Covenant in defense of the Presbyterian Kirk. This rebellion led to the Civil War in both Scotland and England. The victorious Covenanters ousted Episcopalianism until 1661, when Charles II established the Episcopal Church in Scotland. About three hundred ministers refused to serve the new establishment, even though many Presbyterian practices such as synods were kept. Since Episcopalianism was popular only in the northeast, there were several antiepiscopal risings—one in 1679 touched off by the murder of Archbishop James Sharp. After 1688, William III turned to the Presbyterian party because seven of nine Scottish bishops remained loyal to James II. In 1690, Episcopalianism, though still tolerated, was permanently disestablished.

**Scottish Missionary Society.** An agency of the Church of Scotland (Presbyterian) which arose from two associations founded at Edinburgh and Glasgow in 1796. Both groups labored under the shadow of indifference and opposition. In 1824, John Inglis persuaded the General Assembly of the church to establish a mission in India. In 1829, the creation of educational stations in the East set a precedent for similar activities in South Africa, Asia, and the Pacific.

**Scriptorium.** The room of a monastery set apart for the use of copyists in the preparation of manuscripts. Although the copying of manuscripts was intended primarily to provide the monastery with the necessary books to maintain its educational program, the monasteries proved to be of profound benefit to mankind by preserving works of literature from total destruction in the turmoil of the Middle Ages.

**Scriver, Christian** (1629–1693). German Lutheran Pietist. Born near Kiel, he studied theology at Rostock. He served as pastor in Stendal (1653–1667) and Magdeburg (1667–1690), and was court chaplain at Quedlinburg (1690–1693). Scriver is known as an Arndtian Pietist with his strong emphasis on repentance, regeneration, forgiveness, adoption, and union with Christ. He sought to relate personal piety and the Lutheran confessions in an organic relationship that would hold the objective and subjective sides of redemption in balance, insisting that God's work for man must become a reality through the work of the indwelling Holy Spirit. A friend of Philip Spener, he helped prepare the way for Pietism by his critique of contemporary Lutheran orthodoxy while remaining doctrinally orthodox himself. Of his many devotional writings, he is best remembered for his *Treasure of the Soul* (5 parts, 1675–1692).

**Scudder, Ida S.** (1870–1960). American missionary doctor. Following a family tradition, she served as a medical missionary in India. She founded a one-room dispensary in Vellore in 1900. Under her direction, it became a major hospital and medical center. She also established a nursing school and a medical college for women. Her roadside clinics took care of thousands of patients each year. The medical center also became a research center for leprosy.

**Seabury, Samuel** (1729–1796). Episcopalian bishop. Educated at Yale and Edinburgh, he was ordained in 1753 and was sent by the Society for the Propagation of the Gospel as a missionary to New Jersey. He was a devoted Loyalist and was a chaplain in the British army during the American Revolution. In 1784 he was consecrated a bishop while in Scotland and became the first Episcopal bishop in America in 1785, serving the diocese of Connecticut and Rhode Island.

**Sebaste, Forty Martyrs of.** Forty soldiers of the Thundering Legion (the Twelfth Roman Legion, said to have been composed of Christians) put to death c. 320 during the Licinian persecution. Basil of Caesarea and Gregory of Nyssa relate the story of their martyrdom at Sebaste, where they were left naked to die on a frozen pond, tempted by hot baths on the banks of the pond to renounce their faith and save themselves. A heathen soldier of the guard who was converted took the place of one apostate. The remains of the martyrs were recovered by the empress Pulcheria.

**Second Great Awakening.** Early in the 19th century, religious revivals occurred almost simultaneously in different parts of the country. In New England, evangelical Congregationalists and Methodists were effective revivalists. Revivals occurred in Virginia at the Presbyterian colleges of Hampden-Sidney and Washington. At Yale College, Timothy Dwight considered preaching a part of his work as college president. In 1802, one third of the student body was converted under his preaching in the college chapel. Dwight found revivalism a successful means of fighting "infidelity" among his students. This was indicative of the change that came about in revivalism during the Second Awakening. It was developed as a technique to induce religious conversion.

In Kentucky, the revival had its inspiration in James McGready, a fiery Presbyterian minister who moved to Logan County from North Carolina in 1796. He became pastor of three small congregations there. His fervent preaching and diligent pastoral work had immediate results among his congregations. In 1797, a revival broke out among his parishioners at Gaspar River. In 1800, the culmination of the Cumberland revival was reached. A four-day meeting was held at Red River in June. Three Presbyterian ministers, William Hodges, John Rankin, William McGee, and a Methodist minister, John McGee, assisted McGready. With continual exhorting by the ministers, the emotional pitch of the meetings rose steadily. News of the revival spread. In July, another "sacramental" service was held at Gaspar River, attended by people from far and wide. During this revival gathering, the people lived in makeshift tents, a distinctive feature of the camp meeting which developed at that time.

The next major camp meeting was held the following year at Cane Ridge in August. The meeting was on an interdenominational basis, with Methodist, Baptist, and Presbyterian clergymen participating, the Methodists and Baptists being particularly enthusiastic about the new means of revival. The response was a large one, with at least ten thousand people in attendance. The extreme emotionalism resulted in physical "exercises" such as falling, running, jumping, and jerking, which were attributed to the Holy Spirit. As the excesses of the revival became more pronounced, so did the opposition. The Presbyterian Church dissolved the Cumberland Presbytery for permitting the excesses and for ordaining ministers without the necessary academic qualifications. The Kentucky revival was followed by two schisms from the Presbyterian Church— the Cumberland Presbytery which became independent and the "New Light" schism under Barton W. Stone. It was the Methodists and Baptists who encouraged the revival and who reaped the largest number of converts. The Methodists adapted the camp meeting for revivalism and continued its use long into the 19th century.

The third phase of the Second Awakening took place in central and western New York where Charles G. Finney was the chief revivalist. He had been trained as a lawyer but gave up his practice for the ministry in 1824 when he was licensed a Presbyterian minister. He preferred itinerant preaching to a settled ministry and soon was traveling about to neighboring communities. The revivals under his leadership did not have the excesses of the Kentucky revival. Finney instituted certain "New Measures," such as the anxious bench, the inquiry room, and the protracted meetings, which were intended to induce conversion in his hearers. He had very successful tours in various cities of the East, including New York and Boston. He adapted his type of revivalism to the urban scene. Many young college graduates copied Finney's methods, and revivalism became widespread. According to Robert Baird, revivals were "a constituent part of the religious system" in America after the Second Awakening of the 19th century.

BIBLIOGRAPHY: J. C. Brauer, *Protestantism in America* (Philadelphia, 1966); W. S. Hudson, *The Great Tradition of the American Churches* (New York, 1953); C. R. Keller, *The Second Great Awakening in Connecticut* (New Haven, 1942); T. Smith, *Revivalism and Social Reform* (New York, 1957); W. W. Sweet, *Religion on the American Frontier: 1783–1840,* 4 vols. (New York, 1964).

**Secretariat for Promoting Christian Unity.** An association created by John XXIII in his *Motu proprio super Dei nutu* and allocution (June 5, 1960) to assist non-Catholics in following the work and accomplishments of the Second Vatican Council, and to facilitate Christian unity. Presided over by Cardinal Bea, it was organized like a Commission and its chief function has been to foster communication between Catholics and non-Catholics, mainly on ecumenical affairs.

**Secular Arm.** In ecclesiastical law the legal and political structure of the state or some other lay authority. Church members could be excommunicated for taking to the secular arm those matters reserved to ecclesiastical courts. Heretics were handed over to the secular arm for punishment, since it seemed inappropriate for the church to impose serious temporal penalties.

**Secular Clergy.** Clerics not members of religious or monastic orders and who therefore do not follow a rule. The term "secular clergy" was first used for priests who lived in the world (*saeculum*). They took no vows, but were bound by oaths of loyalty to their bishop. Canon law forbids secular clergy of the Latin rite to marry, although in recent years dispensations have infrequently been granted to non-Catholic ministers converted after marriage, allowing them to be ordained while continuing in the married state.

**See** (from Latin *sedes*, "seat"). The name applied more generally to the city in which a bishop has his official residence, although specifically it refers to the throne of the bishop located within the cathedral church. The Holy See refers to the papacy and its legal and administrative offices and congregations.

**Seeberg, Reinhold** (1859–1935). German Lutheran theologian. The product of the Baltic province of Livonia, he took his first academic post in Dorpat (1884), then at Erlangen (1889), and finally at Berlin (1898) in practical theology. Seeberg looked upon himself as Lutheran and rooted his theology in the confessions but maintained a free approach to the received theological formulations. Though he played little part in the affairs of the state church, he was active in voluntary religious associations, particularly in the Inner Mission and Christian Socialism movements.

**Seekers.** One of several radical sects on the edge of Puritanism in 17th-century England. Meeting in small groups, they felt that no true church existed, and awaited the future appearance of one, authenticated by new apostles. Their roots may go back to earlier Arian Separatists (the Legatines), but they flourished in the unsettled 1640's. In the 1650's many became Quakers. The final views of Roger Williams were of this type.

**Seipel, Ignaz** (1876–1932). Austrian Roman Catholic statesman-priest. Ordained in 1899, Seipel lectured at Salzburg (1909) and Vienna (1917). Shortly thereafter he entered politics. In 1918 he was minister of social welfare under the last royal government; in 1919, deputy in constituting the national assembly supporting moderate federalism; later, a member of the national council. During the first coalition government after 1919, Seipel opposed intimate alliance between Christian Socialists and Social Democrats. After Johann Schober resigned, Austrian policy under Seipel moved to the right. Chairman of Christian Socialists from 1921 to 1930, he was chancellor of Austria from 1922 to 1924 and 1926 to 1929. During the 1922 inflation he rescued Austria through foreign loans, with bank notes independent of the government. His social legislation, social reform, and treaties consolidated Austrian resources. A pact with Pan-Germans enabled him to create an antisocialist majority. He was minister of foreign affairs in 1930. His scholarly writings include an edition (with Heinrich Lammash) of Hugo Grotius on international law. He never appeared in public without clerical dress, and was hailed by the Roman hierarchy as one who lived the statesman-priest role according to canon law. Some of his sermons and speeches were recently issued by R. Blüml, *Im Dienst des Wortes* (Vienna, c. 1955).

**Selina, Countess.** See HUNTINGDON, COUNTESS OF.

**Selivanov.** See SKOPTSY.

**Selwyn, George Augustus** (1809–1878). Anglican missionary bishop. Educated at St. John's, Cambridge, and ordained in 1833, he became missionary bishop of New Zealand in 1841. A Tractarian, he opposed the view that a civil letters patent could give him power to ordain. He was largely responsible for the extension and organization of the Anglican Church in New Zealand. Returning home in 1867, he became bishop of Lichfield in 1868. Selwyn College was founded in his memory in 1881.

**Semler, Johann Salomo** (1725–1791). German Protestant theologian. Semler held the chair of theology at Halle from 1752. A Pietist, he moved to neological rationalism, seeking to renew the church by rational inquiry. He did important translation work and also worked in hermeneutics, history, dogmatics, ethics, archaeology, and numismatics. Semler was a pioneer in textual criticism. He restricted reason's role in supernatural things and argued for conservatism in public religion.

**Seneca, Lucius Annaeus** (c. 4 B.C.–A.D. 65). Stoic philosopher, author, politician, and tutor of the emperor Nero. He finally committed suicide by order of Nero because he apparently was involved in a conspiracy against his ex-pupil. His writings express Roman Stoic doctrines, especially ethical, which were not often reflected in his life. In the 4th century, Christians composed a dossier of letters supposedly exchanged by Seneca with the apostle Paul.

**Sentences.** The designation for a whole genus of medieval theological and philosophical works, but also taken to refer specifically to the best known of such works, viz., the *Sententiarum libri quatuor* (*Four Books of Sentences*) of Peter Lombard (d. c. 1160), bishop of Paris. Taking their name from the Latin for a formally expressed opinion, the *Sentences* gave form and direction to the commentaries on discordant opinions, Biblical texts, decretals, and so on. Influenced by Peter Abelard's *Sic et non,* Lombard's work attempted to resolve theologically important issues after presenting the conflicting evidence for opposing contentions. His *Sentences* were divided into four books concerning: (1) the Trinity; (2) created things; (3) the nature of Christ, the incarnation, redemption, the mystery of grace; (4) the sacraments and the last ends of man. This work remained the accepted theological treatise throughout the Middle Ages, finally being superseded by the more complete and more rigorously organized *Summa theologiae* of Thomas Aquinas. The appearance of Aquinas' *Summa* did not summarily end the significance of Lombard's *Sentences,* however, for they continued to be the basis of various Scholastic exercises and a model for the organization of material.

**Separation of Church and State** (United States). This separation has been called the central ideological fact of American history. Together with the closely related development of religious liberty and denominational pluralism, such a distinction in a politically homogeneous society was unique in Western Christendom. Traditionally, Christians assumed the necessity of legal coercion, ecclesiastical establishment, and identification of church membership with a national population on the grounds that man as sinner would not normally accept or openly receive the means of grace, much less a personal conversion. It was also believed that the effectiveness of civil government and the orderliness of society depended upon religious uniformity. State compulsion was conceived not as an evil but as a necessary good for the salvation of souls and the welfare of the state. The earliest European colonial experiments in North America brought this pattern of religious establishment with them. Jamestown (1607, Anglican), Massachusetts Bay (1620, Puritan), and New Netherland (1624, Dutch Reformed) each considered a single, organic state church, or church state, to be the desirable arrangement. This assumption was challenged, however, from a number of directions in the 17th- and 18th-century American colonial milieu. Roger Williams in Rhode Island and William Penn in Pennsylvania preached religious freedom on principle. Cecil Calvert preached toleration in Maryland for economic expediency as did the Dutch very soon in New Netherland. The Great Awakening, deistic philosophy, and the Revolution all tended to break down religious provincialism in the 18th-century colonies and make colonists aware of the possibility and necessity of a pluralistic society. Thus in the United States, through Article VI of the Constitution (1789), the First Amendment of the Bill of Rights (1791), and the Due Process Clause of the Fourteenth Amendment (1868), legal coercion was universally rejected. This was based on the assumption that man was essentially good and free, able not only to choose his own salvation, but even to discriminate between competing religious claims. Separation meant modified ideologies, institutions, and practices for both church and state. The religious bodies lost financial support and coercive power, and tasted the almost unique experience of self-government. They could no longer depend upon the state to provide them with new members. This "voluntaryism" meant that the religious bodies were compelled to build their own financial resources, devise an ecclesiastical discipline, actively seek converts, and become primarily missionary and evangelizing societies. Separation also came to mean a specialized role for Christianity in society, in contrast with the traditional ideal of universal Christian responsibility for civilization. Secular solution to social and political conflicts came to be widely accepted by Christians as appropriate and workable. The role of religion in a secular society has not yet been entirely clarified, whether moral, political, educational, or ideological. Separation intensified a Puritan-oriented tendency on the part of the denominations to view outward forms as of secondary importance and matters of ecclesiology, theology, and piety have consequently become unrelated religious activities. The denominations have come to stress an individualistic and private religious experience while Christian diversity is accepted as a perpetual condition.

Religious bodies have sometimes tended to pay homage to the currents of social and cultural customs in order to win adherents. Religious growth sometimes came to be closely associated with an ability to bring denominational interests and goals into harmony with those of society. Denominations have in some cases become representatives of "culture religion," yet without being coerced to do so by the state. They have gained freedom from interference by the state but sometimes seem to stand in bondage to popular tastes. For the state, separation has meant that religion can no longer provide the explicit ideological rationale for its goals and existence that it has traditionally provided, and secular explanations must be devised. The First Amendment prohibited Congress from interfering with religious freedom either directly or by the establishment of a national church, but this applied only to the Federal Government, and in some states establishment or semiestablishment continued until far into the 19th century (Connecticut, 1818; Massachusetts, 1833; New Hampshire, 1876). Not until 1934 did the Supreme Court specify religious liberty in the states under the Fourteenth Amendment, although since 1925 it has been clear that neither the states nor the Federal Government could invade private religious liberty arbitrarily. The Jehovah's Witnesses case of 1940 reinforced these decisions. In recent years separation has also been interpreted to prohibit states from using tax money or tax-supported facilities to aid religion directly, though indirect aid to parochial schools in the form of bus transportation (1947) and free lunches (1946) has been approved. In 1962 and 1963 separation was applied to forbid the use of any officially prescribed prayers or communal Bible-reading in public schools. There has been a fluidity in the historical development of separation that is not always clearly understood, and most American denominations have not formulated a comprehensive and synthetic position on separation, religious liberty, and voluntaryism.

BIBLIOGRAPHY: W. S. Hudson, *The Great Tradition of the American Churches* (New York, 1953); W. H. Marnell, *The First Amendment: The History of Religious Freedom in America* (Garden City, 1964); S. E. Mead, *The Lively Experiment* (New York, 1963); J. H. Nichols, *Democracy and the Churches* (Philadelphia, 1951); A. P. Stokes and L. Pfeffer, *Church and State in the United States* (New York, 1964); J. F. Wilson (ed.), *Church and State in American History* (Boston, 1965).

**Separatism.** The policy of those Puritan churchmen who were not satisfied with the Elizabethan Settlement after 1559 and therefore formed congregations separate from the Establishment. They were generally radical in their desire to be rid of "the filthy rags of Popery" and wanted to carry forward the reform of the church without "tarrying for anie," especially not for the magistrate (see BROWNE, ROBERT). While the conforming or Presbyterian Puritans wanted to stay within the Established Church and seek reforms, the Separatists sought to withdraw and found their own "true congregations" according to the Word of God.

**Sequence.** A rhythmical prose or metrical hymn, originating in the High Middle Ages, which was derived from the musical prolongation (*sequentia*) of the last vowel of the Alleluia used responsively between Epistle and Gospel at certain festal Masses. Of the hundreds in use before the Reformation only four ("Victimae Paschali," at Easter; "Veni, Sancte Spiritus," at Pentecost; "Lauda Sion," at Corpus Christi; "Dies Irae," at All Souls') survived the reform of the Missal under Pius V, and another ("Stabat Mater," on the two Feasts of Our Lady's Seven Sorrows) was added in 1727.

**Serampore College.** A school located in West Bengal, India, founded in 1818 by William Carey to educate ministers. The king of Denmark in 1827 granted a charter giving power to confer all degrees. Originally Baptist, the college was reconstituted on interdenominational lines in 1910, the charter was revived and recognized by the Bengal Legislative Act of 1918, and other theological schools were represented in the Senate. Through a syllabus and examinations, students of these schools receive Serampore B.D. and M.Th. degrees.

**Seraphim of Sarov** (1759–1833). One of the best-known "holy teachers" of modern Russia. The son of a merchant, he embraced the religious life when eighteen years of age and pursued the vigorous Eastern ascetic tradition. In 1825 he opened his doors to the world after seventeen years of seclusion. An unending stream of pilgrims soon made their way to the isolated monastery of Sarov. At times it was said that as many as four thousand to five thousand people came to his door daily, where they found an ascetic-looking holy man dressed in white. He heard many of their confessions, counseled with others on their problems, and was also reputed to have the gift of healing.

**Serapion** (d. 211). Bishop of Antioch (with jurisdiction as far as Rhossus, thirty miles away). He actively opposed Montanism and wrote a dissuasive against conversion to Judaism. On a visit to Rhossus he approved the apocryphal Gospel of Peter; on returning to Antioch he read it more carefully, conferred with Docetist users of the book, and sent a list of unorthodox passages back to Rhossus. Antioch, like Rome, was becoming a metropolitan. (See Palut.)

**Serapion of Thmuis** (d. after 360). Fourth-century Christian prelate. After living as a monk and companion of Antony of Egypt, he became bishop of Thmuis (c. 339). He was a friend and protégé of Athanasius, who sent him on an embassy to Constantius and wrote him letters on the Spirit. His own writings include a treatise against the Manichees and a correspondence with Apollinarius during his orthodox period. The Sacramentary bearing his name is a compilation, the origin of which may be traceable to him.

**Serbian Orthodox Church.** An autocephalous member of the Eastern Orthodox communion tracing its origins back beyond the first archbishop, Sava, named in 1219. The medieval Serbian monarch, warrior, and lawgiver, Stephen Dushan, assigned the rank of patriarch to the metropolitan at Pech. In 1389, Serbs were made tributary to the Turkish sultan after their defeat at Kosovo. Their patriarchate was abolished in 1765 and they were returned to the religious sway of Constantinople. Prelates were Phanariot (residents of Constantinople), Greeks who too often were ignorant both of the language and customs of the Serbs. When Serbia won the right to its own dynasty in 1830, Prince Milosh Obrenovitch was able to secure (1832) autonomy for the church. It did not become autocephalous until 1879 after the final recognition of Serbian independence by the Congress of Berlin treaty. When Yugoslavia was united at the close of 1918, the church was enlarged by the consolidation of six former separate jurisdictions (e.g., Montenegro). The rank of patriarch was restored at Belgrade in 1920. The Serbian Orthodox Church resisted the Axis during World War II. Marshal Tito in 1955 stated that Communist Yugoslavia aimed to drive the church from public life. Yet his representatives attended the enthronment at Pech of the Serbian patriarch (May 29, 1961), hinting at a *détente*.

**Sergiev, John** (1821–1908). Russian priest, better known as Father John of Kronshtadt.

He was considered a saint even during his lifetime, a unique distinction in Eastern Orthodoxy, for he was not a monk but a married secular priest whose reputation for spirituality and healing brought Russians of all classes to his door for assistance. A great teacher and practitioner of prayer, Father John is the author of *My Life in Christ,* a work translated into many languages and read faithfully to this day.

**Sergius** (Sergij of Radonež) (c. 1314–c. 1392). The most revered of Russian saints. Born at Rostov, he lived in Radonež, near Moscow, until 1335, when he retreated to a hermit's life in the forests. Disciples began to gather around him, and at the wish of the patriarch of Constantinople he founded near Moscow the monastery of the Holy Trinity, which became the most celebrated monastic community in Russia and the first of many such foundations. Sergius was a respected and influential adviser to the grand duke of Moscow, but refused the offer of the metropolitan see of Moscow in 1378.

**Sergius I** (d. 701). Pope from 687. Born in Antioch and educated at Palermo, he baptized Caedwalla, king of Wessex, in 689. He supported the English mission to Frisia, consecrating Willibrord as archbishop of the Frisians in 695. The attempt of the emperor to enforce the decrees of the Trullan Synod (692) were resisted by Sergius. When imperial officials attempted to remove him to Constantinople, he was rescued by the Roman people.

**Serra, Junípero** (1713–1784). Spanish Franciscan missionary in California. Entering the order in 1730, Serra became professor of philosophy at the Lullian University of Palma. In 1750 he arrived in Mexico City to serve the Apostolic College of San Fernando. For nine years he was missionary to the Sierra Gorda Indians, translating the Catechism. In 1767, as *presidente,* he became the guiding force in the mission to Upper and Lower California. Eventually twenty-one missions were founded; Serra was personally responsible for San Diego (1769), San Carlos (1770), San Antonio, San Gabriel (1771), San Luis Obispo (1772), San Francisco de Assisi, San Juan Capistrano (1776), Santa Clara (1777), San Buenaventura (1782). His preaching was extraordinary, and included pounding his breast with a stone, scourging himself, and applying a lighted torch to his chest, to move people to penance. By 1783, six thousand Indians were baptized and fifty-three hundred confirmed. Serra was also instrumental in improving farming and living conditions. He experienced difficulties with local authorities over his actions, but vindicated himself to the viceroy in *Representacion* (1773). Enabled to administer confirmation in 1778, he was nevertheless prevented from doing so until 1780. Serra was noted for his executive ability and profound piety. His *Diario* gives an account of early missions in Spanish Mexico and California.

**Servetus, Michael** (1511–1553). Spanish physician and heretic. As a brilliant young student, Servetus discovered that the Nicene doctrine of the Trinity used non-Biblical terms, and after study of the Bible and the ante-Nicene fathers he formulated another view, rich in Eucharistic and baptismal theology. He published his views in 1531 and again in 1553, which led to his execution in Geneva as a heretic. He held that the Spirit, only a power and not a person, infiltered the seed of the Word, the heavenly flesh, into Jesus so that Christ became the natural Son of God and the fullness of God. An early modalism, denying the eternal generation of the Word, gave way to a view of the eternity of the Word which was also eternal Light and Substance, God's idea of perfect Man, progressively being incarnated until the world's eventual deification and God's eventual mundification. The incarnation occurred in men through an inner and outer baptism (at thirty, by immersion) resulting in the believer's salvation from spiritual and physical death, from distorted knowledge and propensity to hatred. The believer was further nourished in the Eucharist by Christ's celestial flesh. Faith began with devotion to Christ rather than with adherence to the fallen, Constantinian, Trinitarian church. Servetus was also an anatomist and geographer, and urged that the Bible be understood in its historical context. His most notable scientific achievement was his discovery of the pulmonary circulation of the blood.

**Servites** (*or* Order of the Servants of Mary). A mendicant order founded by seven prominent Florentines who began to live as hermits in 1233. Gradually their community grew into the order which was officially sanctioned in 1304. The members wear a black habit and follow the Augustinian Rule. Under Philip Benizi (1233–1285), the order began extensive mission work. There are also contemplative nuns within the order, and a conventual third order.

**Servus Servorum Dei** ("Servant of the Servants of God"). A title referring to the pope, generally used in official documents after the time of Gregory VII. The title was first used by Gregory I.

**Seton, Elizabeth Ann Bayley** (1774–1821). American religious. Upon the death of her husband, William Magee Seton, Elizabeth became a convert to Roman Catholicism (1805). She founded and was the first mother superior of the Sisters of Charity in the United States.

**Settlement Houses.** Centers set up in congested city areas to provide educational, recreational, medical, etc., services for underprivileged people. These institutions helped create a new attitude toward charity and social justice among the Protestant churches in the post-Civil War period, a new direction in the response of the churches and the people of wealth who often dominated them to the conditions of immigrants and poor laborers in the cities. Isolated from the scenes of social injustice and unrest, most Protestants maintained the traditional attitude which regarded individual charity as sufficient to alleviate the conditions of the poor. The new direction was indicated by the establishment of Toynbee Hall in London in 1884. Whereas earlier missionaries had lived in the better parts of town, the group at Toynbee Hall made their home in the slums in order to gain firsthand knowledge of the needs of those they hoped to serve. Jane Addams visited Toynbee Hall and returned to Chicago to establish Hull House in 1889, a project that eventually attracted worldwide attention. Graham Taylor's Chicago Commons Social Settlement was another pioneer settlement in the United States.

The object of the settlement was not only to allow workers to participate full time in the life of the slum community but also, as Jane Addams envisioned it, to become a model and a catalyst for social action and community cooperation. The settlement served as school, church, library, bathhouse, theater, art gallery, bank, and hospital, but primarily as a center where the disintegrated life of a slum community could give way to social interaction.

The success of the pioneer settlements led to the founding of similar institutions in most major cities. They were usually established in connection with either a university or a seminary, in order that students might gain experimental knowledge of social problems on which rational projects of reform and institutionalized social justice could be based.

**Seventh-day Adventists.** A religious denomination that grew out of the ministry of William Miller. This group is a conservative, legalistic, premillennial body which emphasizes the observance of Saturday as the Sabbath and acknowledges the inspiration of Ellen G. White. William Miller and Mrs. White were 19th-century Americans who believed that Christ would return in 1844. The Adventists began by rationalizing the Biblical passages which they felt had been fulfilled then. However, they were not formally organized until 1863. They now believe that the only prophetic texts waiting to be fulfilled concern their church and its ministry. When the Adventist message has been proclaimed throughout the world and their church has been built to its predestined size, then the end of the age will come. Besides their prophetic interests, the Adventists believe in soul sleep until the resurrection of the dead, when the faithful will be rewarded while the wicked will be destroyed. Adventists practice baptism by total immersion and have a congregational church polity tempered by local and national conferences. The group has a heavy commitment to missions, printing, and education. There are approximately 3,326 Seventh-day Adventist churches with 370,688 members in the United States, and the worldwide membership is believed to be approximately twice this figure.

**Severian** (flourished c. 400). Bishop of Gabala (Syria). He is chiefly remembered as a leading exegete of the Antiochene reaction to allegorical exegesis. He seems to have been a pupil of Diodorus of Tarsus (as evidenced by large fragments of a *Commentary to all the Epistles of St. Paul* in Biblical catenae). About thirty of his homilies are extant, including six on the Hexaemeron and a set of nine in Armenian. Most of his surviving writings have been attributed to Chrysostom.

**Severinus** (d. 482). Apostle of Noricum (Austria). After the death of Attila (453) he moved into the Roman province of Noricum and founded two monasteries. While the sons of Attila were fighting among themselves, Severinus won the respect of the barbarians and the Romans by bringing material aid and by moderating the ferocity of the destruction in this conflict. Odoacer is said to have asked the blessing of Severinus with regard to his plans to invade Italy.

**Severus of Antioch** (c. 460–538). Leading theologian of the Monophysites. He was born in Pisidia, studied at Alexandria and Beirut, and was early interested in theology, though he was not baptized until 488. After his baptism he became a monk in Egypt, then lived at Constantinople as a representative of his party, and in 512 was made patriarch of Antioch. His letters give a vivid picture of the human problems of church life in an age of conflict. On the accession of Justin I in 518 he was expelled from Antioch and took refuge in Egypt—though also at times visiting Constantinople, for instance, for the unsuccessful religious colloquy of 536 between Monophysites and Chalcedonians. The more extreme party represented by Julian of Halicarnassus predominated for a time, but Severus was the ranking Monophysite until his death, and his theology came to prevail, especially in Syria. He was equally opposed to any obscuring of the humanity of Christ and to any separation of the divine and human natures—in fact, he seems to differ only verbally from contemporary Chalcedonians such as Leontius of Byzantium. Many of his works—letters, sermons, and treatises—which are lost in Greek are preserved in Syriac translations.

**Sext.** The brief worship consisting of psalms, hymn, short lesson, and collect, said at the sixth hour (about twelve o'clock) in monasteries. Private prayer at noon is an ancient and widespread custom (also in Islam). Peter prays at that time in Acts 10:9. Like Terce and None, it is a "little hour" which is meant to bring to periodic formulation the constant prayer of a Christian's daily activity.

**Sextus, Sayings of.** A collection of proverbs compiled by a Christian at the end of the 2d century, setting forth a mixture of Neo-Pythagorean and Christian concepts about God and the spiritual (ascetic) life. First quoted by Origen (e.g., *Contra Celsum* 8. 30), they were translated into Latin by Rufinus, who ascribed them to the Roman bishop Sixtus II. Jerome ridiculed Rufinus' view and insisted that they were Pythagorean.

**Shaftesbury, Earl of.** See ASHLEY COOPER, ANTHONY.

**Shakers.** A communal, pacifistic sect from England also known as the United Society of Believers in Christ's Second Appearing, the Millennial Church, and the Alethians. Of Quaker origin, the sect was founded by Jane and James Wardley in 1747 and later dominated by "Mother" Ann Lee. Persecuted and under the guidance of a "revelation," Ann Lee and eight followers emigrated to America in 1774 and settled near Watervliet, N.Y. Revivalism produced converts, and in 1787 the first Shaker society was formed at Lebanon, N.Y. By the time of the Kentucky revival (1800–1804) there were Shakers in New York, Massachusetts, Connecticut, Kentucky, Ohio, and Indiana. Mostly noted for celibacy, communism, and the unique worship that gave them their name, Shakers held that God was both male and female, as were Adam and the angels and spirits as well. Christ, one of the superior spirits, appeared in Jesus as the male principle. In Mother Ann the female principle of Christ was manifested, and in her the promise of the Second Coming was fulfilled. The millennium began with the forming of the Shaker Church. Shaker communism was characterized by celibacy, confession of sin, common property, faith healing, and separation from the world. Worldly goods were repudiated and self-sufficiency encouraged. A shift from agriculture to manufacturing caused some internal controversy. In 1874 there were 2,415 members in 58 communities. By 1905 fewer than 1,000 members existed, and in 1950 there were less than 100 in five communities.

**Shakespeare, John Howard** (1857–1928). Baptist minister and leader in England. John Shakespeare held a pastorate in Norwich for fifteen years, but his primary contribution was to be in the field of organization. He became secretary of the Baptist Union in 1898, a position he held for twenty years. Under his guidance, the Union developed into an effective organization, and Shakespeare came to be recognized as a man of ability and influence. He was responsible to a large extent for the establishment of the Baptist World Alliance in 1905. During World War I, as president of the National Free Church Council, he broke through British tradition so that Baptist and other evangelical chaplains could be appointed to minister to the army. Shakespeare was continually stressing the importance of the Baptists' abandoning their tradition of autonomous congregations and uniting for mutual benefits and support. Largely through his efforts, the Federal Council of the Evangelical Free Churches was founded in 1919, with Shakespeare as its first moderator. In his strong desire for an ecumenical dialogue not only between various branches of the Baptist Church but among all Protestants, he expressed himself as willing to make numerous concessions, even that of accepting reordination from bishops of the Church of England. Few of Shakespeare's fellow Baptists were willing to follow him such a distance toward reunion, and many of his efforts were thwarted as a result of their reticence. His book *The Churches at the Crossroads,* published in 1918, presents an impassioned plea for the ecumenical movement in Protestantism.

**Sharp, Granville** (1735–1813). English philanthropist and social reformer. He spent most of his adult life working for the freedom of the slaves. His defense of the Negro slave James Somerset led to the Somerset decision (1772), by which it was declared "that as soon as any slave sets his foot upon English territory, he becomes free." He conceived the idea of a colony for liberated slaves which later materialized in the settlement of Sierra Leone. During the last years of his life he took a prominent part in founding the British and Foreign Bible Society.

**Sharp, James** (c. 1618–1679). Scottish churchman devoted to the cause of royal supremacy and episcopacy in Scotland. In 1637, Sharp graduated M.A. from King's College, Aberdeen. At the outbreak of the covenanting strife he went to Oxford, possibly having been expelled for refusing to take the covenanting oath. Aberdeen was the center of episcopalian sentiment in Scotland, and Sharp was drawn to the episcopalian view of church order. Just before he was to take episcopal orders he was forced by illness to return to Scotland and to St. Leonard's College. In 1648 he became minister at Crail. In the great schism between Resolutioners and Protesters he supported the resolution of 1650 and soon became prominent in the debate. He was arrested by Cromwell and spent eight months in the Tower. Sharp was involved in the restoration of Charles II and was used by the king in his plan to restore episcopacy in Scotland. While lulling presbyterian suspicions, he played a double role which became apparent when in 1661, Parliament established episcopacy, and Sharp was consecrated archbishop of St. Andrews. His measures to curb the covenanting spirit were severe, and he refused to consider Leighton's plan to blend presbyterianism and episcopacy. He became an object of intense hatred and his murder was an act of retribution by some men of Fife.

**Sheldon, Charles Monroe** (1857–1946). Congregational clergyman and author. Sheldon gained fame as a writer while he served as pastor in Vermont and Kansas. His most famous book, *In His Steps* (1896), sold 25 million copies and aroused national demand for social reform. An effort in 1900 to edit the *Topeka Daily Capital* "just as Jesus would have done it" created nationwide interest. From 1920 to 1925 he edited the *Christian Herald.*

**Shenoute** (c. 360–450). Abbot for many years of the White Monastery near Akhmîm in Upper Egypt, which followed a strict form of the Rule of Pachomius. His attacks on paganism, vigorous guidance of monks and laity, and organization of relief after Bedouin raids made him a national hero of the Egyptian Church. His writings (letters and sermons) are the chief monuments of original Christian literature in Coptic.

**Shepard, Thomas** (c. 1605–1649). New England Puritan preacher. After going to Boston from England in 1635 he served the church at Cambridge and was active in the controversies of the day. He was a member of the Cambridge Synod of 1648 which adopted a confession of faith and plan of church government for New England Congregationalism. Among his many interests was a concern for the conversion of the Indians.

**Shields, Thomas Todhunter** (1873–1955). Canadian Baptist. He was educated in Bristol, England. After ordination in 1897 he became minister at the Baptist Church, Delhi, Ontario (1897–1900). Thereafter he was minister at the Wentworth Baptist Church, Hamilton (1900–1903), the Adelaide Street Baptist Church, London, Ontario (1903–1910), and the Jarvis Street Church, Toronto, Ontario (1910–1955). In 1922 he founded *The Gospel Witness,* a controversial fundamentalist paper. He was president of the Baptist Bible Union of North America (1923–1930) and president of the Toronto Baptist Seminary (1927–1955). He was also a member of the board of governors of McMaster University for eight years.

**Sibylline Oracles.** Oracles that were ascribed to various Sibylline prophetesses and circulated in the Hellenistic world, and in the 2d century B.C. such oracles in Greek hexameters composed by Jewish writers. Christians (especially between A.D. 80 and 180) added other oracles to the Jewish collection. The writings presented apocalyptic prophecies in Sibylline form and became so popular among Christians that their opponents called them "Sibyllists."

**Sic et Non.** A collection of texts from the Bible and from the commentaries of the fathers compiled by Abelard about 1122. Abelard juxtaposed contradictory texts to serve as exercises to train his students in logic. The texts collected in the main body of the work are a valuable compendium of the writings of the fathers available to 12th-century scholars. It is the Preface, however, that has become famous, for in it Abelard taught that the key to knowledge was doubt, since doubt moved one to inquiry and inquiry led to truth.

**Sicilian Vespers.** A revolt of the Sicilians against Charles of Anjou, so named because it broke out in Palermo at Vespers on Easter Monday, March 30, 1282. The rebels, aided by the intervention of the Aragonese king, completely destroyed the Angevin authority on the island, wrecking Charles's plans for an invasion of the Byzantine Empire. Recently it has been shown that the Byzantine emperor Michael VIII Palaeologus secretly subsidized the Sicilian malcontents and the Aragonese king.

**Sickingen, Franz von** (1481–1523). A powerful member of the German Estate of Knights which had gradually lost its political, military, and social status with the decline of feudalism and the rise of mercenary armies under the command of ecclesiastical and secular princes. He and other knights saw in the Reformation an opportunity to advance their political aim of reducing the influence of the territorial princes by furthering a national movement, at the same time enhancing their own position by freeing the Empire from the domination of the pope and his servants, the ecclesiastical princes. Thus he offered Luther asylum both before and after the Diet of Worms, an offer that Luther rejected. In 1522, Sickingen led an army of knights against the archbishop of Trier but was repulsed. The following year he was killed when the archbishop besieged his castle at Landstuhl and crushed the knights' revolt. Luther, who had dedicated his work *On Confession* (1522) to Sickingen, deplored the use of force and political means which only served to compromise the Reformation as a spiritual movement. Opinion is divided over whether Sickingen's enthusiasm for the Reformation was genuine or whether he sought through it to secularize the wealth of the church for the economic, political, and social benefit of the knights.

**Sidonius Apollinaris** (c. 439–c. 480). Early Christian bishop, politician, and writer. A prominent landholder of Clermont in central Gaul, he wrote poems reflecting the life of a cultured Roman layman. They include eulogies of several of the shadowy Western emperors of the 460's. One of them, Avitus, was Sidonius' father-in-law; another, the emperor Anthemius, made Sidonius prefect of Rome in 468. On returning to Gaul, he found Clermont threatened by the advancing power of the Visigoths. Shortly, probably in 471, the citizens chose him as their bishop, looking for a civil protector as well as a pastor. Trying in vain to prevent the fall of Clermont, or at least to smooth the transition to Gothic rule, he was for a time imprisoned by the Visigothic king Euric. He soon returned to Clermont to end his days in peace, probably not long after 480. As a bishop he turned from poetry to prose; his nine books of letters reflect his considerable acquaintance among both Gallo-Romans, lay and clerical, and Goths. As a churchman he was conscientious rather than conspicuously devout, as a writer correct rather than brilliant; but his writings are an important source for the social life of this transitional period, including its ecclesiastical aspects.

**Siegmund-Schultze, Friedrich** (1885–    ). German ecumenical figure. Siegmund-Schultze established and controlled the influential Student Lebensgemeinschaft (1911), assumed leadership of the Berlin youth welfare office (1917), and became honorary professor of youth science on the Berlin faculty (1926). In 1933 he moved to Switzerland to aid German refugees, especially Jewish. He was named director of the social-educational seminary at Dortmund, and honorary professor at Münster (1948). Active in ecumenical affairs after 1914, Siegmund-Schultze established the ecumenical archives in Soest in 1959. He edited *Eiche* (1912–1932), and the *Ökumenische Jahrbuch* until 1937.

**Sieveking, Amalie** (1794–1859). German social reformer. The daughter of a well-to-do family from Hamburg, Germany, she was appalled by the social conditions of her time and founded a school for the poor in 1813. She nursed victims of the cholera epidemic in 1831 and founded a League of Women for the Care of the Poor and the Sick in 1832. She refused important positions of leadership in church and government in order to pursue her own fight against poverty and disease, and was a champion of the Christian Women's Movement in Germany.

**Siger of Brabant** (c. 1240–c. 1284). Aristotelian rationalist and early defender of the autonomy of philosophy. He studied at Paris and became a master in 1265, professing monopsychism and the eternity of matter. Attacked by Thomas Aquinas and Bonaventure, condemned by the bishop, and cited before the Inquisition, he fled to the Curia at Orvieto, where he was cleared of charges of heresy but forced to remain. He was murdered by his clerk in a fit of insanity.

**Sigismund II Augustus** (1520–1572). King of Poland and Lithuania. Sigismund, the last of the Jagellon line, succeeded his father in 1548. He was sympathetic to the ideals of humanism as well as to the Reformation, and during his reign many of the educated classes espoused Calvinism. Eventually, however, political unrest among the nobles led him to take the side of the Roman Catholic bishops; in 1564 he accepted the decrees of the Council of Trent from the papal legate. Even though non-Roman groups received religious freedom the year after Sigismund died, they were never able to present a united front.

**Sigismund III** (Sigismund Vasa) (1566–1632). King of Poland and Sweden. He was the son of John III of Sweden and Princess Catherine of Poland. A staunch Roman Catholic, he became king of Poland in 1587, encouraged the Jesuits in their work with the people, and did everything he could to aid the eventual reunion of the Ruthenian Orthodox with Rome (see BREST-LITOVSK, UNION OF). His piety sometimes outweighed his prudence and in 1592 he was indicted by the Polish Diet for granting Polish property to Austria. Two years later he received the Swedish crown (1594) but refused to support the national Lutheran religion. As a result he was not admitted into the country and the regent, his uncle (Charles IX), eventually took over the throne (1604). In Poland the reign of Sigismund marked the virtual destruction of the Reformed Church as an organized body.

**Sigtuna Foundation.** An organization established in Sweden by Manfred Björkquist in 1915 for the creative encounter of church and culture. It is located on Lake Mäler just north of Stockholm. There is a large library, schools, and a conference center where problems of society are discussed in a Christian framework. Dramas are performed in summer, especially those by Olov Hartman, the present director.

**Silesius, Angelus** (1624–1677). Pen name used by the mystical poet and controversialist Johannes Scheffler. He was led to the Catholic faith by his reading of Jakob Boehme and the church fathers. His chief fame rests on his mystical poems published as *Heilige Seelenlust* and *Der cherubinische Wandersmann*. Many of his poems have found a place in both Protestant and Roman Catholic hymnals.

**Simeon, Charles** (1759–1836). Evangelical Anglican rector and preacher, a leader of the early 19th-century Low Church party. Chided by opponents as "more a Church-man than a Gospel-man," he held the cure of Holy Trinity, Cambridge, for half a century. Simeon was a friend of the British and Foreign Bible Society and an organizer of the Church Missionary Society (antislavery, Bible circulation, mission aid). Extensive writings reflect his attachment to the Anglican order and ordinances.

**Simeon of Thessalonica** (d. 1429). Byzantine archbishop, theologian, and liturgist. Of his preepiscopal life nothing is known save his fervor as a monk. A significant author in his own day, he wrote widely on doctrinal and liturgical matters, his main work being a *Dialogue Against All Heresies and on the One Faith*. He expounded the creeds, explained the Greek ritual, and controverted Turks, Jews, and the Church of Rome.

**Simeon Stylites** (c. 390–459). First and most famous of the pillar hermits. He became an anchorite near Antioch before the age of twenty. Some ten years later he took up his abode on a pillar, low at first, but gradually increased to 60 or 70 feet. Here, never descending, he lived until his death in 459, widely influencing the religious and even the political life of his time by his preaching and teaching.

**Simon de Montfort** (d. 1218). Crusader against the Albigenses. The fourth of his line, he took the cross in 1199 and set out upon the ill-starred Fourth Crusade. The inheritor of the earldom of Leicester, England, through his mother, Simon became in 1208 the agent of the papacy and the French Crown as leader of the "crusade" against the Albigensian heretics in southern France. He was noted for his cruelty in the suppression of these "enemies of the church." He died in the siege of Toulouse.

**Simony.** The intended or consummated buying or selling of spiritual objects, or of temporal objects to which a spiritual value has become attached. The term is derived from Acts 8:18–24, in which Simon Magus offered to pay Peter for the gift of the Holy Spirit. The apocryphal Apostolic Canons (late 4th century, Syria) decreed that any cleric who had obtained orders through money payment should be deposed as Simon Magus had been by Peter. The Council of Chalcedon (451) condemned as simony the ordinations, or the provision of offices, obtained by money. The simoniac and any cleric connected with the transaction were to be deposed. If one of the parties was a layman, he was to be excommunicated. The decrees against simony were reiterated in the local councils of the following centuries. In 787, a new dimension was added; the decrees against simony were applied to heads of monasteries who demanded payment from those seeking to be members of the community. Simony was one of the three great evils attacked by the church reformers of the 11th century. The decrees against simony were embodied by Gratian in his Code of Canon Law. The Third and Fourth Lateran Councils and the Council of Trent repeated the prohibitions against the abuse. Pius IX deleted the penalties against simoniacal ordinations. The current legislation may be found in Canons 727–730 of the Roman Church.

**Simplicianus** (d. 400). Bishop of Milan from 397 until his death. He had been tutor to Ambrose, moving to Milan from Rome to prepare his pupil for baptism and ordination upon his election as bishop in 373. Upon Ambrose's death, Simplicianus succeeded him in the see. He was instrumental in the conversions of Victorinus and Augustine (who acknowledges his debt to Simplicianus in his *Confessions*, Book 8).

**Simplicius** (d. 483). Pope from 468. He was born at Tivoli. During his reign, the imperial authority was overthrown in the West and the government taken over by Odoacer. In the controversies with the Monophysites, he defended the Chalcedonian Formula, resisting attempts by the emperor Zeno to enforce theological unity with his Henoticon. Disagreement over this document forced a schism between Rome and Constantinople which lasted until 519 (see ACACIAN SCHISM).

**Simpson, Matthew** (1811–1884). Methodist bishop. Born in Cadiz, Ohio, he entered the ministry with little formal education, rising rapidly and becoming president of Indiana Asbury College (later DePauw). He was active in political life and spoke out on social issues, including slavery. During the Civil War he was a friend of Lincoln and Stanton and expressed himself effectively in support of the Union cause.

**Sin.** As part of the whole problem of evil, the doctrine of sin has been perennially discussed throughout Christian history. Sometimes said to be the only Christian doctrine capable of empirical exhibition, sin—its nature and its origin—has defied simple description. It has all the mystery of the familiar.

Four general types of description may be observed. A characteristically Socratic description of the flaws in man's acts attributes them to ignorance. If, as is argued, "no man ever willingly does less than the good he knows," then a defective act is the simple consequence of defective knowledge. Doubtless, given this view, men bear the cost of their ignorance, but ignorance is no morally culpable condition. Here is no talk of guilt, and the principal means to overcome the problem is education. With this view there is no need for any idea of a fall from perfection.

A second view—one which might be called Platonic and which is influential among the Christian fathers—sees the flaw as a privation of the good. The argument depends, perhaps, upon the assertion that unmitigated evil is simply impossible. One thus obtains the axiom: "To the extent that it exists, everything is good." Utter evil simply cannot exist. Sin, therefore, is a condition in which man falls away from a goodness that is his proper end.

Among Christian fathers, this view of evil as privation was combined with the Biblical accounts of the fall of men and of angels, and one gains the picture of a universe which, as a whole, is falling away and stands in need of redemption. Subsequent to Adam an individual sins because of the tendency of the cosmos. That the falling away never becomes complete is witness to God's work as preserver and redeemer.

Church fathers given to this view were influenced by classical Greek thought to the extent that they made a great deal of Christ as Savior by teaching men about the error of their ways. Yet it was obvious to them that given so radical a view, sin was not to be remedied as if it were simply ignorance of the good to be sought. There is, accordingly, a more radical view of redemption as found, for example, in Athanasius and Anselm.

A third view often complements the second. It is one seemingly most Biblical, and it might today be characterized as existential. It is that view of sin which is expressed in Augustine's self-admission that he never committed a sin unwillingly. This is the view of sin as a flawed will. Socrates could not understand how it might be possible for a man not to will to do the good that he knows. The apostle Paul speaks for this Biblical tradition in asserting that there can be a conflict between knowledge and will. This third view is most illuminated by the doctrine of the Fall.

It seems clear that a privation from the good may take place by small degrees. The initial deflection from a creature's proper end may be so slight as to be imperceptible. When, however, the flaw is a rebellious will, the initial act of rebellion is the complete characterization of the individual: man cannot lose his innocence by degrees. Similarly, redemption is not by degrees. It is this view of sin which accords with the Biblical images having to do with the substitution of an innocent victim in place of the guilty one.

Yet, while this view of sin is compatible with the Biblical ideas of sin's extreme nature, there has been a continual insistence that so total a view of sin leads to moral indifference. This is in large part the issue at stake in the noteworthy controversy between Augustine and Pelagius. Pelagius felt that man, if of totally corrupt will, could not be a responsible moral agent. Since, however, man is spoken of as a responsible agent, his will must be free. For Augustine, on the contrary, man was completely dependent upon God to overcome the radical defect stemming from the fall of Adam. Those who would agree with Augustine are often bothered by his tendency to suggest that the consequences of Adam's fall were communicated to subsequent generations through the act of procreation.

Pelagius' views were condemned finally by the Second Council of Orange (529). His concerns, however, were to a degree perpetuated in the continuous tendency to speak primarily of sins rather than of sin. An individual could thus be required to examine his life, the nature of his acts, and amend those which were in need of amendment. While such a practice was not defective in moral seriousness, it frequently led to an excessive concern for self-analysis which was called scrupulosity. There was the further possibility, frequently exhibited, of developing a works righteousness.

It was this tendency, clearly evidenced throughout the late Middle Ages, which precipitated the Reformation by way of Luther's protest. Here one of the classic dilemmas of Christian history arises: A proper understanding of divine grace is accompanied by a profound conviction concerning the radical nature of man's sin—this, as commonly misconstrued, leads to moral indifferentism; on the other hand, the attempt to inculcate moral seriousness by a consideration of the nature of man's acts leads often to the crassest sort of doctrine of salvation by works.

A fourth view, continuously characterized as heretical, has been influential throughout the history of the church. Probably of Persian origin, it is the view that holds man to be a soul of divine origin imprisoned in a material body. The body is the source of all depraved appetites. This dualist view is frequently named for the Manichaeans, who were its influential advocates in the 3d and 4th centuries. Augustine was a Manichaean prior to his conversion, and elements of this doctrine are sometimes thought to be present in his later work —as in his notion that sin is transmitted by the act of procreation.

As has already been indicated, any discussion over the extent to which man is tainted by sin must inevitably involve also the issue of human freedom, and it is in these terms that the debate has frequently been conducted. The 17th-century debates between Arminians and Calvinists are an example.

Although the nature of sin is thus open to discussion and has been the topic for occasional council decrees, one cannot speak of any increment or specification of church teaching on the matter. The advance of psychology, however, has led to much speculation, and attempts have frequently been made to find ways of speaking of sin in psychological terms. Freudian terminology was most often particularly useful for speaking of sin in a radical fashion, but the attempts often were more Manichaean than orthodox.

Recent theology, while adding no new definitions, has generally chosen to speak of sin in social terms. The early fathers recognized, of course, that sin had social consequences. Against their general practice of finding the origin of sin in a personal act, however, recent theologians have tended to speak of sin as social in both origin and consequence. It is possible to suggest, for example, that Adam's fall was social in just this fashion: not only was the primal communion with God vitiated, but the relation between man and woman was at the same time damaged, and the element of shame arises as a sign of the damaging of these relationships.

Not only is this emphasis compatible with earlier teaching, it constitutes a rediscovery of some Old Testament ways of thinking about man: man is a psychosomatic unity who finds meaning to life in a rich variety of social relationships. The radical nature of Christian teaching about sin now becomes clear: sin is the loss of man's relationship with God, and at the same time his alienation from his own ends as a man. The Biblically holistic view of man is here evidenced. To be redeemed by Christ is to find the healing of all relationships. One thus overcomes some of the simplistic errors of earlier times which suggested that a man's relationship with God could be restored apart from his reconciliation with his fellows.

BIBLIOGRAPHY: S. Freud, *The Future of an Illusion* (Garden City, 1957); S. Kierkegaard, *The Concept of Dread* (Princeton, 1944); R. Niebuhr, *The Nature and Destiny of Man*, Vol. I (New York, 1964); D. E. Roberts, *Psychotherapy and a Christian View of Man* (New York, 1950); P. Schoonenberg, *Man and Sin* (Notre Dame, 1965).

**Singulari Nos.** Encyclical letter of Pope Gregory XVI, issued on June 25, 1834. It was a sequel to the earlier attack upon L'Avenir movement and the Abbé de Lamennais contained in the pope's *Mirari vos* (1832). Occasioned by the publication of Lamennais' *Paroles d'un croyant*, the pope condemned once more in *Singulari nos* the "liberties" advocated by Lamennais. The influence of Metternich and the legitimatist powers here seems obvious.

**Siricius** (c. 334–399). Pope, succeeding Damasus, from 384. He advanced the development of papal authority, issuing (in his Epistle to Himerius of Tarragona) the first papal decretals. He appointed the bishop of Thessalonica his vicar in Illyria for the defense of papal authority against encroachment by Constantinople. Siricius' pontificate also saw the last attempt at a revival of paganism in Rome (392–394) and the condemnation of Jovinian (c. 390).

**Sirmium, Council of** (357). Actually the second council to meet in Sirmium (the first was in 351), convened in 357 under the leadership of Germinius, bishop of Sirmium, and Valens and Ursacius, sometime personal disciples of Arius. It was here that Arianism received its extreme expression. In a creed that Hilary of Poitiers described as the *Exemplum blasphemiae apud Sirmium* (hence its common designation as "the blasphemy of Sirmium") the Arians forbade the description of the relation of the Father and the Son by the terms "substance" or "essence" in any form, "for this cause and reason, that it is not contained in the divine Scriptures and that it is beyond human knowledge." The creed also emphatically asserts the superiority of the Father and the subjection of the Son, "along with all the things which the Father subjected to Himself." This synod actually proved to be a turning point in the Arian controversy, provoking the moderate party to a countermeeting at Ancyra which issued anathemas covering all the extreme Arian doctrines. The resulting "Homoean" compromise, framed at Sirmium in May of 359, proved unstable after the death of the Arian emperor Constantius (361), and the return to Nicene orthodoxy grew steadily over the next twenty years until finally reaffirmed at Constantinople (381).

**Sirmond, Jacques** (1559–1651). French Jesuit scholar. He taught classical languages in Paris for a number of years and in 1590 became private secretary to the general of the Jesuit Order, Aquaviva, in Rome, where he became acquainted with Bellarmine, Baronius, and other Italian intellectuals. In 1608 Sirmond returned to France, became rector of Clermont, the Jesuit college in Paris (1617), and confessor to Louis XIII (1637–1643). He published numerous works: editions of Greek and Latin Christian writings, an edition of the early councils of France, and a dissertation rejecting the traditional identification of Dionysius the Areopagite and Dionysius (Denys) of Paris. In his ecclesiology Sirmond favored Gallicanism.

**Sisters of Charity.** Although this designation applies to a whole family of Roman Catholic religious orders for women, the best known and most numerous (c. forty-five thousand members today) of these orders is that congregation established by Vincent de Paul and Louise de Marillac in 1633. This sisterhood devotes itself to the performance of the corporal works of mercy, specifically among the poor.

**Sistine Chapel.** The private chapel of the popes in the Vatican Palace. Built for Sixtus IV in 1473, it is used for the celebration of most important papal functions, except for those held in St. Peter's Basilica itself. The cardinals' election of a new pope occurs in the Sistine Chapel. The chapel is noted for its choir and especially for its frescoes by Michelangelo. Particularly impressive is Michelangelo's *The Last Judgment*, which covers the altar wall.

**Six Articles.** The manifesto, issued at the instigation of Henry VIII in 1539, of the conservative principles of the "Henrician reaction," forbidding the furtherance of reformation beyond renunciation of papal supremacy. Conformity was required on each of six controversial issues: belief in transubstantiation, Communion in one kind, compulsory clerical celibacy, permanent obligation of vows of chastity (even after the dissolution of the monasteries), private Masses, and auricular confession.

**Sixtus** (Xystus) **II** (d. 258). Pope from 257. During the persecution of Valerian, which was directed especially against the leaders of the church, Sixtus was arrested in one of the cemeteries with four of his deacons and put to death on Aug. 6, 258 (see LAWRENCE).

**Sixtus IV** (Francesco della Rovere, 1414–1484). Pope from 1471. The son of a poor family, Sixtus entered the Franciscan Order, eventually becoming general of the order. Upon his election as pope, he was determined to make the papacy a great temporal power. For this reason, he became deeply involved in the internal affairs of the Italian states. During his reign, Italy was racked by intrigues and wars, with the opponents changing sides constantly. He made nepotism a regular part of his administration, elevating seven of his relatives to the cardinalate. One of them, a nephew, later became Julius II. Unfortunately, many of his relatives were unworthy of such preferment.

Art and learning flourished in the reign of Sixtus. He was the builder of the Sistine Chapel, which Michelangelo was to make famous. He was also responsible for the great frescoes in the Vatican Library, which he reestablished.

Sixtus made an effort as well to quiet the discontented elements in the church who were calling for reform. Under his direction the Waldenses of northern Italy were persecuted. He sanctioned the use of the Inquisition in Spain and its possessions in 1478. He annulled the decrees of the Council of Constance (1414–1418). Dominated by secular interests and largely unconcerned with abuses in the church, Sixtus added to the discontent of reform-minded churchmen.

**Sixtus V** (Felice Peretti, 1521–1590). Pope from 1585. Born in poverty he entered a Franciscan monastery at the age of twelve. At Rome from 1552, he was made inquisitor general in the Venetian Republic in 1557. However, disputes caused by the severity and zeal that were to characterize his reign caused his recall in 1560. Pius V made him vicar apostolic of the Franciscans, bishop in 1566, and cardinal in 1570. During the pontificate of Gregory XIII, whom he disliked, he remained in retirement (1579–1585), editing the works of Ambrose and discreetly watching the political events that finally led to his election as pope in 1585. Immediately he regrouped the temporal holdings of the papacy, and, putting into practice his favorite principle that riches as well as severity are necessary for good government, he inaugurated a financial reform that was to develop the papacy from bankruptcy to one of the richest kingdoms in Europe, despite an enormous outlay for new buildings. He also completely overhauled the central administration of the Roman Church so that a proper delegation of authority would effectively enforce the decrees of the Council of Trent. Both achievements earned him acclaim as a founder of the Roman Catholic Reformation, or Counter-Reformation. His death in 1590 saved Bellarmine's book on controversies from condemnation, and the Jesuits from drastic constitutional revisions.

**Skoptsy.** Russian dissident sect originating in the 18th century in reaction to the orgiastic tendencies of the Khlysty. Early leader Selivanov preached that sexual drives were the source of sin, hindering the progress of people toward God; the only way to avoid temptations of the flesh was by making it impossible for people to sin. The sect practiced emasculation; hence their name Skoptsy ("the Castrated").

**Skovoroda, Gregory Savvich** (1722–1794). Russian philosopher. He was influenced by Western thought which he absorbed at the

Kiev Academy and during his travels in the West. He taught for several years in theological colleges, but by 1765 he had become a free ecclesiastical thinker. He insisted on the right of free creative activity within a basic loyalty to the Russian Orthodox Church. His thought was deeply rooted in Scripture, with strong moral and mystical overtones.

**Slavonic, Old Church.** A dialect of Old Slavonic which became the customary liturgical language of the Orthodox Slavic Churches. The dialect represents an early stage in the linguistic development when regional differences were less prominent. It seems to have been the common dialect of Macedonia and Bulgaria. The alphabet was devised in 855 by Cyril who, with his companion Methodius, translated the Byzantine liturgy, the New Testament, and the Psalter. The Old Russian Chronicle was written in Church Slavonic.

**Slavophiles.** A group of Russian intellectuals who, though without any formal organization or definite political program, were often harassed by the czarist regime. Their ideology was based on the belief in the superiority of Russian Orthodoxy and the historical world mission of Russia. Most noted of the Slavophiles were Aleksei S. Khomiakov, Ivan and Peter Kireyevski, Konstantin and Ivan Aksakov, and George Samarin. They were prominent in Moscow in the decades between 1840 and 1860.

**Sleidan, John** (c. 1505–1556). Historian of the Reformation. Considered the greatest historian of his time, Sleidan studied at a number of universities, and probably at Liège adopted Protestant opinions. He did some minor corresponding and diplomatic work for French interests before settling in Strasbourg in 1542. He was active in the Reformation there, and came under the attention of Martin Bucer, who in 1544 suggested to Philip of Hesse that Sleidan be appointed a salaried historian of the Reformation. His custom was to copy all papers bearing upon the Reformation to which he had access, and he made a good start at Strasbourg. The first volume of his history came out in 1545, after which the Smalcald War interrupted the work, and he continued his writing in England. He received a pension from Edward VI, but returned to the Continent. In 1554 he was appointed professor at Strasbourg, and the same year finished his second volume, but financial difficulties delayed its publication, and he died almost penniless. His work, entitled *Commentaries on the Religious and Political History of Charles V,* was most impartial—so much so that it pleased almost no one. Although not analytical or interpretative, it is a free-flowing history which is still valuable for its wealth of important documents.

**Smalcald Articles.** Confessional statement by Martin Luther. When Pope Paul III summoned a general council for May, 1537, at Mantua, Elector John Frederick of Saxony called for an assembly of the Smalcald League in February, 1537, to decide on the propriety of attending (in response to the pope's express invitation). Luther was asked to state the League's beliefs, stipulating matters that could be discussed with the Roman Catholics at Trent. He drew up the articles in three sections: (1) those dealing with the majesty of God as presented in the ancient creeds; (2) those treating of Christ's redemption, which included justification by faith, denounced Romanist practices (especially the Mass), and identified the pope as Antichrist; (3) and those which touch on matters open for discussion: redemption, sin, law, repentance, gospel, sacraments, power of the keys, confession, vocation, the church, monastic vows, and human ordinances. The elector was pleased at the result, but Melanchthon, disliking the attack against the papacy, expressed his reservations in a *Tract on the Power and Primacy of the Pope.* At Smalcald, Melanchthon's *Tract* was read and adopted. Luther, who was ill at the time, did not have his articles read, but they were subscribed by the theologians (though not by the princes). They were elevated to confessional status in 1544, called the Smalcald Articles after 1553, and included in the Book of Concord (1580) with Melanchthon's *Tract* added as an appendix, his authorship of it forgotten. Today, the Smalcald Articles, with the *Tract,* are recognized as one of the six Lutheran confessional documents.

**Smalcald League.** A defensive alliance of German Lutheran states and cities formed after the Diet of Augsburg (1530) against the threat of force by imperial armies. The immediate threat was dispelled and on Zwingli's death (October, 1531) many southern German Protestants also joined the League, which won a truce from the emperor in 1532. Internal dissension led to defeat in the Smalcald War (1546–1547) at Mühlberg.

**Small, Albion Woodbury** (1854–1926). Sociologist. A Baptist minister's son, he was educated at Colby College, Newton Theological Institution, Berlin, Leipzig, and Johns Hopkins (Ph.D., 1889). In 1881 he became professor of history and political economy at Colby and in 1889 its president. There he began teaching courses in the new field of sociology. In 1892 he was made head of the first sociology department at the new University of Chicago, where he continued until death, being after 1904 also dean of the Graduate School of Arts, Literature, and Science. He was one of the organizers of the American Sociological Society in 1905, and founder (1895) and until death editor of the *American Journal of Sociology*. His teaching and writing contributed greatly toward making the University of Chicago a center of the Social Gospel.

**Small Catechism, Luther's.** Published in 1529 to meet the need for a simple textbook for both adults and children that would contain the essentials of the Christian faith. It was divided into five parts (Ten Commandments, Creed, Lord's Prayer, Baptism, and Lord's Supper) and, with the Large Catechism, became a part of the Book of Concord (1580). Translated into many foreign languages, it is used as a manual of instruction in preparation for the Lutheran rite of confirmation.

**Smalley, John** (1734–1820). Congregational clergyman. A graduate of Yale College (1756), he studied theology with Joseph Bellamy, and was ordained (1758) to the pastorate of the church in New Britain, Conn. He opposed the Halfway Covenant and the Separatists, and defended the New England Theology in his writings, among which were published *Natural and Moral Inability* (1769) and *Discourses* (1803, 1814). Among his most illustrious theological students were Nathanael Emmons and Oliver Ellsworth, who became Chief Justice of the Supreme Court.

**Smectymnuus.** A pseudonymous pamphlet by five Puritan writers who jointly entered into controversy with Bishop Joseph Hall over episcopacy. It was published under the name formed from the combined initials of the five authors: Stephen Marshall, Edward Calamy, Thomas Young, Matthew Newcomen, and William Spurstow. They argued that bishops were not of divine origin, and if retained, must be reduced to apostolic simplicity.

**Smend, Julius** (1857–1930). German Protestant theologian. He studied at Bonn, Halle, and Göttingen, became pastor at Paderborn, Bonn, and Siegen, and professor of practical theology at Strasbourg (1893). The author of several books on theology, he was a disciple of Albrecht Ritschl. He was joint editor with Friedrich Spitta of the *Monatsschrift für Gottesdienst und kirchliche Kunst* from 1895.

**Smith, Adam** (1723–1790). Political economist. Educated at the University of Glasgow,

Smith early came under the influence of Francis Hutcheson, whose teachings on morals and economics are seen reflected in Smith's mature writings. After Glasgow, Smith studied at Oxford and then returned to Scotland where he lectured on English literature until elected to the chair of logic at Glasgow in 1751. In 1752 he succeeded to the chair of moral philosophy and was subsequently appointed vice-rector in 1762. The next year he resigned his position and became traveling tutor to the young Henry Scott, third duke of Buccleuch. During his travels on the Continent, Smith came to know David Hume and met Voltaire, Robert Holcot, Turgot, André Morellet, and François Quesnay. After the murder of Scott, Smith returned to Scotland and began to write his *Wealth of Nations*, his most influential book, published in 1776. He argued that society is so constituted that each man promotes the interests of all by attending to his own interests. Smith was a theist who placed great emphasis upon final causes. Basically unorthodox in his faith, he shared the rationalism of the philosophers of his time. As a reward for his suggestions about taxation, Smith was made commissioner of customs in 1777 and in recognition of his fame was appointed lord rector of Glasgow University in 1787.

**Smith, George Adam** (1856–1942). Scottish Old Testament scholar. He sought to unite scientific scholarship and devout reverence. After study in Scotland and Germany he traveled in Palestine, Egypt, and Syria. He was professor at Free Church College, then principal at the University of Aberdeen. His two volumes on Isaiah won him fame. He wrote extensively, lectured widely, and filled responsible positions for his church and his country.

**Smith, Gerald Birney** (1868–1929). Baptist theologian at the University of Chicago from 1900. He stressed experience as the basis of theology and emphasized the role of science and democratic principles in theological reconstruction. He edited the *American Journal of Theology* (1909–1920) and the *Journal of Theology* (1921–1929). Typical works were *Practical Theology* (1903) and *Social Idealism and the Changing Theology* (1913). He was influenced by the Ritschlian Johann Wilhelm Herrmann.

**Smith, Henry Boynton** (1815–1877). American Presbyterian. Intellectual leader of New School Presbyterianism and moderator in 1863 of its General Assembly, Boynton brought about reunion in 1869. A "liberal Edwardsian," he taught at Union Theological

Seminary, New York City (1850–1874). Study at Berlin and Halle led him to champion historical criticism and translate the works of Gieseler and Hagenbach. From 1859 he edited the *American Theological Review*.

**Smith, Henry Preserved** (1847–1927). Presbyterian minister and theological professor. Born in Troy, Ohio, he graduated from Amherst College (1869) and Lane Seminary (1872). As a professor at Lane he defended Charles Briggs's views on higher criticism, and was suspended from the ministry. He later taught at Amherst College, Meadville Theological Seminary, and was librarian and professor of Hebrew at Union Theological Seminary, New York City.

**Smith, Joseph** (1805–1844). Founder of the Church of Jesus Christ of Latter-day Saints, or Mormons. Joseph Smith's family were part of the great Yankee migrations from New England into New York at the beginning of the 19th century. The family on both his mother's and his father's sides had deep roots in New England, but they were not prosperous. The move to Palmyra, N.Y., did not change their economic circumstances, and Joseph has been described as a ragged boy. The area into which the Smiths moved in 1816 was not frontier territory, but a prospering, settled community which became even more prosperous with the opening of the Erie Canal in 1825. Palmyra in 1820 was not simply a farming community but possessed woolen manufacturies, flour and paper mills, a blast furnace, and a six-hundred-volume library. The land lying along the Erie Canal has been often referred to as the "burned-over district." Religious excitement during the decade of the 1820's swept this area like a prarie fire. Many movements sprang up in addition to the Mormons—the revivals of Charles Finney, the communitarianism of John Humphrey Noyes, the Shakers, Millerites, and Rappites. The Smith family was prone to religious fervor of this type and also spent time looking for buried treasure with divining rods and "peek" stones, a kind of natural rock crystal. It was in this environment that Joseph began to have visions which eventually directed him to a hillside where he discovered golden plates covered with mysterious writing. He showed these plates to only a very small group of witnesses, and nothing much is known about them. With supernatural assistance, Joseph claimed, he was able to translate the writing on the tablets and present it to the world as the Book of Mormon. With the completion of the book, an angel, it is said, snatched away the plates, but the divine revelations did not cease. Upon these revelations and upon the teachings of the Book of Mormon, the Church of Jesus Christ of Latter-day Saints was founded. Many have doubted whether Smith had the ability to write the Book of Mormon. Mormons, of course, are not troubled by this problem, since they believe the book was translated at the dictate of God. But others, for whom this explanation has not proved adequate, have looked to men in Smith's circle of acquaintances and disciples for a source. In any case, neither the book nor the church prospered in New York, and Smith decided in 1831 to move farther west. The church became established successfully in Kirtland, Ohio, Far West, Mo., and Nauvoo, Ill. A great many converts were added to the church in Kirtland, and a community established in which all resources were held in common by a band of elders and trustees. Smith continued to direct his followers by means of revelations which became increasingly frequent and matter-of-fact. In 1836 financial troubles began to mount, and Smith experimented in the founding of a bank in order to bail the community out of its difficulties. Because the state refused to license his inadequately backed institution, Smith founded what he called an antibank. The ruse did not prevent the antibank's collapse along with many other banks of the country in the panic of 1837. His own followers turned on him, furious for having been stripped of all their assets, and forced him to flee with a band of followers to Missouri, where other Mormons were living. In Missouri the Mormons were compelled to move three times by irate residents who were alarmed at their concerted action and their claims to eventual ownership of the whole state. The Mormons finally crossed the Mississippi into Illinois and founded Nauvoo, at the time of Smith's death the largest city in Illinois. The years from 1839 to 1844 were among the most successful of Smith's career. He obtained a charter from the state which made him virtually king of a separate domain. Leaders of both parties, including Lincoln and Douglas, courted him— for he dictated the votes of all of his followers. He obtained a revelation permitting polygamy among leaders of the church, however, and, though kept virtually secret, this instigated another attack upon the community by non-Mormons from neighboring towns. Joseph and his brother submitted to arrest, and were murdered by a mob in the Carthage jail on June 27, 1844.

BIBLIOGRAPHY: F. Brodie, *No Man Knows My History* (New York, 1946); W. Cross, *The Burned-over District* (Ithaca, 1950); L. M. Smith, *Biographical Sketches of Joseph*

*Smith* (Lamoni, Iowa, 1908); A. F. Tyler, *Freedom's Ferment* (New York, 1962); R. B. West, *The Kingdom of the Saints* (New York, 1957); *The Book of Mormon*.

**Smith, Preserved** (1880–1941). Well-known American historian whose works dealt with the Reformation period. Smith received the B.A. from Amherst in 1901, the M.A. from Columbia in 1902 and the Ph.D. in 1907. He taught at Williams College, Amherst, and Harvard, and was professor of history at Cornell from 1922. His books include *The Life and Letters of Martin Luther* (1911), *The Age of the Reformation* (1920), *Erasmus— A Study of His Life, Ideals, and Place in History* (1923), and a *History of Modern Culture* (2 vols., 1930–1934).

**Smith, Rodney** (Gipsy Smith) (1860–1947). British evangelist. Born in a gipsy tent near Epping Forest, England, he was converted in 1876 and for a short time served in the Salvation Army. An unconventional preacher in the tradition of Dwight L. Moody, he avoided sensationalism and appealed to his hearers in a direct, personal way, using gospel solos in his work. He made several tours of the United States as well as of Australia and South Africa.

**Smith, William** (1727–1803). Episcopal clergyman and first provost of the College and Academy of Philadelphia (later the University of Pennsylvania). Born and educated in Scotland, Smith came to America in 1751 and developed new patterns of liberal education as provost of the College. He favored reconciliation between Britain and the American colonies, and, after the Revolution, played an active part in reorganizing the Episcopal Church in the United States.

**Smith, William Robertson** (1846–1894). Scottish Biblical critic and Orientalist. He was professor of Oriental languages and Biblical exegesis at the Free College, Aberdeen, in 1870 and in 1875 he joined the Old Testament panel of the Revised Version. His articles in the *Encyclopædia Britannica* led to his expulsion from Aberdeen in 1881. He became a Cambridge don in 1885. In *The Old Testament and the Jewish Church* (1881) he espoused Pentateuchal criticism, and in *The Religion of the Semites* (1889), the concept of sacrifice as fellowship.

**Smyth, John** (c. 1554–1612). The man generally reckoned as founder of the English Baptists. Starting as a clergyman in the Church of England, he moved to Independency, ending as a Baptist. A graduate of Christ's College, Cambridge, he was ordained by the bishop of Lincoln. To avoid conforming, he decided not to take a living, but became lecturer in Lincoln in 1600. Six years after, Smyth left the Anglicans and joined the Gainsborough Separatists, who chose him as their pastor. Persecution caused the congregation to emigrate to Amsterdam. There, Smyth's study of the New Testament convinced him that the Bible knew nothing of infant baptism, but proved rather that the ordinance was to be administered on the profession of repentance. Smyth baptized by affusion first himself, then his followers. Critics castigated him as a self-baptizer (or "se-baptist"), asking him why he did not go to the Waterland Mennonites. Immediately, he opened communications and made application to join the Dutch group. Thomas Helwys and about ten others refused to follow. During the negotiations, Smyth drew up a declaration of faith in which he maintained an Arminian position and in which he espoused the idea of freedom of conscience. He became ill and died in 1612, but through Helwys the group of English Baptists that he had started grew into one of the major denominations.

**Sobor.** See SYNODS, RUSSIAN ORTHODOX.

**Sobriquets.** Epithets or fanciful appellations, in the Middle Ages customarily bestowed upon great scholars, particularly theologians and lawyers, symbolizing their achievements or qualities. In medieval literature, these sobriquets were often used in place of the proper names. Some examples are: The Angelic Doctor (Thomas Aquinas), The Mellifluous Doctor (Bernard of Clairvaux), The Subtle Doctor (Duns Scotus), The Scholastic Doctor (Abelard and others).

**Social Gospel.** A movement, chiefly among American liberal Protestants, to Christianize society by applying the Biblical principles of love and justice to such institutions as the family, the state, and the economy—seeking to redeem corporate as well as individual life. The dates for its major phase were about 1870 to 1918.

Christianity's traditional concern for the needy, based on the teaching and example of Jesus, had become largely a matter of charity to individuals in the late 19th century. There were, however, many instances of previous concern for the social conditions that produced needy individuals: the Old Testament prophets, medieval rules for a "just price," Puritan social regulations, abolitionism, and movements for peace, temperance, and other reforms that flourished before the Civil War. American Protestantism was not generally reform-minded after the Civil War, but a series of social crises (i.e., the depression of 1873 and the labor strife of 1877) gradually aroused them until Progressive politics and the Social Gospel claimed many by the early 1900's. A sense of justice and a fear of socialism caused a search for solutions to the problems of "robber baron" industrialism and slum-ridden urbanization. Workers claimed the churches unfairly sided with wealthy businessmen, and indeed Protestantism seemed in danger of losing all of labor's loyalty. Europe had faced these problems earlier, and thoughtful Americans began to study the ideas of reformers such as Adolf von Harnack, Giuseppe Mazzini, J. F. D. Maurice, Charles Kingsley, and Ruskin. This background combined with Enlightenment humanism, the liberal theology of men such as Horace Bushnell, Theodore T. Munger, and William Clarke, the new science of sociology, and the work of groups such as the Y.M.C.A. to produce the Social Gospel.

The first modern statements of the Social Gospel were too advanced to be widely influential. In 1851, Stephen Colwell's book *New Themes for the Protestant Clergy* sounded a Social Gospel note that suffered the fate of being ahead of its times. Even the brilliant *Christian Sociology* of J. H. W. Stuckenberg in 1880 went largely unnoticed. But progress had been made in the 1870's. Massachusetts especially was stirred by the reform preaching of Joseph Cook and the Christian Labor Union of Jesse Jones and Edward Rogers. The acknowledged "father" of the Social Gospel, Washington Gladden, published the first of his many Social Gospel books in 1876.

In the 1880's increasing numbers of Christians sought solutions to labor problems on a basis of realistic social science—for immigration, business monopoly, and a decline in real wages had increased tensions. Social gospelers tended to support labor unions, and Gladden helped found the American Economic Association. Josiah Strong became a famous Social Gospel leader after his 1885 book *Our Country* aroused many to the crisis of Christianity's responsibility for social problems.

The Kingdom of God on earth was emphasized in the 1890's, and Christian organizations were formed to further it. George D. Herron for a time received considerable attention with a Social Gospel that began with self-sacrifice and ended with a radical reconstruction of society. The chief channel of the Social Gospel to the laity was the Social Gospel novel, such as William Stead's *If Christ Came to Chicago* and Charles Sheldon's *In His Steps* (which sold over twenty-five million copies). Also to endure was the institution of Labor Sunday, 1890.

The most flourishing time for the Social Gospel was in the 20th century before World War I. The mature Social Gospel benefited from and helped shape Progressivism, sociology, ecumenism, and modern interpretations of the social teachings of Jesus. The latter stressed love and respect for personality. By these standards laissez-faire industrialism, with its sweatshops and child labor, was unchristian and in need of basic reform at the least. The Social Gospel's most effective spokesman emerged in 1907 when Walter Rauschenbusch published *Christianity and the Social Crisis*.

The concerns of the Social Gospel had broadened from labor to urbanization, family life, and the increased role of government. Some social gospelers also worked for disarmament, interracial justice, and prohibition, though these were less characteristic of the movement as a whole, which, like society at large, saw the socioeconomic problems of industrialism as the chief crisis of the day.

Techniques developed by the Social Gospel were largely those of education, social service, and political reform. "Institutional" churches were founded in depressed areas to provide the poor with opportunities for wholesome recreation and to show the relevance of Christianity to modern life through services such as legal aid. Many of the settlement houses also had a religious orientation. Denominational agencies were formed to preach the Social Gospel and urge reforms. Unofficial groups such as the Church Association for the Advancement of the Interests of Labor had been active since the 1880's. In the early 1900's the denominations most influenced by the Social Gospel—Baptists, Congregationalists, Episcopalians, Methodists, Presbyterians, and Unitarians—organized official social welfare commissions, and most major denominations eventually showed some organized concern. Geographically, the Social Gospel was strongest in the Northeast and the Midwest.

Most significant was the strength of the Social Gospel in the Federal Council of Churches, which adopted most of the Methodist "Social Creed" in its first year (1908), calling for protection of workers physically and socially, increased leisure, higher wages, the abolition of sweatshops and child labor.

Though there were significant variations and degrees of liberalism, the general thought of the Social Gospel may be summarized as having these key ideas: Laissez-faire capitalism represents the selfish law of the jungle, not the Christian way of cooperation. A Christian motive for business is service, not merely profit. Justice, not subsistence charity, is the Christian ethic in wages as in other matters.

Since sin is more than personal vice, and since environment so largely shapes personality, social structures that produce unhealthy environments are sinful. People, including workers, must be treated as humans, not commodities. Salvation is social, but it is evangelical as well as reformist. Individualism, economic and religious, tends dangerously toward selfishness, which contradicts the Biblical ideals of the Kingdom of God. God is immanent in the world, working through men. Society is interdependent and requires active Christian brotherliness. Application of the teachings of Jesus and the prophets can bring the Kingdom of God into being on earth. The time to act is now.

The term "Social Gospel" derives from a magazine of that name published by the Christian Commonwealth Colony (1897–1900), though it was not commonly used until after 1900—the earlier designation being "social Christianity."

Key leaders of the Social Gospel, aside from those noted above, include Lyman Abbott, W. D. P. Bliss, Richard Ely, Charles Henderson, Shailer Mathews, Francis G. Peabody, Newman Smyth, Charles Stelzle, Alva Taylor, and Graham Taylor.

The Social Gospel naturally was related to secular developments. Many social gospelers were sympathetic to a Christianized socialism but few Social Gospel advocates were Socialists politically. The reform Progressivism of Theodore Roosevelt and Woodrow Wilson was more congenial to most. The two movements shared ideas and leadership, greatly influencing each other.

In 1918, Gladden and Rauschenbusch died. The interests of most Americans were turned from social reform to the war and then to trying to forget it. Prohibition absorbed most of the remaining reform energies. The social gospelers who continued optimistic were challenged by realistic critics such as the neoorthodox theologians. Disillusion and a religious depression that preceded the economic one produced a decline of impact. The Social Gospel was kept alive, however, emerging in new, more realistic, relativistic, international, ecumenical, and theological forms with the New Deal and World War II.

Recent Church involvement in civil rights, antipoverty, and antiwar movements is related to the Social Gospel—as is the "Secular City" philosophy—but the relationship is not agreed upon, aside from the foundation of Christian concern for social justice. Though a minority movement, especially among laymen, the Social Gospel was very influential. It has been called America's leading contribution to Christian thought.

BIBLIOGRAPHY: R. T. Handy (ed.), *The Social Gospel in America: 1870–1920* (New York, 1966); C. H. Hopkins, *The Rise of the Social Gospel in American Protestantism: 1660–1935* (New Haven, 1940); H. F. May, *Protestant Churches and Industrial America* (New York, 1949); D. B. Meyer, *The Protestant Search for Political Realism: 1919–1941* (Berkeley and Los Angeles, 1960); R. Miller, *American Protestantism and Social Issues* (Chapel Hill, N.C., 1958).

**Society for Promoting Christian Knowledge** (S.P.C.K.). An Anglican society for the publication and distribution of religious books and literature. It was directly connected with the work of Dr. Thomas Bray, who was appointed by the bishop of London in 1695 to act as commissary for the Anglican churches in the American colonies. Those interested in assisting Bray in his efforts to provide libraries for the American clergy organized the society in 1698 and secured a royal charter in 1701. In the 18th century the society promoted schools for the study of the catechism, helped organize charity schools for poor children in England, and set up lending libraries in local parishes. For a time it supported mission work in eastern India and assisted the missionary work of John and Charles Wesley in the colony of Georgia (1735–1738). The society has printed and sold books, tracts, and Anglican prayer books, as well as films and filmstrips. It has published works in most of the major European languages as well as in African and Asian languages in those areas where Anglican missions have been active. The S.P.C.K. has provided chaplains for British emigrants overseas, as well as Bibles and prayer books for the armed forces. It operates bookstores in Britain and in British territories overseas.

**Society for the Propagation of the Gospel** in foreign parts (S.P.G.). Anglican missionary society founded in 1701, to further work begun by the Society for Promoting Christian Knowledge. Its dual purpose was to provide the ministrations of the Church of England for overseas British subjects and to evangelize non-Christian peoples. Instrumental in promoting Anglicanism in American colonies, it now supports work in sixty overseas dioceses and mission areas.

**Society of Friends.** See QUAKERS.

**Society of Jesus.** See JESUS, SOCIETY OF.

**Society of St. John the Evangelist** (*or* Cowley Fathers). Anglican society of missionary priests founded in 1865 by Richard M. Benson (1824–1915), vicar of St. James's, Cowley. The object of this oldest Anglican society for men of religion is a life of discipline and prayers under monastic vows. They are dedicated to education. Divided into English, American, and Canadian congregations, they have also established houses in India and South Africa.

**Society of the Divine Word.** A Roman Catholic religious order for men (priests and brothers) engaged in missionary activity in Africa, Australia, South America, the southern United States, and Asia. The order was founded in Holland in 1875 by Fr. Arnold Janssen, and has become one of the best-known and most numerous of Catholic mission societies. There are over fifty thousand professed members of the order today.

**Socinianism.** A rationalistic theology of the 16th century named after Laelius and Faustus Socinus. The Sozzini family of Siena moved from leadership in Italian jurisprudence of the 15th century to leadership in 16th-century radical Christianity. Laelius Sozzini (1525–1562) and his nephew Faustus (1539–1604) were the intellectual shapers of a unitarianism that long posed questions to orthodoxy and was for a time the faith of a continuing community in Poland. Both Laelius and Faustus Socinus (the Latinized forms of their names) held to the natural mortality of the soul and regarded the sacraments as signs and not seals. They respected the capacity of human rationality. Laelius traveled in Reformation centers in a spirit of devout inquiry (which Calvin saw as an unwholesome tentativeness), formulating questions to which Faustus gave answers. Faustus accepted the Scriptures as revelation from God, but held that nothing in them could be contrary to reason, though some things were above reason, such as the affirmation of God as creator. The difficulties in Scripture are best understood by the morally enlightened, and it must be considered that God progressively discloses himself in history.

Faustus sought to rethink Christian faith in the face of Paduan naturalism. Man's problem, he felt, was the need to be saved from extinction at death. All men, including Adam before the Fall and Christ, were subject to death, which is natural and not a punishment for sin. Christ was different from other men only in an unusual affinity for relationship to God. This affinity was attested by his virgin birth and by his miracles and signs, and he was divinely taught after his baptism. God raised Christ from the dead and exalted him in the ascension to participation in divine power, giving to him rulership over the world until his Second Advent and declaring thereby the eventual victory of God's essential loving-kindness to his creatures in purposing to save them from individual extinction in death to eternal life. Though Christ was not preexistent, he was to be adored because of his divine adoptive office. Eternal life was to be conferred on those who sincerely understood the teachings of the Scriptures and lived in imitation of Christ according to Scriptural teachings of love and concern for all men, while the unrighteous remained in extinction. Faustus Socinus removed the ontological underpinnings of traditional theology. God did not require an infinite satisfaction, and sin was not so deep a corruption. God's raising of Christ to divine status was not retroactive to his life, so that the doctrine of the two natures is without foundation. God's justice guides all men individually in living justly.

Though Socinus respected the moral earnestness of the Racovians among whom he found himself after 1579, he could not agree to the solemn rite of Baptism which they required. True baptism, he thought, was an inner experience requiring no water, though its presence could be signified in this way. The church was present wherever virtue was manifest as love and concern for one's fellowman. Socinus defended the Racovians' separation of the community of the faithful from participation in civil government, and ably expressed their concern for a simple and disciplined life. By the time he died in 1604 his views were largely accepted by the Polish Minor Church with its center in Raków. The Racovian Catechism of 1605, formulated and published by his followers as part of an extensive educative effort, embodied his views, though adding immersionist baptism, so that a continuing church community resulted. Latin, German, Dutch, and English translations led to a wide circulation of his views in the following century. There was an estimated total of 125 congregations in the Polish history of Socinianism. Their polity resembled that of the Reformed Churches, and the use of church discipline in the common life was tempered by Socinus' ideal of rationality and the Anabaptist distaste for coercion. Increasing public persecution inspired by Jesuits led to the banishment of the Socinians in 1658. The following decades saw scattered groups of exiles slowly dwindling. Socinianism lived on mostly as a chapter in the history of religious ideas rather than as a social movement in itself, though a small group still existed in Transylvania in the 20th century.

BIBLIOGRAPHY: S. Kot, *Socinianism in Poland* (Boston, 1957); E. Wilbur, *A History of Unitarianism* (Cambridge, Mass., 1946).

**Socrates** (c. 469–399 B.C.). Greek philosopher. His life and teaching are known to us chiefly through the writings of Plato and somewhat less through those of Xenophon. His dialectical search for truth led to his martyrdom. His identification of knowledge with goodness made him respected by many of the fathers: Justin and other Apologists regarded him as practically a Christian.

**Socrates Scholasticus** (c. 380–450). Greek church historian. His *Ecclesiastical History,* in seven books, was written as a continuation of Eusebius and is divided into periods according to the reigns of emperors. His sources include Rufinus, Gelasius of Caesarea, Athanasius (in the second edition), Sabinus of Heraclea, and Timotheus of Berytus. His work exists also in Syriac and Armenian translations.

**Söderblom, Nathan** (1866–1931). Swedish Lutheran theologian, professor of church history, and ecumenical leader. Born at Trönö and educated at Uppsala and Paris, he was ordained in 1893. In 1914 he was named primate of the Church of Sweden as archbishop of Uppsala; in 1930 he was awarded the Nobel Peace Prize. Söderblom was a prominent supporter of the reunion movement and the leading figure in the Christian Conference on Life and Work, which met in Stockholm in 1925. This ecumenical gathering, representing all principal Christian churches except Roman Catholicism, was his greatest accomplishment. The theme of the Conference, "Unity in Christ," reflected his desire to organize the practical cooperation of the Christian churches, especially in social problems, without consideration of doctrinal differences. His religion was essentially constructive, and he believed that the Christian churches should become more deeply concerned with social and ethical questions. His important works are translated into English, and they include *The Nature of Revelation* (1903) and *The Living God* (1933).

**Sohm, Rudolph** (1841–1917). German Lutheran jurist. Born at Rostock, he studied law there, at Berlin, and at Heidelberg. He taught at Göttingen, Freiburg, Strasbourg, and Leipzig, laying the foundations for modern church law in Germany. He held that ecclesiastical law is incompatible with the true nature of the church, that there is no such thing as a legally constituted individual congregation, and that local congregations are actually the total church in visible reality.

**Sokolov, Timofei** (Tikhon Zadonskii) (1724–1783). Russian theologian. After serving as bishop of Voronezh, where he organized a seminary, he resigned his bishopric and retired to a provincial monastery. Here he shunned human society except for the poor and oppressed. He was the author of *On the True Christianity* and *A Spiritual Treasure Collected from the World* and was regarded as representative of Russian kenoticism.

**Solemn League and Covenant.** An agreement between the English and Scottish Parliaments in 1643. Riding the crest of a great popular movement, Scottish leaders, civil and ecclesiastical, had signed the National Covenant in 1638. This pledge to uphold Presbyterianism and resist prelacy was in defiance of Charles I and the Stuart designs to restore episcopacy. But Charles was having trouble in England with a rebellious Parliament and a church coming to admire the Scottish system. To placate the Scots, Charles went to Holyrood and gave his royal assent to the full establishment of Presbyterianism in Scotland. When civil war broke out in England, however, the Scots were not securely in the king's support. The reforming zeal of the Covenanters could not resist the invitation of English ministers for a meeting at Westminster to effect the full reformation of the English Church and union with the Church of Scotland. The General Assembly in 1643 drafted a treaty in religious language whereby the two countries and churches might be leagued. It was called "A Solemn League and Covenant, for reformation and defence of religion, the honour and happiness of the king, and the peace and safety of the three kingdoms of Scotland, England, and Ireland." The League swore to protect the Reformed religion and to achieve the reformation of the English Church, presumably on the Scottish pattern. The English approved and signed the League and the Scots entered the civil strife against the king.

**Soloviev, Vladimir Sergeevich** (1853–1900). Russian philosopher and religious thinker, also a poet of distinction. Soloviev was a central and leading figure in the intellectual life of Russia in his time. The spectacular "religious renaissance" in Russia in the first decades of this century was due mainly to the inspiring impact of his thought. He shared with Dostoevsky a concern for religious revival and renewal, believing them to be the only basis for the solution of social and cultural problems. Philosophically, Soloviev stood in the tradition of German idealism, especially that of Schelling's later period and partly that of Schopenhauer, but his main inspiration was Christian. At the center of his religious metaphysics was the concept of "Godmanhood"— a reality disclosed in the person of Christ and to be completed in the fullness of mankind. His most distinctive idea was that of Divine Sophia, the Wisdom of God, conceived as an eternal prototype and root of all existence. It was a peculiar version of Christian Platonism.

Having strong practical concerns, Soloviev envisaged the restoration of a unified culture and society. This had to begin within the European community with a reconciliation between the Orthodox East and the Roman West. He never paid much attention to the world of the Reformation. For a time he dreamed of an alliance between the Russian Empire and the Church of Rome. The schism between East and West was for him but a superficial historical split—the church was still one, still undivided in its basic structure and sacramental life. For that reason, he felt himself a member of both communions at once. His unionist pleading was badly misunderstood by Orthodox and Roman Catholics alike. He finally realized the utopian nature of his dream and abandoned it. During his last years he was full of apocalyptic forebodings and spoke of the collapse of European history and of the approaching end of all history.

**Somaschi.** Members of the Order of Somascha, a religious congregation formed in 1532 by Jerome Emiliani (1481–1537) to take care of the poor and the sick and to provide shelter for orphans. It was Jerome's wish that the Somaschi live, eat, and dress the way the people did with whom they worked, and he himself contracted a fatal disease from one of his patients. When he died, the group almost dissolved, but Gambarana, the new superior, managed to keep them together. For a few years they were absorbed by the Theatines, but in 1568, Pope Pius V made them an autonomous religious order.

**Somerset, Edward Seymour, Duke of** (c. 1506–1552). Protector of England (1547–1550). The brother of Jane Seymour (third queen of Henry VIII and mother of Edward VI), he became "squire of the body" to King Henry (1529), viscount of Beauchamp on Henry's marriage to his sister (1536), earl of Hertford on Edward's birth (1537), and duke of Somerset upon Henry's death and the accession of Edward (1547). Somerset was then chosen as "the Protector" by the Council of Regency, and for some two years was virtually the ruler of England. In the wake of the unsuccessful attempts of Henry to unify Scotland

and England and to espouse Edward to Mary Queen of Scots, Somerset's own more conciliatory plan to win the Scots also failed, but it was the model for the eventual settlement. In matters religious, he secured the repeal of all heresy and treason laws made after Edward III, but the chaos produced by his policy of free discussion and toleration forced him to effect the enactment of the first Act of Uniformity (1549) prescribing a Book of Common Prayer which was an artful compromise between the old faith and the new learning. He fell victim (1550) to a curious coalition of Roman Catholics who resented the Prayer Book, Protestants who wanted more reform, and wealthy landowners hostile to his agrarian policy, all under the leadership of Warwick (later Northumberland) who was to succeed him as Protector. A trial for treason having failed, he was executed on forged royal instructions for the lesser crime of having attempted a change of government.

**Sonderbund** (1843). An alliance of the seven Roman Catholic cantons of Switzerland. Suppression of the monasteries in Aargau canton in 1843 led the seven Catholic cantons (Uri, Schwyz, Unterwalden, Lucerne, Zug, Fribourg, and the Valais) to form a Sonderbund ("separate league") on Aug. 31, 1843, and to issue a manifesto demanding the reopening of all suppressed monasteries. The Jesuits were invited to return and given special privileges, and in December, 1845, the Sonderbund became a military confederation. In 1847 the league was defeated in the field and the Jesuits once more were expelled.

**Sorbonne.** A college of the old University of Paris, originally founded c. 1257 as the Maison de Sorbonne, a house for poor theological students, by Robert de Sorbon, the confessor of Louis IX. It became noted for academic excellence throughout the world. Its masters were frequently consulted on theological issues. From 1554 until its suppression in 1792, it was the theological faculty of the university. After its revival in 1808, it was a center of Gallicanism. It was finally suppressed in 1882, although the name is still commonly applied to the entire university.

**Sorssky, Nil.** See JOSEPH OF VOLOKOLAMSK.

**Soto, Dominic de** (1494–1560). Spanish Dominican. He entered the Dominican Order when he was thirty (1524) and later taught theology at the University of Salamanca as "second" professor for several years (1532–1549). In 1545, Charles V sent De Soto to the Council of Trent as his personal theologian. At Trent he wrote his *De natura et gratia* presenting the Thomistic notion of original sin and grace. In 1552 he was given the "first" chair of theology at Salamanca as successor to Cano.

**South Africa, Christian Council of.** An organization founded in 1936 as successor to the General Missionary Conference of South Africa (1904). It resulted from a conference called at Bloemfontein in 1934 by John R. Mott as chairman of the International Missionary Council. The Christian Council was an effective ecumenical agent of the churches until the Dutch churches withdrew over the government's policy of apartheid and the opposition of the English churches to it.

**South India, Church of.** See CHURCH OF SOUTH INDIA.

**South India United Church.** A body formed in 1908 by the merger of the General Union of the United Churches in South India and the Presbyterian churches in South India. The former was a 1905 union of the London Missionary Society and the American Board churches, and the latter a union of the Reformed Church in America and the Church of Scotland congregations, formed in 1901. In 1919 the Malabar Church of the Basel Mission joined. This church united with Anglicans and Methodists to create the Church of South India in 1947.

**Southwell, Robert** (c. 1561–1595). Jesuit poet and missioner. He was born in Norfolk and educated at Douai and Paris, entering the Roman novitiate of the Society of Jesus in 1578. In 1584 he was ordained, the same year that an act was passed which forbade English subjects who had taken priest's orders since the queen's accession from remaining in England. Despite this, two years later he asked to be sent to England as a missionary with Fr. Henry Garnett. He ministered to persecuted Roman Catholics and in 1589 was chaplain to the countess of Arundel, whose husband had been imprisoned for treason. In 1592, Southwell was captured by Richard Topcliffe, racked thirteen times in an effort to obtain evidence about other priests, imprisoned three years, and executed at Tyburn. His best-known poem is "The Burning Babe." He was beatified in 1929.

**Sozomen** (5th century). Greek church historian and contemporary of Socrates Scholasticus. His nine-book history, from which half of the last book is lost, covers the same period as Socrates' history does but attempts to be more impartial and rhetorical. Uncritical of his sources, Sozomen has been accused of various heresies. Of his earlier work, which parallels that of Eusebius of Caesarea, neither the original twelve books nor the epitome in two books is extant.

**Spalatin** (Burckhardt), **George** (1484–1545). An important Reformation figure in Saxony. Ordained in 1508, trained as a humanist at Erfurt, he became tutor of Elector Frederick's nephew, John Frederick (1511), and soon handled all the elector's correspondence. He was the first to interpret Luther to the elector. A key supporter of Luther, he supervised the publication of many of his works and was himself a prolific writer and good historian. His correspondence is invaluable for Reformation studies.

**Spalding, Johann Joachim** (1714–1804). German Lutheran theologian. Born at Tribsees and educated at Rostock, he was pastor of Lassahn and Berlin. His importance lies in his attempt to harmonize the tenets of the *Aufklärung* with the divine truths of Christianity. His theological liberalism exposed him to much attack, and in 1786 he was forced to resign his state offices on the accession of Frederick William II.

**Spalding, John Lancaster** (1840–1916). Roman Catholic bishop and educator. After study at Rome and Louvain and serving parishes in Louisville, Ky., and New York City he became bishop of Peoria, Ill., in 1877. He was thereafter active in the Irish colonization movement, a leader in founding the Catholic University of America in Washington, D.C., and a prolific writer, publishing several books and articles.

**Spangenberg, Augustus Gottlieb** (1704–1792). Moravian churchman. Educated at Jena, Spangenberg came under the influence of Zinzendorf about 1728. He lectured at Jena while continuing relations with Herrnhut. Called to the theological faculty at the University of Halle in 1732, he left within a year due to antagonism over his adherence to the Moravian community. He then formally joined the Brethren and traveled to America for Zinzendorf to begin a pioneer missionary enterprise in Georgia and in Pennsylvania, where he served almost thirty years. In Savannah in 1736, Governor Oglethorpe introduced John Wesley to him, a meeting that Wesley noted in his *Journal*, for they became friends. In Europe from 1739 to 1744 (including England), Spangenberg returned to organize the community at Bethlehem, Pa., as a bishop after 1744. He served as Zinzendorf's European apologete (1749), but returned to America (1751–1753, and 1754). Spangenberg consolidated the work of Zinzendorf, and prepared the latter's biography after returning to Europe in 1762.

**Speer, Robert Elliott** (1867–1947). Presbyterian missionary statesman. He was born at Huntingdon, Pa., and educated at Phillips Academy and Princeton University (1889). In his second year at Princeton Seminary he was appointed secretary of the Board of Foreign Missions, Presbyterian Church U.S.A., a post he held from 1891 to 1937. He was active in interdenominational causes. In 1927 he served as moderator of the Presbyterian General Assembly.

**Spencer, Herbert** (1820–1903). English philosopher. Originally he was a railway engineer, but subsequently devoted his attention to questions of a political and social nature. From 1848 to 1853, he was subeditor of the *Economist* magazine. In 1851 his *Social Statics* appeared. It was an attempt to base his views on a coherent set of first principles, by combining induction with deduction. In his *Principles of Psychology* (1855), he described the so-called intuitions of the individual as reflections of racial experience. In discussing the problems of beginnings and endings, he denied that philosophy could afford any convincing explanations; instead, mankind could only worship at the altar of the Unknown and the Unknowable. His *First Principles* (1862) asserted the relativity of knowledge; the human mind must necessarily confine itself to the perception of phenomena rather than noumena. In seeking the root principle of phenomenal experience, Spencer defined his theory of evolution as the integration of matter and the dissipation of motion, with matter passing from an indefinite and incoherent homogeneity to a definite, coherent homogeneity. Here he indicated how the earth had evolved from its nebulous to its present stage. His *Principles of Biology* (2 vols., 1864, 1867) represented the application of his hypothesis to the structure and fundamental complexities of plant and animal life.

**Spencer, John** (1630–1693). English Hebrew scholar. After graduating from Corpus Christi, Cambridge, he became a university preacher. He served as rector of Landbeach in Cambridgeshire for a while, then was elected to the position of master of Corpus Christi College in 1667. Being closely connected with the university for the rest of his life, he contributed to the Cambridge University collection of verse on the death of the queen dowager in 1669. He was vice-chancellor for one term (1673–1674), and three years later became dean of Ely Cathedral. His most significant contribution came through his scholarly work as theologian and Hebraist. It was he who first drew the connection between the Hebrew religion and the religions of kindred Semitic races. His main work, *De legibus Hebraeorum* ("On the Laws of the Hebrews"), laid the foundations for the future study of comparative religions. His feat is even more remarkable when one realizes that his sources were so limited. For the next two centuries, the scholars in that field largely developed and extended those concepts which Spencer had laid down in the 17th century.

**Spener, Philip Jacob** (1635–1705). A leader of German Pietism. He was born in Alsace and attended the University of Strasbourg. After completing his courses in 1659, he spent two years in travel, visiting Geneva, where he came under the influence of Jean de Labadie, a zealous French Reformed preacher with a bent toward mysticism. Spener later returned to Strasbourg, where he was ordained and finished his doctoral dissertation. Although trained for teaching, he received a call in 1666 to serve as senior minister at Frankfurt.

While serving this city, Spener became dissatisfied with contemporary 17th-century Christianity and worked out his Pietistic program. He called for a greater use of Scripture, more involvement of the laity in the work of the church, increased emphasis on good works in Christianity, stringent piety for ministers, and more preaching on the spiritual life. These suggestions were published in an influential book called *Pia desideria* ("Pious Wishes," (1675). Spener's proposals for reform became the object of discussion in a large-scale pamphlet literature.

The initial success of his suggestions waned, however, when the implications of his ideas became clear. Clergymen felt threatened by the incursion of laity; professors of theology disliked being told that they needed to emphasize the heart as much as the head; and others resented change from the familiar Protestant scholasticism which had settled over Germany. Spener himself became concerned when little groups who followed his ideas tended to develop into churches apart from the main state church and he even wrote a pamphlet condemning Separatism in an effort to combat this tendency.

In 1686, after twenty years at Frankfurt, Spener took the post of court preacher to Elector John George III of Saxony. Although much about his five-year stay at Dresden was unhappy, he did make the acquaintance of August Hermann Francke (1663–1727) who was to succeed him as the leader of the German Pietist movement. Spener moved again in 1691 and became an executive in the Lutheran church at Berlin where he remained until his death, carrying on a vigorous defense of the spreading Pietist movement. Among the strong accusations brought against the Pietists were those of the University of Wittenberg which claimed that the movement was guilty of at least 284 heresies.

Spener's letters, papers, and writings have been gathered into eight volumes and present a rather full view of his work. He did not argue with the more orthodox theologians of his day but he put a heavier emphasis on those doctrines which played a direct part in personal religious experience. Spener felt that controversy with the Reformed Church was unnecessary, even though he could not accept the Calvinist doctrine of predestination. His reform ideas involved the rejection of the Scholastic tradition of the late Middle Ages. Pietism places a larger emphasis on regeneration than on justification. There is an interest in the anthropological aspects of salvation rather than in the doctrinal side. It has been pointed out that Spener's ideas were influential in the experience of Nicholas Zinzendorf (1700–1760), founder of the Moravian Church, and through the Moravians on John Wesley (1703–1791), who founded the Methodist Church and emphasized experiential perfection.

BIBLIOGRAPHY: P. J. Spener, *Pia desideria* (Philadelphia, 1964); J. T. McNeill, *Modern Christian Movements* (Philadelphia, 1954); M. E. Richard, *P. J. Spener and His Work* (Philadelphia, 1893); F. E. Stoeffler, *The Rise of Evangelical Pietism* (Leiden, 1965).

**Spengler, Oswald** (1880–1936). German philosopher of history. Between 1911 and 1922 in Munich he composed and revised the two-volume work for which he is chiefly known: *The Decline of the West* (English translation, 1926–1928). Its gloomy, fatalistic prognosis received immediate recognition when published during and after the collapse of the German forces in World War I. He claimed that he owed "everything" to Goethe and to Nietzsche, although his organic theory of the rise and fall of civilizations is more like that of G. B. Vico before him and Arnold Toynbee after him.

**Speyer, Diets of** (1526 and 1529). Emperor Charles V wanted strict enforcement of the 1521 Edict of Worms (see WORMS, DIET OF) and eradication of Lutheranism in Germany, but his war with the pope enabled the Lutheran municipal and princely estates, led by Elector John Frederick of Saxony and Landgrave Philip of Hesse, to press for elim-

ination of churchly abuses at the Diet in 1526. They won the right of princes to order religious affairs in their own territories; they also called for a free council on German soil and the setting aside of the Edict of Worms. These acts formed the legal basis for continuing the work of reform in their territories, but the effective religious division of Germany dates from this Diet.

By 1529, when a further Diet met at Speyer, the emperor had defeated his enemies and was in a position to press his religious demands. A largely Roman Catholic commission asked for the abrogation of the 1526 resolutions and for enforcement of the Edict of Worms. When this proposed legislation had been passed, the evangelical estates lodged an oral protest on April 19, and a written one the next day, declaring that they could not abandon the resolutions of 1526 or the principles of their religion. Because of this protest, the label "protestant" was attached to the Lutherans and later to other evangelical groups.

**Spinola, Christoph Royas de** (1626–1695). Roman Catholic unionist. Entering the Franciscan Order at Cologne, Spinola eventually became provincial curator and general definitor. He assumed the bishopric of Knin (Yugoslavia) in 1666, and of Vienna Neustadt in 1685. He worked actively for church union (writing a tract, *Concordia christiana*), and supported the efforts of Molanus and Leibnitz. After 1671 he visited Protestant princes for the emperor, and became the authorized agent for unity questions in 1695, but he accomplished little without the Curia's support. His plan for a Vienna dialogue failed because of Protestant distrust.

**Spinoza, Baruch** (1632–1677). Dutch philosopher. He was born in Amsterdam of a Portuguese Jewish family and educated in both religious and secular lore. The study of Descartes and the physical sciences caused him to accept views that led to his excommunication at the age of twenty-four from the Jewish synagogue. He became a lens grinder, lived quietly near The Hague and produced his philosophic works. Among the more important of these are *Tract on God and Man and His Happiness*, *Theological-Political Tract*, and *Ethics Demonstrated with Geometrical Order*. In 1673, he refused an opportunity to become professor of philosophy at the University of Heidelberg because it would restrict his freedom. Spinoza adopted the mathematical method of Descartes but rejected the Cartesian dualism between the material world and the immaterial mind. Matter and mind, he taught, are both aspects of God and have no existence apart from him. God is not an individual but one absolute, infinite, and all-present substance which is known by thought and extension. Spinoza's pantheism, as his system came to be called, left no room for the orthodox understanding of God. He denied the inspiration of the Bible, the efficacy of prayer, and miracles. He did believe, however, in the immortality of the soul as a kind of absorption into an impersonal, all-present soul of God.

**Spiritual Exercises.** A handbook of meditations by Ignatius Loyola. Originating in the mystical experiences of Ignatius while at Loyola in 1521, and taking more explicit shape during his life at Manresa in 1522, the *Exercises* were revised and expanded during the greater part of his life. In their final form, of which the earliest extant text is dated 1541, they are a concise handbook for one who is to guide others to find the will of God in regard to their lives, and to confirm them in the resolution to follow that will. The book stresses the activity of the exercitant; the exercises are to be "performed" to obtain the desired result. There are four "weeks" of meditations: (1) on sin and its consequences, to reform the deformed; (2) on Christ's life on earth, to conform the reformed; (3) on Christ's passion, to confirm the conformed; (4) on the risen life, to transform the confirmed. Throughout the book are suggestions for the ascetical life, instructions on prayer, the avoidance of scrupulosity, the evaluation of impulses and motives, and the rules for "thinking with the Church." At the request of Francis Borgia they were examined by papal censors and given solemn approbation by Pope Paul III in 1548. Their widespread good effects caused later popes to prescribe them, especially for candidates for orders.

**Spiritual Franciscans.** Even during the lifetime of Francis of Assisi a dispute arose over the possession of material wealth by his followers. The Spiritual Franciscans insisted on a return to the austerity required by the rule. In 1230 the decretal *Quo elongati* permitted the corporate possession of wealth, but the Spirituals continued to insist on evangelical poverty. Bonaventure offered a compromise solution whereby the friars would be permitted only the use of such things as were necessary for their work. Nicholas III ratified this suggestion in *Exiit qui seminat* (1279), but it was rejected by the Spirituals. In 1317, John XXII condemned them and burned four intransigents as heretics (here they were first called Fraticelli), enjoining obedience under threat of excommunication. Louis of Bavaria was

sympathetic to their cause, and William of Occam became their literary champion. In 1323 the papal bull *Cum inter nonnullos* declared absolute poverty to be heretical. The Conventuals, those permitting wealth, were supported by FitzRalph in *De pauperie salvatoris*. The views of the Spirituals were taken over by the Friars of the Spiritual Observance (Observants). The works of Joachim of Flora were influential among the Spirituals.

**Spiritualism.** Throughout the history of the church there have been instances of protest against orthodox ecclesiastical forces by those who appeal directly to the Holy Spirit, bypassing or minimizing the norms or authority of Jesus Christ, the visible institution, or creeds. The emphasis on the Spirit is linked variously to apocalypticism, the periodization of history, voluntary poverty, theocratic programs, mysticism and other forms of inner piety, humanistic rationalism, and anti-Trinitarianism. These diverse and sometimes unrelated phenomena, because of their common appeal to the Spirit, are often designated by the term "Spiritualism."

The prototype of Spiritualism is Montanism, a movement stemming from a Phyrgian convert to Christianity, Montanus, who in about A.D. 171 declared that he was the promised Paraclete of the Gospel of John. He and his "prophetesses," Prisca and Maximilla, purported to utter spiritual prophecies enjoining an ecstatic speaking in tongues, a rigorist morality to the point of martyrdom, a strict church discipline with respect to those who had lapsed under persecution, and the fallenness of the general church. They declared that the New Jerusalem would soon descend on Phrygia, to which the faithful should gather.

A medieval outbreak of Spiritualism was stimulated by the Flemish Tanchelm (or Tanquelin), who appeared as a revolutionary leader in Zeeland, Brabant, Utrecht, and Antwerp in about 1110. Starting from a message of protest against the wealth and immorality of the clergy, he moved on to declare that he possessed the Holy Spirit, to the same degree that Christ did and that he was, like Christ, God. His following was large and endured for a number of years after his death (c. 1115). He had numerous counterparts and imitators in the ensuing decades, but the next major Spiritualist figure was Joachim of Flora (d. 1202). Joachim did not appeal to a spiritual source outside Scripture but instead claimed to find the exegetical clue to Scripture in the notion of the periodization of history in three successive stages: the Age of the Father, or Law; the Age of the Son, or Gospel; and the

Age of the Spirit, in which the "everlasting gospel" replaces the precepts of the New Testament. The Joachite message of the new age of the Spirit was to be reflected not only in the Spiritual Franciscans but also in the secular thinkers Auguste Comte and Karl Marx.

The Spiritual Franciscans were followers of Francis of Assisi who deplored the second-generation tendency to soften if not reverse the early Franciscan program of poverty. John of Parma, Peter John Olivi, and Jacopone da Todi gave 14th-century inspiration to the Fraticelli, the Beghards, and the Beguines.

Among the Reformers, Spiritualism was evident as early as 1521, when Andreas Carlstadt celebrated a radically Protestant Communion service, stressing the supremacy of the Spirit over the letter. At about the same time the three "Zwickau prophets" claimed spirit possession and direct revelation, as did the revolutionary Thomas Müntzer (d. 1525). Kaspar Schwenkfeld manifested Spiritualist tendencies in his rejection of any redemptive character to the outward rite of even believers' baptism, and Melchior Hofmann, also in Strasbourg in 1529, rejected Lutheran ecclesiastical views of the Lord's Supper and engaged in a spiritualizing exegesis tending toward apocalypticism. In the same year there came to Strasbourg yet another Spiritualist, Sebastian Franck, who was moving from Lutheranism, with its rejection of Anabaptism and Spiritualism, to an avowed Spiritualism in which he advocated the elimination of audible prayer, preaching, ceremonies, sacraments, and ordination in favor of a purely invisible church. Diverse outcroppings of 16th-century Protestant Spiritualism are seen also in Prussia, Silesia, Poland, the Netherlands, and Switzerland.

A notable and enduring Spiritualism appeared in George Fox (d. 1691), whose doctrine of the Inner Light became a central tenet of the Society of Friends (Quakers).

The term "spiritualism" is used also for the idea of communication with departed spirits. See the following article.

BIBLIOGRAPHY: G. H. Williams, *The Radical Reformation* (Philadelphia, 1962).

**Spiritualism in America.** Spiritualism, or spiritism, as it is sometimes called, is the belief that the spirits of the dead or departed communicate with the living. The belief resembles aspects of the Christian's confession of a "communion of saints," ministers to a human longing and curiosity to know that there is life after death, and sometimes represents a refined form of animism, reported,

e.g., from Haiti and among North American Indians. Although the modern movement owes something to Emmanuel Swedenborg, Franz Mesmer, and A. J. Davis, author of *Principles of Nature, Her Divine Revelations, and a Voice to Mankind* (1847), interest was stimulated by the strange communications to Margaret and Kate Fox, children of Hydesville, N.Y., who were said to be able to decode rappings from spirits in 1848. Interest spread not only among the uneducated and presumably more credulous but also among distinguished persons, e.g., Alfred Russel Wallace, Arthur Conan Doyle, Oliver Lodge, William James, James Hyslop, Morton Prince. According to the National Spiritualist Association of Churches, formed in 1893, followers affirm among other beliefs in a Declaration of Principles, the existence of "Infinite Intelligence," the "existence and personal identity of the individual" after death, and that "communication with the so-called dead is a fact, scientifically proven by the phenomena of spiritualism." Communication in spiritualism usually takes place through mediums at seances. As indicated in the *Spiritualist Manual* (7th ed., 1944), there is much variety in types of mediumship, e.g., in the use of trances, simple repetition of messages, reporting of visual occurrences, and decoding a wide range of physical phenomena. Spiritualists have gathered in churches and camps and in a Federation of Spiritual Churches and Association (1944). In the 1960's, spiritualists numbered approximately 250,000 in England, and in the United States nearly 180,000.

There has been a continued quest for adequate means of research through experimental studies in extrasensory perception, including telepathy, clairvoyance, and precognition. The Society for Psychical Research was formed in London in 1882. More recent experiments have been carried out by J. B. Rhine at the Parapsychology Laboratory, Duke University (1934), and in other places in America and Europe. Obviously, the claims of spiritualists lend themselves readily to imposture, and such experiments in parapsychology attempt to detect error, deliberate trickery, and self-delusion, as well as to investigate the problem with which spiritualism is concerned. The Holy Office of the Roman Catholic Church condemned spiritistic practices in 1898, although it permitted scientific investigation of extrasensory phenomena.

**Spitta, Friedrich** (1852–1924). German Protestant theologian. A professor of New Testament at Bonn, Strasbourg, and Göttingen, he was joint editor from 1895 with Julius

Smend of *Monatsschrift für Gottesdienst und kirchliche Kunst*. His best-known works are *Zur Geschichte und Litteratur des Urchristentums* (3 vols., 1893–1907) and *Das Johannes-Evangelium als Quelle der Geschichte Jesu* (1910).

**Spottiswoode, John** (1565–1639). Scottish churchman and historian. Having studied at the University of Glasgow under Andrew and James Melville, this son of one of the "superintendents" of the Kirk began his ministerial career as a strict adherent to the principles of presbyterianism. As the relations between Kirk and king became strained he veered toward the king and prelacy. He accompanied James VI to London in 1603 and was used by the new monarch of England to attempt to integrate the Church of Scotland and the English Church. James could not tolerate the idea that ministers should dictate to the nation in civil matters, so Spottiswoode became James's agent and an Erastian of the strictest type. He was advanced in Scotland. In 1605 he was made a member of the Privy Council. He became bishop of Glasgow, and in 1615 archbishop of St. Andrews. He presided over several assemblies of the Church of Scotland at which unpopular measures of the king were adopted, including the Five Articles of Perth in 1618. He was also very high in the favor of Charles I, whom he crowned at Holyrood in 1633. He observed the riots that resulted from the introduction of the new liturgy and sought to modify the king's demands. In 1638 the National Covenant was approved, and Spottiswoode fled. His best-known literary work is a history of the Church of Scotland.

**Sprague, William Buell** (1795–1876). Congregational clergyman. Graduated from Yale College in 1815 and Princeton Seminary in 1819, he was ordained and installed in the Congregational Church of West Springfield, Mass., in 1819 and served that congregation until he was called to the Second Presbyterian Church of Albany, N.Y., where he remained for forty years. Sprague published *Annals of the American Pulpit* and numerous other works.

**Springfield Presbytery.** A New Light body in Kentucky and Ohio founded by Barton W. Stone and four friends, when opposition to their revivals caused them to withdraw from the Presbyterian Synod of Kentucky in September, 1803. In June, 1804, it was dissolved in favor of a looser congregational body called simply the "Christian Church," which is one of the sources of the present denomination of that name.

**Spurgeon, Charles Haddon** (1834–1892). English Baptist preacher. The descendant of several generations of Independent ministers, he became a Baptist preacher in 1850. He was pastor of the Baptist congregation at Waterbeach (1852) and at the Metropolitan Tabernacle in Newington (1854). A devout Calvinist, he had a bitter controversy (1864) with the Evangelical party of the Established Church for advocating baptismal regeneration. The quarrel led to a rupture with the Baptist Union (1887).

**Stability, Vow of.** A promise given by all monks living under the Benedictine Rule to remain until death connected with the monastery where they initially entered their order. Benedict (c. 480–c. 543) included this vow in his rule, voiding the earlier practice which allowed monks to change monasteries at will. The vow contributed to the unification, organization, and continuity of Western monasticism and through it was furthered Benedict's own concept of the monastery as a large family with the abbot as father.

**Staël-Holstein, Auguste-Louis de** (1790–1827). Son of the famous Anne Louise Germaine, baroness of Staël-Holstein. Educated at a Protestant school in Geneva, Staël moved to Paris to complete his education in political science, economics, and philosophy. He fled to Switzerland under Napoleon's wrath, and then to England, where he made the acquaintance of political figures such as William Wilberforce. Returning to Coppet in 1814, he engaged in politics and again aroused the irritation of Napoleon. An active Protestant and head of the Bible society, he was a benevolent philanthropist. He edited a number of his mother's works.

**Stahl, Friedrich Julius** (1802–1861). German Protestant ecclesiastical jurist and statesman. The son of Jewish parents, he became a Christian in 1819. He studied law at Würzburg, Heidelberg, and Erlangen. He was professor of ecclesiastical law at Erlangen (1832), Würzburg (1833), and Berlin (1840). A prominent leader in the Conservative Party, both in politics and in religious affairs, he held high positions in the Prussian Government and Church.

**Stained Glass.** Decorative glass colored by any of several techniques. The origin of the art is lost in antiquity, but it seems to have entered Europe from Egypt. Stained glass has been widely used in scenic church windows since the 10th century. An important feature of Romanesque architecture, it came to its highest expression in the Gothic period of the

13th and 14th centuries. Its popularity in the present era is demonstrated by the acclaim that has greeted Marc Chagall's "Jerusalem Windows."

**Stanislaus** (1030–1079). Roman Catholic prelate. Born of Polish nobility, he was educated at Gnesen and in 1072 was elected bishop of Kraków. He rebuked the king, Boleslav II, for his personal immorality, finally excommunicating him. The king then attacked and killed Stanislaus while the bishop was celebrating Mass. The details of the story are questionable, and it has been asserted that Stanislaus was put to death for treason against the king. He is known as the patron saint of Poland.

**Stankevich, Nicolai Vladimirovich** (1813–1840). Leader of a philosophic circle of students in Moscow in the 1830's and an ardent adherent of German idealistic philosophy. Like his fellow members of the intelligentsia under the repressive regime of Czar Nicholas I, Stankevich felt that the search for abstract truths would provide guides for practical life on both the personal and sociopolitical levels.

**Stapleton, Thomas** (1535–1598). Roman Catholic controversialist. A fellow of New College, Oxford, he left England upon Elizabeth's accession, traveling to Louvain and Paris to study theology. In 1563 he refused to take the oath that would permit him to return to England. He retired permanently to Louvain, sojourning for three years at Douai to help William Allen found the English College there. In 1590, Philip II appointed him professor of Scripture at Louvain. His works include a translation of Bede's *History of the Church in England* and the *Apology of Staphylus and Hosius,* as well as many controversial treatises written in Latin.

**Starets** (pl., *startsi*). In Russian, literally, an "elder"; actually a religious leader possessed of particular holiness and of special charismatic powers. A major institution in Russian popular religion, the *starets* was generally a monk and resided in or near a monastery where he performed a pastoral function for the tens of thousands of pilgrims who sought him out. Best known to Western Christians through Dostoevsky's character Father Zossima in *The Brothers Karamazov,* these confessor wonder-workers played a major role in the Russian spiritual revival of the late 19th century.

**Staupitz, John** (c. 1469–1524). German theologian, vicar-general of the Augustinian Observantist congregations in Germany, and dean of the theological faculty at Wittenberg.

He became the spiritual adviser of Luther when the latter came to Wittenberg in 1508. Staupitz directed Luther to the Scriptures and induced him to study for the doctorate in theology. Later, Luther praised Staupitz for having led him into a knowledge of the grace of God. The emphasis which Staupitz put on humility as the way to Christian perfection left a strong imprint on Luther's early thought.

**Stearns, Shubal** (1706–1771). Baptist clergyman. Boston born, little educated, he was ordained a Baptist minister in 1751. He worked in Virginia and in 1755 began a Baptist congregation at Sandy Creek, N.C., out of which emerged the Sandy Creek Association of Separatist Baptists. An ardent revivalist, he contributed greatly to the growth of Baptists in the South, especially during the 1760's.

**Stein, Lorenz von** (1815–1890). German political theorist and economist. Influenced by Fichte and Hegel, Stein was professor of constitutional law and national economy at Kiel (1846–1851); in 1855 he moved to Vienna to teach. He was ennobled in 1868. Stein deplored the Germanic emphasis on the state to the detriment of society. Even before Marx he recognized the implications of the social questions that arose from industrialism. His *Der Sozialismus und Kommunismus des heutigen Frankreich* (1842), a pioneer study, distinguished the socioeconomic from the politico-governmental sphere of life.

**Steinbart, Gotthelf Samuel** (1738–1809). Eclectic German rationalist. Influenced by S. J. Baumgarten, Wilhelm Teller, J. G. Toellner, Locke, and Voltaire, Steinbart taught theology and philosophy at Frankfurt an der Oder (1774) and administered the orphanage and seminary. Allowing some validity to revelation, he criticized the Old Testament conception of God and resultant atonement theory, and urged instead reasoned reliance on God's love; Jesus taught "virtues" as the way to bliss. His major work was *System der reinen Philosophie oder Glückseitslehre.*

**Steinkopf, Karl Friedrich Adolf** (1773–1859). German churchman. Secretary of the Basel Christentumsgesellschaft (1795–1800) and cofounder of the Basel Missionary Society, Steinkopf served a Lutheran congregation in London after 1801. He visited Europe for the British and Foreign Bible Society and the Religious Tract Society in 1812, 1815, and 1820, actively organizing European Bible societies and obtaining financial aid for Roman Catholic societies. After the Apocrypha conflict he returned to London in 1826 to work with the Society.

**Steinmetz, Johann Adam** (1689–1762). German Lutheran pastor and educator. He was called in 1732 as general superintendent of the duchy of Magdeburg and abbot of the Bergen Cloister. Under the influence of Halle Pietism, he developed a cloister school that attracted students from influential families. A journal, *Theologia pastoralis practica,* was published by him from 1737 to 1758. He is given credit as an important link between German Pietists and American churchmen. A Pietist hymnal (1738) is another of his publications.

**Stelzle, Charles** (1869–1941). Presbyterian minister and sociologist. He grew up on New York's poverty-stricken East Side and worked as a machinist for eight years. Then he entered the ministry to bring the gospel to the workingman. In 1903 he became secretary of the Department of Church and Labor of the Presbyterian Church U.S.A. In 1910 he founded Labor Temple on New York's East Side, which he made into a famous institutional church.

**Stephanus Gobarus** (6th century). A writer about 575. He is known only from excerpts in the *Myriobiblion* of Photius, which show that he collected opinions of the early fathers, apparently in order to illustrate their disagreements. Adolf von Harnack compared his work with the *Sic et non* of Peter Abelard, but it is difficult to prove that Gobarus possessed Abelard's theological sophistication. The collection is of some value because of the lost documents recorded in it.

**Stephen I** (d. 257). Pope from 254. He is best known for his vigorous defense against Cyprian of the Roman tradition of the validity of heretical or schismatic Baptism. Stephen's efforts to enforce this position throughout the church are one of the first attempts to claim universal authority for the Roman see, but with his death at the beginning of the persecution of Valerian the controversy remained in suspense.

**Stephen II** (III) (d. 757). Pope from 752. Since a predecessor named Stephen died before consecration, and is not always included in papal lists, this pope is counted as either the second or the third Stephen. The Lombard king Aistulf began a siege on Rome, forcing Stephen to seek aid first from Constantinople, then from the Frankish king Pepin III. In 754, Stephen crowned Pepin and his sons in return for the granting of political authority over central Italy (the Donation of Pepin). The Franks entered Italy and subdued the Lombards. Stephen died shortly thereafter.

**Stephen Harding** (d. 1134). Third abbot of Cîteaux. An Englishman, he became a monk at Molesme, leaving in 1098 with Robert to form the new community in France at Cîteaux. He was elected abbot in 1109, which office he held when Bernard and thirty companions entered the monastery. His regulations for the early Cistercian houses were incorporated into the *Charta Caritatis,* which for some time was attributed entirely to him. His personal asceticism is reflected in the early history of the Cistercian Order.

**Stephen of Hungary** (c. 975–1038). The "Apostle of Hungary." With his father, Duke Geza, he was converted by Adalbert of Prague. In 997 he succeeded his father and began to incorporate the Hungarians under his rule. In 1001 he received a royal crown from Pope Sylvester II, becoming the first king of Hungary. He established bishoprics and monasteries throughout the kingdom while ruthlessly suppressing paganism. He is regarded as the patron saint of Hungary.

**Stephen of Muret** (c. 1050–1124). Founder of the hermitic Order of Grandmont. He was the son of a French nobleman, but the details of his life are now lost amid legend. He gathered around him an austere religious community in the desert of Muret, near Limoges (c. 1110), modeled after the discipline of the Calabrian hermits. Following his death, his disciples moved the foundation to Grandmont. A rule attributed to him was not written until after his death.

**Sternhold, Thomas** (d. 1549). English versifier of the Psalter. His initial collection of metrical psalms, rendered in ballad rhythm and dedicated to Edward VI, was supplemented first by John Hopkins and later by other writers, the entire Psalter being issued by John Day in 1562, as an appendix to the Book of Common Prayer. The collection, often called the Old Version, was generally known as "Sternhold and Hopkins," and achieved great popularity in both England and Scotland.

**Sterry, Peter** (c. 1613–1672). Oliver Cromwell's chaplain. A graduate of Emmanuel College, Cambridge, a member of the Westminster Assembly, and chaplain to Lady Brooke in 1644, Sterry was an intimate of Sir Henry Vane and Richard Baxter. He was voted preacher to the council of state. Out of favor after Cromwell's death, he lived in London as a tutor and writer. By nature mystical, and strongly influenced by Jakob Boehme, Sterry was at once Platonist and Puritan.

**Stewart, Charles James** (1775–1837). Anglican bishop of Quebec. He was born in

England and educated at Oxford, receiving his B.A. degree in 1795 and his M.A. in 1799. In 1807 he undertook work in Canada on behalf of the Society for the Propagation of the Gospel. After several years of missionary activities, he was selected to succeed Jacob Mountain as bishop of Quebec (1825).

**Stiles, Ezra** (1727–1795). Congregational clergyman. Graduating from Yale in 1746, he was a tutor there beginning in 1749 for six years. During that time he also studied law and after admission to the bar in 1753 had a two-year part-time practice. In 1755 he was ordained and installed pastor of the Second Congregational Church, Newport, R.I., which he served for twenty-one years. While at Newport he was a librarian, studied Hebrew and several other languages, had an important part in the founding of Rhode Island College (Brown University), carried on a voluminous correspondence, and became generally recognized as the most learned man in New England. He is also said to have predicted as early as 1765 that the colonies would one day declare their independence. In March, 1776, the war forced him to flee from Newport and in May, 1777, he became pastor at Portsmouth, N.H. The following September he was elected president of Yale and was installed in July, 1778. He led Yale during some of its most turbulent years, also teaching church history and theology. He was a prolific writer and left unfinished an *Ecclesiastical History of New England* and other manuscripts. His diary and papers, now published, are of great historical value.

**Stillingfleet, Edward** (1635–1699). Scholar and bishop of Worcester. He graduated from St. John's College, Cambridge, and was ordained by Ralph Browning, deprived bishop of Exeter. After receiving the rectory of Sutton, Bedfordshire, he published a book, *Irenicum,* arguing for a compromise between Episcopalians and Presbyterians. Three years later in 1662 he published *Origines sacrae,* which asserted the divinity of the Scriptures by historical argument. This was followed in two years by the polemical anti-Roman Catholic, *A Rational Account of the Grounds of the Protestant Religion.* These works justly brought him wide acknowledgment, and a number of posts were given him, including a canonry in Canterbury Cathedral in 1669. He became archdeacon of London in 1677 and soon gained wide attention as a preacher. Although in favor with the Establishment, he remained on good terms with the nonconformists, whom he befriended on more than one occasion. In 1678, he was made dean of St.

Paul's, where he wrote *Origines Britannicae* (published in 1685), an investigation of the origins of Christianity in Britain. Disturbed by the religious policy of James II, he was in favor at once after the Revolution (1689) and was installed as bishop of Worcester. An able bishop, he was prominent in his own day, though his written works have not endured the test of time.

**Stockholm Conference** (1925). At the end of World War I, plans were made to convene an international conference of church leaders to consider proper Christian attitudes and approaches to ethical problems facing the postwar world. The Universal Christian Conference on Life and Work met in Stockholm, Aug. 19–30, 1925, attended by over 500 delegates of some 91 church bodies from 37 nations, to seek ways of applying the gospel in all areas of human life. The conference members, suspending all problems of Faith and Order, directed attention to moral questions in the economic, social, and political realms. In a concluding "Message," the Conference expressed the collective view that the church, in its concern for human welfare and personality, should involve itself in economic and industrial problems. Opposition to social and moral evils such as slums, alcohol, and crime was strongly declared, and the need to work for their extirpation stressed. Deploring racial discrimination and war, the Conference emphasized the responsibility of the church to promote brotherhood and international cooperation. The "Message" was not binding on the participating churches, leaving each to act suitably in its own sociopolitical context. The deliberations were continued at the Oxford (1937) and Amsterdam (1948) Conferences.

**Stoddard, Solomon** (1643–1729). Congregational clergyman at Northampton, Mass. (1672–1729). He was a leader in the movement to grant full church membership and both ordinances to those who, though destitute of a conversion experience, exhibited godliness, which was contrary to New England Covenant Theology. This "Stoddardeanism," vigorously opposed by the Mathers, and later by Stoddard's grandson Jonathan Edwards, became prevalent in the Connecticut Valley, even into the 18th century.

**Stoecker, Adolf** (1835–1908). Protestant minister, politician, and social reformer, less a creative thinker than a man of practical affairs. From 1874 court preacher in Berlin, he encountered extensive religious apathy and social problems which he sought to stem with a political party, founded in 1878, an effort to apply the principles of the gospel to the problems of the day. After his election to the German diet in 1881 he became the spokesman with increasing frequency for a vehement anti-Semitism.

**Stoglav, Council of.** See COUNCIL OF 1551.

**Stoicism.** A school of philosophy founded by Zeno of Citium (d. 264 B.C.). It was espoused by such men as Cleanthes and Chrysippus among the Greeks and Brutus, Cato, Cicero, Seneca, Epictetus, and Marcus Aurelius among the Romans. Its materialism is the source of Tertullian's corporeal doctrine of the soul. The Christian doctrine of the Logos is related to the Stoic concept of the *spermatikos logos*. The theism and high moral standards of the Stoics made them appeal to early Christians more than any other pagans except Plato, and extensive use of Stoic sources occurs, for example, in the Alexandrians Clement and Origen and in the Latin writers Ambrose and Augustine.

**Stolz, Alban** (1808–1883). German Roman Catholic theologian and writer. A student of Johann Hirscher, ordained as vicar in Rotenfels (1833), Stolz taught religion at Bruchsal (1835), and theology and pedagogy at Freiburg (1847). He was known chiefly for *Kalender für Zeit und Ewigkeit* (1843 ff.), widely circulated among Protestants as well as Roman Catholics; it contained meditations and travelogues. His satirical writings showed sharp perceptive ability, and at times a mystical inclination.

**Stone, Barton Warren** (1772–1844). Frontier evangelist. Converted to Presbyterianism in North Carolina, he preached in Tennessee and in 1798 was ordained pastor of Cane Ridge and Concord, Ky. James McGready's revivals two hundred miles south in Logan County spread to Cane Ridge through his preaching, and beginning in August, 1801, huge camp meetings were held with thousands in attendance. Opposition developed in the Synod of Kentucky against the emotionalism of the revivals and their implicit denial of Calvinism, and Stone and others feared repressive measures and severe disciplining. Stone, having had doubts about Calvinism since before his ordination anyway, with four friends withdrew in 1803 and set up the independent Springfield Presbytery. It was dissolved, however, in 1804, and its congregations continued under the nonsectarian title "Christian," with each congregation fully sovereign. Stone met Alexander Campbell in 1824, and in 1832 merged with some of Campbell's followers in Kentucky. About fifty "Christian" congregations, approximately half of the total, went into the union with the Disciples of Christ. This union Stone called "the very noblest act of my life." In 1834 he moved to Jacksonville, Ill., and continued his traveling, preaching, and writing.

**Storch, Nicholas.** See ZWICKAU PROPHETS.

**Stowe, Harriet Beecher** (1811–1896). American author. Daughter of Lyman Beecher, she was heir to the same Calvinistic tradition that produced a generation of Beechers devoted to religion and public service. Her contributions lie in the realm of literature. For thirty years she averaged a book a year. *Uncle Tom's Cabin* (1852) ranks as the most important antislavery propaganda published in America. Later novels examine New England life, presenting a realistic picture of the relationship between religion and personality, and are a source for understanding post-Edwardsian piety.

**Strabo, Walafrid.** See WALAFRID STRABO.

**Strachan, John** (1778–1867). Canadian Anglican bishop. He was born at Aberdeen, Scotland, and educated at the University of Aberdeen (M.A., 1796) and St. Andrews. He came to Canada in 1799 and taught school at Kingston and Cornwall. After his ordination in 1803 he was appointed rector of Cornwall, and in 1812 he became rector of York. In 1818 he was appointed to the Executive Council, and to the Legislative Council of Upper Canada in 1820. He became first president of King's College in 1827, and in 1852 founded the University of Trinity College, Toronto. He was appointed first bishop of Toronto in 1839.

**Strauss, David Friedrich** (1808–1874). German theologian and writer. Born at Ludwigsburg, he studied theology and philosophy at Tübingen and Berlin. He was deeply influenced by the teachings of F. D. E. Schleiermacher and G. W. F. Hegel, an influence fully developed in his famous *Das Leben Jesu* (1835). In this book Strauss applied the concept of myth to theological work and argued that the whole gospel tradition was only the "historical garb fashioned for primitive Christian ideas by naïve poetic mythmakers and consolidated in an historical personality." The development of early Christianity was to be understood in terms of the Hegelian dialectic; the gospel was thus a myth employed to glorify the foundations and founder of Christianity. Strauss's work had a profound influence on subsequent German theology in the 19th century, leading to the formation of three theological parties: positive, mediating, and liberal. Strauss himself became the center of a storm of protest and was forced to leave the teaching profession to earn his livelihood. In later life he rejected Christianity entirely in favor of scientific materialism.

**Strigel, Victorinus** (1524–1569). German theologian and Melanchthonian. Strigel was instructor successively at Wittenberg, Magdeburg, Erfurt, and Jena. He was attacked by Flacius for synergism and publicly defended himself before Duke John Frederick in 1560. He moved to Leipzig, where he found himself under attack again. In the Palatinate, he accepted the Reformed view of the Lord's Supper (1567) and taught at Heidelberg. He wrote widely on philosophy, philology, history, and theology, and produced a Bible commentary.

**Strong, Augustus Hopkins** (1836–1921). Baptist pastor and educator. After an education at Yale and at Rochester Theological Seminary and a year of study at Berlin, Strong was ordained in the Baptist ministry in 1861. He served churches in Massachusetts and Ohio until 1872, when he became president and professor of Biblical theology at Rochester. He encouraged his students to do independent work in historical theology and to go beyond his own conservative position. He is remembered today for his work on theology as reflected in 19th-century literature.

**Strong, Josiah** (1847–1916). Congregational clergyman and prominent Social Gospel exponent. Strong came to national attention in 1885 with the publication of *Our Country,* a pioneer sociological treatise. He sounded the note of crisis in the dangers inherent in the concentration of wealth, class distinctions, the discontents of labor, slums, immigration, and a gross materialism that was corrupting public morals. He challenged the churches to become the "conscience of the social organism." Influenced by Horace Bushnell's theology, Strong emphasized the earthly Kingdom, to be perpetuated by the churches in interdenominational fellowship. Their task was to reconcile socialism and individualism, social responsibility and property rights. In 1886, Strong was appointed secretary of the American Evangelical Alliance. In 1898 he resigned to form the League for Social Service (American Institute for Social Service in 1902). In 1904 he organized the British Institute of Social Service. He was coeditor of *The Kingdom* (1894–1899), the most influential Social Gospel journal of its day. Strong was influential in the formation of the Federal Council of Churches and helped make the Chautauqua movement a forum for the Social Gospel. Important works included *The New Era* (1893), *The Twentieth Century City* (1898), *Religious Movements for Social Betterment* (1900), and *The Challenge of the City* (1907).

**Strossmayer, Joseph Georg** (1815–1905). German Roman Catholic bishop. Born in Croatia, ordained priest in 1838, he became professor of canon law at Vienna (1847) and bishop of Djakovo in 1850. At the Vatican Council of 1869–1870 he joined with J. H. Reinkens to attack papal infallibility and to defend Protestantism. After several years of opposition, he finally published the Vatican decrees in his diocesan journal. Despite his German ancestry, he was a strong pan-Slavist.

**Stuart, Charles** (*known as* "the Young Pretender") (1720–1788). Grandson of James II and eldest son of James Edward, the Old Pretender. Handsome and adventurous, he was called Bonnie Prince Charlie by his Scottish supporters. Raised in exile, he led the Jacobite revolt of 1745, invading England after winning most of Scotland. Final defeat came at Culloden in April, 1746, ending the last serious threat to the settlement of 1688–1689. Charles then returned to exile.

**Stuart, John** (1740–1811). Episcopal missionary. He was born at Paxton, Pa., and educated at the College of Philadelphia and the University of Pennsylvania (B.A., 1763; M.A., 1770; D.D., 1799). After being ordained by the Church of England in 1770, he was sent as a missionary to the Mohawks at Fort Hunter, N.Y., and went to Canada during the American Revolution. He taught school at Montreal between 1781 and 1785. Thereafter he became the first Church of England missionary to the "Western Settlements" and the rector of St. George's Church, Kingston, in 1785.

**Stuart, Moses** (1780–1852). American Biblical scholar. Educated at Yale, Stuart fell under the influence of Timothy Dwight and returned to New Haven as a tutor. He was ordained in 1806 and four years later went to Andover Seminary as professor of sacred literature. Lacking scholarly training, he taught himself Hebrew and in 1821 published the first American Hebrew grammar. His contributions also include work in Greek and German. Through a series of commentaries, he introduced Americans to new trends in German Biblical scholarship. He produced more than forty books and pamphlets and gained an international reputation as a Biblical scholar.

**Student Christian Movement.** Generally, the total student Christian enterprise including many organizations. Its beginnings as a movement are associated with the Y.M.C.A., which was founded in London (1844) and adapted as a student organization in 1858. Formal plans for an intercollegiate Y.M.C.A. were inaugurated in 1877 in America. The Y.W.C.A., with beginnings in 1858, formed a national student organization in 1886. The development of the Student Volunteer Movement from 1887 provided another element. This movement spread from America to Europe and around the world. In 1895 these and other student Christian organizations from around the world joined to form the World's Student Christian Federation under John R. Mott. The Student Christian Movement is international and interfaith. It has been associated with the spread of Christianity and with the rise and development of the modern ecumenical movement for which it has provided many leaders.

Specifically, "Student Christian Movement" is the name adopted by the British segment of the worldwide movement. It developed out of various student movements active late in the last century. The SCM operates a press publishing Christian literature for students, arranges study groups, and sponsors Christian fellowship activities.

**Student Volunteer Movement.** An association of students concerned with Christian mission. The origin of the movement is dated from a gathering of students at the Mt. Hermon school near Northfield, Mass., in 1886, under the sponsorship of Dwight L. Moody. The meeting took the direction of missionary concern and enlisted 100 volunteers for foreign missions. Concern spread and through the work of Robert P. Wilder, 2,106 volunteers were enlisted in 1887. In 1888 a continuing organization with the name Student Volunteers for Foreign Missions was established with John R. Mott as chairman.

The slogan of the organization was "The evangelization of the world in this generation." The movement soon spread to Europe and ultimately over the world. In 1892 the international Student Volunteer Missionary Union was formed, enlarging the scope of the original organization.

With growing interest in home missions, the movement in 1945 changed its name to Student Volunteer Movement for Christian Missions. The association continues to foster missionary interest on college campuses by arranging for visits of furloughed missionaries, by the distribution of missionary literature, and by the encouragement of student missionary conferences and campus fellowships.

**Studium.** A monastery founded in 463 by the former Roman consul Studius in the western precincts of Constantinople. It was estab-

lished as a house of Acoemeti ("sleepless ones," who carry out the ideal of Ps. 34:1 by the continual offering of the Divine Office), which rose to prominence in the late 8th century when Theodore and his uncle Plato brought their monastic community from Saccudium (798). Adapting the rule of Basil under Theodore's leadership, the monastery expanded rapidly (some seven hundred monks) and became the model for Byzantine monasticism during its golden age (from the 9th to the 11th century). From it was founded Lavra, the cenobitic community on Mt. Athos (963). To Byzantine church life this community contributed its monastic rule (*Constitutiones studitanae*), a large number of liturgical hymns including the Canons, and a continuing effect upon spiritual life (e.g., even the Hesychast movement began as a protest against Studite monasticism, as seen in Simeon, the New Theologian, d. 1022). Destroyed by the crusaders in 1204 and rebuilt in 1290, the monastery fell to the Turks in 1453. They had destroyed all of it by 1555 except the monastery church of St. John the Baptist which is presently a mosque.

**Studium Generale.** The term first applied to the institution which later became the university. It was made up of a faculty of arts and at least one graduate faculty of law, medicine, or theology. The graduate of the *studium* was granted the privilege of teaching anywhere. The more famous *studia* were Paris in the arts and theology, Salerno in medicine, and Bologna in law.

**Stundists.** A group of evangelical Russian Protestants who came into being in the 1860's through contact with German colonists, usually Mennonites, who settled in the Ukraine. Their name derives from their custom of reading the Bible during their leisure hours (cf. German *Stunden* and Russian *štundisty*). By 1909 they had grown to a quarter of a million adherents and in that year they joined other Baptists to form the Union of Evangelical Christians.

**Sturm, Johannes** (1507–1589). German Protestant Reformer and educationalist. He studied at Louvain, was later converted by Bucer and went to Strasbourg in 1537 to help further the Reformation. He organized a school along humanist lines in 1538 which was to serve as the model for Calvin's Geneva Academy. In 1581 he was banished by the Gnesio-Lutherans because of his unionistic sympathies, but was later permitted to return.

**Suárez, Francisco** (1548–1617). Leader of the rebirth of Scholasticism in the 16th century, one of the greatest theologians of the Society of Jesus. Suárez was born in Granada to a family of jurists. He studied law in Salamanca, where in 1564 he entered the Society, studying philosophy and theology until 1570. From 1571 he was instructor and professor of philosophy in Segovia, Valladolid, and briefly in Rome. From 1585 he taught theology at Alcalá and Salamanca; in 1597 Philip II appointed him *professor primarius* at Coimbra. He died at Lisbon after a hard and simple life of study.

Though within the general Scholastic framework, the philosophicotheological system resulting from his work was to found a school all its own, called Suarezianism, whose philosophical groundwork was to be used for more than a century in most European universities both Roman Catholic and Protestant. Although essentially he followed Aristotle and Aquinas, he incorporated the results of a critical evaluation of Duns Scotus and later Scholasticism, and the thrust of his thinking was away from excessive multiplication of intellectual principles toward simpler concepts about experienced beings. Thus, the principle of individuation is simply the concreteness of an individual thing, which in turn is the direct object of intellectual knowledge; moreover, there is no real distinction between the whatness and the existence of the creature. The main theological tenets of Suárez may be summarized: the sin of the fallen angels was their ambition for the hypostatic union; God would have become man even if Adam had not sinned; it is possible to hold one and the same truth scientifically and by faith; the content of the act of faith includes belief in divine authority; the Eucharist is constituted by transubstantiation.

His principal philosophical work is the *Disputationes metaphysicae*. Although he had intended to write a full commentary on the *Summa* of Thomas Aquinas, he was interrupted by his general and Pope Paul V, who ordered him to write apologetic works. The two results were *De virtute et statu religionis* (4 vols., 1608–1625), and *Defensio fidei* (1613), a work against the Anglican theology and the oath of supremacy and divine right theory of King James I. It was burned at London by royal command and prohibited by the Parlement of Paris in 1614. *De vera intelligentia auxilii efficacis* (1605; published 1655) embodied his stand in the controversy concerning the relationship between divine grace, the human will, and predestination. Called "congruism," it was a position only slightly modifying that of Molina.

Suárez' most original contributions were in his political theory and legal philosophy, principally contained in the *Defensio, De legibus* (1612), and *De bello et de Indies*. In refuting the theory of the divine right of authority, he maintains that the original holder of political authority is the people itself. Therefore all constitutions can be only of positive law, not of divine or of natural law, and the state ideally is founded by the explicit consent of its founders. Against the Aristotelian theory of "natural slavery" he argues strongly for the natural rights of the human person, such as life, liberty, and prosperity.

He was critical of most of the practices of the Spanish colonists in the Indies; for him these countries were sovereign states, members of the community of nations, and thus legally equal to Spain. In fact, neither pope, emperor, nor Christian princes had the right to invade or conquer a foreign land on the grounds of the backwardness of its citizens or the propagation of Christianity. He based these statements on what he called for the first time the *jus inter gentes,* a body of public international law resting on natural law and containing customary and treaty law.

His collected works were published in twenty-three volumes at Venice (1740–1751), and in twenty-eight volumes at Paris (1856–1878), although neither publication is complete.

BIBLIOGRAPHY: R. Brouillard, "Suárez," *Dictionnaire de Théologie Catholique,* Vol. XIV, cols. 2638–2728 (15 vols., 1903–1950).

**Subintroductae.** Women who lived under a vow of chastity with male ascetics in spiritual marriage. The custom probably goes back as far as the 2d century (not to I Cor. 7:36–38), since Hermas seems to know of it. Obviously imprudent, it was attacked by Cyprian, Chrysostom, and Athanasius, among others, and was condemned by the Councils of Elvira (Canon 27) in 306, Ancyra (Canon 19) in 314, and Nicaea (Canon 3) in 325.

**Suetonius** (Gaius Suetonius Tranquillus) (c. 69–after 121). Biographer and historian. He was a Roman knight and secretary *ab epistulis* to the emperor Hadrian, probably during 119 to 121. He is best known for his *Lives of the Caesars,* published in 120. These biographies, lively and vivid, begin with Julius Caesar and end with Domitian. They contain one certain mention of Christians (in Nero's reign these men, "given to a new and mischievous superstition," were punished) and one possible allusion (Claudius expelled from Rome the Jews who were rioting "at the instigation of Chrestus").

**Suger** (c. 1081–1151). Abbot of St.-Denis, near Paris, from 1122. Entering the abbey as an oblate (c. 1091), he was a fellow student of Louis VI of France. His public career began in 1106 as secretary to the abbot, then provost of Berneval (1107) and of Toury (1109); he was named king's emissary to the court of Pope Gelasius II at Maguelonne (1118), and to Rome as emissary to Callistus II (1121). Elected as abbot during his absence, he was ordained priest (1122) and took office. The following year he attended the First Lateran Council and there came to the serious attention of the pope. Although he expended much effort in the succeeding years on reorganizing the life and administration of his abbey and enhancing its fabric, he was also a most powerful and influential figure in public life as adviser to Louis VII and furthered his efforts to strengthen the French Crown against the feudal barons. Though Suger opposed the Second Crusade, Louis made him regent of France in his own absence. Among Suger's literary remains are eulogistic but temperate biographies of Louis VI and VII, a detailed account of the consecration of the abbey church rebuilt from 1135 as the first Gothic structure, a long narrative of his administration of the abbey, and a treatise designed to reconcile the conflicting claims of church and state based upon the *Celestial Hierarchy* of Pseudo-Dionysius the Areopagite, whom Suger considered the patron saint not only of his abbey but of himself as well.

**Suhard, Emmanuel** (1874–1949). French cardinal. Ordained in 1898, Suhard became bishop of Bayeux-Lisieux in 1928, archbishop of Reims in 1930, cardinal in 1935, and archbishop of Paris in 1940. His concern was particularly for two classes, the proletariat and the intellectual. He encouraged the "worker priests," establishing the Mission de Paris for the former and the Centre Intellectuel des Catholiques Français for the latter.

**Sully, Maximilien de Béthune, Duc de** (1560–1641). Probably the ablest and best known of the ministers of Henry IV of France. As a governor and minister under the Protestant heir, Sully encouraged Henry to give up Protestantism to gain the nation, though he himself would not renounce his Protestantism. He ably returned order to the chaotic finances of France after the Wars of Religion.

**Sulpicians** (*or* Society of Priests of St.-Sulpice). A congregation of Roman Catholic secular priests, without vows, founded by Jean-Jacques Olier, curé of the Paris Church of St.-Sulpice, in 1642. The Sulpicians' chief work is seminary education. By 1789 the congregation had thirty-six houses in France, and though dissolved by the Revolution, it was set up again in 1814. Sulpician seminaries were founded in Canada in 1692 and in the United States (St. Mary's in Baltimore) in 1792. The Paris house of the congregation was, until the beginning of the 20th century, the best seminary in France; many British, Irish, and American clergy were trained there. In general, the spirituality of the Sulpicians followed that of Cardinal Bérulle. Until the Revolution they were Gallican but anti-Jansenist in sympathies; subsequently they tended to oppose Lammenais and Modernism.

**Summa Contra Gentiles.** Theological treatise by Thomas Aquinas. It was written during the years 1259 to 1264, said to have been at the request of Raymond of Peñafort, who wanted a defense of the Christian faith to be used against the threat of Islam in Spain. In challenging pantheistic philosophy with an orderly summary of the faith, Thomas Aquinas' apologetic distinguished the twofold order of religious truths: supernatural, or revealed, truth (faith), and natural, or demonstrated, truth (science).

**Summa Theologiae.** The best-known work of the prince of the medieval Schoolmen, Thomas Aquinas (1225–1274), the *Doctor Angelicus* or *Doctor Communis*. The *Summa theologiae* is an intellectual Cathedral of Chartres. It is an allegory in words of the medieval Christian's conception of the meaning of God's revelation of love to man, just as Chartres is an allegory of the same matter in stone. Faced with the same problem that had confronted the medieval Moslem and Jewish communities, i.e., that of reconciling the practice of faith with the practice of consistent rational thought as set forth in ancient Greece (particularly by Aristotle and Plato), the Christian community produced in Aquinas' *Summa* its great medieval synthesis of reason and revelation. Begun after 1265, and never actually completed, the *Summa theologiae* considers first the nature of *sacra doctrina* (theology) and its distinction from philosophy. Preferring Aristotle to Plato, and emphasizing the importance of the intellect rather than the will as a human faculty, Aquinas moved the Christian world from its Platonic-Augustinian bases to a more realist-intellectualist position. From a firm theological foundation, Aquinas considered the problems presented by philosophy, and brought Athens a bit closer to Jerusalem than Tertullian might have thought possible.

**Sumner, William Graham** (1840–1910). Episcopalian clergyman and educator. After completing his studies at Yale he was called there to the new chair of political and social sciences in 1872 and remained until his death. He was a distinguished teacher and lecturer. He advocated free economy and opposed economic liberalism. In 1900 he advocated a peace movement. One of his most famous books was *Folkways,* published in 1907.

**Sundar Singh** (1889–c. 1929). Indian Christian. Born at Rampur, Punjab, India, to a wealthy Sikh family, he attended a Presbyterian mission school. Although he at first hated Christianity, he saw a vision of Christ and was converted (1904). Educated for the Anglican priesthood, he could not conform to foreign ways and became a Christian Sadhu, teaching the gospel in Indian fashion. His fame as a mystic spread, and in 1920 and 1922 he spoke in England, Europe, America, and Australia. He made several evangelistic trips into forbidden Tibet and disappeared there in 1929.

**Sunday, Billy** (William Ashley Sunday) (1862–1935). American revivalist. Sunday was raised near Ames, Iowa, and first came to prominence as a professional baseball player in Chicago. It was there in 1886 that he was converted in the Pacific Garden Mission. He became interested in church work, joined the Jefferson Park Presbyterian Church, and attended Bible classes at the Y.M.C.A.—his only formal religious training; when later in his career he was ordained, the committee seems to have made its decision largely on the basis of his past record as a revivalist. In 1891, Sunday gave up a lucrative baseball contract to work for the Y.M.C.A., but when he couldn't make ends meet on the small salary, he accepted a job as assistant to J. Wilbur Chapman, one of the successful revivalists of the day. Two years later Chapman retired to a pastorate, and Sunday, with only a few sermons and not much more confidence, accepted an offer to conduct a revival of his own in Garner, Iowa. He was unsure of himself for several years, imitating the style of Chapman or some other revivalist, but when he finally did things his own way, his performances were beyond imitation.

All restraint and solemnity were forgotten as Sunday preached. Calling himself "a rube of rubes," he spoke in slang, abusive expletives near profanity, and excessively flowery descriptions. In retelling the story of David's killing of Goliath he said that David put one of the stones in his sling, threw it, and "socked Goliath in the coco between the lamps, and he went down for the count." When he produced a description such as "the red-nosed, buttermilk-eyed, beetle-browed, peanut-brained, stall-fed, old saloon keeper," the audiences usually applauded. These words were accompanied by bodily gyrations of dizzying variety and speed. He would pound the pulpit, jump on a chair or on the pulpit itself, fight both sides of a boxing match or duel, and, as one of his most famous acts, portray the sinner trying to get into heaven the way a baseball player tries to steal "home," only to be called "out" by God, the umpire. Many claimed that Sunday was capable of outdrawing and outacting any vaudeville troupe in America. In his obituary in *The New York Times,* he was called "the greatest high-pressure and mass conversion Christian evangelist that America or the world has known." His successful career led through most of the larger towns of the Midwest and then after 1913, into most of the larger metropolises of the United States. As has been true of so many revivalists, his greatest challenge and success came in New York City, where in 1917 he claimed to have won 98,264 converts. Although this was the largest number of converts Sunday ever recorded, he was, in fact, proportionately more successful in cities with fewer than ten thousand people. In these relatively small towns, he quite regularly could win 20 percent of the population.

The astonishing record of conversions leads one to wonder just what Sunday's converts were converted to. The answer seems to be many things and, quite frequently, nothing at all. Many people did join the churches after his campaigns, but many who signed decision cards were already church members, had no intention of joining, or were simply marching in a large parade to the front of the tabernacle. Sunday frequently won converts to American patriotism, hatred of the Germans (during World War I), and especially prohibition. Some historians have argued that the passage of the Eighteenth Amendment to the Constitution (which enacted prohibition) contributed significantly to Sunday's loss of popularity after 1920. He had made the attack on liquor the mainstay of his campaign for many years: "Booze" was his most famous sermon and the song "De Brewer's Big Horses" was a great favorite. Americans after 1920 were not in a mood to reform much more of anything—the world, their town, or themselves. Invitations came less frequently from the big cities, and gradually Sunday fell out of the public eye. He ended his life preaching in the same small Midwestern towns in which he had begun thirty-five years before, unable to understand why his magic no longer worked.

BIBLIOGRAPHY: W. T. Ellis, *Billy Sunday: The Man and His Message* (Philadelphia, 1936); W. G. McLoughlin, *Billy Sunday Was His Real Name* (Chicago, 1955); and *Modern Revivalism* (New York, 1959).

**Sunday School Association, International.** See INTERNATIONAL SUNDAY SCHOOL ASSOCIATION.

**Sunday School Movement.** The antecedent of the modern Sunday school movement is the work of Robert Raikes (1735–1811) of Gloucester, England. Seeking to ameliorate the social plight of the poor, which he attributed chiefly to ignorance, Raikes recruited pupils between the ages of six and fourteen from the streets and with a hired teacher opened the first Sunday school in 1780. Reading, writing, and religion were the subjects taught.

About the same time, America was also discovering the need for the Sunday school. In the Southern colonies, where the English pattern prevailed, education for the poor was of no concern beyond that provided by the apprentice system. Although parochial schools were predominant in the Middle colonies, and in New England religiously oriented common schools were operated, the great majority of citizens had no access to learning. Moreover, the coming of the Enlightenment in all its manifestations produced a secularization of education that separated religion from general learning. The Sunday school offered a practical answer to both secularization and the need for additional educational facilities.

The first American Sunday school based on Raikes's model was begun in 1785 in the home of William Elliot of Accomac Co., in Virginia. The following year Bishop Francis Asbury of the Methodist Church established a second, and by 1790 his denomination recommended Sunday schools for all children. The Methodists, however, were not successful in the venture and like most other denominations, developed little serious interest in Sunday schools until after the War of 1812.

The lay character of Raikes's early schools was transmitted to America as well as their combination of rudimentary education and religion, and for approximately forty years laymen dominated the Sunday school movement in this country. As local Sunday schools began to appear, voluntary nonsectarian societies were organized to promote and support them. The First Day or Sabbath School Society of Philadelphia was formed in 1790, and for years afterward operated a successful and extensive educational program among the poor of that city. Other major cities had similar groups. The period from 1816 to 1858 was the golden age for such organizations. In May, 1824, the American Sunday School Union emerged to give national direction to the movement. Under the leadership of laymen, it was designed to aid all Sunday schools by providing superior curriculum materials and assisting teachers to employ improved methods of instruction. Prior to this time the normal lesson material was the Catechism coupled with the Bible as a source of readings. Memorization was the standard teaching method. The American "Union" made uniform and selected lessons available as well as other resources such as Bible dictionaries and low cost libraries. It also sponsored Sunday school conventions to inspire and educate those involved, and its missionaries founded literally thousands of new Sunday schools.

The year 1825 also marked the "Babel Era," so named because of the flood of diverse Sunday school materials which were put on the market. Because the various denominations were reluctant to entrust religious education entirely to laymen, and because they were anxious to have their unique points of view presented, they began to establish their own Sunday schools. Eventually they came to dominate the movement. After 1858, the American "Union" gave way to the National Convention whose rise, along with the later International Conventions, put an end to the Babel Era. They operated until 1914.

After World War I the leadership of the Sunday school movement was almost entirely in the hands of professional religious workers. The rise of liberal theology with its emphasis on religious education provided new vigor for the Sunday school in the postwar years.

BIBLIOGRAPHY: A. A. Brown, *A History of Religious Education in Recent Times* (New York, 1923); E. M. Fergusson, *Historic Chapters in Christian Education in America* (New York, 1935); E. Rice, *The Sunday School Movement: 1780–1917, and the American Sunday School Union: 1817–1917* (Philadelphia, 1917).

**Sunday School Society.** Interdenominational Society for the Support and Encouragement of Sunday Schools in the Different Counties of England, popularly known as the Sunday School Society, formed in London, Sept. 7, 1785, under the leadership of Robert Raikes and William Fox. The purpose of the Society was to provide free weekly instruction in reading to the poor, and to make available an agency for specifically Christian nurture. The basic textbook was the Bible, taught by salaried instructors in conveniently located classrooms. While a number of Sunday schools had been in operation prior to 1785, notably those led by Raikes and Hannah More, the Society was the first organization established to promote and extend Sunday schools throughout England. It was instrumental in the formation of 3,730 schools with over 300,000 members. Its success inspired a more general Sunday school movement, including formation of other societies such as the London Sunday School Union (1803). After twenty-seven years of operation the Society, even after ending the policy of paying teachers, was exhausted financially. It rejected the option of trying to retain solvency by selling Bibles to the poor, and chose instead to dissolve itself rather than abandon its free literature policy. Its work, however, was carried on by other agencies.

**Superintendents.** In general, Protestant ministers with supervision of churches within a certain territory or district. In Scotland the Reformers sought to develop the function of the bishop superintendent. In the First Book of Discipline (1560) the role of the superintendent was detailed. Each of ten districts was to have a superintendent. He was to be an active minister, to travel through the district regularly, to preach, to plant and erect new churches, to supervise ministers, and in many ways to admonish, correct, and strengthen. His election would be by vote of the ministers of the district who had selected him from among several ministers nominated by ministers, elders, deacons, magistrates, or town councils. In his work and life the superintendent would be under the scrutiny of ministers in his own and neighboring districts. The system was never fully operative or effective and did not long survive the adoption of the Second Book of Discipline in 1581 when the government of the Kirk was forming into a system of presbyteries.

The system of superintendents was tried in Germany. In general it was the duty of the prince to appoint the superintendents (or visitors) who exercised oversight over the doctrine and worship of churches and pastors and were directly responsible to the prince. The Lutheran system of superintendents was based on the right of the prince to control and direct the external fortunes of the church. The Scottish superintendents were less civil administrators and more pastors, and were directly answerable to the General Assembly.

**Supralapsarianism.** A distinction arising in Dutch Calvinist theology in the 16th century relating to the order of the decrees of God in relation to the Fall. In opposition to infralapsarianism, this viewpoint maintains that the decrees of election and reprobation preceded the decrees of creation and the Fall. Election thus underlies the decree of the Fall. Supralapsarianism sees the Fall as an "active" decree of God, yet maintains as staunchly as infralapsarianism that God is not the author of sin.

**Supremacy Acts** (1534 and 1559). In English church history, the declarations of the monarch's sovereignty in ecclesiastical affairs. Although the king had been recognized *de facto* supreme head of the Church of England by the ordinaries since their submission in 1532, not until 1534 did Parliament pass the Supremacy Act naming Henry VIII "only supreme head in earth of the Church of England, called *Anglicana Ecclesia.*" Repealed under Mary in 1554, the act was restored by Elizabeth's Supremacy Act of 1559, which modified the title ("supreme governor") but continued the responsibility.

**Supreme Ecclesiastical Council** (Russia). In line with Stalin's new policy of *rapprochement* with the Russian Orthodox Church, the Supreme Ecclesiastical Council was created by the Soviet Government in October, 1943. The Council's avowed purpose was to further a closer and more amicable relationship between the state and the church. An adjunct to the Council of People's Commissars, the Ecclesiastical Council in effect is a department of state for religious affairs. The Council arranges for theological education, and to it must be sent all petitions for the reopening or construction of churches and all nominations to episcopal office. (See SYNODS, RUSSIAN ORTHODOX.)

**Suso, Heinrich** (c. 1300–1366). German mystic. He was born von Berg, but took his mother's name. Educated at Constance and Cologne, he entered the Dominican Order and was a disciple of Meister Eckhart. At forty, he abandoned the severe asceticism that had marked his life and began to preach throughout Swabia. Two works are outstanding: *The Little Book of Truth* and *The Little Book of Eternal Wisdom.* Both treat of mysticism, the first speculatively and the second practically.

**Swabian Syngram.** A profession of faith signed in 1525 by Lutheran pastors of Swabia as a response to the Eucharistic theology of Oecolampadius. It was composed by Johann Brenz, based on Luther's doctrine of God's Word as the cause of the Eucharistic presence. It emphasizes the bodily presence of Christ in the Sacrament, though only for those who have faith; and it is noteworthy that in the discussion surrounding this document the question of the ubiquity of Christ's glorified body was first raised.

**Sweden, Conversion of.** The first Swedish contacts with Christianity came through commerce and Viking expeditions. Concentrated efforts began when Louis the Pious (814–840) sent Ansgar from the diocese of Hamburg. Pagan opposition hampered his work, so that actual conversion was largely the result of later efforts by English missionaries. Church organization was firmly established in the 12th century with Uppsala as the archepiscopal see.

**Swedenborg** (Svedberg), **Emanuel** (1688–1772). Swedish scientist, philosopher, and theologian. He was born at Stockholm and educated at Uppsala, becoming professor of theology at Uppsala and bishop of Skara. Swedenborg's religious thought evolved from materialism to mysticism. In his early life, especially in his *Prodromus philosophiae ratiocinantis de infinito et causa finali creationis* (1734), he attempted to prove that the universe had a fundamentally spiritual substance. Between 1736 and 1745, however, he underwent a profound mystical conversion. He became conscious of a mystical union with God in which Christ called him to become His prophet, and to disseminate the doctrines of the "New Church." In 1747 he began an intensive study of the Bible and Hebrew; he now lived continually "in the world of the spirit," and in his numerous writings he described his visions of heaven and hell. Swedenborg regarded himself as a prophet of a spiritual fraternity that would be revealed by a second advent, and he believed that life on earth was only a preparation for the world of the spirit. He is sometimes described as a spiritualist "medium," but this label is erroneous, for he was a devout, mystical theologian. He had many devoted followers in Sweden, France, and England. (See CHURCH OF THE NEW JERUSALEM.)

**Swift, Jonathan** (1667–1745). British satirist and dean of St. Patrick's, Dublin (1713). He was born in Dublin, educated at Trinity College and Oxford, and ordained priest in 1695. Although he was a consistent supporter of the Church of England, he was a Whig in politics and was persuaded to write against the Occasional Conformity Act (1708). Although he was not an Irish patriot, he bitterly assailed the English mismanagement of Ireland. He despised injustice and employed his great powers of irony to condemn religious and economic exploitation of Ireland by English-men. In his *Proposal for the Universal Use of Irish Manufactures* (1720) he urged an Irish boycott of English goods; in his *Drapier Letters* (1724) he attacked the Crown for making extravagant profits from the control of the Irish currency; in his *Modest Proposal for Preventing the Children of Poor People from Being a Burden to their Parents or the Country* (1729) he condemned the economic policy of the English Government. Swift's powers of enforcing momentuous truth by ludicrous exaggeration were used to religious ends in his *Argument to Prove the Inconvenience of Abolishing Christianity* (1708). His fame rests upon the popularity of his satirical *Gulliver's Travels* (1726).

**Swiss Brethren.** See GREBEL, CONRAD; BLAUROCK, GEORGE; HUBMAIER, BALTHASAR.

**Swiss Federation of Protestant Churches.** A body founded in 1920, directly continuing the Evangelical Diet, which for three centuries until 1858 united the separate cantonal churches, and its successor, the Conference of Swiss Protestant Churches (1858–1920). Its members are the cantonal state churches, the cantonal free churches, and the Methodist Church. The Federation represents all the churches in relation to government and holds membership in the World Council of Churches for the cantonal state churches.

**Syllabus of Errors.** Eighty propositions containing "the principal errors of our time" condemned by Pius IX (Dec. 8, 1864), accompanied by the encyclical *Quanta Cura*. As early as 1849, Gioacchino Vincenzo Pecci (later Leo XIII) requested a condemnation of modern errors. In 1851, *La Civiltà Cattolica* asked for an explicit condemnation of rationalism. O. P. Gerbet issued his *Instruction pastorale,* consisting of eighty-five propositions against popular errors, in 1860. Pius IX established a commission to utilize Gerbet's theses. Sixty-one theses were laid before the bishops on June 8, 1862, and the assembly gave approval to Pius IX's condemnation of *Maxima quidem*. This condemnation and its approval served as immediate precursors of the Syllabus. Bilio's commission was entrusted with the final formulation of eighty errors to be condemned. The Syllabus included thirty of the sixty-one errors listed before the bishops in 1862. The encyclical accompanying the Syllabus announced a jubilee year in 1865, but the Syllabus was not signed by the pope. Reaction to the Syllabus varied. Belgians feared infringement of constitutional rights. Gladstone attacked it, while Newman called for a *schola theologorum* to interpret it. Doellinger said that it verged on the comic.

Papers in France and Germany called the Syllabus a "definitive divorce of the Church from the modern world." Other journalists suggested that Pius was prepared to suppress the steam engine and the gas light. F. A. P. Dupanloup issued *The September Convention and the Encyclical of December 8* in January, 1865, called the "antisyllabus" by ultramontanists. He exposed erroneous interpretations of the Syllabus, and was praised by 630 bishops. Clemens Schrader offered a strictly ultramontane exposition of the Syllabus with minimal concern for the historical roots of each thesis. He was lauded by Pius IX. Subsequent interpretations of the Syllabus were as important as the document itself. Undoubtedly it struck a blow at liberalism in its many facets.

**Sylvester** (d. 335). Pope from 314. He is chiefly remembered because of a late legend that he baptized Constantine and received the Donation of Constantine as a reward for curing the emperor of leprosy. It is known that two presbyters represented him at the Council of Arles (314)—although the "report" of the Council to Sylvester is probably spurious—and that he was also represented at the Council of Nicaea (325) by two presbyters.

**Sylvester II** (Gerbert, c. 945–1003). Pope from 999. Born in Auvergne, educated at the monastery of Aurillac, and in Barcelona, Cordova, and Seville, he excelled in mathematics and natural science. He was appointed a teacher in the cathedral school of Reims by Archbishop Adalbero. His elevation to the see of Reims as Adalbero's successor was contested and ultimately nullified by a synod (Causeiense) in 995. Gerbert then entered the service of Emperor Otto III, becoming his teacher. In 998 he was appointed archbishop of Ravenna, and in 999 he became the first French pope.

Papal-imperial relations were harmonious during his pontificate. He was active in mission work, establishing a metropolitan for Poland at Gnesen, for Hungary at Gran, and in 1000 he gave the title of king to Stephen of Hungary, appointing him papal vicar. He was also active in maintaining strict discipline against concubinage of the clergy and against simony. He is especially known as a central figure of the Ottonian Renaissance, his encyclopedic learning causing some contemporaries to suspect him of magic. In philosophy he was attracted by dialectics, and in science he allegedly invented the pendulum clock, represented the earth as a globe, experimented with steam, and may have introduced Arabic numerals to western Europe.

**Symeon of Mesopotamia** (4th century). The outstanding theologian of the Messalian ascetics. This extremely austere sect originated in Mesopotamia, and quickly spread to Syria and Asia Minor, teaching a complete rejection of all worldly pursuits, including work. In Symeon, however, rejection of the world is less emphasized, greater weight being given to an active concern for others. Messalianism was condemned as heretical at the Synod of Side and the Council of Ephesus. Symeon's writings have come down to us camouflaged as the work of Macarius the Egyptian.

**Symmachian Forgeries.** A group of spurious documents drawn up during the troubled pontificate of Pope Symmachus (498–514) to support the doctrine that the Roman pontiff cannot be judged by any man. By being later included in the *Liber pontificalis* they obtained wide circulation and exercised much influence. Together with other forgeries such as the Donation of Constantine and the pseudo-Isidorian decretals, they were contributing factors, though by no means the only ones, in strengthening the claims of the Roman papacy.

**Symmachus** (d. 514). Pope from 498. His accession was disputed by a minority of the populace supporting Laurentius. Bringing false charges against Symmachus, they succeeded in weakening his support. Although he was confirmed by the "Palmary Synod" (assembled by the Gothic king Theodoric, 501), the conflict continued until 506. Symmachus spent his remaining years struggling against the Manichaeans and the Henoticon of Zeno, a focus of conflict with Constantinople.

**Syncellus, George** (flourished c. 800). Byzantine chronicler, designated *syncellus* ("cellmate") of the Byzantine patriarch Tarasius (d. 806). When Tarasius died, Syncellus compiled a *Chronography* from creation to Diocletian (285), more a chronological table than a history, helpful in solving early Greek chronology problems because he used and thus preserved no longer extant earlier sources. At his request, his friend Theophanes continued the chronicle to the year 813.

**Synergistic Controversy.** A debate within 16th-century Lutheranism. Synergism is the view that man cooperates to a certain degree with God in the work of salvation. Luther's early writings stressed the wholly divine nature of salvation, with God as the initiator and the redeeming activity of Christ as the wholly adequate means of securing salvation for man. However, as early as 1527, Melanchthon, in a gloss on Colossians, as in his 1532 commentary on Romans, asked whether there may be something in man that causes some men to be saved and others condemned. He could not attribute this to any arbitrary decision of God. He concluded that after God had offered forgiveness and the Holy Spirit, then man's will accepted or rejected the proffered gifts. The controversy broke out during the Leipzig Interim (1548–1552), in which many concessions had been made to Roman Catholic practices. Matthias Flacius of Magdeburg attacked Melanchthon bitterly, insisting that man was "a resisting knotty piece unfit for the hewer." Melanchthon defended himself before Elector August, but Flacius continued his attack. Victorinus Strigel took up Melanchthon's defense after his teacher's death, but no satisfactory settlement was reached until the Formula of Concord (1577), which finally decided against Melanchthon's synergism but (perhaps inconsistently) avoided the predestinarianism of his opponents.

**Synesius** (c. 370–413). Christian prelate and Neoplatonic philosopher. A startling figure among the fathers of the church, Synesius was a country gentleman of the province of Cyrene, west of Egypt. His early works include essays in popular philosophy and such elegant trifles as *Praise of Baldness*. If baptized, he was only a nominal churchman. Surprisingly, he was a friend of both Christian and pagan leaders at Alexandria, the patriarch Theophilus and the philosopher Hypatia. From 399 to 402 he represented his fellow citizens at the court of Constantinople; in 410 the people of Ptolemaïs called him to the episcopate, with a view to civic as much as to spiritual leadership. He accepted with some reservations—he would not abandon his Platonic view of the resurrection, nor leave the wife whom "God and the law and the sacred hand of Theophilus" had given him. As bishop he rose to his duties and seems at last to have found a personal faith; his hymns register a shift from Neoplatonic theism to Christian devotion. He protected the people against an oppressive governor and organized their defense against the Bedouin of the desert. His life ended in tragedy—his wife and sons died, and he expected to perish in the ruin of Cyrene. The city was spared this fate, however, and long remembered him as the good philosopher bishop.

**Synod.** (1) An assembly for deliberation regarding church matters, usually on the local or provincial level. (2) A structure of church government which in Europe is often the political authority that orders parish life, and in America is usually organized by parishes themselves for mutual assistance and governance. Some Protestants believe the synod is a divinely ordained pattern of church government given in the New Testament.

**Synods, Russian Orthodox** (1917, 1943, 1945). After the destruction of the czarist regime in 1917 the Russian Orthodox Church found it necessary to reorganize and reaccommodate itself to the revolutionary government. A synod (Russian, *sobor*) of the entire church was called in August, 1917, to deal with these problems. Anxious to reassert its independence from the state and to stem the tide of radicalism (particularly Bolshevism), the *sobor* reinstated the patriarchate (abolished by Czar Peter the Great) and put forth various anti-Bolshevik proclamations. This anti-Bolshevik propaganda did not cease after Lenin came to power in October, and it is in part a cause of the hostile attitude of the Soviet state and its persecution of the church during the next two decades.

A more lenient attitude toward the church on the part of the Communist Government appeared during the Second World War, and a *rapprochement* between church and state was finally achieved. The *sobor* of 1943, which met to elect a new patriarch, had the goodwill and the support of Stalin; in turn it issued a statement urging all Orthodox to support the war effort and the regime.

The *sobor* of 1945 put the seal on this new harmonious relationship between the Soviet state and the church. The government furnished transportation not only for all Russian delegates but for representatives from other countries who attended (the patriarchs of Alexandria and Antioch, representatives of the patriarchs of Constantinople and Jerusalem, and prelates from Yugoslavia, Romania, and North America). The chairman of the newly established governmental Supreme Ecclesiastical Council attended the opening sessions, and praising the church for its patriotism during the German invasion, pledged his government's continued goodwill and assistance. The *sobor* then proclaimed its gratitude to the state and the church's support, and prayers for the "beloved leader of the Soviet state," Joseph Stalin.

**Syrian Christians.** There are two churches in Syria, an orthodox Catholic Church in union with Rome (Melkites), and a Monophysite body called the Jacobite Church. After Chalcedon the Monophysite body refused to accept the Council's decision and the "dogmatic letter" of Leo I. Taking its name from Jacob Baradai (6th century), the Jacobite Church lost heavily to Islam especially c. 640 and in the 13th and 14th centuries. Moslems contributed greatly to internal discord, but the church had good relations with the crusaders. There were several attempts to unite with Rome, notably in 1237, 1247, and after Florence. The Jacobite Church is strongest in the west Syrian countryside. It suffered heavily during World War I at the hands of the Turks, but held a reform synod in 1930 at Mosul. A recent energetic patriarch was Ephrem Barsum (d. 1957). The Jacobites follow the Antiochene rite in Syriac, and number about 100,-000. The Jacobites were active in southern India when the Jesuits and Capuchins established a Uniate body there in 1626. Until c. 1599 many Jacobites in India had been in union with Rome, but then the Portuguese attempted to Latinize them. This resulted in the secession of many Malabar Jacobites in 1653, though a large number of Jacobites remained in full communion with Rome and elected a Roman Catholic bishop in 1656. The dissident party revolted and a hundred-year persecution ensued. Eventually many Jacobites turned to the Chaldean rite, but the Malabar Jacobite Church remained strong. Meanwhile, in Syria, Michael Garweh (d. 1801) became the first Uniate patriarch. He ruled from Lebanon. Five Jacobite bishops, including Matthew Nakar (1832), went over to Rome (1820–1850). World War I interfered greatly with Roman Catholic gains. The present patriarchal residence is in Beirut. Priests are generally celibate. The Jacobite metropolitan of Beirut, Mar Yohanna Gandur, went over to Rome in 1950. Present Uniat Syrians number about 80,000. The Maronites, another Uniate body, have been in union with Rome since about 1181.

**Syrian Orthodox Church of Malabar.** The origins of Christianity in India remain obscure, although local tradition unanimously maintains that the Church in Malabar, on the southwest Indian coast, was founded by the apostle Thomas, who is held in special veneration. Historians, however, are inclined to ascribe an East Syrian foundation, for when "discovered" by the Portuguese in the beginning of the 16th century, the Malabar Church used Syriac in worship, a Chaldean liturgy, and paid obedience to the Nestorian catholicos in Babylon. With the Portuguese came Roman missionaries, who were received as brethren until they attempted forcible Latinization. This movement reached its apex at the Synod of Diamper (1599), when obedience to Rome was secured, but not without the assistance of Portuguese arms. Opposition soon broke out, especially after the murder of Bishop Ahatella, when the majority of the Malabars withdrew

from Rome. Renewed contacts with other Eastern Christians became possible after the Dutch expelled the Portuguese missionaries in 1633. A new hierarchy was then supplied by the Syrian (Jacobite) patriarch at Holm who assumed spiritual authority over the Malabar Church.

Although marred by later divisions, much internal dissension, and further complicated during the British occupation which encouraged Anglican missionaries, the Malabar Church has displayed renewed life and activity. It is actively engaged in the World Council of Churches and has revived contacts with the Eastern Orthodox Churches.

**Syrian Protestant Church** (*also called the* Protestant Millet). Originally begun and supported by several Protestant missionary denominations, the church was at first an unrecognized Christian minority in a Moslem environment. With the growth of nationalism under the French mandate of 1920 to 1940, the Syrian Protestant community took over from the American missionaries and obtained official government recognition by the formation of a synod and a federation of all Protestant denominations which then became a millet (the "religious community" upon which each person's religious, political, and social life depends) independent of foreign control.

# T

**Tabernacle** (from Latin for "tent"). The canopied receptacle for the reserved Sacrament, set on the middle of the high altar in all except monastic and cathedral churches. It began to replace the sacrament house and the hanging pyx in the 16th century, and since 1863 is the only manner of reservation permitted in the Roman Catholic Church, except for a few churches specifically exempted by papal indult.

**Taborites.** A radical group within the Hussite following. They received their name from the town of Tabor, located near Prague, which was their headquarters. Their members were artisans and peasants under the military leadership of a noble, Jan Žižka of Trocnov. They united with the rest of the Hussites to defend the Bohemian countryside. Much of their success in offensive and defensive maneuvers from 1420 to 1431 was due to Žižka's ingenious use of farm wagons for barricades and a movable cannon. The Taborites were concerned with economic and social as well as religious reforms. Communistic living was attempted but met with little success. Although the Taborites subscribed to the Articles of Prague of 1420, they were greatly influenced by the writings of Wycliffe and by groups of Picards, Catharists, and Waldenses. They rejected purgatory, all sacraments except Baptism and Communion, transubstantiation, veneration of the saints, and all holy days except Sundays and fast days. They abolished vestments, statues, and altars, and used only the Bohemian tongue in their worship service, which consisted of hymns, prayers of offering, readings from Sacred Scripture, preaching, and Communion. Their bishops were elected by the priests, and they had no offices other than deacon, priest, and bishop. (See BOHEMIAN BRETHREN.)

**Taché, Alexandre Antonin** (1823–1894). Canadian Roman Catholic bishop. He was born at Rivière du Loup, Lower Canada, and educated at the College of St. Hyacinthe and the Theological Seminary of Montreal. He became a novice in the Oblate Order in 1844, and was sent as a missionary the following year to the Red River Settlement. Having been consecrated coadjutor bishop of St. Boniface in 1851, he became the second bishop of St. Boniface in 1853. In 1871 he was created archbishop and metropolitan of St. Boniface. He helped to restore order after the Red River Rebellion of 1869, and played a major role in the early stages of the Manitoba Separate Schools controversy.

**Tacitus, Cornelius** (c. 55–c. 120). Roman historian. He was the author of *Dialogue on Orators; Life of Agricola,* a biography of his father-in-law; *Germania; Historiae;* and *Annales.* Among the earliest witnesses to Christianity in secular literature is his *Annales* (15.44), wherein he cites Nero's persecution of the Christians, whom he made scapegoats for the fire in Rome (A.D. 64); Tacitus believes them innocent of this charge, although he calls their religion a pernicious superstition (*exitabilis superstitio*).

**Tagore, Rabindranath** (1861–1941). Indian poet. He was born in Calcutta, descendant of Hindu Brahma Samaj leaders, and educated in India and England. He founded Shantiniketan (1901), now Visva-Bharati University. Interpreting Indian spirituality throughout the world, he sought to build spiritual unity of man on love, self-giving labor, and world brotherhood within the Great Soul. He wrote mystical poems, i.e., *Song Offerings (Gitanjali),* in Bengali and English. His published works fill twenty-eight volumes.

**Taille, Maurice de la** (1872–1933). French Jesuit professor of dogmatic theology at the Gregorian University, Rome (1919–1933). His masterpiece was *Mysterium fidei,* a three-volume study of the Mass, the most important contribution to Eucharistic theology since the First Vatican Council (1869–1870). He saw a unity in Christ's sacrifice, beginning in oblation at the Last Supper, achieving immolation on Calvary, and continuation in the Mass.

**Taiping** ("Great Peace"). The name given to the mid-19th-century Chinese rebellion which combined agrarian unrest, anti-Manchu feeling, and confused Christian elements. The leader was an unsuccessful civil service candidate who founded a Society for the Worship of God with the tenets of God as Father, Jesus as Elder Brother, and himself as Younger Brother. Gaining thousands of converts, the movement spread from Canton to Peking and cost perhaps twenty million lives between 1848 and 1865 before being suppressed.

**Tait, Archibald Campbell** (1811–1882). Archbishop of Canterbury. While a fellow at Balliol College, Oxford, this former Scotch Presbyterian protested against Newman's Tract 90 and opposed Anglo-Catholicism all of his life. In 1842 he became headmaster of Rugby and in 1849 dean of Carlisle. Made bishop of London in 1856, he was known as a strong Broad Churchman, although he objected to *Essays and Reviews* (1860). In 1868 he became archbishop, in which office he was known as an earnestly religious man, fearless and strong in dealing with issues, opposed to Catholicism and favorably inclined toward liberalism.

**Taizé Community.** Taizé is a community of Protestant monks devoted to the task of reconciling Christians with one another. Established in 1944 at Taizé near the secularized monastery of Cluny in the old dukedom of Burgundy, Taizé was the inspiration of a small group of theology students centering around the present prior, Roger Schutz. The members take the traditional monastic vows of poverty, celibacy, obedience.

**Talleyrand** (Charles Maurice de Talleyrand-Périgord) (1754–1838). Statesman from one of the first families of France. Barred from the profession of arms by a childhood injury, he entered the church, and though he read and approved Voltaire, he became bishop of Autun (1789). He joined the democratic side of the Revolution at the right time and for the next forty-five years displayed such a remarkable genius for adapting himself to the changing regimes in France that he not only survived but held influential offices in virtually all of them, rendering significant service as well. A brilliant diplomat, he largely arranged the Restoration (1814) and preserved France from extreme vengeance at the Congress of Vienna. Through it all he remained the cultivated, cynical, brilliantly perceptive aristocrat of the ancien régime. At the very end, he once again submitted to the church.

**Talmage, Thomas de Witt** (1832–1902). Dutch Reformed and Presbyterian clergyman. After three Reformed pastorates he moved in 1869 to Central Presbyterian Church, Brooklyn, N.Y., where his unusual preaching style and his old-fashioned message drew some of the largest audiences ever to hear a preacher in America. A series of three tabernacles built for him were each destroyed by fire. After 1890 he edited the *Christian Herald*.

**Talmud.** A "fence around Torah," with a collection of commentary on the law of Moses and the sayings of the great rabbis, which has been the object of deep veneration among the Jewish people ever since the early years of the Christian era. The Talmud has been one of the major factors in preserving both the identity of the Jewish people under persecution and their passion for learning, logic, humor, and faith. There are two Talmuds: the larger, the Babylonian, and the Palestinian. They contain two parts: the Mishnah, a collection of law based on Torah; and the Gemara (which differs in the two Talmuds), commentaries on the Mishnah.

**Tappan, Arthur** (1786–1865), and **Lewis** (1788–1873). Merchant philanthropist organizers of the American and Foreign Antislavery Society. The sons of a Calvinist family in Northampton, Mass., they entered business in their teens and amassed substantial fortunes. Committed to a broad doctrine of stewardship, the brothers supported reforms in education and gave of their administrative talents and wealth to various associations which made up the "benevolent empire." They were especially active in antislavery reform.

**Taschereau, Elzéar Alexandre** (1820–1898). Canadian Roman Catholic bishop. Born at St. Marie de la Beauce, Lower Canada, he was educated at the Quebec Seminary and was ordained in 1842. He became a professor, then director and finally superior of the Quebec Seminary. He was vicar-general of the diocese of Quebec in 1862, and in 1871 was consecrated sixteenth bishop and sixth archbishop of Quebec. In 1886 he became the first Canadian cardinal of the Roman Catholic Church.

**Tasso, Torquato** (1544–1595). Italian poet. His greatest work was *Gerusalemme liberata* (finished in 1575), an epic of the First Crusade. About 1575 he was assailed by religious scruples and turned from a life of passion to one of remorse. Tasso had an extremely sensitive nature and was seriously affected by criticism against his writing. His patron, Alphonso II of Ferrara, twice found it necessary to have him committed to an asylum and when he was finally released, Tasso spent his time wandering from one court to another seeking sympathy.

**Tatian** (2d century). Syrian Apologist, literary critic, and heretical theologian of the late 2d century. First an ardent student of Greek rhetoric and according to himself very famous, Tatian was a pupil of Justin at Rome. After about 165 he returned to Syria where he wrote: (1) a treatise *On Animals,* now lost, to show that man without the divine spark is no different from the beasts that perish; (2) the *Oration Against the Greeks,* a bitter attack (perhaps in 176 or 177) on the Greco-Roman culture to which he had previously been devoted; (3) the *Diatessaron,* a harmony of the four Gospels based chiefly on the supposedly apostolic Matthew and John (the earliest fragment was found in Greek at Dura-on-the-Euphrates in 1934); and (4) a lost treatise *On Perfection According to the Savior,* in which he interpreted Paul as advocating celibacy for all Christians. According to Irenaeus, Tatian was the founder of the Encratites. He has sometimes been regarded as a Docetist, but since he speaks of Jesus as "the God who suffered," this accusation seems unfounded. His *Oration* was quoted by Clement of Alexandria and Eusebius, but later it was preserved only in one 10th-century manuscript and a few copies of it (first published in 1546). The *Diatessaron,* after usurping the place of the Gospels in Syria, was suppressed during the 5th century and now survives only in translations, chiefly in Oriental languages.

**Tauler, John** (c. 1300–1361). Medieval mystic. Born in Strasbourg, the son of a wealthy man, he rejected his patrimony to enter the Dominican Order (c. 1314) under Meister Eckhart. He studied at Cologne, but whether he studied at Paris or not is debated. A professor of the Strasbourg Dominican *studium,* Tauler preceded his community to Basel, where they fled from the antipapal authorities who supported Louis IV of Bavaria in his dispute with the pope. He returned to Strasbourg (1347–1348), only to see conventual discipline decline before a series of catastrophies: papal interdict and exile, the Black Death, the Basel earthquake of 1356. In the last decade of his life, he and Heinrich von Nördlingen preached widely and effectively. His exhortations to repentance and his outspoken denunciations brought persecution, and yet his influence was great. His writings are mostly sermons in German in a simple style aimed at drawing the people to union with God. This 14th-century Dominican was read and reread by Luther. In 1879 the Dominican scholar Heinrich Denifle separated Tauler's true works from the many spurious editions current until then.

**Tausen, Hans** (1494–1561). Danish Lutheran Reformer. He studied at Wittenberg and introduced the Reformation to Viborg in 1525. He was given a letter of protection by Frederick I allowing him to continue to preach unmolested. In 1529 he began preaching in Copenhagen, where he drew large enthusiastic crowds with his sermons and evangelical worship services. At the Diet of Copenhagen (1530) a confession of faith was drawn up by the Lutheran preachers for a public disputation, but the Roman Catholic bishops refused to debate in the vernacular before the populace, thus discrediting themselves. Tausen has long been credited with drawing up the Forty-three Articles of the Copenhagen Confession, but recent research indicates a close parallel to the Malmøbook of Peder Laurentsen. In 1533, Tausen's protector died and at the instigation of Bishop Rönne, he was convicted of blasphemy and ordered to leave Copenhagen. The enraged populace would have killed the bishop had not Tausen personally intervened. So impressed was Rönne by this act that he allowed Tausen to continue to preach. During the civil war following King Frederick's death, his son Christian, a zealous Lutheran, was proclaimed king in 1535, and Tausen's worries were then over. One of the first acts of Christian III was to introduce the Reformation by royal decree. Tausen was sent to the Roman Catholic stronghold of Roskilde and in 1542 was appointed bishop of Ribe.

**Taxes, Church.** Revenue used in support of established churches. Gradual separation of church and state (with independent rights for the former), changing economic and social conditions in the early 19th century, and decreasing revenues brought about church taxes in Germany. Both state and church tax laws were required for church taxes in the German Evangelical Church, but only state law was required for Roman Catholic church taxes except for a time in Prussia and Hesse.

In Prussia, the Rhenish-Westphalian Church constitution of March 5, 1835, assessed evangelical members a specified tax. This action was a pattern for later laws in Hesse on April 23, 1875, in Württemberg on June 14, 1887, in Baden on July 26, 1888, in Bavaria on May 28, 1892, and in Saxony-Weimar on Feb. 24, 1894. These tax laws were repeatedly amended by church and state assemblies. At the fall of the ecclesiastical hierarchy in 1918, church taxes assumed new importance for the financial structure of the German Church. Taxes currently are levied for both local and territorial churches, but since 1956 church taxes in Germany have become contributions. The administration of church taxes is an ecclesiastical affair. In the German Republic all churches have given over the administration of taxes to finance authorities except in the Bavarian territorial church. Taxes in Germany have been severely criticized, although they remain the church's greatest source of income. In Scandinavian countries, church taxes demonstrate the dependence of church on state. The Established Church in England levies no tax, but in spite of the repeal of the Test and Corporation Acts (1828), English free churches have continued to pay church rates supporting the Established Church.

**Taylor, Graham** (1851–1938). Dutch Reformed and Congregational clergyman and educator. A pastor's son, he was educated at Rutgers and Reformed Theological Seminary in New Brunswick, N.J., and was ordained in 1873. He served the Reformed Church in Hopewell, N.Y., from 1873 to 1880 and the Fourth Congregational Church, Hartford, Conn., from 1880 to 1892. In 1892 he became professor of social economics at Chicago Theological Seminary, which position he held until his death. After 1903 he also lectured at the University of Chicago. He was an eminent teacher known especially for his courses on the social teachings of Jesus. In 1894 he founded the Chicago Commons Social Settlement and headed it until he died. He was author of several books and articles and is remembered as one of the prominent exponents of the Social Gospel.

**Taylor, James Hudson** (1832–1905). An English missionary in China (1853–1860, with the not very successful Chinese Evangelization Society). In 1865, he organized the China Inland Mission, later the most successful mission in China, designed to reach areas away from the coast. It was interdenominational in character, paying no salaries, making no fund appeals (depending on the Lord—

hence, "faith mission"), conservative in theology, concerned with evangelism primarily. Taylor retained control of the Mission, returning to China in 1866 and attracting large numbers of missionaries from abroad.

**Taylor, Jeremy** (1613–1667). Anglican bishop of Down and Connor, Ireland, and administrator of Dromore. After his education at Cambridge, he was made Laud's own chaplain and was soon appointed chaplain in ordinary to Charles I. In 1638, Taylor was installed as rector at Uppingham, Rutland, where he diligently cared for his parish. While serving with the Royal Army, he was captured in 1645, then released. With his family he lived for a while at Golden Grove, Carmarthenshire, and there wrote three of his best works: *A Discourse of the Liberty of Prophesying, Holy Living,* and *Holy Dying.* The first work argues for toleration. Reason is the ultimate judge of religion, and since reason is an individual attribute, it is wrong to persecute for unorthodox beliefs. Further, people who live good lives cannot be heretics. This treatise did much to form the English mind on the subject, but it did not prevent Taylor himself from suppressing Presbyterians in his diocese after the Restoration (1660). In 1657 the death of two sons so shattered him that he never completely recovered his former serenity. In 1660 he was in London, signed the Royalist "declaration," and was promoted to the see of Down and Connor when episcopacy was restored. His life in the Irish see was intolerable, for he could not adequately handle either the Presbyterian or Roman Catholic dissenters. He begged to be relieved, but his pleas were not granted. He died from a fever in 1667. Not greatly distinguished as a theologian, he was remembered chiefly for his devotional classics on holy living and dying.

**Taylor, Nathaniel William** (1786–1858). American minister and first professor of theology at Yale Divinity School. He was one of the last champions of the New England Theology. He spent all of his life in Connecticut, being born in New Milford, educated at Yale, and after theological training in the household of Yale's president, Timothy Dwight, called to the pastorate of the First Church of Christ of New Haven. His sermons produced a powerful effect on his congregation and revivals were regular occurrences. In appearance Taylor was strikingly handsome; in pulpit manner he was rigorously logical, but warm and animated as well—in fact, he was known to become so caught up in his subject that he spoke with tears running down his face.

In 1822, the Divinity School was established at Yale, and Taylor was named its first professor of theology. He continued the traditional New England Calvinist emphasis upon man's sinful depravity and complete dependence upon God's grace in electing to save sinners. Taylor did, however, attempt to reconstruct man's moral ability and freedom to such an extent that he could give some theological justification to the emphasis that was being placed upon the initiative of the sinner in the Second Great Awakening. His was one of the last attempts to hold together the older Calvinist emphasis upon God's activity and the newer revivalist emphasis upon man's activity. Those among his students who also became theologians (Horace Bushnell, Leonard Bacon, and Theodore T. Munger) found it necessary to begin their work on a new foundation.

**"Te Deum."** A Latin hymn of praise to God, so called from its first words, "We praise thee, O God." In the Roman Catholic Church it is part of the office of Matins during certain seasons of the Christian year. In addition, it is used upon other occasions when a hymn of thanksgiving is in order. Some Protestant churches also use the "Te Deum" as part of their liturgies.

**Teelinck, Willem** (1579–1629). Reformed theologian of the Netherlands. After studying law, Teelinck visited England and was influenced by pietistic Puritans. He studied theology at Leiden (1604) and assumed pastorates in Haamstede (1606) and Middelburg (1612). Called the "reformed Thomas à Kempis" by Voetius, he was active in the "Second Reformation." His pious, at times mystical, sermons attracted and stirred many. His writings were effective; *Ecce homo* was an early call for missions among the Reformed.

**Teilhard de Chardin, Pierre** (1881–1955). French Jesuit, distinguished geologist and paleontologist. He was decorated for gallantry in World War I. After taking his doctorate at the Sorbonne he did research in China from 1923 to 1945. A discoverer of the fossilized Peking man, Teilhard developed a controversial theory of evolution which sought to reconcile science and religion. Because of censure from Rome, his books *The Phenomenon of Man* and *The Divine Milieu* were not published until after his death.

**Telemachus** (d. 391). An Eastern monk known to us only through the history of Theodoret and a mention in the Hieronymian *Martyrology,* where his name is Almachius.

He is credited with moving the emperor Honorius to abolish the gladiatorial combats in Rome. Theodoret says that Telemachus was killed by enraged spectators on Jan. 1, 391, when he entered the arena seeking to stop the bloodshed by personally separating the combatants.

**Telesio, Bernardino** (1508–1588). Italian philosopher and scientist who led a scholarly protest movement against the accepted authority of abstract reason in southern Italy. He was born at Cosenza, near Naples, and after studying at the Universities of Milan, Padua, and Rome, returned to his birthplace to found an anti-Aristotelian academy. He spent the remainder of his life lecturing and writing on philosophic themes. His most enduring work, *De natura rerum juxta propria principia,* appeared in two parts, in 1565 and 1587 respectively, and was supplemented by a large number of scientific and philosophical works of subsidiary importance. After his death in 1588, his books were placed on the Index. Working as a natural philosopher, Telesio concluded that all truth came through the senses and that the soul itself was material. The church objected to his teachings because he diminished the role of God in creation, reduced man to the same status as all the rest of nature and denied him the power to seek truth by faith and abstract reason. However, Telesio's empiricism directly and deeply influenced the philosophers Thomas Campanella and Giordano Bruno in the 16th century and to a lesser extent Francis Bacon and Thomas Hobbes in the 17th.

**Teller, Wilhelm Abraham** (1734–1804). German Lutheran rationalist. Born and educated at Leipzig, he was pastor, superintendent, and professor of theology at Helmstedt. As a leader of the *Aufklärung,* he attempted to apply reason to Christianity. He rejected original sin, the natures of Christ, and the Trinity. His views provoked opposition, but in 1767 he accepted the position of superior consistorial councilor at Berlin under the protection of Frederick the Great.

**Temperance Movement.** Biblical teachings on the temperate use of alcoholic drink attracted little general notice until distilled liquors became cheap and widely available in northern Europe during the 18th century. Widespread drunkenness produced a variety of problems and attracted increasing concern. The Wesleys opposed the selling or the drinking of distilled liquors in 1743. Philadelphia physician Benjamin Rush published his famed pamphlet, *An Inquiry Into the Effects of Spirituous Liquors on the Human Body and Mind,* in 1784.

In 1800 the temperance movement began in America with the circulation of an abstinence pledge in Virginia. Local efforts multiplied, and became national in the American Temperance Society, founded in 1826; in ten years it was committed to total abstinence with the inclusion of fermented drinks in its pledge. After the Washingtonian revival, led by reformed drunkards, the new goal became legal prohibition, which was first realized in Maine in 1851. The founding of the Prohibition Party in 1869, the Women's Christian Temperance Union in 1874, and the Anti-Saloon League in 1893 added support, and by 1902 every state required temperance instruction in the public schools. At first primarily propaganda, such instruction has continued to the present time and has gained stature with the decline of contention and the increase of scientific knowledge.

The Eighteenth Amendment (1920) established nationwide prohibition of intoxicating liquors. Enacted in the last burst of Progressive reformist energy, it proved impossible to enforce in the relaxed climate of the 1920's. The temperance effort sagged after victory, as leaders transferred responsibility to the state. Prohibition was the only cause that enjoyed the support of both modernists and fundamentalists, and their quarrels during the 1920's destroyed the continued cooperation needed to help it work. Since the Eighteenth Amendment was repealed in 1933, the temperance movement has come to stress education, rehabilitation of alcoholics, and moderate regulatory legislation.

In England, a 19th-century temperance movement sprang from the individualistic moral tendencies of Methodism and the Evangelical party within the Church of England. The work of Thomas Chalmers in Scotland produced a religious awakening in that country at the beginning of the 19th century, and a Scottish temperance movement followed in the wake of revival. Temperance movements occurred in the Scandinavian countries during the 19th century, notably in Denmark, where temperance was part of the Inner Mission movement led by Vilhelm Beck.

**Tempier, Étienne** (d. 1279). Bishop of Paris from 1268. Determined to maintain discipline over the university, he condemned in 1270 various propositions being taught by the Averroists, and when asked by Pope John XXI in 1277 to report on erroneous doctrines in the arts faculty, he hurriedly listed 219, including some ideas derived from Thomas Aquinas.

Thereafter the whole rationalist movement went on the defensive and a long Augustinian reaction triumphed in philosophy.

**Templars.** The military order founded in Jerusalem by Hugues de Payens in 1119 to provide protection for pilgrims visiting the Holy Land. Baldwin II gave Hugues and seven comrades quarters in a wing of his palace in the temple area, from whence the name Templars. At first a Benedictine Order, they soon became independent, responsible only to the pope. The Templars were made up of knights of noble birth; sergeants from the middle classes; and clerics, who had charge of non-military affairs. The knights wore white tunics, the sergeants black, both with a red cross. With the commendation of Bernard, their fame spread across Europe, where many chapters sprang up. Because of their ubiquity and strength, they became the chief bankers of the crusading era and acquired immense wealth. In the Holy Land they formed the core of the Christian armies and became a major political force in the power struggles within the Christian domains during the 13th century. With the other military orders, the Hospitalers and the Teutonic Knights, they became the chief landowners in the Latin kingdom of Jerusalem. After the fall of Acre in 1291 the Templars made their headquarters on Cyprus, but were suppressed on charges of heresy and immorality by Philip IV of France in 1310, and in 1312 forever by Pope Clement V.

**Temple, Frederick** (1821–1902). Archbishop of Canterbury. He was educated at Balliol College, Oxford, and ordained in 1846. In 1858 he became headmaster of Rugby and creatively set new traditions. He was appointed bishop of Exeter in 1869 after stormy debate over his association with rationalism. In 1884 he gave the Bampton Lectures. As archbishop of Canterbury (1896–1902) he was sensitive to the working man. Intelligent and industrious, he was dedicated to Christian higher education and church unity.

**Temple, William** (1881–1944). Archbishop of Canterbury. A son of Frederick Temple, archbishop of Canterbury, William was educated at Rugby, Oxford, and on the Continent. He was early active in the Workers' Educational Association and in 1908, having overcome certain theological difficulties, was ordained in the Church of England. While headmaster of Repton he contributed to *Foundations* (1912) and in 1914 moved to St. James's, Piccadilly. In 1915 he was appointed honorary chaplain to the king and the next year married Frances Gertrude Acland. His first major book, *Mens Creatrix* (1917),

presented the philosophical foundations for theism. He was much involved in plans for the revitalization of the church and in line with his concerns resigned his benefice to give full time to the Life and Liberty movement. In 1920 he was made bishop of Manchester, and as bishop published *Christus Veritas* (1924), chaired the international Conference on Christian Politics, Economics, and Citizenship, and gave leadership to the growing ecumenical movement. He was chairman of the Edinburgh Conference (1937) and was instrumental in the founding of the British Council of Churches. In 1929 he was made archbishop of York and was widely known as a champion of social and economic justice, a main force in the development of the World Council of Churches, and an important theologian, publishing his most prestigious work, *Nature, Man and God* (1934). In 1942 he became archbishop of Canterbury, and in the remaining two years participated in the reform of British education, provided moral leadership for his nation in the midst of bitter war and began to shift, theologically, from philosophical and incarnational thinking to a theology of redemption.

**Temporal-Spiritual Relations.** The relationship between church and state has seldom been harmonious, for each has traditionally sought to command the ultimate loyalty of its members. This conflict of interests can be observed at the very beginnings of Christianity in the persecution of Christians by the Roman state. To the Romans the Christians were traitors bent upon the destruction of the state—through their avowed allegiance to an authority other than Rome, their refusal to serve in the army or to participate in the official functions of the state, above all their refusal to do obeisance to the state by casting incense before the statue of the emperor.

With the conversion of the emperor Constantine I (312–337) to Christianity a new phase in temporal-spiritual relations was reached. The state now turned from repression of the church to favoritism, but Constantine and his successors kept the church under strict imperial supervision, intervening in doctrinal disputes and carefully keeping watch on ecclesiastical personnel. The church on its part, grateful for toleration and the favor of the emperor, cheerfully accepted this new relationship and sought to use the state to further Christian ends, such as the extirpation of paganism and heresy. Indeed, Athanasius chided Constantine not for his intervention in the Arian controversy but for his laxity in not using all the power of the state to suppress Arian beliefs.

In the Byzantine East the domination of the state over the church continued down to the end of the Byzantine Empire in 1453. The Byzantine Church might almost be viewed as a department of state, for the emperor was clearly the administrative head of the church with the power of appointment of bishops, of translating bishops, and of creating or abolishing metropolitan sees. Yet even the docile Byzantine Church opposed emperors when it believed they had overstepped their authority, as when the Isaurian emperors (717–867) unsuccessfully sought to impose iconoclasm on the church or when the Palaeologian emperors (1261–1453) tried to bring about ecclesiastical union with Rome.

In the West the conflict between church and state waxed hot throughout much of the medieval period, for the Western Church would claim superiority over the temporal authority. The precedent for this was set by Ambrose (d. 397), who denied the emperor Theodosius I Communion until that monarch had done penance for certain acts he had committed. Nevertheless, throughout the early medieval period the church tended to become subordinate to the various Germanic kings. Even the papacy had to turn to the Frankish king Charlemagne for protection, and in consequence it accepted that monarch's domination of the church. Later in the 10th and 11th centuries the church in the Holy Roman Empire became deeply tied up with the secular power through its administrative services to the emperors.

The Western ideal for the relationship of church and state was expressed by Pope Gelasius I (d. 496). According to his theory, the spiritual and temporal powers ("swords") are entrusted to two distinct authorities—the pope and the emperor—each of whom derives his power from God and each of whom is supreme within his own sphere. Both powers are to cooperate to achieve the perfect Christian commonwealth. However, the Gelasian theory was soon turned against the state; the popes claimed that since the ultimate goal of all men, including princes, is salvation, the spiritual sword is necessarily superior to the secular sword. Therefore, secular authority must bow to the authority of the church and must be used at the behest of the church. From these papal claims resulted the monumental struggle between the popes and the secular princes, particularly the Holy Roman Emperors, with the ultimate triumph of the medieval papacy over the temporal authorities.

The emergence of the new dynastic states and the Protestant Reformation, however, militated against the subordination of the state to the church. Protestantism tended to accept domination of the church by the secular authority, and the ambitious dynastic princes, seeking to extend their power, insisted that the church—be it Protestant or Roman Catholic —within their territories must heed the wishes of the state. The end result was the creation of national churches subsidized and supervised by the secular government. As a result of the American Revolution another theory of church-state relations emerged, that of complete separation of temporal and spiritual authority. This theory, however, does not prevail throughout most of the Christian world. To a greater or lesser degree the pattern of national churches still obtains.

BIBLIOGRAPHY: L. Duchesne, *Early History of the Christian Church* (New York, 1913); A. C. Flick, *Rise of the Medieval Church* (New York, 1909); E. R. Goodenough, *The Church in the Roman Empire* (New York, 1931); P. Hughes, *A Popular History of the Catholic Church* (New York, 1947); K. S. Latourette, *History of Christianity* (New York, 1953); P. Smith, *The Age of the Reformation* (reissue, New York, 1962).

**Ten Articles** (1536). The first doctrinal statement of the English Church after the repudiation of papal supremacy. The Articles, adopted in 1536 by Convocation at Henry VIII's desire, are (probably deliberately) ambiguous in their total effect: such matters as the mode of the Eucharistic presence, the relation between faith and works, and the use of images are treated in a manner acceptable to the less rigid on both Catholic and Protestant sides. (See BISHOPS' BOOK.)

**Tengstrom, Jaako** (1755–1832). Finnish Lutheran poet, historian, statesman, and archbishop. Tengstrom taught theology at Turken (1790–1803). Bishop of Turken in 1803, he was elevated to the first archbishopric of Finland in 1817. He cofounded the Finnish Bible Society in 1812, and dedicated the University of Helsinki in 1817. Tengstrom played a statesman's role in the reconstruction following 1809, wrote poetry, and translated classic poets. As a church historian he wrote several biographies. Theologically he was somewhat rationalistic.

**Tennent, William** (1673–1745), and **Gilbert** (1703–1764). Presbyterian clergymen. Coming from Ireland, William served parishes in New York and Pennsylvania. In 1726 he began to train young men for the ministry in his own home in Neshaminy, Pa. In 1736 he built the famous Log College, where his son,

Gilbert, and several other leading revivalists were educated. Gilbert's revivals in New Jersey were part of the First Great Awakening and contributed to the Presbyterian schism of 1741.

**Terce.** One of the little "hours" or "offices" of prayer in the Roman Breviary. It was derived from the practice of the synagogue and the early church and developed through monastic worship. Acts 2:15 indicates that the Spirit's descent occurred at the third hour, *hora tertia,* which is noted in the hymn. Like Sext and None, Terce is brief, containing psalms, a hymn, a short lesson, and a collect. Nine o'clock is the modern counterpart to the third hour.

**Teresa of Ávila** (Teresa de Cepeda y Ahumada, 1515–1582). Spanish mystic. Born in the Castilian town of Ávila, Teresa was one of eleven children and the favorite of her aristocratic father. In 1531 she was sent as a boarder to an Augustinian convent in Ávila; about five years later she entered the Carmelite Convent of the Incarnation. Severe ill-health partially paralyzed the young nun for years. A vivacious, happy personality, Teresa was a favorite at the Incarnation, where for twenty years she lived according to the mitigated Carmelite rule, enjoying a well-appointed suite, entertaining friends and relations, and frequently leaving the cloister to visit aristocratic ladies. Such a life caused increasing storms of conscience, however, and in 1555 Teresa underwent her "second conversion." She gave herself over to mental prayer in which she began to experience God's presence in the "prayer of quiet" and of "union" together with occasional locutions and visions. In 1559, she experienced "transverberation" in which an angel with a fire-tipped lance seemed to pierce her heart. Although she had turned to the learned direction of the Jesuits, she met at this time Peter of Alcántara, the Discalced (i.e., "Barefoot") Franciscan reformer, remarkable for gentle ways and austere penance. From him perhaps came the ideas of a discalced reform of Carmel, a return to the rule of Fray Hugo written in 1248 and mitigated by Pope Eugenius IV in 1432. Teresa dreamed of a small convent where a few nuns might observe the primitive rule. To her dreams were added specific divine commands until she gained the approval of her Jesuit confessor, Baltasar Álvarez and her provincial, Gregorio Fernandez. As plans progressed, the nuns of the Incarnation felt their way of life threatened and the people of Ávila grumbled at having another convent to support. The provincial withdrew his support, but Doña Guiomar de Ulloa, a friend, went to Rome and obtained from the pope permission for Teresa to found a convent and to write binding rules. The little convent of St. Joseph's was founded in 1562, but only in 1565 was it established according to Teresa's idea of poverty, i.e., made dependent upon alms and the limited industry of the nuns. Teresa's reform began to spread in 1567 when the general of the Carmelite order, P. Rossi (Rubeo), visited Spain to enforce Trent's decrees. Displeased by general laxity, he approved the reform and authorized Teresa to found more houses, including two for men. During the second foundation of nuns at Medina del Campo, Teresa met Fray John of St. Matias, who was to become John of the Cross, one of the first men to join the reform and Teresa's "son and father." The rest of Teresa's life was spent traveling over Spain in springless carts through blistering heat and unmitigated cold to found, visit, comfort, and strengthen thirty houses of the reform. She had to contend with jealousy, suspicion, ecclesiastical censure, accusations of false mysticism which in Counter-Reformation Spain could mean trial by the Inquisition, as well as misunderstanding of the reform itself. She corresponded with and gained the support of Philip II. During such intense activity Teresa continued her contemplative prayer and, in addition, fought continual ill-health. She wished to hide in an obscure corner and give herself to silence and contemplation, but the difficulties of foundations and of the reform itself kept her moving until her death at Alba de Tormes on Oct. 4, 1582.

Teresa was one of Spain's greatest literary geniuses. Her works display the psychological insight, common sense, charm, gaiety, humor, and love that still elicit affection and respect for this great mystic. Two of her works are autobiographical: the *Life,* written at the request of her directors, and the *Book of Foundations.* Two other books were written for her nuns: *The Way of Perfection* (1566) and *The Interior Castle* (1577). The latter is the mature work of a great contemplative and traces the way of prayer from conversion to the ecstasy of "spiritual marriage" or "transforming union." Her spirit is strong; she demands courage and renunciation, with gentle charity for others. Energy, not lethargy, should be the result of contemplation as well as obedience and a sense of humor that is the cure for self-conceit about a personal state of prayer. Teresa was canonized by Gregory XV in 1622.

BIBLIOGRAPHY: T. Dicken, *The Crucible of Love* (New York, 1963); E. A. Peers, *Mother of Carmel* (London, 1946).

**Tersteegen, Gerhard** (1697–1769). German Reformed mystic, best known as a hymn writer. After a dramatic conversion he submitted to a life of devotion, living ascetically. In time he gave himself to the care of souls and was widely sought as a spiritual counselor. His translations and writings are extensive. His hymns, more than one hundred, were at first included only in pietistic collections, but later came to be received generally. Among them are "God Reveals His Presence" and "God Calling Yet! Shall I Not Hear?"

**Tertiary.** A member of a third order of one of the mendicant orders (Dominicans, Franciscans, or Carmelites). They were founded as a way in which the laity could participate in the work and spirituality of the order. Formed into chapters under the direction of priests of the order, tertiaries are bound by a discipline, recite an office, undergo a novitiate, but do not profess vows. Some tertiaries live a communal life in a convent and are known as tertiaries regular.

**Tertullian** (Quintus Septimius Florens Tertullianus) (c. 160–c. 220). African church father and Montanist. Tertullian was the first major theologian to write in Latin and may be called the founder of ecclesiastical Latin. He wrote apologetic, polemical, and ascetic works, and was a pioneer in much theological formulation.

He was a Carthaginian, and his father was a Roman official, either a proconsul or a centurion, so he was probably a Roman rather than a native. Christianity stayed in the cities in Africa and found its converts among the urban minority. Although Carthage probably encompassed three quarters of a million citizens at the time, they were only the administrative superstructure over the vast indigenous agricultural population. Tertullian's education was excellent; he could write equally well in Latin or Greek and was familiar with philosophy, literature, history, physiology, logic, and psychology. He traveled at some time in his life to Rome, Greece, and the Middle East. He was believed to have been a lawyer, and some even identify him with the jurist Tertullian whose writings are cited in the digests of the Corpus Juris Civilis.

The date of his conversion is deduced from the fact that his *Apology* was written in 197, and it seems unlikely that so outspoken a man as Tertullian could have been a Christian long without having written something about it. The reasons for his conversion must be inferred from his writings. It is possible that he heard the "testimony of the soul naturally Christian" of which he writes so eloquently. Some scholars think guilt feelings over a misspent youth were a factor. A major cause must have been the spectacular heroism of Christian martyrs.

Jerome says that he was a priest, although he never says so himself. We know that he was married, because he wrote two treatises to his wife, one asking her not to remarry if he predeceased her, and the other asking her at least to marry a Christian if she did remarry.

Tertullian was a rigorist; perhaps the rigorism of the Christians is what first attracted him to them. This single-minded asceticism accounts for his lapse into Montanism. African Montanism differed from the Phrygian original in several ways. It did not hold a theory of prophetic rather than apostolic succession, it was not so ecstatic, and it gave women a less spectacular role in church. The African Montanists also did not think that martyrs could give absolution, although they considered them steadfast under persecution. On all other points Montanists were strictly orthodox Christians. Tertullian may have regarded himself as a Puritan Catholic. For a long time Tertullian seems to have led the ascetic minority in the church at Carthage but finally parted from the less strict members of the same congregation. About 207 he became the head of a small Montanist community in Carthage. Augustine tells us that even the Montanists were not strict enough for Tertullian, and so he began a sect of his own which lasted until Augustine's day. Tertullian's difference with Montanism was probably over his Stoic doctrine of the corporeality of the soul. He was said to have lived to a great age.

Although some authorities divide the works of Tertullian into Catholic and Montanist writings, this breakdown is not very helpful. The Catholic works were more scrupulous than was customary and the books written after his apostasy were often the beginning of orthodox formulation on the subjects with which they dealt. A more fruitful set of categories is the following: (1) apologetic, (2) polemic, and (3) ascetic.

1. *Apologetic works.* Tertullian has been called "the last of the Greek apologists" as well as the "father of Latin theology." His *To the Heathen* and *Apology* show why. They were both written in 197, but the greater finish of the latter and its allusions to the revolt of Albinus reveal it to be the later work. *To the Heathen* is in two books, the first of which says that Christians should not be punished for their convictions, but should be judged upon the basis of their upright actions. Chris-

tians are defended against the charges current in that period. The second book follows Varro's division of the gods into those of the philosophers, those of the poets, and those of the nations. Thus a pagan writer furnishes Tertullian with ammunition against pagan religion. The *Apology* is an expansion of *To the Heathen* and, dedicated to the provincial governors instead of the masses, is a much more polished piece of work. One of Tertullian's few works that can be called charming is his *Testimony of the Soul,* which was also written in 197 and is only six chapters long. It is an early presentation of the "argument from general consent" for the existence of God. *To Scapula* is addressed to the proconsul of Africa (211–213) who persecuted Christians and put many to death. In it Tertullian says that he is not so much interested in protecting Christians, who do not fear death, as in protecting Romans from the guilt of murder. In the work is a plea for freedom of religion. *Against the Jews* in the authentic first part draws heavily on Justin Martyr's *Dialogue with Trypho,* and the second half is an inept rehash, probably by a disciple, of Tertullian's third book *Against Marcion.*

2. *Polemic works. The Prescription of Heretics* invokes the device of Roman law called the *praescriptio* by which one side in a suit denies the relevance of the other side's allegations. The object is to read the opponent out of court before he is given a hearing. The argument of Tertullian is that since the Scriptures are the Catholic Church's book, heretics violate the church's property rights in quoting the Bible against the church. In essence it is the argument that Catholicism still uses against Protestantism, namely, that those nearest to the events of the foundation of the church and the writing of the Holy Scriptures probably understand them best because of the interpretation passed on to them by the apostles. Although often considered to be mere authoritarianism, this argument was the only sort of historical appeal possible at the time of Tertullian.

The longest of Tertullian's works is his thorough treatise in five books *Against Marcion.* It is our main source for knowledge about Marcion and from it Marcion's canon of the New Testament and his *Antitheses* have been reconstructed. The first of the five books on Marcion is devoted to demonstrating that "God is not if he is not one," and the second to showing that the Maker of the world is the same as the loving God revealed in Christ. The third book shows how Christ is the fulfillment of Old Testament prophecy. The fourth book is an extended commentary on Luke as the fifth is a commentary on the Pauline corpus, the two books proving that Marcion's own canon reveals the Old Testament God to be the God of Christ.

Tertullian wrote against Hermogenes, who believed in the eternity of matter, and summarized previous attacks on the Valentinians. *On Baptism* was written to oppose Quintilla, who taught that the sacrament was unnecessary; it is the only work on the subject before Nicaea. The *Scorpiace* compares Gnostics to scorpions and says that martyrdom is the antidote to their sting. *On the Flesh of Christ* and *The Resurrection of the Flesh* are strong polemics against Docetism. The Praxeas against whom Tertullian wrote may be the pope Callistus, who appears to have espoused monarchian views; "Praxeas" could mean "busybody." It is in this treatise that Tertullian introduces most of the terms to be used in Western formulations of the doctrine of the Trinity (a term first employed by him). He was the first to write of three persons and one substance. *On the Soul* arose in refutation of contemporary errors, but it contains the Stoic doctrine of the corporeality of the soul, which was probably the distinctive doctrine of the Tertullianists.

3. *Ascetic works.* The sixteen extant works of ascetic theology all betray the rigorism of Tertullian, which led him into Montanism. *Ad martyres* is written to Christians in prison awaiting martyrdom and encourages them by telling them that their death will be the means by which they escape the prison of the world. *De spectaculis,* of which there was a Greek edition, shows by historical and ethical argument that Christians were not to attend the public games. In *De cultu feminarum,* Tertullian joined most of the Puritans in history in condemning feminine fashions as immodest. His *De oratione* is the oldest surviving commentary on the Lord's Prayer. In *De patientia* he praises a virtue for which he admits a nostalgic longing. His treatise on repentance is an important source for the history of the penitential system. In *De exhortatione castitatis* he defines marriage as legitimate debauchery and, in his treatise on the subject, he makes it clear that he considers monogamy to consist of one marriage only, with no remarriage where a partner has died. He feels that it is idolatry for Christians to wear the military crown. Flight to avoid persecution is forbidden. Any trade connected with idolatry is disallowed. In *De pudicitia* he develops a penitential theory more rigorous than its earlier Catholic expression. Finally he showed his break with pagan culture by adopting the philosopher's mantle instead of the toga as his

dress, and he wrote his shortest work in defense of this practice.

BIBLIOGRAPHY: Tertullian, *Treatise Against Hermogenes,* ed. by J. H. Waszink (Westminster, Md., 1956); A. Roberts and J. Donaldson (eds.), *The Ante-Nicene Fathers,* Vols. 3–4 (Grand Rapids, 1951).

R. A. Norris, Jr., *God and World in Early Christian Theology* (New York, 1967); R. E. Roberts, *The Theology of Tertullian* (London, 1924); B. B. Warfield, *Studies in Tertullian and Augustine* (New York, 1930).

**Test Act.** A law that made the holding of public offices in England dependent upon taking Communion in the Church of England. It was enacted by the English Parliament in 1672 (25 Car. II. c.2), and was entitled "An act for preventing dangers which may happen from popish recusants." According to the act, public officials were required to take an oath of supremacy, to subscribe to a declaration against transubstantiation, and to receive the Sacrament within three months after taking office. The act was suspended with the passing of the Catholic Emancipation Act in 1829 and was specifically repealed in 1863.

**Testaments of the Twelve Patriarchs.** A Hebrew writing, extant only in translations, in imitation of the so-called Testament of Jacob (Gen., ch. 49). Each of the twelve books is a testament by one of Jacob's sons said to have been given to his descendants from his deathbed. Originating from a Maccabean milieu in the 2d century B.C., the Testaments are full of ex post facto prophecies, successively augmented with anti-Maccabean and Christian interpolations.

**Testamentum Domini.** A church order in the form of the Lord's last legacy to his church, actually based on the Apostolic Tradition of Hippolytus, with additions that reflect the more elaborate liturgical practices of a church in Asia Minor or Syria c. 375. Lost in the original Greek, it was preserved in a Syriac translation, which was published in 1899 by the Syrian Catholic patriarch Ephraim Rahmani.

**Testem Benevolentiae** (Jan. 22, 1899). The letter of Leo XIII to James Cardinal Gibbons censuring "Americanism" as a "phantom heresy." Some French clerics alleged that American prelates taught that the church should adapt itself to the modern age, relax faith (to speed conversions), place natural above supernatural virtue, deemphasize religious vows, and export "American" methods to Europe. Gibbons protested that these views were not held.

**Tetrapolitan Confession.** The oldest German Reformed confession, written in 1530 (also called Strasbourg Confession and Swabian Confession). It was prepared by Martin Bucer with the help of Wolfgang Capito and Caspar Hedio in the name of the four imperial cities of Strasbourg, Constance, Memmingen, and Lindau. Composed during the Diet of Augsburg, it was presented to the emperor after the Lutheran Confession and Zwingli's Confession, but was opposed and misinterpreted by members of the Diet. The authors wrote an apology in reply. The confession resembles the Lutheran Confession of Augsburg in its doctrine, arrangement, and spirit of moderation. It differs especially in its strong emphasis upon the supreme authority of Scripture, on which the Lutheran Confession is silent. The statement on the Lord's Supper is couched in ambiguous language, evidently intended to avoid the conflict between Lutheran and Zwinglian views. This confession was the first attempt at a union symbol for all Protestants. Its failure foreshadowed the widening breach between the Lutheran and Reformed positions. The four cities later signed the Lutheran Confession in order to join the Smalcald League. Bucer, however, remained true to his confession, reconfessing it in his last will and upon his deathbed.

**Tetzel, John** (c. 1465–1519). German Dominican who was made an indulgence preacher to provide income for building St. Peter's in Rome and whose work near Wittenberg incited Luther to write his Ninety-five Theses. Tetzel won a bitter reproach from the pope's envoy and the scorn of the local populace. Although he received some support for his reply to Luther, the whole affair left him ruined in both spirit and body. Certainly Tetzel's teaching pandered to popular superstition and his manner of preaching was overly flamboyant, but his defects of character may have been exaggerated and (as Luther himself recognized in a letter of comfort to the dying man) he could not be made the scapegoat for the scandal over indulgences.

**Teutonic Order.** A German religious military order of knights, priests, and laymen. The order originated through the efforts of citizens of Bremen and Lübeck to establish a field hospital at the siege of Acre (1190) during the Third Crusade. It was formally confirmed by Pope Clement III in 1199 and soon became involved in the conquest of pagan lands. In 1226 the Holy Roman Emperor Frederick II gave Prussia to the Teutonic Grand Master Hermann of Salza on condition that the order subjugate the territory for the Empire and the church. The knights completed the conquest by 1283 and encouraged the immigration of German settlers. From early in the 13th century the order had attempted, with little success, to extend its authority over pagan Lithuania. Finally, in 1386, the Lithuanian king Jagello formed an alliance with Poland against the order and at the battle of Tannenberg (1410) the power of the knights was broken. Ironically, the price of the alliance was the Lithuanian acceptance of Christianity. By 1466 the knights had lost all their territory except East Prussia which they administered for Poland. In 1525, when Grand Master Albert of Prussia was converted to Protestantism through Luther's influence, the members who remained Catholic moved to Mergentheim. Napoleon dissolved the order in Germany in 1805, but it continued in Austria, where in 1929 it was limited to religious work mostly in schools and hospitals. In 1966 the order had ninety-seven members.

**Thailand, Church of Christ In.** A body formed by the union of the North and South Siam Presbyteries (Presbyterian Church U.S.A.), the Disciples churches in the Nakhon Pathom area, and some Baptist churches dating from the very early mission in the country. The constituting assembly was April 7–11, 1934. The Marburger Mission affiliated in 1953, and the reconstituted American Baptist Mission works in close relation. In 1962 the community numbered 23,636.

**Theatines.** A religious order founded in 1524 by Gaetano da Thiene (Cajetan), Boniface da Colle, and Gian Pietro Carafa (later Pope Paul IV). The name was taken from Chieti (Theate), in central Italy, where Carafa was bishop. The rule of the Theatines, based on the rule of Augustine and approved by Clement VII, guaranteed a life of strict austerity, and the Theatines hoped that by their efforts the religious life of priests and laity could be revived. They are noted for the bishops and popes they gave to the Counter-Reformation.

**Theban Legion.** According to the *Passio Agaunensium martyrum* of Eucherius of Lyons, an entire Christian legion from the Thebaid (Upper Nile valley), commanded by Maurice, was massacred (c. 286) by the emperor Maximian at Agaunum (now St. Maurice-en-Valais) for refusing to participate in pagan sacrificial rites. Although unhistorical in this form, the story may have had some historical roots. The martydom is the subject of a famous painting by El Greco.

**Theocracy.** The form of political organization in which God himself is acknowledged as head of the state. Where such acknowledgment is genuine, the divine will is the prime concern of legislators, laws are both civil and religious obligations, and religious and political institutions are intimately conjoined. Since God's purposes and will for the state must be interpreted, religious functionaries may well achieve high political influence or even rule; theocratic government may become a hierocracy. Where the divine will is embodied in fixed teaching, theocratic ideals may become recognized goals and purposes of society without requiring clerical rule.

States purporting to enjoy divine governance were common in the ancient world (as in Egypt and Mesopotamia), where the ruler served as oracle, representative, or even incarnation of the god. In modern times theocratic ideas have been exemplified in Tibetan Lamaism and in Islam. Theocracy has proved to be an important theme throughout Judeo-Christian history. The term appears to have been invented (by analogy with "aristocracy" and "democracy") by the Hellenistic Jew Josephus (*Against Apion*, 2. 16), to describe the political system of the Hebrews. A theocratic tradition of Old Testament interpretation has since viewed Jehovah as supreme ruler of Israel, making known his will through priests, judges, and prophets, as well as through Moses and the law. That the institution of the monarchy disturbed this system of divine sovereignty was inferred from the Gideon and Samuel stories (Judg. 8:23; I Sam. 8:7), but kings were nonetheless to be regarded as God's vicegerents. After the exile and the disappearance of the monarchy, theocracy was vindicated in the hierocratic government set up in the restored nation.

In the early church, isolation from political power, persecution, and vivid anticipations of Christ's return and kingly rule placed theocratic concepts closer to eschatology than to political thought. But in the Middle Ages the dominance of religion and the central position of the church awakened theocratic impulses at several levels. In central Italy the papacy established an actual territorial sovereignty which endured until Italian unification in the 19th century. More importantly, ecclesiastical claims to authority in politics and society fostered the development of classic papal theory, evident in Gelasius I's doctrine of the two powers and invoked with mixed success by such great pontiffs as Gregory VII, Innocent III, and Boniface VIII. Against such claims secular rulers at length evolved divine right concepts by which God's authority was made the basis of princely government. Medieval heresies, criticizing contemporary church and society, sometimes envisioned a perfect theocratic order (often with millennial overtones) and sought to anticipate its coming in the practices of the heretical community.

Reformation doctrine generally taught the independent authority but close mutual relationship of church and state; with different functions they were still bound in common service to the gospel. Practically, Lutheran Germany evinced much subordination of the church to the state, but in Calvin's Geneva and Reformed churches everywhere theocratic ideas were prominent. The church was the obedient community under godly discipline and with a ruling as well as preaching ministry. The state, no less than the church, was bound by the divine will revealed in Scripture. This outlook required the church's independence of state control but not a clerical ascendancy (though this sometimes occurred). The Anabaptists' legalism, radical ethic, and discipline also stirred some theocratic impulses. Although as pacifists they ordinarily offered no challenge to the state, the theocratic constitution at Münster (1534) combined magistracy and spiritual power in a brief but disastrous experiment.

In modern history British Protestantism has been notably receptive to theocratic views. The Scottish Kirk has nourished a national tradition of judging political issues by religious and moral criteria—a muted echo of Andrew Melville's teaching that King James VI was subject to King Jesus and to the pledge by 17th-century Covenanters to take God's Word as their government. English Puritanism was essentially theocratic, and its various forms express different solutions to the problem of securing respect for God's will in church and society. Accordingly, the Puritan Revolution was rich in theocratic experiment, conservatively in Presbyterian and Independent projects for godly magistracy and more radically in Cromwell's rule, the Little Parliament (1653), and Fifth Monarchy and sectarian agitation. (Even the early Quakers, rejecting worldly compromises, sought by spiritual means a society perfectly responsive to divine will.) After some eclipse, Puritan theocratic themes partially revived in altered form in the Victorian "Nonconformist Conscience," where the doctrine that what is morally wrong cannot be politically right served as a formula for political action.

Theocratic loyalties have also strongly influenced American religious history. New England apologists, such as John Cotton and John Eliot, proclaimed theocratic government in Massachusetts. Franchise restriction to church members, Scriptural legalism, and dedication of rulers to God's service supported this outlook, though magisterial and clerical functions were carefully distinguished. Jeopardized by the Enlightenment and the American Revolution, these ideas revived in the Second Great Awakening with new techniques based on revivals, moral crusades, and voluntary societies. They long continued to influence both conservatives and progressives in 19th-century Protestantism. The American West with its freedom and opportunity for sectarian perfectionism also harbored theocratic ideas, apparent in the Oneida community, the Rappites, Shakers, Mormons, and others. While the 20th century offers little encouragement to theocratic projects of government, either in the United States or elsewhere, some modern sects (such as Jehovah's Witnesses) continue to testify for a theocratic order.

BIBLIOGRAPHY: J. Bright, *The Kingdom of God* (Nashville, 1953); H. Frankfort, *Kingship and the Gods* (Chicago, 1948); H. R. Niebuhr, *The Kingdom of God in America* (New York, 1937); G. Tellenbach, *Church, State, and Christian Society at the Time of the Investiture Contest* (Oxford, 1940); E. Troeltsch, *The Social Teaching of the Christian Churches,* 2 vols. (New York, 1960).

**Theodora** (c. 508–548). Wife of Justinian I, emperor of the Eastern Roman Empire. She was an actress before her marriage to Justinian in 523. During the remaining years of her life, she exerted a considerable influence on her husband in political and religious affairs. A strong supporter of Monophysitism, she brought about the consecration of two Monophysite monks in 543. One of them, Jacob Baradai, was responsible for the establishing of the Jacobites in Syria.

**Theodore** (c. 350–c. 427). Bishop of Mopsuestia in Cilicia from 392. He was a leading representative of the Antiochene School of theologians and exegetes. Educated in Antioch, he attended the school of the pagan rhetorician Libanius together with John Chrysostom, and under the latter's influence entered the monastic life. After a brief lapse from this initial resolution, he returned to his monastery, again at the urging of Chrysostom. There he remained, first as a pupil of Diodore of Tarsus, then as a teacher in his own right, until his election as bishop of Mopsuestia. Of his later career, apart from his literary activity, little is known. He visited Constantinople at least once, as one of a group of bishops assembled to settle a disputed succession to the see of Bostra. It is recorded also that at a later date, he extended hospitality to the Pelagian leader Julian of Eclanum, only to consent to the latter's condemnation at a synod held shortly after Julian had departed. Theodore died on the eve of the Nestorian controversy. Though he was condemned by the Council of Constantinople in 553 for having held the Nestorian view that there are two "persons" in Christ, Theodore enjoyed during his lifetime the reputation of an orthodox teacher. He was the accepted theological authority for those Orientals who, having agreed to the condemnation of Nestorius, adhered nevertheless to the view that there are two natures in Christ; and it was in the course of the controversy that grew up after the Council of Ephesus (431) that his name was introduced into the Christological debate and his reputation became a storm center of argument. While he lived, Theodore was an effective opponent of both Arian and Apollinarian doctrine as well as a prolific author of Scriptural commentaries. Of his dogmatic works, only scattered fragments remain. His *Catechetical Lectures* have been recovered in Syriac version, and much of his exegetical work is available, whether in the original Greek or in Latin or Syriac version. In his exegesis, Theodore followed the Antiochene tradition of literal and typological interpretation, repudiating the allegorical method associated with Origen and the school of Alexandria. It was his settled conviction that the several books of the Bible must be understood against the historical background of the times in and for which they were written. This led him to curtail drastically the number of Old Testament passages that might legitimately be accepted as straightforward messianic prophecy, even though he was prepared to admit that many passages which had customarily been read in this sense might be applied to Christ by analogy. Against Apollinarius, Theodore developed the typically Antiochene emphasis on the completeness of Christ's humanity. He explained the incarnation as a moral union effected by the initiative of divine grace and perfected in the consequent human obedience of the "assumed Man." Thus in his view the single "person" of the Redeemer is constituted by the divine Son's gracious indwelling of the Man Jesus—an indwelling generically like his indwelling of the prophets and apostles, but specifically different and therefore unique in that Christ alone is the one in whom the Word dwells "as in a son." This Christological point of view issues in a strong distinction between the divine and the human "natures" of Christ, which is reflected in Theodore's exegetical habit of assigning sayings and deeds of Christ to "the Man" different from those assigned to the divine Son. It is also closely connected with Theodore's doctrine of man, according to which man is essentially a free agent and sin is a deliberate, free disobedience to divine precept which is nourished and multiplied by the weakness of a mortal and mutable nature. Because of his sin, man's redemption requires the direct action of God; but in order to be the redemption of man, it requires to be worked in and through the free obedience of a human agent. This insistence on the rational freedom of man, which lies at the root of Theodore's Christological dualism, is also the source of the charge of Pelagianism which has not infrequently been brought against him.

**Theodore of Raïthu** (6th century). A monk and presbyter in the monastery of Raïthu in the mid-6th century. The only theological work definitely known to be his is a defense of the Christological positions of Chalcedon and Cyril of Alexandria. This *Proparaskeuē*, after outlining the opposed extremes of Mani and Paul of Samosata, Apollinarius and Theodore of Mopsuestia, and Nestorius and Eutyches, proceeds to its principal concern, an attack on the Monophysites Severus of Antioch and Julian of Halicarnassus.

**Theodore of Studium** (759–826). A Byzantine monastic reformer, widely venerated in the East. He became abbot of Saccudium in Bythynia, but was banished to Thessalonica after excommunicating Emperor Constantine VI for an uncanonical second marriage. After Constantine's death in 797 he refounded the monastery of Studium in Constantinople, which became a famous center of monastic study and reform. Most of Theodore's later life was spent in exile because of his uncompromising zeal against the iconoclasts, whom later emperors favored.

**Theodore of Tarsus** (c. 602–690). Greek priest and archbishop of Canterbury. Theodore was educated in Tarsus and Athens in both religious and secular subjects. Little is known of his life before he became archbishop of Canterbury in 668 at the age of sixty-six. He was recommended for the post by the African monk Hadrian after the English candidate, Wighard, died in Rome before his consecration. Theodore was consecrated by Pope Vitalian and went to England with Hadrian and the English monk Benedict Biscop. Although the Synod of Whitby in 664 had ruled in favor of Roman Church practices over Celtic customs, it was largely through the work of Theodore that the English Church was united with Rome. Upon his arrival in

668 he visited throughout the country and then began to reform and organize the church. He laid the foundations for the parish system, created new dioceses, consecrated bishops, and was interested in education and Christian morals. In 673 he presided over the Synod of Hertford which ruled against certain persistent Celtic customs and in 680 he presided over the Synod of Hatfield which drew up and sent to Rome a statement of the English Church's orthodoxy. Under Theodore, who labored until his death at the age of eighty-eight, the English Church was unified, organized under the archbishop of Canterbury, and firmly bound to Rome.

**Theodoret** (c. 393–c. 458). Bishop of Cyrrhus. Born in Antioch and early attached to the ascetic life, he entered the monastery of Nicerte outside Antioch in 416. There he remained until 423, when against his will he was made bishop of Cyrrhus. There, until his death, he carried on a notable pastoral ministry. Historian, Apologist, and an exegete of the Antiochene school, Theodoret is best known for his stand in the Christological debate of his time, which he entered with a refutation of Cyril of Alexandria's anathematisms against Nestorius. At the Council of Ephesus (431) he aligned himself with the dissident Orientals and declined to sign the condemnation of Nestorius. He continued to write against the Cyrillian position, even refusing for some time to sign the Formulary of Reunion (433), which he may have written. He was deposed by the "Robber Council" of Ephesus (449). Restored by the emperor Marcian, he attended the Council of Chalcedon (451), where he agreed reluctantly to condemn Nestorius. His works against Cyril and the Ephesian Council were condemned at Constantinople (553), but in his later years Theodoret had probably renounced Nestorianism and adopted a more orthodox point of view.

**Theodoric** (c. 455–526). Ostrogoth ruler. He spent his early years as a hostage in Constantinople. King of the Ostrogoths from the death of his father, Theudemir (c. 475), he overthrew the usurper Odoacer at the behest of his former enemy, the emperor Zeno, and became king of Italy in 493. Ruling from Ravenna until his death in 526, Theodoric brought peace and prosperity to his kingdoms, observing a careful impartiality toward both Catholics and his own Ostrogothic Arians.

**Theodosius I the Great** (c. 346–395). Eastern Roman Emperor from 379. He was born in Spain, the son of another Theodosius who had distinguished himself as a general in the service of Valentinian. Theodosius gained renown for his defeat of a Sarmatian invasion of Moesia in 374. After the death of Valens at the battle of Adrianople, he was summoned by Gratian to head the Eastern Empire, and was proclaimed Augustus in January, 379. His military skill and diplomacy enabled him to pacify the Goths who had overrun the Balkan peninsula—in part by settling large numbers of the barbarians within the Empire. The problems of his reign were complicated by the instability of the imperial succession in the West, where he was twice forced to intervene to frustrate usurpers. The son of orthodox Christian parents, Theodosius fostered the final settlement of the Trinitarian issue at the Council of Constantinople (381) and made Christianity the sole official religion of the Empire. In a series of edicts, he forbade Christian heretics to assemble in cities and ordered pagan temples to be overthrown in the lands under his control. He died in Milan shortly after establishing his son Honorius as Emperor of the West.

**Theodosius II** (401–450). Eastern Roman Emperor from 408. He passed the first part of his reign as a minor, when the Empire was directed by his sister Pulcheria and the prefect Anthemius. He was responsible for the promulgation of the Theodosian Code, and played a somewhat shifting role in the Nestorian and Eutychian controversies. His reign was marked by Hunnish invasions of the Balkans, dealt with by tribute payment.

**Theodotus of Ancyra** (d. c. 445). Bishop of Ancyra (Ankara) in the 5th century. Once a personal disciple of Nestorius, he made a strong attack against him at the first session of the Council of Ephesus (431), and was counteranathematized by the Nestorians at Tarsus the following year. His works included *Six Books Against Nestorius,* an *Exposition of the Symbol of Nicaea,* and several sermons. Of these only the *Exposition* and some sermons are extant.

**Theodotus of Byzantium** (2d century). One of the earliest dynamic (Adoptianist) monarchians, influenced, some think, by the Alogi of Asia Minor. Theodotus (variously styled the Cobbler, Tanner, or Currier) came to Rome from Byzantium c. 190. He was excommunicated by Pope Victor for teaching that Jesus became the Christ at his baptism. His teaching was continued by Theodotus the Money Changer, among others. Some Theodotians simply denied Christ's divinity; others held that he became divine at his resurrection.

**Theodulf of Orléans** (c. 750–821). Ecclesiastic and scholar. Born in Spain, he was named by Charlemagne to be abbot of Fleury and bishop of Orléans. He took part in several missions for the emperor and instituted numerous liturgical reforms. The author of several theological works, he also composed poems and hymns, including "All Glory, Laud, and Honor." He was implicated in the rebellion of Bernard of Italy against Louis the Pious and was deposed and exiled.

**Theognostus** (d. c. 282). Probably head of the school at Alexandria (248–282) as successor of Dionysius. His principal work, the *Outlines* (described by Photius; fragments in Athanasius and Gregory of Nyssa), was almost entirely based on the doctrines of Origen and reveals how rigidly conservative the school became. His Christology was largely based on Proverbs and the Wisdom of Solomon.

**Theologia Germanica** (c. 1350). An anonymous mystical treatise, the printing of which Luther supervised in 1518. Luther's preface warns the reader not to be put off by "its bad German, or its crabbed and uncouth words," since its contents are rich: "Next to the Bible and St. Augustine, no book has ever come into my hands from which I have learnt, or would wish to learn, more of what God, and Christ, and man and all things are." Luther found in it vindication for his "new" German theology, and during his lifetime it went into seventeen editions. In 1850 a second manuscript was found at Würzburg. It dates from 1497 and states that the author was "a priest and a warden in the house of the Teutonic Order in Frankfurt." According to its teaching, the creature "is no true substance, but is an accident, or a brightness, . . . and has no substance except in the fire whence the brightness flowed forth, such as the sun." The fall of man is his self-assertiveness, his craving to possess. The incarnation is redemptive, since man could not without God, and God should not without man, effect salvation. Sanctification is a repetition of the redemptive incarnation to the extent that God is given and takes over all that is in man until no "mine" (i.e., no assertion of the self) exists.

**Theopaschites** ("those who believe that God suffered"). A group of 6th-century Monophysites who, basing their teaching on Proclus of Constantinople (d. 446), said that one of the Trinity had been crucified. The name had already been used by Nestorius as the title of a dialogue attacking Cyril of Alexandria. In the 6th-century controversy the formula was upheld by the emperor Justinian but rejected by the bishops of Constantinople and Rome.

**Theophilus** (2d century). Bishop of Antioch during the reign of Commodus (180–192). Nothing is known of his life; his surviving works consist of three books addressed to a certain Autolycus. The first defends Christians against the accusation of godlessness, attacks pagan deities, explains the name Christian as derived from chrism, and argues for resurrection. The second criticizes unreliable Greek authors and explains the inspiration and the accuracy of Old Testament history, beginning with creation. The third attacks Greek writers again and praises the Old Testament law given by Moses; then comes a "proof" that Moses was older than any Greek writers, along with a chronology of world history up to 180.

The work of Theophilus gives significant evidence for the influence of Jewish (especially but not exclusively Hellenistic) writers on Christian thought at Antioch in his time; his theology (much of which can be read only between the lines of his work) is based primarily on the Old Testament, though he regards some New Testament writings as Scripture. His attacks on Greco-Roman culture reflect the methods of the skeptics, as does his interpretation of faith as required in all human activities. Several of his leading ideas about the Logos (Christ) were later appropriated by Irenaeus and Tertullian, neither of whom mentioned him, but his work was rarely copied and survives only in an 11th-century manuscript and a 16th-century copy of it.

**Theophilus of Alexandria** (d. 412). Bishop of Alexandria from 385. Although described by most historians as violent, unscrupulous, and ambitious, he is commemorated as a saint by the Coptic and Syriac churches. He is remembered chiefly for the extirpation of paganism from Egypt (391), his condemnation of Origen (401), and his role in the deposition and exile of John Chrysostom (403). Gibbon's evaluation of him as "the perpetual enemy of peace and virtue, a bold, bad man, whose hands were alternately polluted with gold and with blood" may be extreme, and most information about him comes from his enemies, but it would nevertheless seem that the picture usually presented is not unrealistic. Certainly much of his episcopate was spent in furthering the prestige of his see, often in unscrupulous ways. Theophilus exercised a powerful influence on all the political affairs of his day, bringing to them an intellect and vigor whose impressiveness is not diminished by his personal ambitions. Theophilus was considered a father of the church by Arnobius, Theodoret, and Leo the Great, among others. He left a considerable volume of writing, little of which is extant. The Prologue of an Easter Table, several epistles, Paschal letters, and homilies remain, mostly in translations.

**Theosophy.** A system of belief about God and the world claiming a special insight into divine nature and often associated with mysticism. It was decisively influenced by Jakob Boehme, the 17th-century Lutheran mystic, and through him by the Kabbalah, Neoplatonism, Meister Eckhart, and Paracelsus. Boehme sought to reconcile ontological evil with an all-powerful God. The objectives of theosophy include the establishment of a universal brotherhood of mankind, the study of comparative religion and philosophy, and a systematic investigation of "occultism," the psychic character of existence. In America, theosophy is associated with the Theosophical Society founded in 1875 by Mme. Helena P. Blavatsky and Col. Henry S. Olcott. Upon Blavatsky's death in 1891, internal conflict caused a split, and the dominant group was led by William Q. Judge. Blavatsky claimed contact with the mahatmas in Tibet, who possessed secret and ancient wisdom. In them man's spiritual nature was believed to be so highly developed that it possessed total control over natural forces in the universe, thus becoming capable of the miraculous. Modern theosophy lays emphasis upon reincarnation through successions of earthly lives, based upon Indian Brahmanic and Buddhistic teachings of Karma. The saying, "A man is born into the world he has made," expresses their doctrine of the inevitable law of moral causality. Theosophy also seeks reconciliation to a morally incomprehensible cosmic justice.

**Thérèse of Lisieux** (Thérèse Martin, 1873–1897). French Carmelite nun. One of the most popular of those proclaimed saints by the Roman Catholic Church (canonized as the Little Flower in 1925), Thérèse had a paradoxical career. Though she lived much of her life in the seclusion of a Carmelite convent, she was subsequently declared the patroness of the Catholic missions. Her "Little Way" became a popular spiritual method.

**Thesaurus Meritorum.** The doctrine upon which the practice of distributing and selling indulgences was based. Alexander of Hales (d. 1245) defined thesaurus meritorum as a "treasury of spiritual merits accumulated from the abundant works and merits of Christ and the saints which suffice to pay off the debts of the living." From this treasury the medieval church granted indulgences, that is, the remission of temporal punishment which men, even after the absolution of their sins, otherwise would have had to incur.

**Thierry of Chartres** (d. after 1151). A master at Chartres. He left that school for Paris c. 1134. He may have succeeded Gilbert de La Porrée as chancellor of Chartres in 1142. His work, *Heptateuchon*, is a collection of texts related to the seven liberal arts. The treatise *On the Seven Days* is an attempt to explain the account of the Creation in Genesis by recourse to the physical data found in Chalcidius' commentary on Plato's *Timaeus*.

**Third Rome.** A title claimed from the early 16th century for the Muscovite dukedom (later, under Ivan IV, the Muscovite czardom). It expressed the belief that Moscow, which under Ivan III had thrown off the Tartar yoke in 1480, had succeeded Rome and Constantinople (the "New" or "second Rome") as the custodian of the orthodox Christian faith, the grand duke being the true Christian prince. Old Rome had allegedly fallen into heresy; the Byzantine Church had compromised its claims by submitting to the pope at the Council of Ferrara-Florence (1439), and Constantinople had fallen to the Turkish Moslems (1453). The title seems to have been used first in the reign (1505–1533) of Basil (Vasily) III, father of Ivan IV the Terrible. It was again invoked when Moscow was granted the status of patriarchate by Jeremiah II of Constantinople (1589).

**Thirty-nine Articles.** The set of doctrinal statements finally adopted by Convocation (1563) and Parliament (1571), as a definition of the English Church's position with respect to the religious questions disputed in the 16th century. The adoption of the Thirty-nine Articles is the final stage of a process to be traced historically to the separation of the English Church from Rome (1533). In the context of negotiations with the Lutheran princes from 1535, a list of Ten Articles was drawn up (1536) and adopted with royal authority by Convocation. A year later a book of instruction based on the Ten Articles and called *The Institution of a Christen Man* (Bishops' Book) reasserted seven sacraments (against the three of Ten Articles) while stressing justification by faith. Though never published, the Thirteen Articles were composed in 1538, becoming the vehicle whereby the language of the Augsburg Confession entered the later articles. In 1539, the Act of Six Articles swung back in the Catholic direction. By royal authority in 1543, a revision of the Bishops' Book was made the standard of doctrine under the title *Necessary Doctrine and Erudition for any Christian Man* (King's Book). The two Prayer Books, the conservative one of 1549 and the more reforming one of 1552, are indicative of a tendency in the Church of England, and a revision of the Thirteen Articles, comprising the Forty-two Articles, was promulgated with Edward's authority in June, 1553. Their effect was short-lived, since he died in July and they were suspended during Mary's reign.

When Elizabeth succeeded in 1558, Archbishop Parker drew up Eleven Articles which were intended to cast a broad net for both Catholics and Reformed (1559). These articles were not published, only circulated. At the meeting of Convocation in 1563, the old Forty-two Articles were presented with four deleted, four added, and some seventeen modified. Of this list, Convocation passed all but three, but the queen, before accepting them, deleted Article 29 (because anti-Roman) and prefaced Article 20 (on the authority of the church). In 1571, Parliament required subscription to all thirty-nine by the clergy and degree candidates at the universities. The latter were relieved of this requirement in the 19th century, and since 1865 the clergy affirm that the doctrine in the Articles is consonant with Scripture and promise not to teach contrary to the Articles. The Thirty-nine Articles were adopted by the Church of Ireland in 1635, by the synod of the Scottish Episcopal Church in 1804, and introduced into the Prayer Book by the General Convention of the Episcopal Church in the U.S. in 1801 without requirement of subscription.

Not a timely confession of faith but embodying the Church of England's response to the Reformation, the Articles reflect that controversy and are to be interpreted in the light of it. Their character is demonstrated by a brief summary of the contents: (1) Arts. 1–5 set forth briefly and without exposition or comment the fundamental truths of the Christian faith in Trinitarian form; (2) Arts. 6–8 assert the Scriptures to be the rule of faith and relate the creeds thereto; (3) Arts. 9–18 discuss individual religion in terms of sin and grace responding to the Reformation issues raised on this particular; (4) Arts. 19–36 discuss, though not in separate order, the church and the sacraments with special reference to differences of the Church of England from the Roman Church; (5) Arts. 37–39 relate church and state, defining the Establishment. In the early years of the Oxford movement an intense controversy was set in motion over the meaning of the Articles by Tract 90, which was written by John Henry Newman. To the utter dismay of more conservative Tractarians, he claimed to be able to read the Articles in consonance with the dogmas of the Council of Trent. Newman became a Roman Catholic,

and the controversy subsided, but not without damage to the cause of the Tractarians. The archaic language of the Articles and their impertinency if not obsoleteness has fed a growing agitation for an updating, a complete overhaul, or even a discarding of the Articles.

BIBLIOGRAPHY: H. E. W. Turner (ed.), *The Articles of the Church of England* (London, 1964); E. J. Bicknell, *A Theological Introduction to the Thirty-nine Articles*, 3d ed. (London, 1955); B. J. Kidd, *The 39 Articles*, 5th ed. (1925); W. R. Matthews, *The Thirty-nine Articles* (1961).

**Thirty Years' War** (1618–1648). Conflict between Protestant and Roman Catholic powers in central Europe. Actually a series of four wars (known as the Bohemian, Danish, Swedish, and French periods), the war began primarily as a religious conflict, but political goals soon came to dominate it. Once the war started, the ambitions of the Hapsburg house in Germany, and the intervention of Denmark, Sweden, and France caused an indefinite extension of hostilities and an alteration of the basic motivations.

The first period of the Thirty Years' War (1618–1623) began when the outraged Protestants of Bohemia revolted against their Roman Catholic Hapsburg ruler who had violated a charter of 1609 that granted them freedom of worship. In 1619 they deposed the emperor, Ferdinand II, and chose as their king Frederick, the Protestant elector of the Palatinate. The Bohemians, however, deserted by the Protestant "Union," were quickly subdued by Ferdinand, who called upon Spain and the Catholic League for assistance. In the wake of the Roman Catholic victory, the Counter-Reformation was vigorously implemented. Ferdinand next subdued the Palatinate territory of Frederick, giving the Upper Palatinate and its electoral title to Maximilian of Bavaria.

The second period (1625–1629) commenced when Christian IV (1588–1648) of Denmark assumed the role of defender of the faith with the promised support of France and England, neither of whom desired to see a strong Hapsburg monarch in Germany. Christian IV also sought to protect and possibly even enhance his own German holdings, especially in Lower Saxony. He stood no chance, however, against the combined army of Wallenstein and Tilly. As they drove him out of Germany and into the Jutland peninsula, he was fortunate that they did not have a navy to pursue him over to the Danish islands to which he had fled. In 1629 he was happy to sign the Peace of Lübeck, which allowed him to retain his original holdings basically intact.

At this juncture the third period (1630–1635) of the war ensued with the advent of Gustavus Adolphus and his highly trained, well-disciplined, and religiously motivated Swedish army on the German shores of Pomerania. At the Battle of Breitenfeld (1631), Gustavus Adolphus scored a brilliant victory over the previously invincible Tilly. The next year he followed up his victory by occupying Munich and devastating Bavaria. The "Lion of the North" then turned toward Vienna and the army of Wallenstein which he met at Lützen. Here the Swedish army was again victorious, but the death of their king in battle proved irreparable and in 1635 Sweden sought to withdraw honorably from the conflict.

Cardinal Richelieu of France, seeing the weakened condition of the Hapsburg monarchy, and determined to crush it once and for all, ordered the French army to attack in 1635, thus initiating the fourth and final period of the war. By no stretch of the imagination could the conflict now be considered a religious war. Germany became the battlefield in the struggle for supremacy between Bourbon France and Hapsburg Austria–Spain. Finally, after years of indecisive conflict, the various parties sat down at Münster and Osnabrück in Westphalia for the first modern peace conference and eventually signed the Peace of Westphalia in 1648. Germany lay prostrate and was set back culturally, economically, and politically for many years. The Holy Roman Empire had received its deathblow, and people in general were determined never again to fight another war in the name of religion.

BIBLIOGRAPHY: A. Bailly, *The Cardinal Dictator: A Portrait of Richelieu* (London, 1936); P. Frischauer, *The Imperial Crown* (London, 1939); S. R. Gardiner, *The Thirty Years' War* (London, 1912); M. Roberts, *Gustavus Adolphus* (New York, 1953); C. V. Wedgwood, *The Thirty Years War* (London, 1938; reissued Garden City, 1961).

**Tholuck, Friedrich August Gottreu** (1799–1877). Mediating German theologian. After his education at Breslau and Berlin, Pietist friends and J. A. W. Neander led him to faith in God, Pietism, and theology. He was professor of theology at the University of Halle for forty-nine years. His influential apologetical writings and Bible commentaries, his effective teaching, preaching, and pastoral work among students did much to check the spread of rationalism in Germany. He was a representative of the *Vermittlungstheologie*.

**Thomas, Norman Mattoon** (1884–1968). Perennial Presidential candidate of the Socialist Party of the United States from 1928 to 1948. Thomas was ordained a Presbyterian minister in 1911. He criticized the nationalistic fervor of the churches in World War I and resigned his pastorate. He became a pacifist and joined the Socialist Party. A founder of the American Civil Liberties Union, he was also active in the Fellowship of Reconciliation. Thomas was a moderate socialist, not a Marxist, and was anti-Soviet. An advocate of the League of Nations, he encouraged pacifism and neutralism in America during World War II. The author of many books, Thomas considered himself an "old-fashioned Socialist."

**Thomas à Kempis** (Thomas Hamerken, c. 1380–1471). German monk and devotional writer. Born in Kempen, he was sent with his brother John to the Deventer school founded by Gerhard Groote, and there studied under Florentius Radewyns. In 1399 he went to Zwolle and the convent of Mt. St. Agnes, where John was already prior. Professed as an Augustinian canon in 1407, he was ordained in 1413 and became subprior in 1425. His authorship of the *Imitation of Christ* is admitted by a majority of scholars.

**Thomas Aquinas.** See AQUINAS, THOMAS.

**Thomasius, Christian** (1655–1728). Jurist, scholar, and founder of the University of Halle. By insisting on the necessity of critical and free inquiry, rather than the reliance on authoritative statements, he aided in the introduction of the spirit of the Enlightenment in Germany. His *Fundamenta juris naturae ac gentium* (1705) defined common sense as the source of natural law, an orientation that allowed him to advance persuasive arguments against torture and the persecution of "witches."

**Thomism.** The name given to a school of philosophy that follows the main positions elaborated by Thomas Aquinas (c. 1225–1274). Thomas is given credit for having "baptized" Aristotle, some of whose writings had appeared in Arabic translations in Europe in the late 12th and early 13th centuries and caused much dismay among Christian theologians. Under the influence of Averroës' commentaries on Aristotle a school of Christian rationalists grew up in opposition to the far more ancient and acceptable Augustinian-Franciscan school of "fideists." In the *Summa theologiae*, the *Summa contra Gentiles*, and in his lesser-known works, Aquinas took up the task of reconciling Christian revelation with the philosophy of Aristotle. His philosophy has been called that of a "critical realist." Eschewing Platonism and Augustinian illuminationism, Aquinas insisted that our knowledge originates in sensations of a physical world that man's reason is equipped to know. Natural reason was adequate for a knowledge of God's existence, but this knowledge was completed and perfected by the Christian revelation. Thomism, though nearly disappearing in the 17th and 18th centuries, was reborn at the insistence of popes such as Leo XIII and Pius X, by whom it was made *the* Catholic philosophy.

**Thompson, Charles L.** (1839–1924). Presbyterian clergyman. Ordained in 1861, he was pastor in Juneau and Janesville, Wis., in Cincinnati, Chicago, Pittsburgh, Kansas City, and from 1888 to 1898 at Madison Avenue Presbyterian Church in New York City. From 1898 until his death he was secretary of the Presbyterian Board of Home Missions and after 1908 also chairman of the Home Missions Council. He wrote several useful books.

**Thoreau, Henry David** (1817–1862). Social critic, essayist, naturalist, and transcendentalist. Thoreau gave up teaching to become a lecturer and author. He was closely associated with the leaders of transcendentalism. Professionally a surveyor, Thoreau sought life and reality through nature. After 1841 he had the concept of a return to nature and took up residence at Walden Pond from July 4, 1845, until his arrest for nonpayment of the poll tax on Sept. 6, 1847. Out of this experience appeared the famous essay "Civil Disobedience." His intimate relationship with nature led to the publication of *Walden* (1854), his most famous work. *Excursions* (1863) was also a paean of nature. After 1847, Thoreau became increasingly critical of commercialism, urbanization, and industrialization. Distrustful of society, he was suspicious of reformers. *Walden,* appearing as harmless natural science, disarmed opponents while striking blows at the superficialities of society and civil government. Thoreau repudiated slavery and in 1859 was one of the first to champion the cause of John Brown. A romantic, pantheist, and unconventional social critic, Thoreau was a uniquely unsentimental and keen observer, but totally unsystematic. Many of his works were published posthumously, notably his *Journal.*

**Thorlakson, Gudbranur** (1541–1627). Icelandic Lutheran bishop from 1571. He established Lutheranism in Iceland following the death of Jon Arason (the only Roman Catholic bishop in Scandinavia to die as a martyr). Thorlakson set up a printing press and published ninety works in Icelandic, including the Bible (1584), a hymnbook (1589), and works by Palladius and Niels Hemmingsen. He also introduced Luther's Catechism and the rite of confirmation to the Church of Iceland.

**Thorn, Colloquy of** (1645). A conference called by Vladislav IV, the king of Poland (1632–1648), to prevent religious strife between Roman Catholics and Protestants. It failed to achieve its goal and only deepened the disharmony among the Protestants. The activities of Georg Calixtus and the unilateral discussions between the Reformed and the Roman Catholics aroused Lutheran suspicions and initiated the syncretistic controversies.

**Thorndike, Herbert** (1598–1672). Anglican divine. Graduated from Trinity College, Cambridge, he held various posts there prior to 1641, including university preacher, tutor, deputy public orator, Hebrew lecturer, and senior bursar, specializing in theology, and Oriental and rabbinical literature. In 1641 appeared his first tract, *Discourse of the Government of Churches,* in which he argued for the primitive origins of episcopacy in the apostolic age. With the Civil War and its aftermath, Thorndike lived in an unsettled state, producing some polemical tracts. A most important scholarly work appeared at this time (1657), Walton's *Polyglot Bible,* for which Thorndike contributed the Syriac portion. He then turned himself to his most important treatise, the *Epilogue* (1659), in which he argued that the church must use as its basis the discipline and the teaching of the primitive Catholic Church. His aim was not so much directed abroad as at the English scene, where he sought to bring the parties to unity. He was unable, however, to gather the divergent forces to his side. With the Restoration, his fellowship at Trinity was restored, where he continued to push for his settlement. Going into semiretirement in 1667, he continued his literary activity until his death.

**Thornton, Henry** (1760–1815). Philanthropist and economist. He was the son of John Thornton of Clapham Common, England, a wealthy supporter of the early English Evangelicals. With little education, Henry entered upon a banking career in which he continued through all of his life. In 1782 he was elected a member of Parliament for Southwark and retained this seat for the rest of his life. In Parliament he was considered a financial expert. He refused to join any political party, but sympathized with the French Revolution in its early stages. He separated himself from many Protestants by voting for Catholic emancipation. He was a most influential member of the Clapham Sect, a loose confederation of Evangelicals that gathered around William Wilberforce and met at Thornton's home.

He was related by marriage to Wilberforce, whose wife was Thornton's aunt, and Thornton supported the Parliamentary leader's antislave trade activities. He was instrumental in the formation of the Sierra Leone Company and was treasurer of the Society for Missions to Africa and the East (the forerunner of the Church Missionary Society) and of the British and Foreign Bible Society. He actively supported the educational adventures of Hannah More. Known for his evangelical piety, Thornton composed prayers and edited various religious tracts.

**Thornwell, James Henley** (1812–1862). Southern Presbyterian preacher, polemicist, and educator. He studied at South Carolina College and after a brief sojourn at Andover and Harvard, he returned to South Carolina, where he served as a pastor and was connected with his alma mater as professor, chaplain, and president (1851–1855). He founded the *Southern Presbyterian Review* (1847), was an active secessionist after the election of Lincoln, and helped establish the Presbyterian Church in the Confederate States of America.

**Thou, Jacques Auguste de** (1553–1617). French diplomat, historian, and book collector. He was made councilor of state in 1588, helped to reconcile Henry III with Henry of Navarre, entered the latter's service on his accession as Henry IV, became grand master of the royal library in 1598, and in the same year helped to prepare the Edict of Nantes. Thou was Gallican to the core and stopped the publication of the decrees of Trent in France. His major historical work, *Historiae sui temporis* (5 vols., 1620), was put on the Index. In it he gave a history, chiefly of France from 1546 to 1607, written from a standpoint favorable to Henry IV and hostile to the Guises.

**Three Chapters.** In the hope of reconciling the Monophysites, the emperor Justinian was persuaded (c. 544) to issue an edict condemning (1) Theodore of Mopsuestia (d. c. 427), who seemed to carry the doctrine of two natures in Christ to a Nestorian extreme; (2) certain writings of Theodoret; and (3) a letter of Ibas of Edessa to Maris the Persian (*i.e.,* Mar X, a Persian bishop), similarly suspect. For convenience, these three items are referred to, from the divisions of the edict, as the "Three Chapters." Justinian secured their condemnation by the Fifth Ecumenical Council (Second Council of Constantinople) in 553. Its pronouncements bring into the Orthodox tradition several developments of Monophysite thought—e.g., the idea of divine suffering expressed in the phrase "one of the

Trinity suffered in the flesh"—but respect the authority of Chalcedon. If theologically useful, the Council was politically a failure. It had no effect on Monophysites, and was widely opposed in the Latin Church. Pope Vigilius confirmed its decisions, but in protest a number of bishops of northern Italy, especially in areas that fell under Lombard rule after 568, broke away in the Istrian schism, which lasted until about 700, and has left a trace in the honorary title of patriarch used in the Middle Ages by the archbishops of Aquileia and Grado, from the latter of whom it passed in 1451 to the archbishop of Venice.

**Three-Self Movement.** The Chinese Communist government-sponsored body for uniting and controlling the Protestant churches. The name is derived from the old mission goal for churches, "self-governing, self-supporting, and self-propagating," and stresses independence. Organized in 1951, it replaced both the denominations and the National Christian Council of China. Wu Yao-Tsung of the Y.M.C.A. has been the leading figure in the movement.

**Thundering Legion.** According to Apollinaris of Hierapolis, a legion about to be attacked on the Danube was suffering from thirst. The prayers of the legionaries, all Christian, resulted in a rainstorm that also put the enemy to flight. The legion was given the title *Fulminatrix* ("thundering"). The same event is ascribed by pagan writers either to the prayer of Marcus Aurelius or to the work of an Egyptian magician. No doubt there were Christians in the legion, but its title (actually *Fulminata*) goes back to the days of Augustus.

**Tikhon** (Vasili Ivanovitch Belyavin, c. 1865–1925). Russian Orthodox prelate. Elected (1917) first patriarch of the Russian Church after 1921, he sought autonomy for the church under the Soviet regime. Resistance to state encroachments, especially confiscation of church property, led to temporary imprisonment, during which church leaders yielded to the state, defeating his hopes for autonomy. Upon his release he sought, until his death, a compatible mode of church life within the state.

**Tillich, Paul Johannes** (1886–1965). Preacher, teacher, theologian, and philosopher. Tillich was influenced by Schelling, Kierkegaard, Nietzsche, Marx, Freud, and Martin Kaehler. A product of the Lutheran piety of the Evangelical Church of Prussia, he was trained at Berlin, Tübingen, Halle, Dresden, and Frankfurt. Though Tillich was established as a rising philosopher in Germany, conflict with Nazism led to his emigration to the United States in 1933, where he taught at Union Theological Seminary (New York City) and Columbia University until 1955. From 1955 to 1962 he taught at Harvard and afterward at the Divinity School of the University of Chicago. Noted for his philosophical existentialism and theology of history, Tillich sought to clarify the meaning of Christianity in the light of the needs and dilemmas of modern secular man. His *Systematic Theology* (3 vols., 1951–1963) stated that Protestant theology can, "without losing its Christian foundations, incorporate strictly scientific methods, a critical philosophy, and a realistic understanding of men and society, and powerful ethical principles and motives." Tillich rejected any gulf between philosophy and theology, and dealt with the relation of God, man, and the world through his concepts of "ultimate reality," "being itself," and "ultimate concern." Late in his career he sought to reconstruct his theological formulations along the lines of the "history of religions" movement of Wach and Eliade. His works include *The Interpretation of History* (1936); *The Protestant Era* (1948); *The Shaking of the Foundations* (1948); *The Courage to Be* (1952); *Love, Power, and Justice* (1954); *The New Being* (1955); and *Christianity and the Encounter of the World Religions* (1963). Through these writings, and as a teacher, Tillich was particularly influential as an interpreter of the Christian faith to American culture.

**Tillotson, John** (1630–1694). Archbishop of Canterbury from 1691. He was the son of Robert Tillotson, a member of a Congregational church in 1645. While John Tillotson was at Clare Hall, Cambridge, he leaned toward Calvinism, and had much affection for nonconformity. Early impressed by Chillingworth's *Religion of Protestants*, and by John Wilkins, master of Trinity College, at the Restoration, he was associated with the Presbyterians until the Act of Uniformity (1662). In 1663 he was elected preacher at Lincoln's Inn, and the year after was appointed Tuesday lecturer at St. Lawrence Jewry. Even at this time, it seems that he gave Communion to some who remained seated, and he refused to bow at the name "Jesus." He carefully developed his ability as preacher, regaining the art from the Puritans for the Anglican Church. His published sermons attracted widespread attention and admiration. During the Restoration, he sought to broaden the English Establishment to include some of the nonconformists, but little was accomplished until the

advent of William and Mary, when a bill for comprehension made considerable progress, but was finally rejected by the church Convocation. Tolerant of both nonjurors and nonconformists, and generous in his charity, he characterized the ideal of a Broad Church which became more prominent in succeeding generations. After long hesitation, he accepted the archbishopric of Canterbury in 1691 (as Sancroft's successor), but he held the office briefly and without distinction.

**Timothy Aelurus** (d. 477). Monophysite claimant to the see of Alexandria from 457. Banished after the riots that marked his accession, he led his party from exile until he returned to Alexandria during the usurpation of Basiliscus after the accession of Zeno. His amusing nickname, "the cat" (or perhaps "weasel"), allegedly from his slinking into monasteries to gain support, should not obscure his importance as a theologian who largely determined the future position of the Monophysites.

**Timothy of Constantinople** (d. 518). Patriarch. When Macedonius II, pro-Chalcedonian patriarch of Constantinople, was humiliatingly deposed by the emperor Anastasius I in 511, Timothy, who was keeper of the treasures of the Great Church and a presbyter disliked by the Chalcedonians, was elevated in his place. At first only uncertainly Monophysite, he attempted to introduce the Monophysitic addition to the Trisagion (512), accepted the condemnation of Chalcedon by the Synod of Tyre (514–515), and died a convinced Monophysite. Among his other acts was the requirement of regular recitation of the purely Nicene Creed in the Liturgy, previously done only on Good Friday.

**Tindal, Matthew** (1655–1733). Deist and author. Tindal, who considered himself a "Christian deist," created a furore among orthodox Christians. Publication of one book resulted in his arrest, along with printer and publisher; another was burned in public by order of the House of Commons. Tindal's most significant answer to critics was *Christianity as Old as the Creation or The Gospel a Republication of the Religion of Nature* (1730). In this "Bible of deism," he argued that the gospel reinforces the immutable laws of nature and reason.

**Tindaro, Mariano Rampolla del.** See RAMPOLLA, COUNT MARIANO DEL TINDARO.

**Tischendorf, Lobegott Friedrich Konstantin von** (1815–1874). German Biblical scholar. In Paris from 1840 to 1843, Tischendorf lectured at Leipzig in 1845 and became professor in

1851. While traveling in the East (1844) he visited St. Catherine's monastery on Mt. Sinai. In the library he noticed a basketful of manuscript pages written in an extremely ancient Greek hand. He was given forty-three leaves containing part of the Old Testament, but discovered that two basketsful of manuscripts had previously been burned. These first sheets of what became known as the Codex Sinaiticus he published after presenting them to Frederick August of Saxony. He returned again (1853) to the monastery, but the monks were cautious. In 1859 he visited under the patronage of Alexander II of Russia and viewed 199 leaves of the Sinaiticus (part of the Old Testament, and the entire New Testament), but could not buy the work. In Cairo he advised the monastery superior to give the manuscript to the czar, patron of the Greek Church. The monks consented, and Tischendorf took the manuscript (15 by 13½ inches, 4 columns) to Russia and published it as a 4th-century document. In 1843 he viewed the unpublished Vaticanus for six hours; in 1867 he published the best edition to date. During 1843 to 1845 he deciphered elements of a difficult palimpsest, the *Ephraemi*. His publication of texts provided a sound base for textual criticism. His eighth edition of the New Testament (1869–1872), though relying too heavily on the Sinaiticus, remains the standard collection of evidence for the Greek New Testament text with its extensive apparatus. Tischendorf also issued the New Testament Apocrypha, and wrote several minor apologetic works.

**Tithes.** Contributions or taxes consisting of a tenth part of some specific thing, paid in kind or in money, usually in support of religious establishments. From patristic times churchmen stressed that on the basis of Biblical texts all Christians were morally obliged to tithe their entire income as an essential part of their recognition of God's sovereign rights and of the dedication of themselves and their goods to him. Although this primitive ecclesiastical tithe disappeared in the Christian East, it became well established in the West that tithes must be paid regularly into the hands of the clergy so that they would have the wherewithal to perform the corporal works of mercy in the name of the Christian community.

The Carolingian kings, Pepin III and Charlemagne, enforced these ancient customs as a matter of uniform public policy but subsequent canonical legislation added the support of churches and the clergy to the traditional charitable use of tithes. Such an innovation was justified as freeing the clergy from economic preoccupations for the sake of Word and Sacrament. In the course of time, however, episcopal control of tithes and their steadily increasing use for the erection and maintaining of churches overshadowed their original purpose. Once their special character of being used exclusively for charity was obscured, the encroachment on the rights of the poor was continuous. By the 12th century, tithes were simply a form of clerical revenue.

**Titian** (Tiziano Vecelli) (c. 1477–1576). Foremost of the Venetian artists and the last great painter of the Italian Renaissance. One of the most prolific artists of all time, Titian left great numbers of paintings, some with secular and some with religious themes. His famous *Assumption of the Virgin* is an example of the latter. He gained a large part of his immense reputation by executing the portraits of popes, cardinals, dukes, and doges.

**Titus of Bostra** (4th century). Bishop. He was ordered expelled from his see by the emperor Julian the Apostate in an attempt to foment dissension among the Christians of that city. The attempt failed, however, and in the following year (363), as bishop of Bostra, Titus took part in a synod at Antioch that ratified the Nicene Creed. Titus' principal work is a treatise against the Manichaeans. Fragments of a commentary on Luke and a sermon on the Epiphany also remain.

**Tocqueville, Alexis Charles Clérel de** (1805–1859). French statesman and writer. He was born at Verneuil, the great-grandson of Malesherbes, the defender of Louis XIV. Under the Second Republic, Tocqueville was a member of the Constituent Assembly and vice-president of the Legislative Assembly. After the establishment of the Second Empire he returned to private life and undertook his work *L'Ancien régime et la révolution,* of which only the first part appeared (1856). His fame, however, rests upon his celebrated book *La Démocratie en Amérique.* This work, the first volume of which appeared in 1835 and the second in 1840, resulted from a journey to America in 1831. In religious thought Tocqueville was greatly influenced by Montesquieu's belief that Christianity was a powerful moral force. He held that democracy could exist only by seeking a moral support in religion and that religion could prosper only by accommodating itself to democracy. Although a Catholic, he attacked the doctrinal, disciplinary, and liturgical exactions of Roman Catholicism and advocated reforms.

**Toellner, Johann Gottlieb** (1724–1774). German theologian. A student of Baumgarten's at Halle, Toellner lectured at Frankfurt an der Oder in 1756 and became philosophy professor in 1760. He held that natural religion was sufficient for blessedness, but was surmounted by Christianity; that the teaching of Jesus embodied all Christian truth; that the doctrine of the Trinity was valueless; and that there was no original sin. Revelation was limited; one must distinguish between Scripture and the word of God, and assign relative value to church confessions (*Unterricht von symbolischen Büchern*).

**Toland, John** (1670–1722). English deist. Born in Ireland, he left Roman Catholicism for Protestantism and was educated at Glasgow, Oxford, and Leiden. A hack writer and political pamphleteer, he wrote a life of Milton, travel pieces, and Whig tracts. His major work, which started the deist controversy and for which he was persecuted, was *Christianity not Mysterious: Or a Treatise Shewing That There is Nothing in the Gospel Contrary to Reason nor Above it* (1696). In this he claimed to be following John Locke in arguing that since Christianity was a replication of things known less clearly and firmly by reason, it could contain nothing less than the purely rational. Locke, however, repudiated Toland. To Toland, reason is the only possible ground of certainty and the mind can only assent to the clear and proved. A doctrine not apparent to reason would be nonsensical, for the mind could not even form an idea of it. To the orthodox this seemed to be an attack upon Christianity as revelation of supernatural "mysteries," and many replies followed. Also among his deistic writings are *Nazarenus* (1718), on the Ebionites, suggesting that the original simple moral precepts of Christianity were corrupted by priests and philosophers, and *Pantheisticon* (1720), a dialogue presenting pantheism.

**Toleration.** See RELIGIOUS LIBERTY.

**Toleration Act** (Austria). An edict issued by Joseph II in October, 1781, which granted important religious concessions to Protestants. In addition to certain political rights (right to hold office), Protestants were given religious toleration, the right not to be forced to take oaths opposed to religious convictions, and the right to be released from observing Catholic feast days. Protestant marriages were placed under the secular courts.

**Toleration Act** (England). An act of the English Parliament (1689) exempting Trinitarian Protestant Dissenters from penal legislation and allowing freedom of worship if they registered their meeting places and if their ministers subscribed to a loyalty oath and the doctrinal parts of the Thirty-nine Articles. It rewarded Dissent for its role in the Glorious Revolution but also doomed hopes for a more inclusive Established Church. Civil disabilities remained.

**Tolstoy, Leo** (1828–1910). Russian writer and social critic. Born of a well-to-do family, he studied at the University of Kazan but left to enlist in the army. His experiences during the Crimean War led him to write *Tales from Sevastopol* (1855), which describes the horrors of war. After thirteen years he resigned from the army, traveled in western Europe and returned to his ancestral estate. On his lands he tried various social and educational reforms. The serfs were freed and Tolstoy worked side by side with them in the field. Schools were established where the peasant children could get an education. In the years that followed, his two most famous novels appeared: *War and Peace* (1866) and *Anna Karenina* (1875–1877). The latter part of his life was spent in moral and religious speculation. The guide to Tolstoy's religion was a literal understanding of the Gospels purged of their miraculous content. This belief can be resolved into five commandments: pacifism, chastity, rejection of oaths, refusal to serve as magistrate, and love of one's enemies. This last point is most crucial, for the increase of love would lead to the establishment of God's Kingdom on earth. Traditional Christian ideas such as the deity of Christ, the atonement, and immortality were rejected by Tolstoy.

**Tonsure.** The shaving of the head as a rite of admission to the clerical state required of all except English and American Roman Catholic clergy. It was begun as part of monasticism in the 5th century and extended to all clergy in the 6th and 7th centuries. Three types of tonsure have been known: Western—shaving the whole crown, leaving only a fringe of hair symbolizing the crown of thorns; Pauline or Eastern—shaving the entire head; and Celtic—shaving the hair in front of a line extending over the head from ear to ear.

**Torquemada, Juan de** (1388–1468). Spanish Dominican theologian. Born in Valladolid, Spain, Torquemada (Johannes de Turrecremata) entered the Dominican monastery in that town, eventually becoming prior. Noted for his piety and learning, he received the doctor's degree at Paris in 1423, and quickly earned a reputation as a theologian. While a young man, he had attended the Council of Constance, but his name is chiefly connected with the Councils of Basel and Ferrara-Florence. Eugenius IV sent Torquemada as a theological delegate to the Council of Basel (1431). With zeal and dialectical skill, he defended papal authority against the concept of conciliar authority. The pope was superior to, and not to be judged by, any council. When Basel deposed Eugenius IV in 1438, Torquemada led the dissenting faction in the formation of the rival Council of Ferrara-Florence. In 1439, Eugenius IV made Torquemada a cardinal, calling him the "Defender of the Faith."

During 1448 and 1449, Torquemada wrote a work (*Summa de ecclesia*) on the seat of authority in the church that foreshadowed the ultramontantist position: The pope exercises authority over all Christians. As the representative of Christ, he is the source of all authority on earth, both the spiritual and the temporal, which he delegates to civil rulers. Considered the foremost theologian of his day, Torquemada was a possible candidate for the papacy in both 1458 and 1464.

**Torquemada, Tomás de** (1420–1498). Spanish inquisitor. A nephew of the theologian Juan de Torquemada, Tomás early in life entered a Dominican monastery. Content to remain a simple friar, Torquemada refused every ecclesiastical advancement. In 1483, however, he was appointed to the office that was to make his name famous: Grand Inquisitor of Castile and Aragon. The Inquisition was established by Pope Sixtus IV in bulls of 1478 and 1483. Its primary purpose was to discover and destroy heresy. Under Torquemada the Inquisition received its definitive form, being directed by a Grand Inquisitor and a council that was charged with general oversight. Individual inquisitors sought out heretics and brought them to trial. In 1484, Torquemada wrote a handbook of twenty-eight articles for the guidance of the inquisitors. The primary targets were the Jews and the Moslems who had confessed the Christian faith rather than be expelled from Spain. Under Torquemada the Inquisition became the most powerful force in Spain next to the Crown, with which, however, it worked very closely, given the intimate connection of political and religious interests at the time.

**Torrey, Reuben Archer** (1856–1928). American Bible teacher and evangelist. Trained at Yale, he later fell under the influence of Dwight L. Moody and left Congregationalism for work as a nondenominational, itinerant evangelist. He made a number of worldwide trips and devoted himself to prophetic Bible study, producing more than forty books on the subject. He was connected with a number of Bible schools, including the Moody Institute and the Bible Institute of Los Angeles.

**Toynbee Hall.** The first of many settlement houses established in England in the later 19th century. It grew out of the concern of some Oxford undergraduates for understanding the problems of the urban workers. Organized in 1884, it was dedicated to the memory of Arnold Toynbee (1852–1883), the brilliant economic historian who had called for an awakened conscience of the British privileged classes. Canon Samuel Barnett and his wife were the first directors. The idea was picked up and expanded in the United States.

**Tractarians.** See ANGLO-CATHOLIC MOVEMENT.

***Tractatus Origenis.*** A series of twenty homilies in 10th- and 12th-century manuscripts attributed to Origen. They were first published in 1900 by Battifol and Wilmart, who thought they were Novatian works of the 4th century. Most scholars now accept Morin's theory that they were by Bishop Gregory of Elvira. His Luciferian antipathy to Arian penitents would resemble Novatian antagonism to those who were weak in the face of persecution.

**Traditors.** Those who under persecution surrendered to the authorities Scriptures for which they were responsible, sacred vessels, or the names of other Christians. The term came to have theological importance in the Donatist controversy following the Diocletian persecution. According to the Donatists, traditors lost their sacramental authority by their betrayal of trust. The Donatists therefore refused to recognize Caecilian as bishop of Carthage on the ground that his consecrators were traditors.

**Traherne, Thomas** (c. 1634–1674). One of the English metaphysical poets. A graduate of Oxford, he published only one book in his lifetime. Friends put out two other volumes of his devotional prose posthumously. Almost forgotten, his poetry remained in manuscript form until discovered in the 20th century, when interest was renewed. His meditations are rich, giving evidence of deep religious experience within the Anglicanism of this period.

**Trajan** (53–117). Roman emperor from 98. During his reign the Empire was expanded to the East and reached its peak geographically. Answering a letter from Pliny the Younger, Trajan held that Christians were not to be sought out and that anonymous accusations were not to be accepted. If accused, tried, and convicted (of being Christians), however, they were to be punished. The Apologists in vain criticized the presupposition that Christianity was illegal.

**Transcendentalism.** An optimistic, mystic, and naturalistic state of mind rather than a system of thought, it has had a wide influence on American literature, philosophy, and religion. Based on English romanticism (Coleridge, Wordsworth, Carlyle) and German philosophical idealism, it found Calvinistic orthodoxy too harsh and Unitarian rationalism too arid. It emphasized individual apprehension of experience as sacred, unique, and authoritative. Man was part of the divine essence and his innate ideas transcended all sense experience. Man's instinctive insights, based on the mystic unity of God, nature, and man, permitted the discovery of truth without reference to dogma and established authority. Never an organized movement, it was centered in the Transcendental Club, which first met in 1836. It participated in the unsuccessful Brook Farm community (1840–1846) and published *The Dial* (1840–1844) quarterly. Ralph Waldo Emerson was the central figure, and his essay *Nature* (1836) the most representative document, together with the *Essays* (1841, 1844) and his addresses "The American Scholar" (1837) and "The Divinity School Address" (1838). Henry David Thoreau was the most uncompromising figure, as demonstrated in *Civil Disobedience* (1849) and *Walden* (1854). Theodore Parker sought to reconcile Christian revelation with human intuition by stressing four fundamentals: the existence of God, moral obligation, Christ's sacrifice, and the promise of salvation. Other important figures included Orestes Brownson, Bronson Alcott, Margaret Fuller, and James F. Clarke. Transcendentalism was viewed by orthodoxy as the inevitable result of antinomianism and Unitarianism, and by liberalism as emancipation from the confines of traditional religion. Misinterpreted as exotic and idyllic, it was a positive criticism of materialism and capitalistic society in America.

**Transept.** The transverse part of a church with a ground plan in the form of a cross. The ends of the transept are normally square, but occasionally are semicircular. In most cases, there is only one transept in a church; however, sometimes, especially in England, there are two.

**Translatio Imperii.** Legendary right by which popes exerted power over the Holy Roman Empire. In 1200, Pope Innocent III first expressed it in choosing Otto IV, nephew of Richard the Lion-Hearted, over Philip, son of Frederick I Barbarossa, as emperor. Innocent asserted that the Holy See had taken the Empire from the Greeks and given it to the Germans and retained the right to appoint or remove an emperor. The "Translation of the Empire" theory remained part of the controversy between Vatican and Empire through the 17th century.

**Translation of Relics.** The transfer of newly discovered remains of early saints to other sites. It was a prominent feature of church life in the 4th and 5th centuries. Concern for relics, already manifest in the 2d century, increased early in the 4th century when the empress Helena is said to have discovered the cross of Jesus in Palestine, where even in pre-Christian times the tombs of Old Testament persons were highly regarded. Within a few years the bones of Timothy, Andrew, and Luke were discovered and brought to Constantinople. Under Julian the Apostate the tomb of John the Baptist at Sebaste was wrecked; his head, however, reached Constantinople in 391. In 415 the bones of Stephen were found, while about 450 the relics of Ignatius were brought within the city of Antioch. In 452 another head of the Baptist was discovered, and in 458, the bones of Barnabas—on Cyprus, where the church wished to be free of Antioch. In earlier times the possession of relics was regarded as supporting the authenticity and authority of local tradition; thus Polycrates of Ephesus argued against Rome on the ground that Asia possessed ancient tombs, while Gaius of Rome argued against Montanists that both Peter and Paul were buried at Rome. A shrine probably related to Peter has been discovered under the Vatican.

**Transubstantiation.** The Roman Catholic doctrine of the change that takes place in the bread and the wine during the Mass. It is essentially an attempt to interpret the manner in which Christ is present in the Lord's Supper. Instead of understanding Christ's words at the Last Supper ("This is my body. . . . This is my blood") in a figurative sense, transubstantiation seeks to maintain their literal meaning. Making use of philosophical concepts, the doctrine asserts that the bread and the wine, at the words of the celebrant, undergo a "substantial conversion." That is to say that while the bread and the wine continue in their natural form, in substance they become in reality the very body and blood of Jesus Christ. The concept of transubstantiation was applied to the Lord's Supper during the 12th century and was proclaimed as an essential part of the faith by the

Fourth Lateran Council in 1215. It was not until the 13th century, however, that it received the classical formulation which has continued to the present. In the 16th century, the Council of Trent reasserted transubstantiation over against Protestant doctrines ranging from a Real Presence to merely symbolic presence.

**Travers, Walter** (c. 1548–1635). Puritan divine. After graduation from Christ's College, Cambridge, he traveled on the Continent, where, in Geneva, he met Beza who became his close friend. He published at La Rochelle in 1574 his famous treatise *Of Ecclesiastical Discipline,* which became the model of Presbyterian government. In 1578, Travers became the pastor of the English merchants in Antwerp, being ordained by Thomas Cartwright and others. He was soon back in England, acting as domestic chaplain to Lord Burghley and tutor to his son, Robert Cecil. In 1581, he was appointed afternoon lecturer at the Temple. Three years later at the Lambeth Conference, he was the main spokesman for the Puritan minority, urging reform of the liturgy. Though he was nominated as master of the Temple, Richard Hooker received the appointment, for Travers refused to be reordained. About 1585, the Puritans began to take measures to establish a voluntary Presbyterian discipline within the Church of England. Travers was asked to draft an organization. He drew up two sketches that were later translated as *A Directory of Church Government Anciently Contended For,* the standard for Presbyterian organization. He taught in the University of St. Andrews, was appointed as provost of Trinity College, Dublin, and retired in 1598.

**Traversari, Ambrogio** (c. 1386–1439). Scholarly Italian Camaldolensian monk. He was one of the first Westerners to learn Greek and Hebrew during the Renaissance. He was the only clerical member of a group of Florentine humanists known as the "circle of Santo Spirito." His greatest scholarly contribution was his translation of the Greek fathers into Latin. In 1431 he became general of his order and devoted the remainder of his life to ecclesiastical reform.

**Treaty of Lunéville.** The peace treaty signed by Austria and France on Feb. 9, 1801, which confirmed Napoleon Bonaparte's control of Italy and western Germany. With Austria passive, Prussia neutral, and Russia friendly, Napoleon established French supremacy in Europe. The treaty deeply influenced the papacy to come to political and religious terms with the French state in the Concordat of 1801.

**Tremellius, John** (1510–1580). Old Testament scholar. The son of a Ferrarese Jew, Tremellius was converted to Christianity in 1540 through Cardinal Pole, embraced Protestantism in 1541, and the same year fled Italy with Peter Martyr. He occupied academic positions at Oxford, Cambridge, and Heidelberg. A strong Calvinist, he was expelled by the Lutheran count palatine in 1577. Probably his greatest work was a translation of the Bible into Latin.

**Trent, Council of** (1545–1563). Roman Catholic synod, reckoned as the Nineteenth Ecumenical Council by the Church of Rome. Although the later 15th and early 16th centuries saw much European agitation for an ecumenical council to solve the prevailing difficulties, great delay was caused by quarrels between Pope Clement VII and Emperor Charles V concerning the conditions of a council and by the national interests of European rulers. Finally, by the bull *Laetare Hierusalem* (Nov. 19, 1544), Pope Paul III fixed the opening date for March 15, 1545, in Trent and stated the tasks: to settle the religious dispute by doctrinal decisions, to reform ecclesiastical abuses, and to begin a crusade against the infidels. In February, 1545, Cardinals Giovanni del Monte, Marcello Cervini, and Reginald Pole were appointed to be the presiding papal legates. Differences between pope and emperor again caused delay. The pope saw the Council as a means of strengthening Roman Catholicism against heresy, while the emperor, to unite Christianity, desired doctrinal decisions to be postponed until a discussion with the Protestants. At last, however, the pope convened the Council on Dec. 13, 1545.

The procedural decisions reached by the first three sessions were to treat doctrine and reform simultaneously and to vote by individuals rather than by nations, thereby giving the Italians more power. The Council pronounced on Scripture and tradition (Session IV), original sin (Session V), justification (Session VI), and the sacraments, particularly baptism and confession (Session VII). But the seeming outbreak of an epidemic in Trent provoked a decision (March 11, 1547) to move to Bologna, although the emperor and some bishops remained behind. Nothing was accomplished at Bologna except the decision to adjourn, reached on June 2.

To keep alive the possibility of reconciliation between the two faiths the emperor secured and promulgated (June 3, 1548) an interim agreement. Although affairs worsened because of Pope Paul III's refusal to reconvene the Council, his death (Nov. 10, 1549) changed matters. The new pope, Julius III, the former cardinal legate Giovanni del Monte, proclaimed the second session by the bull *Quum ad tollenda* (Nov. 14, 1550), and the Council reconvened on May 1, 1551, but the alignment of personnel had changed. The French king had forbidden the attendance of his bishops, the Spaniards assumed an independent attitude backed by the emperor, the Jesuits were represented by Lainez and Salmeron, and Protestant representatives made a brief appearance. Practically nothing was accomplished toward reconciliation because the first session had already made many doctrinal decisions, and, although the bishops were prepared to discuss the Mass, ordinations, and reform, they considered the issues of the first session settled. The session was, moreover, curtailed by the revolt of Maurice of Saxony (March 20, 1552), and after treating the Lord's Supper (Session XIII), and the sacraments of penance and Extreme Unction (Session XIV), it was suspended on April 23, 1552.

During the next ten years, the Peace of Augsburg (1555), which granted equality to Protestant and Roman Catholic estates, left little to be desired by the Lutherans. The pressure to convene for interior reform, however, especially from the French and Spanish, caused Pius IV to announce a reopening for Jan. 18, 1562, by the bull *Ad ecclesiae regimen* (Nov. 29, 1560). The feuds caused by the French and Spanish reform demands, which included decentralization, brought about a break in the sessions from September, 1562, to July, 1563, but papal diplomacy broke the force of the attack and remained in control. The session pronounced on the Lord's Supper *sub utraque specie* (Session XXI), the sacrifice of the Mass (Session XXII), the sacrament of ordination (Session XXIII), of marriage (Session XXIV), purgatory, and the veneration of saints, relics, and images. The final session closed the Council on Dec. 4, 1563, and Pius IV ratified its enactments by the bull *Benedictus Deus* (Jan. 26, 1564).

The Council was controlled throughout by the Roman legates; its doctrinal emphasis strengthened Roman Catholicism against the Protestant Reformers. Its structural reforms showed advances, though not enough provision was made for their implementation. However, the strong positions of Trent demonstrated the inward life of Roman Catholicism; they have exercised great influence on its thinking to the present day. It is well to note, however, that because of the wide divergences of opinion on doctrinal matters even within the Roman Church, this Council undertook less to speak positively than to lay down the limits that no Roman Catholic might transgress. Nor did the Council state expressly that the various reformers had in fact transgressed these limits. Hence, as a careful reading of its decrees makes clear, considerable latitude of opinion was allowed for, particularly as regards justification and the relationship of Scripture and tradition, a fact that has made Trent the subject of renewed interest in 20th-century ecumenical discussion.

BIBLIOGRAPHY: H. J. Schroeder (tr.), *Canons and Decrees of the Council of Trent* (St. Louis, 1941); H. Jedin, *A History of the Council of Trent* (New York, 1957).

**Tridentine Profession** (*or* Creed of Pius IV). A profession of faith based on the doctrinal decrees of the Council of Trent. Among the tasks left to Pope Pius IV by the Council of Trent was the composition of a binding formula of faith for all Roman Catholic dignitaries and teachers. It was promulgated in 1564 and was binding upon all priests and teachers in Roman Catholic seminaries, colleges, and universities. The first of its twelve articles contains the Nicene Creed, the remaining eleven a summary of the doctrines of Trent and an oath of allegiance to the pope as vicar of Christ.

**Triers.** A commission set up by Parliamentary act of 1654, appointed by Oliver Cromwell, as an examining body to pass on the fitness and ability of preachers and lecturers named to fill vacant benefices. It consisted of 29 clerics and 9 laymen, of which 5 were a quorum for an affirmative and 9 for a negative vote. Its task was to ensure the admission of competent ministers to benefices and to exclude "weak, scandalous, popish, and ill-affected persons."

**Trinitarians** (*or* Order of the Most Holy Trinity). A mendicant order founded in 1198 chiefly for the purpose of ransoming captives and slaves. The members followed the Augustinian rule, and wore a white habit with a red and blue cross on the scapular and cape. In the late 16th century, a discalced reform was begun, which is the sole surviving branch of the original order. An affiliated order of women also exists at present.

**Trivium.** The medieval name for the three elementary disciplines of the seven liberal arts. The trivium consisted of grammar, which included the study of classical literature; rhetoric, which also included logic; and dialectic, or philosophy.

**Troeltsch, Ernst** (1865–1923). German Protestant philosopher and theologian. Educated at Berlin and Göttingen, he served as a minister before becoming a professor at Heidelberg and Berlin. Strongly influenced by Ritschl and Schleiermacher, he was the leading theologian of the religiohistorical school. He felt that religion is affected by social culture, but he tempered this view by emphasizing human freedom in the shaping of religion. At the close of World War I, Troeltsch entered politics and was appointed minister of education in the German federal cabinet. His major works, *Christian Thought* and *The Social Teachings of the Christian Churches*, appeared in 1923.

The explanation of church and sect that he presented in his work, though often criticized, is still used by sociologists of religion. Among the distinctions he makes between the church and the sect are that the former tends to accept the social order and dominate the masses while the latter insists on individualistic attitudes toward salvation and fellowship. The sect is usually composed of the lower social classes and tends to be hostile or indifferent to the state. The fact that the church is built on the upper classes emphasizes a morality on good terms with the world. A sect relies on the Sermon on the Mount and stresses the apocalyptic opposition of the Kingdom of God to all secular interests. Troeltsch suggests that if the terms "church" and "sect" are not to a person's liking, he may use the expressions "institutional" and "voluntary" churches.

**Trollope, Anthony** (1815–1882). Prolific English novelist, many of whose books deal with the bucolic clerical life of Victorian England. In his best-known series, called *Chronicles of Barsetshire*, Trollope explored in six comedies of manners the hypocrisies of ecclesiastical life. In *The Vicar of Bullhampton* he turned social reformer, dealing seriously with the problem of Victorian Christianity's sexual standards and with the delicate balance of clerical duty to be one's brother's keeper as opposed to the vice of meddling in the lives of one's fellow Christians.

**Truce of God** (*Treuga Dei*). An extension of the Peace of God restricting warfare during specific periods, first from Vespers on Saturday to sunrise on Monday (11th century) and then during feast or fast periods such as Holy Week and later Lent and Advent. Sponsored by the Cluniacs in the 11th century to curtail war, to protect the peasantry during planting and harvesting, and to protect merchants and pilgrims in their travels, the Truce was more highly developed in Germany than in France.

**Trullan Synod** (Quinisext, 692). The Sixth Ecumenical Council (680) had established harmony between the Byzantine Empire and Rome, but shortly thereafter relations were again strained over papal claims to ecclesiastical supremacy. In 691, Emperor Justinian II summoned a council that met in the imperial banqueting hall (*in trullo*) at Constantinople. This Council was meant to complete the work of the Fifth and Sixth Ecumenical Councils and is therefore also known as the *Penthektē*, *Quinisextum*, or Fifth-sixth, Council. Rome was not represented at this Council, and Pope Sergius rejected its acts because of certain canons (e.g., prohibition of Saturday fast, permission for priests to marry) that appeared to be aimed at Roman practices. The most serious objection made by Sergius was to a canon giving the patriarch of Constantinople equal status with the pope. Justinian's attempt to enforce these canons by having Sergius arrested and brought to Constantinople was thwarted by the Roman populace aided by Italian soldiers.

**Trusteeism** (*or* Trustee System). A system originating in 1785 in the actions of a board of trustees of the Roman Catholic Church of New York City who maintained their right as property owners of a church site to select or dismiss their own clergy. The idea of trusteeism spread, and a number of churches for a time resisted the authority of the bishops, often when a priest of one nationality was assigned to a congregation predominantly of another. Some parishes actually left the church. The movement was defeated largely through the efforts of John England, first bishop of Charleston; Bishop Francis Patrick Kenrick, of Philadelphia, who ended trusteeism in his diocese by the use of an interdict (1831) on St. Mary's Church; and Bishop John Hughes, who was engaged in the battle against the lay trustee system while a priest at St. Mary's, and who finally abolished it after he became bishop of New York in 1838.

**Tübingen School.** A name applied to two distinct but related groups of historical scholars whose work emanated from their association with the University of Tübingen in Württemberg. Ferdinand Christian Baur (1792–1860) may be taken as the outstanding figure in the Protestant group, and Johann Adam Moehler (1796–1838) as his counterpart in the Catholic camp. Under the influence of the critical method of Leopold von Ranke (1795–1886), the philosophical dialectic of G. W. F. Hegel (1770–1831), and developments in philological method, the scholars at Tübingen began to apply the concept of development to the history of dogma and to treat the Sacred Scriptures with neither greater nor less respect than secular documents. By thus historicizing the study of theology, they introduced a new and startling element into 19th-century Christianity: the influence of time upon form. Baur's *Symbolik und Mythologie* (1824–1825) suggested the direction in which the school would move. Moehler's *Symbolik* and his *Einheit in der Kirche* showed the church as something vital, not something that the categories of philosophers could ultimately capture. Baur's insistence on applying Hegelian methodology worked ill for his "school," but the Catholic school found successors to Moehler in Staudenmaier and Karl Josef von Hefele.

**Tuckney, Anthony** (1599–1670). Puritan divine. After completing his studies at Emmanuel College, Cambridge, Tuckney succeeded his cousin, John Cotton, as vicar of Boston, England. A member of the Westminster Assembly, he was chairman of the committee that prepared the Shorter Catechism, and the Decalogue section of the Larger Catechism was mostly his work. After holding various positions at Cambridge following the Assembly, he was retired at the Restoration.

**Tulchan Bishops.** Those appointed in the Reformed Presbyterian Church of Scotland in 1572 who were willing to give the larger part of the revenues of their dioceses to lay patrons obtaining appointments for them. The situation came about when the earl of Morton, Scotland's regent, undertook to increase revenue for the state by appointing bishops to benefices that had been established under the old system of hierarchy. These new prelates could claim the full revenue of the benefice but must turn over most of it to the state. Since the word "tulchan" indicated a calfskin stuffed with straw to deceive a cow into giving milk, popular wit called the new appointees "tulchan bishops."

**Tunstall, Cuthbert** (1474–1559). English bishop and conservative figure during the Reformation. Tunstall was a proponent neither of the New Learning nor of the Protestant doctrines spreading from the Continent in the 1520's. His first prominence ecclesiastically was as Archbishop Warham's chancellor, and politically as a negotiator for Henry VIII. He was made bishop of London in 1522 and in 1530 translated to Durham, where he also served as president of the Council of the North. Tunstall's wavering on the issues of Henry's divorce and of the royal supremacy have earned him, perhaps unjustly, something of the reputation of a trimmer. However, under Edward VI he tried steadily to restrain Protestantizing tendencies, and was imprisoned

in 1551 for his opposition. During the Marian reaction he was restored to his see and was conspicuously clement in his treatment of Protestants accused before him of heresy. On Elizabeth's accession he was deprived again, and spent his last months in the custody of Archbishop Parker.

**Twelve Articles of the Peasants.** The "charter" of the Peasants' War (1524–1526). From many lists of grievances, Lotzar or, more probably, Schappeler, friend of Zwingli, drafted the Articles, which were adopted at Memmingen on March 7, 1525. The preamble denied that the peasants were abolishing established spiritual or temporal authority. Love, peace, patience, and unity were their aim. Their very reasonable demands were: (1) to make their own choice of pastors to serve their community, or to dismiss the unseemly; (2) to suggest that the great tithes be used for the poor, or in emergencies for war; (3) to abolish small tithes, since God created the beasts of the field for all to enjoy; (4) to be villeins (serfs) no longer, since Christ freed all, though they would obey elected authority; (5) the right to take ground game and fowl, and fish in flowing water; (6) the restoration of woods, meadows, and plowlands to the community; (7) to remove new services demanded of them; (8) to be paid for services rendered; (9) the establishment of just rents; (10) the consistent administration of justice; (11) the abolition of death dues that ruined widows and orphans; (12) to test all grievances by the Word of God; if wrong, they would submit, and they asked the same of the nobility. Luther approved the Articles but denounced insurrection as a means of obtaining their aims.

**Tyconius** (d. c. 400). Donatist theologian who met increasing difficulty after 370 because of his writings. Excommunicated by a Donatist synod at Carthage c. 378 as a proponent of Catholic views on church and sacraments, Tyconius refused to join the Catholic camp. His exposition of salvation used the antithesis of law and grace and stressed the element of faith. Augustine quoted part of Tyconius' *Liber regularum* in his *De doctrina christiana*, and his "two kingdom" concept owed something to Tyconius. Part of Tyconius' commentary on Revelation is preserved by Beatus and Primasius. The commentary rejected both historical and chiliastic interpretations in favor of a strong spiritual exegesis.

**Tyndale (Tindale), William** (c. 1494–1536). English translator of the Bible, important both for his Biblical work and as a prototype of early Puritanism. He was willing to violate the law in order to bring about reformation, but within the limits of passive resistance. He worked closely with the merchants of London, and he placed central importance on the Bible. All these characteristics typified Puritanism of the Tudor period. Tyndale graduated from Magdalen Hall, Oxford (M.A., 1515). He then moved to Cambridge, where he pursued his interest in the Erasmian tradition of humanism. In 1523 he journeyed to London to obtain support for translating the Bible into English, as had been previously advocated by numerous humanists. Lutheranism had altered the climate, and Tyndale met vigorous resistance. Since Germany furnished both the freedom and the facilities to carry out the project, he sailed for Hamburg in 1524. He completed a translation of the New Testament, began printing it in Cologne, finished the printing in Worms (1526), and shipped copies back to England. With the major work completed, Tyndale then wrote some tracts advocating reformation. He began working on the Old Testament, but was betrayed in 1535 in Antwerp and executed the following year. His scholarship became the basis of much subsequent English translation. Strongly influenced by Martin Luther, Tyndale inclined toward the Swiss on the divisive issue of the Lord's Supper.

**Type** (648). Edict of Constans II, emperor of the Eastern Roman Empire, forbidding discussion of Monothelism. Since the Ecthesis (638) had decreed that Christ was one will, controversy had raged within the church. Constans issued the Type or Typus ("Outline of the Faith"), which endeavored to silence all opposition to Monothelism under threat of severe punishment. When Pope Martin I resisted the doctrine expressed in the decree, Constans ordered him seized and brought to Constantinople. Here the pontiff was imprisoned, and subsequently he was exiled to the Crimea, where he died.

**Tyrrell, George** (1861–1909). English modernist theologian. The best known of the English Catholic modernists, Tyrrell was received into the Roman Catholic Church in 1879, becoming a Jesuit novice a year later. He studied theology and philosophy at Stonyhurst, and for a while was an ardent Thomist. After missionary work in England and teaching philosophy at the Jesuit college at Stonyhurst, Tyrrell began the composition of those works, at first quite orthodox, which were to gain him his reputation and secure his condemnation by the church. *Nova et vetera* (1897), *Hard Sayings* (1898), and *On External Religion* (1899) were followed by the less acceptable *Lex orandi* (1903), *Lex credendi* (1906), and the pseudonymous *The Church and the Future* (1903). Difficulties arising over the questions involved in theological considerations of hell and the relations between faith and culture led to his formal dismissal from the Society of Jesus in 1906. He saw revelation as a nominalist, and from an evolutionary point of view. He felt that each generation had to cut its own path toward the ultimately real by means of new symbols. His great enemy was "theologism," the idea that words could encapsulate reality. With his untimely death, the modernist movement perished.

# U

**Ubiquity.** The divine attribute of omnipresence. The term "ubiquity" became important in the Eucharistic debates of the Reformation. Zwingli denied the presence of the body of Christ in the Lord's Supper because it could be only in heaven at God's right hand. Luther replied that the right hand of God, his power, was everywhere (ubiquitous) and therefore in the Supper. Johann Brenz defended Luther's views (1559), and the Formula of Concord (1577) recognized the ubiquity of Christ's body without defining it.

**Udall, John** (c. 1560–1592). English Puritan. He graduated from Trinity College, Cambridge, where he became a close friend of John Penry. He took holy orders and became curate at Kingston. Three volumes of sermons were published from his ministry there in 1584. Two years later the bishop of Winchester summoned him to appear before the High Commission for preaching Puritan ideas, and he was convicted. Soon restored, after this experience he intensified his zeal. In 1588 he persuaded the Puritan printer Waldegrave to publish a fiery anonymous tract, *The State of the Church of England.* A second anonymous tract, entitled *A Demonstration of the Truth of that Discipline which Christ hath Prescribed,* appeared the same year. About the same time, the Marprelate Tracts began to appear (1588–1589), and it seems that Udall furnished some material for the first, though the evidence is obscure. In any case, his preaching and literary activities (suspected or real) displeased the authorities, who in 1589 summoned him to London. He was accused of being the author of the two tracts, which he refused to deny under oath; thereupon he was sentenced to death. Though pardoned in 1592, he died before his release. He is also remembered for his authorship of the scholarly Hebrew dictionary included in his *Key to the Holy Tongue.*

**Ukrainian Orthodox Church.** A communion represented by five jurisdictions: Ukrainian Orthodox Church of America (Ecumenical Patriarchate), Ukrainian Orthodox Church of the United States of America, Holy Ukrainian Autocephalic Orthodox Church in Exile, Ukrainian Autocephalic Jurisdiction, and Ukrainian Orthodox Church of Canada. It traces its origins to the baptism of Prince Vladimir of Kiev (c. 989). After considering Roman Catholicism, Judaism, and even Islam, Vladimir chose to accept the faith of the Greek Orthodox Church.

Kiev became the ecclesiastical and cultural metropolis of Russia and received Greek missionaries and hierarchs from Byzantium. These were later reinforced by South Slavs, especially Bulgarians, who brought with them the literary and religious legacy of Cyril and Methodius. Kiev remained the Christian center of all Russia until the Mongol conquest (1240). Later, the center shifted to Vladimir in the north and finally to Moscow (1326).

The Ukraine, however, was liberated from the Mongols, not by a Russian state, but by Lithuania, whose later union with Catholic Poland created some difficulties for the Orthodox populations. Except for a minority that joined the Uniate movement sponsored by Poland and implemented by the Jesuits at the Council of Brest-Litovsk (1596), the vast majority of the Ukrainians remained faithful to the Orthodox Church and continued under the jurdisdiction of the patriarchate of Constantinople until they were incorporated into the Russian Church (1687). A separate Ukrainian Orthodox Church appeared among refugee Ukrainians only after World War I, first in western Europe and later in the Americas.

**Ulfilas** (c. 311–383). Apostle to the Visigoths. A Cappadocian, probably of Gothic descent, he was educated in Constantinople, where in 341 he was consecrated a bishop by Eusebius of Nicomedia. He traveled as a missionary among the Goths, translating the Bible into Gothic. He was a member of the Arian party and thus converted the Goths to Arian, not Catholic, Christianity. Therefore, when the Goths entered western Europe, they were already Christian.

**Ultramontanism.** Roman Catholic movement that advocated centralization of power in the papacy and opposed conciliar or nationalist decentralization. "Old" ultramontanism struggled to free the papacy from secular control, as in the investiture conflict. This theory was challenged at Constance but was supported by Bellarmine in the 17th century. "New" ultramontanism was born in France at the turn of the 19th century, after Bourbon restoration. As an alternative to Gallicanism, Chateaubriand, Louis Bonald, and Joseph de Maistre (*Du Pape,* 1819) held that renewal of the church depended on centralized authority in papal hands. Until the middle of the century French ultramontanism was joined with liberal Catholicism. Lammenais, Montalambert, and preachers such as Lacordaire and De Ravignan contended that popular freedom depended on the pope's power. French devotional movements (Sacred Heart, Marian worship and miracles, Lourdes) contributed to the movement's strength. By the middle of the century, Veuillot, Guéranger, and others divorced the movement from liberal Catholicism. Belgium became an ultramontane state with the country's independence. In England, W. G. Ward and H. E. Manning promoted theological ultramontanism. Active ultramontanists in Germany included the "Circle of Mainz," issuing from De Maistre, Archbishop Frey in Würzburg, A. Räss, and N. Weiss (published *Der Katholik* c. 1830), J. J. Goerres in Munich, and C. A. Von Droste-Vischering in Cologne. The Katholikentag and Bishops Conferences were ultramontane. German ultramontanism had become political by 1850, and the Kulturkampf hardened the movement. Unilateral papal acts, including the declaration of the Immaculate Conception (1854) and the Syllabus of Errors (1864), were well received by ultramontanists everywhere. The Roman Jesuit paper *Civiltà Cattolica* was strongly ultramontane. The Vatican Council (1869–1870) and its dogma of papal infallibility climaxed the neo-ultramontane movement.

**Umayyads.** The first dynasty to gain control of Mohammed's empire (661) after his death and early struggles to establish a succession. Founding their capital at Damascus, the Umayyads created a government based on Hellenistic-Roman administration. Internally, they fostered learning and science while spreading the message of Mohammed and acquiring considerable territory. In 762, this dynasty fell to the Abbassids, although a surviving branch, having established Moslem rule in Spain in 756, paved the way for the Moorish culture there.

**Unam Sanctum.** The bull issued on Nov. 18, 1303, by Pope Boniface VIII (1294–1303), usually taken to mark the zenith of claims on behalf of a conception of papal monarchy and the right of the church to intervene in secular affairs. His pontificate stood at the end of a century of tremendous influence and towering aspiration on the part of the papacy, and on the very edge of its precipitate decline. Ever since the aspirations adumbrated by Pope Gregory VII (1073–1085), the papacy had followed a course of action continually inspired by a belief in the papal possession of the *plenitudo potestatis* ("fullness of power") supposedly given to the popes as vicars of Christ through Peter. *Unam sanctam* is the capstone of such a development. The historical circumstances surrounding the issuance of the bull are concerned with the protracted struggle between the papacy and the French monarch Philip IV the Fair (1285–1314) over issues such as the taxation of the clergy and the jurisdiction of civil or national courts over high ecclesiastics. The bull itself speaks of the "one holy catholic and apostolic church, outside of which there is neither salvation nor remission of sins," descants upon the spiritual and temporal authority of the popes, and ends with the insistence that all men are subject to the papacy.

**Unamuno y Jugo, Miguel de** (1864–1936). Spanish existentialist. He attended the University of Madrid, studying philosophy and the humanities. Later he was professor of the history of the Castilian language at the University of Salamanca and became rector of the institution in 1901. In the troubled years of Spanish history during our century he often experienced persecution. He was relieved of his position as rector because of his sympathy with the Allies in World War I and was later exiled to one of the Canary Islands for opposing the dictatorship of Rivera. After escaping from his place of exile and living in France, he returned to Spain and served the Spanish Republic briefly before his death. Unamuno's two best-known works are *The Tragic Sense of Life* and *The Agony of Christianity*. In these he tries to show the inadequacies of the closed systems of dogmatic theology which both Protestants and Roman Catholics had developed after the Reformation. Canon law disturbed Unamuno, for he felt that the church had taken too much of the attitude of the old Roman Empire. Faith, in his opinion, came through trials of anguish and doubt rather than through rationality. In the final analysis the most important feature of Christianity is the hopeless and frustrating dialectic of faith versus reason. God is needed to give man a reason for existence. Unamuno's idea of the tragic necessity for faith finds parallels in the thought of Martin Luther and Søren Kierkegaard.

**Unanimous Consent of the Fathers.** From the beginning the church looked for authority for its dogmas in the traditional teaching of the fathers. This idea was most clearly formulated by Vincent of Lérins (flourished 430), who defined the Catholic faith as "what has everywhere, always, by all, been believed." Although this dictum was perhaps understood literally for centuries, Abelard demonstrated the fact that there was no such unanimity among the fathers, even upon very important issues, in his *Sic et non* ("Yes and No"), which listed contrary statements of the fathers in parallel columns. Although this doctrine is still maintained in the Roman Catholic Church, it is now interpreted so as not to require verbal agreement, but only a "moral" unanimity.

**Una Sancta Movement.** Roman Catholic movement seeking unity in the church. Paul Couturier (1881–1953) and the Mechelen (Malines) Conversations of the 1920's provided impetus for the movement in France, and Lambert Beauduin (d. 1960) established a union cloister in Amay. The German branch arose from new reformational studies and the common suffering under Hitler. In 1928, M. J. Metzger (d. 1944) established a brotherhood like Couturier's in Germany. Ecumenical circles followed in Berlin, Munich, Leipzig, Bielefeld, Kassel, and Frankfurt, with terminological clarification a primary objective. Thomas Sartory, editor of *Una Sancta,* became a leader. After the Vatican placed the movement under diocesan control, a Roman Catholic bishop established the Möhler Institute in Paderborn (1957) as an ecumenical research center. Other institutes followed. Conferences and organizations have arisen in Italy, England, Ireland, and the United States. Several *Festschriften* have been jointly published by Roman Catholic and Protestant officials.

**Uniate.** A term describing those Eastern Christians who have accepted union with the Roman see. The Armenians of Cilicia first entered into union with Rome in 1198, but the union became permanent in 1749 when the Armenian patriarchate of Cilicia was established. The Armenian rite Catholic Poles accepted union with Rome in 1635. The first mention of Georgian Uniates occurs in 1328. In the 16th century the Chaldeans, a Nestorian group, accepted union (1551), and in 1564 the Albanians of Byzantine rite in Italy accepted union with Rome. The most successful of the ecclesiastical unions was that with the Ruthenian Church, the Union of Brest-Litovsk

(1596). In the 17th century union with the Roman Church was accepted by Syrians (1661), with the election of the first Catholic patriarch. In 1697 under the leadership of Bishop Theophilus the Romanian Uniate Church came into existence. The Melkites also began a movement toward union in the 17th century, but this union was firmly established when Cyril IV was elected patriarch for the Catholic Melkites in 1724. In the 18th century, Copts, led by the Coptic bishop of Jerusalem, accepted union with the Roman Church. A Bulgarian Uniate Church came into existence in the 19th century in 1839, but the Bulgarian Uniate received their own bishop only in 1911. Finally, in 1930 the Malankar Jacobites, led by Mar Ivanios and Mar Theophilus, embraced union with the Roman Church.

**Uniformity, Acts of.** The Parliamentary enactments whereby the use of the Book of Common Prayer and attendance at Anglican services were prescribed. There were four such acts. The first, in 1549 (under Edward VI), imposed the Prayer Book of that year, with penalities for nonconformity, to be meted out by the ecclesiastical courts. The second, in 1552 (also under Edward), aimed to enforce attendance at services according to the more "reformed" second Prayer Book, since the 1549 Book was thought susceptible of too conservative an interpretation. Worship at non-Anglican services was made a punishable offense for laity as well as for clergy. The third act was passed in 1559 (under Elizabeth), the legislation under Queen Mary having repealed the second act. Certain changes from the 1552 book were stipulated, the ornaments (i.e., church furnishings and vesture of ministers) of the 1549 book were ordered, and lay absence from church was to be punished by fines to be used for the poor. The fourth act, in 1662 (under Charles II), enforced the reestablishment of Anglicanism (after the Puritan Revolution) and conformity to the Prayer Book of that year, to which all ministers had to assent. Ministers not episcopally ordained by August were to be deprived of their churches. A large number of ministers, perhaps about two thousand, lost their livings in this way (the so-called Great Ejection). The stringency of uniformity required was relaxed by various acts of toleration from 1689 to 1871.

*Unigenitus.* The title of two important papal bulls. The first, by Clement VI (1343), was regarded as approving the dogmatic teaching on indulgences popular in the late medieval period, and was one of the authorities over which Cardinal Cajetan and Luther quar-

reled at Augsburg in 1518 (see Luther's account in *Acta Augustana*). The second was Clement XI's bull condemning the Jansenist Quesnel, especially the one hundred and one propositions from his *Moral Reflections on the New Testament*. The bull was issued on Sept. 8, 1713, in response to pressure from the Jesuits and Louis XIV, who had long opposed Jansenism and whose passion for unity (*un roi, une foi, une loi*) extended to religious uniformity. The bull failed to achieve its purpose, for it contributed to permanent schism in Utrecht and to the continuation of both religious and constitutional struggle in France.

**Unitarianism.** A religious movement stressing the unipersonality of God in opposition to Trinitarianism. Modern Unitarianism has had three main centers of development: (1) the Socinian movement in Poland, now almost dead; (2) English anti-Trinitarianism of the 17th century onward, arising through rationalist Calvinism and Enlightenment religion; and (3) somewhat independently of England, the breakup of New England Calvinist covenant theology. Socinianism was indirectly influential in England. More important was the simplification of Christianity to a "natural religion" on which all might agree. Herbert of Cherbury, Hugo Grotius, William Chillingworth, and others contributed on this point. John Biddle (1615–1662) is often regarded as the father of English Unitarianism. In the instruction and worship that he fostered, there was no prayer to Christ, and a denial of the deity of the Holy Spirit. Socinian supernaturalist Christology was further left behind where Locke's view was adopted that the miracles of Christ are not self-evident proofs of his divinity but are to be judged by his doctrine. After the Act of Uniformity of 1662, dissenting chapels were often instituted in a noncreedally specific way, so that in the following century and a half changing doctrines led about two hundred of them to become Unitarian. From 1691 to 1705 a series of tracts sponsored by Thomas Firmin spread Unitarian ideas, stirring countermeasures by Parliament. Many first became Arminians, emphasizing the freedom of man and the goodness of God, and Arians, denying the eternity of the Son. Unitarianism did not become a distinct movement until about 1800. Joseph Priestly (1733–1804) lent much weight to a simple humanitarian understanding of Jesus, while his acquaintance, Theophilus Lindsey (1723–1808), an Anglican priest, opened a storefront Unitarian chapel in London in 1774 using a modified Anglican liturgy in worship. In 1791 a Unitarian society for promoting Christian knowledge was organized by Thomas Belsham. In 1825 it was strong enough to unite with other societies to form the British and Foreign Unitarian Association. The Scriptures were still regarded as authoritative, and the miracles, resurrection, Messiahship, and Second Advent of Christ still held to. The influence of James Martineau (1805–1900) led to a more rigorous subjection of the Bible to rational criteria, so that revelation came to be seen as an appeal to conscience and to purity of morals through persons rather than as communication of divine truths. Martineau's view that Jesus expressed within human limits the righteousness and love of God to which all men might aspire and so attain a full communion of the human spirit with the divine gained wide acceptance, and a number of able spokesmen for Unitarianism appeared in the 19th century.

In America the denial of the Trinity was sparked by a similar movement of thought. Jonathan Mayhew raised public questions about it in 1755. King's Chapel in Boston became a Unitarian fellowship in 1785, using some of Lindsey's liturgical changes. The growth of a liberal party, not yet explicitly Unitarian, led to a capture of Harvard College in 1805 and the formation of Harvard Divinity School in 1816. In 1825 an American Unitarian Association was formed under the unofficial leadership of William Ellery Channing, and many Congregational churches in New England became members of it. In 1865 a national conference defined Unitarianism more closely, and in 1961 the Association was united with the Universalists to form the Unitarian Universalist Association.

More important than a simple denial of the Trinity to modern Unitarianism is a belief in the goodness of man and respect for human achievements such as those in science, so that no savior coequal with God is needed but only the benign influence of moral heroes such as Jesus, leading to a life of love to God and love in brotherhood to one's fellowman. The traditional view of the atonement is made superfluous by the goodness of God which does not require satisfaction for shortcomings but only seeks to guide men to goodness. Freedom of belief has been prominent among Unitarians; Ralph Waldo Emerson and O. B. Frothingham (and others more recently) protested a Unitarian orthodoxy. Unitarian piety emphasizes practical morality and ethical concerns; its worship is often on the intellectual and formal side.

BIBLIOGRAPHY: G. W. Cooke, *American Unitarianism* (Boston, 1902); O. B. Frothingham, *Boston Unitarianism: 1820–1850* (New York, 1890); D. Parke (ed.), *The Epic of Unitarianism* (Boston, 1957); S. Persons, *Free Religion* (New Haven, 1947).

**Unitas Fratrum.** See BOHEMIAN BRETHREN.

**United Brethren in Christ.** An evangelical denomination founded by Philip William Otterbein and Martin Boehm in Frederick County, Md., in 1800. Otterbein, a pastor of the German Reformed Church, emigrated to Pennsylvania in 1752. Pietistically inclined, Otterbein worked with the Mennonite Martin Boehm among German settlers in Pennsylvania, Maryland, and Virginia. In 1774, Otterbein organized an independent congregation in Baltimore. Other German Pietist clergy joined with him, and in 1800 held a conference establishing the United Brethren in Christ. Otterbein and Boehm were elected bishops. The first general conference was held in 1815 and produced a confession of faith and a book of discipline, both printed in English and German. Sometimes called the "German phase of Methodism in America," United Brethren theology was Arminian. It also emphasized the doctrines of the Trinity, the authority of Scripture, justification, regeneration, Sabbatarianism, and the future state. Polity was similar to Methodism, but the office of elder was the only ministerial order. In 1889 a dispute over changes in polity and membership in secret societies led to division, the majority forming the Church of the United Brethren in Christ and the minority the Church of the United Brethren in Christ (Old Constitution). In 1946 the majority body united with the Evangelical Church, also of Pietist inclinations, to form The Evangelical United Brethren Church. In 1968 The Evangelical United Brethren Church merged with The Methodist Church to form The United Methodist Church.

**United Secession Church.** Eighteenth-century predecessor of the United Presbyterian Church. In 1733 Dissenters against the national church in Scotland, led by Ebenezer and Ralph Erskine, formed independent congregations. They soon were divided over an oath of allegiance to the Established Church required of burgesses. Reunited in 1820, they formed the United Secession Church, representing 280 congregations. Advocating the personal element in religious experience, they protested against "Moderatism" and other practices of the national church. In 1847, a majority of members of the United Secession Church and the Relief Church formed the United Presbyterian Church.

**Universalism.** The doctrine that all people will eventually be saved. In the United States it gave rise to a new denomination known as the Universalist Church of America. Although the doctrine had been taught by some since the ancient church, the origins of the denomination are to be traced to George de Bonneville of Pennsylvania and to John Murray, a New England preacher who was greatly influenced by English Universalism. In 1779, Murray founded the first Universalist congregation in Gloucester, Mass. The first convention (1790) was held in Philadelphia, producing a statement of faith and a plan for church government. After 1794, Hosea Ballou became the leading Universalist theologian, his *Treatise on Atonement* being the classical Universalist document. His influence led Universalism in America in a more liberal direction by a denial of the Trinity, the divinity of Christ, the depravity of man, hell, miracles, and a sacrificial atonement. In 1803, 1899, and 1935 the denomination adopted statements of faith in accordance with these views, although no creedal subscription was required of its members. In May, 1961, the Universalists merged with Unitarianism in the new Unitarian Universalist Association.

**Universals.** Philosophic term applied to general or abstract concepts which represents the elements common to individuals of the same genus or species. Whether there was an extramental reality corresponding to a universal and what its relationship was to the individuals it classified was the first purely philosophical problem discussed in the Middle Ages. Starting with an examination of the relation of intellectual concepts, which are abstract and general, to extramental reality, which is individual, the debate broadened out to consider the whole epistemological problem of the relation of thought to reality. The starting point was Boethius' commentary on Porphyry's introduction to Aristotle's *Categories*. He quoted Porphyry as remarking that he refused to state at present whether genera and species were subsistent entities, or whether they consisted in concepts alone; if subsisting, whether they were material or immaterial; and, further, whether they were separate from sensible objects or not. Boethius, however, attempted solutions to these problems. He pointed out that there are two ways in which an idea may be formed so that its content is not found in extramental objects exactly as it exists in the idea. One may join man and horse together arbitrarily to form the idea of a centaur, or one may form the idea of a line. Though no mere line exists in nature, the idea is not false as the centaur is, because bodies involve lines and all that has been done is to isolate a line and consider it

apart from its body. Composition, as in the case of the centaur, produces a false idea; but abstraction produces an idea that is true, even though the thing conceived does not exist extramentally in a state of separation. Genera and species are such ideas, formed by abstraction. The idea of *humanity* is abstracted from individual men, and this likeness is the idea of the species. The idea of the genus is formed by considering the likeness of several species. Consequently, genera and species exist in individuals, but as thought they are universals. They subsist in sensible things, but are understood separately from bodies. Though extramentally there is only one subject for both genus and species, i.e., the individual, they can be considered separately, just as the same line can be seen as being both concave and convex. Thus Boethius suggested the Aristotelian solution, but did not propose it as his own. He went on to add that Plato believed that genera and species and other universals not only were known separately from bodies but also existed and subsisted outside them. "I have no intention," he added "of deciding which of these opinions is true, for that rests with a higher philosophy." When he did give his own view, in the *Consolation of Philosophy,* Boethius declared flatly for the Platonic explanation. The greater popularity of this work and the overwhelming influence of Augustine's Neoplatonism were probably decisive in ensuring that until the 12th century exaggerated realism would prevail. Not until Abelard, criticizing both Roscellinus and William of Champeaux, asserted that universals were neither subjective constructions nor things, but names of qualities immanent in many things, was there a return to the position of moderate realism implied in Boethius' account of Aristotle. Abelard argued that universals were formed by abstraction, which freed the object considered of all its individuality. Through such universals one was enabled to see what was in the object, though not *as* it was in the object. Thus while denying exaggerated realism, Abelard did not deny the objective foundation of the universal concept. He had come by sheer logical acumen to the position of Aristotle, even though ignorant of most of his important works. The availability of these works in the following century reinforced his view. On the basis of the *De anima,* and its analysis of the human mind, Avicenna had introduced a refinement of terminology which clarified Aristotle's solution in a way that Boethius had not. By distinguishing between the universal *ante rem* (as an idea in the divine mind), the universal *in re* (existing in the individual), and the universal *post rem* (as a concept in the human mind), Avicenna greatly facilitated an understanding of Aristotle's view, and his enormous influence on 13th-century philosophy ensured that moderate realism would be advocated by most thinkers, since logically, metaphysically, and psychologically it was the most compatible with the systems of Christian Aristotelianism. With Occam's denial that logic had any connection with extramental reality, however, the discussion was closed for the rest of the Middle Ages.

BIBLIOGRAPHY: R. I. Aaron, *The Theory of Universals* (Oxford, 1952); M. H. Carré, *Realists and Nominalists* (New York, 1946); É. Gilson, *The Spirit of Medieval Philosophy* (New York, 1936).

**Universities.** The modern university system is a product of the Middle Ages. Individual schools and teachers had always existed, but the apparatus of faculties, teaching licenses, prescribed books, and degrees dates only from the 12th and 13th centuries. The term *universitas* simply means a body of people and was so used in the earliest days. There could thus be a guild of teachers, as at Paris, or a guild of students, as at Bologna. These bodies made the rules in matters which interested them, such as the admission of a teacher to the *jus docendi* at Paris or the restriction of a teacher's departure from town as at Bologna. In early days, the word *studium* or *studium generale*—the place for obtaining education—corresponded more closely to the modern university than did the medieval term *universitas*.

The first universities had diverse origins. Some, such as Paris, arose from cathedral schools. Others were founded by individual rulers, such as Naples, founded by Frederick II in 1224. Some were founded by towns, and in some cases a secession from an already established university produced a new one, as was the case with Padua and perhaps with Oxford. No modern university originated in a monastic school.

The right to call a school a university depends upon the definition accepted as to what a university is in the modern sense. Salerno had a college for the education of physicians as early as the 10th century but did not teach the liberal arts. Bologna taught both civil and canon law, thus originating the degree Doctor of Laws, but it was not permitted to teach theology as a separate subject until 1360.

Early universities did not provide for the residence of students. Halls of residence grew up in time at Paris and Oxford, but in most towns students had to find their own lodgings.

The universities satisfied the need for a secular education in the liberal arts, in civil law, or in medicine. It is likely that more than half of the students did not take degrees, coming simply to hear a great teacher. With no entrance requirements, many students doubtless overestimated their abilities to keep up with the courses offered. The university idea grew in importance, however, and by the end of the Middle Ages there were at least eighty of them. The greatest number of courses was always in the liberal arts, and it is an error to regard the universities as simply the preserve of the theologians. Because of the importance of theology, the teaching of it in a new and untried university was not encouraged. It is likely that only Paris, Toulouse (founded by Gregory IX), Oxford, and Salamanca taught theology in the 13th century. Before beginning theology, a student would have had to complete the course in the arts, taking as long as five or six years. While the 12th century produced a revival of humanism, the undergraduate course of the student in the 13th century although nominally based on the old trivium and quadrivium was dominated by the new dialectic, and as the century drew on, the *Organon* of Aristotle became the chief intellectual fare. If the student survived this and proved his abilities in public disputations in Latin, he might then be permitted to graduate and do theology. This meant some six years for his first degree in divinity and another six for his doctorate in sacred theology. The courses would be based mainly on the Bible and the *Sentences* of Peter Lombard. Consequently, civil law and canon law were more popular subjects of study than theology. It is likely that logic and law did something to quench the literary humanism of the previous century.

The universities had immense prestige, and if originating in a cathedral school, usually managed to shake off the yoke of the chancellor of the diocese, who was in charge of education. There was little interference with the freedom of teaching and no suppression of scientific investigation, though there was a tendency to defer to written authorities without adequate criticism of them.

BIBLIOGRAPHY: J. L. Daly, *The Medieval University: 1200–1400* (New York, 1961); L. J. Paetow, *The Arts Course at Medieval Universities, with Special Reference to Grammar and Rhetoric* (Urbana-Champaign, 1910); H. Rashdall, *The Universities of Europe in the Middle Ages* (Oxford, 1936).

**University Test Acts** (1871). An English law removing the application of tests requiring conformity to the Church of England for nondivinity students, fellows, and masters at the Universities of Oxford, Cambridge, and Durham. The Act of Uniformity (1662), part of the so-called Clarendon Code, had required of all students, fellows, and masters at those universities that they denounce transubstantiation, subscribe to the Thirty-nine Articles, and partake of the Sacrament in the Church of England.

**Univers Religieux, L'.** French Catholic journal of opinion (1833–1914). Its most famous editor was Louis Veuillot (1813–1883), who from 1845 vigorously championed the spiritual and temporal claims of the Holy See. Suppressed (1860) by Napoleon III for attacks on Victor Emmanuel II of Sardinia-Piedmont, L'Univers reappeared (1867) to defend papal infallibility before the First Vatican Council. Disputes occurred when it rallied to the Third Republic, and the end came with World War I.

**Urban II** (Otto di Lagery, c. 1042–1099). Pope from 1088. Once a student of Bruno at Reims, later a monk of Cluny, he became a cardinal bishop after 1078. Because Rome was held by the emperor's antipope, he could not enter the city until 1090. Forced to flee, he returned again in 1094. He continued the reforms of Gregory VII, holding two Councils in 1095 at Piacenza and Clermont. At the latter he preached the First Crusade. He died before learning of the capture of Jerusalem by the crusaders.

**Urban V** (Guillaume de Grimoard, 1310–1370). Pope at Avignon from 1362. A native of France, Urban was one of the great canon lawyers of the 14th century. As a diplomat, he served in the Curia of the Avignon popes. Although not a cardinal, Urban was elected pope in 1362 as a compromise candidate agreed upon by rival factions within the College of Cardinals.

The most pressing problem facing Urban at the beginning of his reign was the worsening condition of Rome and central Italy which had fallen into complete chaos in the absence of the popes. In order to alleviate these intolerable conditions, Urban was the first of the Avignon popes to return to Rome. Arriving in April, 1367, Urban remained in Rome until September, 1370. He began the restoration of the city.

During this time, the Eastern Roman Emperor John V Palaeologus sought aid against the Turkish pressure on his eastern frontier. Denouncing the Schism between the Eastern and Roman Churches, John V submitted publicly to Urban's authority, but his plea for aid went unheeded.

Under constant French pressure to return to Avignon, Urban finally consented. Though warned by Bridget of Sweden of his early death if he left Rome, Urban returned in 1370 and died in December.

**Urban VI** (Bartolomeo Prignano, 1318–1389). Pope from 1378. In 1377, Gregory XI returned to Rome, ending the residence of the popes in the French city of Avignon. When, after Gregory's death in 1378, the College of Cardinals met in Rome to elect a successor, the people of Rome demanded an Italian pope, threatening the cardinals and insisting that a new pope must be elected quickly. Fearful of the crowd outside, the cardinals elected Prignano pope. Almost at once, Urban came into conflict with the cardinals. He adamantly refused to go to Avignon. Possessing little tact or prudence, he pushed his program of reform. Increasingly alienated from the pope, the cardinals began to regret his election. Finally, they declared his election invalid, stating that he had been chosen under improper conditions. On Sept. 20, 1378, the cardinals proceeded to elect a new pope, the Frenchman Clement VII. This was the beginning of the Great Schism. France, Spain, and Scotland submitted to Clement; England, Germany, and northern Italy submitted to Urban. Although a saintly, learned man, Urban was unable to resolve the crisis, and the Schism continued.

**Urban VII** (Giovanni Battista Castagna, 1521–1590). Pope. Born in Rome of a noble Genoan family, he served with distinction as a diplomat in the papal service. In 1553 he was made archbishop of Rossano, and took part in the Council of Trent. In 1583 he was made a cardinal, and in 1590 was elected pope. After only twelve days' reign, however, he died of malaria.

**Urban VIII** (Maffeo Barberini, 1568–1644). Pope from 1623. Born in Florence of a noble family, he studied with the Jesuits of the Roman College and obtained a doctorate in law at Pisa (1589). After serving in the Roman Curia, he was sent to France as legate in 1604, being made cardinal in 1606 in recognition of his successful dealings with Henry IV. He was made bishop of Spoleto (1608), then legate to Bologna (1617), and in 1623 was elected pope. His policy with regard to the Thirty Years' War appears to have been to avoid taking sides, and he has been reproached for spending on the fortification of the Papal States the money he might have given to the Hapsburgs. He sought, through Henrietta

Maria, to obtain the return of England to the Roman Church, but when Charles I asked for funds to use in arming himself against Parliament, the pope demanded his conversion in return, and nothing was achieved. Though a Latinist of some merit himself, Urban approved, in 1632, a hastily reworked reform of the breviary. Nepotism made his relatives rich, but involved him in a senseless war with the duke of Parma. In 1639 he moved to prohibit slavery in some of the Spanish and Portuguese colonies. During his pontificate came the second trial of Galileo, and in 1642 he condemned Jansen's *Augustinus*. Urban also concerned himself with various architectural projects in and around Rome, including the summer residence at Castel Gandolfo.

**Ursula.** A legendary British princess who was supposedly martyred near Cologne while returning with eleven thousand virgins from a pilgrimage to Rome. A popular legend in the Middle Ages, it seems to have no support except for a 4th-century inscription found near Cologne vaguely referring to the site of the martyrdom of some virgins. The discovery in 1106 of an ancient cemetery near the Church of St. Ursula provided impetus for the cult, as well as numerous relics.

**Ursulines.** A Roman Catholic teaching order. In 1535, twelve women, calling themselves "The Company of Saint Ursula," gathering under the leadership of Angela Merici, were given episcopal approval to educate young women and to care for the sick and needy. Pope Paul III approved them in 1544, and in 1572 Gregory XIII declared them a religious order under the rule of Augustine, making them the first teaching order of women in the Roman Church. The order spread rapidly, especially in France. In 1639, Mme. de la Peltrie, a wealthy widow, sailed with three Ursulines to answer a Canadian appeal for groups of religious women to Christianize Indian girls. The first convent was founded at Quebec under the mystic Marie Guyard, "Mary of the Incarnation." French initiative also brought Mother Marie Franchepain and ten companions to New Orleans in 1727, making them the earliest such group in the United States. They established ten mission centers for the conversion of the Indians of the Rocky Mountains. At the invitation of Pope Leo XIII, the order held a world congress at Rome in 1900 and centralized their work by founding the Roman Union of Ursulines, although there are still significant independent communities. Today they head many boarding and day schools, and, in the United States, a number of colleges.

**Ussher, James** (1581–1656). Archbishop of Armagh. Educated at Trinity College, Dublin, he became professor of divinity there in 1607 and vice-chancellor in 1614. In 1621 he became bishop of Meath and in 1625 was translated to Armagh. He was on friendly terms with Archbishop Laud but in 1641 was advocating a modified episcopacy. After the Irish rebellion (1641) he resided in England, argued against the treatment of the king by Parliament and was respected by Cromwell, who upon Ussher's death gave him a state funeral in Westminster Abbey. Ussher was a profound scholar, did pioneering work on the letters of Ignatius of Antioch, wrote much controversial literature, and was known as a man of genuine piety.

**Usury.** Now applied only to the practice of lending money at excessive rates of interest, usury originally meant any instance of lending money at interest. It was the common opinion in the ancient world that lending money for profit was wrong, for money was looked upon only as a means of exchange and not as a commodity in itself. This point of view was taken over by the church. It was reasoned that if a man, particularly a fellow Christian, needed money, he should be the object of charity and not a source of profit. Thus canon law in the early Middle Ages unequivocally condemned usury. It was for this reason that the great banking families of the Middle Ages, the Rothschilds and the Fuggers, were Jewish and as such not subject to canon law. As the European economy became more complex, the church was forced to moderate its views somewhat. The Fourth Lateran Council of 1215 condemned only excessive interest. But the view that money should not be lent at interest continued into the Reformation era. Martin Luther took an ambiguous position. In his sermons of 1518 he condemned usury as an unmitigated evil. But in a treatise "On Interest" he defended lending money at interest, providing the rate was not excessive and the whole transaction had a "clean appearance" (*hübschen Schein*). John Calvin approved of charging moderate interest in certain instances. Needless to say, the church in the modern period does not condemn lending money at reasonable rates of interest.

**Utraquists.** The more moderate group within the Hussite following (see CALIXTINES). Their membership came largely from the high nobility and the masters of the University of Prague. They were ready to compromise to achieve reconciliation with the Roman Church but refused to submit without reservation. They insisted on Communion in both kinds (*sub utraque specie,* hence their name) and demanded the abolition of certain abuses among the clergy.

**Utrecht Constitution** (1938). Provisional constitution of the World Council of Churches adopted at Utrecht, May 9–12, 1938, by the "Committee of Fourteen" (seven from Life and Work and seven from Faith and Order), together with some ninety consulting delegates. It provided for council meetings on specific subjects (Life and Work), and retained a minimal "basis" of Faith and Order (churches "accepting our Lord Jesus Christ as God and Saviour"). Basis, membership, functions, authority, organizations, appointments, other ecumenical organizations, and amendments were included articles. "Churches" were defined in amendment as "such denominations as are composed of local autonomous churches."

# V

**Valdés, Alphonso de** (c. 1500–1532). Spanish humanist. He brought the ideas of Erasmus into his country and was also the chancellor of Emperor Charles V. After the capture and pillage of Rome in 1527, he wrote the dialogue *Lactantius,* violently attacking the pope as a warmonger and deceiver and calling the fate of Rome "God's judgment." Valdés negotiated with Melanchthon at the Diet of Augsburg (1530) in a conciliatory spirit, but that he was more a statesman and a humanist than a sympathizer with the Protestant Reformers was shown only a year later when he congratulated the Roman Catholics on their victory in Switzerland over Zwingli. Juan de Valdés was his twin brother.

**Valdés, Juan de** (c. 1500–1541). Spanish-born leader of a group of liberal Italian Catholics. Like his twin brother, Alphonso, he was educated in Spain as a humanist scholar. Exiled from Spain because of his political views, he came to Naples in 1534 and soon became the center of a religious circle that included lay men and women from important families as well as many noted clerics. His teaching and writing emphasized the inner, spiritual nature of all religious living, often to the detriment of external doctrines and institutions. Despite charges that he was a Lutheran or Socinian, however, he remained a faithful Roman Catholic devoted to the purification of the Church of Rome, blending a deep piety with the clarity and tolerance of Erasmian humanism. After his death, his writings were condemned by Rome, and many of his followers were tried for heresy. Some of them did become Protestants; two of them, Bernardino Ochino and Peter Martyr, made the ideas of Valdés important for the Reformation in England.

**Valence, Synod of** (855). A synod of bishops that met at Valence in January of 855 to try the bishop of that city for misconduct. The primary action taken was to condemn the chapters of the Synods of Quiercy, thereby upholding the doctrine of double predestination as taught by Gottschalk. Other canons passed related to the selection and consecration of bishops, the preservation of church property, and the regulation of excommunication and penance.

**Valentine.** A martyr on the Via Flaminia during the persecution of Claudius (c. 269). The Roman martyrology seems to indicate that there were two men of that name who met death in the same way, during the same year, and on the same road. One was the bishop of Terni and the other a priest of Rome. Probably legends associated with both men merged, creating the subsequent confusion. The earliest trace of the custom of celebrating Valentine's Day is in a letter written in 1477 (*Paston Letters,* No. 783). According to this letter, there is no relationship between the custom and the ancient martyr legend.

**Valentinus** (2d century). Founder of the important Gnostic sect that bears his name (Valentinians). Chief sources for his life are Epiphanius and Irenaeus. According to them, he was born and educated in Egypt, beginning his teaching there. Then followed a period in Rome (c. 136–c. 165) during which he seceded from the church. After this he may have moved on to Cyprus. Fragments of his writings are preserved in Clement of Alexandria and Hippolytus; the Gospel of Truth and Epistle to Rheginos of the Jung Codex (discovered in 1952) are possibly the work of Valentinus. Also extant are some writings of his disciples Heracleon and Ptolemaeus. Valentinus' teaching, a highly eclectic dualism, was based on a hierarchy of personifications of the divine attributes (aeons) which were always paired as male and female, constituting in their totality the pleroma, the spiritual world. In an eternal prototype of redemption, Christ and the Holy Spirit issue from one of the highest aeons, Mind. This procession was called forth by the "temptation" of Wisdom, which in the purity of the pleroma amounted to a sort of "fall." Another consequence of this fall was the creation of the world and man. But man still has a spiritual seed within, and it is to redeem this that Christ descends from the pleroma to give the gnosis by which those who are capable are led into the pleroma, their true home.

**Valerian** (c. 190–c. 260). Roman emperor from 253. At the beginning of his reign, he was favorable to the Christians, many of whom lived in his palace. In 257, Macrianus, an Egyptian, persuaded Valerian that the presence of Christians in the palace made it impossible to predict the future. Valerian therefore instituted the death penalty for the clergy and compelled the laity to worship Roman gods. Cyprian died in this persecution. Valerian's policy was to exterminate Christianity by striking at the leaders. In 260 he was captured by the Persians, at which time his son, Gallienus, stopped the persecution.

**Valerian** (d. c. 460). First a monk at Lérins and later bishop of Cemele (Cimiez). Valerian attended the Synods of Riez (439) and Vaison (442) as protector of the jurisdictional prerogatives of the archbishop of Arles and the abbot of Lérins. He concurred with Leo I's *Epistola dogmatica ad Flavianum* and was an addressee of two of Leo's writings. Extant are his *Epistola ad monachos* and twenty homilies that discuss moral and ascetical topics.

**Valla, Lorenzo** (c. 1405–1457). Italian humanist in whom Renaissance literary criticism reached its fullest development. Born and reared in Rome, Valla led a wandering life. He studied and taught at various places, finally returning to Rome in 1447 to serve the remainder of his life as secretary to Pope Nicholas V. Valla possessed a widely ranging critical sense and a combative spirit that often brought him into conflict with philosophers, theologians, and sometimes the papacy. He offended theologians by exposing various ancient writings as spurious, even daring to question whether the apostles really wrote the Apostles' Creed. In 1440, he combined historical with philological criticism to demonstrate that the document by which papal claims to territorial sovereignty in Italy were justified, the Donation of Constantine, was an 8th-century forgery. This work aroused the ire of many churchmen, even though it was of little practical importance, since the papacy had not made use of the Donation for some time. Valla contributed heavily to the development of the historicogrammatical school of linguistic scholarship with his textual criticism of the New Testament and his *Elegantiarum Latinae linguae libri sex,* a systematic survey of correct classical usage based on the best available sources. Valla's works later exerted a strong influence on both Erasmus and Martin Luther.

**Vallombrosa.** A monastery, the motherhouse of the Vallombrosan Order, located near Florence. It was founded c. 1036 by John Gualbert, incorporating into the Benedictine pattern many elements from the eremitic life: perpetual silence, strict enclosure, and absolute poverty. They used lay brothers to work the fields. The order still exists in small numbers at present in Italy, although the house at Vallombrosa has been closed.

**Vane, Henry** (1613–1662). English Puritan statesman. Educated at Oxford, Vane was for a short period governor of Massachusetts (1690). Returning to England, he resisted Archbishop Laud in Parliament and took part in the framing of the Solemn League and Covenant. He served in Oliver Cromwell's Council of State but eventually fell from favor because of his disagreement with Cromwell's use of force. Nevertheless, at the Restoration he was executed.

**Vatican.** A hill in Rome located on the west bank of the Tiber, where in early imperial times the Circus of Nero was located. Thought to be the site of the crucifixion and burial of Peter, it was from earliest Christian times a special shrine. A church was constructed there by Constantine and later a papal residence established. Until the removal of the papacy to Avignon in 1308, the Vatican was the occasional residence of the popes, the customary residence being at the Lateran. After the return to Rome in 1378, the residence of the popes was on the Vatican. An extensive program of rebuilding was begun in 1447 which climaxed in the dedication of the new Basilica of St. Peter in 1626. This new complex of buildings became the administrative and residential center of the papal court. The Sistine Chapel, named for Pope Sixtus IV, was completed in 1481. Courts, loggias, and staircases were completed by Alexander VI, Julius II, Leo X, and Paul III. The Vatican today includes the Basilica, the Papal Palace, the Vatican Library (completed in 1821), the Pio-Clementine Library (built by Clement XIV and Pius VI), and numerous other buildings providing living quarters and services for the residents of the Vatican. The Lateran Treaty of 1929 made the Vatican an independent state headed by the pope. Two Ecumenical Councils have been held at the Vatican (1896–1870 and 1962–1965).

**Vatican Council I** (1869–1870). The first Council of the Vatican is looked upon by the Roman Catholic Church as the Twentieth Ecumenical Council of the Christian Church. The last such Council prior to Vatican I was that of Trent (1545–1563). Thus, when the Council was proclaimed on June 26, 1867, there had been no Ecumenical Council for over three hundred years, a space of time unparalleled in the history of the Church.

Whatever might be said to the contrary, Vatican I has the decided reputation of being a Council of "reaction." Pope Pius IX (1846–1878), whose nascent "liberal" tendencies had been frustrated by the Revolutionary movement of 1848, had issued his encyclical *Quanta cura* on Dec. 8, 1864. To this was attached the so-called Syllabus of Errors, which left no doubt as to where the papacy stood, particularly on such issues as those involving liberalism and modern civilization. Thus both before and after the bull *Aeterni patris* (July 29, 1868) summoning the Council, there was great concern both within and without the church as to the reactionary direction such a meeting might take. The Syllabus, the suspicion that the question of papal infallibility would be inserted in the schema of the Council, and the growing suspicion that there were those who would attempt to have this "doctrine" accepted by acclamation, sharpened distinctions already present between two schools of thought in the church which might be called "Cisalpine" and "ultramontane." With their roots in Gallicanism and the particularist traditions of regional churches, the Cisalpines such as the Munich theologian and church historian Doellinger; Dupanloup, bishop of Orléans; and Strossmayer, bishop of Djakovo in Bosnia, hoped for the omission of the infallibility, either on the grounds that it was "inopportune" (Dupanloup) or else a historical fabrication (Doellinger). The ultramontanes, on the other hand—men such as Manning of Westminster (England), Bishop Pie of Poitiers, and Senestrey of Ratisbon—wished for a strong statement of papal supremacy and infallibility. Their school of thought had come into prominence after the French Revolution when the romantic conservatism of René de Chateaubriand, coupled with the fideism and traditionalism of Joseph de Maistre and Louis de Bonald, cast a seductive halo about the archauthoritarian position of the papacy. The ultramontane cause was served arduously by Louis Veuillot and his acidulous *L'Univers,* as well as by the Jesuits of *La Civiltà Cattolica* in Rome.

The Council opened in baroque splendor on Dec. 8, 1869—the Feast of the Immaculate Conception of the Blessed Virgin Mary, which dogma Pius IX had uniquely proclaimed fifteen years before. Five theological commissions had prepared numerous schema for the consideration of the Council. However, only the two Constitutions *Dogmatica de fide* and *De ecclesia Christi* were actually voted on and proclaimed in the seven months during which the Council sat. The Constitution on Dogma, directed particularly against rationalism, presented no difficulty. However, the "Inopportunists" were unable to prevent the insertion of the question of infallibility into the *Schema de ecclesia,* and the issue was brought to a final "trial" vote, after much rephrasing of the draft, on July 13, 1870. At that time there were 451 who voted *placet,* 88 *non placet,* and 62 *placet juxta modum.* The doctrine, more circumscribed than initially proposed, was solemnly proclaimed by Pius IX on July 18, 1870. Dupanloup and the "Inopportunists" had left Rome rather than vote on this occasion, and all the ecclesiastics present on the 18th voted *placet* except the bishops of Cajazzo (Italy) and Little Rock, Ark. (U.S.A.). The onset of the Franco-Prussian War put an end to the sitting of the Council, which was suspended (but never formally terminated) on Oct. 20, 1870, after Italian troops took Rome.

BIBLIOGRAPHY: J. B. Bury, *History of the Papacy in the 19th Century* (New York, 1964); C. Butler, *The Vatican Council,* 2 vols. (London, 1936); H. E. Manning, *The Vatican Council* (New York, 1871).

**Vatican Council II** (Oct. 11, 1962, to Dec. 8, 1965). Ninety-two years after the proroguing of the First Council of the Vatican by Pope IX, the unfinished work of the church was taken up once more at an ecumenical council. In the extraordinary person of Pope John XXIII the Roman Catholic Church had finally found a man of charity, mercy, and peace under whose inspiration Vatican II would not only proceed to the disciplinary reforms untouched by Vatican I but move forward toward the work of reconciling Christian to Christian, man to man, a task particularly necessary in a world growing smaller and yet more fragmented.

The summoning of this twenty-first Ecumenical Council was first mentioned to the College of Cardinals by Pope John on Jan. 25, 1959. The encyclical letter *Ad Petri Cathedram* (June 29, 1959) specified the problems with which the Council would be concerned. Truth, unity, and peace, all under the aegis of love, were the general concerns of the pope. Perhaps the scandal of disunity among Christians bothered him most of all. To this work then, the Council would be directed. The encyclical also called for a general examination of conscience on the part of Christians regarding the practical application to daily life of the norms of Christian morality; expressed concern for missionary activity; and spoke again and again of the necessity of binding up the wounds caused by the divisions of mankind. Throughout the document the conciliatory spirit of the pope can be felt. It breathes the word *aggiornamento.* The church has the obligation of meeting the modern world on reasonable grounds. To facilitate such a meeting, the pope mentioned on Nov. 14, 1960, that the formulation of new dogma would not be a task of the coming Council. Vatican II would be concerned with "discipline," with the removal of all unnecessary or antiquated barriers that might prevent the church from encouraging the acquisition of truth, unity, and peace among men.

The bull convoking the Council was issued on Dec. 25, 1961. Ten commissions and two secretariats prepared the schematic material for the consideration of the Council fathers. The work of the Council was spread over four sessions (Oct. 11 to Dec. 8, 1962; Sept. 29 to Dec. 4, 1963; Sept. 14 to Nov. 21, 1964; Sept. 14 to Dec. 8, 1965). The death of Pope John XXIII on June 3, 1963, between the first and the second session, did not interrupt its work, which was continued unabated by Pope John's successor, Paul VI. The results of the four sessions were issued in sixteen conciliar statements—two on the church, two on priests, and one each on revelation, the liturgy, the instruments of social communication, ecumenism, the episcopate, religious life, the laity, missions, education, non-Christians, Eastern Churches, and religious freedom.

Though it would be impossible to arrange hierarchically the sixteen statements according to a scheme of "importance," the pastoral constitution on the church in the modern world (*Gaudium et spes,* proclaimed on Dec. 7, 1965), echoing the spirit of Pope John's two encyclicals (*Mater et Magistra,* May 15, 1961, and *Pacem in Terris,* April 11, 1963), would seem to be that document by the implementation of which the work of the Ecumenical Council will stand or fall. Again, the "Decree on the Bishops' Pastoral Office in the Church" (*Christus Dominus,* promulgated on Oct. 28, 1965) returned some symmetry to a hierarchical structure unbalanced by the First Vatican Council's decrees regarding the supremacy and infallibility of the pope. On Dec. 8, 1965, the Council was terminated by Pope Paul VI.

BIBLIOGRAPHY: W. M. Abbott (ed.), *The Documents of Vatican II* (New York, 1966); and *Twelve Council Fathers* (New York, 1963); G. Baum, *The Teachings of the Second Vatican Council* (Glen Rock, N.J., 1966); G. C. Berkouwer, *The Second Vatican Council and the New Catholicism* (Grand Rapids, 1964); H. Küng, *The Council: Reform and Reunion* (New York, 1961); G. A. Lindbeck (ed.), *Dialogue on the Way* (Minneapolis, 1965).

**Vatke, Johann Karl Wilhelm** (1806–1882). German Old Testament scholar and speculator. Vatke was unsalaried lecturer at Berlin in 1830, and lecturer in 1837. He was closely allied with D. F. Strauss, and at odds with E. W. Hengstenberg. His *Die biblische Theologie* (1835) offered the first historicocritical presentation of Old Testament theology. His judgment of P as the latest Pentateuchal writer was later vindicated. Vatke moved gradually from Hegel to Kant in his experiential theory. Following Hegel, his mentor, he gave impetus to the study of comparative religions.

**Vaud, Free Church of.** A free church organized in the French-speaking Swiss canton of Vaud, next to Geneva, in 1846 by 150 clergymen who left the Reformed State Church. An evangelical revival, opposed by the established church, led to the schism. The cause of the free group was ably championed by Alexandre Vinet (1797–1847), an influential Swiss theologian who drafted a constitution for the church.

**Vaughan, Henry** (1622–1695). Poet from Wales. He attended Oxford for a while, studied law, and then turned to medicine. About 1650, he experienced a spiritual transformation after which his poetry assumed a mystical, reflective, devotional character. He was deeply influenced by George Herbert, sharing both the evident religious dedication and the less praiseworthy literary tricks and conceits. *Silex scintillans* is his best work.

**Vaughan, Herbert** (1832–1903). Roman Catholic cardinal. He was born into a royalist and Catholic English family and had as an uncle William Vaughan, bishop of Plymouth. Educated at Stonyhurst, Brugelette in Belgium, Downside, and Rome, he was ordained in 1854. After some time as vice-president of St. Edmund's, Ware, Vaughan set out to raise money for the founding of a college to train Catholic missionaries in England. He sought funds in the Republic of New Granada, in California, and in South America. Vaughan was recalled to England by Cardinal Manning and arrived in 1865 with funds that were supplemented by friends and enabled him to establish St. Joseph's College, Mill Hill, whose graduates were to work among the Negro people of the United States. During the controversies surrounding the First Vatican Council, Vaughan supported the ultramontane cause through the *Tablet,* which he edited for three years. In 1872 he was made bishop of Salford and in 1892 archbishop of Westminster. In 1893 he became a cardinal. Always ready to promote Catholic education on every level, Vaughan sought for and achieved permission from Rome for Roman Catholics to attend the English universities. He was also known for his part in the debate concerning the validity of Anglican orders and was the chief founder of Westminster Cathedral in London.

**Vault.** An arched structure used in architecture for ceilings or roofs. Its chief advantage is that it distributes the weight to the side walls and does not require center supports, even when covering a rather large area. The vault was a dominant feature of medieval church architecture. There are several types of vaults, among them the barrel vault, which is the simplest, and the groin vault, formed when barrel vaults meet at right angles.

**Vázquez, Gabriel** (1549–1604). Spanish Jesuit theologian who taught in several universities in his native land and for a few years in Rome. He gained a reputation for his knowledge of the different schools of theology and most notably for his study of Augustine and Aquinas. On the doctrine of grace he was a Molinist, and wrote against Suárez and his "congruistic" theory. In moral theology, Vázquez was an early champion of probabilism.

**Veit, Friedrich** (1861–1948). German Lutheran churchman. Educated at Erlangen and Leipzig, Veit was itinerant preacher in Upper Bavaria (1884–1886), missionary in Munich (1887), pastor in Schwarzenbach, pastor in Munich (1892), dean (1905), member of consistory (1915), and president of the Bavarian Church (1917). He negotiated a concordat with Bavaria, and created a new church order in 1920. He became president of the Bavarian Lutheran Church in 1921, and in 1924 president of the German Federation of Evangelical Churches, of which he was a strong supporter. He was involved in hymnal and agenda revisions before his retirement in 1933.

**Velichkovsky, Paisi** (1722–1794). Russian monk. He joined the community of Mt. Athos and later became abbot of the Niamets monastery in Moldavia. He kindled a spiritual revival, drawing inspiration from the early fathers and ascetics which issued in mystical piety and a cultivation of the art of spiritual direction. He influenced the Russian Orthodox Church by translating Greek ascetic works into Slavonic and through disciples who popularized his principles in Russia.

**Venantius Fortunatus** (c. 535–605). One of the last of the ancient Latin poets. He left Italy in 565 on a pilgrimage to Tours, and became chaplain to the Convent of the Holy Cross founded by Queen Radegunde at Poitiers. His writings are mainly elegant occasional verses, but he rises to greater heights in the processional hymns "Vexilla regis prodeunt" and "Pange lingua gloriosi," written in 569 for the reception of a fragment of the true cross, and the Easter verses, "Salve festa dies." He died in 605 after a few years as bishop of Poitiers.

**Veneration of Relics.** The reverence paid to the relics of saints. These relics include the bones, ashes, garments, personal possessions such as books and furnishings, and many other objects which at some time have been in contact with the bodies of the saints. According to Catholic doctrine, these relics are to be envisioned with a veneration that does not give its attention to the objects themselves but rather to the saints they commemorate. Particularly, the veneration is to focus upon the saints' bodies, because it was their bodies which had once been the temples of the Holy Spirit and it is their bodies which are one day to be wedded to the glorious body of Jesus Christ. The doctrine also associates miraculous powers with the relics of saints; it does not suggest, however, that miracles are indeed caused by the relics themselves but rather that the relics have merely been the occasion of God's working miracles. In this connection too it should be emphasized that a clear distinction is drawn between worship paid to God and reverence to the relics of a saint. Christians traditionally have loved the saints and honored their relics, but they have worshiped only the Christ. The veneration of relics can be traced back to the early stage of Christianity, and its entire history demonstrates a sustained and dynamic faith. (See RELIQUARY.)

**Veneration of the True Cross.** The cross rarely appeared at all as a Christian symbol until the fourth century. At this time, there arose a legend of the finding of the true cross in Jerusalem by Helena, the mother of Constantine, who built a church on the site of the newly discovered tomb of Christ. Neither in his letter offering to build the church nor in the account of the Pilgrim of Bordeaux (333), nor in the several works of Eusebius is there any mention of the cross. To a catechetical lecture (350) of Cyril of Jerusalem we owe the observation that the true cross had been in possession of the Jerusalem church for some time and that relics of it "had already been scattered" abroad. Shortly after, the pilgrim Aetheria testifies to veneration of the true cross on Good Friday in Jerusalem. Whatever may be the value of the legend of the discovery of the cross, it spurred devotion to the true cross and within the century were to be found relics of it in both Rome and Constantinople. Queen Radegunde of the Franks (d. 587) had a relic of it at her convent in Poitiers which inspired Venantius Fortunatus to write the hymn "Vexilla regis prodeunt." In later years relics of the cross were to be discovered throughout western Europe, in Italy, in France, and in Germany where they occupy positions of increasing importance in the cult of relics.

**"Veni, Creator Spiritus."** An anonymous 9th-century hymn of seven stanzas, possibly by Rabanus Maurus (c. 776–856), calling for an intervention of the Holy Spirit in the life of the church and of the individual Christian. It is filled with creative, Pentecostal expectancy in the transforming and enriching power of the Spirit. In the Roman rite it is used for the Vespers of Pentecost, at all ordinations, confirmations, and the dedication of churches.

**Venn, Henry** (1725–1797). Evangelical clergyman of the Church of England. A deeply pious churchman who sought to follow in the tradition of William Law, he was successively a curate at the Evangelical center at Clapham, vicar of Huddersfield, and of Gelling, and author of the popular book *The Complete Duty of Man* (1763). His son, John Venn (1759–1813), shared his father's convictions, was appointed rector of Clapham in 1793, and was a founder of the Church Missionary Society.

**Vergil the Necromancer.** Roman poet. Although Vergil was the best-known Latin poet of the Middle Ages, his fame from the 12th century onward rested on his alleged reputation for magic, which may come from the *Fourth Eclogue,* the *Eighth Eclogue,* or the use of the *Aeneid* as an instrument for divination. The legend probably originates with John of Salisbury (*Policraticus*) and is expanded in such works as *De naturis rerum* of Alexander of Neckham (d. 1217). Various forms of it were collected (c. 1499) in French and spread into vernacular literature of the next century. The legend found a home in Naples, where Vergil was known as the city's protector.

**Vespers.** An office of worship for sunset or evening. The monastic form is parallel to Lauds. The Reformers combined Compline with Vespers to make Evening Prayer. The common structure consists of psalms with Gloria Patri, hymn, lessons, canticle (Magnificat or the Nunc Dimittis from Compline), and prayers that include the Kyrie, the Lord's Prayer, and collects. As an office it is basically meditative in contrast to the proclamation and presentation of the Eucharist.

**Vestiarian** (*or* Vestments) **Controversy.** A controversy over clerical dress that arose after the Elizabethan Settlement in 1559 and the passing of the new Act of Uniformity and the "ornaments rubric" in the Book of Common Prayer (1559). The act restored "such ornaments as were in use by authority of Parliament in the second year of King Edward VI." This referred to the vestments prescribed for Holy Communion by the Book of Common Prayer of 1549, namely, the alb and the cope. (The Book of 1552 had abolished alb and cope, and left only the rochet for the bishops, and the surplice for priests and deacons.) The Marian exiles, who had lived on the Continent for six years, returned and, after their tutelage in Geneva, Strasbourg, and elsewhere were profoundly dissatisfied with the state of ecclesiastical affairs in England, especially in the matter of vestments, which they came to regard as the "rags of popery" because worn at the Roman Mass. The controversy that ensued was bitter as Puritan and anti-Puritan argued for and against vestments. The bishops were charged with enforcing the act, but there was widespread disobedience in the ranks. The Puritans were hoping for a thorough purgation of the church from all vestiges of the papacy, and the bishops found it impossible to enforce even a minimum of conformity among all the clergy. Archbishop Parker attempted to enforce just this minimum by his *Advertisements* (1566), which were issued on the archbishop's own authority and did not seem to have royal sanction. They called, among other things, for use of the surplice, a garment that was not associated with the Mass. Despite Parker's goodwill, the fact remained that many of the bishops were Puritan, or sympathetic to that cause, and thus the proposals were not entirely successful. (For the earlier vestiarian controversy under Edward VI, see HOOPER, JOHN.

**Vestments, Church.** See ECCLESIASTICAL VESTMENTS.

**Vestries.** A body of persons entrusted in the Church of England and in the Protestant Episcopal Church with the administration of parish temporal affairs. The vestries became the center for lay control of the established

Anglican Church in colonial Virginia. Created by statute in 1641, they were responsible for the organization of parish life, including finances and social welfare. After 1660 the Virginia vestries became self-perpetuating closed corporations. Seldom did they follow legal requirements in presenting ministers for induction by the royal governor, but kept them on a year-to-year contractual basis. These practices became so entrenched that in the 18th century the parish vestries were a source of opposition to an American episcopate.

**Veto Act.** Legislation passed by the General Assembly of the Church of Scotland in 1834 aimed at curbing the abuses of patronage. It held that no pastor could be forced upon a congregation contrary to its wishes and stipulated that if a majority of the male heads of families in a vacant congregation disapproved of a ministerial candidate, it would be deemed sufficient ground for the presbytery to reject such a person. The act was declared illegal, since it violated the Patronage Act of 1712. The unresolved dispute led to the eventual Disruption of the Church of Scotland in 1843.

**Veuillot, Louis François** (1813–1883). Roman Catholic journalist and pamphleteer. As a young writer in Rome and Paris, Veuillot struggled with the meaning of politics and religion. He became a militant advocate of ultramontane Catholicism, a fierce foe of liberalism. His most effective writing was for the lay Catholic journal *L'Univers Religieux*. He defended the liberty of the Roman Church in France and the temporal power of the pope, proclaiming Roman Catholicism as the answer to European problems.

**Vianney, Jean-Baptiste Marie** (1786–1859). French priest. In 1818 he was made parish priest at Ars, a small village near Lyons. There he displayed an aptitude for the direction of souls, soon attracting visitors from all over France and eventually from many other countries as well. By 1855 the annual influx of pilgrims to Ars reached an estimated twenty thousand and Vianney spent from sixteen to eighteen hours a day in the confessional. In 1925 he was canonized.

**Victor I** (d. 199). Pope from 189. The first Roman bishop to bear a Latin name, Victor markedly strengthened the Roman primacy during his episcopate, making considerable use of the weapon of excommunication. The first to be expelled was apparently the Adoptianist Theodotus of Byzantium. Victor also asked local synods to convene and discuss the Quartodeciman question; upon learning that almost every other church was in agreement with Roman usage, he excommunicated the entire church of Asia Minor along with its leader, Polycrates of Ephesus. Irenaeus and others wrote him to urge greater consideration, love, and concern for unity; these writers do not seem to have questioned his authority. It seems likely that after Victor's action the Asian church abandoned its traditional usage, since there is no record of its being maintained there at a later date. It is possible that Victor also excommunicated Montanists, though the Roman bishop involved may have been Eleutherius. According to later legend he summoned Theophilus of Alexandria (d. 412) to Rome. The real power of Victor was extensive enough. Later Adoptianists claimed that he had shared their views, but their claim is refuted by his excommunication of Theodotus. He was probably not a martyr, in spite of late legend.

**Victor II** (Gebhard, d. 1057). Pope from 1055. Son of a Swabian baron, he was appointed bishop of Eichstätt and became an adviser to Henry III. He was nominated to the papacy by the emperor in 1055 to succeed Leo IX, whose program of reform he continued. In 1056 while in Germany, he was appointed by the dying emperor to be guardian of young Henry IV. His opportunity to wield influence as guardian was cut short by his sudden death in Italy in 1057.

**Victorines.** A multinational group of 12th-century exegetes, commentators, poets, and spiritual writers who were canons of the abbey church of St.-Victor in the suburbs of Paris (founded 1110). Aiming at a balance between the life of cloistered religious and devotion to scholarship, these quasi-chaplains to the students of Paris worked to achieve a synthesis of all the new learning and the dialectic of the schools with the traditional wisdom of the fathers so that all knowledge would serve contemplation and the experience of God.

Their most renowned members were the Breton, Adam of St.-Victor (d. 1172), the lyric poet and composer of the finest sequences of the medieval liturgy; Hugh of St.-Victor (d. 1141), the grand expositor of a methodology of Bible study in his *Didascalicon* and the author of one of the first systematico-historical *summas* of salvation history, *De sacramentis Christianae fidei*; and his two most important pupils, the Scot, Richard of St.-Victor (d. 1173), who concentrated on the spiritual and mystical exposition of Scripture, and the Englishman, Andrew of St.-Victor (d. 1175), who preferred the careful literal study of the Biblical texts.

**Victorinus, Gaius Marius** (4th century). Latin writer. Born in Africa, he became famous in Rome as a rhetorician, and was honored with a statue in the forum of Trajan. He wrote commentaries on Cicero's philosophical works, and translated Aristotle's *Categories* and *Syntax* into Latin. His translations of Porphyry and other Neoplatonic authors became the means by which the West was instructed in this school. Gradually he was convinced by the church's teaching and was baptized (c. 354), much to the amazement of pagan Rome and to the gratification of the Christians. He espoused the cause of the *homoousion,* but his theological arguments thread a maze of Neoplatonic thought and are obscure and confusing. Occasionally he anticipates positions later taken by Augustine, who much admired him and may have followed his exposition of the Pauline doctrine of justification by faith. Perhaps because of the obscurity of his thought, Victorinus was never venerated as a saint. It may be Augustine's appreciation of his work and life that caused his writings to be preserved. In addition to theological and philosophical work, Victorinus composed a set of commentaries on Paul's letters and wrote three hymns to the Trinity. In 362 he resigned his position as a rhetorician under the oppressive measures of Julian.

**Victorinus of Pettau** (d. c. 304). First known bishop of Pettau (modern Poetovio) who apparently died under Diocletian. Strategically located geographically, Victorinus exposed the Latin Church to Greek exegetical method and substance. He relied on Irenaeus, Hippolytus, Papias, and especially Origen. Only a commentary on Revelation by him is fully extant; fragments of a Matthew commentary recently discovered are not mentioned by Jerome. In its first edition the Revelation commentary was chiliastic and ponderous, and until 1916 only Jerome's greatly revised copy was known. The chiliasm of a tract on creation, *De fabrica mundi,* probably contributed to Victorinus' condemnation in the *Decretum Gelasianum.*

**Victor of Capua** (d. 554). Bishop of Capua from 541. Most of his writings survive only in fragments. These include treatises on Noah's Ark and the resurrection, and a Pascal cycle. His best-known work, however, is intact. This is the Codex Fuldensis, a Latin New Testament in which the Gospels are arranged in a harmony based on the *Diatessaron* of Tatian but with the wording of the Vulgate.

**Victor of Vita** (late 5th century). Bishop of Vita in North Africa. He is best known for his *Historia persecutionis Africanae provinciae,* written from exile shortly after 484. This account of the persecution of the African Catholics by the Arian Vandals gives a clear picture of North African civilization in this period (429–484). It contains an official list (the *Notitiae Africae*) of Catholic bishops of the country.

**Vienne, Council of** (1311–1312). The Fifteenth Ecumenical council. It was called by Pope Clement V under pressure from Philip IV the Fair of France to consider the charge of heresy against the late Pope Boniface VIII, and the suppression of the Knights Templars (the principal military-religious order of the Middle Ages) as well as confiscation of their properties. The king used the threat of a posthumous trial against Boniface's alleged crimes in order to get the consent of the pope to the Templars' dissolution. The Council was convened on Oct. 16, 1311, with a select three hundred churchmen in attendance. To evade condemnation of Boniface, Clement V suppressed the Order of the Temple by the papal bull *Vox in excelsio* explaining that he was acting not as a trial judge but as an administrator in the fullness of his apostolic authority. Clement resisted the king in the matter of the Templars' property, giving the fortune to the order of the Knights Hospitalers and to the three military orders in Spain. In addition to the principal considerations, the Council voted decrees by which to put an end to disputes within the Franciscan Order as to the meaning of Francis' teachings. It ruled on the duties of bishops, the layman's usurpation of church jurisdiction, and principles governing the issuing of benefices. It is unfortunate that the official records of the Council of Vienne have not survived.

**Vigilius** (d. 555). Pope from 537. His election was determined by the emperor Justinian's representatives at Rome after the forcible removal of his predecessor, Silverius, but Virgilius turned out to be not wholly subservient. Taken to Constantinople in 546, he at first accepted and then opposed Justinian's condemnation of the Three Chapters. The Fifth General Council was held without him in 553, but he confirmed its decisions later. On his way back to Rome he died in Sicily.

**Villehardouin, Geoffrey of** (c. 1160–c. 1213). Marshall of Champagne, witness and participant of the Fourth Crusade. His account of its history, beginning with the preaching of the Crusade by Fulk de Neuilly, ends with the death of Boniface of Montferrat, and has been completed by Henry of Valenciennes. The narrative is sober, clear, and reliable, although it suffers from his studied defense of the Crusade's leaders, whose motives are never questioned. His work is possibly the earliest French prose extant.

**Vilmar, August Friedrich Christian** (1800–1868). German Lutheran churchman and theologian. As a student at Marburg he lost his faith for a time under the influence of rationalism. Later he became acting superintendent of the church of Hesse (1851–1855) and in 1855 was appointed professor of theology at Marburg. He espoused High Church principles, combining an insistence on the authority and autonomy of the church, sacramentalism, and the divine right of the clergy, with a strict Lutheran confessionalism.

**Vincent de Paul** (c. 1580–1660). Founder of the Lazarists. Born in southwestern France, he began his studies for the priesthood at Dax in 1595, continued them in Toulouse, and was ordained in 1600. He obtained a baccalaureate in theology at Toulouse in 1604, and a licentiate in canon law at Paris in 1623. There is a legend that from 1605 to 1607 he was a captive of the Moors, but its authenticity is doubtful. From 1613 to 1625 he served as chaplain and tutor for the family of the general of the king's galleys. For a short time in 1617 he also served as parish priest of the village of Châtillon-des-Dombes, with the result that he vowed to devote himself to the service of the poor. To this end he formed a group of secular priests, the Lazarists, or Congregation of the Mission, to preach to the poor, especially in the countryside, and to conduct spiritual exercises for the clergy. With Louise de Marillac, he founded, in 1633, the Daughters of Charity, a sisterhood devoted to charitable works, the first women religious to live outside the cloister. He was also a member of the Conseil de Conscience (1643–1652), the advisory committee on clerical appointments in all France. He belonged to the French school of spirituality; influenced by Bérulle and Francis of Sales, he stressed total creaturely dependence and the incarnation in his preaching and writing. He died, widely revered, in Paris in 1660, and was canonized in 1737.

**Vincent Ferrer** (c. 1350–1419) Spanish Dominican preacher. Vincent was born at Valencia, Spain, entered the Dominican Order in 1367, and studied at Barcelona and Toulouse. From 1385 to 1390 he taught theology at the cathedral school of Valencia. He served as confessor for Queen Yolanda of Aragon until he became confessor for Benedict XIII in 1395. From 1399 to 1409 he successfully preached on missionary journeys through western Europe. He helped end the Western Schism before he died.

**Vincentians.** See LAZARISTS.

**Vincent of Beauvais** (c. 1190–1264). One of the first and most famous Parisian Dominicans. He spent most of his life in close association with the interests and labors of the great Christian king Louis of France. As part of an immense educational design to rescue man from his intellectual and moral darkness, Vincent labored to produce three important anthologies that would summarize the inherited wisdom of the past, both pagan and Christian, and make it accessible to "moderns," kings and politicians in particular.

The compilation of the *Speculum majus* or *Great Triple Mirror* (published c. 1256–1259) made him the greatest encyclopedist of the Middle Ages and earned him the epithet *Laboriosissimus*. The first book alone, the *Speculum doctrinale*, contained seventeen books divided into 2,374 chapters—a summary of all the scholastic knowledge of the age. The *Naturale* and the *Historiale* were similar collections of pertinent material.

At the request of Queen Margaret he also produced a treatise to facilitate the education of her own and other noble children (*De eruditione filiorum nobilium*), and ten years later (c. 1260) he edited a much larger anthology, *De morali principis institutione,* for the ethical instruction of princes, courtiers, and all others in public life.

**Vincent of Lérins** (d. before 450). Priest and monk of the island monastery of Lérins near Nice. In the controversy growing out of that between Augustine and Pelagius, he was a semi-Pelagian. An early work in which he opposed Augustine, *Objectiones,* is no longer extant, but it occasioned a refutation by Prosper of Aquitaine entitled *Responsiones ad capitula objectionum Vincentianarum.* His later works include two *Commonitoria* (books of instructions), written in 434. Of these only the first has been preserved, together with an extract from both made by the author. Written under the pseudonym Peregrinus, they were intended as a handbook for distinguishing what was the true Catholic faith in the controversy. Although he does not specifically mention Augustine, in the first *Commonitorium* he condemns Augustine's doctrine of grace as a novelty. It is in this work (*Com.* 2. 3) that he lays down the threefold test of Catholicity known as the Vincentian Canon: *Quod ubique, quod semper, quod ab omnibus creditum est* ("What has everywhere, always, by all, been believed"). This canon is meant as a yardstick to distinguish between false and true doctrine on the basis of ecumenicity, antiquity, and common consent. Ultimate authority for him was Holy Scripture as interpreted according to "the ecclesiastical and catholic sense."

**Vines, Richard** (c. 1600–1656). Puritan divine and proficient Greek scholar. Educated at Magdalene College, Cambridge, he became a schoolmaster at Hinckley, Leicestershire, in 1624, and later was presented to the rectories in two Warwickshire towns, Weddington and Caldecote. In 1642, he was chosen as an "orthodox divine" whom Parliament could consult on religious matters. Nominated to the Westminster Assembly, he moved to London. The following year the earl of Manchester had him appointed master of Pembroke Hall, Cambridge, against his wishes. While maintaining his position in the Assembly, he assumed his duties at the college. Although he started with buildings in disrepair and no students, his reputation was sufficient to attract a number of men. The Westminster Assembly placed Vines on the Confession of Faith committee, but his real interest lay with the problem of church government, in which he preferred presbyterianism. During the discussion with Charles I on the Isle of Wight, Vines developed a respect for the king and attended him at the royal execution. When Parliament called for allegiance to the existing government without king or House of Lords, Vines refused, and was ejected from his positions. A Puritan of prodigious learning and wide toleration for his day, he was highly respected among his contemporaries.

**Vinet, Alexandre** (1797–1847). French-speaking Protestant writer. Prominent in the mid-19th-century Swiss religious awakening which occurred against the background of the prevailing rationalism of the established church, Vinet was known as the Schleiermacher of French Protestantism. He led in the 1845 formation of the Free Church of Vaud, and defended this action in a series of statements on religious liberty.

**Viret, Pierre** (1511–1571). Swiss Reformer. He studied theology at Paris, but was converted to Protestantism by Farel (1531). From that time forward Viret was Farel's close associate, as he was later to be to Calvin. He was active in the coming of the Reformation to Geneva, and after 1536 began his activities in Lausanne. Failing to implant Calvinist discipline in Bernese Vaud in 1558, he traveled about France assisting the French Reformed.

**Visigothic Christianity in Spain.** Of the Germanic tribes that settled in Roman western Europe during the 4th and 5th centuries, the Visigoths, next to the Franks, were undoubtedly the most important. Euric (c. 467–c. 485), perhaps their greatest king, established a state that extended from the Loire to the Straits of Gibraltar. He seemed well on the way toward establishing a kingdom that would include all of Gaul and Spain, but this was not to be.

While resident in the Balkans in the 4th century, the Visigoths had been converted to Arianism and had retained that faith even after it had been crushed throughout the Roman world. They were therefore looked upon as heretics by the Romanized inhabitants of Gaul and Spain who opposed their mastery and rejoiced when they were driven from Gaul by the Frankish king Clovis in 507. Thereafter, their dominion was limited largely to the Iberian peninsula.

Even in Spain, however, the Visigoths were long unable to maintain political control without constant struggle. They were often at war with Constantinople and the Suevi, who continued to hold large areas of the peninsula, and they were frequently faced with Catholic revolts in their own territories. Yet gradually they extended their frontiers to include all of Iberia, and when King Recared accepted Roman Catholicism for himself and his court in 589, the great Arian-Orthodox controversy was put to rest.

After Recared's conversion Visigothic society experienced a period of prominence and cultural development under the orthodox church and clergy. Isidore of Seville (560–636), the great savant of the age, produced his *Etymologies,* an encyclopedic compendium of the knowledge of the day, and a *History of the Goths.* It was he, too, who founded schools and seminaries and completed the so-called Mozarabic liturgy. Isidore was only one, however, of an outstanding generation of churchmen whose activities and ideas were made famous by a series of Councils held at Toledo, the Visigothic capital after 534. The Councils of Toledo were of major importance to the Visigothic kingdom and to the Spanish Christian states that succeeded it. The Councils, composed of both clerics and nobles, laid down principles for the good government of secular society, though they were primarily concerned with religious and doctrinal matters. The Fourth Council established rules regarding royal election, and subsequent Councils attempted to strengthen royal authority.

It should not be imagined that the councils were true legislative bodies, though they were often consulted by the kings. Yet if Visigothic monarchs were not dominated by the Councils, they were certainly greatly influenced by the clergy who expressed themselves through the Councils. This is clearly shown by the content of Visigothic laws and legal codes which developed from Recared on. Under Recceswinth (653–672), Visigothic and Roman laws were brought together to form a new legal code, the *Liber judiciorum,* which clearly shows the influence of Christian thought as understood by the orthodox clerics of the 7th century. So important was this code that it continued to serve under the name of the *Fuero Juzgo* as the basis of secular law among Spanish Christians throughout the Middle Ages.

Unfortunately, the Visigoths failed to establish anything approximating a stable form of royal government and the clergy, usually zealous and devout, also numbered among themselves persons who were spiritually lax and grossly ignorant. More serious than either of these factors, however, was the severe persecution of the Jews begun by King Sisebut and sanctioned by the church, for the Jews, a large and wealthy minority, welcomed and supported the Moorish invasion of 711. Yet even after the collapse of the Visigothic kingdom the church survived and continued to maintain its vigor under Islamic domination as well as in Christian Spain. And it was not until the 11th century that the ancient Mozarabic liturgy was replaced throughout Spain by that of Rome.

BIBLIOGRAPHY: J. B. Bury, *History of the Later Roman Empire* (London, 1923); C. A. Scott, *Ulfilas: Apostle of the Goths* (Cambridge, 1885); A. K. Ziegler, *Church and State in Visigothic Spain* (Washington, 1930).

**Visitandines** (*or* Order of the Visitation of Holy Mary). A religious order of women. It was formed in 1610 by Francis of Sales and Jane Frances of Chantal (1572–1641) to supply a religious and communal way of life for those unable or unwilling to undergo the severities common in religious orders. Emphasis was placed on poverty, spiritual exercises, and such virtues as kindness and gentleness rather than upon beds of dirt or wood, midnight vigils, continual abstinence, and lengthy fasts. Francis intended the main work of the order to be that of visiting the sick and the poor (hence the name). This was unheard of in women's orders at that time, so he was persuaded to turn it into a contemplative order.

**Visitations, Episcopal.** A periodic, formal, canonical visit by a bishop or his delegate to each parish, school, monastery, or other institution under his jurisdiction to ascertain the temporal and spiritual condition of the diocese. During the Middle Ages the ideal practice

was to conduct one visitation every three years. Although such periodic visitations can be traced as early as the 6th century, Charlemagne's general capitulary for the *missi* of 802 assisted in spreading the practice and bringing to it uniformity of procedure. The formalities of the inquiry later became the basis for inquisitorial procedures, and some scholars see its influence on the concept of communal responsibility for indicting local transgressors of the law. Bishops were forbidden to enter exempt institutions, most of which were under the direct jurisdiction of the pope. The Third Lateran Council (1179) sought to regulate the retinue of bishops on visitation (Canon 4), since the demands of hospitality had become burdensome to those who were being visited. Ordinarily the bishop's justice in dealing with infractions of moral or ecclesiastical law was final, but an elaborate system of appeals developed for those who wished to carry litigation farther. Probably the most complete register of medieval episcopal visitations available today is that of Eudes of Rouen (1200–1276) in the Columbia University *Records of Civilization* series (LXXII).

**Visser 't Hooft, Willem Adolf** (1900– ). Dutch Reformed churchman and renowned ecumenical leader. Born in Haarlem, Holland, he studied theology at Leiden University. He served as secretary of the World Alliance of Y.M.C.A.'s (1924–1931), general secretary of the World Student Christian Federation (1931–1938), and general secretary of the World Council of Churches (1938–1966), though World War II interrupted the actual formation of the World Council of Churches until 1948. He is the author of numerous books dealing with ecumenism and the church's role in modern society as well as the editor of *The Ecumenical Review.*

**Vitalian** (d. 672). Pope from 657. He attempted to steer a cautious course during the Monothelete controversy. The ascendant heretical party in Constantinople later removed his name from their diptychs for his orthodox position. In 668 he consecrated Theodore of Tarsus and appointed him archbishop of Canterbury.

**Vitringa, Campegius** (c. 1659–1722). Dutch Reformed Old Testament scholar. In 1681 he became professor of Oriental Languages at the University of Franeker and later was appointed to the theological faculty. Firmly committed to the Calvinism of Dort, he held views of the Scriptures that were conservative, although he conceded a measure of freedom in the sphere of textual criticism.

The author of several books, he was chiefly noted for his two-volume commentary on Isaiah.

**Vittoria, Francisco de** (c. 1485–1546). The first figure in an important renaissance of Thomism in Spain. Trained in both theology and philosophy, in 1526 he was given a major professorship at the University of Salamanca, where he drew around himself a group of scholars devoted to the critical realism of Thomas Aquinas in opposition to all forms of nominalism and illuminism, emphasizing not the Scholastic subtleties of Thomism but its practical concreteness. This focus not only led Vittoria into active political life as a counselor on Spanish affairs for Charles V, but also prompted the particular work for which he is best known—his defense of the political rights of the Indians of America in which he set forth principles that were to become cornerstones for international law. Theoretically, he argued that natural law applies to nations as well as to individuals and that for the purposes of international law the various nations could be seen to constitute a single commonwealth. Practically, he claimed for the natives the same political rights that European citizens possessed, and denied the moral validity of all forms of imperialism.

**Vladimir** (956–1015). First Christian ruler of Russia (from 980). Although a grandson of Olga, he was raised a pagan by his father. He became prince of Kiev in 980, and after an outburst of fervent paganism, decided to seek a new religion. He chose Orthodoxy and married a Byzantine princess in 989. He proceeded to impose the new faith upon his subjects. He took steps to educate a Russian clergy that he used in civil capacities, since they were the only literates. He died while preparing to drive a pagan son from Novgorod.

**Voetius, Gisbert** (1589–1676). Dutch Reformed theologian. A delegate to the Synod of Dort, he was a consistent defender of Calvinist orthodoxy. From 1634 until his death he taught theology at Utrecht. He was an early representative of Pietism in Holland and favored a church more independent of the state. A seasoned controversialist, he did battle against Arminianism, Roman Catholicism, the Cartesian philosophy, and the covenant theology of Cocceius.

**Voltaire** (*pen name of* François Marie Arouet) (1694–1778). French writer educated by the Jesuits. His first play *Œdipe* (1716) met with great success and launched him on the road to literary greatness. From 1726 to 1729 he was forced to live in exile in England, where he was profoundly influenced by deism and the writings of Newton and Locke. His *Letters Concerning the English Nation* (1734) abound with admiration for English institutions. This work was burned in Paris, and he found it expedient to flee to Cirey in Lorraine, where he lived with Mme. de Châtelet until 1749. During this period he penned some of his best works. By the middle of the 18th century, Voltaire had become the greatest literary celebrity in Europe. In 1750 he moved to the court of Frederick the Great in Prussia. Though they admired each other, their personalities clashed and after two years Voltaire returned to France, where he settled near the Swiss border at Ferney in 1758. During this last period of his life, he launched a vigorous attack on the Catholic Church which he called "the infamy." Through satire and wit he sneered at the institutions of the church in which he saw nothing but hypocrisy, deceit, and superstition. At the same time he courageously defended innocent victims of tyranny and sought progressive reforms. Though often accused of atheism, he believed in a deistic God and sought a primitive natural religion based on simple morality which rejected all external authority whether the Bible or the church. Though he never lived to see it, he profoundly influenced the French mind in directions that became apparent during the French Revolution.

**Voluntaryism.** The principle of voluntary support of religious systems and institutions rather than state assistance for such purposes. This term is applied to the special situation of church-state relationships which prevail in the United States. It is not to be confused with voluntarism, the philosophical theory that asserts the will as the fundamental principle of reality. Voluntaryism means that all churches are equal before the law, that all churches and ecclesiastical activity are supported freely and voluntarily by the people apart from any financial support by the state. Voluntaryism was the direct consequence of the establishment of religious liberty in the United States. It was something totally new in Christian history. From the time of Constantine in the early 4th century to the end of the 18th century the Christian church had been supported by and sustained by the state. It was not the intention of the Puritans or the Pilgrims to establish religious liberty in America. When it came, the clergymen, with the exception of the Baptists and the Quakers, were shocked. They felt that religious liberty meant the destruction of the Christian churches, for Christians did not see how churches could exist without the financial and legal support of the state. Not only did the churches survive under voluntary support, but they flourished in a way unmatched by any church-state system.

Robert Baird, in 1843, was the first historian to point out the importance of voluntaryism for the history of Christianity in America. He saw it as the most distinguishing characteristic of the churches in America in contrast to the churches everywhere else in the world. The center of voluntaryism is that nobody can be forced to join or support any religious movement. Under voluntaryism the very form of the church changed. The church was not an institution into which all people were born within the boundaries of a given state. It did not have the support of the law and the state. The church was composed of a group of people who voluntarily joined together to form an organization to pursue in common certain particular goals or objectives. This meant that there were many churches and religious organizations both competing against yet also cooperating with one another. The presence of many voluntary religious groups created a situation called pluralism. The fact that voluntary religious groups defined themselves primarily in terms of given objectives and tangible goals gave a distinctive caste to their religiousness. Though theology continued to play a role, voluntaryism tended to play down theological developments at the expense of activism. Theology was, in a sense, simply affirmed or taken for granted. The major effort and energy of the voluntary organization was put into the action and the goals of that organization. The voluntary group had to organize itself, rule itself, find support for itself, and seek to influence the world toward its goals. Activism became one of voluntaryism's special marks. Every effort was made to develop missions—home and foreign—to establish and maintain reform, charity, and educational institutions. These together became the objective goals to which the voluntary organizations dedicated themselves. Through work for these goals the voluntary organizations were given specific meaning, purpose, and justification. Activism became the special mark of voluntaryism rather than theological formulation or cultural formation. Also, the laity came to play a special role in voluntaryism. It was difficult for clericalism to prevail long in such a system. Voluntaryism depended on the participation and leadership of the laity, for without their presence and participation the clergy or the churches could not survive. Laity not only led in the organization and day-to-day work of the local church

groups, they also provided a good deal of the leadership and the funds for the national associations that carried through reform, works of mercy, and educational programs. Thus voluntaryism shaped religion in America and represented the initial way in which Christianity responded to the modern world which was rapidly becoming secular.

BIBLIOGRAPHY: R. Baird, *Religion in America* (New York, 1856); W. S. Hudson, *The Great Tradition of the American Churches* (New York, 1953); S. E. Mead, *The Lively Experiment* (New York, 1963); M. B. Powell (ed.), *The Voluntary Church* (New York, 1967).

**Volunteers of America.** A religious social welfare organization, founded in 1896 by Ballington Booth (1859–1940) as a result of a schism in Salvation Army leadership. Focusing attention on urban social problems, the organization assists in the rehabilitation of convicts, provides medical aid for the poor and for unwed mothers, and operates churches and Sunday schools as well.

**Vonifatievich, Stephen** (flourished c. 1650). Russian churchman. He was a member of a Zealots of the Faith group which sought to replace mechanical church ritual with a more personal and emotional service linking clergy and laity. Associated with Archpriest Avvakum, he joined him in denouncing revision of Russian church books and ceremonies according to Greek models. These upholders of national piety were anathematized by a Church Council in 1667, thus launching Russian schism.

**Vorstius, Conrad** (1569–1622). Dutch Arminian theologian. Appointed to replace Arminius at the University of Leiden upon the latter's death in 1609, he came under extreme criticism and pressures from Dutch, German, and English Calvinists, and was dismissed in 1612 by the States General. He was among those condemned by the Synod of Dort as a heretic and banished from the country. He was a prolific writer for the Arminian viewpoint.

**Voss, Gerhard Jan** (1577–1649). Dutch humanist, theologian, and grammarian. While teaching at Leiden, he was in the midst of the Arminian controversy but refused to take sides. Criticized by the partisans, he was removed from his position but was later reappointed as professor of oratory and chronology (1622). In 1632 he moved to a professorship in church history at Amsterdam. He was best known to subsequent generations as the author of a Latin grammar that was the standard in the Netherlands for over two centuries. In the field of church history his most important contributions were his studies on the ancient creeds (1642); it was Voss who exposed the legendary attribution of the third ecumenical creed to Athanasius.

**Vulgate.** A Latin version of the Scriptures prepared almost entirely by Jerome in the 4th century. Pope Damasus commissioned Jerome to make a new Latin translation of the Bible to replace the many diverse and often defective versions then current. This work occupied Jerome from 382 until about 405. All of the Old Testament was translated from the Hebrew, but duplicate translations (notably of The Psalms, which was the more popular in later times) were made of some parts from the Septuagint. The version that became common in the medieval West was largely that of Jerome. The Council of Trent endorsed a corrected version of the Vulgate as the standard text for Roman Catholics (which was published in 1592—the Clementine Vulgate). The Douay English version was made from the Vulgate.

**Wackenroder, Wilhelm Heinrich** (1773–1798). Early romantic writer. Wackenroder developed an intimate friendship with Ludwig Tieck, who studied with him at Erlangen and Göttingen and accompanied him to Nuremberg (1793) in search of medieval art treasures. Wackenroder was devoted to medieval Christian art (especially early Italian), but he urged tolerance for primitive Christian works. He gave art the function of religion, and referred to art museums as churches. He published little, but widened the cultural horizons of later generations.

**Wadding, Luke** (1588–1657). Franciscan theologian and historian. A native of Waterford, Ireland, Wadding joined the Franciscans in Portugal and was educated at Lisbon and Coimbra. He supervised the training of Irish Roman Catholic clergy at Salamanca and Rome. In 1639 he brought out a complete edition of the works of Duns Scotus; from 1625 to 1654 he composed his *Annales ordinis minorum,* an important history of the beginnings of his order.

**Wagner, Richard** (1813–1883). German composer. He wrote musical drama of intense seriousness for the purpose of "representing the perfect nature of man." He turned music away from the human voice to the expressive strength of the symphonic orchestra. The singers that he used were supposed to fit into the orchestral background. Wagnerianism became a musical and philosophical cult popular with such extreme groups as the Nazis. Some of his more famous operas are *Tannhäuser, Lohengrin, Der Ring des Nibelungen, Die Meistersinger von Nürnberg,* and *Parsifal.*

**Wake, William** (1657–1737). Archbishop of Canterbury. Educated at Oxford, Wake was chaplain to the English ambassador at Paris, canon of Christ Church, Oxford, dean of Exeter, and bishop of Lincoln. In 1716 he became archbishop and demonstrated his broad convictions by negotiating, unsuccessfully, for a reunion of the Church of England and the French Church, and by seeking to meet some of the demands of the nonconformists. Among his writings are *Principles of the Christian Religion* (1700) and *The State of the Church and Clergy of England* (1703).

**Walafrid Strabo** (from Latin *strabus,* "squint-eyed") (c. 808–849). German monk and theological writer. He was educated at Reichenau, and studied under Rabanus Maurus at Fulda, where he was a friend of Gottschalk. He became abbot of Reichenau in 838. Though he was involved politically in the struggles of Charlemagne's successors against Charles the Bald, his voluminous theological and scientific writings in both prose and poetic form make him an outstanding exemplar of the second generation of the Carolingian Renaissance. His book on liturgical and other customs of the era is a primary source for this period.

**Walch, Johann Georg** (1693–1775). German Lutheran theologian. Born at Jena, he was educated at Leipzig and became professor of philosophy at Jena (1718). He was a member of the orthodox school, without, however, becoming hostile to Pietism. Among his many works are philosophical and theological manuals. His most important contribution was a twenty-four volume edition of Martin Luther's works. Two of his sons, J. E. I. Walch and C. W. F. Walch, were also distinguished theologians.

**Waldenses.** An Italian Protestant religious group. They probably had their origins among the followers of Peter Waldo, a Lyons merchant, who about 1170 sold his possessions and took up a life of poverty as a wandering preacher. These Poor Men of Lyons, who were interested in cleansing the church of its worldliness, formed communities on the French side of the Alps. Their reforming views soon attracted the church's opposition, and despite attempts to receive recognition, they were excommunicated by the Council of Verona (1184). Forced to organize on their own, they appointed ministers who used Waldo's translation of the New Testament. They rejected the majority of the seven sacraments and gave new meanings to those they retained. They rejected belief in purgatory, miracles, invocation of saints, fasts, and abstinences, and refused to take oaths. Although they grew in numbers, they soon became the objects of enduring persecution. They suffered in the crusade launched by Pope Innocent III against the Albigenses in 1209 and were later sought out by the Inquisition. Though often scattered, the majority continued to live in the Alpine valleys of the borders between France, Switzerland, and Italy. They contacted various Reformation leaders and in 1532 issued a new Confession of Faith that marked them as a Reformed Protestant group. Persecutions continued, however, and it was not until the mid-19th century that they enjoyed relative religious and political freedom. Their membership is about twenty thousand and they are located primarily in Piedmont, though they have congregations elsewhere in Italy, in South America, and in New York City.

**Waldenström, Paul Peter** (1838–1917). Swedish theologian and educator, leader of the free church movement in Sweden. In 1878 he and his followers founded the Swedish Mission Covenant Church. It began as a missionary fellowship but ultimately became the largest free church group in Sweden. In 1882 he resigned from the Lutheran State Church of Sweden and in 1904 became the official head of the Swedish Mission Covenant Church. Influenced by Albrecht Ritschl, he sought to defend his controversial moralistic doctrine of the atonement while at the same time championing an evangelical, conservative Biblical theology.

**Wales, Church of.** Christianity in Wales goes back to at least the 4th century when Roman missionaries were active in Wales. The land was Christianized by Celtic Christians in the following centuries, monasteries were founded, and the influence of saints such as David, Deiniol, and Asaph was strongly felt. The advent of the Roman mission to Britain with Augustine of Canterbury at the beginning of the 7th century marked the start of the effort to bring the Welsh Church into submission to the Roman see, which was effected by the 12th century. The Reformation of the 16th century was on the whole successful in Wales, and the church there was brought under the control of the Crown. Puritanism grew slowly in Wales,

and during the Civil War of the 17th century Wales was Royalist and High Church. After the Restoration, church life declined, largely due to neglect, pluralism, and nonresidency. The Methodist separation in 1811 was a heavy blow to the Established Church, dissent then growing rapidly. Such events among others led to the disestablishment of the Church of Wales in 1920. It is now organized as a separate province of the Anglican Communion, the six bishops being appointed by representative electors, one of the six being chosen as archbishop. Disestablishment marked the beginning of a resurgence of life in the Church of Wales.

**Wallin, Johan Olof** (1779–1839). Swedish Lutheran archbishop and hymnologist. Born at Stora Tuna, he was educated at Uppsala and ordained in 1806. He became primate of the Church of Sweden and archbishop of Uppsala in 1837. His chief claim to fame, however, lies in his great gifts as a hymn writer. His *Hymnbook* (1819) completely revised the Swedish Psalmbook and remained unaltered for over one hundred years.

**Walpurga** (c. 710–779). English abbess. She was the sister of Willibald, the first bishop of Eichstätt in Bavaria. She joined the mission of Boniface to Germany and eventually became head of the double monastery of Heidenheim, where she died. The night of May 1, the date of the transfer of her bodily remains to Eichstätt, came to be known as Walpurgis Night, and in German folklore (e.g., Goethe's *Faust*, Part 1) was associated with witches' sabbaths and similar superstitions.

**Walsingham.** A chapel near Norwich founded in the reign of Edward the Confessor, which later was incorporated into an Augustinian priory. A shrine to the Virgin Mary, it was the object of many pilgrimages throughout the Middle Ages. Its immense wealth was dispersed and the shrine dismantled in 1538 by order of Henry VIII. In recent times there has been a revival of pilgrimages to the site.

**Walter the Penniless** (d. 1097). Eleventh-century French knight. A disciple of Peter the Hermit, he preached a crusade among the French peasantry, forming an army of fifteen thousand disorganized and untrained followers, which later became known as the Peasants' Crusade. The army gained in numbers as it moved across France and Germany. It caused a disturbance at Belgrade when the local commander was unable to provide food. After a brief stay in Constantinople, the army crossed into Asia Minor, where in the autumn of 1097 it was attacked by Turks. Most of the army, including Walter himself, was killed.

**Walther, Carl Ferdinand Wilhelm** (1811–1887). American Lutheran clergyman. Raised in Saxony and educated at Leipzig, he was ordained in 1837 and became pastor at Bräunsdorf. Discontented with the state church, he landed in St. Louis, Mo., with Martin Stephan and his band in 1839. When Stephan was deposed, Walther became leader of the group and in 1839 opened a school that later became Concordia Seminary. In 1884 he founded the journal *Der Lutheraner*, which served to rally together conservative Lutherans, and in 1847 he became first president of the new German Evangelical Lutheran Synod of Missouri, Ohio, and Other States. He was also first president of the Synodical Conference founded in 1872. An able preacher and polemicist, he was the champion of a rigid confessional Lutheranism. He might well be called the father of the Lutheran Church—Missouri Synod.

**Warburton, William** (1698–1779). Anglican bishop of Gloucester. Educated in the grammar school at Oakham, Rutlandshire, Warburton was apprenticed to an attorney when he decided to seek ordination. Once ordained, he progressed steadily until consecrated bishop in 1759. He was known for his writings, for editions of Shakespeare and Pope, but principally for *The Alliance between Church and State* (1736) and the *Divine Legation of Moses Demonstrated* (1731–1741), both of which involved him in controversy. In *The Alliance*, he justified the existing state of affairs in England and argued that since the state protects the church, the latter in turn surrenders its independence. Perhaps unjustly, he was considered an easygoing, worldly, rough-speaking, not very intelligent prelate.

**Ward, Nathaniel** (c. 1578–1652). English Puritan. Born in England and educated at Emmanuel College, Cambridge, Ward practiced law until a European visit in 1618 exposed him to radical Protestantism and he became a clergyman. Returning to England in 1624, he joined the Puritans and in 1633 was removed by Archbishop Laud. The next year he migrated to Massachusetts Bay, where he preached at Ipswich. He is the author of the "Body of Liberties" (1641), the first codification of Massachusetts law. In 1647 he published an antitoleration tract, *The Simple Cobler of Aggawam in America*. He returned to England to take part in the Civil War.

**Ward, William George** (1812–1882). English Tractarian and Roman Catholic apologist. He was educated at Oxford, where he lectured for a time and came under the influence of the Tractarians. In 1844 he published his controversial *Ideal of a Christian Church, in Comparison with Existing Practice*, in which he upheld the Roman Communion as the highest embodiment of Christianity. In 1845 he was received into the Roman Catholic Church. From 1863 to 1878 he edited the *Dublin Review* and vigorously defended ultramontanism.

**Ware, Henry** (1764–1845). American clergyman. A leader of the liberal forces in New England Congregationalism, he entered Harvard in 1781 and upon graduation began a study for the ministry. He was called to his only parish in Hingham, Mass., in 1787. Selected as a candidate for the Hollis professorship of divinity at Harvard by the liberals, he was openly opposed by the orthodox but finally inaugurated in May, 1805. Following this first public break between liberal and orthodox Calvinists, Ware did not pursue the issue openly until the exchange of publications between himself and Leland Woods from 1820 to 1823, called the "Wood'n Ware Controversy." Ware contended that the question, What is the natural character of man? was the real issue between the Unitarians and the orthodox.

**Warfield, Benjamin Breckinridge** (1851–1921). American Presbyterian theologian. After an undergraduate and theological education at Princeton and study at Leipzig, Warfield taught New Testament at Western Theological Seminary, Pittsburgh (1878–1887), until he succeeded A. A. Hodge at Princeton as professor of theology. As editor of the *Presbyterian and Reformed Review* (1890–1903), and author of twenty books and numerous articles, Warfield carried on the Princeton tradition of scholastic Presbyterian Fundamentalism developed by the Hodges.

**Warham, William** (c. 1450–1532). Archbishop of Canterbury from 1504. Distinguished as a lawyer and as a patron of the New Learning, Warham found the service of Henry VII more congenial than that of Henry VIII. From 1514, Wolsey's prominence as, successively, archbishop of York, cardinal, and papal legate overshadowed Warham's primacy. After Wolsey's fall in 1529, Warham opposed the idea of royal supremacy and died soon after the submission of the clergy.

**Wars of Religion, French** (1562–1598). The Colloquy of Poissy in 1561, though generally fruitless, may have been partly responsible for the Edict of January, 1562, which for the first time gave legal recognition to the French Reformed. They received the privilege of conscience, and the right to worship outside town walls. However, in March of

1562 the Guises perpetrated the Massacre of Vassy, where a church full of unarmed Huguenots was fired upon. The Huguenots quickly retaliated with vandalism on Roman Catholic churches and armed for organized resistance. War was soon in progress, and by 1563 both the duke of Guise and Antoine de Bourbon were dead. The Edict of Amboise ended the struggle, but its terms were favorable only to Huguenot nobles.

Five years of truce were broken by the outbreak of another war, and the activities of the duke of Alva in the Low Countries— a potential threat to the neighboring Huguenots—brought about a third. Huguenot leaders Coligny and the Prince de Condé left the royal court to take refuge in Huguenot-controlled La Rochelle, gathering an army as they went. Condé was killed in the battle of Jarnac, and another defeat soon followed. However, Catherine de' Medici began to be impressed by the Huguenot's tenacity and in the Edict of Saint-Germain (1570) gave them more favorable terms than they had hitherto received. Within each district, permission to worship in two towns was granted.

Coligny returned to court, where he became an influence on King Charles IX, and Charles considered aiding the Reformed in the Low Countries in an effort to set back Philip of Spain. The queen mother Catherine, however, did not find this policy to her liking, and after the marriage of her daughter to Henry of Navarre arranged with the Guises for Coligny's assassination. When this failed, they had no recourse but to exterminate as many Huguenots as possible on the pretext that the Reformed intended to take over the government. The Bartholomew's Day Massacre deprived the Huguenots of most of their leaders, and stunned them, but they were not deterred. More fighting in 1573 and 1576 ended with the Edict of Beaulieu, which allowed Huguenot worship in all towns except Paris and the residence of the Court.

At this point in the Huguenot successes, a new force entered. The Catholic League was formed in 1576 and became active in promoting the Roman cause—with Guise leadership and Spanish money. Initially backing the king, the League became in time more Roman Catholic than French, occasionally opposing the king. Two more wars, each with its concluding peace (1578, 1580), reduced the terms granted to the Huguenots. The crisis came in 1584 when the last brother of King Henry III died. The League of Paris was formed, simply a military conspiracy to keep France ultra Roman Catholic. King Henry was soon fighting the League for control of Paris, but

lost to the frenzied, League-controlled populace. He fled Paris, had the Guise leaders assassinated (1588), and then joined Henry of Navarre, the recognized leader of the Huguenots. Navarre was winning small battles, and the support of the king increased his successes. In 1589, however, King Henry III was assassinated, leaving Navarre heir to the throne—a Protestant king in a Catholic France.

The new king, Henry IV, was deluged with requests and demands that he become Roman Catholic, but he refused. Victories at Arques in 1589 and Ivry in 1590 led him to the siege of Paris later that year, but an army from the Low Countries raised the siege and Henry withdrew. The war dragged on for another three years without decisive issue, until Henry finally decided that the only way to save France from destruction by a never-ending civil war was to become Roman Catholic himself. In July of 1593 he made the conversion, and was crowned the following February. In March he finally entered Paris, welcomed by the people. Now that he was a Roman Catholic, all opposition withered away, and the wars of religion were finally over, though the Huguenots had to wait until 1598 for the Edict of Nantes to define their position legally.

BIBLIOGRAPHY: H. D. Sedgwick, *Henry of Navarre* (Indianapolis, 1930); J. W. Thompson, *The Wars of Religion in France: 1559– 1576* (Chicago, 1909).

**Washingtonians.** Members of the Washington Temperance Society. It was founded on April 2, 1840, in Chase's Tavern, Baltimore, when six drunkards took a comprehensive pledge of their own devising and proclaimed as their objective the salvation of drunkards by reformed drunkards. The movement spread rapidly but suffered from a lack of coordination, many of its members drifting off into other temperance societies. The movement was not basically religious, although it used religious language and took on characteristics of the frontier revivals, being led by evangelists such as J. H. W. Hawkins and John B. Gough.

**Watson, John** (1847–1939). Canadian educator. He was born in Glasgow, Scotland, and educated at the University of Glasgow (M.A., 1872; LL.D., 1880). Appointed professor of logic, metaphysics, and ethics at Queen's University, Kingston, Canada, in 1872, he was made vice-principal of Queen's in 1901. He was a charter member of the Royal Society of Canada and the author of numerous works on philosophical and religious themes.

**Watts, Isaac** (1674–1748). English non-conformist. He became the pastor of an Independent congregation in London, but in 1712 resigned and devoted much time to writing. He is regarded as the founder of English hymnody. The *Hymns* appeared in 1707 and the *Psalms of David* in 1719. The *Psalms* were free paraphrases rather than metrical versions, and some, e.g., "O God, Our Help in Ages Past," are still widely used. He wrote some six hundred hymns, including a volume of children's hymns.

**Wayland, Francis** (1796–1865). Moralist and educator. He attempted to apply theistic ethics to contemporary life. As president of Brown University (1827–1855) he succeeded in implementing many of his ideas. Trained at Union College and Andover, Wayland served the First Baptist Church of Boston (1821–1826). His texts on moral philosophy (1835) and political economy (1837) were standard works for more than a generation.

**Wearmouth** and **Jarrow.** Twin monasteries founded in 7th-century England by Benedict Biscop. Jarrow, where Bede lived most of his life, was dedicated to Paul, and Wearmouth to Peter. Bede tells us that Benedict brought vessels, vestments, relics, and paintings from Rome, importing glassmakers from Gaul (an innovation) for windows and lighting. Both were destroyed by the Danes in the 9th century and the sites lay unused until the 11th-century revival.

**Weber, Max** (1864–1920). German sociologist. A university professor, he wrote extensively, touching many subjects, including religion. In his famous essay, *The Protestant Ethic and the Spirit of Capitalism,* Weber asserts the significance of religious and ethical ideas, setting forth the thesis that Calvinism, associating moral obligation with business success, provided a climate that contributed to the rise of modern capitalism.

**Wee Frees.** The small minority group in the Free Church of Scotland who declined to enter the United Free Church formed by the union in 1900 of the Free Church of Scotland and the United Presbyterian Church. The courts awarded the Wee Frees, as constituting the legal Free Church, all the properties of that body. An act of Parliament in 1905, however, overturned this decision and apportioned the property according to membership and ability to make effective use of it.

**Wegscheider, Julius August Ludwig** (1771–1849). German rationalistic theologian. Born at Kublingen, he became professor at Göttingen and Halle. Under the influence of Kant's rational analysis of religion and morals, he wrote numerous theological works in which he rejected everything in Christian doctrine that did not stand the test of reason. His rejection of many tenets of orthodox Christianity brought charges of heresy against him, but he was acquitted.

**Weigel, Valentin** (1533–1588). Lutheran pastor and mystic. He studied at Leipzig and Wittenberg and became pastor in the small Saxon town of Zschopau in 1567. Although he subscribed to the Formula of Concord, his writings published posthumously reveal mystical and pantheistic concepts wholly at variance with the teaching of his church. Influenced apparently by Plato and the medieval mystics, he expressed ideas which in turn found a hearing among the admirers of Jakob Boehme and the Rosicrucians.

**Weiss, Johannes** (1863–1914). German Protestant theologian. In 1890 he became a professor at Göttingen and in 1892 published *The Preaching of Jesus Concerning the Kingdom of God,* which established his reputation. In contrast to the "historical Jesus" of the liberals, he called attention to the eschatological element in the Gospels. In 1908 he was appointed professor of New Testament at Heidelberg. His major work, *The History of Primitive Christianity,* was still unfinished at his death.

**Weisse, Christian Hermann** (1801–1866). German rationalist theologian and professor of philosophy at Leipzig. Under the influence of Jakob Boehme and F. W. J. Schelling, he developed an elaborate ethical theism in close relation with Christian doctrines. The concept of religious freedom was his central position, and he argued that although God is bound to the logical and mathematical laws of existence, he is still free within that structure.

**Weitling, Wilhelm** (1808–1871). German religious socialist. As an orphan, Weitling received Roman Catholic instruction until he was twelve. Later, during his productive career (1838–1844), he wished to be counted a Christian, but his credentials were questionable. In Paris he joined a secret German society, mixing primitive Christianity and perceptive industrial insights, and prophesying Christian communism under brotherhood. In Switzerland he befriended A. Becker, organized workingmen's societies, at times suffered messianic delusions, published a socialistic Christian periodical in Geneva, and urged socialism via the gospel. In *Die Garantien der Harmonie und Freiheit* he defied irreligious materialism; a personal clash with Marx occurred in Brussels (1847) after Weitling had been arrested in Zurich (1843) and banished. He moved to America (1848) and passed into oblivion.

**Weizsäcker, Karl Heinrich von** (1822–1899). German Lutheran theologian and professor of church history. Born at Oehringen, educated at Tübingen, he entered the ministry in 1848 and became professor (1868) and chancellor (1890) at Tübingen. His most important books, notably *Die christliche Kirche im apostolischen Zeitalter* (1886), concerned the history of early Christianity, which he believed centered around the mystical-idealistic element in the Fourth Gospel.

**Weld, Theodore Dwight** (1803–1895). Abolitionist. A Congregational pastor's son, he grew up near Utica, N.Y., where he was influenced by Charles Finney and was for two years one of his evangelists. He was absorbed in the temperance crusade for a time but after 1830 became an abolitionist. His work was done primarily in the West, where he was perhaps the leading figure in the antislavery movement. He is credited with having won to the cause the Beecher family (including Henry Ward and Harriet, whose *Uncle Tom's Cabin* grew out of one of his tracts) and several important political figures. He was the chief writer and trainer of personnel for the American Anti-Slavery Society and in 1841 to 1843 assisted John Quincey Adams in his abolitionist campaigns in Congress. After 1843 he retired to the more quiet life of preacher and teacher.

**Wellhausen, Julius** (1844–1918). German Old Testament scholar and historian. He taught at Göttingen, Halle, and Marburg. In his *History of Israel* (1878) he supported and developed the thesis of Karl Graf that in the Priestly Code was to be found the latest element in the Hexateuch. In the Old Testament as a whole, the Prophetic Books were said to precede the Law, with The Psalms coming last of all. His views encountered vigorous opposition but for a time gained widespread recognition.

**Welsh Calvinistic Methodists.** One of the denominations that grew out of George Whitefield's ministry. In 1795, persecution caused the group to leave the Church of England. By 1823 a confession of faith was published based on the Westminster Confession. There is a heavy emphasis on revival preaching within this sect, with a church polity involving features of Congregationalism and Presbyterianism. There are approximately 1,500 churches in this group, with 150,000 communicants.

**Wenceslas** (c. 907–929). Bohemian ruler and martyr. He received a Christian education from his grandmother Ludmilla and took over the government (c. 922). He sought to improve Bohemia's relations with Western nations, especially Germany. This policy, coupled with resentment from Bohemian pagans, probably caused his murder by his brother Boleslav. He was soon venerated as Bohemia's patron saint and was later the inspiration of the familiar Christmas carol.

**Werkmeister, Leonhard** (1745–1823). German Roman Catholic reformer. He became a Benedictine in 1764 or 1765 and assumed the name Benedict Maria. In 1769 he was ordained a priest and worked among the poor in Neresheim. He taught at Freising (1772–1774, 1778–1780) and was director of studies at Neresheim (1780–1784), court preacher in Stuttgart (1784–1794 or 1795), pastor in Steinbach by Esslingen (1796). Frederick II in 1807 named him to his spiritual council and to the Oberkirchenrat in 1817. Werkmeister urged the reform of the Roman catechism, spiritual offices, and liturgy (he issued a German Mass and Protestant hymns) while he was court preacher, but he was retired at the death of Karl Eugen, count of Württemberg. Most of his writings appeared anonymously.

**Wesley, Charles** (1707–1788). Eighteenth child of Samuel and Susannah, and younger brother of John Wesley. He entered Christ Church, Oxford, in 1726, the same year that John had become a fellow of Lincoln College. Displaying unusual religious zeal, he persuaded several undergraduates to undertake a strict regime of religious observance with him. The group was derisively labeled "Methodist" by other students. The name endured, attaching itself to the later Wesleyan movement. Ordained in 1735, Charles went to Georgia with John as secretary to Colonel Oglethorpe, the governor. His health suffered under the hardships of colonial life, and he returned to England in 1736. John followed in 1738. On Whitsunday (May 21), 1738, Charles was converted from a legalistic to an evangelical faith. He became a strong ally of his brother, who was converted in the same year. John was the preacher and leader of the evangelical revival, while Charles was its poet. Widely regarded as the greatest of Protestant hymn writers, he composed over 5,500 hymns. Charles disapproved of his brother's ordinations and never dissociated himself from the Church of England. Married to Sarah Gwynne in 1749, he settled in Bristol. In 1771 he moved to London, where he died on March 29, 1788.

**Wesley, John** (1703–1791). Leader in the 18th-century Evangelical Revival in England and founder of Methodism. The 15th child of the Anglican clergyman Samuel Wesley, he was born at the rectory of Epworth, England. John's early training was under the close supervision of his mother, the former Susannah Annesley. The continuing influence of this unusual woman over the life of her famous son may be regarded as an important factor in shaping his career. In 1714, Wesley entered the Charterhouse School in London, where he remained until in 1720 he was elected to Christ Church, Oxford University. He graduated A.B. in 1724 and, at the advice of his father, accepted deacon's orders in the following year. In 1726 he was elected a fellow at Lincoln College, Oxford, a dignity that he enjoyed until his marriage a quarter of a century later. It was at this time that he first came into contact with writings of a mystical bent: Thomas à Kempis' *Imitation of Christ* and Jeremy Taylor's *Holy Living* and *Holy Dying*. Graduating M.A. early in 1727, he took up duties as curate at Epworth that summer, where he remained for two years because of his father's incapacity. While at Epworth he was ordained a presbyter (1728) and came into contact with the work of William Law, later coming to know Law himself (1732). Upon his return to Oxford late in 1729, Wesley found a small group of scholars and fellows who at first met on Sunday evenings and later every evening for study and religious edification. This group, which became known as the "Holy Club," had a particular interest in the resurrection of what they conceived to be primitive Christianity. They studied the Greek New Testament, fasted on Wednesdays and Fridays, partook of the Sacrament weekly, and had a particular interest in visiting sick persons and prisoners. Wesley soon became the recognized leader of this group which, because of its emphasis on regularity in observances, became known as the Methodists.

Soon after their father's death in 1735 the brothers John and Charles sailed to Georgia in America, where John was to work as a missionary to Indians. On shipboard he came into contact with Moravian emigrants and was deeply moved by their personal faith. Though not allowed to work among Indians, Wesley ministered to the English community in Georgia and maintained a close contact with the Moravians, who were led by A. G. Spangenberg. Directly as a result of his conflict with

Miss Sophia Hopkey, by whom he had been rejected, and indirectly as a result of general dissatisfaction with his High Church opinions and practices, it was necessary for Wesley to return to England late in 1737. Soon after his arrival in England he met Peter Boehler, a Moravian minister, who led him into his conversion experience on Wednesday, May 24, 1738, when his "heart was strangely warmed" during the reading of Luthers' *Preface to the Epistle to the Romans* at Aldersgate, London. Though he visited Herrnhut, Germany, shortly thereafter, he broke relations with the Moravians within two years. In 1739 he began to establish his United Societies and late in that year gathered his followers at the Foundery in Moorfields, London. Herein lay the action from which Methodism sprung. At the insistence of his friend George Whitefield, he began to preach in the open air to masses of industrial laborers.

During the following decade the movement gained its basic form and spread under the leadership of Wesley throughout the British Isles (Ireland, 1747; Scotland, 1751). It has been calculated that during his fifty-two-year itinerancy, he averaged 4,000 miles annually, or traveled 208,000 miles in all, preaching some 40,000 sermons. The success of his work rested on his ability to enlist and organize the services of others. Early in his career he began to use "lay preachers" whose task was to carry out the work of the semimilitary order of which Wesley was undisputed head.

Faced with an inadequate supply of ordained men and convinced that there was no essential difference between a presbyter and a bishop, Wesley "set apart" Thomas Coke (1784) as superintendent for the American work (officially begun in 1768). The next year he ordained others for work in Scotland. This was followed by numerous other ordinations.

During the last decade of his life Wesley attempted to provide both for the fulfillment of his lifelong wish that his followers should remain with the Anglican Communion and that his work should not be destroyed because of his death. In the latter of these he succeeded, but in the former he did not.

The theology of Wesley is marked by a powerful emphasis upon Christ's universal atonement. All who accepted Christ would be saved, and to those who sought diligently after holiness of life, complete deliverance from sin was a fruitful promise. Early in his career (1740) he had broken with Whitefield over the matter of predestination, and although a personal reconciliation took place only two years later, Wesley continued to stress his Arminianism. His *Explanatory Notes Upon* the New Testament and *Standard Sermons* (4 vols.) are looked upon as official statements of his doctrine, but his hymns and those of his brother Charles also constitute a rich statement of his theology.

BIBLIOGRAPHY: J. Wesley, *Standard Sermons*, 2 vols., ed. by E. H. Sugden (London, 1921); N. Curnock (ed.), *The Journal of the Rev. John Wesley*, 8 vols. (London, 1909–1916); A. C. Outler (ed.), *John Wesley* (New York, 1964).

W. R. Cannon, *The Theology of John Wesley* (New York, 1946); M. L. Edwards, *John Wesley and the Eighteenth Century* (London, 1933); H. Lindström, *Wesley and Sanctification* (Stockholm, 1946); M. Schmidt, *John Wesley: A Theological Biography*, Vol. 1 (Nashville, 1963).

**Wesley, Samuel** (1662–1735). Anglican cleric and father of John and Charles Wesley. Son of a nonconformist minister, he received his early education at nonconformist academies. He conformed to Anglicanism, received a B.A. from Oxford (1688), and was ordained priest in 1690. Wesley became rector of Epworth, Lincolnshire, in 1695. Frequently elected to Convocation, he also won a small measure of fame for his prose and poetic writings.

**Wessel.** See GANSFORT, WESSEL.

**Wessenberg, Ignaz Heinrich Karl von** (1774–1860). German Roman Catholic. As vicar-general in Constance he labored to improve moral and educational standards. He urged the revival of church councils and at the Congress of Vienna strove unsuccessfully to secure the establishment of a national German Catholic Church. His activities were resented at Rome. When the pope vetoed his appointment as administrator of the diocese of Constance in 1827, he soon retired to private life.

**West, Stephen** (1735–1819). Congregational clergyman. Graduated from Yale College in 1755, he studied theology with Timothy Woodbridge and was ordained pastor of the church and missionary to the Indians at Stockbridge, Mass., in 1759, succeeding Jonathan Edwards. He was a close friend of Samuel Hopkins and became an advocate of Edwardsian theology, publishing numerous works, including *Essay on Moral Agency* (1772) and *Essay on the Scripture Doctrine of the Atonement* (1785). He taught many theological students, among them John Thornton Kirkland, president of Harvard College. He was a trustee of Williams College at the time of its incorporation, and assisted in forming the Creed and Associate Statutes of Andover Theological Seminary.

**Westcott, Brooke Foss** (1825–1901). Anglican bishop and theologian. Westcott was regius professor of divinity at Cambridge, a position he retained after being consecrated bishop of Durham in 1890. His wide interests included psychical research, reform of theological studies, foreign missions, and social affairs (he was first president of the Christian Social Union). His most significant contributions to theological literature were an edition of the Greek New Testament (with F. J. A. Hort, 1881) and commentaries on the Gospel of John and on the epistles of John.

**Western Church.** See ROMAN CATHOLICISM.

**Westminster Abbey.** On the "island" of Thorney in the Thames the saintly Edward the Confessor (1042–1066) refounded or enlarged the Benedictine establishment of St. Peter's in Westminster. Subsequently, the almost equally pious monarch Henry III (1216–1272) rebuilt the Confessor's church. The site of almost every coronation since 1066, and the place of burial for many illustrious Englishmen, the Abbey has become the mother church of the English-speaking world.

**Westminster Assembly.** A council, gathered from 1643 until 1653 (without formal dissolution) to advise the Long Parliament on a religious settlement for England. Membership consisted of 121 divines and 30 lay assessors (ten lords and twenty commoners). Eight Scottish commissioners were invited to be present as advisers because Parliament had promised to reform the English Church along Scottish lines in exchange for military aid against Charles I. Though the members were largely agreed on matters of doctrine, factions within the Assembly made agreement on church polity difficult. The Scots wanted England to duplicate their form of government (*jure divino* Presbyterianism). The English Presbyterians were not all willing to follow the Scots in every respect, but most of them did want a presbyterianism with enforced uniformity. The few Independents protested against such an establishment, while the Episcopalians, advocates of a rival establishment, failed to attend the discussions. The Assembly did not have power to decide, but had to submit its recommendations to Parliament: although there were Erastians among the divines, the two bodies disagreed as to whether Parliament or the church should be responsible for church order and discipline. In 1644 the Assembly completed the Form of Presbyterial Church Government and the Directory of Public Worship. In 1646 the Confession of Faith was completed, and in 1647 the Larger Catechism and the Shorter Catechism (see WESTMINSTER STANDARDS). Though the Assembly failed to Presbyterianize England, the Confession and Shorter Catechism were a lasting heritage for the Presbyterian world, still influential at mid-20th century.

**Westminster Confession.** The Confession of Faith of the Westminster Assembly. The Assembly was originally commissioned to revise the Thirty-nine Articles, but the Scottish alliance of Parliament required the drafting of a new confession, which contained thirty-three chapters. The Assembly did not disapprove of the Thirty-nine Articles, but desired to see them sharpened along the lines of the Lambeth Articles, and it is clear that they were greatly influenced by both the order and the content of the Irish Articles of Archbishop Ussher. Completed in December, 1646, the Confession was approved by the English Parliament (with some alterations) in June, 1647, by the Scots General Assembly in August, and by the Scots Parliament in February, 1649. Apparently the English makers of the Confession did not intend it to be imposed as an inflexible doctrinal test, but this is in fact how it came to be used, especially in Scotland. In American Presbyterianism it has been modified from time to time (notably in its teaching on the relations of church and state), but it still remains a doctrinal standard. The Confession has also exercised a powerful influence in the English-speaking world outside of Presbyterianism: it provided the basis for the Congregationalist Savoy Declaration, the Particular Baptist Confession of 1677, and the General Baptist Orthodox Creed of 1678. The doctrinal position of the Westminster Confession may be characterized as Scholastic, Puritan Calvinism. The conflict with Arminianism has elevated the divine decrees (predestination) to a prominence they did not have in Calvin's *Institutes,* and the strong Christocentric character of the Reformation gospel is somewhat overshadowed by a Scholastic framework compounded of predestinarianism and the covenant theology. Characteristic of the Puritan mind are the strong interest in the subjective operations of grace on the individual soul and the identification (which Calvin had rejected) of the Lord's Day as the Christian Sabbath.

**Westminster Standards.** The comprehensive name for the various formularies produced by the Westminster Assembly, including (in the order of their completion), the Directory for the Public Worship of God (1644), the Form of Government (1644), the Confession of Faith (1646), and the Larger Catechism and the Shorter Catechism (1647). The Directory, intended to replace the Book of Common Prayer, was not a closely prescribed liturgy, but an order of service and a general guide for the prayers. The Form of Government detailed the Presbyterian system of polity. The Larger Catechism proved too ponderous for usefulness, but the Shorter Catechism, well known for its opening affirmation that "man's chief end is to glorify God," has enjoyed an influence comparable to that of Luther's Small Catechism and the Heidelberg Catechism. (For the doctrinal position of the Westminster Standards, see WESTMINSTER CONFESSION.)

**Westphal, Joachim** (c. 1510–1574). German Lutheran theologian. He studied under Luther and Melanchthon at Wittenberg and was a teacher at Hamburg, Wittenberg, and Jena before becoming pastor and finally superintendent at Hamburg. Active in controversies of the time, he was motivated by his primary concern about the Lord's Supper to warn against the influence of Calvinist and Zwinglian teaching. A 1552 tract roused Calvin and opened a widespread Eucharistic controversy.

**Westphalia, Peace of** (1648). The settlement that brought the Thirty Years' War to an end. It was the first attempt in modern history to settle European problems by a general meeting of nations and it regulated the religious and political affairs of Europe for years to come.

The most important territorial provisions were the following: (1) Sweden acquired Western Pomerania, Stettin, Bremen, and Verden; (2) France obtained Alsace (excluding Strasbourg), Metz, Toul, Verdun, and Pinerolo; (3) Brandenburg received Eastern Pomerania; (4) Bavaria retained the Upper Palatinate; (5) Saxony kept Lusatia; (6) the Lower Palatinate was restored to the legitimate ruler, Charles Louis; (7) Switzerland and Holland were recognized as independent and sovereign states.

Politically, the treaty marked a significant decline in the concept of universal government and gave impetus to the growing importance of the territorial states by granting virtual independence and sovereign power to the 343 states of the Holy Roman Empire. Each state could enter into treaties and alliances with foreign powers without seeking the counsel or consent of the emperor or central diet. Further, France and Sweden, which now held territory in the Empire, were given the right to vote in the imperial diet.

The religious issues which had largely triggered the war but which had nearly been lost sight of were settled by a compromise and accepted by the war-weary people of Europe. The settlement called for a reaffirmation of the Peace of Augsburg and its principle of *Cuius regio, eius religio,* only now extended to include the Calvinists. January 1, 1624, became the test date for possession of ecclesiastical lands. The treaty did not establish religious toleration, nor did it give legal recognition to Anabaptists. It did help to disentangle religion from political interests. Religion became increasingly a matter of individual conscience. Princes became less inclined to expel religious dissenters for the sake of conformity, and people became used to the idea that various faiths could and should live side by side in peace.

**Wettstein, Johann Jakob** (1693–1754). Early scholar in New Testament textual criticism. He toured Europe collecting New Testament manuscripts and made the first formal list of Greek New Testament manuscripts in accessible collections. In 1751 he published an edition of the Greek New Testament with commentary comparing the New Testament with the literature of Judaism and classical paganism. His home church at Basel often accused him of Socinian heresy.

**Wheelock, Eleazar** (1711–1779). Congregational clergyman. Becoming a pastor in 1735 he participated actively in the Great Awakening in Connecticut. He is better remembered, however, as the founder in 1754 of Moor's Charity School, which developed in 1769 into Dartmouth College, a school for Indians and whites interested in doing missionary work among the Indians. He was president of Dartmouth until his death.

**Whichcote, Benjamin** (1609–1683). Cambridge Platonist. Born in Shropshire, Whichcote studied at Cambridge and was ordained in 1636. For twenty years as Sunday afternoon lecturer at Cambridge he exercised a wide influence. Among his pupils were the Cambridge Platonists John Smith, Ralph Cudworth, and Henry More. In 1644 he was made provost of King's College, Cambridge, which post he lost at the Restoration. Midway between Puritan and High Church sympathies, he adhered to the Act of Uniformity. His thought emphasized the importance along with revelation, of those truths discoverable by reason alone.

**Whiston, William** (1667–1752). English rationalist. A disciple of Newton, he was professor of mathematics at Cambridge from 1703 to 1710. His major work, *Primitive Christianity Revived* (1711), sought to show that the accepted doctrine of the Trinity was not in harmony with Scripture nor the faith of the early church, which he conceived to be Arian. His most successful accomplishment was a translation of Josephus' works which was published in 1737. In 1747 he left the Anglican Communion and became a Baptist.

**Whitaker, William** (1548–1595). English Calvinistic divine. Born in the vicinity of Manchester, Whitaker studied at Cambridge and became regius professor of divinity there in 1580, and headmaster of St. John's College in 1586. He was a staunch Calvinist and wrote refutations of the books of Thomas Stapleton and Cardinal Bellarmine. He was the principal author of the Lambeth Articles, which, however, were modified somewhat by John Whitgift.

**Whitby, Synod of** (664). A meeting in northern England, with King Oswy presiding, called to determine whether Celtic or Roman customs should prevail in the church. The main question was the date of Easter, but other matters such as the style of tonsure were discussed. Oswy and the delegates eventually ruled in favor of the Roman customs. Although the English Church thus repudiated Celtic influences, it was many years before the old customs disappeared.

**White, William** (1748–1836). American Episcopal bishop. Ordained deacon in London in 1770 and priest in 1772, White became rector of Christ Church, Philadelphia. An ardent patriot during the Revolution, he was a leading advocate of a national Episcopal church, and published *The Case of the Episcopal Churches in the United States Considered* (1782). White was instrumental in devising a constitution for the new Protestant Episcopal Church which was adopted in 1785 and revised in 1789. He introduced the novel principle for Episcopalians of a laity equal to the clergy in legislation. With William Smith, White was responsible for the American revision of the Book of Common Prayer. Elected bishop of the newly formed Philadelphia diocese in 1786, he was consecrated in England in 1787 and became presiding bishop in 1796. The leading Episcopal controversialist and apologist, White was himself conciliatory but not latitudinarian. He sought cooperation with other denominations and promoted benevolent societies, including a Sunday school, despite hostility. He helped train a generation of churchmen, including W. A. Muhlenberg, J. H. Hobart, and Jackson Kemper. Other writings included the effective *Comparative views of the Controversy between the Calvinists and the Arminians* (1817) and the autobiographical *Memoirs of the Protestant Episcopal Church in the United States of America* (1820).

**White Fathers** (*originally* Missionaries of Our Lady of Africa of Algeria). A Roman Catholic missionary order founded in 1868 by Cardinal Charles Lavigerie, then the archbishop of Algeria. Stressing adaptation to the ways of the people being evangelized, the order received its common name from the fact that the religious garb chosen was patterned after that of the Moslem population of Algeria. Professed members of the order take an oath to bind themselves to work for the conversion of Africa. Although the initial work of the White Fathers was done in the Sahara, in 1878 they were sent to Equatorial Africa and eventually established mission stations in what was then known as the Belgian Congo, Mozambique, Ruanda-Urundi, Kenya, Uganda, Tanganyika, the Gold Coast, and the French Sudan. There are both priests and religious brothers in the order, and a related society of sisters. The White Fathers are probably the best known and perhaps the most numerous of the Roman Catholic mission societies working in Africa. In the mid-1950's there were almost 1,900 priests professed in the society and over 1,400 sisters. Brothers numbered only about 400. At the same time, they operated more than 5,000 schools, not counting the almost innumerable "Bush schools." They have fortunately seen to the creation of a native clergy.

**Whitefield, George** (1714–1770). The most widely known and most controversial preacher of the Evangelical Revival in both Great Britain and America. He founded no sect but gave growth to every English Protestant denomination with Calvinist leanings.

He was born and raised in the Bell Inn, Gloucester. His widowed mother supervised his early education. Although he had done creditably with Latin classics and excellently with rhetoric, he was withdrawn from school at the age of fifteen in order to serve as drawer in the Inn. Four years later he was accepted into Pembroke College, Oxford, as a servitor. He joined the Holy Club and became acquainted with Charles and John Wesley. During Lent in 1735 strict abstinence and inward conflicts led him to despair, followed by a feeling of deliverance, three years before John Wesley's similarly heart-warming experience. He accepted ordination in the Church of England, and although only twenty-one years of age, preached immediately thereafter with great success throughout Gloucestershire and in some of the leading churches of London. In the following year he was graduated from Oxford. Whitefield followed John Wesley as a missionary to Georgia in 1738. During his initial three months' stay he conceived of the idea of an orphanage. The needs of the developing orphanage drove him throughout Great Britain and British America seeking funds during the rest of his life. When he returned to London, he was immensely successful as an evangelist. He initiated the practice of preaching in the open and persuaded Wesley to do likewise. During the next four years he visited almost every population center in the English-speaking world. In New Jersey and New England his preaching brought to a climax the Great Awakening begun by Theodore Frelinghuysen, Gilbert Tennent, and Jonathan Edwards. He similarly supported and extended the awakenings in Wales initiated by Howel Harris and Daniel Rowland, and those in Scotland under William McCulloch and James Robe.

Selina, Countess of Huntingdon, appointed Whitefield one of her chaplains at large in 1748 and he maintained a regular correspondence with her until his death. In 1753 he compiled a hymnbook and in 1756 a chapel was built for his use on Tottenham Court Road in London, but his itinerancy prevented a continuous ministry there. Crossing the Atlantic seven times, he repeatedly visited every American colony from Maine to Georgia, as well as Scotland, Wales, many parts of England and, less frequently, Ireland. Whitefield preached about eighteen thousand times, averaging ten sermons a week until his death of asthma in Newburyport, Mass., at the age of fifty-six.

Whitefield's preaching was graphic and emotional, with a ready profusion of extemporaneous language accompanied by singularly appropriate gestures. He charmed the multitudes. Benjamin Franklin, in his *Autobiography*, wrote: "He had a loud and clear voice, and articulated his words so perfectly that he might be heard and understood at a great distance, especially as his auditors observed the most perfect silence." He used the Bible extensively in leading men and women through repentance to faith. Although adhering to a Calvinist doctrine of predestination, he did not hesitate to offer Christ to everyone. The experience of new birth was all-important. By that experience a man might be assured of salvation and enabled to progress in holiness. Whitefield was informal, almost conversational, yet bold and direct when addressing himself to all classes, races, and ages, applying his message to their separate interests and needs. He wept profusely in the pulpit, prayed spontaneously, and convinced his hearers of his earnest sincerity and concern for their salvation. Among those influenced by him were Horace Walpole, David Hume, Lord Chesterfield, Lord Littleton, Samuel Foote, David Garrick, Lord Bolingbroke, and untold numbers of common working men and women, Negroes, Indians, gentlemen and ladies.

BIBLIOGRAPHY: G. Whitefield, *Journals* (London, 1960); A. D. Belden, *George Whitefield the Awakener* (New York, 1953); S. C. Henry, *George Whitefield: Wayfaring Witness* (New York, 1957); R. Philip, *The Life and Times of the Rev. George Whitefield* (London, 1838); L. Tyerman, *The Life of the Rev. George Whitefield*, 2 vols. (London, 1876–1877).

**Whitehead, Alfred North** (1861–1947). English mathematician and philosopher. Whitehead taught at Trinity College, Cambridge, and University College and Imperial College of Science and Technology, University of London, before becoming professor of philosophy at Harvard (1924–1937). He used symbols as a means of expression and was deeply concerned with religion. "The discoveries of modern science supply a basis for regenerative philosophy." In *Process and Reality* (1929), he sought the elimination of all dualisms and the reconciliation of realistic and conceptual views of philosophy. Whitehead proposed the "philosophy of organism," "the becoming, the being and the relatedness of actual entities." Whitehead's attempt to realign and integrate science and religion influenced Sir James Jeans, Robert A. Millikan, Sir Arthur Eddington, and the Chicago school of theology. Other works were *Science and the Modern World* (1925), *Religion in the Making* (1926), and *Adventures of Ideas* (1933).

**Whitgift, John** (c. 1530–1604). Archbishop of Canterbury from 1583. The son of a Lincolnshire merchant, Whitgift was educated in London and at Cambridge (Queens' College and Pembroke Hall), where he was influenced by Nicholas Ridley and John Bradford. His advancement at Cambridge was rapid: fellow of Peterhouse at twenty-five, Lady Margaret professor of divinity at thirty-three, regius professor and master of Pembroke Hall four years later, master of Trinity and vice-chancellor, 1570. Whitgift may be said to have been instrumental in enforcing the Elizabethan Settlement at Cambridge. He promulgated new statutes for the university, and successfully resisted Thomas Cartwright, the leader of the Puritan faction opposed to acquiescence in the

ecclesiastical ordering of Elizabeth's regime.

As a loyal defender of the Establishment, Whitgift was chosen to answer the anonymous tract, *An Admonition to the Parliament* (actually written by John Field and Thomas Wilcox, but instigated by Cartwright), the appearance of which in 1572 marked the height of the Puritan agitation for reform of the Church of England on the Genevan model. A *Second Admonition* appeared a few months later, before Whitgift's *Answere* could be published. The controversy was prolonged by Cartwright's *Replye to an answere* in 1573; and this in turn provoked Whitgift's *Defense of the Answere* (1574), an enormous volume containing a defense of Anglicanism which has been called a precursor of Richard Hooker's. By now Whitgift was marked for high preferment, and in 1577 was made bishop of Worcester. There he opposed both Roman Catholic recusants and Puritans, especially the "prophesyings" of the latter—meetings for Biblical exposition and exhortation which provided a potential basis for a classis organization of the church along Presbyterian lines. Archbishop Grindal's sympathy with these prophesyings was responsible for his loss of royal support, and by the time he died in 1583 no real leadership had been coming from Canterbury for several years.

Whitgift's translation to the primacy in that year marked a return to close and effective cooperation between archbishop and queen. With Elizabeth's backing, Whitgift was able to resist the pressures in both Council and Parliament for ecclesiastical reforms along Puritan lines. The Eleven Articles of 1583 allowed no compromise with the provisions of the *Advertisements* of 1566, and clarified ambiguities in the Canons of 1571. Whitgift used the Ecclesiastical Commission, or High Commission Court, effectively and vigorously, though without the vindictiveness that Puritan historiography ascribed to him. The last ten years of his archiepiscopate were marked by comparative tranquillity, and the quiet ascendancy of divines of a new stamp, such as Richard Bancroft, Lancelot Andrewes and William Laud, who were to lead the Church of England during the reign of James I.

The controversy surrounding the Lambeth Articles of 1595 marks the last real effort of the Puritan party to make a rigid Calvinism the official theology of the Church of England. When Peter Baro opposed his fellow Cambridge professor William Whitaker and other arch-Calvinist divines, Whitgift assisted in the preparation of nine uncompromisingly predestinarian articles that reflected probably his own theological views and certainly his concern for peace within the University of Cambridge. The Articles lacked any official authorization and were displeasing to Elizabeth because they imparted too much of a partisan confessional bias to Anglicanism, however, and Whitgift suppressed them. His role in their promulgation contributed to the unfavorable character some later historians gave him, that of being too much a time server to favor the Puritan reforms in polity which would seem consistent with his Calvinist theology.

Whitgift's inner convictions are almost as enigmatic as those of his queen. Certainly he was concerned with the well-being of the church, with the standards—both spiritual and educational—of its clergy, and with its internal harmony. His great benefaction of a school and almshouse at Croydon seems to indicate a man of traditional piety.

BIBLIOGRAPHY: V. J. K. Brook, *John Whitgift and the English Church* (New York, 1957); P. M. Dawley, *John Whitgift and the English Reformation* (New York, 1954).

**Whitman, Marcus** (1802–1847). Presbyterian physician and American Board missionary. In 1836 he led a party to the Oregon wilderness, where he and his wife, Narcissa, established an effective mission to the Cayuse Indians. Eleven years later the tribe, enraged by a measles epidemic, murdered the missionaries. The legend that Whitman saved this territory for the United States has been revised by historians, but he remains a courageous Western pioneer whose death and example stimulated interest in and emigration to the Pacific Northwest. A Marcus Whitman National Monument is now located near Walla Walla, Washington.

**Whittingham, William** (c. 1524–1579). Puritan dean of Durham. A graduate of Christ's Church, Oxford, and a Marian exile, he worked with John Knox in the English congregation at Frankfurt and was its chief historian. In Geneva, he helped produce the Geneva, or "Breeches," Bible, and translated a number of psalms for the metrical Psalter. As dean of Durham, he protested against "popish apparel," but conformed under pressure.

**Whittingham, William Rollinson** (1805–1879). Fourth Protestant Episcopal bishop of Maryland (elected 1840). Born in New York City, he was educated at General Theological Seminary. In the decade before his election, he served a parish and later taught church history at his alma mater. He was a man of vast learning and a respected preacher. His episcopate was troubled by opposition to his High Church Anglo-Catholicism, administrative problems in a largely rural diocese, and political strife attending the Civil War era.

**Whole Duty of Man, The.** An English devotional manual, published probably in 1657, which was enormously influential in the subsequent hundred and fifty years (28th edition, 1790). Its authorship is not definitely known, but Richard Allestree is a strong probability. The book is directed toward Sunday reading, for which it was, in a Sabbatarian age, eminently suitable. Eschewing speculative theology, it stressed the concept of duty as the basis of Christian life.

**Wichern, Johann Hinrich** (1808–1881). German Lutheran pastor and social reformer. A significant and unique figure in German church history. He had tremendous social concern but no understanding of the causes of social and economic problems. It was his belief that the prevalence of poverty, crime, and disease among the industrial masses was caused by sin and lack of religion. Pietist in background and outlook, he believed that personal religion, especially Christian love, would solve all economic and social inequities. Theologically and politically he was a strong Lutheran conservative supporting the views of the dominant Prussian landowners. Yet he had great concern for the poor. In 1833 he founded *Rauhes Haus* in Hamburg to rehabilitate and educate delinquent youths. This venture became a model for similar institutions in Germany. Wichern became spokesman for rescue homes, orphanages, hospitals, and prison reform throughout Germany. In 1848 he persuaded the Kirchentag to establish the Inner Mission, which had two purposes: to organize formally German Protestant charities, and to revitalize Christian witness among the industrial masses. Against the prevailing clericalism of the day, he utilized the laity in his charitable and evangelistic programs. The Inner Mission continues to function in Germany today.

**Wieland, Christoph Martin** (1733–1813). German author. Raised in pietistic surroundings and influenced by F. G. Klopstock, Wieland studied at Tübingen (1750). He went to Zurich in 1752, and tutored there in 1754 and in Bern in 1755. He taught at Biberach (1760–1769), then taught philosophy at Erfurt. After 1772 he lived in Weimar except during 1797 to 1809 when he was in Osmannstädt. Called the "German Voltaire," Wieland was influenced in his poetry by French and English Enlightenment thinkers, especially Voltaire and Shaftesbury. His works were an embodiment of rich German rococo style. He created an adequate literary expression for the German Enlightenment, and strongly opposed religious enthusiasm. Especially important was his *Agathon*.

**Wieman, Henry Nelson** (1884–    ). American theologian. Born in Richhill, Mo., he studied at San Francisco Theological Seminary, then in Germany and at Harvard University (Ph.D., 1917). He taught at Occidental College for ten years and then at the University of Chicago Divinity School for twenty years. As a liberal theologian he represented the extreme left. His theistic naturalism began with presuppositions derived from 20th-century culture rather than from historic Christianity.

**Wieselgren, Peter** (1800–1887). Swedish Lutheran pastor and temperance leader. He crusaded against the Swedish propensity for alcoholic beverages, especially brandy. As a schoolboy he organized the first temperance society; as a pastor he preached temperance and founded societies throughout Sweden. The chief results were winning the support of King Oscar I in the 1840's and a law in 1854 forbidding private distilleries and imposing a heavy tax on brandy.

**Wilberforce, Robert** (1802–1857). English cleric and defector from the Church of England to the Roman communion. He was the son of William, and the brother of Samuel and Henry Wilberforce. A fellow and tutor of Oriel College, Oxford (1826–1831), he was well acquainted with John Henry Newman and Richard Hurrell Froude. While archdeacon of the East Riding (1841–1854) he became confessor to Henry Edward Manning, who was also to defect to Rome. Increasingly affected by doubts concerning the royal supremacy as he wrote and studied subjects of concern to the extreme Tractarians, in August, 1854, he resigned his position and by November had decided to be received into the Roman Church in Paris. Hesitating to proceed to orders at first, he overcame his irresolution and entered seminary in Rome (1855) but died before he could be ordained.

**Wilberforce, Samuel** (1805–1873). Anglican bishop. A son of William Wilberforce, he was educated at Oxford, ordained deacon in 1828, then served as rector on the Isle of Wight, where he achieved his reputation as an eloquent and progressive clergyman. In 1841 the prince consort appointed Wilberforce a royal chaplain. He became dean of Westminster and bishop of Oxford in 1845, bishop of Winchester in 1869. Wilberforce established Cuddesdon Theological College (1854), en-

couraged education among the poor, and sponsored the formation of Anglican sisterhoods.

**Wilberforce, William** (1759–1833). Anglican Evangelical, philanthropist, and member of the Clapham Sect. Elected to Parliament in 1780, he spearheaded the campaign against Negro slavery. After several reverses, in 1807 he succeeded in obtaining an act of Parliament abolishing the slave trade within the British Empire. He retired in 1825, his protégé, Thomas Buxton, pushing through a law abolishing slavery itself in 1833. Wilberforce also supported Catholic emancipation, an open-door policy for Christian missions in India, and assisted in the formation of the Church Missionary Society, the British and Foreign Bible Society, and the Society for Bettering the Conditions of the Poor.

**Wilfrid** (634–709). English bishop. After receiving his education at Lindisfarne, Canterbury, and Rome he became abbot of a monastery at Ripon and a defender of papal authority and Roman Church customs. At the Synod of Whitby (664) he successfully argued the superiority of these usages over Celtic customs. Soon afterward Wilfrid was consecrated bishop of York and experienced several political and ecclesiastical disputes before retirement to the Ripon monastery.

**Willard, Frances E.** (1839–1898). Social reformer. A teacher from 1860, she served as president of Evanston College for Ladies from 1871 to 1874, when she resigned to join the rising temperance movement. In 1879 she became a national officer of the W.C.T.U. and in 1891 world president of that organization. Temperance lecture tours took her to every state in the Union. She also helped to organize the political Prohibition Party.

**Willehad** (d. 789). Bishop of Bremen. A Northumbrian, educated at York, he went as a missionary to Frisia in 765. In 780 he was sent by Charlemagne to preach in Saxony, but had to curtail this work because of the Saxon rebellion in 782. After a visit to Rome and a brief retirement at Echternach, he was recalled to the Saxon mission. In 787 he was consecrated as the first bishop of Bremen. There he died in 789, a few days after dedicating his cathedral church.

**William I** (*sometimes called* "the Great") (1797–1888). Prussian king and German emperor from 1871. He was born in 1797, fought against Napoleon, and was well instructed in military affairs. Although a staunch supporter of the royal prerogative, when he became king in 1861 he could live with the 1850 Prussian constitution. He was neither as romantic nor as reactionary as his brother Frederick William IV, whom he had succeeded. He determinedly supported Otto von Bismarck, whom he named minister of foreign affairs in 1862. He saw Prussia (dearer to him than the imperial crown) led from successful war to successful war by Bismarck until proclamation of the German Empire at Versailles, Jan. 18, 1871. Bismarck held the post of imperial chancellor in unified Germany as long as the old kaiser lived. Though William was a stout Lutheran, he understood that not all his subjects were. Hence his first Prussian minister had been a Catholic. British diplomat Lord Frederick Hamilton wrote that William "looked an emperor, every inch of him." His son Frederick III married a daughter of Queen Victoria. His grandson was William II. William I may be regarded as anchor to the Iron Chancellor's ship of state. Without this Hohenzollern monarch, the latter's diplomatic and domestic triumphs would have been impossible.

**William II** (1859–1941). German emperor from 1888 to 1918. Grandson of both Queen Victoria and William I, he had a modest education and apprenticeship of only three months as crown prince. Anxious to direct state policy, he quarreled with the chancellor, Bismarck, and ousted him in 1890. Gifted with a quick mind, though no tact, William II contributed to the international tensions of the early 20th century. He was a devout Lutheran and a devoted father to six sons.

**William III** (1650–1702). King of England from 1689 and prince of Orange. He was the only and posthumous son of William II, Prince of Orange, and Mary, daughter of Charles I of England. After William II's death the house of Orange was overthrown, and the Netherlands was ruled by an oligarchy from one of the seven provinces, Holland. William grew up among enemies, maturing into a cold and artful man. In 1672, Louis XIV invaded the Dutch Republic, and the States General made William stadtholder, captain general, and admiral for life. From this time forward William's primary goal was the defeat of Louis XIV. It was partially to gain England's support in this struggle that he accepted the English throne, launching a "bloodless" invasion at Torbay on Nov. 5, 1688. Already a Stuart on his mother's side, he had married Mary, eldest daughter of James II, in November, 1677, and was crowned as joint sovereign with her on Feb. 13, 1689. His own undoubted Protestantism and his near relationship to the Stuarts provided both Whig and Tory leaders with a viable alternative to the Roman Catholic James II. William's major accomplishments

were in foreign affairs, where he led the successful coalition against Louis XIV, culminating with the War of Spanish Succession and the Treaty of Utrecht. Never in good health, he did not live to see the triumph of his foreign policy, dying on March 8, 1702.

**William of Champeaux** (c. 1070–1121). Theologian. Born at Champeaux, he studied under Manegold of Lautenbach at Paris, under Anselm at Laon, and under Roscellinus at Compiègne. He taught at Notre Dame in Paris from 1095, becoming rector of the schools in 1103. Attacked by Abelard, he retired as a canon to the priory of St.-Victor, where his theological teaching laid the basis of the Victorine tradition. He was made bishop of Châlons-sur-Marne in 1113. Together with the abbot of Cluny he was appointed by Pope Callistus II in 1119 to negotiate with the emperor Henry V on episcopal investitures at Strasbourg and Mouzon. In his early teaching of logic he advocated ultrarealism, maintaining that the same essential nature was wholly present at the same time in each individual member of the species. After Abelard's criticism, which showed that this view led to pantheism, he adopted the indifference theory, saying that the same nature was present in individuals in a state of undifferentiation. His teaching in moral theology, found in his *Sententiae,* followed Anselm of Laon, dealing with grace and predestination, law, simony, and particularly marriage, in a generally Augustinian spirit. These ideas were far more influential than his logic and were greatly admired by Bernard, one of his close friends.

**William of Malmesbury** (c. 1090–c. 1143). English historian. A descendant of both English and Norman families, William, the librarian of the great monastic establishment at Malmesbury, looked upon himself as a successor to the Anglo-Saxon historian, the Venerable Bede (c. 672–735). In the judgment of posterity, William has generally been accepted as a worthy heir to Bede's mantle. His search for sources, his attempt at historical objectivity, and his ability to write well have endeared him to commentators in ages subsequent to his own. A voluminous writer, William composed or translated the lives of the Anglo-Saxon saints Dunstan, Wulfstan, and Adhelm, and wrote several exegetical and devotional works. He is best remembered, however, for three histories: the *Gesta regum Anglorum* (a record of the kings of England from the Anglo-Saxon conquest); the *Gesta pontificum Anglorum* (an account of members of the English hierarchy from the coming of Augustine); and the *Historia novella* (or

"Modern History"), which takes up the account of English history where the *Gesta regum Anglorum* ended, and describes the turmoil of the civil wars between Stephen and Mathilda. William had as his patron Robert, earl of Gloucester, an illegitimate son of King Henry I, one of the most important participants in this civil strife.

**William of Moerbeke** (c. 1215–1286). Well-known translator from the Greek, and a close friend of Thomas Aquinas. His careful literal translation of Aristotle's *Politics* appeared in 1260, followed by *Metaphysics* and a succession of editions of the works of other Greek authors and a number of Aristotelian commentators. Certain translations were made at the request of Aquinas. By translating Proclus and showing him to be the author of *Liber de causis,* he enabled Aquinas to distinguish Aristotle from the Neoplatonic accretions of the Arab commentators. He was made archbishop of Corinth (1278).

**William of Norwich** (c. 1132–1144). An alleged martyr whose murder in 1144 was attributed by the populace to Jewish ritual murder. The story was accepted by monks at Norwich who buried the body in their chapter house and fostered the cultus. Since local authorities took no action against local Jews, the assumption is that the murder was in no way related to them. Other legends existed about Christian boys slain by Jews. None seems to have had any factual basis.

**William of Orange** (*also called* William I *and* William the Silent) (1533–1584). Hero of Dutch independence. He was brought up in a devout Lutheran home, but became nominally Roman Catholic in order to inherit the domain of Orange. When King Philip II of Spain sent the duke of Alva to the Netherlands to subjugate the rebellious Dutch, William quietly left for Germany. He commissioned the "sea beggars" to prey on Spanish shipping and, having organized a small army, invaded the Netherlands from the east in 1568. The support of the common people finally enabled him to establish a toehold from which the duke of Alva could not displace him. Philip was forced to remove Alva in 1573 and to replace him with a more moderate regent. The Reformed faith became identified with the fight for independence. William himself espoused the Reformed faith in 1573. In 1576, the Pacification of Ghent established the Reformed faith in the Netherlands and removed the Inquisition. This milestone is a profound tribute to William's generalship and diplomacy. Through his influence an increasing freedom of conscience was allowed in the

Netherlands, which became an asylum for the persecuted from all over Europe. In 1581, Philip published a ban against William as a traitor and outlaw and offered a reward for his capture, dead or alive. William replied with his famous apology, and the northern provinces retaliated by proclaiming their independence from Spain. He died in 1584, the victim of an assassin's bullet.

**William of Tyre** (c. 1130–c. 1185). French prelate and chronicler. The son of European parents, he was born in Palestine, but studied in Europe. He was commissioned by King Amaury of Jerusalem to write a history of his reign. In 1175, William became archbishop of Tyre and attended the Third Lateran Council. He also wrote a history of the First Crusade, covering the period to 1184, which remains the primary source for the history of the crusader states.

**Williams, Charles Walter Stansby** (1886–1945). English writer and scholar. Most of his adult life was spent as an editor of the Oxford University Press. He became the center of a literary group which included T. S. Eliot, W. H. Auden, C. S. Lewis, and Dorothy Sayers. A devout member of the Church of England, he wrote novels that are profoundly Christian, combining interest in religion and the supernatural with sensational plots. Among his best-known novels are *War in Heaven* (1930), *Descent Into Hell* (1937), and *All Hallows' Eve* (1944).

**Williams, Sir George** (1821–1905). English evangelical and social reformer. In 1844 he founded the Y.M.C.A. to benefit young workingmen. Within a short time, branch organizations were set up in Scotland, Ireland, India, America, and France. From 1855, when he presided over the first world's Y.M.C.A. conference, to the end of his life, Williams promoted the activities of the association.

**Williams, Roger** (c. 1603–1683). Left-wing Puritan, exponent of religious liberty, and founder of Rhode Island. A Cambridge graduate, Williams emigrated to Massachusetts Bay in 1631. He gained the lasting enmity of the Massachusetts authorities by his advocacy of separatism, his opposition to civil enforcement of religious uniformity, and his repudiation of civil oaths. He served briefly at Plymouth and in 1634 became pastor of the Salem church in defiance of the General Court. He further alienated the authorities by attacking their expropriation of Indian lands. In 1635 he was tried for sedition and banished. In 1636 he founded Providence on land purchased from the Indians, established religious liberty, and made it a haven for those with unorthodox and radical religious views. At the same time, his personal spiritual pilgrimage led him to become a Baptist and by 1639 a Seeker. Williams gained fame as a pamphleteer, notably in *The Bloody Tenet of Persecution* (1644). Wrongly characterized as a skeptic and freethinker, Williams' theology and piety remained essentially Puritan and Calvinistic. He opposed Presbyterian attempts at uniformity in England on the basis that civil authority had no power in religious matters and that religious persecution had no Biblical sanctions. His views were based essentially on the "two kingdom" concept of society. Although both were ordained by God, church government and civil government were distinct entities. Both had their own "ministries" responsible directly to God, the civil to God as creator and the ecclesiastical to God as redeemer. Williams thus negated the traditional concept that ecclesiastical uniformity was essential to political uniformity and that civil power was derived from church order. Besides endorsing separation of church and state, Williams pioneered in democratic government by insisting that God had ordained that "the *Soveraigne, originall,* and *foundation* of *civill power* lies in the *people.*"

**Willibald** (c. 700–786). English missionary and bishop. Following a monastic education, he went on journeys to Rome (722) and Jerusalem (724). By 730 he had returned to the Benedictine abbey of Monte Cassino, where he spent the next ten years. Pope Gregory III then sent him to Germany at the request of Boniface, to whom he was related. In 742, Boniface consecrated him bishop of Eichstätt and he served in Germany, along with his brother and sister, for the rest of his life.

**Willibrord** (658–739). English monk, archbishop, and missionary; the "Apostle of the Frisians." Willibrord received his early training at the monastery at Ripon under Abbot Wilfrid. In 678 he moved to an Irish monastery where he stayed twelve years and was ordained a priest. His first missionary journey was in 690 when he and eleven others went to Frisia (Holland and Belgium). He traveled to Rome in 693 to seek papal support for his work and on a second visit two years later Pope Sergius consecrated him archbishop of the Frisians. Willibrord also received the support of the Frankish ruler Pepin of Héristal, who gave him land at Utrecht for his cathedral. In 698 he established the monastery of Echternach in Luxembourg and it became an important center for training missionaries. His friendship with Pepin caused him to be viewed with suspicion by the pagan Frisian king Radbod, who feared a complete Frankish conquest of his lands. When Pepin died in 714, Radbod seized the opportunity to regain some of his lost territory and drove out Willibrord. The archbishop, however, was soon restored to Utrecht by Pepin's son, Charles Martel. During his lifetime he also took short missionary journeys to Denmark and Germany and for a time Boniface, later to become the best-known English missionary to Europe, worked with him. Willibrord continued his missionary work until his death.

**Windesheim.** Location of a community of Augustinian canons founded by Radewyns and others near Zwolle, the Netherlands, in 1386. The house was approved by Boniface IX in 1395 and, being itself a fruit of the *devotio moderna,* provided an important complement to the lay community of the Brethren of the Common Life at Deventer. Under the leadership of Radewyns, Vos, and Busch the principles of Windesheim piety and learning were widely disseminated in the Netherlands, Germany, and Switzerland. Daughter houses were founded, from one of which came the famous *Imitation of Christ*; and, though the Dutch houses were closed at the time of the Reformation, elsewhere the movement survived into the 19th century.

**Windischmann, Friedrich Heinrich Hugo** (1811–1861). Roman Catholic Orientalist and exegete. Son of philosopher Karl Windischmann, Friedrich became an expert Orientalist after studies at Bonn, Munich, and Venice. Ordained in 1836, he taught canon law and New Testament at Freising in 1838 and 1839. He entered into conflict with civil authorities as vicar-general of Munich (1846–1856), but led the way toward a concordat with Bavaria. His writings, including *Vindiciae petrinae* and numerous exegetical works, also took issue with F. C. Baur.

**Windthorst, Ludwig** (1812–1891). German Roman Catholic political leader. A barrister who served for several years as minister of justice for Hannover, he became in 1871 the leader of the Roman Catholic Center Party in the new German empire. He was a skillful debater and parliamentarian, guiding his party in opposing Bismarck's centralizing policies and through the trials of the Kulturkampf. Not all their aims were achieved, but the Center Party was consolidated as a decisive force in German politics.

**Winebrenner, John** (1797–1860). American religious leader. He was born in Maryland and studied at Dickinson College in Carlisle,

Pa., becoming a pastor in the German Reformed Church (1820–1825). In the latter year he severed connections with that church body and in 1830 organized the General Eldership of the Churches of God. He was noted for his revivalist preaching and opposed the use of creeds and non-Scriptural names. He sought the restoration of primitive apostolic purity as the remedy for sectarianism. The General Eldership is noted for its practice of foot washing.

**Winstanley, Gerrard.** See DIGGERS.

**Winthrop, John** (1588–1649). Governor of Massachusetts. Born near Groton, Suffolk, he attended Trinity College, Cambridge. Becoming convinced that God's wrath was sure to fall on England, he viewed Massachusetts as a place of refuge for Englishmen, and a shelter for the remnant to establish the pure church. Elected governor, he set out at the head of the migration on March 30, 1630. The charter left the government of the plantation in the hands of the members of the company; but on Oct. 19 of the same year the franchise was extended to all citizen freemen who were members of the church, which gave political rights to a much larger percentage of the people than in England and proved a momentous step toward democracy. While he sought to maintain purity, he was also determined to retain charity, and was accused by some of being too lenient. His position is reflected in his attitude toward Roger Williams. Though he seems to have approved Williams' sentence, he maintained friendship with him. Commissioners responsible for his statue in the American capitol said, "His mind, more than any other, arranged the social state of Massachusetts; Massachusetts moulded the society of New England."

**Wirth, Hermann** (1885–    ). German scholar of prehistory. For many years Wirth lived as a private teacher in Marburg, although he lectured at Berlin (1909–1919). In his writings and lectures he sought to demonstrate that the high race migrated from Arctic regions to America with no less force than it moved to points south and east. In religion he argued that there was an early monotheism and faith in a world creator. His opinions have found little acceptance among specialists. He was associated with the "German Christian" movement during the era of National Socialism.

**Wise, John** (1652–1725). Congregational clergyman. While pastor at Ipswich, Mass. (1680–1725), he gained fame for his forceful writing in favor of democracy and Congregational polity. In 1687 he was temporarily defrocked for resisting the despotic Governor Andros and had a part in the reorganization after his removal. After 1710 he was largely responsible for the defeat of the Mathers' Massachusetts Proposals.

**Wiseman, Nicholas Patrick Stephen** (1802–1865). English Roman Catholic prelate. Born of Irish emigrant parents in Seville, Spain, Wiseman was educated at Ushaw College (England) and at the English College, Rome, of which he became rector in 1828. Upon the reestablishment of the English Roman Catholic hierarchy by Pope Pius IX in 1850, Wiseman was made first archbishop of Westminster, and a cardinal of the church.

**Wishart, George** (c. 1513–1546). Scottish Reformation preacher and martyr. With an M.A. gained at the University of Aberdeen, Wishart returned as schoolmaster to his native Montrose. Deeply interested in religion, he was summoned by the bishop of Brechin and charged with heresy, possibly because he taught the New Testament in Greek. He fled the country but within a year had been convicted of heresy in Bristol. This time he went to Germany and Switzerland (c. 1540) and became closely associated with the progress of reformation there. He translated the Helvetic Confession from Latin into English. In 1543 he assumed a post at Cambridge and that same year returned to Scotland with the embassy which had been to London to propose the marriage of Prince Edward with Mary. It has never been proved that he was the Wishart who offered the English government a plan for getting rid of Cardinal Beaton. In Scotland, Wishart began a career of preaching upon reformation themes that kept him in constant trouble and danger. When churches were closed to him he took to the fields. During this time John Knox became devotedly attached to the cause for which Wishart fought as he denounced errors and abuses in the church. Wishart was arrested by Bothwell, tried for heresy by Cardinal Beaton on Feb. 28, 1546, and burned at the stake the next day.

**Witchcraft Trials at Salem** (Massachusetts Bay). In the 17th century, witches were anticipated just as Indian raids were, and witchcraft was as real an offense as murder or treason. Though Cotton Mather and other leading divines urged caution on "spectral evidence," the court of Salem, William Stoughton presiding, felt that no innocent person could be a specter, that those who were so accused were guilty, and only one witness was necessary for accusations. Some complained of torments by dead persons, and several women were accused by ten young girls of having bewitched them. The hysteria spread, and in a few months hundreds were imprisoned and tried, and twenty put to death in 1692. Mary Easty's refusal to plead guilty pointed out the paradox that New England faced—that those who confessed witchcraft went free and those who denied it were punished. This threat to basic ethics led to widespread reaction. The executions ended on October 3, upon the publication of Increase Mather's *Cases of Conscience Concerning Evil Spirits.* On October 15, Cotton Mather's *The Wonders of the Invisible World* attempted to explain the trials as part of New England's sins and God's retribution. By May, 1693, all prisoners charged with witchcraft were freed by Governor Phelps. Criticism of the trials included Samuel Willard's *Miscellany Observations respecting Witchcraft* (1693) and John Hale's *Nature of Witchcraft* (1698).

**Witherspoon, John** (1723–1794). Presbyterian clergyman. A Scottish immigrant, he became the sixth president of the College of New Jersey (Princeton) in 1768. In 1776 he was elected to the Continental Congress, where he was an avid proponent of independence. He was the only clergyman to sign the Declaration of Independence. He was the moderator of the first Presbyterian General Assembly, held in 1789.

**Wittenberg Concord** (1536). An agreement between the Saxon Lutherans and the Protestants of southern Germany on the Lord's Supper, the culmination of discussions begun by Martin Bucer in 1530. At Augsburg the Saxons had asserted their disagreement with the Swiss and the southern Germans, but Bucer pressed for a united evangelical position. In 1532 adherents of the Tetrapolitan Confession were allowed to join the Smalcald League. The Stuttgart Concord of August, 1534, and the Cassel Agreement between Melanchthon and Bucer in December, 1534, brought the Saxons and southern Germans closer together, as did an agreement between Luther and the city of Augsburg in July, 1535. A series of conferences in May, 1536, first in Eisenach and then in Wittenberg, led to a final agreement at the end of May. Luther and Bucer had been drawing closer together during this period, and the Concord was signed with nearly complete agreement on the presence of Christ's body with the sacramental bread. The only unsettled point revolved around ubiquity. However, this unsettled question, which had prevented agreement at Marburg in 1529, also prevented the Swiss Protestants from accepting the Concord. A Zurich synod challenged the Concord and Luther renewed his attack against Zwingli, now dead.

**Wittig** (Witting), **Victor** (1825–1906). A founder of Swedish Methodism. Emigrating to the United States, he became editor of *Sändebudet,* the periodical of Swedish Methodism in America. In the 1860's he visited Sweden and won recognition as a Methodist preacher. In 1868, the Methodist Missionary Society in America gave Wittig the responsibility of developing Methodism in Sweden. He helped establish the first Methodist chapel in Sweden at Karlskroner in 1870.

**Wizenmann, Thomas** (1759–1787). German poet and thinker. Educated at Tübingen in theology and philosophy, Wizenmann was influenced by the writings of J. A. Bengel, F. C. Oetinger, J. G. von Herder, and J. C. Lavater, and by personal acquaintance with J. M. Hahn and F. H. Jacobi. Unlike Jacobi, he anchored religious belief in historical facts, but worked independently of both orthodoxy and neology. His works included *Göttliche Entwicklung des Satans,* and *Die Resultate der Jakobischen und Mendelsohnschen Philosophie.*

**Wobbermin, Georg** (1869–1943). German religious philosopher. A *Privatdocent* in Berlin (1898), Wobbermin was successively professor at Marburg (1906), Breslau (1907), Heidelberg (1915), Göttingen (1922), and Berlin (1935). As a student of Julius Kaftan he was interested in the transcendental-philosophical foundations of religion. He urged a return to Schleiermacher's points of departure, and was known for his "religiopsychological method." Wobbermin attempted to coordinate psychological and historical aspects in religion. Among his many works was *The Nature of Religion* (1921; English translation, 1933).

**Wöllner, Johann Christof** (1732–1800). Prussian pastor and minister of public worship in the reign of Frederick William II (1786–1797). Although an ordained Lutheran minister, he joined the esoteric Rosicrucian order, and founded a lodge of which the crown prince Frederick William became a member. Wöllner gained strong influence over Frederick, especially after he became king. During Frederick's reign Wöllner dominated much of Prussia's domestic policy. In 1788 he drew up and had the king publish an edict on the "Constitutional Status of Religion in the German States" in which Wöllner revealed his strong dislike for the Enlightenment and for rationalistic tendencies in religion. Although the first part of the edict codified already existing religious toleration in Germany, the second part sought to impose an antiquated strict orthodoxy on all Protestant clergy, university professors, and schoolmasters. Freedom of discussion and thought in religion were abrogated. He particularly censured Kant for perverting pure Christian doctrine and so aided in the retirement of the renowned philosopher. After some early success, enforcement of the edict was strongly opposed by the clergy and aristocracy. In the next reign Wöllner was retired without a pension.

**Wolff, Christian** (1679–1754). A leader of the German Enlightenment who taught at Leipzig, Halle, and Marburg. He held that that alone is true which can be demonstrated by reason. Reason shows us that God exists and what his attributes are. Revelation cannot contradict reason. Miracles are possible, but not probable. Expelled from Halle in 1723 because of his radical views, he taught at Marburg until he was reinstated at Halle by Frederick the Great in 1740.

**Wolsey, Thomas** (c. 1474–1530). The last great medieval ecclesiastic statesman of England. After the beginnings of an academic career at Oxford, Wolsey became involved in diplomatic and government service, being made a privy councilor as early as 1511. Once his usefulness to Henry VIII had been established—he became virtually vicegerent of the kingdom—his rise was meteoric: within ten years he was bishop of Lincoln, of Bath and Wells, of Durham (and later, Winchester), archbishop of York, cardinal, lord chancellor, papal legate. At least twice he was considered for the papacy. His wealth, his haughtiness, and the magnificence of his style of living brought him many enemies, particularly among the nobility. However, his adeptness in the intricacies of foreign politics in the 1520's, coupled with his administrative ability, made him invaluable to the king. One failure, however, defeated him: papal permission for him to adjudicate the matter of Henry's divorce proved finally impossible to obtain; and Anne Boleyn's faction, then in the ascendant, turned on Wolsey. He fell in 1529 and was left with only the archbishopric of York. The following year he was accused of treason, but died before he could be put to trial.

**Woman's Christian Temperance Union.** An organization founded at Cleveland, Ohio, in 1874, which developed from a women's crusade against the saloon. The W.C.T.U. throve under the leadership of Frances E. Willard from 1879 to 1898. Promoting the idea that all drinking was morally wrong, bringing poverty to the home and crime to society, the

Union obtained laws in every state requiring public school temperance instruction by 1902. Influential in the formation of the World Woman's Temperance Union in 1883, now active in seventy nations, the W.C.T.U. has also promoted woman suffrage, prison reform, world peace, child-labor laws, and antivice crusades.

**Woolman, John** (1720–1772). Quaker leader. Little educated, he began a traveling ministry at the age of twenty-three. Visits to Virginia amplified earlier antislavery feelings, and after 1746 he crusaded against slavery. In 1769, New Jersey put a high duty on slaves imported, and in 1776 the Philadelphia Yearly Meeting rejected slaveowners, both due largely to his influence. His *Journal* greatly influenced later abolitionists.

**Woolston, Thomas** (1669–1733). English deist. He denounced the appeal to miracles in support of Christianity. His *Six Discourses on the Miracles of Our Saviour* appeared between 1727 and 1729. His aim was to demonstrate that miracles could have no real evidential value, but the tenor of the work was to discredit the miraculous and supernatural elements in Christianity. Woolston was indicted for blasphemy, convicted, and punished by fine and imprisonment.

**Wordsworth, William** (1770–1850). English poet. During his youth, Wordsworth rejected the church and sympathized with French revolutionaries. Through his influence on Coleridge, with whom he published the *Lyrical Ballads* in 1798, his romanticism made an impact on 19th-century Anglican theology and social ethics. His chief characteristics as a poet were his ability to bring out the emotional and spiritual meanings in persons and events and his art of investing nature with spiritual qualities. In his mature years he turned toward religious orthodoxy and produced some of his most appreciated works (*The Prelude* and *Ode on Intimations of Immortality*). He was made poet laureate in 1843.

**Worker Priests** (*prêtres-ouvriers*). A noteworthy, controversial French Catholic spiritual and social experiment during and after World War II. Priests donned the workingman's garb, took blue-collar jobs, and sought to bring laborers back to traditional faith. They said Mass, heard confessions, and carried out pastoral duties in their spare time. The theory was that a workers' mission should use up-to-date methods to re-Christianize France, that no priest could claim a true knowledge of the proletariat unless he lived the same life with all its concomitant hardships and sufferings. By identification with "progressive" forces the clergy would prove that they were not mere agents of the bourgeoisie. Impetus for the worker priests came from the abbé Henri Godin, who (with Abbé Yves Daniel), influenced by Pius XI's *Rerum ecclesiae,* exposed in a book, *France, Pays de Mission?* (1943), the spiritual poverty of the unchurched anticlerical Communist-leaning masses. Also, Abbé Jacques Loew made a helpful case study of the affairs of Marseilles longshoremen. Both priests tried to restore belief to their proletarian comrades by toiling alongside them. Soon other worker priests in blue smocks instead of black soutanes did the same, even following to Nazi slave-labor camps. Priests did not necessarily identify themselves to their fellow laborers until questioned. The Mission de Paris sponsored the movement. It was sustained by Cardinal Archbishop Emmanuel Suhard and blessed on his deathbed. Its superior, Abbé Jacques Hollande, emphasized gradualism; results could require generations. The project flourished to 1953, when there were about 100 priests of this cast (out of 40,000 in France) with a score, including members of the regular clergy, working in Paris alone. "Freebooters of God" to their admirers and "Stalinist priests" to their detractors, the worker priests were generally favored by the French hierarchy who saw them as Christian witnesses responding to a genuine need. Sometimes the offices of religion were conducted with laymen present who had little more than Baptism. Criticism of the program came after May 28, 1952, when two worker priests were arrested during the Leftist riots against NATO Gen. Matthew Ridgway, symbol of America's participation in the Korean War. Papal nuncio Angelo Roncalli (soon to be John XXIII), middleman between the French clergy and Rome, presumably reported to the Vatican that he was disturbed over certain worker priest practices: Mass at (then) uncanonical hours, union cards and offices, working-style blouses, promiscuity of tenement dwellings, breakdown of discipline, and support for the Marxist class struggle. In effect, were the workers being turned to faith or the priests to Communism? Giuseppe Cardinal Pizzardo (1953) expressed the decision of the Holy See, which, as modified after intervention by the French hierarchy, was: postponement of further seminary training for worker priests, limitation of their labor in factories to three hours a day, resignation from unions, and housing with other priests. Many worker priests submitted, a few deserted to marriage or Communism, and one carried on a mission among Arabs at Nazareth, Israel. When Maurice Cardinal Feltin of Paris (1959) asked John XXIII for revival, permission for the scheme was withdrawn entirely, save for priests and seminarians serving as "apostles" in proletarian parishes—*with* but not *of* the masses. French prelates again begged renewal after Paul VI became pope. In the fall of 1965 reinstitution was admitted for three years. The name was changed to "working priests" (*prêtres au travail*) and union memberships but not offices were allowed. Three hundred fifty priests could enroll in the program with a dozen scheduled for missions in the Americas. At the end of the term, review would be made and decision on continuation taken.

BIBLIOGRAPHY: W. Bosworth, *Catholicism and Crisis in Modern France* (Princeton, 1962); J. Petrie, *The Worker Priests* (London, 1956); M. Ward, *France Pagan? The Mission of Abbé Godin* (New York, 1949).

**World Alliance of Reformed Churches.** One of the strongest worldwide denominational cooperative bodies, founded in 1875. Membership is open to "any Church organized on Presbyterian principles which holds the supreme authority of the Scriptures of the Old and New Testaments in matters of faith and morals, and whose creed is in harmony with the consensus of the Reformed Confessions." Meetings of its General Council have been held in Scotland, England, Ireland, Wales, Switzerland, Canada, the United States, and Brazil. These conferences are held every two or three years if the international situation permits. Each Reformed denomination is represented in this Council by two delegates for every 100 congregations, up to 500 congregations, and then by one representative for every 500 churches. There are various geographical subdivisions within the alliance.

The organization's purpose is purely advisory "to confer on matters of common interest and to further the ends for which the church has been constituted." In recent years this has been an important instrument for relating the Presbyterian and Reformed Churches to the ecumenical movement. The Alliance publishes a periodical called *The Presbyterian World* and the *Proceedings* of each General Council meeting.

**World Convention of Churches of Christ.** The world fellowship of denominations affiliated with the Disciples of Christ and Churches of Christ. Created in 1930 in Washington, D.C., the convention has met since in England (1935), the United States (1947), Australia (1952), Canada (1955), Scotland (1960), and Puerto Rico (1965). Its purpose is limited to fellowship, with no ecclesiastical or administrative responsibilites. Some two million persons are considered members, preponderantly in the United States.

**World Council of Churches.** An organization formally constituted in 1948. The current ecumenical movement began in the last century with the World Missionary Movement. Interdenominational missionary conferences were held, culminating with the World Missionary Conference at Edinburgh in 1910. Before this conference adjourned, it appointed a continuation committee which, under the leadership of John R. Mott, founded a number of national Christian councils. These efforts were merged in 1921 with the creation of an International Missionary Council which in turn sponsored a number of missionary conferences such as those in Jerusalem (1928) and Madras (1938).

Inspired by the World Missionary Conference with the thought of a reunited Christendom, Charles H. Brent, missionary bishop of the Philippine Islands of the Protestant Episcopal Church, persuaded the conference of his denomination to call a World Conference on Faith and Order. Because of World War I, this conference at Lausanne, Switzerland, attended by delegates of major Protestant and Orthodox groups did not meet until 1927. A second meeting, held in 1937 at Edinburgh, discussed the doctrine of grace, the Word of God, the ministry and sacraments, and the church's unity in life and worship.

Another group that fostered the growth of ecumenical feeling was the Life and Work movement that grew out of the ministry of Archbishop Nathan Söderblom of Sweden. His suggestion of having an ecumenical council to "consider urgent practical tasks before the church" resulted in the first Universal Christian Conference on Life and Work at Stockholm in 1925. The conference made a valuable survey of the social needs of the world, but the meeting witnessed a clash between German theologians who felt the principal duty of the church was the preaching of salvation and performance of works of charity and the Americans who felt it necessary to preach a "social gospel." The Continuation Committee appointed by this conference formed the Universal Christian Council for Life and Work in 1930. A second Conference met at Oxford in 1937 and recommended the establishment of a world conference of churches. They issued a *Message* that discussed the responsibility of the church in a world threatened again by war and repression.

Other proposals for cooperation between the churches had been made since World War I. It has been suggested that the organization of the League of Nations had its effect on these plans for a league of churches. The most persistent proposal in the decade of the 1930's was to merge the "Faith and Order" and "Life and Work" movements. It was useful to unite these bodies because of an overlapping of activity, a shortage of support due to the depression, and the necessity to bring together doctrinal and practical issues in the face of a militant nationalistic totalitarian ideology. Several leaders in the movements, including William Adams Brown, Joseph H. Oldham, and William Temple, worked toward uniting the groups. The plan that was decided upon was to ask the churches to send representatives to create a church council. Both of the Conferences agreed to this plan and a council of church leaders met at Utrecht in 1938 to agree on a constitution and set a date for the first meeting. World War II forced the postponement of this meeting but it influenced the movement in more favorable ways, for as Christians of many nations worked through the ecumenical fellowship to help refugees and prisoners of war they learned to cooperate with each other, a lesson that was not forgotten once peace returned to Europe.

Then, in 1948 at Amsterdam the constituting Assembly of the World Council of Churches was held. For two weeks, 351 delegates from 147 churches in 44 countries met to form the organization. Despite the fact that the Roman Catholic Church, the Russian Orthodox Church, the Southern Baptists, and the Missouri Synod Lutherans refused to attend, this was the most comprehensive Christian assembly yet to convene. The Council was described by its constitution as "a fellowship of churches which accept our Lord Jesus Christ as God and Saviour." The functions of the council were to be to: (1) carry on the work of the two world movements for Faith and Order and Life and Work, (2) facilitate common action by the churches, (3) promote cooperation in study, (4) foster the growth of ecumenical consciousness in the members of all churches, (5) establish relations with denominational federations, and (6) call world conferences on specific subjects as occasion requires. The Council did not intend to be a superchurch, for its constitution stated that it "shall offer counsel and provide opportunity of united action in matters of common interest," but "the World Council shall not legislate for the churches; nor shall it act for them in any manner except as indicated above or as may hereafter be specified by the constituent Churches." The Council operates through a representative assembly appointed by the churches, which meets every five years. A central committee of 100 members, which meets annually, and an executive committee carry out the assembly's decisions. Some of the early leaders elected at Amsterdam were John R. Mott, honorary president; G. Bromley Oxnam, one of the active presidents; and W. A. Visser 't Hooft, general secretary. The theme for discussion at the first meeting was "Man's Disorder and God's Design."

A second assembly was held at Evanston in 1954 to discuss the theme "Christ—the Hope of the World." This topic was divided into six subthemes including "our oneness in Christ and our disunity as churches, the mission of the Church to those outside her life, the responsible society in a world perspective, Christians in the struggle for a world community, the church amid social and ethnic tensions, and the Christian in his vocation." Some organizational changes were also made at this meeting and the officers and Continuation Committee were elected. A third assembly met at New Delhi in 1961 based on the theme "Jesus Christ, the Light of the World." At this meeting the International Missionary Council merged with the World Council of Churches, the Russian Orthodox Church joined the Council, and observers were present from the Roman Catholic Church. All major Protestant and Orthodox bodies were now represented in the group, which comprised about 200 churches.

The World Council engages in many activities besides the calling of periodic assemblies of churchmen. These are coordinated by the General Secretary and include ecumenical studies, ecumenical action, interchurch aid, refugee and world service, world missions, and evangelism. The work in each of these areas is furthered by various departments and commissions. The Council also maintains at Bossey near Geneva a study center for advanced education in the area of ecumenical studies and lay leadership training and publishes *The Ecumenical Review* (quarterly), *Ecumenical Press Service,* and various departmental bulletins and reports.

In 1966, Eugene Carson Blake, former stated clerk of The United Presbyterian Church in the U.S.A., became the general secretary of the World Council of Churches. The prospects for greater growth in an ecumenical direction seem favorable with the increased participation of the Orthodox Churches since 1961 and the mounting Roman Catholic interest. Two major American Protestant groups (the Southern Baptist Convention and The Lutheran Church—Missouri Synod) still remain outside the Council. There has also been a trend toward regional groupings within the movement as evidenced by the formation among the "younger" churches of Asia and Africa of the East Asia Conference and the All African Conference of Churches.

BIBLIOGRAPHY: P. C. Crow, *The Ecumenical Movement in Bibliographical Outline* (New York, 1965); D. P. Gaines, *The World Council of Churches: A Study of Its Background and History* (Peterborough, N.H., 1966); J. T. McNeill, *Unitive Protestantism* (Richmond, 1964); R. Rouse and S. C. Neill (eds.), *A History of the Ecumenical Movement: 1517–1948* (2d ed. rev., Philadelphia, 1967).

**World's Parliament of Religions.** A body that met at the Chicago World's Fair, Sept. 10–27, 1893, representatives from most of the major world religions attending. They surveyed religious achievements of the 19th century and discussed common aims and grounds for union. The Brotherhood of Christian Unity was an ecumenical outgrowth of the Parliament.

**World Student Christian Federation.** An association organized in Sweden in 1895 by John R. Mott and others, the parent body of some thirty national student Christian movements. Its aims are: (1) the proclamation of the authority and universality of Jesus Christ; (2) interconfessional cooperation; (3) the independence and individuality of member groups; and (4) the unity of the national movements. The Federation has contributed many leaders to the ecumenical movement, and was the first to enlist the participation of Eastern Orthodoxy.

**Worms, Concordat of** (1122). An agreement between Callistus II and Henry V of Germany terminating the quarrel over investitures. Callistus agreed that the election of bishops and abbots in the German kingdom should take place in the presence of the king, who had the duty of preventing simoniacs or other unsuited men from being elected. The elected would receive the regalia by accepting the scepter from the king, after which a bishop would invest him with ring and staff. Bishops and abbots elected in Burgundy and Italy would receive the regalia from Henry within six months of their election. Henry surrendered the right of investiture with ring and staff, and restored the temporalities to the see of Rome which had been confiscated by his father or himself. The papalists maintained that the agreement was a personal one, effective only in the lifetime of Callistus; the imperialists argued that the agreement was binding on successors of both. In practice, the right of the king to control the higher clergy was guaranteed by his presence at the elections in Germany. The papacy had won its claim over investiture. The question of investiture ceased to be a controversy after this concordat.

**Worms, Conference of** (1540–1541). The second of three conferences between Roman Catholic and Protestant theologians, called by Emperor Charles V in a last attempt to achieve religious reconciliation in the Empire. At Hagenau (1540) nothing was achieved. Eleven representatives on each side met at Worms (Nov. 25, 1540) and chose Johann Eck and Melanchthon as their spokesmen. They eventually agreed on the doctrine of original sin, then decided (Jan. 18, 1541) to transfer the conference to Ratisbon (Regensburg), where the imperial diet was to meet.

**Worms, Diet of** (1521). The German Imperial Parliament at which Martin Luther appeared before Emperor Charles V. The Diet lasted from Jan. 27 to May 25. Luther appeared briefly on April 17. On the 18th he refused to recant unless convinced by Scripture or plain argument, concluding, according to tradition: "Here I stand. I cannot do otherwise. God help me. Amen." The emperor decided against Luther, who left on April 26. On May 25 the Edict of Worms was published condemning his teachings.

**Worms, Synod of** (1122). A local church council called by Pope Callistus II. It is important for the Concordat of Worms, which was a compromise settlement of the investiture controversy between the papacy and the German emperors.

**Worship.** The characteristic rites or practices of any religion which express reverence. In this use of the word neither a god nor a liturgy is absolutely necessary. Man's religious practice will be outlined here in this broad sense, giving special attention to Christian examples.

Acts of worship arise out of varied thoughts and feelings. As acts or patterns of action they achieve independence of their original motivation. First we shall look at the subjective causes of worship, then turn to the types of structures by which one or many persons can give expression to their feelings.

I. The inner motivation to worship. (1) Rudolf Otto in *The Idea of the Holy* describes the feeling of *awe* before the fascinating and fearful "other" which is both the primary cause and basic experience of worship. The spon-taneous wonder we feel in the presence of great power or beauty is the closest profane counterpart. The immediate experience of the numinous leaves one speechless, but many acts of worship are permeated by this fundamental reverence. Awe is transformed into love when the object of worship is a savior or a beneficent anthropomorphic figure.

(2) The joy of life, the feeling of well-being, is also a cause of worship as *celebration*. Groups experience an exhilaration at harvest, victory, the remembrance of a beneficial event in the past, or the recognition of an act of God. The gathering overflows in song and dance. The anxieties of man are transcended and selfhood is lost in frenzies of happiness and indulgence.

(3) Man's desire to come to terms with the world produces the attitude of worship characterized by the proverb *Do ut des* ("I give, that you may give"). In this spirit one may give things to the god or even coerce and "control" the universe by the power of ritual. The same contractual or purposive approach can be used for the relief of some ill.

(4) *Times of transition* in life usually call for ritual recognition. Birth, death, puberty, marriage, and the entrance upon a life of religious or political leadership are times of special importance and danger. Therefore, men turn to their deepest frame of reference for validation. Worship is similarly incorporated into the beginning of important public events.

(5) Man wants to *participate in reality*. Ritually he joins himself with the rhythms of the universe or the power of fertility. He reverences family and society. He searches to know the basic meaning of existence. Although modern man does many of these things through the sciences, there yet remain areas of life that can be entered only with reverence.

The types of worship and their forms are variously suited to and produced by one or more of the subjective aspects listed above. It is necessary, however, to realize that individuals or groups can use a form of worship for a purpose at variance with its inherent structure and tone. The new purpose can be religious also or it can be profane (e.g., magic spells are often liturgical formulas).

II. Types of worship. (1) *Devotion* or adoration is expressed in song and ceremonies of respect. Poetry, ecstatic utterance, and even glossolalia serve as forms for the expression of love and awe. Sometimes an image of the adored one is addressed, served, and caressed as a concrete expression of praise. The ceremonies of respect for gods and kings are interchangeable. Offerings, from flowers to human lives, can be expressions of gratitude. Christians have expressed devotion in hymns and psalms, rosaries, processions and pilgrimages, reverence for the sacramental elements, kneeling and bowing, and some kinds of prayers.

(2) *Supplication* most often takes the form of prayer, for example, the litany. The presentation of need can be seen in hymns and blessings, the latter being the ritual assumption that the desired effect is present (e.g., the bridal couple is blessed with the desire that their union will be holy).

(3) *Liturgy* includes many devotional aspects but the term here designates a different type of worship. Liturgy is the representation of sacred realities in a dramatic mode. Many religions celebrate liturgically the creation of the world or the cycle of life and nature. In Christianity it is the historic upper room and by extension the whole life and death of Christ that is rehearsed in the Mass or Communion service. Sacramental meals are frequent aspects of liturgies, for in them the worshiper participates in the reality that is being celebrated. The following components of liturgical worship are also present in other types but have their fullest meaning here: (*a*) A special place, a consecrated space that is marked off from the rest of the world, can be temporary or a permanent temple. (*b*) A new kind of time, e.g., the liturgical year, is an indication of the intention of transcending time in worship. Man desires to be united with the past or the eternally present. A holiday or feast illustrates a liturgical conception of time, in which certain times are more important than others because of the event that is remembered. (*c*) Entrance into the special place and time of the liturgy is marked by washing or confession and absolution. (*d*) Since the liturgy is an extraordinary situation, one's best clothing or specially prepared apparel is worn. (*e*) Exalted speech, chant, and song, which need not be totally understandable, contribute to the supramundane nature of liturgy. (*f*) Stylized and prescribed actions, a form of dance, extend the ritual to the body as well as the mind. (*g*) The sacred is focalized in some way, e.g., the altar, a sacrificial animal, the leader of the liturgy, an image, a mountain, or a stone. (*h*) Everyone in a liturgy is a part of the dramatic action, but there is a differentiation of function between leader, choir, acolytes, etc. Many of these elements can be seen in drama or opera, dance, and games, because liturgy is the origin of all of them.

The rites in which the transitional points of life are marked are extensions of liturgy to specific situations. Many of the same elements and the same kind of reference to a transcendent meaning are present.

(4) *Meditation* or the cultivation of certain mental and emotional states is a type of worship more individual than liturgy. In Christianity the monastic offices, growing out of some of the practices of the early church, represent this type. Psalms, hymns, readings, and prayers can also be parts of liturgy, but the total effect and purpose of Matins, Vespers, or the little offices is the development of a personal harmony with God. Prayer and meditation alone is the same thing but without the formal aspects that group action demands.

(5) *Spiritual exercises* are a way of attaining the same goals as meditation but with the help of various disciplines. Such forms of worship include fasting, voluntary poverty, celibacy, regular confession, and obedience to a spiritual father.

(6) *Teaching and learning* are forms of worship when they are involved with the communication of sacred events or wisdom concerning the ultimate purpose and meaning of life. Charismatic preaching is in its own way a re-creation of holy realities. Thus the sermon and the reading of Paul's letters are an aspect of worship.

(7) In its broadest sense worship is to be recognized in *acts of love* for mankind. Thus the good deed can be a prayer and the picket line can be a modern rite by which one serves God through care for the neighbor.

BIBLIOGRAPHY: Y. Brilioth, *Eucharistic Faith and Practice* (London, 1956); G. Dix, *The Shape of the Liturgy* (London, 1945); F. Heiler, *Prayer* (New York, 1932); R. Paquier, *Dynamics of Worship* (Philadelphia, 1967); G. Parrinder, *Worship in the World's Religions* (New York, 1961); E. Underhill, *Worship* (New York, 1937); J.-J. von Allman, *Worship: Its Theology and Practice* (New York, 1965).

**Worthies, Nine.** Those deemed in the late Middle Ages the worthiest of all men. The list consisted of three Jews (Joshua, King David, and Judas Maccabaeus); three pagans (Hector, Alexander the Great, and Julius Caesar); and three Christians (King Arthur, the emperor Charlemagne, and Godfrey of Bouillon, leader of the First Crusade, which captured Jerusalem in 1099). They were men of marvelous deeds, and examples of chivalry, love, prowess, courtesy, courage, and faith. One of the best-known references to them is in Caxton's original preface to *Le Morte d'Arthur* of Sir Thomas Malory.

**Wrede, Wilhelm** (1859–1906). German New Testament scholar. Born at Breslau, he was educated at Leipzig and Göttingen and became professor at Breslau (1893–1906). In his two most important books, *Das Messias-geheimnis in den Evangelein* (1901) and *Paulus* (1907), he argued that Paul radically changed the teachings of Jesus Christ into ecclesiastical orthodoxy and that Jesus never claimed to be the Messiah of later New Testament stories.

**Wren, Christopher** (1632–1723). English architect of St. Paul's Cathedral, London. Born in East Knoyle, Wiltshire, he attended Wadham College, Oxford (1646–1650). Made a fellow of All Souls College, Oxford (1653), and professor of astronomy at Gresham College, London (1657), he became Savilian professor of astronomy at Oxford (1660). In 1661 he became assistant, and later full surveyor general of the royal works, a post that he held for over fifty years.

Knighted in 1673, he was one of the founders of the Royal Society, serving as president from 1680 to 1682. A very competent geometrician and mathematician, Wren was noted primarily for his architectural achievements. The Great Fire (1666) gave him the opportunity of rebuilding many of London's public buildings. He was then famous for designs such as the Chapel of Pembroke College, Cambridge (1663, commissioned by his uncle, Bishop Matthew Wren), and the Sheldonian Theatre, Oxford (1664). Wren had already been picked to redesign St. Paul's, but the fire allowed him to rebuild it completely (1675–1716). In addition, he built fifty-two churches and thirty-six company halls in the city. Chelsea Hospital (1682), Trinity College Library, Cambridge (1677), and Tom Tower, Christ Church, Oxford, are among his most famous works outside London. Wren also sat in Parliament for many years, beginning in 1685.

**Wulfstan** (Wulstan) (c. 1009–1095). Anglo-Saxon bishop of Worcester from 1062, and saint. Educated in the monastic schools of Evesham and Peterborough, he was ordained priest at Worcester c. 1038, and served thereafter as cathedral prior. He succeeded Aldred as bishop, proving a devout and tireless minister who, because of his local standing, was one of the few churchmen left undisturbed at the Norman Conquest. He worked notably for the suppression of the trade in foreign slaves. He outlived both the Conqueror and his Norman archbishop Lanfranc, and assisted at the consecration of Anselm. The legend of his illiteracy seems ill-founded.

**Wunderle, Georg** (1881–1950). Roman Catholic philosopher and theologian. Ordained in 1905, Wunderle lectured in philosophy at Eichstätt (1913) and received the chair of apologetics and comparative religions at Würz-

burg (1916). He became professor of Eastern Christianity in 1947. In his religiophilosophical, historical, psychological, and pedagogical writings, and in his studies of the Eastern Church, he worked to synthesize Roman Catholic faith and contemporary knowledge.

**Wundt, Wilhelm Max** (1832–1920). German physiologist and philosopher. Born at Neckarau and educated at Tübingen, Heidelberg, and Berlin, he became professor of philosophy and psychology at Zurich (1874), Heidelberg (1875), and Leipzig (1876). His greatest fame rests upon his contributions to psychology, and his books *Der Spiritismus* (1879) and *Philosophische Studien* (1883) are of interest to theology because of their relation to psychology.

**Württemberg Confession** (1551). A statement of Protestant beliefs compiled by Johann Brenz for presentation at the Council of Trent (1552). The confession was rejected when Brenz and others who had traveled to Trent were not allowed to be heard in a public session. Also known as the Swabian Confession, it became, along with the Augsburg Confession, the doctrinal standard for the Reformation in Württemberg and later also contributed to the Thirty-nine Articles of the Anglican Church.

**Wycliffe** (Wyclyf), **John** (c. 1325–1384). English philosopher and reformer. Little is known of the early life of Wycliffe, who was born in Yorkshire and educated at Oxford in the 1340's. He received his doctorate in theology in 1372. Though granted a number of academic and ecclesiastical positions, not until 1374 did he achieve public notice, and he was then some fifty years old. He was sent to Bruges to discuss the papal feudatory demands on England with representatives of Gregory XI. At this time he became identified with an anticlerical party led by John of Gaunt, duke of Lancaster, the king's fourth son. Wycliffe also preached in London, where his attacks against abuses in the hierarchy received popular attention. Because of his association with the Lancastrian party, attempts to rebuke and silence him were unsuccessful. An appearance at St. Paul's before the bishop of London, Courtenay, resulted in a dispute between Lancaster and the bishop (1377). A papal bull of the same year had equally little effect, since Oxford favored Wycliffe, and a council of doctors stated that the eighteen propositions singled out in the bull were not erroneous. In his "Protest" (1378), Wycliffe defended the propositions, which contained the substance of his teaching at that time, and about 1379 he began to send out scholars and laymen to the countryside to preach and to read the Bible to the people. Translations of the Bible into English began to be made to fill the demand.

Not until 1380 did Wycliffe meet serious opposition to his theological views. At this time, however, he clarified and expanded his thoughts on the Eucharist in an attack on the doctrine of transubstantiation, and the University of Oxford condemned his teachings. Deprived now of Lancaster's patronage and forced to give up preaching, he retired to Lutterworth and spent his time writing. He died there in 1384.

Wycliffe began with a defense of the national interests against the claims of the French (Avignon) papacy, and he was led to question the authority upon which those claims were based. His search for a basis of authority led him to the Sacred Scriptures, and he concluded that they alone possessed finality. The decisions of the papacy and the general councils were under the "law of God." He then went on to conclude that since the popes had no authority from Christ, who did not ordain the papacy, the popes were Antichrists. He questioned monastic ownership of property and defended the evangelical poverty of the Franciscan Spirituals. He bitterly attacked the secular possessions and endowments of the church at large and urged a return to apostolic poverty. In his reform measures Wycliffe wanted the clergy to be unconditionally stripped of their wealth and their full attention given to spiritual matters. By his doctrine of "lordship," or "dominion," he provided the civil powers with a reason for disendowment of the church, arguing that clerical possessions were held in trust from God and were therefore forfeited by those who were not in the state of grace.

Wycliffe's emphasis on the authority of Sacred Scripture and his hostility to sacerdotal power led him to question the sacramental system: confirmation he rejected as unscriptural, and ordination he carefully circumscribed. In his doctrine of the Eucharist he claimed to have recovered the authentic teaching of the Catholic Church before the innovating error of transubstantiation. The body of Christ is present in the sacred sign of bread, which retains its nature as bread but "sacramentally" becomes the body of Christ. He did not mean to deny the doctrine of the Real Presence, but combined it with a theory of "remanence," according to which the elements remain naturally bread and wine, though they become efficacious signs of Christ's presence. Further, Wycliffe distrusted elaborate symbolism and encouraged a return to simplicity in ritual and church decoration and a rejection of the veneration of saints and their relics. He retained the concept of an ordained mediating priesthood, but of priests who lived a life of apostolic simplicity.

The teachings of Wycliffe had much popular appeal, for their principles were readily applicable to contemporary social, economic, and political conditions. John of Gaunt found him a useful ally, and Wycliffe's ideas were even blamed for the Peasants' Revolt of 1381. Wycliffe, however, remained primarily interested in religious questions. Indeed, although he was the initiator of a popular religious movement (Lollardy), he was very much the professional academician, and his political involvements were confined to the last turbulent decade of his life. Before 1370 he had already completed a treatise on logic and an ambitious philosophical *Summa,* and he had embarked on an equally ambitious *Summa* of theology. Many of his theological writings of the period following the journey to Bruges (1374) were not mere occasional treatises, but were designated by Wycliffe as parts of this *Summa theologica.* Wycliffe ranks, in fact, not only as a distinguished Reformer and political thinker, but as one of the outstanding philosopher theologians of the 14th century.

BIBLIOGRAPHY: E. A. Block, *John Wyclif: Radical Dissenter* (San Diego, 1962); K. B. McFarlane, *John Wycliffe and the Beginnings of English Nonconformity* (London, 1952); J. Stacey, *Wyclif and Reform* (London, 1964); H. B. Workman, *John Wyclif* (London, 1926).

# X

**Ximenes, Francisco** (1436–1517). Spanish cardinal. Ximenes was one of the foremost figures of Spanish history, deeply involved in the religious, political, and intellectual life of Spain. He resided in Rome for a period, after which his involvement in Spain's religious affairs began when he was appointed confessor to Queen Isabella in 1492. A man of strong piety and simple life, Ximenes refused ecclesiastical appointments. Much to his dismay, he was made archbishop of Toledo in 1495 by Alexander VI. He accepted the post, but only on the direct appeal of the pope. In 1507 at the request of Ferdinand of Aragon, Julius II made Ximenes a cardinal. His manner of life continued unchanged in spite of these appointments. He was even reprimanded by Alexander VI for neglecting the pomp of his office.

Ximenes was an ardent reformer and a zealous missionary. He reformed the monastic houses and the Spanish Franciscans, rooting out heresy and restoring the rigor of the monastic rule. His greatest concern was for the conversion of the non-Christian peoples of Spain: the Jews and the Moors. With the expulsion of the Jews in 1492, the Moors were the largest non-Christian minority in Spain. Originally, after the fall of Granada, the Moors were granted religious liberty. In 1502, as a result of Ximenes' efforts, the Moors who refused to accept Christianity were ordered expelled from all of Spain except Aragon. A series of bloody revolts followed. Although the price of such religious uniformity was high, Ximenes persisted in his policy. At the same time, the Inquisition under the feared Torquemada was at the height of its power. Ximenes himself was appointed Grand Inquisitor of Castile in 1507, in which capacity he sought to alleviate the evils of the institution.

Ximenes was also involved in the political affairs of Spain. As archbishop of Toledo and primate of Spain, he served as chancellor of Castile. Twice he was regent: first, of Castile in 1504 after the death of Isabella, and second, of Spain in 1516 and 1517 after the death of Ferdinand and during the absence of Charles V. As regent of Spain, Ximenes moved the capital from Guadalupe to Madrid. At his urging, the Spanish standing army was developed, which made Spain a land, as well as a naval, power. In 1509, Ximenes himself led an army that took the city of Oran on the North African coast by direct assault.

Spanish expansion into non-Christian lands served not only to increase Spain's empire, but also to provide a means of converting non-Christian peoples of these lands. For this reason, Spain's colonies in the New World were a source of concern to Ximenes. He attempted to mitigate the evils of slavery. Missionaries were sent under his direction to convert and care for the native populations. Non-Catholics—descendants of the Moors and Jews—were prohibited from going to the New World.

The world of scholarship was not neglected by Ximenes. He was himself a scholar and a patron of learning. He founded the great University of Alcalá in 1499. His greatest scholarly achievement, however, was the publication of a multilingual Bible called the Complutensian Polyglot (from the Latin name of Alcalá). Ximenes conceived the idea in 1502 and worked upon it until his death in 1517. The Old Testament consisted of the Latin, Greek, and Hebrew texts printed side by side.

This, the first Christian edition of the Old Testament in Hebrew, was used by William Tyndale in his English translation of the Old Testament. The New Testament (printed in 1514, but not circulated until 1522) contained the Greek and Latin texts. It had been preceded by Erasmus' hastily published edition of the New Testament in Greek in 1516. Dedicated to Leo X, the Polyglot was finally published in 1522 after Ximenes' death. Bound in six large volumes, only six hundred copies were printed, which severely limited the degree of use. Nonetheless, Ximenes and his assistants had led the way in preparing an edition of the Bible in its original languages.

Religion, politics, and learning—Ximenes was active in all these spheres. As such, he was one of the architects of Spain's golden age in the 16th century.

BIBLIOGRAPHY: J. P. R. Lyell, *Cardinal Ximenes* (London, 1917).

# Y

**Yaroslavski, Emil** (1878–1943). Russian Communist. Active in the Bolshevik Revolution in Moscow (1917), Yaroslavski became a leading figure in the League of the Militant Godless, an organization established by Lenin's regime to spread antireligious propaganda against the Russian Orthodox Church. Later, for his support of Stalin during the interparty stuggle following Lenin's death, Yaroslavski was made a member of the Central Committee of the Communist Party. He is recognized in Russia as the semiofficial historian of the Communist Party, and his works are considered to be the correct interpretations of party history.

**Yavorsky, Stefan** (1658–1722). Russian churchman; acting patriarch from 1700 to 1721. A convert to Roman Catholicism in his youth, he remained under strong Catholic influence after returning to Orthodoxy. He was the author of *The Rock of Faith*, an attack upon Protestantism. He opposed Peter the Great and Theofan Prokopovich in their abolition of the patriarchate and subjugation of the church to the Russian state by means of the establishment of the Holy Synod.

**Young, Brigham** (1801–1877). Second president of The Church of Jesus Christ of Latter-day Saints (Mormons). A product of the "burned-over district" in New York, Young was a Methodist in 1823 and was baptized a Mormon in 1832 after intensive study of the Book of Mormon. The most successful missionary in the East, Young led converts to Kirtland, Ohio, in 1833, became third in seniority in the Quorum of the Twelve Apostles in 1835, and in 1838 the senior member, second only to Smith. Young directed the move to Nauvoo, Ill., in 1838, a mission to England in 1839 and 1840, and by 1841 was the *de facto* leader of Mormonism. With Smith's death in 1844, Young avoided collapse of the sect and secured a fanatical loyalty. The Mormon exodus to Deseret, the valley of the Great Salt Lake, began in 1846 and 1847. Young sought total isolation for the sake of independent Mormon development. With scientific city planning, an agrarian culture, autocratic control, and a self-sufficient economy, Young transformed Smith's sacerdotal system into a successful social entity. Though he added little to Mormon beliefs, Young stressed the unity of the sect, polygamy (after 1844), and insisted that the Kingdom must first be built on earth. Young overcame famine and economic distress in 1854 and 1855, but bowed to a blood purge in 1856 and 1857. Regaining control in 1857, he established Mormon self-consciousness even as its political and economic powers were lost to United States expansion.

**Young, Egerton Ryerson** (1840–1909). Canadian Methodist. Born at Crosby, Upper Canada, he was educated at the Provincial Normal School, Toronto, where he taught for several years. In 1867 he was ordained by the Methodist Church, and in the following year was sent as a missionary to the Northwest, where he remained until 1876. From 1876 to 1888 he served various churches in Ontario. He wrote numerous books based on his experience in the Northwest.

**Young Men's Christian Association.** A society begun in London, June 6, 1844, by George Williams (1821–1905) and twelve coworkers to improve "the spiritual condition of the young men engaged in the drapery and other trades." Since that time it has expanded its purpose to encompass meeting the needs of body, mind, and spirit, and come to number associations in over eighty countries around the world. As a movement, it was the product of the evangelistic zeal of the 19th century and an urban environment. From the outset to the present the Y.M.C.A. has been a voluntary lay movement that regards itself as an auxiliary of the Christian church but without affiliation with any particular branch of it. Although its origins were Protestant, urban, and white collar, it has been able to function successfully under Catholic or non-

Christian leaders and to serve all parts of society.

The appeal of the organization was almost instantaneous. Within the first year it had employed a full-time official; early in its history, rooms were rented and its "home away from home" emphasis begun. Bible classes were started in 1847. Before the death of its founder it was worldwide. In 1855, nearly one hundred representatives from nine different countries met in Paris and formed the World Alliance of the Y.M.C.A. Its executive, the Central International Committee, was formed in 1878. The now famous "Paris Basis" opened membership to those who believed in "Jesus Christ as their God and Savior" and who desired to associate their efforts "for the extension of His Kingdom amongst young men." The motto of the World Alliance, "That they all may be one—that the world may believe," gives adequate expression to the self-understanding of the Y.M.C.A.

The movement came to North America in 1851 with associations being organized independently, but almost simultaneously, in Montreal and Boston. Since then the American branch has had the greatest influence in shaping the world Y.M.C.A. In no area was this more pronounced than in foreign service. The Student Y.M.C.A., born on the campuses of the Universities of Virginia and Michigan in 1858, spawned the Student Volunteer Movement, whose efforts enabled the American Y.M.C.A. to aid groups in thirty-one countries. Moreover, the program developed in New York City by Robert R. McBurney became the model for local associations throughout the world. This was the "fourfold program" to develop the spiritual, social, mental, and physical capacities of members. Its heart was a building that provided facilities for each aspect of the emphasis.

The last quarter of the 19th century witnessed significant advances to provide the movement with adequate property and to establish trained secretaries and directors of local organizations on a full-time basis. Special services were also extended to seamen, railroad men, and Negroes. The two World Wars provided the Y.M.C.A. with an opportunity to serve men in the Armed Forces, prisoners of war, and refugees. Its success, especially during World War I, opened parts of the world to it that had previously been closed.

As the departments multiplied, however, the specifically religious aspects of the Y's program declined. This may also have been due to the growing interfaith character of its membership. At present the organization is perplexed as to how to maintain open membership without compromising the integrity of its Christian heritage, but it may well be that the lay character and deep ecumenical spirit of the Y.M.C.A. will make it of greater service to the present than it has been in the past.

BIBLIOGRAPHY: C. H. Hopkins, *History of the Y.M.C.A. in North America* (New York, 1951); K. S. Latourette, *World Service: A History of the Foreign Work and World Service of the Young Men's Christian Associations of the United States and Canada* (New York, 1957); J. R. Mott, *Addresses and Papers*, Vols. 3–4 (New York, 1947); C. P. Shedd, *History of the World's Alliance of the Young Men's Christian Association* (London, 1955).

**Young Women's Christian Association.** Formed from separate groups organized in England in 1855 by Miss Emma Robarts and Mrs. Arthur Kinnaird, the Y.W.C.A. has grown to include more than three million members in over seventy lands. With membership now open to all girls and women who accept its purposes, the Y.W.C.A.'s world organization is concerned primarily with literacy and learning, health and nutrition, vocational training and the rights of women.

**Youth for Christ.** A youth evangelism movement. Its leaders trace its origins to the National Young Life Campaign of London in 1911. At its height, during the 1940's and 1950's, it conducted rallies in fifty to sixty different countries annually. The Youth for Christ International was organized in 1945. Some of its leaders were Charles Templeton, Torrey Johnson, Stratton Shufelt, and Billy Graham.

# Z

**Zabarella, Francesco** (1360–1417). Canon lawyer. A native of Padua, Francesco studied jurisprudence at Bologna and Florence, completing his studies in 1385. He received the minor orders in the same year and then pursued an academic career at Florence (1385–1390) and Padua (1390–1410). While he was in Padua, Francesco's interest turned to diplomacy and he went on several missions for the government of that city-state. In 1404 he was sent to France to persuade Charles VII to aid Padua against Venice. However, when Venice annexed Padua, Francesco gave his allegiance to the conqueror, and in 1409 he was sent to the Council of Pisa as councilor for the Venetian legate. Francesco was then made bishop of Florence by Pope John XXIII in 1410. A year later he was appointed cardinal

deacon (he never received major orders). From this time on Francesco was deeply involved in the affairs of John XXIII and the Council of Constance. He was sent by John to Emperor Sigismund to arrange the place of the new council and later encouraged John to resign from the papacy to ensure the success of Constance. His conciliarist position was that of a moderate, as is seen in his treatise *De schismate*. He died in Constance while attending the Council.

**Zacharias Rhetor** (c. 470–540). Monophysite writer. In his youth a student at Alexandria and member of an ascetic brotherhood, he later became a lawyer at Constantinople. He was the author of the lives of Severus of Antioch and other Monophysite leaders, and a chronicle (lost but used by later writers) for the years from 450 to 491. He is an important source for the history of the period as viewed by Monophysites. Only by mistake has he been identified with the anti-Monophysite Zacharias who was bishop of Mytilene in 536.

**Zahn, Theodor von** (1838–1933). German Lutheran theologian. Born at Mors, educated at Erlangen, Basel, and Berlin, he became professor of the New Testament at Kiel (1877), Erlangen (1878), and Leipzig (1888). His numerous scholarly works are characterized by great erudition and thoroughness. He was a representative of the conservative tendency in Biblical research, and defended the authenticity of the Bible and the early church tradition.

**Zedlitz, Karl Abraham Freiherr von** (1731–1793). German statesman and educator. Zedlitz entered Prussian juridical service in 1755. In 1770 he became privy state and juridical minister in Berlin, and after 1771 assumed control of the department of church and school affairs. As one of Frederick's influential ministers, Zedlitz advanced the cause of village schools, and in 1787 established the nonclassical teaching staff.

**Zeisberger, David** (1721–1808). Moravian missionary. He was trained at Herrnhut and emigrated to America in 1738. For over sixty years, from 1745 until his death, Zeisberger labored among the American Indians in New England, North Carolina, Pennsylvania, Ohio, Michigan, and Canada. He mastered several Indian dialects and established a number of Christian Indian villages, most of which were destroyed in the upheavals of the period. His *Diary* was published in 1885.

**Zeller, Christian Heinrich** (1779–1860). German hymnologist and educator. Born at

Entrigen and educated at Tübingen, in 1820 he began teaching neglected children at Beuggen and spent the rest of his life perfecting and writing on systems of pedagogy. He was also a contributor of many hymns to church hymnals.

**Zenana Bible and Medical Mission.** An organization known today as the Bible and Missionary Fellowship. It was founded in 1852 as a union society of Anglicans and Dissenters to assist the Calcutta Normal School. The original name was the India Female Normal School and Instruction Society. It was the pioneer English agency for work for women and children by single women, and it has influenced the development of the faith mission movement. Its missions are in northern India.

**Zenana Missionary Society.** A separate organization formed under the auspices of the Church of England on April 10, 1880, although the work itself dates back a half century earlier. Male missionaries of the Church Missionary Society and other groups were not permitted to enter the zenanas where the women in Indian households were secluded. Women missionaries were therefore recruited for this work. When the society was formed, thirty-two women were transferred to the new organization which assumed work on sixteen stations. They became involved in evangelistic, educational, and medical work as well as in work with the blind and deaf-mutes and industrial missions for those who were ostracized as a result of their conversion. In 1958 the Church Missionary Society and the Zenana Missionary Society merged.

**Zeno** (c. 450–491). Roman emperor of the East from 474. An Isaurian soldier, originally named Tarasicodissa, he changed his name on becoming son-in-law and heir to the emperor Leo I. In 475–476 he was driven from Constantinople by a usurper, Basiliscus, who appealed to the support of the Monophysites. On his return Zeno restored the Chalcedonian patriarchs at Antioch and Alexandria, but gradually adopted the idea of strengthening the unity of the Empire by a religious compromise. The result was the Henoticon ("Decree of Union"), issued in 482, probably drafted by Zeno's ecclesiastical adviser, the patriarch Acacius of Constantinople. It affirmed the common faith in one Christ, God and man, and condemned those who had taught otherwise "at Chalcedon or any other Synod." On this basis communion was established with the Monophysite claimants, Peter Mongus of Alexandria and Peter the Fuller of Antioch. The Henoticon was condemned at Rome, however, because it condemned Chalcedon implicitly (see ACACIAN SCHISM), and by extreme Monophysites because it did not do so explicitly. The effort at compromise thus caused confusion rather than union; however, the Henoticon, increasingly interpreted in a Monophysite sense, remained the official confession of the Empire under Zeno and his successor Anastasius (491–518).

**Zeno of Verona** (d. c. 375). Bishop. Little is known of this Zeno except that he was born in Africa and became bishop of Verona in 362. There is a historically valueless biography of him which was written in the 8th century by Coronatus, a priest of Verona. Zeno's sermons, virtually unknown until the Middle Ages, are reminiscent of Cyprian and Tertullian. A legend holds that he used to fish in the Adige River and is therefore symbolically represented as holding a fishing rod.

**Zephyrinus** (d. 217). Bishop of Rome from 199. According to Hippolytus, he was both ignorant and avaricious, and was under the control of Callistus, his successor, whom he "set over the cemetery"—apparently the principal possession of the Roman Church. Adoptianists accused him of falsifying the traditional confession; Hippolytus says that he acknowledged "one God, Jesus Christ," but he sometimes condemned similar views. It is hard to judge his episcopate when nothing but criticism survives.

**Ziegenbalg, Bartholomeus** (1683–1719). First Protestant missionary of the modern era. He went as a Lutheran missionary from Halle to the Danish colony of Tranquebar in India at the request of Frederick IV of Denmark. Landing in 1706, and despite opposition from Danish officials, he began mission work. He learned Tamil, prepared a grammar and lexicons, and translated the Scriptures. In spite of an early death, Ziegenbalg's work persisted, supported by German Pietists and finances from Denmark and England.

**Zinzendorf, Nicholas Ludwig, Count von** (1700–1760). Moravian leader responsible for revitalizing the Unity of the Brethren (Moravians). Of Pietist parents, he spent his school years at the Halle Paedagogium (1710–1716), but prepared in law for a public career at Wittenberg (1719). Keener on religious revival than on politics, he retired from public life in 1728. Early travels to Holland and France led to friendship with Cardinal L. A. de Noailles and a growing vision of Christian unity through small fellowships not separatist but transcending confessional lines. In 1720, he bought an estate in Berthelsdorf, made it a refuge for persecuted Brethren, and called it Herrnhut. He established a printing press with which the movement was furthered by tractates, catechisms, a weekly paper, and a hymnal—the latter two he wrote and on the others he was a collaborator. Forced to separatism by circumstances external to the movement, he was consecrated a bishop, but after internal polity strife, he laid aside the office. After two generally unhappy years in North America (1741–1743) he returned to Germany, thence to England to rethink his theology (1749–1755). He spent the rest of his life in visiting Brethren communities at home and abroad. Theologically self-taught, he wrote numerous tracts stressing "Heart Religion," Christocentric piety, and reawakened zeal for a servant-missionary church informed by love. Though Pietist by origin and early education, he transcended these beginnings to find a new position much nearer Luther.

**Zirkel, Gregor** (1762–1817). Roman Catholic theologian. Ordained in 1786, Zirkel taught at Würzburg (1795) and declined a call to Königsberg (1800). As suffragan bishop (1802) he struggled with the Bavarian electoral government for the rights of bishops (1803–1806). He served as adviser during Tuscan rule (1805–1814). His church-political writings were important. Under the influence of Kantian rationalism during his early years, Zirkel returned to positive Roman Catholic theology at the turn of the century. At his death he had been named bishop of Speyer.

**Žižka, Jan.** See TABORITES.

**Zoeckler, Otto** (1833–1906). German Lutheran theologian. Born at Grunberg, educated at Giessen, Halle, Erlangen, and Berlin, he became professor of theology at Giessen (1863) and Greifswald (1866). He viewed everything from the scientific-historical perspective and wrote numerous scholarly apologetic historical studies on Christian theology and church history. He is often described as the father of scientific apologetics.

**Zoeckler, Theodore** (1867–1949). Evangelical churchman. A missionary to Jews (1890) and pastor in Stanislau (1891), Zoeckler opened a home for children (1896), and soon a school. He entered into association with a deaconess house and worked vigorously in the Austrian inner mission. Fleeing to Gallneukirchen during World War I, he returned to Stanislau to nurture his institutions. As a leader of the church of the Augsburg and Helvetic Confessions, he united six evangelical churches in Poland to form the

Council of Evangelical Churches in 1926. In 1939 he reestablished his institutions in Germany.

**Zoe Movement.** A brotherhood of theologians within the Greek Orthodox Church engaged in widely varied activities for church renewal. Founded about 1910 by Father Eusebius Matthopolous, the movement proper numbers about 150, of whom 34 are priests. Nearly all have earned advanced theological degrees. Although members observe monastic discipline, they take no formal vows, and may leave the brotherhood at any time. They usually spend one month in the central house and the rest of the year in the program activities. The basic aim of Zoe ("Life") is the enlargement of Christian truth, life, and culture throughout Greece. One method is by publications. Their periodical *Zoe* has a distribution of 175,000 per week. A scholarly journal *Aktines,* designed to serve intellectuals, is published in 15,000 monthly copies. Other periodicals are aimed at children, families, teachers, and important vocational groups. More than 650,000 copies of their edition of the New Testament have been circulated. Education is another main emphasis, from grade schools through theological schools. More than 2,500 catechetical schools enrolled 170,000 pupils in 1955, with additional courses to prepare religious teachers. There is a technical school that combines trade skills with Christian instruction. Closely connected with Zoe are several cooperative Christian corporations of intellectuals, women, students, youth, and teachers. All endeavor to permeate culture and combat secularism. Zoe also tries to reach people directly through sermons, lectures, and discussion groups in villages and factories.

**Zollikofer, Georg Joachim** (1730–1788). German preacher and hymnologist. Born at St. Gall and educated locally, he became minister at Murten, Monstein, and Inesburg, and pastor of the Reformed Church at Leipzig (1758). His fame rests upon his literate sermons and his hymns. His theology has been described as rational supernaturalistic; his chief theological works are *Anreden und Gebete* (1777) and *Andachtsübungen und Gebete zum Privatgebrauche* (1785).

**Zosimus** (d. 418). Pope for just over twenty months before his death. Zosimus' brief reign was characterized by strong papal claims accompanied by blunders that repeatedly forced reversal of his policies. He himself had to retract (in his *Epistola tractoria*) his approval of Pelagianism. His attempt to override Gallican metropolitical rights was abandoned by his successor, Boniface. Though the *Epistola tractoria* is lost, several other letters of his are extant.

**Zosimus** (late 5th or early 6th century). Greek historian. Zosimus was a lawyer connected with the treasury at Constantinople. His *Historia Romana* in six books gives the history of the Roman emperors to 410. While the earlier histories are brief and sketchy, his work is detailed from 270 forward. Zosimus' viewpoint is that of an honest and intelligent pagan historian, and provides a valuable contrast to ecclesiastical sources.

**Zwemer, Samuel M.** (1867–1952). American Presbyterian missionary and educator. Serving as a missionary in the Middle East from 1890 to 1929, he earned the title of "the modern apostle to the Moslem world." Later he taught at Princeton Seminary and was editor of *The Moslem World*. As a teacher and writer, he produced a number of volumes on missions and comparative religion.

**Zwickau Prophets.** German radical reformers. Three men from Zwickau, an industrial city in Saxony and a center of sectarianism, visited Wittenberg in 1521. Sharply critical of ceremonial expression of faith, especially infant baptism, they recommended revelatory dreams and visions. Their chiliasm was related to pressing social problems. The prophets—Thomas Drechsel, Nicholas Storch, and Marcus Stübner—influenced Müntzer in Zwickau but failed to persuade the Wittenbergers.

**Zwingli, Ulrich** (1484–1531). The initiator of Protestantism in German Switzerland and the first theologian of the Reformed tradition. Zwingli was born on Jan. 1, 1484, at Wildhaus, about forty miles from Zurich, where his father was village mayor. He studied for two years each at Basel and Berne and four years at Vienna, then in 1502 returned to Basel, where he first seriously encountered the New Testament, as well as Thomas Aquinas and Aristotle. He took the degree of Bachelor of Arts in 1504 and Master of Arts in 1506. Soon ordained a priest and appointed vicar at Glarus, he ministered for ten years while continuing his study of the fathers and secular history, struggling against his sensuality, and opposing mercenary recruitment. In 1513 and 1515 he served briefly as chaplain to Swiss forces in Italy, and in 1516 accepted a position as preacher at Einsiedeln. At the end of 1518 he was invited to serve the principal church of Zurich.

Zwingli's early preaching at Zurich was devoted to expounding the words and miracles of Jesus, and he came to see a contrast between the gospel and the rules of the Roman Church. He was impressed by Luther's writings, but hoped to avoid a decisive clash with Rome. In 1522 he defended workmen and priests who had eaten meat during Lent. Also, that spring he secretly married Anna Reinhard Meyer, a widow; the union was formalized two years later, shortly before the birth of the first of their four children. Refused a review of church practice by his bishop, Zwingli turned to the town council. In 1523 it called a meeting of citizens and clerics to consider his Sixty-seven Theses, which proclaimed the gospel the only source of truth and denied validity to any practice (e.g., papal supremacy, the Mass as sacrifice, pilgrimages, clerical celibacy, monastic orders) not specified by the New Testament. The council drafted a resolution in Zwingli's favor, and the reform of Zurich began. Within two years the Latin Mass was replaced by a German Eucharist, with the minister facing the congregation across an ordinary table, the churches were cleared of images, pilgrimages were discontinued, monasteries and convents were secularized and the proceeds devoted to social welfare. At the same time Zwingli wrote the first comprehensive Protestant manifesto, *Commentary on True and False Religion* (1525).

Divergences soon developed between Zwingli and others interested in reform. Through the humanist writings of Erasmus he had heard the call back to the Scriptural sources of Christianity, a criticism of church abuses, and the idea of faith as trust. As Zwingli grew more convinced of divine control over his own life and all human affairs, and more zealous in transforming religious practice, the two men were separated theologically and temperamentally. On the other hand, having broken with Rome, Zwingli and the council saw the city's religious unity as essential, and could not tolerate a vocal Anabaptist minority that arose in 1523. The baptism of infants was ordered, rebaptism prohibited, and death by drowning decreed for those who persisted in defiance; by 1527 the opposition was eliminated. Conflict with Luther over the nature of Christ's presence in the Eucharist began in 1524, evoking a multitude of letters and pamphlets of increasing vehemence on both sides, until an impasse was admitted in 1529 when the two principals met at Marburg.

In the meantime the struggle against Roman Catholicism continued. Five cantons of the Swiss Confederation dissociated themselves from the reform, and at the Diet of Baden in

1526, which Zwingli disdained to attend, a huge majority of delegates supported them. In 1528, however, Zwingli appeared at Berne for a public debate and won a resounding victory, gaining Zurich the support of another Swiss state and assuring the permanence of reform in Switzerland. As the continuing hostility of the Roman Catholic cantons limited both Zurich's territorial ambitions and the expansion of the reform movement, however, Zwingli increasingly identified religious and political interests, believing that war was inevitable and maintaining an illusory hope of winning Francis I of France to the Protestant cause. When war finally broke out on Oct. 11, 1531, Zurich was inadequately prepared, its outnumbered forces were shattered at Kappel, and Zwingli was among the dead. In Zurich his aggressive political policies were repudiated, but the ecclesiastical reform was continued and consolidated by Bullinger.

In addition to the Theses and the *Commentary*, Zwingli's theological writings include major treatises on Baptism (1525), the Eucharist (1526), and Providence (1530); *Fidei Ratio* (1530); and *An Exposition of the Faith* (1531). All were born of controversy and were loosely constructed. Their theological value lies primarily in their acute reasoning and in various insights that were left to others to round out systematically.

Historically, the most important Zwinglian doctrine was his radical view of the Eucharist, in which he distinguished the material elements, representing the body and blood of Christ, from the spiritual presence of Christ, i.e., the free activity of God in the heart of the believer coming to the Lord's Table. Without the recipient's faith the elements had no power; they were not means of grace to effect faith. The Words of Institution, "This is my body," were understood figuratively on the grounds that a thoroughgoing literalism was impossible and that John, ch. 6, equated eating the Bread of Life with believing in Christ. For Zwingli, the sacrament had a fourfold function: to commemorate Christ's self-sacrifice as a satisfaction for sins, to strengthen the believer's faith in redemption, to identify the individual with the community of faith, and to enlist the senses in behalf of obedience.

Zwingli held Baptism to be a covenant sign pledging the believer to discipleship and gathering him into the church; it symbolized but could not provide pardon and inward cleansing. He argued that as the New Testament parallel to circumcision, infant baptism pertained to the family, which together with the pastor was responsible for the instruction of the child. He also insisted that John baptized infants. He did not base infant baptism on the fact of original sin, which he understood as inclination toward sin but not as guilt. He held that any Christian baptism was valid, even if performed by "papal heretics," and that the alleged case of rebaptism in Acts, ch. 19, was based on a misinterpretation of the text.

The dualistic emphasis of Zwingli's sacramental doctrine is also reflected elsewhere in his thought. In his view the divine Word comprised both the Scriptural text, correctly interpreted, and the internal operation of the Spirit. He distinguished carefully the divine and human natures of Christ, attributing various words and works to each. He saw the church as invisible and visible: invisible in the sense that it consisted of the elect, known only to God and themselves; visible in the sense that it included all who claimed to be Christians and exercised its authority (by the aid of civil government) over the hostile and insolent.

BIBLIOGRAPHY: G. W. Bromiley (ed.), *Zwingli and Bullinger* (The Library of Christian Classics, Vol. XXIV, Philadelphia, 1953); S. M. Jackson, *et al.* (eds.), *The Latin Works of Huldreich Zwingli*, 3 vols. (New York, 1912; Philadelphia, 1922, 1929).

J. Courvoisier, *Zwingli: A Reformed Theologian* (Richmond, 1963); O. Farner, *Zwingli the Reformer* (New York, 1952); S. M. Jackson, *Huldreich Zwingli* (New York, 1901); J. Rilliet, *Zwingli: Third Man of the Reformation* (Philadelphia, 1964).